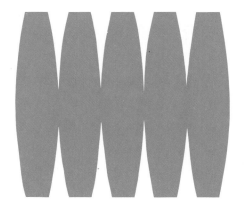

RAND McNALLY
GOODE'S WORLD ATLAS
16th Edition

EDWARD B. ESPENSHADE, JR., *Editor*
Professor Emeritus of Geography
Northwestern University

JOEL L. MORRISON, *Senior Consultant*
Professor of Geography
University of Wisconsin

RAND McNALLY & COMPANY / Chicago • New York • San Francisco

Photo credits:
Figures 22, 23—United States Geological Survey;
Figures 1, 2, 18, 19, 20—National Aeronautics & Space Administration.

Identification of cover photos (left to right): Southern Peru; Northern Baja California; Lethbridge, Alberta; Miami, Florida; Canyonlands, Southeastern Utah

Third printing, Revised 1983
Copyright © 1982
by Rand McNally & Company

Copyright ©
1922, 1923, 1932, 1933,
1937, 1939, 1943, 1946,
1949, 1954, 1957, 1960,
1964, 1970, 1974, 1978
by Rand McNally & Company

Formerly Goode's School Atlas

Made in U.S.A.

Library of Congress Catalog Card Number: 81-51412

contents

regional section

**regional thematic maps / environment maps /
physical-political reference maps**

acknowledgments

This is the sixteenth edition of the Rand McNally *Goode's World Atlas* which was first published sixty years ago. The name of Dr. J. Paul Goode, the original editor and distinguished cartographer who designed the early editions, has been retained to affirm the high standards which all those who have participated in the preparation of the book during these years have sought to attain.

Through the years, general-reference maps coverage has been expanded; the number of thematic maps has been increased and their kinds extended; and systematic improvements in symbolism, cartographic presentation, and map production and printing have been incorporated.

In this edition, the introductory section on maps has been expanded to include imagery. Seven new world thematic maps cover the topics of nutrition and health. Eighteen new continental thematic maps treat energy sources, water resources, natural hazards, landform regions, ethnic groups, and political change. Continuing a policy of periodic revision, most of the thematic maps and graphs have been revised. The Pinyin transliteration system has been used for the maps of China, and a map of New Zealand has been added to the reference-map section. Added to the tabular section is a new World Political Information Table. The Pronouncing Index, Major Cities Map Index, and other tabular material have been reset to aid in their use. The additions and the other revisions, which reflect a changing world, increase the usefulness of the Rand McNally *Goode's World Atlas* as a standard major world reference atlas.

Sources

Every effort was made to assemble the latest and most authentic source materials to use in this edition. In the general physical-political maps, data from national and state surveys, recent military maps, and hydrographic charts were utilized. Source materials for the specialized maps were even more varied. They included both published and unpublished items in the form of maps, descriptions in articles and books, statistics, and correspondence with geographers and others. To the various agencies and organizations, official and unofficial, that cooperated, appreciation and thanks are expressed. Noteworthy among these organizations and agencies were: The United Nations (for demographic and trade statistics); the Food and Agriculture Organization of The United Nations (for production statistics on livestock, crops, and forest products and for statistics on world trade); the Population Reference Bureau (for population data); the Office of the Geographer, Department of State (for the map "Surface Transport Facilities" and other items); the office of Foreign Agricultural Relations, Department of Agriculture (for information on crop and livestock production and distribution); the Bureau of Mines, Department of the Interior (for information on mineral production); various branches of the national military establishment and the Weather Bureau, Department of Commerce (for information on temperature, wind, pressure, and ocean currents); the Maritime Commission and the Department of Commerce

(for statistics on ocean trade); the American Geographical Society (for use of its library and permission to use the Miller cylindrical projection); the University of Chicago Press, owners of the copyright (for permission to use Goode's Homolosine equal-area projection); the McGraw-Hill Book Company (for cooperation in permitting the use of Glenn Trewartha's map of climatic regions and Petterssen's diagram of zones of precipitation); the Association of American Geographers (for permission to use Richard Murphy's map of landforms); and publications of the World Bank (for nutrition, health, and economic information).

Other Acknowledgments

The variety and complexity of the problems involved in the preparation of a world atlas make highly desirable the participation of specialists in the fields concerned. In the preparation of the new edition of the Rand McNally *Goode's World Atlas,* the editors have been ably assisted by several such experts. They express their deep appreciation and thanks to all of them. They are particularly indebted to the cooperating experts listed herein, who have assumed primary responsibility for certain maps.

The editors thank the entire Cartographic and Design staff of Rand McNally & Company for their continued outstanding contributions.

JOEL L. MORRISON
University of Wisconsin

EDWARD B. ESPENSHADE, JR.
Northwestern University

Cooperating Experts

A. W. KUCHLER
Department of Geography
University of Kansas

RICHARD E. MURPHY
Professor of Geography
University of New Mexico

ERWIN RAISZ
Late Cartographer
Cambridge, Massachusetts

GLENN T. TREWARTHA
Department of Geography
University of Wisconsin

DERWENT WHITTLESEY
Late Professor of Geography
Harvard University

BOGDAN ZABORSKI
Professor of Geography (Emeritus)
University of Ottawa

introduction: maps and imagery

The map is a unique means of recording and communicating geographic information. By reducing the world to a smaller scale, it enables us to see regions of the earth well beyond our ordinary range of vision. Thus, a map represents one of the most convenient, accurate, and effective ways to learn about size, distance, direction, and the geographic features of our planet.

An atlas is a collection of general reference maps and thematic maps (maps that depict specialized information) along with related graphic and statistical data. Whether readers are interested in the political boundaries of the Middle East or in the distribution of oil reserves, an atlas is an indispensable aid to understanding the many facets of our complex earth and the general course of world events.

The maps in *Goode's World Atlas* are grouped into four sections, beginning with World Thematic Maps, portraying the distribution of climatic regions, raw materials, landforms, and other major worldwide features. The second section, Major Cities Maps, focuses on individual cities and their environs. The main body of the atlas is the Regional Section, providing detailed physical-political reference maps for all inhabited land areas. Finally, the section Ocean Floor Maps vividly depicts the terrain beneath the world's seas.

Geographical tables and indexes complete the atlas, providing comparative data, a glossary of foreign geographical terms, an index for the major cities maps, and a universal pronouncing index for place-names on the general reference maps. Each of the four map sections contains a separate introduction and appropriate legends to help readers understand and interpret the material.

CARTOGRAPHIC COMMUNICATION:
Mapmakers, Maps, and the Reader

To communicate information through a map, cartographers must assemble the geographic data, use their personal perception of the world to select the relevant information, and apply graphic techniques to produce the map. Readers must then be able to interpret the mapped data and relate it to their own experience and need for information. Thus, the success of any map depends on both the cartographer's and the map reader's knowledge and perception of the world and on their common understanding of a map's purpose and limitations.

Maps can present an almost infinite variety of information about our world. However, when reduced to fundamentals, the map shows only existence, associative existence, and spatially associated existence. *Existence* refers simply to the notation on a map that a point or area exists. *Associative existence* implies adding an absolute or relative quantity to the identified point or area (e.g., its elevation or annual rainfall). *Spatially associated existence* indicates spatial relationships between points or areas (e.g., distances and directions between cities)

Technological advances in gathering geographic information through satellites and high-altitude photography have greatly expanded the cartographer's ability to collect data and create accurate maps. These pictures and images enable us to see the world through infrared, radar, and other spectral wavelengths. The images created can be used as background for maps or manipulated to show us totally new ways of viewing natural and human patterns and landforms on the earth's surface.

The ability to understand maps and related imagery depends first on the reader's skill at recognizing how a curved, three-dimensional world is symbolized on a flat, two-dimensional map. Normally, we view the world horizontally (that is, our line of vision parallels the horizon), at an eye level about five and one-half to six feet above the ground. Images appear directly in front and to either side of us, with our eyes encompassing all details as nonselectively as a camera. Less frequently, when we are atop a high platform or in an airplane, we view the world obliquely, as shown in Figure 1, in which both vertical and horizontal facets of objects can be seen. And only those persons at very high altitudes will view the world at a vertical angle (Figure 2). Yet maps are based on our ability to visualize the world from an overhead, or vertical, perspective.

A map differs from a purely vertical photograph in two important respects. First, in contrast to the single focal point of a photograph, a map is created as if the viewer were directly overhead at all points (see Figure 3). Second, just as our brains select from the myriad items in our field of vision those objects of interest or importance to us, so each map presents only those details necessary for a particular purpose—a map is not an inventory of all that is visible. Selectivity is one of a map's most important and useful characteristics.

Imagery gained from high altitudes and satellites can have properties of both photographs and maps, for it can show complex detail or selected features; but its focal point may be that of neither a photograph nor a map. Because these remotely sensed images often look odd or unfamiliar, map readers need more-detailed explanations to help them interpret the information.

Skill in reading maps is basically a matter of practice, but a fundamental grasp of cartographic principles and the symbols, scales, and projections commonly employed in creating maps is essential to comprehensive map use.

Map Data

When creating a map, the cartographer must select the objects and information to be shown, evaluate their relative importance, and find some way to simplify their form. The combined process is called *cartographic generalization*. In attempting to generalize data, the cartographer is limited by the purpose of the map, its scale, the technical methods used to produce it, and the accuracy and reliability of the data. Because a well-drawn map creates an aura of truth and exactness, the cartographer should caution the reader against interpreting the generalized data too literally.

Figure 1. Oblique aerial photograph of New York City.

Figure 2. High-altitude vertical photograph of New York City area.

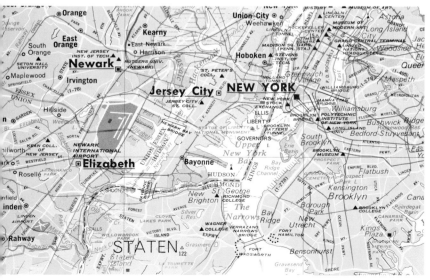

Figure 3. Map of New York City and environs.

Cartographic generalization consists of simplification, classification, symbolization, and induction.

Simplification involves omitting details that will clutter the map and confuse the reader. The degree of simplification depends on the purpose and scale of the map. If the cartographer is creating a detailed map of Canada and merely wants to show the location of the United States, he or she can draw a simplified outline of the country. However, if the map requires a precise identification of the states in New England and the Great Lakes region, the mapmaker will have to draw a more detailed outline, still being careful not to distract the reader from the main features of the Canadian map.

Classification of data is a way of reducing the information to a form that can be easily presented on a map. For example, portraying precise urban populations in the United States would require using as many different symbols as there are cities. Instead, the cartographer groups cities into population categories and assigns a distinct symbol to each one. With the help of a legend, the reader can easily decode the classifications (for an example, see page 51).

Symbolization of information depends largely on the nature of the original data. Information can be *nominal* (showing differences in kind, such as land versus water, grassland versus forest); or *ordinal* (showing relative differences in quantities as well as kind, such as *major* versus *minor* ore deposits); or *interval* (degrees of temperature, inches of rainfall) or *ratio* (population densities), both expressing quantitative details about the data being mapped.

Cartographers use various shapes, colors, or patterns to symbolize these categories of data, and the particular nature of the information being communicated often determines how it is symbolized. Population density, for example, can be shown by the use of small dots or different intensities of color. However, if nominal data is being portrayed—for instance, the desert and fertile areas of Egypt—the mapmaker may want to use a different method of symbolizing the data, perhaps pattern symbols. The color, size, and style of type used for the different elements on a map are also important to symbolization.

Induction is the term cartographers use to describe the process whereby more information is represented on a map than is actually supplied by the original data. For instance, in creating a rainfall map, a cartographer may start with precise rainfall records for relatively few points on the map. After deciding the interval categories into which the data will be divided (e.g., thirty inches or more, fifteen to thirty inches, under fifteen inches), the mapmaker infers from the particular data points that nearby places receive the same or nearly the same amount of rainfall and draws the lines that distinguish the various rainfall regions accordingly. Obviously, generalizations arrived at through induction can never be as precise as the real-world patterns they represent. The map will only tell the reader that all the cities in a given area received about the same amount of rainfall; it will not tell exactly how much rain fell in any particular city in any particular time period.

Cartographers must also be aware of the map reader's perceptual limitations and preferences. During the past two decades, numerous experiments have helped determine how much information readers actually glean from a map and how symbols, colors, and shapes are recognized and interpreted. As a result, cartographers now have a better idea of what kind of rectangle to use; what type of layout or lettering suggests qualities such as power, stability, movement; and what colors are most appropriate.

Map Scale

Since part or all of the earth's surface may be portrayed on a single page of an atlas, the reader's first question should be: What is the relation of map size to the area represented? This proportional relationship is known as the *scale* of a map.

Scale is expressed as a ratio between the distance or area on the map and the same distance or area on the earth. The map scale is commonly represented in three ways: (1) as a simple fraction or ratio called the representative fraction, or RF; (2) as a written statement of map distance in relation to earth distance; and (3) as a graphic representation or a bar scale. All three forms of scale for distances are expressed on Maps A–D.

The RF is usually written as 1:62,500 (as in Map A), where 1 always refers to a unit of distance on the map. The ratio means that 1 centimeter or 1 millimeter or 1 foot on the map represents 62,500 centimeters or millimeters or feet on the earth's surface. The units of measure on both sides of the ratio must always be the same.

Maps may also include a *written statement* expressing distances in terms more familiar to the reader. In Map A the scale 1:62,500 is expressed as being (approximately) 1 inch to 1 mile; that is, 1 inch on the map represents roughly 1 mile on the earth's surface.

The *graphic scale* for distances is usually a bar scale, as shown in Maps A–D. A bar scale is normally subdivided, enabling the reader to measure distance directly on the map.

An *area scale* can also be used, in which one unit of area (square inches, square centimeters) is proportional to the same square units on the earth. The scale may be expressed as either $1:62,500^2$ or 1 to the square of 62,500. Area scales are used when the transformation of the globe to the flat map has been made so that areas are represented in true relation to their respective area on the earth.

When comparing map scales, it is helpful to remember that the *larger* the scale (see Map A) the smaller the area represented and the greater the amount of detail that a map can include. The *smaller* the scale (see Maps B, C, D) the larger the area covered and the less detail that can be presented.

Large-scale maps are useful when readers need such detailed information as the location of roadways, major buildings, city plans, and the like. On a smaller scale, the reader is able to place cities in relation to one another and recognize other prominent features of the region. At the smallest scale, the reader can get a broad view of several states and an idea of the total area. Finer details cannot be shown.

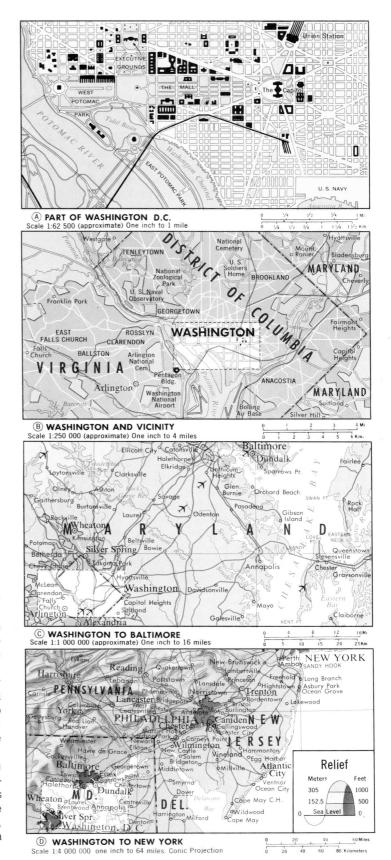

(A) **PART OF WASHINGTON D.C.**
Scale 1:62 500 (approximate) One inch to 1 mile

(B) **WASHINGTON AND VICINITY**
Scale 1:250 000 (approximate) One inch to 4 miles

(C) **WASHINGTON TO BALTIMORE**
Scale 1:1 000 000 (approximate) One inch to 16 miles

(D) **WASHINGTON TO NEW YORK**
Scale 1:4 000 000 one inch to 64 miles. Conic Projection

Map Projections

Every cartographer is faced with the problem of transforming the curved surface of the earth onto a flat plane with a minimum of distortion. The systematic transformation of locations on the earth (spherical surface) to locations on a map (flat surface) is called projection.

It is not possible to represent on a flat map the spatial relationships of angle, distance, direction, and area that only a globe can show faithfully. As a result, projection systems inevitably involve some distortion. On large-scale maps representing a few square miles, the distortion is generally negligible. But on maps depicting large countries, continents, or the entire world, the amount of distortion can be significant. Some maps of the Western Hemisphere, because of their projection, incorrectly portray Canada and Alaska as larger than the United States and Mexico, while South America looks considerably smaller than its northern neighbors.

One of the more practical ways map readers can become aware of projection distortions and learn how to make allowances for them is to compare the projection grid of a flat map with the grid of a globe. Some important characteristics of the globe grid are found listed on page xii.

There are an infinite number of possible map projections, all of which distort one or more of the characteristics of the globe in varying degrees. The projection system that a cartographer chooses depends on the size and location of the area being projected and the purpose of the map. In this atlas, most of the maps are drawn on projections that give a consistent area scale; good land and ocean shape; parallels that are parallel; and as consistent a linear scale as possible throughout the projection.

The transformation process is actually a mathematical one, but to aid in visualizing this process, it is helpful to consider the earth reduced to the scale of the intended map and then projected onto a simple geometric shape—a cylinder, cone, or plane. These geometric forms are then flattened to two dimensions to produce cylindrical, conic, and plane projections (see Figures 4, 5, and 6). Some of the projection systems used in this atlas are described on the following pages. By comparing these systems with the characteristics of a globe grid, readers can gain a clearer understanding of map distortion.

Mercator: This transformation—bearing the name of a famous sixteenth century cartographer—is conformal; that is, land masses are represented in their true shapes. Thus, for every point on the map, the angles shown are correct in every direction within a limited area. To achieve this, the projection increases latitudinal and longitudinal distances away from the equator. As a result, land *shapes* are correct, but their *areas* are distorted. The farther away from the equator, the greater the area distortion. For example, on a Mercator map, Alaska appears far larger than Mexico, whereas in fact Mexico's land area is greater. The Mercator projection is used in nautical navigation, because a line connecting any two points gives the compass direction between them. (See Figure 4.)

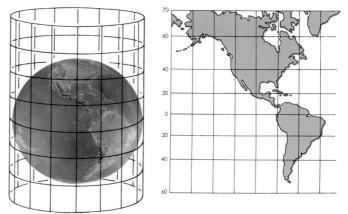

Figure 4. Mercator Projection (right), based upon the projection of the globe onto a cylinder.

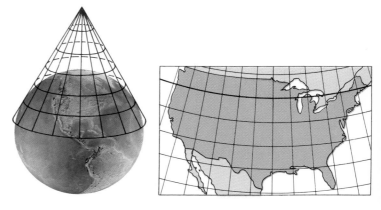

Figure 5. Projection of the globe onto a cone and a resultant Conic Projection.

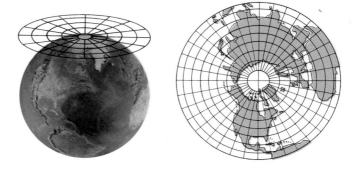

Figure 6. Lambert Equal-Area Projection (right), which assumes the projection of the globe onto a plane surface.

Conic: In this transformation—a globe projected onto a tangent cone—meridians of longitude appear as straight lines, and lines of latitude appear as parallel arcs. The parallel of tangency (that is, where the cone is presumed to touch the globe) is called a standard parallel. In this projection, distortion increases in bands away from the standard parallel. Conic projections are helpful in depicting middle-latitude areas of east-west extension. (See Figure 5.)

Lambert Equal Area *(polar case):* This projection assumes a plane touching the globe at a single point. It shows true distances close to the center (the tangent point) but increasingly distorted ones away from it. The equal-area quality (showing land areas in their correct proportion) is maintained throughout; but in regions away from the center, distortion of shape increases. (See Figure 6.)

Miller Cylindrical: O. M. Miller suggested a modification to the Mercator projection to lessen the severe area distortion in the higher latitudes. The Miller projection is neither conformal nor equal-area. Thus, while shapes are less accurate than on the Mercator, the exaggeration of *size* of areas has been somewhat decreased. The Miller cylindrical is useful for showing the entire world in a rectangular format. (See Figure 7.)

Mollweide Homolographic: The Mollweide is an equal-area projection; the least distorted areas are ovals centered just above and below the center of the projection. Distance distortions increase toward the edges of the map. The Mollweide is used for world-distribution maps where a pleasing oval look is desired along with the equal-area quality. It is one of the bases used in the Goode's Interrupted Homolosine projection. (See Figure 8.)

Sinusoidal, or Sanson-Flamsteed: In this equal-area projection the scale is the same along all parallels and the central meridian. Distortion of shapes is less along the two main axes of the projection but increases markedly toward the edges. Maps depicting areas such as South America or Africa can make good use of the Sinusoidal's favorable characteristics by situating the land masses along the central meridian, where the shapes will be virtually undistorted. The Sinusoidal is also one of the bases used in the Goode's Interrupted Homolosine. (See Figure 9.)

Goode's Interrupted Homolosine: An equal-area projection, Goode's is composed of the Sinusoidal grid from the equator to about 40° N and 40° S latitudes; beyond these latitudes, the Mollweide is used. This grid is interrupted so that land masses can be projected with a minimum of shape distortion by positioning each section on a separate central meridian. Thus, the shapes as well as the sizes of land masses are represented with a high degree of fidelity. Oceans can also be positioned in this manner. (See Figure 10.)

Robinson: This recently devised transformation is a projection that serves as a compromise of all the distortions that can occur on a world map. Though no single attribute is maintained, the projection minimizes visually disturbing distortions. As a result, the continental outlines "look" appropriate.

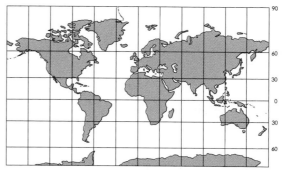

Figure 7.   Miller Cylindrical Projection.

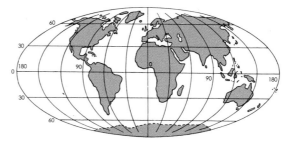

Figure 8.   Mollweide Homolographic Projection.

Figure 9.   Sinusoidal Projection.

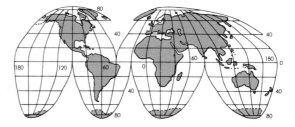

Figure 10.   Goode's Interrupted Homolosine Projection.

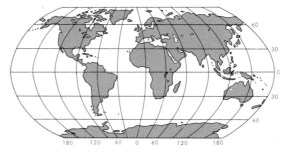

Figure 11.   Robinson Projection.

Bonne: This equal-area transformation is mathematically related to the Sinusoidal. Distances are true along all parallels and the central meridian. Farther out from the central meridian, however, the increasing obliqueness of the grid's angles distorts shape and distance. This limits the area that can be usefully projected. Bonne projections, like conics, are best employed for relatively small areas in middle latitudes. (See Figure 12.)

Conic with Two Standard Parallels: The linear scale of this projection is consistent along two standard parallels instead of only one as in the simple conic. Since the spacing of the other parallels is reduced somewhat between the standard parallels and progressively enlarged beyond them, the projection does not exhibit the equal-area property. Careful selection of the standard parallels, however, provides good representation of limited areas. Like the Bonne projection, this system is widely used for areas in middle latitudes. (See Figure 13.)

Polyconic: In this system, the globe is projected onto a series of strips taken from tangent cones. Parallels are nonconcentric circles, and each is divided equally by the meridians, as on the globe. While distances along the straight central meridian are true, they are increasingly exaggerated along the curving meridians. Likewise, general representation of areas and shapes is good near the central meridian but progressively distorted away from it. Polyconic projections are used for middle-latitude areas to minimize all distortions and were employed for large-scale topographic maps. (See Figure 14.)

Lambert Conformal Conic: This conformal transformation system usually employs two standard parallels. Distortion increases away from the standard parallels, being greatest at the edges of the map. It is useful for projecting elongated east-west areas in the middle latitudes and is ideal for depicting the forty-eight contiguous states. It is also widely used for aeronautical and meteorological charts. (See Figure 15.)

Lambert Equal Area *(oblique and polar cases):* This equal-area projection can be centered at any point on the earth's surface, perpendicular to a line drawn through the globe. It maintains correct angles to all points on the map from its center (point of tangency), but distances become progressively distorted toward the edges. It is most useful for roughly circular areas or areas whose dimensions are nearly equal in two perpendicular directions.

The two most common forms of the Lambert projection are the oblique and the polar, shown in Figures 6 and 16. Although the meridians and parallels for the forms are different, the distortion characteristics are the same.

Important characteristics of the globe grid

1. All meridians of longitude are equal in length and meet at the Poles.
2. All lines of latitude are parallel and equally spaced on meridians.
3. The length, or circumference, of the parallels of latitude decreases as one moves from the equator to the Poles. For instance, the circumference of the parallel at 60° latitude is one-half the circumference of the equator.
4. Meridians of longitude are equally spaced on each parallel, but the distance between them decreases toward the Poles.
5. All parallels and meridians meet at right angles.

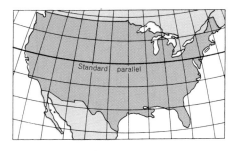

Figure 12.
Bonne Projection.

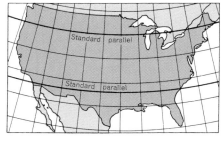

Figure 13.
Conic Projection with Two Standard Parallels.

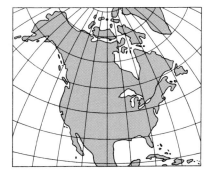

Figure 14.
Polyconic Projection.

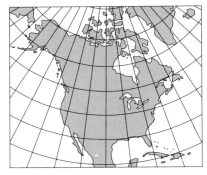

Figure 15.
Lambert Conformal Conic Projection.

Figure 16.
Lambert Equal-Area Projection (oblique case).

REMOTELY SENSED IMAGERY

Recent technological advances have greatly expanded our ability to "see" surface features on the earth. *Remote sensing* can be defined as gathering and recording from a distance information about many types of geographic features. Human beings have been using a form of remote sensing for thousands of years. To gather information about terrain, people have climbed trees or hilltops and used their eyes, ears, and even their sense of smell to detect what lay in the distance. Now, with highly sophisticated cameras and electronic sensing equipment as our remote sensors, we can learn a great deal more about our world than we have been able to gather with our physical senses.

Remote sensing is based on two fundamental principles. First, each type of surface material (rock, soil, vegetation) absorbs and reflects solar energy in a characteristic manner. In addition, a certain amount of internal energy is emitted by each surface. Remote-sensing instruments can detect this absorbed, reflected, and emitted energy and produce photographs or images.

Second, while the human eye is sensitive to only a small portion of the electromagnetic spectrum (shown as A in the top illustration of Figure 17), remote-sensing instruments can work in longer and shorter wavelengths, generally in the infrared and radar, or microwave, regions. These areas of the spectrum are often referred to as bands.

In remote-sensing photography, the most commonly used bands, in addition to those in the visible spectrum, are the near-infrared bands of 0.7 to 0.8μ (micrometers) and 0.8 to 1.1μ. Infrared photography has proved invaluable in studying agricultural areas. Since healthy plants reflect a considerable amount of near-infrared light, high-altitude photographs using this band of the spectrum can detect diseased vegetation before the problem is visible to the naked eye.

Multispectral photographic techniques are also being used. In this type of remote sensing, reflected energy from a surface is isolated into a number of given wavelength bands (shown in the bottom illustration of Figure 17). Each band can be separately recorded on film, or bands can be recorded simultaneously. These restricted wavelengths include a blue band of 0.4 to 0.5μ, a green band of 0.5 to 0.6μ, and a red band of 0.6 to 0.7μ. Scientists can select various band widths in order to highlight certain features within an area. The photographs in Figure 18 demonstrate the different effects that multispectral photography can produce and the types of information that can be revealed.

Thermal infrared (shown as B in the top illustration in Figure 17) and radar, or microwave, (shown as C) have also been important for gathering geographical data. Thermal imagery records the temperatures of surface features and is collected through electronic sensing instruments, not by cameras. These images show "hot spots" in lakes, rivers, and coastal areas where waste discharges are affecting the water temperature. Thermal-infrared sensing can also pick up animal populations that may be camouflaged to the naked eye. Heat loss from buildings can also be measured.

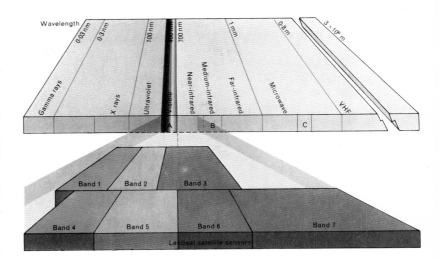

Figure 17. Top: The electromagnetic spectrum.

Bottom: Visible portion of the spectrum.

0.7 to 0.8μ band: Black-and-white, infrared.

0.8 to 0.9μ band: Black-and-white, infrared.

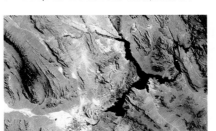

0.5 to 0.8 μ band: Color infrared.

0.4 to 0.7μ band: Color.

0.6 to 0.7μ band: Black-and-white, visible.

0.5 to 0.6μ band: Black-and-white, visible.

Figure 18. Images taken over Lake Mead, Colorado, by a multispectral camera. Each of the images has been derived from a different wavelength band of the spectrum.

Figure 19. Landsat (satellite) image of southeastern Colorado.

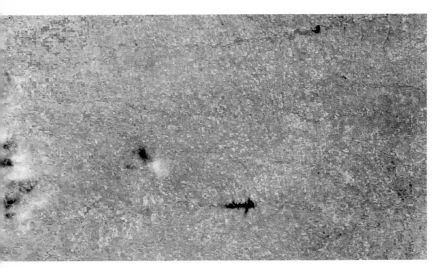

Figure 20. Landsat (satellite) image of western Kansas.

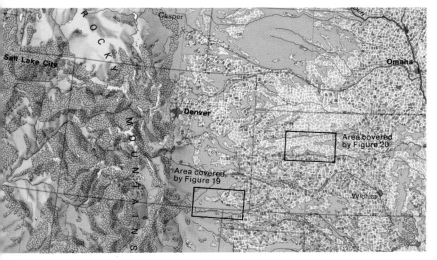

Figure 21. Land use (environment) map derived by using information from the satellite images in Figures 19 and 20.

Radar differs from other sensing methods in that a signal is sent out by the sensor, and the intensity of the reflected "echo" is recorded electronically. (The images may then be printed as a photograph.) Radar has the advantage of being unaffected by weather conditions, and in areas with persistent cloud cover it has proved to be the most reliable instrument available. This type of remote sensing can record surface relief features with remarkable accuracy. It is also useful in searching for mineral deposits and in detecting the types and extent of land ice, sea ice, and groundwater.

Landsat

Perhaps the most well-known examples of remotely sensed imagery are the pictures gathered by the Landsat satellites. Originally known as ERTS (Earth Resource Technology Satellite), Landsat 1 was launched in 1972 and functioned until 1979. Landsat 2 and Landsat 3—launched in 1975 and 1978, respectively—are still collecting data.

These satellites carry a system that views the earth in two visible and two near-infrared bands. The images are gathered electronically by sensors that scan the terrain directly beneath the satellite and record energy from individual areas on the ground. The size of these areas is determined by the spot size, or resolution capacity, of the optical scanner on board the satellite.

The smallest individual area distinguished by the scanner is called a picture element, or *pixel*. Each Landsat pixel covers about an acre of the earth's surface, with approximately 7,800,000 pixels composing each image (an image covers 115 x 115 mi or 185 x 185 km). The pixels are recorded as digits and transmitted to a ground receiving station. The digits represent brightness values and are stored in a computer as four separate arrays, one for each band of the visible and near-infrared light used. The digits can be electronically manipulated to produce false-color pictures like those shown in Figure 19 and Figure 20. A single Landsat satellite can gather some thirty million bits of data for each frame in about twenty-five seconds.

This form of data gathering has a number of advantages over conventional photography. Chiefly, the digits can be computer enhanced to bring out specific features more clearly and reveal subtle changes that may not appear on a conventional photograph of the same area.

Scientists are still discovering new uses for Landsat images. The uniform orbits of the Landsat satellites allow for coverage of the same terrain every eighteen days. As a result, the scanners can detect changes in crops, vegetation, and farming patterns; damage resulting from earthquakes, hurricanes, floods, and fires; and movements of desert sands, erosion patterns, and levels of some pollutants discharged into waterways.

Landsat images are particularly helpful to cartographers in correcting existing maps or creating new ones, as the striking resemblance between the environmental map (Figure 21) and the two pictures above it shows.

High-Altitude Imagery

Cartographers also benefit from the increased use of high-altitude photography. Figure 22 is a good example of an infrared photograph taken with a high-altitude camera mounted in an aircraft. The imagery gathered is limited by the sensitivity of the film, which can record only in the 0.3 to 1.1μ range of the spectrum. Even within this range, and using only black-and-white film, the data collected can be used to generate highly accurate 1:24,000 topographic maps, such as the one shown in Figure 23. Side benefits of this form of photography can be the production of orthophotomaps and digital elevation models (DEM). A DEM is composed of a set of equally spaced surface elevations for an area of the earth.

High-altitude photographs, like satellite pictures, can be used to monitor changes. Often these pictures will record shifts in land use, transportation lines, erosion, drainage patterns, soil characteristics, and surface structures.

Although *Goode's World Atlas* does not employ topographic maps, they are used as a reference source for the volume. High-altitude photography makes it possible to update such features as highway networks, metropolitan areas, the shape and flow of rivers and lakes, ocean currents, and ice formations.

Recent and future technological advances in collecting geographic information promise to make the cartographer's job somewhat easier. More important, these advances will allow us to give the atlas user more-detailed and up-to-date knowledge about our world and the impact of human activity around the globe.

Joel L. Morrison
University of Wisconsin

Edward B. Espenshade, Jr.
Northwestern University

Figure 22.   High-altitude infrared image of the Goodland, Kansas, area.

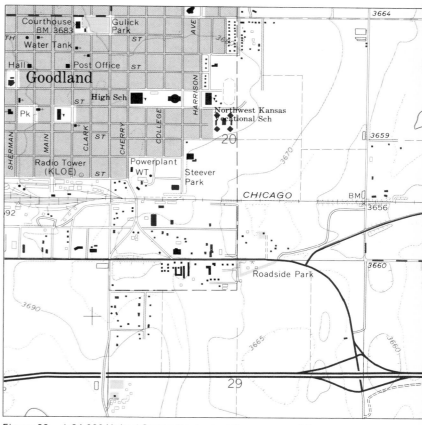

Figure 23.   1:24,000 United States Geological Survey map of the Goodland, Kansas, area.

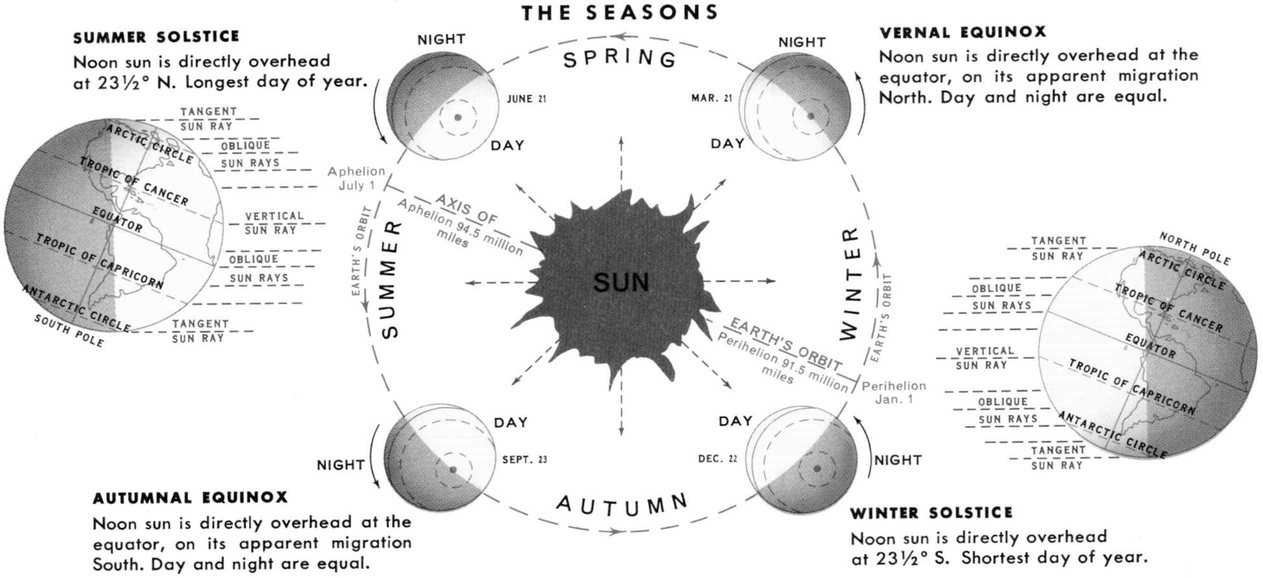

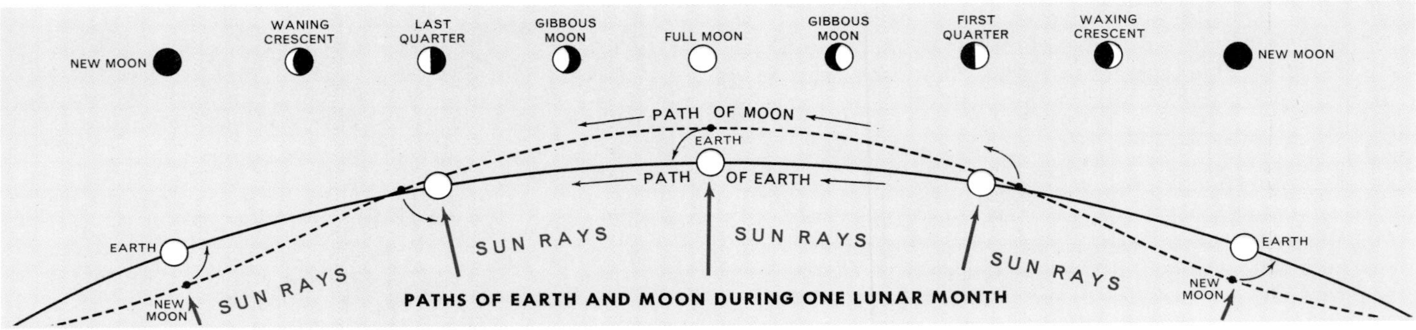

THE SEASONS

SUMMER SOLSTICE
Noon sun is directly overhead at 23½° N. Longest day of year.

TANGENT SUN RAY
ARCTIC CIRCLE
OBLIQUE SUN RAYS
TROPIC OF CANCER
EQUATOR — VERTICAL SUN RAY
TROPIC OF CAPRICORN — OBLIQUE SUN RAYS
ANTARCTIC CIRCLE — TANGENT SUN RAY
SOUTH POLE

SPRING
NIGHT — JUNE 21 — DAY
NIGHT — MAR. 21 — DAY

Aphelion July 1
AXIS OF
Aphelion 94.5 million miles
EARTH'S ORBIT

SUMMER
SUN
WINTER

EARTH'S ORBIT
Perihelion 91.5 million miles
Perihelion Jan. 1

NIGHT — SEPT. 23 — DAY
DAY — DEC. 22 — NIGHT

AUTUMN

VERNAL EQUINOX
Noon sun is directly overhead at the equator, on its apparent migration North. Day and night are equal.

TANGENT SUN RAY — NORTH POLE
ARCTIC CIRCLE
OBLIQUE SUN RAYS — TROPIC OF CANCER
EQUATOR
VERTICAL SUN RAY — TROPIC OF CAPRICORN
OBLIQUE SUN RAYS — ANTARCTIC CIRCLE
TANGENT SUN RAY

AUTUMNAL EQUINOX
Noon sun is directly overhead at the equator, on its apparent migration South. Day and night are equal.

WINTER SOLSTICE
Noon sun is directly overhead at 23½° S. Shortest day of year.

NEW MOON | WANING CRESCENT | LAST QUARTER | GIBBOUS MOON | FULL MOON | GIBBOUS MOON | FIRST QUARTER | WAXING CRESCENT | NEW MOON

PATH OF MOON
EARTH
PATH OF EARTH
EARTH — SUN RAYS — SUN RAYS — SUN RAYS — EARTH
NEW MOON — NEW MOON

PATHS OF EARTH AND MOON DURING ONE LUNAR MONTH

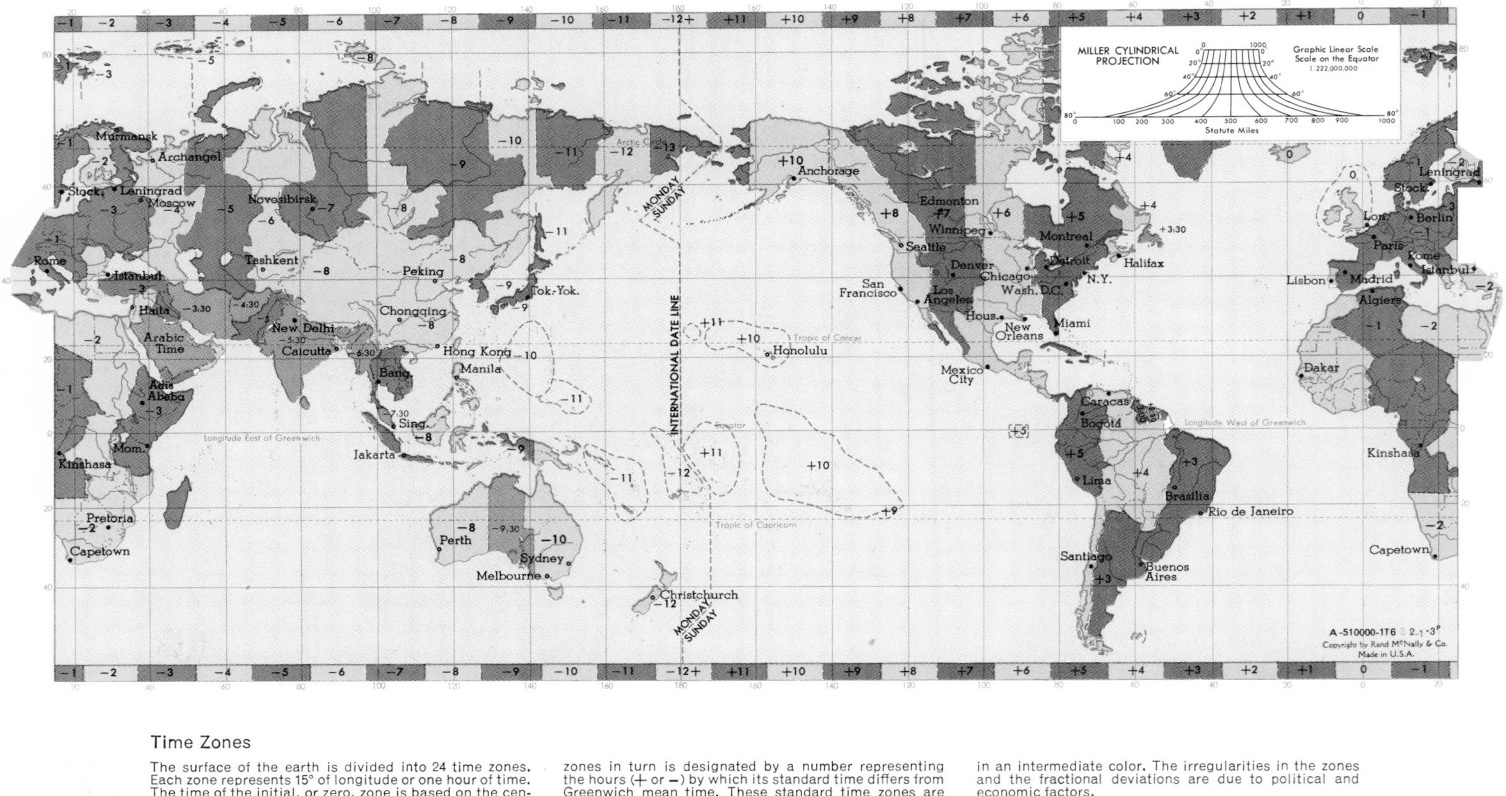

MILLER CYLINDRICAL PROJECTION
Graphic Linear Scale
Scale on the Equator 1:222,000,000
Statute Miles

Time Zones

The surface of the earth is divided into 24 time zones. Each zone represents 15° of longitude or one hour of time. The time of the initial, or zero, zone is based on the central meridian of Greenwich and is adopted eastward and westward for a distance of 7½° of longitude. Each of the zones in turn is designated by a number representing the hours (+ or –) by which its standard time differs from Greenwich mean time. These standard time zones are indicated by bands of orange and yellow. Areas which have a fractional deviation from standard time are shown in an intermediate color. The irregularities in the zones and the fractional deviations are due to political and economic factors.

(Revised to 1980. After U.S. Defense Mapping Agency)

world thematic maps

This section of the atlas consists of more than sixty thematic maps presenting world patterns and distributions. Together with accompanying graphs, these maps communicate basic information on mineral resources, agricultural products, trade, transportation, and other selected aspects of the natural and cultural geographical environment.

A thematic map uses symbols to show certain characteristics of, generally, one class of geographical information. This "theme" of a thematic map is presented upon a background of basic locational information—coastline, country boundaries, major drainage, etc. The map's primary concern is to communicate visually basic impressions of the distribution of the theme. For instance, on page 39 the distribution of cattle shown by point symbols impresses the reader with relative densities—the distribution of cattle is much more uniform throughout the United States than it is in China, and cattle are more numerous in the United States than in China.

Although it is possible to use a thematic map to obtain exact values of a quantity or commodity, it is not the purpose intended, any more than a thematic map is intended to be used to give precise distances from New York to Moscow. If one seeks precise statistics for each country, he may consult the bar graph on the map or a statistical table.

The map on this page is an example of a special class of thematic maps called cartograms. The cartogram assigns to a named earth region an area based on some value other than land surface area. In the cartogram below the areas assigned are proportional to their countries' populations and tinted according to their rate of natural increase. The result of mapping on this base is a meaningful way of portraying this distribution since natural increase is causally related to existing size of population. On the other hand, natural increase is not causally related to earth area. In the other thematic maps in this atlas, relative earth sizes have been considered when presenting the distributions.

Real and hypothetical geographical distributions of interest to man are practically limitless but can be classed into point, line, area, or volume information relative to a specific location or area in the world. The thematic map, in communicating these fundamental classes of information, utilizes point, line, and area symbols. The symbols may be employed to show *qualitative* differences (differences in *kind*) of a certain category of information and may also show *quantitative* differences in the information (differences in *amount*). For example, the natural-vegetation map (page 16) was based upon information gathered by many observations over a period of time. It utilizes area symbols (color and pattern) to show the difference in the *kind* of vegetation as well as the extent. Quantitative factual information was shown on the annual-precipitation map, page 14, by means of isohyets (lines connecting points of equal rainfall). Also, area symbols were employed to show the intervals between the lines. In each of these thematic maps, there is one primary theme, or subject; the map communicates the information far better than volumes of words and tables could.

One of the most important aspects of the thematic-map section is use of the different maps to show comparisons and relationships among the distributions of various types of geographical information. For example, the relationship of dense population (page 20) to areas of intensive subsistence agriculture (page 30) and to manufacturing and commerce (page 28) is an important geographic concept.

The statistics communicated by the maps and graphs in this section are intended to give an idea of the relative importance of countries in the distributions mapped. The maps are not intended to take the place of statistical reference works. No single year affords a realistic base for production, trade, and certain economic and demographic statistics. Therefore, averages of data for three or four years have been used. Together with the maps, the averages and percentages provide the student with a realistic idea of the importance of specific areas.

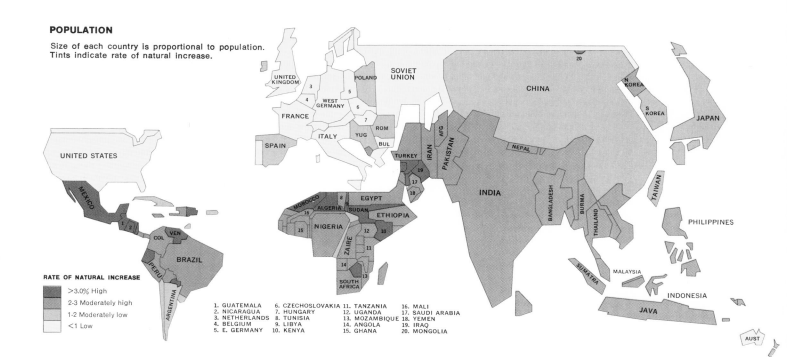

POPULATION

Size of each country is proportional to population.
Tints indicate rate of natural increase.

RATE OF NATURAL INCREASE

- >3.0% High
- 2-3 Moderately high
- 1-2 Moderately low
- <1 Low

1. GUATEMALA	6. CZECHOSLOVAKIA	11. TANZANIA
2. NICARAGUA	7. HUNGARY	12. UGANDA
3. NETHERLANDS	8. TUNISIA	13. MOZAMBIQUE
4. BELGIUM	9. LIBYA	14. ANGOLA
5. E. GERMANY	10. KENYA	15. GHANA

16. MALI	
17. SAUDI ARABIA	
18. YEMEN	
19. IRAQ	
20. MONGOLIA	

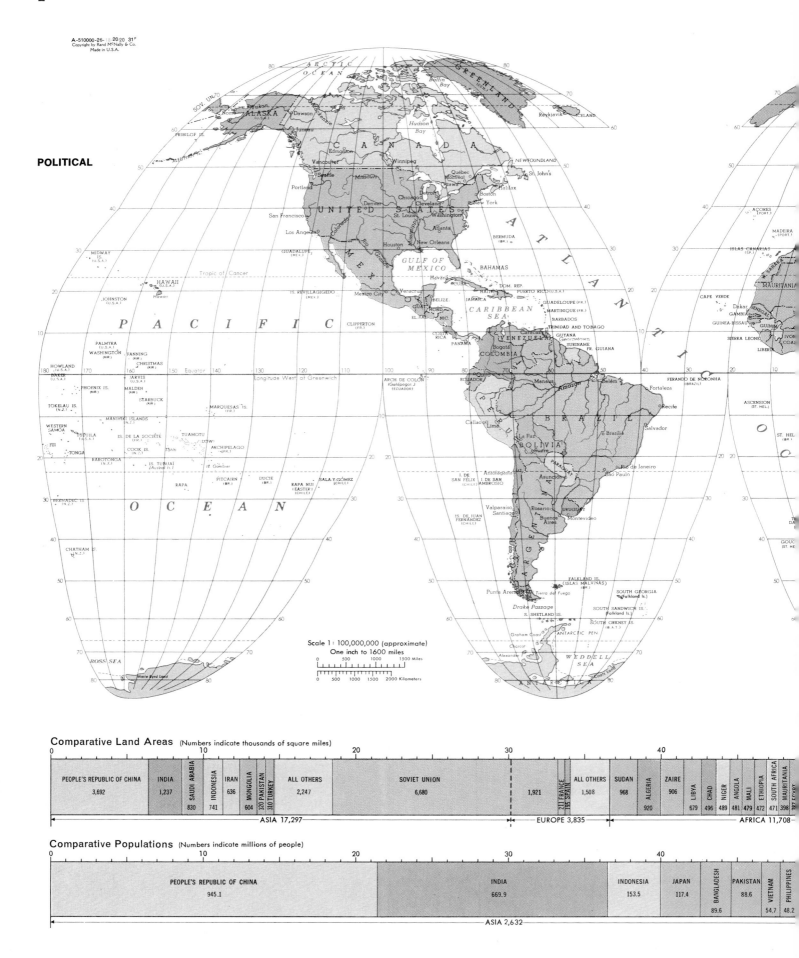

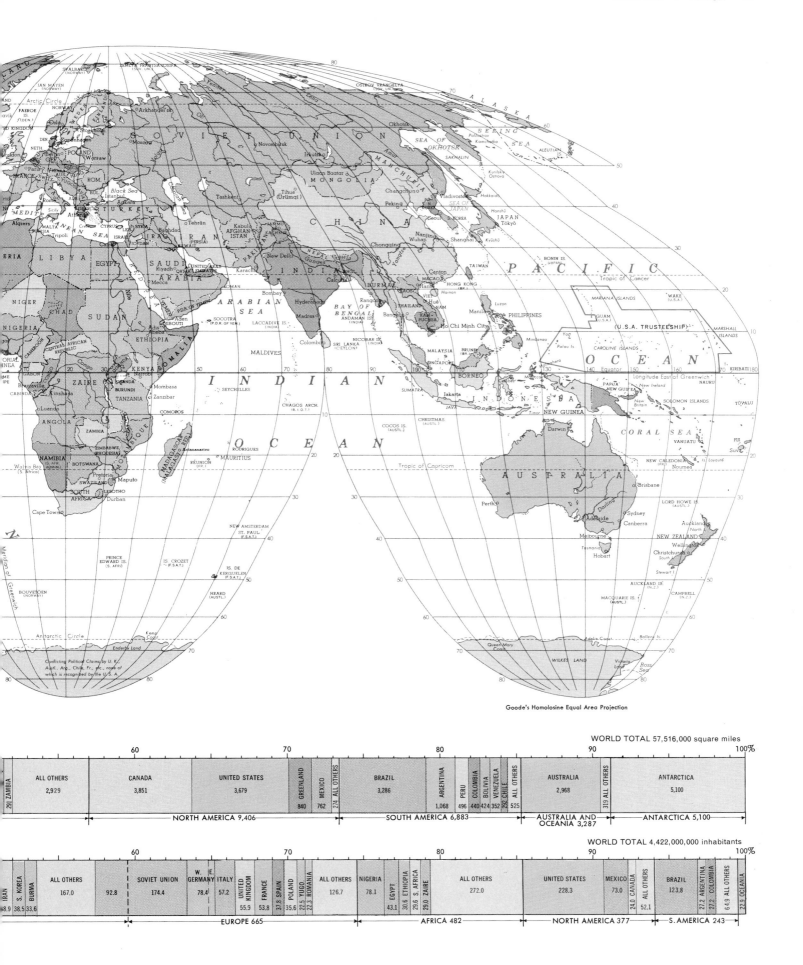

Goode's Homolosine Equal Area Projection

WORLD TOTAL 57,516,000 square miles

	60	70		80		90	100%

| ZAMBIA 291 | ALL OTHERS 2,929 | CANADA 3,851 | UNITED STATES 3,679 | GREENLAND 840 | MEXICO 762 | ALL OTHERS 274 | BRAZIL 3,286 | ARGENTINA 1,068 | PERU 496 | COLOMBIA 440 | BOLIVIA 424 | VENEZUELA 352 | CHILE 292 | ALL OTHERS 525 | AUSTRALIA 2,968 | ALL OTHERS 319 | ANTARCTICA 5,100 |

NORTH AMERICA 9,406 — SOUTH AMERICA 6,883 — AUSTRALIA AND OCEANIA 3,287 — ANTARCTICA 5,100

WORLD TOTAL 4,422,000,000 inhabitants

	60	70		80		90	100%

| IRAN 48.9 | S. KOREA 38.5 | BURMA 33.6 | ALL OTHERS 167.0 | 92.8 | SOVIET UNION 174.4 | W. GERMANY 78.4 | E. ITALY 57.2 | UNITED KINGDOM 55.9 | FRANCE 53.8 | SPAIN 37.8 | POLAND 35.6 | YUGO 22.5 | ROMANIA 22.3 | ALL OTHERS 126.7 | NIGERIA 78.1 | EGYPT 43.1 | ETHIOPIA 30.6 | S. AFRICA 29.6 | ZAIRE 29.0 | ALL OTHERS 272.0 | UNITED STATES 228.3 | MEXICO 73.0 | CANADA 24.0 | ALL OTHERS 52.1 | BRAZIL 123.8 | ARGENTINA 27.2 | COLOMBIA 27.2 | ALL OTHERS 64.9 | OCEANIA 22.9 |

EUROPE 665 — AFRICA 482 — NORTH AMERICA 377 — S. AMERICA 243

A-510000-76 -4-12-19
Copyright by Rand McNally & Co.
Made in U.S.A.

PHYSICAL

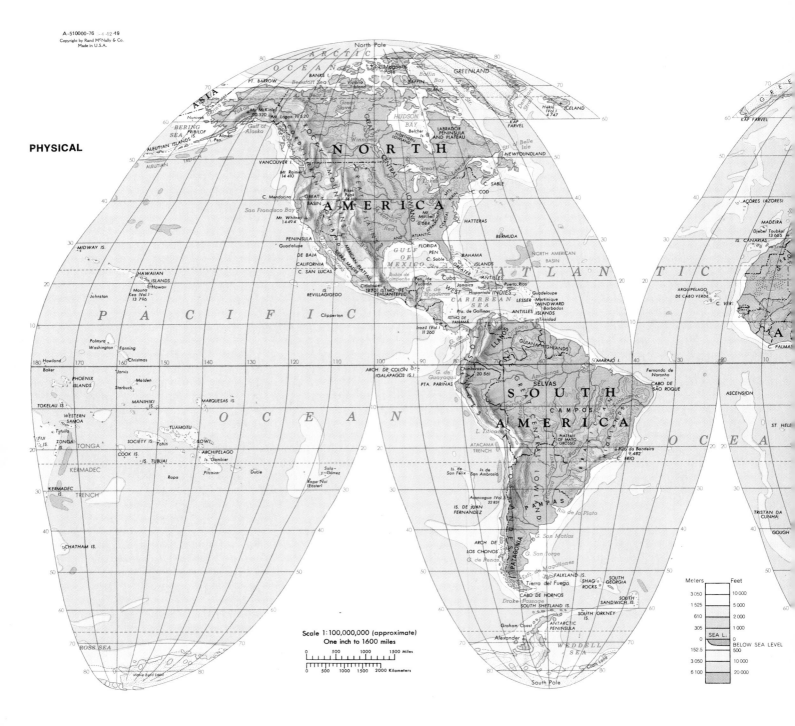

Scale 1:100,000,000 (approximate)
One inch to 1600 miles

Meters	Feet	
3 050	10 000	
1 525	5 000	
610	2 000	
305	1 000	
0 SEA L.	0	
		BELOW SEA LEVEL
152.5	500	
3 050	10 000	
6 100	20 000	

Land Elevations in Profile

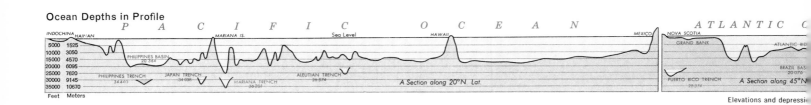

Ocean Depths in Profile

Elevations and depressi

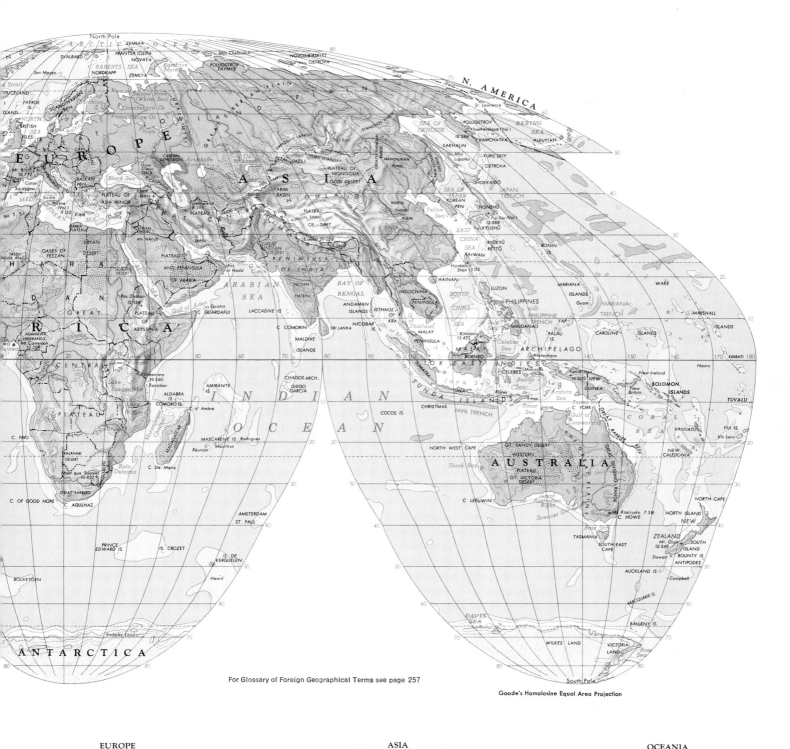

For Glossary of Foreign Geographical Terms see page 257

Goode's Homolosine Equal Area Projection

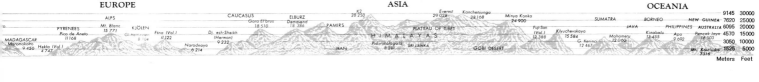

EUROPE   ASIA   OCEANIA

K2	Everest	Kanchenjunga							9145	30000
28 250	29 028	28 168	Minya Konka				NEW GUINEA	7620	25000
24 900			SUMATRA	BORNEO	PHILIPPINES	AUSTRALIA	6095	20000

ALPS   CAUCASUS   ELBURZ

| | | | | | | | | | | | | |
| | | | | | | | | | | | Meters | Feet |

Mt. Blanc 15 771   Gora El'brus 18 510   Demavend 18 386   PAMIRS   PLATEAU OF TIBET   Fuji-San (Vol.) 12 388   JAVA   Kinabalu 13 455   Apo 9 692   Puncak Jaya 4570 15000

PYRENEES   KJÖLEN   HIMALAYAS   Klyuchevskaya 15 584   Mahameru 12 000   3050 10000

Pico de Aneto 11 168   Glittertinnen 8 104   Etna (Vol.) 11 122   Dj. esh-Sheikh (Hermon) 9 232   IRAN   GOBI DESERT   G. Kerinci 12 467   Mt. Kosciusko 7316   1525 5000

MADAGASCAR   Narodnaya 6 214   Pidurutalagala 8 281   SRI LANKA

Maromokotro 9 450   Hekla (Vol.) 4 747

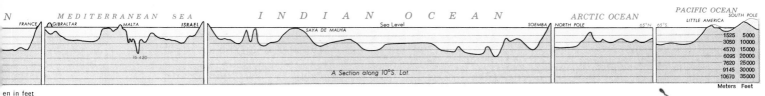

MEDITERRANEAN SEA   INDIAN OCEAN   ARCTIC OCEAN   PACIFIC OCEAN

FRANCE   GIBRALTAR   MALTA   ISRAEL   SAYA DE MALHA   Sea Level   SOEMBA   NORTH POLE   65°N.   65°S.   SOUTH POLE   LITTLE AMERICA

1525	5000
3050	10000
4570	15000
6095	20000
7620	25000
9145	30000
10670	35000

16 420   A Section along 10°S. Lat.   Meters   Feet

en in feet

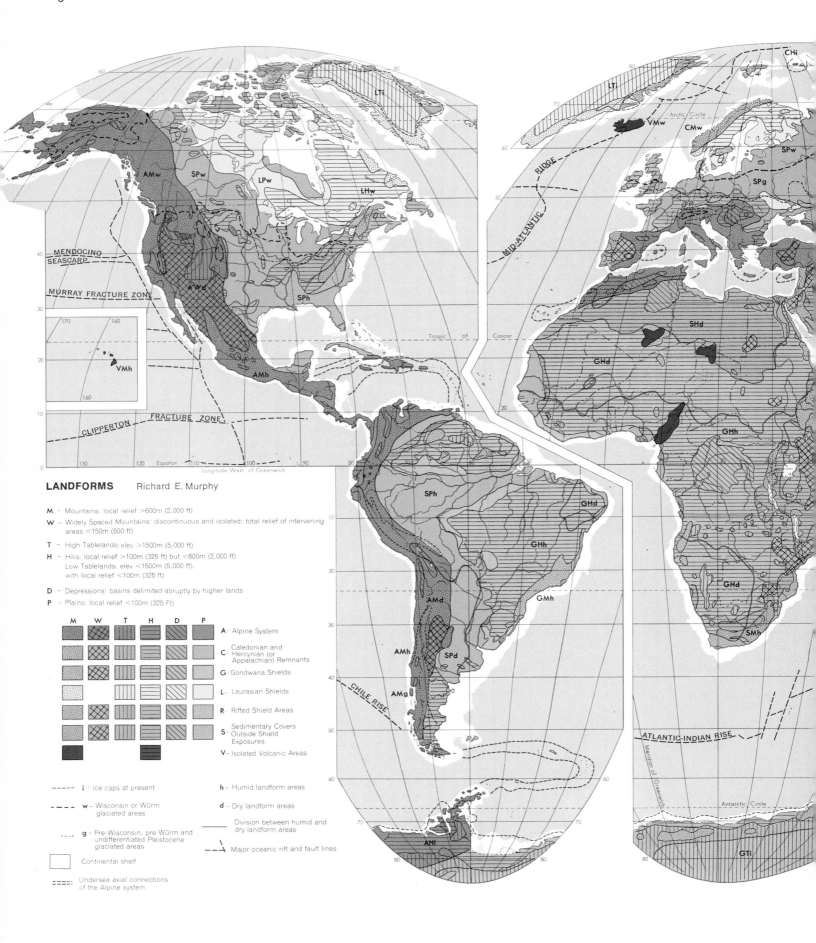

6

LANDFORMS   Richard E. Murphy

M – Mountains: local relief >600m (2,000 ft)

W – Widely Spaced Mountains: discontinuous and isolated; total relief of intervening areas <150m (500 ft)

T – High Tablelands: elev >1500m (5,000 ft)

H – Hills: local relief >100m (325 ft) but <600m (2,000 ft)
Low Tablelands: elev <1500m (5,000 ft), with local relief <100m (325 ft)

D – Depressions: basins delimited abruptly by higher lands

P – Plains: local relief <100m (325 Ft)

M   W   T   H   D   P

A – Alpine System

C – Caledonian and Hercynian (or Appalachian) Remnants

G – Gondwana Shields

L – Laurasian Shields

R – Rifted Shield Areas

S – Sedimentary Covers Outside Shield Exposures

V – Isolated Volcanic Areas

- - - - -   i – Ice caps at present

- - - -   w – Wisconsin or Würm glaciated areas

- - - -   g – Pre-Wisconsin, pre-Würm and undifferentiated Pleistocene glaciated areas

☐   Continental shelf

=====   Undersea axial connections of the Alpine system

h – Humid landform areas

d – Dry landform areas

——   Division between humid and dry landform areas

⌐   Major oceanic rift and fault lines

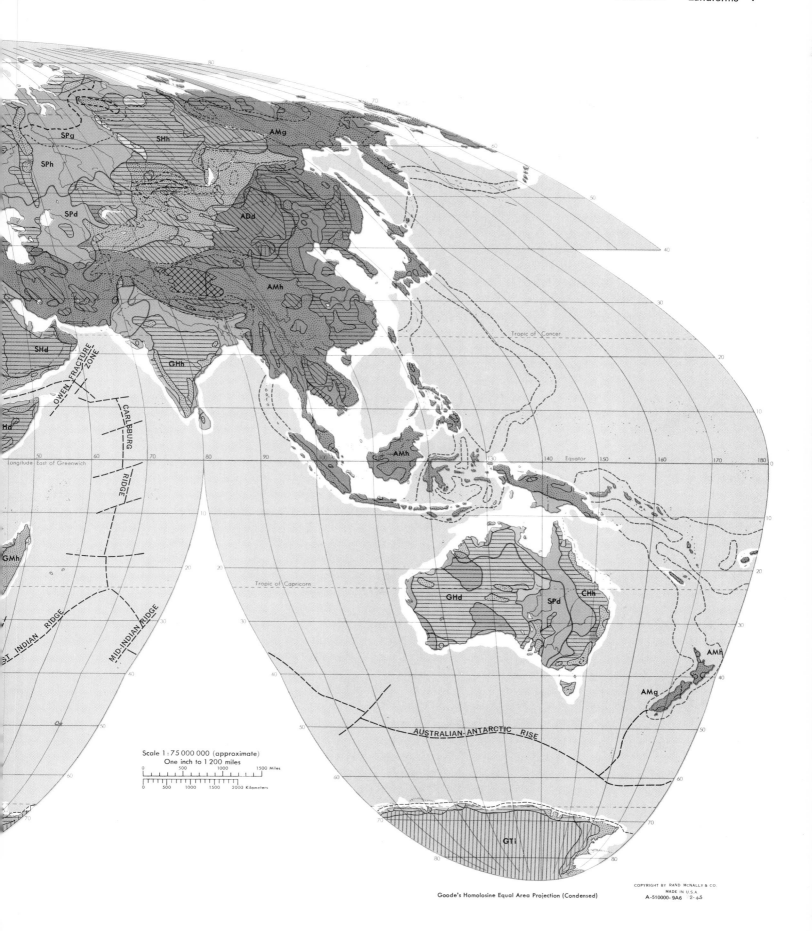

SPg
SPh
SHh
AMg
SPd
ADd
AMh
SHd
GHh
OWEN FRACTURE ZONE
CARLSBURG RIDGE
Hd
Longitude East of Greenwich
AMh
Tropic of Cancer
Equator
GMh
ST INDIAN RIDGE
MID-INDIAN RIDGE
Tropic of Capricorn
GHd
SPd
CHh
AMh
AMg
AUSTRALIAN-ANTARCTIC RISE
GTi

Scale 1:75 000 000 (approximate)
One inch to 1 200 miles

0   500   1000   1500 Miles

0   500   1000   1500   2000 Kilometers

Goode's Homolosine Equal Area Projection (Condensed)

8

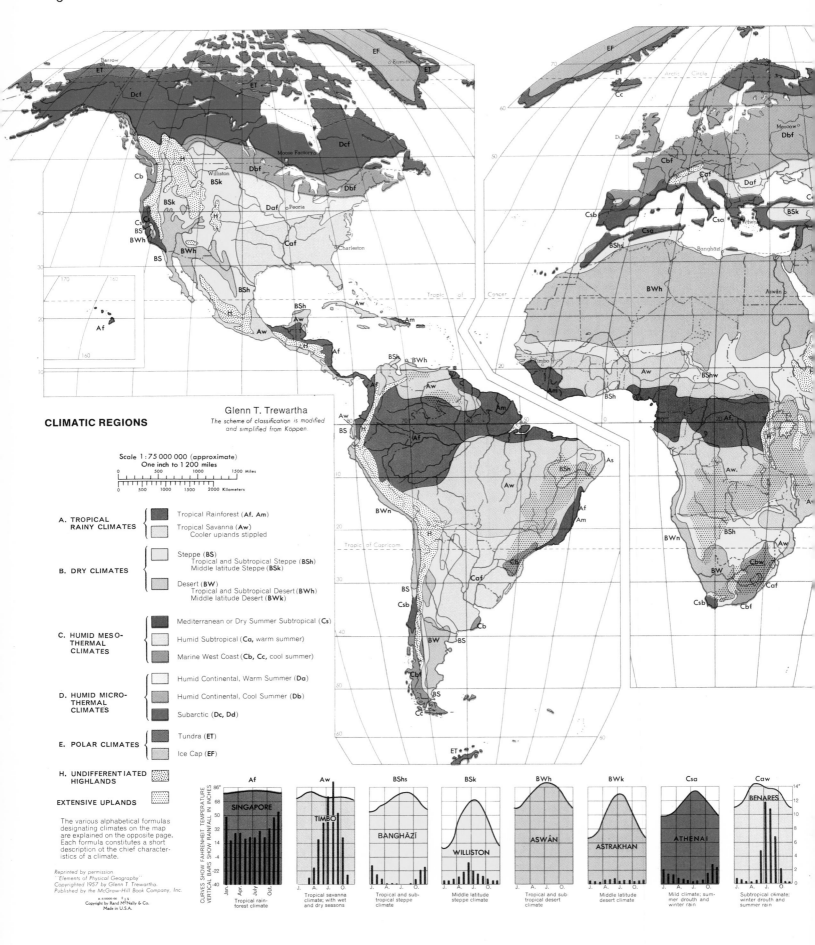

CLIMATIC REGIONS

Glenn T. Trewartha
The scheme of classification is modified and simplified from Köppen

Scale 1:75 000 000 (approximate)
One inch to 1 200 miles

A. TROPICAL RAINY CLIMATES	Tropical Rainforest (**Af, Am**)
	Tropical Savanna (**Aw**) Cooler uplands stippled
B. DRY CLIMATES	Steppe (**BS**) Tropical and Subtropical Steppe (**BSh**) Middle latitude Steppe (**BSk**)
	Desert (**BW**) Tropical and Subtropical Desert (**BWh**) Middle latitude Desert (**BWk**)
C. HUMID MESO-THERMAL CLIMATES	Mediterranean or Dry Summer Subtropical (**Cs**)
	Humid Subtropical (**Ca**, warm summer)
	Marine West Coast (**Cb, Cc,** cool summer)
D. HUMID MICRO-THERMAL CLIMATES	Humid Continental, Warm Summer (**Da**)
	Humid Continental, Cool Summer (**Db**)
	Subarctic (**Dc, Dd**)
E. POLAR CLIMATES	Tundra (**ET**)
	Ice Cap (**EF**)
H. UNDIFFERENTIATED HIGHLANDS	
EXTENSIVE UPLANDS	

The various alphabetical formulas designating climates on the map are explained on the opposite page. Each formula constitutes a short description of the chief character-istics of a climate.

CURVES SHOW FAHRENHEIT TEMPERATURE
VERTICAL BARS SHOW RAINFALL IN INCHES

Af — SINGAPORE — Tropical rain-forest climate

Aw — TIMBO — Tropical savanna climate; with wet and dry seasons

BShs — BANGHAZI — Tropical and sub-tropical steppe climate

BSk — WILLISTON — Middle latitude steppe climate

BWh — ASWÂN — Tropical and sub-tropical desert climate

BWk — ASTRAKHAN — Middle latitude desert climate

Csa — ATHENAI — Mild climate; summer drouth and winter rain

Caw — BENARES — Subtropical climate; winter drouth and summer rain

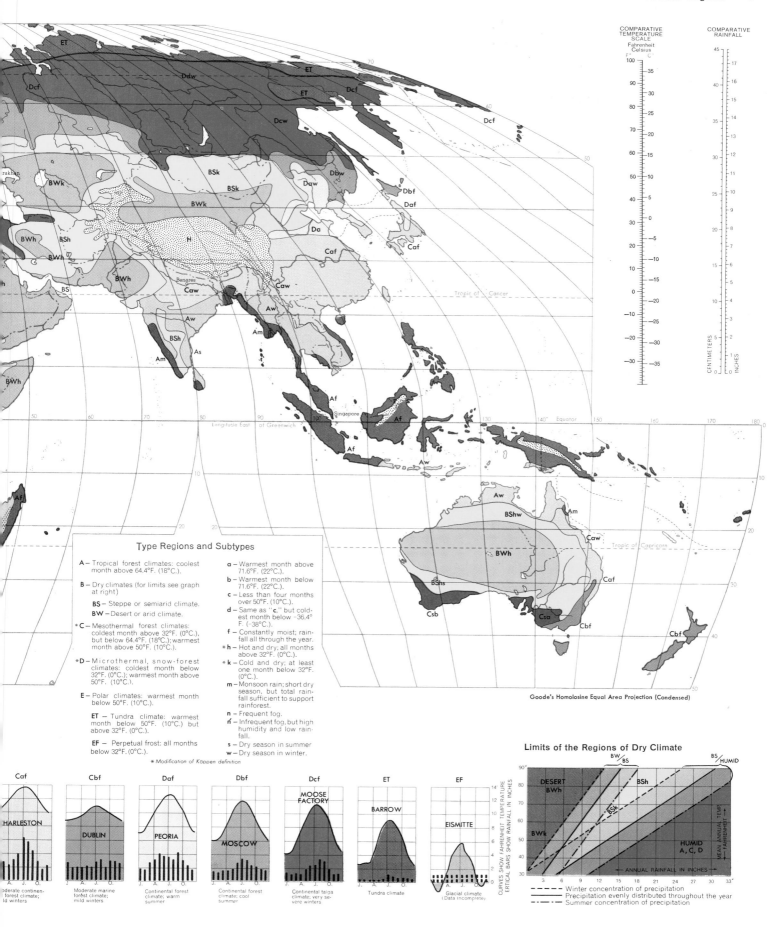

COMPARATIVE
TEMPERATURE
SCALE
Fahrenheit
Celsius

COMPARATIVE
RAINFALL

Goode's Homolosine Equal Area Projection (Condensed)

Type Regions and Subtypes

A – Tropical forest climates: coolest month above 64.4°F. (18°C.).

B – Dry climates (for limits see graph at right)

   BS – Steppe or semiarid climate.

   BW – Desert or arid climate.

*__**C**__ – Mesothermal forest climates: coldest month above 32°F. (0°C.), but below 64.4°F. (18°C.); warmest month above 50°F. (10°C.).

*__**D**__ – Microthermal, snow-forest climates: coldest month below 32°F. (0°C.); warmest month above 50°F. (10°C.).

E – Polar climates: warmest month below 50°F. (10°C.).

   ET – Tundra climate: warmest month below 50°F. (10°C.) but above 32°F. (0°C.).

   EF – Perpetual frost: all months below 32°F. (0°C.).

   Modification of Köppen definition

a – Warmest month above 71.6°F. (22°C.).

b – Warmest month below 71.6°F. (22°C.).

c – Less than four months over 50°F. (10°C.).

d – Same as "c," but coldest month below –36.4° F. (–38°C.).

f – Constantly moist; rainfall all through the year.

*__**h**__ – Hot and dry; all months above 32°F. (0°C.).

*__**k**__ – Cold and dry; at least one month below 32°F. (0°C.).

m – Monsoon rain; short dry season, but total rainfall sufficient to support rainforest.

n – Frequent fog.

n' – Infrequent fog, but high humidity and low rainfall.

s – Dry season in summer

w – Dry season in winter

Limits of the Regions of Dry Climate

– – – Winter concentration of precipitation
——— Precipitation evenly distributed throughout the year
–·–·– Summer concentration of precipitation

Caf
HARLESTON
Moderate continen-
tal forest climate;
mild winters

Cbf
DUBLIN
Moderate marine
forest climate;
mild winters

Daf
PEORIA
Continental forest
climate; warm
summer

Dbf
MOSCOW
Continental forest
climate; cool
summer

Dcf
MOOSE
FACTORY
Continental taiga
climate; very se-
vere winters

ET
BARROW
Tundra climate

EF
EISMITTE
Glacial climate
(Data incomplete)

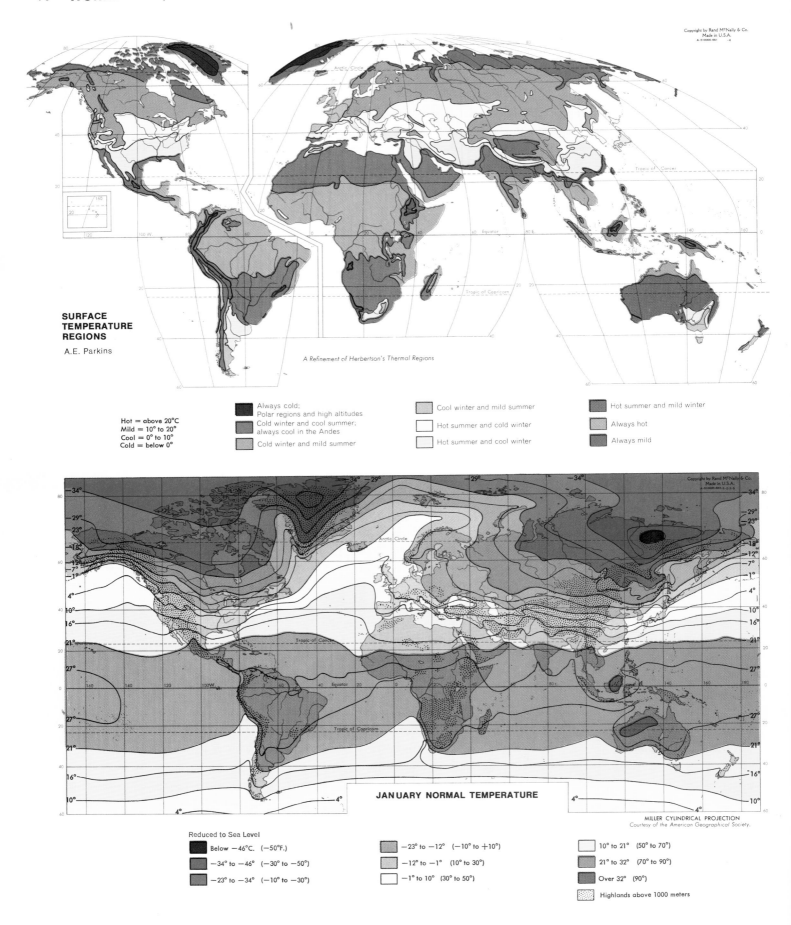

SURFACE TEMPERATURE REGIONS

A.E. Parkins

A Refinement of Herbertson's Thermal Regions

Hot = above 20°C
Mild = 10° to 20°
Cool = 0° to 10°
Cold = below 0°

Always cold;
Polar regions and high altitudes

Cold winter and cool summer;
always cool in the Andes

Cold winter and mild summer

Cool winter and mild summer

Hot summer and cold winter

Hot summer and cool winter

Hot summer and mild winter

Always hot

Always mild

JANUARY NORMAL TEMPERATURE

MILLER CYLINDRICAL PROJECTION
Courtesy of the American Geographical Society.

Reduced to Sea Level

Below −46°C. (−50°F.)

−34° to −46° (−30° to −50°)

−23° to −34° (−10° to −30°)

−23° to −12° (−10° to +10°)

−12° to −1° (10° to 30°)

−1° to 10° (30° to 50°)

10° to 21° (50° to 70°)

21° to 32° (70° to 90°)

Over 32° (90°)

Highlands above 1000 meters

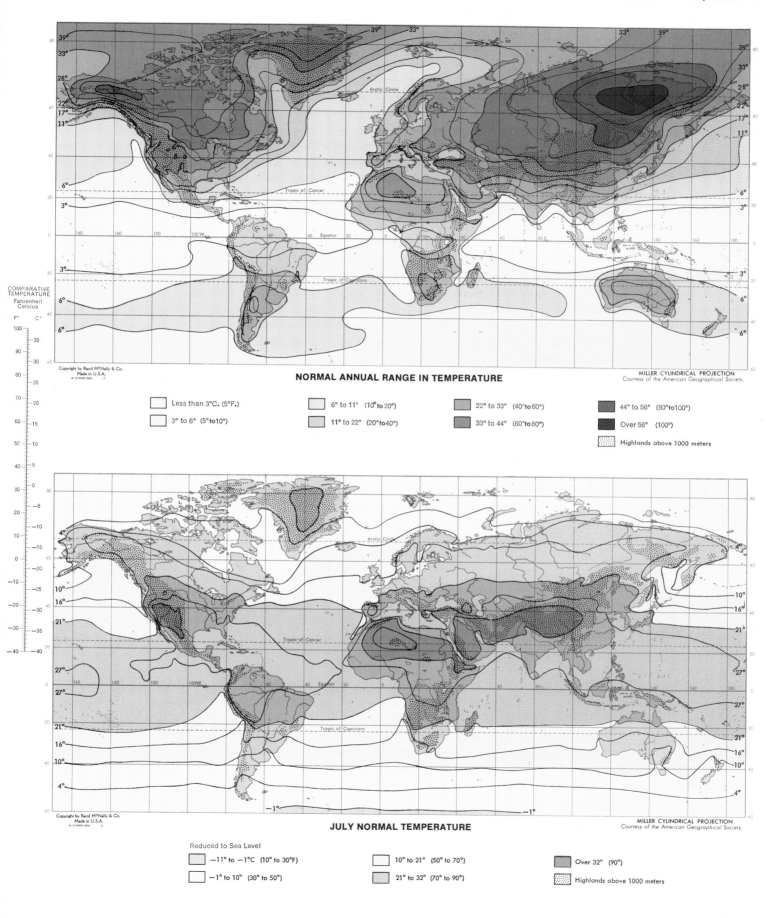

NORMAL ANNUAL RANGE IN TEMPERATURE

MILLER CYLINDRICAL PROJECTION
Courtesy of the American Geographical Society.

Copyright by Rand McNally & Co.
Made in U.S.A.
A-510000-662- -5

COMPARATIVE
TEMPERATURE
Fahrenheit
Celsius

| | Less than 3°C. (5°F.) | | 6° to 11° (10° to 20°) | | 22° to 33° (40° to 60°) | | 44° to 56° (80° to 100°) |

| | 3° to 6° (5° to 10°) | | 11° to 22° (20° to 40°) | | 33° to 44° (60° to 80°) | | Over 56° (100°) |

Highlands above 1000 meters

JULY NORMAL TEMPERATURE

MILLER CYLINDRICAL PROJECTION
Courtesy of the American Geographical Society.

Copyright by Rand McNally & Co.
Made in U.S.A.
A-510000-664- -5

Reduced to Sea Level

| | −11° to −1°C (10° to 30°F) | | 10° to 21° (50° to 70°) | | Over 32° (90°) |

| | −1° to 10° (30° to 50°) | | 21° to 32° (70° to 90°) | | Highlands above 1000 meters |

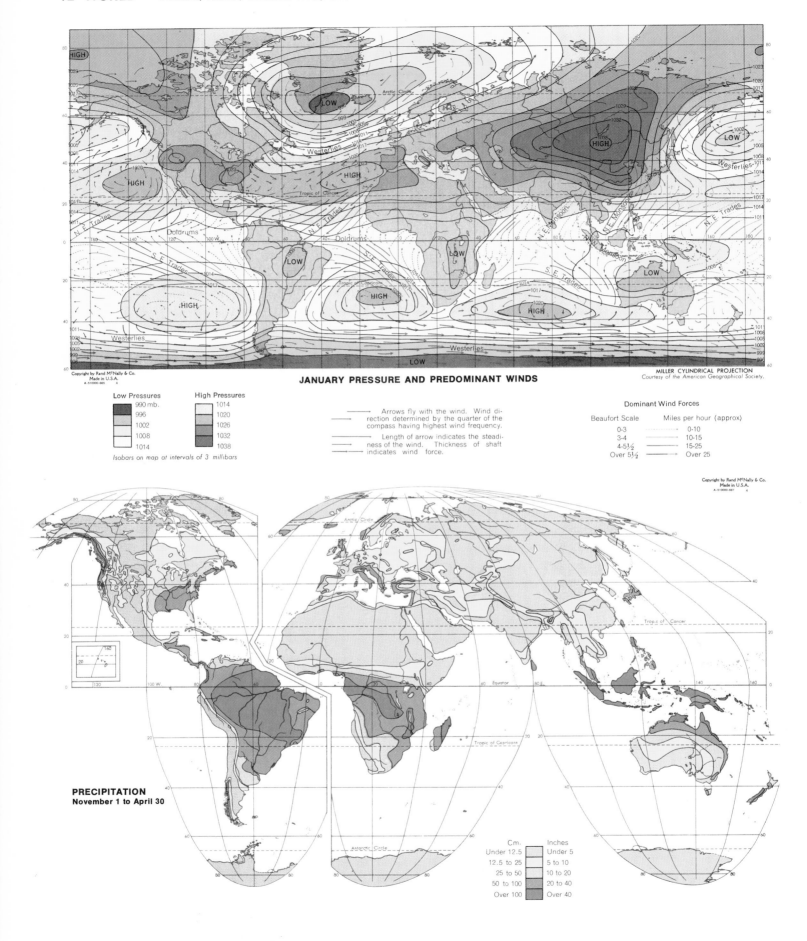

JANUARY PRESSURE AND PREDOMINANT WINDS

MILLER CYLINDRICAL PROJECTION
Courtesy of the American Geographical Society.

Copyright by Rand McNally & Co.
Made in U.S.A.
A-510000-665   4

Low Pressures	High Pressures
990 mb.	1014
996	1020
1002	1026
1008	1032
1014	1038

Isobars on map at intervals of 3 millibars

Arrows fly with the wind. Wind direction determined by the quarter of the compass having highest wind frequency.

Length of arrow indicates the steadiness of the wind. Thickness of shaft indicates wind force.

Dominant Wind Forces

Beaufort Scale	Miles per hour (approx)
0-3	0-10
3-4	10-15
4-5½	15-25
Over 5½	Over 25

Copyright by Rand McNally & Co.
Made in U.S.A.
A-510000-667   4

PRECIPITATION
November 1 to April 30

Cm.	Inches
Under 12.5	Under 5
12.5 to 25	5 to 10
25 to 50	10 to 20
50 to 100	20 to 40
Over 100	Over 40

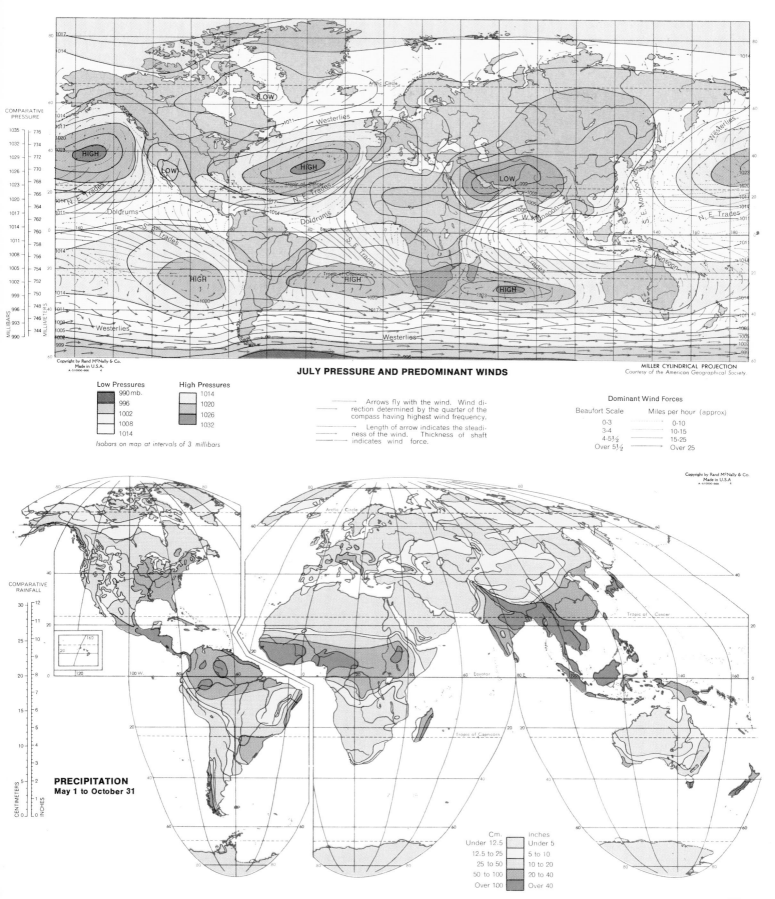

JULY PRESSURE AND PREDOMINANT WINDS

MILLER CYLINDRICAL PROJECTION
Courtesy of the American Geographical Society.

COMPARATIVE PRESSURE

MILLIBARS	MILLIMETERS
1035	776
1032	774
1029	772
1026	770
1023	768
1020	766
1017	764
1014	762
1011	760
1008	758
1005	754
1002	752
999	750
996	748
993	746
990	744

Copyright by Rand McNally & Co.
Made in U.S.A.
A-510000-666   4

Low Pressures
990 mb.
996
1002
1008
1014

High Pressures
1014
1020
1026
1032

Isobars on map at intervals of 3 millibars

Arrows fly with the wind. Wind direction determined by the quarter of the compass having highest wind frequency.

Length of arrow indicates the steadiness of the wind. Thickness of shaft indicates wind force.

Dominant Wind Forces

Beaufort Scale	Miles per hour (approx)
0-3	0-10
3-4	10-15
4-5½	15-25
Over 5½	Over 25

COMPARATIVE RAINFALL

CENTIMETERS	INCHES
30	12
	11
	10
25	9
20	8
	7
15	6
	5
10	4
	3
5	2
	1
0	0

Copyright by Rand McNally & Co.
Made in U.S.A
A-510000-668   4

PRECIPITATION
May 1 to October 31

Cm.	Inches
Under 12.5	Under 5
12.5 to 25	5 to 10
25 to 50	10 to 20
50 to 100	20 to 40
Over 100	Over 40

**ANNUAL
PRECIPITATION
AND OCEAN
CURRENTS**

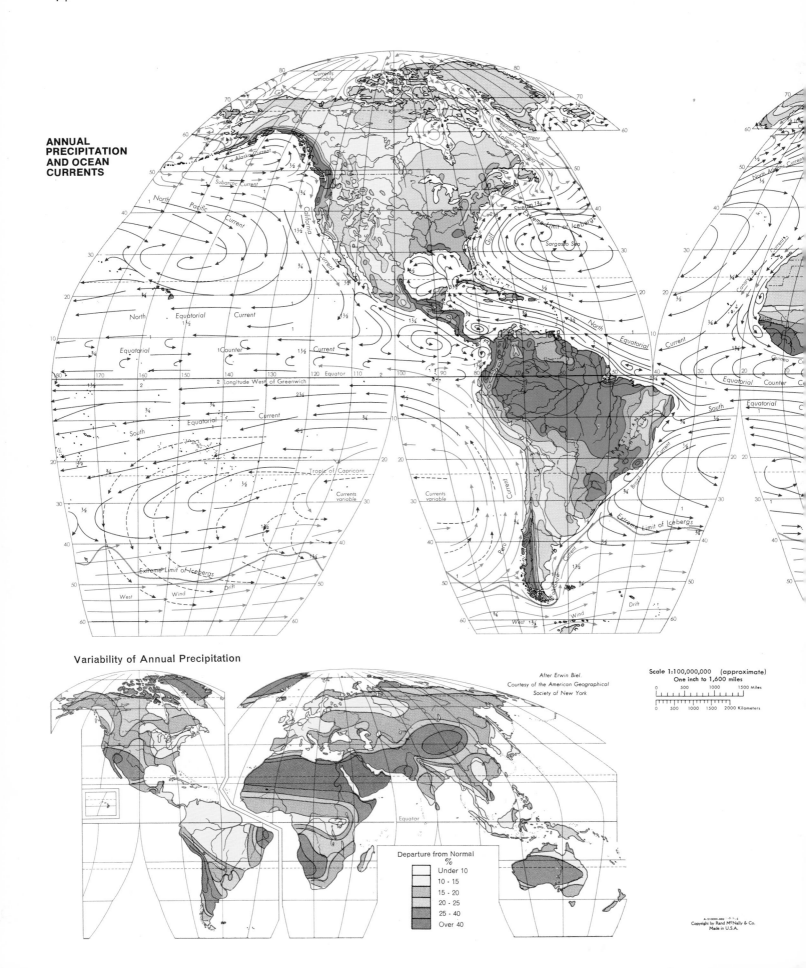

Variability of Annual Precipitation

After Erwin Biel.
Courtesy of the American Geographical
Society of New York

Scale 1:100,000,000 (approximate)
One inch to 1,600 miles

0   500   1000   1500 Miles

0   500   1000   1500   2000 Kilometers

Departure from Normal
%
Under 10
10 - 15
15 - 20
20 - 25
25 - 40
Over 40

A-510000-680 -3 7-4
Copyright by Rand McNally & Co.
Made in U.S.A.

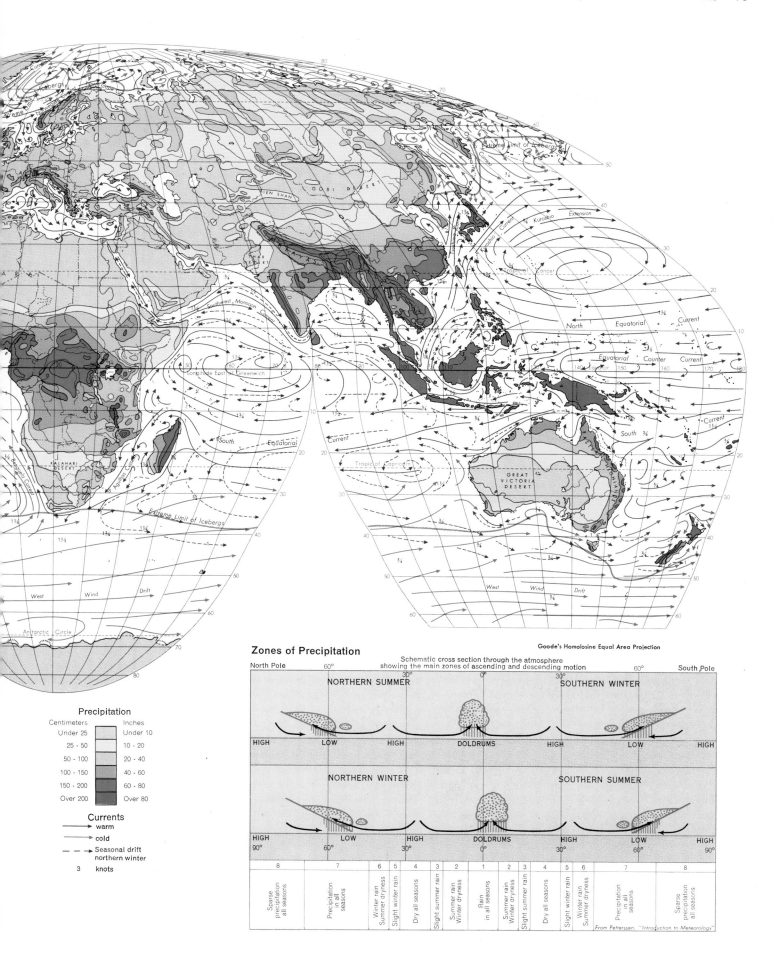

Precipitation

Centimeters		Inches
Under 25		Under 10
25 - 50		10 - 20
50 - 100		20 - 40
100 - 150		40 - 60
150 - 200		60 - 80
Over 200		Over 80

Currents

→ warm
→ cold
‑‑→ Seasonal drift
     northern winter
3   knots

Goode's Homolosine Equal Area Projection

Zones of Precipitation

Schematic cross section through the atmosphere
showing the main zones of ascending and descending motion

North Pole   60°   30°   0°   30°   60°   South Pole

NORTHERN SUMMER   SOUTHERN WINTER

HIGH   LOW   HIGH   DOLDRUMS   HIGH   LOW   HIGH

NORTHERN WINTER   SOUTHERN SUMMER

HIGH   LOW   HIGH   DOLDRUMS   HIGH   LOW   HIGH
90°   60°   30°   0°   30°   60°   90°

8	7	6	5	4	3	2	1	2	3	4	5	6	7	8
Sparse precipitation all seasons	Precipitation in all seasons	Winter rain Summer dryness	Slight winter rain	Dry all seasons	Slight summer rain	Summer rain Winter dryness	Rain in all seasons	Summer rain Winter dryness	Slight summer rain	Dry all seasons	Slight winter rain	Winter rain Summer dryness	Precipitation in all seasons	Sparse precipitation all seasons

From Petterssen, "Introduction to Meteorology"

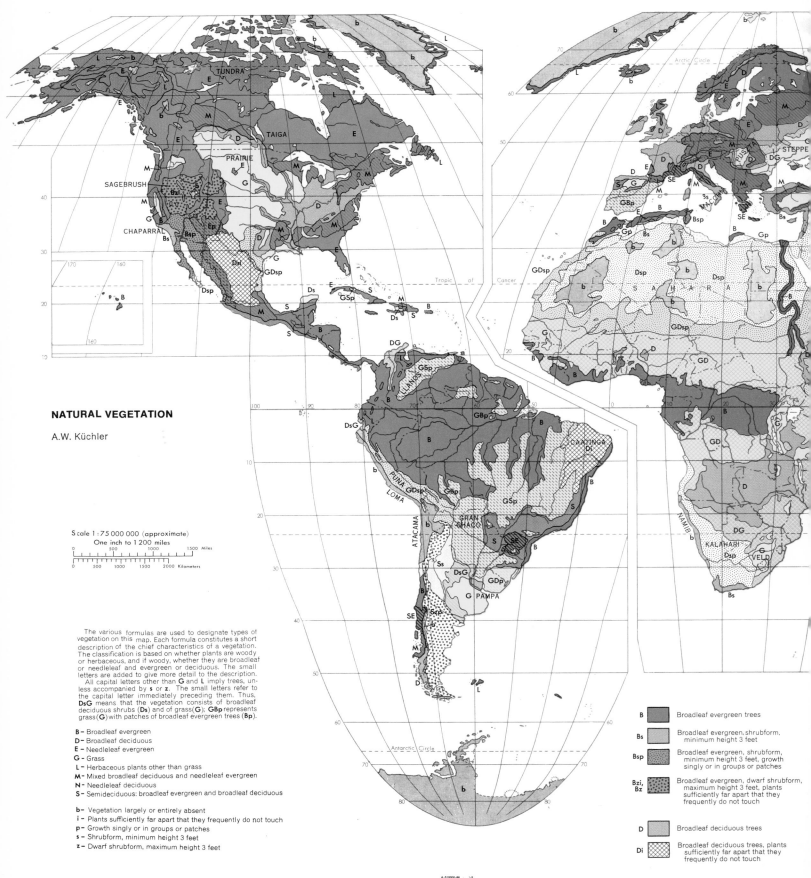

NATURAL VEGETATION

A.W. Küchler

Scale 1 : 75 000 000 (approximate)
One inch to 1 200 miles

```
0    500    1000    1500  Miles
0  500  1000  1500  2000  Kilometers
```

The various formulas are used to designate types of vegetation on this map. Each formula constitutes a short description of the chief characteristics of a vegetation. The classification is based on whether plants are woody or herbaceous, and if woody, whether they are broadleaf or needleleaf and evergreen or deciduous. The small letters are added to give more detail to the description.

All capital letters other than **G** and **L** imply trees, unless accompanied by **s** or **z**. The small letters refer to the capital letter immediately preceding them. Thus, **DsG** means that the vegetation consists of broadleaf deciduous shrubs (**Ds**) and of grass (**G**); **GBp** represents grass (**G**) with patches of broadleaf evergreen trees (**Bp**).

B – Broadleaf evergreen
D – Broadleaf deciduous
E – Needleleaf evergreen
G – Grass
L – Herbaceous plants other than grass
M – Mixed broadleaf deciduous and needleleaf evergreen
N – Needleleaf deciduous
S – Semideciduous: broadleaf evergreen and broadleaf deciduous

b – Vegetation largely or entirely absent
i – Plants sufficiently far apart that they frequently do not touch
p – Growth singly or in groups or patches
s – Shrubform, minimum height 3 feet
z – Dwarf shrubform, maximum height 3 feet

B	Broadleaf evergreen trees
Bs	Broadleaf evergreen, shrubform, minimum height 3 feet
Bsp	Broadleaf evergreen, shrubform, minimum height 3 feet, growth singly or in groups or patches
Bzi, Bz	Broadleaf evergreen, dwarf shrubform, maximum height 3 feet, plants sufficiently far apart that they frequently do not touch
D	Broadleaf deciduous trees
Di	Broadleaf deciduous trees, plants sufficiently far apart that they frequently do not touch

Goode's Homolosine
Equal Area Projection
(Condensed)

		Broadleaf deciduous, shrubform, minimum height 3 feet
		Broadleaf deciduous, shrubform, minimum height 3 feet, plants sufficiently far apart that they frequently do not touch
		Broadleaf deciduous, shrubform, minimum height 3 feet, growth singly or in groups or patches
		Broadleaf deciduous, dwarf shrubform, maximum height 3 feet, growth singly or in groups or patches
		Broadleaf deciduous, shrubform, minimum height 3 feet / Grass and other herbaceous plants
		Broadleaf deciduous trees / Grass and other herbaceous plants
		Broadleaf deciduous trees / Broadleaf evergreen, shrubform, minimum height 3 feet

E		Needleleaf evergreen trees
Ep		Needleleaf evergreen trees, growth singly or in groups or patches
G		Grass and other herbaceous plants
Gp		Grass and other herbaceous plants, growth singly or in groups or patches
GBp		Grass and other herbaceous plants / Broadleaf evergreen trees, growth singly or in groups or patches
GD		Grass and other herbaceous plants / Broadleaf deciduous trees
GDp		Grass and other herbaceous plants / Broadleaf deciduous trees, growth singly or in groups or patches

GDsp		Grass and other herbaceous plants / Broadleaf deciduous, shrubform, minimum height 3 feet, growth singly or in groups or patches
GSp		Grass and other herbaceous plants / Semideciduous: broadleaf evergreen and broadleaf deciduous trees, growth singly or in groups or patches
L		Herbaceous plants other than grass
M		Mixed: broadleaf deciduous and needleleaf evergreen trees
N		Needleleaf deciduous trees
ND		Needleleaf deciduous trees / Broadleaf deciduous trees

S		Semideciduous: broadleaf evergreen and broadleaf deciduous trees
Ss		Sem-deciduous: broadleaf evergreen and broadleaf deciduous, shrubform, minimum height 3 feet
SsG		Semideciduous: broadleaf evergreen and broadleaf deciduous, shrubform, minimum height 3 feet / Grass and other herbaceous plants
Szp		Semideciduous: broadleaf evergreen and broadleaf deciduous, dwarf shrubform, maximum height 3 feet, growth singly or in groups or patches
SE		Semideciduous: broadleaf evergreen and broadleaf deciduous trees / Needleleaf evergreen trees
b		Vegetation largely or entirely absent

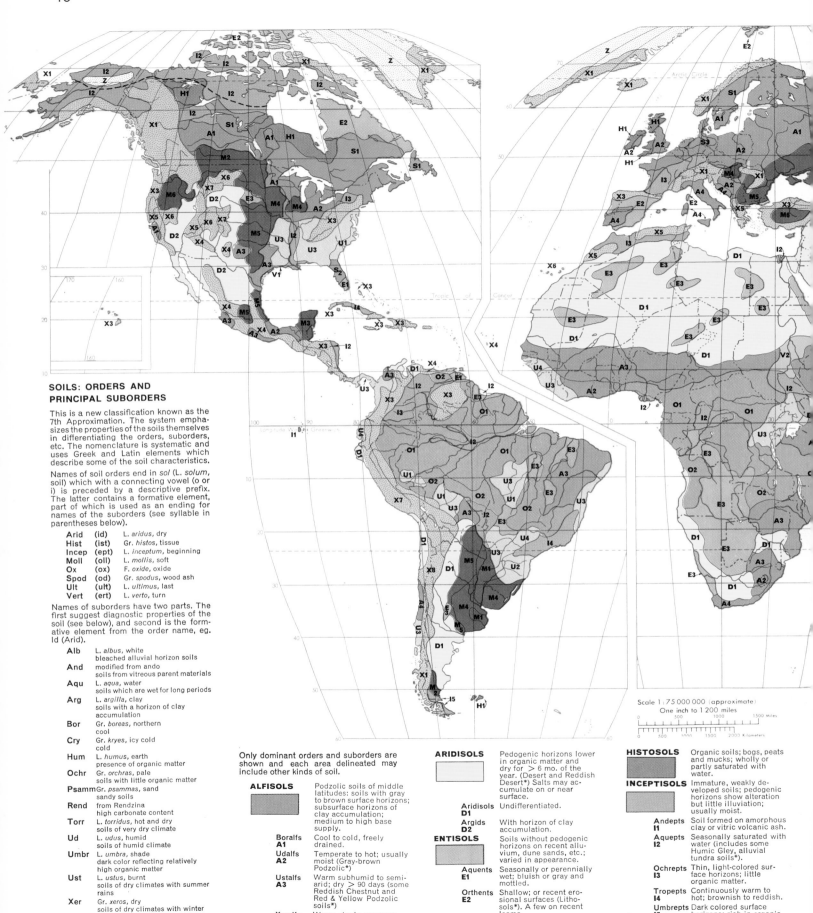

18

SOILS: ORDERS AND PRINCIPAL SUBORDERS

This is a new classification known as the 7th Approximation. The system emphasizes the properties of the soils themselves in differentiating the orders, suborders, etc. The nomenclature is systematic and uses Greek and Latin elements which describe some of the soil characteristics.

Names of soil orders end in *sol* (L. *solum*, soil) which with a connecting vowel (o or i) is preceded by a descriptive prefix. The latter contains a formative element, part of which is used as an ending for names of the suborders (see syllable in parentheses below).

Arid	(id)	L. *aridus*, dry
Hist	(ist)	Gr. *histos*, tissue
Incep	(ept)	L. *inceptum*, beginning
Moll	(oll)	L. *mollis*, soft
Ox	(ox)	F. *oxide*, oxide
Spod	(od)	Gr. *spodus*, wood ash
Ult	(ult)	L. *ultimus*, last
Vert	(ert)	L. *verto*, turn

Names of suborders have two parts. The first suggest diagnostic properties of the soil (see below), and second is the formative element from the order name, eg. Id (Arid).

Alb	L. *albus*, white bleached alluvial horizon soils
And	modified from ando soils from vitreous parent materials
Aqu	L. *aqua*, water soils which are wet for long periods
Arg	L. *argilla*, clay soils with a horizon of clay accumulation
Bor	Gr. *boreas*, northern cool
Cry	Gr. *kryes*, icy cold cold
Hum	L. *humus*, earth presence of organic matter
Ochr	Gr. *orchras*, pale soils with little organic matter
Psamm	Gr. *psammas*, sand sandy soils
Rend	from Rendzina high carbonate content
Torr	L. *torridus*, hot and dry soils of very dry climate
Ud	L. *udus*, humid soils of humid climate
Umbr	L. *umbra*, shade dark color reflecting relatively high organic matter
Ust	L. *ustus*, burnt soils of dry climates with summer rains
Xer	Gr. *xeros*, dry soils of dry climates with winter rains

Only dominant orders and suborders are shown and each area delineated may include other kinds of soil.

ALFISOLS
Podzolic soils of middle latitudes: soils with gray to brown surface horizons; subsurface horizons of clay accumulation; medium to high base supply.

Boralfs A1	Cool to cold, freely drained.
Udalfs A2	Temperate to hot; usually moist (Gray-brown Podzolic*)
Ustalfs A3	Warm subhumid to semi-arid; dry > 90 days (some Reddish Chestnut and Red & Yellow Podzolic soils*)
Xeralfs A4	Warm, dry in summer; moist in winter.

ARIDISOLS
Pedogenic horizons lower in organic matter and dry for > 6 mo. of the year. (Desert and Reddish Desert*) Salts may accumulate on or near surface.

Aridisols D1	Undifferentiated.
Argids D2	With horizon of clay accumulation.

ENTISOLS
Soils without pedogenic horizons on recent alluvium, dune sands, etc.; varied in appearance.

Aquents E1	Seasonally or perennially wet; bluish or gray and mottled.
Orthents E2	Shallow; or recent erosional surfaces (Lithosols*). A few on recent loams.
Psamments E3	Sandy soils on shifting and stabilized sands.

HISTOSOLS
Organic soils; bogs, peats and mucks; wholly or partly saturated with water.

INCEPTISOLS
Immature, weakly developed soils; pedogenic horizons show alteration but little illuviation; usually moist.

Andepts I1	Soil formed on amorphous clay or vitric volcanic ash.
Aquepts I2	Seasonally saturated with water (includes some Humic Gley, alluvial tundra soils*).
Ochrepts I3	Thin, light-colored surface horizons; little organic matter.
Tropepts I4	Continuously warm to hot; brownish to reddish.
Umbrepts I5	Dark colored surface horizons; rich in organic matter; medium to low base supply.

Scale 1 : 75 000 000 (approximate)
One inch to 1 200 miles

Goode's Homolosine Equal Area Projection (Condensed)

Copyright by Rand McNally & Co.
Made in U.S.A.
A-510000-761= -2-2-2

- - - - - Limit of continuous permafrost

*Terms refer to Great Soils Group terminology.

MOLLISOLS Soils of the steppe (incl. Chernozem and Chestnut soils*). Thick, black organic rich surface horizons and high base supply.

Albolls **M1** Seasonally saturated with water; light gray subsurface horizon.

Borolls **M2** Cool or cold (incl. some Chernozem, Chestnut and Brown soils*).

Rendolls **M3** Formed on highly calcareous parent materials (Rendzina*).

Udolls **M4** Temperate to warm; usually moist (Prairie soils*).

Ustolls **M5** Temperate to hot; dry for > 90 days (incl. some Chestnut and Brown soils*).

Xerolls **M6** Cool to warm; dry in summer; moist in winter.

OXISOLS Deeply weathered tropical and subtropical soils (Laterites*); rich in sesquioxides of iron and aluminum; low in nutrients; limited productivity without fertilizer.

Orthox **O1** Hot and nearly always moist.

Ustox **O2** Warm or hot; dry for long periods but moist > 90 consecutive days.

SPODOSOLS Soils with a subsurface accumulation of amorphous materials overlaid by a light colored, leached sandy horizon.

Spodosols **S1** Undifferentiated (mostly high latitudes).

Aquods **S2** Seasonally saturated with water; sandy parent materials.

Humods **S3** Considerable accumulations of organic matter in subsurface horizon.

Orthods **S4** With subsurface accumulations of iron, aluminum and organic matter (Podzols*).

ULTISOLS Soils with some subsurface clay accumulation; low base supply; usually moist and low in inorganic matter; usually moist and low in organic matter; can be productive with fertilization.

Aquults **U1** Seasonally saturated with water; subsurface gray or mottled horizon.

Humults **U2** High in organic matter; dark colored; moist, warm to temperate all year.

Udults **U3** Low in organic matter; moist, temperate to hot (Red-Yellow Podzolic; some Reddish-Brown Lateritic soils*).

Ustults **U4** Warm to hot; dry > 90 days.

VERTISOLS Soils with high content of swelling clays; deep, wide cracks in dry periods dark colored.

Uderts **V1** Usually moist; cracks open < 90 days.

Usterts **V2** Cracks open > 90 days; difficult to till (Black tropical soils*).

MOUNTAIN SOILS Soils with various moisture and temperature regimes; steep slopes and variable relief and elevation; soils vary greatly within short distance.

X1 Cryic great groups of Entisols, Inceptisols and Spodosols.

X2 Boralfs and Cryic groups of Entisols and Inceptisols.

X3 Udic great groups of Alfisols, Entisols and Ultisols; Inceptisols.

X4 Ustic great groups of Alfisols, Entisols, Inceptisols, Mollisols and Ultisols.

X5 Xeric great groups of Alfisols, Entisols, Inceptisols, Mollisols and Ultisols.

X6 Torric great groups of Entisols; Aridisols.

X7 Ustic and cryic great groups of Alfisols, Entisols; Inceptisols and Mollisols; ustic great groups of Ultisols; cryic great groups of Spodosols.

X8 Aridisols; torric and cryic great groups of Entisols, and cryic great groups of Spodosols and Inceptisols.

Z Areas with little or no soil; icefields, and rugged mountain.

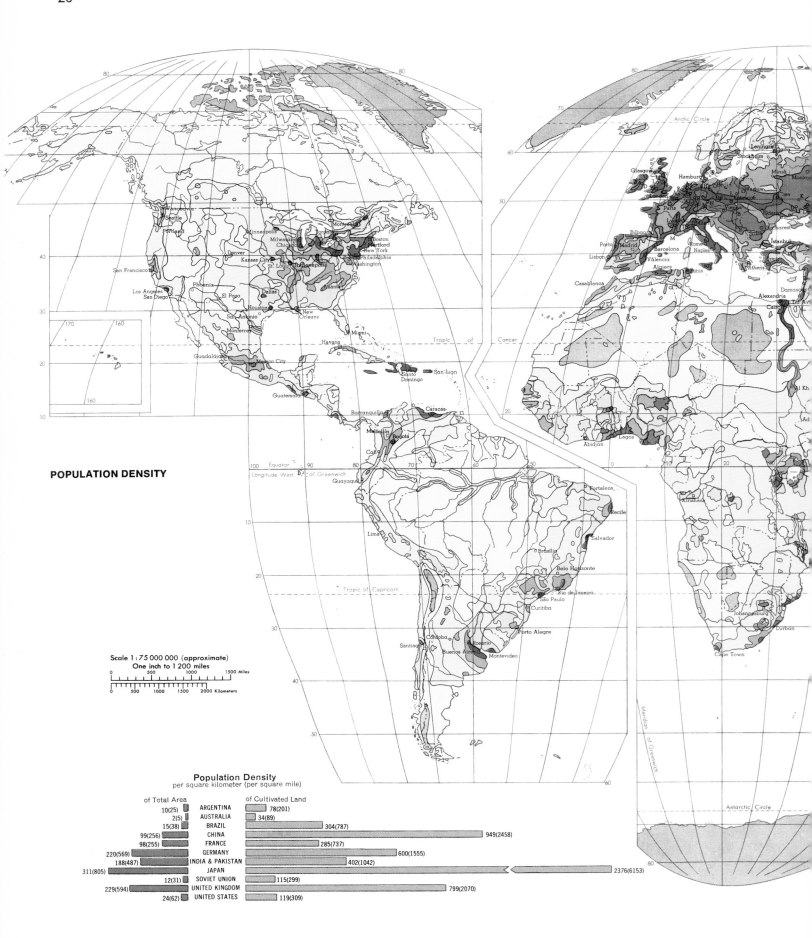

POPULATION DENSITY

Scale 1 : 75 000 000 (approximate)
One inch to 1 200 miles

0 500 1000 1500 Miles

0 500 1000 1500 2000 Kilometers

Population Density
per square kilometer (per square mile)

of Total Area		of Cultivated Land	
10(25)	ARGENTINA	78(201)	
2(5)	AUSTRALIA	34(89)	
15(38)	BRAZIL	304(787)	
99(256)	CHINA	949(2458)	
98(255)	FRANCE	285(737)	
220(569)	GERMANY	600(1555)	
188(487)	INDIA & PAKISTAN	402(1042)	
311(805)	JAPAN	2376(6153)	
12(31)	SOVIET UNION	115(299)	
229(594)	UNITED KINGDOM	799(2070)	
24(62)	UNITED STATES	119(309)	

Goode's Homolosine Equal Area Projection (Condensed)

Per Sq. Km. | Per Sq. Mile
Uninhabited | Uninhabited
Under 1 | Under 2
1-10 | 2-25
10-25 | 25-60
25-50 | 60-125
50-100 | 125-250
Over 100 | Over 250

□ Metropolitan areas over 2,000,000 population
○ Metropolitan areas 1,000,000 to 2,000,000 population

*Not all cities are named and some
are identified by initial letter only.*

Rural/Urban Population Ratios

Rural		Urban
20%	ARGENTINA	80%
14	AUSTRALIA	86
39	BRAZIL	61
24	CANADA	76
74	CHINA	26
27	FRANCE	73
79	INDIA	21
24	JAPAN	76
38	SOVIET UNION	62
55	TURKEY	45
22	UNITED KINGDOM	78
26	UNITED STATES	74

A-510000-16 -6-3-8 *
Copyright by Rand McNally & Co.
Made in U.S.A.

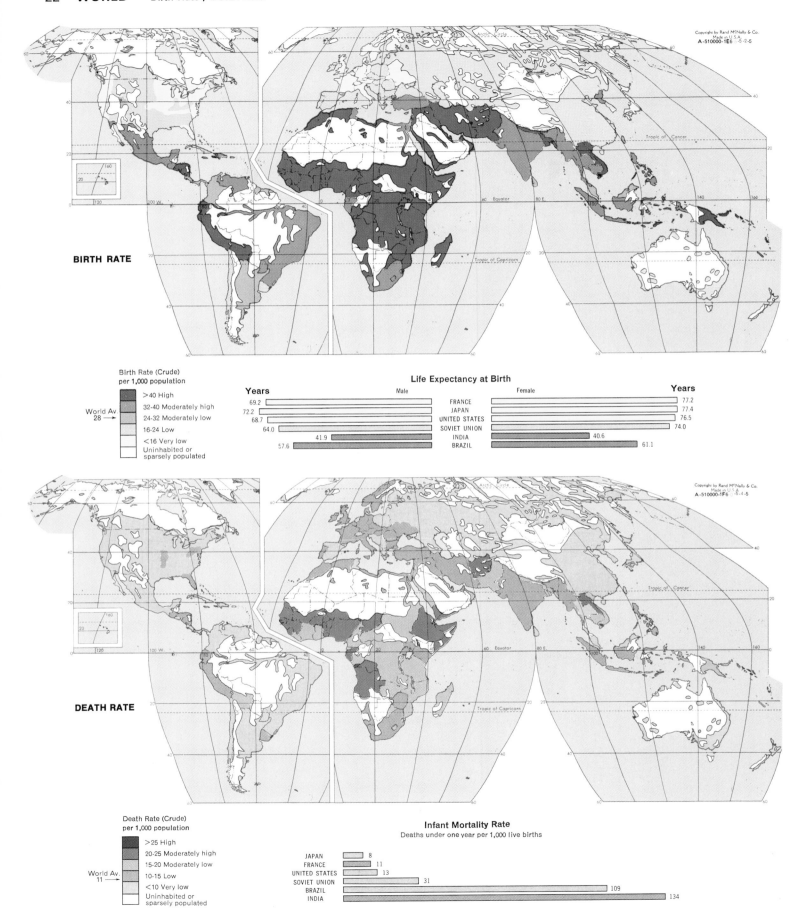

BIRTH RATE

Birth Rate (Crude)
per 1,000 population

>40 High
32-40 Moderately high
World Av. 28 → 24-32 Moderately low
16-24 Low
<16 Very low
Uninhabited or sparsely populated

Life Expectancy at Birth

Years	Male		Female	Years
		FRANCE		77.2
69.2		JAPAN		77.4
72.2		UNITED STATES		76.5
68.7		SOVIET UNION		74.0
64.0		INDIA		
41.9		BRAZIL	40.6	
57.6			61.1	

DEATH RATE

Death Rate (Crude)
per 1,000 population

>25 High
20-25 Moderately high
15-20 Moderately low
World Av. 11 → 10-15 Low
<10 Very low
Uninhabited or sparsely populated

Infant Mortality Rate
Deaths under one year per 1,000 live births

JAPAN	8
FRANCE	11
UNITED STATES	13
SOVIET UNION	31
BRAZIL	109
INDIA	134

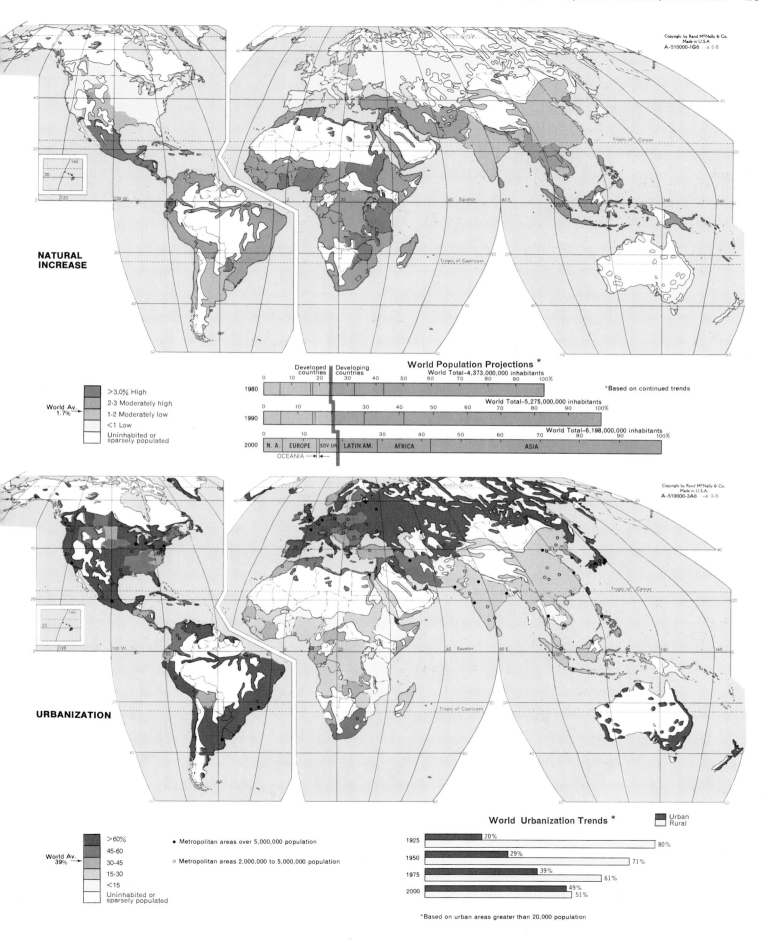

NATURAL INCREASE

>3.0% High
2-3 Moderately high
1-2 Moderately low
<1 Low
Uninhabited or sparsely populated

World Av. 1.7%

World Population Projections *

Developed countries   Developing countries

*Based on continued trends

1980   World Total–4,373,000,000 inhabitants

1990   World Total–5,275,000,000 inhabitants

2000   World Total–6,198,000,000 inhabitants

N. A.   EUROPE   SOV. UN.   LATIN AM.   AFRICA   ASIA

OCEANIA

URBANIZATION

>60%
45-60
30-45
15-30
<15
Uninhabited or sparsely populated

World Av. 39%

• Metropolitan areas over 5,000,000 population

○ Metropolitan areas 2,000,000 to 5,000,000 population

World Urbanization Trends *

Urban
Rural

1925   20%   80%
1950   29%   71%
1975   39%   61%
2000   49%   51%

*Based on urban areas greater than 20,000 population

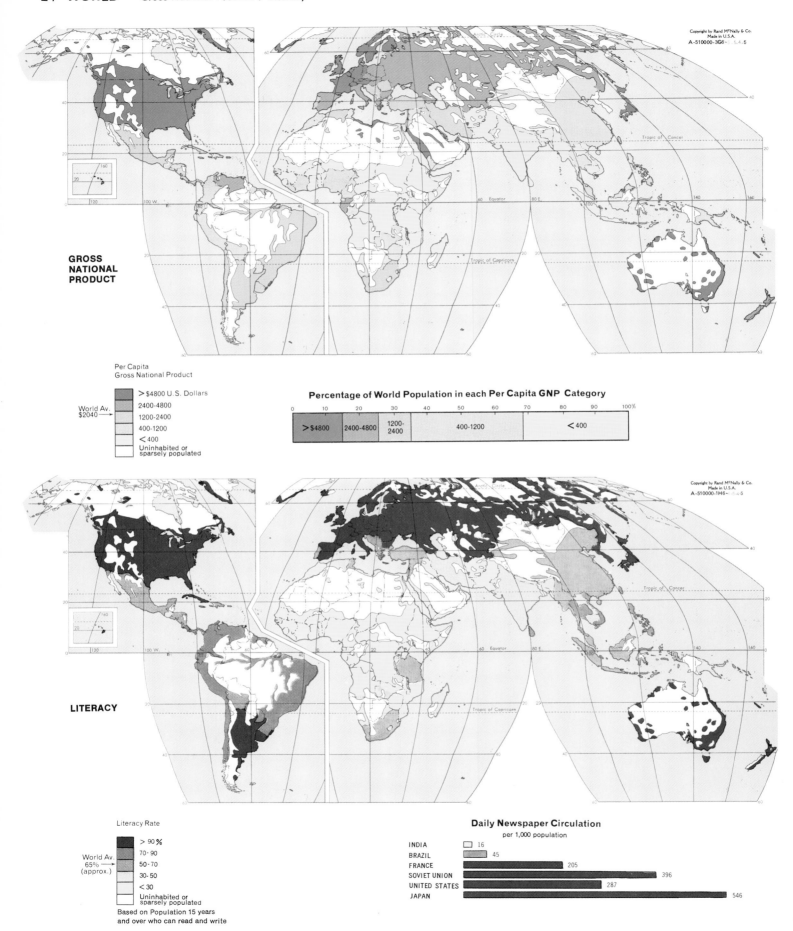

Copyright by Rand McNally & Co.
Made in U.S.A.
A-510000-3G6~ 5.4.5

**GROSS
NATIONAL
PRODUCT**

Per Capita
Gross National Product

> $4800 U.S. Dollars
2400-4800
World Av.
$2040 → 1200-2400
400-1200
< 400
Uninhabited or
sparsely populated

Percentage of World Population in each Per Capita GNP Category

0   10   20   30   40   50   60   70   80   90   100%

| > $4800 | 2400-4800 | 1200-2400 | 400-1200 | < 400 |

Copyright by Rand McNally & Co.
Made in U.S.A.
A-510000-1H6~ 5.4.5

LITERACY

Literacy Rate

> 90 %
70-90
World Av.
65% → 50-70
(approx.)
30-50
< 30
Uninhabited or
sparsely populated

Based on Population 15 years
and over who can read and write

Daily Newspaper Circulation
per 1,000 population

INDIA	16
BRAZIL	45
FRANCE	205
SOVIET UNION	396
UNITED STATES	287
JAPAN	546

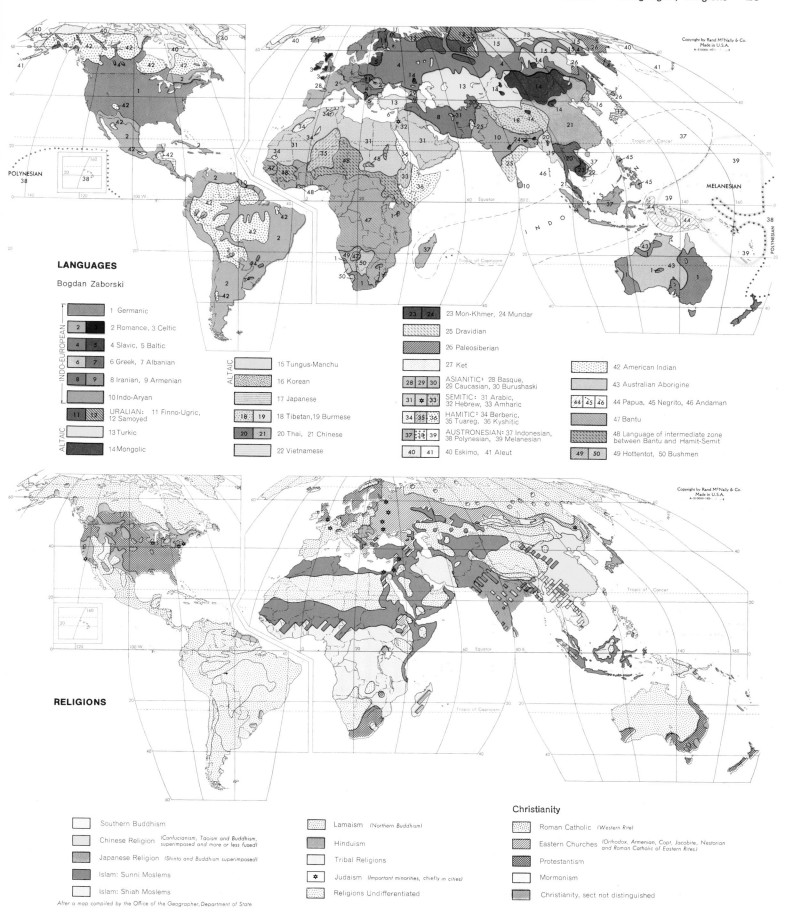

LANGUAGES

Bogdan Zaborski

Copyright by Rand McNally & Co.
Made in U.S.A.
A-510000-161-

INDO-EUROPEAN
	1 Germanic
2 3	2 Romance, 3 Celtic
4 5	4 Slavic, 5 Baltic
6 7	6 Greek, 7 Albanian
8 9	8 Iranian, 9 Armenian
	10 Indo-Aryan

URALIAN: 11 Finno-Ugric,
12 Samoyed

ALTAIC
13	Turkic
14	Mongolic
15	Tungus-Manchu
16	Korean
17	Japanese
18 19	18 Tibetan, 19 Burmese
20 21	20 Thai, 21 Chinese
22	Vietnamese

23 24   23 Mon-Khmer, 24 Mundar
25   25 Dravidian
26   26 Paleosiberian
27   27 Ket
28 29 30   **ASIANITIC:** 28 Basque,
29 Caucasian, 30 Burushaski
31 ✿ 33   **SEMITIC:** 31 Arabic,
32 Hebrew, 33 Amharic
34 35 36   **HAMITIC:** 34 Berberic,
35 Tuareg, 36 Kyshitic
37 38 39   **AUSTRONESIAN:** 37 Indonesian,
38 Polynesian, 39 Melanesian
40 41   40 Eskimo, 41 Aleut

42 American Indian
43 Australian Aborigine
44 45 46   44 Papua, 45 Negrito, 46 Andaman
47 Bantu
48 Language of intermediate zone
between Bantu and Hamit-Semit
49 50   49 Hottentot, 50 Bushmen

RELIGIONS

Copyright by Rand McNally & Co.
Made in U.S.A.
A-510000-162-

	Southern Buddhism
	Chinese Religion *(Confucianism, Taoism and Buddhism, superimposed and more or less fused)*
	Japanese Religion *(Shinto and Buddhism superimposed)*
	Islam: Sunni Moslems
	Islam: Shiah Moslems

	Lamaism *(Northern Buddhism)*
	Hinduism
	Tribal Religions
✿	Judaism *(Important minorities, chiefly in cities)*
	Religions Undifferentiated

Christianity

	Roman Catholic *(Western Rite)*
	Eastern Churches *(Orthodox, Armenian, Copt, Jacobite, Nestorian and Roman Catholic of Eastern Rites.)*
	Protestantism
	Mormonism
	Christianity, sect not distinguished

After a map compiled by the Office of the Geographer, Department of State

CALORIE SUPPLY

Note: Size of each country is proportional to population

Calorie supply per capita
(percentage of requirements*)

≥120% Well above requirements
110 to 120 Above requirements
100 to 110 Adequate nutrition
90 to 100 Some malnutrition
<90 Serious malnutrition and/or hunger
n.a. Data not available

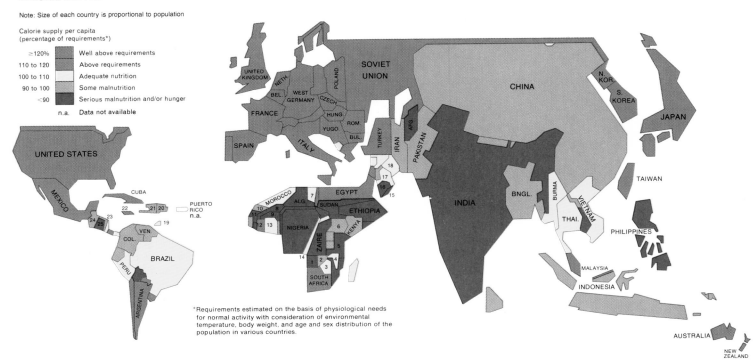

*Requirements estimated on the basis of physiological needs for normal activity with consideration of environmental temperature, body weight, and age and sex distribution of the population in various countries.

1. ANGOLA	6. UGANDA	11. GUINEA	16. YEMEN	21. HAITI
2. ZAMBIA	7. TUNISIA	12. IVORY COAST	17. SAUDI ARABIA	22. JAMAICA
3. ZIMBABWE	8. MALI	13. GHANA	18. IRAQ	23. HONDURAS
4. MALAWI	9. UPPER VOLTA	14. CAMEROON	19. TRIN. & TOBAGO	24. GUATEMALA
5. TANZANIA	10. SENEGAL	15. P.D.R. YEMEN	20. DOM. REPUBLIC	25. EL SALVADOR

© 1982 Rand McNally & Co.
Made in U.S.A.
A-510000-1V6 -1 -1-1

PROTEIN CONSUMPTION

Note: size of each country is proportional to population

n.a. Data not available

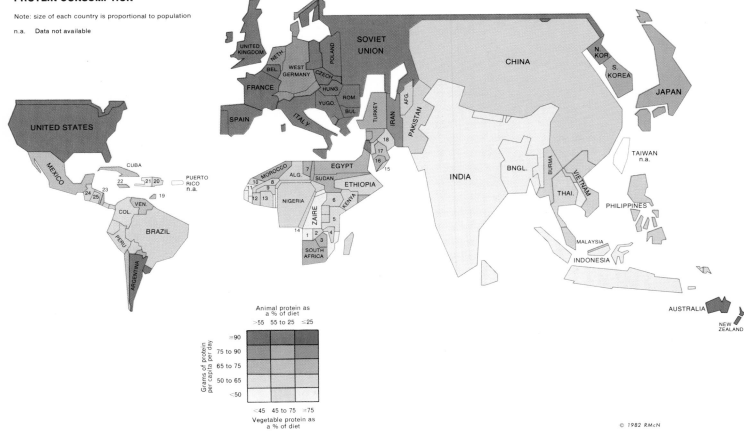

Animal protein as
a % of diet
>55 55 to 25 ≤25

Grams of protein
per capita per day
≥90
75 to 90
65 to 75
50 to 65
<50

<45 45 to 75 ≥75
Vegetable protein as
a % of diet

© 1982 RMcN

PHYSICIANS

Note: Size of each country is proportional to population

Population per physician

- <1000
- 1000 to 6000
- 6000 to 18000
- ≥18000
- n.a.   Data not available

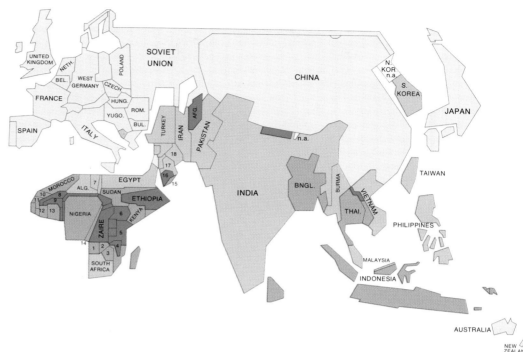

1. ANGOLA	6. UGANDA	11. GUINEA	16. YEMEN	21. HAITI
2. ZAMBIA	7. TUNISIA	12. IVORY COAST	17. SAUDI ARABIA	22. JAMAICA
3. ZIMBABWE	8. MALI	13. GHANA	18. IRAQ	23. HONDURAS
4. MALAWI	9. UPPER VOLTA	14. CAMEROON	19. TRIN. & TOBAGO	24. GUATEMALA
5. TANZANIA	10. SENEGAL	15. P.D.R. YEMEN	20. DOM. REPUBLIC	25. EL SALVADOR

© 1982 Rand McNally & Co.
Made in U.S.A.
A-510000-1L6   -1-1-1

LIFE EXPECTANCY

Note: Size of each country is proportional to population

Life expectancy at birth

- ≥70 years
- 60 to 70
- 50 to 60
- <50

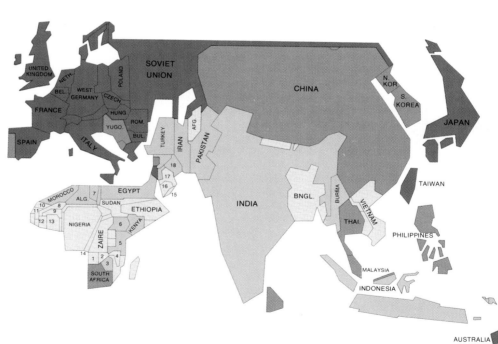

Deaths by Age Group as a % of Total Deaths

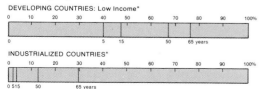

DEVELOPING COUNTRIES: Low Income*

INDUSTRIALIZED COUNTRIES*

Life Expectancy at Birth

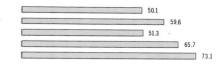

DEVELOPING: Low Income*	50.1
DEVELOPING: Middle Income*	59.6
OIL EXPORTING*	51.3
CENTRALLY PLANNED*	65.7
INDUSTRIALIZED*	73.1

*as defined by the World Bank

© 1982 RMcN.

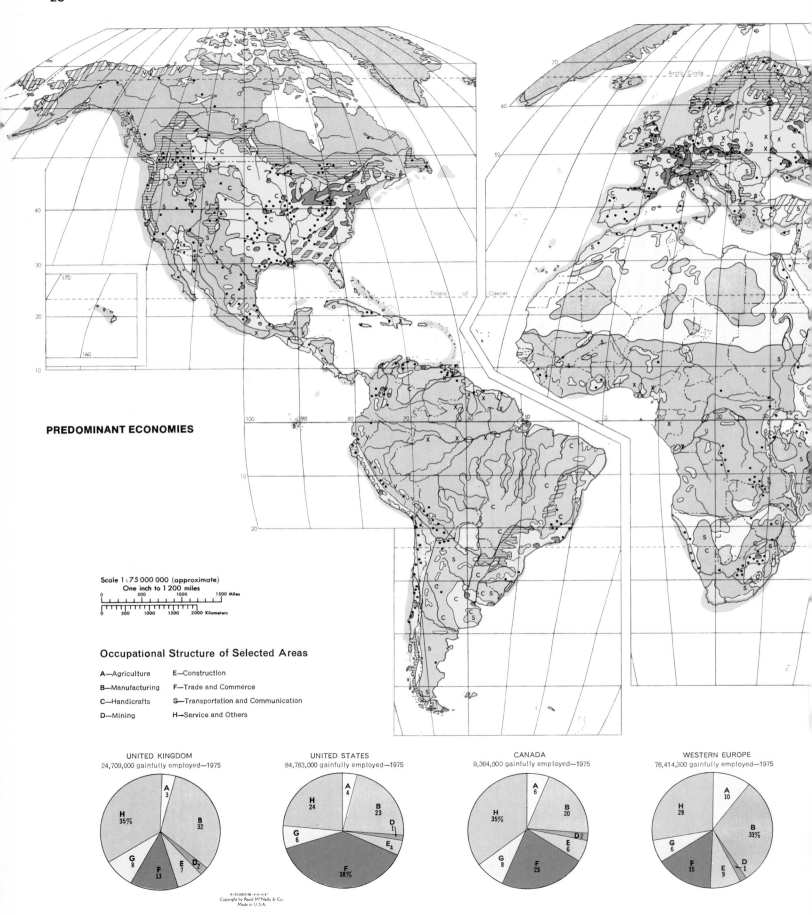

PREDOMINANT ECONOMIES

Scale 1:75 000 000 (approximate)
One inch to 1 200 miles

Occupational Structure of Selected Areas

A—Agriculture   E—Construction

B—Manufacturing   F—Trade and Commerce

C—Handicrafts   G—Transportation and Communication

D—Mining   H—Service and Others

UNITED KINGDOM
24,709,000 gainfully employed—1975

H 35% · B 32 · A 3 · G 8 · F 13 · E 7 · D 2

UNITED STATES
84,783,000 gainfully employed—1975

H 24 · A 4 · B 23 · D 1 · E 4 · F 38% · G 6

CANADA
9,364,000 gainfully employed—1975

H 35% · A 6 · B 20 · D 2 · E 6 · F 23 · G 8

WESTERN EUROPE
76,414,300 gainfully employed—1975

H 28 · A 10 · B 31% · D 1 · E 9 · F 15 · G 6

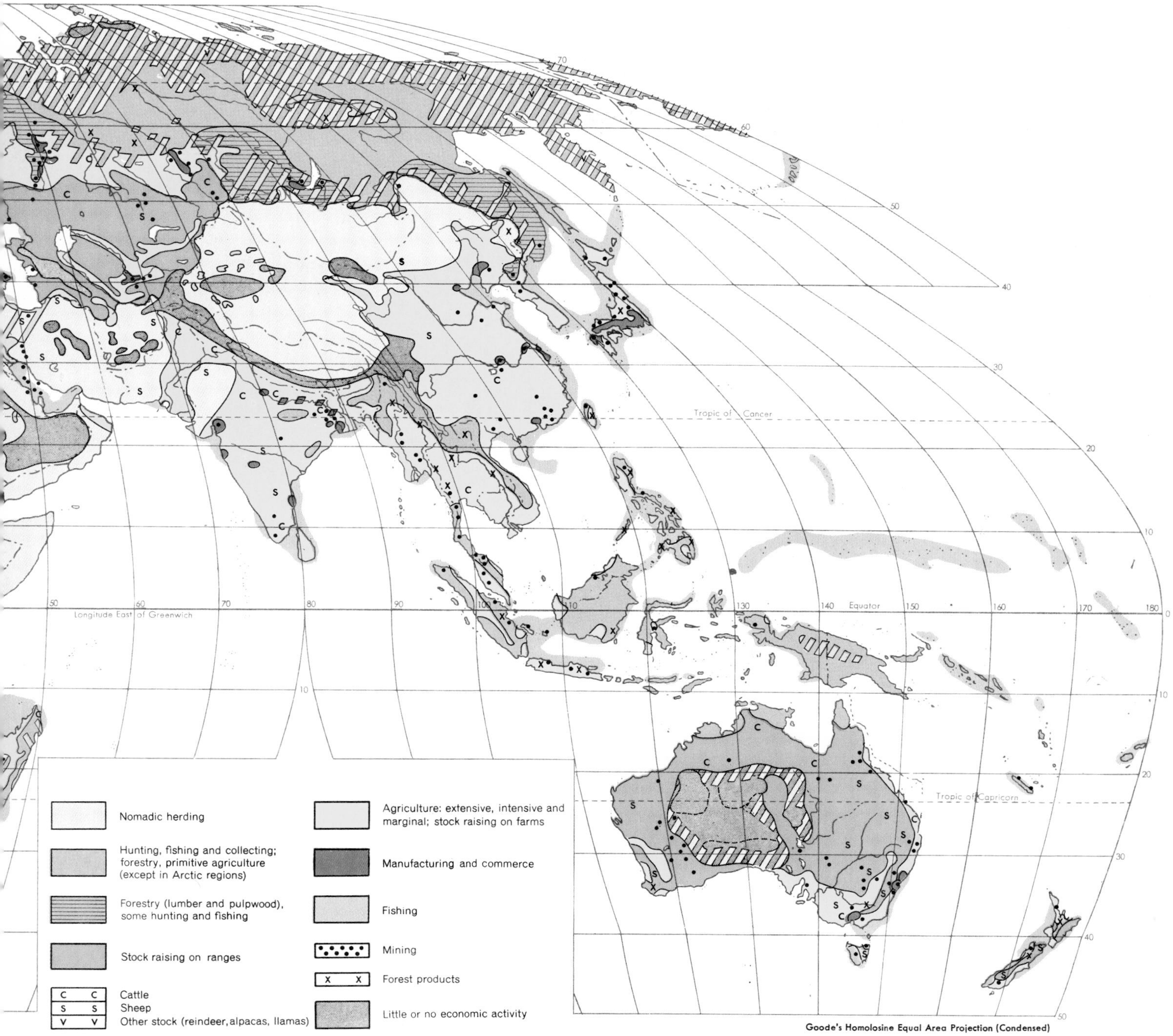
Tropic of Cancer
Tropic of Capricorn
Equator
Longitude East of Greenwich
Nomadic herding
Hunting, fishing and collecting; forestry, primitive agriculture (except in Arctic regions)
Forestry (lumber and pulpwood), some hunting and fishing
Stock raising on ranges
C C Cattle
S S Sheep
V V Other stock (reindeer, alpacas, llamas)
Agriculture: extensive, intensive and marginal; stock raising on farms
Manufacturing and commerce
Fishing
Mining
X X Forest products
Little or no economic activity

Goode's Homolosine Equal Area Projection (Condensed)

SOVIET UNION
...094,000 gainfully employed—1975

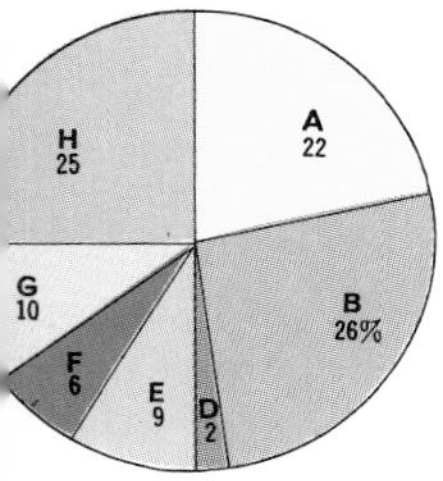
A 22
B 26%
D 2
E 9
F 6
G 10
H 25

BRAZIL
29,545,400 gainfully employed—1970

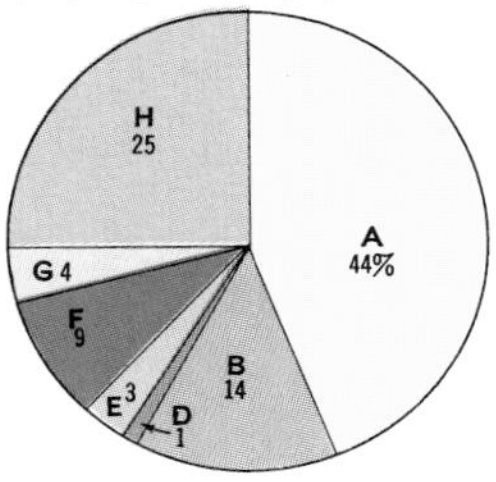
A 44%
B 14
D 1
E 3
F 9
G 4
H 25

INDIA
180,373,000 gainfully employed—1973

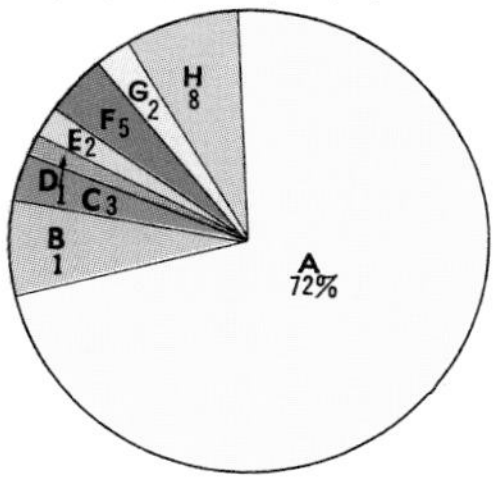
A 72%
B 1
C 3
D 1
E 2
F 5
G 2
H 8

CHINA
270,000,000 gainfully employed—Est. 1970

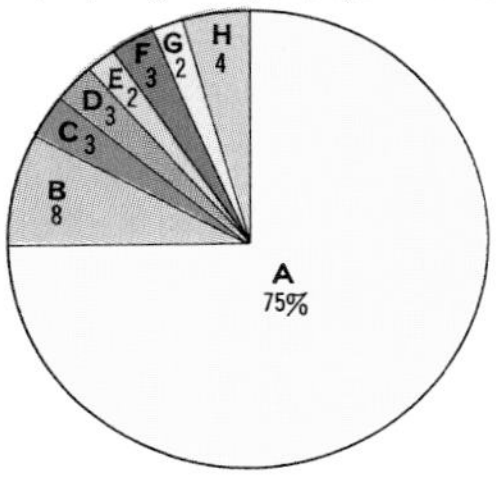
A 75%
B 8
C 3
D 3
E 2
F 3
G 2
H 4

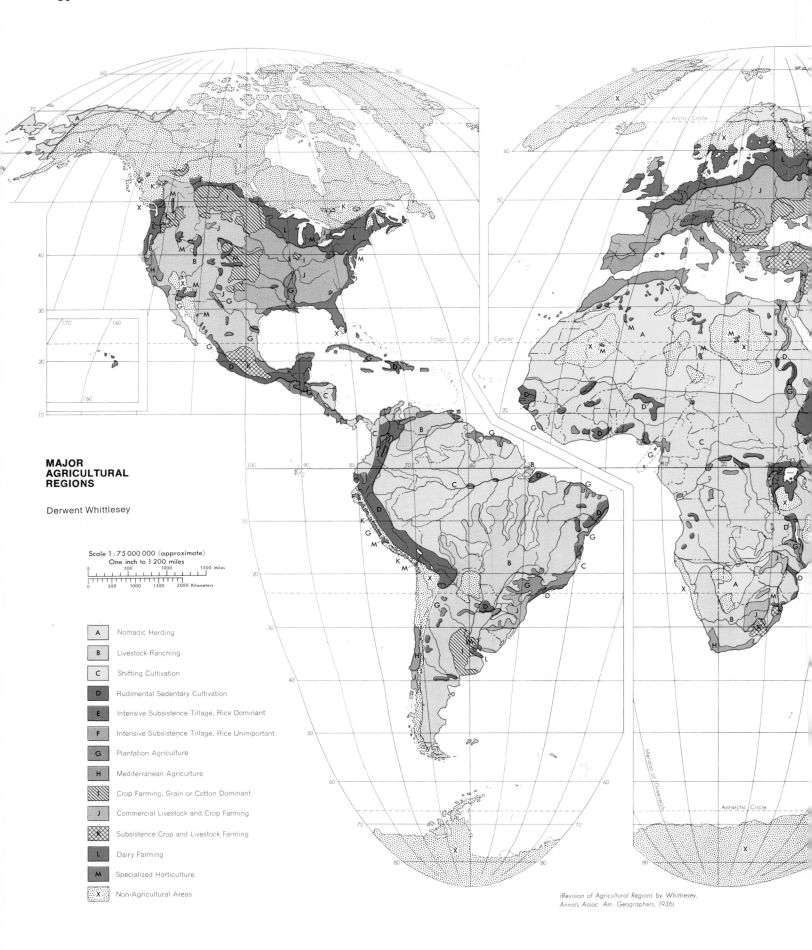

**MAJOR
AGRICULTURAL
REGIONS**

Derwent Whittlesey

Scale 1 : 75 000 000 (approximate)
One inch to 1 200 miles

A	Nomadic Herding
B	Livestock Ranching
C	Shifting Cultivation
D	Rudimental Sedentary Cultivation
E	Intensive Subsistence Tillage, Rice Dominant
F	Intensive Subsistence Tillage, Rice Unimportant
G	Plantation Agriculture
H	Mediterranean Agriculture
I	Crop Farming, Grain or Cotton Dominant
J	Commercial Livestock and Crop Farming
K	Subsistence Crop and Livestock Farming
L	Dairy Farming
M	Specialized Horticulture
X	Non-Agricultural Areas

(Revision of Agricultural Regions by Whittlesey,
Annals Assoc. Am. Geographers, 1936)

Goode's Homolosine Equal Area Projection (Condensed)

A-510000-562-2-3-4°
Copyright by Rand M°Nally & Co.
Made in U.S.A.

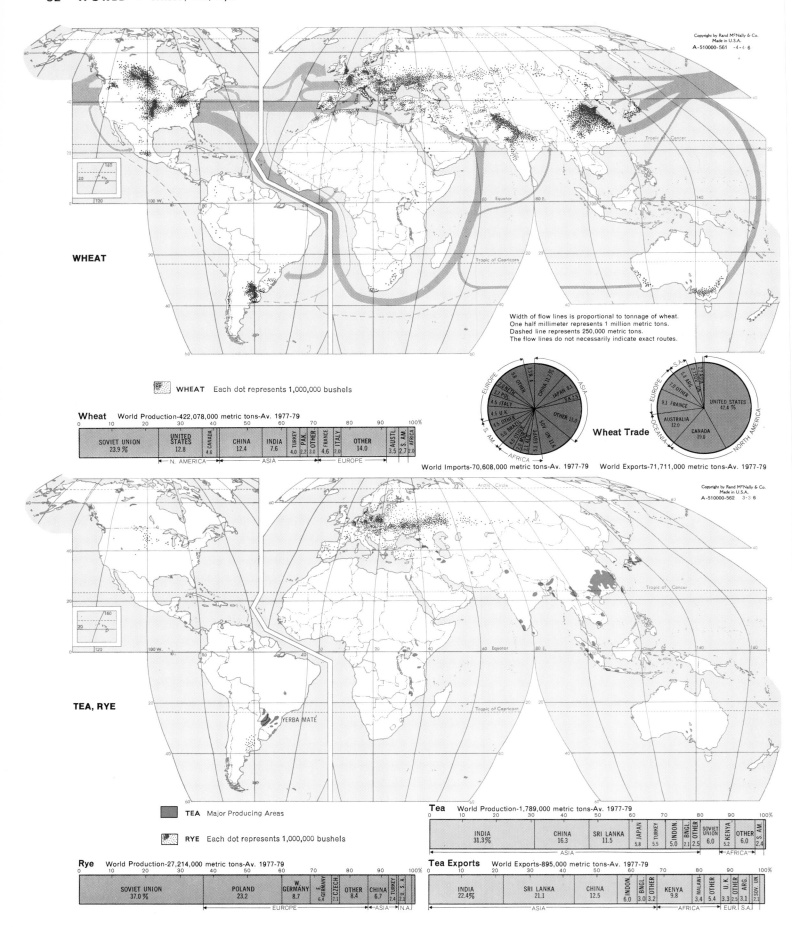

WHEAT

WHEAT   Each dot represents 1,000,000 bushels

Wheat   World Production-422,078,000 metric tons-Av. 1977-79

0	10	20	30	40	50	60	70	80	90	100%		
SOVIET UNION 23.9 %			UNITED STATES 12.8	CANADA 4.6	CHINA 12.4	INDIA 7.6	TURKEY 4.0	PAK. 2.2 OTHER 3.0	FRANCE 4.6	ITALY 2.0	OTHER 14.0	AUSTL. 3.5 S. AM. 2.7 AFRICA 2.0

◄ N. AMERICA ► ◄ ASIA ► ◄ EUROPE ►

Width of flow lines is proportional to tonnage of wheat.
One half millimeter represents 1 million metric tons.
Dashed line represents 250,000 metric tons.
The flow lines do not necessarily indicate exact routes.

Wheat Trade

World Imports-70,608,000 metric tons-Av. 1977-79

World Exports-71,711,000 metric tons-Av. 1977-79

TEA, RYE

YERBA MATÉ

TEA   Major Producing Areas

RYE   Each dot represents 1,000,000 bushels

Tea   World Production-1,789,000 metric tons-Av. 1977-79

0	10	20	30	40	50	60	70	80	90	100%	
INDIA 31.3%			CHINA 16.3	SRI LANKA 11.5	JAPAN 5.8	TURKEY 5.5	INDON. 5.0	BNGL. 2.1 OTHER	SOVIET UNION 6.0	KENYA 5.2 OTHER 6.0	S. AM. 2.4

◄ ASIA ► ◄ AFRICA ►

Tea Exports   World Exports-895,000 metric tons-Av. 1977-79

0	10	20	30	40	50	60	70	80	90	100%	
INDIA 22.4%			SRI LANKA 21.1	CHINA 12.5	INDON. 6.0	BNGL. 3.0 OTHER 3.2	KENYA 9.8	MALAWI 3.4 OTHER 5.4	U.K. 3.3 OTHER 2.5	ARG. 3.1 SOV. UN. 2.1	

◄ ASIA ► ◄ AFRICA ► EUR. S.A.

Rye   World Production-27,214,000 metric tons-Av. 1977-79

0	10	20	30	40	50	60	70	80	90	100%	
SOVIET UNION 37.0 %			POLAND 23.2	W. GERMANY 8.7	E. GERMANY 6.4	CZECH 2.1	OTHER 8.4	CHINA 6.7	TURKEY 2.4 U.S.A. 2.8		

◄ EUROPE ► ◄ ASIA ► N.A.

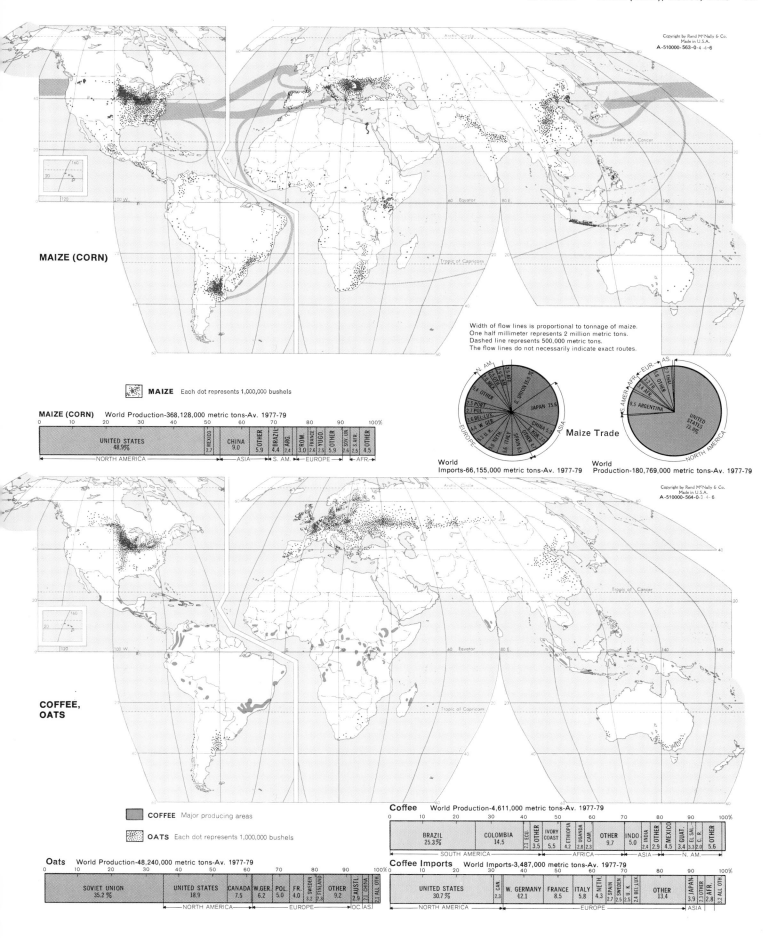

MAIZE (CORN)

Width of flow lines is proportional to tonnage of maize.
One half millimeter represents 2 million metric tons.
Dashed line represents 500,000 metric tons.
The flow lines do not necessarily indicate exact routes.

Maize Trade

World
Imports-66,155,000 metric tons-Av. 1977-79

World
Production-180,769,000 metric tons-Av. 1977-79

MAIZE Each dot represents 1,000,000 bushels

MAIZE (CORN) World Production-368,128,000 metric tons-Av. 1977-79

0	10	20	30	40	50	60	70	80	90	100%

UNITED STATES 48.9%	MEXICO 2.7	CHINA 9.0	OTHER 5.9	BRAZIL 4.4	ARG. 2.4	ROM. 3.0	FRANCE 2.6	YUGO. 2.5	OTHER 5.9	SOV. UN. 2.6	S. AFR. 2.5	OTHER 4.5

NORTH AMERICA | ASIA | S. AM. | EUROPE | AFR.

COFFEE, OATS

COFFEE Major producing areas

OATS Each dot represents 1,000,000 bushels

Coffee World Production-4,611,000 metric tons-Av. 1977-79

0	10	20	30	40	50	60	70	80	90	100%

BRAZIL 25.3%	COLOMBIA 14.5	ECU. 2.1	OTHER 3.5	IVORY COAST 5.5	ETHIOPA 4.2	UGANDA 4.2	CAM. 2.3	OTHER 9.7	INDO. 5.0	INDIA 2.4	MEXICO 4.5	GUAT. 3.4	EL SAL. 3.3	C. R. 2.0	OTHER 5.6

SOUTH AMERICA | AFRICA | ASIA | N. AM.

Coffee Imports World Imports-3,487,000 metric tons-Av. 1977-79

0	10	20	30	40	50	60	70	80	90	100%

UNITED STATES 30.7%	CAN. 2.3	W. GERMANY 12.1	FRANCE 8.5	ITALY 5.8	NETH. 4.3	SPAIN 2.7	SWEDEN 2.5	U.K. 2.4	BEL.LUX 2.4	OTHER 13.4	JAPAN 3.9	AFR. 2.3	ALL OTH. 3.2

NORTH AMERICA | EUROPE | ASIA

Oats World Production-48,240,000 metric tons-Av. 1977-79

0	10	20	30	40	50	60	70	80	90	100%

SOVIET UNION 35.2%	UNITED STATES 18.9	CANADA 7.5	W.GER. 6.2	POL. 5.0	FR. 4.0	SWEDEN 3.2	FINLAND 2.3	OTHER 9.2	AUSTL. 2.7	CHINA 2.1	ALL OTH.

NORTH AMERICA | EUROPE | OC. AS.

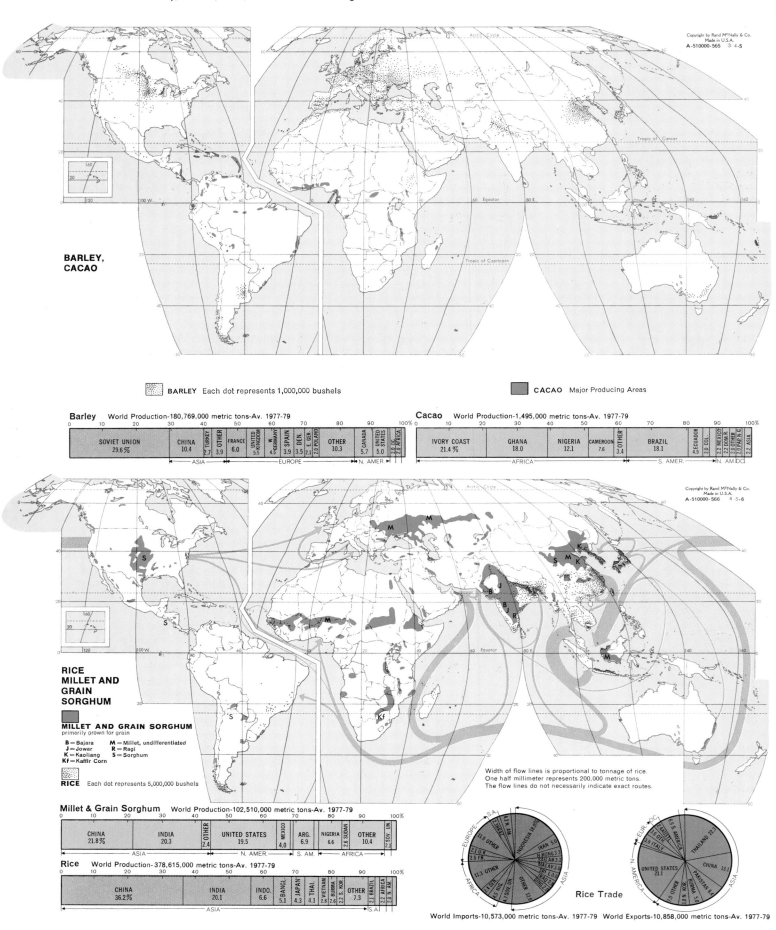

BARLEY, CACAO

BARLEY Each dot represents 1,000,000 bushels

CACAO Major Producing Areas

Barley World Production-180,769,000 metric tons-Av. 1977-79

0	10	20	30	40	50	60	70	80	90	100%
SOVIET UNION 29.6%			CHINA 10.4	TURKEY 2.7	OTHER 3.9	FRANCE 6.0	UNITED KINGDOM 5.5	W. GERMANY 4.5	SPAIN 3.9	DEN. 3.5	E. GER. 2.1	POLAND 2.0	OTHER 10.3	CANADA 5.7	UNITED STATES 3.0 OC.	AFRICA 2.0

← ASIA → ← EUROPE → ← N. AMER. →

Cacao World Production-1,495,000 metric tons-Av. 1977-79

0	10	20	30	40	50	60	70	80	90	100%
IVORY COAST 21.4%		GHANA 18.0	NIGERIA 12.1	CAMEROON 7.6	OTHER 3.4	BRAZIL 18.1	ECUADOR 4.9	COL. 2.0	MEXICO 2.2	DOM. R. 2.2	OTHER 2.0	PAP. N. G. 2.0	ASIA 2.2

← AFRICA → ← S. AMER. → ← N. AM. OC. →

RICE MILLET AND GRAIN SORGHUM

MILLET AND GRAIN SORGHUM
primarily grown for grain

B = Bajara   M = Millet, undifferentiated
J = Jowar   R = Ragi
K = Kaoliang   S = Sorghum
Kf = Kaffir Corn

RICE Each dot represents 5,000,000 bushels

Width of flow lines is proportional to tonnage of rice.
One half millimeter represents 200,000 metric tons.
The flow lines do not necessarily indicate exact routes.

Millet & Grain Sorghum World Production-102,510,000 metric tons-Av. 1977-79

0	10	20	30	40	50	60	70	80	90	100%
CHINA 21.8%		INDIA 20.3	OTHER 2.4	UNITED STATES 19.5	MEXICO 4.0	ARG. 6.9	NIGERIA 6.6	SUDAN 2.6	OTHER 10.4	SOV. UN. 2.1

← ASIA → ← N. AMER. → ← S. AM. → ← AFRICA →

Rice World Production-378,615,000 metric tons-Av. 1977-79

0	10	20	30	40	50	60	70	80	90	100%
CHINA 36.2%			INDIA 20.1	INDO. 6.6	BANGL. 5.1	JAPAN 4.3	THAI. 4.1	VIETNAM 2.6	BURMA 2.6	S. KOR. 2.2	OTHER 7.3	BRAZIL 2.1	AFRICA 2.2	N. AM.

← ASIA → ← S.A. →

Rice Trade

World Imports-10,573,000 metric tons-Av. 1977-79   World Exports-10,858,000 metric tons-Av. 1977-79

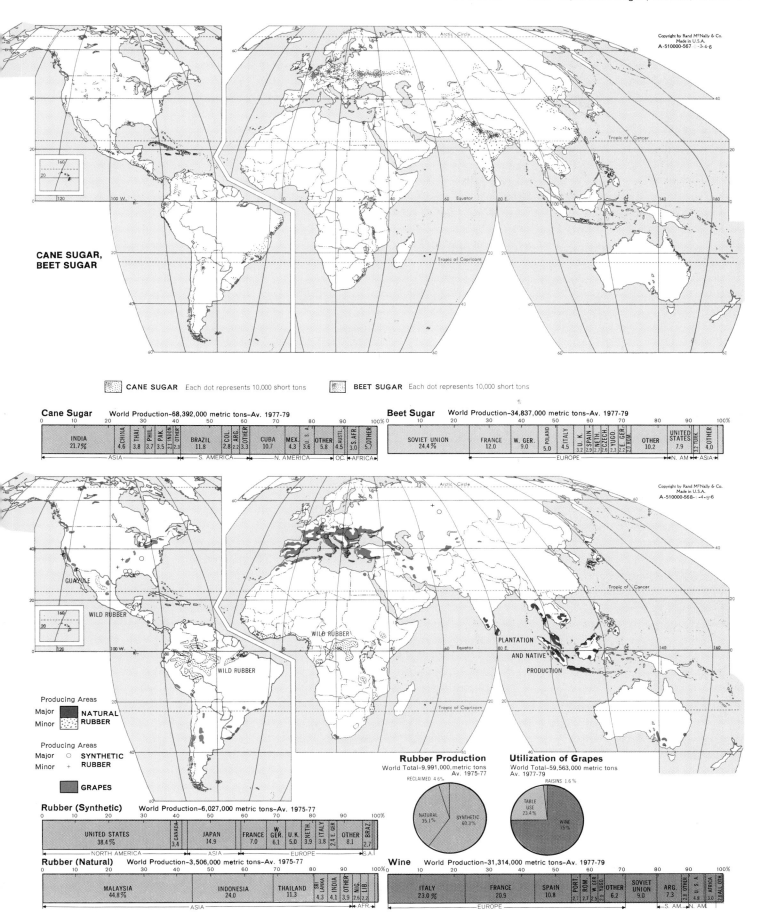

CANE SUGAR, BEET SUGAR

CANE SUGAR Each dot represents 10,000 short tons

BEET SUGAR Each dot represents 10,000 short tons

Cane Sugar World Production–68,392,000 metric tons–Av. 1977-79

| INDIA 21.7% | CHINA 4.6 | THAI. 3.8 | PHIL. 3.7 | PAK. 3.5 | INDON 2.1 | OTHER 2.3 | BRAZIL 11.8 | COL. 2.8 | ARG. 2.2 | OTHER 3.3 | CUBA 10.7 | MEX. 4.3 | U.S.A. 3.6 | OTHER 5.8 | AUSTL. 4.5 | S.AFR. 3.0 | OTHER 5.7 |

ASIA — S. AMERICA — N. AMERICA — OC. — AFRICA

Beet Sugar World Production–34,837,000 metric tons–Av. 1977-79

| SOVIET UNION 24.4% | FRANCE 12.0 | W. GER. 9.0 | POLAND 5.0 | ITALY 4.5 | U.K. 3.2 | SPAIN 2.9 | NETH. 2.7 | CZECH. 2.6 | YUGO. 2.3 | E. GER. 2.2 | ROM. 2.0 | OTHER 10.2 | UNITED STATES 7.9 | TURK. 3.2 | OTHER 4.0 |

EUROPE — N. AM — ASIA

GUAYULE

WILD RUBBER

WILD RUBBER

WILD RUBBER

PLANTATION

AND NATIVE

PRODUCTION

Producing Areas
Major / Minor   NATURAL RUBBER

Producing Areas
Major ○ / Minor +   SYNTHETIC RUBBER

GRAPES

Rubber Production
World Total–9,991,000 metric tons
Av. 1975-77

RECLAIMED 4.6%
NATURAL 35.1%
SYNTHETIC 60.3%

Utilization of Grapes
World Total–59,563,000 metric tons
Av. 1977-79

RAISINS 1.6%
TABLE USE 23.4%
WINE 75%

Rubber (Synthetic) World Production–6,027,000 metric tons–Av. 1975-77

| UNITED STATES 38.4% | CANADA 3.4 | JAPAN 14.9 | FRANCE 7.0 | W. GER. 6.1 | U.K. 5.0 | NETH. 3.9 | ITALY 3.8 | E.GER. 2.4 | OTHER 8.1 | BRAZ. 2.7 |

NORTH AMERICA — ASIA — EUROPE — S.A.

Rubber (Natural) World Production–3,506,000 metric tons–Av. 1975-77

| MALAYSIA 44.8% | INDONESIA 24.0 | THAILAND 11.3 | SRI LANKA 4.3 | INDIA 4.1 | OTHER 3.9 | NIG. 2.6 | LIB. 2.2 |

ASIA — AFR.

Wine World Production–31,314,000 metric tons–Av. 1977-79

| ITALY 23.0% | FRANCE 20.9 | SPAIN 10.8 | PORT. 2.7 | ROM. 2.7 | W.GER. 2.6 | YUGO. 2.0 | OTHER 6.2 | SOVIET UNION 9.0 | ARG. 7.3 | U.S.A. 4.8 | AFRICA 3.0 | ALL OTH 2.2 |

EUROPE — S. AM. — N. AM.

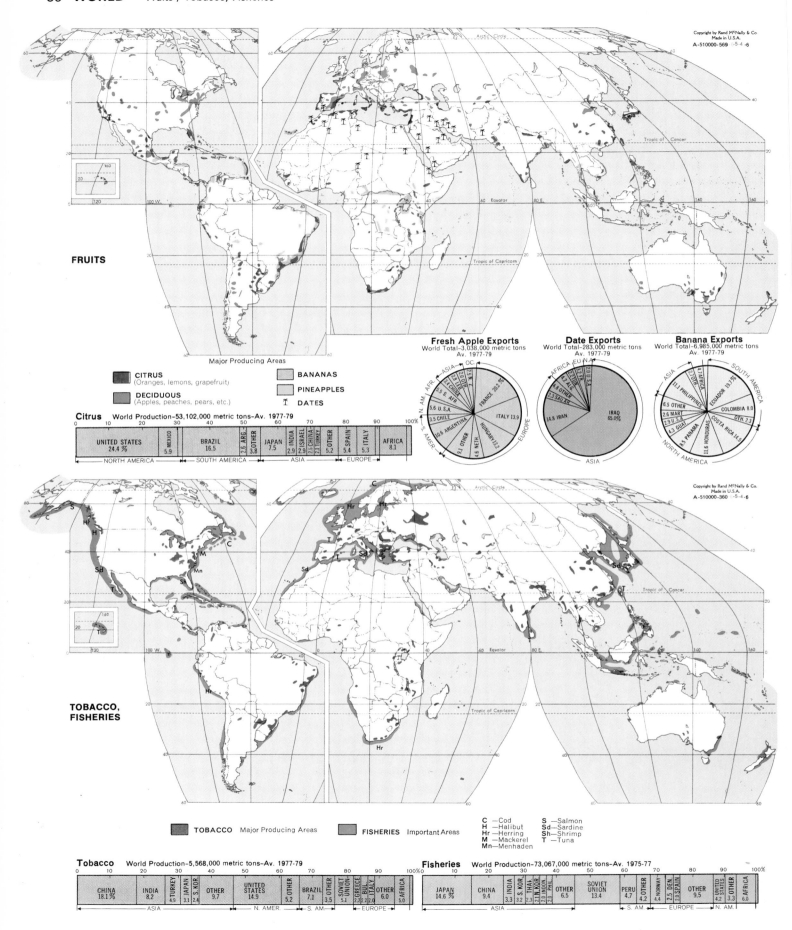

FRUITS

Major Producing Areas

	CITRUS (Oranges, lemons, grapefruit)
	DECIDUOUS (Apples, peaches, pears, etc.)
	BANANAS
	PINEAPPLES
⚘	DATES

Citrus World Production-53,102,000 metric tons-Av. 1977-79

UNITED STATES 24.4 %	MEXICO 5.9	BRAZIL 16.5	ARG. 2.6	OTHER 3.8	JAPAN 7.5	INDIA 2.9	ISRAEL 2.9	CHINA 2.5	TURKEY 2.1	OTHER 5.2	SPAIN 5.4	ITALY 5.3	AFRICA 8.1
NORTH AMERICA		SOUTH AMERICA			ASIA						EUROPE		

Fresh Apple Exports
World Total-3,038,000 metric tons
Av. 1977-79

FRANCE 20.1 %
ITALY 13.9
HUNGARY 12.2
NETH. 4.6
OTHER 9.1
ARGENTINA 10.5
CHILE 3.5
U.S.A. 5.6
S. AFR. 5.5
CHINA 2.8
LEB. 2.4
N.Z. 2.0
OTHER

Date Exports
World Total-283,000 metric tons
Av. 1977-79

IRAQ 65.0%
IRAN 14.8
SAU. AR. 2.3
ALG. 4.2
OTHER 4.8
U.S. 2.4
FR. 2.2
OTHER

Banana Exports
World Total-6,985,000 metric tons
Av. 1977-79

ECUADOR 19.7%
COLOMBIA 8.0
COSTA RICA 14.5
HONDURAS 11.6
PANAMA 8.5
GUAT. 4.3
U.S.A. 2.9
MART. 2.6
OTHER 6.5
PHILIPPINES 11.1
OTHER 2.7
OTH. 2.3

TOBACCO, FISHERIES

| | TOBACCO Major Producing Areas |
| | FISHERIES Important Areas |

C —Cod	S —Salmon
H —Halibut	Sd—Sardine
Hr —Herring	Sh—Shrimp
M —Mackerel	T —Tuna
Mn—Menhaden	

Tobacco World Production-5,568,000 metric tons-Av. 1977-79

CHINA 18.1%	INDIA 8.2	TURKEY 4.9	JAPAN 3.1	S. KOR 2.4	OTHER 9.7	UNITED STATES 14.9	OTHER 5.2	BRAZIL 7.1	SOVIET UNION 3.5	GREECE 5.1	BUL. 2.2	ITALY 2.2	OTHER 6.0	AFRICA 5.0
ASIA						N. AMER.		S. AM.		EUROPE				

Fisheries World Production-73,067,000 metric tons-Av. 1975-77

JAPAN 14.6 %	CHINA 9.4	INDIA 3.3	S. KOR. 3.2	THAI. 2.3	N.KOR 2.1	INDON. 2.0	PHIL. 2.0	OTHER 6.5	SOVIET UNION 13.4	PERU 4.7	OTHER 4.2	NORWAY 4.4	DEN. 2.5	SPAIN 2.0	OTHER 9.5	UNITED STATES 4.2	OTHER 3.3	AFRICA 6.0
ASIA										S. AM.		EUROPE				N. AM.		

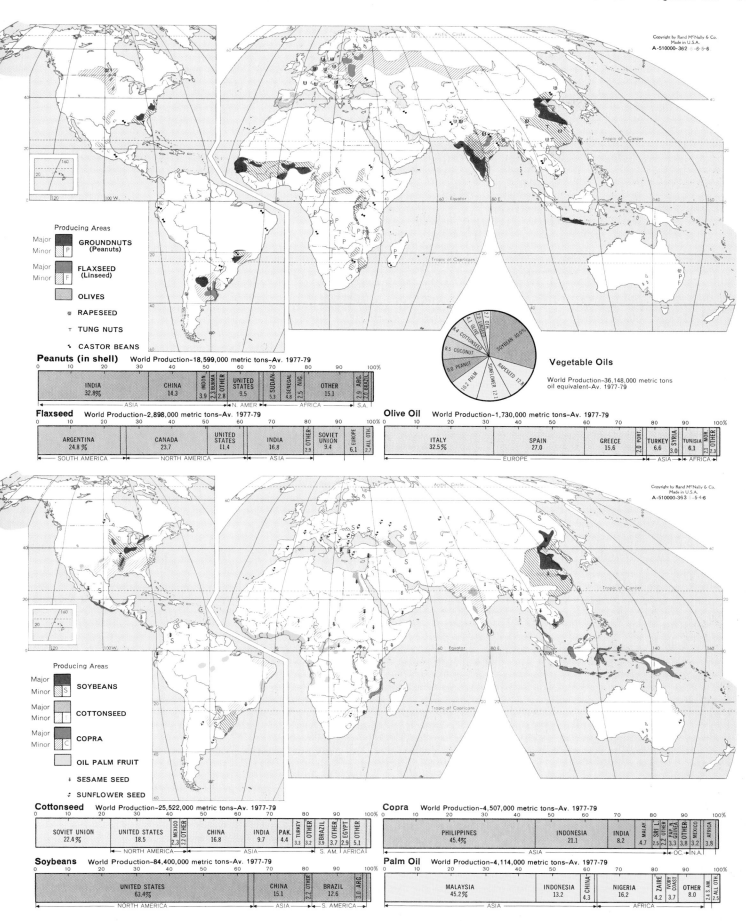

Producing Areas

Major	Minor	
■	P	GROUNDNUTS (Peanuts)
■	F	FLAXSEED (Linseed)
■		OLIVES

ш RAPESEED

т TUNG NUTS

ь CASTOR BEANS

Vegetable Oils

World Production—36,148,000 metric tons
oil equivalent—Av. 1977-79

Pie chart: SOYBEAN 30.6, RAPESEED 13.8, SUNFLOWER 12.1, PALM 10.2, PEANUT 9.0, COCONUT 8.5, COTTONSEED 8.4, OLIVE 4.1, LINSEED 2.8, OTH. 2.7

Peanuts (in shell) World Production—18,599,000 metric tons—Av. 1977-79

0	10	20	30	40	50	60	70	80	90	100%

| INDIA 32.8% | CHINA 14.3 | INDON. 3.9 | BURMA 2.3 | OTHER 2.8 | UNITED STATES 9.5 | SUDAN 5.3 | SENEGAL 4.8 | NIG. 2.5 | OTHER 15.1 | ARG. 2.9 | BRAZIL 2.0 |

ASIA ———— N. AMER. ———— AFRICA ———— S.A.

Flaxseed World Production—2,898,000 metric tons—Av. 1977-79

0	10	20	30	40	50	60	70	80	90	100%

| ARGENTINA 24.8% | CANADA 23.7 | UNITED STATES 11.4 | INDIA 16.8 | OTHER 2.9 | SOVIET UNION 9.4 | EUROPE 6.1 | ALL OTH. 2.7 |

SOUTH AMERICA ———— NORTH AMERICA ———— ASIA

Olive Oil World Production—1,730,000 metric tons—Av. 1977-79

0	10	20	30	40	50	60	70	80	90	100%

| ITALY 32.5% | SPAIN 27.0 | GREECE 15.6 | PORT. 2.0 | TURKEY 6.6 | SYRIA 3.0 | TUNISIA 6.1 | MOR. 2.1 | OTHER 2.3 |

EUROPE ———— ASIA ———— AFRICA

Producing Areas

Major	Minor	
■	S	SOYBEANS
■		COTTONSEED
■	C	COPRA

□ OIL PALM FRUIT

ь SESAME SEED

ь SUNFLOWER SEED

Cottonseed World Production—25,522,000 metric tons—Av. 1977-79

0	10	20	30	40	50	60	70	80	90	100%

| SOVIET UNION 22.4% | UNITED STATES 18.5 | MEXICO 2.3 | OTHER 2.2 | CHINA 16.8 | INDIA 9.7 | PAK. 4.4 | TURKEY 3.3 | OTHER 2.2 | BRAZIL 3.9 | OTHER 3.7 | EGYPT 2.9 | OTHER 5.1 |

NORTH AMERICA ———— ASIA ———— S. AM. | AFRICA

Soybeans World Production—84,400,000 metric tons—Av. 1977-79

0	10	20	30	40	50	60	70	80	90	100%

| UNITED STATES 63.4% | CHINA 15.1 | OTHER 2.2 | BRAZIL 12.6 | ARG. 3.0 |

NORTH AMERICA ———— ASIA ———— S. AMERICA

Copra World Production—4,507,000 metric tons—Av. 1977-79

0	10	20	30	40	50	60	70	80	90	100%

| PHILIPPINES 45.4% | INDONESIA 21.1 | INDIA 8.2 | MALAY. 4.7 | SRI L. 2.5 | PAP. N. GUINEA 3.3 | OTHER 3.8 | MEXICO 3.8 | AFRICA 3.8 |

ASIA ———— OC. | N.A.

Palm Oil World Production—4,114,000 metric tons—Av. 1977-79

0	10	20	30	40	50	60	70	80	90	100%

| MALAYSIA 45.2% | INDONESIA 13.2 | CHINA 4.3 | NIGERIA 16.2 | ZAIRE 4.2 | IVORY COAST 3.7 | OTHER 8.0 | S. AM. 2.4 | ALL OTH. 2.5 |

ASIA ———— AFRICA

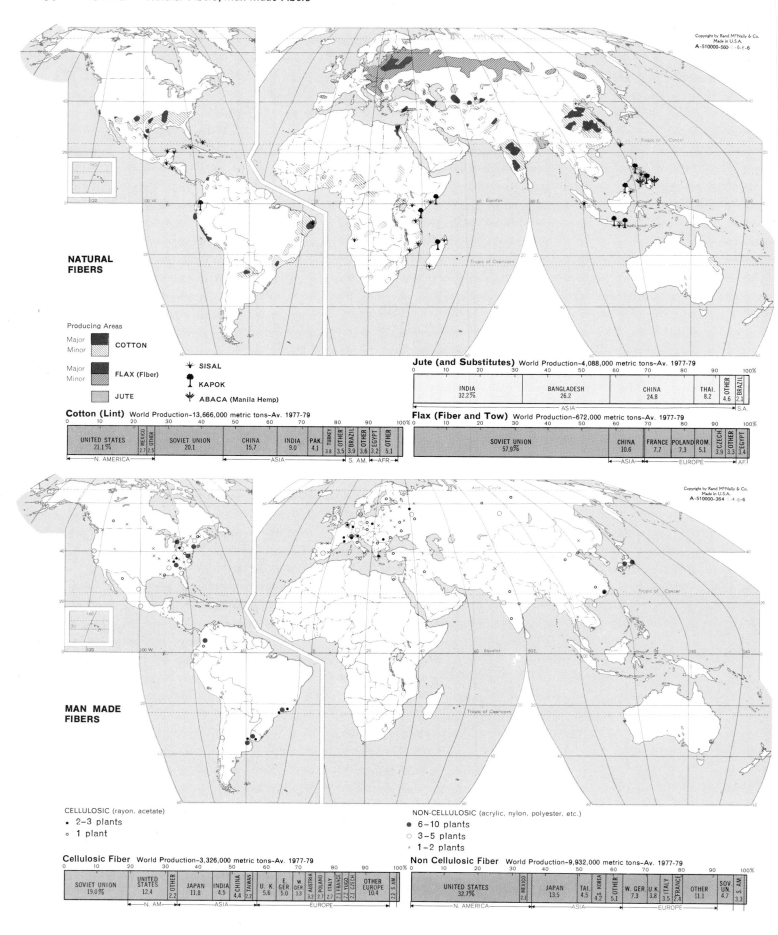

NATURAL FIBERS

Producing Areas

Major	COTTON
Minor	
Major	FLAX (Fiber)
Minor	
	JUTE

✷ SISAL

♣ KAPOK

✸ ABACA (Manila Hemp)

Cotton (Lint) World Production–13,666,000 metric tons–Av. 1977-79

0	10	20	30	40	50	60	70	80	90	100%
UNITED STATES 21.1%		MEXICO 2.7	OTHER 2.5	SOVIET UNION 20.1		CHINA 15.7		INDIA 9.0	PAK. 4.1	TURKEY 3.8	OTHER 3.5	BRAZIL 3.9	OTHER 3.6	EGYPT 3.2	OTHER 5.1

N. AMERICA — ASIA — S. AM. — AFR.

Jute (and Substitutes) World Production–4,088,000 metric tons–Av. 1977-79

0	10	20	30	40	50	60	70	80	90	100%
INDIA 32.2%			BANGLADESH 26.2		CHINA 24.8		THAI. 8.2	OTHER 4.6	BRAZIL 2.1

ASIA — S.A.

Flax (Fiber and Tow) World Production–672,000 metric tons–Av. 1977-79

0	10	20	30	40	50	60	70	80	90	100%
SOVIET UNION 57.9%						CHINA 10.6	FRANCE 7.7	POLAND 7.3	ROM. 5.1	CZECH 3.9	OTHER 3.3	EGYPT 3.4

ASIA — EUROPE — AF.

MAN MADE FIBERS

CELLULOSIC (rayon, acetate)
● 2–3 plants
○ 1 plant

NON-CELLULOSIC (acrylic, nylon, polyester, etc.)
● 6–10 plants
○ 3–5 plants
✕ 1–2 plants

Cellulosic Fiber World Production–3,326,000 metric tons–Av. 1977-79

0	10	20	30	40	50	60	70	80	90	100%
SOVIET UNION 19.0%		UNITED STATES 12.4	OTHER 2.2	JAPAN 11.8	INDIA 4.5	CHINA 4.4	TAIWAN 2.2	U.K. 5.6	E. GER. 5.0	W GER. 3.3	AUSTRIA 3.2	POLAND 2.7	ITALY 2.7	FRANCE 2.3	YUGO 2.2	CZECH 2.1	OTHER EUROPE 10.4	S. AM 2.2

N. AM. — ASIA — EUROPE

Non Cellulosic Fiber World Production–9,932,000 metric tons–Av. 1977-79

0	10	20	30	40	50	60	70	80	90	100%
UNITED STATES 32.7%			MEXICO 2.1	JAPAN 13.5		TAI. 4.5	KOREA 4.2	OTHER 5.1	W. GER. 7.3	U.K. 3.8	ITALY 3.5	FRANCE 2.4	OTHER 11.1	SOV. UN. 4.7	S. AM. 3.3

N. AMERICA — ASIA — EUROPE

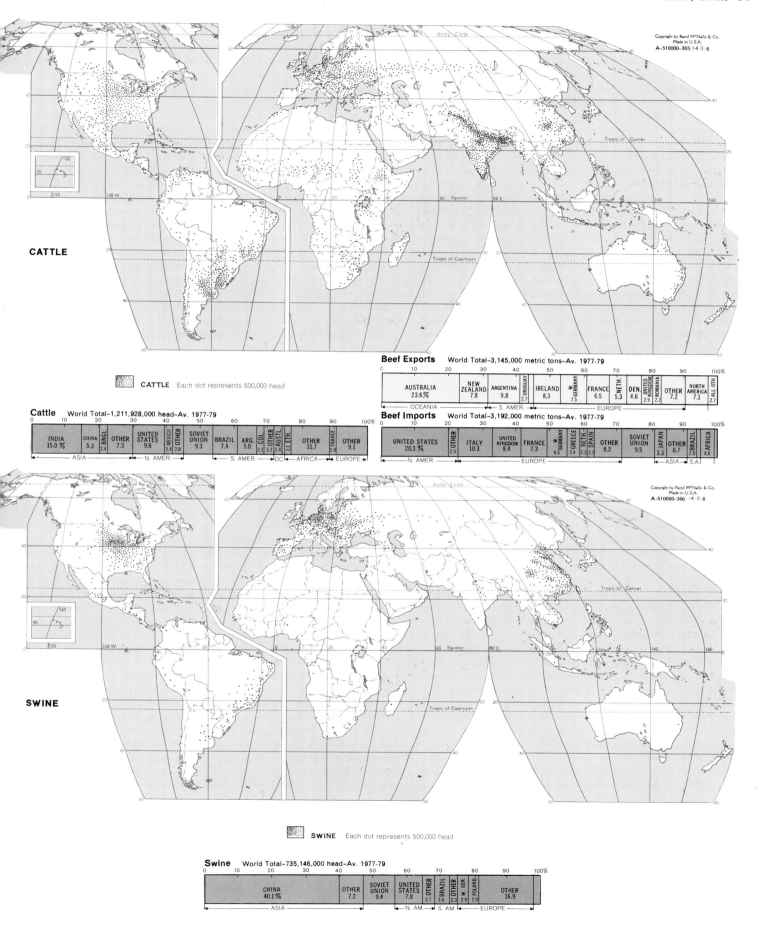

CATTLE

CATTLE   Each dot represents 500,000 head

Cattle   World Total–1,211,928,000 head–Av. 1977-79

INDIA 15.0%	CHINA 5.3	BNGL. 2.4	OTHER 7.3	UNITED STATES 9.6	MEXICO 2.4	OTHER 2.8	SOVIET UNION 9.3	BRAZIL 7.4	ARG. 5.0	COL. 2.1	OTHER 3.3	AUSTL. 2.1	ETH. 2.1	OTHER 11.7	FRANCE 2.0	OTHER 9.1
ASIA				N. AMER.				S. AMER.				OC	AFRICA		EUROPE	

Beef Exports   World Total–3,145,000 metric tons–Av. 1977-79

AUSTRALIA 23.6%	NEW ZEALAND 7.8	ARGENTINA 9.8	URUGUAY 2.7	IRELAND 8.3	W. GERMANY 7.5	FRANCE 6.5	NETH. 5.3	DEN. 4.6	UNITED KINGDOM 2.9	ROMANIA 2.7	OTHER 7.2	NORTH AMERICA 7.1	ALL OTH. 2.7
OCEANIA		S. AMER.		EUROPE									

Beef Imports   World Total–3,192,000 metric tons–Av. 1977-79

UNITED STATES 20.3%	OTHER 2.5	ITALY 10.3	UNITED KINGDOM 8.4	FRANCE 7.3	W. GERMANY 6.5	GREECE 3.4	NETH. 2.3	SPAIN 2.1	OTHER 8.2	SOVIET UNION 9.5	JAPAN 3.3	OTHER 6.7	BRAZIL 2.3	AFRICA 4.5
N. AMER.		EUROPE									ASIA		S.A.	

SWINE

SWINE   Each dot represents 500,000 head

Swine   World Total–735,146,000 head–Av. 1977-79

CHINA 40.1%	OTHER 7.2	SOVIET UNION 9.4	UNITED STATES 7.8	OTHER 3.7	BRAZIL 5.0	OTHER 2.3	W. GER. 2.9	POLAND 2.9	OTHER 16.9
ASIA		N. AM.			S. AM.		EUROPE		

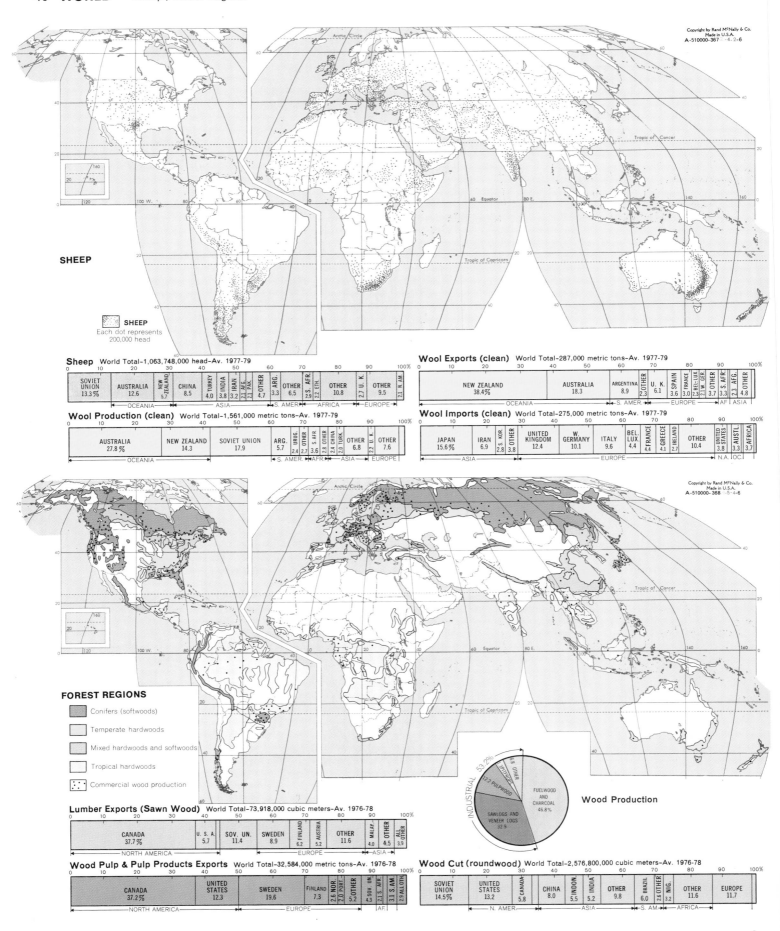

SHEEP

SHEEP
Each dot represents
200,000 head

Sheep World Total–1,063,748,000 head–Av. 1977-79

0	10	20	30	40	50	60	70	80	90	100%

| SOVIET UNION 13.3% | AUSTRALIA 12.6 | NEW ZEALAND 5.7 | CHINA 8.5 | TURKEY 4.0 | INDIA 3.8 | IRAN 3.2 | AFG. 2.1 | PAK. 2.1 | OTHER 4.7 | ARG. 3.3 | OTHER 6.5 | S. AFR. 2.9 | ETH. 2.2 | OTHER 10.8 | U.K. 2.7 | OTHER 9.5 | N. AM. 2.1 |

OCEANIA — ASIA — S. AMER. — AFRICA — EUROPE

Wool Production (clean) World Total–1,561,000 metric tons–Av. 1977-79

0	10	20	30	40	50	60	70	80	90	100%

| AUSTRALIA 27.8% | NEW ZEALAND 14.3 | SOVIET UNION 17.9 | ARG. 5.7 | URUG. 2.4 | OTHER 2.7 | S. AFR. 3.6 | CHINA 2.4 | OTHER 2.8 | OTHER 6.8 | U.K. 2.0 | OTHER 7.6 |

OCEANIA — S. AMER. — AFR — ASIA — EUROPE

Wool Exports (clean) World Total–287,000 metric tons–Av. 1977-79

0	10	20	30	40	50	60	70	80	90	100%

| NEW ZEALAND 38.4% | AUSTRALIA 18.3 | ARGENTINA 8.9 | OTHER 2.3 | U.K. 6.1 | SPAIN 3.6 | FRANCE 3.0 | BEL-LUX 2.1 | W. GER. 2.3 | OTHER 3.7 | S. AFR. 3.3 | AF 2.3 | AFG. 4.8 |

OCEANIA — S. AMER. — EUROPE — AF — ASIA

Wool Imports (clean) World Total–275,000 metric tons–Av. 1977-79

0	10	20	30	40	50	60	70	80	90	100%

| JAPAN 15.6% | IRAN 6.9 | S. KOR. 2.8 | OTHER 3.8 | UNITED KINGDOM 12.4 | W. GERMANY 10.1 | ITALY 9.6 | BEL. LUX. 4.4 | FRANCE 4.4 | GREECE 4.1 | IRELAND 2.7 | OTHER 10.4 | UNITED STATES 3.8 | AUSTL. 3.3 | AFRICA 3.7 |

ASIA — EUROPE — N.A. — OC

FOREST REGIONS

- Conifers (softwoods)
- Temperate hardwoods
- Mixed hardwoods and softwoods
- Tropical hardwoods
- Commercial wood production

Wood Production

Pie chart:
- INDUSTRIAL 53.2%
- OTHER 6.8
- PULPWOOD 13.5
- PULPWOOD 2.2
- SAWLOGS AND VENEER LOGS 32.9
- FUELWOOD AND CHARCOAL 46.8%

Lumber Exports (Sawn Wood) World Total–73,918,000 cubic meters–Av. 1976-78

0	10	20	30	40	50	60	70	80	90	100%

| CANADA 37.7% | U.S.A. 5.7 | SOV. UN. 11.4 | SWEDEN 8.9 | FINLAND 6.2 | AUSTRIA 5.2 | OTHER 11.6 | MALAY. 4.0 | OTHER 4.5 | ALL OTHER 3.9 |

NORTH AMERICA — EUROPE — ASIA

Wood Pulp & Pulp Products Exports World Total–32,584,000 metric tons–Av. 1976-78

0	10	20	30	40	50	60	70	80	90	100%

| CANADA 37.2% | UNITED STATES 12.3 | SWEDEN 19.6 | FINLAND 7.3 | NOR. 2.6 | PORT. 2.0 | OTHER 5.2 | SOV. UN. 5.2 | S. AFR. 2.1 | S. AM. 3.1 | ALL OTH. 2.9 |

NORTH AMERICA — EUROPE — AF.

Wood Cut (roundwood) World Total–2,576,800,000 cubic meters–Av. 1976-78

0	10	20	30	40	50	60	70	80	90	100%

| SOVIET UNION 14.5% | UNITED STATES 13.2 | CANADA 5.8 | CHINA 8.0 | INDON. 5.5 | INDIA 5.2 | OTHER 9.8 | BRAZIL 6.0 | OTHER 2.6 | NIG. 3.2 | OTHER 11.6 | EUROPE 11.7 |

N. AMER. — ASIA — S. AM — AFRICA

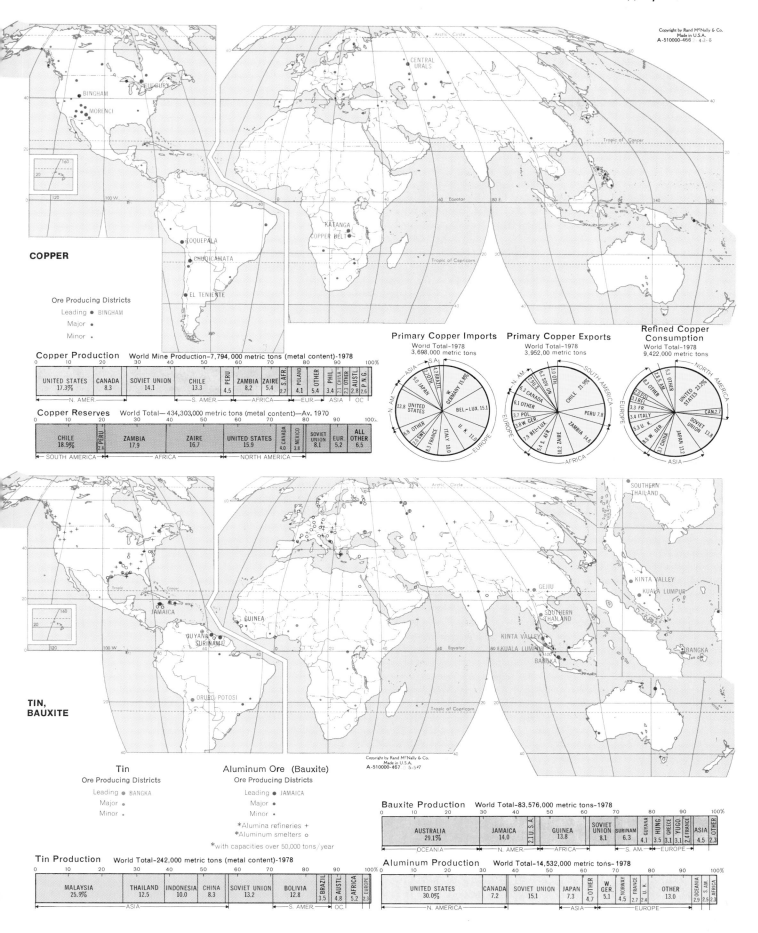

COPPER

Ore Producing Districts

Leading ● BINGHAM

Major ●

Minor ●

Copper Production World Mine Production–7,794,000 metric tons (metal content)-1978

UNITED STATES 17.3%	CANADA 8.3	SOVIET UNION 14.1	CHILE 13.3	PERU 4.5	ZAMBIA 8.2	ZAIRE 5.4	S. AFR. 2.7	POLAND 4.1	OTHER 5.4	PHIL. 3.4	CHINA 2.1	OTHER 2.3	AUSTL. 2.8	P.N.G. 2.6
N. AMER.			S. AMER.		AFRICA			EUR.		ASIA			OC	

Copper Reserves World Total— 434,303,000 metric tons (metal content)—Av. 1970

CHILE 18.9%	PERU 2.4	ZAMBIA 17.9	ZAIRE 16.7	UNITED STATES 15.9	CANADA 4.0	MEXICO 3.8	SOVIET UNION 8.1	EUR. 5.2	ALL OTHER 6.5
SOUTH AMERICA		AFRICA		NORTH AMERICA					

Primary Copper Imports
World Total-1978
3,698,000 metric tons

S. Ai
4.2 BRAZIL
2.7 OTH.
9.0 JAPAN
ASIA
N. AM.
W. GERMANY 15.9%
13.8 UNITED STATES
BEL.–LUX. 15.1
16.8 OTHER
2.0 SWE.
ITALY 10.0
8.3 FRANCE
U.K. 11.0
EUROPE

Primary Copper Exports
World Total-1978
3,952,00 metric tons

SOUTH AMERICA
3.0 OTH.
6.2 SOV. UN.
20.3
6.3 CANADA
N. AM.
CHILE 21.9%
6.1 OTHER
3.8 W. GER.
7.9 BEL.–LUX.
PERU 7.8
5.4 S. AFR.
POL
ZAMBIA 14.6
10.2 ZAIRE
AFRICA
EUROPE

Refined Copper Consumption
World Total-1978
9,422,000 metric tons

NORTH AMERICA
5.3 OTHER
2.8 S. AM.
2.0 POL.
3.1 BEL.
UNITED STATES 23.2%
3.3 FR.
3.4 ITALY
CAN. 2.7
5.3 U.K.
SOVIET UNION 13.8
5.5 W. GER.
6.3 CHINA
JAPAN 13.2
ASIA

TIN, BAUXITE

Tin
Ore Producing Districts

Leading ● BANGKA

Major ●

Minor ●

Aluminum Ore (Bauxite)
Ore Producing Districts

Leading ● JAMAICA

Major ●

Minor ●

*Alumina refineries +
*Aluminum smelters o

*with capacities over 50,000 tons/year

Bauxite Production World Total-83,576,000 metric tons-1978

AUSTRALIA 29.1%	JAMAICA 14.0	U.S.A. 2.1	GUINEA 13.8	SOVIET UNION 8.1	SURINAM 6.3	GUYANA 4.1	HUNG. 3.5	GREECE 3.1	YUGO. 3.1	FRANCE 2.4	ASIA 4.5	OTHER
OCEANIA	N. AMER.		AFRICA		S. AM.		EUROPE					

Tin Production World Total-242,000 metric tons (metal content)-1978

MALAYSIA 25.9%	THAILAND 12.5	INDONESIA 10.0	CHINA 8.3	SOVIET UNION 13.2	BOLIVIA 12.8	BRAZIL 3.5	AUSTL. 4.8	AFRICA 5.2	EUROPE 2.3
ASIA						S. AMER.	OC.		

Aluminum Production World Total-14,532,000 metric tons-1978

UNITED STATES 30.0%	CANADA 7.2	SOVIET UNION 15.1	JAPAN 7.3	W. GER. 4.7	NORWAY 5.1	FRANCE 4.5	U.K. 2.7	OTHER 13.0	OCEANIA 2.9	S. AM 2.5	AFRICA 2.3
N. AMERICA		ASIA		EUROPE							

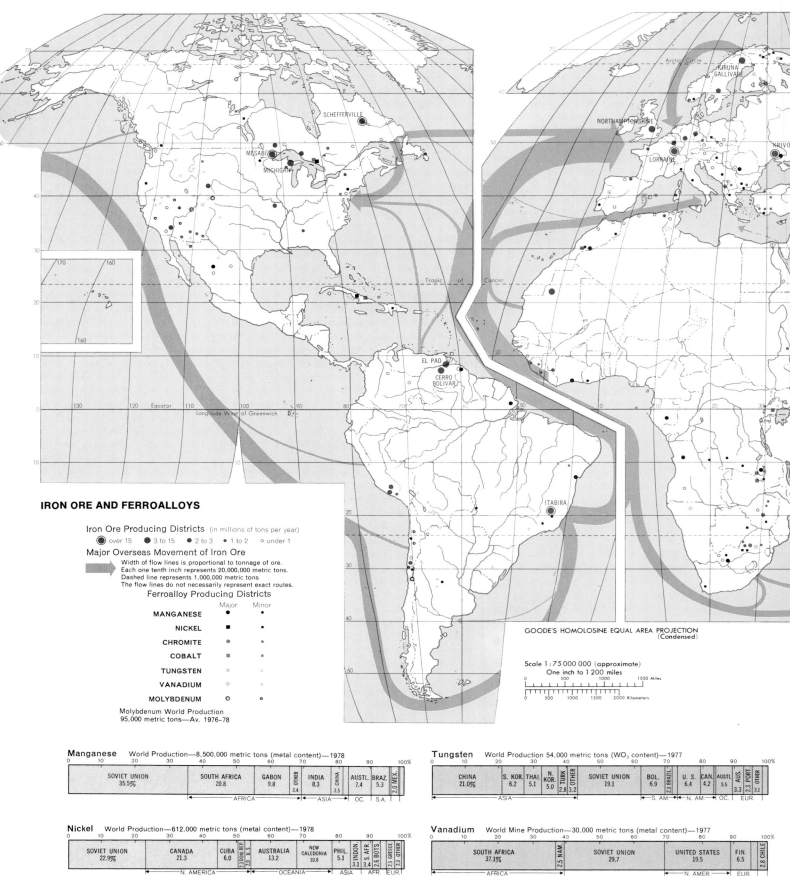

IRON ORE AND FERROALLOYS

Iron Ore Producing Districts (in millions of tons per year)

● over 15 ● 3 to 15 ● 2 to 3 ● 1 to 2 ○ under 1

Major Overseas Movement of Iron Ore

Width of flow lines is proportional to tonnage of ore.
Each one tenth inch represents 20,000,000 metric tons.
Dashed line represents 1,000,000 metric tons
The flow lines do not necessarily represent exact routes.

Ferroalloy Producing Districts

	Major	Minor
MANGANESE	●	●
NICKEL	■	■
CHROMITE	●	●
COBALT	■	■
TUNGSTEN	●	●
VANADIUM	■	■
MOLYBDENUM	○	○

Molybdenum World Production
95,000 metric tons—Av. 1976-78

GOODE'S HOMOLOSINE EQUAL AREA PROJECTION
(Condensed)

Scale 1 : 75 000 000 (approximate)
One inch to 1 200 miles

0   500   1000   1500 Miles

0   500   1000   1500   2000 Kilometers

Manganese World Production—8,500,000 metric tons (metal content)—1978

SOVIET UNION 35.5%	SOUTH AFRICA 20.8	GABON 9.8	OTHER 3.4	INDIA 8.3	CHINA 3.5	AUSTL. 7.4	BRAZ. 5.3	MEX. 2.0

AFRICA — ASIA — OC. — S.A.

Tungsten World Production 54,000 metric tons (WO₃ content)—1977

CHINA 21.0%	S. KOR. 6.2	THAI. 5.1	N. KOR. 5.0	TURK 2.8	OTHER 3.2	SOVIET UNION 19.1	BOL. 6.9	BRAZIL 2.3	U. S. 6.4	CAN. 4.2	AUSTL. 5.5	AUS. 3.3	PORT. 2.3	OTHER 3.1

ASIA — S. AM. — N. AM. — OC. — EUR.

Nickel World Production—612,000 metric tons (metal content)—1978

SOVIET UNION 22.9%	CANADA 21.3	CUBA 6.0	DOM. REP. 2.3	U.S. 2.0	AUSTRALIA 13.2	NEW CALEDONIA 10.8	PHIL. 5.1	INDON. 3.1	S. AFR. 2.6	BOTS. 2.6	GREECE 2.5	OTHER 2.3

N. AMERICA — OCEANIA — ASIA — AFR. — EUR.

Vanadium World Mine Production—30,000 metric tons (metal content)—1977

SOUTH AFRICA 37.1%	NAM. 2.5	SOVIET UNION 29.7	UNITED STATES 19.5	FIN. 6.5	CHILE 2.8

AFRICA — N. AMER. — EUR.

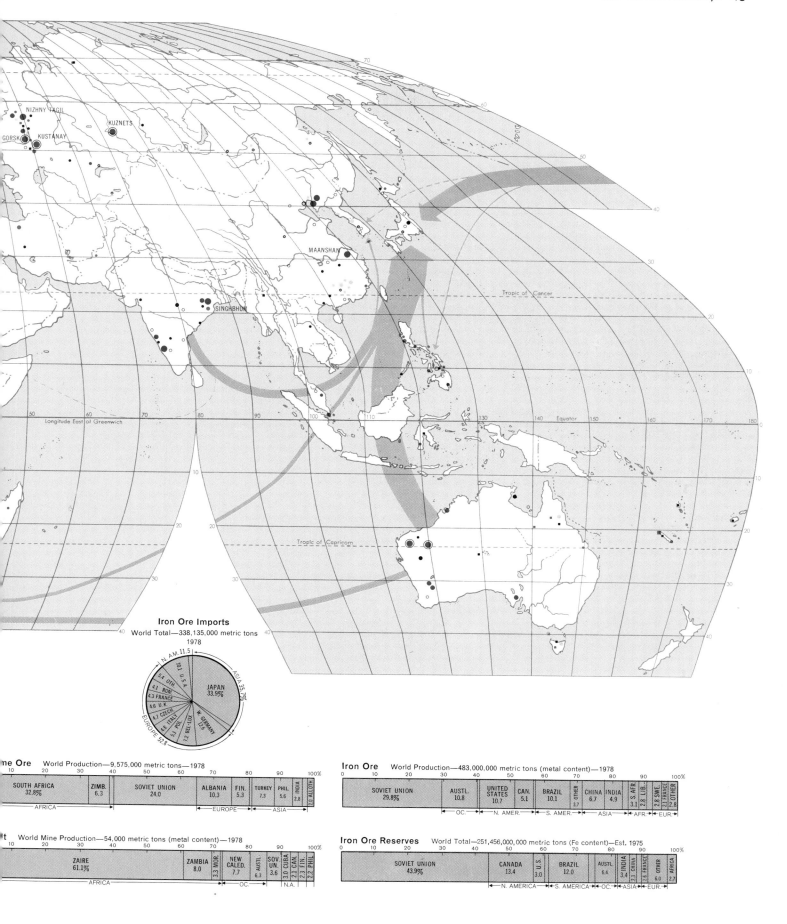

Iron Ore Imports
World Total—338,135,000 metric tons
1978

N. AM. 11.5
10.1 U.S.A
5.4 OTH.
4.1 ROM.
4.3 FRANCE
4.6 U.K.
4.7 CZECH.
4.8 POL.
5.1 ITALY
7.2 BEL-LUX
W. GERMANY 12.8
EUROPE 52.8
JAPAN 33.9%
ASIA 35.7%

ne Ore World Production—9,575,000 metric tons—1978

SOUTH AFRICA 32.8%	ZIMB. 6.3	SOVIET UNION 24.0	ALBANIA 10.3	FIN. 5.3	TURKEY 7.3	PHIL. 5.6	INDIA 2.8	2.0 ALLOTH.	
AFRICA			EUROPE		ASIA				

Iron Ore World Production—483,000,000 metric tons (metal content)—1978

SOVIET UNION 29.8%	AUSTL. 10.8	UNITED STATES 10.7	CAN. 5.1	BRAZIL 10.1	OTHER 3.7	CHINA 6.7	INDIA 4.9	S. AFR. 3.1	2.8 LIB.	2.8 SWE. 2.1 FRANCE	OTHER 2.8
	OC.	N. AMER.		S. AMER.		ASIA		AFR.		EUR.	

t World Mine Production—54,000 metric tons (metal content)—1978

ZAIRE 61.1%	ZAMBIA 8.0	3.3 MOR.	NEW CALED. 7.7	AUSTL. 6.3	SOV. UN. 3.6	CUBA 3.0	CAN. 2.1	FIN. 2.3	PHIL. 2.2
AFRICA			OC.		N.A.				

Iron Ore Reserves World Total—251,456,000,000 metric tons (Fe content)—Est. 1975

SOVIET UNION 43.9%	CANADA 13.4	U.S. 3.0	BRAZIL 12.0	AUSTL. 6.4	INDIA 2.3	CHINA	FRANCE 2.6	OTHER 6.0	AFRICA 2.7
	N. AMERICA		S. AMERICA	OC.	ASIA		EUR.		

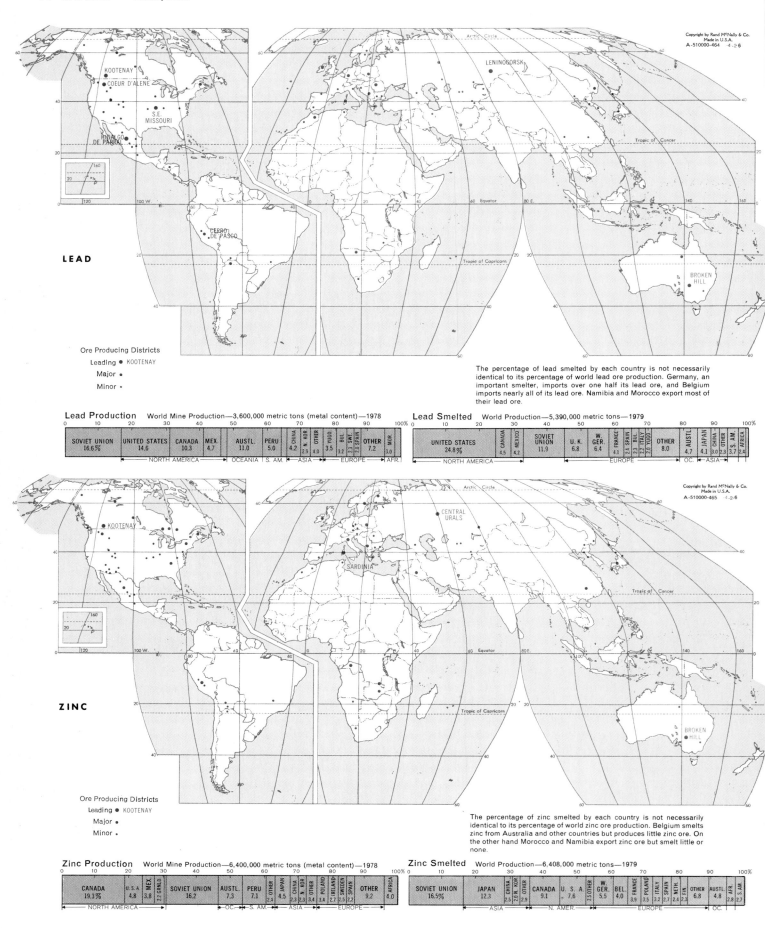

LEAD

Ore Producing Districts

Leading ● KOOTENAY

Major •

Minor ·

The percentage of lead smelted by each country is not necessarily identical to its percentage of world lead ore production. Germany, an important smelter, imports over one half its lead ore, and Belgium imports nearly all of its lead ore. Namibia and Morocco export most of their lead ore.

Lead Production World Mine Production—3,600,000 metric tons (metal content)—1978

SOVIET UNION 16.6%	UNITED STATES 14.6	CANADA 10.3	MEX. 4.7	AUSTL. 11.0	PERU 5.0	CHINA 4.2	N. KOR. 2.5	OTHER 4.0	YUGO 3.5	BUL. 3.4	SWE. 2.3	SPAIN 2.0	OTHER 7.2	MOR. 3.0
NORTH AMERICA				OCEANIA	S. AM.	ASIA			EUROPE					AFR.

Lead Smelted World Production—5,390,000 metric tons—1979

UNITED STATES 24.8%	CANADA 4.5	MEXICO 4.2	SOVIET UNION 11.9	U.K. 6.8	W. GER. 6.4	FRANCE 4.1	SPAIN 2.4	BUL. 2.3	ITALY 2.2	YUGO 2.0	OTHER 8.0	AUSTL. 4.7	JAPAN 4.1	CHINA 3.0	S. AM. 2.3	AFRICA 2.4
NORTH AMERICA			EUROPE									OC.	ASIA			

ZINC

Ore Producing Districts

Leading ● KOOTENAY

Major •

Minor ·

The percentage of zinc smelted by each country is not necessarily identical to its percentage of world zinc ore production. Belgium smelts zinc from Australia and other countries but produces little zinc ore. On the other hand Morocco and Namibia export zinc ore but smelt little or none.

Zinc Production World Mine Production—6,400,000 metric tons (metal content)—1978

CANADA 19.3%	U.S.A. 4.8	MEX. 3.8	GRNLD. 2.2	SOVIET UNION 16.2	AUSTL. 7.3	PERU 7.1	OTHER 2.4	JAPAN 4.5	CHINA 4.0	N. KOR. 3.4	OTHER 3.4	POLAND 3.4	IRELAND 2.7	SWEDEN 2.3	SPAIN 2.2	OTHER 9.2	AFRICA 4.0
NORTH AMERICA					OC.	S. AM.		ASIA				EUROPE					

Zinc Smelted World Production—6,408,000 metric tons—1979

SOVIET UNION 16.5%	JAPAN 12.3	CHINA 2.6	N. KOR. 2.6	OTHER 2.9	CANADA 9.1	U.S.A. 7.6	OTHER 2.5	W. GER. 5.5	BEL. 4.0	FRANCE 3.9	POLAND 3.2	ITALY 3.2	SPAIN 2.9	NETH. 2.3	FIN. 2.3	OTHER 6.8	AUSTL. 4.8	AFR. 2.8	S. AM. 2.7
ASIA					N. AMER.			EUROPE									OC.		

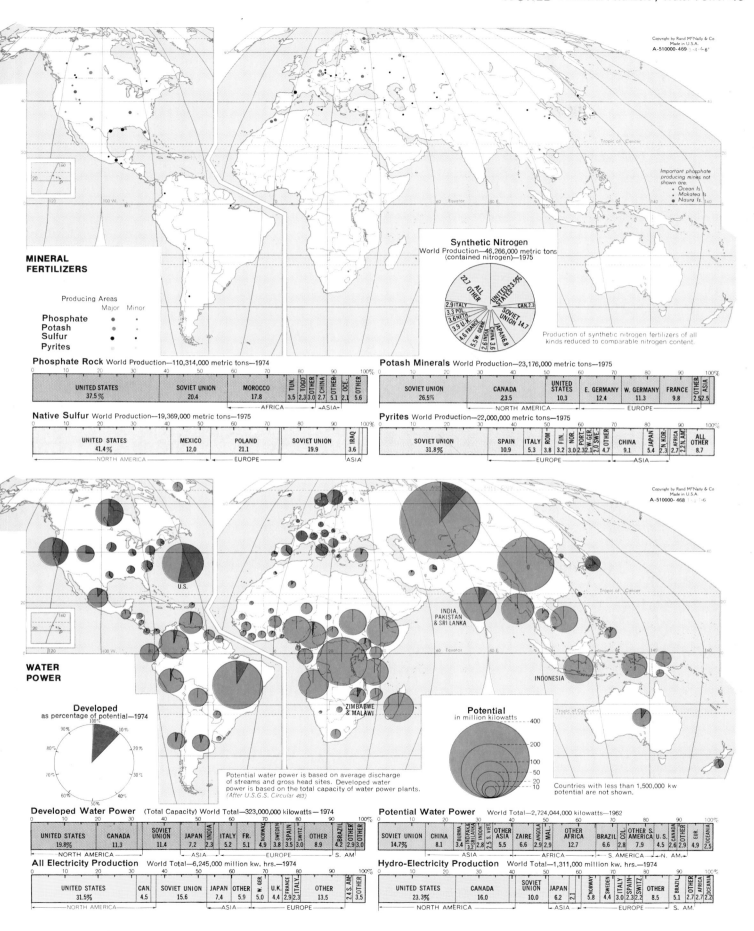

Important phosphate
producing mines not
shown are:
• Ocean Is
▲ Makatea Is
● Nauru Is.

MINERAL FERTILIZERS

Producing Areas

	Major	Minor
Phosphate		
Potash		
Sulfur		
Pyrites		

Synthetic Nitrogen
World Production—46,266,000 metric tons
(contained nitrogen)—1975

Production of synthetic nitrogen fertilizers of all
kinds reduced to comparable nitrogen content.

Phosphate Rock World Production—110,314,000 metric tons—1974

UNITED STATES 37.5%	SOVIET UNION 20.4	MOROCCO 17.8	TUN. 3.5	TOGO 2.3	OTHER 3.0	CHINA 2.7	OTHER 5.1	OCE. 2.1	OTHER 5.6

AFRICA — ASIA

Potash Minerals World Production—23,176,000 metric tons—1975

SOVIET UNION 26.5%	CANADA 23.5	UNITED STATES 10.3	E. GERMANY 12.4	W. GERMANY 11.3	FRANCE 9.8	OTHER 2.5	ASIA 2.5

NORTH AMERICA — EUROPE

Native Sulfur World Production—19,369,000 metric tons—1975

UNITED STATES 41.4%	MEXICO 12.0	POLAND 21.1	SOVIET UNION 19.9	IRAQ 3.6

NORTH AMERICA — EUROPE — ASIA

Pyrites World Production—22,000,000 metric tons—1975

SOVIET UNION 31.8%	SPAIN 10.9	ITALY 5.3	ROM 3.8	FIN 3.2	NOR. 3.0	PORT. 2.3	W. GER. 2.1	SWE. 2.0	OTHER 4.7	CHINA 9.1	JAPAN 5.4	N. KOR. 2.3	AFRICA 2.7	N. AM. 2.2	ALL OTHER 8.7

EUROPE — ASIA

WATER POWER

Developed
as percentage of potential—1974

Potential water power is based on average discharge
of streams and gross head sites. Developed water
power is based on the total capacity of water power plants.
(After U.S.G.S. Circular 483)

Potential
in million kilowatts

— 400
— 200
— 100
— 50
— 20
— 10

Countries with less than 1,500,000 kw
potential are not shown.

Developed Water Power (Total Capacity) World Total—323,000,000 kilowatts—1974

UNITED STATES 19.8%	CANADA 11.3	SOVIET UNION 11.4	JAPAN 7.2	INDIA 2.3	ITALY 5.2	FR. 5.1	NORWAY 4.9	SWEDEN 3.5	SWITZ. 3.0	OTHER 8.9	BRAZIL 4.2	OTHER 2.9	OTHER 3.1

NORTH AMERICA — ASIA — EUROPE — S. AM

Potential Water Power World Total—2,724,044,000 kilowatts—1962

SOVIET UNION 14.7%	CHINA 8.1	BURMA 3.4	INDIA-PAK & SRI LANKA 3.2	INDO. 2.8	S. VIET. 2.5	OTHER ASIA 5.5	ZAIRE 6.6	ANGOLA 2.9	MAL. 2.9	OTHER AFRICA 12.7	BRAZIL 6.6	COL. 2.8	OTHER S. AMERICA 7.9	U.S. 4.5	CANADA 2.6	OTHER 2.9	EUR. 4.9	OCEANIA 2.5

ASIA — AFRICA — S. AMERICA — N. AM.

All Electricity Production World Total—6,245,000 million kw. hrs.—1974

UNITED STATES 31.5%	CAN. 4.5	SOVIET UNION 15.6	JAPAN 7.4	OTHER 5.9	W. GER. 5.0	U.K. 4.4	FRANCE 2.9	ITALY 2.3	OTHER 13.5	S. AM 2.4	OTHER 3.5

NORTH AMERICA — ASIA — EUROPE

Hydro-Electricity Production World Total—1,311,000 million kw. hrs.—1974

UNITED STATES 23.3%	CANADA 16.0	SOVIET UNION 10.0	JAPAN 6.2	2.1	NORWAY 5.8	SWEDEN 4.4	ITALY 3.0	SPAIN 2.3	SWITZ. 2.2	OTHER 8.5	BRAZIL 5.1	OTHER 2.7	AFRICA 2.7	OCEANIA 2.2

NORTH AMERICA — ASIA — EUROPE — S. AM.

U.S.

INDIA, PAKISTAN & SRI LANKA

INDONESIA

ZIMBABWE & MALAWI

MEXICO

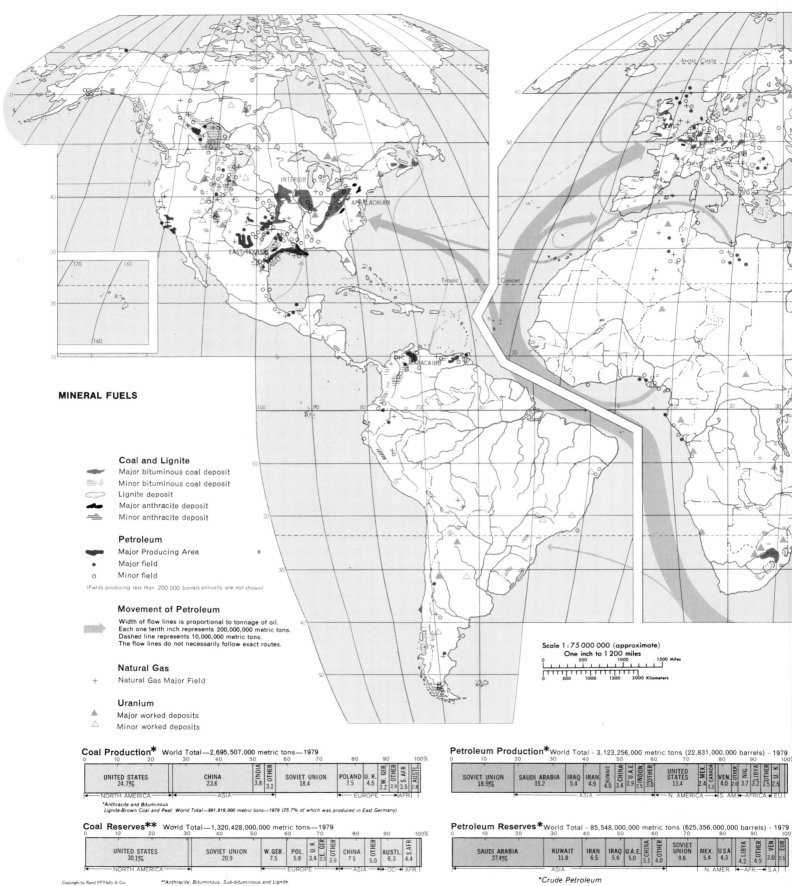

Arctic Circle

INTERIOR

APPALACHIAN

EAST TEXAS GULF

Tropic of Cancer

SILESIA

MARACAIBO

MINERAL FUELS

Coal and Lignite

Major bituminous coal deposit

Minor bituminous coal deposit

Lignite deposit

Major anthracite deposit

Minor anthracite deposit

Petroleum

Major Producing Area

• Major field

○ Minor field

(Fields producing less than 200,000 barrels annually are not shown)

Movement of Petroleum

Width of flow lines is proportional to tonnage of oil.
Each one tenth inch represents 200,000,000 metric tons.
Dashed line represents 10,000,000 metric tons.
The flow lines do not necessarily follow exact routes.

Natural Gas

+ Natural Gas Major Field

Uranium

▲ Major worked deposits

△ Minor worked deposits

Scale 1:75 000 000 (approximate)
One inch to 1 200 miles

0   500   1000   1500 Miles

0   500   1000   1500   2000 Kilometers

Coal Production* World Total—2,695,507,000 metric tons—1979

0	10	20	30	40	50	60	70	80	90	100%

| UNITED STATES 24.7% | CHINA 23.6 | INDIA 3.8 | OTHER 3.1 | SOVIET UNION 18.4 | POLAND 7.5 | U.K. 4.5 | W. GER. 3.2 | OTHER 2.9 | S. AFR. 3.5 | AUSTL. 2.8 |

◄——NORTH AMERICA——► ◄————ASIA————► ◄————EUROPE————► ◄AFR.►

*Anthracite and Bituminous
Lignite-Brown Coal and Peat: World Total—991,819,000 metric tons—1979 (25.7% of which was produced in East Germany)

Coal Reserves** World Total—1,320,428,000,000 metric tons—1979

0	10	20	30	40	50	60	70	80	90	100%

| UNITED STATES 30.1% | SOVIET UNION 20.9 | W. GER. 7.5 | POL. 5.8 | U.K. 3.4 | E. GER. 3.9 | CHINA 7.5 | OTHER 5.0 | AUSTL. 6.3 | S. AFR. 4.4 |

◄——NORTH AMERICA——► ◄————EUROPE————► ◄———ASIA———► ◄OC.► ◄AFR.►

Petroleum Production* World Total - 3,123,256,000 metric tons (22,831,000,000 barrels) - 1979

0	10	20	30	40	50	60	70	80	90	100%

| SOVIET UNION 18.9% | SAUDI ARABIA 15.2 | IRAQ 5.4 | IRAN 4.9 | KUWAIT 4.0 | CHINA 3.4 | U.A.E. 2.9 | INDON. 3.0 | OTHER | UNITED STATES 13.4 | MEX. 2.4 | CANADA 2.3 | VEN. 4.0 | NIG. 3.7 | LIBYA 3.5 | OTHER | U.K. 2.5 |

◄————————————ASIA————————————► ◄——N. AMERICA——► ◄S. AM.► ◄AFRICA► ◄EU►

Petroleum Reserves* World Total - 85,548,000,000 metric tons (625,356,000,000 barrels) - 1979

0	10	20	30	40	50	60	70	80	90	100%

| SAUDI ARABIA 27.4% | KUWAIT 11.8 | IRAN 6.5 | IRAQ 5.6 | U.A.E. 5.0 | CHINA 3.1 | OTHER 4.0 | SOVIET UNION 9.6 | MEX. 5.4 | USA 4.3 | LIBYA 4.2 | OTHER 4.9 | VEN. 3.7 | S.A. 2.5 |

◄————————————ASIA————————————► ◄——N. AMER.——► ◄AFR.► ◄S.A.►

*Crude Petroleum

**Anthracite, Bituminous, Sub-bituminous and Lignite

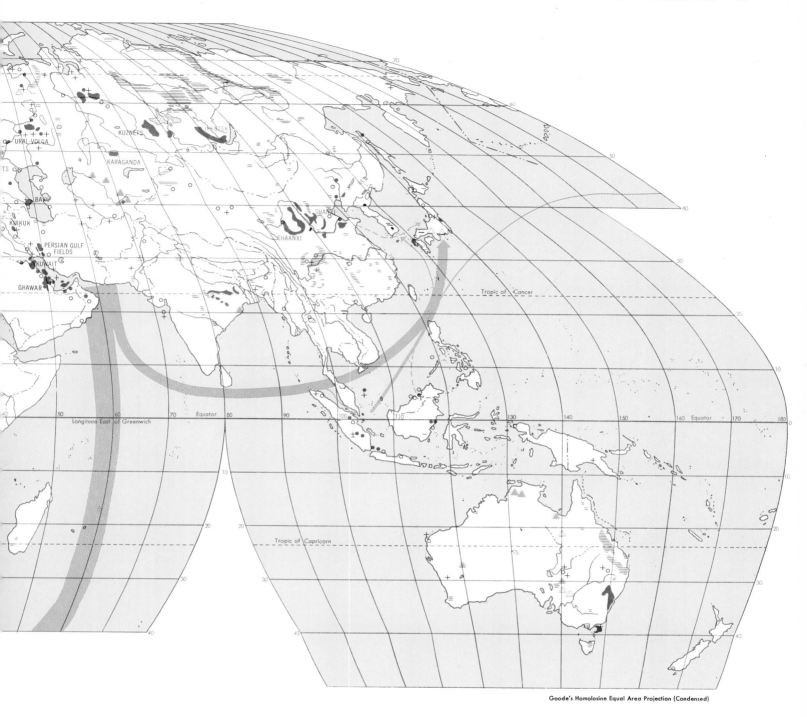

KUZNETS

URAL-VOLGA

KARAGANDA

TS

BAKU

KIRKUK

PERSIAN GULF
FIELDS

KUWAIT

GHAWAR

SHANXI

SHAANXI

70

60

50

40

30

Tropic of Cancer

20

10

50   60   70   *Equator*   80   90   100   110   120   130   140   150   160   *Equator*   170   180

Longitude East of Greenwich

10

Tropic of Capricorn

20

30

40

Goode's Homolosine Equal Area Projection (Condensed)

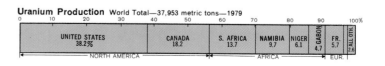

ral Gas Production World Total—1,456,000,000,000 cubic meters—1979

10	20	30	40	50	60	70	80	90	100%

UNITED STATES 39.0%	CAN. 5.8	SOVIET UNION 26.3	NETH. 6.2	ROM. 2.8	U.K. 2.6	OTHER 6.0	ASIA 5.6	S. AM. 2.1

—— NORTH AMERICA ——   —— EUROPE ——

ral Gas Reserves World Total—70,391,000,000,000 cubic meters—1979

10	20	30	40	50	60	70	80	90	100%

SOVIET UNION 36.6%	IRAN 14.9	SAUDI ARABIA 5.1	OTHER 10.9	U.S. 7.8	CAN. 3.6	MEX. 2.5	ALG. 4.0	NIGERIA 2.0	NETH. 2.3	OTHER 3.6	S. AM 3.4

—— ASIA ——   N. AMER.   AFR.   EUR.

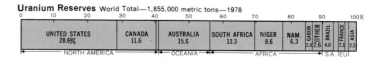

Uranium Production World Total—37,953 metric tons—1979

10	20	30	40	50	60	70	80	90	100%

UNITED STATES 38.2%	CANADA 18.2	S. AFRICA 13.7	NAMIBIA 9.7	NIGER 6.1	GABON 4.7	FR. 5.7	ALL OTH.

—— NORTH AMERICA ——   —— AFRICA ——   EUR.

Uranium Reserves World Total—1,855,000 metric tons—1978

10	20	30	40	50	60	70	80	90	100%

UNITED STATES 28.6%	CANADA 11.6	AUSTRALIA 15.6	SOUTH AFRICA 13.3	NIGER 8.6	NAM. 6.3	GABON 2.0	OTHER 4.0	BRAZIL 4.0	FRANCE 2.1	ASIA 2.2

—— NORTH AMERICA ——   OCEANIA   —— AFRICA ——   S.A. EUR.

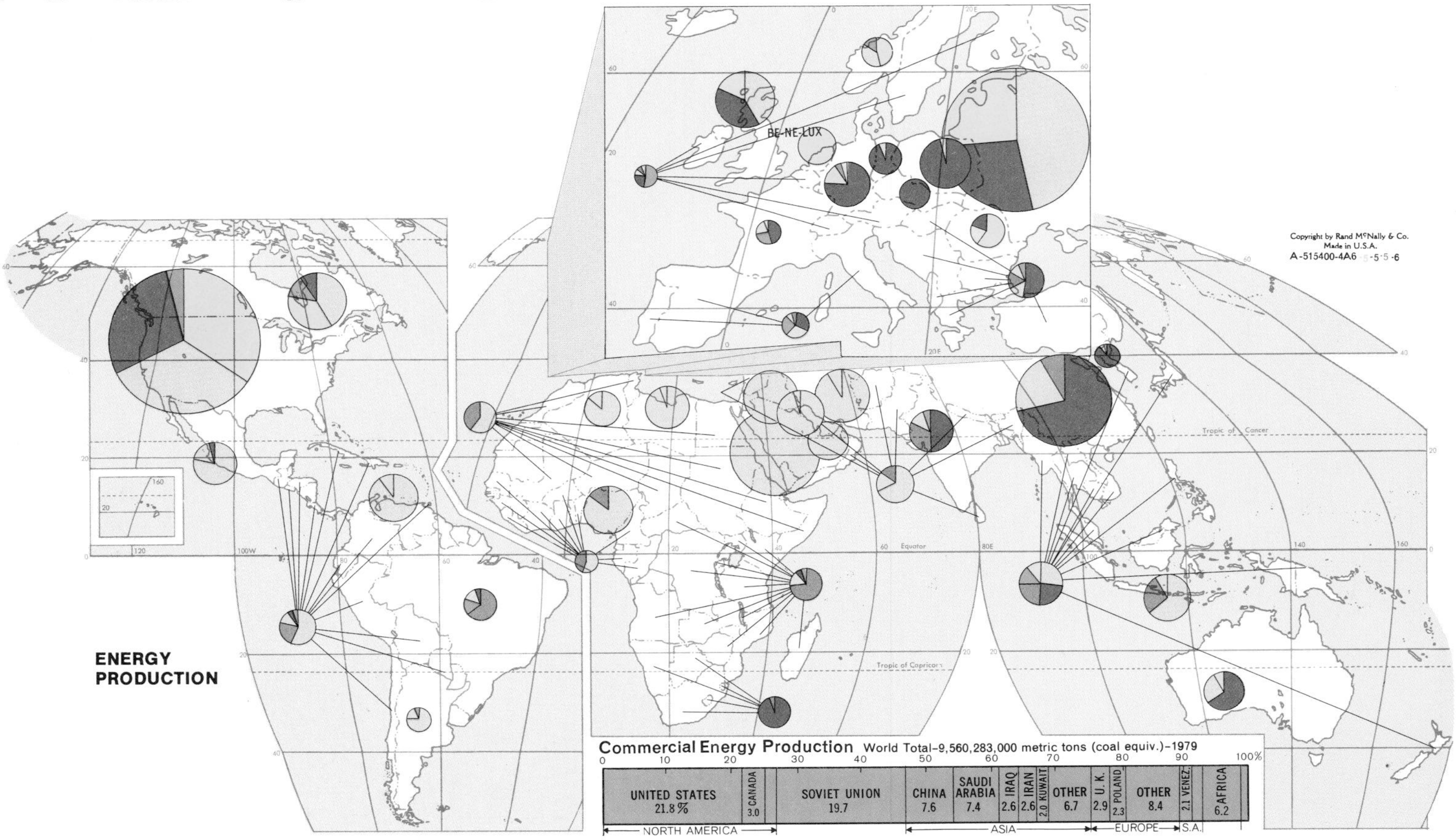

ENERGY PRODUCTION

Commercial Energy Production World Total–9,560,283,000 metric tons (coal equiv.)–1979

| 0 | 10 | 20 | 30 | 40 | 50 | 60 | 70 | 80 | 90 | 100% |

| UNITED STATES 21.8% | CANADA 3.0 | SOVIET UNION 19.7 | CHINA 7.6 | SAUDI ARABIA 7.4 | IRAQ 2.6 | IRAN 2.6 | KUWAIT 2.0 | OTHER 6.7 | U.K. 2.9 | POLAND 2.3 | OTHER 8.4 | VENEZ. 2.1 | AFRICA 6.2 |

NORTH AMERICA — ASIA — EUROPE — S.A.

Volume of Energy
in millions of metric tons
(Coal equivalent)–1979

— 2,500
— 1,000
— 500
— 250
— 100
— 40

Volume data is not shown for countries with less than
1 million metric tons (coal equivalent)

Composition of Energy

Commercial Energy

| Solid fuels | Liquid fuels | Natural and imported gas | Hydro, nuclear & imported electricity | Other |

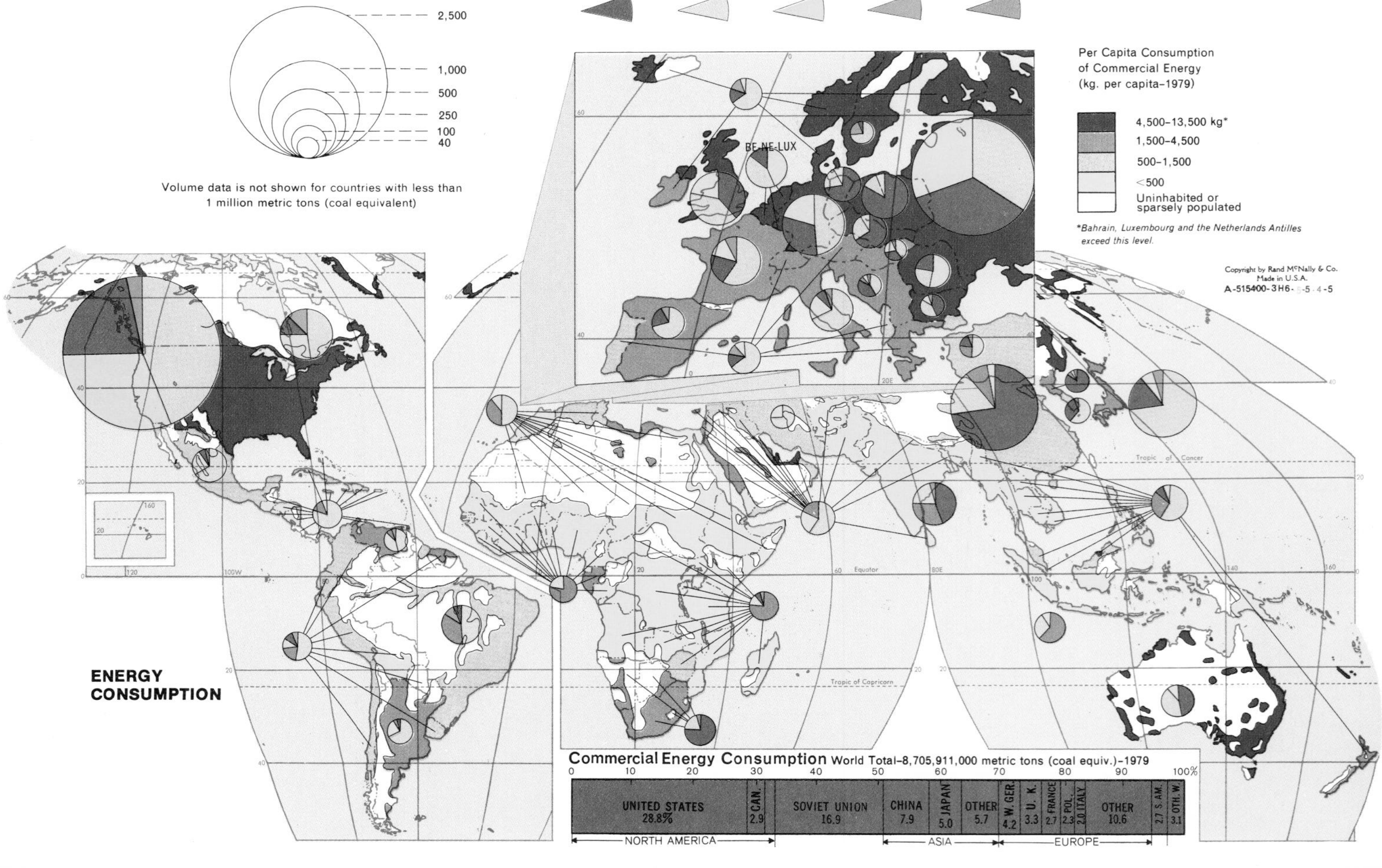

Per Capita Consumption
of Commercial Energy
(kg. per capita–1979)

4,500–13,500 kg*
1,500–4,500
500–1,500
<500
Uninhabited or
sparsely populated

*Bahrain, Luxembourg and the Netherlands Antilles
exceed this level.

ENERGY CONSUMPTION

Commercial Energy Consumption World Total–8,705,911,000 metric tons (coal equiv.)–1979

| 0 | 10 | 20 | 30 | 40 | 50 | 60 | 70 | 80 | 90 | 100% |

| UNITED STATES 28.8% | CAN. 2.9 | SOVIET UNION 16.9 | CHINA 7.9 | JAPAN 5.7 | OTHER 5.7 | W. GER. 4.2 | U.K. 3.3 | FRANCE 2.7 | POL. 2.7 | ITALY 2.0 | OTHER 10.6 | S. AM. 2.7 | OTH. W. 3.1 |

NORTH AMERICA — ASIA — EUROPE

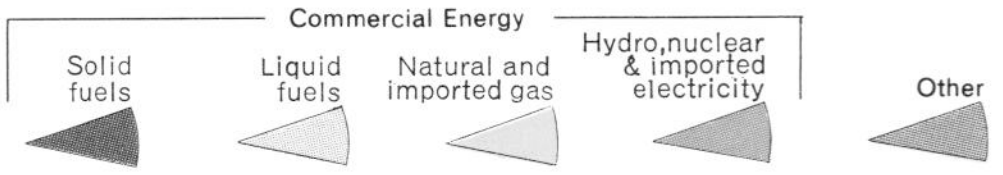

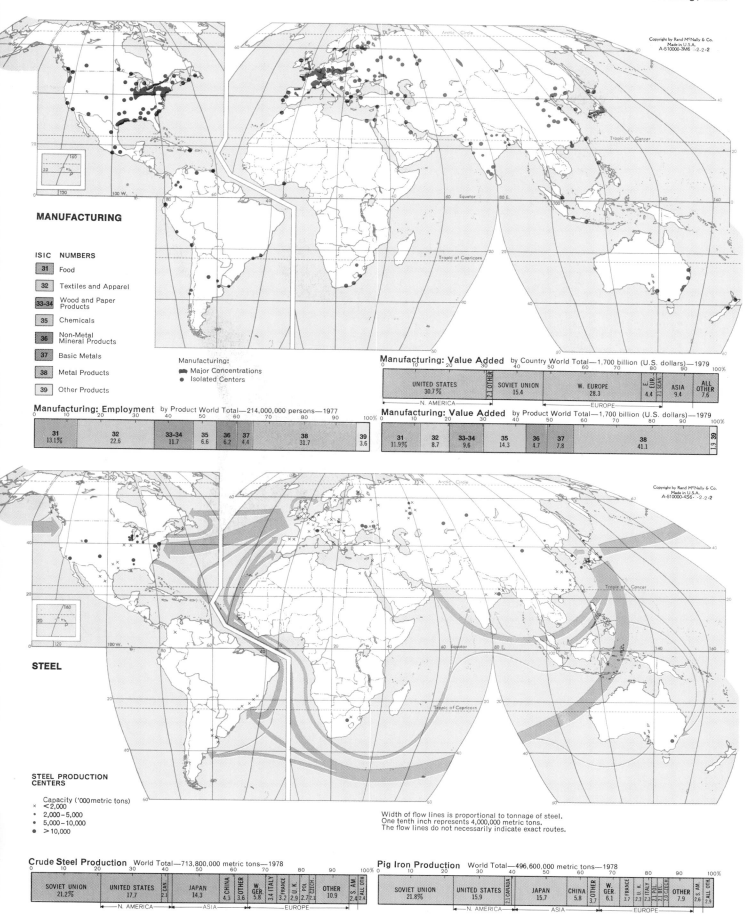

MANUFACTURING

ISIC NUMBERS

31	Food
32	Textiles and Apparel
33-34	Wood and Paper Products
35	Chemicals
36	Non-Metal Mineral Products
37	Basic Metals
38	Metal Products
39	Other Products

Manufacturing:
- Major Concentrations
- Isolated Centers

Manufacturing: Value Added by Country World Total—1,700 billion (U.S. dollars)—1979

UNITED STATES 30.7%	OTHER 2.1	SOVIET UNION 15.4	W. EUROPE 28.3	E. EUR. 4.4	SCAN. 2.1	ASIA 9.4	ALL OTHER 7.6
N. AMERICA			EUROPE				

Manufacturing: Employment by Product World Total—214,000,000 persons—1977

31 13.1%	32 22.6	33-34 11.7	35 6.6	36 6.2	37 4.4	38 31.7	39 3.6

Manufacturing: Value Added by Product World Total—1,700 billion (U.S. dollars)—1979

31 11.9%	32 8.7	33-34 9.6	35 14.3	36 4.7	37 7.8	38 41.1	39 1.9

STEEL

STEEL PRODUCTION CENTERS

Capacity ('000 metric tons)
- × <2,000
- • 2,000–5,000
- • 5,000–10,000
- • >10,000

Width of flow lines is proportional to tonnage of steel.
One tenth inch represents 4,000,000 metric tons.
The flow lines do not necessarily indicate exact routes.

Crude Steel Production World Total—713,800,000 metric tons—1978

SOVIET UNION 21.2%	UNITED STATES 17.7	CAN. 2.1	JAPAN 14.3	CHINA 4.3	OTHER 3.6	W. GER. 5.8	ITALY 3.4	FRANCE 3.2	U.K. 2.9	POL 2.7	CZECH 2.1	OTHER 10.9	S. AM. 2.4	ALL OTH 2.4
	N. AMERICA		ASIA			EUROPE								

Pig Iron Production World Total—496,600,000 metric tons—1978

SOVIET UNION 21.8%	UNITED STATES 15.9	CANADA 2.1	JAPAN 15.7	CHINA 5.8	OTHER 3.7	W. GER. 6.1	FRANCE 3.7	U.K. 2.3	ITALY 2.1	POL 2.1	CZECH 2.1	OTHER 7.9	S. AM. 2.6	ALL OTH 2.9
	N. AMERICA		ASIA			EUROPE								

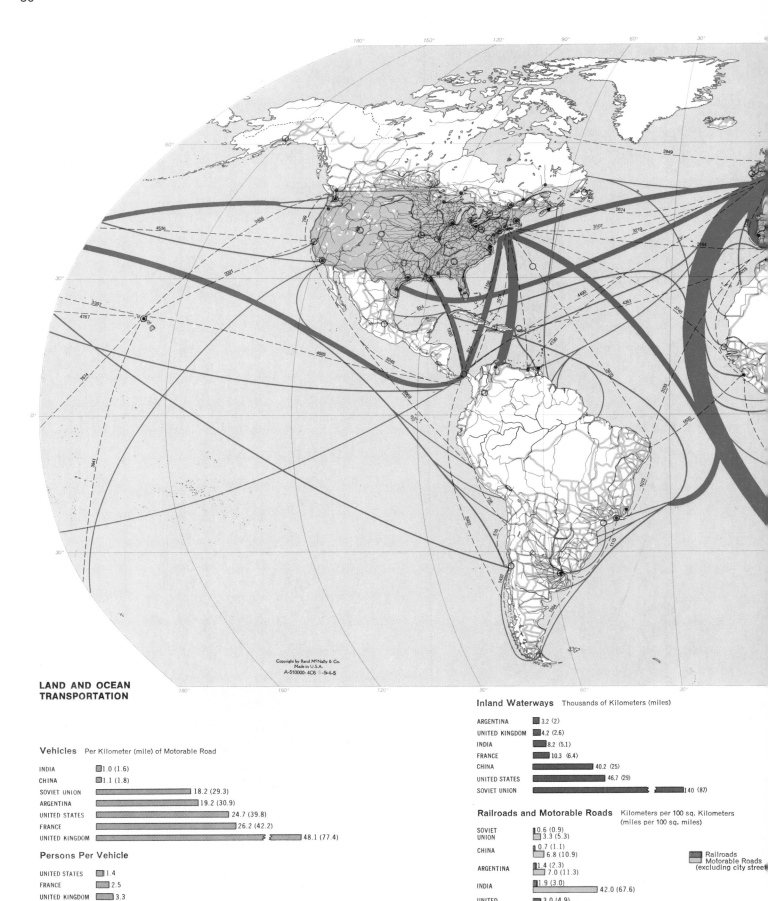

Copyright by Rand McNally & Co.
Made in U.S.A.
A-510000-4C6 -5-4-5

LAND AND OCEAN TRANSPORTATION

Vehicles Per Kilometer (mile) of Motorable Road

INDIA   1.0 (1.6)
CHINA   1.1 (1.8)
SOVIET UNION   18.2 (29.3)
ARGENTINA   19.2 (30.9)
UNITED STATES   24.7 (39.8)
FRANCE   26.2 (42.2)
UNITED KINGDOM   48.1 (77.4)

Persons Per Vehicle

UNITED STATES   1.4
FRANCE   2.5
UNITED KINGDOM   3.3
ARGENTINA   6.8
SOVIET UNION   19
INDIA   485
CHINA   1125

Inland Waterways Thousands of Kilometers (miles)

ARGENTINA   3.2 (2)
UNITED KINGDOM   4.2 (2.6)
INDIA   8.2 (5.1)
FRANCE   10.3 (6.4)
CHINA   40.2 (25)
UNITED STATES   46.7 (29)
SOVIET UNION   140 (87)

Railroads and Motorable Roads Kilometers per 100 sq. Kilometers
(miles per 100 sq. miles)

SOVIET UNION   0.6 (0.9)
                 3.3 (5.3)
CHINA   0.7 (1.1)
                 6.8 (10.9)
ARGENTINA   1.4 (2.3)
                 7.0 (11.3)
INDIA   1.9 (3.0)
                 42.0 (67.6)
UNITED STATES   3.0 (4.9)
                 67.0 (107.9)
FRANCE   6.4 (10.2)
                 146.0 (2
UNITED KINGDOM   7.5 (12.0)
                 153.

Railroads
Motorable Roads
(excluding city street

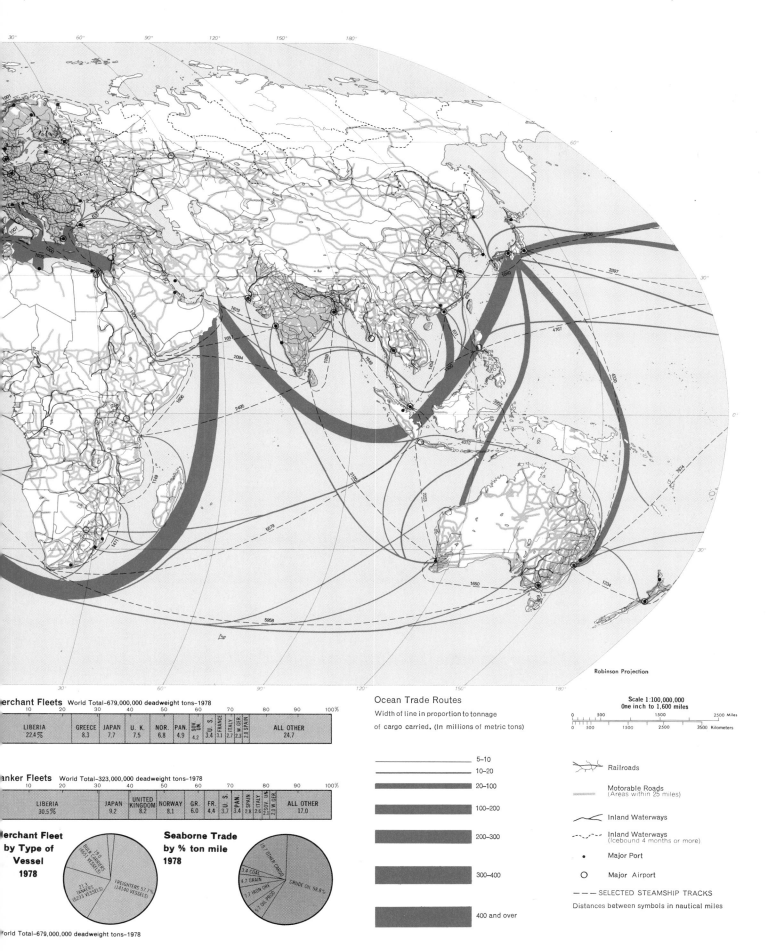

Robinson Projection

Merchant Fleets World Total–679,000,000 deadweight tons–1978

	10	20	30	40	50	60	70	80	90	100%

| LIBERIA 22.4% | GREECE 8.3 | JAPAN 7.7 | U. K. 7.5 | NOR. 6.8 | PAN. 4.9 | SOV. UN. 4.2 | U. S. 3.4 | FRANCE 3.1 | ITALY 2.7 | W. GER. 2.3 | SPAIN 2.0 | ALL OTHER 24.7 |

Tanker Fleets World Total–323,000,000 deadweight tons–1978

	10	20	30	40	50	60	70	80	90	100%

| LIBERIA 30.5% | JAPAN 9.2 | UNITED KINGDOM 8.2 | NORWAY 8.1 | GR. 6.0 | FR. 4.4 | U. S. 3.7 | PAN. 3.4 | SPAIN 2.8 | ITALY 2.6 | SOV UN. 2.1 | W.GER. 2.0 | ALL OTHER 17.0 |

Merchant Fleet by Type of Vessel 1978

BULK CARRIERS 19.0 (1651 VESSELS)
TANKERS 21.3 (5233 VESSELS)
FREIGHTERS 57.7% (14140 VESSELS)

World Total–679,000,000 deadweight tons–1978

Seaborne Trade by % ton mile 1978

CRUDE OIL 58.5%
OIL/OTHER CARGO 19.0
GRAIN 4.7
COAL 3.4
IRON ORE 7.7
OIL PROD. 6.7

Ocean Trade Routes

Width of line in proportion to tonnage of cargo carried. (In millions of metric tons)

	5–10
	10–20
	20–100
	100–200
	200–300
	300–400
	400 and over

Scale 1:100,000,000
One inch to 1,600 miles

0   500   1500   2500 Miles
0   500   1500   2500   3500 Kilometers

Railroads

Motorable Roads (Areas within 25 miles)

Inland Waterways

Inland Waterways (Icebound 4 months or more)

• Major Port

○ Major Airport

– – – SELECTED STEAMSHIP TRACKS

Distances between symbols in nautical miles

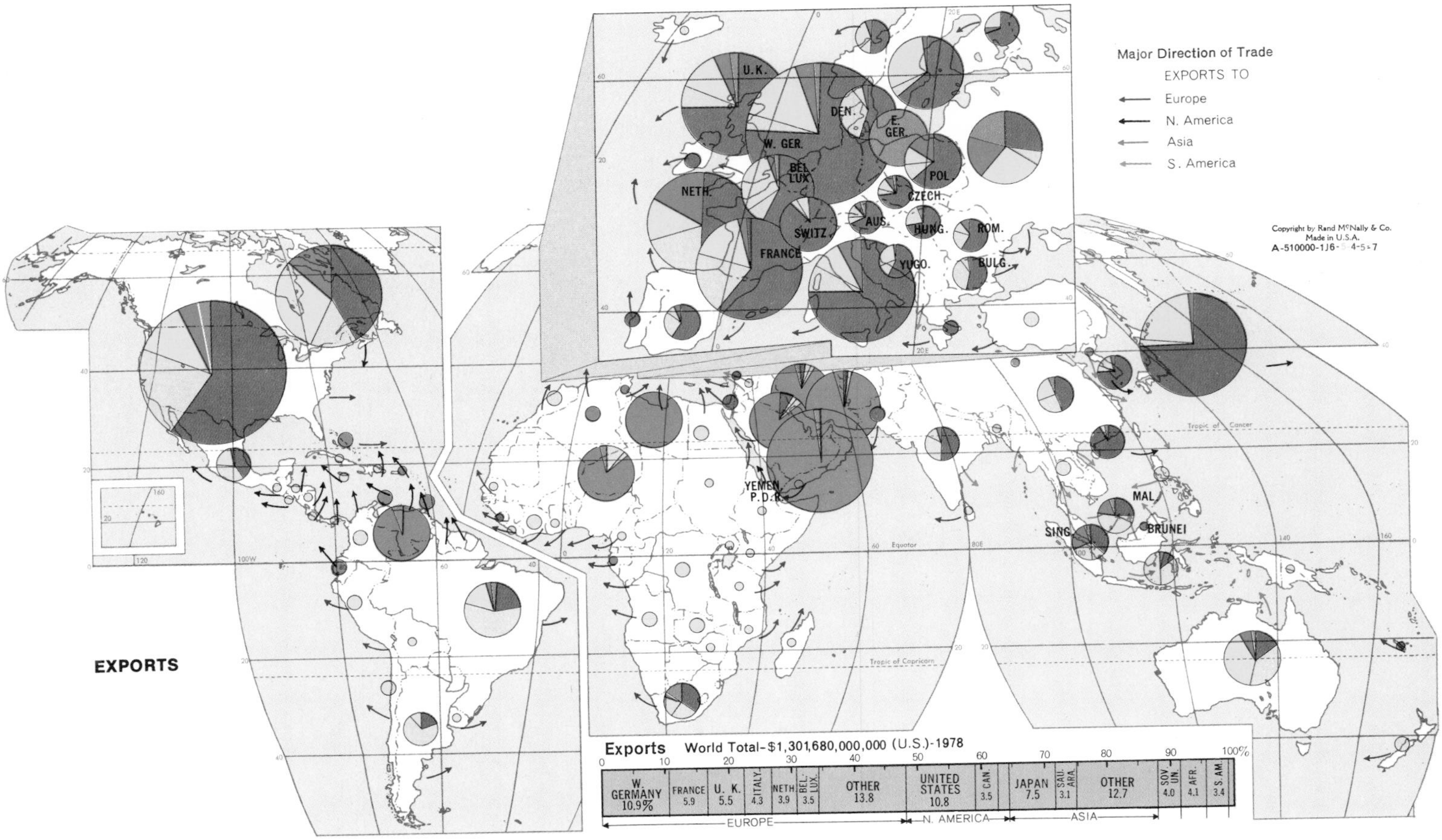
Major Direction of Trade
EXPORTS TO
Europe
N. America
Asia
S. America
U.K.
DEN.
E. GER.
W. GER.
BEL. LUX.
POL.
NETH.
CZECH.
SWITZ.
AUS.
HUNG.
ROM.
FRANCE
YUGO.
BULG.
YEMEN P.D.R.
MAL.
BRUNEI
SING.
Tropic of Cancer
Equator
Tropic of Capricorn
Exports World Total-$1,301,680,000,000 (U.S.)-1978
W. GERMANY 10.9%
FRANCE 5.9
U. K. 5.5
ITALY 4.3
NETH 3.9
BEL. LUX. 3.5
OTHER 13.8
UNITED STATES 10.8
CAN 3.5
JAPAN 7.5
SAU. ARA 3.1
OTHER 12.7
SOV. UN. 4.0
AFR. 4.1
S. AM. 3.4
EUROPE
N. AMERICA
ASIA

EXPORTS

Composition of Trade
(Data based on 1974)

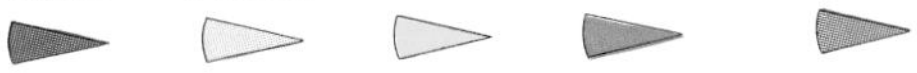
Manufactured Articles
Food, bev. & tobacco
Raw Materials
Fuel & Related Prod.
All other or undifferentiated

Volume of Trade
(in millions of U.S. dollars)
(1974)

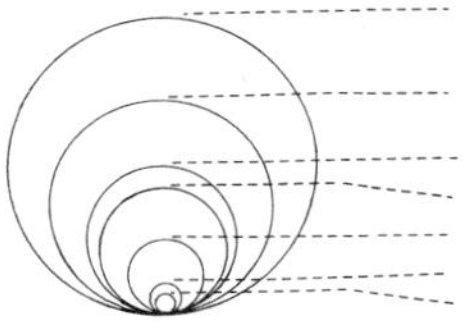
75,000–100,000
30,000–75,000
15,000–30,000
7,500–15,000
3,000–7,500
1,000–3,000
0–1,000

If volume of trade is less than three billion dollars color indicates major class only

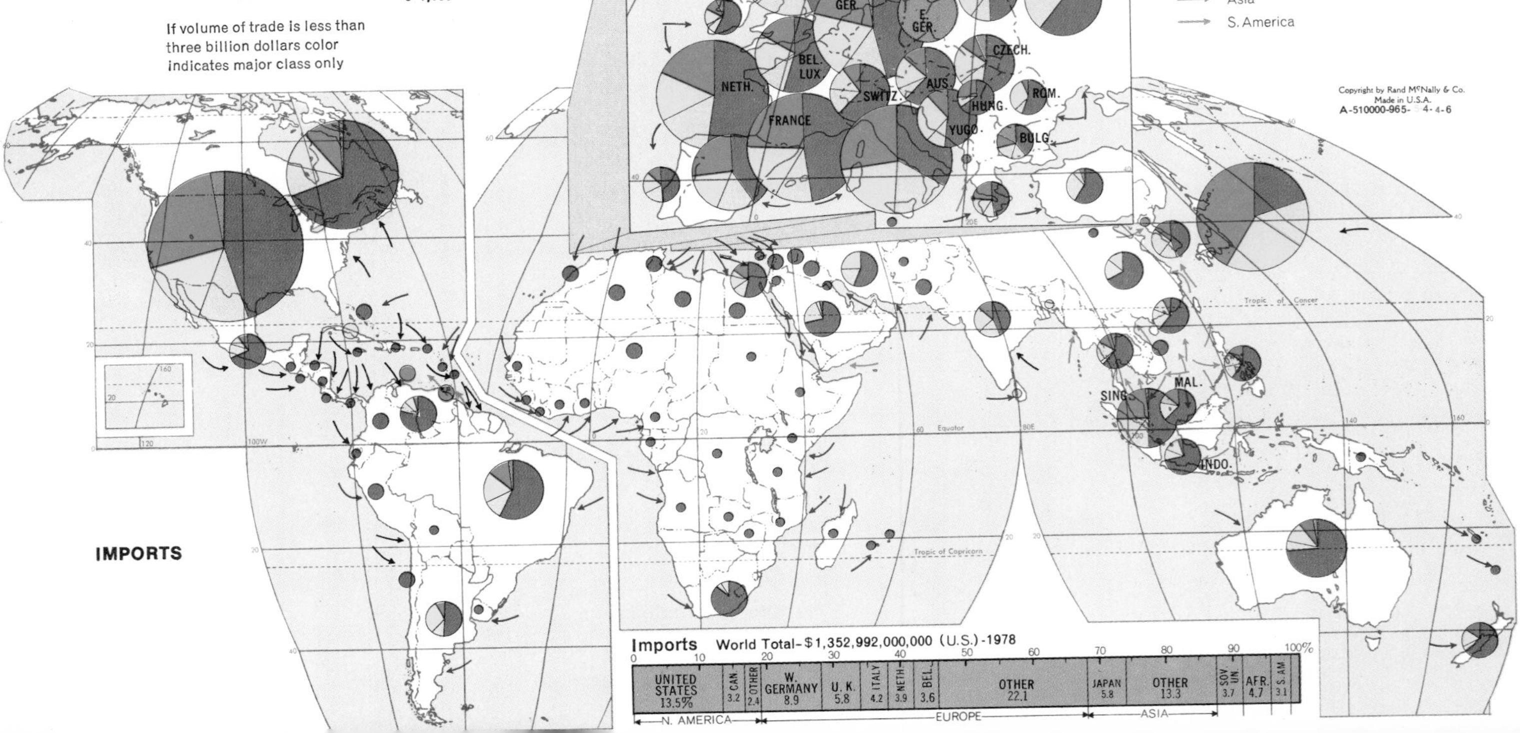
Major Direction of Trade
IMPORTS FROM
Europe
N. America
Asia
S. America
U.K.
DEN.
POL.
W. GER.
E. GER.
BEL. LUX.
CZECH.
NETH.
SWITZ.
AUS.
ROM.
FRANCE
HUNG.
YUGO.
BULG.
SING.
MAL.
INDO.
Tropic of Cancer
Equator
Tropic of Capricorn
Imports World Total-$1,352,992,000,000 (U.S.)-1978
UNITED STATES 13.5%
CAN. 3.2
OTHER 2.4
W. GERMANY 8.9
U. K. 5.8
ITALY 4.2
NETH. 3.9
BEL. 3.6
OTHER 22.1
JAPAN 5.8
OTHER 13.3
SOV. UN 3.7
AFR. 4.7
S. AM 3.1
N. AMERICA
EUROPE
ASIA

IMPORTS

major cities maps

This section consists of 62 maps of the world's most populous metropolitan areas. In order to make comparison easier, all the metropolitan areas are shown at the same scale, 1:300,000.

Detailed urban maps are an important reference requirement for a world atlas. The names of many large settlements, towns, suburbs, and neighborhoods can be located on these large-scale maps. From a thematic standpoint the maps show generalized land-use patterns. Included were the total urban extent, major industrial areas, parks, public land, wooded areas, airports, shopping centers, streets, and railroads. A special effort was made to portray the various metropolitan areas in a manner as standard and comparable as possible. (For the symbols used, see the legend below.)

Notable differences occur in the forms of cities. In most of North America these forms were conditioned by a rectangular pattern of streets; land-use zones (residential, commercial, industrial) are well defined. The basic structure of most European cities is noticeably different and more complex; street patterns are irregular and zones are less well defined. In Asia, Africa, and South America the form tends to be even more irregular and complex. Widespread dispersion of craft and trade activities has lessened zonation, there may be cities with no identifiable city centers, and sometimes there may be dual centers (old and modern). Higher population densities result in more limited, compact urban places in these areas of the world.

A separate index of the metropolitan-area maps' place-names starts on page 244.

Inhabited Localities

The symbol represents the number of inhabitants within the locality

- · 0—10,000
- ○ 10,000—25,000
- ◉ 25,000—100,000
- ▣ 100,000—250,000
- ▆ 250,000—1,000,000
- ■ >1,000,000

The size of type indicates the relative economic and political importance of the locality

Écommoy		
Trouville	**St.-Denis**	
Lisieux	**PARIS**	

Hollywood	Section of a City,
Westminster	Neighborhood
Northland ■	
Center	Major Shopping Center

Urban Area (area of continuous industrial, commercial, and residential development)

Major Industrial Area

Wooded Area

Political Boundaries

International (First-order political unit)

▬ ▪ ▬ ▪ Demarcated, Undemarcated, and Administrative

▬ ▪ ▪ ▬ Demarcation Line

Internal

State, Province, etc. (Second-order political unit)

County, Oblast, etc. (Third-order political unit)

Okrug, Kreis, etc. (Fourth-order political unit)

- - - - - - City or Municipality (may appear in combination with another boundary symbol)

Capitals of Political Units

BUDAPEST	Independent Nation
Recife	State, Province, etc.
White Plains	County, Oblast, etc.
Iserlohn	Okrug, Kreis, etc.

Transportation

Road

Primary

Secondary

Tertiary

Railway

CANADIAN NATIONAL — Primary

Secondary

Rapid Transit

Airport

LONDON (HEATHROW) AIRPORT

Rail or Air Terminal

■ SÜD BAHNHOF

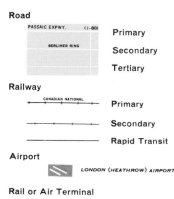

REICHS-BRÜCKE — Bridge

Tunnel

GREAT ST. BERNARD TUNNEL

Houston Ship Channel — Shipping Channel

Canal du Midi — Navigable Canal

TO MALMÖ — Ferry

Hydrographic Features

Shoreline

Undefined or Fluctuating Shoreline

Amur — River, Stream

Intermittent Stream

Rapids, Falls

SALTO ÁNGEL — Navigable Canal

Canal du Midi

Irrigation or Drainage Canal

Los Angeles Aqueduct — Aqueduct

Pier, Breakwater

GREAT BARRIER REEF — Reef

L. Victoria — Lake, Reservoir

Intermittent Lake

The Everglades — Swamp

Miscellaneous Cultural Features

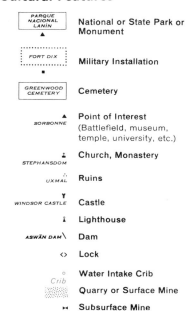

PARQUE NACIONAL LANÍN
▲ — National or State Park or Monument

FORT DIX — Military Installation

GREENWOOD CEMETERY — Cemetery

▲ SORBONNE — Point of Interest (Battlefield, museum, temple, university, etc.)

♱ STEPHANSDOM — Church, Monastery

∴ UXMAL — Ruins

♜ WINDSOR CASTLE — Castle

⚲ — Lighthouse

ASWĀN DAM — Dam

<> — Lock

○ Crib — Water Intake Crib

▒ — Quarry or Surface Mine

⋈ — Subsurface Mine

Topographic Features

Mt. Kenya 5199 △ — Elevation Above Sea Level

Elevations are given in meters

⋆ — Rock

A N D E S Mountain Range, Plateau,
KUNLUNSHANMAI Valley, etc.

BAFFIN ISLAND — Island

POLUOSTROV KAMČATKA — Peninsula, Cape, Point, etc.
CABO DE HORNOS

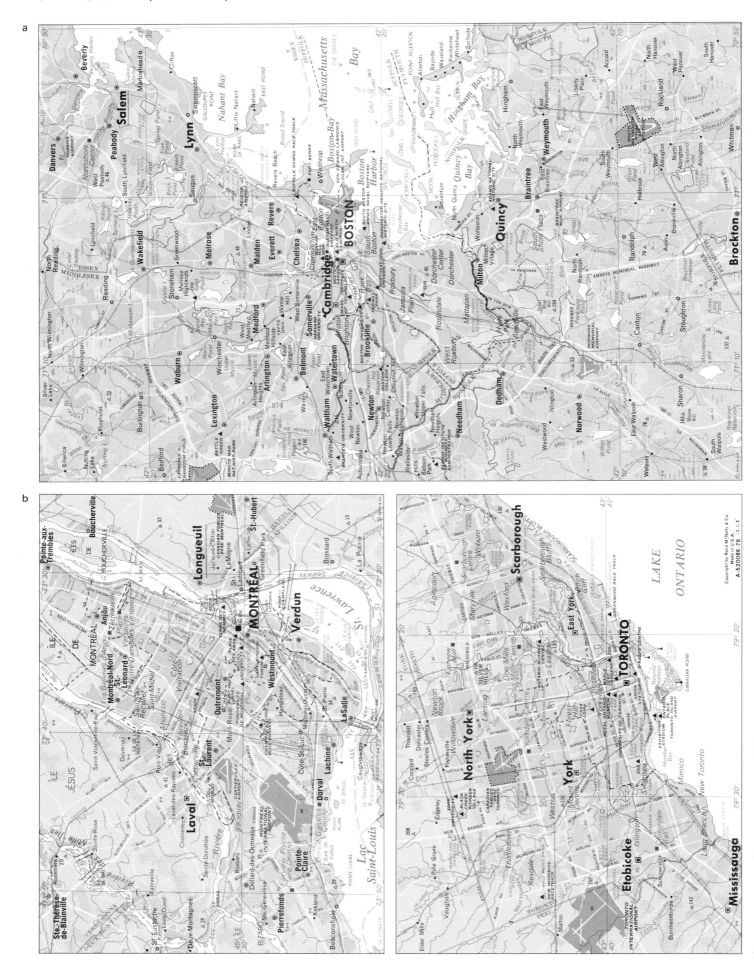

Scale 1:300,000; one inch to 4.7 miles.

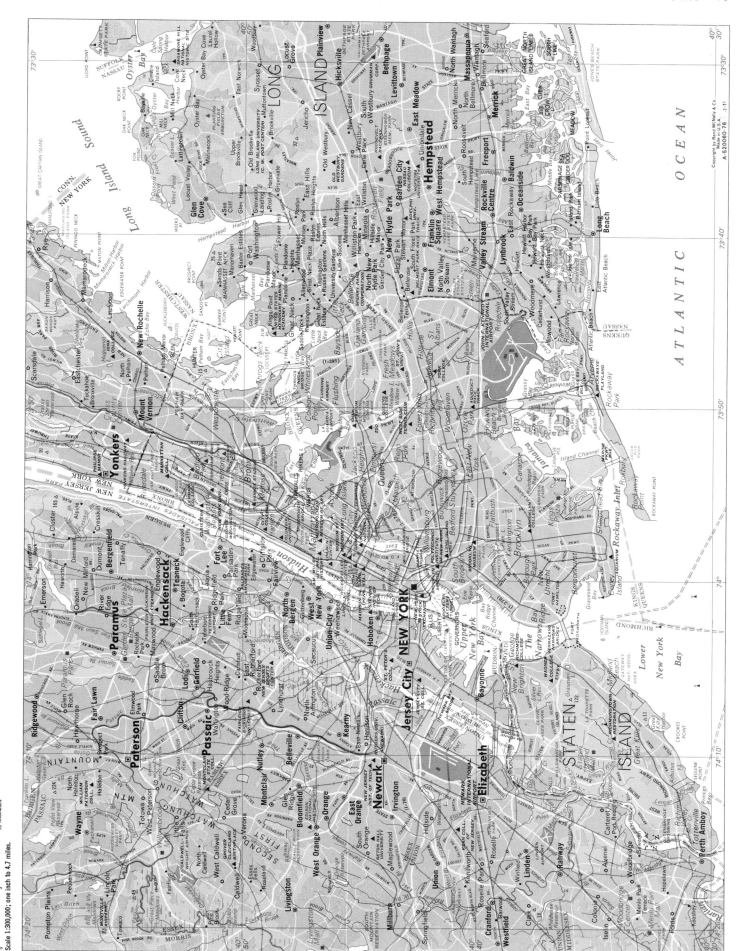

Scale 1:300,000; one inch to 4.7 miles.

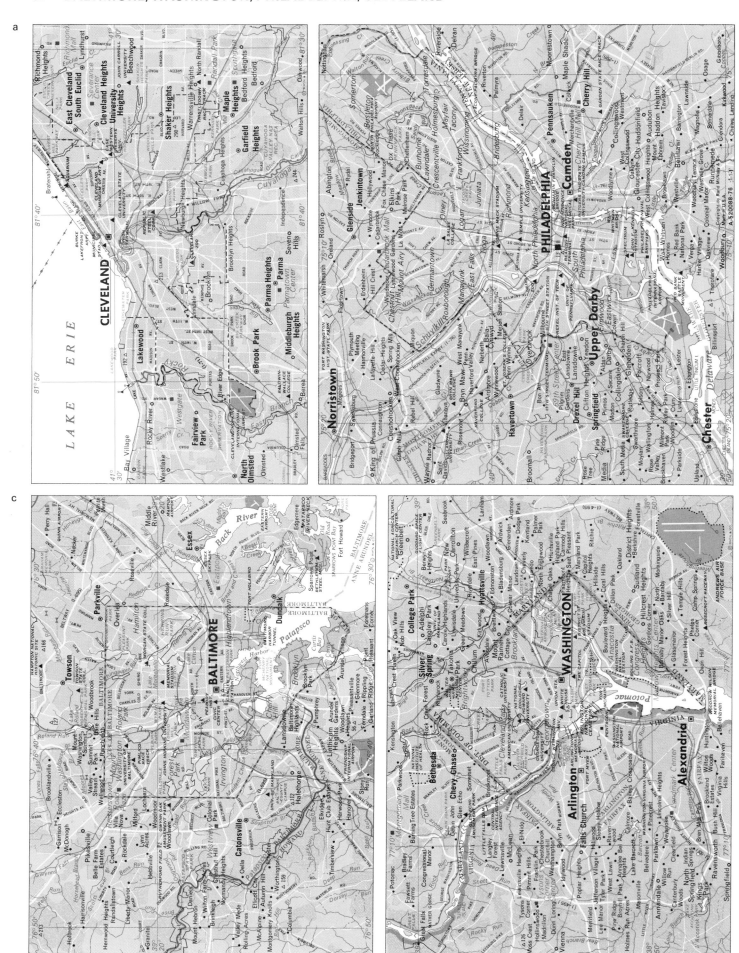

Scale 1:300,000; one inch to 4.7 miles.

a

Niagara Falls
△188
American Falls
Horseshoe Falls
NEW YORK
ONTARIO
NIAGARA
Chippawa
Sandy Beach
Edgewater
GRAND ISLAND
North Grand Island Bridge
North Tonawanda
Tonawanda Channel
Tonawanda
Grandyle
Falconwood
Grand Island
Ferry Village
Town of Tonawanda
Amherst
Kenmore
STATE UNIV. OF NEW YORK
Getzville
Ellicott
Snyder
Stevensville
Black Creek
Niagara
FORT ERIE RACE TRACK
Fort Erie
Peace Bridge
Bertie Bay
Erie Beach
BUFFALO
BUFFALO COAST GUARD BASE
Ridgeway
Wavecrest
Crystal Beach
Abino Bay
WINDMILL POINT
Cheektowaga
Sloan
Thruway Plaza
West Seneca
LAKE
CANADA
UNITED STATES
ERIE
BETHLEHEM STEEL MILL
STONY POINT
Lackawanna
Woodlawn Beach

b

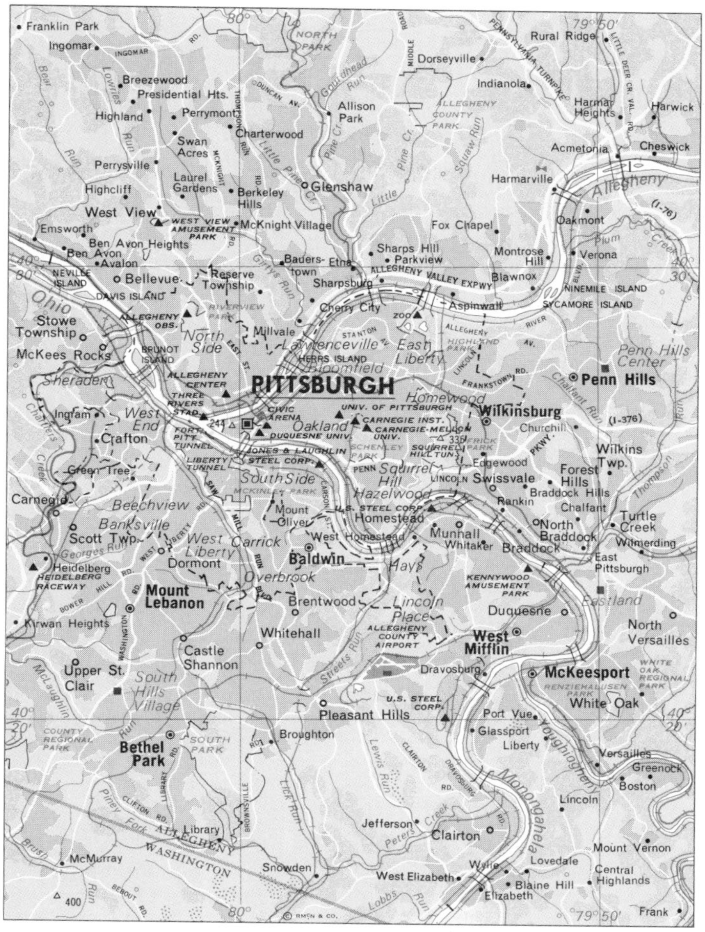

Franklin Park
Ingomar
Breezewood
Presidential Hts.
Highland
Perrymont
Charterwood
Allison Park
Indianola
Dorseyville
Rural Ridge
Harmar Heights
Harwick
Acmetonia
Cheswick
Perrysville
Highcliff
Laurel Gardens
Berkeley Hills
Glenshaw
Harmarville
Montrose Hill
Verona
Fox Chapel
West View
WEST VIEW AMUSEMENT PARK
McKnight Village
Sharps Hill
Emsworth
Ben Avon Heights
Ben Avon
Avalon
Bellevue
Reserve Township
Etna
Sharpsburg
Blawnox
Neville
NINEMILE ISLAND
SYCAMORE ISLAND
Ohio
Stowe Township
DAVIS ISLAND
Millvale
Lawrenceville
East Liberty
Aspinwall
Cherry City
McKees Rocks
Sherader
North Side
ALLEGHENY CENTER
THREE RIVERS STAD.
PITTSBURGH
Homewood
Penn Hills
Ingram
West End
CIVIC ARENA
UNIV. OF PITTSBURGH
CARNEGIE INST.
Wilkinsburg
Crafton
FORT PITT TUNNEL
DUQUESNE UNIV.
CARNEGIE-MELLON UNIV.
Churchill
Green Tree
LIBERTY TUNNEL
Oakland
SQUIRREL HILL TUN.
Edgewood
Swissvale
Carnegie
Beechview
South Side
Squirrel Hill
Lincoln Place
Forest Hills
Wilkins Twp.
Banksville
West Liberty
Hazelwood
Rankin
Braddock Hills
Chalfant
Scott Twp.
Mount Oliver
U.S. STEEL CORP.
Homestead
North Braddock
Turtle Creek
Heidelberg
HEIDELBERG RACEWAY
Dormont
West Carrick
Overbrook
West Homestead
Munhall
Whitaker
Braddock
Wilmerding
Kirwan Heights
Mount Lebanon
Brentwood
Lincoln Place
Hays
KENNYWOOD AMUSEMENT PARK
East Pittsburgh
Whitehall
ALLEGHENY COUNTY AIRPORT
Dravosburg
Duquesne
Eastland
Upper St. Clair
Castle Shannon
SOUTH HILLS VILLAGE
West Mifflin
North Versailles
Bethel Park
SOUTH PARK
Broughton
Pleasant Hills
U.S. STEEL CORP.
Port Vue
Liberty
McKeesport
White Oak
Glassport
Versailles
Boston
McMurray
Library
Lincoln
Greenock
Jefferson
Clairton
Elizabeth
West Elizabeth
Blaine Hill
Mount Vernon
Central Highlands
WASHINGTON
Snowden
△400
Frank

c

Wolverine Lake
Walled Lake
Wing Lake Shores
Birmingham
GRAND PRIX AIRPORT
Oakland Mall
McKINLEY AIRPORT
△188
Fraser
Novi
Walled Lake
△282
Bloomfield Village
Clawson
△194
Red Run
Macomb Mall
Franklin
Beverly Hills
Bingham Farms
Berkley
Madison Heights
GENERAL MOTORS TECHNICAL CENTER
Warren
Roseville
Farmington Hills
△266
LAWRENCE INSTITUTE OF TECHNOLOGY
Lathrup Village
Royal Oak
Universal Mall
(I-696)
Center Line
St. Clair Shores
Farmington
Southfield
Huntington Woods
DETROIT ZOOLOGICAL PARK
Ten Mile
HAZEL PARK RACE TRACK
East Detroit
St. Clair
Oak Park
Pleasant Ridge
Ferndale
Hazel Park
Eastland
GAUKLER POINT
Clarenceville
Royal Oak Township
Northland
MACOMB
WAYNE
Grosse Pointe Woods
OAKLAND
WAYNE
Northville
Livonia Mall
Redford Township
MICHIGAN STATE FAIR GROUNDS
PALMER PARK
Harper Woods
Grosse Pointe Shores
Northville Downs
Redford
UNIV. OF DETROIT
Grosse Pointe Farms
△235
Livonia
Brightmoor
Highland Park
DETROIT CITY AIRPORT
Plymouth
DETROIT RACE COURSE
(I-96)
Strathmoor
Hamtramck
CHRYSLER CORP. HAMTRAMCK PLANT
Grosse Pointe
WONDERLAND CENTER
△196
MIDDLE ROUGE PARKWAY
191
WARREN
DETROIT INST. OF ARTS
WAYNE STATE UNIV.
Grosse Pointe Park
METTETAL AIRPORT
HOLLIDAY PARK
WESTLAND CENTER
OLYMPIA STADIUM
BELLE ISLE
△205
Westland
Dearborn Heights
△186
FORD FIELD
Dearborn
TIGER STADIUM
DETROIT
AMTRAK STA.
COBO HALL
DOSSIN GREAT LAKES MUSEUM
PECHE ISLE
Garden City
FORD MUSEUM GREENFIELD VILLAGE
FORD MOTOR CO. ROUGE PLANT
FORT WAYNE MILITARY MUSEUM
AMBASSADOR BRIDGE
UNIV. OF WINDSOR
DETROIT-WINDSOR TUNNEL
Windsor
Riverside
St. Clair Beach
Tecumseh
Inkster
Delray
MICHIGAN
UNITED STATES
ONTARIO
CANADA
Wayne
Melvindale
River Rouge
GREAT LAKES STEEL WORKS
△183
Devonshire Plaza
WINDSOR AIRPORT
Sheldon
Allen Park
Lincoln Park
Ecorse
WINDSOR RACEWAY
DETROIT METROPOLITAN WAYNE COUNTY AIRPORT
Romulus
Taylor
La Salle
FIGHTING ISLAND
MACDONALD CARTIER FREEWAY

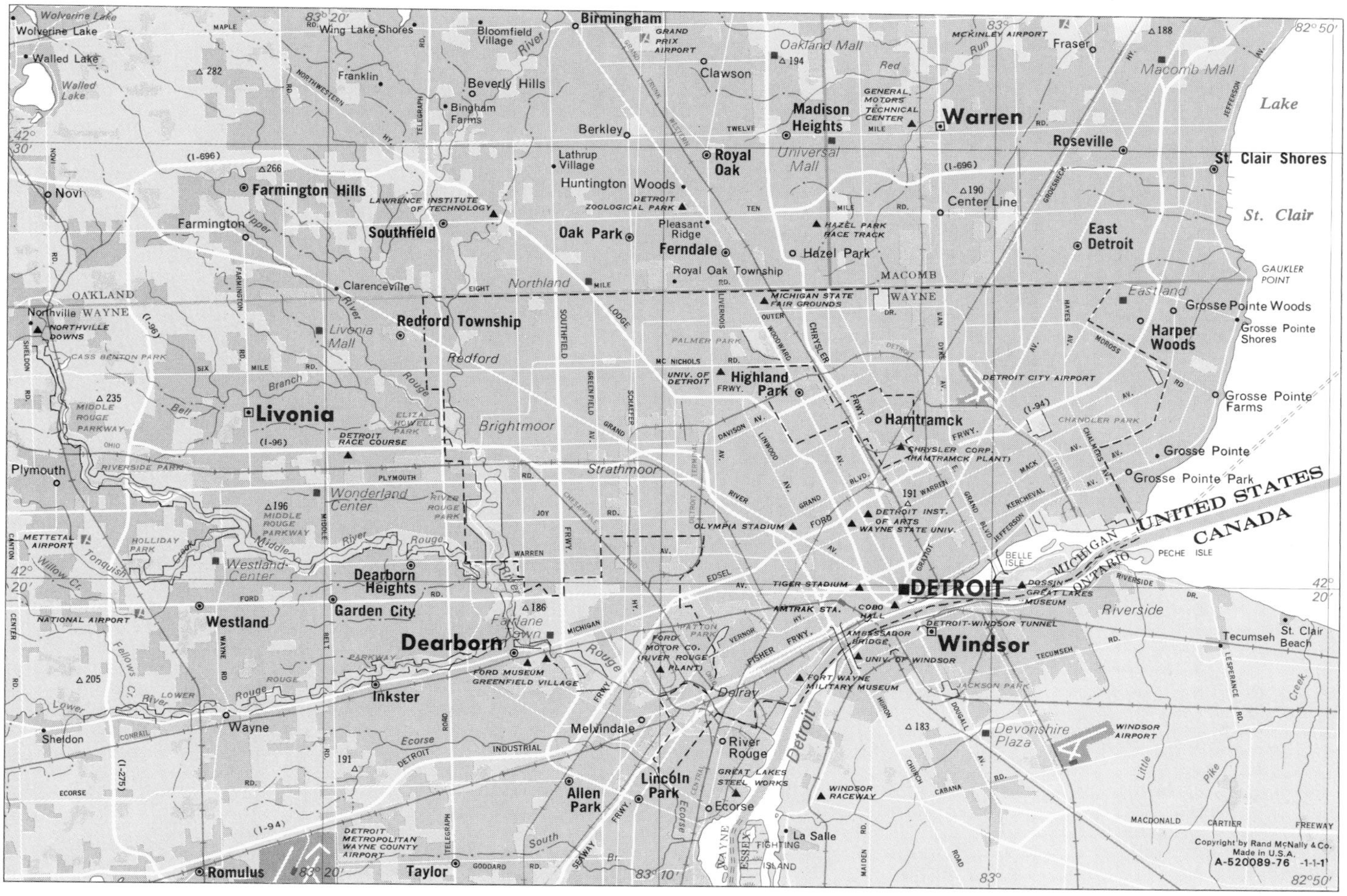

Scale 1:300,000; one inch to 4.7 miles.
0 5 10 Kilometers

Copyright by Rand McNally & Co.
Made in U.S.A.
A-520089-76 -1-1-1

Scale 1:300,000; one inch to 4.7 miles.

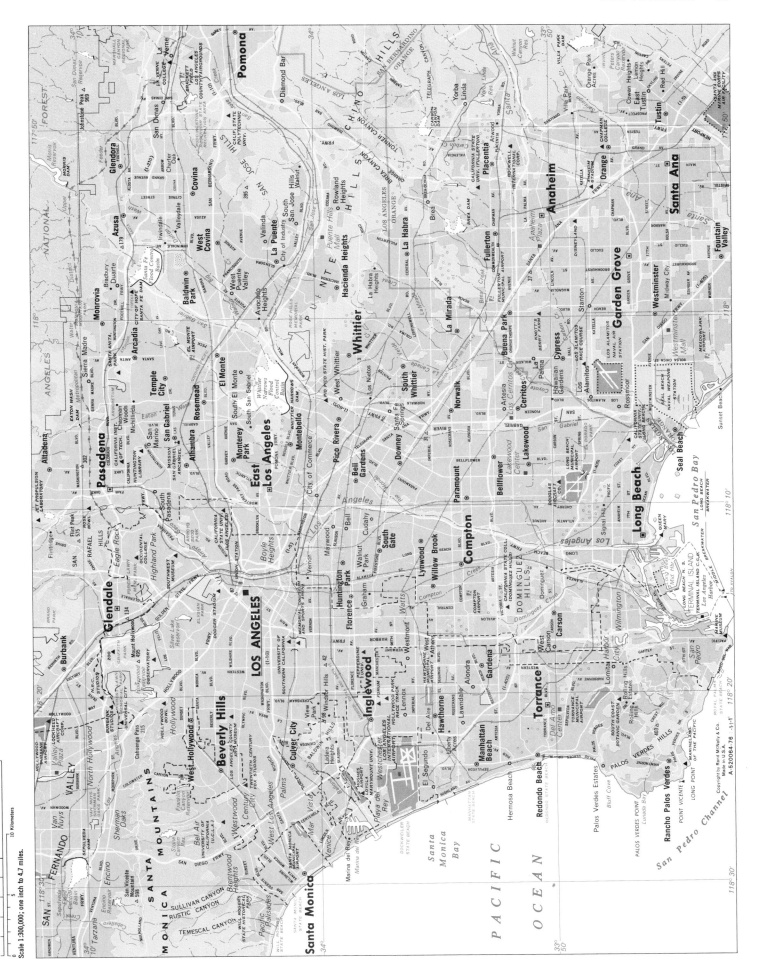

Scale 1:300,000; one inch to 4.7 miles.

a
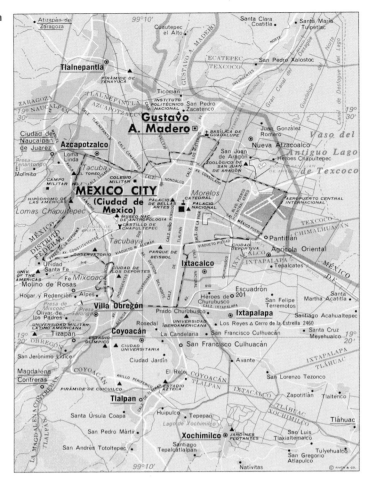

b

c
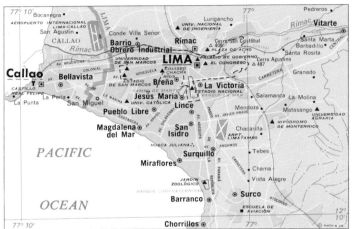

d
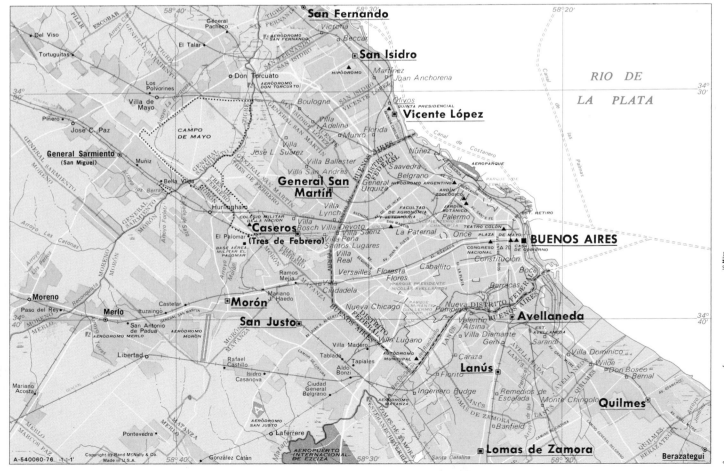

Scale 1:300,000; one inch to 4.7 miles.

10 Miles

10 Kilometers

a
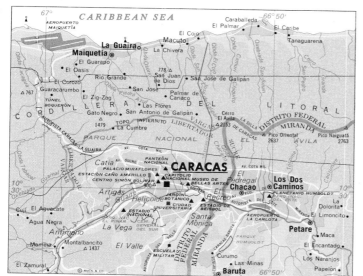

b

c
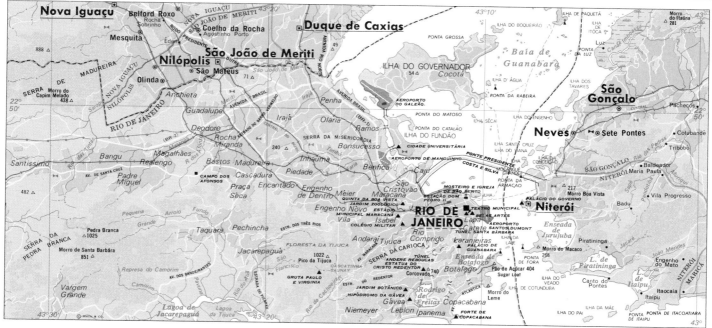

d

Scale 1:300,000; one inch to 4.7 miles.

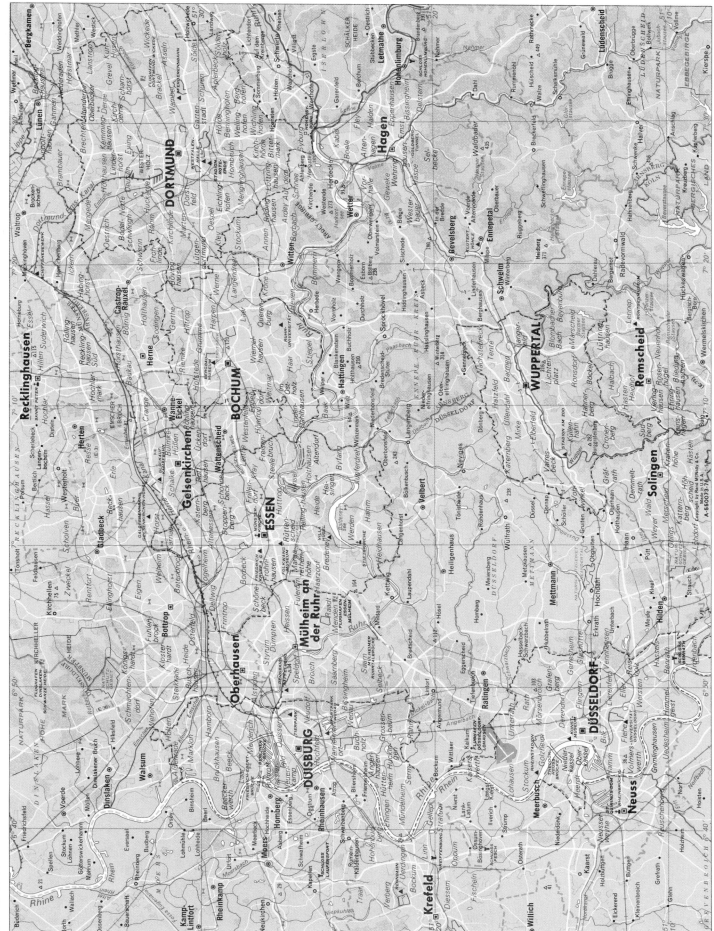

Scale 1:300,000; one inch to 4.7 miles.

a

b

c

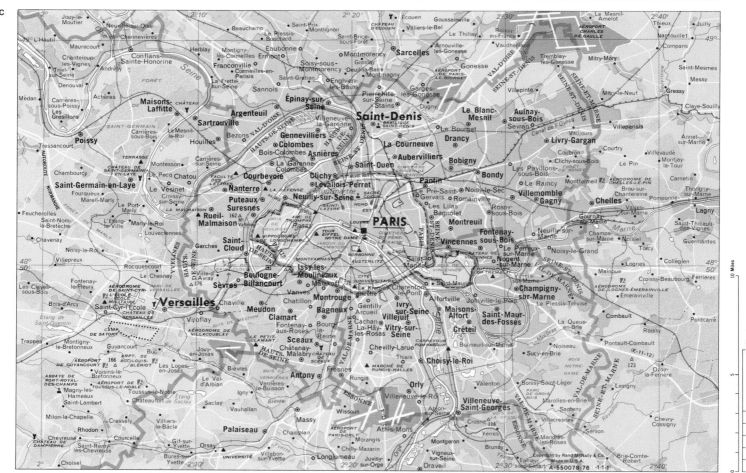

Scale 1:300,000; one inch to 4.7 miles.

a

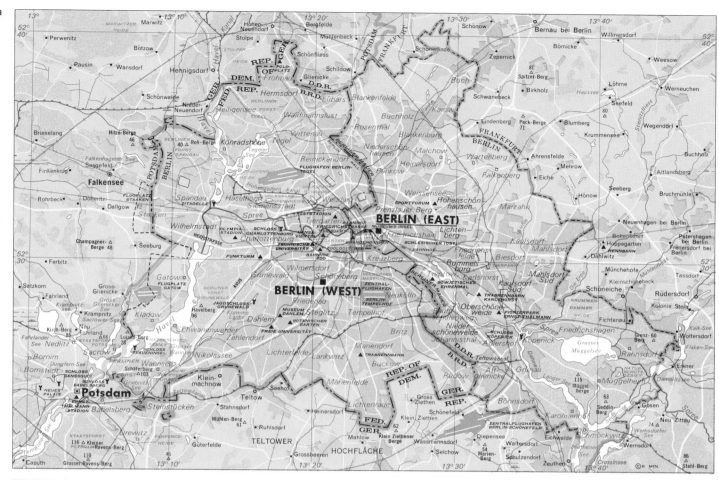

b
c

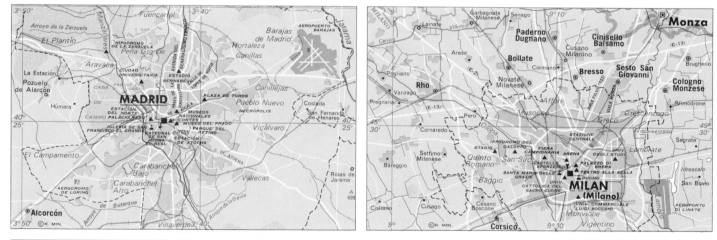

d
e

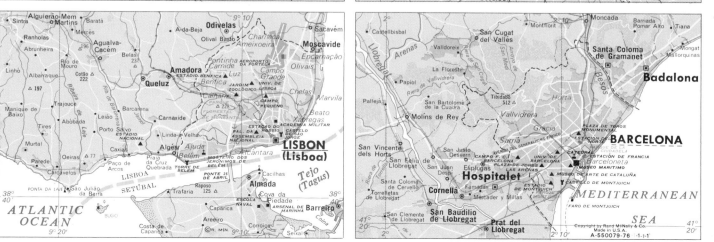

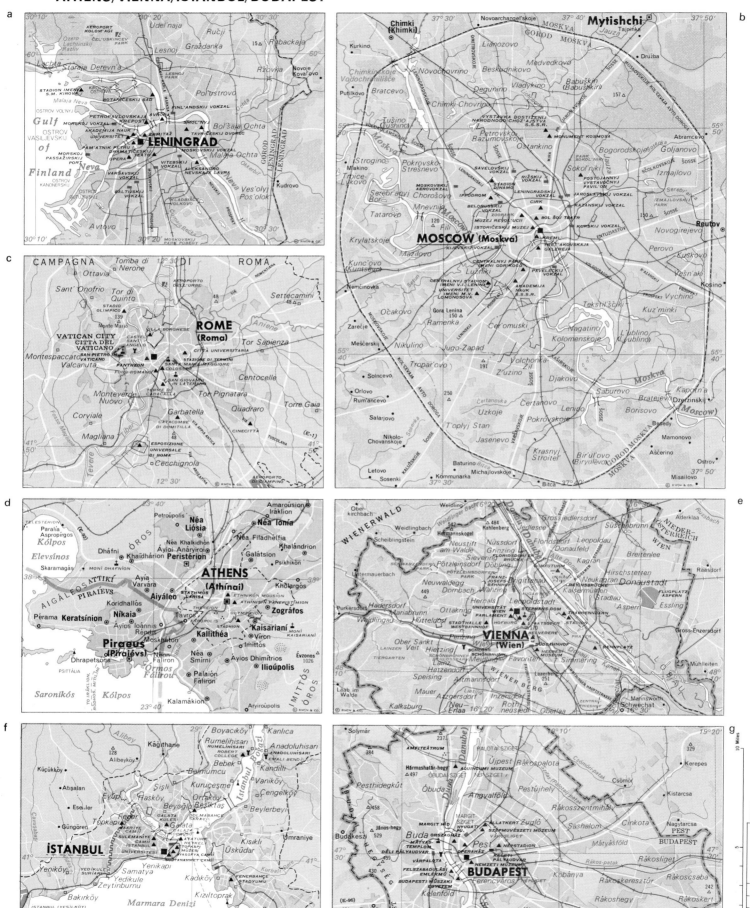

Scale 1:300,000; one inch to 4.7 miles.

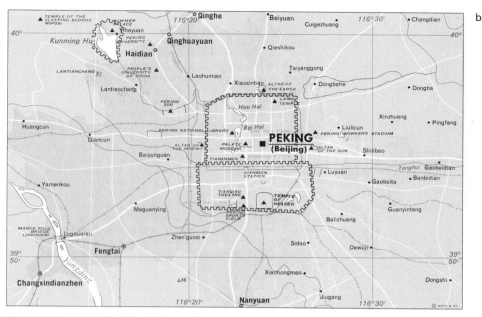

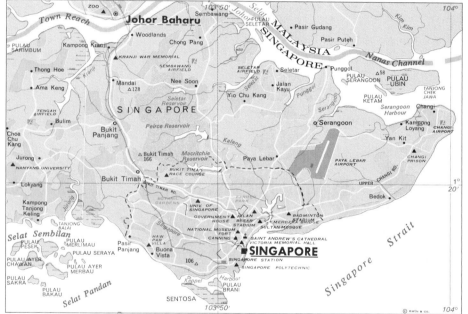

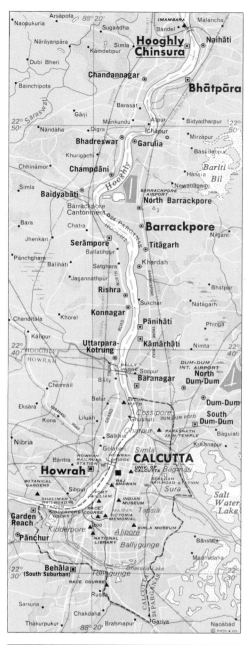

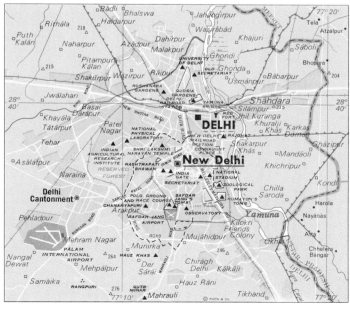

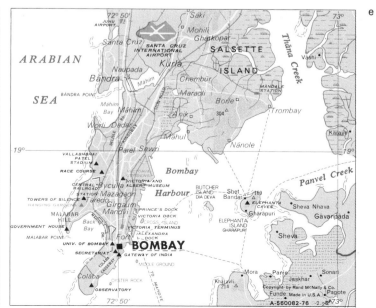

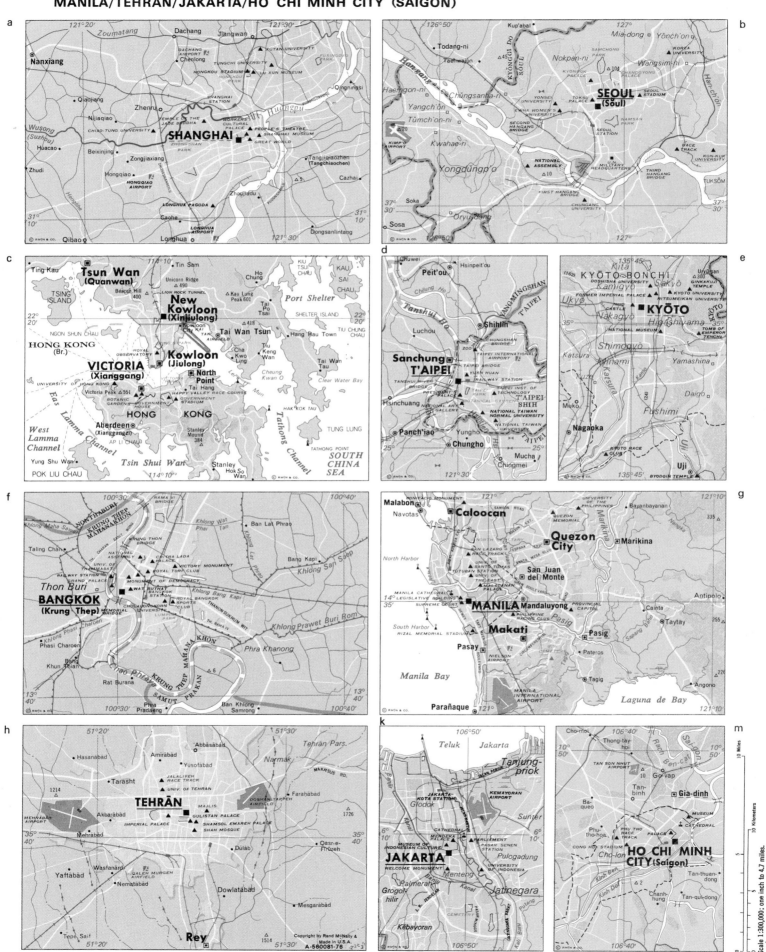

a

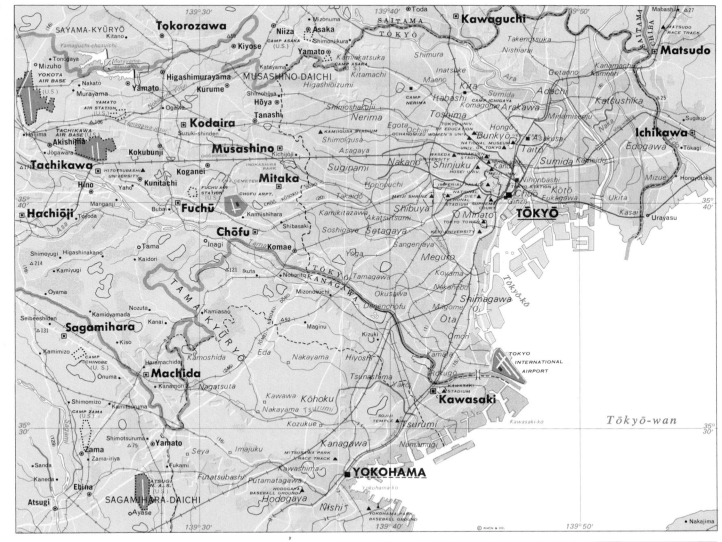

b

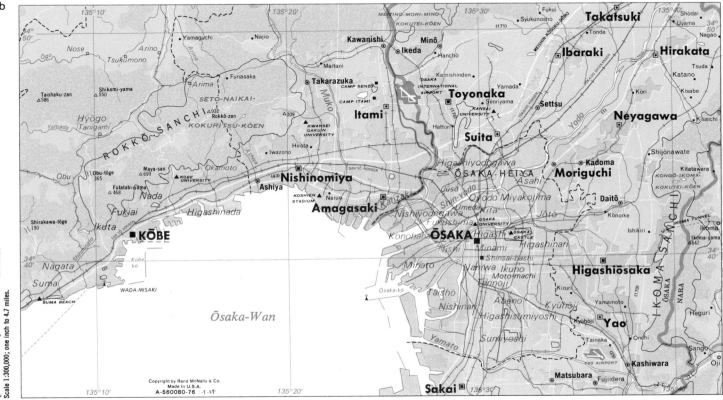

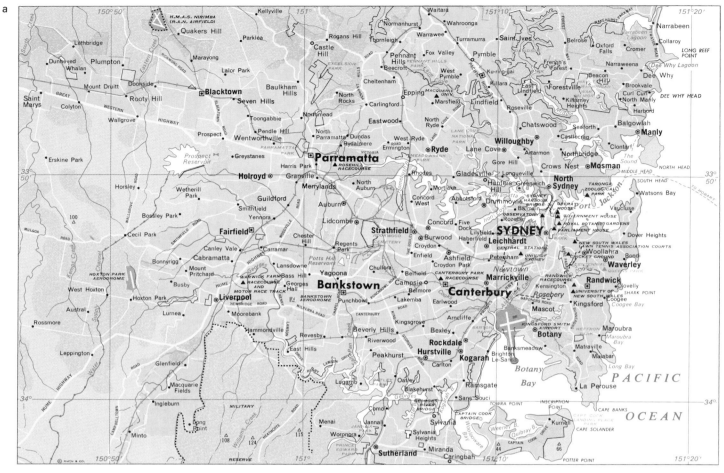

regional section

physical-political reference maps

Basic continental and regional coverage of the world's land areas is provided by the following section of physical-political reference maps. The section falls into a continental arrangement: North America, South America, Europe, Asia, Australia, and Africa. (Introducing each regional reference-map section are basic thematic maps and the environment maps.)

To aid the student in acquiring concepts of the relative sizes of continents and of some of the countries and regions, uniform scales for comparable areas were used so far as possible. Continental maps are at a uniform scale of 1:40,000,000. In addition, most of the world is covered by a series of regional maps at scales of 1:16,000,000 and 1:12,000,000.

Maps at 1:10,000,000 provide even greater detail for parts of Europe, Africa, and Southeast Asia. The United States, parts of Canada, and much of Europe and the Soviet Union are mapped at 1:4,000,000. Seventy-six urbanized areas are shown at 1:1,000,000. The new, separate metropolitan-area section contains larger-scale maps of selected urban areas.

Many of the symbols used are self-explanatory. A complete legend below provides a key to the symbols on the reference maps in this atlas.

General elevation above sea level is shown by layer tints for altitudinal zones, each of which has a different hue and is defined by a generalized contour line. A legend is given on each map, reflecting this color gradation.

The surface configuration is represented by hill-shading, which gives the three-dimensional impression of landforms. This terrain representation is superimposed on the layer tints to convey a realistic and readily visualized impression of the surface. The combination of altitudinal tints and hill-shading best shows elevation, relief, steepness of slope, and ruggedness of terrain.

If the world used one alphabet and one language, no particular difficulty would arise in understanding place-names. However, some of the people of the world, the Chinese and the Japanese, for example, use nonalphabetic languages. Their symbols are transliterated into the Roman alphabet. In this atlas a "local-name" policy generally was used for naming cities and towns and all local topographic and water features. However, for a few major cities the Anglicized name was preferred and the local name given in parentheses, for instance, Moscow (*Moskva*), Vienna (*Wien*), Cologne (*Köln*). In countries where more than one official language is used, a name is in the dominant local language. The generic parts of local names for topographic and water features are self-explanatory in many cases because of the associated map symbols or type styles. A complete list of foreign generic names is given in the Glossary, on page 257.

Place-names on the reference maps are listed in the Pronouncing Index, which is a distinctive feature of *Goode's World Atlas*.

Physical-Political Reference Map Legend

Cultural Features

Political Boundaries

(over water)	International (Demarcated, Undemarcated, and Administrative)
	Disputed de facto
	Disputed de-jure
	Indefinite or Undefined
(over water)	Secondary, State, Provincial, etc.
	Parks, Indian Reservations
	City Limits / Urbanized Areas
▫	Neighborhoods, Sections of City

Populated Places

⊙	1,000,000 and over
◎	250,000 to 1,000,000
⊙	100,000 to 250,000
•	25,000 to 100,000
○	0 to 25,000
TŌKYŌ	National Capitals
Boise	Secondary Capitals

Note: On maps at 1:20,000,000 and smaller the town symbols do not follow the specific population classification shown above. On all maps, type size indicates the relative importance of the city.

Transportation

	Railroads
	Railroads On 1:1,000,000 scale maps
	Railroad Ferries
	Roads
Major	On 1:1,000,000 scale maps
Other	
Major	On 1:4,000,000 scale maps
Other	
	On other scale maps
	Caravan Routes
✈	Airports

Other Cultural Features

	Dams
	Pipelines
▲	Pyramids
∴	Ruins

Land Features

△	Peaks, Spot Heights
=	Passes
	Sand
	Contours

Water Features

Lakes and Reservoirs

	Fresh Water
	Fresh Water: Intermittent
	Salt Water
	Salt Water: Intermittent

Other Water Features

	Salt Basins, Flats
	Swamps
	Ice Caps and Glaciers
	Rivers
	Intermittent Rivers
	Aqueducts and Canals
	Ship Channels
	Falls
	Rapids
	Springs
△	Water Depths
	Fishing Banks
	Sand Bars
	Reefs

environment maps

The environment-map series shows the general nature of the environment, whether natural or modified by man. The appearance and/or general activity which characterize an area were the conditions for its being classified in one of the map categories. Inclusion in a category was determined largely by the percent of the area covered by urban development, crops (including pasture), trees, or grass. On these small-scale maps, no attempt was made to depict specific crops or the productivity of the area.

Ten major environments were depicted and the categories identified and described in the legend below. The colors and patterns for each category were chosen to illustrate the results of man's activity. Hill shading was used to show land configuration. Together, these design elements create a visual impression of the surface environment.

Naturally, when mapping any distribution it is necessary to limit the number of categories. Therefore, some gradations of meaning exist within the limits of the chosen categories. For example, the grassland, grazing-land category identifies the lush pampas of Argentina and the savanna of Africa as well as the steppes of the Soviet Union. Furthermore, in areas of cropland certain enclaves which might not be defined as cropland are included within the boundary. Tracts such as these, through the process of generalization were included within the boundary of the dominant environment surrounding them. Finally, it should be pointed out that boundaries on these maps, as on all maps, are never absolute but mark the center of transitional zones between categories.

Actual urban shapes were shown where metropolitan areas are of a large areal extent. A red dot indicates concentrated urbanized development where actual shapes would be indistinguishable at the map scale. Black dots were used to locate selected places important as locational reference points.

From these maps one may make comprehensive observations about the extent and distribution of the major world environments. For example, the urban areas of the world are limited in extent, although over 40 percent of the world's population lives in these areas. Together, the categories of cropland and cropland associated with woodland or grazing land apply to relatively small portions of the earth's surface. Conversely, vast areas of each continent show man's limited influence on the natural environment. The barren lands, wasteland, and tundra, the sparse grass and steppe land, and the tropical rain forests are notable in this respect.

Use of the environment-series maps with the world and continental thematic maps of population, landforms, transportation, and gross national product, for instance, allows further insights into the nature of the world's major environments.

Environment Map Legend

URBAN
Major areas of contiguous residential, commercial, and industrial development.

CROPLAND
Cultivated land predominates (includes pasture, irrigated land, and land in crop rotation).

CROPLAND AND WOODLAND
Cultivated land interrupted by small wooded areas.

CROPLAND AND GRAZING LAND
Cultivated land with grassland and rangeland.

GRASSLAND, GRAZING LAND
Extensive grassland and rangeland with little or no cropland.

· OASIS
Important small areas of cultivation within grassland or wasteland.

FOREST, WOODLAND
Extensive wooded areas with little or no cropland.

SWAMP, MARSHLAND
Extensive wetland areas (includes mangroves).

TUNDRA
Areas of lichen, shrubs, small trees, and wetland.

SHRUB, SPARSE GRASS; WASTELAND
Desert shrub and short grass, growing singly or in patches. Wasteland includes sand, salt flats, etc. (Extensive wastelands shown by pattern).

BARREN LAND
Icefields, glaciers, permanent snow, with exposed rock.

· Selected cities as points of reference.

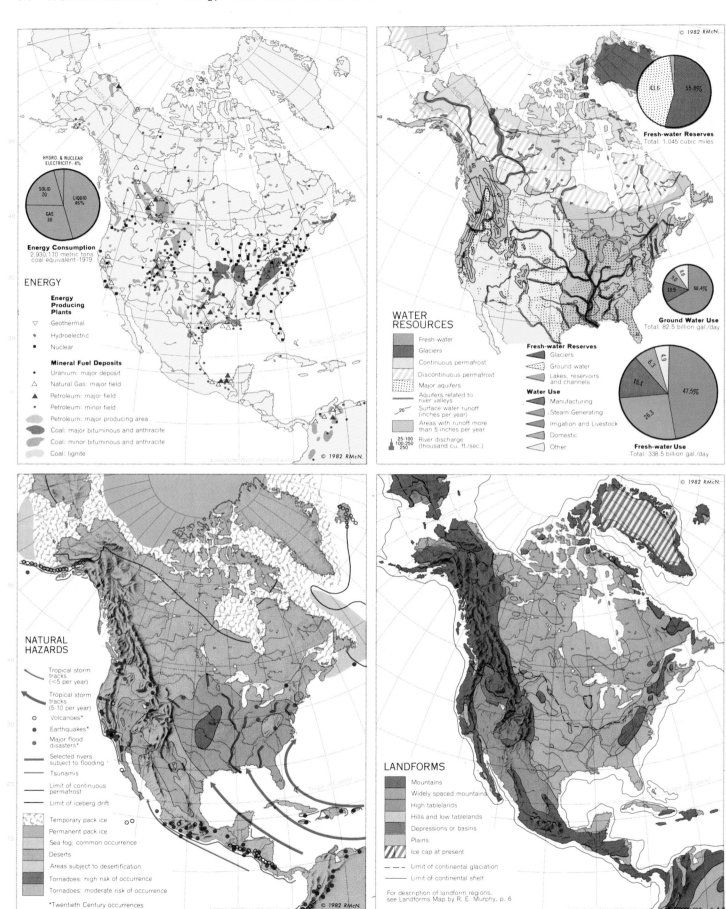

© 1982 RMcN.

ENERGY

HYDRO. & NUCLEAR
ELECTRICITY – 4%

SOLID
20

GAS
30

LIQUID
46%

Energy Consumption
2,930,170 metric tons
coal equivalent–1979

Energy Producing Plants

▽ Geothermal

• Hydroelectric

■ Nuclear

Mineral Fuel Deposits

• Uranium: major deposit

△ Natural Gas: major field

▲ Petroleum: major field

• Petroleum: minor field

Petroleum: major producing area

Coal: major bituminous and anthracite

Coal: minor bituminous and anthracite

Coal: lignite

© 1982 RMcN.

WATER RESOURCES

Fresh-water

Glaciers

Continuous permafrost

Discontinuous permafrost

Major aquifers

Aquifers related to river valleys

—20— Surface water runoff (inches per year)

Areas with runoff more than 5 inches per year

25-100
100-250
250
River discharge (thousand cu. ft./sec.)

43.6   55.8%

Fresh-water Reserves
Total: 1,045 cubic miles

8.6
9.0
13.9   68.4%

Ground Water Use
Total: 82.5 billion gal./day

4.9
6.3
15.1   47.5%
26.3

Fresh-water Use
Total: 338.5 billion gal./day

Fresh-water Reserves

◁ Glaciers

◁ Ground water

◁ Lakes, reservoirs and channels

Water Use

◁ Manufacturing

◁ Steam Generating

◁ Irrigation and Livestock

◁ Domestic

◁ Other

NATURAL HAZARDS

Tropical storm tracks (<5 per year)

Tropical storm tracks (5-10 per year)

○ Volcanoes*

● Earthquakes*

● Major flood disasters*

Selected rivers subject to flooding

Tsunamis

Limit of continuous permafrost

Limit of iceberg drift

Temporary pack ice

Permanent pack ice

Sea fog: common occurrence

Deserts

Areas subject to desertification

Tornadoes: high risk of occurrence

Tornadoes: moderate risk of occurrence

*Twentieth Century occurrences

© 1982 RMcN.

LANDFORMS

Mountains

Widely spaced mountains

High tablelands

Hills and low tablelands

Depressions or basins

Plains

Ice cap at present

– – – Limit of continental glaciation

—— Limit of continental shelf

For description of landform regions,
see Landforms Map by R. E. Murphy, p. 6

© 1982 RMcN.

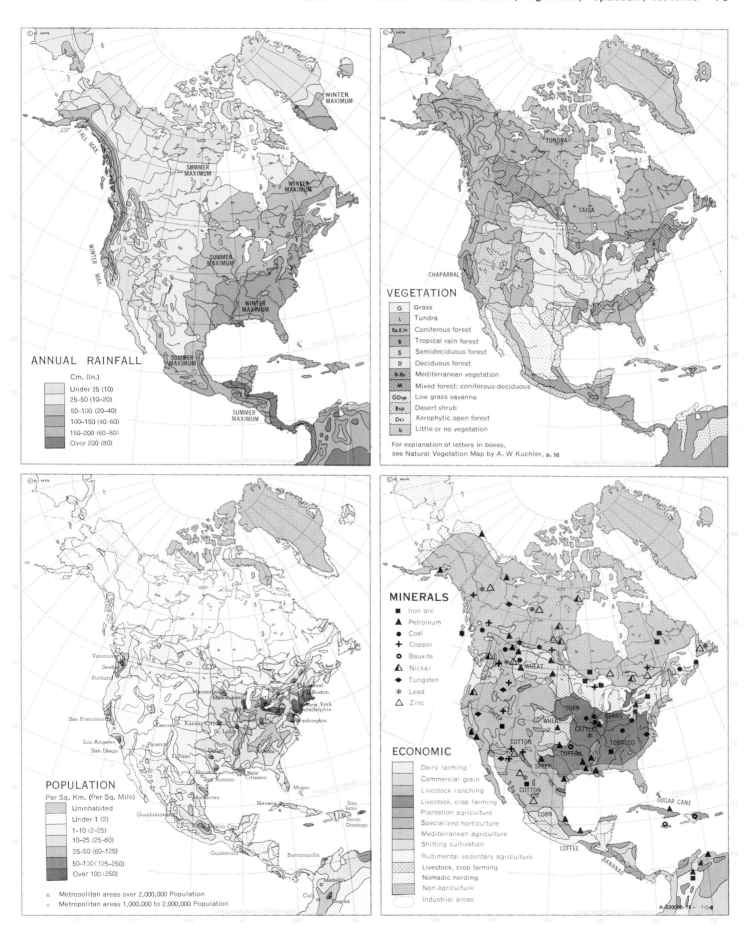

ANNUAL RAINFALL

Cm. (In.)

- Under 25 (10)
- 25–50 (10–20)
- 50–100 (20–40)
- 100–150 (40–60)
- 150–200 (60–80)
- Over 200 (80)

VEGETATION

G	Grass
L	Tundra
Ep.E.N	Coniferous forest
B	Tropical rain forest
S	Semideciduous forest
D	Deciduous forest
B–Bs	Mediterranean vegetation
M	Mixed forest: coniferous-deciduous
GDsp	Low grass savanna
Bsp	Desert shrub
Dsi	Xerophytic open forest
b	Little or no vegetation

For explanation of letters in boxes,
see Natural Vegetation Map by A. W Kuchler, **p. 16**

POPULATION

Per Sq. Km. (Per Sq. Mile)

- Uninhabited
- Under 1 (2)
- 1–10 (2–25)
- 10–25 (25–60)
- 25–50 (60–125)
- 50–100 (125–250)
- Over 100 (250)

▫ Metropolitan areas over 2,000,000 Population
◦ Metropolitan areas 1,000,000 to 2,000,000 Population

MINERALS

- ■ Iron ore
- ▲ Petroleum
- ● Coal
- + Copper
- ◦ Bauxite
- △ Nickel
- ◆ Tungsten
- ✳ Lead
- △ Zinc

ECONOMIC

- Dairy farming
- Commercial grain
- Livestock ranching
- Livestock, crop farming
- Plantation agriculture
- Specialized horticulture
- Mediterranean agriculture
- Shifting cultivation
- Rudimental sedentary agriculture
- Livestock, crop farming
- Nomadic herding
- Non agriculture
- Industrial areas

A-520000-16 - 1-2-8

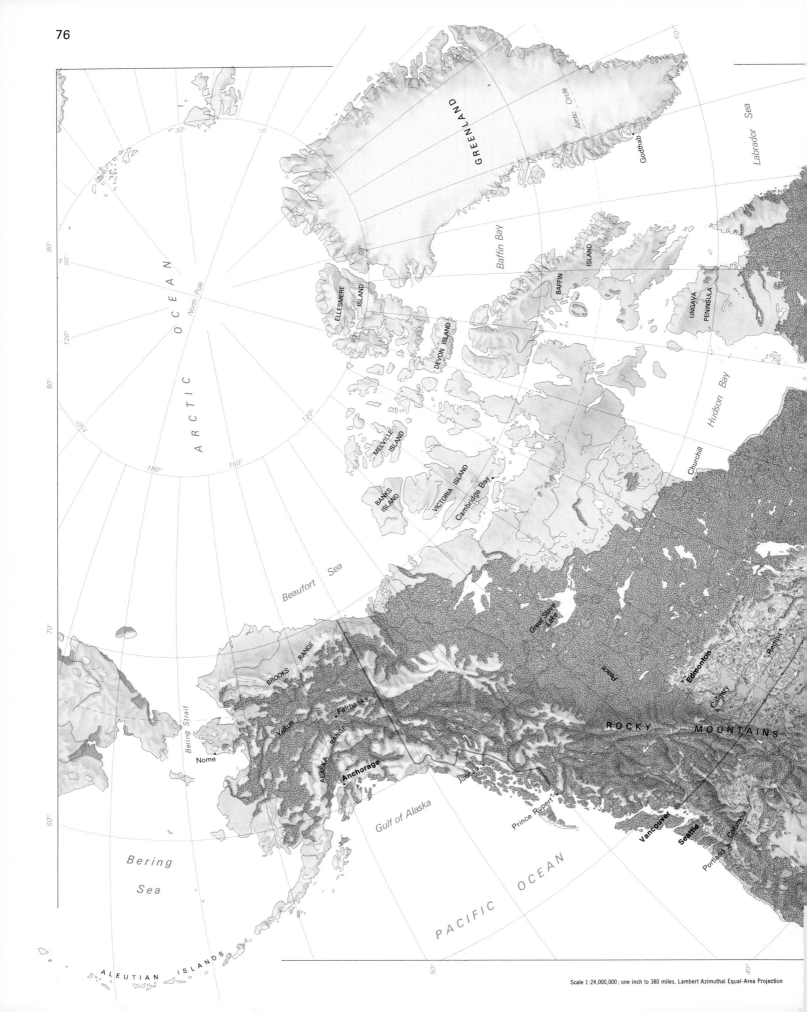

GREENLAND

Godthab

Arctic Circle

Labrador Sea

Baffin Bay

A R C T I C   O C E A N

North Pole

O C E A N

ELLESMERE ISLAND

DEVON ISLAND

BAFFIN ISLAND

UNGAVA PENINSULA

MELVILLE ISLAND

Hudson Bay

VICTORIA ISLAND

Cambridge Bay

Churchill

BANKS ISLAND

Beaufort Sea

Great Slave Lake

Peace

Regina

Edmonton

BROOKS RANGE

Calgary

Bering Strait

Fairbanks

Yukon

R O C K Y   M O U N T A I N S

Nome

ALASKA RANGE

Anchorage

Juneau

Prince Rupert

Gulf of Alaska

Vancouver

Seattle

Bering Sea

British Columbia

Portland

P A C I F I C   O C E A N

A L E U T I A N   I S L A N D S

Scale 1:24,000,000; one inch to 380 miles. Lambert Azimuthal Equal-Area Projection

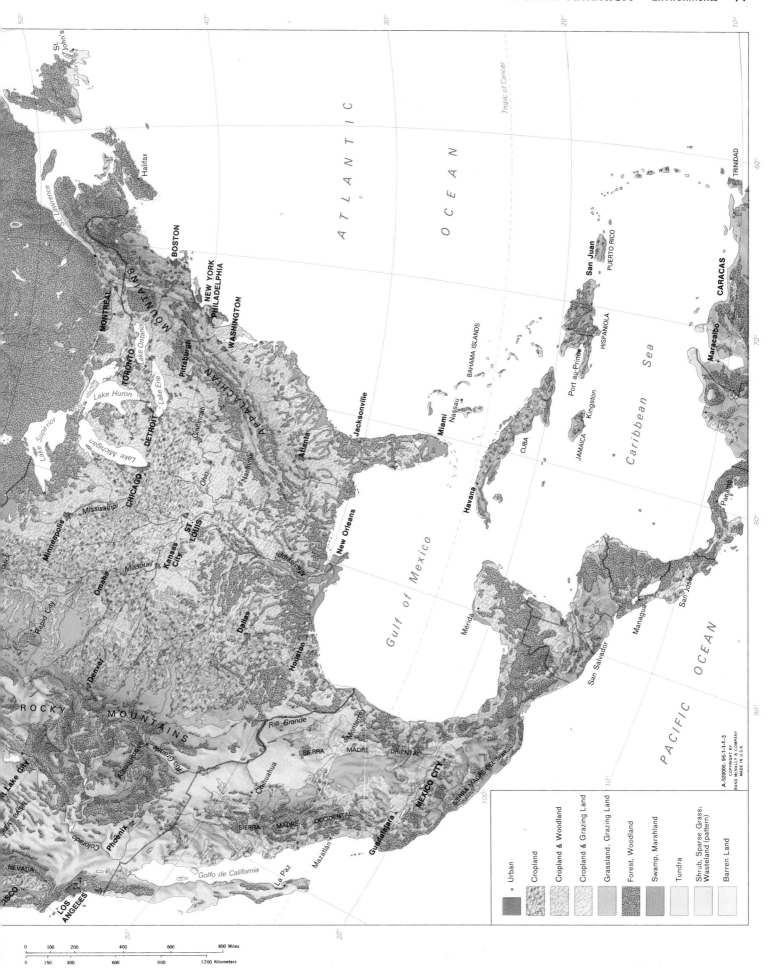

Urban
Cropland
Cropland & Woodland
Cropland & Grazing Land
Grassland, Grazing Land
Forest, Woodland
Swamp, Marshland
Tundra
Shrub, Sparse Grass, Wasteland (pattern)
Barren Land

A-520000-96-1-1-1-3
COPYRIGHT BY
RAND McNALLY & COMPANY
MADE IN U.S.A.

0   100   200   400   600   800 Miles
0   150   300   600   900   1200 Kilometers

PACIFIC

OCEAN

45°

125°

40°

35°

30°

PACIFIC

OCEAN

120°

25°

115°

110°

Vancouver

Seattle

Spokane

Portland

Columbia

CASCADE RANGE

Medford

Boise

Reno

GREAT BASIN

SIERRA

NEVADA

Fresno

SAN
FRANCISCO

Las Vegas

Colorado

LOS ANGELES

San Diego

Phoenix

Hermosillo

Gulf of California

ROCKY MOUNTAINS

Calgary

Regina

Bismarck

Billings

Rapid City

Casper

Great Salt
Lake

Salt Lake City

Denver

Albuquerque

El Paso

Odessa

Chihuahua

SIERRA MADRE OCCIDENTAL

Torreon

Rio Grande

Monterrey

San Antonio

SIERRA MADRE ORIENTAL

Rio Grande

Red

Oklahoma
City

Amarillo

Wichita

Omaha

Missouri

Lake Winnipeg

Winn

Omah

D

Gulf of Mexico

ATLANTIC OCEAN

	Urban
	Cropland
	Cropland & Woodland
	Cropland & Grazing Land
	Grassland, Grazing Land
	Forest, Woodland
	Swamp, Marshland
	Shrub, Sparse Grass, Wasteland (pattern)
	Barren Land

Scale 1:12,000,000; one inch to 190 miles. Polyconic Projection   0   50   100   200   300   400 Miles

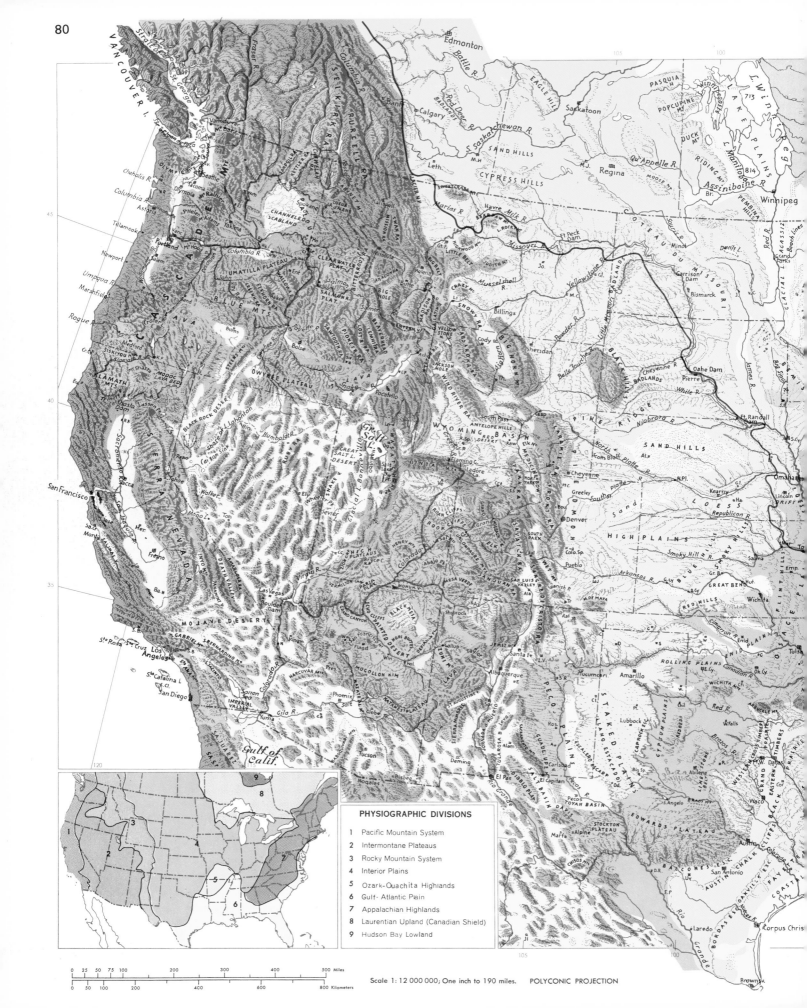

PHYSIOGRAPHIC DIVISIONS

1 Pacific Mountain System
2 Intermontane Plateaus
3 Rocky Mountain System
4 Interior Plains
5 Ozark-Ouachita Highlands
6 Gulf- Atlantic Plain
7 Appalachian Highlands
8 Laurentian Upland (Canadian Shield)
9 Hudson Bay Lowland

```
0  25 50 75 100        200           300            400             500 Miles
0  50  100       200          400             600               800 Kilometers
```

Scale 1: 12 000 000; One inch to 190 miles.   POLYCONIC PROJECTION

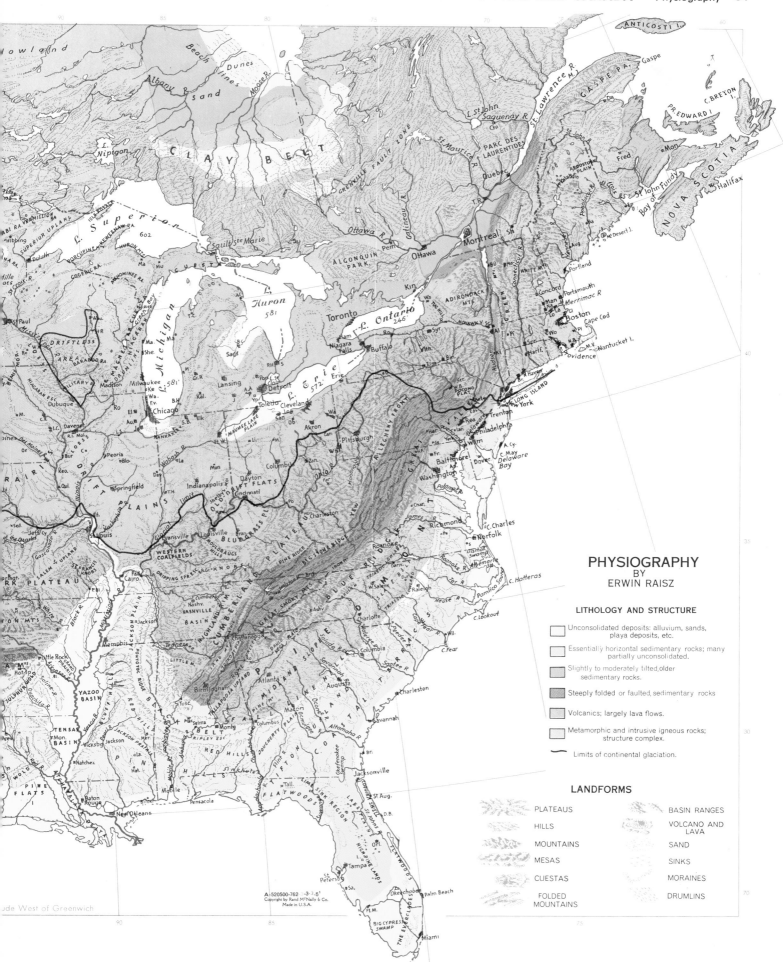

PHYSIOGRAPHY
BY
ERWIN RAISZ

LITHOLOGY AND STRUCTURE

Unconsolidated deposits: alluvium, sands, playa deposits, etc.

Essentially horizontal sedimentary rocks; many partially unconsolidated.

Slightly to moderately tilted, older sedimentary rocks.

Steeply folded or faulted, sedimentary rocks

Volcanics; largely lava flows.

Metamorphic and intrusive igneous rocks; structure complex.

Limits of continental glaciation.

LANDFORMS

PLATEAUS   BASIN RANGES

HILLS   VOLCANO AND LAVA

MOUNTAINS   SAND

MESAS   SINKS

CUESTAS   MORAINES

FOLDED MOUNTAINS   DRUMLINS

A-520500-762 · -3-3.5'
Copyright by Rand McNally & Co.
Made in U.S.A.

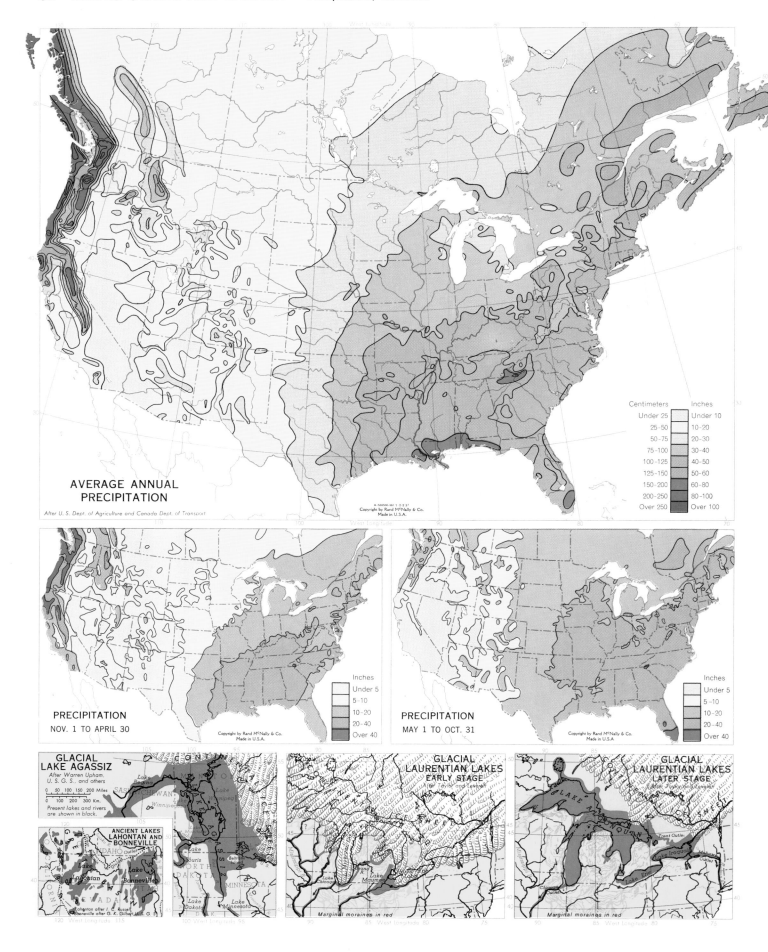

AVERAGE ANNUAL PRECIPITATION

After U. S. Dept. of Agriculture and Canada Dept. of Transport

A-520500-161 1 -2-2 31
Copyright by Rand McNally & Co.
Made in U.S.A.

Centimeters	Inches
Under 25	Under 10
25–50	10–20
50–75	20–30
75–100	30–40
100–125	40–50
125–150	50–60
150–200	60–80
200–250	80–100
Over 250	Over 100

PRECIPITATION
NOV. 1 TO APRIL 30

Copyright by Rand McNally & Co.
Made in U.S.A.

Inches
Under 5
5–10
10–20
20–40
Over 40

PRECIPITATION
MAY 1 TO OCT. 31

Copyright by Rand McNally & Co.
Made in U.S.A.

Inches
Under 5
5–10
10–20
20–40
Over 40

GLACIAL LAKE AGASSIZ
After Warren Upham,
U. S. G. S. and others

0   50 100 150 200 Miles
0 100 200 300 Km.
Present lakes and rivers
are shown in black.

ANCIENT LAKES LAHONTAN AND BONNEVILLE
Lahontan after I. C. Russell
Bonneville after G. K. Gilbert, U.S. G. S.

GLACIAL LAURENTIAN LAKES EARLY STAGE
After Taylor and Leverett

Marginal moraines in red

GLACIAL LAURENTIAN LAKES LATER STAGE
After Taylor and Leverett

Marginal moraines in red

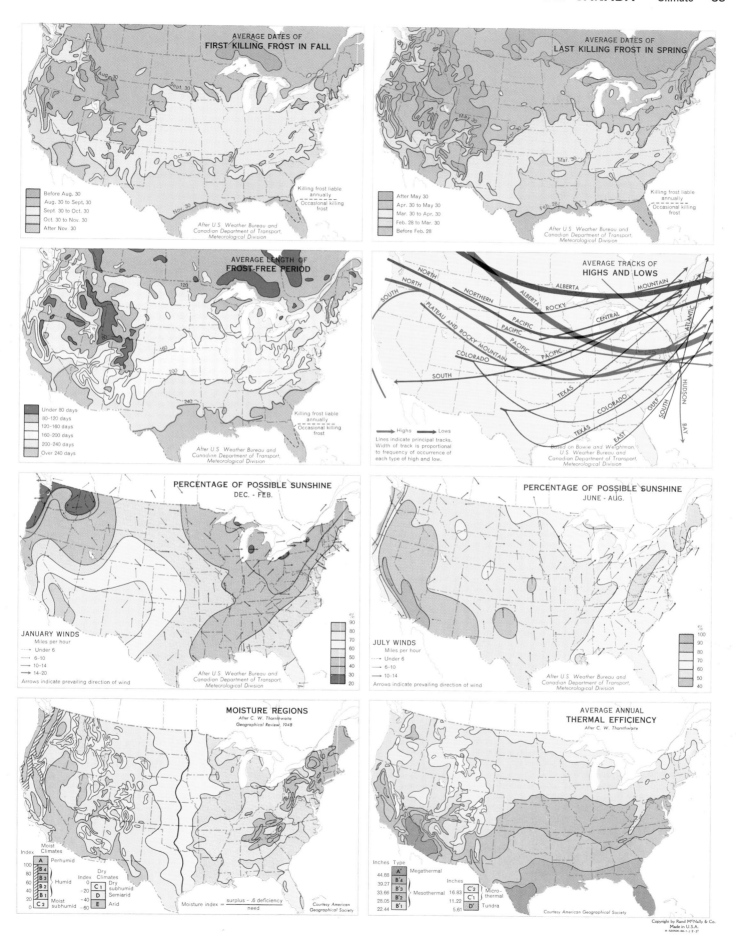

AVERAGE DATES OF
FIRST KILLING FROST IN FALL

Aug. 30
Sept. 30
Oct. 30
Nov. 30

Before Aug. 30
Aug. 30 to Sept. 30
Sept. 30 to Oct. 30
Oct. 30 to Nov. 30
After Nov. 30

Killing frost liable
annually
Occasional killing
frost

After U.S. Weather Bureau and
Canadian Department of Transport,
Meteorological Division

AVERAGE DATES OF
LAST KILLING FROST IN SPRING

May 30
Apr. 30
Mar. 30
Feb. 28

After May 30
Apr. 30 to May 30
Mar. 30 to Apr. 30
Feb. 28 to Mar. 30
Before Feb. 28

Killing frost liable
annually
Occasional killing
frost

After U.S. Weather Bureau and
Canadian Department of Transport,
Meteorological Division

AVERAGE LENGTH OF
FROST-FREE PERIOD

120
160
200
240

Under 80 days
80-120 days
120-160 days
160-200 days
200-240 days
Over 240 days

Killing frost liable
annually
Occasional killing
frost

After U.S. Weather Bureau and
Canadian Department of Transport,
Meteorological Division

AVERAGE TRACKS OF
HIGHS AND LOWS

NORTH
NORTH
SOUTH
NORTHERN
ALBERTA
ROCKY
MOUNTAIN
PLATEAU AND ROCKY MOUNTAIN
PACIFIC
PACIFIC
PACIFIC
PACIFIC
CENTRAL
ATLANTIC
COLORADO
SOUTH
TEXAS
COLORADO
HUDSON
BAY
SOUTH
GULF
TEXAS
EAST

Highs   Lows

Lines indicate principal tracks.
Width of track is proportional
to frequency of occurrence of
each type of high and low.

Based on Bowie and Weightman,
U.S. Weather Bureau and
Canadian Department of Transport,
Meteorological Division

PERCENTAGE OF POSSIBLE SUNSHINE
DEC. - FEB.

JANUARY WINDS
Miles per hour
Under 6
6-10
10-14
14-20
Arrows indicate prevailing direction of wind

%
90
80
70
60
50
40
30
20

After U.S. Weather Bureau and
Canadian Department of Transport,
Meteorological Division

PERCENTAGE OF POSSIBLE SUNSHINE
JUNE - AUG.

JULY WINDS
Miles per hour
Under 6
6-10
10-14
Arrows indicate prevailing direction of wind

%
100
90
80
70
60
50
40

After U.S. Weather Bureau and
Canadian Department of Transport,
Meteorological Division

MOISTURE REGIONS
After C. W. Thornthwaite
Geographical Review, 1948

Moist
Climates
100   A   Perhumid
80   B4
60   B3   } Humid
40   B2
20   B1
0   C2   } Moist
subhumid

Dry Climates
Index
0   C1   Dry
subhumid
-20   D   Semiarid
-40
-60   E   Arid

Moisture index = surplus - .6 deficiency
need

Courtesy American
Geographical Society

AVERAGE ANNUAL
THERMAL EFFICIENCY
After C. W. Thornthwaite

Inches Type
44.88   A'   Megathermal
39.27   B'4
33.66   B'3   } Mesothermal
28.05   B'2
22.44   B'1

Inches
16.83   C'2
11.22   C'1   } Micro-
thermal
5.61   D'   Tundra

Courtesy American
Geographical Society

84

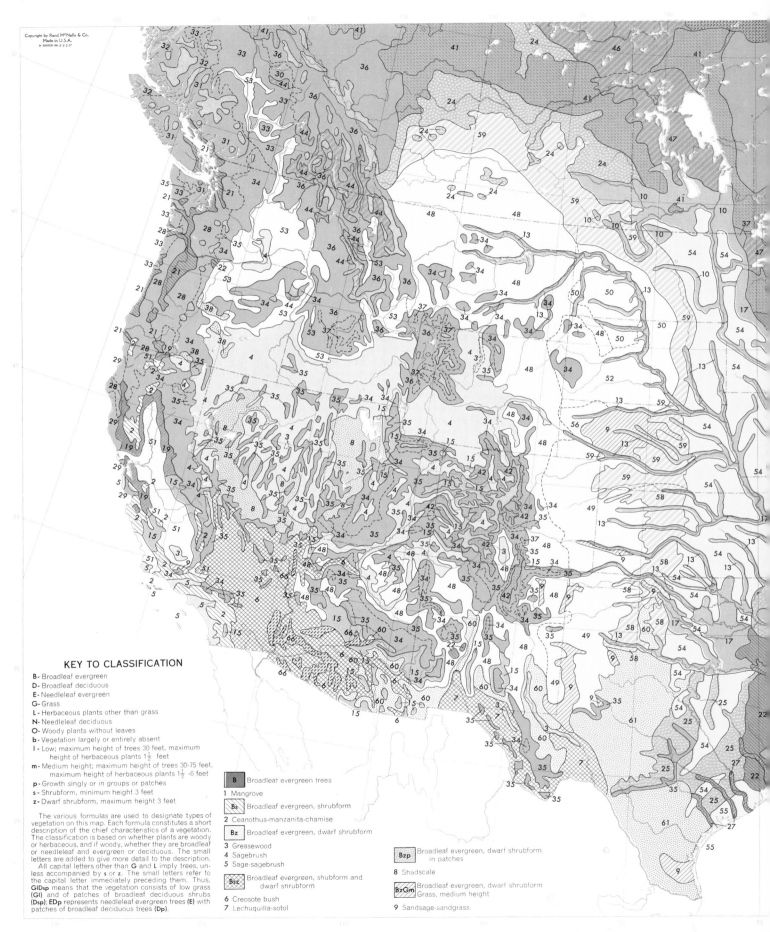

KEY TO CLASSIFICATION

B - Broadleaf evergreen
D - Broadleaf deciduous
E - Needleleaf evergreen
G - Grass
L - Herbaceous plants other than grass
N - Needleleaf deciduous
O - Woody plants without leaves
b - Vegetation largely or entirely absent
l - Low; maximum height of trees 30 feet, maximum
  height of herbaceous plants 1½ feet
m - Medium height; maximum height of trees 30-75 feet,
  maximum height of herbaceous plants 1½ -6 feet
p - Growth singly or in groups or patches
s - Shrubform, minimum height 3 feet
z - Dwarf shrubform, maximum height 3 feet

  The various formulas are used to designate types of
vegetation on this map. Each formula constitutes a short
description of the chief characteristics of a vegetation.
The classification is based on whether plants are woody
or herbaceous, and if woody, whether they are broadleaf
or needleleaf and evergreen or deciduous. The small
letters are added to give more detail to the description.
  All capital letters other than **G** and **L** imply trees, unless accompanied by **s** or **z**. The small letters refer to
the capital letter immediately preceding them. Thus,
GlDsp means that the vegetation consists of low grass
(**Gl**) and of patches of broadleaf deciduous shrubs
(**Dsp**); **EDp** represents needleleaf evergreen trees (**E**) with
patches of broadleaf deciduous trees (**Dp**).

B Broadleaf evergreen trees	
1 Mangrove	
Bs Broadleaf evergreen, shrubform	
2 Ceanothus-manzanita-chamise	
Bz Broadleaf evergreen, dwarf shrubform	
3 Greasewood	
4 Sagebrush	
5 Sage-sagebrush	
Bsz Broadleaf evergreen, shubform and dwarf shrubform	
6 Creosote bush	
7 Lechuquilla-sotol	

Bzp Broadleaf evergreen, dwarf shrubform, in patches

8 Shadscale

Bzp Gm Broadleaf evergreen, dwarf shrubform Grass, medium height

9 Sandsage-sandgrass

0 25 50 75 100   200   300   400   500 Miles

0 50 100   200   400   600   800 Kilometers

Scale 1:14 000 000; One inch to 220

Copyright by Rand McNally & Co.
Made in U.S.A.
A-520500 IM-2-2-21'

NATURAL VEGETATION
BY A. W. KÜCHLER

Based on "A Physiognomic Classification of Vegetation"
Annals of the Assoc. of American Geographers, Vol. 39, September, 1949

D Broadleaf deciduous trees

10 Aspen-oak
11 Beech-maple
12 Beech-tulip tree-maple-basswood
13 Cottonwood-willow
14 Maple-basswood
15 Oak
16 Oak-ash-maple
17 Oak-hickory
18 Oak-tulip tree

DB Broadleaf deciduous trees
Broadleaf evergreen trees

19 Oak-madrone

DE Broadleaf deciduous trees
Needleleaf evergreen trees

20 Maple-yellow birch-hemlock-pine
21 Oak-Douglas fir
22 Oak-pine
23 Maple-beech-hemlock

D / Gmp Broadleaf deciduous trees
Grass, medium height, in patches

24 Aspen-needle grass-wheat grass
25 Oak-hickory-bluestem

DN Broadleaf deciduous trees
Needleleaf deciduous trees

26 Bay trees-bald cypress
27 Tupelo-gum-bald cypress

E Needleleaf evergreen trees

28 Douglas fir
29 Douglas fir-redwood
30 Hemlock-arbor vitae
31 Hemlock-arbor vitae-Douglas fir
32 Hemlock-arbor vitae-fir
33 Hemlock-spruce
34 Pine
35 Pine-juniper
36 Pine-spruce
37 Spruce-fir

Esp Needleleaf evergreen, shrubform,
in patches

38 Juniper

EDp Needleleaf evergreen trees
Broadleaf deciduous trees, in patches

39 Douglas fir-pine-aspen
40 Pine-spruce-birch
41 Spruce-aspen
42 Spruce-fir-aspen
43 Spruce-poplar-birch

EN Needleleaf evergreen trees
Needleleaf deciduous trees

44 Hemlock-arbor vitae-Douglas fir-larch
45 Pine-bald cypress
46 Pine-spruce-larch
47 Spruce-larch

Gl Grass, low

48 Grama grass
49 Grama grass-buffalo grass
50 Grama grass-needle grass
51 Needle grass-blue grass
52 Wheat grass
53 Wheat grass-blue grass

Gm Grass, medium height

54 Bluestem
55 Broom grass-water grass
56 Marsh grass
57 Saw grass

Gml Grass, medium and low height

58 Bluestem-bunch grass
59 Needle grass-wheat grass

Gl / Dsp Grass, low
Broadleaf deciduous, shrubform, in patches

60 Bunch grass-oak

Gm / Dsp Grass, medium height
Broadleaf deciduous, shrubform, in patches

61 Mesquite grass-mesquite

L Herbaceous plants other than grass

62 Lichens, etc.

LEp Herbaceous plants other than grass
Needleleaf evergreen trees, in patches

63 Lichens-spruce

LEp / Np Herbaceous plants other than grass
Needleleaf evergreen trees, in patches
Needleleaf deciduous trees, in patches

64 Lichens-spruce-larch

N Needleleaf deciduous trees

65 Bald cypress

Op Woody plants without leaves, in patches

66 Palo verde-cacti-ocotillo

b Vegetation largely or entirely absent

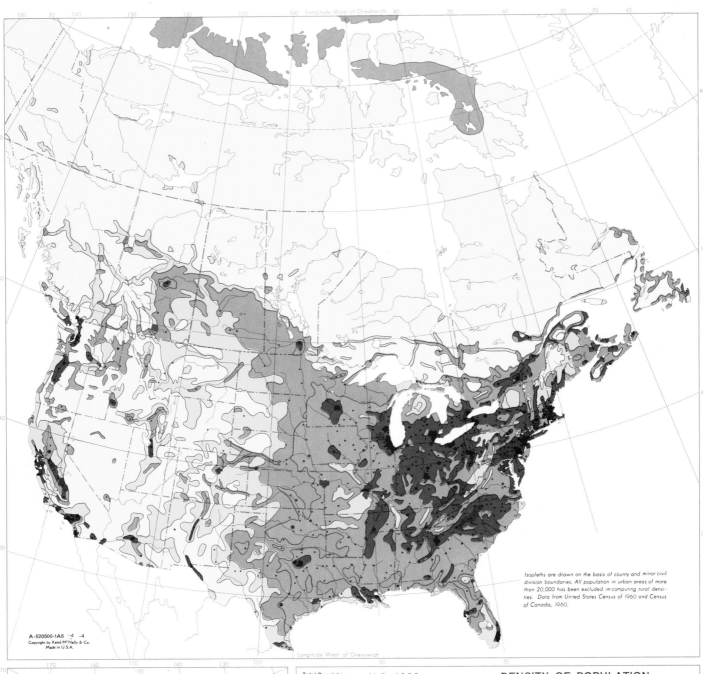

Isopleths are drawn on the basis of county and minor civil division boundaries. All population in urban areas of more than 20,000 has been excluded in computing rural densities. Data from United States Census of 1960 and Census of Canada, 1960.

A-520500-1A6 -4 -4
Copyright by Rand McNally & Co.
Made in U.S.A.

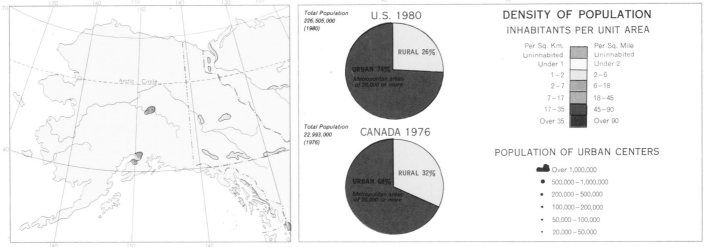

Total Population
226,505,000
(1980)

U.S. 1980

RURAL 26%

URBAN 74%
*Metropolitan areas
of 20,000 or more*

Total Population
22,993,000
(1976)

CANADA 1976

RURAL 32%

URBAN 68%
*Metropolitan areas
of 20,000 or more*

DENSITY OF POPULATION
INHABITANTS PER UNIT AREA

Per Sq. Km.	Per Sq. Mile
Uninhabited	Uninhabited
Under 1	Under 2
1 – 2	2 – 6
2 – 7	6 – 18
7 – 17	18 – 45
17 – 35	45 – 90
Over 35	Over 90

POPULATION OF URBAN CENTERS

Over 1,000,000
500,000 – 1,000,000
200,000 – 500,000
100,000 – 200,000
50,000 – 100,000
20,000 – 50,000

Scale 1: 32 000 000; One inch to 500 miles. LAMBERT CONFORMAL CONIC PROJECTION

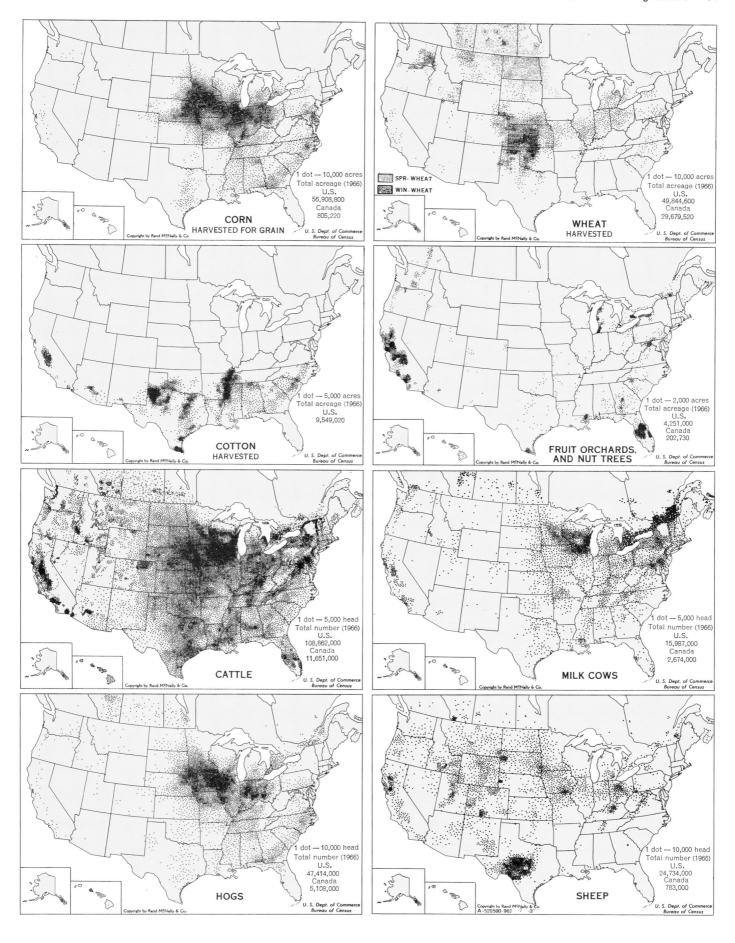

CORN
HARVESTED FOR GRAIN

1 dot — 10,000 acres
Total acreage (1966)
U.S.
56,908,800
Canada
805,220

Copyright by Rand McNally & Co.

U. S. Dept. of Commerce
Bureau of Census

SPR. WHEAT
WIN. WHEAT

WHEAT
HARVESTED

1 dot — 10,000 acres
Total acreage (1966)
U.S.
49,844,800
Canada
29,679,520

Copyright by Rand McNally & Co.

U. S. Dept. of Commerce
Bureau of Census

COTTON
HARVESTED

1 dot — 5,000 acres
Total acreage (1966)
U.S.
9,549,020

Copyright by Rand McNally & Co.

U. S. Dept. of Commerce
Bureau of Census

FRUIT ORCHARDS,
AND NUT TREES

1 dot — 2,000 acres
Total acreage (1966)
U.S.
4,251,000
Canada
202,730

Copyright by Rand McNally & Co.

U. S. Dept. of Commerce
Bureau of Census

CATTLE

1 dot — 5,000 head
Total number (1966)
U.S.
108,862,000
Canada
11,651,000

Copyright by Rand McNally & Co.

U. S. Dept. of Commerce
Bureau of Census

MILK COWS

1 dot — 5,000 head
Total number (1966)
U.S.
15,987,000
Canada
2,674,000

Copyright by Rand McNally & Co.

U. S. Dept. of Commerce
Bureau of Census

HOGS

1 dot — 10,000 head
Total number (1966)
U.S.
47,414,000
Canada
5,108,000

Copyright by Rand McNally & Co.

U. S. Dept. of Commerce
Bureau of Census

SHEEP

1 dot — 10,000 head
Total number (1966)
U.S.
24,734,000
Canada
783,000

Copyright by Rand McNally & Co.
A-520500-962   -3-

U. S. Dept. of Commerce
Bureau of Census

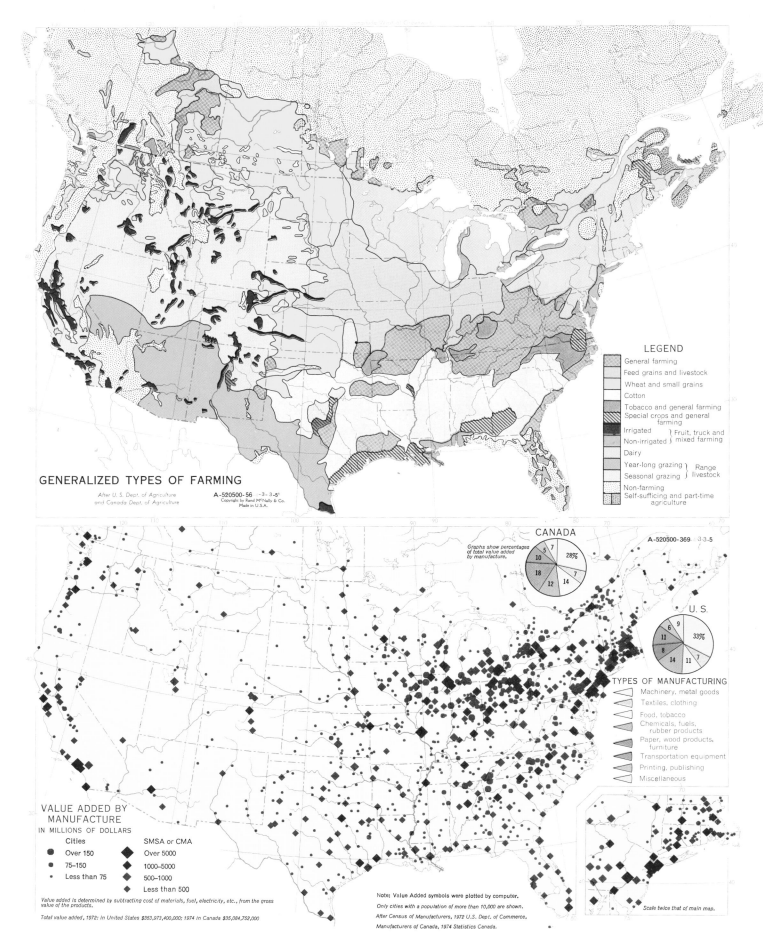

GENERALIZED TYPES OF FARMING

*After U. S. Dept. of Agriculture
and Canada Dept. of Agriculture*

A-520500-56 -3-3-5¹
Copyright by Rand McNally & Co.
Made in U.S.A.

LEGEND

General farming
Feed grains and livestock
Wheat and small grains
Cotton
Tobacco and general farming
Special crops and general farming
Irrigated } Fruit, truck and
Non-irrigated } mixed farming
Dairy
Year-long grazing } Range
Seasonal grazing } livestock
Non-farming
Self-sufficing and part-time agriculture

CANADA

A-520500-369 -3-3-5

Graphs show percentages of total value added by manufacture.

28%
7 5
10
18
12 14

U. S.

33%
6 9
11 7
8 14 11

TYPES OF MANUFACTURING

Machinery, metal goods
Textiles, clothing
Food, tobacco
Chemicals, fuels, rubber products
Paper, wood products, furniture
Transportation equipment
Printing, publishing
Miscellaneous

VALUE ADDED BY MANUFACTURE

IN MILLIONS OF DOLLARS

Cities	SMSA or CMA
Over 150	Over 5000
75–150	1000–5000
Less than 75	500–1000
	Less than 500

Value added is determined by subtracting cost of materials, fuel, electricity, etc., from the gross value of the products.

Total value added, 1972: In United States $353,973,400,000; 1974 in Canada $35,084,752,000

Note: Value Added symbols were plotted by computer.

Only cities with a population of more than 10,000 are shown.

*After Census of Manufacturers, 1972 U.S. Dept. of Commerce,
Manufacturers of Canada, 1974 Statistics Canada.*

Scale twice that of main map.

Scale 1: 28 000 000; One inch to 440 miles. LAMBERT CONFORMAL CONIC PROJECTION

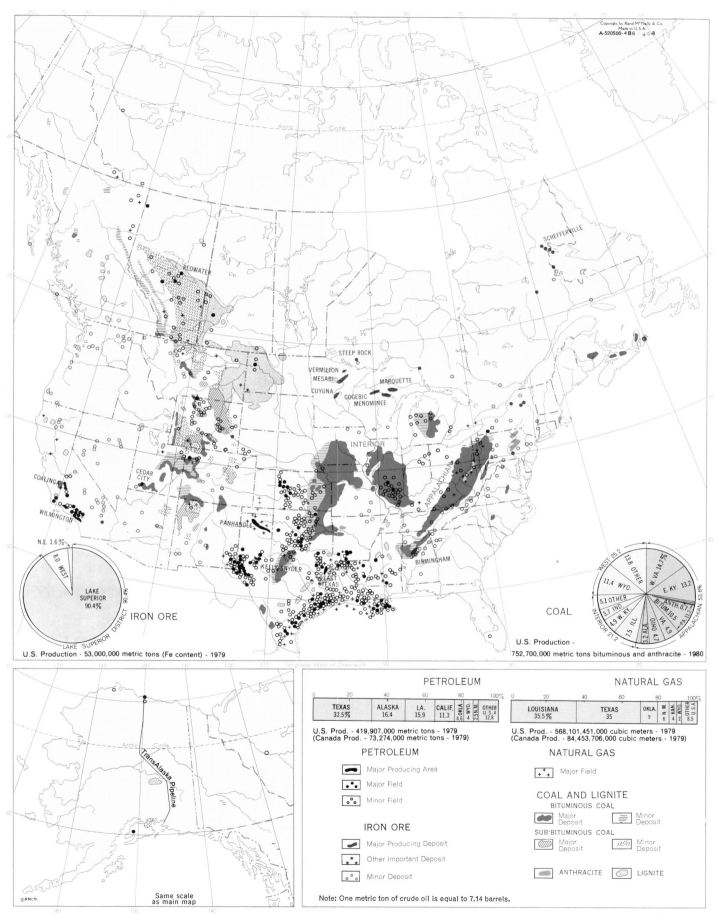

Copyright by Rand McNally & Co.
Made in U.S.A.
A-520500-4 B 6. g-5-8

REDWATER

SCHEFFERVILLE

STEEP ROCK
VERMILION
MESABI
CUYUNA
GOGEBIC
MENOMINEE
MARQUETTE

INTERIOR

COALINGA

CEDAR CITY

WILMINGTON

APPALACHIAN

PANHANDLE

KELLY SNYDER

EAST TEXAS

BIRMINGHAM

IRON ORE

N.E. 1.6%
8.0 WEST
LAKE SUPERIOR 90.4%
LAKE SUPERIOR DISTRICT 90.4%

U.S. Production - 53,000,000 metric tons (Fe content) - 1979

COAL

WEST 25.2 | 13.8 OTHER | W. VA. 14.7%
11.4 WYO. | E. KY 13.2
5.1 OTHER | ANTH. 0.7 | BITUM 10.5
INTERIOR 21.2 | 3.7 IND. | PA. 9.7 | APPALACHIAN 53.6%
4.9 W. KY. | VA. 4.9
7.5 ILL. | OHIO 4.7
3.2 ALA

U.S. Production - 752,700,000 metric tons bituminous and anthracite - 1980

TransAlaska Pipeline

Arctic Circle

Same scale as main map

©RMCN.

PETROLEUM

0	20	40	60	80	100%

| TEXAS 32.5% | ALASKA 16.4 | LA. 15.9 | CALIF. 11.3 | OKLA. 4.6 | WYO. | 2.5 N.M. | OTHER U.S.A 12.8 |

U.S. Prod. - 419,907,000 metric tons - 1979
(Canada Prod. - 73,274,000 metric tons - 1979)

NATURAL GAS

0	20	40	60	80	100%

| LOUISIANA 35.5% | TEXAS 35 | OKLA. 9 | N.M. 6 | KAN. 4 | WYO. 2 | OTHER U.S.A. 8.5 |

U.S. Prod. - 568,101,451,000 cubic meters - 1979
(Canada Prod. - 84,453,706,000 cubic meters - 1979)

PETROLEUM

- Major Producing Area
- Major Field
- Minor Field

IRON ORE

- Major Producing Deposit
- Other Important Deposit
- Minor Deposit

NATURAL GAS

- Major Field

COAL AND LIGNITE

BITUMINOUS COAL
- Major Deposit
- Minor Deposit

SUB-BITUMINOUS COAL
- Major Deposit
- Minor Deposit

- ANTHRACITE
- LIGNITE

Note: One metric ton of crude oil is equal to 7.14 barrels.

Scale 1: 32 000 000; One inch to 500 miles.   LAMBERT CONFORMAL CONIC PROJECTION

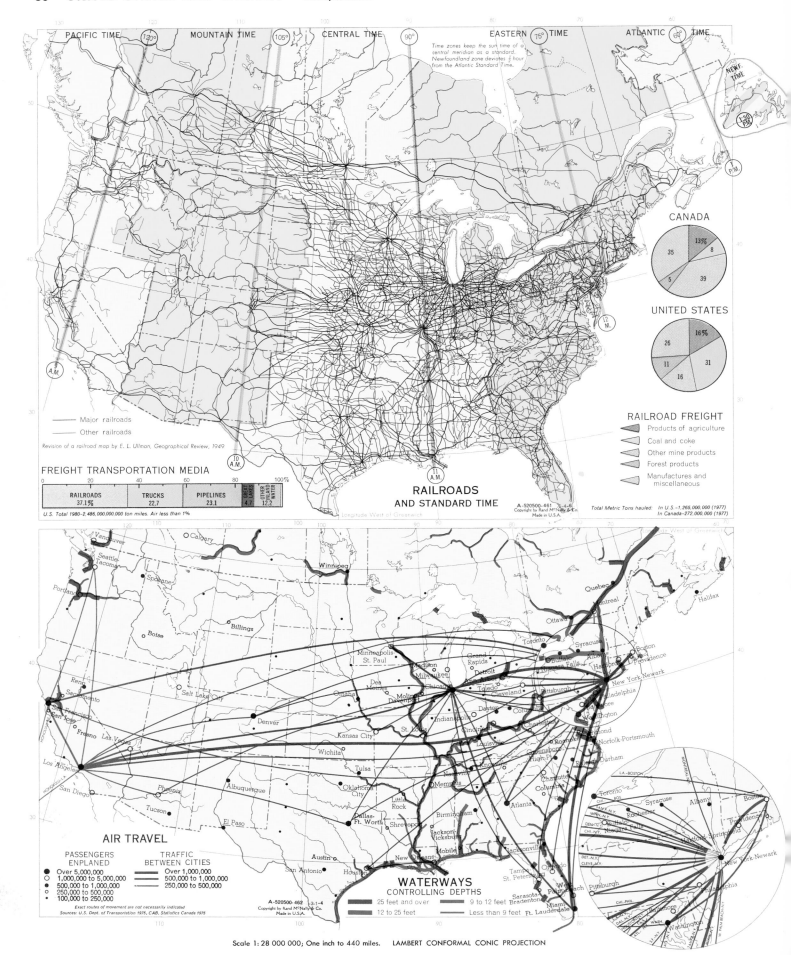

RAILROADS
AND STANDARD TIME

FREIGHT TRANSPORTATION MEDIA

| RAILROADS 37.1% | TRUCKS 22.7 | PIPELINES 23.1 | GREAT LAKES 4.7 | OTHER INLAND WATER 12.2 |

U.S. Total 1980–2,486,000,000,000 ton miles. Air less than 1%

Major railroads
Other railroads

Revision of a railroad map by E. L. Ullman, Geographical Review, 1949

CANADA

UNITED STATES

RAILROAD FREIGHT
Products of agriculture
Coal and coke
Other mine products
Forest products
Manufactures and miscellaneous

Total Metric Tons hauled: In U.S.–1,265,000,000 (1977)
In Canada–272,000,000 (1977)

AIR TRAVEL

PASSENGERS ENPLANED
● Over 5,000,000
○ 1,000,000 to 5,000,000
○ 500,000 to 1,000,000
○ 250,000 to 500,000
· 100,000 to 250,000

TRAFFIC BETWEEN CITIES
Over 1,000,000
500,000 to 1,000,000
250,000 to 500,000

Exact routes of movement are not necessarily indicated
Sources: U.S. Dept. of Transportation 1975, CAB, Statistics Canada 1975

WATERWAYS
CONTROLLING DEPTHS
25 feet and over
12 to 25 feet
9 to 12 feet
Less than 9 feet

Scale 1: 28 000 000; One inch to 440 miles.   LAMBERT CONFORMAL CONIC PROJECTION

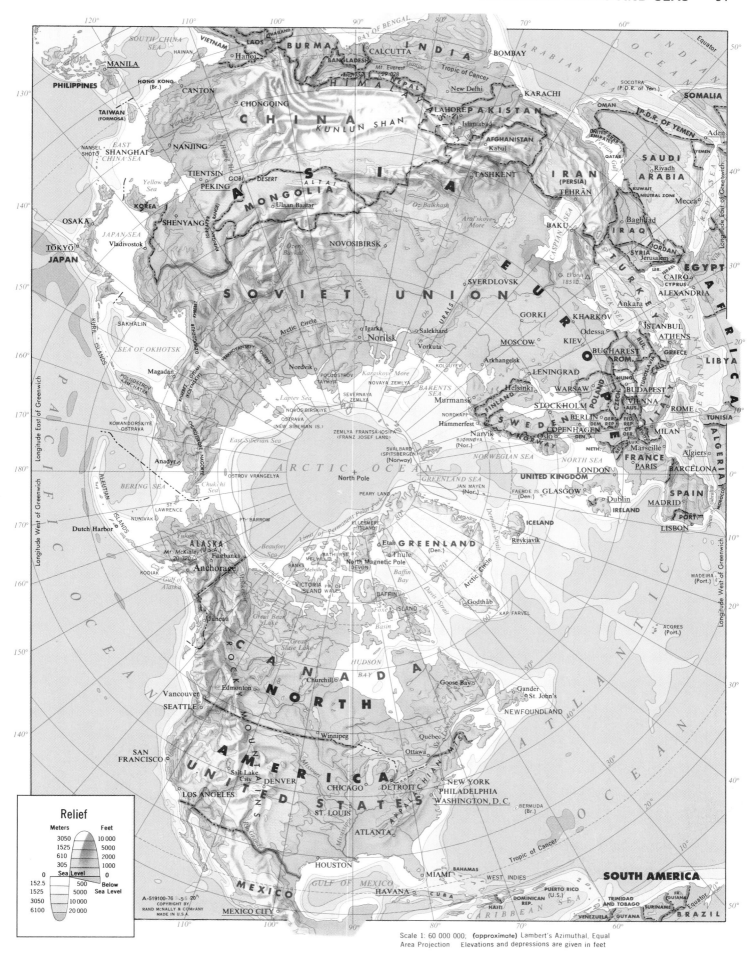

Relief

Meters		Feet
3050		10 000
1525		5000
610		2000
305		1000
Sea Level		0
0	500	Below
152.5		Sea Level
1525	5000	
3050	10 000	
6100	20 000	

A-519100-76
COPYRIGHT BY
RAND MCNALLY & COMPANY
MADE IN U.S.A.

Scale 1: 60 000 000; (approximate) Lambert's Azimuthal, Equal
Area Projection   Elevations and depressions are given in feet

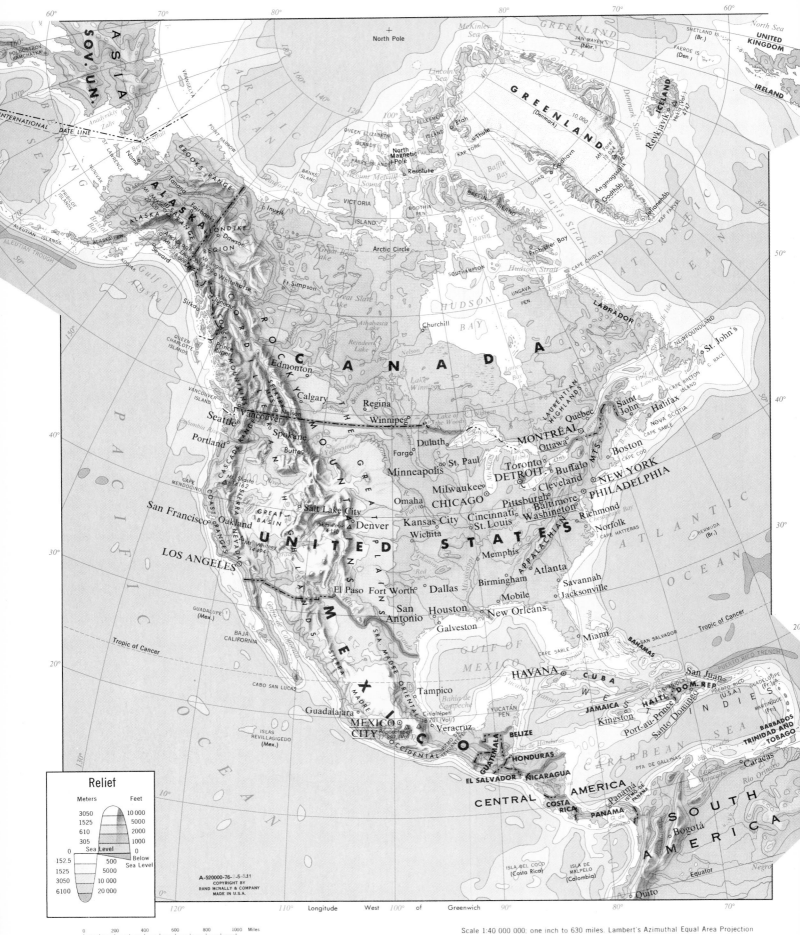

60°   70°   80°   North Sea   70°   60°

ASIA SOV. UN.

GREENLAND SEA

SHETLAND IS. (Br.)   UNITED KINGDOM

North Pole

McKinley Sea

JAN MAYEN (Nor.)

FAEROE IS. (Den.)

IRELAND

POLUOSTROV KAMCHATKA   Anadyrskiy Zaliv   WRANGELYA   POINT BARROW   North Pole

INTERNATIONAL DATE LINE

St. LAWRENCE   Nome   Inuvik   BROOKS RANGE

Lincoln Sea   ELLESMERE   Etah   Thule   KAP YORK

GREENLAND (Denmark)   10,000   Mt. Forel   11,024

ICELAND   Reykjavik   Hekla (Vol.) 4757

PRIBILOF ISLANDS   NUNIVAK   ST. LAWRENCE   Nome   ALASKA   Fairbanks   KLONDIKE   Dawson   REGION

QUEEN ELIZABETH ISLANDS   PARRY ISLANDS   Viscount Melville Sound   Resolute   North Magnetic Pole

Angmagssalik   Godthåb   KAP FARVEL

ALEUTIAN ISLANDS   Kodiak   Seward   Whitehorse   ALASKA RANGE

BANKS ISLAND   VICTORIA ISLAND   BOOTHIA PEN.

Baffin Bay   DISKO   Godhavn

ALEUTIAN TROUGH   Gulf of Alaska   Sitka   Juneau   PRINCE RUPERT

Beaufort Sea   Ft. Simpson   Great Bear Lake

BAFFIN ISLAND   Foxe Basin   Frobisher Bay   CAPE CHIDLEY

ATLANTIC OCEAN

QUEEN CHARLOTTE ISLANDS   VANCOUVER ISLAND   COAST RANGE   Prince Rupert

Arctic Circle   Great Slave Lake   Athabasca Lake   Reindeer Lake

Hudson Strait   UNGAVA PEN.   Ungava Bay   LABRADOR

CANADA   Edmonton   Calgary   Nelson   THE   Churchill

HUDSON BAY   Southampton   CAPE CHIDLEY

NEWFOUNDLAND   St. John's   C. RACE

Seattle   Vancouver   Spokane   Regina   Winnipeg   Lake of the Woods   Lake Winnipeg

Saskatchewan

LAURENTIAN HIGHLANDS   Québec   Saint John   Halifax   NOVA SCOTIA   CAPE BRETON ISLAND

Portland   Butte   Yellowstone   Fargo   Duluth   St. Paul   Minneapolis

MONTREAL   Ottawa   Toronto   DETROIT   Buffalo   Boston   CAPE COD

APPALACHIAN MTS.

Salt Lake City   Denver   Omaha   CHICAGO   Milwaukee   Cleveland   NEW YORK   PHILADELPHIA

San Francisco   Oakland   Pikes Peak 14,110   Wichita   Kansas City   St. Louis   Cincinnati   Pittsburgh   Baltimore   Washington   Richmond

GREAT BASIN   SIERRA NEVADA   Mt. Whitney 14,494

UNITED   STATES   Norfolk   CAPE HATTERAS   BERMUDA (Br.)

LOS ANGELES   COAST RANGES   GREAT   PLAINS   Memphis   Atlanta   APPALACHIANS

El Paso   Fort Worth   Dallas   Birmingham   Savannah

GUADALUPE (Mex.)   San Antonio   Houston   Mobile   Jacksonville

Tropic of Cancer   BAJA CALIFORNIA   Galveston   New Orleans   GULF OF MEXICO   Miami   BAHAMAS   SAN SALVADOR   Tropic of Cancer

CABO SAN LUCAS   Tampico   Bahia de Campeche   YUCATÁN PEN.   HAVANA   CUBA   San Juan   PUERTO RICO (U.S.A.)   GUADELOUPE (Fr.)

ISLAS REVILLAGIGEDO (Mex.)   Guadalajara   SIERRA MADRE ORIENTAL   Citlaltépetl 18,701 (Vol.)   Veracruz

MEXICO   M E X I C O   MEXICO CITY   Popocatépetl   BELIZE   Golfo de Honduras   JAMAICA   Kingston   HAITI   DOM. REP.   Port-au-Prince   Santo Domingo   MARTINIQUE (Fr.)   BARBADOS

SIERRA MADRE DEL SUR   GUATEMALA   HONDURAS   EL SALVADOR   NICARAGUA   CARIBBEAN   SEA   TRINIDAD AND TOBAGO

PACIFIC   OCEAN   CENTRAL   AMERICA   COSTA RICA   PANAMA   PTA DE GALLINAS   Caracas

ISLA DEL COCO (Costa Rica)   ISLA DE MALPELO (Colombia)   Bogotá   SOUTH   AMERICA

Quito   Equator   Rio Negro

Relief

Meters		Feet
3050		10 000
1525		5000
610		2000
305		1000
0	Sea Level	0
152.5		500 Below Sea Level
1525		5000
3050		10 000
6100		20 000

A-520000-76- -5--5-11
COPYRIGHT BY
RAND McNALLY & COMPANY
MADE IN U.S.A.

120°   110°   Longitude   West   100°   of   Greenwich   90°   80°   70°

0   200   400   600   800   1000 Miles
0   400   800   1200   1600 Kilometers

Scale 1:40 000 000: one inch to 630 miles. Lambert's Azimuthal Equal Area Projection
Elevations and depressions are given in feet

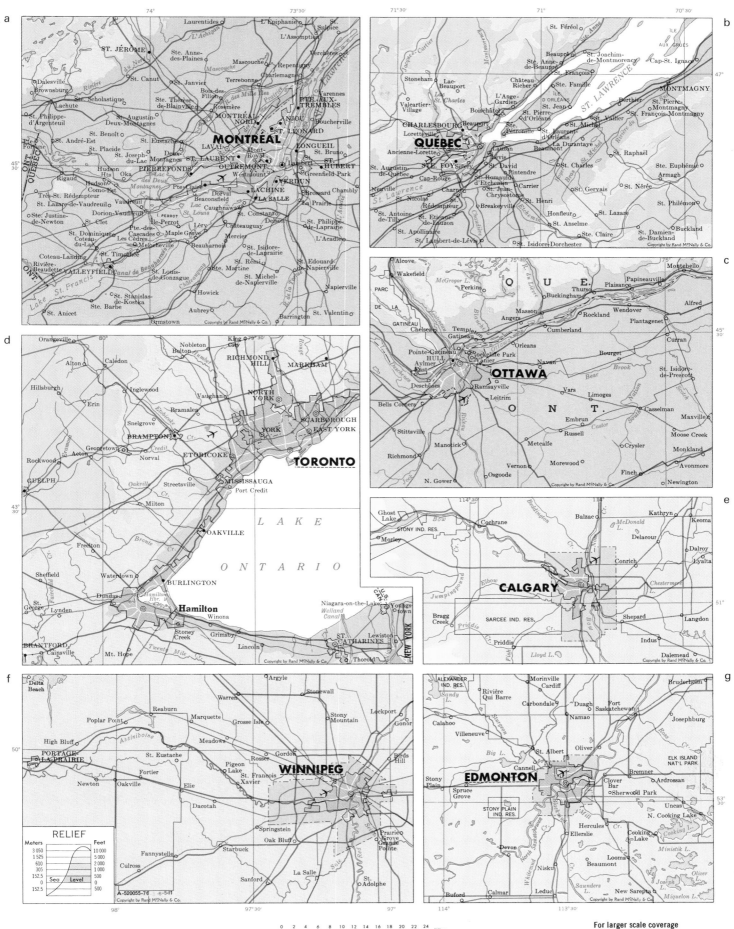

Scale 1:1 000 000; One inch to 16 miles.
Elevations and depressions are given in feet.

RELIEF

Meters		Feet
3 050		10 000
1 525		5 000
610		2 000
305		1 000
152.5		500
0	Sea Level	0
152.5		500

A-520055-76 -6-5-11

Miles
0 2 4 6 8 10 12 14 16 18 20 22 24
Kilometers
0 4 8 12 16 20 24 28 32 36 40

For larger scale coverage
of Montréal and Toronto
see page 54.

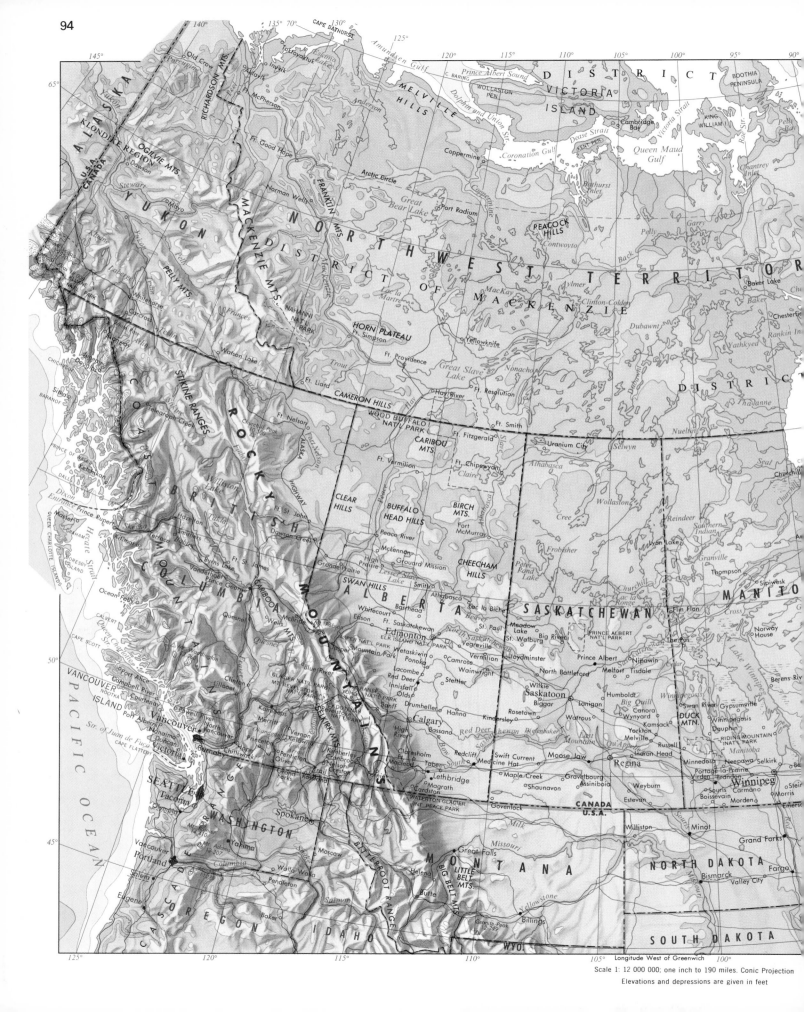

Scale 1: 12 000 000; one inch to 190 miles. Conic Projection

Elevations and depressions are given in feet

a

Same scale as main map

QUEBEC

CAPE BAULD

Gulf of

St. Lawrence

GROS MORNE NAT'L PARK
Deer Lake
Corner Brook
Stephenville
Botwood
Grand Falls
Windsor
Gander
Bonavista

LONG RANGE MTS.
Twillingate

TERRA NOVA NAT'L PARK

NEWFOUNDLAND

St. George's
Trinity

CHANNEL-PORT-AUX-BASQUES

CAPE RAY
CAPE NORTH
CAPE BRETON ISLAND

Grand Bank
Burin
Fortune Bay
Placentia Bay

St. John's

ST. PIERRE AND MIQUELON (Fr.)

ATLANTIC OCEAN

FRANKLIN

BAFFIN ISLAND

MELVILLE PENINSULA

Foxe Basin

Arctic Circle

Foxe Channel

SOUTHAMPTON ISLAND

Foxe Peninsula

KEEWATIN

HUDSON BAY

All islands within bays and straits lie within Northwest Territories.

PENINSULE D'UNGAVA

Ungava Bay

TORNGAT MTS.

NEW FOUNDLAND

LABRADOR

MTS. OTISH

QUEBEC

James Bay

Ft. George

Ft. Albany

Moosonee

ONTARIO

Coral Rapids
Fraserdale

Hearst

Armstrong Sta.
Nakina
Geraldton
Longlac
Kapuskasing
Cochrane
Iroquois Falls
Timmins
Kirkland Lake
Cobalt
Matheson

Thunder Bay

Lake Superior

Marathon
MICHIPICOTEN
Blind River
Sault Ste. Marie
Thessalon

Sudbury
North Bay
Sturgeon Falls

MICHIGAN

Escanaba
Marquette
Sault Ste. Marie

Georgian Bay

MANITOULIN

Lake Huron

WISCONSIN

Duluth
Superior

Green Bay

Madison

MILWAUKEE

CHICAGO

Toledo

DETROIT

Windsor
Lansing
Flint
Saginaw
Grand Rapids

ONTARIO

Lake Erie

London
Sarnia
Chatham
St. Thomas
Port Huron

Kitchener
TORONTO
Hamilton
St. Catharines
Niagara
BUFFALO

Owen Sound
Wiarton
Kincardine

Barrie
Midland
Orillia
Lindsay
Oshawa
Whitby
Peterborough
Cobourg
Trenton

Lake Ontario
Rochester
NEW YORK

MONTREAL
Ottawa
Hull
Pembroke
Renfrew
Smiths Falls
Brockville
Kingston
Alexandria Bay
Ogdensburg

Laval
Valleyfield

Trois Rivières
Shawinigan
Joliette
Sorel
Drummondville

Québec
Lévis

Sherbrooke
Granby

MAINE

VERMONT
NEW HAMPSHIRE
MASS.
CONN.
R.I.

Hartford
Providence

Albany

PENNSYLVANIA

Scranton
Newark
NEW YORK
N.J.

BOSTON

ATLANTIC OCEAN

Portland

CANADA U.S.A.

Woodstock
Edmundston
Rivière-du-Loup

Matane
Rimouski
Campbellton
Carleton

Gaspé
CHIC-CHOCS MTS.

ILES DE LA MADELEINE

PRINCE EDWARD ISLAND
P.E.I.
Charlottetown
Summerside

NEW BRUNSWICK

Fredericton
Moncton
Chatham
Newcastle
Richibucto
Sussex
Saint John
St. Andrews
St. Stephen

Amherst
Truro
Springhill
New Glasgow
Sydney
Sydney Mines
New Waterford
Glace Bay

NOVA SCOTIA

Halifax
Dartmouth
Windsor
Kentville
Bridgewater
Lunenburg
Liverpool
Shelburne
Yarmouth

Gulf of St. Lawrence

ILE D'ANTICOSTI

Sept-Iles
Natashquan

MEALY MTS.

Goose Bay
Churchill Falls

Nain
Hopedale
Makkovik
Rigolet
Cartwright
Battle Harbour

Hamilton Inlet

Strait of Belle Isle

LONG RANGE MTS.

GROS MORNE NAT'L PARK
Corner Brook
Stephenville
St. George's

Ft. Chimo

Hebron

Schefferville

Lac Bienville

Chibougamau
St. Félicien
Roberval
Chambord
Jonquière
Chicoutimi
La Malbaie
St. Paul's

Dolbeau
Alma
Kenogami
Arvida

Chandler
New Carlisle

Betsiamites

La Sarre
Amos
Senneterre
Rouyn
Val-d'Or
Noranda
Malartic

Ville-Marie
Temiscaming
Mattawa

Chapleau

Relief

Meters		Feet
3050		10 000
1525		5000
610		2000
305		1000
152.5		500
0	Sea Level	0
152.5		500
1525		5000
3050		10 000

A-520200-76
COPYRIGHT BY
RAND McNALLY & COMPANY
MADE IN U.S.A.

0 25 50 75 100   200   300   400   500 Miles

0   100   200   300   400   600   800 Kilometers

PACIFIC OCEAN

Relief

Meters		Feet
3050		10 000
1525		5000
610		2000
305		1000
152.5		500
0	Sea Level	0
152.5		500
1525		5000

A-520220-76- 6-5-7
COPYRIGHT BY
RAND McNALLY & COMPANY
MADE IN U.S.A.

Continued on pages 114-115

Longitude West of Greenwich

Scale 1:4 000 000; one inch to 64 miles. Conic Projection

Elevations and depressions are given in feet.

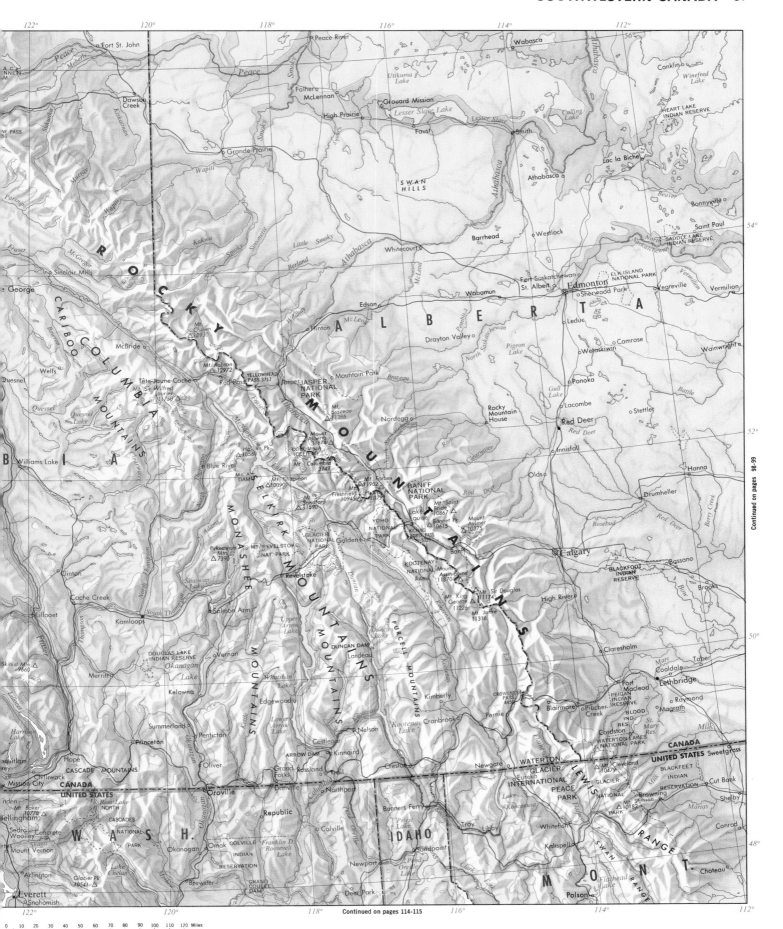

Continued on pages 98-99

Continued on pages 114-115

0 10 20 30 40 50 60 70 80 90 100 110 120 Miles

0   20   40   60   80   100   120   140   160   180   200 Kilometers

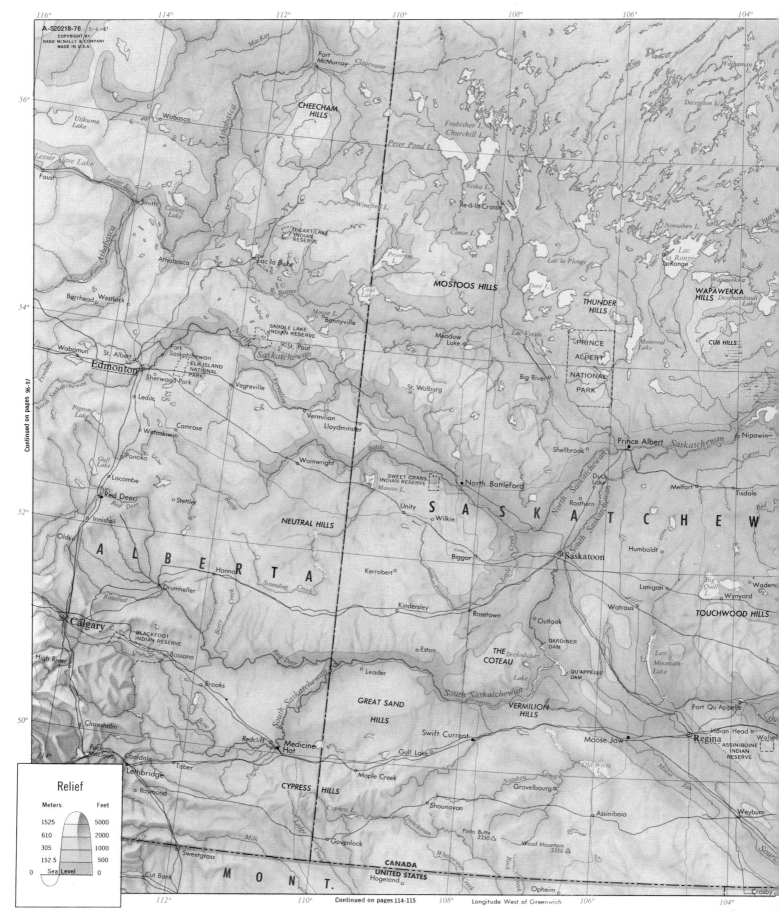

Continued on pages 96-97

Continued on pages 114-115

Longitude West of Greenwich

Scale 1:4 000 000; one inch to 64 miles. Conic Projection
Elevations and depressions are given in feet.

Relief

Meters	Feet
1525	5000
610	2000
305	1000
152.5	500
0 Sea Level	0

A-520218-76   5-4-61
COPYRIGHT BY
RAND McNALLY & COMPANY
MADE IN U.S.A.

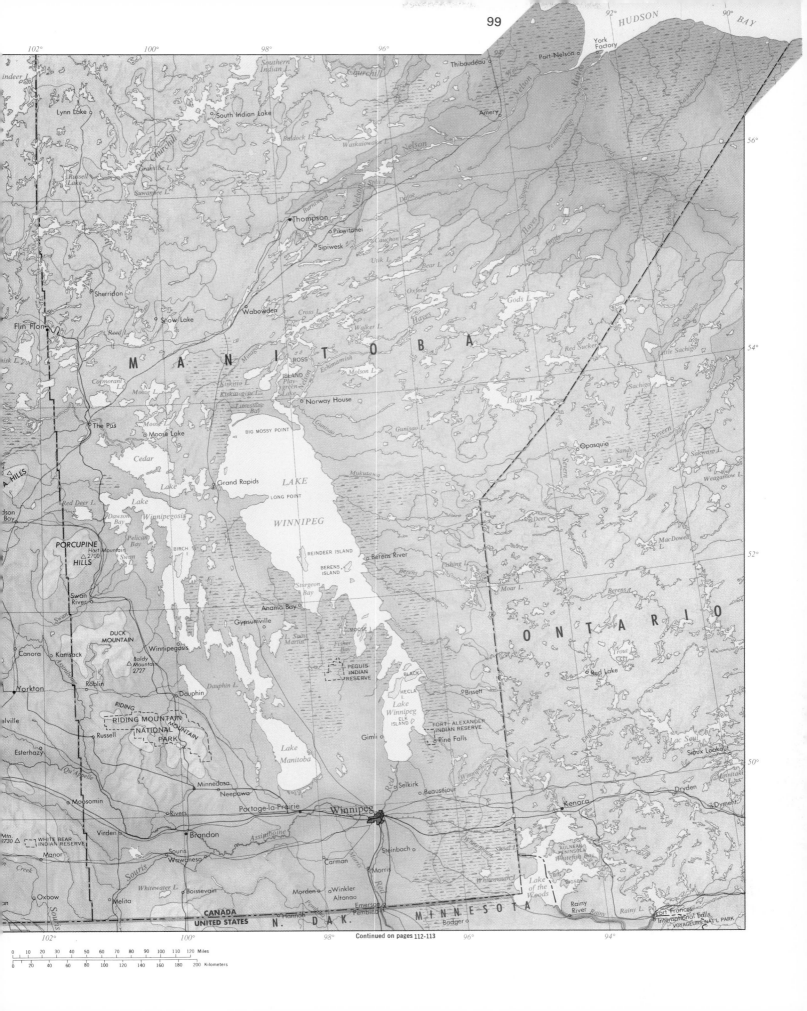

HUDSON   BAY

York
Factory
Port Nelson
Thibaudeau
Amery

Churchill

Southern
Indian L.

Lynn Lake

South Indian Lake

Baldock L.

Waskaiowaka L.

Nelson

Kakachuwi

Granville L.

Russell
Lake

Suwannee L.

Burntwood

Split L.

Deloe

Thompson
Pikwitonei
Sipiwesk
Cauchon L.

Utik L.
Bear L.

Pennywemet

Hayes

Sherridon

Wabowden
Cross L.

Oxford
L.

Gods L.

God's

Hayes

Red Sucker L.

Little Sachigo

Flin Flon

Snow Lake

Reed L.

M A N I T O B A

Walker L.

Echimamish

Molson L.

Island L.

Sachigo

Cormorant
L.

Moose L.

Kiskitto L.

Kiskittogisu L.

ROSS

ISLAND
Playgreen
Lake

Norway House

Limestone
Bay

Gunisao

Gunisao L.

Opasquia
Sand

Severn

Severn

The Pas

Moose Lake

Cedar
Lake

BIG MOSSY POINT

LAKE

Mukutawa

Island L.

Weagamow L.

Red Deer L.

Lake
Winnipegosis

Dawson
Bay

Grand Rapids

LONG POINT

O N T A R I O

Deer
L.

MacDowell

PORCUPINE
Hart Mountain
△ 2700
HILLS

Pelican
Bay

Swan
L.

BIRCH
I.

WINNIPEG

REINDEER ISLAND

Trout

Swan
River

DUCK
MOUNTAIN

Baldy
Mountain
△ 2727

Winnipegosis

Dauphin L.

St. Saint
Martin

BERENS
ISLAND

Berens River

Berens

Fishing I.

Moar
L.

Berens

Canora
Kamsack

Roblin

Anama Bay

Gypsumville

Sturgeon
Bay

Fisher
Bay

MOOSE I.

Red Lake

Yorkton

Dauphin

RIDING MOUNTAIN

RIDING
MOUNTAIN

NATIONAL
PARK

PEGUIS
INDIAN
RESERVE

HECLA
I.

BLACK I.

Bissett

Lac Seul

Esterhazy

Russell

Lake
Manitoba

Lake
Winnipeg

ELK
ISLAND

FORT ALEXANDER
INDIAN RESERVE

Sioux Lookout

Winnitaki

Qu'Appelle

Minnedosa

Gimli

Pine Falls

Minnedosa

Neepawa

Selkirk

Beauséjour

Kenora

Dryden

Dymeht

Moosomin

Rivers

Winnipeg

English

Portage-la-Prairie

Virden

Brandon

Assiniboine

Mtn. △
2730

WHITE BEAR
INDIAN RESERVE

Souris

Wawanesa

Steinbach

Shoal L.

AULNEAU
PENINSULA
Whitefish Bay

Turtle

Manor

Carman

Morris

Whitemouth

Creek

Oxbow

Melita

Souris

Whitewater L.

Boissevain

Morden

Winkler
Altona

Morris

Lake
of the
Woods

EHGSBY

Rainy
River

Souris

CANADA
UNITED STATES

Hannah

N. DAK.

Emerson
Pembina

Badger o

MINNESOTA

Rainy L.

Rainy

International Falls

Fort Frances

VOYAGEURS NAT'L PARK

Continued on pages 112-113

0 10 20 30 40 50 60 70 80 90 100 110 120 Miles

0   20   40   60   80   100   120   140   160   180   200 Kilometers

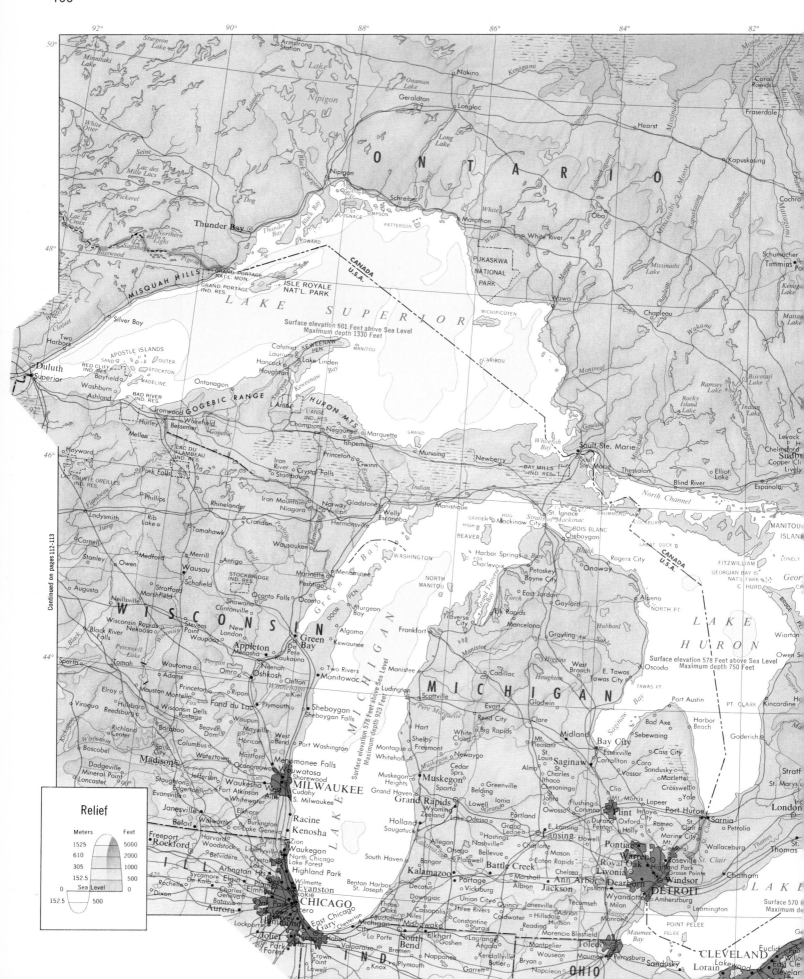

A-520221-76   6-7-11
COPYRIGHT BY
RAND McNALLY & COMPANY
MADE IN U.S.A.

Continued on pages 102-103

QUEBEC

LAKE ONTARIO
Surface 245 Feet above Sea Level
Maximum depth 802 Feet

NEW YORK

ADIRONDACK MTS.

VERMONT

NEW HAMPSHIRE

MAINE

MASS.

CONN.

R.I.

APPALACHIAN MTS.

CATSKILL MTS.

Scale 1:4 000 000; one inch to 64 miles. Conic Projection
Elevations and depressions are given in feet

Longitude West of Greenwich

Continued on pages 108-109

0 10 20 30 40 50 60 70 80 90 100 110 120 Miles
0   20   40   60   80   100   120   140   160   180 200 Kilometers

Continued on pages 108-109

Scale 1:4 000 000; one inch to 64 miles. Conic Projection
Elevations and depressions are given in feet.

Longitude West of Greenwich

Relief

Meters		Feet
1525		5000
610		2000
305		1000
152.5		500
0	Sea Level	0
152.5		500
1525		5000

Scale 1:1 000 000

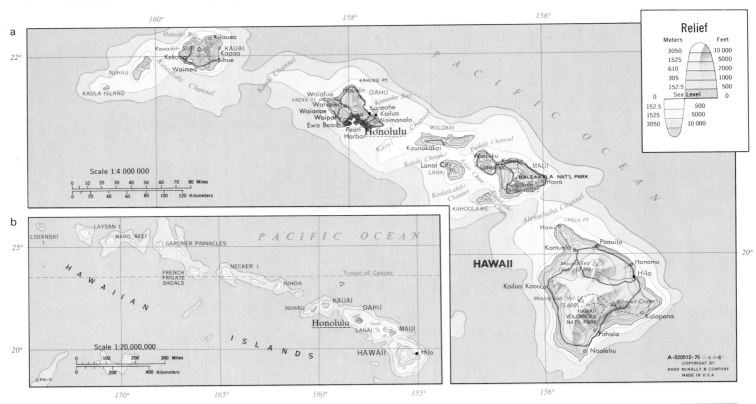

a

A-520512-76 0-4-4-5
COPYRIGHT BY
RAND MCNALLY & COMPANY
MADE IN U.S.A.

Relief

Meters	Feet
3050	10 000
1525	5000
610	2000
305	1000
152.5	500
0 Sea Level	0
152.5	500
1525	5000
3050	10 000

Scale 1:4 000 000

HAWAII

b

Scale 1:20,000,000

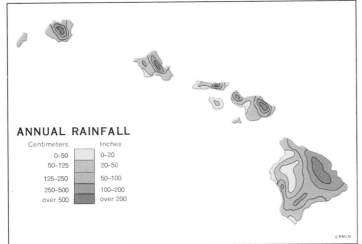

ANNUAL RAINFALL

Centimeters	Inches
0–50	0–20
50–125	20–50
125–250	50–100
250–500	100–200
over 500	over 200

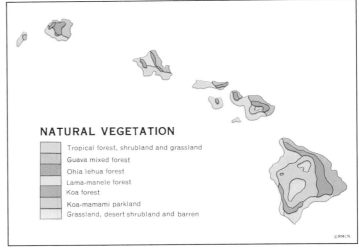

NATURAL VEGETATION

Tropical forest, shrubland and grassland
Guava mixed forest
Ohia lehua forest
Lama-manele forest
Koa forest
Koa-mamami parkland
Grassland, desert shrubland and barren

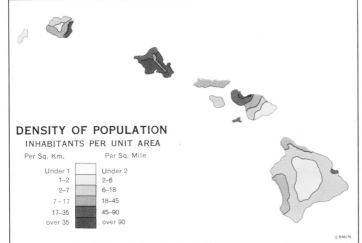

DENSITY OF POPULATION
INHABITANTS PER UNIT AREA

Per Sq. Km.	Per Sq. Mile
Under 1	Under 2
1–2	2–6
2–7	6–18
7–17	18–45
17–35	45–90
over 35	over 90

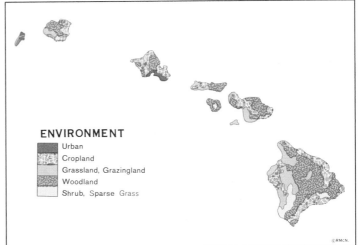

ENVIRONMENT

Urban
Cropland
Grassland, Grazingland
Woodland
Shrub, Sparse Grass

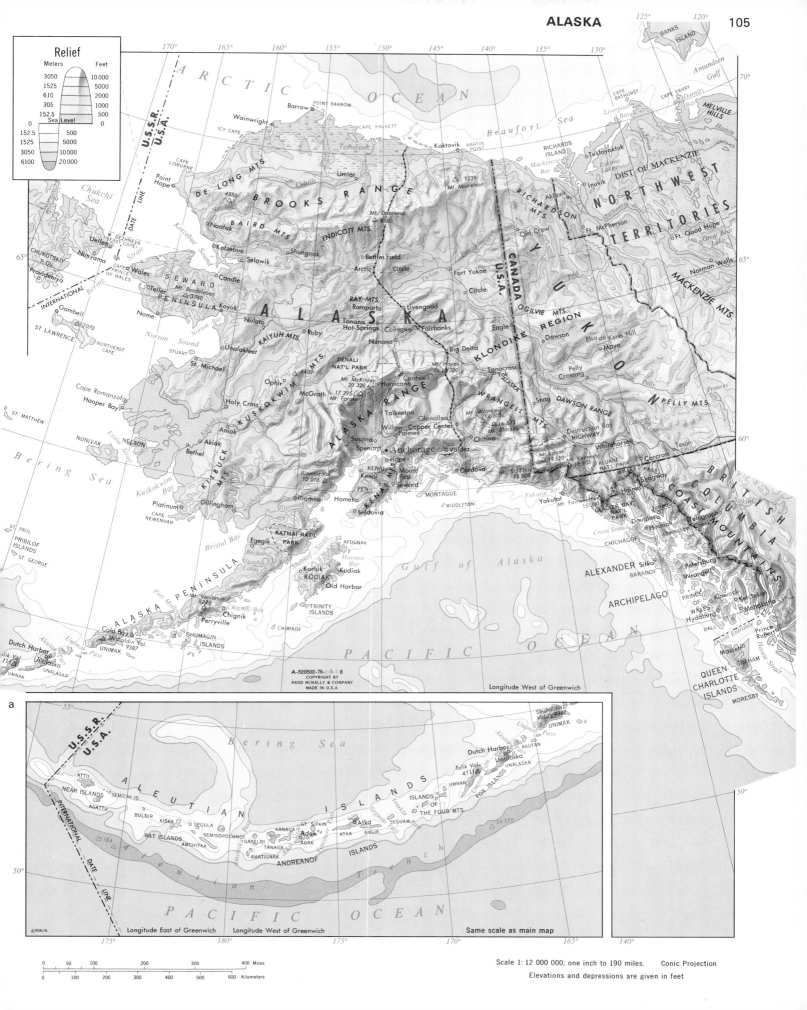

Relief

Meters	Feet
3050	10 000
1525	5000
610	2000
305	1000
152.5	500
0 Sea Level	0
152.5	500
1525	5000
3050	10 000
6100	20 000

A-520502-76-2-5-5 8
COPYRIGHT BY
RAND McNALLY & COMPANY
MADE IN U.S.A.

Longitude West of Greenwich

Longitude East of Greenwich   Longitude West of Greenwich   Same scale as main map

©RMcN

Scale 1: 12 000 000; one inch to 190 miles.   Conic Projection

Elevations and depressions are given in feet

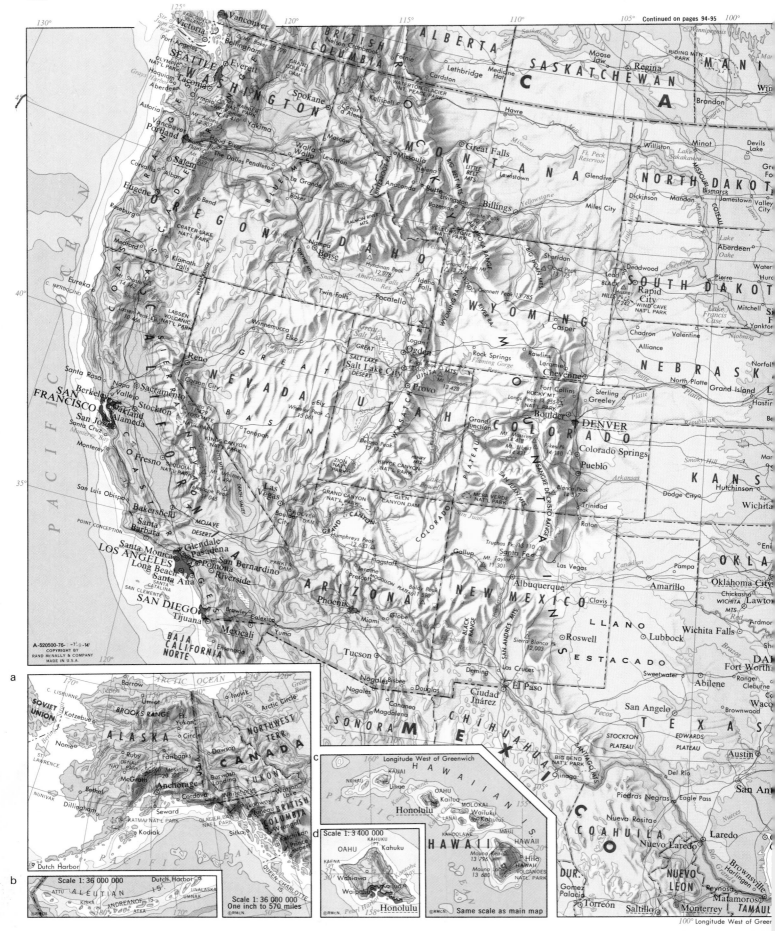

Continued on pages 94-95

Scale 1:12 000 000; one inch to 190 miles. Polyconic Projec

Elevations and depressions are given in feet

100° Longitude West of Gree

Relief

Meters	Feet
3050	10 000
1525	5000
610	2000
305	1000
152.5	500
0 Sea Level	0 Sea Level
152.5	500
1525	5000
3050	10 000
6100	20 000
	Below Sea Level

Cities and Towns

0 to 50,000   500,000 to 1,000,000

50,000 to 500,000   1,000,000 and over

Cities and Towns

0 to 50,000   500,000 to 1,000,000

50,000 to 500,000   1,000,000 and over

Longitude West of Greenwich

Continued on pages 112-113

Continued on pages 124-125

Scale 1:4 000 000; one inch to 64 miles. Conic Projection
Elevations and depressions are given in feet

Continued on pages 100-101

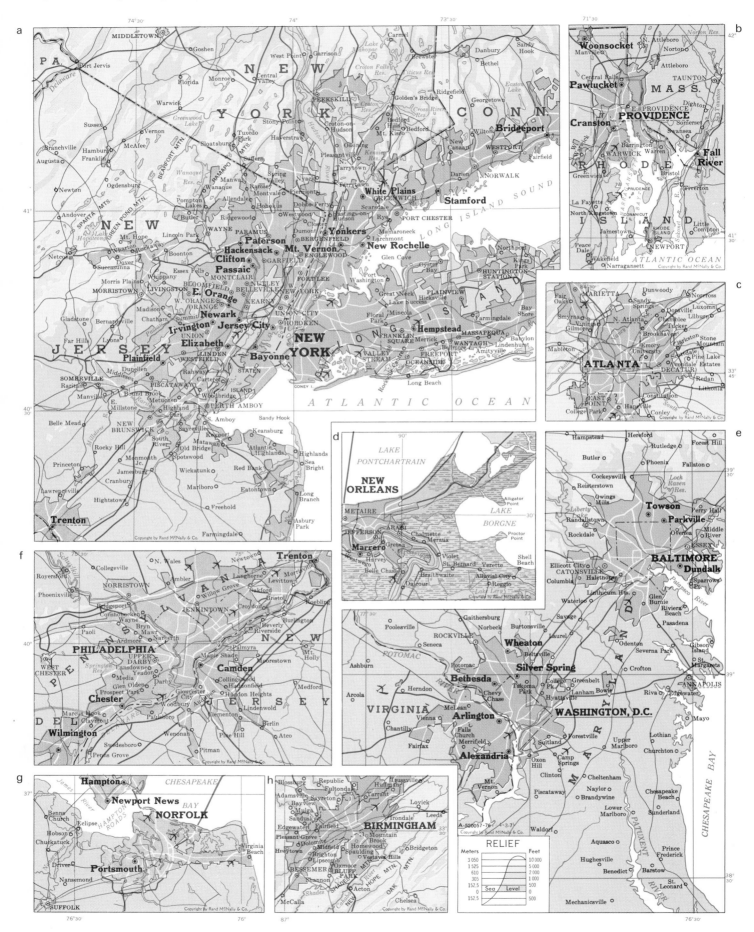

Scale 1:1 000 000; One inch to 16 miles.
Elevations and depressions are given in feet.

For larger scale coverage of New York, Baltimore, Washington, D. C. and Philadelphia see pages 55 and 56.

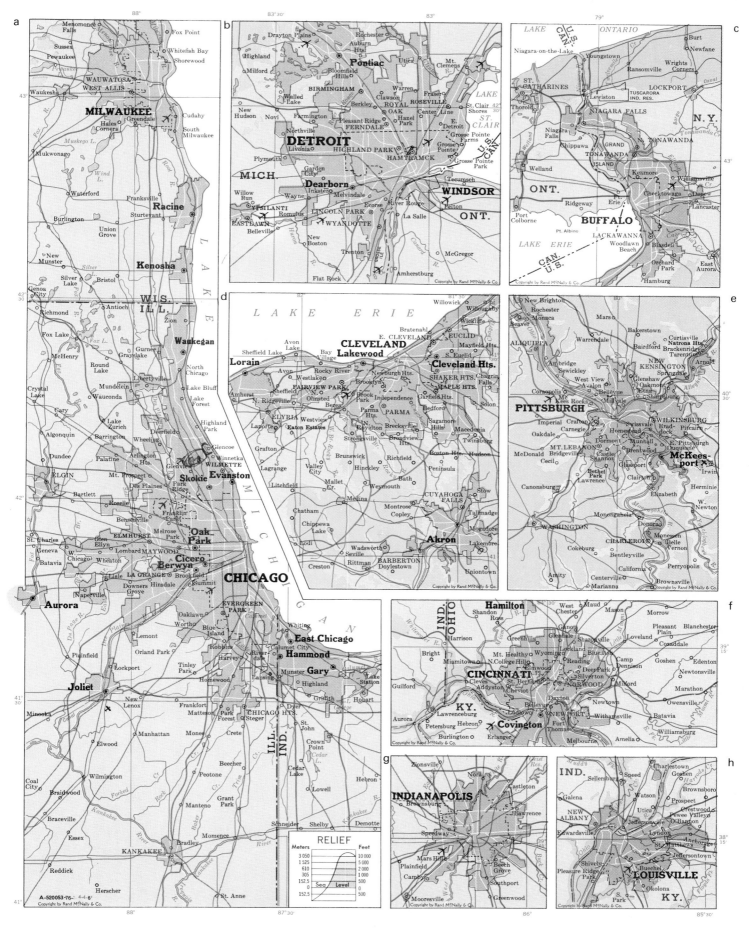

Scale 1:1 000 000; One inch to 16 miles.
Elevations and depressions are given in feet.

For larger scale coverage
of Chicago see page 58.

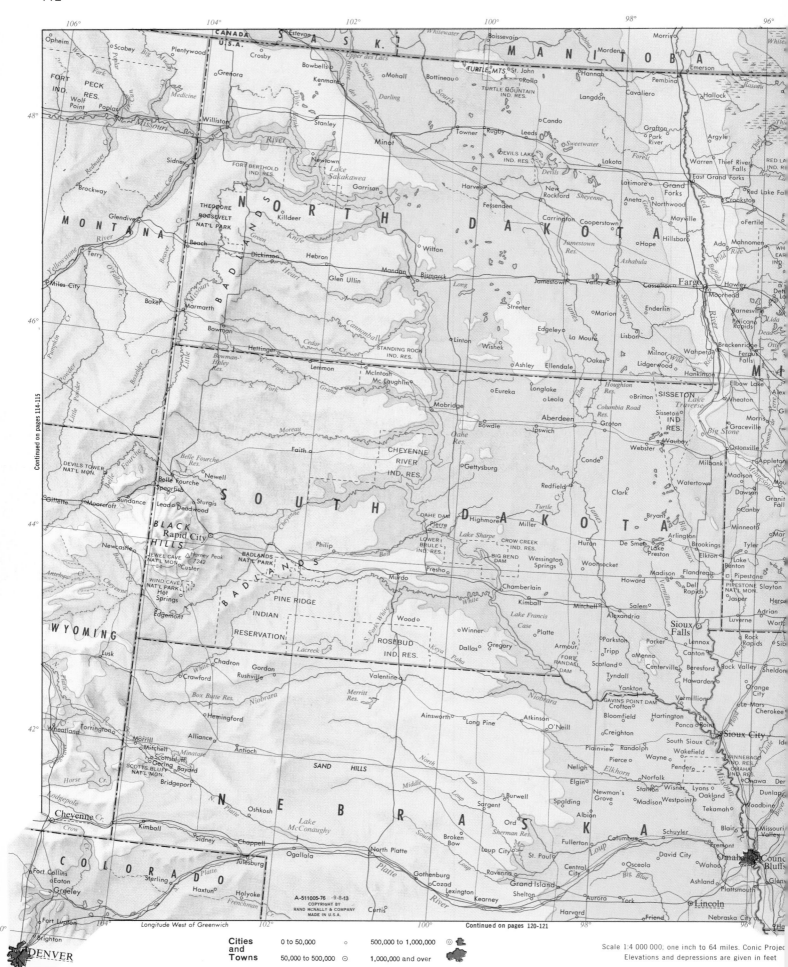

CANADA
U.S.A.

MANITOBA

SASK.

MONTANA

NORTH DAKOTA

SOUTH DAKOTA

WYOMING

NEBRASKA

COLORADO

DENVER

A-511005-76 -9-8-13
COPYRIGHT BY
RAND McNALLY & COMPANY
MADE IN U.S.A.

Longitude West of Greenwich

Cities
and
Towns

0 to 50,000   o   500,000 to 1,000,000   ◎

50,000 to 500,000   ⊙   1,000,000 and over

Scale 1:4 000 000; one inch to 64 miles. Conic Projec
Elevations and depressions are given in feet

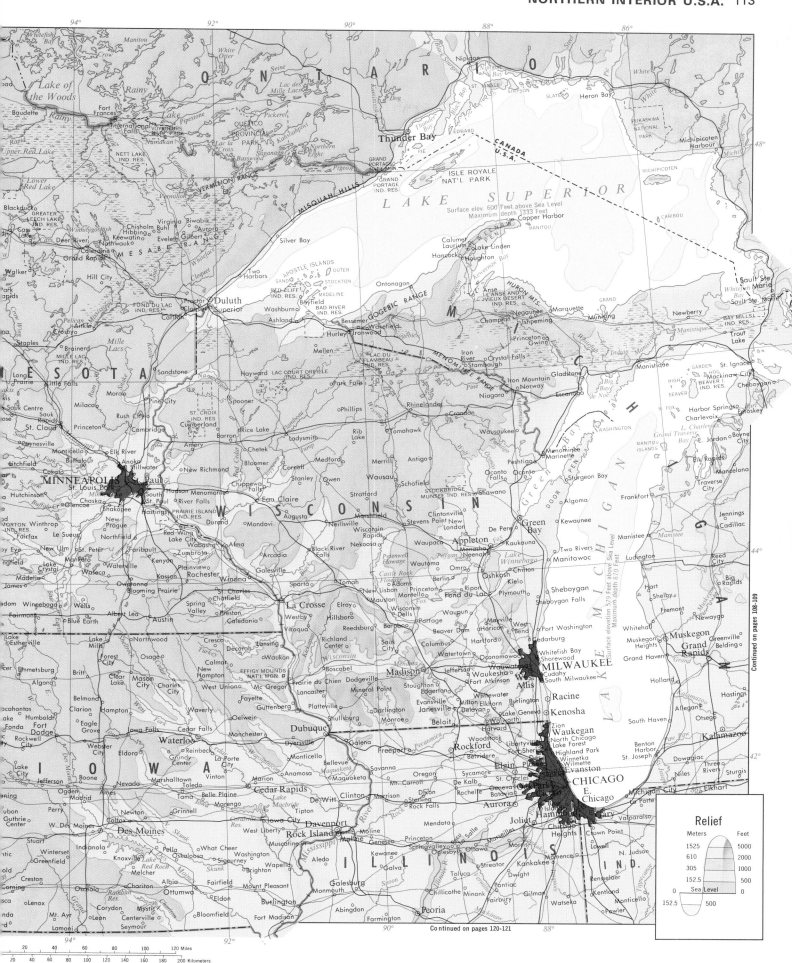

Continued on pages 108-109

Continued on pages 120-121

Relief

Meters	Feet
1525	5000
610	2000
305	1000
152.5	500
0 Sea Level	0
152.5	500

20 40 60 80 100 120 Miles
20 40 60 80 100 120 140 160 180 200 Kilometers

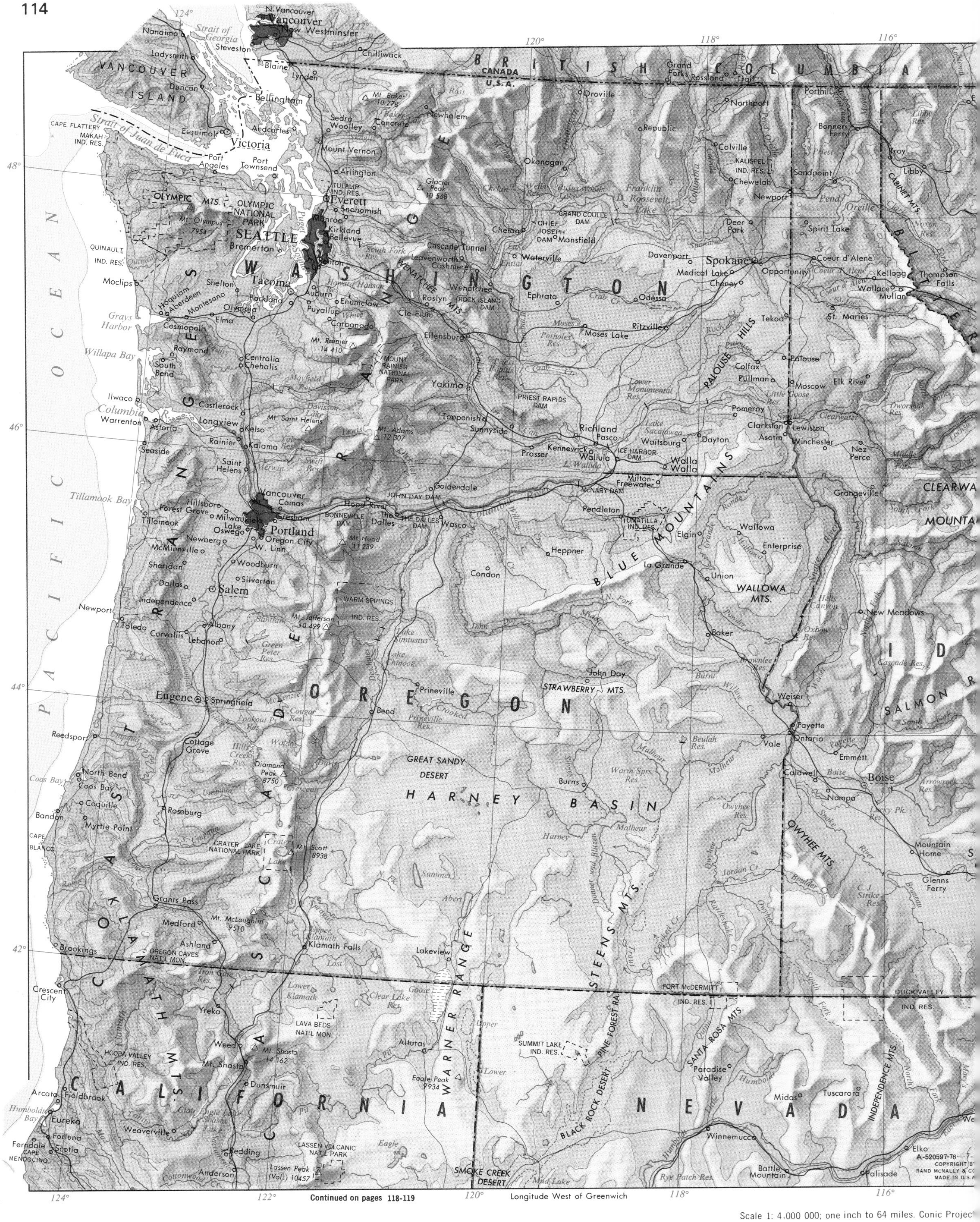

114

BRITISH COLUMBIA
CANADA
U.S.A.

VANCOUVER ISLAND
Nanaimo
Ladysmith
Duncan
Esquimalt
Victoria
Port Angeles
Port Townsend

Strait of Georgia
N. Vancouver
Vancouver
New Westminster
Steveston
Blaine
Lynden
Chilliwack

Bellingham
Anacortes
Sedro Woolley
Concrete
Mt. Baker 10,778
Newhalem
Ross

Grand Forks
Rossland
Trail
Porthill
Northport
Libby Res.
Troy
Libby
CABINET MTS.

Oroville
Republic
Colville
KALISPEL IND. RES.
Chewelah
Sandpoint
Bonners Ferry

CAPE FLATTERY
MAKAH IND. RES.

OLYMPIC MTS.
OLYMPIC NATIONAL PARK
Mt. Olympus 7954
QUINAULT IND. RES.

Arlington
Mount Vernon
Glacier Peak 10,568

Okanogan
Wells
Chelan
Waterville
Mansfield
GRAND COULEE DAM
CHIEF JOSEPH DAM

Davenport
Spokane
Medical Lake
Cheney
Opportunity
Coeur d'Alene
Kellogg
Wallace
Mullan
Thompson Falls

Everett
Snohomish
Monroe
Kirkland
Bellevue
SEATTLE
Bremerton
Tacoma
Shelton
Puget Sound

WASHINGTON

Cascade Tunnel
Leavenworth
Cashmere
WENATCHEE MTS.
Wenatchee
ROCK ISLAND DAM

Ephrata
Moses Lake
Ritzville
St. Maries
Tekoa
Deer Park
Spirit Lake
Pend Oreille

Auburn
Enumclaw
Puyallup
Carbonado
Cle Elum
Roslyn
Ellensburg

PALOUSE HILLS
Colfax
Palouse
Pullman
Moscow
Elk River
Dworshak Res.

Olympia
Packwood
Centralia
Chehalis
Mt. Rainier 14,410
MOUNT RAINIER NATIONAL PARK
Yakima

Potholes Res.
Crab Cr.
Odessa
Moses
Lower Monumental Res.
Little Goose
Pomeroy
Clearwater

Hoquiam
Aberdeen
Montesano
Cosmopolis
Elma
Raymond
South Bend
Grays Harbor
Willapa Bay

Toppenish
Sunnyside
PRIEST RAPIDS DAM
Priest Rapids Res.

Richland
Pasco
Kennewick
Prosser
Wallula
L. Wallula
ICE HARBOR DAM
Waitsburg
Dayton
Walla Walla
Clarkston
Lewiston
Asotin
Winchester
Nez Perce

Mt. St. Helens
Mt. Adams 12,307
Goldendale
JOHN DAY DAM
McNARY DAM
Milton-Freewater

Castlerock
Longview
Kelso
Rainier
Kalama
Saint Helens

Astoria
Warrenton
Columbia
Seaside

PACIFIC OCEAN

Tillamook Bay
Tillamook
Forest Grove
Hillsboro
Milwaukie
Lake Oswego
Portland
Oregon City
W. Linn
Vancouver
Camas
Washougal
BONNEVILLE DAM
Hood River
The Dalles
THE DALLES DAM
Wasco

Pendleton
UMATILLA IND. RES.
Elgin
La Grande
Union
Wallowa
Enterprise
WALLOWA MTS.
Hells Canyon

McMinnville
Newberg
Sheridan
Dallas
Woodburn
Silverton
Salem
Independence
Albany
Lebanon
Corvallis
Toledo
Newport

WARM SPRINGS IND. RES.
Mt. Jefferson 10,499
Lake Simtustus
Lake Chinook

Condon
Heppner
John Day
BLUE MOUNTAINS
N. Fork
Baker
Oxbow Res.
Brownlee Res.
New Meadows
Cascade Res.

OREGON

Green Peter Res.
Eugene
Springfield
McKenzie R.
Lookout Point Res.
Hills Creek Res.
Cottage Grove
Diamond Peak 8750
Crescent

Prineville
Bend
Crooked
Prineville Res.
Strawberry Mts.
John Day
Burnt
Willow Cr.

Weiser
Payette
Vale
Ontario
Emmett
Caldwell
Boise
Nampa
Arrowrock Res.

SALMON R.
IDAHO

Reedsport
North Bend
Coos Bay
Coquille
Bandon
Myrtle Point
CAPE BLANCO

GREAT SANDY DESERT
HARNEY BASIN
Burns
Harney
Malheur
Warm Sprs. Res.
Malheur
Beulah Res.
Lucky Pk. Res.

Umpqua
Roseburg
CRATER LAKE NATIONAL PARK
Crater Lake
Mt. Scott 8938
Cougar Res.

OWYHEE MTS.
Owyhee
Jordan Cr.
Mountain Home
Glenns Ferry
C.J. Strike Res.

COAST RANGE
KLAMATH MTS.
Grants Pass
Medford
Ashland
OREGON CAVES NAT'L MON.
Mt. McLoughlin 9510
Upper Klamath Lake
Klamath Falls
Lost

Summer
Abert
Lakeview
WARNER RANGE
STEENS MTS.
Donner und Blitzen
Black Rock Desert
FORT McDERMITT IND. RES.
PINE FOREST RA.
SANTA ROSA MTS.
Paradise Valley
Midas
Tuscarora
INDEPENDENCE MTS.

Brookings
Crescent City
CALIFORNIA
CASCADE RANGE
Yreka
Weed
Mt. Shasta 14,162
Dunsmuir
LAVA BEDS NAT'L MON.
Lower Klamath
Clear Lake Res.
Goose Lake
Alturas
Eagle Peak 9934
Lower
SUMMIT LAKE IND. RES.
DUCK VALLEY IND. RES.

Arcata
Fieldbrook
Eureka
Fortuna
Ferndale
CAPE MENDOCINO
Humboldt Bay
Scotia
Weaverville
Redding
Anderson
Clair Engle Lake
Shasta Lake
LASSEN VOLCANIC NAT'L PARK
Lassen Peak (Vol.) 10,457
Eagle
Pit
NEVADA
Winnemucca
Battle Mountain
Palisade
Elko
Humboldt
Rye Patch Res.
SMOKE CREEK DESERT
Mud Lake

A-520597-76
COPYRIGHT B
RAND McNALLY & CO
MADE IN U.S.A.

Continued on pages 118-119
Longitude West of Greenwich

Scale 1: 4,000,000; one inch to 64 miles. Conic Projec
Elevations and depressions are given in feet

Continued on pages 112-113

Continued on pages 118-119

Relief

Meters	Feet
3050	10000
1525	5000
610	2000
305	1000
152.5	500
0	Sea Level	0
1525	500

Cities and Towns

0 to 50,000   500,000 to 1,000,000

50,000 to 500,000   1,000,000 and over

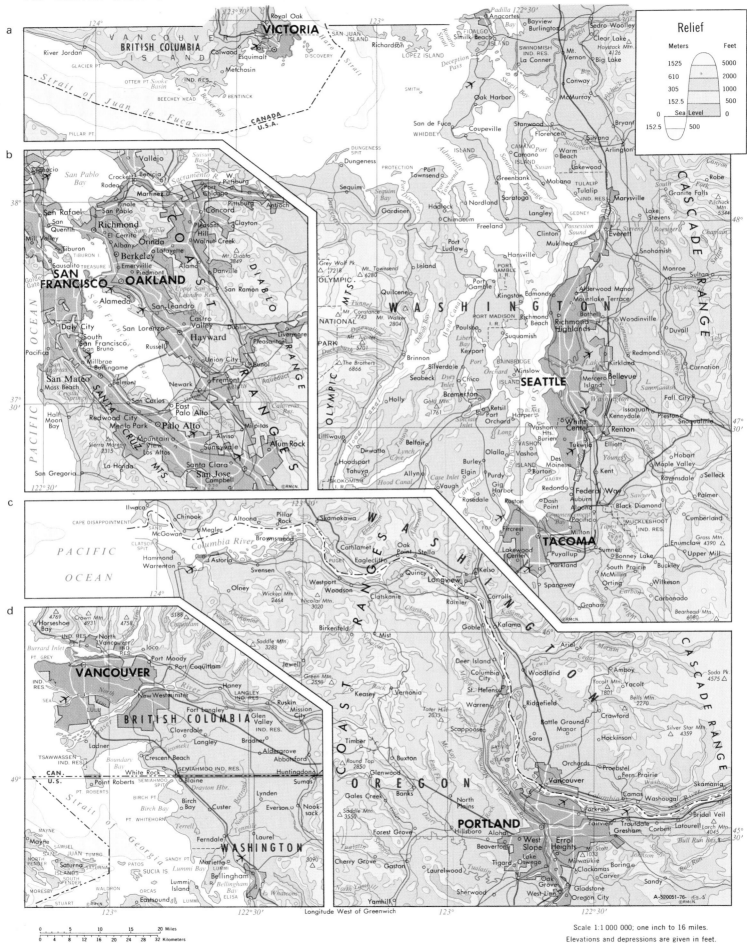

Relief

Meters		Feet
1525		5000
610		2000
305		1000
152.5		500
0	Sea Level	0
152.5		500

Scale 1:1 000 000; one inch to 16 miles.
Elevations and depressions are given in feet.

Longitude West of Greenwich

0   5   10   15   20 Miles
0 4 8 12 16 20 24 28 32 Kilometers

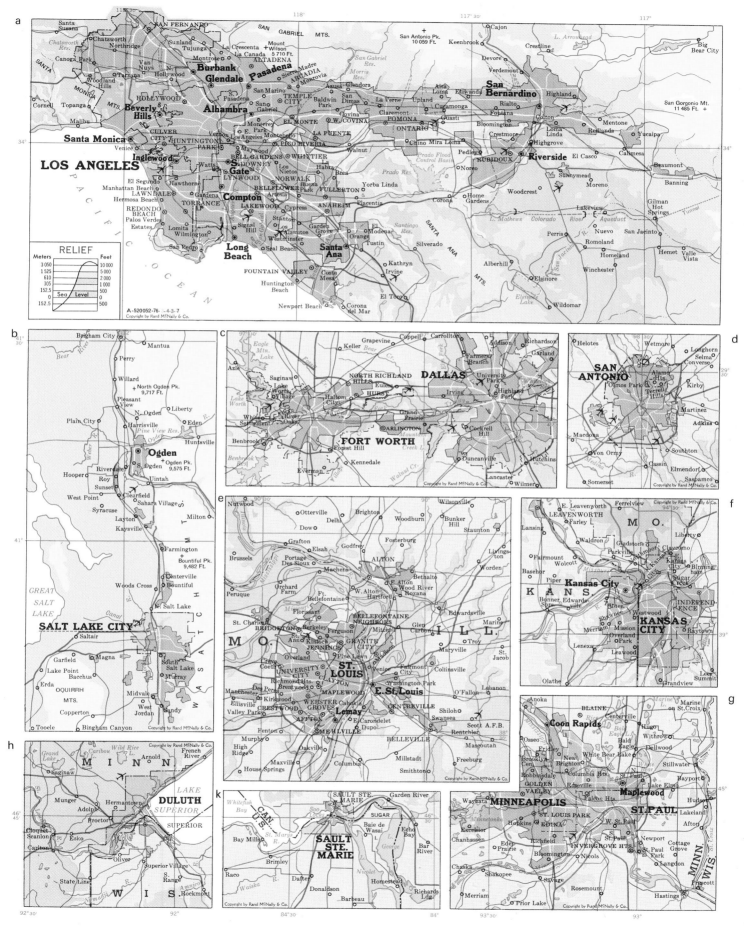

a

Santa Susana · Santa Susana
Chatsworth Northridge
Chatsworth Res. SAN FERNANDO
Canoga Park Sunland Tujunga
Woodland Hills Van Nuys Hollywood
Topanga Tarzana La Crescenta La Canada Mount + Wilson 5 710 Ft.
SANTA Cornell MONICA MTS. **Burbank**
Malibu **Glendale** **Pasadena**
Beverly Hills HOLLYWOOD Sierra Madre Monrovia
Alhambra Pasadena San Marino ARCADIA Azusa Glendora
34° **Santa Monica** TEMPLE CITY Baldwin San Dimas La Verne Upland
CULVER CITY San Gabriel E. Park El Monte Covina W. COVINA Claremont Pomona
Venice HUNTINGTON PARK Monterey Park ONTARIO
Inglewood Vernon Montebello Pico Rivera
LOS ANGELES Maywood WHITTIER Walnut
El Segundo Watts Bell Gardens DOWNEY La Habra Brea
Manhattan Beach Hawthorne Gardena S. Gate LYNWOOD NORWALK Buena Park FULLERTON
LAWNDALE Artesia
Hermosa Beach **Compton** BELLFLOWER LAKEWOOD Cypress ANAHEIM Placentia
REDONDO BEACH TORRANCE Stanton Garden Grove
Palos Verdes Estates Lomita Wilmington Los Alamitos Westminster Orange Tustin
San Pedro **Long Beach** Signal Hill Seal Beach **Santa Ana**
FOUNTAIN VALLEY Costa Mesa
Huntington Beach Irvine
PACIFIC OCEAN Newport Beach Corona del Mar El Toro

San Antonio Pk. 10 059 Ft. Cajon
Keenbrook Crestline L. Arrowhead
Devore Verdemont Big Bear City
San Gabriel Res. Morris Res. **San Bernardino** San Gorgonio Mt. 11 485 Ft. +
Alta Loma Etiwanda Highland
Cucamonga Rialto Fontana Mentone
Guasti Colton Loma Linda Redlands Yucaipa
Chino Mira Loma Bloomington Crestmore Highgrove
RUBIDOUX **Riverside** El Casco Calimesa
Prado Flood Control Basin Pedley Noreo Beaumont
Prado Res. Home Gardens Sunnymead Moreno Banning
Corona Woodcrest Gilman Hot Springs
Santiago Res. Lakeview Tunnel
Silverado L. Mathews Colorado River Aqueduct
SANTA Perris Romoland San Jacinto Hemet Valle Vista Winchester
Kathryn ANA Nuevo Homeland
Alberhill MTS. Elsinore Elsinore Lake Wildomar

RELIEF
Meters / Feet
3 050 / 10 000
1 525 / 5 000
610 / 2 000
305 / 1 000
152.5 / 500
Sea Level / 0
152.5 / 500
A-520052-76- -4-3-7 Copyright by Rand McNally & Co.

b
41° 30′
Brigham City Mantua
Bear River Perry
Willard North Ogden Pk. 9,717 Ft.
Plain City Pleasant View N. Ogden Liberty
Harrisville Eden
Pine View Res. Huntsville
Ogden + Ogden Pk. 9,575 Ft.
Hooper Riverdale Roy Ogden Uintah
Sunset
West Point Clearfield Sahara Village
Syracuse Layton
41° Kaysville
Milton
Farmington + Bountiful Pk. 9,482 Ft.
GREAT SALT LAKE Centerville Bountiful
Woods Cross
N. Salt Lake
SALT LAKE CITY
Saltair
Garfield Magna South Salt Lake Murray
Lake Point Bacchus
Erda OQUIRRH Midvale
Copperton MTS. West Jordan Sandy
Tooele Bingham Canyon
Copyright by Rand McNally & Co.

c
97° 30′
Eagle Mtn. Lake Grapevine Coppell Carrollton Addison Richardson
Keller Bear Farmers Branch Garland
Azle Saginaw NORTH RICHLAND HILLS University Park
Lake Worth Village Haltom City HURST **DALLAS** Highland Park
Euless Irving
White Settlement Oaks **FORT WORTH** Grand Prairie Cockrell Hill
Benbrook ARLINGTON Mountain Creek L.
Forest Hill
Kennedale Duncanville
Everman Lancaster Wilmer
Copyright by Rand McNally & Co.

d
98° 30′
Helotes Wetmore Longhorn
29° 30′ Selma Converse
SAN ANTONIO Alamo Hts. Kirby
Olmos Park Terrell Hills Martinez
Macdona Adkins
Von Ormy Southton
Cassin Elmendorf
Somerset Saspamco
Copyright by Rand McNally & Co.

e
90° 30′
Nutwood Otterville Brighton Wilsonville
Delhi Woodburn
Grafton Elsah Dow Bunker Hill
Brussels Godfrey Fosterburg Staunton
Portage Des Sioux Machens Living-
Peruque Orchard Farm E. Alton ston
Ft. Bellefontaine W. Alton Bethalto
Worden
St. Charles Florissant Wood River Roxana
Hartford Edwardsville
BRIDGETON Berkeley ILL.
M O. Ferguson Mitchell Marine
Anna Kinlock JENNINGS GRANITE CITY Glen Carbon
Overland Pine Lawn Maryville
Creve Coeur UNIVERSITY CITY Venice Fairmont City Troy
Richmond Hts. Clayton **ST. LOUIS** St. Jacob
Des Peres Brentwood Collinsville
Manchester MAPLEWOOD E. ST. Louis Washington Park Lebanon
Ellisville WEBSTER GROVES Cahokia O'Fallon
Valley Park CRESTWOOD **Lemay** CENTREVILLE Shiloh
AFFTON Swansea
Fenton E. Carondelet Scott A.F.B.
Murphy MEHLVILLE Dupo Rentchler
High Ridge Oakville BELLEVILLE
Maxville Millstadt Mascoutah
House Springs Columbia Freeburg
Smithton
Copyright by Rand McNally & Co.

f
94° 30′
E. Leavenworth Ferrelview
LEAVENWORTH Farley **M O.**
Lansing Gladstone Liberty
Fairmount Wolcott Parkville Claycomo
Basehor Piper **Kansas City** Sugar Creek Birming-ham
Bonner Springs Edwards-ville Westwood KANS. INDEPENDENCE
Shawnee Merriam Mission **KANSAS CITY** Raytown
Lenexa Overland Park Leawood
39° Olathe Grandview Lee's Summit
Copyright by Rand McNally & Co.

g
93° 30′
Marine on St. Croix
Anoka BLAINE Centerville Marine
Coon Rapids Hugo Withrow Dellwood
Osseo Fridley Bald Eagle L.
Brooklyn Cen. New Brighton White Bear Lake Stillwater
Robbinsdale Columbia Hts. Bayport
Wayzata GOLDEN VALLEY Roseville **MAPLEWOOD** Lake Elmo
ST. LOUIS PARK St. Paul 45°
Excelsior **MINNEAPOLIS** Falcon Hts. Afton
Hopkins EDINA Hudson
Chanhassen St. Paul Newport Lakeland
Eden Prairie Richfield INVER GROVE HTS. W. St. Paul Cottage Grove
Chaska Bloomington Nicols St. Paul Park Langdon
Shakopee Savage MINN. WIS.
Prior Lake Rosemount Prescott
Merriam Hastings

h
92° 30′
Grand Lake Caribou Wild Rice L.
Saginaw Arnold French River
M I N N.
Munger Hermantown DULUTH
Adolph Proctor LAKE SUPERIOR
Cloquet SUPERIOR
Scanlon Esko
Carlton Oliver 46° 45′
Superior Village
State Line
Range Rockmont
W I S.

k
84° 30′
SAULT STE. MARIE Garden River
Whitefish Bay CAN. U.S. Soo Locks
St. Marys R. 46° SUGAR
Bay Mills Baie de Wasai Echo Bay
SAULT STE. MARIE Bar River
L. George
Raco Dafter
Brimley Nicolet
Waiska Donaldson Homestead Richards Ldg.
Barbeau
Copyright by Rand McNally & Co.

0 2 4 6 8 10 12 14 16 18 20 22 24 Miles
0 4 8 12 16 20 24 28 32 36 40 Kilometers

Scale 1:1 000 000; One inch to 16 miles.
Elevations and depressions are given in feet.

For larger scale coverage of Los Angeles see page 59.

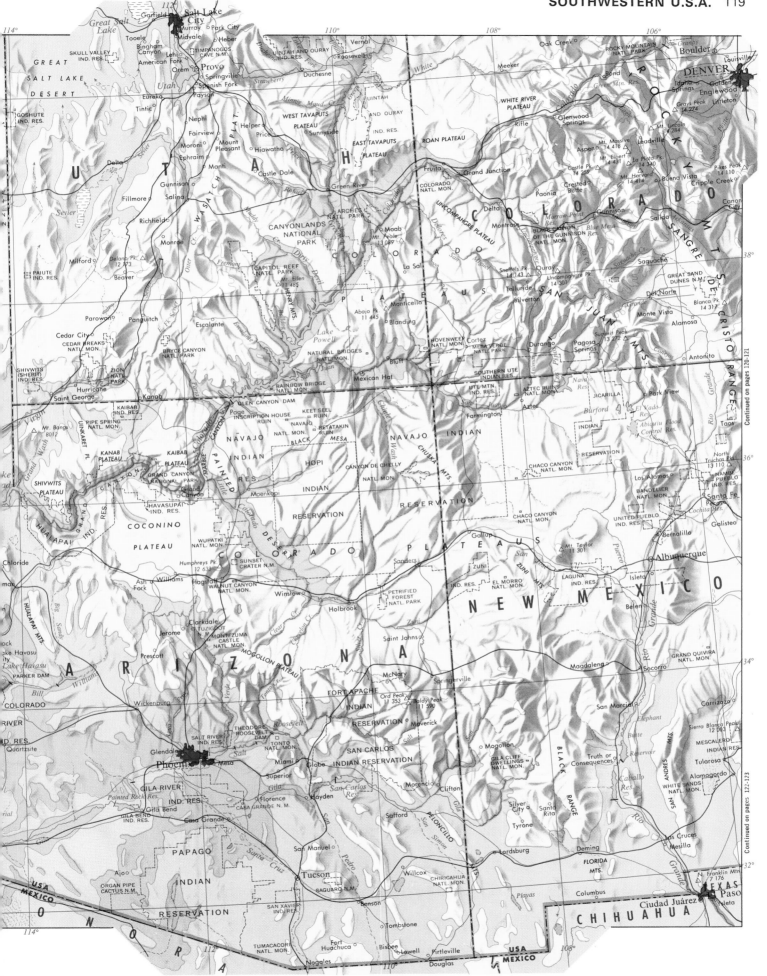

Continued on pages 120-121
Continued on pages 122-173

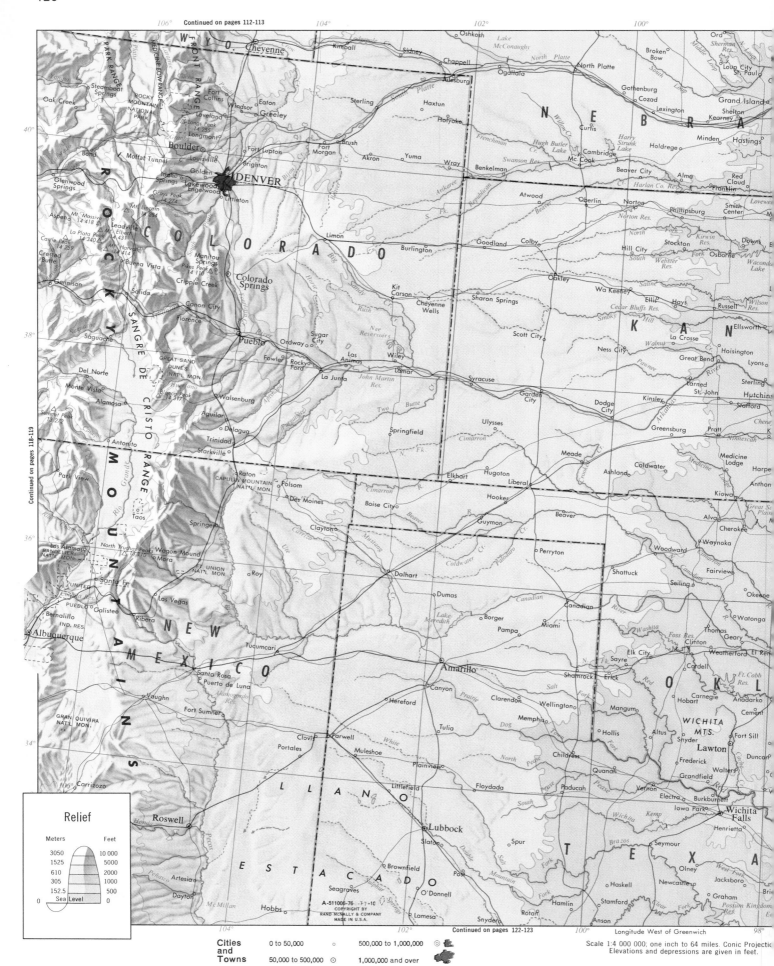

120

Continued on pages 112-113

Continued on pages 118-119

W Y O.

Cheyenne

Kimball

Sidney

Oshkosh

Lake McConaughy

Ord

Sherman Res.

Middle Loop

Chappell

North Platte

North Platte

Broken Bow

Loup City

St. Paul

Julesburg

Ogallala

Gothenburg

Grand Island

N E B R A

Sterling

Haxtun

Cozad

Lexington

Shelton

Kearney

Minden

Hastings

Holyoke

Curtis

Harry Strunk Lake

Holdrege

Brush

Akron

Yuma

Wray

Frenchman

Hugh Butler Lake

Swanson Res.

Cambridge

Mc Cook

Beaver City

Alma

Red Cloud

Franklin

Fort Collins

Windsor

Eaton

Greeley

Steamboat Springs

Oak Creek

P A R K R A N G E

M E D I C I N E B O W R A N G E

F R O N T R A N G E

Fort Lupton

Fort Morgan

Benkelman

Harlan Co. Res.

Lovewer

Bond

R O C K Y M O U N T A I N N A T I O N A L P A R K

Longs Peak 14,255

Longmont

Boulder

Louisville

Brighton

Moffat Tunnel

Golden

Idaho Springs

DENVER

Lakewood

Englewood

Littleton

Limon

Burlington

Goodland

Colby

Atwood

Oberlin

Norton

Phillipsburg

Smith Center

Loveland

Grays Peak 14,274

Glenwood Springs

Aspen

Mt. Massive 14,418

Mt. Lincoln 14,284

La Plata Peak 14,340

Mt. Elbert 14,431

Mt. Harvard 14,414

Leadville

Pikes Peak 14,110

Manitou Springs

Buena Vista

Norton Res.

North Fork

Hill City

Stockton

Kirwin Res.

Osborne

Downs

Castle Peak 14,259

Crested Butte

Cripple Creek

Colorado Springs

C O L O R A D O

Kit Carson

Cheyenne Wells

Sharon Springs

Scott City

Oakley

Wa Keeney

Saline

Ellis

Hays

Russell

Cedar Bluffs Res.

Smoky

Hill

Wilson Res.

Ellsworth

Gunnison

Salida

Canon City

Florence

Pueblo

Ordway

Sugar City

Nee Reservoirs

Rush

Ness City

La Crosse

Great Bend

Hoisington

Lyons

Saguache

Del Norte

Monte Vista

Alamosa

G R E A T S A N D D U N E S N A T L M O N.

Blanca Peak 14,317

Fowler

Rocky Ford

Las Animas

Wiley

Lamar

Syracuse

Garden City

Dodge City

Kinsley

Walnut

Larned

St. John

Pawnee

Stafford

Sterling

Hutchins

Summit Peak 13,272

S A N G R E D E C R I S T O R A N G E

La Junta

John Martin Res.

Butte

Two

Arkansas

Greensburg

Pratt

Medicine

Ninnescah

Chene

Walsenburg

Aguilar

Delagua

Trinidad

Starkville

Springfield

Cimarron

N. Fk.

Ulysses

Meade

Coldwater

Ashland

Medicine Lodge

Harpe

R O C K Y

Park View

Antonito

C A P U L I N M O U N T A I N N A T L M O N.

Raton

Folsom

Des Moines

Elkhart

Hugoton

Liberal

Kiowa

Anthon

M O U N T A I N S

Taos

Springer

Clayton

Boise City

Hooker

Guymon

Beaver

Alva

Cherokee

Waynoka

North Truchas Peaks 13,110

Wagon Mound

Mora

U N I O N N A T L M O N.

Roy

Carrizo

Ute

Perryton

Woodward

Fairview

Los Alamos

B A N D E L I E R N A T L M O N.

Santa Fe

Las Vegas

Dalhart

Coldwater

Paloduro

Shattuck

Seiling

Okeene

P U E B L O I N D. R E S.

Galisteo

Ribera

Dumas

Canadian

Canadian

River

Washita

Thomas

Geary

Watonga

Bernalillo

Albuquerque

Tucumcari

Lake Meredith

Borger

Pampa

Miami

Foss Res.

Clinton

Weatherford

El Ren

N E W

Santa Rosa

Puerto de Luna

Amarillo

N. Fk.

Elk City

Sayre

Erick

Cardell

Ft. Cobb Res.

O K L A

Vaughn

Canyon

Hereford

Prairie

Clarendon

Wellington

Salt

Fork

Shamrock

Memphis

Mangum

Hobart

Carnegie

Anadarko

Cement

M E X I C O

Fort Sumner

Hollis

Altus

Snyder

Fort Sill

W I C H I T A M T S.

Lawton

G R A N Q U I V I R A N A T L M O N.

Clovis

Farwell

Tulia

Dog

Childress

Quanah

Frederick

Walters

Duncar

Carrizozo

Portales

Muleshoe

White

Plainview

Red

Grandfield

M O U N T A I N S

Roswell

L L A N O

Littlefield

Floydada

Paducah

Pease

Vernon

Electra

Iowa Park

Burkburnett

Wichita Falls

Lubbock

Spur

Brazos

Seymour

Henrietta

Olney

Jacksboro

E S T A C A D O

Slaton

Salt

Fork

Double

Kemp

T E X A

Brownfield

Post

McMillan

Penasco

Artesia

Dayton

Seagraves

O'Donnell

Hamlin

Stamford

Newcastle

Graham

Possum Kingdom Res.

Hobbs

P. Lamesa

Rotan

Snyder

Anson

Haskell

Clear

Fork

Sulphur

A-511006-76—7-7-10

COPYRIGHT BY

RAND McNALLY & COMPANY

MADE IN U.S.A.

Continued on pages 122-123

Longitude West of Greenwich

Relief

Meters		Feet
3050		10 000
1525		5000
610		2000
305		1000
152.5		500
0	Sea Level	0

Cities and Towns

0 to 50,000 ○

50,000 to 500,000 ⊙

500,000 to 1,000,000 ◎

1,000,000 and over

Scale 1:4 000 000; one inch to 64 miles. Conic Projection

Elevations and depressions are given in feet.

Continued on pages 112-113 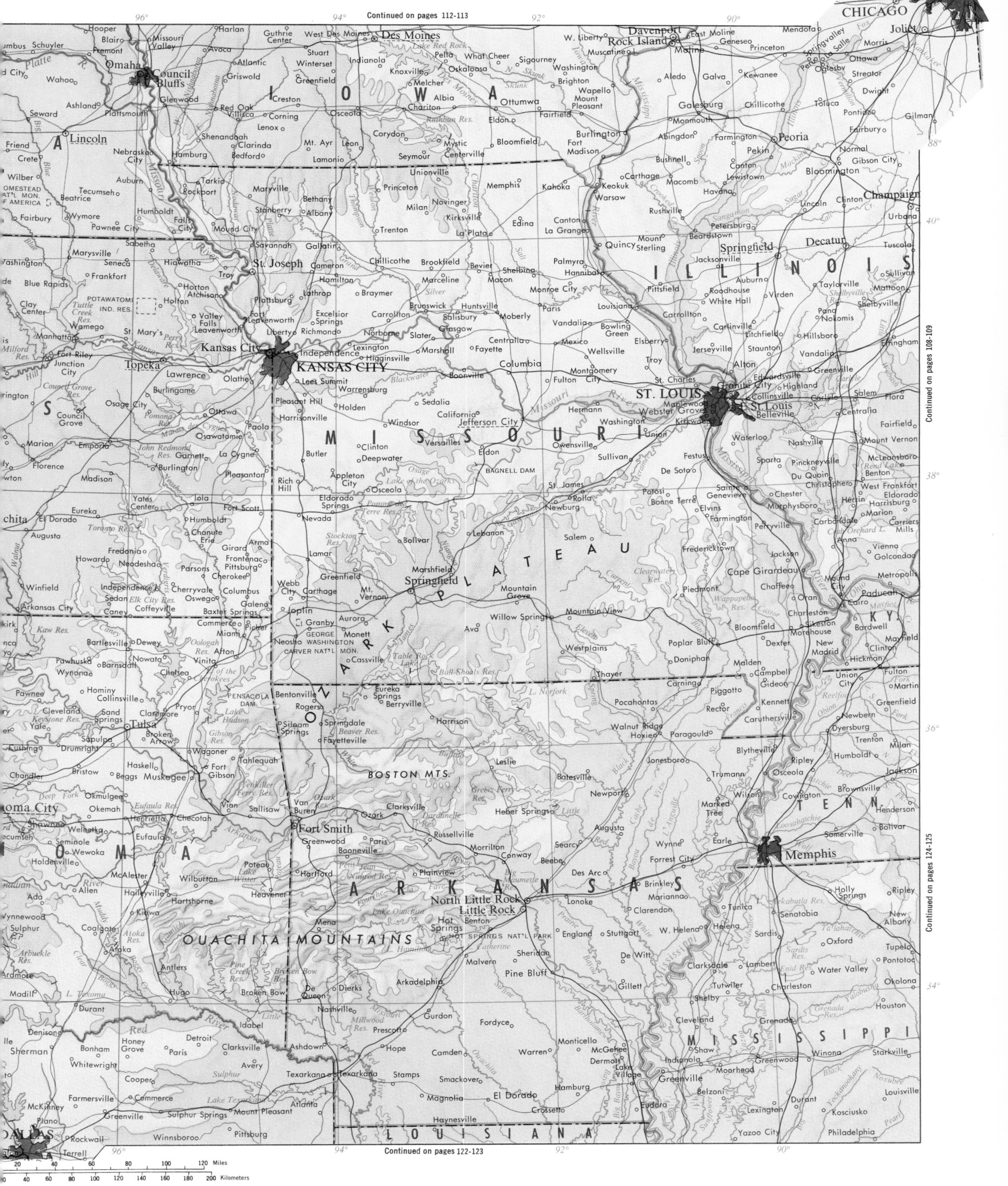
Continued on pages 108-109
Continued on pages 124-125
Continued on pages 122-123

Aurora
CHICAGO
Joliet

IOWA

ILLINOIS

MISSOURI

INDIANA (KY.)

TENN.

ARKANSAS

OKLAHOMA

MISSISSIPPI

LOUISIANA

OZARK PLATEAU

BOSTON MTS.

OUACHITA MOUNTAINS

Omaha
Council Bluffs
Lincoln
Des Moines
West Des Moines
Davenport
Rock Island
East Moline
Moline

St. Joseph
Kansas City
KANSAS CITY
Topeka
Lawrence
Tulsa
Fort Smith
Little Rock
North Little Rock
Hot Springs
HOT SPRINGS NAT'L PARK
Springfield
ST. LOUIS
E. ST. LOUIS
Memphis
Peoria
Springfield
Decatur
Champaign

Red River

Missouri River

Mississippi

Arkansas River

20 40 60 80 100 120 Miles
40 80 120 160 200 Kilometers

96°   94°   92°   90°   88°
40°   38°   36°   34°

NEW MEXICO

Alamogordo
Alamo Pk.
7820
WHITE SANDS
NAT'L MON.
Penasco
Artesia
Dayton
McMillan
O'Donnell
Seagraves
Newcastle
Haskell
Graham
Carlsbad
Hobbs
Seminole
Lamesa
Rotan
Hamlin
Stamford
Mineral W
CARLSBAD
CAVERNS
NAT'L PARK
Wind Mtn.
7278
32°
N. Franklin Mtn.
7176
Red Bluff Res.
Big Spring
Snyder
Roscoe
Sweetwater
Merkel
Abilene
Ranger
Thur
Eastland
Cisco
Desdem
GUADALUPE MTS.
Guadalupe
8751
Midland
Stanton
Colorado
City
Baird
Gorman
Dublin
El Paso
Ysleta
Wink
Odessa
Winters
Ballinger
De Leon
Ciudad Juárez
Pecos
Sterling City
Coleman
Fabens
Toyah
North
Colorado
Santa Anna
Brownwood
Ham
Guadalupe
Sierra Blanca
Pecos
Concho
Middle
Concho
San Angelo
Brownwood
Procter Res. Leon
Comanche
Van Horn
Nasworthy
Goldthw
Villa
Ahumada
Eagle Pk.
7496
DAVIS MTS.
McCamey
Concho
Eden
Brady
San Saba
Buchanan
Baldy Peak
8382
Fort Stockton
EDWARDS
Menard
Mason
Llano
Llano
Lom
Marfa
Alpine
STOCKTON
Big
Canyon
Sonora
Junction
San Saba
Coyame
Cathedral Mt
6860
SANTIAGO MTS.
PLATEAU
Sanderson
PLATEAU
Rocksprings
Fredericksburg
Chinati Pk.
7730
Ojinaga
Presidio
Pecos
U.S.A.
MEXICO
SERRANÍAS
Kerrville
San
Cuchillo Parado
BIG BEND
NAT'L PARK
Emory Pk.
7835
DEL BURRO
Amistad
Res.
Camp Wood
Boerne
New Braunfels
Medina
Chihuahua
Aldama
Del Rio
Villa Acuña
Brackettville
Honda
Sabinal
San Antonio
Uvalde
Floresville
CHIHUAHUA
Meoqui
Jiménez
Piedras Negras
Fuente
Eagle Pass
Crystal City
Poteet
Pearsall
Pleasanton
Naica
SIERRA
Zaragoza
Morelos
Nava
Carrizo Springs
Asherton
28°
Gigantes
Jaco
Allende
Guerrero
Cotulla
Fowlerton
George
West
San Pedro
Toronto
COAHUILA
Rosales
Encinal
Corpus C
Ciudad Camargo
(Santa Rosalia)
MADRE
Muzquiz
San Juan de Sabinas
Hidalgo
Dolores
San Diego
Sierra Mojada
BOLSÓN
Laguna de
la Leche
Progreso
Presa de
D. Martin
Laredo
Nuevo Laredo
Mirando City
Premont
Hidalgo
del Parral
Jimenez
DE
Sacramento
San Buenaventura
Nadadores
Abasolo
Lampazos
Hebbronville
Falfurrias
Valle de Allende
Villa Lopez
Rey
MAPIMI
Cuatro Ciénegas
Nadadores
Zapata
Guerrero
Santa Barbara
Escalon
ORIENTAL
Monclova
Bustamante
Villaldama
Sabinas Hidalgo
Mier
Riogrande
Rosario
Villa Coronado
Villa
Ocampo
MEXICO
Aguaguas
Camargo
26°
Indé
Mapimí
Paredon
Garcia
Cerralvo
General Zuazua
Los Herreras
Reynosa
Santa Cruz
Sacramento
San Pedro de
las Colonias
Laguna de
Mayran
Salinas Victoria
NUEVO
Presa de
Azucar
Rodeo
Gómez Palacio
Lerdo
Torreón
Matamoros
Laguna de
Viesca
Ramos Arizpe
Monterrey
Santa Catarina
Cadereyta Jiménez
China
Nazas
Viesca
Parras
General Cepeda
Saltillo
Arteaga
Villa de Aldende
Montemorelos
San Luis del
Cordero
DURANGO
Cuencame
LEON
Galeana
San Juan del Río
Gomez Farias
Linares
Burgos
San
Fernando
Laguna de
Santiaguillo
San Juan de
Guadalupe
Mazapil
Concepción
del Oro
Santa Clara
ZACATECAS
Villagrán
San Carlos
Cruillas
TAMAULI
Durango
Juan Aldama

Continued on pages 120-121
Continued on pages 128-129

Relief

Meters		Feet
1525		5000
610		2000
305		1000
152.5		500
0	Sea Level	0
152.5		500
1525		5000
3050		10 000

Longitude West of Greenwich

Scale 1:4 000 000; one inch to 64 miles. Conic Projecti
Elevations and depressions are given in feet

Continued on pages 120-121

Continued on pages 124-125

ARK.

MISSISSIPPI

LOUISIANA

GULF OF MEXICO

DALLAS

Fort Worth

HOUSTON

Galveston

Shreveport

Baton Rouge

New Orleans

Jackson

Vicksburg

Waco

Corpus Christi

Brownsville
Matamoros

a

HOUSTON

West University Place
Bellaire
Pasadena
Jacinto City
Galena Pk.
Baytown
La Porte
South Houston
Genoa
Missouri City
Pearland
Arcola
Friendswood
Manvel
League City
Dickinson
Alvin
Algoa
Alta Loma
Sandy Point
Hitchcock
Liverpool
Danbury
Angleton
Bastrop

Texas City
La Marque
Port Bolivar
Galveston

GALVESTON BAY
EAST BAY
BOLIVAR PENINSULA
WEST BAY
GALVESTON ISLAND
GULF OF MEXICO

Crosby
Sheldon
Highlands
Mont Belvieu
Wallisville
Hankamer
Anahuac
Turtle Bay
Channelview
Smith Point
High Island

Scale 1:1 000 000

A-511007-76-

COPYRIGHT BY
RAND McNALLY & COMPANY
MADE IN U.S.A.

©RMcN

Cities and Towns	0 to 50,000	500,000 to 1,000,000
	50,000 to 500,000	1,000,000 and over

Continued on pages 108-109

Continued on pages 120-121

Continued on pages 122-123

ILL.

MISSOURI

KENTUCKAY

TENNESSEE

ARKANSAS

Memphis

Nashville

Knoxville

Chattanooga

MISSISSIPPI

ALABAMA

GEOR

Birmingham

ATLANTA

Atlanta

Tuscaloosa

Montgomery

Columbus

Jackson

LOUISIANA

Macon

Baton Rouge

New Orleans

Mobile

Pensacola

F L O R I

GULF OF MEXICO

CHANDELEUR
ISLANDS

A-520598-76-
COPYRIGHT BY
RAND McNALLY & COMPANY
MADE IN U.S.A.

Longitude West of Greenwich

Scale 1:4 000 000; one inch to 64 miles. Conic Projection
Elevations and depressions are given in feet

Relief

Meters		Feet
1525		5000
610		2000
305		1000
152.5		500
0	Sea Level	0
152.5		500
1525		5000

Same scale as main map

a

Cities
and
Towns

0 to 50,000	○	500,000 to 1,000,000	◎
50,000 to 500,000	⊙	1,000,000 and over	

20 30 40 50 60 70 80 90 100 110 120 Miles
20 40 60 80 100 120 140 160 180 200 Kilometers

©RMcN.

126

Scale 1:16 000 000; one inch to 250 miles. Polyconic Projec

Elevations and depressions are given in feet

b

PUERTO RICO

ATLANTIC OCEAN

Aguadilla · Arecibo · San Juan · Bayamón
PTA. HIGUERO · Utuado · Caguas · Fajardo · CEBEZAS DE SAN JUAN · St. Thomas · TORTOLA (Br. h.)
Mayagüez · Coamo · Coyey · Humacao · CULEBRA · Charlotte Amalie · ST. JOHN (U.S.A.)
CABO ROJO · Ponce · Salinas · Guayama · Vieques · VIEQUES · ST. CROIX

CARIBBEAN SEA · Christiansted SAINT CROIX (U.S.A.)

Scale 1:4 000 000

0 10 20 30   40 Miles
0 10 20 30 40 50 60 Kilometers

©RMCN

c

ST. THOMAS

LITTLE HANS LOLLICK
INNER BRASS · OUTER BRASS · HANS LOLLICK
STORMY PT. · PICARA PT. · GRASS CAY
ST. THOMAS (U.S.A.) · THATCH CAY
Crown Mt. 1558 · Charlotte Amalie (St. Thomas) · Nadir
WATER · FLAMINGO PT. · St. Thomas Harbor

©RMCN   Scale 1:500 000

Relief

Meters		Feet
3050		10 000
1525		5000
610		2000
305		1000
152.5		500
0	Sea Level	0
152.5		500
1525		5000
3050		10 000
6100		20 000

Longitude West of Greenwich

50	100	200	300	400	500 Miles
100	200	400	600		800 Kilometers

Cities and Towns

0 to 50,000 ∘   500,000 to 1,000,000 ⊚

50,000 to 500,000 ⊙   1,000,000 and over

Continued on pages 122-123

Longitude West of Greenwich

Scale 1:4 000 000; one inch to 64 miles. Conic Projection
Elevations and depressions are given in feet

Relief

Meters		Feet
3050		10 000
1525		5000
610		2000
305		1000
152.5		500
0	Sea Level	0
152.5		500
1525		5000
3050		10 000

A-531695-76- 6-5-12
COPYRIGHT BY
RAND McNALLY & COMPANY
MADE IN U.S.A.

Cities and Towns

0 to 50,000   o
50,000 to 500,000   ⊙
500,000 to 1,000,000   ◎
1,000,000 and over

For larger scale coverage
of Mexico City see page 60.

Continued on pages 130-131

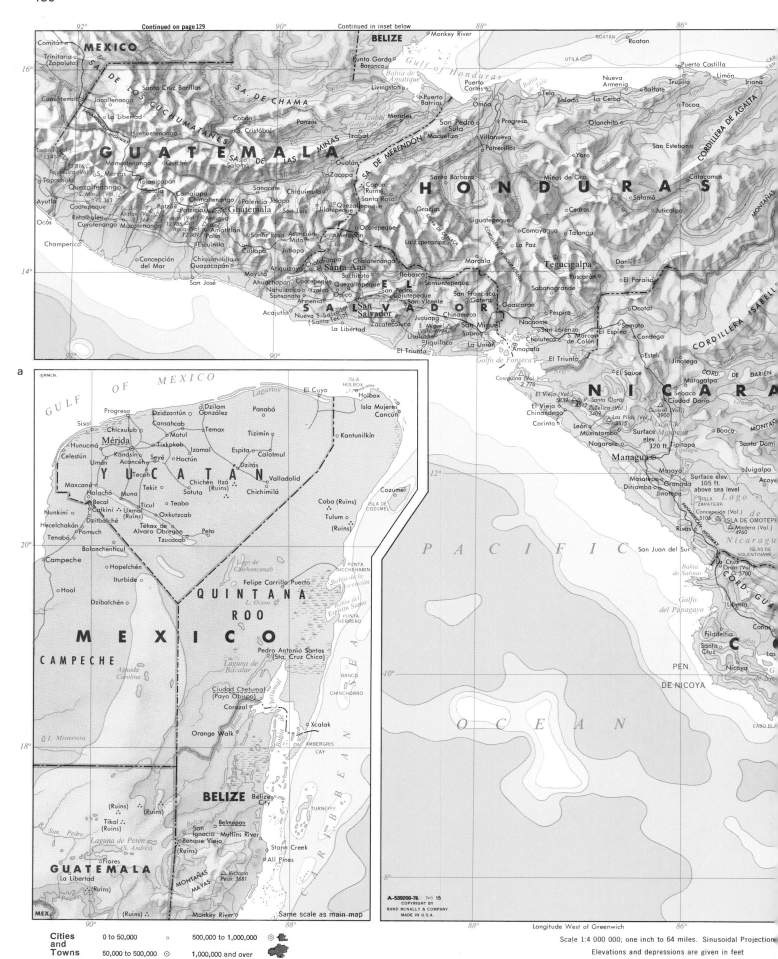

Continued on page 129 Continued in inset below

MEXICO

BELIZE

GUATEMALA

HONDURAS

EL SALVADOR

NICARA

a ®RMcN.

GULF OF MEXICO

YUCATAN

QUINTANA ROO

MEXICO

CAMPECHE

BELIZE

GUATEMALA

PACIFIC OCEAN

CARIBBEAN

MEX.

Same scale as main map

A-539200-76 7•5 15
COPYRIGHT BY
RAND McNALLY & COMPANY
MADE IN U.S.A.

Longitude West of Greenwich

Scale 1:4 000 000; one inch to 64 miles. Sinusoidal Projection

Elevations and depressions are given in feet

Cities and Towns

| 0 to 50,000 | o | 500,000 to 1,000,000 | ◎ |
| 50,000 to 500,000 | ⊙ | 1,000,000 and over | |

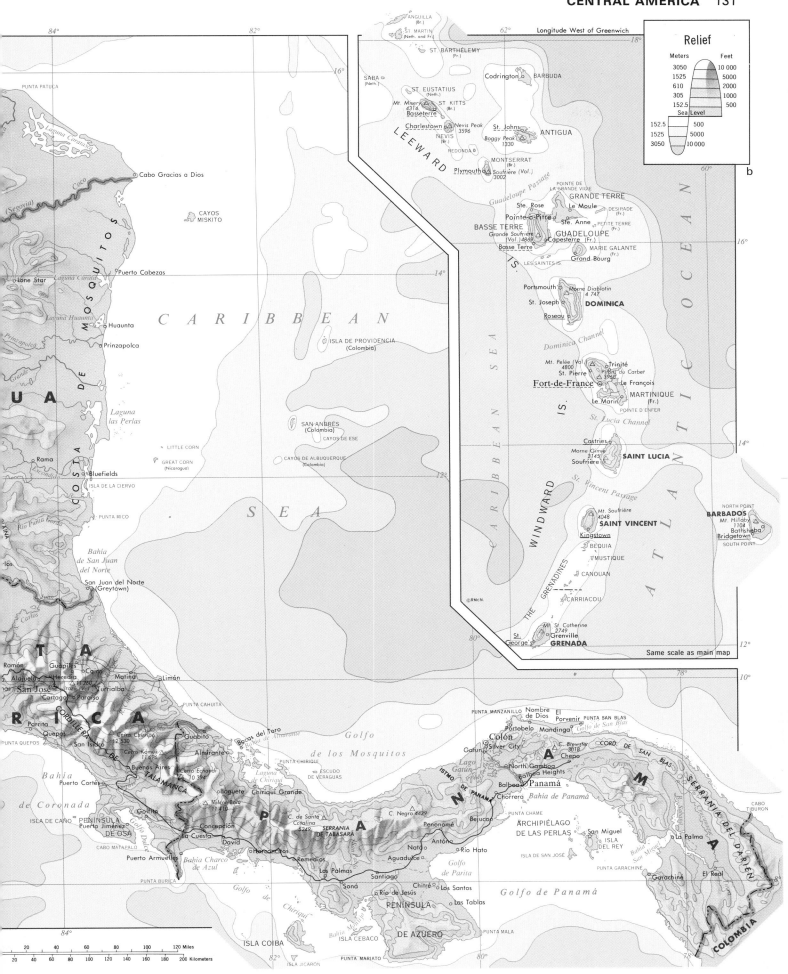

PUNTA PATUCA

Cabo Gracias a Dios

Coco
(Segovia)

CAYOS
MISKITO

Puerto Cabezas

Lone Star
Huaunta

Laguna Caratasca

Laguna Huaunta

Prinzapolca

Prinzapolca

U A

M O S Q U I T O S

C O S T A   D E

C A R I B B E A N

ISLA DE PROVIDENCIA
(Colombia)

Laguna
las Perlas

Rama

Bluefields

ISLA DE LA CIERVO

Escondida

Río Punta Gorda

PUNTA MICO

LITTLE CORN

GREAT CORN
(Nicaragua)

SAN-ANDRÉS
(Colombia)
CAYOS DE ESE

CAYOS DE ALBUQUERQUE
(Colombia)

S E A

Bahía
de San Juan
del Norte

San Juan del Norte
(Greytown)

Carlos

Juan

Ios

Longitude West of Greenwich

ANGUILLA
ST. MARTIN
(Neth. and Fr.)

ST. BARTHÉLEMY
(Fr.)

SABA
(Neth.)

Codrington   BARBUDA

ST. EUSTATIUS
(Neth.)

Mt. Misery   ST. KITTS
4314   (Br.)
Basseterre

Charlestown   Nevis Peak   St. Johns
NEVIS   3596   ANTIGUA
(Br.)
Boggy Peak
1330   REDONDA

L E E W A R D

MONTSERRAT
(Br.)

Plymouth   Soufrière (Vol.)
3002

POINTE DE
LA GRANDE VIGIE

Guadeloupe Passage

GRANDE TERRE

Ste. Rose   Le Moule   DÉSIRADE
(Fr.)

Pointe-à-Pitre   Ste. Anne   PETITE TERRE
(Fr.)

BASSE TERRE

Grande Soufrière   Capesterre (Fr.)
(Vol.)4869   GUADELOUPE
Basse Terre   MARIE GALANTE
(Fr.)
LES SAINTES IS.   Grand Bourg

Portsmouth   Morne Diablotin
4 747
St. Joseph   DOMINICA

Roseau

Dominica Channel

Mt. Pelée (Vol.)
4800   Trinité
St. Pierre   Piton du Carbet
3960
Fort-de-France   Le François
MARTINIQUE
(Fr.)
Le Marin
POINTE D'ENFER

St. Lucia Channel

Castries

Morne Gimie   SAINT LUCIA
3145
Soufrière

St. Vincent Passage

Mt. Soufrière
4048
SAINT VINCENT

Kingstown

BEQUIA

MUSTIQUE

CANOUAN

CARRIACOU

Mt. St. Catherine
2749
Grenville
St. George's   GRENADA

C A R I B B E A N   S E A

W I N D W A R D   I S.

T H E   G R E N A D I N E S

A T L A N T I C   O C E A N

NORTH POINT
BARBADOS
Mt. Hillaby
1104   Bathsheba
Bridgetown
SOUTH POINT

©RMcN.

Same scale as main map

Ramón   Guápiles   Cairo

Alajuela   Heredia

San José   Irazú Vol.   Turrialba
11 260
Cartago   Paraíso

Parrita

Quepos

PUNTA QUEPOS

San Isidro

Matina   Limón

PUNTA CAHUITA

T A

R I C A

C A

Cerro Chirripó
12 530
Cerro Kómuk
11 696

Buenos Aires   Cerro Echandi
10 354

Bahía
de   Puerto Cortés
Coronada

ISLA DE CAÑO

PENÍNSULA
Puerto Jiménez
DE OSA

CABO MATAPALO

Puerto Armuelles

PUNTA BURICA

C O R D I L L E R A   D E   T A L A M A N C A

Guábito

Bocas del Toro
Bahía de Almirante

Almirante

PUNTA CHIRIQUÍ

Chiriquí Grande

Báguete

Bagueté

Volcán Barú
11 410

Golfito

Concepción

La Cuesta   David

Horconcitos

Remedios

Las Palmas

Golfo   de

Chiriquí

Laguna
de Chiriquí

ESCUDO
DE VERAGUAS

Golfo

de los Mosquitos

C. de Santa
Catalina
5249   C. Negro 4429

SERRANÍA
DE TABASARÁ

P A N

Santiago

Soná

Río de Jesús

PENÍNSULA

DE AZUERO

Chitré   Los Santos

Las Tablas

Bahía Muntijo

ISLA CEBACO

PUNTA MALA

ISLA COIBA

ISLA JICARÓN

PUNTA MARIATO

PUNTA MANZANILLO
Nombre   El
de Dios   Porvenir   PUNTA SAN BLAS

Portobelo   Mandinga   Golfo de San Blas

Colón

Gatún   Silver City   C. Brewster
3018
Chepo

North Gamboa

Lago   Balboa Heights
Gatún

Balboa   Panamá

ISTMO DE PANAMÁ

Chorrera   Bahía de Panamá

PUNTA CHAME

Bejuco

Penonomé

Antón   Río Hato

Natá   Aguadulce

Golfo
de Parita

Golfo de Panamá

A

M

A

CORD. DE SAN

SERRANÍA DEL DARIÉN

Chepo

ARCHIPIÉLAGO
DE LAS PERLAS

San Miguel
ISLA
DEL REY

ISLA DE SAN JOSÉ

PUNTA GARACHINÉ

Bahía
San Miguel

Garachiné

El Real

La Palma

CABO
TIBURÓN

COLOMBIA

Sambú

Relief

Meters	Feet
3050	10 000
1525	5000
610	2000
305	1000
152.5	500
Sea Level	
152.5	500
1525	5000
3050	10 000

20   40   60   80   100   120 Miles
20   40   60   80   100   120   140   160   180   200 Kilometers

FLORIDA

GULF

OF

MEXICO

Relief

Meters		Feet
3050		10 000
1525		5000
610		2000
305		1000
152.5		500
0	Sea Level	0
152.5		500
1525		5000
3050		10 000
6100		20 000

Delray Beach
Fort Lauderdale
Dania
Miami Beach
MIAMI

LITTLE BAHAMA BANK
GREAT SALE CAY
LITTLE ABACO
West End
Freeport
GRAND BAHAMA
PINDER POINT
SETTLEMENT PT.
Whale Cay Channels
Marsh Harbour
GREAT ABACO
Cross Harbor
Cornwall
ELBOW CAY
Pelican Harbor
Cherokee Sound

Northwest Providence Channel

GREAT ISAAC
BROTHERS
LITTLE ISAAC
MORES
GORDA CAY
Crossing Rocks

NORTH BIMINI
SOUTH BIMINI
Barnett Harbor
N. CAT CAY
Dollar Harbor
RIDING ROCKS
GREAT STIRRUP CAY
GREAT HARBOUR CAY
BERRY ISLANDS
FRAZIERS HOG CAY
WHALE CAY
BONDS CAY
SOUTHWEST PT.
Northeast Providence Channel
BRIDGE
ROYAL
CURL

ORANGE CAY

JOULTER'S CAYS
Nicolls Town
Staniard Creek
SIMMS PT.
WILLIAMS
Nassau
PARADISE
NEW PROVIDENCE
SHIP CHANNEL CAY
HIGHBORNE CAY

ANDROS ISLAND
North Bight
Middle Bight
South Bight
Turner Sound

SALVADOR PT.
SNAP PT.
GREEN CAY
BOOBY ROC
TONGUE OF THE OCEAN
SHROUD CA

Straits of Florida

SANIBEL
Naples
Big Cypress Swamp
SEMINOLE IND. RES.
CAPE ROMANO
Everglades
TEN THOUSAND ISLANDS
EVERGLADES
EVERGLADES NATIONAL PARK
Homestead
THE EVERGLADES
Biscayne Bay
Whitewater Bay
CAPE SABLE
Florida Bay
KEY LARGO
FLORIDA KEYS
Key West
PINE IS.
MARQUESAS KEYS
DRY TORTUGAS

Santaren Channel

DOG ROCKS
DAMAS CAYS
NORTH ELBOW CAYS
CAY SAL BANK
CAY SAL
ANGUILLA CAYS
HURRICANE FLATS
CURLY CUT CAYS

Nicholas Channel

Tropic of Cancer

Bahía Honda
HAVANA
CIUDAD DE LA HABANA
Marianao
Regla
Guanabacoa
Guanajay
San Antonio de los Baños
Bauta
Candelaria
Pan de Guajaibón 2532
Santa Lucía
ARCHIPIÉLAGO DE LOS COLORADOS
PORGANOS
Consolación del Sur
SIERRA DE LOS ORGANOS
PINAR DEL RIO
VUELTA
Pinar del Río
San Juan y Martínez
Guane
Mantua
Bahía de Guadiana
PEN. DE GUANAHACABIBES
CABO FRANCES
CABO CORRIENTES
CABO PEPE
PTA. FRANCES
Ensenada de Cortés
CAYOS DE SAN FELIPE
CAYOS DE LOS INDIOS
Nueva Gerona
ISLA DE LA JUVENTUD
Santa Fé
CAYOS LAGUNA
ISLAS DE MANGLES
ARCHIPIÉLAGO DE LOS CANARREOS
CAYOS DE JUAN LUIS
Ensenada de la Siguanea
PUNTA GORDA
CAYOS INGLES
PENÍNSULA DE ZAPATA
Ensenada de la Broa
CAYO DE DIOS
GOLFO DE BATABANÓ
Berucal
Güira de Melena
Batabanó
Alquízar
HABANA
Güines
Unión de Reyes
Bolondrón
Navajas
Jagüey Grande
Colón
Pedro Betancourt
Alacranes
MATANZAS
Jovellanos
Cárdenas
Corralillo
Martí
Quemado de Güines
Sagua la Grande
Santo Domingo
Rodas
Aguada de Pasajeros
Lajas
Cruces
Palmira
CIENFUEGOS
Cienfuegos
Bahía de Cienfuegos
Casilda
Trinidad
SIERRA DE TRINIDAD
Pico San Juan 1156
Tunas de Zaza
Santa Clara
VILLA CLARA
Santa Esperanza
Camajuaní
Zulueta
Yaguajay
Remedios
Caibarién
Placetas
Florida
Fomento
SANCTI SPIRITUS
Sancti Spíritus
Jatibonico
Ciego de Ávila
Morón
CIEGO DE AVILA
Júcaro
CAMAGÜEY
Camagüey
Minas
Santa Lucía
San Pedro
Santa Cruz del Sur
GOLFO DE GUACANAYABO
Campechuela
Guayabal
Manzanillo
Niquero
GRANMA
SIERRA
Pico Ojo del Toro 1746
CABO CRUZ
LAS TUNAS
Victoria de las Tunas
Nuevitas
Puerto Pad
CAYO COCO
CAYO GUAJABA
CAYO SABINAL
Bahía de Nue
CAYO SANTA MARIA
CAYO CRUZ
CAYO ROMANO
CAYO LOBOS
Laguna de Leche
ARCHIPIÉLAGO DE SABANA
CAYO BLANCOS
Bahía de Cárdenas
Bahía de Santa Clara
Bahía Matanzas
CAYO FRAGOSO
Bahía Buena Vista
Bahía Perros
Laguna La Guira

Old Bahama Channel

Bahía de Cochinos
CAYOS DE DIOS
Golfo de Cazones
CAYO LARGO
BANCO JARDINES
CAYO ROSARIO
CAYO CANTILES
BANCO XAGUA
Ensenada de la Broa
CAYOS CINCO BALAS
CAYOS DE LAS DOCE LEGUAS
CAYOS ANA MARIA
LABERINTO DE LAS DOCE LEGUAS
Canal de Caballones

CARIBBEAN

CAYMAN ISLANDS
LITTLE CAYMAN
CAYMAN BRAC
(Br.)
Georgetown
GRAND CAYMAN

SEA

Montego Bay
Falmouth
St. Ann's Bay
GALINA
Lucea
SOUTH NEGRIL PT.
Savanna la Mar
JAMAICA
Mt. Denham 2256
Annotto Bay
Port M
Black River
Spanish
May Pen
Kingst
GT. PEDRO BLUFF
PORTLAND PT.
Portland PT.

Tropic of Cancer

Longitude West of Greenwich

A-533200-76 | 6-4-9'
COPYRIGHT BY
RAND McNALLY & COMPANY
MADE IN U.S.A.

Cities and Towns

| 0 to 50,000 | o | 500,000 to 1,000,000 | ◎ |
| 50,000 to 500,000 | ⊙ | 1,000,000 and over | |

Scale 1:4 000 000; one inch to 64 miles. Conic Projection
Elevations and depressions are given in feet.

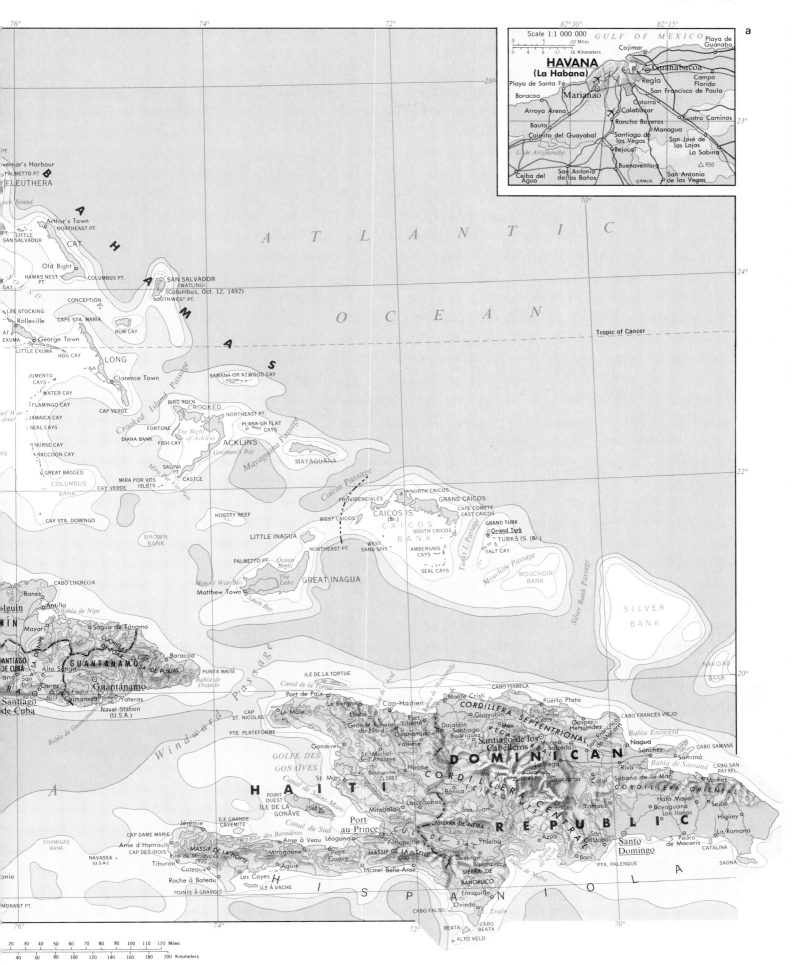

Scale 1:1 000 000

GULF OF MEXICO

HAVANA
(La Habana)

Playa de Guanabo
Cojimar
Guanabacoa
Regla
Campo Florido
Playa de Santa Fé
Baracoa
Marianao
Cotorro
San Francisco de Paula
Arroya Arena
Calabazar
Cuatro Caminos
Bauta
Rancho Boyeros
Managua
Caimito del Guayabal
Santiago de las Vegas
San José de las Lajas
La Sabina
Bejucal
△950
Ceiba del Agua
San Antonio de los Baños
Buenaventura
San Antonio de las Vegas
©RMcN.

A T L A N T I C

O C E A N

Governor's Harbour
PALMETTO PT.
ELEUTHERA
Rock Sound

Arthur's Town
NORTHEAST PT.
LITTLE SAN SALVADOR
CAT
Old Bight
HAWKS NEST PT.
COLUMBUS PT.
SAN SALVADOR
(WATLING)
(Columbus, Oct. 12, 1492)
SOUTHWEST PT.
B A H A M A S

LEE STOCKING
CONCEPTION
Rolleville
CAPE STA. MARIA
RUM CAY
George Town
EXUMA
LITTLE EXUMA
HOG CAY
LONG
Clarence Town
SAMANA OR ATWOOD CAY
JUMENTO CAYS
WATER CAY
BIRD ROCK
CROOKED
NORTHEAST PT.
FLAMINGO CAY
CAP VERDE
FORTUNE
PLANA OR FLAT CAYS
JAMAICA CAY
The Bight of Acklins
SEAL CAYS
DIANA BANK
FISH CAY
ACKLINS
Abraham's Bay
NURSE CAY
SALINA PT.
MIRA POR VOS
CASTLE
MAYAGUANA
RACCOON CAY
CAY VERDE
Mira por Vos Pass
Mayaguana Passage
GREAT RAGGED
MIRA POR VOS ISLETS
COLUMBUS BANK
CAY STA. DOMINGO

Caicos Passage

PROVIDENCIALES
NORTH CAICOS
HOGSTY REEF
WEST CAICOS
GRAND CAICOS
CAICOS IS.
(Br.)
CAPE COMETE
EAST CAICOS
BROWN BANK
LITTLE INAGUA
CAICOS BANK
SOUTH CAICOS
GRAND TURK
Grand Turk
NORTHEAST PT.
WEST SAND SPIT
AMBERGRIS CAYS
TURKS IS. (Br.)
SALT CAY
PALMETTO PT.
SEAL CAYS
Ocean Bight
The Lake
GREAT INAGUA
Mouchoir Passage
Man of War Bay
MOUCHOIR BANK
Matthew Town
South Bay

Tropic of Cancer

SILVER BANK

CABO LUCRECIA
Banes
Antilla
Bahia de Nipe
Holguin
Mayari
Sagua de Tánamo
CUCHILLAS DE TOA
SA. DE NIPE
Baracoa
3100
SANTIAGO DE CUBA
Alto Songo
SA. DE PURIAL
GUANTÁNAMO
PUNTA MAISI
Bahia de Ovando
San Luis
Caney
Guantánamo
ILE DE LA TORTUE
CABO ISABELA
Gran Piedra
Santiago de Cuba
6470
Yateras
CANAL de la Tortue
Monte Cristi
Puerto Plata
CABO FRANCÉS VIEJO
Caimanera
Naval Station (U.S.A.)
Port de Paix
Le Borgne
Cap-Haitien
CORDILLERA SEPTENTRIONAL
Pico Diego
Gasper Hernández
NAVIDAD BANK
Bahia de Guantánamo
CAP ST. NICOLAS
Le Môle
Limbé
Fort Liberté
Guayubin
Mao
Gros Morne
Santiago
San Francisco de Macoris
Windward Passage
PTE. PLATEFORME
Grande Rivière du Nord
Dajabón
Santiago Rodriguez
Santiago de los Caballeros
Salcedo
Nagua
CABO SAMANA
Gonaives
Ouanaminthe
Valliere
La Vega
Riva
Bahia Escosesa
St. Michel de l'Atalaye
VEGA
Bahia de Samana
CABO SAN RAFAEL
GOLFE DES GONAÏVES
Hinche
DOMINICAN
Salto
Sánchez
Miches
St. Marc
Pic Bonhomme
5883
CORDILLERA CENTRAL
Pico Duarte
10 417
Jarabacoa
Cotui
Sabana de la Mar
CABO SAMANA
HAITI
Mte. Tina 7434
CORDILLERA ORIENTAL
POINT OUEST
ILE DE LA GONÂVE
Mirebalais
Lascahobas
Banica
Mte. Tina
8785
Yamasa
Bayaguana
Seibo
ILE GRANDE CAYEMITE
2546
San Juan
Hato Mayor
Los Llanos
Higüey
Jérémie
Canal du Sud
Port-au-Prince
Petionville
REPUBLIC
Azua
San Cristobal
Bani
S. Pedro de Macoris
La Romana
CAP DAME MARIE
Anse d'Hainault
MASSIF DE LA HOTTE
Pico de Macaya
7920
Léogane
CUL DE SAC
SIERRA DE NEIBA
Lago Enriquillo
Neiba
Santo Domingo
CATALINA
CAP DES IROIS
Tiburon
Miragoane
Petit Goave
MASSIF DE LA SELLE
2795
Duverge
Barahona
PTA. PALENQUE
SAONA
Coteaux
Aquin
Les Cayes
ILE À VACHE
Jacmel
Belle-Anse
SIERRA DE BAHORUCO
Enriquillo
Bahia de Neiba
FORMIGAS BANK
NAVASSA (U.S.A.)
Roche à Bateau
POINTE À GRAVOIS
CABO FALSO
Oviedo
H I S P A N I O L A
MORANT PT.
BEATA
CABO BEATA
ALTO VELO

20 30 40 50 60 70 80 90 100 110 120 Miles
40 60 80 100 120 140 160 180 200 Kilometers

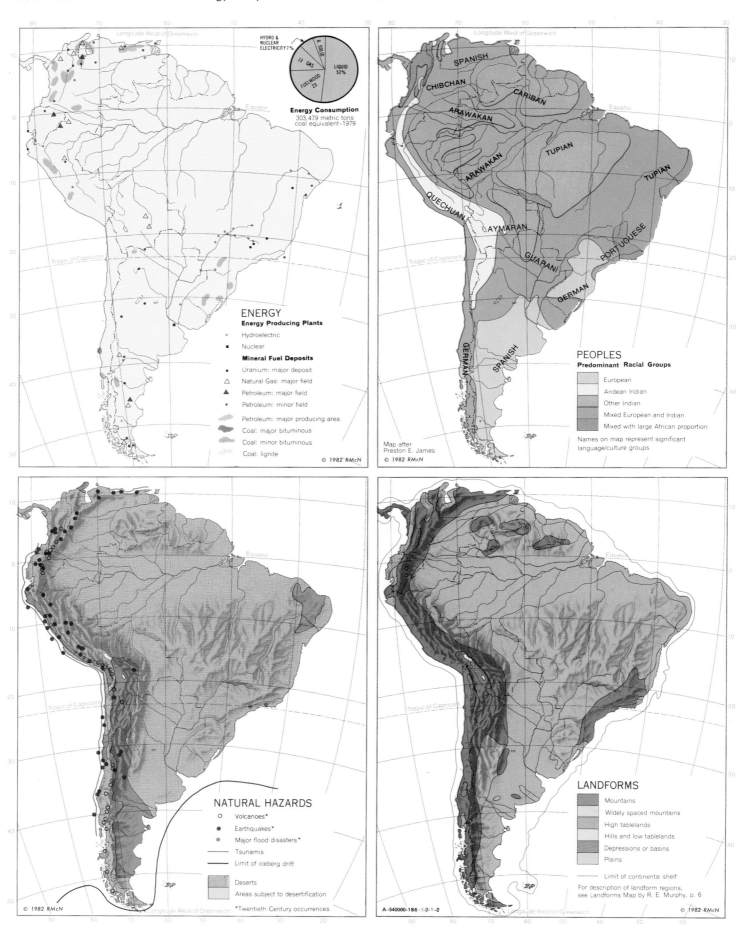

ENERGY

Energy Producing Plants

- ● Hydroelectric
- ■ Nuclear

Mineral Fuel Deposits

- · Uranium: major deposit
- △ Natural Gas: major field
- ▲ Petroleum: major field
- ● Petroleum: minor field
- Petroleum: major producing area
- Coal: major bituminous
- Coal: minor bituminous
- Coal: lignite

© 1982 RMcN

HYDRO & NUCLEAR ELECTRICITY 7%
SOLID 6
GAS 13
FUELWOOD 23
LIQUID 52%

Energy Consumption
303,479 metric tons
coal equivalent-1979

PEOPLES
Predominant Racial Groups

- European
- Andean Indian
- Other Indian
- Mixed European and Indian
- Mixed with large African proportion

Names on map represent significant
language/culture groups

Map after
Preston E. James
© 1982 RMcN

NATURAL HAZARDS

- ○ Volcanoes*
- ● Earthquakes*
- ● Major flood disasters*
- — Tsunamis
- — Limit of iceberg drift
- Deserts
- Areas subject to desertification

© 1982 RMcN

*Twentieth Century occurrences

LANDFORMS

- Mountains
- Widely spaced mountains
- High tablelands
- Hills and low tablelands
- Depressions or basins
- Plains

— Limit of continental shelf

For description of landform regions,
see Landforms Map by R. E. Murphy, p. 6

A-540000-1S6-1-2-1-2   © 1982 RMcN

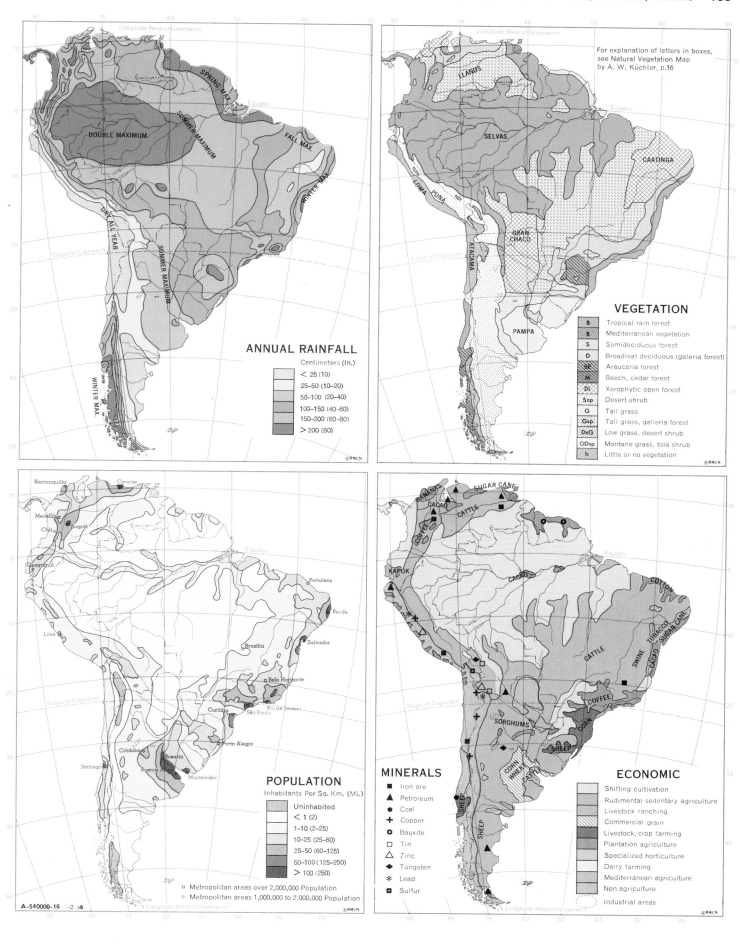

ANNUAL RAINFALL

Centimeters (In.)

- < 25 (10)
- 25–50 (10–20)
- 50–100 (20–40)
- 100–150 (40–60)
- 150–200 (60–80)
- > 200 (80)

VEGETATION

For explanation of letters in boxes, see Natural Vegetation Map by A. W. Küchler, p.16

- **B** Tropical rain forest
- **B** Mediterranean vegetation
- **S** Semideciduous forest
- **D** Broadleaf deciduous (galeria forest)
- **BE** Araucaria forest
- **M** Beech, cedar forest
- **Di** Xerophytic open forest
- **Szp** Desert shrub
- **G** Tall grass
- **Gsp** Tall grass, galleria forest
- **DsG** Low grass, desert shrub
- **GDsp** Montane grass, tola shrub
- **b** Little or no vegetation

POPULATION

Inhabitants Per Sq. Km. (Mi.)

- Uninhabited
- < 1 (2)
- 1–10 (2–25)
- 10–25 (25–60)
- 25–50 (60–125)
- 50–100 (125–250)
- > 100 (250)

□ Metropolitan areas over 2,000,000 Population
○ Metropolitan areas 1,000,000 to 2,000,000 Population

MINERALS

- ■ Iron ore
- ▲ Petroleum
- ● Coal
- ✛ Copper
- ◉ Bauxite
- □ Tin
- △ Zinc
- ◆ Tungsten
- ✳ Lead
- ▣ Sulfur

ECONOMIC

- Shifting cultivation
- Rudimental sedentary agriculture
- Livestock ranching
- Commercial grain
- Livestock, crop farming
- Plantation agriculture
- Specialized horticulture
- Dairy farming
- Mediterranean agriculture
- Non agriculture
- Industrial areas

A-540000-16 -2 36

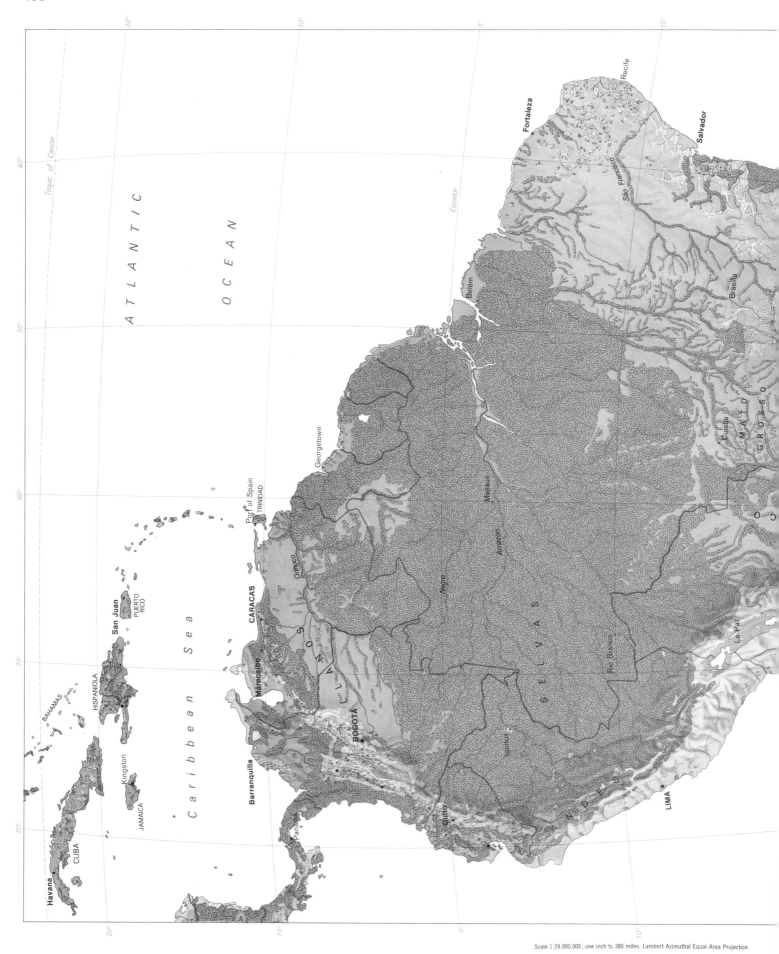

Tropic of Cancer

40°

Equator

50°

A T L A N T I C

O C E A N

60°

70°

80°

Recife

Fortaleza

Salvador

São Francisco

Belém

Brasília

Cuiabá

M A T O

G R O S S O

Georgetown

Port of Spain
TRINIDAD

Manaus

Amazon

Negro

S E L V A S

Rio Branco

La Paz

Orinoco

San Juan

PUERTO
RICO

BAHAMAS

HISPANIOLA

CARACAS

Maracaibo

Kingston

JAMAICA

Barranquilla

BOGOTÁ

Iquitos

A N D E S

LIMA

Havana

CUBA

Panama

Quito

C a r i b b e a n   S e a

20°

10°

0°

10°

Scale 1:24,000,000; one inch to 380 miles. Lambert Azimuthal Equal-Area Projection

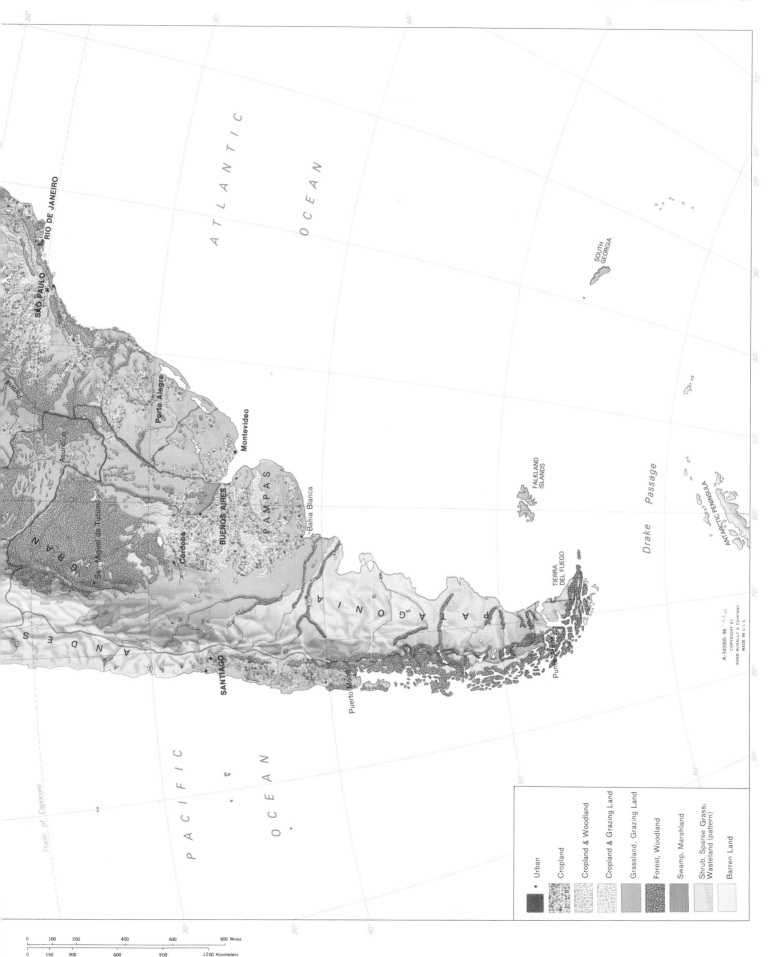

ATLANTIC

OCEAN

RIO DE JANEIRO

SÃO PAULO

Porto Alegre

Asunción

Montevideo

SOUTH
GEORGIA

San Miguel de Tucumán

BUENOS AIRES

PAMPAS

Córdoba

Bahia Blanca

FALKLAND
ISLANDS

GRAN

Drake   Passage

ANTARCTIC PENINSULA

P A T A G O N I A

TIERRA
DEL FUEGO

ANDES

SANTIAGO

Punta Arenas

Puerto Montt

PACIFIC

OCEAN

Tropic of Capricorn

A-540000-96   -1, 1, -3
COPYRIGHT BY
RAND McNALLY & COMPANY
MADE IN U.S.A.

- Urban
- Cropland
- Cropland & Woodland
- Cropland & Grazing Land
- Grassland, Grazing Land
- Forest, Woodland
- Swamp, Marshland
- Shrub, Sparse Grass,
  Wasteland (pattern)
- Barren Land

| 0 | 100 | 200 | 400 | 600 | 800 Miles |

| 0 | 150 | 300 | 600 | 900 | 1200 Kilometers |

Scale 1:40 000 000; one inch to 630 miles. Lambert's Azimuthal, Equal Area Projection
Elevations and depressions are given in feet

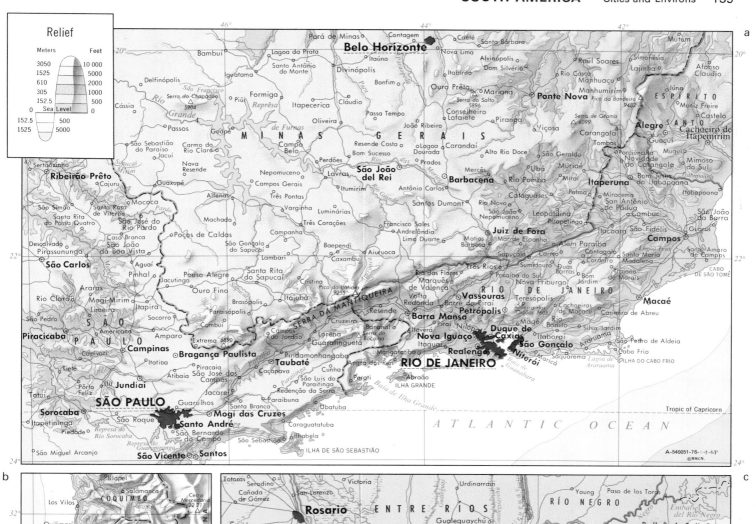

a

Relief

Meters		Feet
3050		10 000
1525		5000
610		2000
305		1000
152.5		500
Sea Level		0
152.5		500
1525		5000

Belo Horizonte

MINAS GERAIS

ESPIRITO SANTO

Ribeirão Prêto

Ponte Nova

Alegre
Cachoeiro de Itapemirim

São Carlos

São João del Rei

Barbacena

Itaperuna

São Paulo

Juiz de Fora

Campos

Piracicaba

Campinas

Bragança Paulista

Vassouras

RIO DE JANEIRO

Macaé

Jundiaí

Taubaté

Barra Mansa

Petrópolis

Duque de Caxias

São Gonçalo

SÃO PAULO

Nova Iguaçu

Itaguaí

Realengo

Niterói

Sorocaba

Mogi das Cruzes

Santo André

São Bernardo do Campo

RIO DE JANEIRO

Tropic of Capricorn

ATLANTIC OCEAN

São Vicente

Santos

ILHA DE SÃO SEBASTIÃO

A-540051-76—7-4-71
©RMCN

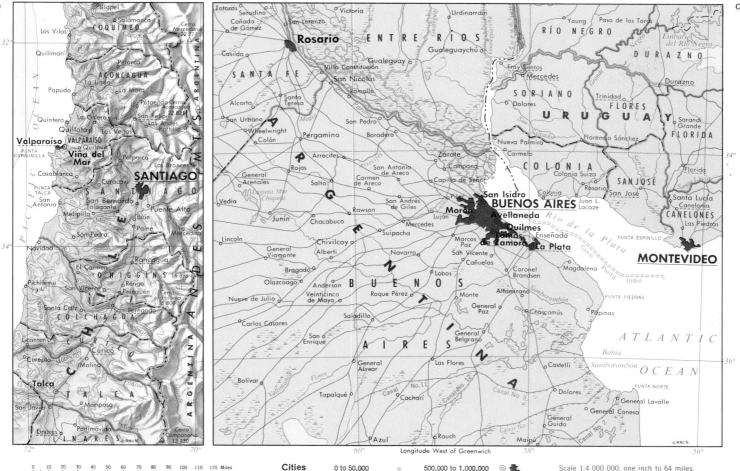

b

c

ARGENTINA

COQUIMBO

ACONCAGUA

Rosario

ENTRE RIOS

RÍO NEGRO

DURAZNO

SANTA FE

URUGUAY

FLORES

FLORIDA

Valparaíso

VALPARAISO

Viña del Mar

SORIANO

Durazno

SANTIAGO

SAN JOSÉ

COLONIA

O'HIGGINS

BUENOS AIRES

San Isidro

Morón

Avellaneda

Quilmes

Lomas de Zamora

La Plata

MONTEVIDEO

Rio de la Plata

CANELONES

Las Piedras

COLCHAGUA

CURICÓ

Talca

TALCA

LINARES

BUENOS AIRES

ARGENTINA

ATLANTIC OCEAN

Bahía Samborombón

Longitude West of Greenwich

©RMCN

| 0 | 10 | 20 | 30 | 40 | 50 | 60 | 70 | 80 | 90 | 100 | 110 | 120 Miles |
| 0 | 20 | 40 | 60 | 80 | 100 | 120 | 140 | 160 | 180 | 200 Kilometers |

Cities and Towns

| 0 to 50,000 | ○ | 500,000 to 1,000,000 | ◉ |
| 50,000 to 500,000 | ⊙ | 1,000,000 and over | ▨ |

Scale 1:4 000 000; one inch to 64 miles.
Elevations and depressions are given in feet.

140

NICARAGUA
EL SALVADOR

Managua • Bluefields

León •
San Juan del Sur •
San Juan del Norte
(Greytown)

Puntarenas •
San José •
Limón •

CARIBBEAN SEA

Irazú (Vol)
11,260
Bocas del Toro

David •
Golfo Dulce

Golfo de los Mosquitos

ISTMO DE PANAMA
Colón •
Panamá •
Golfo de Panamá
Golfo del Darién

COIBA

PENINSULA DE AZUERO

CABO CORRIENTES

ISLA DEL COCO
(Costa Rica)

ISLA DE MALPELO
(Colombia)

PACIFIC OCEAN

PTA DE GALLINAS
PENÍNSULA DE GUAJIRA
Ríohacha
Santa Marta
Puerto Colombia • Ciénaga
Barranquilla
Sabanalarga •
Cartagena •
Sincelejo •
Montería •
Turbo •

Maracaibo
Cabimas
Lago de Maracaibo

ARUBA (Neth.) CURAÇAO (Neth.) BONAIRE (Neth.)
Willemstad
ISLAS LOS ROQUES
ORCHILA
La Asunción ISLA DE MARGARITA
Puerto Cabello
Maiquetía CARACAS
La Guaira
Barcelona
Cumaná

VENEZUELA

Cúcuta •
San Cristóbal •
Bucaramanga
Barquisimeto
Valencia
San Carlos

Medellín

BOGOTÁ

COLOMBIA

Buenaventura •
Cali •
Palmira •
Popayán •

Neiva •

Pasto •
Tulcán •
Ipiales •

Quito •
ECUADOR
Ambato •
Guayaquil •
Cuenca •

Iquitos •

Chiclayo •
Trujillo •
Chimbote •

PERU

Callao •
LIMA •

Cuzco •

Arequipa •
La Paz
BOLIVIA
Sucre •
Potosí •

Tropic of Capricorn

CHILE
Antofagasta •

ARGENT.

Cities and Towns
0 to 50,000 •
50,000 to 500,000 ⊙
500,000 to 1,000,000 ◎
1,000,000 and over

Scale 1:16 000 000, one inch to 250 miles. Sinusoidal Pro
Elevations and depressions are given in feet

b

TRINIDAD AND TOBAGO

CARIBBEAN SEA

Tocuyo de la Costa
Chichiriviche
Cayo Sombrero
Tucacas
Golfo Triste
Puerto Cabello
Morón
Montalbán Guacara
Miranda
San Joaquín
Valencia
Lago de Valencia
Güigüe
Villa de Cura
San Sebastián
Tinaquillo
COJEDES
San Juan de los Morros
Parapara
Camatagua
Dos Caminos
Barbacoas

CARACAS
Maiquetía
Carayaca
La Sabana
La Guaira
Naiguatá
Petare
Santa Lucía
DISTRITO FEDERAL
Pico Cenizal 2988
Pico Naiguatá 9072
Maracay
Los Teques
La Victoria
Cagua
Santa Teresa
MIRANDA
Ocumare del Tuy
San Francisco de Macaira
Altagracia de Orituco
GUARICO
Valle de Guanape
Onoto
Aragua de Barcelona

ISLA DE MARGARITA
Boca del Pozo   2303
PUNTA ARENAS
Punta de Piedras
NUEVA ESPARTA
ISLA CUBAGUA
PUNTA DE ARAYA
Manicuare
Cumaná
Las Vegas
SUCRE
Puerto La Cruz
Guanta
Barcelona
ANZOÁTEGUI

Scale 1:4 000 000
0 10 20 30 40 Miles
0 10 20 30 40 50 60 Kilometers
©R.M.C.N.

Port of Spain
TRINIDAD
Boca Grande
Morawhanna
Georgetown
Bártica
Rosignol
New Amsterdam
Wismar
Rockstone
Skeldon
Totness
Paramaribo
Nieuw Nickerie
Paranam
Moengo
St. Laurent
Albina
Sinnamary
ILE DU DIABLE (DEVIL'S I.)
Cayenne
Saint-Georges

GUYANA
WILHELMINA GEBERGTE
SURINAME
FRENCH GUIANA
ACARAÍ MTS.
TUMUC-HUMAC MTS.
CABO ORANGE

Amapá
AMAPÁ (TER.)
Mazagão
ILHA CAVIANA

ATLANTIC OCEAN

Equator

Manaus (Manáos)
Parintins
Itacoatiara
TUPINAMBARANAS
Maués
Borba
Itaituba
Santarém
Óbidos
Alenquer
Faro
Breves
ILHA DE MARAJÓ
Gurupá
Belém (Pará)
Abaetetuba
Cametá
Marapanim
Bragança
Cururupu
São Luís (Maranhão)
Alcântara
Rosário
Tutóia
Camocim
Acaraú
Viana
Itapecurú-Mirim
Parnaíba
Sobral
FORTALEZA (Ceará)
Maranguape
Baturité
Ipu
Aracati
Areia Branca
Macau
CABO DE SÃO ROQUE
ARQUIPÉLAGO FERNANDO DE NORONHA (Brazil)
ATOL DAS ROCAS (Brazil)

Altamira
Tucuruí
PARÁ
SERRA DOS CARAJÁS
São João do Araguaia
Araguatins
Tocantinópolis
Carolina
Riachão
Grajaú
Barra do Corda
Mirador
Floriano
Loreto
Balsas
Santa Filomena
Parnaguá
MARANHÃO
Teresina
Monção
Brejo
Barras
Codó
Caxias
Pedreiras
Campo Maior
PIAUÍ
Oeiras
Amarante
Paulistana
São Raimundo Nonato
Picos
Crateús
Senador Pompeu
Iguatu
Icó
CEARÁ
Russas
Mossoró
Currais Novos
RIO GRANDE DO NORTE
Ceará-Mirim
Novo Cruz
Natal
Campina Grande
Juazeiro do Norte
Crato
Flores
PARAÍBA
João Pessoa (Paraíba)
Nazaré da Mata
Jaboatão
Caruaru
Olinda
RECIFE (Pernambuco)
SERRA DO ARARIPE
Granito
Cabrobó
PLANALTO DA BORBOREMA
PERNAMBUCO
Garanhuns
Palmares
Pôrto de Pedras
Juàzeiro
Sertânia
TABOLEIRO
ALAGOAS
Palmeira dos Indios
Maceió
Propriá
Corúripe
Penedo
SERGIPE
Jeremoabo
Senhor do Bonfim
Itabaiana
Aracaju
Serrinha
São Cristóvão
Inhambupe
BAHIA
Jacobina
Morro do Chapéu
Feira de Santana
Catu
Santo Amaro
Cachoeira
Nazaré
SALVADOR (Bahia)
Lençóis
Mucugê
Alagoinhas

B R A Z I L

CHAPADA DOS PARECIS
SERRA DOS PARECIS
Diamantino
Rosário Oeste
Cuiabá
MATO GROSSO
CHAPADA DE MATO GROSSO
SA. DA TAQUARA
SERRA DO TOMBADOR
SERRA DO NORTE
SERRA FORMOSA
SERRA DO RONCADOR
SERRA DO ESTRONDO
SERRA DO GURUPI
CHAP. DAS MANGABEIRAS
Pôrto Nacional
ILHA DO BANANAL
Natividade
Barra
SERRA DO PIAUÍ
SERRA GERAL DE GOIÁS
GOIÁS
Barreiras
Correntina
Carinhanha
Januária
Bom Jesus da Lapa
Caetité
Condeúba
Vitória da Conquista
Jequié
Ilhéus
Itabuna
Canavieiras
Belmonte
Pôrto Seguro
SERRA DO ESPINHAÇO
ARQUIPÉLAGO DOS ABROLHOS
Caravelas
SERRA DO CAIAPÓ
SERRA DAS ARARAS
Cáceres
Barão de Melgaço
Mato Grosso
Pilar de Goiás
Cavalcante
Pirenópolis
Goiânia
Anápolis
Luziânia
Silvânia
Bela Vista de Goiás
Formosa
Brasília
D.F.
São Francisco
Montes Claros
Grão Mogol
Pirapora
Paracatu
Ipameri
Catalão
Araguari
Pedra Azul
Teófilo Otoni
Diamantina
Peçanha
São Mateus
MINAS GERAIS
SA. DOS AIMORÉS
Rio Pardo de Minas
Minas Novas
Curvelo
Corinto
Gov. Valadares
Colatina
Vitória
ESPÍRITO SANTO
Aracruz
Guarapari
Cachoeiro do Itapemirim

Corumbá
Puerto Suárez
El Roboré
San José
La Gaiba
Mato Grosso
PARAGUAY
Bahía Negra
Fuerte Olimpo
Pôrto Murtinho
Mariscal Estigarribia
Puerto Casado
Puerto Pinasco
Pedro Juan Caballero
Ponta Porã
Concepción
Horqueta
Belén
Coxim
Aquidauana
Nioaque
Bella Vista
Campo Grande
Três Lagoas
Presidente Epitácio
Araçatuba
Marília
Bauru
Assis
Londrina
Jacarèzinho
PARANÁ
Guaíra
Pôrto Mendes
Ponta Grossa
Guarapuava
Ituiutaba
Paranaíba
Itapira
Uberlândia
Uberaba
Araxá
Patrocínio
Araguari
Pará de Minas
Sete Lagoas
BELO HORIZONTE
Sta. Bárbara
Pico da Bandeira 9481
Divinópolis
Conselheiro Lafaiete
Barbacena
Ponte Nova
São João del Rei
Juiz de Fora
Campos
Nova Friburgo
Petrópolis
RIO DE JANEIRO
Niterói
CABO FRIO
Nova Iguaçu
SÃO PAULO
São José do Rio Preto
Franca
Ribeirão Prêto
Pouso Alegre
Varginha
Araraquara
São Carlos
Rio Claro
Piracicaba
Botucatu
Sorocaba
Campinas
Jundiaí
Taubaté
Santos
São Vicente
Mogi das Cruzes
Itapetininga
Itararé
Castro
Curitiba

Tropic of Capricorn

Continued on page 142

0 50 100 200 300 400 500 Miles
0 100 200 400 600 800 Kilometers

Relief		
Meters		Feet
3050		10 000
1525		5000
610		2000
305		1000
152.5		500
0	Sea Level	0
152.5		500
1525		5000
3050		10 000
6100		20 000

Continued on pages 140-141

a

BUENOS AIRES

Scale 1:1 000 000

b

RIO DE JANEIRO

Scale 1:1 000 000

Relief

Meters	Feet
3050	10 000
1525	5000
610	2000
305	1000
152.5	500
0 Sea Level	0
152.5	500 Below
1525	5000 Sea Level
3050	10 000
6100	20 000

FALKLAND IS.
(ISLAS MALVINAS)
(Br.)

A-549200-76
COPYRIGHT BY
RAND M?NALLY & COMPANY
MADE IN U.S.A.

Longitude West of Greenwich

Scale 1:16 000 000; one inch to 250 miles. Sinusoidal Projection
Elevations and depressions are given in feet

For larger scale coverage of Buenos Aires,
Rio de Janeiro, and São Paulo see pages 60 and 61

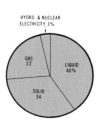

HYDRO. & NUCLEAR
ELECTRICITY 3%

GAS
22

LIQUID
40%

SOLID
34

Energy Consumption
3,699,305 metric tons
coal equivalent–1979

ENERGY

Energy Producing Plants

▽ Geothermal

• Hydroelectric

■ Nuclear

Mineral Fuel Deposits

• Uranium: major deposit

△ Natural Gas: major field

▲ Petroleum: major field

• Petroleum: minor field

Petroleum: major producing area

Coal: major bituminous and anthracite

Coal: minor bituminous and anthracite

Coal: lignite

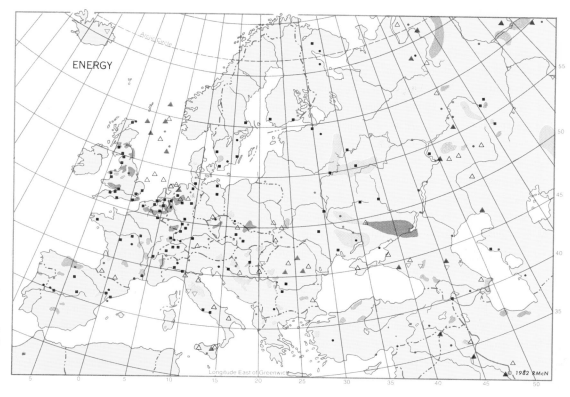

ENERGY

NATURAL HAZARDS

○ Volcanoes*

● Earthquakes*

● Major flood disasters*

—— Tsunamis

—— Limit of iceberg drift

Temporary pack ice

Areas subject to desertification

*Twentieth Century occurrences

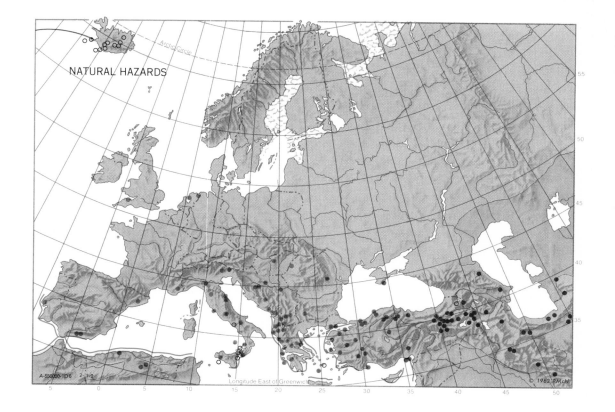

NATURAL HAZARDS

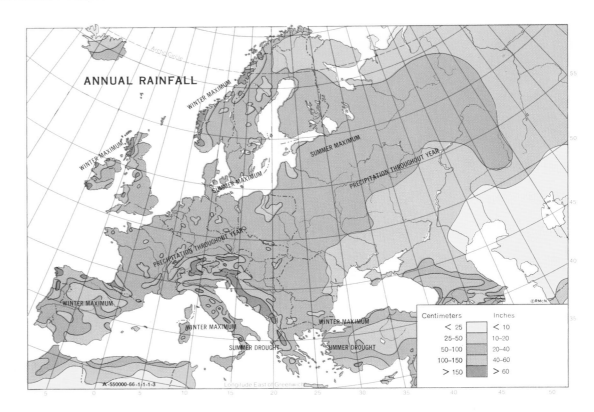

ANNUAL RAINFALL

WINTER MAXIMUM

WINTER MAXIMUM

WINTER MAXIMUM

SUMMER MAXIMUM

SUMMER MAXIMUM

PRECIPITATION THROUGHOUT YEAR

PRECIPITATION THROUGHOUT YEAR

WINTER MAXIMUM

WINTER MAXIMUM

WINTER MAXIMUM

SUMMER DROUGHT

SUMMER DROUGHT

Arctic Circle

Longitude East of Greenwich

A-550000-66-1-1-1-3

©RMcN

Centimeters	Inches
< 25	< 10
25–50	10–20
50–100	20–40
100–150	40–60
> 150	> 60

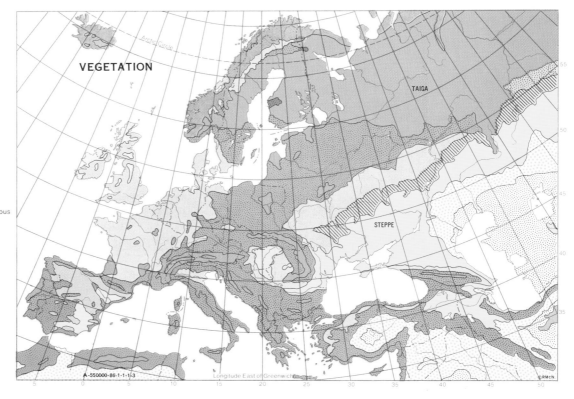

VEGETATION

TAIGA

STEPPE

Arctic Circle

Longitude East of Greenwich

A-550000-86-1-1-1-3

©RMcN

VEGETATION

E	Coniferous forest
B, Bs	Mediterranean vegetation
M	Mixed forest: coniferous-deciduous
S	Semi-deciduous forest
D	Deciduous forest
DG	Wooded steppe
G	Grass (steppe)
Gp	Short grass
Dsp	Desert shrub
L	Heath and moor
L	Alpine vegetation, tundra
b	Little or no vegetation

For explanation of letters in boxes,
see Natural Vegetation Map
by A. W. Kuchler, p. 16

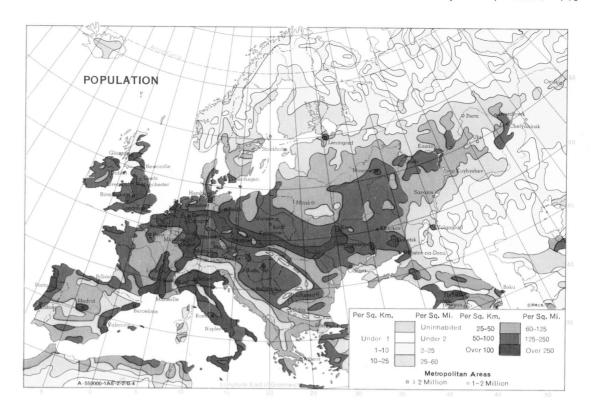

POPULATION

Per Sq. Km.	Per Sq. Mi.	Per Sq. Km.	Per Sq. Mi.
	Uninhabited	25–50	60–125
Under 1	Under 2	50–100	125–250
1–10	2–25	Over 100	Over 250
10–25	25–60		

Metropolitan Areas
□ > 2 Million   ○ 1–2 Million

A-550000-1A6-2-2-0-4

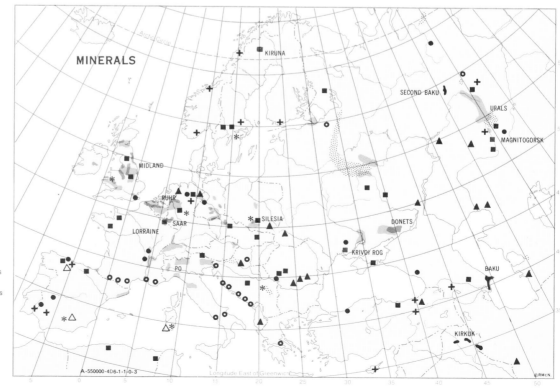

MINERALS

MINERALS

Industrial areas
Major coal deposits
Major petroleum deposits
Lignite deposits
▲ Minor petroleum deposits
● Minor coal deposits
■ Major iron ore
■ Minor iron ore
✳ Lead
○ Bauxite
△ Zinc
✛ Copper

A-550000-4D6-1-1-0-3

146

Legend:
- Urban
- Cropland
- Cropland & Woodland
- Cropland & Grazing Land
- Grassland, Grazing Land
- Forest, Woodland
- Swamp, Marshland
- Tundra
- Shrub, Sparse Grass, Wasteland (pattern)
- Barren Land
- • Oasis

Reykjavik

ATLANTIC

OCEAN

Narvik
Trondheim
Bergen
Oslo
Göteborg
Copenhagen
Glasgow
Belfast
MANCHESTER
Dublin
LONDON
Amsterdam
Hamburg
BERLIN
Antwerp
Essen
Leipzig
Frankfurt
PARIS
Seine
Loire
Strasbourg
Prague
Brest
Munich
VIENNA
Zürich
Lyon
Rhône
MILAN
Venice
Genoa
La Coruña
Bordeaux
Garonne
Bilbao
PYRENEES
Douro
MADRID
Ebro
Lisbon
Marseille
BARCELONA
Sevilla
CORSICA
ROME
SARDINIA
Naples
ISLAS BALEARES
Tanger
Algiers
Oran
ATLAS MOUNTAINS
Casablanca
Tunis
Palermo
SICILY
MALTA

North Sea

Gulf of Bothnia

Helsinki
LENINGRAD
Tallinn
Stockholm
Riga
Baltic Sea
Kaliningrad
Minsk
Oder
Warsaw
Prip
Elbe
Kraków
L'vov
Danube
Tisza
BUDAPEST
CARPATHIANS
Zagreb
Sava
Belgrade
Bucharest
Danube
Sofia
Adriatic Sea
Tirane
Tyrrhenian Sea
Aegean Sea
Athens
Mediterranean Sea
CRETE

Bay of Biscay

ALPS

North Sea

Longitude West of Greenwich   Longitude East of Greenwich

Scale 1: 16,000,000; one inch to 250 miles. Conic Projection

0   50 100   200   300   400   500 Miles
0   100   200   400   600   800 Kilometers

Nar'yan-Mar
Ob
Novosibirsk
Irtysh
Omsk
Archangelsk
URALS
SVERDLOVSK
Karaganda
Perm'
Pechora
Vologda
Kirov
Ufa
Balkhash
Kama
Volga
Kazan'
Magnitogorsk
Gorkiy
Kzyl-Orda
Kuybyshev
Orsk
Syr-Dar'ya
MOSCOW
Volga
Ural
Tula
Aral'skoye
More
(Aral Sea)
PESKI
KYZYLKUM
Saratov
DEPRESSION
CASPIAN
Khar'kov
DEPRESSION
VOLGOGRAD
Don
Amu Dar'ya
Dnepropetrovsk
Donetsk
Volga
Astrakhan
PESKI KARAKUMY
Dnepr
MANYCH
DEPRESSION
Odessa
Krasnodar
Ashkhabad
C a s p i a n
CAUCASUS   MTS.
BAKU
S e a
TBILISI
B l a c k   S e a
Yerevan
NBUL
Ankara
ELBURZ   MTS.
TEHRAN
DASHT-E-KAVIR
TOROS
ATA DAG
Kerman
Nicosia
Tigris
CYPRUS
ZAGROS
Euphrates
MOUNTAINS
Beirut
Baghdad
Abādān

ICELAND

Lava
Ice

ATLANTIC OCEAN

Arctic Circle

Nord Cape

LAPPLAND

Narvik

Kiruna

Ingre Basin

Knobs

LOWLAND

Muskeg Driftland

Rock and Drift Coast

Northern Driftland

Granite Upland

Moraine Region

Elongat

Lake

Gulf of Bothnia

Faeröerne

Sogne Fiord

Shetland Is.

Trondh

Sylarna

Ostersund

Clay

Dovre

Ostersund

Østerdalen

Bergen

Hardanger Fiord

Gudbrandsdalen

Hallingdal

Numedal

Oslo

Vänern Basin

Helsinki

Gulf of Finland

Stav

Orkney Is.

NW. HIGHL'DS

Dr. Orsa Ring

Vänern Glacial Channel

Malar Basin

Stockholm

Riga

Nor Lowland

NORTH SEA

GRAMPIAN Mts.

Gt.

Ed.

SO. HIGHLANDS

Skagerrak

Kattegat

Moraine

Southern Driftland

Gotland

Öland

Cuestas

Lowland

Peipu

Dau

656 feet

Boa

LAKE DIST.

PENNINE CHAIN

Shannon Va.

Wicklow Mts.

Snowden

Cleveland Hills

Elbe R.

Weser R.

Kiel

Copenhagen

Skåne Plain

BALTIC SEA

Niemen R.

Vilnyus

Kau.

Limit of Glaciation

Exmoor

WELSH HIGHL'DS

Cotswold

Chiltern Hills

E. Anglian Hl.

London

N. Downs

S. Downs

Amsterdam

Hague

Rhine R.

dunes

NETHERLANDS

Ant.

Br.

DUNES

Hamburg

Baltic Lakes

Oder R.

Berlin

Po

Danzig

Mazurian Lakes

Mazovian Plain

Warsaw

BALTIC LAKE PLAINS

Brest

Sw

Łódź

Łysa Gory

Lublin Plateau

Mo

English Channel

Dartmoor

Cotentin

Seine R.

L.H.

ARMORICAN MASSIF

Loire R.

Nan.

PARIS BASIN

Orl.

CHAMPAGNE LOWL'D

Flandrian Plain

Ardenne

Eifel

Westerwald

Sauerland

Taunus

Vogelsbg.

Rhon

Thuringian For.

ORE M

Dr.

SILESIAN PLAIN

SUDETES

Wr.

Galician Basin

Pr.

Cracow

Lvov

PODOLI

To

Gra

Bor

Bordeaux

AQUITANIAN LOWL'D

dunes

Landes

Lot

CENTRAL MASSIVE

Lova

Lyons

St.

CAUSSES PLAT.

CEVENNES

Loire R.

Garonne R.

LOIRE BASIN

MORVAN PLAT.

LANGRES PLAT.

Hunsruck

Lorrain.

LORRAIN BASIN

Vosges

Black Forest

Schwabian Jura

Frank

stu.

str.

JURA

SWISS

Nur.

BAVARIAN BASIN

Austrian Plain

Mun.

alps

Bohemian For.

Bohemian Basin

Prague

Pl.

Moravian Hills

Tatry

Vienna

Little Alfold

Budapest

Biharm

Cluj

Transylvanian Basin

CANTABRIAN Mts.

Douro R.

LEON OLD CASTILIAN BASIN

Sa Estrela

Sal.

Guadarrama

Sª de Gredos

Madrid

EBRO BASIN

CATALAN Mts.

Pa

Ebro R.

Costa Brava

Barcelona

Tar.

Po R.

Milan

Turin

Venice

Trieste

Riviera

Genoa

Monaco

PO VALLEY

ADRIATIC

KAPELA KARST

DINARIC ALPS

ABRUZZI

APULIAN V.

Zagreb

Papuk

Sava R.

Mt. Maree

Belgrade

Sava R.

WALLACHIAN P

Iron Gate

Danube R.

Danubian Plai

BALKAN

Kosova Polje

ANTIBALKANS

Skopje

Rila M

RODOPE M

Bay of Biscay

LEON OLD CASTILIAN BASIN

Guadiana R.

Sa. MORENA

NEW CAST.

BALANCHA BASIN

Luciana

Toledo

ANDALUSIAN LOWL'D

Seville

Sd Segura

Sª Filabres

Sa Nevada

Valencia

Cor.

Cart.

BALEARIC ISLANDS

CORSICA

SARDINIA

TYRRHENIAN SEA

VOLCANIC BELT

Rome

Naples

Vesuvius

Mt. Gargano

MURGE PLAT.

Lipari Volcanoes

Palermo

SICILY

Etna

CALABRIAN Mts.

IONIAN SEA

Lisbon

Tagus R.

Tangiers

Strait of Gibraltar

Gib.

Mal.

Ce.

Marseilles

Fl.

Nis

Sof

Less

Morava R.

Maritza R.

Vardar R.

Larissa

PINDUS Mts.

Olympus

Athens

CRE

Rabat

Cas.

RIF ATLAS

COASTAL PLAIN

Fes

Mel.

Oran

TELL ATLAS

Algiers

Bône

Biz.

Tunis

Malta

MEDITERRANEAN SEA

MOROCCO MESETA

MIDDLE ATLAS

MOULOUYA BASIN

HIGH PLATEAUS

HIGH ATLAS

SAHARAN ATLAS

Biskra

JEB. AURES

TUNISIAN ATLAS

Sousse

656 feet

Longitude West of Greenwich   Longitude East of Greenwich

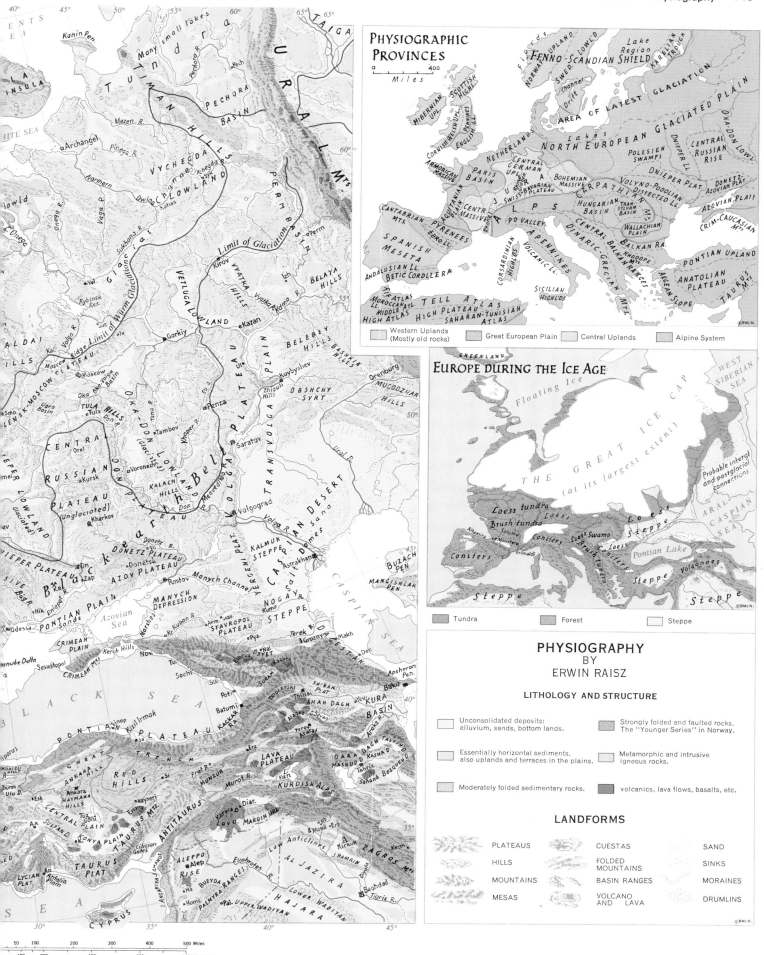

PHYSIOGRAPHIC PROVINCES

0   400
Miles

FENNO-SCANDIAN SHIELD

AREA OF LATEST GLACIATION

NORTH EUROPEAN GLACIATED PLAIN

Scottish Highl.
Hibernian Upl.
Cornish Welsh Upl.
Pennines
English L.
Netherlands
Armorican Massive
Paris Basin
Central German Upl.
Aquitanian Basin
Central Massives
Bohemian Massive
Bavarian Plateau
Swiss Plateau
ALPS
Pyrenees
Cantabrian Mts.
Ebro L.L.
PO VALLEY
APENNINES
Spanish Meseta
Andalusian L.L.
Betic Cordillera
Corsardinian Highlds
Volcanic L.L.
Sicilian Highlds
Carpathian Mts.
Volyno-Podolian Dissected L.L.
Hungarian Basin
Transylvan. Basin
Central Balkan Ra.
Dinaric-Grecian Ranges
Wallachian Plain
Rhodope Mts.
Aegean Slope
Polesien Swamps
Dnieper Plat.
Dnieper L.L.
Donetz-Azovian Plat.
Azovian Plain
Crim-Caucasian Mts.
Pontian Upland
Central Russian Rise
Oka-Don Lowld.

High Atlas
Middle Atlas
Morocca Atl.
Tell Atlas
High Plateau
Saharan-Tunisian Atlas
Tif Atlas L.L.

Anatolian Plateau
Taurus Mts.

| Western Uplands (Mostly old rocks) | Great European Plain | Central Uplands | Alpine System |

©R.M.C.N.

EUROPE DURING THE ICE AGE

GREENLAND
Floating Ice
WEST SIBERIAN SEA
THE GREAT ICE CAP (at its largest extent)
Probable interglacial and postglacial connections
ARAL
CASPIAN SEA
Loess tundra
Brush tundra
Altamira
Solutre
Le Moustier
Grimaldi
Conifers
Loess
Loess Swamp
Conifers
Loess Steppe
Pontian Lake
Brush tundra
Steppe
Volcanoes
Steppe
Steppe
Conifers

| Tundra | Forest | Steppe |

©R.M.C.N.

PHYSIOGRAPHY
BY
ERWIN RAISZ

LITHOLOGY AND STRUCTURE

Unconsolidated deposits: alluvium, sands, bottom lands.

Strongly folded and faulted rocks. The "Younger Series" in Norway.

Essentially horizontal sediments, also uplands and terraces in the plains.

Metamorphic and intrusive igneous rocks.

Moderately folded sedimentary rocks.

volcanics, lava flows, basalts, etc.

LANDFORMS

PLATEAUS	CUESTAS	SAND
HILLS	FOLDED MOUNTAINS	SINKS
MOUNTAINS	BASIN RANGES	MORAINES
MESAS	VOLCANO AND LAVA	DRUMLINS

©R.M.C.N.

EUROPE LANGUAGES

BY

BOGDAN ZABORSKI

Scale 1:16,500,000; one inch to 260 miles Conic Projection

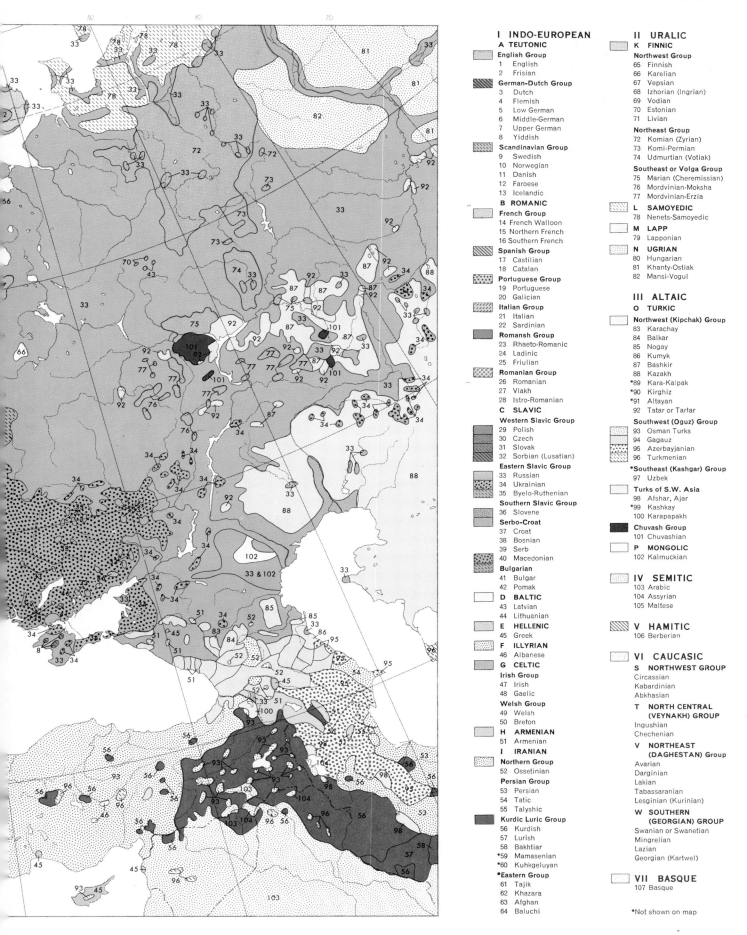

I INDO-EUROPEAN

A TEUTONIC
English Group
1 English
2 Frisian
German-Dutch Group
3 Dutch
4 Flemish
5 Low German
6 Middle-German
7 Upper German
8 Yiddish
Scandinavian Group
9 Swedish
10 Norwegian
11 Danish
12 Faroese
13 Icelandic
B ROMANIC
French Group
14 French Walloon
15 Northern French
16 Southern French
Spanish Group
17 Castilian
18 Catalan
Portuguese Group
19 Portuguese
20 Galician
Italian Group
21 Italian
22 Sardinian
Romansh Group
23 Rhaeto-Romanic
24 Ladinic
25 Friulian
Romanian Group
26 Romanian
27 Vlakh
28 Istro-Romanian
C SLAVIC
Western Slavic Group
29 Polish
30 Czech
31 Slovak
32 Sorbian (Lusatian)
Eastern Slavic Group
33 Russian
34 Ukrainian
35 Byelo-Ruthenian
Southern Slavic Group
36 Slovene
Serbo-Croat
37 Croat
38 Bosnian
39 Serb
40 Macedonian
Bulgarian
41 Bulgar
42 Pomak
D BALTIC
43 Latvian
44 Lithuanian
E HELLENIC
45 Greek
F ILLYRIAN
46 Albanese
G CELTIC
Irish Group
47 Irish
48 Gaelic
Welsh Group
49 Welsh
50 Breton
H ARMENIAN
51 Armenian
I IRANIAN
Northern Group
52 Ossetinian
Persian Group
53 Persian
54 Tatic
55 Talyshic
Kurdic Luric Group
56 Kurdish
57 Lurish
58 Bakhtiar
*59 Mamasenian
*60 Kuhkgeluyan
*Eastern Group
61 Tajik
62 Khazara
63 Afghan
64 Baluchi

II URALIC

K FINNIC
Northwest Group
65 Finnish
66 Karelian
67 Vepsian
68 Izhorian (Ingrian)
69 Vodian
70 Estonian
71 Livian
Northeast Group
72 Komian (Zyrian)
73 Komi-Permian
74 Udmurtian (Votiak)
Southeast or Volga Group
75 Marian (Cheremissian)
76 Mordvinian-Moksha
77 Mordvinian-Erzia
L SAMOYEDIC
78 Nenets-Samoyedic
M LAPP
79 Lapponian
N UGRIAN
80 Hungarian
81 Khanty-Ostiak
82 Mansi-Vogul

III ALTAIC

O TURKIC
Northwest (Kipchak) Group
83 Karachay
84 Balkar
85 Nogay
86 Kumyk
87 Bashkir
88 Kazakh
*89 Kara-Kalpak
*90 Kirghiz
*91 Altayan
92 Tatar or Tartar
Southwest (Oguz) Group
93 Osman Turks
94 Gagauz
95 Azerbayjanian
96 Turkmenian
*Southeast (Kashgar) Group
97 Uzbek
Turks of S.W. Asia
98 Afshar, Ajar
*99 Kashkay
100 Karapapakh
Chuvash Group
101 Chuvashian
P MONGOLIC
102 Kalmuckian

IV SEMITIC
103 Arabic
104 Assyrian
105 Maltese

V HAMITIC
106 Berberian

VI CAUCASIC

S NORTHWEST GROUP
Circassian
Kabardinian
Abkhasian
T NORTH CENTRAL (VEYNAKH) GROUP
Ingushian
Chechenian
V NORTHEAST (DAGHESTAN) Group
Avarian
Darginian
Lakian
Tabassaranian
Lesginian (Kurinian)
W SOUTHERN (GEORGIAN) GROUP
Swanian or Swanetian
Mingrelian
Lazian
Georgian (Kartwel)

VII BASQUE
107 Basque

*Not shown on map

Relief

Meters	Feet
3050	10 000
1525	5000
610	2000
305	1000
152.5	500
Sea Level	Sea Level
0	0
152.5	500	Below
1525	5000	Sea Level
3050	10 000

Longitude West of Greenwich   Longitude East of Greenwich   Continued on pages 220-221

Scale 1: 16 000 000; one inch to 250 miles. Conic Projection
Elevations and depressions are given in feet

| 0 | 50 | 100 | 200 | 300 | 400 | 500 Miles |

| 0 | 100 | 200 | 400 | 600 | 800 Kilometers |

Continued on pages 178-179

Continued on pages 192-193

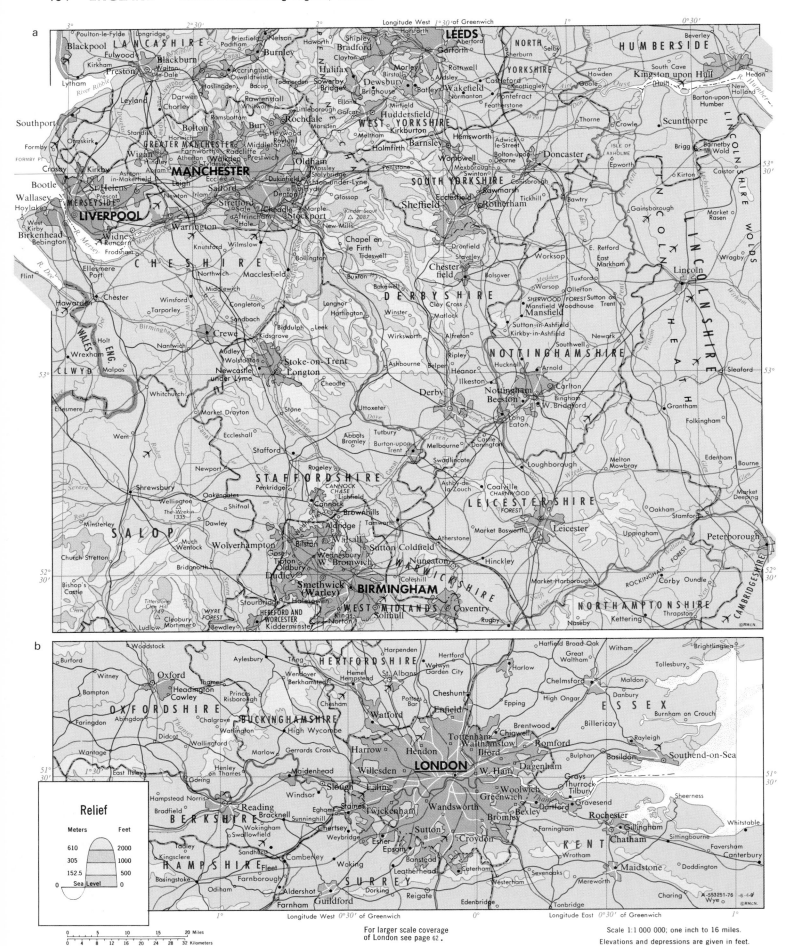

For larger scale coverage
of London see page 62 .

Scale 1:1 000 000; one inch to 16 miles.

Elevations and depressions are given in feet.

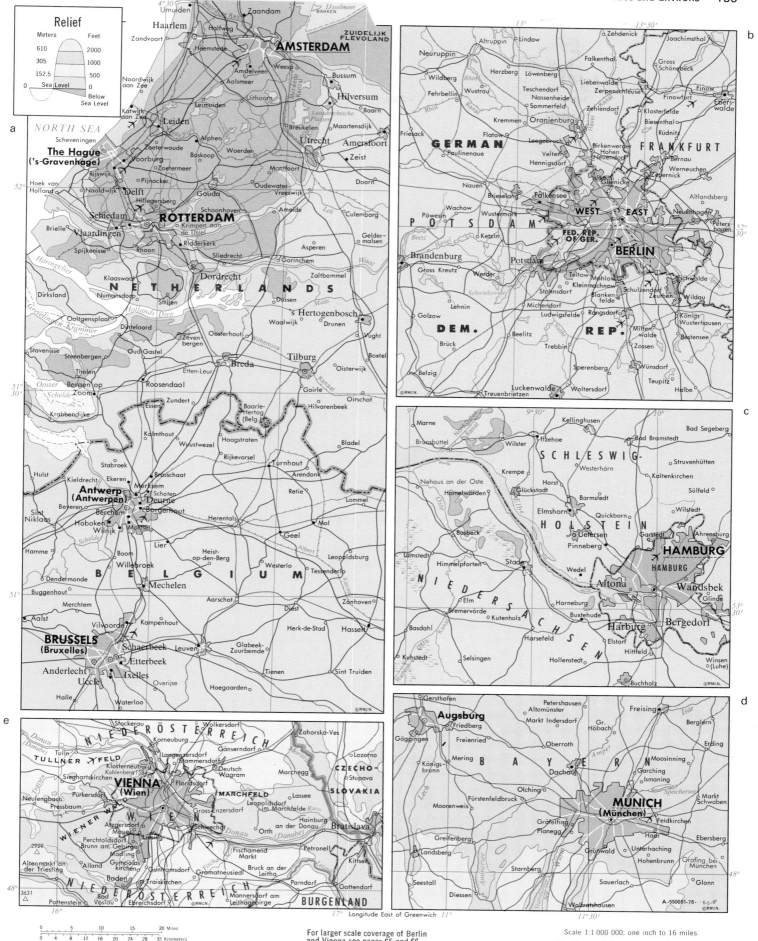

Relief

Meters	Feet
610	2000
305	1000
152.5	500
0	Sea Level	0
	Below Sea Level

a

NORTH SEA

IJmuiden
Zaandam
Haarlem
Zandvoort
Heemstede
Halfweg
Noordwijk aan Zee
Amstelveen
Aalsmeer
Uithoorn
AMSTERDAM
Weesp
Bussum
Hilversum
Baarn
Katwijk aan Zee
Leiden
Leimuiden
Maartensdijk
Amersfoort
Scheveningen
Voorburg
Alphen
Woerden
Utrecht
Zeist
The Hague ('s-Gravenhage)
Zoeterwoude
Boskoop
Zoetermeer
Montfoort
Doorn
Rijswijk
Pijnacker
Oudewater
Vreeswijk
Hoek van Holland
Naaldwijk
Delft
Hillegersberg
Gouda
Schoonhoven
Amerde
Culemborg
Schiedam
ROTTERDAM
Krimpen aan de IJssel
Asperen
Gelder-malsen
Brielle
Vlaardingen
Ridderkerk
Sliedrecht
Gorinchem
Zaltbommel
Spijkenisse
Rhoon
NETHERLANDS
Klaaswaal
Numansdorp
Dordrecht
Dussen
Waal
Stavenisse
Steenbergen
Oud Gastel
Strijen
Hollands Diep
Waalwijk
Drunen
's Hertogenbosch
Dirksland
Oosterhout
Vught
Ooltgensplaat
Dinteloord
Zeven-bergen
Etten-Leur
Breda
Tilburg
Boxtel
Ooster Schelde
Bergen op Zoom
Roosendaal
Oisterwijk
Tholen
Krabbendijke
Zundert
Goirle
Oirschot
Essen
Baarle-Hertog (Belg.)
Hilvarenbeek
Kalmthout
Hoogstraten
Bladel
Wuustwezel
Rijkevorsel
Brasschaat
Turnhout
Arendonk
Hulst
Stabroek
Schoten
Retie
Lommel
Kieldrecht
Ekeren
Merksem
Deurne
Beveren
Antwerp (Antwerpen)
Borgerhout
Herentals
Mol
Sint Niklaas
Hoboken
Berchem
Mortsel
Geel
Hamme
Wilrijk
Lier
Boom
Heist-op-den-Berg
Westerlo
Leopoldsburg
Dendermonde
Willebroek
BELGIUM
Tessenderlo
Buggenhout
Mechelen
Hasselt
Aalst
Merchtem
Aarschot
Zonhoven
Vilvoorde
Kampenhout
Diest
Herk-de-Stad
BRUSSELS (Bruxelles)
Schaerbeek
Leuven
Glabbeek-Zuurbemde
Anderlecht
Etterbeek
Tienen
Sint Truiden
Uccle
Ixelles
Halle
Overijse
Hoegaarden
Waterloo

e

Donau (Danube)
Stockerau
Wolkersdorf
NIEDERÖSTERREICH
Zahorska-Ves
Korneuburg
Tulln
Langenzersdorf
Gänserndorf
TULLNER FELD
Klosterneuburg
Stammersdorf
Lozorno
Sieghartskirchen
Kahlenberg 1584
Deutsch Wagram
Stupava
CZECHO-
Neulengbach
Floridsdorf
Marchegg
VIENNA (Wien)
SLOVAKIA
Pressbaum
Purkersdorf
MARCHFELD
Lassee
Bratislava
Pressbaum
WIENER WALD
Atzgersdorf
Mauer
Gross-Enzersdorf
Leopoldsdorf im Marchfelde
Perchtoldsdorf
Liesing
Hainburg an der Donau
Brunn am Gebirge
Schwechat
Orth
Petronell
2929
Gumpolds-kirchen
Fischamend Markt
Altenmarkt an der Triesting
Baden
Guntramsdorf
Bruck an der Leitha
Kittsee
Alland
Bad Vöslau
Gramatneusiedl
Parndorf
NIEDERÖSTERREICH
Traiskirchen
Mannersdorf am Leithagebirge
Gattendorf
3631
Pottenstein
Ebreichsdorf
BURGENLAND

b

Neuruppin
Altruppin
Lindow
Zehdenick
Joachimsthal
Wildberg
Herzberg
Löwenberg
Falkenthal
Gross Schönebeck
Fehrbellin
Wustrau
Teschendorf
Liebenwalde
Zerpenschleuse
Finowfurt
Finow
Eberswalde
GERMAN
Nassenheide
Sommerfeld
Zehlendorf
Klosterfelde
Kremmen
Oranienburg
Birkenwerder
Hohen Neuendorf
Biesenthal
Rüdnitz
Friesack
Flatow
Leegebruch
Bernau
Werneuchen
Nauen
Brieselang
Velten
Hennigsdorf
Glienicke
Zepernick
Wachow
WEST
EAST
Neuenhagen
POTSDAM
Wustermark
Falkensee
FRANKFURT
Päwesin
Ketzin
Altlandsberg
Beetz
FED. REP. OF GER.
Peters-hagen
Brandenburg
Werder
BERLIN
Gross Kreutz
Potsdam
Teltow
Mahlow
Eichwalde
Lehnin
Kleinmachnow
Schulzendorf
Zeuthen
Wildau
Golzow
Stahnsdorf
Blankenfelde
DEM.
Michendorf
Ludwigsfelde
Rangsdorf
Königs Wusterhausen
Brück
Beelitz
Mitten-walde
Bestensee
Belzig
Trebbin
Zossen
REP.
Wünsdorf
Sperenberg
Teupitz
Luckenwalde
Woltersdorf
Halbe
Treuenbrietzen

c

Marne
Kellinghusen
Bad Segeberg
Brunsbüttel
Wilster
Itzehoe
Bad Bramstedt
SCHLESWIG-
Westerhörn
Struvenhütten
Nehaus an der Oste
Krempe
Kaltenkirchen
Horst
Barmstedt
Sülfeld
Glückstadt
Hamelwörden
Elmshorn
Quickborn
Wilstedt
HOLSTEIN
Basbeck
Uetersen
Garstedt
Ahrensburg
Pinneberg
Lamstedt
Stade
HAMBURG
Himmelpforten
Wedel
HAMBURG
NIEDERSACHSEN
Altona
Wandsbek
Bremervörde
Horneburg
Glinde
Basdahl
Kutenholz
Buxtehude
Harburg
Bergedorf
Harsefeld
Elstorf
Kuhstedt
Selsingen
Hollenstedt
Hittfeld
Winsen (Luhe)
Buchholz

d

Gersthofen
Petershausen
Altomünster
Freising
Augsburg
Friedberg
Markt Indersdorf
Gr. Höbach
Bergkirchen
Göggingen
Freienried
Oberroth
Moosinning
Königs-brunn
Mering
Garching
Dachau
Ismaning
BAYERN
Olching
Erding
Moorenweis
Fürstenfeldbruck
MUNICH (München)
Feldkirchen
Greifenberg
Gräfelfing
Planegg
Haar
Ebersberg
Landsberg
Grünwald
Unterhaching
Hohenbrunn
Grafing bei München
Starnberg
Seestall
Sauerlach
Glonn
Diessen
Wolfratshausen

A-550051-76 — 6-6-9[?]

Scale 1:1 000 000; one inch to 16 miles.
Elevations and depressions are given in feet.

Longitude East of Greenwich

ICELAND

NORWEGIAN SEA

ARCTIC OCEAN

Arctic Circle

NORWAY

SWEDEN

FINLAND

SOVIET UNION

LAPLAND

Murmansk

GULF OF BOTHNIA

Helsinki

Tampere

Turku

STOCKHOLM

Uppsala

Norrköping

Linköping

Göteborg

Borås

Oslo

Bergen

Stavanger

Trondheim

DENMARK

COPENHAGEN

København

Odense

Esbjerg

Århus

Ålborg

BALTIC SEA

Tallinn

Riga

Kaliningrad

Gdańsk

Gdynia

Klaipėda

Liepāja

NORTH SEA

UNITED KINGDOM

SCOTLAND

Aberdeen

Dundee

Edinburgh

GLASGOW

Newcastle upon Tyne

Sunderland

Middlesbrough

Hartlepool

Carlisle

Belfast

NORTHERN IRELAND

IRELAND

BRITISH ISLES

HEBRIDES

SHETLAND IS. (Br.)

ORKNEY IS. (Br.)

FAEROE IS. (Den.)

Tórshavn

JAN MAYEN (Nor.)

Reykjavík

ATLANTIC OCEAN

DOGGER BANK

Relief

Meters	Feet
3050	10 000
1525	5000
610	2000
305	1000
152.5	500
0	Sea Level
152.5	Below Sea Level 500
1525	5000
3050	10 000

Scale 1: 10 000 000; one inch to 160 miles. Conic Projection

Elevations and depressions are given in feet

CZECHOSLOVAKIA
GERMANY, FEDERAL REPUBLIC OF
FRANCE
SPAIN
PORTUGAL
SWITZERLAND
ITALY
YUGOSLAVIA
HUNGARY
ALBANIA
ALGERIA
MOROCCO
TUNISIA
ENGLAND

BUDAPEST
VIENNA
PRAGUE
MUNICH
STUTTGART
FRANKFURT
COLOGNE
DÜSSELDORF
ESSEN
BRUSSELS
AMSTERDAM
The Hague
Rotterdam
LONDON
PARIS
Versailles
Orléans
Bordeaux
Toulouse
MONACO
Marseille
Toulon
Cannes
Nice
BARCELONA
ANDORRA
MADRID
Toledo
Valencia
Murcia
Cartagena
Almería
Málaga
Sevilla
Cádiz
LISBON
Porto
Coimbra
NAPLES
ROME
Vatican City
Palermo
Catania
Siracusa
Messina
Reggio di Calabria
Taranto
Brindisi
Bari
CORSICA (Fr.)
SARDINIA (It.)
Cagliari
Sassari
MALTA
Tirana
Algiers (Alger)
Oran
Constantine
Tunis
Bizerte
Tangiers
Melilla (Sp.)
Ceuta (Sp.)
Gibraltar (Br.)
Tétouan

ADRIATIC SEA
TYRRHENIAN SEA
LIGURIAN SEA
IONIAN SEA
MEDITERRANEAN SEA
BAY OF BISCAY
ENGLISH CHANNEL
BALEARES (Sp.)
MALLORCA
MENORCA
IBIZA
Palma

ATLAS MOUNTAINS
SIERRA MORENA
SIERRA NEVADA
CORDILLERA CANTABRICA

Longitude East of Greenwich
Longitude West of Greenwich

50   100   150   200   250   300 Miles
100   200   300   400   500 Kilometers

158

a

Same scale as main map

ATLANTIC

SHETLAND
St. Magnus Bay
ISLANDS
(Br.)
MAINLAND
Lerwick
FOULA
YELL

OCEAN
FAIR
ISLAND
SUMBURGH. HD.

WESTRAY
ROUSAY
N. RONALDSAY
SANDAY
STRONSAY
ORKNEY
Kirkwall
MAINLAND
ISLANDS
HOY
S. RONALDSAY
(Br.)
Pentland
Firth
DUNCANSBY HD.
Thurso
SCOTLAND

©RMCN.

Relief

Meters   Feet
610   2000
305   1000
152.5   500
0   Sea Level 0
152.5   500
1525 Below   5000
      Sea Level

A-559700-76 -8-7-13
COPYRIGHT BY
RAND McNALLY & COMPANY
MADE IN U.S.A.

Longitude West of Greenwich

Scale 1: 4 000 000; one inch to 64 miles. Conic Projec
Elevations and depressions are given in feet

10 20 30 40 50 60 70 80 90 100 110 120 Miles
20 40 60 80 100 120 140 160 180 200 Kilometers

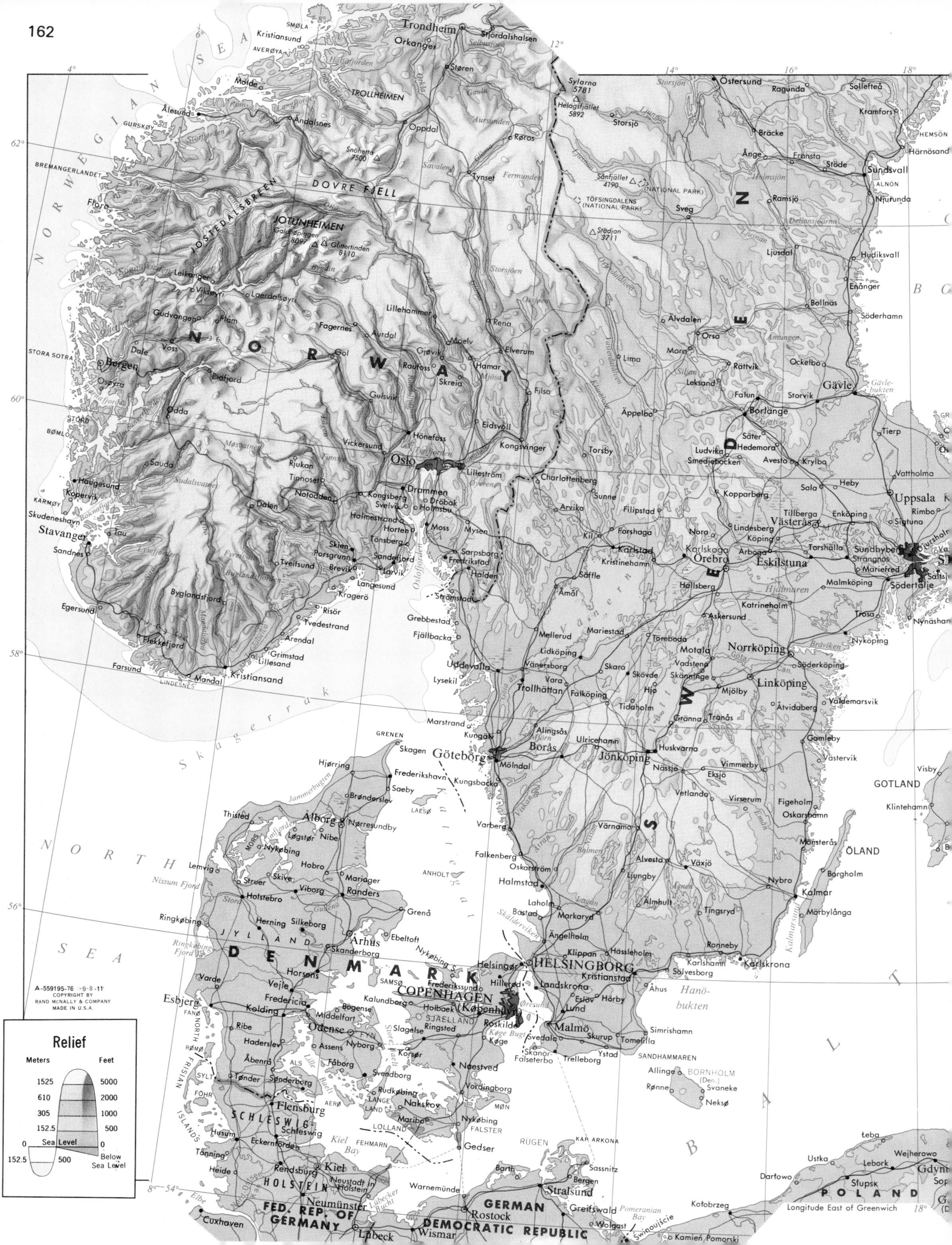
NORWEGIAN SEA
NORWAY
SWEDEN
DENMARK
NORTH SEA
Skagerrak
Kattegat
BALTIC
DOVRE FJELL
JOTUNHEIMEN
JOSTEDALSBREEN
TROLLHEIMEN
Galdhøpiggen 8097
Glittertinden 8110
Snøhetta 7500
Sylarna 5781
Helagsfjället 5892
Sånfjället 4190 (NATIONAL PARK)
TÖFSINGDALENS (NATIONAL PARK)
Stadjan 3711
Trondheim
Kristiansund
Orkanger
Støren
Molde
Ålesund
Åndalsnes
Oppdal
Røros
Tynset
Florø
Leikanger
Vikøyri
Laerdalsøyri
Gudvangen
Flåm
Fagernes
Aurdal
Lillehammer
Rena
Moelv
Gjøvik
Raufoss
Hamar
Elverum
Skreia
Bergen
Dale
Voss
Eidfjord
Os
Odda
Gulsvik
Hønefoss
Eidsvoll
Kongsvinger
Vickersund
Oslo
Lillestrøm
Rjukan
Tinnoset
Notodden
Kongsberg
Drammen
Drøbak
Svelvik
Holmestrand
Horten
Tønsberg
Moss
Mysen
Sarpsborg
Fredrikstad
Halden
Skien
Porsgrunn
Brevik
Sandefjord
Larvik
Langesund
Kragerø
Risør
Tvedestrand
Arendal
Grimstad
Lillesand
Kristiansand
Mandal
Farsund
Flekkefjord
Egersund
Stavanger
Sandnes
Haugesund
Kopervik
Skudeneshavn
Sauda
Dalen
Tveitsund
Byglandsfjord
LINDESNES
Östersund
Ragunda
Sollefteå
Kramfors
Härnösand
Bräcke
Ånge
Fränsta
Stöde
Sundsvall
Njurunda
Ramsjö
Sveg
Storsjö
Ljusdal
Hudiksvall
Enånger
Bollnäs
Söderhamn
Älvdalen
Orsa
Mora
Rättvik
Ockelbo
Gävle
Lima
Leksand
Falun
Storvik
Borlänge
Säter
Hedemora
Tierp
Ludvika
Smedjebacken
Avesta
Krylbo
Vattholma
Torsby
Charlottenberg
Sunne
Arvika
Filipstad
Kopparberg
Sala
Heby
Uppsala
Rimbo
Sigtuna
Tillberga
Enköping
Västerås
Lindesberg
Köping
Nora
Forshaga
Kil
Karlstad
Kristinehamn
Karlskoga
Örebro
Arboga
Eskilstuna
Torshälla
Sundbyberg
Strängnäs
Mariefred
Södertälje
Saltsjö
Malmköping
Säffle
Åmål
Hallsberg
Katrineholm
Askersund
Trosa
Nynäshamn
Mellerud
Mariestad
Töreboda
Nyköping
Lidköping
Vänersborg
Motala
Norrköping
Söderköping
Skara
Skövde
Vadstena
Skänninge
Linköping
Mjölby
Vara
Trollhättan
Falköping
Hjo
Tidaholm
Åtvidaberg
Valdemarsvik
Uddevalla
Lysekil
Strömstad
Grebbestad
Fjällbacka
Marstrand
Kungälv
Alingsås
Ulricehamn
Gränna
Tranås
Göteborg
Borås
Jönköping
Huskvarna
Gamleby
Västervik
Mölndal
Kungsbacka
Nässjö
Eksjö
Vimmerby
Vetlanda
Virserum
Figeholm
Oskarshamn
Visby
GOTLAND
Klintehamn
Varberg
Värnamo
Mönsterås
ÖLAND
Falkenberg
Oskarström
Alvesta
Växjö
Borgholm
Halmstad
Ljungby
Nybro
Kalmar
Laholm
Båstad
Markaryd
Älmhult
Tingsryd
Mörbylånga
Ängelholm
Klippan
Hässleholm
Ronneby
Karlshamn
Karlskrona
Sölvesborg
Helsingør
HELSINGBORG
Kristianstad
Åhus
Hanöbukten
Landskrona
Eslöv
Hörby
Lund
Malmö
Svedala
Skurup
Tomelilla
Simrishamn
Ystad
Trelleborg
Skanör-Falsterbo
SANDHAMMAREN
BORNHOLM (Den.)
Allinge
Rønne
Svaneke
Nexø
GRENEN
Skagen
Hjørring
Frederikshavn
Saeby
Brønderslev
LAESØ
Thisted
Ålborg
Nørresundby
Løgstør
Nibe
Nykøbing
Hobro
Lemvig
Struer
Skive
Viborg
Mariager
Randers
Holstebro
Grenå
Ringkøbing
Herning
Silkeborg
Århus
Ebeltoft
Skanderborg
ANHOLT
JYLLAND
Horsens
Varde
Vejle
Esbjerg
Fredericia
Kolding
SAMSØ
Frederikssund
Hillerød
COPENHAGEN (København)
Kalundborg
Holbaek
Roskilde
Køge
Bogense
Middelfart
Odense
FYN
SJAELLAND
Ringsted
Slagelse
Ribe
Haderslev
Assens
Nyborg
Korsør
Naestved
Åbenrå
Fåborg
ALS
Svendborg
Tønder
Sønderborg
Vordingborg
Rudkøbing
LANGELAND
Nakskov
MØN
Maribo
LOLLAND
Nykøbing
FALSTER
Gedser
FANØ
RØMØ
SYLT
FÖHR
NORTH FRISIAN ISLANDS
Flensburg
SCHLESWIG
Schleswig
Husum
Eckernförde
Tönning
Heide
Rendsburg
Kiel
Neustadt in Holstein
HOLSTEIN
Neumünster
FEHMARN
RÜGEN
KAP ARKONA
Sassnitz
Bergen
Barth
Stralsund
Greifswald
Warnemünde
Rostock
Wismar
Lübeck
Cuxhaven
Wolgast
Świnoujście
Kamień Pomorski
Kołobrzeg
Darłowo
Ustka
Słupsk
Lebork
Łeba
Wejherowo
Gdynia
POLAND
FED. REP. OF GERMANY
GERMAN DEMOCRATIC REPUBLIC
Longitude East of Greenwich
A-559195-76 -9-8-11
COPYRIGHT BY RAND MCNALLY & COMPANY MADE IN U.S.A.
Relief
Meters
Feet
1525
5000
610
2000
305
1000
152.5
500
0
Sea Level
0
152.5
500
Below Sea Level

Scale 1:4 000 000; one inch to 64 miles. Conic Projection
Elevations and depressions are given in feet.

NORTH SEA

DENMARK

BALTI C

SCHLESWIG-HOLSTEIN

Flensburg • Schleswig • Husum • Rendsburg • Eckernförde • Kiel • Neustadt in Holstein

Svendborg • Langeland • Rudkøbing • Nakskov • Nykøbing FALSTER • Gedser • MØN • LOLLAND

Sassnitz • RÜGEN • Bergen • Stralsund • Barth • Rostock • Greifswald • Wolgast

FRISIAN ISLANDS • HELGOLAND • Norderney • Wangerooge • Cuxhaven

Wilhelmshaven • Bremerhaven • Stade • HAMBURG • Lübeck • Wismar • Schwerin

MECKLENBURG

GERMAN DEMOCRATIC REPUBLIC (EAST GERMANY)

NETHERLANDS • AMSTERDAM • Groningen • Leeuwarden • Utrecht • Arnhem • Nijmegen

Oldenburg • Bremen • Delmenhorst • Verden • NIEDERSACHSEN • Celle • Uelzen

LÜNEBURGER HEIDE • Hannover • Braunschweig • Wolfsburg • Magdeburg • BRANDENBURG

Neubrandenburg • Neustrelitz • Neu Ruppin • Oranienburg • Potsdam • BERLIN • East Berlin • Frankfurt an der Oder

FEDERAL REPUBLIC

Münster • Osnabrück • Bielefeld • Herford • Detmold • Paderborn • Hildesheim

DÜSSELDORF • ESSEN • Dortmund • Duisburg • Bochum • Hagen • Wuppertal • Solingen

MÖNCHENGLADBACH • COLOGNE (Köln) • Bonn • Aachen • NORDRHEIN

Kassel • Göttingen • Nordhausen • HARZ • Halle • Leipzig • Dessau • Wittenberg • Cottbus

WESTFALEN • Siegen • Marburg an der Lahn • Giessen • WESTERWALD

THÜRINGEN • Eisenach • Gotha • Erfurt • Weimar • Jena • Gera • Zwickau

Dresden • Bautzen • Görlitz • Meissen • Freiberg • Karl-Marx-Stadt • ERZGEBIRGE

GERMANY

Koblenz • Wiesbaden • FRANKFURT AM MAIN • Hanau • Offenbach • Darmstadt

Mainz • HESSEN • Fulda • Schweinfurt • Würzburg • Bamberg • Bayreuth • Hof

RHEINLAND-PFALZ • LUXEMBOURG • Trier • SAARLAND • Saarbrücken • Kaiserslautern

Worms • Mannheim • Heidelberg • ODENWALD • Speyer • Ludwigshafen

(WEST GERMANY) • Karlsruhe • Pforzheim • STUTTGART • Esslingen • Ludwigsburg

Erlangen • Fürth • Nürnberg • Schwabach • Amberg • Weiden • Regensburg

FRANCE • Strasbourg • Baden-Baden • Tübingen • Reutlingen • Ulm • Neu Ulm

BADEN • WÜRTTEMBERG • Heidenheim • Augsburg • Ingolstadt • Landshut

BAYERN (BAVARIA) • Straubing • Passau • Deggendorf

Freiburg • SCHWARZWALD • Tuttlingen • Ravensburg • Kempten • Memmingen

Basel • Schaffhausen • Konstanz • Friedrichshafen • Lindau • Bregenz • MUNICH (München)

Dachau • Freising • Rosenheim • Bad Tölz • Traunstein • Salzburg • Linz

SWITZERLAND • Zürich • Sankt Gallen • VORARLBERG • Feldkirch • Bludenz

LIECHTENSTEIN • Innsbruck • Kufstein • SALZBURG • OBERÖSTERREICH • Wels • Steyr

VIENNA (Wien) • St. Pölten • Wiener Neustadt

A U S T R I A • Schwaz • HOHE TAUERN • NIEDERE TAUERN • STEIERMARK

KÄRNTEN • Villach • Klagenfurt • Leoben • Bruck • Graz

Bolzano • Trento • Merano • Udine • YUGOSLAVIA • Maribor

BÖHMERWALD (BOHEMIAN FOREST) • Plzeň • PRAGUE (Praha) • Kladno • Kolín

C Z E C H O S L O V A K I A • BOHEMIA • České Budějovice • Tábor • Jihlava • Brno

Litoměřice • Most • Teplice • Ústí nad Labem • Liberec • Jelenia Góra • Wałbrzych

Hradec Králové • Pardubice

P O L A N D • Szczecin (Stettin) • Stargard Szczeciński • Gorzów Wlkp. • Zielona Góra

Legnica • POMERANIA

Scale 1:4 000 000; one inch to 64 miles. Conic Projection
Elevations and depressions are given in feet.

Continued on pages 166-167
Continued on pages 170-171

Longitude East of Greenwich

COPYRIGHT BY RAND McNALLY & COMPANY, MADE IN U.S.A.

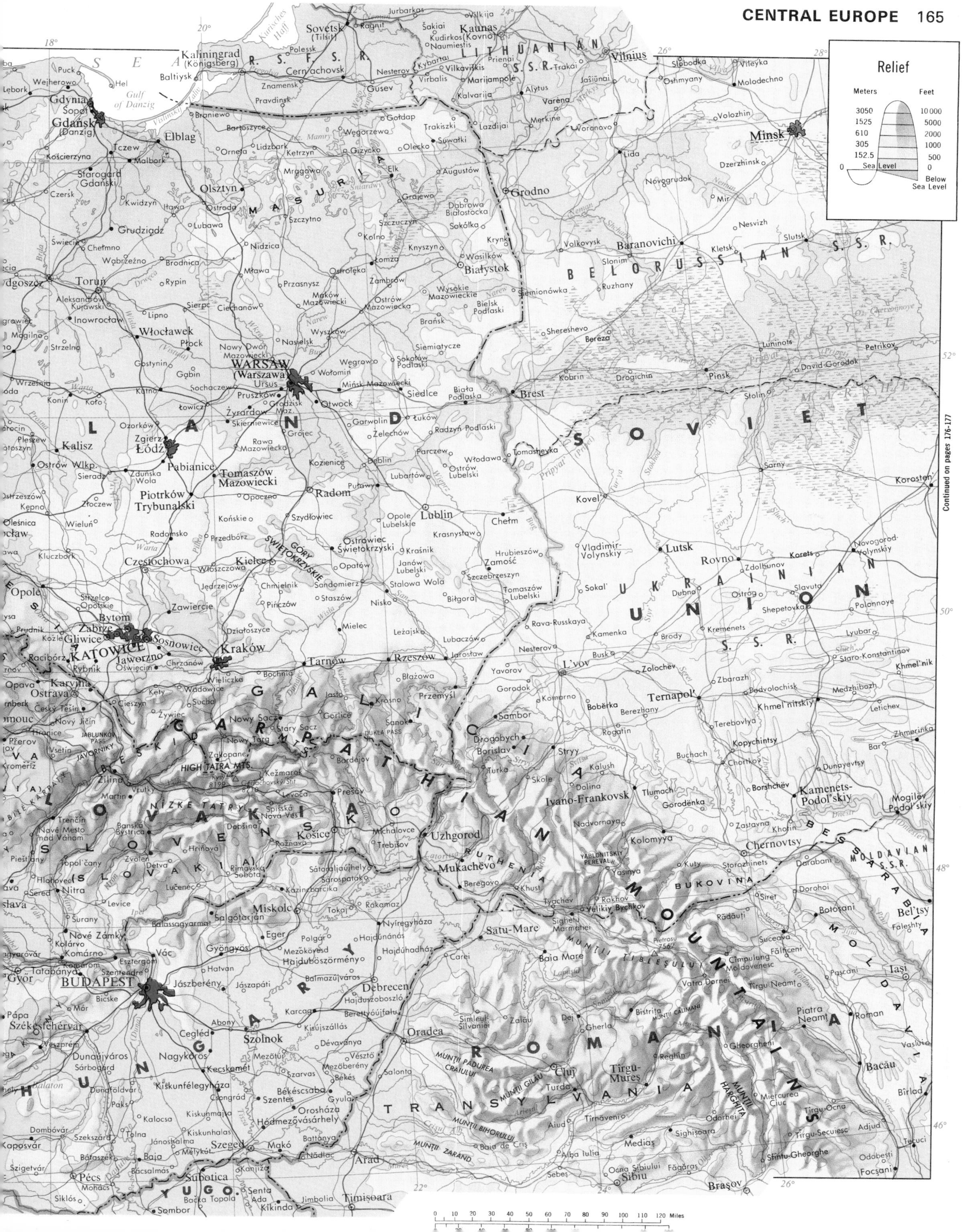

Relief

Meters	Feet
3050	10 000
1525	5000
610	2000
305	1000
152.5	500
0 Sea Level	Sea Level
	Below Sea Level

Continued on pages 176-177

SEA

Gulf of Danzig

R.S.F.S.R.

LITHUANIAN S.S.R.

Vilnius

Minsk

BELORUSSIAN S.S.R.

SOVIET

UNION

UKRAINIAN S.S.R.

P O L A N D

Kaliningrad (Königsberg)

Sovetsk (Tilsit)

Kaunas

Gdynia
Sopot
Gdańsk (Danzig)
Puck
Wejherowo
Hel
Baltiysk
Lebork
Elblag
Malbork
Tczew
Starogard Gdański
Kościerzyna
Czersk
Świecie
Chełmno
Grudziądz
Toruń
Bydgoszcz
Olsztyn
Szczytno
Nidzica
Mława
Ciechanów
Płock
Włocławek
Warsaw (Warszawa)
Łódź
Pabianice
Zgierz
Kalisz
Radom
Lublin
Kielce
Częstochowa
Katowice
Kraków
Tarnów
Rzeszów
Przemyśl
L'vov
Ternopol
Lutsk
Rovno
Kovel
Brest
Białystok
Grodno
Pinsk
Baranovichi
Minsk

MASURIA

GALICIA

CARPATHIAN MOUNTAINS

SLOVAKIA

HIGH TATRA MTS.

HUNGARY

BUDAPEST

Miskolc
Debrecen
Szeged
Arad
Oradea

ROMANIA

TRANSYLVANIA

Cluj
Tirgu-Mures
Sibiu
Braşov
Bacău
Iaşi

BUKOVINA

Chernovtsy

MOLDAVIAN S.S.R.

YUGO.

0 10 20 30 40 50 60 70 80 90 100 110 120 Miles

Relief

Meters		Feet
3050		10 000
1525		5000
610		2000
305		1000
152.5		500
Sea Level		0
152.5		500
1525		5000

UNITED KINGDOM

Honiton · Exeter · Dorchester · Poole · Southampton · Worthing · Hove · Folkestone · Dover · Dunkerque · Roeselare · Gent · Aalst · Mechelen

BELGIUM · BRUSSE

Launceston · Exmouth · Weymouth · Bournemouth · Cowes · Newport · ISLE OF WIGHT · Portsmouth · Chichester · Brighton · Lewes · Hastings · Bexhill · Eastbourne · Boulogne-sur-Mer · Étaples · Berck · Calais · St. Omer · Armentières · Ieper · Kortrijk · Anderlecht · Nivelles

Plymouth · Torquay (Torbay) · Dartmouth · START POINT

ENGLISH

CHANNEL

Str. of Dover

Lille · Tourcoing · Roubaix · Valenciennes · Mons · Charleroi

Béthune · Bruay-en-Artois · Douai · Denain · Hautmont · Maubeuge

Arras · Crécy-en-Ponthieu · Albert · Bapaume · Cambrai · Fourmies · Hirson

C. DE LA HAGUE · ALDERNEY · GUERNSEY · St. Peter Port · SARK · CHANNEL ISLANDS (Br.) · JERSEY · St. Helier

Cherbourg · PTE. DE BARFLEUR · Valognes · Carentan · Baie de la Seine · Bayeux · Saint-Lô · Caen · Lisieux · Trouville · Honfleur · Pont-Audemer · Rouen · Gisors · Beauvais · Compiègne · Creil · Soissons · Laon · Rethel · Vouziers · ARGONN

Fécamp · Bolbec · Yvetot · Le Havre · Elbeuf · Louviers · Vernon · Mantes-la-Jolie · Pontoise · Meaux · Château-Thierry · Épernay · Reims · Châlons-sur-Marne · Vitry-le-François

St. Valéry-sur-Somme · Dieppe · Le Tréport · Neufchâtel-en-Bray · Montdidier · Roye · Amiens · Corbie · Péronne · St. Quentin · Charleville-Mézières · Sedan

PICARDIE · PAYS DE BRAY

NORMANDIE · Conde · Flers · COLLINES DE NORMANDIE · Argentan · L'Aigle · Dreux · Évreux · St. Germain-en-Laye · Versailles · Boulogne-Billancourt · Corbeil-Essonnes · Romilly-sur-Seine · Arcis-sur-Aube · Joinville · Troyes

St. Pol-de-Léon · Morlaix · Guingamp · St. Brieuc · Dinard · St. Malo · Golfe de St. Malo · Granville · Avranches · Fougères · Vitré · Alençon · Nogent-le-Rotrou · Chartres · Rambouillet · Étampes · Fontainebleau · Montereau-faut-Yonne · Nemours · Sens · Joigny · Auxerre · Montbard

I. D'OUESSANT · Landerneau · MTS. D'ARRÉE · Carhaix-Plouguer · Quimper · BRETAGNE · Pontivy · Montfort · Rennes · Laval · Le Mans · Sablé-sur-Sarthe · La Flèche · Vendôme · Blois · Orléans · Gien · Briare · Cosne-sur-Loire · Clamecy · Avallon · MORVAN · Dijon · CÔTE D'OR

Brest · Douarnenez · Audierne · PTE. DU RAZ · Pont-l'Abbé · Concarneau · ÎLES DE GLÉNAN · ÎLE DE GROIX · Lorient · Hennebont · Vannes · Redon · Châteaubriant · Châteaugontier · SOLOGNE · Romorantin-Lanthenay · Nevers · Autun · Le Creusot

Quimperlé · Ploërmel · Château-Gontier · Sablé · La Flèche

ÎLE DE NOIRMOUTIER · Pornic · Nantes · Angers · Trélazé · Saumur · Tours · Amboise · Vierzon · Mehun-sur-Yèvre · Bourges · St. Amand-Mont Rond · Paray-le-Monial · Cluny

Quiberon · BELLE-ÎLE · St. Nazaire · Chemillé · Cholet · Thouars · Loudun · Chinon · Loches · Descartes · Issoudun · St. Florent-sur-Cher · Montceau

FRANCE

ÎLE D'YEU · L. de Grand Lieu · La Roche-sur-Yon · Bressuire · Parthenay · HAUTEURS DE GÂTINE · Châtellerault · Le Blanc · Argenton-sur-Creuse · Châteauroux · Châteaumeillant · Moulins · Digoin

Les Sables-d'Olonne · Fontenay-le-Comte · Luçon · Poitiers · Montmorillon · Montluçon · Commentry · Vichy · Roanne · Villefranche

ÎLE DE RÉ · La Rochelle · Surgères · Rochefort · St. Jean-d'Angély · Ruffec · Confolens · Guéret · Aubusson · Riom · Thiers · Tarare

BAY OF BISCAY · Marennes · La Tremblade · Saintes · Cognac · Charente · Royan · Barbezieux · Angoulême · St. Junien · Limoges · Ussel · Issoire · AUVERGNE · Clermont-Ferrand · Villeurbanne

ÎLE D'OLÉRON · Jonzac · PLATEAUX DU LIMOUSIN · St. Yrieix-la-Perche · Bort-les-Orgues · Puy de Sancy 6185 · Ambert · Montbrison · St. Chamond · Firminy · St. Étienne · Annonay · Yssingeaux

Blaye-et-Ste. Luce · Coutras · Périgueux · Brive-la-Gaillarde · Tulle · Argentat · Murat · Plomb du Cantal 6076 · St. Flour · Le Puy · Romans · VALEN

Blanquefort · Mérignac · Pessac · Libourne · Dordogne · MASSIF · Mt. Mézenc 5751 · Privas · Aubenas · Le Teil

Arcachon · Bassin d'Arcachon · Bègles · Bordeaux · Bergerac · Salat-la-Canéda · Aurillac · CENTRAL · Langogne

La Teste-de-Buch · Étang de Cazaux · La Réole · Marmande · Lot · Cahors · Figeac · Decazeville · Aubin · Mende · Alès · Bagnols-sur-Cèze

Étang de Carcans · LANDES · Langon · Tonneins · Villeneuve-sur-Lot · Villefranche-de-Rouergue · Rodez · Millau · Avignon

Labouheyre · Étang de Biscarosse · Agen · Moissac · Castelsarrasin · Carmaux · Gaillac · Albi · St. Affrique · CÉVENNES · Vigan · Lodève · Nîmes · Beaucaire

Nérac · Condom · Montauban · GASCOGNE · Mont-de-Marsan · Aire-sur-l'Adour · Auch · Toulouse · Castres · Bédarieux · Montpellier · Lunel

Dax · Adour · Tarbes · Muret · Baziège · Castelnaudary · Pézenas · Béziers · Sète

Biarritz · Bayonne · Salies-de-Béarn · Pau · St. Gaudens · Pamiers · Carcassonne · Narbonne · Agde · Golfe du

St. Jean-de-Luz · Irún · Oloron-Ste. Marie · Lourdes · Bagnères-de-Bigorre · St. Girons · Foix · Limoux · Sigean

Ronceveaux · Laruns · Bagnères-de-Luchon · Tarascon · Quillan · Rivesaltes · Perpignan

Pamplona · Jaca · Mt. Perdido 11007 · Pico de Aneta 11168 · ANDORRA · Andorra · Ax-les-Thermes · Prades · Céret · Port Vendres

Tafalla · Boltaña · PYRÉNÉES · SPAIN · Longitude West of Greenwich · Longitude East of Greenwich · C. DE CREUS

A-550900-76-87-8-10¹
COPYRIGHT BY
RAND McNALLY & COMPANY
MADE IN U.S.A.

a

Miramas · Équilles · Aix-en-Provence · St. Chamas · Istres · Berre-l'Étang · Cognac · Gardanne · Simiane · Étang de Berre · Marignane · Vitrolles · Port-de-Bouc · Martigues · Lavéra · Châteauneuf · L'Estaque · Allauch · La Couronne · Carry-le-Rouet · Penne-sur-Huveaune · Carro · Sausset-les-Pins · Marseille · Mazargues · La Madrague · COL DE LA GINESTE 1073

Golfe du Lion

MEDITERRANEAN SEA

Scale 1:1 000 000

0 · 5 · 10 Miles
0 · 4 · 8 · 12 · 16 Kilometers

©RMcN.

Scale 1:4 000 000; one inch to 64 miles. Conic Projecti
Elevations and depressions are given in feet

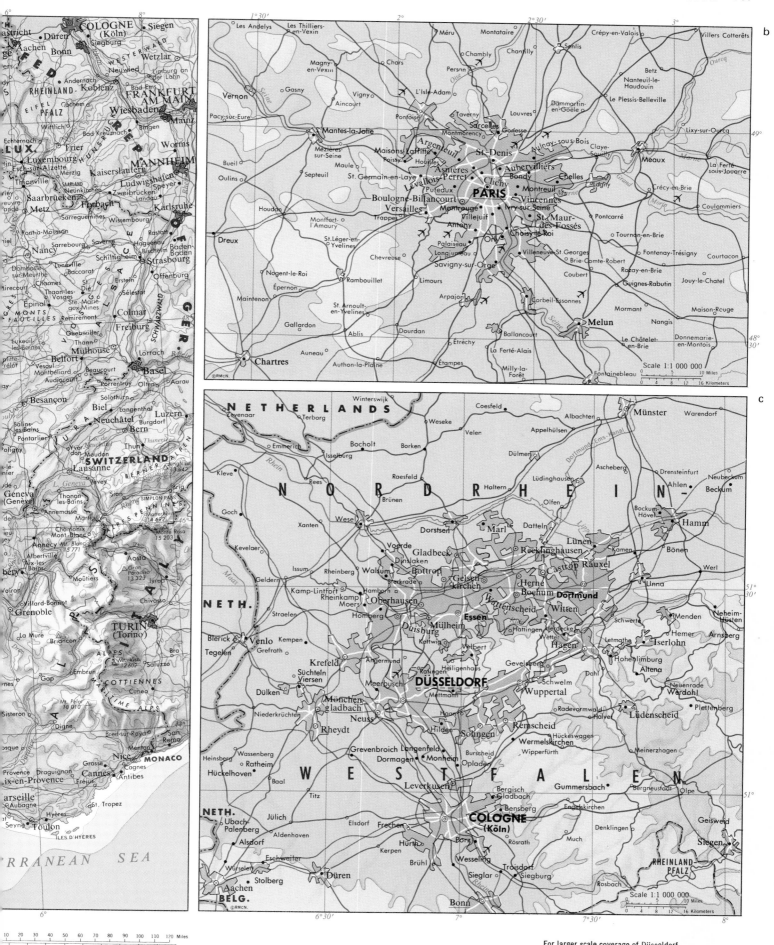

b

c

For larger scale coverage of Düsseldorf and Paris see pages 63 and 64.

Scale 1:4 000 000, one inch to 64 miles. Conic Projection
Elevations and depressions are given in feet

Longitude West of Greenwich

Main map (Spain, Portugal, France, Algeria)

FRANCE

Marsan · Condom · Gaillac · Albi
Pau · Tarbes · Auch · Verdun · Gimone · Baïse · Castres · Bédarieux · Montpellier
· Oloron · Lourdes · St. Gaudens · Toulouse · Muret · Castelnaudary · Pézenas · Méze · Lodève · Sète
· St. Girons · Pamiers · Carcassonne · Limoux · Béziers · Narbonne · Martigues · Miramas · Arles
PYRÉNÉES · St. Girons · Foix · Quillan · Rivesaltes · Sigean · Golfe du Lion
· Bagnères-de-Bigorre · Bagnères-de-Luchon · Pico de Aneto 10720 · Ax-les-Thermes · Prades · Perpignan · Port Vendres
· Puerto de Somport 5354 · ANDORRA · Andorra · Céret · CABO DE CREUS
· Boltaña · Ripoll · Olot · Golfo de Rosas
· SA. DE GUARA · Huesca · Barbastro · Berga · Manlleu · Vich · Gerona · La Bisbal
· Monzón · Balaguer · Manresa · Granollers · San Feliú de Guixols
· Tamarite de Litera · Lérida · Tárrega · Igualada · Sabadell · Tarrasa · Mataró · Calella
· Sariñena · Fraga · Barjas Blancas · Montblanch · Vilafranca del Panadés · Sabadell · Badalona
· Caspe · Alcañiz · Gandesa · Valls · Reus · BARCELONA
· Villanueva y Geltrú · Tarragona
· Morella · Tortosa · Amposta · CABO DE TORTOSA
· San Mateo · Alcanar · Vinaroz · Benicarló
· Peñagolosa 5952 · Torreblanca
CATALUÑA
· Castellón de la Plana · Villarreal · Burriana · COLUMBRETES · BALEARIC SEA
· Onda · Vall de Uxó · ISLAS BALEARES (Sp) · MENORCA (MINORCA)
· Liria · Sagunto · Golfo de Valencia · Ciudadela · Mahón
· Valencia · Catarroja · Pollensa · Ba. de Alcudia
· Sueca · Cullera · Sóller · La Puebla · Inca
· Játiva · Gandía · Oliva · Palma · Manacor · Felanitx
· Onteniente · Pego · Denia · Jávea · Ba. de Palma · Santany
· Alcoy · Cocentaina · CABO DE LA NAO · MALLORCA (MAJORCA) · CAPE SALINAS
· Jijona · Villajoyosa · IBIZA (IVIZA) · CABRERA
· Alicante · San Antonio Abad · Sta. Eulalia del Río
· Elche · Ibiza · FORMENTERA
· Segura · Mar Menor · CABO DE PALOS
· Torrevieja · MEDITERRANEAN SEA

ALGERIA
· Mostaganem · FERRAT · Arzew · Oued Rhiou · Dellys
· Oued Tlelat · Mohammadia · Mascara · ATLAS MOUNTAINS · Algiers (Alger) · Boudouaou
· Sebkra d'Oran · Ighil Izane · Rhiou · Cherchell · Boufarik · El Arba
· Tagdempt · Ksar Chellala · Ténès · El Affroun · Blida · Bouira
· Mercier-Lacombe · Carnot · Miliana · Médéa · Saur el Ghozlane
· Zahrez Chergui · Ksar el Boukhari · Sidi Aïssa
· Aïn Oussera · Bouira-Sahary

Longitude East of Greenwich

20 40 60 80 100 120 Miles
20 40 60 80 100 120 140 160 180 200 Kilometers

a. Madrid
S. Lorenzo de El Escorial · SA. DEL HOYO 4606 · Colmenar Viejo · Fuente el Saz · Algete
El Escorial · Galapagar · S. Sebastián de los Reyes · Alcobendas
Valdemorillo · Las Rozas de Madrid · El Pardo · Barajas de Madrid · Torrejón de Ardoz · Alcalá de Henares
Pozuelo de Alarcón · Fuencarral · S. Fernando de Henares
Brunete · **MADRID** · Vicálvaro · Campo Real
Villaviciosa de Odón · Alcorcón · Vallecas · Arganda
Navalcarnero · Leganés · Móstoles · Getafe · Loeches · Valdilecha · Carabaña
Parla · Pinto · S. Martín de la Vega · Morata de Tajuña · Tielmes · Perales de Tajuña
Scale 1:1 000 000
0 4 8 12 16 Miles
0 4 8 12 16 Kilometers ©RMcN

b. Lisbon
Mafra · Cheleiros · Alhandra · Samora Correia
São João das Lampas · Montelavar · Almargem do Bispo · Alverca
Colares · Sintra · Loures · Sacavém a Moscavide
CABO DA ROCA · Queluz · Odivelas · Alcóchete
Alcabideche · Barcarena · Amadora · **LISBON (Lisboa)** · Montijo
Cascais · Estoril · Carnaxide · Oeiras · Rio Tejo · Almada · Moita
ATLANTIC OCEAN · Costa de Caparica · Barreiro · Seixal · Alhos Vedros · Pinhal Novo
· Coina · Palmela
· Setúbal
Scale 1:1 000 000
0 5 10 Miles
0 4 8 12 16 Kilometers
9°30' · CABO ESPICHEL · Sesimbra · Ba. de Setúbal · Rio Sado · 9° · Comporta ©RMcN

c. Naples
Frattamaggiore · Acerra · Nola · Avellino
Marano di Napoli · Afragola · Pomigliano d'Arco · Monteforte Irpino
NAPLES (Napoli) · Somma Vesuviana · S. Giuseppe Vesuviano 3710
Pozzuoli · Bacoli · Portici · Vesuvio 3842 · Sarno · Mercato S. Severino
I. DI PROCIDA · C. MISENO · Torre del Greco · Nocera Inf. · Cava dei Tirreni
Procida · Torre Annunziata · Pompeii Ruins · Angri · Salerno
Forio · Ischia 2585 · Castellammare di Stabia · Gragnano
I. D'ISCHIA · Golfo di Napoli · TYRRHENIAN SEA · Sorrento · Amalfi
Scale 1:1 000 000
0 5 10 Miles
0 4 8 12 16 Kilometers · I. DI CAPRI 1932 · Capri · PUNTA CAMPANELLA · Golfo di Salerno ©RMcN

d. Rome
Pyrgi · Monterotondo
Caere · Cerveteri · Veio · Mentana · Guidonia
Ladispoli · **ROME (Roma)** · Tivoli · Villa Adriana
Fregene · **VATICAN CITY** · Zagarolo
Fiumicino · Frascati
Ostia Antica · Marino · COLLI ALBANI 3114 · Genzano di Roma
Lido di Roma · Laurentum · Albano Laziale
Pomezia · Lanúvio · Velletri
TYRRHENIAN SEA · Aprilia · Cisterna di Latina
AGRO PONTINO
Scale 1:1 000 000
0 5 10 Miles
0 4 8 12 16 Kilometers · Anzio · Nettuno ©RMcN

For larger scale coverage of Lisbon, Madrid, and Rome see pages 65 and 66.

Continued on pages 164-165

Continued on pages 166-167

Scale 1:4 000 000; one inch to 64 miles. Conic Projection
Elevations and depressions are given in feet

Relief

Feet 5000 2000 1000 500 0
Meters 1525 610 305 152.5 Sea Level
0 152.5 500

Cities and Towns

0 to 50,000 500,000 to 1,000,000
50,000 to 500,000 1,000,000 and over

Scale 1:4 000 000; one inch to 64 miles. Conic Proje
Elevations and depressions are given in feet

Scale 1:20 000 000; one inch to 315 mil
Lambert's Azimuthal, Equal Area Projec
Elevations and depressions are given in

Cities
and
Towns

0 to 50,000   500,000 to 1,000,000
50,000 to 500,000   1,000,000 and over

Ohskaya Guba

WESTERN SIBERIAN LOWLAND

KARA SEA

Kara Strait

KHREBET PAY-KHOY

NOVAYA ZEMLYA

PECHORA BASIN

Vorkuta

Arctic Circle

URAL

U R A L   M T S.

PECHORA

Ust'-Tsil'ma

Pechora

MALOZEMEL'SKAYA TUNDRA

Nar'yan-Mar

KARA SEA

ARCTIC OCEAN

BARENTS SEA

KOLGUYEV

P-OV KANIN

M KANIN NOS

KOMI A.S.S.R.

Ukhta

Syktyvkar

Kotlas

Mezen'

Pinega

Arkhangel'sk (Arkhangel)

Northern Dvina

Shenkursk

Vel'sk

Velikiy Ustyug

Solvychegodsk

Nikol'sk

WHITE SEA

KOL'SKIY P-OV (KOLA PEN)

Onega

Lake Onega

Onega

Kargopol'

Vytegra

Pudozh

NORWAY

NORD KAPP

MAGERØY

SORØY

Hammerfest

Vardø

Vadsø

Kirkenes

Pechenga

Polyarnyy

Murmansk

Monchegorsk

Kandalaksha

Kirovsk

LAPLAND

Lake Onega

Medvezhegorsk

Petrozavodsk

KARELIAN A.S.S.R.

Kem'

Belomorsk

Segezha

SWEDEN

FINLAND

Oulu

Kuopio

Tampere

Helsinki

GULF OF FINLAND

Vyborg

Kronshtadt

Pushkin

LENINGRAD

Novgorod

Pskov

ESTONIAN S.S.R.

Tallinn

Tartu

Pärnu

Narva

BALTIC SEA

HIIUMAA (DAGÖ)

SAAREMAA (EZEL)

LATVIAN S.S.R.

Riga

LITHUANIAN S.S.R.

Klaipeda

Šiauliai

Kaunas

Vilnius

RUSSIAN S.F.S.R.

MOSCOW (Moskva)

GORKI

Dzerzhinsk

Vladimir

Kovrov

Murom

Ryazan'

Kolomna

Serpukhov

Podol'sk

Rybinsk

Yaroslavl'

Rostov

Ivanovo

Kostroma

Kirov

Vologda

Cherepovets

Kalinin (Tver')

Smolensk

Minsk

VALDAI HILLS

Velikiye Luki

Vitebsk

TATAR A.S.S.R.

Kazan'

CHUVASH A.S.S.R.

Cheboksary

MARI A.S.S.R.

Yoshkar-Ola

UDMURT A.S.S.R.

Izhevsk

Glazov

SVERDLOVSK

BASHKIR A.S.S.R.

Ufa

Chelyabinsk

Nizhniy Tagil

Perm'

Magnitogorsk

Continued on pages 156-157

Relief

Feet: 10000 5000 2000 1000 500 0 Below Sea Level

Meters: 3050 1525 610 305 152.5 0 Sea Level 152.5 1525 3050 500 5000 10000

0 50 100 150 200 250 300 Miles

0 100 200 300 400 500 Kilometers

Scale 1:10 000 000; one inch to 160 miles. Conic Projection
Elevations and depressions are given in feet.

Continued on pages 158-159

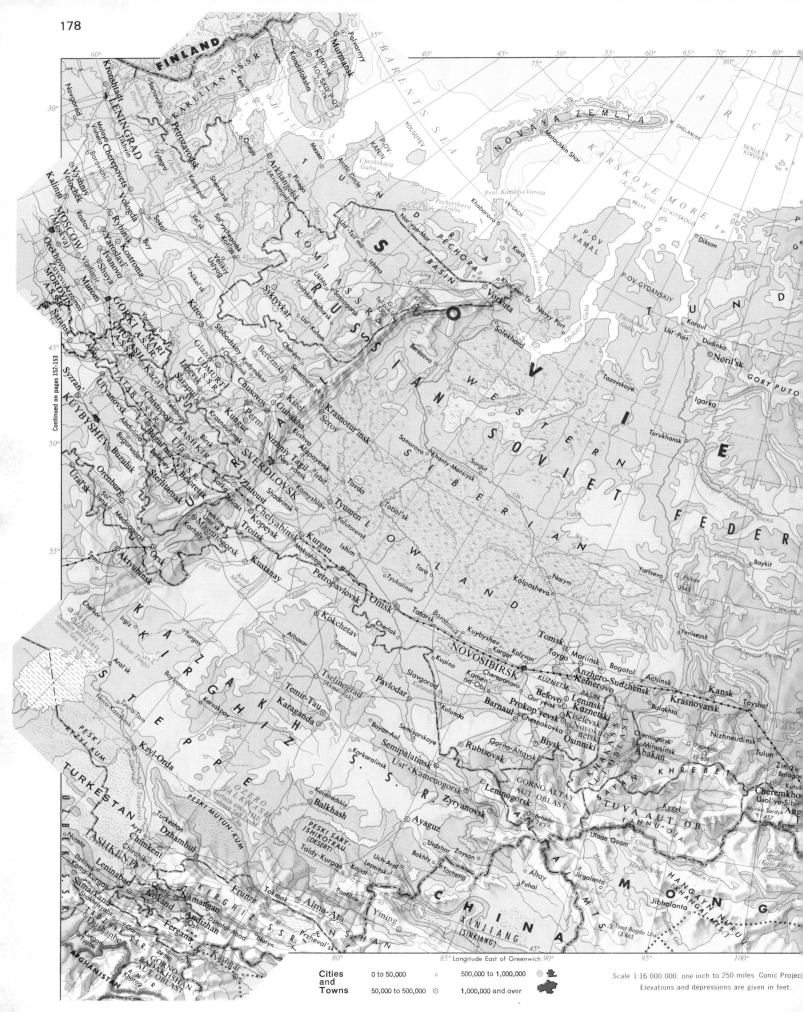

Relief

Meters	Feet
3050	10 000
1525	5000
610	2000
305	1000
152.5	500
0	Sea Level
152.5	500
1525	5000
3050	10 000

A-579300-76
COPYRIGHT BY
RAND M¢NALLY & COMPANY
MADE IN U.S.A.

Continued on pages 194-195

50 100   200   300   400   500 Miles
100   200   400   600   800 Kilometers

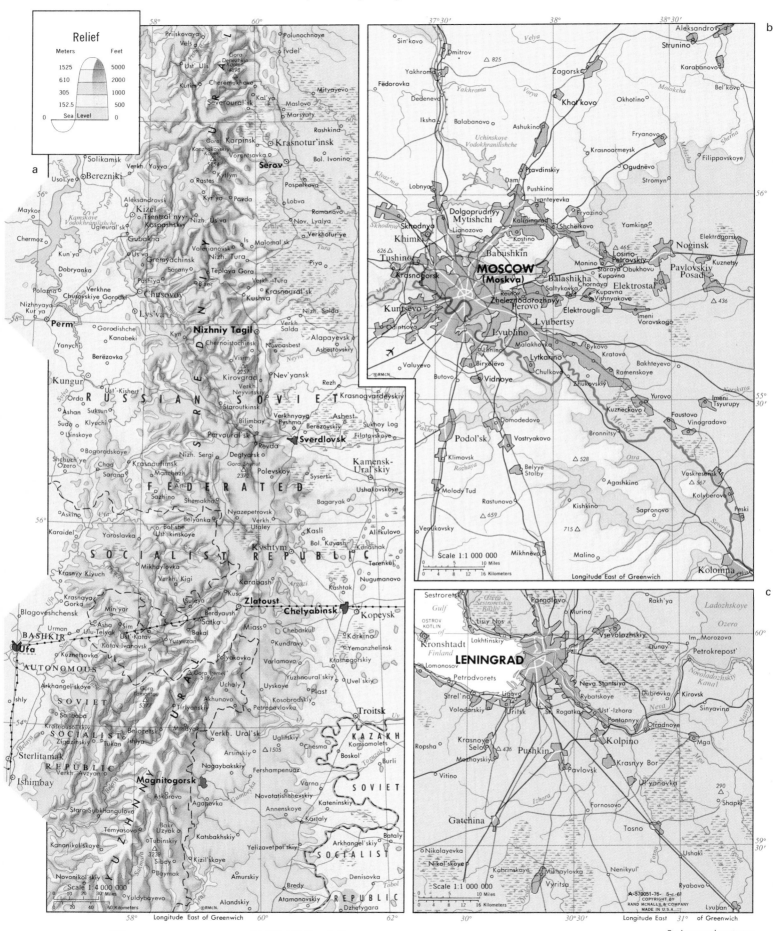

Relief

Meters	Feet
1525	5000
610	2000
305	1000
152.5	500
Sea Level	0

Scale 1:4 000 000

Scale 1:1 000 000

Scale 1:1 000 000

Longitude East of Greenwich

Longitude East of Greenwich

Longitude East of Greenwich

Cities and Towns

| | 0 to 50,000 | 500,000 to 1,000,000 |
| | 50,000 to 500,000 | 1,000,000 and over |

For larger scale coverage of Moscow see page 66.

A-570051-76 6-1-61
COPYRIGHT BY
RAND McNALLY & COMPANY
MADE IN U.S.A.

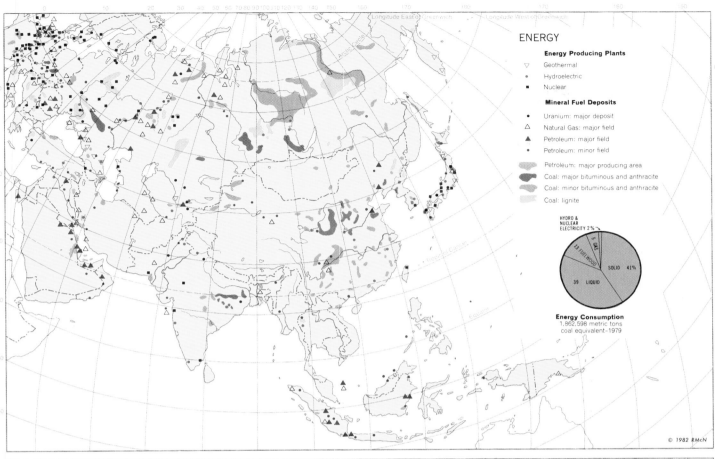

ENERGY

Energy Producing Plants

▽ Geothermal

• Hydroelectric

■ Nuclear

Mineral Fuel Deposits

• Uranium: major deposit

△ Natural Gas: major field

▲ Petroleum: major field

• Petroleum: minor field

Petroleum: major producing area

Coal: major bituminous and anthracite

Coal: minor bituminous and anthracite

Coal: lignite

HYDRO &
NUCLEAR
ELECTRICITY 2%

GAS 5

13 FUELWOOD

SOLID 41%

39 LIQUID

Energy Consumption
1,862,598 metric tons
coal equivalent-1979

© 1982 RMcN

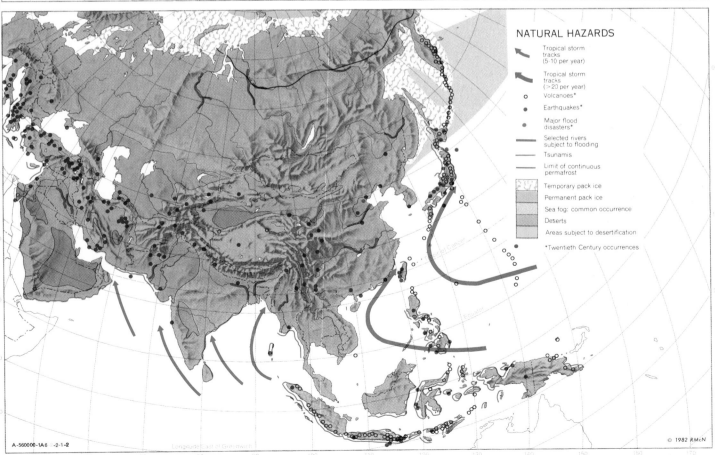

NATURAL HAZARDS

Tropical storm
tracks
(5-10 per year)

Tropical storm
tracks
(>20 per year)

○ Volcanoes*

• Earthquakes*

• Major flood
disasters*

Selected rivers
subject to flooding

Tsunamis

Limit of continuous
permafrost

Temporary pack ice

Permanent pack ice

Sea fog: common occurrence

Deserts

Areas subject to desertification

*Twentieth Century occurrences

A-560000-1A6 -2-1-2

© 1982 RMcN

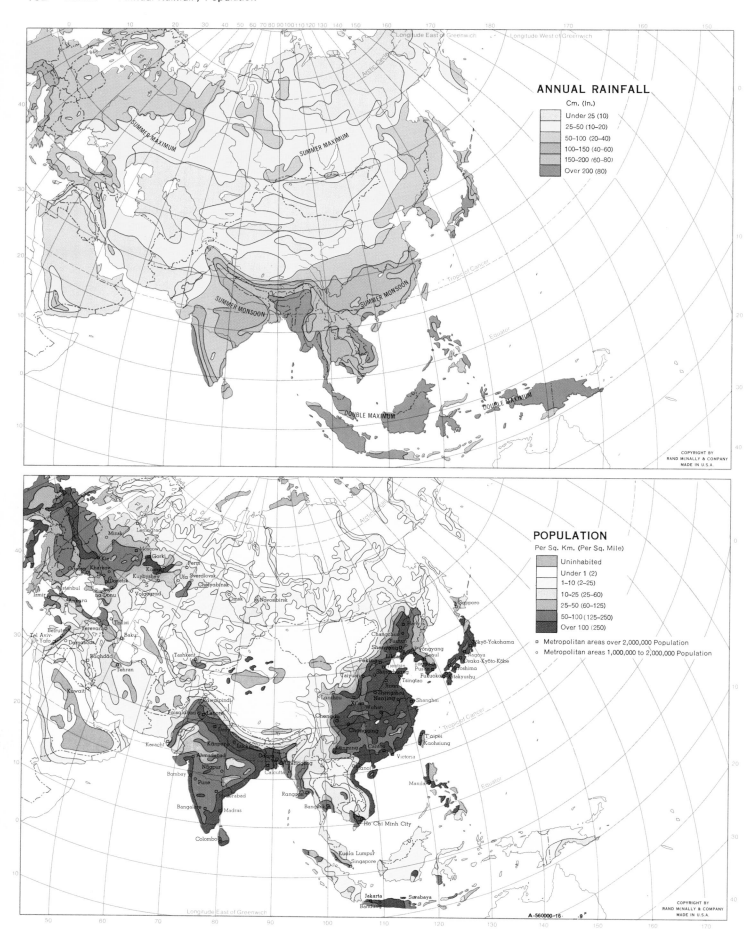

ANNUAL RAINFALL

Cm. (In.)

Under 25 (10)
25–50 (10–20)
50–100 (20–40)
100–150 (40–60)
150–200 (60–80)
Over 200 (80)

POPULATION

Per Sq. Km. (Per Sq. Mile)

Uninhabited
Under 1 (2)
1–10 (2–25)
10–25 (25–60)
25–50 (60–125)
50–100 (125–250)
Over 100 (250)

□ Metropolitan areas over 2,000,000 Population
○ Metropolitan areas 1,000,000 to 2,000,000 Population

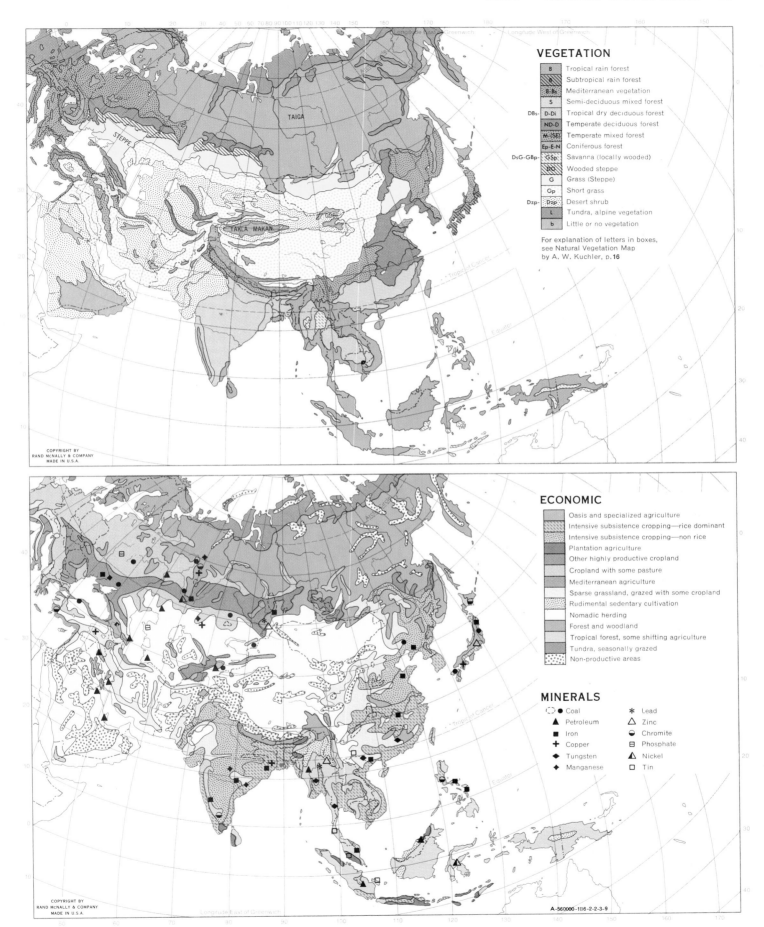

VEGETATION

B	Tropical rain forest
B	Subtropical rain forest
B-Bs	Mediterranean vegetation
S	Semi-deciduous mixed forest
DBs- D-Di	Tropical dry deciduous forest
ND-D	Temperate deciduous forest
M-(SE)	Temperate mixed forest
Ep-E-N	Coniferous forest
DsG-GBp- GSp	Savanna (locally wooded)
BG	Wooded steppe
G	Grass (Steppe)
Gp	Short grass
Dzp- Dzp	Desert shrub
L	Tundra, alpine vegetation
b	Little or no vegetation

For explanation of letters in boxes,
see Natural Vegetation Map
by A. W. Kuchler, p.16

ECONOMIC

	Oasis and specialized agriculture
	Intensive subsistence cropping—rice dominant
	Intensive subsistence cropping—non rice
	Plantation agriculture
	Other highly productive cropland
	Cropland with some pasture
	Mediterranean agriculture
	Sparse grassland, grazed with some cropland
	Rudimental sedentary cultivation
	Nomadic herding
	Forest and woodland
	Tropical forest, some shifting agriculture
	Tundra, seasonally grazed
	Non-productive areas

MINERALS

●	Coal	✳	Lead
▲	Petroleum	△	Zinc
■	Iron	◖	Chromite
✚	Copper	⊟	Phosphate
◆	Tungsten	▲	Nickel
◆	Manganese	☐	Tin

A-560000-1B6-2-2-3-9

184

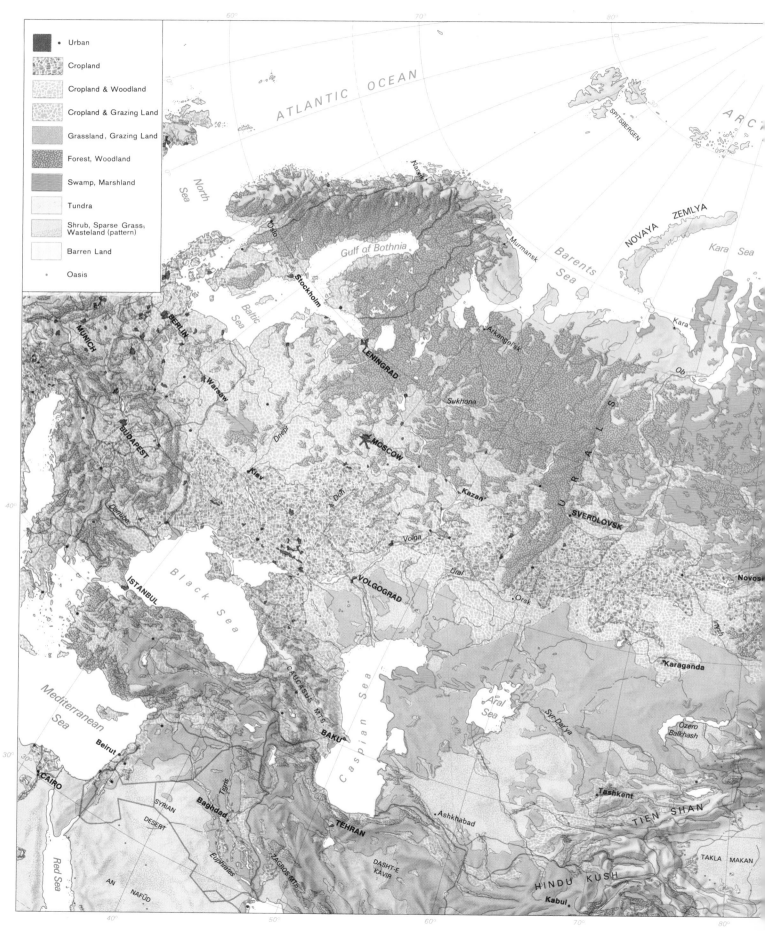

Legend:
- Urban
- Cropland
- Cropland & Woodland
- Cropland & Grazing Land
- Grassland, Grazing Land
- Forest, Woodland
- Swamp, Marshland
- Tundra
- Shrub, Sparse Grass, Wasteland (pattern)
- Barren Land
- • Oasis

Labels on map:

ATLANTIC OCEAN

North Sea

SPITSBERGEN

ARC...

NOVAYA ZEMLYA

Kara Sea

Barents Sea

Murmansk

Narvik

Oslo

Gulf of Bothnia

Arkangel'sk

Kara

Stockholm

Baltic Sea

LENINGRAD

Ob

BERLIN

MUNICH

Warsaw

Sukhona

U R A L S

MOSCOW

BUDAPEST

Dnepr

Kiev

Don

Kazan

SVERDLOVSK

Danube

Volga

Ural

Novosi...

Orsk

VOLGOGRAD

ISTANBUL

Black Sea

Karaganda

CAUCASUS MT'S

Aral Sea

Irtysh

Mediterranean Sea

BAKU

Caspian Sea

Ozero Balkhash

Syr-Darya

Beirut

Tashkent

CAIRO

Tigris

Baghdad

Ashkhabad

SYRIAN

TEHRAN

TIEN SHAN

Red Sea

DESERT

Euphrates

ZAGROS MTS

DASHT-E KAVIR

TAKLA MAKAN

AN NAFUD

HINDU KUSH

Kabul

CEAN

East Siberian Sea

Anadyrskiy Zaliv

Bering Sea

Laptev Sea

Nordvik

Ambarchik

KHREBET GYDAN

Magadan

POLUOSTROV KAMCHATKA

Petropavlovsk-Kamchatskiy

GORY PUTORANA

Olenëk

Lena

Yakutsk

Sea of Okhotsk

Tura

Lena

SAKHALIN

Komsomol'sk-na-Amure

Amur

Krasnoyarsk

GREATER KHINGAN RANGE

Argun

HOKKAIDŌ

Lake Baikal

Sapporo

Irkutsk

Harbin

Vladivostok

HONSHŪ

Ulaan Baatar

Sea of Japan

TOKYO

ALTAI MTS.

SHENYANG

SEOUL

GOBI (DESERT)

Urumqi

PEKING

Yellow Sea

KYŪSHŪ

Huang-Ho

Zhengzhou

East China Sea

PACIFIC OCEAN

SHANGHAI

SHAN

A-568500-96 -1-1-3
COPYRIGHT BY
RAND McNALLY & COMPANY
MADE IN U.S.A.

0 100 200 400 600 800 Miles
0 150 300 600 900 1200 Kilometers

Mediterranean Sea

CAUCASUS MTS.

Caspian Sea

Aral Sea

Syr-Dar'ya

Karaganda

Ozero Balkhash

BAKU

Beirut

CAIRO

Tigris

SYRIAN DESERT

Baghdad

Euphrates

ZAGROS MTS.

TEHRAN

Ashkhabad

Tashkent

TIEN SHAN

DASHT-E KAVIR

TAKLA MAKAN

HINDU KUSH

AN NAFŪD

Red Sea

Persian Gulf

•Kermān

Kabul

Rawalpindi

PLA

Indus

•Mecca

•Riyadh

DELHI

Muscat

KARACHI

AR RUB' AL KHĀLĪ

DANAKIL

•Aden

Gulf of Aden

•Berbera

Arabian Sea

Nāgpur

BOMBAY

WESTERN GHATS

EASTERN GHAT

MADRAS

•Calicut

SRI LA

Colombo

INDIAN OCEAN

Scale 1:24,000,000; one inch to 380 miles. Lambert Azimuthal Equal-Area Projection

Legend:

- ■ • Urban
- Cropland
- Cropland & Woodland
- Cropland & Grazing Land
- Grassland, Grazing Land
- Forest, Woodland
- Swamp, Marshland
- Tundra
- Shrub, Sparse Grass; Wasteland (pattern)
- Barren Land
- • Oasis

HONSHŪ

Sea
of
Japan

TOKYO

Vladivostok

Harbin

GREATER
KHINGAN RA.

SHENYANG

SEOUL

KYŪSHŪ

PACIFIC

OCEAN

Ulaan Baatar

GOBI (DESERT)

Ürümqi

PEKING

Yellow

Sea

East
China
Sea

30°

ALTA:
MTS

AN

Zhengzhou

SHANGHAI

140°

40°

BET

WUHAN

CHONGQING

Huang He

20°

Tropic of Cancer

T'aipei

TAIWAN

Philippine

Sea

130°

Mekong

M A L A Y A S

Brahmaputra

Kunming

CANTON

7ES

Hanoi

HAINAN DAO

Mandalay

Salween

Mekong

Cebu

MANILA

10°

CUTTA

Bay of

Bengal

Salween

Rangoon

BANGKOK

South

China

MINDANAO

Kota Kinabalu

Celebes

Sea

Manado

Andaman

Sea

HO CHI MINH CITY

Sea

0°

Medan

Kuching

BORNEO

CELEBES

SINGAPORE

120°

S U M A T R A

Ujung Pandang

Equator

Java Sea

10°

JAKARTA

JAVA

90°   100°

0   100   200   400   600   800 Miles

0 150   300   450   600   750   900   1200 Kilometers

10°

120°

188

Continued on page 218

Relief

Meters		Feet
3050		10 000
1525		5000
610		2000
305		1000
0	Sea Level	0
		Below
152.5		500 Sea Level
1525		5000
3050		10 000
6100		20 000

A-519695-76 -512-10 23ʰ
COPYRIGHT BY
RAND MCNALLY & COMPANY
MADE IN U.S.A.

Scale 1:40 000 000; one inch to 630 miles. Lambert's Azimuthal, Equal Area Projection
Elevations and depressions are given in feet

a

CYPRUS

Néa Páfos
Ólimbos 33°
6401
Lárnax
Kólpos 34°
Lárnakos
AKR PIDÁLION
Episkopi
Lemesós
AKR. GÁTAS

Longitude 35° East of Greenwich 36°

Halba
Tarābulus
(Tripoli)
Al Quṣayr
Al Hirmil
Al Batrūn
Zgharta
Amyūn Jotal
Jubayl (Byblos)
Ba'labakk

34°
8625

Beirut
(Bayrūt)
Jūniyah
Ad Dāmūr
Zahlah
Az Zabdānī
Ṣaydā
(Sidon)
Jazzin
Damascus Dūmā
Rāshayyā (Dimashq)
Al Kiswah

SYRIA

Ṣūr
(Tyre)
Marj 'Uyūn
Tibnīn
Qiryat Shemona
Al Qunayṭirah
Nahariyya
3962 Zefat
As Suwaydā'
'Akko
636
Haifa
(Hefa)
Teverya
Nazerat
Dar'ā

MEDITERRANEAN

SEA

Afula
Bet She'an
Irbid
Hadera
Jenin
Netanya
Ṭūlkarm
Jarash
Al Mafraq
Herzliyya
Shechem
(Ruins)
Petah Tiqwa
Nabulus
Tel Aviv-Yafo
As Salt
Rishon leZiyyon
Ariha
Amman
Rehovot (Jericho)
Jerusalem
Ashdod
Ma'daba
Qiryat
Bayt Laḥm
Zuwayzā
Ashqelon
Gat (Bethlehem)
Al Khalīl
Dhibān
(Hebron)

Areas occupied by Israel since June 1967

Gaza
(Ghazzah)
Al Mazra'ah
Mahaṭṭat al
Khān Yūnus
Be'er Sheva
Al Karak
Qaṭrānah
Port Said (Būr Sa'īd)
Rafah
Sderot
'Arad
Al Mazār
Khalīj aṭ
Tīnah
Sabkhat al
Bardawil
Dimona
At Ṭafīlah
Al 'Arīsh
Sedom
Mahaṭṭat Jurf
ad Darāwīsh
Rummānah
Ḥaṣor Shivta
(Ruins)
Ash Shawbak
Al Qanṭarah
Qezi'at
Petra
(Ruins)
Daphnae
(Ruins)
Ismailia
Wādī Mūsā
Ma'ān
(Al Ismā'īliyah)
Ra's Abū Qurūn
JABAL
NEGEV
Fā'id
3578
YU 'ALLIQ
QA' AL JAFR
Great Bitter
Al Qusaymah
Lake
EGYPT
Ath Thamad
3513
Suez
An Nakhl
(As Suways)
MITLA PASS
Ra's an Naqb
Al Kuntillah
Mahaṭṭat
'Aqabat al Hijāzīyah
Jabal Ramm
5755
Eilat
4136
JABAL AL
JALĀLAH
JABAL AT TĪH
Al 'Aqabah
Mahaṭṭat
AL BAHRĪYAH
ar Ramlah
JABAL AL 'AJMAH
3789
Al Mudawwarah
Bi'r Zafarānah
Ra's al Junaynah
3335
Haql
Abū Zanīmah
Nuwaybi' al
SAUDI ARABIA
4833
SINAI PEN.
Muzayyinat
JABAL MAZHAFAH
JABAL AL JALĀLAT
(SHIBH JAZĪRAT SĪNĀ')
6232
AL QIBLĪYAH

Scale 1:4 000 000
0 10 20 30 40 50 Miles
0 20 40 60 80 Kilometers

b

Kuala Lumpur
Kelang
PAHANG
Merchong
Scale 1:4 000 000
0 10 20 30 40 50 Miles
Port Kelang
Kajang
Kuala Klawang
0 20 40 60 80 Kilometers
SELANGOR
Gunong Telapa
Burok
3915
Rahau
TIOMAN
Telok Datok
Gunong Kajang
3444
NEGERI SEMBILAN
Sepang
Rantau
Seremban
Rompin
PEMANGGIL
Port Dickson
Rembau
Gemas
Padang Endau
Tampin
Segamat
Gunong Besar
AUR
CAPE RACHADO
Alor Gajah
Jasin
Mt. Ophir
3403
Gunong Besar
Labis
MALAYSIA
Mersing
2002
SOUTH
TINGGI
Melaka
MELAKA
Panchor
Paloh
(Malacca)
MALAY
Bandar
JOHOR
CHINA
Maharani
Keluang
3312
Gunong Blumut
Jumrah
RUPAT
Telukletyak
Rengam
PENINSULA
Ayer
SEA
Batupanjang
Batu
Hitam
Layang Layang
Dumai
Pahat
Kota Tinggi
TANJONG
Bengkalis
BENGKALIS
Pontian Kechil
Johor
TANJONG
Bukitbatu
Baharu
JAMUNIA
Ketamputih
SINGAPORE
Pinggir
Kudap
SINGAPORE
TANJONG
SUMATRA
1837
BATAM
TANJUNG
Telesung
KARIMUN
KEPULAUAN RIAU
BERAKIT
INDONESIA
BESAR
Tanjungpinang
1181
RIAU
Tanjunbalai
RANGSANG
Serangpung
BINTAN
341
Buatan
Siaksriinderapura
TEBINGTINGGI
Minas
KUNDUR

Longitude East of Greenwich

NORTH AMERICA
M. DEZHNEVA
(EAST CAPE)
Bering Str.
CHUKOTSKIY
POLUOSTROV
Arctic Circle
VRANGELYA
(WRANGEL)
PRIBILOF IS
(USA)
SIBERIAN
KHREBET
KORYAKSKIY
(USA)
SEA
KOMANDORSKIYE OSTROVA
West Longitude
(Sov. Union)
KHREBET GYDAN
BERING
170°
Okhotsk
ALEUTIAN ISLANDS
(USA)
SEA
East Longitude
180°
O Yakutsk
Petropavlovsk-
Kamchatskiy
170°
M. LOPATKA
SEA OF
OKHOTSK
KURIL ISLANDS
(Sov. Union)
160°
Komsomolsk
Blagoveshchensk
SAKHALIN
HOKKAIDO
Sovetskaya Gavan
Hakodate
MANCHURIA
Khabarovsk
150°
HARBIN
PACIFIC
Tropic of Cancer
JAPAN
CHANGCHUN
Jilin
Vladivostok
SEA OF
OCEAN
SHENYANG
JAPAN
Sendai
NORTH
TOKYO
Pyongyang
KOREA
YOKOHAMA
SEOUL
KYOTO
SOUTH
KOBE **OSAKA**
TSINGTAO
KITAKYUSHU Shikoku
Nagasaki
KYUSHU
NANJING
EAST
SHANGHAI
CHINA
140°
WUHAN
SEA
NANSEI SHOTO
T'AIPEI
Fuzhou
TAIWAN
Amoy
(FORMOSA)
PHILIPPINE
CANTON
SEA
Swatow
HONG KONG
Macau
VICTORIA
HAINAN DAO
LUZON
SOUTH CHINA SEA
PHILIPPINES
Quezon City
SAMAR
MANILA
Mindoro
LEYTE
PHILIPPINE
TRENCH
PANAY
NEGROS
MINDANAO
HO CHI
MINH CITY
(Saigon)
PALAWAN
Kota Kinabalu
Sandakan
SULU
SEA
CELEBES
SEA
HALMAHERA
NEW
GUINEA
BRUNEI
MALAYSIA
BORNEO
Kuching
CELEBES
Equator

0 200 400 600 800 1000 Miles
0 400 800 1200 1600 Kilometers

190

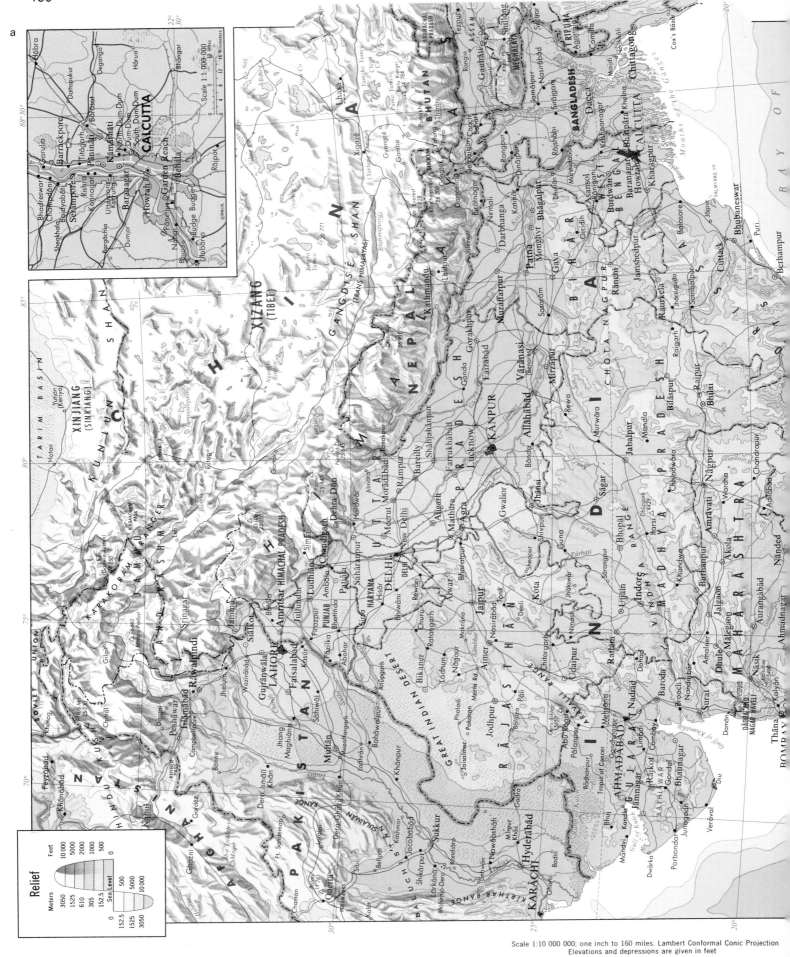

Scale 1:10 000 000; one inch to 160 miles. Lambert Conformal Conic Projection
Elevations and depressions are given in feet

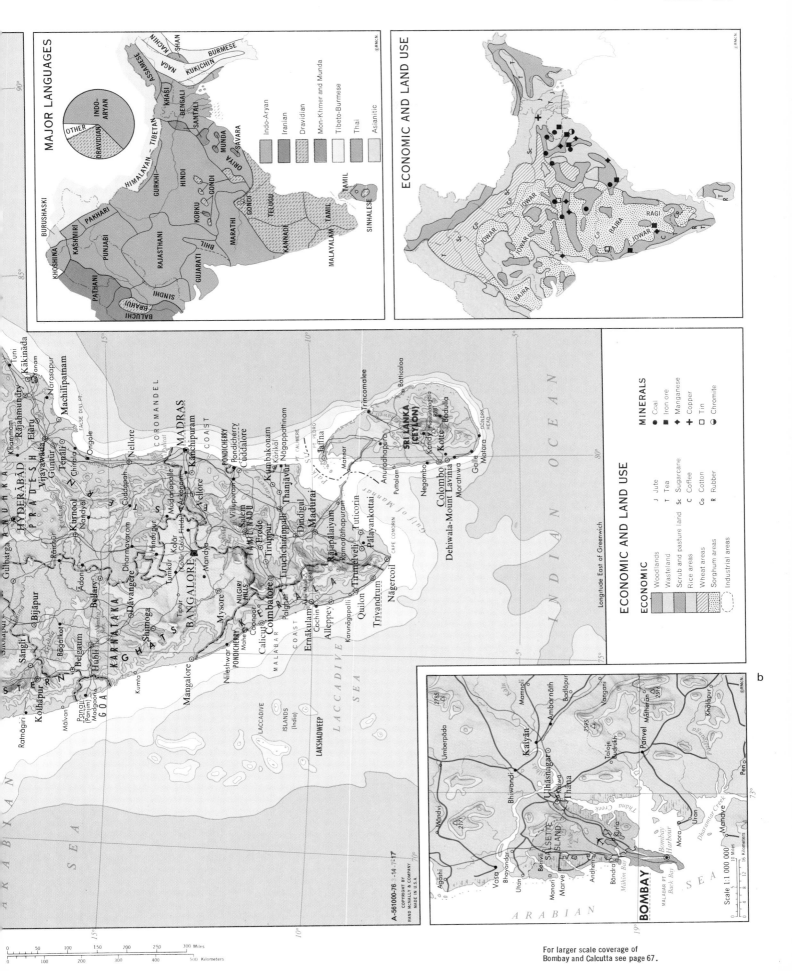

For larger scale coverage of
Bombay and Calcutta see page 67.

BLACK SEA

İstanbul Boğazı (Bosporus)
İstanbul
Üsküdar
Mudanya
Bursa
Kütahya
Eskişehir
Ankara
İzmir
Bergama
Aydın
Muğla
Afyon
Kütahya
Konya
Mersin
Adana
Tarsus
İskenderun
Antakya
Gaziantep

Zonguldak
Kastamonu
Sinop
Çankırı
Merzifon
Samsun
Yozgat
Çorum
Giresun
Sivas
Erzincan
Trabzon
Kayseri
Malatya
Elâzığ
Diyarbakır
Siverek
Maraş
Urfa

Ordzhonikidze
Grozny
Poti
Kutaisi
Batumi
GEORGIAN S.S.R.
Tbilisi
Leninakan
Kars
Yerevan
ARMENIAN S.S.R.
CAUCASUS MTS.
AZERBAYDZHAN S.S.R.
Kirovabad
Baku

CASPIAN SEA
Shevchenko
Fort Shevchenko
Makhachkala
Derbent

KAZAKH
ARAL'SK
MORE (Aral Sea)
Kungrad
Chimbay
PLATO UST'-URT
PESKI KYZYL (DESERT)
Nukus
Khiva
Turtkul'
TURKESTAN
S.S.R.
PESKI KARAKUMY (DESERT)
Chardzhou
Bukhara

SOVIET UNION
TURKMEN S.S.R.

CYPRUS
Nicosia
MEDITERRANEAN SEA

Tarābulus (Tripoli)
Lādhiqīyah (Latakia)
LEBANON
Beirut
Şaydā (Sidon)
Haifa
ISRAEL
Tel Aviv-Yafo
Jerusalem
Gaza
Rashīd
Damietta
Port Said (Būr Sa'īd)
ALEXANDRIA (Al Iskandarīyah)
CAIRO (Al Qāhirah)
Suez (As Suways)

Aleppo
Ḥamāh
SYRIA
Ḥimṣ
Damascus (Dimashq)
As Suwaydā
Amman
JORDAN
Ar Ramādī
Palmyra (Ruins)
Dayr az Zawr
Abū Kamāl
Tikrīt
BAGHDAD
Karbalā
An Najaf
Babylon (Ruins)
Al Mawṣil
Nineveh (Ruins)
As Sulaymānīyah
Irbīl
Kirkūk
KURDISTAN

Van Gölü
Van
Bitlis
Khvoy
Tabrīz
Ardabīl
Orūmīyeh
Miāneh
Lenkoran
Bandar-e Anzalī
Rasht
Bandar-e Torkman
Chikishlyar
Bābol
Gorgān
Qazvīn
ELBURZ MTS.
Qolleh-ye Damāvand
TEHRAN
Qom
Hamadān
Kermānshāh
Kangāvar
Sanandaj
Zanjān

Nabīt-Dag
Krasnovodsk
Bojnūrd
KOPPEH DĀGH
Ashkhabad
Gorgān
Emāmshahr
Neyshābūr
Mashhad
Herāt
Kushka
Mary

ZAGROS MTS.
Arāk
Borūjerd
Kāshān
DASHT-E KAVIR DESERT
Dāmghān
Bejestān
Ferdows
Qāyen
AFGHANISTAN

Dezfūl
Shūshtar
Masjed Soleymān
Ahvāz
Khorramshahr
Abādān
Bandar-e Khomeynī
Kāzerūn
Borāzjān
Būshehr
Shīrāz
Persepolis (Ruins)
Eṣfahān
Shahreżā
Yazd
Bāfq
PLATEAU OF IRAN
Birjand
Farāh

IRAN
Daryācheh-ye Namak
Daryācheh-ye Bakhtegān
Rafsanjān
Kermān
Zāhedān
Khāsh
Bampūr
Rīgān

Jahrom
Lār
Bandar 'Abbās
Qeshm
QESHM (Hormuz)
Bandar-e Lengeh
Jāsk
Chāh Bahār
Gwādar

An Nāfūd
Al Jawf
Sakākah
Rafḥā
Badanah
Neutral Zone
Al Qayṣūmah
Tayma
Khaybar
JABAL SHAMMAR
Ḥā'il
Buraydah
'Unayzah
Sudayr
Ash Shaqrā
NAJD
AD DAHNĀ
AL ḤASĀ
KUWAIT
Kuwait (Al Kuwayt)

An Nāṣirīyah
Al Baṣrah

Dammām
Az Zahrān (Dhahran)
Al Qaṭīf
Al Hufūf
BAHRAIN
Al Manāmah
QATAR
Ad Dawḥah
Abū Ẓaby
UNITED ARAB EMIRATES
Ajman
Dubayy
Al Buraymī
OMAN
JABAL AL AKHDAR
Jabal ash Shām
Muscat
Maṭraḥ
Al Khābūrah
Sūr
RA'S AL ḤADD

RA'S AT TANNŪRAH
PERSIAN GULF
GULF OF OMAN

SAUDI ARABIA
HIJAZ
AL ḤIJĀZ
Al Madīnah (Medina)
Yanbu
RED SEA
Jiddah
Mecca (Makkah)
Aṭ Ṭā'if
AL AFLAJ
Ad Dilam
Riyadh (Ar Riyāḍ)
AD DAHY
NAFŪD
Al Mubarraz
JABAL TUWAYQ
Wādī ad Dawāsir
Al Lidām
Al Khurmah
Qal'at Bīshah
AR RUB' AL KHĀLĪ
OMAN
RA'S AL MADRAKAH

EGYPT
SINAI
Al 'Aqabah
Ma'ān
Al Karak
SYRIAN DESERT
AT TURAYF

Būr Safājah
Al Quşayr
RA'S BANĀS

SUDAN
Būr Sūdān
Sawākin
Ṭawkar
Al Qunfudhah
Abhā
NAJRAN
Najran
JAZA IR FARASAN
Qīzān
Abū 'Arīsh
Ṣa'dah
San'ā'
YEMEN
Al Ḥudaydah
Ḥodār Shu'ayb
RAMLAT AS SAB'ATAYN
Shibām
Tarīm
Say'ūn
Al Ḥawṭah
ḤADRAMAWT
Al Mukallā
Ash Shiḥr
Sayḥūt
RA'S FARTAK
Mirbāṭ
P.D.R. OF YEMEN
KHŪRYĀN-MŪRYĀN (Oman)
RA'S AL MADRAKAH

Kassalā
Keren (Massawa)
Akordat
Sebderat
Asmera
Adi Ugri
ETHIOPIA
DAHLAK ARCH
KAMARĀN (P.D.R. of Yemen)
Al Luḥayyah
Madīnat ash Sha'b
Aden
Shuqrah
Al Makhā (Mocha)
Zabīd
Ta'izz
Mawza

DJIBOUTI
Djibouti
Tadjoura
Zeila
Berbera
SOMALIA
GULF OF ADEN
SUQUTRA (SOCOTRA) (P.D.R. of Yemen)
Hadibu

ARABIAN SEA

Relief

Meters		Feet
3050		10 000
1525		5000
610		2000
305		1000
152.5		500
0	Sea Level	0
152.5	Below Sea Level	500
1525		5000
3050		10 000

Areas occupied by Israel since June 1967

ADMINISTR. BDY.

Continued on pages 220-221

Tropic of Cancer

A-569400-76 42-12-22
COPYRIGHT BY
RAND McNALLY & COMPANY
MADE IN U.S.A.

Scale 1:16 000 000; one inch to 250 miles. Polyconic Projection
Elevations and depressions are given in feet

Longitude East of Greenwich

a

on pages 178-179

Scale 1:4 000 000

AFGHANISTAN
PAKISTAN

Jalalabad
Dargai
MORGA RA.
KHYBER PASS
Charsadda
Peshawar

b

Scale 1:40 000 000

AFGHANISTAN
PAKISTAN
CHINA
XIZAGN (TIBET)

JAMMU AND KASHMIR
HIMACHAL PRADESH
PUNJAB
HARYANA
UTTAR PRADESH
NEPAL
SIKKIM
BHUTAN
ARUNACHAL PRADESH
ASSAM
NAGALAND
RAJASTHAN
BIHAR
MEGHALAYA
BANGLADESH
WEST BENGAL
MIZORAM
GUJARAT
MADHYA PRADESH
ORISSA
BURMA

Tropic of Cancer

MAHARASHTRA

ARABIAN SEA

KARNATAKA
ANDHRA PRADESH
BAY OF BENGAL

KERALA
TAMIL NADU

SRI LANKA (CEYLON)

INDIA · POLITICAL

1-TRIPURA
2-MANIPUR
3-LAKSHADWEEP
4-DELHI
5-DADRA AND NAGAR HAVELI
6-PONDICHERRY
7-GOA, DAMAN, AND DIU

Continued on pages 188-189

c

Tiruchchirappalli
Ernakulam
KERALA
Alleppey
Quilon
Trivandrum
CAPE COMORIN

Thanjavur
TAMIL NADU
Madurai
Tuticorin
Tirunelveli

Nagappattinam
Jaffna
Mannar
Trincomalee
Anuradhapura
Puttalam
Kandy

SRI LANKA (CEYLON)
Colombo

INDIAN OCEAN

DONDRA HEAD
Galle
Matara

Same scale as main map

Scale bars:
0 50 100 200 300 400 500 Miles
0 100 200 400 600 800 Kilometers

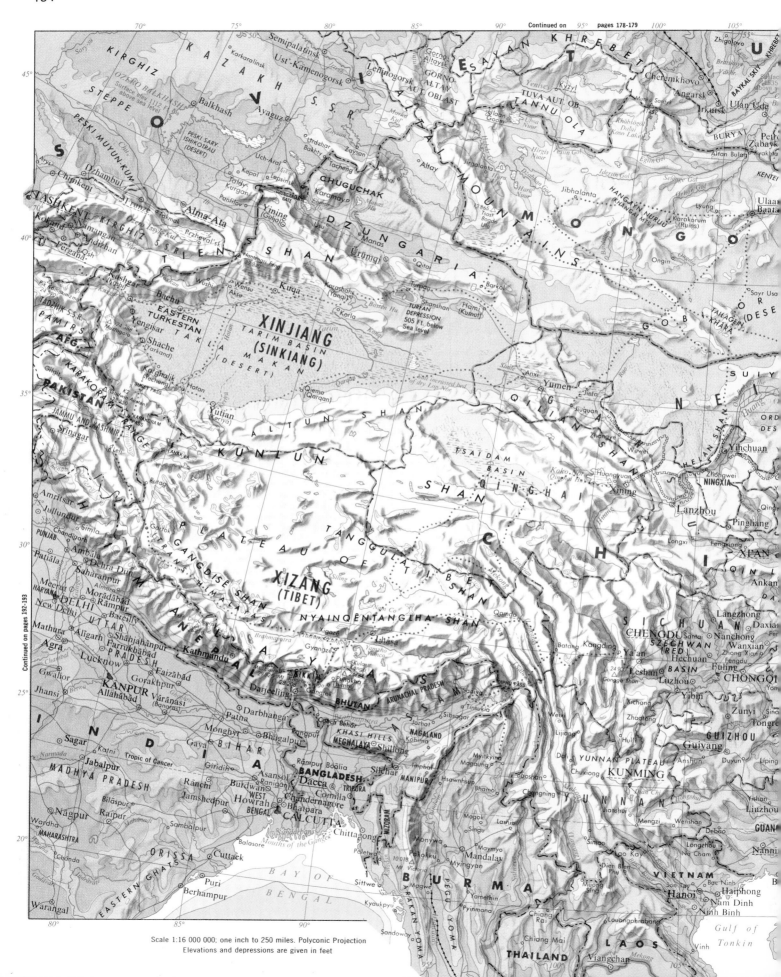

Continued on pages 178-179

Continued on pages 192-193

Scale 1:16 000 000; one inch to 250 miles. Polyconic Projection
Elevations and depressions are given in feet

Chinese Provinces,
Autonomous Regions (AR)
and Municipalities (M)

Conventional Form	—	Pinyin Form
Anhwei	—	Anhui
Chekiang	—	Zhejiang
Fukien	—	Fujian
Heilungkiang	—	Heilongjiang
Honan	—	Henan
Hopeh	—	Hebei
Hunan	—	Hunan
Hupeh	—	Hubei
Inner Mongolia (AR)	—	Nei Monggol
Kansu	—	Gansu
Kiangsi	—	Jiangxi
Kiangsu	—	Jiangsu
Kirin	—	Jilin
Kwangsi (AR)	—	Guangxi
Kwangtung	—	Guangdong
Kweichow	—	Guizhou
Liaoning	—	Liaoning
Ningsia Hui (AR)	—	Ningxia
Peking (M)	—	Beijing
Shanghai (M)	—	Shanghai
Shansi	—	Shanxi
Shantung	—	Shandong
Shensi	—	Shaanxi
Sinkiang (AR)	—	Xinjiang
Szechwan	—	Sichuan
Tibet (AR)	—	Xizang
Tientsin (M)	—	Tianjin
Tsinghai	—	Qinghai
Yunnan	—	Yunnan

A-569700-76--11-6-19°
COPYRIGHT BY
RAND McNALLY & COMPANY
MADE IN U.S.A.

Relief

Meters	Feet
3050	10 000
1525	5000
610	2000
305	1000
152.5	500
0 Sea Level	Sea Level 0
152.5	500 Below
1525	5000 Sea Level
3050	10 000
6100	20 000

Continued on pages 202-203

Longitude East of Greenwich

0   50   100   200   300   400   500 Miles
0   100   200   400   600   800 Kilometers

Cities
and   0 to 50,000   o   500,000 to 1,000,000   ⊚
Towns   50,000 to 500,000   ⊙   1,000,000 and over

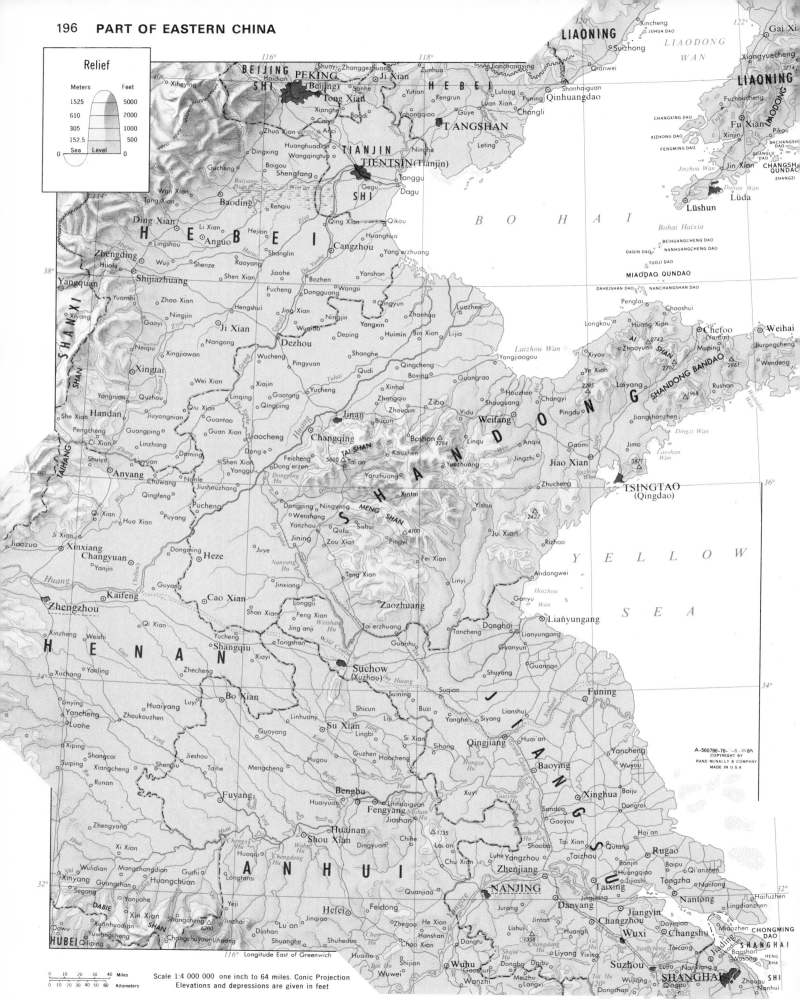

Relief

Meters	Feet
1525	5000
610	2000
305	1000
152.5	500
0 Sea Level	0

LIAONING

LIAODONG WAN

Gai Xi

Xincheng Juhua Dao

Suzhong Qianwei

LIAONING

Xiongyuecheng

LIAODONG

Changxing Dao

Fuzhoucheng

Fu Xian Pikou

XIZHONG DAO Xinjin

FENGMING DAO DACHANGSH

GUANGLU DAO

CHANGSH QUNDAO

Jin Xian Zhangzi

Jinzhou Wan CHANGSH

Dalian Wan

Lüshun Lüda

BEIHUANGCHENG DAO

DAQIN DAO NANHUANGCHENG DAO

TUOJI DAO

MIAODAO QUNDAO

DAHEISHAN DAO NANCHANGSHAN DAO

Penglai Chaoshui

Longkou Huang Xian Chefoo (Yantai) Weihai

AI SHAN 2743 Muping Jiurongcheng

Zhaoyuan 2707

Laiyang 2861 Wendeng

2285 Pingdu SHANDONG BANDAO 1968 Rushan

Jiangshanzhen Dingzi Wan

Gaomi Jimo

Jiao Xian 3871 Laoshan Wan

Jinzhou Wan

Zhucheng TSINGTAO (Qingdao)

BEIJING SHI PEKING (Beijing)

Xiheying Haidian Shunyi Zhanggezhuang Zunhua Jianchangying

Ji Xian HEBEI Shanhaiguan

Tong Xian Sanhe Yutian Fengrun Lulong Funing Qinhuangdao

Xianghe Baodi Yahongqiao Guye Changli

Caiyu Anci TANGSHAN Leting

Zhuo Xian Huanghuadian Ninghe

Dingxing Wangqingtuo Dagu

Gucheng Baigou Shengfang TIANJIN Tanggu

Baiyang Dian Wen'an Wa SHI

Wan Xian Baoding Renqiu

Tang Xian

Ding Xian Li Xian Hejian Qing Xian Qikou BOHAI

Lingshou Anguo Huanghua

Zhengding Wuji Shenze Raoyang Shanglin Yang'erzhuang

Huolu Shijiazhuang Shen Xian Jiaohe Yanshan Luozhen

Yangquan Yuanshi Zhao Xian Ningjin Da Yunhe Bozhen Qingyun Zhanhua

Xiyang Gaoyi Hengshui Jing Xian Wuqiao Yangxin Huimin Lijia

Neiqiu Xingjiawan Fucheng Deping Bin Xian

Xingtai Nangong Dongguang Ningjin Xinhai Guangrao

Ji Xian Dezhou Qingcheng Boxing Shouguang Houzhen

Wei Xian Xiajin Wucheng Pingyuan Shanghe Zhangqiu Zibo Yidu Weifang

Quzhou Gaotang Qinghe Yucheng Qudi Zhoucun Linqu Anqiu Jingzhi

She Xian Handan Liaocheng Dong'e JINAN Bucun Boshan 3284 Kouzhen Yuezhuang

Pengcheng Guangping Guan Xian Changqing TAI SHAN 5600 Tai'an Xintai

Ci Xian Linzhang Daming Shen Xian Yanggu Feicheng Dong'erzhuang Yanzhuang

Anyang Chuwang Nanle Jiushouzhang Dongping Hu Dawen Meng Shan Yishui

Qingfeng Pucheng Dongping Ningyang Sishui 4100 Pingyi

Qi Xian Hua Xian Puyang Wenshang Qufu Fei Xian Linyi

Jiaozuo Xinxiang Guyang Yanzhou Zou Xian 2427 Ju Xian

Ji Xian Changyuan Dongming Juye Jining Teng Xian Rizhao

Zhengzhou Yanjin Heze Nanyang Hu Andongwei

Kaifeng Cao Xian Longgu Zaozhuang Ganyu Lianyungang

HENAN Qi Xian Shan Xian Feng Xian Weishan Hu Tai'erzhuang Haizhou Wan

Weishi Shangqiu Jing'anji Guanhu Tancheng Donghai Lianyungang

Xinzheng Yucheng Xiayi Tongshan Donghai Guannan

Xuchang Zhecheng SUCHOW (Xuzhou) Suining Suqian Funing

Linying Luyi Bo Xian Shicun Buzi Lianshui Huai'an

Yancheng Huaiyang Zhoukouzhen Linhuaji Liji Yanghe Siyang JIANGSU

Luohe Guoyang Su Xian Lingbi Si Xian Sihong Qingjiang Yancheng

Xiping Shangcai Jieshou Taihe Guzhen Haocheng Hongze Hu Wuyou

Suiping Xiangcheng Shendui Hugou Baoying

Runan Mengcheng Beifei Hai'an

Zhengyang Fuyang Bengbu Linhuaiguan Xuyi Xinghua Baiju Dongtai

Xi Xian Chengqi Hu Fengyang Jiashan Gaoyou Hu Sanduo

Wulidian ANHUI Huainan Shou Xian Dingyuan Chihe Gaoyou Rugao

Mangzhangdian Huoqiu Chengdong Hu Lai'an Luhe Yangzhou Banjin Baipu Qi'anzhen

Gushi Longtansi Shuanghe Chu Xian Zhenjiang Huangqiao Jijiashi Tangzha Nantong

Xinyang Yanjiahe Yeji Quanjiao JIANGSU Taixing Haifuzhen

Segang Yanji Feidong NANJING Danyang Jiangyin Lingdianzhen

Huangchuan Xin Xian Shangcheng Jinzhai Lu'an Jinqiao Jurong Jintan Changzhou Dayiqiao Miaozhen CHONGMING DAO

DABIE Chengzhuyuanthu Lihuang HEFEI Zhegao He Xian Hanshan Lishui Huangli Wuxi Changshu HENG SHA

Dawu Xuanhuadian Changzhuyuan Dushan Shuanghe Dangtu Shijiu Hu Changdang Hu Yixing Suzhou Kunshan Luija Nanxiang Jiading

HUBEI Qiliping Chao Xian Chop Xian Wuhe Shijian Dongba Dipu SHANGHAI SHI

Huaibin Shijiu Changdang Liyang Wusong

Wuhu Gaoshun Meizhou Wanzhi Langxi Tai Hu Wujiang SHANGHAI Zhoup Nanhui

Dongshan 20°

0 10 20 30 40 Miles
0 10 20 30 40 50 60 Kilometers

Scale 1:4 000 000 one inch to 64 miles. Conic Projection
Elevations and depressions are given in feet

A-560796-76- -6.4 66
COPYRIGHT BY
RAND McNALLY & COMPANY
MADE IN U.S.A.

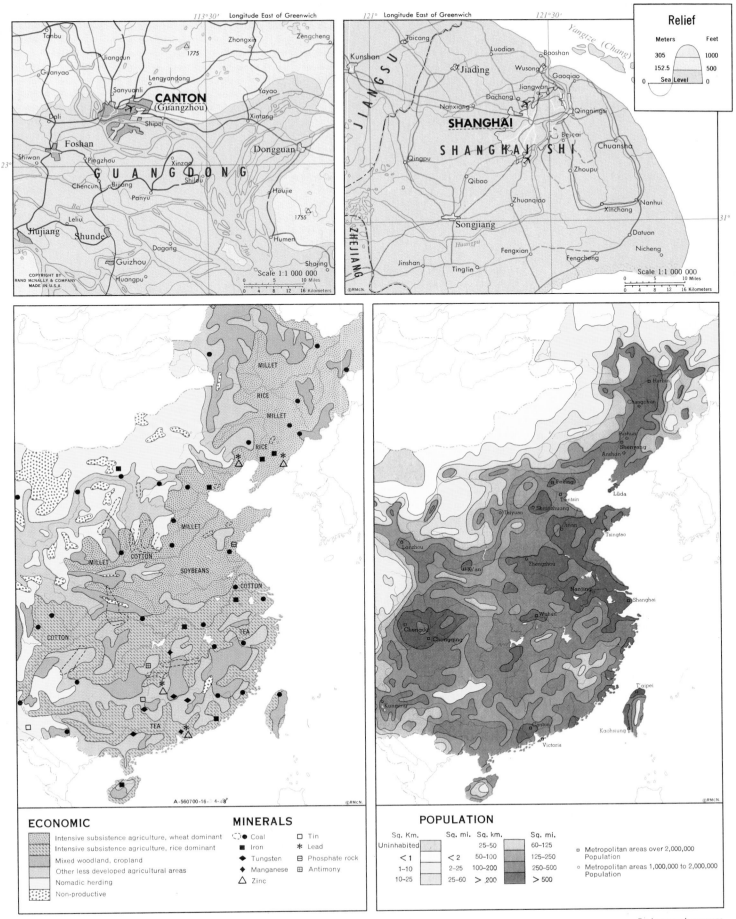

CANTON (Guangzhou)

Tanbu · Jianggun · Zhongxin · Zengcheng · 1775 · Guanyao · Lengyandong · Jiangcun · Sanyuanli · Yayao · Dali · Shipai · Xintang · Foshan · Dongguan · Shiwan · Pingzhou · Xinzao · Houjie · Chencun · Bijiang · Shilou · 1755 · Panyu · Dagang · Humen · Hujiang · Shunde · Guizhou · Huangpu · Shajing

Bei · Longitude East of Greenwich 113°30′

GUANGDONG · 23°

Scale 1:1 000 000
0 4 8 12 16 Kilometers
0 5 Miles

COPYRIGHT BY
RAND McNALLY & COMPANY
MADE IN U.S.A.

SHANGHAI

Longitude East of Greenwich 121° · 121°30′ · Yangtze (Chang)

Kunshan · Taicang · Luodian · Baoshan · Jiading · Wusong · Gaoqiao · Jiangwan · Nanxiang · Dachang · Qingningsi · **SHANGHAI** · Beicar · Chuansha · Qingpu · **SHANGHAI SHI** · Qibao · Zhoupu · Zhuanqiao · Xinchang · Nanhui · Songjiang · Datuan · Jinshan · Fengxian · Fengcheng · Nicheng · Tinglin

JIANGSU · ZHEJIANG · Huangpu · 31°

Scale 1:1 000 000
0 4 8 12 16 Kilometers
0 4 8 12 16 Miles

©RMCN.

Relief

Meters		Feet
305		1000
152.5		500
0	Sea Level	0

ECONOMIC

- Intensive subsistence agriculture, wheat dominant
- Intensive subsistence agriculture, rice dominant
- Mixed woodland, cropland
- Other less developed agricultural areas
- Nomadic herding
- Non-productive

MILLET · RICE · MILLET · RICE · MILLET · COTTON · SOYBEANS · COTTON · MILLET · COTTON · TEA · TEA

A-560700-16- 4-48

©RMCN.

MINERALS

- ◖● Coal
- ■ Iron
- ◆ Tungsten
- ◆ Manganese
- △ Zinc
- □ Tin
- ✳ Lead
- ⊟ Phosphate rock
- ⊞ Antimony

POPULATION

Sq. Km.	Sq. mi.	Sq. km.	Sq. mi.
Uninhabited		25–50	60–125
< 1	< 2	50–100	125–250
1–10	2–25	100–200	250–500
10–25	25–60	> 200	> 500

□ Metropolitan areas over 2,000,000 Population
○ Metropolitan areas 1,000,000 to 2,000,000 Population

Harbin · Changchun · Fushun · Shenyang · Anshun · Peking · Tientsin · Lüda · Lanzhou · Thiyuan · Shihchiazhuang · Jinan · Taingtao · Xi'an · Zhengzhou · Nanjing · Shanghai · Wuhan · Chengdu · Chongqing · T'aipei · Kunming · Canton · Kaohsiung · Victoria

For larger scale coverage
of Shanghai see page 68

Continued on page 200

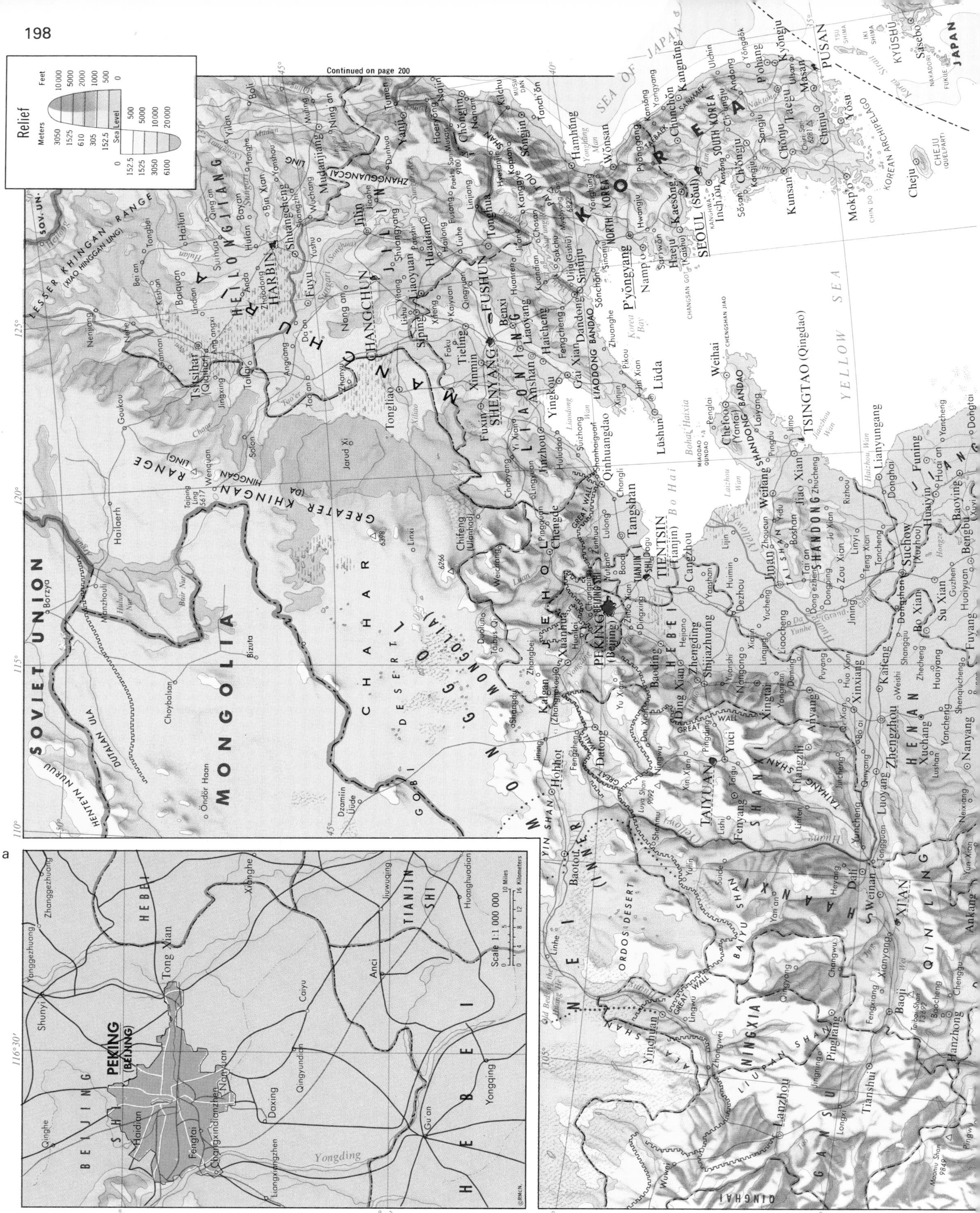

Relief

Meters	Feet
3050	10000
1525	5000
610	2000
305	1000
152.5	500
Sea Level	0

0	0
152.5	500
1525	5000
3050	10000
6100	20000

SOVIET UNION

MONGOLIA

GOBI DESERT

CHAHAR

GREATER KHINGAN RANGE (DA HINGGAN LING)

LESSER KHINGAN RANGE (XIAO HINGGAN LING)

HEILONGJIANG

HARBIN

CHANGCHUN

SHENYANG

FUSHUN

LIAONING

HEBEI

SHANXI

SHAANXI

SHANDONG

HENAN

GANSU

NINGXIA

NEI MONGGOL (INNER MONGOLIA)

ORDOS DESERT

QINGHAI

QINLING

KOREA

NORTH KOREA

SOUTH KOREA

Pyŏngyang

SEOUL (Sŏul)

PUSAN

JAPAN

KYUSHU

CHEJU (QUELPART)

KOREAN ARCHIPELAGO

SEA OF JAPAN

YELLOW SEA

Bo Hai

Korea Bay

PEKING (BEIJING)

TIENTSIN (Tianjin)

TAIYUAN

XIAN

TSINGTAO (Qingdao)

Tangshan

Qinhuangdao

Chengde

LIAODONG BANDAO

SHANDONG BANDAO

GREAT WALL

Lanzhou

a

BEIJING SHI

HEBEI

TIANJIN SHI

PEKING (BEIJING)

Haidian

Fengtai

Tong Xian

Shunyi

Zhanggezhuang

Qinghe

Nankou

Daxing

Caiyu

Anci

Qingundian

Gu'an

Yongqing

Yongding

Scale 1:1 000 000

10 Miles

16 Kilometers

Cities and Towns

0 to 50,000	500,000 to 1,000,000
50,000 to 500,000	1,000,000 and over

For larger scale coverage of Peking see page 67.

Scale 1:10 000 000; one inch to 160 miles. Lambert Conformal Conic Projection
Elevations and depressions are given in feet

Longitude East of Greenwich

CHINA

E A S T   C H I N A   S E A

NANSEI-SHOTO (RYUKYU ISLANDS)

JAPAN

Tropic of Cancer

SAKISHIMA-GUNTO

IRIOMOTE-JIMA

P H I L I P P I N E   S E A

TAIWAN (FORMOSA)

T'AIPEI
Chilung (Kirin)
Ilan
Suao
Hualien
Hsincha
Miaoli
Taichung
Changhua
Chai
T'aitung
Tainan
Kaohsiung
P'ingtung
Hengch'un

Formosa Strait

PESCADORES

BATAN ISLANDS
BATAN I.
C. ENGANO

Luzon Strait

Balintang Channel

Babuyan Channel

BABUYAN ISLANDS

Bashi Channel

LUZON

Aparri
Claveria
Bacarra
Laoag
Batac
Vigan
San Fernando
Baguio
Lingayen
Dagupan
Camiling
Tarlac
Cabanatuan
Subic
Mariveles
MANILA
Quezon City
Cavite
San Pablo
Lipa
Batangas
Lubang
Marinduque

CATANDUANES
YOG PT
PALANAN PT
Casiguran
Baler
Polillo
POLILLO

PHILIPPINES

S O U T H   C H I N A   S E A

DONGSHA DAO (China)

HSISHA CH'ÜNTAO (China)

ZHEJIANG
Shanghai
Songjiang
Jiaxing
Hangzhou
Shaoxing
Ningbo
Jinhua
Wenzhou
Qu Xian
Linhai
Lishui

FUJIAN
Fuzhou
Nanping
Quanzhou
Amoy (Xiamen)
Zhangzhou
Swatow (Shantou)
Chaoyang
Chao'an
Mei Xian

WUYI SHAN
JIANGXI
Nanchang
Qingjiang
Ji'an
Ganzhou
Pingxiang

HUNAN
Changsha
Xiangtan
Hengyang
Shaoyang
Zhuzhou
Lingling
Chenzhou

HUBEI
WUHAN
Wuchang
Hanyang
Hankou
Shashi
Yichang

GUANGDONG
CANTON (Guangzhou)
Kowloon
HONG KONG
VICTORIA
Macau (Port.)
Zhujiang Kou
Foshan
Jiangmen
Taishan
Yangjiang
Zhanjiang
Maoming
Dianbai

HAINAN DAO
Haikou
Qiongshan
Wenchang
Qionghai
Danxian
Dongfang
Yaxian
Ya Xian

LEIZHOU BANDAO
Beihai
Hepu

GUANGXI
Nanning
Liuzhou
Guilin
Wuzhou
Hechi
Baise

GUIZHOU
Guiyang
Zunyi
Anshun

YUNNAN
KUNMING

SICHUAN
SZECHWAN
Chongqing
CHONGQING
Neijiang
Luzhou

V I E T N A M
Hanoi
Haiphong
Nam Dinh
Ninh Binh
Thanh-Hoa
Vinh
Dong Hoi
Hue
Da Nang (Tourane)

ANNAMITIC CORDILLERA

LAOS

THAILAND

KAMPUCHEA

Gulf of Tonkin

Scale:
0   50   100   150   200   250   300 Miles
0   100   200   300   400   500 Kilometers

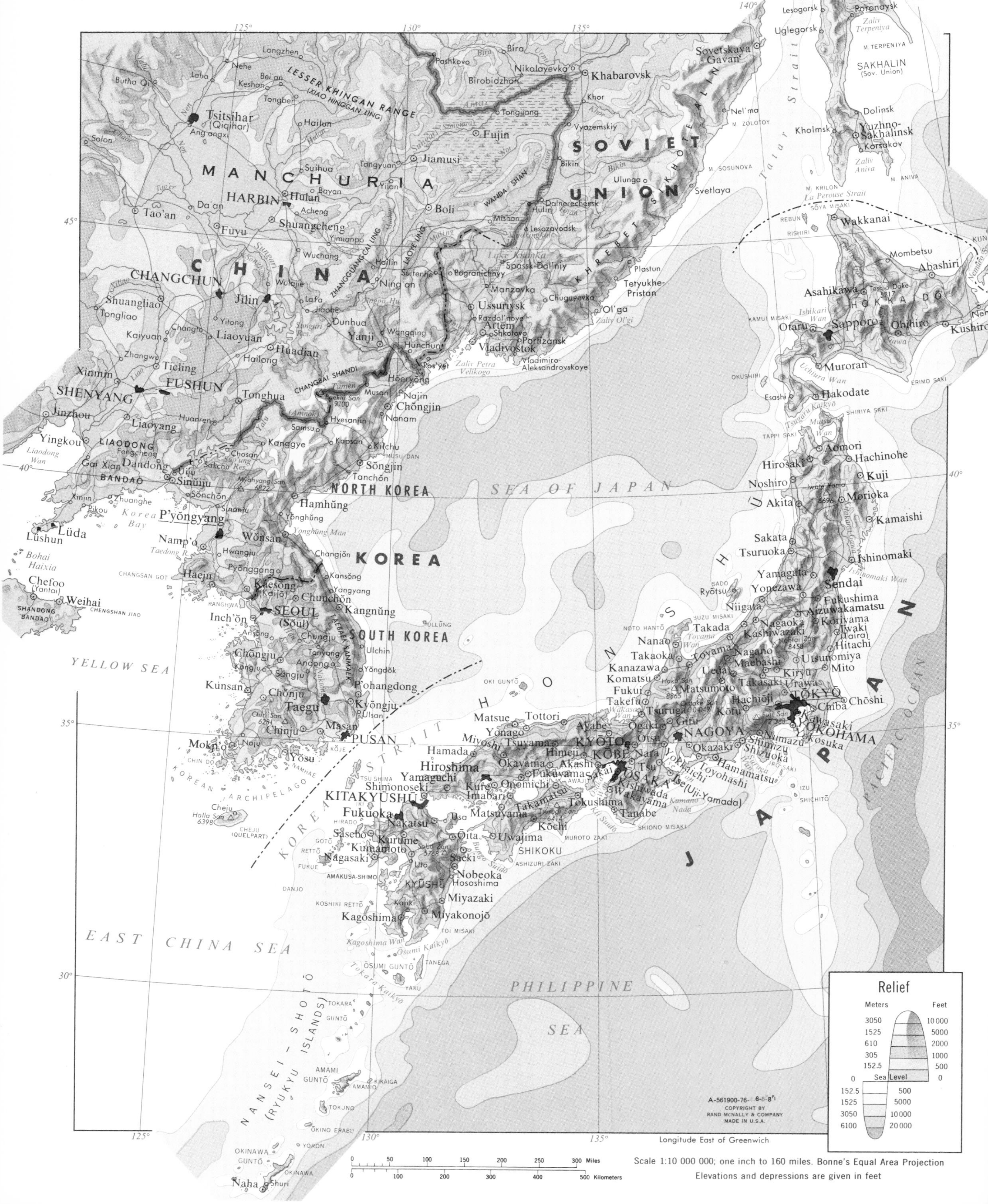

SOVIET UNION

MANCHURIA

CHINA

LESSER KHINGAN RANGE (XIAO HINGGAN LING)

Longzhen
Nehe
Laha
Butha Qi
Bei'an
Keshan
Nikolayevka
Pashkovo
Bira
Bira
Birobidzhan
Khabarovsk
Sovetskaya Gavan'
SAKHALIN (Sov. Union)
Lesogorsk
Uglegorsk
Potronaysk
Zaliv Terpeniya
M. TERPENIYA
Nehe
Nen
Tongbei
Hailun
Tangyuan
Jiamusi
Fujin
Khor
Tongjiang
Nel'ma
M. ZOLOTOY
Dolinsk
Yuzhno-Sakhalinsk
Korsakov
Zaliv Aniva
Tsitsihar (Qiqihar)
Hulan
Suihua
Bayan
Yilan
Boli
Bikin
Vyazemskiy
Svetlaya
La Perouse Strait
SOYA MISAKI
Kholmsk
M. KRILON
REBUN
RISHIRI
Wakkanai
Mombetsu

HARBIN
Da'an
Acheng
Shuangcheng
Yimianpo
Mudanjiang
Mishan
Lesozavodsk
Plastun
Abashiri
Tao'an
Fuyu
Wuchang
Hailin
Lake Khanka
Spassk-Dal'niy
Asahikawa
HOKKAIDO
Tashiro Dake
CHANGCHUN
Jilin
Yitong
Jiaohe
Dunhua
Zhangguangcai Ling
Suifenhe
Pogranichnyy
Manzovka
Chuguyevka
Ol'ga
Zaliv Ol'gi
Kamui Misaki
Otaru
Sapporo
Obihiro
Kushiro
OKUSHIRI
Shuangliao
Tongliao
Changtu
Liaoyuan
Lafa
Ning'an
Wangqing
Hunchun
Yanji
Razdol'noye
Artem
Shkotovo
Vladivostok
Partizansk
Vladimiro-Aleksandrovskoye
Uchiura Wan
Muroran
Kaiyuan
Huadian
Hailong
Huanren
Ussuriysk
Pos'yet
Hoeryong
Musan
Zaliv Petra Velikogo
Esashi
Hakodate
Shiriya Saki
Xinmin
Tieling
Tonghua
Tumen
Najin
Chongjin
Nanam
Noshiro
Aomori
Hachinohe
SHENYANG
FUSHUN
Jinzhou
Liaoyang
Changbai Shan
Hyesanjin
Kapsan
Kilchu
MUSU DAN
Hiroshima
Akita
Morioka
Kuji
Yingkou
LIAODONG
Fengcheng
Kanggye
Samsu
Tanchon
Songjin
Kamaishi
Liaodong Wan
Gai Xian
Dandong
Uiju
Chosan
Sup'ung Res.
NORTH KOREA
Sakata
Tsuruoka
Yamagata
Sendai
Ishinomaki
Ishinomaki Wan
Lushun
Lüda
Xinjin
Pikou
Zhuanghe
Sinuiju
Sonchon
Chonghyongang Res.
Hamhung
Yonghung
Yonghung Man
Yamagata
Yonezawa
Niigata
Fukushima
Aizuwakamatsu
Koriyama
Iwaki (Taira)
Bohai Haixia
Chefoo (Yantai)
KOREA BAY
P'yongyang
Namp'o
Taedong R.
Wonsan
Changjon
Hwangju
Ryotsu
SADO
Nagaoka
Kashiwazaki
Hitachi
SHANDONG BANDAO
Weihai
CHENGSHAN JIAO
Haeju
CHANGSAN GOT
Kaesong (Kaijo)
Pyonggang
Kumgang San
Kansong
KANGHWA
Chunchon
Yangyang
ULLUNG
NOTO HANTO
Nanao
Takada
Toyama
Nagano
Maebashi
Takasaki
Urawa
Utsunomiya
Mito
YELLOW SEA
SEOUL (Soul)
Inch'on
Anseong
Chongju
Chungju
Tanyang
Ulchin
Kanazawa
Komatsu
Toyama
Ueda
Kiryu
Hachioji
TOKYO
Chiba
Choshi
SOUTH KOREA
Chonan
Ansong
Sangju
Yongdok
OKI GUNTO
Fukui
Takefu
Matsumoto
Kofu
Fuji San
KAWASAKI
YOKOHAMA
Kunsan
Chonju
Taegu
Kyongju
Ulsan
P'ohangdong
Matsue
Tottori
Ayabe
KYOTO
Gifu
OGAKI
NAGOYA
Yokkaichi
Yokosuka
Chiri San
Chinju
Masan
PUSAN
Yonago
Tsuyama
Himeji
Nara
Otsu
Tsu
Okazaki
Toyohashi
Hamamatsu
Shimizu
IZU
SHICHITO
Mokp'o
Naju
Yosu
Miyoshi
Hamada
Okayama
Akashi
KOBE
OSAKA
Ise (Uji-Yamada)
Kumano Nada
Cheju
Halla San
Hiroshima
Yamaguchi
Kure
Fukuyama
Onomichi
Imabari
AWAJI
Kishiwada
Wakayama
Tanabe
Shimonoseki
KITAKYUSHU
IKI
Imabari
Matsuyama
Takamatsu
Tokushima
Kii Suido
SHIONO MISAKI
Fukuoka
HIRADO
Usa
Nakatsu
Kochi
SHIKOKU
Muroto Zaki
Saseho
Goto Retto
Kurume
Kumamoto
Oita
Uwajima
Ashizuri Zaki
Nagasaki
FUKUE
Uto
Saiki
Nobeoka
Hososhima
AMAKUSA-SHIMO
KYUSHU
DANJO
KOSHIKI RETTO
Kajiki
Miyazaki
Miyakonojo
Kagoshima
TANEGA
YAKU
KEY ISLANDS
Kagoshima Wan
OSUMI GUNTO
TOI MISAKI
OSUMI KAIKYO

EAST CHINA SEA

SEA OF JAPAN

PACIFIC OCEAN

KOREA STRAIT

TSUSHIMA

KOREAN ARCHIPELAGO

PHILIPPINE SEA

NANSEI-SHOTO (RYUKYU ISLANDS)

TOKARA GUNTO
TOKARA KAIKYO
AMAMI GUNTO
AMAMI
KIKAIGA
TOKUNO
OKINAWA GUNTO
OKINO ERABU
YORON
OKINAWA
Naha
Shuri

YELLOW SEA
Bohai Haixia

Longitude East of Greenwich

A-561900-76   6-6-8
COPYRIGHT BY
RAND McNALLY & COMPANY
MADE IN U.S.A.

Scale 1:10 000 000; one inch to 160 miles. Bonne's Equal Area Projection
Elevations and depressions are given in feet

| 0 | 50 | 100 | 150 | 200 | 250 | 300 Miles |
| 0 | 100 | 200 | 300 | 400 | | 500 Kilometers |

Relief

Meters		Feet
3050		10 000
1525		5000
610		2000
305		1000
152.5		500
0	Sea Level	0
152.5		500
1525		5000
3050		10 000
6100		20 000

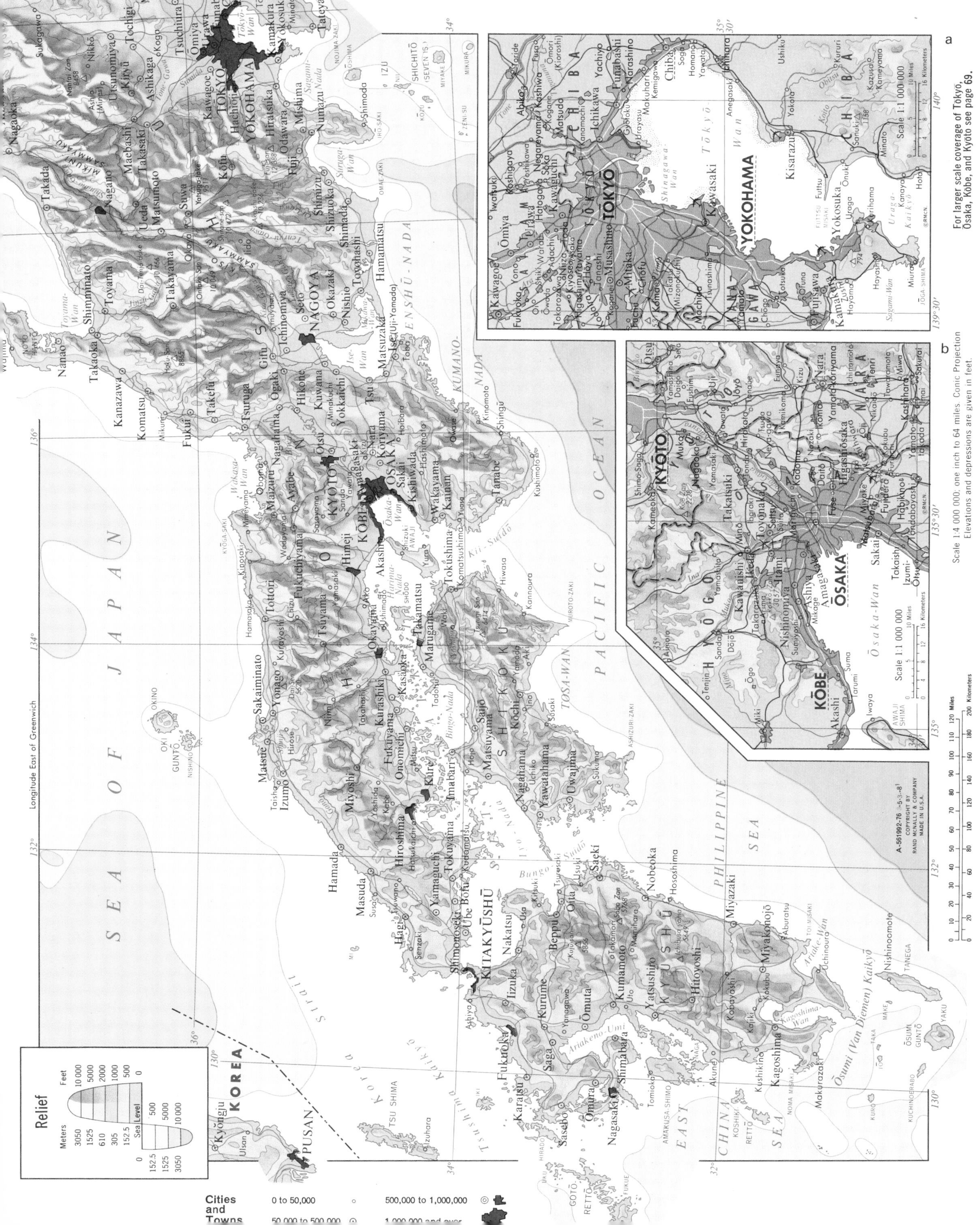

a

For larger scale coverage of Tōkyō,
Osaka, Kōbe, and Kyoto see page 69.

Scale 1:1 000 000

TŌKYŌ

YOKOHAMA

CHIBA

KANAGAWA

Tōkyō-Wan

b

Scale 1:4 000 000: one inch to 64 miles. Conic Projection
Elevations and depressions are given in feet.

KYOTO

ŌSAKA

KŌBE

HYŌGO

NARA

Scale 1:1 000 000

Ōsaka-Wan

SEA OF JAPAN

KOREA

PUSAN

Kyŏngju

Ulsan

PACIFIC OCEAN

PHILIPPINE SEA

EAST CHINA SEA

NAGOYA

KYOTO

OSAKA

KOBE

Himeji

TOKYO

YOKOHAMA

Chiba

HONSHU

SHIKOKU

KYUSHU

KITAKYŪSHŪ

Fukuoka

Nagasaki

Kagoshima

Hiroshima

Okayama

Takamatsu

Kōchi

Matsuyama

Ōita

Beppu

Kumamoto

Miyazaki

ENSHŪ-NADA

KUMANO-NADA

TOSA-WAN

Longitude East of Greenwich

A-561992-76 ·-5-3-87
COPYRIGHT BY
RAND McNALLY & COMPANY
MADE IN U.S.A.

Relief

Meters	Feet
3050	10 000
1525	5000
610	2000
305	1000
152.5	500
0	Sea Level 0
152.5	500
1525	5000
3050	10 000

Cities
and
Towns

0 to 50,000   500,000 to 1,000,000

50,000 to 500,000   1,000,000 and over

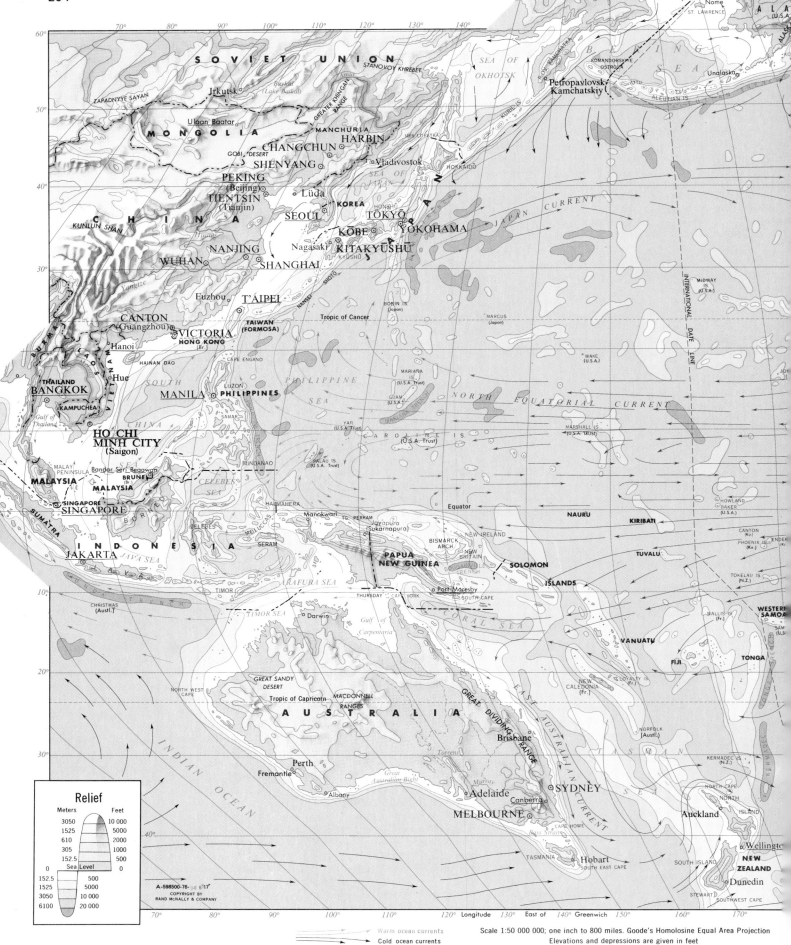

Relief

Meters		Feet
3050		10 000
1525		5000
610		2000
305		1000
152.5		500
0	Sea Level	0
152.5		500
1525		5000
3050		10 000
6100		20 000

A-598500-76
COPYRIGHT BY
RAND McNALLY & COMPANY

Warm ocean currents
Cold ocean currents

Scale 1:50 000 000; one inch to 800 miles. Goode's Homolosine Equal Area Projection
Elevations and depressions are given in feet

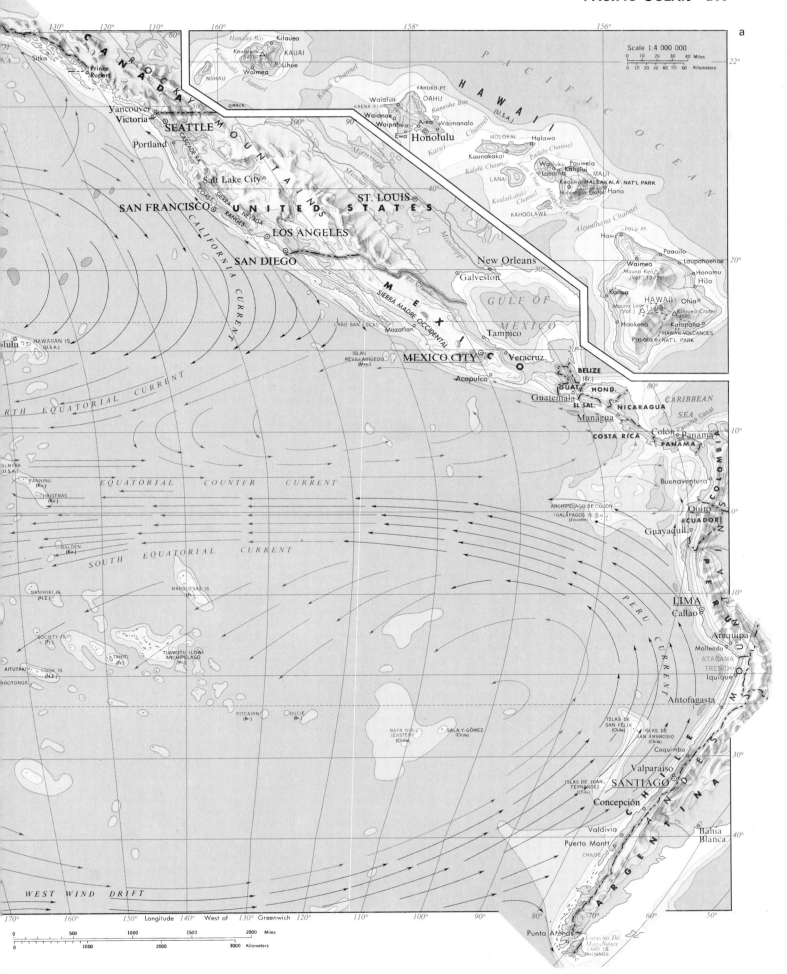

a

Scale 1:4 000 000

0 10 20 30 40 Miles
0 10 20 30 40 50 60 Kilometers

CANADA

ROCKY MOUNTAINS

CASCADE RA.

SIERRA NEVADA

COAST RANGES

CALIFORNIA CURRENT

UNITED STATES

SIERRA MADRE OCCIDENTAL

MEXICO

GULF OF MEXICO

CARIBBEAN SEA

NORTH EQUATORIAL CURRENT

EQUATORIAL COUNTER CURRENT

SOUTH EQUATORIAL CURRENT

PERU CURRENT

CHILE

ANDES

ARGENTINA

WEST WIND DRIFT

Sitka
Prince Rupert
Vancouver
Victoria
SEATTLE
Portland
Salt Lake City
SAN FRANCISCO
LOS ANGELES
SAN DIEGO
ST. LOUIS
New Orleans
Galveston
CABO SAN LUCAS
Mazatlan
Tampico
ISLAS REVILLAGIGEDO (Mex.)
MEXICO CITY
Veracruz
Acapulco
BELIZE (Br.)
GUAT. HOND.
Guatemala
EL SAL. NICARAGUA
Managua
COSTA RICA
Colón
Panama
PANAMA
COLOMBIA
Buenaventura
Quito
ECUADOR
Guayaquil
ARCHIPELAGO DE COLON
GALÁPAGOS IS. (Ecuador)
LIMA
Callao
Arequipa
Mollendo
ATACAMA TRENCH
Iquique
Antofagasta
ISLAS DE SAN FELIX (Chile)
ISLAS DE SAN AMBROSIO (Chile)
Coquimbo
Valparaiso
ISLAS DE JUAN FERNANDEZ (Chile)
SANTIAGO
Concepción
Valdivia
Puerto Montt
CHILOE
Bahía Blanca
Punta Arenas
Estrecho De Magallanes
CABO DE HORNOS

HAWAIIAN IS. (U.S.A.)
ALMYRA (U.S.A.)
FANNING (Kir.)
CHRISTMAS (Kir.)
MALDEN (Kir.)
MANIHIKI IS. (N.Z.)
MARQUESAS IS. (Fr.)
AITUTAKI COOK IS. (N.Z.)
Rarotonga
SOCIETY IS. (Fr.)
TAHITI (Fr.)
TUAMOTU (LOW) ARCHIPELAGO (Fr.)
PITCAIRN (Br.)
DUCIE (Br.)
RAPA NUI (EASTER) (Chile)
SALA-Y-GÓMEZ (Chile)

KAUAI
Hanalei Bay
Kilauea
Kawaikini 5170
Kekaha
Kauakahi
Waimea
Lihue
NIIHAU
Kauai Channel
OAHU
KAHUKU PT.
Waialua
KAENA PT.
Waianae
Waipahu
Ewa
Honolulu
Aiea
Waimanalo
Kaneohe Bay
Kaiwi Channel
MOLOKAI
Kaunakakai
Halawa
Kalohi Channel
LANAI
Wailuku
Pauwela
Kahului
Lahaina
MAUI
Keokea
HALEAKALA NAT'L PARK
Haleakala Crater
Hana
Kealaikahiki Channel
KAHOOLAWE
Alenuihaha Channel
UPOLU PT.
Hawi
Waimea
Mauna Kea (Vol.) 13,796
Paauilo
Laupahoehoe
Honomu
Hilo
Kailua
Ohia
HAWAII
Mauna Loa (Vol.) 13,680
Kilauea Crater 4090
Hookena
Kalapana
Pahala
HAWAII VOLCANOES NAT'L PARK

PACIFIC OCEAN

170° 160° 150° Longitude 140° West of 130° Greenwich 120° 110° 100° 90° 80° 70° 60° 50°

0   500   1000   1500   2000 Miles
0   1000   2000   3000 Kilometers

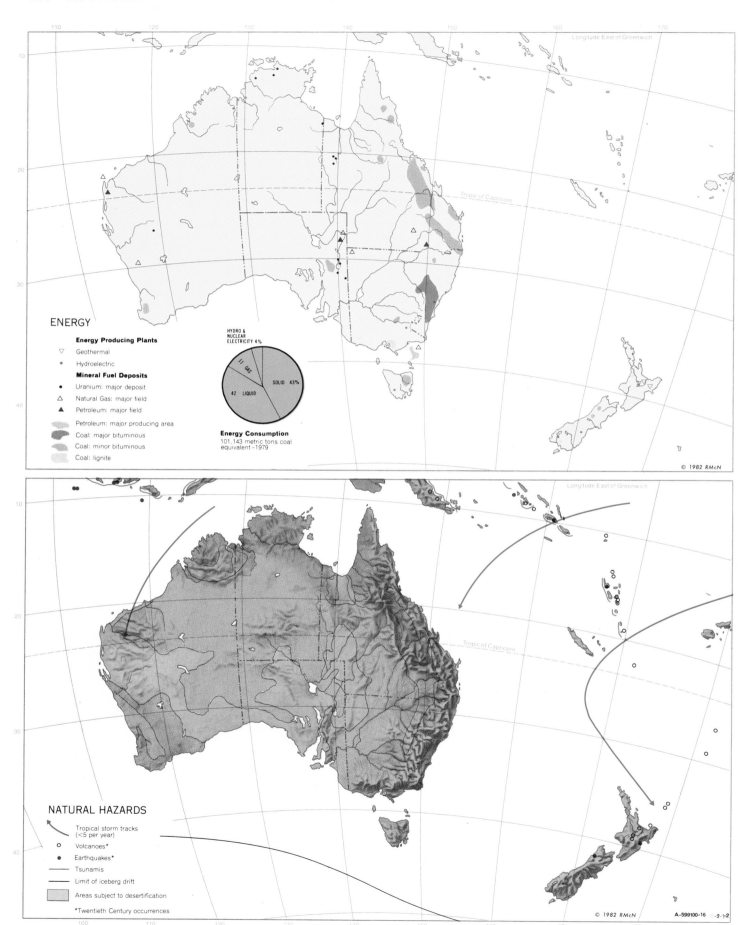

ENERGY

Energy Producing Plants

▽ Geothermal

• Hydroelectric

Mineral Fuel Deposits

• Uranium: major deposit

△ Natural Gas: major field

▲ Petroleum: major field

Petroleum: major producing area

Coal: major bituminous

Coal: minor bituminous

Coal: lignite

HYDRO &
NUCLEAR
ELECTRICITY 4%

GAS 11

SOLID 43%

LIQUID 42

Energy Consumption
101,143 metric tons coal
equivalent - 1979

© 1982 RMcN

NATURAL HAZARDS

↘ Tropical storm tracks
(<5 per year)

○ Volcanoes*

• Earthquakes*

— Tsunamis

— Limit of iceberg drift

Areas subject to desertification

*Twentieth Century occurrences

© 1982 RMcN   A-599100-16   -2-1-2

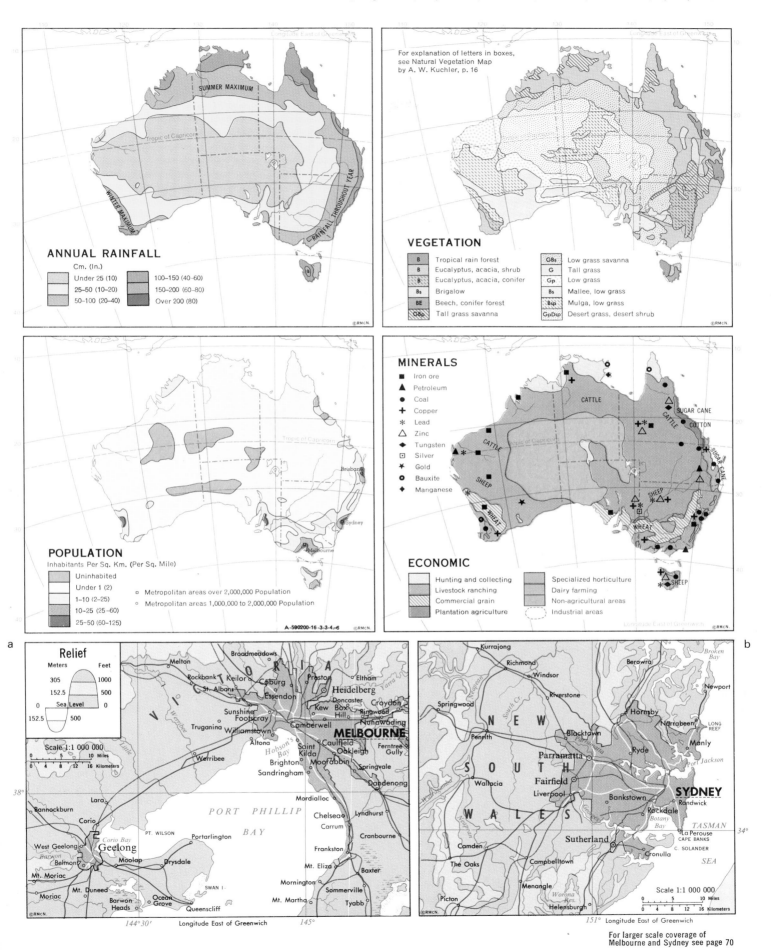

ANNUAL RAINFALL

Cm. (In.)

- Under 25 (10)
- 25–50 (10–20)
- 50–100 (20–40)
- 100–150 (40–60)
- 150–200 (60–80)
- Over 200 (80)

VEGETATION

For explanation of letters in boxes,
see Natural Vegetation Map
by A. W. Kuchler, p. 16

B	Tropical rain forest	GBs	Low grass savanna
B	Eucalyptus, acacia, shrub	G	Tall grass
B	Eucalyptus, acacia, conifer	Gp	Low grass
Bs	Brigalow	Bs	Mallee, low grass
BE	Beech, conifer forest	Bsp	Mulga, low grass
GBp	Tall grass savanna	GpDsp	Desert grass, desert shrub

POPULATION

Inhabitants Per Sq. Km. (Per Sq. Mile)

- Uninhabited
- Under 1 (2)
- 1–10 (2–25)
- 10–25 (25–60)
- 25–50 (60–125)

▫ Metropolitan areas over 2,000,000 Population
◦ Metropolitan areas 1,000,000 to 2,000,000 Population

A-590200-16-3-3-4.-6

MINERALS

- ■ Iron ore
- ▲ Petroleum
- ● Coal
- ＋ Copper
- ＊ Lead
- △ Zinc
- ◆ Tungsten
- ▣ Silver
- ✳ Gold
- ◎ Bauxite
- ◆ Manganese

ECONOMIC

- Hunting and collecting
- Livestock ranching
- Commercial grain
- Plantation agriculture
- Specialized horticulture
- Dairy farming
- Non-agricultural areas
- Industrial areas

a

Relief

Meters		Feet
305		1000
152.5		500
0	Sea Level	0
152.5		500

Scale 1:1 000 000

0   4   8   12   16 Kilometers
0   5   10 Miles

MELBOURNE

144°30'   Longitude East of Greenwich   145°

b

Scale 1:1 000 000

0   4   8   12   16 Kilometers
0   5   10 Miles

SYDNEY

151° Longitude East of Greenwich

For larger scale coverage of
Melbourne and Sydney see page 70

Legend:

- Urban
- Cropland
- Cropland & Woodland
- Cropland & Grazing Land
- Grassland, Grazing Land
- Forest, Woodland
- Swamp, Marshland
- Shrub, Sparse Grass; Wasteland (pattern)
- Barren Land

SINGAPORE

BORNEO

CELEBES

SERAM

SUMATRA

Palembang

Banjarmasin

Java Sea

Ujung Pandang

JAKARTA

Surabaya

Arafura Sea

JAVA

SUMBA

TIMOR

Timor Sea

Darwin

Gulf of Carpentaria

INDIAN OCEAN

KIMBERLEY PLATEAU

Daly

Victoria

Broome

Fitzroy

Mount Isa

GREAT SANDY DESERT

Alice Springs

GIBSON DESERT

SIMPSON DESERT

GREA ARTESI BASI

Carnarvon

Tropic of Capricorn

GREAT VICTORIA DESERT

Lake Eyre

Kalgoorlie

NULLARBOR PLAIN

Lake Gairdner

Broken Hill

Great Australian Bight

FLINDERS RANGES

DARLING RA.

Murray

Perth

Adelaide

INDIAN OCEAN

Scale 1:24,000,000; one inch to 380 miles. Lambert Azimuthal Equal-Area Projection

KIRIBATI

Equator

P A C I F I C   O C E A N

NEW BRITAIN

resby

SOLOMON ISLANDS

Coral   Sea

airns

Townsville

VANUATU

SAMOA ISLANDS

Pago Pago

FIJI
ISLANDS

Suva

Rockhampton

NEW
CALEDONIA

ÎLES
LOYAUTÉ

Nouméa

TONGA ISLANDS

RANGE

Brisbane

GREAT DIVIDING RANGE

SYDNEY

Canberra

Tasman   Sea

P A C I F I C

MELBOURNE

Auckland

NORTH ISLAND

O C E A N

TASMANIA

Hobart

SOUTHERN ALPS

Wellington

Christchurch

SOUTH ISLAND

STEWART
ISLAND

Dunedin

A-590200-96 -1- 7
COPYRIGHT BY
RAND MCNALLY & COMPANY
MADE IN U.S.A.

| 0 | 100 | 200 | 400 | 600 | 800 Miles |

| 0 | 150 | 300 | 600 | 900 | 1200 Kilometers |

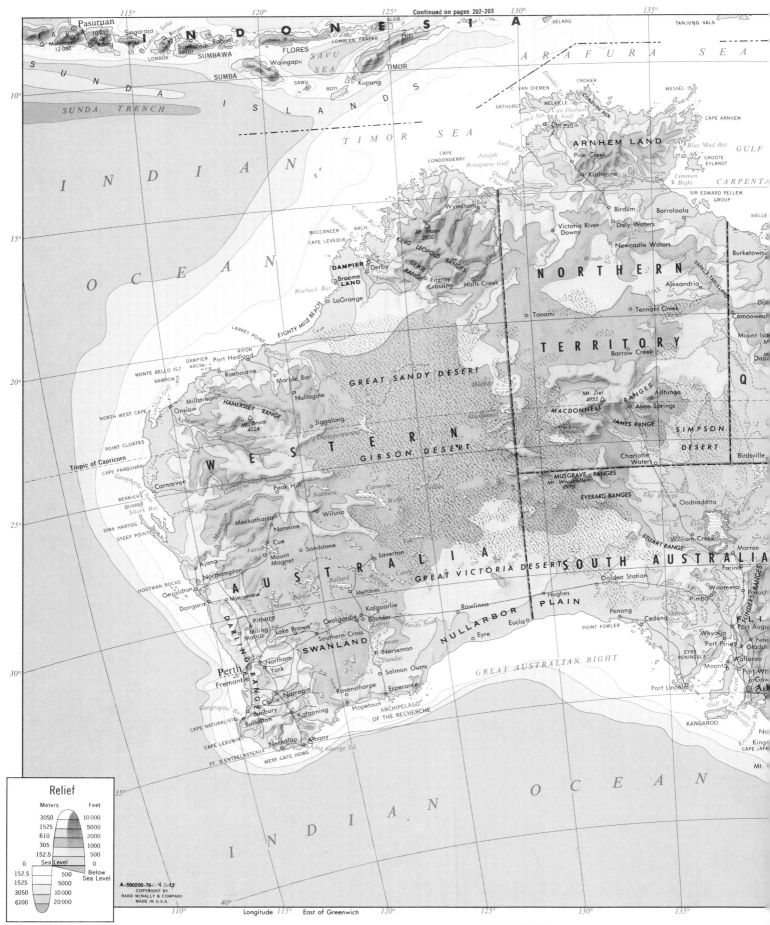

210

Continued on pages 202-203

S U N D A   I S L A N D S

INDONESIA

Pasuruan

SAVU Mahameru 10932 Rinjani
G. 12060 G. Raung

Singaraja Lombok Selat
LOMBOK Rinjani 225
Sumbawa Besar Raba
SUMBAWA FLORES
SUMBA Waingapu
SAWU Savu Sea
ROTI Kupang

ALOR
LOMBLEN PANTAR
DILI
TIMOR

SELARU

ARAFURA SEA

TANJUNG VALS

C. VAN DIEMEN CROKER
Dundas Str.
MELVILLE Coburg Pen. WESSEL IS.
Van Diemen Bathurst Gulf
Darwin Clarence Str.
Anson Bay Queen Chan.
Pine Creek
Katherine

CAPE ARNHEM

Blue Mud Bay
Groote Eylandt
Limmen Bight
SIR EDWARD PELLEW GROUP

ARNHEM LAND

WELLE
GULF

CARPENTA

TIMOR   SEA

CAPE LONDONDERRY
Joseph Bonaparte Gulf

Wyndham
Mt. Hann 2800

KING LEOPOLD RANGES

Victoria River Downs

Birdum
Daly Waters
Newcastle Waters

Borroloola

Alexandria

Burketown

BUCCANEER ARCH.
CAPE LEVEQUE
Sunday Str.
King Sd.

Collier Bay

DAMPIER Derby GEIKIE RANGE Fitzroy
LAND Broome Crossing Halls Creek
Roebuck Bay Fitzroy

Sturt Cr.

NORTHERN

Tanami

Tennant Creek

Camooweal
Mount Isa
Daje
Do

Q

LaGrange
EIGHTY MILE BEACH
LARREY POINT

GREAT SANDY DESERT

TERRITORY

Barrow Creek

RIPON Port Hedland DeGrey
DAMPIER ARCH. Roebourne
MONTE BELLO IS. BARROW Marble Bar
NORTH WEST CAPE

Nullagine

HAMERSLEY RANGE
Millstream Mt. Bruce 4024
Onslow

W E S T E R N

Mt. Ziel 4955
MACDONNELL RANGES Arltunga
Alice Springs
JAMES RANGE

SIMPSON
DESERT

Birdsville

POINT CLOATES

Jiggalong

GIBSON DESERT

Disappointment

Charlotte
Waters

Tropic of Capricorn
CAPE FARQUHAR
Carnarvon
Gascoyne

Peak Hill

Nabberu

Carnegie

MUSGRAVE RANGES
Mt. Woodroffe 4970
EVERARD RANGES

Oodnadatta

The Alberga

BERNIER I.
DORRE I. Shark Bay
DIRK HARTOG
STEEP POINT

Meekatharra
Nannine
Cue

Wiluna

Sandstone

STUART RANGE

William Creek

Marree

Welf
Carey

A U S T R A L I A

Austin Mount Magnet

Laverton

GREAT VICTORIA DESERT
SOUTH AUSTRALIA

Farina

Ajana
Northampton
HOUTMAN ROCKS
Geraldton
Dongara

Ballard
Menzies

Rawlinna

Coldea Station

Woomera
Pimba
Parach

Mingenew
Moore
Pithara
Miling
Moora Lake Brown

Kalgoorlie
Coolgardie Boulder
Goddards Soak

NULLARBOR PLAIN
Rawlinna
Eucla
Eyre

Hughes

Penong
POINT FOWLER
Ceduna

Everard
Gairdner

Whyalla
Port Pirie

EYRE
PENINSULA

FLI
Port Augu
Pete

Perth
Fremantle

Southern Cross
SWANLAND
Cowan
Norseman
Dundas
Salmon Gums

GREAT AUSTRALIAN BIGHT

Port Lincoln

Moonta
Port
Gaw

Geographe Bay
Bunbury
Busselton
CAPE NATURALISTE
CAPE LEEUWIN

Northam York
Collie Narrogin
Katanning
Hopetoun

Ravensthorpe Esperance
ARCHIPELAGO OF THE RECHERCHE

KANGAROO

Ad

Nornalup Albany
PT. D'ENTRECASTEAUX King George Sd.
WEST CAPE HOWE

Na
Kings
CAPE JAFF
Mt.

I N D I A N   O C E A N

Longitude 115° East of Greenwich

Scale 1:16 000 000; one inch to 250 miles. Lambert's Azimuthal, Equal Area Project
Elevations and depressions are given in feet

Relief

Meters		Feet
3050		10 000
1525		5000
610		2000
305		1000
152.5		500
0	Sea Level	0
152.5		500
1525	Below Sea Level	5000
3050		10 000
6100		20 000

PAPUA NEW GUINEA

Mt. Albert Edward
13 100
Buna

Mt. Victoria
13 363
Port Moresby
OWEN STANLEY RA.
SOUTH CAPE
Samarai

Torrès Strait
BANKS
HORN I.
CAPE YORK

TROBRIAND IS.
WOODLARK
D'ENTRECASTEAUX
ISLANDS
LOUISIADE
ARCHIPELAGO
TAGULA
ROSSEL

CHOISEUL
VELLA
LAVELLA
NEW
GEORGIA
RENDOVA
RUSSELL IS.
GUADALCANAL
SANTA ISABEL
MALAITA
FLORIDA
HONIARA
HULAGI
SAN CRISTÓBAL

SOLOMON ISLANDS

RENNELL

SANTA CRUZ
ISLANDS

TORRES IS.
BANKS
ISLANDS

ESPÍRITU SANTO
MAEWO
PENTECOST
MALEKULA
AMBRIM
EPI
EFATE
Vila

VANUATU

EROMANGA
TANA
ANEITYUM

CAPE
YORK
PENINSULA

CAPE MELVILLE
OSPREY REEF

C O R A L   S E A

HOLMES
REEFS
WILLIS IS.

FLINDERS
REEFS

LIHOU REEFS

TREGROSSE IS.

MARION REEF

ÎLES CHESTERFIELD
(Fr.)

ÎLES BÉLEP

OUVÉA
LIFOU
ÎLES LOYAUTÉ
(French)
MARE

**NEW
CALEDONIA**
(Fr.)
Nouméa
ÎLE DES PINS

P A C I F I C   O C E A N

ATHERTON
PLATEAU

Mt. Bartle Frere
3287

Cairns
Mungana
Croydon
Forsayth
Ingham
Gilbert
Mitchell

GREAT BARRIER REEF

GREAT   DIVIDING   RANGE
GREGORY RANGE

Charters Towers
Richmond
Hughenden
Townsville
HINCHINBROOK I.
Halifax Bay

Bowen
WHITSUNDAY IS.
Mt. Dalrymple
4190
Mackay
Répulse Bay
CUMBERLAND IS.

NORTHUMBERLAND IS.
SWAIN REEFS

WRECK REEFS

QUEENSLAND

Kynuna
Winton
Clermont
Emerald
Dingo
BUCKLAND TABLELAND

CONNORS RANGE
Clarke Ra.

Rockhampton
Mount Morgan
CURTIS
Gladstone

CAPRICORN CHANNEL

Langreach
Barcaldine
Jericho
Blackall
Tambo

Thomson
Barcoo

Quilpie
Charleville
Roma

Thargomindah
Cunnamulla
St. George
DARLING
DOWNS
Dalby
Toowoomba
Warwick
Ipswich
Brisbane
N. STRADBROKE I.
Southport

G R E A T   D I V I D I N G   R A N G E

Hungerford
Dirranbandi
Mungindi
Moree
Inverell
Glen Innes
Tenterfield
NEW
ENGLAND
RANGE
Grafton
Lismore

Bundaberg
Hervey Bay
SANDY CAPE
Maryborough
FRASER I.
Gympie

Tropic of Capricorn

25°
30°

Bourke
Brewarrina
Walgett
Narrabri
Tamworth
Armidale
The Round Mountain
3300
Kempsey

N E W   S O U T H   W A L E S

Wilcannia
Cobar
Nyngan
Coonamble
Dubbo
WARRUMBUNGLE RA.
LIVERPOOL RA.
Port Macquarie

Broken Hill
Wyalong
West Wyalong
Forbes
Bathurst
Lithgow
Orange
BLUE MTS.
Maitland
Newcastle
SYDNEY
Wollongong
Botany Bay

P A C I F I C   O C E A N

LORD HOWE I.
(NEW S. WALES)

Wentworth
Hay
Narrandera
Wagga Wagga
Goulburn
Jervis Bay

RIVERINA
MURRAY
BARRIER RANGE

Deniliquin
Albury
Cooma
AUSTL. CAP. TER.
Canberra
Kosciusko
7316
SNOWY MTS.
Bega
Bombala

Kerang
Echuca
Benalla
GREAT
DIVIDING
Bairnsdale
CAPE HOWE

Bendigo
Maryborough
MELBOURNE
NINETY MILE BEACH

V I C T O R I A
Ballarat
Geelong
Warrnambool
CAPE OTWAY
Port Phillip
Wonthaggi
WILSON'S PROMONTORY

T A S M A N   S E A

35°

FURNEAUX GROUP
CAPE BARREN
FLINDERS I.

HUNTER IS.
KING I.
BASS STRAIT

Burnie
Ulverstone
Devonport
Strahan
MT.
5305

TASMANIA
Launceston
New Norfolk
Hobart
BRUNY I.
SOUTH EAST CAPE

40°

**NEW
ZEALAND**

NORTH CAPE
Kaitaia
Russell

P A C I F I C   O C E A N

GREAT
BARRIER
Devonport
HAURAKI GULF
Auckland
NORTH ISLAND
Hamilton
Bay of
Plenty
EAST CAPE

34°
38°

North Taranaki Bight
New Plymouth
C. EGMONT
South
Taranaki Bight
Wanganui
Gisborne
HAWKE BAY
Napier
Hastings
Palmerston North

T A S M A N   S E A

CAPE
FAREWELL
Tasman
Bay
Nelson
Lower Hutt
Wellington
Cook Strait

Karamea Bight
CAPE FOULWIND
Greymouth
Hokitika

SOUTH ISLAND
SOUTHERN ALPS
MT.
COOK
12 349

Pegasus Bay
Christchurch
Canterbury Bight
Timaru

CASCADE PT.
RESOLUTION
ISLAND
Dunedin
CAPE SAUNDERS

Invercargill
STEWART ISLAND
Foveaux Strait
SOUTHWEST
CAPE

P A C I F I C   O C E A N

42°
46°

168°   172°   176°   180°

Same scale as main map

---

0   50   100   200   300   400   500 Miles
0   100   200   400   600   800 Kilometers

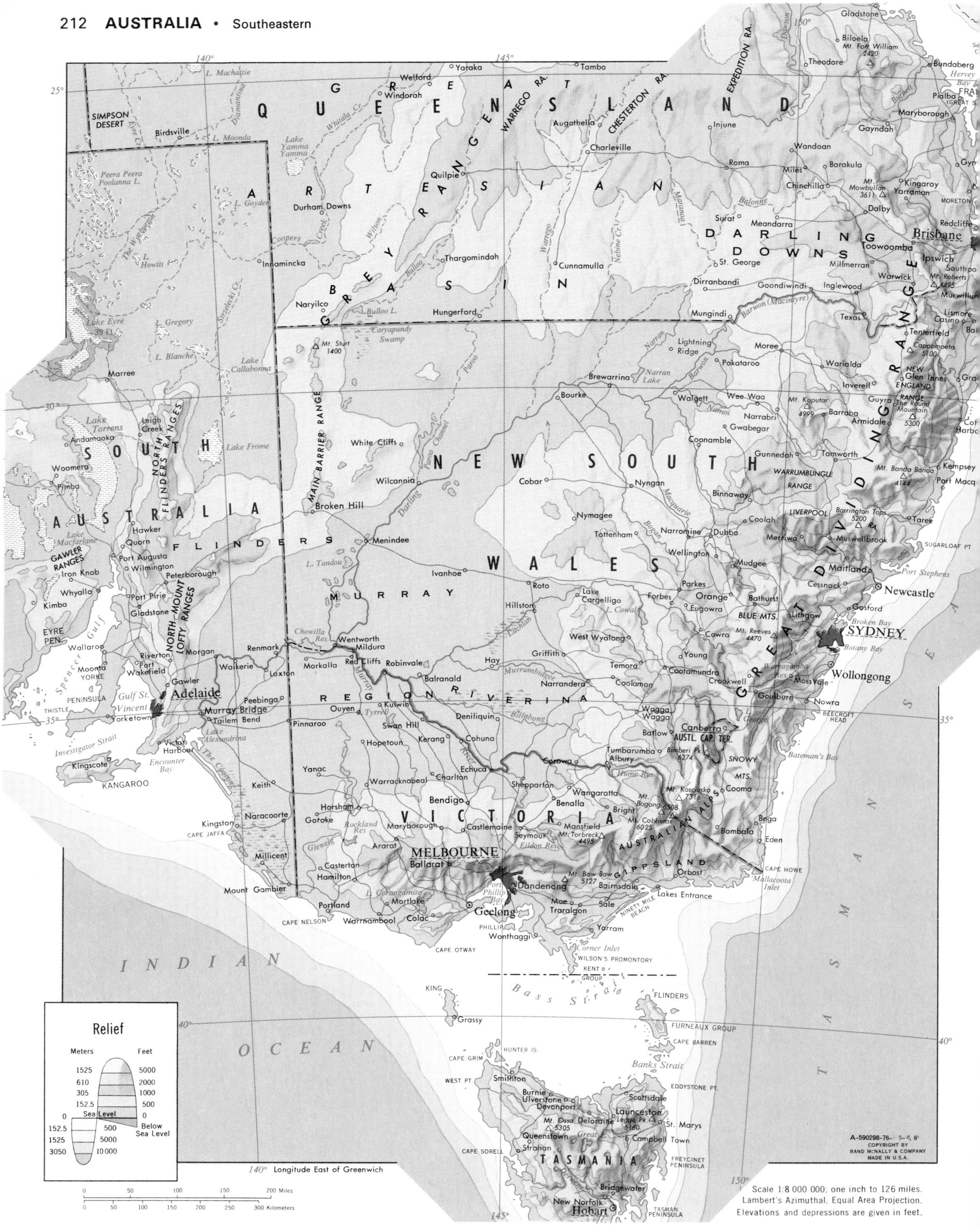

QUEENSLAND

GREAT DIVIDING RANGE

GREAT ARTESIAN BASIN

GREY RANGE

SOUTH AUSTRALIA

NORTH FLINDERS RANGES

FLINDERS RANGES

NORTH MOUNT LOFTY RANGES

GAWLER RANGES

EYRE PEN.

NEW SOUTH WALES

MAIN BARRIER RANGE

MURRAY

RIVERINA

REGION

WARRUMBUNGLE RANGE

LIVERPOOL RANGE

NEW ENGLAND

THE ROUND MOUNTAIN

BLUE MTS.

DARLING DOWNS

MORETON

VICTORIA

GIPPSLAND

AUSTRALIAN ALPS

SNOWY MTS.

AUSTL. CAP. TER.

KANGAROO

THISTLE

YORKE PENINSULA

BEECROFT HEAD

SUGARLOAF PT.

INDIAN OCEAN

TASMANIA

TASMAN SEA

Bass Strait

KING

FLINDERS

FURNEAUX GROUP

CAPE BARREN

HUNTER IS.

Banks Strait

KENT GROUP

WILSON'S PROMONTORY

Corner Inlet

NINETY MILE BEACH

Cities and towns:
Brisbane, Ipswich, Redcliffe, Southport, Toowoomba, Warwick, Dalby, Kingaroy, Yarraman, Maryborough, Gayndah, Wandoan, Barakula, Chinchilla, Miles, Millmerran, Goondiwindi, Inglewood, Texas, Lismore, Casino, Tenterfield, Cooroopa, Glen Innes, Inverell, Warialda, Armidale, Guyra, Barraba, Gwabegar, Kempsey, Port Macquarie, Tamworth, Gunnedah, Coonabarabran, Coonamble, Narrabri, Walgett, Wee Waa, Narromine, Dubbo, Wellington, Mudgee, Merriwa, Muswellbrook, Maitland, Cessnock, Newcastle, Gosford, Taree, Broken Bay, SYDNEY, Botany Bay, Wollongong, Port Stephens

Surat, St. George, Dirranbandi, Mungindi, Lightning Ridge, Moree, Pokataroo, Brewarrina, Bourke, Cobar, Nymagee, Nyngan, Cootamundra, Young, Cowra, Orange, Bathurst, Lithgow, Canberra, Goulburn, Crookwell, Moss Vale, Nowra, Bateman's Bay

St. George, Cunnamulla, Hungerford, Thargomindah, Quilpie, Windorah, Welford, Yaraka, Tambo, Augathella, Charleville, Injune, Roma

Naryilco, Innamincka, Birdsville, Durham Downs, Coopers Creek

Marree, Andamooka, Leigh Creek, Hawker, Quorn, Port Augusta, Wilmington, Peterborough, Woomera, Pimba, Iron Knob, Whyalla, Kimba, Wallaroo, Moonta, Port Pirie, Gladstone, Port Wakefield, Riverton, Kingscote, Victor Harbour, Yorketown, Murray Bridge, Tailem Bend, Adelaide, Gawler, Peebinga, Pinnaroo, Keith, Naracoorte, Kingston, Millicent, Mount Gambier, Portland, Warrnambool

Renmark, Morgan, Waikerie, Loxton, Mildura, Wentworth, Red Cliffs, Morkalla, Robinvale, Balranald, Hillston, Hay, Griffith, Narrandera, Deniliquin, Cohuna, Swan Hill, Kerang, Echuca, Corowa, Albury, Tumbarumba, Wagga Wagga, Batlow, Cooma, Bombala, Eden, Bega, Orbost, Bairnsdale, Sale, Lakes Entrance, Yarram, Traralgon, Moe, Wonthaggi, Colac, Geelong, Dandenong, MELBOURNE, Ballarat, Ararat, Horsham, Hamilton, Casterton, Mortlake, Nhill

White Cliffs, Wilcannia, Menindee, Ivanhoe, Broken Hill, Tibooburra, L. Tandou

Lake Eyre 39 Ft., Lake Torrens, Lake Frome, Lake Callabonna, Lake Blanche, Lake Gregory, L. Macfarlane, Lake Gairdner

Launceston, Devonport, Burnie, Ulverstone, Smithton, Scottsdale, St. Marys, Deloraine, Campbell Town, Queenstown, Strahan, Bridgewater, New Norfolk, Hobart

Mt. Ossa 5305, Legge Pk. 5160, Mt. Kosciusko 7316, Mt. Bogong 6508, Mt. Cobberas 6025, Mt. Torbreck 4495, Mt. Baw Baw 5127, Bimberi Pk. 6274, Mt. Kaputar 4999, Mt. Banda Banda 4144, Barrington Tops 5200, Mt. Reeves 4470, Cappoompeta 5100, Mt. Mowbullan 3611, Mt. Roberts 4495, Mt. Fort William 2420, Mt. Shirt 1400

CAPE OTWAY, CAPE NELSON, CAPE JAFFA, CAPE GRIM, WEST PT., CAPE SORELL, FREYCINET PENINSULA, EDDYSTONE PT., CAPE BARREN, TASMAN PENINSULA, CAPE HOWE, Mallacoota Inlet

A-590298-76- 5-6, 8'
COPYRIGHT BY
RAND McNALLY & COMPANY
MADE IN U.S.A.

Scale 1:8 000 000; one inch to 126 miles.
Lambert's Azimuthal, Equal Area Projection.
Elevations and depressions are given in feet.

140° Longitude East of Greenwich

Relief

Meters	Feet
1525	5000
610	2000
305	1000
152.5	500
0 Sea Level	0
152.5	500 Below Sea Level
1525	5000
3050	10 000

0   50   100   150   200 Miles
0   50   100   150   200   250   300 Kilometers

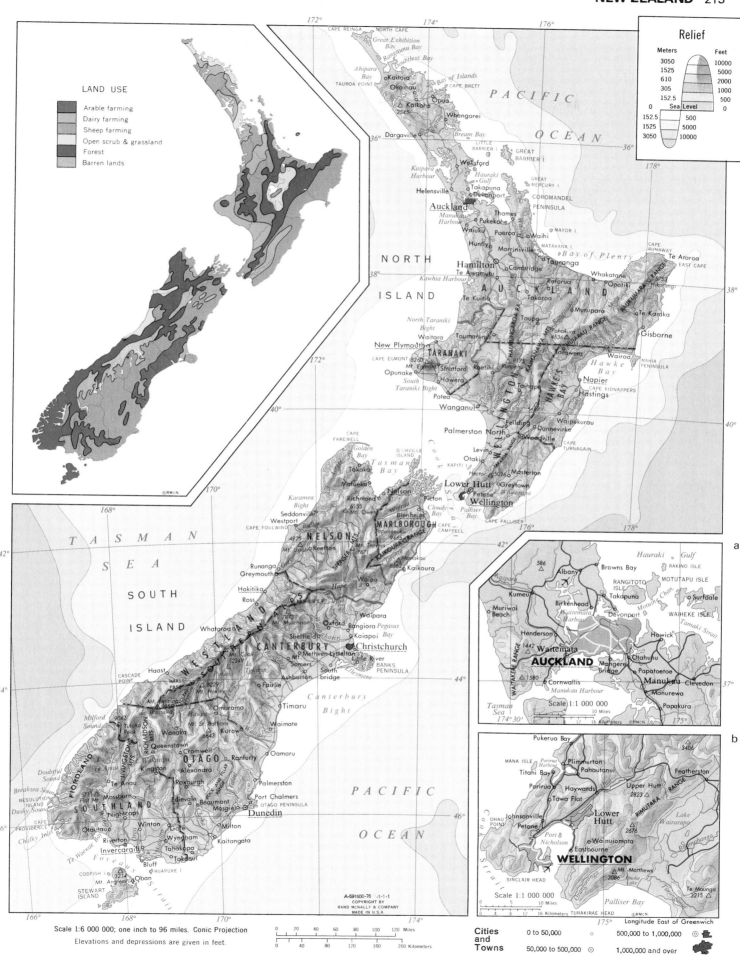

LAND USE

- Arable farming
- Dairy farming
- Sheep farming
- Open scrub & grassland
- Forest
- Barren lands

Relief

Meters		Feet
3050		10000
1525		5000
610		2000
305		1000
152.5		500
0	Sea Level	0
152.5		500
1525		5000
3050		10000

PACIFIC OCEAN

NORTH ISLAND

TASMAN SEA

SOUTH ISLAND

PACIFIC OCEAN

Scale 1:6 000 000; one inch to 96 miles. Conic Projection
Elevations and depressions are given in feet.

A-591600-76   -1-1-1
COPYRIGHT BY
RAND McNALLY & COMPANY
MADE IN U.S.A.

Scale 1:1 000 000

Cities and Towns

0 to 50,000	500,000 to 1,000,000
50,000 to 500,000	1,000,000 and over

Longitude East of Greenwich

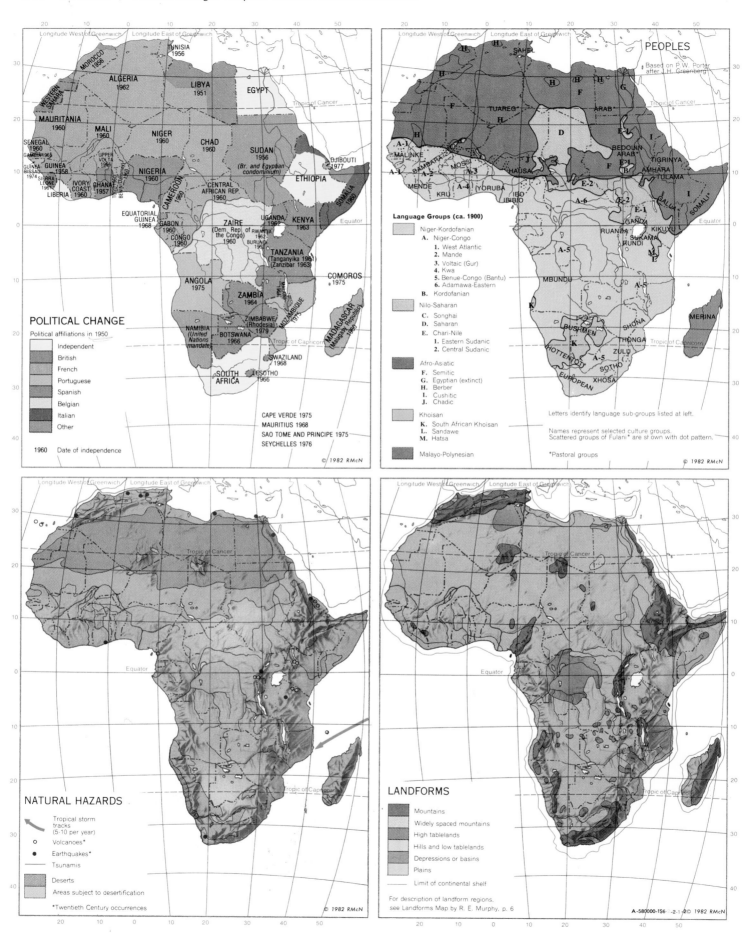

POLITICAL CHANGE

Political affiliations in 1950

- Independent
- British
- French
- Portuguese
- Spanish
- Belgian
- Italian
- Other

1960 Date of independence

CAPE VERDE 1975
MAURITIUS 1968
SAO TOME AND PRINCIPE 1975
SEYCHELLES 1976

© 1982 RMcN

PEOPLES

Based on P. W. Porter
after J. H. Greenberg

Language Groups (ca. 1900)

Niger-Kordofanian
  A. Niger-Congo
    1. West Atlantic
    2. Mande
    3. Voltaic (Gur)
    4. Kwa
    5. Benue-Congo (Bantu)
    6. Adamawa-Eastern
  B. Kordofanian

Nilo-Saharan
  C. Songhai
  D. Saharan
  E. Chari-Nile
    1. Eastern Sudanic
    2. Central Sudanic

Afro-Asiatic
  F. Semitic
  G. Egyptian (extinct)
  H. Berber
  I. Cushitic
  J. Chadic

Khoisan
  K. South African Khoisan
  L. Sandawe
  M. Hatsa

Malayo-Polynesian

Letters identify language sub-groups listed at left.

Names represent selected culture groups.
Scattered groups of Fulani* are shown with dot pattern.

*Pastoral groups

© 1982 RMcN

NATURAL HAZARDS

→ Tropical storm tracks (5-10 per year)
○ Volcanoes*
● Earthquakes*
— Tsunamis

- Deserts
- Areas subject to desertification

*Twentieth Century occurrences

© 1982 RMcN

LANDFORMS

- Mountains
- Widely spaced mountains
- High tablelands
- Hills and low tablelands
- Depressions or basins
- Plains

— Limit of continental shelf

For description of landform regions,
see Landforms Map by R. E. Murphy, p. 6

A-580000-1S6 -2-1-2© 1982 RMcN

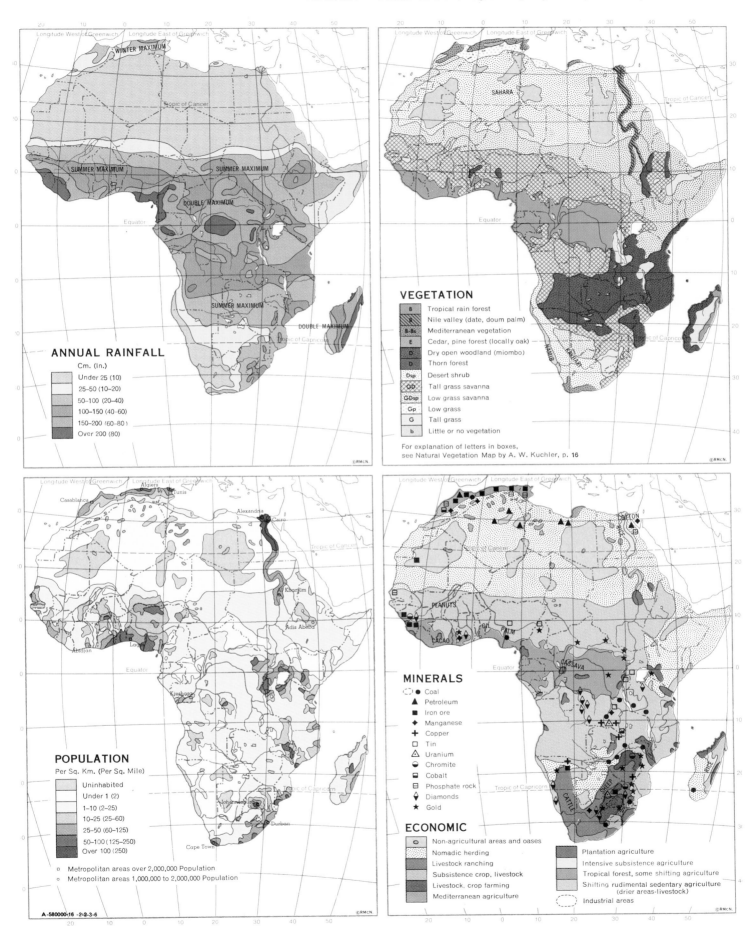

ANNUAL RAINFALL

Cm. (In.)

- Under 25 (10)
- 25–50 (10–20)
- 50–100 (20–40)
- 100–150 (40–60)
- 150–200 (60–80)
- Over 200 (80)

VEGETATION

B	Tropical rain forest
Bₙ	Nile valley (date, doum palm)
B-Bₓ	Mediterranean vegetation
E	Cedar, pine forest (locally oak)
D	Dry open woodland (miombo)
Dₜ	Thorn forest
Dsp	Desert shrub
GD	Tall grass savanna
GDsp	Low grass savanna
Gp	Low grass
G	Tall grass
b	Little or no vegetation

For explanation of letters in boxes,
see Natural Vegetation Map by A. W. Kuchler, p. 16

POPULATION

Per Sq. Km. (Per Sq. Mile)

- Uninhabited
- Under 1 (2)
- 1–10 (2–25)
- 10–25 (25–60)
- 25–50 (60–125)
- 50–100 (125–250)
- Over 100 (250)

□ Metropolitan areas over 2,000,000 Population
○ Metropolitan areas 1,000,000 to 2,000,000 Population

A-580000-16 -2-2-3-6

MINERALS

- ⬭ ● Coal
- ▲ Petroleum
- ■ Iron ore
- ◆ Manganese
- ✛ Copper
- □ Tin
- △ Uranium
- ○ Chromite
- ▱ Cobalt
- ⊟ Phosphate rock
- ⬧ Diamonds
- ★ Gold

ECONOMIC

- ⬭ Non-agricultural areas and oases
- Nomadic herding
- Livestock ranching
- Subsistence crop, livestock
- Livestock, crop farming
- Mediterranean agriculture
- Plantation agriculture
- Intensive subsistence agriculture
- Tropical forest, some shifting agriculture
- Shifting rudimental sedentary agriculture (drier areas-livestock)
- ⬭ Industrial areas

BERLIN
LONDON
PARIS
MADRID

ALPS
ROME
PYRENEES
Casablanca

ATLAS
MOUNTAINS
Algiers
Tunis
Tripoli

CORSICA
SARDINIA
SICILY
MALTA

Mediterranean Sea

Athens
CRETE

Alexandria
CAIRO
ARABIAN DESERT
Nile
Lake Nasser
NUBIAN DESERT
Nile

Banghāzī

LIBYAN DESERT

S A H A R A

GRAND ERG OCCIDENTAL
GRAND ERG ORIENTAL
AHAGGAR
Tamanrasset
ADRAR DES IFORAS

TIBESTI
ENNEDI

CANARY ISLANDS
El Aaiun

EL DJOUF
Tombouctou
Niger
Bamako

Lake Chad
Ndjamena
Kano

Niger
Lagos
Lake Volta
Abidjan

Yaoundé

Gulf of Guinea

ATLANTIC OCEAN
Tropic of Cancer

Dakar
CAPE VERDE ISLANDS
Freetown

ATLANTIC OCEAN

Red Sea

Scale 1:24,000,000; one inch to 380 miles. Lambert Azimuthal Equal-Area Projection

Legend:

- Urban
- Cropland
- Cropland & Woodland
- Cropland & Grazing Land
- Grassland, Grazing Land
- Forest, Woodland
- Swamp, Marshland
- Shrub, Sparse Grass; Wasteland (pattern)
- Barren Land
- • Oasis

Gulf of Aden

Aden

Berbera

DANAKIL

Asmera

Blue Nile

Adis Abeba

White Nile

Mountain Nile

Muqdisho

SEYCHELLES

INDIAN OCEAN

Equator

Nairobi

Dar es Salaam

Lake Victoria

COMORO ISLANDS

Moçambique Channel

Antananarivo

MADAGASCAR

Tropic of Capricorn

Uele

Kisangani

Lake Tanganyika

Lake Nyasa

Blantyre

Ubangi

Congo (Zaire)

Kasai

Lubumbashi

Salisbury

Lusaka

Congo (Zaire)

Kinshasa

Zambezi

Luanda

Limpopo

Durban

Johannesburg

KALAHARI DESERT

Orange

Windhoek

NAMIB DESERT

Orange

INDIAN OCEAN

Cape Town

A-580000-96 -2-2-3

Scale:
0 100 200 400 600 800 Miles
0 150 300 600 900 1200 Kilometers

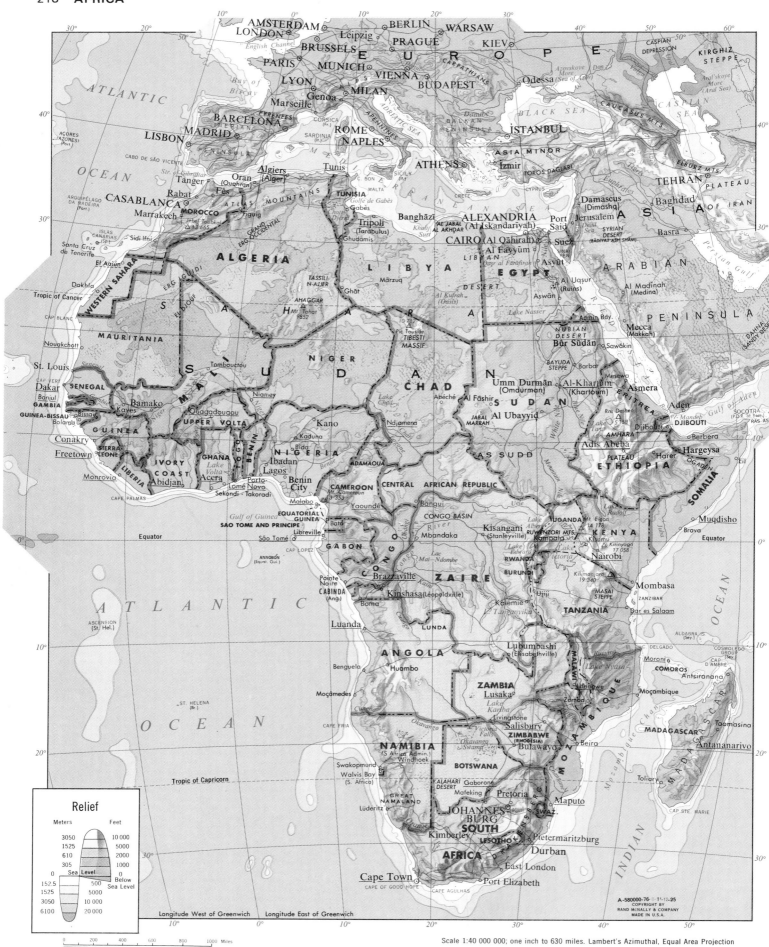

Scale 1:40 000 000; one inch to 630 miles. Lambert's Azimuthal, Equal Area Projection
Elevations and depressions are given in feet.

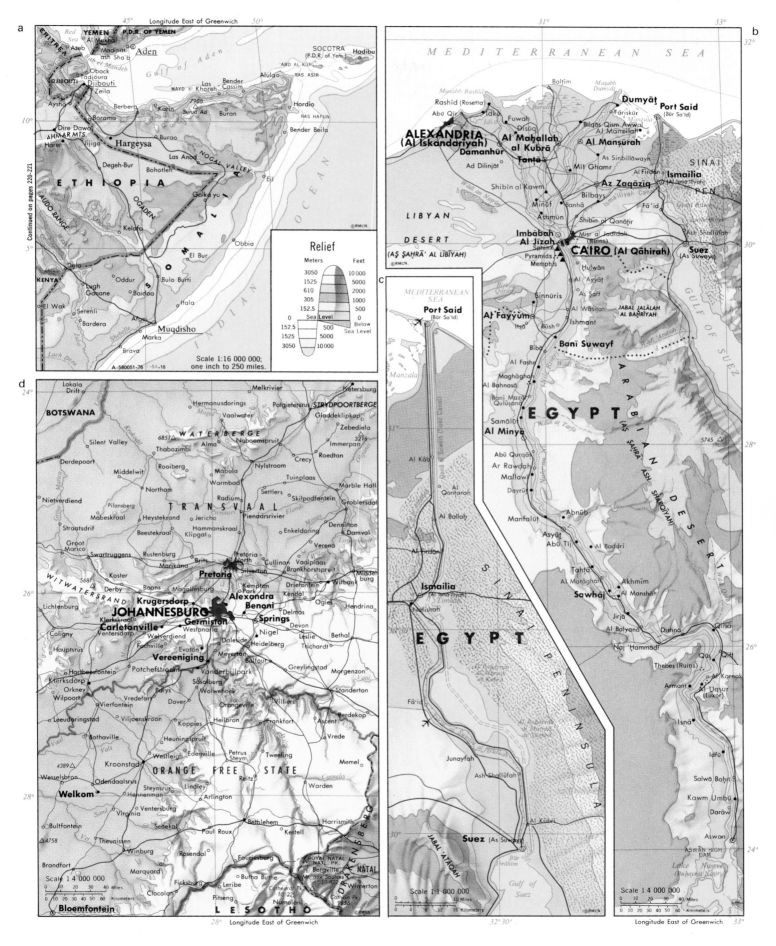

a

Longitude East of Greenwich

Red Sea
ERITREA
YEMEN
P.D.R. OF YEMEN
Aseb
El Mukha
Madinat
ash Sha'b
Aden
SOCOTRA
(P.D.R. of Yem.)
HADIBU
ABD AL-KURI
RAS ASIR
Obock
Tadjoura
Djibouti
DJIBOUTI
Zeila
MAYD I.
Alula
Bender
Cassim
Berbera
Las Khoreh
Aysha
Borama
Karin
7900
Surud Ad
Hordio
Bender Beila
Dire Dawa
AHMAR MTS.
Burao
Harer
Jijiga
Hargeysa
Las Anod
Degeh-Bur
Bohotleh
Eil
ETHIOPIA
OGADEN
NOGAL VALLEY
Galka yo
Kelafo
Obbia
AUDO RANGE
Dolo
El Bur
KENYA
Lugh Ganane
Oddur
Bulo Burti
El Wak
Baidoa
Serenli
Itala
Bardera
Afgoi
Muqdisho
Marka
Brava
Lach Dera
SOMALI
Shebelle
INDIAN OCEAN
Gulf of Aden
Bab el Mandeb

©RMCN

Relief

Meters	Feet
3050	10 000
1525	5000
610	2000
305	1000
152.5	500
0 Sea Level	0 Sea Level
152.5	500 Below
1525	5000
3050	10 000

Scale 1:16 000 000;
one inch to 250 miles.

A-580051-76 -54-18

Continued on pages 220-221

b

MEDITERRANEAN SEA

Masabb Rashid
Baltim
Masabb Dumyat
Rashid (Rosetta)
Disuq
Burullus
Dumyat
Port Said (Bur Sa'id)
Abu Qir
Fariskur
Idku
Fuwah
Bilqas Qism Awwal
Al Manzilah
ALEXANDRIA (Al Iskandariyah)
Al Mahallah al Kubra
Al Mansurah
Mit Ghamr
As Sinbillawayn
Al Firdan
Ismailia (Al Ismā'īlīyah)
SINAI
Damanhur
Tanta
Ad Dilinjat
Shibin al Kawm
Az Zaqaziq
Wadi an Natrun
Minuf
Banha
Bilbays
Ismā'īlīyah Canal
Fa'id
LIBYAN
Ashmun
Shibin al Qanatir
DESERT
Imbabah
Al Jizah
Misr al Jadidah
Ash Shallufah
(AS SAHRA' AL LIBIYAH)
Sphinx
CAIRO (Al Qahirah)
Suez (As Suways)
Pyramids
Memphis
Hulwan
Al 'Ayyat
GULF OF SUEZ
Sinnuris
As Saff
Al Fayyum
Al Wasitah
JABAL JALALAH AL BAHRIYAH
Itsa
Bush
Ishmant
Biba
Bani Suwayf
ARABIAN
Al Fashn
Wadi Arabah
Maghaghah
Al Bahnasa
Bani Mazar
Qulusna
Samalut
Al Minya
DESERT
Abu Qurqas
Ar Rawdah
5745
Mallawi
Dayrut
(AS SAHRA' ASH SHARQIYAH)
Abnub
Manfalut
Asyut
Al Firdan
Abu Tij
EGYPT
Al Badari
Tahta
Al Mata'nah
Akhmim
Al Manshah
Sawhaj
Jirja
Al Balyana
Dishna
Qina
Naj' Hammadi
Qus
Thebes (Ruins)
Al Karnak
Armant
Al Uqsur (Luxor)
Isna
Idfu
Salwa Bahri
Kawm Umbu
Daraw
ASWAN HIGH DAM
Aswan
Lake Nasser (Buhayrat Nasir)
Qift

©RMCN

c

MEDITERRANEAN SEA

Port Said (Bur Sa'id)
Manzala
Al Kab
Al Qantarah
Al Ballah
Al Firdan
Qana al Suways (Suez Canal)
Ismailia (Al Ismā'īlīyah)
Timsah
SINAI PENINSULA
Nifishah
EGYPT
Fa'id
Junayfah
Al Buhayrah al Murrah al Kubra
Ash Shallufah
Al Kubri
Suez (As Suways)
Bur Ibrahim
JABAL 'ATAQAH
Gulf of Suez

Scale 1:1 000 000
0 5 10 Miles
0 8 16 Kilometers

©RMCN

d

BOTSWANA
Lokala Drift
Melkrivier
Pietersburg
Hermanusdorings
Potgietersrus
STRYDPOORTBERGE
Vaalwater
Gladdeklipkop
6851
WATERBERGE
Zebediela
Silent Valley
Alma
Naboomspruit
Thabazimbi
Immerpan
3216
Derdepoort
Rooiberg
Nylstroom
Mabula
Crecy
Middelwit
Warmbad
Roedtan
Pilansberg
Northam
Radium
Tuinplaas
Settlers
Marble Hall
Mabeskraal
Jericho
Skilpadfontein
Groblersdal
Groot Marico
Heystekrand
Hammanskraal
Swartruggens
Klipgat
Dennilton
Rustenburg
Marikana
Brits
Pretoria North
Cullinan
Vaalplaas
Darnall
Koster
Boons
Magaliesburg
Silverton
Bronkhorstspruit
Enkeldoring
Verena
Derby
PRETORIA
Witbank
Middelburg
Krugersdorp
Kempton Park
Driefontein
Ogies
Lichtenburg
ALEXANDRA
Kendal
Hendrina
WITWATERSRAND
5681
JOHANNESBURG
Benoni
Delmas
Germiston
Springs
Coligny
Carletonville
Westonaria
Nigel
Devon
Leslie
Bethal
Hauptrus
Fochville
Daleside
Ventersdorp
Heidelberg
Trichardt
Klerksdorp
Wolverdiend
Evaton
Meyerton
Balfour
Greylingstad
Morgenzon
Orkney
Vereeniging
Vanderbijlpark
Wilpoort
Vredefort
Sasolburg
Parys
Wolwehoek
Standerton
Leeudoringstad
Viljoenskroon
Dover
Villiers
Perdekop
Vierfontein
Koppies
Orangeville
Ascent
Bothaville
Edenville
Heilbron
Frankfort
Vrede
Memel
Wesselsbron
4389
Westleigh
Reitz
Tweeling
Kroonstad
Petrus Steyn
Warden
Odendaalsrus
Lindley
Welkom
Ventersburg
Arlington
Virginia
Steynsrus
ORANGE FREE STATE
Hennenman
Bultfontein
Winburg
Senekal
Bethlehem
Harrismith
Brandfort
4758
Theunissen
Paul Roux
Kestell
DRAKENSBERG
Marquard
Rosendal
Fouriesburg
ROYAL NATAL NAT'L. PK.
Bergville
Winterton
NATAL
Ficksburg
Clocolan
Leribe
Butha Buthe
Bergville
Cathedral Pk. 10 822
Cathkin Pk. 9856
BLOEMFONTEIN
Numataal
Pitseng
LESOTHO

Scale 1:4 000 000
0 10 20 30 40 Miles
0 10 20 30 40 50 60 Kilometers

Scale 1:4 000 000
0 10 20 30 40 Miles
0 10 20 30 40 50 60 Kilometers

©RMCN

Longitude East of Greenwich
Longitude East of Greenwich

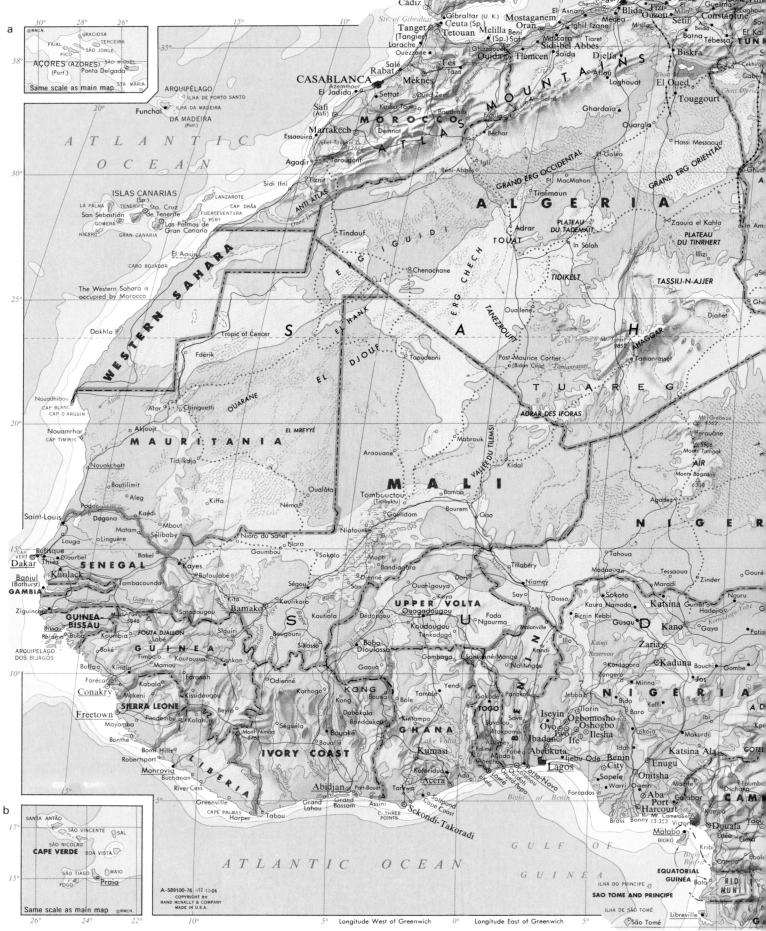

220

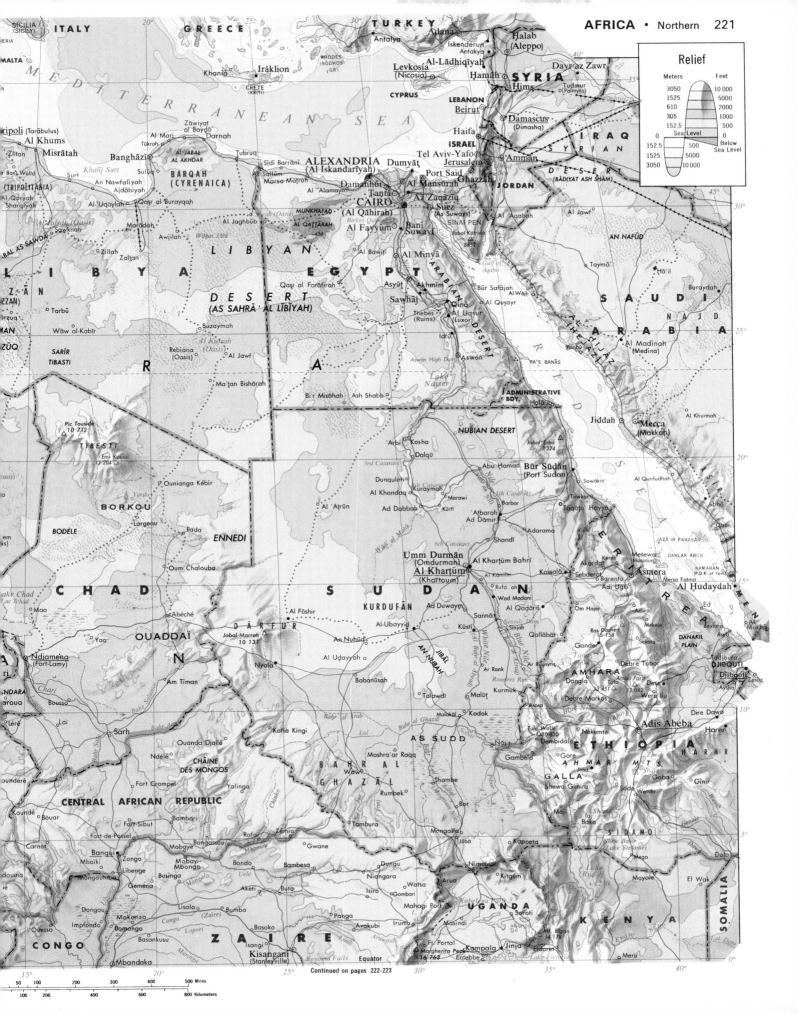

SICILIA (SICILY)   ITALY   GREECE   TURKEY

MALTA

CRETE (KRITI)

Antalya   Adana   Iskenderun   Ḥalab (Aleppo)
RHODES (RÓDHOS) (GR)   Antakya
Khania   Iráklion   Al-Lādhiqīyah   Dayr az Zawr
Levkosía (Nicosia)   SYRIA
CYPRUS   Ḥamāh   Tudmur (Palmyra)
LEBANON   Ḥimṣ
Beirut
Tripoli (Tarābulus)   Haifa   Damascus (Dimashq)   IRAQ
Al Khums   Zāwiyat al Baydā   Tel Aviv-Yafo   SYRIAN
Miṣrātah   Darnah   Jerusalem   'Ammān
Banghāzī   AL JABAL AL AKHDAR   ISRAEL   JORDAN   DESERT (BĀDIYAT ASH SHĀM)
Zliten
Bani Walid   Tūkrah
(TRIPOLITANIA)   BARQAH (CYRENAICA)   Sīdī Barrānī   Port Said   Ghazzah
Al Qaryah ash Shargīyah   An Nawfalīyah   Sallūm   Marsa Maṭrūḥ   Damanhūr   Az Zaqāzīq   Al 'Aqabah   Al Jawf
Surt   Ajdābiyā   Tanṭā   Al Manṣūrah   Suez (As Suways)
Qaṣr al Burayqah   Al 'Alamayn   CAIRO (Al Qāhirah)   Al 'Aqabah
Marādah   (Oasis)   MUNKHAFAD   Bani Suwayf   Al 'Aqabah   AN NAFŪD
Sawknah   Al Jaghbūb   AL QAṬṬĀRAH   Al Fayyūm   Birket Qārūn   SINAI PEN.   Taymā'
Zillah   Awjilah   Jabal Katrino   SAUDI
Zaltan   8652

LIBYAN   EGYPT   Al Minyā   Ḥā'il   Buraydah
JABAL AS SAWDA   Al Bawiti   ARABIAN   Taymā'
Tarbū   Qaṣr al Farāfirah   Asyūṭ   Akhmīm   Būr Safājah   Al Wajh
DESERT (AS SAHRĀ AL LĪBĪYAH)   Sawhāj   Qinā   Al Quṣayr   ARABIA
Wāw al-Kabīr   Thebes (Ruins)   Al Uqsur (Luxor)   SAUDI
Būzaymah   Idfū   NAJD
SARĪR   Al Kufrah (Oasis)   Rebiana (Oasis)   Aswān High Dam   Yanbu'   Al Madīnah (Medina)
TIBESTI   Al Jawf   Aswān   RA'S BANĀS   HIJAZ
Ma'tan Bishārah   Lake Nasser

Bi'r Misāhah   Ash Shabb   ADMINISTRATIVE BDY.   Ḥalā'ib   Jiddah   Mecca (Makkah)   Al Khurmah
Pic Toussidé 10 712   NUBIAN DESERT   Jabal Erba 7 274
Emi Koussi 11 204   'Arbi   Kosha   Al Qunfudhah
TIBESTI   Dalqū
Ounianga Kébir   3rd Cataract   Abu Ḥamad   Abhā
BORKOU   Dunqulah   Kuraymah   Marawi   Gizan
BODÉLE   Largeau   Al Khandaq   JAZĀ'IR FARASĀN
Fada   Ad Dabbah   Kūrti   Barbar   DAHLAK ARCH.
Oum Chalouba   ENNEDI   Al 'Atrūn   Atbarah   (Y.D.R. of Yemen)
Lake Chad   Wādi al Malik   Ad Dāmir   Meṣewa (Maṣaua)   KAMARAN
Lac Tchad   Mao   Adarama   Akordat   KAMARAN
Wādi Ḥowar   6th Cataract   Shandi   Kassalā   Sebderat   Asmera   Al Ḥudaydah
CHAD   SUDAN   Umm Durmān (Omdurman)   Al Kharṭūm Bahrī   Kassalā   Adi Ugri   YEMEN
Abéché   Al Fāshir   Al Kharṭūm (Khartoum)   Al Kāmilin   Barentu   Al Mukhā
OUADDAÏ   DĀRFŪR   Rufa'a   Om Hajer
Yao   Jabal Marrah 10 131   KURDUFAN   Ad Duwaym   Wad Madani   Ed
Ndjamena (Fort-Lamy)   Am Timan   Al-Ubayyid   Al Qaḍārif   Qallābāt   Gonder   Adwa   DANAKIL PLAIN
An Nuhūd   Sannār   Ras Dashen 15 158   Mekele   Beylul
Nyala   JIBĀL   Sennar Dam   Sekota   Assab
Al Uḍayyah   AN NUBAH   Kūsti   Sinjah   Amba Farit 12 451   DJIBOUTI
Babanūsah   White Nile   Ar Rank   Qallābāt   AMHARA   Debre Tabor   Djibouti   Zeila
DĀRFŪR   Talawdi   Bahr al Jabal   Tulu Wallel 10 830   Dangla   Tato   Desē   Aysha
Malūṭ   Kurmuk   Debre Markos   Weré Ilu   Dire Dawa
Sarh   Kafia Kingi   Lol   Malakāl   Kodok   Asosa   Blue Nile   Nekemte   Harer
Ouanda Djallé   Bahr al Arab   Nāsir   Dembidolo   Harar
CHAÎNE DES MONGOS   BAHR AL GHAZĀL   Mashra'ar Raqq   Gore   ETHIOPIA   HARAR
Yalinga   Shambe   Gambela   Jima   Goba   Ginir
CENTRAL AFRICAN REPUBLIC   Rumbek   Bor   AHMAR MTS.
Bambari   AS SUDD   GALLA   Soda   Wendo
Fort-Sibut   Tambura   Mengalla   Shewa Gimira   Maji   SIDAMO
Bouar   Fort-de-Possel   Rafaï   Zémio   Jāba   Shewa Bahir (Lake Stefanie)   Mega   Moyale
Carnot   Gwane   Kapoeta   Bake
Koundé   Mobaye   Bangassou   Dungu   Nimule   Moyale   El Wak
Bangui   Zongo   Mbaïki   Libenge   Bondo   Bambesa   Arua   Kitgum   Dolo
Mongoumba   Gemena   Businga   Mangala   Uele   Mahagi Port   UGANDA   KENYA
Dongou   Lisala   Bumba   Niangara   Watsa   Masindi   Soroti   Mt. Elgon 14 178   Meru
Impfondo   Makanza   Isiro   Gombari   Ft. Portal   Kampala   Jinja   Eldoret
CONGO   Bomongo   Basoko   Buta   Aketi   Kisangani (Stanleyville)   Boyoma Falls   Entebbe   Lake Victoria
Mbandaka   ZAIRE   Lopori   Maringa   Congo (Zaïre)   Equator   Margherita Peak 16 763

Continued on pages 222-223

MEDITERRANEAN SEA

0   50   100   200   300   400   500 Miles
0   100   200   400   600   800 Kilometers

Continued on pages 222-223

Relief

Meters		Feet
3050		10 000
1525		5000
610		2000
305		1000
152.5		500
0	Sea Level	0
152.5		500
1525	Below	5000
3050	Sea Level	10 000

Continued on pages 220-221

Inset map (a):

CAPE TOWN

Scale 1:1 000 000

0 5 10 Miles

0 4 8 12 16 Kilometers

A-589200-76 12-11-22
COPYRIGHT BY
RAND McNALLY & COMPANY
MADE IN U.S.A.

Scale 1:16 000 000; one inch to 250 miles. Sinusoidal Projection
Elevations and depressions are given in feet

0 50 100 200 300 400 500 Miles
0 100 200 400 600 800 Kilometers

b

SOMALIA
Kismayo
Equator

Nairobi
NYA
Ft. Hall
17,058
Kilimanjaro

Witu
Lamu
Bur Gavo

Malindi
Takaungu

Mombasa
Vanga
Lushoto
Tanga
PEMBA ISLAND
Pangani

Zanzibar
ZANZIBAR
Bagamoyo
Dar es Salaam

Morogoro
Kisaki
MAFIA

Utete
Kilwa Kivinje

Lindi

Mikindani
CABO DELGADO
Masasi

Mocímboa da Praia
Ibo
Lúrio

Pemba
Memba
Nacala

Moçambique

Moroni
COMOROS
GRANDE COMORE
MOHÉLI
ANJOUAN
Dzaoudzi
MAYOTTE (Fr.)

ÎLES GLORIEUSES (Fr.)
CAP D'AMBRE
Antsiranano
NOSY BE
Vohimarina

ALDABRA IS. (Sey.)
COSMOLEDO GROUP (Sey.)

I N D I A N

Maroantsetra
Maromokotra

CAP SAINT-ANDRÉ
Helodrano Antongila
NOSY BORAHA

Mahajanga
Mandritsara

ILHA ANGOCHE
António Enes

Besalampy
ÎLE JUAN DE NOVA (Fr.)
Ambatondrazaka
Fenoarivo

NOSY BARREN
Maintirano
Toamasina

MADAGASCAR
Moramanga
Vatomandry

Antananarivo
Antsirabe
Mahanoro

Morondava
Ambositra

BASSAS DA INDIA (Fr.)
Fianarantsoa
Mananjary

EUROPA (Fr.)
Morombe
Manakara
Ivohibe

MOZAMBIQUE CHANNEL
Ihosy
Farafangana

Toliary
Betroka

Tranomaro
Farodofay

CAP STE. MARIE

Pretoria
Pretoria North
Cullinan
Wolhuterskop
Jacksonstuin
MAGALIESBERG
Harbeespoort
Swartspruit
Kosmos
Haribeespoortdam
Silverton
Rayton
Skeerpoort
Voortrekkerhoogte
4549
Hennopsrivier
Valhalla
Lyttelton
Tierpoort
Magalies
WITWATERSBERG
Irene
Riederdam
Sesmyl
Foothills
Olievenhoutpoort
4602
Halfway House
Bapsfontein
Tarlton
Kaalfontein
Kempton Park
Krugersdorp
Modderfontein
Putfontein
JOHANNESBURG
Alexandra
Randfontein
Roodepoort
Discovery
Edenvale
5725
Florida
Primrose
5557
Maraisburg
Boksburg **Benoni**
Brakpan
Scale 1:1 000 000
Orlando
Turffontein
Rosetten
ville
Germiston
0 4 8 12 16 Kilometers
Prinville
Alberton
WITWATERSRAND
Springs

10 Miles
0 4 8 12 16 Kilometers

c

Arlington
Dannhauser
Glencoe
Dundee
Mahlabatini
Paul Roux
Bethlehem
Harrismith
Wasbank
Nqutu
Senekal
Kestell
Royal Natal Nat'l. Pk.
Wahba
Falls
Pomeroy
Babanango
ORANGE FREE STATE
Clarens
ROYAL NATAL NAT'L. PK.
Ladysmith
Nkandla
Melmoth
Fouriesburg
10,822
Ms Oux Sources
Bergville
Tugela
Ficksburg
Butha Buthe
Winterton
Colenso
Tugela Ferry
Eshowe
Clocolan
Leribe
Cathedral Pk.
9856
Weenen
Kranskop
Greytown
Pitseng
Cathkin Pk.
10,438
Mooirivier
Mapumulo
Teyateyaneng
MALOTI MTS.
Machache
9464
Mokhotlong
Thabana Ntlenyana
11,425
New Hanover
Dalton
Stanger
LESOTHO
Roma
Impendle
Howick
Nhlosini
5851
Wartburg
Pietermaritzburg
10,159
Bulwer
Richmond
Camperdown
Verulam
Underberg
Pinetown
Durban
Creighton
Mid Illovo
Isipingo
8326
Donnybrook
Mohale's Hoek
Orange
The Twins
Swartberg
7619
Zastron
Qacha's Nek
3820
Franklin
Umkomaas
DRAKENSBERG
Umzimkulu
Umzinto
Quthing
Matatiele
Cedarville
Scottburgh
9684
7426
Mt. Currie
7297
Kokstad
Harding
Park Rynie
Herschel
Ben Macdhui
Sezela
Witberg
7853
Mount Fletcher
Mount Ayliff
Umtentweni
Lady Grey
9846
Bizana
Port Shepstone
Rhodes
Mount Frere
Tabankulu
Uvongo Beach
Barkly East
Maclear
Flagstaff
Margate
Jamestown
Qumbu
Lusikisiki
Port Edward
Rossouw
Ugie
8430
Elliot
Tsolo
Libode
Molteno
Dordrecht
Indwe
Cala
Umtata
Port St. Johns
STORMBERG
Ngqeleni
Steÿnsburg
Engcobo
RAME HEAD
Lady Frere
Tsomo
Mqanduli
Waverly
Queenstown
Cofimvaba
Idutywa
Elliotdale
Tarkastad
Ngamakwe
Cradock
Tylden
Willowvale
Whittlesea
Carthcart
SOUTH
Butterworth
BANKBERG
WINTERBERG
Seymour
Stutterheim
Kentani
6606
7778
CAPE
Frankfort
Pearston
Adelaide
Keiskammahoek
Toleng
Kei Mouth
Somerset East
Bedford
Fort Alice
Berlin
Morgan's Bay
Fort Beaufort
Breidbach
Gonubie
Riebeek-Oos
King William Town
East London
SUURBERGE
Alicedale
Grahamstown
Kidd's Beach
Kirkwood
Salem
Hamburg
Adda
Bathurst
Alexandria
Port Alfred (Kowie)
Uitenhage
SAINT CROIX ISLAND
BIRD ISLAND
Port Elizabeth
KAAP RECIFE

Scale 1:4 000 000
0 10 20 30 40 Miles
0 10 20 30 40 50 60 Kilometers

I N D I A N

O C E A N

AFRICA

NATAL

MOZAMBIQUE CHANNEL

Tsiribihina

Mangoky

Onilahy

Manambovo

Relief

Meters		Feet
3050		10 000
1525		5000
610		2000
305		1000
152.5		500
0	Sea Level	0
152.5		500
1525		5000
3050		10 000

224

WESTERN SAHARA

PUNTILLA
NEGRA
CABO
BARBAS
CAP BLANC
Nouadhibou
ÎLE TIDRA
CAP TIMIRIS
Nouamrhar

Fdérik
▲ Kediet Ijill
Tichla

MAKTEÏR

OUARANE

EL DJOUF

S A H A R A

Post Maurice Co
(Bidon Cinq)
TANEZROU
TA N'AHENE

Bordj le Prieur

MAURITANIA

ADRAR SOTUF

ADÂFER EL ABIOD

EL MREYYE

TIMETRINE
MONTS

Atar

Akjoujt

Nouakchott

TRARZA

Sebkha de
N'dhamcha

Tidjikdja

Moudjéria

AOUKÂR

AKLÉ 'ÂOUÂNA

Araouane

AZAOUAD

Aguelhok

Anefis in-
Darane

VALLÉE DU TILEMSI

Rosso
Dagana

Saint-Louis
Louga
Thiès

CAP
VERT

Dakar
Rufisque

CAPE
SAINT MARY

Banjul
(Bathurst)

GAMBIA

CAP ROXO

GUINEA-
BISSAU

ARQUIPÉLAGO
DOS
BIJAGÓS

Bissau

Sédhiou
Eticoga

Kaédi
Matam

SENEGAL

Linguère

Ranérou

Diourbel
Touba

Kaolack

Sokona

Kolda

Bignona
Ziguinchor

Manjaka

Kabot

Kiffa

Diéma

Kayes

Naye

Tambacounda

Bafoulabé

Médina Gonasse

PARC
NATIONAL
DU NIOKOLO
KOBA

Goumbati
△ 1 368

Kita

Koblouguidi

Ayoun el Atrous

Néma

Didiéni

Ballé

FERLO

Nioro du Sahel

Goumbou

Kogoni

Lac Faguibine

Tombouctou
(Timbuktu)

Niger

Taoussa

Lac Do

Gao

Ansongo

Hombori

Dauentza

M A L I

Kona

Mati

Mopti

Djibo

Aribinda

Koro

Ouahigouya

Kaya

Téra

Dori

Niamtougou

Taoussa

SUDAN

UPPER VOLTA

Satadougou

Massif Du
Tamgué
△ 1 046

Gamble

Tombadonkéa

Danea

Labé

Dinguiraye

Télimélé

Dabola

Fria

Boffa

Conakry

Mamou

Kindia

Forécariah

Makéni

SIERRA
LEONE

Freetown

Moyamba

Lunsar

Bo

Kenema

Pendembu

Bendu

Benthe

SHERBRO ISLAND

TURNERS
PENINSULA

CAPE MOUNT

Robertsport

Brewerville

Monrovia

Buchanan

LIBERIA

Loma
Mansa
Tingi
▲
6 080

Kissidougou

Faranah

GUINEA

Koundara

Bakoye

Bafing

Satadougou

Niger

Siguiri

Kankan

Kouroussa

Bamako

Koulikoro

Banamba

Ségou

Bla

San

Sido

Koutiala

Sikasso

Bobo Dioulasso

Banfora

Niélé

Tingréla

Korhogo

Ferkéssédougou

Bouna

PARK
NATIONAL
DE BOUNA

Bole

Wa

Lawra

Lokosse

Walewale

Gushiago

Yendi

Bassa

Kaédougou

Ouarkoye

Boromo

Houndé

Dédougou

Léo

Pô

Bawku

Bolgatanga

Nahtinga

PARC
NAT.
DE LA BÉNÉE

Madiori

Sansanne-
Mango

Dapango

Bati

Diébolo

Forêt
Classée
Du Fazao
△ 873

TOGO

Palimé

Atakpamé

Hohoe

Lake
Volta

Sunyani

Mampang

Kumasi

Obuasi

Bibiani

Dunkwa

Nkawkaw

Akwatia

Koforidua

Nsawam

Accra

Tema

Anloga

Lomé

White
Volta

Tamale

Salaga

Kintampo

Wenchi

GHANA

Techiman

Ejura

Ouelle

Bouaké

IVORY COAST

Séguéla

Katiola

Bandoukou

Bouaflé

Dimbokro

Agnibilékrou

Abengourou

Adzopé

Agboville

Divo

Gagnoa

Abidjan

Grand-Bassam

Lagune
Ebrié

Sassandra

CAPE THREE
POINTS

Sekondi-Takoradi

Cape Coast

Winneba

GULF OF

Odienné

Boundiali

Niakaramandougou

Man

Mount
Kahoué
△ 3 658

Danané

Duékoué

Daloa

Guiglo

Duabo

Mont
Niénokoué
△ 2 044

Greenville

Tabou

Harper

Cape
Palmas

Touba

Beyla

Pic De Tio
934

Kérouané

Biankouma

Séguéla

Nzérékoré

Yamou

Sanniquellié

Gbarnga

Ganta

Tchien

Sassandra

MT. NIMBA
NAT. PARK

Sankanbiriwa
6 080

Kabala

Kambia

Port Loko

Zimmi

Cavally

Cestos

ATLANTIC OCEAN

Relief

Meters	Feet
3050	10 000
1525	5000
610	2000
305	1000
152.5	500
0	Sea Level 0
152.5	500
1525	5000
3050	10 000

Scale 1:10,000,000; one inch to 160 miles. Lambert Azimuthal Equal Area Projection
Elevations and depressions are given in feet.

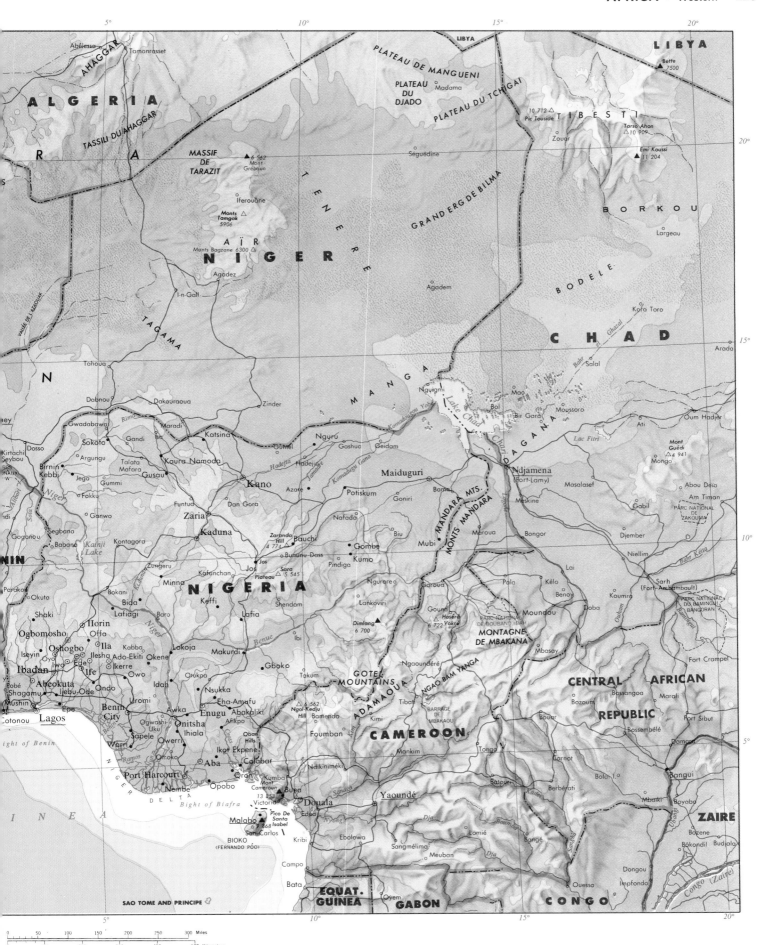

AHAGGAR
Abélessa   Tamanrasset
ALGERIA
TASSILI DU AHAGGAR
R
A
MASSIF DE TARAZIT   ▲ 6 562 Mont Grébaun
Iferouâne
Monts Tamgak 5906
AÏR
Monts Bagzane 6300 △
Agadez
I-n-Gall
N I G E R
TAGAMA
VALLÉE DE L'AZAOUAK
N
Tahoua
Dabnou   Dakouraoua   Zinder
Rima
...ney
Gwadabawa   Maradi
Dosso   Sokoto   Gandi   Isa   Gumel   Ngyru   Gashua   Geidam
Kirtachi Seybou   Argungu   Talata Mafara   Kaura Namoda   Katsina
Birnin Kebbi   Jega   Gummi   Gusau   Hadejia   Hadejia
Fokku   Funtua   Dan Gora   Kano   Azare   Potiskum   Goniri
Niger   Ganwo
Segbana   Babana   Kontagora   Kaduna   Zaranda Hill 4 774   Bauchi   Nafada   Biu
Gogonou   Kainji Lake   Zungeru   Jos Plateau   Sara 5 545   Bununu Dass   Gombe   Mubi
Parakou   Okuta   Bokani   Minna   Kafanchan   Jos   Pindiga   Kumo
Okuta   Bida   Keffi   NIGERIA   Ngureo
Shaki   Lafiagi   Baro   Lafia   Shendam   Lankoviri
Ogbomosho   Ilorin   Offa   Makurdi   Ibi
Oshogbo   Ila   Kabba   Okene   Benue   Gboko   Takum
Iseyin   Ede   Ikerre   Owo   Orukpa   GOTEL MOUNTAINS
Ibadan   Ife   Ondo   Idah   Nsukka   ▲ 4 562 Ngol Kedju Hill   Bamenda
Abeokuta   Ijebu-Ode   Uromi   Awka   Enugu   Abakaliki   ADAMAOUA   Kimi
Shagamu   Benin City   Onitsha   Afikpo   Foumban   CAMEROON
Mushin   Epe   Ogwashi Uku   Ihiala   Oban Hills   Mankim
Cotonou   Lagos   Sapele   Owerri   Cross   Ndikiniméki
Warri   Omoko   Ikot Ekpene   Calabar   Kumba
Ramos   Aba   Oron   Mont Cameroun 13 353   Buea   Douala
Port Harcourt   Opobo   Victoria   Edea
Nembe   DELTA   Malabo   Pico De Santa Isabel   Kribi
NIGER   Bight of Biafra   San Carlos   BIOKO (FERNANDO PÓO)   Ebolowa
GUINEA   Campo   Yaoundé   Sangmélima   Meuban
Bata   EQUAT. GUINEA   Oyem   GABON   Dja
SAO TOME AND PRINCIPE

LIBYA
PLATEAU DE MANGUENI
PLATEAU DU DJADO   Madama
PLATEAU DU TCHIGAI
LIBYA   Bette 7500
10 712 △ Pic Touside   TIBESTI   Tarso Ahon △ 10 909
Zouar   Emi Koussi ▲ 11 204
Séguédine
TENERE
BORKOU
Largeau
GRAND ERG DE BILMA
Agadem   BODELE   Kora Toro
CHAD   Arada
MANGA   Nguigmi   Mao   Bir Gara   Moussoro   Ati   Oum Hadjer
Komadugou Yobe   Lake Chad   Bol   DAGANA   Lac Fitri   Mont Guédi 4 941
Maiduguri   Bama   Ndjamena (Fort-Lamy)   Masalasef   Mongo   Abou Deïa
Komadugou Gana   MANDARA MTS.   Meskine   Gabil   Am Timan
MONTS MANDARA   Maroua   Bongor   Djember   PARC NATIONAL DE ZAKOUMA
Garoua   Lai   Niellim   Bahr Keita
Gouna   Pala   Kélo   Koumra   Sarh (Fort-Archambault)
Hosère 6 722 Yokre   PARC NATIONAL DE BOUBA-NDJIDAH   Moundou   Doba   PARC NATIONAL DU BAMINGUI BANGORAN
MONTAGNE DE MBAKANA   Benoy   Ouham   Fort Crampel
Ngaoundéré   BARRAGE DE MBAKAOU   Mbasay
NGAO BAM YANGA   CENTRAL   Bossangoa   Marali
Tibati   Bouar   Bozoum   AFRICAN   Bossembélé   Fort Sibut
Tongo   REPUBLIC   Carnot   Bossembélé   Damara
Batoun   Bola I.   Bangui
Berbérati   Mbaïki   Boyaba   ZAIRE
Bangé   Bozene   Bökondil   Budjala
Dongou   Impfondo
Ouesso   CONGO   Congo (Zaïre)

CENTRAL AFRICAN REPUBLIC

Fort de Possel
Boali
Bangui

NIGERIA
Opobo
Mont Cameroun
13 353
Douala
Buea
Edéa
Yaoundé
Bight of Biafra
Malabo
San Carlos
BIOKO
(FERNANDO PÓO)
Doumé
Batoua
Berbérati
Bolai I.
Kongbo
Bangassou
Mbaïki
Bayabo
Mongoumba
Bosobolo
Gemena
Businga
Bodalang
Yandongi
Aketi
Buta
Bumba

EQUATORIAL GUINEA
Kribi
Campo
Bata
Ebolowa
Sangmelima
Yokadouma
Lomié
Moloundou
Bangé
Souanké
Ouésso
Dongou
Impfondo
Bomongo
Lisala
Simba
Risanga
(Stanleyville)
Benga

SÃO TOMÉ AND PRÍNCIPE
PRÍNCIPE
CABO SAN JUAN
Acalayong
Benito
Oyem
Mekambo
Djoua
Djokoumatombi
Lokoti
Lifanga
Mange
Isangi
Basoko

ISLA DE CORISCO
MONTS DE CRISTAL
Makokou
Lebango
Likouala
Mbandaka
(Coquilhatville)
Boende
Tshuapa
Ekoli

São Tomé
SÃO TOMÉ
Libreville
Kango
Booué
Equator
CONGO
Owando
Bikoro
Lac Tumba
Bakangu
Yayama
Litoke
Ekoli

CAP LOPEZ
Port-Gentil
Bifoum
GABON
Lambaréné
Sébé
St. François de Boundji
Gamboma
Kiri
Inongo
Lac Mai-Ndombe
Monkoto
Ekanga
ZAIRE

Omboué
Movila
Mount Iboundji
5 184
Koula-Moutou
Franceville
Mbindo
Fimi
Lokolama
Esambo
Kato

Petit Loango
Mossendjo
3 412
Monts De La Lékéti
Diambala
Bandundu
Makaw
Lukenie
Dekese
Sankuru

Tchibanga
Sibiti
Kindanba
Bandundu
Kwa
Tiebo (Port-Francqui)
Domionga

Mayumba
Madingou
Brazzaville
Stanley Pool
Kwango
Kwilu
Mai-Manimba
Kikwit
Lusambo

Madingo
Loubomo
Kinshasa
(Léopoldville)
Kisantu
Demba
Mbuji-M
(Bakwang)

Pointe-Noire
Tshela
Chûtes De Livingstone
(Livingstone Falls)
Mbanza-Ngungu
Popokabaka
Kilembe
Djokupunda
Bulunga
Kananga
(Luluabourg)
Tshikapa
Kanda-Kanda

CABINDA
(Ang.)
Cabinda
Boma
Matadi
Noqui
Kimvula
Kitenda
Kwenge
Kahemba

PONTA DO PADRÃO
Santo António do Zaire
SERRA DO CONGO
São Salvador do Congo
Quimbele
Damba
Kibenga
Portugália
Chicapa
Luachimo

Ambrizete
Mabala
Uíge
Marimba
Quimbonge
Caluango
Sambungo
Papanga

Ambriz
Caxito
Quela
Cuilo
Kam

Luanda
Duque de Bragança
Malanje
KATANGA
Kangowa

PONTA DAS PALMEIRINHAS
Catete
Barra do Dande
Dondo
Nova Gaia
Cacolo
Teixeira de Sousa
Malonga
Naso

PARQUE NACIONAL DE QUIÇAMA
ATLANTIC
CABO DAS TRÊS PONTAS
Porto Amboim
Mussende
Saútar
Lucano
PARQUE NACIONAL DA CAMEIA
Calunda
Lomw

OCEAN
Novo Redondo
Gabela
Cela
Calucinga
ANGOLA
Coemba
Cangombe
Curunga
KASHIJI PLAIN
Chitokoloki

Lobito
Covelo
Alto-Uama
Kuito
Langui-Bungo
Mussuma
LIUWA PLAIN
Mongu

Benguela
SERRA CAMBONDA
SERRA MOCO
8 596
Huambo
(Nova Lisboa)
Chitembo
Chá Pungana
Ninda
BAROTSE PLAIN
Nangweshi

SERRA DO CHILENGUE
Caconda
Cacula
Caluquembe
Menongue
Lungo
Mavinga

CABO DE SANTA MARTA
São Nicolau
SERRA DA NEVE
Chá Pungana

PONTA ALBINA
Mocâmedes
Lubango
PARQUE NACIONAL DO BIKUAR
Folgares
Cassinga
Caiundo
SILOANA PLAINS

PONTA DA MARCA
Baía dos Tigres
PARQUE NACIONAL DO IONA
Chianje
Cahama
Cuando
Cuangar
Sambuio

Foz do Cunene
Oncócua
Cuamato
Melunga
CAPRIVI STRIP
Kasika

Enana Falls
Ruacana Falls
NAMIBIA
BOTS.

Relief

Meters	Feet
3050	10 000
1525	5000
610	2000
305	1000
152.5	500
Sea Level	0
152.5	500
1525	5000
3050	10 000

Scale 1:10,000,000; one inch to 160 miles. Lambert Azimuthal Equal Area Projection
Elevations and depressions are given in feet.

SUDAN ETHIOPIA

UGANDA

KENYA

SOMALIA

RWANDA

BURUNDI

TANZANIA

ZAIRE

ZAMBIA

MALAWI

MOZAMBIQUE

ZIMBABWE (RHODESIA)

COMOROS

INDIAN OCEAN

Nairobi
Kampala
Dar es Salaam
Mombasa
Zanzibar
Lusaka
Lilongwe
Blantyre
Lubumbashi (Elisabethville)

Lake Victoria
Lake Tanganyika
Lake Nyasa
Lake Rukwa
Lake Bangweulu
Lake Kariba

Copyright by Rand McNally & Co.
Made in U.S.A.
A-589500-76 -3-3 9

0   50   100   150   200   250   300 Miles
0   100   200   300   400   500 Kilometers

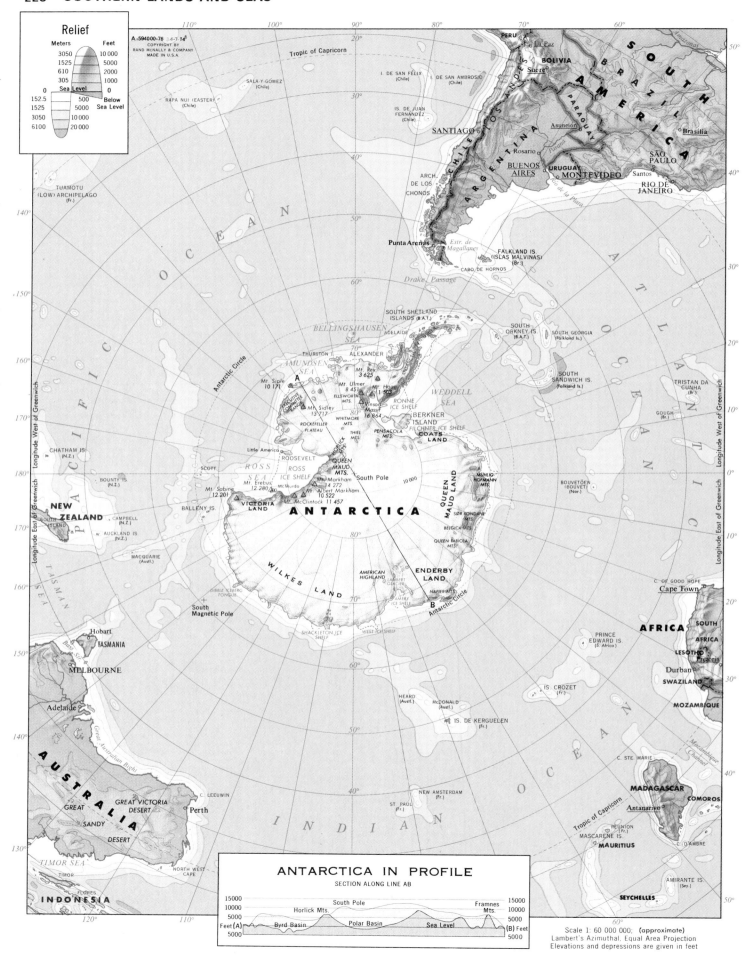

Relief

Meters		Feet
3050		10 000
1525		5000
610		2000
305		1000
0	Sea Level	0
152.5		500
		Below
1525		Sea Level
		5000
3050		10 000
6100		20 000

A -594000-76   3-4-7-14¹
COPYRIGHT BY
RAND McNALLY & COMPANY
MADE IN U.S.A.

ANTARCTICA IN PROFILE
SECTION ALONG LINE AB

Scale 1: 60 000 000; (approximate)
Lambert's Azimuthal, Equal Area Projection
Elevations and depressions are given in feet

ocean floor maps

The maps in this section convey an impression of the physical nature of the world's ocean floors. In general, colors used are those thought to exist on the ocean floors. For continental shelves or shallow inland seas grayish-green was used to correspond to terrigenous oozes, sediments washed from the continental areas. In deeper parts of the oceans calcareous oozes derived from the skeletons of marine life appear in white, and the fine mud from land is red. In the Atlantic materials accumulate relatively rapidly, have a high iron content, and thus are brighter red than elsewhere. Slower sedimentation in the Pacific and Indian oceans results in more manganese and hence darker colors. Undersea ridges were shown in black to suggest recent upwelling of molten rock. Small salt-and-pepper patches portray areas where manganese nodules are found. Around certain islands white was used to show coral reefs. Differences in relief were shown by relief-shading.

Many different features on the ocean floor are recognizable. Towering mountain ranges, vast canyons, broad plains, and a variety of other physiographic forms exceed in magnitude those found on the continents. One of the more pronounced is the Mid-Atlantic Ridge, a chain of mountains bisecting the Atlantic Ocean. One distinct characteristic of this ridge is a trough that runs along the entire center, in effect producing twin ridge lines. Away from the center there are parallel and lower crests, while at right angles to the crests are numerous fracture zones.

Measurements of temperatures and magnetism indicate that the troughs in the Mid-Atlantic Ridge are younger in age than the paralleling crests, whose ages increase with distance from the center. It is believed that the central troughs mark a line where molten materials from the earth's interior rise to the ocean floor, where they form gigantic plates that move slowly apart. This theory suggests that continents are moving away from each other, having been a single landmass in ancient times. The matching curves of the Atlantic shorelines of South America and Africa have long been cited as support for such conjecture. The map below shows the worldwide distribution of the gigantic plates on the ocean floor.

Where the subsea plates meet certain continental areas or island chains, they plunge downward to replenish inner-earth materials and form trenches of profound depths. Along the northern and western edges of the Pacific Ocean several lines of such gutters include some of the deepest known spots—Mariana Trench, Tonga Trench, Kuril Trench. Deep trenches also parallel the western coasts of Central and South America, the northern coast of Puerto Rico and the Virgin Islands, and other coastal areas. Other identifiable features include the great submarine canyons that lead from the edges of the continents; seamounts that rise above the ocean floors; and the continental shelves, which appear to be underwater extensions of landmasses and which vary in shape from narrow fringes to broad plains.

World-Wide Distribution of Tectonic Plates

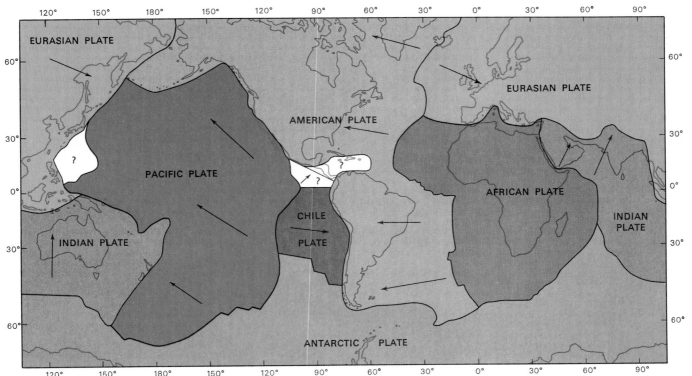

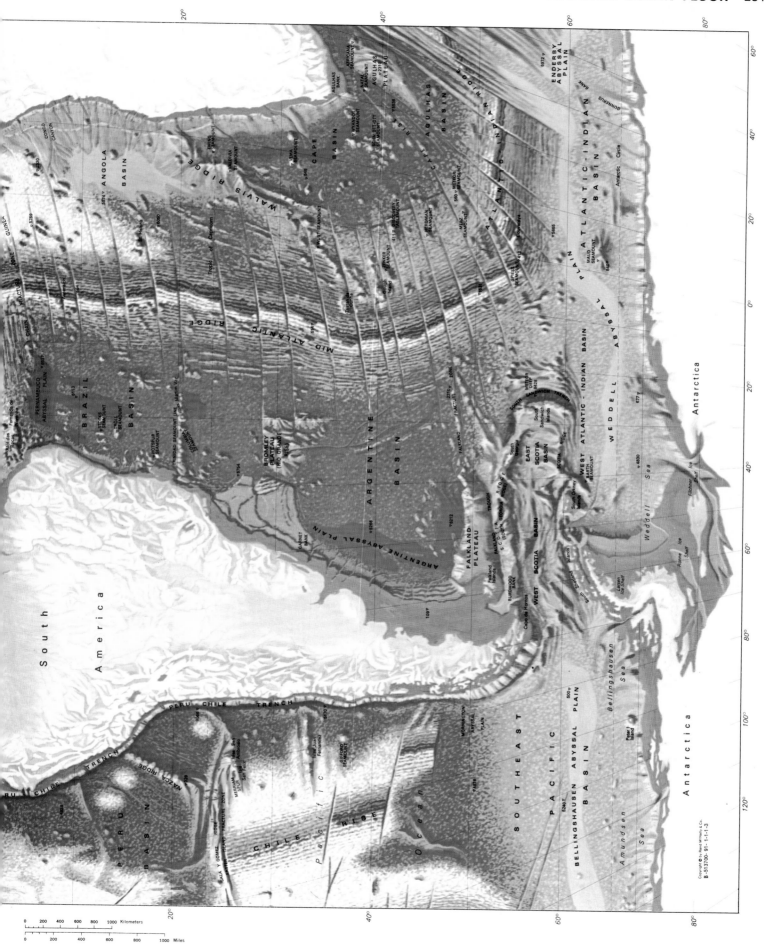

0   200   400   600   800   1000 Kilometers

0   200   400   600   800   1000 Miles

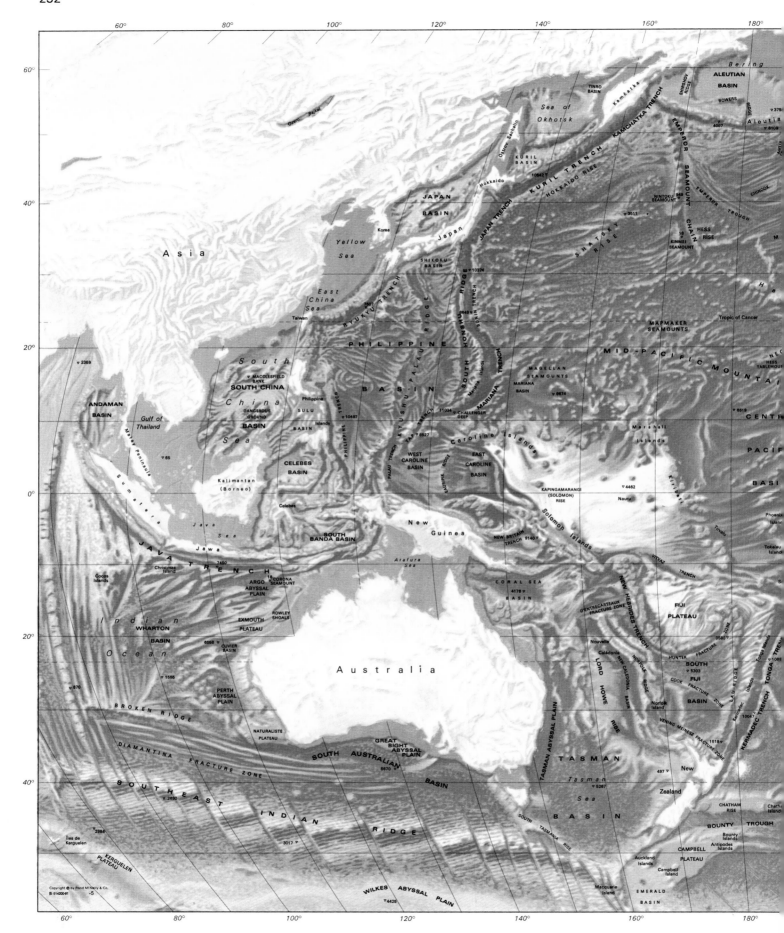

Scale 1:58 000 000; one inch to 900 miles (approx.)
Modified Cylindrical Projection   ▽ Depths in meters.

ALEUTIAN TRENCH
KODIAK
GUYOT
(SEAMOUNT)
ALASKA
ABYSSAL
PLAIN
ALEUTIAN
SAL PLAIN
▽ 5257
TUFTS
ABYSSAL
PLAIN
▽ 3826
27 ▽ MURA
GORDA FRACTURE
CAPE BLANCO
FRACTURE ZONE
CASCADIA

FRACTURE ZONE
R.O
N.O
FRACTURE
ZONE
PIONEER FRACTURE ZONE
DELGADA
FAN
MONTEREY
FAN

MUSICIANS
SEAMOUNTS
▽ 6288
MURRAY
FRACTURE
ZONE
▽ 3006

MOLOKAI FRACTURE ZONE
Isla de
Guadalupe
CEDROS
BANK

5120 ▽
BAJA CALIFORNIA

North America

HAWAIIAN FRACTURE ZONE
MOLOKAI
▽ 1755
SEAMOUNT
PROVINCE

PENSACOLA ▽
SEAMOUNT
1057 ▽

CLARION FRACTURE ZONE
EAST

CLARION
PACIFIC
BASIN
4809 ▽ ZONE
480
SUITCASE
SEAMOUNTS
SEAMOUNT
RIVERA FRACTURE
ZONE
Islas de
Revillagigedo
OROZCO
FRACTURE ZONE
MIDDLE
MATHEMATICIANS
GROUP

CHRISTMAS RIDGE

dge Islands
MOLOKAI

▽ 5720
CLIPPERTON FRACTURE ZONE

Ile
Clipperton
SIQUEIROS FRACTURE
ZONE
TEHUANTEPEC
RIDGE
AMERICA

6689 ▽

GUATEMALA
BASIN
▽ 4086

5349 ▽
20 ▽ GERMAINE
BANK

Christmas
Island
Equator

GALAPAGOS FRACTURE
ZONE
GALAPAGOS
RISE
Galapagos
Islands
CARNEGIE RIDGE

Iles
Marquises
▽ 5029
5465 ▽
5851 ▽
EAST PACIFIC RISE (ALBATROSS CORDILLERA)

COCOS RIDGE
PANAMA
▽ 4201
Isla del
Malpelo

PERU
BASIN
▽ 4389

▽ 7314
Iles de la
Société
Tahiti
Iles
Tuamotu
MARQUESAS FRACTURE ZONE
BAUER FRACTURE ZONE

Cook Islands

Iles Tubai
of Capricorn
▽ 4525

NAZCA RIDGE
329
8066 ▽

Pitcairn
Island
SALA Y GOMEZ RIDGE
Sala y Gomez
Isla de
Pascua
(Easter Island)
EASTER ISLAND FRACTURE ZONE
Isla
San Felix
Isla San
Ambrosio

Rapa
CHILE
BASIN

▽ 1088
SOUTHWEST PACIFIC BASIN
▽ 3841
Islas Juan
Fernandez

EAST PACIFIC RISE (ALBATROSS CORDILLERA)
CHALLENGER FRACTURE ZONE
GIFFORD
SEAMOUNT

FERNANDEZ FRACTURE ZONE

▽ 4766
3977 ▽
▽ 1447

PERU-CHILE TRENCH

South America

SOUTHEAST
PACIFIC
BASIN
▽ 4876

ELTANIN FRACTURE ZONE

Atlantic
Ocean
109 ▽

Falkland
Islands
FALKLAND
PLATEAU 50°

SCOTIA RIDGE
(SOUTH GEORGIA RIDGE)

WEST SCOTIA BASIN

Gulf of
Mexico
MEXICO BASIN
SIGSBEE
KNOLLS ▽ 4023
Mexico
CAMPECHE
BANK
WEST FLORIDA SHELF
BLAKE PLATEAU

Hudson
Bay
Great
Lakes
▽ 331
LABRADOR
BASIN

NORTH
AMERICAN
BASIN
▽ 6392

CAYMAN TRENCH
Caribbean
Sea
BEATA RIDGE
11

NORTH
AMERICA

160° 140° 120° 100° 80° 60° 40°
60°
40°
20°
0°
20°
40°

0 400 800 1200 Kilometers
0 400 800 1200 Miles

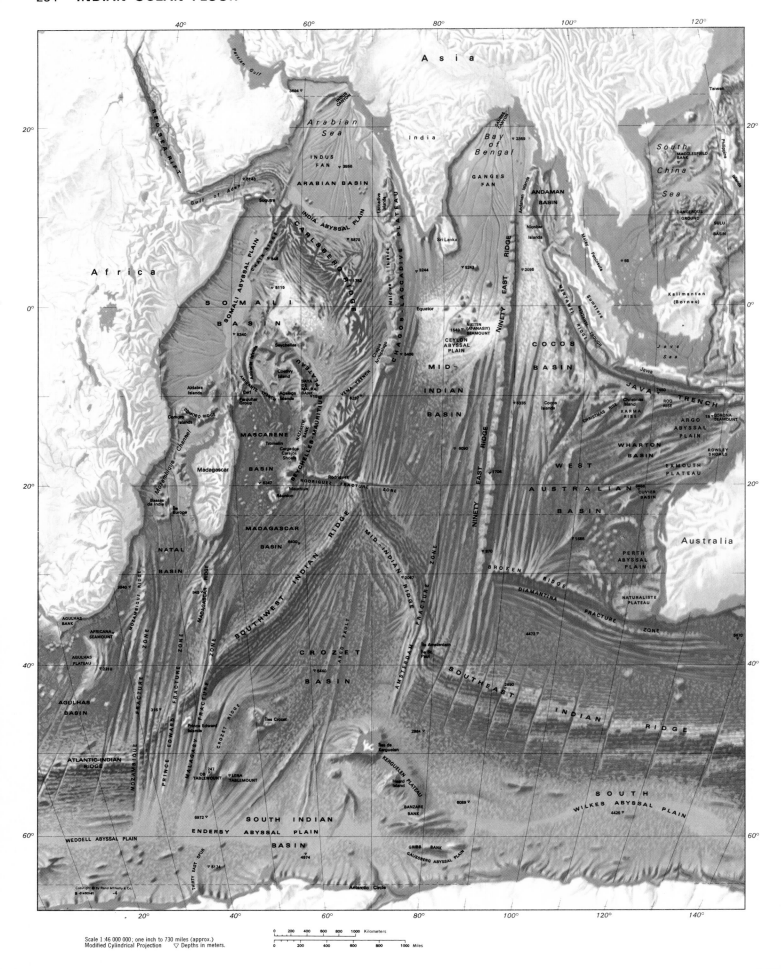

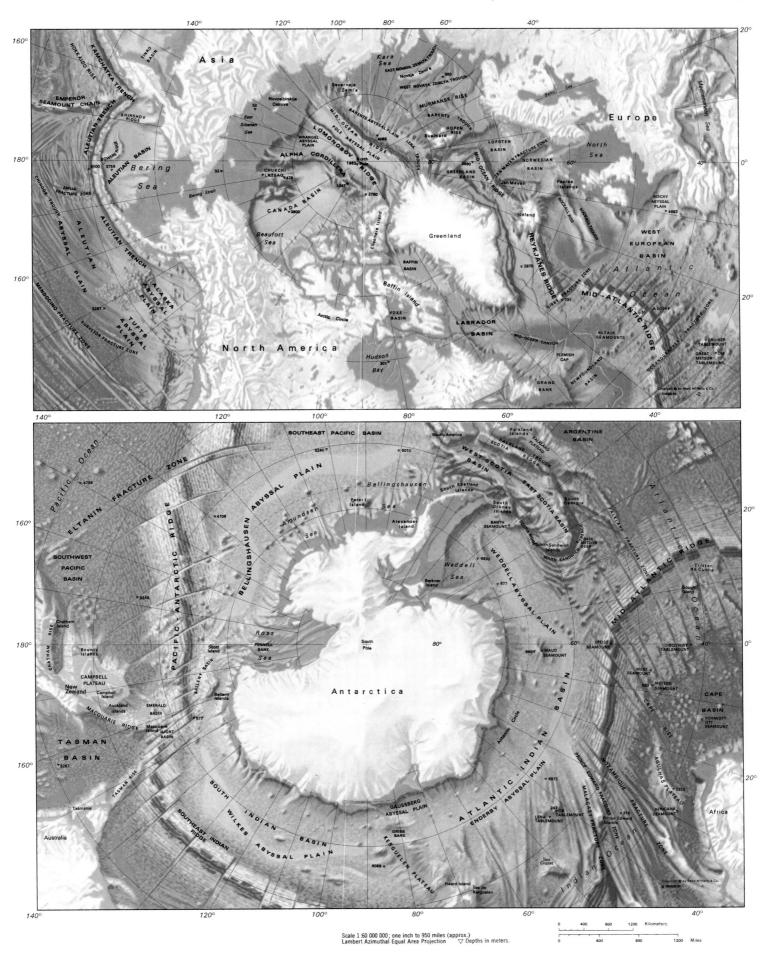

ARCTIC OCEAN FLOOR (top map)

Asia

Europe

North America

Greenland

Seas and waters: Kara Sea, Bering Sea, Beaufort Sea, Baffin Bay, Foxe Basin, Hudson Bay, North Sea, Baltic Sea, Mediterranean Sea, Norwegian Sea, Atlantic Ocean

HOKKAIDO RISE
KAMCHATKA TRENCH
EMPEROR SEAMOUNT CHAIN
TINRO BASIN
ALEUTIAN TRENCH
SHIRSHOV RIDGE
BOWERS
ALEUTIAN BASIN
9100 3758
Bering Sea
32
East Siberian Sea
Novosibirskije Ostrova
CHINOOK TROUGH
AMLIA FRACTURE ZONE
MENDOCINO FRACTURE ZONE
SURVEYOR FRACTURE ZONE
ALEUTIAN ABYSSAL PLAIN
ALEUTIAN TRENCH
ALASKA ABYSSAL PLAIN
TUFTS ABYSSAL PLAIN
5267
32
CHUKCHI PLATEAU 475
Bering Strait
CANADA BASIN 3800
ALPHA CORDILLERA
LOMONOSOV RIDGE
MID-OCEAN RIDGE 4085
POLE ABYSSAL PLAIN
WRANGEL ABYSSAL PLAIN
BARENTS ABYSSAL PLAIN
North 1863 1447
2750
Severnaja Zeml'a
Novaja Zeml'a
EAST NOVAYA ZEMLYA TROUGH
WEST NOVAYA ZEMLYA TROUGH 300
MURMANSK RISE
BARENTS TROUGH
LENA TROUGH
HOPEN RISE
Svalbard
LOFOTEN BASIN
MID-OCEAN RIDGE 3890
GREENLAND BASIN
JAN MAYEN FRACTURE ZONE
NORWEGIAN BASIN
Jan Mayen
Faeroe Islands
MOHN RIDGE
VORING PLATEAU
Iceland
REYKJANES RIDGE 2875
NORTH SEA
BISCAY ABYSSAL PLAIN 4693
WEST EUROPEAN BASIN
Atlantic Ocean
MID-ATLANTIC RIDGE
GIBBS FRACTURE ZONE 731
A 20308
OCEANOGRAPHER FRACTURE ZONE
CRUISER TABLEMOUNT
GREAT METEOR TABLEMOUNT 269
Beaufort Sea
Ellesmere Island
BAFFIN BASIN
Baffin Island
Arctic Circle
FOXE BASIN
Hudson Bay 301
LABRADOR BASIN
MID-OCEAN CANYON
FLEMISH CAP
NEWFOUNDLAND BASIN
ALTAIR SEAMOUNTS
GRAND BANK
Copyright © by Rand McNally & Co.

SOUTH POLAR OCEAN FLOOR (bottom map)

Antarctica

Australia

New Zealand

South America

Africa

Pacific Ocean
Atlantic Ocean
Indian Ocean

SOUTHEAST PACIFIC BASIN 5240 5010
ELTANIN FRACTURE ZONE
4755
4706
PACIFIC-ANTARCTIC RIDGE
BELLINGSHAUSEN ABYSSAL PLAIN
Amundsen Sea
Bellingshausen Sea
Peter I Island
Alexander Island
SOUTHWEST PACIFIC BASIN
5240
Chatham Island
Bounty Islands
CHATHAM RISE
CAMPBELL PLATEAU
New Zealand
Campbell Island
Auckland Islands
EMERALD BASIN
MACQUARIE RIDGE
Macquarie Island 677
BALLENY BASIN
Scott Island
PENNELL BANK
Ross Sea
Ross
Balleny Islands
BALLENY BASIN
EMPEROR BASIN
TASMAN BASIN 5267
Tasmania
TASMAN RISE
SOUTHEAST INDIAN RIDGE
SOUTH INDIAN BASIN
WILKES ABYSSAL PLAIN
GAUSSBERG ABYSSAL PLAIN
GRIBB BANK
KERGUELEN PLATEAU
5089
Heard Island
Iles de Kerguelen
Iles Crozet 316
Prince Edward Islands
MALAGASY FRACTURE ZONE
MOZAMBIQUE FRACTURE ZONE
CAPE RISE
AGULHAS PLATEAU 2310
AFRICANA SEAMOUNT
CAPE BASIN
SCHMIDT-OTT SEAMOUNT
ATLANTIC-INDIAN BASIN 6972
ENDERBY ABYSSAL PLAIN
ATLANTIC-INDIAN RIDGE
PRINCE EDWARD FRACTURE ZONE
247 OB TABLEMOUNT
LENA TABLEMOUNT
SPIESS SEAMOUNT
MAUD SEAMOUNT 840
DISCOVERY TABLEMOUNT
MERZ SEAMOUNT 660
METEOR SEAMOUNT
South Pole
80°
Weddell Sea
Berkner Island
WEDDELL ABYSSAL PLAIN 677
4830
Barth Island
BARTH SEAMOUNT
South Orkney Islands
South Shetland Islands
WEST SCOTIA BASIN
SCOTIA RIDGE
EAST SCOTIA BASIN
South Georgia
SOUTH SANDWICH TRENCH
SOUTH SANDWICH ISLANDS 8428 METEOR DEEP
Falkland Islands
FALKLAND PLATEAU
FALKLAND TROUGH
ARGENTINE BASIN
FALKLAND FRACTURE ZONE
MID-ATLANTIC RIDGE
Tristan da Cunha
Gough Island
Antarctic Circle
Copyright © by Rand McNally & Co.

Scale 1:60 000 000; one inch to 950 miles (approx.)
Lambert Azimuthal Equal Area Projection   ▽ Depths in meters.

Kilometers: 0 400 800 1200
Miles: 0 400 800 1200

introduction
geographical tables
major cities map index
pronouncing index

In the pages which follow, the editors of the atlas have provided factual information of geographic interest on the world, the continents, individual foreign countries, and many other political and physiographic units. Presented in tabular form, these pages are designed to supplement the Goode's maps with data not readily available from the maps themselves. Here will be found the answers to many of the questions raised by those who use the atlas, particularly questions that ask "how large?" "how many?" and "where?".

The first table is the "World Political Information Table". For each political or physiographic unit listed, the table specifies the latest estimated population, area in square miles, population density, capital, largest city, and principal languages. In addition, the table briefly describes the political or administrative status of the units listed and classifies them into major types.

The second table is entitled "World Comparisons". Here are the basic facts about the earth's measurements, the highest and lowest points on earth, and the areas of the continents. Also included are listings of the world's major physical features — mountains, oceans and seas, lakes, rivers, and islands. Each list includes the outstanding features in each category.

"Principal Cities of the World," the last table in the section, is arranged alphabetically and includes the more important and the largest urban centers. It also shows the most recent urban and metropolitan population figures. Following the geographical tables is an index containing a selection of places which appear on the major cities maps located in the front of the atlas. This special index provides the atlas user a convenient format with which to study the world urban areas.

Next are information tables to aid the reader in understanding the maps and the index. The "Glossary of Foreign Geographical Terms" is a multiple-language table listing the foreign geographic word, its language(s), and the English equivalent. Also included is a list of abbreviations for terms used primarily in the indexes, but which appear on the maps as well. Further, there is a pronunciation guide to letters and symbols used in the index.

The "Pronouncing Index" contains information designed to assist the reader at all levels of research. The entry gives the proper map page reference, the latitude-longitude coordinates, the country or continent in which the place is located, and how the local residents pronounce the name.

World Political Information Table

This table lists all countries and dependencies in the world, U.S. States, Canadian provinces, and other important regions and political subdivisions. Besides specifying the form of government for all political areas, the table classifies them into six groups according to their political status. Units labeled **A** are independent sovereign nations. (Several of these are designated as members of the British Commonwealth of Nations.) Units labeled **B** are independent as regards internal affairs, but for purposes of foreign affairs they are under the protection of another country. Units labeled **C** are colonies, overseas territories, dependencies, etc., of other countries. Together the **A**, **B**, and **C** areas comprise practically the entire inhabited area of the world. The areas labeled **D** are physically separate units, such as groups of islands, which are *not* separate countries, but form part of a nation or dependency. Units labeled **E** are States, provinces, Soviet Republics, or similar major administrative subdivisions of important countries. Units in the table with no letter designation are regions or other areas that do not constitute separate political units by themselves.

REGION OR POLITICAL DIVISION	Area* Sq. Mi.	Est. Pop. 1/1/81	Pop. Per. Sq. Mi.	Form of Government and Ruling Power		Capital; Largest City (if other)	Predominant Languages
Aden, see Yemen, P.D.R. of							
Afars & Issas, see Djibouti							
Afghanistan†	250,000	15,055,000	60	Socialist Republic	A	Kābul	Dari, Pushtu
Africa	11,708,000	482,400,000	41			...; Cairo	
Alabama	51,609	3,920,000	76	State (U.S.)	E	Montgomery; Birmingham	English
Alaska	589,759	405,000	0.7	State (U.S.)	E	Juneau; Anchorage	English, Indian, Eskimo
Albania†	11,100	2,725,000	245	Socialist Republic	A	Tiranë	Albanian
Alberta	255,285	1,920,000	7.5	Province (Canada)	E	Edmonton	English
Algeria†	919,595	20,050,000	22	Socialist Republic	A	Algiers (Alger)	Arabic, French, Berber
American Samoa	76	33,000	434	Unincorporated Territory (U.S.)	C	Pago Pago	Samoan, English
Andaman & Nicobar Is.	3,202	195,000	61	Territory (India)	D	Port Blair	Andaman, Nicobar Malay
Andorra	175	39,000	223	Co-Principality (Spanish and French protection)	B	Andorra	Spanish, French
Angola†	481,353	7,155,000	15	Socialist Republic	A	Luanda	Portuguese, native languages
Anguilla	34	7,700	226	Associated State (U.K.)	B	The Valley; South Hill	English
Antarctica	5,405,000						
Antigua (incl. Barbuda)	170	75,000	441	Parliamentary State (Comm. of Nations)	A	St. Johns	English
Arabian Peninsula	1,159,500	20,155,000	17			...; Kuwait	Arabic
Argentina†	1,068,301	27,235,000	25	Federal Republic	A	Buenos Aires	Spanish
Arizona	113,909	2,740,000	24	State (U.S.)	E	Phoenix	English
Arkansas	53,104	2,300,000	43	State (U.S.)	E	Little Rock	English
Armenian S.S.R.	11,506	3,075,000	267	Soviet Socialist Republic (Sov. Un.)	E	Yerevan	Armenian, Russian
Aruba	75	65,000	867	Division of Netherlands Antilles (Neth.)	D	Oranjestad	Dutch, Spanish, English, Papiamento
Ascension	34	1,000	29	Dependency of St. Helena (U.K.)	C	Georgetown	English
Asia	17,297,000	2,631,600,000	152			...; Tōkyō	
Australia†	2,967,909	14,680,000	4.9	Parliamentary State (Federal) (Commonwealth of Nations)	A	Canberra; Sydney	English
Australian Capital Territory	939	235,000	250	Territory (Australia)	E	Canberra	English
Austria†	32,375	7,500,000	232	Federal Republic	A	Vienna (Wien)	German
Azerbaydzhan S.S.R.	33,436	6,145,000	184	Soviet Socialist Republic (Sov. Un.)	E	Baku	Turkish, Russian, Armenian
Azores (Açores)	902	296,000	328	Part of Portugal (3 Districts)	D	...; Ponta Delgada	Portuguese
Baden-Württemberg	13,804	9,250,000	670	State (Federal Republic of Germany)	E	Stuttgart	German
Bahamas†	5,382	250,000	46	Parliamentary State (Commonwealth of Nations)	A	Nassau	English
Bahrain†	256	285,000	1,113	Constitutional Monarchy	A	Al Manāmah	Arabic, English
Balearic Is. (Islas Baleares)	1,936	700,000	362	Part of Spain (Baleares Province)	D	Palma de Mallorca	Spanish
Baltic Republics	67,182	7,565,000	113	Soviet Union		...; Riga	Lithuanian, Latvian, Estonian, Russia
Bangladesh†	55,598	89,595,000	1,611	Republic (Commonwealth of Nations)	A	Dacca	Bangla, English
Barbados†	166	275,000	1,657	Parliamentary State (Commonwealth of Nations)	A	Bridgetown	English
Basutoland, see Lesotho							
Bavaria (Bayern)	27,238	10,920,000	401	State (Federal Republic of Germany)	E	Munich (München)	German
Bechuanaland, see Botswana							
Belgium†	11,781	9,800,000	837	Constitutional Monarchy	A	Brussels (Bruxelles)	French, Dutch (Flemish), German
Belize†(British Honduras)	8,866	165,000	19	Parliamentary State (Commonwealth of Nations)	A	Belmopan; Belize City	English, Spanish, Indian languages
Benelux	80,155	24,400,000	121			...; Brussels	Native languages, French
Belorussian S.S.R.	28,672	9,725,000	851	Soviet Socialist Republic (Sov. Un.)	E	Minsk	Byelorussian, Polish, Russian
Benin†	43,484	3,610,000	83	Socialist Republic	A	Porto Novo; Cotonou	Dutch, French, Luxembourgish
Berlin (West)	185	1,910,000	10,324	State (Federal Republic of Germany)	E	Berlin (West)	German
Bermuda	21	61,000	2,905	Colony (U.K.)	C	Hamilton	English
Bhutan†	18,147	1,340,000	74	Monarchy (Indian protection)	B	Thimbu	Druk-ke, Nepalese dialects
Bioko	785	92,000	117	Part of Equatorial Guinea	D	Malabo	Spanish, native languages, English
Bolivia†	424,164	5,640,000	13	Republic	A	Sucre and La Paz; La Paz	Spanish, Quechua, Aymara
Borneo, Indonesian (Kalimantan)	208,287	6,754,000	32	Part of Indonesia	D	...; Banjarmasin	Indonesian
Botswana (Bechuanaland)†	231,805	870,000	3.8	Republic (Commonwealth of Nations)	A	Gaborone	Setswana, English
Brazil†	3,286,487	123,795,000	38	Federal Republic	A	Brasília; São Paulo	Portuguese
Bremen	156	680,000	4,359	State (Federal Republic of Germany)	E	Bremen	German
British Antarctic Territory (excl. Antarctic mainland)	2,040	Winter pop. 85	0.04	Colony (U.K.)	C	Administered from Stanley, Falkland Islands	English
British Columbia	366,355	2,595,000	7.1	Province (Canada)	E	Victoria; Vancouver	English
British Guiana, see Guyana							
British Indian Ocean Territory	23			Conony (U.K.)	C	Administered from London	
Brunei	2,226	230,000	103	Constitutional Monarchy (U.K. protection)	B	Bandar Seri Begawan (Brunei)	Malay, Chinese, English
Bulgaria†	42,823	9,110,000	213	Socialist Republic	A	Sofia (Sofiya)	Bulgarian
Burma†	261,228	33,585,000	129	Socialist Republic	A	Rangoon	Burmese, English
Burundi (Urundi)†	10,747	4,560,000	424	Republic	A	Bujumbura	Kirundi, French, Swahili
California	158,694	23,850,000	150	State (U.S.)	E	Sacramento; Los Angeles	English
Cambodia, see Kampuchea							
Cameroon†	183,569	8,525,000	46	Republic	A	Yaoundé; Douala	English, French, native languages
Canada†	3,831,033	24,005,000	6.3	Parliamentary State (Federal) (Commonwealth of Nations)	A	Ottawa; Montréal	English, French
Canary Is. (Islas Canarias)	2,808	1,605,000	372	Part of Spain (2 Provinces)	D	Las Palmas de Gran Canaria	Spanish
Cape Verde†	1,557	330,000	212	Republic	A	Praia; Mindelo	Portuguese, Crioula
Caroline Is.	446	89,000	200	Part of U.S. Pacific Is. Trust Ter. (4 Districts)	D	Koror	Malay-Polynesian languages, English
Cayman Is.	100	18,000	180	Colony (U.K.)	C	Georgetown	English
Celebes (Sulawesi)	73,057	11,206,000	153	Part of Indonesia	D	...; Ujung Pandang	Bahasa Indonesia, Malay-Polynesian languages
Central African Republic†	240,535	2,020,000	8.4	Republic	A	Bangui	French, Sangho
Central America	202,000	23,100,000	114			...; Guatemala	Spanish, Indian languages
Central Asia, Soviet	493,090	25,915,000	53	Soviet Union		...; Tashkent	Uzbek, Russian, Kirghiz, Turkoman, Tadzhik
Ceylon, see Sri Lanka							
Chad†	495,755	4,585,000	9.2	Republic	A	Ndjamena (Fort-Lamy)	French, native languages
Channel Is. (Guernsey, Jersey, etc.)	75	132,000	1,760			...; St. Helier	English, French

† Member of the United Nations (1980).
* Areas include inland water.

238

REGION OR POLITICAL DIVISION	Area* Sq. Mi.	Est. Pop. 1/1/81	Pop. Per. Sq. Mi.	Form of Government and Ruling Power		Capital; Largest City (if other)	Predominant Languages
Chile†	292,135	11,065,000	38	Republic	A	Santiago	Spanish
China (excl. Taiwan)†	3,691,500	945,130,000	236	Socialist Republic	A	Peking (Beijing); Shanghai	Chinese dialects
China (Nationalist), see Taiwan							
Christmas I. (Indian Ocean)	54	3,400	63	External Territory (Australia)	C	....; Flying Fish Cove	Chinese, Malay, English
Cocos (Keeling) Is.	5.4	300	56	External Territory (Australia)	C		Malay, English
Colombia†	439,737	27,225,000	62	Republic	A	Bogotá	Spanish
Colorado	104,248	2,910,000	28	State (U.S.)	E	Denver	English
Commonwealth of Nations	10,667,000	1,072,691,000	101			....; London	
Comoros†	838	335,000	400	Republic	A	Moroni	Swahili, French, Arabic
Congo†	132,047	1,550,000	12	Socialist Republic	A	Brazzaville	French, native languages
Congo, The, see Zaire							
Connecticut	5,009	3,130,000	625	State (U.S.)	E	Hartford	English
Cook Is.	91	16,000	176	Self-governing Territory (New Zealand)	B	Avarua	Malay-Polynesian languages, English
Corsica	3,352	200,000	60	Part of France (2 Departments)	D	....; Ajaccio	French, Italian
Costa Rica†	19,730	2,300,000	117	Republic	A	San José	Spanish
Cuba†	44,218	9,700,000	219	Socialist Republic	A	Havana (La Habana)	Spanish
Curaçao	171	165,000	965	Division of Netherlands Antilles (Neth.)	D	Willemstad	Dutch, Spanish, English, Papiamento
Cyprus†	3,572	640,000	179	Republic (Commonwealth of Nations)	A	Nicosia	Greek, Turkish, English
Czechoslovakia†	49,374	15,420,000	312	Socialist Republic	A	Prague (Praha)	Czech, Slovak, Hungarian
Dahomey, see Benin							
Delaware	2,057	600,000	292	State (U.S.)	E	Dover; Wilmington	English
Denmark†	16,631	5,145,000	309	Constitutional Monarchy	A	Copenhagen (København)	Danish
Denmark and Possessions	857,175	5,239,000	6.1			Copenhagen	Danish, Faroese, Eskimo
District of Columbia	67	640,000	9,552	District (U.S.)	E	Washington	English
Djibouti†	8,880	121,000	14	Republic	A	Djibouti	Somali, French, Afar, Arabic
Dominica†	290	83,000	286	Republic (Commonwealth of Nations)	A	Roseau	English, French
Dominican Republic†	18,704	5,515,000	295	Republic	A	Santo Domingo	Spanish
Ecuador†	109,483	8,625,000	79	Republic	A	Quito; Guayaquil	Spanish, Quechua
Egypt (United Arab Republic)†	‡‡386,900	43,135,000	111	Socialist Republic	A	Cairo (Al Qâhirah)	Arabic, English, French
Ellice Is., see Tuvalu							
El Salvador†	8,124	4,590,000	565	Republic	A	San Salvador	Spanish
England (excl. Monmouthshire)	50,362	46,465,000	923	United Kingdom		....; London	English
England & Wales	58,381	49,250,000	844	Administrative division of United Kingdom	E	London	English, Welsh
Equatorial Guinea†	10,831	370,000	34	Republic	A	Malabo	Spanish, English, native languages
Estonian S.S.R.	17,413	1,525,000	88	Soviet Socialist Republic (Sov. Un.)	E	Tallinn	Estonian, Russian
Ethiopia†	472,434	30,645,000	65	Monarchy	A	Adis Abeba	Amharic, Arabic, native languages
Eurasia	21,132,000	3,296,200,000	156			....; Tōkyō	
Europe	3,835,000	664,600,000	173			....; London	
Faeroe Is.	540	43,000	80	Part of Danish Realm	B	Tórshavn	Danish, Faroese
Falkland Is. (excl. Deps.)	4,700	2,000	0.4	Colony (U.K.)	C	Stanley	English
Fernando Poo, see Bioko							
Fiji†	7,055	635,000	90	Parliamentary State (Commonwealth of Nations)	A	Suva	English, Fijian, Hindustani
Finland†	130,129	4,785,000	37	Republic	A	Helsinki	Finnish, Swedish
Florida	58,560	9,950,000	170	State (U.S.)	E	Tallahassee; Miami	English
France†	211,208	53,780,000	255	Republic	A	Paris	French
France and Possessions	260,661	55,330,000	212			Paris	French
Franklin	549,253	8,000	0.01	District of Northwest Territories (Canada)	E	....; Frobisher Bay	English, Eskimo, Indian
French Guiana	35,135	63,000	1.8	Overseas Department (France)	C	Cayenne	French
French Polynesia	1,544	150,000	97	Overseas Territory (France)	C	Papeete	Malay-Polynesian languages, French
French Somaliland, see Djibouti							
French Southern & Antarctic Ter. (excl. Adélie Coast)	3,000	200	0.07	Overseas Territory (France)	C		French
French West Indies	1,112	630,000	567			Fort-de-France	French
Gabon†	103,347	555,000	5.4	Republic	A	Libreville	French, native languages
Galapagos Is. (Colón, Archipiélago de)	3,075	5,800	1.9	Province (Ecuador)	D	Puerto Baquerizo Moreno	Spanish
Gambia†	4,361	610,000	140	Republic (Commonwealth of Nations)	A	Banjul (Bathurst)	English, native languages
Georgia	58,876	5,505,000	94	State (U.S.)	E	Atlanta	English
Georgian S.S.R.	26,911	5,105,000	190	Soviet Socialist Republic (Sov. Union)	E	Tbilisi	Georgic, Armenian, Russian
Germany (Entire)	137,772	78,405,000	569			....; Essen	German
German Democratic Republic (East Germany)†	41,768	16,715,000	400	Socialist Republic	A	Berlin (East)	German
Germany, Federal Republic of (West Germany)†	96,004	61,690,000	643	Federal Republic	A	Bonn; Essen	German
Ghana†	92,100	11,835,000	129	Republic (Commonwealth of Nations)	A	Accra	English, native languages
Gibraltar	2.3	30,000	13,043	Colony (U.K.)	C	Gibraltar	Spanish, English
Gilbert Is., see Kiribati							
Great Britain & Northern Ireland, see United Kingdom							
Greece†	50,944	9,565,000	188	Republic	A	Athens (Athínai)	Greek
Greenland	840,004	51,000	0.06	Part or Danish Realm	B	Godthåb	Danish, Eskimo
Grenada†	133	114,000	857	Parliamentary State (Commonwealth of Nations)	A	St. George's	English
Guadeloupe (incl. Dependencies)	687	320,000	466	Overseas Department (France)	C	Basse-Terre; Pointe-à-Pitre	French, Creole
Guam	212	107,000	505	Unincorporated Territory (U.S.)	C	Agana	English, Chamorro
Guatemala†	42,042	7,685,000	183	Republic	A	Guatemala	Spanish, Indian languages
Guernsey (incl. Dependencies)	30	55,000	1,833	Bailiwick (U.K.)	C	St. Peter Port	English, French
Guinea†	94,926	5,070,000	53	Republic	A	Conakry	Native languages, French
Guinea-Bissau†	13,948	805,000	58	Republic	A	Bissau	Native languages, Portuguese
Guyana†	83,000	921,000	11	Republic (Commonwealth of Nations)	A	Georgetown	English
Haiti†	10,714	5,040,000	470	Republic	A	Port-au-Prince	Creole, French
Hamburg	289	1,665,000	5,761	State (Federal Republic of Germany)	E	Hamburg	German
Hawaii	6,450	970,000	150	State (U.S.)	E	Honolulu	English, Japanese, Hawaiian
Hesse (Hessen)	8,152	5,615,000	689	State (Federal Republic of Germany)	E	Wiesbaden; Frankfurt am Main	German
Hispaniola	29,418	10,555,000	359			....; Port-au-Prince	French, Spanish, Creole
Holland, see Netherlands							
Honduras†	43,277	3,750,000	87	Republic	A	Tegucigalpa	Spanish
Hong Kong	410	5,265,000	12,841	Colony (U.K.)	C	Victoria	Chinese, English
Hungary†	35,920	10,945,000	305	Socialist Republic	A	Budapest	Hungarian
Iceland†	39,769	229,000	5.8	Republic	A	Reykjavík	Icelandic
Idaho	83,557	950,000	11	State (U.S.)	E	Boise	English
Illinois	57,926	11,505,000	199	State (U.S.)	E	Springfield; Chicago	English
India (incl. part of Jammu and Kashmir)†	1,237,061	669,860,000	541	Federal Socialist Republic (Commonwealth of Nations)	A	New Delhi; Calcutta	Hindi and other Indo-Aryan languages, Dravidian languages, English
Indiana	36,519	5,530,000	151	State (U.S.)	E	Indianapolis	English
Indonesia (incl. West Irian)†	741,034	153,510,000	207	Republic	A	Jakarta	Bahasa Indonesia (Indonesian), English
Iowa	56,290	2,935,000	52	State (U.S.)	E	Des Moines	English
Iran (Persia)†	636,296	38,940,000	61	Republic	A	Tehrān	Farsi, Turkish, Kurdish, Arabic
Iraq†	167,925	13,230,000	79	Socialist Republic	A	Baghdād	Arabic, Kurdish
Ireland†	27,136	3,455,000	127	Republic	A	Dublin	English, Irish Gaelic
Isle of Man	227	66,000	291	Self-governing Territory (U.K.)	B	Douglas	English
Israel†	‡‡7,848△	3,920,000	499	Republic	A	Jerusalem; Tel Aviv-Yafo	Hebrew, Arabic, English

† Member of the United Nations (1980).
‡‡ Areas for Egypt, Israel, Jordan and Syria do not reflect de facto changes which took place since 1967.
△ Population excludes 1,100,000 people in territories administered by Israel.
* Areas include inland water.

REGION OR POLITICAL DIVISION	Area* Sq. Mi.	Est. Pop. 1/1/81	Pop. Per Sq. Mi.	Form of Government and Ruling Power		Capital; Largest City (if other)	Predominant Languages
Italy†	116,318	57,230,000	492	Republic	A	Rome (Roma); Milan (Milano)	Italian
Ivory Coast†	123,847	8,390,000	68	Republic	A	Abidjan	French, native languages
Jamaica†	4,244	2,210,000	521	Parliamentary State (Commonwealth of Nations)	A	Kingston	English
Japan†	145,709	117,360,000	805	Constitutional Monarchy	A	Tōkyō	Japanese
Java (Jawa) (incl. Madura)	51,038	96,251,000	1,886	Part of Indonesia	D	.........; Jakarta	Bahasa Indonesia, Chinese, English
Jersey	45	77,000	1,711	Bailiwick (U.K.)	C	St. Helier	English, French
Jordan†	‡‡37,738	2,925,000	78	Constitutional Monarchy	A	Ammān	Arabic, English
Kampuchea†	69,898	6,810,000	97	Socialist Republic	A	Phnom Penh	Khmer (Cambodian)
Kansas	82,264	2,380,000	29	State (U.S.)	E	Topeka; Wichita	English
Kashmir, Jammu &	86,024	9,700,000	113	In dispute (India & Pakistan)		Srīnagar and Jammu; Srīnagar	Kashmiri, Punjabi
Kazakh S.S.R.	1,049,155	14,960,000	14	Soviet Socialist Republic (Sov. Un.)	E	Alma-Ata	Turkish, Russian
Keewatin	228,160	5,000	0.02	District of Northwest Territories (Canada)	E	Baker Lake	English, Eskimo, Indian
Kentucky	40,395	3,690,000	91	State (U.S.)	E	Frankfort; Louisville	English
Kenya†	224,961	16,035,000	71	Republic (Commonwealth of Nations)	A	Nairobi	English, Swahili, native languages
Kerguelen Is.	2,700	90	0.03	Part of French Southern & Antarctic Ter. (Fr.)	D		French
Kirghiz S.S.R.	76,641	3,580,000	47	Soviet Socialist Republic (Sov. Un.)	E	Frunze	Turkish, Farsi, Russian
Kiribati (Gilbert Is.)	291	59,000	203	Republic (Commonwealth of Nations)	A	Bairiki	Gilbertese, English
Korea (Entire)	85,052‡	56,585,000	665			.........; Seoul (Sŏul)	Korean
Korea, North	46,540	18,115,000	389	Socialist Republic	A	P'yŏngyang	Korean
Korea, South	38,025	38,470,000	1,012	Republic	A	Seoul (Sŏul)	Korean, English
Kuwait†	6,880	1,380,000	201	Constitutional Monarchy	A	Kuwait (Al Kuwayt)	Arabic
Labrador	112,826	35,000	0.3	Part of Newfoundland Province (Canada)		.........; Labrador City	English, Eskimo
Laos†	91,429	3,760,000	41	Socialist Republic	A	Viangchan	Lao, French
Latin America	7,938,600	367,960,000	46			.........; Mexico City	Spanish, Portuguese
Latvian S.S.R.	24,595	2,565,000	104	Soviet Socialist Republic (Sov. Un.)	E	Rīga	Latvian, Russian
Lebanon†	4,015	3,205,000	798	Republic	A	Beirut (Bayrūt)	Arabic, French, English
Lesotho (Basutoland)†	11,720	1,360,000	116	Monarchy (Commonwealth of Nations)	A	Maseru	Sesotho, English
Liberia†	43,000	1,890,000	44	Republic	A	Monrovia	Native languages, English
Libya†	679,362	3,030,000	4.5	Socialist Republic	A	Tripoli	Arabic
Liechtenstein	61	26,000	426	Constitutional Monarchy	A	Vaduz	German
Lithuanian S.S.R.	25,174	3,475,000	138	Soviet Socialist Republic (Sov. Un.)	E	Vilnius	Lithuanian, Polish, Russian
Louisiana	48,523	4,235,000	87	State (U.S.)	E	Baton Rouge; New Orleans	English
Lower Saxony (Niedersachsen)	18,308	7,280,000	398	State (Federal Republic of Germany)	E	Hannover	German
Luxembourg†	999	370,000	370	Constitutional Monarchy	A	Luxembourg	Luxembourgish, French, German
Macau	6.0	295,000	49,167	Overseas Province (Portugal)	C	Macau	Chinese dialects
Macías Nguema Biyogo, see Bioko							
Mackenzie	527,490	36,000	0.07	District of Northwest Territories (Canada)	E	.........; Yellowknife	English, Eskimo, Indian
Madagascar (Malagasy Republic)†	226,658	8,835,000	39	Republic	A	Antananarivo	French, Malagasy
Madeira Is. (Arquipélago da Madeira)	307	269,000	876	Part of Portugal (Funchal District)	D	Funchal	Portuguese
Maine	33,215	1,135,000	34	State (U.S.)	E	Augusta; Portland	English
Malawi (Nyasaland)†	45,747	6,045,000	132	Republic (Commonwealth of Nations)	A	Lilongwe; Blantyre	Chichewa, English
Malaya	50,700	11,943,000	236	Part of Malaysia		.........; Kuala Lumpur	Malay, Chinese, English, Tamil
Malaysia†	128,430	14,185,000	110	Constitutional Monarchy (Comm. of Nations)	A	Kuala Lumpur	Malay, Chinese, English
Maldives†	115	155,000	1,348	Republic	A	Male	Arabic, Divehi
Mali†	478,766	6,735,000	14	Republic	A	Bamako	French, Bambara
Malta†	122	360,000	2,951	Republic (Commonwealth of Nations)	A	Valletta	English, Maltese
Manitoba	251,000	1,055,000	4.2	Province (Canada)	E	Winnipeg	English
Marianna Is. (excl. Guam)	183	17,000	93	District of U.S. Pacific Is. Trust Ter.	D	Saipan (island); Chalon Kamoa	Malay-Polynesian languages, English
Maritime Provinces (excl. Newfoundland)	51,963	1,705,000	33	Canada		.........; Halifax	English
Marshall Is.	70	30,000	429	District of U.S. Pacific Is. Trust Ter.	D	Majuro (island); Ebeye	Malay-Polynesian languages, English
Martinique	425	310,000	729	Overseas Department (France)	C	Fort-de-France	French, Creole
Maryland	10,577	4,250,000	402	State (U.S.)	E	Annapolis; Baltimore	English
Massachusetts	8,257	5,780,000	700	State (U.S.)	E	Boston	English
Mauritania†	397,955	1,655,000	4.2	Republic	A	Nouakchott	Arabic, French
Mauritius (incl. Dependencies)†	790	960,000	1,215	Parliamentary State (Commonwealth of Nations)	A	Port Louis	French, Creole, English
Mayotte	144	50,000	347	Overseas Department (France)	C	.........; Dzaoudzi	Swahili, French
Mexico†	761,604	73,010,000	96	Federal Republic	A	Mexico City	Spanish
Michigan	96,791	9,330,000	96	State (U.S.)	E	Lansing; Detroit	English
Middle America	1,055,600	124,860,000	118			.........; Mexico City	Spanish, English
Midway Is.	2.0	1,500	750	Unincorporated Territory (U.S.)	C	Administered from Washington, D.C.	English
Minnesota	86,280	4,110,000	48	State (U.S.)	E	St. Paul; Minneapolis	English
Mississippi	47,716	2,540,000	53	State (U.S.)	E	Jackson	English
Missouri	69,686	4,955,000	71	State (U.S.)	E	Jefferson City; St. Louis	English
Moldavian S.S.R.	13,012	4,010,000	308	Soviet Socialist Republic (Sov. Un.)	E	Kishinëv	Moldavian, Russian, Ukrainian
Monaco	0.6	25,000	41,667	Constitutional Monarchy	A	Monaco	French, Italian, English, Monegasque
Mongolia†	604,250	1,690,000	2.8	Socialist Republic	A	Ulaan Baatar	Khalka Mongol
Montana	147,138	790,000	5.4	State (U.S.)	E	Helena; Billings	English
Montserrat	40	11,000	275	Colony (U.K.)	C	Plymouth	English
Morocco (excl. Western Sahara)†	172,414	20,465,000	119	Constitutional Monarchy	A	Rabat; Casablanca	Arabic, Berber, French
Mozambique†	302,329	15,590,000	52	Socialist Republic	A	Maputo	Portuguese, native languages
Namibia (excl. Walvis Bay)	318,261	1,035,000	3.3	Under South African Administration**	C	Windhoek	Afrikaans, German, native languages
Nauru	8.2	7,700	939	Republic (Commonwealth of Nations)	A	Uaboe District; . . .	Nauruan, English
Nebraska	77,227	1,580,000	20	State (U.S.)	E	Lincoln; Omaha	English
Nepal†	54,362	15,155,000	279	Constitutional Monarchy	A	Kathmandu	Nepali, Tibeto-Burman languages
Netherlands†	15,892	14,170,000	892	Constitutional Monarchy	A	Amsterdam and The Hague ('s-Gravenhage); Amsterdam	Dutch
Netherlands and Possessions	16,275	14,425,000	886			Amsterdam and The Hague; Amsterdam	Dutch, English, Papiamento
Netherlands Antilles	383	255,000	666	Self-governing Territory (Netherlands)	B	Willemstad	Dutch, Spanish, English, Papiamento
Netherlands Guiana, see Suriname							
Nevada	110,541	805,000	7.3	State (U.S.)	E	Carson City; Las Vegas	English
New Brunswick	28,354	720,000	25	Province (Canada)	E	Fredericton; Saint John	English, French
New Caledonia (incl. Deps.)	7,358	139,000	19	Overseas Territory (France)	C	Nouméa	Malay-Polynesian languages, French
New England	66,608	12,440,000	187	United States		.........; Boston	English
Newfoundland	156,185	575,000	3.7	Province (Canada)	E	St. John's	English
Newfoundland (excl. Labrador)	43,359	540,000	12	Part of New foundland Province, Canada	D	.........; St. John's	English
New Hampshire	9,304	925,000	99	State (U.S.)	E	Concord; Manchester	English
New Hebrides, see Vanuatu							
New Jersey	7,836	7,420,000	947	State (U.S.)	E	Trenton; Newark	English
New Mexico	121,667	1,310,000	11	State (U.S.)	E	Santa Fe; Albuquerque	English, Spanish
New South Wales	309,433	5,170,000	17	State (Australia)	E	Sydney	English
New York	53,203	17,690,000	333	State (U.S.)	E	Albany; New York	English

† Member of the United Nations (1980).   ‡ Includes 487 sq. miles of demilitarized zone, not included in North or South Korea figures.
‡ Areas for Egypt, Israel, Jordan, and Syria do not reflect de facto changes which took place since 1967.
* The United Nations declared an end to the mandate of South Africa over Namibia in October 1966. Administration of the territory by South Africa is not recognized by the United Nations.
* Areas include inland water.

REGION OR POLITICAL DIVISION	Area* Sq. Mi.	Est. Pop. 1/1/81	Pop. Per Sq. Mi.	Form of Government and Ruling Power		Capital; Largest City (if other)	Predominant Languages
New Zealand†	103,883	3,125,000	30	Parliamentary State (Commonwealth of Nations)	A	Wellington; Auckland	English, Maori
Nicaragua†	50,193	2,610,000	52	Republic	A	Managua	Spanish
Niedersachsen, see Lower Saxony							
Niger†	489,191	5,380,000	11	Republic	A	Niamey	French, Hausa, native languages
Nigeria†	356,669	78,135,000	219	Federal Republic (Commonwealth of Nations)	A	Lagos	Hausa, Ibo, Yoruba, English
Niue	102	3,100	30	Self-governing Territory (New Zealand)	B	Alofi	Malay-Polynesian languages, English
Norfolk Island	14	2,300	164	External Territory (Australia)	C	Kingston	English
North America	9,406,000	377,400,000	40			; New York	
North Bornea, see Sabah							
North Carolina	52,586	5,920,000	113	State (U.S.)	E	Raleigh; Charlotte	English
North Dakota	70,665	660,000	9.3	State (U.S.)	E	Bismarck; Fargo	English
Northern Ireland	5,452	1,545,000	283	Administrative division of United Kingdom	E	Belfast	English
Northern Rhodesia, see Zambia							
Northern Territory	520,280	120,000	0.2	Territory (Australia)	E	Darwin	English, Aboriginal languages
North Polar Regions							
North Rhine-Westphalia (Nordrhein-Westfalen)	13,154	17,090,000	1,299	State (Federal Republic of Germany)	E	Düsseldorf; Essen	German
Northwest Territories	1,304,903	49,000	0.04	Territory (Canada)	E	Yellowknife	English, Eskimo, Indian
Norway†	125,056	4,095,000	33	Constitutional Monarchy	A	Oslo	Norwegian (Riksmål and Landsmål)
Nova Scotia	21,425	865,000	40	Province (Canada)	E	Halifax	English
Nyasaland, see Malawi							
Oceania (incl. Australia)	3,287,000	22,900,000	7.0			; Sydney	
Ohio	44,679	10,880,000	244	State (U.S.)	E	Columbus; Cleveland	English
Oklahoma	69,919	3,050,000	44	State (U.S.)	E	Oklahoma City	English
Oman†	82,030	900,000	11	Monarchy	A	Muscat; Maṭraḥ	Arabic
Ontario	412,582	8,640,000	21	Province (Canada)	E	Toronto	English
Oregon	96,981	2,650,000	27	State (U.S.)	E	Salem; Portland	English
Orkney Is.	376	19,000	51	Part of Scotland, U.K. (orkney Island Area)	D	Kirkwall	English
Pacific Islands Trust Territory	699	136,000	195	Administered by U.S.	C	Saipan (island); Ebeye	Malay-Polynesian languages, English
Pakistan (incl. part of Jammu and Kashmir)†	319,867	88,610,000	277	Federal Republic	A	Islāmābād; Karāchi	Urdu, English, Punjabi
Pakistan, East, see Bangladesh							
Panama†	29,762	2,000,000	67	Republic	A	Panamá	Spanish, English
Papua New Guinea†	178,703	3,210,000	18	Parliamentary State (Commonwealth of Nations)	A	Port Moresby	Papuan and Negreto languages, English
Paraguay†	157,048	3,100,000	20	Republic	A	Asunción	Spanish, Guarani
Pennsylvania	46,068	11,955,000	260	State (U.S.)	E	Harrisburg; Philadelphia	English
Persia, see Iran							
Peru†	496,224	17,995,000	36	Republic	A	Lima	Spanish, Quechua, Aymara
Philippines†	115,831	48,200,000	416	Republic	A	Manila	Pilipino, English, Spanish
Pitcairn (excl. Dependencies)	1.8	65	36	Colony (U.K.)	C	Adamstown	English
Poland†	120,728	35,645,000	295	Socialist Republic	A	Warsaw (Warszawa); Katowice	Polish
Portugal†	34,340	9,980,000	291	Republic	A	Lisbon (Lisboa)	Portuguese
Portugal and Possessions	34,346	10,275,000	299			Lisbon (Lisboa)	Portuguese
Portuguese Guinea, see Guinea-Bissau							
Prairie Provinces	757,985	3,945,000	5.2	Canada		; Winnipeg	English
Prince Edward Island	2,184	120,000	55	Province (Canada)	E	Charlottetown	English
Puerto Rico	3,435	3,223,000	938	Commonwealth (U.S.)	B	San Juan	Spanish, English
Qatar†	4,247	225,000	53	Monarchy	A	Ad Dawhah	Arabic, English
Quebec	594,860	6,480,000	11	Province (Canada)	E	Québec; Montréal	French, English
Queensland	667,000	2,230,000	3.3	State (Australia)	E	Brisbane	English
Reunion	969	500,000	516	Overseas Department (France)	C	St. Denis	French
Rhineland-Palatinate (Rheinland-Pfalz)	7,660	3,640,000	475	State (Federal Republic of Germany)	E	Mainz	German
Rhode Island	1,214	955,000	787	State (U.S.)	E	Providence	English
Rhodesia, see Zimbabwe							
Rio Muni, see Equatorial Guinea							
Rodrigues	42	29,000	690	Part of Mauritius (U.K.)	D	Port Mathurin	English, French
Romania†	91,699	22,345,000	244	Socialist Republic	A	Bucharest (Bucureşti)	Romanian, Hungarian, German
Russian S.F.S.R.	6,592,846	140,030,000	21	Soviet Federated Socialist Republic (Sov. Un.)	E	Moscow (Moskva)	Russian, Finno-Ugric languages, Farsi, Turkish, Mongolian
Russian S.F.S.R. in Europe	1,527,350	102,440,000	67	Soviet Union		; Moscow	Russian, Finno-Ugric languages
Rwanda†	10,169	4,780,000	470	Republic	A	Kigali	French, Kinyarwanda
Saar (Saarland)	993	1,050,000	1,057	State (Federal Republic of Germany)	E	Saarbrücken	German
Sabah (North Borneo)	29,388	964,000	33	Administrative division of Malaysia	E	Kota Kinabalu; Sandakan	Malay, Chinese, English, native languages
St. Helena (incl. Dependencies)	162	6,800	42	Colony (U.K.)	C	Jamestown	English
St. Kitts-Nevis	104	53,000	510	Associated State (U.K.)	B	Basseterre	English
Saint Lucia†	238	124,000	521	Parliamentary State (Commonwealth of Nations)	A	Castries	English
St. Pierre & Miquelon	93	6,200	67	Overseas Department (France)	C	St.-Pierre	French
St. Vincent†	150	126,000	840	Parliamentary State (Commonwealth of Nations)	A	Kingstown	English
Samoa (Entire)	1,173	193,000	165			; Apia	Samoan, English
San Marino	24	22,000	917	Republic	A	San Marino	Italian
Sao Tome & Principe†	372	87,000	234	Republic	A	São Tomé	Portuguese, native languages
Sarawak	48,342	1,277,000	26	Administrative division of Malaysia	E	Kuching	Malay, Chinese, English, native languages
Sardinia	9,301	1,600,000	172	Part of Italy (Sardegna Autonomous Region)	D	Cagliari	Italian
Saskatchewan	251,700	960,000	3.8	Province (Canada)	E	Regina	English
Saudi Arabia†	830,000	8,465,000	10	Monarchy	A	Riyadh	Arabic
Scandinavia (incl. Finland and Iceland)	510,000	22,612,000	44			; Copenhagen (København)	Swedish, Danish, Norwegian, Finnish, Icelandic
Schleswig-Holstein	6,065	2,590,000	427	State (Federal Republic of Germany)	E	Kiel	German
Scotland	30,416	5,150,000	169	Administrative division of United Kingdom	E	Edinburgh; Glasgow	English, Scots Gaelic
Senegal†	75,955	5,725,000	75	Republic	A	Dakar	Wolof, French, native languages
Seychelles†	171	67,000	392	Republic (Commonwealth of Nations)	A	Victoria	French, Creole, English
Shetland Is.	551	23,000	42	Part of Scotland, U.K. (Shetland Island Area)	D	Lerwick	English
Siam, see Thailand							
Sicily	9,926	5,035,000	507	Part of Italy (Sicilia Autonomous Region)	D	Palermo	Italian
Sierra Leone†	27,925	4,125,000	148	Republic (Commonwealth of Nations)	A	Freetown	English, native languages
Singapore†	224	2,465,000	11,004	Republic (Commonwealth of Nations)	A	Singapore	Chinese, Malay, English, Tamil
Soloman Is.†	11,500	225,000	20	Parliamentary State (Commonwealth of Nations)	A	Honiara	Malay-Polynesian languages, English
Somalia†	246,200	4,535,000	18	Socialist Republic	A	Mugdisho	Somali, Arabic, English, Italian
South Africa (incl. Walvis Bay)†	471,447	29,645,000	63	Republic	A	Pretoria and Cape Town; Johannesburg	English, Afrikaans, native languages
South America	6,883,000	243,100,000	35			; São Paulo	
South Australia	380,070	1,305,000	3.4	State (Australia)	E	Adelaide	English

† Member of the United Nations (1980).
* Areas include inland water.

REGION OR POLITICAL DIVISION	Area* Sq. Mi.	Est. Pop. 1/1/81	Pop. Per. Sq. Mi.	Form of Government and Ruling Power		Capital; Largest City (if other)	Predominant Languages
South Carolina	31,055	3,140,000	101	State (U.S.)	E	Columbia; Charleston	English
South Dakota	77,047	695,000	9.0	State (U.S.)	E	Pierre; Sioux Falls	English
Southern Rhodesia, see Zimbabwe							
South Georgia (incl. Dependencies)	1,580	20	0.01	Dependency of Falkland Is. (U.K.)	C		English, Norwegian
South West Africa, see Namibia							
Soviet Union (Union of Soviet Socialist Republics)†	8,600,383	267,190,000	31	Federal Soviet Republic	A	Moscow (Moskva)	Russian and other Slavic languages, various Altaic and Indo-European languages
Soviet Union in Europe	1,920,789	174,400,000	91	Soviet Union		; Moscow	Russian and other Slavic languages
Spain†	194,882	37,790,000	194	Constitutional Monarchy	A	Madrid	Spanish
Spain and Possessions	194,894	37,921,000	195			Madrid	Spanish
Spanish North Africa	12	131,000	10,917	Five Possessions (no central government) (Spain)	C	; Ceuta	Spanish, Arabic, Berber
Spanish Sahara, see Western Sahara							
Sri Lanka (Ceylon)†	25,097	15,470,000	616	Socialist Republic (Commonwealth of Nations)	A	Colombo	Sinhala, Tamil, English
Sudan†	967,500	18,630,000	19	Republic	A	Al Kharţum	Arabic, native languages, English
Sumatra (Sumatera)	182,860	28,092,000	154	Part of Indonesia	D	; Medan	Bahasa Indonesia, English, Chinese
Suriname†	63,037	425,000	6.7	Republic	A	Paramaribo	Dutch, English, Sranang Tongo
Svalbard and Jan Mayen	24,101	Winter pop. 3,000	0.1	Dependencies (Norway)	C	; Longyearbyen	Norwegian, Russian
Swaziland†	6,704	565,000	84	Monarchy (Commonwealth of Nations)	A	Mbabane	English, siSwati
Sweden†	173,780	8,315,000	48	Constitutional Monarchy	A	Stockholm	Swedish
Switzerland	15,943	6,230,000	391	Federal Republic	A	Bern; Zürich	German, French, Italian
Syria†	‡‡71,498	8,735,000	122	Socialist Republic	A	Damascus (Dimashq)	Arabic
Tadzhik S.S.R.	55,251	3,875,000	70	Soviet Socialist Republic (Sov. Un.)	E	Dushanbe	Tadzhik, Turkish, Russian
Taiwan (Formosa) (Nationalist China)	13,895	18,055,000	1,299	Republic	A	T'aipei	Chinese dialects
Tanganyika, see Tanzania							
Tanzania (Tanganyika & Zanzibar)†	364,900	18,785,000	51	Republic (Commonwealth of Nations)	A	Dar es Salaam	Swahili, English, native languages
Tasmania	26,383	425,000	16	State (Australia)	E	Hobart	English
Tennessee	42,244	4,625,000	109	State (U.S.)	E	Nashville; Memphis	English
Texas	267,339	14,335,000	54	State (U.S.)	E	Austin; Dallas	English, Spanish
Thailand (Siam)†	198,114	47,845,000	242	Constitutional Monarchy	A	Bangkok (Krung Thep)	Thai
Tibet (Xizang)	471,700	1,700,000	3.6	Autonomous Region (China)	E	Lhasa	Tibetan dialects
Togo†	21,925	2,565,000	117	Republic	A	Lomé	Native languages, French
Tokelau (Union Is.)	3.9	1,600	410	Island Territory (New Zealand)	C	; Fakaofo	Malay-Polynesian languages, English
Tonga	270	97,000	359	Monarchy (Commonwealth of Nations)	A	Nukualofa	Tongan, English
Transcaucasia	71,853	14,325,000	199	Soviet Union		; Baku	Russian, Armenian, Georgic, Turkish
Trinidad & Tobago†	1,980	920,000	465	Republic (Commonwealth of Nations)	A	Port of Spain	English
Tristan da Cunha	40	300	7.5	Dependency of St. Helena (U.K.)	C	Edinburgh	English
Trucial States, see United Arab Emirates							
Tunisia†	63,170	6,410,000	101	Republic	A	Tunis	Arabic, French
Turkey†	300,948	45,955,000	153	Republic	A	Ankara; İstanbul	Turkish, Kurdish, Arabic
Turkey in Europe	9,175	3,965,000	432	Turkey		; İstanbul	Turkish
Turkmen S.S.R.	188,456	2,805,000	15	Soviet Socialist Republic (Sov. Un.)	E	Ashkhabad	Turkish, Russian
Turks & Caicos Is.	166	6,700	40	Colony (U.K.)	C	Grand Turk	English
Tuvalu (Ellice Is.)	10	7,500	750	Parliamentary State (Commonwealth of Nations)	C	Funafuti	Malay-Polynesian languages, English
Uganda†	91,134	13,875,000	152	Republic (Commonwealth of Nations)	A	Kampala	English, Swahili, Luganda
Ukrainian S.S.R.†	233,000	50,660,000	217	Federal Socialist Republic (Sov. Un.)	E	Kiev	Ukrainian, Russian
Union of Soviet Socialist Republics, see Soviet Union							
United Arab Emirates†	32,278	1,055,000	33	Federation of Monarchs	A	Abū Ẓaby; Dubayy	Arabic, English
United Arab Republic, see Egypt							
United Kingdom†	94,249	55,945,000	594	Constitutional Monarchy (Commonwealth of Nations)	A	London	English, Welsh, Gaelic
United Kingdom & Possessions	113,676	62,075,000	540			London	English, Welsh, Gaelic, native languages
United States†	3,678,896	228,340,000	62	Federal Republic	A	Washington; New York	English
United States and Possessions	3,683,456	231,941,000	63			Washington; New York	English, Spanish
Upper Volta†	105,869	6,995,000	66	Republic	A	Ouagadougou	French, native languages
Uruguay†	68,037	2,900,000	43	Republic	A	Montevideo	Spanish
Utah	84,916	1,470,000	17	State (U.S.)	E	Salt Lake City	English
Uzbek S.S.R.	172,742	15,655,000	91	Soviet Socialist Republic (Sov. Un.)	E	Tashkent	Turkish, Sart, Russian
Vanuatu (New Hebrides)	5,714	118,000	21	Parliamentary State (Commonwealth of Nations)	A	Vila	Bislama, French, English
Vatican City (Holy See)	0.2	1,000	5,000	Ecclesiastical State	A	Vatican City	Italian, Latin
Venezuela†	352,144	14,115,000	40	Federal Republic	A	Caracas	Spanish
Vermont	9,609	515,000	54	State (U.S.)	E	Montpelier; Burlington	English
Victoria	87,884	3,920,000	45	State (Australia)	E	Melbourne	English
Vietnam†	127,242	54,720,000	430	Socialist Republic	A	Ha-noi; Ho Chi Minh City (Saigon)	Vietnamese
Virginia	40,817	5,385,000	132	State (U.S.)	E	Richmond; Norfolk	English
Virgin Is., British	59	14,000	237	Colony (U.K.)	C	Road Town	English
Virgin Is. (U.S.)	133	100,000	752	Unincorporated Territory (U.S.)	C	Charlotte Amalie	English
Wake I.	3.0	200	67	Unincorporated Territory (U.S.)	C	Administered from Washington, D.C.	English
Wales (incl. Monmouthshire)	8,019	2,785,000	347	United Kingdom		Cardiff	English, Welsh
Wellis & Futuna	98	12,000	122	Overseas Territory (France)	C	Mata-Utu	Malay-Polynesian languages, French
Washington	68,192	4,160,000	61	State (U.S.)	E	Olympia; Seattle	English
Western Australia	975,920	1,275,000	1.3	State (Australia)	E	Perth	English
Western Sahara	102,703	185,000	1.8	Occupied by Morocco		El Aaiún	Arabic
Western Samoa†	1,097	160,000	146	Constitutional Monarchy (Comm. of Nations)	A	Apia	Samoan, English
West Indies	92,000	28,750,000	313			; Havana	Spanish, English, French, Creole
West Virginia	24,181	1,965,000	81	State (U.S.)	E	Charleston; Huntington	English
White Russia, see Belorussian S.S.R.							
Wisconsin	66,216	4,740,000	72	State (U.S.)	E	Madison; Milwaukee	English
World	57,821,000	4,422,000,000	76			; Tōkyō	
Wyoming	97,914	475,000	4.9	State (U.S.)	E	Cheyenne; Casper	English
Yemen†	75,290	5,995,000	80	Republic	A	Şan'ā'	Arabic
Yemen, People's Democratic Republic of,†	128,560	1,850,000	14	Socialist Republic	A	Aden	Arabic
Yugoslovia†	98,766	22,450,000	227	Socialist Federal Republic	A	Belgrade (Beograd)	Serbo-Croatian, Slovenian, Macedonian
Yukon Territory	186,300	26,000	0.1	Territory (Canada)	E	Whitehorse	English, Eskimo, Indian
Zaire (Congo, The)†	905,567	29,050,000	32	Republic	A	Kinshasa	French, Lingala, native languages
Zambia (Northern Rhodesia)†	290,586	5,915,000	20	Republic (Commonwealth of Nations)	A	Lusaka	English, native languages
Zanzibar	950	535,000	563	Part of Tanzania	D	; Zanzibar	Swahili, English, native languages
Zimbabwe (Rhodesia)†	150,804	7,465,000	50	Republic (Commonwealth of Nations)	A	Salisbury	English, native languages

† Member of the United Nations (1980).
*Areas include inland water.

world comparisons

General Information

Equatorial diameter of the earth, 7,926.68 miles
Polar diameter of the earth, 7,899.99 miles
Diameter of the mean sphere of the earth, 7,918.78 miles
Equatorial circumference of the earth, 24,901.46 miles
Polar circumference of the earth, 24,859.73 miles
Mean distance from the earth to the sun, 92,900,000 miles
Mean distance from the earth to the moon, 238,857 miles
Total area of the earth, 196,940,400 square miles

Highest elevation on the earth's surface, Mt. Everest, Asia, 29,028 feet
Lowest elevation on the earth's land surface, shores of the Dead Sea, Asia—1,296 feet
Grestest known depth of the ocean, south of the Mariana Islands, Pacific Ocean, 36,201 feet
Total land area of the earth, including inland water and Antarctica, 57,821,000 square miles.

Area of Africa, 11,708,000 square miles
Area of Antarctica, 5,405,000 square miles
Area of Asia, 17,297,000 square miles
Area of Europe, 3,835,000 square miles
Area of North America, 9,406,000 square miles
Area of Oceania, incl. Australia, 3,287,000 square miles
Area of South America, 6,883,000 square miles
Population of the earth (est. 1/1/81), 4,422,000,000

Principal Islands and Their Areas

ISLAND	Area (Sq. Mi.)
Baffin, Arctic Region	183,810
Banks, Arctic Region	23,230
Borneo, Asia	288,243
Bougainville, Oceania	3,880
Celebes, Indonesia	73,057
Corsica, Mediterranean Sea	3,352
Crete, Mediterranean Sea	3,217
Cuba, West Indies	44,218
Cyprus, Mediterranean Sea	3,572
Devon, Arctic Region	20,861
Ellesmere, Arctic Region	82,119
Great Britain, Europe	88,787
Greenland, Arctic Region	840,004
Hainan, South China Sea	13,127
Hawaii, Oceania	4,030
Hispaniola, West Indies	29,418
Hokkaidō, Japan	29,950
Honshū, Japan	88,930
Iceland, Arctic Region	39,769
Ireland, Europe	32,588
Jamacia, West Indies	4,244
Jawa (Java), Indonesia	50,745
Kyūshū, Japan	16,215
Luzon, Philippines	40,814
Madagascar, Indian Ocean	226,658
Melville, Arctic Region	16,141
Mindanao, Philippines	36,906
Mindoro, Philippines	3,794
Negros, Philippines	4,903
New Britain, Oceania	14,592
New Caledonia, Oceania	5,671
Newfoundland, Canada	43,359
New Guinea, Oceania	316,856
North East Land, Arctic Region	6,350
North Island (New Zealand), Oceania	44,281
Novaya Zemlya, Arctic Region	31,390
Palawan, Philippines	4,500
Panay, Philippines	4,448
Prince of Wales, Arctic Region	12,830
Puerto Rico, West Indies	3,435
Sakhalin, Soviet Union	29,344
Samar, Philippines	5,124
Sardinia, Mediterranean Sea	9,301
Seram, Indonesia	6,046
Sicily, Mediterranean Sea	9,926
Shikoku, Japan	7,245
Somerset, Arctic Region	9,370
Southampton, Hudson Bay	15,700
South Island (New Zealand) Oceania	58,093
Sri Lanka, Indian Ocean	25,097
Sumatra, Indonesia	182,860
T'aiwan (Formosa), China Sea	13,895
Tasmania, Australia	26,383
Tierra del Fuego, S.A.	18,600
Timor, Asia	13,094
Vancouver, Canada	12,408
Victoria, Arctic Region	81,930
Vrangelya, Arctic Region	2,819
West Spitsbergen, Arctic Region	15,260

Principal Lakes, Oceans, Seas, and Their Areas

LAKE Country	Area (Sq. Mi.)
Aral'skoye More (Aral Sea), Sov. Un	26,518
Arctic O.	5,427,000
Athabasca, L., Can	3,120
Atlantic O.	31,744,000
Balkhash, Ozero (L.), Sov. Un	6,678
Baltic Sea, Eur.	163,000
Baykal, Ozero (L.) Sov. Un	12,159
Bering Sea, Asia-N.A.	876,000
Black Sea, Eur.-Asia	178,000
Caribbean Sea, N.A.-S.A.	750,000
Caspian Sea, Sov. Un.	152,084
Chad, L., Chad-Cam.-Nig.	6,300
East China Sea, Asia	482,000
Erie, L., U.S.-Can.	9,940
Eyre, L., Austl.	3,700
Gairdner, L., Austl.	1,500
Great Bear L., Can.	12,275
Great Salt L., U.S.	1,700
Great Slave L., Can.	10,980
Hudson Bay, Can.	476,000
Huron, L., U.S.-Can.	23,010
Indian O	28,371,000
Japan, Sea of, Asia	389,000
Koko Nor (Qinghai Hu) (L.), China	1,650
Ladozhskoye Ozero (Lake Ladoga), Sov. Un.	7,092
Mai-Ndombe, L., Zaire	1,700
Manitoba, L., Can.	1,817
Mediterranean Sea., Eur.-Afr.-Asia	967,000
Mexico, G, of., N.A.	596,000
Michigan, L., U.S	22,400
Nicaragua, Largo de (L.), Nic.	2,972
North Sea, Eur.	222,000
Nyasa, L., Mwi.-Moz.-Tan	10,900
Okhotsk, Sea of, Pac. O.	590,000
Onezhskoye Ozero (Lake Onega), Sov. Un.	3,821
Ontario, L., U.S.-Can.	7,540
Pacific O.	63,855,000
Red Sea, Afr.-Asia	169,000
Rudolf, L., Ken.-Eth.	2,473
Superior, L., U.S.-Can.	31,820
Tanganyika, L., Tan.-Zaire-Bdi.-Zam.	10,965
Titicaca, **Lago** (L.), Bol.-Peru	3,500
Torrens, L., Austl.	2,200
Vänern, L., Swe.	2,156
Van Gölü (L.), Tur.	1,470
Victoria, L., Tan.-Ken.-Ug.	26,828
Winnipeg, L., Can.	9,465
Winnipegosis, L., Can.	2,103
Yellow Sea, China	480,000

Principal Mountains and Their Heights

MOUNTAIN Country	Elev. (Ft.)
Aconcagua, Argentina	22,831
Albert Edward, Papua New Guinea	13,1000
Altar, Ecuador	17,451
Annapurna, Nepal	26,504
Antizana, Ecuador	18,714
Antofalla, Argentina	20,013
Apo, Philippines	9,692
Ararat, Turkey	16,804
Azufre (Lastarria), Chile	18,701
Bandeira, Brazil	9,482
Barú, Panama	11,410
Belukha, Soviet Union	14,783
Blanc, France-Italy	15,771
Blanca, Colorado, U.S.	14,317
Bolívar (La Columna), Venezuela	16,411
Bona, Alaska, U.S.	16,421
Borah, Idaho, U.S.	12,662
Cameroun, Cam	13,353
Cayambe, Ecuador	18,996
Chimborazo, Ecuador	20,561
Citlaltépetl, Mexico	18,701
Colima, Mexico	13,993
Cook, New Zealand	12,349
Cotopaxi, Ecuador	19,347
Cristóbal Colón, Colombia	19,029
Damāvand, Iran	18,934
Dhaulagiri, Nepal	26,810
Dos Conos, Argentina	19,357
Dykh-Tau, Soviet Union	17,070
Elbert, Colorado, U.S.	14,431
El'brus, Soviet Union	18,510
Elgon, Kenya	14,178
Erciyeş, Turkey	12,848
Erebus, Antarctica	12,280
Etna, Italy	11,122
Everest, Nepal-China	29,028
Finsteraarhorn, Switzerland	14,022
Foraker, Alaska, U.S.	17,395
Fuji San, Japan	12,388
Gasherbrum, Pak	26,470
Glittertinden, Norway	8,104
Gongga Shan, China	24,900
Gosainthan, China	26,291
Gran Paradiso, Italy	13,323
Gunnbjørns, Greenland	12,139
Gurla Mandhata, China	25,354
Hantengri Geng (China-Soviet Union)	22,940
Hekla, Iceland	4,747
Hood, Oregon, U.S.	11,239
Hsinkao, Taiwan	13,113
Huascarán, Peru	22,205
Huila, Colombia	18,865
Hvannadalshnukur, Iceland	6,952
Illimani, Bolivia	21,151
Incahuasi, Argentina-Chile	21,719
Injasuti, S. Afr	11,182
Iztaccíhuatl, Mexico	17,343
Jaya, **Puncak**, Indonesia	16,503
Jungfrau, Switzerland	13,668
K2 (Godwin Austen), Pak	28,250
Kailas, China (Tibet)	22,031
Kāmet, India	25,447
Kanchenjunga, Nepal-India	28,208
Karisimbi, Zaire-Rwanda	14,787
Kazbek, Soviet Union	16,558
Kerinci, Indonesia	12,467
Kilimanjaro, Tanzania	19,340
Kinabalu, Malaysia	13,455
Kirinyaga, Kenya	17,058
Klyuchevskaya, Soviet Union	15,584
Kommunizma, Soviet Union	24,590
Korab, Albania	9,026
Kosciusko, Australia	7,316
Koussi, Chad	11,204
Kwanmo, Korea	8,337
Lassen, California, U.S.	10,457
Lenin Pk., Soviet Union	23,406
Leuser, Indonesia	11,178
Llullaillaco, Argentina-Chile	22,146
Logan, Canada	19,520
Loz, Saudi Arabia	8,461
McKinley, Alaska, U.S.	20,320
Makālu, China-Nepal	27,824
Margherita, Zaire-Uganda	16,763
Markham, Antarctica	14,272
Maromokotro, Madagascar	9,436
Matterhorn, Switz.-Italy	14,685
Mauna Kea, Hawaii, U.S.	13,796
Mauna Loa, Hawaii, U.S.	13,680
Mercedario, Argentina	22,211
Meru, Tanzania	14,978
Midi d'Ossau, Pic du France	10,322
Misti, Volcán, Peru	19,098
Mitchell, North Carolina, U.S.	6,684
Musala, Bulgaria	9,592
Muztagata, China	24,388
Namcha Barwa, China	25,443
Nanda Devi, India	25,645
Nanga Parbat, Pak.	26,660
Negoi, Romania	8,344
Neiges, Piton des, Reunion	10,069
Ojos del Salado, Argentina-Chile	22,572
Ólimbos, Greece	9,550
Orohena, Tahiti	7,352
Paricutín, Mexico	9,213
Pelée, Martinique	4,800
Pico, Cape Verde	9,281
Pidurutalagala, Sri Lanka	8,281
Pikes Peak, Colorado, U.S.	14,110
Pissis, Argentina	22,241
Pobeda, China-Soviet Union	24,406
Popocatépetl, Mexico	17,887
Pulog, Philippines	9,612
Rainier, Washington, U.S.	14,410
Rakaposhi, Pak	25,550
Ras Dashen, Ethiopia	15,158
Rinjani, Indonesia	12,225
Rosa, Monte, Italy-Switzerland	15,200
Ruapehu, New Zealand	9,175
St. Elias, U.S.-Canada	18,008
Sajama, Bolivia	21,391
Sanford, Alaska, U.S.	16,237
Sangay, Ecuador	17,159
Sa'uda, Lebanon	10,131
Semeru, Indonesia	12,060
Shām, Oman	9,902
Shasta, California, U.S.	14,162
Shkhara, Soviet Union	16,594
Sources, Mt. aux, Lesotho-S. Afr.	10,822
Thabana Ntlenyana, Lesotho	11,425
Tirich Mīr, Pak.	25,230
Tocorpuri, Bolivia-Chile	19,137
Toubkal, Morocco	13,661
Trikora, Puncak, Indonesia	15,584
Tupungato, Argentina-Chile	22,310
Ulugh Muztagh, China	25,338
Vesuvio (Vesuvius), Italy	3,842
Victoria, Papau New Guinea	13,363
Vinson Massif, Ant	16,864
Waddington, Canada	13,260
Weisshorn, Switzerland	14,780
Whitney, California, U.S.	14,494
Wrangell, Alaska, U.S.	14,005
Yerupaja, Peru	21,765

Principal Rivers and Their Lengths

RIVER Continent	Length (Mi.)
Albany, North America	610
Aldan, Asia	1,392
Amazonas, South America	3,900
Amu Dar'ya (Oxus), Asia	1,628
Amur, Asia	2,802
Araguaia, South America	1,630
Arkansas, North America	1,450
Athabasca, North America	765
Back, North America	605
Brahmaputra, Asia	1,800
Branco, South America	580
Brazos, North America	870
Canadian, North America	906
Churchill, North America	1,000
Colorado, North America	1,450
Columbia, North America	1,214
Congo (Zaïre), Africa	2,900
Cumberland, North America	687
Danube, Europe	1,770
Darling, Australia	1,750
Dnepr (Dnieper), Europe	1,420
Dnestr (Dniester), Europe	876
Don, Europe	1,224
Donets, Europe	735
Elbe, Europe	720
Euphrates, Asia	1,675
Fraser, North America	850
Gambia, Africa	680
Ganges, Asia	1,550
Gila, North America	630
Godāvari, Asia	930
Huang (Yellow), Asia	2,903
Indus, Asia	1,980
Irrawaddy, Asia	1,425
Japurá, South America	1,400
Juruá, South America	1,250
Kama, Europe	1,261
Kolyma, Asia	1,615
Lena, Asia	2,653
Loire, Europe	625
Mackenzie, North America	2,635
Madeira, South America	2,060
Magdalena, South America	950
Marañón, South America	1,000
Mekong, Asia	2,600
Meuse, Europe	575
Mississippi, North America	2,348
Mississippi-Missouri-Red Rock, North America	3,860
Missouri-Red Rock, North America	2,683
Murray, Australia	1,600
Negro, South America	1,305
Nelson, North America	1,600
Neman, Europe	582
Niger, Africa	2,590
Nile, Africa	4,132
Ob'-Irtysh, Asia	3,461
Oder, Europe	565
Ohio, North America	981
Oka, Europe	920
Orange, Africa	1,155
Orinoco, South America	1,800
Ottawa, North America	696
Paraguay, South America	1,290
Paraná, South America	2,450
Paranaíba, South America	850
Peace, North America	1,195
Pechora, Europe	1,118
Pecos, North America	735
Pilcomayo, South America	1,550
Plata-Paraguay, South America	2,300
Purús, South America	1,900
Red, North America	1,018
Rhine, Europe	820
Rhône, Europe	500
Rio Grande, North America	1,885
Roosevelt, South America	950
St. Lawrence, North America	1,900
Salado, South America	870
Salween, Asia	1,730
São Francisco, South America	1,800
Saskatchewan, North America	1,205
Sava, Europe	585
Sénégal, Africa	1,000
Snake, North America	1,038
Sungari (Songhua), Asia	1,140
Syr-Dar'ya, Asia	1,653
Tagus (Tajo, Tejo), Europe	625
Tennessee, North America	652
Tigris, Asia	1,150
Tisza, Europe	607
Tobol, Asia	1,093
Tocantins, South America	1,640
Ucayali, South America	1,220
Ural, Europe	1,522
Uruguay, South America	1,025
Verkhnyaya Tunguska (Angara), Asia	1,549
Vilyuy, Asia	1,513
Volga, Europe	2,293
White, North America	690
Wisla (Vistula), Europe	630
Xi, Asia	1,590
Xingú, South America	1,230
Yangtze, Asia	3,430
Yellowstone, North America	671
Yenisey, Asia	2,566
Yukon, North America	1,800
Zambezi, Africa	1,650

Principal cities of the world

Abidjan, Ivory Coast	1,100,000
Accra, Ghana (738,498)	633,880
Adelaide, Australia (933,300)	13,400
Adis Abebə, Ethiopia	1,125,340
Ahmadābād, India (1,950,000)	1,585,544
Aleppo (Halab), Syria	878,000
Alexandria (Al Iskandarīyah), Egypt (2,850,000)	2,409,000
Algiers (Alger), Algeria (1,800,000)	1,503,720
Al Khartūm (Khartoum). Sudan, (790,000)	333,921
Alma-Ata, Soviet Union (970,000)	928,000
Ammān, Jordan	648,587
Amsterdam, Netherlands (1,810,000)	716,919
Ankara (Angora), Turkey (2,290,000)	2,203,729
Anshan, China	1,050,000
Antwerp (Antwerpen), Belgium (1,105,000)	194,073
Asunción, Paraguay (655,000)	463,700
Athens (Athínai), Greece (2,540,241)	867,023
Atlanta, Georgia (1,932,100)	425,022
Auckland, New Zealand (775,000)	147,600
Baghdād, Iraq (2,183,800)	1,300,000
Baku, Soviet Union (1,800,000)	1,030,000
Baltimore, Maryland (1,875,800)	786,775
Bandung, Indonesia (1,250,000)	1,201,730
Bangalore, India (1,750,000)	1,540,741
Bangkok (Krung Thep), Thailand (3,375,000)	3,133,834
Barcelona, Spain (3,975,000)	1,902,713
Beirut, Lebanon (1,010,000)	474,870
Belfast, No. Ireland (710,00)	354,400
Belgrade (Beograd), Yugoslavia (1,150,000)	770,140
Belo Horizonte, Brazil (1,945,000)	1,557,464
Berlin, East, Ger. Dem. Rep. (*Berlin)	1,128,983
Berlin, West, Fed. Rep. of Ger. (3,775,000)	1,902,250
Bilbao, Spain (995,000)	452,921
Birmingham, England (2,660,000)	1,033,900
Bogotá, Colombia (4,150,000)	4,067,000
Bombay, India (6,750,000)	5,970,575
Bonn, Fed. Rep. of Ger. (555,000)	286,184
Boston, Massachusetts (3,733,700)	562,994
Brasília, Brazil (750,000)	350,000
Bremen, Fed. Rep. of Ger (800,000)	556,128
Brisbane, Australia (1,014,700)	702,000
Brussels (Bruxelles), Belgium (2,400,000)	143,957
Bucharest (Bucureşti), Romania (2,050,000)	1,858,418
Budapest, Hungary (2,600,000)	2,060,000
Buenos Aires, Argentina (10,300,000)	2,978,000
Buffalo, New York (1,152,200)	357,870
Cairo (Al Qāhirah), Egypt (8,500,000)	5,278,000
Calcutta, India (9,100,000)	3,148,746
Cali, Colombia (1,340,000)	1,293,000
Canberra, Australia (241,500)	221,000
Canton (Guangzhou), China	2,500,000
Cape Town, South Africa (1,125,000)	697,514
Caracas, Venezuela (2,475,000)	1,658,500
Cardiff, Wales (625,000)	282,000
Casablanca, Morocco (1,575,000)	1,506,373
Changchun, China	1,300,000
Chelyabinsk, Soviet Union (1,215,000)	1,042,000
Chengdu, China	1,800,000
Chicago, Illinois (7,733,900)	3,005,072
Chongqing (Chungking), China	2,900,000
Cincinnati, Ohio (1,467,900)	385,457
Cleveland, Ohio (2,214,300)	573,822
Cologne (Köln), Fed. Rep. of Ger. (1,815,000)	976,136
Colombo, Sri Lanka (1,540,00)	616,000
Columbus, Ohio (939,600)	564,871
Copenhagen (København), Denmark (1,470,000)	498,850
Dacca, Bangladesh (2,750,000)	1,563,517
Dakar, Senegal	798,792
Dallas, Texas (2,803,000)	904,078
Damascus (Dimashq), Syria (1,550,000)	1,156,000
Dar es Salaam, Tanzania	870,000
Delhi, India (4,500,000)	3,706,558
Denver, Colorado (1,411,300)	491,396
Detroit, Michigan (4,387,000)	1,203,339
Dnepropetrovsk, Soviet Union (1,460,000)	1,083,000
Donetsk (Stalino), Soviet Union (2,075,000)	1,032,000
Dresden, Ger. Dem. Rep. (640,000)	514,508
Dublin (Baile Atha Cliath), Ireland (1,110,000)	544,586
Durban, South Africa (1,040,000)	736,852
Düsseldorf, Fed. Rep. of Ger. (1,225,000)	594,770
Edinburgh, Scotland (635,000)	455,126
Essen, Fed. Rep. of Ger. (5,125,000)	652,501
Florence (Firenze), Italy (660,000)	462,690
Fortaleza, Brazil (1,175,000)	1,109,837
Frankfurt am Main, Fed. Rep. of Ger. (1,880,000)	628,203
Fukuoka, Japan (1,575,000)	1,088,617
Fushun, China	1,150,000
Gdańsk (Danzig), Poland (820,000)	449,200
Geneva (Génève), Switzerland (425,000)	151,100
Genoa (Genova), Italy (855,000)	782,476
Glasgow, Scotland (1,830,00)	794,316
Gorki (Gorkiy), Soviet Union (1,900,000)	1,358,000
Guadalajara, Mexico (2,350,000)	1,813,100
Guatemala, Guatemala (945,000)	717,322
Guayaquil, Ecuador	1,022,010
Hamburg, Fed. Rep. of Ger. (2,260,000)	1,653,043
Hannover, Fed. Rep. of Ger. (1,005,000)	535,854
Ha-noi, Vietnam	1,600,000
Harbin, China	2,400,000
Hartford, Connecticut (1,055,200)	136,392
Havana (La Habana), Cuba (2,000,000)	1,961,674
Helsinki, Finland (885,000)	484,879
Hiroshima, Japan (1,525,000)	899,394
Ho Chi Minh City (Saigon), Vietnam (2,750,000)	1,804,900
Honolulu, Hawaii (762,000)	324,871
Houston, Texas (2,674,900)	1,594,086
Hyderābād, India (2,000,000)	1,607,396
Ibadan, Nigeria	847,000
Indianapolis, Indiana (1,099,300)	700,807
Irkutsk, Soviet Union	561,000
İstanbul, Turkey (4,765,000)	2,853,539
İzmir, Turkey (1,190,000)	753,749
Jakarta (Batavia), Indonesia (6,500,000)	6,400,000
Jerusalem, Israel (420,000)	398,200
Jinan, China	1,125,000
Johannesburg, South Africa (2,550,000)	654,232
Kābul, Afghanistan	749,000
Kānpur, India (1,320,000)	1,154, 388
Kansas City, Missouri (1,248,200)	448,159
Kaohsiung, Taiwan (1,480,000)	1,172,977
Karāchi, Pakistan (4,500,000)	2,800,000
Kathmandu, Nepal (215,000)	150,402
Katowice, Poland (2,590,000)	351,300
Kawasaki, Japan (*Tōkyō)	1,040,698
Kazan', Soviet Union (1,050,000)	1,002,000
Khar'kov, Soviet Union (1,750,000)	1,464,000
Kiev, Soviet Union (2,430,000)	2,192,000
Kingston, Jamaica	665,050
Kinshasa, Zaire	2,202,000
Kitakyūshū, Japan (1,515,000)	1,065,084
Kōbe, Japan (*Ōsaka)	1,367,392
Kowloon, Hong Kong (*Victoria)	749,600
Kuala Lumpur, Malaysia (750,000)	451,728
Kunming, China	1,225,000
Kuwait (Al Kuwayt), Kuwait (780,000)	78,116
Kuybyshev, Soviet Union (1,440,000)	1,226,000
Kyōto, Japan (*Osaka)	1,472,993
Lagos, Nigeria (1,450,000)	1,060,800
Lahore, Pakistan (2,200,000)	2,022,577
Lanzhou, China	950,000
La Paz, Bolivia	654,713
Leeds, England (1,540,000)	724,300
Leipzig, Ger. Dem. Rep. (710,000)	563,980
Leningrad, Soviet Union (5,360,000)	4,119,000
Liège, Belgium (765,000)	220,183
Lille, France (1,015,000)	172,280
Lima, Peru (3,350,000)	340,339
LIsbon (Lisboa), Portugal (1,950,000)	829,900
Liverpool, England (1,535,000)	520,200
Łódź, Poland (1,025,000)	830,800
London, England (11,050,000)	6,877.100
Los Angeles, California (9,798,800)	2,966,763
Louisville, Kentucky (877,300)	298,451
Luanda, Angola	475,328
Lucknow, India (840,000)	749,239
Lüda (Dairen), China (1,700,000†)	1,100,000
Lyon, France (1,170,660)	456,716
Madras, India (3,200,000)	2,469,449
Madrid, Spain (4,415,000)	3,367,438
Managua, Nicaragua	552,900
Manchester, England (2,800,000)	479,100
Manila, Philippines (5,500,000)	1,479,116
Mannheim, Fed. Rep. of Ger. (1,395,000)	303,247
Maracaibo, Venezuela	651,574
Marseille, France (1,070,912)	908,600
Mecca (Makkah), Saudi Arabia	366,801
Medellín, Colombia (2,025,000)	1,477,000
Melbourne, Australia (2,739,700)	65,800
Memphis, Tennessee (804,400)	646,356
Mexico City, Mexico (14,400,000)	8,988,200
Miami, Florida (2,627,900)	346,931
Milan (Milano), Italy (3,800,000)	1,677,109
Milwaukee, Wisconsin (1,357,500)	636,212
Minneapolis, Minnesota (1,973,500)	370,951
Minsk, Soviet Union (1,330,000)	1,295,000
Monterrey, Mexico (1,925,000)	1,054,000
Montevideo, Uruguay (1,350,000)	1,229,748
Montréal, Canada (2,802,485)	1,080,546
Moscow (Moskva), Soviet Union (11,950,000)	7,915,000
Munich (München), Fed. Rep. of Ger. (1,940,000)	1,299,693
Nagoya, Japan (3,700,000)	2,087,884
Nāgpur, India (950,000)	866,076
Nairobi, Kenya	835,000
Nanjing, China	1,800,000
Naples (Napoli), Italy (2,740,000)	1,223,228
Newcastle upon Tyne, England (1,295,000)	287,300
New Delhi, India (*Delhi)	301,801
New Orleans, Louisiana (1,173,200)	557,482
New York, New York (16,519,000)	7,071,030
Norfolk, Virginia (788,800)	219,214
Novosibirsk, Soviet Union (1,460,000)	1,328,000
Nürnberg, Fed. Rep. of Ger. (1,025,000)	484,184
Odessa, Soviet Union (1,120,000)	1,057,000
Oklahoma City, Oklahoma (737,900)	403,213
Omsk, Soviet Union (1,040,000)	1,028,000
Osaka, Japan (15,200,000)	2,648,158
Oslo, Norway (725,000)	454,819
Ottawa, Canada (693,288)	304,462
Palermo, Italy	693,949
Panamá, Panama (645,000)	439,800
Paris, France (9,450,000)	2,050,500
Peking (Beijing), China (8,000,000†)	5,400,000
Perm' Soviet Union (1,075,000)	1,008,000
Perth, Australia (883,600)	88,850
Philadelphia, Pennsylvania (5,135,200)	1,688,210
Phnom Penh, Kampuchea	393,995
Phoenix, Arizona (1,484,900)	764,911
Pittsburgh, Pennsylvania (2,162,000)	423,938
Port-au-Prince, Haiti (800,000)	745,700
Portland, Oregon (1,211,700)	366,383
Porto (Oporto), Portugal (1,150,000)	335,700
Porto Alegre, Brazil (1,760,000)	1 043,964
Prague (Praha), Czechoslovakia (1,275,000)	1,193,345
Pretoria, South Africa (575,000)	545,450
Providence, Rhode Island (896,800)	156,804
Pune, India (1,175,000)	856,105
Pusan, Korea (South)	2,879,570
P'yŏngyang, Korea (North)	840,000
Québec, Canada (542,158)	177,082
Quezon City, Philippines (*Manila)	956,864
Quito, Ecuador	742,858
Rabat, Morocco (540,000)	367,620
Rangoon, Burma (3,000,000)	2,276,000
Rawalpindi, Pakistan (725,000)	372,919
Recife (Pernambuco), Brazil (2,100,000)	1,249,821
Rīga, Soviet Union (920,000)	843,000
Rio de Janerio, Brazil (8,235,000)	4,857,716
Riyadh, Saudi Arabia	666,840
Rochester, New York (808,700)	241,741
Rome (Roma), Italy (3,195,000)	2,911,671
Rosario, Argentina (975,000)	810,000
Rostov-na-Donu, Soviet Union (1,075,000)	946,000
Rotterdam, Netherlands (1,085,000)	579,194
Sacramento, California (843,600)	275,741
St. Louis, Missouri (2,208,000)	453,085
St. Paul, Minnesota (*Minneapolis)	270,230
Salisbury, Zimbabwe (633,000)	118,500
Salt Lake City, Utah (679,400)	163,033
Salvador, Brazil (1,270,000)	1,237,373
San Antonio, Texas (1,007,400)	785,410
San Diego, California (1,595,000)	875,504
San Francisco, California (4,631,200)	678,974
San José, Costa Rica (519,400)	239,800
San Juan, Puerto Rico (1,535,000)	422,701
San Salvador, El Salvador (720,000)	397,100
Santiago, Chile (2,925,000)	517,473
Santo Domingo, Dominican Rep.	979,608
São Paulo, Brazil (9,900,000)	7,198,608
Sapporo, Japan (1,450,000)	1,401,758
Saratov, Soviet Union (1,090,000)	864,000
Seattle, Washington (2,068,600)	493,846
Seoul (Sŏul), Korea (South) (10,775,000)	8,114,000
Shanghai, China (11,300,000†)	8,100,000
Sheffield, England (705,000)	544,200
Shenyang (Mukden), China	3,300,000
Singapore, Singapore (2,600,000)	2,390,800
Sofia (Sofiya), Bulgaria (1,133,733)	1,047,920
Stockholm, Sweden (1,384,310)	649,384
Stuttgart, Fed. Rep. of Ger. (1,935,000)	581,989
Suchow (Xuzhou), China	800,000
Surabaya, Indonesia (1,400,000)	1,332,249
Sverdlovsk, Soviet Union (1,450,000)	1,225,000
Sydney, Australia (3,193,300)	49,750
Taegu, Korea (South)	1,487,098
T'aipei, Taiwan (3,825,000)	2,196,237
Taiyuan, China	1,350,000
Tashkent, Soviet Union (2,015,000)	1,816,000
Tbilisi, Soviet Union (1,240,000)	1,080,000
Tegucigalpa, Honduras	316,800
Tehrān, Iran (4,700,000)	4,496,159
Tel Aviv-Yafo, Israel (1,350,000)	336.300
The Hague ('s-Gravenhage), Netherlands (775,000)	456,886
Tientsin (Tianjin), China (7,000,000†)	4,500,000
Tiranë, Albania	192,300
Tōkyō, Japan (25,800,000)	8,349,209
Toronto, Canada (2,803,101)	633,318
Tripoli (Tarābulus), Libya	264,000
Tsingtao (Qingdao), China	1,200,000
Tsitsihar (Qiqihar), China	850,000
Tunis, Tunisia (915,000)	550,404
Turin (Torino), Italy (1,670,000)	1,160,686
Ufa, Soviet Union (1,000,000)	986,000
Ulaan Baatar, Mongolia	287,000
Valencia, Spain (1,140,000)	750,994
Valparaíso, Chile (530,000)	250,358
Vancouver, Canada (1,166,348)	410,188
Venice (Venezia), Italy (445,000)	355,865
Victoria, Hong Kong (3,975,000)	1,026,870
Vienna (Wien), Austria (1,925,000)	1,572,300
Vladivostok, Soviet Union	558,000
Volgograd (Stalingrad), Soviet Union (1,230,000)	939,000
Warsaw (Warszawa), Poland (2,080,000)	1,576,600
Washington, D.C. (3,181,400)	637,651
Wellington, New Zealand (349,900)	137,600
Winnipeg, Canada (578,217)	560,874
Wuhan, China	3,000,000
Wuppertal, Fed. Rep. of Ger. (870,000)	394,605
Xi'an, China	1,900,000
Yerevan, Soviet Union (1,155,000)	1,036,000
Yokohama, Japan (*Tōkyō)	2,773,322
Zagreb, Yugoslavia	566,084
Zhengzhou, China	1,100,000
Zürich, Switzerland (780,000)	374,200

Metropolitan area populations are shown in parentheses.
* City is located within the metropolitan area of another city; for example, **Kyōto**, Japan (*Ōsaka).
† Population of entire municipality or district, including rural area.

major cities map index

This index includes the more important cities, towns and other localities that appear on the maps on pages 54–71. For a complete list of abbreviations, see page 258. If a page contains several maps, a lowercase letter identifies the particular map to which the entry is indexed.

PLACE	PAGE	Lat.°′	Long.°′
'Abbāsābād	68h	35.44 N	51.25 E
Abbey Wood (Neigh.)	62	51.29 N	0.08 E
Abbots Langley	62	51.43 N	0.25 W
'abd al-Shāhīd	71a	29.55 N	31.13 E
Aberdeen (Xianggangzi)	68c	22.15 N	114.09 E
Abington	56b	40.07 N	75.08 W
Ablon-sur-Seine	64c	48.43 N	2.25 E
Abóbada	65d	38.43 N	9.20 W
Abramcevo	66b	55.50 N	37.50 E
Abridge	62	51.39 N	0.07 E
Abrunheira	65d	38.46 N	9.21 W
Abū an-Numrus	71a	29.57 N	31.12 E
Abū Şir Pyramids (P. Int.)	71a	29.54 N	31.12 E
Accord	54a	42.10 N	70.53 W
Acton (Neigh.)	62	51.30 N	0.16 W
Adachi (Neigh.)	69a	35.45 N	139.48 E
Addington	62	51.18 N	0.23 E
Addlestone	62	51.22 N	0.30 W
Ad-Duqqī	71a	30.04 N	31.15 E
Adelphi	56d	39.00 N	76.58 W
Aderklaa	66e	48.17 N	16.32 E
Adlershof (Neigh.)	65a	52.26 N	13.33 E
Agege	71d	6.37 N	3.20 E
Agincourt (Neigh.)	54c	43.48 N	79.17 W
Agostinho Pôrto	61c	22.47 S	43.23 W
Agrícola Oriental	60a	19.24 N	99.05 W
Aguacate	60b	22.59 N	81.49 W
Agualva-Cacém	65d	38.46 N	9.18 W
Ahlenberg	63	51.25 N	7.28 E
Ahrensfelde	65a	52.35 N	13.35 E
Ahuntsic (Neigh.)	54b	45.33 N	73.39 W
Aigburth (Neigh.)	64b	53.22 N	2.55 W
Ainsworth	64b	53.35 N	2.22 W
Aintree	64b	53.29 N	2.56 W
Airport West	70b	37.44 S	144.53 E
Aiyáleo	66d	37.59 N	23.41 E
Ajuda (Neigh.)	65d	38.43 N	9.12 W
Akbarābād	68h	35.41 N	51.21 E
Akishima	69a	35.41 N	139.22 E
Akrópolis (P. Int.)	66d	37.58 N	23.43 E
Alaguntan	71d	6.26 N	3.30 E
Alameda	58b	37.46 N	122.16 W
Albany	58b	37.53 N	122.18 W
Albany Park (Neigh.)	58a	41.58 N	87.43 W
Al-Barājīl	71a	30.04 N	31.09 E
Albertfalva (Neigh.)	66g	47.27 N	19.02 E
Alberton	71b	26.16 S	28.08 E
Albertson	55	40.46 N	73.39 W
Albertville (Neigh.)	71b	26.10 S	27.59 E
Albion	70b	37.47 S	144.49 E
Alcântara (Neigh.)	65d	38.42 N	9.10 W
Aldeia	61d	23.30 S	46.51 E
Aldeia de Carapicuiba	61d	23.35 S	46.48 W
Aldenham	62	51.40 N	0.21 W
Aldenrade (Neigh.)	63	51.31 N	6.44 E
Alexandra	71b	26.06 S	28.05 E
Alexandria	56d	38.48 N	77.03 W
Alfortville	64c	48.49 N	2.25 E
Algés	65d	38.42 N	9.13 W
Alguierão-Mem Martins	65d	38.48 N	9.20 W
Alhambra	59	34.06 N	118.08 W
Al-Hawāmidīyah	71a	29.54 N	31.15 E
Alipore (Neigh.)	67a	22.31 N	88.18 E
Al-Jīzah (Giza)	71a	30.01 N	31.13 E
Al-Kunayyisah	71a	29.59 N	31.11 E
Allegheny (R.)	57b	40.27 N	80.00 W
Allen Park	57c	42.15 N	83.13 W
Allerton	54a	42.18 N	70.53 W
Allerton (Neigh.)	64b	53.22 N	2.53 W
Allison Park	57b	40.34 N	79.57 W
Al-Imām (Neigh.)	71a	30.01 N	31.10 E
Allston (Neigh.)	54a	42.22 N	71.08 W
Almada	65d	38.41 N	9.09 W
Al-Manāwāt	71a	29.55 N	31.14 E
Al-Marj (Neigh.)	71a	30.09 N	31.20 E
Alondra	59	33.54 N	118.19 W
Alpine	55	40.56 N	73.56 W
Alsip	58a	41.40 N	87.44 W
Altadena	59	34.12 N	118.08 W
Altar of Heaven (P. Int.)	67b	39.53 N	116.25 E
Altar of the Earth (P. Int.)	67b	39.57 N	116.24 E
Altar of the Moon (P. Int.)	67b	39.55 N	116.20 E
Altar of the Sun (P. Int.)	67b	39.54 N	116.27 E
Altenderne Oberbecker (Neigh.)	63	51.35 N	7.33 E
Altenessen (Neigh.)	63	51.29 N	7.00 E
Altenhagen (Neigh.)	63	51.22 N	7.28 E
Altenvoerde	63	51.18 N	7.22 E

PLACE	PAGE	Lat.°′	Long.°′
Altlünun	63	51.38 N	7.31 E
Altmannsdorf (Neigh.)	66e	48.10 N	16.20 E
Alto da Moóca (Neigh.)	61d	23.34 S	46.35 W
Altona	70b	37.52 S	144.50 E
Altona North	70b	37.50 S	144.51 E
Altrincham	64b	53.24 N	2.21 W
Alvanley	64b	53.16 N	2.45 W
Amadora	65d	38.45 N	9.14 W
Amagasaki	69b	34.43 N	135.25 E
Ama Keng	67c	1.24 N	103.42 E
Amaroúsion	66d	38.03 N	23.49 E
Ameixoera (Neigh.)	65d	38.47 N	9.10 W
Amersham	62	51.40 N	0.38 W
Amherst	57a	42.58 N	78.48 W
Anacostia (Neigh.)	56d	38.52 N	76.59 W
Anadoluhisarı (P. Int.)	66f	41.04 N	29.03 E
Anaheim	59	33.51 N	117.57 W
Andrésy	64c	48.59 N	2.04 E
Andrews Air Force Base (P. Int.)	56d	38.48 N	76.52 W
Angerhausen (Neigh.)	63	51.23 N	6.44 E
Angermund	63	51.20 N	6.47 E
Angono	68g	14.31 N	121.08 E
Angyalföld (Neigh.)	66g	47.33 N	19.05 E
Anik (Neigh.)	67e	19.02 N	72.53 E
Anjou	54b	45.36 N	73.33 W
Annandale	56d	38.50 N	77.12 W
An-Narrānīyah	71a	29.58 N	31.10 E
Annen (Neigh.)	63	51.27 N	7.22 E
Annet-sur-Marne	64c	48.56 N	2.43 E
Anschlag	63	51.10 N	7.29 E
Antiguo Lago de Texcoco, Vaso del (L.)	60a	19.30 N	99.00 W
Antímano (Neigh.)	61a	10.28 N	66.59 W
Antony	64c	48.45 N	2.18 E
Antwerp	71b	26.06 S	28.10 E
Apese (Neigh.)	71d	6.25 N	3.25 E
Aplerbeck (Neigh.)	63	51.29 N	7.33 E
Apoquindo	61b	33.24 S	70.32 W
Ara (R.)	69a	35.39 N	139.51 E
Arakawa (Neigh.)	69a	35.47 N	139.44 E
Arakpur (Neigh.)	67d	28.35 N	77.10 E
Aravaca (Neigh.)	65b	40.28 N	3.46 W
Arcadia	59	34.08 N	118.01 W
Arc de Triomphe (P. Int.)	64c	48.53 N	2.17 E
Arcueil	64c	48.48 N	2.20 E
Ardey (Neigh.)	63	51.26 N	7.23 E
Ardmore, Md.	56d	38.56 N	76.52 W
Ardmore, Pa.	56b	40.01 N	75.18 W
Areeiro	65d	38.39 N	9.12 W
Argenteuil	64c	48.57 N	2.15 E
Arima (Neigh.)	69b	34.48 N	135.15 E
Arino (Neigh.)	69b	34.50 N	135.14 E
Arlington, Ma.	54a	42.25 N	71.09 W
Arlington, Va.	56d	38.52 N	77.05 W
Arlington National Cemetery (P. Int.)	56d	38.53 N	77.04 W
Arnouville-lès-Gonesse	64c	49.00 N	2.25 E
Arroyo Arenas	60b	23.02 N	82.28 W
Artarmon	70a	33.49 S	151.11 E
Arteria	59	33.52 N	118.05 W
Artigas (Neigh.)	61a	10.30 N	66.56 W
Arundel Gardens	56c	39.13 N	76.37 W
Arundel Village	56c	39.13 N	76.36 W
Asaka	69a	35.48 N	139.36 E
Asālafpur (Neigh.)	67d	28.38 N	77.05 E
Ashfield	70a	33.53 S	151.08 E
Ashford	62	51.26 N	0.27 W
Ashiya	69b	34.43 N	135.17 E
Ashley	64b	53.21 N	2.20 W
Ashley Green	62	51.44 N	0.35 W
Ashtead	62	51.19 N	0.18 W
Ashton-under-Lyne	64b	53.29 N	2.06 W
Ashton upon Mersey	64b	53.26 N	2.19 W
Asnières [-sur-Seine]	64c	48.55 N	2.17 E
Aspern (Neigh.)	66e	48.13 N	16.29 E
Aspinwall	57b	40.30 N	79.55 W
Asseln (Neigh.)	63	51.32 N	7.35 E
Astley Bridge	64b	53.36 N	2.26 W
Astoria (Neigh.)	55	40.46 N	73.55 W
Athens (Athínai)	66d	37.58 N	23.43 E
Athis-Mons	64c	48.43 N	2.24 E
Atizapán de Zaragoza	60a	19.33 N	99.15 W
Atlantic Beach	55	40.35 N	73.44 W
Atsugi	69a	35.27 N	139.22 E
Atta	67d	28.34 N	77.20 E
At-Talibīyah	71a	30.00 N	31.11 E
Atzalpur	67d	28.43 N	77.21 E
Atzgersdorf (Neigh.)	66e	48.09 N	16.18 E
Aubervilliers	64c	48.55 N	2.23 E

PLACE	PAGE	Lat.°′	Long.°′
Auburn	70a	33.51 S	151.02 E
Auburndale	54a	42.21 N	71.22 W
Auckland Park (Neigh.)	71b	26.11 S	28.00 E
Audenshaw	64b	53.28 N	2.08 W
Audobon	56b	40.07 N	75.27 W
Auf dem Kreinberge	63	51.27 N	7.36 E
Auf dem Schnee (Neigh.)	63	51.26 N	7.25 E
Aughton	64b	53.32 N	2.56 W
Aughton Park	64b	53.33 N	2.53 W
Aulnay-sous-Bois	64c	48.57 N	2.31 E
Austerlitz (P. Int.)	64c	48.50 N	2.22 E
Austin (Neigh.)	58a	41.54 N	87.45 W
Austral	70a	33.56 S	150.48 E
Avalon	57b	40.30 N	80.04 W
Avanley	64b	53.16 N	2.45 W
Aveley	62	51.30 N	0.16 E
Avellaneda	60d	34.40 S	58.20 W
Avenel	55	40.35 N	74.17 W
Avocado Heights	59	34.03 N	118.00 W
Avondale Heights	70b	37.46 S	144.51 E
Awīn	68h	35.48 N	51.24 E
Awsīm	71a	30.07 N	31.08 E
Ayase	69a	35.26 N	139.26 E
Ayía Varvára	66d	37.59 N	23.39 E
Azādpur (Neigh.)	67d	28.43 N	77.11 E
Azcapotzalco	60a	19.28 N	99.12 W
Azusa	59	34.08 N	117.55 W
Az-Zamālik (Neigh.)	71a	30.04 N	31.13 E

B

PLACE	PAGE	Lat.°′	Long.°′
Baak	63	51.25 N	7.10 E
Bābarpur (Neigh.)	67d	28.41 N	77.17 E
Babelsberg (Neigh.)	65a	52.24 N	13.05 E
Babson Park	54a	42.18 N	71.23 W
Babuškin (Neigh.)	66b	55.52 N	37.42 E
Back Bay (Neigh.)	54a	42.21 N	71.05 W
Back B.	67e	18.56 N	72.49 E
Bacongo	71c	4.18 S	15.16 E
Badalona	65e	41.27 N	2.15 E
Badger's Mount	62	51.20 N	0.09 E
Bādli	67d	28.45 N	77.09 E
Baerl	63	51.29 N	6.41 E
Bagneux	64c	48.48 N	2.18 E
Bagnolet	64c	48.52 N	2.25 E
Bahtīm	71a	30.08 N	31.17 E
Baidyabāti	67a	22.47 N	88.20 E
Baileys Crossroads	56d	38.51 N	77.08 W
Bainchipota	67a	22.52 N	88.16 E
Baiyunguan	67b	39.54 N	116.19 E
Baker Street	62	51.30 N	0.21 E
Bakırköy (Neigh.)	66f	40.59 N	28.52 E
Bala-Cynwyd	56b	40.00 N	75.14 W
Baldwin, NY	55	40.39 N	73.37 W
Baldwin, Pa.	57b	40.23 N	79.58 W
Baldwin Park	59	34.06 N	117.58 W
Balgowlah	70a	33.48 S	151.16 E
Bālihāti	67a	22.44 N	88.19 E
Balizhuang	67b	39.52 N	116.28 E
Ballabhpur	67a	22.44 N	88.21 E
Ballenato, Punta (C.)	60b	23.06 N	82.30 W
Ballygunge (Neigh.)	67a	22.31 N	88.21 E
Balmain	70a	33.51 S	151.11 E
Baltimore	56c	39.17 N	76.37 W
Baltimore Highlands	56c	39.14 N	76.38 W
Balwyn	70b	37.49 S	145.05 E
Banbidian	67b	39.54 N	116.32 E
Bāndel	67a	22.56 N	88.22 E
Bandir C.	68k	6.11 S	106.49 E
Bāndra (Neigh.)	67e	19.03 N	72.49 E
Bang Khun Thian	68f	13.42 N	100.28 E
Bangkok (Krung Thep)	68f	13.45 N	100.31 E
Bangu (Neigh.)	61c	22.52 S	44.27 W
Banī Majdūl	71a	30.02 N	31.07 E
Ban Khlong Samrong	68f	13.39 N	100.36 E
Banks, C.	70a	34.00 S	151.15 E
Banksmeadow	70a	33.58 S	151.13 E
Bankstown	70a	33.55 S	151.02 E
Ban Lat Phrao	68f	13.47 N	100.36 E
Banstala	67a	22.32 N	88.25 E
Banstead	62	51.19 N	0.12 W
Ba-queo	68m	10.48 N	106.38 E
Bara	67a	22.46 N	88.17 E
Baragwanth	71b	26.16 S	27.59 E
Barajas de Madrid (Neigh.)	65b	40.28 N	3.35 E
Baranagar	67a	22.38 N	88.22 E
Bārāsat	67a	22.51 N	88.22 E

PLACE	PAGE	Lat.°′	Long.°′
Barcarena	65d	38.44 N	9.17 W
Barcelona	65e	41.23 N	2.11 E
Barcelona (Neigh.)	65b	40.22 N	3.34 E
Barcroft, Lake (Res.)	56d	38.51 N	77.09 W
Bare Hills	56c	39.23 N	76.40 W
Bariti Bil (L.)	67a	22.48 N	88.26 E
Barking (Neigh.)	62	51.33 N	0.06 E
Barkingside (Neigh.)	62	51.36 N	0.05 E
Barmen (Neigh.)	63	51.17 N	7.13 E
Barnes (Neigh.)	62	51.28 N	0.15 W
Barnston	64b	53.21 N	3.05 W
Barnum Island	55	40.36 N	73.39 W
Barracas (Neigh.)	60d	34.38 S	58.22 W
Barrackpore	67a	22.46 N	88.21 E
Barrackpore Cantonment	67a	22.46 N	88.22 E
Barra Funda (Neigh.)	61d	23.31 S	46.39 W
Barrancas	61b	33.27 S	70.46 W
Barranco	60c	12.09 S	77.02 W
Barreiro	65d	38.40 N	9.05 W
Barriada Pomar Alto	65e	41.29 N	2.14 E
Barrington	56b	39.52 N	75.04 W
Barrio Obrero Industrial	60c	12.04 S	77.04 W
Baruta	61a	10.26 N	66.53 W
Basai Dārāpur (Neigh.)	67d	28.40 N	77.08 E
Bashtīl	71a	30.05 N	31.11 E
Basildon	62	51.35 N	0.25 E
Bass Hill	70a	33.54 S	151.00 E
Bāsudebpur	67a	22.49 N	88.25 E
Batenbrock (Neigh.)	63	51.31 N	6.57 E
Battersea (Neigh.)	62	51.28 N	0.10 W
Bauernschaft	63	51.34 N	6.33 E
Bauerstown	57b	40.30 N	79.59 W
Baukau (Neigh.)	63	51.33 N	7.12 E
Baulkham Hills	70a	33.46 S	151.00 E
Baumschulenweg (Neigh.)	65a	52.28 N	13.29 E
Bayford	62	51.46 N	0.06 W
Bayonne	55	40.41 N	74.07 W
Bay Park	55	40.38 N	73.40 W
Bay Ridge (Neigh.)	55	40.37 N	74.02 W
Bayside	54a	42.18 N	70.53 W
Bayside (Neigh.)	55	40.46 N	73.46 W
Bayswater	70b	37.51 S	145.16 E
Bayswater North	70b	37.49 S	145.17 E
Bayview (Neigh.)	58b	37.44 N	122.23 W
Bay Village	56a	41.29 N	81.55 W
Bayville	55	40.54 N	73.33 W
Beachwood	56a	41.34 N	81.28 W
Beacon Hill	70a	33.45 S	151.15 E
Beacon H.	68c	22.21 N	114.09 E
Beaconsfield	54b	45.26 N	73.50 W
Bean	62	51.25 N	0.17 E
Beato (Neigh.)	65d	38.44 N	9.06 W
Bebek (Neigh.)	66f	41.04 N	29.02 E
Bebington	64b	53.23 N	3.01 W
Beccar (Neigh.)	60d	34.28 S	58.31 W
Beckenham (Neigh.)	62	51.24 N	0.02 W
Beddington (Neigh.)	62	51.22 N	0.08 W
Bedford, Ma.	54a	42.29 N	71.17 W
Bedford, Oh.	56a	41.23 N	81.32 W
Bedford Heights	56a	41.22 N	81.30 W
Bedford Park	58a	41.46 N	87.49 W
Bedford Park (Neigh.)	55	40.52 N	73.53 W
Bedford-Stuyvesant (Neigh.)	55	40.41 N	73.55 W
Bedmond	62	51.43 N	0.25 W
Bedok	67c	1.19 N	103.57 E
Beechview (Neigh.)	57b	40.25 N	80.02 W
Beeck (Neigh.)	63	51.29 N	6.44 E
Beeckerwerth (Neigh.)	63	51.29 N	6.41 E
Behāla (South Suburban)	67a	22.31 N	88.19 E
Beiyuan	67b	40.01 N	116.24 E
Bel Air	56d	38.52 N	77.10 W
Bel Air (Neigh.)	59	34.05 N	118.27 W
Belas	65d	38.47 N	9.16 W
Bela Vista (Neigh.)	61d	23.33 S	46.38 W
Belém (Neigh.)	65d	38.42 N	9.12 W
Belènzinho (Neigh.)	61d	23.32 S	46.35 W
Belford Roxo	61c	22.46 S	43.24 W
Belgrano (Neigh.)	60d	34.34 S	58.28 W
Belgrave	70b	37.55 S	145.21 E
Bell	59	33.58 N	118.11 W
Bella Vista, Arg.	60d	34.32 S	58.40 W
Bellavista, Chile	61b	33.31 S	70.37 W
Bellavista, Peru	60c	12.04 S	77.08 W
Belle Farm Estates	56c	39.23 N	76.45 W
Bellehaven	56d	38.47 N	77.04 W
Bellerose	55	40.44 N	73.43 W
Belleville	55	40.48 N	74.09 W
Bellevue	57b	40.30 N	80.03 W
Bellflower	59	33.53 N	118.07 W

PLACE	PAGE	Lat.°′	Long.°′
Bell Gardens	59	33.58 N	118.09 W
Bellmawr	56b	39.51 N	75.06 W
Bellmore	55	40.40 N	73.32 W
Bello	60b	23.07 N	82.24 W
Bellwood	58a	41.53 N	87.52 W
Belmont, Ca.	58b	37.31 N	122.17 W
Belmont, Ma.	54a	42.24 N	71.10 W
Belmore	70a	33.55 S	151.05 E
Belot	60b	23.08 N	82.19 W
Belvedere, Ca.	58b	37.52 N	122.28 W
Belvedere, Va.	56d	38.50 N	77.10 W
Belvedere (Neigh.)	62	51.29 N	0.09 E
Belvedere (P. Int.)	66e	48.11 N	16.23 E
Ben Avon	57b	40.31 N	80.05 W
Benfica (Neigh.), Braz.	61c	22.53 S	43.15 W
Benfica (Neigh.), Port.	65d	38.45 N	9.12 W
Bennettswood	70b	37.51 S	145.07 E
Benninghofen (Neigh.)	63	51.29 N	7.31 E
Benoni	71b	26.12 S	28.18 E
Benoni South	71b	26.13 S	28.18 E
Benrath (Neigh.)	63	51.10 N	6.52 E
Bensenville	58a	41.57 N	87.57 W
Bensonhurst (Neigh.)	55	40.35 N	73.59 E
Bentleigh	70b	37.55 S	145.02 E
Berazategui	60d	34.45 S	58.12 W
Berchum	63	51.23 N	7.32 E
Berea	56a	41.22 N	81.52 W
Bergenfield	55	40.55 N	74.00 W
Bergfelde	65a	52.40 N	13.19 E
Berghausen	63	51.18 N	7.17 E
Bergholtz	57a	43.06 N	78.53 W
Bergisch-Born	63	51.09 N	7.15 E
Bergkamen	63	51.38 N	7.38 E
Berkeley, Ca.	58b	37.57 N	122.18 W
Berkeley, Il.	58a	41.53 N	87.55 W
Berkeley Hills	57b	40.32 N	80.00 W
Berkhamsted	62	51.46 N	0.35 W
Berkley	57c	42.31 N	83.10 W
Berlin (East)	65a	52.30 N	13.25 E
Berlin (West)	65a	52.30 N	13.20 E
Bernau bei Berlin	65a	52.40 N	13.35 E
Bertlich	63	51.37 N	7.04 E
Berwyn	58a	41.50 N	87.47 W
Berwyn Heights	56d	38.59 N	76.54 W
Besedy	66b	55.37 N	37.47 E
Beşiktaş (Neigh.)	66f	41.03 N	29.01 E
Beskudnikovo (Neigh.)	66b	55.52 N	37.34 E
Besòs (R.)	65e	41.25 N	2.04 E
Bethel Park	57b	40.18 N	80.02 W
Bethesda	56d	38.59 N	77.06 W
Bethnal Green (Neigh.)	62	51.32 N	0.03 W
Bethpage	55	40.45 N	73.29 W
Betsham	62	51.25 N	0.19 E
Beverly	54a	42.33 N	70.53 W
Beverly Hills, Austl.	70a	33.57 S	151.05 E
Beverly Hills, Ca.	59	34.03 N	118.26 W
Beverly Hills, Mi.	57c	42.32 N	83.15 W
Bexley	70a	33.57 S	151.08 E
Bexley (Neigh.)	62	51.26 N	0.10 E
Beyenburg (Neigh.)	63	51.15 N	7.18 E
Beylerbeyi (Neigh.)	66f	41.03 N	29.03 E
Beyoğlu (Neigh.)	66f	41.02 N	28.59 E
Bezons	64c	48.56 N	2.13 E
Bhadreswar	67a	22.50 N	88.21 E
Bhalswa (Neigh.)	67d	28.44 N	77.10 E
Bhātpāra	67a	22.52 N	88.24 E
Bhopura	67d	28.42 N	77.20 E
Bickerstaffe	64b	53.32 N	2.50 W
Bickley (Neigh.)	62	51.24 N	0.03 E
Bidston	64b	53.24 N	3.05 W
Biesdorf (Neigh.)	65a	52.31 N	13.33 E
Bièvres	64c	48.45 N	2.13 E
Big Cr.	56a	41.27 N	81.41 W
Biggin Hill (Neigh.)	62	51.18 N	0.04 E
Billericay	62	51.38 N	0.25 E
Billingsport	56b	39.51 N	75.14 W
Bingham Farms	57c	42.32 N	83.16 W
Binh-dong	68m	10.43 N	106.39 E
Binsheim	63	51.31 N	6.42 E
Birch	64b	53.34 N	2.13 W
Birkenhead	64b	53.24 N	3.02 W
Birkholz	65a	52.38 N	13.34 E
Birling	62	51.19 N	0.25 E
Birmingham	57c	42.33 N	83.15 W
Bissingheim (Neigh.)	63	51.24 N	6.49 E
Bittermark (Neigh.)	63	51.27 N	7.28 E
Blackburn	70b	37.49 S	145.09 E
Black Creek Pioneer Village (P. Int.)	54c	43.47 N	79.32 W
Blackley (Neigh.)	64b	53.31 N	2.13 W
Blackmore	62	51.41 N	0.19 E
Black Rock	70b	37.59 S	145.01 E
Black Springs	70b	37.46 S	145.19 E
Blacktown	70a	33.46 S	150.55 E
Bladensburg	56d	38.56 N	76.55 W
Blaine Hill	57b	40.16 N	79.53 W
Blakang Mati (I.)	67c	1.15 N	103.50 E
Blakehurst	70a	33.59 S	151.07 E
Blankenburg (Neigh.)	65a	52.35 N	13.28 E
Blankenfelde (Neigh.)	65a	52.37 N	13.23 E
Blankenstein	63	51.24 N	7.14 E
Blawnox	57b	40.29 N	79.52 W
Bliedinghausen (Neigh.)	63	51.09 N	7.12 E
Bliersheim	63	51.23 N	6.43 E
Blombacher Bach (Neigh.)	63	51.15 N	7.14 E
Bloomfield	55	40.48 N	74.12 W
Bloomfield Village	57c	42.33 N	83.15 W
Blue Island	58a	41.40 N	87.41 W
Blue Mosque (P. Int.)	71a	30.02 N	31.15 E
Bobbingworth	62	51.44 N	0.13 E

PLACE	PAGE	Lat.°′	Long.°′
Bobigny	64c	48.54 N	2.27 E
Boca (Neigh.)	60d	34.38 S	58.21 W
Bocanegra	60c	12.01 S	77.07 W
Bochum	63	51.28 N	7.13 E
Böckel (Neigh.)	63	51.13 N	7.12 E
Bockum	63	51.20 N	6.44 E
Bockum (Neigh.)	63	51.21 N	6.38 E
Bodelschwingh (Neigh.)	63	51.33 N	7.22 E
Bogorodskoje (Neigh.)	66b	55.49 N	37.44 E
Bogota	55	40.53 N	74.02 W
Böhnsdorf (Neigh.)	65a	52.24 N	13.33 E
Bois-Colombes	64c	48.55 N	2.16 E
Boissy-Saint-Léger	64c	48.45 N	2.31 E
Boksburg	71b	26.12 S	28.14 E
Boksburg North	71b	26.12 S	28.15 E
Boksburg South	71b	26.14 S	28.15 E
Boksburg West	71b	26.13 S	28.14 E
Bölkenbusch	63	51.21 N	7.06 E
Bollate	65c	45.33 N	9.07 E
Bollensdorf	65a	52.31 N	13.43 E
Bollington	64b	53.22 N	2.25 W
Bollwerk	63	51.10 N	7.35 E
Bol'šaja Ochta (Neigh.)	66a	59.57 N	30.25 E
Bol'šoj Teatr (P. Int.)	66b	55.46 N	37.37 E
Bolton	64b	53.35 N	2.26 W
Bombay	67e	18.58 N	72.50 E
Bommerholz	63	51.23 N	7.18 E
Bommern (Neigh.)	63	51.25 N	7.20 E
Bom Retiro (Neigh.)	61d	23.32 S	46.38 W
Bon Air	56b	39.58 N	75.19 W
Bondi	70a	33.53 S	151.17 E
Bondy	64c	48.54 N	2.28 E
Bonneuil-sur-Marne	64c	48.46 N	2.29 E
Bonnyrigg	70a	33.54 S	150.54 E
Bonsucesso (Neigh.)	61c	22.52 S	43.15 W
Boothstown	64b	53.30 N	2.25 W
Bootle	64b	53.28 N	3.00 W
Booysens (Neigh.)	71b	26.14 S	28.01 E
Borbeck (Neigh.)	63	51.29 N	6.57 E
Bordeaux	71b	26.06 S	28.01 E
Bordeaux (Neigh.)	54b	45.33 N	73.41 W
Borehamwood	62	51.40 N	0.16 W
Borle (Neigh.)	67e	19.02 N	72.55 E
Bornim (Neigh.)	65a	52.26 N	13.00 E
Bornstedt (Neigh.)	65a	52.25 N	13.02 E
Borough Green	62	51.17 N	0.19 E
Borough Park (Neigh.)	55	40.38 N	74.00 W
Borth	63	51.36 N	6.33 E
Bossley Park	70a	33.52 S	150.54 E
Bostanci (Neigh.)	66f	40.57 N	29.05 E
Boston, Ma.	54a	42.21 N	71.04 W
Boston, Pa.	57b	40.18 N	79.49 W
Boston B.	54a	42.22 N	70.54 W
Boston Garden (P. Int.)	54a	42.22 N	71.04 W
Boston Har.	54a	42.20 N	70.58 W
Botafogo (Neigh.)	61c	22.57 S	43.11 W
Botafogo, Enseada de (B.)	61c	22.57 S	43.10 W
Botany	70a	33.57 S	151.12 E
Botany Bay (Neigh.)	62	51.41 N	0.07 W
Botany B.	70a	33.59 S	151.12 E
Bottrop	63	51.31 N	6.55 E
Bötzow	65a	52.39 N	13.08 E
Boucherville	54b	45.36 N	73.27 W
Boucherville, Îles de (Is.)	54b	45.37 N	73.28 W
Boukiéro	71c	4.12 S	15.18 E
Boulogne (Neigh.)	60d	34.31 S	58.34 W
Boulogne-Billancourt	64c	48.50 N	2.15 E
Bourg-la-Reine	64c	48.47 N	2.19 E
Bournebridge	62	51.38 N	0.11 E
Bourne End	62	51.45 N	0.32 W
Bövinghausen (Neigh.)	63	51.31 N	7.19 E
Bowdon	64b	53.23 N	2.22 W
Box Hill	70b	37.49 S	145.08 E
Boxmoor	62	51.45 N	0.29 W
Boyacıköy (Neigh.)	66f	41.06 N	29.02 E
Braddock	57b	40.25 N	79.50 W
Braddock Hills	57b	40.25 N	79.51 W
Bradshaw	64b	53.36 N	2.24 W
Braintree	54a	42.13 N	71.00 W
Brakpan	71b	26.14 S	28.22 E
Bramhall	64b	53.22 N	2.10 W
Bradenburger Tor (P. Int.)	65a	52.31 N	13.23 E
Bratcevo (Neigh.)	66b	55.51 N	37.24 E
Bratenahl	56a	41.35 N	81.33 W
Braybrook	70b	37.47 S	144.51 E
Brazzaville	71c	4.16 S	15.17 E
Brea	59	33.55 N	117.54 W
Brecheten (Neigh.)	63	51.35 N	7.28 E
Breckerfeld	63	51.16 N	7.28 E
Bredbury	64b	53.25 N	2.06 W
Bredell	71b	26.05 S	28.17 E
Bredeney (Neigh.)	63	51.24 N	6.59 E
Bredenscheid-Stüter	63	51.22 N	7.11 E
Breezewood	57b	40.34 N	80.03 W
Breitscheid	63	51.22 N	6.52 E
Breña	60c	12.04 S	77.04 W
Bren Mar Park	56d	38.48 N	77.09 W
Brentford (Neigh.)	62	51.29 N	0.18 W
Brenthurst	71b	26.16 S	28.23 E
Brentwood, Eng.	62	51.38 N	0.18 E
Brentwood, Md.	56d	38.56 N	76.57 W
Brentwood, Pa.	57b	40.22 N	79.59 W
Brentwood Heights (Neigh.)	59	34.04 N	118.30 W
Brentwood Park	71b	26.08 S	28.18 E
Bresso	65c	45.32 N	9.11 E
Bridesburg (Neigh.)	56b	40.00 N	75.04 W
Bridgeport	56b	40.06 N	75.21 W

PLACE	PAGE	Lat.°′	Long.°′
Bridgeport (Neigh.)	58a	41.51 N	87.39 W
Bridgeview	58a	41.45 N	87.48 W
Brie-Comte-Robert	64c	48.41 N	2.37 E
Brightmoor (Neigh.)	57c	42.24 N	83.14 W
Brighton	70b	37.55 S	145.00 E
Brighton (Neigh.)	54a	42.21 N	71.08 W
Brighton Le-Sands	70a	33.58 S	151.09 E
Brightwood (Neigh.)	56d	38.58 N	77.02 W
Brigittenau (Neigh.)	66e	48.14 N	16.22 E
Brilyn Park	56d	38.54 N	77.10 W
Brindley Heath	62	51.12 N	0.03 W
Brinkleigh	56c	39.18 N	76.50 W
Brisbane	58b	37.41 N	122.24 W
Broadheath	64b	53.24 N	2.21 W
Broadley Common	62	51.45 N	0.04 E
Broadmeadows	70b	37.40 S	144.54 E
Broadmoor	58b	37.41 N	122.29 W
Brockenscheidt	63	51.38 N	7.25 E
Brockton	54a	42.05 N	71.01 W
Broich (Neigh.)	63	51.25 N	6.51 E
Bromborough	64b	53.19 N	2.59 W
Bromley (Neigh.)	62	51.24 N	0.02 E
Bromley Common (Neigh.)	62	51.22 N	0.03 E
Bronx (Neigh.)	55	40.49 N	73.56 W
Bronxville	55	40.56 N	73.50 W
Brookfield	58a	41.49 N	87.51 W
Brookhaven	56b	39.52 N	75.23 W
Brookland (Neigh.)	56d	38.56 N	76.59 W
Brooklandville	56c	39.26 N	76.41 W
Brooklawn	56b	39.53 N	75.08 W
Brookline	54a	42.21 N	71.07 W
Brooklyn	56a	41.25 N	81.49 W
Brooklyn (Neigh.)	56c	39.14 N	76.36 W
Brooklyn Heights	56a	41.24 N	81.40 W
Brooklyn Park	56c	39.14 N	76.36 W
Brookmans Park	62	51.43 N	0.12 W
Brookmont	56d	38.57 N	77.07 W
Brook Park	56a	41.24 N	81.48 W
Brook Street	62	51.37 N	0.17 E
Brookvale	70a	33.46 S	151.17 E
Brookville, Ma.	54a	42.08 N	71.01 W
Brookville, NY	55	40.49 N	73.35 W
Bromall	56b	39.59 N	75.22 W
Broomfield	62	51.14 N	0.38 E
Brossard	54b	45.26 N	73.29 W
Broughton	57b	40.21 N	79.59 W
Brou-sur-Chantereine	64c	48.53 N	2.38 E
Broxbourne	62	51.45 N	0.01 W
Bruchmühle	65a	52.33 N	13.47 E
Bruckhausen (Neigh.)	63	51.29 N	6.44 E
Brügge	63	51.13 N	7.34 E
Brugherio	65c	45.33 N	9.18 E
Brunoy	64c	48.42 N	2.30 E
Brunswick	70b	37.46 S	144.58 E
Bryn Mawr	56b	40.01 N	75.19 W
Buc	64c	48.46 N	2.08 E
Buch (Neigh.)	65a	52.38 N	13.30 E
Buchholz	65a	52.35 N	13.47 E
Buchholz (Neigh.), F.R.G.	63	51.23 N	6.46 E
Buchholz (Neigh.), G.D.R.	65a	52.36 N	13.26 E
Buckhorn Island State Park (P. Int.)	57a	43.03 N	78.59 W
Buckingham Palace (P. Int.)	62	51.30 N	0.08 W
Buckow (Neigh.)	65a	52.25 N	13.26 E
Buda (Neigh.)	66g	47.30 N	19.02 E
Budai-hegység (Mts.)	66g	47.31 N	19.57 E
Budakeszi	66g	47.31 N	18.56 E
Budaörs	66g	47.27 N	18.58 E
Budapest	66g	47.30 N	19.05 E
Budberg	63	51.32 N	6.38 E
Büderich	63	51.37 N	6.34 E
Buderus	63	51.33 N	7.38 E
Buena Park	59	33.52 N	118.00 W
Buenos Aires	60d	34.36 S	58.27 W
Buer (Neigh.)	63	51.36 N	7.03 E
Buffalo	57a	42.54 N	78.53 W
Buffalo Har.	57a	42.51 N	78.52 W
Bukit Panjang	67c	1.23 N	103.46 E
Bukit Timah	67c	1.20 N	103.47 E
Bulim	67c	1.23 N	103.43 E
Bulmke-Hüllen (Neigh.)	63	51.31 N	7.06 E
Bulpham	62	51.33 N	0.22 E
Bumbles Green	62	51.44 N	0.02 E
Bundoora	70b	37.42 S	145.04 E
Bunker Hill Monument (P. Int.)	54a	42.22 N	71.04 W
Bunkyō (Neigh.)	69a	35.43 N	139.45 E
Buona Vista	67c	1.16 N	103.47 E
Burbank	59	34.12 N	118.18 W
Bures-sur-Yvette	64c	48.42 N	2.10 E
Burg	63	51.08 N	7.09 E
Burger Township	71b	26.05 S	27.46 E
Burgh Heath	62	51.18 N	0.13 W
Burholme (Neigh.)	56b	40.03 N	75.05 W
Burlingame	58b	37.35 N	122.22 W
Burlington	54a	42.30 N	71.12 W
Burnage	64b	53.26 N	2.12 W
Burnham	58a	41.39 N	87.34 W
Burnhamthorpe	54c	43.37 N	79.36 W
Burning Tree Estates	56d	39.01 N	77.12 W
Burrowhill	62	51.21 N	0.36 W
Burr Ridge	58a	41.46 N	87.55 W
Burton	64b	53.16 N	3.01 W
Burwood, Austl.	70b	37.51 S	145.06 E
Bury	64b	53.36 N	2.17 W
Busby	70a	33.54 S	150.53 E
Buschhausen (Neigh.)	63	51.30 N	6.51 E
Bushey	62	51.39 N	0.22 W
Bushey Heath	62	51.38 N	0.20 W
Bush Hill	56d	38.48 N	77.07 W

PLACE	PAGE	Lat.°′	Long.°′
Bushwick (Neigh.)	55	40.42 N	73.55 W
Bustleton (Neigh.)	56b	40.05 N	75.02 W
Butantã (Neigh.)	61d	23.34 S	46.43 W
Butendorf (Neigh.)	63	51.33 N	6.59 E
Büttgen	63	51.12 N	6.36 E
Byculla (Neigh.)	67e	18.58 N	72.49 E
Byfang (Neigh.)	63	51.24 N	7.06 E
Byfleet	62	51.20 N	0.29 W
Bymea Bay	70a	34.03 S	151.06 E

C

PLACE	PAGE	Lat.°′	Long.°′
Caballito (Neigh.)	60d	34.37 S	58.27 W
Cabin John	56d	38.58 N	77.09 W
Cabramatta	70a	33.54 S	150.56 E
Cachan	64c	48.48 N	2.20 E
Cacilhas	65d	38.41 N	9.09 W
Cadishead	64b	53.25 N	2.26 W
Cairo (Al-Qāhirah)	71a	30.03 N	31.15 E
Caju (Neigh.)	61c	22.53 S	43.13 W
Calabazar	60b	23.01 N	82.22 W
Calcutta	67a	22.32 N	88.22 E
Caldwell	55	40.51 N	74.17 W
Calhariz (Neigh.)	65d	38.44 N	9.12 W
California, University of (U.C.L.A.) (P. Int.)	59	34.04 N	118.26 W
Callao	60c	12.02 S	77.05 W
Caloocan	68g	14.39 N	120.59 E
Calumet, L.	58a	41.41 N	87.35 W
Calumet City	58a	41.37 N	87.31 W
Calumet Park	58a	41.44 N	87.33 W
Calumet Sag Chan.	58a	41.42 N	87.57 W
Camberwell	70b	37.50 S	145.04 E
Cambridge	54a	42.22 N	71.06 W
Cambuci (Neigh.)	61d	23.34 S	46.37 W
Camden	56b	39.57 N	75.07 W
Camden (Neigh.)	62	51.33 N	0.10 W
Campbellfield	70b	37.41 S	144.57 E
Campo Grande (Neigh.)	65d	38.45 N	9.09 W
Campsie	70a	33.55 S	151.06 E
Camp Springs	56d	38.48 N	76.55 W
Canarsie (Neigh.)	55	40.38 N	73.53 W
Canillas (Neigh.)	65b	40.28 N	3.38 W
Canillejas (Neigh.)	65b	40.27 N	3.37 W
Canoga Park (Neigh.)	59	34.12 N	118.35 W
Canterbury, Austl.	70b	37.49 S	145.05 E
Canterbury Woods	56d	38.49 N	77.15 W
Canto do Pontes	61c	22.58 S	43.04 W
Canton	54a	42.09 N	71.09 W
Canyon	58b	37.49 N	122.09 W
Capão Redondo (Neigh.)	61d	23.40 S	46.46 W
Caparica	65d	38.40 N	9.12 W
Capenhurst	64b	53.15 N	2.57 W
Capitol Heights	56d	38.53 N	76.55 W
Capitol View	56d	39.01 N	77.04 W
Captain Cook Bridge (P. Int.)	70a	34.00 S	151.08 E
Capuáva	61d	23.39 S	46.29 W
Caputh	65a	52.21 N	13.00 E
Caraballeda	61a	10.37 N	66.50 W
Carabanchel Alto (Neigh.)	65b	40.22 N	3.45 W
Carabanchel Bajo (Neigh.)	65b	40.23 N	3.47 W
Caracas	61a	10.30 N	66.56 W
Carapicuíba	61d	23.31 S	46.50 W
Caringbah	70a	34.03 S	151.08 E
Carlingford	70a	33.47 S	151.03 E
Carlstadt	55	40.50 N	74.06 W
Carnaxide	65d	38.43 N	9.15 W
Carnegie Institute (P. Int.)	57b	40.27 N	79.57 W
Carnetin	64c	48.54 N	2.42 E
Carnide (Neigh.)	65d	38.46 N	9.11 W
Carrières-sous-Bois	64c	48.57 N	2.07 E
Carrières-sous-Poissy	64c	48.57 N	2.03 E
Carrières-sur-Seine	64c	48.55 N	2.11 E
Carrington	64b	53.26 N	2.24 W
Carshalton (Neigh.)	62	51.22 N	0.10 W
Carson	59	33.50 N	118.16 W
Carsondale	56d	38.57 N	76.50 W
Carteret	55	40.35 N	74.13 W
Casa Loma (P. Int.)	54c	43.41 N	79.25 W
Caseros (Tres de Febrero)	60d	34.36 S	58.33 W
Castellbisbal	65e	41.29 N	1.59 E
Castlecrag	70a	33.48 S	151.13 E
Castle Hill	70a	33.44 S	151.00 E
Castle Shannon	57b	40.22 N	80.02 W
Castleton	64b	53.35 N	2.11 W
Castrop-Rauxel	63	51.34 N	7.19 E
Cataluña, Museo de Arte de (P. Int.)	65e	41.23 N	2.09 E
Caterham	62	51.17 N	0.04 W
Catete (Neigh.)	61c	22.55 S	43.10 W
Catford (Neigh.)	62	51.27 N	0.01 W
Catia (Neigh.)	61a	10.31 N	66.57 W
Catonsville	56c	39.16 N	76.44 W
Caughnawaga	54b	45.25 N	73.41 W
Caulfield	70b	37.53 S	145.03 E
Caxias	65d	38.42 N	9.16 W
Cecchignola (Neigh.)	66c	41.49 N	12.29 E
Cecil Park	70a	33.52 S	150.51 E
Cedarbrook	56b	40.05 N	75.10 W
Cedar Grove	55	40.51 N	74.14 W
Cedar Heights	56b	40.05 N	75.17 W
Cedarhurst	55	40.38 N	73.44 W

PLACE	PAGE	Lat.°′	Long.°′
Dümpten (Neigh.)	63	51.27 N	6.54 E
Dundalk	56c	39.15 N	76.31 W
Dundas	70a	33.48 S	151.02 E
Dunham Town	64b	53.23 N	2.24 W
Dunheved	70a	33.45 S	150.47 E
Dunn Loring	56d	38.53 N	77.14 W
Dunton Green	62	51.18 N	0.11 E
Dunton Wayletts	62	51.35 N	0.24 E
Dunvegan	71b	26.09 S	28.09 E
Duomo (P. Int.)	65c	45.27 N	9.11 E
Duque de Caxias	61c	22.47 S	43.18 W
Duquesne	57b	40.21 N	79.51 W
Durban Roodepoort Deep Gold Mines (P. Int.)	71b	26.10 S	27.51 E
Durchholz	63	51.23 N	7.17 E
Düssel	63	51.16 N	7.03 E
Düsseldorf	63	51.12 N	6.47 E
Dzeržinskij	66b	55.38 N	37.50 E

E

PLACE	PAGE	Lat.°′	Long.°′
Eagle Rock (Neigh.)	59	34.09 N	118.12 W
Ealing (Neigh.)	62	51.31 N	0.20 W
East (R.)	55	40.48 N	73.48 W
East Arlington	54a	42.25 N	71.08 W
East Barnet (Neigh.)	62	51.38 N	0.09 W
East Bedfont (Neigh.)	62	51.27 N	0.26 W
East Braintree	54a	42.13 N	70.58 W
East Burwood	70b	37.51 S	145.09 E
Eastbury	62	51.37 N	0.25 W
Eastchester	55	40.57 N	73.49 W
East Cleveland	56a	41.32 N	81.35 W
Eastcote (Neigh.)	62	51.35 N	0.24 W
East Detroit	57c	42.28 N	82.56 W
Eastern Native (Neigh.)	71b	26.13 S	28.05 E
East Falls (Neigh.)	56b	40.01 N	75.11 W
Eastham	64b	53.19 N	2.58 W
East Ham (Neigh.)	62	51.32 N	0.03 E
East Hills, Austl.	70a	33.58 S	150.59 E
East Hills, NY	55	40.47 N	73.38 W
East Lamma Chan.	68c	22.15 N	114.07 E
East Lansdowne	56b	39.56 N	75.16 W
East Liberty (Neigh.)	57b	40.27 N	79.55 W
East Lindfield	70a	33.46 S	151.11 E
East Los Angeles	59	34.01 N	118.09 W
East Malling	62	51.17 N	0.26 E
East Meadow	55	40.43 N	73.34 W
East Molesey	62	51.24 N	0.21 W
East Newark	55	40.45 N	74.10 W
East New York (Neigh.)	55	40.40 N	73.53 W
East Norwich	55	40.50 N	73.32 W
East Orange	55	40.46 N	74.13 W
East Pittsburgh	57b	40.24 N	79.48 W
East Richmond	58b	37.57 N	122.19 W
East Rockaway	55	40.39 N	73.40 W
East Tilbury	62	51.28 N	0.26 E
East Tustin	59	33.46 N	117.49 W
East Walpole	54a	42.10 N	71.13 W
East Watertown	54a	42.22 N	71.10 W
East Weymouth	54a	42.13 N	70.55 W
Eastwick (Neigh.)	56b	39.55 N	75.14 W
East Wickham (Neigh.)	62	51.28 N	0.07 E
Eastwood	70a	33.48 S	151.05 E
East York	54c	43.41 N	79.20 W
Eaubonne	64c	49.00 N	2.17 E
Ebina	69a	35.26 N	139.25 E
Ebute-ikorodu	71d	6.37 N	3.30 E
Eccles	64b	53.29 N	2.21 W
Eccleston, Eng.	64b	53.27 N	2.47 W
Eccleston, Md	56c	39.24 N	76.44 W
Ecorse	57c	42.15 N	83.09 W
Eda (Neigh.)	69a	35.34 N	139.34 E
Éden	61c	22.48 S	43.24 W
Edendale	71b	26.09 S	28.09 E
Edenvale	71b	26.08 S	28.09 E
Edenvale Location	71b	26.08 S	28.11 E
Edge Hill (Neigh.)	64b	53.24 N	2.57 W
Edgemere	56c	39.14 N	76.27 W
Edgewater, NJ.	55	40.50 N	73.58 W
Edgewater, NY	57a	43.03 N	78.55 W
Edgware (Neigh.)	62	51.37 N	0.17 W
Edgworth	64b	53.39 N	2.24 W
Edison Park (Neigh.)	58a	42.01 N	87.49 W
Edmonston	56d	38.57 N	76.56 W
Edmonton (Neigh.)	62	51.37 N	0.04 W
Edo (R.)	69a	35.41 N	139.53 E
Edogawa (Neigh.)	69a	35.42 N	139.52 E
Egham	62	51.26 N	0.34 W
Egota (Neigh.)	69a	35.43 N	139.40 E
Ehingen (Neigh.)	63	51.22 N	6.42 E
Ehringhausen	63	51.11 N	7.33 E
Ehringhausen (Neigh.)	63	51.09 N	7.11 E
Eiche	65a	52.34 N	13.36 E
Eichlinghofen (Neigh.)	63	51.29 N	7.24 E
Eichwalde	65a	52.22 N	13.37 E
Eickerend	63	51.13 N	6.34 E
Eiffel, Tour (P. Int.)	64c	48.51 N	2.18 E
Eigen (Neigh.)	63	51.33 N	6.57 E
Eilpe (Neigh.)	63	51.21 N	7.29 E
Eksāra	67a	22.38 N	88.17 E
El Aguacate	61a	10.28 N	66.59 W
Elandsfontein	71b	26.10 S	28.12 E
Elberfeld (Neigh.)	63	51.16 N	7.08 E
El Calvario (Neigh.)	60b	23.05 N	82.20 W
El Campamento (Neigh.)	65b	40.24 N	3.46 W
El Caribe	61a	10.37 N	66.49 W
El Cerrito	58b	37.55 N	122.18 W
El Cojo	61a	10.37 N	66.53 W
El Corozo	61a	10.35 N	66.58 W
El Cotorro	60b	23.03 N	82.16 W
Elder Mills	54c	43.49 N	79.38 W
El Encantado	61a	10.27 N	66.47 W
Elephanta I. (Ghārp̄ uri)	67e	18.57 N	72.55 W
El Granada	58b	37.30 N	122.28 W
El Guarapo	61a	10.36 N	66.58 W
Elizabeth, N.J.	55	40.40 N	74.11 W
Elizabeth, Pa.	57b	40.16 N	79.53 W
Elkins Park	56b	40.05 N	75.08 W
Elkridge	56c	39.13 N	76.42 W
Ellesmere Park	64b	53.29 N	2.20 W
Ellesmere Port	64b	53.17 N	2.54 W
Ellicott City	56c	39.16 N	76.48 W
El Limoncito	61a	10.29 N	66.47 W
Ellinghorst (Neigh.)	63	51.34 N	6.57 E
Elmhurst	58a	41.53 N	87.56 W
Elmhurst (Neigh.)	55	40.44 N	73.53 W
El Molinito	60a	19.27 N	99.15 W
Elmont	55	40.42 N	73.42 W
Elmwood (Neigh.)	56b	39.56 N	75.14 W
Elmwood Park	58a	41.55 N	87.49 W
El Palmar	61a	10.38 N	66.52 W
El Pedregal (Neigh.)	61a	10.30 N	66.51 W
El Plantío (Neigh.)	65b	40.28 N	3.49 W
El Recreo (Neigh.)	61a	10.30 N	66.53 W
El Reloj	60a	19.18 N	99.08 W
El Rincón de La Florida	61b	33.33 S	70.34 W
Elsburg	71b	26.15 S	28.12 E
El Segundo	59	33.55 N	118.24 W
Elsey	63	51.22 N	7.34 E
Elstree	62	51.39 N	0.16 W
Eltham (Neigh.)	62	51.27 N	0.04 E
Elton	64b	53.16 N	2.49 W
El Toreo (P. Int.)	60a	19.27 N	99.13 W
El Valle (Neigh.)	61a	10.27 N	66.55 W
El Zamural	61a	10.27 N	67.00 W
El Zig-Zag	61a	10.33 N	66.58 W
Embu	61d	23.39 S	46.51 W
Émerainville	64c	48.49 N	2.37 E
Emerson	55	40.58 N	74.02 W
Emeryville	58b	37.50 N	122.17 W
Emmarentia (Neigh.)	71b	26.10 S	28.01 E
Emst (Neigh.)	63	51.21 N	7.30 E
Emsworth	57b	40.30 N	80.04 W
Encarnação (Neigh.)	65d	38.47 N	9.06 W
Encino (Neigh.)	59	34.09 N	118.30 W
Enfield	70a	33.53 S	151.06 E
Engenho de Dentro (Neigh.)	61c	22.54 S	43.18 W
Engenho do Mato	61c	22.52 S	43.01 W
Engenho Nôvo (Neigh.)	61c	22.55 S	43.17 W
Enghien-les-Bains	64c	48.58 N	2.19 E
Englefield Green	62	51.26 N	0.35 W
Englewood	55	40.54 N	73.59 W
Englewood (Neigh.)	58a	41.47 N	87.39 W
Englewood Cliffs	55	40.53 N	73.57 W
Ennepetal	63	51.18 N	7.22 E
Épinay-sous-Sénart	64c	48.42 N	2.31 E
Épinay-sur-Seine	64c	48.57 N	2.19 E
Eppendorf (Neigh.)	63	51.27 N	7.11 E
Eppenhausen (Neigh.)	63	51.21 N	7.31 E
Epping, Austl.	70a	33.46 S	151.05 E
Epping, Eng.	62	51.43 N	0.07 E
Epping Green, Eng	62	51.44 N	0.05 E
Epping Upland	62	51.43 N	0.06 E
Epsom	62	51.20 N	0.16 W
Erenköy (Neigh.)	66f	40.58 N	29.04 E
Ergste	63	51.25 N	7.34 E
Erith (Neigh.)	62	51.29 N	0.10 E
Erkrath	63	51.13 N	6.55 E
Erle (Neigh.)	63	51.33 N	7.05 E
Ermont	64c	48.59 N	2.16 E
Erskine Park	70a	33.49 S	150.47 E
Esborn	63	51.23 N	7.20 E
Escuadrón 201	60a	19.22 N	99.06 W
Esher	62	51.23 N	0.22 W
Esplugas	65e	41.23 N	2.06 E
Essel (Neigh.)	63	51.37 N	7.15 E
Essen	63	51.28 N	7.01 E
Essenberg	63	51.26 N	6.42 E
Essendon	70b	37.46 S	144.55 E
Essex	56c	39.18 N	76.29 W
Essex Fells	55	40.50 N	74.17 W
Essington	56b	39.52 N	75.18 W
Essling (Neigh.)	66e	48.13 N	16.32 E
Estrella, Cerro de la (Mtn.)	60a	19.21 N	99.05 W
Etna	57b	40.30 N	79.57 W
Etobicoke	54c	43.39 N	79.34 W
Eton	62	51.31 N	0.37 W
Evanston	58a	42.02 N	87.42 W
Everett	54a	42.24 N	71.03 W
Evergreen Park	58a	41.43 N	87.42 W
Everton (Neigh.)	64b	53.25 N	2.58 W
Eving (Neigh.)	63	51.33 N	7.29 E
Ewell	62	51.21 N	0.15 W
Ewu	71d	6.33 N	3.19 E
Eynsford	62	51.22 N	0.13 E
Eyüp (Neigh.)	66f	41.03 N	28.55 E
Ezbekīyah (Neigh.)	71a	30.03 N	31.15 E

F

PLACE	PAGE	Lat.°′	Long.°′
Fabreville (Neigh.)	54b	45.34 N	73.50 W
Fahrland	65a	52.28 N	13.01 E
Failsworth	64b	53.31 N	2.09 W
Fairfield, Austl.	70a	33.52 S	150.57 E
Fairfield, NJ.	55	40.53 N	74.17 W
Fairhaven	56d	38.47 N	77.05 W
Fair Lawn	55	40.56 N	74.07 W
Fairlee	56d	38.52 N	77.16 W
Fairmount Heights	56d	38.54 N	76.55 W
Fairseat	62	51.30 N	0.20 E
Fairview	55	40.49 N	74.00 W
Fairview Park	56a	41.27 N	81.51 W
Falkensee	65a	52.33 N	13.04 E
Falls Church	56d	38.53 N	77.11 W
Famadas	65e	41.21 N	2.05 E
Farazād	68h	35.47 N	51.21 E
Farmington	57c	42.28 N	83.22 W
Farmington Hills	57c	42.28 N	83.23 W
Farnborough (Neigh.)	62	51.21 N	0.04 E
Farningham	62	51.23 N	0.13 E
Farnworth	64b	53.33 N	2.24 W
Far Rockaway (Neigh.)	55	40.36 N	73.45 W
Favoriten (Neigh.)	66e	48.11 N	16.23 E
Fawkham Green	62	51.22 N	0.17 E
Fawkner	70b	37.43 S	144.58 E
Fawsett Farms	56d	38.59 N	77.14 W
Fengtai	67b	39.51 N	116.16 E
Ferbitz	65a	52.30 N	13.01 E
Ferencváros (Neigh.)	66g	47.28 N	19.06 E
Ferndale, Md.	56c	39.11 N	76.38 W
Ferndale, Mi.	57c	42.28 N	83.08 W
Ferny Creek	70b	37.53 S	145.21 E
Ferraz de Vasconcelos	61d	23.32 S	46.22 W
Ferrières	64c	48.49 N	2.42 E
Ferry Village	57a	43.58 N	78.57 W
Fetcham	62	51.17 N	0.22 W
Fichtenau	65a	52.27 N	13.42 E
Fiddlers Hamlet	62	51.41 N	0.08 E
Fili (Neigh.)	66b	55.45 N	37.31 E
Finaalspan	71b	26.17 S	28.15 E
Finchley (Neigh.)	62	51.36 N	0.10 W
Finkenkrug	65a	52.34 N	13.03 E
Firgrove	64b	53.37 N	2.08 W
Fischeln (Neigh.)	63	51.18 N	6.35 E
Fisherman's Wharf (P. Int.)	58b	37.48 N	122.25 W
Fisherville	54c	43.47 N	79.28 W
Fishpool	64b	53.35 N	2.17 W
Fitzroy	70b	37.48 S	144.59 E
Five Dock	70a	33.52 S	151.08 E
Flatbush (Neigh.)	55	40.39 N	73.56 W
Flaunden	62	51.42 N	0.32 W
Flehe (Neigh.)	63	51.12 N	6.47 E
Fley (Neigh.)	63	51.23 N	7.30 E
Flingern (Neigh.)	63	51.14 N	6.49 E
Floral Park	55	40.43 N	73.42 W
Florence	59	33.58 N	118.15 W
Florentia	71b	26.16 S	28.08 E
Flores (Neigh.)	60d	34.38 S	58.28 W
Floresta (Neigh.)	60d	34.38 S	58.29 W
Florida	71b	26.11 S	27.55 E
Flotantes, Jardínes (P. Int.)	60a	19.16 N	99.06 W
Flourtown	56b	40.07 N	75.13 W
Flower Hill	55	40.49 N	73.41 W
Flushing (Neigh.)	55	40.45 N	73.49 W
Folcroft	56b	39.54 N	75.17 W
Folsom	56b	39.54 N	75.19 W
Fontainebleau	71b	26.07 S	27.59 E
Fontenay-aux-Roses	64c	48.47 N	2.17 E
Fontenay-le-Fleury	64c	48.49 N	2.30 E
Fontenay-sous-Bois	64c	48.51 N	2.29 E
Footscray	70b	37.48 S	144.54 E
Fora, Ponta de (C.)	61c	22.57 S	43.07 W
Forbidden City (P. Int.)	67b	39.55 N	116.23 E
Fordham University (P. Int.)	55	40.51 N	73.53 W
Fords	55	40.32 N	74.19 W
Fordsburg (Neigh.)	71b	26.13 S	28.02 E
Forest Gate (Neigh.)	62	51.33 N	0.02 E
Forest Heights	56d	38.49 N	77.00 W
Forest Hill	70b	37.50 S	145.11 E
Forest Hill (Neigh.)	54c	43.42 N	79.24 W
Forest Hills	57b	40.26 N	79.52 W
Forest Hills (Neigh.)	55	40.42 N	73.51 W
Forest Park	58a	41.53 N	87.50 W
Forest Park (Neigh.)	56c	39.19 N	76.41 W
Forestville, Austl.	70a	33.46 S	151.13 E
Forestville, Md.	56d	38.50 N	76.52 W
Formby	64b	53.34 N	3.05 W
Formby Pt.	64b	53.33 N	3.06 W
Fort (Neigh.)	67e	18.56 N	72.50 E
Fort Erie	57a	42.54 N	78.56 W
Fort Howard	56c	39.12 N	76.27 W
Fort Lee	55	40.51 N	73.58 W
Fort McHenry National Monument (P. Int.)	56c	39.16 N	76.35 W
Fort McNair (P. Int.)	56d	38.52 N	77.04 W
Fort Wayne Military Museum (P. Int.)	57c	42.18 N	83.06 W
Fort William (P. Int.)	67a	22.33 N	88.20 E
Foster City	58b	37.34 N	122.16 W
Fourqueux	64c	48.53 N	2.04 E
Fox Chapel	57b	40.30 N	79.55 W
Fox Valley	70a	33.45 S	151.06 E
Franconville	64c	48.59 N	2.14 E
Frank	57b	40.16 N	79.48 W
Frankby	64b	53.22 N	3.08 W
Frankford (Neigh.)	56b	40.01 N	75.05 W
Franklin	57c	42.31 N	83.18 W
Franklin Park, Il.	58a	41.56 N	87.49 W
Franklin Park, Pa.	57b	40.35 N	80.06 W
Franklin Park, Va.	56d	38.55 N	77.09 W
Franklin Roosevelt Park (Neigh.)	71b	26.09 S	27.59 E
Franklin Square	55	40.43 N	73.40 W
Fraser	57c	42.32 N	82.57 W
Fredersdorf bei Berlin	65a	52.31 N	13.44 E
Freeport	55	40.39 N	73.35 W
Freisenbruch (Neigh.)	63	51.27 N	7.06 E
French's Forest	70a	33.45 S	151.14 E
Freshfield	64b	53.34 N	3.04 W
Fresh Meadows (Neigh.)	55	40.44 N	73.48 W
Friedenau (Neigh.)	65a	52.28 N	13.20 E
Friedrichsfeld	63	51.38 N	6.39 E
Friedrichsfelde (Neigh.)	65a	52.31 N	13.31 E
Friedrichshagen (Neigh.)	65a	52.27 N	13.38 E
Friedrichshain (Neigh.)	65a	52.31 N	13.27 E
Friemersheim	63	51.23 N	6.42 E
Friends Colony (Neigh.)	67d	28.34 N	77.16 E
Friendship International Arpt.	56c	39.11 N	76.40 W
Friern Barnet (Neigh.)	62	51.37 N	0.10 W
Frillendorf (Neigh.)	63	51.28 N	7.05 E
Frodsham	64b	53.18 N	2.44 W
Frohnau (Neigh.)	65a	52.38 N	13.18 E
Frohnhausen (Neigh.)	63	51.27 N	6.58 E
Fryerning	62	51.41 N	0.22 E
Fuchū	69a	35.40 N	139.29 E
Fuencarral (Neigh.)	65b	40.30 N	3.41 W
Fuhlenbrock (Neigh.)	63	51.32 N	6.54 E
Fujiidera	69b	34.34 N	135.36 E
Fukagawa (Neigh.)	69a	35.40 N	139.48 E
Fukui (Neigh.)	69b	34.42 N	135.12 E
Fukushima (Neigh.)	69b	34.42 N	135.29 E
Fulerum (Neigh.)	63	51.26 N	6.57 E
Fullerton	59	33.52 N	117.55 W
Fulmer	62	51.33 N	0.34 W
Funasaka	69b	34.49 N	135.17 E
Fundão, Ilha do (I.)	61c	22.51 S	43.14 W
Funde	67e	18.54 N	72.58 E
Futatsubashi	69a	35.29 N	139.30 E
Fyfield	62	51.45 N	0.16 E

G

PLACE	PAGE	Lat.°′	Long.°′
Gagny	64c	48.53 N	2.32 E
Gahmen (Neigh.)	63	51.36 N	7.32 E
Galata (Neigh.)	66f	41.01 N	28.58 E
Galata Köprüsü (P. Int.)	66f	41.00 N	28.57 E
Galátsion	66d	38.01 N	23.45 E
Galvin	70b	37.51 S	144.49 E
Gaobaita	67b	39.53 N	116.30 E
Gaobeidian	67b	39.54 N	116.33 E
Garbagnate Milanese	65c	45.35 N	9.05 E
Garbatella (Neigh.)	66c	41.52 N	12.29 E
Garches	64c	48.51 N	2.11 E
Gardena	59	33.53 N	118.19 W
Garden City, Mi.	57c	42.20 N	83.20 W
Garden City, NY.	55	40.43 N	73.37 W
Garden City Park	55	40.44 N	73.40 W
Garden Grove	59	33.46 N	117.57 W
Garden Reach	67a	22.33 N	88.17 E
Garenfeld	63	51.24 N	7.31 E
Garfield	55	40.53 N	74.07 W
Garfield Heights	56a	41.26 N	81.37 W
Garges-lès-Gonesse	64c	48.58 N	2.25 E
Garland	56c	39.11 N	76.39 W
Garrison	56c	39.24 N	76.45 W
Garston	62	51.41 N	0.23 W
Garston (Neigh.)	64b	53.21 N	2.53 W
Gartenstadt (Neigh.)	63	51.30 N	7.26 E
Garulia	67a	22.49 N	88.22 E
Garwood	55	40.39 N	74.19 W
Gateacre (Neigh.)	64b	53.23 N	2.51 W
Gateway of India (P. Int.)	67e	18.55 N	72.50 E
Gatley	64b	53.23 N	2.14 W
Gato Negro	61a	10.33 N	66.57 W
Gāvanpāda	67e	18.57 N	73.01 E
Gávea (Neigh.)	61c	22.58 S	43.14 W
Gayton	64b	53.19 N	3.06 W
Gee Cross	64b	53.26 N	2.04 W
Gellep-Stratum (Neigh.)	63	51.20 N	6.41 E
Gellibrand, Pt.	70b	37.52 S	144.54 E
Gelsenkirchen	63	51.31 N	7.07 E
General Pacheco	60d	34.28 S	58.40 W
General San Martín	60d	34.35 S	58.30 W
General Sarmiento (San Miguel)	60d	34.33 S	58.43 W
General Urquiza (Neigh.)	60d	34.34 S	58.29 W
Gennebreck	63	51.19 N	7.12 E
Gennevilliers	64c	48.56 N	2.18 E
Gentilly	64c	48.49 N	2.21 E
Georges Hall	70a	33.55 S	150.59 E
Georgetown (Neigh.)	56d	38.54 N	77.03 W
Georgetown University (P. Int.)	56d	38.54 N	77.04 W

PLACE	PAGE	Lat.°′	Long.°′
Gerdview	71b	26.10 S	28.11 E
Gerli (Neigh.)	60d	34.41 S	58.23 W
Germantown (Neigh.)	56b	40.03 N	75.11 W
Germiston	71b	26.15 S	28.05 E
Gerrards Cross	62	51.35 N	0.34 W
Getafe	65b	40.18 N	3.43 W
Getzville	57a	43.01 N	78.46 W
Gevelsberg	63	51.19 N	7.20 E
Geweke (Neigh.)	63	51.22 N	7.25 E
Ghārāpuri	67e	18.54 N	72.56 E
Ghātkopar (Neigh.)	67e	19.05 N	72.54 E
Ghāzipur (Neigh.)	67d	28.38 N	77.19 E
Ghonda (Neigh.)	67d	28.41 N	77.16 E
Ghondi (Neigh.)	67d	28.42 N	77.16 E
Ghushuri	67a	22.37 N	88.22 E
Gia-dinh	68m	10.48 N	106.42 E
Gibbsboro	56b	39.50 N	74.58 W
Gibraltar Pt.	54c	43.36 N	79.23 W
Gidea Park (Neigh.)	62	51.35 N	0.12 E
Gif-sur-Yvette	64c	48.42 N	2.08 E
Ginza (Neigh.)	69a	35.40 N	139.47 E
Girgaum (Neigh.)	67e	18.57 N	72.48 E
Giza Pyramids (P. Int.)	71a	29.59 N	31.08 E
Gladbeck	63	51.34 N	6.59 E
Gladesville	70a	33.50 S	151.08 E
Gladwyne	56b	40.02 N	75.17 W
Glashütte (Neigh.)	63	51.13 N	6.52 E
Glassmanor	56d	38.49 N	76.59 W
Glassport	57b	40.19 N	79.54 W
Glehn	63	51.10 N	6.35 E
Glenarden	56d	38.56 N	76.52 W
Glen Cove	55	40.52 N	73.37 W
Glendale	59	34.10 N	118.17 W
Glendora, Ca.	59	34.08 N	117.52 W
Glendora, NJ.	56b	39.50 N	75.04 W
Glen Echo	56d	38.58 N	77.08 W
Glenfield	70a	33.58 S	150.54 E
Glen Head	55	40.50 N	73.37 W
Glenhuntly	70b	37.54 S	145.03 E
Glenmore	56c	39.11 N	76.36 W
Glenolden	56b	39.54 N	75.17 W
Glen Ridge	55	40.49 N	74.13 W
Glen Rock	55	40.58 N	74.08 W
Glenroy	70b	37.42 S	144.55 E
Glenshaw	57b	40.31 N	79.57 W
Glenside	56b	40.06 N	75.09 W
Glenview	58a	42.04 N	87.48 W
Glen Waverley	70b	37.53 S	145.10 E
Glenwood Landing	55	40.50 N	73.39 W
Glienicke	65a	52.37 N	13.19 E
Gloucester City	56b	39.54 N	75.07 W
Goff's Oak	62	51.43 N	0.05 W
Golabāri	67a	22.36 N	88.20 E
Golden Gate (Str.)	58b	37.49 N	122.29 W
Golders Green (Neigh.)	62	51.35 N	0.12 W
Golf	58a	42.03 N	87.48 W
Golf Park Terrace	58a	42.03 N	87.51 W
Gonesse	64c	48.59 N	2.27 E
González Catán	60d	34.46 S	58.39 W
Gordons Corner	56d	39.50 N	76.57 W
Gore Hill	70a	33.49 S	151.11 E
Gorton (Neigh.)	64b	53.27 N	2.10 W
Gosen	65a	52.24 N	13.43 E
Gotanno (Neigh.)	69a	35.46 N	139.49 E
Götterswickerhamm	63	51.35 N	6.40 E
Göttin	65a	52.27 N	12.54 E
Gournay-sur-Marne	64c	48.52 N	2.34 E
Goussainville	64c	49.01 N	2.28 E
Go-vap	68m	10.49 N	106.42 E
Governador, Ilha do (I.)	61c	22.48 S	43.12 W
Grafenberg (Neigh.)	63	51.14 N	6.50 E
Gran Canal del Desagüe (Can.)	60a	19.29 N	99.05 W
Grand Island	57a	43.01 N	78.58 W
Grand I.	57a	43.02 N	78.58 W
Grandyle	57a	43.00 N	78.57 W
Grange Hill	62	51.37 N	0.05 E
Granite	56c	39.21 N	76.51 W
Grant Park (P. Int.)	58a	41.52 N	87.37 W
Granville	70a	33.50 S	151.01 E
Grassendale (Neigh.)	64b	53.21 N	2.54 W
Gravesend	62	51.27 N	0.24 E
Grays	62	51.29 N	0.20 E
Greasby	64b	53.23 N	3.07 W
Great Altcar	64b	53.33 N	3.01 W
Great Bookham	62	51.16 N	0.22 W
Great Burstead	62	51.36 N	0.25 E
Great Crosby	64b	53.29 N	3.01 W
Great Falls	56d	39.00 N	77.17 W
Great Kills (Neigh.)	55	40.33 N	74.10 W
Great Neck	55	40.47 N	73.44 W
Great Oxney Green	62	51.44 N	0.25 E
Great Parndon	62	51.45 N	0.05 E
Great Sutton	64b	53.17 N	2.56 W
Great Warley	62	51.35 N	0.17 E
Greco (Neigh.)	65c	45.30 N	9.13 E
Greenbelt	56d	39.01 N	76.53 W
Greenbrae	58b	37.57 N	122.31 W
Greenfield Park	54b	45.29 N	73.29 W
Greenhithe	62	51.27 N	0.17 E
Green Meadows	56d	38.58 N	76.57 W
Greenmount	64b	53.37 N	2.20 W
Greensborough	70b	37.42 S	145.06 E
Greenside (Neigh.)	71b	26.09 S	28.01 E
Greenstead	62	51.42 N	0.14 E
Green Street	62	51.40 N	0.16 W
Green Street Green (Neigh.)	62	51.21 N	0.04 E
Greenvale	55	40.49 N	73.38 W
Greenwich	70a	33.50 S	151.11 E
Greenwich (Neigh.)	62	51.28 N	0.02 E
Greenwich Observatory (P. Int.)	62	51.28 N	0.00
Greenwich Village (Neigh.)	55	40.44 N	74.00 W
Greenwood	54a	42.29 N	71.04 W
Greiffenburg (P. Int.)	63	51.20 N	6.38 E
Grevel (Neigh.)	63	51.34 N	7.33 E
Greystanes	70a	33.49 S	150.58 E
Grimlinghausen (Neigh.)	63	51.10 N	6.44 E
Grinzing (Neigh.)	66e	48.15 N	16.21 E
Grossbeeren	65a	52.21 N	13.18 E
Grossenbaum (Neigh.)	63	51.22 N	6.47 E
Gross-Enzersdorf	66e	48.12 N	16.33 E
Grosse Pointe	57c	42.24 N	82.55 W
Grosse Pointe Farms	57c	42.25 N	82.53 W
Grosse Pointe Park	57c	42.23 N	82.56 W
Grosse Pointe Woods	57c	42.27 N	82.55 W
Grossjedlersdorf (Neigh.)	66e	48.17 N	16.25 E
Gross Ziethen	65a	52.24 N	13.27 E
Gruiten	63	51.14 N	7.01 E
Grumme (Neigh.)	63	51.30 N	7.14 E
Grünau (Neigh.)	65a	52.25 N	13.34 E
Grünewald	63	51.13 N	7.37 E
Grunewald (Neigh.)	65a	52.30 N	13.17 E
Guadalupe, Basílica de (P. Int.)	60a	19.29 N	99.07 W
Guaianazes (Neigh.)	61d	23.33 S	46.25 W
Guaire (R.)	61a	10.25 N	66.46 W
Guanabacoa	60b	23.07 N	82.18 W
Guanabara, Baía de (B.)	61c	22.50 S	43.10 W
Guanyintang	67b	39.52 N	116.31 E
Guaracarumbo	61a	10.34 N	66.59 W
Guarulhos	61d	23.28 S	46.32 W
Guermantes	64c	48.51 N	2.42 E
Guildford	70a	33.51 S	150.59 E
Gulph Mills	56b	40.04 N	75.21 W
Gustavo A. Madero	60a	19.29 N	99.07 W
Guttenberg	55	40.48 N	74.01 W
Guyancourt	64c	48.46 N	2.04 E

H

PLACE	PAGE	Lat.°′	Long.°′
Haan	63	51.11 N	7.00 E
Haar (Neigh.)	63	51.26 N	7.13 E
Haberfield	70a	33.53 S	151.08 E
Hachiōji	69a	35.39 N	139.20 E
Hacienda Heights	59	33.58 N	117.58 W
Hackensack	55	40.53 N	74.03 W
Hacketts	62	51.45 N	0.05 W
Hackney (Neigh.)	62	51.33 N	0.03 W
Haddonfield	56b	39.54 N	75.02 W
Haddon Heights	56b	39.52 N	75.02 W
Hadersdorf (Neigh.)	66e	48.13 N	16.14 E
Hadfield	70b	37.42 S	144.56 E
Haemgon-ni (Neigh.)	68b	37.35 N	126.49 E
Hagen	63	51.22 N	7.28 E
Hahnenberg	63	51.12 N	7.24 E
Haidārpur (Neigh.)	67d	28.43 N	77.09 E
Haidian	67b	39.59 N	116.18 E
Haijima	69a	35.42 N	139.21 E
Hainault (Neigh.)	62	51.36 N	0.06 E
Halden (Neigh.)	63	51.23 N	7.31 E
Hale, Eng.	64b	53.23 N	2.21 W
Halebarns	64b	53.22 N	2.19 W
Haledon	55	40.56 N	74.11 W
Halethorpe	56c	39.15 N	76.41 W
Halewood	64b	53.22 N	2.49 W
Haliç (B.)	66f	41.02 N	28.58 E
Hallam	70b	38.01 S	145.06 E
Halstead	62	51.20 N	0.08 E
Halver	63	51.11 N	7.30 E
Ham (Neigh.)	62	51.26 N	0.19 W
Hamberg	71b	26.11 S	27.53 E
Hamborn (Neigh.)	63	51.29 N	6.46 E
Hamm (Neigh.), F.R.G.	63	51.12 N	6.44 E
Hammersmith (Neigh.)	62	51.30 N	0.14 W
Hammond	58a	41.36 N	87.30 W
Hammondville	70a	33.57 S	150.57 E
Hampstead (Neigh.)	62	51.33 N	0.11 W
Hampstead Heath (P. Int.)	62	51.34 N	0.10 W
Hampton	70b	37.56 S	145.00 E
Hampton (Neigh.)	62	51.25 N	0.22 W
Hampton National Historic Site (P. Int.)	56c	39.25 N	76.35 W
Hamtramck	57c	42.24 N	83.03 W
Handforth	64b	53.21 N	2.13 W
Han-gang (R.)	68b	37.36 N	126.47 E
Hang Hau Town	68c	22.19 N	114.16 E
Hanover	56c	39.11 N	76.42 W
Hanworth (Neigh.)	62	51.26 N	0.23 W
Hapsford	64b	53.16 N	2.48 W
Haramachida	69a	35.33 N	139.27 E
Harbor City (Neigh.)	59	33.48 N	118.17 W
Harbord	70a	33.45 S	151.26 E
Harbor Isle	55	40.36 N	73.40 W
Harefield (Neigh.)	62	51.36 N	0.29 W
Haringey (Neigh.)	62	51.35 N	0.07 W
Harker Village	56b	39.51 N	75.09 W
Harlem (Neigh.)	55	40.49 N	73.56 W
Harlesden (Neigh.)	62	51.32 N	0.15 W
Harlington (Neigh.)	62	51.29 N	0.26 W
Harmar Heights	57b	40.33 N	79.49 W
Harmarville	57b	40.32 N	79.51 W
Harola	67d	28.36 N	77.19 E
Harold Hill (Neigh.)	62	51.36 N	0.13 E
Harold Wood (Neigh.)	62	51.36 N	0.14 E
Harpen (Neigh.)	63	51.29 N	7.16 E
Harper Woods	57c	42.24 N	82.55 W
Harpurhey (Neigh.)	64b	53.31 N	2.13 W
Harrison, NJ.	55	40.45 N	74.10 W
Harrison, NY.	55	40.58 N	73.43 W
Harrisonville	56c	39.23 N	77.50 W
Harris Park	70a	33.49 S	151.01 E
Harrow (Neigh.)	62	51.35 N	0.21 W
Harrow on the Hill (Neigh.)	62	51.34 N	0.20 W
Hartley	62	51.23 N	0.19 E
Harvel	62	51.21 N	0.22 E
Harvey	58a	41.37 N	87.39 W
Harwick	57b	40.34 N	79.48 W
Harwood, Eng.	64b	53.35 N	2.23 W
Harwood, Md.	56c	38.52 N	76.37 W
Harwood Heights	58a	41.59 N	87.48 W
Harwood Park	56c	39.12 N	76.44 W
Hasanābād	68h	35.44 N	51.19 E
Hasbrouck Heights	55	40.52 N	74.04 W
Haskayne	64b	53.34 N	2.58 W
Hasköy (Neigh.)	66f	41.02 N	28.58 E
Hasselbeck-Schwarzbach	63	51.16 N	6.53 E
Hassels (Neigh.)	63	51.10 N	6.53 E
Hasslinghausen	63	51.20 N	7.17 E
Hästen (Neigh.), F.R.G.	63	51.09 N	7.06 E
Hasten (Neigh.), F.R.G.	63	51.12 N	7.09 E
Hastingwood	62	51.45 N	0.09 E
Hattingen	63	51.23 N	7.10 E
Hatton (Neigh.)	62	51.28 N	0.25 W
Hattori	69b	34.46 N	135.27 E
Hatzfeld (Neigh.)	63	51.17 N	7.11 E
Haughton Green	64b	53.27 N	2.06 W
Hauz Rāni (Neigh.)	67d	28.32 N	77.13 E
Havana	60b	23.08 N	82.22 W
Havel-Kanal (Can.)	65a	52.36 N	13.12 E
Haverford	56b	40.01 N	75.18 W
Havering (Neigh.)	62	51.34 N	0.14 E
Havering-atte-Bower (Neigh.)	62	51.37 N	0.11 E
Havering's Grove	62	51.38 N	0.23 E
Havertown	56b	39.59 N	75.18 W
Hawaiian Gardens	59	33.50 N	118.04 W
Hawf, Jabal (Hills)	71a	29.55 N	31.21 E
Hawley	62	51.25 N	0.14 E
Haworth	55	40.58 N	73.59 W
Hawthorn	70b	37.49 S	145.02 E
Hawthorne, Ca.	59	33.55 N	118.21 W
Hawthorne, NJ.	55	40.57 N	74.09 W
Hayes (Neigh.), Eng.	62	51.23 N	0.01 E
Hazel Grove	64b	53.23 N	2.08 W
Headley	62	51.17 N	0.16 W
Heald Green	64b	53.22 N	2.14 W
Heathmont	70b	37.49 S	145.15 E
Heaton Moor	64b	53.25 N	2.11 W
Heaverham	62	51.18 N	0.15 E
Heaviley	64b	53.24 N	2.09 W
Hebbville	56c	39.20 N	77.46 W
Heerdt (Neigh.)	63	51.13 N	6.43 E
Heide (Neigh.), F.R.G.	63	51.31 N	6.52 E
Heidelberg, Austl.	70b	37.45 S	145.04 E
Heidelberg, Pa.	57b	40.23 N	80.05 W
Heil	63	51.38 N	7.35 E
Heiligenhaus	63	51.19 N	6.59 E
Heiligensee (Neigh.)	65a	52.36 N	13.13 E
Heinersdorf	65a	52.23 N	13.20 E
Heinersdorf (Neigh.)	65a	52.34 N	13.27 E
Heisingen (Neigh.)	63	51.25 N	7.04 E
Heliopolis, see Misr al-Jadīdah (Neigh.)	71a	30.06 N	31.20 E
Heliopolis (P. Int.)	71a	30.08 N	31.17 E
Helsby	64a	53.16 N	2.46 W
Hemel Hempstead	62	51.46 N	0.28 W
Hempstead	55	40.42 N	73.37 W
Hennigsdorf	65a	52.38 N	13.13 E
Herbede	63	51.25 N	7.16 E
Herdecke	63	51.24 N	7.26 E
Hermannskogel (Mtn.)	66e	48.16 N	16.18 E
Hermosa Beach	59	33.52 N	118.24 W
Hermsdorf (Neigh.)	65a	52.37 N	13.18 E
Hernals (Neigh.)	66e	48.13 N	16.20 E
Herne	63	51.32 N	7.13 E
Hernwood Heights	56c	39.22 N	77.50 W
Héroes Chapultepec	60a	19.28 N	99.04 W
Héroes de Churubusco	60a	19.22 N	99.06 W
Herongate	62	51.36 N	0.21 E
Heronsgate	62	51.38 N	0.31 W
Hersham	62	51.22 N	0.23 W
Herten	63	51.35 N	7.07 E
Heswall	64b	53.20 N	3.06 W
Hetzendorf (Neigh.)	66e	48.10 N	16.18 E
Heven (Neigh.)	63	51.26 N	7.17 E
Hewlett	55	40.38 N	73.42 W
Hewlett Harbor	55	40.38 N	73.41 W
Hextable	62	51.25 N	0.11 E
Heywood	64b	53.36 N	2.13 W
Hickory Hills	58a	41.43 N	87.49 W
Hicksville	55	40.46 N	73.32 W
Hiddinghausen	63	51.22 N	7.17 E
Hiesfeld	63	51.33 N	6.46 E
Hietzing (Neigh.)	66e	48.11 N	16.18 E
Higashi (Neigh.)	69b	34.41 N	135.31 E
Higashimurayama	69a	35.46 N	139.29 E
Higashinada (Neigh.)	69b	34.43 N	135.16 E
Higashinakano	69a	35.38 N	139.25 E
Higashinari (Neigh.)	69b	34.40 N	135.33 E
Higashiōizumi (Neigh.)	69a	35.45 N	139.36 E
Higashiōsaka	69b	34.39 N	135.35 E
Higashisumiyoshi (Neigh.)	69b	34.37 N	135.32 E
Higashiyama (Neigh.)	68e	34.52 N	135.48 E
Higashiyodogawa (Neigh.)	69b	34.44 N	135.29 E
Higham Upshire	62	51.26 N	0.28 E
High Beach	62	51.39 N	0.02 E
Highcliff	57b	40.32 N	80.03 W
Higher Broughton (Neigh.)	64b	53.30 N	2.15 W
Highland	57b	40.33 N	80.04 W
Highland Park, Md.	56d	38.54 N	76.54 W
Highland Park, Mi.	57c	42.24 N	83.06 W
Highlands North (Neigh.)	71b	26.09 S	28.05 E
High Laver	62	51.45 N	0.13 E
High Ongar	62	51.43 N	0.16 E
Hightown	64b	53.32 N	3.04 W
Hilden	63	51.10 N	6.56 E
Hillbrow (Neigh.)	71b	26.11 S	28.03 E
Hill Crest	56b	40.05 N	75.11 W
Hillcrest Heights	56d	38.52 N	76.57 W
Hillen (Neigh.)	63	51.37 N	7.13 E
Hillingdon (Neigh.)	62	51.32 N	0.27 W
Hillside	56d	38.52 N	76.55 W
Hillside (Neigh.)	55	40.42 N	73.47 W
Hillwood	56d	38.52 N	77.10 W
Hiltrop (Neigh.)	63	51.30 N	7.15 E
Himmelgeist (Neigh.)	63	51.10 N	6.49 E
Hingham	54a	42.14 N	70.53 W
Hingham	54a	42.17 N	70.55 W
Hino	69a	35.41 N	139.24 E
Hinsdale	58a	41.48 N	87.56 W
Hinsel (Neigh.)	63	51.26 N	7.05 E
Hirota	69b	34.45 N	135.21 E
Hirschstetten (Neigh.)	66e	48.14 N	16.29 E
Hither Green (Neigh.)	62	51.27 N	0.01 W
Hoboken	55	40.45 N	74.03 W
Hobsons B.	70b	37.51 S	144.56 E
Hochdahl	63	51.13 N	6.56 E
Hochheide	63	51.27 N	6.41 E
Ho Chi Minh City (Saigon)	68m	10.45 N	106.40 E
Hochlar (Neigh.)	63	51.36 N	7.10 E
Höchsten	63	51.27 N	7.29 E
Hodgkins	58a	41.46 N	87.51 W
Hofburg (P. Int.)	66e	48.12 N	16.22 E
Hogar y Redención	60a	19.22 N	99.13 W
Hohenlimburg	63	51.21 N	7.35 E
Hohen-Neuendorf	65a	52.40 N	13.16 E
Hohenschönhausen (Neigh.)	65a	52.33 N	13.30 E
Hohensyburg (P. Int.)	63	51.25 N	7.29 E
Höhscheid (Neigh.)	63	51.09 N	7.04 E
Hoisten	63	51.08 N	6.42 E
Holborn (Neigh.)	62	51.31 N	0.07 W
Holbrook	54a	42.09 N	71.01 W
Hollins	64b	53.34 N	2.17 W
Hollis (Neigh.)	55	40.43 N	73.46 W
Hollywood (Neigh.)	59	34.06 N	118.21 W
Hollywood Bowl (P. Int.)	59	34.07 N	118.20 W
Holmes	56b	39.54 N	75.19 W
Holmes Run Acres	56d	38.51 N	77.13 W
Holroyd	70a	33.50 S	150.58 E
Holten (Neigh.)	63	51.31 N	6.48 E
Holthausen (Neigh.)	63	51.34 N	7.26 E
Holzen	63	51.26 N	7.31 E
Holzheim	63	51.09 N	6.39 E
Holzwickede	63	51.30 N	7.36 E
Homberg, F.R.G.	63	51.28 N	6.43 E
Homestead	57b	40.24 N	79.54 W
Hometown	58a	41.44 N	87.44 W
Homewood (Neigh.)	57b	40.27 N	79.54 W
Höntrop (Neigh.)	63	51.27 N	7.08 E
Hooghly (R.)	67a	22.33 N	88.15 E
Hooghly-Chinsura	67a	22.54 N	88.24 E
Hooton	64b	53.18 N	2.57 W
Hoppegarten	65a	52.31 N	13.40 E
Hörde (Neigh.)	63	51.29 N	7.30 E
Horinouchi (Neigh.)	69a	35.41 N	139.40 E
Hornchurch (Neigh.)	62	51.34 N	0.12 E
Horndon on the Hill	62	51.31 N	0.25 E
Horneburg	63	51.38 N	7.18 E
Horn Hill	62	51.37 N	0.32 W
Hornsby	70a	33.42 S	150.06 E
Hornsey (Neigh.)	62	51.35 N	0.07 W
Horsell	62	51.19 N	0.34 W
Horsley	70a	33.51 S	150.51 E
Horst (Neigh.)	63	51.32 N	7.02 E
Horsthausen (Neigh.)	63	51.33 N	7.13 E
Horstmar (Neigh.)	63	51.36 N	7.33 E
Hortaleza (Neigh.)	65b	40.28 N	3.39 W
Horton Kirby	62	51.23 N	0.15 E
Hösel	63	51.19 N	6.54 E
Hospitalet	65e	41.22 N	2.08 E
Hough Green	64b	53.23 N	2.47 W
Houilles	64c	48.56 N	2.11 E
Hounslow (Neigh.)	62	51.29 N	0.22 W
Howard Beach (Neigh.)	55	40.40 N	73.51 W
Howrah	67a	22.35 N	88.20 E
Howrah Bridge (P. Int.)	67a	22.35 N	88.21 E
Hoxton Park	70a	33.55 S	150.51 E
Hōya	69a	35.43 N	139.34 E
Hsinchuang	68d	25.02 N	121.26 E
Huangcun	67b	39.56 N	116.11 E
Huangpu (R.)	68a	31.18 N	121.33 E
Hubbelrath	63	51.16 N	6.55 E
Hückeswagen	63	51.08 N	7.20 E
Hudson (R.)	55	40.42 N	74.02 W

PLACE	PAGE	Lat.°'	Long.°'
Hügel, Villa (P. Int.)	63	51.25 N	7.01 E
Huipulco	60a	19.17 N	99.09 W
Hülscheid	63	51.16 N	7.34 E
Humber (R.)	54c	43.38 N	79.28 W
Humboldt, Planetario (P. Int.)	61a	10.30 N	66.50 W
Hunters Hill	70a	33.50 S	151.09 E
Huntington	56d	38.48 N	77.15 W
Huntington Park	59	33.59 N	118.13 W
Huntington Woods	57c	42.29 N	83.10 W
Hunt's Cross (Neigh.)	64b	53.21 N	2.51 W
Huntsville	56d	38.55 N	76.54 W
Hurlingham	60d	34.36 S	58.38 W
Hurstville	70a	33.58 S	151.06 E
Husen (Neigh.)	63	51.33 N	7.36 E
Hütteldorf (Neigh.)	66e	48.12 N	16.16 E
Hüttenheim (Neigh.)	63	51.22 N	6.43 E
Hutton	62	51.38 N	0.22 E
Huttrop (Neigh.)	63	51.27 N	7.03 E
Hyattsville	56d	38.56 N	76.56 W
Hyde	64b	53.27 N	2.04 W
Hyde Park (Neigh.)	58a	41.48 N	87.36 W
Hyōgo (Neigh.)	69b	34.47 N	135.10 E
Hythe End	62	51.27 N	0.32 W

I

PLACE	PAGE	Lat.°'	Long.°'
Ibaraki	69b	34.49 N	135.34 E
Iberoamericana, Universidad (P. Int.)	60a	19.21 N	99.08 W
Ibese	71d	6.33 N	3.29 E
Ibirapuera (Neigh.)	61d	23.37 S	46.40 W
Ichāpur	67a	22.50 N	88.24 E
Ichikawa	69a	35.44 N	139.55 E
Ickenham (Neigh.)	62	51.34 N	0.27 W
Ickern (Neigh.)	63	51.36 N	7.21 E
Iddo (Neigh.)	71d	6.28 N	3.23 E
Idylwood	56d	38.54 N	77.12 W
Iganmu (Neigh.)	71d	6.29 N	3.22 E
Igbobi	71d	6.32 N	3.22 E
Ightham	62	51.17 N	0.17 E
Ikeda	69b	34.49 N	135.25 E
Ikeja	71d	6.36 N	3.21 E
Ikoma	69b	34.41 N	135.42 E
Ikorodu	71d	6.37 N	3.31 E
Ikoyi (Neigh.)	71d	6.27 N	3.26 E
Ikoyi I.	71d	6.27 N	3.26 E
Ikuno (Neigh.)	69b	34.39 N	135.33 E
Ikuta (Neigh.)	69b	34.42 N	135.11 E
Ilchester	56c	39.15 N	76.46 W
Île-Cadieux	54b	45.25 N	74.01 W
Ilioúpolis	66d	37.56 N	23.45 E
Illovo	71b	26.08 S	28.03 E
Ilverich	63	51.17 N	6.42 E
Imbābah	71a	30.04 N	31.13 E
Inagi	69a	35.38 N	139.30 E
Inatsuke (Neigh.)	69a	35.46 N	139.43 E
Ince	64b	53.17 N	2.49 W
Ince Blundell	64b	53.31 N	3.02 W
Independence	56a	41.23 N	81.39 W
Independence National Historical Park (P. Int.)	56b	39.57 N	75.09 W
In der Bredde	63	51.20 N	7.23 E
India Gate (P. Int.)	67d	28.37 N	77.18 E
Indian Head Park	58a	41.47 N	87.54 W
Indianola	57b	40.34 N	79.51 W
Indianópolis (Neigh.)	61d	23.36 S	46.38 W
Indian Springs	56d	38.49 N	77.10 W
Indonesian Culture, Museum of (P. Int.)	68k	6.09 N	106.49 E
Industria (Neigh.)	71b	26.12 S	27.59 E
Ingatestone	62	51.41 N	0.22 E
Ingeniero Budge (Neigh.)	60d	34.43 S	58.28 W
Ingleburn	70a	34.00 S	150.52 E
Ingleside (Neigh.)	58b	37.43 N	122.28 W
Inglewood	59	33.58 N	118.21 W
Ingomar	57b	40.35 N	80.05 W
Ingram	57b	40.26 N	80.04 W
Ingrave	62	51.36 N	0.21 E
Inkster	57c	42.17 N	83.17 W
Inwood	55	40.37 N	73.45 W
Inzersdorf (Neigh.)	66e	48.09 N	16.21 E
Ipanema (Neigh.)	61c	22.59 S	43.12 W
Irby	64b	53.21 N	3.07 W
Irlam	64b	53.28 N	2.25 W
Iron Cove (B.)	70a	33.52 S	151.10 E
Irving Park (Neigh.)	58a	41.57 N	87.43 W
Irvington (Neigh.)	56c	39.17 N	76.41 W
Isando	71b	26.09 S	28.12 E
Iselin	55	40.34 N	74.19 W
Isidro Casanova	60d	34.42 S	58.35 W
Island Park	55	40.36 N	73.40 W
Isleworth (Neigh.)	62	51.28 N	0.20 W
Islington (Neigh.), Can.	54c	43.39 N	79.32 W
Islington (Neigh.), Eng.	62	51.34 N	0.06 W
Ismā'īlīyah (Neigh.)	71a	30.03 N	31.14 E
Issy-les-Moulineaux	64c	48.49 N	2.17 E
Istanbul	66f	41.01 N	28.58 E
Istead Rise	62	51.24 N	0.22 E
Itaipu	61c	22.58 S	43.02 W
Itaipu, Ponta de (C.)	61c	22.59 S	43.03 W
Itami	69b	34.46 N	135.25 E
Itaquaquecetuba	61d	23.29 S	46.21 W
Itire	71d	6.31 N	3.21 E
Ituzaingó	60d	34.40 S	58.40 W
Iupeba	61d	23.41 S	46.22 W
Ivanhoe	70b	37.46 S	145.03 E
Iver	62	51.31 N	0.30 W
Iver Heath	62	51.32 N	0.31 W
Ivry-sur-Seine	64c	48.49 N	2.23 E
Ixtacalco	60a	19.23 N	99.07 W
Ixtapalapa	60a	19.21 N	99.06 W

J

PLACE	PAGE	Lat.°'	Long.°'
Jabavu	71b	26.15 S	27.53 E
Jacarepaguá (Neigh.)	61c	22.56 S	43.20 W
Jackson, Port (B.)	70a	33.50 S	151.16 E
Jackson Heights (Neigh.)	55	40.45 N	73.53 W
Jacomino	60b	23.06 N	82.20 W
Jade Buddha, Temple of the (Yufosi) (P. Int.)	68a	31.14 N	121.26 E
Jakarta	68k	6.10 S	106.48 E
Jamaica B.	55	40.36 N	73.51 W
Jamālīyah (Neigh.)	71a	30.03 N	31.16 E
Jameson Raid Memorial (P. Int.)	71b	26.11 S	27.49 E
Jardim Paulista (Neigh.)	61d	23.35 S	46.40 W
Jardines del Pedregal de San Angel	60a	19.18 N	99.13 W
Jasenevo (Neigh.)	66b	55.36 N	37.33 E
Jazīrat Muhammad	71a	30.07 N	31.12 E
Jedlesee (Neigh.)	66e	48.16 N	16.23 E
Jefferson	57b	39.56 N	80.04 W
Jefferson Park (Neigh.)	58a	41.59 N	87.46 W
Jenkintown	56b	40.06 N	75.08 W
Jericho	55	40.48 N	73.32 W
Jersey City	55	40.44 N	74.02 W
Jésus, Île (I.)	54b	45.35 N	73.45 W
Jesús del Monte (Neigh.)	60b	23.06 N	82.22 W
Jesús María	60c	12.04 S	77.04 W
Jhenkāri	67a	22.46 N	88.18 E
Jhil Kuranga (Neigh.)	67d	28.40 N	77.17 E
Jiangwan	68a	31.18 N	121.29 E
Jiugang	67b	39.49 N	116.27 E
Johannesburg	71b	26.15 S	28.00 E
Johannisthal (Neigh.)	65a	52.26 N	13.30 E
John Carroll University (P. Int.)	56a	41.29 N	81.32 W
John F. Kennedy International Arpt.	55	40.38 N	73.47 W
Johns Hopkins University (P. Int.)	56c	39.20 N	76.37 W
Johor Baharu	67c	1.27 N	103.45 E
Johor, Selat (Str.)	67c	1.28 N	103.48 E
Joinville-le-Pont	64c	48.49 N	2.28 E
José C. Paz	60d	34.32 S	58.44 W
Jouy-en-Josas	64c	48.46 N	2.10 E
Juan Anchorena (Neigh.)	60d	34.29 S	58.30 W
Juan González Romero	60a	19.30 N	99.04 W
Jugo-Zapad (Neigh.)	66b	55.40 N	37.32 E
Juilly	64c	49.01 N	2.42 E
Juniata (Neigh.)	56b	40.01 N	75.07 W
Jurong	67c	1.21 N	103.42 E
Justice	58a	41.45 N	87.50 W
Juvisy-sur-Orge	64c	48.41 N	2.23 E
Jwālahari (Neigh.)	67d	28.40 N	77.06 E

K

PLACE	PAGE	Lat.°'	Long.°'
Kaarst	63	51.14 N	6.37 E
Kabel (Neigh.)	63	51.24 N	7.29 E
Kadıköy (Neigh.)	66f	40.59 N	29.01 E
Kadoma	69b	34.44 N	135.35 E
Kagran (Neigh.)	66e	48.15 N	16.27 E
Kaidori	69a	35.37 N	139.27 E
Kaisariani	66d	37.58 N	23.47 E
Kaisermühlen (Neigh.)	66e	48.14 N	16.26 E
Kaiserwerth (Neigh.)	63	51.18 N	6.44 E
Kalamákion	66d	37.55 N	23.43 E
Kalina (Neigh.)	71c	4.18 S	15.16 E
Kālkāji (Neigh.)	67d	28.33 N	77.16 E
Kalksburg (Neigh.)	66e	48.08 N	16.15 E
Kalkum	63	51.18 N	6.46 E
Kallithéa	66d	37.57 N	23.42 E
Kāmārhāti	67a	22.40 N	88.22 E
Kamata (Neigh.)	69a	35.33 N	139.43 E
Kāmdebpur	67a	22.54 N	88.20 E
Kameari (Neigh.)	69a	35.46 N	139.51 E
Kameido (Neigh.)	69a	35.42 N	139.50 E
Kamiakatsuka (Neigh.)	69a	35.46 N	139.39 E
Kamiasao	69a	35.35 N	139.30 E
Kamiishihara	69a	35.39 N	139.32 E
Kamikitazawa (Neigh.)	69a	35.40 N	139.38 E
Kamioyamada	69a	35.35 N	139.24 E
Kamitsuruma	69a	35.31 N	139.25 E
Kamoshida (Neigh.)	69a	35.34 N	139.30 E
Kamp-Lintfort	63	51.30 N	6.31 E
Kampong Kranji	67c	1.26 N	103.46 E
Kampong Loyang	67c	1.22 N	103.58 E
Kampong Tanjong Keling	67c	1.18 N	103.42 E
Kanai	69a	35.35 N	139.28 E
Kanamachi (Neigh.)	69a	35.56 N	139.53 E
Kanamori	69a	35.32 N	139.28 E
Kangaroo Ground	70b	37.41 S	145.13 E
Kanzaki (R.)	69b	34.42 N	135.25 E
Kapellen	63	51.25 N	6.35 E
Kapotn'a (Neigh.)	66b	55.38 N	37.48 E
Karave	67e	19.01 N	73.01 E
Karkar Dūmān (Neigh.)	67d	28.39 N	77.18 E
Karnap	63	51.09 N	6.56 E
Karolinenhof (Neigh.)	65a	52.23 N	13.38 E
Kasai (Neigh.)	69a	35.39 N	139.53 E
Kashiwara	69b	34.35 N	135.37 E
Kasslerfeld (Neigh.)	63	51.26 N	6.45 E
Katano	69b	34.48 N	135.42 E
Katayama (Neigh.)	69a	35.46 N	139.34 E
Katernberg (Neigh.), F.R.G.	63	51.29 N	7.04 E
Katsura (R.)	68e	34.53 N	135.42 E
Katsushika (Neigh.)	69a	35.43 N	139.51 E
Katternberg (Neigh.)	63	51.09 N	7.02 E
Kaulsdorf-Süd (Neigh.)	65a	52.29 N	13.34 E
Kawaguchi	69a	35.48 N	139.43 E
Kawanishi	69b	34.49 N	135.24 E
Kawasaki	69a	35.32 N	139.43 E
Kawashima (Neigh.)	69a	35.28 N	139.35 E
Kearny	55	40.46 N	74.09 W
Kearsley	64b	53.32 N	2.23 W
Kebayoram (Neigh.)	68k	6.12 S	106.46 E
Keilor	70b	37.43 S	144.50 E
Kelenföld (Neigh.)	66g	47.28 N	19.03 E
Kellyville	70a	33.43 S	150.57 E
Kelvedon Hatch	62	51.40 N	0.16 E
Kemminghausen (Neigh.)	63	51.34 N	7.29 E
Kempton Park	71b	26.06 S	28.14 E
Kemsing	62	51.18 N	0.14 E
Kenberma	54a	42.17 N	70.52 W
Kenilworth, Il.	58a	42.05 N	87.43 W
Kenilworth, NJ.	55	40.41 N	74.18 W
Kenley (Neigh.)	62	51.19 N	0.06 W
Kenmore	57a	42.58 N	78.53 W
Kensington, Austl.	70a	33.55 S	151.14 E
Kensington, Ca.	58b	37.54 N	122.16 W
Kensington, Md.	56d	39.02 N	77.03 W
Kensington (Neigh.), NY.	55	40.39 N	73.58 W
Kensington (Neigh.), Pa.	56b	39.58 N	75.08 W
Kensington (Neigh.), S. Afr.	71b	26.12 S	28.06 E
Kensington and Chelsea (Neigh.)	62	51.29 N	0.11 W
Kentland	56d	38.55 N	76.53 W
Keon Park	70b	37.42 S	145.01 E
Keratsínion	66d	37.58 N	23.37 E
Kettwig	63	51.22 N	6.56 E
Kew, Austl.	70b	37.49 S	145.02 E
Kew, S. Afr.	71b	26.08 S	28.06 E
Kew Gardens (P. Int.)	62	51.28 N	0.18 W
Khaïdhárion	66d	37.33 N	22.53 E
Khajuri (Neigh.)	67d	28.43 N	77.16 E
Khalándrion	66d	38.01 N	23.48 E
Khardah	67a	22.44 N	88.22 E
Khayāla (Neigh.)	67d	28.40 N	77.06 E
Khichripur (Neigh.)	67d	28.37 N	77.19 E
Kholargós	66d	38.00 N	23.48 E
Khorel	67a	22.42 N	88.19 E
Kibouendé	71c	4.19 S	15.11 E
Kichijōji	69a	35.42 N	139.35 E
Kidderpore (Neigh.)	67a	22.31 N	88.19 E
Kierspe	63	51.08 N	7.35 E
Killara	70a	33.46 S	151.09 E
Killarney Heights	70a	33.46 S	151.13 E
Kilokri (Neigh.)	67d	28.35 N	77.16 E
King George's Res.	62	51.39 N	0.01 W
King of Prussia	56b	40.05 N	75.23 W
Kingsbury (Neigh.)	62	51.35 N	0.17 W
Kingsdown	62	51.21 N	0.17 E
Kingsford	70a	33.56 S	151.14 E
Kingsgrove	70a	33.57 S	151.06 E
Kings Langley	62	51.43 N	0.28 W
Kings Park	56d	38.48 N	77.15 W
Kings Point	55	40.49 N	73.45 W
Kingston upon Thames (Neigh.)	62	51.25 N	0.19 W
Kinshasa (Léopoldville)	71c	4.18 S	15.18 E
Kinshasa-Est (Neigh.)	71c	4.18 S	15.18 E
Kinshasa-Quest (Neigh.)	71c	4.20 S	15.15 E
Kintamo, Rapides de	71c	4.19 S	15.15 E
Kintsana	71c	4.19 S	15.10 E
Kirchderne (Neigh.)	63	51.33 N	7.30 E
Kirchende	63	51.25 N	7.26 E
Kirchhellen	63	51.36 N	6.55 E
Kirchhellen Heide (For.)	63	51.36 N	6.53 E
Kirchhörde (Neigh.)	63	51.27 N	7.27 E
Kirchlinde (Neigh.)	63	51.32 N	7.22 E
Kirdāsah	71a	30.02 N	31.07 E
Kirkby	64b	53.29 N	2.54 W
Kirkdale (Neigh.)	64b	53.26 N	2.59 W
Kirkland	54b	45.27 N	73.52 W
Kirkwood	56d	38.57 N	76.58 W
Kirwan Heights	57b	40.22 N	80.06 W
Kishar Bāla	68h	35.49 N	51.13 E
Kısıklı (Neigh.)	66f	41.01 N	29.03 E
Kiso	69a	35.34 N	139.26 E
Kistarcsa	66g	47.33 N	19.16 E
Kita (Neigh.)	69a	35.45 N	139.44 E
Kitamachi (Neigh.)	69a	35.46 N	139.39 E
Kitamba (Neigh.)	71c	4.19 S	15.14 E
Kitatawara	69b	34.44 N	135.42 E
Kiyose	69a	35.47 N	139.32 E
Kizuki	69a	35.34 N	139.40 E
Kizuri	69b	34.39 N	135.34 E
Kledering (Neigh.)	66e	48.08 N	16.26 E
Kleef	63	51.11 N	6.56 E
Kleinbeeren	65a	52.22 N	13.20 E
Klein Elandsvlei	71b	26.09 S	27.39 E
Kleinebroich	63	51.12 N	6.35 E
Kleinmachnow	65a	52.24 N	13.15 E
Klein Ziethen	65a	52.23 N	13.27 E
Kley (Neigh.)	63	51.30 N	7.22 E
Klip (R.)	71b	26.16 S	27.49 E
Klippoortje	71b	26.17 S	28.14 E
Kliptown	71b	26.17 S	27.53 E
Knockholt	62	51.18 N	0.06 E
Knockholt Pound	62	51.19 N	0.08 E
Knoppiesfontein	71b	26.05 S	28.25 E
Knott's Berry Farm (P. Int.)	59	33.50 N	118.00 W
Knotty Ash (Neigh.)	64b	53.25 N	2.54 W
Knowsley	64b	53.27 N	2.51 W
Knowsley Hall (P. Int.)	64b	53.26 N	2.50 W
Knox	70b	37.53 S	145.18 E
Kōbe	69b	34.41 N	135.10 E
Kodaira	69a	35.44 N	139.29 E
Koganei	69a	35.42 N	139.32 E
Kogarah	70a	33.58 S	151.08 E
Kokubunji	69a	35.42 N	139.29 E
Kolomenskoje (Neigh.)	66b	55.40 N	37.41 E
Kolonie Stolp	65a	52.28 N	13.46 E
Komae	69a	35.38 N	139.35 E
Komagome (Neigh.)	69a	35.44 N	139.45 E
Kondli (Neigh.)	67d	28.37 N	77.19 E
Königshardt (Neigh.)	63	51.33 N	6.51 E
Konnagar	67a	22.42 N	88.22 E
Konohana (Neigh.)	69b	34.41 N	135.16 E
Kōnoike	69b	34.42 N	135.37 E
Kooyong	70b	37.50 S	145.02 E
Kōri	69b	34.47 N	135.39 E
Koridhallós	66d	37.59 N	23.39 E
Kosino	66b	55.43 N	37.52 E
Kosmosa, Monument (P. Int.)	66b	55.49 N	37.38 E
Kōtō (Neigh.)	69a	35.41 N	139.48 E
Kowloon (Jiulong)	68c	22.18 N	114.10 E
Kowloon City	68c	22.19 N	114.11 E
Kozukue (Neigh.)	69a	35.30 N	139.36 E
Krahenhöhe (Neigh.)	63	51.10 N	7.06 E
Krampnitz	65a	52.28 N	13.04 E
Krasnyj Stroitel' (Neigh.)	66b	55.35 N	37.37 E
Kray (Neigh.)	63	51.28 N	7.05 E
Krefeld	63	51.20 N	6.34 E
Kreml' (P. Int.)	66b	55.45 N	37.37 E
Kreuzberg	63	51.09 N	7.27 E
Kreuzberg (Neigh.)	65a	52.30 N	13.23 E
Krishnapur	67a	22.36 N	88.26 E
Krugersdorp	71b	26.05 S	27.35 E
Krugersdorp West	71b	26.06 S	27.45 E
Krummenerl	63	51.05 N	7.45 E
Krummensee	65a	52.36 N	13.42 E
Krylatskoje (Neigh.)	66b	55.45 N	37.26 E
Küçükbakkal	66f	40.58 N	29.06 E
Kudbrooke (Neigh.)	62	51.28 N	0.03 E
Küllenhahn (Neigh.)	63	51.14 N	7.08 E
Kunitachi	69a	35.41 N	139.26 E
Kupferdreh (Neigh.)	63	51.23 N	7.05 E
Ku-ring-gai	70a	33.45 S	151.08 E
Kurl (Neigh.)	63	51.35 N	7.35 E
Kurla (Neigh.)	67e	19.05 N	72.53 E
Kurnell	70a	34.01 S	151.13 E
Kuruçeşme (Neigh.)	66f	41.03 N	29.02 E
Kurume	69a	35.45 N	139.32 E
Kuskovo (Neigh.)	66b	55.44 N	37.49 E
Kuz'minki (Neigh.)	66b	55.42 N	37.48 E
Kwa-Thema	71b	26.18 S	28.23 E
Kyōto	68e	35.00 N	135.45 E
Kyūhōji (Neigh.)	69b	34.38 N	135.35 E

L

PLACE	PAGE	Lat.°'	Long.°'
Laab im Walde	66e	48.09 N	16.11 E
Laaken (Neigh.)	63	51.15 N	7.15 E
La Bandera	61b	33.34 S	70.39 W
La Boissière	64c	48.46 N	1.59 E
La Canada	59	34.12 N	118.12 W
La Candelaria	60a	19.20 N	99.09 W
Lachine	54c	45.26 N	73.40 W
Lachta (Neigh.)	66a	60.00 N	30.09 E
La Cisterna	61b	33.33 S	70.41 W
Lackawanna	57a	42.49 N	78.50 W
La Courneuve	64c	48.56 N	2.23 E
La Dolorita	61a	10.29 N	66.47 W
Lafayette Hill	56b	40.05 N	75.15 W
Laferrere	60d	34.45 S	58.35 W
Laflèche	54b	45.30 N	73.28 W
La Floresta	65e	41.27 N	2.04 E
La Florida	61b	33.33 S	70.34 W
La Frette-sur-Seine	64c	48.58 N	2.11 E
La Garenne-Colombes	64c	48.55 N	2.15 E
Lagny	64c	48.52 N	2.43 E
Lagos	71d	6.27 N	3.24 E
La Grange	58a	41.49 N	87.55 W
La Grange Highlands	58a	41.48 N	87.53 W
La Grange Park	58a	41.50 N	87.52 W
La Granja	61b	33.32 S	70.39 W
La Guaira	61a	10.36 N	66.56 W
La Guardia Arpt.	55	40.46 N	73.53 W

PLACE	PAGE	Lat.°′	Long.°′
Mayfair (Neigh.), S. Afr.	71b	26.12 S	28.01 E
Mayfair West (Neigh.)	71b	26.12 S	28.00 E
Maywood, Ca.	59	33.59 N	118.11 W
Maywood, Il.	58a	41.53 N	87.51 W
Maywood, NJ.	55	40.56 N	74.04 W
Mazilovo (Neigh.)	66b	55.44 N	37.26 E
Mazorra	60b	23.01 N	82.24 W
Meadowlands	71b	26.13 S	27.54 E
Meckinghoven	63	51.37 N	7.19 E
Medford	54a	42.25 N	71.07 W
Medford Hillside	54a	42.24 N	71.07 W
Media	56b	39.54 N	75.23 W
Medvedkovo (Neigh.)	66b	55.53 N	37.38 E
Meerbusch	63	51.15 N	6.41 E
Meguro (Neigh.)	69a	35.38 N	139.42 E
Mehpālpur (Neigh.)	67d	28.33 N	77.08 E
Mehrābād	68h	35.40 N	51.20 E
Mehram Nagar (Neigh.)	67d	28.34 N	77.07 E
Mehrow	65a	52.34 N	13.37 E
Mehrum	63	51.35 N	6.37 E
Meide	63	51.11 N	6.55 E
Meiderich (Neigh.)	63	51.28 N	6.46 E
Meidling (Neigh.)	66e	48.11 N	16.20 E
Meiersberg	63	51.17 N	6.57 E
Meiji Shrine (P. Int.)	69a	35.41 N	139.42 E
Melbourne	70b	37.49 S	144.58 E
Melling	64b	53.30 N	2.56 W
Melrose	54a	42.27 N	71.04 W
Melrose Highlands	54a	42.28 N	71.04 W
Melrose Park	58a	41.54 N	87.51 W
Menden (Neigh.)	63	51.24 N	6.54 E
Mengede (Neigh.)	63	51.34 N	7.23 E
Menglinghausen (Neigh.)	63	51.28 N	7.25 E
Menlo Park Terrace	55	40.32 N	74.20 W
Mentone	70b	37.59 S	145.05 E
Meopham	62	51.22 N	0.22 E
Meopham Station	62	51.23 N	0.21 E
Mercader y Millás	65e	41.21 N	2.05 E
Mercês	65d	38.47 N	9.19 W
Merdeka Palace (P. Int.)	68k	6.10 S	106.49 E
Mere	64b	53.20 N	2.25 W
Meredale	71b	26.17 S	27.59 E
Merion Station	56b	40.00 N	75.15 W
Merlo	60d	34.40 S	58.45 W
Merlynston	70b	37.43 S	144.58 E
Merri (Cr.)	70b	37.48 S	145.01 E
Merrick	55	40.40 N	73.33 W
Merrifield	56d	38.52 N	77.14 W
Merrionette Park	58a	41.41 N	87.42 W
Merrylands	70a	33.50 S	150.59 E
Merscheid (Neigh.)	63	51.10 N	7.01 E
Mersey (R.)	64b	53.26 N	3.01 W
Merton (Neigh.)	62	51.25 N	0.12 W
Meščerskij	66b	55.40 S	37.25 E
Mesquita	61c	22.48 S	43.26 W
Messy	64c	48.58 N	2.42 E
Metropolitan Museum of Art (P. Int.)	55	40.47 N	73.58 W
Mettmann	63	51.15 N	6.58 E
Meudon	64c	48.48 N	2.14 E
Mexico City (Ciudad de México)	60a	19.24 N	99.09 W
Mia-dong (Neigh.)	68b	37.37 N	127.01 E
Michajlovskoje	66b	55.35 N	37.35 E
Michillinda	59	34.07 N	118.05 W
Middleburgh Heights	56a	41.22 N	81.48 W
Middle River	56c	39.19 N	76.27 W
Middleton	64b	53.33 N	2.13 W
Midland Beach (Neigh.)	55	40.34 N	74.05 W
Midlothian	58a	41.38 N	87.42 W
Midway	71b	26.18 S	27.51 E
Midway City	59	33.45 N	118.00 W
Milan (Milano)	65c	45.28 N	9.12 E
Milford	56c	39.21 N	76.44 W
Millbourne	56b	39.58 N	75.15 W
Millbrae	58b	37.36 N	122.24 W
Millburn	55	40.44 N	74.20 W
Mill Green	62	51.41 N	0.22 E
Mill Hill (Neigh.)	62	51.37 N	0.13 W
Mill Neck	55	40.52 N	73.34 W
Millvale	57b	40.29 N	79.58 W
Mill Valley	58b	37.54 N	122.32 W
Milmont Park	56b	39.53 N	75.20 W
Milnrow	64b	53.37 N	2.06 W
Milon-la-Chapelle	64c	48.44 N	2.03 E
Milspe	63	51.18 N	7.21 E
Milton	54a	42.15 N	71.05 W
Minami (Neigh.), Jap.	68e	34.58 N	135.45 E
Minamisenju (Neigh.)	69a	35.44 N	139.48 E
Minato (Neigh.), Jap.	69a	35.39 N	139.45 E
Minato (Neigh.), Jap.	69b	34.39 N	135.26 E
Mineola	55	40.45 N	73.38 W
Minō	69b	34.50 N	135.28 E
Mintard	63	51.22 N	6.54 E
Minto	70a	34.01 S	150.51 E
Miquon	56b	40.04 N	75.16 W
Miraflores	60c	12.08 S	77.03 W
Miramar (Neigh.)	60b	23.07 N	82.25 W
Miranda	70a	34.02 S	151.06 E
Mirzāpur	67a	22.50 N	88.24 E
Misailovo	66b	55.34 N	37.49 E
Misr al-Jadīdah (Heliopolis) (Neigh.)	71a	30.06 N	31.20 E
Mişr al-Qadīmah (Old Cairo) (Neigh.)	71a	30.00 N	31.14 E
Mississauga	54c	43.35 N	79.37 W
Mitaka	69a	35.40 N	139.33 E
Mitcham	70b	37.49 S	145.12 E
Mitcham (Neigh.)	62	51.24 N	0.10 W
Mitry-Mory	64c	48.59 N	2.37 E
Mitte (Neigh.)	65a	52.31 N	13.24 E
Mixcoac (Neigh.)	60a	19.23 N	99.12 W
Miyakojima (Neigh.)	69b	34.43 N	135.33 E
Mizonokuchi	69a	35.36 N	139.37 E
Mizonuma	69a	35.48 N	139.36 E
Mizue (Neigh.)	69a	35.41 N	139.54 E
Mizuho	69a	35.46 N	139.21 E
Mnevniki (Neigh.)	66b	55.45 N	37.28 E
Moba	71d	6.27 N	3.28 E
Modderbee	71b	26.10 S	28.24 E
Modderfontein	71b	26.06 S	28.09 E
Modjeska	59	33.43 N	117.37 W
Mödling	66e	48.05 N	16.17 E
Moers	63	51.27 N	6.37 E
Mofolo	71b	26.14 S	27.53 E
Mohili (Neigh.)	67e	19.06 N	72.53 E
Molino de Rosas	60a	19.22 N	99.13 W
Molíns de Rey	65e	41.25 N	2.01 E
Möllen	63	51.35 N	6.42 E
Moncada	65e	41.29 N	2.11 E
Mondeor	71b	26.17 S	28.00 E
Mongat	65e	41.28 N	2.17 E
Monken Hadley (Neigh.)	62	51.40 N	0.11 W
Monongahela (R.)	57b	40.27 N	80.00 W
Monrovia	59	34.09 N	118.03 W
Montalbancito	61a	10.28 N	66.59 W
Montara	58b	37.33 N	122.31 W
Montclair, Ca.	59	34.06 N	117.41 W
Montclair, NJ.	55	40.49 N	74.13 W
Montebello	59	34.01 N	118.06 W
Monte Chingolo (Neigh.)	60d	34.45 S	58.20 W
Monterey Park	59	34.04 N	118.07 W
Montespaccato (Neigh.)	66c	41.54 N	12.23 E
Monteverde Nuovo (Neigh.)	66c	41.51 N	12.27 E
Montfermeil	64c	48.54 N	2.34 E
Montflorit	65e	41.29 N	2.08 E
Montgeron	64c	48.42 N	2.27 E
Montgomery Knolls	56c	39.14 N	76.48 W
Montigny-le-Bretonneux	64c	48.46 N	2.02 E
Montigny-lés-Cormeilles	64c	48.59 N	2.12 E
Montjuich, Castillo de (P. Int.)	65e	41.22 N	2.10 E
Montmagny	64c	48.58 N	2.21 E
Montmartre (Neigh.)	64c	48.53 N	2.21 E
Montmorency, Austl.	70b	37.43 S	145.07 E
Montmorency, Fr.	64c	49.00 N	2.20 E
Montréal	54b	45.31 N	73.34 W
Montréal-Nord	54b	45.36 N	73.38 W
Montréal-Quest	54b	45.27 N	73.39 W
Montreuil	64c	48.52 N	2.27 E
Montrose	70b	37.49 S	145.21 E
Montrose Hill	57b	40.30 N	79.51 W
Montrouge	64c	48.49 N	2.19 E
Mont-Royal	54b	45.31 N	73.39 W
Monza	65c	45.35 N	9.16 E
Moóca (Neigh.)	61d	23.33 S	46.35 W
Moonachie	55	40.50 N	74.03 W
Moorabbin	70b	37.56 S	145.02 E
Moorebank	70a	33.56 S	150.56 E
Moorestown	56b	39.58 N	74.57 W
Mooroolbark	70b	37.47 S	145.19 E
Moorside	64b	53.34 N	2.04 W
Morangis	64c	48.42 N	2.20 E
Mordialloc	70b	38.00 S	145.05 E
Morelos (Neigh.)	60a	19.27 N	99.07 W
Moreno	60d	34.39 S	58.48 W
Moreton	64b	53.24 N	3.07 W
Moriguchi	69b	34.44 N	135.34 E
Morivione (Neigh.)	65c	45.26 N	9.12 E
Morley Green	64b	53.20 N	2.16 W
Morningside	56d	38.50 N	76.53 W
Morón	60d	34.39 S	58.37 W
Morro, Castillo del (P. Int.)	60b	23.09 N	82.21 W
Mörsenbroich (Neigh.)	63	51.15 N	6.48 E
Mortlake	70a	33.51 S	151.07 E
Mortlake (Neigh.)	62	51.28 N	0.16 W
Morton	56b	39.55 N	75.20 W
Morton Grove	58a	42.02 N	87.47 W
Moscavide	65d	38.47 N	9.06 W
Moscow (Moskva)	66b	55.45 N	37.35 E
Moskháton	66d	37.57 N	23.41 E
Mosman	70a	33.49 S	151.14 E
Moss Bank	64b	53.29 N	2.44 W
Moss Beach	58b	37.32 N	122.31 W
Moss Crest	56d	38.55 N	77.15 W
Mossley	64b	53.32 N	2.02 W
Mossley Hill (Neigh.)	64b	53.23 N	2.55 W
Mottingham (Neigh.)	62	51.26 N	0.03 E
Mount Baldy	59	34.14 N	117.40 W
Mount Dennis (Neigh.)	54c	43.42 N	79.30 W
Mount Druitt	70a	33.46 S	150.49 E
Mount Ephraim	56b	39.53 N	75.06 W
Mount Greenwood (Neigh.)	58a	41.42 N	87.43 W
Mount Hebron	56c	39.18 N	76.50 W
Mount Lebanon	57b	40.23 N	80.03 W
Mountnessing	62	51.39 N	0.21 E
Mount Oliver	57b	40.28 N	79.59 W
Mount Pritchard	70a	33.54 S	150.54 E
Mount Prospect	58a	42.04 N	87.56 W
Mount Rainier	56d	38.56 N	76.58 W
Mount Vernon, NY	55	40.54 N	73.50 W
Mount Vernon, Pa.	57b	40.17 N	79.48 W
Mount Washington (Neigh.)	56c	39.22 N	76.40 W
Mount Washington Summit	56c	39.23 N	76.40 W
Mount Waverley	70b	37.53 S	145.08 E
Moylan	56b	39.54 N	75.23 W
Mucking	62	51.30 N	0.26 E
Mühlenbeck	65a	52.40 N	13.22 E
Mühleiten	66e	48.10 N	16.34 E
Mujāhidpur (Neigh.)	67d	28.34 N	77.13 E
Mukō	68e	34.56 N	135.42 E
Mülheim an der Ruhr	63	51.24 N	6.54 E
Münchehofe	65a	52.30 N	13.40 E
Mündelheim (Neigh.)	63	51.21 N	6.41 E
Munhall	57b	40.24 N	79.53 W
Munirka (Neigh.)	67d	28.34 N	77.10 E
Munro (Neigh.)	60d	34.32 S	58.31 W
Murayama	69a	35.45 N	139.23 E
Murtal	65d	38.42 N	9.22 W
Musashino	69a	35.42 N	139.34 E
Mushin	71d	6.32 N	3.22 E
Musturud	71a	30.08 N	31.17 E
Mytischi	66b	55.55 N	37.46 E
N			
Nächstebreck (Neigh.)	63	51.18 N	7.14 E
Nagao	69b	34.50 N	135.43 E
Nagaoka	68e	34.55 N	135.42 E
Nagata (Neigh.)	69b	34.40 N	135.09 E
Nagatino (Neigh.)	66b	55.41 N	37.41 E
Nagatsuta (Neigh.)	69a	35.32 N	139.30 E
Nagytarcsa	66g	47.32 N	19.17 E
Nahaut	54a	42.25 N	70.55 W
Nahant B.	54a	42.27 N	70.55 W
Nahmer	63	51.20 N	7.35 E
Nāhyā	71a	30.03 N	31.07 E
Naihāti	67a	22.54 N	88.25 E
Naka (R.)	69a	35.39 N	139.51 E
Nakagyō (Neigh.)	68e	35.01 N	135.45 E
Nakajima	69a	35.26 N	139.56 E
Nakanobu (Neigh.)	69a	35.36 N	139.43 E
Namamugi (Neigh.)	69a	35.29 N	139.41 E
Nancefield	71b	26.17 S	27.53 E
Naniwa (Neigh.)	69b	34.39 N	135.30 E
Nānole (Neigh.)	67e	19.01 N	72.55 E
Nanterre	64c	48.53 N	2.12 E
Nantouillet	64c	49.00 N	2.42 E
Nanxiang	68a	31.17 N	121.18 E
Nanyuan	67b	39.48 N	116.23 E
Naoābād	67a	22.28 N	88.27 E
Naopukuria	67a	22.55 N	88.16 E
Nārāyanpāra	67a	22.54 N	88.19 E
Narberth	56b	40.01 N	75.18 W
Narrabeen	70a	33.43 S	151.18 E
Narraweena	70a	33.45 S	151.16 E
Narre Warren North	70b	37.59 S	145.19 E
Naruo	69b	34.43 N	135.23 E
Nātāgarh	67a	22.42 N	88.25 E
Natalspruit	71b	26.19 S	28.09 E
National Park	56b	39.51 N	75.12 W
Naupada (Neigh.)	67e	19.04 N	72.50 E
Navestock	62	51.39 N	0.13 E
Navestock Side	62	51.39 N	0.16 E
Navotas	68g	14.40 N	120.57 E
Nayābās	67d	28.45 N	77.19 E
Nazlat as-Sammān	71a	29.59 N	31.08 E
Nazlat Khalīfah	71a	30.01 N	31.10 E
Ndjili (Neigh.)	71c	4.20 S	15.22 E
Néa Ionía	66d	38.02 N	23.45 E
Néa Liósia	66d	38.02 N	23.42 E
Near North Side (Neigh.)	58a	41.54 N	87.38 W
Néa Smírni	66d	37.57 N	23.43 E
Nedlitz (Neigh.)	65a	52.26 N	13.03 E
Needham	54a	42.17 N	71.14 W
Needham Heights	54a	41.28 N	71.14 W
Nee Soon	67c	1.24 N	103.49 E
Nematābād	68h	35.38 N	51.12 E
Nemčinovka	66b	55.43 N	37.23 E
Néon Psikhikón	66d	38.00 N	23.47 E
Ness	64b	53.17 N	3.03 W
Neston	64b	53.18 N	3.04 W
Netherton	64b	53.30 N	2.58 W
Nette (Neigh.)	63	51.33 N	7.25 E
Neudorf (Neigh.)	63	51.25 N	6.47 E
Neuenhagen bei Berlin	65a	52.32 N	13.41 E
Neuenhof (Neigh.)	63	51.10 N	7.13 E
Neuenkamp (Neigh.)	63	51.26 N	6.44 E
Neu-Erlaa (Neigh.)	66e	48.08 N	16.19 E
Neu Fahrland	65a	52.26 N	13.03 E
Neuilly-sur-Marne	64c	48.51 N	2.32 E
Neuilly-sur-Seine	64c	48.53 N	2.16 E
Neukirchen-Vluyn	63	51.27 N	6.33 E
Neuss	63	51.12 N	6.41 E
Neusserweyhe (Neigh.)	63	51.13 N	6.39 E
Neustift am Walde (Neigh.)	66e	48.15 N	16.18 E
Neuville-sur-Oise	64c	49.01 N	2.04 E
Neuwaldegg (Neigh.)	66e	48.14 N	16.17 E
Neva (R.)	66a	59.55 N	30.15 E
Neves	61c	22.51 S	43.06 W
Neviges	63	51.19 N	7.05 E
Neville I.	57b	40.31 N	80.08 W
Newabāgam	67a	22.48 N	88.24 E
New Addington (Neigh.)	62	51.21 N	0.01 W
Newark	55	40.44 N	74.10 W
New Brighton	64b	53.26 N	3.03 W
New Brighton (Neigh.)	55	40.38 N	74.06 W
Newburgh Heights	56a	41.27 N	81.40 W
New Carrollton	56d	35.58 N	76.53 W
Newclare (Neigh.)	71b	26.11 S	27.58 E
New Delhi	67d	28.36 N	77.12 E
New Eltham (Neigh.)	62	51.26 N	0.04 E
New Ferry	64b	53.22 N	2.59 W
Newgate Street	62	51.44 N	0.07 W
Newham (Neigh.)	62	51.32 N	0.03 E
New Hey	64b	50.36 N	2.06 W
New Hyde Park	55	40.44 N	73.41 W
New Hythe	62	51.19 N	0.27 E
New Kowloon (Xinjiulong)	68c	22.20 N	114.10 E
New Lagos (Neigh.)	71d	6.30 N	3.22 E
Newmarket	71b	26.17 S	28.08 E
New Milford	55	40.56 N	74.01 W
Newport	70b	37.51 S	144.53 E
New Redruth	71b	26.16 S	28.07 E
New Rochelle	55	40.55 N	73.47 W
Newton	54a	42.21 N	71.11 W
Newton Brook (Neigh.)	54c	43.48 N	79.24 W
Newton Highlands	54a	41.19 N	71.13 W
Newton Lower Falls	54a	42.19 N	71.23 W
Newton Upper Falls	54a	42.19 N	71.13 W
Newtonville	54a	42.21 N	71.13 W
Newton (Neigh.)	70a	33.54 S	151.11 E
New Utrecht (Neigh.)	55	40.36 N	73.59 W
New York	55	40.43 N	74.01 W
Neyagawa	69b	34.46 N	135.38 E
Ngamouéri	71c	4.14 S	15.14 E
Ngombe	71c	4.24 S	15.11 E
Niagara Falls, Can.	57a	43.06 N	79.04 W
Niagara Falls, NY	57a	43.06 N	79.02 W
Niederaden (Neigh.)	63	51.36 N	7.34 E
Niederbonsfeld	63	51.23 N	7.08 E
Niederdonk	63	51.14 N	6.41 E
Niederelfringhausen	63	51.21 N	7.10 E
Nieder-Neuendorf	65a	52.37 N	13.12 E
Niederschöneweide (Neigh.)	65a	52.27 N	13.31 E
Niederschönhausen (Neigh.)	65a	52.35 N	13.23 E
Niemeyer (Neigh.)	61c	23.00 S	43.15 W
Nierst	63	51.19 N	6.43 E
Nihonbashi (Neigh.)	69a	35.41 N	139.47 E
Niiza	69a	35.48 N	139.34 E
Níkaia	66d	37.58 N	23.39 E
Nikolo-Chovanskoje	66b	55.36 N	37.27 E
Niles	58a	42.01 N	87.49 W
Nilgani	67a	22.46 N	88.26 E
Nilópolis	61c	22.49 S	43.25 W
Nine Ashes	62	51.42 N	0.18 E
Nishi	69b	34.41 N	135.30 E
Nishinari (Neigh.)	69b	34.38 N	135.28 E
Nishionmiya	69b	34.43 N	135.20 E
Nishiyodogawa (Neigh.)	69b	34.42 N	135.27 E
Niterói	61c	22.53 S	43.07 W
Noborito	69a	35.37 N	139.34 E
Nogent-sur-Marne	64c	48.50 N	2.29 E
Noisy-le-Grand	64c	48.51 N	2.33 E
Noisy-le-Roi	64c	48.51 N	2.04 E
Noisy-le-Sec	64c	48.53 N	2.28 E
Nonantum	54a	42.20 N	71.12 W
Norden	64b	53.38 N	2.13 W
Norf	63	51.09 N	6.43 E
Normandy Heights	56c	39.17 N	76.48 W
Normanhurst	70a	33.43 S	151.06 E
Norridge	58a	41.57 N	87.49 W
Norristown	56b	40.07 N	75.21 W
North Abington	54a	42.08 N	70.57 W
North Arlington	55	40.47 N	74.08 W
North Auburn	70a	33.50 S	151.02 E
North Balwyn	70b	37.48 S	145.05 E
North Barnaby	56d	38.49 N	76.57 W
North Barrackpore	67a	22.46 N	88.22 E
North Beach (Neigh.)	58b	37.48 N	122.25 W
North Bellmore	55	40.41 N	73.32 W
North Bergen	55	40.48 N	74.01 W
North Box Hill	70b	37.48 S	145.07 E
North Braddock	57b	40.24 N	79.52 W
Northbridge	70a	33.49 S	151.13 E
North Caldwell	55	40.52 N	74.16 W
Northcliff (Neigh.)	71b	26.09 S	27.58 E
Northcote	70b	37.46 S	145.00 E
North Downs (Plat.)	62	51.10 N	0.10 E
North Dum-Dum	67a	22.38 N	88.23 E
North Englewood	56d	38.55 N	76.55 W
North Essendon	70b	37.45 S	144.54 E
Northfield	58a	42.06 N	87.46 W
North Fitzroy	70b	37.47 S	144.59 E
Northfleet	62	51.27 N	0.21 E
North Germiston	71b	26.14 S	28.09 E
North Haledon	55	40.58 N	74.11 W
North Hanover	54a	42.09 N	70.52 W
North Hills	55	40.47 N	73.41 W
North Hollywood (Neigh.)	59	34.10 N	118.23 W
Northlake	58a	41.55 N	87.54 W
North Manly	70a	33.46 S	151.16 E
Northmead, Austl.	70a	33.47 S	151.00 E
Northmead, S. Afr.	71b	26.10 S	28.20 E
North Merrick	55	40.41 N	73.34 W
North Ockendon (Neigh.)	62	51.32 N	0.18 E
North Olmsted	56a	41.25 N	81.56 W
North Parramatta	70a	33.48 S	151.00 E
North Philadelphia (Neigh.)	56b	39.58 N	75.09 W
North Point	68c	22.17 N	114.12 E
North Quincy	54a	42.17 N	71.01 W
North Randolph	54a	42.12 N	71.04 W

PLACE	PAGE	Lat.°′	Long.°′
Tehrān	68h	35.40 N	51.26 E
Tekstil'ščiki (Neigh.)	66b	55.42 N	37.44 E
Tela	67d	28.44 N	77.20 E
Teltow	65a	52.23 N	13.16 E
Teltower Hochfläche (Plat.)	65a	52.22 N	13.20 E
Tempelhof (Neigh.)	65a	52.28 N	13.23 E
Temple City	59	34.07 N	118.03 W
Temple Hills	56d	38.49 N	76.57 W
Temple of Heaven (P. Int.)	67b	39.53 N	116.25 E
Templestowe	70b	37.45 S	145.07 E
Temple University (P. Int.)	56b	39.59 N	75.09 W
Tenafly	55	40.56 N	73.58 W
Tennōji (Neigh.)	69b	34.39 N	135.31 E
Tepalcates	60a	19.23 N	99.04 W
Tepepan	60a	19.16 N	99.08 W
Terminal I.	59	33.45 N	118.15 W
Teterboro	55	40.52 N	74.03 W
Tevere (Tiber) (R.)	66c	41.49 N	12.25 E
Thākurpukur	67a	22.28 N	88.19 E
Thames (R.)	62	51.30 N	0.29 E
Thames Ditton	62	51.23 N	0.21 W
Thāna Cr.	67e	19.00 N	72.57 E
Thatto Heath	64b	53.26 N	2.45 W
The Basin	70b	37.51 S	145.19 E
The Capital (P. Int.)	56d	38.53 N	77.00 W
The Narrows (Str.)	55	40.37 N	74.03 W
The Oval (P. Int.)	62	51.29 N	0.07 W
The Sound (Str.)	70a	33.49 S	151.17 E
Theydon Bois	62	51.40 N	0.06 E
Thiais	64c	48.46 N	2.23 E
Thier	63	51.05 N	7.22 E
Thistletown (Neigh.)	54c	43.44 N	79.33 W
Thomaston	55	40.47 N	73.43 W
Thomastown	70b	37.41 S	145.01 E
Thon Buri (Neigh.)	68f	13.43 N	100.29 E
Thong	62	51.24 N	0.24 E
Thong Hoe	67c	1.25 N	103.42 E
Thong-tay-hoi	68m	10.50 N	106.39 E
Thorigny-sur-Marne	64c	48.53 N	2.42 E
Thornbury	70b	37.45 S	145.00 E
Thornhill	71b	26.07 S	28.09 E
Thornleigh	70a	33.44 S	151.05 E
Thornton	64b	53.30 N	3.00 W
Thornton Hough	64b	53.19 N	3.03 W
Thornton-le-Moors	64b	53.16 N	2.50 W
Thornwood Common	62	51.43 N	0.08 E
Tiburon	58b	36.04 N	119.19 W
Tiefenbroich	63	51.18 N	6.49 E
Tiergarten (Neigh.)	65a	52.31 N	13.21 E
Tiergarten (P. Int.)	65a	52.31 N	13.21 E
Tietê (R.)	61d	23.29 S	46.51 W
Tilbury	62	51.28 N	0.23 E
Timberview	56c	39.13 N	76.45 W
Times Square (P. Int.)	55	40.45 N	74.00 W
Timperley	64b	53.24 N	2.19 W
Ting Kau	68c	22.23 N	114.04 E
Tioga (Neigh.)	56b	40.00 N	75.10 W
Tires	65d	38.43 N	9.21 W
Titāgarh	67a	22.45 N	88.22 E
Tiu Keng Wan	68c	22.18 N	114.15 E
Tizapán	60a	19.20 N	99.13 W
Tláhuac	60a	19.16 N	99.00 W
Tlalnepantla	60a	19.33 N	99.12 W
Tlalpan	60a	19.17 N	99.10 W
Tlaltenco	60a	19.17 N	99.01 W
Toda	69a	35.48 N	139.41 E
Tokorozawa	69a	35.47 N	139.28 E
Toksu Palace (P. Int.)	68b	37.35 N	126.58 E
Tōkyō	69a	35.42 N	139.46 E
Tollygunge (Neigh.)	67a	22.30 N	88.21 E
Tolworth (Neigh.)	62	51.23 N	0.17 W
Tombs of the Caliphs (P. Int.)	71a	30.03 N	31.17 E
Tonawanda	57a	43.01 N	78.53 W
Tonawanda, Town of	57a	42.59 N	78.52 W
Tonawanda Cr.	57a	43.02 N	78.53 W
Tonda	69b	34.50 N	135.36 E
Tönsholt	63	51.38 N	6.58 E
Toongabbie	70a	33.47 S	150.57 E
Toot Hill	62	51.42 N	0.12 E
Topkapi (Neigh.)	66f	41.02 N	28.54 E
Topkapi Müzesi (P. Int.)	66f	41.00 N	28.59 E
T'oplyj Stan (Neigh.)	66b	55.37 N	37.30 E
Top of Hebers	64b	53.34 N	2.12 W
Toppings	64b	53.37 N	2.25 W
Torcy	64c	48.51 N	2.39 E
Tor di Quinto (Neigh.)	66c	41.56 N	12.28 E
Toronto	54c	43.39 N	79.23 W
Tor Pignatara (Neigh.)	66c	41.52 N	12.32 E
Torrance	59	33.50 N	118.19 W
Torrellas de Llobregat	65e	41.21 N	1.59 E
Tor Sapienza (Neigh.)	66c	41.54 N	12.35 E
Tortuguitas	60d	34.28 S	58.45 W
Toshima (Neigh.)	69a	35.44 N	139.43 E
Totowa	55	40.54 N	74.13 W
Tottenham (Neigh.)	62	51.35 N	0.04 W
Tottenville (Neigh.)	55	40.31 N	74.15 W
Totteridge (Neigh.)	62	51.38 N	0.12 W
Tottington	64b	53.37 N	2.20 W
Toussus-le-Noble	64c	48.45 N	2.07 E
Towaco	55	40.56 N	74.21 W
Tower Hamlets (Neigh.)	62	51.32 N	0.03 W
Tower of London (P. Int.)	62	51.30 N	0.05 W
Towers of Silence (P. Int.)	67e	18.58 N	72.48 E
Town Reach (Str.)	67c	1.28 N	103.44 E
Towson	56c	39.24 N	76.36 W
Toyoda	69a	35.39 N	139.23 E
Toyonaka	69b	34.47 N	135.28 E
Traar (Neigh.)	63	51.23 N	6.36 E
Trafaria	65d	38.40 N	9.14 W
Trafford Park	64b	53.28 N	2.20 W
Tranmere	64b	53.23 N	3.01 W
Trappes	64c	48.47 N	2.00 E
Tremblay-lès-Gonnesse	64c	48.59 N	2.34 E
Tremont (Neigh.)	55	40.51 N	73.55 W
Treptow (Neigh.)	65a	52.29 N	13.29 E
Tressancourt	64c	48.55 N	2.00 E
Triel-sur-Seine	64c	48.59 N	2.00 E
Tring	62	51.48 N	0.40 W
Troice-Lykovo (Neigh.)	66b	55.47 N	37.24 E
Trombay (Neigh.)	67e	19.02 N	72.57 E
Tropar'ovo (Neigh.)	66b	55.39 N	37.29 E
Trottiscliffe	62	51.19 N	0.21 E
Troyville (Neigh.)	71b	26.12 S	28.04 E
Tsing I.	68c	22.21 N	114.05 E
Tsin Shui Wan (B.)	68c	22.13 N	114.10 E
Tsuda	69b	34.49 N	135.43 E
Tsukumono (Neigh.)	69b	34.50 N	135.11 E
Tsunashima (Neigh.)	69a	35.32 N	139.38 E
Tsu Wan (Quanwan)	68c	22.22 N	114.07 E
Tsurumi (R.)	69a	35.29 N	139.41 E
Tuckahoe	55	40.57 N	73.50 W
Tullamarine	70b	37.41 S	144.52 E
Turffontein (Neigh.)	71b	26.15 S	28.02 E
Turranmurra	70a	33.44 S	151.08 E
Turtle Creek	57b	40.25 N	79.49 W
Tustin	59	33.45 N	117.49 W
Tuxedo	56d	38.55 N	76.55 W
Twickenham (Neigh.)	62	51.27 N	0.20 W
Tyler Park	56d	38.52 N	77.12 W
Tysons Corner	56d	38.55 N	77.14 W
U			
Ückendorf (Neigh.)	63	51.30 N	7.07 E
Uedesheim (Neigh.)	63	51.10 N	6.48 E
Uerdingen (Neigh.)	63	51.21 N	6.39 E
Uji	68e	34.53 N	135.48 E
Ukita (Neigh.)	69a	35.40 N	139.52 E
Üllendahl (Neigh.)	63	51.19 N	7.18 E
Unidad Sante Fe	60a	19.23 N	99.15 W
Union	55	40.42 N	74.16 W
Union City	55	40.46 N	74.02 W
Uniondale	55	40.43 N	73.36 W
United Nations Headquarters (P. Int.)	55	40.45 N	73.58 W
University Heights	56a	41.30 N	81.32 W
University Park	56d	38.58 N	76.57 W
Untermauerbach	66e	48.14 N	16.12 E
Upholland	64b	53.33 N	2.44 W
Upland	56b	39.51 N	75.23 W
Upper Brookville	55	40.51 N	73.34 W
Upper Darby	56b	39.58 N	75.16 W
Upper Ferntree Gully	70b	37.54 S	145.19 E
Upper New York B.	55	40.41 N	74.03 W
Upper Saint Clair	57b	40.21 N	80.05 W
Upper Tooting (Neigh.)	62	51.26 N	0.10 W
Upton, Eng.	62	51.30 N	0.35 W
Uptown (Neigh.)	58a	41.58 N	87.40 W
Upwey	70b	37.54 S	145.20 E
Urayasu	69a	35.39 N	139.54 E
Urmston	64b	53.27 N	2.21 W
Üsküdar (Neigh.)	66f	41.01 N	29.03 E
Usmānpur (Neigh.)	67d	28.41 N	77.15 E
Utfort	63	51.28 N	6.38 E
Utinga	61d	23.38 S	46.32 W
Uttarpara-Kotrung	67a	22.40 N	88.21 E
Uxbridge (Neigh.)	62	51.33 N	0.29 W
Uyama	69b	34.50 N	135.41 E
V			
Vaires-sur-Marne	64c	48.52 N	2.39 E
Valcanuta (Neigh.)	66c	41.53 N	12.25 E
Valentín Alsina (Neigh.)	60d	34.40 S	58.25 W
Valérien, Mont (Hill)	64c	48.53 N	2.13 E
Valldoreix	65e	41.28 N	2.04 E
Vallecas (Neigh.)	65b	40.23 N	3.37 W
Valleydale	59	34.06 N	117.56 W
Valley Mede	56c	39.17 N	76.50 W
Valley Stream, Md.	56c	39.23 N	76.41 W
Valley Stream, NY.	55	40.40 N	73.42 W
Vaniköy (Neigh.)	66f	41.04 N	29.04 E
Van Nuys (Neigh.)	59	34.11 N	118.26 W
Vanves	64c	48.50 N	2.18 E
Vanzago	65c	45.32 N	9.00 E
Vargem Grande (Neigh.)	61c	22.59 S	43.29 W
Várpalota (P. Int.)	66g	47.30 N	19.02 E
Vasiljevskij, Ostrov (I.)	66a	59.56 N	30.15 E
Vatican City (Città del Vaticano)	66c	41.54 N	12.27 E
Vaucluse	70a	33.51 S	151.17 E
Vaughan	54c	43.47 N	79.36 W
Vauhallan	64c	48.44 N	2.12 E
Vaujours	64c	48.56 N	2.35 E
Velbert	63	51.20 N	7.02 E
Venice (Neigh.)	59	34.00 N	118.29 W
Vennhausen (Neigh.)	63	51.13 N	6.51 E
Venterspos Location	71b	26.18 S	27.42 E
Verberg (Neigh.)	63	51.22 N	6.36 E
Verdun	54c	45.27 N	73.34 W
Verga	56b	39.52 N	75.10 W
Vermont	70b	37.50 S	145.12 E
Verona, NJ.	55	40.50 N	74.12 W
Verona, Pa.	57b	40.30 N	79.50 W
Verrières-le-Buisson	64c	48.45 N	2.16 E
Versailles, Fr.	64c	48.48 N	2.08 E
Versailles, Pa.	57b	40.21 N	79.51 W
Versailles (Neigh.)	60d	34.38 S	58.31 W
Versailles, Château de (P. Int.)	64c	48.48 N	2.07 E
Verulamium (P. Int.)	62	51.45 N	0.22 W
Vešn'aki (Neigh.)	66b	55.44 N	37.49 E
Vicálvaro (Neigh.)	65b	40.24 N	3.36 W
Vicente López	60d	34.32 S	58.29 W
Victoria (Xianggang)	68c	22.17 N	114.09 E
Victoria (Neigh.)	60d	34.28 S	58.31 W
Victoria I.	71c	6.26 N	3.26 E
Victoria Lawn Tennis Association Courts (P. Int.)	70b	37.51 S	145.02 E
Victoria Peak (Mtn.)	68c	22.17 N	114.08 E
Victoria Station (P. Int.)	64b	53.29 N	2.15 W
Vienna (Wien), Aus.	66e	48.13 N	16.20 E
Vienna, Va	56d	38.29 N	75.49 W
Vieringhausen (Neigh.)	63	51.11 N	7.10 E
View Park	59	34.00 N	118.21 W
Vigentino (Neigh.)	65c	45.25 N	9.11 E
Vila Augusta	61d	23.28 S	46.32 W
Vila Boacaya (Neigh.)	61d	23.29 S	46.44 W
Vila Guilherme (Neigh.)	61d	23.30 S	46.36 W
Vila Isabel (Neigh.)	61c	22.55 S	43.15 W
Vila Jaguára (Neigh.)	61d	23.31 S	46.45 W
Vila Madalena (Neigh.)	61d	23.33 S	46.42 W
Vila Mariana (Neigh.)	61d	23.35 S	46.38 W
Vila Progresso	61c	22.55 S	43.03 W
Vila Prudente (Neigh.)	61d	23.35 S	46.33 W
Villa Adelina (Neigh.)	60d	34.31 S	58.32 W
Villa Borghese (P. Int.)	66c	41.55 N	12.29 E
Villa Bosch (Neigh.)	60d	34.36 S	58.34 W
Villa Ciudadela (Neigh.)	60d	34.38 S	58.34 W
Villa de Mayo	60d	34.31 S	58.41 W
Villa Devoto (Neigh.)	60d	34.36 S	58.31 W
Villa Diamante (Neigh.)	60d	34.41 S	58.26 W
Villa Domínico (Neigh.)	60d	34.41 S	58.20 W
Villa José L. Suárez (Neigh.)	60d	34.32 S	58.34 W
Villa Lugano (Neigh.)	60d	34.41 S	58.28 W
Villa Lynch (Neigh.)	60d	34.36 S	58.32 W
Villa Madero	60d	34.41 S	58.30 W
Villa Nova, Md.	56c	39.21 N	76.44 W
Villanova, Pa.	56b	40.02 N	75.21 W
Villa Obregón	60a	19.21 N	99.12 W
Villa Real (Neigh.)	60d	34.37 S	58.31 W
Villa Sáenz Peña (Neigh.)	60d	34.46 S	58.31 W
Villa San Andrés (Neigh.)	60d	34.33 S	58.32 W
Villa Santos Lugares (Neigh.)	60d	34.36 S	58.32 W
Villa Turdera (Neigh.)	60d	34.48 S	58.25 W
Villaverde (Neigh.)	65b	40.21 N	3.42 W
Villebon-sur-Yvette	64c	48.42 N	2.15 E
Villecresnes	64c	48.43 N	2.32 E
Ville-d'Avray	64c	48.50 N	2.11 E
Villejuif	64c	48.48 N	2.22 E
Villemomble	64c	48.53 N	2.31 E
Villeneuve-la-Garenne	64c	48.56 N	2.20 E
Villeneuve-le-Roi	64c	48.44 N	2.25 E
Villeneuve-Saint-Georges	64c	48.44 N	2.27 E
Villeparisis	64c	48.56 N	2.37 E
Villevaudé	64c	48.55 N	2.39 E
Villiers-le-Bâcle	64c	48.44 N	2.08 E
Villiers-le-Bel	64c	49.00 N	2.23 E
Villiers-sur-Marne	64c	48.50 N	2.33 E
Vincennes	64c	48.51 N	2.26 E
Vincennes, Château de (P. Int.)	64c	48.51 N	2.26 E
Virgen del San Cristóbal (P. Int.)	61b	33.26 S	70.39 W
Virginia Hills	56d	38.47 N	77.06 W
Virginia Water	62	51.24 N	0.34 W
Viroflay	64c	48.48 N	2.10 E
Víron	66d	37.57 N	23.45 E
Vitacura	61b	33.24 S	70.36 W
Vitarte	60c	12.02 S	76.54 W
Vitry-sur-Seine	64c	48.48 N	2.24 E
Vladykino (Neigh.)	66b	55.52 N	37.36 E
Voerde, F.R.G.	63	51.35 N	6.41 E
Voesch	63	51.24 N	6.26 E
Vogelheim (Neigh.)	63	51.29 N	6.59 E
Vohwinkel (Neigh.)	63	51.14 N	7.09 E
Voisins-le-Bretonneux	64c	48.45 N	2.03 E
Volchonka-Zil (Neigh.)	66b	55.40 N	37.37 E
Vollme	63	51.10 N	7.36 E
Volmarstein	63	51.22 N	7.23 E
Volmerswerth (Neigh.)	63	51.11 N	6.46 E
Vorhalle (Neigh.)	63	51.23 N	7.28 E
Vormholz	63	51.24 N	7.18 E
W			
Wadeville	71b	26.16 S	28.11 E
Währing (Neigh.)	66e	48.14 N	16.21 E
Wahroonga	70a	33.43 S	150.07 E
Waidmannslust (Neigh.)	65a	52.36 N	13.20 E
Waitara	70a	33.43 S	150.06 E
Wakefield	54a	42.30 N	71.04 W
Waldbauer (Neigh.)	63	51.18 N	7.28 E
Walkden	64b	53.32 N	2.24 W
Wallach	63	51.35 N	6.34 E
Wallasey	64b	53.26 N	3.03 W
Wallgrove	70a	33.47 S	150.51 E
Wallingford	56b	39.54 N	75.22 W
Wallington	55	40.51 N	74.07 W
Wallington (Neigh.)	62	51.21 N	0.09 W
Walmersley	64b	53.37 N	2.18 W
Walnut	59	34.01 N	117.51 W
Walnut Park	59	33.58 N	118.13 W
Walpole	54a	42.08 N	71.15 W
Walsum	63	51.32 N	6.41 E
Walter Reed Army Medical Center (P. Int.)	56d	38.58 N	77.02 W
Waltersdorf	65a	52.22 N	13.35 E
Waltham	54a	42.23 N	71.14 W
Waltham Forest (Neigh.)	62	51.35 N	0.01 W
Walthamstow (Neigh.)	62	51.35 N	0.01 W
Walton	62	51.24 N	0.25 W
Walton on the Hill	62	51.17 N	0.15 W
Waltrop	63	51.37 N	7.23 E
Walt Whitman Homes	56b	39.52 N	75.11 W
Walze	63	51.16 N	7.31 E
Wambel (Neigh.)	63	51.32 N	7.32 E
Wandhofen	63	51.26 N	7.33 E
Wandsworth (Neigh.)	62	51.27 N	0.11 W
Wangsim-ni (Neigh.)	68b	37.36 N	127.03 E
Wanheimerort (Neigh.)	63	51.24 N	6.46 E
Wanne-Eickel	63	51.32 N	7.09 E
Wannsee (Neigh.)	65a	52.25 N	13.09 E
Wansdorf	65a	52.38 N	13.05 E
Wanstead (Neigh.)	62	51.34 N	0.02 E
Wantagh	55	40.40 N	73.30 W
Wantirna	70b	37.51 S	145.14 E
Wantirna South	70b	37.52 S	145.14 E
Ward	68h	35.48 N	51.10 E
Wardle	64b	53.39 N	2.08 W
Warlingham	62	51.19 N	0.04 W
War Memorial Stadium (P. Int.)	57a	42.54 N	78.52 W
Warrandyte	70b	37.45 S	145.13 E
Warrandyte South	70b	37.46 S	145.14 E
Warrāq al-'Arab	71a	30.06 N	31.12 E
Warrāq al-Hadar	71a	30.06 N	31.13 E
Warrāq al-Hadar wa Ambūtbah wa Mīt an-Naṣārā	71a	30.06 N	31.13 E
Warrawee	70a	33.44 S	151.07 E
Warren	57c	42.28 N	83.01 W
Warrensville Heights	56a	41.26 N	81.29 W
Wartenberg (Neigh.)	65a	52.34 N	13.31 E
Waseda University (P. Int.)	69a	35.42 N	139.43 E
Washington	56d	38.54 N	77.01 W
Washington Monument (P. Int.)	56d	38.53 N	77.03 W
Washington National Arpt.	56d	38.51 N	77.02 W
Wassmannsdorf	65a	52.22 N	13.28 E
Waterloo	64b	53.28 N	3.02 W
Watertown	54a	42.22 N	71.11 W
Watford	62	51.40 N	0.25 W
Watsonia	70b	37.43 S	145.05 E
Watsons Bay	70a	33.51 S	151.17 E
Wattenscheid	63	51.29 N	7.08 E
Watts (Neigh.)	59	33.56 N	118.15 W
Wattville	71b	26.13 S	28.18 E
Waveland	54a	42.17 N	70.53 W
Waverley	70a	33.54 S	151.16 E
Waverly	54a	42.23 N	71.11 W
Wayne, NJ.	55	40.55 N	74.17 W
Wayne, Pa.	56b	40.03 N	75.23 W
Wazīrābād (Neigh.)	67d	28.43 N	77.14 E
Wāzirpur (Neigh.)	67d	28.41 N	77.10 E
Wealdstone (Neigh.)	62	51.36 N	0.20 W
Wedau (Neigh.)	63	51.24 N	6.48 E
Wedding (Neigh.)	65a	52.33 N	13.22 E
Weddinghofen	63	51.36 N	7.37 E
Weehawken	55	40.46 N	74.01 W
Weesow	65a	52.39 N	13.43 E
Wegendorf	65a	52.36 N	13.45 E
Wehofen (Neigh.)	63	51.32 N	6.46 E
Wehringhausen (Neigh.)	63	51.21 N	7.27 E
Weidling	66e	48.17 N	16.19 E
Weidlingau (Neigh.)	66e	48.13 N	16.13 E
Weidlingbach	66e	48.16 N	16.15 E
Weitmar (Neigh.)	63	51.27 N	7.12 E
Welcome Monument (P. Int.)	68k	6.11 S	106.49 E
Welhamgreen	62	51.44 N	0.13 W
Welheim (Neigh.)	63	51.32 N	6.59 E

glossary of foreign geographical terms

Annam . . . Annamese
Arab . . . Arabic
Bantu . . . Bantu
Bur . . . Burmese
Camb . . . Cambodian
Celt . . . Celtic
Chn . . . Chinese
Czech . . . Czech
Dan . . . Danish
Du . . . Dutch
Fin . . . Finnish
Fr . . . French
Ger . . . German
Gr . . . Greek
Hung . . . Hungarian
Ice . . . Icelandic
India . . . India
Indian . . . American Indian
Indon . . . Indonesian
It . . . Italian
Jap . . . Japanese
Kor . . . Korean
Mal . . . Malayan
Mong . . . Mongolian
Nor . . . Norwegian
Per . . . Persian
Pol . . . Polish
Port . . . Portuguese
Rom . . . Romanian
Rus . . . Russian
Siam . . . Siamese
So. Slav . . . Southern Slavonic
Sp . . . Spanish
Swe . . . Swedish
Tib . . . Tibetan
Tur . . . Turkish
Yugo . . . Yugoslav

å, Nor., Swe . . . brook, river
aa, Dan., Nor . . . brook
aas, Dan., Nor . . . ridge
āb, Per . . . water, river
abad, India, Per . . . town, city
ada, Tur . . . island
adrar, Berber . . . mountain
air, Indon . . . stream
akrotírion, Gr . . . cape
älf, Swe . . . river
alp, Ger . . . mountain
altipiano, It . . . plateau
alto, Sp . . . height
archipel, Fr . . . archipelago
archipiélago, Sp . . . archipelago
arquipélago, Port . . . archipelago
arroyo, Sp . . . brook, stream
ås, Nor., Swe . . . ridge
austral, Sp . . . southern
baai, Du . . . bay
bab, Arab . . . gate, port
bach, Ger . . . brook, stream
backe, Swe . . . hill
bad, Ger . . . bath, spa
bahía, Sp . . . bay, gulf
bahr, Arab . . . river, sea, lake
baia, It . . . bay, gulf
baía, Port . . . bay
baie, Fr . . . bay, gulf
bajo, Sp . . . depression
bak, Indon . . . stream
bakke, Dan., Nor . . . hill
balkan, Tur . . . mountain range
bana, Jap . . . point, cape
banco, Sp . . . bank
bandar, Mal., Per. . . . town, port, harbor
bang, Siam . . . village
bassin, Fr . . . basin
batang, Indon., Mal . . . river
ben, Celt . . . mountain, summit
bender, Arab . . . harbor, port
bereg, Rus . . . coast, shore
berg, Du., Ger., Nor., Swe. . . . mountain, hill
bir, Arab . . . well
birkat, Arab . . . lake, pond, pool
bit, Arab . . . house
bjaerg, Dan., Nor . . . mountain
bocche, It . . . mouth
boğazı, Tur . . . strait
bois, Fr . . . forest, wood
boloto, Rus . . . marsh
bolsón, Sp. . . . flat-floored desert valley
boreal, Sp . . . northern
borg, Dan., Nor., Swe . . . castle, town
borgo, It . . . town, suburb
bosch, Du . . . forest, wood
bouche, Fr . . . river mouth
bourg, Fr . . . town, borough
bro, Dan., Nor., Swe . . . bridge
brücke, Ger . . . bridge
bucht, Ger . . . bay, bight
bugt, Dan., Nor., Swe . . . bay, gulf
bulu, Indon . . . mountain
burg, Du., Ger . . . castle, town
buri, Siam . . . town
burun, burnu, Tur . . . cape
by, Dan., Nor., Swe . . . village
caatinga, Port. (Brazil) . . . open brushland
cabezo, Sp . . . summit
cabo, Port., Sp . . . cape
campo, It., Port., Sp . . . plain, field
campos, Port. (Brazil) . . . plains
cañón, Sp . . . canyon
cap, Fr . . . cape
capo, It . . . cape
casa, It., Port., Sp . . . house
castello, It., Port . . . castle, fort
castillo, Sp . . . castle
càte, Fr . . . hill
çay, Tur . . . stream, river
cayo, Sp . . . rock, shoal, islet
cerro, Sp . . . mountain, hill
champ, Fr . . . field
chang, Chn . . . village, middle
château, Fr . . . castle
chen, Chn . . . market town
chiang, Chn . . . river
chott, Arab . . . salt lake
chou, Chn. . . . capital of district; island
chu, Tib . . . water, stream
cidade, Port . . . town, city
cima, Sp . . . summit, peak
città, It . . . town, city
ciudad, Sp . . . town, city
cochilha, Port . . . ridge
col, Fr . . . pass
colina, Sp . . . hill
cordillera, Sp . . . mountain chain
costa, It., Port., Sp . . . coast
côte, Fr . . . coast
cuchilla, Sp . . . mountain ridge
dağ, Tur . . . mountain(s)
dake, Jap . . . peak, summit
dal, Dan., Du., Nor., Swe . . . valley
dan, Kor . . . point, cape
danau, Indon . . . lake
dar, Arab . . . house, abode, country
darya, Per . . . river, sea
dasht, Per . . . plain, desert
deniz, Tur . . . sea
désert, Fr . . . desert
deserto, It . . . desert
desierto, Sp . . . desert
détroit, Fr . . . strait
dijk, Du . . . dam, dike
djebel, Arab . . . mountain
do, Kor . . . island
dorf, Ger . . . village
dorp, Du . . . village
duin, Du . . . dune
dzong, Tib. . . . fort, administrative capital
eau, Fr . . . water
ecuador, Sp . . . equator
eiland, Du . . . island
elv, Dan., Nor . . . river, stream
embalse, Sp . . . reservoir
erg, Arab . . . dune, sandy desert
est, Fr., It . . . east
estado, Sp . . . state
este, Port., Sp . . . east
estrecho, Sp . . . strait
étang, Fr . . . pond, lake
état, Fr . . . state
eyjar, Ice . . . islands
feld, Ger . . . field, plain
festung, Ger . . . fortress
fiume, It . . . river
fjäll, Swe . . . mountain
fjärd, Swe . . . bay, inlet
fjeld, Nor . . . mountain, hill
fjord, Dan., Nor . . . fiord, inlet
fjördur, Ice . . . fiord, inlet
fleuve, Fr . . . river
flod, Dan., Swe . . . river
flói, Ice . . . bay, marshland
fluss, Ger . . . river
foce, It . . . river mouth
fontein, Du . . . a spring
forêt, Fr . . . forest
fors, Swe . . . waterfall
forst, Ger . . . forest
fos, Dan., Nor . . . waterfall
fu, Chn . . . town, residence
fuente, Sp . . . spring, fountain
fuerte, Sp . . . fort
furt, Ger . . . ford
gang, Kor . . . stream, river
gangri, Tib . . . mountain
gat, Dan., Nor . . . channel
gàve, Fr . . . stream
gawa, Jap . . . river
gebergte, Du . . . mountain range
gebiet, Ger . . . district, territory
gebirge, Ger . . . mountains
ghat, India . . . pass, mountain range
gobi, Mong . . . desert
gol, Mong . . . river
göl, gölü, Tur . . . lake
golf, Du., Ger . . . gulf, bay
golfe, Fr . . . gulf, bay
golfo, It., Port., Sp . . . gulf, bay
gomba, gompa, Tib . . . monastery
gora, Rus., So. Slav . . . mountain
góra, Pol . . . mountain
gorod, Rus . . . town
grad, Rus., So. Slav . . . town
guba, Rus . . . bay, gulf
gundung, Indon . . . mountain
guntō, Jap . . . archipelago
gunung, Mal . . . mountain
haf, Swe . . . sea, ocean
hafen, Ger . . . port, harbor
haff, Ger . . . gulf, inland sea
hai, Chn . . . sea, lake
hama, Jap . . . beach, shore
hamada, Arab . . . rocky plateau
hamn, Swe . . . harbor
hāmūn, Per . . . swampy lake, plain
hantō, Jap . . . peninsula
hassi, Arab . . . well, spring
haus, Ger . . . house
haut, Fr . . . summit, top
hav, Dan., Nor . . . sea, ocean
havn, Dan., Nor . . . harbor, port
havre, Fr . . . harbor, port
háza, Hung . . . house, dwelling of
heim, Ger . . . hamlet, home
hem, Swe . . . hamlet, home
higashi, Jap . . . east
hisar, Tur . . . fortress
hissar, Arab . . . fort
ho, Chn . . . river
hoek, Du . . . cape
hof, Ger . . . court, farmhouse
höfn, Ice . . . harbor
hoku, Jap . . . north
holm, Dan., Nor., Swe . . . island
hora, Czech . . . mountain
horn, Ger . . . peak
hoved, Dan., Nor . . . cape
hsien, Chn . . . district, district capital
hu, Chn . . . lake
hügel, Ger . . . hill
huk, Dan., Swe . . . point
hus, Dan., Nor., Swe . . . house
île, Fr . . . island
ilha, Port . . . island
indsö, Dan., Nor . . . lake
insel, Ger . . . island
insjö, Swe . . . lake
irmak, irmagi, Tur . . . river
isla, Sp . . . island
isola, It . . . island
istmo, It., Sp . . . isthmus
järvi, jaur, Fin . . . lake
jebel, Arab . . . mountain
jima, Jap . . . island
jökel, Nor . . . glacier
joki, Fin . . . river
jökull, Ice . . . glacier
kaap, Du . . . cape
kai, Jap . . . bay, gulf, sea
kaikyō, Jap . . . channel, strait
kalat, Per . . . castle, fortress
kale, Tur . . . fort
kali, Mal . . . creek, river
kand, Per . . . village
kang, Chn . . . mountain ridge; village
kap, Dan., Ger . . . cape
kapp, Nor., Swe . . . cape
kasr, Arab . . . fort, castle
kawa, Jap . . . river
kefr, Arab . . . village
kei, Jap . . . creek, river
ken, Jap . . . prefecture
khor, Arab . . . bay, inlet
khrebet, Rus . . . mountain range
kiang, Chn . . . large river
king, Chn . . . capital city, town
kita, Jap . . . north
ko, Jap . . . lake
köbstad, Dan . . . market-town
kol, Mong . . . lake
kólpos, Gr . . . gulf
kong, Chn . . . river
kopf, Ger . . . head, summit, peak
köpstad, Swe . . . market-town
körfezi, Tur . . . gulf
kosa, Rus . . . spit
kou, Chn . . . river mouth
köy, Tur . . . village
kraal, Du. (Africa) . . . native village
ksar, Arab . . . fortified village
kuala, Mal . . . bay, river mouth
kuh, Per . . . mountain
kum, Tur . . . sand
kuppe, Ger . . . summit
küste, Ger . . . coast
kyo, Jap . . . town, capital
la, Tib . . . mountain pass
labuan, Mal . . . anchorage, port
lac, Fr . . . lake
lago, It., Port., Sp . . . lake
lagoa, Port . . . lake, marsh
laguna, It., Port., Sp . . . lagoon, lake
lahti, Fin . . . bay, gulf
län, Swe . . . county
landsby, Dan., Nor . . . village
liehtao, Chn . . . archipelago
liman, Tur . . . bay, port
ling, Chn . . . pass, ridge, mountain
llanos, Sp . . . plains
loch, Celt. (Scotland) . . . lake, bay
loma, Sp . . . long, low hill
lough, Celt. (Ireland) . . . lake, bay
machi, Jap . . . town
man, Kor . . . bay
mar, Port., Sp . . . sea
mare, It., Rom . . . sea
marisma, Sp . . . marsh, swamp
mark, Ger . . . boundary, limit
massif, Fr . . . block of mountains
mato, Port . . . forest, thicket
me, Siam . . . river
meer, Du., Ger . . . lake, sea
mer, Fr . . . sea
mesa, Sp . . . flat-topped mountain
meseta, Sp . . . plateau
mina, Port., Sp . . . mine
minami, Jap . . . south
minato, Jap . . . harbor, haven
misaki, Jap . . . cape, headland
mont, Fr . . . mount, mountain
montagna, It . . . mountain
montagne, Fr . . . mountain
montaña, Sp . . . mountain
monte, It., Port., Sp. . . . mount, mountain
more, Rus., So. Slav . . . sea
morro, Port., Sp . . . hill, bluff
mühle, Ger . . . mill
mund, Ger . . . mouth, opening
mündung, Ger . . . river mouth
mura, Jap . . . township
myit, Bur . . . river
mys, Rus . . . cape
nada, Jap . . . sea
nadi, India . . . river, creek
naes, Dan., Nor . . . cape
nafud, Arab . . . desert of sand dunes
nagar, India . . . town, city
nahr, Arab . . . river
nam, Siam . . . river, water
nan, Chn., Jap . . . south
näs, Nor., Swe . . . cape
nez, Fr . . . point, cape
nishi, nisi, Jap . . . west
njarga, Fin . . . peninsula
nong, Siam . . . marsh
noord, Du . . . north
nor, Mong . . . lake
nord, Dan., Fr., Ger., It., Nor., Swe . . . north
norte, Port., Sp . . . north
nos, Rus . . . cape
nyasa, Bantu . . . lake
ö, Dan., Nor., Swe . . . island
occidental, Sp . . . western
ocna, Rom . . . salt mine
odde, Dan., Nor . . . point, cape
oeste, Port., Sp . . . west
oka, Jap . . . hill
oost, Du . . . east
oriental, Sp . . . eastern
óros, Gr . . . mountain
ost, Ger., Swe . . . east
öster, Dan., Nor., Swe . . . eastern
ostrov, Rus . . . island
oued, Arab . . . river, stream
ouest, Fr . . . west
ozero, Rus . . . lake
pää, Fin . . . mountain
padang, Mal . . . plain, field
pampas, Sp. (Argentina) . . . grassy plains
pará, Indian (Brazil) . . . river
pas, Fr . . . channel, passage
paso, Sp . . . mountain pass, passage
passo, It., Port. . . . mountain pass, passage, strait
patam, India . . . city, town
pei, Chn . . . north
pélagos, Gr . . . open sea
pegunungan, Indon . . . mountains
peña, Sp . . . rock
peresheyek, Rus . . . isthmus
pertuis, Fr . . . strait
peski, Rus . . . desert
pic, Fr . . . mountain peak
pico, Port., Sp . . . mountain peak
piedra, Sp . . . stone, rock
ping, Chn . . . plain, flat
planalto, Port . . . plateau
planina, Yugo . . . mountains
playa, Sp . . . shore, beach
pnom, Camb . . . mountain
pointe, Fr . . . point
polder, Du., Ger . . . reclaimed marsh
polje, So. Slav . . . plain, field
poluostrov, Rus . . . peninsula
pont, Fr . . . bridge
ponta, Port . . . point, headland
ponte, It., Port . . . bridge
pore, India . . . city, town
porthmós, Gr . . . strait
porto, It., Port . . . port, harbor
potamós, Gr . . . river
p'ov, Rus . . . peninsula
prado, Sp . . . field, meadow
presqu'île, Fr . . . peninsula
proliv, Rus . . . strait
pu, Chn . . . commercial village
pueblo, Sp . . . town, village
puerto, Sp . . . port, harbor
pulau, Indon . . . island
punkt, Ger . . . point
punt, Du . . . point
punta, It., Sp . . . point
pur, India . . . city, town
puy, Fr . . . peak
qal'a, qal'at, Arab . . . fort, village
qasr, Arab . . . fort, castle
rann, India . . . wasteland
ra's, Arab . . . cape, head
reka, Rus., So. Slav . . . river
represa, Port . . . reservoir
rettō, Jap . . . island chain
ría, Sp . . . estuary
ribeira, Port . . . stream
ribeirão, Port . . . river
rio, It., Port . . . stream, river
río, Sp . . . river
rivière, Fr . . . river
roca, Sp . . . rock
rt, Yugo . . . cape
rūd, Per . . . river
saari, Fin . . . island
sable, Fr . . . sand
sahara, Arab . . . desert, plain
saki, Jap . . . cape
sal, Sp . . . salt
salar, Sp . . . salt flat, salt lake
salto, Sp . . . waterfall
san, Jap., Kor . . . mountain, hill
sat, satul, Rom . . . village
schloss, Ger . . . castle
sebkha, Arab . . . salt marsh
see, Ger . . . lake, sea
şehir, Tur . . . town, city
selat, Indon . . . stream
selvas, Port. (Brazil) . . . tropical rain forests
seno, Sp . . . bay
serra, Port . . . mountain chain
serranía, Sp . . . mountain ridge
seto, Jap . . . strait
severnaya, Rus . . . northern
shahr, Per . . . town, city
shan, Chn . . . mountain, hill, island
shatt, Arab . . . river
shi, Jap . . . city
shima, Jap . . . island
shōtō, Jap . . . archipelago
si, Chn . . . west, western
sierra, Sp . . . mountain range
sjö, Nor., Swe . . . lake, sea
sö, Dan., Nor . . . lake, sea
söder, södra, Swe . . . south
song, Annam . . . river
sopka, Rus . . . peak, volcano
source, Fr . . . a spring
spitze, Ger . . . summit, point
staat, Ger . . . state
stad, Dan., Du., Nor., Swe. . . . city, town
stadt, Ger . . . city, town
stato, It . . . state
step', Rus . . . treeless plain, steppe
straat, Du . . . strait
strand, Dan., Du., Ger., Nor., Swe . . . shore, beach
stretto, It . . . strait
strom, Ger . . . river, stream
ström, Dan., Nor., Swe. . . . stream, river
stroom, Du . . . stream, river
su, suyu, Tur . . . water, river
sud, Fr., Sp . . . south
süd, Ger . . . south
suidō, Jap . . . channel
sul, Port . . . south
sund, Dan., Nor., Swe . . . sound
sungai, sungei, Indon., Mal . . . river
sur, Sp . . . south
syd, Dan., Nor., Swe . . . south
tafelland, Ger . . . plateau
take, Jap . . . peak, summit
tal, Ger . . . valley
tanjung, tanjong, Mal . . . cape
tao, Chn . . . island
târg, târgul, Rom . . . market, town
tell, Arab . . . hill
teluk, Indon . . . bay, gulf
terra, It . . . land
terre, Fr . . . earth, land
thal, Ger . . . valley
tierra, Sp . . . earth, land
tō, Jap . . . east; island
tonle, Camb . . . river, lake
top, Du . . . peak
torp, Swe . . . hamlet, cottage
tsangpo, Tib . . . river
tsi, Chn . . . village, borough
tso, Tib . . . lake
tsu, Jap . . . harbor, port
tundra, Rus . . . treeless arctic plains
tung, Chn . . . east
tuz, Tur . . . salt
udde, Swe . . . cape
ufer, Ger . . . shore, riverbank
ujung, Indon . . . point, cape
umi, Jap . . . sea, gulf
ura, Jap . . . bay, coast, creek
ust'ye, Rus . . . river mouth
valle, It., Port., Sp . . . valley
vallée, Fr . . . valley
valli, It . . . lake
vár, Hung . . . fortress
város, Hung . . . town
varoš, So. Slav . . . town
veld, Du . . . open plain, field
verkh, Rus . . . top, summit
ves, Czech . . . village
vest, Dan., Nor., Swe . . . west
vik, Swe . . . cove, bay
vila, Port . . . town
villa, Sp . . . town
villar, Sp . . . village, hamlet
ville, Fr . . . town, city
vostok, Rus . . . east
wad, wādī, Arab. . . . intermittent stream
wald, Ger . . . forest, woodland
wan, Chn., Jap . . . bay, gulf
weiler, Ger . . . hamlet, village
westersch, Du . . . western
wüste, Ger . . . desert
yama, Jap . . . mountain
yarimada, Tur . . . peninsula
yug, Rus . . . south
zaki, Jap . . . cape
zaliv, Rus . . . bay, gulf
zapad, Rus . . . west
zee, Du . . . sea
zemlya, Rus . . . land
zuid, Du . . . south

abbreviations of geographical names and terms

Afg. . . . . Afghanistan
Afr. . . . . Africa
Ak. . . . . Alaska
Al. . . . . Alabama
Alb. . . . . Albania
Alg. . . . . Algeria
And. . . . . Andorra
Ang. . . . . Angola
Ant. . . . . Antarctica
Ar. . . . . Arkansas
Arch. . . . . Archipelago
Arc. O. . . . . Arctic Ocean
Arg. . . . . Argentina
A. S. S. R. Autonomous Soviet
. . . . Socialist Republic
Atl. O. . . . . Atlantic Ocean
Aus. . . . . Austria
Austl. . . . . Australia
Aut. . . . . Autonomous
Az. . . . . Arizona

B. . . . . Bay, Bahia
Ba. . . . . Bahamas
B.A.T. . . . . . . British Antarctic
. . . . Territory
Bngl. . . . . Bangladesh
Barb. . . . . Barbados
Bdy. . . . . Boundary
Bel. . . . . Belgium
Bg. . . . . Berg
Bhu. . . . . Bhutan
Bk. . . . . Bank
Bol. . . . . Bolivia
Bots. . . . . Botswana
Br. . . . . British
Braz. . . . . Brazil
Bru. . . . . Brunei
Bul. . . . . Bulgaria
Bur. . . . . Burma

C. . . . . Cerro, Cape
Ca. . . . . California
Cam. . . . . Cameroon
Can. . . . . Canal, Canada
Can. Is. . . . . Canary Is.
Cen. Afr. Rep. . . . . Central African
. . . . Republic
Chan. . . . . Channel
Co. . . . . County, Colorado
Col. . . . . Colombia
Con. . . . . Congo
Comm. . . . . Commonwealth
C. R. . . . . Costa Rica
Cr. . . . . Creek
Ct. . . . . Connecticut
C. V. . . . . Cape Verde
Czech. . . . . Czechoslovakia

DC . . . . . . District of Columbia
De. . . . . Delaware
Den. . . . . Denmark
Dept. . . . . Department
Des. . . . . Desert
D. F. . . . . Distrito Federal
Dist. . . . . District
Div. . . . . Division
Dom. Rep. . . . Dominican Republic

E. . . . . East
Ec. . . . . Ecuador
Eng. . . . . England
Equat. Gui. . . . . Equatorial Guinea
Eth. . . . . Ethiopia
Eur. . . . . Europe

Faer. . . . . Faeroe Is.
Falk. Is. . . . . Falkland Is.
Fd. . . . . Fjord
Fed. Rep. of Ger., F.R.G.
. . Federal Republic of Germany
Fin. . . . . Finland
Fk. . . . . Fork
Fl. . . . . Florida
For. . . . . Forest
Fr. . . . . France
Fr. Gu. . . . . French Guiana
Ft. . . . . Fort

G. . . . . Golfo, Gulf
Ga. . . . . Georgia
Gam. . . . . Gambia
Ger. Dem. Rep., G.D.R. . . . . .
. . . German Democratic Republic
Gib. . . . . Gibraltar
Grc. . . . . Greece
Grnld. . . . . Greenland
Gt. . . . . Great
Gt. Brit. . . . . Great Britain
Guad. . . . . Guadeloupe
Guat. . . . . Guatemala
Gui. . . . . Guinea
Guy. . . . . Guyana

Hai. . . . . Haiti
Har., Hbr. . . . . Harbor, Harbour

Hd. . . . . Head
Hi. . . . . Hawaii
Hond. . . . . Honduras
Hts. . . . . Heights
Hung. . . . . Hungary

I. . . . . Island
Ia. . . . . Iowa
Ice. . . . . Iceland
Id. . . . . Idaho
Il. . . . . Illinois
In. . . . . Inset, Indiana
Ind. O. . . . . Indian Ocean
Indon. . . . . Indonesia
Ind. Res. . . . Indian Reservation
Int., Intl. . . . . International
Ire. . . . . Ireland
Is. . . . . Islands
Isr. . . . . Israel
Isth. . . . . Isthmus
It. . . . . Italy

Jam. . . . . Jamaica
Jap. . . . . Japan
Jc. . . . . Junction

Kamp. . . . . Kampuchea
Ken. . . . . Kenya
Km. . . . . Kilometer, Kilometers
Kor. . . . . Korea
Ks. . . . . Kansas
Kuw. . . . . Kuwait
Ky. . . . . Kentucky

L. . . . . Lago, Lake, Loch, Lough
La. . . . . Louisiana
Lat. . . . . Latitude
Leb. . . . . Lebanon
Leso. . . . . Lesotho
Lib. . . . . Liberia
Liech. . . . . Liechtenstein
Long. . . . . Longitude
Lux. . . . . Luxembourg

M. . . . . Mile, Miles
Ma. . . . . Massachusetts
Mad. . . . . Madagascar
Mad. Is. . . . . Madeira Islands
Mala. . . . . Malaysia
Mand. . . . . Mandate
Mart. . . . . Martinique
Max. . . . . Maximum
Max. surf. elev. . . . . . Maximum
. . . . surface elevation
Md. . . . . Maryland
Me. . . . . Maine
Medit. . . . . Mediterranean
Mex. . . . . Mexico
Mi. . . . Mile, Miles, Michigan
Mn. . . . . Minnesota
Mo. . . . . Missouri
Mong. . . . . Mongolia
Mor. . . . . Morocco
Moz. . . . . Mozambique
Ms. . . . . Mississippi
Mt. . . . . . . Mount, Montana
Mtn. . . . . Mountain
Mts. . . . . Mountains

N. A. . . . . North America
Natl. . . . . National
Natl. Mon. . . National Monument
Ne. . . . . Nebraska
NC . . . . North Carolina
N. Cal. . . . . New Caledonia
ND . . . . North Dakota
Neigh. . . . . Neighborhood
Nep. . . . . Nepal
Neth. . . . . Netherlands
NH . . . . New Hampshire
Nic. . . . . Nicaragua
Nig. . . . . Nigeria
N. Ire. . . . . Northern Ireland
NJ . . . . New Jersey
NM . . . . New Mexico
Nor. . . . . Norway
Nv. . . . . Nevada
NY . . . . New York
N. Z. . . . . New Zealand

O. . . . . Ocean
Obs. . . . . Observatory
Oh. . . . . Ohio
Ok. . . . . Oklahoma
Om. . . . . Oman
Or. . . . . Oregon
O-va. . . . . Ostrova

P. . . . . Pass
Pa. . . . . Pennsylvania
Pac. O. . . . . Pacific Ocean
Pak. . . . . Pakistan
Pan. . . . . Panama

Pap. N. Gui. Papua New Guinea
Par. . . . . Paraguay
Pass. . . . . Passage
P.D.R. of Yem. . . . . . . Yemen,
. . . . People's Democratic
. . . . Republic of
Pen. . . . . Peninsula
Phil. . . . . Philippines
P. Int. . . . . . Point of Interest
Pk. . . . . Peak, Park
Plat. . . . . Plateau
Pln. . . . . Plain
Pol. . . . . Poland
Port. . . . . Portugal
P-Ov. . . . . Poluostrov
P. R. . . . . Puerto Rico
Prov. . . . . Province
Pt. . . . . Point
Pta. . . . . Punta
Pte. . . . . Pointe

R. . . . . . River, Rio, Rivière
Ra. . . . . Range, Ranges
Reg. . . . . Region
Rep. . . . . Republic
Res. . . . Reservation, Reservoir
Rf. . . . . Reef
RI . . . . Rhode Island
Rom. . . . . Romania
R. R. . . . . Railroad
R. S. F. S. R. . . . Russian Soviet
Federated Socialist Republic
Rw. . . . . Rwanda
Ry. . . . . Railway
Rys. . . . . Railways

S. . . . . . San, Santo, South
Sa. . . . . Serra, Sierra
S. A. . . . . South America
S. Afr. . . . . South Africa
Sal. . . . . El Salvador
Sau. Ar. . . . . Saudi Arabia
SC . . . . South Carolina
Scot. . . . . Scotland
SD . . . . South Dakota
Sd. . . . . Sound
S. L. . . . . Sierra Leone
Sol. Is. . . . . Solomon Is.
Som. . . . . Somalia
Sov. Un. . . . . Soviet Union
Sp. . . . . Spain
Spr., Sprs. . . . Spring, Springs
S. S. R. Soviet Socialist Republic
St. . . . . Saint
Sta. . . . . Santa
Ste. . . . . Sainte
Str. . . . . Strait
Strm. . . . . Stream
Sud. . . . . Sudan
Sur. . . . . Surinam
Swaz. . . . . Swaziland
Swe. . . . . Sweden
Switz. . . . . Switzerland
Swp. . . . . Swamp
Syr. . . . . Syria

Tan. . . . . Tanzania
Tas. . . . . Tasmania
Ter. . . . . Territory
Thai. . . . . Thailand
Tn. . . . . Tennessee
Trin. . . . . Trinidad and Tobago
Tun. . . . . Tunisia
Tur. . . . . Turkey
Tx. . . . . Texas

U.A.E. . . . . United Arab Emirates
Ug. . . . . Uganda
U. K. . . . . United Kingdom
of Gt. Brit. and N. Ire.
Ur. . . . . Uruguay
U. S., U. S. A. . . . United States
of America
Ut. . . . . Utah

Va. . . . . Virginia
Val. . . . . Valley
Vdkhr. . . . . . Vodokhranilishche
Ven. . . . . Venezuela
Viet. . . . . Vietnam
Vir. Is. . . . . Virgin Is.
Vol. . . . . Volcano
Vt. . . . . Vermont

Wa. . . . . Washington
Wi. . . . . Wisconsin
W. Sah. . . . . Western Sahara
W. Sam. . . . . Western Samoa
WV . . . . West Virginia
Wy. . . . . Wyoming

Yugo. . . . . Yugoslavia

Zimb. . . . . Zimbabwe

pronunciation of geographical names

key to the sound values of letters and symbols used in the index to indicate pronunciation

ă – ăt, căt, băttle
ā̇ – ā̇ppeal, finā̇l
ā – rāte, elāte
â – inanimâte, senâte
ä – cälm, ärm
à – àsk, bàth
a̍ – ma̍rine, sofa̍ (short neutral or inde-
. . . terminate sound)
â – fâre, prepâre
ch – church, choose
dh – as th in other, either
ē – bē, ēve
ė – crėate, ėvent
ĕ – bĕt, ĕnd
ĕ̇ – recĕ̇nt (short neutral or indeterminate sound)
ẽ – cratẽr, cindẽr
g – gō, gāme
gh – gutteral g
ĭ – wĭll, bĭt
ĭ̇ – short neutral or indeterminate sound
ī – rīde, bīte
к – gutteral k as ch in German ich
ng – sing
ŋ – baŋk, liŋger
N – indicates nasalized preceding vowel
ŏ – nŏd, ŏdd
ŏ̇ – cŏ̇mmit, cŏ̇nnect
ō – ōld, bōld
ȯ – ȯbey, hȯtel
ô – ôrder, nôrth
oi – boil
o͞o – fo͞od, ro͞ot
o͝o – fo͝ot, wo͝od
ou – thou, out
s – as in soft, so, sane
sh – dish, finish
th – thin, thick
ū – pūre, cūre
ŭ̇ – ŭ̇nite, ŭ̇sûrp
û – ûrn, fûr
ŭ – stŭd, ŭp
ü – as in French tu
ŭ̇ – circŭ̇s, sŭ̇bmit
zh – as z in azure
' – indeterminate vowel sound

In many cases the spelling of foreign geographic names does not even remotely indicate the pronunciation to an American, i. e., Słupsk in Poland is pronounced swo͞opsk; Jujuy in Argentina is pronounced ho͞o-hwē'; La Spezia in Italy is lä-spē'zyä.

This condition is hardly surprising, however, when we consider that in our own language Worcester, Massachusetts, is pronounced wo͝os'tẽr; Sioux City, Iowa, so͞o sĭ'tĭ; Schuylkill Haven, Pennsylvania, sko͞ol'kĭl hä-vĕn; Poughkeepsie, New York, pŏ-kĭp'se.

The indication of pronunciation of geographic names presents several peculiar problems:

1. Many foreign tongues use sounds that are not present in the English language and which an American cannot normally articulate. Thus, though the nearest English equivalent sound has been indicated, only approximate results are possible.

2. There are several dialects in each foreign tongue which cause variation in the local pronunciation of names. This also occurs in identical names in the various divisions of a great language group, as the Slavic or the Latin.

3. Within the United States there are marked differences in pronunciation, not only of local geographic names, but also of common words, indicating that the sound and tone values for letters as well as the placing of the emphasis vary considerably from one part of the country to another.

4. A number of different letter and diacritical combinations could be used to indicate essentially the same or approximate pronunciations.

Some variation in pronunciation other than that indicated in this index may be encountered, but such a difference does not necessarily indicate that either is in error, and in many cases it is a matter of individual choice as to which is preferred. In fact, an exact indication of pronunciation of many foreign names using English letters and diacritical marks is extremely difficult and sometimes impossible.

pronouncing index
over 30,000 geographical names

This universal index includes in a single alphabetical list the important names that appear on the reference maps. The place name is followed by the country or continent in which it is located, the pronunciation of the name, the page number of the map on which it appears, and the approximate geographic coordinates.

Local official names are used on the maps for nearly all cities and towns, with the exception of about 50 major world cities for which Anglicized conventional names have been preferred. For these exceptions, the index gives a cross-reference to the official local names.

The system of alphabetizing used in the index is standard. When more than one name (including political and physical names) with the same spelling is shown, the order of precedence is as follows: first, place names; second, political divisions; and third, physical features.

An explanation of the pronunciation system for names appears on the facing page.

If a place is indexed to an inset map, the page number is followed by a lower-case letter which refers to the appropriate inset on that page.

Each country name is followed by the continent in which it is located. Each place in the U.S. is identified by the state. All other places are identified by the country in which each is located.

Names of political and administrative subdivisions are followed by descriptive terms (Dist., Reg., Prov., State, etc.). Descriptive terms (Str., Is., Mtn., etc.) also appear after the names of physical features and points of interest.

A key to the abbreviations used for country and state names, descriptive terms, and other items in the index appears on the facing page.

PLACE (Pronunciation)	PAGE	Lat. °′	Long. °′
Aachen, F.R.G. (ä′kĕn)	167c	50.46 N	6.07 E
Aalen, F.R.G. (ä′lĕn)	164	48.49 N	10.08 E
Aalsmeer, Neth.	155a	52.16 N	4.44 E
Aalst, Bel.	155a	50.58 N	4.00 E
Aarau, Switz. (är′ou)	164	47.22 N	8.03 E
Aarschot, Bel.	155a	50.59 N	4.51 E
Aba, Nig.	225	5.06 N	7.21 E
Aba, Zaïre	227	3.52 N	30.14 E
Ābādān, Iran (ä-bŭ-dän′)	192	30.15 N	48.30 E
Abaetetuba, Braz. (ä′bä-ĕ-tĕ-tōō′bä)	141	1.44 S	48.45 W
Abajo Pk., Ut. (ä-bä′hō)	119	37.51 N	109.28 W
Abakaliki, Nig.	225	6.21 N	8.06 E
Abakan, Sov. Un. (ŭ-bá-kän′)	178	53.43 N	91.28 E
Abakan (R.), Sov. Un.	178	53.00 N	91.06 E
Abancay, Peru (ä-bän-kä′ē)	140	13.44 S	72.46 W
Abashiri, Jap. (ä-bä-shē′rē)	200	44.00 N	144.13 E
Abasolo, Mex. (ä-bä-sō′lō)	128	24.05 N	98.24 W
Abasolo, Mex.	122	27.13 N	101.25 W
Abay (R.), see Blue Nile			
Abaya L., Eth. (ä-bä′yä)	221	6.24 N	38.22 E
'Abbāsah, Tur'at al (Can.), Egypt	219c	30.45 N	32.15 E
Abbeville, Al. (ăb′ē-vĭl)	124	31.35 N	85.15 W
Abbeville, Fr. (ȧb-vēl′)	166	50.08 N	1.49 E
Abbeville, Ga. (ăb′ē-vĭl)	124	31.53 N	83.23 W
Abbeville, La.	123	29.59 N	92.07 W
Abbeville, SC	125	34.09 N	82.25 W
Abbiategrasso, It. (äb-byä′tä-gräs′sō)	170	45.23 N	8.52 E
Abbots Bromley, Eng. (ăb′ŭts brŭm′lē)	154	52.49 N	1.52 W
Abbotsford, Can. (ăb′ŭts-fĕrd)	116d	49.03 N	122.17 W
Abd Al Kuri (I.), P.D.R. of Yem. (äbd-ĕl-kōō′rē)	219a	12.12 N	51.00 E
Abdulino, Sov. Un. (ȧb-dōō-lē′nō)	176	53.40 N	53.45 E
Abéché, Chad (ä-bĕ-shä′)	221	13.48 N	20.39 E
Abengourou, Ivory Coast	224	6.44 N	3.29 W
Åbenrå, Den. (ô′bĕn-rô)	162	55.03 N	9.20 E
Abeokuta, Nig. (ä-bā-ô-kōō′tä)	225	7.10 N	3.26 E
Abercorn, see Mbala			
Aberdare, Wales (ăb-ēr-dâr′)	160	51.45 N	3.35 W
Aberdeen, Ms. (ăb-ēr-dēn′)	124	33.49 N	88.33 W
Aberdeen, Scot.	160	57.10 N	2.05 W
Aberdeen, SD	112	45.28 N	98.29 W
Aberdeen, Wa.	114	47.00 N	123.48 W
Aberford, Eng. (ăb′ēr-fērd)	154	53.49 N	1.21 W
Abergavenny, Wales (ăb′ēr-gȧ-vĕn′ĭ)	160	51.45 N	3.05 W
Abert L., Or. (ä′bĕrt)	114	42.39 N	120.24 W
Aberystwyth, Wales (ă-bĕr-ĭst′wĭth)	160	52.25 N	4.04 W
Abhā, Sau. Ar.	192	17.47 N	42.29 E
Abidjan, Ivory Coast (ä-bēd-zhäN′)	224	5.19 N	4.02 W
Abiko, Jap. (ä-bē-kō)	201a	35.53 N	140.01 E
Abilene, Ks. (ăb′ĭ-lēn)	121	38.54 N	97.12 W
Abilene, Tx.	122	32.25 N	99.45 W
Abingdon, Eng.	154b	51.38 N	1.17 W
Abingdon, Il. (ăb′ĭng-dŭn)	113	40.48 N	90.21 W
Abingdon, Va.	125	36.42 N	81.57 W
Abington, Ma. (ăb′ĭng-tŭn)	103a	42.07 N	70.57 W
Abiquiu Res., NM	119	36.26 N	106.42 W
Abitibi (L.), Can. (ăb-ĭ-tĭb′ĭ)	95	48.27 N	80.20 W
Abitibi (R.), Can.	95	49.30 N	81.10 W
Abkhaz A.S.S.R., Sov. Un.	177	43.10 N	40.45 E
Ablis, Fr. (ȧ-blē′)	167b	48.31 N	1.50 E
Abnūb, Egypt (äb-nōōb′)	219b	27.18 N	31.11 E
Åbo, see Turku			
Abohar, India	190	30.12 N	74.13 E
Aboisso, Ivory Coast	224	5.28 N	3.12 W
Abomey, Benin (ȧb-ô-mā′)	225	7.11 N	1.59 E
Abony, Hung. (ŏ′bô-ny′)	165	47.12 N	20.00 E
Abou Deïa, Chad	225	11.27 N	19.17 E
Abra (R.), Phil (ä′brä)	203a	17.16 N	120.38 E
Abraão, Braz. (äbrä-ouN′)	139a	23.10 S	44.10 W
Abraham's B., Ba.	133	22.20 N	73.50 W
Abram, Eng. (ā′brăm)	154	53.31 N	2.36 W
Abrantes, Port. (ä-brän′tĕs)	168	39.28 N	8.13 W
Abrolhos, Arquipélago dos (Arch.), Braz. (ä-rōōĕ-pĕ′lä-gô dôs ä-brô′l-yōs)	141	17.58 S	38.40 W
Abruka (I.), Sov. Un. (ä-brōō′kȧ)	163	58.09 N	22.30 E
Abruzzi E Molise (Reg.), It. (ä-brōōt′sē, mô′lē-zā)	170	42.10 N	13.55 E
Absaroka Ra. (Mts.), Wy. (ăb-sä-rô-kä)	115	44.50 N	109.47 W
Abu Road, India	190	24.38 N	72.45 E
Abū Arīsh, Sau. Ar. (ä-bōō á-rēsh′)	192	16.48 N	43.00 E
Abū Ḥamad, Sud. (ä′bōō hä′-mĕd)	221	19.37 N	33.21 E
Abū Kamāl, Syr.	192	34.45 N	40.46 E
Abunā (R.), Bol-Braz. (ä-bōō-nä′)	140	10.25 S	67.00 W
Abū Qīr, Egypt (ä′bōō kēr′)	219b	31.18 N	30.06 E
Abū Qurqāş, Egypt (ä′bōō kōōr-käs′)	219b	27.57 N	30.51 E
Abū Qurūn, Ra's (Mtn.), Egypt	189a	30.22 N	33.32 E
Aburatsu, Jap. (ä′bōō-rät′sōō)	201	31.33 N	131.20 E
Abū Tīj, Egypt	219b	27.03 N	31.19 E
Abū Zaby, U.A.E.	192	24.15 N	54.28 E
Abū Zanīmah, Egypt	189a	29.03 N	33.08 E
Abyad, Al-Bahr al- (R.), see White Nile			
Abyy, Sov. Un.	179	68.24 N	134.00 E
Acacias, Col. (ä-kä′sēäs)	140a	3.59 N	73.44 W
Acadia Natl. Park, Me. (ȧ-kā′dĬ-ȧ)	102	44.19 N	68.01 W
Acajutla, Sal. (ä-kä-hōōt′lä)	130	13.37 N	89.50 W
Acala, Mex. (ä-kä′lä)	129	16.38 N	92.49 W
Acalayong, Equat. Gui.	226	1.05 N	9.40 E
Acámbaro, Mex. (ä-käm′bä-rō)	128	20.03 N	100.42 W
Acancéh, Mex. (ä-kän-sĕ′)	130a	20.50 N	89.27 W
Acapetlahuaya, Mex. (ä-kä-pĕt′lä-hwä′yä)	128	18.24 N	100.04 W
Acaponeta, Mex. (ä-kä-pô-nā′tä)	128	22.31 N	105.25 W
Acaponeta (R.), Mex.	128	22.47 N	105.23 W
Acapulco, Mex. (ä-kä-pōōl′kô)	128	16.49 N	99.57 W
Acaraí Mts., Braz.	141	1.30 N	57.40 W
Acaraú, Braz. (ä-kárhä-ōō′)	141	2.55 S	40.04 W
Acarigua, Ven. (ä-kä-rē′gwä)	140	9.29 N	69.11 W
Acatlán de Osorio, Mex. (ä-kät-län′dä ō-sō′rē-ō)	128	18.11 N	98.04 W
Acatzingo de Hidalgo, Mex. (ä-kät-zēŋ′gô dä ē-dhäl′gō)	129	18.58 N	97.47 W
Acayucan, Mex. (ä-kä-yōō′kän)	129	17.56 N	94.55 W
Accoville, WV (ăk′kô-vĭl)	108	37.45 N	81.50 W
Accra, Ghana (ä′krä)	224	5.33 N	0.13 W
Accrington, Eng. (ăk′rĭng-tŭn)	154	53.45 N	2.22 W
Acerra, It. (ä-chĕ′r-rä)	169c	40.42 N	14.22 E
Achacachi, Bol. (ä-chä-kä′chē)	140	16.11 S	68.32 W
Acheng, China (ä′chĕng)	200	45.32 N	126.59 E
Achill I., Ire. (ä-chĭl′)	160	53.55 N	10.05 W
Achinsk, Sov. Un. (ä-chēnsk′)	178	56.13 N	90.32 E
Acireale, It. (ä-chē-rä-ä′lä)	170	37.37 N	15.12 E
Ackia Battle Ground Natl. Mon., Ms. (ä-kyū′)	124	34.22 N	89.05 W
Acklins (I.), Ba. (ăk′lĭns)	133	22.30 N	73.55 W
Acklins, The Bight of (B.), Ba.	133	22.35 N	74.20 W
Acolman, Mex. (ä-kōl-mä′n)	129a	19.38 N	98.56 W
Aconcagua (Prov.), Chile (ä-kôn-kä′gwä)	139b	32.20 S	71.00 W
Aconcagua, Cerro (Mtn.), Arg.	139b	32.38 S	70.00 W
Aconcagua (R.), Chile	139b	32.43 S	70.53 W
Açores (Azores) (Is.), Atl. O. (ä-zō′rĕs) (ȧ-zōrz′)	220a	37.44 N	29.25 W
Acoyapa, Nic. (ä-kô-yä′pä)	130	11.54 N	85.11 W
Acqui, It. (äk′kwē)	170	44.41 N	8.22 E
Acre (State), Braz. (ä′krä)	140	8.40 S	70.45 W
Acre (R.), Braz.	140	10.33 S	68.34 W
Acton, Al. (ăk′tŭn)	110h	33.21 N	86.49 W
Acton, Can.	93d	43.38 N	80.02 W
Acton, Ma.	103a	42.29 N	71.26 W
Actopan, Mex. (äk-tô-pän′)	128	20.16 N	98.57 W
Actópan (R.), Mex. (äk-tō′pän)	129	19.25 N	96.31 W
Acuitzio del Canje, Mex. (ä-kwēt′zĕ-ō dĕl kän′hĕ)	128	19.28 N	101.21 W
Acul, Baie de l' (B.), Hai. (ä-kōōl′)	133	19.55 N	72.20 W
Ada, Mn. (ā′dü)	112	47.17 N	96.32 W
Ada, Oh.	108	40.45 N	83.45 W
Ada, Ok.	121	34.45 N	96.43 W
Ada, Yugo. (ä′dä)	171	45.48 N	20.06 E
Adachi, Jap.	201a	35.50 N	39.36 E
Adak (I.), Ak. (ä-däk′)	105a	56.50 N	176.48 W
Adak, Ak.	105a	51.40 N	176.28 W
Adak Str., Ak.	105a	51.42 N	177.16 W
Adalia, see Antalya			
Adamaoua (Mts.), Cam.-Nig.	225	6.30 N	11.50 E
Adams (R.), Can.	97	51.30 N	119.20 W
Adams, Ma. (ăd′ămz)	109	42.35 N	73.10 W
Adams, Wi.	113	43.55 N	89.48 W
Adams, Mt., Wa.	114	46.15 N	121.19 W
Adamsville, Al. (ăd′ămz-vĭl)	110h	33.36 N	86.57 W
Adana, Tur. (ä′dä-nä)	177	37.05 N	35.20 E
Adapazari, Tur. (ä-dä-pä-zä′rē)	177	40.45 N	30.20 E
Adarama, Sud. (ä-dä-rä′mä)	221	17.11 N	34.56 E
Adda (R.), It. (äd′dä)	170	45.43 N	9.31 E
Ad Dabbah, Sud.	221	18.04 N	30.58 E
Ad Dahnā (Des.), Sau. Ar.	192	26.05 N	47.15 E
Ad-Dāmir, Sud. (ad-dä′mĕr)	221	17.38 N	33.57 E
Ad Dammān, Sau. Ar.	192	26.27 N	49.59 E
Ad Dāmūr, Leb.	189a	33.44 N	35.27 E
Ad Dawhah, Qatar	192	25.02 N	51.28 E
Ad Dilam, Sau. Ar.	192	23.47 N	47.03 E
Ad Dilinjāt, Egypt	219b	30.48 N	30.32 E
Addison, Tx. (ä′dĭ-sŭn)	117c	32.58 N	96.50 W
Addo, S. Afr. (ädō)	223c	33.33 S	25.43 E
Ad Duwaym, Sud. (dōō-äm′)	221	13.56 N	32.22 E
Addyston, Oh. (ä′dĕ-stŭn)	111f	39.09 N	84.42 W
Adel, Ga. (ä-dĕl′)	124	31.08 N	83.55 W
Adelaide, Austl. (ăd′ĕ-lād)	212	34.46 S	139.08 E
Adelaide, S. Afr. (ăd-ĕl′äd)	223c	32.41 S	26.07 E
Adelaide I., Ant.	228	67.15 S	68.40 W
Aden, P.D.R. of Yem. (ä′dĕn)	192	12.48 N	45.00 E
Aden, G. of, Asia	192	11.45 N	45.45 E
Adi, Pulau (I.), Indon. (ä′dē)	203	4.25 S	133.52 E
Adige (R.), It. (ä′dē-jä)	170	46.38 N	10.43 E
Adige R., Aus.-Switz.	158	46.34 N	10.51 E

260 Adilābād – Alboran

PLACE (Pronunciation)	PAGE	Lat. °′	Long. °′
Adilābād, India (ŭ-dĭl-ä-bäd′)	190	19.47 N	78.30 E
Adirondack, Mts., NY (ăd-ĭ-rŏn′dăk)	109	43.45 N	74.40 W
Adis Abeba, Eth.	221	9.00 N	38.44 E
Adi Ugri, Eth. (ä-dē ōō′grē)	221	14.54 N	38.52 E
Adjud, Rom. (äd′zhōōd)	165	46.05 N	27.12 E
Adkins, Tx.	117d	29.22 N	98.18 W
Admiralty (I.), Ak.	105	57.50 N	133.50 W
Admiralty Inlet, Wa. (ăd′mĭrål-tē)	116a	48.10 N	122.45 W
Admiralty Is., Pap. N. Gui.	203	1.40 S	146.45 E
Ado-Ekiti, Nig.	225	7.38 N	5.12 E
Adolph, Mn. (ā′dolf)	117h	46.47 N	92.17 W
Ādoni, India	191	15.42 N	77.18 E
Adour (R.), Fr. (å-dōōr′)	166	43.43 N	0.38 W
Adra, Sp. (ä′drä)	168	36.45 N	3.02 W
Adrano, It. (ä-drä′nō)	170	37.42 N	14.52 E
Adria, It. (ä′drē-ä)	170	45.03 N	12.01 E
Adrian, Mi. (ā′drĭ-ăn)	108	41.55 N	84.00 W
Adrian, Mn.	112	43.39 N	95.56 W
Adrianople, see Edirne			
Adriatic Sea, Eur.	170	43.30 N	14.27 E
Adrir, Alg.	220	27.53 N	0.15 W
Adwa, Eth.	221	14.02 N	38.58 E
Adwick-le-Street, Eng. (ăd′wĭk-lê-strēt′)	154	53.35 N	1.11 W
Adycha (R.), Sov. Un. (ä′dĭ-chå)	179	66.11 N	136.45 E
Adzhamka, Sov. Un. (åd-zhäm′kå)	173	48.33 N	32.28 E
Adzopé, Ivory Coast	224	6.06 N	3.52 W
Adz′va (R.), Sov. Un. (ädz′vå)	176	67.00 N	59.20 E
Aegean Sea, Asia-Eur. (ē-jē′ăn)	159	39.04 N	24.56 E
Aerø (I.), Den. (âr′ö)	161	54.52 N	10.22 E
Affton, Mo.	117e	38.33 N	90.20 W
Afghanistan, Asia (ăf-găn-ĭ-stăn′)	188	33.00 N	63.00 E
Afgoi, Som. (äf-gô′ĭ)	219a	2.08 N	45.08 E
Afikpo, Nig.	225	5.53 N	7.56 E
Aflou, Alg. (ä-flōō′)	220	33.59 N	2.04 E
Afognak (I.), Ak. (ä-fŏg-nåk′)	105	58.28 N	151.35 W
Afragola, It. (ä-frå′gō-lä)	169c	40.40 N	14.19 E
Africa (ăf′rĭ-kå)	218		
Afton, Mn. (ăf′tŭn)	117g	44.54 N	92.47 W
Afton, Ok.	121	36.42 N	94.56 W
Afton, Wy.	115	42.42 N	110.52 W
'Afula, Isr. (ä-fōō′lå)	189a	32.36 N	35.17 E
Afyon, Tur. (ä-fē-ōn)	177	38.45 N	30.20 E
Agadem, Niger (ä′gå-dĕm)	225	16.50 N	13.17 E
Agadez, Niger (ä′gå-dĕs)	225	16.58 N	7.59 E
Agadir, Mor. (ä-gå-dēr)	220	30.30 N	9.37 W
Agalta, Cord. de (Mts.), Hond. (kôr-dĕl-yĕ′rä-dĕ-ä-gä′l-tä)	130	15.15 N	85.42 W
Agapovka, Sov. Un. (ä-gä-pôv′kä)	180a	53.18 N	59.10 E
Agartala, India	190	23.53 N	91.22 E
Agāshi, India	191b	19.28 N	72.46 E
Agashkino, Sov. Un. (á-gäsh′kĭ-nô)	180b	55.18 N	38.13 E
Agattu (I.), Ak. (å′gä-tōō)	105a	52.14 N	173.40 E
Agayman, Sov. Un. (á-gä-ē-män′)	173	46.39 N	34.20 E
Agboville, Ivory Coast	224	5.56 N	4.13 W
Agdam, Sov. Un. (äg′dăm)	177	40.00 N	47.00 E
Agde, Fr. (ägd)	166	43.19 N	3.30 E
Agen, Fr. (å-zhäN′)	166	44.13 N	0.31 E
Aginskoye, Sov. Un. (ä-hĭn′skô-yĕ)	179	51.15 N	113.15 E
Agno, Phil. (äg′nō)	203a	16.07 N	119.49 E
Agno (R.), Phil.	203a	15.42 N	120.28 E
Agnone, It. (än-yō′nā)	170	41.49 N	14.23 E
Agogo, Ghana	224	6.47 N	1.04 W
Agra, India (ä′grä)	190	27.18 N	78.00 E
Agri (R.), It. (ä′grē)	170	40.15 N	16.21 E
Agrínion, Grc. (á-grē′nyôn)	171	38.38 N	21.06 E
Agua (Vol.), Guat. (ä′gwä)	130	14.28 N	90.43 W
Agua Blanca, Río (R.), Mex. (rē′ō-ä-gwä-blä′n-kä)	128	21.46 N	102.54 W
Agua Brava, Laguna de (L.), Mex. (lä-gōō′nä-dĕ-ä′gwä-brä′vä)	128	22.04 N	105.40 W
Agua Caliente Ind. Res., Ca. (ä′gwä kal-yĕn′tä)	118	33.50 N	116.24 W
Aguada, Cuba (ä-gwä′då)	132	22.25 N	80.50 W
Aguada L., Mex.	130a	18.46 N	89.40 W
Aguadas, Col. (ä-gwä′dás)	140a	5.37 N	75.27 W
Aguadilla, P.R. (ä-gwä-dēl′yä)	127b	18.27 N	67.10 W
Aguadulce, Pan. (ä-gwä-dōōl′sä)	131	8.15 N	80.33 W
Agua Escondida, Meseta de (Plat.), Mex. (mĕ-sĕ′tä-dĕ-ä′gwä-ĕs-kôn-dē′dä)	129	16.54 N	91.35 W
Agua Fria (R.), Az. (ä′gwä frē-ä)	119	33.43 N	112.22 W
Aguai, Braz. (ägwä-ē′)	139a	22.04 S	46.57 W
Agualeguas, Mex. (ä-gwä-lä′gwäs)	122	26.19 N	99.33 W
Aguanaval, R., Mex. (ä-guä-nä-väl′)	122	25.12 N	103.28 W
Aguán R., Hond. (ä-gwä′n)	130	15.22 N	87.00 W
Aguanus (R.), Can. (ä-gwä′nŭs)	103	50.45 N	62.03 W
Aguascalientes, Mex. (ä′gwäs-käl-yĕn′täs)	128	21.52 N	102.17 W
Aguascalientes (State), Mex.	128	22.00 N	102.18 W
Águeda, Port. (ä-gwā′då)	168	40.36 N	8.26 W
Agueda (R.), Sp. (ä-gē-dä)	168	40.50 N	6.44 W
Aguelhok, Mali	224	19.28 N	0.52 E
Aguilar, Co. (ä-gē-lär′)	120	37.24 N	104.38 W
Aguilar, Sp.	168	37.32 N	4.39 W
Aguilas, Sp. (ä-gē-läs)	168	37.26 N	1.35 W
Aguililla, Mex. (ä-gē-lēl-yä)	128	18.44 N	102.44 W
Aguililla (R.), Mex.	128	18.30 N	102.48 W
Aguja, Pta. (Pt.), Peru (pŭn′tä á-gōō′ hä)	140	6.00 S	81.15 W
Agulhas, C., S. Afr. (ä-gōōl′yäs)	222	34.47 S	20.00 E
Agusan (R.), Phil. (ä-gōō′sän)	203	8.12 N	126.07 E
Ahaggar (Mts.), Alg. (á-há-gär′)	220	23.14 N	6.00 E
Ahlen, F.R.G. (ä′lĕn)	167c	51.45 N	7.52 E
Ahmadābād, India (ŭ-mĕd-ā-bād′)	190	23.04 N	72.38 E
Ahmadnagar, India (ä′mûd-nŭ-gŭr)	190	19.09 N	74.45 E
Ahmar Mts., Eth.	219a	9.22 N	42.00 E
Ahoskie, NC (ā-hŏs′kē)	125	36.15 N	77.00 W
Ahrensburg, F.R.G. (ä′rĕns-bōōrg)	155c	53.40 N	10.14 E
Ahrweiler, F.R.G. (är′vī-lĕr)	164	50.34 N	7.05 E
Ähtärinjärvi (L.), Fin.	163	62.46 N	24.25 E
Ahuacatlán, Mex. (ä-wä-kät-län′)	128	21.05 N	104.28 W
Ahuachapan, Sal. (ä-wä-chä-pän′)	130	13.57 N	89.53 W
Ahualulco, Mex. (ä-wä-lōōl′kō)	128	20.43 N	103.57 W
Ahuatempan, Mex. (ä-wä-tĕm-pän)	128	18.11 N	98.02 W
Åhus, Swe. (ô′hōōs)	162	55.56 N	14.19 E
Ahvāz, Iran	192	31.15 N	48.54 E
Ahvenanmaa (Åland Is.), Fin. (ä′vĕ-nån-mô) (ô′länd)	163	60.36 N	19.55 E
Aiea, Hi.	104a	21.18 N	157.52 W
Aiken, SC (ā′kĕn)	125	33.32 N	81.43 W
Aimorès, Serra dos (Mts.), Braz. (sĕ′r-rä-dôs-ī-mō-rĕ′s)	141	17.40 S	42.38 W
Aimoto, Jap. (ī-mô-tō)	201b	34.59 N	135.09 E
Aïn Beïtda, Alg. (ä′ēn bā-dä′)	220	35.57 N	7.25 E
Aincourt, Fr. (âN-kōō′r)	167b	49.04 N	1.47 E
Aïn Oussera, Alg. (ĕn ōō-sā-rà)	169	35.25 N	2.50 E
Aïn Salah, Alg.	220	27.13 N	2.22 E
Ainsworth, Ne. (ānz′wûrth)	112	42.32 N	99.51 W
Aïn Témouchent, Alg. (ä′ēntĕ-mōō-shaN′)	157	35.20 N	1.23 W
Aipe, Col. (ī′pĕ)	140a	3.13 N	75.15 W
Aïr (Mts.), Niger	225	18.00 N	8.30 E
Aire (R.), Eng.	154	53.42 N	1.00 W
Aire-sur-l'Adour, Fr. (âr)	166	43.42 N	0.17 W
Airhitam, Selat (Str.), Indon.	189b	0.58 N	102.38 E
Aisne (R.), Fr. (ĕn)	166	49.28 N	3.32 E
Aitape, Pap. N. Gui. (ä-ē-tä′på)	203	3.00 S	142.10 E
Aitkin, Mn. (āt′kĭn)	113	46.32 N	93.43 W
Aitolikón, Grc. (å-tō′lĭ-kôn)	171	38.27 N	21.21 E
Aitos, Bul. (ä-ē′tōs)	171	42.42 N	27.17 E
Aitutaki (I.), Cook Is. (ī-tōō-tä′kē)	205	19.00 S	162.00 W
Aiud, Rom. (ä′ē-ōōd)	165	46.19 N	23.40 E
Aiuruoca, Braz. (äē′ōō-rōō′-kä)	139a	21.57 S	44.36 W
Aiuruoca (R.), Braz.	139a	22.11 S	44.35 W
Aix-en-Provence, Fr. (ĕks-prô-văNs)	166a	43.32 N	5.27 E
Aix-les-Bains, Fr. (ĕks′-lā-baN′)	167	45.42 N	5.56 E
Aíyina, Grc.	171	37.37 N	22.12 E
Aíyina (I.), Grc.	171	37.43 N	23.35 E
Aíyion, Grc.	171	38.13 N	22.04 E
Aizpute, Sov. Un. (ä′ēz-pōō-tĕ)	163	56.44 N	21.37 E
Aizuwakamatsu, Jap.	201	37.27 N	139.51 E
Ajaccio, Fr. (ä-yät′chō)	170	41.55 N	8.42 E
Ajalpan, Mex. (ä-häl′pän)	129	18.21 N	97.14 W
Ajana, Austl. (ăj-ăn′ĕr)	210	28.00 S	114.45 E
Ajax Mt., Mt. (ā′jăks)	115	45.19 N	113.43 W
Ajdābiyah, Libya	221	30.56 N	20.16 E
Ajmah, Jabal al (Mts.), Egypt	189a	29.12 N	34.03 E
Ajman, U.A.E.	192	25.15 N	54.30 E
Ajmer, India (ŭj-mēr′)	190	26.26 N	74.42 E
Ajo, Az. (ä′hô)	119	32.20 N	112.55 W
Ajuchitlán del Progreso, Mex. (ä-hōō-chet-lån′)	128	18.11 N	100.32 W
Ajusco, Mex. (ä-hōō′s-kō)	129a	19.13 N	99.12 W
Ajusco, Cerro (Mtn.), Mex. (sĕ′r-rô-ä-hōō′s-kō)	129a	19.12 N	99.16 W
Akaishi-dake (Mtn.), Jap. (ä-kī-shē dä′kā)	201	35.30 N	138.00 E
Akashi, Jap. (ä′kä-shē)	201b	34.38 N	134.59 E
Aketi, Zaire (ä-kå-tē)	226	2.44 N	23.46 E
Akhaltsikhe, Sov. Un. (äkä′l-tsĭ-kĕ)	177	41.40 N	42.50 E
Akhdar, Al Jabal al (Mts.), Libya	221	32.00 N	22.00 E
Akhelóös (R.), Grc. (ä-hĕ′lô-ōs)	171	38.45 N	21.26 E
Akhisar, Tur. (äk-hĭs-sär′)	177	38.58 N	27.58 E
Akhtarskaya, Bukhta (B.), Sov. Un. (bōōk′tä äK-tär′skå-yå)	173	45.53 N	38.22 E
Akhtopol, Bul. (äK′tô-pōl)	171	42.08 N	27.54 E
Akhtyrka, Sov. Un. (äK-tür′kå)	173	50.18 N	34.53 E
Akhunovo, Sov. Un. (ä-kû′nô-vô)	180a	54.13 N	59.36 E
Aki, Jap. (ä′kē)	201	33.31 N	133.51 E
Akiak, Ak. (äk′yåk)	105	61.00 N	161.02 W
Akimiski (I.), Can. (ä-kĭ-mĭ′skĭ)	95	52.54 N	80.22 W
Akita, Jap. (ä′kē-tä)	200	39.40 N	140.12 E
Akjoujt, Mauritania	224	19.45 N	14.23 W
'Akko, Isr.	189a	32.56 N	35.05 E
Aklavik, Can. (äk′lä-vĭk)	94	68.28 N	135.26 W
'Aklé'Âouâna (Dunes), Mali-Mauritania	224	18.07 N	6.00 W
Ako, Jap. (ä′kō)	201	34.44 N	134.22 E
Akola, India (á-kô′lä)	190	20.47 N	77.00 E
Akordat, Eth.	221	15.34 N	37.54 E
Akpatok (I.), Can. (åk′på-tŏk)	95	60.30 N	67.10 W
Akranes, Ice.	156	64.18 N	21.40 W
Akron, Co. (ăk′rŭn)	120	40.09 N	103.14 W
Akron, Oh.	111d	41.05 N	81.30 W
Aksaray, Tur. (äk-så-rī′)	177	38.30 N	34.05 E
Aksehir, Tur. (äk′shå-hēr)	177	38.20 N	31.20 E
Aksehir (L.), Tur.	177	38.40 N	31.30 E
Aksha, Sov.Un. (äk′shå)	179	50.28 N	113.00 E
Aksu, China (ä-kū-sōō)	194	41.29 N	80.15 E
Aktyubinsk, Sov. Un. (äk′tyōō-bĕnsk)	177	50.20 N	57.00 E
Akune, Jap. (ä′kōō-nå)	201	32.03 N	130.16 E
Akureyri, Ice. (ä-kōō-rå′rē)	156	65.39 N	18.01 W
Akutan (I.), Ak. (ä-kōō-tän′)	105a	53.58 N	169.54 W
Akwatia, Ghana	224	6.04 N	0.49 W
Alabama (State), U.S. (ăl-å-băm′å)	107	32.50 N	87.30 W
Alabama (R.), Al.	124	31.20 N	87.39 W
Alabat (I.), Phil. (ä-lä-bät′)	203a	14.14 N	122.05 E
Alacam, Tur. (ä-lä-chäm′)	177	41.30 N	35.40 E
Alacranes, Cuba (ä-lä-krä′nås)	132	22.45 N	81.35 W
Al Aflaj (Des.), Sau. Ar.	192	24.00 N	44.47 E
Alagôas (State), Braz. (ä-lä-gō′äzh)	141	9.50 S	36.33 W
Alagoinhas, Braz. (ä-lä-gō-ēn′yäzh)	141	12.13 S	38.12 W
Alagón, Sp. (ä-lä-gōn′)	168	41.46 N	1.07 W
Alagón (R.), Sp.	168	39.53 N	6.42 W
Alahuatán (R.), Mex. (ä-lä-wä-tà′n)	128	18.30 N	100.00 W
Alajuela, C.R. (ä-lä-hwa′lä)	131	10.01 N	84.14 W
Alajuela, L., Pan.	126a	9.15 N	79.34 W
Alakol (L.), Sov. Un.	178	45.45 N	81.13 E
Alalakeiki Chan., Hi. (ä-lä-lä-kā′kē)	104a	20.40 N	156.30 W
Al 'Alamayn, Egypt	221	30.53 N	28.52 E
Alameda, Ca. (ăl-å-mā′då)	116b	37.46 N	122.15 W
Alameda (R.), Ca.	116b	37.36 N	122.02 W
Alaminos, Phil. (ä-lä-mē′nôs)	203a	16.09 N	119.58 E
Al 'Amirīyah, Egypt	159	31.01 N	29.52 E
Alamo, Ca. (ă′lå-mō)	116b	37.51 N	122.02 W
Alamo, Mex. (ä′lä-mô)	129	20.55 N	97.41 W
Alamo, Nv. (ă′lå-mō)	118	37.22 N	115.10 W
Alamo, R., Mex. (ä′lä-mô)	122	26.33 N	99.35 W
Alamogordo, NM (ăl-å-mō-gôr′dō)	119	32.55 N	106.00 W
Alamo Heights, Tx. (ă′lå-mō)	117d	29.28 N	98.27 W
Alamo Pk., NM (ă′lå-mō pēk)	122	32.50 N	105.55 W
Alamosa, Co. (ăl-å-mō′så)	119	37.25 N	105.50 W
Alandskiy, Sov. Un. (ä-länt′skĭ)	180a	52.14 N	59.48 E
Alanga Arba, Ken.	227	0.07 N	40.25 E
Alanya, Tur.	177	36.40 N	32.10 E
Alaotra (L.), Mad. (ä-lä-ō′trå)	223	17.15 S	48.17 E
Alapayevsk, Sov. Un. (ä-lä-pä′yĕfsk)	180a	57.50 N	61.35 E
Al 'Aqabah, Jordan	189a	29.32 N	35.00 E
Alaquines, Mex. (ä-lå-kē′nås)	128	22.07 N	99.35 W
Al 'Arīsh, Egypt (ä-rēsh′)	189a	31.08 N	33.48 E
Alaska (State), U.S. (å-lăs′kå)	106a	64.00 N	150.00 W
Alaska, G. of, Ak.	105	57.42 N	147.40 W
Alaska Hy., Ak.	105	63.00 N	142.00 W
Alaska Pen., Ak.	105	55.50 N	162.10 W
Alaska Ra., Ak.	105	62.00 N	152.18 W
Al-'Atrūn, Sud.	221	18.13 N	26.44 E
Alatyr′, Sov.Un. (ä′lä-tür)	176	54.55 N	46.30 E
Alausí, Ec. (å-lou-sē′)	140	2.15 S	78.45 W
Al 'Ayyāṭ, Egypt (ä-ē-yät′)	219b	29.38 N	31.18 E
Alba, It. (äl′bä)	170	44.41 N	8.02 E
Albacete, Sp. (äl-bä-thā′tā)	168	39.00 N	1.49 W
Albachten, F.R.G. (äl-bå′K-tĕn)	167c	51.55 N	7.31 E
Al Badārī, Egypt	219b	26.59 N	31.29 E
Alba de Tormes, Sp. (äl-bå dā tôr′mās)	168	40.48 N	5.28 W
Al Bahnasā, Egypt	219b	28.35 N	30.30 E
Alba Iulia, Rom. (äl-bä yōō′lyå)	165	46.05 N	23.32 E
Al Ballah, Egypt (bä′lä)	219c	30.46 N	32.20 E
Al Balyanā, Egypt	219b	26.12 N	32.00 E
Albani, Colli (Mtn.), It.	169d	41.46 N	12.45 E
Albania, Eur. (ăl-bā′nĭ-å)	152	41.45 N	20.00 E
Albano, Lago (L.), It. (lä′-gō äl-bä′nō)	169d	41.45 N	12.44 E
Albano Laziale, It. (äl-bä′nō lät-zē-ä′lā)	169d	41.44 N	12.43 E
Albany, Austl. (ôl′bå-nĭ)	210	35.00 S	118.00 E
Albany, Ca.	116b	37.54 N	122.18 W
Albany, Ga.	124	31.35 N	84.10 W
Albany, Mo.	121	40.14 N	94.18 W
Albany, NY	109	42.40 N	73.50 W
Albany, Or.	114	44.38 N	123.06 W
Albany (R.), Can.	95	51.45 N	83.30 W
Al Başrah, Iraq	192	30.35 N	47.59 E
Al Batrūn, Leb. (bä-trōōn′)	189a	34.16 N	35.39 E
Al Bawīţī, Egypt	221	28.19 N	29.00 E
Albemarle, NC (ăl′bē-märl)	125	35.24 N	80.36 W
Albemarle Sd., NC	125	36.00 N	76.17 W
Albenga, It. (äl-bĕŋ′gä)	170	44.04 N	8.13 E
Alberche (R.), Sp. (äl-bĕr′chå)	168	40.08 N	4.19 W
Alberga, The (R.), Austl. (ăl-bŭr′gå)	210	27.15 S	135.00 E
Albergaria a-Velha, Port. (äl-bĕr-gá-rē′ á-ä-väl′yå)	168	40.47 N	8.31 W
Alberhill, Ca. (ăl′bĕr-hĭl)	117a	33.43 N	117.23 W
Albert, Fr. (ăl-bâr′)	166	50.00 N	2.49 E
Albert (L.), Afr. (ăl′bĕrt) (ál-bâr′)	227	1.50 N	30.40 E
Albert, Parc Natl. (Natl. Pk.), Zaire	227	0.05 N	29.30 E
Alberta (Prov.), Can. (ăl-bŭr′tå)	94	54.33 N	117.10 W
Alberta, Mt., Can.	97	52.18 N	117.28 W
Albert Edward, Mt., Pap. N. Gui. (ăl′bērt ĕd′wērd)	203	8.25 S	147.25 E
Alberti, Arg. (ál-bĕ′r-tē)	139c	35.01 S	60.16 W
Albert Kanaal (Can.), Bel.	155a	51.07 N	5.07 E
Albert Lea, Mn. (ăl′bērt lē′)	113	43.38 N	93.24 W
Albert Nile (R.), Ug.	227	3.25 N	31.35 E
Alberton, Can. (ăl′bēr-tŭn)	102	46.49 N	64.04 W
Alberton, S. Afr.	223b	26.16 S	28.08 E
Albertville, Al. (ăl′bērt-vĭl)	124	34.15 N	86.10 W
Albertville, Fr. (ál-bêr-vēl′)	167	45.42 N	6.25 E
Albertville, see Kalemie			
Albi, Fr. (äl-bē′)	166	43.54 N	2.07 E
Albia, Ia. (ăl-bĭ-å)	113	41.01 N	92.44 W
Albina, Sur. (äl-bē′nä)	141	5.30 N	54.33 W
Albina, Ponta (Pt.), Ang.	226	15.51 S	11.44 E
Albino, Pt., Can. (äl-bē′nō)	111c	42.50 N	79.05 W
Albion, Mi. (ăl′bĭ-ŭn)	108	42.15 N	84.50 W
Albion, Ne.	112	41.42 N	98.00 W
Albion, NY	109	43.15 N	78.10 W
Alboran, Isla del (I.), Sp. (ē′s-lä-dĕl-äl-bō-rä′n)	168	35.58 N	3.02 W

ăt; finăl; rāte; senāte; ärm; åsk; sofå; fâre; ch-choose; dh-as th in other; bē; ēvent; bĕt; recĕnt; cratēr; g-gō; gh-guttural g; bĭt; ĭ-short neutral; rīde; K-guttural k as ch in German ich;

PLACE (Pronunciation)	PAGE	Lat. °′	Long. °′
Ålborg, Den. (ôl'bŏr)	162	57.02 N	9.55 E
Al Buḩayrah al Murrah al Kubrá (Great Bitter) (Salt L.), Egypt	219c	30.24 N	32.27 E
Al Buḩayrah al Murrah aş Şughrá (Little Bitter) (Salt L.), Egypt	219c	30.10 N	32.36 E
Albuquerque, NM (ăl-bŭ-kûr'kē)	119	35.05 N	106.40 W
Albuquerque, Cayus de (I.), Col. (ăl-bŭ-kûr'kē)	131	12.12 N	81.24 W
Al Buraymī, Om.	192	23.45 N	55.39 E
Alburquerque, Sp. (äl-bo͞or-kĕr'kā)	168	39.13 N	6.58 W
Albury, Austl. (ôl'bĕr-ē)	212	36.00 S	147.00 E
Alcabideche, Port. (äl-kȧ-bē-dā'chå)	169b	38.43 N	9.24 W
Alcácer do Sal, Port. (äl-kä'sĕr do͞o säl')	168	38.24 N	8.33 W
Alcalá de Henares, Sp. (äl-kä-lä' dā ā-na'räs)	169a	40.29 N	3.22 W
Alcalá la Real, Sp. (äl-kä-lä'lä rā-äl')	168	37.27 N	3.57 W
Alcamo, It. (äl'kȧ-mō)	170	37.58 N	13.03 E
Alcanadre (R.), Sp. (äl-kä-nä'drå)	169	41.41 N	0.18 W
Alcanar, Sp. (äl-kä-när')	169	40.35 N	0.27 E
Alcañiz, Sp. (äl-kän-yēth')	169	41.03 N	0.08 W
Alcântara, Braz. (äl-kän'tȧ-rȧ)	141	2.17 S	44.29 W
Alcaraz, Sp. (äl-kä-räth')	168	38.39 N	2.28 W
Alcaudete, Sp. (äl-kou-dhā'tā)	168	37.38 N	4.05 W
Alcázar de San Juan, Sp. (äl-kä'thär dā sän hwän')	168	39.22 N	3.12 W
Alcira, Sp. (ä-thē'rä)	169	39.09 N	0.26 W
Alcoa, Tn. (ăl-kō'ȧ)	124	35.45 N	84.00 W
Alcobendas, Sp. (äl-kō-bĕn'dȧs)	169a	40.32 N	3.39 W
Alcochete, Port. (äl-kō-chā'ta)	169b	38.45 N	8.58 W
Alcorón, Sp. (äl-kô-rō'n)	169a	40.22 N	3.50 W
Alcorta, Arg. (äl-kôr'tä)	139c	33.32 S	61.08 W
Alcova Res., Wy. (ăl-kō'vȧ)	115	42.31 N	106.33 W
Alcove, Can. (ăl-kōv')	93c	45.41 N	75.55 W
Alcoy, Sp. (äl-koi')	169	38.42 N	0.30 W
Alcudia, Bahia de (B.), Sp. (bä-ē'ä-dĕ-äl-ko͞o-dhē'ä)	169	39.48 N	3.20 E
Aldabra Is., Afr. (äl-dä'brä)	223	9.16 S	46.17 E
Aldama, Mex. (äl-dä'mä)	128	22.54 N	98.04 W
Aldama, Mex.	122	28.50 N	105.54 W
Aldan, Sov.Un.	179	58.46 N	125.19 E
Aldan (R.), Sov. Un.	179	63.30 N	132.14 E
Aldan Plat., Sov. Un.	179	57.42 N	130.28 E
Aldanskaya, Sov. Un.	179	61.52 N	135.29 E
Aldenhoven, F.R.G. (äl'dĕn-hō'vĕn)	167c	50.54 N	6.18 E
Aldergrove, Can. (ôl'dēr-grōv)	116d	49.03 N	122.28 W
Alderney (I.), Guernsey (ôl'dēr-nĭ)	166	49.43 N	2.11 W
Aldershot, Eng. (ôl'dēr-shŏt)	154b	51.14 N	0.46 W
Alderson, WV (ôl-dēr-sŭn)	108	37.40 N	80.40 W
Alderwood Manor, Wa. (ôl'dēr-wo͝od măn'ŏr)	116a	47.49 N	122.18 W
Aldridge-Brownhills, Eng.	154	52.38 N	1.55 W
Aledo, Il. (ȧ-le'dō)	121	41.12 N	90.47 W
Aleg, Mauritania	224	17.03 N	13.55 W
Alegre, Braz. (ȧlĕ'grĕ)	139a	20.41 S	41.32 W
Alegre (R.), Braz.	142b	22.22 S	43.34 W
Alegrete, Braz. (ä-lå-grā'tā)	142	29.46 S	55.44 W
Aleksandrov, Sov. Un. (ä-lyĕk-sän' drôf)	180b	56.24 N	38.45 E
Aleksandrovsk, Sov. Un. (ä-lyĕk-sän'drôfsk)	180a	59.11 N	57.36 E
Aleksandrovsk, Sov. Un.	179	51.02 N	142.21 E
Aleksandrów Kujawski, Pol. (ä-lĕk-säh'dro͞ov ko͞o-yav'skē)	165	52.54 N	18.45 E
Alekseyevka, Sov. Un. (ä-lyĕk-sä-yĕf'kȧ)	173	50.39 N	38.40 E
Aleksin, Sov. Un. (ä-lyĕk-sēn)	172	54.31 N	37.07 E
Aleksinac, Yugo. (ä-lyĕk-sē-nȧk')	171	43.33 N	21.42 E
Alem Paraíba, Braz. (ä-lĕ'm-pȧ-rȧē'bȧ)	139a	21.54 S	42.40 W
Alençon, Fr. (ȧ-lăɴ-sôɴ')	166	48.26 N	0.08 E
Alenquer, Braz. (ä-lĕŋ-kĕr')	141	1.58 S	54.44 W
Alenquer, Port.	168	39.04 N	9.01 W
Alentjo (Reg.), Port. (ä-lĕŋ-tä'zho͞o)	168	38.05 N	7.45 W
Alenuihaha Chan., Hi. (ä'lå-no͞o-ē-hä'hä)	104a	20.20 N	156.05 W
Aleppo, Syr. (ȧ-lĕp-ō)	159	36.10 N	37.18 E
Alès, Fr. (ä-lĕs')	166	44.07 N	4.06 E
Alessandria, It. (ä-lĕs-sän'drē-ä)	170	44.53 N	8.35 E
Alessio, see Lesh			
Ålesund, Nor. (ô'lĕ-so͞on')	162	62.28 N	6.14 E
Aleutian Is., Ak. (ȧ-lu'shăn)	105a	52.40 N	177.30 W
Aleutian Trench, Ak.	105a	50.40 N	177.10 E
Alevina, Mys (C.), Sov. Un.	179	58.49 N	151.44 E
Alexander Arch., Ak. (ăl-ĕg-zăn'dēr)	105	57.05 N	138.10 W
Alexander City, Al.	124	32.55 N	85.55 W
Alexander Ind. Res., Can.	93g	53.47 N	114.00 W
Alexander I., Ant.	228	71.00 S	71.00 W
Alexandra, S. Afr. (ăl-ex-ăn'drȧ)	223b	26.07 S	28.07 E
Alexandria, Austl. (ăl-ĕg-zăn'drĭ-ȧ)	210	19.00 S	136.56 E
Alexandria, Can.	109	45.50 N	74.35 W
Alexandria, In.	108	40.20 N	85.20 W
Alexandria, La.	123	31.18 N	92.28 W
Alexandria, Mn.	112	45.53 N	95.23 W
Alexandria, Rom.	171	43.55 N	25.21 E
Alexandria, S. Afr. (ăl-ĕx-ăn-drĭ-ȧ)	223c	33.40 S	26.26 E
Alexandria, SD	112	43.39 N	97.45 W
Alexandria, Va. (ăl-ĕg-zăn'drĭ-ȧ)	110e	38.50 N	77.05 W
Alexandria, see Al Iskandarīyah			
Alexandria Bay, NY	109	44.20 N	75.55 W
Alexandroúpolis (Dedeagats), Grc. (ä-lĕk-sän-dro͞o'pō-lĭs) (de'dĕ-ä-gäts)	171	40.41 N	25.51 E
Alfaro, Sp. (äl-färō)	168	42.08 N	1.43 W
Al-Fāshir, Sud. (fä'shēr)	221	13.38 N	25.21 E
Al Fashn, Egypt	219b	28.47 N	30.53 E
Al Fayyūm, Egypt	221	29.14 N	30.48 E
Alfenas, Braz. (äl-fĕ'nȧs)	139a	21.26 S	45.55 W
Alfiós (R.), Grc.	171	37.33 N	21.50 E
Al Firdān, Egypt (fer-dän')	219b	30.43 N	32.20 E
Alfonso Claudio, Braz. (äl-fōn'sô-klou'dēô)	139a	20.05 S	41.05 W
Alfred, Can. (ăl'frĕd)	93c	45.34 N	74.52 W
Alfreton, Eng. (ăl'fēr-tŭn)	154	53.06 N	1.23 W
Algarve (Reg.), Port. (äl-gär'vĕ)	168	37.15 N	8.12 W
Algeciras, Sp. (äl-hā-thē'räs)	168	36.08 N	5.25 W
Alger (Algiers), Alg. (äl-zhā') (ăl-jēr)	220	36.51 N	2.56 E
Algeria, Afr. (ăl-gē'rĭ-ȧ)	218	28.45 N	1.00 E
Algete, Sp. (äl-hā'tā)	169a	40.36 N	3.30 W
Alghero, It. (äl-gâ'rō)	170	40.32 N	8.22 E
Algiers, see Alger			
Algoa, Tx. (ăl-gō'ȧ)	123a	29.24 N	95.11 W
Algoabaai (B.), S. Afr. (ăl'gōȧ)	223c	33.51 S	24.50 E
Algoma, Wa.	116a	47.17 N	122.15 W
Algoma, Wi.	113	44.38 N	87.29 W
Algona, Ia.	113	43.04 N	94.11 W
Algonac, Mi. (ăl'gô-năk)	108	42.35 N	82.30 W
Algonquin, Il. (ăl-gŏŋ'kwĭn)	111a	42.10 N	88.17 W
Algonquin Provincial Park, Can.	109	45.50 N	78.20 W
Alhama de Granada, Sp. (äl-hä'mä)	168	37.00 N	3.59 W
Alhama de Murcia, Sp.	168	37.50 N	1.24 W
Alhambra, Ca. (ăl-hăm'brȧ)	117a	34.05 N	118.08 W
Al Ḩammām, Egypt	159	30.46 N	29.42 E
Alhandra, Port. (äl-yän'drȧ)	169b	38.55 N	9.01 W
Al Hasā (Plain), Sau. Ar.	192	27.00 N	47.48 E
Alhaurín, Sp. (ä-lou-rēn')	168	36.40 N	4.40 W
Al Ḩijāz (Reg.), Sau. Ar.	192	23.45 N	39.08 E
Al Hirmil, Leb.	189a	34.23 N	36.22 E
Al-Hoceima, Sp.	168	35.15 N	3.55 W
Alhos Vedros, Port. (äl'yōs'vä'drōs)	169b	38.39 N	9.02 W
Alhucemas, Baie d' (B.), Mor.	168	35.18 N	3.50 W
Al Hudaydah, Yemen	192	14.43 N	43.03 E
Al Hufūf, Sau. Ar.	192	25.15 N	49.43 E
Aliákmon (R.), Grc. (äl-ē-ȧk'mōn)	171	40.26 N	22.17 E
Alibori (R.), Benin	225	11.40 N	2.55 E
Alicante, Sp. (ä-lē-kän'tä)	169	38.20 N	0.30 W
Alice, S. Afr. (ăl-ĭs)	223c	32.47 S	26.51 E
Alice, Tx. (ăl'ĭs)	122	27.45 N	98.04 W
Alice, Punta (Pt.), It. (ä-lē'chĕ)	171	39.23 N	17.10 E
Alice Arm, Can.	96	55.29 N	129.29 W
Alicedale, S. Afr. (ăl'ĭs-dăl)	223c	33.18 S	26.04 E
Alice Springs, Austl. (ăl'ĭs)	210	23.38 S	133.56 E
Alicudi (I.), It. (ä-lē-ko͞o'dē)	170	38.34 N	14.21 E
Alifkulovo, Sov. Un. (ä-lĭf-kû'lô-vô)	180a	55.57 N	62.06 E
Alīgarh, India (ä-lē-gŭr')	190	27.58 N	78.08 E
Alingsås, Swe. (ȧ'lĭŋ-sôs)	162	57.57 N	12.30 E
Aliquippa, Pa. (ăl-ĭ-kwĭp'ȧ)	111e	40.37 N	80.15 W
Al Iskandarīyah (Alexandria), Egypt	219b	31.12 N	29.58 E
Al Ismā'ī-līyah, see Ismailia			
Aliwal North, S. Afr. (ä-lē-wäl')	222	31.09 S	28.26 E
Al-Jabal Al-Akhḑar (Mts.), Om.	192	23.30 N	56.43 W
Al Jafr, Qa'al (L.), Jordan	189a	30.15 N	36.24 E
Al Jaghbūb, Libya	221	29.46 N	24.32 E
Al Jawf, Libya	221	24.14 N	23.15 E
Al Jawf, Sau. Ar.	192	29.45 N	39.30 E
Aljezur, Port. (äl-zhä-zo͞or')	168	37.18 N	8.52 W
Al Jīzah, Egypt	219b	30.01 N	31.12 E
Al Jufrah (Oasis), Libya	220	29.30 N	15.16 E
Aljustrel, Port. (äl-zho͞o-strĕl')	168	37.44 N	8.23 W
Al Kāb, Egypt	219c	30.56 N	32.19 E
Al Kāmilīn, Sud. (käm-lĕn')	221	15.09 N	33.06 E
Al Karak, Jordan (kĕ-räk')	189a	31.11 N	35.42 E
Al Karnak, Egypt (kär'nak)	219b	25.42 N	32.43 E
Al Khābūrah, Om.	192	23.45 N	57.30 E
Al Khalīl (Hebron), Jordan	189a	31.31 N	35.07 E
Al Khandaq, Sud. (kän-dăk')	221	18.38 N	30.29 E
Al Kharţūm (Khartoum), Sud. (kär-to͞om')	221	15.34 N	32.36 E
Al Kharţūm Baḩrī, Sud.	221	15.43 N	32.41 E
Al Khums, Libya	221	32.35 N	14.10 E
Al Khurmah, Sau. Ar.	192	21.37 N	41.44 E
Al Kiswah, Syr.	189a	33.31 N	36.13 E
Alkmaar, Neth. (älk-mär')	161	52.39 N	4.42 E
Al Kūbrī, Egypt (ko͞o'brē)	219c	30.01 N	32.35 E
Al Kufrah (Oasis), Libya	221	24.45 N	22.45 E
Al Kuntillah, Egypt	189a	29.59 N	34.42 E
Al Kuwayt (Kuwait), Kuw. (ko͞o-wit)	192	29.04 N	47.59 E
Al Lādhiqīyah (Latakia), Syr.	159	35.32 N	35.51 E
Allagash (R.), Me. (ăl'ȧ-găsh)	102	46.50 N	69.24 W
Allāhābād, India (ŭl-ŭ-hä-bäd')	190	25.32 N	81.53 E
All American Can., Ca. (âl ȧ-mĕr'ĭ-kăn)	118	32.43 N	115.12 W
Alland, Aus.	155e	48.04 N	16.05 E
Allariz, Sp. (äl-yä-rēth')	168	42.10 N	7.48 W
Allatoona (R.), Ga. (ăl'ȧ-to͞on'ȧ)	124	34.05 N	84.57 W
Allauch, Fr. (ä-lĕ'o͞o)	166a	43.21 N	5.30 E
Allaykha, Sov.Un. (ä-lī'ĸȧ)	179	70.32 N	148.53 E
Allegan, Mi. (ăl'ē-găn)	100	42.30 N	85.55 W
Allegany Ind. Res., NY (ăl-ē-gā'nĭ)	109	42.05 N	78.55 W
Allegheny (R.), Pa.	109	41.10 N	79.20 W
Allegheny Front (Mts.), U.S.	109	38.12 N	80.03 W
Allegheny Mts., U.S.	107	37.35 N	81.55 W
Allegheny Plat, U.S.	108	39.00 N	81.15 W
Allegheny Res., Pa.	109	41.50 N	78.55 W
Allen, Ok. (ăl'ĕn)	121	34.51 N	96.26 W
Allen, Lough (B.), Ire. (lŏk ăl'ĕn)	160	54.07 N	8.09 W
Allendale, NJ (ăl'ĕn-dāl)	110a	41.02 N	74.08 W
Allendale, SC	125	33.00 N	81.19 W
Allende, Mex. (äl-yĕn'då)	129	18.23 N	92.49 W
Allende, Mex.	122	28.20 N	100.50 W
Allentown, Pa. (ăl'en-toun)	109	40.35 N	75.30 W
Alleppey, India (ȧ-lĕp'ē)	191	9.33 N	76.22 E
Aller R., F.R.G. (äl'ēr)	164	52.43 N	9.50 E
Alliance, Ne. (ȧ-lī'ăns)	112	42.06 N	102.53 W
Alliance, Oh.	108	40.55 N	81.10 W
Al Lidām, Sau.Ar.	192	20.45 N	44.12 E
Allier (R.), Fr. (ȧ-lyā')	166	46.43 N	3.03 E
Alligator Pt., La. (ăl'ĭ-gā-tēr)	110d	30.57 N	89.41 W
Allinge, Den. (äl'ĭŋ-ĕ)	162	55.16 N	14.48 E
All Pines, Belize (ôl pīnz)	130a	16.55 N	88.15 W
Al Luḩayyah, Yemen	192	15.58 N	42.48 E
Alluvial City, La.	110d	29.51 N	89.42 W
Allyn, Wa. (ăl'ĭn)	116a	47.23 N	122.51 W
Alma, Can. (ăl'mȧ)	102	45.36 N	64.59 W
Alma, Can.	102	48.29 N	71.42 W
Alma, Ga.	125	31.33 N	82.31 W
Alma, Mi.	108	43.25 N	84.40 W
Alma, Ne.	120	40.08 N	99.21 W
Alma, S. Afr.	219d	24.30 S	28.05 E
Alma, Wi.	113	44.21 N	91.57 W
Alma-Ata, Sov. Un. (ăl'mȧ ȧ'tȧ)	178	43.19 N	77.08 E
Al Mabrak (R.), Sau. Ar.	189a	29.16 N	35.12 E
Almada, Port. (äl-mä'dä)	169b	38.40 N	9.09 W
Almadén, Sp. (äl-mȧ-dhān')	168	38.47 N	4.50 W
Al Madīnah (Medina), Sau. Ar.	192	24.26 N	39.42 E
Al Mafraq, Jordan	189a	32.21 N	36.13 E
Almagre, Laguna (L.), Mex. (lä-go͞o'nä-äl-mä'grē)	129	23.48 N	97.45 W
Almagro, Sp. (äl-mä'grō)	168	38.52 N	3.41 W
Al Maḩallah al Kubrā, Egypt	219b	31.00 N	31.10 E
Al Manāmah, Bahrain	192	26.01 N	50.33 E
Almanor (R.), Ca. (ăl-măn'ôr)	118	40.11 N	121.20 W
Almansa, Sp. (äl-män'sä)	168	38.52 N	1.09 W
Al Manshāh, Egypt	219b	26.31 N	31.46 E
Almansor (R.), Port. (äl-män-sôr)	168	38.41 N	8.27 W
Al Manşūrah, Egypt	219b	31.02 N	31.25 E
Al Manzilah, Egypt (män'za-la)	219b	31.09 N	32.05 E
Almanzora (R.), Sp. (äl-män-thō'rä)	168	37.20 N	2.25 W
Al Marāghah, Egypt	219b	26.41 N	31.35 E
Almargem do Bispo, Port. (äl-mär-zhĕɴ)	169b	38.51 N	9.16 W
Al-Marj, Libya	221	32.44 N	21.08 E
Al Maşīrah (I.), Om.	192	20.43 N	58.58 E
Al Mawsil, Iraq	192	36.00 N	42.53 E
Almazán, Sp. (äl-mä-thän')	168	41.30 N	2.33 W
Al Mazār, Jordan	189a	31.04 N	35.41 E
Al Mazra'ah, Jordan	189a	31.17 N	35.33 E
Almeirim, Port. (äl-māī-rēɴ')	168	39.13 N	8.31 W
Almelo, Neth. (äl'mē-lō)	161	52.20 N	6.42 E
Almendra, Embalse de (Res.), Sp.	168	41.15 N	6.10 W
Almendralejo, Sp. (äl-mān-drä-lā'hō)	168	38.43 N	6.24 W
Almería, Sp. (äl-mā-rē'ä)	168	36.52 N	2.28 W
Almería, Golfo de (G.), Sp. (gôl-fô-dĕ-äl-māī-reɴ')	168	36.45 N	2.26 W
Älmhult, Swe. (ĕlm'ho͝olt)	162	56.35 N	14.08 E
Almina, Pta., Mor. (äl-mē'nä)	168	35.58 N	5.17 W
Al Minyā, Egypt	219b	28.04 N	30.45 E
Almirante, Pan. (äl-mē-rän'tä)	131	9.18 N	82.24 W
Almirante, Bahía de (B.), Pan. (bä-ē'ä-dĕ-äl-mē-rän'tā)	131	9.22 N	82.07 W
Almirós, Grc.	171	39.13 N	22.47 E
Almodóvar del Campo, Sp. (äl-mō-dhō'vär)	168	38.43 N	4.10 W
Almoi, India	190	29.41 N	79.42 E
Almoloya, Mex. (äl-mō-lō'yä)	128	19.32 N	99.44 W
Almoloya, Mex.	129a	19.11 N	99.28 W
Almonte, Can. (ăl-mŏn'tē)	109	45.15 N	76.15 W
Almonte, Sp. (äl-mōn'tā)	168	37.16 N	6.32 W
Almonte (R.), Sp.	168	39.35 N	5.50 W
Almora, India	190	29.20 N	79.40 E
Al Mubarraz, Sau.Ar.	192	22.31 N	46.27 E
Al Mudawwarah, Jordan	189a	29.20 N	36.01 E
Al Mukallā, P.D.R. of Yem.	192	14.27 N	49.05 E
Al Mukhā, Yemen	192	13.43 N	43.27 E
Almuñécar, Sp. (äl-mo͞on-yā'kär)	168	36.44 N	3.43 W
Alnön (I.), Swe.	162	62.20 N	17.39 E
Aloha, Or. (ä'lô-hä)	116c	45.29 N	122.52 W
Alor, Pulau (I.), Indon. (ä'lôr)	203	8.07 S	125.00 E
Álora, Sp. (ä'lô-rä)	168	36.49 N	4.42 W
Alor Gajah, Mala	189b	2.23 N	102.13 E
Alor Setar, Mala. (ä'lôr stär)	202	6.10 N	100.16 E
Alouette (R.), Can. (ä-lo͞o-ĕt')	116d	49.16 N	122.32 W
Alpena, Mi. (ăl-pē'nȧ)	108	45.05 N	83.30 W
Alphen, Neth.	155a	52.07 N	4.38 E
Alpiarça, Port. (äl-pyär'sȧ)	168	39.38 N	8.37 W
Alpine, Tx. (ăl'pīn)	122	30.21 N	103.41 W
Alps (Mts.), Eur. (ălps)	158	46.18 N	8.42 E
Alpujarra, Col. (äl-po͞o-ĸȧ'rȧ)	140a	3.23 N	74.56 W
Alpujarras (Mts.), Sp. (äl-po͞o-här'räs)	168	36.55 N	3.25 W
Al Qaḑārif, Sud.	221	14.03 N	35.11 E
Al Qāhirah (Cairo), Egypt	219b	30.00 N	31.17 E
Al Qanţarah, Egypt	219c	30.51 N	32.20 E
Al Qaryah ash Sharqīyah, Libya	221	30.36 N	13.13 E
Al Qaţīf, Sau. Ar.	192	26.30 N	50.00 E
Al Qayşūmah, Sau. Ar.	192	28.15 N	46.20 E
Al Qunaytirah, Syr.	189a	33.09 N	35.49 E
Al Qunfudhah, Sau. Ar.	192	19.08 N	41.05 E

PLACE (Pronunciation)	PAGE	Lat. °′	Long. °′
Al Quşaymah, Egypt	189a	30.40 N	34.23 E
Al Quşayr, Egypt	221	26.14 N	34.11 E
Al Qusayr, Egypt	189a	34.32 N	36.33 E
Als (I.), Den. (äls)	162	55.06 N	9.40 E
Alsace (Reg.), Fr. (äl-sá's)	167	48.25 N	7.24 E
Al Shan (Mts.), China (äī'shän)	196	37.27 N	120.35 E
Altadena, Ca. (ăl-tä-dē'nä)	117a	34.12 N	118.08 W
Alta Gracia, Arg. (äl'tä grä'sē-ä)	142	31.41 S	64.19 W
Altagracia, Ven.	140	10.42 N	71.34 W
Altagracia de Orituco, Ven. (ä'l-tá-grá'sēä-dē-ôrē-tōō'kô)	141b	9.53 N	66.22 W
Altai Mts., Asia (äl'tī')	194	49.11 N	87.15 E
Alta Loma, Ca. (ăl'tă lō'mä)	117a	34.07 N	117.35 W
Alta Loma, Tx. (ăl'tá lō-má)	123a	29.22 N	95.05 W
Altamaha (R.), Ga. (ôl-tá-má-hô')	125	31.50 N	82.00 W
Altamira, Braz. (äl-tä-mē'rä)	141	3.13 S	52.14 W
Altamira, Mex.	129	22.25 N	97.55 W
Altamirano, Arg. (äl-tä-mē-rä'nō)	142	35.26 S	58.12 W
Altamura, It. (äl-tä-mōō'rä)	170	40.40 N	16.35 E
Altan Bulag, Mong.	179	50.18 N	106.31 E
Altavista, Va. (äl-tä-vĭs'tá)	125	37.08 N	79.14 W
Altay, China (äl-tā)	194	47.52 N	86.50 E
Altenburg, G.D.R. (äl-tĕn-bōōrgh)	164	50.59 N	12.27 E
Altenmarkt an der Triesting, Aus.	155e	48.02 N	16.00 E
Alter do Chão, Port. (äl-tĕr'dōō shäN'ōN)	168	39.13 N	7.38 W
Altiplanicie Mexicana (Plat.), Mex. (äl-tē-plä-nē'syĕ-mĕ-κē-kä-nä)	128	22.38 N	102.33 W
Altiplano (Plat.), Bol. (äl-tē-plá'nō)	140	18.38 S	68.20 W
Altlandsberg, G.D.R. (ält länts'bĕrgh)	155b	52.34 N	13.44 E
Alto, La. (ăl'tō)	123	32.21 N	91.52 W
Alto Marañón, Rio (R.), Peru (rē'ō-ál'tô-mä-rän-yō'n)	140	8.18 S	77.13 W
Alto Molócuè, Moz.	227	15.38 S	37.42 E
Altomünster, F.R.G. (äl'tō-mün'stĕr)	155d	48.24 N	11.16 E
Alton, Can. (ôl'tŭn)	93d	43.52 N	80.05 W
Alton, Il.	117e	38.53 N	90.11 W
Altona, Austl.	207a	37.52 S	144.50 E
Altona, Can.	99	49.06 N	97.33 W
Altona, F.R.G. (äl'tō-ná)	155c	53.33 N	9.54 E
Altoona, Al. (ăl-tōō'ná)	124	34.01 N	86.15 W
Altoona, Pa.	109	40.25 N	78.25 W
Altoona, Wa.	116c	46.16 N	123.39 W
Alto Rio Doce, Braz. (äl'tô-rē'ô-dō'sĕ)	139a	21.02 S	43.23 W
Alto Songo, Cuba (äl-fō-sôŋ'gō)	133	20.10 N	75.45 W
Altotonga, Mex. (äl-tō-tôŋ'gä)	129	19.44 N	97.13 W
Alto-Uama, Ang.	226	12.14 S	15.33 E
Alto Velo (I.), Dom. Rep. (äl-tô-vĕ'lō)	133	17.30 N	71.35 W
Altrincham, Eng. (ôl'trĭng-ăm)	154	53.18 N	2.21 W
Altruppin, G.D.R. (ält rōō'ppēn)	155b	52.56 N	12.50 E
Altun Shan (Mts.), China (äl-tōōn shän)	194	36.58 N	85.09 E
Alturas, Ca. (ăl-tōō'rás)	114	41.29 N	120.33 W
Alturas, Serra das (Mts.), Port. (sĕ'r-rä-däs-äl-tōō'räs)	168	40.43 N	7.48 W
Altus, Ok. (ăl'tŭs)	120	34.38 N	99.20 W
Al-Ubayyiḍ, Sud.	221	13.15 N	30.15 E
Al-Uḍayyah, Sud.	221	12.06 N	28.16 E
Al-'Ugaylah, Libya	221	30.15 N	19.07 E
Alūksne, Sov. Un. (ä'lōōks-nĕ)	172	57.24 N	27.04 E
'Alula, Som. (ä-lōō'lä)	219a	11.53 N	50.40 E
Alumette I., Can. (á-lü-mĕt')	109	45.50 N	77.00 W
Alum Rock, Ca.	116b	37.23 N	121.50 W
Al Uqşur (Luxor), Egypt	219b	25.38 N	32.59 E
Alushta, Sov. Un. (ä'lshōō-tá)	173	44.39 N	34.23 E
Alva, Ok. (ăl'vá)	120	36.46 N	98.41 W
Alvarado, Mex. (äl-vä-rä'dhō)	129	18.48 N	95.45 W
Alvarado, Luguna de (L.), Mex. (lä-gōō'nä-dĕ-äl-vä-rá'dô)	129	18.44 N	96.45 W
Älvdalen, Swe. (ĕlv'dä-lĕn)	162	61.14 N	14.04 E
Alverca, Port. (al-vĕr'ká)	169b	38.53 N	9.02 W
Alvesta, Swe. (äl-vĕs'tä)	162	56.55 N	14.29 E
Alvin, Tx. (ăl'vĭn)	123a	29.25 N	95.14 W
Alvinópolis, Braz. (äl-vēnō'pō-lēs)	139a	20.07 S	43.03 W
Alviso, Ca. (ăl-vī'sō)	116b	37.26 N	121.59 W
Al Wajh, Sau. Ar.	192	26.15 N	36.32 E
Alwar, India (ŭl'wŭr)	190	27.39 N	76.39 E
Al Wāsiţah, Egypt	219b	29.21 N	31.15 E
Alytus, Sov. Un. (ä'lē-tōōs)	163	54.25 N	24.05 E
Almacuzac (R.), Mex. (ä-mä-kōō-zák)	128	18.00 N	99.03 W
Amadeus, (L.), Austl. (ăm-á-dē'ŭs)	210	24.30 S	131.25 E
Amadjuak (L.), Can. (ä-mädj'wăk)	95	64.50 N	69.20 W
Amagasaki, Jap. (ä'mä-gä-sä'kē)	201b	34.43 N	135.25 E
Amakusa-Shimo (I.), Jap. (ämä-kōō'sä shē-mō)	201	32.24 N	129.35 E
Åmål, Swe. (ô'môl)	162	59.05 N	12.40 E
Amalfi, Col. (ä'mä'l-fē)	140a	6.55 N	75.04 W
Amalfi, It. (ä-mä'l-fē)	169c	40.23 N	14.36 E
Amaliás, Grc. (á-mäl'yás)	171	37.48 N	21.23 E
Amalner, India	190	21.07 N	75.06 E
Amambaí, Serra de (Mts.), Braz.	141	20.06 S	57.08 W
Amami Guntō (Is.), Jap. (ä'mä'mē gōōn'tō')	200	28.25 N	129.00 E
Amamio (I.), Jap. (ä-mä'mē-ō)	200	28.10 N	129.55 E
Amapá, Braz. (ä-mä-pá')	141	2.14 N	50.48 W
Amapá (Ter.) **Braz.**	141	1.15 N	52.15 W
Amapala, Hond. (ä-mä-pä'lä)	130	13.16 N	87.39 W
Amarante, Braz. (ä-mä-rän'tä)	141	6.17 S	42.43 W
Amargosa (R.), Ca. (á'mär-gō'sá)	118	35.55 N	116.45 W
Amarillo, Tx. (ăm-á-rĭl'ō)	120	35.14 N	101.49 W

PLACE (Pronunciation)	PAGE	Lat. °′	Long. °′
Amaro, Mt., It. (ä-mä'rō)	170	42.07 N	14.07 E
Amasya, Tur. (ä-mä'sē-á)	177	40.40 N	35.50 E
Amatenango, Mex. (ä-mä-tä-naŋ'gō)	129	16.30 N	92.29 W
Amatignak (I.), Ak. (ä-má'tē-näk)	105a	51.12 N	178.30 W
Amatique, Bahía de (B.), Belize-Guat. (bä-ē'ä-dĕ-ä-mä-tē'kä)	130	15.58 N	88.50 W
Amatitlán, Guat. (ä-mä-tē-tlän')	130	14.27 N	90.39 W
Amatlán de Cañas, Mex. (ä-mät-län'dā kän-yäs)	128	20.50 N	104.22 W
Amazonas (State), Braz. (ä-mä-thō'näs)	140	4.15 S	64.30 W
Amazonas, Rio (R.), Braz. (rē'ō-ä-mä-thō'näs)	141	2.03 S	53.18 W
Ambāla, India (ŭm-bä'lŭ)	190	30.31 N	76.48 E
Ambalema, Col. (äm-bä-lā'mä)	140a	4.47 N	74.45 W
Ambarchik, Sov. Un. (ŭm-bär'chĭk)	179	69.39 N	162.18 E
Ambarnāth, India	191b	19.12 N	73.10 E
Ambato, Ec. (äm-bä'tō)	140	1.15 S	78.30 W
Ambatondrazaka, Mad.	223	17.58 S	48.43 E
Amberg, F.R.G. (äm'bĕrgh)	164	49.26 N	11.51 E
Ambergris Cay (I.), Belize (ăm'bēr-grēs kāz)	130	18.04 N	87.43 W
Ambergris Cays (Is.), Turks & Caicos Is.	133	21.20 N	71.40 W
Ambérieu-en-Bugey, Fr. (äN-bā-rē-u')	167	45.57 N	5.21 E
Ambert, Fr. (äN-bĕr')	166	45.32 N	3.41 E
Ambil I., Phil. (äm'bēl)	203a	13.51 N	120.25 E
Ambler, Pa. (ăm'blēr)	110f	40.09 N	75.13 W
Amboise, Fr. (äN-bwăz')	166	47.25 N	0.56 E
Ambon, Indon.	203	3.45 S	128.17 E
Ambon, Pulau (I.), Indon.	203	4.50 S	128.45 E
Ambositra, Mad. (äN-bô-sē'trä)	223	20.31 S	47.28 E
Amboy, Il. (ăm'boi)	108	41.41 N	89.15 W
Amboy, Wa.	116c	45.55 N	122.27 W
Ambre, Cap d' (C.), Mad.	223	12.06 S	49.15 E
Ambridge, Pa. (ăm'brĭdj)	111e	40.36 N	80.13 W
Ambrim (I.), Vanuatu	211	16.25 S	168.15 E
Ambriz, Ang.	226	7.50 S	13.06 E
Ambrizete, Ang.	226	7.14 S	12.52 E
Amchitka (I.), Ak. (ăm-chĭt'ká)	105a	51.25 N	178.10 E
Amchitka Pass., Ak.	105a	51.30 N	179.36 W
Amealco, Mex. (ä-mä-äl'kō)	128	20.12 N	100.08 W
Ameca, Mex. (ä-mĕ'kä)	128	20.34 N	104.02 W
Amecameca, Mex. (ä-må-kä-mā'kä)	129a	19.06 N	98.46 W
Ameide, Neth.	155a	51.57 N	4.57 E
Ameland (I.), Neth.	161	53.29 N	5.54 E
Amelia, Oh. (á-mĕl'yá)	111f	39.01 N	84.12 W
American (R.), Ca. (á-mĕr'ĭ-kăn)	118	38.43 N	120.45 W
Americana, Braz. (ä-mĕ-rē-kä'ná)	139a	22.46 S	47.19 W
American Falls, Id. (á-mĕ-ĭ-kăn)	115	42.45 N	112.53 W
American Falls Res., Id.	115	42.56 N	113.18 W
American Fork, Ut.	119	40.20 N	111.50 W
American Highland, Ant.	228	72.00 S	79.00 E
Americus, Ga. (á-mĕr'ĭ-kŭs)	124	32.04 N	84.15 W
Amersfoort, Neth. (ä'mĕrz-fōrt)	155a	52.08 N	5.23 E
Amery, Can. (ā'mēr-ē)	99	56.34 N	94.03 W
Amery, Wi.	113	45.19 N	92.24 W
Ames, Ia. (āmz)	113	42.00 N	93.36 W
Amesbury, Ma. (āmz'bēr-ē)	103a	42.51 N	70.56 W
Amfissa, Grc. (ám-fĭ'sá)	171	38.32 N	22.26 E
Amga, Sov. Un. (ŭm-gä')	179	61.08 N	132.09 E
Amga (R.), Sov. Un.	179	61.41 N	133.11 E
Amgun (R.), Sov. Un.	179	53.33 N	137.57 E
Amhara (Prov.), Eth. (äm-hä'rä)	221	11.30 N	36.45 E
Amherst, Can. (ăm'hērst)	102	45.49 N	64.14 W
Amherst, Oh.	111d	41.24 N	82.13 W
Amherst (I.), Can.	101	44.08 N	76.45 W
Amiens, Fr. (ä-myäN')	166	49.54 N	2.18 E
Amirante Is., Sey.	228	6.02 S	52.30 E
Amisk L., Can.	99	54.35 N	102.13 W
Amistad Res., Tx.	122	29.20 N	101.00 W
Amite, La. (ă-mēt')	123	30.43 N	90.32 W
Amite R., La.	123	30.45 N	90.48 W
Amity, Pa. (ăm'ĭ-tĭ)	111e	40.02 N	80.11 W
Amityville, NY (ăm'ĭ-tĭ-vĭl)	110a	40.41 N	73.24 W
Amlia (I.), Ak. (á'mlēä)	105a	52.00 N	173.28 W
'Ammān, Jordan (äm'mán)	189a	31.57 N	35.57 E
Ammersee (L.), F.R.G. (äm'mĕr)	155d	48.00 N	11.08 E
Amnicon R., Wi. (ăm'nė-kŏn)	117h	46.35 N	91.56 W
Amnok (R.), **see Yalu**			
Amorgós (I.), Grc. (ä-môr'gōs)	171	36.47 N	25.47 E
Amory, Ms. (ām'o-rē)	124	33.58 N	88.27 W
Amos, Can. (ā'mŭs)	101	48.31 N	78.04 W
Amoy, see Xiamen			
Amparo, Braz. (äm-pa'-rô)	139a	22.43 S	46.44 W
Amper R., F.R.G. (äm'pĕr)	155d	48.18 N	11.32 E
Amposta, Sp. (äm-pōs'tä)	169	40.42 N	0.34 E
Amqui, Can.	102	48.28 N	67.28 W
Amrāvati, India	190	20.58 N	77.47 E
Amritsar, India (ŭm-rĭt'sŭr)	190	31.43 N	74.52 E
Amstelveen, Neth.	155a	52.18 N	4.51 E
Amsterdam, Neth. (äm-stĕr-däm')	155a	52.21 N	4.52 E
Amsterdam, NY (ăm'stĕr-dăm)	109	42.55 N	74.10 W
Amstetten, Aus. (äm'stĕt-ĕn)	164	48.09 N	14.53 E
Am Timan, Chad (äm'tē-män')	221	11.18 N	20.30 E
Amu Darya (R.), Asia (ä-mōō-dä'rēä)	192	40.40 N	62.00 E
Amukta Pass., Ak. (ä-mōōk'tá)	105a	52.30 N	172.00 W
Amundsen G., Can. (ä'mŭn-sĕn)	94	70.17 N	123.28 W
Amundsen Sea, Ant.	228	72.00 S	110.00 W
Amungen (L.), Swe.	162	61.07 N	16.00 E
Amurskiy, Sov. Un. (ä-mûr'skĭ)	180a	52.35 N	59.36 E

PLACE (Pronunciation)	PAGE	Lat. °′	Long. °′
Amurskiy, Zaliv (B.), Sov. Un. (zä'lĭf ä-mōōr'skĭ)	200	43.20 N	131.40 E
Amusgos (San Pedro), Mex. (ä-mōō's-gôs) (sän-pē'drō)	128	16.39 N	98.09 W
Amuyao, Mt., Phil. (ä-mōō-yä'ō)	203a	17.04 N	121.09 E
Amvrakikos Kólpos (G.), Grc.	171	39.00 N	21.00 E
Amyun, Leb.	189a	34.18 N	35.48 E
Anabar (R.), Sov. Un. (ăn-á-bär')	179	71.15 N	113.00 E
Anaco, Ven. (ä-ná'kô)	141b	9.29 N	64.27 W
Anaconda, Mt. (ăn-á-kŏn'dá)	115	46.07 N	112.55 W
Anacortes, Wa. (ăn-á-kôr'tĕz)	116a	48.30 N	122.37 W
Anadarko, Ok. (ăn-á-där'kō)	120	35.05 N	98.14 W
Anadyr', Sov.Un. (ŭ-ná-dĭr')	179	64.47 N	177.01 E
Anadyr (R.), Sov. Un.	179	65.30 N	172.45 E
Anadyrskiy Zaliv (B.), Sov. Un.	189	64.10 N	178.00 W
Anaheim, Ca. (ăn'á-hīm)	117a	33.50 N	117.55 W
Anahuac, Tx. (ä-nä'wăk)	123a	29.46 N	94.41 W
Ānai Mudi (Mtn.), India	191	10.10 N	77.00 E
Anama Bay, Can.	99	51.56 N	98.05 W
Ana María, Cayos (Is.), Cuba (kä'yōs-ä'ná má-rē'á)	132	21.55 N	78.50 W
Anambas, Kepulauan (Is.), Indon. (ä-näm-bäs)	202	2.41 N	106.38 E
Anamosa, Ia. (ăn-á-mō'sá)	113	42.06 N	91.18 W
Anan'yev, Sov. Un. (á-nä'nyĕf)	173	47.43 N	29.59 E
Anapa, Sov. Un. (á-nä'pä)	173	44.54 N	37.19 E
Anápolis, Braz. (ä-ná'pō-lēs)	141	16.17 S	48.47 W
Añatuya, Arg. (á-nyä-tōō'yá)	142	28.22 S	62.45 W
Anchieta, Braz. (án-chyĕ'tä)	142b	22.49 S	43.24 W
Ancholme (R.), Eng. (ăn'chŭm)	154	53.28 N	0.27 W
Anchorage, Ak. (ăŋ'kēr-āj)	105	61.12 N	149.48 W
Anchorage, Ky.	111b	38.16 N	85.32 W
Anci, China (än-tsŭ)	198a	39.31 N	116.41 E
Ancienne-Lorette, Can. (äN-syĕn' lō-rĕt')	93b	46.48 N	71.21 W
Ancon, Pan. (ăŋ-kōn')	126a	8.55 N	79.32 W
Ancona, It. (än-kō'nä)	170	43.37 N	13.32 E
Ancud, Chile (äŋ-kōōdh')	142	41.52 S	73.45 W
Ancud, G. de, Chile (gôl-fô-dĕ-äŋ-kōōdh')	142	41.15 S	73.00 W
Anda, China	198	46.20 N	125.20 E
Andalgalá, Arg. (á'n-däl-gá-lá')	142	27.35 S	66.14 W
Åndalsnes, Nor.	162	62.33 N	7.46 E
Andalucia (Reg.), Sp. (än-dä-lōō-sē'á)	168	37.35 N	5.40 W
Andalusia, Al. (ăn-dá-lōō'zhĭá)	124	31.19 N	86.19 W
Andaman Is., Andaman & Nicobar Is. (ăn-dá-măn')	202	11.38 N	92.17 E
Andaman Sea, Asia	202	12.44 N	95.45 E
Andarax (R.), Sp.	168	37.00 N	2.40 W
Anderlecht, Bel. (än'dĕr-lĕkt)	155a	50.49 N	4.16 E
Andernach, F.R.G. (än'dĕr-näk)	164	50.25 N	7.23 E
Anderson, Arg. (á'n-dĕr-sōn)	139c	35.15 S	60.15 W
Anderson, Ca. (ăn'dēr-sŭn)	114	40.28 N	122.19 W
Anderson, In.	108	40.05 N	85.50 W
Anderson, SC	125	34.30 N	82.40 W
Anderson (R.), Can.	94	68.32 N	125.12 W
Andes Mts., S. A. (ăn'dēz) (än'dās)	138	13.00 S	75.00 W
Andheri (Neigh.), India	191b	19.08 N	72.50 E
Andhra Pradesh (State), India	191	16.00 N	79.00 E
Andikíthira (I.), Grc.	159	35.50 N	23.20 E
Andizhan, Sov. Un. (än-dē-zhän')	178	40.51 N	72.39 E
Andong, Kor. (än'dŭng')	200	36.31 N	128.42 E
Andongwei, China (än-dôŋ-wā)	196	35.08 N	119.19 E
Andorra, And. (än-dôr'rä)	169	42.38 N	1.30 E
Andorra, Eur.	157	42.30 N	2.00 E
Andover, Ma. (ăn'dô-vēr)	103a	42.39 N	71.08 W
Andover, NJ	110a	40.59 N	74.45 W
Andøya (I.), Nor. (änd-ûê)	156	69.12 N	14.58 E
Andreanof Is., Ak. (än-drå-ä'nôf)	105a	51.10 N	177.00 W
Andrelândia, Braz. (än-drĕ-lá'n-dyá)	139a	21.45 S	44.18 W
Andrew Johnson Natl. Mon., Tn. (ăn'drōō jŏn'sŭn)	124	36.15 N	82.55 W
Andrews, NC (ăn'drōōz)	124	35.12 N	83.48 W
Andrews, SC	125	33.25 N	79.32 W
Andreyevka, Sov. Un. (än-drå-yĕf'ká)	173	48.03 N	37.03 E
Andria, It. (än'drē-ä)	170	41.17 N	15.55 E
Andros, Grc. (än'dhrôs)	171	37.50 N	24.54 E
Andros I., Ba. (ăn'drŏs)	132	24.30 N	78.00 W
Ándros (I.), Grc. (än'drôs)	171	37.59 N	24.55 E
Androscoggin (R.), Me. (ăn-drŭs-kŏg'ĭn)	102	44.25 N	70.45 W
Anefis i-n-Darane, Mali	224	18.03 N	0.36 E
Anegasaki, Jap. (ä'nå-gä-sä'kē)	201a	35.29 N	140.02 E
Aneityum (I.), Vanuatu (ä-nå-ē'tē-ŭm)	211	20.15 S	169.49 E
Aneta, ND (á-nē'tá)	112	47.41 N	97.57 W
Angamacutiro, Mex. (än'gä-mä-kōō-tē'rô)	128	20.08 N	101.44 W
Angangueo, Mex. (än-gäŋ'gwå-ō)	128	19.36 N	100.18 W
Ang'angxi, China (äŋ-äŋ-shyē)	198	47.05 N	123.58 E
Angara (R.), **see Verkhnyaya, Tunguska**			
Angarsk, Sov. Un.	178	52.48 N	104.15 E
Ange, Swe. (ông'å)	162	62.31 N	15.39 E
Angel, Salto (Falls), Ven. (säl'tō-á'n-hĕl)	140	5.44 N	62.27 W
Angel De La Guarda (I.), Mex. (á'n-hĕl-dĕ-lä-gwä'r-dä)	126	29.30 N	113.00 W
Angeles, Phil. (än'hå-lās)	203a	15.09 N	120.35 E
Ängelholm, Swe. (ĕng'ĕl-hôlm)	162	56.14 N	12.50 E
Angelina R., Tx. (ăn-jē lē'ná)	123	31.30 N	94.53 W
Angels Camp, Ca. (ān'jĕls kămp')	118	38.03 N	120.33 W

264 Areia Branca – Atacama

PLACE (Pronunciation)	PAGE	Lat. °'	Long. °'
Areia Branca, Braz. (ä-rĕ'yä-brä'n-kä)	141	4.58 S	37.02 W
Arena, Pt., Ca. (ä-rā'nȧ)	118	38.57 N	123.40 W
Arenas, Punta (Pt.), Ven. (po͞on'tä-rĕ'näs)	141b	10.57 N	64.24 W
Arenas de San Pedro, Sp. (ä-rā'nås dā sän pā'drō)	168	40.12 N	5.04 W
Arendal, Nor. (ä'rĕn-däl)	162	58.29 N	8.44 E
Arendonk, Bel.	155a	51.19 N	5.07 E
Arequipa, Peru (ä-rå-kē'pä)	140	16.27 S	71.30 W
Arezzo, It. (ä-rĕt'sō)	170	43.28 N	11.54 E
Arga (R.), Sp. (är'gä)	168	42.35 N	1.55 W
Arganda, Sp. (är-gän'dä)	169a	40.18 N	3.27 W
Argazi (L.), Sov. Un. (är'gä-zĭ)	180a	55.24 N	60.37 E
Argazi R., Sov. Un.	180a	55.33 N	57.30 E
Argentan, Fr. (år-zhäN-täN')	166	48.45 N	0.01 W
Argentat, Fr. (år-zhäN-tä')	166	45.07 N	1.57 E
Argenteuil, Fr. (är-zhäN-tû'y')	167b	48.56 N	2.15 E
Argentina, S.A. (är-jĕn-tē'nȧ)	138	35.30 S	67.00 W
Argentino (L.), Arg. (är-Kĕn-tē'nō)	142	50.15 S	72.45 W
Argenton-sur-Creuse, Fr. (är-zhäN'tôN-sür-krôs)	166	46.34 N	1.28 E
Argeş (R.), Rom. (år'zhĕsh)	171	44.27 N	25.22 E
Argolikos Kólpos (G.), Grc.	171	37.20 N	23.00 E
Argonne (Mts.), Fr. (ä'r-gôn)	166	49.21 N	5.54 E
Argos, Grc. (är'gŏs)	171	37.38 N	22.45 E
Argostólion, Grc. (är-gŏs-tô'lē-ŏn)	171	38.10 N	20.30 E
Arguello, Pt., Ca. (är-gwĕl'yō)	118	34.35 N	120.40 W
Argun R., China-Sov. Un. (år-go͞on')	179	50.15 N	118.45 E
Argungu, Nig.	225	12.45 N	4.31 E
Argyle, Can. (är'gīl)	93f	50.11 N	97.27 W
Argyle, Mn.	112	48.21 N	96.48 W
Århus, Den. (ôr'ho͞os)	162	56.09 N	10.10 E
Ariakeno-Umi (Sea), Jap. (ä-rē'ä-Kä'nō o͞o'nē)	201	33.03 N	130.18 E
Ariake-Wan (B.), Jap. (ä'rē-ä'kä wän)	201	31.19 N	131.15 E
Ariano, It. (ä-rē-ä'nō)	170	41.09 N	15.11 E
Ariari (R.), Col. (ä-ryà'rē)	140a	3.34 N	73.42 W
Aribinda, Upper Volta	224	14.14 N	0.52 W
Arica, Chile (ä-rē'kä)	140	18.34 S	70.14 W
Arichat, Can. (ä-rĭ-shät')	103	45.31 N	61.01 W
Ariège (R.), Fr. (å-rē-ĕzh')	166	43.26 N	1.29 E
Ariel, Wa. (â'rĭ-ĕl)	116c	45.57 N	122.34 W
Arieşul (R.), Rom. (ä-rē-ā'sho͞ol)	165	46.25 N	23.15 E
Ariguanabo, L. de, Cuba (lä'gô-dĕ-ä-rē-gwä-nä'bô)	133a	22.17 N	82.33 W
Arīḥā (Jericho), Jordan	189a	31.51 N	35.28 E
Arikaree (R.), Co. (ä-rĭ-kȧ-rē')	120	39.51 N	102.18 W
Arima, Jap. (ä'rē-mä')	201b	34.48 N	135.16 E
Aringay, Phil. (ä-rĭŋ-gä'ē)	203a	16.25 N	120.20 E
Arinos (R.), Braz. (ä-rē'nŏzsh)	141	12.09 S	56.49 W
Aripuanã (R.), Braz. (ä-rē-pwän'yȧ)	141	7.06 S	60.29 W
'Arīsh, Wādī al (R.), Egypt (å-rēsh')	189a	30.36 N	34.07 E
Aristazabal I., Can.	96	52.30 N	129.20 W
Arizona (State), U.S. (ăr-ĭ-zō'nȧ)	106	34.00 N	113.00 W
Arjona, Sp. (är-hō'nä)	168	37.58 N	4.03 W
Arka (R.), Sov. Un.	179	60.12 N	142.30 E
Arkabutla Res., Ms. (är-kȧ-bŭt'lȧ)	124	34.48 N	90.00 W
Arkadelphia, Ar. (är-kȧ-dĕl'fĭ-ȧ)	121	34.06 N	93.05 W
Arkansas (State), U.S. (är'kăn-sô) (är-kăn'sȧs)	107	34.50 N	93.40 W
Arkansas City, Ks.	121	37.04 N	97.02 W
Arkansas R., Ok.	121	35.20 N	94.56 W
Arkhangelsk (Archangel), Sov. Un. (år-Kän'gĕlsk)	176	64.30 N	40.25 E
Arkhangel'skiy, Sov. Un. (är-kän-gĕl'skĭ)	180a	52.52 N	61.53 E
Arkhangel'skoye, Sov. Un. (är-kän-gĕl'skô-yĕ)	180a	54.25 N	56.48 E
Arklow, Ire. (ärk'lō)	160	52.47 N	6.10 W
Arkona, Kap (C.), G.D.R. (är'kō-nä)	162	54.43 N	13.43 E
Arkonam, India (ăr-kō-näm')	191	13.05 N	79.43 E
Arlanza (R.), Sp. (är-län-thä')	168	42.08 N	3.45 W
Arlanzón (R.), Sp. (är-län-thōn')	168	42.12 N	3.58 W
Arlberg Tun., Aus. (ärl'bĕrgh)	164	47.05 N	10.15 E
Arles, Fr. (ärl)	166	43.42 N	4.38 E
Arlington, Ga. (är'lĭng-tun')	124	31.25 N	84.42 W
Arlington, Ma.	103a	42.26 N	71.13 W
Arlington, SD (är'lēng-tŭn)	112	44.23 N	97.09 W
Arlington, Tx. (är'lĭng-tŭn)	117c	32.44 N	97.07 W
Arlington, S. Afr.	219d	28.02 S	27.52 E
Arlington, Vt.	109	43.05 N	73.05 W
Arlington, Va.	110e	38.55 N	77.10 W
Arlington, Wa.	116a	48.11 N	122.08 W
Arlington Heights, Il. (är'lēng-tŭn-hī'ts)	111a	42.05 N	87.59 W
Arltunga, Austl. (ärl-to͞oŋ'gȧ)	210	23.19 S	134.45 E
Arma, Ks. (är'mȧ)	121	37.34 N	94.43 W
Armagh, Can. (är-mä') (är-mäK')	93b	46.45 N	70.36 W
Armagh, N. Ire.	160	54.21 N	6.25 W
Armant, Egypt (är-mänt')	219b	25.37 N	32.32 E
Armaro, Col. (är-má'rō)	140a	4.58 N	74.54 W
Armavir, Sov. Un. (år-må-vĭr')	177	45.00 N	41.00 E
Armenia, Col. (är-mē'nē-ä)	140a	4.33 N	75.40 W
Armenia, Sal. (är-mā'nē-ä)	130	13.44 N	89.31 W
Armenian, S. S. R., Sov. Un.	174	41.00 N	44.39 E
Armentières, Fr. (år-mäN-tyâr')	166	50.43 N	2.53 E
Armeria, Rio de (R.), Mex. (rē'ō-dĕ-är-mā-rē'ä)	128	19.36 N	104.10 W
Armherstburg, Can. (ärm'hĕrst-bo͝orgh)	111b	42.06 N	83.06 W
Armidale, Austl. (är'mĭ-dāl)	212	30.27 S	151.50 E
Armour, SD (är'mēr)	112	43.18 N	98.21 W
Armstrong Station, Can. (ärm'strŏng)	100	50.21 N	89.00 W
Armyansk, Sov. Un. (ärm'yånsk)	173	46.06 N	33.42 E
Arnedo, Sp. (är-nā'dō)	168	42.12 N	2.03 W
Arnhem, Neth. (ärn'hĕm)	161	51.58 N	5.56 E
Arnhem, C., Austl.	210	12.15 S	137.00 E
Arnhem Land, (Reg.), Austl. (ärn'hĕm-lănd)	210	13.15 S	133.00 E
Arno (R.), It. (ä'r-nô)	170	43.45 N	10.42 E
Arnold, Eng. (är'nŭld)	154	53.00 N	1.08 W
Arnold, Mn. (är'nūld)	117h	46.53 N	92.06 W
Arnold, Pa.	111e	40.35 N	79.45 W
Arnprior, Can. (ärn-prī'ēr)	109	45.25 N	76.20 W
Arnsberg, F.R.G. (ärns'bĕrgh)	161	51.25 N	8.02 E
Arnstadt, G.D.R. (ärn'shtät)	164	50.51 N	10.57 E
Aroab, Namibia (är'ō-ȧb)	222	25.40 S	19.45 E
Aroostook (R.), Me. (ȧ-ro͞os'to͝ok)	102	46.44 N	68.15 W
Aroroy, Phil. (ä-rô-rō'ē)	203a	12.30 N	123.24 E
Arpajon, Fr. (är-pä-jō'n)	167b	48.35 N	2.15 E
Arpoador, Ponta do (Pt.), Braz. (pô'n-tä-dō-är'pôä-dō'r)	142b	22.59 S	43.11 W
Arraiolos, Port. (är-rī-ō'lōzh)	168	38.47 N	7.59 W
Ar Ramādī, Iraq	192	33.30 N	43.12 E
Arran, Island of, Scot. (ă'răn)	160	55.25 N	5.25 W
Ar Rank, Sud.	221	11.45 N	32.53 E
Arras, Fr. (å-räs')	166	50.21 N	2.40 E
Ar Rawḍah, Egypt	219b	27.47 N	30.52 E
Arrecifes, Arg. (är-rå-sē'fås)	139c	34.03 S	60.05 W
Arrecifes (R.), Arg.	139c	34.07 S	59.50 W
Arrée, Mts. d', Fr. (är-rā')	166	48.27 N	4.00 W
Arriaga, Mex. (är-rēä'gä)	129	16.15 N	93.54 W
Ar Riyāḍ, see Riyadh			
Arrone (R.), It.	169d	41.57 N	12.17 E
Arrowhead, L., Ca. (lăk ăr'ōhĕd)	117a	34.17 N	117.13 W
Arrow R., Mt. (ăr'ō)	115	47.29 N	109.53 W
Arrowrock Res., Id. (ăr'ō-rŏk)	114	43.40 N	115.30 W
Arroya Arena, Cuba (är-rô'yä-rĕ'nä)	133a	23.01 N	82.30 W
Arroyo de la Luz, Sp. (är-rō'yō-dĕ-lä-lo͞o'z)	168	39.39 N	6.46 W
Arroyo Grande (R.), Mex. (är-rô'yō-grä'n-dĕ)	128	23.30 N	98.45 W
Arroyo Seco, Mex. (är-rō'yō sä'kō)	128	21.31 N	99.44 W
Ar Rub' Al Khālī (Des.), Sau. Ar.	192	20.30 N	49.15 E
Ar-Ruşayriş, Sud.	221	11.38 N	34.42 E
Arsen'yev, Sov. Un.	179	44.13 N	133.32 E
Arsinskiy, Sov. Un. (är-sĭn'skĭ)	180a	53.46 N	59.54 E
Árta, Grc. (är'tä)	171	39.08 N	21.02 E
Arteaga, Mex. (är-tä-ä'gä)	122	25.28 N	100.50 W
Artëm, Sov. Un. (år-tyôm')	179	43.28 N	132.29 E
Artemisa, Cuba (är-tå-mē'sä)	132	22.50 N	82.45 W
Artëmovsk, Sov. Un. (år-tyŏm'ŏfsk)	173	48.37 N	38.00 E
Artesia, NM (är-tē'sĭ-ȧ)	120	32.44 N	104.23 W
Artesian Basin, The, Austl. (är-tē'zhăn)	212	26.45 S	141.40 E
Arthabaska, Can.	102	46.03 N	71.54 W
Arthur's Town, Ba.	133	24.40 N	75.40 W
Arti, Sov. Un. (är'tĭ)	180a	56.20 N	58.38 E
Artibonite (R.), Hai. (är-tē-bô-nē'tä)	133	19.00 N	72.25 W
Aru, Kepulauan (Is.), Indon.	203	6.20 S	133.00 E
Arua, Ug. (ä'ro͞o-ä)	227	3.01 N	30.55 E
Aruba, (I.), Neth. Antilles (ä-ro͞o'bȧ)	140	12.29 N	70.00 W
Arunachal Pradesh (Union Ter.), India	194	27.35 N	92.56 E
Arusha, Tan. (ȧ-ro͞o'shä)	227	3.22 S	36.41 E
Arvida, Can.	101	48.26 N	71.11 W
Arvika, Swe. (är-vē'kȧ)	162	59.41 N	12.35 E
Arzamas, Sov. Un. (är-zä-mäs')	176	55.20 N	43.52 E
Arzew, Alg. (är-zå-o͞o')	169	35.50 N	0.20 W
Arzua, Sp. (är-tho͞o'ä)	168	42.54 N	8.19 W
As, Czech. (äsh')	164	50.12 N	12.13 E
Asahi-Gawa (Strm.), Jap. (ȧ-sä'hē-gä'wä)	201	35.01 N	133.40 E
Asahikawa, Jap.	200	43.50 N	142.09 E
Asaka, Jap. (ä-sä'kä)	201a	35.47 N	139.36 E
Asansol, India	190	23.45 N	86.58 E
Asbest, Sov. Un. (äs-bĕst')	180a	57.02 N	61.28 E
Asbestos, Can. (ăs-bĕs'tŏs)	102	45.49 N	71.52 W
Asbestovskiy, Sov. Un.	180a	57.46 N	61.23 E
Asbury Park, NJ (ăz'bĕr-ĭ)	110a	40.13 N	74.01 W
Ascención, Bahía de la (B.), Mex. (bä-ē'ä-dĕ-lä-äs-sĕn-sē-ōn')	130a	19.39 N	87.30 W
Ascensión, Mex. (äs-sĕn-sē-ōn')	128	24.21 N	99.54 W
Ascension (I.), Atl. O. (ȧ-sĕn'shŭn)	218	8.00 S	13.00 W
Ascent, S. Afr. (ăs-ĕnt')	219d	27.14 S	29.06 E
Aschaffenburg, F.R.G. (ä-shäf'ĕn-bo͝orgh)	164	49.58 N	9.12 E
Ascheberg, F.R.G. (ä'shĕ-bĕrg)	167c	51.47 N	7.38 E
Aschersleben, G.D.R. (äsh'ĕrs-lā-bĕn)	164	51.46 N	11.28 E
Ascoli Piceno, It. (äs'kô-lēpē-chā'nō)	170	42.50 N	13.55 E
Aseb, Eth.	219a	12.52 N	43.39 E
Asenovgrad, Bul.	171	42.00 N	24.49 E
Aseri, Sov. Un. (ȧ'sĕ-rĭ)	172	59.26 N	26.58 E
Asfi, see Safi			
Asha, Sov. Un. (ä'shä)	180a	55.01 N	57.17 E
Ashabula (L.), ND (ăsh'ȧ-bū-lä)	112	47.07 N	97.51 W
Ashan, Sov. Un. (ä'shän)	180a	57.08 N	56.25 E
Ashbourne, Eng. (ăsh'bŭrn)	154	53.01 N	1.44 W
Ashburn, Ga. (ăsh'bŭrn)	124	31.42 N	83.42 W
Ashburn, Va.	110e	39.02 N	77.30 W
Ashburton (R.), Austl. (ăsh'bûr-tŭn)	210	22.30 S	115.30 E
Ashby-de-la-Zouch, Eng. (ăsh'bĭ-dē-lȧ zo͞osh')	154	52.44 N	1.23 W
Ashdod, Isr.	189a	31.46 N	34.39 E
Ashdown, Ar. (ăsh'doun)	121	33.41 N	94.07 W
Asheboro, NC (ăsh'bŭr-ô)	125	35.41 N	79.50 W
Asherton, Tx. (ăsh'ēr-tŭn)	122	28.26 N	99.45 W
Asheville, NC (ăsh'vĭl)	125	35.35 N	82.35 W
Ash Fork, Az.	119	35.13 N	112.29 W
Ashikaga, Jap. (ä'shē-kä'gȧ)	201	36.22 N	139.26 E
Ashiya, Jap. (ä'shē-yä')	201	33.54 N	130.40 E
Ashiya, Jap.	201b	34.44 N	135.18 E
Ashizuri-Zaki (Pt.), Jap. (ä-shē-zo͞o-rē zä-kē)	201	32.43 N	133.04 E
Ashkhabad, Sov. Un. (ŭsh-kä-bät')	153	39.45 N	58.13 E
Ashland, Al. (ăsh'lȧnd)	124	33.15 N	85.50 W
Ashland, Ks.	120	37.11 N	99.46 W
Ashland, Ky.	108	38.25 N	82.40 W
Ashland, Me.	102	46.37 N	68.26 W
Ashland, Ma.	103a	42.16 N	71.28 W
Ashland, Ne.	112	41.02 N	96.23 W
Ashland, Oh.	108	40.50 N	82.15 W
Ashland, Or.	114	42.12 N	122.42 W
Ashland, Pa.	109	40.45 N	76.20 W
Ashland, Wi.	113	46.34 N	90.55 W
Ashley, ND (ăsh'lē)	112	46.03 N	99.23 W
Ashley, Pa.	109	41.15 N	75.55 W
Ashmore Rf., Indon. (ăsh'mōr)	202	12.08 S	122.45 E
Ashmūn, Egypt (åsh-mo͞on')	219b	30.19 N	30.57 E
Ashqelon, Isr. (äsh'kĕ-lōn)	189a	31.40 N	34.36 E
Ash Shabb, Egypt (shĕb)	221	22.34 N	29.52 E
Ash Shallūfah, Egypt (shäl'lo͞o-fä)	219c	30.09 N	32.33 E
Ash Shaqrā', Sau. Ar.	192	25.10 N	45.08 E
Ash Shawbak, Jordan	189a	30.31 N	35.35 E
Ash Shiḥr, P.D.R. of Yem.	192	14.45 N	49.32 E
Ashtabula, Oh. (ăsh-tȧ-bū'lȧ)	108	41.55 N	80.50 W
Ashton, Id. (ăsh'tŭn)	115	44.04 N	111.28 W
Ashton-in-Makerfield, Eng. (ăsh'tŭn-ĭn-māk'ēr-fēld)	154	53.29 N	2.39 W
Ashton-under-Lyne, Eng. (ăsh'tŭn-ŭn-dēr-līn')	154	53.29 N	2.04 W
Ashuanipi (L.), Can. (ăsh-wȧ-nĭp'ĭ)	95	52.40 N	67.42 W
Ashukino, Sov. Un. (ȧ-sho͞o'kinô)	180b	56.10 N	37.57 E
Asia (ā'zhȧ)	188		
Asia Minor, Asia (ā'zhȧ)	153	38.18 N	31.18 E
Asientos, Mex. (ä-sē-ĕn'tŏs)	128	22.13 N	102.05 W
Asilah, Mor.	168	35.30 N	6.05 W
Asinara, Golfo dell' (G.), It. (gôl'fô-dĕl-ä-sē-nä'rä)	170	40.58 N	8.28 E
Asinara (I.), It.	170	41.02 N	8.22 E
Asīr (Reg.), Sau. Ar. (ä-sēr')	192	19.30 N	42.00 E
Asir, Ras (C.), Som.	219a	11.55 N	51.30 E
Askarovo, Sov. Un. (äs-kä-rō'vô)	180a	53.21 N	58.32 E
Askersund, Swe. (äs'kĕr-so͞ond)	162	58.43 N	14.53 E
Askino, Sov. Un. (äs'kĭ-nô)	180a	56.06 N	56.29 E
Asmera, Eth. (äs-mä'rä)	221	15.17 N	38.56 E
Asnieres, Fr. (ä-nyâr')	167b	48.55 N	2.18 E
Asosa, Eth.	221	10.13 N	34.28 E
Asotin, Wa. (ȧ-sō'tĭn)	114	46.19 N	117.01 W
Aspen, Co. (ăs'pĕn)	119	39.15 N	106.55 W
Asperen, Neth.	155a	51.52 N	5.07 E
Aspy B., Can. (ăs'pē)	103	46.55 N	60.25 W
Aş Şaff, Egypt	219b	29.33 N	31.23 E
Aş Şahrā' al Lībīyah, see Libyan Des.			
Aş Şaḥrā' ash Sharqīyah, see Arabian Des.			
As Sallūm, Egypt	221	31.34 N	25.09 E
As Salt, Jordan	189a	32.02 N	35.44 E
Assam (State), India (ăs-săm')	190	26.00 N	91.00 E
Assens, Den. (äs'sĕns)	162	55.16 N	9.54 E
As Sinbillāwayn, Egypt	219b	30.53 N	31.37 E
Assini, Ivory Coast. (ȧ-sē-nē')	220	4.52 N	3.16 W
Assiniboia, Can.	98	49.38 N	105.59 W
Assiniboine (R.), Can. (ă-sĭn'ĭ-boin)	98	50.03 N	97.57 W
Assiniboine, Mt., Can.	97	50.52 N	115.39 W
Assis, Braz. (ä-sē's)	141	22.39 S	50.21 W
Assisi, It.	170	43.04 N	12.37 E
As-Sudd (Reg.), Sud.	221	8.45 N	30.45 E
As Sulaymānīyah, Iraq	192	35.47 N	45.23 E
As Suwaydā', Syr.	192	32.41 N	36.41 E
As Suways (Suez), Egypt	219c	29.58 N	32.34 E
Astakós, Grc. (äs'tä-kôs)	171	38.42 N	21.00 E
Astara, Sov. Un.	177	38.30 N	48.50 E
Asti, It. (äs'tē)	170	44.54 N	8.12 E
Astipálaia (I.), Grc.	159	36.31 N	26.19 E
Astorga, Sp. (äs-tôr'gä)	168	42.28 N	6.03 W
Astoria, Or. (ăs-tō'rĭ-ȧ)	116c	46.11 N	123.51 W
Astrakhan' Sov. Un. (äs-trȧ-kän')	177	46.15 N	48.00 E
Astrida, Rw. (äs-trē'dȧ)	222	2.37 S	29.48 E
Asturias (Reg.), Sp. (äs-to͞o'ryäs)	168	43.21 N	6.00 W
Asunción, Par. (ä-so͞on-syōn')	142	25.25 S	57.30 W
Asunción, see Ixtaltepec			
Asunción, see Nochixtlán			
Asunción Mita, Guat. (ä-so͞on-syō'n-mē'tä)	130	14.19 N	89.43 W
Åsunden (L.), Swe. (ô'so͞on-dĕn)	161	57.46 N	13.16 E
Aswān, Egypt (ä-swän')	219b	24.05 N	32.57 E
Aswān High Dam, Egypt	219b	23.58 N	32.53 E
Asyūṭ, Egypt (ä-syo͞ot')	219b	27.10 N	31.10 E
Atacama, Puna de (Reg.), Chile (po͞o'nä-dĕ-ätä-kȧ'mä)	142	23.15 S	68.45 W
Atacama, Puna de (Plat.), Bol. (po͞o'nä-dĕ-ä-tä-kȧ'mä)	140	21.35 S	66.58 W
Atacama, Desierto de (Des.), Chile-Peru (dĕ-syĕ'r-tô-dĕ-ä-tä-kȧ'mä)	138	23.50 S	69.00 W
Atacama, Salar de (L.), Chile (sȧ-lär'dĕ-ätä-kȧ'mä)	142	23.38 S	68.15 W

ăt; finȧl; rāte; senāte; ärm; åsk; sofȧ; fâre; ch-choose; dh-as th in other; bē; ēvent; bĕt; recĕnt; cratēr; g-gō; gh-guttural g; bĭt; ĭ-short neutral; rīde; K-guttural k as ch in German ich;

PRONOUNCING INDEX

Atacama Trench – Babanango 265

PLACE (Pronunciation)	PAGE	Lat. °′	Long. °′
Atacama Trench, S.A.	142	25.00 S	71.30 W
Ataco, Col. (ä-tá'kō)	140a	3.36 N	75.22 W
Atacora, Chaîne de l' (Mts.), Benin	224	10.15 N	1.15 E
Atā 'itah, Jabal al (Mts.), Jordan	189a	30.48 N	35.19 E
Atakpamé, Togo (ä'täk-pá-mā')	224	7.32 N	1.08 E
Atamanovskiy, Sov. Un. (ä-tä-mä'nôv-skĭ)	180a	52.15 N	60.47 E
'Atāqah, Jabal (Mts.), Egypt	219c	29.59 N	32.20 E
Atar, Mauritania (ä-tär')	220	20.45 N	13.16 W
Atascadero, Ca. (ăt-ăs-kȧ-dâ'rō)	118	35.29 N	120.40 W
Atascosa R., Tx. (ăt-ăs-kō'sȧ)	122	28.50 N	98.17 W
Atauro, Ilha de (I.), Indon. (dĕ-ä-tä'ōō-rô)	203	8.20 S	126.15 E
'Aţbarah, Sud. (ät'bȧ-rä)	221	17.45 N	33.15 E
Atbara R., Sud.	221	17.14 N	34.27 E
Atbasar, Sov. Un. (ät'bä-sär')	178	51.42 N	68.28 E
Atchafalaya B., La. (ăch-ȧ-fȧ-lī'ȧ)	123	29.25 N	91.30 W
Atchafalaya R., La.	123	30.53 N	91.51 W
Atchison, Ks. (ăch'ĭ-sŭn)	121	39.33 N	95.08 W
Atco, NJ (ăt'kō)	110f	39.46 N	74.53 W
Atempan, Mex. (ä-tĕm-pá'n)	129	19.49 N	97.25 W
Atenguillo (R.), Mex. (ä-tĕn-gē'l-yô)	128	20.18 N	104.35 W
Athabasca, Can. (ăth-ȧ-băs'kȧ)	94	54.43 N	113.17 W
Athabasca (L.), Can.	94	59.04 N	109.10 W
Athabasca (R.), Can.	97	56.00 N	112.35 W
Athens, Al. (ăth'ĕnz)	124	34.47 N	86.58 W
Athens, Ga.	124	33.55 N	83.24 W
Athens, Oh.	108	39.20 N	82.10 W
Athens, Pa.	109	42.00 N	76.30 W
Athens, Tn.	124	35.26 N	84.36 W
Athens, Tx.	123	32.13 N	95.51 W
Athens, see Athínai			
Atherstone, Eng. (ăth'ēr-stŭn)	154	52.34 N	1.33 W
Atherton, Eng. (ăth'ēr-tŭn)	154	53.32 N	2.29 W
Atherton Plat., Austl. (ădh-ēr-tŏn)	211	17.00 S	144.30 E
Athi (R.), Ken. (ä'tē)	227	2.43 S	38.30 E
Athínai (Athens), Grc. (ä-thē'nĕ)	171	38.00 N	23.38 E
Athlone, Ire. (ăth-lōn')	160	53.24 N	7.30 W
Athos (Mtn.), Grc. (ăth'ŏs)	171	40.10 N	24.15 E
Ath Thamad, Egypt	189a	29.41 N	34.17 E
Athy, Ire. (ȧ-thī)	160	52.59 N	7.08 W
Ati, Chad	225	13.13 N	18.20 E
Atibaia, Braz. (ä-tē-bá'yȧ)	139a	23.08 S	46.32 W
Atikonak (L.), Can.	95	52.34 N	63.49 W
Atimonan, Phil. (ä-tē-mō'nän)	203a	13.59 N	121.56 E
Atiquizaya, Sal. (ä'tē-kē-zä'yä)	130	14.00 N	89.42 W
Atitlan (Vol.), Guat. (ä-tē-tlän')	130	14.35 N	91.11 W
Atitlan L., Guat. (ä-tē-tlän')	130	14.38 N	91.23 W
Atizapán, Mex. (ä'tē-zá-pän')	129a	19.33 N	99.16 W
Atka, Ak. (ăt'kȧ)	105a	52.18 N	174.18 W
Atka (I.), Ak.	105a	51.58 N	174.30 W
Atkarsk, Sov. Un. (åt-kärsk')	177	51.50 N	45.00 E
Atkinson, Ne. (ăt'kĭn-sŭn)	112	42.32 N	98.58 W
Atlanta, Ga. (ăt-lăn'tȧ)	110c	33.45 N	84.23 W
Atlanta, Tx.	121	33.09 N	94.09 W
Atlantic, Ia. (ăt-lăn'tĭk)	113	41.23 N	94.58 W
Atlantic, NC	125	34.54 N	76.20 W
Atlantic Highlands, NJ	110a	40.25 N	74.04 W
Atlantic City, NJ	109	39.20 N	74.30 W
Atlantic O.	4		
Atlas Mts., Alg.-Mor. (ăt'lăs)	220	31.22 N	4.57 W
Atliaca, Mex. (ät-lē-ä'kä)	128	17.38 N	99.24 W
Atlin (L.), Can. (ăt'lĭn)	94	59.34 N	133.20 W
Atlixco, Mex. (ät-lēz'kō)	128	18.52 N	98.27 W
Atmore, Al. (ăt'mōr)	124	31.01 N	87.31 W
Atoka, Ok. (ȧ-tō'kȧ)	121	34.23 N	96.07 W
Atoka Res., Ok.	121	34.30 N	96.05 W
Atotonilco el Alto, Mex. (ä'tô-tô-nēl'kō ĕl äl'tō)	128	20.35 N	102.32 W
Atotonilco el Grande, Mex. (ä'tô-tô-nēl-kō ĕl grän'dā)	128	20.17 N	98.41 W
Atoui R., Mauritania-W. Sah. (ȧ-tōō-ē')	220	21.00 N	15.32 W
Atoyac, Mex. (ä-tô-yäk')	128	20.01 N	103.28 W
Atoyac (R.), Mex.	129	16.27 N	97.28 W
Atoyac (R.), Mex.	128	18.35 N	98.16 W
Atoyac de Alvarez, Mex. (ä-tô-yäk'dā äl'vä-rāz)	128	17.13 N	100.29 W
Atoyatempan, Mex. (ä-tō'yá-tĕm-pän')	129	18.47 N	97.54 W
Atrak (R.), Iran	192	37.45 N	56.30 E
Atran (R.), Swe.	162	57.02 N	12.43 E
Atrato, Rio (R.), Col. (rē'ō-ä-trä'tō)	140	7.15 N	77.18 W
Atrato (R.), Col. (ä-trä'tō)	140a	5.48 N	76.19 W
Aţ Ţafīlah, Jordan (tä-fē'la)	189a	30.50 N	35.36 E
Aţ Ţā'if, Sau. Ar.	192	21.03 N	41.00 E
Attalla, Al. (ȧ-tăl'yȧ)	124	34.01 N	86.05 W
Attawapiskat (R.), Can. (ăt'ȧ-wȧ-pĭs'kăt)	95	52.31 N	86.22 W
Attersee (L.) (Kammer), Aus.	164	47.57 N	13.25 E
Attica, NY (ăt'ĭ-kȧ)	109	42.55 N	78.15 W
Attleboro, Ma. (ăt''l-bŭr-ô)	110b	41.56 N	71.15 W
Attow, Ben (Mtn.), Scot. (bĕn ăt'tô)	160	57.15 N	5.25 W
Attoyac Bay, Tx. (ă-toi'yăk)	123	31.45 N	94.23 W
Attu (I.), Ak. (ät-tōō')	105a	53.08 N	173.18 E
Aţ Ţūr, Egypt	159	28.09 N	33.47 E
Aţ Ţurayf, Sau. Ar.	192	31.32 N	38.30 E
Åtvidaberg, Swe. (ôt-vē'dá-bĕrgh)	162	58.12 N	15.55 E
Atwood, Ks. (ăt'wood)	120	39.48 N	101.06 W
Atzcapotzalco, Mex. (ät'zkä-pô-tzäl'kō)	129a	19.29 N	99.11 W
Atzgersdorf, Aus.	155e	48.10 N	16.17 E
Auau Chan., Hi. (ä'ōō-ä'ōō)	104a	20.55 N	156.50 W
Aubagne, Fr. (ō-bän'y')	167	43.18 N	5.34 E
Aube (R.), Fr. (ōb)	166	48.42 N	3.49 E
Aubenas, Fr. (ōb-nä')	166	44.37 N	4.22 E
Aubervilliers, Fr. (ō-bĕr-vē-yā')	167b	48.54 N	2.23 E
Aubin, Fr. (ō-băN')	166	44.29 N	2.12 E
Aubrey, Can. (ô-brē')	93a	45.08 N	73.47 W
Auburn, Al. (ô'bŭrn)	124	32.35 N	85.26 W
Auburn, Ca.	118	38.52 N	121.05 W
Auburn, Il.	121	39.36 N	89.46 W
Auburn, In.	108	41.20 N	85.05 W
Auburn, Me.	102	44.04 N	70.24 W
Auburn, Ma.	103a	42.11 N	71.51 W
Auburn, Ne.	121	40.23 N	95.50 W
Auburn, NY	109	42.55 N	76.35 W
Auburn, Wa.	116a	47.18 N	122.14 W
Auburn Hts., Mi.	111b	42.37 N	83.13 W
Aubusson, Fr. (ō-bü-sôN')	166	45.57 N	2.10 E
Auch, Fr. (ōsh)	166	43.38 N	0.35 E
Aucilla (R.), Fl.-Ga. (ô-sĭl'ȧ)	124	30.15 N	83.55 W
Auckland, N.Z. (ôk'lănd)	213	36.53 S	174.45 E
Auckland Is., N.Z.	228	50.30 S	166.30 E
Aude (R.), Fr. (ōd)	166	42.55 N	2.08 E
Audierne, Fr. (ō-dyĕrn')	166	48.02 N	4.31 W
Audincourt, Fr. (ō-dăn-kōōr')	167	47.30 N	6.49 W
Audley, Eng. (ôd'lĭ)	154	53.03 N	2.18 W
Audo Ra., Eth.	219a	6.58 N	41.18 E
Audubon, Ia. (ô'dōō-bŏn)	113	41.43 N	94.57 W
Audubon, NJ	110f	39.54 N	75.04 W
Aue, G.D.R. (ou'ē)	164	50.35 N	12.44 E
Augathella, Austl. (ôr'gȧ'thē-lȧ)	212	25.49 S	146.40 E
Augrabiesvalle (Falls), S. Afr.	222	28.30 S	20.00 E
Augsburg, F.R.G. (ouks'bōōrgh)	155d	48.23 N	10.55 E
Augusta, Ar. (ô-gŭs'tȧ)	121	35.16 N	91.21 W
Augusta, Ga.	125	33.26 N	82.00 W
Augusta, Ks.	121	37.41 N	96.58 W
Augusta, Ky.	108	38.45 N	84.00 W
Augusta, Me.	102	44.19 N	69.42 W
Augusta, NJ	110a	41.07 N	74.44 W
Augusta, Wi.	113	44.40 N	91.09 W
Augustow, Pol. (ou-gōōs'tōōf)	165	53.52 N	23.00 E
Aulnay-sous-Bois, Fr. (ō-nĕ'sōō-bwä')	167b	48.56 N	2.30 E
Aulne (R.), Fr. (ōn)	166	48.08 N	3.53 W
Auneau, Fr. (ō-nĕü)	167b	48.28 N	1.45 E
Auob (R.), Namibia (ä'wŏb)	222	25.00 S	19.00 E
Aur (I.), Mala.	189b	2.27 N	104.51 E
Aura, Fin.	163	60.38 N	22.32 E
Aurangābād, India (ou-rŭŋ-gä-bäd')	190	19.56 N	75.19 E
Aurdal, Nor. (äûr-däl)	162	60.54 N	9.24 E
Aurès, Massif de l' (Mts.), Alg.	158	35.16 N	5.53 E
Aurillac, Fr. (ō-rē-yák')	166	44.57 N	2.27 E
Aurora, Can.	101	43.59 N	79.25 W
Aurora, Il. (ô-rō'rȧ)	111a	41.45 N	88.18 W
Aurora, In.	111f	39.04 N	84.55 W
Aurora, Mn.	113	47.31 N	92.17 W
Aurora, Mo.	121	36.58 N	93.42 W
Aurora, Ne.	120	40.54 N	98.01 W
Aursunden (L.), Nor. (äûr-sûndĕn)	162	62.42 N	11.10 E
Au Sable (R.), Mi. (ô-sä'b'l)	108	44.40 N	84.25 W
Ausable (R.), NY	109	44.25 N	73.50 W
Austin, Mn. (ôs'tĭn)	113	43.40 N	92.58 W
Austin, Nv.	118	39.30 N	117.05 W
Austin, Tx.	123	30.15 N	97.42 W
Austin (L.), Austl.	210	27.45 S	117.30 E
Austin Bayou, Tx. (ôs'tĭn bī-ōō')	123a	29.17 N	95.21 W
Australia, (ôs-trā'lĭ-ȧ)	210		
Australian Alps (Mts.), Austl.	212	37.10 S	147.55 E
Australian Capital Ter., Austl. (ôs-trā'lĭ-ăn)	212	35.30 S	148.40 E
Austria, Eur. (ôs'trĭ-ȧ)	152	47.15 N	11.53 E
Authon-la-Plaine, Fr. (ō-tôN-lä-plĕ'n)	167b	48.27 N	1.58 E
Autlán, Mex. (ä-ōōt-län')	128	19.47 N	104.24 W
Autun, Fr. (ō-tŭN')	166	46.58 N	4.14 E
Auvergne (Mts.), Fr. (ō-vĕrn'y')	166	45.12 N	2.31 E
Auxerre, Fr. (ō-sâr')	166	47.48 N	3.32 E
Ava, Mo. (ā'vȧ)	121	36.56 N	92.40 W
Avakubi, Zaire (ä-vá-kōō'bē)	227	1.20 N	27.34 E
Avallon, Fr. (ȧ-vá-lôN')	166	47.30 N	3.58 E
Avalon, Pa. (ăv'ȧ-lŏn)	111e	40.31 N	80.05 W
Avalon, Ca.	118	33.21 N	118.22 W
Aveiro, Port. (ä-vä'rōō)	168	40.38 N	8.38 W
Avelar, Braz. (ä'vē-lá'r)	142b	22.20 S	43.25 W
Avellaneda, Arg. (ä-vĕl-yä-nä'dhä)	142a	34.25 S	58.23 W
Avellino, It. (ä-vĕl-lē'nō)	169c	40.40 N	14.46 E
Averøya (I.), Nor. (ävĕr-ûē)	162	63.40 N	7.16 E
Aversa, It. (ä-vĕr'sä)	170	40.58 N	14.13 E
Avery, Tx. (ā'vēr-ĭ)	121	33.34 N	94.46 W
Avesta, Swe. (ä-vĕs'tä)	162	60.16 N	16.09 E
Aveyron (R.), Fr. (ä-vā-rôN)	166	44.07 N	1.45 E
Avezzano, It. (ä-vät-sä'nō)	170	42.03 N	13.27 E
Avigliano, It. (ä-vēl-yä'nō)	170	40.45 N	15.44 E
Avignon, Fr. (ȧ-vē-nyôN')	166	43.55 N	4.50 E
Ávila, Sp. (ä-vē-lä)	168	40.39 N	4.42 W
Avilés, Sp. (ä-vē-lās')	168	43.33 N	5.55 W
Avoca, Ia. (ȧ-vō'kȧ)	121	41.29 N	95.16 W
Avon, Ct. (ā'vŏn)	109	41.40 N	72.50 W
Avon, Ma. (ā'vŏn)	103a	42.08 N	71.03 W
Avon, Oh.	111d	41.27 N	82.02 W
Avon (R.), Eng. (ā'vŭn)	160	52.05 N	1.55 W
Avondale, Ga.	110c	33.47 N	84.16 W
Avon Lake, Oh.	111d	41.31 N	82.01 W
Avonmore, Can. (ä'vôN-mōr)	93c	45.11 N	74.58 W
Avon Park, Fl. (ā'vŏn pärk')	125a	27.35 N	81.29 W
Avranches, Fr. (á-vräNsh')	166	48.43 N	1.34 W
Awaji-Shima (I.), Jap. (ä'wä-jē shē-mä)	201b	34.32 N	135.02 E
Awe, Loch (L.), Scot. (lŏK ôr)	160	56.22 N	5.04 W
Awjilah, Libya	221	29.07 N	21.21 E
Ax-les-Thermes, Fr. (äks'lā tĕrm')	166	42.43 N	1.50 E
Axochiapan, Mex. (äks-ō-chyä'pän)	128	18.29 N	98.49 W
Ay (R.), Sov. Un.	176	55.55 N	57.55 E
Ayabe, Jap. (ä'yä-bĕ)	201	35.16 N	135.17 E
Ayachi, Arin' (Mtn.), Mor.	158	32.29 N	4.57 W
Ayacucho, Arg. (ä-yä-kōō'chō)	142	37.05 S	58.30 W
Ayacucho, Peru	140	12.12 S	74.03 W
Ayaguz, Sov. Un. (ä-yá-gōōz')	178	48.00 N	80.12 E
Ayamonte, Sp. (ä-yä-mō'n-tĕ)	168	37.14 N	7.28 W
Ayan, Sov. Un. (ä-yän')	179	56.26 N	138.18 E
Ayata, Bol. (ä-yä'tä)	140	15.17 S	68.43 W
Ayaviri, Peru (ä-yä-vē'rē)	140	14.46 S	70.38 W
Aydar (R.), Sov. Un. (ī-där')	173	49.15 N	38.48 E
Ayden, NC (ā'dĕn)	125	35.27 N	77.25 W
Aydın, Tur. (āīy-dĕn)	177	37.40 N	27.40 E
Ayer, Ma. (âr)	103a	42.33 N	71.36 W
Ayer Hitam, Mala.	189b	1.55 N	103.11 E
Ayiassos, Grc.	171	39.06 N	26.25 E
Áyion Óros (Mount Athos) (Reg.), Grc.	171	40.20 N	24.15 E
Áyios Evstrátios (I.), Grc.	171	39.30 N	24.58 E
Ayíou Orous, Kólpos (G.), Grc.	171	40.15 N	24.00 E
Aylesbury, Eng. (ālz'bēr-ĭ)	154b	51.47 N	0.49 W
Aylmer (L.), Can. (āl'mēr)	94	64.27 N	108.22 W
Aylmer, Mt., Can.	97	51.19 N	115.26 W
Aylmer East, Can. (āl'mēr)	93c	45.24 N	75.50 W
Ayo el Chico, Mex. (ä'yō el chē'kō)	128	20.31 N	102.21 W
Ayon (I.), Sov. Un. (ī-ôn')	179	69.50 N	168.40 E
Ayorou, Niger	224	14.44 N	0.55 E
Ayotla, Mex. (ä-yōt'lä)	129a	19.18 N	98.55 W
Ayoun el Atrous, Mauritania	224	16.40 N	9.37 W
Ayr, Scot. (âr)	160	55.27 N	4.40 W
Aysha, Eth.	219a	10.48 N	42.32 E
Ayutla, Guat. (ä-yōōt'lä)	130	14.44 N	92.11 W
Ayutla, Mex.	128	16.50 N	99.16 W
Ayutla, Mex.	128	20.09 N	104.20 W
Ayvalik, Tur. (āīy-wă-lĭk)	171	39.19 N	26.40 E
Azaouad (Dunes), Mali	224	18.00 N	3.20 W
Azaouak, Vallée de l' (Val.), Mali	225	15.50 N	3.10 E
Azare, Nig.	225	11.40 N	10.11 E
Azemmour, Mor. (á-zē-mōōr')	220	33.20 N	8.21 W
Azerbaydzhan (Azerbaijan) (S.S.R.), Sov. Un. (ä'zēr-bä-ē-jän')	174	40.38 N	47.25 E
Azle, Tx. (áz'lē)	117c	35.54 N	97.33 W
Azogues, Ec. (ä-sō'gās)	140	2.47 S	78.45 W
Azores (Is.), see **Açores**			
Azov, Sov. Un. (á-zôf') (ä-zôf)	173	47.07 N	39.19 E
Azov, Sea of, see **Azovskoye More**			
Azovskoye More (Sea of Azov), Sov. Un. (á-zôf'skô-yĕ mô'rĕ)	173	46.00 N	36.20 E
Azoyú, Mex. (ä-zô-yōō')	128	16.42 N	98.46 W
Azraq, Al-Bahr al- (R.), see **Blue Nile**			
Aztec, NM (ăz'tĕk)	119	36.40 N	108.00 W
Aztec Ruins Natl. Mon., NM	119	36.50 N	108.00 W
Azua, Dom. Rep. (ä'swä)	133	18.30 N	70.45 W
Azuaga, Sp. (ä-thwä'gä)	168	38.15 N	5.42 W
Azuero, Peninsula de (Pen.), Pan. (ä-swā'rō)	131	7.30 N	80.34 W
Azucar, Presa de (Res.), Mex. (prĕ'sä-dĕ-ä-zōō'kär)	122	26.06 N	98.44 W
Azufre, Cerro (Copiapó) (Vol.), Chile (sĕr'rō ä-sōō'frā) (kō-pē-äpō')	142	26.10 S	69.00 W
Azul, Arg. (ä-sōōl')	139c	36.46 S	59.51 W
Azul, Sierra (Mts.), Mex. (sē-ĕ'r-rä-zōō'l)	128	23.20 N	98.28 W
Azul, Cordillera (Mts.), Peru (kô'r-dē-lyĕ'rä-zōō'l)	140	7.15 S	75.30 W
Azusa, Ca. (ä-zōō'sȧ)	117a	34.08 N	117.55 W
Az Zabdānī, Syr.	189a	33.45 N	36.06 E
Az̧ Z̧ahrān (Dhahran, Sau. Ar. (dā-rän')	192	26.13 N	50.00 E
Az Zaqāzīq, Egypt	219b	30.36 N	31.36 E
Az Zarqā', Jordan	189a	32.03 N	36.07 E
Az Zawiyah, Libya	221	32.28 N	11.55 E

B

PLACE (Pronunciation)	PAGE	Lat. °′	Long. °′
Baal, F.R.G. (bäl)	167c	51.02 N	6.17 E
Baao, Phil. (bä'ō)	203a	13.27 N	123.22 E
Baarle-Hertog, Bel.	155a	51.26 N	4.57 E
Baarn, Neth.	155a	52.12 N	5.18 E
Babaeski, Tur. (bä'bä-ĕs'kĭ)	171	41.25 N	27.05 E
Babahoyo, Ec. (bä-bä-ō'yō)	140	1.56 S	79.24 W
Babana, Nig.	225	10.36 N	3.50 E
Babanango, S. Afr.	223c	28.24 S	31.11 E

ng-sing; ŋ-baŋk; N-nasalized n; nŏd; cŏmmit; ōld; ôbey; ôrder; oi-boil; fōōd; fŏŏt; ou-out; s-soft; sh-dish; th-thin; pūre; ûnite; ûrn; stŭd; circŭs; ü-as in French tu; '-indeterminate vowel.

266 Babanūsah – Bandar Maharani

PLACE (Pronunciation)	PAGE	Lat. °′	Long. °′
Babanūsah, Sud.	221	11.30 N	27.55 E
Babar, Pulau (I.), Indon. (bä'bär)	203	7.50 S	129.15 E
Bab-el-Mandeb, Str. of, Afr.-Asia (bäb'ĕl män-dĕb')	219a	13.17 N	42.49 E
Babia, Arroyo de la, Mex. (är-rō'yō dā lä bä'bē-ȧ)	122	28.26 N	101.50 W
Babine (R.), Can.	96	55.10 N	127.00 W
Babine L., Can. (băb'ēn)	96	54.45 N	126.00 W
Bābol, Iran	192	36.30 N	52.48 E
Babushkin, Sov. Un. (bä'bo͞osh-kĭn)	179	51.47 N	106.08 W
Babushkin, Sov. Un.	180b	55.52 N	37.42 E
Babuyan Is., Phil. (bä-bo͞o-yän')	202	19.30 N	122.38 E
Babyak, Bul. (bäb'zhȧk)	171	41.59 N	23.42 E
Babylon, NY (băb'ĭ-lŏn)	110a	40.42 N	73.19 W
Babylon (Ruins), Iraq	192	32.15 N	45.23 E
Bacalar, Laguna de (L.), Mex. (lä-go͞o-nä-dĕ-bä-kä-lär')	130a	18.50 N	88.31 W
Bacan, Pulau (I.), Indon.	203	0.30 S	127.00 E
Bacarra, Phil. (bä-kär'rä)	199	18.22 N	120.40 E
Bacău, Rom.	165	46.34 N	27.00 E
Baccarat, Fr. (bȧ-kȧ-rȧ')	167	48.29 N	6.42 E
Bacchus, Ut. (băk'ŭs)	117b	40.40 N	112.06 W
Bachajón, Mex. (bä-chä-hōn')	129	17.08 N	92.18 W
Bachu, China (bä-cho͞o)	194	39.50 N	78.23 E
Back (R.), Can.	94	65.30 N	104.15 W
Bačka Palanka, Yugo. (bäch'kä pälän-kä)	171	45.14 N	19.24 E
Bačka Topola, Yugo. (bäch'kä tô'pô-lä')	171	45.48 N	19.38 E
Back Bay, India (băk)	191b	18.55 N	72.45 E
Backstairs Pass., Austl. (băk-stârs')	210	35.50 S	138.15 E
Bac Ninh, Viet. (bäk'nēn'')	199	21.10 N	106.02 E
Baco, Mt., Phil. (bä'kō)	203a	12.50 N	121.11 E
Bacoli, It. (bä-kō-lē')	169c	40.33 N	14.05 E
Bacolod, Phil. (bä-kō'lōd)	202	10.42 N	123.03 E
Bácsalmás, Hung. (bäch'ôl-mäs)	165	46.07 N	19.18 E
Bacup, Eng. (băk'ŭp)	154	53.42 N	2.12 W
Bad (R.), SD (băd)	112	44.04 N	100.58 W
Badajoz, Sp. (bä-dhä-hōth')	168	38.52 N	6.56 W
Badalona, Sp. (bä-dhä-lō'nä)	169	41.27 N	2.15 E
Badanah, Sau. Ar.	192	30.49 N	40.45 E
Bad Axe, Mi. (băd' ăks)	108	43.50 N	82.55 W
Bad Bramstedt, F.R.G. (bät bräm'shtĕt)	155c	53.55 N	9.53 E
Bad Ems, F.R.G. (bät ĕms)	167	50.20 N	7.45 E
Baden, Aus. (bä'dĕn)	155e	48.00 N	16.14 E
Baden, Switz.	164	47.28 N	8.17 E
Baden-Baden, F.R.G. (bä'dĕn-bä'dĕn)	164	48.46 N	8.11 E
Baden Württemberg (State), F.R.G. (bä'dĕn vür'tĕm-bĕrgh)	164	48.38 N	9.00 E
Bad Freienwalde, G.D.R. (bät frī'ĕn-väl'dĕ)	164	52.47 N	14.00 E
Bad Hersfeld, F.R.G. (bät hĕrsh'fĕlt)	164	50.53 N	9.43 E
Bad Homberg, F.R.G. (bät hōm'bĕrgh)	161	50.14 N	8.35 E
Badin, NC (bă'dĭn)	125	35.23 N	80.08 W
Badīn, Pak.	190	24.47 N	69.51 E
Bad Ischl, Aus. (bät ĭsh''l)	164	47.46 N	13.37 E
Bad Kissingen, F.R.G. (bät kĭs'ĭng-ĕn)	164	50.12 N	10.05 E
Bad Kreuznach, F.R.G. (bät kroits'näk)	164	49.52 N	7.53 E
Badlands (Reg.), ND (băd' lănds)	112	46.43 N	103.22 W
Badlands (Reg.), SD	112	43.43 N	102.36 W
Badlands Natl. Park, SD	112	43.56 N	102.37 W
Badlāpur, India	191b	19.12 N	73.12 E
Badogo, Mali	224	11.02 N	8.13 W
Bad Oldeslow, F.R.G. (bät ōl'dĕs-lōē)	164	53.48 N	10.21 E
Bad Reichenhall, F.R.G. (bät rī'ĸĕn-häl)	164	47.43 N	12.53 E
Bad River Ind. Res., Wi. (băd)	113	46.41 N	90.36 W
Bad Segeberg, F.R.G. (bät sĕ'gĕ-bo͞orgh)	155c	53.56 N	10.18 E
Bad Tölz, F.R.G. (bät tûltz)	164	47.46 N	11.35 E
Badulla, Sri Lanka	191	6.55 N	81.07 E
Bad Vöslau, Aus.	155e	47.58 N	16.13 E
Badwater Cr., Wy. (băd'wô-tĕr)	115	43.13 N	107.55 W
Baena, Sp. (bä-ā'nä)	168	37.38 N	4.20 W
Baependi, Braz. (bä-å-pĕn'dĭ)	139a	21.57 S	44.51 W
Baffin B., Can. (băf'ĭn)	92	72.00 N	65.00 W
Baffin B., Tx.	123	27.11 N	97.35 W
Baffin I., Can.	92	67.20 N	71.00 W
Bafoulabé, Mali (bä-fo͞o-lä-bā')	224	13.48 N	10.50 W
Bāfq, Iran (bäfk)	192	31.48 N	55.23 E
Bafra, Tur. (bäf'rä)	177	41.30 N	35.50 E
Bagabag, Phil. (bä-gä-bäg')	203a	16.38 N	121.16 E
Bāgalkot, India	191	16.14 N	75.40 E
Bagamoyo, Tan. (bä-gä-mō'yō)	227	6.26 S	38.54 E
Bagaryak, Sov. Un. (bȧ-gȧr-yäk')	180a	56.13 N	61.32 E
Bagbele, Zaire	227	4.21 N	29.17 E
Bagé, Braz. (bä-zhā')	142	31.17 S	54.07 W
Baghdād, Iraq (bȧgh-dȧd') (băg'dăd)	192	33.14 N	44.22 E
Bagheria, It. (bä-gâ-rē'ä)	170	38.03 N	13.32 E
Bagley, Mn. (băg'lē)	112	47.31 N	95.24 W
Bagnara, It. (bän-yä'rä)	170	38.17 N	15.52 E
Bagnell Dam, Mo. (băg'nĕl)	121	38.13 N	92.40 W
Bagnères-de-Bigorre, Fr. (bän-yâr'dē-bē-gor')	166	43.40 N	0.70 E
Bagnères-de-Luchon, Fr. (bän-yâr' dē-lu chôɴ')	166	42.46 N	0.36 E
Bagnols-sur-Ceze, Fr. (bä-nyôl')	166	44.09 N	4.37 E
Bagoé R., Mali (bȧ-gô'å)	220	12.22 N	6.34 W
Baguio, Phil. (bä-gē-ō')	203a	16.24 N	120.36 E
Bagzane, Monts (Mtn.), Niger	225	18.40 N	8.40 E
Bahamas, N.A. (bȧ-hā'mȧs)	127	26.15 N	76.00 W
Bahau, Mala.	189b	2.48 N	102.25 E
Bahāwalpur, Pak. (bŭ-hä'wŭl-po͞or)	190	29.29 N	71.41 E
Bahi Swp., Tan.	227	6.05 S	35.10 E
Bahia, see Salvador			
Bahia (State), Braz.	141	11.05 S	43.00 W
Bahía, Islas de la (I.), Hond. (ē's-läs-dĕ-lä-bä-ē'ä)	126	16.15 N	86.30 W
Bahía Blanca, Arg. (bä-ē'ä blän'kä)	142	38.45 S	62.07 W
Bahía de Caráquez, Ec. (bä-e'ä dā kä-rä'kĕz)	140	0.45 S	80.29 W
Bahía Negra, Par. (bä-ē'ä nā'grä)	141	20.11 S	58.05 W
Bahias, Cabo dos (C.), Arg. (kȧ'bô-dôs-bä-ē'äs)	142	44.55 S	65.35 W
Bahoruco, Sierra de (Mts.), Dom. Rep. (sē-ĕ'r-rä-dĕ-bä-ô-ro͞o'kô)	133	18.10 N	71.25 W
Bahrain, Asia (bä-rān')	192	26.15 N	51.17 E
Bahr al Ghazāl (Prov.), Sud. (bär ĕl ghä-zäl')	221	7.56 N	27.15 E
Bahrīyah (Oasis), Egypt (bȧ-hȧ-rē'yä)	159	28.34 N	29.01 E
Bahrīyah, Jabal Jalālah al (Plat.), Egypt	189a	29.15 N	32.20 E
Baia de Criş, Rom. (bä'yä dā krēs')	165	46.11 N	22.40 E
Baia dos Tigres, Ang.	226	16.36 S	11.43 E
Baia Mare, Rom. (bä'yä mä'rä)	165	47.40 N	23.35 E
Baidoa, Som.	219a	3.19 N	44.20 E
Baidyabāti, India	190a	22.47 N	88.21 E
Baie-Comeau, Can.	102	49.13 N	68.10 W
Baie de Wasai, Mi. (bā dē wä-sä'ē)	117k	46.27 N	84.15 W
Baie-St. Paul, Can. (bā'sănt-pôl')	101	47.27 N	70.30 W
Baigou, China (bī-gō)	196	39.08 N	116.02 E
Baihe, China (bī-hŭ)	198	32.30 N	110.15 E
Bai Hu (L.), China (bī-ho͞o)	196	31.22 N	117.38 E
Baiju, China (bī-jyo͞o)	196	33.04 N	120.17 E
Baikal Mts., see Baykal'skiy Khrebet			
Baikal. L., see Baykal, Ozero			
Baile Átha Cliath (Dublin), Ire. (bō'lĕō'hŏclē'ōh)	160	53.20 N	6.15 W
Bailén, Sp. (bä-ē-lān')	168	38.05 N	3.48 W
Băileşti, Rom. (bă-ĭ-lĕsh'tē)	171	44.01 N	23.21 E
Bainbridge, Ga. (bān'brĭj)	124	30.52 N	84.35 W
Bainbridge I., Wa.	116a	47.39 N	122.32 W
Baipu, China (bī-po͞o)	196	32.15 N	120.47 E
Baiquan, China (bī-chyuäŋ)	198	47.22 N	126.00 E
Baird, Tx. (bârd)	122	32.22 N	99.28 W
Bairdford, Pa. (bârd'fōrd)	111e	40.37 N	79.53 W
Baird Mts., Ak.	105	67.35 N	160.10 W
Bairnsdale, Austl. (bârnz'dāl)	212	37.50 S	147.39 E
Baïse (R.), Fr. (bȧ-ēz')	166	43.52 N	0.23 E
Baiyang Dian (L.), China (bī-yäŋ-dĭĕn)	196	39.00 N	115.45 E
Baiyu Shan (Mts.), China (bī-yo͞o shän)	198	37.02 N	108.30 E
Baja, Hung. (bŏ'yŏ)	165	46.11 N	18.55 E
Baja California Norte (State), Mex. (bä-hä)	126	30.15 N	117.25 W
Baja California Sur (State), Mex.	126	26.00 N	113.30 W
Bakal, Sov. Un. (bä'kȧl)	180a	54.57 N	58.50 E
Baker, Mt. (bā'kĕr)	115	46.21 N	104.12 W
Baker, Or.	114	44.46 N	117.52 W
Baker (I.), Oceania	204	1.00 N	176.00 W
Baker (L.), Can.	94	63.51 N	96.10 W
Baker, Mt., Wa.	114	48.46 N	121.52 W
Baker Cr., Il.	111a	41.13 N	87.47 W
Bakersfield, Ca. (bā'kĕrz-fēld)	118	35.23 N	119.00 W
Bakerstown, Pa. (bā'kerz-toun)	111e	40.39 N	79.56 W
Bakewell, Eng. (bāk'wĕl)	154	53.12 N	1.40 W
Bakhchisaray, Sov. Un. (bȧĸ'chĕ-sȧ-rī')	173	44.46 N	33.54 E
Bakhmach, Sov. Un. (bȧĸ-mäch')	173	51.09 N	32.47 E
Bakhtegan, Daryācheh-ye (L.), Iran	192	29.29 N	54.31 E
Bakhteyevo, Sov. Un. (bȧk-tyĕ'yĕ-vô)	180b	55.35 N	38.32 E
Bako, Eth. (bä'kö)	221	5.47 N	36.39 E
Bakony (Mts.), Hung. (bȧ-kōn'y')	165	46.57 N	17.30 E
Bakoye (R.), Mali (bȧ-kô'ē)	224	12.47 N	9.35 W
Bakr Uzyak, Sov. Un. (bȧkr o͞oz'yȧk)	180a	52.59 N	58.43 E
Baku, Sov. Un. (bȧ-ko͞o')	177	40.28 N	49.45 E
Bakwanga, see Mbuji-Mayi			
Balabac I., Phil. (bä'lä-bäk)	202	8.00 N	116.28 E
Balabac Str., Indon.-Phil.	202	7.23 N	116.30 E
Ba'labakk, Leb.	189a	34.00 N	36.13 E
Balabanovo, Sov. Un. (bȧ-lȧ-bä'nô-vô)	180b	56.10 N	37.44 E
Balagansk, Sov. Un. (bä-lä-gänsk')	178	53.58 N	103.09 E
Balaguer, Sp. (bä-lä-gĕr')	169	41.48 N	0.50 E
Balakhta, Sov. Un. (bȧ'lȧk-tȧ')	178	55.22 N	91.43 E
Balakleya, Sov. Un. (bȧ'lȧ-klā'yȧ)	173	49.28 N	36.51 E
Balakovo, Sov. Un. (bȧ'lȧ-kô'vō)	177	52.00 N	47.40 E
Balancán, Mex. (bä-läŋ-kän')	129	17.47 N	91.32 W
Balanga, Phil. (bä-läŋ'gä)	203a	14.41 N	120.31 E
Balashikha, Sov. Un. (bȧ-lä'shĭ-kȧ)	180b	55.48 N	37.58 E
Balashov, Sov. Un. (bȧ'lȧ-shôf)	177	51.30 N	43.00 E
Balasore, India (bä-lȧ-sōr')	190	21.38 N	86.59 E
Balassagyarmat, Hung. (bô'lôsh-shô-dyôr'mŏt)	165	48.04 N	19.19 E
Balaton L., Hung. (bô'lô-tôn)	165	46.47 N	17.55 E
Balayan, Phil. (bä-lä-yän')	203a	13.56 N	120.44 E
Balayan B., Phil.	203a	13.46 N	120.46 E
Balboa Heights, Pan. (bäl-bô'ä)	131	8.59 N	79.33 W
Balboa Mt., Pan.	126a	9.05 N	79.44 W
Balcarce, Arg. (bäl-kär'sā)	142	37.49 S	58.17 W
Balchik, Bul.	171	43.24 N	28.13 E
Bald Eagle, Mn. (bôld ē'g'l)	117g	45.06 N	93.01 W
Bald Eagle L., Mn.	117g	45.08 N	93.03 W
Baldock L., Can.	99	56.33 N	97.57 W
Baldwin Park, Ca. (bôld'wĭn)	117a	34.05 N	117.58 W
Baldwinsville, NY (bôld'wĭns-vĭl)	109	43.10 N	76.20 W
Baldy Mtn., Can.	99	51.28 N	100.44 W
Baldy Pk., Az. (bôl'dē)	119	33.55 N	109.35 W
Baldy Pk., Tx. (bôl'dē pēk)	122	30.38 N	104.11 W
Baleares, Islas (Balearic Is.), Sp. (e's-läs bä-lĕ-ä'rĕs)	169	39.25 N	1.28 E
Balearic Is., see Baleares, Islas			
Balearic Sea., Eur. (băl-ē-ăr'ĭk)	169	39.40 N	1.05 E
Baleine, Grande Rivière de la (R.), Can.	95	54.45 N	74.20 W
Baler, Phil. (bä-lar')	203a	15.46 N	121.33 E
Baler B., Phil.	203a	15.51 N	121.40 E
Balesin (I.), Phil.	203a	14.28 N	122.10 E
Baley, Sov. Un. (bȧl-yä')	179	51.29 N	116.12 E
Balfate, Hond. (bäl-fä'tē)	130	15.48 N	86.24 W
Balfour, S. Afr. (băl'fo͞or)	219d	26.41 S	28.37 E
Bali (I.), Indon. (bä'lē)	202	8.00 S	115.22 E
Balikesir, Tur. (balĭk'īysĭr)	177	39.40 N	27.50 E
Balikpapan, Indon. (bä'lĕk-pä'pän)	202	1.13 S	116.52 E
Balintang Chan., Phil. (bä-lĭn-täng')	202	19.50 N	121.08 E
Balkan Mts., see Stara Planina			
Balkh, Afg. (bälk)	193	36.48 N	66.50 E
Balkhash, Sov. Un. (bȧl-käsh')	178	46.58 N	75.00 E
Balkhash, Ozero (L.), Sov. Un.	178	45.58 N	72.15 E
Balki, Sov. Un. (bäl'kĭ)	173	47.22 N	34.56 E
Ballancourt, Fr. (bä-äɴ-ko͞or')	167b	48.31 N	2.23 E
Ballarat, Austl. (băl'ȧ-răt)	212	37.37 S	144.00 E
Ballard (L.), Austl. (băl'ȧrd)	210	29.15 S	120.45 E
Ballater, Scot. (băl'ȧ-tĕr)	160	57.05 N	3.06 W
Ballé, Mali	224	15.20 N	8.35 W
Balleny Is., Ant. (băl'ĕ nē)	228	67.00 S	164.00 E
Ballina, Austl. (băl-ĭ-nä')	212	28.50 S	153.35 E
Ballina, Ire.	160	54.06 N	9.05 W
Ballinasloe, Ire. (băl'ĭ-nȧ-slō')	160	53.20 N	8.09 W
Ballinger, Tx. (băl'ĭn-jĕr)	122	31.45 N	99.58 W
Ballston Spa, NY (bôls'tŭn spä')	109	43.05 N	73.50 W
Balmazújváros, Hung. (bŏl'mŏz-o͞o'y'vä'rōsh)	165	47.35 N	21.23 E
Balobe, Zaire	227	0.05 N	28.00 E
Balonne (R.), Austl. (băl-ōn')	212	27.00 S	149.10 E
Bālotra, India	190	25.56 N	72.12 E
Balranald, Austl. (băl'-rȧn-ăld)	212	34.42 S	143.30 E
Balş, Rom. (bälsh)	171	44.21 N	24.05 E
Balsam (L.), Can. (bôl'sȧm)	109	44.30 N	78.50 W
Balsas, Braz. (bäl'säs)	141	7.09 S	46.04 W
Balsas (R.), Mex.	126	18.00 N	103.00 W
Balta, Sov. Un. (bȧl'tȧ)	173	47.57 N	29.38 E
Baltic Sea, Eur. (bôl'tĭk)	156	55.20 N	16.50 E
Baltīm, Egypt (bȧl-tēm')	219b	31.33 N	31.04 E
Baltimore, Md. (bôl'tĭ-môr)	110e	39.20 N	76.38 W
Baltiysk, Sov. Un. (bäl-tēysk')	163	54.40 N	19.55 E
Baluarte, Río del, Mex. (rē'ō-dĕl-bä-lo͞o-ä'r-tē)	128	23.09 N	105.42 W
Baluchistān (Reg.), Pak. (bȧ-lo͞o-chĭ-stän')	193	27.30 N	65.30 E
Balzac, Can. (bôl'zăk)	93e	51.10 N	114.01 W
Bama, Nig.	225	11.30 N	13.41 E
Bamako, Mali (bä-mä-kō')	224	12.39 N	8.00 W
Bambang, Phil. (bäm-bäng')	203a	16.24 N	121.08 E
Bambari, Cen. Afr. Rep. (bäm-bȧ-rē)	221	5.44 N	20.40 E
Bamberg, F.R.G. (bäm'bĕrgh)	164	49.53 N	10.52 E
Bamberg, SC (băm'bûrg)	125	33.17 N	81.04 W
Bambuí, Braz. (bä'm-bo͞o-ē)	139a	20.01 S	45.59 W
Bamenda, Cam.	225	5.56 N	10.10 E
Bamingui (R.), Cen. Afr. Rep.	225	7.35 N	19.45 E
Bamingui Bangoran, Parc Nat'l. du (Natl. Park), Cen. Afr. Rep.	225	8.05 N	19.35 E
Bampton, Eng. (băm'tŭn)	154b	51.42 N	1.33 W
Bampūr, Iran (bŭm-po͞or')	192	27.15 N	60.22 E
Bam Yanga, Ngao (Mts.), Cam.	225	8.20 N	14.40 E
Banahao, Mt., Phil. (bä-nä-hä'ô)	203a	14.04 N	121.45 E
Banalia, Zaire	226	1.33 N	25.20 E
Banamba, Mali	224	13.33 N	7.27 W
Bananal, Braz. (bä-nä-näl')	139a	22.42 S	44.17 W
Bananal, Ilha do (I.), Braz. (ē'lä-dô-bä-nä-näl')	141	12.09 S	50.27 W
Banās (R.), India (băn-äs')	190	25.20 N	74.51 E
Banās, Ra's (C.), Egypt	221	23.48 N	36.39 E
Banat (Reg.), Rom.-Yugo. (bä-nät')	171	45.35 N	21.05 E
Bancroft, Can. (băn'krŏft)	109	45.05 N	77.55 W
Bancroft, see Chililabombwe			
Bānda, India (bän'dä)	190	25.36 N	80.21 E
Banda, Kepulauan (Is.), Indon.	203	4.40 S	129.56 E
Banda Aceh, Indon.	202	5.10 N	95.10 E
Banda Banda, Mt., Austl. (băn'dȧ băn'dȧ)	212	31.09 S	152.15 E
Banda Laut (Banda Sea), Indon.	203	6.05 S	127.28 E
Bandama Blanc (R.), Ivory Coast (bän-dä'mä)	224	6.15 N	5.00 W
Bandar Abbās, Iran (bän-där' ȧb-bäs')	192	27.04 N	56.22 E
Bandar-e Khomeynī, Iran	192	30.27 N	48.45 E
Bandar-e Lengeh, Iran	192	26.44 N	54.47 E
Bandar-e Torkman, Iran	192	37.05 N	54.08 E
Bandar Maharani, Mala. (bän-där' mä-hä-rä'nē)	189b	2.02 N	102.34 E

PRONOUNCING INDEX

Bandar Seri Begawan – Bathurst 267

PLACE (Pronunciation)	PAGE	Lat. °′	Long. °′
Bandar Seri Begawan, Bru.	207	5.00 N	114.59 E
Bande, Sp.	168	42.02 N	7.58 W
Bandeira, Pico da (Pk.), Braz. (pĕ′kōō dä bän dā′rä)	139a	20.27 S	41.47 W
Bandelier Natl. Mon., NM (băn-dĕ-lēr′)	119	35.50 N	106.45 W
Banderas, Bahía de (B.), Mex. (bä-ē′ä dĕ bän-dĕ′räs)	128	20.38 N	105.35 W
Bandirma, Tur. (bän-dĭr′mȧ)	177	40.25 N	27.50 E
Bandon, Or. (băn′dŭn)	114	43.06 N	124.25 W
Bāndra (Neigh), India	191b	19.04 N	72.49 E
Bandundu, Zaire	226	3.18 S	17.20 E
Bandung, Indon.	207	7.00 S	107.22 E
Banes, Cuba (bä′näs)	133	21.00 N	75.45 W
Banff, Can. (bănf)	97	51.10 N	115.34 W
Banff, Scot.	160	57.39 N	2.37 W
Banff Natl. Park, Can.	97	51.38 N	116.22 W
Bánfield, Arg. (bȧ′n-fyĕ′ld)	142a	34.44 S	58.24 W
Banfora, Upper Volta	224	10.38 N	4.46 W
Bangalore, India (băŋ′gȧ′lôr)	191	13.03 N	77.39 E
Bangassou, Cen. Afr. Rep. (bäɴ-gȧ-sōō′)	221	4.47 N	22.49 E
Bangé, Cam.	225	3.01 N	15.07 E
Bangeta, Mt., Pap. N. Gui.	203	6.20 S	147.00 E
Banggai, Kepulauan (Is.), Indon. (bäng-gī′)	203	1.05 N	123.45 E
Banggi, Pulau (I.), Mala.	202	7.12 N	117.10 E
Banghāzī, Libya (bĕn-gä′zē)	221	32.08 N	20.06 E
Bangka (I.), Indon. (băŋ′kȧ)	202	2.24 S	106.55 E
Bangkalan, Indon. (bäng-kȧ-län′)	202	6.07 S	112.50 E
Bangkok, see Krung Thep			
Bangladesh, Asia	193	24.15 N	90.00 E
Bangong Co (L.), China (bäŋ-gôŋ tswo)	190	33.40 N	79.30 E
Bangor, Me. (băn′gēr)	102	44.47 N	68.47 W
Bangor, Mi.	108	42.20 N	86.05 W
Bangor, Pa.	109	40.55 N	75.10 W
Bangor, Wales (băŋ′ēr) (băŋ′ōr)	160	53.13 N	4.05 W
Bangs, Mt., Az. (băngs)	119	36.45 N	113.50 W
Bangued, Phil. (bän-gād′)	203a	17.36 N	120.38 E
Bangui, Cen. Afr. Rep. (bäɴ-gē′)	225	4.22 N	18.35 E
Bangweulu, L., Zambia (băng-wē-ōō′lōō)	227	10.55 S	30.10 E
Bangweulu Swp., Zambia	227	11.25 S	30.10 E
Banhā, Egypt	219b	30.24 N	31.11 E
Bani, Dom. Rep. (bä′-nē)	133	18.15 N	70.25 W
Bani, Phil. (bä′nē)	203a	16.11 N	119.51 E
Bani (R.), Mali	224	13.07 N	6.15 W
Bánica, Dom. Rep. (bä′-nē-kä)	133	19.00 N	71.35 W
Banī Mazār, Egypt	219b	28.29 N	30.48 E
Banī Suwayf, Egypt	219b	29.05 N	31.06 E
Banjak, Kepulauan (I.), Indon.	202	2.08 N	97.15 E
Banja Luka, Yugo. (bän-yä-lōō′kȧ)	170	44.45 N	17.11 E
Banjarmasin, Indon. (bän-jĕr-mä′sĕn)	202	3.18 S	114.32 E
Banjin, China (bän-jyĭn)	196	32.23 N	120.14 E
Banjul (Bathurst), Gam.	224	13.28 N	16.39 W
Bankberg (Mts.), S. Afr. (bȧŋk′bûrg)	223c	32.18 S	25.15 E
Banks, Or. (bănks)	116c	45.37 N	123.07 W
Banks (Is.), Austl.	211	10.10 S	143.08 E
Banks, C., Austl.	207b	34.01 S	151.17 E
Banks I., Can.	96	53.25 N	130.10 W
Banks I., Can.	92	73.00 N	123.00 W
Banks Is., Vanuatu	211	13.38 S	168.23 E
Banks Pen., N.Z.	213	43.45 S	172.20 E
Banks Str., Austl.	212	40.45 S	148.00 E
Bann (R.), N. Ire. (băn)	160	54.50 N	6.29 W
Banning, Ca. (băn′ĭng)	117a	33.56 N	116.53 W
Bannister (R.), Va. (băn′ĭs-tēr)	125	36.45 N	79.17 W
Bannockburn, Austl.	207a	38.03 S	144.11 E
Bannu, Pak.	190	33.03 N	70.39 E
Baños, Ec. (bä′-nyôs)	140	1.30 S	78.22 W
Banská Bystrica, Czech. (bän′skä bē′strē-tzä)	165	48.46 N	19.10 E
Bansko, Bul. (bän′skō)	171	41.51 N	23.33 E
Banstead, Eng. (băn′stĕd)	154b	51.18 N	0.09 W
Banton, Phil. (bän-tōn′)	203a	12.54 N	121.55 E
Bantry, Ire. (băn′trĭ)	160	51.39 N	9.30 W
Bantry B., Ire.	160	51.25 N	10.09 W
Banyuwangi, Indon. (bän-jōō-wäŋ′gē)	202	8.15 S	114.15 E
Baocheng, China (bou-chŭŋ)	198	33.15 N	106.58 E
Baodi, China (bou-dē)	196	39.44 N	117.19 E
Baoding, China (bou-dĭŋ)	196	38.52 N	115.31 E
Baoji, China (bou-jyĕ)	198	34.10 N	106.58 E
Baoshan, China (bou-shän)	194	25.14 N	99.03 E
Baoshan, China	197b	31.25 N	121.29 E
Baotou, China (bou-tō)	198	40.28 N	110.10 E
Baoying, China (bou-yĭŋ)	196	33.14 N	119.20 E
Bapsfontein, S. Afr. (băps-fŏn-tān′)	223b	26.01 S	28.26 E
Baqueroncito, Col. (bä-kĕ-rô′n-sē-tō)	140a	3.18 N	74.40 W
Bar, Sov. Un. (bär)	173	49.02 N	27.44 E
Barabinsk, Sov. Un. (bȧ′rȧ-bĭnsk)	178	55.18 N	78.00 E
Baraboo, Wi. (bâr′ȧ-bōō)	113	43.29 N	89.44 W
Baracoa, Cuba (bä-rä-kō′ä)	133	20.20 N	74.25 W
Baracoa, Cuba	133a	23.03 N	82.34 W
Baradeo, Arg. (bä-rä-dĕ′ŏ)	139c	33.50 S	59.30 W
Baradères, Baie des (B.), Hai (bä-rä-dâr′)	133	18.35 N	73.35 W
Barahona, Dom. Rep. (bä-rä-ô′nä)	133	18.15 N	71.10 W
Barajas de Madrid, Sp. (bä-rä′häs dä mä-drēdh′)	169a	40.28 N	3.35 W
Baranagar, India	190a	22.38 N	88.25 E
Baranco, Belize (bä-räŋ′kō)	130	16.01 N	88.55 W
Baranof (I.), Ak. (bä-rä′nôf)	105	56.48 N	136.08 W
Baranovichi, Sov. Un. (bä′rä-nô-vē′chē)	165	53.08 N	25.59 E
Baranpauh, Indon.	189b	0.40 N	103.28 E
Barão de Juperanã, Braz. (bä-rou′ɴ-dĕ-zhōō-pe-rȧ′nȧ)	142b	22.21 S	43.41 W
Barão de Melgaço, Braz. (bä-rouɴ-dĕ-mĕl-gä′sō)	141	16.12 S	55.48 W
Bārāsat, India	190a	22.42 N	88.29 E
Barataria B., La.	123	29.13 N	89.90 W
Baraya, Col. (bä-rȧ′yä)	140a	3.10 N	75.04 W
Barbacena, Braz. (bär-bä-sā′nȧ)	139a	21.15 S	43.46 W
Barbacoas, Col. (bär-bä-kō′äs)	140	1.39 N	78.12 W
Barbacoas, Ven. (bä-bä-kō′äs)	141b	9.30 N	66.58 W
Barbados, N.A. (bär-bā′dōz)	127	13.30 N	59.00 W
Barbar, Sud.	221	18.11 N	34.00 E
Barbastro, Sp. (bär-bäs′trō)	169	42.05 N	0.05 E
Barbeau, Mi. (bȧr-bō′)	117k	46.17 N	84.16 W
Barberton, Oh. (bär′bēr-tŭn)	111d	41.01 N	81.37 W
Barberton, S. Afr.	222	25.48 S	31.04 E
Barbezieux, Fr. (bärb′zyû′)	166	45.30 N	0.11 W
Barbosa, Col. (bär-bô′-sȧ)	140a	6.26 N	75.19 W
Barbourville, Ky.	124	36.52 N	83.58 W
Barboursville, WV (bär′bērs-vĭl)	108	38.20 N	82.20 W
Barbuda (I.), Antigua (bär-bōō′dȧ)	127	17.45 N	61.15 W
Barcaldine, Austl. (bär′kôl-dīn)	211	23.33 S	145.17 E
Barcarena, Port. (bär-kä-rĕ′-nä)	169b	38.29 N	9.17 W
Barcarrota, Sp. (bär-kär-rō′tä)	168	38.31 N	6.50 W
Barcellona, It. (bä-chĕl-lō′nä)	170	38.07 N	15.15 E
Barcelona, Sp. (bär-thȧ-lō′nä)	169	41.25 N	2.08 E
Barcelona, Ven. (bär-sȧ-lō′nä)	141b	10.09 N	64.41 W
Barcelos, Braz. (bär-sĕ′lôs)	140	1.04 S	63.00 W
Barcelos, Port. (bär-thȧ′lōs)	168e	41.34 N	8.39 W
Bardar-e Pahlavī, Iran	192	37.16 N	49.15 E
Bardawīl, Sabkhat al (B.), Egypt	189a	31.20 N	33.24 E
Bardejov, Czech. (bär′dyĕ-yôf)	165	49.18 N	21.18 E
Bardera, Som. (bär-dā′rä)	219a	2.13 N	42.24 E
Bardsey I., Wales (bärd′sē)	160	52.45 N	4.50 W
Bardstown, Ky. (bärds′toun)	108	37.50 N	85.30 W
Bardwell, Ky. (bärd′wĕl)	124	36.51 N	88.57 W
Barents Sea, Sov. Un. (bä′rĕnts)	174	72.14 N	37.28 E
Barentu, Eth. (bä-rĕn′tōō)	221	15.06 N	37.39 E
Barfleur, Pte. de (Pt.), Fr. (bär-flûr′)	166	49.43 N	1.17 W
Barguzin, Sov. Un. (bär′gōō-zĭn)	179	53.44 N	109.28 E
Bar Harbor, Me. (bär här′bēr)	102	44.22 N	68.13 W
Bari, It. (bä′rē)	170	41.08 N	16.53 E
Barinas, Ven. (bä-rē′näs)	140	8.36 N	70.14 W
Baring, C., Can. (bâr′ĭng)	94	70.07 N	119.48 W
Barisan, Pegunungan (Mts.), Indon. (bä-rē-sän′)	202	2.38 S	101.45 E
Barito (Strm.), Indon. (bä-rē′tō)	202	2.10 S	114.38 E
Barka (R.), Eth.	221	16.44 N	37.34 E
Barkley Sd., Can.	96	48.53 N	125.20 W
Barkly East, S. Afr. (bärk′lē ēst)	223c	30.58 S	27.37 E
Barkly Tableland (Plat.), Austl. (bär′klē)	210	18.15 S	137.05 E
Barkol, China (bär-kûl)	194	43.43 N	92.50 E
Bar-le-Duc, Fr. (bär-lē-dük′)	166	48.47 N	5.05 E
Barlee (L.), Austl. (bär-lē′)	210	29.45 S	119.00 E
Barletta, It. (bär-lĕt′tä)	170	41.19 N	16.20 E
Barmstedt, F.R.G. (bärm′shtĕt)	155c	53.47 N	9.46 E
Barnaul, Sov. Un. (bär-nä-ōōl′)	178	53.18 N	83.23 E
Barnesboro, Pa. (bärnz′bēr-ô)	109	40.45 N	78.50 W
Barnesville, Ga. (bärnz′vĭl)	124	33.03 N	84.10 W
Barnesville, Mn.	112	46.38 N	96.25 W
Barnesville, Oh.	108	39.55 N	81.10 W
Barnet, Vt. (bär′nĕt)	109	44.20 N	72.00 W
Barnetby le Wold, Eng. (bär′nĕt-bī)	154	53.34 N	0.26 W
Barnett Hbr., Ba.	132	25.40 N	79.20 W
Barnsdall, Ok. (bärnz′dôl)	121	36.38 N	96.14 W
Barnsley, Eng. (bärnz′lĭ)	154	53.33 N	1.29 W
Barnstaple, Eng. (bärn′stā-p′l)	160	51.06 N	4.05 W
Barnwell, SC (bärn′wĕl)	125	33.14 N	81.23 W
Baro, Nig. (bä′rô)	225	8.37 N	6.25 E
Bāro (R.), Eth.	221	7.40 N	34.17 E
Baroda, India (bär-rō′dä)	190	22.21 N	73.12 E
Barotse Pln., Zambia	226	15.50 S	22.55 E
Barqah (Cyrenaica) (Prov.), Libya	221	31.09 N	21.45 E
Barquisimeto, Ven. (bär-kē-sē-mā′tō)	140	10.04 N	69.16 W
Barra, Braz. (bär′rä)	141	11.04 S	43.11 W
Barraba, Austl.	212	30.22 S	150.36 E
Barra do Corda, Braz. (bär′rä dōō cōr-dä)	141	5.33 S	45.13 W
Barra Mansa, Braz. (bär′rä män′sä)	139a	22.35 S	44.09 W
Barrancabermeja, Col. (bär-räŋ′kä-bēr-mā′hä)	140	7.06 N	73.49 W
Barranquilla, Col. (bär-rän-kēl′yä)	140	10.57 N	75.00 W
Barras, Braz. (bä′r-räs)	141	4.13 S	42.14 W
Barre, Vt. (băr′ē)	109	44.15 N	72.30 W
Barre do Piraí, Braz. (bär′rē-dô-pē′rä-ē′)	139a	22.30 S	43.49 W
Barreiras, Braz. (bär-rā′räs)	141	12.13 S	44.59 W
Barreiro, Port. (bär-rĕ′ē-rōō)	169b	38.39 N	9.05 W
Barren, C., Austl. (băr′ĕn)	212	40.20 S	149.00 E
Barren, Nosy (Is.), Mad.	223	18.18 S	43.57 E
Barren (R.), Ky.	124	37.00 N	86.20 W
Barretos, Braz. (bär-rā′tōs)	141	20.40 S	48.36 W
Barrhead, Can. (băr-hĕd) (bär′ĭd)	97	54.08 N	114.24 W
Barrie, Can. (băr′ĭ)	109	44.25 N	79.45 W
Barrington, Can. (bă-rĕng-tŏn)	93a	45.07 N	73.35 W
Barrington, Il.	111a	42.09 N	88.08 W
Barrington, RI	110b	41.44 N	71.16 W
Barrington Tops (Mtn.), Austl.	212	32.00 S	151.25 E
Bar River, Can. (bär)	117k	46.27 N	84.02 W
Barron, Wi. (băr′ŭn)	113	45.24 N	91.51 W
Barrow, Ak. (băr′ō)	105	71.20 N	156.00 W
Barrow (I.), Austl.	210	20.50 S	115.00 E
Barrow Creek, Austl.	210	21.23 S	133.55 E
Barrow-in-Furness, Eng.	160	54.10 N	3.15 W
Barrow Pt., Ak.	105	71.20 N	156.00 W
Barrow R., Ire. (bȧ-rȧ)	160	52.35 N	7.05 W
Barstow, Ca. (bär′stō)	118	34.53 N	117.03 W
Barstow, Md.	110e	38.32 N	76.37 W
Barth, G.D.R. (bärt)	164	54.20 N	12.43 E
Bartholomew Bayou, Ar. (bär-thŏl′ō-mū bī-ōō′)	121	33.53 N	91.45 W
Barthurst, Can. (băr-thŭrst′)	102	47.38 N	65.40 W
Bartica, Guy (bär′tĭ-kȧ)	141	6.23 N	58.32 W
Bartin, Tur. (bär′tĭn)	177	41.35 N	32.12 E
Bartle Frere, Mt., Austl. (bärt″l frēr′)	211	17.30 S	145.46 E
Bartlesville, Ok. (bär′tlz-vĭl)	121	36.44 N	95.58 W
Bartlett, Il. (bärt′lĕt)	111a	41.59 N	88.11 W
Bartlett, Tx.	123	30.48 N	97.25 W
Barton, Vt. (bär′tŭn)	109	44.45 N	72.05 W
Barton-upon-Humber, Eng. (bär′tŭn-ŭp′ŏn-hŭm′bēr)	154	53.41 N	0.26 W
Bartoszyce, Pol. (bär-tô-shĭ′tsȧ)	165	54.15 N	20.50 E
Bartow, Fl. (bär′tō)	125a	27.51 N	81.50 W
Barú, Volcán (Vol.), Pan.	131	8.48 N	82.37 W
Barvenkovo, Sov. Un. (bär′vĕn-kô′vô)	173	48.55 N	36.59 E
Barwon (R.), Austl. (bär′wŭn)	212	29.45 S	148.25 E
Barwon Heads, Austl.	207a	38.17 S	144.29 E
Barycz R., Pol. (bä′rĭch)	164	51.30 N	16.38 E
Basankusu, Zaire (bä-sän-kōō′sōō)	221	1.14 N	19.45 E
Basbeck, F.R.G. (bäs′bĕk)	155c	53.40 N	9.11 E
Basdahl, F.R.G. (bäs′däl)	155c	53.27 N	9.00 E
Basehor, Ks. (bās′hôr)	117f	39.08 N	94.55 W
Basel, Switz. (bä′z′l)	164	47.32 N	7.35 E
Bashee (R.), S. Afr. (bă-shē′)	223c	31.47 S	28.25 E
Bashi Chan, Phil. (băsh′ē)	199	21.20 N	120.22 E
Bashkir (A.S.S.R.), Sov. Un. (băsh-kēr′)	176	54.12 N	57.15 E
Bashtanka, Sov. Un. (bȧsh-tän′kȧ)	173	47.32 N	32.31 E
Basilan I., Phil.	202	6.37 N	122.07 E
Basilicata (Reg.), It. (bä-zē-lē-kä′tä)	170	40.30 N	15.55 E
Basin, Wy. (bā′sĭn)	115	44.22 N	108.02 W
Basingstoke, Eng. (bä′zĭng-stōk)	154b	51.14 N	1.06 W
Baška, Yugo. (bäsh′ka)	170	44.58 N	14.44 E
Baskale, Tur. (bäsh-kä′lĕ)	177	38.10 N	44.00 E
Baskatong Res., Can.	101	46.50 N	75.50 W
Baskunchak (L.), Sov. Un.	177	48.20 N	46.40 E
Basoko, Zaire (bȧ-sō′kō)	221	0.52 N	23.50 E
Bassano, Can. (băs-săn′ō)	97	50.47 N	112.28 W
Bassano del Grappa, It.	170	45.46 N	11.44 E
Bassari, Togo	224	9.15 N	0.47 E
Bassas da India (I.), Afr. (bäs′säs dä ēn′dē-ȧ)	223	21.23 S	39.42 E
Bassein, Bur. (bŭ-sēn′)	202	16.46 N	94.47 E
Basse Terre, Guad. (bȧs′ târ′)	131b	16.00 N	61.43 W
Basseterre, St. Kitts-Nevis	131b	17.20 N	62.42 W
Basse Terre I., Guad.	131b	16.10 N	62.14 W
Bassett, Va. (băs′sĕt)	125	36.45 N	81.58 W
Bass Is., Oh. (băs)	108	41.40 N	82.50 W
Bass Str., Austl.	212	39.40 S	145.40 E
Basswood (L.), Can.-Mn. (băs′wŏŏd)	113	48.10 N	91.36 W
Båstad, Swe. (bô′stät)	162	56.26 N	12.46 E
Bastia, Fr. (bäs′tē-ä)	170	42.43 N	9.27 E
Bastogne, Bel. (bäs-tôn′y′)	161	50.02 N	5.45 E
Bastrop, La. (băs′trŭp)	123	32.47 N	91.55 W
Bastrop, Tx.	123	30.08 N	97.18 W
Bastrop Bayou, Tx.	123a	29.07 N	95.22 W
Bata, Equat.Gui. (bä′tä)	226	1.51 N	9.45 E
Batabanó, Cuba (bä-tä-bä-nō′)	132	22.45 N	82.20 W
Batabano, Golfo, de (G.), Cuba (gôl-fô-dĕ-bä-tä-bȧ′nô)	132	22.10 N	83.05 W
Batāla, India	190	31.54 N	75.18 E
Bataly, Sov. Un. (bȧ-tä′lĭ)	180a	52.51 N	62.03 E
Batam I., Indon. (bä-täm′)	189b	1.03 N	104.00 E
Batan Is., Phil. (bä-tän′)	199	20.58 N	122.20 E
Batang, China (bä-täŋ)	194	30.08 N	99.00 E
Batangan, C., Viet.	199	15.18 N	109.10 E
Batangas, Phil. (bä-tän′gäs)	203a	13.45 N	121.04 E
Bátaszék, Hung. (bä′tȧ-sĕk)	165	46.07 N	18.40 E
Batavia, Il. (bȧ-tā′vĭ-ȧ)	111a	41.51 N	88.18 W
Batavia, NY	109	43.00 N	78.15 W
Batavia, Oh.	111f	39.05 N	84.10 W
Bataysk, Sov. Un. (bȧ-tīsk′)	173	47.08 N	39.44 E
Bătdâmbâng, Kamp. (băt-tȧm-bȧng′)	202	13.14 N	103.15 E
Batesburg, SC (bāts′bûrg)	125	33.53 N	81.34 W
Batesville, Ar. (bāts′vĭl)	121	35.46 N	91.39 W
Batesville, In.	108	39.15 N	85.15 W
Batesville, Ms.	124	34.17 N	89.55 W
Batetska, Sov. Un. (bȧ-tĕ′tskȧ)	172	58.36 N	30.21 E
Bath, Can. (bȧth)	102	46.31 N	67.36 W
Bath, Eng.	160	51.24 N	2.20 W
Bath, Me.	102	43.54 N	69.50 W
Bath, NY	109	42.25 N	77.20 W
Bath, Oh.	111d	41.11 N	81.38 W
Bathsheba, Barb.	131b	13.13 N	60.30 W
Bathurst, Austl. (băth′ŭrst)	211	33.28 S	149.30 E

ng-sing; ŋ-baŋk; ɴ-nasalized n; nŏd; cŏmmit; ōld; ôbey; ôrder; oi-boil; fōōd; fŏŏt; ou-out; s-soft; sh-dish; th-thin; pūre; ůnite; ûrn; stŭd; circŭs; ü-as in French tu; ′-indeterminate vowel.

PLACE (Pronunciation)	PAGE	Lat. °′	Long. °′
Bathurst, S. Afr. (băt-hûrst)	223c	33.26 S	26.53 E
Bathurst, see Banjul			
Bathurst, C., Can. (băth'rst)	105	70.33 N	127.55 W
Bathurst (I.), Austl.	210	11.19 S	130.13 E
Bathurst Inlet, Can.	94	68.10 N	108.00 W
Batia, Benin	224	10.54 N	1.29 E
Batian (I.), Indon.	203	1.07 S	127.52 E
Bāţlāq-E Gāvkhūnī (L.), Iran	192	31.40 N	52.48 E
Batley, Eng. (băt'lĭ)	154	53.43 N	1.37 W
Batna, Alg. (bät'nä)	220	35.41 N	6.12 E
Baton Rouge, La. (băt'ŭn ro͞ozh')	123	30.28 N	91.10 W
Batouri, Cam.	225	4.26 N	14.22 E
Batticaloa, Sri Lanka	191	8.40 N	81.10 E
Battle (R.), Can.	97	52.20 N	111.59 W
Battle (R.), Can.	98	53.05 N	109.40 W
Battle Creek, Mi. (băt''l krēk')	108	42.20 N	85.15 W
Battle Ground, Wa. (băt''l ground)	116c	45.47 N	122.32 W
Battle Harbour, Can. (băt''l här'bēr)	95	52.17 N	55.33 W
Battle Mountain, Nv.	114	40.40 N	116.56 W
Battonya, Hung. (bät-tô'nyä)	165	46.17 N	21.00 E
Batu Kepulauan (I.), Indon. (bä'to͞o)	202	0.10 S	99.55 E
Batumi, Sov. Un. (bŭ-to͞o'mē)	177	41.40 N	41.30 E
Batu Pahat., Mala.	189b	1.51 N	102.56 E
Batupanjang, Indon.	189b	1.42 N	101.35 E
Baturité, Braz. (bä-to͞o-rē-tā')	141	4.16 S	38.47 W
Bauang, Phil. (bä'wăng)	203a	16.31 N	120.19 E
Bauchi, Nig. (bà-o͞o'chē)	225	10.19 N	9.50 E
Baudouinville, Zaire (bō-dwăn-vēl')	222	7.12 S	29.39 E
Bauld, C. Can.	103	51.38 N	55.25 W
Bāuria, India	190a	22.29 N	88.08 E
Bauru, Braz. (bou-ro͞o')	141	22.21 S	48.57 W
Bauska, Sov. Un. (bou'skà)	163	56.24 N	24.12 E
Bauta, Cuba (bá'o͞o-tä)	133a	22.14 N	82.33 W
Bautzen, G.D.R. (bout'sĕn)	164	51.11 N	14.27 E
Bavaria (State), **see Bayern**			
Baw Baw, Mt., Austl. (bá-bá)	212	37.50 S	146.17 E
Bawean, Pulau (I.), Indon. (bá'vē-än)	202	5.50 S	112.40 E
Bawtry, Eng. (bôtrĭ)	154	53.26 N	1.01 W
Baxley, Ga. (băks'lĭ)	125	31.47 N	82.22 W
Baxter, Austl. (Băks'tēr)	207a	38.12 S	145.10 E
Baxter Springs, Ks. (băks'tēr sprĭngs')	121	37.01 N	94.44 W
Bayaguana, Dom. Rep. (bä-yä-gwä'nä)	133	18.45 N	69.40 W
Bay al Kabīr Wadi (R.), Libya	158	29.52 N	14.28 E
Bayambang, Phil. (bä-yäm-băng')	203a	15.50 N	120.26 E
Bayamo, Cuba (bä-yä'mō)	132	20.25 N	76.35 W
Bayamón, P.R.	127b	18.27 N	66.13 W
Bayan, China (bä-yän)	198	46.00 N	127.20 E
Bayan-Aul, Sov. Un. (bä'yän-oul')	178	50.43 N	75.37 E
Bayard, Ne. (bā'ērd)	112	41.45 N	103.20 W
Bayard, WV	109	39.15 N	79.20 W
Bayburt, Tur. (bä'ĭ-bo͝ort)	177	40.15 N	40.10 E
Bay City, Mi. (bā)	108	43.35 N	83.55 W
Bay City, Tx.	123	28.59 N	95.58 W
Baydarag Gol (R.), Mong.	194	46.09 N	98.52 E
Baydaratskaya Guba (B.), Sov. Un.	176	69.20 N	66.10 E
Bay de Verde, Can.	103	48.05 N	52.54 W
Bayern (Bavaria) (State), F.R.G. (bī'ērn) (bá-vâ-rĭ-à)	164	49.00 N	11.16 E
Bayeux, Fr. (bá-yû')	166	49.19 N	0.41 W
Bayfield, Wi. (bā'fēld)	113	46.48 N	90.51 W
Baykal, Ozero (Baikal, L.), Sov. Un. (bī'käl') (bī'kôl)	179	53.00 N	109.28 E
Baykals'kiy Khrebet (Baikal Mts.), Sov. Un.	179	53.30 N	102.00 E
Baykit, Sov. Un. (bī-kēt')	178	61.43 N	96.39 E
Baykonur, Sov. Un. (bī-kô-no͞or')	178	47.46 N	66.11 E
Baymak, Sov. Un. (bäy'mäk)	180a	52.35 N	58.21 E
Bay Mills, Mi. (bā mĭlls)	117k	46.27 N	84.36 W
Bay Mills Ind. Res., Mi.	113	46.19 N	85.03 W
Bay Minette, Al. (bā'mĭn-ĕt')	124	30.52 N	87.44 W
Bayombong, Phil. (bä-yôm-bông')	203a	16.28 N	121.09 E
Bayonne, Fr. (bá-yôn')	166	43.28 N	1.30 W
Bayonne, NJ (bā-yōn')	110a	40.40 N	74.07 W
Bayou Bodcau Res., La. (bī'yo͞o bŏd'кō)	123	32.49 N	93.22 W
Bayport, Mn. (bā'pōrt)	117g	45.02 N	92.46 W
Bayramic, Tur.	171	39.48 N	26.35 E
Bayreuth, F.R.G. (bī-roit')	164	49.56 N	11.35 E
Bay Roberts, Can. (bā rŏb'ērts)	103	47.36 N	53.16 W
Bayrūt, see Beirut			
Bays, L. of, Can. (bās)	109	45.15 N	79.00 W
Bay St. Louis, Ms. (bā' sânt lo͞o'ĭs)	124	30.19 N	89.20 W
Bay Shore, NY (bā' shôr)	110a	40.44 N	73.15 W
Bayt Lahm (Bethlehem), Jordan (bĕth'lē-hĕm)	189a	31.42 N	35.13 E
Baytown, Tx. (bā'town)	123a	29.44 N	95.01 W
Bayview, Al. (bā'vū)	110h	33.34 N	86.59 W
Bayview, Wa.	116a	48.29 N	122.28 W
Bay Village, Oh. (bā)	111d	41.29 N	81.56 W
Baza, Sp. (bä'thä)	168	37.29 N	2.46 W
Baza, Sierra de (Mts.), Sp.	168	37.19 N	2.48 W
Bazar-Dyuzi (Mt.), Sov. Un. (bä'zár-dyo͞oz'ē)	177	41.20 N	47.40 E
Bazaruto, Ilha do (I.), Moz. (bä-zä-ro͞o'tō)	222	21.42 S	36.10 E
Baziège, Fr.	166	43.25 N	1.41 E
Be,Nosy (I.), Mad.	223	13.14 S	47.28 E
Beach, ND (bēch)	112	46.55 N	104.00 W
Beachy Head, Eng. (bēchē hĕd)	161	50.40 N	0.25 E
Beacon, NY (bē'kŭn)	109	41.30 N	73.55 W
Beaconsfield, Can. (bē'kŭnz-fēld)	93a	45.26 N	73.51 W

PLACE (Pronunciation)	PAGE	Lat. °′	Long. °′
Beafort Mtn., NJ (bē'fōrt)	110a	41.08 N	74.23 W
Beals Cr., Tx. (bēls)	122	32.10 N	101.14 W
Bear Brook (R.), Can.	93c	45.24 N	75.15 W
Bear Creek, Mt. (bâr krēk)	115	45.11 N	109.07 W
Bear Cr., Al. (bâr)	124	34.27 N	88.00 W
Bear Cr., Tx.	117c	32.56 N	97.09 W
Beardstown, Il. (bērds'toun)	121	40.01 N	90.26 W
Bearhead Mtn., Wa. (bâr'hĕd)	116a	47.01 N	121.49 W
Bear (L.), Id.-Ut.	115	41.56 N	111.10 W
Bear L., Can.	99	55.08 N	96.00 W
Bear R., Id.	115	42.17 N	111.42 W
Bear R., Ut.	117b	41.28 N	112.10 W
Beas de Segura, Sp. (bā'äs dā sä-go͞o'rä)	168	38.16 N	2.53 W
Beata (I.), Dom. Rep. (bē-ä'tä)	133	17.40 N	71.40 W
Beata, Cabo (C.), Dom. Rep. (kä'bô-bē-ä'tä)	133	17.40 N	71.20 W
Beatrice, Ne. (bē'á-trĭs)	121	40.16 N	96.45 W
Beatty, Nv. (bēt'ē)	118	36.58 N	116.48 W
Beattyville, Ky. (bēt'ē-vĭl)	108	37.35 N	83.40 W
Beaucaire, Fr. (bō-kâr')	166	43.49 N	4.37 E
Beaucourt, Fr. (bō-ko͞or')	167	47.30 N	6.54 E
Beaufort, NC (bō'frt)	125	34.43 N	76.40 W
Beaufort, SC	125	32.25 N	80.40 W
Beaufort Sea, Ak.	105	70.30 N	138.40 W
Beaufort West, S. Afr.	222	32.20 S	22.45 E
Beauharnois, Can. (bō-är-nwä')	93a	45.23 N	73.52 W
Beaumont, Ca. (bō'mŏnt)	117a	33.57 N	116.57 W
Beaumont, Can.	93g	53.22 N	113.18 W
Beaumont, Can.	93b	46.50 N	71.01 W
Beaumont, Tx.	123	30.05 N	94.06 W
Beaune, Fr. (bōn)	166	47.02 N	4.49 E
Beauport, Can. (bō-pôr')	93b	46.52 N	71.11 W
Beaupré, Can. (bō-prā')	93b	47.03 N	70.53 W
Beauséjour, Can.	99	50.04 N	96.33 W
Beauvais, Fr. (bō-vĕ')	166	49.25 N	2.05 E
Beaver, Ok. (bē'vēr)	120	36.46 N	100.31 W
Beaver, Pa.	111e	40.42 N	80.18 W
Beaver, Ut.	119	38.15 N	112.40 W
Beaver (I.), Mi.	108	45.40 N	85.30 W
Beaver (R.), Can.	98	54.20 N	111.10 W
Beaver City, Ne.	120	40.08 N	99.52 W
Beaver Cr., Co.	120	39.42 N	103.37 W
Beaver Cr., Ks.	120	39.44 N	101.05 W
Beaver Cr., Mt.	112	46.45 N	104.18 W
Beaver Cr., Wy.	112	43.46 N	104.25 W
Beaver Dam, Wi.	113	43.29 N	88.50 W
Beaverhead Mts., Mt. (bē'vēr-hĕd)	115	44.33 N	112.59 W
Beaverhead R., Mt.	115	45.25 N	112.35 W
Beaver Ind. Res., Mi.	108	45.40 N	85.30 W
Beaverton, Or. (bē'vēr-tŭn)	116c	45.29 N	122.49 W
Bebará', Col. (bĕ-bä-rá')	140a	6.07 N	76.39 W
Bebington, Eng. (bē'bĭng-tŭn)	154	53.20 N	2.59 W
Bečej, Yugo. (bĕ'chā)	171	45.36 N	20.03 E
Becerreá, Sp. (bā-thā'rē-ä)	168	42.49 N	7.12 W
Béchar, Alg.	220	31.39 N	2.14 W
Becharof (L.), Ak. (bĕk-á-rôf)	105	57.58 N	156.58 W
Becher B., Can. (bēch'ēr)	116a	48.18 N	123.37 W
Beckley, WV (bĕk'lĭ)	108	37.40 N	81.15 W
Bédarieux, Fr. (bā-dá-ryû')	166	43.36 N	3.11 E
Beddington Cr., Can. (bĕd'ĕng tŭn)	93e	51.14 N	114.13 W
Bedford, Can. (bĕd'fērd)	109	45.10 N	73.00 W
Bedford, Eng.	160	52.10 N	0.25 W
Bedford, In.	108	38.50 N	86.30 W
Bedford, Ia.	113	40.40 N	94.41 W
Bedford, Ma.	103a	42.30 N	71.17 W
Bedford, NY	110a	41.12 N	73.38 W
Bedford, Oh.	111d	41.23 N	81.32 W
Bedford, Pa.	109	40.05 N	78.20 W
Bedford, S. Afr.	223c	32.43 S	26.19 E
Bedford, Va.	125	37.19 N	79.27 W
Bedford Hills, NY	110a	41.14 N	73.41 W
Beebe, Ar. (bē'bē)	121	35.04 N	91.54 W
Beecher, Il. (bē'chŭr)	111a	41.20 N	87.38 W
Beechey Hd., Can. (bē'chĭ hĕd)	116a	48.19 N	123.40 W
Beech Grove, In. (bēch grōv)	111g	39.43 N	86.05 W
Beecroft Hd., Austl. (bē'krûft)	212	35.03 S	151.15 E
Beelitz, G.D.R. (bĕ'lētz)	155b	52.14 N	12.59 E
Be'er Sheva', Isr. (bēr-shĕ'bá)	189a	31.15 N	34.48 E
Be'er Sheva' (R.), Isr.	189a	31.23 N	34.30 E
Beestekraal, S. Afr.	219d	25.22 S	27.34 E
Beeston, Eng. (bēs't'n)	154	52.55 N	1.11 W
Beetz R., G.D.R. (bĕtz)	155b	52.28 N	12.37 E
Beeville, Tx. (bē'vĭl)	123	28.24 N	97.44 W
Bega, Austl. (bā'gá)	212	36.50 S	149.49 E
Beggs, Ok. (bĕgz)	121	35.46 N	96.06 W
Bègles, Fr. (bĕ'gl')	166	44.47 N	0.34 W
Begoro, Ghana	224	6.23 N	0.23 W
Behala, India	190a	22.31 N	88.19 E
Behm Can., Ak.	96	55.41 N	131.35 W
Bei (R.), China (bā)	197a	22.54 N	113.08 E
Bei'an, China (bā-än)	198	48.05 N	126.26 E
Beicai, China (bā-tsī)	197b	31.12 N	121.33 E
Beifei (R.), China (bā-fā)	196	33.14 N	117.03 E
Beihai, China (bā-hī)	199	21.30 N	109.10 E
Beihuangcheng Dao (I.), China (bā-hŭäŋ-chŭŋ dou)	196	38.23 N	120.55 E
Beijing (Peking), China (bā-jyĭŋ)	198a	39.55 N	116.23 E
Beijing Shi (Mun.), China (bā-jyĭŋ shr)	196	40.07 N	116.00 E
Beira, Moz. (bā'rá)	222	19.45 N	34.58 E
Beira (Reg.), Port. (bĕ'y-rä)	168	40.38 N	8.00 W
Beirut (Bayrūt), Leb. (bā-ro͞ot')	189a	33.53 N	35.30 E

PLACE (Pronunciation)	PAGE	Lat. °′	Long. °′
Beja, Port. (bä'zhä)	168	38.03 N	7.53 W
Béja, Tun.	157	36.52 N	9.20 E
Bejaïa (Bougie), Alg.	220	36.46 N	5.00 E
Bejar, Sp.	168	40.25 N	5.43 W
Bejestān, Iran	192	34.30 N	58.22 E
Bejucal, Cuba (bā-ho͞o-käl')	133a	22.08 N	82.23 W
Bejuco, Pan. (bĕ-кo͞o'kō)	131	8.37 N	79.54 W
Békés, Hung. (bā'kāsh)	165	46.45 N	21.08 E
Békéscsaba, Hung. (bā'kāsh-chô'bô)	165	46.39 N	21.06 E
Beketova, Sov. Un. (bĕk'e-to'vá)	195	53.23 N	125.21 E
Bela Crkva, Yugo. (bĕ'lä tsĕrk'vä)	171	44.53 N	21.25 E
Belalcázar, Sp. (bāl-ä-kä'thär)	168	38.35 N	5.12 W
Bela Vista de Goia's, Braz.	141	16.57 S	48.47 W
Belawan, Indon. (bå-lä'wan)	202	3.43 N	98.43 E
Belaya (R.), Sov. Un. (byĕ'lī-yá)	176	52.30 N	56.15 E
Belaya Tserkov', Sov. Un. (byĕ'lī-yá tsĕr'kôf)	173	49.48 N	30.09 E
Belcher Is., Can. (bĕl'chēr)	95	56.20 N	80.40 W
Belding, Mi. (bĕl'dĭng)	108	43.05 N	85.25 W
Belebey, Sov. Un. (byĕ'lĕ-bā'ĭ)	176	54.00 N	54.10 E
Belém (Pará), Braz. (bå-lĕɴ') (pä-rä)	141	1.18 S	48.27 W
Belen, NM (bĕ-lån')	119	34.40 N	106.45 W
Belén, Par. (bā-lān')	142	23.30 S	57.09 W
Bélep, Isles (Is.), N. Cal.	211	19.30 S	160.32 E
Belëv, Sov. Un. (byĕl'yĕf)	172	53.49 N	36.06 E
Belfair, Wa. (bĕl'far)	116a	47.27 N	122.50 W
Belfast, Me. (bĕl'fåst)	102	44.25 N	69.01 W
Belfast, N. Ire.	160	54.36 N	5.45 W
Belfast, Lough (B.), Ire. (lŏк bĕl'fåst)	160	54.45 N	6.00 W
Belfort, Fr. (bå-fôr')	167	47.40 N	7.50 E
Belgaum, India	191	15.57 N	74.32 E
Belgium, Eur. (bĕl'jĭ-ŭm)	152	51.00 N	2.52 E
Belgorod, Sov. Un. (byĕl'gŭ-rut)	173	50.36 N	36.32 E
Belgorod (Oblast), Sov. Un.	173	50.40 N	36.42 E
Belgorod Dnestrovskiy, Sov. Un. (byĕl'gŭ-rŭd nyĕs-trôf'skē)	173	46.09 N	30.19 E
Belgrade, see Beograd			
Belhaven, NC (bĕl'hā-vĕn)	125	35.33 N	76.37 W
Belington, WV (bĕl'ĭng-tŭn)	109	39.00 N	79.55 W
Beli Timok (R.), Yugo. (bĕ'lē tē'mōk)	171	43.35 N	22.13 E
Belitung (I.), Indon.	202	3.30 S	107.30 E
Belize City, Belize (bĕ-lēz')	130a	17.31 N	88.10 W
Belize, N.A.	126	17.00 N	88.40 W
Belize R., Belize	130a	17.16 N	88.56 W
Bel'kovo, Sov. Un. (byĕl'kô-vô)	180b	56.15 N	38.49 E
Bel'kovskiy (I.), Sov. Un. (byĕl-kôf'skĭ)	179	75.52 N	133.00 E
Bell (I.), Can. (bĕl)	103	50.45 N	55.35 W
Bell (R.), Can.	101	49.25 N	77.15 W
Bella Bella, Can.	96	52.10 N	128.07 W
Bella Coola, Can.	96	52.22 N	126.46 W
Bellaire, Oh. (bĕl-âr')	108	40.00 N	80.45 W
Bellaire, Tx.	123a	29.43 N	95.28 W
Bellary, India (bĕl-lä'rē)	191	15.15 N	76.56 E
Bella Union, Ur. (bĕ'l-yä-o͞o-nyō'n)	142	30.18 S	57.26 W
Bella Vista, Arg. (bā'lyá vēs'tá)	142	27.07 S	65.14 W
Bella Vista, Arg.	142	28.35 S	58.53 W
Bella Vista, Arg.	142a	34.18 S	58.41 W
Bella Vista, Braz.	141	22.16 S	56.14 W
Belle-Anse, Hai	133	18.15 N	72.00 W
Belle B., Can. (bĕl)	103	47.35 N	55.15 W
Belle Chasse, La. (bĕl shäs')	110d	29.52 N	90.00 W
Bellefontaine, Oh. (bĕl-fŏn'tån)	108	40.25 N	83.50 W
Bellefontaine Neighbors, Mo.	117e	38.46 N	90.13 W
Belle Fourche, SD (bĕl' fo͞orsh')	112	44.28 N	103.50 W
Belle Fourche (R.), Wy.	112	44.29 N	104.40 W
Belle Fourche Res., SD	112	44.51 N	103.44 W
Bellegarde, Fr. (bĕl-gärd')	167	46.06 N	5.50 E
Belle Glade, Fl. (bĕl glād)	125a	26.39 N	80.37 W
Belle-Île (I.), Fr. (bĕlēl')	166	47.15 N	3.30 W
Belle Isle, Str. of, Can.	103	51.35 N	56.30 W
Belle Mead, NJ (bĕl mēd)	110a	40.28 N	74.40 W
Belleoram, Can.	103	47.31 N	55.25 W
Belle Plaine, Ia. (bĕl plān')	113	41.52 N	92.19 W
Belle Vernon, Pa. (bĕl vûr'nŭn)	111e	40.08 N	79.52 W
Belleville, Can. (bĕl'vĭl)	109	44.15 N	77.25 W
Belleville, Il.	117e	38.31 N	89.59 W
Belleville, Ks.	121	39.49 N	97.37 W
Belleville, Mi.	111b	42.12 N	83.29 W
Belleville, NJ	110a	40.47 N	74.09 W
Bellevue, Ia. (bĕl'vū)	113	42.14 N	90.26 W
Bellevue, Ky.	111f	39.06 N	84.29 W
Bellevue, Mi.	108	42.30 N	85.00 W
Bellevue, Oh.	108	41.15 N	82.45 W
Bellevue, Pa.	111e	40.30 N	80.04 W
Bellevue, Wa.	116a	47.37 N	122.12 W
Belley, Fr. (bĕ-lē')	167	45.46 N	5.41 E
Bellflower, Ca. (bĕl-flou'ēr)	117a	33.53 N	118.08 W
Bell Gardens, Ca.	117a	33.59 N	118.11 W
Bellingham, Ma. (bĕl'ĭng-hăm)	103a	42.05 N	71.28 W
Bellingham, Wa.	116d	48.46 N	122.29 W
Bellingham B., Wa.	116d	48.44 N	122.34 W
Bellingshausen Sea, Ant. (bĕl'ĭngz houz'n)	228	72.00 S	80.30 W
Bellinzona, Switz. (bĕl-ĭn-tsō'nä)	170	46.10 N	9.09 E
Bell I., Can.	103	50.44 N	55.35 W
Bellmore, NY (bĕl-mōr)	110a	40.40 N	73.31 W
Bello, Col. (bĕ'l-yō)	140a	6.20 N	75.33 W
Bellow Falls, Vt. (bĕl'ōz fôls)	109	43.10 N	72.30 W
Bellpat, Pak.	190	29.08 N	68.00 E
Bell Pen., Can.	95	63.50 N	81.16 W
Bells Corners, Can.	93c	45.20 N	75.49 W

ăt; finăl; rāte; senåte; ärm; åsk; sofá; fâre; ch-choose; dh-as th in other; bē; ēvent; bĕt; recĕnt; cratēr; g-gō; gh-guttural g; bĭt; ĭ-short neutral; rīde; к-guttural k as ch in German ich;

PRONOUNCING INDEX Bells Mtn. – Bienville 269

PLACE (Pronunciation)	PAGE	Lat. °′	Long. °′
Bells Mtn., Wa. (bĕls)	116c	45.50 N	122.21 W
Belluno, It. (bĕl-lōō'nō)	170	46.08 N	12.14 E
Bell Ville, Arg. (bĕl vēl')	142	32.33 S	62.36 W
Bellville, S.Afr.	222a	33.54 S	18.38 E
Bellville, Tx. (bĕl'vĭl)	123	29.57 N	96.15 W
Bélmez, Sp. (bĕl'mĕth)	168	38.17 N	5.17 W
Belmond, Ia. (bĕl'mŏnd)	113	42.49 N	93.37 W
Belmont, Ca.	116b	37.34 N	122.18 W
Belmonte, Braz. (bĕl-mōn'tȧ)	141	15.58 S	38.47 W
Belmopan, Belize	126	17.15 N	88.47 W
Belogorsk, Sov.Un.	179	51.09 N	128.32 E
Belo Horizonte, Braz. (bĕ'lôre-sô'n-tĕ)	139a	19.54 S	43.56 W
Beloit, Ks. (bē-loit')	120	39.26 N	98.06 W
Beloit, Wi.	113	42.31 N	89.04 W
Belomorsk, Sov.Un. (byĕl-ô-môrsk')	176	64.30 N	34.42 E
Belopol'ye, Sov.Un. (byĕ'lô-pôl'yĕ)	173	51.10 N	34.19 E
Beloretsk, Sov.Un. (byĕ'lô-rĕtsk)	180a	53.58 N	58.25 E
Belorussian (S.S.R.), Sov.Un.	174	53.30 N	25.33 E
Belosarayskaya, Kosa (C.), Sov.Un. (kô-sä'byĕ'lô-sä-räy'skä'yä)	173	46.43 N	37.18 E
Belovo, Sov.Un. (byĕ'lŭ-vû)	178	54.17 N	86.23 E
Belovodsk, Sov.Un. (byĕ-lŭ-vôdsk')	173	49.12 N	39.36 E
Beloye (L.), Sov.Un.	176	60.10 N	38.05 E
Belozersk, Sov.Un. (byĕ-lŭ-zyôrsk')	176	60.00 N	38.00 E
Belper, Eng. (bĕl'pēr)	154	53.01 N	1.28 W
Belt, Mt. (bĕlt)	115	47.11 N	110.58 W
Belt Cr., Mt.	115	47.19 N	110.58 W
Belton, Tx. (bĕl'tŭn)	123	31.04 N	97.27 W
Belton L., Tx.	123	31.15 N	97.35 W
Beltsville, Md. (belts-vĭl)	110e	39.03 N	76.56 W
Bel'tsy, Sov.Un. (bĕl'tsē)	173	47.47 N	27.57 E
Belukha, Gol'tsy (Mtn.), Sov.Un.	178	49.47 N	86.23 E
Belvidere, Il. (bĕl-vē-dēr')	113	42.14 N	88.52 W
Belvidere, NJ	109	40.50 N	75.05 W
Belyando (R.), Austl. (bĕl-yăn'dō)	211	22.09 S	146.48 E
Belyanka, Sov. Un. (byĕl'yȧn-kȧ)	180a	56.04 N	59.16 E
Belynichi, Sov. Un. (byĕl-ĭ-nĭ'chĭ)	172	54.02 N	29.42 E
Belyy, Sov. Un. (byĕ'lē)	172	55.52 N	32.58 E
Belyy (I.), Sov. Un.	178	73.19 N	72.00 E
Belyye Stolby, Sov. Un. (byĕ'lĭ-ye stôl'bĭ)	180b	55.20 N	37.52 E
Belzig, G.D.R. (bĕl'tsēg)	155b	52.08 N	12.35 E
Belzoni, Ms. (bĕl-zō'nē)	124	33.09 N	90.30 W
Bembe, Ang. (bĕN'bĕ)	222	7.00 S	14.20 E
Bembézar (R.), Sp. (bĕm-bā-thär')	168	38.00 N	5.18 W
Bemidji, Mn. (bē-mĭj'ĭ)	113	47.28 N	94.54 W
Bena Dibele, Zaire (bĕn'ȧ dē-bĕ'lĕ)	222	4.00 S	22.49 E
Benalla, Austl. (bĕn-ăl'ȧ)	212	36.30 S	146.00 E
Benares, see Vārānasi			
Benavente, Sp. (bā-nä-vĕn'tā)	168	42.01 N	5.43 W
Benbrook, Tx. (bĕn'brŏŏk)	117c	32.41 N	97.27 W
Benbrook Res., Tx.	117c	32.35 N	97.30 W
Bend, Or. (bĕnd)	114	44.04 N	121.17 W
Bendeleben, Mt., Ak. (bĕn-dĕl-bĕn)	105	65.18 N	163.45 W
Bender Beila, Som.	219a	9.40 N	50.45 E
Bender Cassim, Som.	219a	11.19 N	49.10 E
Bendery, Sov. Un. (bĕn-dyĕ're)	173	46.49 N	29.29 E
Bendigo, Austl. (bĕn'dĭ-gō)	212	36.39 S	144.20 E
Benedict, Md. (bĕnĕ'dĭct)	110e	38.31 N	76.41 W
Benešov, Czech. (bĕn'ĕ-shôf)	164	49.48 N	14.40 E
Benevento, It. (bā-nā-vĕn'tō)	170	41.08 N	14.46 E
Bengal, B. of, Asia (bĕn-gôl')	188	17.30 N	87.00 E
Bengamisa, Zaire	226	0.57 N	25.10 E
Bengbu, China (bŭŋ-bōō)	196	32.52 N	117.22 E
Bengkalis, Indon. (bĕng-kä'lĭs)	189b	1.29 N	102.06 E
Bengkulu, Indon.	202	3.46 S	102.18 E
Benguela, Ang. (bĕn-gĕl'ȧ)	226	12.35 S	13.25 E
Beni (R.), Bol. (bā'nē)	140	13.41 S	67.30 W
Beni-Abbès, Alg. (bā'nē ä-bĕs')	220	30.11 N	2.13 W
Benicarló, Sp. (bā-nē-kär-lō')	169	40.26 N	0.25 E
Benicia, Ca. (bē-nĭsh'ĭ-ȧ)	116b	38.03 N	122.09 W
Benin, Afr.	218	8.00 N	2.00 E
Benin (R.), Nig. (bĕn-ēn')	225	5.55 N	5.15 E
Benin City, Nig.	225	6.19 N	5.41 E
Beni Saf, Alg. (bā'nē säf')	220	35.23 N	1.20 W
Benito (R.), Equat. Gui.	226	1.35 N	10.45 E
Benkelman, Ne. (bĕn-kĕl-mȧn)	120	40.05 N	101.35 W
Benkovac, Yugo. (bĕn'kō-vȧts)	170	44.02 N	15.41 E
Ben Macdhui (Mtn.), Leso-S. Afr. (bĕn măk-dōō'ē)	223c	30.38 S	27.54 E
Bennettsville, SC (bĕn'ĕts vĭl)	125	34.35 N	79.41 W
Bennington, Vt. (bĕn'ĭng-tŭn)	109	42.55 N	73.15 W
Benns Church, Va. (bĕnz' chûrch')	110g	36.47 N	76.35 W
Benoni, S. Afr. (bĕ-nō'nĭ)	223b	26.11 S	28.19 E
Benoy, Chad	225	8.59 N	16.19 E
Benque Viejo, Belize (bĕn-kĕ bĭē'hō)	130a	17.07 N	89.07 W
Bensberg, F.R.G.	167c	50.58 N	7.09 E
Bensenville, Il. (bĕn'sĕn-vĭl)	111a	41.57 N	87.56 W
Bensheim, F.R.G. (bĕns-hīm)	164	49.42 N	8.38 E
Benson, Az. (bĕn-sŭn)	119	32.00 N	110.20 W
Benson, Mn.	112	45.18 N	95.36 W
Bentleyville, Pa. (bent'lē vĭl)	111e	40.07 N	80.01 W
Benton, Ar. (bĕn'tŭn)	121	34.34 N	92.34 W
Benton, Ca.	118	37.44 N	118.22 W
Benton, Can.	102	45.59 N	67.36 W
Benton, Il.	108	38.00 N	88.55 W
Benton Harbor, Mi. (bĕn'tŭn här'bēr)	108	42.05 N	86.30 W
Bentonville, Ar. (bĕn'tŭn-vĭl)	121	36.22 N	94.11 W
Benue (R.), Nig. (bā'nōō-ȧ)	225	7.55 N	8.55 E
Benut (R.), Mala.	189b	1.43 N	103.20 E
Benwood, WV (bĕn-wŏŏd)	108	39.55 N	80.45 W
Benxi, China (bŭn-shyĕ)	198	41.25 N	123.50 E
Beograd (Belgrade), Yugo. (bĕ-ô'gràd) (bĕl'gräd)	171	44.48 N	20.32 E
Beppu, Jap. (bĕ'pōō)	201	33.16 N	131.30 E
Bequia I., N.A. (bĕk-ē'ä)	131b	13.00 N	61.08 W
Berakit, Tanjung (C.), Indon.	189b	1.16 N	104.44 E
Berat, Alb. (bĕ-rät')	171	40.43 N	19.59 E
Berau, Teluk (B.), Indon.	203	2.22 S	131.40 E
Berazategui, Arg. (bĕ-rä-zä'tĕ-gē)	142a	34.46 S	58.14 W
Berbera, Som. (bûr'bûr-ȧ)	219a	10.25 N	45.05 E
Berbérati, Cen. Afr. Rep.	225	4.16 N	15.47 E
Berck, Fr. (bĕrk)	166	50.26 N	1.36 E
Berd'ansk, Sov. Un.	159	46.45 N	36.47 E
Berdichev, Sov. Un. (bĕ-dē'chĕf)	173	49.53 N	28.32 E
Berdyanskaya, Kosa (C.), Sov. Un. (kô-sä' bĕ-dyän'skä-yä)	173	46.38 N	36.42 E
Berdyaush, Sov. Un. (bĕr'dyàûsh)	180a	55.10 N	59.12 E
Berea, Ky. (bĕ-rē'ȧ)	124	37.30 N	84.19 W
Berea, Oh.	111d	41.22 N	81.51 W
Beregovo, Sov. Un. (bĕ'rĕ-gô-vô)	165	48.13 N	22.40 E
Bereku, Tan.	227	4.27 S	35.44 E
Berens (R.), Can. (bĕr'enz)	99	52.15 N	96.30 W
Berens I., Can.	99	52.18 N	97.40 W
Berens River, Can.	99	52.22 N	97.02 W
Beresford, SD (bĕr'ĕs-fērd)	112	43.05 N	96.46 W
Berettyóújfalu, Hung. (bĕ'rĕt-tyō-ōō'y'fô-lōō)	165	47.14 N	21.33 E
Berëza, Sov.Un. (bĕ-rā'zȧ)	165	52.29 N	24.59 E
Berezhany, Sov.Un. (bĕr-yĕ'zhȧ-nĕ)	165	49.25 N	24.58 E
Berezina (R.), Sov.Un. (bĕr-yĕ'zē-nȧ)	172	53.20 N	29.05 E
Berezino, Sov.Un. (bĕr-yä'zē-nô)	172	53.51 N	28.54 E
Berezna, Sov.Un. (bĕr-yôz'nȧ)	173	51.32 N	31.47 E
Bereznegovata, Sov.Un.	173	47.19 N	32.58 E
Berezniki, Sov.Un. (bĕr-yôz'nyĕ-kē)	180a	59.25 N	56.46 E
Berëzovka, Sov.Un. (bĕr-yôz'ôf-kȧ)	173	47.12 N	30.56 E
Berëzovka, Sov.Un.	180a	57.35 N	57.19 E
Berëzovo, Sov.Un. (bĭr-yô'zē-vû)	176	64.10 N	65.10 E
Berëzovskiy, Sov.Un. (bĕr-yô'zôf-skĭ)	180a	56.54 N	60.47 E
Berga, Sp. (bĕr'gä)	169	42.05 N	1.52 E
Bergama, Tur. (bĕr'gä-mä)	177	39.08 N	27.09 E
Bergamo, It. (bĕr'gä-mō)	170	45.43 N	9.41 E
Bergantin, Ven. (bĕr-gän-tē'n)	141b	10.04 N	64.23 W
Bergedorf, F.R.G. (bĕr'gē-dôrf)	155c	53.29 N	10.12 E
Bergen, G.D.R. (bĕr'gĕn)	164	54.26 N	13.26 E
Bergen, Nor.	162	60.24 N	5.20 E
Bergenfield, NJ	110a	40.55 N	73.59 W
Bergen op Zoom, Neth.	155a	51.29 N	4.16 E
Bergerac, Fr. (bĕr-zhē-ràk')	166	44.49 N	0.28 E
Bergisch Gladbach, F.R.G. (bĕrg'ĭsh-glät'bäk)	167c	50.59 N	7.08 E
Berglern, F.R.G. (bĕrgh'lĕrn)	155d	48.24 N	11.55 E
Bergneustadt, F.R.G.	167c	51.01 N	7.39 E
Bergville, S.Afr. (bĕrg'vĭl)	223c	28.46 S	29.22 E
Berhampur, India	190	19.19 N	84.48 E
Bering Sea, Asia-N.A. (bē'rĭng)	92	58.00 N	175.00 W
Bering Str., Ak.	105	64.50 N	169.50 W
Berislav, Sov.Un. (byĕr'ĭ-slàf)	173	46.49 N	33.24 E
Berja, Sp. (bĕr'hä)	168	36.50 N	2.56 W
Berkeley, Ca. (bûrk'lĭ)	116b	37.52 N	122.17 W
Berkeley, Mo.	117e	38.45 N	90.20 W
Berkeley Springs, WV (bûrk'lĭ sprĭngz)	109	39.40 N	78.10 W
Berkhamsted, Eng. (bĕk'hȧm'stĕd)	154b	51.44 N	0.34 W
Berkley, Mi. (bûrk'lĭ)	111b	42.30 N	83.10 W
Berkovitsa, Bul. (bĕ-kō'vĕ-tsȧ)	171	43.14 N	23.08 E
Barkshire (Co.), Eng.	154b	51.23 N	1.07 W
Berland (R.), Can.	97	54.00 N	117.10 W
Berlenga (Is.), Port. (bĕr-lĕn'gäzh)	168	39.25 N	9.33 W
Berlin, East, G.D.R. (bĕr-lēn')	155b	52.31 N	13.28 E
Berlin, West, F.R.G.	155b	52.31 N	13.20 E
Berlin, NH (bûr-lĭn)	109	44.25 N	71.10 W
Berlin, NJ	110f	39.47 N	74.56 W
Berlin, S.Afr. (bĕr-lĭn)	223c	32.53 S	27.36 E
Berlin, Wi. (bûr-lĭn')	113	43.58 N	88.58 W
Bermejo (R.), Arg. (bĕr-mā'hō)	142	25.05 S	61.00 W
Bermeo, Sp. (bĕr-mā'yō)	168	43.23 N	2.43 W
Bermuda (I.), N.A.	127	32.20 N	65.45 W
Bern, Switz. (bĕrn)	164	46.55 N	7.25 E
Bernal, Arg. (bĕr-näl')	142a	34.27 S	58.17 W
Bernalillo, NM (bĕr-nä-lē'yō)	119	35.20 N	106.30 W
Bernard (L.), Can. (bĕr-närd')	109	45.45 N	79.25 W
Bernardsville, NJ (bŭr nȧrds'vĭl)	110a	40.43 N	74.34 W
Bernau, G.D.R. (bĕr'nou)	155b	52.40 N	13.35 E
Bernburg, G.D.R. (bĕrn'bŏŏrgh)	164	51.48 N	11.43 E
Berndorf, Aus. (bĕrn'dôrf)	164	47.57 N	16.05 E
Berne, In. (bûrn)	108	40.40 N	84.55 W
Berner Alpen (Mts.), Switz.	164	46.29 N	7.30 E
Bernier (I.), Austl. (bĕr-nēr')	210	24.58 S	113.15 E
Bernina Pizzo (Pk.), Switz.	164	46.23 N	9.58 E
Bero (R.), Ang.	226	15.10 S	12.20 E
Beroun, Czech. (bā'rōn)	164	49.57 N	14.03 E
Berounka R., Czech. (bĕ-rōn'kȧ)	164	49.53 N	13.40 E
Berowra, Austl.	207b	33.36 S	151.10 E
Berre, Étang de (L.), Fr. (ā-tôN' dĕ bâr')	166a	43.27 N	5.07 E
Berre-l' Étang, Fr. (bâr'lā-tôN')	166a	43.28 N	5.11 E
Berriane, Alg. (bĕr-ē-äN')	158	32.50 N	3.49 E
Berriozabal, Mex. (bā'rēō-zä-bäl')	129	16.47 N	93.16 W
Berry Creek (R.), Can.	97	51.15 N	111.40 W
Berryessa (R.), Ca. (bĕ'rĭ ĕs'ȧ)	118	38.35 N	122.33 W
Berry Is., Ba.	132	25.40 N	77.50 W
Berryville, Ar. (bĕr'ē-vĭl)	121	36.21 N	93.34 W
Bershad', Sov.Un. (byĕr'shät)	173	48.22 N	29.31 E
Berthier, Can.	93b	46.56 N	70.44 W
Bertrand (R.), Wa. (bûr'trȧnd)	116d	48.58 N	122.31 W
Berwick, Pa. (bûr'wĭk)	109	41.05 N	76.10 W
Berwick-upon-Tweed, Eng. (bûr'ĭk)	160	55.45 N	2.01 W
Berwyn, Il. (bûr'wĭn)	111a	41.49 N	87.47 W
Besalampy, Mad. (bĕz-ȧ-lȧm-pē')	223	16.48 S	40.40 E
Besançon, Fr. (bĕ-säN-sôn)	167	47.14 N	6.02 E
Besar, Gunong (Mt.), Mala.	189b	2.31 N	103.09 E
Besed' (R.), Sov.Un. (byĕ'syĕt)	172	52.58 N	31.36 E
Beshenkovichi, Sov.Un. (byĕ'shĕn-kōvĕ'chĭ)	172	55.04 N	29.29 E
Beskid (Mts.), Czech.-Pol.	165	49.23 N	19.00 E
Bességes, Fr. (bĕ-sĕzh')	166	44.20 N	4.07 E
Bessemer, Al. (bĕs'ē-mēr)	110h	33.24 N	86.58 W
Bessemer, Mi.	113	46.29 N	90.04 W
Bessemer City, NC	125	35.16 N	81.17 W
Bestensee, G.D.R. (bĕs'tĕn-zā)	155b	51.15 N	13.39 E
Betanzos, Sp. (bĕ-tän'thōs)	168	43.18 N	8.14 W
Betatakin Ruin, Az. (bĕt-ȧ-tăk'ĭn)	119	36.40 N	110.29 W
Bethal, S.Afr. (bĕth'ăl)	219d	26.27 S	29.28 E
Bethalto, Il. (bȧ-thăl'tō)	117e	38.54 N	90.03 W
Bethanien, Namibia	222	26.20 S	16.10 E
Bethany, Mo.	121	40.15 N	94.04 W
Bethel, Ak. (bĕth'ĕl)	105	60.50 N	161.50 W
Bethel, Ct.	110a	41.22 N	73.24 W
Bethel, Vt.	109	43.50 N	72.40 W
Bethel Park, Pa.	111e	40.19 N	80.02 W
Bethesda, Md. (bĕ-thĕs'dȧ)	110e	39.00 N	77.10 W
Bethlehem, Pa. (bĕth'lē-hĕm)	109	40.40 N	75.25 W
Bethlehem, S.Afr.	219d	28.14 S	28.18 E
Bethlehem, see Bayt Lahm			
Béthune, Fr. (bā-tün')	166	50.32 N	2.37 E
Betroka, Mad. (bĕ-trŏk'ȧ)	223	23.13 S	46.17 E
Bet She'an, Isr.	189a	32.30 N	35.30 E
Betsiamites, Can.	102	48.57 N	68.36 W
Betsiamites, (R.), Can.	102	49.11 N	69.20 W
Betsiboka (R.), Mad. (bĕt-sĭ-bō'kȧ)	223	16.47 S	46.45 E
Bettles Field, Ak. (bĕt'tŭls)	105	66.58 N	151.48 W
Betwa (R.), India (bĕt'wȧ)	190	25.00 N	77.37 E
Betz, Fr. (bĕ)	167b	49.09 N	2.58 E
Beveren, Bel.	155a	51.13 N	4.14 E
Beverly, Eng. (bĕv'ēr-lĭ)	154	53.50 N	0.25 W
Beverly, Ma.	103a	42.34 N	70.53 W
Beverly, NJ	110f	40.03 N	74.56 W
Beverly Hills, Ca.	117a	34.05 N	118.24 W
Bevier, Mo. (bē-vēr')	121	39.44 N	92.36 W
Bewdley, Eng. (būd'lĭ)	154	52.22 N	2.19 W
Bexhill, Eng. (bĕks'hĭl)	161	50.49 N	0.25 E
Bexley, Eng. (bĕks'ly)	154b	51.26 N	0.09 E
Beyla, Gui. (bā'lȧ)	224	8.41 N	8.37 W
Beylul, Eth.	221	13.15 N	42.21 E
Beypazari, Tur. (bā-pȧ-zä'rĭ)	177	40.10 N	31.40 E
Beyşehir, Tur. (bā-shĕ'h'r)	177	38.00 N	31.45 E
Beyşehir Gölü (L.), Turk.	177	38.00 N	31.30 E
Beysugskiy, Liman (B.), Sov.Un. (lĭ-män' bĕy-sōōg'skĭ)	173	46.07 N	38.35 E
Bezhetsk, Sov.Un. (byĕ-zhĕtsk')	172	57.46 N	36.40 E
Bezhitsa, Sov.Un. (byĕ-zhĭ'tsȧ)	172	53.19 N	34.18 E
Béziers, Fr. (bā-zyā')	166	43.21 N	3.12 E
Bhadreswar, India	190a	22.49 N	88.22 E
Bhāgalpur, India (bä'gŭl-pōōr)	190	25.15 N	86.59 E
Bhamo, Bur. (bŭ-mō')	194	24.00 N	96.15 E
Bhāngar, India	190a	22.30 N	88.36 E
Bharatpur, India (bĕrt'pōōr)	190	27.21 N	77.33 E
Bhatinda, India (bŭ-tĭn-dȧ)	190	30.19 N	74.56 E
Bhaunagar, India (bäv-nŭg'ŭr)	190	21.45 N	72.58 E
Bhayandar, India	191a	19.20 N	72.50 E
Bhilai, India	190	21.14 N	81.23 E
Bhīma (R.), India (bē'mȧ)	190	17.15 N	75.55 E
Bhiwandi, India	191a	19.18 N	73.03 E
Bhiwāni, India	190	28.53 N	76.08 E
Bhopāl, India (bô-päl)	190	23.20 N	77.25 E
Bhubaneswar, India (bōō-bû-nāsh'vûr)	190	20.21 N	85.53 E
Bhuj, India (bōōj)	190	23.22 N	69.39 E
Bhutan, Asia (bōō-tän')	193	27.15 N	90.30 E
Biafra, Bight of, Afr.	226	4.05 N	7.10 E
Biak (I.), Indon. (bē'ăk)	203	1.00 S	136.00 E
Biała Podlaska, Pol. (byä'wȧ pŏd-läs'kä)	165	52.01 N	23.08 E
Białogard, Pol. (byä-wō'gärd)	164	54.00 N	16.01 E
Białystok, Pol. (byä-wĭs'tŏk)	165	53.08 N	23.12 E
Biankouma, Ivory Coast	224	7.44 N	7.37 W
Biarritz, Fr. (byä-rēts')	166	43.27 N	1.39 W
Bibā, Egypt (bē'bȧ)	219b	28.54 N	30.59 E
Bibb City, Ga. (bĭb' sĭ'tē)	124	32.31 N	84.56 W
Biberach, F.R.G. (bē'bĕräk)	164	48.06 N	9.49 E
Bibiani, Ghana	224	6.28 N	2.20 W
Bic, Can. (bĭk)	102	48.22 N	68.42 W
Bicknell, In. (bĭk'nĕl)	108	38.45 N	87.20 W
Bicske, Hung. (bĭsh'kĕ)	165	47.29 N	18.38 E
Bida, Nig. (bē'dä)	225	9.05 N	6.01 E
Biddeford, Me. (bĭd'ē-fērd)	102	43.29 N	70.29 W
Biddulph, Eng. (bĭd'ŭlf)	154	53.07 N	2.10 W
Bidon Cinq, see Post Maurice Cortier			
Biebrza R., Pol. (byĕb'zhȧ)	165	53.18 N	22.25 E
Biel, Switz. (bēl)	164	47.09 N	7.12 E
Bielefeld, F.R.G. (bē'lĕ-fĕlt)	164	52.01 N	8.35 E
Biella, It. (byĕl'lä)	170	45.34 N	8.05 E
Bielsk Podlaski, Pol. (byĕlsk pŭd-lä'skĭ)	165	52.47 N	23.14 E
Bien Hoa, Viet.	202	10.59 N	106.49 E
Bienville, Lac (L.), Can.	95	55.32 N	72.45 W

ng-sing; ŋ-baŋk; N-nasalized n; nŏd; cŏmmit; ōld; ôbey; ôrder; oi-boil; fōōd; fŏŏt; ou-out; s-soft; sh-dish; th-thin; pūre; ûnite; ûrn; stŭd; circŭs; ü-as in French tu; '-indeterminate vowel.

ăt; fīnăl; rāte; senāte; ärm; ásk; sofá; fâre; ch-choose; dh-as th in other; bĕ; ĕvent; bĕt; recĕnt; cratēr; g-gō; gh-guttural g; bīt; ĭ-short neutral; rīde; ᴋ-guttural k as ch in German ich;

PRONOUNCING INDEX

Blue Island – Bosanski Novi 271

PLACE (Pronunciation)	PAGE	Lat. °′	Long. °′
Blue Island, Il.	111a	41.39 N	87.41 W
Blue Mesa Res., Co.	119	38.25 N	107.00 W
Blue Mts., Austl.	212	33.35 S	149.00 E
Blue Mts., Jam.	132	18.05 N	76.35 W
Blue Mts., Or.	114	45.15 N	118.50 W
Blue Mud B., Austl. (bloo mŭd)	210	13.20 S	136.45 E
Blue Nile (Abay) (R.), Eth. (á-bä'ē)	221	9.45 N	37.23 E
Blue Nile (Al-Bahr al-Azraq) (R.), Sud. (bärĕlaz-räk')	221	12.50 N	34.10 E
Blue Rapids, Ks. (bloo răp'ĭdz)	121	39.40 N	96.41 W
Blue Ridge (Mts.), U.S. (bloo rĭj)	107	35.30 N	82.50 W
Blue River, Can.	97	52.05 N	119.17 W
Blue R., Mo.	117f	38.55 N	94.33 W
Bluff, Ut.	119	37.18 N	109.34 W
Bluff Park, Al.	110h	33.24 N	86.52 W
Bluffton, In. (blŭf-tŭn)	108	40.40 N	85.15 W
Bluffton, Oh.	108	40.50 N	83.55 W
Blumenau, Braz. (bloo'mĕn-ou)	142	26.53 S	48.58 W
Blumut, Gunong (Mt.), Mala.	189b	2.03 N	103.34 E
Blyth, Eng. (blīth)	160	55.03 N	1.34 W
Blythe, Ca.	118	33.37 N	114.37 W
Blytheville, Ar. (blīth'vĭl)	121	35.55 N	89.51 W
Bo, S.L.	224	7.56 N	11.21 W
Boac, Phil.	203a	13.26 N	121.50 E
Boaco, Nic. (bô-ä'kō)	130	12.24 N	85.41 W
Bo'ai, China (bwo-ī)	198	35.10 N	113.08 E
Boa Vista do Rio Branco, Braz. (bō'ä vēsh'tä doo rē'oo brän'koo)	141	2.46 N	60.45 W
Boa Vista I., C.V. (bō-ä-vēsh'tá)	220b	16.01 N	23.52 W
Bobĕrka, Sov.Un. (bō'bĕr-ká)	165	49.36 N	24.18 E
Bobo Dioulasso, Upper Volta (bō'bō-dyoo-làs-sō')	224	11.12 N	4.18 W
Bobr, Sov.Un. (bô'b'r)	172	54.19 N	29.11 E
Bóbr (R.), Pol. (bŭ'br)	164	51.44 N	15.13 E
Bobrinets, Sov.Un. (bô'brē-nyĭts)	173	48.04 N	32.10 E
Bobrov, Sov.Un. (bŭb-rôf')	173	51.07 N	40.01 E
Bobrovitsa, Sov.Un. (bŭb-rô'vē-tsá)	173	50.43 N	31.27 E
Bobruysk, Sov.Un. (bŏ-broo'ĭsk)	172	53.07 N	29.13 E
Boca del Pozo, Ven. (bô-kä-dĕl-pô'zō)	141b	11.00 N	64.21 W
Boca de Uchire, Ven. (bô-kä-dĕ-oo-chē'rĕ)	141b	10.09 N	65.27 W
Bocaina, Serra da (Mtn.), Braz. (sĕ'r-rä-dá-bô-kä'ē-nä)	139a	22.47 S	44.39 W
Bocas, Mex. (bō'käs)	128	22.29 N	101.03 W
Bocas del Toro, Pan. (bō'käs dĕl tō'rō)	131	9.24 N	82.15 W
Bochnia, Pol. (bōĸ'nyä)	165	49.58 N	20.28 E
Bocholt, F.R.G. (bō'ĸôlt)	167c	51.50 N	6.37 E
Bochum, F.R.G.-o(bō'ĸoom)	167c	51.29 N	7.13 E
Bockum-Hövel, F.R.G. (bō'ĸoom-hû'fĕl)	167c	51.41 N	7.45 E
Bodalang, Zaire	226	3.14 N	22.14 E
Bodaybo, Sov.Un. (bō-dī'bō)	179	57.12 N	114.46 E
Bodele (Depression), Chad. (bō-då-lā')	225	16.45 N	17.05 E
Boden, Swe.	156	65.51 N	21.29 E
Bodensee (L.), F.R.G.-Switz. (bō'dĕn zā)	164	47.48 N	9.22 E
Bodmin, Eng. (bŏd'mĭn)	160	50.29 N	4.45 W
Bodmin Moor, Eng. (bŏd'mĭn moor)	160	50.36 N	4.43 W
Bodø, Nor. (bôd'û)	156	67.13 N	14.19 E
Bodrum, Tur.	177	37.10 N	27.07 E
Boende, Zaire (bô-ĕn'då)	226	0.13 S	20.52 E
Boerne, Tx. (bō'ĕrn)	122	29.49 N	98.44 W
Boesmans (R.), S.Afr.	223c	33.29 S	26.09 E
Boeuf R., La. (bĕf)	123	32.23 N	91.57 W
Boffa, Gui. (bôf'á)	224	10.10 N	14.02 W
Bōfu, Jap. (bō'foo)	201	34.03 N	131.35 E
Bogalusa, La. (bō-gá-loo'sá)	123	30.48 N	89.52 W
Bogan (R.), Austl. (bô'gĕn)	212	32.10 S	147.40 E
Bogense, Den. (bô'gĕn-sĕ)	162	55.34 N	10.09 E
Boggy Pk., Antigua (bŏg'ĭ-pēk)	131b	17.03 N	61.50 W
Bogodukhov, Sov.Un. (bō-gō-doo'ĸôf)	173	50.10 N	35.31 E
Bogong, Mt., Austl.	212	36.50 S	147.15 E
Bogor, Indon.	202	6.45 S	106.45 E
Bogoroditsk, Sov.Un. (bō-gŏ'rô-dĭtsk)	172	53.48 N	38.06 E
Bogorodsk, Sov.Un.	176	56.02 N	43.40 E
Bogorodskoye, Sov.Un. (bō-gō-rôd'skô-yĕ)	180a	56.43 N	56.53 E
Bogotá, Col. (bō-gō-tä')	140a	4.38 N	74.06 W
Bogotá, Rio (R.), Col. (rē'ō-bō-gō-tä')	140a	4.27 N	74.38 W
Bogotol, Sov.Un. (bŏ'gō-tŏl)	178	56.15 N	89.45 E
Bogoyavlenskoye, Sov.Un. (bŏ'gō-yäf'lĕn-skō'yĕ)	173	48.46 N	33.19 E
Boguchar, Sov.Un. (bō'goo-chär)	177	49.40 N	41.00 E
Boguete, Pan. (bō-gĕ'tĕ)	131	8.54 N	82.29 W
Boguslav, Sov.Un. (bō'goo-släf)	173	49.34 N	30.51 W
Bohai Haixia (Str.), China (bwo-hī hī-shyä)	198	38.05 N	121.40 E
Bohain-en-Vermandois, Fr. (bô-ăN-ŏN-vâr-mäN-dwä')	166	49.58 N	3.22 E
Bohemia (Prov.), see Cechy			
Bohemian For., F.R.G. (bô-hē'mĭ-ăn)	164	49.35 N	12.27 E
Bohol (I.), Phil. (bô-hôl')	203	9.28 N	124.35 E
Bohom, Mex. (bô-ô'm)	129	16.47 N	92.42 W
Bohotleh, Som. (bô-hŏt'lĕ)	219a	8.15 N	46.20 E
Boiestown, Can. (boiz'toun)	102	46.27 N	66.25 W
Bois Blanc (I.), Mi. (boi' blăŋk)	108	45.45 N	84.30 W
Boischâtel, Can. (bwä-shä-tĕl')	93b	46.54 N	71.08 W
Bois-des-Filion, Can. (boo-ä'dĕ-fē-yōN')	93a	45.40 N	73.46 W
Boise, Id. (boi'zē)	114	43.38 N	116.12 W
Boise (R.), Id.	114	43.43 N	116.30 W
Boise City, Ok.	120	36.42 N	102.30 W
Boissevain, Can. (bois'vān)	99	49.14 N	100.03 W
Bojador, Cabo (C.), W.Sah. (ká'bô-bō-hä-dōr') (bŏj-á-dōr')	220	26.21 N	16.08 W
Bojnūrd, Iran	192	37.29 N	57.13 E
Bokani, Nig.	225	9.26 N	5.13 E
Boké, Gui. (bō-kā')	220	10.58 N	14.15 W
Boknafjorden (Fd.), Nor.	162	59.12 N	5.37 E
Boksburg, S.Afr. (bŏĸs'bûrgh)	223b	26.13 N	28.15 E
Bokungu, Zaire	226	0.41 S	22.19 E
Bol, Chad	225	13.28 N	14.43 E
Bolai I., Cen.Afr.Rep.	225	4.20 N	17.21 E
Bolama, Guinea-Bissau (bô-lä'mä)	220	11.34 S	15.41 W
Bolan (Mt.), Pak. (bô-län')	190	30.13 N	67.09 E
Bolaños, Mex. (bō-län'yôs)	128	21.40 N	103.48 W
Bolaños (R.), Mex.	128	21.26 N	103.54 W
Bolan P., Pak.	190	29.50 N	67.10 E
Bolbec, Fr. (bôl-bĕk')	166	49.37 N	0.26 E
Bole, Ghana (bō'lå)	224	9.02 N	2.29 W
Bolesławiec, Pol. (bō-lĕ-slä'vyĕts)	164	51.15 N	15.35 E
Bolgatanga, Ghana	224	10.46 N	0.52 W
Bolgrad, Sov.Un. (bŏl-grát)	173	45.41 N	28.38 E
Boli, China (bwo-lē)	198	45.40 N	130.38 E
Bolinao, Phil. (bō-lē-nä'ô)	203a	16.24 N	119.53 E
Bolívar, Arg. (bô-lē'vär)	139c	36.15 S	61.05 W
Bolívar, Col.	140	1.46 N	76.58 W
Bolivar, Mo. (bŏl'ĭ-vár)	121	37.37 N	93.22 W
Bolivar, Tn.	124	35.14 N	88.56 W
Bolívar (La Columna) (Mtn.), Ven. (bô-lē'vär) (lä-kô-loo'm-nä)	140	8.44 N	70.54 W
Bolivar Pen., Tx. (bŏl'ĭ-vár)	123a	29.25 N	94.40 W
Bolivia, S.A. (bō-lĭv'ĭ-á)	138	17.00 S	64.00 W
Bolkhov, Sov. Un. (bŏl-ĸôf')	172	53.27 N	35.59 E
Bollin (R.), Eng. (bŏl'ĭn)	154	53.18 N	2.11 W
Bollington, Eng. (bôl'ĭng-tŭn)	154	53.18 N	2.06 W
Bollnäs, Swe. (bôl'nĕs)	162	61.22 N	16.20 E
Bolmen (L.), Swe. (bôl'mĕn)	162	56.58 N	13.25 E
Bolobo, Zaire (bō'lô-bô)	222	2.14 S	16.18 E
Bologna, It. (bô-lōn'yä)	170	44.30 N	11.18 E
Bologoye, Sov. Un. (bŏ-lŏ-gô'yĕ)	172	57.52 N	34.02 E
Bolonchenticul, Mex. (bô-lôn-chĕn-tē-koo'l)	130a	20.03 N	89.47 W
Bolondrón, Cuba (bô-lôn-drōn')	132	22.45 N	81.25 W
Bolseno, Lago di (L.), It. (lä'gō-dē-bôl-sā'nô)	170	42.35 N	11.40 E
Bol'shaya Anyuy (R.), Sov. Un.	179	67.58 N	161.15 E
Bol'shaya Chuva (R.), Sov. Un.	179	58.15 N	111.13 E
Bol'shaya Kinel' (R.), Sov. Un.	176	53.20 N	52.40 E
Bol'shaya Lepetikha, Sov. Un. (bŏl-shá'yá'lyĕ'phyĕ-tē'ĸá)	173	47.11 N	33.58 E
Bol'shaya Viska, Sov. Un. (vĭs-kä')	173	48.34 N	31.54 E
Bol'shaya Vradiyevka, Sov. Un. (vrá-dyĕf'ká)	173	47.51 N	30.38 E
Bol'she Ust'ikinskoye, Sov. Un. (bŏl'she oos-tyĭ-kĕn'skô-yĕ)	180a	55.58 N	58.18 E
Bol'shoy Begichëv (I.), Sov. Un.	179	74.30 N	114.40 E
Bol'shoye Ivonino, Sov. Un. (ĭ-vô'nĭ-nô)	180a	59.41 N	61.12 E
Bol'shoy Kuyash, Sov. Un. (bŏl'-shôy koo'yásh)	180a	55.52 N	61.07 E
Bolshoy Tokmak, Sov. Un. (bŏl-shôy' tôk-mäk')	173	47.17 N	35.48 E
Bolsover, Eng. (bōl'zō-vĕr)	154	53.14 N	1.17 W
Boltaña, Sp. (bôl-tä'nä)	169	42.28 N	0.03 E
Bolton, Can. (bōl'tŭn)	93d	43.53 N	79.44 W
Bolton, Eng.	154	53.35 N	2.26 W
Bolton-upon-Dearne, Eng. (bōl'tŭn-ŭp'ŏn-dûrn)	154	53.31 N	1.19 W
Bolu, Tur. (bō'loo)	177	40.45 N	31.45 E
Bolva (R.), Sov. Un. (bôl'vä)	172	53.30 N	34.30 E
Bolvadin, Tur. (bŏl-vä-dēn')	177	38.50 N	30.50 E
Bolzano, It. (bôl-tsä'nō)	170	46.31 N	11.22 E
Boma, Zaire (bō'mä)	226	5.51 S	13.03 E
Bombala, Austl. (bŭm-bä'lă)	212	36.55 S	149.07 E
Bombay, India (bŏm-bā')	191b	18.58 N	72.50 E
Bombay Hbr., India	191b	18.55 N	72.52 E
Bomi Hills, Lib.	220	7.00 N	11.00 W
Bom Jardim, Braz. (bôn zhär-dēN')	139a	22.10 S	42.25 W
Bom Jesus do Itabapoana, Braz. (bôN-zhĕ-soo's-dô-ē-tá'bä-pô-á'nä)	139a	21.08 S	41.51 W
Bømlo (I.), Nor. (bûmlô)	162	59.47 N	4.57 E
Bomongo, Zaire	226	1.22 N	18.21 E
Bom Sucesso, Braz. (bôn-soo-sĕ'sô)	139a	21.02 S	44.44 W
Bomu (R.), see Mbomou			
Bon, C., Tun. (bôN)	157	37.04 N	11.13 E
Bonaire (I.), Neth. Antilles (bô-når')	140	12.10 N	68.15 W
Bonavista, Can. (bŏ-ná-vĭs'tá)	103	48.39 N	53.07 W
Bonavista B., Can.	103	48.45 N	53.20 W
Bond, Co. (bŏnd)	120	39.53 N	106.40 W
Bondo, Zaire (bôn'dô)	226	3.49 N	23.40 E
Bondoc Pen., Phil. (bôn-dŏk')	203a	13.24 N	122.30 E
Bondoukou, Ivory Coast (bŏn-doo'koo)	224	8.02 N	2.48 W
Bonds Cay (I.), Ba. (bŏnds kē)	132	25.30 N	77.45 W
Bône, see Annaba			
Bone, Teluk (G.), Indon.	202	4.09 S	121.00 E
Bonete, Cerro (Mt.), Arg. (bô'nĕtĕh çĕrrô)	142	27.50 S	68.35 W
Bonfim, Braz. (bôN-fē'N)	139a	20.20 S	44.15 W
Bongor, Chad.	225	10.17 N	15.22 E
Bong Son, Viet.	199	14.20 N	109.10 E
Bonham, Tx. (bŏn'ăm)	121	33.35 N	96.09 W
Bonhomme, Pic (Pk.), Hai.	133	19.10 N	72.20 W
Bonifacio, Fr. (bō-nē-fä'chō)	170	41.23 N	9.10 E
Bonifacio, Str. of., Eur.	170	41.14 N	9.02 E
Bonifay, Fl. (bŏn-ĭ-fā')	124	30.46 N	85.40 W
Bonin Is., Asia (bō'nĭn)	204	26.30 N	141.00 E
Bonn, F.R.G. (bôn)	167c	50.44 N	7.06 E
Bonne B., Can. (bŏn)	103	49.33 N	57.55 W
Bonners Ferry, Id. (bon'erz fĕr'ĭ)	114	48.41 N	116.19 W
Bonner Springs, Ks. (bŏn'ēr sprĭngz)	117f	39.04 N	94.52 W
Bonne Terre, Mo. (bŏn târ')	121	37.55 N	90.32 W
Bonnet Pk., Can. (bŏn'ĭt)	97	51.26 N	115.53 W
Bonneville Dam, Or.-Wa. (bŏn'ē-vĭl)	114	45.37 N	121.57 W
Bonnie B., Can. (bŏn'ē)	103	49.38 N	58.15 W
Bonny, Nig. (bŏn'ē)	220	4.29 N	7.13 E
Bonny Lake, Wa. (bŏn'ē lăk)	116a	47.11 N	122.11 W
Bonnyville, Can. (bŏn'e-vĭl)	97	54.16 N	110.44 W
Bonorva, It. (bô-nŏr'vä)	170	40.26 N	8.46 E
Bonthain, Indon. (bôn-tīn')	202	5.30 S	119.52 E
Bonthe, S.L.	224	7.32 N	12.30 W
Bontoc, Phil. (bôn-tŏk')	203a	17.10 N	121.01 E
Booby Rocks (I.), Ba. (boo'bĭ rŏks)	132	23.55 N	77.00 W
Booker T. Washington Natl. Mon., Va. (bŏŏk'ēr tē wŏsh'ĭng-tŭn)	125	37.07 N	79.45 W
Boom, Bel.	155a	51.05 N	4.22 E
Boone, Ia. (boon)	113	42.04 N	93.51 W
Booneville, Ar. (boon'vĭl)	121	35.09 N	93.54 W
Booneville, Ky.	108	37.25 N	83.40 W
Booneville, Ms.	124	34.37 N	88.35 W
Boons, S. Afr.	219d	25.59 S	27.15 E
Boonton, NJ (boon'tŭn)	110a	40.54 N	74.24 W
Boonville, In.	108	38.00 N	87.15 W
Boonville, Mo.	121	38.57 N	92.44 W
Boothbay Harbor, Me. (booth'bā här'bĕr)	102	43.51 N	69.39 W
Boothia, G. of, Can. (boo'thĭ-á)	95	69.04 N	86.04 W
Boothia Pen., Can.	92	73.30 N	95.00 W
Bootle, Eng. (boot'l)	154	53.29 N	3.02 W
Booué, Gabon	226	0.06 S	11.56 E
Bor, Sud. (bôr)	221	6.13 N	31.35 E
Bor, Tur. (bōr)	177	37.50 N	34.40 E
Boraha, Nosy (I.), Mad.	223	16.58 S	50.15 E
Borah Pk., Id. (bō'rá)	115	44.12 N	113.47 W
Borama, Som. (bôr-á-mă)	219a	10.05 N	43.08 E
Borås, Swe. (boo'rōs)	162	57.43 N	12.55 E
Borāzjān, Iran (bō-räz-jän')	192	29.13 N	51.13 E
Borba, Braz. (bôr'bä)	141	4.23 S	59.31 W
Borborema, Planalto da (Plat.), Braz. (plä-năl'tô-dä-bôr-bô-rĕ'mä)	141	7.35 S	36.40 W
Bordeaux, Fr. (bôr-dō')	166	44.50 N	0.37 W
Bordentown, NJ (bôr'dĕn-toun)	109	40.05 N	74.40 W
Bordj-bou-Arréridj, Alg. (bôrj-boo-ä-rä-rĕj')	157	36.03 N	4.48 E
Borgå, Fin. (bôr'gō)	163	60.26 N	25.41 E
Borgarnes, Ice.	156	64.31 N	21.40 W
Borger, Tx. (bôr'gĕr)	120	35.40 N	101.23 W
Borgholm, Swe. (bôrg-hōlm')	162	56.52 N	16.40 E
Borgne (L.), La. (bôrn'y')	123	30.03 N	89.36 W
Borgomanero, It. (bôr'gō-mä-nâ'rō)	170	45.40 N	8.28 E
Borgo Val di Taro, It. (bô'r-zhō-väl-dē-tá'rō)	170	44.29 N	9.44 E
Boring, Or. (bōring)	116c	45.26 N	122.22 W
Borislav, Sov. Un. (bô'rĭs-lôf)	165	49.17 N	23.24 E
Borisoglebsk, Sov. Un. (bŏ-rē sô-glyĕpsk')	177	51.20 N	42.00 E
Borisov, Sov. Un. (bŏ-rē'sôf)	172	54.16 N	28.33 E
Borisovka, Sov. Un. (bŏ-rē-sôf'ká)	173	50.38 N	36.00 E
Borispol', Sov. Un. (bo-rĭs'pol)	173	50.17 N	30.54 E
Borivli, India	191b	19.15 N	72.48 E
Borja, Sp. (bôr'hä)	168	41.50 N	1.33 W
Borjas Blancas, Sp. (bô'r-ĸäs-blä'n-käs)	169	41.29 N	0.53 E
Borken, F.R.G. (bōr'kĕn)	167c	51.50 N	6.51 E
Borkou (Reg.), Chad. (bôr-koo')	221	18.11 N	18.28 E
Borkum I., F.R.G. (bōr'koom)	164	53.31 N	6.50 E
Borlänge, Swe. (bôr-lĕŋ'gĕ)	162	60.30 N	15.24 E
Borneo (I.), Asia (bôr'nē-ō)	202	0.25 N	112.39 E
Bornholm (I.), Den. (bôrn-hôlm)	162	55.16 N	15.15 E
Borodayevka, Sov. Un.	173	48.44 N	34.09 E
Boromlya, Sov. Un. (bŏ-rôm''l-yä)	173	50.36 N	34.58 E
Boromo, Upper Volta	224	11.45 N	2.56 W
Borovan, Bul. (bŏ-rô-vän')	171	43.24 N	23.47 E
Borovichi, Sov. Un. (bŏ-rô-vē'chē)	172	58.22 N	33.56 E
Borovsk, Sov. Un. (bô'rŏvsk)	172	55.13 N	36.26 E
Borracha, Isla la (I.), Ven. (ē's-lä-lá-bôr-rá'chä)	141b	10.18 N	64.44 W
Borroloola, Austl. (bŏr-rô-loo'lá)	210	16.15 S	136.19 E
Borshchëv, Sov. Un. (bôrsh-chyôf')	165	48.47 N	26.04 E
Bort-les-Orgues, Fr. (bôr-lā-zôrg)	166	45.26 N	2.26 E
Borūjerd, Iran	192	33.45 N	48.53 E
Borzna, Sov. Un. (bôrz'ná)	173	51.15 N	32.26 E
Borzya, Sov. Un. (bôrz'yá)	179	50.37 N	116.53 E
Bosa, It. (bō'sä)	170	40.18 N	8.34 E
Bosanska Dubica, Yugo. (bō'sän-skä doo'bĭt-sä)	170	45.10 N	16.49 E
Bosanska Gradiška, Yugo. (bō'sän-skä grä-dĭsh'kä)	170	45.08 N	17.15 E
Bosanski Novi, Yugo. (bō's sän-skĭ nō'vē)	170	45.00 N	16.22 E

272 Bosanski Petrovac – Brighton

PLACE (Pronunciation)	PAGE	Lat. °′	Long. °′
Bosanski Petrovac, Yugo. (bō'sän-skĭ pĕt'rō-väts)	170	44.33 N	16.23 E
Bosanski Šamac, Yugo. (bō'sän-skĭ shä'mäts)	171	45.03 N	18.30 E
Boscobel, Wi. (bŏs'kō-bĕl)	113	43.08 N	90.44 W
Bose, China (bwo-sŭ)	199	24.00 N	106.38 E
Boshän, China (bwo-shan)	196	36.32 N	117.51 E
Boskol, Sov. Un. (bås-kôl')	180a	53.45 N	61.17 E
Boskoop, Neth.	155a	52.04 N	4.39 E
Boskovice, Czech. (bŏs'kō-vē-tsĕ)	164	49.26 N	16.37 E
Bosna (R.), Yugo.	171	44.19 N	17.54 E
Bosnia (Reg.), Yugo. (bŏs'nĭ-ȧ)	171	44.17 N	16.58 E
Bosobolo, Zaire	226	4.11 N	19.54 E
Bosporous (Str.), see İstanbul Boğazi			
Bossangoa , Cen. Afr. Rep.	225	6.29 N	17.27 E
Bossembélé, Cen. Afr. Rep.	225	5.16 N	17.39 E
Bossier City, La. (bŏsh'ēr)	123	32.31 N	93.42 W
Bosten Hu (L.), China (bwo-stŭn ho͞o)	194	42.06 N	88.01 E
Boston, Ga. (bôs'tŭn)	124	30.47 N	83.47 W
Boston, Ma.	103a	42.15 N	71.07 W
Boston Heights, Oh.	111d	41.15 N	81.30 W
Boston Mts., Ar.	121	35.46 N	93.32 W
Botany B., Austl. (bŏt'ȧ-nĭ)	207b	33.58 S	151.11 E
Botevgrad, Bul.	171	42.54 N	23.41 E
Bothaville, S. Afr. (bō'tä-vĭl)	219d	27.24 S	26.38 E
Bothell, Wa. (bŏth'ĕl)	116a	47.46 N	122.12 W
Bothnia, G. of, Eur. (bŏth'nĭ-ȧ)	156	63.40 N	21.30 E
Botosani, Rom. (bō-tō-shän'ĭ)	165	47.46 N	26.40 E
Botswana, Afr. (bŏtswănă)	218	22.10 S	23.13 E
Bottineau, ND (bŏt-ĭ-nō')	112	48.48 N	100.28 W
Bottrop, F.R.G. (bōt'trōp)	167c	51.31 N	6.56 E
Botucatú, Braz. (bō-to͞o-kä-to͞o')	141	22.50 S	48.23 W
Botwood, Can. (bŏt'wo͝od)	103	49.08 N	55.21 W
Bouafle, Ivory Coast (bo͞o-ȧ-flā')	224	6.59 N	5.45 W
Bouaké, Ivory Coast (bo͞o-ȧ-kā')	224	7.41 N	5.00 W
Bouar , Cen. Afr. Rep. (bo͞o-är)	225	5.57 N	15.36 E
Bou Areg, Sebkha (Marsh), Mor.	168	35.09 N	3.02 W
Boubandjidah, Parc Natl. de (Natl. Pk.), Cam.	225	8.20 N	14.40 E
Boucherville, Can. (bo͞o-shȧ-vēl')	93a	45.37 N	73.27 W
Boucle du Baoulé, Parc Natl. de la (Natl. Pk.), Mali	224	13.50 N	9.15 W
Boudenib, Mor. (bo͞o-dĕ-nĕb')	220	32.14 N	3.04 W
Boudette, Mn. (bo͞o-dĕt)	113	48.42 N	94.34 W
Boudouaou, Alg.	169	36.44 N	3.25 E
Boufarik, Alg. (bo͞o-fȧ-rēk')	169	36.35 N	2.55 E
Bougainville Trench, Oceania (bo͞o-gäN-vēl')	204	7.00 S	152.00 E
Bougie, see Bejaïa			
Bougouni, Mali (bo͞o-go͞o-nē')	220	11.27 N	7.30 W
Bouïra, Alg. (boo-ē'rȧ)	158	36.25 N	3.55 E
Bouïra-Sahary, Alg. (bwē-rȧ sȧ'ȧ-rē)	169	35.16 N	3.23 E
Bouka (R.), Gui.	224	11.05 N	10.40 W
Boulder, Austl. (bōl'dēr)	210	31.00 S	121.40 E
Boulder, Co.	120	40.02 N	105.19 W
Boulder (R.), Mt.	115	46.10 N	112.07 W
Boulder City, Nv.	118	35.57 N	114.50 W
Boulder Cr., Id.	114	42.53 N	116.49 W
Boulder Pk., Id.	115	43.53 N	114.33 W
Boulogne-Billancourt, Fr. (bo͞o-lôn'y'-bē-yäN-ko͞or')	167b	48.50 N	2.14 E
Boulogne-sur-Mer, Fr. (bo͞o-lôn'y-sür-mâr')	166	50.44 N	1.37 E
Boumba (R.), Cam.	225	3.20 N	14.40 E
Bouna, Ivory Coast (bo͞o-nä')	224	9.16 N	3.00 W
Bouna, Park Natl. de (Natl. Pk.), Ivory Coast	224	9.20 N	3.35 W
Boundary B., Can. (boun'dȧ-rĭ)	116d	49.03 N	122.59 W
Boundary Pk., Nv.	118	37.52 N	118.20 W
Bound Brook, NJ (bound bro͝ok)	110a	40.34 N	74.32 W
Bountiful, Ut. (boun'tĭ-fo͝ol)	117b	40.55 N	111.53 W
Bountiful Pk., Ut. (boun'tĭ-fo͝ol)	117b	40.58 N	111.49 W
Bounty Is., N.Z.	228	47.42 S	179.05 E
Bourem, Mali (bo͞o-rĕm')	220	16.43 N	0.15 W
Bourg-en-Bresse, Fr. (bo͞or-gĕN-brĕs')	166	46.12 N	5.13 E
Bourges, Fr. (bo͞orzh)	166	47.06 N	2.22 E
Bourget, Can. (bo͞or-zhĕ')	93c	45.26 N	75.09 W
Bourgoin, Fr. (bo͞or-gwăN')	167	45.46 N	5.17 E
Bourke, Austl. (bŭrk)	212	30.10 S	146.00 E
Bourne, Eng. (bōrn)	154	52.46 N	0.22 W
Bournemouth, Eng. (bôrn'mŭth)	160	50.44 N	1.55 W
Bou Saâda, Alg. (bo͞o-sä'dȧ)	158	35.13 N	4.17 E
Bousso, Chad. (bo͞o-sô')	221	10.33 N	16.45 E
Boutilimit, Mauritania (bo͞o-tē-lē-mē')	220	17.30 N	14.54 W
Bouvert (I.), see **Bouvetøen**			
Bouvetøen (Bouvert) (I.), Alt. O.	228	54.26 S	3.24 E
Bow (R.), Can. (bō)	97	50.35 N	112.15 W
Bowbells, ND (bō'bĕls)	112	48.50 N	102.16 W
Bowdle, SD (bōd''l)	112	45.28 N	99.42 W
Bowen, Austl. (bō'ĕn)	211	20.02 S	148.14 E
Bowie, Md. (bo͞o'ĭ) (bō'ē)	110e	38.59 N	76.47 W
Bowie, Tx.	120	33.34 N	97.50 W
Bowling Green, Ky. (bōlĭng grēn)	124	37.00 N	86.26 W
Bowling Green, Mo.	121	39.19 N	91.09 W
Bowling Green, Oh.	108	41.25 N	83.40 W
Bowman, ND (bō'măn)	112	46.11 N	103.23 W
Bowron (R.), Can. (bō'rŭn)	97	53.20 N	121.10 W
Boxelder Cr., Mt. (bŏks'ĕl-dēr)	112	45.35 N	104.28 W
Boxelder Cr., Mt.	115	47.17 N	108.37 W
Bo Xian, China (bwo shyĕn)	196	33.52 N	115.47 E
Boxing, China (bwo-shyĭŋ)	196	37.09 N	118.08 E
Boxtel, Neth.	155a	51.40 N	5.21 E
Boyabo, Zaire	226	3.43 N	18.46 E
Boyang, China (bwo-yäŋ)	199	29.00 N	116.42 E
Boyer (R.), Can. (boi'ēr)	93b	46.26 N	70.56 W
Boyer (R.), Ia.	112	41.45 N	95.36 W
Boyle, Ire. (boil)	160	53.59 N	8.15 W
Boyne City, Mi.	108	45.15 N	85.05 W
Boyne (R.), Ire. (boin)	160	53.40 N	6.40 W
Boyoma Falls, Zaire	226	0.30 N	25.12 E
Bozcaada, Tur. (bōz-cä'dä)	171	39.50 N	26.05 E
Bozca Ada (I.), Tur.	171	39.50 N	26.00 E
Bozeman, Mt. (bōz'măn)	115	45.41 N	111.00 W
Bozene, Zaire	226	2.56 N	19.12 E
Bozhen, China (bwo-jŭn)	196	38.05 N	116.35 E
Bozoum, Cen. Afr. Rep.	225	6.19 N	16.23 E
Bra, It. (brä)	170	44.41 N	7.52 E
Brač (I.), Yugo. (bräch)	170	43.18 N	16.36 E
Bracciano, Lago di (L.), It. (lä'gō-dē-brä-chä'nō)	170	42.05 N	12.00 E
Bracebridge, Can. (brās'brĭj)	109	45.05 N	79.20 W
Braceville, Il. (brās'vĭl)	111a	41.13 N	88.16 W
Bräcke, Swe. (brĕk'kĕ)	162	62.44 N	15.28 E
Brackenridge, Pa. (brăk'ĕn-rĭj)	111e	40.37 N	79.44 W
Brackettville, Tx. (brăk'ĕt-vĭl)	122	29.19 N	100.24 W
Braço Maior (R.), Braz.	141	11.00 S	51.00 W
Braço Menor (R.), Braz. (brä'zō-mĕ-nō'r)	141	11.38 S	50.00 W
Bradano (R.), It. (brä-dä'nō)	170	40.43 N	16.22 E
Braddock, Pa. (brăd'ŭk)	111e	40.24 N	79.52 W
Bradenton, Fl. (brā'dĕn-tŭn)	125a	27.28 N	82.35 W
Bradfield, Eng. (brăd'fēld)	154b	51.25 N	1.08 W
Bradford, Eng. (brăd'fērd)	154	53.47 N	1.44 W
Bradford, Oh.	108	40.10 N	84.30 W
Bradford, Pa.	109	42.00 N	78.40 W
Bradley, Il. (brăd'lĭ)	111a	41.09 N	87.52 W
Bradner, Can. (brăd'nēr)	116d	49.05 N	122.26 W
Brady, Tx. (brā'dĭ)	122	31.09 N	99.21 W
Braga, Port. (brä'gä)	168	41.20 N	8.25 W
Bragado, Arg. (brä-gä'dō)	139c	35.07 S	60.28 W
Bragança, Braz. (brä-gän'sä)	141	1.02 S	46.50 W
Bragança, Port.	168	41.48 N	6.46 W
Bragança Paulista, Braz. (brä-gän'sä-pä'o͞o-lē's-tȧ)	139a	22.58 S	46.31 W
Bragg Creek, Can. (brăg)	93e	50.57 N	114.35 W
Brahmaputra (R.), India (brä'mȧ-po͞o'trȧ)	193	26.45 N	92.45 E
Brāhui (Mts.), Pak.	193	28.32 N	66.15 E
Braidwood, Il. (brād'wo͝od)	111a	41.16 N	88.13 W
Brăila, Rom. (brē'ēlȧ)	173	45.15 N	27.58 E
Brainerd, Mn. (brān'ērd)	113	46.20 N	94.09 W
Braintree, Ma. (brān'trē)	103a	42.14 N	71.00 W
Braithwaite, La. (brĭth'wĭt)	110d	29.52 N	89.57 W
Brakpan, S. Afr. (brăk'păn)	223b	26.15 S	28.22 E
Bralorne, Can. (brā'lôrn)	96	50.47 N	122.49 W
Bramalea, Can.	93d	43.48 N	79.41 W
Brampton, Can. (brămp'tŭn)	93d	43.41 N	79.46 W
Branca, Pedra (Mtn.), Braz. (pĕ'drä-brä'N-kä)	142b	22.55 S	43.28 W
Branchville, NJ (branch'vĭl)	110a	41.09 S	74.44 W
Branchville, SC	125	33.17 N	80.48 W
Branco (R.), Braz. (bräŋ'kō)	141	2.21 N	60.38 W
Brandberg (Mtn.), Namibia	222	21.15 S	14.15 E
Brandenburg, G.D.R. (brän'dĕn-bo͝orgh)	155b	52.25 N	12.33 E
Brandenburg (Reg.), G.D.R.	164	52.12 N	13.31 E
Brandfort, S. Afr. (brăn'd-fôrt)	219d	28.42 S	26.29 E
Brandon, Can. (brăn'dŭn)	99	49.50 N	99.57 W
Brandon, Vt.	109	43.45 N	73.05 W
Brandon Mtn., Ire. (brăn-dŏn)	160	52.15 N	10.12 W
Brandywine, Md. (brăndĭ'wīn)	110e	38.42 N	76.51 W
Branford, Ct. (brăn'fērd)	109	41.15 N	72.50 W
Braniewo, Pol. (brä-nyĕ'vô)	165	54.23 N	19.50 E
Brańsk, Pol. (brän' sk)	165	52.44 N	22.51 E
Brantford, Can. (brănt'fērd)	93d	43.09 N	80.17 W
Bras d'Or L., Can. (brä-dôr')	103	45.52 N	60.50 W
Brasília, Braz. (brä-sē'lvä)	141	15.49 S	47.39 W
Brasilia Legal (Fordlândia), **Braz.** (brä-sē'lyä-lē-gäl) (fô'rd-län-dyä)	141	3.45 S	55.46 W
Brasópolis, Braz. (brä-sô'pô-lēs)	139a	22.30 S	45.36 W
Braşov (Oraşul-Stalin), **Rom.**	171	45.39 N	25.35 E
Brass, Nig. (brăs)	220	4.28 N	6.28 E
Bras St. Michel (R.), Can.	93b	46.47 N	70.51 W
Brasschaat, Bel. (bräs'ĸät)	155a	51.19 N	4.30 E
Bratenahl, Oh. (bră'tĕn-ôl)	111d	41.34 N	81.36 W
Bratislava, Czech. (brä'tĭs-lä-vä)	155e	48.09 N	17.07 E
Bratsk, Sov. Un. (brätsk)	178	56.10 N	102.04 E
Bratskoye Vdkhr. (Res.), Sov. Un.	178	56.10 N	102.05 E
Bratslav, Sov. Un. (brät'slȧf)	173	48.48 N	28.59 E
Brattleboro, Vt. (brăt''l-bŭr-ô)	109	42.50 N	72.35 W
Braunau, Aus. (brou'nou)	164	48.15 N	13.05 E
Braunschweig, F.R.G. (broun'shvīgh)	164	52.16 N	10.32 E
Brava, Som. (brä'vä)	219a	1.20 N	44.00 E
Bråviken (R.), Swe.	162	58.40 N	16.40 E
Bravo del Norte, Rio (R.), **see Grande, Rio**			
Brawley, Ca. (brô'lĭ)	118	32.59 N	115.32 W
Bray, Ire. (brā)	160	53.10 N	6.05 W
Braymer, Mo. (brā'mēr)	121	39.34 N	93.47 W
Brays Bay, Tx. (brās'bĭ'yo͞o)	123a	29.41 N	95.33 W
Brazeau, Mt., Can. (bră-zō')	97	52.33 N	117.21 W
Brazeau (R.), Can.	97	52.55 N	116.10 W
Brazil, In. (brȧ-zĭl')	108	39.30 N	87.00 W
Brazil, S.A.	138	9.00 S	53.00 W
Brazilian Highlands (Mts.), Braz. (brȧ zĭl yăn hī-lăndz)	138	14.00 S	48.00 W
Brazos (R.), U.S. (brä'zōs)	106	33.10 N	98.50 W
Brazos (R.), Clear Fk., Tx.	122	32.56 N	99.14 W
Brazos (R.), Double Mountain Fk., Tx.	120	33.23 N	101.21 W
Brazos (R.), Salt Fk., Tx. (sôlt fôrk)	120	33.20 N	110.57 W
Brazzaville, Con. (brȧ-zȧ-vēl')	226	4.16 S	15.17 E
Brčko, Yugo. (bĕrch'kō)	171	44.54 N	18.46 E
Brda R., Pol. (bĕr-dä)	165	53.18 N	17.55 E
Brea, Ca. (brē'ȧ)	117a	33.55 N	117.54 W
Breakeyville, Can.	93b	46.40 N	71.13 W
Breckenridge, Mn. (brĕk'ĕn-rĭj)	112	46.17 N	96.35 W
Breckenridge, Tx.	122	32.46 N	98.53 W
Brecksville, Oh. (brĕks'vĭl)	111d	41.19 N	81.38 W
Břeclav, Czech. (brzhĕl'läf)	164	48.46 N	16.54 E
Breda, Neth. (brā-dä')	155a	51.35 N	4.47 E
Bredasdorp, S. Afr. (brā'das-dôrp)	222	34.15 S	20.00 E
Bredy, Sov. Un. (brĕ'dĭ)	180a	52.25 N	60.23 E
Bregenz, Aus. (brā'gĕnts)	164	47.30 N	9.46 E
Bregovo, Bul. (brĕ'gō-vô)	171	44.07 N	22.45 E
Breidbach, S. Afr. (brēd'băk)	223c	32.54 S	27.26 E
Breiðafjördur (Fd.), Ice.	156	65.15 N	22.50 W
Breil-sur-Roya, Fr. (brĕ'y')	167	43.57 N	7.36 E
Brejo, Braz. (brā'zho͞o)	141	3.33 S	42.46 W
Bremangerlandet (I.), Nor.	162	61.51 N	4.25 E
Bremen, F.R.G. (brā-mĕn)	164	53.05 N	8.50 E
Bremen, In. (brē'mĕn)	108	41.25 N	86.05 W
Bremerhaven, F.R.G. (brām-ēr-hä'fĕn)	164	53.33 N	8.38 E
Bremerton, Wa. (brĕm'ēr-tŭn)	116a	47.34 N	122.38 W
Bremervörde, F.R.G. (brĕ'mēr-fûr-dĕ)	155c	53.29 N	9.09 E
Bremner, Can. (brĕm'nēr)	93g	53.34 N	113.14 W
Bremond, Tx. (brĕm'ŭnd)	123	31.11 N	96.40 W
Brenham, Tx. (brĕn'ăm)	123	30.10 N	96.24 W
Brenner P., Aus.-It. (brĕn'ēr)	164	47.00 N	11.30 E
Brentwood, Eng. (brĕnt'wo͝od)	154b	51.37 N	0.18 E
Brentwood, Md.	109	39.00 N	76.55 W
Brentwood, Mo.	117e	38.37 N	90.21 W
Brentwood, Pa.	111e	40.22 N	79.59 W
Brescia, It. (brā'shä)	170	45.33 N	10.15 E
Bressanone, It. (brĕs-sä-nō'nā)	170	46.42 N	11.40 E
Bressuire, Fr. (grĕ-swēr')	166	46.49 N	0.14 W
Brest, Fr. (brĕst)	166	48.24 N	4.30 W
Brest, Sov. Un.	165	52.06 N	23.43 E
Brest (Oblast), Sov. Un.	172	52.30 N	26.50 E
Bretagne (Reg.), Fr. (brĕ-tän'yĕ)	166	48.00 N	3.00 W
Breton, Pertvis (Str.), Fr. (pâr-twĕ'brĕ-tôN')	166	46.18 N	1.43 W
Breton Sd., La. (brĕt'ŭn)	124	29.38 N	89.15 W
Breukelen, Neth.	155a	52.09 N	5.00 E
Brevard, NC (brē-värd')	124	35.14 N	82.45 W
Breves, Braz. (brā'vĕzh)	141	1.32 S	50.13 W
Brevik, Nor. (brĕ'vĕk)	162	59.04 N	9.39 E
Brewarrina, Austl. (bro͞o-ēr-rē'nȧ)	212	29.54 S	146.50 E
Brewer, Me. (bro͞o'ēr)	102	44.46 N	68.46 W
Brewerville, Lib.	224	6.26 N	10.47 W
Brewster, NY (bro͞o'stēr)	110a	41.23 N	73.38 W
Brewster, Cerro (Mtn.), Pan. (sĕ'r-rô-bro͞o'stēr)	131	9.19 N	79.15 W
Brewton, Al. (bro͞o'tŭn)	124	31.06 N	87.04 W
Brežice, Yugo. (brĕ'zhē-tsĕ)	170	45.55 N	15.37 E
Breznik, Bul. (brĕs'nĕk)	171	42.44 N	22.55 E
Briancon, Fr. (brē-äN-sôN')	167	44.54 N	6.39 E
Briare, Fr. (brē-är')	166	47.40 N	2.46 E
Bridal Veil, Or. (brīd'ăl vāl)	116c	45.33 N	122.10 W
Bridge Pt., Ba. (brĭj)	132	25.35 N	76.40 W
Bridgeport, Al. (brĭj'pôrt)	124	34.55 N	85.42 W
Bridgeport, Ct.	110a	41.12 N	73.12 W
Bridgeport, IL.	108	38.40 N	87.45 W
Bridgeport, Ne.	112	41.40 N	103.06 W
Bridgeport, Oh.	108	40.00 N	80.45 W
Bridgeport, Pa.	110f	40.06 N	75.21 W
Bridgeport, Tx.	120	33.13 N	97.46 W
Bridgeton, Al. (brĭj'tŭn)	110h	33.27 N	86.39 W
Bridgeton, Mo.	117e	38.45 N	90.23 W
Bridgeton, NJ	109	39.30 N	75.15 W
Bridgetown, Can.	102	44.51 N	65.18 W
Bridgetown, Barb. (brĭj' toun)	131b	13.08 N	59.37 W
Bridgeville, Pa. (brĭj'vĭl)	111e	40.22 N	80.07 W
Bridgewater, Austl. (brĭj'wô-tēr)	212	42.50 S	147.28 E
Bridgewater, Can.	102	44.23 N	64.31 W
Bridgnorth, Eng. (brĭj'nôrth)	154	52.32 N	2.25 W
Bridgton, Me. (brĭj'tŭn)	102	44.04 N	70.45 W
Bridlington, Eng. (brĭd'lĭng-tŭn)	160	54.06 N	0.10 W
Brie-Comte-Robert, Fr. (brē-ĸôNt-ē-rō-bâr')	167b	48.42 N	2.37 E
Brielle, Neth.	155a	51.54 N	4.08 E
Brierfield, Al. (brī'ēr-fēld)	124	33.01 N	86.55 W
Brierfield, Eng. (brī'ēr fēld)	154	53.49 N	2.14 W
Brier I., Can. (brī'ēr)	102	44.16 N	66.24 W
Brieselang, G.D.R. (brē'zĕ-läng)	155b	52.36 N	12.59 E
Briey, Fr. (brē-ĕ')	167	49.15 N	5.57 E
Brig, Switz. (brēg)	164	46.17 N	7.59 E
Brigg, Eng. (brĭg)	154	53.33 N	0.29 W
Brigham City, Ut. (brĭg'ăm)	117b	41.31 N	112.01 W
Brighouse, Eng. (brĭg'hous)	154	53.42 N	1.47 W
Bright, Austl. (brīt)	212	36.43 S	147.00 E
Bright, In. (brīt)	111f	39.13 N	84.51 W
Brightlingsea, Eng. (brī't-lĭng-sē)	154b	51.50 N	1.00 E
Brighton, Al. (brīt'ŭn)	110h	33.27 N	86.56 W

PRONOUNCING INDEX

Brighton – Burketown 273

PLACE (Pronunciation)	PAGE	Lat. °′	Long. °′
Brighton, Co.	120	39.58 N	104.49 W
Brighton, Eng.	160	50.47 N	0.07 W
Brighton, Il.	117e	39.03 N	90.08 W
Brighton, Ia.	113	41.11 N	91.47 W
Brihuega, Sp. (brē-wā'gä)	168	40.32 N	2.52 W
Brimley, Mi. (brĭm'lē)	117k	46.24 N	84.34 W
Brindisi, It. (brēn'dē-zē)	171	40.38 N	17.57 E
Brinje, Yugo. (brēn'yĕ)	170	45.00 N	15.08 E
Brinkley, Ar. (brĭŋk'lĭ)	121	34.52 N	91.12 W
Brinnon, Wa. (brĭn'ŭn)	116a	47.41 N	122.54 W
Brion (I.), Can. (brē-ôN')	103	47.47 N	61.29 W
Brioude, Fr. (brē-o͞od')	166	45.18 N	3.22 E
Brisbane, Austl. (brĭz'bān)	212	27.30 S	153.10 E
Bristol, Ct. (brĭs'tŭl)	109	41.40 N	72.55 W
Bristol, Eng.	160	51.29 N	2.39 W
Bristol, Pa.	110f	40.06 N	74.51 W
Bristol, RI	110b	41.41 N	71.14 W
Bristol, Tn.	125	36.35 N	82.10 W
Bristol, Vt.	109	44.10 N	73.00 W
Bristol, Va.	125	36.36 N	82.00 W
Bristol, Wi.	111a	42.32 N	88.04 W
Bristol B., Ak.	105	58.05 N	158.54 W
Bristol Chan., Eng.	160	51.20 N	3.47 W
Bristow, Ok. (brĭs'tō)	121	35.50 N	96.25 W
British Columbia (Prov.), Can. (brĭt'ĭsh kŏl'ŭm-bĭ-ȧ)	94	56.00 N	124.53 W
Brits, S. Afr.	219d	25.39 S	27.47 E
Britstown, S. Afr. (brĭts'toun)	222	30.30 S	23.40 E
Britt, Ia. (brĭt)	113	43.05 N	93.47 W
Britton, SD (brĭt'ŭn)	112	45.47 N	97.44 W
Brive-la-Gaillarde, Fr. (brēv-lä-gī-yärd'ē)	166	45.10 N	1.31 E
Briviesca, Sp. (brē-vyās'kä)	168	42.34 N	3.21 W
Brno, Czech. (b'r'nô)	164	49.18 N	16.37 E
Broa, Ensenada de la (B.), Cuba (ĕn-sĕ-nä'dä-dĕ-lä-brō'ä)	132	22.30 N	82.00 W
Broach, India	190	21.47 N	72.58 E
Broad (R.), Ga. (brôd)	124	34.15 N	83.14 W
Broad (R.), NC	125	35.38 N	82.40 W
Broadmeadows, Austl. (brôd'mĕd-ōz)	207a	37.40 S	144.53 E
Broadview Heights, Oh. (brôd'vū)	111d	41.18 N	81.41 W
Brockport, NY (brŏk'pōrt)	109	43.15 N	77.55 W
Brockton, Ma. (brŏk'tŭn)	103a	42.04 N	71.01 W
Brockville, Can. (brŏk'vĭl)	101	44.35 N	75.40 W
Brockway, Mt. (brŏk'wā)	115	47.24 N	105.41 W
Brodnica, Pol. (brôd'nĭt-sȧ)	165	53.16 N	19.26 E
Brody, Sov. Un. (brô'dĭ)	165	50.05 N	25.10 E
Broken Arrow, Ok. (brō'kĕn ăr'ō)	121	36.03 N	95.48 W
Broken B., Austl.	207b	33.34 S	151.20 E
Broken Bow, Ne. (brō'kĕn bō)	112	41.24 N	99.37 W
Broken Bow, Ok.	121	34.02 N	94.43 W
Broken Hill, Austl. (brōk'ĕn)	212	31.55 S	141.35 E
Broken Hill, see Kabwe			
Bromley, Eng. (brŭm'lĭ)	154b	51.23 N	0.01 E
Bromptonville, Can. (brŭmp'tŭn-vĭl)	109	45.30 N	72.00 W
Brønderslev, Den. (brûn'dĕr-slĕv)	162	57.15 N	9.56 E
Bronkhorstspruit, S. Afr.	219d	25.50 S	28.48 E
Bronnitsy, Sov. Un. (brô-nyĭ'tsĭ)	180b	55.26 N	38.16 E
Bronson, Mi. (brŏn'sŭn)	108	41.55 N	85.15 W
Bronte Cr., Can.	93d	43.25 N	79.53 W
Brood (R.), SC (bro͞od)	125	34.46 N	81.25 W
Brookfield, Il. (bro͝ok'fēld)	111a	41.49 N	87.51 W
Brookfield, Mo.	121	39.45 N	93.04 W
Brookhaven, Ga. (bro͝ok'hāv'n)	110c	33.52 N	84.21 W
Brookhaven, Ms.	124	31.35 N	90.26 W
Brookings, Or. (bro͝ok'ĭngs)	114	42.04 N	124.16 W
Brookings, SD	112	44.18 N	96.47 W
Brookline, Ma. (bro͝ok'līn)	103a	42.20 N	71.08 W
Brookline, NH	103a	42.44 N	71.37 W
Brooklyn, Oh. (bro͝ok'lĭn)	111d	41.26 N	81.44 W
Brooklyn Center, Mn.	117g	45.05 N	93.21 W
Brook Park, Oh. (bro͝ok)	111d	41.24 N	81.50 W
Brooks, Can.	97	50.35 N	111.53 W
Brooks Ra., Ak. (bro͝oks)	105	68.20 N	159.00 W
Brooksville, Fl. (bro͝oks'vĭl)	125a	28.32 N	82.28 W
Brookville, In. (bro͝ok'vĭl)	108	39.20 N	85.00 W
Brookville, Pa.	109	41.10 N	79.00 W
Brookwood, Al. (bro͝ok'wo͝od)	124	33.15 N	87.17 W
Broome, Austl. (bro͞om)	210	18.00 S	122.15 E
Brossard, Can.	93a	45.26 N	73.28 W
Brothers (Is.), Ba. (brŭd'hĕrs)	132	26.05 N	79.00 W
Broumov, Czech. (bro͞o'môf)	164	50.33 N	15.55 E
Brown Bk., Ba.	133	21.30 N	74.35 W
Brownfield, Tx. (broun'fēld)	120	33.11 N	102.16 W
Browning, Mt. (broun'ĭng)	115	48.37 N	113.05 W
Brownsboro, Ky. (brounz'bô-rô)	111h	38.22 N	85.30 W
Brownsburg, Can. (brouns'bûrg)	93a	45.40 N	74.24 W
Brownsburg, In.	111g	39.51 N	86.23 W
Brownsmead, Or. (brounz'-mēd)	116c	46.13 N	123.33 W
Brownstown, In. (brounz'toun)	108	38.50 N	86.00 W
Brownsville, Pa. (brounz'vĭl)	111e	40.01 N	79.53 W
Brownsville, Tn.	124	35.35 N	89.15 W
Brownsville, Tx.	123	25.55 N	97.30 W
Brownville Junction, Me. (broun'vĭl)	102	45.20 N	69.04 W
Brownwood, Tx. (broun'wo͝od)	122	31.44 N	98.58 W
Brownwood (L.), Tx.	122	31.55 N	99.15 W
Brozas, Sp. (brō'thäs)	168	39.37 N	6.44 W
Bruce, Mt., Austl. (bro͞os)	210	22.35 S	118.15 E
Bruce Pen, Can.	108	44.50 N	81.20 W
Bruceton, Tn. (bro͞os'tŭn)	124	36.02 N	88.14 W
Bruchsal, F.R.G. (bro͝ok'zäl)	164	49.08 N	8.34 E
Bruck, Aus. (bro͝ok)	164	47.25 N	15.14 E
Brück, G.D.R. (brük)	155b	52.12 N	12.45 E
Bruck an der Leitha, Aus.	155e	48.01 N	16.47 E
Bruderheim, Can. (bro͞o'dĕr-hīm)	93g	53.47 N	112.56 W
Brugge, Bel.	161	51.13 N	3.05 E
Brühl, F.R.G. (brül)	167c	50.49 N	6.54 E
Bruneau (R.), Id. (bro͞o-nō')	114	42.47 N	115.43 W
Brunei, Asia (bro͞o-nī')	202	4.52 N	113.38 E
Brünen, F.R.G. (brü'nĕn)	167c	51.43 N	6.41 E
Brunete, Sp. (bro͞o-nā'tā)	169a	40.24 N	4.00 W
Brunette (I.), Can. (bro͞o-nĕt')	103	47.16 N	55.54 W
Brunn am Gebirge, Aus. (bro͞on'äm gĕ-bĭr'gĕ)	155e	48.07 N	16.18 E
Brunsbüttel, F.R.G. (bro͞ons'büt-tĕl)	155c	53.58 N	9.10 E
Brunswick, Ga. (brŭnz'wĭk)	125	31.08 N	81.30 W
Brunswick, Me.	102	43.54 N	69.57 W
Brunswick, Md.	109	39.20 N	77.35 W
Brunswick, Mo.	121	39.25 N	93.07 W
Brunswick, Oh.	111d	41.14 N	81.50 W
Brunswick, Pen. de, Chile	142	53.25 S	71.15 W
Bruny (I.), Austl. (bro͞o'nē)	211	43.30 S	147.50 E
Brush, Co. (brŭsh)	120	40.14 N	103.40 W
Brusque, Braz. (bro͞o's-ko͞oĕ)	142	27.15 S	48.45 W
Brussels, Il. (brŭs'ĕls)	117e	38.57 N	90.36 W
Brussels, see Bruxelles			
Bruxelles (Brussels), Bel. (brü-sĕl') (brŭs'ĕls)	155a	50.51 N	4.21 E
Bryan, Oh. (brī'ăn)	108	41.25 N	84.30 W
Bryan, Tx.	123	30.40 N	96.22 W
Bryansk, Sov. Un. (b'r-yänsk')	172	53.12 N	34.23 E
Bryansk (Oblast), Sov. Un.	172	52.43 N	32.25 E
Bryant, SD (brī'ănt)	112	44.35 N	97.29 W
Bryant, Wa.	116a	48.14 N	122.10 W
Bryce Canyon Natl. Park, Ut. (brīs)	119	37.35 N	112.15 W
Bryn Mawr, Pa. (brĭn mär')	110f	40.02 N	75.20 W
Bryson City, NC (brīs'ŭn)	124	35.25 N	83.25 W
Bryukhovetskaya, Sov. Un. (b'ryŭk'ô-vyĕt-skä'yä)	173	45.56 N	38.58 E
Buatan, Indon.	189b	0.45 N	101.49 E
Buba, Guinea-Bissau (bo͞o'bȧ)	220	11.39 N	14.58 W
Bucaramanga, Col. (bo͞o-kä'rä-mäŋ'gä)	140	7.12 N	73.14 W
Buccaneer Arch, Austl. (bŭk-ȧ-nēr')	210	16.05 S	122.00 E
Buchach, Sov. Un. (bo͞o'chäch)	165	49.04 N	25.25 E
Buchanan, Lib. (bū-kăn'ăn)	224	5.57 N	10.02 W
Buchanan, Mi.	108	41.50 N	86.25 W
Buchanan (L.), Austl. (bû-kân'nŏn)	211	21.40 S	145.00 E
Buchanan (L.), Tx. (bû-kăn'ăn)	122	30.55 N	98.40 W
Buchans, Can.	103	48.49 N	56.52 W
Bucharest, see București			
Buchholtz, F.R.G. (bo͝ok'hōltz)	155c	53.19 N	9.53 E
Buck Cr., In. (bŭk)	111g	39.43 N	85.58 W
Buckhannon, WV (bŭk-hăn'ŭn)	109	39.00 N	80.10 W
Buckhaven, Scot. (bŭk-hā'v'n)	160	56.10 N	3.10 W
Buckie, Scot. (bŭk'ĭ)	160	57.40 N	2.50 W
Buckingham, Can. (bŭk'ĭng-ăm)	93c	45.35 N	75.25 W
Buckingham (R.), India (bŭk'ĭng-ăm)	190	15.18 N	79.50 E
Buckinghamshire (Co.), Eng.	154b	51.45 N	0.48 W
Buckland, Can. (bŭk'lănd)	93b	46.37 N	70.33 W
Buckland Tableland (Reg.), Austl.	211	24.31 S	148.00 E
Buckley, Wa. (buk'lē)	116a	47.10 N	122.02 W
Bucksport, Me. (bŭks'pôrt)	102	44.35 N	68.47 W
Buctouche, Can. (bük-to͞osh')	102	46.28 N	64.43 W
Bucun, China (bo͞o-tso͞on)	196	36.38 N	117.26 E
București (Bucharest), Rom. (bo͞o-ko͞o-rĕsh'tĭ) (bo͞o-kȧ-rĕst')	171	44.23 N	26.10 E
Bucyrus, Oh. (bū-sī'rŭs)	108	40.50 N	82.55 W
Budapest, Hung. (bo͞o'dȧ-pĕsht')	165	47.30 N	19.05 E
Budge Budge, India	190a	22.28 N	88.08 E
Budjala, Zaire	226	2.39 N	19.42 E
Buea, Cam.	225	4.09 N	9.14 E
Buechel, Ky. (bē-chûl')	111h	38.12 N	85.38 W
Bueil, Fr. (bwā')	167b	48.55 N	1.27 E
Buena Park, Ca. (bwā'nȧ pärk)	117a	33.52 N	118.00 W
Buenaventura, Col. (bwā'nä-vĕn-to͞o'rä)	140	3.46 N	77.09 W
Buenaventura, Cuba	133a	22.49 N	82.22 W
Buenaventura, Bahía de (B.), Col. (bä-ē'ä-dĕ-bwā'nä-vĕn-to͞o'rä)	140	3.45 N	79.23 W
Buena Vista, Co. (bū'nȧ vĭs'tȧ)	120	38.51 N	106.07 W
Buena Vista, Ga.	124	32.15 N	84.30 W
Buena Vista, Va.	109	37.45 N	79.20 W
Buena Vista, Bahía (B.), Cuba (bä-ē'ä-bwĕ-nä-vē's-tä)	132	22.30 N	79.10 W
Buena Vista Lake Res., Ca. (bū'nȧ vĭs'tȧ)	118	35.14 N	119.17 W
Buendia, Embalse de (Res.), Sp.	168	40.30 N	2.45 W
Buenos Aires, Arg. (bwā'nōs ī'rās)	142	34.20 S	58.30 W
Buenos Aires, Col.	140a	3.01 N	76.34 W
Buenos Aires, C. R.	131	9.10 N	83.21 W
Buenos Aires (Prov.), Arg.	142	36.15 S	61.45 W
Buenos Aires (L.), Arg.-Chile	142	46.30 S	72.15 W
Buffalo, Mn. (buf'ȧ lō)	113	45.10 N	93.50 W
Buffalo, NY	111c	42.54 N	78.51 W
Buffalo, Tx.	123	31.28 N	96.04 W
Buffalo, Wy.	115	44.19 N	106.42 W
Buffalo (R.), Ar.	121	35.56 N	92.58 W
Buffalo (R.), S. Afr.	223c	28.35 S	30.27 E
Buffalo (R.), Tn.	124	35.24 N	87.10 W
Buffalo Bayou, Tx.	123a	29.46 N	95.32 W
Buffalo Cr., Mn.	113	44.46 N	94.28 W
Buffalo Head Hills, Can.	94	57.16 N	116.18 W
Buford, Can. (bū'fûrd)	93g	53.15 N	113.55 W
Buford, Ga. (bū'fērd)	124	34.05 N	84.00 W
Bug (R.), Pol. (bo͞og)	165	52.29 N	21.20 E
Bug (R.), Sov. Un. (bo͝ok)	173	48.12 N	30.13 E
Buga, Col. (bo͞o'gä)	140a	3.54 N	76.17 W
Buggenhout, Bel.	155a	51.01 N	4.10 E
Buggs Island L., NC-Va.	125	36.30 N	78.38 W
Buglandsfjorden (Fd.), Nor.	162	58.53 N	7.55 E
Bugojno, Yugo. (bo͞o-gō ĭ nô)	170	44.03 N	17.28 E
Bugul'ma, Sov. Un. (bo͞o-go͞ol'mȧ)	176	54.40 N	52.40 E
Buguruslan, Sov. Un. (bo͞o-go͞o-ro͞os-lan')	176	53.30 N	52.32 E
Buhi, Phil. (bo͞o'ē)	203a	13.26 N	123.31 E
Buhl, Id. (būl)	114	42.36 N	114.45 W
Buhl, Mn.	113	47.28 N	92.49 W
Buin, Chile (bo͞o-ēn')	139b	33.44 S	70.44 W
Buinaksk, Sov. Un. (bo͞o'ē-näksk)	177	42.40 N	47.20 E
Buir Nur (L.), China-Mong. (bo͞o-ēr no͞or)	198	47.50 N	117.00 E
Bujalance, Sp. (bo͞o-hä-län'thā)	168	37.54 N	4.22 W
Bujumbura, Burundi	227	3.23 S	29.22 E
Bukama, Zaire (bo͞o-kä'mä)	222	9.08 S	26.00 E
Bukavu, Zaire	227	2.30 S	28.52 E
Bukhara, Sov. Un. (bo͞o-kä'rä)	153	39.31 N	64.22 E
Bukitbatu, Indon.	189b	1.25 N	101.58 E
Bukittingg, Indon.	202	0.25 S	100.28 E
Bukoba, Tan.	227	1.20 S	31.49 E
Bukovina (Reg.), Sov. Un. (bo͞o-kô'vĭ-nȧ)	165	48.06 N	25.20 E
Bula, Indon. (bo͞o'lä)	203	3.00 S	130.30 E
Bulalacao, Phil. (bo͞o-lä-lä'kä-ō)	203a	12.30 N	121.20 E
Bulawayo, Zimb. (bo͞o-lȧ-wä'yō)	222	20.12 S	28.43 E
Buldir (I.), Ak. (bŭl dĭr)	105a	52.22 N	175.50 E
Bulgaria, Eur. (bo͝ol-gā'rĭ-ă)	152	42.12 N	24.13 E
Bulkley Ra., Can. (bŭlk'lē)	96	54.30 N	127.30 W
Bullaque (R.), Sp. (bo͞o-lä'kā)	168	39.15 N	4.13 W
Bullas, Sp. (bo͞ol'yäs)	168	38.07 N	1.48 W
Bulldog Cr., Ut. (bŭl'dŏg')	119	37.45 N	110.55 W
Bull Harbour, Can. (hăr'bēr)	96	50.45 N	127.55 W
Bull Head (Mtn.), Jam.	132	18.10 N	77.15 W
Bulloo (R.), Austl. (bŭ-lo͞o')	211	25.23 S	143.30 E
Bull Run (R.), Or. (bo͝ol)	116c	45.26 N	122.11 W
Bull Run Res., Or.	116c	45.29 N	122.11 W
Bull Shoals Res., Ar.-Mo. (bo͝ol shōlz)	121	36.35 N	92.57 W
Bulo Burti, Som. (bo͞o'lō bo͞or'tĭ)	219a	3.53 N	45.30 E
Bulphan, Eng. (bo͝ol'făn)	154b	51.33 N	0.21 E
Bultfontein, S. Afr. (bo͝olt'fōn-tān')	219d	28.18 S	26.10 E
Bulun, Sov. Un. (bo͞o-lo͞on')	179	70.48 N	127.27 E
Bulungu, Zaire (bo͞o-lo͞oŋ'go͞o)	226	6.04 S	21.54 E
Bulwer, S. Afr. (bo͝ol-wēr)	223c	29.49 S	29.48 E
Bumba, Zaire (bo͞om'bȧ)	226	2.11 N	22.28 E
Bumire I., Tan.	227	1.40 S	32.05 E
Buna, Pap. N. Gui. (bo͞o'nȧ)	203	8.58 S	148.38 E
Bunbury, Austl. (bŭn'bŭrĭ)	210	33.25 S	115.45 E
Bundaberg, Austl. (bŭn'dȧ-bûrg)	212	24.45 S	152.18 E
Bungo-Suidō (Chan.), Jap. (bo͞oŋ'gō so͞o-ē'dō)	201	33.26 N	131.54 E
Bunguran Utara, Kepulauan (Is.), Indon.	202	.322 N	108.00 E
Bunia, Zaire	227	1.34 N	30.15 E
Bunker Hill, Il. (bŭnk'ēr hĭl)	117e	39.03 N	89.57 W
Bunkie, La. (bŭŋ'kĭ)	123	30.55 N	92.10 W
Bun Plns, Ken.	227	0.55 N	40.35 E
Bununu Dass, Nig.	225	10.00 N	9.31 E
Buor-Khaya, Guba (B.), Sov. Un.	179	71.45 N	131.00 E
Buor Khaya, Mys (C.), Sov. Un.	179	71.47 N	133.22 E
Bura, Ken.	227	1.06 S	39.57 E
Buran, Som. (bûr'ăn)	219a	10.38 N	48.30 E
Burao, Som.	219a	9.20 N	45.45 E
Buraydah, Sau. Ar.	192	26.23 N	44.14 E
Burbank, Ca. (bûr'bănk)	117a	34.11 N	118.19 W
Burdekin (R.), Austl. (bûr'dē-kĭn)	211	19.22 S	145.07 E
Burdur, Tur. (bo͞or-do͞or')	177	37.50 N	30.15 E
Burdwān, India (bo͝od-wän')	190	23.29 N	87.53 E
Bureinskiy, Khrebet (Mts.), Sov. Un.	179	51.15 N	133.30 E
Bureya, Sov. Un. (bo͞orā'ȧ)	179	49.55 N	130.00 E
Bureya (R.), Sov. Un. (bo͞o-rā'yä)	179	51.00 N	130.14 E
Burford, Eng. (bûr-fērd)	154b	51.46 N	1.38 W
Burford (L.), NM	119	36.37 N	107.21 W
Burgas, Bul. (bo͝or-gäs')	171	42.29 N	27.30 E
Burgas, Gulf of, Bul.	159	42.30 N	27.40 E
Bur Gavo, Som.	223	1.14 S	41.47 E
Burgaw, NC (bûr'gô)	125	34.31 N	77.56 W
Burgdorf, Switz. (bo͞org'dôrf)	164	47.04 N	7.37 E
Burgenland (State), Aus.	155e	47.58 N	16.57 E
Burgeo, Can.	103	47.36 N	57.34 W
Burgess, Va.	109	37.53 N	76.21 W
Burgos, Mex. (bo͞or'gōs)	122	24.57 N	98.47 W
Burgos, Phil.	203a	16.03 N	119.52 E
Burgos, Sp. (bo͞o'r-gôs)	168	42.20 N	3.44 W
Burgsvik, Swe. (bo͞orgs'vĭk)	162	57.04 N	18.18 E
Burhānpur, India (bo͞or'hän-po͞or)	190	21.26 N	76.08 E
Burias I., Phil. (bo͞o'rē-äs)	203a	12.56 N	122.56 E
Burias Pass, Phil. (bo͞o'rē-äs)	203a	13.04 N	123.11 E
Burica, Punta (Pt.), Pan. (po͞o'n-tä-bo͞o'rē-kä)	131	8.02 N	83.12 W
Burien, Wa. (bū'rĭ-ĕn)	116a	47.28 N	122.20 W
Burin, Can. (bûr'ĭn)	103	47.02 N	55.10 W
Burin Pen., Can.	103	47.00 N	55.40 W
Burkburnett, Tx. (bûrk-bûr'nĕt)	120	34.04 N	98.35 W
Burke, Vt. (bûrk)	109	44.40 N	72.00 W
Burke Chan., Can.	96	52.07 N	127.38 W
Burketown, Austl. (bûrk'toun)	210	17.50 S	139.30 E

274 Burley – Calimesa

PLACE (Pronunciation)	PAGE	Lat. °′	Long. °′
Burley, Id. (bûr'lĭ)	115	42.31 N	113.48 W
Burley, Wa.	116a	47.25 N	122.38 W
Burli, Sov. Un.	180a	53.36 N	61.55 E
Burlingame, Ca. (bûr'lĭn-găm)	116b	37.35 N	122.22 W
Burlingame, KS.	121	38.45 N	95.49 W
Burlington, Can. (bûr'lĭng-tŭn)	93d	43.19 N	79.48 W
Burlington, Co.	120	39.17 N	102.26 W
Burlington, Ia.	113	40.48 N	91.05 W
Burlington, Ks.	121	38.10 N	95.46 W
Burlington, Ky.	111f	39.01 N	84.44 W
Burlington, Ma.	103a	42.31 N	71.13 W
Burlington, NJ	110f	40.04 N	74.52 W
Burlington, NC	125	36.05 N	79.26 W
Burlington, Vt.	109	44.30 N	73.15 W
Burlington, Wa.	116a	48.28 N	122.20 W
Burlington, Wi.	111a	42.41 N	88.16 W
Burma, Asia (bûr'mȧ)	188	21.00 N	95.15 E
Burnaby, Can.	96	49.14 N	122.58 W
Burnet, Tx. (bûrn'ĕt)	122	30.46 N	98.14 W
Burnham on Crouch, Eng. (bûrn'ăm-ŏn-krouch)	154b	51.38 N	0.48 E
Burnie, Austl. (bûr'nē)	212	41.15 S	146.05 E
Burnley, Eng. (bûrn'lē)	154	53.47 N	2.19 W
Burns, Or. (bûrnz)	114	43.35 N	119.05 W
Burnside, Ky. (bûrn'sīd)	124	36.57 N	84.33 W
Burns Lake, Can. (bûrnz lăk)	96	54.14 N	125.46 W
Burnsville, Can. (bûrnz'vĭl)	102	47.44 N	65.07 W
Burnt R., Or. (bûrnt)	114	44.26 N	117.53 W
Burntwood (R.), Can.	99	55.53 N	97.30 W
Burrard Inlet, Can. (bûr'ȧrd)	116d	49.19 N	123.15 W
Burriana, Sp. (bo͞or-rē-ȧ'nä)	169	39.53 N	0.05 W
Bursa, Tur. (bo͞or'sȧ)	177	40.10 N	28.10 E
Būr Safājah, Egypt	221	26.57 N	33.56 E
Būr Sa'īd (Port Said), Egypt	219c	31.15 N	32.19 E
Burscheid, F.R.G. (bo͞or'shīd)	167c	51.05 N	7.07 E
Būr Sūdān (Port Sudan), Sud. (so͞o-dän')	221	19.30 N	37.10 E
Burt, NY (bŭrt)	111c	43.19 N	78.45 W
Burt (L.), Mi. (bŭrt)	108	45.25 N	84.45 W
Burton, Wa. (bûr'tŭn)	116a	47.24 N	122.28 W
Burton Res., Ga.	124	34.46 N	83.40 W
Burtonsville, Md. (bûrtŏns-vil)	110e	39.07 N	76.57 W
Burton-upon-Trent, Eng. (bûr'tŭn-ŭp'-ŏn-trĕnt)	154	52.48 N	1.37 W
Buru (I.), Indon.	203	3.30 S	126.30 E
Burullus (L.), Egypt	219b	31.20 N	30.58 E
Burundi, Afr.	218	3.00 S	29.30 E
Burwell, Ne. (bûr'wĕl)	112	41.46 N	99.08 W
Bury, Eng. (bĕr'ĭ)	154	53.36 N	2.17 W
Buryat A.S.S.R., Sov. Un.	179	55.15 N	112.00 E
Bury St. Edmunds, Eng. (bĕr'ĭ-sānt ĕd'mŭndz)	161	52.14 N	0.44 E
Burzaco, Arg. (bo͞or-zȧ'kô)	142a	34.35 S	58.23 W
Busanga Swp., Zambia	227	14.10 S	25.50 E
Bush, Egypt (bo͞osh)	219b	29.13 N	31.08 E
Būshehr, Iran	192	28.48 N	50.53 E
Bushmanland (Reg.), S. Afr. (bo͞osh-măn lănd)	222	29.15 S	18.45 E
Bushnell, Il. (bo͞osh'nĕl)	121	40.33 N	90.28 W
Businga, Zaire (bo͞o-siŋ'gȧ)	226	3.20 N	20.53 E
Busira (R.), Zaire	226	0.05 S	19.20 E
Busk, Sov. Un. (bo͞o'sk)	165	49.58 N	24.39 E
Busselton, Austl. (bŭs'l-tŭn)	210	33.40 S	115.30 E
Bussum, Neth.	155a	52.16 N	5.10 E
Bustamante, Mex. (bo͞os-tȧ-män'tȧ)	122	26.34 N	100.30 W
Busto Arsizio, It. (bo͞os'tō är-sēd'zē-ō)	170	45.47 N	8.51 E
Busuanga (I.), Phil. (bo͞o-swäŋ'gä)	203a	12.20 N	119.43 E
Buta, Zaire (bo͞o'tȧ)	226	2.48 N	24.44 E
Butha Buthe, Leso. (bo͞o-thȧ-bo͞o'thȧ)	223c	28.49 S	28.16 E
Butha Qi, **China** (bo͞o-thä chē)	200	47.59 N	122.56 E
Butler, Al. (bŭt'lẽr)	124	32.05 N	88.10 W
Butler, In.	108	41.25 N	84.50 W
Butler, Md.	110e	39.32 N	76.46 W
Butler, NJ	110a	41.00 N	74.20 W
Butler, Pa.	109	40.50 N	79.55 W
Butovo, Sov. Un. (bo͞o-tô'vô)	180b	55.33 N	37.36 E
Butsha, Zaire	227	0.57 N	29.13 E
Buttahatchie (R.), Al.-Ms. (bŭt-ȧ-hăch'ē)	124	34.02 N	88.05 W
Butte, Mt. (būt)	115	46.00 N	112.31 W
Butterworth, S. Afr. (bŭ tẽr'wûrth)	223c	32.20 S	28.09 E
Butt of Lewis (C.), Scot. (bŭt ŏv lū'ĭs)	160	58.34 N	6.15 W
Butuan, Phil. (bo͞o-to͞o'än)	203	8.40 N	125.33 E
Butung (I.), Indon.	202	5.00 S	122.55 E
Buturlinovka, Sov. Un. (bo͞o-to͞o'lē-nôf'ka)	173	50.47 N	40.35 E
Buxtehude, F.R.G. (bo͞oks-tĕ-ho͞o'dĕ)	155c	53.29 N	9.42 E
Buxton, Eng. (bŭks't'n)	154	53.15 N	1.55 W
Buxton, Or.	116c	45.41 N	123.11 W
Buy, Sov. Un. (bwē)	176	58.30 N	41.48 E
Buzău, Rom. (bo͞o-zĕ'o͞o)	171	45.09 N	26.51 E
Buzău (R.), Rom.	173	45.17 N	27.22 E
Buzaymah, Libya	221	25.14 N	22.13 E
Buzi, China (bo͞o-dz)	196	33.48 N	118.13 E
Buzuluk, Sov. Un. (bo͞o-zo͞o-lo͝ok')	177	52.50 N	52.10 E
Bwendi, Zaire	227	4.01 N	26.41 E
Byala, Bul.	171	43.26 N	25.44 E
Byala Slatina, Bul. (byä'la slä'tēnä)	171	43.26 N	23.56 E
Byblos, see Jubayl			
Bydogoszcz, Pol. (bĭd'gôshch)	165	53.07 N	18.00 E
Byesville, Oh. (bīz-vĭl)	108	39.55 N	81.35 W
Bygdin (L.), Nor. (bügh-dĕn')	162	61.24 N	8.31 E
Byglandsfjord, Nor. (bügh'lănds-fyôr)	162	58.40 N	7.49 E
Bykhovo, Sov. Un. (bĭ-ĸô'vô)	172	53.32 N	30.15 E
Bykovo, Sov. Un. (bĭ-kô'vô)	180b	55.38 N	38.05 E
Byrranga, Gory (Mts.), Sov. Un.	178	74.15 N	94.28 E
Bytantay (R.), Sov. Un. (byän'tăy)	179	68.15 N	132.15 E
Bytom, Pol. (bĭ'tŭm)	165	50.21 N	18.55 E
Bytosh', Sov. Un. (bĭ-tôsh')	172	53.48 N	34.06 E
Bytow, Pol. (bĭ'tŭf)	165	54.10 N	17.30 E
C			
Caazapá, Par. (kä-zä-pä')	142	26.14 S	56.18 W
Cabagan, Phil. (kä-bä-gän')	203a	17.27 N	121.50 E
Cabalete (I.), Phil. (kä-bä-lā'tȧ)	203a	14.19 N	122.00 E
Caballones, Canal de (Chan.), Cuba (kä-nä'l-dĕ-kä-bäl-yô'nĕs)	132	20.45 N	79.20 W
Caballo Res., NM (kä-bä-lyō')	119	33.00 N	107.20 W
Cabanatuan, Phil. (kä-bä-nä-twän')	203a	15.30 N	120.56 E
Cabano, Can. (kä-bä-nō')	102	47.41 N	68.54 W
Cabarruyan (I.), Phil. (kä-bä-ro͞o'yän)	203a	16.21 N	120.10 E
Cabedelo, Braz. (kä-bē-dā'lo͞o)	141	6.58 S	34.49 W
Cabeza, Arrecife (Reef), Mex. (är-rē-sē'fē-kä-bē-zä)	129	19.07 N	95.52 W
Cabeza del Buey, Sp. (kȧ-bā'thä dĕl bwā')	168	38.43 N	5.18 W
Cabimas, Ven. (kä-bē'mäs)	140	10.21 N	71.27 W
Cabinda, Ang. (kä-bĭn'dȧ)	218	5.10 S	10.00 E
Cabinda, Ang.	226	5.33 S	12.12 E
Cabinet Mts., Mt. (kăb'ĭ-nĕt)	114	48.13 N	115.52 W
Cabo Frio, Braz. (kä'bô-frē'ô)	139a	22.53 S	42.02 W
Cabo Frio, Ilha do, Braz. (ē'lä-dô-kä'bô frē'ô)	139a	23.01 S	42.00 W
Cabonga Res., Can.	101	47.25 N	76.35 W
Cabot Hd., Can. (kăb'ŭt)	108	45.15 N	81.20 W
Cabot Str., Can. (kăb'ŭt)	103	47.35 N	60.00 W
Cabra, Sp. (käb'rä)	168	37.28 N	4.29 W
Cabra I., Phil.	203a	13.55 N	119.55 E
Cabrera (I.), Sp. (kä-brā'rä)	169	39.08 N	2.57 E
Cabrera, Sierra de la (Mts.), Sp.	168	42.15 N	6.45 W
Cabriel (R.), Sp. (kä-brē-ĕl')	168	39.25 N	1.20 W
Cabrillo Natl. Mon., Ca. (kä-brēl'yō)	118a	32.41 N	117.03 W
Cabrobó, Braz. (kä-brō-bô')	141	8.34 S	39.13 W
Cabuçu (R.), Braz. (kä-bo͞o'-so͞o)	142b	22.57 S	43.36 W
Cabugao, Phil. (kä-bo͞o'gä-ô)	203a	17.48 N	120.28 E
Čačak, Yugo. (chä'chȧk)	171	43.51 N	20.22 E
Caçapava, Braz. (kä'sä-pȧ'vä)	139a	23.05 S	45.52 W
Cáceres, Braz. (kȧ'sē-rĕs)	141	16.11 S	57.32 W
Cáceres, Sp. (kȧ'thȧ-rās)	168	39.28 N	6.20 W
Cachapoal (R.), Chile (kä-chä-pô-ȧ'l)	139b	34.23 S	70.19 W
Cacharí, Arg. (kä-chä-rē')	139c	36.23 S	59.29 W
Cache (R.), Ar. (kȧsh)	121	35.24 N	91.12 W
Cache Creek, Can.	97	50.48 N	121.19 W
Cache Cr., Can. (kȧsh)	118	38.53 N	122.24 W
Cache la Poudre (R.), Co. (kȧsh lȧ po͞od'r')	120	40.43 N	105.39 W
Cachi, Nevados de (Pk.), Arg. (nĕ-vȧ'dôs-dĕ-kȧ'chē)	142	25.05 S	66.40 W
Cachinal, Chile (kä-chē-näl')	142	24.57 S	69.33 W
Cachoeira, Braz. (kä-shô-ā'rä)	141	12.32 S	38.47 W
Cachoeira do Sul, Braz. (kä-shô-ā'rä-dô-so͞o'l)	142	30.02 S	52.49 W
Cachoeiras de Macacu, Braz. (kä-shô-ā'räs-dĕ-mä-kä'ko͞o)	139a	22.28 S	42.39 W
Cachoeiro de Itapemirim, Braz. (kä-shô-ā'rô-dĕ-ē'tä-pĕmē-rē'ɴ)	139a	20.51 S	41.06 W
Cacolo, Ang.	226	10.07 S	19.17 E
Caconda, Ang. (kä-kōn'dä)	226	13.43 S	15.06 E
Cacouna, Can.	102	47.54 N	69.31 W
Cacula, Ang.	226	14.29 S	14.10 E
Caddo (L.), La.-Tx. (kăd'ō)	123	32.37 N	94.15 W
Cadereyta, Mex. (kä-dȧ-rā'tä)	128	20.42 N	99.47 W
Cadereyta Jimenez, Mex. (kä-dä-rā'tä hē-mā'näz)	122	25.36 N	99.59 W
Cadi, Sierra de (Mts.), Sp. (sē-ĕ'r-rä-dĕ-kä'dē)	169	42.17 N	1.34 E
Cadillac, Mi. (kăd'ĭ-lăk)	108	44.15 N	85.25 W
Cadiz, Ca. (kā'dĭz)	118	34.33 N	115.30 W
Cadiz, Oh.	108	40.15 N	81.00 W
Cádiz, Sp. (kȧ'dēz)	168	36.34 N	6.20 W
Cádiz, Golfo de (G.), Sp. (gôl-fô-dĕ-kȧ'dēz)	168	36.50 N	7.00 W
Caen, Fr. (käɴ)	166	49.13 N	0.22 W
Caernarfon, Wales	160	53.08 N	4.17 W
Caernarfon B., Wales	160	53.09 N	4.56 W
Caeté, Braz. (kä'ē-tē')	139a	19.53 S	43.41 W
Caetité, Braz. (kä-ā-tē-tā')	141	14.02 S	42.14 W
Cagayan, Phil. (kä-gä-yän')	203	8.13 N	124.30 E
Cagayan (R.), Phil.	202	16.45 N	121.55 E
Cagayan Is., Phil.	202	9.40 N	120.30 E
Cagayan Sulu (I.), Phil. (kä-gä-yän so͞o'lo͞o)	202	7.00 N	118.30 E
Cagli, It. (käl'yē)	170	43.35 N	12.40 E
Cagliari, It. (käl'yä-rē)	170	39.16 N	9.08 E
Cagliari, Golfo di (G.), It. (gôl-fô-dē-käl'yä-rē)	170	39.08 N	9.12 E
Cagnes, Fr. (kän'y')	167	43.40 N	7.14 E
Cagua, Ven. (kä'gwä)	141b	10.12 N	67.27 W
Caguas, P.R. (kä'gwäs)	127b	18.12 N	66.01 W
Cahaba (R.), Al. (kȧ hä-bä)	124	32.50 N	87.15 W
Cahama, Ang. (kä-ȧ'mä)	226	16.17 S	14.19 E
Cahokia, Il. (kȧ-hō'kĭ-ȧ)	117e	38.34 N	90.11 W
Cahora-Bassa (Gorge), Moz.	227	15.40 S	32.50 E
Cahors, Fr. (kȧ-ôr')	166	44.27 N	1.27 E
Cahuacán, Mex. (kä-wä-kä'n)	129a	19.38 N	99.25 W
Cahuita, Punta (Pt.), C.R. (po͞o'n-tä-kä-wē'tȧ)	131	9.47 N	82.41 W
Caiapó, Serra do (Mts.), Braz. (sĕ'r-rä-dô-kä-yä-pô')	141	17.52 S	52.37 W
Caibarién, Cuba (kī-bä-rē-ĕn')	132	22.35 N	79.30 W
Caicedonia, Col. (kī-sē-dô-nēä)	140a	4.21 N	75.48 W
Caicos Bk., Ba. (kī'kōs)	133	21.35 N	72.00 W
Caicos Is., Turks & Caicos Is.	133	21.45 N	71.50 W
Caicos Passage (Str.), Ba.	133	21.55 N	72.45 W
Caillou B., La. (kȧ-yo͞o')	123	29.07 N	91.00 W
Caimanera, Cuba (kī-mä-nā'rä)	133	20.00 N	75.10 W
Caiman Pt., Phil. (kī'mȧn)	203a	15.56 N	119.33 E
Caimito, (R.), Pan. (kä-ē-mē'tô)	126a	8.50 N	79.45 W
Caimito del Guayabal, Cuba (kä-ē-mē'tō-dĕl-gwä-yä-bä'l)	133a	22.42 N	82.36 W
Cairns, Austl. (kârnz)	211	17.02 S	145.49 E
Cairo, C.R. (kī'rô)	131	10.06 N	83.47 W
Cairo, see Al Qāhirah			
Cairo, Ga. (kā'rō)	124	30.48 N	84.12 W
Cairo, Il.	121	36.59 N	89.11 W
Caistor, Eng. (kȧs'tẽr)	154	53.30 N	0.20 W
Caiundo, Ang.	226	15.46 S	17.28 E
Caiyu, China (tsī-yo͞o)	198a	39.39 N	116.36 E
Cajamarca, Col. (kä-ĸä-mȧ'r-kä)	140	4.25 N	75.25 W
Cajamarca, Peru (kä-hä-mär'kä)	140	7.16 S	78.30 W
Čajniče, Yugo. (chī'nĭ-chĕ)	171	43.32 N	19.04 E
Cajon, Ca. (kȧ-hōn')	117a	34.18 N	117.28 W
Cajuru, Braz. (kȧ-zho͞o'ro͞o)	139a	21.17 S	47.17 W
Čakovec, Yugo. (chȧ'kō-vĕts)	170	46.23 N	16.27 E
Cala, S. Afr. (cä-lȧ)	223c	31.33 S	27.41 E
Calabar, Nig. (kăl-ȧ-bär')	225	4.57 N	8.19 E
Calabazar, Cuba (kä-lä-bä-zä'r)	133a	23.02 N	82.25 W
Calabozo, Ven. (kä-lä-bō'zō)	140	8.48 N	67.27 W
Calabria (Reg.), It. (kä-lä'brē-ä)	170	39.26 N	16.23 E
Calafat, Rom. (kȧ-lȧ-fȧt')	171	43.59 N	22.56 E
Calaguas Is., Phil. (kä-läg'wäs)	203a	14.30 N	123.06 E
Calahoo, Can. (kȧ-lȧ-ho͞o')	93g	53.42 N	113.58 W
Calahorra, Sp. (kä-lä-ôr'rä)	168	42.18 N	1.58 W
Calais, Fr. (kȧ-lĕ')	166	50.56 N	1.51 E
Calais, Me.	102	45.11 N	67.15 W
Calama, Chile (kä-lä'mä)	142	22.17 S	68.58 W
Calamar, Col. (kä-lä-mär')	140	10.24 N	75.00 W
Calamar, Col.	140	1.55 N	72.33 W
Calamba, Phil. (kä-läm'bä)	203a	14.12 N	121.10 E
Calamian Group (Is.), Phil. (kä-lä-myän')	202	12.14 N	118.38 E
Calañas, Sp. (kä-län'yäs)	168	37.41 N	6.52 W
Calanda, Sp.	169	40.53 N	0.20 W
Calapan, Phil. (kä-lä-pän')	203a	13.25 N	121.11 E
Călăraşi, Rom. (kŭ-lŭ-răsh'ĭ)	159	44.09 N	27.20 E
Calatayud, Sp. (kä-lä-tä-yo͞odh')	168	41.23 N	1.37 W
Calauag B., Phil.	203a	14.07 N	122.10 E
Calaveras Res., Ca. (kăl-ȧ-vēr'ăs)	116b	37.29 N	121.47 W
Calavite, C., Phil. (kä-lä-vē'tä)	203a	13.29 N	120.00 E
Calcasieu (R.), La. (kăl'kȧ-shū)	123	30.22 N	93.08 W
Calcasieu L., La.	123	29.58 N	93.08 W
Calcutta, India (kăl-kŭt'ȧ)	190a	22.32 N	88.22 E
Caldas, Col. (kȧ'l-däs)	140a	6.06 N	75.38 W
Caldas (Dept.), Col.	140a	5.20 N	75.38 W
Caldas da Rainha, Port. (käl'däs dä rīn'yȧ)	168	39.25 N	9.08 W
Calder (R.), Eng. (kôl'dẽr)	154	53.39 N	1.30 W
Caldera, Chile (käl-dȧ'rä)	142	27.02 S	70.53 W
Calder Can., Eng.	154	53.48 N	2.25 W
Caldwell, Id. (kôld'wĕl)	114	43.40 N	116.43 W
Caldwell, Ks.	121	37.04 N	97.36 W
Caldwell, Oh.	108	39.40 N	81.30 W
Caldwell, Tx.	123	30.30 N	96.40 W
Caledon, Can. (kăl'ē-dŏn)	93d	43.52 N	79.59 W
Caledonia, Mn. (kăl-ē-dō'nĭ-ȧ)	113	43.38 N	91.31 W
Calella, Sp. (kä-lĕl'yä)	169	41.37 N	2.39 E
Calera Victor Rosales, Mex. (kä-lā'rä-vē'k-tôr-rō-sȧ'lĕs)	128	22.57 N	102.42 W
Calexico, Ca. (kȧ-lĕk'sĭ-kō)	118	32.41 N	115.30 W
Calgary, Can. (kăl'gȧ-rĭ)	93e	51.03 N	114.05 W
Calhoun, Ga. (kăl-ho͞on')	124	34.30 N	84.56 W
Cali, Col. (kä'lē)	140a	3.26 N	76.30 W
Calicut, India (kăl'ĭ-kŭt)	191	11.19 N	75.49 E
Caliente, Nv. (käl-yĕn'tä)	119	37.38 N	114.30 W
California, Mo. (kăl-ĭ-fôr'nĭ-ȧ)	121	38.38 N	92.38 W
California, Pa.	111e	40.03 N	79.53 W
California (State), U.S.	106	38.10 N	121.20 W
California, Golfo de (G.), Mex. (gôl-fô-dĕ-kä-lē-fôr-nyä)	126	30.30 N	113.45 W
Călimani, Munţii (Mts.), Rom.	165	47.05 N	24.47 E
Calimere, Pt., India	191	10.20 N	80.20 E
Calimesa, Ca. (kă-lĭ-mā'sȧ)	117a	34.00 N	117.04 W

PRONOUNCING INDEX

Calipatria – Carata 275

PLACE (Pronunciation)	PAGE	Lat. °′	Long. °′
Calipatria, Ca. (kăl-ĭ-pàt′rĭ-ȧ)	118	33.03 N	115.30 W
Calkini, Mex. (käl-kē-nē′)	129	20.21 N	90.06 W
Callabonna, L., Austl. (călă′bŏnȧ)	212	29.35 S	140.28 E
Callao, Peru (käl-yä′ô)	140	12.02 S	77.07 W
Calling (L.), Can. (kôl′ĭng)	97	55.15 N	113.12 W
Calmar, Can. (kăl′mär)	93g	53.16 N	113.49 W
Calmar, Ia.	113	43.12 N	91.54 W
Calnalí, Mex. (käl-nä-lē′)	128	20.53 N	98.34 W
Calooshatchee (R.), Fl. (kȧ-loo-sȧ-hăch′ē)	125a	26.45 N	81.41 W
Calotmul, Mex. (kä-lôt-mo͞ol)	130a	20.58 N	88.11 W
Calpulalpan, Mex. (käl-po͞o-lȧl′pän)	128	19.35 N	98.33 W
Caltagirone, It. (käl-tä-jē-rō′nā)	170	37.14 N	14.32 E
Caltanissetta, It. (käl-tä-nē-sĕt′tä)	170	37.30 N	14.02 E
Caluango, Ang.	226	8.21 S	19.40 E
Calucinga, Ang.	226	11.18 S	16.12 E
Calumet, Mi. (kă-lū-mĕt′)	113	47.15 N	88.29 W
Calumet, L., Il.	111a	41.43 N	87.36 W
Calumet City, Il.	111a	41.37 N	87.33 W
Calunda, Ang.	226	12.06 S	23.23 E
Caluquembe, Ang.	226	13.47 S	14.44 E
Calvert, Tx. (kăl′vẽrt)	123	30.59 N	96.41 W
Calvert I., Can.	96	51.35 N	128.00 W
Calvi, Fr. (käl′vē)	170	42.33 N	8.35 E
Calvillo, Mex. (käl-vēl′yō)	128	21.51 N	102.44 E
Calvinia, S. Afr. (kăl-vĭn′ĭ-ȧ)	222	31.20 S	19.50 E
Cam (R.), Eng. (kăm)	160	52.15 N	0.05 E
Camagüey, Cuba (kä-mä-gwā′)	132	21.25 N	78.00 W
Camagüey (Prov.), Cuba	132	21.30 N	78.10 W
Camajuani, Cuba (kä-mä-hwä′nē)	132	22.25 N	79.50 W
Camaná, Peru (kä-mä′nä)	140	16.37 S	72.33 W
Camano, Wa. (kä-mä′no)	116a	48.10 N	122.32 W
Camano I., Wa.	116a	48.11 N	122.29 W
Camargo, Mex. (kä-mär gō)	122	26.19 N	98.49 W
Camarón, Cabo (C.), Hond. (kȧ′bô-kä-mä-rōn′)	130	16.06 N	85.05 W
Camas, Wa. (kăm′ȧs)	116c	45.36 N	122.24 W
Camas Cr., Id.	115	44.10 N	112.09 W
Camatagua, Ven. (kä-mä-tá′gwä)	141b	9.49 N	66.55 W
Ca-Mau, Mui (Pt.), Viet.	202	8.36 N	104.43 E
Cambay, India (kăm-bā′)	190	22.22 N	72.39 E
Cambonda, Serra (Mts.), Ang.	226	12.10 S	14.15 E
Camborne, Eng. (kăm′bôrn)	160	50.15 N	5.28 W
Cambrai, Fr. (käN-brĕ′)	166	50.10 N	3.15 E
Cambrian Mts., Wales (kăm′brĭ-ăn)	160	52.05 N	4.05 W
Cambridge, Eng. (kām′brĭj)	160	52.12 N	0.11 E
Cambridge, Md.	109	38.35 N	76.10 W
Cambridge, Mn.	113	45.35 N	93.14 W
Cambridge, Ma.	103a	42.23 N	71.07 W
Cambridge, Ne.	120	40.17 N	100.10 W
Cambridge, Oh.	108	40.00 N	81.35 W
Cambridge Bay, Can.	94	69.15 N	105.00 W
Cambridge City, In.	108	39.45 N	85.15 W
Cambridgeshire (Co.), Eng.	154	52.26 N	0.19 W
Cambuci, Braz. (käm-bo͞o′sē)	139a	21.35 S	41.54 W
Cambuí, Braz. (käm-bo͞o-ē′)	139a	22.38 S	46.02 W
Camby, In. (kăm′bē)	111g	39.40 N	86.19 W
Camden, Al. (kăm′dĕn)	124	31.58 N	87.15 W
Camden, Ar.	121	33.36 N	92.49 W
Camden, Austl.	207b	34.03 S	150.42 E
Camden, Me.	102	44.11 N	69.05 W
Camden, NJ	110f	39.56 N	75.06 W
Camden, SC	125	34.14 N	80.37 W
Cameia, Parque Nacional da (Natl. Pk.), Ang.	226	11.40 S	21.20 E
Cameron, Mo. (kăm′ẽr-ŭn)	121	39.44 N	94.14 W
Cameron, Tx.	123	30.52 N	96.57 W
Cameron, WV	108	39.40 N	80.35 W
Cameron Hills, Can.	94	60.13 N	120.20 W
Cameroon, Afr.	218	5.48 N	11.00 E
Cameroun, Mont (Mtn.), Cam.	225	4.12 N	9.11 E
Cametá, Braz. (kä-mā-tä′)	141	1.14 S	49.30 W
Camiling, Phil. (kä-mē-lĭng′)	203a	15.42 N	120.24 E
Camilla, Ga. (kȧ-mĭl′ȧ)	124	31.13 N	84.12 W
Caminha, Port. (kä-mēn′yȧ)	168	41.52 N	8.44 W
Camoçim, Braz. (kä-mô-sēN′)	141	2.56 S	40.55 W
Camooweal, Austl.	210	20.00 S	138.13 E
Campana, Arg. (käm-pä′nä)	139c	34.10 S	58.58 W
Campana (I.), Chile (käm-pän′yä)	142	48.20 S	75.15 W
Campanario, Sp. (kä-pä-nä′rē-ō)	168	38.51 N	5.36 W
Campanella, Punta (C.), It. (po͞o′n-tä-käm-pä-nĕ′lä)	169c	40.20 N	14.21 E
Campanha, Braz. (käm-pän-yăN′)	139a	21.51 S	45.24 W
Campania (Reg.), It. (käm-pän′yä)	170	41.00 N	14.40 E
Campbell, Ca. (kăm′bĕl)	116b	37.17 N	121.57 W
Campbell, Mo.	121	36.29 N	90.04 W
Campbell (Is.), N.Z.	228	52.30 S	169.00 E
Campbellpore, Pak.	190	33.49 N	72.24 E
Campbell River, Can.	96	50.01 N	125.15 W
Campbellsville, Ky. (kăm′bĕlz-vĭl)	124	37.19 N	85.20 W
Campbellton, Can. (kăm′bĕl-tŭn)	102	48.00 N	66.40 W
Campbelltown, Austl. (kăm′bĕl-toun)	207b	34.04 S	150.49 E
Campbelltown, Scot. (kăm′b′l-toun)	160	55.25 N	5.50 W
Camp Dennison, Oh. (dĕ′nĭ-sŏn)	111f	39.12 N	84.17 W
Campeche, Mex. (käm-pā′chā)	129	19.51 N	90.32 W
Campeche (State), Mex.	126	18.55 N	90.20 W
Campeche, Bahía de (B.), Mex. (bä-ē′ä-dĕ-käm-pā′chā)	126	19.30 N	93.40 W
Campechuela, Cuba (käm-pā-chwā′lä)	132	20.15 N	77.15 W
Camperdown, S. Afr. (kăm′pẽr-doun)	223c	29.14 S	30.33 E
Campina Grande, Braz. (käm-pē′nä grän′dĕ)	141	7.15 S	35.49 W
Campinas, Braz. (käm-pē′näzh)	139a	22.53 S	47.03 W
Camp Ind. Res., Ca. (kămp)	118	32.39 N	116.26 W
Campo, Cam. (käm′pō)	225	2.22 N	9.49 E
Campoalegre, Col. (kä′m-pô-àlĕ′grĕ)	140	2.34 N	75.20 W
Campobasso, It. (käm′pô-bäs′sō)	170	41.35 N	14.39 E
Campo Belo, Braz.	139a	20.52 S	45.15 W
Campo de Criptana, Sp. (käm′pō dā krēp-tä′nä)	168	39.24 N	3.09 W
Campo Florido, Cuba (kä′m-pō flō-rē′dō)	133a	23.07 N	82.07 W
Campo Grande, Braz. (käm-po͞o grän′dĕ)	141	20.28 S	54.32 W
Campo Grande, Braz.	142b	22.54 S	43.33 W
Campo Maior, Braz. (käm-po͞o mä-yôr′)	141	4.48 S	42.12 W
Campo Maior, Port.	168	39.03 N	7.06 W
Campo Real, Sp. (käm′pô rā-äl′)	169a	40.21 N	3.23 W
Campos, Braz. (kä′m-pôs)	139a	21.46 S	41.19 W
Campos do Jordão, Braz. (kä′m-pôs-dô-zhôr-dou′N)	139a	22.45 S	45.35 W
Campos Gerais, Braz. (kä′m-pôs-zhĕ-rà′es)	139a	21.17 S	45.43 W
Camps Bay, S. Afr. (kămps)	222a	33.57 S	18.22 E
Camp Springs, Md. (cămp sprĭngz)	110e	38.48 N	76.55 W
Camp Wood, Tx. (kămp wo͝od)	122	29.39 N	100.02 W
Camrose, Can. (kăm-rōz)	98	53.01 N	112.50 W
Camu (R.), Dom. Rep. (kä′mo͞o)	133	19.05 N	70.15 W
Canada, N.A. (kăn′ȧ-dȧ)	92	50.00 N	100.00 W
Canada B., Can.	103	50.43 N	56.10 W
Cañada de Gómez, Arg. (kä-nyä′dä-dĕ-gô′mĕz)	139c	32.49 S	61.24 W
Canadian, Tx. (kȧ-nā′dĭ-ăn)	120	35.54 N	100.24 W
Canadian R., Ok.	121	34.53 N	97.06 W
Canajoharie, NY (kăn-ȧ-jô-hăr′ē)	109	42.55 N	74.35 W
Çanakkale, Tur. (chä-näk-kä′lĕ)	171	40.10 N	26.26 E
Çanakkale Boğazi (Dardanelles) (Str.), Tur. (chä-näk-kä′lĕ) (där-dȧ-nĕlz′)	171	40.05 N	25.50 E
Canandaigua, NY (kăn-ăn-dā′gwȧ)	109	42.55 N	77.20 W
Canandaigua (L.), NY	109	42.45 N	77.20 W
Cananea, Mex. (kä-nä-nĕ′ä)	126	31.00 N	110.20 W
Canarias, Islas (Is.), Sp. (ē′s-läs-kä-nä′ryäs)	220	29.15 N	16.30 W
Canarreos, Arch. de los (Is.), Cuba (är-chē-pyĕ′lä-gô-dĕ-lôs-kä-när-rĕ′ōs)	132	21.35 N	82.20 W
Cañas, C.R. (kä′-nyäs)	130	10.26 N	85.06 W
Cañasgordas, Col. (kä′nyäs-gô′r-däs)	140a	6.44 N	76.01 W
Cañas R., C.R.	130	10.20 N	85.21 W
Canastota, NY (kăn-ȧs-tō′tȧ)	109	43.05 N	75.45 W
Canastra, Serra de (Mts.), Braz. (sĕ′r-rä-dĕ-kä-nä′s-trä)	141	19.53 S	46.57 W
Canatlán, Mex. (kä-nät-län′)	122	24.30 N	104.45 W
Canaveral, C., Fl.	125a	28.30 N	80.23 W
Canavieiras, Braz. (kä-nà-vē-ā′räs)	141	15.40 S	38.49 W
Canberra, Austl. (kăn′bĕr-ȧ)	212	35.21 S	149.10 E
Canby, Mn. (kăn′bĭ)	112	44.43 N	96.15 W
Canchyauya, Cerros de (Mts.), Peru (sĕ′r-rôs-dĕ-kän-cho͞o-ȧ′ïä)	140	7.30 S	74.30 W
Cancuc, Mex. (kän-ko͞ok)	129	16.58 N	92.17 W
Cancún, Mex.	130a	21.25 N	86.50 W
Candelaria, Cuba (kän-dĕ-lä′ryä)	132	22.45 N	82.55 W
Candelaria, Phil. (kän-dā-lä′rē-ä)	203a	15.39 N	119.55 E
Candelaria (R.), Mex. (kän-dĕ-lä-ryä)	129	18.25 N	91.21 W
Candeleda, Sp. (kän-dhā-lā′dhä)	168	40.09 N	5.18 W
Candia, see Iráklion			
Candle, Ak. (kăn′d′l)	105	65.00 N	162.04 W
Cando, ND (kăn′dō)	112	48.27 N	99.13 W
Candon, Phil. (kän-dōn′)	203a	17.13 N	120.26 E
Canelones, Ur. (kä-nĕ-lô-nĕs)	139c	34.32 S	56.19 W
Canelones (Dept.), Ur.	139c	34.34 S	56.15 W
Cañete, Peru (kän-yā′tā)	140	13.06 S	76.17 W
Caney, Cuba (kä-nā′) (kā′nĭ)	133	20.05 N	75.45 W
Caney, Ks. (kā′nĭ)	121	37.00 N	95.57 W
Caney (R.), Tn.	124	36.10 N	85.50 W
Cangas, Sp. (kän′gäs)	168	42.15 N	8.43 W
Cangas de Narcea, Sp. (kä′n-gäs-dĕ-när-sĕ-ä)	168	43.08 N	6.36 W
Cangombe, Ang.	226	13.40 S	19.54 E
Cangzhou, China (tsäŋ-jō)	196	38.21 N	116.53 E
Caniapiscau (L.), Can.	95	54.10 N	71.13 E
Caniapiscau (R.), Can.	95	57.00 N	68.45 W
Canicatti, It. (kä-nē-kät′tē)	170	37.18 N	13.58 E
Cañitas, Mex. (kän-yē′täs)	128	23.38 N	102.44 W
Çankırı, Tur. (chän-kē′rē)	177	40.40 N	33.40 E
Cannell, Can.	93g	53.35 N	113.38 W
Cannelton, In. (kăn′ĕl-tŭn)	108	37.55 N	86.45 W
Cannes, Fr. (kán)	167	43.34 N	7.05 E
Canning, Can. (kăn′ĭng)	102	45.09 N	64.25 W
Cannock, Eng. (kăn′ŭk)	154	52.41 N	2.02 W
Cannock Chase (Reg.), Eng. (kăn′ŭk chās)	154	52.43 N	1.54 W
Cannon (R.), Mn. (kăn′ŭn)	113	44.18 N	93.24 W
Cannonball (R.), ND (kăn′ŭn-bäl)	112	46.17 N	101.35 W
Caño, Isla de (I.), C.R. (ē′s-lä-dĕ-kä′nō)	131	8.38 N	84.00 W
Canoe (R.), Can. (kȧ-no͞o)	97	52.20 N	119.00 W
Canoga Park, Ca. (kä-nō′gȧ)	117a	34.07 N	118.36 W
Canon City, Co. (kăn′yŭn)	120	38.27 N	105.16 W
Canonsburg, Pa. (kăn′ŭnz-bûrg)	111e	40.16 N	80.11 W
Canoochee (R.), Ga. (kȧ-no͞o′chē)	125	32.25 N	82.11 W
Canora, Can. (kȧ-nōrȧ)	99	51.37 N	102.26 W
Canosa, It. (kä-nō′sä)	170	41.14 N	16.03 E
Canouan (I.), St. Vincent	131b	12.44 N	61.10 W
Cansaheab, Mex. (kän-sä-ĕ-äb)	130a	21.11 N	89.05 W
Canso, Can. (kăn′sō)	103	45.20 N	61.00 W
Canso, C., Can.	103	45.21 N	60.46 W
Canso, Str. of, Can.	103	45.37 N	61.25 W
Cantabrica, Cordillera (Mts.),Sp. (kôr-dēl-yĕ′rä-kan-tä′brē-kä)	168	43.05 N	6.05 W
Cantagalo, Braz. (kän-tä-gá′lo)	139a	21.59 S	42.22 W
Cantanhede, Port. (kän-täN-yä′dā)	168	40.22 N	8.35 W
Canterbury, Eng. (kăn′tẽr-bẽr-ē)	154b	51.17 N	1.06 E
Canterbury Bight, N.Z.	211a	44.15 S	172.08 E
Cantiles, Cayo (I.), Cuba (ky-ō-kän-tē′lås)	132	21.40 N	82.00 W
Canton, Ga.	124	34.13 N	84.29 W
Canton, Il.	121	40.34 N	90.02 W
Canton, Ma.	103a	42.09 N	71.09 W
Canton, Ms.	124	32.36 N	90.01 W
Canton, Mo.	121	40.08 N	91.33 W
Canton, NC	124	35.32 N	82.50 W
Canton, Oh.	108	40.50 N	81.25 W
Canton, Pa.	109	41.50 N	76.45 W
Canton, SD	112	43.17 N	96.37 W
Canton, see Guangzhou			
Canton (I.), Oceania	204	3.50 S	174.00 W
Cantu, It. (kän-to͞o′)	170	45.43 N	9.09 E
Cañuelas, Arg. (kä-nyo͞oĕ′-läs)	139c	35.03 S	58.45 W
Canumã (R.), Braz. (kä-no͞o-mà′)	141	6.20 S	58.57 W
Canyon, Tx. (kăn′yŭn)	120	34.59 N	101.57 W
Canyon (R.), Wa.	116a	48.09 N	121.48 W
Canyon De Chelly Natl. Mon., Az.	119	36.14 N	110.00 W
Canyonlands Natl. Park, Ut.	119	38.10 N	110.00 W
Cao Xian, China (tsou shyĕn)	196	34.48 N	115.33 E
Capalonga, Phil. (kä-pä-lōŋ′gä)	203a	14.20 N	122.30 E
Capannori, It. (kä-pän′nô-rē)	170	43.50 N	10.30 E
Capaya (R.), Ven. (kä-pä-ïä)	141b	10.28 N	66.15 W
Cap-Chat, Can. (kȧp-shä′)	95	48.02 N	65.20 W
Cap-de-la-Madeleine, Can. (kȧp dē lȧ mȧ-d′lĕn′)	102	46.23 N	72.30 W
Cape (Prov.), S. Afr. (kāp)	222	31.50 S	21.15 E
Cape Breton (I.), Can. (kāp brĕt′ŭn)	103	45.48 N	59.50 W
Cape Breton Highlands Natl. Park, Can.	103	46.45 N	60.45 W
Cape Charles, Va. (kāp chärlz)	125	37.13 N	76.02 W
Cape Coast, Ghana	224	5.05 N	1.15 W
Cape Fear (R.), NC (kāp fēr)	125	34.43 N	78.41 W
Cape Flats, S. Afr. (kāp flăts)	222a	34.01 S	18.37 E
Cape Girardeau, Mo. (jē-rär-dō′)	121	37.17 N	89.32 W
Cape May, NJ (kāp mā)	109	38.55 N	74.50 W
Cape May C.H., NJ	109	39.05 N	75.00 W
Cape Romanzof, Ak. (rō′ män zôf)	105	61.50 N	165.45 W
Capesterre, Guad.	131b	16.02 N	61.37 W
Cape Tormentine, Can.	102	46.08 N	63.47 W
Cape Town, S. Afr. (kāp toun)	222a	33.48 S	18.28 E
Cape Verde, Afr.	220b	15.48 N	26.02 W
Cape York Pen., Austl. (kāp yôrk)	211	12.30 S	142.35 E
Cap-Haïtien, Hai. (kȧp ȧ-ē-syăN′)	133	19.45 N	72.15 W
Capilla de Señor, Arg. (kä-pēl′yä dā sän-yôr′)	139c	34.18 S	59.07 W
Capitachouane, (R.), Can.	101	47.50 N	76.45 W
Capitol Reef Natl. Park, Ut. (kăp′ĭ-tŏl)	119	38.15 N	111.10 W
Capivari, Braz. (kä-pē-vá′rē)	139a	22.59 S	47.29 W
Capivari (R.), Braz.	142b	22.39 S	43.19 W
Capoompeta (Mtn.), Austl. (kȧ-po͞om-pē′tȧ)	212	29.15 S	152.12 E
Capraia (I.), It. (kä-prä′yä)	170	43.02 N	9.51 E
Caprara Pt., It. (kä-prä′rä)	170	41.08 N	8.20 E
Capreol, Can.	100	46.43 N	80.56 W
Caprera (I.), It. (kä-prā′rä)	170	41.12 N	9.28 E
Capri, It.	169c	40.18 N	14.16 E
Capri, I. di, It. (ē′-sō-lä-dē-kä′prē)	169c	40.19 N	14.10 E
Capricorn Chan., Austl. (kăp′rĭ-kôrn)	211	22.27 S	151.24 E
Caprivi Strip (Reg.), Namibia	222	18.00 S	22.00 E
Cap-Rouge, Can. (kȧp ro͞ozh′)	93b	46.45 N	71.21 W
Cap-St. Ignace, Can. (kĭp săN-tē-nyás′)	93b	47.02 N	70.27 W
Capua, It. (kä′pwä)	170	41.07 N	14.14 E
Capulhuac, Mex. (kä-po͞ol-hwäk′)	128	19.33 N	99.43 W
Capulin Mountain Natl. Mon., NM (kȧ-pū′lĭn)	120	36.15 N	103.58 W
Capultitlán, Mex. (kä-po͞o′l-tē-tlȧ′n)	129a	19.15 N	99.40 W
Caquetá (R.), Col. (kä-kä-tä′)	140	0.23 S	73.22 W
Carabaña, Sp. (kä-rä-bän′yä)	169a	40.16 N	3.15 W
Carabobo (State), Ven. (kä-rä-bô′-bô)	141b	10.07 N	68.06 W
Caracal, Rom. (kȧ-rȧ-kȧl′)	171	44.06 N	24.22 E
Caracas, Ven. (kä-rä′käs)	141b	10.30 N	66.58 W
Carácuaro de Morelos, Mex. (kä-rä′kwä-rō-dĕ-mô-rĕ-lôs)	128	18.44 N	101.04 W
Caraguatatuba, Braz. (kä-rä-gwä-tȧ-to͞o′bä)	139a	23.37 S	45.26 W
Carajás, Serra dos (Mts.), Braz. (sĕ′r-rä-dôs-kä-rä-zhá′s)	141	5.58 S	51.45 W
Caramanta, Cerro (Mtn.), Col. (sĕ′r-rô-kä-rä-mȧ′n-tä)	140a	5.29 N	76.01 W
Caramarca, Arg. (kä-rä-mȧ′r-kä)	142	28.29 S	65.45 W
Carandaí, Braz. (kä-rän-dȧē′)	139a	20.57 S	43.47 W
Carangola, Braz. (kä-rän′gō′lä)	139a	20.46 S	42.02 W
Caransebeş, Rom. (kȧ-rȧn-sä′bĕsh)	171	45.24 N	22.13 E
Caraquet, Can. (kă-rȧ-kĕt′)	102	47.48 N	64.57 W
Carata, Laguna (L.), Nic. (lä-go͞o′nä-kä-rä′tä)	131	13.59 N	83.41 W

ng-sing; ŋ-baŋk; N-nasalized n; nŏd; cŏmmit; ōld; ôbey; ôrder; oi-boil; fo͞od; fo͝ot; ou-out; s-soft; sh-dish; th-thin; pūre; ûnite; ûrn; stŭd; circŭs; ü-as in French tu; ′-indeterminate vowel.

276 Caratasca – Catskill

PLACE (Pronunciation)	PAGE	Lat. °′	Long. °′
Caratasca, Laguna (L.), Hond. (lä-goo͞'nä-kä-rä-täs'kä)	131	15.20 N	83.45 W
Caravaca, Sp. (kä-rä-vä'kä)	168	38.05 N	1.51 W
Caravelas, Braz. (kä-rä-vĕl'äzh)	141	17.46 S	39.06 W
Carayaca, Ven. (kà-rä-ī'ä'kä)	141b	10.32 N	67.07 W
Caràzinho, Braz. (kä-rà'zē-nyŏ)	142	28.22 S	52.33 W
Carballino, Sp. (kär-bäl-yē'nō)	168	42.26 N	8.04 W
Carballo, Sp. (kär-bäl'yō)	168	43.13 N	8.40 W
Carbon (R.), Wa. (kär'bŏn)	116a	47.06 N	122.08 W
Carbonado, Wa. (kär-bō-nä'dō)	116a	47.05 N	122.03 W
Carbonara, C., It. (kär-bō-nä'rä)	170	39.08 N	9.33 E
Carbondale, Can. (kär'bŏn-dāl)	93g	53.45 N	113.32 W
Carbondale, Il.	121	37.42 N	89.12 W
Carbondale, Pa.	109	41.35 N	75.30 W
Carbonear, Can. (kär-bō-nēr')	103	47.45 N	53.14 W
Carbon Hill, Al. (kär'bŏn hĭl)	124	33.53 N	87.34 W
Carcagente, Sp. (kär-kä-hĕn'tā)	169	39.09 N	0.29 W
Carcans, Étang de (L.), Fr. (ā-taN-dĕ-kär-kän)	166	45.12 N	1.00 W
Carcassonne, Fr. (kȧr-kȧ-sôn')	166	43.12 N	2.23 E
Carcross, Can. (kär'krôs)	94	60.18 N	134.54 W
Cárdenas, Cuba (kär'dā-näs)	132	23.00 N	81.10 W
Cárdenas, Mex. (kȧ'r-dĕ-näs)	129	17.59 N	93.23 W
Cárdenas, Mex.	128	22.01 N	99.38 W
Cardenas, Bahía de (B.), Cuba (bä-ē'ä-dĕ-kär'dā-näs)	132	23.10 N	81.10 W
Cardiff, Can. (kär'dĭf)	93g	53.46 N	113.36 W
Cardiff, Wales	160	51.30 N	3.18 W
Cardigan, Wales (kär'dĭ-găn)	160	52.05 N	4.40 W
Cardigan B., Wales	160	52.35 N	4.40 W
Cardston, Can. (kärds'tŭn)	97	49.12 N	113.18 W
Carei, Rom. (kä-rē')	165	47.42 N	22.28 E
Carentan, Fr. (kä-rôN-täN')	166	49.19 N	1.14 W
Carey, Oh. (kā'rē)	108	40.55 N	83.25 W
Carey (L.), Austl. (kâr'ē)	210	29.20 S	123.35 E
Carhaix-Plouguer, Fr. (kär-ĕ')	166	48.17 N	3.37 W
Caribbean Sea, N.A.-S.A. (kăr-ĭ-bē'ăn)	127	14.30 N	75.30 W
Caribe, Arroyo (R.), Mex. (är-ro'ï-kä-rē'bĕ)	129	18.18 N	90.38 W
Cariboo Mts., Can. (kă'rĭ-boo͞)	97	53.00 N	121.00 W
Caribou, Me.	102	46.51 N	68.01 W
Caribou (I.), Can.	100	47.22 N	85.42 W
Caribou L., Mn.	117h	46.54 N	92.16 W
Caribou Mts., Can.	94	59.20 N	115.30 W
Carinhanha, Braz. (kä-rĭ-nyän'yä)	141	14.14 S	43.44 W
Carini, It. (kä-rē'nē)	170	38.09 N	13.10 E
Carinthia (State), see **Kärnten**			
Carleton Place, Can. (kärl'tŭn)	101	45.15 N	76.10 W
Carletonville, S. Afr.	219d	26.20 S	27.23 E
Carlinville, Il. (kär'lĭn-vĭl)	121	39.16 N	89.52 W
Carlisle, Eng. (kär-lĭl')	160	54.54 N	3.03 W
Carlisle, Ky.	108	38.20 N	84.00 W
Carlisle, Pa.	109	40.10 N	77.15 W
Carloforte, It. (kär'lō-fôr-tå)	170	39.11 N	8.28 E
Carlos Casares, Arg. (kär-lôs-kä-sà'rēs)	139c	35.38 S	61.17 W
Carlow, Ire. (kär'lō)	160	52.50 N	7.00 W
Carlsbad, NM (kärlz'băd)	122	32.24 N	104.12 W
Carlsbad Caverns Nat'l Park, NM	122	32.08 N	104.30 W
Carlton, Eng. (kärl'tŭn)	154	52.58 N	1.05 W
Carlton, Mn.	117h	46.40 N	92.26 W
Carlton Center, Mi. (kärl'tŭn sĕn'tēr)	108	42.45 N	85.20 W
Carlyle, Il. (kärlīl')	121	38.37 N	89.23 W
Carmagnolo, It. (kär-mä-nyô'lä)	170	44.52 N	7.48 E
Carman, Can. (kär'mȧn)	99	49.32 N	98.00 W
Carmarthen, Wales (kär-mär'thĕn)	160	51.50 N	4.20 W
Carmarthen B., Wales (kär-mär'thĕn)	160	51.33 N	4.50 W
Carmaux, Fr. (kȧr-mō')	166	44.05 N	2.09 E
Carmel, NY (kär'mĕl)	110a	41.25 N	73.42 W
Carmelo, Ur. (kär-mĕ'lo)	139c	33.59 S	58.15 W
Carmen, Isla del (I.), Mex. (ē's-lä-dĕl-kȧ'r-mĕn)	129	18.43 N	91.40 W
Carmen, Laguna del (L.), Mex. (lä-goo͞'nä-dĕl-kȧ'r-mĕn)	129	18.15 N	93.26 W
Carmen de Areco, Arg. (kär'mĕn' dā ä-rā'kō)	139c	34.21 S	59.50 W
Carmen de Patagones, Arg. (kȧ'r-mĕn-dĕ-pä-tä-gô'nĕs)	142	41.00 S	63.00 W
Carmi, Il. (kär'mī)	108	38.05 N	88.10 W
Carmo, Braz. (kȧ'r-mô)	139a	21.57 S	42.06 W
Carmo do Rio Clara, Braz. (kȧ'r-mô-dô-rē'ô-klä'rä)	139a	20.57 S	46.04 W
Carmona, Sp.	168	37.28 N	5.38 W
Carnarvon, Austl. (kär-när'vŭn)	210	24.45 S	113.45 E
Carnarvon, S. Afr.	222	31.00 S	22.15 E
Carnation, Wa. (kär-nā'shŭn)	116a	47.39 N	121.55 W
Carnaxide, Port. (kär-nä-shē'dĕ)	169b	38.44 N	9.15 W
Carndonagh, Ire. (kärn-dō-nä')	160	55.15 N	7.15 W
Carnegie, Ok. (kär-nĕg'ĭ)	120	35.06 N	98.38 W
Carnegie, Pa.	111e	40.24 N	80.06 W
Carneys Point, NJ (kär'nēs)	109	39.45 N	75.25 W
Carnic Alps (Mts.), Aus.-It.	164	46.43 N	12.38 E
Carnot, Alg. (kär nō')	169	36.15 N	1.40 E
Carnot, Cen. Afr. Rep.	225	5.00 N	15.52 E
Carnsore Pt., Ire. (kärn'sôr)	160	52.10 N	6.16 W
Caro, Mi. (kā'rō)	108	43.30 N	83.25 W
Carolina, Braz. (kä-rô-lē'nä)	141	7.26 S	47.16 W
Carolina, S. Afr. (kăr-ô-lī'nȧ)	222	26.07 S	30.09 E
Carolina (L.), Mex. (kä-rō-lē'nä)	130a	18.41 N	89.40 W
Caroline Is., Pac. Is. Trust Ter. (kăr'ô-līn)	204	9.30 N	143.00 E
Caroni (R.), Ven. (kä-rō'nē)	140	5.49 N	62.57 W
Carora, Ven. (kä-rō'rä)	140	10.09 N	70.12 W
Carpathians (Mts.), Eur. (kär-pā'thĭ-ăn)	159	49.23 N	20.14 E
Carpaţii Meridionali (Transylvanian Alps) (Mts.), Rom.	171	45.30 N	23.30 E
Carpentaria, G. of, Austl. (kär-pĕn-târ'ĭȧ)	210	14.45 S	138.50 E
Carpentras, Fr. (kär-päN-träs')	166	44.04 N	5.01 E
Carpi, It.	170	44.48 N	10.54 E
Carabelle, Fl. (kăr'ȧ-bĕl)	124	29.50 N	84.40 W
Carrauntoohil, Ire. (kă-răn-too͞'ĭl)	160	52.01 N	9.48 W
Carrara, It. (kä-rä'rä)	170	44.05 N	10.05 E
Carretas, Punta (Pt.), Peru (poo͞'n-tä-kär-rē'tĕ'räs)	140	14.15 S	76.25 W
Carriacou (I.), Grenada (kăr-ē-ȧ-koo͞')	131b	12.28 N	61.20 W
Carrick-on-Sur, Ire. (kăr'-ĭk)	160	52.20 N	7.35 W
Carrier, Can. (kăr'ĭ-ēr)	93b	46.43 N	71.05 W
Carriere, Ms. (kȧ-rēr')	124	30.37 N	89.37 W
Carriers Mills, Il. (kăr'ĭ-ērs)	108	37.40 N	88.40 W
Carrington, ND (kăr'ĭng-tŭn)	112	47.26 N	99.06 W
Carr Inlet, Wa. (kăr ĭn'lĕt)	116a	47.20 N	122.42 W
Carrion Crow Hbr., Ba. (kăr'ĭŭn krō)	132	26.35 N	77.55 W
Carrión de los Condes, Sp. (kär-rē-ōn' dā los kōn'dās)	168	42.20 N	4.35 W
Carrizo Cr., NM (kär-rē'zō)	120	36.22 N	103.39 W
Carrizo Springs, Tx.	122	28.32 N	99.51 W
Carrizozo, NM (kär-rē-zō'zō)	119	33.40 N	105.55 W
Carroll, Ia. (kăr'ŭl)	113	42.03 N	94.51 W
Carrollton, Ga. (kăr-ŭl-tŭn)	124	33.35 N	84.05 W
Carrollton, Il.	121	39.18 N	90.22 W
Carrollton, Ky.	108	38.45 N	85.15 W
Carrollton, Mi.	108	43.30 N	83.55 W
Carrollton, Mo.	121	39.21 N	93.29 W
Carrollton, Oh.	108	40.35 N	81.10 W
Carrollton, Tx.	117c	32.58 N	96.53 W
Carrols, Wa. (kăr'ŭlz)	116c	46.05 N	122.51 W
Carron (L.), Scot. (kȧ'rŭn)	160	57.25 N	5.25 W
Carrot (R.), Can.	98	53.12 N	103.50 W
Carry-le-Rouet, Fr. (kä-rē'lĕ-roo͞-ā')	166a	43.20 N	5.10 E
Carsamba, Tur. (chär-shäm'bä)	177	41.05 N	36.40 E
Carson (R.), Nv. (kär'sŭn)	118	39.15 N	119.25 W
Carson City, Nv.	118	39.10 N	119.45 W
Carson Sink, Nv.	118	39.51 N	118.25 W
Cartagena, Col. (kär-tä-hā'nä)	140	10.30 N	75.40 W
Cartagena, Sp. (kär-tä-Kĕ'nä)	169	37.46 N	1.00 W
Cartago, Col. (kär-tä'gō)	140a	4.44 N	75.54 W
Cartago, C. R.	131	9.52 N	83.56 W
Cartaxo, Port. (kär-tä'shō)	168	39.10 N	8.48 W
Carteret, NJ (kär'tē-ret)	110a	40.35 N	74.13 W
Cartersville, Ga. (kär'tērs-vĭl)	124	34.09 N	84.47 W
Carthage, Il. (kär'thāj)	121	40.27 N	91.09 W
Carthage, Mo.	121	37.10 N	94.18 W
Carthage, NY	109	44.00 N	75.45 W
Carthage, NC	125	35.22 N	79.25 W
Carthage, Tx.	123	32.09 N	94.20 W
Carthage, Tun.	220	37.04 N	10.18 E
Carthcart, S. Afr. (cärth-cȧ't)	223c	32.18 S	27.11 E
Cartwright, Can. (kärt'rít)	95	53.36 N	57.00 W
Caruaru, Braz. (kä-roo͞-ä-roo͞')	141	8.19 S	35.52 W
Carúpano, Ven. (kä-roo͞'pä-nō)	140	10.45 N	63.21 W
Caruthersville, Mo. (kȧ-rŭdh'ērz-vĭl)	121	36.09 N	89.41 W
Carver, Or. (kärv'ēr)	116c	45.24 N	122.30 W
Carvoeiro, Cabo (C.), Port. (kȧ'bō-kär-vô-ĕ'y-rō)	168	39.22 N	9.24 W
Cary, Il. (kă'rē)	111a	42.13 N	88.14 W
Casablanca, Chile (kä-sä-bläŋ'kä)	139b	33.19 S	71.24 W
Casablanca, Mor.	220	33.32 N	7.41 W
Casa Branca, Braz. (kȧ'sä-brä'N-kä)	139a	21.47 S	47.04 W
Casa Grande, Az. (kä'sä grän'dā)	119	32.50 N	111.45 W
Casa Grande Natl. Mon., Az.	119	33.00 N	111.33 W
Casale Monferrato, It. (kä-sä'lā)	170	45.08 N	8.26 E
Casalmaggiore, It. (kä-säl-mäd-jō'rā)	170	45.00 N	10.24 E
Casamance (R.), Senegal (kä-sä-mäNs')	224	12.43 N	16.00 W
Cascade Pt., N.Z. (kăs-kād')	213	43.59 S	168.23 E
Cascade Ra., U.S.	106	42.50 N	122.20 W
Cascade Tun., Wa.	114	47.41 N	120.53 W
Cascais, Port. (käs-kȧ-ēzh)	169b	38.42 N	9.25 W
Case Inlet, Wa. (kās)	116a	47.22 N	122.47 W
Caseros, Arg. (kä-sā'rôs)	142a	34.35 S	58.34 W
Caserta, It. (kä-zĕr'tä)	170	41.04 N	14.21 E
Casey, Il. (kā'sĭ)	108	39.20 N	88.00 W
Cashmere, Wa. (kăsh'mĭr)	114	47.30 N	120.28 W
Casiguran, Phil. (käs-sē-goo͞'rän)	203a	16.15 N	122.10 E
Casiguran Sd., Phil.	203a	16.02 N	121.51 E
Casilda, Arg. (kä-sē'l-dä)	139c	33.02 S	61.11 W
Casilda, Cuba	132	21.50 N	80.00 W
Casimiro de Abreu, Braz. (kä'sē-mē'ro-dĕ-ȧ-brĕ'oo͞)	139a	22.30 S	42.11 W
Casino, Austl. (kȧ-sē'nō)	212	28.35 S	153.10 E
Casiquiare (R.), Ven. (kä-sē-kyä'rä)	140	2.11 N	66.15 W
Caspe, Sp. (käs'pā)	169	41.18 N	0.02 W
Casper, Wy. (kăs'pēr)	115	42.51 N	106.18 W
Caspian Dep., Sov. Un. (kăs'pĭ-ȧn)	176	47.40 N	52.35 E
Caspian Sea, Asia	174	40.00 N	52.00 E
Cass, WV (kăs)	109	38.25 N	79.55 W
Cass (L.), Mn.	113	47.23 N	94.28 W
Cassai (R.), Ang. (kä-sä'ē)	226	7.30 S	21.45 E
Cass City, Mi. (kăs)	108	43.35 N	83.10 W
Casselman, Can. (kăs''l-mȧn)	93c	45.18 N	75.05 W
Casselton, ND (kăs''l-tŭn)	112	46.53 N	97.14 W
Cássia, Braz. (kȧ'syä)	139a	20.36 S	46.53 W
Cassin, Tx. (kăs'ĭn)	117d	29.16 N	98.29 W
Cassinga, Ang. (kä-sĭŋ'gä)	222	15.05 S	16.15 E
Cassino, It. (käs-sē'nō)	170	41.30 N	13.50 E
Cass Lake, Mn. (kăs)	113	47.23 N	94.37 W
Cassopolis, Mi. (kăs-ŏ'pô-lĭs)	108	41.55 N	86.00 W
Cassville, Mo. (kăs'vĭl)	121	36.41 N	93.52 W
Castanheira de Pêra, Port. (käs-tän-yā'rä-dĕ-pĕ'rä)	168	40.00 N	8.07 W
Castellammare di Stabia, It. (käs-tĕl-läm-mä'rā-dē-stä'byä)	169c	40.26 N	14.29 E
Castelli, Arg. (kȧs-tĕ'zhē)	139c	36.07 S	57.48 W
Castellón de la Plana, Sp. (käs-tĕl-yō'n-dĕ-lä-plä'nä)	169	39.59 N	0.05 W
Castelnaudary, Fr. (kȧs'tĕl-nō-dȧ-rē')	166	43.20 N	1.57 E
Castelo, Braz. (käs-tĕ'lō)	139a	21.37 S	41.13 W
Castelo Branco, Port. (käs-tā'lō bräŋ'koo͞)	168	39.48 N	7.37 W
Castelo de Vide, Port. (käs-tā'lo͞o dĭ vē'dĭ)	168	39.25 N	7.25 W
Castelsarrasin, Fr. (kȧs'tĕl-sȧ-rȧ-zăN')	166	44.03 N	1.05 E
Castelvetrano, It. (käs'tĕl-vē-trä'nō)	170	37.43 N	12.50 E
Castilla, Peru (kȧs-tē'l-yä)	140	5.18 S	80.40 W
Castilla La Nueva (Reg.), Sp. (käs-tēl'yä lä nwä'vȧ)	168	39.15 N	3.55 W
Castilla La Vieja (Reg.), Sp. (käs-tēl'yä lä vyä'hä)	168	40.48 N	4.24 W
Castillo De San Marcos Natl. Mon., Fl. (kȧs-tē'lyä de-sän mär-kōs)	125	29.55 N	81.25 W
Castle (I.), Ba. (kȧs''l)	133	22.05 N	74.20 W
Castlebar, Ire. (kȧs''l-bär)	160	53.55 N	9.15 W
Castle Dale, Ut. (kȧs'l dāl)	119	39.15 N	111.00 W
Castle Donington, Eng. (dŏn'ĭng-tŭn)	154	52.50 N	1.21 W
Castleford, Eng. (kȧs'l-fērd)	154	53.43 N	1.21 W
Castlegar, Can. (kȧs''l-gär)	97	49.19 N	117.40 W
Castlemaine, Austl. (käs''l-mān)	212	37.05 S	114.10 E
Castle Pk., Co.	119	39.00 N	106.50 W
Castlerock, Wa. (kȧs''l-rŏk)	114	46.17 N	122.53 W
Castle Rock Flowage (Res.), Wi.	113	44.03 N	89.48 W
Castle Shannon, Pa. (shăn'ŭn)	111e	40.22 N	80.02 W
Castleton, In. (kȧs''l-tŏn)	111g	39.54 N	86.03 W
Castor (R.), Can (kăs'tôr)	93c	45.16 N	75.14 W
Castor (R.), Mo.	121	36.59 N	89.53 W
Castres, Fr. (kȧs'tr')	166	43.36 N	2.13 E
Castries, St. Lucia (kȧs-trē')	131b	14.01 N	61.00 W
Castro, Braz. (käs'troo͞)	142	24.56 S	50.00 W
Castro, Chile (käs'tro)	142	42.27 S	73.48 W
Castro Daire, Port. (käs'troo͞ dīr'ĭ)	168	40.56 N	7.57 W
Castro del Río, Sp. (käs-trô-dĕl rē'ō)	168	37.42 N	4.28 W
Castrop Rauxel, F.R.G. (käs'trōp rou'ksĕl)	167c	51.33 N	7.19 E
Castro Urdiales, Sp. (käs'trō o͞or-dyä'lâs)	168	43.23 N	3.11 W
Castro Valley, Ca.	116b	37.42 N	122.05 W
Castro Verde, Port. (käs-trō vĕr'dĕ)	168	37.43 N	8.05 W
Castrovillari, It. (käs'trō-vēl-lyä'rē)	170	39.48 N	16.11 E
Castuera, Sp. (käs-too͞-ā'rä)	168	38.43 N	5.33 W
Casula, Moz.	227	15.25 S	33.40 E
Cat (I.), Ba.	133	25.30 N	75.30 W
Catacamas, Hond. (kä-tä-kȧ'mäs)	130	14.52 N	85.55 W
Cataguases, Braz. (kä-tä-gwȧ'sĕs)	139a	21.23 S	42.42 W
Catahoula (L.), La. (kăt-ȧ-ho͞o'lȧ)	123	31.35 N	92.20 W
Catalão, Braz. (kä-tä-louN')	141	18.09 S	47.42 W
Catalina (I.), Dom. Rep. (kä-tä-lē'nä)	133	18.20 N	69.00 W
Cataluma (Reg.), Sp. (kä-tä-lo͞o'mä)	169	41.23 N	0.50 E
Catamarca (Prov.), Arg. (kä-tä-mär'kä)	142	27.15 S	67.15 W
Catanduanes I., Phil. (kä-tän-dwä'nĕs)	203	13.55 N	125.00 E
Catanduva, Braz. (kä-tȧn-do͞o'vä)	141	21.12 S	48.47 W
Catania, It. (kä-tä'nyä)	170	37.30 N	15.09 E
Catania, Golfo di (G.), It. (gôl-fô-dē-kä-tä'nyä)	170	37.24 N	15.28 E
Catanaun, Phil. (kä-tä-nä'wän)	203a	13.36 N	122.20 E
Catanzaro, It. (kä-tän-dzä'rō)	170	38.53 N	16.34 E
Catarroja, Sp. (kä-tär-rō'hä)	169	39.24 N	0.25 W
Catawba (L.), SC	125	35.02 N	81.21 W
Catawba (R.), NC (kȧ-tô'bȧ)	125	35.25 N	80.55 W
Catazajá, Laguna de (L.), Mex. (lä-goo͞'nä-dĕ-kä-tä-zä-hȧ')	129	17.45 N	92.03 W
Catbalogan, Phil. (kät-bä-lō'gän)	203	11.45 N	124.52 E
Catemaco, Mex. (kä-tä-mä'kō)	129	18.26 N	95.06 W
Catemaco, Lago (L.), Mex. (lä'gô-kä-tä-mä'kō)	129	18.23 N	95.04 W
Caterham, Eng. (kā'tēr-ŭm)	154b	51.16 N	0.04 W
Catete, Ang. (kä-tĕ'tĕ)	226	9.06 S	13.43 E
Cathedral Mt., Tx. (kȧ-thē'drăl)	122	30.09 N	103.46 W
Cathedral Pk., S. Afr. (kȧ-thē'drăl)	223c	28.53 S	29.04 E
Catherine, L., Ar. (kă-thēr-ĭn)	121	34.26 N	92.47 W
Cathkin Pk., S. Afr. (kăth'kĭn)	223c	29.08 S	29.22 E
Cathlamet, Wa. (kăth-lăm'ĕt)	116c	46.12 N	123.22 W
Catlettsburg, Ky. (kăt'lĕts-bûrg)	108	38.20 N	82.35 W
Catoche, C., Mex. (kä-tô'chĕ)	126	21.30 N	87.15 W
Catonsville, Md. (kā'tŭnz-vĭl)	110e	39.16 N	76.45 W
Catorce, Mex. (kä-tôr'sȧ)	128	23.41 N	100.51 W
Catskill, NY (kăts'kĭl)	109	42.15 N	73.50 W
Catskill Mts., NY	109	42.20 N	74.35 W

PRONOUNCING INDEX
Cattaraugus Ind. Res. – Chaoshui 277

PLACE (Pronunciation)	PAGE	Lat. °′	Long. °′
Cattaraugus Ind. Res., NY (kăt'tă-rā-gŭs)	109	42.30 N	79.05 W
Catu, Braz. (kȧ-tōō)	141	12.26 S	38.12 W
Catuala, Ang.	226	16.29 S	19.03 E
Catumbela (R.), Ang. (kä'tŏm-bĕl'ȧ)	226	12.40 S	14.10 E
Cauayan, Phil. (kou-ä'yän)	203a	16.56 N	121.46 E
Cauca (R.), Col. (kou'kä)	140	7.30 N	75.26 W
Caucagua, Ven. (käōō-kȧ'gwä)	141b	10.17 N	66.22 W
Caucasus Mts., Sov. Un. (kô'kȧ-sŭs)	177	43.20 N	42.00 E
Cauchon L., Can. (kô-shŏn')	99	55.25 N	96.30 W
Caughnawaga, Can.	93a	45.24 N	73.41 W
Caulonia, It. (kou-lō'nyä)	170	38.24 N	16.22 E
Cauquenes, Chile (kou-kā'nās)	142	35.54 S	72.14 W
Caura (R.), Ven. (kou'rä)	140	6.48 N	64.40 W
Causapscal, Can.	102	48.22 N	67.14 W
Caution, C., Can. (kô'shŭn)	96	51.10 N	127.47 W
Cauto (R.), Cuba (kou'tō)	133	20.33 N	76.20 W
Cauvery (R.), India	190	11.15 N	78.06 E
Cava, Braz. (kȧ'vä)	142b	22.41 S	43.26 W
Cava de' Tirreni, It. (kä'vä-dĕ-tēr-rĕ'nē)	169c	40.27 N	14.43 E
Cávado (R.), Port. (kä-vä'dō)	168	41.43 N	8.08 W
Cavalcante, Braz. (kä-väl-kän'tā)	141	13.45 S	47.33 W
Cavalier, ND (kăv-ȧ-lēr')	112	48.45 N	97.39 W
Cavally (R.), Ivory Coast-Lib.	224	4.40 N	7.30 W
Cavan, Ire. (kăv'ăn)	160	54.01 N	7.00 W
Cavarzere, It. (kä-vär'dzā-rā)	170	45.08 N	12.06 E
Cavendish, Vt. (kăv'ĕn-dĭsh)	109	43.25 N	72.35 W
Caviana, Ilha (I.), Braz. (kä-vyä'nä)	141	0.45 N	49.33 W
Cavite, Phil. (kä-vē'tä)	203a	14.30 N	120.54 E
Caxambu, Braz. (kä-shä'm-bōō)	139a	22.00 S	44.45 W
Caxias, Braz. (kä'shē-äzh)	141	4.48 S	43.16 W
Caxias do Sul, Braz. (kä'shē-äzh-dô-sōō'l)	142	29.13 S	51.03 W
Caxito, Ang. (kä-shē'tōō)	226	8.33 S	13.36 E
Cayambe, Ec. (kȧ-īä'm-bĕ)	140	0.03 N	79.09 W
Cayenne, Fr. Gu. (kā-ĕn')	141	4.56 N	52.18 W
Cayetano Rubio, Mex. (kä-yĕ-tä-nô-rōō'byô)	128	20.37 N	100.21 W
Cayey, P. R.	127b	18.05 N	66.12 W
Cayman Brac (I.), Cayman Is. (kī-män' brăk)	132	19.45 N	79.50 W
Cayman Is., N. A.	132	19.30 N	80.30 W
Cay Sal Bk., Ba. (kē-săl)	132	23.55 N	80.20 W
Cayuga (L.), NY (kā-yōō'gȧ)	109	42.35 N	76.35 W
Cazalla de la Sierra, Sp. (kä-thäl'yä-dĕ-lä-sē-ĕ'r-rä)	168	37.55 N	5.48 W
Cazaux, Étang de (L.), Fr. (ā-tăN' dĕ kä-zō')	166	44.32 N	0.59 W
Cazenovia, NY (kăz-ē-nō'vĭ-ȧ)	109	42.55 N	75.50 W
Cazenovia Cr., NY	111c	42.49 N	78.45 W
Čazma, Yugo. (chäz'mä)	170	45.44 N	16.39 E
Cazombo, Ang. (kä-zô'm-bô)	222	12.25 N	22.40 E
Cazones (R.), Mex. (kä-zŏ'nĕs)	129	20.37 N	97.28 W
Cazones, Ensenada de (B.), Cuba (ĕn-sĕ-nä-dä-dĕ-kä-zŏ'nās)	132	22.05 N	81.30 W
Cazones, Golfo de (G.), Cuba (gôl-fô-dĕ-kä-zŏ'nās)	132	23.55 N	81.15 W
Cazorla, Sp. (kä-thôr'lä)	168	37.55 N	2.58 W
Cea (R.), Sp. (thā'ä)	168	42.18 N	5.10 W
Ceará, see Fortaleza			
Ceará (State), Braz. (sā-ä-rä')	141	5.13 S	39.43 W
Ceará-Mirim, Braz. (sā-ä-rä'mē-rē'N)	141	6.00 S	35.13 W
Cebaco, Isla (I.), Pan. (ē's-lä-sä-bä'kō)	131	7.27 N	81.08 W
Cebolla Cr., Co. (sē-bōl'yä)	119	38.15 N	107.10 W
Cebreros, Sp. (sĕ-brĕ'rôs)	168	40.28 N	4.28 W
Cebu, Phil. (sā-bōō')	203	10.22 N	123.49 E
Čechy (Bohemia) (Prov.), Czech. (bô-hē'mĭ-ȧ)	164	49.51 N	13.55 E
Cecil, Pa. (sē'sĭl)	111e	40.20 N	80.10 W
Cedar (R.), Ia.	113	42.23 N	92.07 W
Cedar (R.), Wa.	116c	45.56 N	122.32 W
Cedar (R.) West Fk., Ia.	113	42.49 N	93.10 W
Cedar Bayou, Tx.	123a	29.54 N	94.58 W
Cedar Breaks Natl. Mon., Ut.	119	37.35 N	112.55 W
Cedarburg, Wi. (sē'dēr bûrg)	113	43.23 N	88.00 W
Cedar City, Ut.	119	37.40 N	113.10 W
Cedar Cr., ND	112	46.05 N	102.10 W
Cedar Falls, Ia.	113	42.31 N	92.29 W
Cedar Keys, Fl.	124	29.06 N	83.03 W
Cedar Lake, In.	111a	41.22 N	87.27 W
Cedar L., In.	111a	41.23 N	87.25 W
Cedar Rapids, Ia.	113	42.00 N	91.43 W
Cedar Springs, Mi.	108	43.15 N	85.40 W
Cedartown, Ga. (sē'dēr-toun)	124	34.00 N	85.15 W
Cedarville, S. Afr. (cēdår'vĭl)	223c	30.23 S	29.04 E
Cedral, Mex. (sā-dräl')	128	23.47 N	100.42 W
Cedros, Hond. (sā'drôs)	130	14.36 N	87.07 W
Cedros (I.), Mex.	126	28.10 N	115.10 W
Ceduna, Austl. (sē-dōō'nȧ)	210	32.15 S	133.55 E
Cefalù, It. (chā-fä-lōō')	170	38.01 N	14.01 E
Cega (R.), Sp. (thā'gä)	168	41.25 N	4.27 W
Cegléd, Hung. (tsā'glād)	165	47.10 N	19.49 E
Ceglie, It. (chĕ'lyĕ)	171	40.39 N	17.32 E
Cehegín, Sp. (thā-å-hēn')	168	38.05 N	1.48 W
Ceiba del Agua, Cuba (sā'bä-dĕl-ä'gwä)	133a	22.08 N	82.38 W
Cekhira, Tun.	220	34.17 N	10.00 E
Cela, Ang. (sĕ-lȧ)	226	11.25 S	15.07 E
Celaya, Mex. (sā-lä'yä)	128	20.33 N	100.49 W
Celebes (Sulawesi) (I.), Indon.	202	2.15 S	120.30 E
Celebes Sea, Indon.	202	3.45 N	121.52 E
Celestún, Mex. (sĕ-lĕs-tōō'n)	130a	20.57 N	90.18 W
Celina, Oh. (sĕlī'na)	108	40.30 N	84.35 W
Celje, Yugo. (tsĕl'yĕ)	170	46.13 N	15.17 E
Celle, F.R.G. (tsĕl'ē)	164	52.37 N	10.05 E
Cement, Ok. (sē-mĕnt')	120	34.56 N	98.07 W
Cenderawasih Teluk (B.), Indon.	203	2.20 S	135.30 E
Ceniza, Pico (Mtn.), Ven. (pē'kô-sĕ-nē'zä)	141b	10.24 N	67.26 W
Center, Tx. (sĕn'tēr)	123	31.50 N	94.10 W
Centerhill Res., Tn. (sĕn'tēr-hĭl)	124	36.02 N	86.00 W
Center Line, Mi. (sĕn'tēr līn)	111b	42.29 N	83.01 W
Centerville, Ia. (sĕn'tēr-vĭl)	113	40.44 N	92.48 W
Centerville, Mn.	117g	45.10 N	93.03 W
Centerville, Pa.	111e	40.02 N	79.58 W
Centerville, SD	112	43.07 N	96.56 W
Centerville, Ut.	117b	40.55 N	111.53 W
Central, Cordillera (Mts.), Bol. (kôr-dēl-yĕ'rä-sĕn-trä'l)	140	19.18 S	65.29 W
Central, Cordillera (Mts.), Col.	140a	3.58 N	75.55 W
Central, Cordillera (Cibao Mts.), Dom. Rep. (kôr-dēl-yä'rä sĕn'träl) (sē-bä'ô)	133	19.05 N	71.30 W
Central Cordillera (Mts.), Phil. (kôr-dēl-yĕ'rä-sĕn'träl)	203a	17.05 N	120.55 E
Central African Republic, Afr.	218	7.50 N	21.00 E
Central America, N. A. (ä-mĕr'ĭ-kȧ)	126	10.45 N	87.15 W
Central City, Ky. (sĕn'trȧl)	124	37.15 N	87.09 W
Central City, Ne. (sĕn'tral sĭ'tĭ)	112	41.07 N	98.00 W
Central Falls, RI (sĕn'tral fôlz)	110b	41.54 N	71.23 W
Centralia, Il. (sĕn-trā'lĭ-ȧ)	108	38.35 N	89.05 W
Centralia, Mo.	121	39.11 N	92.07 W
Centralia, Wa.	114	46.42 N	122.58 W
Central Plat, Sov. Un.	176	55.00 N	33.30 E
Central Valley, NY	110a	41.19 N	74.07 W
Centreville, Il. (sĕn'tēr-vĭl)	117e	38.33 N	90.06 W
Centreville, Md.	109	39.05 N	76.05 W
Century, Fl. (sĕn'tů-rĭ)	124	30.57 N	87.15 W
Cephalonia (I.), see Kefallinéa			
Céret, Fr. (sā-rĕ')	166	42.29 N	2.47 E
Ceretè, Col. (sĕ-rĕ-tĕ')	140	8.56 N	75.58 W
Cerignola, It. (chā-rē-nyô'lä)	170	41.16 N	15.55 E
Cerknica, Yugo. (tsĕr'knē-tsȧ)	170	45.48 N	14.21 E
Cern'achovsk, Sov. Un. (chĕr-nyä'Kôfsk)	163	55.38 N	21.17 E
Cerralvo, Mex. (sĕr-räl'vō)	122	26.05 N	99.37 W
Cerralvo (I.), Mex.	126	24.00 N	109.59 W
Cerrito, Col. (sĕr-rē'-tô)	140	3.41 N	76.17 W
Cerritos, Mex. (sĕr-rē'tôs)	128	22.26 N	100.16 W
Cerro de Pasco, Peru (sĕr'rō dā päs'kō)	140	10.45 S	76.14 W
Cerro Gordo, Arroyo de, Mex. (är-rô-yô-dĕ-sĕ'r-rô-gôr-dô)	122	26.12 N	104.06 W
Certegui, Col. (sĕr-tĕ'gē)	140a	5.21 N	76.35 W
Cervantes, Phil. (sĕr-vän'tās)	203a	16.59 N	120.42 E
Cervera del Río Alhama, Sp. (thĕr-vā'rä dĕl rē'ō-äl-ä'mä)	168	42.02 N	1.55 W
Cerveteri, It. (chĕr-vĕ'tĕ-rē)	169d	42.00 N	12.06 E
Cesena, It. (chĕ'sĕ-nä)	170	44.08 N	12.16 E
Cēsis, Sov. Un. (sā'sĭs)	163	57.19 N	25.17 E
Česká Lípa, Czech. (chĕs'kä lē'pa)	164	50.41 N	14.31 E
České Budějovice, Czech. (chĕs'kā bōō'dyĕ-yô-vēt-sĕ)	164	49.00 N	14.30 E
Českomoravaska Vysočina (Mts.), Czech.	164	49.21 N	15.40 E
Český Těšín, Czech.	165	49.43 N	18.22 E
Cesme, Tur. (chĕsh'mĕ)	171	38.20 N	26.20 E
Cessnock, Austl.	212	32.58 S	151.15 E
Cestos (R.), Lib.	224	5.40 N	9.25 W
Cetinje, Yugo. (tsĕt'in-yĕ)	171	42.23 N	18.55 E
Ceuta (Sp.), Aft. (thā-ōō'tä)	220	36.04 N	5.36 W
Cévennes (Reg.), Fr. (sā-vĕn')	166	44.20 N	3.48 E
Ceyhan (R.), Tur.	159	37.19 N	36.06 E
Ceylon, see Sri Lanka			
Chabot (L.), Ca. (sha'bŏt)	116b	37.44 N	122.06 W
Chacabuco, Arg. (chä-kä-bōō'kō)	139c	34.37 S	60.27 W
Chacaltianguis, Mex. (chä-käl-tē-äŋ'gwĕs)	129	18.18 N	95.50 W
Chachapoyas, Peru (chä-chä-poi'yäs)	140	6.16 S	77.48 W
Chaco (Prov.), Arg. (chä'kō)	142	26.00 S	60.45 W
Chaco Canyon Natl. Mon., NM (chä'kô)	119	35.38 N	108.06 W
Chad, Sov. Un. (chäd)	180a	56.33 N	57.11 E
Chad, Afr.	218	17.48 N	19.00 E
Chad, L., Afr.	225	13.55 N	13.40 E
Chadbourn, NC (chăd'bŭn)	125	34.19 N	78.55 W
Chadron, Ne. (chăd'rŭn)	112	42.50 N	103.10 W
Chafarinas (C.), Mor.	168	35.08 N	2.20 W
Chaffee, Mo. (chăf'ē)	121	37.10 N	89.39 W
Chāgal Hills, Afg.-Pak.	192	29.15 N	63.28 E
Chagodoshcha (R.), Sov. Un. (chä-gō-dôsh-chä)	172	59.08 N	35.13 E
Chagres R., Pan. (chä'grĕs)	131	9.18 N	79.22 W
Chagrin R., Oh. (shȧ'grĭn)	111d	41.34 N	81.24 W
Chagrin Falls, Oh. (shȧ'grĭn fôls)	111d	41.26 N	81.23 W
Chahar (Reg.), China (chä-här)	198	44.25 N	115.00 E
Chāh Bahār, Iran (chä'h' bä'här)	192	25.18 N	60.45 E
Chake Chake, Tan.	227	5.15 S	39.46 E
Chalatenango, Sal. (chäl-ä-tĕ-näŋ'gō)	130	14.04 N	88.54 W
Chalbi Des., Ken.	227	3.40 N	36.50 E
Chalcatongo, Mex. (chäl-kä-tôŋ'gō)	129	17.04 N	97.41 W
Chalchihuites, Mex. (chäl-chē-wē'tås)	128	23.28 N	103.57 W
Chalchuapa, Sal. (chäl-chwä'pä)	130	14.01 N	89.39 W
Chalchyn (R.), China-Mong. (chäl-chyn)	179	48.00 N	118.45 E
Chalco, Mex. (chäl-kō)	129a	19.15 N	98.54 W
Chaleur B., Can. (shȧ-lûr')	102	47.58 N	65.33 W
Chalgrove, Eng. (chăl'grôv)	154b	51.38 N	1.05 W
Chaling, China (chä'lĭng)	199	27.00 N	113.31 E
Chalmette, La. (shăl-mĕt')	110d	29.57 N	89.57 W
Châlons-sur-Marne, Fr. (shȧ-lôN'sür-märn)	166	48.57 N	4.23 E
Chalon-sur-Saône, Fr.	166	46.47 N	4.54 E
Chaltel, Cerro (Mtn.), Arg.-Chile (sĕ'r-rô-chäl'tĕl)	142	48.10 S	73.18 W
Chama (R.), NM (chä'mä)	119	36.19 N	106.31 W
Chama, Sierra de (Mts.), Guat. (sē-ĕ'r-rä-dĕ-chä-mä)	130	15.48 N	90.20 W
Chamama, Malawi	227	12.55 S	33.43 E
Chaman, Pak. (chŭm-än')	190	30.58 N	66.21 E
Chambal (R.), India (chŭm-bäl')	190	26.05 N	76.37 E
Chamberlain, SD (chäm'bĕr-lĭn)	112	43.48 N	99.21 W
Chamberlain (L.), Me.	102	46.15 N	69.10 W
Chambersburg, Pa. (chām'bērz-bûrg)	109	40.00 N	77.40 W
Chambéry, Fr. (shäm-bā-rē')	167	45.35 N	5.54 E
Chambeshi (R.), Zambia	227	10.35 S	31.20 E
Chamblee, Ga. (chăm-blē')	110c	33.55 N	84.18 W
Chambly, Can. (shäN-blē')	93a	45.27 N	73.17 W
Chambly, Fr.	167b	49.11 N	2.14 E
Chambord, Can.	95	48.22 N	72.01 W
Chame, Punta (Pt.), Pan. (pōō'n-tä-chä'mȧ)	131	8.41 N	79.27 W
Chamelecón (R.), Hond. (chä-mĕ-lĕ-kô'n)	130	15.09 N	88.42 W
Chamonix-Mont-Blanc, Fr. (shȧ-mô-nē')	167	45.55 N	6.50 E
Champagne (Reg.), Fr. (shäm-pän'yĕ)	166	48.53 N	4.48 E
Champaign, Il. (shăm-pān')	108	40.10 N	88.15 W
Champdāni, India	190b	22.48 N	88.21 E
Champerico, Guat. (chäm-pȧ-rē'kō)	130	14.18 N	91.55 W
Champion, Mi. (chăm'pĭ-ŭn)	113	46.30 N	87.59 W
Champlain, L., NY-Vt. (shăm-plān')	109	44.45 N	73.20 W
Champlitte-et-le-Prálot, Fr. (shäN-plēt')	167	47.38 N	5.28 E
Champotón, Mex. (chäm-pō-tōn')	129	19.21 N	90.43 W
Champotón (R.), Mex.	129	19.19 N	90.15 W
Chañaral, Chile (chän-yä-räl')	142	26.20 S	70.46 W
Chandeleur Is., La. (shăn-dĕ-lōōr')	124	29.53 N	88.35 W
Chandeleur Sd., La.	124	29.47 N	89.08 W
Chandīgarh, India	190	30.51 N	77.13 E
Chandler, Can. (chăn'dlēr)	95	48.21 N	64.41 W
Chandler, Ok.	121	35.42 N	96.52 W
Chandrapur, India	190	19.58 N	79.21 E
Chang (R.), see Yangtze			
Changane (R.), Moz.	222	22.42 S	32.46 E
Changara, Moz.	227	16.54 S	33.14 E
Changchun, China (chäŋ-chōōn)	198	43.55 N	125.25 E
Changdang Hu (L.), China (chäŋ-däŋ hōō)	196	31.37 N	119.29 E
Changde, China (chäŋ-dŭ)	199	29.00 N	111.38 E
Changhua, Taiwan (chäng'hwä')	199	24.02 N	120.32 E
Changjŏn, Kor. (chäng'jŭn')	200	38.40 N	128.05 E
Changli, China (chäŋ-lē)	196	39.46 N	119.10 E
Changning, China (chäŋ-nĭŋ)	194	24.34 N	99.49 E
Changping, China (chäŋ-pĭŋ)	198	40.12 N	116.10 E
Changqing, China (chäŋ-chyĭŋ)	196	36.33 N	116.42 E
Changsan Cot (I.), Kor.	200	38.06 N	124.50 E
Changsha, China (chäŋ-shä)	199	28.20 N	113.00 E
Changshan Quandao (Is.), China (chäŋ-shän chyōōn-dou)	196	39.08 N	122.26 E
Changshu, China (chäŋ-shōō)	196	31.40 N	120.45 E
Changting, China	199	25.50 N	116.18 E
Changtu, China	200	43.00 N	124.02 E
Changwu, China (chäng'wōō')	198	35.12 N	107.45 E
Changxindianzhen, China (chäŋ-shyĭn-diĕn-jŭn)	198a	39.49 N	116.12 E
Changxing Dǎo (I.), China (chäŋ-shyĭŋ dou)	196	39.38 N	121.10 E
Changyi, China (chäŋ-yē)	196	36.51 N	119.23 E
Changyuan, China (chyäŋ-yuän)	196	35.10 N	114.41 E
Changzhi, China (chäŋ-jr)	198	35.58 N	112.58 E
Changzhou, China (chäŋ-jō)	196	31.47 N	119.56 E
Changzhuyuan, China (chäŋ-jōō-yuän)	196	31.33 N	115.17 E
Chanhassen, Mn. (shăn'hăs-sĕn)	117g	44.52 N	93.32 W
Channel Is., Eur. (chăn'ĕl)	152	49.15 N	3.30 W
Channel-Port-aux-Basques, Can.	103	47.35 N	59.11 W
Channelview, Tx. (chăn'elvū)	123a	29.46 N	95.07 W
Chantada, Sp. (chän-tä'dä)	168	42.38 N	7.36 W
Chanthaburi, Thai.	202	12.37 N	102.04 E
Chantilly, Fr. (shäN-tē-yē')	167b	49.12 N	2.30 E
Chantilly, Va. (shăn'tĭlē)	110e	38.53 N	77.26 W
Chantrey Inlet, Can. (chăn-trē)	94	67.49 N	95.00 W
Chanute, Ks. (shȧ-nōōt')	121	37.41 N	95.27 W
Chany (L.), Sov. Un. (chä'nē)	178	54.15 N	77.31 E
Chao'an, China (chou-än)	199	23.48 N	116.35 E
Chao Hu (L.), China (chou hōō)	196	31.31 N	117.28 E
Chao Hu (L.), China	199	31.45 N	116.59 E
Chao Phraya, (R.), Thai.	202	16.13 N	99.33 E
Chaor (R.), China (chou-r)	198	47.20 N	121.40 E
Chaoshui, China (chou-shwā)	196	37.43 N	120.56 E

278 Chao Xian – Chi-Chocs. Mts.

PLACE (Pronunciation)	PAGE	Lat. °′	Long. °′
Chao Xian, China (chou shyĕn)	196	31.37 N	117.50 E
Chaoyang, China (chou-yäŋ)	199	23.18 N	116.32 E
Chaoyang, China	198	41.32 N	120.20 E
Chapada, Serra da (Mts.), Braz. (sĕ′r-rä-dä-shä-pä′dä)	141	14.57 S	54.34 W
Chapadão, Serra do (Mtn.), Braz. (sĕ′r-rä-dô-shä-pä-dou′ɴ)	139a	20.31 S	46.20 W
Chapala, Mex. (chä-pä′lä)	128	20.18 N	103.10 W
Chapala, Lago de (L.), Mex. (lä′gô-dĕ-chä-pä′lä)	128	20.14 N	103.02 W
Chapalagana (R.), Mex. (chä-pä-lä-gä′nä)	128	22.11 N	104.09 W
Chaparral, Col. (chä-pär-rá′l)	140a	3.44 N	75.28 W
Chapayevsk, Sov. Un. (châ-pī′ĕfsk)	177	53.00 N	49.30 E
Chapel Hill, NC (chăp′′l hĭl)	125	35.55 N	79.05 W
Chaplain (L.), Wa. (chăp′lĭn)	116a	47.58 N	121.50 W
Chapleau, Can. (chăp-lō′)	95	47.43 N	83.28 W
Chapman, Mt., Can. (chăp′măn)	97	51.50 N	118.20 W
Chapman's B., S. Afr. (chăp′măns bă)	222a	34.06 S	18.17 E
Chappell, Ne. (chă-pĕl′)	112	41.06 N	102.29 W
Chapultenango, Mex. (chä-pōōl-tē-näŋ′gō)	129	17.19 N	93.08 W
Chá Pungana, Ang.	226	13.44 S	18.39 E
Charcas, Mex. (chär′käs)	128	23.09 N	101.09 W
Charco de Azul, Bahía (B.), Pan. (bä-ē′ä-chä′r-kō-dĕ-ä-zōō′l)	131	8.14 N	82.45 W
Chardzhou, Sov. Un. (chĕr-jō′ōō)	153	38.52 N	63.37 E
Charente (R.), Fr. (shà-räɴt′)	166	45.48 N	0.28 W
Chari (R.), Chad (shä-rē′)	225	12.45 N	14.55 E
Charing, Eng. (chă′rĭng)	154b	51.13 N	0.49 E
Chariton, Ia. (châr′ĭ-tŭn)	113	41.02 N	93.16 W
Chariton (R.), Mo.	121	40.24 N	92.38 W
Charlemagne, Can. (shärl-mäny′)	93a	45.43 N	73.29 W
Charleroi, Bel. (shàr-lē-rwä′)	161	50.25 N	4.35 E
Charleroi, Pa. (shär′lē-roi)	111e	40.08 N	79.54 W
Charles, C., Va. (chärlz)	125	37.05 N	75.48 W
Charlesbourg, Can. (shàrl-bōōr′)	93b	46.51 N	71.16 W
Charles City, Ia. (chärlz)	113	43.03 N	92.40 W
Charleston, Il. (chärlz′tŭn)	108	39.30 N	88.10 W
Charleston, Ms.	124	34.00 N	90.02 W
Charleston, Mo.	121	36.53 N	89.20 W
Charleston, SC	125	32.47 N	79.56 W
Charleston, WV	108	38.20 N	81.35 W
Charlestown, In. (chärlz′toun)	111h	38.46 N	85.39 W
Charlestown, St. Kitts-Nevis	131b	17.10 N	62.32 W
Charleville, Austl. (chär′lē-vĭl)	212	26.16 S	146.28 E
Charleville Mézières, Fr. (shärl-vĕl′)	166	49.48 N	4.41 E
Charlevoix, Mi. (shär′lē-voi)	108	45.20 N	85.15 W
Charlevoix, L., Mi.	113	45.17 N	85.43 W
Charlotte, Mi. (shär′lŏt)	108	42.35 N	84.50 W
Charlotte, NC	125	35.15 N	80.50 W
Charlotte Amalie (St. Thomas), Virgin Is. (U.S.A.) (shär-lŏt′ĕ ä-mä′lĭ-á)	127c	18.21 N	64.54 W
Charlotte L., Can.	96	52.07 N	125.30 W
Charlotte Hbr., Fl.	125a	26.49 N	82.00 W
Charlottenberg, Swe. (shär-lŭt′ĕn-bĕrg)	162	59.53 N	12.17 E
Charlottesville, Va. (shär′lŏtz-vĭl)	109	38.00 N	78.25 W
Charlottetown, Can. (shär′lŏt-toun)	103	46.14 N	63.08 W
Charlotte Waters, Austl. (shär′lŏt)	210	26.00 S	134.50 E
Charmes, Fr. (shärm)	167	48.23 N	6.19 E
Charnwood For., Eng. (chärn′wo͝od)	154	52.42 N	1.15 W
Charny, Can. (shär-nē′)	93b	46.43 N	71.16 W
Chars, Fr. (shär)	167b	49.09 N	1.57 E
Chārsadda, Pak. (chŭr-sä′dä)	193a	34.17 N	71.43 E
Charters Towers, Austl. (chär′tērz)	211	20.03 S	146.20 E
Chartres, Fr. (shärt′r′)	167b	48.26 N	1.29 E
Chascomús, Arg. (chäs-kō-mōōs′)	139c	35.32 S	58.01 W
Chase City, Va. (chās)	125	36.45 N	78.27 W
Chashniki, Sov. Un. (chăsh′nyē-kē)	172	54.51 N	29.08 E
Chaska, Mn. (chăs′kà)	117g	44.48 N	93.36 W
Châteaubriant, Fr. (shä-tō-brē-äɴ′)	166	47.43 N	1.23 W
Châteaudun, Fr. (shä-tō-däɴ′)	166	48.04 N	1.23 E
Château-Gontier, Fr. (chá-tō′gôɴ′tyā′)	166	47.48 N	0.43 W
Châteauguay, Can. (chá-tō-gā)	93a	45.22 N	73.45 W
Châteauguay (R.), Can.	93a	45.13 N	73.51 W
Châteauneault, Fr.	166a	43.23 N	5.11 E
Château-Renault, Fr. (shá-tō-rē-nō′)	166	47.36 N	0.57 E
Château-Richer, Can. (shá-tō′rē-shā′)	93b	47.00 N	71.01 W
Châteauroux, Fr. (shá-tō-rōō′)	166	46.47 N	1.39 E
Château-Thierry, Fr. (shá-tō′ty-ĕr-rē′)	166	49.03 N	3.22 E
Châtellerault, Fr. (shä-tĕl-rō′)	166	46.48 N	0.31 E
Chatfield, Mn. (chăt′fēld)	113	43.50 N	92.10 W
Chatham, Can. (chăt′ăm)	100	42.25 N	82.10 W
Chatham, Can.	102	47.02 N	65.28 W
Chatham, Eng. (chăt′ŭm)	154b	51.23 N	0.32 E
Chatham, NJ (chăt′ăm)	110a	40.44 N	74.23 W
Chatham, Oh.	111d	41.06 N	82.01 W
Chatham Is., N. Z.	204	44.00 S	178.00 W
Chatham Sd., Can.	96	54.32 N	130.35 W
Chatham Str., Ak.	105	57.00 N	134.40 W
Chatsworth, Ca. (chătz′wûrth)	117a	34.16 N	118.36 W
Chatsworth Res., Ca.	117a	34.15 N	118.41 W
Chattahoochee, Fl. (chăt-tá-hōō′ chee)	124	30.42 N	84.47 W
Chattahoochee (R.), Al.-Ga.	124	31.17 N	85.10 W
Chattanooga, Tn. (chăt-á-nōō′gá)	124	35.01 N	85.15 W
Chattooga (R.), Ga.-SC (chá-tōō′gá)	124	34.47 N	83.13 W
Chaudière (R.), Can. (shō-dyĕr′)	101	46.26 N	71.10 W
Chaumont, Fr. (shō-môɴ′)	166	48.08 N	5.07 E
Chaunskaya Guba (B.), Sov. Un.	179	69.15 N	170.00 E
Chauny, Fr. (shō-nē′)	166	49.40 N	3.09 E
Chau-phu, Kamp.	202	10.49 N	104.57 E
Chausy, Sov. Un. (chou′sĭ)	172	53.57 N	30.58 E
Chautauqua (L.), NY (shá-tô′kwá)	109	42.10 N	79.25 W
Chavaniga, Sov. Un.	176	66.02 N	37.50 E
Chaves, Port. (chä′vĕzh)	168	41.44 N	7.30 W
Chavinda, Mex. (chä-vē′n-dä)	128	20.01 N	102.27 W
Chazumba, Mex. (chä-zōōm′bä)	129	18.11 N	97.41 W
Cheadle, Eng. (chē′d′l)	154	52.59 N	1.59 W
Cheat R.), WV (chēt)	109	39.35 N	79.40 W
Cheb, Czech. (ĸĕb)	164	50.05 N	12.23 E
Chebarkul, Sov. Un. (chĕ-bár-kûl′)	180a	54.59 N	60.22 E
Cheboksary, Svo. Un. (chyĕ-bôk-sä′rĕ)	176	56.00 N	47.20 E
Cheboygan, Mi. (shē-boi′găn)	108	45.40 N	84.30 W
Chech, Erg (Dune), Alg.	220	24.45 N	2.07 W
Chechen′ (I.), Sov. Un. (chyĕch′ĕn)	177	44.00 N	48.10 E
Checotah, Ok. (chē-kō′tá)	121	35.27 N	95.32 W
Chedabucto B., Can. (chĕd-á-bŭk-tō)	103	45.23 N	61.10 W
Cheduba I., Bur.	202	18.45 N	93.01 E
Cheecham Hills, Can. (chēē′hăm)	98	56.20 N	111.10 W
Cheektowaga, NY (chēk-tō-wä′gá)	111c	42.54 N	78.46 W
Chefoo (Yantai), China (yän-tī)	196	37.32 N	121.22 E
Chehalis, Wa. (chē-hā′lĭs)	114	46.39 N	122.58 W
Chehalis R., Wa.	114	46.47 N	123.17 W
Cheju, Kor. (chĕ′jōō′)	200	33.29 N	126.40 E
Cheju (Quelpart) (I.), Kor.	200	33.20 N	126.25 E
Chekalin, Sov. Un. (chĕ-kä′lĭn)	172	54.05 N	36.13 E
Chela, Serra da (Mts.), Ang. (sĕr′rá dä shä′lá)	222	15.30 S	13.30 E
Chelan, Wa. (chē-lăn′)	114	47.51 N	119.59 W
Chelan (L.), Wa.	114	48.09 N	120.20 W
Cheleiros, Port. (shĕ-la′rōzh)	169b	38.54 N	9.19 W
Chelia (Mtn.), Alg.	157	35.22 N	6.47 E
Chéliff (R.), Alg. (shā-lēf)	169	36.17 N	1.22 E
Chelkar, Sov. Un. (chyĕl′kär)	178	47.52 N	59.41 E
Chelkar (L.), Sov. Un.	177	50.30 N	51.30 E
Chelkar Tengiz (L.), Sov. Un. (chyĕl′kär tĕn′yēz)	178	47.42 N	61.45 E
Chelm, Pol. (ĸĕlm)	165	51.08 N	23.30 E
Chelmno, Pol. (ĸĕlm′nō)	165	53.20 N	18.25 E
Chelmsford, Can.	100	46.35 N	81.12 W
Chelmsford, Eng. (chĕlm′s-fĕrd)	154b	51.44 N	0.28 E
Chelmsford, Ma.	103a	42.36 N	71.21 W
Chelsea, Al. (chĕl′sē)	110h	33.20 N	86.38 W
Chelsea, Austl.	207a	38.05 S	145.08 E
Chelsea, Can.	93c	45.30 N	75.46 W
Chelsea, Ma.	103a	42.23 N	71.02 W
Chelsea, Mi.	108	42.20 N	84.00 W
Chelsea, Ok.	121	36.32 N	95.23 W
Cheltenham, Eng. (chĕlt′nŭm)	160	51.57 N	2.06 W
Cheltenham, Md. (chĕltĕn-hăm)	110e	38.45 N	76.50 W
Chelva, Sp. (chĕl′vä)	169	39.43 N	1.00 W
Chelyabinsk, Sov. Un. (chĕl-yä-bĕnsk′)	180a	55.10 N	61.25 E
Chelyuskin, Mys (C.), Sov. Un. (chĕl-yōōs′-kĭn)	179	77.45 N	104.45 E
Chemba, Moz.	227	17.08 S	34.52 E
Chemillé, Fr. (shē-mē-yā′)	166	47.13 N	0.46 W
Chemnitz, see Karl-Marx-Stadt			
Chemung (R.), NY (shē-mŭng)	109	42.20 N	77.25 W
Chĕn, Gora (Mtn.), Sov. Un.	179	65.13 N	142.12 E
Chenāb (R.), Pak. (chē-näb)	190	31.33 N	72.28 E
Chenachane, Alg. (shē-ná-shän′)	220	26.14 N	4.14 W
Chencun, China (chŭn-tsōōn)	197a	22.58 N	113.14 E
Cheney, Wa. (chē′nā)	114	47.29 N	117.34 W
Chengde, China (chŭŋ-dŭ)	198	40.50 N	117.50 E
Chengdong Hu (L.), China (chŭŋ-dôŋ hōō)	196	32.22 N	116.32 E
Chengdu, China (chŭŋ-dōō)	199	30.30 N	104.10 E
Chenggu, China (chŭŋ-gōō)	198	33.05 N	107.25 E
Chenghai, China (chŭŋ-hī)	199	23.22 N	116.40 E
Chengshan, Jiao (C.), China (jyou chŭŋ-shän)	198	37.28 N	122.40 E
Chengxi Hu (L.), China (chŭŋ-shyē hōō)	196	32.31 N	116.04 E
Chen Xian, China (chŭn-shyĕn)	199	25.40 N	113.00 E
Chepén, Peru (chĕ-pĕ′n)	140	7.17 S	79.24 W
Chepo, Pan. (chā′pō)	131	9.12 N	79.06 W
Chepo R., Pan.	131	9.10 N	78.36 W
Cher (R.), Fr. (shâr)	166	47.14 N	1.34 E
Cherán, Mex. (chā-rän′)	128	19.41 N	101.54 W
Cherangany Hills, Ken.	227	1.25 N	35.20 E
Cheraw, SC (chē′rô)	125	34.40 N	79.52 W
Cherbourg, Fr. (shär-bōōr′)	166	49.39 N	1.43 W
Cherchell, Alg. (shĕr-shĕl′)	220	36.38 N	2.09 E
Cherdyn′, Sov. Un. (chĕr-dyĕn′)	176	60.25 N	56.32 E
Cheremkhovo, Sov. Un. (chĕr′yĕm-kô-vō)	178	52.58 N	103.18 E
Cherëmukhovo, Sov. Un. (chĕr-yĕ-mû-kô-vô)	180a	60.20 N	60.00 E
Cherepanovo, Sov. Un. (chĕr′yĕ pä-nô′vō)	178	54.13 N	83.18 E
Cherepovets, Sov. Un. (chĕr-yĕ-pô′vyĕtz)	172	59.08 N	37.59 E
Chereya, Sov. Un. (chĕr-ā′yä)	172	54.38 N	29.16 E
Chergui, Chott ech (L.), Alg. (chĕr gē)	158	34.12 N	0.10 W
Chergui (I.), Tun.	158	34.50 N	11.40 E
Cherikov, Sov. Un. (chĕ′rē-kôf)	172	53.34 N	31.22 E
Cherkassy, Sov. Un. (chĕr-kå′sĭ)	173	49.26 N	32.03 E
Cherkassy (Oblast), Sov. Un.	173	48.58 N	30.55 E
Cherlak, Sov. Un. (chĭr-läk′)	178	54.04 N	74.28 E
Chermoz, Sov. Un. (chĕr-môz′)	180a	58.47 N	56.08 E
Chern′, Sov. Un. (chĕrn)	172	53.28 N	36.49 E
Chërnaya Kalitva (R.), Sov. Un. (chôr′ná yá ká-lēt′vá)	173	50.15 N	39.16 E
Chernigov, Sov. Un. (chĕr-nē′gôf)	173	51.28 N	31.18 E
Chernigov (Oblast), Sov. Un. (chĕr-nē′gôf)	173	51.23 N	31.15 E
Chernigovka, Sov. Un.	173	47.08 N	36.20 E
Chernobay, Sov. Un. (chĕr-nō-bī′)	173	49.41 N	32.24 E
Chernobyl′, Sov. Un. (chĕr-nō-bĭl′)	173	51.17 N	30.14 E
Chernogorsk, Sov. Un. (chĕr-nŏ-gôrsk′)	178	54.01 N	91.07 E
Chernoistochinsk, Sov. Un. (chĕr-nôy-stô′chĭnsk)	180a	57.44 N	59.55 E
Chërnomorskoye, Sov. Un. (chĕr-nō-môr′skô-yĕ)	173	45.29 N	32.43 E
Chernovtsy (Cernăuti), Sov. Un. (chĭr-nôf′tsĕ) (chĕr-nou′tsĕ)	165	48.18 N	25.56 E
Chernyanka, Sov. Un. (chĕrn-yäŋ′kä)	173	50.56 N	37.48 E
Cherokee, Ia. (chĕr-ô-kē′)	112	42.43 N	95.33 W
Cherokee, Ks.	121	37.21 N	94.50 W
Cherokee, Ok.	120	36.44 N	98.22 W
Cherokee (L.), Tn.	124	36.22 N	83.22 W
Cherokee Indian Res., NC	124	35.33 N	83.12 W
Cherokee Sound Ba.	132	26.15 N	76.55 W
Cherokees, L. of the, Ok. (chĕr-ô-kēz′)	121	36.32 N	95.14 W
Cherryfield, Me. (chĕr′ĭ-fēld)	102	44.37 N	67.56 W
Cherry Grove, Or.	116c	45.27 N	123.15 W
Cherryvale, Ks.	121	37.16 N	95.33 W
Cherryville, NC (chĕr′ĭ-vĭl)	125	35.32 N	81.22 W
Cherskogo, Khrebet (Mts.), Sov. Un.	179	66.15 N	138.30 E
Cherven′, Sov. Un. (chĕr′vyĕn)	172	53.43 N	28.26 E
Chervonoye (L.), Sov. Un. (chĕr-vô′nô-yĕ)	172	52.24 N	28.12 E
Chesaning, Mi. (chĕs′á-nĭng)	108	43.10 N	84.10 W
Chesapeake, Va. (chĕs′á-pēk)	110g	36.48 N	76.16 W
Chesapeake B., Md.	109	38.20 N	76.15 W
Chesapeake Beach, Md.	110e	38.42 N	76.33 W
Chesham, Eng. (chĕsh′ŭm)	154b	51.41 N	0.37 W
Cheshire, Mi. (chĕsh′ĭr)	108	42.25 N	86.00 W
Cheshire (Co.), Eng.	154	53.16 N	2.30 W
Chëshskaya Guba (B.), Sov. Un.	176	67.25 N	46.00 E
Chesma, Sov. Un. (chĕs′má)	180a	53.50 N	60.42 E
Chesnokovka, Sov. Un. (chĕs-nŏ-kôf′ká)	178	53.28 N	83.41 E
Chester, Eng. (chĕs′tēr)	154	53.12 N	2.53 W
Chester, Il.	121	37.54 N	89.48 W
Chester, Pa.	110f	39.51 N	75.22 W
Chester, SC	125	34.42 N	81.11 W
Chester, Va.	125	37.20 N	77.24 W
Chester, WV	108	40.35 N	80.30 W
Chesterfield, Eng. (chĕs′tēr-fēld)	154	53.14 N	1.26 W
Chesterfield, Îles, N. Cal.	211	19.38 S	160.08 E
Chesterfield (Inlet), Can.	94	63.59 N	92.09 W
Chesterfield Inlet, Can.	94	63.19 N	91.11 W
Chestermere L., Can. (chĕs′tē-mēr)	93e	51.03 N	113.45 W
Chesterton, In. (chĕs′tēr-tŭn)	108	41.35 N	87.05 W
Chestertown, Md. (chĕs′tēr-toun)	109	39.15 N	76.05 W
Chesuncook (L.), Me. (chĕs′ŭn-ko͝ok)	102	46.03 N	69.40 W
Chetek, Wi. (chĕ′tĕk)	113	45.18 N	91.41 W
Chetumal, Bahía de (B.), Belize (bä-ē-ä dĕ chĕt-ōō-mäl′)	130a	18.07 N	88.05 W
Chevelon Cr., Az. (shĕv′á-lŏn)	119	34.35 N	111.00 W
Cheviot, Oh. (shĕv′ĭ-ŭt)	111f	39.10 N	84.37 W
Chevreuse, Fr. (shĕ-vrûz′)	167b	48.42 N	2.02 E
Chevy Chase, Md. (shĕvĭ chās)	110e	38.58 N	77.06 W
Chew Bahir (Lake Stefanie), Eth. (stĕf-a-nē)	221	4.46 N	37.31 E
Chewelah, Wa. (chē-wē′lä)	114	48.17 N	117.42 W
Cheyenne, Wy. (shī-ĕn′)	112	41.10 N	104.49 W
Cheyenne (R.), SD	112	44.20 N	102.15 W
Cheyenne River Ind. Res., SD	112	45.07 N	100.46 W
Cheyenne Wells, Co.	120	38.46 N	102.21 W
Chhindwāra, India	190	22.08 N	78.57 E
Chiai, Taiwan (chī′ī′)	199	23.28 N	120.28 E
Chiang Mai, Thai.	194	18.38 N	98.44 E
Chiang Rai, Thai.	202	19.53 N	99.48 E
Chianje, Ang.	226	15.45 S	13.48 E
Chiapa, Rio de (R.), Mex. (rē′ō-dĕ-chē-ä′pä)	130	16.00 N	92.20 W
Chiapa de Corzo, Mex. (chē-ä′pä dä kôr′zō)	129	16.44 N	93.01 W
Chiapas (State), Mex. (chē-ä′päs)	126	17.10 N	93.00 W
Chiapas, Cordilla de (Mts.), Mex. (kôr-dĕl-yĕ′rä-dĕ-chyá′räs)	129	15.55 N	93.15 W
Chiari, It. (kyä′rē)	170	45.31 N	9.57 E
Chiasso, Switz.	164	45.50 N	8.57 E
Chiautla, Mex. (chyä-ōōt′lä)	128	18.16 N	98.37 W
Chiavari, It. (kyä-vä′rē)	170	44.18 N	9.21 E
Chiba, Jap. (chē′bä)	201a	35.37 N	140.08 E
Chiba (Pref.), Jap.	201a	35.47 N	140.02 E
Chibougamau, Can. (chē-bōō′gä-mou)	101	49.57 N	74.23 W
Chibougamau (L.), Can.	101	49.53 N	74.21 W
Chicago, Il. (shĭ-kô-gō) (chĭ-kä′gō)	111a	41.49 N	87.37 W
Chicago Heights, Il.	111a	41.30 N	87.38 W
Chicapa (R.), Ang. (chē-kä′pä)	226	7.45 S	20.25 E
Chicbul, Mex. (chēk-bōō′l)	129	18.45 N	90.56 W
Chic-Chocs, Mts., Can.	102	48.38 N	66.37 W

ăt; finăl; rāte; senăte; ärm; åsk; sofá; fâre; ch-choose; dh-as th in other; bē; ėvent; bĕt; recĕnt; cratēr; g-gō; gh-guttural g; bĭt; ĭ-short neutral; rīde; ĸ-guttural k as ch in German ich;

PRONOUNCING INDEX

Chichagof – Cinto 279

PLACE (Pronunciation)	PAGE	Lat. °′	Long. °′
Chichagof (I.), Ak. (chē-chä'gôf)	105	57.50 N	137.00 W
Chichâncanab, Lago de (L.), Mex. (lä'gô-dĕ-chē-chän-kä-nä'b)	130a	19.50 N	88.28 W
Chichen Itzá (Ruins), Mex. (chē-chĕ'n-ē-tsä')	130a	20.38 N	88.35 W
Chichester, Eng. (chĭch'ĕs-tẽr)	160	50.50 N	0.55 W
Chichimila, Mex. (chē-chē-mē'lä)	130a	20.36 N	88.14 W
Chichiriviche, Ven. (chē-chē-rē-vē-chĕ)	141b	10.56 N	68.17 W
Chickamauga, Ga. (chĭk-ȧ-mô'gȧ)	124	34.50 N	85.15 W
Chickamauga, (L.), Tn.	124	35.18 N	85.22 W
Chickasawhay (R.), Ms. (chĭk-ȧ-sô'wā)	124	31.45 N	88.45 W
Chickasha, Ok. (chĭk'ȧ-shā)	120	35.04 N	97.56 W
Chiclana de la Frontera, Sp. (chē-klä'nä)	168	36.25 N	6.09 W
Chiclayo, Peru (chē-klä'yō)	140	6.46 S	79.50 W
Chico, Ca. (chē'kō)	118	39.43 N	121.51 W
Chico, Wa.	116a	47.37 N	122.43 W
Chico (R.), Arg.	142	44.30 S	66.00 W
Chico (R.), Arg.	142	49.15 S	69.30 W
Chico (R.), Phil.	203a	17.33 N	121.24 E
Chicoa, Moz.	227	15.37 S	32.24 E
Chicoloapan, Mex. (chē-kō-lwä'pän)	129a	19.24 N	98.54 W
Chiconautla, Mex. (chē-kō-nä-o͞o'tlä)	129a	19.39 N	99.01 W
Chicontepec, Mex. (chē-kōn'tĕ-pĕk')	128	20.58 N	98.08 W
Chicopee, Ma. (chĭk'ō-pē)	109	42.10 N	72.35 W
Chicoutimi, Can. (shē-ko͞o'tē-mē')	101	48.26 N	71.04 W
Chicxulub, Mex. (chēk-so͞o-lo͞o'b)	130a	21.10 N	89.30 W
Chidley, C., Can. (chĭd'lĭ)	95	60.32 N	63.56 W
Chief Joseph Dam, Wa.	114	48.00 N	119.39 W
Chiefland, Fl. (chēf'lȧnd)	124	29.30 N	82.50 W
Chiemsee (L.), F.R.G. (ĸēm zā)	164	47.58 N	12.20 E
Chieri, It. (kyâ'rē)	170	45.03 N	7.48 E
Chieti, It. (kyĕ'tē)	170	42.22 N	14.22 E
Chifeng (Ulanhad), China (chr-fŭŋ)	198	42.18 N	118.52 E
Chigirin, Sov. Un. (chē-gē'rĕn)	173	49.02 N	32.39 E
Chignanuapan, Mex. (chē'g-ŋä-nwä-pá'n)	128	19.49 N	98.02 W
Chignecto B., Can. (shĭg-nĕk'tō)	102	45.33 N	64.50 W
Chignik, Ak. (chĭg'nĭk)	105	56.14 N	158.12 W
Chignik B., Ak.	105	56.18 N	157.22 W
Chigu Co (L.), China (chr-go͞o tswo)	190	28.55 N	91.47 E
Chihe, China (chr-hŭ)	196	32.32 N	117.57 E
Chihuahua, Mex. (chē-wä'wä)	122	28.37 N	106.06 W
Chihuahua (State), Mex.	126	29.00 N	107.30 W
Chikishlyar, Sov. Un. (chē-kēsh-lyär')	177	37.40 N	53.50 E
Chilanga, Zambia	227	15.34 S	28.17 E
Chilapa, Mex. (chē-lä'pä)	128	17.34 N	99.14 W
Chilchota, Mex. (chēl-chō'tä)	128	19.40 N	102.04 W
Chilcotin (R.), Can. (chĭl-kō'tĭn)	96	52.20 N	124.15 W
Childress, Tx. (chīld'rĕs)	120	34.26 N	100.11 W
Chile, S.A. (chē'lā)	138	35.00 S	72.00 W
Chilecito, Arg. (chē-lā-sē'tō)	142	29.06 S	67.25 W
Chilengue, Serra do (Mts.), Ang.	226	13.20 S	15.00 E
Chilí, Pico de (Pk.), Col. (pē'kō-dĕ chē-lē')	140a	4.14 N	75.38 W
Chilibre, Pan. (chē-lē'brĕ)	126a	9.09 N	79.37 W
Chililabombwe (Bancroft), Zambia	227	12.18 S	27.43 E
Chilka (L.), India	190	19.26 N	85.42 E
Chilko (R.), Can. (chĭl'kō)	96	51.53 N	123.53 W
Chilko L., Can.	96	51.20 N	124.05 W
Chillán, Chile (chēl-yän')	142	36.44 S	72.06 W
Chillicothe, Il. (chĭl-ĭ-kŏth'ē)	108	41.55 N	89.30 W
Chillicothe, Mo.	121	39.46 N	93.32 W
Chillicothe, Oh.	108	39.20 N	83.00 W
Chilliwack, Can. (chĭl'ĭ-wăk)	97	49.10 N	121.57 W
Chiloé, Isla de (I.), Chile (ē's-lä-dĕ-chē-lô-ā')	142	43.00 S	75.00 W
Chilpancingo, Mex. (chēl-pän-sēŋ'gō)	128	17.32 N	99.30 W
Chilton, Wi. (chĭl'tŭn)	113	44.00 N	88.12 W
Chilung (Kirin), Taiwan (chĭ'lung)	199	25.02 N	121.48 E
Chilwa, L. Malawi-Moz.	227	15.12 S	36.30 E
Chimacum, Wa. (chĭm'ä-kŭm)	116a	48.01 N	122.47 W
Chimalpa, Mex. (chē-mäl'pä)	129a	19.26 N	99.22 W
Chimaltenango, Guat. (chē-mäl-tĕ-näŋ'gō)	130	14.39 N	90.48 W
Chimaltitan, Mex. (chēmäl-tē-tän')	128	21.36 N	103.50 W
Chimbay, Sov. Un. (chĭm-bī')	153	43.00 N	59.44 E
Chimborazo (Mtn.), Ec. (chēm-bô-rä'zō)	140	1.35 S	78.45 W
Chimbote, Peru (chēm-bō'tå)	140	9.02 S	78.33 W
Chimkent, Sov. Un. (chĭm-kĕnt)	178	42.17 N	69.42 E
China, Asia (chī'nȧ)	188	36.45 N	93.00 E
China, Mex. (chē'nä)	122	25.43 N	99.13 W
Chinameca, Sal. (Chē-nä-mā'kä)	130	13.31 N	88.18 W
Chinandega, Nic. (chē-nän-dā'gä)	130	12.38 N	87.08 W
Chinati Pk., Tx. (chĭ-nä'tē)	122	29.56 N	104.29 W
Chincha Alta, Peru (chĭn'chä äl'tä)	140	13.24 S	76.04 W
Chinchas, Islas (Is.), Peru (ē's-läs-chē'n-chäs)	140	11.27 S	79.05 W
Chinchilla, Austl. (chĭn-chĭl'ȧ)	212	26.44 S	150.36 E
Chinchorro, Banco (Bk.), Mex. (bä'n-kō-chēn-chô'r-rō)	130a	18.43 N	87.25 W
Chincilla de Monte Aragon, Sp.	168	38.54 N	1.43 W
Chinde, Moz. (shĕn'dĕ)	222	17.39 S	36.34 E
Chin Do (I.), Kor.	200	34.30 N	125.43 E
Chindwin R., Bur. (chĭn-dwĭn)	194	23.30 N	94.34 E
Chingola, Zambia (chĭng-gōlä)	227	12.32 S	27.52 E
Chinguar, Ang. (chĭng-gär)	222	12.35 S	16.15 E
Chinguetti, Mauritania (chēŋ-gĕt'ē)	220	20.34 N	12.34 W
Chinju, Kor. (chĭn'jo͞o)	200	35.13 N	128.10 E
Chinko (R.), Cen. Afr. Rep. (shĭn'kô)	221	6.37 N	24.31 E
Chinmen, see Quemoy			
Chino, Ca. (chē'nō)	117a	34.01 N	117.42 W
Chinon, Fr. (shē-nôɴ')	166	47.09 N	0.13 E
Chinook, Mt. (shĭn-o͝ok')	115	48.35 N	109.15 W
Chinook, Wa. (shĭn-o͝ok')	116c	46.17 N	123.57 W
Chinsali, Zambia	227	10.34 S	32.03 E
Chinteche, Malawi (chĭn-tĕ'chĕ)	222	11.48 S	34.14 E
Chioggia, It. (kyôd'jä)	170	45.12 N	12.17 E
Chipata, Zambia	227	13.39 S	32.40 E
Chipera, Moz. (zhē-pĕ'rä)	222	15.16 S	32.30 E
Chipley, Fl. (chĭp'lĭ)	124	30.45 N	85.33 W
Chipman, Can. (chĭp'mȧn)	102	46.11 N	65.53 W
Chipola (R.), Fl. (chĭ-pō'lȧ)	124	30.40 N	85.14 W
Chippawa, Can. (chĭp'ē-wä)	111c	43.03 N	79.03 W
Chippewa (R.), Mn. (chĭp'ē-wä)	112	45.07 N	95.41 W
Chippewa (R.), Wi.	113	45.07 N	91.19 W
Chippewa Falls, Wi.	113	44.55 N	91.26 W
Chippewa Lake, Oh.	111d	41.04 N	81.54 W
Chiputneticook L., Can. (chĭ-po͞ot-nĕt'ĭ-ko͝ok)	102	45.47 N	67.45 W
Chiquimula, Guat. (chē-kē-mo͞o'lä)	130	14.47 N	89.31 W
Chiquimulilla, Guat. (chē-kē-mo͞o-lē'l-yä)	130	14.08 N	90.23 W
Chiquinquira, Col. (chē-kēŋ'kē-rä')	140	5.33 N	73.49 W
Chiquita, Laguna Mar (L.), Arg. (lä-go͞o'nä-mär-chē-kē'tä)	139c	34.25 S	61.10 W
Chirald, India	191	15.52 N	80.22 E
Chirchik, Sov. Un. (chĭr-chēk')	178	41.28 N	69.18 E
Chire (R.), Moz.	227	17.15 S	35.25 E
Chiricahua Natl. Mon., Az. (chĭ-rä-cä'hwä)	119	32.02 N	109.18 W
Chirikof (I.), Ak. (chĭ'rĭ-kôf)	105	55.50 N	155.35 W
Chiriquí, Golfo de (G.), Pan. (gôl-fô-dĕ-chē-rē-kē')	131	7.56 N	82.18 W
Chiriquí, Laguna de (L.), Pan. (lä-go͞o'nä-dĕ-chē-rē-kē')	131	9.06 N	82.02 W
Chiriqui, Punta (Pt.), Pan. (po͞o'n-tä-chē-rē-kē')	131	9.13 N	81.39 W
Chiriquí Grande, Pan. (chē-rē-kē' grän'dā)	131	8.57 N	82.08 W
Chiri San (Mt.), Kor. (chĭ'rĭ-sän')	200	35.20 N	127.39 E
Chiromo, Malawi	222	16.34 S	35.13 E
Chirpan, Bul.	171	42.12 N	25.19 E
Chirripó, Cerro (Mtn.), C. R. (chē-rē'pō)	131	9.30 N	83.31 W
Chirripo, Rio (R.), C. R.	131	9.50 N	83.20 W
Chisholm, Mn. (chĭz'ŭm)	113	47.28 N	92.53 W
Chistopol', Sov. Un. (chĭs-tô'pôl-y')	176	55.18 N	50.30 E
Chita, Sov. Un. (chē-tá')	179	52.09 N	113.39 E
Chitambo, Zambia	227	12.55 S	30.39 E
Chitembo, Ang.	226	13.34 S	16.40 E
Chitina, Ak. (chĭ-tē'nȧ)	105	61.28 N	144.35 W
Chitokoloki, Zambia	226	13.50 S	23.13 E
Chitorgarh, India	190	24.59 N	74.42 E
Chitrāl, Pak. (chē-träl')	190	35.58 N	71.48 E
Chitré, Pan. (chē'trâ)	131	7.59 N	80.26 W
Chittagong, Bngl. (chĭt-á-gông')	190	22.26 N	90.51 E
Chiumbe (R.), Ang. (chē-o͞om'bå)	226	9.05 S	21.00 E
Chivasso, It. (kē-väs'sō)	170	45.13 N	7.52 E
Chivilcoy, Arg. (chē-vēl-koi')	139c	34.51 S	60.03 W
Chixoy (R.), Guat. (chē-ĸoi')	130	15.40 N	90.35 W
Chizu, Jap. (chē-zo͞o')	201	35.16 N	134.15 E
Chloride, Az. (klō'rīd)	119	35.25 N	114.15 W
Chmielnik, Pol. (ĸmyĕl'nĕĸ)	165	50.36 N	20.46 E
Choapa (R.), Chile (chô-á'pä)	139b	31.56 S	70.48 W
Chocó (Dept.), Col. (chô-kô')	140a	5.33 N	76.28 W
Choctawhatchee, B., Fl. (chôk-tô-hăch'ē)	124	30.15 N	86.32 W
Choctawhatchee (R.), Fl.-Ga.	124	30.37 N	85.56 W
Chodziez, Pol. (ĸôj'yĕsh)	164	52.59 N	16.55 E
Choele Choel, Arg. (chô-ĕ'lĕ-chôĕ'l)	142	39.14 S	66.46 W
Chōfu, Jap. (chō'fo͞o')	201a	35.39 N	139.33 E
Chōgo, Jap. (chō-gō)	201a	35.25 N	139.28 E
Choiseul, (I.), Sol. Is. (shwä-zûl')	211	7.30 S	157.30 E
Chojnice, Pol. (ĸōi-nē-tsĕ)	165	53.41 N	17.34 E
Cholet, Fr. (shô-lĕ')	166	47.06 N	0.54 W
Cholula, Mex. (chō-lo͞o'lä)	128	19.04 N	98.19 W
Choluteca, Hond. (chō-lo͞o-tā'kä)	130	13.18 N	87.12 W
Choluteco (R.), Hond.-Nic.	130	13.34 N	86.59 W
Chomutov, Czech. (kō'mo͞o-tôf)	164	50.27 N	13.23 E
Chona (R.), Sov. Un. (chō'nä)	179	60.45 N	109.15 E
Chone, Ec. (chô'nĕ)	140	0.48 S	80.06 W
Chŏngjin, Kor. (chŭng-jĭn')	200	41.48 N	129.46 E
Chŏngju, Kor. (chŭng-jo͞o')	200	36.35 N	127.30 E
Chongming Dao (I.), China (chôŋ-mĭŋ dou)	199	31.40 N	122.30 E
Chongqing, China (chôŋ-chyĭŋ)	199	29.38 N	107.30 E
Chŏnju, Kor. (chŭn-jo͞o')	200	35.48 N	127.08 E
Chorley, Eng. (chôr'lĭ)	154	53.40 N	2.38 W
Chornaya, Sov. Un.	180b	55.45 N	38.04 E
Chorrillos, Peru (chôr-rē'l-yōs)	140	12.17 S	76.55 W
Chortkov, Sov. Un. (chôrt'kôf)	165	49.01 N	25.48 E
Chosan, Kor. (chō-sän')	200	40.44 N	125.48 E
Chosen, Fl. (chō'z'n)	125a	26.41 N	80.41 W
Chōshi, Jap. (chō'shē)	200	35.40 N	140.55 E
Choszczno, Pol. (chôsh'chnô)	164	53.10 N	15.25 E
Chota Nagpur (Reg.), India	190	23.40 N	82.50 E
Choteau, Mt. (shō'tō)	115	47.51 N	112.10 W
Chowan (R.), NC (chô-wän')	125	36.13 N	76.46 W
Chowilla Res., Austl.	212	34.05 S	141.20 E
Chown, Mt., Can. (choun)	97	53.24 N	119.22 W
Choybalsan, Mong.	198	47.50 N	114.15 E
Christchurch, N.Z. (krīst'chûrch)	213	43.30 S	172.38 E
Christian (I.), Can. (krĭs'chăn)	108	44.50 N	80.00 W
Christiansburg, Va. (krĭs'chănz-bûrg)	125	37.08 N	80.25 W
Christiansted, Vir. Is. (U.S.A.)	127b	17.45 N	64.44 W
Christmas (I.), Oceania,	205	2.20 N	157.40 W
Christmas I., Austl.	202	10.35 S	105.40 E
Christopher, Il. (krĭs'tô-fẽr)	121	37.58 N	89.04 W
Chrudim, Czech. (ĸro͞o'dyĕm)	164	49.57 N	15.46 E
Chrzanów, Pol. (ĸzhä'no͞of)	165	50.08 N	19.24 E
Chuansha, China (chůän-shä)	197b	31.12 N	121.41 E
Chubut (Prov.), Arg. (cho͞o-bo͞ot')	142	44.00 S	69.15 W
Chubut (R.), Arg. (cho͞o-bo͞ot')	142	43.05 S	69.00 W
Chuckatuck, Va. (chŭck á-tŭck)	110g	36.51 N	76.35 W
Chucunaque (R.), Pan. (cho͞o-ko͞o-nä'kâ)	131	8.36 N	77.48 W
Chudovo, Sov. Un. (cho͞o'dô-vô)	172	59.03 N	31.56 E
Chudskoye Oz. (Peipus, L.), Sov. Un. (cho͞ot'skô-yĕ)	172	58.43 N	26.45 E
Chuguchak (Reg.), China (cho͞o'go͞o-chäk')	194	46.09 N	83.58 E
Chuguyev, Sov. Un. (cho͞o'go͞o-yĕf)	173	49.52 N	36.40 E
Chuguyevka, Sov. Un. (cho͞o-go͞o'yĕf-kȧ)	200	43.58 N	133.49 E
Chugwater Cr., Wy. (chŭg'wô-tẽr)	112	41.43 N	104.54 W
Chukot Natl. Okrug (Reg.), Sov. Un.	179	68.15 N	170.00 E
Chukotskiy (Chukot) P-Ov (Pen.), Sov. Un.	179	66.12 N	175.00 W
Chukotskoye Nagor'ye (Mts.), Sov. Un.	179	66.00 N	166.00 E
Chula Vista, Ca. (cho͞o'lá vĭs'tá)	118a	32.38 N	117.05 W
Chulkovo, Sov. Un. (cho͞ol-kô vô)	180b	55.33 N	38.04 E
Chulucanas, Peru (cho͞o-lo͞o-kä'näs)	140	5.13 S	80.13 W
Chulum (R.), Sov. Un.	178	57.52 N	84.45 E
Chumikan, Sov. Un. (cho͞o-mē-kän')	179	54.47 N	135.09 E
Chun'an, China (cho͞on-än)	199	29.38 N	119.00 E
Chunchŏn, Kor. (cho͞on-chŭn')	200	37.51 N	127.46 E
Chungju, Kor. (chŭng'jo͞o')	200	37.00 N	128.19 E
Chunya, Tan.	227	8.32 S	33.25 E
Chunya (R.), Sov. Un. (cho͞on'yä')	178	61.45 N	101.28 E
Chuquicamata, Chile (cho͞o-kē-kä-mä'tä)	142	22.08 S	68.57 W
Chur, Switz. (ko͞or)	164	46.51 N	9.32 E
Churchill, Can. (chûrch'ĭl)	94	58.50 N	94.10 W
Churchill, C., Can.	94	59.07 N	93.50 W
Churchill (R.), Can.	99	57.20 N	96.30 W
Churchill Falls, Can.	95	53.35 N	64.27 W
Churchill L., Can.	98	56.12 N	108.40 W
Churchill Pk., Can.	94	58.10 N	125.14 W
Church Stretton, Eng. (chûrch strĕt'ŭn)	154	52.32 N	2.49 W
Churchton, Md.	110e	38.49 N	76.33 W
Churu, India	190	28.22 N	75.00 E
Churumuco, Mex. (cho͞o-ro͞o-mo͞o'kō)	128	18.39 N	101.40 W
Chuska Mts., Az.-NM (chŭs-kȧ)	119	36.21 N	109.11 W
Chusovaya R., Sov. Un. (cho͞o-sô-vä'yȧ)	180a	58.08 N	58.35 E
Chusovoy, Sov. Un. (cho͞o-sô-vôy')	180a	58.18 N	57.50 E
Chust, Sov. Un. (cho͞ost)	178	41.05 N	71.28 E
Chuvash A. S. S. R., Sov. Un. (cho͞o'vȧsh)	176	55.45 N	46.00 E
Chuviscar (R.), Mex. (cho͞o-vēs-kär')	122	28.34 N	105.36 W
Chuwang, China (cho͞o-wäŋ)	196	36.08 N	114.53 E
Chu Xian, China (cho͞o shyĕn)	196	32.19 N	118.19 E
Chuxiong, China (cho͞o-shyôŋ)	194	25.19 N	101.34 E
Cicero, Il. (sĭs'ẽr-ō)	111a	41.50 N	87.46 W
Cide, Pur. (jē'dĕ)	177	41.50 N	33.00 E
Ciechanów, Pol. (tsyĕ-kä'no͞of)	165	52.52 N	20.39 E
Ciego de Avila, Cuba (syā'gō dā ä'vē-lä)	132	21.50 N	78.45 W
Ciego de Avila (Prov.), Cuba	132	22.00 N	78.40 W
Ciempozuelos, Sp. (thyĕm-pô-thwā'lōs)	168	40.09 N	3.36 W
Ciénaga, Col. (syā'nä-gä)	140	11.01 N	74.15 W
Cienfuegos, Cuba (syĕn-fwā'gōs)	132	22.10 N	80.30 W
Cienfuegos (Prov.), Cuba	132	22.15 N	80.40 W
Cienfuegos, Bahía (B.), Cuba (bä-ē'ä-syĕn-fwā'gōs)	132	22.00 N	80.35 W
Ciervo, Isla de la (I.), Nic. (ē's-lä-dĕ-lä-syĕ'r-vō)	131	11.56 N	83.20 W
Cieszyn, Pol. (tsyĕ'shĕn)	165	49.47 N	18.45 E
Cieza, Sp. (thyā'thä)	168	38.13 N	1.25 W
Cigüela (R.), Sp.	168	39.53 N	2.54 W
Cihuatlán, Mex. (sē-wä-tlá'n)	128	19.13 N	104.36 W
Cihuatlán (R.), Mex.	128	19.11 N	104.30 W
Cijara, Embalse de (Res.), Sp.	168	39.25 N	5.00 W
Cilician Gates P.), Tur.	177	37.30 N	35.30 E
Cimarron (R.), North Fk., Co.	120	37.13 N	102.30 W
Cimarron R., U.S. (sĭm-ȧ-rōn')	106	36.26 N	98.27 W
Cîmpina, Rom.	171	45.08 N	25.47 E
Cîmpulung, Rom.	171	45.15 N	25.03 E
Cîmpulung Moldovenesc, Rom.	165	47.31 N	25.36 E
Cinca (R.), Sp. (thēŋ'kä)	169	42.09 N	0.08 E
Cincinnati, Oh. (sĭn-sĭ-nát'ĭ)	111f	39.08 N	84.30 W
Cinco Balas, Cayos (Is.), Cuba (kä'yōs-thēŋ'kō bä'läs)	132	21.05 N	79.25 W
Cintalapa, Mex. (sĕn-tä-lä'pä)	129	16.41 N	93.44 W
Cinto, Mt., Fr. (chēn'tō)	170	42.24 N	8.54 E

ng-sing; ŋ-baŋk; ɴ-nasalized n; nŏd; cŏmmit; ōld; ôbey; ôrder; oi-boil; fo͞od; fo͝ot; ou-out; s-soft; sh-dish; th-thin; pūre; ûnite; ûrn; stŭd; circŭs; ü-as in French tu; '-indeterminate vowel.

PLACE (Pronunciation)	PAGE	Lat. °'	Long. °'
Circle, Ak. (sûr'k'l)	105	65.49 N	144.22 W
Circleville, Oh. (sûr'k'lvĭl)	108	39.35 N	83.00 W
Cirebon, Indon.	202	6.50 S	108.33 E
Cisco, Tx. (sĭs'kō)	122	32.23 N	98.57 W
Cisneros, Col. (sēs-nĕ'rôs)	140a	6.33 N	75.05 W
Cisterna di Latina, It. (chēs-tĕ'r-nä-dē-lä-tē'nä)	169d	41.36 N	12.53 E
Cistierna, Sp. (thēs-tyĕr'nä)	168	42.48 N	5.08 W
Citlaltépetl (Vol.), Mex. (sē-tlăl-tĕ'pĕtl)	129	19.04 N	97.14 W
Citronelle, Al. (cĭt-rô'nĕl)	124	31.05 N	88.15 W
Cittadella, It. (chēt-tä-dĕl'lä)	170	45.39 N	11.51 E
Città di Castello, It. (chēt-tä'dē käs-tĕl'lō)	170	43.27 N	12.17 E
Ciudad Altamirano, Mex. (syōō-dä'd-äl-tä-mē-rä'nō)	128	18.24 N	100.38 W
Ciudad Bolívar, Ven. (syōō-dhädh' bô-lē'vär)	140	8.07 N	63.41 W
Ciudad Camargo (Santa Rosalia), Mex. (syōō-dhädh' kä-mär'gō) (sän'tà rō-sä'lēä)	122	27.42 N	105.10 W
Ciudad Chetumal (Payo Obispo), Mex. (syōō-dhädh' chĕt-ōō-mäl) (pä'yō ô-bēs'pō)	130a	18.30 N	88.17 W
Ciudad Darío, Nic. (syōō-dhädh'dä'rē-ō)	130	12.44 N	86.08 W
Ciudad de la Habana (Prov.), Cuba	132	23.20 N	82.10 W
Ciudad de las Casas, Mex. (syōō-dä'd-dē-lä-kà'säs)	129	16.44 N	92.39 W
Ciudad del Carmen, Mex. (syōō-dä'd-dĕl-kà'r-mĕn)	129	18.39 N	91.49 W
Ciudad del Maíz, Mex. (syōō-dhädh'del mä-ēz')	128	22.24 N	99.37 W
Ciudad de Valles, Mex. (syōō-dhädh'dā väl'yās)	128	21.59 N	99.02 W
Ciudadela, Sp. (thyōō-dhä-dhā'lä)	169	40.00 N	3.52 E
Ciudad Fernández, Mex. (syōō-dhädh'fĕr-nän'dĕz)	128	21.56 N	100.03 W
Ciudad García Mex. (syōō-dhädh'gär-sē'ä)	128	22.39 N	103.02 W
Ciudad Guayana Ven.	140	8.30 N	62.45 W
Ciudad Guzmán, Mex. (syōō-dhädh'gōōz-män)	128	19.40 N	103.29 W
Ciudad Hidalgo, Mex. (syōō-dä'd-ē-dä'l-gō)	128	19.41 N	100.35 W
Ciudad Juárez, Mex. (syōō-dhädh hwä'räz)	123	31.44 N	106.28 W
Ciudad Madero, Mex. (syōō-dä'd-mä-dĕ'rô)	129	22.16 N	97.52 W
Ciudad Mante, Mex. (syōō-dä'd-màn'tĕ)	128	22.34 N	98.58 W
Ciudad Manuel Doblado, Mex. (syōō-dä'd-män-wäl'dō-blä'dō)	128	20.43 N	101.57 W
Ciudad Obregón, Mex. (syōō-dhädh-ô-brē-gô'n)	126	27.40 N	109.58 W
Ciudad Real, Sp. (thyōō-dhädh'rā-äl')	168	38.59 N	3.55 W
Ciudad Rodrigo, Sp. (thyōō-dhädh'rô-drē'gō)	168	40.38 N	6.34 W
Ciudad Serdán, Mex. (syōō-dä'd-sĕr-dà'n)	129	18.58 N	97.26 W
Ciudad Victoria, Mex. (syōō-dhädh'vēk-tō'rē-ä)	128	23.43 N	99.09 W
Civitavecchia, It. (chē'vē-tä-vĕk'kyä)	170	42.06 N	11.49 E
Ci Xian, China (tsē shyĕn)	196	36.22 N	114.23 E
Clackamas, Or. (klăc-kà'măs)	116c	45.25 N	122.34 W
Claire (L.), Can. (klâr)	94	58.33 N	113.16 W
Clair Engle L., Ca.	114	40.51 N	122.41 W
Clairton, Pa. (klârtŭn)	111e	40.17 N	79.53 W
Clanton, Al. (klăn'tŭn)	124	32.50 N	86.38 W
Clare, Mi. (klâr)	108	43.50 N	84.45 W
Clare I., Ire.	160	53.46 N	10.00 W
Claremont, Ca. (klâr'mŏnt)	117a	34.06 N	117.43 W
Claremont, NH (klâr'mŏnt)	109	43.20 N	72.20 W
Claremont, WV	108	37.55 N	81.00 W
Claremore, Ok. (klâr'mōr)	121	36.16 N	95.37 W
Claremorris, Ire. (klâr-mŏr'ĭs)	160	53.46 N	9.05 W
Clarence Str., Ak.	96	55.25 N	132.00 W
Clarence Str., Austl. (klăr'ĕns)	210	12.15 S	130.05 E
Clarence Town, Ba.	133	23.05 N	75.00 W
Clarendon, Ar. (klăr'ĕn-dŭn)	121	34.42 N	91.17 W
Clarendon, Tx.	120	34.55 N	100.52 W
Clarens, S. Afr. (clâ-rēns)	223c	28.34 S	28.26 E
Claresholm, Can. (klâr'ĕs-hōlm)	98	50.02 N	113.35 W
Clarinda, Ia. (klà-rĭn'dà)	113	40.42 N	95.00 W
Clarines, Ven. (klä-rē'nĕs)	141b	9.57 N	65.10 W
Clarion, Ia. (klăr'ĭ-ŭn)	113	42.43 N	93.45 W
Clarion, Pa.	109	41.10 N	79.25 W
Clark, SD (klärk)	112	44.52 N	97.45 W
Clark, Pt, Can.	108	44.05 N	81.50 W
Clarke City, Can.	102	50.12 N	66.38 W
Clarkdale, Az (klärk-dāl)	119	34.45 N	112.05 W
Clarke Ra, Austl.	211	20.30 S	148.00 E
Clark Fork (R.), Mt.	115	47.50 N	115.35 W
Clark Hill Res., Ga.-SC (klärk-hĭl)	125	33.50 N	82.35 W
Clarksburg, WV (klärkz'bûrg)	109	39.15 N	80.20 W
Clarksdale, Ms. (klärks-dāl)	124	34.10 N	90.31 W
Clark's Harbour, Can. (klärks)	102	43.26 N	65.38 W
Clarkston, Ga. (klärks'tŭn)	110c	33.49 N	84.15 W
Clarkston, Wa.	114	46.24 N	117.01 W
Clarksville, Ar. (klärks-vĭl)	121	35.28 N	93.26 W
Clarksville, Tn.	124	36.30 N	87.23 W
Clarksville, Tx.	121	33.37 N	95.02 W
Clatskanie, Or.	116c	46.04 N	123.11 W
Clatskanie (R.), Or. (klăt-skā'nē)	116c	46.06 N	123.11 W
Clatsop Spit, Or. (klăt-sŏp)	116c	46.13 N	124.04 W
Cláudio, Braz. (klou'-dēō)	139a	20.26 S	44.44 W
Claveria, Phil. (klä-vå-rē'ä)	199	18.38 N	121.08 E
Clawson, Mi. (klô's'n)	111b	42.32 N	83.09 W
Claxton, Ga. (klăks'tŭn)	125	32.07 N	81.54 W
Clay, Ky. (klā)	124	37.28 N	87.50 W
Clay Center, Ks. (klā sĕn'tēr)	121	39.23 N	97.08 W
Clay City, Ky. (klā sĭ'tĭ)	108	37.50 N	83.55 W
Claycomo, Mo. (kla-kō'mo)	113f	39.12 N	94.30 W
Clay Cross, Eng. (klā krŏs)	154	53.10 N	1.25 W
Claye-Souilly, Fr. (klĕ-sōō-yē')	167b	48.56 N	2.43 E
Claymont, De. (klā-mŏnt)	110f	39.48 N	75.28 W
Clayton, Al. (klā'tŭn)	124	31.52 N	85.25 W
Clayton, Ca.	116b	37.56 N	121.56 W
Clayton, Eng.	154	53.47 N	1.49 W
Clayton, Mo.	117e	38.39 N	90.20 W
Clayton, NM	120	36.26 N	103.12 W
Clayton, NC	125	35.40 N	78.27 W
Clear (L.), Ca.	118	39.05 N	122.50 W
Clear Boggy Cr., Ok. (klēr bŏg'ĭ krēk)	121	34.21 N	96.22 W
Clear Cr., Az.	119	34.40 N	111.05 W
Clear Cr., Tx.	123a	29.34 N	95.13 W
Clear Cr., Wy.	115	44.35 N	106.20 W
Clearfield, Pa. (klēr-fēld)	109	41.00 N	78.25 W
Clearfield, Ut.	117b	41.07 N	112.01 W
Clear Hills, Can.	94	57.11 N	119.20 W
Clear Lake, Ia.	113	43.09 N	93.23 W
Clear Lake, Wa.	116a	48.27 N	122.14 W
Clear Lake Res., Ca.	114	41.53 N	121.00 W
Clearwater, Fl. (klēr-wô'tēr)	125a	27.43 N	82.45 W
Clearwater (R.), Can.	97	52.00 N	114.50 W
Clearwater (R.), Can.	97	52.00 N	120.10 W
Clearwater (R.), Can.	98	56.10 N	110.40 W
Clearwater (R.), Id.	114	46.27 N	116.33 W
Clearwater (R.) Middle Fork, Id.	114	46.10 N	115.48 W
Clearwater (R.) North Fork, Id.	114	46.34 N	116.08 W
Clearwater (R.) South Fork, Id.	114	45.46 N	115.53 W
Clearwater Mts., Id.	114	45.56 N	115.15 W
Clearwater Res., Mo.	121	37.20 N	91.04 W
Cleburne, Tx. (klē'bŭrn)	123	32.21 N	97.23 W
Cle Elum, Wa. (klē ĕl'ŭm)	114	47.12 N	120.55 W
Clementon, NJ (klē'mĕn-tŭn)	110f	39.49 N	75.00 W
Cleobury Mortimer, Eng. (klēō-bĕr'ĭ môr'tĭ-mēr)	154	52.22 N	2.29 W
Clermont, Austl. (klēr'mŏnt)	211	23.02 S	147.46 E
Clermont, Can.	102	47.45 N	70.20 W
Clermont-Ferrand, Fr. (klĕr-môn'fĕr-rän')	166	45.47 N	3.03 E
Cleveland, Ms. (klēv'lănd)	124	33.45 N	90.42 W
Cleveland, Oh.	111d	41.30 N	81.42 W
Cleveland, Ok.	121	36.18 N	96.28 W
Cleveland, Tn.	124	35.09 N	84.52 W
Cleveland, Tx.	123	30.18 N	95.05 W
Cleveland Heights, Oh.	111d	41.30 N	81.35 W
Cleveland Pen., Ak.	96	55.45 N	132.00 W
Cleves, Oh. (klē'vĕs)	111f	39.10 N	84.45 W
Clew B., Ire. (klōō)	160	53.47 N	9.45 W
Clewiston, Fl. (klē'wis-tŭn)	125a	26.44 N	80.55 W
Clichy, Fr. (klē-shē')	167b	48.54 N	2.18 E
Clifden, Ire. (klĭf'dĕn)	160	53.31 N	10.04 W
Clifton, Az. (klĭf'tŭn)	119	33.05 N	109.20 W
Clifton, NJ	110a	40.52 N	74.09 W
Clifton, SC	125	35.00 N	81.47 W
Clifton, Tx.	123	31.45 N	97.31 W
Clifton Forge, Va.	109	37.50 N	79.50 W
Clinch (R.), Tn.-Va. (klĭnch)	124	36.30 N	83.19 W
Clingmans Dome (Mtn.), NC (klĭng'măns dōm)	124	35.37 N	83.26 W
Clinton, Can. (klĭn-'tŭn)	97	51.05 N	121.35 W
Clinton, Il.	108	40.10 N	88.55 W
Clinton, In.	108	39.40 N	87.25 W
Clinton, Ia.	113	41.50 N	90.13 W
Clinton, Ky.	124	36.39 N	88.56 W
Clinton, Md.	110e	38.46 N	76.54 W
Clinton, Ma.	103a	42.25 N	71.41 W
Clinton, Mo.	121	38.23 N	93.46 W
Clinton, NC	125	35.58 N	78.20 W
Clinton, Ok.	120	35.31 N	98.56 W
Clinton, SC	125	34.27 N	81.53 W
Clinton, Tn.	124	36.05 N	84.08 W
Clinton, Wa.	116a	47.59 N	122.22 W
Clinton-Colden (L.), Can.	94	63.58 N	106.34 W
Clinton R., Mi.	111b	42.36 N	83.00 W
Clintonville, Wi. (klĭn'tŭn-vĭl)	113	44.37 N	88.46 W
Clio, Mi. (klē'ō)	108	43.10 N	83.45 W
Cloates, Pt., Austl. (klōts)	210	22.47 S	113.45 E
Clocolan, S. Afr.	219d	28.56 S	27.35 E
Clonakilty B., Ire. (klŏn-à-kĭltē)	160	51.30 N	8.50 W
Cloncurry, Austl. (klŏn-kŭr'ē)	210	20.58 S	140.42 E
Clonmel, Ire. (klŏn-mĕl)	160	52.21 N	7.45 W
Cloquet, Mn. (klô-kā')	117h	46.42 N	92.28 W
Closter, NJ (klōs'tēr)	110a	40.58 N	73.57 W
Cloud Pk., Wy. (kloud)	115	44.23 N	107.11 W
Clover, SC (klō'vēr)	125	35.08 N	81.08 W
Clover Bar, Can. (klō'vēr băr)	93g	53.34 N	113.20 W
Cloverdale, Ca. (klō'vēr-dāl)	118	38.47 N	123.03 W
Cloverdale, Can.	116d	49.06 N	122.44 W
Cloverport, Ky. (klō'vēr pōrt)	108	37.50 N	86.35 W
Clovis, NM (klō'vĭs)	120	34.24 N	103.11 W
Cluj, Rom. (klōōzh)	165	46.46 N	23.34 E
Clun (R.), Eng. (klŭn)	154	52.25 N	2.56 W
Cluny, Fr. (klü-nē')	166	46.27 N	4.40 E
Clutha (R.), N.Z. (klōō'thà)	213	45.52 S	169.30 E
Clwyd (Co.), Wales	154	53.01 N	2.59 W
Clyde, Ks.	121	39.34 N	97.23 W
Clyde, Oh.	108	41.15 N	83.00 W
Clyde (R.), Scot.	160	55.35 N	3.50 W
Clyde, Firth of, Scot. (fûrth ŏv klīd)	160	55.28 N	5.01 W
Côa (R.), Port. (kō'ä)	168	40.28 N	6.55 W
Coacalco, Mex. (kō-ä-käl'kō)	129a	19.37 N	99.06 W
Coachella, Can., Ca. (kō'chĕl-là)	118	33.15 N	115.25 W
Coahuayana, Rio de (R.), Mex. (rē'ō-dĕ-kô-ä-wä-yà'nä)	128	19.00 N	103.33 W
Coahuayutla, Mex. (kō'ä-wī-yōōt'lä)	128	18.19 N	101.44 W
Coahuila (State), Mex. (kō-ä-wē'lä)	126	27.30 N	103.00 W
Coal City, Il. (kōl sĭ'tĭ)	111a	41.17 N	88.17 W
Coalcomán, Rio de (R.), Mex. (rē'ō-dĕ-kō-äl-kō-män')	128	18.45 N	103.15 W
Coalcomán, Sierra de (Mts.), Mex. (svĕr'rä dā kō-äl-kō-män')	128	18.30 N	102.45 W
Coalcomán de Matamoros, Mex. (kō-äl-kō-män'dä mä-tä-mō'rōs)	128	18.46 N	103.10 W
Coaldale, Can. (kōl'dāl)	98	49.43 N	112.37 W
Coaldale, Nv.	118	38.02 N	117.57 W
Coalgate, Ok. (kōl'gāt)	121	34.44 N	96.13 W
Coal Grove, Oh. (kōl grōv)	108	38.20 N	82.40 W
Coalinga, Ca. (kō-à-lĭŋ'gà)	118	36.09 N	120.23 W
Coalville, Eng. (kōl'vĭl)	154	52.43 N	1.21 W
Coamo, P.R. (kō-ä'mō)	127b	18.05 N	66.21 W
Coari, Braz. (kō-är'ē)	140	4.06 S	63.10 W
Coast Mts., Can. (kōst)	96	54.10 N	128.00 W
Coast Ranges (Mts.), U.S.	106	41.28 N	123.30 W
Coatepec, Mex. (kō-ä-tā-pĕk)	128	19.23 N	98.44 W
Coatepec, Mex.	129	19.26 N	96.56 W
Coatepec, Mex.	129d	19.08 N	99.25 W
Coatepeque, Guat. (kō-ä-tā-pā'kā)	130	14.40 N	91.52 W
Coatepeque, Sal.	130	13.56 N	89.30 W
Coatesville, Pa. (kōts'vĭl)	109	40.00 N	75.50 W
Coatetelco, Mex. (kō-ä-tā-tĕl'kō)	128	18.43 N	99.47 W
Coaticook, Can. (kō'tĭ-kōōk)	109	45.10 N	71.55 W
Coatlinchán, Mex. (kô-ä-tlē'n-chä'n)	129a	19.26 N	98.52 W
Coats (I.), Can. (kōts)	95	62.23 N	82.11 W
Coats Land (Reg.), Ant.	228	74.00 S	30.00 W
Coatzacoalcos (Puerto México), Mex. (kō-ät'zä-kō-äl'kōs) (pwĕ'r-tô-mĕ'-kē-kô)	129	18.09 N	94.26 W
Coatzacoalcos (R.), Mex.	129	17.40 N	94.41 W
Coba (Ruins), Mex. (kô'bä)	130a	20.23 N	87.23 W
Cobalt, Can. (kō'bôlt)	95	47.21 N	79.40 W
Cobán, Guat. (kō-bän')	130	15.28 N	90.19 W
Cobar, Austl.	212	31.28 S	145.50 E
Cobberas, Mt., Austl. (cŏ-bēr-ăs)	212	36.45 S	148.15 E
Cobequid Mts., Can.	102	45.35 N	64.10 W
Cobh, Ire. (kôv)	160	51.52 N	8.09 W
Cobija, Bol. (kō-bē'hä)	140	11.12 S	68.49 W
Cobourg, Can. (kō'bōōrgh)	109	43.55 N	78.05 W
Cobre (R.), Jam. (kō'brā)	132	18.05 N	77.00 W
Cóbuè, Moz.	227	12.04 S	34.50 E
Coburg, F.R.G. (kō'bōōrg)	164	50.16 N	10.57 E
Cocentaina, Sp. (kō-thān-tä-ē'nà)	169	38.44 N	0.27 W
Cochabamba, Bol. (kō-chä-bäm'bà)	140	17.30 S	66.08 W
Cochem, F.R.G. (kō'kĕm)	167	50.10 N	7.06 E
Cochin, India (kō-chĭn')	191	9.58 N	76.19 E
Cochinos, Bahia (B.), Cuba (bä-ē'ä-kô-chē'nōs)	132	22.05 N	81.10 W
Cochinos Bks., Ba.	133	22.20 N	76.15 W
Cochita Res., NM	119	35.45 N	106.10 W
Cochran, Ga. (kŏk'răn)	124	32.23 N	83.23 W
Cochrane, Can. (kŏk'răn)	95	49.01 N	81.06 W
Cochrane, Can.	93e	51.11 N	114.28 W
Cockburn (I.), Can. (kŏk-bûrn)	108	45.55 N	83.25 W
Cockeysville, Md. (kŏk'ĭz-vĭl)	110e	39.30 N	76.40 W
Cockrell Hill, Tx. (kŏk'rĕl)	117c	32.44 N	96.53 W
Coco (Segovia) (R.), Hond.-Nic. (kō-kō) (sē-gô'vyä)	131	14.55 N	83.45 W
Coco, Cayo (I.), Cuba (kä'-yō-kō'kō)	132	22.30 S	78.30 W
Coco, Isla del (I.), C.R. (ē's-lä-dĕl-kô-kô)	126	5.33 N	87.02 W
Cocoa, Fl. (kō'kō)	125a	28.21 N	80.44 W
Cocoa Beach, Fl.	125a	28.20 N	80.35 W
Cocoli, Pan. (kŏ-kô'lē)	126a	8.58 N	79.36 W
Coconino, Plat., Az. (kō kō nē'nō)	119	35.45 N	112.28 W
Cocos (Keeling) Is., Oceania (kō'kôs) (kē'ling)	7	11.50 S	90.50 E
Coco Solito, Pan. (kô-kô-sŏ-lē'tō)	126a	9.21 N	79.53 W
Cocula, Mex. (kō-kōō'lä)	128	20.23 N	103.47 W
Cocula (R.), Mex.	128	18.17 N	99.11 W
Codajás, Braz. (kō-dä-häzh')	140	3.44 S	62.09 W
Codera, Cabo (C.), Ven. (kà'bô-kō-dĕ'rä)	141b	10.35 N	66.06 W
Codó, Braz. (kō-dō')	141	4.21 S	43.52 W
Codogno, It. (kô-dō'nyō)	170	45.08 N	9.43 E
Codrington, Antigua (kŏd'rĭng-tŭn)	131	17.39 N	61.49 W
Cody, Wy. (kō'dĭ)	11	44.31 N	109.02 W
Coemba, Ang.	226	12.08 S	18.05 E
Coesfeld, F.R.G. (kûs'fĕld)	167c	51.56 N	7.10 E
Coeur d' Alene, Id. (kûr dá-lān')	114	47.43 N	116.35 W
Coeur d' Alene (L.), Id.	114	47.32 N	116.39 W
Coeur d' Alene (R.), Id.	114	47.26 N	116.35 W
Coffeyville, Ks. (kŏf'ĭ-vĭl)	121	37.01 N	95.38 W
Coff's Harbour, Austl.	212	30.20 S	153.10 E
Cofimvaba, S. Afr. (căfĭm'vä-bà)	223c	32.01 S	27.37 E
Coghinas (R.), It. (kō'gē-nàs)	170	40.31 N	9.00 E
Cognac, Fr. (kôn-yak')	166	45.41 N	0.22 W
Cohasset, Ma. (kō-hăs'ĕt)	103a	42.14 N	70.48 W
Cohoes, NY (kô-hōz')	109	42.50 N	73.40 W

ăt; finăl; rāte; senâte; ärm; ȧsk; sofȧ; fâre; ch-choose; dh-as th in other; bē; ēvent; bĕt; recĕnt; cratēr; g-gō; gh-guttural g; bĭt; ĭ-short neutral; rīde; K-guttural k as ch in German ich;

PLACE (Pronunciation)	PAGE	Lat. °′	Long. °′
Coig (R.), Arg. (kô'ĕk)	142	51.15 N	71.00 W
Coimbatore, India (kō-ĕm-bȧ-tôr')	191	11.03 N	76.56 E
Coimbra, Port. (kô-ēm'brä)	168	40.14 N	8.23 W
Coín, Sp. (kô-ēn')	168	36.40 N	4.45 W
Coina, Port. (kô-ē'nȧ)	169b	38.35 N	9.03 W
Coina (R.), Port. (kô'y-nä)	169b	38.35 N	9.02 W
Coipasa, Salar de (Salt Flat), Chile (sä-lä'r-dĕ-koi-pä'-sä)	140	19.12 S	69.13 W
Coixtlahuaca, Mex. (kō-ēks'tlä-wä'kä)	129	17.42 N	97.17 W
Cojedes (State), Ven. (kô-kĕ'dĕs)	141b	9.50 N	68.21 W
Cojimar, Cuba (kō-hē-mär')	133a	23.10 N	82.19 W
Cojutepeque, Sal. (kô-hōō-tĕ-pā'kå)	130	13.45 N	88.50 W
Cokato, Mn. (kô-kā'tō)	113	45.03 N	94.11 W
Cokeburg, Pa. (kōk bŭgh)	111e	40.06 N	80.03 W
Colac, Austl. (kŏ'lăc)	212	38.25 S	143.40 E
Colares, Port. (kô-lä'rĕs)	169b	38.47 N	9.27 W
Colatina, Braz. (kô-lä-tē'nä)	141	19.33 S	40.42 W
Colby, Ks. (kōl'bĭ)	120	39.23 N	101.04 W
Colchagua (Prov.), Chile (kôl-chá'gwä)	139b	34.42 S	71.24 W
Colchester, Eng. (kōl'chĕs-tẽr)	161	51.52 N	0.50 E
Cold L., Can. (kōld)	98	54.33 N	110.05 W
Coldwater, Ks. (kōld'wô-tẽr)	120	37.14 N	99.21 W
Coldwater, Mi.	108	41.55 N	85.00 W
Coldwater (R.), Ms.	124	34.25 N	90.12 W
Coldwater Cr., Tx.	120	36.10 N	101.45 W
Coleman, Tx. (kōl'mȧn)	122	31.50 N	99.25 W
Colenso, S.Afr. (kŏ-lĕnz'ō)	223c	28.48 S	29.49 E
Coleraine, Mn. (kōl-rān')	113	47.16 N	93.29 W
Coleraine, N. Ire.	160	55.08 N	6.40 W
Coleshill, Eng. (kōlz'hĭl)	154	52.30 N	1.42 W
Colfax, Ia. (kōl'făks)	113	41.40 N	93.13 W
Colfax, La.	123	31.31 N	92.42 W
Colfax, Wa.	114	46.53 N	117.21 W
Colhué Huapi (L.), Arg. (kôl-wā'ōōá'pē)	142	45.30 S	68.45 W
Coligny, S.Afr.	219d	26.20 S	26.18 E
Colima, Mex. (kōlē'mä)	128	19.13 N	103.45 W
Colima (State), Mex.	128	19.10 N	104.00 W
Colima, Nevado de (Mtn.), Mex. (nĕ-vä'dô-dĕ-kô-lē'mä)	128	19.30 N	103.38 W
Coll (I.), Scot. (kŏl)	160	56.42 N	6.23 W
College, Ak.	105	64.43 N	147.50 W
College Park, Ga. (kŏl'ĕj)	110c	33.39 N	84.27 W
College Park, Md.	110e	38.59 N	76.58 W
Collegeville, Pa. (kŏl'ĕj-vĭl)	110f	40.11 N	75.27 W
Collie, Austl. (kŏl'ē)	210	33.20 S	116.20 E
Collier B., Austl. (kŏl-yẽr)	210	15.30 S	123.30 E
Collingswood, NJ (kŏl'ĭngz-wŏŏd)	110f	39.54 N	75.04 W
Collingwood, Can.	108	44.30 N	80.20 W
Collins, Ms. (kŏl'ĭns)	124	31.40 N	89.34 W
Collinsville, Il. (kŏl'ĭnz-vĭl)	117e	38.41 N	89.59 W
Collinsville, Ok.	121	36.21 N	95.50 W
Collo, Alg. (kôl'ō)	220	37.02 N	6.29 E
Colmar, Fr. (kôl'mär)	167	48.03 N	7.25 E
Colmenar de Oreja, Sp. (kôl-mā-när'dāōrā'hä)	168	40.06 N	3.25 W
Colmenar Viejo, Sp. (kôl-mā-när'vyā'hō)	169a	40.40 N	3.46 W
Cologne, see Köln			
Colombia, Col. (kô-lôm'bē-ä)	140a	3.23 N	74.48 W
Colombia, S.A.	138	3.30 N	72.30 W
Colombo, Sri Lanka (kō-lôm'bō)	191	6.58 N	79.52 W
Colón, Arg. (kō-lōn')	139c	33.55 S	61.08 W
Colón, Cuba (kô-lō'n)	132	22.45 N	80.55 W
Colón, Mex. (kō-lōn')	128	20.46 N	100.02 W
Colón, Pan. (kô-lō'n)	126a	9.22 N	79.54 W
Colon, Arch. de (Galápagos Is.), Ec. (är-chē-pyĕ'l-ȧgô-dĕ-kō-lōn') (gä-lä'pägôs)	140	0.10 S	87.45 W
Colōn, Montañas de (Mts.), Hond. (môn-tä'n-yäs-dĕ-kô-lô'n)	131	14.58 N	84.39 W
Colonia, Ur. (kō-lō'nē-ä)	139c	34.27 S	57.50 W
Colonia (Dept.), Ur.	139c	34.08 S	57.50 W
Colonia Suiza, Ur. (kô-lô'nēä-sōōē'zä)	139c	34.17 S	57.15 W
Colonna, Capo (C.), It.	171	39.02 N	17.15 E
Colonsay (I.), Scot. (kŏl-ôn-sā')	160	56.08 N	6.08 E
Coloradas, Lomas (Hills), Arg. (lô'mäs-kō-lō-rä'däs)	142	43.30 S	68.00 W
Colorado (State), U.S.	106	39.30 N	106.55 W
Colorado (R.), Tx.	123	30.08 N	97.33 W
Colorado City, Tx. (kŏl-ô-rä'dō sĭ'tĭ)	122	32.24 N	100.50 W
Colorado, Rio (R.), Arg.	142	38.30 S	66.00 W
Colorado Natl. Mon., Co.	119	39.00 N	108.40 W
Colorado Plat, U.S.	106	36.20 N	109.25 W
Colorado R., U.S.	106	36.25 N	112.00 W
Colorado River Aqueducts, Ca.	118	33.38 N	115.43 W
Colorado River Ind. Res., Az.	119	34.03 N	114.02 W
Colorados, Arch. de los (Is.), Cuba (är-chē-pyĕ'lä-gô-dĕ-lôs-kō-lō-rä'dōs)	132	22.25 N	84.25 W
Colorado Springs, Co. (kŏl-ô-rä'dō)	120	38.49 N	104.48 W
Colotepec (R.), Mex. (kô-lô'tĕ-pĕk)	129	15.56 N	96.57 W
Colotlán, Mex. (kô-lô-tlän')	128	22.06 N	103.14 W
Colotlán (R.), Mex.	128	22.09 N	103.17 W
Colquechaca, Bol. (kôl-kā-chä'kä)	140	18.47 S	66.02 W
Colstrip, Mt. (kōl'strip)	115	45.54 N	106.38 W
Colton, Ca. (kōl'tŭn)	117a	34.04 N	117.20 W
Columbia, Il. (kō-lŭm'bĭ-ȧ)	117e	38.26 N	90.12 W
Columbia, Ky.	124	37.06 N	85.15 W
Columbia, Md.	110e	39.15 N	76.51 W
Columbia, Ms.	124	31.15 N	89.49 W
Columbia, Mo.	121	38.55 N	92.19 W
Columbia, Pa.	109	40.00 N	76.25 W
Columbia, SC	125	34.00 N	81.00 W
Columbia, TN.	124	35.36 N	87.02 W
Columbia, Mt., Can.	97	52.09 N	117.25 W
Columbia (R.), Can.	97	51.30 N	119.00 W
Columbia (R.), Can.-U.S.	94	46.20 N	123.00 W
Columbia City, In.	108	41.10 N	85.30 W
Columbia City, Or.	116c	45.53 N	112.49 W
Columbia Heights, Mn.	117g	45.03 N	93.15 W
Columbia Icefield, Can.	97	52.08 N	117.26 W
Columbia Mts., Can.	97	51.30 N	118.30 W
Columbiana, Al. (kô-ŭm-bĭ-ă'nȧ)	124	33.10 N	86.35 W
Columbretes (I.), Sp. (kô-lōōm-brē'tĕs)	169	39.54 N	0.54 E
Columbus, Ga. (kô-lŭm'bŭs)	124	32.29 N	84.56 W
Columbus, In.	108	39.15 N	85.55 W
Columbus, Ks.	121	37.10 N	94.50 W
Columbus, Ms.	124	33.30 N	88.25 W
Columbus, Mt.	115	45.39 N	109.15 W
Columbus, Ne.	112	41.25 N	97.25 W
Columbus, NM	119	31.50 N	107.40 W
Columbus, Oh.	108	40.00 N	83.00 W
Columbus, Tx.	123	29.44 N	96.34 W
Columbus, Wi.	113	43.20 N	89.01 W
Columbus Bk., Ba. (kô-lŭm'bŭs)	133	22.05 N	75.30 W
Columbus Grove, Oh.	108	40.55 N	84.05 W
Columbus Pt., Ba.	133	24.10 N	75.15 W
Colusa, Ca. (kô-lū'sȧ)	118	39.12 N	122.01 W
Colville, Wa. (kŏl'vĭl)	114	48.33 N	117.53 W
Colville (R.), Ak.	105	69.00 N	156.25 W
Colville R, Wa.	114	48.25 N	117.58 W
Colvos Pass., Wa. (kōl'vōs)	116a	47.24 N	122.32 W
Colwood, Can. (kŏl'wŏŏd)	116a	48.26 N	123.30 W
Comacchio, It. (kô-mäk'kyō)	170	44.42 N	12.12 E
Comala, Mex. (kō-mä-lä')	128	19.22 N	103.47 W
Comalapa, Guat. (kō-mä-lä'-pä)	130	14.43 N	90.56 W
Comalcalco, Mex. (kō-mäl-käl'kō)	129	18.16 N	93.13 W
Comanche, Ok. (kô-măn'chē)	120	34.20 N	97.58 W
Comanche, Tx.	122	31.54 N	98.37 W
Comanche Cr., Tx.	122	31.02 N	102.47 W
Comayagua, Hond. (kō-mä-yä'gwä)	130	14.24 N	87.36 W
Combahee (R.), SC (kŏm-bȧ-hē')	125	32.42 N	80.40 W
Comer, Ga. (kŭm'ẽr)	124	34.02 N	83.07 W
Comete, C., Turks & Caicos (kô-mā'tā)	133	21.45 N	71.25 W
Comilla, Bngl. (kō-mĭl'ä)	190	23.33 N	91.17 E
Comino, C., It. (kô-mē'nō)	170	40.30 N	9.48 E
Comitán, Mex. (kô-mē-tän')	130	16.16 N	92.09 W
Commencement B., Wa. (kŏ-mĕns'mĕnt bā)	116a	47.17 N	122.21 W
Commentry, Fr. (kô-mäN-trē')	166	46.16 N	2.44 E
Commerce, Ga. (kŏm'ẽrs)	124	34.10 N	83.27 W
Commerce, Ok.	121	36.57 N	94.54 W
Commerce, Tx.	121	33.15 N	95.52 W
Como, It. (kō'mō)	170	45.48 N	9.03 E
Como, Lago di (L.), It. (lä'gō-dē-kō'mō)	170	46.00 N	9.30 E
Comodoro Rivadavia, Arg. (kō'mô-dō'rô rē-vä-dä 'vē-ä)	142	45.47 S	67.31 W
Como-Est, Can.	93a	45.27 N	74.08 W
Comonfort, Mex. (kô-mōn-fô'rt)	128	20.43 N	100.47 W
Comorin C., India (kŏ'mô-rĭn)	191	8.05 N	78.05 E
Comoros, Afr.	218	12.30 S	42.45 E
Comox, Can. (kō'mŏks)	96	49.40 N	124.55 W
Compainalá, Mex. (kôm-pä-ē-nä-lä')	129	17.05 N	93.11 W
Companario, Cerro (Mtn.), Arg.-Chile (sĕ'r-rô-kôm-pä-nä'ryō)	139b	35.54 S	70.23 W
Compiègne, Fr. (kôN-pyĕn'y')	166	49.25 N	2.49 E
Comporta, Port. (kôm-pôr'tȧ)	169b	38.24 N	8.48 W
Compostela, Mex. (kôm-pô-stā'lä)	128	21.41 N	104.54 W
Compton, Ca. (kŏmpt'tŭn)	117a	33.54 N	118.14 W
Cona (R.), Ga. (kô-nȧ)	124	34.40 N	84.51 W
Conakry, Gui. (kô-nȧ-krē')	224	9.31 N	13.43 W
Conanicut (I.), RI (kŏn'ȧ-nĭ-kŭt)	110b	41.34 N	71.20 W
Concarneau, Fr. (kôN-kär-nō')	166	47.54 N	3.52 W
Concepción, Bol. (kôn-sĕp'syōn')	141	15.47 S	61.08 W
Concepción, Chile	142	36.51 S	72.59 W
Concepción, Pan.	131	8.31 N	82.38 W
Concepción, Par.	142	23.29 S	57.18 W
Concepcion, Phil.	203a	15.19 N	120.40 E
Concepción (R.), Mex.	126	30.25 N	112.20 W
Concepción (Vol.), Nic.	130	11.36 N	85.43 W
Concepción del Mar, Guat. (kôn-sĕp-syōn'dĕl mär')	130	14.07 N	91.23 W
Concepción del Oro, Mex. (kôn-sĕp-syōn' dĕl ō'rō)	122	24.39 N	101.24 W
Concepción del Uruguay, Arg. (kôn-sĕp-syô'n-dĕl-ōō-rōō-gwī')	142	32.31 S	58.10 W
Conception (I.), Ba.	133	23.50 N	75.05 W
Conception, Pt., Ca.	118	34.27 N	120.28 W
Conception B., Can. (kŏn-sĕp'shŭn)	103	47.50 N	52.50 W
Concho (R.), Tx. (kŏn'chō)	122	31.34 N	100.00 W
Conchos (R.), Mex. (kōn'chōs)	122	25.03 N	99.00 W
Conchos (R.), Mex.	122	29.08 N	105.02 W
Concord, Ca. (kŏŋ'kŏrd)	116b	37.58 N	122.02 W
Concord, Ma.	103a	42.28 N	71.21 W
Concord, NH	109	43.10 N	71.30 W
Concord, NC	125	35.23 N	80.11 W
Concordia, Arg. (kŏn-kôr'dĭ-ȧ)	142	31.18 S	57.59 W
Concordia, Col.	140a	6.04 N	75.54 W
Concordia, Ks.	121	39.32 N	97.39 W
Concordia, Mex. (kôn-kô'r-dyä)	128	23.17 N	106.06 W
Concrete, Wa. (kŏn-'krēt)	114	48.33 N	121.44 W
Conde, Fr.	166	48.50 N	0.36 W
Conde, SD (kŏn-dē')	112	45.10 N	98.06 W
Condega, Nic. (kŏn-dĕ'gä)	130	13.20 N	86.27 W
Condeúba, Braz. (kōn-dā-ōō'bä)	141	14.47 S	41.44 W
Condom, Fr.	166	43.58 N	0.22 E
Condon, Or. (kŏn'dŭn)	114	45.14 N	120.10 W
Conecun (R.), Al. (kô-nē'kŭ)	124	31.05 N	86.52 W
Conegliano, It. (kō-nål-yä'nō)	170	45.59 N	12.17 E
Conejos (R.), Co. (kô-nā'hōs)	119	37.07 N	106.19 W
Conemaugh, Pa. (kŏn'ē-mô)	109	40.25 N	78.50 W
Coney I., NY (kō'nĭ)	110a	40.34 N	73.27 W
Confolens, Fr. (kôN-fä-läN')	166	46.01 N	0.41 E
Congaree (R.), SC (kŏŋ-gȧ-rē')	125	33.53 N	80.55 W
Conghua, China (tsôŋ-hwä)	199	23.30 N	113.40 E
Congleton, Eng. (kŏŋ'g'l-tŭn)	154	53.10 N	2.13 W
Congo, Afr. (kŏn'gō)	218	3.00 S	13.48 E
Congo (Zaire) (R.), Afr.	226	1.10 N	18.25 E
Congo, Serra do (Mts.), Ang.	226	6.25 S	18.30 E
Congo, The, see Zaire			
Congo Basin, Zaire	218	2.47 N	20.58 E
Conisbrough, Eng. (kŏn'ĭs-bŭr-ō)	154	53.29 N	1.13 W
Coniston, Can.	101	46.29 N	80.51 W
Conklin, Can. (kŏŋk'lĭn)	97	55.38 N	111.05 W
Conley, Ga. (kŏn'lĭ)	110c	33.38 N	84.19 W
Conn, Lough (L.), Ire. (lŏk kŏn)	160	53.56 N	9.25 W
Connacht (Reg.), Ire. (cŏn'åt)	160	53.50 N	8.45 W
Conneaut, Oh. (kŏn-ē-ôt')	108	41.55 N	80.35 W
Connecticut (State), U.S. (kŏ-nĕt'ĭ-kŭt)	107	41.40 N	73.10 W
Connecticut R., U.S.	109	43.55 N	72.15 W
Connellsville, Pa. (kŏn'nĕlz-vĭl)	109	40.00 N	79.40 W
Connemara (Mts.), Ire. (kŏn-nē-mȧ'rȧ)	160	53.30 N	9.54 W
Connersville, In. (kŏn'ẽrz-vĭl)	108	39.35 N	85.10 W
Connors Ra., Austl. (kŏn'nŏrs)	211	22.15 S	149.00 E
Conrad, Mt. (kŏn'răd)	115	48.11 N	111.56 W
Conrich, Can. (kŏn'rĭch)	93e	51.06 N	113.51 W
Conroe, Tx. (kŏn'rō)	123	30.18 N	95.23 W
Conselheiro Lafaiete, Braz. (kôn-sĕ-lā'rô-lȧ-fā'ē-tĕ)	139a	20.40 S	43.46 W
Conshohocken, Pa. (kŏn-shō-hŏk'ĕn)	110f	40.04 N	75.18 W
Consolación del Sur, Cuba (kôn-sô-lä-syōn')	132	22.30 N	83.55 W
Con Son (Is.), Viet.	202	8.30 N	106.28 E
Constance, Mt., Wa. (kŏn'stȧns)	116a	47.46 N	123.08 W
Constanţa, Rom. (kōn-stån'tsȧ)	159	44.12 N	28.36 E
Constantina, Sp. (kŏn-stän-tē'nä)	168	37.52 N	5.39 W
Constantine, Alg. (kôN-stäN'tēn')	220	36.28 N	6.38 E
Constantine, Mi. (kŏn'stăn-tēn)	108	41.50 N	85.40 W
Constitución, Chile (kôn'stĭ-tōō-syōn')	142	35.24 S	72.25 W
Constitution, Ga. (kŏn-stĭ-tū'shŭn)	110c	33.41 N	84.20 W
Contagem, Braz. (kôn-tá'zhĕm)	139a	19.54 S	44.05 W
Contepec, Mex. (kōn-tĕ-pĕk')	128	20.04 N	100.07 W
Contreras, Mex. (kôn-trĕ'räs)	129a	19.18 N	99.14 W
Contwoyto (L.), Can.	94	65.42 N	110.50 W
Converse, Tx. (kŏn'vẽrs)	117d	29.31 N	98.17 W
Conway, Ar. (kŏn'wā)	121	35.06 N	92.27 W
Conway, NH	109	44.00 N	71.10 W
Conway, SC	125	33.49 N	79.01 W
Conway, Wa.	116a	48.20 N	122.20 W
Conyers, Ga. (kŏn'yŏrz)	124	33.41 N	84.01 W
Cooch Behār, India (kōōch bē-här')	190	26.25 N	89.34 E
Cook, C., Can. (kŏŏk)	96	50.08 N	127.55 W
Cook, Mt., N.Z.	213	43.27 S	170.13 E
Cookeville, Tn. (kŏŏk'vĭl)	124	36.07 N	85.30 W
Cooking Lake, Can. (kŏŏk'ĭng)	93g	53.10 N	113.08 W
Cooking L., Can.	93g	53.25 N	113.02 W
Cook Inlet, Ak.	105	60.50 N	151.38 W
Cook Is., Oceania	205	19.20 S	158.00 W
Cook Str., N.Z.	213	40.37 S	174.15 E
Cooktown, Austl. (kŏŏk'toun)	211	15.40 S	145.20 E
Cooleemee, NC (kōō-lē'mē)	125	35.50 N	80.32 W
Coolgardie, Austl. (kōōl-gär'dē)	210	31.00 S	121.25 E
Cooma, Austl. (kōō'mȧ)	212	36.22 S	149.10 E
Coonamble, Austl. (kōō-năm'b'l)	212	31.00 S	148.30 E
Coonoort, India	191	10.22 N	76.15 E
Coon Rapids, Mn. (kōōn)	117g	45.09 N	93.17 W
Cooper, Tx. (kōōp'ẽr)	121	33.23 N	95.40 W
Cooper Center, Ak. (kōōp'ẽr sĕn'tẽr)	105	61.54 N	15.30 W
Coopers Cr., Austl. (kōō'pẽrz)	212	27.32 N	141.19 E
Cooperstown, NY (kōōp'ẽrs-toun)	109	42.45 N	74.55 W
Cooperstown, ND	112	47.26 N	98.07 W
Coorong, The (L.), Austl. (kōō'rŏng)	212	36.07 N	319.45 E
Coosa, Al. (kōō'sȧ)	124	32.43 N	86.25 W
Coosa (R.), Al.	124	34.00 N	86.00 W
Coosawattee (R.), Ga. (kōō-sȧ-wôt'ē)	124	34.37 N	84.45 W
Coos Bay, Or. (kōōs)	114	43.21 N	124.12 W
Coos B., Or.	114	43.19 N	124.40 W
Cootamundra, Austl. (kōōtȧ-mŭnd'rȧ)	212	34.25 S	148.00 E
Copacabana, Braz. (kō'pä-kȧ-bá'nä)	142b	22.57 S	43.11 W
Copalita (R.), Mex. (kō-pä-lē'tä)	129	15.55 N	96.06 W
Copán (Ruins), Hond. (kō-pän')	130	14.50 N	89.10 W
Copano B., Tx. (kō-păn'ō)	123	28.08 N	97.25 W
Copenhagen, see København			
Copiapó, Chile (kō-pyä-pō')	142	27.16 S	70.28 W
Copley, Oh. (kŏp'lē)	111d	41.06 N	81.38 W
Copparo, It. (kôp-pä'rō)	170	44.53 N	11.50 E
Coppell, Tx. (kŏp'pĕl)	117c	32.57 N	97.00 W
Copper (R.), Ak. (kŏp'ẽr)	105	62.38 N	145.00 W
Copper Cliff, Can.	100	46.28 N	81.04 W
Copper Harbor, Mi.	113	47.27 N	87.53 W

PLACE (Pronunciation)	PAGE	Lat. °′	Long. °′
Copperhill, Tn. (kŏp'ẽr hĭl)	124	35.00 N	84.22 W
Coppermine, Can. (kŏp'ẽr-mīn)	94	67.46 N	115.19 W
Copper Mtn., Ak.	96	55.14 N	132.36 W
Copperinine (R.), Can.	94	66.48 N	114.59 W
Copperton, Ut. (kŏp'ẽr-tŭn)	117b	40.34 N	112.06 W
Coquilhatville, see Mbandaka			
Coquilee, Or. (kô-kēl')	114	43.11 N	124.11 W
Coquimbo, Chile (kô-kēm'bō)	142	29.58 S	71.31 W
Coquimbo (Prov.), Chile	139b	31.50 S	71.05 W
Coquitlam (L.) (kō-kwĭt-lăm)	116d	49.23 N	122.44 W
Corabia, Rom. (kō-rä'bĭ-à)	171	43.45 N	24.29 E
Coracora, Peru (kō'rä-kō'rä)	140	15.12 S	73.42 W
Coral Gables, Fl.	125a	25.43 N	80.14 W
Coral Rapids, Can. (kŏr'ăl)	100	50.18 N	81.49 W
Coral Sea, Oceania (kŏr'ăl)	204	13.30 S	150.00 E
Coralville Res., Ia.	113	41.45 N	91.50 W
Corangamite, L., Austl. (cŏr-ăŋg'á-mīt)	212	38.05 S	142.55 E
Coraopolis, Pa. (kō-rä-ŏp'ô-lĭs)	111e	40.30 N	80.09 W
Corato, It. (kô'rä-tô)	170	41.08 N	16.28 E
Corbeil-Essonnes, Fr. (kôr-bā'yĕ-sŏn')	167b	48.31 N	2.29 E
Corbett, Or. (kôr'bĕt)	116c	45.31 N	122.17 W
Corbie, Fr. (kôr-bē')	166	49.55 N	2.27 E
Corbin, Ky. (kôr'bĭn)	124	36.55 N	84.06 W
Corby, Eng. (kôr'bĭ)	154	52.29 N	0.38 W
Corcovado (Mtn.(, Braz. (kôr-kô-vä'dōō)	142b	22.57 S	43.13 W
Corcovado, Golfo (G.), Chile (kôr-kô-vä'dhō)	142	43.40 S	75.00 W
Cordeiro, Braz. (kôr-dā'rō)	139a	22.03 S	42.22 W
Cordele, Ga. (kôr-dēl')	124	31.55 N	83.50 W
Cordell, Ok. (kôr-dĕl')	120	35.19 N	98.58 W
Cordilleran Highlands (Reg.), N.A. (kōr dĭl'lŭr ăn)	92	55.00 N	125.00 W
Córdoba, Arg. (kôr'dô-vä)	142	30.20 S	64.03 W
Córdoba, Mex. (kô'r-dô-bä)	129	18.53 N	96.54 W
Córdoba, Sp. (kô'r-dô-bä)	168	37.55 N	4.45 W
Córdoba (Prov.), Arg. (kôr'dô-vä)	142	32.00 S	64.00 W
Córdoba, Sa. de (Mts.), Arg.	142	31.15 S	64.30 W
Cordova, Al. (kôr'dô-và)	124	33.45 N	86.22 W
Cordova, Ak. (kôr'dô-vä)	105	60.34 N	145.38 W
Cordova B., Ak.	96	54.55 N	132.35 W
Corfu (I.), see Kérkira			
Corigliano, It. (kō-rē-lyä'nō)	170	39.35 N	16.30 E
Corinth, Ms. (kŏr'ĭnth)	124	34.55 N	88.30 W
Corinth, see Kórinthos			
Corinto, Braz. (kô-rē'n-tō)	141	18.20 S	44.16 W
Corinto, Col.	140a	3.09 N	76.12 W
Corinto, Nic. (kŏr-ĭn'to)	130	12.30 N	87.12 W
Corio, Austl.	207a	38.05 S	144.22 E
Corio B., Austl.	207a	38.07 S	144.25 E
Corisco, Isla de (I.), Equat. Gui.	226	0.50 N	8.40 E
Cork, Ire. (kôrk)	160	51.54 N	8.25 W
Cork Hbr., Ire.	160	51.44 N	8.15 W
Corleone, It. (kôr-lā-ō'nā)	170	37.48 N	13.18 E
Cormorant L., Can.	99	54.13 N	100.47 W
Cornelia, Ga. (kôr-nē'lyà)	124	34.31 N	83.30 W
Cornelis (R.), S. Afr. (kôr-nē'lĭs)	219d	27.48 S	29.15 E
Cornell, Ca. (kôr-nĕl')	117a	34.06 N	118.46 W
Cornell, Wi.	113	45.10 N	91.10 W
Corner Brook, Can. (kôr'nẽr)	103	48.57 N	57.57 W
Corner Inlet, Austl.	212	38.55 S	146.45 E
Corning, Ar. (kôr'nĭng)	121	36.26 N	90.35 W
Corning, Ia.	113	40.58 N	94.40 W
Corning, NY	109	42.10 N	77.05 W
Corno, Monte (Mtn.), It. (kôr'nō)	170	42.28 N	13.37 E
Cornwall, Ba.	132	25.55 N	77.15 W
Cornwall, Can. (kôrn'wôl)	109	45.05 N	74.35 W
Coro, Ven. (kō'rō)	140	11.22 N	69.43 W
Corocoro, Bol. (kō-rō-kō'rō)	140	17.15 S	68.21 W
Coromandel Coast, India (kŏr-ō-man'dĕl)	191	13.30 N	80.30 E
Coromandel Pen., N.Z.	211a	36.50 S	176.00 E
Corona, Al. (kō-rō'nà)	124	33.42 N	87.28 W
Corona, Ca.	117a	33.52 N	117.34 W
Coronada, Bahía de (B.), C.R. (bä-ē'ä-dĕ-kô-rô-nä'dō)	131	8.47 N	84.04 W
Corona del Mar, Ca. (kô-rō'nà dĕl mär)	117a	33.36 N	117.53 W
Coronado, Ca. (kŏr-ô-nä'dō)	118a	32.42 N	117.12 W
Coronation G., Can. (kŏr-ô-nā'shŭn)	94	68.07 N	112.50 W
Coronel, Chile (kō-rō-nĕl')	142	37.00 S	73.10 W
Coronel Brandsen, Arg. (kŏ-rô-nĕl-brà'nd-sĕn)	139c	35.09 S	58.15 W
Coronel Dorrego, Arg. (kŏ-rô-nĕl-dôr-rē'gō)	142	38.43 S	61.16 W
Coronel Oviedo, Par. (kŏ-rô-nĕl-ô-vē'dô)	142	25.28 S	56.22 W
Coronel Pringles, Arg. (kŏ-rô-nĕl-prēn'glĕs)	142	37.54 S	61.22 W
Coronel Suárez, Arg. (kŏ-rô-nĕl-swä'rās)	142	37.27 S	61.49 W
Corowa, Austl. (cŏr-ŏwă)	212	36.02 S	146.23 E
Corozal, Belize (cŏr-ŏth-äl')	130a	18.25 N	88.23 W
Corpus Christi, Tx. (kôr'pŭs krĭstē)	123	27.48 N	97.24 W
Corpus Christi B., Tx.	123	27.47 N	97.14 W
Corpus Christi L., Tx.	122	28.08 N	98.20 W
Corral, Chile (kô-räl')	142	39.57 S	73.15 W
Corral de Almaguer, Sp. (kô-räl'dā äl-mä-gâr')	168	39.45 N	3.10 W
Corralillo, Cuba (kô-rä-lē-yō)	132	28.00 N	80.40 W
Corregidor I, Phil. (kô-rā-hē-dōr')	203a	14.21 N	120.25 E
Correntina, Braz. (kô-rĕn-tē-nà)	141	13.18 S	44.33 W
Corrib, Lough (L.), Ire. (lŏk kŏr'ĭb)	160	53.56 N	9.19 W
Corrientes, Arg. (kō-ryĕn'tās)	142	27.25 S	58.39 W
Corrientes (Prov.)	142	28.45 S	58.00 W
Corrientes, Cabo (C.), Col. (ká'bô-kō-ryĕn'tās)	140	5.34 N	77.35 W
Corrientes, Cabo (C.), Cuba (ká'bô-kôr-rē-ĕn'tĕs)	132	21.50 N	84.25 W
Corrientes, Cabo (C.), Mex.	128	20.25 N	105.41 W
Corse, C., Fr. (kôrs)	170	42.59 N	9.19 E
Corsica (I.), Fr. (kô'r-sē-kä)	170	42.10 N	8.55 E
Corsicana, Tx. (kôr-sĭ-kăn'à)	123	32.06 N	96.28 W
Cortazar, Mex. (kôr-tä-zär)	128	20.30 N	100.57 W
Corte, Fr. (kôr'tå)	170	42.18 N	9.10 E
Cortegana, Sp. (kôr-tå-gä'nä)	168	37.54 N	6.48 W
Cortés, Ensenada de (B.), Cuba (ĕn-sĕ-nä-dä-dĕ-kôr-tās')	132	22.05 N	83.45 W
Cortez, Co.	119	37.21 N	108.35 W
Cortland, NY (kôrt'lănd)	109	42.35 N	76.10 W
Cortona, It. (kôr-tō'nä)	170	43.16 N	12.00 E
Corubal (R.), Guinea-Bissau	224	11.43 N	14.40 W
Coruche, Port. (kô-rōō'she)	168	38.58 N	8.34 W
Coruh (R.), Tur. (chō-rōōk')	177	40.30 N	41.10 E
Corum, Tur. (chō-rōōm')	177	40.34 N	34.45 E
Corumbá, Braz. (kō-rōōm-bä')	141	19.01 S	57.28 W
Corunna, Mi. (kô-rŭn'à)	108	43.00 N	84.05 W
Coruripe, Braz. (kō-rōō-rē'pĭ)	141	10.09 S	36.13 W
Corvallis, Or. (kŏr-văl'ĭs)	114	44.34 N	123.17 W
Corve (R.), Eng. (kôr'vê)	154	52.28 N	2.43 W
Corry, Pa. (kŏr'ĭ)	109	41.55 N	79.40 W
Corydon, In. (kŏr'ĭ-dŭn)	108	38.10 N	86.05 W
Corydon, Ia.	113	40.45 N	93.20 W
Corydon, Ky.	108	37.45 N	87.40 W
Cosamaloápan, Mex. (kô-sà-mä-lwä'pän)	129	18.21 N	95.48 W
Coscomatepec, Mex. (kôs'kōmä-tĕ-pĕk')	129	19.04 N	97.03 W
Cosenza, It. (kô-zĕnt'sä)	170	39.18 N	16.15 E
Coshocton, Oh. (kô-shŏk'tŭn)	108	40.15 N	81.55 W
Cosigüina (Vol.), Nic.	108	12.59 N	83.35 W
Cosmoledo Group (Is.), Afr. (kŏs-mô-lā'dō)	223	9.42 S	47.45 E
Cosmopolis, Wa. (kŏz-mŏp'ô-lĭs)	114	46.58 N	123.47 W
Cosne-sur-Loire, Fr. (kōn-sür-lwär')	166	47.25 N	2.57 E
Cosoleacaque, Mex. (kō sō lā-ä-kä'kē)	129	18.01 N	94.38 W
Costa de Caparica, Port.	169b	38.40 N	9.12 W
Costa Mesa, Ca. (kŏs'tà mā'sà)	117a	33.39 N	118.54 W
Costa Rica, N.A. (kŏs'tà rē'kà)	127	10.30 N	84.30 W
Cosumnes (R.), Ca. (kō-sŭm'nĕz)	118	38.21 N	121.17 W
Cotabambas, Peru (kō-tä-bäm'bäs)	140	13.49 S	72.17 W
Cotabato, Phil. (kō-tä-bä'tō)	203	7.06 N	124.13 E
Cotaxtla, Mex. (kō-täs'tlä)	129	18.49 N	96.22 W
Cotaxtla (R.), Mex.	129	18.54 N	96.21 W
Coteau-du-Lac, Can. (cō-tō'dü-lăk)	93a	45.17 N	74.11 W
Coteau-Landing, Can.	93a	45.15 N	74.13 W
Coteaux, Hai.	133	18.15 N	74.05 W
Côe d'Or (hill), Fr. (kōr-dōr')	166	47.02 N	4.35 E
Cotija de la Paz, Mex. (kô-tē'-ĸä-dĕ-lä-pà'z)	128	19.46 N	102.43 W
Cotonou, Benin (kô-tô-nōō')	225	6.21 N	2.26 E
Cotopaxi (Mtn.), Ec. (kō-tô-păk'sē)	140	0.40 S	78.26 W
Cotorro, Cuba (kô-tôr-rō)	133a	23.03 N	82.17 W
Cotswold Hills, Eng. (kŭtz'wōld)	160	51.35 N	2.16 W
Cottage Grove, Mn. (kŏt'åj grōv)	117g	44.50 N	92.52 W
Cottage Grove, Or.	114	43.48 N	123.04 W
Cottbus, G.D.R. (kōt'bōōs)	164	51.47 N	14.20 E
Cottienes Alps (Mts.), Fr.-It.	167	44.46 N	7.02 E
Cottonwood (R.), Mn. (kŏt'ŭn-wŏŏd)	112	44.25 N	95.35 W
Cottonwood Cr., Ca.	114	40.24 N	122.50 W
Cotuí, Dom. Rep. (kô-tōō'-ē)	133	19.05 N	70.10 W
Cotulla, Tx. (kō-tŭl'là)	122	28.26 N	99.14 W
Coubert, Fr. (kōō-bâr')	167b	48.40 N	2.43 E
Coudersport, Pa. (kou'dẽrz-port)	109	41.45 N	78.00 W
Coudres, Île aux (I.), Can.	102	47.17 N	70.12 W
Coulommiers, Fr. (kōō-lô-myā')	167b	48.49 N	3.05 E
Coulto, Serra do (Mts.), Braz. (sĕ'r-rä-dô-kô-ōō'tô)	142b	22.33 S	43.27 W
Council Bluffs, Ia. (koun'sĭl blŭf)	112	41.16 N	95.53 W
Council Grove, Ks. (koun'sĭl grōv)	121	38.39 N	96.30 W
Coupeville, Wa. (kōōp'vĭl)	116a	48.13 N	122.41 W
Courantyne (R.), Guy.-Sur. (kôr'ăntĭn)	141	4.28 N	57.42 W
Courtenay, Can. (cōōrt-nā')	96	49.41 N	125.00 W
Coushatta, La. (kou-shăt'à)	123	32.02 N	93.21 W
Coutras, Fr. (kōō-trá')	166	45.02 N	0.07 W
Covelo, Ang.	226	12.06 S	13.55 E
Coventry, Eng. (kŭv'ĕn-trĭ)	154	52.25 N	1.29 W
Covilhã, Port. (kô-vēl'yăɴ)	168	40.18 N	7.29 W
Covina, Ca. (kô-vē'nà)	117a	34.06 N	117.54 W
Covington, Ga. (kŭv'ĭng-tŭn)	124	33.36 N	83.50 W
Covington, In.	108	40.10 N	87.15 W
Covington, Ky.	111f	39.05 N	84.31 W
Covington, La.	123	30.30 N	90.06 W
Covington, Oh.	108	40.10 N	84.20 W
Covington, Ok.	121	36.18 N	97.32 W
Covington, Tn.	124	35.33 N	89.40 W
Covington, Va.	109	37.50 N	80.00 W
Cowal, L., Austl. (kou'ăl)	212	33.30 S	147.10 E
Cowan, (L.), Austl. (kou'ăn)	210	32.00 S	122.30 E
Cowansville, Can.	102	45.13 N	72.47 W
Cow Cr., Or. (kou)	114	42.45 N	123.35 W
Cowes, Eng. (kouz)	160	50.43 N	1.25 W
Cowichan L., Can.	96	48.54 N	124.20 W
Cowlitz (R.), Wa. (kou'lĭts)	114	46.30 N	122.45 W
Cowra, Austl. (kou'rà)	212	33.50 S	148.33 E
Coxim, Braz. (kō-shēɴ')	141	18.32 S	54.43 W
Coxquihui, Mex. (kōz-kē-wē')	129	20.10 N	97.34 W
Cox's Bāzār, Bngl.	190	21.32 N	92.00 E
Coyaima, Col. (kô-yaē'mä)	140a	3.48 N	75.11 W
Coyame, Mex. (kō-yä'mā)	122	29.26 N	105.05 W
Coyanosa Draw, Tx. (kŏ yá-nō'sä)	122	30.55 N	103.07 W
Coyoacán, Mex. (kô-yô-á-kän')	129a	19.21 N	99.10 W
Coyote (R.), Ca. (kī'ōt)	116b	37.37 N	121.57 W
Coyuca de Benítez, Mex. (kō-yōō'kä dā bā-nē'tāz)	128	17.04 N	100.06 W
Coyuca de Catalán, Mex. (kō-yōō'kä dā kä-tä-län')	128	18.19 N	100.41 W
Coyutla, Mex. (kō-yōō'tlä)	129	20.13 N	97.40 W
Cozad, Ne. (kō'zăd)	120	40.53 N	99.59 W
Cozaddale, Oh. (kô-zăd-dāl)	111f	39.16 N	84.09 W
Cozoyoapan Mex. (kŏ-zō-yô-ä-pá'n)	128	16.45 N	98.17 W
Cozumel, Mex. (kŏ-zōō-mĕ'l)	130a	20.31 N	86.55 W
Cozumel, Isla de (I.), Mex. (ē's-lä-dĕ-kō-zōō-mĕ'l)	130a	20.26 N	87.10 W
Crab Cr., Wa. (krăb)	114	46.47 N	119.43 W
Crab Cr., Wa.	114	47.21 N	119.09 W
Cradock, S. Afr. (krä'dŭk)	223c	32.12 S	25.38 E
Crafton, Pa. (krăf'tŭn)	111e	40.26 N	80.04 W
Craig, Co. (krāg)	115	40.32 N	107.31 W
Craiova, Rom. (krá-yō'vá)	171	44.18 N	23.50 E
Cranberry (L.), NY (krăn'bĕr-ĭ)	109	44.10 N	74.50 W
Cranbourne, Austl.	207a	38.07 S	145.16 E
Cranbrook, Can. (krăn'brŏŏk)	97	49.31 N	115.46 W
Cranbury, NJ (krăn'bē-rĭ)	110a	40.19 N	74.31 W
Crandon, Wi. (krăn'dŭn)	113	45.35 N	88.55 W
Cranston, RI (krăns'tŭn)	110b	41.46 N	71.25 W
Crater L., Or. (krā'tẽr)	114	43.00 N	122.08 W
Crater Lake Natl. Park, Or.	114	42.58 N	122.40 W
Craters of the Moon Natl. Mon., Id. (krā'tẽr)	115	43.28 N	113.15 W
Crateús, Braz. (krä-tå-ōōzh')	141	5.09 S	40.35 W
Crato, Braz. (krä'tōō)	141	7.19 S	39.13 W
Crawford, Ne. (krô'fẽrd)	112	42.41 N	103.25 W
Crawford, Wa.	116c	45.49 N	122.24 W
Crawfordsville, In. (krô'fẽrdz-vĭl)	108	40.00 N	86.55 W
Crazy Mts., Mt. (krā'zĭ)	115	46.11 N	110.25 W
Crazy Woman Cr., Wy.	115	44.08 N	106.40 W
Crecy, S. Afr. (krē-sē)	219d	24.38 S	28.52 E
Crécy-en-Brie, Fr. (krā-sē'-ĕɴ-brē')	167b	48.52 N	2.55 E
Crécy-en-Ponthieu, Fr.	166	50.13 N	1.48 E
Credit (R.), Can.	93d	43.41 N	79.55 W
Cree (L.), Can. (krē)	94	57.35 N	107.52 W
Creighton, Ne. (krā'tŭn)	112	42.27 N	97.54 W
Creighton, S. Afr. (cre-tŏn)	223c	30.02 S	28.52 E
Creil, Fr. (krĕ'y')	166	49.18 N	2.28 E
Crema, It. (krā'mä)	170	45.21 N	9.53 E
Cremona, It. (krā-mō'nä)	170	45.09 N	10.02 E
Crépy-en-Valois, Fr. (krā-pē'ĕɴ-vä-lwä')	167b	49.14 N	2.53 E
Cres, Yugo. (Tsrĕs)	170	44.58 N	14.21 E
Cres (I.), Yugo.	170	44.50 N	14.31 E
Crescent (L.), Fl. (krĕs'ĕnt)	125	29.33 N	81.30 W
Crescent (L.), Or.	114	43.25 N	121.58 W
Crescent Beach, Can.	116d	49.03 N	122.58 W
Crescent City, Ca. (krĕs'ĕnt)	114	41.46 N	124.13 W
Crescent City, Fl.	125	29.26 N	81.35 W
Cresco, Ia. (krĕs'kō)	113	43.23 N	92.07 W
Crested Butte, Co. (krĕst'ĕd būt)	119	38.50 N	107.00 W
Crestline, Ca. (krĕst-lĭn)	117a	34.15 N	117.17 W
Crestline, Oh.	108	40.50 N	82.40 W
Crestmore, Ca. (krĕst'môr)	117a	34.02 N	117.23 W
Creston, Can. (krĕs'tŭn)	97	49.06 N	116.31 W
Creston, Ia.	113	41.04 N	94.22 W
Creston, Oh.	111d	40.59 N	81.54 W
Crestview, Fl. (krĕst'vū)	124	30.44 N	86.35 W
Crestwood, Ky. (krĕst'wŏŏd)	111h	38.20 N	85.28 W
Crestwood, Mo.	117e	38.33 N	90.23 W
Crete, Il. (krēt)	111a	41.26 N	87.38 W
Crete, Ne.	121	40.38 N	96.56 W
Crete (I.), Grc.	170a	35.15 N	24.30 E
Creus, Cabo de (C.), Sp. (kä'-bô-dĕ-krĕ-ōōs)	169	42.16 N	3.18 E
Creuse (R.), Fr. (krûz)	166	46.51 N	0.49 E
Creve Coeur, Mo. (krēv kōōr)	117e	38.40 N	90.27 W
Crevillente, Sp. (krā-vē-lyĕn'tā)	169	38.12 N	0.48 W
Crewe, Eng. (krōō)	154	53.06 N	2.27 W
Crewe, Va.	125	37.09 N	78.08 W
Crimea P-Ov (Pen.), see Krymskiy			
Crimmitschau, G.D.R. (krĭm'ĭt-shou)	164	50.49 N	12.22 E
Cripple Creek, Co. (krĭp''l)	120	38.44 N	105.12 W
Crisfield, Md. (krĭs-fēld)	109	38.00 N	75.50 W
Cristal, Monts de (Mts.), Gabon	226	0.50 N	10.30 E
Cristina, Braz. (krĕs-tē'-nä)	139a	22.13 S	45.15 W
Cristobal Colón, Pico (Pk.), Col. (pē'kō-krĕs-tô'bäl-kō-lōn')	140	11.00 N	74.00 W
Crişul Alb (R.), Rom. (krē'shōōl ălb)	165	46.20 N	22.15 E
Crna (R.), Yugo. (ts'r'ná)	171	41.03 N	21.46 E
Črna Gora (Montenegro)(Reg.), Yugo. (ts'r-ná-gō'rá) (môn-tå-nā'grō) (môn-tē-nē'grō)	171	42.55 N	18.52 E
Črnomelj, Yugo. (ch'r'nō-māl')	170	45.35 N	15.11 E
Croatia (Reg.), see Hrvatska			
Crockett, Ca. (krŏk'ĕt)	116b	38.03 N	122.14 W
Crockett, Tx.	123	31.19 N	95.28 W
Crofton, Md.	110e	39.01 N	76.43 W
Crofton, Ne.	112	42.44 N	97.32 W
Croix, Lac la (L.), Can.-Mn. (läk lä krōō-ä')	113	48.19 N	91.53 W

ăt; finăl; rāte; senåte; ärm; ȧsk; sofȧ; fâre; ch-choose; dh-as th in other; bē; ēvent; bĕt; recĕnt; cratẽr; g-gō; gh-guttural g; bĭt; ĭ-short neutral; rīde; ĸ-guttural k as ch in German ich;

PLACE (Pronunciation)	PAGE	Lat. °′	Long. °′
Croker (I.), Austl. (krō'kȧ)	210	10.45 S	132.25 E
Cronulla, Austl. (krō-nŭl'ȧ)	207b	34.03 S	151.09 E
Crooked (I.), Ba.	133	22.45 N	74.10 W
Crooked (L.), Can.	103	48.25 N	56.05 W
Crooked (R.), Can.	96	54.30 N	122.55 W
Crooked (R.), Or.	114	44.07 N	120.30 W
Crooked Cr., Il. (kro͝ok'ĕd)	121	40.21 N	90.49 W
Crooked Cr., Or.	114	42.23 N	118.14 W
Crooked Island Passage (Str.), Ba.	133	22.40 N	74.50 W
Crookston, Mn. (kro͝oks'tŭn)	112	47.44 N	96.35 W
Crooksville, Oh. (kro͝oks'vĭl)	108	39.45 N	82.05 W
Crosby, Mn. (krôz'bĭ)	113	46.29 N	93.58 W
Crosby, ND	112	48.55 N	103.18 W
Crosby, Tx.	123a	29.55 N	95.04 W
Cross (L.), Can. (krôs)	109	44.55 N	76.55 W
Cross (L.), La.	123	32.33 N	93.58 W
Cross (R.), Nig.	225	5.35 N	8.05 E
Cross City, Fl.	124	29.55 N	83.25 W
Crossett, Ar. (krôs'ĕt)	121	33.08 N	92.00 W
Cross Hbr., Ba.	132	25.55 N	77.105 W
Cross Lake, Can.	99	54.37 N	97.47 W
Cross L., Can.	99	54.45 N	97.30 W
Cross River Res., NY (krôs)	110a	41.14 N	73.34 W
Cross Sd., Ak. (krŏs)	105	58.12 N	137.20 W
Crosswell, Mi. (krŏz'wĕl)	108	43.15 N	82.35 W
Crotch (R.), Can.	101	45.02 N	76.55 W
Crotone, It. (krō-tô'nĕ)	171	39.05 N	17.08 E
Croton Falls Res., NY (krōtŭn)	110a	41.22 N	73.44 W
Croton-on-Hudson, NY (krō'tŭn-ŏn hŭd'sŭn)	110a	41.12 N	73.53 W
Crow (L.), Can.	113	49.13 N	93.29 W
Crow Agency, Mt.	115	45.36 N	107.27 W
Crow Cr., Co.	120	41.08 N	104.25 W
Crow Creek Ind. Res., SD	112	44.17 N	99.17 W
Crow Ind. Res., Mt. (krō)	115	45.26 N	108.12 W
Crowle, Eng. (kroul)	154	53.36 N	0.49 W
Crowley, La. (krou'lē)	123	30.13 N	92.22 W
Crown Mtn., Vir.Is.(U.S.A.)	127c	18.22 N	64.58 W
Crown Mtn., Can. (kroun)	116d	49.24 N	123.05 W
Crown Point, In. (kroun point')	111a	41.25 N	87.22 W
Crown Point, NY	109	44.00 N	73.25 W
Crowsnest P., Can.	97	49.39 N	114.45 W
Crow Wing (R.), Mn. (krō)	113	44.50 N	94.01 W
Crow Wing (R.), Mn.	113	46.42 N	94.48 W
Crow Wing (R.),North Fork, Mn.	113	45.16 N	94.28 W
Crow Wing (R.),South Fork, Mn.	113	44.59 N	94.42 W
Croydon, Austl. (kroi'dŭn)	211	18.15 S	142.15 E
Croydon, Austl.	207a	37.48 S	145.17 E
Croydon, Eng.	154b	51.22 N	0.06 W
Croydon, Pa.	110f	40.05 N	74.55 W
Crozet Is., Ind. O. (krō-zĕ')	228	46.20 S	51.30 E
Cruces, Cuba (kro͞o'sås)	132	22.20 N	80.20 W
Cruces, Arroyo de, Mex. (är-rō'yô-dĕ-kro͞o'sĕs)	122	26.17 N	104.32 W
Cruillas, Mex. (kro͞o-ēl'yäs)	122	24.45 N	98.31 W
Cruz, Cabo (C.), Cuba (kä'-bô-kro͞oz)	132	19.50 N	77.45 W
Cruz, Cayo (I.), Cuba (kä'yō-kro͞oz)	132	22.15 N	77.50 W
Cruz Alta, Braz. (kro͞oz äl'tä)	142	28.41 S	54.02 W
Cruz del Eje, Arg. (kro͞o's-dĕl-ĕ-kĕ)	142	30.46 S	64.45 W
Cruzeiro, Braz. (kro͞o-zä'ro͞o)	139a	22.36 S	44.57 W
Cruzeiro do Sul, Braz. (kro͞o-zä'ro͞o do͞o so͞ol)	140	7.34 S	72.40 W
Crysler, Can.	93c	45.13 N	75.09 W
Crystal City, Tx. (krĭs'tăl sĭ'tĭ)	122	28.40 N	99.90 W
Crystal Falls, Mi. (krĭs'tăl fôls)	113	46.06 N	88.21 W
Crystal Lake, Il. (krĭs'tăl lāk)	111a	42.15 N	88.18 W
Crystal Springs, Ms. (krĭs'tăl sprĭngz)	124	31.58 N	90.20 W
Crystal Sprs., Ca.	116b	37.31 N	122.26 W
Csongrád, Hung. (chôn'gräd)	165	46.42 N	20.09 E
Csorna, Hung. (chôr'nä)	165	47.39 N	17.11 E
Cúa, Ven. (ko͞o'ä)	141b	10.10 N	66.54 W
Cuajimalpa, Mex. (kwä-hē-mäl'pä)	129a	19.21 N	99.18 W
Cuale, Sierra del (Mts.), Mex. (sē-ĕ'r-rä-dĕl-kwä'lĕ)	128	20.20 N	104.58 W
Cuamato, Ang. (kwä-mä'tō)	226	17.05 S	15.09 E
Cuando, Ang. (kwän'dō)	226	16.32 S	22.07 E
Cuando (R.), Ang.	226	16.50 S	22.40 E
Cuangar, Ang.	226	17.36 S	18.39 E
Cuango (Kwango) (R.), Afr. (kwäŋ'gō)	226	6.35 S	16.50 E
Cuanza (R.), Ang. (kwän'zä)	226	9.05 S	13.15 E
Cuarto Saladillo (R.), Arg. (kwär'tō-sä-lä-dē'l-yō)	142	33.00 S	63.25 W
Cuatro Caminos, Cuba (kwä'trô-kä-mē'nôs)	133a	23.01 N	82.13 W
Cuatro Ciénegas, Mex. (kwä'trō syā'nā-gās)	122	26.59 N	102.03 W
Cuauhtemoc, Mex. (kwä-o͞o-tē-mōk')	130	15.43 N	91.57 W
Cuautepec, Mex. (kwä-o͞o-tē-pĕk)	128	16.41 N	99.04 W
Cuautepec, Mex.	128	20.01 N	98.19 W
Cuautitlán, Mex. (kwä-o͞o-tēt-län')	129a	19.40 N	99.12 W
Cuautla, Mex. (kwä-o͞o'tlä)	128	18.47 N	98.57 W
Cuba, Port. (ko͞o'bȧ)	168	38.10 N	7.55 W
Cuba, N.A. (kū'bȧ)	127	22.00 N	79.00 W
Cubagua, Isla (I.), Ven. (ē's-lä-ko͞o-bä'gwä)	141b	10.48 N	64.10 W
Cubango (Okavango)(R.), Ang.-Namibia (ko͞o-bäŋ'gō)	226	17.10 S	18.20 E
Cub Hills, Can. (kŭb)	98	54.20 N	104.30 W
Cucamonga, Ca. (ko͞o-kȧ-mōŋ'gȧ)	117a	34.05 N	117.35 W
Cuchi, Ang.	222	14.40 S	16.50 E
Cuchillo Parado, Mex. (ko͞o-chē'lyô pä-rä'dō)	122	29.26 N	104.52 W
Cuchumatanes, Sierra de los (Mts.), Guat.	130	15.35 N	91.10 W
Cúcuta, Col. (ko͞o'ko͞o-tä)	140	7.56 N	72.30 W
Cudahy, Wi. (kŭd'ȧ-hĭ)	111a	42.57 N	87.52 W
Cuddalore, India (kŭd ȧ-lōr')	191	11.49 N	79.46 E
Cuddapah, India (kŭd'ȧ-pä)	191	14.31 N	78.52 E
Cue, Austl. (kū)	210	27.30 S	118.10 E
Cuéllar, Sp. (kwā'lyär')	168e	41.24 N	4.15 W
Cuenca, Ec. (kwĕn'kä)	140	2.52 S	78.54 W
Cuenca, Sp.	168	40.05 N	2.07 W
Cuenca, Sierra de (Mts.), Sp. (sē-ĕ'r-rä-dĕ-kwĕ'n-kä)	168	40.02 N	1.50 W
Cuencame, Mex. (kwĕn-kä-mā')	122	24.52 N	103.42 W
Cuerámaro, Mex. (kwā-rä'mä-rô)	128	20.39 N	101.44 W
Cuernavaca, Mex. (kwĕr-nä-vä'kä)	129a	18.55 N	99.15 W
Cuero, Tx. (kwā'rō)	123	29.05 N	97.16 W
Cuetzalá del Progreso, Mex. (kwĕt-zä-lä dĕl prō-grā'sō)	128	18.07 N	99.51 W
Cuetzalan del Progreso, Mex. (kwĕt-zä-län dĕl prō-grā'sō)	129	20.02 N	97.33 W
Cuevas del Almanzora, Sp. (kwĕ'väs-dĕl-äl-män-zō-rä)	168	37.19 N	1.54 W
Cuglieri, It. (ko͞o-lyā'rĕ)	170	40.11 N	8.37 E
Cuiabá, Braz. (ko͞o-yä-bä')	141	15.33 S	56.03 W
Cuicatlán, Mex. (kwē-kä-tlän')	129	17.46 N	96.57 W
Cuilapa, Guat. (ko͞o-ē-lä'pä)	130	14.16 N	90.20 W
Cuilo (R.), Ang.	226	9.15 S	19.30 E
Cuito (R.), Ang. (ko͞o-ē-'tō)	226	14.15 S	19.00 E
Cuitzeo, Mex. (kwēt'zā-ō)	128	19.57 N	101.11 W
Cuitzeo, Laguna de (L.), Mex. (lä-o͞o'nä-dĕ-kwēt'zā-ō)	128	19.58 N	101.05 W
Cul de Sac (R.), Dom. Rep.-Hai. (ko͞o'l-dĕ-sä'k)	133	18.35 N	72.05 W
Culebra, (I.), P.R. (ko͞o-lā'brä)	127b	18.19 N	65.32 W
Culemborg, Neth.	155a	51.57 N	5.14 E
Culgoa (R.), Austl. (kŭl-gō'ȧ)	211	29.21 S	147.00 E
Culiacán, Mex. (ko͞o-lyä-kȧ'n)	126	24.45 N	107.30 W
Culion, Phil. (ko͞o-lē-ōn')	202	11.43 N	119.58 E
Cúllar de Baza, Sp. (ko͞o'l-yär-dĕ-bä'zä)	168	37.36 N	2.35 W
Cullera, Sp. (ko͞ol-yā'rä)	169	39.12 N	0.15 W
Cullinan, S. Afr. (ko͞o'lĭ-nån)	223b	25.41 S	28.32 E
Cullman, Ala. (kŭl'măn)	124	34.10 N	86.50 W
Culpeper, Va. (kŭl'pĕp-ĕr)	109	38.30 N	77.55 W
Culcross, Can. (kŭl'rôs)	93f	49.43 N	97.54 W
Culver, In. (kŭl'vĕr)	108	41.15 N	86.25 W
Culver City, Ca.	117a	34.00 N	118.23 W
Cumaná, Ven. (ko͞o-mä-nä')	141b	10.28 N	64.10 W
Cumberland, Can. (kŭm'bĕr-lănd)	93c	45.31 N	75.25 W
Cumberland, Md.	109	39.40 N	78.40 W
Cumberland, Wa.	116a	47.17 N	121.55 W
Cumberland, Wi.	113	45.31 N	92.01 W
Cumberland (R.), U.S.	124	36.45 N	85.33 W
Cumberland, L., Ky.	124	36.55 N	85.20 W
Cumberland Is., Austl.	211	20.20 S	149.46 E
Cumberland Pen., Can.	95	65.59 N	64.05 W
Cumberland Plat., Tn.	124	35.25 N	85.30 W
Cumberland Sd., Can.	95	65.27 N	65.44 W
Cundinamarca (Dept.), Col. (ko͞on-dē-nä-mä'r-kȧ)	140a	4.57 N	74.27 W
Cunduacán, Mex. (ko͞on-do͞o-ȧ-kän')	129	18.04 N	93.23 W
Cunene (Kunene)(R.), Ang.-Namibia	226	17.05 S	12.35 E
Cuneo, It. (ko͞o'nā-ō)	170	44.24 N	7.31 E
Cunha, Braz. (ko͞o'nyȧ)	139a	23.05 S	44.56 W
Cunnamulla, Austl. (kŭn-ȧ-mŭl-ȧ)	212	28.00 S	145.55 E
Cupula, Pico (Mtn.) (pē'kō-ko͞o'po͞o-lä)	126	24.45 N	111.10 W
Cuquío, Mex. (ko͞o-kē'ō)	128	20.55 N	103.03 W
Curaçao (I.), Neth. Antilles (ko͞o-rä-sä'ō)	140	12.12 N	68.58 W
Curacautín, Chile (kä-rä-kao͞o-tē'n)	142	38.25 S	71.53 W
Curacaví, Chile (ko͞o-rä-kä-vē')	139b	33.23 S	71.09 W
Curaumilla, Punta (Pt.), Chile (ko͞o-rou-mē'lyä)	139b	33.05 S	71.44 W
Curepto, Chile (ko͞o-rĕp-tō)	139b	35.06 S	72.02 W
Curicó, Chile (ko͞o-rē-kō')	139b	34.57 S	71.14 W
Curicó (Prov.), Chile	139b	34.55 S	71.15 W
Curitiba, Braz. (ko͞o-rē-tē'bȧ)	142	25.20 S	49.15 W
Curly Cut Cays (I.), Ba.	132	23.40 N	77.40 W
Currais Novos, Braz. (ko͞or-rä'ĕs nō-vōs)	141	6.02 S	36.39 W
Curran, Can. (kŭ-räN')	93c	45.30 N	74.59 W
Current (I.), Ba. (kŭ-rĕnt)	132	25.20 N	76.50 W
Current (R.), Mo. (kûr'ĕnt)	121	37.18 N	91.21 W
Currie, Mt., S. Afr. (kŭ-rē)	223c	30.28 S	29.23 E
Currituck Sd., NC (kûr'ĭ-tŭk)	125	36.27 N	75.42 W
Curtea-de-Argeş, Rom. (ko͞or'tĕ-ä dĕ är'zhĕsh)	171	45.09 N	24.40 E
Curtis, Ne. (kûr'tĭs)	120	40.36 N	100.29 W
Curtis (I.), Austl.	211	23.38 S	151.43 E
Curtisville, Pa. (kûr'tĭs-vĭl)	111e	40.38 N	79.50 W
Curuá (R.), Braz. (ko͞o-ro͞o-ä')	141	6.26 S	54.39 W
Čurug, Yugo. (cho͞o'ro͞og)	171	45.27 N	20.26 E
Curunga, Ang.	226	12.51 S	21.12 E
Curupira, Serra (Mts.), Braz.-Ven. (sĕr'rȧ ko͞o-ro͞o-pē'rȧ)	140	1.00 N	65.30 W
Cururupu, Braz. (ko͞o-ro͞o-ro͞o-po͞o')	141	1.40 S	44.56 W
Curuzú Cuatiá, Arg. (ko͞o-ro͞o-zo͞o' kwä-tē-ä')	142	29.45 S	57.58 W
Curvelo, Braz. (ko͞or-vĕl'o͞o)	141	18.47 S	44.14 W
Cushing, Ok. (kŭsh'ĭng)	121	35.58 N	96.46 W
Custer, SD (kŭs'tĕr)	112	43.46 N	103.36 W
Custer, Wa.	116d	48.55 N	122.39 W
Custer Battlefield Nat'l Mon., Mt. (kŭs'tĕr băt''l-fēld)	115	45.44 N	107.15 W
Cut Bank, Mt. (kŭt bănk)	115	48.38 N	112.19 W
Cuthbert, Ga. (kŭth'bĕrt)	124	31.47 N	84.48 W
Cuttack, India (kŭ-tăk')	190	20.38 N	85.53 E
Cutzamala (R.), Mex. (ko͞o-tzä-mä-lä')	128	18.57 N	100.41 W
Cutzamalá de Pinzón, Mex. (ko͞o-tzä-mä-lä'dĕ-pēn-zô'n)	128	18.28 N	100.36 W
Cuvo (R.), Ang. (ko͞o'vō)	226	10.55 S	14.00 E
Cuxhaven, F.R.G. (ko͝oks'hä-fĕn)	164	53.51 N	8.43 E
Cuyahoga Falls, Oh.	111d	41.08 N	81.29 W
Cuyahoga R., Oh. (kī-ȧ-hō'gȧ)	111d	41.22 N	81.38 W
Cuyapaire Ind. Res., Ca. (kū-yȧ-pâr)	118	32.46 N	116.20 W
Cuyo Is., Phil. (ko͞o'yō)	202	10.54 N	120.08 E
Cuyotenango, Guat. (ko͞o-yō-tĕ-näŋ'gō)	130	14.30 N	91.35 W
Cuyuni (R.), Guy.-Ven. (ko͞o-yo͞o'nē)	141	6.40 N	60.44 W
Cuyutlán, Mex. (ko͞o-yo͞o-tlän')	128	18.54 N	104.04 W
Cuzco, Peru	140	13.36 S	71.52 W
Cynthiana, Ky. (sĭn-thĭ-ăn'ȧ)	108	38.20 N	84.20 W
Cypress, Ca. (sī'prĕs)	117a	33.50 N	118.03 W
Cypress Hills, Can.	98	49.40 N	110.20 W
Cypress L., Can.	98	49.28 N	109.43 W
Cyprus, Asia (sī'prŭs)	188	35.00 N	31.00 E
Cyrenaica (Prov.), see Barqah			
Czechoslovakia, Eur. (chĕk'ō-slō-vä'kĭ-ȧ)	152	49.28 N	16.00 E
Czersk, Pol. (chĕrsk)	165	53.47 N	17.58 E
Częstochowa, Pol. (chăN-stō KÔ'vȧ)	165	50.49 N	19.10 E

D

PLACE (Pronunciation)	PAGE	Lat. °′	Long. °′
Da'an, China (dä-än)	198	45.25 N	124.22 E
Dabakala, Ivory Coast (dä-bä-kä'lä)	220	8.16 N	4.36 W
Daba Shan (Mts.), China (dä-bä shän)	198	32.25 N	108.20 E
Dabeiba, Col. (dä-bā'bä)	140a	7.01 N	76.16 W
Dabie Shan (Mts.), China (dä-bĭē shän)	199	31.40 N	114.50 E
Dabnou, Niger	225	14.09 N	5.22 E
Dabob B., Wa. (dā'bŏb)	116a	47.50 N	122.50 W
Dabola, Gui.	224	10.45 N	11.07 W
Dąbrowa Białostocka, Pol. (dôN-brō'vä)	165	53.37 N	23.18 E
Dacca, Bngl. (dä'kä) (dăk'ȧ)	190	23.45 N	90.29 E
Dachang, China (dä-chäŋ)	197b	31.18 N	121.25 E
Dachangshan Dao (I.), China (dä-chäŋ-shän dou)	196	39.21 N	122.31 E
Dachau, F.R.G. (dä'KOU)	155d	48.16 N	11.26 E
Dacotah, Can. (dȧ-kō'tȧ)	93f	49.52 N	97.38 W
Dade City, Fl. (dād)	125a	28.22 N	82.09 W
Dadeville, Al. (dād'vĭl)	124	32.48 N	85.44 W
Dādra & Nagar Haveli (Union Ter.), India	190	20.00 N	73.00 E
Dadu (R.), China (dä-do͞o)	199	29.20 N	103.03 E
Daet (Mtn.), Phil. (dä'ăt)	203a	14.07 N	122.59 E
Dafoe (R.), Can.	99	55.50 N	95.50 W
Dafter, Mi. (dăf'tĕr)	117k	46.21 N	84.26 W
Dagana, Senegal (dä-gä'nä)	224	16.31 N	15.30 W
Dagana (Reg.) Chad	225	12.20 N	15.15 E
Dagang, China (dä-gäŋ)	197a	22.48 N	113.24 E
Dagda, Sov. Un. (dȧg'dȧ)	172	56.04 N	27.30 E
Dagenham, Eng. (dăg'ĕn-ăm)	154b	51.32 N	0.09 E
Dagestan (Reg.), Sov. Un. (dä-gĕs-tän')	177	43.40 N	46.10 E
Daggett, Ca. (dăg'ĕt)	118	34.50 N	116.52 W
Dagu, China (dä-go͞o)	196	39.00 N	117.42 E
Dagu (R.), China	196	36.29 N	120.06 E
Dagupan, Phil. (dä-go͞o'pän)	203a	16.02 N	120.20 E
Daheishan Dao (I.), China (dä-hā-shän dou)	196	37.57 N	120.37 E
Da Hinggan Ling, see Greater Khingan Range			
Dahl, F.R.G. (däl)	167c	51.18 N	7.33 E
Dahlak Arch. (Is.), Eth.	221	15.45 N	40.30 E
Dahomey, see Benin			
Daibu, China (dī-bo͞o)	196	31.22 N	119.29 E
Daigo, Jap. (dī-gō)	201b	34.57 N	135.49 E
Daimiel Manzanares, Sp. (dī-myĕl'män-zä-nä'rĕs)	168	39.05 N	3.36 W
Dairy (R.), Or. (dâr'ĭ)	116c	45.33 N	123.04 W
Dairy (R.), East Fk. Or.	116c	45.40 N	123.03 W
Dai-Sen (Mtn.), Jap. (dī'sĕn')	201	35.22 N	133.35 E
Dai-Tenjo-dake (Mtn.), Jap. (dī-tĕn'jō dä-KÄ)	201	36.21 N	137.38 E
Daitō, Jap.	201b	34.42 N	135.38 E
Daiyun Shan (Mtn.), China (dī-yo͞on shän)	199	25.40 N	118.08 E
Dajabón, Dom. Rep. (dä-KÄ-bō'n)	133	19.35 N	71.40 W
Dajarra, Austl. (dȧ-jăr'ȧ)	210	21.45 S	139.30 E
Dakar, Senegal (dȧ-kär')	224	14.40 N	17.26 W
Dakhla, W. Sah.	220	23.45 N	16.04 W

ng-sing; ŋ-baŋk; N-nasalized n; nŏd; cŏmmit; ōld; ôbey; ôrder; oi-boil; fo͞od; fo͝ot; ou-out; s-soft; sh-dish; th-thin; pūre; ûnite; ûrn; stŭd; circŭs; ü-as in French tu; '-indeterminate vowel.

284 Dakouraoua – Delmas

PLACE (Pronunciation)	PAGE	Lat. °'	Long. °'
Dakouraoua, Niger	225	13.58 N	6.15 E
Dakovica, Yugo.	171	42.33 N	20.28 E
Dalälven (R.), Swe.	162	60.26 N	15.50 E
Dalatando, Ang.	226	9.18 S	14.54 E
Dalby, Austl. (dôl'bē)	212	27.10 S	151.15 E
Dalcour, La. (dăl-kour)	110d	29.49 N	89.59 W
Dale, Nor. (dä'lĕ)	162	60.35 N	5.55 E
Dale Hollow (L.), Tn. (dāl hŏl'ō)	124	36.33 N	85.03 W
Dalemead, Can. (dä'lē-mēd)	93e	50.53 N	113.38 W
Dalen, Nor. (dä'lĕn)	162	59.28 N	8.01 E
Daleside, S. Afr. (dāl'sīd)	219d	26.30 S	28.03 E
Dalesville, Can. (dālz'vĭl)	93a	45.42 N	74.23 W
Daley Waters, Austl. (dā lē)	210	16.15 S	133.30 E
Dalhart, Tx. (dăl härt)	120	36.04 N	102.32 W
Dalhousie, Can. (dăl-hōō'zē)	102	48.04 N	66.23 W
Dali, China (dä-lē)	197a	23.27 N	113.06 E
Dali, China	194	26.00 N	100.08 E
Dali, China	194	35.00 N	109.38 E
Dalian Wan (B.), China (dä-lĭĕn wän)	196	38.55 N	121.50 E
Dalías, Sp. (dä-lē'äs)	168	36.49 N	2.50 W
Dall (I.), Ak. (dăl)	105	54.50 N	133.10 W
Dallas, Or. (dăl'lȧs)	114	44.55 N	123.20 W
Dallas, SD	112	43.13 N	99.34 W
Dallas, Tx.	117c	32.45 N	96.48 W
Dalles Dam, Or.	114	45.36 N	121.08 W
Dall I., Ak.	96	54.50 N	132.55 W
Dalmacija (Reg.), Yugo. (däl-mä'tsē-yä)	170	43.25 N	16.37 E
Dalnerechensk, Sov. Un.	179	46.07 N	133.21 E
Daloa, Ivory Coast	224	6.53 N	6.27 W
Dalqū, Sud. (dĕl'gō)	221	20.07 N	30.41 E
Dalroy, Can. (dăl'roi)	93e	51.07 N	113.39 W
Dalrymple, Mt., Austl. (dăl'rĭm-p'l)	211	21.14 S	148.46 E
Dalton, Ga. (dôl'tŭn)	124	34.46 N	84.58 W
Dalton, S. Afr. (dôl'tŏn)	223c	29.21 S	30.41 E
Daly (R.), Austl. (dā'lĭ)	210	14.15 S	131.15 E
Daly City, Ca. (dā'lē)	116b	37.42 N	122.27 W
Damān, India	190	20.32 N	72.53 E
Damanhûr, Egypt (dä-män-hōōr')	219b	30.59 N	30.31 E
Damar, Pulau (I.), Indon.	203	7.15 S	129.15 E
Damara Rep., Cen. Afr. Rep.	225	4.58 N	18.42 E
Damaraland (Reg.), Namibia (dă'mȧ-rȧ-lănd)	222	22.15 S	16.15 E
Damas Cays (Is.), Ba. (dä'mäs)	132	23.50 N	79.50 W
Damascus, see Dimashq			
Damāvand (Mtn.), Iran	177	36.05 N	52.05 E
Damba, Ang. (däm'bä)	226	6.41 S	15.08 E
Dame Marie, Cap (C.), Hai. (dăm mȧrē')	133	18.35 N	74.50 W
Dāmghān, Iran (dām-gān')	192	35.50 N	54.15 E
Daming, China (dä-mĭŋ)	196	36.15 N	115.09 E
Dammartin-en-Goële, Fr. (däN-mär-tăN-äN-gō-ĕl')	167b	49.03 N	2.40 E
Dampier, Selat (Str.), Indon. (dăm'pēr)	203	0.40 S	131.15 E
Dampier Arch, Austl. (däN-pyâr')	210	20.15 S	116.25 E
Dampier Land (Pen.), Austl.	210	17.30 S	122.25 E
Dan (R.), NC (dăn)	125	36.26 N	79.40 W
Danakil Pln., Eth.	221	12.45 N	41.01 E
Danané, Ivory Coast	224	7.16 N	8.09 W
Da Nang (Tourane), Viet.	199	16.08 N	108.22 E
Danbury, Ct. (dăn'bēr-ĭ)	110a	41.23 N	73.27 W
Danbury, Eng.	154b	51.42 N	0.34 E
Danbury, Tx.	123a	29.14 N	95.22 W
Dandenong, Austl. (dăn'dē-nông)	207a	37.59 S	145.13 E
Dandong, China (dän-dôŋ)	198	40.10 N	124.30 E
Dane (R.), Eng. (dān)	154	53.11 N	2.14 W
Danea, Gui.	224	11.27 N	13.12 W
Danforth, Me.	102	45.38 N	67.53 W
Dangla, Eth.	221	11.17 N	37.00 E
Dan Gora, Nig.	225	11.30 N	8.09 E
Dangtu, China (däŋ-tōō)	196	31.35 N	118.28 E
Dani, Upper Volta	224	13.43 N	0.10 W
Dania, Fl. (dā'nĭ-ȧ)	125a	26.01 N	80.10 W
Danilov, Sov. Un. (dä'nē-lôf)	172	58.12 N	40.08 E
Danissa Hills, Ken.	227	3.20 N	40.55 E
Dankov, Sov. Un. (däŋ'kôf)	172	53.17 N	39.09 E
Danlí, Hond. (dän'lē)	130	14.02 N	86.35 W
Dannemora, NY (dăn-ē-mō'rȧ)	109	44.45 N	73.45 W
Dannhauser, S. Afr. (dän'hou-zēr)	223c	28.07 S	30.04 E
Dansville, NY (dănz'vĭl)	109	42.30 N	77.40 W
Danube, Mouths of the, Rom. (dăn'ūb)	173	45.13 N	29.37 E
Danube (Donau,Duna)(R.), Eur.	164	48.35 N	10.38 E
Danvers, Ma. (dăn'vērz)	103a	42.34 N	70.57 W
Danville, Ca. (dăn'vĭl)	116b	37.49 N	122.00 W
Danville, Il.	108	40.10 N	87.35 W
Danville, In.	108	39.45 N	86.30 W
Danville, Ky.	108	37.35 N	84.50 W
Danville, Pa.	109	41.00 N	76.35 W
Danville, Va.	125	36.35 N	79.24 W
Dan Xian, China (dän shyĕn)	199	19.30 N	109.38 E
Danyang, China (dän-yäŋ)	196	32.01 N	119.32 E
Danzig, G. of, Pol. (dän'tsĭk)	156	54.41 N	19.01 E
Dao Xian, China (dou shyĕn)	199	25.35 N	111.27 E
Daphnae (Ruins), Egypt	189a	30.43 N	32.12 E
Dapango, Upper Volta	224	10.52 N	0.12 E
Daqin Dao (I.), China (dä-chyĭn dou)	196	38.18 N	120.50 E
Dar'ā, Syria	189a	32.37 N	36.07 E
Darabani, Rom. (dă-rȧ-băn'ĭ)	165	48.13 N	26.38 E
Daraj, Libya	220	30.12 N	10.14 E
Darāw, Egypt (dȧ-rä'ōō)	219b	24.24 N	32.56 E
Darbhanga, India (dŭr-bŭŋ'gä)	190	26.03 N	85.09 E
Darby, Pa. (där'bĭ)	110f	39.55 N	75.16 W
Darby (I.), Ba.	133	23.50 N	76.20 W
Dardanelles (Str.), see Çanakkale Boğazi			
Dar es Salaam, Tan. (där ĕs sȧ-läm')	227	6.48 S	39.17 E
Dārfūr (Prov.), Sud. (där-fōōr')	221	13.21 N	23.46 E
Dargai, Pak. (dŭr-gä'ē)	193a	34.35 N	72.00 E
D'Arguin, Cap (C.), Mauritania	220	20.28 N	17.46 W
Darien, Col. (dā-rĭ-ĕn')	140a	3.56 N	76.30 W
Darien, Ct. (dâ-rē-ĕn')	110a	41.04 N	73.28 W
Darién, Cordillera de (Mts.), Nic.	130	13.00 N	85.42 W
Darién, Golfo del (G.), N.A.-S.A. (gôl-fô-dĕl-dä-rĭ-ĕn')	140	9.36 N	77.54 W
Darien, Serrania del (Ra.), Pan. (sĕr-ä-nē'ä dĕl dä-rē-ĕn')	131	8.13 N	77.28 W
Darjeeling, India (dŭr-jē'lĭng)	190	27.05 N	88.16 E
Darling(L.), ND (där'lĭng)	112	48.35 N	101.25 W
Darling (R.), Austl.	212	31.50 S	143.20 E
Darling Downs (Reg.), Austl.	212	27.22 S	150.00 E
Darling Ra, Austl.	210	30.30 S	115.45 E
Darlington, Eng. (där'lĭng-tŭn)	160	54.32 N	1.35 W
Darlington, SC	125	34.15 N	79.52 W
Darlington, Wi.	113	42.41 N	90.06 W
Darłowo, Pol. (där-lô'vô)	164	54.26 N	16.23 E
Darmstadt, F.R.G. (därm'shtät)	164	49.53 N	8.40 E
Darnah, Libya	221	32.44 N	22.41 E
Darnley B., Ak. (därn'lē)	105	70.00 N	124.00 W
Daroca, Sp. (dä-rō-kä)	168	41.08 N	1.24 W
Dartmoor, Eng. (därt'mōōr)	160	50.35 N	4.05 W
Dartmouth, Can. (därt'mŭth)	102	44.40 N	63.34 W
Dartmouth, Eng.	160	50.33 N	3.28 W
Daru I., Pap. N. Gui. (dä'rōō)	203	9.04 S	143.21 E
Daruvar, Yugo. (där'rōō-vär)	170	45.37 N	17.16 E
Darwen, Eng. (där'wĕn)	154	53.42 N	2.28 W
Darwin, Austl. (där'wĭn)	210	12.25 S	131.00 E
Darwin, Cordillera (Mts.), Chile-Arg. (kôr-dēl-yĕ'rä-där'wĕn)	142	54.40 S	69.30 W
Dash Point, Wa. (dăsh)	116a	47.19 N	122.25 W
Dasht (R.), Pak. (dŭsht)	192	25.30 N	62.30 E
Dasht-e Kavīr Des., Iran (dŭsht-ē-ka-vēr')	192	34.41 N	53.30 E
Dasht-e-Lūt (Des.), Iran (dȧ'sht-ē-lōōt)	192	31.47 N	58.38 E
Dasol B., Phil. (dä-sōl')	203a	15.53 N	119.40 E
Datian Ding (Mtn.), China (dä-tĭĕn dĭŋ)	199	22.25 N	111.20 E
Datong, China (dä-tôŋ)	198	40.00 N	113.30 E
Dattapukur, India	190a	22.45 N	88.32 E
Datteln, F.R.G. (dät'tĕln)	167c	51.39 N	7.20 E
Datu, Tandjung (C.), Indon.	202	2.08 N	110.15 E
Datuan, China (dä-tūän)	197b	30.57 N	121.43 E
Daugava (R.), Sov. Un.	163	56.40 N	24.40 E
Daugavpils, Sov. Un. (dá'ōō-gäv-pēls)	172	55.52 N	26.32 E
Dauphin, Can. (dô'fĭn)	99	51.09 N	100.00 W
Dauphin L., Can.	99	51.17 N	99.48 W
Dāvangere, India	191	14.30 N	75.55 E
Davao, Phil. (dä'vä-ô)	203	7.05 N	125.30 E
Davao G., Phil.	203	6.30 N	125.45 E
Davenport, Ia. (dăv'ĕn-pōrt)	113	41.34 N	90.38 W
Davenport, Wa.	114	47.39 N	118.07 W
David, Pan. (dä-vēdh')	131	8.27 N	82.27 W
David City, Ne. (dā'vĭd)	112	41.15 N	97.10 W
David-Gorodok, Sov. Un. (dȧ-vēt' gō-rō'dôk)	165	52.02 N	27.14 E
Davis, Ok. (dā'vĭs)	121	34.34 N	97.08 W
Davis, WV	109	39.15 N	79.25 W
Davis L., Or.	114	43.38 N	121.43 W
Davis Mts., Tx.	122	30.45 N	104.17 W
Davis Str., Can.	92	66.00 N	60.00 W
Davisson Lake (Res.), Wa.	114	46.20 N	122.10 W
Davlekanovo, Sov. Un.	176	54.15 N	55.05 E
Davos, Switz. (dä'vōs)	164	46.47 N	9.50 E
Dawa (R.), Eth.	221	4.34 N	41.34 E
Dawāsir, Wādī ad (R.), Sau. Ar.	192	20.48 N	44.07 E
Dawen (R.), China (dä-wŭn)	196	35.58 N	116.53 E
Dawley, Eng. (dô'lĭ)	154	52.38 N	2.28 W
Dawna Ra., Bur. (dô'nȧ)	202	17.02 N	98.01 E
Dawson, Can. (dô'sŭn)	105	64.04 N	139.22 W
Dawson, Ga.	124	31.45 N	84.29 W
Dawson, Mn.	112	44.54 N	96.03 W
Dawson (R.), Austl.	212	24.20 S	149.45 E
Dawson B., Can.	99	52.55 N	100.50 W
Dawson Creek, Can.	97	55.46 N	120.14 W
Dawson Ra., Can.	105	62.15 N	138.10 W
Dawson Springs, Ky.	124	37.10 N	87.40 W
Dawu, China (dä-wōō)	196	31.33 N	114.07 E
Dax, Fr. (dȧks)	166	43.42 N	1.06 W
Daxian, China (dä-shyĕn)	199	31.12 N	107.30 E
Daxing, China (dä-shyĭŋ)	198a	39.44 N	116.19 E
Dayiqiao, China (dä-yē-chyou)	196	31.43 N	120.40 E
Dayr az Zawr, Syr. (dȧ-ēr'ez-zôr')	192	35.15 N	40.01 E
Dayrūṭ, Egypt	219b	27.33 N	30.48 E
Dayton, Ky. (dā'tŭn)	111f	39.07 N	84.28 W
Dayton, NM	120	32.44 N	104.23 W
Dayton, Oh.	108	39.54 N	84.15 W
Dayton, Tn.	124	35.30 N	85.00 W
Dayton, Tx.	123	30.03 N	94.53 W
Dayton, Wa.	114	46.18 N	117.59 W
Daytona Beach, Fl. (dā-tō'nȧ)	125	29.11 N	81.02 W
Dayu, China (dä-yōō)	199	25.20 N	114.20 E
Da Yunhe (Grand Canal), China (dä yōōn-hŭ)	196	34.23 N	117.57 E
Dayville, Ct. (dā'vĭl)	109	41.50 N	71.55 W
De Aar, S. Afr. (dē-är')	222	30.45 S	24.05 E
Dead (L.), Mn. (dĕd)	112	46.28 N	96.00 W
Dead Sea, Isr.-Jordan	189a	31.30 N	35.30 E
Deadwood, SD (dĕd'wŏŏd)	112	44.23 N	103.43 W
Deal Island, Md. (dēl-ī'lȧnd)	109	38.10 N	75.55 W
Dean (R.), Can. (dēn)	96	52.45 N	125.30 W
Dean Chan, Can.	96	52.33 N	127.13 W
Deán Funes, Arg. (dĕ-ȧ'n-fōō-nĕs)	142	30.26 S	64.12 W
Dearborn, Mi. (dēr'bŭrn)	111b	42.18 N	83.15 W
Dearg, Ben (Mtn.), Scot. (bĕn dŭrg)	160	57.48 N	4.59 W
Dease Str., Can. (dēz)	94	68.50 N	108.20 W
Death Valley, Ca.-Nv.	118	36.55 N	117.12 W
Death Valley Junction, Ca.	118	36.18 N	116.26 W
Death Valley Natl. Mon., Ca.	118	36.34 N	117.00 W
Debal'tsevo, Sov. Un. (dyĕb'äl-tsyĕ'vô)	173	48.23 N	38.29 E
Debao, China (dŭ-bou)	199	23.18 N	106.40 E
Debar (Dibra), Yugo. (dĕ'bär) (dĕ'brä)	171	41.31 N	20.32 E
Dęblin, Pol. (däN'blĭn)	165	51.34 N	21.49 E
Dębno, Pol. (dĕb-nô')	164	52.47 N	13.43 E
Debo, Lac (L.), Mali	224	15.15 N	4.40 W
Debrecen, Hung. (dĕ'brĕ-tsĕn)	165	47.32 N	21.40 E
Debre Markos, Eth.	221	10.15 N	37.45 E
Debre Tabor, Eth.	221	11.57 N	38.09 E
Decatur, Al. (dē-kā'tŭr)	124	34.35 N	87.00 W
Decatur, Ga.	110c	33.47 N	84.18 W
Decatur, Il.	121	39.50 N	88.59 W
Decatur, In.	108	40.50 N	84.55 W
Decatur, Mi.	108	42.10 N	86.00 W
Decatur, Tx.	120	33.14 N	97.33 W
Decazeville, Fr. (dē-käz'vēl')	166	44.33 N	2.16 E
Deccan (Plat.), India (dĕk'ăn)	190	19.05 N	76.40 E
Deception L., Can.	98	56.33 N	104.15 W
Deception P., Wa. (dē-sĕp'shŭn)	116a	48.24 N	122.44 W
Děčín, Czech. (dyĕ'chēn)	164	50.47 N	14.14 E
Decorah, Ia. (dē-kō'rȧ)	113	43.18 N	91.48 W
Dedeagats, see Alexandroúpolis			
Dedenevo, Sov. Un. (dyĕ-dyĕ'nyĕ-vô)	180b	56.14 N	37.31 E
Dedham, Ma. (dĕd'ăm)	103a	42.15 N	71.11 W
Dedo do Deus (Mt.), Braz. (dĕ-dô-dô-dĕ'ōōs)	142b	22.30 S	43.02 W
Dédougou, Upper Volta (dā-dōō-gōō')	224	12.38 N	3.28 W
Dee (R.), Scot.	160	57.05 N	2.25 W
Deep River, Can.	101	46.06 N	77.20 W
Deep (R.), NC (dēp)	125	35.36 N	79.32 W
Deep Fk. (R.), OK.	121	35.35 N	96.42 W
Deepwater, Mo. (dep-wô-tēr)	121	38.15 N	93.46 W
Deerfield, IL. (dēr'fēld)	111a	42.10 N	87.51 W
Deer (I.), Me.	102	44.07 N	68.38 W
Deer Island, Or.	116c	45.56 N	122.51 W
Deer Lake, Can.	103	49.10 N	57.25 W
Deer L., Can.	99	52.40 N	94.30 W
Deer Lodge, Mt. (dēr lŏj)	115	46.23 N	112.42 W
Deer Park, Oh.	111f	39.12 N	84.24 W
Deer Park, Wa.	114	47.58 N	117.28 W
Deer River, Mn.	113	47.20 N	93.49 W
Defiance, Oh. (dē-fī'ăns)	108	41.15 N	84.20 W
DeFuniak Springs, Fl. (dē fū'nĭ-ăk)	124	30.42 N	86.06 W
Deganga, India	190a	22.41 N	88.41 E
Degeh-Bur, Eth.	219a	8.10 N	43.25 E
Deggendorf, F.R.G. (dĕ'ghĕn-dôrf)	164	48.50 N	12.59 E
Degollado, Mex. (dā-gô-lyä'dō)	128	20.27 N	102.11 W
DeGrey (R.), Austl. (dē grā')	210	20.20 S	119.25 E
Degtyarsk, Sov. Un. (dĕg-ty'arsk)	180a	56.42 N	60.05 E
Dehiwala-Mount Lavinia, Sri Lanka	191	6.47 N	79.55 E
Dehra Dūn, India (dā'rŭ)	190	30.09 N	78.07 E
Dehua, China (dŭ-hwä)	199	25.30 N	118.15 E
Dej, Rom. (dāzh)	165	47.09 N	23.53 E
De Kalb, Il. (dē kălb')	113	41.54 N	88.46 W
Dekese, Zaire	226	3.27 S	21.24 E
Delacour, Can. (dĕ-lä-kōōr')	93e	51.09 N	113.45 W
Delagua, Co. (dĕl-ä'gwä)	120	37.19 N	104.42 W
De Land, Fl. (dē lănd')	125	29.00 N	81.19 W
Delano, Ca. (dĕl'ȧ-nō)	118	35.47 N	119.15 W
Delano Pk., Ut.	119	38.25 N	112.25 W
Delavan, Wi. (dĕl'ȧ-văn)	113	42.39 N	88.38 W
Delaware, Oh. (dĕl'ȧ-wâr)	108	40.15 N	83.05 W
Delaware (State), U.S.	107	38.40 N	75.30 W
Delaware (R.), Ks.	121	39.45 N	95.47 W
Delaware (R.), U.S.	109	41.50 N	75.20 W
Delaware B., De.-NJ	109	39.05 N	75.10 W
Delaware Res., Oh.	108	40.30 N	83.05 E
Delémont, Switz. (dē-lā-môN')	164	47.21 N	7.18 E
De Leon, Tx. (dē lē-ŏn')	122	32.06 N	98.33 W
Delfinópolis, Braz. (dĕl-fē'nô'pō'-lĕs)	139a	20.20 S	46.50 W
Delft, Neth. (dĕlft)	155a	52.01 N	4.20 E
Delfzijl, Neth.	161	53.20 N	6.50 E
Delgada Pta. (Pt.), Arg. (pōō'n-tä-dĕl-gä'dä)	142	43.46 S	63.46 W
Delgado, Cabo (C.), Moz. (kȧ'bô-dĕl-gä'dō)	227	10.40 S	40.35 E
Delhi, Il. (dĕl'hī)	117e	39.03 N	90.16 W
Delhi, India	190	28.54 N	77.13 E
Delhi, La.	123	32.26 N	91.29 W
Delhi (State), India	190	28.30 N	76.50 E
Delitzsch, G.D.R. (dā'lĭch)	164	51.32 N	12.18 E
Dell Rapids, SD (dĕl)	112	43.50 N	96.43 W
Dellwood, Mn. (dĕl'wŏŏd)	117g	45.05 N	92.58 W
Dellys, Ag. (dĕ'lēs')	220	36.59 N	3.40 E
Del Mar, Ca. (dĕl mär')	118a	32.57 N	117.16 W
Delmas, S. Afr. (dĕl'mȧs)	219d	26.08 S	28.43 E

ăt; finȧl; rāte; senȧte; ärm; ȧsk; sofȧ; fâre; ch-choose; dh-as th in other; bē; ėvent; bĕt; recĕnt; cratēr; g-gō; gh-guttural g; bĭt; ĭ-short neutral; rīde; K-guttural k as ch in German ich;

PRONOUNCING INDEX

Delmenhorst – Dnepropetrovsk 285

PLACE (Pronunciation)	PAGE	Lat. °′	Long. °′
Delmenhorst, F.R.G. (dĕl′mĕn-hôrst)	164	53.03 N	8.38 E
Del Norte, Co. (dĕl nôrt′)	119	37.40 N	106.25 W
De-Longa (I.), Sov. Un.	179	76.30 N	153.00 E
De Long Mts., Ak. (dē′lŏng)	105	68.38 N	162.30 W
Deloraine, Austl. (dĕ-lŭ-rān)	212	41.30 S	146.40 E
Delphi, In. (dĕl′fī)	108	40.35 N	86.40 W
Delphos, Oh. (dĕl′fŏs)	108	40.50 N	84.20 W
Delray Beach, Fl. (dĕl-rā′)	125a	26.27 N	80.05 W
Del Rio, Tx. (dĕl rē′ō)	122	29.21 N	100.52 W
Delson, Can. (dĕl′sŭn)	93a	45.24 N	73.32 W
Delta, Co.	119	38.45 N	108.05 W
Delta, Ut.	119	39.20 N	112.35 W
Delta Beach, Can.	93f	50.10 N	98.20 W
Delta Mendota Can., Ca.	118	37.10 N	121.02 W
Delvine, Alb. (dĕl′vē-nȧ)	171	39.58 N	20.10 E
Dëma (R.), Sov. Un. (dyĕm′ä)	176	53.40 N	54.30 E
Demba, Zaire	226	5.30 S	22.16 E
Dembidolo, Eth.	221	8.46 N	34.46 E
Demidov, Sov. Un. (dzyĕ′mē-dô′f)	172	55.16 N	31.32 E
Deming, NM (dĕm′ĭng)	119	32.15 N	107.45 W
Demmin, G.D.R. (dĕm′mēn)	164	53.54 N	13.04 E
Demnat, Mor. (dĕm-nät)	220	31.58 N	7.03 W
Demopolis, Al. (dē-mŏp′ô-lĭs)	124	32.30 N	87.50 W
Demotte, In. (dē′mŏt)	111a	41.12 N	87.13 W
Dempo, Gunung (Vol.), Indon. (dĕm′pô)	202	4.04 S	103.11 E
Dem′yanka (R.), Sov. Un. (dyĕm-yän′kä)	178	59.07 N	72.58 E
Demyansk, Sov. Un. (dyĕm-yänsk′)	172	57.39 N	32.26 E
Denain, Fr. (dē-năN′)	166	50.23 N	3.21 E
Denali Natl. Park, Ak.	105	63.48 N	153.02 W
Denbigh, Wales (dĕn′bĭ)	160	53.15 N	3.25 W
Dendermonde, Bel.	155a	51.02 N	4.04 E
Dendron, Va. (dĕn′drŭn)	125	37.02 N	76.53 W
Denezhkin Kamen, Gora (Mtn.), Sov. Un. (dzyě-ŋĕ′zhkĕn kȧmĭēŋ)	180a	60.26 N	59.35 E
D′Enfer, Pointe (Pt.), Mart.	131b	14.21 N	60.48 W
Denham, Mt., Jam.	132	18.20 N	77.30 W
Den Helder, Neth. (dĕn hĕl′dĕr)	161	52.55 N	5.45 E
Denia, Sp. (dā′nyä)	169	38.48 N	0.06 E
Deniliquin, Austl. (dĕ-nĭl′ĭ-kwĭn)	212	35.20 S	144.52 E
Denison, Ia. (dĕn′ĭ-sŭn)	112	42.01 N	95.22 W
Denison, Tx.	121	33.45 N	97.02 W
Denisovka, Sov. Un. (dĕ-nē′sof-kȧ)	180a	52.26 N	61.45 E
Denizli, Tur. (dĕn-ĭz-lē′)	177	37.40 N	29.10 E
Denklingen, F.R.G. (dĕn′klēn-gĕn)	167c	50.54 N	7.40 E
Denmark, SC (dĕn′märk)	125	33.18 N	81.09 W
Denmark, Eur.	152	56.14 N	8.30 E
Denmark Str., Grnld.	92	66.30 N	27.00 W
Dennilton, S. Afr. (dĕn-ĭl-tŭn)	219d	25.18 S	29.13 E
Dennison, Oh. (dĕn′ĭ-sŭn)	108	40.25 N	81.20 W
Denpasar, Indon.	202	8.35 S	115.10 E
Denton, Eng. (dĕn′tŭn)	154	53.27 N	2.07 W
Denton, Md.	109	38.55 N	75.50 W
Denton, Tx.	121	33.12 N	97.06 W
D′Entrecasteaux, Pt., Austl. (däN-tr′kȧs-tō′)	210	34.50 S	114.45 E
D′Entrecasteaux Is., Pap. N. Gui. (däN-tr′-lȧs-tō′)	203	9.45 S	152.00 E
Denver, Co. (dĕn′vẽr)	120	39.44 N	104.59 W
Deoli, India	190	25.52 N	75.23 E
De Pere, Wi. (dē pēr′)	113	44.25 N	88.04 W
Depew, NY (dē-pū′)	111c	42.55 N	78.43 W
Deping, China (dŭ-pĭŋ)	196	37.28 N	116.57 E
Depue, Il. (dē pū)	108	41.15 N	89.55 W
De Queen, Ar. (dē kwēn′)	121	34.02 N	94.21 W
De Quincy, La. (dē kwĭn′sĭ)	123	30.27 N	93.27 W
Dera Ghāzi Khān, Pak. (dā′rŭ gä-zē′ κan′)	190	30.09 N	70.39 E
Dera Ismāīl Khān, Pak. (dā′rŭ ĭs-mä-ēl′ κän′)	190	31.55 N	70.51 E
Derbent, Sov. Un. (dĕr-bĕnt′)	177	42.00 N	48.10 E
Derby, Austl. (där′bē) (dûr′bē)	210	17.20 S	123.40 E
Derby, Ct. (dûr′bē)	109	41.20 N	73.05 W
Derby, Eng. (där′bē)	154	52.55 N	1.29 W
Derby, S. Afr. (där′bĭ)	219d	25.55 S	27.02 E
Derbyshire (Co.), Eng.	154	53.11 N	1.30 W
Derdepoort, S. Afr.	219d	24.39 S	26.21 E
Dere, Lak (R.), Ken.	227	0.45 N	40.15 E
Derg, Lough (L.), Ire. (lŏk dĕrg)	160	53.00 N	8.09 W
De Ridder, La. (dē rĭd′ẽr)	123	30.50 N	93.18 W
Dermott, Ar. (dûr′mŏt)	121	33.32 N	91.24 W
Derry, NH (dâr′ĭ)	103a	42.53 N	71.22 W
Derventa, Yugo. (dĕr′ven-tȧ)	171	45.58 N	17.58 E
Derwent (R.), Austl. (dĕr′wĕnt)	212	42.21 S	146.30 E
Derwent (R.), Eng.	154	52.54 N	1.24 W
Des Arc, Ar. (dāz ärk′)	121	34.59 N	91.31 W
Descalvado, Braz. (dĕs-käl-vȧ-dô)	139a	21.55 S	47.37 W
Descartes, Fr.	166	46.58 N	0.42 E
Deschambault L., Can.	98	54.40 N	103.35 W
Deschênes, Can.	93c	45.23 N	75.47 W
Deschenes, L., Can.	93c	54.25 N	75.53 W
Deschutes R., Or. (dā-shōōt′)	114	44.25 N	121.21 W
Desdemona, Tx. (dĕz-dē-mō′nȧ)	122	32.16 N	98.33 W
Dese, Eth.	221	11.00 N	39.51 E
Deseado, Rio (R.), Arg. (rē-ō-dā-sā-ä′dhō)	142	46.50 S	67.45 W
Desirade I., Guad. (dā-zē-räs′)	131b	16.21 N	60.51 W
De Smet, SD (dē smĕt′)	112	44.23 N	97.33 W
Des Moines, Ia. (dē moin′)	113	41.35 N	93.37 W
Des Moines, NM	120	36.42 N	103.48 W
Des Moines, Wa.	116a	46.24 N	122.20 W
Des Moines (R.), U.S.	107	43.45 N	94.20 W
Desna (R.), Sov. Un. (dyĕs-nȧ′)	173	51.05 N	31.03 E
Desolación (I.), Chile (dĕ-sô-lä-syō′n)	142	53.05 S	74.00 W
De Soto, Mo. (dē sŏ′tō)	121	38.07 N	90.32 W
Des Peres, Mo. (dĕs pĕr′ĕs)	117e	38.36 N	90.26 W
Des Plaines, Il. (dĕs plānz′)	111a	42.02 N	87.54 W
Des Plaines R., Il.	111a	41.39 N	87.56 W
Dessau, G.D.R. (dĕs′ou)	164	51.50 N	12.15 E
Detmold, G.D.R. (dĕt′mōld)	164	51.57 N	8.55 E
Detroit, Mi. (dē-troit′)	111b	42.22 N	83.10 W
Detroit, Tx.	121	33.41 N	95.16 W
Detroit Lakes, Mn. (dē-troit′lākz)	112	46.48 N	95.51 W
Detva, Czech. (dyĕt′vȧ)	165	48.32 N	19.21 E
Deurne, Bel.	155a	51.13 N	4.27 E
Deutsch Wagram, Aus.	155e	48.19 N	16.34 E
Deux-Montagnes, Can. (dû mōN-tăny′)	93a	45.33 N	73.54 W
Deux Montagnes, Lac des (L.), Can.	93a	45.28 N	74.00 W
Deva, Rom. (dā′vä)	171	45.52 N	22.52 E
Dévaványa, Hung. (dā′vô-vän-yô)	165	47.01 N	20.58 E
Develi, Tur. (dĕ′vȧ-lē)	177	38.20 N	35.10 E
Deventer, Neth. (dĕv′ĕn-tẽr)	161	52.14 N	6.07 E
Devils (L.), ND (dĕv″lz)	112	47.57 N	99.04 W
Devils (R.), Tx.	122	29.55 N	101.10 W
Devils I., see Diable, Ile du			
Devils Lake, ND	106	48.10 N	98.55 W
Devils Lake Ind. Res., ND	112	48.08 N	99.40 W
Devils Postpile Natl. Mon., Ca.	118	37.42 N	119.12 W
Devils Tower Natl. Mon., Wy.	115	44.38 N	105.07 W
Devoll (R.), Alb.	171	40.55 N	20.10 E
Devon, Can.	93g	53.23 N	113.43 W
Devon, S. Afr. (dĕv′ŭn)	219d	26.23 S	28.47 E
Devonport, Austl. (dĕv′ŭn-pôrt)	212	41.20 S	146.30 E
Devonport, N.Z.	211a	36.50 S	174.45 E
Devore, Ca. (dē-vôr′)	117a	34.13 N	117.24 W
Dewatto, Wa. (dē-wȧt′ō)	116a	47.27 N	123.04 W
Dewey, Ok. (dū′ĭ)	121	36.48 N	95.55 W
De Witt, Ar. (dē wĭt′)	121	34.17 N	91.22 W
De Witt, Ia.	113	41.46 N	90.34 W
Dewsbury, Eng. (dūz′bẽr-ĭ)	154	53.42 N	1.39 W
Dexter, Me. (dĕks′tẽr)	102	45.01 N	69.19 W
Dexter, Mo.	121	36.46 N	89.56 W
Dexter (L.), Fl.	125	29.07 N	81.24 W
Dezfūl, Iran	192	32.14 N	48.37 E
Dezhnëva, Mys (East Cape), Sov. Un. (dyĕzh′nyĭf)	189	68.00 N	172.00 W
Dezhou, China (dŭ-jō)	196	37.28 N	116.17 E
Dhahran, see Aẕ Ẕahrān			
Dharamtar Cr., India	191b	18.49 N	72.54 E
Dharmavaram, India	191	14.32 N	77.43 E
Dhaulāgiri (Mtn.), Nep. (dou-lȧ-gē′rē)	190	28.42 N	83.31 E
Dhenoúsa (I.), Grc.	171	37.09 N	25.53 E
Dhībān, Jordan	189a	31.30 N	35.46 E
Dhidhimótikhon, Grc.	171	41.20 N	26.27 E
Dhodhekánisos (Dodecanese) (Is.), Grc.	171	38.00 N	26.10 E
Dhule, India	190	20.58 N	74.43 E
Día (I.), Grc. (dē′ä)	170a	35.27 N	25.17 E
Diable, Ile du (Devils I.), Fr. Gu.	141	5.15 N	57.10 W
Diablo, Mt., Ca. (dyä′blō)	116b	37.52 N	121.55 W
Diablo Heights, Pan. (dyȧ′blō)	126a	8.58 N	79.34 W
Diablo Range (Mts.), Ca.	116b	37.47 N	121.50 W
Diaca, Moz.	227	11.30 S	39.59 E
Diaka (R.), Mali	224	14.40 N	5.00 E
Diamantina, Braz.	141	18.14 S	43.32 W
Diamantina (R.), Austl. (dī′man-tē′nȧ)	210	25.38 S	139.53 E
Diamantino, Braz. (dē-ȧ-män-tē′no)	141	14.22 S	56.23 W
Diamond Pk., Or.	114	43.32 N	122.08 W
Diana Bk., Ba. (dī′ăn′ȧ)	133	22.30 N	74.45 W
Dianbai, China (dĭĕn-bī)	199	21.30 N	111.20 E
Dian Chi (L.), China (dĭĕn chē)	199	24.58 N	103.18 E
Dibra, see Debar			
Dickinson, ND (dĭk′ĭn-sŭn)	112	46.52 N	102.49 W
Dickinson, Tx. (dĭk′ĭn-sŭn)	123a	29.28 N	95.02 W
Dickinson Bayou, Tx.	123a	29.26 N	95.08 W
Dickson, Tn. (dĭk′sŭn)	124	36.03 N	87.24 W
Dickson City, Pa.	109	41.25 N	75.40 W
Dicle (R.), Tur. (dĭj′lȧ)	177	37.50 N	40.40 E
Didcot, Eng. (dĭd′cŏt)	154b	51.35 N	1.15 W
Didiéni, Mali	224	13.53 N	8.06 W
Die, Fr. (dē)	167	44.45 N	5.22 E
Diefenbaker (Res.), Can.	94	51.20 N	108.10 W
Diefenbaker L., Can.	98	51.00 N	106.55 W
Diego de Ocampo, Pico (Pk.), Dom. Rep. (pē′-kô-dyĕ′gô-dĕ-ô-kä′m-pô)	133	19.40 N	70.45 W
Diego Ramirez, Islas (Is.), Chile (dē ä′gō rä-mē′räz)	142	56.15 S	70.15 W
Diéma, Mali	224	14.32 N	9.12 W
Dien Bien Phu, Viet.	194	21.38 N	102.49 E
Dieppe, Can. (dē-ĕp′)	102	46.06 N	64.45 W
Dieppe, Fr.	166	49.54 N	1.05 E
Dierks, Ar. (dērks)	121	34.06 N	94.02 W
Diessen, F.R.G. (dēs′sĕn)	155d	47.57 N	11.06 E
Diest, Bel.	155a	50.59 N	5.05 E
Digby, Can. (dĭg′bĭ)	102	44.37 N	65.46 W
Dighton, Ma. (dī-tŭn)	110b	41.49 N	71.05 W
Digne, Fr. (dēn′y′)	167	44.07 N	6.16 E
Digoin, Fr. (dē-gwăN′)	166	46.28 N	4.06 E
Digul (R.), Indon.	203	7.00 S	140.27 E
Dijohan Pt., Phil. (dē-kō-än)	203a	16.24 N	122.25 E
Dijon, Fr. (dē-zhōN′)	166	47.21 N	5.02 E
Dikson, Sov. Un. (dĭk′sŏn)	178	73.30 N	80.35 E
Dikwa, Nig. (dē′kwä)	221	12.06 N	13.53 E
Dili, Indon. (dĭl′ē)	203	8.35 S	125.35 E
Di Linosa I., It. (dē-lē-nô′sä)	158	36.01 N	12.43 E
Dilizhan, Sov. Un.	177	40.45 N	45.00 E
Dillingham, Ak. (dĭl′ĕng-hăm)	105	59.10 N	158.38 W
Dillon, Mt. (dĭl′ŭn)	115	45.12 N	112.40 W
Dillon, SC	125	34.24 N	79.28 W
Dillon Res., Oh.	108	40.05 N	82.05 W
Dilolo, Zaire (dē-lō′lō)	222	10.19 S	22.23 E
Dimashq (Damascus), Syr. (dȧ-măs′kŭs)	192	33.31 N	36.18 E
Dimbokro, Ivory Coast	224	6.39 N	4.42 W
Dimbovita (R.), Rom.	171	44.43 N	25.41 E
Dimitrovo, see Pernik			
Dimlang (Mtn.), Nig.	225	8.24 N	11.47 E
Dimona, Isr.	189a	31.03 N	35.01 E
Dinagate (I.), Phil.	203	10.15 N	126.15 E
Dinājpur, Bngl.	190	25.38 N	87.39 E
Dinan, Fr. (dē-näN′)	166	48.27 N	2.03 W
Dinant, Bel. (dē-näN′)	161	50.17 N	4.50 E
Dinara (Mts.), Yugo. (dē′nä-rä)	170	43.50 N	16.15 E
Dinard, Fr.	166	48.38 N	2.04 W
Dindigul, India	191	10.25 N	78.03 E
Dingalan B., Phil. (dĭŋ-gä′län)	203a	15.19 N	121.33 E
Dingle, Ire. (dĭng″l)	160	52.10 N	10.13 W
Dingle B., Ire.	160	52.02 N	10.15 W
Dingo, Austl. (dĭŋ′gō)	211	23.45 S	149.26 E
Dinguiraye, Gui.	224	11.18 N	10.43 W
Dingwall, Scot. (dĭng′wôl)	160	57.37 N	4.23 W
Ding Xian, China (dĭŋ shyĕn)	196	38.30 N	115.00 E
Dingxing, China (dĭŋ-shyĭŋ)	196	39.18 N	115.50 E
Dingyuan, China (dĭŋ-yūän)	196	32.32 N	117.40 E
Dingzi Wan (B.), China	196	36.33 N	121.06 E
Dinosaur Natl. Mon., Co.-Ut. (dī′nō-sôr)	115	40.45 N	109.17 W
Dinslaken, F.R.G. (dēns′lä-kĕn)	167c	51.33 N	6.44 E
Dinteloord, Neth.	155a	51.38 N	4.21 E
Dinuba, Ca. (dī-nū′bȧ)	118	36.33 N	119.29 W
Dios, Cayo de (I.), Cuba (kä′yō-dĕ-dē-ōs′)	132	22.05 N	83.05 W
Diourbel, Senegal (dē-ōōr-bĕl′)	224	14.40 N	16.15 W
Diphu Pass, China (dĭ-pōō)	193	28.15 N	96.45 E
Diquis (R.), C.R. (dē-kēs′)	131	8.59 N	83.24 W
Dire Dawa, Eth.	219a	9.40 N	41.47 E
Diriamba, Nic. (dēr-yäm′bä)	130	11.52 N	86.15 W
Dirk Hartog (I.), Austl.	210	26.25 S	113.15 E
Dirksland, Neth.	155a	51.45 N	4.04 E
Dirranbandi, Austl. (dĭ-rȧ-băn′dē)	212	28.24 S	148.29 E
Dirty Devil (R.), Ut. (dûr′tĭ dĕv″l)	119	38.20 N	110.30 W
Disappointment (L.), Austl.	210	23.20 S	120.20 E
Disappointment, C., Wa. (dĭs′ȧ-point′ment)	116c	46.16 N	124.11 W
D′Ischia, I., It. (dē′sh-kyä)	169c	40.26 N	13.55 E
Discovery, S. Afr. (dĭs-kŭv′ẽr-ĭ)	223b	26.10 S	27.53 E
Discovery (Is.), Can. (dĭs-kŭv′ẽr-ē)	116a	48.25 N	123.13 W
Dishnā, Egypt (dēsh′nȧ)	219b	26.08 N	32.27 E
Disko (I.), Grnld. (dĭs′kō)	92	70.00 N	54.00 W
Dismal Swp., NC-Va. (dĭz′măl)	125	36.35 N	76.34 W
Disna, Sov. Un. (dēs′nȧ)	172	55.34 N	28.15 E
Dispur, India	190	26.00 N	91.50 E
Disraëli, Can. (dĭs-rā′lĭ)	102	45.53 N	71.23 W
District of Columbia, U.S.	107	38.50 N	77.00 W
Distrito Federal (Dist.), Braz. (dēs-trē′tô-fē-dĕ-rä′l)	141	15.49 S	47.39 W
Distrito Federal (Dist.), Mex.	129	19.14 N	99.08 W
Disūq, Egypt (dē-sōōk′)	219b	31.07 N	30.41 E
Diu, India (dē′ōō)	190	20.48 N	70.58 E
Divilacan B., Phil. (dē-vē-lä′kän)	203a	17.26 N	122.25 E
Divinópolis, Braz. (dē-vē-nô′pô-lēs)	139a	20.10 S	44.53 W
Divo, Ivory Coast	224	5.50 N	5.22 W
Dixon, Il. (dĭks′ŭn)	113	41.50 N	89.30 W
Dixon Entrance, Ak.-Can.	96	54.25 N	132.00 W
Diyarbakir, Tur. (dē-yär-bĕk′ĭr)	177	38.00 N	40.10 E
Dja (R.), Cam.	225	3.25 N	13.17 E
Djambala, Con.	226	2.33 S	14.45 E
Djanet, Alg.	220	24.29 N	9.26 E
Djebob (Mtn.), Ghana	224	8.20 N	0.37 E
Djedi (R.), Alg.	158	34.18 N	4.39 E
Djelfa, Alg. (jĕl′fä)	220	34.40 N	3.17 E
Djember, Chad.	225	10.25 N	17.50 E
Djerba, Île de (I.), Tun.	158	33.53 N	11.26 E
Djerid, Chott (L.), Tun. (jĕr′ĭd)	220	33.15 N	8.29 E
Djibasso, Upper Volta	224	13.07 N	4.10 W
Djibo, Upper Volta	224	14.06 N	1.38 W
Djibouti, Djibouti (jē-bōō-tē′)	219a	11.34 N	43.00 E
Djibouti, Afr.	218	11.35 N	48.08 E
Djokoumatombi, Con.	226	0.47 N	15.22 E
Djokupunda, Zaire	226	5.27 S	20.58 E
Djoua (R.), Con.-Gabon	226	1.25 N	13.40 E
Djursholm, Swe. (djōōrs′hōlm)	162	59.26 N	18.01 E
Dmitriyevka, Sov. Un. (d′mē-trē-yĕf′kȧ)	173	47.57 N	38.56 E
Dmitriyev-L′govskiy, Sov. Un. (d′mē′trĭ-yĕf l′gôf′skĭ)	173	52.07 N	35.05 E
Dmitrov, Sov. Un. (d′mē′trôf)	180b	56.21 N	37.32 E
Dmitrovsk, Sov. Un. (d′mē′trôfsk)	172	52.30 N	35.10 E
Dnepr (Dnieper) (R.), Sov. Un. (nē′pẽr)	173	46.47 N	32.57 E
Dneprodzerzhinsk, Sov. Un. (d′nyĕp′rô-zẽr-shĭnsk)	173	48.32 N	34.38 E
Dneprodzerzhinskoye Vdkhr. (Res.), Sov. Un.	174	49.00 N	34.10 E
Dnepropetrovsk, Sov. Un. (d′nyĕp′rô-pȧ-trôfsk)	173	48.23 N	34.10 E
Dnepropetrovsk (Oblast), Sov. Un.	173	48.15 N	34.08 E

286 Dnepr Zaliv – Duitama

PLACE (Pronunciation)	PAGE	Lat. °′	Long. °′
Dnepr Zaliv (B.), Sov. Un. (dnyĕp'r zȧ'lĭf)	173	46.33 N	31.45 E
Dnestr (Dniester) (R.), Sov. Un. (nēst'rōōl) (nēs'tēr)	173	48.21 N	28.10 E
Dnestrovskiy Liman (B), Sov. Un.	173	46.13 N	29.50 E
Dnieper (R.), see Dnepr			
Dniester (R.), see Dnestr			
Dno, Sov.Un. (d'nô')	172	57.49 N	29.59 E
Do, Lac (L.), Mali	224	15.50 N	2.20 W
Doba, Chad	225	8.39 N	16.51 E
Dobbs Ferry, NY (dŏbz'fĕ'rē)	110a	41.01 N	73.53 W
Dobbyn, Austl. (dŏb'ĭn)	210	19.45 S	140.02 E
Dobele, Sov.Un. (dŏ'bĕ-lĕ)	163	56.37 N	23.18 E
Döbeln, G.D.R. (dû'bĕln)	164	51.08 N	13.07 E
Doberai Jazirah (Pen.), Indon.	203	1.25 S	133.15 E
Dobo, Indon.	203	6.00 S	134.18 E
Doboj, Yugo. (dō'boi)	171	44.42 N	18.04 E
Dobryanka, Sov. Un. (dôb-ryän'kȧ)	180a	58.27 N	56.26 E
Dobšina, Czech. (dôp'shē-nä)	165	48.48 N	20.25 E
Doce (R.), Braz. (dō'sä)	141	19.01 S	42.14 W
Doce Leguas, Cayos de las (Is.), Cuba (kä'yōs-dĕ-läs-dō-sĕ-lĕ'gwäs)	132	20.55 N	79.05 W
Doctor Arroyo, Mex. (dôk-tōr' är-rō'yō)	128	23.41 N	100.10 W
Dr. Ir. W. J. van Blommestein Meer (Res.), Sur.	141	4.45 N	55.05 W
Doddington, Eng. (dŏd'dĭng-tŏn)	154b	51.17 N	0.47 E
Dodecanese (S.), see Dhodhekánisos			
Dodge City, Ks. (dŏj)	120	37.44 N	100.01 W
Dodgeville, Wi. (dŏj'vĭl)	113	42.58 N	90.07 W
Dodoma, Tan. (dō'dō-mȧ)	227	6.11 S	35.45 E
Dog (L.), Can. (dŏg)	113	48.42 N	89.24 W
Dogger Bk., Eur. (dŏg'gēr)	161	55.07 N	2.25 E
Dogubayazit, Tur.	177	39.35 N	44.00 E
Dohad, India	190	22.52 N	74.18 E
Doiran (L), Grc.	171	41.10 N	23.00 E
Dōjō, Jap. (dō-jō)	201b	34.51 N	135.14 E
Dokshitsy, Sov. Un. (dôk-shētsē)	172	54.53 N	27.49 E
Dolbeau, Can.	101	48.52 N	72.16 W
Dole, Fr. (dōl)	167	47.07 N	5.28 E
Dolgaya, Kosa (C.), Sov. Un. (kô'sȧ dôl-gä'yä)	173	46.42 N	37.42 E
Dolgeville, NY	109	43.10 N	74.45 W
Dolgiy (I.), Sov. Un.	176	69.20 N	59.20 E
Dolgoprudnyy, Sov. Un.	180b	55.57 N	37.33 E
Dolina, Sov. Un. (dô-lyē'nä)	165	48.57 N	24.01 E
Dolinsk, Sov. Un. (dȧ-lēnsk')	200	47.29 N	142.31 E
Dollar Hbr, Ba.	132	25.30 N	79.15 W
Dolo, Som.	221	4.01 N	42.14 E
Dolomite, Al. (dŏl'ō-mīt)	110h	33.28 N	86.57 W
Dolomiti, Alpi (Mts.), It. (äl-pē-dō-lō'mē-tē)	170	46.16 N	11.43 E
Dolores, Arg. (dō-lō'rĕs)	139c	36.20 S	57.42 W
Dolores, Col.	140a	3.33 N	74.54 W
Dolores, Phil. (dō-lō-rĕs)	203a	17.40 N	120.43 E
Dolores, Tx. (dō-lō'rĕs)	122	27.42 N	99.47 W
Dolores, Ur.	139c	33.32 S	58.15 W
Dolores (R.), Co.-Ut.	119	38.35 N	108.50 W
Dolores Hidalgo, Mex. (dō-lō'rĕs-ē-däl'gō)	128	21.09 N	100.56 W
Dolphin and Union Str., Can. (dŏl'fĭn ūn'yŭn)	94	69.22 N	117.10 W
Domažlice, Czech. (dō'mäzh-lē-tsĕ)	164	49.27 N	12.55 E
Dombasle-sur-Meurthe, Fr. (dôN-bäl')	167	48.38 N	6.18 E
Dombóvár, Hung. (dŏm'bō-vär)	165	46.22 N	18.08 E
Domeyko, Cordillera (Mts.), Chile (kôr-dēl-yĕ'rä-dô-mā'kō)	140	20.50 S	69.02 W
Dominica, N.A. (dŏ-mĭ-nē'kȧ)	127	15.30 N	60.45 W
Dominica Chan., N.A.	131b	15.00 N	61.30 W
Dominican Republic, N.A. (dō-mĭn'ĭ-kăn)	127	19.00 N	70.45 W
Dominion, Can. (dō-mĭn'yŭn)	103	46.13 N	60.01 W
Domiongo, Zaire	226	4.37 S	21.15 E
Domodedovo, Sov. Un. (dô-mô-dyĕ'do-vô)	180b	55.27 N	37.45 E
Dom Silvério, Braz. (doN-sēl-vĕ'ryō)	139a	20.09 S	42.57 W
Don (R.), Eng. (dŏn)	154	53.27 N	1.34 W
Don (R.), Eng.	154	53.39 N	0.58 W
Don (R.), Scot.	160	57.19 N	2.39 W
Don (R.), Sov.Un.	174	49.50 N	41.30 E
Donaldson, Mi. (dŏn'ăl-sŭn)	117k	46.19 N	84.22 W
Donaldsonville, La. (dŏn'ăld-sŭn-vĭl)	123	30.05 N	90.58 W
Donalsonville, Ga.	124	31.02 N	84.50 W
Donau (R.), See Danube			
Donawitz, Aus. (dō'nȧ-vĭts)	164	47.23 N	15.05 E
Don Benito, Sp. (dōn'bā-nē'tō)	168	38.55 N	6.08 W
Doncaster, Austl. (doŋ'kăs-tēr)	207a	37.47 S	145.08 E
Doncaster, Eng. (doŋ'kăs-tēr)	154	53.32 N	1.07 W
Dondo, Ang. (dōn'dō)	226	9.38 S	14.25 E
Dondo, Moz.	222	19.33 S	34.47 E
Dondra Hd., Sri Lanka	191	5.52 N	80.52 E
Donegal, Ire. (dŏn-ē-gôl')	160	54.44 N	8.05 W
Donegal Bay, Ire. (dŏn-ē-gôl')	160	54.35 N	8.36 W
Donets (R.), Sov. Un. (dō-nyĕts')	173	48.48 N	38.42 E
Donets Coal Basin (Reg.), Sov. Un. (dō-nyĕts')	173	48.15 N	38.50 E
Donetsk (Oblast), Sov. Un.	173	47.55 N	37.40 E
Donetsk (Stalino), Sov. Un. (dō-nyĕts'k) (stä'lĭ-nō)	173	48.00 N	37.35 E
Dong (R.), China (dôŋ)	195	34.13 N	115.08 E
Dongara, Austl. (dôn-gă'rȧ)	210	29.15 S	115.00 E
Dongba, China (dôŋ-bä)	196	31.40 N	119.02 E
Dong'e, China (dôŋ-ŭ)	196	36.21 N	116.14 E
Dong'erzen, China (dôŋ-är-dzŭn)	196	36.11 N	116.16 E
Dongfang, China (dôŋ-fäŋ)	199	19.08 N	108.42 E
Donggala, Indon. (dôn-gä'lä)	202	0.45 S	119.32 E
Dongguan, China (dôŋ-gûän)	197a	23.03 N	113.46 E
Dongguang, China (dôŋ-gûäŋ)	196	37.54 N	116.33 E
Donghai, China (dôŋ-hī)	196	34.35 N	119.05 E
Dong Hoi, Viet. (dông-hô-ē')	199	17.25 N	106.42 E
Dongming, China (dôŋ-mĭŋ)	196	35.16 N	115.06 E
Dongo, Ang. (dôŋ'gō)	222	14.45 S	15.30 E
Dongon Pt., Phil (dông-ôn')	203a	12.43 N	120.35 E
Dongou, Con. (dôŋ-gōō')	226	2.02 N	18.04 E
Dongping, China (dôŋ-pĭŋ)	196	35.50 N	116.24 E
Dongping Hu (L.), China (dôŋ-pĭŋ hōō)	196	36.06 N	116.24 E
Dongsha Dao (I.), see Pratas			
Dongshan, China (doŋ-shän)	196	31.05 N	120.24 E
Dongtai, China	196	32.51 N	120.20 E
Dongting Hu (L.), China (dôŋ-tĭŋ hōō)	199	29.10 N	112.30 E
Dongxiang, China (dôŋ-shyän)	199	28.18 N	116.38 E
Doniphan, Mo. (dŏn'ĭ-făn)	121	36.37 N	90.50 W
Donji Vakuf, Yugo. (dōn'yĭ väk'ōōf)	170	44.08 N	17.25 E
Don Martin, Presa de (Res.), Mex. (prĕ'sä-dĕ-dôn-mär-tē'n)	122	27.35 N	100.38 W
Donnacona, Can.	102	46.40 N	71.46 W
Donnemarie-en-Montois, Fr. (dôn-mä-rē'ĕN-môN-twä')	167b	48.29 N	3.09 E
Donner und Blitzen (R.), Or. (dŏn'ēr ōōnt'blĭ'tsĕn)	114	42.45 N	118.57 W
Donnybrook, S. Afr. (dŏ-nĭ-brŏŏk)	223c	29.56 S	29.54 E
Donora, Pa. (dŏ-nō'rȧ)	111e	40.10 N	79.51 W
Doonerak, Mt., Ak. (dōō'nē-răk)	105	68.00 N	150.34 W
Doorn, Neth.	155a	52.02 N	5.21 E
Door Pen., Wi. (dōr)	113	44.40 N	87.36 W
Dora Baltea (R.), It. (dō'rä bäl'tä-ä)	170	45.40 N	7.34 E
Doraville, Ga. (dō'rȧ-vĭl)	110c	33.54 N	84.17 W
Dorchester, Eng. (dôr'chĕs-tēr)	160	50.45 N	2.34 W
Dordogne (R.), Fr. (dôr-dôn'yĕ)	166	44.53 N	0.16 E
Dordrecht, Neth. (dôr'drĕKt)	155a	51.48 N	4.39 E
Dordrecht, S. Afr. (dô'drĕKt)	223c	31.24 S	27.06 E
Dorgali, It. (dôr'gä-lē)	170	40.18 N	9.37 E
Doré L., Can.	98	54.31 N	107.06 W
Dorion-Vaudreuil, Can. (dôr-yō)	93a	45.23 N	74.01 W
Dorking, Eng. (dôr'kĭng)	154b	51.12 N	0.20 W
D'Orleans, Ile (I.), Can. (yl dōr-lē-äN')	93b	46.56 N	71.00 W
Dormont, Pa. (dôr'mŏnt)	111e	40.24 N	80.02 W
Dornbirn, Aus. (dôrn'bērn)	164	47.24 N	9.45 E
Dornoch, Scot. (dôr'nŏK)	160	57.55 N	4.01 W
Dornoch Firth, Scot. (dôr'nŏK fûrth)	160	57.55 N	3.55 W
Dorogobuzh, Sov. Un. (dôrôgô'-bōō'zh)	172	54.57 N	33.18 E
Dorohoi, Rom. (dō-rō-hoi')	165	47.57 N	26.28 E
Dorpat, see Tartu			
Dorre (I.), Austl. (dôr)	210	25.19 S	113.10 E
Dorstsen, F.R.G.	167c	51.40 N	6.58 E
Dortmund, F.R.G. (dôrt'mōōnt)	167c	51.31 N	7.28 E
Dortmund-Ems-Kanal (Can.), F.R.G. (dôrt'mōōnd-ĕms'kä-näl')	167c	51.50 N	7.25 E
Dörtyol, Tur. (dûrt'yôl)	177	36.50 N	36.20 E
Dorval, Can. (dôr-vȧl')	93a	45.26 N	73.44 W
Dos Caminos, Ven. (dôs-kä-mē'nôs)	141b	9.38 N	67.17 W
Dosewallips (R.), Wa. (dō'sē-wäl'lĭps)	116a	47.45 N	123.04 W
Dos Hermanas, Sp. (dōsĕr-mä'näs)	168	37.17 N	5.56 W
Dosso, Niger (dôs-ō')	225	13.03 N	3.12 E
Dothan, Al. (dō'thăn)	124	31.13 N	85.23 W
Douai, Fr. (dōō-ā')	166	50.23 N	3.04 E
Douala, Cam. (dōō-ä'lä)	225	4.03 N	9.42 E
Douarnenez, Fr. (dōō-är nē-nĕs')	166	48.06 N	4.18 W
Double Bayou, Tx. (dŭb''l bī'yōō)	123a	29.40 N	94.38 W
Douentza, Mali	224	15.00 N	2.57 W
Douglas, Ak. (dŭg'lăs)	105	58.18 N	134.35 W
Douglas, Ar.	119	31.20 N	109.30 W
Douglas, Ga.	124	31.30 N	82.53 W
Douglas, Isle of Man (dŭg'lăs)	160	54.10 N	4.24 W
Douglas, Wy. (dŭg'lăs)	115	42.45 N	105.21 W
Douglas (R.), Eng. (dŭg'lăs)	154	53.38 N	2.48 W
Douglas (R.), Tn. (dŭg'lăs)	124	36.00 N	83.35 W
Douglas Chan., Can.	96	53.30 N	129.12 W
Douglas Lake Ind. Res., Can.	97	50.10 N	120.49 W
Douglasville, Ga. (dŭg'lăs-vĭl)	124	33.45 N	84.47 W
Doumé, Cam. (dōō-mā')	221	4.41 N	13.26 E
Dourada, Serra (Mts.), Braz. (sĕ'r-rä-dôōō-rȧ'dȧ)	141	15.11 S	49.57 W
Dourdan, Fr. (dōōr-däN')	167b	48.32 N	2.01 E
Douro (R.), Port. (dô'ōō-rō)	168	41.03 N	8.12 W
Dove (R.), Eng. (dŭv)	154	52.53 N	1.47 W
Dover, De. (dō vēr)	109	39.10 N	75.30 W
Dover, Eng.	161	51.08 N	1.19 E
Dover, NH	109	43.15 N	71.00 W
Dover, NJ	110a	40.53 N	74.33 W
Dover, Oh.	108	40.35 N	81.30 W
Dover, S. Afr.	219d	27.05 S	27.44 E
Dover, Str. of, Eur.	161	50.50 N	1.15 W
Dover-Foxcroft, Me. (dō'vēr fŏks'krôft)	102	45.10 N	69.15 W
Dovlekanovo, Sov. Un. (dŏv'lyĕk-ȧ-nô-vô)	176	54.15 N	55.05 E
Dovre Fjell (Plat.), Nor. (dŏv'rĕ fyĕl')	162	62.03 N	8.36 E
Dow, Il. (dou)	117e	39.01 N	90.20 W
Dowagiac, Mi. (dō-wô'jăk)	108	42.00 N	86.05 W
Downers Grove, Il. (dou'nērz grōv)	111a	41.48 N	88.00 W
Downey, Ca. (dou'nĭ)	117a	33.56 N	118.08 W
Downieville, Ca. (dou'nĭ-nĭl)	118	39.35 N	120.48 W
Downs, Ks. (dounz)	120	39.29 N	98.32 W
Doylestown, Oh. (doilz'toun)	111d	40.58 N	81.43 W
Drâa, C., Mor. (drȧ)	220	28.39 N	12.15 W
Drâa, Oued (R.), Mor.	220	28.00 N	9.31 W
Drabov, Sov. Un. (drä'bôf)	173	49.57 N	32.14 E
Drac (R.), Fr. (dräK)	167	44.50 N	5.47 E
Dracut, Ma. (drä'kŭt)	103a	42.40 N	71.19 W
Draganovo, Bul. (drä-gä-nō'vô)	171	43.13 N	25.45 E
Drăgăşani, Rom. (drä-gȧ-shän'ĭ)	171	44.39 N	24.18 E
Draguignan, Fr. (drä-gēn-yäN')	167	43.35 N	6.28 E
Drakensberg (Mts.), Leso-S.Afr. (drä'kĕnz-bĕrgh)	222	29.15 S	29.07 E
Drake Passage, S.A.-Ant. (dräk păs'ĭj)	138	57.00 S	65.00 W
Dráma, Grc. (drä'mä)	171	41.09 N	24.10 E
Drammen, Nor. (dräm'ĕn)	162	59.45 N	10.15 E
Drau (R.), Aus. (drou)	164	46.44 N	13.45 E
Drava (R.), Yugo. (drä'vä)	170	46.37 N	15.17 E
Dravograd, Yugo. (drä'vô-gräd')	170	46.37 N	15.01 E
Drawsko Pomorskie, Pol. (dräv'skō pō-mōr'skyĕ)	164	53.31 N	15.50 E
Drayton Hbr., Wa. (drā'tŭn)	116d	48.58 N	122.40 W
Drayton Plains, Mi.	111b	42.41 N	83.23 W
Drayton Valley, Can.	97	53.13 N	114.59 W
Drensteinfurt, F.R.G. (drĕn'shtīn-fōōrt)	167c	51.47 N	7.44 E
Dresden, G.D.R. (drās'dĕn)	164	51.05 N	13.45 E
Dreux, Fr. (drû)	167b	48.44 N	1.24 E
Driefontein, S. Afr.	219d	25.53 S	29.10 E
Drin (R.), Alb. (drēn)	171	42.13 N	20.13 E
Drina (R.), Yugo. (drē'nä)	171	44.09 N	19.30 E
Drinit, Pelgi (B.), Alb.	171	41.42 N	19.17 E
Drissa, Sov. Un. (drĭs'sä)	172	55.48 N	27.59 E
Drissa (R.), Sov. Un.	172	55.44 N	28.58 E
Driver, Va.	110g	36.50 N	76.30 W
Dröbak, Nor. (drû'bäk)	162	59.40 N	10.35 E
Drobeta-Turnu-Severin, Rom. (sĕ-vĕ-rēn')	171	43.54 N	24.49 E
Drogheda, Ire. (drŏ'hē-dȧ)	160	53.43 N	6.15 W
Drogichin, Sov. Un. (drō-gē'chĭn)	165	52.10 N	25.11 E
Drogobych, Sov. Un. (drŏ-hō'bĭch)	165	49.21 N	23.31 E
Drôme (R.), Fr. (drōm)	166	44.42 N	4.53 E
Dronfield, Eng. (drŏn'fēld)	154	53.18 N	1.28 W
Drumheller, Can. (drŭm-hĕl-ēr)	97	51.28 N	112.42 W
Drummond (I.), Mi. (drŭm'ŭnd)	108	46.00 N	83.50 W
Drummondville, Can. (drŭm'ŭnd-vĭl)	102	45.53 N	72.33 W
Drumright, Ok. (drŭm'rīt)	121	35.59 N	96.37 W
Drunen, Neth.	155a	51.41 N	5.10 E
Drut' (R.), Sov.Un. (drōōt)	172	53.40 N	29.45 E
Druya, Sov.Un. (drōō'yȧ)	172	55.45 N	27.26 E
Drweca R., Pol. (d'r-văn'tsȧ)	165	53.06 N	19.13 E
Dryden, Can. (drī-dĕn)	95	49.47 N	92.50 W
Drysdale, Austl.	207a	38.11 S	144.34 E
Dry Tortugas (I.), Fl. (tôr-tōō'gäz)	125a	24.37 N	82.45 W
Dschang, Cam. (dshäng)	220	5.34 N	10.09 E
Duabo, Lib.	224	5.40 N	8.05 W
Duagh, Can.	93g	53.43 N	113.24 W
Duarte, Pico (Mtn.), Dom. Rep. (dŭ'ärtēh pēcō)	127	19.00 N	71.00 W
Duas Barras, Braz. (dōō'äs-bȧ'r-räs)	139a	22.03 S	42.30 W
Dubawnt (L.), Can. (dōō-bônt')	94	63.27 N	103.30 W
Dubawnt (R.), Can.	94	61.30 N	103.49 W
Dubayy, U.A.E.	192	25.18 N	55.26 E
Dubbo, Austl. (dŭb'ō)	212	32.20 S	148.42 E
Dubie, Zaire	227	8.33 S	28.32 E
Dublin, Ca. (dŭb'lĭn)	116b	37.42 N	121.56 W
Dublin, Ga.	124	32.33 N	82.55 W
Dublin, see Baile Átha Cliath			
Dublin, Tx.	122	32.05 N	98.20 W
Dubno, Sov.Un. (dōō'b-nô)	165	50.24 N	25.44 E
Du Bois, Pa. (dōō-bois')	109	41.10 N	78.45 W
Dubossary, Sov. Un. (dōō-bŏ-sä'rĭ)	173	47.16 N	29.11 E
Dubovka, Sov. Un. (dōō-bôf'kȧ)	177	49.00 N	44.50 E
Dubrovka, Sov. Un. (dōō-brôf'kȧ)	180c	59.51 N	30.56 E
Dubrovnik (Ragusa), Yugo. (dōō'brôv-nĕk) (rä-gōō'sä)	171	42.40 N	18.10 E
Dubrovno, Sov. Un. (dōō-brôf'nō)	172	54.39 N	30.54 E
Dubuque, Ia. (dōō-būk')	113	42.30 N	90.43 W
Duchesne, Ut. (dōō-shān')	119	40.12 N	110.23 W
Duchesne (R.), Ut.	119	40.20 N	110.50 W
Duchess, Austl. (dŭch'ĕs)	210	21.30 S	139.55 E
Ducie I., Oceania (dü-sē')	205	25.30 S	126.20 W
Duck (R.), Tn.	124	35.55 N	87.40 W
Duckabush (R.), Wa. (dŭk'ȧ-bōōsh)	116a	47.41 N	123.09 W
Duck Lake, Can.	98	52.47 N	106.13 W
Duck Mtn., Can.	99	51.35 N	101.00 W
Ducktown, Tn. (dŭk'toun)	124	35.03 N	84.20 W
Duck Valley Ind. Res., Id.-Nv.	114	42.02 N	115.49 W
Duckwater Pk., Nv. (dŭk-wô-tēr)	118	39.00 N	115.31 W
Duda (R.), Col. (dōō'dä)	140a	3.25 N	74.23 W
Dudinka, Sov. Un. (dōō-dĭn'kȧ)	178	69.15 N	85.42 E
Dudley, Eng. (dŭd'lĭ)	154	52.28 N	2.07 E
Duékoué, Ivory Coast	224	6.45 N	7.21 W
Duero (R.), Sp. (dwĕ'rō)	168	41.30 N	5.10 W
Dugger, In. (dŭg'ēr)	108	39.00 N	87.10 W
Dugi Otok (I.), Yugo. (dōō'gē o'tôk)	170	44.03 N	14.40 E
Duisburg, F.R.G. (dōō'ĭs-bōōrgh)	167c	51.26 N	6.46 E
Duitama, Col. (dōōē-tä'mä)	140	5.48 N	73.09 W

ăt; finȧl; rāte; senāte; ärm; ȧsk; sofȧ; fâre; ch-choose; dh-as th in other; bē; ēvent; bĕt; recĕnt; cratēr; g-gō; gh-guttural g; bĭt; ĭ-short neutral; rīde; K-guttural k as ch in German ich;

PRONOUNCING INDEX

Dukhovshchina – Edgeley 287

PLACE (Pronunciation)	PAGE	Lat. °′	Long. °′
Dukhovshchina, Sov. Un. (do͞o-ĸôfsh-'chĕná)	172	55.13 N	32.26 E
Dukinfield, Eng. (dŭk'ĭn-fēld)	154	53.28 N	2.05 W
Dukla P., Pol. (do͞o'klä)	165	49.25 N	21.44 E
Dulce, Golfo (G.), C.R. (gôl'fô do͞ol'sä)	131	8.25 N	83.13 W
Dulcigno, see Ulcinj			
Dülken, F.G.R. (dül'kĕn)	167c	51.15 N	6.21 E
Dülmen, F.R.G. (dül'mĕn)	167c	51.50 N	7.17 E
Duluth, Mn. (do͞o-lo͞oth')	117h	46.50 N	92.07 W
Dūmā, Syria	189a	33.34 N	36.17 E
Dumaguete City, Phil. (do͞o-mä-gā'tā)	203	9.14 N	123.15 E
Dumai, Indon.	189b	1.39 N	101.30 E
Dumali Pt., Phil. (do͞o-mä'lē)	203a	13.07 N	121.42 E
Dumas, Tx.	120	35.52 N	101.58 W
Dumbarton, Scot. (dŭm'bär-tŭn)	160	56.00 N	4.35 W
Dum-Dum, India	190a	22.37 N	88.25 E
Dumfries, Scot. (dŭm-frēs')	160	54.05 N	3.40 W
Dumjor, India	190a	22.37 N	88.14 E
Dumont, NJ (do͞o'mŏnt)	110a	40.56 N	74.00 W
Dumyâț, Egypt	219b	31.22 N	31.50 E
Dumyâț, Maşabb (Chan.), Egypt	219b	31.36 N	31.45 E
Duna (R.), Hung. (do͞o'nä)	165	46.07 N	18.45 E
Duna (R.), see Danube			
Dunaföldvär, Hung. (do͞o'nô-fûld'vär)	165a	46.48 N	18.55 E
Dunajec (R.), Pol. (do͞o-nä'yĕts)	165	49.52 N	20.53 E
Dunaújváros, Hung.	165	46.57 N	18.55 E
Dunay, Sov. Un. (do͞o'nī)	180c	59.59 N	30.57 E
Dunayevtsy, Sov. Un. (do͞o-nä'yĕf-tsĭ)	173	48.52 N	26.51 E
Dunbar, WV	108	38.20 N	81.45 W
Duncan, Can. (dŭŋ'kăn)	96	48.47 N	123.42 W
Duncan, Ok.	120	34.29 N	97.56 W
Duncan (R.), Can.	97	50.30 N	116.45 W
Duncan Dam, Can.	97	50.15 N	116.55 W
Duncan L, Can.	97	50.20 N	117.00 W
Duncansby Hd., Scot. (dŭn'kănz-bĭ)	160a	58.40 N	3.01 W
Duncanville, Tx. (dŭn'kăn-vĭl)	117c	32.39 N	96.55 W
Dundalk, Ire. (dŭn'kôk)	160	54.00 N	6.18 W
Dundalk, Md.	110e	39.16 N	76.31 W
Dundalk B., Ire. (dŭn'dôk)	160	53.55 N	6.15 W
Dundas, Can. (dŭn-dăs')	93d	43.16 N	79.58 W
Dundas (L.), Austl. (dŭn-dăs)	210	32.15 S	122.00 E
Dundas I., Can.	96	54.33 N	130.55 W
Dundas Str., Austl.	210	10.35 S	131.15 E
Dundee, Il. (dŭn-dē)	111a	42.06 N	88.17 W
Dundee, Scot	160	56.30 N	2.55 W
Dundee, S. Afr	223c	28.14 S	30.16 E
Dundrum B., Ire. (dŭn-drŭm')	160	54.13 N	5.47 W
Dundedin, Fl. (dŭn-ē'dĭn)	125a	28.00 N	82.43 W
Dunedin, N.Z.	211a	45.48 S	170.32 E
Dunellen, NJ (dŭn-ĕl'l'n)	110a	40.36 N	74.28 W
Dunfermline, Scot. (dŭn-fĕrm'lĭn)	160	56.05 N	3.30 W
Dungarvan, Ire. (dŭn-gar'văn)	160	52.06 N	7.50 W
Dungeness, Wa. (dŭnj-nĕs')	116a	48.09 N	123.07 W
Dungeness (R.), Wa.	116a	48.03 N	123.10 W
Dungeness Spit, Wa.	116a	48.11 N	123.03 W
Dunhua, China (do͞on-hwä)	198	48.18 N	128.10 E
Dunkerque, Fr. (dŭɴ-kĕrk')	166	51.02 N	2.37 E
Dunkirk, In. (dŭn'kûrk)	108	40.20 N	85.25 W
Dunkirk, NY	109	42.30 N	79.20 W
Dunkwa, Ghana	224	5.22 N	1.12 W
Dun Laoghaire, Ire. (dŭn-lā'rĕ)	160	53.16 N	6.09 W
Dunlap, Ia. (dŭn'lăp)	112	41.53 N	95.33 W
Dunlap, Tn.	124	35.23 N	85.23 W
Dunmore, Pa. (dŭn'mōr)	109	41.25 N	75.30 W
Dunn, NC (dŭn)	125	35.18 N	78.37 W
Dunnellon, Fl. (dŭn-ĕl'ŏn)	125	29.02 N	82.28 W
Dunnville, Can. (dŭn'vĭl)	109	42.55 N	79.40 W
Dunqulah, Sud.	221	19.21 N	30.19 E
Dunsmuir, Ca. (dŭnz'mūr)	114	41.08 N	122.17 W
Dunwoody, Ga. (dŭn-wo͝od'ĭ)	110c	33.57 N	84.20 W
Duolun, China (dwô-lo͞on)	198	42.12 N	116.15 E
Du Page R., Il. (do͞o pāj)	111a	41.41 N	88.11 W
Du Page R., E. Br., Il.	111a	41.49 N	88.05 W
Du Page R., W. Br., Il.	111a	41.48 N	88.10 W
Dupax, Phil. (do͞o'päks)	203a	16.16 N	121.06 E
Dupo, Il. (dū'pō)	117e	38.31 N	90.12 W
Duque de Bragança, Ang. (do͞o'kå dā brä-gäɴ'sä)	226	9.06 S	15.57 E
Duque de Caxias, Braz. (do͞o'kĕ-dĕ-kå'shyås)	142b	22.46 S	43.18 W
Duquesne, Pa. (do͞o-kān')	111e	40.22 N	79.51 W
Du Quoin, Il. (do͞o-kwoin')	121	38.01 N	89.14 W
Durance (R.), Fr. (dü-räɴs')	167	43.46 N	5.52 E
Durand, Mi. (dŭ-rănd')	108	42.50 N	84.00 W
Durand, Wi.	113	44.37 N	91.58 W
Durango, Co. (do͞o-răŋ'gō)	119	37.15 N	107.55 W
Durango, Mex. (do͞o-rä'n-gô)	128	24.02 N	104.42 W
Durango (State), Mex.	126	25.00 N	106.00 W
Durant, Ms. (dŭ-rănt')	124	33.05 N	89.50 W
Durant, Ok.	121	33.59 N	96.23 W
Duratón (R.), Sp. (do͞o-rä-tôn')	168	41.55 N	3.55 W
Durazno, Ur. (do͞o-räz'nō)	139c	33.21 S	56.31 W
Durazno (Dept.), Ur.	139c	33.00 S	56.35 W
Durban, S. Afr. (dûr'băn)	223c	29.48 S	31.00 E
Durbanville, S. Afr. (dûr-băn'vĭl)	222a	33.50 S	18.39 E
Durbe, Sov. Un. (do͞or'bĕ)	163	56.36 N	21.24 E
Durdevac, Yugo.(dûr'dyĕ-väts')	170	46.03 N	17.03 E
Düren, F.R.G. (dü'rĕn)	167c	50.48 N	6.30 E
Durham, Eng. (dûr'ăm)	160	54.47 N	1.46 W
Durham, NC	125	36.00 N	78.55 W
Durham Downs, Austl.	212	27.30 S	141.55 E
Durrës, Alb. (do͞or'ĕs)	171	41.19 N	19.27 E
Duryea, Pa. (do͞or-yā')	109	41.20 N	75.50 W
Dushan, China (do͞o-shän)	199	25.50 N	107.42 E
Dushan, China	196	31.38 N	116.16 E
Dushanbe, Sov. Un.	193	38.30 N	68.45 E
Düsseldorf, F.R.G. (düs'ĕl-dôrf)	167c	51.14 N	6.47 E
Dussen, Neth.	155a	51.43 N	4.58 E
Dutalan Ula (Mtn.), Mong.	198	49.25 N	112.40 E
Dutch Harbor, Ak. (dŭch här'bēr)	105a	53.58 N	166.30 W
Duvall, Wa. (do͞o'vâl)	116a	47.44 N	121.59 W
Duvergé, Dom. Rep. (do͞o-vĕr-hĕ')	133	18.20 N	71.20 W
Duwamish (R.), Wa. (do͞o-wăm'ĭsh)	116a	47.24 N	122.18 W
Duyun, China (do͞o-yo͞on)	199	26.18 N	107.40 E
Dvina, Western, (R.), see **Zapadnaya Dvina**			
Dvinskaya Guba (G.), Sov. Un.	176	65.10 N	38.40 E
Dvür Králové, Czech. (dvo͞or' krä'lô-vâ)	164	50.28 N	15.43 E
Dwārka, India	190	22.18 N	68.59 E
Dwight, Il. (dwīt)	108	41.00 N	88.20 W
Dworshak Res, Id.	114	46.45 N	115.50 W
Dyat'kovo, Sov. Un. (dyät'kō-vō)	172	53.36 N	34.19 E
Dyer, In. (dī'ēr)	111a	41.30 N	87.31 W
Dyersburg, Tn. (dī'ērz-bûrg)	124	36.02 N	89.23 W
Dyersville, Ia. (dī'ērz-vĭl)	113	42.28 N	91.09 W
Dyes Inlet, Wa. (dīz)	116a	47.37 N	122.45 W
Dyment, Can. (dī'mĕnt)	99	49.37 N	92.19 W
Dzabhan Gol (R.), Mong.	194	48.19 N	94.08 E
Dzamiin Üüde, Mong.	198	44.38 N	111.32 E
Dzaoudzi, Mayotte (dzou'dzĭ)	223	12.44 S	45.15 E
Dzaudzhikau, Sov. Un. (dzou-jĭ-kou')	153	48.00 N	44.52 E
Dzerzhinsk, Sov. Un. (dzhĕr-zhĭnsk')	173	48.24 N	37.58 E
Dzerzhinsk, Sov. Un.	172	53.41 N	27.14 E
Dzerzhinsk, Sov. Un.	176	56.20 N	43.50 E
Dzhalal-Abad, Sov. Un. (jȧ-läl'ȧ-bät')	178	41.13 N	73.35 E
Dzhambul, Sov. Un. (dzhäm-bo͞ol')	178	42.51 N	71.29 E
Dzhankoy, Sov. Un. (dzhän'koi)	173	45.43 N	34.22 E
Dzhetygara, Sov. Un. (dzhĕt'-gä'rȧ)	180a	52.12 N	61.18 E
Dzhizak, Sov. Un. (dzhĕ'zäk)	178	40.13 N	67.58 E
Dzhugdzhur Khrebet (Mts.), Sov. Un. (jo͞og-jo͞or')	179	56.15 N	137.00 E
Dzialoszyce, Pol. (jyä-wō-shē'tsĕ)	165	50.21 N	20.22 E
Dzibalchén, Mex. (zē-bäl-chĕ'n)	130a	19.25 N	89.39 W
Dzidzantún, Mex. (zĕd-zän-to͞o'n)	130a	21.18 N	89.00 W
Dzierzoniów, Pol. (dzyĕr-zhôn'yŭf)	164	50.44 N	16.38 E
Dzilam González, Mex. (zē-lä'm-gôn-zä'lĕz)	130a	21.21 N	88.53 W
Dzitás, Mex. (zē-tà's)	130a	20.47 N	88.32 W
Dzitbalché, Mex. (dzēt-bäl-chā')	130a	20.18 N	90.03 W
Dzungaria (Reg.), China (dzo͞oŋ-gä'rĭ-ȧ)	194	44.39 N	86.13 E
Dzungarian Gate (P.), China	194	45.00 N	88.00 E

E

PLACE (Pronunciation)	PAGE	Lat. °′	Long. °′
Eagle, Ak (ē'g'l)	105	64.42 N	141.20 W
Eagle, WV	108	38.10 N	81.20 W
Eagle (R.), Co.	119	39.32 N	106.28 W
Eaglecliff, Wa (ē'gl-klĭf)	116c	46.10 N	123.13 W
Eagle Cr., In.	111g	39.54 N	86.17 W
Eagle Grove, Ia.	113	42.39 N	93.55 W
Eagle Lake, Me.	102	47.03 N	68.38 W
Eagle Lake, Tx.	123	29.37 N	96.20 W
Eagle L., Ca.	114	40.45 N	120.52 W
Eagle Mountain L., Tx.	117c	32.56 N	97.27 W
Eagle Pass, Tx.	122	28.49 N	100.30 W
Eagle Pk, Ca.	114	41.18 N	120.11 W
Ealing, Eng. (ē'lĭng)	154b	51.29 N	0.19 W
Earle, Ar. (ûrl)	121	35.14 N	90.28 W
Earlington, Ky. (ûr'lĭng-tŭn)	124	37.15 N	87.31 W
Easley, SC (ēz'lĭ)	125	34.48 N	82.37 W
East, Mt., Pan.	126a	9.09 N	79.46 W
East Alton, Il. (ôl'tŭn)	117e	38.53 N	90.08 W
East Angus, Can. (ăŋ'gŭs)	101	45.35 N	71.40 W
East Aurora, NY (ô-rō'rȧ)	111c	42.46 N	78.38 W
East B, Tx	123a	29.30 N	94.41 W
East Berlin, G.D.R. (bĕr-lēn')	155b	52.31 N	13.28 E
East Bernstadt, Ky (bûrn'stăt)	124	37.09 N	84.08 W
Eastbourne, Eng. (ēst'bôrn)	161	50.48 N	0.16 E
East Caicos (I.), Turk & Caicos Is. (kī'kōs)	133	21.40 N	71.35 W
East Cape (C.), N.Z.	213	37.37 S	178.33 E
East Cape, see **Dezhneva, Mys**			
East Carondelet, Il. (kȧ-rŏn'dĕ-lĕt)	117e	38.33 N	90.14 W
East Chicago, In. (shĭ-kô'gō)	111a	41.39 N	87.29 W
East China Sea, Asia	195	30.28 N	125.52 E
East Cleveland, Oh (klēv'lănd)	111d	41.33 N	81.35 W
East Cote Blanche B., La. (kōt bläɴsh')	123	29.30 N	92.07 W
East Des Moines (R.), Ia. (dē moin')	113	42.57 N	94.17 W
East Detroit, Mi (dē-troit')	111b	42.28 N	82.57 W
Easter (I.), see **Rapa Nui**			
Eastern Ghāts (Mts.), India	191	13.50 N	78.45 E
Eastern Turkestan (Reg), China (to͞or-kĕ-stän')(tûr-kĕ-stăn')	194	39.40 N	78.20 E
East Grand Forks, Mn. (grănd fôrks)	112	47.56 N	97.02 W
East Greenwich, RI (grĭn'ĭj)	110b	41.40 N	71.27 W
Easthampton, Ma. (ēst-hămp'tŭn)	109	42.15 N	72.45 W
East Hartford, Ct (härt'fērd)	109	41.45 N	72.35 W
East Helena, Mt. (hĕ-hē'nȧ)	115	46.31 N	111.50 W
East Ilsley, Eng. (ĭl'slē)	154b	51.30 N	1.18 W
East Jordan, Mi. (jôr'dăn)	108	45.05 N	85.05 W
East Kansas City, Mo. (kăn'zȧs)	117f	39.09 N	94.30 W
Eastland, Tx (ēst'lănd)	122	32.24 N	98.47 W
East Lansing, Mi (lăn'sĭng)	108	42.45 N	84.30 W
Eastlawn, Mi	111b	42.15 N	83.35 W
East Leavenworth, Mo (lĕv'ĕn-wûrth)	117f	39.18 N	94.50 W
East Liverpool, Oh. (lĭv'ēr-po͞ol)	108	40.40 N	80.35 W
East London, S. Afr. (lŭn'dŭn)	223c	33.02 S	27.54 E
East Los Angeles, Ca (lōs ăŋ'hȧ-lās)	117a	34.01 N	118.09 W
Eastmain (R.), Can. (ēst'măn)	95	52.12 N	73.19 W
Eastman, Ga. (ēst'măn)	124	32.10 N	83.11 W
East Millstone, NJ (mĭl'stōn)	110a	40.30 N	74.35 W
East Moline, Il. (mô-lēn')	113	41.31 N	90.28 W
East Nishnabotna R.), Ia. (nĭsh-nȧ-bŏt'nȧ)	119	40.53 N	95.23 W
Easton, Md. (ēs'tŭn)	109	72.45 N	76.05 W
Easton, Pa.	109	40.45 N	75.15 W
Easton L, Ct.	110a	41.18 N	73.17 W
East Orange, NJ (ŏr'ĕnj)	110a	40.46 N	74.12 W
East Palo Alto, Ca	116b	37.27 N	122.07 W
East Peoria, Il. (pē-ō'rĭ-ȧ)	108	40.40 N	89.30 W
East Pittsburgh, Pa (pĭts'bûrg)	111e	40.24 N	79.50 W
East Point, Ga.	110c	33.41 N	84.27 W
Eastport, Me. (ēst'pōrt)	102	44.53 N	67.01 W
East Providence, RI (prŏv'ĭ-dĕns)	110b	41.49 N	71.22 W
East Retford, Eng. (rĕt'fērd)	154	53.19 N	0.56 W
East Rochester, NY (rŏch'ĕs-tēr)	109	43.10 N	77.30 W
East St. Louis, Il. (sănt lo͞o'ĭs)(lo͞o-ĭ)	117e	38.38 N	90.10 W
East Siberian Sea, Sov. Un. (sī-bĭr'y'n)	174	73.00 N	153.28 E
Eastsound, Wa. (ēst-sound)	116d	48.42 N	122.42 W
East Stroudsburg, Pa (stroudz'bûrg)	109	41.00 N	75.10 W
East Syracuse, NY (sĭr'ȧ-kūs)	109	43.05 N	76.00 W
East Tavaputs.Plat., Ut. (tă-vă'-pŭts)	119	39.25 N	109.45 W
East Tawas, Mi (tô'wȧs)	108	44.15 N	83.30 W
East Walker (R.), Nv (wôk'ēr)	118	38.36 N	119.02 W
East York, Can.	93d	43.41 S	79.20 W
Eaton, Co. (ē'tŭn)	111	40.31 N	104.42 W
Eaton, Oh.	108	39.45 N	84.40 W
Eaton Estates, Oh.	111d	41.19 N	82.01 W
Eaton Rapids, Mi. (răp'ĭdz)	108	42.30 N	84.40 W
Eatonton, Ga. (ē'tŭn-tŭn)	124	33.20 N	83.24 W
Eatontown, NJ (ē'tŭn-toun)	110a	40.18 N	74.04 W
Eau Claire, Wi. (ō klâr')	113	44.47 N	91.32 W
Ebeltoft, Den. (ĕ'bĕl-tŭft)	162	56.11 N	10.39 E
Ebensburg, Pa.	109	40.29 N	78.44 W
Ebersberg, F.R.G. (ĕ'bērs-bĕrgh)	155d	48.05 N	11.58 E
Ebingen, F.R.G. (ā'bĭng-ĕn)	164	48.13 N	9.04 E
Ebinur Hu (L.), China (ä-bē-no͞or ho͞o)	194	45.09 N	83.15 E
Eboli, It. (ĕb'ô-lē)	170	40.38 N	15.04 E
Ebolowa, Cam.	225	2.54 N	11.09 E
Ebreichsdorf, Aus.	155e	47.58 N	16.24 E
Ebrie, Lagune (Lagoon), Ivory Coast	224	5.20 N	4.50 W
Ebro (R.), Sp. (ā'brō)	169	41.30 N	0.35 W
Eccles, Eng. (ĕk''lz)	154	53.29 N	2.20 W
Eccles, WV	108	37.45 N	81.10 W
Eccleshall, Eng. (ĕk''lz-hôl)	154	52.51 N	2.15 W
Eceabat (Maidos), Tur.	171	40.10 N	26.21 E
Echague, Phil. (ā-chä'gwä)	203a	16.43 N	121.40 E
Echandi, Cerro (Mt.), Pan. (sĕ'r-rō-ĕ-chä'nd)	131	9.05 N	82.51 W
Echimamish (R.), Can.	99	54.15 N	97.30 W
Echo Bay, Can. (ĕk'ō)	117k	46.29 N	84.04 W
Echoing (R.), Can. (ĕk'ō-ĭng)	99	55.15 N	91.30 W
Echternach, Lux. (ĕk'tēr-näk)	167	49.48 N	6.25 E
Echuca, Austl. (ē-cho͞o'kȧ)	212	36.10 S	144.47 E
Écija, Sp. (ā'thē-hä)	168	37.20 N	5.07 W
Eckernförde, F.R.G.	164	54.27 N	9.51 E
Eclipse, Va (ē-klĭps')	110g	36.55 N	76.29 W
Ecorse, Mi (ē-kôrs')	111b	42.15 N	83.09 W
Ecuador, S.A. (ĕk'wȧ-dôr)	138	0.00 N	78.30 W
Ed, Eth.	221	13.57 N	41.37 E
Eddyville, Ky. (ĕd'ĭ-vĭl)	124	37.03 N	88.03 W
Ede, Nig.	225	7.44 N	4.27 E
Edéa, Cam. (ĕ-dā'ä)	225	3.48 N	10.08 E
Eden, Tx.	122	31.13 N	99.51 W
Eden, Ut.	117b	41.18 N	111.49 W
Eden (R.), Eng. (ē'dĕn)	160	54.40 N	2.35 W
Edenbridge, Eng. (ē'dĕn-brĭj)	154b	51.11 N	0.05 E
Edenham, Eng. (ē'd'n-ăm)	154	52.46 N	0.25 W
Eden Prairie, Mn. (prâr'ĭ)	117g	44.51 N	93.29 W
Edenton, NC (ē'dĕn-tŭn)	125	36.02 N	76.37 W
Edenton, Oh	111f	39.14 N	84.02 W
Edenvale, S. Afr. (ēd'ĕn-văl)	223b	29.06 N	28.10 E
Edenville, S. Afr. (ē'd'n-vĭl)	219d	27.33 S	27.42 E
Eder R., F.R.G. (ā'dēr)	164	51.05 N	8.52 E
Edgefield, SC (ĕj'fēld)	125	33.52 N	81.55 W
Edgeley, ND (ĕj'lĭ)	112	46.24 N	98.43 W

288 Edgemont – Emmons Mt.

PLACE (Pronunciation)	PAGE	Lat. °′	Long. °′
Edgemont, SD (ĕj′mŏnt)	112	43.19 N	103.50 W
Edgerton, Wi. (ĕj′ẽr-tŭn)	113	42.49 N	89.06 W
Edgewater, Al. (ĕj-wô-tẽr)	110h	33.31 N	86.52 W
Edgewater, Md.	110e	38.58 N	76.35 W
Edgewood, Can. (ĕj′wo͝od)	97	49.47 N	118.08 W
Édhessa, Grc.	171	40.48 N	22.04 E
Edina, Mn. (ė-dī′nȧ)	117g	44.55 N	93.20 W
Edina, Mo.	121	40.10 N	92.11 W
Edinburg, In. (ĕd″n-bûrg)	108	39.20 N	85.55 W
Edinburg, Tx.	122	26.18 N	98.08 W
Edinburgh, Scot. (ĕd″n-bŭr-ō)	160	55.57 N	3.10 W
Edirne (Adrianople), Tur. (ĕ-dĭr′nĕ)(ā-drĭ-ăn-ō′p′l)	171	41.41 N	26.35 E
Edisto, (R.), SC (ĕd′ĭs-tō)	125	33.10 N	80.50 W
Edisto (R.), North Fk., SC	125	33.42 N	81.24 W
Edisto (R.), South Fk., SC	125	33.43 N	81.35 W
Edisto Island, SC	125	32.32 N	80.20 W
Edmond, Ok. (ĕd′mŭnd)	121	35.39 N	97.29 W
Edmonds, Wa. (ĕd′mŭndz)	116a	47.49 N	122.23 W
Edmonton, Can.	93g	53.33 N	113.28 W
Edmundston, Can. (ĕd′mŭn-stŭn)	102	47.22 N	68.20 W
Edna, Tx. (ĕd′nȧ)	123	28.59 N	96.39 W
Edremit, Tur. (ĕd-rĕ-mēt′)	171	39.35 N	27.00 E
Edremit Körfezi (G.), Tur.	171	39.28 N	26.35 E
Edson, Can. (ĕd′sŭn)	97	53.35 N	116.26 W
Edward (I.), Can. (ĕd′wẽrd)	100	48.21 N	88.29 W
Edward (L.), Zaire	227	0.25 S	29.40 E
Edwardsville, Il. (ĕd′wẽrdz-vĭl)	117e	38.49 N	89.58 W
Edwardsville, In	111h	38.17 N	85.53 W
Edwardsville, Ks.	117f	39.04 N	94.49 W
Eel (R.), Ca. (ēl)	114	40.39 N	124.15 W
Eel (R.), In.	108	40.50 N	85.55 W
Efate (I.), Vanuatu (ā-fä′tä)	211	18.02 S	168.29 E
Effigy Mounds Natl. Mon., Ia. (ĕf′ĭ-jŭ mounds)	113	43.04 N	91.15 W
Effingham, Il. (ĕf′ĭng-hăm)	108	39.05 N	88.30 W
Ega (R.), Sp. (ā′gä)	168	42.40 N	2.20 W
Egadi, Isole (Is.), It. (ė′sō-lĕ-ĕ′gä-dē)	170	38.01 N	12.00 E
Egea de los Caballeros, Sp. (ā-kā′ȧ dā lōs kä-bäl-yā′rōs)	168	42.07 N	1.05 W
Egegik, Ak. (ĕg′ĕ-jĭt)	105	58.10 N	157.22 W
Eger, Hung. (ĕ gĕr)	165	47.53 N	20.24 E
Egersund, Nor. (ĕ′ghĕr-so͞on′)	162	58.29 N	6.01 E
Egg Harbor, NJ (ĕg här′bẽr)	109	39.30 N	74.35 W
Egham, Eng. (ĕg′ŭm)	154b	51.24 N	0.33 W
Egiin Gol. (R.), Mong. (ā-gēn′)	194	49.41 N	100.40 E
Egmont, C., N.Z. (ĕg′mŏnt)	213	39.18 S	173.49 E
Egridir Gölü (L.), Tur. (ā-rĭ-dĭr′)	177	38.10 N	30.00 E
Eguilles, Fr (ĕ-gwē′)	166a	43.34 N	5.21 E
Egypt, Afr. (ē′jĭpt)	218	26.58 N	27.01 E
Eha-Amufu, Nig.	225	6.40 N	7.46 E
Eibar, Sp. (ā′ē-bär)	168	43.12 N	2.20 W
Eichstätt, F.R.G. (īk′shtät)	164	48.54 N	11.14 E
Eichwalde, G.D.R. (īĸ′väl-dĕ)	155b	52.22 N	13.37 E
Eidfjord, Nor. (ĕĭd′fyōr)	162	60.28 N	7.04 E
Eidsvoll, Nor. (īdhs′vôl)	162	60.19 N	11.15 E
Eifel (Plat), F.R.G. (ī′fĕl)	164	50.08 N	6.30 E
Eighty Mile Beach, Austl.	210	20.45 S	121.00 E
Eil, Som.	219a	7.53 N	49.45 E
Eilenburg, G.D.R. (ī′lĕn-bo͞orgh)	164	51.27 N	12.38 E
Eilliot, S. Afr.	223c	31.19 S	27.52 E
Einbeck, F.R.G. (īn′bĕk)	164	51.49 N	9.52 E
Eindhoven, Neth. (īnd′hō-vĕn)	161	51.29 N	5.20 E
Eirunepé, Braz. (ā-ro͞o-nĕ-pĕ′)	140	6.37 S	69.58 W
Eisenach, G.D.R. (ī′zĕn-äĸ)	164	50.58 N	10.18 E
Eisenhüttenstadt, G.D.R.	164	52.08 N	14.40 E
Eisleben, G.D.R. (īs′lā′bĕn)	164	51.31 N	11.33 E
Ejura, Ghana	224	7.23 N	1.22 W
Ejutla de Crespo, Mex. (ā-ho͞ot′lä dā krās′pō)	129	16.34 N	96.44 W
Ekanga, Zaire	226	2.23 S	23.14 E
Ekenäs (Tammisaari), Fin. (ĕ′kĕ-nâs)(tȧm′ĭ-sä′rĭ)	163	59.59 N	23.25 E
Ekeren, Bel.	155a	51.17 N	4.27 E
Ekoli, Zaire	226	0.23 S	24.16 E
Eksjö, Swe. (ĕk′shû)	162	57.41 N	14.55 E
El Aaiún, W. Sah.	220	26.45 N	13.15 W
El Affroun, Alg. (ĕl ȧf-froun′)	169	36.28 N	2.38 E
Elands (R.), S. Afr. (ēlănds)	223c	31.48 S	26.09 E
Elands (R.), S. Afr.	219d	25.11 S	28.52 E
El Arahal, Sp. (ĕl ä-rä-äl′)	168	37.17 N	5.32 W
El Arba, Alg.	169	36.35 N	3.10 E
El Asnam, (Orléansville) Alg.	158	36.14 N	1.32 E
Elat, Isr.	189a	29.34 N	34.57 E
Elâzig, Tur. (ĕl-ä′zēz)	177	38.40 N	39.00 E
Elba, Al. (ĕl′bȧ)	124	31.25 N	86.01 W
Elba, Isolad′ (I.), It. (ē-sō lä-d-ĕl′bȧ)	170d	42.42 N	10.25 E
El Banco, Col. (ĕl băn′cō)	140	8.58 N	74.01 W
El Barco de Valdeorras, Sp (ĕl bär′kō)	168	42.26 N	6.58 W
Elbansan, Alb. (ĕl-bä-sän′)	171	41.08 N	20.05 E
El Bayadh, Alg.	158	33.42 N	1.06 E
Elbe (Labe)(R.), Czech.-G.D.R. (ĕl′bĕ)(lä′bĕ)	164	53.47 N	9.20 E
Elbert, Mt., Co. (ĕl′bērt)	119	39.05 N	106.25 W
Elberton, Ga. (ĕl′bĕr-tŭn)	124	34.05 N	82.53 W
Elbeuf, Fr. (ĕl-bûf′)	166	49.16 N	0.59 E
Elbistan, Tur. (ēl-bē-stän′)	177	38.20 N	37.10 E
Elblag, Pol. (ĕl′bläŋg)	165	54.11 N	19.25 E
El Bonillo, Sp. (ĕl bō-nēl′yō)	168	38.56 N	2.31 W
Elbow (R.), Can. (ĕl′bō)	93e	51.03 N	114.24 W
Elbow Cay (I.), Ba	132	26.25 N	77.55 W
Elbow Lake, Mn.	112	46.00 N	95.59 W
El′brus, Gora (Mt.), Sov. Un. (ĕl′bro͞os′)	177	43.20 N	42.25 E
El Bur, Som	219a	4.35 N	46.40 E
El Burgo de Osma, Sp.	168	41.35 N	3.02 W
Elburz Mts., Iran, (ĕl′bo͞orz′)	177	36.30 N	51.00 E
El Cajon, Ca.	118a	32.48 N	116.58 W
El Cajon, Col (ĕl-kä-kô′n)	140a	4.50 N	76.35 W
El Cambur, Ven. (käm-bo͞or′)	141b	10.24 N	68.06 W
El Campo, Tx. (kăm′pō)	123	29.13 N	96.17 W
El Carmen, Chile (kȧ′r-mĕn)	139b	34.14 S	71.23 W
El Carmen, Col. (kȧ′r-mĕn)	140	9.54 N	75.12 W
El Casco, Ca. (kăs′kō)	117a	33.59 N	117.08 W
El Centro, Ca. (sĕn′trō)	118	32.47 N	115.33 W
El Cerrito, Ca. (sĕr-rē′tō)	116b	37.55 N	122.19 W
Elche, Sp. (ĕl′chā)	169	38.15 N	0.42 W
El Cuyo, Mex.	130a	21.30 N	87.42 W
Elda, Sp. (ĕl′dä)	169	38.28 N	0.44 W
El Djouf (Des.), Mauritania (ĕl djo͞of)	220	21.45 N	7.05 W
Eldon, Ia. (ĕl-dŭn)	113	40.55 N	92.15 W
Eldon, Mo.	119	38.21 N	92.36 W
Eldora, Ia. (ĕl-dō′rȧ)	113	42.21 N	93.08 W
El Dorado, Ar. (ĕl dō-rä′dō)	121	33.13 N	92.39 W
Eldorado, Il.	108	37.50 N	88.30 W
El Dorado, Ks.	121	37.49 N	96.51 W
Eldorado Springs, Mo. (sprĭngz)	121	37.51 N	94.02 W
Eldoret, Ken. (ĕl-dō-rĕt′)	227	0.31 N	35.17 E
El Ebano, Mex. (ā-bä′nō)	128	22.13 N	98.26 W
Electra, Tx. (ē-lĕk′trȧ)	120	34.02 N	98.54 W
Electric Pk., Mt. (ē-lĕk′trĭk)	115	45.03 N	110.52 W
Elektrogorsk, Sov. Un. (ĕl-yĕk′trô-gôrsk)	180b	55.53 N	38.48 E
Elektrostal, Sov. Un. (ĕl-yĕk′trō-stȧl)	180b	55.47 N	38.27 E
Elektrougli, Sov. Un.	180b	55.43 N	38.13 E
Elephant Butte Res., NM (ĕl′ē-fănt būt)	119	33.25 N	107.10 W
El Escorial, Sp (ĕl-ĕs-kō-ryä′l)	169a	40.38 N	4.08 W
El Espino, Nic. (ĕl-ĕs-pē′nŏ)	130	13.26 N	86.48 W
Eleuthera (I.), Ba. (ē-lū′thēr-ȧ)	133	25.05 N	76.10 W
Eleuthera Pt., Ba.	133	24.35 N	76.05 W
Eleven Point (R.), Mo. (ē-lĕv′ĕn)	121	36.53 N	91.39 W
El Ferrol, Sp. (fā-rōl′)	168	43.30 N	8.12 W
Elgin, Il (ĕl′jĭn)	111a	42.03 N	88.16 W
Elgin, Ne.	112	41.58 N	98.04 W
Elgin, Or.	114	45.34 N	117.58 W
Elgin, Scot.	160	57.40 N	3.30 W
Elgin, Tx.	123	30.21 N	97.22 W
Elgin, Wa.	116a	47.23 N	122.42 W
El Goléa, Alg. (gō-lā-ä′)	220	30.39 N	2.52 E
Elgon, Mt., Ken. (ĕl′gŏn)	227	1.00 N	34.25 E
El Grullo, Mex. (gro͞ol-yō)	128	19.46 N	104.10 W
El Guapo, Ven. (gwȧ′pō)	141b	10.07 N	66.00 W
El Hank (Bluffs), Mauritania-Mali	114	23.44 N	6.45 W
El Hatillo, Ven. (ä-tē′l-yō)	141b	10.08 N	65.13 W
Elie, Can. (ē′lē)	93f	49.55 N	97.45 W
Elila (R.), Zaire (ĕ-lē′lȧ)	227	3.00 S	26.50 E
Elisa (I.), Wa. (ē-lī′sȧ)	116d	48.43 N	122.37 W
Élisabethville, see Lubumbashi			
Elisenvaara, Sov. Un. (ā-lē′sĕn-vä′rȧ)	163	61.25 N	29.46 E
Elizabeth, La. (ē-lĭz′ȧ-bĕth)	123	30.50 N	92.47 W
Elizabeth, NJ	110a	40.40 N	74.13 W
Elizabeth, Pa.	111e	40.16 N	79.53 W
Elizabeth City, NC	125	36.15 N	76.15 W
Elizabethton, Tn (ē-lĭz-ȧ-bĕth′tŭn)	125	36.19 N	82.12 W
Elizabethtown, Ky. (ē-lĭz′ă-bĕth-toun)	108	37.40 N	85.55 W
El Jadida, Mor.	220	33.14 N	8.34 W
Elk, Pol.	165	53.53 N	22.23 E
Elk (R.), Can.	97	50.00 N	115.00 W
Elk (R.), Tn.	124	35.05 N	86.36 W
Elk (R.), WV	108	38.30 N	81.05 W
El Kairouan, Tun. (kĕr-o͞o-än)	220	35.46 N	10.04 E
El Kala, Alg.	157	36.52 N	8.23 E
Elk City, Ok. (ĕlk)	120	35.23 N	99.23 W
El Kef, Tun. (xĕf′)	157	36.14 N	8.42 E
Elkhart, In. (ĕlk′härt)	108	41.40 N	86.00 W
Elkhart, Ks.	120	37.00 N	101.54 W
Elkhart, Tx	123	31.38 N	95.35 W
Elkhorn, Wi (ĕlk′hôrn)	113	42.39 N	88.32 W
Elkhorn (R.), Ne.	112	42.06 N	97.46 W
Elkin, NC (ĕl′kĭn)	125	36.15 N	80.50 W
Elkins, WV (ĕl′kĭnz)	109	38.55 N	79.50 W
Elk I, Can.	99	50.45 N	96.32 W
Elk Island Natl. Park, Can. (ĕlk ī′lănd)	97	53.37 N	112.45 W
Elko, Nv. (ĕl′kō)	114	40.51 N	115.46 W
Elk Point, SD	112	42.41 N	96.41 W
Elk Rapids, Mi. (răp′ĭdz)	108	44.55 N	85.25 W
Elk River, Id. (rĭv′ẽr)	114	46.47 N	116.11 W
Elk River, Mn.	113	45.17 N	93.33 W
Elkton, Ky. (ĕlk′tŭn)	124	36.47 N	87.08 W
Elkton, Md.	109	39.35 N	75.50 W
Elkton, SD	112	44.15 N	96.28 W
Elland, Eng. (el′ănd)	154	53.41 N	1.50 W
Ellen, Mt., Ut. (ĕl′ĕn)	119	38.05 N	110.50 W
Ellendale, ND (ĕl′ĕn-dāl)	112	46.01 N	98.33 W
Ellensburg, Wa. (ĕl′ĕnz-bûrg)	114	47.00 N	120.31 W
Ellenville, NY (ĕl′ĕn-vĭl)	109	41.40 N	74.25 W
Ellerslie, Can. (ĕl′ẽrz-lē)	93g	53.25 N	113.30 W
Ellesmere, Eng. (ĕlz′mẽr)	154	52.55 N	2.54 W
Ellesmere I, Can.	92	81.00 N	80.00 W
Ellesmere Port, Eng.	154	53.17 N	2.54 W
Ellice Is., see Tuvalu			
Ellicott City, Md. (ĕl′ĭ-kŏt sĭ′tē)	110e	39.16 N	76.48 W
Ellicott Cr., NY	111c	43.00 N	78.46 W
Elliotdale, S. Afr. (ĕl-ĭ-ŏt′dāl)	223c	31.58 S	28.42 E
Elliot Lake, Can.	100	46.23 N	82.39 W
Elliot, Wa. (el′ĭ-ŭt)	116a	47.28 N	122.08 W
Ellis, Ks. (ĕl′ĭs)	120	38.56 N	99.34 W
Ellisville, Ms. (ĕl′ĭs-vĭl)	124	31.37 N	89.10 W
Ellisville, Mo.	117e	38.35 N	90.35 W
Ellsworth, Ks. (ĕlz′wûrth)	120	38.43 N	98.14 W
Ellsworth, Me.	102	44.33 N	68.26 W
Ellsworth Highland, Ant.	228	77.00 S	90.00 W
Ellwangen, F.R.G. (ĕl′väŋ-gĕn)	164	48.47 N	10.08 E
Elm, F.R.G. (ĕlm)	155c	53.31 N	9.13 E
Elm (R.), SD	112	45.47 N	98.28 W
Elm (R.), WV	108	38.30 N	81.05 W
Elma, Wa. (ĕl′mȧ)	114	47.02 N	123.20 W
El Mahdia, Tun (mä-dē′a)(mä′dē-ȧ)	157	35.30 N	11.09 E
Elm Cr, Tx.	121	33.34 N	97.25 W
Elmendorf, Tx (ĕl′mĕn-dôrf)	117d	29.16 N	98.20 W
Elm Fork, Tx. (ĕlm fôrk)	117c	32.55 N	96.56 W
Elmhurst, Il (ĕlm′hûrst)	111a	41.54 N	87.56 W
El Milia, Alg. (mē′ä)	220	36.30 N	6.16 E
Elmira, NY (ĕl-mī′rȧ)	109	42.05 N	76.50 W
Elmira Heights, NY	109	42.10 N	76.50 W
El Misti (Vol.), Peru (mē′s-tē)	140	16.04 S	71.20 W
El Modena, Ca (mō-dē′nō)	117a	33.47 N	117.48 W
El Monte, Ca. (mōn′tā)	117a	34.04 N	118.02 W
El Morro Natl. Mon., NM	119	35.05 N	108.20 W
El Mreyyé (Des.), Mauritania	224	19.15 N	7.50 W
Elmshorn, F.R.G. (ĕlms′hôrn)	155c	53.45 N	9.39 E
Elmwood Place, Oh. (ĕlm′wo͝od plās)	111f	39.11 N	84.30 W
Elokomin (R.), Wa. (ē-lō′kō-mĭn)	116c	46.16 N	123.16 W
El Oro, Mex. (ô-rō)	128	19.49 N	100.04 W
El Oued, Alg. (wĕd′)	220	33.23 N	6.49 E
El Pao, Ven. (ĕl pȧ′ō)	140	8.08 N	62.37 W
El Paraíso, Hond. (pä-rä-ē′sō)	130	13.55 N	86.35 W
El Pardo, Sp. (pä′r-dō)	169a	40.31 N	3.47 W
El Paso, Tx. (pas′ō)	122	31.47 N	106.27 W
El Pilar, Ven. (pē-lä′r)	141b	9.56 N	64.48 W
El Porvenir, Pan. (pōr-vä-nēr′)	131	9.34 N	78.55 W
El Puerto de Sta. María, Sp. (pwĕr tō dā sän tä mä-rē′ä)	168	36.36 N	6.18 W
El Real, Pan. (rā-äl)	131	8.07 N	77.43 W
El Reno, Ok. (rē′nō)	120	35.31 N	97.57 W
El Roboré, Bol. (rô-bō-rĕ′)	141	18.23 S	59.43 W
Elroy, Wi. (ĕl′roi)	113	43.44 N	90.17 W
Elsa, Can.	105	63.55 N	135.25 W
Elsah, Il. (ĕl′zȧ)	117e	38.57 N	90.22 W
El Salto, Mex. (säl′tō)	128	22.48 N	105.22 W
El Salvador, N.A.	126	14.00 N	89.30 W
El Sauce, Nic. (ĕl-sȧ′o͞o-sĕ)	130	13.00 N	86.40 W
Elsberry, Mo. (ēlz′bĕr-ĭ)	121	39.09 N	90.44 W
Elsdorf, F.R.G. (ĕls′dōrf)	167c	50.56 N	6.35 E
El Segundo, Ca (sēgŭn′dō)	117a	33.55 N	118.24 W
Elsinore, Ca. (ĕl′sĭ-nôr)	117a	33.40 N	117.19 W
Elsinore L., Ca	117a	33.38 N	117.21 W
Elstorf, F.R.G. (ĕls′tōrf)	155c	53.25 N	9.48 E
Eltham, Austl. (ĕl′thăm)	207	37.43 S	145.08 E
El Tigre, Ven. (tē′grĕ)	140	8.49 N	64.15 W
El′ton (L.), Sov. Un.	177	49.10 N	47.00 E
El Toro, Ca. (tō′rō)	117a	33.37 N	117.42 W
El Triunfo, Hond. (ĕl-trē-o͞o′n-fô)	130	13.06 N	87.00 W
El Triunfo, Sal.	130	13.17 N	88.32 W
Elūru, India	193	16.44 N	80.09 E
El Vado Res, NM	119	36.37 N	106.30 W
Elvas, Port. (ĕl′väzh)	168	38.53 N	7.11 W
Elverum, Nor. (ĕl′vĕ-ro͞om)	162	60.53 N	11.33 E
El Viego, Nic. (ĕl-vyĕ′ĸō)	130	12.10 N	87.10 W
El Viejo (Vol.), Nic.	130	12.44 N	87.03 W
Elvins, Mo. (ĕl′vĭnz)	121	37.49 N	90.31 W
El Wak, Ken. (wäk′)	221	3.00 N	41.00 E
Elwood, Il. (ĕ′wo͝od)	111a	41.24 N	88.07 W
Elwood, In.	108	40.15 N	85.50 W
Ely, Eng. (ē′lĭ)	161	52.25 N	0.17 E
Ely, Mn.	113	47.54 N	91.53 W
Ely, Nv.	118	39.16 N	114.53 W
Elyria, Oh. (ē-lĭr′ĭ-ȧ)	111d	41.22 N	82.07 W
Ema (R.), Sov. Un. (ā′mȧ)	163	58.25 N	27.00 E
Emån (R.), Swe.	162	57.15 N	15.46 E
Emba (R.), Sov. Un. (yĕm′bȧ)	177	46.50 N	54.10 E
Embalse Guri (L.), Ven.	140	7.30 N	63.00 W
Embarrass (R.), Il. (ĕm-băr′ăs)	108	39.15 N	88.05 W
Embrun, Can. (ĕm′brŭn)	93c	45.16 N	75.17 W
Embrun, Fr. (äɴ-brûɴ′)	167	44.35 N	6.32 E
Embu, Ken.	227	0.32 S	37.27 E
Emden, F.R.G. (ĕm′dĕn)	164	53.21 N	7.15 E
Emerald, Austl. (ĕm′ẽr-ăld)	211	28.34 S	148.00 E
Emerson, Can. (ĕm′ẽr-sŭn)	99	49.00 N	97.12 W
Emeryville, Ca (ĕm′ẽr-ĭ-vĭl)	116b	37.50 N	122.17 W
Emi Koussi, (Mtn.), Chad (ā′mē ĸo͞o-sē′)	225	19.50 N	18.30 E
Emilia-Romagna (Reg.), It. (ē-mēl′yä rô-mȧ′n-yä)	170	44.35 N	10.48 E
Emiliano Zapata, Mex. (ĕ-mē-lyȧ′nō-zä-pȧ′tȧ)	129	17.45 N	91.46 W
Eminence, Ky. (ĕm′ĭ-nĕns)	108	38.25 N	85.15 W
Emira I., Pap. N. Gui. (ā-mē-rä′)	203	1.40 S	150.28 E
Emmen, Neth. (ĕm′ĕn)	161	52.48 N	6.55 E
Emmerich, F.R.G. (ĕm′ẽr-ĭk)	167c	51.51 N	6.16 E
Emmetsburg, Ia. (ĕm′ĕts-bûrg)	113	43.07 N	94.41 W
Emmett, Id. (ĕm′ĕt)	114	43.53 N	116.30 W
Emmons Mt., Ut. (ĕm′ŭnz)	115	40.43 N	110.20 W

ăt; finăl; rāte; senāte; ärm; ȧsk; sofȧ; fâre; ch-choose; dh-as th in other; bē; ēvent; bĕt; recĕnt; cratẽr; g-gō; gh-guttural g; bĭt; ĭ-short neutral; rīde; ĸ-guttural k as ch in German ich;

PLACE (Pronunciation)	PAGE	Lat. °′	Long. °′
Emory Pk., Tx. (ĕ'mō-rē pĕk)	122	29.13 N	103.20 W
Empoli, It. (ām'pô-lē)	170	43.43 N	10.55 E
Emporia, Ks. (ĕm-pō'rĭ-*á*)	121	38.24 N	96.11 W
Emporia, Va.	125	37.40 N	77.34 W
Emporium, Pa. (ĕm-pō'rĭ-*ŭ*m)	109	41.30 N	78.15 W
Ems R., F.R.G. (ĕms)	164	52.52 N	7.16 E
Ems-Weser (Can.), F.R.G. (vā'zĕr)	164	52.23 N	8.11 E
Enånger, Swe. (ĕn-ôn̦'gĕr)	164	61.36 N	16.55 E
Encantada, Cerro de la (Mtn.), Mex. (sĕ'r-rô-dĕ-lä-ĕn-kän-tä'dä)	126	31.58 N	115.15 W
Encanto, C., Phil. (ĕn-kän'tō)	203a	15.44 N	121.46 E
Encarnación, Par. (ĕn-kär-nä-syōn')	142	27.26 S	55.52 W
Encarnación de Diaz, Mex. (ĕn-kär-nä-syōn dā dē'äz)	128	21.34 N	102.15 W
Encinal, Tx. (ĕn'sĭ-nôl)	122	28.02 N	99.22 W
Encontrados, Ven. (ĕn-kōn-trä'dōs)	140	9.01 N	72.10 W
Encounter B., Austl. (ĕn-koun'tĕr)	212	35.50 S	138.45 E
Endako (R.), Can.	96	54.05 N	125.30 W
Endau (R.), Mala.	189b	2.29 N	103.40 E
Enderbury (I.), Oceania (ĕn'dĕr-bûrĭ)	204	2.00 S	107.50 W
Enderby Land (Reg.), Ant. (ĕn'dĕr bĭ)	228	72.00 S	52.00 E
Enderlin, ND (ĕn'dĕr-lĭn)	112	46.38 N	97.37 W
Endicott, NY (ĕn'dĭ-k*ŏ*t)	109	42.05 N	76.00 W
Endicott Mts., Ak.	105	67.30 N	153.45 W
Enez, Tur.	171	40.42 N	26.05 E
Enfield, Ct. (ĕn'fēld)	109	41.55 N	72.35 W
Enfield, Eng.	154b	51.38 N	0.06 W
Enfield, NC	125	36.10 N	77.41 W
Engang, Cabo (C.), Dom.Rep. (ká'-bô- ĕn-gä-nō)	133	18.40 N	68.30 W
Engcobo, S. Afr. (ĕŋg-cô-bô)	223c	31.41 S	27.59 E
Engel's, Sov. Un. (ĕn'gĕls)	177	51.20 N	45.40 E
Engelskirchen, F.R.G. (ĕn'gĕls-kĕr'ĸĕn)	167c	50.59 N	7.25 E
Englewood, Co. (ĕn'g'l-wo͝od)	120	39.39 N	105.00 W
Enggano, Pulau (I.), Indon. (ĕng-gä'nō)	202	5.22 S	102.18 E
England, Ar. (ĭŋ'gl*ă*nd)	121	34.33 N	91.58 W
England (Reg.), U.K. (ĭŋ'gl*ă*nd)	160	51.35 N	1.40 W
Engleė, Can. (ĕn-gleē)	103	50.44 N	56.06 W
Englewood, NJ	110a	40.54 N	73.59 W
English, In. (ĭn'glĭsh)	108	38.15 N	86.25 W
English (R.), Can.	95	50.31 N	94.12 W
English Chan, Eng.	157	49.45 N	3.06 W
Énguera, Sp. (ān'gārä)	169	38.58 N	0.42 W
Enid, Ok. (ē'nĭd)	120	36.25 N	97.52 W
Enid Res., Ms.	124	34.13 N	89.47 W
Enkeldoorn, Zimb. (ĕŋ'k'l-do͞orn)	222	19.59 S	30.58 E
Enkeldoring, S. Afr (ĕŋ'k'l-dôr-ĭng)	219d	25.24 S	28.43 E
Enköping, Swe. (ĕn'kû-pĭng)	162	59.39 N	17.05 E
Ennedi (Plat.), Chad (ĕn-nĕd'ē)	221	16.45 N	22.45 E
Ennis, Ire. (ĕn'ĭs)	160	52.54 N	9.05 W
Ennis, Tx.	123	32.20 N	96.38 W
Enniscorthy, Ire. (ĕn-ĭs-kôr'thĭ)	160	52.33 N	6.27 W
Enniskillen, N. Ire (ĕn-ĭs-kĭl'ĕn)	160	54.20 N	7.25 W
Enns (R.), Aus. (ĕns)	164	47.37 N	14.35 E
Enoree, SC (ē-nō'rē)	125	34.43 N	81.58 W
Enoree (R.), SC	125	34.35 N	81.55 W
Enriquillo, Dom. Rep. (ĕn-rē-kē'l-yō)	133	17.55 N	71.15 W
Enriquillo, Lago (L.), Dom. Rep. (lä'gō-ĕn-rē-kē'l-yō)	133	18.35 N	71.35 W
Enschede, Neth. (ĕns'ĸā-d*ĕ*)	161	52.10 N	6.50 E
Ensenada, Mex. (ĕn-sĕ-nä'dä)	126	32.00 N	116.30 W
Enseñada, Arg.	139c	34.50 S	57.55 W
Enshi, China (ŭn-shr)	199x	30.18 N	109.25 E
Enshū-Nada (Sea), Jap. (ĕn'sho͞o nä-dä)	201	34.25 N	137.14 E
Entebbe, Ug. (ĕn-tĕb'ĕ)	227	0.04 N	32.28 E
Enterprise, Al. (ĕn'tĕr-prīz)	124	31.20 N	85.50 W
Enterprise, Or.	114	45.25 N	117.16 W
Entiat, L, Wa.	114	45.43 N	120.11 W
Entraygues, Fr. (ĕɴ-trĕg')	166	44.39 N	2.33 E
Entre-Rios, Moz. (ĕn-trā rē'ōs)	227	14.57 S	37.20 E
Entre Rios (Prov.), Arg.	142	31.30 S	59.00 W
Enugu, Nig. (ĕ-no͞o'go͞o)	225	6.27 N	7.27 E
Enumclaw, Wa. (ĕn'ŭm-klô)	116a	47.12 N	121.59 W
Envigado, Col. (ĕn-vē-gá'dô)	140a	6.10 N	75.34 W
Eolie, Isole (Is.), It. (ĕ'ô-lē-ē-ô'lyĕ)	170	38.43 N	14.43 E
Epe, Nig.	225	6.37 N	3.59 E
Epernay, Fr. (ā-pĕr-nĕ')	166	49.02 N	3.54 E
Épernon, Fr. (ā-pĕr-nôɴ')	167b	48.36 N	1.41 E
Ephraim, Ut. (ē'frā-ĭm)	119	39.20 N	111.40 W
Ephrata, Wa. (ĕfrā'tá)	114	47.18 N	119.35 W
Epi, Vanuatu (ā'pē)	211	16.59 S	168.29 E
Épila, Sp. (ā'pē-lä)	168	41.38 N	1.15 W
Épinal, Fr. (ā-pē-nál')	167	48.11 N	6.27 E
Episkopi, Cyprus	189a	34.38 N	32.55 E
Epping, Eng. (ĕp'ĭng)	154b	51.41 N	0.06 E
Epupa Falls, Ang.	226	17.00 S	13.05 E
Epworth, Eng. (ĕp'wûrth)	154	53.31 N	0.50 W
Equatorial Guinea, Afr.	220	2.00 N	7.15 E
Eramosa (R.), Can. (ĕr-*á*-mō's*á*)	93d	43.39 N	80.08 W
Erba, Jabal (Mtn.), Sud. (ĕr-bá)	221	20.53 N	36.45 E
Erciyeş Daği (Mtn.), Tur.	159	38.30 N	35.36 E
Erda, Ut. (ĕr'dä)	117b	40.41 N	112.17 W
Erding, F.R.G. (ĕr'dēng)	155d	48.19 N	11.54 E
Erechim, Braz. (ĕ-rĕ-shē'ɴ)	142	27.43 S	52.11 W
Ereğli, Tur. (ĕ-rā'ĭ-le)	177	37.40 N	34.00 E
Ereğli, Tur.	177	41.15 N	31.25 E
Erfurt, G.D.R. (ĕr'fo͞ort)	164	50.59 N	11.04 E
Ergene (R.), Tur. (ĕr'gĕ-nĕ)	171	41.17 N	26.50 E
Erges (R.), Port.-Sp. (ĕr'-zhĕs)	168	39.45 N	7.01 W
Ergļi, Sov. Un.	163	56.54 N	25.38 E
Eria (R.), Sp. (å-rē'ä)	168	42.10 N	6.08 W
Erick, Ok. (âr'ĭk)	120	35.14 N	99.51 W
Erie, Ks. (ē'rĭ)	121	37.35 N	95.17 W
Erie, Pa.	109	42.05 N	80.05 W
Erie, L., U.S.-Can.	107	42.15 N	81.25 W
Erimo Saki (C.), Jap. (ā'rē-mō sä-kē)	200	41.53 N	143.20 E
Erin, Can. (ĕ'rĭn)	93d	43.46 N	80.04 W
Eritrea (Reg.), Eth. (ā-rē-trā'á)	221	16.15 N	38.30 E
Erlangen, F.R.G. (ĕr'läng-*ĕ*n)	164	49.36 N	11.03 E
Erlanger, Ky. (ĕr'lăng-ĕr)	111f	39.01 N	84.36 W
Ermoúpolis, Grc.	171	37.30 N	24.56 E
Ernākulam, India	191	9.58 N	76.23 E
Erne, Upper Lough (L.), N. Ire. (lŏk ûrn)	160	54.20 N	7.24 W
Erne, Lower Lough (L.), Ire.	160	54.30 N	7.40 W
Erode, India	191	11.20 N	77.45 E
Eromanga (I.), Vanuatu	211	18.58 S	169.18 E
Eros, La. (ē'rōs)	123	32.23 N	92.22 W
Errego, Moz.	227	16.02 S	37.14 E
Errigal (Mtn.), Ire. (ĕr-ĭ-gôl')	160	55.02 N	8.07 W
Errol Heights, Or.	116c	45.29 N	122.38 W
Erstein, Fr. (ĕr'shtīn)	167	48.27 N	7.40 E
Erwin, NC (ûr'wĭn)	125	35.16 N	78.40 W
Erwin, Tn.	125	36.07 N	82.25 W
Erzgebirge (Ore.Mts.), G.D.R. (ĕrts'gĕ-bē'gĕ)	164	50.29 N	12.40 E
Erzincan, Tur. (ĕr-zĭn-jän')	177	39.50 N	39.30 E
Erzurum, Tur. (ĕrz'ro͞om')	177	39.55 N	41.10 E
Esambo, Zaire	226	3.40 S	23.24 E
Esashi, Jap. (ĕs'ä-shē)	200	41.50 N	140.10 E
Esbjerg, Den. (ĕs'byĕrgh)	162	55.29 N	8.25 E
Escalante, Ut. (ĕs-kȧ-lăn'tē)	119	37.50 N	111.40 W
Escalante (R.), Ut.	119	37.40 N	111.20 W
Escalón, Mex.	122	26.45 N	104.20 W
Escambia (R.), Fl. (ĕs-kăm'bĭ-*á*)	124	30.38 N	87.20 W
Escanaba, Mi. (ĕs-k*á*-nô'b*á*)	113	45.44 N	87.05 W
Escanaba (R.), Mi.	113	46.10 N	87.22 W
Escarpada Point, Phil.	202	18.40 N	122.45 E
Esch-sur-Alzette, Lux.	167	49.32 N	6.21 E
Eschwege, F.R.G. (ĕsh'vā-gē)	164	51.11 N	10.02 E
Eschweiler, F.R.G. (ĕsh'vī-lĕr)	167c	50.49 N	6.15 E
Escocesá, Bahia (B.), Dom. Rep. (bä-ē'ä-ĕs-kō-sĕ'sä)	133	19.25 N	69.40 W
Escondido, Ca. (ĕs-k*ŏ*n-dē'dō)	118	33.07 N	117.00 W
Escondido, Rio (R.), Mex. (rē'ō-ĕs-kōn-dē'dô)	122	28.30 N	100.45 W
Escondido R, Nic.	131	12.04 N	84.09 W
Escudo de Veraguas I., Pan. (ĕs-ko͞o'dä dā vā-rä'gwäs)	131	9.07 N	81.25 W
Escuinapa, Mex. (ĕs-kwē-nä'pä)	128	22.49 N	105.44 W
Escuintla, Guat. (ĕs-kwēn'tlä)	130	14.16 N	90.47 W
Escuintla, Mex.	129	15.20 N	92.45 W
Ese, Cayos de (I.), Col.	131	12.24 N	81.07 W
Esfahān, Iran	192	32.38 N	51.30 E
Esgueva (R.), Sp. (ĕs-gĕ'vä)	168	41.48 N	4.10 W
Eshowe, S. Afr. (ĕsh'ô-wē)	223c	28.54 S	31.28 E
Esiama, Ghana	224	4.56 N	2.21 W
Eskdale, WV (ĕsk'dāl)	108	38.05 N	81.25 W
Eskifjördur, Ice. (ĕs'kē-fyûr'do͞or)	156	65.04 N	14.01 W
Eskilstuna, Swe. (å'shĕl-stü-na)	162	59.23 N	16.28 E
Eskimo Lakes (L.), Can. (es'kĭ-mō)	94	69.40 N	130.10 W
Eskişehir, Tur. (ĕs-kē-shĕ'h'r)	177	39.40 N	30.20 E
Esko, Mn. (ĕs'kô)	117h	46.27 N	92.22 W
Esla (R.), Sp. (ĕs-lä)	168	41.50 N	5.48 W
Eslöv, Swe. (ĕs'lûv)	162	55.50 N	13.17 E
Esmeraldas, Ec. (ĕs-mā-räl'däs)	140	0.58 N	79.45 W
Espada, Punta (Pt.), Dom. Rep. (po͞o'n-tä-ĕs-pä'dä)	133	18.30 N	68.30 W
Espanola, Can. (ĕs-p*á*-nō'l*á*)	100	46.11 N	81.59 W
Esparta, C.R. (ĕs-pär'tä)	131	9.59 N	84.40 W
Esperance, Austl. (ĕs'pē-r*ă*ns)	210	33.45 S	122.07 E
Esperanza, Cuba (ĕs-pĕ-rä'n-zä)	132	22.30 N	80.10 W
Espichel, Cabo (C.), Port. (ká'bō-ĕs-pē-shĕl')	169b	38.25 N	9.13 W
Espinal, Col. (ĕs-pē-näl')	140a	4.10 N	74.53 W
Espinhaço, Serra do (Mts.), Braz. (sĕ'r-rä-dô-ĕs-pē-ná-sô)	141	16.06 S	44.56 W
Espinillo, Punta (Pt.), Ur. (po͞o'n-tä-ĕs-pē-nē'l-yô)	139c	34.49 S	56.27 W
Espírito Santo, Braz. (ĕs-pē'rē-tô-sän'tô)	141	20.27 S	40.18 W
Espírito Santo (State), Braz.	141	19.57 S	40.58 W
Espíritu Santo, Bahia del (B.), Mex. (bä-ē'ä-dĕl-ĕs-pē'rē-to͞o-sän'tô)	130a	19.25 N	87.28 W
Espiritu Santo (I.), Vanuatu (ĕs-pē'rē-to͞o sän'tō)	211	15.45 S	166.50 E
Espita, Mex. (ĕs-pē'tä)	130a	20.57 N	88.22 W
Espoo, Fin.	163	60.13 N	24.41 E
Esposende, Port. (ĕs-pō-zĕn'dā)	168	41.33 N	8.45 W
Esquel, Arg. (ĕs-kĕ'l)	142	42.47 S	71.22 W
Esquimalt, Can. (ĕs-kwī'mŏlt)	116a	48.26 N	123.24 W
Essaouira, Mor.	220	31.34 N	9.44 W
Essen, Bel.	155a	51.28 N	4.27 E
Essen, F.R.G. (ĕs'sĕn)	167c	51.26 N	6.59 E
Essequibo (R.), Guy. (ĕs-ā-kē'bō)	141	4.26 N	58.17 W
Essex, Il.	111a	41.11 N	88.11 W
Essex, Md.	110e	39.19 N	76.29 W
Essex, Ma.	103a	42.38 N	70.47 W
Essex, Vt.	109	44.30 N	73.05 W
Essex Fells, NJ (ĕs'*ĕ*ks fĕlz)	110a	40.50 N	74.16 W
Essexville, Mi. (ĕs'*ĕ*ks-vĭl)	108	43.35 N	83.50 W
Esslingen, F.R.G. (ĕs'slēn-gĕn)	164	48.45 N	9.19 E
Estacado, Llano (Plain), U.S. (yá-nō ĕs-t*á*c*á*-dō')	106	33.50 N	103.20 W
Estados, Isla de los, S.A.	142	55.05 S	63.00 W
Estância, Braz. (ĕs-tän'sĭ-ä)	141	11.17 S	37.18 W
Estarreja, Port. (ĕ-tär-rā'zhä)	168	40.44 N	8.39 W
Estats, Pique d' (Pk.), Fr.	169	42.43 N	1.30 E
Estcourt, S. Afr. (ĕst-coort)	223c	29.04 S	29.53 E
Este, It. (ĕs'tā)	170	45.13 N	11.40 E
Estelí, Nic. (ĕs-tā-lē')	130	13.10 N	86.23 W
Estella, Sp. (ĕs-tāl'yä)	168	42.40 N	2.01 W
Estepa, Sp. (ĕs-tā'pä)	168	37.18 N	4.54 W
Estepona, Sp. (ĕs-tā-pō'nä)	168	36.26 N	5.08 W
Esterhazy, Can. (ĕs'tĕr-hā-zē)	99	50.40 N	102.08 W
Esteros, B., Ca. (ĕs-tā'rōs)	118	35.22 N	121.04 W
Estevan, Can. (ē-stē'v*ă*n)	98	49.07 N	103.05 W
Estevan Group (Is.), Can.	96	53.05 N	129.40 W
Estherville, Ia. (ĕs'tĕr-vĭl)	113	43.24 N	94.49 W
Estill, SC (ĕs'tĭl)	125	32.46 N	81.15 W
Eston, Can.	98	51.10 N	108.45 W
Estonian S.S.R., Sov. Un. (ĕs-tō'nĭ-ăn)	174	59.10 N	25.00 E
Estoril, Port. (ĕs-tô-rĕl')	169b	38.45 N	9.24 W
Estrêla (R.), Braz. (ĕs-trĕ'lä)	142b	22.39 S	43.16 W
Estrêla, Serra da (Mts.), Port. (sĕr'rá dä ĕs-trā'l*á*)	168	40.25 N	7.45 W
Estremadura (Reg.), Port. (ĕs-trā-mä-do͞o'r*á*)	168	41.35 N	8.36 W
Estremoz, Port. (ĕs-trā-mōzh')	168	38.50 N	7.35
Estrondo, Serra do (Mts.), Braz. (sĕr'r' do͞o ĕs-trôn'do͞o)	141	9.52 S	48.56 W
Esumba, Île (I.), Zaire	226	2.00 N	21.12 E
Esztergom, Hung. (ĕs'tĕr-gōm)	165	47.46 N	18.45 E
Etah, Grnld. (ē't*á*)	92	78.20 N	72.42 W
Étampes, Fr. (ā-täɴp')	167b	48.26 N	2.09 E
Étaples, Fr. (ā-täp'l')	166	50.32 N	1.38 E
Etchemin (R.), Can. (ĕch'ĕ-mĭn)	93b	46.39 N	71.03 W
Ethiopia, Afr. (ē-thē-ō'pē-á)	218	7.53 N	37.55 E
Eticoga, Guinea-Bissau	224	11.09 N	16.08 W
Etiwanda, Ca. (ĕ-tĭ-wän'd*á*)	117a	34.07 N	117.31 W
Etlatongo, see San Mateo			
Etna, Pa. (ĕt'n*á*)	111e	40.30 N	79.55 W
Etna, Mt. (Vol.), It.	170	37.48 N	15.00 E
Etobicoke, Can.	93d	43.39 N	79.34 W
Etobicoke Cr., Can.	93d	43.44 N	79.48 W
Etolin Str., Ak. (ĕt ō lĭn)	105	60.35 N	165.40 W
Etorofu (I.), see Iturop			
Etoshapan (L.), Namibia (ētō'shä)	222	19.07 S	15.30 E
Etowah, Tn. (ĕt'ô-wä)	124	35.18 N	84.31 W
Etowah (R.), Ga.	124	34.23 N	84.19 W
Étréchy, Fr. (ā-trā-shē')	167b	48.29 N	2.12 E
Etten-Leur, Neth.	155a	51.34 N	4.38 E
Etterbeek, Bel. (ĕt'ĕr-băk)	155a	50.51 N	4.24 E
Etzatlán, Mex. (ĕt-zä-tlän')	128	20.44 N	104.04 W
Eucla, Austl. (ū'klá)	210	31.45 S	128.50 E
Euclid, Oh. (ū'klĭd)	111d	41.34 N	81.32 W
Eudora, Ar. (u-dō'rá)	121	33.07 N	91.16 W
Eufaula, Al. (û-fô'l*á*)	124	31.53 N	85.09 W
Eufaula, Ok.	121	35.16 N	95.35 W
Eufaula Res., Ok.	121	35.00 N	94.45 W
Eugene, Or. (û-jĕn')	114	44.02 N	123.06 W
Euless, Tx. (ū'lĕs)	117c	32.50 N	97.05 W
Eunice, La. (ū'nĭs)	123	30.30 N	92.25 W
Eupen, Bel. (oi'pĕn)	161	50.39 N	6.05 E
Euphrates (R.), Asia (û-frā'tēz)	192	36.00 N	39.30 E
Eure (R.), Fr. (ûr)	166	49.03 N	1.22 E
Eureka, Ca. (û-rē'ká)	114	40.45 N	124.10 W
Eureka, Ks.	121	37.48 N	96.17 W
Eureka, Mt.	114	48.53 N	115.07 W
Eureka, Nv.	118	39.33 N	115.58 W
Eureka, SD	112	45.46 N	99.38 W
Eureka, Ut.	119	39.55 N	112.10 W
Eureka Springs, Ar.	121	36.24 N	93.43 W
Eurgun (Mtn.), Iran	192	28.47 N	57.00 E
Europe, (ū'rŭp)	152		
Eustis, Fl. (ūs'tĭs)	125	28.50 N	81.41 W
Eutaw, Al. (ū-tâ)	124	32.48 N	87.50 W
Eutsuk L., Can. (o͞ot'sŭk)	96	53.20 N	126.44 W
Evanston, Il. (ĕv'*ă*n-stŭn)	111a	42.03 N	87.41 W
Evanston, Wy.	115	41.17 N	111.02 W
Evansville, In. (ĕv'*ă*nz-vĭl)	108	38.00 N	87.30 W
Evansville, Wi.	113	42.46 N	89.19 W
Evart, Mi. (ĕv'ĕrt)	108	43.55 N	85.10 W
Evaton, S. Afr. (ĕv'*á*-t*ŏ*n)	219d	26.32 S	27.53 E
Eveleth, Mn. (ĕv'ē-lĕth)	113	47.27 N	92.35 W
Everard (L.), Austl. (ĕv'ĕr-ârd)	210	36.20 S	134.10 E
Everard Ra., Austl.	210	27.15 S	132.00 E
Everest, Mt., Nep.-China (ĕv'ĕr-ĕst)	190	28.00 N	86.57 E
Everett, Ma. (ĕv'ĕr-ĕt)	103a	42.24 N	71.03 W
Everett, Wa. (ĕv'ĕr-ĕt)	116a	47.59 N	122.11 W
Everett Mts., Can.	95	62.34 N	68.00 W
Everglades, Fl. (ĕv'ĕr-glādz)	125a	25.50 N	81.25 W
Everglades, The (Swp.), Fl.	132	25.35 N	80.55 W
Everglades Natl. Park, Fl.	125a	25.39 N	80.57 W
Evergreen, Al. (ĕv'ĕr-grēn)	124	31.25 N	87.56 W
Evergreen Park, Il.	111a	41.44 N	87.42 W
Everman, Tx. (ĕv'ĕr-m*ă*n)	117c	32.38 N	97.17 W
Everson, Wa. (ĕv'ĕr-s*ŭ*n)	116d	48.55 N	122.21 W
Évora, Port. (ĕv'ô-rä)	168	38.35 N	7.54 W
Évreux, Fr. (ā-vrû')	166	49.02 N	1.11 E
Evrótas (R.), Grc. (ĕv-rō'täs)	171	37.15 N	22.17 E
Évvoia (I.), Grc.	171	38.38 N	23.45 E
Ewa Beach, Hi. (ē'wä)	104	21.17 N	158.03 E
Ewaso Ng'iro (R.), Ken.	221	0.59 N	37.47 E
Excelsior, Mn. (ĕk-sel'sĭ-ŏr)	117g	44.54 N	93.35 W

290 Excelsior Springs – Filadelfia

PLACE (Pronunciation)	PAGE	Lat. °′	Long. °′
Excelsior Springs, Mo.	121	39.20 N	94.13 W
Exe (R.), Eng. (ěks)	160	50.57 N	3.37 W
Exeter, Ca. (ěk'sē-tēr)	118	36.18 N	119.09 W
Exeter, Eng.	160	50.45 N	3.33 W
Exeter, NH	109	43.00 N	71.00 W
Exmoor, Eng. (ěks'mo͞or)	160	51.10 N	3.55 W
Exmouth, Eng. (ěks'mŭth)	160	50.40 N	3.20 W
Exmouth, G., Austl.	210	21.45 S	114.30 E
Exploits (R.), Can. (ěks-ploits')	103	48.50 N	56.15 W
Extórrax (R.), Mex. (ěx-tó'răx)	128	21.04 N	99.39 W
Extrema, Braz. (ěsh-trě'mä)	139a	22.52 S	46.19 W
Extremadura (Reg.), Sp. (ěks-trā-mä-doo'rä)	168	38.43 N	6.30 W
Exuma Sd, Ba. (ěk-so͞o'mä)	133	24.20 N	76.20 W
Eyasi, L., Tan. (å-yä'sē)	227	3.25 S	34.55 E
Eyjafjördur (Fd.), Ice.	156	66.21 N	18.20 W
Eyrarbakki, Ice.	156	63.51 N	20.52 W
Eyre, Austl. (âr)	210	32.15 S	126.20 E
Eyre (L.), Austl.	212	28.43 S	137.50 E
Eyre Pen, Austl.	210	33.30 S	136.00 E
Ezeiza, Arg. (ě-zā'zä)	142a	34.36 S	58.31 W
Ezine, Tur. (å'zĭ-nå)	171	39.47 N	26.18 E

F

PLACE (Pronunciation)	PAGE	Lat. °′	Long. °′
Fabens, Tx. (fā'běnz)	122	31.30 N	106.07 W
Fåborg, Den. (fô'bôrg)	162	55.06 N	10.19 E
Fabriano, It. (fä-brē-ä'nô)	170	43.20 N	12.55 E
Facatativá, Col. (fä-kä-tä-tē-vá')	140a	4.49 N	74.09 W
Fada, Chad (fä'dä)	221	17.06 N	21.18 E
Fada Ngourma, Upper Volta (fä'dä''n go͞or'mä)	224	12.04 N	0.21 E
Faddeya (I.), Sov. Un. (fád-yä')	179	76.12 N	145.00 E
Faenza, It. (fä-ěnd'zä)	170	44.16 N	11.53 E
Faeroe Is., Eur. (fā'rō)	152	62.00 N	5.45 W
Fafe, Port. (fä'fā)	168	41.30 N	8.10 W
Fafen (R.), Eth.	219a	8.15 N	42.40 E
Făgăras, Rom. (fá-gä'răsh)	171	45.50 N	24.55 E
Fagerness, Nor. (fä'ghēr-nĕs)	162	61.00 N	9.10 E
Fagnano (L.), Arg.-Chile (fäk-nä'nô)	142	54.35 S	68.20 W
Faguibine, Lac (L.), Mali	224	16.50 N	4.20 W
Faial I., Acores (fä-yä'l)	220a	38.40 N	29.19 W
Fā'id, Egypt (fä-yēd')	219c	30.19 N	32.18 E
Fairbanks, Ak. (fâr'bănks)	105	64.50 N	147.48 W
Fairbury, Il. (fâr'bĕr-ĭ)	108	40.45 N	88.25 W
Fairbury, Ne.	121	40.09 N	97.11 W
Fairchild Cr., Can. (fâr'chīld)	93d	43.18 N	80.10 W
Fairfax, Mn. (fâr'făks)	113	44.29 N	94.44 W
Fairfax, SC	125	32.29 N	81.13 W
Fairfax, Va.	110e	38.51 N	77.20 W
Fairfield, Al. (fâr'fēld)	110h	33.30 N	86.50 W
Fairfield, Austl.	207b	33.52 S	150.57 E
Fairfield, Ct.	110a	41.08 N	73.22 W
Fairfield, Il.	108	38.25 N	88.20 W
Fairfield, Ia.	113	41.00 N	91.59 W
Fairfield, Me.	102	44.35 N	69.38 W
Fairhaven, Ma. (fâr-hā'věn)	109	41.35 N	70.55 W
Fair Haven, Vt.	109	43.35 N	73.15 W
Fair I., Scot. (fâr)	160a	59.34 N	1.41 W
Fairmont, Mn. (fâr'mŏnt)	113	43.39 N	94.26 W
Fairmont, WV	109	39.30 N	80.10 W
Fairmont City, Il.	117e	38.39 N	90.05 W
Fairmount, In.	108	40.25 N	85.45 W
Fairmount, Ks.	117f	39.12 N	95.55 W
Fair Oaks, Ga. (fâr ōks)	110c	33.56 N	84.33 W
Fairport, NY (fâr'pōrt)	109	43.05 N	77.30 W
Fairport Harbor, Oh.	108	41.45 N	81.15 W
Fairview, Ok. (fâr'vū)	120	36.16 N	98.28 W
Fairview, Or.	116c	45.32 N	112.26 W
Fairview, Ut.	119	39.35 N	111.30 W
Fairview Park, Oh.	111d	41.27 N	81.52 W
Fairweather, Mt., Can. (fâr-wĕdh'ēr)	105	59.12 N	137.22 W
Faisalabad, Pak.	190	31.29 N	73.06 E
Faith, SD (fāth)	112	45.02 N	120.02 W
Faizābād, India	190	26.50 N	82.17 E
Fajardo, P.R.	127b	18.20 N	65.40 W
Fakfak, Indon.	203	2.56 S	132.25 E
Faku, China (fä-ko͞o)	198	42.28 N	123.20 E
Falalise, C., Viet.	199	19.20 N	106.18 E
Falcón (State), Ven. (fäl-kô'n)	141b	11.00 N	68.28 W
Falconer, NY (fô'k'n-ēr)	109	42.10 N	79.10 W
Falcon Heights, Mn. (fô'k'n)	117g	44.59 N	93.10 W
Falcon Res., Tx. (fôk'n)	122	26.47 N	99.03 W
Falemé (R.), Afr. (fá-lā-mā')	224	13.40 N	12.00 W
Faleshty, Sov. Un. (fä-lăsh'tĭ)	173	47.33 N	27.46 E
Falfurrias, Tx. (fäl'fo͞o-rē'ás)	122	27.15 N	98.08 W
Falher, Can. (fäl'ēr)	97	55.44 N	117.12 W
Falkenberg, Swe. (fäl'kĕn-bĕrgh)	162	56.54 N	12.25 E
Falkensee, G.D.R. (fäl'kĕn-zā)	155b	52.34 N	13.05 E
Falkenthal, G.D.R. (fäl'kĕn-täl)	155b	52.54 N	13.18 E
Falkirk, Scot. (fôl'kûrk)	160	55.59 N	3.55 W
Falkland Is., S.A. (fôk'lănd)	142	50.45 S	61.00 W
Falköping, Swe. (fäl'chûp-ĭng)	162	58.09 N	13.30 E
Fall City, Wa.	116a	47.34 N	121.53 W
Fall Cr., In. (fôl)	111g	39.52 N	86.04 W
Fallon, Nv. (făl'ŭn)	118	39.30 N	118.48 W
Fall River, Ma.	110b	41.42 N	71.07 W
Falls Church, Va. (fălz chûrch)	110e	38.53 N	77.10 W
Falls City, Ne.	121	40.04 N	95.37 W
Fallston, Md. (fâls'ton)	110e	39.32 N	76.26 W
Falmouth, Eng. (făl'mŭth)	160	50.08 N	5.04 W
Falmouth, Jam.	132	18.30 N	77.40 W
Falmouth, Ky.	108	38.40 N	84.20 W
False (B.), see **Valsbaai**			
False Divi Pt., India	189	15.45 N	80.50 E
Falso, Cabo (C.), Dom.Rep. (ká'bô-fál-sô)	133	17.45 N	71.55 W
Falster (I.), Den. (fäls'tēr)	162	54.48 N	11.58 E
Fălticeni, Rom. (fŭl-tē-chān'y')	165	47.27 N	26.17 E
Falun, Swe. (fä-lo͞on')	162	60.38 N	15.35 E
Famagusta, Cyprus (fä-mä-go͞os'tä)	159	35.08 N	33.59 E
Famatina, Sierra de (Mts.), Arg. (sē-ĕ'r-rà-dē-fä-mä-tē'nä)	142	29.00 S	67.50 W
Fang Xian, China (fäŋ-shyĕn)	199	32.05 N	110.45 E
Fanning (I.), Oceania (făn'ĭng)	205	4.20 N	159.00 W
Fannystelle, Can. (făn'ĭ-stĕl)	93f	49.45 N	97.46 W
Fano, It. (fä'nō)	170	43.49 N	13.01 E
Fanø (I.), Den. (fän'û)	162	55.24 N	8.10 E
Farafangana, Mad. (fä-rä-fäŋ-gä'nä)	223	21.18 S	47.59 E
Farāh, Afg. (fä-rä')	192	32.15 N	62.13 E
Farallón, Punta (Pt.), Mex. (po͞o'n-tä-fä-rä-lōn)	128	19.21 N	105.03 W
Faranah, Gui (fä-rä'nä)	224	10.02 N	10.44 W
Farasān, Jaza'ir (Is.), Eth.	221	16.45 N	41.08 E
Faregh, Wadi al (R.), Libya (wädē ĕl fä-rĕg')	159	30.10 N	19.34 E
Farewell, C., N.Z. (fâr-wĕl')	213	40.37 S	172.40 E
Fargo, ND (fär'gō)	112	46.53 N	96.48 W
Far Hills, NJ (fär hĭlz)	110a	40.41 N	74.38 W
Faribault, Mn. (fâ'rĭ-bō)	113	44.19 N	93.16 W
Farilhões (Is.), Port. (fä-rē-lyôɴzh')	168	39.28 N	9.32 W
Faringdon, Eng. (fă'rĭng-dŏn)	154b	51.38 N	1.35 W
Fāriskūr, Egypt (fä-rēs-ko͞or')	219b	31.19 N	31.46 E
Farit, Amba (Mt.), Eth.	221	10.51 N	37.52 E
Farley, Mo (fär'lē)	117f	39.16 N	94.49 W
Farmers Branch, Tx. (fär'mērz branch)	117c	32.56 N	96.53 W
Farmersburg, In. (fär'mērz-bûrg)	108	39.15 N	87.25 W
Farmersville, Tx. (fär'mērz-vĭl)	121	33.11 N	96.22 W
Farmingdale, NJ (färm'ĕng-dāl)	110a	40.11 N	74.10 W
Farmingdale, NY	110a	40.44 N	73.26 W
Farmingham, Ma. (färm-ĭng-hăm)	103a	42.17 N	71.25 W
Farmington, Il. (färm-ĭng-tŭn)	121	40.42 N	90.01 W
Farmington, Me.	102	44.40 N	70.10 W
Farmington, Mi.	111b	42.28 N	83.23 W
Farmington, Mo.	121	37.46 N	90.26 W
Farmington, NM	119	36.40 N	108.10 W
Farmington, Ut.	117b	40.59 N	111.53 W
Farmville, NC (färm-vĭl)	125	35.35 N	77.35 W
Farmville, Va.	125	37.15 N	78.23 W
Farnborough, Eng. (färn'bŭr-ô)	154b	51.15 N	0.45 W
Farne (I.), Eng. (färn)	160	55.40 N	1.32 W
Farnham, Can. (fär'năm)	109	45.15 N	72.55 W
Farningham, Eng. (fär'nĭng-ŭm)	154	51.22 N	0.14 E
Farnworth, Eng. (färn'wŭrth)	154	53.34 N	2.24 W
Faro, Braz. (fä'ro͞o)	141	2.05 S	56.32 W
Faro, Port.	168	37.01 N	7.57 W
Farodofay, Mad.	223	24.59 S	46.58 E
Fåron (I.), Swe.	163	57.57 N	19.10 E
Farquhar, C., Austl. (fär'kwàr)	210	23.50 S	112.55 E
Farrell, Pa. (făr'ĕl)	108	41.10 N	80.30 W
Farrukhābād, India (fŭ-ro͞ok-hä-bäd')	190	27.29 N	79.35 E
Fársala (Pharsalus), Grc.	171	39.18 N	22.25 E
Farsund, Nor. (fär'so͞on)	162	58.05 N	6.47 E
Fartura, Serra da (Mts.), Braz. (sĕ'r-rä-dà-fär-to͞o'rä)	142	26.40 S	53.15 W
Farvel, Kap (C.), Grnld.	92	60.00 N	44.00 W
Farwell, Tx. (fär'wĕl)	120	34.24 N	103.03 W
Fasano, It. (fä-zä'nō)	171	40.50 N	17.22 E
Fastov, Sov. Un. (fäs'tôf)	173	50.04 N	29.57 E
Fatëzh, Sov. Un.	173	52.06 N	35.51 E
Fatima, Port.	168	39.36 N	9.36 E
Fatsa, Tur. (fät'sä)	177	40.50 N	37.30 E
Faucilles, Monts. (Mts.), Fr. (môɴ' fō-sēl')	167	48.07 N	6.13 E
Fauske, Nor.	156	67.15 N	15.24 E
Faust, Can. (foust)	97	55.19 N	115.38 W
Faustovo, Sov. Un.	180b	55.27 N	38.29 E
Faversham, Eng. (fă'vēr-sh'm)	154b	51.19 N	0.54 E
Faxaflói (B.), Ice.	156	64.33 N	22.40 W
Fayette, Al. (fâ-yĕt')	124	33.40 N	87.54 W
Fayette, Ia.	113	42.49 N	91.49 W
Fayette, Ms.	124	31.43 N	91.00 W
Fayette, Mo.	121	39.09 N	92.41 W
Fayetteville, Ar. (fâ-yĕt'vĭl)	121	36.03 N	94.08 W
Fayetteville, NC	125	35.02 N	78.54 W
Fayetteville, Tn.	124	35.10 N	86.33 W
Fazao, Forêt Classée du (For.), Togo	224	8.50 N	0.40 E
Fazilka, India	190	30.30 N	74.02 E
Fazzān (Fezzan) (Prov.), Libya	221	26.45 N	13.01 E
Fdérik, Mauritania	220	22.45 N	12.38 W
Fear, C., NC (fēr)	125	33.52 N	77.48 W
Feather (R.), Ca. (fĕth'ēr)	118	38.56 N	121.41 W
Feather, Middle Fk. of (R.), Ca.	118	39.49 N	121.10 W
Feather, North Fk. of (R.), Ca.	118	40.00 N	121.20 W
Featherstone, Eng. (fĕdh'ēr stŭn)	154	53.39 N	1.21 W
Fécamp, Fr. (fā-käɴ')	166	49.45 N	0.20 E
Federal, Distrito (Dist.), Ven. (dēs-trē'tô-fē-dē-rä'l)	141b	10.34 N	66.55 W
Federal Way, Wa.	116a	47.20 N	122.20 W
Fëdorovka, Sov. Un. (fyô'dō-rôf-kà)	180b	56.15 N	37.14 E
Fehmarn I., F.R.G. (fā'märn)	164	54.28 N	11.15 E
Fehrbellin, G.D.R. (fĕr'bĕl-lĕn)	155b	52.49 N	12.46 E
Feia, Logoa (L.), Braz. (lô-gôä-fĕ'yä)	139a	21.54 S	41.45 W
Feicheng, China (fā-chŭŋ)	196	36.18 N	116.45 E
Feidong, China (fā-dôŋ)	196	31.53 N	117.28 E
Feira de Santana, Braz. (fĕ'ê-rä dā sänt-än'ä)	141	12.16 S	38.46 W
Fei Xian, China (fā-shyĕn)	196	35.17 N	117.59 E
Felanitx, Sp. (fā-lä-nēch')	169	39.29 N	3.09 E
Feldkirch, Aus. (fĕlt'kĭrk)	164	47.15 N	9.36 E
Feldkirchen, F.R.G. (fĕld'kēr-ĸĕn)	155d	48.09 N	11.44 E
Felipe Carrillo Puerto, Mex. (fĕ-lē'pĕ-kär-rē'l-yô-pwĕ'r-tô)	130a	19.36 N	88.04 W
Feltre, It. (fĕl'trā)	170	46.02 N	11.56 E
Femunden (L.), Nor.	162	62.17 N	11.40 E
Fengcheng, China (fŭŋ-chŭŋ)	198	40.28 N	124.03 E
Fengcheng, China	197b	30.55 N	121.38 E
Fengdu, China (fŭŋ-do͞o)	199	29.58 N	107.50 E
Fengjie, China (fŭŋ-jyĕ)	199	31.02 N	109.30 E
Fengming Dao (I.), China (fŭŋ-mĭŋ dou)	196	39.19 N	121.15 E
Fengrun, China (fŭŋ-ro͞on)	196	39.51 N	118.06 E
Fengtai, China (fŭŋ-tī)	198a	39.51 N	116.19 E
Fengxian, China (fŭŋ-shyĕn)	197b	30.55 N	121.26 E
Feng Xian, China	196	34.41 N	116.36 E
Fengxiang, China (fŭŋ-shyäŋ)	198	34.25 N	107.20 E
Fengyang, China (fŭng'yäng')	196	32.55 N	117.32 E
Fengzhen, China (fŭŋ-jŭn)	198	40.28 N	113.20 E
Fenimore, Pass. Ak. (fĕn-ĭ-mōr)	105a	51.40 N	175.38 W
Fenoarivo, Mad.	223	17.30 S	49.31 E
Fenton, Mi. (fĕn-tŭn)	108	42.50 N	83.40 W
Fenton, Mo.	117e	38.31 N	90.27 W
Fenyang, China	198	37.20 N	111.48 E
Feodosiya (Kefe), Sov. Un. (fĕ-ô-dō'sē'yȧ) (kyĕ'fĕ)	173	45.02 N	35.21 E
Ferdows, Iran	192	34.00 N	58.13 E
Ferentino, It. (fā-rĕn-tē'nō)	170	41.42 N	13.18 E
Fergana, Sov. Un.	178	40.16 N	72.07 E
Fergus Falls, Mn. (fûr'gŭs)	112	46.17 N	96.03 W
Ferguson, Mo. (fûr-gŭ-sŭn)	117e	38.45 N	90.18 W
Ferkéssédougou, Ivory Coast	224	9.36 N	5.12 W
Fermo, It. (fĕr'mō)	170	43.10 N	13.43 E
Fermoselle, Sp. (fĕr-mō-sāl'yȧ)	168	41.20 N	6.23 W
Fermoy, Ire. (fûr-moi')	160	52.05 N	8.06 W
Fernandina Beach, Fl. (fûr-năn-dē'nȧ)	125	30.38 N	81.29 W
Fernando de Noronha, Arquipélago (Arch.), Braz. (är-kē-pĕ'lä-gô-fĕr-nän-dō-dĕ-nô-rō'n-yä)	141	3.50 S	33.15 W
Fernando Póo (I.), see **Bioko**			
Fernān-Núñez, Sp. (fĕr-nän'no͞on'yăth)	168	37.42 N	4.43 W
Fernão Veloso, Baia de (B.), Moz.	227	14.20 S	40.55 E
Ferndale, Ca. (fûrn'dāl)	114	40.34 N	124.18 W
Ferndale, Mi.	111b	42.27 N	83.08 W
Ferndale, Wa.	116d	48.51 N	122.36 W
Fernie, Can. (fûr'nĭ)	97	49.30 N	115.03 W
Fern Prairie, Wa. (fûrn prâr'ĭ)	116c	45.38 N	122.25 W
Ferntree Gully, Austl.	207a	37.53 S	145.18 E
Ferrara, It. (fĕr-rä'rä)	170	44.50 N	11.37 E
Ferrat, Cap (C.), Alg. (kăp fĕr-răt)	169	35.49 N	0.29 W
Ferreira do Alentejo, Port. (fĕr-rĕ'ê-rä do͞o ä-lĕɴ-tā'zho͞o)	168	38.03 N	8.06 W
Ferreira do Zezere, Port (fĕr-rĕ'ê-rä do͞o zā-zä'rĕ)	168	39.49 N	8.17 W
Ferrelview, Mo. (fĕr'rĕl-vū)	117f	39.18 N	94.40 W
Ferreñafe, Peru (fĕr-rĕn-yȧ'fĕ)	140	6.38 S	79.48 W
Ferriday, La. (fĕr'ĭ-dā)	123	31.38 N	91.33 W
Fershampenuaz, Sov. Un. (fĕr-shàm'pĕn-wäz)	180a	53.32 N	59.50 E
Fertile, Mn. (fur'tĭl)	112	47.33 N	96.18 W
Fès, Mor. (fĕs)	220	34.08 N	5.00 W
Fessenden, ND (fĕs'ĕn-dĕn)	112	47.39 N	99.40 W
Festus, Mo. (fĕst'ŭs)	121	38.12 N	90.22 W
Fethiye, Turk. (fĕt-hē'yĕ)	177	36.40 N	29.05 E
Feuilles, Rivière aux (R.), Can.	95	58.30 N	70.50 W
Fezzan (Prov.), see **Fazzān**			
Ffestiniog, Wales	160	52.59 N	3.58 W
Fianarantsoa, Mad. (fyȧ-nä'rȧn-tsō'ȧ)	223	21.21 S	47.15 E
Ficksburg, S. Afr (fĭks'bûrg)	219d	28.53 S	27.53 E
Fidalgo I., Wa. (fĭ-dăl'gō)	116a	48.28 N	122.39 W
Fieldbrook, Ca. (fēld'bro͝ok)	116	40.59 N	124.02 W
Fier, Alb. (fyĕr)	171	40.43 N	19.34 E
Fife Ness (C.), Scot. (fīf'nes')	160	56.15 N	2.19 W
Fifth Cataract, Sud.	221	18.27 N	33.38 E
Figeac, Fr. (fē-zhȧk')	166	44.37 N	2.02 E
Figeholm, Swe. (fē-ghĕ-hōlm)	162	57.24 N	16.33 E
Figueira da Foz, Port. (fē-gwĕy-rä-dà-fô'z)	168	40.10 N	8.50 W
Figuig, Mor.	220	32.20 N	1.30 W
Fiji, Oceania (fē'jē)	204	18.40 S	175.00 E
Filadelfia, C.R. (fĭl-ȧ-dĕl'fĭ-ȧ)	130	10.26 N	85.37 W

PRONOUNCING INDEX

Filatovskoye – Fort Sandeman 291

PLACE (Pronunciation)	PAGE	Lat. °′	Long. °′
Filatovskoye, Sov. Un. (fĭ-lä'tôf-skô-yĕ)	180a	56.49 N	62.20 E
Filbert, WV (fĭl'bẽrt)	125	37.18 N	81.29 W
Filchner Ice Shelf, Ant. (fĭlk'nẽr)	228	80.00 S	35.00 W
Filiatrá, Grc.	171	37.10 N	21.35 E
Filicudi (I.), It. (fē'le-kōō'dē)	170	38.34 N	14.39 E
Filigas (R.), Tur.	159	41.10 N	32.53 E
Filippovskoye, Sov. Un. (fĭ-lĭ-pôf'skô-yĕ)	180b	56.06 N	38.38 E
Filipstad, Swe. (fĭl'ĭps-städh)	162	59.44 N	14.09 E
Fillmore, Ut. (fĭl'môr)	119	39.00 N	112.20 W
Filsa, Nor.	162	60.35 N	12.03 E
Fimi (R.), Zaire	226	2.43 S	17.50 E
Finch, Can. (fĭnch)	93c	45.09 N	75.06 W
Findlay, Oh. (fĭnd'lā)	108	41.05 N	83.40 W
Fingoe, Moz.	227	15.12 S	31.50 E
Finisterre, Cabo de (C.), Sp. (ká'bô-dĕ-fĭn-ĭs-târ')	168	42.52 N	9.48 W
Finke (R.), Austl. (fĭŋ'kē)	210	25.25 S	134.30 E
Finland, Eur. (fĭn'lănd)	152	62.45 N	26.13 E
Finland, G. of, Eur. (fĭn'lănd)	163	59.35 N	23.35 E
Finlandia, Col. (fēn-lä'n-dēä)	140a	4.38 N	75.39 W
Finlay (R.), Can. (fĭn'lā)	94	57.45 N	125.30 W
Finow, G.D.R. (fē'nōv)	155b	52.50 N	13.44 E
Finowfurt, G.D.R. (fē'nō-fōōrt)	155b	52.50 N	13.41 E
Finsterwalde, G.D.R. (fĭn'stẽr-väl-dē)	164	51.38 N	13.42 E
Firat (R.), Tur. (fē-rät')	177	39.40 N	38.30 E
Fircrest, Wa. (fûr'krĕst)	116a	47.14 N	122.31 W
Firenze (Florence), It. (fē-rĕnt'sä)	170	43.47 N	11.15 E
Firenzuola, It. (fē-rĕnt-swô'lä)	170	44.08 N	11.21 E
Firozpur, India	190	30.58 N	74.39 E
Fischa (R.), Aus.	155e	48.04 N	16.33 E
Fischamend Markt, Aus.	155e	48.07 N	16.37 E
Fish (R.), Namibia (fĭsh)	222	27.30 S	17.45 E
Fish Cay (I.), Ba.	133	22.30 N	74.20 W
Fish Cr., Can. (fĭsh)	93e	50.52 N	114.21 W
Fisher, La. (fĭsh'ẽr)	123	31.28 N	93.30 W
Fisher B., Can.	99	51.30 N	97.16 W
Fisher Chan, Can.	96	52.10 N	127.42 W
Fisher Str., Can.	95	62.43 N	84.28 W
Fishing L., Can. (fĭsh'ĭng)	99	52.07 N	95.25 W
Fitchburg, Ma. (fĭch'bûrg)	103a	42.35 N	71.48 W
Fitri, Lac (L.), Chad	225	12.50 N	17.28 E
Fitzgerald, Ga. (fĭts-jĕr'ăld)	124	31.42 N	83.17 W
Fitz Hugh Sd., Can. (fĭts hū)	96	51.40 N	127.57 W
Fitzroy (R.), Austl. (fĭts-roi')	210	18.00 S	124.05 E
Fitzroy (R.), Austl.	211	23.45 S	150.02 E
Fitzroy Crossing, Austl.	210	18.08 S	126.00 E
Fitzwilliam (I.), Can. (fĭts-wĭl'yŭm)	108	45.30 N	81.45 W
Fiume, see Rijeka			
Fiumicino, It. (fyōō-mē-chē'nô)	169d	41.47 N	12.19 E
Fjällbacka, Swe. (fyĕl'bäk-à)	162	58.37 N	11.17 E
Flåm, Nor. (flôm)	162	60.15 N	7.01 E
Flagstaff, Az. (flăg-stáf)	119	35.15 N	111.40 W
Flagstaff, S. Afr. (flăg'stäf)	223c	31.06 S	29.31 E
Flagstaff (L.), Me. (flăg-stáf)	109	45.05 N	70.30 W
Flalow, G.D.R. (flä'lōv)	155b	52.44 N	12.58 E
Flambeau (R.), Wi. (flăm-bō')	113	45.32 N	91.05 W
Flaming Gorge Res., Wy.	115	41.13 N	109.30 W
Flamingo, Fl. (flá-mĭŋ'gô)	125	25.10 N	80.55 W
Flamingo Cay (I.), Ba. (flá-mĭŋ'gô)	133	22.50 N	75.50 W
Flamingo Pt, Vir. Is. (U.S.A.)	127c	18.19 N	65.00 W
Flanders (Reg.), Fr. (flăn'dẽrz)	161	50.53 N	2.29 E
Flandreau, SD (flăn'drō)	112	44.02 N	96.35 W
Flathead (R.), Can.	97	49.30 N	114.30 W
Flathead L., Mt. (flăt'hĕd)	115	47.57 N	114.20 W
Flathead R., Mt.	115	48.45 N	114.20 W
Flathead R., Middle Fork, Mt.	115	48.30 N	113.47 W
Flathead R., South Fork, Mt.	115	48.05 N	113.45 W
Flat Rock, Mi. (flăt rŏk)	111b	42.06 N	83.17 W
Flattery C., Wa. (flăt'ẽr-ĭ)	114	48.22 N	125.45 W
Flat Willow Cr., Mt. (flat wĭl'ô)	115	46.45 N	108.47 W
Flekkefjord, Nor. (flăk'kĕ-fyôr)	162	58.19 N	6.38 E
Flemingsburg, Ky. (flĕm'ĭngz-bûrg)	108	38.25 N	83.45 W
Flensburg, F.R.G. (flĕns'bōōrgh)	164	54.48 N	9.27 E
Flers, Fr. (flĕr)	166	48.43 N	0.37 W
Fletcher, NC	125	35.26 N	82.30 W
Flinders (Reg.), Austl. (flĭn'dẽrz)	210	32.15 S	138.45 E
Flinders (I.), Austl.	212	39.35 S	148.10 E
Flinders (R.), Austl.	211	18.48 S	141.07 E
Flinders Rfs., Austl.	211	17.30 S	149.02 E
Flin Flon, Can. (flĭn flŏn)	108	54.46 N	101.53 W
Flint, Wales	154	53.15 N	3.07 W
Flint, Mi.	108	43.00 N	83.45 W
Flint (R.), Ga. (flĭnt)	124	31.25 N	84.15 W
Flora, Il. (flō'rá)	108	38.40 N	88.25 W
Flora, In.	108	40.25 N	86.30 W
Florala, Al. (flŏr-ăl'á)	124	31.01 N	86.19 W
Floral Park, NY (flôr'ăl pärk)	110a	40.42 N	73.42 W
Florence, Al. (flŏr'ĕns)	124	34.46 N	87.40 W
Florence, Az.	119	33.00 N	111.25 W
Florence, Co.	120	38.23 N	105.08 W
Florence, Ks.	121	38.14 N	96.56 W
Florence, SC	125	34.10 N	79.45 W
Florence, Wa.	116a	48.13 N	122.21 W
Florence, see Firenze			
Florencia, Col. (flō-rĕn'sē-á)	140	1.31 N	75.13 W
Florencio Sanchez, Ur. (flō-rĕn-sĕō-sá'n-chĕz)	139c	33.52 S	57.24 W
Florencio Varela, Arg. (flō-rĕn'sē-o vä-rā'lä)	142a	34.34 S	58.16 W
Flores, Braz. (flō'rĕzh)	141	7.57 S	37.48 W
Flores, Guat.	130a	16.53 N	89.54 W
Flores (Dept.), Ur.	139c	33.33 S	57.00 W
Flores (I.), Indon.	202	8.14 S	121.08 E
Flores (R.), Arg.	139c	36.13 S	60.28 W
Flores Laut (Flores Sea), Indon.	202	7.09 N	120.30 E
Floresville, Tx. (flō'rĕs-vĭl)	122	29.10 N	98.08 W
Floriano, Braz. (flō-rà-ä'nōō)	141	6.17 S	42.58 W
Florianópolis, Braz. (flō-rē-ä-nō'pō-lēs)	142	27.30 S	48.30 W
Florida, Col. (flō-rē'dä)	140a	3.20 N	76.12 W
Florida, Cuba	132	22.10 N	79.50 W
Florida, NY (flŏr'ĭ-dá)	110a	41.20 N	74.21 W
Florida, S. Afr.	223b	26.11 S	27.56 E
Florida, Ur. (flō-rē-dhä)	139c	34.06 S	56.14 W
Florida, (State), U.S. (flŏr'ĭ-dá)	107	30.30 N	84.40 W
Florida (Dept.), Ur. (flô-rē'dhä)	139c	33.48 S	56.15 W
Florida (I.), Sol. Is.	211	8.56 S	159.45 E
Florida, Strs. of, N.A.	132	24.10 N	81.00 W
Florida B., Fl. (flŏr'ĭ-dá)	125a	24.55 N	80.55 W
Florida Keys (Is.), Fl.	125a	24.33 N	81.20 W
Florida Mts., NM	119	32.10 N	107.35 W
Florido, R., Mex. (flō-rē'dō)	122	27.21 N	104.48 W
Floridsdorf, Aus. (flô'rĭds-dôrf)	155e	48.16 N	16.25 E
Florina, Grc. (flô-rē'nä)	171	40.48 N	21.24 E
Florissant, Mo. (flŏr'ĭ-sănt)	117e	38.47 N	90.20 W
Florø, Nor. (flô'ü)	162	61.36 N	5.01 E
Floyd (R.), Ia. (floid)	112	42.38 N	96.15 W
Floydada, Tx. (floi-dā'dá)	120	33.59 N	101.19 W
Floyds Fk. (R.), Ky. (floi-dz)	111h	38.08 N	85.30 W
Flumendosa, R., It. (flōō-mĕn-dô'sä)	170	39.45 N	9.18 E
Flushing, Mi. (flûsh'ĭng)	108	43.05 N	83.50 W
Fly (R.), Pap. N. Gui. (flī)	203	8.00 S	141.45 E
Foča, Yugo. (fō'chä)	171	43.29 N	18.48 E
Fochville, S. Afr. (fōk'vĭl)	219d	26.29 S	27.29 E
Focsani, Rom. (fōk-shä'nē)	165	45.41 N	27.17 E
Fogang, China (fwo-gäŋ)	199	23.50 N	113.35 E
Foggia, It. (fôd'jä)	170	41.30 N	15.34 E
Fogo, Can. (fō'gō)	101	49.43 N	54.17 W
Fogo I, Can.	101	49.40 N	54.13 W
Fogo I, C.V.	220b	14.46 N	24.51 W
Fohnsdorf, Aus. (fōns'dôrf)	164	47.13 N	14.40 E
Föhr I., F.R.G. (fûr)	164	54.47 N	8.30 E
Foix, Fr. (fwä)	166	42.58 N	1.34 E
Fokku, Nig.	225	11.40 N	4.31 E
Folgares, Ang.	226	14.54 S	15.08 E
Foligno, It. (fô-lēn'yō)	170	42.58 N	12.41 E
Folkeston, Eng.	161	51.05 N	1.18 E
Folkingham, Eng. (fō'kĭng-ăm)	154	52.53 N	0.24 W
Folkston, Ga.	125	30.50 N	82.01 W
Folsom, NM (fōl'sŭm)	120	36.47 N	103.56 W
Folsom City, Ca.	118	38.40 N	121.10 W
Fomento, Cuba (fō-mĕ'n-tō)	132	21.35 N	78.20 W
Fómeque, Col. (fō'mĕ-kĕ)	140a	4.29 N	73.52 W
Fonda, Ia. (fŏn'dá)	113	42.33 N	94.51 W
Fond du Lac, Wi. (fŏn dū lăk')	113	43.47 N	88.29 W
Fond du Lac Ind. Res., Mn.	113	46.44 N	93.04 W
Fondi, It. (fōn'dē)	170	41.23 N	13.25 E
Fonsagrada, Sp. (fōn-sä-grä'dhä)	168	43.08 N	7.07 W
Fonseca, Golfo de (G.), Hond. (gôl-fô-dĕ-fôn-sä'kä)	130	13.09 N	87.55 W
Fontainebleau, Fr. (fôɴ-tĕn-blō')	167b	48.24 N	2.42 E
Fontana, Ca. (fŏn-tă'nà)	117a	34.06 N	117.27 W
Fonte Boa, Braz. (fōn'tā bō'á)	140	2.32 S	66.05 W
Fontenay-le-Comte, Fr. (fôɴt-nĕ'lē-kôɴt')	166	46.28 N	0.53 W
Fontenay-Trésigny, Fr. (fôɴ-te-hā' tra-sēn-yē')	167b	48.43 N	2.53 E
Fontenelle Res., Wy.	115	42.05 N	110.05 W
Fontera, Punta (Pt.), Mex. (pōō'n-tä-fôn-tĕ'rä)	129	18.36 N	92.43 W
Fontibón, Col. (fōn-tē-bôn')	140a	4.42 N	74.09 W
Fontur (Pt.), Ice.	156	66.21 N	14.02 W
Foothills, S. Afr. (fōōt-hĭls)	223b	25.55 S	27.36 E
Foraker, Mt., Ak. (fôr'á-kẽr)	105	62.40 N	152.40 W
Forbach, Fr. (fôr'bäĸ)	167	49.12 N	6.54 E
Forbes, Austl. (fôrbz)	212	33.24 S	148.05 E
Forbes, Mt., Can.	97	51.52 N	116.56 W
Forchheim, F.R.G. (fôrĸ'hīm)	164	49.43 N	11.05 E
Fordlândia, see Brasília Legal			
Fordyce, Ar. (fôr'dīs)	121	33.48 N	92.24 W
Forecariah, Gui. (fōr-kà-rē'ä')	224	9.26 N	13.06 W
Forel, Mt., Grnld.	92	65.50 N	37.41 W
Forest, Ms. (fŏr'ĕst)	124	32.22 N	89.29 W
Forest (R.), ND	112	48.08 N	97.45 W
Forest City, Ia.	113	43.14 N	93.40 W
Forest City, NC	125	35.20 N	81.52 W
Forest City, Pa.	109	41.35 N	75.30 W
Forest Grove, Or. (grōv)	116c	45.31 N	123.07 W
Forest Hill, Md.	110e	39.35 N	76.26 W
Forest Hill, Tx.	117c	32.40 N	97.16 W
Forestville, Can. (fŏr'ĕst-vĭl)	102	48.45 N	69.06 W
Forestville, Md.	110e	38.51 N	76.55 W
Forez, Mts. du, Fr. (môɴ dü fô-rā')	166	44.55 N	3.43 E
Forfar, Scot. (fôr'fár)	160	57.10 N	2.55 W
Forillon, Parc Natl. (Natl. Pk.), Can.	102	48.50 N	64.05 W
Forio (Mtn.), It. (fô'ryō)	169c	40.29 N	13.55 E
Forked Cr., Il. (fôrk'd)	111a	41.16 N	88.01 W
Forked Deer (R.), Tn.	120	35.53 N	89.29 W
Forli, It. (fôr-lē')	170	44.13 N	12.03 E
Formby, Eng. (fôrm'bē)	154	53.34 N	3.04 W
Formby Pt., Eng.	154	53.33 N	3.06 W
Formentera, Isla de (I.), Sp. (ē's-lä-dĕ-fôr-mĕn-tā'rä)	169	38.43 N	1.25 E
Formiga, Braz. (fôr-mē'gá)	139a	20.27 S	45.25 W
Formigas Bk., N.A. (fōr-mē'gäs)	133	18.30 N	75.40 W
Formosa, Arg. (fôr-mō'sä)	142	27.25 S	58.12 W
Formosa, Braz.	141	15.32 S	47.10 W
Formosa (Prov.), Arg.	142	24.30 S	60.45 W
Formosa B, Ken.	227	2.45 S	40.30 E
Formosa (I.), see Taiwan			
Formosa, Serra (Mts.), Braz. (sĕ'r-rä)	141	12.59 S	55.11 W
Formosa Str., Asia (fôr-mō'sá)	189	24.30 N	120.00 E
Fornosovo, Sov. Un. (fôr-nô'sô vô)	180c	59.35 N	30.34 E
Forrest City, Ar. (for'ĕst sĭ'tĭ)	121	35.00 N	90.46 W
Forsayth, Austl. (fôr-sīth')	211	18.33 S	143.42 E
Forshaga, Swe. (fôrs'hä'gä)	162	59.34 N	13.25 E
Forst, G.D.R. (fôrst)	164	51.45 N	14.38 E
Forsyth, Ga. (fôr-sīth')	124	33.02 N	83.56 W
Forsyth, Mt.	115	46.15 N	106.41 W
Fort Albany, Can. (fôrt ôl'bá nĭ)	95	52.20 N	81.30 W
Fort Alexander Ind. Res., Can.	99	50.27 N	96.15 W
Fortaleza (Ceará), Braz. (fôr'tä-lā'zà) (sä-ä-rä')	141	3.35 S	38.31 W
Fort Apache Ind. Res., Az. (á-păch'ē)	119	34.02 N	110.27 W
Fort Atkinson, Wi. (ăt'kĭn-sŭn)	113	42.55 N	88.46 W
Fort Beaufort, S. Afr. (bō'fôrt)	223c	32.47 S	26.39 E
Fort Bellefontaine, Mo. (bĕl-fŏn-tān')	117e	38.50 N	90.15 W
Fort Benton, Mt. (bĕn'tŭn)	115	47.51 N	110.40 W
Fort Berthold Ind. Res., ND (bẽrth'ōld)	112	47.47 N	103.28 W
Fort Branch, In. (brănch)	108	38.15 N	87.35 W
Fort Chipewyan, Can.	94	58.46 N	111.15 W
Fort Cobb Res., Ok.	120	35.12 N	98.28 W
Fort Collins, Co. (kŏl'ĭns)	120	40.36 N	105.04 W
Fort Crampel, Cen. Afr. Rep. (krám-pĕl')	225	6.59 N	19.11 E
Fort-de-France, Mart. (dē fräɴs)	131b	14.37 N	61.06 W
Fort Deposit, Al. (dē-pŏz'ĭt)	124	31.58 N	86.35 W
Fort-de-Possel, Cen. Afr. Rep. (dē pô-sĕl')	221	5.03 N	19.11 E
Fort Dodge, Ia. (dŏj)	113	42.31 N	94.10 W
Fort Edward, NY (wẽrd)	109	43.15 N	73.30 W
Fort Erie, Can. (ē'rĭ)	111c	42.55 N	78.56 W
Fortescue (R.), Austl. (fôr'tĕs-kū)	210	21.25 S	116.50 E
Fort Fairfield, Me. (fâr'fēld)	102	46.46 N	67.53 W
Fort Fitzgerald, Can. (fĭts-jĕr'ăld)	94	59.48 N	111.50 W
Fort Frances, Can. (frăn'sĕs)	99	48.36 N	93.24 W
Fort Frederica Natl. Mon., Ga. (frĕd'ē-rĭ-kà)	125	31.13 N	85.25 W
Fort Gaines, Ga. (gānz)	124	31.35 N	85.03 W
Fort George, Can. (jôrj)	95	53.40 N	78.58 W
Fort Gibson, Ok. (gĭb'sŭn)	121	35.50 N	95.13 W
Fort Good Hope, Can. (gŏŏd hōp)	94	66.19 N	128.52 W
Forth, Firth of, Scot. (fûrth ŏv fôrth)	160	56.04 N	3.03 W
Fort Hall, Ken. (hôl)	221	0.47 S	37.13 E
Fort Hall Ind. Res., Id.	115	43.02 N	112.21 W
Fort Huachuca, Az. (wä-chōō'kä)	119	31.30 N	110.25 W
Fortier, Can. (fôr'tyā')	93f	49.56 N	97.55 W
Fort Jameson, Zambia (jām'sŭn)	222	13.35 S	32.43 E
Fort Jefferson Natl. Mon., Fl. (jĕf'ẽr-sŭn)	125a	24.42 N	83.02 W
Fort Johnston, Malawi	222	14.16 S	35.14 E
Fort Kent, Me. (kĕnt)	102	47.14 N	68.37 W
Fort Langley, Can. (lăng'lĭ)	116d	49.10 N	122.35 W
Fort Lauderdale, Fl. (lô'dẽr-dāl)	125a	26.07 N	80.09 W
Fort Lee, NJ	110a	40.50 N	73.58 W
Fort Liard, Can.	94	60.16 N	123.34 W
Fort Liberté, Hai. (lē-bĕr-tā')	133	19.40 N	71.50 W
Fort Louden (R.), Tn. (fôrt lou'dĕn)	124	35.52 N	84.10 W
Fort Lupton, Co. (lŭp'tŭn)	120	40.04 N	104.54 W
Fort McDermitt Ind. Res., Or. (măk dẽr'mĭt)	114	42.04 N	118.07 W
Fort Macleod, Can. (mà-kloud')	97	49.43 N	113.25 W
Fort MacMahon, Alg. (mák mà-ôɴ')	220	29.55 N	1.49 E
Fort McMurray, Can. (măk-mŭr'ĭ)	98	56.44 N	111.23 W
Fort McPherson, Can. (măk-fŭr's'n)	94	67.37 N	134.59 W
Fort Madison, Ia. (măd'ĭ-sŭn)	113	40.40 N	91.17 W
Fort Matanzas, Fl. (mä-tän'zäs)	125	29.39 N	81.17 W
Fort Meade, Fl. (mēd)	125a	27.45 N	81.48 W
Fort Mill, SC (mĭl)	125	35.03 N	80.57 W
Fort Miribel, Alg. (mē-rē-bĕl')	158	28.50 N	2.51 E
Fort Mohave Ind. Res., Ca. (mô-hä'vâ)	118	34.59 N	115.02 W
Fort Morgan, Co. (môr'găn)	120	40.14 N	103.49 W
Fort Myers, Fl. (mī'ẽrz)	125a	26.36 N	81.45 W
Fort Nelson, Can. (nĕl'sŭn)	94	58.57 N	122.30 W
Fort Nelson (R.), Can. (nĕl'sŭn)	94	58.44 N	122.20 W
Fort Payne, Al. (pān)	124	34.26 N	85.41 W
Fort Peck, Mt. (pĕk)	115	47.58 N	106.30 W
Fort Peck Ind. Res., Mt.	112	48.22 N	105.40 W
Fort Peck Res., Mt.	115	47.52 N	106.59 W
Fort Pierce, Fl. (pērs)	125a	27.25 N	80.20 W
Fort Portal, Ug. (pôr'tăl)	227	0.40 N	30.16 E
Fort Providence, Can. (prŏv'ĭ-dĕns)	94	61.27 N	117.59 W
Fort Pulaski Natl. Mon., Ga. (pu-lăs'kĭ)	125	31.59 N	80.56 W
Fort Qu'Appelle, Can.	98	50.46 N	103.55 W
Fort Randall Dam, U.S.	112	42.48 N	98.35 W
Fort Resolution, Can. (rĕz'ô-lū'shŭn)	94	61.08 N	113.42 W
Fort Riley, Ks. (rī'lĭ)	121	39.05 N	96.46 W
Fort St. James, Can. (fôrt sānt jāmz)	96	54.26 N	124.15 W
Fort St. John, Can. (sānt jŏn)	97	56.15 N	120.51 W
Fort Sandeman, Pak. (săn'da-măn)	190	31.28 N	69.29 E

ng-sing; ŋ-baŋk; ɴ-nasalized n; nŏd; cŏmmit; ōld; ôbey; ôrder; oi-boil; fōōd; fŏŏt; ou-out; s-soft; sh-dish; th-thin; pūre; ûnite; ûrn; stŭd; circŭs; ü-as in French tu; '-indeterminate vowel.

292 Fort Saskatchewan – Fushun

PLACE (Pronunciation)	PAGE	Lat. °′	Long. °′
Fort Saskatchewan, Can. (sās-kăt'chōō-ân)	93g	53.43 N	113.13 W
Fort Scott, Ks. (skŏt)	121	37.50 N	94.43 W
Fort Severn, Can. (sĕv'ērn)	95	56.58 N	87.50 W
Fort Shevchenko, Sov. Un. (shĕv-chĕn'kô)	177	44.30 N	50.18 E
Fort Sibut, Cen. Afr. Rep. (fôr sē-bü')	225	5.44 N	19.05 E
Fort Sill, Ok. (fôrt sĭl)	120	34.41 N	98.25 W
Fort Simpson, Can. (sĭmp'sŭn)	94	61.52 N	121.48 W
Fort Smith, Ar. (smĭth)	121	35.23 N	94.24 W
Fort Smith, Can.	94	60.09 N	112.08 W
Fort Stockton, Tx. (stŏk'tŭn)	122	30.54 N	102.51 W
Fort Sumner, NM (sŭm'nēr)	120	34.30 N	104.17 W
Fort Sumter Natl. Mon., SC (sŭm'tēr)	125	32.43 N	79.54 W
Fort Thomas, Ky. (tŏm'ăs)	111f	39.05 N	84.27 W
Fortuna, Ca. (fôr-tū'nȧ)	114	40.36 N	124.10 W
Fortune, Can. (fôr'tůn)	103	47.04 N	55.51 W
Fortune (I.), Ba.	133	22.35 N	74.20 W
Fortune B, Can.	103	47.25 N	55.25 W
Fort Union Natl. Mon., NM (ūn'yŭn)	120	35.51 N	104.57 W
Fort Valley, Ga. (văl'ĭ)	124	32.33 N	83.53 W
Fort Vermilion, Can. (vēr-mĭl'yŭn)	94	58.23 N	115.50 W
Fort Victoria, Zimb.	222	20.07 S	30.47 E
Fortville, In. (fôrt-vĭl)	108	40.00 N	85.50 W
Fort Wayne, In. (wān)	108	41.00 N	85.10 W
Fort William, Scot. (wĭl'yŭm)	160	56.50 N	3.00 W
Fort William, Mt., Austl. (wĭ'ĭ-ăm)	212	24.45 S	151.15 E
Fort Worth, Tx. (wûrth)	117c	32.45 N	97.20 W
Fort Yukon, Ak. (yōō'kŏn)	105	66.30 N	145.00 W
Fort Yuma Ind. Res., Ca. (yōō'mä)	118	32.54 N	114.47 W
Foshan, China	197a	23.02 N	113.07 E
Fossano, It. (fôs-sä'nō)	170	44.34 N	7.42 E
Fossil Cr., Tx. (fŏs-ĭl)	117c	32.53 N	97.19 W
Fossombrone, It. (fôs-sôm-brō'nā)	170	43.41 N	12.48 E
Foss Res., Ok.	120	35.38 N	99.11 W
Fosston, Mn. (fôs'tŭn)	112	47.34 N	95.44 W
Fosterburg, Il. (fôs'tēr-bûrg)	117e	38.58 N	90.04 W
Fostoria, Oh. (fŏs-tō'rĭ-ȧ)	108	41.10 N	83.20 W
Fougéres, Fr. (fōō-zhâr')	166	48.23 N	1.14 W
Foula (I.), Scot. (fou'lȧ)	160a	60.08 N	2.04 W
Foulwind, C., N.Z. (foul'wĭnd)	213	41.45 S	171.00 E
Foumban, Cam. (fōōm-bän')	225	5.43 N	10.55 E
Fountain Cr., Co. (foun'tĭn)	120	38.36 N	104.37 W
Fountain Valley, Ca.	117a	33.42 N	117.57 W
Fourche le Fave (R.), Ar. (fōōrsh lä fāv')	121	34.46 N	93.45 W
Fouriesburg, S. Afr. (fōō'rēz-bûrg)	219d	28.38 S	28.13 E
Fourmies, Fr. (fōōr-mē')	166	50.01 N	4.01 E
Four Mts., Is. of the, Ak. (fōr)	105a	52.58 N	170.40 W
Fourth Cataract, Sud.	221	18.52 N	32.07 E
Fouta Djallon (Mts.), Gui. (fōō'tä jä-lôɴ)	220	11.37 N	12.29 W
Foveaux Str., N.Z. (fō-vō')	213	46.30 S	167.43 E
Fowler, Co. (foul'ēr)	120	38.04 N	104.02 W
Fowler, In.	108	40.35 N	87.20 W
Fowler, Pt., Austl.	210	32.05 S	132.30 E
Fowlerton, Tx. (foul'ēr-tŭn)	122	28.26 N	98.48 W
Fox (I.), Wa. (fŏks)	116a	47.15 N	122.08 W
Fox (R.), Il.	113	41.35 N	88.43 W
Fox, (R.), Wi.	113	44.18 N	88.23 W
Foxboro, Ma. (fŏks'bŭrō)	103a	42.04 N	71.15 W
Foxe Basin, Can. (fŏks)	94	67.35 N	79.21 W
Foxe Chan, Can.	95	64.30 N	79.23 W
Foxe Pen, Can.	95	64.57 N	77.26 W
Fox Is., Ak. (fŏks)	105a	53.04 N	167.30 W
Fox Lake, Il. (lăk)	111a	42.24 N	88.11 W
Fox L., Il.	111a	42.24 N	88.07 W
Fox Point, Wi.	111a	43.10 N	87.54 W
Foyle, Lough (B.), Ire. (lŏk foil')	160	55.07 N	7.08 W
Foz do Cunene, Ang.	226	17.16 S	11.50 E
Fraga, Sp. (frä'gä)	169	41.31 N	0.20 E
Fragoso, Cayo (I.), Cuba (kä'yō-frä-gō'sō)	132	22.45 N	79.30 W
Franca, Braz. (frä'n-kä)	141	20.28 S	47.20 W
Francavilla, It. (fräŋ-kä-vēl'lä)	171	40.32 N	17.37 E
France, Eur. (frȧns)	152	46.39 N	0.47 E
Frances (L.), Can. (frăn'sĭs)	94	61.27 N	128.28 W
Frances, Cabo (C.), Cuba (kä'bô-frän-sĕ's)	132	21.55 N	84.05 W
Frances, Punta (Pt.), Cuba (pōō'n-tä-frän-sĕ's)	132	21.45 N	83.10 W
Frances Viejo, Cabo (C.), Dom. Rep. (kä'bô-frän'sās vyā'hô)	133	19.40 N	69.35 W
Franceville, Gabon (fräɴs-vēl')	226	1.38 S	13.35 E
Francis Case, L., SD (frăn'sĭs)	112	43.15 N	99.00 W
Francisco Sales, Braz. (frän-sē's-kô-sá'lĕs)	139a	21.42 S	44.26 W
Francistown, Bots. (frăn'sĭs-toun)	222	21.17 S	27.28 E
Frankfort, Il. (frăŋk'fŭrt)	111a	41.30 N	87.51 W
Frankfort, In.	108	40.15 N	86.30 W
Frankfort, Ks.	121	39.42 N	96.27 W
Frankfort, Ky.	108	38.10 N	84.55 W
Frankfort, Mi.	108	44.40 N	86.15 W
Frankfort, NY	109	43.05 N	75.05 W
Frankfort, S. Afr	219d	27.17 S	28.30 E
Frankfort, S. Afr. (frănk'fŏrt)	223c	32.43 S	27.28 E
Frankfurt (Dist.), G.D.R. (fräŋk'fōōrt)	155b	52.42 N	13.37 E
Frankfurt am Main, F.R.G.	164	50.07 N	8.40 E
Frankfurt an der Oder, G.D.R.	164	52.20 N	14.31 E
Franklin, In. (frănk'lĭn)	108	39.25 N	86.00 W
Franklin, Ky.	124	36.42 N	86.34 W

PLACE (Pronunciation)	PAGE	Lat. °′	Long. °′
Franklin, La.	123	29.47 N	91.31 W
Franklin, Ma.	103a	42.05 N	71.24 W
Franklin, Ne.	120	40.06 N	99.01 W
Franklin, NH	109	43.25 N	71.40 W
Franklin, NJ	110a	41.08 N	74.35 W
Franklin, Oh.	108	39.30 N	84.20 W
Franklin, Pa.	109	41.25 N	79.50 W
Franklin, Tn.	124	35.54 N	86.54 W
Franklin, S. Afr.	223c	30.19 S	29.28 E
Franklin, Va.	125	36.41 N	76.57 W
Franklin, Dist. of, Can.	94	70.46 N	105.22 W
Franklin (L.), Nv.	118	40.23 N	115.10 W
Franklin D. Roosevelt L., Wa.	114	48.12 N	118.43 W
Franklin Mts., Can.	94	65.36 N	125.55 W
Franklin Park, Il.	111a	41.56 N	87.53 W
Franklin Square, NY	110a	40.43 N	73.40 W
Franklinton, La. (frăŋk'lĭn-tŭn)	123	30.49 N	90.09 W
Frankston, Austl.	207a	38.09 S	145.08 E
Franksville, Wi. (frănkz'vĭl)	111a	42.46 N	87.55 W
Fransta, Swe.	162	62.30 N	16.04 E
Franz Josef Land (Is.), see Zemlya Frantsa Iosifa			
Frascati, It. (fräs-kä'tē)	169d	41.49 N	12.45 E
Fraser, Mi. (frā'zēr)	111b	42.32 N	82.57 W
Fraser (Great Sandy) (I.), Austl. (frā'zēr)	212	25.12 S	153.00 E
Fraser (R.), Can.	96	52.20 N	122.35 W
Fraserburgh, Scot. (frā'zēr-bûrg)	160	57.40 N	2.01 W
Fraser Plateau, Can.	96	51.30 N	122.00 W
Frattamaggiore, It. (frät-tä-mäg-zhyô'rĕ)	169c	40.41 N	14.16 E
Fray Bentos, Ur. (frī bĕn'tōs)	139c	33.10 S	58.19 W
Frazee, Mn. (frå-zē')	112	46.42 N	95.43 W
Fraziers Hog Cay (I.), Ba.	132	25.25 N	77.55 W
Frechen, F.R.G. (frĕ'ĸĕn)	167c	50.54 N	6.49 E
Fredericia, Den. (frĕdh-ĕ-rē'tsē-ȧ)	162	55.35 N	9.45 E
Frederick, Md. (frĕd'ēr-ĭk)	109	39.25 N	77.25 W
Frederick, Ok.	120	34.23 N	99.01 W
Frederick House (R.), Can.	100	49.05 N	81.20 W
Fredericksburg, Tx. (frĕd'ēr-ĭkz-bûrg)	122	30.16 N	98.52 W
Fredericksburg, Va.	109	38.20 N	77.30 W
Fredericktown, Mo. (frĕd'ēr-ĭk-toun)	121	37.32 N	90.16 W
Fredericton, Can. (frĕd'ēr-ĭk-tŭn)	102	45.48 N	66.39 W
Frederikshavn, Den. (frĕdh'ĕ-rĕks-houn)	162	57.27 N	10.31 E
Frederikssund, Den. (frĕdh'ĕ-rĕks-sōōn)	162	55.51 N	12.04 E
Fredonia, Col. (frē-dō'nyȧ)	140a	5.55 N	75.40 W
Fredonia, Ks. (frē-dō'nĭ-ȧ)	121	36.31 N	95.50 W
Fredonia, NY	109	42.25 N	79.20 W
Fredrikstad, Nor. (frĕdh'rĕks-städ)	162	59.14 N	10.58 E
Freeburg, Il. (frē'bûrg)	117e	38.26 N	89.59 W
Freehold, NJ (frē'hōld)	110a	40.15 N	74.16 W
Freeland, Pa. (frē'lȧnd)	110	41.00 N	75.50 W
Freeland, Wa.	116a	48.01 N	122.32 W
Freels, C., Can. (frēlz)	103	46.37 N	53.45 W
Freelton, Can. (frēl'tŭn)	93d	43.24 N	80.02 W
Freeport, Ba.	132	26.30 N	78.45 W
Freeport, Il. (frē'pōrt)	113	42.19 N	89.30 W
Freeport, NY	110a	40.39 N	73.35 W
Freeport, Tx.	117	28.56 N	95.21 W
Freetown, S.L. (frē'toun)	224	8.30 N	13.15 W
Fregenal de la Sierra, Sp. (frā-hå-näl' dā lä syĕr'rä)	168	38.09 N	6.40 W
Fregene, It. (frĕ-zhĕ'-nĕ)	169d	41.52 N	12.12 E
Freiberg, G.D.R. (frī'bĕrgh)	164	50.54 N	13.18 E
Freiburg, G.D.R.	164	48.00 N	7.50 E
Freienried, F.R.G. (frī'ĕn-rēd)	155d	48.20 N	11.08 E
Freirina, Chile (frå-ĭ-rē'nä)	142	28.35 S	71.26 W
Freising, F.R.G. (frī'zĭng)	155d	48.25 N	11.45 E
Fréjus, Fr. (frā-zhüs')	167	43.28 N	6.46 E
Fremantle, Austl. (frē'măn-t'l)	210	32.03 S	116.05 E
Fremont, Ca. (frē-mŏnt')	116b	37.33 N	122.00 W
Fremont, Mi.	108	43.25 N	85.55 W
Fremont, Ne.	112	41.26 N	96.30 W
Fremont, Oh.	108	41.20 N	83.05 W
Fremont (R.), Ut.	119	38.20 N	111.30 W
Fremont Pk., Wy.	115	43.05 N	109.35 W
French Broad (R.), Tn.-NC (frĕnch brôd)	124	35.59 N	83.01 W
French Frigate Shoals (Rocks), Hi.	104b	23.30 N	167.10 W
French Guiana, S.A. (gē-ä'nä)	138	4.20 N	53.00 W
French Lick, In. (frĕnch lĭk)	108	38.35 N	86.35 W
Frenchman (R.), Can.	98	49.25 N	108.30 W
Frenchman Cr., Mt. (frĕnch-mȧn)	115	48.51 N	107.20 W
Frenchman Cr., Ne.	120	40.24 N	101.50 W
Frenchman Flat, Nv.	118	36.55 N	116.11 W
French River, Mn.	117h	46.54 N	91.54 W
Freshfield, Mt., Can. (frĕsh'fēld)	97	51.44 N	116.57 W
Fresnillo, Mex. (frås-nēl'yō)	128	23.10 N	102.52 W
Fresno, Ca. (frĕz'nō)	118	36.43 N	119.47 W
Fresno, Col. (frĕs'nō)	140a	5.10 N	75.01 W
Fresno (R.), Ca. (frĕz'nō)	118	37.00 N	120.24 W
Fresno Slough, Ca.	118	36.39 N	120.12 W
Freudenstadt, F.R.G. (froi'den-shtät)	164	48.28 N	8.26 E
Freycinet Pen., Austl. (frā-sē-nĕ')	212	42.13 S	148.56 E
Fria (R.), Az. (frē-ä)	119	34.03 N	112.12 W
Fria, C., Namibia (frĭȧ)	222	18.15 S	12.10 E
Fria, Gui.	224	10.05 N	13.32 W
Frias, Arg. (frē-äs)	142	28.43 S	65.03 W
Fribourg, Switz. (frē-bōōr')	164	46.48 N	7.07 E
Fridley, Mn. (frĭd'lĭ)	117g	45.05 N	93.16 W

PLACE (Pronunciation)	PAGE	Lat. °′	Long. °′
Frieburg, F.R.G. (frī'bōōrgh)	164	47.59 N	7.50 E
Friedberg, F.R.G. (frēd'bĕrgh)	155d	48.22 N	11.00 E
Friedland, G.D.R. (frēt'länt)	164	53.39 N	13.34 E
Friedrichshafen, F.R.G. (frē-drĕks-häf'ĕn)	164	47.39 N	9.28 E
Friend, Ne. (frĕnd)	121	40.40 N	97.16 W
Friendswood, Tx. (frĕnds'wŏŏd)	123a	29.31 N	95.11 W
Fries, Va. (frēz)	125	36.42 N	80.59 W
Friesack, G.D.R. (frē'säk)	155b	52.44 N	12.35 E
Frio, Cabo (C.), Braz. (kä'bō-frē'ō)	141	22.58 S	42.08 W
Frio R, Tx.	122	29.00 N	99.15 W
Frisian (Is.), Neth. (frē'zhăn)	161	53.30 N	5.20 E
Friuli-Venezia Giulia (Reg.), It.	170	46.20 N	13.20 E
Frobisher L., Can. (frŏb'ĭsh'ēr)	98	56.25 N	108.20 W
Frobisher Bay, Can.	95	63.48 N	68.31 W
Frobisher B., Can.	95	62.49 N	66.41 W
Frodsham, Eng. (frŏdz'ăm)	154	53.18 N	2.48 W
Frohavet (Sea), Nor.	156	63.49 N	9.12 E
Frome, L., Austl. (frōōm)	212	30.40 S	140.13 E
Frontenac, Ks. (frŏn'tē-năk)	121	37.27 N	94.41 W
Frontera, Mex. (frôn-tā'rä)	129	18.34 N	92.38 W
Front Ra., Wy. (frŭnt)	115	42.17 N	105.53 W
Front Royal, Va. (frŭnt)	109	38.55 N	78.10 W
Frosinone, It. (frō-zē-nō'nå)	170	41.38 N	13.22 E
Frostburg, Md. (frôst'bûrg)	109	39.40 N	78.55 W
Fruita, Co. (frōōt-ȧ)	119	39.10 N	108.45 W
Frunze, Sov.Un. (frōōn'zĕ)	178	42.49 N	74.42 E
Fryanovo, Sov.Un. (f'ryä'nô-vô)	180b	56.08 N	38.28 E
Fryazino, Sov.Un. (f'ryä'zĭ-nô)	180b	55.58 N	38.05 E
Frydlant, Czech. (frēd'länt)	164	50.56 N	15.05 E
Fucheng, China (fōō-chŭŋ)	196	37.53 N	116.08 E
Fuchu, Jap. (fōō'chōō)	201a	35.41 N	139.29 E
Fuchun (R.), China (fōō-chōōn)	199	29.50 N	120.00 E
Fuego (Vol.), Guat. (fwā'gō)	130	14.29 N	90.52 W
Fuencarral, Sp. (fuān-kär-räl')	169a	40.29 N	3.42 W
Fuensalida, Sp. (fwān-sä-lē'dä)	168	40.04 N	4.15 W
Fuente, Mex. (fwĕ'n-tĕ')	122	28.39 N	100.34 W
Fuente de Cantos, Sp. (fwĕn'tā dā kän'tōs)	168	38.15 N	6.18 W
Fuente el Saz, Sp. (fwĕn'tå ĕl säth')	169a	40.39 N	3.30 W
Fuenteobejuna, Sp.	168	38.15 N	5.30 W
Fuentesaúco, Sp. (fwĕn-tå-sä-ōō'kō)	168	41.18 N	5.25 W
Fuerte, Rio del (R.), Mex. (rē'ō-dĕl-fōō-ĕ'r-tĕ)	126	26.15 N	108.50 W
Fuerte Olimpo, Par. (fwĕr'tå ō-lēm-pō)	141	21.10 S	57.49 W
Fuerteventura I., Can.Is. (fwĕr'tå-vĕn-tōō'rä)	220	28.24 N	13.21 W
Fuhai, China	194	47.01 N	87.07 E
Fuji, Jap. (jōō'jē)	201	35.11 N	138.44 E
Fuji (R.), Jap.	201	35.20 N	138.23 E
Fujian (Prov.), China (fōō-jyĕn)	195	25.40 N	117.30 E
Fujidera, Jap.	201	34.34 N	135.37 E
Fujin, China (fōō-jyĭn)	195	47.13 N	132.11 E
Fuji-san (Mtn.), Jap. (fōō'jē sän)	201	35.23 N	138.44 E
Fujisawa, Jap. (fōō'jē-sä'wa)	201a	35.20 N	139.29 E
Fukuchiyama, Jap. (fōō'kōō-chē-yä'ma)	201	35.18 N	135.07 E
Fukue (I.), Jap. (fōō-kōō'ā)	201	32.40 N	129.02 E
Fukui, Jap. (fōō'kōō-ē)	201	36.05 N	136.14 E
Fukuoka, Jap. (fōō'kōō-ō'kȧ)	201	33.35 N	130.23 E
Fukuoka, Jap.	201a	31.52 N	139.31 E
Fukushima, Jap. (fōō'kōō-shē'mȧ)	200	37.45 N	140.29 E
Fukuyama, Jap. (fōō'kōō-yä'mȧ)	201	34.31 N	133.21 E
Fūlādī, Kūh-e (Mtn.), Afg.	193	34.38 N	67.55 E
Fulda R., F.R.G. (fōōl'dä)	164	51.05 N	9.40 E
Fuling, China (fōō-lĭŋ)	199	29.40 N	107.30 E
Fullerton, Ca. (fōōl'ēr-tŭn)	117a	33.53 N	117.56 W
Fullerton, La.	123	31.00 N	93.00 W
Fullerton, Ne.	112	41.21 N	97.59 W
Fulton, Ky. (fŭl'tŭn)	124	36.30 N	88.53 W
Fulton, Mo.	121	38.51 N	91.56 W
Fulton, NY	109	43.20 N	76.25 W
Fultondale, Al. (fŭl'tŭn-dāl)	110h	33.37 N	86.48 W
Funabashi, Jap. (fōō'nä-bä'shē)	201a	35.43 N	139.59 E
Funaya, Jap. (fōō-nä'yä)	201b	34.45 N	135.52 E
Funchal, Mad.Is. (fōōn-shäl')	220	32.41 N	16.15 W
Fundación, Col. (fōōn-dä-syō'n)	140	10.43 N	74.13 W
Fundão, Port. (fōōn-douɴ')	168	40.08 N	7.32 W
Fundy, B. of, Can. (fŭn'dĭ)	100	45.00 N	66.00 W
Fundy Natl.Park, Can.	100	45.38 N	65.00 W
Funing, China, (fōō-nĭŋ)	196	33.55 N	119.54 E
Funing, China	196	39.55 N	119.16 E
Funing Wan. (B.), China	199	26.48 N	120.35 E
Funtua, Nig.	225	11.31 N	7.17 E
Furancungo, Moz.	227	14.55 S	33.35 E
Furbero, Mex. (fōōr-bĕ'rô)	129	20.21 N	97.32 W
Furmanov, Sov.Un. (fûr-mä'nôf)	172	57.14 N	41.11 E
Furnas, Reprêsa de (Res.), Braz.	142b	21.00 S	46.00 W
Furneaux Group (Is.), Austl. (fûr'nō)	211	40.15 S	146.27 E
Fürstenfeld, Aus. (für'stĕn-fĕlt)	164	47.02 N	16.03 E
Fürstenfeldbruck, F.R.G. (fur'stĕn-fĕld'brŏŏk)	155d	48.11 N	11.16 E
Fürstenwalde, G.D.R. (für'stĕn-väl-dĕ)	164	52.21 N	14.04 E
Fürth, F.R.G. (fürt)	164	49.28 N	11.03 E
Furuichi, Jap. (fōō'rōō-ē'chē)	201b	34.33 N	135.37 E
Fusa, Jap. (fōō'sä)	201a	35.52 N	140.08 E
Fusagasugá, Col. (fōō-sä-gä-sōō-gá')	140a	4.22 N	74.22 W
Fuse, Jap.	201b	34.40 N	135.43 E
Fushimi, Jap. (fōō'shē-mē)	201b	34.57 N	135.47 E
Fushun, China (fōō'shōōn')	198	41.50 N	124.00 E

PRONOUNCING INDEX

Fusong – Gel'myazov 293

PLACE (Pronunciation)	PAGE	Lat. °'	Long. °'
Fusong, China (fo͞o-soŋ)	198	42.12 N	127.12 E
Futtsu, Jap. (fo͞o'tso͞o')	201a	35.19 N	139.49 E
Futtsu Misaki (C.), Jap. (fo͞ot'tso͞o' mē-sä'kē)	201a	35.19 N	139.46 E
Fuwah, Egypt (fo͞o'wȧ)	219b	31.13 N	30.35 E
Fu Xian, China (fo͞o shyĕn)	196	39.36 N	121.59 E
Fuxin, China (fo͞o-shyĭn)	198	42.05 N	121.40 E
Fuyang, China	199	30.10 N	119.58 E
Fuyang, China (fo͞o-yäŋ)	196	32.53 N	115.48 E
Fuyang (R.), China (fo͞o-yäŋ)	196	36.59 N	114.48 E
Fuyu, China (fo͞o-yo͞o)	198	45.20 N	125.00 E
Fuzhou, China (fo͞o-jō)	199	26.02 N	119.18 E
Fuzhou (R.), China	196	39.38 N	121.43 E
Fuzhoucheng, China (fo͞o-jō-chŭŋ)	196	39.46 N	121.44 E
Fyn (I.), Den. (fü''n)	162	55.24 N	10.33 E
Fyne, Loch (L.), Scot. (fīn)	160	56.14 N	5.10 W
Fyresvatn (L.), Nor.	162	59.04 N	7.55 E
G			
Gabela, Ang.	226	10.48 S	14.20 E
Gaborone, Bots.	222	24.28 S	25.59 E
Gabès, Tun. (gä'bĕs)	220	33.51 N	10.04 E
Gabès, Golfe de (G.), Tun.	220	32.22 N	10.59 E
Gabil, Chad	225	11.09 N	18.12 E
Gabin, Pol (gōɴ'bĕn)	165	52.23 N	19.47 E
Gabon, Afr. (gȧ-bôɴ')	218	0.30 S	10.45 E
Gabriel R., Tx. (gā'brĭ-ĕl)	123	30.38 N	97.15 W
Gabrovo, Bul. (gäb'rô-vō)	171	42.52 N	25.19 E
Gachetá, Col. (gä-chā'tä)	140a	4.50 N	73.36 W
Gacko, Yugo. (gäts'kô)	171	43.10 N	18.34 E
Gadsden, Al. (gădz'dĕn)	124	34.00 N	86.00 W
Gadyach, Sov.Un. (gäd-yäch')	173	50.22 N	33.59 E
Găeşti, Rom. (gä-yĕsh'tē)	171	44.43 N	25.21 E
Gaeta, It. (gä-ā'tä)	170	41.18 N	13.34 E
Gaffney, SC (găf'nĭ)	125	35.04 N	81.47 W
Gafsa, Tun. (gäf'sä)	220	34.16 N	8.37 E
Gagarin, Sov.Un.	172	55.32 N	34.58 E
Gagnoa, Ivory Coast	224	6.08 N	5.56 W
Gagrary (I.), Phil. (gä-grä-rē)	203a	13.23 N	123.58 E
Gaillac-sur-Tarn, Fr. (gȧ-yäk'sür-tärn')	152	43.54 N	1.52 E
Gaillard Cut, Pan. (gä-ēl-yä'rd)	126a	9.03 N	79.42 W
Gainesville, Fl. (gānz'vĭl)	125	29.40 N	82.20 W
Gainesville, Ga.	124	34.16 N	83.48 W
Gainesville, Tx.	121	33.38 N	97.08 W
Gainsborough, Eng. (gānz'bŭr-ô)	154	53.23 N	0.46 W
Gairdner, L., Austl. (gârd'nēr)	212	32.20 S	136.30 E
Gaithersburg, Md. (gā'thērs'bûrg)	110e	39.08 N	77.13 W
Gai Xian, China (gī-shyĕn)	196	40.25 N	122.20 E
Galana (R.), Ken.	227	3.00 S	39.30 E
Galapagar, Sp. (gä-lä-pä-gär')	169a	40.36 N	4.00 W
Galápagos Is., see Colon, Arch. de			
Galaria (R.), It.	169d	41.58 N	12.21 E
Galashiels, Scot. (găl-ȧ-shēlz)	160	55.40 N	2.57 W
Galati, Rom. (gȧ-lätz'ĭ)	173	45.25 N	28.05 E
Galatina, It. (gä-lä-tē'nä)	171	40.10 N	18.12 E
Galaxídhion, Grc.	171	38.26 N	22.22 E
Galdhopiggen (Mtn.), Nor.	162	61.37 N	8.17 E
Galeana, Mex. (gä-lå-ä'nä)	122	24.50 N	100.04 W
Galena, Il. (gȧ-lē'nȧ)	113	42.26 N	90.27 W
Galena, In.	111h	38.21 N	85.55 W
Galená, Ks.	121	37.06 N	94.39 W
Galena Pk., Tx.	123a	29.44 N	95.14 W
Galera, Cerro (Mtn.), Pan. (sĕ'r-rô-gä-lĕ'rä)	126a	8.55 N	79.38 W
Galeras (Vol.), Col. (gä-lĕ'räs)	140	0.57 N	77.27 W
Gales (R.), Or. (gālz)	116c	45.33 N	123.11 W
Galesburg, Il. (gālz'bûrg)	121	40.56 N	90.21 W
Galesville, Wi. (gālz'vĭl)	113	44.04 N	91.22 W
Galeton, Pa. (gāl'tŭn)	109	41.45 N	77.40 W
Galich, Sov.Un. (gäl'ich)	176	58.20 N	42.38 E
Galicia (Reg.), Pol.-Sov.Un. (gȧ-lĭsh'ĭ-ȧ)	165	49.48 N	21.05 E
Galicia (Reg.), Sp. (gä-lē'thyä)	168	43.35 N	8.03 W
Galilee (L.), Austl. (găl'ĭ-lē)	211	22.23 S	145.09 E
Galilee, Sea of, Isr.	189a	32.53 N	35.45 E
Galina Pt., Jam. (gä-lē'nä)	132	18.25 N	76.50 W
Galion, Oh. (găl'ĭ-ŭn)	127	40.45 N	82.50 W
Galisteo, NM (gä-lĭs-tā'ō)	121	35.20 N	106.00 W
Galite, La. I., Alg. (gä-lēt)	157	37.36 N	8.03 E
Galka'yo, Som.	219a	7.00 N	47.30 E
Galla (Prov.), Eth. (gäl'lä)	221	7.22 N	35.28 E
Gallarate, It. (gäl-lä-rä'tā)	170	45.37 N	8.48 E
Gallardon, Fr. (gä-lär-dôɴ')	167b	48.31 N	1.40 E
Gallatin, Mo. (găl'ȧ-tĭn)	121	39.55 N	93.58 W
Gallatin, Tn.	124	36.23 N	86.28 W
Gallatin R., Mt.	115	45.12 N	111.10 W
Galle, Sri Lanka (gäl)	191	6.13 N	80.10 E
Gállego (R.), Sp. (gäl-yā'gō)	169	42.27 N	0.37 W
Gallinas, Pta. de (Pt.), Col. (gä-lyē'näs)	140	12.10 N	72.10 W
Gallipoli, It. (gäl-lē'pô-lē)	171	40.03 N	17.58 E
Gallipoli, see Gelibolu			
Gallipoli Pen., Tur.	171	40.23 N	25.10 E
Gallipolis, Oh. (găl-ĭ-pô-lēs)	108	38.50 N	82.10 W
Gällivare, Swe. (yĕl-ĭ-vär'ĕ)	156	68.06 N	20.29 E
Gallo (R.), Sp. (gäl'yō)	168	40.43 N	1.42 W
Gallup, NM (găl'ŭp)	121	35.30 N	108.45 W
Galnale Doria R., Eth.	221	5.35 N	40.26 E
Galt, Can.	108	43.22 N	80.19 W
Galty Mts., Ire.	160	52.19 N	8.20 W
Galva, Il. (găl'vȧ)	121	41.11 N	90.02 W
Galveston, Tx. (găl'vĕs-tŭn)	123a	29.18 N	94.48 W
Galveston B, Tx.	123	29.39 N	94.45 W
Galveston I, Tx.	123a	29.12 N	94.53 W
Galway, Ire.	160	53.16 N	9.05 W
Galway B., Ire. (gôl'wā)	160	53.10 N	9.47 W
Gamba, China (gäm-bä)	190	28.23 N	89.42 E
Gambaga, Ghana (gäm-bä'gä)	224	10.32 N	0.26 W
Gambela, Eth. (găm-bā'lȧ)	221	8.15 N	34.33 E
Gambia, Afr. (găm'bē-ȧ)	220	13.38 N	19.38 W
Gambia (R.), (Gambie), Afr.	224	13.20 N	15.55 W
Gambie (R.), (Gambia), Afr.	224	13.20 N	15.55 W
Gamboma, Con. (gäm-bō'mä)	226	1.53 S	15.51 E
Gamleby, Swe. (gäm'lĕ-bü)	162	57.54 N	16.20 E
Gan (R.), China (gän)	199	26.50 N	115.00 E
Gandak (R.), India	190	26.37 N	84.22 E
Gander, Can. (găn'dēr)	103	48.57 N	54.34 W
Gander (R.), Can.	103	49.10 N	54.35 W
Gander L., Can.	103	48.55 N	55.40 W
Gandhinagar, India	190	23.30 N	72.47 E
Gandi, Nig.	225	12.55 N	5.49 E
Gandía, Sp. (gän-dē'ä)	169	38.56 N	0.10 W
Gangdisê Shan (Trans Himalayas)(Mts.), China (gäŋ-dē-sŭ shän) (trăns-hĭ-mä-lȧ-yȧs)	194	30.25 N	83.43 E
Ganges, Mouths of, India (găn'jēz)	190	21.18 N	88.40 E
Ganges (R.), India (găn'jēz)	190	24.32 N	87.58 E
Gangi, It. (gän'jē)	170	37.48 N	14.15 E
Gangtok, India	194	27.15 N	88.30 E
Gannan, China (gän-nän)	198	47.50 N	123.30 E
Gannett Pk., Wy. (găn'ĕt)	115	43.10 N	109.38 W
Gano, Oh. (g'nō)	111f	39.18 N	84.24 W
Gänserndorf, Aus.	155e	48.21 N	16.43 E
Gansu (Prov.), China (gän-so͞o)	194	38.50 N	101.10 E
Ganwo, Nig.	225	11.13 N	4.42 E
Ganyu, China (gän-yo͞o)	196	34.52 N	119.07 E
Ganzhou, China (gän-jō)	199	25.50 N	114.30 E
Gao, Mali (gä'ō)	224	16.16 N	0.03 W
Gao'an, China (gou-än)	199	28.30 N	115.02 E
Gaomi, China, (gou-mē)	196	36.23 N	119.46 E
Gaoqiao, China (gou-chyou)	197b	31.21 N	121.35 E
Gaoshun, China (gou-sho͞on)	196	31.22 N	118.50 E
Gaotang, China (gou-täŋ)	196	36.52 N	116.12 E
Gaoyao, China (gou-you)	199	23.08 N	112.25 E
Gaoyi, China (gou-yē)	196	37.37 N	114.39 E
Gaoyou, China (gou-yō)	196	32.46 N	119.26 E
Gaoyou Hu (L.), China (gou-yō ho͞o)	196	32.59 N	119.04 E
Gap, Fr. (gȧp)	167	44.34 N	6.08 E
Gapan, Phil. (gä-pän)	203a	15.18 N	120.56 E
Garachiné, Pan. (gä-rä-chē'nå)	131	8.02 N	78.22 W
Garachiné, Punta (Pt.), Pan. (po͞o'n-tä-gä-rä-chē'nå)	131	8.08 N	78.35 W
Garanhuns, Braz. (gä-rän-yo͞oɴsh')	141	8.49 S	36.28 W
Garber, Ok. (gär'bēr)	121	36.28 N	97.35 W
Garching, F.R.G. (gär'kĕng)	155d	48.15 N	11.39 E
Garcia, Mex. (gär-sē'ä)	122	25.90 N	100.37 W
Garcia de la Cadena, Mex. (dē-lä-kä-dē-nä)	128	21.14 N	103.26 W
Garda, Lago di (L.), It. (lä-gō-dē-gär'dä)	170	45.43 N	10.26 E
Gardanne, Fr. (gár-dán')	166a	43.28 N	5.29 E
Gardelegen, G.D.R. (gär-dē-lå'ghĕn)	164	52.32 N	11.22 E
Garden (I.), Mi. (gär'd'n)	108	45.50 N	85.50 W
Gardena, Ca. (gär-dē'nå)	117a	33.53 N	118.19 W
Garden City, Mi.	111b	42.20 N	83.21 W
Garden City, Ks.	120	37.58 N	100.52 W
Garden Grove, Ca. (gär'd'n grōv)	117a	33.47 N	117.56 W
Garden' Reach., India	190a	22.33 N	88.17 E
Garden River, Can.	117k	46.33 N	84.10 W
Gardēz, Afg.	190	33.43 N	69.09 E
Gardiner, Me. (gärd'nēr)	102	44.12 N	69.46 W
Gardiner, Mt.	115	45.03 N	110.43 W
Gardiner, Wa.	116a	48.03 N	122.55 W
Gardiner Dam, Can.	98	51.17 N	106.51 W
Gardner, Ma.	109	42.35 N	72.00 W
Gardner, Can., Can.	96	53.28 N	128.15 W
Gardner Pinnacles (Rocks), Hi.	104b	25.10 N	167.00 W
Gareloi (I.), Ak. (gär-lo͞o-ä')	105a	51.40 N	178.48 W
Garfield, NJ (gär'fēld)	110a	40.53 N	74.06 W
Garfield, Ut.	117b	40.45 N	112.10 W
Garfield Heights, Oh	111d	41.25 N	81.36 W
Gargaliánoi, Grc. (gär-gä-lyä'nē)	171	37.07 N	21.50 E
Gargždai, Sov.Un. (gärgzh'dī)	163	55.43 N	20.09 E
Garibaldi, Mt., Can. (gâr-ĭ-băl'dē)	96	49.51 N	123.01 W
Garin, Arg. (gä-rē'n)	142a	34.10 S	58.44 W
Garissa, Ken.	227	0.28 S	39.38 E
Garland, Tx. (gär'lănd)	117c	32.55 N	96.39 W
Garland, Ut.	115	41.45 N	112.10 W
Garm, Sov.Un.	178	39.12 N	70.28 E
Garmisch-Partenkirchen, F.R.G. (gär'mēsh pär'tĕn-kēr'kĕn)	164	47.38 N	11.10 E
Garnett, Ks. (gär'nĕt)	121	38.16 N	95.15 W
Garonne Rivière (R.), Fr. (gȧ-rôn)	166	44.43 N	0.25 W
Garoua, Cam. (gär'wä)	225	9.18 N	13.24 E
Garrett, In. (găr'ĕt)	108	41.20 N	85.10 W
Garrison, NY (găr'ĭ-sŭn)	110a	41.23 N	73.57 W
Garrison, ND	112	47.38 N	101.24 W
Garrovillas, Sp. (gä-rô-vēl'yäs)	168	39.42 N	6.30 W
Garry (L.), Can. (găr'ĭ)	94	66.16 N	99.23 W
Garsen, Ken.	227	2.16 S	40.07 E
Garson, Can.	102	46.34 N	80.52 W
Garstedt, F.R.G. (gär'shtĕt)	155c	53.40 N	9.58 E
Gartok, China (gär-tŏk')	190	31.11 N	80.35 E
Garulia, India	190a	22.48 N	88.23 E
Garwolin, Pol. (gär-vō'lēn)	165	51.54 N	21.40 E
Gary, In. (gā'rĭ)	111a	41.35 N	87.21 W
Garza-Little Elm Res., Tx.	123	33.16 N	96.54 W
Garzón, Col. (gär-thōn')	140	2.13 N	75.44 W
Gasan, Phil. (gä-sän')	203a	13.19 N	121.52 E
Gasan-Kuli, Sov.Un.	177	37.25 N	53.55 E
Gas City, In. (găs)	108	40.30 N	85.40 W
Gascogne, (Reg.), Fr. (gäs-kôn'yĕ)	166	43.45 N	1.49 W
Gasconade (R.), Mo. (găs-kô-nād')	121	37.46 N	92.15 W
Gascoyne, (R.), Austl. (găs-koin')	210	25.15 S	117.00 E
Gashland, Mo. (găsh'-lănd)	117f	39.15 N	94.35 W
Gashua, Nig.	225	12.54 N	11.00 E
Gasny, Fr. (gäs-nē')	167b	49.05 N	1.36 E
Gaspé, Can.	102	48.50 N	64.29 W
Gaspé, Baie de (B.), Can. (gas'pā)(gäs-pā')	102	48.35 N	63.45 W
Gaspé, Cape de (C.), Can.	102	48.45 N	63.34 W
Gaspé, Péninsule de (Pen.), Can.	102	48.23 N	65.42 W
Gasper Hernandez, Dom.Rep. (gäs-pär' ĕr-nän'dăth)	133	19.40 N	70.15 W
Gassaway, WV (găs'ȧ-wā)	108	38.40 N	80.45 W
Gaston, Or. (găs'tŭn)	116c	45.26 N	123.08 W
Gastonia, NC (găs-tô'nĭ-ȧ)	125	35.15 N	81.14 W
Gastre, Arg. (gäs-trĕ)	142	42.12 S	68.50 W
Gata, Cabo de (C.), Sp. (ká'bô-dĕ-gä'tä)	168	36.42 N	2.00 W
Gata, Sierra de (Mts.), Sp. (syĕr'rȧ dä gä'tä)	168	40.12 N	6.39 W
Gátes, Akrotírion (C.), Cyprus	189a	34.30 N	33.15 E
Gatchina, Sov.Un. (gä-chē'nȧ)	180c	59.33 N	30.08 E
Gateshead, Eng. (gāts'hĕd)	160	54.56 N	1.38 W
Gatesville, Mex. (gāts'vĭl)	123	31.26 N	97.34 W
Gâtine, Hauteurs de (Hills), Fr.	166	46.40 N	0.50 W
Gatineau, Can. (gá'tē-nō)	93c	45.29 N	75.38 W
Gatineau (R.), Can.	93c	45.45 N	75.50 W
Gatineau, Parc de la (Natl. Pk.), Can.	93c	45.32 N	75.53 W
Gatooma, Zimb. (gå-to͞o'mä)	227	18.21 S	29.55 E
Gattendorf, Aus.	155e	48.01 N	17.00 E
Gatun, Pan. (gä-to͞on')	126a	9.16 N	79.25 W
Gatún, L., Pan.	126a	9.13 N	79.24 W
Gatun (R.), Pan.	126a	9.21 N	79.10 W
Gatun Locks, Pan.	126a	9.16 N	79.27 W
Gauhāti, India	190	26.09 N	91.51 E
Gauja (R.), Sov.Un. (gå'o͞o-yȧ)	163	57.10 N	24.30 E
Gaula (R.), Nor.	162	62.55 N	10.45 E
Gauttier-Gebergte (Mts.), Indon. (gō-tyā')	203	2.30 S	138.45 E
Gávdhos (I.), Grc. (gäv'dôs)	170a	34.48 N	24.08 E
Gavins Point Dam, Ne. (gă'-vĭns)	112	42.47 N	97.47 W
Gävle, Swe. (yĕv'lĕ)	162	60.40 N	17.07 E
Gavle-bukten (B.), Swe.	162	60.45 N	17.30 E
Gavrilov Posad, Sov.Un. (gá'vrē-lôf'ka po-sát)	172	56.34 N	40.09 E
Gavrilov-Yam, Sov.Un. (gá'vrē-lôf yäm')	172	57.17 N	39.49 E
Gawler, Austl. (gô'lēr)	212	34.35 S	138.47 E
Gawler Ra., Austl.	212	32.35 S	136.30 E
Gaya, India (gŭ'yä)(gī'ȧ)	190	24.53 N	85.00 E
Gaya, Nig. (gä'yä)	220	11.58 N	9.05 E
Gaylord, Mi. (gā'lôrd)	108	45.00 N	84.35 W
Gayndah, Austl. (gān'dȧh)	212	25.43 S	151.33 E
Gaysin, Sov.Un.	173	48.46 N	29.22 E
Gaza, see Ghazzah			
Gaziantep, Tur. (gä-zē-än'tĕp)	177	37.10 N	37.30 E
Gbarnga, Lib.	224	7.00 N	9.29 W
Gdańsk (Danzig), Pol. (g'dänsk)(dän'tsĕg)	165	54.20 N	18.40 E
Gdov, Sov.Un. (g'dôf')	172	58.44 N	27.51 E
Gdynia, Pol. (g'dĕn'yä)	165	54.29 N	18.30 E
Geary, Ok. (gē'rĭ)	120	35.36 N	98.19 W
Géba (R.), Guinea-Bissau	224	12.25 N	14.35 W
Gebo, Wy. (gĕb'ō)	115	43.49 N	108.13 W
Ged, La. (gĕd)	123	30.07 N	93.36 W
Gediz (R.), Tur.	159	38.44 N	28.45 E
Gedney, (I.), Wa. (gĕd-nē)	116a	48.01 N	122.18 W
Gedser, Den.	164	54.35 N	12.08 E
Geel, Bel.	155a	51.09 N	5.01 E
Geelong, Austl. (jē-lông')	207a	38.06 S	144.13 E
Geelvink-baai (B.), Indon. (gāl'vĭŋk)	203	2.20 S	135.30 E
Gegu, China (gŭ-go͞o)	196	39.00 N	117.30 E
Ge Hu (L.), China (gŭ ho͞o)	196	31.37 N	119.57 E
Geidam, Nig.	225	12.57 N	11.57 E
Geikie Ra., Austl. (gē'kē)	210	17.35 S	125.32 E
Geislingen, F.R.G. (gis'lĭng-ĕn)	164	48.37 N	9.52 E
Geist Res., In. (gēst)	111g	39.57 N	85.59 W
Geita, Tan.	227	2.52 S	32.10 E
Gejiu, China (gŭ-jĭo)	199	23.32 N	102.50 E
Geldermalsen, Neth.	155a	51.53 N	5.18 E
Geldern, F.R.G. (gĕl'dĕrn)	167c	51.31 N	6.20 E
Gelibolu (Gallipoli), Tur. (gĕl-lē'pô-lē)(gĕ-lĭb'ô-lo͞o)	171	40.25 N	26.40 E
Gel'myazov, Sov.Un.	173	49.49 N	31.54 E

ng-sing; ŋ-baŋk; ɴ-nasalized n; nŏd; cŏmmit; ōld; ôbey; ôrder; oi-boil; fo͞od; fo͝ot; ou-out; s-soft; sh-dish; th-thin; pūre; ûnite; ûrn; stŭd; circŭs; ü-as in French tu; '-indeterminate vowel.

294 Gelsenkirchen – Gol

PLACE (Pronunciation)	PAGE	Lat. °′	Long. °′
Gelsenkirchen, F.R.G. (gĕl-zĕn-kĭrk-ĕn)	167c	51.31 N	7.05 E
Gemas, Mala. (jĕm'ás)	189b	2.35 N	102.37 E
Gemena, Zaire	226	3.15 N	19.46 E
Gemlik, Tur. (gĕm'lĭk)	177	40.30 N	29.10 E
Genale (R.), Eth.	219	5.00 N	41.15 E
General Alvear, Arg. (gĕ-nĕ-räl'ál-vĕ-á'r)	139c	36.04 S	60.02 W
General Arenales, Arg. (ä-rĕ-nä'lĕs)	139c	34.19 S	61.16 W
General Belgrano, Arg. (bĕl-grá'nô)	139c	35.45 S	58.32 W
General Cepeda, Mex. (sĕ-pĕ'dä)	122	25.24 N	101.29 W
General Conesa, Arg. (kô-nĕ'sä)	139c	36.30 S	57.19 W
General Guido, Arg. (gē'dô)	139c	36.41 S	57.48 W
General Lavalle, Arg. (lá-vá'l-yĕ)	139c	36.25 S	56.55 W
General Madariaga, Arg. (män-dá-rēá'gä)	142	36.59 S	57.14 W
General Paz, Arg. (pá'z)	139c	35.30 S	58.20 W
General Pedro Antonio Santios, Mex. (pĕ'drô-än-tô'nyô-sän-tyôs)	128	21.37 N	98.58 W
General Pico, Arg. (pē'kô)	142	36.46 S	63.44 W
General Roca, Arg. (rô-kä)	142	39.01 S	67.31 W
General San Martín, Arg. (sän-mar-tē'n)	142a	34.19 S	58.32 W
General Viamonte, Arg. (vēá'môn-tē)	139c	35.01 S	60.59 W
General Zuazua, Mex. (zwä'zwä)	122	25.54 N	100.07 W
Genesee (R.), NY (jĕn-ē-sē')	109	42.25 N	78.10 W
Geneseo, Il. (jē-nĕs'eō)	108	41.28 N	90.11 W
Geneva, Al. (jē-nē'vá)	124	31.03 N	85.50 W
Geneva, Il.	111a	41.53 N	88.18 W
Geneva, Ne.	121	40.32 N	97.37 W
Geneva, NY	109	42.50 N	77.00 W
Geneva, Oh.	108	41.45 N	80.55 W
Geneva, see Génève			
Geneva, L., Switz.	164	46.28 N	6.30 E
Génève (Geneva), Switz. (zhē-nĕv')	164	46.14 N	6.04 E
Genichesk, Sov.Un. (gĕnĕ-chyĕsk')	173	46.11 N	34.47 E
Genil (R.), Sp. (hå-nēl')	168	37.15 N	4.05 W
Genoa, Ne. (jen'ô-á)	121	41.26 N	97.43 W
Genoa, see Genova			
Genoa City, Wi.	111a	42.31 N	88.19 W
Genova (Genoa), It. (jĕn'ō-vä)	170	44.23 N	9.52 E
Genova, Golfo di (G.), It. (gôl-fô-dē-jĕn'ō-vä)	170	44.10 N	8.45 E
Genovesa (I.), Ec. (ĕ's-lä-gē-nō-vē-sä)	126	0.08 N	90.15 W
Gent, Bel.	161	51.05 N	3.40 E
Genthin, G.D.R. (gĕn-tēn')	164	52.24 N	12.10 E
Genzano di Roma, It., (gzhĕnt-zá'-nô-dē-rô'mä)	169d	41.43 N	12.49 E
Geographe B., Austl. (jē-ô-grăf')	210	33.00 S	114.00 E
Geographic Chan., Austl. (jēô'grä-fĭk)	210	24.15 S	112.50 E
Geokchay, Sov. Un. (gē-ôk'chī)	177	40.40 N	47.40 E
George (L.), Fl. (jôr-ĭj)	125	29.10 N	81.50 W
George (L.), NY (jôrj)	109	43.40 N	73.30 W
George L., Can.-U.S. (jôrg)	117k	46.26 N	84.09 W
George, L., In.	111a	41.31 N	87.17 W
George, L., Ug.	227	0.02 N	30.25 E
Georges (R.), Austl.	207b	33.57 S	151.00 E
George Town, Ba.	133	23.30 N	75.50 W
Georgetown, Can. (jôr-ĭj-toun)	103	46.11 N	62.32 W
Georgetown, Can. (jôrg-toun)	93d	43.39 N	79.56 W
Georgetown, Cayman Is.	132	19.20 N	81.20 W
Georgetown, Ct.	110	41.15 N	73.25 W
Georgetown, De.	109	38.40 N	75.20 W
Georgetown, Guy. (jôrj'toun)	141	7.45 N	58.04 W
Georgetown, Il.	108	40.00 N	87.40 W
Georgetown, Ky.	108	38.10 N	84.35 W
George Town, (Pinang), Mala.	202	5.21 N	100.09 E
Georgetown, Md.	109	39.25 N	75.55 W
Georgetown, Ma. (jôrg-toun)	103a	42.43 N	71.00 W
Georgetown, S.C. (jôr-ĭj-toun)	125	33.22 N	79.17 W
Georgetown, Tx. (jôrg-toun)	123	30.37 N	97.40 W
George Washington Birthplace Natl. Mon., Va. (jôrj wŏsh'ĭng-tŭn)	109	38.10 N	77.00 W
George Washington Carver Natl. Mon., Mo. (jôrg wăsh-ĭng-tŭn kär'vēr)	121	36.58 N	94.21 W
George West, Tx.	122	28.20 N	98.07 W
Georgia (State), U.S. (jôr'ji-ă)	107	32.40 N	83.50 W
Georgia, Str. of, Can.	96	49.20 N	124.00 W
Georgia, Str. of, Wa.	116d	48.56 N	123.06 W
Georgian (S.S.R.), Sov. Un.	174	42.17 N	43.00 E
Georgian B., Can.	100	45.15 N	80.50 W
Georgian Bay Is. Natl. Pk, Can.	100	45.20 N	81.40 W
Georgiana, Al. (jôr-jē-än'á)	124	31.39 N	86.44 W
Georgina (R.), Austl. (jôr-jē'ná)	210	22.00 S	138.15 E
Georgiyevsk, Sov. Un. (gyôr-gyĕfsk')	177	44.05 N	43.30 E
Gera, G.D.R. (gā'rä)	164	50.52 N	12.06 E
Geral, Serra (Mts.), Braz. (sĕr'rá zhå-räl')	142	28.30 S	51.00 W
Geral de Goiás, Serra (Mts.), Braz. (zhå-räl'-dĕ-gô-yà's)	159	14.22 S	45.40 W
Geraldton, Austl. (jĕr'ăld-tŭn)	210	28.40 S	114.35 E
Geraldton, Can.	95	49.43 N	87.00 W
Gérgal, Sp. (gĕr'gäl)	168	37.08 N	2.29 E
Gering, Ne. (gē'rĭng)	112	41.49 N	103.41 W
Gerlachovský Štít (Mtn.), Czech.	165	49.12 N	20.08 E
German Democratic Republic, Eur.	152	53.30 N	12.30 E
Germantown, Oh. (jûr'măn-toun)	108	39.35 N	84.25 W
Germany, Federal Republic of, Eur. (jûr'má-nĭ)	152	51.45 N	8.30 E
Germiston, S. Afr. (jûr'mĭs-tŭn)	223b	26.19 S	28.11 E
Gerona, Phil. (hā-rō'nä)	203a	15.36 N	120.36 E
Gerona, Sp. (hĕ-rô'nä)	168	41.55 N	2.48 E
Gerrards Cross, Eng. (jĕr'ards krŏs)	154b	51.34 N	0.33 W
Gers (R.), Fr. (zhĕr)	169	43.25 N	0.30 E
Gersthofen, F.R.G. (gĕrst-hō'fĕn)	155d	48.26 N	10.54 E
Getafe, Sp. (hä-tä'få)	169a	40.19 N	3.44 W
Gettysburg, Pa. (gĕt'ĭs-bûrg)	109	39.50 N	77.15 W
Gettysburg, SD	112	45.01 N	99.59 W
Gevelsberg, F.R.G. (gĕ-fĕls'bĕrgh)	167c	51.18 N	7.20 E
Ghāghra (R.), India	190	27.19 N	81.22 E
Ghana, Afr. (gän'ä)	218	8.00 N	2.00 W
Ghanzi, Bots. (gän'zē)	222	21.30 S	22.00 E
Ghardaïa, Alg. (gär-dä'ē-ä)	220	32.29 N	3.38 E
Gharo, Pak.	190	24.50 N	68.35 E
Ghāt, Libya	220	24.52 N	10.16 E
Ghazāl, Bahr al- (R.), Sud.	221	9.11 N	29.37 E
Ghazal, Bahr el (R.), Chad. (bär ĕl ghä-zäl')	225	14.30 N	17.00 E
Ghaznī, Afg. (gŭz'nē)	190	33.43 N	68.18 E
Ghazzah, Gaza Strip (Gaza)	189a	31.30 N	34.29 E
Gheorgheni, Rom.	165	46.48 N	25.30 E
Gherla, Rom. (gĕr'lä)	165	47.01 N	23.55 E
Ghost Lake, Can.	93e	51.15 N	114.46 W
Ghudāmis, Libya	220	30.07 N	9.26 E
Giannutri, I. di, It. (jän-nōō'trē)	170	42.15 N	11.06 E
Gibara, Cuba (hē-bä'rä)	133	21.05 N	76.10 W
Gibeon, Namibia (gĭb'ē-ŭn)	222	24.45 S	16.40 E
Gibraleón, Sp. (hē-brä-lå-ōn')	168	37.24 N	7.00 W
Gibraltar, Eur. (hē-bräl-tä'r)	157	36.08 N	5.22 W
Gibraltar, Bay of, Sp.	168	35.04 N	5.10 W
Gibraltar, Str. of, Afr.-Eur.	168	35.55 N	5.45 W
Gibson City, Il. (gĭb'sŭn)	108	40.25 N	88.20 W
Gibson Des, Austl.	210	24.45 S	123.15 E
Gibson Island, Md.	110e	39.05 N	76.26 W
Gibson Res., Ok.	121	36.07 N	95.08 W
Giddings, Tx. (gĭd'ĭngz)	123	30.11 N	96.55 W
Gideon, Mo. (gĭd'ē-ŭn)	121	36.27 N	89.56 W
Gien, Fr. (zhē-ăN')	166	47.43 N	2.37 E
Giessen, F.R.G. (gēs'sĕn)	164	50.35 N	8.40 E
Gifu, Jap. (gē'fōō)	201	35.25 N	136.45 E
Gig Harbor, Wa. (gĭg)	116a	47.20 N	122.36 W
Giglio, I. di, It. (jēl'yō)	170	42.23 N	10.55 E
Gijón, Sp. (hē-hōn')	168	43.33 N	5.37 W
Gila (R.), Az. (hē'lá)	119	32.41 N	113.50 W
Gila Bend, Az.	119	32.59 N	112.41 W
Gila Bend Ind. Res., Az.	119	33.02 N	112.48 W
Gila Cliffs Dwellings Natl. Mon., NM	119	33.15 N	108.20 W
Gila River Ind. Res., Az.	119	33.11 N	112.38 W
Gilbert, Mn. (gĭl'bērt)	113	47.27 N	92.29 W
Gilbert (R.), Austl. (gĭl-bĕrt)	211	17.15 S	142.09 E
Gilbert, Mt., Can.	96	50.51 N	124.20 W
Gilboa, Mt., S. Afr. (gĭl-bôá)	223c	29.13 N	30.17 E
Gilford I., Can. (gĭl'fērd)	96	50.45 N	126.25 W
Gilgit, Pak. (gĭl'gĭt)	190	35.58 N	73.48 E
Gil I., Can. (gĭl)	96	53.13 N	129.15 W
Gillen (I.), Austl. (jĭl'ĕn)	210	26.15 S	125.15 E
Gillett, Ar. (jĭ-lĕt')	121	34.07 N	91.22 W
Gillette, Wyo.	115	44.17 N	105.30 W
Gillingham, Eng. (gĭl'ĭng ăm)	154b	51.23 N	0.33 E
Gilman, Il. (gĭl'măn)	108	40.45 N	87.55 W
Gilman Hot Springs, Ca.	117a	33.49 N	116.57 W
Gilmer, Tx. (gĭl'mēr)	123	32.43 N	94.57 W
Gilmore, Ga. (gĭl'môr)	110c	33.51 N	84.29 W
Gilroy, Ca. (gĭl-roi')	118	37.00 N	121.34 W
Giluwe, Mt., Pap. N. Gui.	203	6.04 S	144.00 E
Gimli, Can. (gĭm'lē)	99	50.39 N	97.00 W
Gimone (R.), Fr. (zhē-mōn')	166	43.26 N	0.36 E
Ginir, Eth.	221	7.13 N	40.44 E
Ginosa, It. (jē-nō'zä)	170	40.35 N	16.48 E
Ginzo, Sp. (hēn-thō')	168	42.03 N	7.43 W
Gioia del Colle, It. (jô'yä dĕl kôl'lā)	170	40.48 N	16.55 E
Gi-Paraná (R.), Braz. (zhē-pä-rä-ná')	141	9.33 S	61.35 W
Girard, Ks. (jĭ-rärd')	121	37.30 N	94.50 W
Girardot, Col. (hē-rär-dōt')	140a	4.19 N	75.47 W
Giresun, Tur. (ghĕr'ĕ-sōōn')	177	40.55 N	38.20 E
Giridih, India (jē-rē-dē)	190	24.12 N	81.18 E
Gironde (Est.), Fr. (zhē-rônd')	166	45.31 N	1.00 W
Girvan, Scot. (gûr'văn)	160	55.15 N	5.01 W
Gisborne, N.Z. (gĭz'bŭrn)	213	38.40 S	178.08 E
Gisenyi, Rw.	227	1.43 S	29.15 E
Gisors, Fr. (zhē-zôr')	166	49.19 N	1.47 E
Gitambo, Zaire	226	4.21 N	24.45 E
Gitega, Burundi	222	3.39 S	30.05 E
Giurgui, Rom. (jōōr'jōō)	171	43.53 N	25.58 E
Givet, Fr. (zhē-vĕ')	166	50.80 N	4.47 E
Givors, Fr. (zhē-vôr')	166	45.35 N	4.46 E
Gizhiga, Sov. Un. (gē'zhi-gá)	179	61.59 N	160.46 E
Gizycko, Pol. (gĭ'zhĭ-ko)	165	54.03 N	21.48 E
Gjirokastër, Alb.	171	40.04 N	20.10 E
Gjøvik, Nor. (gyû'vĕk)	162	60.47 N	10.36 E
Glabeek-Zuurbemde, Bel.	155a	50.52 N	4.59 E
Glace Bay, Can. (gläs bā)	103	46.12 N	59.57 W
Glacier Bay Natl. Park, Ak. (glā'shēr)	105	58.40 N	136.50 W
Glacier Natl. Park, Can.	97	51.45 N	117.35 W
Glacier Pk., Wa.	114	48.07 N	121.10 W
Glacier Pt., Can.	116a	48.24 N	123.59 W
Gladbeck, F.R.G. (gläd'bĕk)	167c	51.35 N	6.59 E
Gladdeklipkop, S. Afr.	219d	24.17 S	29.36 E
Gladstone, Austl. (glăd'stŏn)	212	23.45 S	150.00 E
Gladstone, Austl.	212	33.15 S	138.20 E
Gladstone, Mi.	113	45.50 N	87.04 W
Gladstone, NJ	110a	40.43 N	74.39 W
Gladstone, Or.	116c	45.23 N	122.36 W
Gladwin, Mi. (glăd'wĭn)	108	44.00 N	84.25 W
Glåma (R.), Nor.	162	61.22 N	11.02 E
Glamoč, Yugo. (gläm'ôch)	170	44.03 N	16.51 E
Glarus, Switz. (glä'rōōs)	164	47.02 N	9.03 E
Glasgow, Ky.	124	37.00 N	85.55 W
Glasgow, Mo.	121	39.14 N	92.48 W
Glasgow, Mt.	115	48.14 N	106.39 W
Glasgow, Scot. (glás'gō)	160	55.54 N	4.25 W
Glassport, Pa. (glás'pōrt)	111e	40.19 N	79.53 W
Glauchau, G.D.R. (glou'Kou)	164	50.51 N	12.28 E
Glazov, Sov. Un. (glä'zôf)	176	58.05 N	52.52 E
Glen (R.), Eng. (glĕn)	154	52.44 N	0.18 W
Glénan, Îles de (Is.), Fr. (ĕl-dĕ-glā-näN')	166	47.43 N	4.42 W
Glen Burnie, Md. (bûr'nē)	110e	39.10 N	76.38 W
Glen Canyon Dam, Az. (glĕn kăn'yŭn)	119	36.57 N	111.25 W
Glen Carbon, Il. (kär'bŏn)	117e	38.45 N	89.59 W
Glencoe, Il.	111a	42.08 N	87.45 W
Glencoe, Mn. (glĕn'kō)	113	44.44 N	94.07 W
Glencoe, S. Afr. (glĕn-cō)	223c	28.14 S	30.09 E
Glen Cove, NY (kōv)	110a	40.51 N	73.38 W
Glendale, Az. (glĕn'dāl)	119	33.30 N	112.15 W
Glendale, Ca.	117a	34.09 N	118.15 W
Glendale, Oh.	111f	31.16 N	84.22 W
Glendive, Mt. (glĕn'dīv)	115	47.08 N	104.41 W
Glendo, Wy.	115	42.32 N	104.54 W
Glendora, Ca. (glĕn-dō'rá)	117a	34.08 N	117.52 W
Glenelg (R.), Austl.	212	37.20 S	141.30 E
Glen Ellyn, Il. (glĕn ĕl'-lĕn)	111a	41.53 N	88.04 W
Glen Innes, Austl. (ĭn'ĕs)	212	29.45 S	152.02 E
Glenomra, La. (glĕn-mō'rá)	123	30.58 N	92.36 W
Glenns Ferry, Id. (fĕr'ĭ)	114	42.58 N	115.21 W
Glenville, Ga. (glĕn'vĭl)	125	31.55 N	81.56 W
Glen Olden, Pa. (ōl'd'n)	110f	39.54 N	75.17 W
Glenrock, Wy. (glĕn'rŏk)	115	42.50 N	105.53 W
Glens Falls, NY (glĕnz fôlz)	109	43.20 N	73.40 W
Glenshaw, Pa. (glĕn'shô)	111e	40.33 N	79.57 W
Glen Ullin, ND (glĕn'ŭl'ĭn)	112	46.47 N	101.49 W
Glen Valley, Can.	116d	49.09 N	122.30 W
Glenview, IL (glĕn'vū)	111a	42.04 N	87.48 W
Glenwood, Ia.	112	41.03 N	95.44 W
Glenwood, Mn.	112	45.39 N	95.23 W
Glenwood Springs, Co.	119	39.35 N	107.20 W
Glienicke, G.D.R. (glē'nē-kē)	155b	52.38 N	13.19 E
Glinde, F.R.G. (glĕn'dē)	155c	53.32 N	10.13 E
Glittertinden (Mtn.), Nor.	162	61.39 N	8.12 E
Gliwice, Pol. (gwĭ-wĭt'sĕ)	165	50.18 N	18.40 E
Globe, Az. (glōb)	119	33.20 N	110.50 W
Globino, Sov. Un. (glôb'ĕ-nô)	173	49.22 N	33.17 E
Glogów, Pol. (gwō'gōōv)	164	51.40 N	16.04 E
Glommen (R.), Nor. (glôm'ĕn)	162	60.03 N	11.15 E
Glonn, F.R.G. (glônn)	155d	47.59 N	11.52 E
Glorieuses, Îles (Is.), Afr.	223	11.28 S	47.50 E
Glossop, Eng. (glŏs'ŭp)	154	53.26 N	1.57 W
Gloster, Ms. (glŏs'tēr)	124	31.10 N	91.00 W
Gloucester, Eng. (glŏs'tēr)	160	51.54 N	2.11 W
Gloucester, Ma.	103a	42.37 N	70.40 W
Gloucester City, NJ	110f	39.53 N	75.08 W
Glouster, Oh. (glŏs'tēr)	108	39.35 N	82.05 W
Glover I., Can. (glŭv'ēr)	103	48.44 N	57.45 W
Gloversville, NY (glŭv'ērz-vĭl)	109	43.05 N	74.20 W
Glovertown, Can. (glŭv'ēr-toun)	103	48.41 N	54.02 W
Glubokoye, Sov. Un. (glōō-bô-kō'yĕ)	172	55.08 N	27.44 E
Glückstadt, F.R.G. (glük-shtät)	155c	53.47 N	9.25 E
Glukhov, Sov. Un. (glōō'Kôf')	173	51.42 N	33.52 E
Glushkovo, Sov. Un. (glōōsh'kô-vô)	173	51.21 N	34.43 E
Gmünden, Aus. (g'mōōn'dĕn)	164	47.57 N	13.47 E
Gniezno, Pol. (g'nyăz'nô)	165	52.32 N	17.34 E
Gnjilane, Yugo. (gnyē'lä-nĕ)	171	42.28 N	21.27 E
Goa (Ter.), India (gō'á)	191	15.45 N	74.00 E
Goascorán, Hond. (gō-äs'kō-rän')	130	13.37 N	87.43 W
Goba, Eth. (gō'bä)	221	7.17 N	39.58 E
Gobabis, Namibia (gō-bä'bĭs)	222	22.25 S	18.50 E
Gobi or Shamo (Des.), Mong. (gō'be)	194	43.29 N	103.15 E
Goble, Or. (gō'b'l)	116c	46.01 N	122.53 W
Goch, F.R.G. (gôK)	167c	51.35 N	6.10 E
Godāvari (R.), India (gō-dä'vŭ-rē)	190	17.42 N	81.15 E
Goddards Soak (Swp.), Austl. (gŏd'árdz)	210	31.20 S	123.30 E
Goderich, Can. (gōd'rĭch)	108	43.45 N	81.45 W
Godfrey, Il. (gŏd'frē)	117e	38.57 N	90.12 W
Godhavn, Grnld. (gōdh'hâvn)	92	69.15 N	53.30 W
Gods (R.), Can. (gŏdz)	99	55.17 N	93.35 W
Gods Lake, Can.	99	54.40 N	94.09 W
Godthåb, Grnld. (gŏt'hōōb)	92	64.10 N	51.32 W
Godwin Austen (Mtn.), see K2			
Goéland, Lac au (L.), Can.	101	49.47 N	76.41 W
Goffs, Ca. (gôfs)	118	34.57 N	115.06 W
Gogebic (L.), Mi. (gō-gē'bĭk)	113	46.24 N	89.25 W
Gogebic Ra, Mi.	113	46.37 N	89.48 W
Goggingen, F.R.G. (gûg'gĕn-gĕn)	155d	48.21 N	10.53 E
Gogland (I.), Sov. Un.	163	60.04 N	26.55 E
Gogonou, Benin	225	10.50 N	2.50 E
Gogorrón, Mex. (gō-gô-rōn')	128	21.51 N	100.54 W
Goiânia, Braz. (gô-vá'nyä)	141	16.41 S	48.57 W
Goiás, Braz. (gô-yá's)	141	15.57 S	50.10 W
Goiás (State), Braz.	141	12.35 S	48.38 W
Goirle, Neth.	155a	51.31 N	5.06 E
Gökçeada (I.), Tur.	171	40.10 N	25.27 E
Göksu (R.), Tur. (gûk'sōō')	177	36.40 N	33.30 E
Gol, Nor. (gûl)	162	60.58 N	8.54 E

ăt; finăl; rāte; senāte; ärm; àsk; sofá; fâre; ch-choose; dh-as th in other; bē; ēvent; bĕt; recĕnt; cratẽr; g-gō; gh-guttural g; bĭt; ĭ-short neutral; rīde; K-guttural k as ch in German ich;

PLACE (Pronunciation)	PAGE	Lat. °′	Long. °′
Golax, Va. (gō'lăks)	125	36.41 N	80.56 W
Golcar, Eng. (gŏl'kȧr)	154	53.38 N	1.52 W
Golconda, Il. (gŏl-kŏn'dȧ)	121	37.21 N	88.32 W
Gołdap, Pol. (gôl'dăp)	165	54.17 N	22.17 E
Golden, Can.	97	51.18 N	116.58 W
Golden, Co.	120	39.44 N	105.15 W
Goldendale, Wa. (gōl'dĕn-dāl)	114	45.49 N	120.48 W
Golden Gate (Str.), Ca. (gōl'dĕn gāt)	116b	37.48 N	122.32 W
Golden Hinde, Can. (hīnd)	96	49.40 N	125.45 W
Golden's Bridge, NY	110a	41.17 N	73.41 W
Golden Valley, Mn.	117g	44.58 N	93.23 W
Goldfield, Nv. (gōld'fēld)	118	37.42 N	117.15 W
Gold Hill (Mtn.), Pan.	126a	9.03 N	79.08 W
Gold Mtn., Wa. (gōld)	116a	47.33 N	122.48 W
Goldsboro, NC (gōldz-bûr'ô)	125	35.23 N	77.59 W
Goldthwaite, Tx. (gōld'thwāt)	122	31.27 N	98.34 W
Goleniów, Pol. (gō-lĕ-nyŭf')	164	53.33 N	14.51 E
Golets-Purpula, Gol'tsy (Mtn.), Sov. Un.	179	59.08 N	115.22 E
Golfito, C.R. (gōl-fē'tō)	131	8.40 N	83.12 W
Golfo Dulce, see Izabal, L.			
Goliad, Tx. (gō-lĭ-ăd')	123	28.40 N	97.12 W
Golo (R.), Fr.	170	42.28 N	9.18 E
Golo I., Phil. (gō'lō)	203a	13.38 N	120.17 E
Golovchino, Sov. Un. (gō-lôf'chē-nō)	173	50.34 N	35.52 E
Golyamo Konare, Bul. (gō'lă-mō-kō'nä-rĕ)	171	42.16 N	24.33 E
Golzow, G.D.R. (gōl'tsōv)	155b	52.17 N	12.36 E
Gombari, Zaire (go͞om-bä-rē)	227	2.45 N	29.00 E
Gombe, Nig.	225	10.19 N	11.02 E
Gomel', Sov. Un. (go'mĕl')	172	52.20 N	31.03 E
Gomel', Sov. Un. (Oblast)	172	52.18 N	29.00 E
Gomera I., Can. Is. (gô-mä'rä)	220	28.00 N	18.01 W
Gomez Farias, Mex. (gō'măz fä-rē'ȧs)	122	24.59 N	101.02 W
Gómez Palacio, Mex. (pä-lä'syō)	122	25.35 N	103.30 W
Gonaïves, Hai. (gō-nȧ-ēv')	133	19.25 N	72.45 W
Gonaïves, Golfe des (G.), Hai. (gō-nȧ-ēv')	133	19.20 N	73.20 W
Gonâve, Ile De La (I.), Hai. (gô-náv')	133	18.50 N	73.30 W
Gonda, India	190	27.13 N	82.00 E
Gondal, India	190	22.02 N	70.47 E
Gonder, Eth.	221	12.39 N	37.30 E
Gonesse, Fr. (gō-nĕs')	167b	48.59 N	2.28 E
Gongga Shan (Mt.), China (gōŋ-gä shän)	194	29.16 N	101.46 E
Goniri, Nig.	225	11.30 N	12.20 E
Gonō (R.), Jap. (gō'nō)	201	35.00 N	132.25 E
Gonor, Can. (gō'nŏr)	93f	50.04 N	96.57 W
Gonubie, S. Afr. (gŏn'o͞o-bē)	223c	32.56 S	28.02 E
Gonzales, Mex. (gŏn-zä'lĕs)	128	22.47 N	98.26 W
Gonzales, Tx. (gŏn-zä'lĕz)	123	29.31 N	97.25 W
González Catán, Arg. (gōn-zá'lĕz-kä-tá'n)	142a	34.31 S	58.39 W
Good Hope Mtn., Can.	96	51.09 N	124.10 W
Good Hope, C. of, S. Afr. (kāp ov go͝od hōp)	222a	34.21 S	18.29 E
Gooding, Id. (go͝od'ĭng)	114	42.55 N	114.43 W
Goodland, Ind. (go͝od'lȧnd)	108	40.50 N	87.15 W
Goodland, Ks.	120	39.19 N	101.43 W
Goodwood, S. Afr. (go͝od'wo͝od)	222a	33.54 S	18.33 E
Goole, Eng. (go͞ol)	154	53.42 N	0.52 W
Goose (R.), ND	112	47.40 N	97.41 W
Goose Bay, Can.	95	53.19 N	60.33 W
Gooseberry Cr., Wy. (go͞os-bĕr'ĭ)	115	44.04 N	108.35 W
Goose Cr., Id. (go͞os)	115	42.07 N	113.53 W
Goose L., Ca.	114	41.56 N	120.35 W
Gorakhpur, India (gō'rŭk-po͞or)	190	26.45 N	82.39 E
Gorda, Punta (Pt.), Cuba (po͞o'n-tä-gôr-dä)	132	22.25 N	82.10 W
Gorda Cay, Ba. (gôr'dä)	132	26.05 N	77.30 W
Gordon, Can. (gôr'dŭn)	93f	50.00 N	97.20 W
Gordon, Ne.	112	42.47 N	102.14 W
Gore, Eth. (gō'rĕ)	221	8.12 N	35.34 E
Gorgān, Iran	192	36.44 N	54.30 E
Gorgona, Isola di, It. (gôr-gō'nä)	170	43.27 N	9.55 E
Gori, Sov. Un. (gō'rĕ)	177	42.00 N	44.08 E
Gorinchem, Neth. (gō'rĭn-κĕm)	155a	51.50 N	4.59 E
Goring, Eng. (gôr'ĭng)	154b	51.30 N	1.08 W
Gorizia, It. (gô-rē'tsē-yä)	170	44.56 N	13.40 E
Gorki, Sov. Un. (gôr'kē)	176	56.15 N	44.05 E
Gor'kovskoye, Sov. Un.	176	56.38 N	43.40 E
Gor'kovskoye Vdkhr. (Res.), Sov. Un. (gôr-kôf-skô-yĕ)	172	57.38 N	41.18 E
Gorlice, Pol. (gôr-lē'tsĕ)	165	49.38 N	21.11 E
Görlitz, G.D.R. (gŭr'lĭts)	164	51.10 N	15.01 E
Gorlovka, Sov. Un. (gôr'lôf-kȧ)	173	48.17 N	38.03 E
Gorman, Tx. (gôr'măn)	122	32.13 N	98.40 W
Gorna Oryakhovitsa, Bul. (gôr'nä-ôr-yĕk'ô-vē-tsȧ)	171	43.08 N	25.40 E
Gornji Milanovac, Yugo (gôrn'yē-mē'la-nō-väts)	171	44.02 N	20.29 E
Gorno-Altay Aut. Oblast, Sov. Un.	178	51.00 N	86.00 E
Gorno-Altaysk, Sov. Un. (gôr'nŭ'ŭl-tīsk')	178	52.28 N	82.45 E
Gorodënka, Sov. Un. (gō-rô-deŋ'kä)	165	48.40 N	25.30 E
Gorodets (Res.), Sov. Un.	176	57.00 N	43.55 E
Gorodishche, Sov. Un. (gô-rô'dĭsh-chĕ)	180a	57.57 N	57.03 E
Gorodnya, Sov. Un. (gô-rôd''nyä)	173	51.54 N	31.31 E
Gorodok, Sov. Un. (gō-rô-dôk')	165	49.37 N	23.40 E
Gorodok, Sov. Un.	172	55.27 N	29.58 E
Gorodok, Sov. Un.	178	50.30 N	103.58 E

PLACE (Pronunciation)	PAGE	Lat. °′	Long. °′
Gorontalo, Indon. (gō-rōn-tä'lo)	202	0.40 N	123.04 E
Goryn' R., Sov. Un. (gō'rĕn')	165	50.55 N	26.07 E
Gorzow Wielkopolski, Pol. (gō-zho͞ov'vyĕl-ko-pōl'skē)	164	53.44 N	15.15 E
Gosely, Eng.	154	52.33 N	2.10 W
Goshen, In. (gō'shĕn)	108	41.35 N	85.50 W
Goshen, Ky.	111h	38.24 N	85.34 W
Goshen, NY	110a	41.24 N	74.19 W
Goshen, Oh.	111f	39.14 N	84.09 W
Goshute Ind. Res., Ut. (gō-sho͞ot')	119	39.50 N	114.00 W
Goslar, F.R.G. (gôs'lär)	164	51.55 N	10.25 E
Gospa (R.), Ven. (gôs-pä)	141b	9.43 N	64.23 W
Gospić, Yugo. (gôs'pĭch)	170	44.31 N	15.03 E
Gostivar, Yugo. (gos'tē-vär)	171	41.46 N	20.58 E
Gostynin, Pol. (gôs-tē'nĭn)	165	52.24 N	19.30 E
Göta (R.), Swe. (gōĕtä)	162	58.11 N	12.03 E
Göta Kanal (Can.), Swe. (yû'tȧ)	162	58.35 N	15.24 E
Göteborg, Swe. (yû'tĕ-bôrgh)	162	57.39 N	11.56 E
Gotel Mts., Cam.-Nig.	225	7.05 N	11.20 E
Gotera, Sal. (gō-tā'rä)	130	13.41 N	88.06 W
Gotha, G.D.R. (gō'tȧ)	164	50.47 N	10.43 E
Gothenburg, Ne. (gŏth'ĕn-bûrg)	120	40.57 N	100.08 W
Gotland (I.), Swe.	162	57.35 N	17.35 E
Gotō-Rettō (Is.), Jap. (gō'tō rĕt'tō)	201	33.06 N	128.54 E
Gotska Sandön (I.), Swe.	163	58.24 N	19.15 E
Göttingen, F.R.G. (gŭt'ĭng-ĕn)	164	51.32 N	9.57 E
Gouda, Neth. (gou'dä)	155a	52.00 N	4.42 E
Gough (I.), Atl. O. (gŏf)	228	40.00 S	10.00 W
Gouin, Rés, Can.	95	48.15 N	74.15 W
Goukou, China (gō-kō)	198	48.45 N	121.42 E
Goulais (R.), Can.	100	46.45 N	84.10 W
Goulburn, Austl. (gōl'bŭrn)	212	34.47 S	149.40 E
Goumbati (Mtn.), Senegal	224	13.08 N	12.06 W
Goumbou, Mali (go͞om-bo͞o')	224	14.59 N	7.27 W
Gouna, Cam.	225	8.32 N	13.34 E
Goundam, Mali (go͞on-dăɴ')	220	16.29 N	3.37 W
Gouré, Niger (go͞o-ra')	220	13.53 N	10.44 E
Gouverneur, NY (gŭv-ẽr-no͞or')	109	44.20 N	75.25 W
Govenlock, Can. (gŭvĕn-lŏk)	98	49.15 N	109.48 W
Governador Ilhado (I.), Braz. (gô-vĕr-nä-dō-'r-ē-lä'dō)	142b	22.48 S	43.13 W
Governador Portela, Braz. (pōr-tĕ'lä)	142b	22.28 S	43.30 W
Governador Valadares, Braz. (vä-lä-dä'rĕs)	141	18.47 S	41.45 W
Governor's Harbour, Ba.	133	25.15 N	76.15 W
Gowanda, NY (gô-wŏn'dȧ)	109	42.30 N	78.55 W
Goya, Arg. (gō'yä)	142	29.06 S	59.12 W
Goyt (R.), Eng. (goit)	154	53.19 N	2.03 W
Graaff-Reinet, S. Afr. (gräf'rĭ'nĕt)	222	32.10 S	24.40 E
Gracac, Yugo. (grä'chäts)	170	44.16 N	15.50 E
Gračanico, Yugo.	171	44.42 N	18.19 E
Graceville, Fl. (grās'vĭl)	124	30.57 N	85.30 W
Graceville, Mn.	112	45.33 N	96.25 W
Gracias, Hond. (grä'sē-äs)	130	14.35 N	88.37 W
Gracias a Dios, Cabo (C.) (kä'bô-grä-syäs-ä-dyō's)	131	15.00 N	83.13 W
Graciosa I., Açores (grä-syō'sä)	220a	39.07 N	27.30 W
Gradačac, Yugo. (gra-dä'chats)	171	44.50 N	18.28 E
Gradizhsk, Sov. Un. (grä-dēzhsk')	173	49.12 N	33.06 E
Grado, Sp. (grä'dō)	168	43.24 N	6.04 W
Gräfelging, F.R.G. (grä'fĕl-fĕng)	155d	48.07 N	11.27 E
Grafing bei München, F.R.G. (grä'fĕng)	155d	48.03 N	11.58 E
Grafton, Austl. (graf'tŭn)	212	29.38 S	153.05 E
Grafton, Il.	117e	38.58 N	90.26 W
Grafton, Ma.	103a	42.13 N	71.41 W
Grafton, ND	112	48.24 N	97.25 W
Grafton, Oh.	111d	41.16 N	82.04 W
Grafton, WV	109	39.20 N	80.00 W
Gragnano, It. (grän-yä'nô)	169c	40.27 N	14.32 E
Graham, NC (grā'ăm)	125	36.03 N	79.23 W
Graham, Tx.	120	33.07 N	98.34 W
Graham, Wa.	116a	47.03 N	122.18 W
Graham (I.), Can.	94	53.50 N	132.40 W
Grahamstown, S. Afr. (grā'ăms'toun)	223c	33.19 S	26.33 E
Grajaú, Braz. (grá-zhá-o͞o')	141	5.59 S	46.03 W
Grajaú (R.), Braz.	141	4.24 S	46.04 W
Grajewo, Pol. (grä-yä'vo)	165	53.38 N	22.28 E
Grama, Serra de (Mtn.), Braz. (sĕ'r-rä-dĕ-grá'mȧ)	139a	23.42 S	42.28 W
Gramada, Bul. (grä'mä-dä)	171	43.46 N	22.41 E
Gramatneusiedl, Aus.	155e	48.02 N	16.29 E
Grammichele, It. (gräm-mē-kĕ'lā)	170	37.15 N	14.40 E
Grampian Mts., Scot. (grăm'pĭ-ăn)	160	56.30 N	4.55 W
Granada, Nic. (grä-nä'dhä)	130	11.55 N	85.58 W
Granada, Sp. (grä-nä'dä)	168	37.13 N	3.37 W
Gran Bajo (Pln.), Arg. (grán'bä'kō)	142	47.35 S	68.45 W
Granbury, Tx. (grăn'bĕr-ĭ)	123	32.26 N	97.45 W
Granby, Can. (grăn'bĭ)	109	45.30 N	72.40 W
Granby, Mo.	121	36.54 N	94.15 W
Granby (L.), Co.	120	40.07 N	105.40 W
Gran Canaria I., Can. Is. (grän'kä-nä'rē-ä)	220	27.39 N	15.39 W
Gran Chaco (Reg.), Arg.-Par. (grán'chá'kŏ)	142	25.30 S	62.15 W
Grand (I.), Mi.	113	46.37 N	86.38 W
Grand (L.), Can.	102	45.17 N	67.42 W
Grand (L.), Can.	102	66.15 N	45.59 W
Grand (R.), Can.	101	43.45 N	80.20 W
Grand (R.), Mi.	108	42.58 N	85.13 W
Grand (R.), Mo.	121	39.50 N	93.52 W

PLACE (Pronunciation)	PAGE	Lat. °′	Long. °′
Grand (R.), SD	112	45.40 N	101.55 W
Grand (R.), North Fork, SD	112	45.52 N	102.49 W
Grand (R.), South Fork, SD	112	45.38 N	102.56 W
Grand Bahama (I.), Ba.	132	26.35 N	78.30 W
Grand Bank, Can. (grănd băngk)	103	47.06 N	55.47 W
Grand Bassam, Ivory Coast (gräɴ bá-säɴ')	224	5.12 N	3.44 W
Grand Bourg, Guad. (gräɴ bo͞or')	131b	15.54 N	61.20 W
Grand Caicos (I.), Turks & Caicos Is. (grănd kä-ē'kōs)	133	21.45 N	71.50 W
Grand Canal, Ire.	160	53.21 N	7.15 W
Grand Canal, see Da Yunhe			
Grand Canyon, Az. (grănd kăn yŭn)	119	36.05 N	112.10 W
Grand Canyon, Az.	119	35.50 N	113.16 W
Grand Canyon Natl. Park, Az.	119	36.15 N	112.20 W
Grand Cayman (I.), Cayman Is. (kā'măn)	132	19.15 N	81.15 W
Grand Coulee Dam, Wa. (ko͞o'lē)	114	47.58 N	119.28 W
Grande (R.), Chili	139b	35.25 S	70.14 W
Grande, (R.), Mex.	129	17.37 N	96.41 W
Grande (R.), Ur.	139c	33.19 S	57.15 W
Grande, Bahía (B.), Arg. (bä-ē'ä-grán'dĕ)	142	50.45 S	68.00 W
Grande, Boca (Est.), Ven. (bō'kä-grä'n-dĕ)	141	8.46 N	60.17 W
Grande, Ciri (R.), Pan. (sē'rē-grä'n'dĕ)	126a	8.55 N	80.04 W
Grande, Cuchilla (Mts.), Ur. (ko͞o-chē'l-yä)	142	33.00 S	55.15 W
Grande, Ilha (I.), Braz. (grän'dĕ)	139a	23.11 S	44.14 W
Grande, Rio (R.), Bol.	140	16.49 S	63.19 W
Grande, Rio (R.), Braz.	141	19.48 S	49.54 W
Grande, Rio (R.), (Bravo del Norte, Rio), Mex.-U.S. (grăn'dȧ)	106	26.50 N	99.10 W
Grande, Salinas (F.), Arg. (sä-lē'näs)	142	29.45 S	65.00 W
Grande, Salto (Falls), Braz. (säl-tô)	141	16.18 S	39.38 W
Grande Cayemite, Ile (I.), Hai.	133	18.45 N	73.45 W
Grande Comore, Comoros (grä'n-dĕ-kô-mô-rĕ)	223	11.44 S	42.38 E
Grande de Otoro, Hond. (grä'da dā ô-tō'rô)	130	14.42 N	88.21 W
Grande Pointe, Can. (grănd point')	93f	49.47 N	97.03 W
Grande Prairie, Can. (prâr'ĭ)	97	55.10 N	118.48 W
Grande R., Nic. (grän'dĕ)	131	13.01 N	84.21 W
Grand Erg Occidental (Dunes), Alg.	220	29.37 N	6.04 E
Grande Rivière du Nord, Hai. (rē-vyâr' dü nôr')	133	19.35 N	72.10 W
Grande Ronde R., Or. (rŏnd')	114	45.32 N	117.52 W
Gran Desierto (Des.), Mex. (grän-dĕ-syĕ'r-tô)	118	32.14 N	114.28 W
Grande Soufriere Vol., Guad. (so͞o-frē-âr')	131b	16.06 N	61.42 W
Grande Terre I., Guad. (târ')	131b	16.28 N	61.13 W
Grande Vigie, Pointe de la (Pt.), Guad. (gräɴd vē-gē')	131b	16.32 N	61.25 W
Grand Falls, Can. (fôlz)	103	48.56 N	55.40 W
Grandfather, Mt., NC (grănd-fä-thẽr)	99	36.07 N	81.48 W
Grandfield, Ok. (grănd'fēld)	120	34.13 N	98.39 W
Grand Forks, Can. (fôrks)	97	49.02 N	118.27 W
Grand Forks, ND	112	47.55 N	97.05 W
Grand Haven, Mi (hā'v'n)	108	43.05 N	86.15 W
Grand Island, Ne. (ī'lȧnd)	120	40.56 N	98.20 W
Grand I, NY	111c	43.03 N	78.58 W
Grand Junction, Co. (jŭngk'shŭn)	119	39.05 N	108.35 W
Grand L., Can. (lăk)	103	49.00 N	57.10 W
Grand L., La.	123	29.57 N	91.25 W
Grand L., Mn.	117h	46.54 N	92.26 W
Grand Ledge, Mi. (lĕj)	108	42.45 N	84.50 W
Grand Lieu, L. de, Fr. (gräɴ'-lyû)	166	46.00 N	1.45 W
Grand Manan (I.), Can. (mȧ-năn)	102	44.40 N	66.50 W
Grand Mère, Can. (gräɴ mâr')	101	46.36 N	72.43 W
Grand Morin (R.), Fr. (mô-raɴ')	167b	48.23 N	2.19 E
Grândola, Port. (grăɴ'dô-lȧ)	168	38.10 N	8.36 W
Grand Portage Ind. Res., Mn. (pōr'tĭj)	113	47.54 N	89.34 W
Grand Portage Natl. Mon., Mi.	113	47.59 N	89.47 W
Grand Prairie, Tx. (prĕ'rē)	117c	32.45 N	97.00 W
Grand Quivira Natl. Mon., NM (kē-vē'rȧ)	119	34.10 N	106.05 W
Grand Rapids, Can.	99	53.08 N	99.20 W
Grand Rapids, Mi. (răp'ĭdz)	108	43.00 N	85.45 W
Grand Rapids, Mn.	113	47.16 N	93.33 W
Grand Rapids Forebay (Res.), Can.	99	53.10 N	100.00 W
Grand-Riviere, Can.	102	48.26 N	64.30 W
Grand Teton Mt., Wy.	115	43.46 N	110.50 W
Grand Teton Natl. Park, Wy. (tē'tŏn)	115	43.54 N	110.15 W
Grand Traverse B., Mi. (trăv'ẽrs)	108	45.00 N	85.30 W
Grand Turk, Turks & Caicos Is. (tûrk)	133	21.30 N	71.10 W
Grand Turk (I.), Turks & Caicos Is.	123	21.30 N	71.10 W
Grandview, Mo. (grănd'vyo͞o)	117f	38.53 N	94.32 W
Grand Wash (R.), Az. (wŏsh)	119	36.20 N	113.52 W
Granger, Wy. (grān'jẽr)	115	41.37 N	109.58 W
Grangeville, Id. (grānj'vĭl)	114	45.56 N	116.08 W
Granite City, Il. (grăn'ĭt sĭt'ĭ)	117e	38.42 N	90.09 W
Granite Falls, Mn. (fôlz)	112	44.46 N	95.34 W
Granite Falls, NC	125	35.49 N	81.25 W
Granite Falls, Wa.	116a	48.05 N	121.59 W
Granite L., Can.	103	48.01 N	57.00 W
Granite Pk., Mt.	115	45.13 N	109.48 W
Graniteville, SC (grăn'ĭt-vĭl)	125	33.35 N	81.50 W
Granito, Braz. (grä-nē'tō)	141	7.39 S	39.34 W
Granma (Prov.), Cuba	132	20.10 N	76.50 W

296 Granna – Guadeloupe Pass

PLACE (Pronunciation)	PAGE	Lat. °′	Long. °′
Gränna, Swe. (grĕn′á)	162	58.02 N	14.38 E
Granollers, Sp. (grä-nôl-yĕrs′)	169e	41.36 N	2.19 E
Gran Pajonal (Marsh), Peru (grä′n-pä-κô-näl′)	140	11.14 S	71.45 W
Gran Piedra (Mtn.), Cuba (grän-pyĕ′drä)	123	20.00 N	75.40 W
Grantham, Eng. (grăn′tǎm)	154	52.54 N	0.38 W
Grant Park, Il. (grănt pärk)	111a	41.14 N	87.39 W
Grants Pass, Or. (grànts pàs)	114	42.26 N	123.20 W
Granville, Fr. (grän-vēl′)	166	48.52 N	1.35 W
Granville, NY (grăn′vĭl)	109	43.25 N	73.15 W
Granville (L.), Can.	99	56.18 N	100.30 W
Grão Mogol, Braz. (grouN′ mōō-gôl′)	141	16.34 S	42.35 W
Grapevine, Tx. (grāp′vīn)	117c	32.56 N	97.05 W
Gräso (I.), Swe.	162	60.30 N	18.35 E
Grass (R.), NY	109	44.45 N	75.10 W
Grass Cay (I.), Vir. Is.(U.S.A.)	127c	18.22 N	64.50 W
Grasse, Fr. (gräs)	167	43.39 N	6.57 E
Grass Mtn., Wa. (gràs)	116a	47.13 N	121.48 W
Grates Pt., Can. (grāts)	103	48.09 N	52.57 W
Gravelbourg, Can. (grăv′ĕl-bôrg)	98	49.53 N	106.34 W
Gravesend, Eng. (grāvz′ĕnd′)	154b	51.26 N	0.22 E
Gravina, It. (grä-vē′nä)	170	40.48 N	16.27 E
Gravois, Pte., Hai. (grà-vwä′)	133	18.00 N	74.20 W
Gray, Fr. (grâ)	167	47.26 N	5.35 E
Grayling, Mi. (grā′lĭng)	108	44.40 N	84.40 W
Grayslake, Il. (grāz′lāk)	111a	42.20 N	88.20 W
Grays Pk., Co. (grāz)	120	39.29 N	105.52 W
Grayvoron, Sov. Un. (grá-ē′vô-rôn)	173	50.28 N	35.41 E
Graz, Aus. (gräts)	164	47.05 N	15.26 E
Great Abaco (I.), Ba. (ä′bä-kō)	132	26.30 N	77.05 W
Great Artesian Basin (Reg.), Austl. (är-tēzh-ǎn bā-sĭn)	211	23.16 S	143.37 E
Great Australian Bight, Austl. (ôs-trā′lĭ-ǎn bīt)	210	33.30 S	127.00 E
Great Bahama Bk., Ba (bǎ-hā′mǎ)	132	25.00 N	78.50 W
Great Barrier (I.), N.Z. (băr′ĭ-ēr)	213	37.00 S	175.31 E
Great Barrier Rf., Austl. (bá-rĭ-ēr rēf)	211	16.43 S	146.34 E
Great Basin, U.S. (grāt bā′s′n)	106	40.08 N	117.10 W
Great Bear L., Can. (bâr)	94	66.10 N	119.53 W
Great Bend, Ks. (bĕnd)	120	38.41 N	98.46 W
Great Bitter, see Al Buḩayrah al Murrah al Kubrā			
Great Blasket I., Ire. (blàs′kĕt)	160	52.05 N	10.55 W
Great Britain, U.K. (brĭt′n)	152	56.53 N	0.02 W
Great Corn I., Nic.	131	12.10 N	82.54 W
Great Divide Basin, Wyo. (dĭ-vīd′ bā′s′n)	115	42.10 N	108.10 W
Great Dividing Ra., Austl. (dĭ-vī-dĭng rānj)	211	35.16 S	146.38 E
Great Duck (I.), Can. (dŭk)	100	45.40 N	83.22 W
Greater Khingan Range (Da Hinggan Ling), China (dä hĭŋ-gän lĭŋ)	198	46.30 N	120.00 E
Greater Leech Ind. Res., Mn. (grāt′ēr lēch)	113	47.39 N	94.27 W
Greater Manchester (Co.), Eng.	154	53.34 N	2.41 W
Greater Sunda Is., Indon.	202	4.00 S	108.00 E
Great Exuma (I.), Ba. (ĕk-sōō′mä)	133	23.35 N	76.00 W
Great Falls, Mt. (fôlz)	115	47.30 N	111.15 W
Great Falls, SC	125	34.32 N	80.53 W
Great Guana Cay (I.), Ba. (gwä′nä)	133	24.00 N	76.20 W
Great Harbor Cay (I.), Ba. (kē)	132	25.45 N	77.50 W
Great Inagua (I.), Ba. (ē-nä′gwä)	133	21.00 N	73.15 W
Great Indian Des., India	190	27.35 N	71.37 E
Great Isaac (I.), Ba. (ī′zák)	132	26.05 N	79.05 W
Great Karroo (Mts.), S. Afr. (grāt kǎ′rōō)	222	32.45 S	22.00 E
Great Namaland (Reg.), Namibia	222	25.45 S	16.15 E
Great Neck, NY (nĕk)	110a	40.48 N	73.44 W
Great Nicobar I., Andaman & Nicobar Is. (nĭk-ô-bär′)	202	7.00 N	94.18 E
Great Pedro Bluff (Hd.), Jam.	132	17.50 N	78.05 W
Great Plains, The (Reg.), N.A. (plāns)	92	45.00 N	104.00 W
Great Ragged (I.), Ba.	133	22.10 N	75.45 W
Great Ruaha (R.), Tan.	227	7.45 S	34.50 E
Great St. Bernard Pass, Switz-It. (sānt bĕr-närd′)	170	45.53 N	7.15 E
Great Salt L., Ut. (sôlt lāk)	115	41.19 N	112.48 W
Great Salt Lake Des., U.S.	106	41.00 N	113.30 W
Great Salt Plains Res., Ok.	120	36.56 N	98.14 W
Great Sand Dunes Natl. Mon., Co.	120	37.56 N	105.25 W
Great Sand Hills, Can. (sănd)	98	50.35 N	109.05 W
Great Sandy (I.), see Fraser			
Great Sandy Des., Austl. (săn′dē)	210	21.50 S	123.10 E
Great Sandy Des., Or. (săn′dĭ)	114	43.43 N	120.44 W
Great Sitkin (I.), Ak. (sĭt-kĭn)	105a	52.18 N	176.22 W
Great Slave (L.), Can. (slāv)	94	61.37 N	114.58 W
Great Smoky Mts. Natl. Park, NC-Tn. (smōk-ē)	124	35.43 N	83.20 W
Great Stirrup Cay (I.), Ba. (stĭr-ŭp)	132	25.50 N	77.55 W
Great Victoria Des., Austl. (vĭk-tō′rĭ-ǎ)	210	29.45 S	124.30 E
Great Waltham, Eng. (wôl′thŭm)	154	51.47 N	0.27 E
Great Yarmouth, Eng. (yär-mŭth)	161	52.35 N	1.45 E
Grebbestad, Swe. (grĕb-bĕ-städh)	162	58.42 N	11.15 E
Gréboun, Mont (Mtn.), Niger	225	20.00 N	8.35 E
Gredos, Sierra de (Mts.) (syĕr′rä dā grā′dōs)	168	40.13 N	5.30 W
Greece, Eur. (grēs)	152	39.00 N	21.30 E
Greeley, Co. (grē′lĭ)	120	40.25 N	104.41 W
Green (R.), Ky (grēn)	124	37.13 N	86.30 W
Green (R.), ND	112	47.05 N	103.05 W
Green (R.), U.S.	106	38.30 N	110.10 W
Green (R.), Ut.	119	38.30 N	110.05 W
Green (R.), Wa.	116a	47.17 N	121.57 W
Greenbank, Wa. (grēn′bănk)	116a	48.06 N	122.35 W
Green Bayou, Tx.	123a	29.53 N	95.13 W
Green Bay, Wi.	113	44.30 N	88.04 W
Green B., U.S.	107	44.55 N	87.40 W
Greenbelt, Md. (grēn′bĕlt)	110e	38.59 N	76.53 W
Greencastle, In. (grēn-kás′′l)	108	39.40 N	86.50 W
Green Cay (I.)	132	24.05 N	77.10 W
Green Cove Springs, Fl. (kōv)	125	29.56 N	81.42 W
Greendale, Wi. (grēn′dāl)	111a	42.56 N	87.59 W
Greenfield, In. (grēn′fēld)	108	39.45 N	85.40 W
Greenfield, Ia.	113	41.16 N	94.30 W
Greenfield, Ma.	109	42.35 N	72.35 W
Greenfield, Mo.	121	37.23 N	93.48 W
Greenfield, Oh.	108	39.15 N	83.25 W
Greenfield, Tn.	124	36.08 N	88.45 W
Greenfield Park, Can.	93a	45.29 N	73.29 W
Greenhills, Oh. (grēn-hĭls)	111f	39.16 N	84.31 W
Greenland, N.A. (grēn′lǎnd)	92	74.00 N	40.00 W
Green Mtn., Or.	116c	45.52 N	123.24 W
Green Mountain Res., Co.	119	39.50 N	106.20 W
Green Mts., Vt.	109	43.10 N	73.05 W
Greenock, Scot. (grēn′ŭk)	160	55.55 N	4.45 W
Green Pond Mtn., NJ (pŏnd)	110a	41.00 N	74.32 W
Greenport, NY	109	41.06 N	72.22 W
Green River, Ut. (grēn rĭv′ēr)	119	39.00 N	110.05 W
Green River, Wy.	115	41.32 N	109.26 W
Green R., Blacks Fk, Wy.	115	41.08 N	110.27 W
Green R., Hams Fk., Wy.	115	41.55 N	110.40 W
Greensboro, Al. (grēnz′bŭro)	124	32.42 N	87.36 W
Greensboro, Ga. (grēns-bûr′ô)	124	33.34 N	83.11 W
Greensboro, NC	125	36.04 N	79.45 W
Greensburg, In. (grēnz′bûrg)	108	39.20 N	85.30 W
Greensburg, Ks. (grēns-bûrg)	120	37.36 N	99.17 W
Greensburg, Pa.	109	40.20 N	79.30 W
Greenville, Al. (grēn′vĭl)	124	31.49 N	86.39 W
Greenville, Il.	121	38.52 N	89.22 W
Greenville, Ky.	124	37.11 N	87.11 W
Greenville, Lib.	224	5.01 N	9.03 W
Greenville, Me.	102	45.26 N	69.35 W
Greenville, Mi.	108	43.10 N	85.25 W
Greenville, Ms.	124	33.25 N	91.00 W
Greenville, NC	125	35.35 N	77.22 W
Greenville, Oh.	108	40.05 N	84.35 W
Greenville, Pa.	108	41.20 N	80.25 W
Greenville, SC	125	34.50 N	82.25 W
Greenville, Tn.	124	36.08 N	82.50 W
Greenville, Tx.	121	33.09 N	96.07 W
Greenwich, Ct.	110a	41.01 N	73.37 W
Greenwich, Eng. (grĭn′ĭj)	154b	51.28 N	0.00
Greenwood, Ar. (grēn-wŏŏd)	121	35.13 N	94.15 W
Greenwood, In.	111g	39.37 N	86.07 W
Greenwood, Ms.	124	33.30 N	90.09 W
Greenwood, SC	125	34.10 N	82.10 W
Greenwood (R.), SC	125	34.17 N	81.55 W
Greenwood L., NY	110a	41.13 N	74.20 W
Greer, SC (grēr)	125	34.55 N	81.56 W
Grefrath, F.R.G. (grĕf′rät)	167c	51.20 N	6.21 E
Gregory, SD (grĕg′ô-rĭ)	112	43.12 N	99.27 W
Gregory, L., Austl. (grĕg′ô-rē)	212	29.47 S	139.15 E
Gregory Ra., Austl.	211	19.23 S	143.45 E
Greifenberg, F.R.G. (grī′fĕn-bĕrgh)	155d	48.04 N	11.06 E
Greifswald, G.D.R. (grīfs′vält)	164	54.05 N	13.24 E
Greiz, G.D.R. (grīts)	164	50.39 N	12.14 E
Gremyachinsk, Sov. Un. (grâ′myá-chĭnsk)	180a	58.35 N	57.53 E
Grenå, Den. (grĕn′ô)	162	56.25 N	10.51 E
Grenada, Ms. (grē-nä′da)	124	33.45 N	89.47 W
Grenada, N.A.	127	12.02 N	61.15 W
Grenada Res., Ms.	124	33.52 N	89.30 W
Grenadines, The (Is.), Grenada-St. Vincent (grĕn′ǎ-dēnz)	131b	12.37 N	61.35 W
Grenen (Pt.), Den.	162	57.43 N	10.31 E
Grenoble, Fr. (grē-nô′bl′)	167	45.14 N	5.45 E
Grenora, ND (grē-nō′rǎ)	112	48.38 N	103.55 W
Grenville, Can. (grē-nvĭl)	109	45.40 N	74.35 W
Grenville, Grenada	131b	12.07 N	61.38 W
Gresham, Or. (grĕsh′ǎm)	116c	45.30 N	122.25 W
Gretna, La. (grĕt′nǎ)	110d	29.56 N	90.03 W
Grevelingen Krammer, R., Neth.	155a	51.42 N	4.03 E
Grevená, Grc. (grĕ′vā-nà)	171	40.02 N	21.30 E
Grevenbroich, F.R.G. (grĕ′fen-broik)	167c	51.05 N	6.36 E
Grey (R.), Can. (grā)	103	47.53 N	57.00 W
Grey, Pt., Can.	116d	49.22 N	123.16 W
Greybull, Wy. (grā′bŏŏl)	115	44.28 N	108.05 W
Greybull R., Wy.	115	44.13 N	108.43 W
Greylingstad, S. Afr. (grā-lĭng′shtát)	219d	26.40 S	29.13 E
Greymouth, N.Z. (grā′mouth)	213	42.27 S	171.17 E
Grey Ra., Austl.	212	28.40 S	142.05 E
Greys Hbr., Wa. (grās)	114	46.55 N	124.23 W
Greytown, S. Afr. (grā′toun)	223c	29.07 S	30.38 E
Greytown, see San Juan del Norte			
Grey Wolf Pk., Wa. (grā wŏŏlf)	116a	48.53 N	123.12 W
Gridley, Ca. (grĭd′lĭ)	118	39.22 N	121.43 W
Griffin, Ga. (grĭf′ĭn)	124	33.15 N	84.16 W
Griffith, Austl. (grĭf-ĭth)	212	34.16 S	146.10 E
Griffith, In.	111a	41.31 N	87.26 W
Grigoriopol′, Sov. Un. (grĭ′gor-ĭ-ô′pôl)	173	47.09 N	29.18 E
Grijalva (R.), Mex. (grē-häl′vä)	129	17.25 N	93.23 W
Grim, C., Austl. (grĭm)	212	40.43 S	144.30 E
Grimma, G.D.R. (grĭm′á)	164	51.14 N	12.43 E
Grimsby, Can. (grĭmz′bĭ)	93d	43.11 N	79.33 W
Grímsey (I.), Ice. (grĭms′â)	156	66.30 N	17.50 W
Grimstad, Nor. (grĭm-städh)	162	58.21 N	8.30 E
Grindstone Island, Can.	103	47.25 N	61.51 W
Grinnel, Ia. (grĭ-nĕl′)	113	41.44 N	92.44 W
Griswold, Ia. (grĭz′wǔld)	113	41.11 N	95.05 W
Griva, Sov. Un. (grē′vá)	172	55.51 N	26.31 E
Groais I., Can.	103	50.57 N	55.35 W
Grobina, Sov. Un. (grō′bĭnĭa)	163	56.35 N	21.10 E
Groblersdal, S. Afr.	219d	25.11 S	29.25 E
Grodno, Sov. Un. (grôd′nō)	165	53.40 N	23.49 E
Grodzisk, Pol. (grō′jēsk)	164	52.14 N	16.22 E
Grodzisk Masowiecki, Pol. (grō′jēsk mä-zō-vyĕts′ke)	165	52.06 N	20.40 E
Groesbeck, Tx. (grōs′bĕk)	123	31.32 N	96.31 W
Groix, Île de (I.), Fr. (ēl dē grwä′)	166	47.39 N	3.28 W
Grójec, Pol. (grōō′yĕts)	165	51.53 N	20.52 E
Gronau, F.R.G. (grō′nou)	164	52.12 N	7.05 E
Groningen, Neth. (grō′nĭng-ĕn)	161	53.13 N	6.30 E
Groote Eylandt (I.), Austl. (grō′tē ī′länt)	210	13.50 S	137.30 E
Grootfontein, Namibia (grōt′fōn-tān′)	222	18.15 S	19.30 E
Groot-Kei, S. Afr. (kē)	223c	32.17 S	27.30 E
Grootkop, (Mtn.), S. Afr.	222a	34.11 S	18.23 E
Groot Marico, S. Afr.	219d	25.36 S	26.23 E
Groot R., S. Afr.	219d	25.13 S	26.20 E
Groot-Vis (R.), S. Afr.	223c	33.04 S	36.08 E
Groot Vloer (L.), S. Afr. (grōt′ vlōōr′)	223c	33.00 S	20.16 E
Gros Morne (Mtn.), Can. (grō môrn′)	103	49.36 N	57.48 W
Gros Morne Natl. Pk., Can.	95	49.45 N	59.15 W
Gros Pate (Mtn.), Can.	103	50.16 N	57.25 W
Grosse I., Mi. (grōs)	111b	42.08 N	83.09 W
Grosse Isle, Can. (īl′)	93f	50.04 N	97.27 W
Grossenhain, G.D.R. (grōs′ĕn-hīn)	164	51.17 N	13.33 E
Gross-Enzersdorf, Aus.	155e	48.13 N	16.33 E
Grosse Pointe, Mi. (point′)	111b	42.23 N	82.54 W
Grosse Pointe Farms, Mi. (färm)	111b	42.25 N	82.53 W
Grosse Pointe Park, Mi. (pärk)	111b	42.23 N	82.55 W
Grosseto, It. (grôs-sā′tō)	170	42.46 N	11.09 E
Grossglockner Pk, Aus. (glôk′nēr)	164	47.06 N	12.45 E
Gross Höbach, F.R.G. (hû′bäk)	155d	48.21 N	11.36 E
Gross Kreutz, G.D.R. (kroitz)	155b	52.24 N	12.47 E
Gross Schönebeck, G.D.R. (shō′nē-bĕk)	155b	52.54 N	13.32 E
Gros Ventre R., Wy. (grōvĕn′t′r)	115	43.38 N	110.34 W
Groton, Ct. (grôt′ŭn)	109	41.20 N	72.00 W
Groton, Ma.	103a	42.37 N	71.34 W
Groton, SD	112	45.25 N	98.04 W
Grottaglie, It. (grôt-täl′yā)	171	40.32 N	17.26 E
Grouard Mission, Can.	97	55.31 N	116.09 W
Groveland, Ma. (grōv′land)	103a	42.25 N	71.02 W
Groveton, NH (grōv′tŭn)	109	44.35 N	71.30 W
Groveton, Tx.	123	31.04 N	95.07 W
Groznyy, Sov. Un. (grôz′nĭ)	177	43.20 N	45.40 E
Grudziądz, Pol. (grōō′jyôNts)	165a	53.30 N	18.48 E
Grues, Île aux (I.), Can. (ō grü)	93b	47.05 N	70.32 W
Grumpholds-Kirchen, Aus.	155e	48.03 N	16.17 E
Grundy Center, Ia. (grŭn′dĭ sĕn′tēr)	113	42.22 N	92.45 W
Gruñidora, Mex. (grōō-nyē-dô′rō)	128	24.10 N	101.49 W
Grünwald, F.R.G. (grōōn′väld)	155d	48.04 N	11.34 E
Gryazi, Sov. Un. (gryä′zĭ)	172	52.31 N	39.59 E
Gryazovets, Sov. Un. (gryä′zô-vĕts)	152	58.52 N	40.14 E
Gryfice, Pol. (grĭ-fĭ-tsĕ)	164	53.55 N	15.11 E
Gryfino, Pol. (grĭ′fē-nô)	164	53.16 N	14.30 E
Guabito, Pan. (gwä-bē′tô)	131	9.30 N	82.33 W
Guacanayabo, Golfo de (G.), Cuba (gôl-fô-dē-gwä-kä-nä-yä′bô)	132	20.30 N	77.40 W
Guacara, Ven. (gwá′kä-rä)	141b	10.16 N	67.48 W
Guacarí, Col. (gwä-kä-rē′)	140a	3.45 N	76.20 W
Guaçuí, Braz. (gwä′sōō-ē′)	139a	20.47 S	41.40 W
Guadalajara, Mex. (gwä-dhä-lä-hä′rä)	128	20.41 N	103.21 W
Guadalajara, Sp. (gwä-dä-lä-kä′rä)	168	40.37 N	3.10 W
Guadalcanal, Sp. (gwä-dhäl-kä-näl′)	168	38.05 N	5.48 W
Guadalcanal (I.), Sol. Is.	211	9.48 S	158.43 E
Guadalcázar, Mex. (gwä-dhäl-kä′zär)	128	22.38 N	100.24 W
Guadalete (R.), Sp. (gwä-dhä-lā′tå)	168	38.53 N	5.38 W
Guadalhorce (R.), Sp. (gwä-dhäl-ôr′thā)	168	37.05 N	4.50 W
Guadalimar (R.), Sp. (gwä-dhä-lē-mär′)	168	38.29 N	2.53 W
Guadalope (R.), Sp. (gwä-dä-lô-pē)	169	40.48 N	0.10 W
Guadalquivir, Río (R.), Sp. (rē′ō-gwä-dhäl-kē-vēr′)	168	36.35 N	6.00 W
Guadalupe, Mex.	122	31.23 N	106.06 W
Guadalupe, Sierra de (Mts.), Sp. (syĕr′rä dā gwä-dhä-lōō′pä)	168	39.30 N	5.25 W
Guadalupe I., Mex.	126	29.00 N	118.45 W
Guadalupe Mts., NM-Tx	122	32.00 N	104.55 W
Guadalupe Pk., Tx.	122	31.55 N	104.55 W
Guadalupe R., Tx. (gwä-dhä-lōō′på)	122	29.54 N	99.03 W
Guadarrama, Sierra de (Mts.), Sp. (gwä-dhär-rä′mä)	168	41.00 N	3.40 W
Guadarrama (R.), Sp. (gwä-dhär-rä′mä)	169a	40.34 N	3.58 W
Guadatentin (R.), Sp.	168	37.43 N	1.58 W
Guadeloupe, N.A. (gwä-dē-lōōp)	127	16.40 N	61.10 W
Guadeloupe Pass, N.A.	131b	16.26 N	62.00 W

ăt; finǎl; rāte; senâte; ärm; àsk; sofá; fâre; ch-choose; dh-as th in other; bē; ēvent; bĕt; recĕnt; cratēr; g-gō; gh-guttural g; bĭt; ĭ-short neutral; rīde; κ-guttural k as ch in German ich;

PLACE (Pronunciation)	PAGE	Lat. °′	Long. °′
Guadiana, Bahia de (B.), Cuba (bä-ē'ä-dē-gwä-dhē-ä'nä)	132	22.10 N	84.35 W
Guadiana (R.), Port. (gwä-dvä'nä)	168	37.43 N	7.43 W
Guadiana Alto (R.), Sp. (äl'tö)	168	39.02 N	2.52 W
Guadiana Menor (R.), Sp. (mä'nôr)	168	37.43 N	2.45 W
Guadiaro (R.), Sp. (gwä-dhē-ä rö)	168	37.38 N	5.25 W
Guadiela (R.), Sp. (gwä-dhē-ä'lä)	168	40.27 N	2.05 W
Guadíx, Sp. (gwä-dēsh')	168	37.18 N	3.09 W
Guaira, Braz. (gwä-ē-rä)	141	24.03 s	44.02 W
Guaire (R.), Ven. (gwī'rē)	141b	10.25 N	66.43 W
Guajaba, Cayo (I.), Cuba (kä'yō-gwä-hä'bä)	132	21.50 N	77.35 W
Guajará Mirim, Braz. (gwä-zhä-rä'mē-rěN')	140	10.58 s	65.12 W
Guajira, Pen. de (Pen.), Col.-Ven. (pě-ně'ng-sōō-lä-dě-gwä-Kē'rä)	140	12.35 N	73.00 W
Gualán, Guat. (gwä-län')	130c	15.08 N	89.21 W
Gualeguay, Arg. (gwä-lě-gwä'y)	139c	33.10 s	59.20 W
Gualeguay (R.), Arg.	139c	32.49 s	59.05 W
Gualeguaychú, Arg. (gwä-lä-gwī-chōō')	139c	33.01 s	58.32 W
Gualeguaychú (R.), Arg.	139c	32.58 s	58.27 W
Gualicho, Salina (F.), Arg. (sä-lē'nä-gwä-lē'chō)	142	40.20 s	65.15 W
Guam, Oceania (gwäm)	204	14.00 N	143.20 E
Guaminí, Arg. (gwä-mē-nē')	142	37.02 s	62.21 W
Guamo, Col. (gwä'mō)	140a	4.02 N	74.58 W
Gu'an, China (gōō-än)	198a	39.25 N	116.18 E
Guan (R.), China (gůän)	196	31.56 N	115.19 E
Guanabacoa, Cuba (gwä-nä-bä-kō'ä)	133a	23.08 N	82.19 W
Guanabara, Baia de (B.), Braz.	142b	22.44 s	43.09 W
Guanacaste Cord. (Mts.), C.R. (kôr-děl-yē'rä-gwä-nä-käs'tä)	130	10.54 N	85.27 W
Guanacevi, Mex. (gwä-nä-sě-vē')	126	25.30 N	105.45 W
Guanahacabibes, Pen. de, Cuba (pě-něn-sōō-lä-dě-gwä-nä hä-kä-bē'bäs)	132	21.55 N	84.35 W
Guanajay, Cuba (gwänä-hī')	132	22.55 N	82.40 W
Guanajuato, Mex. (gwä-nä-hwä'tō)	128	21.01 N	101.16 W
Guanajuato (State), Mex.	126	21.00 N	101.00 W
Guanape, Ven. (gwä-nä'pě)	141b	9.55 N	65.32 W
Guanape (R.), Ven.	141b	9.52 N	65.20 W
Guanare, Ven. (gwä-nä'rä)	140	8.57 N	69.47 W
Guanduçu (R.), Braz. (gwä'n-dōō'sōō)	142b	22.50 s	43.40 W
Guane, Cuba (gwä'nä)	132	22.10 N	84.05 W
Guangchang, China (gůän-chän)	199	25.50 N	116.18 E
Guangde, China (gůän-dǔ)	199	30.40 N	119.20 E
Guangdong (Prov.), China (gůän-dòŋ)	195	23.45 N	113.15 E
Guanglu Dao (I.), China (gůän-lōō dou)	196	39.13 N	122.21 E
Guangping, China (gůän-pǐŋ)	196	36.30 N	114.57 E
Guangrao, China (gůän-rou)	196	37.04 N	118.24 E
Guangshan, China (gůän-shän)	196	32.02 N	114.53 E
Guangxi (Aut. Reg.), China (gůän-shyě)	194	24.00 N	108.30 E
Guangzhou (Canton), China (gůän-jō)	197a	23.07 N	113.15 E
Guanhu, China (gůän-hōō)	196	34.26 N	117.59 E
Guannan, China (gůän-nän)	196	34.17 N	119.17 E
Guanta, Ven. (gwän'tä)	141b	10.15 N	64.35 W
Guantanamo, Cuba (gwän-tä'nä-mô)	133	20.10 N	75.10 W
Guantánamo (Prov.), Cuba	133	20.10 N	75.05 W
Guantanamo, Bahía de (B.), Cuba (bä-ē'ä-dě)	133	19.35 N	75.35 W
Guantao, China (gůän-tou)	196	36.39 N	115.25 E
Guan Xian, China (gůän-shyěn)	196	36.30 N	115.28 E
Guanyao, China (gůän-you)	197a	23.13 N	113.04 E
Guanyun, China (gůän-yōōn)	196	34.28 N	119.16 E
Guapé, Braz. (gwä-pě)	139a	20.45 s	45.55 W
Guapiles, C.R. (gwä-pě-lěs)	131	10.05 N	83.54 W
Guapimirim, Braz. (gwä-pě-mē-rě'N)	142b	22.31 s	42.59 W
Guaporé (R.), Bol.-Braz. (gwä-pô-rä')	140	12.11 s	63.47 W
Guaqui, Bol. (gwä'kě)	140	16.42 s	68.47 W
Guara, Sierra de (Mts.), Sp. (sě-ě'r-rä-dě-gwä'rä)	169	42.24 N	0.15 W
Guarabira, Braz. (gwä-rä-bē'rä)	141	6.49 s	35.27 W
Guaranda, Ec. (gwä-rän'dä)	140	1.39 s	78.57 W
Guarapari, Braz. (gwä-rä-pä'rē)	141	20.34 s	40.31 W
Guarapiranga, Represa do (Res.), Braz. (r'ě-prě-sá-dô-gwä'rä-pě-rä'n-gä)	139a	23.45 s	46.44 W
Guarapuava, Braz. (gwä-rä-pwä'vá)	142	25.29 s	51.26 W
Guaratinguetá, Braz. (guä-rä-tIN-gä-tá')	139a	22.49 s	45.10 W
Guarda, Port. (gwär'dä)	168	40.32 N	7.17 W
Guardiato (R.), Sp.	168	38.10 N	5.05 W
Guarena, Sp. (gwä-rā'nyä)	168	38.52 N	6.08 W
Guaribe (R.), Ven. (gwä-rě'bě)	141b	9.48 N	65.17 W
Guárico (State), Ven.	141b	9.42 N	67.25 W
Guárico (R.), Ven.	141b	9.50 N	67.07 W
Guarulhos, Braz. (gwä-rōō'l-yôs)	139a	32.28 s	46.30 W
Guarus, Braz. (gwä'rōōs)	139a	21.44 s	41.19 W
Guasca, Col. (gwäs'kä)	140a	4.52 N	73.52 W
Guasipati, Ven. (gwä-sě-pä'tě)	141	7.26 N	61.57 W
Guastalla, It. (gwäs-täl'lä)	170	44.53 N	10.39 E
Guasti, Ca. (gwäs'tī)	117a	34.04 N	117.35 W
Guatemala, Guat. (guä-tå-mä'lä)	130	14.37 N	90.32 W
Guatemala, N.A.	126	15.45 N	91.45 W
Guatire, Ven. (gwä-tě'rě)	141b	10.28 N	66.34 W
Guaxupé, Braz. (gwä-shōō-pě')	139a	21.18 s	46.42 W
Guayabal, Cuba (gwä-yä-bä'l)	132	20.40 N	77.40 W
Guayalejo (R.), Mex. (gwä-yä-lě'hô)	128	23.24 N	99.09 W
Guayama, P.R. (gwä-yä'mä)	127b	18.00 N	66.08 W
Guayamouc (R.), Hai.	133	19.05 N	72.00 W
Guayaquil, Ec. (gwī-ä-kēl')	140	2.16 s	79.53 W
Guayaquil, Golfo de (G.), Ec. (gôl-fô-dě)	140	3.03 s	82.12 W
Guayare (R.), Col. (gwä-yä'rě)	140	3.35 N	69.28 W
Guaymas, Mex. (gwä'y-mäs)	126	27.49 N	110.58 W
Guayubin, Dom. Rep. (gwä-yōō-bě'n)	133	19.40 N	71.25 W
Guazacapán, Guat. (gwä-zä-kä-pän')	130	14.04 N	90.26 W
Gubakha, Sov. Un. (gōō-bä'kä)	180a	58.53 N	57.35 E
Gubbio, It. (gōōb'byō)	170	43.23 N	12.36 E
Gucheng, China (gōō-chǔŋ)	196	39.09 N	115.43 E
Gudar, Sierra de (Mts.), Sp. (syěr'rä dä gōō'dhär)	169	40.28 N	0.47 W
Gudena (R.), Den.	162	56.20 N	9.47 E
Gudvangen, Nor. (gōōdh'väŋ-gěn)	162	60.52 N	6.45 E
Guebwiller, Fr. (gěb-vě-lâr')	167	47.53 N	7.10 E
Guédi, Mont (Mtn.), Chad	225	12.14 N	18.58 E
Guelma, Alg. (gwěl'mä)	220	36.32 N	7.17 E
Guelph, Can. (gwělf)	93d	43.33 N	80.15 W
Güere (R.), Ven. (gwě'rě)	141b	9.39 N	65.00 W
Guéret, Fr. (gā-rě')	166	46.09 N	1.52 E
Guernsey (I.), Eur. (gûrn'zǐ)	166	49.27 N	2.36 W
Guerrara, Alg. (gěr-rä'rä)	158	32.50 N	4.26 E
Guerrero, Mex. (gěr-rä'rô)	122	26.47 N	99.20 W
Guerrero, Mex.	122	28.20 N	100.24 W
Guerrero (State), Mex.	122	17.45 N	100.15 W
Gueydan, La. (gā'dǎn)	123	30.01 N	92.31 W
Guia de Paçobaíba, Braz. (gwē'ä-dě-pä'kō-bī'bä)	142b	22.42 s	43.10 W
Guiana Highlands (Mts.), Braz.	138	3.20 N	60.00 W
Guichi, China (gwä-chr)	199	30.35 N	117.28 E
Guichicovi (San Juan), Mex. (gwē-chē-kō'vě)	129	16.58 N	95.10 W
Guidonia, It. (gwē-dô'nyä)	169d	42.00 N	12.45 E
Guiglo, Ivory Coast	224	6.33 N	7.29 W
Guignes, Fr. (gēN'yě)	167b	48.38 N	2.48 E
Güigüe, Ven. (gwē'gwě)	141b	10.05 N	67.48 W
Guija, L., Sal. (gē'hä)	130	14.16 N	89.21 W
Guildford, Eng. (gǐl'fěrd)	154b	51.13 N	0.34 W
Guilford, In. (gǐl'fěrd)	111f	39.10 N	84.55 W
Guilin, China (gwä-lǐn)	199	25.18 N	110.22 E
Guimarães, Port. (gē-mä-räNsh')	168	41.27 N	8.22 W
Guinea, Afr. (gǐn'ě)	218	10.48 N	12.28 W
Guinea, G. of, Afr.	218	2.00 N	1.00 E
Guinea-Bissau, Afr. (gǐn'ě)	218	12.00 N	20.00 W
Güines, Cuba (gwē'näs)	132	22.50 N	82.05 W
Guingamp, Fr. (gǎN-gǎN')	166	48.35 N	3.10 W
Güira de Melena, Cuba (gwē'rä dä mä-lā'nä)	132	22.45 N	82.30 W
Güiria, Ven. (gwē-rē'ä)	140	10.43 N	62.16 W
Guir (R.), Mor.-Alg.	158	31.55 N	2.48 W
Guise, Fr. (guěz)	167	49.54 N	3.37 E
Guisisil (Vol.), Nic. (gē-sě-sēl')	130	12.40 N	86.11 W
Guiyang, China (gwä-yäŋ)	199	26.45 N	107.00 E
Guizhou, China (gwä-jō)	197a	22.46 N	113.15 E
Guizhou (Prov.), China	194	27.00 N	106.10 E
Gujarat (State), India	190	22.54 N	79.00 E
Gujānwāla, Pak. (gōōj-rän'va-lá)	190	32.08 N	74.14 E
Gulbarga, India (gōōl-bûr'gà)	191	17.25 N	76.52 E
Gulbene, Sov. Un. (gōōl-bä'ně)	172	57.09 N	26.49 E
Gulfport, Ms. (gǔlf'pōrt)	124	30.24 N	89.05 W
Gulja, see Yining			
Gull Lake, Can.	98	50.10 N	108.25 W
Gull L., Can.	96	52.35 N	114.00 W
Gulu, Ug.	227	2.47 N	32.18 E
Gulyay Pole, Sov. Un.	173	47.39 N	36.12 E
Gumaca, Phil. (gōō-mä-kä')	203a	13.55 N	122.06 E
Gumbeyka R., Sov. Un. (gōōm-běy'ká)	180a	53.20 N	59.42 E
Gumel, Nig.	225	12.39 N	9.22 E
Gummersbach, F.R.G. (gōōm'ěrs-bäk)	164	51.02 N	7.34 E
Gummi, Nig.	225	12.09 N	5.09 E
Gumpoldskirchen, Aus.	155	48.04 N	16.15 E
Guna, India	190	24.44 N	77.17 E
Gunisao (R.), Can. (gǔn-ǐ-sä'ō)	99	53.40 N	97.35 W
Gunisao L., Can.	99	53.54 N	97.58 W
Gunnedah, Austl. (gǔn'ně-dä)	212	31.00 s	150.10 E
Gunnison, Co. (gǔn'ǐ-sǔn)	119	38.33 N	106.56 W
Gunnison, Ut.	119	39.10 N	111.50 W
Gunnison (R.), Col.	119	38.30 N	106.40 W
Guntersville, Al. (gǔn'těrz-vǐl)	124	34.20 N	86.19 W
Guntersville L., Al.	124	34.30 N	86.20 W
Guntramsdorf, Aus.	155e	48.04 N	16.19 E
Guntūr, India (gōōn'tōōr)	191	16.22 N	80.29 E
Guo, China (gwô)	196	33.00 N	117.16 E
Guoyang, China (gwô-yäŋ)	196	33.32 N	116.10 E
Gurdon, Ar. (gûr'dǔn)	123	33.56 N	93.10 W
Gurgucia (R.), Braz. (gōōr-gōō'syä)	141	8.12 s	43.49 W
Gurnee, Il. (gûr'ně)	111a	42.22 N	87.55 W
Gurskøy, (I.), Nor. (gōōrskǔě)	162	62.18 N	5.20 E
Gurupá, Braz. (gōō-rōō-pä')	141	1.28 s	51.32 W
Gurupí, Serra do (Mts.) (sě'r-rä-dô-gōō-rōō-pě')	141	5.32 s	47.02 W
Gurupí (R.), Braz. (gōō-rōō-pě')	141	2.37 s	46.45 W
Guru Sikhar Mt.), India	190	29.42 N	72.50 E
Gur'yev, Sov. Un. (gōōr'yěf)	177	47.10 N	51.50 E
Gur'yevsk, Sov. Un. (gōōr-yǐfsk')	178	54.14 N	86.07 E
Gusau, Nig. (gōō-zä'ōō)	225	12.12 N	6.40 E
Gusev, Sov. Un. (gōō'sěf)	163	54.35 N	22.15 E
Gushi, China	196	32.11 N	115.39 E
Gushiago, Ghana	224	9.55 N	0.12 W
Gusinje, Yugo. (gōō-sēn'yě)	171	42.34 N	19.54 E
Gus'-Khrustal'nyy, Sov. Un. (gōōs-κrōō-stäl'ny)	172	55.39 N	40.41 E
Gustavo A. Madero, Mex. (gōōs-tä'vô-ä-mä-dě'rô)	129a	19.29 N	99.07 W
Güstrow, G.D.R. (gůs'trô)	164	53.48 N	12.12 E
Gütersloh, F.R.G. (gü'těrs-lo)	164	51.54 N	8.22 E
Guthrie, Ok. (gǔth'rǐ)	121	35.52 N	97.26 W
Guthrie Center, Ia.	113	41.41 N	94.33 W
Gutiérrez Zamora, Mex. (gōō-tī-âr'räz zä-mō'rä)	129	20.27 N	97.17 W
Guttenberg, Ia. (gǔt'ěn-bûrg)	113	42.48 N	91.09 W
Guyana, S.A. (gǔy'änä)	138	7.45 N	59.00 W
Guyang, China (gōō-yäŋ)	196	34.56 N	114.57 E
Guye, China (gōō-yü)	196	39.46 N	118.23 E
Guymon, Ok. (gī'mǒn)	120	36.41 N	101.29 W
Guysborough, Can. (gīz'bûr-ô)	103	45.23 N	61.30 W
Guzhen, China (gōō-jǔn)	196	33.20 N	117.18 E
Gvardeysk, Sov. Un. (gvär-děysk')	163	54.39 N	21.11 E
Gwda (R.), Pol.	165	53.21 N	16.52 E
Gwadabawa, Nig.	225	13.20 N	5.15 E
Gwādar, Pak. (gwä'dûr)	192	25.15 N	62.29 E
Gwane, Zaire (gwän)	227	4.43 N	25.50 E
Gwelo, Zimb. (gwä'lô)	222	19.15 s	29.48 E
Gwembe, Zambia	222	16.30 s	27.35 E
Gwinn, Mi. (gwǐn)	113	46.15 N	87.30 W
Gyangzê, China (gyäŋdzú)	194	29.00 N	89.28 E
Gyaring Co. (L.), China (gyä-rǐŋ)	190	30.37 N	88.33 E
Gydan, Khrebet (Kolymskiy), (Mts.), Sov. Un.	179	61.45 N	155.00 E
Gydanskiy, P-Ov (Pen.), Sov. Un.	178	70.42 N	76.03 E
Gympie, Austl. (gǐm'pě)	212	26.20 s	152.50 E
Gyöngyös, Hung. (dyůn'dvůsh)	165	47.47 N	19.55 E
Györ, Hung. (dyůr)	165	47.40 N	17.37 E
Gyōtoku, Jap. (gyō'tô-kōō')	201a	35.42 N	139.56 E
Gypsumville, Can. (jǐp'sǔm'vǐl)	99	51.45 N	98.35 W
Gyula, Hung. (dyōō'lä)	165	46.38 N	21.18 E

H

PLACE (Pronunciation)	PAGE	Lat. °′	Long. °′
Haan, F.R.G. (hän)	167c	51.12 N	7.00 E
Haapamäki, Fin. (häp'ä-mě-kě)	163	62.16 N	24.20 E
Haapsalu, Sov. Un. (häp'sä-lōō)	163	58.56 N	23.33 E
Haar, F.R.G. (här)	155d	48.06 N	11.44 E
Ha 'Arava (Wādī al Jayb), Isr.	189a	30.33 N	35.10 E
Haarlem, Neth. (här'lěm)	155a	52.22 N	4.37 E
Habana (Prov.), Cuba (hä-vä'nä)	132	22.45 N	82.25 W
Habikino, Jap.	201b	34.32 N	135.37 E
Hābra, India	190a	22.49 N	88.38 E
Hachinohe, Jap. (hä'chē-nô'hä)	200	40.29 N	141.40 E
Hachiōji, Jap. (hä'chē-ô'jě)	201	35.39 N	139.18 E
Hackensack, NJ (hǎk'ěn-sǎk)	110a	40.54 N	74.03 W
Haddonfield, NJ (hǎd'ǔn-fěld)	110f	39.53 N	75.02 W
Haddon Heights, NJ (hǎd'ǔn hīts)	110f	39.53 N	75.03 W
Hadejia, Nig. (hä-dā'jä)	225	12.30 N	9.59 E
Hadejia (R.), Nig.	225	12.15 N	9.40 E
Hadera, Isr. (κä-dě'rä)	189a	32.26 N	34.55 E
Haderslev, Den. (hä'dhěrs-lěv)	162	55.17 N	9.28 E
Hadibu, P.D.R. of Yem.	219a	12.40 N	53.50 E
Hadlock, Wa. (hǎd'lŏk)	116a	48.02 N	122.46 W
Hadramawt (Reg.), P.D.R. of Yem.	192	15.22 N	48.40 E
Hadur Shuayb, Jabal (Mtn.), Yemen	192	15.45 N	43.45 E
Haeju, Kor. (hä-jū)	200	38.03 N	125.42 E
Hafnarfjördur, Ice.	156	64.02 N	21.32 W
Hafun, Ras. (C.), Som. (hä-fōōn')	219a	10.15 N	51.35 E
Hageland, Mt. (häge'länd)	115	48.53 N	108.43 W
Hagen, F.R.G. (hä'gěn)	167c	51.21 N	7.29 E
Hagerstown, In. (hä'gěrz-toun)	108	39.55 N	85.10 W
Hagerstown, Md.	109	39.40 N	77.45 W
Hagi, Jap. (hä'gī)	201	34.25 N	131.25 E
Hague, C. de la, Fr. (dě lä äg')	166	49.44 N	1.55 W
Hague, The, see 's Gravenhagen			
Haguenau, Fr. (á-gẽ'nō')	167	48.47 N	7.48 E
Hai'an, China (hī-än)	196	32.35 N	120.25 E
Haibara, Jap. (hä'ē-bä'rä)	201	34.29 N	135.57 E
Haicheng, China (hī-chǔŋ)	198	40.58 N	122.45 E
Haidian, China (hī-dǐěn)	198a	39.59 N	116.17 E
Haifa (Hefa), Isr. (hä'ē-fä)	189a	32.48 N	35.00 E
Haifeng, China (hä'ē-fěŋ)	199	23.00 N	115.20 E
Haifuzhen, China (hä'ē-fōō-jǔn)	196	31.57 N	121.48 E
Haikou, China (hī-kō)	199	20.00 N	110.20 E
Hā'il, Sau. Ar. (hāl)	188	27.30 N	41.47 E
Hailaerh, China	198	49.10 N	118.40 E
Hailey, Id. (hā'lǐ)	115	43.31 N	114.19 W
Haileybury, Can.	101	47.27 N	79.38 W
Haileyville, Ok. (hā'lǐ-vǐl)	121	34.51 N	95.34 W
Hailin, China (hä'ē-lēn)	200	44.31 N	129.11 E
Hailing Dao (I.), China (hī-lǐŋ dou)	199	21.30 N	112.15 E

298 Hailong – Hauterive

PLACE (Pronunciation)	PAGE	Lat. °′	Long. °′
Hailong, China (hī-loŋ)	198	42.32 N	125.52 E
Hailun, China (hä'ē-lo͞on')	198	47.18 N	126.50 E
Hainan Dao (I.), China (hī-nän dou)	199	19.00 N	111.10 E
Hainburg an der Donau, Aus.	155e	48.09 N	16.57 E
Haines, Ak. (hānz)	105	59.10 N	135.38 W
Haines City, Fl.	125a	28.05 N	81.38 W
Haiphong, Viet. (hī'fông')(hä'ēp-hōng)	199	20.52 N	106.40 E
Haiti, N.A. (hā'tĭ)	127	19.00 N	72.15 W
Haizhou Wan (B.), China	198	35.49 N	120.35 E
Hajdúböszormény, Hung. (hôl'do͞o-bû'sûr-män')	165	47.41 N	21.30 E
Hajdúhadház, Hung. (hô'ĭ-do͞o-hôd'häz)	165	47.32 N	21.32 E
Hajdúnánás, Hung. (hô'ĭ-do͞o-nä'näsh)	165	47.52 N	21.27 E
Hajduszoboszló, Hung. (hô'ĭ-do͞o-sô'bôs-lō)	165	47.24 N	21.25 E
Hakodate, Jap. (hä-kō-dä'tā)	200	41.46 N	140.42 E
Haku-San (Mtn.), Jap. (hä'ko͞o-sän')	201	36.11 N	136.45 E
Halachó, Mex. (ä-lä-chō')	129	20.28 N	90.06 W
Halā'ib, Egypt (hä-lä'ēb)	221	22.10 N	36.40 E
Ḩalbā, Leb.	189a	34.33 N	36.03 E
Halbe, G.D.R. (häl'bē)	155b	52.07 N	13.43 E
Halberstadt, G.D.R. (häl'bēr-shtät)	164	51.54 N	11.07 E
Halcon, Mt., Phil. (häl-kōn')	203a	13.19 N	120.55 E
Halden, Nor. (häl'dĕn)	162	59.10 N	11.21 E
Haldensleben, G.D.R.	164	52.18 N	11.23 E
Hale, Eng. (hāl)	154	53.22 N	2.20 W
Haleakala Crater, Hi. (hä'lā-ä'kä-lä)	104a	20.44 N	156.15 W
Haleakala Natl. Park, Hi.	104a	20.46 N	156.00 W
Hales Corners, Wi. (hālz kôr'nērz)	111a	42.56 N	88.03 W
Halesowen, Eng. (hālz'ô-wĕn)	154	52.26 N	2.03 W
Halethorpe, Md. (hāl-thôrp)	110e	39.15 N	76.40 W
Haleyville, Al. (hā'lĭ-vĭl)	124	34.11 N	87.36 W
Half Moon Bay, Ca. (hăf'mo͞on)	116b	37.28 N	122.26 W
Halfway House, S. Afr. (häf-wā hous)	223b	26.00 S	28.08 E
Halfweg, Neth.	155a	52.23 N	4.45 E
Halifax, Can. (hăl'ĭ-fāks)	102	44.39 N	63.36 W
Halifax, Eng.	154	53.44 N	1.52 W
Halifax B., Austl. (hăl'ĭ-făx)	211	18.56 S	147.07 E
Halifax Hbr., Can.	102	44.35 N	63.31 W
Halkett, C., Ak.	105	70.50 N	151.15 W
Hallam Park, Can.	97	52.11 N	118.46 E
Halla San (Mt.), Kor. (häl'lá-sän)	200	33.20 N	126.37 E
Halle, Bel. (häl'lĕ)	155a	50.45 N	4.13 E
Halle, G.D.R.	164	51.30 N	11.59 E
Hallettsville, Tx. (hăl'ĕts-vĭl)	123	29.26 N	96.55 W
Hallock, Mn. (hăl'ŭk)	112	48.46 N	96.57 W
Hall Pen, Can. (hôl)	95	63.14 N	65.40 W
Halls Bayou, Tx.	123a	29.55 N	95.23 W
Hallsberg, Swe. (häls'bĕrgh)	162	59.04 N	15.04 E
Halls Creek, Austl. (hôlz)	210	18.15 S	127.45 E
Halmahera (I.), Indon. (häl-mä-hä'rä)	203	0.45 N	128.45 E
Halmahera, Laut (Halmahera Sea), Indon.	203	1.00 S	129.00 E
Halmstad, Swe. (hälm'städ)	162	56.40 N	12.46 E
Halsafjorden, Nor. (häl'sē fyôrd)	162	63.03 N	8.23 E
Halstead, Ks. (hôl'stĕd)	121	38.02 N	97.36 W
Haltern, F.R.G. (häl'tĕrn)	167c	51.45 N	7.10 E
Haltom City, Tx. (hôl'tŏm)	117c	32.48 N	97.13 W
Halvarenbeek, Neth.	155a	51.29 N	5.10 E
Ḩamāh, Syr. (hä'mä)	159	35.08 N	36.53 E
Hamadān, Iran (hŭ-mŭ-dän')	192	34.45 N	48.07 E
Hamamatsu, Jap. (hä'mä-mät'so͞o)	201	34.41 N	137.43 E
Hamar, Nor. (hä'mär)	162	60.49 N	11.05 E
Hamasaka, Jap. (hä'má-sä'ká)	197	35.57 N	134.27 E
Hamborn, F.R.G. (häm'bōrn)	167c	51.30 N	6.43 E
Hamburg, Ar. (hăm'bûrg)	121	33.15 N	91.49 W
Hamburg, F.R.G. (häm'bo͝orgh)	155c	53.34 N	10.02 E
Hamburg, Ia.	112	40.39 N	95.40 W
Hamburg, NJ	110a	41.09 N	74.35 W
Hamburg, NY	111c	42.44 N	78.51 W
Hamburg, S. Afr. (häm'bûrg)	223c	33.18 S	27.28 E
Hamburg (State), F.R.G.	155c	53.35 N	10.00 E
Hamden, Ct. (hăm'dĕn)	109	41.20 N	72.55 W
Hämeenlinna, Fin. (hĕ'mân-lĭn-ná)	163	61.00 N	24.29 E
Hameln, F.R.G. (hä'mĕln)	164	52.06 N	9.23 E
Hamelwörden, F.R.G. (hä'mĕl-vûr-dĕn)	155c	53.47 N	9.19 E
Hamersley ., Austl. (hăm'ērz-lē)	210	22.15 S	117.50 E
Hamhŭng, Kor. (häm'ho͝ong')	200	39.57 N	127.35 E
Hami (Kumul), China (hä-mē)(kō-mo͞ol')	194	42.58 N	93.14 E
Hamilton, Al.	124	34.09 N	88.01 W
Hamilton, Austl. (hăm'ĭl-tŭn)	212	37.50 S	142.10 E
Hamilton, Can.	93d	43.15 N	79.52 W
Hamilton, Ma.	103a	42.37 N	70.52 W
Hamilton, Mo.	121	39.43 N	93.59 W
Hamilton, Mt.	115	46.15 N	114.09 W
Hamilton, N.Z.	213	37.45 S	175.28 E
Hamilton, Oh.	111f	39.22 N	84.33 W
Hamilton, Tx.	122	31.42 N	98.07 W
Hamilton, L., Ar.	121	34.25 N	93.32 W
Hamilton Hbr., Can.	93d	43.17 N	79.50 W
Hamilton Inlet, Can.	95	54.20 N	56.57 W
Hamina, Fin. (há'mē-ná)	163	60.34 N	27.15 E
Hamlet, NC (hăm'lĕt)	125	35.52 N	79.46 W
Hamlin, Tx. (hăm'lĭn)	120	32.54 N	100.08 W
Hamm, F.R.G. (häm)	167c	51.40 N	7.48 E
Hammanskraal, S. Afr. (hä-mȧns-kräl')	219d	25.24 S	28.17 E
Hamme, Bel.	155a	51.06 N	4.07 E
Hamme-Oste Kanal (Can.), F.R.G. (hä'mē-ōs'tē kä-näl)	155c	53.20 N	8.59 E
Hammerfest, Nor. (hä'mĕr-fĕst)	156	70.38 N	23.59 E
Hammond, In. (hăm'ŭnd)	111a	41.37 N	87.31 W
Hammond, La.	123	30.30 N	90.28 W
Hammond, Or.	116c	46.12 N	123.57 W
Hammonton, NJ (hăm'ŭn-tŭn)	109	39.40 N	74.45 W
Hampden, Me. (hăm'dĕn)	102	44.44 N	68.51 W
Hampshire Downs, Eng. (hămp'shĭr dounz)	160	51.01 N	1.05 W
Hampstead, Md.	110e	39.36 N	76.54 W
Hampstead Norris, Eng. (hămp-stĕd nŏ'rĭs)	154b	51.27 N	1.14 W
Hampton, Can. (hămp'tŭn)	102	45.32 N	65.51 W
Hampton, Ia.	113	42.43 N	93.15 W
Hampton, Va.	110g	37.02 N	76.21 W
Hampton Roads (Inlet), Va.	110g	36.56 N	76.23 W
Ḩamrā, Al- Ḩammadah al- (Plat.), Libya	220	29.39 N	10.53 E
Hamtramck, Mi. (hăm-trăm'ĭk)	111b	42.24 N	83.03 W
Hāmūn-i Māshkel (L.), Pak. (hā-mo͞on'ē māsh-kĕl')	192	28.28 N	64.13 E
Han (R.), China (hän)	199	25.00 N	116.35 E
Han (R.), China	199	31.40 N	112.04 E
Han (R.), Kor.	200	37.10 N	127.40 E
Hana, Hi. (hä'nä)	104a	20.43 N	155.59 W
Hanábana (R.), Cuba (hä-nä-bä'nä)	132	22.30 N	80.55 W
Hanalei B., Hi. (hä-nä-lā'ē)	104a	22.15 N	159.40 W
Hanang (Mtn.), Tan.	227	4.26 S	35.24 E
Hanau, F.R.G. (hä'nou)	164	50.08 N	8.56 E
Hancock, Mi. (hăn'kŏk)	113	47.08 N	88.37 W
Haney, Can. (hā-nē)	97	49.13 N	122.36 W
Hanford, Ca. (hăn'fērd)	118	36.20 N	119.38 W
Hangayn Nuruu (Khangai Mts.), Mong.	194	48.03 N	99.45 E
Hangchou, China (hăng'chō')	199	30.17 N	120.12 E
Hango, Fin. (häŋ'gû)	163	59.49 N	22.56 E
Hangzhou Wan (B.), China (häŋ-jō wän)	199	30.20 N	121.25 E
Handan, China (hän-dän)	196	36.37 N	114.30 E
Hankamer, Tx. (hăn'kȧ-mēr)	123a	29.52 N	94.42 W
Hankinson, ND (häŋ'kĭn-sŭn)	112	46.04 N	96.54 W
Hankou, China (hän-kō)	199	30.42 N	114.22 E
Hann, Mt., Austl. (hän)	210	16.05 S	126.07 E
Hanna, Can. (hăn'ȧ)	97	51.38 N	111.54 W
Hanna, Wy.	115	41.51 N	106.34 W
Hannah, ND	112	48.58 N	98.42 W
Hannibal, Mo. (hăn'ĭ băl)	121	39.42 N	91.22 W
Hannover, F.R.G. (hän-ō'vĕr)	164	52.22 N	9.45 E
Hanö-bukten (B.), Swe.	162	55.54 N	14.55 E
Hanoi, Viet. (hä-noi')	199	21.04 N	105.50 E
Hanover, Can. (hăn'ô-vēr)	108	44.10 N	81.05 W
Hanover, Ma.	103a	42.07 N	70.49 W
Hanover, NH	109	43.45 N	72.15 W
Hanover, Pa.	109	39.50 N	77.00 W
Hanover (I.), Chile	142	51.00 S	74.45 W
Hanshan, China (hän'shän')	196	31.43 N	118.06 E
Hans Lollick (I.), Vir. Is. (U.S.A.) (häns'lôl'ĭk)	127c	18.24 N	64.55 W
Hanson, Ma. (hăn'sŭn)	103a	42.04 N	70.53 W
Hansville, Wa. (hăns'-vĭl)	116a	47.55 N	122.33 W
Hantengri Feng (Mtn.), China (hän-tŭŋ-rē fŭŋ)	194	42.10 N	80.20 E
Hantsport, Can. (hănts'pōrt)	102	45.04 N	64.11 W
Hanyang, China (han'yäng')	199	30.30 N	114.10 E
Hanzhong, China (hän-jôŋ)	198	33.02 N	107.00 E
Haocheng, China (hou-chŭŋ)	196	33.19 N	117.33 E
Haparanda, Swe. (hä-pa-rän'dä)	156	65.54 N	23.57 E
Hapeville, Ga. (hăp'vĭl)	110c	33.39 N	84.25 W
Haql, Sau. Ar.	189a	29.15 N	34.57 E
Har, Laga (R.), Ken.	227	2.15 N	39.30 E
Hara Nuur (L.), Mong.	194	47.47 N	94.01 E
Harar (Prov.), Eth.	221	8.15 N	41.00 E
Hara Usa (L.), Mong.	194	48.00 N	92.32 E
Harbin, China	198	45.40 N	126.30 E
Harbor Beach, Mi. (här'bēr bēch)	108	43.50 N	82.40 W
Harbor Springs, Mi.	108	45.25 N	85.05 W
Harbour Breton, Can. (brĕt'ŭn) (brē-tôɴ')	103	47.29 N	55.48 W
Harbour Grace, Can. (grās)	103	47.32 N	53.13 W
Harburg, F.R.G. (här-bo͝orgh)	155c	53.28 N	9.58 E
Hardangerfjorden (Fd.), Nor. (här-däng'ĕr fyôrd)	162	59.58 N	6.30 E
Hardin, Mt. (här'dĭn)	115	45.44 N	107.36 W
Harding, S. Afr. (här'dĭng)	223c	30.34 S	29.54 E
Harding (L.), Al.-Ga.	124	32.43 N	85.00 W
Hardwār, India (hŭr'dvär)	190	29.56 N	78.06 E
Hardy (R.), Mex. (här'dĭ)	118	32.04 N	115.10 W
Hare B., Can. (hâr)	101	51.18 N	55.50 W
Harer, Eth. (hȧ-rär')	219a	9.43 N	42.10 E
Hargeysa, Som. (här-gā'ē-sȧ)	219a	9.20 N	43.57 E
Harghita, Munții (Mts.), Rom.	165	46.25 N	25.40 E
Harima-Nada (Sea), Jap. (hä'rē-mä nä-dä)	201	34.34 N	134.37 E
Haringvliet (R.), Neth.	155a	51.49 N	4.03 E
Harlan, Ia. (här'lăn)	122	41.40 N	95.10 W
Harlàn, Ky.	124	36.50 N	83.19 W
Harlan Co. Res., Ne.	120	40.03 N	99.51 W
Harlem, Mt. (hár'lĕm)	115	48.33 N	108.50 W
Harlingen, Neth. (här'lĭng-ĕn)	161	53.10 N	5.24 E
Harlingen, Tx.	123	26.12 N	97.42 W
Harlow, Eng. (här'lō)	154b	51.46 N	0.08 E
Harlowton, Mt. (hár'lō-tun)	115	46.26 N	109.50 W
Harmony, In. (här'mô-nĭ)	108	39.35 N	87.00 W
Harney Basin, Or. (här'nĭ)	114	43.26 N	120.19 W
Harney L., Or.	114	43.11 N	119.23 W
Harney Pk., SD	112	43.52 N	103.32 W
Härnosand, Swe. (hĕr-nû-sänd)	162	62.37 N	17.54 E
Haro, Sp. (ä'rō)	168	42.35 N	2.49 W
Haro Str., Can.-U.S. (hă'rō)	116a	48.27 N	123.11 W
Harpenden, Eng. (här'pĕn-d'n)	154b	51.48 N	0.22 W
Harper, Ks. (här'pēr)	120	37.17 N	98.02 W
Harper, Lib.	224	4.25 N	7.43 W
Harper, Wa.	116a	47.31 N	122.32 W
Harpers Ferry, WV (här'pērz)	109	39.20 N	77.45 W
Harricana (R.), Can.	101	50.10 N	78.50 W
Harriman, Tn. (hă'ĭ-mȧn)	124	35.55 N	84.34 W
Harrington, De. (hăr'ĭng-tŭn)	109	38.55 N	75.35 W
Harri Rud (R.), Afg.	192	34.29 N	61.16 E
Harris (I.), Scot. (hăr'ĭs)	160	57.55 N	6.40 W
Harris (L.), Fl.	125a	28.43 N	81.40 W
Harrisburg, Il. (hăr'ĭs-bûrg)	108	37.45 N	88.35 W
Harrisburg, Pa.	109	40.15 N	76.50 W
Harrismith, S. Afr. (hă-rĭs'mĭth)	219d	28.17 S	29.08 E
Harrison, Ar. (hăr'ĭ-sŭn)	121	36.13 N	93.06 W
Harrison, Oh.	111f	39.16 N	84.45 W
Harrison L., Can.	97	49.31 N	121.59 W
Harrisonburg, Va. (hăr'ĭ-sŭn-bûrg)	109	38.30 N	78.50 W
Harrisonville, Mo. (hăr-ĭ-sŭn-vĭl)	121	38.39 N	94.21 W
Harrisville, Ut. (hăr'ĭs-vĭl)	117b	41.17 N	112.00 W
Harrisville, WV	108	39.10 N	81.05 W
Harrodsburg, Ky. (hăr'ŭdz-bûrg)	108	37.45 N	84.50 W
Harrods Cr., Ky. (hăr'ŭdz)	111h	38.24 N	35.33 W
Harrow, Eng. (hăr'ō)	154b	51.34 N	0.21 W
Harsefeld, F.R.G. (här'zē-fĕld')	155c	53.27 N	9.30 E
Harstad, Nor. (här'städh)	156	68.49 N	16.10 E
Hart, Mi. (härt)	108	43.40 N	86.25 W
Hartbeesfontein, S. Afr.	219d	26.46 S	26.25 E
Hartbeespoortdam (L.), S. Afr.	223b	25.47 S	27.43 E
Hartford, Al. (härt'fērd)	124	31.05 N	85.42 W
Hartford, Ar.	121	35.01 N	94.21 W
Hartford, Ct.	109	41.45 N	72.40 W
Hartford, Il.	117e	38.50 N	90.06 W
Hartford, Ky.	124	37.25 N	86.50 W
Hartford, Mi.	108	42.15 N	86.15 W
Hartford, Wi.	113	43.19 N	88.25 W
Hartford City, In.	108	40.35 N	85.25 W
Hartington, Eng. (härt'ĭng-tŭn)	154	53.08 N	1.48 W
Hartington, Ne.	112	42.37 N	97.18 W
Hartland Pt., Eng.	160	51.03 N	4.40 W
Hartlepool, Eng. (här't'l-po͞ol)	160	54.40 N	1.12 W
Hartley, Zimb.	227	18.18 S	30.10 E
Hartley, Ia. (härt'lĭ)	112	43.12 N	95.29 W
Hartley Bay, Can.	96	53.25 N	129.15 W
Hart Mtn., Can. (härt)	99	52.25 N	101.30 W
Hartsbeespoort, S. Afr.	223b	25.44 S	27.51 E
Hartselle, Al. (härt'sĕl)	124	34.24 N	86.55 W
Hartshorne, Ok. (härts'hôrn)	121	34.49 N	95.34 W
Hartsville, SC (härts'vĭl)	125	34.20 N	80.04 W
Hartwell, Ga. (härt'wĕl)	124	34.21 N	82.56 W
Hartwell Res., Ga.	124	34.30 N	83.00 W
Hārua, India	190a	22.36 N	88.40 E
Harvard, Il. (här'vȧrd)	113	42.25 N	88.39 W
Harvard, Ma.	103a	42.30 N	71.35 W
Harvard, Ne.	120	40.36 N	98.08 W
Harvard, Mt., Co.	119	38.55 N	106.20 W
Harvey, Can.	102	45.44 N	64.46 W
Harvey, Il.	111a	41.37 N	87.39 W
Harvey, La.	110d	29.54 N	90.05 W
Harvey, ND	112	47.46 N	99.55 W
Harwich, Eng. (här'wĭch)	161	51.53 N	1.13 E
Haryana (State), India	190	29.00 N	75.45 E
Harz Mts., G.D.R. (härts)	164	51.42 N	10.50 E
Hasā, Wādī al (R.), Jordan	189a	30.55 N	35.50 E
Hashimoto, Jap. (hä'shē-mō'tō)	201	34.19 N	135.37 E
Haskell, Ok. (hăs'kĕl)	121	35.49 N	95.41 W
Haskell, Tx.	120	33.09 N	99.43 W
Haslingden, Eng. (hăz'lĭng dĕn)	154	53.43 N	2.19 W
Hasselt, Bel. (häs'ĕlt)	155a	50.56 N	5.23 E
Hassi Messaoud, Alg.	220	31.17 N	6.13 E
Hasseleholm, Swe. (häs'lĕ-hōlm)	162	56.10 N	13.44 E
Hastings, Eng. (hās'tĭngz)	161	50.52 N	0.28 E
Hastings, Mi.	108	42.40 N	85.20 W
Hastings, Mn.	117g	44.44 N	92.51 W
Hastings, Ne.	120	40.34 N	98.42 W
Hastings, N.Z.	213	39.33 S	176.53 E
Hastings-on-Hudson, NY (ŏn-hŭd'sŭn)	110a	40.59 N	75.53 W
Hatchie (R.), Tn. (hăch'ē)	124	35.28 N	89.14 W
Hațeg, Rom. (kät-säg')	171	45.35 N	22.57 E
Hatfield Broad Oak, Eng. (hăt-fēld brôd ōk)	154	51.50 N	0.14 E
Hatogaya, Jap. (hä'tō-gä-yä)	201a	35.50 N	139.45 E
Hatsukaichi, Jap. (hät'so͞o-kȧ'ē-chē)	201	34.22 N	132.19 E
Hatteras, C., NC (hăt'ēr-ȧs)	125	35.15 N	75.24 W
Hattiesburg, Ms. (hăt'ĭz-bûrg)	124	31.20 N	89.18 W
Hattingen, F.R.G. (hä'tĕn-gĕn)	167c	51.24 N	7.11 E
Hatvan, Hung. (hôt'vôn)	165	47.39 N	19.44 E
Haugesund, Nor. (hou'gē-soon')	162	59.26 N	5.20 E
Haukivesi (L.), Fin. (hou'kē-vē'sē)	163	62.02 N	29.02 E
Haultain (R.), Can.	98	56.15 N	106.35 W
Hauptsrus, S. Afr.	219d	26.35 S	26.16 E
Hauraki, G., N.Z. (hä-o͞o-rä'kē)	213	36.30 S	175.00 E
Haut, Isle au, Me. (hō)	102	44.03 N	68.13 W
Haut Atlas (Mts.), Mor.	158	32.10 N	5.49 W
Hauterive, Can.	102	49.11 N	68.16 W

PRONOUNCING INDEX

Hauula – Hills Creek Res. 299

PLACE (Pronunciation)	PAGE	Lat. °′	Long. °′
Hauula, Hi.	104a	21.37 N	157.45 W
Havana, Il. (hȧ-vă'nȧ)	121	40.17 N	90.02 W
Havana, see La Habana			
Havasu L., Az. (hăv'ȧ-sōō)	119	34.26 N	114.09 W
Havel R., G.D.R. (hä'fĕl)	164	53.09 N	13.10 E
Haverhill, Ma. (hā'vēr-hĭl)	103a	42.46 N	71.05 W
Haverhill, NH	109	44.00 N	72.05 W
Haverstraw, NY (hă'vēr-strô)	110a	41.11 N	73.58 W
Havlíckuv Brod, Czech.	164	49.38 N	15.34 E
Havre-Bouche Boucher, Can. (hăv'rá-bōō-shā')	103	45.42 N	61.30 W
Havre, Mt. (hăv'ēr)	115	48.34 N	109.42 W
Havre de Grace, Md. (hăv'ēr dē grás')	109	39.35 N	76.05 W
Havre-St. Pierre, Can.	103	50.15 N	63.36 W
Haw (R.), NC (hô)	125	36.17 N	79.46 W
Hawaii (State), U.S.	106c	20.00 N	157.40 W
Hawaii (I.), Hi (häw wī'ē)	104b	19.50 N	157.15 W
Hawaiian Is., U.S. (hä-wī'ăn)	106c	22.00 N	158.00 W
Hawaii Volcanoes Natl. Pk., Hi.	104a	19.30 N	155.25 W
Hawarden, Ia. (hā'wár-dĕn)	112	43.00 N	96.28 W
Hawi, Hi. (hä'wē)	104a	20.16 N	155.48 W
Hawick, Scot. (hô'ĭk)	160	55.25 N	2.55 W
Hawke B., N.Z. (hôk)	213	39.17 S	177.20 E
Hawker, Austl. (hô'kēr)	212	31.58 S	138.12 E
Hawkesbury, Can. (hôks'bĕr-ĭ)	109	45.35 N	74.35 W
Hawkinsville, Ga. (hô'kĭnz-vĭl)	124	32.15 N	83.30 W
Hawks Nest Pt., Ba.	133	24.05 N	75.30 W
Hawley, Mn. (hô'lĭ)	112	46.52 N	96.18 W
Haworth, Eng. (hā'wûrth)	154	53.50 N	1.57 W
Hawtah, Sau. Ar.	192	15.58 N	48.26 E
Hawthorne, Ca. (hô'thôrn)	117a	33.55 N	118.22 W
Hawthorne, Nv.	118	38.33 N	118.39 W
Haxtun, Co. (hăks'tŭn)	120	40.39 N	102.38 W
Hay (R.), Austl. (hā)	210	23.00 S	136.45 E
Hay (R.), Can.	94	60.21 N	117.14 W
Hayama, Jap. (hä-yä'mä)	201a	35.16 N	139.35 E
Hayashi, Jap. (hä-yä'shē)	201a	35.13 N	139.38 E
Hayden, Az. (hā'dĕn)	119	33.00 N	110.50 W
Hayes, Mt., Ak. (hāz)	105	63.32 N	146.40 W
Hayes (R.), Can.	109	55.25 N	93.55 W
Haynesville, La. (hānz'vĭl)	123	32.55 N	93.08 W
Hayrabolu, Tur.	171	41.14 N	27.05 E
Hay River, Can.	104	60.50 N	115.53 W
Hays, Ks. (hāz)	120	38.51 N	99.20 W
Haysī, Wādī al (R.), Egypt	189	29.24 N	34.32 E
Haystack Mtn., Wa. (hā-stăk')	116a	48.26 N	122.07 W
Hayward, Ca. (hā'wērd)	116b	37.40 N	122.06 W
Hayward, Wi.	113	46.01 N	91.31 W
Hazard, Ky. (hăz'ărd)	124	37.13 N	83.10 W
Hazelhurst, Ga. (hā'z'l-hûrst)	125	31.50 N	82.36 W
Hazel Park, Mi.	111b	42.28 N	83.06 W
Hazelton, Can. (hā'z'l-tŭn)	96	55.15 N	127.40 W
Hazelton Mts., Can.	96	55.00 N	128.00 W
Hazelhurst, Ms.	124	31.52 N	90.23 W
Hazleton, Pa.	109	41.00 N	76.00 W
Headland, Al. (hĕd'lănd)	124	31.22 N	85.20 W
Healdsburg, Ca. (hēldz'bûrg)	118	38.37 N	122.52 W
Healdton, Ok. (hēld'tŭn)	121	34.13 N	97.28 W
Heanor, Eng. (hēn'ŏr)	154	53.01 N	1.22 W
Heard I., Ind. O. (hûrd)	228	53.10 S	74.35 E
Hearne, Tx. (hûrn)	123	30.53 N	96.35 W
Hearst, Can. (hûrst)	95	49.36 N	83.40 W
Heart (R.), ND (härt)	112	46.46 N	102.34 W
Heart Lake Ind. Res., Can.	97	55.02 N	111.30 W
Heart's Content, Can. (härts kŏn'tĕnt)	103	47.52 N	53.22 W
Heath Pte., Can. (hēth)	103	49.06 N	61.45 W
Heavener, Ok. (hēv'nēr)	121	34.52 N	94.36 W
Hebbronville, Tx. (hē'brŭn-vĭl)	122	27.18 N	98.40 W
Hebei (Prov.), China (hŭ-bā)	195	39.15 N	115.40 E
Heber, Ut. (hē'bēr)	119	40.30 N	111.25 W
Heber Springs, Ar.	121	35.28 N	91.59 W
Hebgen Res., Mt. (hĕb'gĕn)	115	44.47 N	111.38 W
Hebrides, Sea of, Scot.	160	57.00 N	7.00 W
Hebron, Can. (hĕb'rŭn)	95	58.11 N	62.56 W
Hebron, In.	111a	41.19 N	87.13 W
Hebron, Ky.	111f	39.04 N	84.43 W
Hebron, Ne.	121	40.11 N	97.36 W
Hebron, ND	112	46.54 N	102.04 W
Hebron, see Al Khalīl			
Heby, Swe. (hĭ'bü)	162	59.56 N	16.48 E
Hecate Str., Can. (hĕk'ȧ-tē)	96	53.00 N	131.00 W
Hecelchakán, Mex. (ā-sĕl-chä-kän')	129	20.10 N	90.09 W
Hechi, China (hŭ-chr)	199	24.50 N	108.18 E
Hechuan, China (hŭ-chyuän)	199	30.00 N	106.20 E
Hecla I., Can.	99	51.08 N	96.45 W
Hedemora, Swe. (hĭ-dĕ-mō'rä)	162	60.16 N	15.55 E
Hedon, Eng. (hĕ-dŭn)	154	53.44 N	0.12 W
Heemstede, Neth.	155a	52.20 N	4.36 E
Heerlen, Neth.	161	50.55 N	5.58 E
Hefa, see Haifa			
Hefei, China (hŭ-fā)	196	31.51 N	117.15 E
Heflin, Al. (hĕf'lĭn)	124	33.40 N	85.33 W
Heide, F.R.G. (hī'dĕ)	164	54.13 N	9.06 E
Heidelberg, Austl. (hī'dĕl-bûrg)	207	37.45 S	145.04 E
Heidelberg, F.R.G. (hīdĕl-bĕrgh)	164	49.24 N	8.43 E
Heidenheim, F.R.G. (hī'dĕn-hīm)	164	48.41 N	10.09 E
Heilbron, S. Afr. (hĭl'brōn)	219d	27.17 S	27.58 E
Heilbronn, F.R.G. (hīl'brōn)	164	49.09 N	9.16 E
Heiligenhaus, F.R.G. (hī'lē-gĕn-houz)	167c	51.19 N	6.58 E
Heiligenstadt, G.D.R. (hī'lē-gĕn-shtät)	164	51.21 N	10.10 E
Heilong (R.), China-Sov. Un. (hā-loŋ)	198	49.38 N	127.25 E
Heilongjiang, China (hā-lôŋ-jyäŋ)	195	46.36 N	128.07 E
Heinola, Fin. (hā-nō'lȧ)	163	61.13 N	26.03 E
Heinsberg, F.R.G. (hīnz'bĕrgh)	167c	51.04 N	6.07 E
Heist-op-den-Berg, Bel.	155a	51.05 N	4.14 E
Hejaz, see Al Hijāz			
Hejian, China (hŭ-jyĕn)	196	38.28 N	116.05 E
Hel, Pol. (hāl)	165	54.37 N	18.53 E
Helagsfjället (Mtn.), Swe.	162	62.54 N	12.24 E
Helan Shan (Mts.), China (hŭ-län shän)	194	38.02 N	105.20 E
Helena, Ar. (hē-lē'nȧ)	121	34.33 N	90.35 W
Helena, Mt. (hĕ-lē'nȧ)	115	46.35 N	112.01 W
Helensburgh, Austl. (hĕl'ĕnz-bŭr-ô)	207b	34.11 S	150.59 E
Helensburgh, Scot.	160	56.01 N	4.53 W
Helgoland I., F.R.G. (hĕl'gō-länd)	164	54.13 N	7.30 E
Helka (Vol.), Ice. (hĕl'kȧ)	156	63.53 N	19.37 W
Hellier, Ky. (hĕl'yēr)	125	37.16 N	82.27 W
Hellín, Sp. (ĕl-yén')	168	38.30 N	1.40 W
Helmand (R.), Afg. (hĕl'mŭnd)	192	31.00 N	63.48 E
Helmond, Neth. (hĕl'mōnt) (ĕl'môN')	161	51.35 N	5.04 E
Helmstedt, F.R.G. (hĕlm'shtĕt)	164	52.14 N	11.03 E
Helotes, Tx. (hē'lōts)	117d	29.35 N	98.41 W
Helper, Ut. (hĕlp'ēr)	119	39.40 N	110.55 W
Helsingborg, Swe. (hĕl'sĭng-bôrgh)	162	56.04 N	12.40 E
Helsingfors, see Helsinki			
Helsingør, Den. (hĕl-sĭng-ûr')	162	56.03 N	12.33 E
Helsinki (Helsingfors), Fin. (hĕl'sĕn-kē) (hĕl'sĭng-fôrs')	163	60.10 N	24.53 E
Hemel Hempstead, Eng. (hĕm'ĕl hĕmp'stĕd)	154b	51.43 N	0.29 W
Hemer, F.R.G.	167c	51.32 N	7.46 E
Hemet, Ca. (hĕm'ĕt)	117a	33.45 N	116.57 W
Hemingford, Ne. (hĕm'ĭng-fērd)	112	42.21 N	103.30 W
Hemphill, Tx. (hĕmp'hĭl)	123	31.20 N	93.48 W
Hempstead, NY (hĕmp'stĕd)	110a	40.42 N	73.37 W
Hempstead, Tx.	123	30.07 N	96.05 W
Hemse, Swe. (hĕm'sē)	162	57.15 N	18.25 E
Hemsön (I.), Swe.	162	62.43 N	18.22 E
Henan (Prov.), China (hŭ-nän)	195	33.58 N	112.33 E
Henares (R.), Sp. (ā-nä'rās)	168	40.50 N	2.55 W
Henderson, Ky. (hĕn'dēr-sŭn)	108	37.50 N	87.30 W
Henderson, Nv.	118	36.09 N	115.04 W
Henderson, NC	125	36.18 N	78.24 W
Henderson, Tn.	124	35.25 N	88.40 W
Henderson, Tx.	123	32.09 N	94.48 W
Hendersonville, NC (hĕn'dēr-sŭn-vĭl)	125	35.17 N	82.28 W
Hendon, Eng. (hĕn'dŭn)	154b	51.34 N	0.13 W
Hendrina, S. Afr. (hĕn-drē'nȧ)	219d	26.10 S	29.44 E
Hengch'un, Taiwan (hĕng'chŭn')	199	22.00 N	120.42 E
Hengelo, Neth. (hĕngē-lō)	161	52.20 N	6.45 E
Hengshan, China (hĕng'shän')	199	27.20 N	112.40 E
Hengshui, China (hĕng'shōō-ē')	196	37.43 N	115.42 E
Heng Xian, China (hŭŋ shyĕn)	199	22.40 N	104.20 E
Hengyang, China	199	26.58 N	112.30 E
Henley on Thames, Eng. (hĕn'lē ŏn tĕmz)	154b	51.31 N	0.54 W
Henlopen, C., De. (hĕn-lō'pĕn)	109	38.45 N	75.05 W
Hennebont, Fr. (ĕn-bôN')	166	47.47 N	3.16 W
Hennenman, S. Afr.	219d	27.59 S	27.03 E
Hennessey, Ok. (hĕn'ĕ-sĭ)	120	36.04 N	97.53 W
Hennigsdorf, G.D.R. (hĕ'nĕngz-dōrf))	155b	52.39 N	13.12 E
Hennops (R.), S. Afr. (hĕn'ŏps)	223b	25.51 S	27.57 E
Hennopsrivier, S. Afr.	223b	25.50 S	27.59 E
Henrietta, Ok. (hĕn-rĭ-ĕt'ȧ)	121	35.25 N	95.58 W
Henrietta, Tx. (hen-rĭ-ĕ'tȧ)	120	33.47 N	98.11 W
Henrietta Maria, C., Can. (hĕn-rĭ-ĕt'ȧ)	95	55.10 N	82.20 W
Henry Mts., Ut. (hĕn'rĭ)	119	38.55 N	110.45 W
Henteyn Nuruu (Mts.), Sov. Un.	198	49.40 N	111.00 E
Henzada, Bur.	202	17.38 N	95.28 E
Heppner, Or. (hĕp'nēr)	114	45.21 N	119.33 W
Hepu, China (hŭ-pōō)	199	21.28 N	109.10 E
Herāt, Afr. (hĕ-rät')	192	34.28 N	62.13 E
Hercegovina (Reg.), Yugo. (hĕr-tsĕ-gô'vē-nȧ)	171	43.23 N	17.52 E
Hercules, Can.	93g	53.27 N	113.20 W
Herdecke, F.R.G. (hĕr'dĕ-kĕ)	167c	51.24 N	7.26 E
Heredia, C.R. (ā-rā'dhē-ä)	131	10.04 N	84.06 W
Hereford, Eng. (hĕrĕ'fērd)	160	52.05 N	2.44 W
Hereford, Md.	110e	39.35 N	76.42 W
Hereford, Tx. (hĕr'ē-fērd)	120	34.47 N	102.25 W
Hereford and Worcester (Co.), Eng.	154	52.24 N	2.15 W
Herencia, Sp. (å-rān'thē-ä)	168	39.23 N	3.22 W
Herentals, Bel.	155a	51.10 N	4.51 E
Herford, F.R.G. (hĕr'fôrt)	164	52.06 N	8.42 E
Herington, Ks. (hĕr'ĭng-tŭn)	121	38.41 N	96.57 W
Herisau, Switz. (hā'rē-zou)	164	47.23 N	9.18 E
Herk-de-Stad, Bel.	155a	50.56 N	5.13 E
Herkimer, NY (hûr'kĭ-mēr)	109	43.05 N	75.00 W
Hermann, Mo. (hûr'măn)	121	38.41 N	91.27 W
Hermansville, Mi. (hûr'măns-vĭl)	108	45.40 N	87.35 W
Hermantown, Mn. (hēr'măn-toun)	117h	46.46 N	92.12 W
Hermanusdorings, S. Afr.	219d	24.08 S	27.46 E
Herminie, Pa. (hûr-mĭ'nē)	111e	40.16 N	79.45 W
Hermitage B., Can. (hûr'mĭ-tĕj)	103	47.35 N	56.05 W
Hermit Is., Pap. N. Gui. (hûr'mĭt)	203	1.48 S	144.55 E
Hermosa Beach, Ca. (hĕr-mō'sȧ)	117a	33.51 N	118.24 W
Hermosillo, Mex. (ĕr-mô-sē'l-yō)	126	29.00 N	110.57 W
Herndon, Va. (hĕrn'don)	110e	38.58 N	77.22 W
Herne, F.R.G. (hĕr'nĕ)	167c	51.32 N	7.13 E
Herning, Den. (hĕr'nĭng)	162	56.08 N	8.55 E
Heron (L.), Mn. (hĕr'ŭn)	112	43.42 N	95.23 W
Heron Lake, Mn.	112	43.48 N	95.20 W
Herrero, Punta (pt.), Mex. (pōō'n-tä-ĕr-rĕ'rô)	130	19.18 N	87.24 W
Herrin, Il. (hĕr'ĭn)	108	37.50 N	89.00 W
Herschel, S. Afr. (hĕr'-shĕl)	223c	30.37 S	27.12 E
Herscher, Il. (hĕr'shēr)	111a	41.03 N	88.06 W
Herstal, Bel. (hĕr'stäl)	161	50.42 N	5.32 E
Hertford, NC (hûrt'fērd)	125	36.10 N	76.30 W
Hertfordshire (Co.), Eng.	154	51.46 N	0.05 W
Hertzberg, G.D.R. (hĕrtz'bĕrgh)	155b	52.54 N	12.58 E
Hervás, Sp.	168	40.16 N	5.51 W
Herzliyya, Isr.	189a	32.10 N	34.49 E
Hessen, (State), F.R.G. (hĕs'ĕn)	164	50.42 N	9.00 E
Hetch Hetchy Aqueduct, Ca. (hĕtch hĕt'chĭ ăk'wē-dŭkt)	118	37.27 N	120.54 W
Hettinger, ND (hĕt'ĭn-jēr)	112	45.58 N	102.36 W
Heuningspruit, S. Afr.	219d	27.28 S	27.26 E
He Xian, China (hŭ shyĕn)	199	24.20 N	111.28 E
He Xian, China	196	31.44 N	118.20 E
Heyang, China (hŭ-yäŋ)	198	35.18 N	110.18 E
Heystekrand, S. Afr.	219d	25.16 S	27.14 E
Heyuan, China (hŭ-yüän)	199	23.48 N	114.45 E
Heywood, Eng. (hā'wŏŏd)	154	53.36 N	2.12 W
Heze, China (hŭ-dzŭ)	196	35.13 N	115.28 E
Hialeah, Fl. (hī-ȧ-lē'ăh)	125a	25.49 N	80.18 W
Hiawatha, Ks. (hī-ȧ-wô'thȧ)	121	39.50 N	95.33 W
Hiawatha, Ut.	119	39.25 N	111.05 W
Hibbing, Mn. (hĭb'ĭng)	113	47.26 N	92.58 W
Hickman, Ky. (hĭk'măn)	124	34.33 N	89.10 W
Hickory, NC (hĭk'ô-rĭ)	125	35.43 N	81.21 W
Hicksville, NY (hĭks'vĭl)	110a	40.47 N	73.25 W
Hicksville, OH	108	41.15 N	84.45 W
Hico, Tx. (hī'kō)	122	32.00 N	98.02 W
Hidalgo, Mex. (ē-dhäl'gō)	118	24.14 N	99.25 W
Hidalgo, Mex.	122	27.49 N	99.53 W
Hidalgo (State), Mex.	126	20.45 N	99.30 W
Hidalgo del Parral, Mex. (ē-dä'l-gō-dĕl-pär-rá'l)	122	26.55 N	105.40 W
Hidalgo Yalalag, Mex. (ē-dhäl'gō-yä-lä-läg)	129	17.12 N	96.11 W
Hiedelberg, S. Afr.	219d	26.32 S	28.22 E
Hierro I., Can.Is. (yĕ'r-rô)	220	27.37 N	18.29 W
Higashimurayama, Jap.	201a	35.46 N	139.28 E
Higashiōsaka, Jap.	201b	34.40 N	135.44 E
Higgins (L.), Mi. (hĭg'ĭnz)	108	44.20 N	84.45 W
Higginsville, Mo. (hĭg'ĭnz-vĭl)	121	39.05 N	93.44 W
High (I.), Mi.	108	45.45 N	85.45 W
High Bluff, Can.	93f	50.01 N	98.08 W
Highborne Cay, Ba. (hībôrn kē)	132	24.45 N	76.50 W
Highgrove, Ca. (hī'grōv)	117a	34.01 N	117.20 W
High Island, Tx.	123a	29.34 N	94.24 W
Highland, Ca. (hī'lănd)	117a	34.08 N	117.13 W
Highland, Il.	121	38.44 N	89.41 W
Highland, In.	111a	41.33 N	87.28 W
Highland, Mi.	111b	42.38 N	83.37 W
Highland Park, Il.	111a	42.11 N	87.47 W
Highland Park, Mi.	111b	42.24 N	83.06 W
Highland Park, NJ	110a	40.30 N	74.25 W
Highland Park, Tx.	117c	32.49 N	96.48 W
Highlands, NJ (hī-lăndz)	110a	40.24 N	73.59 W
Highlands, Tx.	123a	29.49 N	95.01 W
Highmore, SD (hī'mōr)	112	44.30 N	99.26 W
High Ongar, Eng. (on'gēr)	154b	51.43 N	0.15 E
High Pk., Phil.	203a	51.38 N	120.05 E
High Point, NC	125	35.55 N	80.00 W
High Prairie, Can.	97	55.26 N	116.29 W
High Ridge, Mo.	113e	38.27 N	90.32 W
High River, Can.	97	50.35 N	113.52 W
Highrock (R.), NC (hī'-rŏk)	125	35.40 N	80.15 W
High Springs, Fl.	125	29.48 N	82.38 W
High Tatra Mts., Czech.-Pol.	165	49.15 N	19.40 E
Hightstown, NJ (hīts-toun)	110a	40.16 N	74.32 W
High Wycombe, Eng. (wĭ-kŭm)	154b	51.36 N	0.45 W
Higuero, Pta (Pt.), P.R.	127b	18.21 N	67.11 W
Higuerote, Ven. (ē-gē-rô'tĕ)	141b	10.29 N	66.06 W
Higüey, Dom. Rep. (ē-gwĕ'y)	133	18.40 N	68.45 W
Hiiumaa (D'Ago), Sov. Un. (hē'ōōm-ô)	163	58.47 N	22.05 E
Hikone, Jap. (hē'kô-nĕ)	201	35.15 N	136.15 E
Hildburghausen, G.D.R. (hĭld'bōōrg hou-zĕn)	164	50.26 N	10.45 E
Hilden, F.R.G. (hĕl'dĕn)	167c	51.10 N	6.56 E
Hildesheim, F.R.G. (hĭl'dĕs-hīm)	164	52.08 N	9.56 E
Hillaby, Mt., Barb. (hĭl'ȧ-bĭ)	131b	13.15 N	59.35 W
Hill City, Ks. (hĭl)	120	39.22 N	99.54 W
Hill City, Mn.	113	46.58 N	93.38 W
Hillegersberg, Neth.	155a	51.57 N	4.29 E
Hillerød, Den. (hĕ'lĕ-rûdh)	162	55.56 N	12.17 E
Hillsboro, IL. (hĭlz'bŭr-ō)	121	39.09 N	89.28 W
Hillsboro, Ks.	121	38.22 N	97.11 W
Hillsboro, NH	109	43.05 N	71.55 W
Hillsboro, ND	112	47.23 N	97.05 W
Hillsboro, Oh.	108	39.10 N	83.40 W
Hillsboro, Or.	116c	45.31 N	122.59 W
Hillsboro, Tx.	123	32.01 N	97.06 W
Hillsboro, Wi.	113	43.39 N	90.20 W
Hillsburgh, Can. (hĭlz'bûrg)	93d	43.48 N	80.09 W
Hills Creek Res., Or.	114	43.41 N	122.26 W

ng-sing; ŋ-baŋk; N-nasalized n; nŏd; cŏmmit; ōld; ôbey; ôrder; oi-boil; fōōd; fŏŏt; ou-out; s-soft; sh-dish; th-thin; pūre; ûnite; ûrn; stŭd; circŭs; ü-as in French tu; '-indeterminate vowel.

PLACE (Pronunciation)	PAGE	Lat. °′	Long. °′
Hillsdale, Mi. (hĭls-dāl)	118	41.55 N	84.35 W
Hilo, Hi. (hē'lō)	104a	19.44 N	155.01 W
Hilversum, Neth. (hĭl'vẽr-sŭm)	155a	52.13 N	5.10 E
Himachal Pradesh (State), India	190	36.03 N	77.41 E
Himalaya Mts., Asia (hĭ-mä'lȧ-yȧ)	193	29.30 N	85.02 E
Himeji, Jap. (hē'mȧ-jē)	201	34.50 N	134.42 E
Himmelpforten, F.R.G. (hē'mĕl-pfōr-tĕn)	155c	53.37 N	9.19 E
Hinche, Hai. (hēn'chȧ) (äɴsh)	133	19.10 N	72.05 W
Hinchinbrook (I.), Austl. (hĭn-chĭn-brŏŏk)	211	18.23 S	146.57 W
Hinckley, Eng. (hĭnk'lĭ)	154	52.32 N	1.21 W
Hindley, Eng. (hĭnd'lĭ)	154	53.32 N	2.35 W
Hindu Kush (Mts.), Asia (hĭn'dōō kōōsh')	193	35.15 N	68.44 E
Hindupur, India (hĭn'dōō-pōōr)	191	13.52 N	77.34 E
Hingham, Ma. (hĭng'ăm)	103a	42.14 N	70.53 W
Hinkley, Oh. (hĭnk'-lĭ)	111d	41.14 N	81.45 W
Hinojosa del Duque, Sp. (ē-nō-kō'sä)	168	38.30 N	5.09 W
Hinsdale, Il. (hĭnz'dāl)	111a	41.48 N	87.56 W
Hinton, Can. (hĭn'tŭn)	97	53.25 N	117.34 W
Hinton, WV (hĭn'tŭn)	108	37.40 N	80.55 W
Hirado (I.), Jap. (hē'rä-dō)	201	33.19 N	129.18 E
Hirakata, Jap. (hē'rä-kä'tä)	201b	34.49 N	135.40 E
Hiratsuka, Jap. (hē-rät-sōō'kȧ)	201	35.20 N	139.19 E
Hirgis Nuur (L.), Mong.	194	49.18 N	94.21 E
Hirosaki, Jap. (hē'rō-sä'kē)	200	40.31 N	140.38 E
Hirose, Jap. (hē'rō-sā)	201	35.20 N	133.11 E
Hiroshima, Jap. (hē-rō-shē'mȧ)	201	34.22 N	132.25 E
Hirson, Fr. (ēr-sôɴ')	166	49.54 N	4.00 E
Hisar, India	195	29.15 N	75.47 E
Hispaniola (I.), N.A. (hĭ'spăn-ĭ-ō-lȧ)	127	17.30 N	73.15 W
Hitachi, Jap. (hē-tä'chē)	200	36.42 N	140.47 E
Hitchcock, Tx. (hĭch'kŏk)	123a	29.21 N	95.01 W
Hitdorf, F.R.G. (hēt'dōrf)	167c	51.04 N	6.56 E
Hitoyoshi, Jap. (hē'tô-yō'shē)	201	32.13 N	130.45 E
Hitra (I.), Nor. (hĭträ)	156	63.34 N	7.37 E
Hittefeld, F.R.G. (hē'tĕ-fĕld)	155c	53.23 N	9.59 E
Hiwasa, Jap. (hē'wȧ-sä)	201	33.44 N	134.31 E
Hiwassee (R.), Tn. (hī-wôs'sē)	124	35.10 N	84.35 W
Hjälmaren (L.), Swe.	162	59.07 N	16.05 E
Hjo, Swe. (yō)	162	58.19 N	14.11 E
Hjørring, Den. (jûr'ĭng)	162	57.27 N	9.59 E
Hlohovec, Czech. (hlō'ho-vĕts)	165	48.24 N	17.49 E
Hobart, Austl. (hō'bȧrt)	212	43.00 S	147.30 E
Hobart, In.	111a	41.31 N	87.15 W
Hobart, Ok.	120	35.02 N	99.06 W
Hobart, Wa.	116a	47.25 N	121.58 W
Hobbs, NM (hŏbs)	120	32.41 N	104.04 W
Hobdo Gol (R.), Mong.	194	49.06 N	91.16 E
Hoboken, Bel. (hō'bō-kĕn)	155a	51.11 N	4.20 E
Hoboken, NJ	110a	40.43 N	74.03 W
Hobro, Den. (hô-brô')	162	56.38 N	9.47 E
Hobson, Va. (hŏb'sŭn)	110g	36.54 N	76.31 W
Hobson's B., Austl. (hŏb'sŭnz)	207a	37.54 S	144.45 E
Ho Chi Minh City (Saigon), Viet.	202	10.46 N	106.34 E
Hockinson, Wa. (hŏk'ĭn-sŭn)	116c	45.44 N	122.29 W
Hoctún, Mex. (ôk-tōō'n)	130a	20.52 N	89.10 W
Hodgenville, Ky. (hŏj'ĕn-vĭl)	108	37.35 N	85.45 W
Hodges Hill (Mtn.), Can. (hŏj'ĕz)	101	49.04 N	55.53 W
Hódmezövásárhely, Hung. (hōd'mĕ-zû-vô'shôr-hĕl-y')	165	46.24 N	20.21 E
Hodna, Chott el (L.), Alg.	157	35.20 N	3.27 E
Hodonin, Czech. (hē'dô-nén)	165	48.50 N	17.06 E
Hoegaarden, Bel.	155a	50.46 N	4.55 E
Hoek van Holland, Neth.	155a	51.59 N	4.05 E
Hoeryŏng, Kor. (hwĕr'yŭng)	200	42.28 N	129.39 E
Hof, F.R.G. (hōf)	164	50.19 N	11.55 E
Hofsjökull (Gl.), Ice. (hôfs'yü'kōōl)	156	64.55 N	18.40 W
Hog (I.), Mi.	108	45.50 N	85.20 W
Hogansville, Ga. (hō'gănz-vĭl)	124	33.10 N	84.54 W
Hog Cay (I.), Ba.	133	23.35 N	75.30 W
Hogsty Rf., Ba.	133	21.45 N	73.50 W
Hohenbrunn, F.R.G. (hō'hĕn-brōōn)	155d	48.03 N	11.42 E
Hohenlimburg, F.R.G. (hō'hĕn lĕm'bōōrg)	167c	51.20 N	7.35 E
Hohen Neuendorf, G.D.R. (hō'hĕn noi'ĕn-dōrf)	155b	52.40 N	13.22 E
Hohe Tauern (Mts.), Aus. (hō'ĕ tou'ĕrn)	164	47.11 N	12.12 E
Hohhot, China (hŭ-hōō-tŭ)	198	41.05 N	111.50 E
Hohoe, Ghana	224	7.09 N	0.28 E
Hohokus, NJ (hō-hō-kŭs)	110a	41.01 N	74.08 W
Hoisington, Ks. (hoi'zĭng-tŭn)	120	38.30 N	98.46 W
Hojo, Jap. (hō'jô)	201	33.58 N	132.50 E
Hokitika, N.Z. (hō-kĭ-tē'kä)	213	42.43 S	170.59 E
Hokkaido (I.), Jap. (hôk'kĭ-dō)	200	43.30 N	142.45 E
Holbaek, Den. (hôl'bĕk)	162	55.42 N	11.40 E
Holbox, Mex. (ôl-bŏ'x)	130a	21.33 N	87.19 W
Holbox, Isla (I.), Mex. (ē's-lä-ôl-bŏ'x)	130a	21.40 N	87.21 W
Holbrook, Az. (hōl'brŏŏk)	119	34.55 N	110.15 W
Holbrook, Ma.	103a	42.10 N	71.01 W
Holden, Ma. (hōl'dĕn)	103a	42.21 N	71.51 W
Holden, Mo.	121	38.42 N	94.00 W
Holden, WV	108	37.45 N	82.05 W
Holdenville, Ok. (hōl'dĕn-vĭl)	121	35.05 N	96.25 W
Holdrege, Ne. (hōl'drĕj)	120	40.25 N	99.28 W
Holguín, Cuba (ôl-gēn')	133	20.55 N	76.15 W
Holguín (Prov.), Cuba	133	20.40 N	76.15 W
Holidaysburg, Pa. (hŏl'ĭ-dāz-bûrg)	109	40.30 N	78.30 W
Hollabrunn, Aus.	164	48.33 N	16.04 E
Holland, Mi. (hŏl'ănd)	108	42.45 N	86.10 W
Holland Diep (Chan.), Neth.	155a	51.43 N	4.25 E
Hollenstedt, F.R.G. (hō'lĕn-shtĕt)	155c	53.22 N	9.43 E
Hollis, NH (hŏl'ĭs)	103a	42.30 N	71.29 W
Hollis, Ok.	120	34.39 N	99.56 W
Hollister, Ca. (hŏl'ĭs-tẽr)	118	36.50 N	121.25 W
Holliston, Ma. (hŏl'ĭs-tŭn)	103a	42.12 N	71.25 W
Holly, Mi. (hŏl'ĭ)	108	42.45 N	83.30 W
Holly, Wa.	116a	47.34 N	122.58 W
Holly Springs, Ms. (hŏl'ĭ sprĭngz)	124	34.45 N	89.28 W
Hollywood, Ca. (hŏl'ē-wŏŏd)	117a	34.06 N	118.20 W
Hollywood, Fl.	125a	26.00 N	80.11 W
Holmes Rfs., Austl. (hōmz)	211	16.33 S	148.43 E
Holmestrand, Nor. (hôl'mĕ-strän)	162	59.29 N	10.17 E
Holmsbu, Nor. (hôlms'bōō)	162	59.36 N	10.26 E
Holmsjön (L.), Swe.	162	62.23 N	15.43 E
Holstebro, Den. (hôl'stĕ-brô)	162	56.22 N	8.39 E
Holston (R.), Tn. (hōl'stŭn)	124	36.02 N	83.42 W
Holt, Eng. (hōlt)	154	53.05 N	2.53 W
Holton, Ks. (hōl'tŭn)	121	39.27 N	95.43 W
Holy Cross, Ak. (hō'lĭ krôs)	105	62.10 N	159.40 W
Holyhead, Wales (hŏl'ē-hĕd)	160	53.48 N	4.45 W
Holy I., Eng.	160	55.43 N	1.48 W
Holy I., Wales (hō'lĭ)	160	53.45 N	4.45 W
Holyoke, Co. (hōl'yōk)	120	40.36 N	102.18 W
Holyoke, Ma.	109	42.10 N	72.40 W
Homano, Jap. (hō-mä'nō)	201a	35.33 N	140.08 E
Homberg, F.R.G. (hōm'bĕrgh)	167c	51.27 N	6.42 E
Hombori, Mali	224	15.17 N	1.42 W
Home Gardens, Ca. (hōm gär'd'nz)	117a	33.53 N	117.32 W
Homeland, Ca. (hōm'lănd)	117a	33.44 N	117.07 W
Homer, Ak. (hō'mẽr)	105	59.42 N	151.30 W
Homer, La.	123	32.46 N	93.05 W
Homestead, Fl. (hōm'stĕd)	125a	25.27 N	80.28 W
Homestead, Mi.	117k	46.20 N	84.07 W
Homestead, Pa.	111e	40.29 N	79.55 W
Homestead Natl. Mon. of America, Ne.	122	40.16 N	96.51 W
Homewood, Al. (hōm'wŏŏd)	110h	33.28 N	86.48 W
Homewood, Il.	111a	41.34 N	87.40 W
Hominy, Ok. (hŏm'ĭ-nĭ)	122	36.25 N	96.24 W
Homochiho (R.), Ms. (hō-mō-chĭt'ō)	124	31.23 N	91.15 W
Homs, Syr. (hōms)	159	34.42 N	36.52 E
Honda, Col. (hŏn'dȧ)	140a	5.13 N	74.45 W
Honda, Bahía (B.), Cuba (bä-ē'ä-ô'n-dä)	132	23.10 N	83.20 W
Hondo, Tx.	122	29.20 N	99.08 W
Hondo, Rio (R.), Belize (hon-dō')	130a	18.16 N	88.32 W
Hondo (R.), NM	120	33.22 N	105.06 W
Honduras, N.A. (hŏn-dōō'rȧs)	126	14.30 N	88.00 W
Honduras, Gulf of, N.A.	126	16.30 N	87.30 W
Honea Path, SC (hŭn'ĭ păth)	125	34.25 N	82.16 W
Hönefoss, Nor. (hē'nē-fôs)	162	60.10 N	10.15 E
Honesdale, Pa. (hōnz'dāl)	109	41.30 N	75.15 W
Honey (R.), Ca. (hŭn'ĭ)	118	40.11 N	120.34 W
Honey Grove, Tx. (hŭn'ĭ grōv)	121	33.35 N	95.54 W
Honfleur, Can. (ôɴ-flûr')	93b	46.39 N	70.53 W
Honfleur, Fr. (ôɴ-flûr')	166	49.26 N	0.13 E
Hon Gay, Viet.	199	20.58 N	107.10 E
Hongshui (R.), China (hôŋ-shwā)	199	25.00 N	107.22 E
Honguedo, Détroit d' (Str.), Can.	102	49.08 N	63.45 W
Hongze Hu (L.), China (hôŋ-dzŭ hōō)	196	33.17 N	118.37 E
Honiara, Sol. Is.	211	9.15 S	159.45 E
Honiton, Eng. (hŏn'ĭ-tŏn)	160	50.49 N	3.10 W
Hong Kong, Asia (hŏng' kŏng')	195	21.45 N	115.00 E
Honolulu, Hi. (hŏn-ō-lōō'lōō)	104a	21.18 N	157.50 W
Honomu, Hi. (hŏn'ō-mōō)	104a	19.50 N	155.04 W
Honshū (I.), Jap. (hŏn'shōō)	200	36.50 N	135.20 E
Hood, Mt., Or.	114	45.20 N	121.43 W
Hood Can., Wa. (hŏŏd)	116a	47.45 N	122.45 W
Hood River, Or.	114	45.42 N	121.30 W
Hoodsport, Wa. (hŏŏdz'pōrt)	116a	47.25 N	123.09 W
Hoogly (R.), India (hōōg'lĭ)	190	21.35 N	87.50 E
Hoogstraten, Bel.	155a	51.24 N	4.46 E
Hooker, Ok. (hŏŏk'ẽr)	120	36.49 N	101.13 W
Hool, Mex. (ōō'l)	130a	19.32 N	90.22 W
Hoonah, Ak. (hōō'nä)	105	58.05 N	135.25 W
Hoopa Valley Ind. Res., Ca. (hōō'pȧ)	114	41.18 N	123.35 W
Hooper, Ne. (hŏŏp'ẽr)	121	41.37 N	96.31 W
Hooper, Ut.	117b	41.10 N	112.08 W
Hooper Bay, Ak.	105	61.32 N	166.02 W
Hoopeston, Il. (hōōps'tŭn)	108	40.35 N	87.40 W
Hoosick Falls, NY (hōō'sĭk)	109	42.55 N	73.15 W
Hoover Dam, Nv. (hōō'vẽr)	118	36.00 N	115.06 W
Hopatcong, L., NJ (hō-păt'kong)	110a	40.57 N	74.38 W
Hope, Ak. (hōp)	105	60.54 N	149.48 W
Hope, Ar.	121	33.41 N	93.35 W
Hope, Can.	97	49.23 N	121.26 W
Hope, ND	112	47.17 N	97.45 W
Hope, Ben (Mtn.), Scot. (bĕn hōp)	160	58.25 N	4.25 W
Hopedale, Can. (hōp'dāl)	95	55.26 N	60.11 W
Hopedale, Ma. (hōp'dāl)	103a	42.08 N	71.33 W
Hopelchén, Mex. (o-pĕl-chĕ'n)	130a	19.47 N	89.51 W
Hopes Advance, C., Can. (hōps ăd-vans')	95	61.05 N	69.35 W
Hopetoun, Austl. (hōp'toun)	210	33.50 S	120.15 E
Hopewell, Va. (hōp'wĕl)	125	37.14 N	77.15 W
Hopetown, S. Afr. (hōp'toun)	222	29.35 S	24.10 E
Hopi Ind. Res., Az. (hō'pē)	119	36.20 N	110.30 W
Hopkins, Mn. (hŏp'kĭns)	117g	44.55 N	93.24 W
Hopkinsville, Ky. (hŏp'kĭns-vĭl)	124	36.50 N	87.28 W
Hopkinton, Ma. (hŏp'kĭn-tŭn)	103a	42.14 N	71.31 W
Hoquiam, Wa. (hō'kwĭ-ăm)	114	47.00 N	123.53 W
Horby, Swe. (hûr'bü)	162	55.50 N	13.41 E
Horconcitos, Pan. (ŏr-kôn-sē'-tôs)	131	8.18 N	82.11 W
Hordio, Som.	219a	10.43 N	51.05 E
Horgen, Switz. (hôr'gĕn)	164	47.16 N	8.35 E
Horicon, Wi. (hŏr'ĭ-kŏn)	113	43.26 N	88.40 W
Hormuz, Str. of, Asia (hôr'mŭz')	192	26.30 N	56.30 E
Horn, C., see Hornos, Cabo de			
Horn (Is.), Austl. (hôrn)	211	10.30 S	143.30 E
Hornavan (L.), Swe.	156	65.54 N	16.17 E
Horneburg, F.R.G. (hôr'nĕ-bŏŏrgh)	155c	53.30 N	9.35 E
Hornell, NY (hôr-nĕl')	109	42.10 N	77.40 W
Horn Mts., Can.	94	62.12 N	120.29 W
Hornos, C. de (Horn, C.), Chile (kȧ'-bô-dĕ-ŏ'r-nôs) (kā'p-hŏr'n)	142	56.00 S	67.00 W
Hornsby, Austl. (hôrnz'bĭ)	207b	33.43 S	151.06 E
Horqueta, Par. (ŏr-kĕ'tä)	142	23.20 S	57.00 W
Horse Cr., Co. (hôrs)	120	38.49 N	103.48 W
Horse Cr., Wy.	112	41.33 N	104.39 W
Horse Is., Can.	103	50.11 N	55.45 W
Horsens, Den. (hôrs'ĕns)	162	55.50 N	9.49 E
Horseshoe B., Can. (hôrs-shōō)	116d	49.23 N	123.16 W
Horsforth, Eng. (hôrs'fŭrth)	154	53.50 N	1.38 W
Horsham, Austl. (hôr'shăm) (hôrs'ăm)	212	36.42 S	142.17 E
Horst, F.R.G. (hôrst)	155c	53.49 N	9.37 E
Horten, Nor. (hôr'tĕn)	162	59.26 N	10.27 E
Horton, Ks. (hôr'tŭn)	122	39.38 N	95.32 W
Horton (R.), Ak. (hôr'tŭn)	105	68.38 N	122.00 W
Horwich, Eng. (hŏr'ĭch)	154	53.36 N	2.33 W
Hoséré Vokré (Mtn.), Cam.	225	8.20 N	13.15 E
Hososhima, Jap. (hō'sô-shē'mä)	201	32.25 N	131.40 E
Hoste (I.), Chile (ôs'tä)	142	55.20 S	70.45 W
Hostotipaquillo, Mex. (ôs-tō'tĭ-pä-kēl'yô)	128	21.09 N	104.05 W
Hota, Jap. (hō'tä)	201a	35.08 N	139.50 E
Hotan, China (hwô-tän)	194	37.11 N	79.50 E
Hotan (R.), China	194	39.09 N	81.08 E
Hoto Mayor, Dom. Rep. (ô-tô-mä-yŏ'r)	133	18.45 N	69.10 W
Hot Springs, Ak. (hŏt sprĭngs)	105	65.00 N	150.20 W
Hot Springs, Ar.	121	34.29 N	93.02 W
Hot Springs, SD	112	43.28 N	103.32 W
Hot Springs, Va.	109	38.00 N	79.55 W
Hot Springs Natl. Park, Ar.	121	34.30 N	93.00 W
Hotte, Massif de la (Mts.), Hai.	133	18.25 N	74.00 W
Hotville, Ca. (hŏt'vĭl)	118	32.50 N	115.24 W
Houdan, Fr. (ōō-däɴ')	167b	48.47 N	1.36 E
Houghton, Mi. (hō'tŭn)	113	47.06 N	88.36 W
Houghton, (L.), Mi.	108	44.20 N	84.45 W
Houilles, Fr. (ōō-yĕs')	167b	48.55 N	2.11 E
Houjie, China (hwô-jyĕ)	197a	22.58 N	113.39 E
Houlton, Me. (hōl'tŭn)	102	46.07 N	67.50 W
Houma, La. (hōō'mȧ)	123	29.36 N	90.43 W
Houndé, Upper Volta	224	11.30 N	3.31 W
Housatonic (R.), Ct.-Ma. (hōō-sȧ-tŏn'ĭk)	109	41.50 N	73.25 W
House Springs, Mo. (hous sprĭngs)	117e	38.24 N	90.34 W
Houston, Ms. (hūs'tŭn)	124	33.53 N	89.00 W
Houston, Tx.	123a	29.46 N	95.21 W
Houston Ship Chan., Tx.	123a	29.38 N	94.57 W
Houtbaai, S. Afr.	222a	34.03 S	18.22 E
Houtman Rocks (Is.), Austl. (hout'măn)	210	28.15 S	112.45 E
Houzhen, China (hwô-jŭn)	196	36.59 N	118.59 E
Hove, Eng. (hōv)	160	50.50 N	0.09 W
Hovenweep Natl. Mon., Co.-Ut. (hō'v'n-wēp)	119	37.27 N	108.50 W
Howard, Ks. (hou'ȧrd)	121	37.27 N	96.10 W
Howard, SD	112	44.01 N	97.31 W
Howden, Eng. (hou'dĕn)	154	53.44 N	0.52 W
Howe C., Austl. (hou)	212	37.30 S	150.40 E
Howell, Mi. (hou'ĕl)	108	42.40 N	84.00 W
Howe Sd., Can.	96	49.22 N	123.18 W
Howick, Can. (hou'ĭk)	93a	45.11 N	73.51 W
Howick, S. Afr.	223c	29.29 S	30.16 E
Howland (I.), Oceania (hou'lănd)	204	1.00 N	176.00 W
Howrah, India (hou'rä)	190b	22.33 N	88.20 E
Howse Pk., Can.	97	51.30 N	116.40 W
Howson Pk., Can.	96	54.25 N	127.45 W
Hoxie, Ar. (kŏh'sĭ)	121	36.03 N	91.00 W
Hoy (I.), Scot. (hoi)	160a	58.53 N	3.10 W
Hōya, Jap.	201a	35.45 N	139.35 E
Hoylake, Eng. (hoi-lāk')	154	53.23 N	3.11 W
Hoyo, Sierra del (Mts.), Sp. (sē-ĕ'r-rä-dĕl-ō'yō)	169a	40.39 N	3.56 W
Hradec Králové, Czech. (hrȧ'dĕts krä'lô-vā)	164	50.14 N	15.50 E
Hranice, Czech. (hrän'yĕ-tsĕ)	165	49.33 N	17.45 E
Hrinová, Czech. (hrēn'yô-vä)	165	48.36 N	19.32 E
Hron R., Czech.	165	48.22 N	18.42 E
Hrubieszów, Pol. (hrōō-byä'shōōf)	165	50.48 N	23.54 E
Hrvatska (Croatia) (Reg.), Yugo. (hr-väts'kä)	170	45.24 N	15.18 E
Hsawnhsup, Bur.	194	24.29 N	94.45 E
Hsiaoku Ho (R.), China (sĭou'gōō hū)	196	36.29 N	120.06 E
Hsich'ang, China	199	26.50 N	102.25 E
Hsiliao (R.), China	198	43.23 N	121.40 E
Hsinchiang (Mts.), China	190	41.52 N	81.20 E
Hsinchu, Taiwan (hsĭn'chōō')	199	24.48 N	121.00 E
Hsinkao Shan (Mtn.), Taiwan	199	23.38 N	121.05 E
Huacho, Peru (wä'chō)	140	11.13 S	77.29 W

PRONOUNCING INDEX

Huadian – Ignacio 301

PLACE (Pronunciation)	PAGE	Lat. °′	Long. °′
Huadian, China (hwä-dĭĕn)	198	42.38 N	126.45 E
Huai (R.), China (hwī)	195	32.07 N	114.38 E
Huai'an, China (hwī-än)	196	33.31 N	119.11 E
Huailai, China	198	40.20 N	115.45 E
Huailin, China (hwī-lĭn)	196	31.27 N	117.36 E
Huainan, China	196	32.38 N	117.02 E
Huaiyang, China (ho͞oäī'yang)	196	33.45 N	114.54 E
Huaiyuan, China (hwī-yụ̈än)	196	32.53 N	117.13 E
Huajicori, Mex. (wä-jḗ-kō'rḗ)	128	22.41 N	105.24 W
Huajuapan de León, Mex. (wäj-wä'päm dā lā-ón')	129	17.46 N	97.45 W
Hualapai Ind. Res., Az. (wäl'apī)	119	35.41 N	113.38 W
Hualapai Mts., Az.	119	34.53 N	113.54 W
Hualien, Taiwan (hwä'lyĕn')	199	23.58 N	121.58 E
Huallaga (R.), Peru (wäl-yä'gä)	140	8.12 S	76.34 W
Huamachuco, Peru (wä-mä-cho͞o'kō)	140	7.52 S	78.11 W
Huamantla, Mex. (wä-män'tlȧ)	129	19.18 N	97.54 W
Huambo (Nova Lisboa), Ang.	226	12.44 S	15.47 E
Huamuxtitlán, Mex. (wä-mo͞os-tē-tlän')	128	17.49 N	98.38 W
Huan (R.), China (hụ̈än)	194	36.45 N	106.30 E
Huancavelica, Peru (wän'kä-vā-lē'kä)	140	12.47 S	75.02 W
Huancayo, Peru (wän-kä'yṓ)	140	12.09 S	75.04 W
Huanchaca, Bol. (wän-chä'kä)	140	20.09 S	66.40 W
Huang (Yellow River), China (hụ̈äŋ)	195	35.06 N	113.39 E
Huang, Old Beds of the (Yellow) (R.), China	195	40.28 N	106.34 E
Huangchuan, China (hụ̈äŋ-chụ̈än)	196	32.07 N	115.01 E
Huang He, Old Course of the (R.), China (hụ̈äŋ-hŭ)	196	34.28 N	116.59 E
Huanghua, China (hụ̈äŋ-hwä)	196	38.28 N	117.18 E
Huanghuadian, China (hụ̈äŋ-hwä-dĭĕn)	198a	39.22 N	116.53 E
Huangli, China (ho͞oäɴg'lē)	196	31.39 N	119.42 E
Huangpu, China (hụ̈äŋ-po͞o)	197a	22.44 N	113.20 E
Huangpu (R.), China	197b	30.56 N	121.16 E
Huangqiao, China (hụ̈än-chyou)	196	32.15 N	120.13 E
Huang Xian, China (hụ̈äŋ shyĕn)	196	37.39 N	120.32 E
Huangyuan, China (hụ̈äŋ-yụ̈än)	194	37.00 N	101.01 E
Huanren, China (hụ̈än-rŭn)	198	41.10 N	125.30 E
Huánuco, Peru (wä-no͞o'kṓ)	140	9.50 S	76.17 W
Huánuni, Bol. (wä-no͞o'nē)	140	18.11 S	66.43 W
Huapí, Montañas de (Mts.), Nic. (môn-tä'n-yäs-dĕ-wȧ'pē')	131	12.35 N	84.43 W
Huaquechula, Mex. (wä-kĕ-cho͞o'lä)	128	18.44 N	98.37 W
Huaral, Peru (wä-rä'l)	140	11.28 S	77.11 W
Huarás, Peru (o͞oä'rȧ's)	140	9.32 S	77.29 W
Huascarán, Nevs. (Pk.), Peru (wäs-kä-rän')	140	9.05 S	77.50 W
Huasco, Chile (wäs'kō)	142	28.32 S	71.16 W
Huatla de Jiménez, Mex. (wȧ'tlä-dĕ-ĸē-mĕ'nĕz)	129	18.08 N	96.49 W
Huatlatlauch, Mex. (wä'tlä-tlä-o͞o'ch)	129	18.40 N	98.04 W
Huatusco, Mex. (wä-to͞os'kṓ)	129	19.09 N	96.57 W
Huauchinango, Mex. (wä-o͞o-chḗ-näŋ'gṓ)	128	20.09 N	98.03 W
Huaunta, Nic. (wä-o͞o'n-tä)	131	13.30 N	83.32 W
Huaunta, Laguna (L.), Nic. (lä-go͞o'nä-wä-o͞o'n-tä)	131	13.35 N	83.46 W
Huautla, Mex. (wä-o͞o'tlä)	128	21.04 N	98.13 W
Hua Xian, China (hwä shyĕn)	196	35.34 N	114.32 E
Huaynamota, Rió de (R.), Mex. (rḗ'ō-dĕ-wäy-nä-mŏ'tä)	128	22.10 N	104.36 W
Huazolotitlán (Santa María), **Mex.** (wäzṓ-lṓ-tlē-tlän')	129	16.18 N	97.55 W
Hubbard, NH (hŭb'ĕrd)	103a	42.53 N	71.12 W
Hubbard, Tx.	123	31.53 N	96.46 W
Hubbard (L.), Mi.	108	44.45 N	83.30 W
Hubbard Creek Res., Tx.	122	32.50 N	98.55 W
Hubei (Prov.), China (ho͞o-bā)	195	31.20 N	111.58 E
Hubli, India (ho͞o'blḗ)	191	15.25 N	75.09 E
Hückeswagen, F.R.G. (hü'kĕs-vä'gĕn)	167c	51.09 N	7.20 E
Hucknall, Eng. (hŭk'năl)	154	53.02 N	1.12 W
Huddersfield, Eng. (hŭd'ērz-fēld)	154	53.39 N	1.47 W
Hudiksvall, Swe. (ho͞o'dĭks-väl)	162	61.44 N	17.05 E
Hudson, Can. (hŭd'sŭn)	93a	45.26 N	74.08 W
Hudson, Ma.	103a	42.24 N	71.34 W
Hudson, Mi.	108	41.50 N	84.15 W
Hudson, NY	109	42.15 N	73.45 W
Hudson, Oh.	111d	41.15 N	81.27 W
Hudson, Wi.	117g	44.59 N	92.45 W
Hudson Bay, Can.	99	52.52 N	102.25 W
Hudson B., Can.	95	60.15 N	85.30 W
Hudson Falls, NY	109	43.20 N	73.30 W
Hudson Heights, Can.	93a	45.28 N	74.09 W
Hudson R., NY	108	41.55 N	73.55 W
Hudson Str., Can.	95	63.25 N	74.05 W
Hue, Viet. (ü-ā')	199	16.28 N	107.42 E
Huebra (R.), Sp. (wĕ'brä)	168	40.44 N	6.17 W
Huehuetenango, Guat. (wā-wḗ-tḗ-näŋ'gṓ)	130	15.19 N	91.26 W
Huejotzingo, Mex. (wā-hṓ-tzĭŋ'gō)	128	19.09 N	98.24 W
Huejúcar, Mex. (wā-ho͞o'kär)	128	22.26 N	103.12 W
Huejuquilla el Alto, Mex. (wā-ho͞o-kēl'yä ĕl äl'tō)	128	22.42 N	102.54 W
Huejutla, Mex. (wā-ho͞o'tlä)	128	21.08 N	98.26 W
Huelma, Sp. (wĕl'mä)	168	37.39 N	3.36 W
Huelva, Sp. (wĕl'vä)	168	37.16 N	6.58 W
Huércal-Overa, Sp. (wĕr-käl' ō-vā'rä)	168	37.12 N	1.58 W
Huerfano (R.), Co. (wâr'fȧ-nō)	120	37.41 N	105.13 W
Huésca, Sp. (wĕs-kä)	169	42.07 N	0.25 W
Huéscar, Sp. (wās'kär)	168	37.50 N	2.34 W
Huetamo de Múñez, Mex. (wḗ-tä'mō dā-mo͞on'yĕz)	128	18.34 N	100.53 W
Huete, Sp. (wā'tḗ)	168	40.09 N	2.42 W
Hueycatenango, Mex. (wĕy-kȧ-tĕ-nă'n-gô)	128	17.31 N	99.10 W
Hueytlalpan, Mex. (wā'ī-tlăl'păn)	129	20.03 N	97.41 W
Hueytown, Al.	110h	33.28 N	86.59 W
Huffman, Al. (hŭf'măn)	110h	33.36 N	86.42 W
Hugh Butler (L.), Ne.	120	40.21 N	100.40 W
Hughenden, Austl. (hū'ĕn-dĕn)	211	20.58 S	144.13 E
Hughes, Austl. (hūz)	210	30.45 S	129.30 E
Hughesville, Md.	110e	38.32 N	76.48 W
Hugo, Mn. (hū'gō)	117g	45.10 N	93.00 W
Hugo, Ok.	121	34.01 N	95.32 W
Hugoton, Ks. (hū'gō-tŭn)	120	37.10 N	101.28 W
Hugou, China (ho͞o-gō)	196	33.22 N	117.07 E
Huichapan, Mex. (wē-chä-pän')	128	20.22 N	99.39 W
Huila (Dept.), Col. (wē'lä)	140a	3.10 N	75.20 W
Huila, Nevado de (Pk.), Col. (nĕ-vä-dṓ-de-wē'lä)	140a	2.59 N	76.01 W
Huilai, China	199	23.02 N	116.18 E
Huili, China	199	26.48 N	102.20 E
Huimanguillo, Mex. (wē-män-gēl'yō)	129	17.50 N	93.16 W
Huimin, China (ho͞oĭ mīn)	196	37.29 N	117.32 E
Huitzilac, Mex. (o͞oē't-zē-lä'k)	129a	19.01 N	99.16 W
Huitzitzilingo, Mex. (wē-tzē-tzē-lḗ'n-go)	128	21.11 N	98.42 W
Huitzuco, Mex. (wḗ-tzo͞o'kō)	128	18.16 N	99.20 W
Huixquilucan, Mex. (o͞oē'x-kē-lo͞o-kä'n)	129a	19.21 N	99.22 W
Huixtla, Mex. (wēs'tlä)	129	15.12 N	92.28 W
Huiyang, China	199	23.05 N	114.25 E
Hukou, China (ho͞o-kō)	199	29.58 N	116.20 E
Hulan, China (ho͞o'län')	198	45.58 N	126.32 E
Hulan (R.), China	198	42.20 N	126.30 E
Hulin, China (ho͞o'lĭn')	200	45.45 N	133.25 E
Hull, Can. (hŭl)	93c	45.26 N	75.43 W
Hull, Ma.	103a	42.18 N	70.54 W
Hull (R.), Eng.	154	53.47 N	0.20 W
Hulst, Neth. (ho͝olst)	155a	51.17 N	4.01 E
Huludao, China (ho͞o-lo͞o-dou)	198	40.40 N	122.55 E
Hulun Nur (L.), China (ho͞o-lo͞on no͞or)	198	48.50 N	116.45 E
Ḥulwān, Egypt (hĕl'wän)	219b	29.51 N	31.20 E
Humacao, P.R. (o͞o-mä-kä'ō)	127b	18.09 N	65.49 W
Humaitá, Braz. (o͞o-mä-ē-tä')	128	7.37 S	62.58 W
Humaitá, Par.	140	27.08 S	58.18 W
Humansdorp, S. Afr. (ho͞o'mäns-dôrp)	222	33.57 S	24.45 E
Humbe, Ang. (ho͝om'bâ)	222	16.50 S	14.55 E
Humber (L.), Eng. (hŭm'bēr)	160	53.38 N	0.40 W
Humber (R.), Can.	93d	43.53 N	79.40 W
Humbermouth, Can. (hŭm'bēr-mŭth)	103	48.58 N	57.55 W
Humberside (Co.), Eng.	154	53.47 N	0.36 W
Humble, Tx. (hŭm'b'l)	123	29.58 N	95.15 W
Humboldt, Can. (hŭm'bōlt)	98	52.12 N	105.07 W
Humboldt, Ia.	113	42.43 N	94.11 W
Humboldt, Ks.	121	37.48 N	95.26 W
Humboldt, Ne.	121	40.10 N	95.57 W
Humboldt (R.), U.S.	106	40.30 N	116.50 W
Humboldt B., Ca.	114	40.48 N	124.25 W
Humboldt R., East Fork, Nv.	114	40.59 N	115.21 W
Humboldt R., North Fork, Nv.	114	41.25 N	115.45 W
Humbolt, Tn.	124	35.47 N	88.55 W
Humbolt Ra., Nv.	118	40.12 N	118.16 W
Humbolt Salt Marsh, Nv.	118	39.49 N	117.41 W
Humbolt Sink, Nv.	118	39.58 N	118.54 W
Humen, China (ho͞o-mŭn)	197a	22.49 N	113.39 E
Humphreys Pk., Az. (hŭm'frĭs)	119	35.20 N	111.40 W
Humpolec, Czech. (ho͝om'pō-lĕts)	164	49.33 N	15.21 E
Humuya R., Hond. (o͞o-mo͞o'yä)	130	14.38 N	87.36 W
Hunaflói (B.), Ice. (ho͞o'nä-flṓ'ĭ)	156	65.41 N	20.44 W
Hunan (Prov.), China (ho͞o'nän')	195	28.08 N	111.25 E
Hunchun, China (ho͝on-chụ̈n)	195	42.53 N	130.34 E
Hunedoara, Rom. (ĸo͞o'nĕd-wä'rȧ)	171	45.45 N	22.54 E
Hungary, Eur. (hŭŋ'gȧ-rĭ)	152	46.44 N	17.55 E
Hungerford, Austl. (hŭn'gēr-fērd)	212	28.50 S	144.32 E
Hungry Horse Res., Mt. (hŭŋ'gȧ-rĭ hôrs)	115	48.11 N	113.30 W
Hunsrück (Mts.), F.G.R. (ho͝ons'rûk)	164	49.43 N	7.12 E
Hunte R., F.R.G. (ho͝on'tē)	164	52.45 N	8.26 E
Hunter Is., Austl. (hŭn-tēr)	211	40.33 S	143.36 E
Huntingburg, In. (hŭnt'ĭng-bûrg)	108	38.15 N	86.55 W
Huntingdon, Can. (hŭnt'ĭng-dŭn)	109	45.10 N	74.05 W
Huntingdon, Can.	116d	49.00 N	122.16 W
Huntingdon, Tn.	124	36.00 N	88.23 W
Huntington, In.	108	40.55 N	85.30 W
Huntington, Pa.	109	40.30 N	78.00 W
Huntington, WV	108	38.25 N	82.25 W
Huntington Beach, Ca.	117a	33.39 N	118.00 W
Huntington Park, Ca.	117a	33.59 N	118.14 W
Huntington Station, NY	110a	40.51 N	73.25 W
Huntley, Mt.	115	45.54 N	108.01 W
Huntsville, Al. (hŭnts'vĭl)	124	34.44 N	86.36 W
Huntsville, Can.	109	45.20 N	79.15 W
Huntsville, Mo.	121	39.24 N	92.32 W
Huntsville, Tx.	123	30.44 N	95.34 W
Huntsville, Ut.	117b	41.16 N	111.46 W
Hunucmá, Mex. (ho͞o-no͞ok-mä')	129	21.01 N	89.54 W
Huolu, China (ho͝oŭ lo͞o)	196	38.05 N	114.20 E
Huon G., Pap. N. Gui.	203	7.15 S	147.45 E
Huoqiu, China (hwṓ-chyṓ)	196	32.19 N	116.17 E
Huoshan, China (hwṓ-shän)	199	31.30 N	116.25 E
Ḥuraydin, Wādī (R.), Egypt	189a	30.55 N	34.12 E
Hurd, C., Can. (hûrd)	108	45.15 N	81.45 W
Hurley, Wi. (hûr'lĭ)	113	46.26 N	90.11 W
Hurlingham, Arg. (o͞o'r-lēn-gäm)	142a	34.20 S	58.38 W
Huron, Oh. (hū'rŏn)	108	41.20 N	82.35 W
Huron, SD	112	44.22 N	98.15 W
Huron, L., U. S.-Can. (hū'rŏn)	107	45.15 N	82.40 W
Huron Mts., Mi. (hū'rŏn)	113	46.47 N	87.52 W
Huron R., Mi.	111b	42.12 N	83.26 W
Hurricane, Ak. (hŭr'ĭ-kān)	105	63.00 N	149.30 W
Hurricane, Ut.	119	37.10 N	113.20 W
Hurricane Flats (Shoal), Ba. (hŭ-rĭ-kăn flăts)	132	23.35 N	78,30 W
Húsavik, Ice.	156	66.00 N	17.10 W
Huşi, Rom. (ko͝osh')	173	46.52 N	28.04 E
Huskvarna, Swe. (ho͝osk-vär'nȧ)	162	57.48 N	14.16 E
Hurst, Tx.	117c	32.48 N	97.12 W
Husum, F.R.G. (ho͞o'zo͝om)	164	54.29 N	9.04 E
Hutchins, Tx. (hŭch'ĭnz)	117c	32.38 N	96.43 W
Hutchinson, Ks. (hŭch'ĭn-sŭn)	120	38.02 N	97.56 W
Hutchinson, Mn.	113	44.53 N	94.23 W
Hut'o Ho (R.), China (ho͞o'tō'hō')	198	38.10 N	114.00 E
Huy, Bel. (û-ē') (hû'ḗ)	161	50.33 N	5.14 E
Hvannadalshnúkur (Mtn.), Ice.	156	64.09 N	16.46 W
Hvar (I.), Yugo. (ĸhvär)	170	43.08 N	16.28 E
Hwangju, Kor. (hwäng'jo͞o')	200	38.39 N	125.49 E
Hyattsville, Md. (hī'ăt's-vil)	110e	38.57 N	76.58 W
Hydaburg, Ak. (hī-dă'bûrg)	105	55.12 N	132.49 W
Hyde, Eng. (hīd)	154	53.27 N	2.05 W
Hyderābād, India (hī-dēr-ȧ́-băd')	191	17.29 N	79.28 E
Hyderābād, Pak.	190	25.29 N	68.28 E
Hyderabad (State), India	191	23.29 N	76.50 E
Hyéres, Fr. (ē-ắr')	167	43.09 N	6.08 E
Hyéres, Îles d' (Is.), Fr. (ēl'dyâr')	167	42.57 N	6.17 E
Hyesanjin, Kor. (hyĕ'sän-jĭn')	200	41.11 N	128.12 E
Hymera, In. (hī-mē'rȧ)	108	39.10 N	87.20 W
Hyndman Pk., Id. (hīnd'măn)	115	43.38 N	114.04 W
Hyōgo (Pref.), Jap. (hĭyō'gō)	201b	34.54 N	135.15 E
Hythe, Can.	104	55.20 N	119.33 W

I

PLACE (Pronunciation)	PAGE	Lat. °′	Long. °′
Ia (R.), Jap. (ḗ'ä)	201b	34.54 N	135.34 E
Ialomiţa (R.), Rom.	171	44.37 N	26.42 E
Iasi, Rom. (yä'shḗ)	165	47.10 N	27.40 E
Iba, Phi. (ē'bä)	203a	15.20 N	119.59 E
Ibadan, Nig. (ḗ-bä'dän)	225	7.17 N	3.30 E
Ibagué, Col. (ḗ-bȧ-gā')	140a	4.27 N	75.13 W
Ibar (R.), Yugo. (ē'bär)	171	43.22 N	20.35 E
Ibaraki, Jap. (ē-bä'rä-gē)	201b	34.49 N	135.35 E
Ibarra, Ec. (ḗ-bär'rä)	140	0.19 N	78.08 W
Iberian Pen., Port.-Sp.	218	41.00 N	0.07 W
Iberville, Can. (ḗ-bắr-vēl') (ī'bēr-vĭl)	102	45.14 N	73.01 W
Ibi, Nig. (ē'bḗ)	225	8.12 N	9.45 E
Ibiapaba, Serra da (Mts.), Braz. (sĕ'r-rä-dä-ē-byä-pȧ'bä)	141	3.30 S	40.55 W
Ibiza, Sp. (ḗ-bē'thä)	169	38.55 N	1.24 E
Ibiza, (Iviza) (I.), Sp. (ē-bḗ'zä)	169	39.07 N	1.05 E
Ibo, Moz. (ē'bō)	227	12.20 S	40.35 E
Iboundji, Mont. (Mtn.), Gabon	226	1.08 S	11.48 E
Ibrāhīm, Būr (B.), Egypt	219	29.57 N	32.33 E
Ibrahim, Jabal (Mtn.), Sau. Ar.	192	20.31 N	41.17 E
Ibwe Munyama, Zambia	227	16.09 S	28.34 E
Ica, Peru (ē'kȧ)	140	14.09 S	75.42 W
Icá (R.), Braz. (ē-kȧ')	140	2.56 S	69.12 W
Içana, Braz. (ē-sä'nä)	140	0.15 N	67.19 W
Ice Harbor Dam, Wa.	114	46.15 N	118.54 W
Iceland, Eur. (īs'lănd)	152	65.12 N	19.45 W
Ichibusayama (Mt.), Jap. (ē'chḗ-bo͞o'sȧ-yä'mä)	201	32.19 N	131.08 E
Ichihara, Jap.	201a	35.31 N	140.05 E
Ichikawa, Jap. (ē'chḗ-kä'wä)	201a	35.44 N	139.54 E
Ichinomiya, Jap. (ē'chē-nō-mē'yȧ)	201	35.19 N	136.49 E
Ichinomoto, Jap. (ē-chē'nō-mō-tō)	201b	34.37 N	135.50 E
Ichnya, Sov.Un. (ĭch'nyä)	173	50.47 N	32.23 E
Icó, Braz. (ḗ-kô')	141	6.25 S	38.43 W
Icutú, Cerro (Mtn.), Ven. (sĕ'r-rṓ-ḗ-ko͞o-to͞o')	140	7.07 N	65.30 W
Icy C., Ak. (ī'sĭ)	105	70.20 N	161.40 W
Idabel, Ok. (ī'dȧ-bĕl)	121	33.52 N	94.47 W
Idagrove, Ia. (ī'dȧ-grōv)	112	42.22 N	95.29 W
Idah, Nig. (ē'dä)	225	7.07 N	6.43 E
Idaho (State), U. S. (ī'dȧ-hō)	106	44.00 N	115.10 W
Idaho Falls, Id.	115	43.30 N	112.01 W
Idaho Springs, Co.	120	39.43 N	105.32 W
Idanha-a-Nova, Port. (ḗ-dän'yȧ-ä-nō'vȧ)	168	39.58 N	7.13 W
Ideriin Gol (R.), Mong.	194	48.58 N	98.38 E
Idfū, Egypt (ĕd'fo͞o)	219b	24.57 N	32.53 E
Idhra (I.), Grc.	171	37.20 N	23.30 E
Idi, Indon. (ē'dḗ)	202	4.58 N	97.47 E
Idkū, Egypt (ēd'ko͞o)	219b	31.18 N	30.20 E
Idkū L., Egypt	219b	31.13 N	30.22 E
Idle (R.), Eng. (īd''l)	154	53.22 N	0.56 W
Idriaj, Yugo. (ē'drḗ-ȧ)	170	46.01 N	14.01 E
Idutywa, S. Afr. (ē-do͞o-tī'wȧ)	223c	32.06 S	28.18 E
Ieper, Bel.	161	50.50 N	2.53 E
Ierápetra, Grc.	170a	35.01 N	25.48 E
Iesi, It. (yā'sḗ)	170	43.37 N	13.20 E
Ife, Nig.	225	7.30 N	4.30 E
Iferouâne, Niger (ēf'ro͞o-än')	225	19.04 N	8.24 E
Iforas, Adrar des (Mts.), Alg.-Mali (ä-drär')	225	19.55 N	2.00 E
Igalula, Tan.	227	5.14 S	33.00 E
Igarka, Sov. Un. (ḗ-gär'kȧ)	178	67.22 N	86.16 E
Ighil Izane, Alg.	171	35.43 N	0.43 E
Iglesias, It. (ē-lĕ'syôs)	170	39.20 N	8.34 E
Igli, Alg. (ḗ-glē')	220	30.32 N	2.15 W
Igloolik, Can.	95	69.33 N	81.18 W
Ignacio, Ca. (ĭg-nā'cĭ-ō)	116b	38.05 N	122.32 W

302 Iguaçu – Isle Verte

PLACE (Pronunciation)	PAGE	Lat. °′	Long. °′
Iguaçu (R.), Braz. (ē-gwä-sōō')	142b	22.42 S	43.19 W
Iguala, Mex. (ē-gwä'lä)	128	18.18 N	99.34 W
Igualada, Sp. (ē-gwä-lä'dä)	169	41.35 N	1.38 E
Iguassu (R.), Braz. (ē-gwä-sōō')	142	25.45 S	52.30 W
Iguassu Falls, Braz.	142	25.40 S	54.16 W
Iguatama, Braz. (ē-gwä-tá'mä)	139a	20.13 S	45.40 W
Iguatu, Braz. (ē-gwä-tōō')	141	6.22 S	39.17 W
Iguidi, Erg (Dune), Alg.	220	26.22 N	6.53 W
Iguig, Phil. (ē-gēg')	203a	17.46 N	121.44 E
Ihiala, Nig.	225	5.51 N	6.51 E
Iida, Jap. (ē'ē-dà)	201	35.39 N	137.53 E
Iijoki (R.), Fin. (ē'yō'kĭ)	176	65.28 N	27.00 E
Iizuka, Jap. (ē'ē-zōō-kà)	201	33.39 N	130.39 E
Ijebu-Ode, Nig. (ē-jĕ'bōō ōdå)	225	6.50 N	3.56 E
IJmuiden, Neth.	155a	52.27 N	4.36 E
IJsselmeer (L.), Neth. (ī'sĕl-mâr)	161	52.46 N	5.14 E
Ikaalinen, Fin. (ē'kä-lĭ-nĕn)	163	61.47 N	22.55 E
Ikaría (I.), Grc. (ē-kä'ryà)	171	37.43 N	26.07 E
Ikeda, Jap. (ē'kå-dä)	201b	34.49 N	135.26 E
Ikerre, Nig.	225	7.31 N	5.14 E
Ikhtiman, Bul. (ēk'tē-män)	171	42.26 N	23.49 E
Iki (I.), Jap. (ē'kē)	201	33.46 N	129.44 E
Ikoma, Jap.	201b	34.41 N	135.43 E
Ikoma, Tan. (ē-kō'mä)	222	2.08 S	34.47 E
Iksha, Sov. Un. (ĭk'shà)	180b	56.10 N	37.30 E
Ila, Nig.	225	8.01 N	4.55 E
Ilagen, Phil. (ē-lä'gän)	203a	17.09 N	121.52 E
Ilan, Taiwan (ē'län')	199	24.50 N	121.42 E
Iława, Pol. (ē-lä'và)	165	53.35 N	19.36 E
Île-á-la-Crosse, Can.	98	55.34 N	108.00 W
Ilebo (Port-Franqui), Zaire	226	4.19 S	20.35 E
Ilek, Sov. Un. (ē'lyĕk)	177	51.30 N	53.10 E
Ilek (R.), Sov. Un.	177	51.20 N	53.10 E
Île-Perrot, Can. (yl-pĕ-rōt')	93a	45.21 N	73.54 W
Ilesha, Nig.	225	7.38 N	4.45 E
Ilford, Eng. (ĭl'fērd)	154b	51.33 N	0.06 E
Ilfracombe, Eng. (ĭl-frá-kōōm')	160	51.13 N	4.08 W
Ilhabela, Braz. (ē'lä-bĕ'lä)	139a	23.47 S	45.21 W
Ilha Grande, Baia de (B.), Braz. (ēl'yà grän'dĕ)	139a	23.17 S	44.25 W
Ílhavo, Port. (ēl'yà-vō)	168	40.36 N	8.41 W
Ilhéus, Braz. (ē-lĕ'ōōs)	141	14.52 S	39.00 W
Iliamna, Ak. (ē-lē-ăm'nà)	105	59.45 N	155.05 W
Iliamna (L.), Ak.	105	59.25 N	155.30 W
Iliamna (Vol.), Ak.	105	60.18 N	153.25 W
Ilim (R.), Sov. Un. (ē-lyĕm')	178	57.28 N	103.00 E
Ilimsk, Sov. Un. (ē-lyĕmsk')	178	56.47 N	103.43 E
Ilin I., Phil. (ē-lyĕn')	203a	12.16 N	120.57 E
Il'intsiy, Sov.Un.	173	49.07 N	29.13 E
Ilion, NY (ĭl'ĭ-ŭn)	109	43.00 N	75.05 W
Ili R., Sov. Un. (ē'lē)	194	43.46 N	77.41 E
Ilkeston, Eng. (ĭl'kĕs-tŭn)	154	52.58 N	1.19 W
Illampu, Nevado (Pk.), Bol. (nĕ-vá'dô-ēl-yäm-pōō')	140	15.50 S	68.15 W
Illapel, Chile (ē-zhä-pĕ'l)	139b	31.37 S	71.10 W
Iller R., F.R.G. (ĭl'er)	164	47.52 N	10.06 E
Illimani, Nevado (Pk.), Bol. (nĕ-vá'dô-ēl-yē-mä'nĕ)	140	16.50 S	67.38 W
Illinois (State), U. S. (ĭl-ĭ-noi') (ĭl-ĭ-noiz')	107	40.25 N	90.40 W
Illinois (R.), Il.	121	40.52 N	89.31 W
Illizi, Alg.	220	26.35 N	8.24 E
Il'men', Ozero (L.), Sov. Un. (ô'zĕ-rô el''men'') (ĭl'mĕn)	172	58.18 N	32.00 E
Ilo, Peru	140	17.46 S	71.13 W
Ilobasco, Sal. (ē-lô-bäs'kô)	130	13.57 N	88.46 W
Iloilo, Phil. (ē-lô-ē'lō)	202	10.49 N	122.33 E
Ilopango, L., Sal. (ē-lô-päŋ'gō)	130	13.48 N	88.50 W
Ilorin, Nig. (ē-lō-rēn')	225	8.30 N	4.32 E
Ilūkste, Sov. Un.	172	55.59 N	26.20 E
Ilwaco, Wa. (ĭl-wä'kô)	116c	46.19 N	124.02 W
Ilych (R.), Sov. Un. (ē'l'ĭch)	176	62.30 N	57.30 E
Imabari, Jap. (ē'mä-bä'rē)	201	34.05 N	132.58 E
Imai, Jap. (ē-mī')	201b	34.30 N	135.47 E
Iman (R.), Sov. Un. (ē-män')	200	45.40 N	134.31 E
Imandra (L.), Sov. Un. (ē-män'drá)	176	67.40 N	32.30 E
Imbābah, Egypt (ēm-bä'bà)	219b	30.06 N	31.09 E
Imbarié, Braz. (ēm-bä-ryĕ')	142b	22.38 S	43.13 W
Imeni Morozova, Sov. Un. (ĭm-yĕ'nyĭ mô rô'zô vá)	180c	59.58 N	31.02 E
Imeni Moskvy, Kanal (Moscow Can.), Sov. Un. (ká-näl'ĭm-yă'nĭ mōs-kvĭ)	172	56.33 N	37.15 E
Imeni Tsyurupy, Sov. Un.	180b	55.30 N	38.39 E
Imeni Vorovskogo, Sov. Un.	180b	55.43 N	38.21 E
Imlay City, Mi. (ĭm'lā)	108	43.00 N	83.15 W
Immenstadt, F.R.G. (ĭm'ĕn-shtät)	164	47.34 N	10.12 E
Immerpan, S. Afr. (ĭmĕr-pän)	219d	24.29 S	29.14 E
Imola, It. (ē'mô-lä)	170	44.19 N	11.43 E
Imotski, Yugo. (ē-môts'kē)	170	43.25 N	17.15 E
Impameri, Braz.	141	17.44 S	48.03 W
Impendle, S. Afr. (ĭm-pĕnd'lå)	223c	29.38 S	29.54 E
Imperia, It. (ēm-pā'rē-ä)	170	43.52 N	8.00 E
Imperial, Pa. (ĭm-pē'rĭ-ăl)	111e	40.27 N	80.15 W
Imperial Beach, Ca.	118a	32.34 N	117.08 W
Imperial Res., Az.	119	32.57 N	114.19 W
Imperial Valley, Ca.	118	33.00 N	115.22 W
Impfondo, Con. (ĭmp-fōn'dô)	226	1.37 N	18.04 E
Imphāl, India (ĭmp'hŭl)	193	24.42 N	94.00 E
Ina (R.), Jap. (ē-nä')	201b	34.56 N	135.21 E
Inaja Ind. Res., Ca. (ē-nä'hä)	118	32.56 N	116.37 W
Inari (L.), Fin.	156	69.02 N	26.22 E
Inca, Sp. (ēŋ'kä)	169	39.43 N	2.53 E
Ince Burun (C.), Tur. (ĭn'jå)	177	42.00 N	35.00 E
Inch'ŏn, Kor. (ĭn'chŭn)	200	37.26 N	126.46 E
Incudine, Mt. (Mtn.), Fr. (ēn-kōō-dē'nå) (ăN-kü-dēn')	170	41.53 N	9.17 E
Indalsälven (R.), Swe.	162	62.50 N	16.50 E
Indé, Mex. (ēn'då)	122	25.53 N	105.15 W
Independence, Ks. (ĭn-dē-pĕn'dĕns)	121	37.14 N	95.42 W
Independence, Mo.	117f	39.06 N	94.26 W
Independence, Oh.	111d	41.23 N	81.39 W
Independence, Or.	114	44.49 N	123.13 W

PLACE (Pronunciation)	PAGE	Lat. °′	Long. °′
Independence Mts., Nv.	114	41.15 N	116.02 W
Inder (L.), Sov. Un.	177	48.20 N	52.10 E
India, Asia (ĭn'dĭ-ă)	188	23.00 N	77.30 E
Indian (L.), Mi. (ĭn'dĭ-ăn)	113	46.04 N	86.34 W
Indian (R.), NY	109	44.05 N	75.45 W
Indiana, Pa. (ĭn-dĭ-ăn'ă)	109	40.40 N	79.10 W
Indiana (State), U. S.	107	39.50 N	86.45 W
Indianapolis, In. (ĭn-dĭ-ăn-ăp'ō-lĭs)	111g	39.45 N	86.08 W
Indian Arm (R.), Can. (ĭn'dĭ-ăn ärm)	116d	49.21 N	122.55 W
Indian Head, Can.	98	50.29 N	103.44 W
Indian L., Can.	100	47.00 N	82.00 W
Indian O.	5		
Indianola, Ia. (ĭn-dĭ-ăn-ō'lă)	113	41.22 N	93.33 W
Indianola, Ms.	124	33.29 N	90.35 W
Indigirka (R.), Sov. Un. (ēn-dē-gēr'kà)	179	67.45 N	145.45 E
Indio (R.), Pan. (ē'n-dyô)	126a	9.13 N	78.28 W
Indochina (Reg.), Asia (ĭn-dô-chī'nà)	202	17.22 N	105.18 E
Indonesia, Asia (ĭn'dô-nē-zhă)	202	4.38 S	118.45 E
Indore, India (ĭn-dōr')	190	22.48 N	76.51 E
Indragiri (R.), Indon. (ĭn-drá-jē'rē)	202	0.27 S	102.05 E
Indrāvati (R.), India (ĭn-drŭ-vä'tē)	130	19.15 N	80.54 E
Indre (R.), Fr. (ăN'dr')	166	47.13 N	0.29 E
Indus, Can. (ĭn'dŭs)	93e	50.55 N	113.45 W
Indus (R.), Pak.	190	26.43 N	67.41 E
Indwe, S. Afr. (ĭnd'wå)	223c	31.30 S	27.21 E
Inebolu, Tur. (ē-nå-bō'lōō)	177	41.50 N	33.40 E
Inego, Tur. (ē'nå-gŭ)	177	40.05 N	29.20 E
Infanta, Phil. (ēn-fän'tä)	203a	14.44 N	121.39 E
Infanta, Phil.	203a	15.50 N	119.53 E
Inferror, Laguna (L.), Mex. (lä-gōō'nä-ēn-fēr-rôr)	129	16.18 N	94.40 W
Infiernillo, Presa de (Res.), Mex.	129	18.50 N	101.50 W
Infiesto, Sp. (ēn-fyĕ's-tô)	168	43.21 N	5.24 W
I-n-Gall, Niger	225	16.47 N	6.56 E
Ingersoll, Can. (ĭn'gēr-sŏl)	108	43.05 N	81.00 W
Ingham, Austl. (ĭng'ăm)	211	18.45 S	146.14 E
Ingles, Cayos (Is.), Cuba (kä-yōs-ē'n-glē's)	132	21.55 N	82.35 W
Inglewood, Ca. (ĭn'g'l-wŏŏd)	117a	33.57 N	118.22 W
Inglewood, Can.	93d	43.48 N	79.56 W
Ingoda (R.), Sov. Un. (ēn-gō'dă)	179	51.29 N	112.32 E
Ingolstadt, F.R.G. (ĭŋ'gôl-shtät)	164	48.46 N	11.27 E
Ingul (R.), Sov. Un. (ēn-gōōl')	173	47.22 N	32.52 E
Ingulets (R.), Sov. Un. (ēn-gōōl'yĕts')	173	47.12 N	33.12 E
Ingur (R.), Sov. Un. (ēn-gōōr')	177	42.30 N	42.00 E
Inhambane, Moz. (ēn-äm-bä'-nĕ)	222	23.47 S	35.28 E
Inhambupe, Braz. (ēn-yäm-bōō'pä)	141	11.47 S	38.13 W
Inharrime, Moz. (ēn-yär-rē'mä)	222	24.17 S	35.07 E
Inhomirim, Braz. (ē-nô-mē-rē'N)	142b	22.34 S	43.11 W
Inirida (R.), Col. (ē-nē-rē'dä)	140	2.25 N	70.38 W
Injune, Austl. (ĭn'jōōn)	212	25.52 S	148.30 E
Inkeroinem, Fin. (ĭn'kĕr-oi-nĕn)	163	60.42 N	26.50 E
Inkster, Mi. (ĭngk'stēr)	111b	42.18 N	83.19 W
Innamincka, Austl. (ĭnn-ă'mĭn-kă)	212	27.50 S	140.48 E
Inner Brass (I.), Vir. Is. (U.S.A.) (bräs)	127c	18.23 N	64.58 W
Inner Hebrides (Is.), Scot.	160	57.20 N	6.20 W
Inner Mongolia, (Aut. Reg.), **see Nei Monggol**			
Innisfail, Can.	97	52.02 N	113.57 W
Inn R., F.R.G.-Aus. (ĭn)	164	48.19 N	13.16 E
Innsbruck, Aus. (ĭns'brŏŏk)	164	47.15 N	11.25 E
Ino, Jap. (ē'nō)	201	33.34 N	133.23 E
Inongo, Zaire (ē-nôŋ'gō)	226	1.57 S	18.16 E
Inowroctaw, Pol. (ē-nô-vrôts'läf)	165	52.48 N	18.16 E
In Salah, Alg.	220	27.13 N	2.22 E
Inscription House Ruin, Az. (ĭn'skrĭp-shŭn hous rōō'ĭn)	119	36.45 N	110.47 W
Inter-American Hy., Mex. (ĭn'tēr ă-mĕr'ĭ-kăn)	128	22.30 N	99.08 W
International Falls, Mn. (ĭn'tēr-năsh'ŭn-ăl fôlz)	113	48.34 N	93.26 W
Inuvik, Can.	94	68.40 N	134.10 W
Inuyama, Jap. (ē'nōō-yä'mä)	201	35.24 N	137.01 E
Invercargil, N. Z. (ĭn-vēr-kär'gĭl)	213	46.25 S	68.27 E
Inverel, Austl. (ĭn-vēr-el')	212	29.50 S	151.32 E
Invergrove Hts., Mn. (ĭn'vēr-grōv)	117g	44.51 N	93.01 W
Inverness, Can. (ĭn-vēr-nĕs')	103	46.14 N	61.18 W
Inverness, Fl.	125	28.48 N	82.22 W
Inverness, Scot.	160	57.30 N	4.07 W
Investigator Str., Austl. (ĭn-vĕst'ĭ'gā-tôr)	212	35.33 S	137.00 E
Inyangani, Mt., Zimb. (ēn-yän-gä'nē)	222	18.06 S	32.37 E
Inyokern, Ca.	118	35.39 N	117.51 W
Inyo Mts., Ca. (ĭn'yō)	118	36.55 N	118.04 W
Inzer R., Sov. Un. (ĭn'zĕr)	180a	54.24 N	57.17 E
Inzia (R.), Zaire	226	5.55 S	17.50 E
Iō (I.), Jap. (ē'wō)	201	30.46 N	130.15 E
Ioánnina (Yannina), Grc. (yō-ä'nē-nà) (yä'nē-nà)	171	39.39 N	20.52 E
Ioco, Can.	116d	49.18 N	122.53 W
Iola, Ks. (ī-ō'lă)	121	37.55 N	95.23 W
Iôna, Parque Nacional do (Natl. Pk.), Ang.	226	16.35 S	12.00 E
Ionia, Mi. (ī-ō'nĭ-ă)	108	43.00 N	85.10 W
Ionian Is., Grc. (ī-ō'nĭ-ăn)	171	39.10 N	20.05 E
Ionian Sea, Eur.	159	38.59 N	18.48 E
Íos (I.), Grc. (ī'ŏs)	171	36.48 N	25.25 E
Iowa (State), U.S. (ī'ô-wă)	107	42.05 N	94.20 W
Iowa (R.), Ia.	113	41.55 N	92.20 W
Iowa City, Ia.	113	41.39 N	91.31 W
Iowa Falls, Ia.	113	42.32 N	93.16 W
Iowa Park, Tx.	120	33.57 N	98.39 W
Ipala, Tan.	227	4.30 S	32.53 E
Ípeirus (Reg.), Grc.	171	39.35 N	20.45 E
Ipel' (R.), Czech.-Hung. (ē'pĕl)	165	48.08 N	19.00 E
Ipiales, Col. (ē-pē-ä'lås)	140	0.48 N	77.45 W
Ipoh, Mala.	202	4.45 N	101.05 E
Ipswich, Austl. (ĭps'wĭch)	212	27.40 S	152.50 E
Ipswich, Eng.	161	52.05 N	1.05 E
Ipswich, Ma.	103a	42.41 N	70.50 W
Ipswich, SD	112	45.26 N	99.01 W

PLACE (Pronunciation)	PAGE	Lat. °′	Long. °′
Ipu, Braz. (ē-pōō)	141	4.11 S	40.45 W
Iput' (R.), Sov. Un. (ē-pōōt')	172	52.53 N	31.57 E
Iquique, Chile (ē-kē'kĕ)	140	20.16 S	70.07 W
Iquitos, Peru (ē-kē'tōs)	140	3.39 S	73.18 W
Iráklion (Candia), Grc.	170a	35.20 N	25.10 E
Iran, Asia (ē-rän')	188	31.15 N	53.30 E
Iran, Plat. of, Iran	192	32.28 N	58.00 E
Iran Mts., Mala.	202	2.30 N	114.30 E
Irapuato, Mex. (ē-rä-pwä'tō)	128	20.41 N	101.24 W
Iraq, Asia (ē-räk')	188	32.00 N	42.30 E
Irazu Vol, C.R. (ē-rä-zōō')	131	9.58 N	83.54 W
Irbid, Jordan (ēr-bēd')	189a	32.33 N	35.51 E
Irbil, Iraq	177	36.10 N	44.00 E
Irbit, Sov. Un. (ēr-bēt')	176	57.40 N	63.10 E
Irébou, Zaire (ē-rā'bōō)	222	0.40 S	17.48 E
Ireland, Eur. (īr-lănd)	152	53.33 N	13.00 W
Iremel', Gora (Mt.), Sov. Un. (gà-rä'ĭ-rē'mĕl)	180a	54.32 N	58.52 E
Irene, S. Afr. (ĭ-rē-nē)	223b	25.53 S	28.13 E
Irgiz, Sov. Un. (ĭr-gēz')	178	48.30 N	61.17 E
Irgiz (R.), Sov. Un.	178	49.30 N	60.32 E
Irīgui (Reg.), Mali-Mauritania	224	16.45 N	5.35 W
Iriklinskoye Vdkhr (Res.), Sov. Un.	176	52.20 N	58.50 E
Iringa, Tan. (ē-rĭŋ'gä)	227	7.46 S	35.42 E
Iriomote Jima (I.), Jap. (ērē'-ō-mō-tä)	199	24.20 N	123.30 E
Iriona, Hond. (ē-rē-ō'nä)	130	15.53 N	85.12 W
Irish Sea, Eur. (ī'rĭsh)	160	53.55 N	5.25 W
Irkutsk, Sov. Un. (ĭr-kōōtsk')	178	52.16 N	104.00 E
Irlam, Eng. (ûr'lăm)	154	53.26 N	2.26 W
Irois, Cap des (C.), Hai.	133	18.25 N	74.50 W
Irondale, Al. (ī'ērn-dăl)	110h	33.32 N	86.43 W
Iron Gate (Gorge), Yugo.-Rom.	171	44.43 N	22.32 E
Iron Knob, Austl. (ī-ăn nŏb)	212	32.47 S	137.10 E
Iron Mountain, Mi. (ī'ērn)	113	45.49 N	88.04 W
Iron River, Mi.	113	46.09 N	88.39 W
Ironton, Oh. (ī'ērn-tŭn)	108	38.30 N	82.45 W
Ironwood, Mi. (ī'ērn-wŏŏd)	113	46.28 N	90.10 W
Iroquois (R.), Il.-In. (ĭr'ô-kwoi)	108	40.55 N	87.20 W
Iroquois Falls, Can.	95	48.41 N	80.39 W
Irō-Saki (C.), Jap. (ē'rō sä'kē)	201	34.35 N	138.54 E
Irpen' (R.), Sov. Un. (ĭr-pĕn')	173	50.13 N	29.55 E
Irrawaddy (R.), Bur. (ĭr-ă-wäd'ē)	193	23.27 N	96.25 E
Irtysh (R.), Sov. Un. (ĭr-tĭsh')	178	58.32 N	68.31 E
Irumu, Zaire (ē-rōō'mōō)	221	1.30 N	29.52 E
Irun, Sp. (ē-rōōn')	168	43.20 N	1.47 W
Irvine, Ca. (ûr'vĭn)	117a	33.40 N	117.45 W
Irvine, Scot.	160	55.39 N	4.40 W
Irvine, Ky.	108	37.40 N	84.00 W
Irving, Tx. (ûr'vēng)	117c	32.49 N	96.57 W
Irvington, NJ (ûr'vēng-tŭn)	110a	40.43 N	74.15 W
Irwin, Pa. (ûr'wĭn)	111e	40.19 N	79.42 W
Isa, Nig.	225	13.14 N	6.24 E
Is, Sov. Un. (ēs)	180a	58.48 N	59.44 E
Isaacs, Mt., Pan. (ē-sä-ä'ks)	126a	9.22 N	79.01 W
Isabela (I.), Mex. (ē-sä-bĕ'-lä)	128	21.56 N	105.53 W
Isabela (I.), Ec. (ē-sä-bä'lä)	140	0.47 S	91.35 W
Isabela, Cabo (C.), Dom. Rep. (kä'bô-ē-sä-bĕ'lä)	133	20.00 N	71.00 W
Isabella, Cord. (Mts.), Nic. (kôr-dēl-yĕ'rä-ē-sä-bĕlä)	130	13.20 N	85.37 W
Isabella Ind. Res., Mi. (ĭs-à-bĕl'-lå)	108	43.35 N	84.55 W
Isaccea, Rom. (ē-säk'chä)	173	45.16 N	28.26 E
Ísafjördur, Ice. (ēs'á-fyr-dōōr)	156	66.09 N	22.39 W
Isangi, Zaire (ē-säŋ'gē)	226	0.46 N	24.15 E
Isar R., F.R.G. (ē'zär)	164	48.27 N	12.02 E
Isarco (R.), It. (ē-sär'kō)	170	46.37 N	11.25 E
Isarog, Mt., Phil. (ē-sä-rô-g)	203a	13.40 N	123.23 E
Ischia, It. (ēs'kyä)	169c	40.29 N	13.58 E
Ise (Uji-Yamada), Jap. (ĭs'hē) (û'gē-yä'mä'dà)	201	34.30 N	136.43 E
Iseo, Lago d' (L.), It. (lä-'gō-dē-ē-zĕ'ō)	170	45.50 N	9.55 E
Isère (R.), Fr. (ē-zâr')	167	45.24 N	6.04 E
Iserlohn, F.R.G. (ē'zĕr-lōn)	167c	51.22 N	7.42 E
Isernia, It. (ē-zĕr'nyä)	170	41.35 N	14.14 E
Ise-Wan (B), Jap. (ē'sĕ wän)	201	34.49 N	136.44 E
Iseyin, Nig.	225	7.58 N	3.36 E
Ishikari Wan (B.), Jap. (ē'shē-kä-rē wän)	200	43.30 N	141.05 E
Ishim, Sov. Un. (ĭsh-ĕm')	178	56.07 N	69.13 E
Ishim (R.), Sov. Un.	178	53.17 N	67.45 E
Ishimbay, Sov. Un. (ē-shēm-bī')	180a	53.28 N	56.02 E
Ishinomaki, Jap. (ĭsh-nō-mä'kē)	200	38.22 N	141.22 E
Ishinomaki Wan (B.), Jap. (ē-shē-nō-mä'kē wän)	200	38.10 N	141.40 E
Ishly, Sov. Un. (ĭsh'lĭ)	180a	54.13 N	55.55 E
Ishlya, Sov. Un. (ĭsh'lyà)	180a	53.54 N	57.48 E
Ishmant, Egypt	219b	29.17 N	31.15 E
Ishpeming, Mi. (ĭsh'pē-mĭng)	113	46.28 N	87.42 W
Isipingo, S. Afr. (ĭs-ĭ-pĭŋg-gō)	223c	29.59 S	30.58 E
Isiro (Paulis), Zaire	227	2.47 N	27.37 E
İskenderun, Tur. (ĭs-kĕn'dĕr-ōōn)	177	36.45 N	36.15 E
İskenderun Körfezi (G.), Turk.	159	36.22 N	35.25 E
İskilip, Tur. (ēs'kĭ-lēp')	177	40.40 N	34.30 E
Iskūr (R.), Bul. (ĭs'k'r)	171	43.05 N	23.37 E
Isla-Cristina, Sp. (ī'lä-krē-stē'nä)	168	37.13 N	7.20 W
Islāmābād, Pak.	193	33.55 N	73.05 E
Isla Mujeres, Mex. (ē's-lä-mōō-kĕ'rĕs)	130a	21.25 N	86.53 W
Island L., Can.	99	53.47 N	94.25 W
Islands, B. of, Can. (ī'lăndz)	103	49.10 N	58.15 W
Islay (I.), Scot. (ī'lā)	160	55.55 N	6.35 W
Isle (R.), Fr. (ēl)	166	45.02 N	0.29 E
Isle of Axholme (Reg.), Eng. (ăks'-hōm)	154	53.33 N	0.48 W
Isle of Man, Eur. (măn)	160	54.26 N	4.21 W
Isle Royale Nat'l Park, U. S. (ĭl'roi-ăl')	113	47.57 N	88.37 W
Isleta, NM (ēs-lä'tá) (ī-lĕ'tá)	119	34.55 N	106.45 W
Isle Verte, Can. (ēl vĕrt')	102	48.01 N	69.20 W

ăt; finăl; rāte; senāte; ärm; àsk; sofá; fâre; ch-choose; dh-as th in other; bē; ēvent; bĕt; recĕnt; cratēr; g-gō; gh-guttural g; bĭt; ĭ-short neutral; rīde; K-guttural k as ch in German ich;

PRONOUNCING INDEX

Ismailia – Jeanerette 303

PLACE (Pronunciation)	PAGE	Lat. °′	Long. °′
Ismailia (Al Isma 'īlīyah), Egypt (ēs-mā-ēl'ēȧ)	219c	30.35 N	32.17 E
Ismā'īlīyah Can., Egypt	219c	30.25 N	31.45 E
Ismaning, F.R.G. (ēz'mä-nēng)	155d	48.14 N	11.41 E
Isnā, Egypt (ēs'nȧ)	219b	25.17 N	32.33 E
Isparta, Tur. (ē-spär'tȧ)	177	37.50 N	30.40 E
Israel, Asia	192	32.40 N	34.00 E
Issaquah, Wa. (īz'sȧ-kwăh)	116a	47.32 N	122.02 W
Isselburg, F.R.G. (ē'sĕl-bo͞org)	167c	51.50 N	6.28 E
Issoire, Fr. (ē-swȧr')	166	45.32 N	3.13 E
Issoudun, Fr. (ē-so͞o-dăN')	166	46.56 N	2.00 E
Issum, F.R.G. (ē'so͞om)	167c	51.32 N	6.24 E
Issyk-Kul, Ozero (L.), Sov. Un.	178	42.13 N	76.12 E
Istādeh-ye Moqor, Ab-e (L.), Afg.	190	32.35 N	68.00 E
Istanbul, Tur. (ē-stän-bo͞ol')	177	41.02 N	29.00 E
Istanbul Boğazi (Bosporous) (Str.), Tur.	177	41.10 N	29.10 E
Istiaía, Grc. (ĭs-tyī'yä)	171	38.58 N	23.11 E
Istmina, Col. (ēst-mē'nä)	140a	5.10 N	76.40 W
Istokpoga (L.), Fl. (ĭs-tŏk-pō'gȧ)	125a	27.20 N	81.33 W
Istra (Pen.), Yugo. (ē-strä)	170	45.18 N	13.48 E
Istranca Dağlari (Mts.), Bul.-Turk. (ĭ-strän'jȧ)	171	41.50 N	27.25 E
Istres, Fr. (ēs'tr')	166a	43.30 N	5.00 E
Itá, Par. (ē-tá')	142	25.39 S	57.14 W
Itabaiana, Braz. (ē-tä-bä-yȧ-nä)	141	10.42 S	37.17 W
Itabapoana, Braz. (ē-tä'-bä-pōä'nä)	139a	21.19 S	40.58 W
Itabapoana (R.), Braz.	139a	21.11 S	41.18 W
Itabirito, Braz. (ē-tä-bē-rē'tō)	139a	20.15 S	43.46 W
Itaboraí, Braz. (ē-tä-bō-räē')	139a	22.46 S	42.50 W
Itabuna, Braz. (ē-tä-bo͞o'nȧ)	141	14.47 S	39.17 W
Itacoara, Braz. (ē-tä-kō'ä-rä)	139a	21.41 S	42.04 W
Itacoatiara, Braz. (ē-tȧ-kwȧ-tyä'rȧ)	141	3.03 S	58.18 W
Itaguaí, Braz. (ē-tä-gwä-ē')	139a	22.52 S	43.46 W
Itagüi, Col. (ē-tä'gwē)	140a	6.11 N	75.36 W
Itagui (R.), Braz.	142b	22.53 S	43.43 W
Itaipava, Braz. (ē-tī-pȧ'-vä)	142b	22.23 S	43.09 W
Itaipu, Braz. (ē-tī'po͞o)	142b	22.58 S	43.02 W
Itaituba, Braz. (ē-tä'ĭ-to͞o'bȧ)	141	4.12 S	56.00 W
Itajái, Braz. (ē-tä-zhī')	142	26.52 S	48.39 W
Itajubá, Braz. (ē-tä-zho͞o-bá')	139a	22.26 S	45.27 W
Itala, Som.	219a	2.45 N	46.15 E
Italy, Eur. (ĭt'ȧ-lē)	152	43.58 N	11.14 E
Italy, Tx.	123	32.11 N	96.51 W
Itambi, Braz. (ē-tä'm-bē)	142b	22.44 S	42.57 W
Itami, Jap. (ē'tä'mē')	201b	34.47 N	135.25 E
Itapecerica, Braz. (ē-tä-pĕ-sĕ-rē'kȧ)	139a	21.29 S	45.08 W
Itapecurú (R.), Braz. (ē-tä-pĕ-ko͞o-ro͞o')	141	4.05 S	43.49 W
Itapēcuru-Mirim, Braz. (ē-tä-pĕ'ko͞o-ro͞o-mē-rēN')	141	3.17 S	44.15 W
Itaperuna, Braz. (ē-tȧ-pȧ-ro͞o'nä)	139a	21.12 S	41.53 W
Itapetininga, Braz. (ē-tä-pĕ-tē-nē'N-gä)	139a	23.37 S	48.03 W
Itapira, Braz. (ē-tȧ-pē'rȧ)	141	20.42 S	51.19 W
Itapira, Braz.	139a	21.27 S	46.47 W
Itarsi, India	190	22.43 N	77.45 E
Itasca, Tx. (ī-tăs'kȧ)	123	32.09 N	97.08 W
Itasca (L.), Mn.	113	47.13 N	95.14 W
Itatiaia, Pico da (Pk.), Braz. (pē'-kō-dȧ-ē-tä-tyȧ'ēä)	139a	22.18 S	44.41 W
Itatiba, Braz. (ē-tȧ-tē'bä)	139a	23.01 S	46.48 W
Itaúna, Braz. (ē-tä-o͞o'nä)	139a	20.05 S	44.35 W
Itaverá, Braz. (ē-tä-vē-rá')	139a	22.44 S	44.07 W
Ithaca, Mi. (ĭth'ȧ-kȧ)	108	43.20 N	84.35 W
Ithaca, NY	109	42.25 N	76.30 W
Itháka (I.), Grc. (ē'thä-kē)	171	38.27 N	20.48 E
Itigi, Tan.	227	5.42 S	34.29 E
Itimbiri (R.), Zaire	226	2.40 N	23.30 E
Itoko, Zaire (ē-tō'kō)	222	1.13 S	22.07 E
Itsā, Egypt (ēt'sȧ)	219b	29.13 N	30.47 E
Itu, Braz. (ē-to͞o')	139a	23.16 S	47.16 W
Ituango, Col. (ē-twäṉ'gō)	140a	7.07 N	75.44 W
Ituiutaba, Braz. (ē-to͞o-ēo͞o-tä'bä)	141	18.56 S	49.17 W
Itumirim, Braz. (ē-to͞o-mē-rē'N)	139a	21.20 S	44.51 W
Itundujia Santa Cruz, Mex. (ē-to͞on-do͞o-hē'ä sä'n-tä kro͞o'z)	129	16.50 N	97.43 W
Iturbide, Mex. (ē'to͞or-bē'dhä)	130a	19.38 N	89.31 W
Iturup (Etorofu) (I.), Sov. Un. (ē-to͞o-ro͞op')	179	45.35 N	147.15 E
Ituzaingo, Arg. (ē-to͞o-zä-ē'n-gō)	142a	34.24 S	58.40 W
Itzehoe, F.R.G. (ē'tzē-hō)	155c	53.55 N	9.31 E
Iuka, Ms. (ī-ū'kȧ)	124	34.47 N	88.10 W
Iúna, Braz. (ē-o͞o'-nä)	139a	20.22 S	41.32 W
Iva (R.),	178	53.45 N	99.30 E
Ivanhoe, Austl. (ĭv'ăn-hō)	212	32.53 S	144.10 E
Ivano-Frankovsk, Sov. Un. (ē-vä'nō frän-kôvsk')	165	48.53 N	24.46 E
Ivanovo, Sov. Un. (ē-vä'nô-vō)	172	57.02 N	41.54 E
Ivanovo (Oblast), Sov. Un.	172	56.55 N	40.30 E
Ivanpol', Sov. Un. (ē-văn'pôl)	173	49.51 N	28.11 E
Ivanteyevka, Sov. Un. (ē-vȧn-tyĕ'yĕf-kȧ)	180b	55.58 N	37.56 E
Ivdel', Sov. Un. (ĭv'dyĕl)	180a	60.42 N	60.27 E
Iviza (I.), see Ibiza			
Ivohibé, Mad. (ē-vô-hē-bā')	223	22.28 S	46.59 E
Ivory Coast, Afr.	218	7.43 N	6.30 W
Ivrea, It. (ē-vrē'ä)	170	45.25 N	7.54 E
Ivujivik, Can.	95	62.17 N	77.52 W
Iwaki (Taira), Jap.	200	37.03 N	140.57 E
Iwate Yama (Mt.), Jap. (ē-wä-tē-yä'mä)	200	39.50 N	140.56 E
Iwatsuki, Jap.	201a	35.48 N	139.43 E
Iwaya, Jap. (ē'wȧ-yȧ)	201b	34.35 N	135.01 E
Iwo, Nig.	225	7.38 N	4.11 E
Ixcateopán, Mex. (ēs-kä-tä-ō-pän')	128	18.29 N	99.49 W
Ixelles, Bel.	155a	50.49 N	4.23 E
Ixhuatán (San Francisco), Mex. (ēs-hwä-tän')	129	16.19 N	94.30 W
Ixhautlán, Mex. (ēs-wȧt-län')	128	20.41 N	98.01 W
Ixmiquilpan, Mex. (ēs-mē-kēl'pän)	128	20.30 N	99.12 W
Ixopo, S. Afr.	223c	30.10 S	30.04 E
Ixtacalco, Mex. (ēs-tȧ-käl'kō)	129a	19.23 N	99.07 W
Ixtaltepec (Asunción), Mex. (ēs-täl-tē-pĕk')	129	16.33 N	95.04 W
Ixtapalapa, Mex. (ēs'tä-pä-lä'pä)	129a	19.21 N	99.06 W
Ixtapaluca, Mex. (ēs'tä-pä-lo͞o'kä)	129a	19.18 N	98.53 W
Ixtepec, Mex. (ēks-tĕ'pĕk)	129	16.37 N	95.09 W
Ixtlahuaca, Mex. (ēs-tlä-wä'kä)	129a	19.34 N	99.46 W
Ixtlán de Juárez, Mex. (ēs-tlän' dā hwä'rāz)	129	17.20 N	96.29 W
Ixtlán del Río, Mex. (ēs-tlän'dĕl rē'ō)	128	21.05 N	104.22 W
Iyo-Nada (Sea), Jap. (ē'yō nä-dä)	201	33.33 N	132.07 E
Izabal, Guat. (ē'zä-bäl')	130	15.23 N	89.10 W
Izabal, L. (Golfo Dulce), Guat. (gôl'fō do͞ol'sȧ)	130	15.30 N	89.04 W
Izalco, Sal. (ē-zäl'kō)	130	13.50 N	89.40 W
Izamal, Mex. (ē-zä-mä'l)	130a	20.55 N	89.00 W
Izhevsk, Sov. Un. (ē-zhyĕfsk')	176	56.50 N	53.15 E
Izhma, Sov. Un. (ĭzh'mȧ)	176	65.00 N	54.05 E
Izhma (R.), Sov. Un.	176	64.00 N	53.00 E
Izhora R., Sov. Un. (ēz'hô-rȧ)	180c	59.36 N	30.20 E
Izmail, Sov. Un. (ēz-mȧ-ēl)	173	45.00 N	28.49 E
İzmir, Tur. (ĭz-mēr')	177	38.25 N	27.05 E
İzmir Körfezi (G.), Tur.	171	38.43 N	26.37 E
İzmit, Tur. (ĭz-mēt')	177	40.45 N	29.45 E
Iznajar, Embalse de (Res.), Sp.	168	37.15 N	4.30 W
Iztaccíhuatl (Mtn.), Mex.	129a	19.10 N	98.38 W
Izu (I.), Jap. (ē'zo͞o)	201	34.32 N	139.25 E
Izuhara, Jap. (ē'zo͞o-hä'rä)	201	34.11 N	129.18 E
Izumi-Ōtsu, Jap. (ē'zo͞o-mo͞o ō'tso͞o)	201b	34.30 N	135.24 E
Izumo, Jap. (ē'zo͞o-mō)	201	35.22 N	132.45 E

J

PLACE (Pronunciation)	PAGE	Lat. °′	Long. °′
Jaachimsthal, G.D.R. (yä'kēm-stäl)	155b	52.58 N	13.45 E
Jabal, Bahr al (R.), Sud.	221	7.02 N	30.45 E
Jabalpur, India	190	23.18 N	79.59 E
Jablonec nad Nisou, Czech. (yäb'lō-nyĕts)	164	50.43 N	15.12 E
Jablunkov P., Czech. (yäb'lo͞on-kôf)	165	49.31 N	18.35 E
Jaboatão, Braz. (zhä-bô-à-touN)	141	8.14 S	35.08 W
Jaca, Sp. (hä'kä)	169	42.35 N	0.30 W
Jacala, Mex. (hä-kä'lä)	128	21.01 N	99.11 W
Jacaltenango, Guat. (hä-käl-tē-näṉ'gō)	130	15.39 N	91.41 W
Jacareí, Braz. (zhä-kä-rĕ-ē')	139a	23.19 S	45.57 W
Jacarepaguá, Braz. (zhä-kä-rā'pä-gwä')	142b	22.55 S	43.22 W
Jacarézinho, Braz. (zhä-kä-rĕ'zē-nyō)	141	23.13 S	49.58 W
Jachymov, Czech. (yä'chĭ-môf)	164	50.22 N	12.51 E
Jacinto City, Tx. (hä-sĕn'tō) (jȧ-sĭn'tō)	123a	29.45 N	95.14 W
Jacksboro, Tx. (jăks'bŭr-ō)	120	33.13 N	98.11 W
Jackson, Al. (jăk'sŭn)	124	31.31 N	87.52 W
Jackson, Ca.	118	38.22 N	120.47 W
Jackson, Ga.	124	33.19 N	83.55 W
Jackson, Ky.	124	37.32 N	83.17 W
Jackson, La.	123	30.50 N	91.13 W
Jackson, Mi.	108	42.15 N	84.25 W
Jackson, Mn.	113	43.37 N	95.00 W
Jackson, Ms.	124	32.17 N	90.10 W
Jackson, Mo.	121	37.23 N	89.40 W
Jackson, Oh.	108	39.00 N	82.40 W
Jackson, Tn.	124	35.37 N	88.49 W
Jackson, Port., Austl.	207b	33.50 S	151.18 E
Jackson L., Wy.	115	43.57 N	110.28 W
Jacksonville, Al. (jăk'sŭn-vĭl)	124	33.52 N	85.45 W
Jacksonville, Fl.	125	30.20 N	81.40 W
Jacksonville, Il.	121	39.43 N	90.12 W
Jacksonville, Tx.	123	31.58 N	95.18 W
Jacksonville Beach, Fl.	125	31.18 N	81.25 W
Jacmel, Hai. (zhák-mĕl')	133	18.15 N	72.30 W
Jaco, L., Mex. (hä'kō)	122	27.51 N	103.50 W
Jacobābād, Pak.	190	28.22 N	68.30 E
Jacobina, Braz. (zhä-kô-bē'nȧ)	141	11.13 S	40.30 W
Jacques Cartier, Mt., Can.	102	48.59 N	66.00 W
Jacques-Cartier, (R.), Can.	93b	47.04 N	71.28 W
Jacques Cartier, Détroit de (Str.), Can.	103	50.07 N	63.58 W
Jacquet River, Can. (zhá-kĕ') (jăk'ĕt)	102	47.55 N	66.00 W
Jacuí, Braz. (zhä-ko͞o-ē')	139a	21.03 S	46.43 W
Jacutinga, Braz. (zhȧ-ko͞o-tēn'gä)	139a	21.17 S	46.36 W
Jade B., F.R.G. (yä'dĕ)	164	53.28 N	8.17 E
Jadotville, see Likasi			
Jaén, Peru (Kä-ĕ'n)	140	5.38 S	78.49 W
Jaen, Sp.	168	37.45 N	3.48 W
Jaffa, C., Austl. (jăf'ȧ)	212	36.58 S	139.29 E
Jaffna, Sri Lanka (jäf'nȧ)	191	9.44 N	80.09 E
Jagüey Grande, Cuba (hä'gwā grän'dā)	132	22.35 N	81.05 W
Jahore Str., Mala.	189b	1.22 N	103.37 E
Jahrom, Iran	192	28.30 N	53.28 E
Jaibo (R.), Cuba (hä-ē'bō)	123	20.10 N	75.20 W
Jaipur, India	190	27.00 N	75.50 E
Jaisalmer, India	190	27.00 N	70.54 E
Jajce, Yugo. (yī'tsĕ)	170	44.20 N	17.19 E
Jajpur, India	190	20.49 N	86.37 E
Jakarta, Indon. (yä-kär'tä)	202	6.17 S	106.45 E
Jakobstad, Fin. (yȧ'kôb-stádh)	156	63.33 N	22.31 E
Jalacingo, Mex. (hä-lä-sĭṉ'gō)	129	97.16 N	19.47 W
Jalālābād, Afg. (jŭ-lä-lȧ-bäd)	193a	34.25 N	70.27 E
Jalālah al Baḩrīyah, Jabal, (Mts.), Egypt	219b	29.20 N	32.00 E
Jalapa, Guat. (hä-lä'pȧ)	130	14.38 N	89.58 W
Jalapa de Diaz (San Felipe), Mex. (dā dē-äz') (sän fā-lē'pā)	129	18.06 N	96.33 W
Jalapa del Marqués, Mex. (dĕl mär-kās')	129	16.30 N	95.29 W
Jalapa Enríquez, Mex. (ĕn-rē'käz)	129	19.32 N	96.53 W
Jaleswar, Nep.	190	26.50 N	85.55 E
Jalgaon, India	190	21.08 N	75.33 E
Jalisco, Mex. (hä-lēs'kō)	128	21.27 N	104.54 W
Jalisco (State), Mex.	126	20.07 N	104.45 W
Jalón (R.), Sp. (hä-lōn')	168	41.22 N	1.46 W
Jalostotitlán, Mex. (hä-lōs-tē-tlàn')	128	21.09 N	102.30 W
Jalpa, Mex. (häl'pä)	129	18.12 N	93.06 W
Jalpa, Mex. (häl'pä)	128	21.40 N	103.04 W
Jalpan, Mex. (häl'pän)	128	21.13 N	99.31 W
Jaltepec, Mex. (häl-tå-pĕk')	129	17.20 N	95.15 W
Jaltipan, Mex. (häl-tå-pän')	129	17.59 N	94.42 W
Jaltocan, Mex. (häl-tô-kän')	128	21.08 N	98.32 W
Jālū, Wāḩat (Oasis), Libya	221	28.58 N	21.45 E
Jamaare (R.), Nig.	225	11.50 N	10.10 E
Jamaica, N. A.	127	17.45 N	78.00 W
Jamaica Cay (I.), Ba.	133	22.45 N	75.55 W
Jamālpur, Bngl.	190	24.56 N	89.58 E
Jamay, Mex. (hä-mī')	128	20.16 N	103.43 W
Jambi, Indon. (mäm'bē)	202	1.45 S	103.28 E
James (R.), Mo.	121	36.51 N	93.22 W
James (R.), NC	125	36.07 N	81.48 W
James (R.), U.S.	106	46.25 N	98.55 W
James (R.), Va.	109	37.35 N	77.50 W
James B., Can. (jāmz)	95	53.53 N	80.40 W
Jamesburg, NJ (jāmz'bûrg)	110a	40.21 N	74.26 W
James Pt., Ba.	133	25.20 N	76.30 W
James Ra., Austl.	210	24.15 S	133.30 E
James Ross (I.), Ant.	138	64.20 S	58.20 W
Jamestown, NY (jāmz'toun)	109	42.05 N	79.15 W
Jamestown, ND	112	46.54 N	98.42 W
Jamestown, RI	110b	41.30 N	71.21 W
Jamestown, S. Afr.	223c	31.07 S	26.49 E
Jamestown Res., ND	112	47.16 N	98.40 W
Jamiltepec, Mex. (hä-mēl-tå-pĕk)	129	16.16 N	97.54 W
Jammerbagten (B.), Den.	162	57.20 N	9.28 E
Jammu, India	190	32.50 N	74.52 E
Jammu and Kashmir (Disputed Reg.), India-Pak. (kăsh-mēr')	190	39.10 N	75.05 E
Jāmnagar, India (jäm-nŭ'gŭr)	190	22.33 N	70.03 E
Jamshedpur, India (jäm'shĕd-po͞or)	190	22.52 N	86.11 E
Jamundí, Col. (hä-mo͞o'n-dē')	140a	3.15 N	76.32 W
Jándula (R.), Sp. (hän'do͞o-lȧ)	168	38.28 N	3.52 W
Janesville, Wi. (jānz'vĭl)	113	42.41 N	89.03 W
Janin, Jordon	189a	32.27 N	35.19 E
Jan Mayen (I.), Nor. (yän mī'ĕn)	156	70.59 N	8.05 W
Jánoshalma, Hung. (yä'nôsh-hôl-mō)	165	46.17 N	19.18 E
Janów Lubelski, Pol. (yä'no͞of lū-bĕl'skĭ)	165	50.40 N	22.25 E
Januária, Braz. (zhä-nwä'rē-ä)	141	15.31 S	44.17 W
Japan, Asia (jȧ-păn')	189	36.30 N	133.30 E
Japan, Sea of, Asia (jȧ-păn')	200	40.08 N	132.55 E
Japeri, Braz. (zhȧ-pĕ'rē)	142b	22.38 S	43.40 W
Japurá (R.), Braz. (zhä-po͞o-rä')	140	1.30 S	67.54 W
Jarabacoa, Dom. Rep. (Kä-rä-bä-kō'ä)	123	19.05 N	70.40 W
Jaral del Progreso, Mex. (hä-räl dĕl prō-grä'sō)	128	20.21 N	101.05 W
Jarama (R.), Sp. (hä-rä'mä)	168	40.33 N	3.30 W
Jarash, Jordan	189a	32.17 N	35.53 E
Jardines, Banco (Bk.), Cuba (bä'n-kō-här-dē'nås)	132	21.45 N	81.40 W
Jari (R.), Braz. (zhä-rē)	141	0.28 N	53.00 W
Jarocin, Pol. (yä-rō'tsyēn)	165	51.58 N	17.31 E
Jarosław, Pol. (yȧ-rôs-wȧf)	165	50.01 N	22.41 E
Jarud Xi, China (jya-lo͞o-tŭ shyē)	198	44.35 N	120.40 E
Jasin, Mala.	189b	2.19 N	102.26 E
Jašiūnai, Sov. Un. (dzá-sho͞o-ná'yĕ)	163	54.27 N	25.25 E
Jāsk, Iran (jäsk)	192	25.46 N	57.48 E
Jasło, Pol. (yäs'wō)	165	49.44 N	21.28 E
Jason B., Mala.	189b	1.53 N	104.14 E
Jasonville, In. (jā'sŭn-vĭl)	108	39.10 N	87.15 W
Jasper, Al. (jăs'pẽr)	124	33.50 N	87.17 W
Jasper, Can.	97	52.53 N	118.05 W
Jasper, Fl.	124	30.30 N	82.56 W
Jasper, In.	108	38.20 N	86.55 W
Jasper, Mn.	112	43.51 N	96.22 W
Jasper, Tx.	123	30.55 N	93.59 W
Jasper Natl. Park, Can.	97	53.09 N	117.45 W
Jászapáti, Hung. (yäs'ŏ-pä-tē)	165	47.29 N	20.10 E
Jászberény, Hung.	165	47.30 N	19.56 E
Jatate (R.), Mex. (hä-tä-tä')	129	16.30 N	91.29 W
Jatibonico, Cuba (hä-tē-bō-nē'kō)	132	22.00 N	79.15 W
Játiva, Sp. (hä'tē-vä)	169	38.58 N	0.31 W
Jaú, Braz. (zhȧ-o͞o')	142	22.16 S	48.31 W
Jauja, Peru (Kä-o͞o'K)	140	11.43 S	75.32 W
Jaumave, Mex. (hou-mä'vȧ)	128	23.23 N	99.24 W
Jaunjelgava, Sov. Un. (youn'yĕl'gȧ-vȧ)	163	56.37 N	25.06 E
Java Trench, Indon.	202	9.45 S	107.30 E
Javari (R.), Col.-Peru (Kȧ-vä-rē)	140	4.25 S	72.07 W
Jávea, Sp. (hȧ-vā'ä)	169	38.45 N	0.07 E
Jawa (I.), Indon.	202	8.35 S	111.11 E
Jawa, Laut (Java Sea), Indon.	202	5.10 S	110.30 E
Jawor, Pol. (yä'vôr)	164	51.04 N	16.12 E
Jaworzno, Pol. (yä-vôzh'nō)	165	50.11 N	19.18 E
Jaya, Puncak (Pk.), Indon.	203	4.00 S	131.15 E
Jayapura (Sukarnapura), Indon.	203	2.30 S	140.45 W
Jayb, Wādī al (R.), see Ha 'Arava			
Jazzīn, Leb.	189a	33.34 N	35.37 E
Jeanerette, La. (jĕn-ẽr-et') (zhän-rĕt')	123	29.54 N	91.41 W

ng-sing; ŋ-baŋk; N-nasalized n; nŏd; cŏmmit; ōld; ōbey; ôrder; oi-boil; fo͞od; fo͝ot; ou-out; s-soft; sh-dish; th-thin; pūre; ûnite; ûrn; stŭd; circŭs; ü-as in French tu; '-indeterminate vowel.

PLACE (Pronunciation)	PAGE	Lat. °′	Long. °′
Jebba, Nig. (jĕb'ä)	220	9.07 N	4.46 E
Jeddore L., Can.	103	48.07 N	55.35 W
Jędrzejów, Pol. (yăn-dzhá'yoof)	165	50.38 N	20.18 E
Jefferson, Ga. (jĕf'ĕr-sŭn)	124	34.05 N	83.35 W
Jefferson, la.	113	42.10 N	94.22 W
Jefferson, la.	110d	29.57 N	90.04 W
Jefferson, La.	123	32.47 N	94.21 W
Jefferson, Tx.	123	32.47 N	94.21 W
Jefferson, Wi.	113	42.59 N	88.45 W
Jefferson, Mt., Or.	114	44.41 N	121.50 W
Jefferson City, Mo.	115	38.34 N	92.10 W
Jefferson R., Mt.	115	45.37 N	112.22 W
Jeffersontown, Ky. (jĕf'ĕr-sŭn-toun)	111h	38.11 N	85.34 W
Jeffersonville, In. (jĕf'ĕr-sŭn-vĭl)	111h	38.17 N	85.44 W
Jega, Nig.	225	12.15 N	4.23 E
Jehol (Reg.), China (jē-hŏl)	195	42.31 N	118.12 E
Jeib, Wadi el (R.), Jordan-Isr.	159	30.30 N	35.20 E
Jēkabpils, Sov. Un. (yĕk'áb-pĭls)	163	56.29 N	25.50 E
Jelenia Góra, Pol. (yĕ-lĕn'yá gōō'rä)	164	50.53 N	15.43 E
Jelgava, Sov. Un. (yĕl'gá-vä)	163	56.39 N	23.40 E
Jellico, Tn. (jĕl'ĭ-kō)	124	36.34 N	84.06 W
Jena, G.D.R. (yā'nä)	164	50.55 N	11.37 E
Jenkins, Ky. (jĕŋ'kĭnz)	110f	37.09 N	82.38 W
Jenkintown, Pa. (jĕŋ'kĭn-toun)	110f	40.06 N	75.08 W
Jennings, La. (jĕn'ĭngz)	123	30.14 N	92.40 W
Jennings, Mi.	108	44.20 N	85.20 W
Jennings, Mo.	117e	38.43 N	90.16 W
Jequié, Braz. (zhě-kyě')	141	13.53 s	40.06 W
Jequitinhonha (R.), Braz. (zhě-kē-tēṇ-ō'n-yä)	141	16.47 s	41.19 W
Jérémie, Hai. (zhā-rā-mē')	133	18.40 N	74.10 W
Jeremoabo, Braz. (zhě-rä-mŏ-á'bŏ)	141	10.03 s	38.13 W
Jerez, Punta (Pt.), Mex. (pōō'n-tä-kě-rāz')	129	23.04 N	97.44 W
Jerez de la Frontera, Sp. (kĕ-rãth' dä lä frŏn-tā'rä)	168	36.42 N	6.09 W
Jerez de Los Caballeros, Sp. (kĕ-rath'dä lōs kä-väl-yā'rŏs)	168	38.20 N	6.45 W
Jericho, Austl. (jĕr'ĭ-kō)	211	28.38 s	146.24 E
Jericho, S. Afr. (jĕr-ĭkō')	219d	25.16 N	27.47 E
Jericho, see Arīhā			
Jerome, Az. (jě-rōm')	119	34.45 N	112.10 W
Jerome, Id.	115	42.44 N	114.31 W
Jersey (I.), Eur. (jûr'zĭ)	166	49.13 N	2.07 W
Jersey City, NJ	110a	40.43 N	74.05 W
Jersey Shore, Pa.	109	41.10 N	77.15 W
Jerseyville, Il. (jĕr'zĕ-vĭl)	121	39.07 N	90.18 W
Jerusalem, Isr.-Jordan (jĕ-rōō'sá-lĕm)	189a	31.46 N	35.14 E
Jesup, Ga. (jĕs'ŭp)	125	31.36 N	81.53 W
Jesús Carranza, Mex. (hĕ-sōō's-kär-rá'n-zä)	129	17.26 N	95.01 W
Jewel Cave Natl. Mon., SD	112	43.44 N	103.52 W
Jewel, Or. (jū'ĕl)	116c	45.56 N	123.30 W
Jhālawār, India	190	24.29 N	79.09 E
Jhang Maghiâna, Pak.	190	31.21 N	72.19 E
Jhānsi, India (jän'sē)	190	25.29 N	78.32 E
Jhārsuguda, India	190	22.51 N	86.13 E
Jhelum (R.), Pak. (jā'lŭm)	190	31.40 N	71.51 E
Jiache, China	196	38.03 N	116.18 E
Jiading, China (jyä-chū)	197a	31.23 N	121.15 E
Jialing (R.), China (jyä-lĭŋ)	199	30.30 N	106.20 E
Ji'an, China (jyē-än)	199	27.15 N	115.10 E
Ji'an, China	198	41.00 N	126.04 E
Jianchangying, China (jyĕn-chäṇ-yĭŋ)	196	40.09 N	119.47 E
Jiangcun, China (jyän-tsoon)	197a	23.16 N	113.14 E
Jiangling, China (jyäṇ-lĭṇ)	199	30.30 N	112.10 E
Jiangshanzhen, China (jyäṇ-shän-jûn)	196	36.39 N	120.31 E
Jiangsu (Prov.), China (jyäṇ-sōō)	195	33.45 N	120.30 E
Jiangwan, China (jyäṇ-wän)	197b	31.18 N	121.29 E
Jiangxi (Prov.), China (jyäṇ-shyē)	195	28.15 N	116.00 E
Jiangyin, China (jyäṇ-yĭn)	199	31.54 N	120.15 E
Jianli, China (jyĕn-lē)	199	29.50 N	112.52 E
Jianning, China (jyĕn-nĭṇ)	199	26.50 N	116.55 E
Jian'ou, China (jyĕn-ō)	199	27.10 N	118.18 E
Jianshi, China (jyĕn-shr)	199	30.40 N	109.45 E
Jiaohe, China (jyou-hû)	198	43.40 N	127.20 E
Jiao Xian, China (jyou shyĕn)	196	36.18 N	120.01 E
Jiaozuo, China (jyou-dzwŏ)	196	35.15 N	113.18 E
Jiashan, China	196	32.41 N	118.00 E
Jiaxing, China (jyä-shyĭṇ)	199	30.45 N	120.50 E
Jiayu, China (jyä-yōō)	199	33.00 N	114.00 E
Jiazhou Wan (B.), China (jyä-jō wän)	196	36.10 N	119.55 E
Jibhalanta, Mong.	194	47.49 N	97.00 E
Jicarilla Ind. Res., NM (Kē-kä-rēl'yä)	119	36.45 N	107.00 W
Jicaron, Isla (I.), Pan. (Kē-kä-rōn')	131	7.14 N	81.41 W
Jiddah, Sau. Ar.	192	21.30 N	39.15 E
Jieshou, China	196	33.17 N	115.20 E
Jieyang, China (jyě-yäṇ)	199	23.38 N	116.20 E
Jiggalong, Austl. (jĭg'á-lông)	210	23.20 s	120.45 E
Jiguani, Cuba (Kē-gwä-nē')	133	20.20 N	76.30 W
Jigüey, Bahía (B.), Cuba (bä-ē'ä-Kē'gwä)	132	22.15 N	78.10 W
Jihlava, Czech. (yě'hlä-vä)	164	49.23 N	15.33 E
Jijel, Alg.	157	36.49 N	5.47 E
Jijia (R.), Rom.	165	47.35 N	27.02 E
Jijiashi, China	196	32.10 N	120.17 E
Jijiga, Eth.	219a	9.15 N	42.48 E
Jijona, Sp.	168	38.31 N	0.29 W
Jilf al-Kabīr, Hadabat al (Plat.), Egypt	221	24.09 N	25.29 E
Jilin, China (jyĕ-lĭn)	198	43.58 N	126.40 E
Jilin (Prov.), China	195	44.20 N	124.50 E
Jiloca (R.), Sp. (Kē-lô'kä)	168	41.13 N	1.30 W
Jilotepeque, Guat. (Kē-lô-tĕ-pĕ'kĕ)	130	14.39 N	89.36 W
Jima, Eth.	221	7.41 N	36.52 E
Jimbolia, Rom. (zhĭm-bô'lyä)	171	45.45 N	20.44 E
Jiménez, Mex. (Kē-mā'nāz)	128	24.12 N	98.29 W
Jiménez, Mex.	122	27.09 N	104.55 W
Jiménez, Mex.	122	29.03 N	100.42 W
Jiménez del Téul, Mex. (tĕ-ōō'l)	128	21.28 N	103.51 W
Jimo, China (jyē-mwo)	196	36.22 N	120.28 E
Jim Thorpe, Pa. (jĭm' thôrp')	109	40.50 N	75.45 W
Jinan, China (jyē-nän)	196	36.40 N	117.01 E
Jincheng, China (jyĭn-chŭ)	198	35.30 N	112.50 E
Jindřichův Hradec, Czech. (yēṇ'd'r-zhĭ-kōōf hrä'dĕts)	164	49.09 N	15.02 E
Jing (R.), China (jyĭŋ)	198	34.40 N	108.20 E
Jing'anji, China (jyĭŋ-än-jē)	198	34.30 N	116.55 E
Jingdezhen, China (jyĭŋ-dû-jûn)	199	29.18 N	117.18 E
Jingjiang, China (jyĭŋ-jyäṇ)	196	32.02 N	120.15 E
Jingning, China (jyĭŋ-nĭṇ)	198	35.28 N	105.50 E
Jingpo Hu (L.), China (jyĭŋ-pwo hōō)	198	44.10 N	129.00 E
Jing Xian, China (jyĭŋ shyĕn)	199	26.32 N	109.45 E
Jing Xian, China	196	37.43 N	116.17 E
Jingxing, China	198	47.00 N	123.00 E
Jingzhi, China (jyĭŋ-jr)	196	36.19 N	119.23 E
Jinhua, China (jyĭn-hwä)	199	29.10 N	119.42 E
Jining, China	196	35.26 N	116.34 E
Jining, China	198	41.00 N	113.10 E
Jinja, Ug. (jĭn'jä)	227	0.26 N	33.12 E
Jinotega, Nic. (Kē-nô-tā'gä)	130	13.07 N	86.00 W
Jinotepe, Nic. (Kē-nô-tā'pä)	130	11.52 N	86.12 W
Jinqiao, China (jyĭn-chyou)	196	31.46 N	116.46 E
Jinshan, China (jyĭn-shän)	197b	30.53 N	121.09 E
Jinta, China (jyĭn-tä)	194	40.11 N	98.45 E
Jintan, China (jyĭn-tän)	196	31.47 N	119.34 E
Jin Xian, China (jyĭn shyĕn)	196	39.04 N	121.40 E
Jinxiang, China (jyĭn-shyäṇ)	196	35.03 N	116.20 E
Jinyun, China (jyĭn-yōōn)	199	28.40 N	120.08 E
Jinzhai, China (jyĭn-jī)	196	31.41 N	115.51 E
Jinzhou, China (jyĭn-jō)	198	41.00 N	121.00 E
Jinzhou Wan (B.), China (jyĭn-jō wän)	196	39.07 N	121.17 E
Jinzū-Gawa (Strm.), Jap. (jēn'zōō gä'wä)	201	36.26 N	137.18 E
Jipijapa, Ec. (Kē-pē-hä'pä)	140	1.36 s	80.52 W
Jiquilisco, Sal. (Kē-kē-lē's-kô)	130	13.18 N	88.32 W
Jiquilpan de Juarez, Mex. (Kē-kēl'pän dä hwä'räz)	128	20.00 N	102.43 W
Jiquipilco, Mex. (hē-kē-pē'l-kô)	129a	19.32 N	99.37 W
Jirgalanta, Mong.	194	48.08 N	91.40 E
Jirjā, Egypt (jēr'gä)	219b	26.20 N	31.51 E
Jitotol, Mex. (Kē-tô-tōl')	129	17.03 N	92.54 W
Jiu (R.), Rom.	171	44.45 N	23.17 E
Jiujiang, China (jyô-jyän)	197a	22.50 N	113.02 E
Jiujiang, China	199	29.43 N	116.00 E
Jiuquan, China (jyô-chyän)	194	39.46 N	98.26 E
Jiurongcheng, China (jyô-rôṇ-chûṇ)	196	37.23 N	122.31 E
Jiushouzhang, China (jyô-shō-jäṇ)	196	35.59 N	115.52 E
Jiuwuqing, China (jyô-wōō-chyĭṇ)	198a	32.39 N	116.51 E
Jiuyongqian, China (jyô-yôṇ-nĭĕn)	196	36.41 N	114.46 E
Ji Xian, China (jyĕ shyĕn)	196	35.25 N	114.03 E
Ji Xian, China	196	37.37 N	115.33 E
Ji Xian, China	196	40.03 N	117.25 E
Jiyum (R.), China (jyĕ-yōōm)	196	39.35 N	117.34 E
João Belo, Moz. (zho'un-bĕ'lô)	222	25.00 s	33.45 E
João Pessoa (Paraíba), Braz. (shô-ouṇ' pĕ-sôá') (pä-rä-ē'bá)	141	7.09 s	34.45 W
João Ribeiro, Braz. (zhô-uṇ-rē-bä'rŏ)	139a	20.42 s	44.03 W
Jobabo (R.), Cuba (hô-bä'bä)	132	20.50 N	77.15 W
Jock (R.), Can. (jŏk)	93c	45.08 N	75.51 W
Jocotepec, Mex. (jô-kô-tä-pĕk')	128	20.17 N	103.26 W
Jodar, Sp. (hô'där)	168	37.54 N	3.20 W
Jodhpur, India (hŏd'pōōr)	190	26.23 N	73.00 E
Joensuu, Fin. (yô-ĕn'sōō)	163	62.35 N	29.46 E
Joffre, Mt., Can. (jô'f'r)	97	50.32 N	115.13 W
Jōga-Shima(I.), Jap. (jô'gä shē'mä)	201a	35.07 N	139.37 E
Jõgeva, Sov. Un. (yû'gĕ-vä)	172	58.45 N	26.23 E
Joggins, Can.	100	45.42 N	64.27 W
Johannesburg, S. Afr. (yô-hän'ĕs-bōōrgh)	223b	26.08 s	27.54 E
John Day Dam, Or.	114	45.40 N	120.15 W
John Day R., Or. (jŏn'dā)	114	44.46 N	120.15 W
John Day R., Middle Fork, Or.	114	44.53 N	119.04 W
John Day R., North Fork, Or.	114	45.03 N	118.50 W
John Martin Res., Co. (jŏn mär'tĭn)	120	37.57 N	103.04 W
Johnson (R.), Or. (jŏn'sŭn)	116c	45.27 N	122.20 W
Johnsonburg, Pa.	109	41.30 N	78.40 W
Johnson City, Il.	108	37.50 N	88.55 W
Johnson City, NY	109	42.10 N	76.00 W
Johnson City, Tn.	125	36.17 N	82.23 W
Johnston (I.), Oceania (jŏn'stŭn)	204	17.00 N	168.00 W
Johnstone St., Can.	96	50.25 N	126.00 W
Johnston Falls, Afr.	227	10.35 s	28.50 E
Johnstown, NY (jonz'toun)	109	43.00 N	74.20 W
Johnstown, Pa.	109	40.20 N	78.50 W
Johor (R.), Mala. (jŭ-hôr')	189b	1.39 N	103.52 E
Johor Bahru, Mala. (bä-hū-rōō')	189b	1.28 N	103.46 E
Jõhvi, Sov. Un. (yû'vĭ)	172	59.21 N	27.21 E
Joigny, Fr. (zhwän-yē')	166	47.58 N	3.26 E
Joinville, Braz. (zhwäṇ-vēl')	142	26.18 s	48.47 W
Joinville, Fr.	166	48.28 N	5.05 E
Joinville (I.), Ant.	138	63.00 s	53.30 W
Jojutla, Mex. (hô-hōō'tlä)	128	18.39 N	99.11 W
Jola, Mex. (Kô'lä)	128	21.08 N	104.26 W
Joliet, Il. (jô-lĭ-ĕt')	111a	41.37 N	88.05 W
Joliette, Can. (zhô-lyĕt')	101	46.01 N	73.30 W
Jolo, Phil. (hô-lô)	202	5.59 N	121.05 E
Jolo I., Phil.	202	5.55 N	121.15 E
Jomalig (I.), Phil. (hô-mä'lĕg)	203a	14.44 N	122.34 E
Jomulco, Mex. (hô-mōōl'kô)	128	21.08 N	104.24 W
Jonacatepec, Mex. (hô-nä-kä-tä-pĕk')	128	18.39 N	98.46 W
Jonava, Sov. Un. (yô-nä'vä)	163	55.05 N	24.15 E
Jones, Phil. (jŏnz)	203a	13.56 N	122.05 E
Jones, Phil.	203a	16.35 N	121.39 E
Jonesboro, Ar. (jŏnz'bûrô)	121	35.49 N	90.42 W
Jonesboro, La.	123	32.14 N	92.43 W
Jonesville, La. (jŏnz'vĭl)	123	31.35 N	91.50 W
Jonesville, Mi.	108	42.00 N	84.45 W
Jong (R.), S.L.	224	8.10 N	12.10 W
Joniškis, Sov. Un. (yô'nĭsh-kĭs)	163	56.14 N	23.36 E
Jönköping, Swe. (yûn'chû-pĭng)	162	57.47 N	14.10 E
Jonquiere, Can. (zhôn-kyär')	101	48.25 N	71.15 W
Jonuta, Mex. (hô-nōō'tä)	129	18.07 N	92.09 W
Jonzac, Fr. (zhôṇ-zäk')	166	45.27 N	0.27 W
Joplin, Mo. (jŏp'lĭn)	121	37.05 N	94.31 W
Jordan, Asia (jôr'dăn)	188	30.15 N	38.00 E
Jordan (R.), Jordan	189a	31.58 N	35.36 E
Jordan R., Ut.	117b	40.42 N	111.56 W
Jorhät, India	193	26.43 N	94.16 E
Jorullo, Vol. de, Mex. (vŏl-ká'n-dĕ-hô-rōōl'yô)	128	18.54 N	101.38 W
Jos Plat., Nig. (jŏs)	225	9.53 N	9.05 E
Joseph Bonaparte, G., Austl. (jô'sĕf bŏ'ná-pärt)	210	13.30 s	128.40 E
Josephburg, Can.	93g	53.45 N	113.06 W
Joseph L., Can. (jô'sĕf läk)	93g	53.18 N	113.06 W
Joshua Tree Natl. Mon., Can. (jŏ'shū-á trē)	118	34.02 N	115.53 W
Jos Plat., Nig.	225	9.53 N	9.05 E
Jostedalsbreen (Gl.), Nor. (yôstĕ-däls-brēēn)	162	61.40 N	6.55 E
Jotunheimen (Mts.), Nor.	162	61.44 N	8.11 E
Joulter's Cays (Is.), Ba. (jōl'tērz)	132	25.20 N	78.10 W
Jouy-le-Chatel, Fr. (zhwē-lě-shä-tĕl')	167b	48.40 N	3.07 E
Jovellanos, Cuba (hô-vĕl-yä'nŏs)	132	22.50 N	81.10 W
Jōyō, Jap.	201b	34.51 N	135.48 E
J. Percy Priest Res., Tn.	124	36.00 N	86.45 W
Juan Aldama, Mex. (kōōä'n-äl-dá'mä)	128	24.16 N	103.21 W
Juan de Fuca, Str. of, Wa.-Can. (hwän' dä fōō'kä)	114	48.25 N	124.37 W
Juan de Nova, Ile (I.), Afr.	223	17.18 s	43.07 E
Juan Diaz, (R.), Pan. (Kōōä'n-dē'äz)	126a	9.05 N	79.30 W
Juan Fernández, Islas de (Is.), Chile (ē's-läs-dĕ-hwän' fĕr-nän'däth)	138	33.30 s	79.00 W
Juan L. Lacaze, Ur. (hōōä'n-ē'lĕ-lä-ká'zĕ)	139c	34.25 s	57.28 W
Juan Luis, Cayos de (Is.), Cuba (ka-yŏs-dĕ-hwän lōō-ēs')	132	22.15 N	82.00 W
Juàzeiro, Braz. (zhōōä'zä'rŏ)	141	9.27 s	40.28 W
Juazeiro do Norte, Braz. (zhōōä'zá'rŏ-dŏ-nôr-tē)	141	7.16 s	38.57 W
Juárez, Arg. (hōōá'rĕz)	142	37.42 s	59.46 W
Jūbā, Sud.	221	4.58 N	31.37 E
Juba R., Som. (jōō'bä)	219a	1.30 N	42.25 E
Jubayl (Byblos), Leb. (jōo-bīl')	189a	34.07 N	35.38 E
Júcar (R.), Sp. (hōō'kär)	168	39.10 N	1.22 W
Júcaro, Cuba (hōō'kä-rŏ)	132	21.40 N	78.50 W
Juchipila, Mex. (hōō-chē-pē'lä)	128	21.26 N	103.09 W
Juchitán, Mex. (hōō-chē-tän')	126	16.15 N	95.00 W
Juchitán de Zaragoza, Mex. (hōō-chē-tän' dä thä-rä-gō'thä)	129	16.27 N	95.03 W
Juchitlán, Mex. (hōō-chē-tlän)	128	20.05 N	104.07 W
Jucuapa, Sal. (Kōō-kwä'pä)	130	13.30 N	88.24 W
Judenburg, Aus. (jōō'dĕn-bûrg)	164	47.10 N	14.40 E
Judith R., Mt. (jōō'dĭth)	115	47.20 N	109.36 W
Juhua Dao (I.), China (jōō-hwä dou)	196	40.30 N	120.47 E
Juigalpa, Nic. (hwĕ-gäl'pä)	130	12.02 N	85.24 W
Juist (I.), F.R.G. (yōō'ēst)	161	53.41 N	6.50 E
Juiz de Fora, Braz. (zhōō-ēzh' dä fô'rä)	139a	21.47 s	43.20 W
Jujuy, Arg. (hōō-hwē')	142	24.14 s	65.15 W
Jujuy (Prov.), Arg. (hōō-hwē')	142	23.00 s	65.45 W
Jukskei (R.), S. Afr.	223b	25.58 s	27.58 E
Julesburg, Co. (jōōlz'bûrg)	120	40.59 N	102.16 W
Juliaca, Peru (hōō-lyä'kä)	140	15.26 s	70.12 W
Julian Alps (Mts.), Yugo.	170	46.05 N	14.05 E
Julianehåb, Grnld.	92	60.07 N	46.20 W
Jülich, F.R.G. (yü'lĕk)	167c	50.55 N	6.22 E
Jullundur, India	190	31.29 N	75.39 E
Julpaiguri, India	190	26.35 N	88.48 E
Jumento Cays (Is.), Ba. (hōō-mĕn'tô)	133	23.05 N	75.40 W
Jumilla, Sp. (hōō-mēl'yä)	168	38.28 N	1.20 W
Jump (R.), Wi. (jŭmp)	113	45.18 N	90.53 W
Jumpingpound Cr., Can. (jŭmp-ĭng-pound)	93e	51.01 N	114.34 W
Jumrah, Indon.	189b	1.48 N	101.04 E
Jumundá (R.), Braz. (zhōō-mo͞on-dä')	141	1.33 s	57.42 W
Junāgādh, India (jōō-nä'gŭd)	190	21.33 N	70.25 E
Junayfah, Egypt	219c	30.11 N	32.26 E
Junaynah, Ra's al (Mt.), Egypt	189a	29.02 N	33.58 E
Junction, Tx. (jŭŋk'shŭn)	122	30.29 N	99.48 W
Junction City, Ks.	121	39.01 N	96.49 W
Jundiai, Braz. (zhōōn-dyä-ē')	139a	23.12 s	46.52 W
Juneau, Ak. (jōō'nō)	105	58.25 N	134.30 W
Jungfrau (Pk.), Switz. (yōōng'frou)	166	46.30 N	7.59 E
Junin, Arg. (hōō-nē'n)	139c	34.35 s	60.56 W
Junin, Col.	140a	4.47 N	73.39 W
Juniyah, Leb. (jōō-nē'ĕ)	189a	33.59 N	35.38 E
Jupiter, Mt., Wa.	116a	47.42 N	123.04 W
Jupiter (R.), Can.	103	49.40 N	63.20 W
Jur (R.), Sud. (jōōr)	221	6.38 N	27.52 E
Jura (I.), Scot. (jōō'rä)	160	56.09 N	6.45 W
Jura (Mts.), Switz. (zhü-rä')	167	46.55 N	6.49 E
Jura, Sd. of, Scot. (jōō'rä)	160	55.45 N	5.55 W
Jurbarkas, Sov. Un. (yōōr-bär'käs)	163	55.06 N	22.50 E
Jūrmala, Sov. Un.	163	56.57 N	23.37 E
Jurong, China (jyōō-rôṇ)	196	31.58 N	119.12 E
Juruá (R.), Braz. (zhōō-rōō-ä')	140	5.27 s	67.39 W
Juruena (R.), Braz. (zhōō-rōōě'nä)	141	12.22 s	58.34 W
Jutaí (R.), Braz. (zhōō-tá- y')	140	4.26 s	68.14 W
Jutiapa, Guat. (hōō-tē-ä'pä)	130	14.16 N	89.55 W
Juticalpa, Hond. (hōō-tē-käl'pä)	130	14.35 N	86.17 W
Juventino Rosas, Mex. (Kōō-vĕn-tē'nô-rŏ-säs)	128	20.38 N	101.02 W
Juventud, Isla de la (I.), Cuba	132	21.40 N	82.45 W
Ju Xian, China (jyōō shyĕn)	196	35.35 N	118.50 E

PRONOUNCING INDEX

Juxtahuaca – Karakoram Pass 305

PLACE (Pronunciation)	PAGE	Lat. °′	Long. °′
Juxtahuaca, Mex. (hōōs-tlä-hwä'kä)	128	17.20 N	98.02 W
Južna Morava (R.), Yugo. (ū'zhnä mô'rä-vä)	171	42.30 N	22.00 E
Juye, China (jyōō-yü)	196	35.25 N	116.05 E
Jylland (Reg.), Den.	162	56.04 N	9.00 E
Jyväskylä, Fin. (yü'vĕs-kü-lĕ)	163	62.14 N	25.46 E
K			
Kaabong, Ug.	227	3.31 N	34.08 E
Kaalfontein, S. Afr. (kärl-fōn-tān)	223b	26.02 S	28.16 E
Kaappunt (C.), S. Afr.	222a	34.21 S	18.30 E
Kabaena, Pulau (I.), Indon. (kä-bà-ā'nà)	202	5.35 S	121.07 E
Kabala, S. L. (kà-bà'là)	220	9.43 N	11.39 W
Kabale, Ug.	227	1.15 S	29.59 E
Kabalega Falls, Ug.	227	2.15 N	31.41 E
Kabalo, Zaire (kä-bä'lō)	227	6.03 S	26.55 E
Kabambare, Zaire (kä-bäm-bä'rå)	222	4.47 S	27.45 E
Kabba, Nig.	225	7.50 N	6.03 E
Kabe, Jap. (kä'bā)	201	34.32 N	132.30 E
Kabinakagami (R.), Can.	100	49.00 N	84.15 W
Kabinda, Zaire (kä-bēɴ'dä)	226	6.08 S	24.29 E
Kabompo (R.), Zambia (kà-bôm'pō)	226	14.00 S	23.40 E
Kabongo, Zaire (kà-bông'ō)	222	7.58 S	25.10 E
Kabot, Gui.	224	10.48 N	14.57 W
Kaboudia, Ra's (C.), Tun.	158	35.17 N	11.28 E
Kābul, Afg. (kä'bōōl)	190	34.39 N	69.14 E
Kabul (R.), Asia (kä'bōōl)	193	34.44 N	69.43 E
Kabunda, Zaire	227	12.25 S	29.22 E
Kabwe (Broken Hill), Zambia	227	14.27 S	28.27 E
Kachuga, Sov. Un. (kå-chōō-gå)	179	54.09 N	105.43 E
Kadei (R.), Cam.-Cen. Afr. Rep.	225	4.00 N	15.10 E
Kadiyevka, Sov. Un. (kå-dī-yĕf'kå)	173	48.34 N	38.37 E
Kadnikov, Sov. Un. (käd'nē-kôf)	176	59.30 N	40.10 E
Kadoma, Jap.	201b	34.43 N	135.36 E
Kaduna, Nig. (kä-dōō'nä)	225	10.33 N	7.27 E
Kaduna (R.), Nig.	225	9.30 N	6.00 E
Kaédi, Mauritania (kä-ā-dē')	224	16.09 N	13.30 W
Kaena Pt., Hi. (kä'ā-nä)	104a	21.33 N	158.19 W
Kaesŏng (Kaijo), Kor. (kä'ĕ-sŭng) (kī'jō)	200	38.00 N	126.35 E
Kafanchan, Nig.	225	9.36 N	8.17 E
Kafia Kingi, Sud. (kä'fē-å kiŋ'gē)	221	9.17 N	24.28 E
Kafue, Zambia (kä'fōō)	222	15.45 S	28.17 E
Kafue (R.), Zambia	227	15.45 S	26.30 E
Kafue Flats (Pln.), Zambia	227	16.15 S	26.30 E
Kafue Natl. Pk., Zambia	227	15.00 S	25.35 E
Kafwira, Zaire	227	12.10 S	27.33 E
Kagal'nik (R.), Sov. Un. (kä-gäl''nēk)	173	46.58 N	39.25 E
Kagera (R.), Tan. (kä-gā'rå)	227	1.10 S	31.10 E
Kagoshima, Jap. (kä'gô-shē'må)	201	31.35 N	130.31 E
Kagoshima-Wan (B.), Jap. (kä'gô-shē'mä wän)	201	31.24 N	130.39 E
Kagul, Sov. Un. (ka-gōōl')	173	45.49 N	28.17 E
Kahayan (R.), Indon.	202	1.45 S	113.40 E
Kahemba, Zaire	226	7.17 S	19.00 E
Kahia, Zaire	227	6.21 S	28.24 E
Kahoka, Mo. (kå-hō'kå)	121	40.26 N	91.42 W
Kahoolawe (I), Hi. (kä-hōō-lä'wē)	104a	20.28 N	156.48 W
Kahoué, Mont (Mtn.), Ivory Coast	224	7.06 N	7.15 W
Kahshahpiwi (R.), Can.	113	48.24 N	90.56 W
Kahuku Pt., Hi. (kä-hōō'kōō)	104a	21.50 N	157.50 W
Kahului, Hi.	104a	20.53 N	156.28 W
Kai, Kepulauan (Is.), Indon.	203	5.35 S	132.45 E
Kaiang, Mala.	189b	3.00 N	101.47 E
Kaiashk (R.), Can.	100	49.40 N	89.30 W
Kaibab Ind. Res., Az. (kä'ē-bàb)	119	36.55 N	112.45 W
Kaibab Plat, Az.	119	36.30 N	112.10 W
Kaidu (R.), China (kī-dōō)	194	42.35 N	84.04 E
Kaieteur Fall, Guy. (kī-ĕ-tōōr')	141	4.48 N	59.24 W
Kaifeng, China (kī-fŭŋ)	196	34.48 N	114.22 E
Kaijo, see Kaesong			
Kai Kecil (I.), Indon.	203	5.45 S	132.40 E
Kaikyō, Sōya (Str.), Sov. Un. (sô'yä kä-ĕ'kī-ō)	175	45.45 N	141.20 E
Kailua, Hi. (kä'ē-lōō'ä)	104a	21.18 N	157.43 W
Kailua Kona, Hi.	104a	19.49 N	155.59 W
Kaimana, Indon.	203	3.32 S	133.47 E
Kaimanawa Mts., N.Z.	213	39.10 S	176.00 E
Kainan, Jap. (kä'ē-nän')	201	34.09 N	135.14 E
Kainji L., Nig.	225	10.25 N	4.50 E
Kaiserslautern, F.R.G. (kī-zĕrs-lou'tĕrn)	164	49.26 N	7.46 E
Kaitaia, N. Z. (kä-ē-tä'ē-ä)	213	35.30 S	173.28 E
Kaiwi Chan.,Hi. (käē-wē)	104a	21.10 N	157.38 W
Kaiyuan, China (kū-yuän)	199	23.42 N	103.20 E
Kaiyuan, China	198	42.30 N	124.00 E
Kaiyuh Mts., Ak. (kī-yōō')	105	64.25 N	157.38 W
Kajaani, Fin. (kä'yà-nē)	156	64.15 N	27.16 E
Kajang, Gunong (Mt.), Mala.	189b	2.47 N	104.05 E
Kajiki, Jap. (kä'jē-kē)	201	31.44 N	130.41 E
Kakhovka, Sov. Un. (kä-ĸôf'kå)	173	46.46 N	33.32 E
Kakhovskoye (L.), Sov. Un. (kå-ĸôf'skô-yĕ)	173	47.21 N	33.33 E
Kākināda, India	193	16.58 N	82.18 E
Kaktovik, Ak. (kăk-tō'vĭk)	105	70.08 N	143.51 W
Kakwa (R.), Can. (kăk'wå)	97	54.00 N	118.55 W
Kalach, Sov. Un. (kå-låch')	177	50.15 N	40.55 E
Kaladan (R.), Bur.	194	21.07 N	93.04 E
Kalahari Des., Bots. (kä-lä-hä'rē)	222	23.00 S	22.03 E
Kalama, Wa. (kȧ-lăm'ȧ)	116c	46.01 N	122.50 W
Kalama (R.), Wa.	116c	46.03 N	122.47 W
Kalámai, Grc. (kä-lä-mī')	171	37.04 N	22.08 E
Kalamazoo, Mi. (kăl-ȧ-mȧ-zōō')	108	42.20 N	85.40 W
Kalamazoo (R.), Mi.	108	42.35 N	86.00 W
Kalanchak, Sov. Un. (kä-län-chäk')	173	46.17 N	33.14 E
Kalapana, Hi. (kä-lä-pä'nä)	104a	19.25 N	155.00 W
Kalar (Mtn.), Iran	192	31.43 N	51.41 E
Kalāt, Pak. (kŭ-lät')	190	29.05 N	66.36 E
Kalatoa, Pulau (I.), Indon.	202	7.22 S	122.30 E
Kalemie (Albertville), Zaire	227	5.56 S	29.12 E
Kalgan (Zhangjiakou), China (käl-gän') (jäŋ-jyä-kō)	198	40.45 N	114.58 E
Kalgoorlie, Austl. (kăl-gōōr'lē)	210	30.45 S	121.35 E
Kaliakra, Nos (Pt.), Rom.	159	43.25 N	28.42 E
Kalima, Zaire	227	2.34 S	26.37 E
Kalinin (Tver), Sov. Un. (kä-lē'nĕn) (tvĕr)	172	56.52 N	35.57 E
Kalinin (Oblast), Sov. Un.	172	56.50 N	33.08 E
Kaliningrad (Königsberg), Sov. Un. (kä-lē-nēn'grät) (kû'nĕks-bĕrgh)	163	54.42 N	20.32 E
Kaliningrad, Sov. Un. (kä-lē-nēn'grät)	180b	55.55 N	37.49 E
Kalinkovichi, Sov. Un. (kä-lēn-ko-vē'chē)	173	52.07 N	29.19 E
Kalispel Ind. Res., Wa. (kăl-ĭ-spĕl')	114	48.25 N	117.30 W
Kalispell, Mt. (kăl'ĭ-spĕl)	115	48.12 N	114.18 W
Kalisz, Pol. (kä'lēsh)	165	51.45 N	18.05 E
Kaliua, Tan.	227	5.04 S	31.48 E
Kalixälven (R.), Swe.	156	67.12 N	22.00 E
Kalmar, Swe. (käl'mär)	162	56.40 N	16.19 E
Kalmarsund (Sd.), Swe. (käl'mär)	162	56.30 N	16.17 E
Kal'mius (R.), Sov. Un. (käl''myōōs)	173	47.15 N	37.38 E
Kalmthout, Bel.	155a	51.23 N	4.28 E
Kalmyk A. S. S. R., Sov. Un. (kål'mĭk)	177	46.56 N	46.00 E
Kalocsa, Hung. (kä'lō-chä)	165	46.32 N	19.00 E
Kalohi Chan., Hi. (kä-lō'hī)	104a	20.55 N	157.15 W
Kaloko, Zaire	227	6.47 S	25.48 E
Kalomo, Zambia (kä-lō'mō)	227	17.02 S	26.30 E
Kalsubai Mt., India	190	24.43 N	73.47 E
Kaltenkirchen, F.R.G. (käl'tĕn-kēr-ĸĕn)	155c	53.50 N	9.57 E
Kālu (R.), India	191b	19.18 N	73.14 E
Kaluga, Sov. Un. (kȧ-lōō'gä)	172	54.29 N	36.12 E
Kaluga (Oblast), Sov. Un.	172	54.10 N	34.30 E
Kalundborg, Den. (kȧ-lōōn''bôr')	162	55.42 N	11.07 E
Kalush, Sov. Un. (kä'lōōsh)	165	49.02 N	24.24 E
Kalvarija, Sov. Un. (käl-vä-rē'yȧ)	163	54.24 N	23.17 E
Kalwa, India	191b	19.12 N	72.59 E
Kal'ya, Sov. Un. (käl'yȧ)	180a	60.17 N	59.58 E
Kalyān, India	191b	19.16 N	73.07 E
Kalyazin, Sov. Un. (käl-yȧ'zĕn)	172	57.13 N	37.55 E
Kalyma (R.), Sov. Un.	179	66.32 N	152.46 E
Kama (L.), Sov. Un.	176	55.28 N	51.00 E
Kama (R.), Sov. Un. (kä'mä)	176	56.10 N	53.50 E
Kamaishi, Jap. (kä'mä-ē'shē)	200	39.16 N	142.03 E
Kamakura, Jap. (kä'mä-kōō'rä)	201a	35.19 N	139.33 E
Kamarān (I.), P. D. R. of Yem.	192	15.19 N	41.47 E
Kāmārhāti, India	190a	22.41 N	88.23 E
Kambove, Zaire (käm-bō'vē)	222	10.58 S	26.43 E
Kamchatka, P-Ov (Pen.), Sov. Un.	179	55.19 N	157.45 E
Kamchatka (R.), Sov. Un.	179	54.15 N	158.38 E
Kamen, F.R.G. (kä'mĕn)	167c	51.35 N	7.40 E
Kamenets-Podol'skiy, Sov. Un. (kȧ-mă'nĕts pô-dôl'skĭ)	173	48.41 N	26.34 E
Kamenjak, Rt (C.), Yugo. (ĸä'mĕ-nyäk)	170	44.45 N	13.57 E
Kamenka, Sov. Un. (kä-mĕŋ'kȧ)	173	48.02 N	28.43 E
Kamenka, Sov. Un.	165	50.06 N	24.20 E
Kamen'-na-Obi, Sov. Un. (kä-mĭny'nŭ ô'bē)	178	53.43 N	81.28 E
Kamensk-Shakhtinskiy, Sov. Un. (kä'mĕnsk shäk'tĭn-skĭ)	173	48.17 N	40.16 E
Kamensk-Ural'skiy, Sov. Un. (kä'mĕnsk ōō-räl'skĭ)	180a	56.27 N	61.55 E
Kamenz, G.D.R. (kä'mĕnts)	164	51.16 N	14.05 E
Kameoka, Jap. (kä'mā-ōkä)	201b	35.01 N	135.35 E
Kamet (Mt.), India	190	35.50 N	79.42 E
Kamień Pomorski, Pol.	164	53.57 N	14.48 E
Kamikoma, Jap. (kä'mē-kō'mä)	201b	34.45 N	135.50 E
Kamina, Zaire	226	8.44 S	25.00 E
Kaministikwia (R.), Can. (kȧ-mĭ-nĭ-stĭk'wĭ-ȧ)	113	48.40 N	89.41 W
Kamituga, Zaire	227	3.04 S	28.11 E
Kamloops, Can. (kăm'lōōps)	97	50.40 N	120.20 W
Kampala, Ug. (käm-pä'lä)	227	0.19 N	32.25 E
Kampar (R.), Indon. (käm'pär)	202	0.30 N	101.30 E
Kampene, Zaire	226	3.36 S	26.40 E
Kampenhout, Bel.	155a	50.56 N	4.33 E
Kamp-Lintfort, F.R.G. (kämp-lĕnt'fōrt)	167c	51.30 N	6.34 E
Kâmpóng Saôm, Kamp.	202	10.40 N	103.50 E
Kâmpóng Thum, Kamp. (kŏm'pŏng-tŏm)	202	12.41 N	104.29 E
Kâmpôt, Kamp. (käm'pōt)	202	10.41 N	104.07 E
Kamp R., Aus. (kämp)	164	48.30 N	15.45 E
Kampene, Zaire	226	3.36 S	26.40 E
Kampuchea, Asia	202	12.15 N	104.00 E
Kamsack, Can. (kăm'săk)	99	51.34 N	101.54 W
Kamskoye (Res.), Sov. Un.	176	59.08 N	56.30 E
Kamskoye Vdkhr. (Res.), Sov. Un.	180a	59.03 N	56.48 E
Kamudilo, Zaire	227	7.42 S	27.18 E
Kamuela, Hi.	104a	20.01 N	155.40 W
Kamuk, Cerro (Mt.), C. R. (sĕ'r-rô-kä-mōō'k)	131	9.18 N	83.02 W
Kamu Misaki (C.), Jap. (kä'mōō mē-sä'kē)	200	43.25 N	139.35 E
Kamyshevatskaya, Sov. Un. (kȧ-mwēsh'ĕ-vät'skä-yȧ)	173	46.24 N	37.58 E
Kamyshin, Sov. Un. (kä-mwēsh'ĭn)	177	50.08 N	45.20 E
Kamyshlov, Sov. Un. (kä-mēsh'lôf)	176	56.50 N	62.32 E
Kan (R.), Sov. Un. (kän)	178	56.30 N	94.17 E
Kanab, Ut. (kăn'ăb)	119	37.00 N	112.30 W
Kanab Plat., Az.	119	36.31 N	112.55 W
Kanabeki, Sov. Un. (kȧ-nä'byĕ-kĭ)	180a	57.48 N	57.16 E
Kanaga (I.), Ak. (kă-nä'gă)	105a	52.02 N	177.38 W
Kanagawa (Pref.), Jap. (kä'nä-gä'wä)	201a	35.29 N	139.32 E
Kanā'is, Ra's al (C.), Egypt	159	31.14 N	28.08 E
Kanamachi, Jap. (kä-nä-mä'chē)	201a	35.46 N	139.52 E
Kananga (Luluabourg), Zaire (lōō'lōō-a-bōōrg')	226	6.14 S	22.17 E
Kananikol'skoye, Sov. Un. (kȧ-nȧ-nĭ-kôl'skô-yĕ)	180a	52.48 N	57.29 E
Kanasín, Mex. (kä-nä-sē'n)	130a	20.54 N	89.31 W
Kanatak, Ak. (kă-nă'tŏk)	105	57.35 N	155.48 W
Kanawha (R.), U. S. (kȧ-nô'wȧ)	107	37.55 N	81.50 W
Kanaya, Jap. (kä-nä'yä)	201a	35.10 N	139.49 E
Kanazawa, Jap. (kä'nȧ-zä'wȧ)	201	36.34 N	136.38 E
Kānchenjunga (Mtn.), India-Nep. (kĭn-chĭn-jōōn'gȧ)	190	27.30 N	88.18 E
Kānchipuram, India	191	12.55 N	79.43 E
Kanda Kanda, Zaire (kän'dȧ kän'dȧ)	226	6.56 S	23.36 E
Kandalaksha, Sov. Un. (kȧn-dȧ-lȧk'shȧ)	176	67.10 N	33.05 E
Kandalakshskiy Zaliv (B.), Sov. Un.	176	66.20 N	35.00 E
Kandava, Sov. Un. (kän'dȧ-vȧ)	163	57.03 N	22.45 E
Kandi, Benin (käɴ-dē')	225	11.08 N	2.56 E
Kandiāro, Pak.	190	27.09 N	68.12 E
Kandla, India (kŭnd'lŭ)	190	23.00 N	70.20 E
Kandy, Sri Lanka (kän'dē)	191	7.18 N	80.42 E
Kane, Pa. (kān)	109	41.40 N	78.50 W
Kaneohe, Hi. (kä-nā-ō'hā)	104a	21.25 N	157.47 W
Kaneohe B., Hi.	104a	21.32 N	157.40 W
Kanëv, Sov. Un. (kä-nyôf')	173	49.46 N	31.27 E
Kanevskaya, Sov. Un. (kȧ-nyĕf'skȧ)	173	46.07 N	38.58 E
Kanevskoye Vdkhr. (Res.), Sov. Un.	177	50.10 N	30.40 E
Kangaroo (I.), Austl. (kăŋ-gȧ-rōō')	212	36.05 S	137.05 E
Kangāvar, Iran (kŭŋ'gā-vär)	192	34.37 N	46.45 E
Kangding, China (käŋ-dĭŋ)	194	30.15 N	101.58 E
Kangean, Kepulauan (I.), Indon. (käŋ'gē-än)	202	6.50 S	116.22 E
Kanggye, Kor. (käng'gyē)	200	40.55 N	126.40 E
Kanghwa (I.), Kor. (käng'hwä)	200	37.38 N	126.00 E
Kangnŭng, Kor. (käng'nōō ng)	200	37.42 N	128.50 E
Kango, Gabon (käɴ-gō)	226	0.09 N	10.08 E
Kangowa, Zaire	226	9.55 S	22.48 E
Kanin, P-Ov. (Pen.), Sov. Un. (kȧ-nēn')	176	68.00 N	45.00 E
Kanin Nos, Mys (G.), Sov. Un.	176	68.40 N	44.00 E
Kaningo, Ken.	227	0.49 S	38.32 E
Kanjiža, Yugo. (kä'nyē-zhä)	171	46.05 N	20.02 E
Kankakee, Il. (kăŋ-kȧ-kē')	111a	41.07 N	87.53 W
Kankakee (R.), Il.	108	41.15 N	88.15 W
Kankan, Gui (käɴ-käɴ) (kän-kän')	224	10.23 N	9.18 W
Kannapolis, NC (kăn-ăp'ō-lĭs)	125	35.30 N	80.38 W
Kannoura, Jap. (kä'nō-ōō'rä)	201	33.34 N	134.18 E
Kano, Nig. (kä'nō)	225	12.00 N	8.30 E
Kanonkop (Mtn.), S. Afr.	222a	33.49 S	18.37 E
Kanopolis Res., Ks. (kăn-ŏp'ô-lĭs)	120	38.44 N	98.01 W
Kānpur, India (kän'pûr)	190	26.00 N	82.45 E
Kansas (State), U. S. (kăn'zȧs)	106	38.30 N	99.40 W
Kansas (R.), Ks.	121	39.08 N	95.52 W
Kansas City, Ks.	117f	39.06 N	94.39 W
Kansas City, Mo.	117f	39.05 N	94.35 W
Kansk, Sov. Un.	178	56.14 N	95.43 E
Kansŏng, Kor.	200	38.09 N	128.29 E
Kantang, Thai. (kän'täng')	202	7.26 N	99.28 E
Kantchari, Upper Volta	224	12.29 N	1.31 E
Kantunilkin, Mex. (kän-tōō-nēl-kē'n)	130a	21.07 N	87.30 W
Kanzhakovskiy Kamen Gora, (Mt.), Sov. Un. (kän-zhä'kôvs-kēē kämĭen)	180a	59.38 N	59.12 E
Kaohsiung, Taiwan (kä-ô-syōōng')	199	22.35 N	120.25 E
Kaolack, Senegal	224	14.09 N	16.04 W
Kaouar (Oasis), Niger	221	19.16 N	13.09 E
Kaoyu Hu (L.), China (kä'ō-yōō'hōō)	199	32.42 N	118.40 E
Kapaa, Hi.	104a	22.06 N	159.20 W
Kapal, Sov. Un. (kå-päl')	178	45.13 N	79.08 E
Kapanga, Zaire	226	8.21 S	22.35 E
Kapchagay, Sov. Un.	189	43.55 N	77.45 E
Kapfenberg, Aus. (käp'fĕn-bĕrgh)	164	47.27 N	15.16 E
Kapiri Mposhi, Zambia	227	13.58 S	28.41 E
Kapoeta, Sud.	221	4.45 N	33.35 E
Kaposvár, Hung. (kô'pōsh-vär)	165	46.21 N	17.45 E
Kapsan, Kor. (käp'sän')	200	40.59 N	128.22 E
Kapuskasing, Can.	95	49.28 N	82.22 W
Kapuskasing (R.), Can.	100	48.55 N	82.55 W
Kapustin Yar, Sov. Un. (kä'pōōs-tĕn yär')	177	48.30 N	45.40 E
Kaputar, Mt., Austl. (kă-pû-tăr)	212	30.11 S	150.11 E
Kapuvár, Hung. (kô'pōō-vär)	164	47.35 N	17.02 E
Kara, Sov. Un. (kärȧ)	178	68.42 N	65.30 E
Kara (R.), Sov. Un.	176	68.30 N	65.20 E
Karabanovo, Sov. Un. (kä'rȧ-bȧ-nō-vô)	180b	56.19 N	38.43 E
Karabash, Sov. Un. (kó-rȧ-bäsh')	180a	55.27 N	60.14 E
Kara-Bogaz-Gol, Zaliv (B.), Sov. Un. (kȧ-rä' bŭ-gäs')	177	41.30 N	53.40 E
Karachev, Sov. Un. (kȧ-rȧ-chôf')	172	53.08 N	34.54 E
Karāchi, Pak.	190	24.59 N	68.56 E
Karacumy (Des.), Sov. Un.	153	39.08 N	59.53 E
Karaganda, Sov. Un. (kȧ-rȧ-gän'dä)	178	49.42 N	73.18 E
Karaidel, Sov. Un. (kä'rī-dĕl)	180a	55.52 N	56.54 E
Kara-Khobda (R.), Sov. Un. (kä-rȧ ĸôb'dȧ)	177	50.40 N	55.00 E
Karakoram Pass, India-Pak.	193	35.35 N	77.45 E

ng-sing; ŋ-baŋk; ɴ-nasalized n; nŏd; cŏmmit; ōld; ôbey; ôrder; oi-boil; fōōd; fŏŏt; ou-out; s-soft; sh-dish; th-thin; pūre; ûnite; ûrn; stŭd; circŭs; ü-as in French tu; '-indeterminate vowel.

PLACE (Pronunciation)	PAGE	Lat. °′	Long. °′
Karakoram Ra., India-Pak. (kä'rä kō'ro͞om)	194	35.24 N	76.38 E
Karakorum (Ruins), Mong.	194	47.25 N	102.22 E
Karaköse, Tur. (kä-rä-kŭ'sĕ)	177	39.50 N	43.10 E
Karakumy (Des.), Sov. Un. (kara-kum)	174	40.00 N	57.00 E
Karaman, Tur. (kä-rä-män')	177	37.10 N	33.00 E
Karamay, China (kär-äm-ā)	194	45.37 N	84.53 E
Karamea Bight, N.Z. (kȧ-rȧ-mē'ȧ bīt)	213	41.20 S	171.30 E
Kara Sea, see Karskoye More			
Karashahr (Yanqi), China (kä-rä-shä-är) (yän-chyē)	194	42.14 N	86.28 E
Karatsu, Jap. (kä'rȧ-tso͞o)	201	33.28 N	129.59 E
Karaul, Sov. Un. (kä-rä-o͞ol')	178	70.13 N	83.46 E
Karawanken Mts., Aus.	164	46.32 N	14.07 E
Karabalā', Iraq (kŭr'bȧ-lä)	192	32.31 N	43.58 E
Karcag, Hung. (kär'tsäg)	165	47.18 N	20.58 E
Kardhítsa, Grc.	171	39.23 N	21.57 E
Kärdla, Sov. Un. (kĕrd'lȧ)	163	58.59 N	22.44 E
Karelian (A. S. S. R.), Sov. Un.	174	62.30 N	32.35 E
Karema, Tan.	227	6.49 S	30.26 E
Kargat, Sov. Un. (kär-gät')	178	55.17 N	80.07 E
Karghalik (Yecheng), China (kä-är-gä-lē-kŭ) (yŭ-chŭŋ)	194	37.30 N	79.26 E
Kargopol', Sov. Un. (kär-gō-pōl'')	176	61.30 N	38.50 E
Kariaí, Grc.	171	40.14 N	24.15 E
Kariba, L., Afr.	227	17.15 S	27.55 E
Karibib, Namibia (kȧr'ȧ-bĭb)	222	21.55 S	15.50 E
Kārikāl, India (kä-rē-käl')	191	10.58 N	79.49 E
Karimata, Pulau-Pulau (Is.), Indon. (kä-rē-mä'tȧ)	202	1.08 S	108.10 E
Karimata, Selat (Karimata Strait), Indon.	202	1.00 S	107.10 E
Karimun Besar (I.), Indon.	189b	1.10 N	103.28 E
Karimunjawa, Kepulauan (Is.), Indon. (kä'rē-mo͞on-yä'vä)	202	5.36 S	110.15 E
Karin, Som. (kȧr'ĭn)	219a	10.43 N	45.50 E
Karkaralinsk, Sov. Un. (kär-kär-ä-lēnsk')	178	49.18 N	75.28 E
Karkar I., Pap. N. Gui. (kär'kär)	203	4.50 S	146.45 E
Karkheh (R.), Iran	192	32.45 N	47.50 E
Karkinitskiy Zailv (B.), Sov. Un. (kär-kē-net'skĭ-ē zä'lĭf)	173	45.50 N	32.45 E
Karl-Marx-Stadt (Chemnitz), G.D.R.	164	50.48 N	12.53 E
Karnataka (State), India	191	14.55 N	75.00 E
Karlobag, Yugo. (kär-lō-bäg')	170	44.30 N	15.03 E
Karlovac, Yugo. (kär'lō-vȧts)	170	45.29 N	15.16 E
Karlovka, Sov. Un. (kȧr'lôv-kȧ)	173	49.26 N	35.08 E
Karlovo, Bul. (kär'lō-vō)	171	42.39 N	24.48 E
Karlovy Vary, Czech. (kär'lō-vē vä'rē)	164	50.13 N	12.53 E
Karlshamn, Swe. (kärls'häm)	162	56.11 N	14.50 E
Karlskrona, Swe. (kärls'krō-nä)	162	56.10 N	15.33 E
Karlsruhe, F.R.G. (kärls'ro͞o-ĕ)	164	49.00 N	8.23 E
Karlstad, Swe. (kärl'städ)	162	59.25 N	13.28 E
Karluk, Ak. (kär'lŭk)	105	57.30 N	154.22 W
Karmøy (I.), Nor. (kärm-ûe)	162	59.14 N	5.00 E
Karnobat, Bul. (kär-nō'bät)	171	42.39 N	26.59 E
Kärnten (Carinthia) (State), Aus. (kĕrn'tĕn)	164	46.55 N	13.42 E
Karonga, Malawi (kȧ-rōŋ'gȧ)	222	9.52 S	33.57 E
Kárpathos (I.), Grc.	159	35.34 N	27.26 E
Karpinsk, Sov. Un. (kär'pĭnsk)	180a	59.46 N	60.00 E
Kars, Tur. (kärs)	177	40.35 N	43.00 E
Karsakpay, Sov. Un. (kär-säk-pī')	178	47.47 N	67.07 E
Kārsava, Sov. Un. (kär'sä-vä)	172	56.46 N	27.39 E
Karshi, Sov. Un. (kär'shē)	193	38.30 N	66.08 E
Karskiye Vorota, Proliv (Str.), Sov. Un.	178	70.30 N	58.07 E
Karskoye More (Kara Sea), Sov. Un.	178	74.00 N	68.00 E
Kartaly, Sov. Un. (kȧr'tá lē)	180a	53.05 N	60.40 E
Karunagapalli, India	191	9.09 N	76.34 E
Karvina, Czech.	165	49.50 N	18.30 E
Kasaan, Ak.	96	55.32 N	132.24 E
Kasai (R.), Zaire	226	3.45 S	19.10 E
Kasama, Zambia (kȧ-să'mȧ)	227	10.13 S	31.12 E
Kasanga, Tan. (kȧ-säŋ'gȧ)	227	8.28 S	31.09 E
Kasaoka, Jap. (kä'sȧ-ō'kȧ)	201	34.33 N	133.29 E
Kasba-Tadla, Mor. (käs'bȧ-täd'lȧ)	220	32.37 N	5.57 W
Kasempa, Zambia (kȧ-sĕm'pȧ)	227	13.27 S	25.50 E
Kasenga, Zaire (kȧ-seŋ'gȧ)	227	10.22 S	28.38 E
Kasese, Ug.	227	0.10 N	30.05 E
Kasese, Zaire	227	1.38 S	27.07 E
Kāshān, Iran (kā-shān')	192	33.52 N	51.15 E
Kashgar (Kashi), China (käsh-gär) (kä-shr)	194	39.29 N	76.00 E
Kashi, see Kashgar			
Kashihara, Jap. (kä'shē-hä'rä)	201b	34.31 N	135.48 E
Kashiji Pln. Zambia	226	13.25 S	22.30 E
Kashin, Sov. Un. (kä-shēn')	172	57.20 N	37.38 E
Kashira, Sov. Un. (kä-shē'rȧ)	172	54.49 N	38.11 E
Kashiwa, Jap. (kä'shē-wä)	201a	35.51 N	139.58 E
Kashiwara, Jap.	201b	34.35 N	135.38 E
Kashiwazaki, Jap. (kä'shē-wä-zä'kē)	176	37.06 N	138.17 E
Kashmir (Disputed Reg.), **see Jammu and Kashmir**			
Kashmor, Pak.	190	28.33 N	69.34 E
Kashtak, Sov. Un. (käsh'ták)	180a	55.18 N	61.25 E
Kasimov, Sov. Un. (kȧ-sē'môf)	172	54.56 N	41.23 E
Kaskanak, Ak. (kăs-kă'nāk)	105	60.00 N	158.00 W
Kaskaskia (R.), Il. (kăs-kăs'kĭ-ȧ)	108	39.10 N	88.50 W
Kaskattama (R.), Can. (kăs-kă-tä'mȧ)	99	56.28 N	90.55 W
Kaskinen, see Kaskö			
Kaskö (Kaskinen), Fin. (käs'kû) (käs'kē-nĕn)	163	62.24 N	21.18 E
Kasli, Sov. Un. (käs'lĭ)	180a	55.54 N	60.46 E
Kasongo, Zaire (kä-sōŋ'gō)	222	4.31 S	26.42 E
Kásos (I.), Grc.	159	35.20 N	26.55 E
Kassalā, Sud. (kä-sä'lä)	221	15.26 N	36.28 E
Kassándras, Kólpos (G.), Grc.	171	40.10 N	23.35 E
Kassel, F.R.G. (käs'ĕl)	164	51.19 N	9.30 E
Kasson, Mn. (kăs'ŭn)	113	44.01 N	92.45 W
Kastamonu, Tur. (kä-stȧ-mō'no͞o)	177	41.20 N	33.50 E
Kastoría, Grc. (kȧs-tō'rĭ-ȧ)	171	40.28 N	21.17 E
Kasūr, Pak.	190	31.10 N	74.29 E
Kataba, Zambia	226	16.05 S	25.10 E
Katahdin, Mt., Me. (kȧ-tä'dĭn)	102	45.56 N	68.57 W
Katanga (Reg.), Zaire (kȧ-täŋ'gȧ)	222	8.30 S	25.00 E
Katanning, Austl. (kȧ-tăn'ĭng)	210	33.45 S	117.45 E
Katav-Ivonovski, Sov. Un. (kä'tăf ĭ-vä'nōfsk)	180a	54.46 N	58.13 E
Kateninskiy, Sov. Un. (kȧtyĕ'nĭs-kĭ)	180a	53.12 N	61.05 E
Kateríni, Grc.	171	40.18 N	22.36 E
Katete, Zambia	227	14.05 S	32.07 E
Katherine, Austl. (kăth'ēr-ĭn)	210	14.15 S	132.20 E
Kāthiāwār (Pen.), India (kä'tyȧ-wär')	190	22.10 N	70.20 E
Kathmandu, Nep. (kāt-mān-do͞o')	190	27.49 N	85.21 E
Kathryn, Can. (kăth'rĭn)	93e	51.13 N	113.42 W
Kathryn, Ca.	117a	33.42 N	117.45 W
Katihār, India	190	25.39 N	87.39 E
Katiola, Ivory Coast	224	8.08 N	5.06 W
Katmai Natl. Park, Ak. (kăt'mī)	105	58.38 N	155.00 W
Katompi, Zaire	227	6.11 S	26.20 E
Katopa, Zaire	226	2.45 S	25.06 E
Katowice, Pol.	165	50.15 N	19.00 E
Kātrīnā, Jabal (Mtn.), Egypt	221	28.43 N	34.00 E
Katrineholm, Swe. (kȧ-trē'nĕ-hōlm)	162	59.01 N	16.10 E
Katsbakhskiy, Sov. Un. (kȧts-bäk'skĭ)	180a	52.57 N	59.37 E
Katsina, Nig. (kät'sē-nȧ)	225	13.00 N	7.32 E
Katsura (R.), Jap. (kä'tso͞o-rä)	201b	34.55 N	135.43 E
Katta-Kurgan, Sov. Un. (kȧ-tȧ-ko͝or-gän')	178	39.45 N	66.42 E
Kattegat (Str.), Eur. (kăt'ĕ-gät)	162	56.57 N	11.25 E
Katumba, Zaire	227	7.45 S	25.18 E
Katun' (R.), Sov. Un. (kȧ-to͞on')	178	51.30 N	86.18 E
Katwijkaan Zee, Neth.	155a	52.12 N	4.23 E
Kauai (I.), Hi.	104a	22.09 N	159.15 W
Kauai Chan., Hi. (kä-o͞o-ä'ē)	104a	21.35 N	158.52 W
Kaufbeuren, F.R.G. (kouf'boi-rĕn)	164	47.52 N	10.38 E
Kaufman, Tx. (kôf'măn)	123	32.36 N	96.18 W
Kaukauna, Wi. (kô-kô'nȧ)	113	44.17 N	88.15 W
Kaulakahi Chan., Hi. (kä'o͞o-lȧ-kä'hē)	104a	22.00 N	159.55 W
Kaunakakai, Hi. (kä'o͞o-nȧ-kä'kī)	104a	21.06 N	156.59 W
Kaunas (Kovno), Sov. Un. (kou'nȧs) (kōv'nō)	163	54.42 N	23.54 E
Kaura Namoda, Nig.	225	12.35 N	6.35 E
Kavajë, Alb. (kȧ-vä'yŭ)	171	41.11 N	19.36 E
Kavála, Grc. (kä-vä'lä)	171	40.55 N	24.24 E
Kavieng, Pap. N. Gui. (kä-vē-ĕng')	203	2.44 S	151.02 E
Kawagoe, Jap. (kä-wă-gō'ā)	201a	35.55 N	139.29 E
Kawaguchi, Jap. (kä-wä-go͞o-chē)	201a	35.48 N	139.44 E
Kawaikini (Mtn.), Hi. (kä-wä'ē-kĭ-nī)	104a	22.05 N	159.33 W
Kawanishi, Jap. (kä-wä'nē-shē)	201b	34.49 N	135.26 E
Kawasaki, Jap. (kä-wä-sä'kē)	201a	35.32 N	139.43 E
Kawm Umbū, Egypt	219b	24.30 N	32.59 E
Kaxgar (R.), China	194	39.26 N	74.30 E
Kaya, Upper Volta (kä'yä)	224	13.05 N	1.05 W
Kayan (R.), Indon.	202	1.45 N	115.38 E
Kaycee, Wy. (kā-sē')	115	43.43 N	106.38 W
Kayes, Mali (kāz)	224	14.27 N	11.26 W
Kayseri, Tur. (kī'sĕ-rē)	177	38.45 N	35.20 E
Kaysville, Ut. (kāz'vĭl)	117b	41.02 N	111.56 W
Kazach'ye, Sov. Un.	179	70.46 N	135.47 E
Kazakh S.S.R., Sov. Un. (kȧ-zäk')	174	48.45 N	59.00 E
Kazan', Sov. Un. (kȧ-zän')	176	55.50 N	49.18 E
Kazanka, Sov. Un. (kȧ-zän'kȧ)	173	47.49 N	32.50 E
Kazanlŭk, Bul. (kȧ'zȧn-lēk)	171	42.47 N	25.23 E
Kazatin, Sov. Un.	173	49.43 N	28.50 E
Kazbek, Gora (Mt.), Sov. Un. (kȧz-bĕk')	177	42.45 N	44.30 E
Kāzerūn, Iran	192	29.37 N	51.44 E
Kazincbarcika, Hung. (kô'zĭnts-bôr-tsĭ-ko)	165	48.15 N	20.39 E
Kazungula, Zambia	227	17.45 S	25.20 E
Kazusa Kameyama, Jap. (kä-zo͞o-sä kä-mā'yä-mä)	201a	35.14 N	140.06 E
Kazym (R.), Sov. Un. (kä-zēm')	178	63.30 N	67.41 E
Kéa (I.), Grc.	171	37.36 N	24.13 E
Kealaikahiki Chan., Hi. (kā-ä'lä-ē-kä-hē'kē)	104a	20.38 N	157.00 W
Keansburg, NJ (kēnz'bûrg)	110a	40.26 N	74.08 W
Kearney, Ne. (kär'nĭ)	120	40.42 N	99.05 W
Kearny, NJ	110a	40.46 N	74.09 W
Keasey, Or. (kēz'ĭ)	116c	45.51 N	123.20 W
Keban Gölü (L.), Tur.	177	38.20 N	39.50 E
Kebnekaise Mt., Swe. (kĕp'nĕ-kȧ-ēs'ĕ)	156	67.53 N	18.10 E
Kecskemét, Hung. (kĕch'kĕ-māt)	165	46.52 N	19.42 E
Kedah State, Mala. (kā'dä)	202	6.00 N	100.31 E
Kédainiai, Sov. Un. (kē-dī'nĭ-ī)	163	55.16 N	23.58 E
Kedgwick, Can. (kĕdj'wĭk)	102	47.39 N	67.21 W
Keenbrook, Ca. (kēn'bro͝ok)	117a	34.16 N	117.29 W
Keene, NH (kēn)	109	42.55 N	72.15 W
Keetmanshoop, Namibia (kāt'mȧns-hōp)	222	26.30 S	18.05 E
Keet Seel Ruin, Az. (kēt sēl)	119	36.46 N	110.32 W
Keewatin, Mn. (kē-wä'tĭn)	113	47.24 N	93.03 W
Keewatin, Dist. of, Can.	94	61.26 N	97.54 W
Kefallinía (Cephalonia) (I.), Grc.	171	38.08 N	20.58 E
Kefe, see Feodosiya			
Keffi, Nig. (kĕf'ē)	225	8.51 N	7.52 E
Ke-Ga, Mui (Pt.), Viet.	202	12.58 N	109.50 E
Kei (R.), S. Afr. (kā)	223c	32.57 S	26.50 E
Keila, Sov. Un. (kā'lȧ)	163	59.19 N	24.25 E
Kei Mouth, S. Afr.	223c	32.40 S	28.23 E
Keiskammahoek, S. Afr. (kās'kämä-ho͝ok')	223c	32.42 S	27.11 E
Kéita, Bahr (R.), Chad.	225	9.30 N	19.17 E
Keitele (L.), Fin. (kā'tĕ-lĕ)	163	62.50 N	25.40 E
Kekaha, Hi.	104a	21.57 N	159.42 W
Kelafo, Eth.	219a	5.40 N	44.00 E
Kelang, Mala.	189b	3.20 N	101.27 E
Kelang (R.), Mala.	189b	3.00 N	101.40 E
Kelkit (R.), Tur.	159	40.38 N	37.03 E
Keller, Tx. (kĕl'ēr)	117c	32.56 N	97.15 W
Kellinghusen, F.R.G. (kĕ'lēng-ho͞o-zĕn)	155c	53.57 N	9.43 E
Kellogg, Id. (kĕl'ŏg)	114	47.32 N	116.07 W
Kelme', Sov. Un. (kĕl-mā)	163	55.36 N	22.53 E
Kélo, Chad	225	9.19 N	15.48 E
Kelowna, Can.	97	49.53 N	119.29 W
Kelsey Bay, Can. (kĕl'sē)	96	50.24 N	125.57 W
Kelso, Wa.	116c	46.09 N	122.54 W
Keluang, Mala.	189b	2.01 N	103.19 E
Kem', Sov. Un. (kĕm)	176	65.00 N	34.48 E
Kemah, Tx. (kē'mȧ)	123a	29.32 N	95.01 W
Kemerovo, Sov. Un.	178	55.31 N	86.05 E
Kemi, Fin. (kā'mē)	156	65.48 N	24.38 E
Kemi (R.), Fin.	156	67.02 N	27.50 E
Kemigawa, Jap. (kĕ'mē-gä'wä)	201a	35.38 N	140.07 E
Kemijarvi, Fin. (kā'mē-yĕr-vē)	156	66.48 N	27.21 E
Kemi-joki (L.), Fin.	156	66.37 N	28.13 E
Kemmerer, Wy. (kém'ēr-ēr)	115	41.48 N	110.36 W
Kemp (L.), Tx. (kĕmp)	120	33.55 N	99.22 W
Kempen, F.R.G. (kĕm'pĕn)	167c	51.22 N	6.25 E
Kempsey, Austl. (kĕmp'sē)	212	30.59 S	152.50 E
Kempt (L.), Can. (kĕmpt)	102	47.28 N	74.00 W
Kempten, F.R.G. (kĕmp'tĕn)	164	47.44 N	10.17 E
Kempton Park, S. Afr. (kĕmp'tŏn pärk)	223b	26.07 S	28.29 E
Ken (R.), India	190	25.00 N	79.55 E
Kenai, Ak. (kĕ-nī')	105	60.38 N	151.18 W
Kenai Mts., Ak.	105	60.00 N	150.00 W
Kenai Pen, Ak.	105	64.40 N	150.18 W
Kendal, Eng. (kĕn'dȧl)	160	54.20 N	1.48 W
Kendal, S. Afr.	219d	26.03 S	28.58 E
Kendallville, In. (kĕn'dăl-vĭl)	108	41.25 N	85.20 W
Kenedy, Tx. (kĕn'ĕ-dĭ)	117	28.49 N	97.50 W
Kenema, SL.	224	7.52 N	11.12 W
Kenitra (Port Lyautey), Mor. (kĕ-nē'trȧ)	158	34.21 N	6.34 W
Kenmare, ND (kĕn-mâr')	112	48.41 N	102.05 W
Kenmore, NY (kĕn'mōr)	111c	42.58 N	78.53 W
Kennebec (R.), Me. (kĕn-ē-bĕk')	102	44.23 N	69.48 W
Kennebunk, Me. (kĕn-ē-buŋk')	102	43.24 N	70.33 W
Kennedale, Tx. (kĕn'-ē-dāl)	117c	32.38 N	97.13 W
Kennedy, C., see Canaveral			
Kennedy, Mt., Can.	105	60.25 N	138.50 W
Kenner, La. (kĕn'ēr)	123	29.58 N	90.15 W
Kennett, Mo. (kĕn'ĕt)	121	36.14 N	90.01 W
Kennewick, Wa. (kĕn'ē-wĭk)	114	46.12 N	119.06 W
Kenney Dam, Can.	96	53.37 N	124.58 W
Kennydale, Wa. (kĕn-nē'dāl)	116a	47.31 N	122.12 W
Kénogami, Can. (kĕn-ō'gä-mē)	101	48.26 N	71.14 W
Kenogamissi L., Can.	100	48.15 N	81.31 W
Keno Hill, Can.	105	63.58 N	135.18 W
Kenora, Can. (kē-nō'rȧ)	99	49.47 N	94.29 W
Kenosha, Wi. (kĕ-nō'shȧ)	111a	42.34 N	87.50 W
Kenova, WV (kē-nō'vȧ)	108	38.20 N	82.35 W
Kensico Res., NY (kĕn'sĭ-kō)	110a	41.08 N	73.45 W
Kent, Oh. (kĕnt)	108	41.05 N	81.20 W
Kent, Wa.	116a	47.23 N	122.14 W
Kentani, S. Afr. (kĕnt-änĭ')	223c	32.31 S	28.19 E
Kentei Shan (Mts.), Mong. (kĕn'tĭ'shän')	194	49.25 N	107.51 E
Kentland, In. (kĕnt'lȧnd)	108	40.50 N	87.25 W
Kenton, Oh. (kĕn'tŭn)	108	40.40 N	83.35 W
Kent Pen, Can.	94	68.28 N	108.10 W
Kentucky (State), U. S. (kĕn-tŭk'ĭ)	107	37.30 N	87.35 W
Kentucky (L.), U. S.	107	36.20 N	88.50 W
Kentucky (R.), U. S.	107	38.15 N	85.01 W
Kentwood, La. (kĕnt'wo͝od)	123	30.56 N	90.31 W
Kenya, Afr. (kēn'yȧ)	218	1.00 N	36.53 E
Kenya, Mt., see Kirinyaga			
Kenyon, Mn. (kĕn'yŭn)	113	44.15 N	92.58 W
Keokuk, Ia. (kē'ō-kŭk)	121	40.24 N	91.34 W
Keoma, Can. (kē-ō'mȧ)	93e	51.13 N	113.39 W
Kepenkeck L., Can.	103	48.13 N	54.45 W
Kępno, Pol. (kȧŋ'pnō)	165	51.17 N	17.59 E
Kerala (State), India	191	16.38 N	76.00 E
Kerang, Austl. (kē-răng')	212	35.32 S	143.58 E
Kerch', Sov. Un. (kĕrch)	173	45.20 N	36.26 E
Kerchenskiy Proliv (Str.) (Kerch Str.), Sov. Un. (kĕr-chĕn'skĭ prô'lĭf)	173	45.08 N	36.35 E
Kerempe Burun (C.), Tur.	177	42.00 N	33.20 E
Keren, Eth.	221	15.46 N	38.28 E
Kerguelen, Is. de, Ind. O. (kĕr'gā-lĕn)	228	49.50 S	69.30 E
Kericho, Ken.	227	0.22 S	35.17 E
Kerinci, Gunung (Mtn.), Indon.	202	1.45 S	101.18 E
Keriya (R.), China (kē'rē-yä)	194	37.13 N	81.59 E
Keriya, see Yütian			
Kerkenna, Îles (I.), Tun. (kĕr'kĕn-nä)	221	34.49 N	11.37 E
Kerki, Sov. Un. (kĕr'kē)	193	37.52 N	65.15 E
Kérkira, Grc.	171	39.36 N	19.56 E
Kérkira (I.), Grc.	171	39.33 N	19.36 E
Kermadec Is., N. Z. (kēr-mȧd'ĕk)	204	30.30 S	177.00 E
Kermadec Tonga Trench, Oceania (kēr-mȧd'ĕk tŏŋ'gȧ)	204	23.00 S	172.30 W
Kermān, Iran (kĕr-mān')	192	30.23 N	57.08 E
Kermānshāh, Iran (kĕr-mān-shā')	192	34.01 N	47.00 E
Kern (R.), Ca.	118	35.31 N	118.37 W
Kern, South Fork of (R.), Ca.	118	35.40 N	118.15 W
Kern Can., Ca. (kûrn)	118	36.57 N	119.37 W
Kérouané, Gui.	224	9.16 N	9.01 W
Kerpen, F.R.G. (kĕr'pĕn)	167c	50.52 N	6.42 E
Kerrobert, Can.	98	51.53 N	109.13 W
Kerrville, Tx. (kûr'vĭl)	122	30.02 N	99.07 W
Kerulen (R.), Mong. (kĕr'o͞o-lĕn)	195	47.52 N	113.22 E
Kesagami L., Can.	101	50.23 N	80.15 W
Kesan, Tur. (kĕ'shȧn)	171	40.50 N	26.37 E
Keshan, China (kŭ-shän)	198	48.00 N	126.30 E
Kesour, Monts des (Mts.), Alg.	158	32.51 N	0.30 W
Kestell, S. Afr. (kĕs'tĕl)	219d	28.19 N	28.43 E

PLACE (Pronunciation)	PAGE	Lat. °′	Long. °′
Keszthely, Hung. (kĕst'hĕl-lǐ)	165	46.46 N	17.12 E
Ket' (R.), Sov. Un. (kyĕt)	178	58.30 N	84.15 E
Keta, Ghana	220	6.00 N	1.00 E
Ketamputih, Indon. (kĕ-tà-päng')	189b	1.25 N	102.19 E
Ketapang, Indon. (kĕ-tä-päng')	202	2.00 S	109.57 E
Ketchikan, Ak. (kĕch-ĭ-kán')	96	55.21 N	131.35 W
Ketrzyn, Pol. (kȧŋ't'r-zīn)	165	54.04 N	21.24 E
Kettering, Eng. (kĕt'ēr-ĭng)	154	52.23 N	0.43 W
Kettering, Oh.	108	39.40 N	84.15 W
Kettle (R.), Can.	97	49.40 N	119.00 W
Kettle (R.), Mn. (kĕt''l)	113	46.20 N	92.57 W
Kettwig, F.R.G. (kĕt'vēg)	167c	51.22 N	6.56 E
Kety, Pol. (kȧŋ tǐ)	165	49.54 N	19.16 E
Ketzin, G.D.R. (kě'tzēn)	155b	52.29 N	12.51 E
Keuka (L.), NY (kĕ-ū'kȧ)	109	42.30 N	77.10 W
Kevelaer, F.R.G. (kě'fĕ-lär)	167c	51.35 N	6.15 E
Kewanee, Il. (kĕ-wä'nĕ)	113	41.15 N	89.55 W
Kewaunee, Wi. (kĕ-wô'nĕ)	113	44.27 N	87.33 W
Keweenaw B., Mi. (kě'wě-nô)	113	46.59 N	88.15 W
Keweenaw Pen., Mi.	113	47.28 N	88.12 W
Keya Paha (R.), S.D. (kē-yä pa'hä)	112	43.11 N	100.10 W
Key Largo (I.), Fl.	125a	25.11 N	80.15 W
Keyport, NJ (kē'pōrt)	110a	40.26 N	74.12 W
Keyport, Wa.	116a	47.42 N	122.38 W
Keyser, WV (kī'sēr)	109	39.25 N	79.00 W
Key West, Fl. (kē wěst')	125a	24.31 N	81.47 W
Kežmarok, Czech. (kĕzh'mȧ-rôk)	165	49.10 N	20.27 E
Khabarovo, Sov. Un. (kŭ-bär-ôvô)	178	69.31 N	60.41 E
Khabarovsk, Sov. Un. (kä-bä'rôfsk)	179	48.35 N	135.12 E
Khakass Aut. Oblast, Sov. Un.	178	52.32 N	89.33 E
Khālāpur, India	191b	18.48 N	73.17 E
Khalkidhiki (Pen.), Grc.	171	40.30 N	23.18 E
Khalkis, Grc. (kál'kis)	171	38.28 N	23.38 E
Khal'mer-Yu, Sov. Un. (kŭl-myěr'-yōō)	178	67.52 N	64.25 E
Khalturin, Sov. Un. (käl'tōō-rēn)	176	58.28 N	49.00 E
Khambhāt, G. of, India	190	21.20 N	72.27 E
Khammam, India	191	17.09 N	80.13 E
Khānābād, Afg.	190	36.43 N	69.11 E
Khandwa, India	190	21.53 N	76.22 E
Khangai Mts., see Hangayn Nuruu			
Khanh-Hung, Viet.	202	9.45 N	105.50 E
Khaniá, Grc. (kä-nē'ä)	170a	35.29 N	24.04 E
Khaníon, Kólpos (G.), Grc.	170a	35.35 N	23.55 E
Khanka (L.), Sov. Un. (ĸän'kȧ)	195	45.09 N	133.28 E
Khānpur, Pak.	190	28.42 N	70.42 E
Khanty-Mansiysk, Sov. Un. (ĸŭn-te'mŭn-sěsk')	178	61.02 N	69.01 E
Khān Yūnus, Gaza Strip	189a	31.21 N	34.19 E
Kharagpur, India (kŭ-rŭg'pōōr)	190	22.26 N	87.21 E
Khar'kov, Sov. Un. (ĸär'kôf)	173	50.00 N	36.10 E
Khar'kov (Oblast), Sov. Un.	173	49.33 N	35.55 E
Kharlovka, Sov. Un.	176	68.47 N	37.20 E
Kharmanli, Bul. (ĸär-män'lě)	171	41.54 N	25.55 E
Khartoum, see Al Kharṭūm			
Khāsh, Iran	192	28.08 N	61.08 E
Khāsh (R.), Afg.	192	32.30 N	64.27 E
Khasi Hills, India	190	25.38 N	91.55 E
Khaskovo, Bul. (ĸás'kô-vô)	171	41.56 N	25.32 E
Khatanga, Sov. Un. (ĸȧ-tän'gȧ)	179	71.48 N	101.47 E
Khatangskiy Zaliv (B.), Sov. Un. (kä-täŋ'g-skē)	179	73.45 N	108.30 E
Khemis Miliana, Alg.	157	36.19 N	1.56 E
Kherson, Sov. Un. (ĸĕr-sŏn')	173	46.38 N	32.34 E
Kherson (Oblast), Sov. Un.	173	46.32 N	32.55 E
Khetan (R.), India	190	10.57 N	78.23 E
Khiitola, Sov. Un. (ĸhě'tô-lä)	163	61.14 N	29.40 E
Khimki, Sov. Un. (kěm'kī)	180b	55.54 N	37.27 E
Khíos, Grc. (kē'ôs)	171	38.23 N	26.09 E
Khíos (I.), Grc.	171	38.20 N	25.45 E
Khiva, Sov. Un. (kē'vä)	153	41.15 N	60.30 E
Khmel'nik, Sov. Un.	173	49.34 N	27.58 E
Khmel'nitskiy, Sov. Un. (kmĕ'lně'ts-kěb)	177	49.29 N	26.54 E
Khmel'nitskiy (Oblast), Sov. Un. (ĸměl-nět'skī ôb'làst')	173	49.27 N	26.30 E
Khöbsögol Dalai (Koso Lake), Mong.	194	51.11 N	99.11 E
Kholm, Sov. Un. (ĸôlm)	172	57.09 N	31.07 E
Kholmsk, Sov. Un. (ĸŭlmsk)	179	47.09 N	142.33 E
Khopër (R.), Sov. Un. (ĸô'pĕr)	177	52.00 N	43.00 E
Khor, Sov. Un. (ĸôr')	200	47.50 N	134.52 E
Khor (R.), Sov. Un.	200	47.23 N	135.20 E
Khóra Sfakíon, Grc.	170a	35.12 N	24.10 E
Khorog, Sov. Un. (ĸôr'ôg)	178	37.30 N	71.47 E
Khorog, Sov. Un.	190	37.10 N	71.43 E
Khorol, Sov. Un.	173	49.48 N	33.17 E
Khorol (R.), Sov. Un.	173	49.50 N	33.21 E
Khorramshahr, Iran (ĸô-ram'shär)	192	30.36 N	48.15 E
Khotin, Sov. Un.	173	48.29 N	26.32 E
Khot'kovo, Sov. Un.	180b	56.15 N	38.00 E
Khoybār, Sau. Ar.	192	25.45 N	39.28 E
Khoyniki, Sov. Un.	173	51.54 N	30.00 E
Khulna, Bngl.	190	22.50 N	89.38 E
Khūryān Mūryān (Is.), Om.	192	17.27 N	56.02 E
Khust, Sov. Un. (ĸōōst)	165	48.10 N	23.18 E
Khvalynsk, Sov. Un. (ĸvȧ-līnsk')	177	52.30 N	48.00 E
Khvoy, Iran	192	38.32 N	45.01 E
Khyber Pass, Pak. (kī'bĕr)	193a	34.28 N	71.18 E
Kialwe, Zaire	227	9.22 S	27.08 E
Kiambi, Zaire (kyäm'bĕ)	227	7.20 S	28.01 E
Kiamichi (R.), Ok. (kyä-mē'chĕ)	121	34.31 N	95.34 W
Kianta (L.), Fin. (kyän'tä)	176	65.00 N	28.15 E
Kibenga, Zaire	226	7.55 S	17.35 E
Kibiti, Tan.	227	7.44 S	38.57 E
Kibombo, Zaire	227	3.54 S	25.55 E
Kibondo, Tan.	227	3.35 S	30.42 E
Kičevo, Yugo. (kě'chě-vô)	171	41.30 N	20.59 E
Kickapoo (R.), Wi. (kǐk'à-pōō)	113	43.20 N	90.55 W
Kicking Horse P., Can.	97	51.25 N	116.10 W
Kidal, Mali (kē-dȧl')	220	18.33 N	1.00 E
Kidderminster, Eng. (kǐd'ēr-mǐn-stēr)	154	52.23 N	2.14 W

PLACE (Pronunciation)	PAGE	Lat. °′	Long. °′
Kidd's Beach, S. Afr. (kīdz)	223c	33.09 S	27.43 E
Kidsgrove, Eng. (kǐdz'grōv)	154	53.05 N	2.30 W
Kiel, F.R.G. (kěl)	164	54.19 N	10.08 E
Kiel, Wi.	113	43.52 N	88.04 W
Kiel B., F.R.G.	164	54.33 N	10.19 E
Kiel Can., see Nord-Ostsee Kan.			
Kielce, Pol. (kyĕl'tsě)	165	50.50 N	20.41 E
Kieldrecht, Bel. (kĕl'drĕĸt)	155a	51.17 N	4.09 E
Kiev, see Kiyev			
Kiev (Oblast), Sov. Un. (kē'yĕf) (ôb'làst')	173	50.05 N	30.40 E
Kievskoye Vdkhr. (Res.), Sov. Un.	177	51.00 N	30.20 E
Kiffa, Mauritania (kēf'ȧ)	224	16.37 N	11.24 W
Kigali, Rw. (kě-gä'lĕ)	222	1.59 S	30.05 E
Kigoma, Tan. (kě-gō'mä)	227	4.57 S	29.38 E
Kii-Suido (Chan.), Jap. (kě sōō-ě'dô)	201	33.53 N	134.55 E
Kikaiga (I.), Jap.	200	28.25 N	130.10 E
Kikinda, Yugo. (kē'kĕn-dä)	171	45.49 N	20.30 E
Kikládhes (Is.), Grc.	171	37.30 N	24.45 E
Kikwit, Zaire (kē'kwĕt)	226	5.02 S	18.49 E
Kil, Swe. (kēl)	162	59.30 N	13.15 E
Kilauea, Hi. (kē-lä-ōō-ā'ä)	104a	22.12 N	159.25 W
Kilauea Crater, Hi.	104a	19.28 N	155.18 W
Kilbuck Mts., Ak. (kǐl-bŭk)	105	60.05 N	160.00 W
Kilchu, Kor. (kǐl'chōō)	200	40.59 N	129.23 E
Kildare, Ire. (kǐl-dâr')	159	53.09 N	7.05 W
Kilembe, Zaire	226	5.42 S	19.55 E
Kilgore, Tx.	123	32.23 N	94.53 W
Kilifi, Ken.	227	3.38 S	39.51 E
Kilimanjaro (Mtn.), Tan. (kyl-ě-män-jä'rô)	223	3.09 S	37.19 E
Kilimatinde, Tan. (kǐl-ě-mä-tǐn'dä)	222	5.48 S	34.58 E
Kilindoni, Tan.	227	7.55 S	39.39 E
Kilingi-Nõmme, Sov. Un. (kě'lǐn-gĕ-nŏm'mě)	163	58.08 N	25.03 E
Kilis, Tur. (kē'lēs)	177	36.50 N	37.20 E
Kiliya, Sov. Un. (kē'lyȧ)	173	45.28 N	29.17 E
Kilkenny, Ire. (kǐl-kěn-ĭ)	160	52.40 N	7.30 W
Kilkis, Grc. (kǐl'kǐs)	171	40.59 N	22.51 E
Killala, Ire. (kǐ-lä'lä)	160	54.11 N	9.10 W
Killarney, Ire.	160	52.03 N	9.05 W
Killdeer, ND (kǐl'dēr)	112	47.22 N	102.45 W
Kilmarnock, Scot. (kǐl-mär'nŭk)	160	55.38 N	4.25 W
Kilrush, Ire. (kǐl'rŭsh)	160	52.40 N	9.16 W
Kilwa Kisiwani, Tan.	227	8.58 S	39.30 E
Kilwa Kivinje, Tan.	223	8.43 S	39.18 E
Kim (R.), Cam.	225	5.40 N	11.17 E
Kimamba, Tan.	227	6.47 S	37.08 E
Kimba, Austl. (kǐm'bá)	212	33.08 S	136.25 E
Kimball, Ne. (kǐm-bál)	112	41.14 N	103.41 W
Kimball, SD	112	43.44 N	98.58 W
Kimberley, Austl. (kǐm'bēr-lǐ)	97	49.41 N	115.59 W
Kimberley, S. Afr.	222	28.40 S	24.50 E
Kimi, Cam.	225	6.05 N	11.30 E
Kimi, Grc.	171	38.38 N	24.05 E
Kímolos (I.), Grc. (kě'mô-lôs)	171	36.52 N	24.20 E
Kimry, Sov. Un. (kǐm'rě)	172	56.53 N	37.24 E
Kimvula, Zaire	226	5.44 S	15.58 E
Kinabalu, Gunong (Mtn.), Mala.	202	5.45 N	115.26 E
Kincardine, Can. (kǐn-kär'dǐn)	108	44.10 N	81.15 W
Kinda, Zaire	226	9.18 S	25.04 E
Kindanba, Con.	226	3.44 S	14.31 E
Kinder, La. (kǐn'dēr)	123	30.30 N	92.50 W
Kindersley, Can. (kǐn'dērz-lě)	98	51.27 N	109.10 W
Kindia, Gui. (kǐn'dě-a)	224	10.04 N	12.51 W
Kindu, Zaïre	227	2.57 S	25.56 E
Kinel'-Cherkassy, Sov. Un.	176	53.32 N	51.32 E
Kineshma, Sov. Un. (kě-něsh'má)	172	57.27 N	41.02 E
King (I.), Austl. (kǐng)	212	39.35 S	143.40 E
Kingaroy, Austl. (kǐŋ'gä-roi)	212	26.37 S	151.50 E
King City, Ca. (kǐng sǐ'tǐ)	118	36.14 N	121.08 W
King City, Can.	93d	43.56 N	79.32 W
Kingcome Inlet, Can. (kǐng'kŭm)	96	50.50 N	126.10 W
Kingfisher, Ok. (kǐng'fǐsh-ēr)	97	50.35 N	97.55 W
King George, Mt., Can.	97	50.35 N	115.24 W
King George Sd., Austl. (jörj)	210	35.15 S	118.30 E
Kingisepp, Sov. Un. (kǐŋ-gĕ-sep')	172	59.22 N	28.38 E
King Leopold Ranges, Austl. (lě'ô-pôld)	210	16.25 S	125.00 E
Kingman, Az. (kǐng'măn)	119	35.10 N	114.05 W
Kingman, Ks. (kǐng'măn)	120	37.38 N	98.07 W
Kings (R.), Ca.	118	36.28 N	119.43 W
Kings Canyon Natl. Park, Ca. (kán'yŭn)	118	36.52 N	118.53 W
Kingsclere, Eng. (kǐngs-clēr)	154b	51.18 N	1.15 W
Kingscote, Austl. (kǐngz'kŭt)	212	35.45 S	137.32 E
King's Lynn, Eng. (kǐngz lǐn')	161	52.45 N	0.20 E
Kings Mt., NC (nôr'tŭn)	125	35.13 N	81.30 W
Kings Norton, Eng.	154	52.25 N	1.54 W
King Sd., Austl.	210	16.50 S	123.35 E
Kings Park, NY (kǐngz pärk)	110a	40.53 N	73.16 W
Kings Pk., Ut.	115	40.46 N	110.20 W
Kingsport, Tn. (kǐngz'pōrt)	125	36.33 N	82.36 W
Kingston, Austl. (kǐngz'tŭn)	212	37.52 S	139.52 E
Kingston, Can.	109	44.15 N	76.30 W
Kingston, Jam.	128	18.00 N	76.45 W
Kingston, NY	109	42.00 N	74.00 W
Kingston, Pa.	111	41.15 N	75.50 W
Kingston, Wa.	116a	47.04 N	122.29 W
Kingston upon Hull, Eng.	154	53.45 N	0.25 W
Kingstown, St. Vincent (kǐngz'toun)	131b	13.10 N	61.14 W
Kingstree, SC (kǐngz'trē)	125	33.30 N	79.50 W
Kingsville, Tx. (kǐngz'vǐl)	122	27.32 N	97.52 W
King William I., Can. (kǐng wǐl'yăm)	94	69.25 N	97.00 W
King William's Town, S. Afr. (kǐng-wǐl'-yŭmz-toun)	213c	32.53 S	27.24 E
Kinira (R.), S. Afr.	223c	30.37 S	28.52 E
Kinloch, Mo. (kǐn-lôk)	117e	38.44 N	90.19 W
Kinnaird, Can. (kǐn-ärd')	97	49.17 N	117.39 W
Kinnairds Hd., Scot. (kǐn-ârds'hěd)	160	57.42 N	3.55 W
Kinomoto, Jap. (kě'nō-mōtō)	201	33.53 N	136.07 E
Kinosaki, Jap. (kě'nō-sä'kě)	201	35.38 N	134.47 E

PLACE (Pronunciation)	PAGE	Lat. °′	Long. °′
Kinshasa (Léopoldville), Zaire	226	4.18 S	15.18 E
Kinsley, Ks. (kǐnz'lǐ)	120	37.55 N	99.24 W
Kinston, NC (kǐnz'tŭn)	125	35.15 N	77.35 W
Kintampo, Ghana (kěn-täm'pô)	224	8.03 N	1.43 W
Kintyre (Pen), Scot.	160	55.50 N	5.40 W
Kioroshi, see Ōmori			
Kiowa, Ks. (kī'ô-wä)	120	37.01 N	98.30 W
Kiowa, Ok.	121	34.42 N	95.53 W
Kiparissía, Grc.	171	37.17 N	21.43 E
Kiparissiakós Kólpos (G.), Grc.	171	37.28 N	21.15 E
Kipawa Lac (L.), Can.	101	46.55 N	79.00 W
Kipembawe, Tan. (kē-pěm-bä'wå)	227	7.39 S	33.24 E
Kipengere Ra., Tan.	227	9.10 S	34.00 E
Kipili, Tan.	227	7.26 S	30.36 E
Kipusha, Zaire	227	11.46 N	27.14 E
Kipushi, Zaire	227	11.46 N	27.14 E
Kirby, Tx. (kûr'bǐ)	117d	29.29 N	98.23 W
Kirbyville, Tx. (kûr'bǐ-vǐl)	123	30.39 N	93.54 W
Kirenga (R.), Sov. Un. (kě-rěŋ'gä)	179	56.30 N	103.18 E
Kirensk, Sov. Un. (kě-rěnsk')	179	57.47 N	108.22 E
Kirghiz S. S. R., Sov. Un. (kir-gēz')	174	41.45 N	74.38 E
Kirghiz Steppe (Plain), Sov. Un.	174	49.28 N	57.07 E
Kirgizskiy Khrebet (Kirgiz) (Mts.), Sov. Un.	193	37.58 N	72.23 E
Kiri, Zaire	226	1.27 S	19.00 E
Kiribati, Oceania	204	1.30 S	173.00 E
Kirin, see Chilung			
Kirinyaga (Kenya) (Mtn.), Ken.	227	0.10 S	37.20 E
Kirkby-in-Ashfield, Eng. (kûrk'bē-ǐn-ăsh'fēld)	154	53.06 N	1.16 W
Kirkcaldy, Scot. (kēr-kô'dǐ)	160	56.06 N	3.15 W
Kirkenes, Nor.	158	69.40 N	30.03 E
Kirkham, Eng. (kûrk'ăm)	154	53.47 N	2.53 W
Kirkland, Wa. (kûrk'lànd)	116a	47.41 N	122.12 W
Kirklareli, Tur. (kěrk'lár-ě'lě)	171	41.44 N	27.15 E
Kirksville, Mo. (kûrks'vǐl)	121	40.12 N	92.35 W
Kirkūk, Iraq (kir-kōōk')	192	35.28 N	44.22 E
Kirkwall, Scot. (kûrk'wôl)	160a	58.58 N	2.59 W
Kirkwood, Mo. (kûrk'wood)	117e	38.35 N	90.24 W
Kirkwood, S. Afr.	223c	33.26 S	25.24 E
Kirn, F.R.G. (kěrn)	164	49.47 N	7.23 E
Kirov, Sov. Un.	172	54.04 N	34.19 E
Kirov, Sov. Un.	178	58.35 N	49.35 E
Kirovabad, Sov. Un. (kě-rŭ-vŭ-bät')	177	40.40 N	46.20 E
Kirovgrad, Sov. Un. (kě'rŭ-vŭ-grad')	180a	57.26 N	60.03 E
Kirovograd, Sov. Un. (kě-rŭ-vŭ-grät')	173	48.33 N	32.17 E
Kirovograd (Oblast), Sov. Un.	173	48.23 N	31.10 E
Kirovsk, Sov. Un.	176	67.40 N	33.58 E
Kirovsk, Sov. Un. (kě-rôfsk')	180c	59.52 N	30.59 E
Kirsanov, Sov. Un. (kěr-sä-nôf)	177	52.40 N	42.40 E
Kirsehir, Tur. (kěr-shě'hēr)	177	39.10 N	34.00 E
Kirtachi Seybou, Niger	225	12.48 N	2.29 E
Kīrthar Ra., Pak. (kīr-tūr)	190	27.00 N	67.10 E
Kirton, Eng. (kûr'tŭn)	154	53.29 N	0.35 W
Kiruna, Swe. (kē-rōō'nä)	158	67.49 N	20.08 E
Kirundu, Zaire	227	0.44 S	25.32 E
Kirwin Res., L. (kûr'wǐn)	120	39.34 N	99.04 W
Kiryū, Jap. (kě'rǐ-ōō)	201	36.26 N	139.18 E
Kirzhach, Sov. Un. (kěr-zhák')	172	56.08 N	38.53 E
Kisaki, Tan. (kē-sä'kě)	223	7.37 S	37.43 E
Kisangani (Stanleyville), Zaire	226	0.30 S	25.12 E
Kisarazu, Jap. (kě'sä-rä'zōō)	201a	35.23 N	139.55 E
Kiselëvsk, Sov. Un. (kě-sǐ-lyôfsk')	178	54.05 N	86.19 E
Kishinëv, Sov. Un. (ke-shě-nyôf')	173	47.02 N	28.52 E
Kishiwada, Jap. (kě-shě-wä'dä)	201	34.25 N	135.18 E
Kishkino, Sov. Un. (kěsh'kǐ-nō)	180b	55.15 N	38.04 E
Kisiwani, Tan.	227	4.08 S	37.57 E
Kiska (I.), Ak. (kǐs'kä)	105a	52.08 N	177.10 E
Kiskatinaw (R.), Can.	97	55.10 N	120.20 W
Kiskitto L., Can. (kǐs-kǐ'tô)	99	54.05 N	98.34 W
Kiskittogisu L., Can.	99	54.05 N	99.00 W
Kiskunfélegyháza, Hung. (kǐsh'kōōn-fā'lěd-y'hä'zō)	165	46.42 N	19.52 E
Kiskunhalas, Hung. (kǐsh'kōōn-hô'lôsh)	165	46.24 N	19.26 E
Kiskunmajsa, Hung. (kǐsh'kōōn-mä'shô)	165	46.29 N	19.42 E
Kismayu, Som.	223	0.18 S	42.30 E
Kiso-Gawa (Strm.), Jap. (kě'sō-gä'wä)	201	35.29 N	137.12 E
Kiso-Sammyaku (Mts.), Jap. (kě'sō säm'myä-kōō)	201	35.47 N	137.39 E
Kissamos, Grc.	170a	35.13 N	24.11 E
Kissidougou, Gui. (kě'sě-dōō'gōō)	224	9.11 N	10.06 W
Kissimmee, Fl. (kǐ-sǐm'ě)	125a	28.17 N	81.25 W
Kissimmee (L.), Fl.	125a	27.58 N	81.17 W
Kissimmee (R.), Fl.	125a	27.45 N	81.07 W
Kistrand, Nor. (kě'stränd)	158	70.29 N	25.01 E
Kisujszállás, Hung. (kǐsh'ōō'y'sä'läsh)	165	47.12 N	20.47 E
Kisumu, Ken. (kě'sōō-mōō)	227	0.06 S	34.45 E
Kita, Mali (kě'tä)	224	13.03 N	9.29 W
Kitakami Gawa (R.), Jap. (kě'tä-kä'mē gä-wä)	200	39.20 N	141.10 E
Kitakyūshū, Jap. (kě'tä-kyōō'shōō')	201	34.15 N	130.23 E
Kitale, Ken.	227	1.01 N	35.00 E
Kit Carson, Co.	120	38.46 N	102.48 W
Kitchener, Can. (kǐch'ě-nēr)	108	43.25 N	80.35 W
Kitenda, Zaire	226	6.53 S	17.21 E
Kitgum, Ug. (kǐt'gōōm)	221	3.29 N	33.04 E
Kíthira (I.), Grc.	159	36.15 N	22.56 E
Kíthnos (I.), Grc.	171	37.24 N	24.10 E
Kitimat, Can. (kǐ'tǐ-mät)	96	54.03 N	128.33 W
Kitimat (R.), Can.	96	53.50 N	129.00 W
Kitimat Ra., Can.	96	53.30 N	128.50 W
Kitlope (R.), Can. (kǐt'lôp)	96	53.00 N	128.00 W
Kitsuki, Jap.	201	33.24 N	131.35 E
Kittanning, Pa. (kǐ-tän'ǐng)	109	40.50 N	79.30 W
Kittatinny Mts., NJ (kǐ-tŭ-tǐ'nē)	110a	41.16 N	74.44 W
Kittery, Me. (kǐt'ēr-ǐ)	102	43.07 N	70.45 W

308 Kittsee – Kōzu

PLACE (Pronunciation)	PAGE	Lat. °′	Long. °′
Kittsee, Aus.	155e	48.05 N	17.05 E
Kitty Hawk, NC (kĭt'ē hôk)	125	36.04 N	75.42 W
Kitunda, Tan.	227	6.48 S	33.13 E
Kitwe, Zambia	227	12.49 S	38.13 E
Kitzingen, F.R.G. (kĭt'zĭng-ĕn)	164	49.44 N	10.08 E
Kiunga, Ken.	227	1.45 S	41.29 E
Kivu, Lac (L.), Zaire	227	1.45 S	28.55 E
Kiyev (Kiev), Sov. Un. (kē'yĕf)	177	50.27 N	30.30 E
Kiyose, Jap.	201a	35.47 N	139.32 E
Kizel, Sov. Un. (kē'zĕl)	180a	59.05 N	57.42 E
Kizil Irmak (R.), Tur. (kĭz'ĭl ĭr-mäk')	177	40.15 N	34.00 E
Kizil'skoye, Sov. Un. (kĭz'ĭl-skô-yĕ)	180a	52.43 N	58.53 E
Kizlyar, Sov. Un. (kĭz-lyär')	177	44.00 N	46.50 E
Kizu, Jap. (kē'zōō)	201b	34.43 N	135.49 E
Kizyl Arvat, Sov. Un. (kē'zĭl-ŭr-vät')	153	38.55 N	56.33 E
Klaas Smits (R.), S. Afr.	223c	31.45 S	26.33 E
Klaaswaal, Neth.	155a	51.46 N	4.25 E
Kladno, Czech. (kläd'nō)	164	50.10 N	14.05 E
Klagenfurt, Aust. (klä'gĕn-fŏŏrt)	164	46.38 N	14.19 E
Klaipėda (Memel), Sov. Un. (klī'pā-dȧ) (mā'mĕl)	163	55.43 N	21.10 E
Klamath Falls, Or.	114	42.13 N	121.49 W
Klamath Mts., Ca.	114	42.00 N	123.25 W
Klamath R., Ca.	114	41.40 N	122.25 W
Klarälven (R.), Swe.	162	60.40 N	13.00 E
Klaskanine (R.), Or. (klăs'kā-nīn)	116c	46.02 N	123.43 W
Klatovy, Czech. (klä'tō-vē)	164	49.23 N	13.18 E
Klawock, Ak. (klā'wăk)	105	55.32 N	133.10 W
Kleinmachnow, G.D.R. (klīn-mäĸ'nō)	155b	52.22 N	13.12 E
Klerksdorp, S. Afr. (klĕrks'dôrp)	219d	26.52 S	26.40 E
Klerksraal, S. Afr. (klĕrks'kräl)	219d	26.15 N	27.10 E
Kletnya, Sov. Un. (klyĕt'nyȧ)	172	52.19 N	33.14 E
Kletsk, Sov. Un. (klĕtsk)	172	53.04 N	26.43 E
Kleve, F.R.G. (klĕ'fĕ)	167c	51.47 N	6.09 E
Klickitat R., Wa.	114	46.01 N	121.07 W
Klimovichi, Sov. Un. (klē-mô-vē'chē)	172	53.37 N	31.21 E
Klimovsk, Sov. Un. (klĭ'môfsk)	180b	55.21 N	37.32 E
Klin, Sov. Un. (klēn)	172	56.18 N	36.43 E
Klintehamn, Swe. (klēn'tĕ-häm)	162	57.24 N	18.14 E
Klintsy, Sov. Un. (klĭn'tsĭ)	172	52.46 N	32.14 E
Klip (R.), S. Afr. (klĭp)	219d	27.18 N	29.25 E
Klipgat, S. Afr.	219d	25.26 S	27.57 E
Klippan, Swe. (klyp'pȧn)	162	56.08 N	13.09 E
Ključ, Yugo. (klyōōch)	170	44.32 N	16.48 E
Kłodzko, Pol. (klôd'skô)	164	50.26 N	16.38 E
Klondike Reg., Ak.-Can. (klŏn'dīk)	105	64.12 N	142.38 W
Klosterfelde, G.D.R. (klōs'tĕr-fĕl-dĕ)	155b	52.47 N	13.29 E
Klosterneuburg, Aus. (klōs-tĕr-noi'bŏŏrgh)	155e	48.19 N	16.20 E
Kluane (L.), Can.	94	61.15 N	138.40 W
Kluane Natl. Pk., Can.	94	60.25 N	137.53 W
Kluczbork, Pol. (klōōch'bōrk)	165	50.59 N	18.15 E
Klyaz'ma (R.), Sov. Un. (klyäz'mȧ)	172	55.49 N	39.19 E
Klyuchevskaya (Vol.), Sov. Un. (klyōō-chĕfskä'yä)	179	56.13 N	160.00 E
Klyuchi, Sov. Un. (klyōō'chĭ)	180a	57.03 N	57.20 E
Knezha, Bul. (knyä'zhȧ)	171	43.27 N	24.03 E
Knife (R.), ND (nīf)	112	47.06 N	102.33 W
Knight Inlet, Can. (nīt)	96	50.41 N	125.40 W
Knightstown, In. (nīts'toun)	108	39.45 N	85.30 W
Knin, Yugo. (knēn)	170	44.02 N	16.14 E
Knittelfeld, Aus.	164	47.13 N	14.50 E
Knob Pk., Phil. (nŏb)	203a	12.30 N	121.20 E
Knottingley, Eng. (nŏt'ĭng-lĭ)	154	53.42 N	1.14 W
Knox, In. (nŏks)	108	41.15 N	86.40 W
Knox, C., Can.	96	54.12 N	133.20 W
Knoxville, Ia. (nŏks'vĭl)	113	41.19 N	93.05 W
Knoxville, Tn.	124	35.58 N	83.55 W
Knutsford, Eng. (nŭts'fērd)	154	53.18 N	2.22 W
Knyszyn, Pol. (knĭ'shĭn)	165	53.16 N	22.59 E
Kobayashi, Jap. (kō'bȧ-yä'shē)	201	31.58 N	130.59 E
Kōbe, Jap. (kō'bĕ)	201b	34.30 N	135.10 E
Kobelyaki, Sov. Un. (kō-bĕl-yä'kē)	173	49.11 N	34.12 E
København (Copenhagen), Den. (kû-b'n-houn')	162	55.43 N	12.27 E
Koblenz, F.R.G. (kō'blĕntz)	164	50.18 N	7.36 E
Kobozha (R.), Sov. Un. (kô-bō'zhȧ)	172	58.55 N	35.18 E
Kobrin, Sov. Un. (kō'brĕn')	165	52.13 N	24.23 E
Kobrinskoye, Sov. Un. (kô-brĭn'skô-yĕ)	180c	59.25 N	30.07 E
Kobuk (R.), Ak. (kō'bŭk)	105	66.58 N	158.48 W
Kobuleti, Sov. Un. (kô-bōō-lyä'tē)	177	41.50 N	41.40 E
Kočani, Yugo. (kô'chä-nē)	171	41.54 N	22.25 E
Kočevje, Yugo. (kô'chäv-ye)	170	45.38 N	14.51 E
Kocher R., F.R.G. (kôĸ'ĕr)	164	49.00 N	9.52 E
Kōchi, Jap. (kō'chē)	201	33.35 N	133.32 E
Kodaira, Jap.	201a	35.43 N	139.29 E
Kodiak, Ak. (kō'dyăk)	105	57.50 N	152.30 W
Kodiak (I.), Ak.	105	57.24 N	153.32 W
Kodok, Sud. (ko'dŏk)	221	9.57 N	32.08 E
Koforidua, Ghana (kō fô-rĭ-dōō'ȧ)	224	6.03 N	0.17 W
Kōfu, Jap. (kō'fōō')	201	35.41 N	138.34 E
Koga, Jap. (kō'gȧ)	201	36.13 N	139.40 E
Kogan (R.), Gui.	224	11.30 N	14.05 W
Kogane, Jap. (kō'gä-nā)	201a	35.50 N	139.56 E
Koganei, Jap. (kō'gä-nā)	201a	35.42 N	139.31 E
Køge, Den. (kû'gĕ)	162	55.27 N	12.09 E
Køge Bugt (B.), Den.	162	55.30 N	12.25 E
Kogil'nik (R.), Sov. Un. (kô-gĕl-nēk')	173	46.08 N	29.10 E
Kogoni, Mali	224	14.44 N	6.02 W
Koh-i Baba Mt., Afg.	190	39.39 N	67.09 E
Kohima, India (kô-ē'mȧ)	193	25.45 N	94.41 E
Koito (R.), Jap. (kô'ē-tō)	201a	35.19 N	139.58 E
Kōje (I.), Kor. (kû'jĕ)	200	34.53 N	129.00 E
Kokand, Sov. Un. (kô-känt')	178	40.27 N	71.07 E
Kokchetav, Sov. Un. (kôk'chĕ-tăf)	178	53.15 N	69.13 E
Kokemäenjoki (R.), Fin.	163	61.23 N	22.03 E
Kokhma, Sov. Un. (kôĸ'mȧ)	172	56.57 N	41.08 E
Kokkola, Fin. (kô'kô-lȧ)	156	63.47 N	22.58 E
Kokomo, In. (kō'kō-mō)	108	40.30 N	86.20 W
Koko Nor (Qinghai Hu) (L.), China (kō'kō nor) (chyĭŋ-hī hōō)	194	37.26 N	98.30 E
Kokopo, Pap. N. Gui. (kô-kô'pō)	203	4.25 S	152.27 E
Koksoak (R.), Can. (kôk'sô-ăk)	95	57.42 N	69.50 W
Kokstad, S. Afr. (kôk'shtät)	223c	30.33 S	29.27 E
Kokubu, Jap. (kō'kōō-bōō)	201	31.42 N	130.46 E
Kokuou, Jap. (kō'kōō-ō'ōō)	201b	34.34 N	135.39 E
Kola Pen., see Kol'skiy P-Ov.			
Kolār, (Kolār Gold Fields), India (kōl-är')	191	13.39 N	78.33 E
Kolárvo, Czech. (kōl-árōvō)	165	47.54 N	17.59 E
Kolbio, Ken.	227	1.10 S	41.15 E
Kol'chugino, Sov. Un. (kôl-chōō'gē-nō)	172	56.19 N	39.29 E
Kolda, Sen.	224	12.53 N	14.57 W
Kolding, Den. (kŭl'dĭng)	162	55.29 N	9.24 E
Kole, Zaire (kō'lā)	222	3.19 S	22.46 E
Kolguyev (I.), Sov. Un. (kôl-gōō'yĕf)	176	69.00 N	49.00 E
Kolín, Czech. (kō'lēn)	164	50.01 N	15.11 E
Kolkasrags (Pt.), Sov. Un. (kôl-käs'rägz)	163	57.46 N	22.39 E
Köln (Cologne), F.R.G.	167c	50.56 N	6.57 E
Kolno, Pol. (kôw'nô)	165	53.23 N	21.56 E
Kolo, Pol. (kô'wô)	165	52.11 N	18.37 E
Kołobrzeg, Pol. (kô-lôb'zhĕk)	164	54.10 N	15.35 E
Kolomna, Sov. Un. (kȧl-ôm'nȧ)	180b	55.06 N	38.47 E
Kolomyya, Sov. Un. (kō'lô-mē'yȧ)	165	48.32 N	25.04 E
Kolp' (R.), Sov. Un. (kôlp)	172	59.29 N	35.32 E
Kolpashevo, Sov. Un. (kŭl pȧ shô'vȧ)	178	58.16 N	82.43 E
Kolpino, Sov. Un. (kôl'pē-nô)	180c	59.45 N	30.37 E
Kolpny, Sov. Un. (kôlp'nyē)	172	52.14 N	36.54 E
Kol'skiy P-Ov. (Kola Pen.), Sov. Un.	176	67.15 N	37.40 E
Kolva (R.), Sov. Un.	176	61.00 N	57.00 E
Kolwezi, Zaire (kōl-wĕ'zē)	227	10.43 S	25.28 E
Kolyberovo, Sov. Un. (kô-lĭ-byâ'rô-vô)	180b	55.16 N	38.45 E
Kolyma (R.), Sov. Un.	179	66.30 N	151.45 E
Kolymskiy (Mts.), see Gydan, Khrebet			
Kolyvan', Sov. Un. (kôl-ē-vän')	178	55.28 N	82.59 E
Kom (R.), Cam.-Gabon	226	2.15 N	12.05 E
Komadougou Yobé (R.), Niger-Nig.	225	13.20 N	12.45 E
Komadugu Gana (R.), Nig.	225	12.15 N	11.10 E
Komae, Jap.	201a	35.37 N	139.35 E
Komandorskie Ostrova (Is.), Sov. Un.	91	55.40 N	167.13 E
Komárno, Czech. (kô'mär-nô)	165	47.46 N	18.08 E
Komarno, Sov. Un.	165	49.38 N	23.43 E
Komárom, Hung. (kô'mä-rôm)	165	47.45 N	18.06 E
Komatipoort, S. Afr. (kō-mä'tē-pōrt)	222	25.21 S	32.00 E
Komatsu, Jap. (kō-mät'sōō)	201	36.23 N	136.26 E
Komatsushima, Jap. (kō-mät'sōō-shē'mä)	201	34.04 N	134.32 E
Komeshia, Zaire	227	8.01 S	27.07 E
Komga, S. Afr. (kōm'gȧ)	223c	32.36 S	27.54 E
Komi (A.S.S.R.), Sov. Un. (kômē)	174	61.31 N	53.15 E
Kommetjie, S. Afr.	222a	34.09 S	18.19 E
Kommunizma, Pik (Pk.), Sov. Un.	194	39.46 N	71.23 E
Komoe (R.), Ivory Coast	224	5.40 N	3.40 W
Komotiní, Grc.	171	41.07 N	25.22 E
Komrat, Sov. Un. (kôm-rät')	173	46.17 N	28.38 E
Komsomolets, Sov. Un. (kôm-sô-mô'lĕts)	180a	53.45 N	63.04 E
Komsomolets Zaliv (B.), Sov. Un.	177	45.40 N	52.00 E
Komsomol'sk-na-Amure, Sov. Un. (kŭm-sŭ-môlsk'nŭ-ŭ-mōōr'yĭ)	179	50.46 N	137.14 E
Komsomol'skoye, Sov. Un. (kôm-sô-môl'skô-yĕ)	173	48.42 N	28.44 E
Kona, Mali	224	14.57 N	3.53 W
Konda (R.), Sov. Un. (kôn'dȧ)	176	60.50 N	64.00 E
Kondas R., Sov. Un. (kôn'dȧs)	180a	59.30 N	56.28 E
Kondoa, Tan. (kōn-dō'ȧ)	222	4.52 S	36.00 E
Kondolole, Zaire	227	1.20 N	25.58 E
Kong, Ivory Coast (kông)	220	9.05 N	4.41 W
Kongbo, Cen. Afr. Rep.	226	4.44 N	21.23 E
Kongolo, Zaire (kôŋ'gō'lō)	227	5.23 S	27.00 E
Kongsberg, Nor. (kŭngs'bĕrg)	162	59.40 N	9.36 E
Kongsvinger, Nor. (kŭngs'vĭŋ-gĕr)	162	60.12 N	12.00 E
Koni, Zaire (kō'nē)	222	10.32 S	27.27 E
Königsberg, see Kaliningrad			
Königsbrunn, F.R.G. (kû'nēgs-brōōn)	155d	48.16 N	10.53 E
Königs Wusterhausen, G.D.R. (kû'nēgs vōōs'tĕr-hou-zĕn)	155b	52.18 N	13.38 E
Konin, Pol. (kô'nyĕn)	165	52.11 N	18.17 E
Kónitsa, Grc. (kô'nyē'tsȧ)	171	40.03 N	20.46 E
Konjic, Yugo. (kôn'yĕts)	171	43.38 N	17.59 E
Konju, Kor.	201	36.21 N	127.05 E
Konkouré (R.), Gui.	224	10.30 N	13.25 W
Konnagar, India	190a	22.41 N	88.22 E
Konotop, Sov. Un. (kô-nô-tôp')	173	51.13 N	33.14 E
Konpienga (R.), Upper Volta	224	11.15 N	0.35 E
Konqi (R.), China (kôn-chyē)	194	41.09 N	87.46 E
Końskie, Pol. (koin''skyĕ)	165	51.12 N	20.26 E
Konstantinovka, Sov. Un. (kôn-stán-tē'nôf-kȧ)	173	48.33 N	37.42 E
Konstanz, F.R.G. (kôn'shtänts)	164	47.39 N	9.10 E
Kontagora, Nig. (kōn-tȧ-gō'rä)	225	10.24 N	5.28 E
Konya, Tur. (kōn'yȧ)	177	36.55 N	32.25 E
Kootenay (R.), Can.	97	49.45 N	117.05 W
Kootenay L., Can.	97	49.35 N	116.50 W
Kootenay Natl. Park, Can. (kōō'tē-nā)	94	51.06 N	117.02 W
Kōō-zan (Mtn.), Jap. (kōō'zän)	201b	34.53 N	135.32 E
Kopervik, Nor. (kô'pĕr-vĕk)	162	59.18 N	5.20 E
Kopeysk, Sov. Un. (kô-pāsk')	180a	55.07 N	61.36 E
Köping, Swe. (chû'pĭng)	162	59.32 N	15.58 E
Kopparberg, Swe. (kŏp'pȧr-bĕrgh)	162	59.53 N	15.00 E
Koppeh Dāgh (Mts.), Iran	192	37.28 N	58.29 E
Koppies, S. Afr.	219d	27.15 S	27.35 E
Koprivnica, Yugo. (kô'prēv-nē'tsȧ)	170	46.10 N	16.48 E
Kopychintsy, Sov. Un. (kō-pē-chēn'tsĕ)	165	49.06 N	25.55 E
Korçë, Alb. (kôr'chĕ)	171	40.37 N	20.48 E
Korčula (I.), Yugo. (kôr'chōō-lȧ)	170	42.50 N	17.05 E
Korea B., China-Kor.	200	39.18 N	123.50 E
Korea, Asia (kô-rē'ȧ)	189	38.45 N	130.00 E
Korean Arch., Kor.	200	34.05 N	125.35 E
Korea Str., Kor.-Jap.	200	33.30 N	128.30 E
Korets, Sov. Un. (kô-rĕts')	165	50.35 N	27.13 E
Korhogo, Ivory Coast (kôr-hō'gō)	224	9.27 N	5.38 W
Korinthiakós Kólpos (G.), Grc.	171	38.15 N	22.33 E
Kórinthos (Corinth), Grc. (kô-rēn'thôs) (kŏr'ĭnth)	171	37.56 N	22.54 E
Kōriyama, Jap. (kō'rē-yä'mä)	200	37.18 N	140.25 E
Korkino, Sov. Un. (kôr'kē-nŭ)	180a	54.53 N	61.25 E
Korla, China (kōr-lä)	194	41.37 N	86.03 E
Körmend, Hung. (kûr'mĕnt)	164	47.02 N	16.36 E
Kornat (I.), Yugo. (kôr-nät')	170	43.46 N	15.10 E
Korneuburg, Aus. (kôr'noi-bŏŏrgh)	155e	48.22 N	16.21 E
Koro, Mali	224	14.04 N	3.05 W
Korocha, Sov. Un. (kô-rō'chȧ)	173	50.50 N	37.13 E
Korop, Sov. Un. (kō'rôp)	173	51.33 N	33.54 E
Korosten', Sov. Un. (kô'rôs-tĕn)	173	50.51 N	28.39 E
Korostyshev, Sov. Un. (kô-rôs'tē-shôf)	173	50.19 N	29.05 E
Koro Toro, Chad	225	16.05 N	18.30 E
Korotoyak, Sov. Un. (kô'rô-tô-yák')	173	51.00 N	39.06 E
Korsakov, Sov. Un. (kôr'sȧ-kôf')	179	46.42 N	143.16 E
Korsnäs, Fin. (kôrs'nĕs)	163	62.51 N	21.17 E
Korsør, Den. (kôrs'ûr')	157	55.19 N	11.08 E
Kortrijk, Bel.	161	50.49 N	3.10 E
Koryakskiy Khrebet (Mts.), Sov. Un.	179	62.00 N	168.45 E
Koryukovka, Sov. Un. (kôr-yōō-kôf'kȧ)	173	51.44 N	32.24 E
Kościan, Pol. (kŭsh'tsyán)	164	52.05 N	16.38 E
Kościerzyna, Pol. (kŭsh-tsyĕ-zhē'nȧ)	165	54.08 N	17.59 E
Kosciusko, Ms. (kŏs-ĭ-ŭs'kō)	124	33.04 N	89.35 W
Kosciusko, Mt., Austl.	212	36.26 S	148.20 E
Kosel'sk, Sov. Un. (kō-zĕlsk')	172	54.01 N	35.49 E
Kosha, Sud.	221	20.49 N	30.27 E
Koshigaya, Jap. (kō'shē-gä'yä)	201a	35.53 N	139.48 E
Koshiki-Rettō (Is.), Jap. (kō-shē'kē rĕt'tō)	201	31.51 N	129.40 E
Kosi (R.), India (kō'sē)	190	26.00 N	86.20 E
Košice, Czech. (kō'shē-tsĕ')	165	48.43 N	21.17 E
Kosmos, S. Afr. (kŏz'mŏs)	223b	25.45 S	27.51 E
Kosobrodskiy, Sov. Un. (kä-sô'brôd-skĭ)	180a	54.14 N	60.53 E
Koso Lake, see Khöbsögol Dalai			
Kosovska Mitrovica, Yugo. (kô'sôv-skä' mē'trô-vē-tsä')	171	42.51 N	20.50 E
Kostajnica, Yugo. (kôs'tä-ē-nē'tsȧ)	170	45.14 N	16.32 E
Koster, S. Afr.	219d	25.52 S	26.52 E
Kostino, Sov. Un. (kôs'tĭ-nô)	180b	55.54 N	37.51 E
Kostroma, Sov. Un. (kôs-trô-mȧ')	172	57.46 N	40.55 E
Kostroma (Oblast), Sov. Un.	172	57.50 N	41.10 E
Kostrzyn, Pol. (kôst'chĕn)	164	52.35 N	14.38 E
Kos'va R., Sov. Un. (kôs'vȧ)	180a	58.44 N	57.08 E
Koszalin, Pol. (kô-shä'lĭn)	164	54.12 N	16.10 E
Kőszeg, Hung. (kû'sĕg)	164	47.21 N	16.32 E
Kota, India	190	25.17 N	75.49 E
Kota Baharu, Mala. (kō'tä bä'rōō)	202	6.15 N	102.23 E
Kotabaru, Indon.	202	3.22 S	116.15 E
Kota Kinabalu, Mala.	202	5.55 N	116.05 E
Kota Kota, Malawi (kō-tȧ kō-tȧ)	222	12.52 S	34.16 E
Kota Tinggi, Mala.	189b	1.43 N	103.54 E
Kotel, Bul. (kō-tĕl')	171	42.54 N	26.28 E
Kotel'nich, Sov. Un. (kō-tyĕl'nĕch)	176	58.15 N	48.20 E
Kotel'nyy (I.), Sov. Un. (kō-tyĕl'nē)	179	74.51 N	134.09 E
Kothapur, India	191	16.48 N	74.15 E
Kotka, Fin. (kŏt'kȧ)	163	60.28 N	26.56 E
Kotlas, Sov. Un. (kôt'lȧs)	176	61.10 N	46.50 E
Kotlin, Ostrov (I.), Sov. Un. (ôs-trôf' kôt'lĭn)	180c	60.02 N	29.49 E
Kotor, Yugo. (kō'tôr)	171	42.26 N	18.48 E
Kotorosl' (R.), Sov. Un. (kô-tô'rôsl)	172	57.18 N	39.08 E
Kotor Varoš, Yugo. (kō'tôr vä'rôsh)	170	44.37 N	17.23 E
Kotovsk, Sov. Un. (kô-tôfsk')	173	47.49 N	29.31 E
Kotte, Sri Lanka	191	6.50 N	80.05 E
Kotto (R.), Cen. Afr. Rep.	221	5.17 N	22.04 E
Kotuy (R.), Sov. Un. (kô-tōō')	179	71.00 N	103.15 E
Kotzebue, Ak. (kôt'sē-bōō)	105	66.48 N	162.42 W
Kotzebue Sd., Ak.	105	67.00 N	164.28 W
Koualé, Mali	224	11.24 N	7.01 W
Kouchibouguac Natl. Pk., Can.	102	46.53 N	65.35 W
Koudougou, Upper Volta (kōō-dōō'gōō)	224	12.15 N	2.22 W
Kouilou (R.), Con.	226	4.00 S	12.05 E
Koula-Moutou, Gabon	226	1.08 S	12.29 E
Koulikoro, Mali (kōō-lē-kō'rō)	224	12.53 N	7.33 W
Koulouguidi, Mali	224	13.27 N	17.33 E
Koumra, Chad	225	8.55 N	17.33 E
Koundara, Gui.	224	12.29 N	13.18 W
Koundé, Cen. Afr. Rep. (kōōn-dā')	221	6.08 N	14.32 E
Kounradskiy, Sov. Un. (kŭ-ōōn-rät'skē)	178	47.25 N	75.10 E
Kouroussa, Gui. (kōō-rōō'sä)	224	10.39 N	9.53 W
Koutiala, Mali (kōō-tē-ä'lä)	220	12.29 N	5.29 W
Kouvola, Fin. (kō'ōō-vō-lä)	163	60.51 N	26.40 E
Kouzhen, China (kō-jŭn)	196	36.19 N	117.37 E
Kovda (L.), Sov. Un. (kôv'dȧ)	176	66.45 N	32.00 E
Kovel' Sov. Un. (kō'vĕl)	165	51.13 N	24.45 E
Kovno, see Kaunas			
Kovrov, Sov. Un. (kôv-rôf')	172	56.23 N	41.21 E
Kowie, see Port Alfred			
Kowloon, Hong Kong (kō'lōōn')	199	22.28 N	114.20 E
Koyuk, Ak. (kô-yōōk')	105	65.00 N	161.18 W
Koyukuk (R.), Ak. (kô-yōō'kōōk)	105	66.25 N	153.50 W
Kozáni, Grc.	171	40.16 N	21.51 E
Kozelets, Sov. Un. (kôzĕ-lyĕts)	173	50.53 N	31.07 E
Kozienice, Pol. (kô-zyĕ-nē'tsĕ)	165	51.34 N	21.35 E
Koźle, Pol. (kôzh'lĕ)	165	50.19 N	18.10 E
Kozloduy, Bul. (kŭz'lô-dwē)	171	43.45 N	23.42 E
Kōzu (I.), Jap. (kō'zōō)	201	34.16 N	139.03 E

ăt; finȧl; rāte; senȧte; ärm; ȧsk; sofȧ; fâre; ch-choose; dh-as th in other; bē; ēvent; bĕt; recĕnt; cratẽr; g-gō; gh-guttural g; bĭt; ĭ-short neutral; rīde; ĸ-guttural k as ch in German ich;

PRONOUNCING INDEX
Kra – La Asunción 309

PLACE (Pronunciation)	PAGE	Lat. °′	Long. °′
Kra, Isth. of, Thai.	202	9.30 S	99.45 E
Kraai (R.), S. Afr. (krä'ē)	223c	30.50 S	27.03 E
Krabbendijke, Neth.	155a	51.26 N	4.05 E
Krâchéh, Kamp.	202	12.28 N	106.06 E
Kragerö, Nor. (krä'gĕr-û)	162	58.53 N	9.21 E
Kragujevac, Yugo. (krä'gōō'yĕ-vàts)	171	44.01 N	20.55 E
Kraków, Pol. (krä'kōōf)	165	50.05 N	20.00 E
Kraljevo, Yugo. (kräl'ye-vô)	157	43.39 N	20.48 E
Kramatorsk, Sov. Un. (krà-mä'tôrsk)	173	48.43 N	37.32 E
Kramfors, Swe. (kräm'fôrs)	162	62.54 N	17.49 E
Kranj, Yugo. (krän')	170	46.16 N	14.23 E
Kranskop, S. Afr. (kränz'kŏp)	223c	28.57 S	30.54 E
Krāslava, Sov. Un. (kräs'lä-vä)	172	55.53 N	27.12 E
Kraslice, Czech. (kräs'lē-tsĕ)	164	50.19 N	12.30 E
Kransnaya Gorka, Sov. Un. (kräs'nà-yà gôr'kà)	180a	55.13 N	56.43 E
Krasnaya Sloboda, Sov. Un.	177	48.25 N	44.35 E
Kraśnik, Pol. (kräsh'nĭk)	165	50.53 N	22.15 E
Krasnoarmeysk, Sov. Un. (kräs'nô-àr-maśk')	180b	56.06 N	38.09 E
Krasnoarmeyskoye, Sov. Un.	173	48.19 N	37.04 E
Krasnodar, Sov. Un. (kräs'nô-dàr)	173	45.03 N	38.55 E
Krasnodarskiy (Oblast) Province, Sov. Un. (kràs-nô-där'skĭ ôb'lást)	173	47.28 N	38.13 E
Krasnogorsk, Sov. Un.	180b	55.49 N	37.20 E
Krasnogorskiy, Sov. Un. (kräs-nô-gôr'skĭ)	180a	54.36 N	61.25 E
Krasnograd, Sov. Un. (kräs'nô-grät)	173	49.23 N	35.26 E
Krasnogvardeyskiy, Sov. Un. (krå'sno-gvăr-dzyĕ ĕs-kēē)	180a	57.17 N	62.05 E
Krasnokamsk, Sov. Un. (kräs-nô-kämsk')	176	58.00 N	55.45 E
Krasnokutsk, Sov. Un. (kràs-nô-kōōtsk')	173	50.03 N	35.05 E
Krasnosel'ye, Sov. Un. (kräs'nô-sĕl'yĕ)	173	48.44 N	32.24 E
Krasnoslobodsk, Sov. Un. (kräs'nô-slôbôtsk')	176	54.20 N	43.50 E
Krasnotur'insk, Sov. Un. (krŭs-nŭ-tōō-rensk')	180a	59.47 N	60.15 E
Krasnoufimsk, Sov. Un. (krŭs-nŭ-ōō-fēmsk')	180a	56.38 N	57.46 E
Krasnoural'sk, Sov. Un. (kräs'nô-ōō-rälsk')	180a	58.21 N	60.05 E
Krasnousol'skiy, Sov. Un. (kräs-nô-ōō-sôl'skĭ)	180a	53.53 N	56.30 E
Krasnovishersk, Sov. Un. (kräs-nô-vēshersk')	176	60.22 N	57.20 E
Krasnovodsk, Sov. Un. (kràs-nô-vôtsk')	177	40.00 N	52.50 E
Krasnoyarsk, Sov. Un. (kräs-nô-yàrsk')	178	56.13 N	93.12 E
Krasnoye Selo, Sov. Un. (kräs'nŭ-yŭ sâ'lô)	180c	59.44 N	30.06 E
Krasny Kholm, Sov. Un. (kräs'nē ĸôlm)	172	58.03 N	37.11 E
Krasnystaw, Pol. (kräs-nē-stäf')	165	50.59 N	23.11 E
Krasnyy Bor, Sov. Un. (kräs'nē bôr)	180c	59.41 N	30.40 E
Krasnyy Klyuch, Sov. Un. (kräs'nē'klyûch')	180a	55.24 N	56.43 E
Krasnyy Kut, Sov. Un. (kràs-nē kōōt')	177	50.50 N	47.00 E
Kratovo, Sov. Un. (krä'tô-vô)	180b	55.35 N	38.10 E
Kratovo, Yugo. (krä'tô-vô)	171	42.04 N	22.12 E
Krefeld, F.R.G. (krā'fĕlt)	167c	51.20 N	6.34 E
Kremenchug, Sov. Un. (krĕm'ĕn-chōōgh')	173	49.04 N	33.26 E
Kremenchugskoye (Res.), Sov. Un. (krĕm-ĕn-chōōgh'skô-ye)	173	49.20 N	32.45 E
Kremenets, Sov. Un. (krĕ-mĕn-yĕts')	165	50.06 N	25.43 E
Kremmen, G.D.R. (krĕ'mĕn)	155b	52.45 N	13.02 E
Krempe, F.R.G. (krĕm'pĕ)	155c	53.50 N	9.29 E
Krems, Aus. (krĕms)	164	48.25 N	15.36 E
Krestsy, Sov. Un.	163	58.18 N	32.26 E
Kresttsy, Sov. Un. (kråst'sē)	172	58.16 N	32.25 E
Kretinga, Sov. Un. (krĕ-tĭŋ'gà)	163	55.55 N	21.17 E
Kribi, Cam. (krē'bē)	225	2.57 N	9.55 E
Krichëv, Sov. Un. (krē'chôf)	172	53.44 N	31.39 E
Krilon, Mys (Pt.), Sov. Un. (mĭs krĭl'ŏn)	200	45.58 N	142.00 E
Krimpen aan de IJssel, Neth.	155a	51.55 N	4.34 E
Krishna (R.), India	193	16.23 N	75.00 E
Krishnanagar, India	190	23.29 N	88.33 E
Kristiansand, Nor. (krĭs-tyàn-sän'')	162	58.09 N	7.59 E
Kristianstad, Swe. (krĭs-tyàn-städ')	162	56.02 N	14.09 E
Kristiansund, Nor. (krĭs-tyàn-sōōn'')	162	63.07 N	7.49 E
Kristinehamn, Swe. (krēs-tē'nĕ-häm')	162	59.20 N	14.05 E
Kristinestad, Fin. (krĭs-tē'nĕ-städh)	163	62.16 N	21.28 E
Kriva-Palanka, Yugo. (krē-và-pà-läŋ'kà)	171	42.12 N	22.21 E
Krivoy Rog, Sov. Un. (krē-voi' rôgh')	173	47.54 N	33.22 E
Krivoye Ozero, Sov. Un.	173	47.57 N	30.21 E
Križevci, Yugo. (krē'zhĕv-tsĭ)	170	46.02 N	16.30 E
Krk (I.), Yugo. (k'rk)	170	45.06 N	14.33 E
Krnov, Czech. (k'r'nôf)	165	50.05 N	17.41 E
Krokodil (R.), S. Afr. (krŏ'kŏ-dĭ)	219d	24.25 S	27.08 E
Krolevets, Sov. Un. (krô-lĕ'vyĕts)	173	51.33 N	33.21 E
Kroměříž, Czech. (krô'myĕr-zhĕzh)	165	49.18 N	17.23 E
Kromy, Sov. Un. (krô'mē)	172	52.44 N	35.41 E
Kronshtadt, Sov. Un. (krōn'shtät)	180c	59.59 N	29.47 E
Kroonstad, S. Afr. (krōn'shtät)	219d	27.40 S	27.15 E
Kropotkin, Sov. Un. (krà-pôt'kĭn)	177	45.25 N	40.30 E
Krosno, Pol. (krôs'nô)	165	49.41 N	21.46 E
Krotoszyn, Pol. (krô-tō'shĭn)	165	51.41 N	17.25 E
Krško, Yugo. (k'rsh'kô)	170	45.58 N	15.30 E
Kruger Natl. Park, S. Afr. (krōō'gĕr) (krü'gĕr)	222	23.22 S	30.18 E
Krugersdorp, S. Afr. (krōō'gĕrz-dôrp)	223b	26.06 S	27.46 E
Krujë, Alb. (krōō'yà)	171	41.32 N	19.49 E

PLACE (Pronunciation)	PAGE	Lat. °′	Long. °′
Krung Thep (Bangkok), Thai.	202	13.50 N	100.29 E
Kruševac, Yugo. (krōō'shĕ-vàts)	171	43.34 N	21.21 E
Kruševo, Yugo.	171	41.20 N	21.15 E
Krylbo, Swe. (krül'bô)	162	60.07 N	16.14 E
Krymskaya, Sov. Un. (krĭm'skà-yà)	173	44.58 N	38.01 E
Krymskaya (Oblast), Sov. Un.	173	45.08 N	34.05 E
Krymskiy P-Ov (Crimea) (Pen.), Sov. Un. (krēm-skĭ pô-lōō-ôs'trôf)	173	45.18 N	33.30 E
Krynki, Pol. (krĭn'kē)	165	53.15 N	23.47 E
Kryukov, Sov. Un. (k'r'yōō-kôf')	173	49.02 N	33.26 E
Ksar Chellala, Alg.	169	35.12 N	2.20 E
Ksar el Boukhari, Alg.	169	35.50 N	2.48 E
Ksar-el-Kebir, Mor.	158	35.01 N	5.48 W
Ksar-es-Souk, Mor.	158	31.58 N	4.25 W
K2 (Godwin Austen), Pak. (gŏd wĭn ôs'tĕn)	194	36.06 N	76.38 E
Kuai (R.), China (kōō-ī)	196	33.30 N	116.56 E
Kuala Klawang, Mala.	189b	2.57 N	102.04 E
Kuala Lumpur, Mala. (kwä'lä lōōm-pōōr')	189b	3.08 N	101.42 E
Kuandian, China (kůän-dĭěn)	198	40.40 N	124.50 E
Kuba, Sov. Un. (kōō'bà)	177	41.05 N	48.30 E
Kuban' (R.), Sov. Un. (kōō-bàn'')	173	45.10 N	37.55 E
Kuban (R.), Sov. Un.	177	45.20 N	40.05 E
Kuban R., Sov. Un.	159	45.14 N	38.20 E
Kubenskoye (L.), Sov. Un.	176	59.40 N	39.40 E
Kuching, Mala. (kōō'chĭng)	202	1.30 N	110.26 E
Kuchinoerabo (I.), Jap. (kōō'chē nō ĕr'á-bō)	201	30.31 N	129.53 E
Kudamatsu, Jap. (kōō'dà-mä'tsōō)	201	34.00 N	131.51 E
Kudap, Indon.	189b	1.14 N	102.30 E
Kudat, Mala. (kōō-dät')	202	6.56 N	116.48 E
Kudirkos Naumietis, Sov. Un. (kōōdĭr-kôs nå'ōō-mĕ'tĭs)	163	54.51 N	23.00 E
Kudymkar, Sov. Un. (kōō-dĭm-kär')	178	58.43 N	54.52 E
Kufstein, Aus. (kōōf'shtīn)	164	47.34 N	12.11 E
Kuhstedt, F.R.G. (kōō'shtĕ)	155c	53.23 N	8.58 E
Kuibyshev, see Kuybyshev			
Kuilsrivier, S. Afr.	222a	33.56 S	18.41 E
Kuito, Ang.	226	12.22 S	16.56 E
Kuji, Jap.	201	33.57 N	131.18 E
Kujū-san (Mt.), Jap. (kōō'jōō-sän')	201	33.07 N	131.14 E
Kukës, Alb. (kōō'kĕs)	171	42.03 N	20.25 E
Kula, Bul. (kōō'là)	171	43.52 N	23.13 E
Kula, Tur.	177	38.32 N	28.30 E
Kula Kangri Mt., China	190	33.11 N	90.36 E
Kular, Khrebet (Mts.), Sov. Un. (kōō-lär')	179	69.00 N	131.45 E
Kuldīga, Sov. Un. (kōōl'dē-gà)	163	56.59 N	21.59 E
Kulebaki, Sov. Un. (kōō-lĕ-bäk'ĭ)	176	55.22 N	42.30 E
Kulmbach, F.R.G. (klōōlm'bäĸ)	164	50.07 N	11.28 E
Kulunda, Sov. Un. (kōō-lōōn'dà)	178	52.38 N	74.00 E
Kulundinskoye (L.), Sov. Un.	178	52.45 N	77.18 E
Kum (R.), Kor. (kōōm)	200	36.50 N	127.30 E
Kuma (R.), Sov. Un. (kōō'mä)	177	44.50 N	45.10 E
Kumamoto, Jap. (kōō'mä-mō'tô)	201	32.49 N	130.40 E
Kumano-Nada (Sea), Jap. (kōō-mä'nō nä-dä)	201	34.03 N	136.36 E
Kumanovo, Yugo. (kōō-mä'nô-vô)	171	42.10 N	21.41 E
Kumasi, Ghana (kōō-mä'sē)	224	6.41 N	1.35 W
Kumba, Cam. (kōōm'bà)	225	4.38 N	9.25 E
Kumbakonam, India (kōōm'bŭ-kō'nŭm)	191	10.59 N	79.25 E
Kumkale, Tur.	171	39.59 N	26.10 E
Kumo, Nig.	225	10.03 N	11.13 E
Kumta, India	191	14.19 N	75.28 E
Kumul, see Hami			
Kunashak, Sov. Un. (kû-nä'shàk)	180a	55.43 N	61.35 E
Kunashir (Kunashiri) (I.), Sov. Un. (kōō-nŭ-shēr')	195	44.40 N	145.45 E
Kunashiri (I.), **see Kunashir**			
Kunda, Sov. Un. (kōō'dà)	172	59.30 N	26.28 E
Kundelungu, Plateau des (Plat.), Zaire	218	9.00 S	25.30 E
Kundravy, Sov. Un. (kōōn'drà-vĭ)	180a	54.50 N	60.14 E
Kundur (I.), Indon.	189b	0.49 N	103.20 E
Kunene (Cunene) (R.), Ang.-Namibia	226	17.05 S	12.35 E
Kungälv, Swe. (kŭng'ĕlf)	162	57.53 N	12.01 E
Kungur, Sov. Un. (kōōn-gōōr')	180a	57.27 N	56.53 E
Kungrad, Sov. Un. (kōōn-grät')	153	42.59 N	59.00 E
Kungsbacka, Swe. (kŭngs'bä-kà)	162	57.31 N	12.04 E
Kunlun Shan (Mts.), China (kōōn-lōōn shän)	194	35.26 N	83.09 E
Kunming, China (kōōn-mĭŋ)	199	25.10 N	102.50 E
Kunsan, Kor. (kōōn'sän')	199	35.54 N	126.46 E
Kunshan, China (kōōnshän)	197b	31.23 N	120.57 E
Kuntsëvo, Sov. Un. (kōōn-tsyô'vô)	180b	55.43 N	37.27 E
Kun'ya, Sov. Un.	180a	58.42 N	56.47 E
Kun'ya (R.), Sov. Un. (kōōn'yà)	172	56.45 N	30.53 E
Kuopio, Fin. (kōō-ô'pē-ŏ)	156	62.48 N	28.30 E
Kupa (R.), Yugo.	170	45.32 N	14.50 E
Kupang, Indon.	203	10.14 S	123.37 E
Kupavna, Sov. Un.	180b	55.49 N	38.11 E
Kupino, Sov. Un. (kōō-pĭ'nô)	178	54.00 N	77.47 E
Kupiškis, Sov. Un. (kōō-pĭsh'kĭs)	139	55.50 N	24.55 E
Kupyansk, Sov. Un. (kōōp-yänsk')	173	49.44 N	37.38 E
Kuqa, China (kōō-chyä)	194	41.34 N	82.44 E
Kura (R.), Sov. Un. (kōō'rà)	177	41.10 N	45.40 E
Kurashiki, Jap. (kōō'rä-shē'kē)	201	34.37 N	133.44 E
Kuraymah, Sud.	221	18.34 N	31.49 E
Kurayoshi, Jap. (kōō'rà-yō'shē)	201	35.25 N	133.49 E
Kurdistan (Reg.), Tur.-Iran (kûrd'ĭ-stän)	177	37.40 N	43.30 E
Kurdufān (Prov.), Sud. (kôr-dō-fän')	221	14.08 N	28.39 E
Kŭrdzhali, Bul.	171	41.39 N	25.21 E
Kure, Jap. (kōō'rĕ)	201	34.17 N	132.35 E
Kuressaare, Sov. Un. (kōō'rĕ-sä'rĕ)	163	58.15 N	22.26 E
Kurgan, Sov. Un. (kōōr-gän')	178	55.28 N	65.14 E
Kurgan Tyube, Sov. Un. (kōōr-gän' tyōō'bĕ)	178	38.00 N	68.49 E
Kurihama, Jap. (kōō-rē-hä'mä)	201a	35.14 N	139.42 E
Kuril Is., Sov. Un. (kōō'rĭl)	179	46.20 N	149.30 E

PLACE (Pronunciation)	PAGE	Lat. °′	Long. °′
Kurisches Haff (Bay), Sov. Un.	163	55.10 N	21.08 E
Kurla (Neigh.), India	191b	19.03 N	72.53 E
Kurmuk, Sud. (kōōr'mōōk)	221	10.40 N	34.13 E
Kurnool, India (kōōr-nōōl')	191	16.00 N	78.04 E
Kuro (I.), Jap. (kōō'rô)	201	30.49 N	129.56 E
Kurrajong, Austl.	207b	33.33 S	150.40 E
Kuršenai, Sov. Un. (kōōr'shå-nī)	153	56.01 N	22.56 E
Kursk, Sov. Un. (kōōrsk)	163	51.44 N	36.08 E
Kursk (Oblast), Sov. Un. (kōōrsk)	163	51.30 N	35.13 E
Kuršumlija, Yugo. (kōōr'shōōm'lĭ-yà)	161	43.08 N	21.18 E
Kūrtī, Sud.	221	18.08 N	31.39 E
Kuruman, S. Afr. (kōō-rōō-män')	222	27.25 S	23.30 E
Kurume, Jap. (kōō'rōō-mĕ)	201	33.10 N	130.30 E
Kururi, Jap. (kōō'rōō-rē)	201a	35.17 N	140.05 E
Kusa, Sov. Un. (kōō'sà)	180a	55.19 N	59.27 E
Kushchëvskaya, Sov. Un.	173	46.34 N	39.40 E
Kushikino, Jap. (kōō'shĭ-kē'nō)	201	31.44 N	130.19 E
Kushimoto, Jap. (kōō'shĭ-mō'tō)	201	33.29 N	135.47 E
Kushiro, Jap. (kōō'shē-rō)	200	43.00 N	144.22 E
Kush-Murun (L.), Sov. Un. (kōōsh-mōō-rōōn')	178	52.30 N	64.15 E
Kushum (R.), Sov. Un. (kōō-shōōm')	177	50.30 N	50.40 E
Kushva, Sov. Un. (kōōsh'và)	180a	58.18 N	59.51 E
Kuskokwim (R.), Ak.	105	61.32 N	160.36 W
Kuskokwim B., Ak. (kŭs'kô-kwĭm)	105	59.25 N	163.14 W
Kuskokwim Mts., Ak.	105	62.08 N	158.00 W
Kuskovak, Ak. (kŭs-kō'väk)	105	60.10 N	162.50 W
Kustanay, Sov. Un. (kōōs-tà-nī')	178	53.10 N	63.39 E
Kūstī, Sud.	221	13.09 N	32.39 E
Kütahya, Tur. (kû-tä'hyà)	177	39.20 N	29.50 E
Kutaisi, Sov. Un. (kōō-tŭ-ē'sē)	177	42.15 N	42.40 E
Kutaradja, Indon.	202	5.30 N	95.20 E
Kutch, Gulf of, India	190	22.45 N	68.33 E
Kutch, Rann of (Swp.), India	190	23.59 N	69.13 E
Kutenholz, F.R.G. (kōō'tĕn-hōlts)	155c	53.29 N	9.20 E
Kutim, Sov. Un. (kōō'tĭm)	180a	60.22 N	58.51 E
Kutina, Yugo. (kōō'tē-nà)	170	45.29 N	16.48 E
Kutno, Pol. (kōōt'nô)	165	52.14 N	19.22 E
Kutno (L.), Sov. Un.	176	65.15 N	31.30 E
Kutulik, Sov. Un. (kōō tōō'lyĭk)	177	53.12 N	102.51 E
Kuty, Sov. Un. (kōō'tē)	165	48.16 N	25.12 E
Kuusamo, Fin. (kōō'sà-mô)	156	65.59 N	29.10 E
Kuvshinovo, Sov. Un. (kōōv-shē'nô-vô)	172	57.01 N	34.09 E
Kuwait, see Al Kuwayt			
Kuwait, Asia	188	29.00 N	48.45 E
Kuwana, Jap. (kōō'wà-nà)	201	35.02 N	136.40 E
Kuybyshev, (Kuibyshev), Sov. Un. (kōō'ē-bĭ-shĭf)	176	53.10 N	50.05 E
Kuybyshevskoye (Res.), Sov. Un.	176	53.40 N	49.00 E
Kuzneckovo, Sov. Un.	180b	55.29 N	38.22 E
Kuznetsk, Sov. Un. (kōōz-nyĕtsk')	177	53.00 N	46.30 E
Kuznetsk Basin, Sov. Un.	178	57.15 N	86.15 E
Kuznetsovka, Sov. Un. (kōōz-nyĕt'sôf-kà)	180a	54.41 N	56.40 E
Kuznetsovo, Sov. Un. (kōōz-nyĕt-sô'vô)	172	56.39 N	36.55 E
Kuznetsy, Sov. Un.	180b	55.50 N	38.39 E
Kvarner Zaliv (B.), Yugo. (kvär'nĕr)	170	44.41 N	14.05 E
Kvichak, Ak. (vĭc'-häk)	105	59.00 N	156.48 W
Kwa (R.), Zaire	226	3.00 S	16.45 E
Kwahu Plat., Ghana	224	7.00 N	1.35 W
Kwando (R.), Zambia	226	16.50 S	22.40 E
Kwango (Cuango) (R.), Afr. (kwäng'ō')	226	6.35 S	16.50 E
Kwangwazi, Tan.	227	7.47 S	38.15 E
Kwenge (R.), Zaire (kwĕŋ'gĕ)	226	6.45 S	18.23 E
Kwidzyń, Pol. (kvē'dzĭn)	165	53.45 N	18.56 E
Kwilu (R.), Zaire (kwē'lōō)	226	3.22 S	17.22 E
Kyakhta, Sov. Un. (kyäĸ'ta)	179	51.00 N	107.30 E
Kyayisu (R.), India	190	38.05 N	74.36 E
Kyaukpyu, Bur. (chouk'pyoo')	194	19.19 N	93.33 E
Kybartai, Sov. Un. (kē'bär-tī')	163	54.40 N	22.46 E
Ky Lam, Viet.	199	15.48 N	108.30 E
Kyn, Sov. Un. (kĭn')	180a	51.52 N	58.42 E
Kynuna, Austl. (kī-nōō'nà)	211	21.30 S	142.12 E
Kyoga, L., Ug.	227	1.30 N	32.45 E
Kyōga-Saki (C.), Jap. (kyō'gä sa'kē)	201	35.46 N	135.14 E
Kyŏngju, Kor. (kyŭng'yōō)	200	35.48 N	129.12 E
Kyōto, Jap. (ky 'tō')	201b	35.00 N	135.46 E
Kyōto (Pref.), Jap.	201b	34.56 N	135.42 E
Kyren, Sov. Un. (kĭ-rĕn')	178	51.46 N	102.13 E
Kyrönjoki (R.), Fin.	163	63.03 N	22.20 E
Kyrya, Sov. Un. (kĕr'yà)	180a	59.18 N	59.03 E
Kyshtym, Sov. Un. (kĭsh-tĭm')	180a	55.43 N	60.33 E
Kytlym, Sov. Un. (kĭt'lĭm)	180a	59.30 N	59.15 E
Kyūshū (I.), Jap. (kyōō'shōō')	201	32.27 N	131.03 E
Kyustendil, Bul. (kyōōs-tĕn-dĭl')	171	42.16 N	22.39 E
Kyzyl, Sov. Un. (kĭ zĭl)	178	51.37 N	93.38 E
Kyzyl Kum, Peski (Des.), Sov. Un. (kĭ zĭl kōōm)	153	42.47 N	64.45 E
Kzyl-Orda, Sov. Un. (kzĕl-ôr'dà)	178	44.58 N	65.45 E

L

PLACE (Pronunciation)	PAGE	Lat. °′	Long. °′
Laa, Aus.	164	48.42 N	16.23 E
La Almunia de Doña Godina, Sp. (lä'äl-mōōn'yä dā dō nyä gō-dē'nä)	168	41.29 N	1.22 W
La Asunción, Ven. (lä ä-sōōn-syōn')	140	11.02 N	63.57 W

PLACE (Pronunciation)	PAGE	Lat. °′	Long. °′
La Baie, Can.	101	48.21 N	70.53 W
La Banda, Arg. (lä bän'dä)	142	27.48 S	64.12 W
La Barca, Mex. (lä bär'kȧ)	128	20.17 N	102.33 W
Labé, Gui. (lȧ-bā')	224	11.19 N	12.17 W
Labe (R.), **see Elbe**			
Laberge (L.), Can. (lȧ-bĕrzh')	94	61.08 N	136.42 W
Laberinto de las Doce Leguas (Is.), Cuba (lä-bå-rēn tô dā läs dō'så lā'gwäs)	132	20.40 N	78.35 W
Labinsk, Sov. Un.	177	44.30 N	40.40 E
Labis, Mala. (läb'ĭs)	189b	2.23 N	103.01 E
La Bisbal, Sp. (lä bēs-bäl')	169	41.55 N	3.00 E
Labo, Phil. (lä'bō)	203a	14.11 N	122.49 E
Labo, Mt., Phil.	203a	14.00 N	122.47 E
Labouheyre, Fr. (lȧ-bo͞o-âr')	166	44.14 N	0.58 W
Laboulaye, Arg. (lä-bô'o͞o-lä-yĕ)	142	34.01 S	63.10 W
Labrador (Reg.), Can. (lăb'rȧ-dôr)	95	53.05 N	63.30 W
Labrador Sea, Can.	103	50.38 N	55.00 W
Lábrea, Braz. (lä-brā'ä)	140	7.28 S	64.39 W
Labuan, Pulau (I.), Mala. (lä-bo͞o-än')	202	5.28 N	115.11 E
Labuha, Indon.	203	0.43 S	127.35 E
L'Acadie, Can. (lȧ-kȧ-dē')	93a	45.18 N	73.22 W
L'Acadie (R.), Can.	93a	45.24 N	73.21 W
La Calera, Chile (lä-kä-lĕ-rä)	139b	32.47 S	71.11 W
La Calera, Col.	140a	4.43 N	73.58 W
Lac Allard, Can.	103	50.38 N	63.28 W
La Canada, Ca. (lä kän-yä'dä)	117a	34.13 N	118.12 W
Lacantum (R.), Mex. (lä-kän-to͞o'm)	129	16.13 N	90.52 W
La Carolina, Sp. (lä kä-rō-lē'nä)	168	38.16 N	3.48 W
La Catedral, Cerro (Mtn.), Mex. (sĕ'r-rō-lä-kä-tĕ-drȧ'l)	129a	19.32 N	99.31 W
Lac-Beauport, Can. (läk-bō-pōr')	93b	46.58 N	71.17 W
Laccodive Is., India (lăk'ȧ-dīv)	191	11.00 N	73.02 E
Laccadive Sea, Asia	190	9.10 N	75.17 E
Lac Court Oreille Ind. Res., Wi. (lāk kôrt-ō-rēl) (lȧk ko͝or tô-rā'y')	113	46.04 N	91.18 W
Lac du Flambeau Ind. Res., Wi.	113	46.12 N	89.50 W
La Ceiba, Hond. (lȧ sēbä)	130	15.45 N	86.52 W
La Ceja, Col. (lä-sĕ-ĸä)	140a	6.02 N	75.25 W
Lac-Frontière, Can.	95	46.42 N	70.00 W
Lacha (L.), Sov. Un. (lȧ'chä)	176	61.15 N	39.05 E
La Chaux de Fonds, Switz. (lȧ shō dē-fôɴ')	164	47.07 N	6.47 E
Lach Dera (R.), Som. (läk dā'rä)	219a	0.45 N	41.26 E
L'Achigan (R.), Can. (lä-shē-gäɴ)	93a	45.49 N	73.48 W
Lachine, Can. (lȧ-shēn')	93a	45.26 N	73.40 W
Lachlan (R.), Austl. (läk'lăn)	212	33.54 S	145.15 E
La Chorrera, Pan. (lȧchōr-rā'rä)	126a	8.54 N	79.47 W
Lachute, Can. (lȧ-sho͞ot')	93a	45.39 N	74.20 W
La Ciotat, Fr. (lȧ syō-tȧ')	167	43.13 N	5.35 E
Lackawanna, NY (lak-ȧ-wŏn'á)	111c	42.49 N	78.50 W
Lac la Biche, Can.	97	54.46 N	112.58 W
La Columna (Mtn.), **see Bolivar**			
Lacombe, Can.	97	52.28 N	113.44 W
La Concordià, Mex. (lä-kōn-kô'r-dyä)	129	16.07 N	92.40 W
Laconia, NH (lȧ-kō'nĭ-ȧ)	109	43.30 N	71.30 W
La Conner, Wa. (lȧ kŏn'ēr)	116a	48.23 N	122.30 W
La Coruña, Sp. (lȧ kō-ro͞on'yä)	168	43.20 N	8.20 W
Lacreek (L.), SD (lȧ'krēk)	112	43.04 N	101.46 W
La Cresenta, Ca. (lȧ krĕs'ĕnt-ȧ)	117a	34.14 N	118.13 W
La Cross, Ks. (lȧ-krôs')	120	38.30 N	99.20 W
La Crosse, Wi.	113	43.48 N	91.14 W
La Cruz, C. R. (lä-kro͞o'z)	130	11.05 N	85.37 W
La Cruz, Col. (lȧ kro͞oz')	140	1.37 N	77.00 W
Lacs, Riviere des (R.), ND (rē-vyĕr' de läk)	112	48.30 N	101.45 W
Lac Simard, (L.), Can.	101	47.38 N	78.40 W
La Cuesta, C. R. (lä-kwĕ's-tä)	131	8.32 N	82.51 W
La Culebra, Sierra de (Mts.), Sp. (sē-ĕ'r-rä-dĕ-lä-ko͞o-lĕ-brä)	168	41.52 N	6.21 W
La Cygne, Ks. (lȧ-sēn'y') (lȧ-sēn')	121	38.20 N	94.45 W
Ladd, Il. (lăd)	108	41.25 N	89.25 W
Ladíspoli, It. (lä-dē's-pô-lē)	169d	41.57 N	12.05 E
Ladner, Can. (lăd'nēr)	116d	49.05 N	123.05 W
Lādnun, India (läd'no͞on)	190	27.45 N	74.20 E
Ladoga, Lake, see Ladozhskoye Ozero			
La Dorado, Col. (lä dō-rä'dȧ)	140a	5.28 N	74.42 W
Ladozhskoye Ozero (Ladoga, L.), Sov. Un. (lȧ-dôsh'skô-yē ô'zĕ-rô)	163	60.59 N	31.30 E
La Durantaye, Can. (lä dü-räɴ-tā')	93b	46.51 N	70.51 W
Lady Frere, S. Afr. (lā-dē frâ'r')	223c	31.48 S	27.16 E
Lady Grey, S. Afr.	223c	30.44 S	27.17 E
Ladysmith, Can. (lā'dĭ-smĭth)	96	48.58 N	123.49 W
Ladysmith, S. Afr.	223c	28.38 S	29.48 E
Ladysmith, Wi.	113	45.27 N	91.07 W
Lae, Pap. N. Gui. (lä'ȧ)	203	6.15 S	146.57 E
Laerdalsøyri, Nor.	162	61.08 N	7.26 E
Laesø (I.), Den. (lâs'û)	162	57.17 N	10.57 E
La Esperanza, Hond. (lä ĕs-pȧ-rän'zä)	130	14.20 N	88.21 W
La Estrada, Sp. (lä ĕs-trä'dä)	168	42.42 N	8.29 W
Lafa, China (lä'fä)	200	43.49 N	127.19 E
Lafayette, Al.	124	32.52 N	85.25 W
Lafayette, Ca.	116b	37.53 N	122.07 W
Lafayette, Ga. (lă-fā-yĕt')	124	34.41 N	85.19 W
Lafayette, In.	108	40.25 N	86.55 W
Lafayette, La.	123	30.15 N	92.02 W
La Fayette, RI	110b	41.34 N	71.29 W
La Ferté-Alais, Fr. (lä-fĕr-tā'ä-lā')	167b	48.29 N	2.19 E
La Ferté-sous-Jouarre, Fr. (lȧ fĕr-tā'so͞o-zho͞o-är')	167b	48.56 N	3.07 E
Lafia, Nig.	225	8.30 N	8.30 E
Lafiagi, Nig.	225	8.52 N	5.25 E
La Flèche, Fr. (lȧ flāsh')	166	47.43 N	0.03 W
La Follete, Tn. (lä-fŏl'ĕt)	124	36.23 N	84.07 W
Lafourche, Bay., La. (bă-yo͞o'lȧ-fo͞orsh')	123	29.25 N	90.15 W
La Gaiba, Braz. (lä-gī'bä)	141	17.54 S	57.32 W
Lagan, N. Ire. (lā'găn)	160	54.30 N	6.00 W
Lagan (R.), Swe.	162	56.34 N	13.25 E
Lagarto, R., Pan. (lä-gä'r-tô)	126a	9.08 N	80.05 W
Lagartos L., Mex. (lä-gä'r-tôs)	130a	21.32 N	88.15 W
Lågan (R.), Nor. (lô'ghĕn)	162	59.15 N	9.47 E
Laghouat, Alg. (lä-gwät')	220	33.45 N	2.49 E
Lagny, Fr. (län-yē')	167b	48.53 N	2.41 E
Lagoa da Prata, Braz. (lȧ-gô'ä-dȧ-prä'tȧ)	139a	20.04 S	45.33 W
Lagoa Dourada, Braz. (lȧ-gô'ä-do͞o-rä'dä)	139a	20.55 S	44.03 W
Lagonay, Phil.	203a	13.44 N	123.31 E
Lagonoy G., Phil. (lä-gō-noi')	203a	13.34 N	123.46 E
Lagos, Nig. (lä'gōs)	225	6.27 N	3.24 E
Lagos, Port. (lä'gōzh)	168	37.08 N	8.43 W
Lagos de Moreno, Mex. (lä'gōs dā mō-rā'nō)	128	21.21 N	101.55 W
La Grand' Combe, Fr. (lȧ gräɴ kaɴb')	166	44.12 N	4.03 E
La Grande, Or. (lȧ grănd')	114	45.20 N	118.06 W
La Grande (R.), Can.	95	53.55 N	77.30 W
La Grange, Austl. (lä grānj)	210	18.40 S	122.00 E
La Grange, Ga. (lȧ-grānj')	124	33.01 N	85.00 W
La Grange, Il.	111a	41.49 N	87.53 W
Lagrange, In.	108	41.40 N	85.25 W
La Grange, Ky.	108	38.20 N	85.25 W
La Grange, Mo.	121	40.04 N	91.30 W
Lagrange, Oh.	111d	41.14 N	82.07 W
Lagrange, Tx.	123	29.55 N	96.50 W
La Grita, Ven. (lä grē'tȧ)	140	8.02 N	71.59 W
La Guaira, Ven. (lä gwä'ē-rä)	141b	10.36 N	66.54 W
La Guardia, Sp. (lä gwär'dē-ȧ)	168	41.55 N	8.48 W
Laguna, Braz. (lä-go͞o'nä)	142	28.19 S	48.42 W
Laguna, Cayos (Is.), Cuba (kä'yōs-lä-go͞o'nă)	132	22.15 N	82.45 W
Laguna de Bay (L.), Phil. (lă-go͞o'nă dä bä'ē)	203a	14.24 N	121.13 E
Laguna Ind. Res., NM	119	35.00 N	107.30 W
Lagunillas, Bol. (lä-go͞o-nēl'yäs)	140	19.42 S	63.38 W
Lagunillas, Mex. (lä-go͞o-nē'l-yäs)	128	21.34 N	99.41 W
La Habana (Havana), Cuba (lä-ä-bȧ'nä)	133a	23.08 N	82.23 W
La Habra, Ca. (lȧ hȧb'rȧ)	117a	34.56 N	117.57 W
Lahaina, Hi. (lä-hä'ē-nä)	104a	20.52 N	156.39 W
Laholm, Swe. (lä'hōlm)	162	56.30 N	13.00 E
La Honda, Ca. (lā hôn'dă)	116b	37.20 N	122.16 W
Lahore, Pak. (lä-hōr')	190	32.00 N	74.18 E
Lahr, F.R.G. (lär)	164	48.19 N	7.52 E
Lahti, Fin. (lä'tē)	163	60.59 N	27.39 E
Lai, C., Viet.	199	17.08 N	107.30 E
Lai, Chad.	225	9.29 N	16.18 E
Lai'an, China (lī-än)	196	32.27 N	118.25 E
Laibin, China (lī-bĭn)	199	23.42 N	109.20 E
L'Aigle, Fr. (lĕ'gl')	166	48.45 N	0.37 E
Laisamis, Ken.	227	1.36 N	37.48 E
Laiyang, China (läī'yäɴg)	196	36.59 N	120.42 E
Laizhou Wan (B.), China (lī-jō wän)	196	37.22 N	119.19 E
Laja, Río de la (R.), Mex. (rē'ō-dĕ-lä-lȧ'ĸä)	128	20.17 N	100.57 W
Lajas, Cuba (lä'häs)	132	22.25 N	80.20 W
Lajeado, Braz. (lä-zhĕȧ'dô)	142	29.24 S	51.46 W
Lajes, Braz. (lȧ'zhĕs)	142	27.47 S	50.17 W
Lajinha, Braz. (lä-zhē'nyä)	139a	20.08 S	41.36 W
La Jolla, Ca. (lȧ hoi'yȧ)	118a	32.51 N	117.16 W
La Jolla Ind. Res., Ca.	118	33.19 N	116.21 W
La Junta, Co. (lȧ ho͞on'tȧ)	120	37.59 N	103.35 W
Lake Arthur, La. (är'thŭr)	123	30.06 N	92.40 W
Lake Barkley (Res.), Tn.	124	36.45 N	88.00 W
Lake Benton, Mn. (bĕn'tŭn)	112	44.15 N	96.17 W
Lake Bluff, Il. (blŭf)	111a	42.17 N	87.50 W
Lake Brown, Austl. (broun)	210	31.03 S	118.30 E
Lake Charles, La. (chärlz')	123	30.15 N	93.14 W
Lake City, Fl.	125	30.09 N	82.40 W
Lake City, Ia.	113	42.14 N	94.43 W
Lake City, Mn.	113	44.28 N	92.19 W
Lake City, SC	125	33.57 N	79.45 W
Lake Cowichan, Can. (kou'ĭ-chăn)	96	48.50 N	124.03 W
Lake Crystal, Mn. (krĭs'tȧl)	113	44.05 N	94.12 W
Lake Dist., Eng. (lāk)	160	54.25 N	3.20 W
Lake Elmo, Mn. (ĕlmō)	117g	45.00 N	92.53 W
Lake Forest, Il. (fŏr'ĕst)	111a	42.16 N	87.50 W
Lake Fork (R.), Ut.	119	40.30 N	110.25 W
Lake Geneva, Wi. (jĕ-nē'vȧ)	113	42.36 N	88.28 W
Lake Harbour, Can. (här'bēr)	95	62.43 N	69.40 W
Lake Havasu City, Az.	118	34.27 N	114.22 W
Lake June, Tx. (jo͞on)	117c	32.43 N	96.45 W
Lakeland, Fl. (lāk'lănd)	125a	28.02 N	81.58 W
Lakeland, Ga.	124	31.02 N	83.02 W
Lakeland, Mn.	117g	44.57 N	92.47 W
Lake Linden, Mi. (lĭn'dĕn)	113	47.11 N	88.26 W
Lake Louise, Can. (lo͞o-ēz')	97	51.26 N	116.11 W
Lake Mills, Ia. (mĭlz')	113	43.25 N	93.32 W
Lakemore, Oh. (lāk-mōr)	111d	41.01 N	81.24 W
Lake Odessa, Mi.	108	42.50 N	85.15 W
Lake Oswego, Or. (ŏs-wē'go)	116c	45.25 N	122.40 W
Lake Placid, NY	109	44.17 N	73.59 W
Lake Point, Ut.	117b	40.41 N	112.16 W
Lakeport, Ca. (lāk'pōrt)	118	39.03 N	122.54 W
Lake Preston, SD (prēs'tŭn)	112	44.21 N	97.23 W
Lake Providence, La. (prŏv'ĭ-dĕns)	123	32.48 N	91.12 W
Lake Red Rock (Res.), Ia.	113	41.30 N	93.15 W
Lake Sharpe (Res.), SD	112	44.30 N	100.00 W
Lakeside, Ca. (lāk'sīd)	118a	32.52 N	116.55 W
Lake Station, In.	111a	41.34 N	87.15 W
Lake Stevens, Wa.	116a	48.01 N	122.04 W
Lake Success, NY (sŭk-sĕs')	110a	40.46 N	73.43 W
Lakeview, Ca. (lāk-vū')	117a	33.50 N	117.07 W
Lakeview, Or.	114	42.11 N	120.21 W
Lake Village, Ar.	121	33.20 N	91.17 W
Lake Wales, Fl. (wālz')	125a	27.54 N	81.35 W
Lakewood, Ca. (lāk'wo͝od)	117a	33.50 N	118.09 W
Lakewood, Co.	120	39.44 N	105.06 W
Lakewood, Oh.	111d	41.29 N	81.48 W
Lakewood, Pa.	109	40.05 N	74.10 W
Lakewood, Wa.	116a	48.09 N	122.13 W
Lakewood Center, Wa.	116a	47.10 N	122.31 W
Lake Worth, Fl. (wûrth')	125a	26.37 N	80.04 W
Lake Worth Village, Tx.	117c	32.49 N	97.26 W
Lake Zürich, Il. (tsü'rĭk)	111a	42.11 N	88.05 W
Lakhdenpokh'ya, Sov. Un. (l'ăk-dĭe'npōĸyȧ)	163	61.33 N	30.10 E
Lakhtinskiy, Sov. Un. (lȧk-tĭn'skĭ)	180c	59.59 N	30.10 E
Lakota, ND (lȧ-kō'tȧ)	112	48.04 N	98.21 W
Lakshadweep (State), India	191	10.10 N	72.50 E
La Libertad, Guat. (lä lē-bĕr-tädh')	130	15.31 N	91.44 W
La Libertad, Guat.	130a	16.46 N	90.12 W
La Libertad, Sal.	130	13.29 N	89.20 W
La Ligua, Chile (lä lē'gwä)	139b	32.21 S	71.13 W
Lalín, Sp. (lä-lē'n)	168	42.40 N	8.05 W
La Línea, Sp. (lä lē'nȧ-ä)	168	36.11 N	5.22 W
Lalitpur, Nep.	190	27.23 N	85.24 E
La Louviere, Bel. (lȧ lo͞o-vyâr')	161	50.30 N	4.10 E
La Luz, Mex. (lä lo͞oz')	128	21.04 N	101.19 W
Lama-Kara, Togo	224	9.33 N	1.12 E
La Malbaie, Can. (lȧ mäl-bā')	101	47.39 N	70.10 W
La Mancha (Mts.), Sp. (lä män'chä)	168	38.55 N	4.20 W
Lamar, Co. (lȧ-mär')	120	38.04 N	102.44 W
Lamar, Mo.	121	37.28 N	94.15 W
La Marmora, Pta. (Mtn.), It. (lä-mä'r-mô-rä)	172	40.00 N	9.28 E
La Marque, Tx. (lȧ-märk)	123a	29.23 N	94.58 W
Lamas, Peru (lä'mȧs)	140	6.24 S	76.41 W
Lamballe, Fr. (läɴ-bäl')	166	48.29 N	2.36 W
Lambaréné, Gabon (läɴ-bȧ-rā-nā')	226	0.42 S	10.13 E
Lambari, Braz. (läm-bȧ'rē)	139a	21.58 S	45.22 W
Lambayeque, Peru (läm-bä-yā'kā)	140	6.41 S	79.58 W
Lambert, Ms. (lăm'bērt)	124	34.10 N	90.16 W
Lambertville, NJ (lăm'bērt-vĭl)	109	40.20 N	75.00 W
Lame Deer, Mt. (lām dēr')	115	45.36 N	106.40 W
Lamego, Port. (lä-mā'gō)	168	41.07 N	7.47 W
La Mesa, Ca. (lä mā'sä)	118a	32.46 N	117.01 W
La Mesa, Col.	140a	4.38 N	74.27 W
Lamesa, Tx.	120	32.44 N	101.54 W
Lamía, Grc. (lȧ-mē'ȧ)	171	38.54 N	22.25 E
Lamon B., Phil. (lä-mōn')	203a	14.35 N	121.52 E
La Mora, Chile (lä-mō'rä)	139b	32.28 S	70.56 W
La Moure, ND (lȧ mo͞or')	112	46.23 N	98.17 W
Lampa (R.), Chile (lȧ'm-pä)	139b	33.15 S	70.55 W
Lampasas, Tx. (lăm-păs'ȧs)	122	31.06 N	98.10 W
Lampasas R., Tx.	122	31.18 N	98.08 W
Lampazos, Mex. (läm-pä'zōs)	122	27.03 N	100.30 W
Lampedusa (I.), It. (läm-pā-do͞o'sä)	157	35.29 N	12.58 E
Lamstedt, F.R.G. (läm'shtĕt)	155c	53.38 N	9.06 E
Lamu, Ken. (lä'mo͞o)	227	2.16 S	40.54 E
Lamu I., Ken.	227	2.25 S	40.50 E
La Mure, Fr. (lȧ mür')	167	44.55 N	5.50 E
Lan' (R.), Sov. Un. (lȧn')	172	52.38 N	27.05 E
Lanai (I.), Hi. (lä-nä'ē)	104a	20.48 N	157.06 W
Lanai City, Hi.	104a	20.50 N	156.56 W
Lanak La (P.), China	190	34.40 N	79.50 E
La Nao, Cabo de (C.), Sp. (kȧ'bô-dĕ-lä-nä'ō)	169	38.43 N	0.14 E
Lanark, Scot. (lăn'ȧrk)	160	55.40 N	3.50 W
Lancashire (Co.), Scot. (lăŋ'kȧ-shĭr)	154	53.49 N	2.42 W
Lancaster, Can. (lăŋ'kăs-tēr)	102	45.15 N	66.06 W
Lancaster, Eng.	160	54.04 N	2.55 W
Lancaster, Ky.	108	37.35 N	84.30 W
Lancaster, Ma.	103a	42.28 N	71.40 W
Lancaster, NH	109	44.25 N	71.30 W
Lancaster, NY	111c	42.54 N	78.42 W
Lancaster, Oh.	108	39.40 N	82.35 W
Lancaster, Pa.	109	40.05 N	76.20 W
Lancaster, Tx.	117c	32.36 N	96.45 W
Lancaster, Wi.	113	42.51 N	90.44 W
Lândana, Ang. (län-dä'nä)	222	5.15 S	12.07 E
Landau, F.R.G. (län'dou)	164	49.13 N	8.07 E
Lander, Wy. (lăn'dēr)	115	42.49 N	108.24 W
Landerneau, Fr. (läɴ-dĕr-nō')	166	48.28 N	4.14 W
Landes (Plain), Fr. (läɴd)	166	44.22 N	0.52 W
Landsberg, F.R.G. (länds'bo͞orgh)	155d	48.03 N	10.53 E
Lands End Pt., Eng.	160	50.03 N	5.45 W
Landshut, F.R.G. (länts'ho͞ot)	164	48.32 N	12.09 E
Landskrona, Swe. (lȧns-kro͞o'nȧ)	162	55.51 N	12.47 E
Lanett, Al. (lȧ-nĕt')	124	32.52 N	85.13 W
Langadhás, Grc.	171	40.44 N	24.10 E
Langat (R.), Mala.	189b	2.46 N	101.33 E
Langdon, Can. (lăng'dŭn)	93e	50.58 N	113.40 W
Langdon, Mn.	117g	44.49 N	92.56 W
L'Ange-Gardien, Can. (läɴzh gȧr-dyăɴ')	93b	46.55 N	71.06 W
Langeland (I.), Den.	162	54.52 N	10.46 E
Langenthal, Switz.	167	47.11 N	7.50 E
Langenzersdorf, Aus.	155e	48.30 N	16.22 E
Langesund, Nor. (läng'ĕ-so͞on')	162	58.59 N	9.38 E
Langfjorden (Fd.), Nor.	162	62.40 N	7.45 E
Langhorne, Pa. (lăng'hôrn)	110f	40.10 N	74.55 W
Langia Mts., Ug.	227	3.35 N	33.35 E
Langjökoll (Glacier), Ice. (läng-yû'ko͞ol)	156	64.40 N	20.31 W
Langla Co. (L.), China (läŋ-lä tswo)	190	30.42 N	80.40 E
Langlade (I.), St. Pierre & Miquelon	101	46.50 N	56.20 W
Langley, Can. (lăng'lĭ)	116d	49.06 N	122.39 W
Langley, SC	125	33.32 N	81.52 W
Langley, Wa.	116a	48.02 N	122.25 W
Langley Ind. Res., Can.	116d	49.12 N	122.31 W
Langnau, Switz. (läng'nou)	164	46.56 N	7.46 E
Lagogne, Fr. (laɴ-gōn'y')	166	44.43 N	3.50 E
Langon, Fr. (läɴ-gôɴ')	166	44.34 N	0.16 W
Langres, Fr. (läɴ'gr')	166	47.53 N	5.20 E
Langres, Plateau de (Plat.), Fr. (plä-tō'dĕ-läɴ'grĕ)	166	47.39 N	5.00 E
Langsa, Indon. (läng'sȧ)	202	4.33 N	97.52 E
Lang Son, Viet. (lăng'sŏn')	202	21.52 N	106.42 E
L'Anguille (R.), Ar. (läɴ-gē'y')	121	35.23 N	90.52 W
Langxi, China (läŋ-shyē)	196	31.10 N	119.09 E
Langzhong, China (läŋ-jôŋ)	199	31.40 N	106.05 E
Lanham, Md. (lăn'ăm)	110e	38.58 N	76.54 W
Lanigan, Can. (lăn'ĭ-gȧn)	98	51.52 N	105.02 W

ăt; finăl; rāte; senāte; ärm; ȧsk; sofȧ; fâre; ch-choose; dh-as th in other; bē; ēvent; bĕt; recĕnt; cratẽr; g-gō; gh-guttural g; bĭt; ĭ-short neutral; rīde; ĸ-guttural k as ch in German ich;

PRONOUNCING INDEX

Lankoviri – Lemon Grove 311

PLACE (Pronunciation)	PAGE	Lat. °′	Long. °′
Lankoviri, Nig.	225	9.00 N	11.25 E
Lansdale, Pa. (lănz'dāl)	109	40.20 N	75.15 W
Lansdowne, Pa.	110f	39.57 N	75.17 W
L'Anse, Mi. (lăns)	113	46.43 N	88.28 W
L'Anse and Vieux Desert Ind. Res., Mi.	113	46.41 N	88.12 W
Lansford, Pa. (lănz'fērd)	118	40.50 N	75.50 W
Lansing, Il.	111a	41.34 N	87.33 W
Lansing, Ia.	113	43.22 N	91.16 W
Lansing, Ks.	117f	39.15 N	94.53 W
Lansing, Mi.	108	42.45 N	84.35 W
Lanús, Arg. (lä-nōōs')	142a	34.27 S	58.24 W
Lanusei, It. (lä-nōō-sĕ'y)	170	39.51 N	9.34 E
Lanúvio, It. (lä-nōō'vyô)	169d	41.41 N	12.42 E
Lanzarote I., Can. Is. (län-zȧ-rō'tä)	220	29.04 N	13.03 W
Lanzhou, China (län-jō)	198	35.55 N	103.55 E
Laoag, Phil. (lä-wäg')	202	18.13 N	120.38 E
Lao Ho (R.), China (lä'ō hō')	195	43.37 N	120.05 E
Laon, Fr. (läN)	166	49.36 N	3.35 E
La Oroya, Peru (lä-ô-rō'yă)	140	11.30 S	76.00 W
Laos, Asia (lā-ōs) (lȧ-ōs')	202	20.15 N	102.00 E
Laoshan Wan (B.), China (lou-shän wän)	196	36.21 N	120.48 E
La Palma, Pan. (lä-päl'mä)	131	8.25 N	78.07 W
La Palma, Sp.	168	37.24 N	6.36 W
La Palma I., Can. Is.	220	28.42 N	19.03 W
La Pampa (Prov.), Arg.	142	37.25 S	67.00 W
Lapa Rio Negro, Braz. (lä-pä-rē'ō-nĕ'grō)	142	26.12 S	49.56 W
La Paz, Arg. (lä päz')	142	30.48 S	59.47 W
La Paz, Bol.	141	16.31 S	68.03 W
La Paz, Hond.	130	14.15 N	87.40 W
La Paz, Mex. (lä-pȧ'z)	128	23.39 N	100.44 W
La Paz, Mex.	126	24.00 N	110.15 W
Lapeer, Mi. (lȧ-pēr')	108	43.05 N	83.15 W
La-Penne-sur-Huveaune, Fr. (la-pĕn'sür-ü-vōn')	166a	43.18 N	5.33 E
La Piedad Cabadas, Mex. (lä pyā-dhädh' kä-bä'dhäs)	128	20.20 N	102.04 W
Lapland (Reg.), Eur. (lăp'lȧnd)	156	68.20 N	22.00 E
La Plata, Arg. (lä plä'tä)	139c	34.54 S	57.57 W
La Plata, Mo. (lȧ plā'tȧ)	121	40.03 N	92.28 W
La Plata Pk., Co.	119	39.00 N	106.25 W
La Pocatière, Can. (lä pô-kȧ-tyâr')	102	47.24 N	70.01 W
La Poile B., Can. (lȧ pwäl')	103	47.38 N	58.20 W
La Porte, In. (lȧ pōrt')	108	41.35 N	86.45 W
Laporte, Oh.	111d	41.19 N	82.05 W
La Porte, Tx.	123a	29.40 N	95.01 W
La Porte City, Ia.	113	42.20 N	92.10 W
Lappeenranta, Fin. (lä'pēn-rän'tä)	163	61.04 N	28.08 E
La Prairie, Can. (lȧ-prâ-rē')	93a	45.24 N	73.30 W
Lâpseki, Tur. (läp'sä-kē)	171	40.20 N	26.41 E
Laptev Sea, Sov. Un. (läp'tyĭf)	174	75.39 N	120.00 E
La Puebla, Sp. (lä pwā'blä)	169	39.46 N	3.02 E
La Puebla de Montalbán, Sp. (lä pwā'blä dā mōnt-äl-bän')	168	39.54 N	4.21 W
La Puente, Ca. (pwĕn'tē)	117a	34.01 N	117.57 W
Lapusul (R.), Rom. (lä'pōō-shōōl)	165	47.29 N	23.46 E
La Quiaca, Arg. (lä kē-ä'kä)	142	22.15 S	65.44 W
L'Aquila, It. (lä'kē-lä)	170	42.22 N	13.24 E
Lār, Iran (lär)	192	27.31 N	54.12 E
Lara, Austl.	207a	38.02 S	144.24 E
Larache, Mor. (lä-räsh')	220	35.15 N	6.09 W
Laramie, Wy. (lăr'ȧ-mĭ)	106	41.20 N	105.40 W
Laramie (R.), Co.	120	40.56 N	105.55 W
Larchmont, NY (lärch'mŏnt)	110a	40.56 N	73.46 W
Larch Mtn., Or. (lärch)	116c	45.32 N	122.06 W
Laredo, Sp. (lä-rā'dhō)	168	43.24 N	3.24 W
Laredo, Tx.	122	27.31 N	99.29 W
La Réole, Fr. (lȧ rȧ-ōl')	166	44.37 N	0.03 W
Largeau, Chad (lär-zhō')	225	17.55 N	19.07 E
Largo, Cayo, Cuba (kä'yō-lär'gō)	132	21.40 N	81.30 W
Larimore, ND (lăr'ĭ-môr)	112	47.53 N	97.38 W
Larino, It. (lä-rē'nō)	170	41.48 N	14.54 E
La Rioja, Arg. (lä rē-ōhä)	142	29.18 S	67.42 W
La Rioja (Prov.), Arg. (lä-rē-ō'kä)	142	28.45 S	68.00 W
Lárisa, Grc. (lä'rē-sȧ)	171	39.38 N	22.25 E
Lārkāna, Pak.	190	27.40 N	68.12 E
Lárnakos, Kólpos (B.), Cyprus	189a	36.50 N	33.45 E
Lárnax, Cyprus	189a	34.55 N	33.37 E
Larned, Ks. (lär'nĕd)	120	38.09 N	99.07 W
La Robla, Sp. (lä rōb'lä)	168	42.48 N	5.36 W
La Rochelle, Fr. (lȧ rō-shĕl')	166	46.10 N	1.09 W
La Roche-sur-Yon, Fr. (lȧ rôsh'sür-yôN')	166	46.39 N	1.27 W
La Roda, Sp. (lä rō'dä)	168	39.13 N	2.08 W
La Romona, Dom. Rep. (lä-rä-mô'nä)	133	18.25 N	69.00 W
Larrey Pt., Austl. (lăr'ē)	210	19.15 S	118.15 E
Laruns, Fr. (lȧ-răNs')	166	42.58 N	0.28 W
Larvik, Nor. (lär'vĕk)	162	59.06 N	10.03 E
La Sabana, Ven. (lä-sä-bȧ'nä)	141b	10.38 N	66.24 W
La Sabina, Cuba (lä-sä-bē'nä)	133a	22.10 N	82.07 W
La Sagra (Mtn.), Sp. (lä sä'grä)	168	37.56 N	2.35 E
La Sal, Ut. (lȧ săl')	119	38.10 N	109.20 W
La Salle, Can. (lȧ săl')	111b	42.14 N	83.06 W
La Salle, Can.	93a	45.26 N	73.39 W
La Salle, Can.	93f	49.41 N	97.16 W
La Salle, Il.	108	41.20 N	89.05 W
Las Animas, Co. (lȧs ă'nĭ-mȧs)	120	38.03 N	103.16 W
Las Anod, Som. (läs ăn'ŏd)	219a	8.24 N	47.20 E
La Sarre, Can.	101	48.43 N	79.12 W
Lascahobas, Hai. (läs-kä-ō'bȧs)	133	19.00 N	71.55 W
Las Cruces, Mex. (läs-krōō'sĕs)	129	16.37 N	93.54 W
Las Cruces, NM	119	32.20 N	106.50 W
La Selle, Massif De (Mts.), Hai. (lä'sĕl')	133	18.25 N	72.05 W
La Serena, Chile (lä-sĕ-rĕ'nä)	142	29.55 S	71.24 W
La Seyne, Fr. (lä-sån')	167	43.07 N	5.52 E
Las Flores, Arg. (läs flō'rĕs)	139c	36.01 S	59.07 W
Lashio, Bur. (lăsh'ē-ō)	194	22.58 N	98.03 E
Las Juntas, C. R. (läs-KŌŌ'n-täs)	130	10.15 N	85.00 W
Las Khoreh, Som. (läs KŌ'rȧ)	219a	11.13 N	48.19 E
Las Maismas (Reg.), Sp. (läs-mī's-mäs)	168	37.05 N	6.25 W
La Solana, Sp. (lä-sô-lä-nä)	168a	38.56 N	3.13 W
Las Palmas de Gran Canaria, Can. Is. (läs päl'mäs)	220	28.07 N	15.28 W
Las Palmas, Pan.	131	8.08 N	81.30 W
La Spezia, It. (lä-spĕ'zyä)	170	44.07 N	9.48 E
Las Piedras, Ur. (läs-pyĕ'drȧs)	139c	34.42 S	56.08 W
Las Pilas (Vol.), Nic. (läs-pē'läs)	130	12.32 N	86.43 W
Las Rosas, Mex. (läs rō thäs)	129	16.24 N	92.23 W
Las Rozas de Madrid, Sp. (läs rō'thas dā mä-dhrēd')	169a	40.29 N	3.53 W
Lassee, Aus.	155e	48.14 N	16.50 E
Lassen Pk., Ca. (lăs'ĕn)	114	40.30 N	121.32 W
Lassen Volcanic Natl. Park, Ca.	114	40.43 N	121.35 W
L'Assomption, Can. (lås-sôm-syôN)	93a	45.50 N	73.25 W
Las Tablas, Pan. (läs tä'bläs)	131	7.48 N	80.16 W
Last Mountain (L.), Can. (lȧst moun'tĭn)	98	51.05 N	105.10 W
Lastoursville, Gabon (lȧs-tōōr-vēl')	222	1.00 S	12.49 E
Las Tres Virgenes, Vol., Mex. (vē'r-hĕ-nĕs)	126	26.00 N	111.45 W
Las Tunas (Prov.), Cuba	132	21.05 N	77.00 W
Las Vacas, Mex. (läs-vȧ'käs)	129	16.24 N	95.48 W
Las Vegas, Chile (läs-vĕ'gäs)	139b	30.50 S	70.59 W
Las Vegas, Nv. (läs vā'gäs)	118	36.12 N	115.10 W
Las Vegas, NM	120	35.36 N	105.13 W
Las Vegas, Ven. (läs-vĕ'gäs)	141b	10.26 N	64.08 W
Las Vigas, Mex.	128	19.38 N	97.03 W
Las Vizcachas, Meseta de (Plat.), Arg. (mĕ-sĕ'tä-dĕ-läs-vēz-kä'chȧs)	142	49.35 S	71.00 W
Latacunga, Ec. (lä-tä-kōōŋ'gä)	140	1.02 S	78.33 W
Latakia, see Al Lādhiqīah			
La Teste-de-Buch, Fr. (lä-tĕst-dĕ-büsh)	166	44.38 N	1.11 W
Lathrop, Mo. (lā'thrŭp)	121	39.32 N	94.21 W
Latium (Reg.), see Lazio			
Latoritsa R., Sov. Un. (lȧ-tô'rĭ-tsȧ)	165	48.27 N	22.30 E
Latourell, Or. (lȧ-tou'rĕl)	116c	45.32 N	122.13 W
La Tremblade, Fr. (lä-trĕN-blȧd')	166	45.45 N	1.12 W
Latrobe, Pa. (lȧ-trōb')	109	40.25 N	79.15 W
La Tuque, Can. (lȧ'tük')	95	47.27 N	72.49 W
Lātūr, India (lä-tōōr')	191	18.20 N	76.35 E
Latvian (S. S. R.), Sov. Un.	174	57.28 N	24.29 E
Launceston, Austl. (lôn'sĕs-tŭn)	212	41.35 S	147.22 E
Launceston, Eng. (lôrn'stŏn)	160	50.38 N	4.26 W
La Unión, Chile (lä-ōō-nyō'n)	142	40.15 S	73.04 W
La Unión, Mex. (lä ōōn-nyōn')	128	17.59 N	101.48 W
La Unión, Sal.	130	13.18 N	87.51 W
La Unión, Sp.	169	37.38 N	0.50 W
Laura, Austl. (lôrȧ)	211	15.40 S	144.45 E
Laura, Sov. Un. (lou'rȧ)	172	57.36 N	27.29 E
Laurel, De. (lô'rĕl)	109	38.30 N	75.40 W
Laurel, Md.	110e	39.06 N	76.51 W
Laurel, Ms.	124	31.42 N	89.07 W
Laurel, Mt.	115	45.41 N	108.45 W
Laurel, Wa.	116d	48.52 N	122.29 W
Laurelwood, Or. (lô'rĕl-wŏŏd)	116c	45.25 N	123.05 W
Laurens, SC (lô'rĕnz)	125	34.29 N	82.03 W
Laurentian Highlands (Reg.), Can. (lô'rĕn-tĭ-ȧn)	92	49.00 N	74.50 W
Laurentides, Can. (lô'rĕn-tīdz)	93a	45.51 N	73.46 W
Lauria, It. (lou'rē-ä)	170	40.03 N	15.02 E
Laurinburg, NC (lô'rĭn-bûrg)	125	34.45 N	79.27 W
Laurium, Mi. (lô'rĭ-ŭm)	113	47.13 N	88.28 W
Lausanne, Switz. (lō-zȧn')	164	46.32 N	6.35 E
Laut, Pulau (I.), Indon.	202	3.39 S	116.07 E
Lautaro, Chile (lou-tä'rō)	142	38.40 S	72.24 W
Laut Kecil, Kepulauan (Is.), Indon.	202	4.44 S	115.43 E
Lauzon, Can. (lō-zōN')	93b	46.50 N	71.10 W
Lava Beds Natl. Mon., Ca. (lä'vȧ bĕds)	114	41.38 N	121.44 W
Lavaca R., Tx. (lȧ-văk'ȧ)	123	29.05 N	96.50 W
Lava Hot Springs, Id.	115	42.37 N	111.58 W
Laval, Can.	93a	45.31 N	73.44 W
Laval, Fr. (lä-väl')	166	48.05 N	0.47 W
La Vecilla de Curueno, Sp.	168	42.53 N	5.18 W
La Vega, Dom. Rep. (lä-vĕ'gä)	133	19.15 N	70.35 W
Lavella (I.), Sol. Is.	211	7.50 S	155.45 E
Lavello, It. (lä-vĕl'lō)	170	41.05 N	15.50 E
La Verne, Ca. (lȧ vûrn')	117a	34.06 N	117.46 W
Laverton, Austl. (lā'vēr-tŭn)	210	28.45 S	122.30 E
La Victoria, Ven. (lä vĕk-tō'rē-ä)	141b	10.14 N	67.20 W
Lavonia, Ga. (lȧ-vō'nĭ-ȧ)	124	34.26 N	83.05 W
Lavon Res., Tx.	123	33.06 N	96.20 W
Lavras, Braz. (lä'vräzh)	139a	21.15 S	44.59 W
Lávrion, Grc. (läv'rĭ-ŏn)	171	37.44 N	24.05 E
Lawndale, Ca. (lôn'dāl)	117a	33.54 N	118.22 W
Lawra, Ghana	224	10.39 N	2.52 W
Lawrence, In. (lô'rĕns)	111g	39.59 N	86.01 W
Lawrence, Ks.	121	38.57 N	95.13 W
Lawrence, Ma.	103a	42.42 N	71.09 W
Lawrence, Pa.	111e	40.18 N	80.07 W
Lawrenceburg, In. (lô'rĕns-bûrg)	111f	39.06 N	84.47 W
Lawrenceburg, Ky.	108	38.00 N	85.00 W
Lawrenceburg, Tn.	124	35.13 N	87.20 W
Lawrenceville, Ga. (lô-rĕns-vĭl)	124	33.56 N	83.57 W
Lawrenceville, Il.	108	38.45 N	87.45 W
Lawrenceville, NJ	110a	40.17 N	74.44 W
Lawrenceville, Va.	125	36.43 N	77.52 W
Lawsonia, Md. (lô-sō'nĭ-ȧ)	109	38.00 N	75.50 W
Lawton, Ok. (lô'tŭn)	120	34.36 N	98.25 W
Lawz, Jabal al (Mtn.), Sau. Ar.	192	28.46 N	35.37 E
Layang Layang, Mala. (lä-yäng' lä-yäng')	189b	1.49 N	103.28 E
Laysan (I.), Hi.	105b	26.00 N	171.00 W
Layton, Ut. (lā'tŭn)	117b	41.04 N	111.58 W
Lazdijai, Sov. Un. (läzh'dē-yī')	163	54.12 N	23.35 E
Lazio (Latium) (Reg.), It. (lä'zyô) (lā't-zēōōm)	170	42.05 N	12.25 E
Lead, SD (lēd)	112	44.22 N	103.47 W
Leader, Can.	98	50.55 N	109.32 W
Leadville, Co. (lĕd'vĭl)	120	39.14 N	106.18 W
Leaf (R.), Ms. (lēf)	124	31.43 N	89.20 W
League City, Tx. (lēg)	123a	29.31 N	95.05 W
Leamington, Can. (lĕm'ĭng-tŭn)	108	42.05 N	82.35 W
Leamington, Eng. (lĕ'mĭng-tŭn)	160	52.17 N	1.25 W
Leatherhead, Eng. (lĕdh'ēr-hĕd')	154b	51.17 N	0.20 W
Leavenworth, Ks. (lĕv'ĕn-wûrth)	117f	39.19 N	94.54 W
Leavenworth, Wa.	114	47.35 N	120.39 W
Leawood, Ks. (lē'wŏŏd)	117f	38.58 N	94.37 W
Leba, Pol. (lā'bä)	165	54.45 N	17.34 E
Lebam R., Mala.	189b	1.35 N	104.09 E
Lebango, Con.	226	0.22 N	14.49 E
Lebanon, Il. (lĕb'ȧ-nŭn)	117e	38.36 N	89.49 W
Lebanon, In.	108	40.00 N	86.30 W
Lebanon, Ky.	124	37.32 N	85.15 W
Lebanon, Mo.	121	37.40 N	92.43 W
Lebanon, NH	109	43.40 N	72.15 W
Lebanon, Oh.	108	39.25 N	84.10 W
Lebanon, Or.	114	44.31 N	122.53 W
Lebanon, Pa.	109	40.20 N	76.20 W
Lebanon, Tn.	124	36.10 N	86.16 W
Lebanon, Asia	192	34.00 N	34.00 E
Lebanon Mts., Leb.	159	33.30 N	35.32 E
Lebedin, Sov. Un. (lyĕ'bĕ-dĕn)	173	48.56 N	31.35 E
Lebedin, Sov. Un.	173	50.34 N	34.27 E
Lebedyan', Sov. Un. (lyĕ'bĕ-dyän')	172	53.03 N	39.08 E
Le Blanc, Fr. (lĕ-bläN')	166	46.38 N	0.59 E
Le Borgne, Hai. (lĕ bōrn'y')	133	19.50 N	72.30 W
Lębork, Pol. (lăN-bōōrk')	165	54.33 N	17.46 E
Lebrija, Sp. (lā-brē'hä)	168	36.55 N	6.06 W
Lebú, Chile (lā-bōō')	142	37.35 S	73.37 W
Lecce, It. (lĕt'chā)	171	40.22 N	18.11 E
Lecco, It. (lĕk'kō)	170	45.52 N	9.28 E
Le Châtelet-en-Brie, Fr. (lĕ-shä-tĕ-lā'ĕN-brē')	167b	48.29 N	2.50 E
Leche, Laguna de (L.), Cuba (lä-gōō'nä-dĕ-lĕ'chĕ)	132	22.10 N	78.30 W
Leche, Laguna de la (L.), Mex.	122	27.16 N	102.45 W
Lech R., F.R.G. (lĕk)	164	47.41 N	10.52 E
Lecompte, La.	123	31.06 N	92.25 W
Le Creusot, Fr. (lĕkrû-zô)	166	46.48 N	4.23 E
Ledesma, Sp. (lȧ-dĕs'mä)	168	41.05 N	5.59 W
Leduc, Can. (lĕ-dōōk')	97	53.16 N	113.33 W
Leech (L.), Mn. (lēch)	113	47.06 N	94.16 W
Leeds, Al. (lēdz)	110h	33.33 N	86.33 W
Leeds, Eng.	154	53.48 N	1.33 W
Leeds, ND	112	48.18 N	99.24 W
Leeds and Liverpool Can., Eng. (lĭv'ēr-pōōl)	154	53.36 N	2.38 W
Leegebruch, G.D.R. (lĕh'gĕn-brōōk)	155b	52.43 N	13.12 E
Leek, Eng. (lēk)	154	53.06 N	2.01 W
Leer, F.R.G. (lār)	164	53.14 N	7.27 E
Leesburg, Fl. (lēz'bûrg)	125	28.49 N	81.53 W
Leesburg, Va.	109	39.10 N	77.30 W
Lees Ferry, Az.	119	36.55 N	111.45 W
Lees Summit, Mo.	117f	38.55 N	94.23 W
Lee Stocking (I.), Ba.	133	23.45 N	76.05 W
Leesville, La. (lēz'vĭl)	123	31.09 N	93.17 W
Leetonia, Oh. (lē-tō'nĭ-ȧ)	110	40.50 N	80.45 W
Leeuwarden, Neth. (lā'wär-dĕn)	161	52.12 N	5.50 E
Leeuwin, C., Austl. (lōō'wĭn)	210	34.15 S	114.30 E
Leeward Is., N. A. (lē'wērd)	123	12.25 N	62.15 W
Le Francois, Mart.	131b	14.37 N	60.55 W
Lefroy (L.), Austl. (lē-froi')	210	31.30 S	122.00 E
Leganés, Sp. (lā-gä'nås)	169a	40.20 N	3.46 W
Legazpi, Phil. (lā-gäs'pē)	203a	13.09 N	123.44 E
Legge Pk., Austl. (lĕg)	212	41.33 S	148.10 E
Leghorn, see Livorno			
Legnano, It. (lā-nyä'nō)	170	45.35 N	8.53 E
Legnica, Pol. (lĕk-nĭt'sȧ)	164	51.13 N	16.10 E
Leh, India (lā)	190	34.10 N	77.40 E
Le Havre, Fr. (lē ȧv'r')	166	49.31 N	0.07 E
Lehi, Ut. (lē'hī)	119	40.25 N	111.55 W
Lehman Caves Natl. Mon., Nv. (lē'mȧn)	119	38.54 N	114.08 W
Lehnin, G.D.R. (lĕh'nēn)	155b	52.19 N	12.45 E
Leicester, Eng. (lĕs'tēr)	154	52.37 N	1.08 W
Leicestershire, (Co.), Eng.	154	52.40 N	1.12 W
Leichhardt, (R.), Austl. (līk'härt)	210	18.30 S	139.45 E
Leiden, Neth. (lī'dĕn)	155a	52.09 N	4.29 E
Leigh Creek, Austl. (lē krēk)	212	30.33 S	138.30 E
Leikanger, Nor. (lī'käŋ'gēr)	162	61.11 N	6.51 E
Leimuiden, Neth.	155a	52.13 N	4.40 E
Leine R., F.R.G. (lī'nĕ)	164	51.58 N	9.56 E
Leinster, Ire. (lĕn-stēr)	160	52.45 N	7.19 W
Leipsic, Oh. (līp'sĭk)	108	41.05 N	84.00 W
Leipzig, G.D.R. (līp'tsĭk)	164	51.20 N	12.24 E
Leiria, Port. (lā-rē'ä)	168	39.45 N	8.50 W
Leitchfield, Ky. (lēch'fēld)	124	37.28 N	86.20 W
Leitha (R.), Aus.	155e	48.04 N	16.57 E
Leitrim, Can.	93c	45.20 N	75.36 W
Leizhou Bandao (Pen.), China (lā-jō bän-dou)	199	20.42 N	109.10 E
Lékéti, Monts de la (Mts.), Con.	226	2.34 S	14.17 E
Leksand, Swe. (lĕk'sänd)	162	60.45 N	14.56 E
Leland, Wa. (lē'lȧnd)	116a	47.54 N	122.53 W
Leliu, China (lŭ-lĭō)	197a	22.52 N	113.09 E
Le Locle, Switz. (lē lō'kl')	164	47.03 N	6.43 E
Le Maire, Estrecho de (Str.), Arg. (ĕs-trĕ'chō-dĕ-lĕ-mī'rĕ)	142	55.15 S	65.30 W
Le Mans, Fr. (lē mäN')	166	48.01 N	0.12 E
Le Marin, Mart.	131b	14.28 N	60.55 W
Le Mars, Ia. (lē märz')	112	42.46 N	96.09 W
Lemay, Mo.	117e	38.32 N	90.17 W
Lemery, Phil. (lā-mā-rē')	203a	13.51 S	120.55 E
Lemesós, Cyprus	189a	34.39 N	33.02 E
Lemhi Ra. (Mts.), Id. (lĕm'hī)	115	44.35 N	113.33 W
Lemhi R., Id.	115	44.40 N	113.27 W
Lemmon, SD (lĕm'ŭn)	112	45.55 N	102.10 W
Le Môle, Hai. (lē mōl')	133	19.50 N	73.20 W
Lemon Grove, Ca. (lĕm'ŭn-grōv)	118a	32.44 N	117.02 W

ng-sing; ŋ-baŋk; N-nasalized n; nŏd; cŏmmit; ōld; ōbey; ôrder; oi-boil; fōōd; fŏŏt; ou-out; s-soft; sh-dish; th-thin; pūre; ůnite; ûrn; stŭd; circŭs; ü-as in French tu; '-indeterminate vowel.

312 Lemont – Lingshou

PLACE (Pronunciation)	PAGE	Lat. °′	Long. °′
Lemont, Il. (lē'mŏnt)	111a	41.40 N	87.59 W
Le Moule, Guad. (lē mo͞ol')	131b	16.19 N	61.22 W
Lempa R., Sal. (lĕm'pä)	130	13.20 N	88.46 W
Lemvig, Den. (lĕm'vēgh)	162	56.33 N	8.16 E
Lena, Swe. (lĭ'nä)	162	60.01 N	17.40 E
Lençóes Paulista, Braz. (lĕN-sôNs' pou-lēs'tȧ)	142	22.30 S	48.45 W
Lençóis, Braz. (lĕn-sóis)	141	12.38 S	41.28 W
Lenexa, Ks. (lē'nĕx-ă)	117f	38.58 N	99.44 W
Lenger, Sov. Un. (lyĭn'gyĕr)	153	41.38 N	70.00 E
Lengyandong, China (lŭŋ-yän-dôŋ)	197a	23.12 N	113.21 E
Lenik (R.), Mala.	189b	1.59 N	102.51 E
Leninabad, Sov. Un. (lĕ-nyē-nȧ bät')	178	40.15 N	69.49 E
Leninakan, Sov. Un. (lĕ-nyē-nȧ-kän')	177	40.40 N	43.50 E
Leningrad, Sov. Un. (lyĕ-nēn-grät')	180c	59.57 N	30.20 E
Leningrad (Oblast), Sov. Un.	172	59.15 N	30.30 E
Leningradskaya, Sov. Un. (lyĕ-nĭn-gräd'skȧ-yȧ)	173	46.19 N	39.23 E
Lenino, Sov. Un. (lyĕ'nĭ-nô)	180b	55.37 N	47.41 E
Leninogorsk, Sov. Un. (lyĕ-nĭn ŭ gôrsk')	178	50.29 N	83.25 E
Leninsk, Sov. Un. (lyĕ-nēnsk')	177	48.40 N	45.10 E
Leninsk-Kuznetski, Sov. Un. (lyĕ-nēnsk'ko͞oz-nyĕt'skĭ)	178	54.28 N	86.48 E
Lenkoran', Sov. Un. (lĕn-kô-rän')	177	38.52 N	48.58 E
Lennox, SD (lĕn'ŭks)	112	43.22 N	96.53 W
Lenoir, NC (lē-nōr')	125	35.54 N	81.35 W
Lenoir City, Tn.	124	35.47 N	84.16 W
Lenox, Ia.	113	40.51 N	94.29 W
Léo, Upper Volta	224	11.06 N	2.06 W
Leoben, Aus. (lā-ō'bĕn)	164	47.22 N	15.09 E
Léogane, Hai. (lā-ô-gan')	133	18.30 N	72.35 W
Leola, SD (lē-ō'lȧ)	112	45.43 N	99.55 W
Leominster, Ma. (lĕm'ĭn-stēr)	103a	42.32 N	71.45 W
Leon, Ia. (lē'ŏn)	113	40.43 N	93.44 W
León, Mex. (lā-ōn')	128	21.08 N	101.41 W
León, Nic. (lĕ-ô'n)	130	12.28 N	86.53 W
León, Sp. (lĕ-ô'n)	168	42.38 N	5.33 W
Leon (Reg.), Sp. (lĕ-ô'n)	168	41.18 N	5.50 W
Leonforte, It. (lā-ôn-fôr'tā)	170	37.40 N	14.27 E
Leon R., Tx. (lē'ōn)	122	31.54 N	98.20 W
Leopoldina, Braz. (lā-ô-pôl-dē'nä)	139a	21.32 S	42.38 W
Leopoldsburg, Bel.	155a	51.07 N	5.18 E
Leopoldsdorf im Marchfelde, Aus. (lā'ô-pôlts-dôrf')	155e	48.14 N	16.42 E
Leopold II, L., see Mai-Ndombe			
Léopoldville, see Kinshasa			
Leovo, Sov. Un. (lā-ō'vô)	173	46.30 N	28.16 E
Lepe, Sp. (lā'pā)	168	37.15 N	7.12 W
Lepel', Sov. Un. (lyĕ-pĕl')	172	54.52 N	28.41 E
Leping, China (lŭ-pĭŋ)	199	29.02 N	117.12 E
L'Epiphanie, Can. (lā-pē-fä-nē')	93a	45.51 N	73.29 W
Le Plessis-Belleville, Fr. (lĕ-plĕ-sē'bĕl-vēl')	167b	49.05 N	2.46 E
Lepontine Alpi (Mts.), Switz. (lē-pŏn'tĭn)	164	46.28 N	8.38 E
Lepreau, Can. (lē-prō')	102	45.10 N	66.28 W
Lepsinsh, Sov. Un.	178	45.32 N	80.47 E
Le Puy, Fr. (lē pwē')	166	45.02 N	3.54 E
Lercara Friddi, It. (lĕr-kä'rä)	170	36.47 N	13.36 E
Lerdo, Mex. (lĕr'dō)	122	25.31 N	103.30 W
Léré, Chad (lā-rā')	221	9.42 N	14.14 E
Léré, Mali	224	15.43 N	4.55 W
Leribe, Leso.	223c	28.53 S	28.02 E
Lérida, Sp. (lā'rē-dhä)	169	41.38 N	0.37 E
Lerma, Mex. (lĕr'mä)	129	19.49 N	90.34 W
Lerma, Mex.	129a	19.17 N	99.30 W
Lerma, Sp. (lĕ'r-mä)	168	42.03 N	3.45 W
Lerma (R.), Mex.	128	20.14 N	101.50 W
Le Roy, NY (lē roi')	109	43.00 N	78.00 W
Lerwick, Scot. (lĕr'ĭk) (lûr'wĭk)	160a	60.08 N	1.27 W
Léry, Can. (lā-rī')	93a	45.21 N	73.49 W
Lery, L., La. (lĕ'rē)	110d	29.48 N	89.45 W
Les Andelys, Fr. (lā-zäN-dē-lē')	167b	49.15 N	1.25 E
Les Cayes, Hai.	133	18.15 N	73.45 W
Les Cèdres, Can. (lā-sĕdr'')	93a	45.18 N	74.03 W
Lesh (Alessio), Alb. (lĕshĕ) (ä-lā'sē-ō)	171	41.47 N	19.40 E
Leshan, China (lŭ-shän)	199	29.40 N	103.40 E
Lésina, Lago di (L.), It. (lä'gō dē lā'zē-nä)	170	41.48 N	15.12 E
Leskovac, Yugo. (lĕs'kô-vȧts)	171	43.00 N	21.58 E
Leslie, Ar. (lĕz'lĭ)	121	35.49 N	92.32 W
Leslie, S. Afr.	219d	26.23 S	28.57 E
Lesnoy, Sov. Un. (lĕs'noi)	176	66.45 N	34.45 E
Lesogorsk, Sov. Un. (lyĕs'ô-gôrsk)	200	49.28 N	141.59 E
Lesotho, Afr. (lĕsō'thô)	222	29.45 S	28.07 E
Lesozavodsk, Sov. Un. (lyĕ-sô-zȧ-vôdsk')	200	45.21 N	133.19 E
Les Sables-d'Olonne, Fr. (lā sȧ'bl'dô-lŭn')	166	46.30 N	1.47 W
Les Saintes Is., Guad. (lā-săNt')	131b	15.50 N	61.40 W
Lesser Khingan Range (Xiao Hinggan Ling), China (shyou hĭŋyän lĭŋ)	195	69.50 N	129.26 E
Lesser Slave (R.), Can.	97	55.15 N	114.30 W
Lesser Slave L., Can. (lĕs'ēr slāv)	97	55.25 N	115.30 W
Lesser Sunda Is., Indon.	202	9.00 S	120.00 E
L'Estaque, Fr. (lĕs-täl)	166a	43.22 N	5.20 E
Les Thilliers-en-Vexin, Fr. (lā-tē-yā'ĕN-vĕ-sȧN')	167b	49.19 N	1.36 E
Le Sueur, Mn. (lē so͞or')	113	44.27 N	93.53 W
Lésvos (I.), Grc.	171	39.15 N	25.40 E
Leszno, Pol. (lĕsh'nô)	164	51.51 N	16.35 E
Le Teil, Fr. (lĕ tā'y')	166	44.34 N	4.39 E
Lethbridge, Can. (lĕth'brĭj)	97	49.42 N	112.50 W
Letichev, Sov. Un. (lyĕ-tē-chĕf')	173	49.22 N	27.29 E
Leticia, Col. (lĕ-tē'syȧ)	140	4.04 S	69.57 W
Leting, China (lŭ-tĭŋ)	196	39.26 N	118.53 E
Letmathe, F.R.G. (lĕt'mät-hĕ)	167c	51.22 N	7.37 E
Le Tréport, Fr. (lē-trā'pôr')	166	50.03 N	1.21 E
Leuven, Bel.	155a	50.53 N	4.42 E
Levack, Can.	100	46.38 N	81.23 W
Levádhia, Grc.	171	38.25 N	22.51 E
Levallois-Perret, Fr. (lē-vȧl-wä'pĕ-rĕ')	167b	48.53 N	2.17 E
Levanger, Nor. (lĕ-väng'ĕr)	156	63.42 N	11.01 E
Levanna (Mtn.), Fr.-It. (lā-vä'nä)	170	45.25 N	7.14 E
Leveque, C., Austl. (lē-vĕk')	210	16.26 S	123.08 E
Leverkusen, F.R.G. (lĕ'fĕr-ko͞o-zĕn)	167c	51.01 N	6.59 E
Levice, Czech. (lā'vĕt-sĕ)	165	48.13 N	18.37 E
Levico, It. (lā'vē-kō)	170	46.02 N	11.20 E
Le Vigan, Fr. (lē vē-gäN')	166	43.59 N	3.36 E
Lévis, Can. (lā-vē') (lē'vĭs)	93b	46.49 N	71.11 W
Levittown, Pa. (lĕ'vĭt-toun)	110f	40.08 N	74.50 W
Levkás, Grc. (lyĕfkäs')	171	38.49 N	20.43 E
Levkás (I.), Grc.	171	38.42 N	20.22 E
Levoča, Czech. (lā'vô-chȧ)	165	49.03 N	20.38 E
Levy (L.), Fl. (lē'vĭ)	125	29.31 N	82.23 W
Lewes, De. (lo͞o'ĭs)	109	38.45 N	75.10 W
Lewes, Eng.	160	50.51 N	0.01 E
Lewis, I. of, Scot. (lo͞o'ĭs)	160	58.05 N	6.07 W
Lewis (R.) East Fk., Wa.	116c	45.52 N	122.40 W
Lewisburg, Tn. (lū'ĭs-bûrg)	124	35.27 N	86.47 W
Lewisburg, WV	108	37.50 N	80.20 W
Lewis Hills, Can.	103	48.48 N	58.30 W
Lewisporte, Can. (lū'ĭs-pōrt)	103	49.15 N	55.04 W
Lewis Ra., Mt. (lū'ĭs)	115	48.05 N	113.06 W
Lewis R., Wa.	114	46.05 N	122.09 W
Lewiston, Id. (lū'ĭs-tŭn)	114	46.24 N	116.59 W
Lewiston, Me.	102	44.05 N	70.14 W
Lewiston, NY	111c	43.11 N	79.02 W
Lewiston, Ut.	115	41.58 N	111.51 W
Lewistown, Il. (lū'ĭs-toun)	121	40.23 N	90.06 W
Lewistown, Mt.	115	47.05 N	109.25 W
Lewistown, Pa.	109	40.35 N	77.30 W
Lexington, Ky. (lĕk'sĭng-tŭn)	108	38.05 N	84.30 W
Lexington, Ma.	103a	42.27 N	71.14 W
Lexington, Ms.	124	33.08 N	90.02 W
Lexington, Mo.	121	39.11 N	93.52 W
Lexington, Nb.	120	40.46 N	99.44 W
Lexington, NC	125	35.47 N	80.15 W
Lexington, Tn.	124	35.37 N	88.24 W
Lexington, Va.	109	37.45 N	79.20 W
Leyte (I.), Phil. (lā'tā)	203	10.35 N	125.35 E
Lezajsk, Pol. (lĕ'zhä-ĭsk)	165	50.14 N	22.25 E
Lezha (R.), Sov. Un. (lĕ-zhä')	172	58.59 N	40.27 E
L'gov, Sov. Un. (lgôf)	173	51.42 N	35.15 E
Lhasa, China (läs'ä)	190	29.41 N	91.12 E
Liangxiangzhen, China (lĭäŋ-shyäŋ-jŭn)	198a	39.43 N	116.08 E
Lianjiang, China (lĭĕn-jyäŋ)	199	21.38 N	110.15 E
Lianozovo, Sov. Un. (lĭ-a-nô'zô-vô)	180b	55.54 N	37.36 E
Lianshui, China (lĭĕn-shwā)	196	33.46 N	119.15 E
Lianyungang, China (lĭĕn-yo͞on-gäŋ)	196	34.35 N	119.09 E
Lianyungang, China	196	34.43 N	119.27 E
Liaocheng, China (lĭou-chŭŋ)	196	36.27 N	115.56 E
Liaodong Bandao (Pen.), China (lĭou-dôŋ bän-dou)	196	39.45 N	122.22 E
Liaodong Wan (B.), China (lĭou-dôŋ wäŋ)	198	40.25 N	121.15 E
Liaoning (Prov.), China	195	41.31 N	122.11 E
Liaoyang, China (lyä'ō-yäng')	198	41.18 N	123.10 E
Liaoyuan, China (lĭou-yüän)	198	43.00 N	124.59 E
Liard (R.), Can. (lē-är')	117	59.43 N	126.42 W
Libano, Col. (lē'bȧ-nô)	140a	4.55 N	75.05 W
Libby, Mt. (lĭb'ē)	114	48.27 N	115.35 W
Libenge, Zaire (lē-bĕŋ'gā)	221	3.39 N	18.40 E
Liberal, Ks. (lĭb'ēr-ăl)	120	37.01 N	100.56 W
Liberec, Czech. (lē'bĕr-ĕts)	164	50.45 N	15.06 E
Liberia, Afr. (lī-bē'rĭ-ȧ)	218	6.30 N	9.55 W
Liberia, C. R.	130	10.38 N	85.28 W
Libertad de Orituco, Ven. (lē-bĕr-tä'd-dĕ-ŏ-rē-to͞o'kô)	141b	9.32 N	66.24 W
Liberty, In. (lĭb'ēr-tĭ)	108	39.35 N	84.55 W
Liberty, Mo.	117f	39.15 N	94.25 W
Liberty, SC	125	34.47 N	82.41 W
Liberty, Tx.	123	30.03 N	94.46 W
Liberty, Ut.	117b	41.20 N	111.52 W
Liberty B., Wa.	116a	47.43 N	122.41 W
Liberty L., Md.	110e	39.25 N	76.56 W
Libertyville, Il. (lĭb'ēr-tĭ-vĭl)	111a	42.17 N	87.57 W
Libode, S. Afr. (lĭ-bō'dĕ)	223c	31.33 S	29.03 E
Libón, R., Hai.	133	19.30 N	71.45 W
Libourne, Fr. (lē-bo͞orn')	166	44.55 N	0.12 W
Libres, Mex. (lē'brās)	129	19.26 N	97.41 W
Libreville, Gabon (lē-br'vēl')	226	0.23 N	9.27 E
Liburn, Ga. (lĭb'ûrn)	110c	33.53 N	84.09 W
Libya, Afr. (lĭb'ē-ä)	218	27.38 N	15.00 E
Libyan Des. (Aş Şahrā' al Lībīyah), Libya (lĭb'ē-ăn)	221	28.23 N	23.34 E
Libyan Plat., Egypt	159	30.58 N	26.20 E
Licancábur, Cerro (Mtn.), Chile (sĕ'r-rô-lē-kȧn-kȧ'bo͞or)	142	22.45 S	67.45 W
Licanten, Chile (lē-kän-tĕ'n)	139b	34.58 S	72.00 W
Lichfield, Eng. (lĭch'fēld)	154	52.41 N	1.49 W
Lichinga, Moz.	227	13.18 S	35.14 E
Lichtenburg, S. Afr. (lĭk'tĕn-bĕrgh)	219d	26.09 S	26.10 E
Lick Cr., In. (lĭk)	111g	39.43 N	86.06 W
Licking (R.), Ky. (lĭk'ĭng)	108	38.30 N	84.10 W
Lida, Sov. Un. (lē'dȧ)	165	53.53 N	25.19 E
Lidgerwood, ND (lĭj'ēr-wood)	112	46.04 N	97.10 W
Lidköping, Swe. (lēt'chû-pĭng)	162	58.31 N	13.06 E
Lido di Roma, It. (lē'dô-dē-rô'mä)	169d	41.19 N	12.17 E
Lidzbark, Pol. (lĭts'bärk)	165	54.07 N	20.36 E
Liebenbergsvlei (R.), S. Afr.	219d	27.35 S	28.25 E
Liebenwalde, G.D.R. (lē'bĕn-väl-dĕ)	155b	52.52 N	13.24 E
Liechou Pan-Tao (Pen.), China	199	20.40 N	109.25 E
Liechtenstein, Eur. (lēk'tĕn-shtīn)	157	47.10 N	10.00 E
Liège, Bel. (lē-āzh')	161	50.40 N	5.30 E
Lienyün, China (lĭan'yün)	195	33.10 N	120.01 E
Lienz, Aus. (lē-ĕnts')	164	46.49 N	12.45 E
Liepāja, Sov. Un. (le'pä-yä')	163	56.31 N	20.59 E
Lier, Bel.	155a	51.08 N	4.34 E
Liesing, Aus. (lē'sĭng)	155e	48.09 N	16.17 E
Liestal, Switz. (lēs'täl)	164	47.28 N	7.44 E
Lievre, Riviére du (R.), Can.	109	45.00 N	75.25 W
Lifanga, Zaire	226	0.19 N	21.57 E
Lifou, (I.), N. Cal.	211	21.15 S	167.32 E
Ligao, Phil. (lē-gä'ô)	203a	13.14 N	123.33 E
Lightning Ridge, Austl.	212	29.23 S	147.50 E
Ligonha (R.), Moz. (lē-gō'nyȧ)	223	16.14 S	39.00 E
Ligonier, In. (lĭg-ô-nēr)	108	41.30 N	85.35 W
Ligovo, Sov. Un. (lē'gô-vô)	180c	59.51 N	30.13 E
Liguria (Reg.), It. (lē-go͞o-rē-ä)	170	44.24 N	8.27 E
Ligurian Sea, Eur. (lĭ-gū'rĭ-ăn)	170	43.42 N	8.32 E
Lihou Rfs., Austl. (lē-ho͞o')	211	17.23 S	152.43 E
Lihuang, China (lē'ho͞oäng)	196	31.32 N	115.46 E
Lihue, Hi. (lē-ho͞o'ā)	104a	21.59 N	159.23 W
Lihula, Sov. Un. (lē'ho͞o-lȧ)	163	58.41 N	23.50 E
Liji, China (lē-jyē)	196	33.47 N	117.47 E
Lijiang, China (lē-jyäŋ)	196	27.00 N	100.08 E
Lijin, China (lē-jyĭn)	196	37.30 N	118.15 E
Likasi (Jadotville), Zaire	227	10.59 S	26.44 E
Likhoslavl', Sov. Un. (lyē-kôsläv''l)	172	57.07 N	35.27 E
Likhovka, Sov. Un. (lyē-Kôf'kȧ)	173	48.52 N	33.57 E
Likouala (R.), Con.	226	0.10 S	16.30 E
Lille, Fr. (lēl)	166	50.38 N	3.01 E
Lille Baelt (str.), Den.	162	55.09 N	9.53 E
Lillehammer, Nor. (lēl'ĕ-häm'mĕr)	162	61.07 N	10.25 E
Lillesand, Nor. (lēl'ĕ-sän')	162	58.16 N	8.19 E
Lilleström, Nor. (lēl'ĕ-strûm)	162	59.56 N	11.04 E
Lilliwaup, Wa. (lĭl'ĭ-wŏp)	116a	47.28 N	123.07 W
Lillooet, Can. (lĭ'lo͞o-ĕt)	97	50.30 N	121.55 W
Lillooet (R.), Can.	97	49.50 N	122.10 W
Lilongwe, Malawi (lē-lô-än)	227	13.59 S	33.44 E
Lima, Oh. (lī'mȧ)	108	40.40 N	84.05 W
Lima, Peru (lē'mä)	140	12.06 S	76.55 W
Lima, Swe.	162	60.54 N	13.24 E
Lima (R.), Port.	168	41.45 N	8.22 W
Lima Duarte, Braz. (dwä'r-tĕ)	139a	21.52 S	43.47 W
Lima Res., Mt.	115	44.45 N	112.15 W
Limay (R.), Arg. (lē-mä'ē)	142	39.50 S	69.15 W
Limbazi, Sov. Un. (lēm'bä-zĭ)	163	57.32 N	24.44 E
Limbdi, India	190	22.37 N	71.52 E
Limbé, Hai.	133	19.45 N	72.30 W
Limburg an der Lahn, F.R.G. (lem-bo͞org')	164	50.22 N	8.03 E
Limeira, Braz. (lē-mā'rä)	139a	22.34 S	47.24 W
Limestone Bay, Can. (līm'stōn)	99	53.50 N	98.50 W
Limfjorden (Fd.), Den.	162	56.55 N	8.56 E
Limmen Bght., Austl. (lĭm'ĕn)	210	14.45 S	136.00 E
Limni, Grc. (lēm'nē)	171	38.47 N	23.22 E
Límnos (I.), Grc.	171	39.58 N	24.48 E
Limoges, Can. (lē-môzh')	93c	45.20 N	75.15 W
Limoges, Fr.	166	45.50 N	1.15 E
Limon, Co. (lī'mŏn)	120	39.15 N	103.41 W
Limón, C. R. (lē-mōn')	131	10.01 N	83.02 W
Limón, Hond. (lē-mô'n)	130	15.53 N	85.34 W
Limon (R.), Dom. Rep.	133	18.20 N	71.40 W
Limón B., Pan.	126a	9.21 N	79.58 W
Limours, Fr. (lē-mo͞or')	167b	48.39 N	2.05 E
Limousin, Plateaux du (Plat.), Fr. (plä-tō' dü lē-mo͞o-zȧN')	166	45.44 N	1.09 E
Limoux, Fr. (lē-mo͞o')	166	43.03 N	2.14 E
Limpopo R., Afr. (lĭm-pō'pō)	222	23.15 S	27.46 E
Linares, Chile (lē-nä'rās)	139b	35.51 S	71.35 W
Linares, Mex.	122	24.53 N	99.34 W
Linares, Sp. (lē-nä'rĕs)	168	38.07 N	3.38 W
Linares (Prov.), Chile	139b	35.53 S	71.30 W
Linaro, C., It. (lē-nä'rä)	170	42.02 N	11.53 E
Linchuan, China (lĭn-chüän)	199	27.58 N	116.18 E
Lincoln, Arg. (lĭŋ'kŭn)	139c	34.51 S	61.29 W
Lincoln, Ca.	118	38.51 N	121.19 W
Lincoln, Can.	93d	43.10 N	79.29 W
Lincoln, Eng.	154	53.14 N	0.33 W
Lincoln, Il.	121	40.09 N	89.21 W
Lincoln, Ks.	120	39.02 N	98.08 W
Lincoln, Me.	102	45.23 N	68.31 W
Lincoln, Ma.	103a	42.25 N	71.19 W
Lincoln, Ne.	121	40.49 N	96.43 W
Lincoln, Mt., Co.	120	39.20 N	106.19 W
Lincoln Heath (Reg.), Eng.	154	53.23 N	0.39 W
Lincoln Park, Mi.	111b	42.14 N	83.11 W
Lincoln Park, NJ	110a	40.56 N	74.18 W
Lincolnshire (Co.), Eng.	154	53.12 N	0.29 W
Lincolnshire Wolds (Hills), Eng. (woldz')	160	53.25 N	0.23 W
Lincolnton, NC (lĭŋ'kŭn-tŭn)	125	35.27 N	81.15 W
Lindale, Ga. (lĭn'dāl)	124	34.10 N	85.10 W
Lindau, F.R.G. (lĭn'dou)	164	47.33 N	9.40 E
Linden, Al. (lĭn'dĕn)	124	32.16 N	87.47 W
Linden, Mo.	117f	39.13 N	94.35 W
Linden, NJ	110a	40.39 N	74.14 W
Lindenhurst, NY (lĭn'dĕn-hûrst)	110a	40.41 N	73.23 W
Lindenwold, NJ (lĭn'dĕn-wôld)	110f	39.50 N	75.00 W
Lindesberg, Swe. (lĭn'dĕs-bĕrgh)	162	59.37 N	15.14 E
Lindesnes (C.), Nor. (lĭn'ĕs-nĕs)	161	58.00 N	7.05 E
Lindho, China	198	40.45 N	107.30 E
Lindi, Tan. (lĭn'dē)	227	10.00 S	39.43 E
Lindi R., Zaire	221	1.00 N	27.13 E
Lindian, China (lĭn-dĭĕn)	198	42.08 N	124.59 E
Lindley, S. Afr. (lĭnd'lē)	219d	27.52 S	27.55 E
Lindow, G.D.R. (lēn'dōv)	155b	52.58 N	12.59 E
Lindsay, Can. (lĭn'zē)	109	44.20 N	78.45 W
Lindsay, Ok.	120	34.50 N	97.38 W
Lindsborg, Ks. (lĭnz'bôrg)	120	38.34 N	97.42 W
Lineville, Al. (līn'vĭl)	124	33.18 N	85.45 W
Linfen, China	198	36.00 N	111.38 E
Linga, Kepulauan (Is.), Indon.	202	0.35 S	105.05 E
Lingao, China (lĭn-gou)	199	19.58 N	109.40 E
Lingayen, Phil. (lĭŋ'gä-yān')	203a	16.01 N	120.13 E
Lingayen G., Phil.	203a	16.18 N	120.11 E
Lingbi, China (lĭŋ-bē)	196	33.33 N	117.33 E
Lingdianzhen, China	196	31.52 N	121.28 E
Lingen, F.R.G. (lĭŋ'gĕn)	164	52.32 N	7.20 E
Lingling, China (lĭŋ-lĭŋ)	199	26.10 N	111.40 E
Lingshou, China (lĭŋ-shō)	196	38.21 N	114.41 E

ăt; fināl; rāte; senāte; ärm; ȧsk; sofȧ; fâre; ch-choose; dh-as th in other; bē; ēvent; bĕt; recĕnt; cratēr; g-gō; gh-guttural g; bĭt; ĭ-short neutral; rīde; K-guttural k as ch in German ich;

PRONOUNCING INDEX
Linguère – Long Pt. 313

PLACE (Pronunciation)	PAGE	Lat. °′	Long. °′
Linguère, Senegal (lĭŋ-gĕr′)	224	15.24 N	15.07 W
Lingwu, China	198	38.05 N	106.18 E
Lingyuan, China (lĭŋ-yůän)	198	41.12 N	119.20 E
Linhai, China	199	28.52 N	121.08 E
Linhe, China (lĭn-hŭ)	198	40.49 N	107.45 E
Linhuaiguan, China (lĭn-hwī-gůän)	196	32.55 N	117.38 E
Linhuanji, China (lĭ-hwī-jyē)	196	33.42 N	116.33 E
Linjiangi, China (lĭn-jyäŋ)	198	41.45 N	127.00 E
Linköping, Swe. (lĭn′chû-pĭng)	162	58.25 N	15.35 E
Linnhe, Loch (L.), Scot. (lĭn′ė)	160	56.35 N	4.30 W
Linqing, China (lĭn-chyĭŋ)	196	36.49 N	115.42 E
Linqux, China (lĭn-chyōō)	196	36.31 N	118.33 E
Lins, Braz. (lė′ɴs)	141	21.42 S	49.41 W
Linthicum Heights, Md. (lĭn′thĭ-kŭm)	110e	39.12 N	76.39 W
Linton, In. (lĭn′tŭn)	108	39.05 N	87.15 W
Linton, ND	112	46.16 N	100.15 W
Linwu, China (lĭn′wōō′)	199	25.20 N	112.30 E
Linxi, China (lĭn-shyē)	198	43.30 N	118.02 E
Linyi, China (lĭn-yē)	196	35.04 N	118.21 E
Linying, China (lĭn′yĭng′)	196	33.48 N	113.56 E
Linz, Aus. (lĭnts)	164	48.18 N	14.18 E
Linzhang, China (lĭn-jäŋ)	196	36.19 N	114.40 E
Lipa, Phil. (lė-pä′)	203a	13.55 N	121.10 E
Lipari, It. (lē′pä-rė)	170	38.29 N	15.00 E
Lipari (I.), It.	170	38.32 N	15.04 E
Lipetsk, Sov. Un. (lyē′pĕtsk)	172	52.26 N	39.34 E
Lipetsk, (Oblast), Sov. Un.	172	52.18 N	38.30 E
Liping, China (lē-pĭŋ)	199	26.18 N	109.00 E
Lipno, Pol. (lēp′nȯ)	165	52.50 N	19.12 E
Lippe (R.), F.R.G. (lĭp′ĕ)	161	51.36 N	6.45 E
Lippstadt, F.R.G. (lĭp′shtät)	164	51.39 N	8.20 E
Lipscomb, Al. (lĭp′skŭm)	110h	33.26 N	86.56 W
Liptsy, Sov. Un. (lyēp′tsė)	173	50.11 N	36.25 E
Lipu, China (lē-pōō)	199	24.38 N	110.35 E
Lira, Ug.	227	2.15 N	32.54 E
Liri (R.), It. (lē′rē)	170	41.49 N	13.30 E
Liria, Sp. (lė′ryä)	169	39.35 N	0.34 W
Lisala, Zaire (lė-sä′lä)	226	2.09 N	21.31 E
Lisboa (Lisbon), Port. (lėzh-bō′ä) (lĭz′bŭn)	169b	38.42 N	9.05 W
Lisbon, ND	112	46.21 N	97.43 W
Lisbon, Oh.	108	40.45 N	80.50 W
Lisbon, see Lisboa			
Lisbon Falls, Me.	102	43.59 N	70.03 W
Lisburn, N. Ire. (lĭs′bŭrn)	160	54.35 N	6.05 W
Lisburne, C., Ak.	105	68.20 N	165.40 W
Lishi, China (lē-shr)	198	37.32 N	111.12 E
Lishu, China	198	43.12 N	124.18 E
Lishui, China	199	28.28 N	120.00 E
Lishui, China (lĭ′shwĭ′)	196	31.41 N	119.01 E
Lisianski I., Hi.	105b	25.30 N	174.00 W
Lisieux, Fr. (lē-zyû′)	166	49.10 N	0.13 E
Lisiy Nos, Sov. Un. (lĭ′sĭy-nôs)	180c	60.01 N	30.00 E
Liski, Sov. Un. (lyēs′kė)	173	50.56 N	39.28 E
Lisle, Il. (līl)	111a	41.48 N	88.04 W
L'Isle-Adam, Fr. (lēl-ädäɴ′)	167b	49.05 N	2.13 E
Lismore, Austl. (lĭz′môr)	212	28.48 S	153.18 E
Lister, Mt., Ant. (lĭs′tēr)	228	78.05 S	163.00 E
Litani (R.), Lib.	189a	33.28 N	35.42 E
Litchfield, Il. (lĭch′fēld)	121	39.10 N	89.38 W
Litchfield, Mn.	113	45.08 N	94.34 W
Litchfield, Oh.	111d	41.10 N	82.01 W
Lithgow, Austl. (lĭth′gō)	212	33.23 S	149.31 E
Lithinon Akra (C.), Grc.	170a	34.59 N	24.35 E
Lithonia, Ga. (lĭ-thō′nĭ-ȧ)	110c	33.43 N	84.07 W
Lithuanian S. S. R., Sov. Un. (lĭth-ů-ā-′nĭ-ȧ)	176	55.42 N	23.30 E
Litin, Sov. Un. (lė-tēn)	173	49.16 N	28.11 E
Litókhoron, Grc. (lē′tȯ-ĸō′rôn)	171	40.05 N	22.29 E
Litoko, Zaire,	226	1.13 S	24.47 E
Litoměřice, Czech. (lē′tȯ-myĕr′zhĭ-tsĕ)	164	50.33 N	14.10 E
Litomyšl, Czech. (lē′tȯ-mēsh′l)	164	49.52 N	16.14 E
Litoo, Tan.	227	9.45 S	38.24 E
Little (R.), Austl.	207a	37.54 S	144.27 E
Little (R.), Tn.-Mo.	124	36.28 N	89.39 W
Little R., Tx.	123	30.48 N	96.50 W
Little Abaco (I.), Ba. (ä′bä-kō)	132	26.55 N	77.45 W
Little Abitibi (R.), Can.	100	50.15 N	81.30 W
Little America, Ant.	228	78.30 S	161.30 W
Little Andama I., Andaman & Nicobar Is. (ăn-dȧ-măn′)	202	10.39 N	93.08 E
Little Bahama Bk., Ba. (bȧ-hā′mȧ)	132	26.55 N	78.40 W
Little Belt Mts., Mt. (bĕlt)	115	47.00 N	110.50 W
Little Bighorn R., Mt. (bĭg-hôrn)	115	45.08 N	107.30 W
Little Bitter, see Al Buhayrah al Murrah aş Şughrā			
Little Bitterroot R., Mt. (bĭt′ēr-ōōt)	114	47.45 N	114.45 W
Little Blue (R.), Ne.	120	40.15 N	98.01 W
Little Blue R., Mo. (blōō)	117f	38.52 N	94.25 W
Littleborough, Eng. (lĭt′′l-bŭr-ȯ)	154	53.39 N	2.06 W
Little Calumet R., Il. (kăl-ů-mĕt′)	111a	41.38 N	87.38 W
Little Cayman (I.), Cayman Is. (kā′mȧn)	132	19.40 N	80.05 W
Little Colorado (R.), Az. (kŏl-ȯ-rā′dō)	119	36.05 N	111.35 W
Little Compton, RI (kŏmp′tŏn)	110b	41.31 N	71.07 W
Little Corn I., Nic.	131	12.19 N	82.50 W
Little Exuma (I.), Ba. (ĕk-sōō′mä)	133	23.25 N	75.40 W
Little Falls, Mn. (fôlz)	113	45.58 N	94.23 W
Little Falls, NY	109	43.05 N	74.55 W
Littlefield, Tx. (lĭt′′l-fēld)	120	33.55 N	102.17 W
Little Fork (R.), Mn. (fôrk)	113	48.24 N	93.30 W
Little Hans Lollick (I.), Vir. Is (U.S.A.) (häns lôl′lĭk)	127c	18.25 N	64.54 W
Little Humboldt R., Nv. (hŭm′bōlt)	114	41.10 N	117.40 W
Little Inagua (I.), Ba. (ė-nä′gwä)	133	21.30 N	73.00 W
Little Isaac (I.), Ba. (ī′zȧk)	132	25.55 N	79.00 W
Little Kanawha (R.), WV (kȧ-nô′wȧ)	108	39.05 N	81.30 W
Little Karroo (Mts.), S. Afr. (kä-rōō)	222	33.50 S	21.02 E
Little Mecatina (R.), Can. (mĕ cȧ tĭ nȧ)	95	52.40 N	62.21 W
Little Miami R., Oh. (mī-ăm′ĭ)	111f	39.19 N	84.15 W
Little Minch (Chan.), Scot.	160	57.35 N	6.45 W
Little Missouri (R.), Ar. (mĭ-sōō′rĭ)	121	34.15 N	93.54 W
Little Missouri (R.), SD	112	45.46 N	103.48 W
Little Pee Dee (R.), SC (pē-dē′)	125	34.35 N	79.21 W
Little Powder R., Wy. (pou′dēr)	115	44.51 N	105.20 W
Little Red (R.), Ar. (rĕd)	121	35.25 N	91.55 W
Little Red R., Ok.	121	33.53 N	94.38 W
Little Rock, Ar. (rôk)	121	34.42 N	92.16 W
Little Sachigo L., Can. (să′chĭ-gō)	99	54.09 N	92.11 W
Little San Salvador (I.), Ba. (săn săl′vȧ-dôr)	133	24.35 N	75.55 W
Little Satilla (R.), Ga. (sȧ-tĭl′ȧ)	112	31.43 N	82.47 W
Little Sioux (R.), Ia. (sōō)	112	42.22 N	95.47 W
Little Smoky (R.), Can. (smōk′ĭ)	97	55.10 N	116.55 W
Little Snake R., Co. (snāk)	115	40.40 N	108.21 W
Little Tallapoosa (R.), Al. (tăl-ȧ-pōō′să)	124	32.25 N	85.28 W
Little Tennessee (R.), Tn. (tĕn-ĕ-sē′)	124	35.36 N	84.05 W
Littleton, Co. (lĭt′′l-tŭn)	120	39.34 N	105.01 W
Littleton, Ma.	103a	42.32 N	71.29 W
Littleton, NH	101	44.15 N	71.45 W
Little Wabash (R.), Il. (wô′băsh)	108	38.50 N	88.30 W
Little Wood R., Id. (wŏŏd)	115	43.00 N	114.08 W
Liuhe, China	198	42.10 N	125.38 E
Liuli, Tan.	227	11.05 S	34.38 E
Liup'an Shan (Mts.), China	198	36.20 N	105.30 E
Liuwa Pln., Zambia	226	14.30 S	22.40 E
Liuyang, China (lyōō′yäng′)	199	28.10 N	113.35 E
Liuyuan, China (lĭȯ-yůän)	196	36.09 N	114.37 E
Liuzhou, China (lĭȯ-jō)	199	24.25 N	109.30 E
Līvāni, Sov. Un. (lē′vȧ-nė)	172	56.24 N	26.12 E
Lively, Can.	100	46.26 N	81.09 W
Livengood, Ak. (līv′ĕn-gŏŏd)	105	65.30 N	148.35 W
Live Oak, Fl. (līv′ōk)	124	30.15 N	83.00 W
Livermore, Ca. (lĭv′ēr-mōr)	116b	37.41 N	121.46 W
Livermore, Ky.	108	37.30 N	87.05 W
Liverpool, Austl. (lĭv′ēr-pōōl)	207b	33.55 S	150.56 E
Liverpool, Can.	102	44.02 N	64.41 W
Liverpool, Eng.	154	53.25 N	2.52 W
Liverpool, Tx.	123a	29.18 N	95.17 W
Liverpool B., Can.	105	69.45 N	130.00 W
Liverpool Ra., Austl.	211	31.47 S	31.00 E
Livindo R., Gabon	221	1.09 N	13.30 E
Livingston, Al. (lĭv′ĭng-stŭn)	124	32.35 N	88.09 W
Livingston, Guat.	130	15.50 N	88.45 W
Livingston, Il.	117e	38.58 N	89.51 W
Livingston, Mt.	115	45.40 N	110.35 W
Livingston, NJ	110a	40.47 N	74.20 W
Livingston, Tn.	124	36.23 N	85.20 W
Livingstone, Zambia (lĭv-ĭng-stȯn)	227	17.50 S	25.53 E
Livingstone, Chutes de (Livingstone Falls), Con.-Zaire	226	4.50 S	14.30 E
Livingstone Mts., Tan.	227	9.30 S	34.10 E
Livingstonia, Malawi (lĭv-ĭng-stō′nĭ-ȧ)	227	10.36 S	34.07 E
Livno, Yugo. (lēv′nȯ)	170	43.50 N	17.03 E
Livny, Sov. Un. (lēv′nė)	172	52.28 N	37.36 E
Livonia, Mi. (lĭ-vō-nĭ-ȧ)	111b	42.25 N	83.23 W
Livorno (Leghorn), It. (lė-vôr′nō) (lĕg′hȯrn)	170	43.32 N	11.18 E
Livramento, Braz. (lē-vrȧ-mĕ′n-tô)	142	30.46 S	55.21 W
Li Xian, China (lē shyĕn)	199	29.42 N	111.40 E
Li Xian, China	196	38.30 N	115.38 E
Liyang, China (lē′yäng′)	196	31.30 N	119.29 E
Lizard Pt., Eng. (lĭz′ȧrd)	160	49.55 N	5.09 W
Lizy-sur-Ourcq, Fr. (lēk-sē′sür-ōōrk′)	167b	49.01 N	3.02 E
Ljmuiden, Neth.	155a	52.27 N	4.35 E
Ljubljana, Yugo. (lyōō′blyä′na)	170	46.04 N	14.29 E
Ljubuški, Yugo. (lyōō′bŏŏsh-kė)	170	43.11 N	17.29 E
Ljungan (R.), Swe.	162	62.50 N	13.45 E
Ljungby, Swe. (lyŏŏng′bü)	162	56.49 N	13.56 E
Ljusdal, Swe. (lyōōs′däl)	162	61.50 N	16.11 E
Ljusnan (R.), Swe.	162	61.55 N	15.33 E
Llandudno, Wales (lăn-düd′nō)	160	53.20 N	3.46 W
Llanelli, Wales (lȧ-nĕl′ĭ)	160	51.44 N	4.09 W
Llanes, Sp. (lyä′nås)	168	43.25 N	4.41 W
Llano, Tx. (lä′nō) (lyä′nō)	122	30.45 N	98.41 W
Llano R., Tx.	122	30.38 N	99.04 W
Llanos (Reg.), Col.-Ven. (lyȧ′nŏs)	140	4.00 N	71.15 W
Llera, Mex. (lyā′rä)	128	23.16 N	99.03 W
Llerena, Sp. (lyā-rā′nä)	168	38.14 N	6.02 W
Llobregat (R.), Sp. (lyȯ-brĕ-gät′)	169	41.55 N	1.55 E
Lloyd L., Can. (loid)	93e	50.52 N	114.13 W
Lloydminster, Can.	100	53.17 N	110.00 W
Lluchmayor, Sp. (lyōōch-mä-yȯr′)	169	39.28 N	2.53 E
Llullaillaco (Vol.), Arg. (lyōō-lyī-lyä′kō)	142	24.50 S	68.30 W
Loange (R.), Zaire (lȯ-äŋ′gā)	226	6.10 S	19.40 E
Lobatsi, Bots. (lō-bä′tsē)	222	25.13 S	25.35 E
Lobería, Arg. (lô-bĕ′rē′ä)	142	38.13 S	58.48 W
Lobito, Ang. (lȯ-bē′tō)	226	12.30 S	13.34 E
Lobnya, Sov. Un. (lôb′nyȧ)	180b	56.01 N	37.29 E
Lobo, Phil.	203a	13.39 N	121.14 E
Lobos, Arg. (lō′bȯs)	139c	35.10 S	59.08 W
Lobos, Cayo (I.), Ba. (lō′bȯs)	132	22.25 N	77.40 W
Lobos, Isla de (I.), Mex. (ė′s-lä-dĕ-lô′bōs)	129	21.24 N	97.11 W
Lobos de Tierra (I.), Peru (lô′bō-dĕ-tyĕ′r-rä)	140	6.29 S	80.55 W
Lobva, Sov. Un. (lôb′vȧ)	180a	59.12 N	60.28 E
Lobva R., Sov. Un.	180a	59.14 N	60.17 E
Locarno, Switz. (lȯ-kär′nō)	164	46.10 N	8.43 E
Loches, Fr. (lȯsh)	166	47.08 N	0.56 E
Lochloosa (L.), Fl. (lŏk-lō′sȧ)	125	29.33 N	82.07 W
Loch Raven Res., Md.	110e	39.28 N	76.38 W
Lockeport, Can.	102	43.42 N	65.07 W
Lockhart, SC (lŏk′hȧrt)	125	34.47 N	81.30 W
Lockhart, Tx.	123	29.54 N	97.40 W
Lock Haven, Pa. (lŏk′hā-vĕn)	109	41.05 N	77.30 W
Lockland, Oh. (lŏk′lănd)	111f	39.14 N	84.27 W
Lockport, Can. (lŏk′pōrt)	93f	50.05 N	96.56 W
Lockport, Il.	111a	41.35 N	88.04 W
Lockport, NY	111c	43.11 N	78.43 W
Loc-ninh, Viet. (lōk′nĭng′)	202	12.00 N	106.30 E
Lod, Isr. (lôd)	189a	31.57 N	34.55 E
Lodèye, Fr. (lȯ-dĕv′)	166	43.43 N	3.18 E
Lodeynoye Pole, Sov. Un. (lȯ-dĕy-nô′yĕ)	163	60.43 N	33.24 E
Lodge Cr., Can. (lŏj)	98	49.20 N	110.20 W
Lodge Cr., Mt.	115	48.51 N	109.30 W
Lodgepole Cr., Wy. (lŏj′pōl)	112	41.22 N	104.48 W
Lodhran, Pak.	190	29.40 N	71.39 E
Lodi, Ca. (lō′dī)	118	38.07 N	121.17 W
Lodi, It. (lô′dē)	170	45.18 N	9.30 E
Lodi, Oh. (lō′dī)	111d	41.02 N	82.01 W
Lodosa, Sp. (lȯ-dô′sä)	168	42.27 N	2.04 W
Lodwar, Ken.	227	3.07 N	35.36 E
Łódź, Pol. (wŏŏdzh)	165	51.46 N	19.13 E
Loeches, Sp. (lȯ-āch′ĕs)	169a	40.22 N	3.25 W
Loffa (R.), Lib.	224	7.10 N	10.35 W
Lofoten (Is.), Nor. (lȯ′fō-tĕn)	156	68.26 N	13.42 E
Logăn, Oh. (lō′gȧn)	108	39.35 N	82.25 W
Logan, Ut.	115	41.46 N	111.51 W
Logan, WV	108	37.50 N	82.00 W
Logan, Mt., Can.	94	60.54 N	140.33 W
Logansport, In. (lō′gănz-pōrt)	108	40.45 N	86.25 W
Logone (R.), Afr. (lō-gō′nā) (lȯ-gȯn′)	225	11.15 N	15.10 E
Logroño, Sp. (lȯ-grō′nyō)	168	42.28 N	2.25 W
Logrosán, Sp. (lȯ-grȯ-sän′)	168	39.22 N	5.29 W
Løgstør, Den. (lügh-stûr′)	162	56.56 N	9.15 E
Loir (R.), Fr. (lwȧr)	166	47.40 N	0.07 E
Loire (R.), Fr.	166	47.19 N	1.11 W
Loja, Ec. (lō′hä)	140	3.49 S	79.13 W
Loja, Sp. (lȯ′-kä)	168	37.10 N	4.11 W
Loka, Zaire	226	0.20 N	17.57 E
Lokala Drift, Bots. (lȯ′kä-lȧ drĭft)	219d	24.00 S	26.38 E
Lokandu, Zaire	227	2.31 S	25.47 E
Lokhvitsa, Sov. Un. (lȯĸ-vėt′sȧ)	173	50.21 N	33.16 E
Lokichar, Ken.	227	2.23 N	35.39 E
Lokitaung, Ken.	227	4.16 N	35.45 E
Lokofa-Bokolongo, Zaire	226	0.12 N	19.22 E
Lokoja, Nig. (lȯ-kō′yä)	225	7.47 N	6.45 E
Lokolama, Zaire	226	2.34 S	19.53 E
Lokosso, Upper Volta	224	10.19 N	3.40 W
Lol R., Sud. (lōl)	221	9.06 N	28.09 E
Loliondo, Tan.	227	2.03 S	35.37 E
Lolland, Den. (lôl′än′)	162	54.41 N	11.00 E
Lolo, Mt.	115	46.45 N	114.05 W
Lom, Bul. (lōm)	171	43.48 N	23.15 E
Loma Linda, Ca. (lō′mȧ lĭn′dȧ)	117a	34.04 N	117.16 W
Loma Mansa (Mtn.), S.L.	224	9.13 N	11.07 W
Lomami (R.), Zaire	226	0.50 S	24.40 E
Lomas de Zamora, Arg. (lō′mäs dā zä-mō′rä)	142a	34.31 S	58.24 W
Lombard, Il. (lŏm-bärd)	111a	41.53 N	88.01 W
Lombardia (Reg.), It. (lȯm-bär-dė′ä)	170	45.20 N	9.30 E
Lomblen, Pulau (I.), Indon. (lŏm-blĕn′)	203	8.08 S	123.45 E
Lombok (I.), Indon. (lŏm-bŏk′)	202	9.15 S	116.15 E
Lomé, Togo. (lō-mā′) (lō′mā)	224	6.08 N	1.13 E
Lomela, Zaire (lȯ-mā′lȧ)	222	2.19 S	23.33 E
Lomela (R.), Zaire	226	0.35 S	21.20 E
Lometa, Tx. (lȯ-mē′tȧ)	122	31.10 N	98.25 W
Lomie, Cam. (lȯ-mė-ā′)	225	3.10 N	13.37 E
Lomita, Ca. (lō-mē′tȧ)	117a	33.48 N	118.20 W
Lommel, Bel.	155a	51.14 N	5.21 E
Lommond, Loch (L.), Scot. (lôk lō′mŭnd)	160	56.15 N	4.40 W
Lomonosov, Sov. Un. (lô-mô′nô-sof)	180c	59.54 N	29.47 E
Lompoc, Ca. (lŏm-pōk′)	118	34.39 N	120.30 W
Lomza, Pol. (lôm′zhȧ)	165	53.11 N	22.04 E
Lonaconing, Md. (lō-nă-kō′nĭng)	109	39.35 N	78.55 W
London, Can. (lŭn′dŭn)	108	43.00 N	81.20 W
London, Eng.	154b	51.30 N	0.07 W
London, Ky.	124	37.07 N	84.06 W
London, Oh.	108	39.50 N	83.30 W
Londonderry, Can. (lŭn′dŭn-dĕr-ĭ)	102	45.29 N	63.36 W
Londonderry, N. Ire.	160	55.00 N	7.19 W
Londonderry, C., Austl.	210	13.30 S	127.00 E
Londrina, Braz. (lôn-drē′nä)	141	21.53 S	51.17 W
Lonely (I.), Can. (lōn′lĭ)	108	45.35 N	81.30 W
Lone Pine, Ca.	118	36.36 N	118.03 W
Lone Star, Nic.	131	13.58 N	84.25 W
Long (I.), Ba.	133	23.25 N	75.10 W
Long (I.), Can.	102	44.21 S	66.25 W
Long (L.), ND	112	46.47 N	100.14 W
Long (L.), Wa.	116a	47.29 N	122.36 W
Longa, Ang.	226	14.42 S	18.32 E
Longa (R.), Ang. (lôŋ′gȧ)	226	10.20 S	13.50 E
Long B., SC	125	33.30 N	78.54 W
Long Beach, Ca. (lông bēch)	117a	33.46 N	118.12 W
Long Beach, NY	110a	40.35 N	73.38 W
Long Branch, NJ (lông brȧnch)	110a	40.18 N	73.59 W
Longdon, ND (lông′-dŭn)	112	48.45 N	98.23 W
Long Eaton, Eng. (ē′tŭn)	154	52.54 N	1.16 W
Longford, Ire. (lŏng′fērd)	160	53.43 N	7.40 W
Longgu, China (lȯŋ-gōō)	196	34.52 N	116.48 E
Longhorn, Tx. (lông-hôrn)	117d	29.33 N	98.23 W
Longido, Tan.	227	2.44 S	36.41 E
Long I., Ak.	96	54.54 N	132.45 W
Long I., NY (lông)	109	40.50 N	72.50 W
Long I., Pap. N. Gui.	203	5.10 S	147.30 E
Long Island Sd., Ct.-NY (lông ī′lănd)	109	41.05 N	72.45 W
Longjumeau, Fr. (lôɴ-zhü-mō′)	167b	48.42 N	2.17 E
Longkou, China (lȯŋ-kō)	196	37.39 N	120.21 E
Longlac, Can. (lông′lȧk)	100	49.41 N	86.28 W
Long L., Can.	100	49.10 N	86.45 W
Longlake, SD (lông-lāk)	112	45.52 N	99.06 W
Longmont, Co. (lông′mŏnt)	120	40.11 N	105.07 W
Longnor, Eng. (lông′nȯr)	154	53.11 N	1.52 W
Long Pine, Ne. (lông pīn)	112	42.31 N	99.42 W
Long Pt., Can.	109	42.35 N	80.05 W

ng-sing; ŋ-baŋk; ɴ-nasalized n; nŏd; cŏmmit; ōld; ȯbey; ôrder; oi-boil; fōōd; fŏŏt; ou-out; s-soft; sh-dish; th-thin; pūre; ůnite; ûrn; stŭd; circŭs; ü-as in French tu; ′-indeterminate vowel.

314 Long Pt. – Luso

PLACE (Pronunciation)	PAGE	Lat. °'	Long. °'
Long Pt., Can.	103	48.48 N	58.46 W
Long Pt., Can.	99	53.02 N	98.40 W
Long Point B., Can.	109	42.40 N	80.10 W
Long Prairie, Mn. (lông prâr'ĭ)	113	45.58 N	94.49 W
Long Range Mts., Can.	103	48.00 N	58.30 W
Longreach, Austl. (lông'rēch)	211	23.32 S	144.17 E
Long Reach (R.), Can.	102	45.26 N	66.05 W
Long Rf., Austl.	207b	33.45 S	151.22 E
Longridge, Eng. (lông'rĭj)	154	53.51 N	2.37 W
Longs Pk., Co. (lôngz)	120	40.17 N	105.37 W
Longtansi, China (lôŋ-tä-sz)	196	32.12 N	115.53 E
Longton, Eng. (lông'tŭn)	154	52.59 N	2.08 W
Longueuil, Can. (lôɴ-gû'y')	93a	45.32 N	73.30 W
Longview, Wa. (lông-vū)	116c	46.06 N	123.02 W
Longview, Tx.	123	32.29 N	94.44 W
Longville, La. (lông'vĭl)	123	30.36 N	93.14 W
Longwy, Fr. (lôɴ-wē')	167	49.32 N	6.14 E
Longxi, China (lôŋ-shyē)	198	35.00 N	104.40 E
Long-xuyen, Viet. (loung' so͞o'yĕn)	202	10.31 N	105.28 E
Longzhen, China (lôŋ-jŭn)	179	48.47 N	126.43 E
Longzhou, China (lôŋ-jō)	199	22.20 N	107.02 E
Lonoke, Ar. (lō'nōk)	121	34.48 N	91.52 W
Lons-le-Saunier, Fr. (lôɴ-lē-sō-nyā')	167	46.40 N	5.33 E
Lontue, (R.), Chile (lôn-to͞oĕ')	139b	35.20 S	70.45 W
Looc, Phil. (lō-ōk')	203a	12.16 N	121.59 E
Loogootee, In.	108	38.40 N	86.55 W
Lookout, C., NC (lo͝ok'out)	125	34.34 N	76.38 W
Lookout Pt. Res., Or.	114	43.51 N	122.38 W
Loolmalasin (Mtn.), Tan.	227	3.03 S	35.46 E
Looma, Can. (o͞o'mä)	93g	53.22 N	113.15 W
Loop Head, Ire. (lo͞op)	160	52.32 N	9.59 W
Loosahatchie (R.), Tn. (lōz-à-hă'chē)	124	35.20 N	89.45 W
Loosdrechtsche Plassen (L.), Neth.	155a	52.11 N	5.09 E
Lopatka, Mys (C.), Sov. Un. (lō-pät'kà)	175	51.00 N	156.52 E
Lopez, Cap (C.), Gabon	226	0.37 N	8.43 E
Lopez B., Phil. (lō'päz)	203a	14.04 N	122.00 E
Lopez I, Wa.	116a	48.25 N	122.53 W
Lopori (R.), Zaire (lō-pō'rē)	226	1.35 N	20.43 E
Lora, Sp. (lō'rä)	168	37.40 N	5.31 W
Lorain, Oh. (lō-rān')	111d	41.28 N	82.10 W
Loralai, Pak. (lō-rŭ-lī')	190	30.31 N	68.35 E
Lorca, Sp. (lôr'kä)	168	37.39 N	1.40 W
Lord Howe (I.), Austl. (lôrd hou)	211	31.44 S	157.56 W
Lordsburg, NM (lôrdz'bûrg)	119	32.20 N	108.45 W
Lorena, Braz. (lô-rā'nà)	139a	22.45 S	45.07 W
Loreto, Braz. (lô-rā'tō)	141	7.09 S	45.10 W
Loretteville, Can. (lô-rĕt-vēl')	93b	46.51 N	71.21 W
Lorica, Col. (lô-rē'kä)	140	9.14 N	75.54 W
Lorient, Fr. (lô-rē'äɴ')	166	47.45 N	3.22 W
Lorn, Firth of, Scot. (fûrth ŏv lôrn')	160	56.10 N	6.09 W
Lörrach, F.R.G. (lûr'äĸ)	164	47.36 N	7.38 E
Los Alamitos, Ca. (lōs ăl-à-mē'tōs)	117a	33.48 N	118.04 W
Los Alamos, NM (ăl-à-mōs')	119	35.53 N	106.20 W
Los Altos, Ca. (ăl-tōs')	116b	37.23 N	122.06 W
Los Andes, Chile (än'dĕs)	139b	32.44 S	70.36 W
Los Angeles, Ca. (ăŋ'gĕl-ĕs) (ă'jĕl-ĕs) (äŋ'hā-lās)	117a	34.00 N	118.15 W
Los Angeles, Chile (äŋ'hā-lās)	142	37.27 S	72.15 W
Los Angeles Aqueduct, Ca.	118	35.12 N	118.02 W
Los Angeles R., Ca.	117a	33.50 N	118.13 W
Los Bronces, Chile (lōs brō'n-sĕs)	139b	33.09 S	70.18 W
Loscha R., Id. (lōs'chă)	114	46.20 N	115.11 W
Los Chonos, Archipielago de, Chile (är-chē-pyĕ'lä-gō dĕ lōs chô'nōs)	142	44.35 N	76.15 W
Los Estados, Isla de (I.), Arg. (ē's-lä dĕ lōs ĕs-dōs)	142	54.45 S	64.25 W
Los Gatos, Ca. (gä'tōs)	118	37.13 N	121.59 W
Los Herreras, Mex. (ĕr-rā-räs)	122	25.55 N	99.23 W
Los Ilanos, Dom. Rep. (lōs ē-lä'nōs)	133	18.35 N	69.30 W
Los Indios, Cayos de (Is.), Cuba (kä'vōs dĕ lōs ē'n-dvō's)	132	21.50 N	83.10 W
Lošinj (I.), Yugo.	170	44.35 N	14.34 E
Losino Petrovskiy, Sov. Un.	180b	55.52 N	38.12 E
Los Nietos, Ca. (nyā'tōs)	117a	33.57 N	118.05 W
Los Palacios, Cuba	132	22.35 N	83.15 W
Los Pinos (R.), Co.-NM (pē'nōs)	119	36.58 N	107.35 W
Los Reyes Mex.(rā'yĕs)	128	19.35 N	102.29 W
Los Reyes, Mex.	129a	19.21 N	98.58 W
Los Santos, Pan. (sän'tōs)	131	7.57 N	80.24 W
Los Santos de Maimona Sp. (sän'tōs)	168	38.38 N	6.30 W
Los Teques, Ven. (tĕ'kĕs)	141b	10.22 N	67.04 W
Lost R., Id. (lôst)	115	43.56 N	113.38 W
Lost R, Or.	114	42.07 N	121.30 W
Lost River Mts., Id. (rĭ'vēr)	115	44.23 N	113.48 W
Los Vilos, Chile (vē'lōs)	139b	31.56 S	71.29 W
Lot (R.), Fr. (lôt)	166	44.32 N	1.08 E
Lota, Chile (lō'tä)	142	37.11 S	73.14 W
Lothian, Md. (lōth'ĭăn)	110e	38.50 N	76.38 W
Lotikipi Pln, Ken.	227	4.25 N	34.55 E
Lötschberg Tunnel, Switz.	164	46.26 N	7.54 E
Louangphrabang, Laos (lo͞o-ang'prä-bäng')	202	19.47 N	102.15 E
Loudon, Tn. (lou'dŭn)	124	35.43 N	84.20 W
Loudonville, Oh. (lou'dŭn-vĭl)	108	40.40 N	82.15 W
Loudun, Fr. (lo͞o-dŭɴ')	166	47.03 N	0.00
Louga, Senegal (lo͞o'gä)	224	15.37 N	16.13 W
Loughborough, Eng. (lŭf'bŭr-ô)	154	56.46 N	1.12 W
Louisa, Ky. (lo͞o'ēz-à)	108	38.05 N	82.40 W
Louisade Arch., Pap. N. Gui. (lo͞o-ĭs-äd är-kĭ-pĕl-ĭ-gō)	211	10.44 S	153.58 E
Louisberg, NC (lo͞o'ĭs-bûrg)	125	36.05 N	79.19 W
Louisburg, Can. (lo͞o'ĭs-bourg)	103	45.55 N	59.58 W
Louiseville, Can.	102	46.17 N	72.58 W
Louis XIV, Pte, Can.	95	54.35 N	79.51 W
Louisiana, Mo. (lo͞o-ē-zē-ăn'à)	121	39.24 N	91.03 W
Louisiana (State), U. S.	107	30.50 N	92.50 W
Louis Trichardt, S. Afr. (lo͞o'ĭs trĭch'art)	222	22.52 S	29.53 E
Louisville, Co. (lo͞o'ĭs-vĭl) (lo͞o'ē-vĭl)	120	39.58 N	105.08 W
Louisville, Ga.	125	33.00 N	82.25 W
Louisville, Ky.	111h	38.15 N	85.45 W
Louisville, Ms.	124	33.07 N	89.02 W
Loulé, Port. (lō-lā')	168	37.08 N	8.03 W
Louny, Czech. (lō'nē)	164	50.20 N	13.47 E
Loup (R.), Ne. (lo͞op)	112	41.17 N	97.58 W
Loup City, Ne.	112	41.15 N	98.59 W
Lourdes, Fr. (lo͞ord)	168	43.06 N	0.03 W
Lourenço Marques, see Maputo			
Loures, Port. (lō'rĕzh)	169b	38.49 N	9.10 W
Lousa, Port. (lō'zà)	168	40.05 N	8.12 W
Louth, Eng. (louth)	160	53.27 N	0.02 W
Louviers, Fr. (lo͞o-vyā')	166	49.13 N	1.11 E
Louvres, Fr. (lo͞ov'r')	167b	49.03 N	2.30 E
Lovat', Sov. Un. (lô-vät'y')	172	57.23 N	31.18 E
Lovech, Bul. (lō'vĕts)	171	43.10 N	24.40 E
Loveland, Co. (lŭv'lănd)	120	40.24 N	105.04 W
Loveland, Oh.	111	39.16 N	84.15 W
Lovell, Wy. (lŭv'ĕl)	115	44.50 N	108.23 W
Lovelock, Nv. (lŭv'lŏk)	118	40.10 N	118.37 W
Lovick, Al. (lŭ'vĭk)	110h	33.34 N	86.38 W
Loviisa, Fin. (lô'vē-sá)	163	60.28 N	26.10 E
Low, C., Can. (lō)	95	62.58 N	86.50 W
Lowa, Zaire (lō'wà)	222	1.30 S	27.18 E
Lowell, In.	111a	41.17 N	87.26 W
Lowell, Ma.	103a	42.38 N	71.18 W
Lowell, Mi.	108	42.55 N	85.20 W
Löwenberg, G.D.R. (lû'vĕn-bĕrgh)	155b	52.53 N	13.09 E
Lower Arrow (L.), Can. (ăr'ō)	97	49.40 N	118.80 W
Lower Austria (State), see Niederösterreich			
Lower Brule Ind. Res., SD (brü'lā)	112	44.15 N	100.21 W
Lower Hutt, N.Z. (hŭt)	213	41.55 S	174.55 E
Lower Klamath L., Ca. (klăm'ăth)	114	41.55 N	121.50 W
Lower L., Ca.-Nv.	114	41.21 N	119.53 W
Lower Marlboro, Md. (lō'ēr mărl'bōrō)	110e	38.40 N	76.42 W
Lower Monumental Res., Wa.	114	46.45 N	118.50 W
Lower Otay Res., Ca. (ō'tā)	118a	32.37 N	116.46 W
Lower Red. (L.), Mn. (rĕd)	113	47.58 N	94.31 W
Lower Saxony (State), see Niedersachsen			
Lowestoft, Eng. (lō'stŏft)	161	52.31 N	1.45 E
Łowicz, Pol. (lô'vĭch)	165	52.06 N	19.57 E
Lowville, NY (lou'vĭl)	109	43.45 N	75.30 W
Loxicha (Santa Catarina), Mex. (lô-zē'chä) (sän-tä kä-tä-rē'nä)	129	16.03 N	96.46 W
Loxton, Austl. (lôks'tŭn)	212	34.25 S	140.38 E
Loyauté, Iles, N. Cal.	211	21.17 S	168.16 E
Loznica, Yugo. (lôz'nē-tsà)	171	44.31 N	19.16 E
Lozorno, Czech.	155e	48.21 N	17.03 E
Lozova, Sov. Un. (lô-zô'vá)	173	48.54 N	36.17 E
Lozovatka, Sov. Un. (lô-zô-vät'kä)	173	48.03 N	33.19 E
Lozovaya, Sov. Un. (lô-zo-vä'yä)	173	48.27 N	38.37 E
Lozoya, Canal de, Sp. (kä-nä'l dĕ lō-thō'yä)	169a	40.36 N	3.41 W
Lualaba (R.), Zaire (lo͞o-à-lä'bà)	227	1.00 S	25.45 E
Luama (R.), Zaire (lo͞o'ä-mà)	227	4.17 S	27.45 E
Lu'an, China (lo͞o-än)	196	31.45 N	116.29 E
Luan (R.), China	198	41.25 N	117.15 E
Luanda, Ang. (lo͞o-än'dä)	226	8.48 S	13.14 E
Luanguinga (R.), Ang. (lo͞o-ä-gĭŋ'gà)	222	14.00 S	20.45 E
Luangwa (R.), Zambia (lo͞o-äŋ'gwà)	227	11.25 S	32.55 E
Luanshya, Zambia	227	13.08 S	28.24 E
Luan Xian, China (luăn shyĕn)	196	39.47 N	118.40 E
Luarca, Sp. (lwä'kä)	168	43.33 N	6.30 W
Lubaczów, Pol. (lo͞o-bä'cho͝of)	175	50.08 N	23.10 E
Lubán, Pol. (lo͞o'bän')	164	51.08 N	15.17 E
Lubānas Ezers (L.), Sov. Un. (lo͞o-bä'nás ă'zĕrs)	163	56.48 N	26.30 E
Lubang, Phil. (lo͞o-bäng')	203a	13.49 N	120.07 E
Lubang (Is.), Phil.	203a	13.47 N	119.56 E
Lubango, Ang.	226	14.55 S	13.30 E
Lubao, Phil. (lo͞o-bä'ō)	203a	14.55 N	120.36 E
Lubartow, Pol. (lo͞o-bär'to͞of)	165	51.27 N	22.37 E
Lubawa, Pol. (lo͞o-bä'vä)	165	53.31 N	19.47 E
Lübben, G.D.R. (lüb'ĕn)	164	51.56 N	13.53 E
Lubbock, Tx. (lŭb'ŭk)	120	33.35 N	101.50 W
Lubec, Me. (lū'bĕk)	102	44.49 N	67.01 W
Lübeck, F.R.G. (lü'bĕk)	164	53.53 N	10.42 E
Lübecker Bucht (B.), G.D.R. (lü'bĕ-kĕr bo͞oĸt)	164	54.10 N	11.20 E
Lubilash (R.), Zaire (lo͞o-bē-lash'-)	226	7.35 S	23.55 E
Lubin, Pol. (lyo͞o'bĭn)	164	51.24 N	16.14 E
Lublin, Pol. (lyo͞o'blĕn')	165	51.14 N	22.33 E
Lubny, Sov. Un. (lo͞ob'nē)	173	50.01 N	33.02 E
Lubuagan, Phil. (lo͞o-bwä-gä'n)	203a	17.24 N	121.11 E
Lubudi, Zaire	227	9.57 S	25.58 E
Lubudi (R.), Zaire (lo͞o-bo͞o'dē)	227	9.20 S	25.20 E
Lubumbashi (Elisabethville), Zaire	227	11.40 S	27.28 E
Lucano, Ang.	227	11.16 S	21.38 E
Lucca, It. (lo͞ok'kä)	170	43.51 N	10.29 E
Luce B., Scot. (lūs)	160	54.45 N	4.45 W
Lucea, Jam.	132	18.25 N	78.10 W
Lucena, Phil. (lo͞o-sā'nä)	203a	13.55 N	121.36 E
Lucena, Sp. (lo͞o-thā'nä)	168	37.25 N	4.28 W
Lucena del Cid, Sp. (lo͞o'thā'nä dā thēdh')	169	40.08 N	0.18 W
Lučenec, Czech. (lo͞o'châ-nyĕts)	165	48.19 N	19.41 E
Lucera, It. (lo͞o-châ'rä)	170	41.31 N	15.22 E
Luchi, China	199	28.18 N	110.10 E
Lucin, Ut. (lū-sĕn')	115	41.23 N	113.59 W
Lucipara, Kepulauan (I.), Indon. (lo͞o-sē-pä'rá)	203	5.45 S	128.15 E
Luckenwalde, G.D.R. (lo͞ok-ĕn-väl'dĕ)	155b	52.05 N	13.10 E
Lucknow, India (lŭk'nou)	190	26.54 N	80.58 E
Luçon, Fr. (lü-sôɴ')	166	46.27 N	1.12 W
Lucrecia, Cabo (C.), Cuba (kà'bô-lo͞o-krā'sē-à)	133	21.05 N	75.30 W
Lüda, China (lü-dä)	196	38.54 N	121.35 E
Luda Kamchiya (R.), Bul.	171	42.46 N	27.13 E
Lüdenscheid, F.R.G. (lü'dĕn-shīt)	167c	51.13 N	7.38 E
Lüderitz, Namibia (lü'dĕr-ĭts) (lü'dĕ-rĭts)	222	26.35 S	15.15 E
Lüderitz Bucht (B.), Namibia	222	26.35 S	14.30 E
Ludhiāna, India	190	31.00 N	75.52 E
Lüdinghausen, F.R.G. (lü'dĕng-hou-zĕn)	167c	51.46 N	7.27 E
Ludington, Mi. (lŭd'ĭng-tŭn)	108	44.00 N	86.25 W
Ludlow, Eng. (lŭd'lō)	154	52.22 N	2.43 W
Ludlow, Ky.	111f	39.05 N	84.33 W
Ludvika, Swe. (loodh-vē'kà)	162	60.10 N	15.09 E
Ludwigsburg, F.R.G. (lo͞ot'vĕks-bo͞orgh)	164	48.53 N	9.14 E
Ludwigsfelde, G.D.R. (lo͞od'vēgs-fĕl-dĕ)	155b	52.18 N	13.16 E
Ludwigshafen, F.R.G. (lo͞ot'vĕks-hä'fĕn)	164	49.29 N	8.26 E
Ludwigslust, G.D.R. (lo͞ot'vĕks-lo͞ost)	164	53.18 N	11.31 E
Ludza, Sov. Un. (lo͞od'zá)	172	56.33 N	27.45 E
Luebo, Zaire (lo͞o-ā'bō)	222	5.15 S	21.22 E
Luena, Zaire	227	9.27 S	25.47 E
Lufira (R.), Zaire (lo͞o-fē'rà)	222	9.32 S	27.15 E
Lufkin, Tx. (lŭf'kĭn)	123	31.21 N	94.43 W
Luga, Sov. Un. (lo͞o'gá)	172	58.43 N	29.52 E
Luga (R.), Sov. Un.	172	59.00 N	29.25 E
Lugano, Switz. (lo͞o-gä'nō)	164	46.01 N	8.52 E
Lugenda (R.), Moz. (lo͞o-zhĕn'dä)	227	12.05 S	38.15
Lugh Ganane, Som.	219a	3.38 N	42.35 E
Lugnaquilla Mtn., Ire. (lo͝ok-nà-kwĭ-lá)	160	52.56 N	6.30 W
Lugo, It. (lo͞o'gô)	170	44.28 N	11.57 E
Lugo, Sp. (lo͞o'gō)	168	43.01 N	7.32 W
Lugoj, Rom.	171	45.51 N	21.56 E
Luhe, China (lo͞o-hŭ)	196	32.22 N	118.50 E
Luhe, see Winsen			
Luiana, Ang.	226	17.23 S	23.03 E
Luilaka (R.), Zaire (lo͞o-ē-lä'kà)	222	2.18 S	21.15 E
Luimneach, Ire. (lĭm'năk)	160	52.39 N	8.35 W
Luis Moya, Mex. (lo͞oē's-mô-yä)	128	22.26 N	102.14 W
Luján, Arg. (lo͞o'hän')	139c	34.36 S	59.07 W
Luján (R.), Arg.	139c	34.33 S	58.59 W
Lujchow Pen., China	195	20.40 N	100.30 E
Lujia, China (lo͞o-jyä)	196	31.17 N	120.54 W
Lukanga Swp., Zambia (lo͞o-käŋ'gà)	227	14.30 S	27.25 E
Lukenie (R.), Zaire (lo͞o-kā'yná)	226	3.10 S	19.05 E
Lukolela, Zaire	222	1.03 S	17.01 E
Lukovit, Bul. (lo͞o'kô-vêt')	171	43.13 N	24.07 E
Luków, Pol. (wo͞o'ko͞of)	165	51.57 N	22.25 E
Lukuga (R.), Zaire (lo͞o-ko͞o'gá)	227	5.50 S	27.35 E
Lule (R.), Swe.	176	66.20 N	20.25 E
Luleå, Swe. (lo͞o-lĕ-ô)	156	65.39 N	21.52 E
Lüleburgaz, Tur. (lü'lĕ-bo͞or-gäs')	171	41.25 N	27.23 E
Luling, Tx. (lū'lĭng)	123	29.41 N	97.38 W
Lulong, China (lo͞o-lôŋ)	196	39.54 N	118.53 E
Lulonga (R.), Zaire	226	1.00 N	18.37 E
Lulu (I.), Can. (lū'lo͞o)	116d	49.09 N	123.05 W
Lulua (R.), Zaire (lo͞o'lo͞o-à)	226	15.40 N	22.07 E
Luluabourg, see Kananga			
Lulu I, Ak.	96	55.28 N	133.30 W
Lulu I, Can.	96	49.09 N	123.05 W
Lumajangdong Co. (L.), China (lo͞o-ma-jäŋ-dôŋtswo)	190	34.00 N	81.47 E
Lumber (R.), NC (lŭm'bēr)	125	35.12 N	79.35 W
Lumberton, Ms. (lŭm'bēr-tŭn)	124	31.00 N	89.25 W
Lumberton, NC	125	34.47 N	79.00 W
Luminárias, Braz. (lo͞o-mē-ná'ryäs)	139a	21.32 S	44.53 W
Lummi (I.), Wa.	116d	48.42 N	122.43 W
Lummi B., Wa. (lŭm'ĭ)	116d	48.47 N	122.44 W
Lummi Island, Wa.	116d	48.44 N	122.42 W
Lumwana, Zambia	226	11.50 S	25.10 E
Luna, Phil. (lo͞o'ná)	203a	16.51 N	120.22 E
Lund, Swe. (lŭnd)	162	55.42 N	13.10 E
Lunda (Reg.), Ang. (lo͞on'dá)	218	8.53 S	20.00 E
Lundi (R.), Zimb. (lo͞on'dē)	222	21.09 S	30.10 E
Lundy (I.), Eng. (lŭn'dē)	160	51.12 N	4.50 W
Lüneberger Heide (Reg.), F.R.G. (lü'nĕ-bo͞or-gĕr hī'dĕ)	164	53.08 N	10.00 E
Lüneburg, F.R.G. (lü'nĕ-bo͞orgh)	164	53.16 N	10.25 E
Lunel, Fr. (lü-nĕl')	166	43.41 N	4.07 E
Lünen, F.R.G. (lü'nĕn)	167c	51.36 N	7.30 E
Lunenburg, Can. (lo͞o'nĕn-bûrg)	102	44.23 N	64.19 W
Lunenburg, Ma.	103a	42.36 N	71.44 W
Lunéville, Fr. (lü-nâ-vel')	167	48.37 N	6.29 E
Lunga (R.), Zambia (lo͞oŋ'gà)	222	12.58 S	26.18 E
Lungué-Bungo (R), Ang.	226	13.00 S	21.27 E
Lūni (R), India	190	25.20 N	72.00 E
Luninets (R), Sov. Un. (lo͞o-nēn'yets)	172	52.14 N	26.54 E
Lunsar, S.L.	224	8.41 N	12.32 W
Luodian, China (lwô-dĭĕn)	197a	31.25 N	121.20 E
Luoding, China (lwô-dĭŋ)	199	23.42 N	111.35 E
Luohe, China (lwô-hŭ)	196	33.35 N	114.02 E
Luoyang, China (lwô-yäŋ)	198	34.45 N	112.32 E
Luozhen, China (lwô-jŭn)	196	37.45 N	118.29 E
Luque, Par. (loo'kä)	142	25.18 S	57.17 W
Lūrah (R), Afg.	190	32.10 N	67.20 E
Luray, Va. (lū-rā')	109	38.40 N	78.25 W
Lurgan, N. Ire. (lûr'găn)	160	54.27 N	6.28 W
Lúrio, Moz. (lo͞o'rē-ō)	223	13.17 S	40.29 E
Lúrio (R), Moz.	227	14.00 S	38.45 E
Lusaka, Zaire	227	7.10 S	29.27 E
Lusaka, Zambia (lo͞o-sä'kà)	227	15.25 S	28.17 E
Lusambo, Zaire (lo͞o-säm'bō)	226	4.58 S	23.27 E
Lusanga, Zaire	222	5.13 S	18.43 E
Lusangi, Zaire	227	4.37 S	27.08 E
Lushai Hills, Bur.	190	28.28 N	92.50 E
Lushan, China	198	33.45 N	113.00 E
Lushiko (R), Zaire	226	6.35 S	19.45 E
Lushoto, Tan. (lo͞o-shō'tō)	223	4.47 S	38.17 E
Lüshun, China (lü-shŭn)	196	38.49 N	121.15 E
Lusikisiki, S. Afr. (lo͞o-sē-kē-sē'kē)	223c	31.22 S	29.37 E
Lusk, Wy. (lŭsk)	112	42.46 N	104.27 W
Luso, Ang. (lo͞o'sô)	226	11.45 S	19.55 E

PLACE (Pronunciation)	PAGE	Lat. °′	Long. °′
Lutcher, La. (lŭch'ēr)	123	30.03 N	90.43 W
Luton, Eng. (lū'tŭn)	160	51.55 N	0.28 W
Lutsk, Sov. Un. (lōōtsk)	165	50.45 N	25.20 E
Luverne, Al. (lū-vûn')	124	31.42 N	86.15 W
Luverne, Mn.	112	43.40 N	96.13 W
Luvua (R), Zaire (lōō'vōō-ȧ)	227	7.00 S	27.45 E
Luwingu, Zambia	227	10.15 S	29.55 E
Luxapalila Cr., Al. (lŭk-sȧ-pôl'ĭ-lȧ)	124	33.36 N	88.08 W
Luxembourg, Lux. (lŭk-sĕm-bûrg) (lük sän-bōōr') (look-sĕm-bōōrgh)	167	49.38 N	6.30 E
Luxembourg, Eur.	152	49.30 N	6.22 E
Luxeuil-les-Baines, Fr.	167	47.49 N	6.19 E
Luxomni, Ga. (lŭx'ôm-nĭ)	110c	33.54 N	84.07 W
Luxor, see Al Uqşur			
Luya Shan (Mtn.), China	198	38.50 N	111.40 E
Luyi, China (lōō-yē)	196	33.52 N	115.32 E
Luza (R.), Sov. Un. (lōō'zä)	176	60.30 N	47.10 E
Luzern, Switz. (lōō-tsĕrn)	164	47.03 N	8.18 E
Luzhou, China (lōō-jō)	199	28.58 N	105.25 E
Luziânia, Braz. (lōō-zyȧ'nēȧ)	141	16.17 S	47.44 W
Luzon (I.), Phil. (lōō-zŏn')	202	17.10 N	119.45 E
Luzon Str., Phil.	199	20.40 N	121.00 E
L'vov, Sov. Un. (l'vōōf)	165	49.51 N	24.01 E
Lyakhovskiye (Is.), Sov. Un. (lya'kô'v-skyē)	179	73.45 N	145.15 E
Lyalta, Can.	93e	51.07 N	113.36 W
Lyalya R., Sov. Un. (lyȧ'lyȧ)	180a	58.58 N	60.17 E
Lyaskovets, Bul.	171	43.07 N	25.41 E
Lydenburg, S. Afr. (lī'dĕn-bûrg)	222	25.06 S	30.21 E
Lyell, Mt., Ca. (lī'ĕl)	118	37.44 N	119.22 W
Lykens, Pa. (lī'kĕnz)	109	40.35 N	76.45 W
Lyna R., Pol. (lĭn'ȧ)	165	53.56 N	20.30 E
Lynch, Ky. (lĭnch)	124	36.56 N	82.55 W
Lynchburg, Va. (lĭnch'bûrg)	125	37.23 N	79.08 W
Lynch Cove, Wa. (lĭnch)	116a	47.26 N	122.54 W
Lynden, Can. (lĭn'dĕn)	93d	43.14 N	80.08 W
Lynden, Wa.	116d	48.56 N	122.27 W
Lyndhurst, Austl.	207a	38.03 S	145.14 E
Lyndon, Ky. (lĭn'dŭn)	111h	38.15 N	85.36 W
Lyndonville, Vt. (lĭn'dŭn-vĭl)	109	44.35 N	72.00 W
Lynn, Ma. (lĭn)	103a	42.28 N	70.57 W
Lynn Lake, Can. (lăk)	99	56.51 N	100.30 W
Lynwood, Ca. (lĭn'wood)	117a	33.56 N	118.13 W
Lyon, Fr. (lē-ôɴ')	166	45.44 N	4.52 E
Lyons, Ga. (lī'ŭnz)	125	32.08 N	82.19 W
Lyons, Ks.	120	38.20 N	98.11 W
Lyons, Ne.	112	41.57 N	96.28 W
Lyons, NJ	110a	40.41 N	74.33 W
Lyons, NY	109	43.05 N	77.00 W
Lysefjorden (Fd.), Nor.	162	58.59 N	6.35 E
Lysekil, Swe. (lü'sĕ-kĕl)	162	58.17 N	11.22 E
Lys'va, Sov. Un. (lĭs'vȧ)	180a	58.07 N	57.47 E
Lytham, Eng. (lĭth'ăm)	154	53.44 N	2.58 W
Lytkarino, Sov. Un.	180b	55.25 N	37.55 E
Lyttelton, S. Afr. (lĭt'l'ton)	223b	25.51 S	28.13 E
Lyuban', Sov. Un. (lyōō'bȧn)	180c	59.21 N	31.15 E
Lyubar, Sov. Un. (lyōō'bär)	173	49.56 N	27.44 E
Lyubertsy, Sov. Un. (lyōō'bĕr-tsē)	180b	55.40 N	37.55 E
Lyubim, Sov. Un. (lyōō-bēm')	172	58.24 N	40.39 E
Lyublino, Sov. Un. (lyōōb'lĭ-nô)	180b	55.41 N	37.45 E
Lyudinovo, Sov. Un. (lū-dē'novō)	172	53.52 N	34.28 E
Lyung, Mong.	194	47.58 N	104.52 E
M			
Ma'ān, Jordan (mä-än')	189a	30.12 N	35.45 E
Maartensdijk, Neth.	155a	52.09 N	5.10 E
Maas (R.), Neth.	167c	51.32 N	6.07 E
Maastricht, Neth. (mäs'trĭkt)	161	50.51 N	5.35 E
Mabaia, Ang.	226	7.13 S	14.03 E
Mabana, Wa. (mä-bä-nä)	116a	48.06 N	122.25 W
Mabank, Tx. (mā'bănk)	123	32.21 N	96.05 W
Mabeskraal, S. Afr.	219d	25.12 S	26.47 E
Mableton, Ga. (mā'b'l-tŭn)	110c	33.49 N	84.34 W
Mabrouk, Mali	220	19.27 N	1.16 W
Mabula, S. Afr. (mȧ'bōō-la)	219d	24.49 S	27.59 E
McAdam, Can. (măk-ăd'ăm)	102	45.36 N	67.20 W
Macaé, Braz. (mä-kä-ā')	139a	22.22 S	41.47 W
McAfee, NJ (măk-ȧ'fē)	110a	41.10 N	74.32 W
Macaira (R.), Ven. (mä-kī'rä)	141b	9.37 N	66.16 W
Macalelon, Phil. (mä-kä-lā-lōn')	203a	13.46 N	122.09 E
McAlester, Ok. (măk ăl'ĕs-tēr)	121	34.55 N	95.45 W
McAllen, Tx. (măk-ăl'ĕn)	122	26.12 N	98.14 W
Macapá, Braz. (mä-kä-pä')	141	0.08 N	50.02 W
Macau, Asia (mȧ-kä'ōō)	195	22.00 N	113.00 E
Macau, Braz. (mȧ-kà'ōō)	141	5.12 S	36.34 W
Macaya, Pico de (Pk.), Hai.	133	18.25 N	74.00 W
McBride, Can. (măk-brīd')	97	53.18 N	120.10 W
McCalla, Al. (măk-kăl'lā)	110h	33.20 N	87.00 W
McCamey, Tx. (mȧ-kā'mĭ)	122	31.08 N	102.13 W
McCaysville, Ga. (mȧ-kāz'vĭl)	124	34.57 N	84.21 W
Macclesfield, Eng. (măk''lz-fēld)	154	53.15 N	2.07 W
Macclesfield Can., Eng. (măk''lz-fēld)	154	53.14 N	2.07 W
McColl, SC (mȧ-kōl')	125	34.40 N	79.34 W
McComb, Ms. (mȧ-kōm')	124	31.14 N	90.27 W
McConaughy, L., Ne. (măk kō'nō ĭ')	112	41.24 N	101.40 W
McCook, Ne. (mȧ-kŏŏk')	120	40.13 N	100.37 W
McCormick, SC (mȧ-kôr'mĭk)	125	33.56 N	82.20 W
Macdona, Tx. (măk-dō'nȧ)	117d	29.20 N	98.42 W
McDonald, Pa. (măk-dŏn'ăid)	111e	40.22 N	80.13 W
Macdonald (I.), Austl. (măk-dŏn'ăld)	210	23.40 S	127.40 E
McDonald I, Austl.	228	53.00 S	72.45 E
McDonald L., Can. (măk-dŏn-ăld)	93e	51.12 N	113.53 W
Macdonnell Ra., Austl. (măk-dŏn'ĕl)	210	23.40 S	131.30 E
MacDowell L., Can. (măk-dou ĕl)	99	52.15 N	92.45 W
Macdui, Ben (Mtn.), Scot. (bĕn măk-dōō'ē)	160	57.06 N	3.45 W
Macedonia, Oh. (măs-ē-dō'nĭ-ȧ)	111d	41.19 N	81.30 E
Macedonia (Reg.), Eur. (măs-ē-dō'nĭ-ȧ)	171	41.05 N	22.15 E
Maceió, Braz. (mä-sȧ-yō')	141	9.33 S	35.35 W
Macerata, It. (mä-chā-rä'tä)	170	43.18 N	13.28 E
Macfarlane, L., Austl. (măc'fär-lān)	212	32.10 S	137.00 E
McGehee, Ar. (mȧ-gē')	121	33.39 N	91.22 W
McGill, Nv. (mȧ-gĭl')	118	39.25 N	114.47 W
McGowan, Wa. (măk-gou'ăn)	116c	46.15 N	123.55 W
McGrath, Ak. (măk'grăth)	105	62.58 N	155.20 W
McGregor, Can. (măk-grĕg'ēr)	111b	42.08 N	82.58 W
McGregor, Ia.	113	42.58 N	91.12 W
McGregor, Tx	123	31.26 N	97.23 W
McGregor (R.), Can.	97	54.10 N	121.00 W
McGregor L., Can. (măk-grĕg'ēr)	93c	45.38 N	75.44 W
Machache (Mtn.), Leso.	223c	29.22 S	27.53 E
Machado, Braz. (mä-shá-dô)	139a	21.42 S	45.55 W
Machakos, Ken.	227	1.31 S	37.16 E
Machala, Ec. (mä-chä'lä)	140	3.18 S	78.54 W
McHenry, Il. (măk-hĕn'rĭ)	111a	42.21 N	88.16 W
Machens, Mo. (măk'ĕns)	117e	38.54 N	90.20 W
Machias, Me. (mȧ-chī'ăs)	102	44.22 N	67.29 W
Machida, Jap. (mä-chē'dä)	201a	35.32 N	139.28 E
Machilipatnam, India	191	16.22 N	81.10 E
Machu Picchu, Peru (mä'chōō-pē'k-chōō)	140	13.00 S	72.24 W
Măcin, Rom. (mȧ-chēn')	173	45.15 N	28.09 E
Macina (Depression), Mali	224	14.50 N	4.40 W
McIntosh, SD (măk'ĭn-tŏsh)	112	45.54 N	101.22 W
Mackay, Austl. (mȧ-kī')	211	21.15 S	149.08 E
Mackay, Id. (măk-kā')	115	43.55 N	113.38 W
Mackay (I), Austl. (mȧ-kī')	210	22.30 S	127.45 E
MacKay (L.), Can. (măk-kā')	94	64.10 N	112.35 W
Mackay (R.), Can.	98	56.50 N	112.30 W
McKay (R), Or.	116	45.43 N	123.00 W
McKeesport, Pa. (mȧ-kez'pōrt)	111e	40.21 N	79.51 W
McKees Rocks, Pa. (mȧ-kēz' rŏks)	111e	40.29 N	80.05 W
McKenzie, Tn. (mȧ-kĕn'zĭ)	124	36.07 N	88.30 W
Mackenzie, Dist. of, Can.	94	63.48 N	125.25 W
Mackenzie (R.), Can.	94	63.38 N	124.23 W
Mackenzie B., Ak.	105	69.20 N	137.10 W
Mackenzie Mts., Can. (mȧ-kĕn'zĭ)	94	63.41 N	129.27 W
McKenzie R., Or.	114	44.07 N	122.20 W
Mackinac, Str. of, Mi. (măk'ĭ-nô) (măk'ĭ-năk)	108	45.50 N	84.40 W
Mackinaw (R.), Il.	108	40.35 N	89.25 W
Mackinaw City, Mi. (măk'ĭ-nô)	108	45.45 N	84.45 W
McKinley, Mt., Ak. (mȧ-kĭn'lĭ)	105	63.00 N	151.02 W
McKinney, Tx. (mȧ-kĭn'ĭ)	121	33.12 N	96.35 W
Mackinnon Road, Ken.	227	3.44 S	39.03 E
McLaughlin, SD (măk-lŏf'lĭn)	112	45.48 N	100.45 W
McLean, Va. (măc'lān)	110e	38.56 N	77.11 W
McLeansboro, Il. (mȧ-klānz'bŭr-ō)	108	38.10 N	88.35 W
Macleantown, S. Afr. (măk-lăn'toun)	223c	32.48 S	27.48 E
Maclear, S. Afr. (mȧ-klēr')	223c	31.06 S	28.23 E
McLennan, Can. (măk-lĭn'nȧn)	94	55.42 N	116.54 W
McLeod Lake, Can.	96	54.59 N	123.02 W
McLeod (R), Can.	97	53.45 N	115.15 W
McLoughlin, Mt., Or. (măk-lŏk'lĭn)	114	42.27 N	122.20 W
McMillan L., Tx. (măk-mĭl'ăn)	122	32.40 N	104.09 W
McMillin, Wa. (măk-mĭl'ĭn)	116a	47.08 N	122.14 W
McMinnville, Or. (măk-mĭn'vĭl)	114	45.13 N	123.13 W
McMinnville, Tn.	124	35.41 N	85.47 W
McMurray, Wa. (măk-mŭr'ĭ)	116a	48.19 N	122.15 W
McNary, Az. (măk-nâr'ē)	119	34.10 N	109.55 W
McNary, La.	123	30.58 N	92.32 W
McNary Dam, Or.-Wa.	114	45.57 N	119.15 W
Macomb, Il. (mȧ-kōōm')	121	40.27 N	90.40 W
Mâcon, Fr. (mä-kôɴ)	166	46.19 N	4.51 E
Macon, Ga. (mā'kŏn)	124	32.49 N	83.39 W
Macon, Ms.	124	32.07 N	88.31 W
Macon, Mo.	121	39.42 N	92.29 W
McPherson, Ks. (măk-fŭr's'n)	121	38.21 N	97.41 W
Macquarie (R.), Austl.	212	31.43 S	148.04 E
Macquarie Is., Austl. (mȧ-kwŏr'ē)	228	54.36 S	158.45 E
McRae, Ga. (măk-rā')	124	32.02 N	82.55 W
McRoberts, Ky. (măk-rŏb'ērts)	124	37.12 N	82.40 W
Macuelizo, Hond. (mä-kwē-lē'zō)	130	15.22 N	88.32 W
Ma'dabā, Jordan	189a	31.43 N	34.47 E
Madagascar, Afr. (măd-ȧ-găs'kȧr)	218	18.05 S	43.12 E
Madame (I.), Can. (mȧ-dȧm')	103	45.33 N	61.02 W
Madanapalle, India	191	13.06 N	78.09 E
Madang, Pap. N. Gui. (mä-däng')	203	5.15 S	145.45 E
Madaoua, Niger (mȧ-dou'ȧ)	220	14.04 N	6.03 E
Madawaska (R.), Can. (măd-ȧ-wŏs'kȧ)	109	45.20 N	77.25 W
Madeira, Ilha da (I.), Mad. Is. (mȧ-dā'rȧ)	220	32.41 N	16.15 W
Madeira, Arquipelado da (Is.), Port. (är-kē-pē'lä-gō-dä-mä-dĕý-rä)	220	33.26 N	16.44 W
Madeira (R.), Braz.	140	6.48 S	62.43 W
Madelia, Mn. (mȧ-dē'lĭ-ȧ)	113	44.03 N	94.23 W
Madeline (I.), Wi. (măd'ĕ-lĭn)	113	46.47 N	91.30 W
Madera, Ca. (mȧ-dā'rȧ)	118	36.57 N	120.04 W
Madera (Vol.), Nic.	130	11.27 N	85.30 W
Madgaon, India	191	15.09 N	73.58 E
Madhya Pradesh (State), India (mŭd'vŭ prŭ-dăsh')	190	22.04 N	77.48 E
Madill, Ok. (mȧ-dĭl')	121	34.04 N	96.45 W
Madīnat ash Sha'b, P.D.R. of Yem.	192	12.45 N	44.00 E
Madingo, Con.	226	4.07 S	11.22 E
Madingou, Con.	226	4.09 S	13.34 E
Madison, Fl. (măd'ĭ-sŭn)	124	30.28 N	83.25 W
Madison, Ga.	124	33.34 N	83.29 W
Madison, Il.	117e	38.40 N	90.09 W
Madison, In.	108	38.45 N	85.25 W
Madison, Ks.	121	38.08 N	96.07 W
Madison, Me.	102	44.47 N	69.52 W
Madison, Mn.	112	44.59 N	96.13 W
Madison, Ne.	112	41.49 N	97.27 W
Madison, NJ	110a	40.46 N	74.25 W
Madison, NC	125	36.22 N	79.59 W
Madison, SD	112	44.01 N	97.08 W
Madison, Wi.	113	43.05 N	89.23 W
Madison Res, Mt.	115	45.25 N	111.28 W
Madison R, Mt.	115	45.15 N	111.30 W
Madisonville, Ky. (măd'ĭ-sŭn-vĭl)	108	37.20 N	87.30 W
Madisonville, La.	117	30.22 N	90.10 W
Madisonville, Tx.	117	30.57 N	95.55 W
Madjori, Upper Volta	224	11.26 N	1.15 E
Madona, Sov. Un. (mȧ'dō'nȧ)	172	56.50 N	26.14 E
Madrakah, Ra's al (C.), Om.	192	18.53 N	57.48 E
Madras, India (mȧ-drȧs') (mŭ-drŭs')	191	13.08 N	80.15 E
Madre, Laguna L., Mex. (lä-gōō'nä mä'drā)	117	25.08 N	97.41 W
Madre, Sierra (Mts.), Mex. (sē-ĕ'r-rä-mȧ'drē)	128	15.55 N	92.40 W
Madre, Sierra (Mts.), Phil.	203a	16.40 N	122.10 E
Madre de Dios, Arch., Chile (mȧ'drā dā dē-ōs')	142	50.40 S	76.30 W
Madre de Dios, Rio (R.), Bol. (rē'ō-mä'drā dā dē-ōs')	140	12.07 S	68.02 W
Madre del Sur, Sierra (Mts.), Mex. (sē-ĕ'r-rä-mä'drā dĕlsōōr')	128	17.35 N	100.35 W
Madrid, Ia. (măd'rĭd)	113	41.51 N	93.48 W
Madrid, Sp. (mä-drē'd)	169a	40.26 N	3.42 W
Madridejos, Sp. (mä-dhrē-dhä'hōs)	168	39.29 N	3.32 W
Mad R., Ca. (măd)	114	40.38 N	123.37 W
Mado Gashi, Ken.	227	0.44 N	39.10 E
Madura (I.), Indon. (mȧ-dōō'rä)	202	6.45 S	113.30 E
Madurai, India (mä-dōō'rä)	191	9.57 N	78.04 E
Madureira, Serra do (Mtn.), Braz. (sĕ'r-rä-dô-mä-dōō-rä'rȧ)	142b	22.49 S	43.30 W
Maebashi, Jap. (mä-ē-bä'shē)	201	36.26 N	139.04 E
Maestra, Sierra (Mts.), Cuba (sē-ĕ'r-rȧ-mä-ās'trä)	132	20.05 N	77.05 W
Maewo (I.), Vanuatu	211	15.17 S	168.16 E
Mafeking, S. Afr. (mäf'ē'kĭng)	222	25.46 S	24.45 E
Mafia (I.), Tan. (mä-fē'ä)	227	7.47 S	40.00 E
Mafra, Braz. (mä'frä)	142	26.21 S	49.59 W
Mafra, Port. (mäf'rȧ)	169b	38.56 N	9.20 W
Magadan, Sov. Un. (mȧ-gȧ-dän')	179	59.39 N	150.43 E
Magadan Oblast, Sov. Un.	179	63.00 N	170.30 E
Magadi, Ken.	227	1.54 S	36.17 E
Magadi (L.), Ken. (mȧ-gä'dē)	227	1.50 S	36.00 E
Magalies (R), S. Afr. (mä-gä'lyĕs)	223b	25.51 S	27.42 E
Magaliesberg (Mts.), S. Afr.	223b	25.45 S	27.43 E
Magaliesburg, S. Afr.	219d	26.01 S	27.32 E
Magallanes, Phil. (mä-gäl-yä'nās)	203a	12.48 N	123.52 E
Magallanes, Estrecho de (Str.), Arg.-Chile (ĕs-trĕ'chô-dĕ-mä-gäl-yä'nĕs)	142	52.30 S	68.45 W
Magangué, Col. (mä-gän'gā)	140	9.08 N	74.56 W
Magat (R.), Phil. (mä-gät')	203a	16.45 N	121.16 E
Magdalena, Arg. (mäg-dä-lā'nä)	139c	35.05 S	57.32 W
Magdalena, Bol.	140	13.17 S	63.57 W
Magdalena, Mex.	106	30.34 N	110.50 W
Magdalena, NM	119	34.10 N	107.45 W
Magdalena (I.), Chile	142	44.45 S	73.15 W
Magdalena, Bahia (B.), Mex. (bä-ē'ä-mäg-dä-lā'nä)	126	24.30 N	114.00 W
Magdalena, Rio (R.), Col.	140	7.45 N	74.04 W
Magdalen Is., Can. (măg'dȧ-lĕn)	103	47.27 N	61.25 W
Magdeburg, G.D.R. (mäg'dĕ-bōōrgh)	164	52.07 N	11.39 E
Magé, Braz. (mä-zhā')	142b	22.39 S	43.02 W
Magenta, It. (mȧ-jĕn'tȧ)	170	45.26 N	8.53 E
Magerøya (I.), Nor.	156	71.10 N	24.11 E
Maggiore, Lago (L.), It.	170	46.03 N	8.25 E
Maghāghah, Egypt	219b	28.38 N	30.50 W
Maghnia, Alg.	158	34.52 N	1.40 W
Magiscatzin, Mex. (mä-kēs-kät-zēn')	128	22.48 N	98.42 W
Maglaj, Yugo. (mȧ'glä-ē)	171	44.34 N	18.12 E
Maglić, Yugo. (măg'lēch)	171	43.36 N	20.36 E
Maglie, It. (mäl'yä)	171	40.06 N	18.20 E
Magna, Ut. (măg'nȧ)	117b	40.43 N	112.06 W
Magnitogorsk, Sov. Un. (măg-nyē'tô-gôrsk)	180a	53.26 N	59.05 E
Magnolia, Ar. (măg-nō'lĭ-ȧ)	121	33.16 N	93.13 W
Magnolia, Ms.	124	31.08 N	90.27 W
Magny-en-Vexin, Fr. (mä-nyē'ĕɴ-vĕ-sȧɴ')	167b	49.09 N	1.45 E
Magog, Can. (mȧ-gŏg')	109	45.15 N	72.10 W
Magpie (R.), Can.	100	50.40 N	64.30 W
Magpie Lac (L.), Can.	102	50.55 N	64.39 W
Magpie (R.), Can.	113	48.13 N	84.50 W
Magrath, Can.	97	49.25 N	112.52 W
Magude, Moz. (mä-gōō'dȧ)	222	24.58 S	32.39 E
Magwe, Bur. (mŭg-wā')	194	20.19 N	94.57 E
Mahabād, Iran	177	36.55 N	45.50 E
Mahahi Port, Zaire (mä-hä'gē)	221	2.14 N	31.12 E
Mahajanga, Mad.	223	15.12 S	46.26 E
Mahakam (Strm.), Indon.	202	0.30 S	116.15 E
Mahali Mts., Tan.	227	6.20 S	30.00 E
Mahaly, Mad. (mȧ-hăl-ē')	223	24.09 S	46.20 E
Mahameru, Gunung (Mtn.), Indon.	202	8.00 S	112.50 E
Mahānadi (R.), India (mŭ-hä-nŭd'ē)	190	20.50 N	84.27 E
Mahanoro, Mad. (mȧ-hȧ-nō'rō)	223	19.57 S	48.47 E
Mahanoy City, Pa. (mä-hȧ-noi')	109	40.50 N	76.10 W
Mahārāshtra (State), India	190	19.06 N	75.00 E
Maḩaţţat al Qaţrānah, Jordan	189a	31.15 N	36.04 E
Maḩaţţat 'Aqabat al Hijāzīyah, Jordan	189a	29.45 N	35.55 E
Maḩaţţat ar Ramlah, Jordan	189	29.31 N	35.57 E

ng-sing; ŋ-baŋk; ɴ-nasalized n; nŏd; cŏmmit; ōld; ōbey; ôrder; oi-boil; fōōd; fŏŏt; ou-out; s-soft; sh-dish; th-thin; pūre; ûnite; ûrn; stŭd; circŭs; ü-as in French tu; '-indeterminate vowel.

316 Maḩaţţat Jurf ad Darāwīsh – Mansfield Woodhouse

PLACE (Pronunciation)	PAGE	Lat. °′	Long. °′
Maḩaţţat Jurf ad Darāwīsh, Jordan	189a	30.41 N	35.51 E
Mahavavy (R.), Mad. (mä-hä-vä'vē)	223	17.42 S	46.06 E
Mahaweli (R.), India	190	7.47 N	80.43 E
Mahe, India (mä-ā')	191	11.42 N	75.39 E
Mahenge, Tan. (mä-hĕŋ'gȧ)	227	7.38 S	36.16 E
Mahi (R.), India	190	23.16 N	73.20 E
Māhīm Bay, India	191b	19.03 N	72.45 E
Mahlabatini, S. Afr. (mä'lȧ-bȧ-tē'nē)	223c	28.15 S	31.29 E
Mahlow, G.D.R. (mä'lōv)	155b	52.23 N	13.24 E
Mahnomen, Mn. (mô-nō'mĕn)	112	47.18 N	95.58 W
Mahón, Sp. (mä-ōn')	169	39.52 N	4.15 E
Mahone Bay, Can. (mȧ-hōn')	102	44.27 N	64.23 W
Mahone B., Can.	102	44.30 N	64.15 W
Mahopac, L., NY (mā-hō'păk)	110a	41.24 N	73.45 W
Mahwah, NJ (mȧ-wä')	110a	41.05 N	74.09 W
Maidenhead, Eng. (mād'ĕn-hĕd)	154b	51.30 N	0.44 W
Maidstone, Eng.	154b	51.17 N	0.32 E
Maiduguri, Nig. (mä'ē-dȧ-gōō'rē)	225	11.51 N	13.10 E
Maigualida Sierra (Mts.), Ven. (sē-ĕ'r-rä-mī-gwä'lē-dě)	140	6.30 N	65.50 W
Maijdi, Bngl.	190	22.59 N	91.08 E
Maikop, see Maykop			
Main (R.), F.R.G. (mīn)	164	49.49 N	9.20 E
Main Barrier Ra., Austl. (băr''ēr)	212	31.25 S	141.40 E
Mai-Ndombe, Lac (Leopold II, L.), Zaire	222	2.16 S	19.00 E
Maine (State), U. S. (mān)	107	45.25 N	69.50 W
Mainland (I.), Scot. (män-lănd)	160a	60.19 N	2.40 W
Maintenon, Fr. (măɴ-tē-nôɴ')	167b	48.35 N	1.35 E
Maintirano, Mad. (mä'ēn-tē-rä'nō)	223	18.05 S	44.08 E
Mainz, F.R.G. (mīnts)	164	49.59 N	8.16 E
Maio I., C. V. (mä'yo)	220b	15.15 N	22.50 W
Maipo (R.), Chile (mī'pō)	139b	33.45 S	71.08 W
Maipo (Vol.), Arg.	142	34.08 S	69.51 W
Maipú, Arg. (mī'pōō')	139c	36.51 S	57.54 W
Maiquetía, Ven. (mī-kē-tē'ä)	141b	10.37 N	66.56 W
Maisí, Punta (Pt.), Cuba (pōō'n-tä-mī-sē')	133	20.10 N	74.00 W
Maison-Rouge, Fr. (mā-zôɴ-rōōzh')	167b	48.34 N	3.09 E
Maitland, Austl. (māt'lănd)	212	32.45 S	151.40 E
Maizuru, Jap. (mä-ī'zōō-rōō)	201	35.26 N	135.15 E
Majene, Indon.	202	3.34 S	119.00 E
Maji, Eth.	221	6.14 N	35.34 E
Majorca (I.), see Mallorca			
Makah Ind. Res., Wa. (mȧ kī')	114	48.17 N	124.52 W
Makanya, Tan. (mä-kän'yä)	223	4.15 S	37.49 E
Makanza, Zaire	221	1.42 N	19.08 E
Makarska, Yugo. (mȧ'kär-skȧ)	170	43.17 N	17.05 E
Makar'yev, Sov. Un.	176	57.50 N	43.48 E
Makasar, see Ujung Pandang			
Makasar, Selat (Makassar Strait), Indon.	202	2.00 S	118.07 E
Makaw, Zaire	226	3.29 S	18.19 E
Make (I.), Jap. (mä'kȧ)	201	30.43 N	130.49 E
Makeni, S. L.	224	8.53 N	12.03 W
Makeyevka, Sov. Un. (mŭk-yä'ŭf-kȧ)	173	48.03 N	38.00 E
Makgadikgadi Pans (L.), Bots.	219	20.38 S	21.31 E
Makhachkala, Sov. Un. (mäĸ'äch-kä'lä)	177	43.00 N	47.40 E
Makhaleng (R.), Leso.	223c	29.53 S	27.33 E
Makindu, Ken.	227	2.17 S	37.49 E
Makkah (Mecca), Sau. Ar. (mĕk'ȧ)	192	21.27 N	39.45 E
Makkovik, Can.	95	55.01 N	59.10 W
Makó, Hung. (mô'kō)	165	46.13 N	20.30 E
Makokou, Gabon (mȧ-kô-kōō')	226	0.34 N	12.52 E
Maków Mazowiecki, Pol. (mä'kōov mä-zō-vyĕts'kē)	165	52.51 N	21.07 E
Makuhari, Jap. (mä-kōō-hä'rē)	201a	35.39 N	140.04 E
Makurazaki, Jap. (mä'kōō-rä-zä'kē)	201	31.16 N	130.18 E
Makurdi, Nig.	225	7.45 N	8.32 E
Makushin, Ak. (mȧ-kōō'shĭn)	105	53.57 N	166.28 W
Makushino, Sov. Un. (mȧ-kōō-shē'n'ō)	178	55.03 N	67.43 E
Malabar Coast, India (măl'ȧ-bär)	191	11.19 N	75.33 E
Malabo, Equat. Gui.	226	3.45 N	8.47 E
Malabon, Phil.	203a	14.39 N	120.57 E
Malacca, Str. of, Asia (mȧ-lăk'ȧ)	202	4.15 N	99.44 E
Malad, Id. (mȧ-lăd')	115	42.11 N	112.15 W
Málaga, Col. (mȧ'lä-gä)	140	6.41 N	72.46 W
Málaga, Sp.	168	36.45 N	4.25 W
Malagón, Sp. (mä-lä-gōn')	168	39.12 N	3.52 W
Malaita (I.), Sol. Is. (mȧ-lä'ē-tȧ)	211	8.38 S	161.15 E
Malakāl, Sud. (mȧ-lȧ-käl')	221	9.46 N	31.54 E
Malakhovka, Sov. Un. (mȧ-läk'ôf-kȧ)	180b	55.38 N	38.01 E
Malang, Indon.	202	8.06 S	112.50 E
Malanje, Ang. (mä-läŋ-gȧ)	226	9.32 S	16.20 E
Malanville, Benin	220	12.04 N	3.09 E
Malapedia (R.), Can.	102	48.11 N	67.08 W
Mala Punta (Pt.), Pan. (pōō'n-tä-mä'lä)	131	7.32 N	79.44 W
Mälaren (L.), Swe.	162	59.38 N	16.55 E
Malartic, Can.	95	48.07 N	78.11 W
Malaspina Str. Can. (mäl-ȧ-spē'nȧ)	96	49.44 N	124.20 W
Malatya, Tur. (mȧ-lä'tyȧ)	177	38.30 N	38.15 E
Malawi, Afr.	218	11.15 S	33.45 E
Malawi, L., see Nyasa, L.			
Malaya (Reg.), Mala. (mȧ-lā'yȧ)	202	3.35 N	101.30 E
Malaya Vishera, Sov. Un. (vē-shä'rä)	172	58.51 N	32.13 E
Malay Pen., Asia (mȧ-lā') (mā'lā)	202	7.46 N	101.06 E
Malaysia, Asia (mȧ-lā'zhȧ)	202	4.10 N	101.22 E
Mal B., Ire. (măl)	160	52.51 N	9.45 W
Malbon, Austl. (măl'bŭn)	210	21.15 S	140.30 E
Malbork, Pol. (mäl'bȯrk)	165	54.02 N	19.04 E
Malcabran (R.), Port. (mäl-kä-brän')	169b	38.47 N	8.46 W
Malden, Ma. (môl'dĕn)	103a	42.26 N	71.04 W
Malden, Mo.	121	36.32 N	89.56 W
Malden (I.), Oceania	205	4.20 S	154.30 W
Maldives, Asia	188	4.30 N	71.30 E
Maldon, Eng. (môrl'dŏn)	154b	51.44 N	0.39 E
Maldonado, Ur. (mäl-dŏ-nä'dō)	142	34.54 S	54.57 W
Maldonado, Punta (Pt.), Mex. (pōō'n-tä)	128	16.18 N	98.34 W
Maléa, Ákra (C.), Grc.	171	37.31 N	23.13 E
Mālegaon, India	190	20.35 N	74.30 E
Male Karpaty (Mts.), Czech.	165	48.31 N	17.15 E
Malekula (I.), Vanuatu (mä-lā-kōō'lä)	211	16.44 S	167.45 E
Malhão da Estrêla (Mtn.), Sp. (mäl-you'ɴ-dä-ĕs-trē'lä)	168	40.20 N	7.38 W
Malheur L., Or. (mȧ-lōōr')	114	43.16 N	118.37 W
Malheur R., Or. (mȧ-lōōr')	114	43.45 N	117.41 W
Mali, Afr.	218	15.45 N	0.15 W
Malibu, Ca. (mă'lĭ-bōō)	117a	34.03 N	118.38 W
Malimba, Monts (Mts.), Zaire	227	7.45 S	29.15 E
Malin, Sov. Un. (mȧ-lēn')	173	50.44 N	29.15 E
Malinalco, Mex. (mä-lē-näl'kō)	128	18.54 N	99.31 W
Malinaltepec, Mex. (mä-lē-näl-tā-pĕk')	128	17.01 N	98.41 W
Malindi, Ken. (mä-lēn'dē)	223	3.14 S	40.04 E
Malin Hd., N. Ire.	160	55.23 N	7.24 W
Malindi, Ken.	227	3.13 S	40.07 E
Malino, Sov. Un. (mä'lĭ-nô)	180b	55.07 N	38.12 E
Malinovka, Sov. Un. (mȧ-lē-nôf'kȧ)	173	49.50 N	36.43 E
Malkara, Tur. (mäl'kȧ-rȧ)	171	40.51 N	26.52 E
Malko Tŭrnovo, Bul. (mäl'kō-t'r'nō-vȧ)	171	41.59 N	27.28 E
Mallaig, Scot.	160	56.59 N	5.55 W
Mallawī, Egypt (mȧ-lä'wē)	219b	27.43 S	30.49 E
Mallet Creek, Oh. (măl'ĕt)	111d	41.10 N	81.55 W
Mallorca (Majorca) (I.), Sp. (mäl-yô'r-kä)	169	39.18 N	2.22 E
Mallow, Ire. (măl'ō)	160	52.07 N	9.04 W
Malmédy, Bel. (mȧl-mā-dē')	161	50.25 N	6.01 E
Malmesbury, S. Afr. (mämz'bēr-ĭ)	222	33.30 S	18.35 E
Malmköping, Swe. (mälm'chû'pĭng)	162	59.09 N	16.39 E
Malmö, Swe. (mälm'û)	162	55.36 N	12.58 E
Malmyzh, Sov. Un. (mȧl-mēzh')	179	49.58 N	137.07 E
Malmyzh, Sov. Un.	176	56.30 N	50.48 E
Maloarkhangelsk, Sov. Un. (mä'lô-ár-ĸäŋ'gĕlsk)	172	52.26 N	36.29 E
Malolos, Phil. (mä-lō'lôs)	203a	14.51 N	120.49 E
Malomal'sk, Sov. Un. (mȧ-lô-mälsk'')	180a	58.47 N	59.55 E
Malone, NY (mȧ-lōn')	109	44.50 N	74.20 W
Malonga, Zaire	226	10.24 S	23.10 E
Maloti Mts., Leso	223c	29.00 S	28.29 E
Maloyaroslavets, Sov. Un. (mä'lô-yä-rô-slä-vyĕts)	172	55.01 N	36.25 E
Malozemel'skaya Tundra (Plains), Sov. Un.	176	67.30 N	50.00 E
Malpas, Eng. (măl'pȧz)	142	53.01 N	2.46 W
Malpelo, Isla de (I.), Col. (mäl-pā'lō)	140	3.55 N	81.30 W
Malpeque B., Can. (môl-pĕk')	102	46.30 N	63.47 W
Malta, Mt. (môl'tȧ)	115	48.20 N	107.50 W
Malta, Eur.	152	35.52 N	13.30 E
Maltahöhe, Namibia (mäl'tä-hō'ē)	222	24.45 S	16.45 E
Maltrata, Mex. (mäl-trä'tä)	129	18.48 N	97.16 W
Maluku (Moluccas) (Is.), Indon.	203	2.22 S	128.25 E
Maluku, Laut (Molucca) (Sea), Indon.	203	0.15 N	125.41 E
Malūt, Sud.	221	10.30 N	32.17 E
Mālvan, India	191	16.08 N	73.32 E
Malvern, Ar. (măl'vērn)	121	34.21 N	92.47 W
Malyy Anyuy (R.), Sov. Un.	179	67.52 N	164.30 E
Malyy Lyakhovskiye (I.), Sov. Un.	179	74.15 N	142.30 E
Malyy Tamir (I.), Sov. Un.	179	78.10 N	107.30 E
Mamantel, Mex. (mä-män-tĕl')	129	18.36 N	91.06 W
Mamaroneck, NY (măm'ȧ-rō-nĕk)	110a	40.57 N	73.44 W
Mamau, Gui.	220	10.26 N	12.07 W
Mambasa, Zaire,	227	1.21 N	29.03 E
Mamberamo (R.), Indon. (mäm-bȧ-rä'mō)	203	2.30 S	138.00 E
Mamburao, Phil. (mäm-bōō'rä-ō)	203a	13.14 N	120.35 E
Mamfe, Cam. (mäm'fĕ)	220	5.46 N	9.17 E
Mamihara, Jap. (mä'mē-hä-rä)	201	32.41 N	131.12 E
Mammoth Cave, Ky. (măm'ŏth)	124	37.10 N	86.04 W
Mammoth Cave Natl. Park, Ky.	124	37.20 N	86.21 W
Mammoth Hot Springs, Wy. (măm'ŭth hôt sprĭngz)	115	44.55 N	110.50 W
Mamnoli, India	191b	19.17 N	73.15 E
Mamoré (R.), Bol. (mä-mō-rā')	140	13.19 S	65.27 W
Mampong, Ghana	224	7.04 N	1.24 W
Mamry, Jezioro (L.), Pol. (mäm'rĭ)	165	54.10 N	21.28 E
Man, Ivory Coast	224	7.24 N	7.33 W
Manacor, Sp. (mä-nä-kôr')	169	39.35 N	3.15 E
Manado, Indon.	203	1.29 N	124.50 E
Managua, Cuba (mä-nä'gwä)	133a	22.14 N	82.17 W
Managua, Nic.	130	12.10 N	86.16 W
Managua, Lago de (L.), Nic. (lä'gô-dĕ)	130	12.28 N	86.10 W
Manakara, Mad. (mä-nä-kä'rŭ)	223	22.17 S	48.06 E
Mananara (R.), Mad. (mä-nä-nä'rŭ)	223	23.15 S	48.15 E
Mananjary, Mad. (mä-nän-zhä'rē)	223	20.16 S	48.13 E
Manáos, see Manaus			
Manas, China (mä-nä-sz)	194	44.30 N	86.00 E
Manas (R.), China	194	45.00 N	85.45 E
Manas Hu (L.), China (mä-nä-sŭ hōō)	194	45.49 N	86.08 E
Manassas, Va. (mȧ-năs'ȧs)	109	38.45 N	77.30 W
Manaus (Manáos), Braz. (mä-nä'ōōzh)	141	3.01 S	60.00 W
Mancelona, Mi. (măn-sē-lō'nȧ)	108	44.50 N	85.05 W
Mancha Real, Sp. (män'chä rā-äl')	168	37.48 N	3.37 W
Manchazh, Sov. Un. (män'chȧsh)	180a	56.30 N	58.10 E
Manchester, Ct. (măn'chĕs-tēr)	109	41.45 N	72.30 W
Manchester, Eng.	154	53.28 N	2.14 W
Manchester, Ga.	124	32.50 N	84.37 W
Manchester, Ia.	113	42.30 N	91.30 W
Manchester, Ma.	103a	42.35 N	70.47 W
Manchester, Mo.	117e	38.36 N	90.31 W
Manchester, NH	109	43.00 N	71.30 W
Manchester, Oh.	108	38.40 N	83.35 W
Manchester Ship Canal, Eng.	154	53.20 N	2.40 W
Manchuria (Reg.), China (măn-chōō'rē-ȧ)	195	48.00 N	124.58 E
Mand (R.), Iran	192	28.20 N	52.30 E
Mandal, Nor. (män'däl)	162	58.03 N	7.28 E
Mandalay, Bur. (măn'dȧ-lā)	194	22.00 N	96.08 E
Mandalselva (R.), Nor.	162	58.25 N	7.30 E
Mandan, ND (măn'dăn)	112	46.49 N	100.54 W
Mandara Mts., Cam.-Nig. (män-dä'rä)	225	10.15 N	13.23 E
Mandau Siak (R.), Indon.	189b	1.03 N	101.25 E
Mandimba, Moz.	227	14.21 S	35.39 E
Mandinga, Pan. (män-dĭŋ'gä)	131	9.32 N	79.04 W
Mandla, India	190	22.43 N	80.23 E
Mándra, Grc. (män'drä)	171	38.06 N	23.32 E
Mandritsara, Mad. (mán-drēt-sä'rȧ)	223	15.49 S	48.47 E
Manduria, It. (män-dōō'rē-ä)	171	40.23 N	17.41 E
Mandve, India	191b	18.47 N	72.52 E
Māndvi, India (mŭnd'vē)	191b	19.29 N	72.53 E
Māndvi, India (mŭnd'vē)	190	22.54 N	69.23 E
Mandya, India	191	12.40 N	77.00 E
Manfalūţ, Egypt (män-fȧ-loot')	219b	27.18 N	30.59 E
Manfredonia, It. (män-frā-dô'nyä)	170	41.39 N	15.55 E
Manfredónia, Golfo di (G.), It. (gôl-fô-dē)	170	41.34 N	16.05 E
Mangabeiras, Chap. das (Plains), Braz. (shä-pä'däs-däs-mäŋ-gä-bē'ē-räzh)	141	8.05 S	47.32 W
Manga (Reg.), Niger	225	14.00 N	11.50 E
Mangalore, India (mŭŋ-gŭ-lōr')	191	12.53 N	74.52 E
Mangaratiba, Braz. (män-gä-rä-tē'bȧ)	139a	22.56 S	44.03 W
Mangatarem, Phil. (män'gȧ-tä'rĕm)	203a	15.48 N	120.18 E
Mange, Zaire,	226	0.54 N	20.30 E
Mangkalihat, Tandjoeng (C.), Indon. (mäng'kȧ-lē-hät')	202	1.25 N	119.55 E
Mangles, Islas de, Cuba (ē's-läs-dĕ-män'glās) (măn'g'lz)	132	22.05 N	83.50 W
Mangoky (R.), Mad. (män-gō'kē)	223	22.02 S	44.11 E
Mangole, Pulau (I.), Indon.	203	1.35 S	126.22 E
Mangualde, Port. (män-gwäl'dĕ)	168	40.38 N	7.44 W
Mangueira, L. da (L.), Braz. (män-gā'ē-rȧ)	142	33.15 S	52.45 W
Mangum, Ok. (măŋ'gŭm)	120	34.52 N	99.31 W
Mangyshlak, P-Ov. (Pen.), Sov. Un.	177	44.30 N	50.40 E
Mangzhangdian, China (mäŋ-jäŋ-dĭĕn)	196	32.07 N	114.44 E
Manhattan, Il.	111a	41.25 N	87.29 W
Manhattan, Ks. (măn-hăt'ăn)	121	39.11 N	96.34 W
Manhattan Beach, Ca.	117a	33.53 N	118.24 W
Manhuaçu, Braz. (män-ōōȧ'sōō)	139a	20.17 S	42.01 W
Manhumirim, Braz. (män-ōō-mē-rē'ɴ)	139a	22.02 S	41.57 W
Mania (R.), Mad. (män'yä)	223	19.52 S	46.02 E
Manicoré, Braz. (mä-nē-kō-rā')	141	5.53 S	61.13 W
Manicouagane (R.), Can.	95	50.00 N	68.35 W
Manicouagane, Lac (L.), Can.	95	51.30 N	68.19 W
Manicuare, Ven. (mä-nē-kwä'rē)	141b	10.35 N	64.10 W
Manikuagan, Rivière (R.), Can.	100	49.30 N	68.30 W
Manihiki Is., Oceania (mä'nē-hē'kē)	205	9.40 S	158.00 W
Manila Phil. (mȧ-nĭl'ȧ)	203a	14.37 N	121.00 E
Manila B., Phil.	203a	14.38 N	120.46 E
Manipur (State), India	194	25.00 N	94.00 E
Manisa, Tur. (mä'nē-sȧ)	177	38.40 N	27.30 E
Manistee, Mi. (măn-ĭs-tē')	108	44.15 N	86.20 W
Manistee (R.), Mi	108	44.25 N	85.45 W
Manistique, Mi. (măn-ĭs-tēk')	113	45.58 N	86.16 W
Manistique (L.), Mi	113	46.14 N	85.30 W
Manistique (R.), Mi	113	46.05 N	86.09 W
Manitoba (Prov.), Can. (măn-ĭ-tō'bȧ)	94	55.12 N	97.29 W
Manitoba (L.), Can.	99	51.00 N	98.45 W
Manito L., Can. (măn'ĭ-tō)	98	52.45 N	109.45 W
Manitou (I.), Mi. (măn'ĭ-tōō)	113	47.21 N	87.33 W
Manitou (L.), Can.	113	49.21 N	93.01 W
Manitou Is., Mi.	108	45.05 N	86.00 W
Manitoulin I., Can. (măn-ĭ-tōō'lĭn)	108	45.45 N	81.30 W
Manitou Springs, Co.	120	38.51 N	104.58 W
Manitowoc, Wi. (măn-ĭ-tō-wŏk')	113	44.05 N	87.42 W
Maniwaki, Can.	101	46.23 N	76.00 W
Manizales, Col. (mä-nē-zä'lās)	140a	5.05 N	75.31 W
Manjacaze, Moz. (man'yä-kä'zĕ)	222	24.37 S	33.49 E
Mānjra (R.), India	190	18.18 N	77.00 E
Mankato, Ks. (măn-kā'tō)	120	39.45 N	98.12 W
Mankato, Mn.	113	44.10 N	93.59 W
Mankim, Cam.	225	5.01 N	12.00 E
Manlléu, Sp. (män-lyā'ōō)	169	42.00 N	2.16 E
Mannar, Sri Lanka (mȧ-när')	191	9.48 N	80.03 E
Mannar, G. of, India	191	8.47 N	78.33 E
Mannersdorf am Leithagebirge, Aus.	155e	47.58 N	16.36 E
Mannheim, F.R.G. (măn'hīm)	164	49.30 N	8.31 E
Manning, Ia. (măn'ĭng)	113	41.53 N	95.04 W
Manning, SC	125	33.41 N	80.12 W
Mannington, WV (măn'ĭng-tŭn)	108	39.30 N	80.55 W
Mannu (R.), It. (mä'n-nōō)	170	39.32 N	9.03 E
Mano (R.), Lib.	224	7.00 N	11.25 W
Man of War B., Ba.	123	21.05 N	74.05 W
Man of War Chan, Ba.	123	22.45 N	76.10 W
Manokwari, Indon. (mȧ-nŏk-wä'rē)	203	0.56 S	134.10 E
Manono, Zaire	227	7.18 S	27.25 E
Manor, Can. (măn'ēr)	99	49.36 N	102.05 W
Manor, Wa.	116c	45.45 N	122.36 W
Manori (Neigh.) India	191b	19.13 N	72.43 E
Manosque, Fr. (mȧ-nôsh')	167	43.51 N	5.48 E
Manotick, Can.	93c	45.13 N	75.41 W
Manresa, Sp. (män-rā'sä)	169	41.44 N	1.52 E
Mansa, Zambia	227	11.12 S	28.53 E
Mansabá, Guinea-Bissau	224	12.18 N	15.15 W
Mansel (I.), Can. (măn'sĕl)	95	61.56 N	81.10 W
Manseriche, Pongo de (Water Gap), Peru (pŏ'n-gô-dĕ-män-sĕ-rē'chĕ)	140	4.15 S	77.45 W
Mansfield, Eng. (mănz'fēld)	154	53.08 N	1.12 W
Mansfield, La.	123	32.02 N	93.43 W
Mansfield, Oh.	108	40.45 N	82.30 W
Mansfield, Wa.	114	47.48 N	119.39 W
Mansfield, Mt., Vt.	109	44.30 N	72.45 W
Mansfield Woodhouse, Eng. (wŏŏd-hous)	154	53.08 N	1.12 W

PRONOUNCING INDEX

Manso – Marysville 317

PLACE (Pronunciation)	PAGE	Lat. °'	Long. °'
Manso (R.), Braz.	141	13.30 S	51.45 W
Manta, Ec. (män'tä)	140	1.03 S	80.16 W
Manteno, Il. (măn-tē-nō)	111a	41.15 N	87.50 W
Manteo, NC	125	35.55 N	75.40 W
Mantes-la-Jolie, Fr. (mäNt-ĕ-lä-zhō-lē')	167b	48.59 N	1.42 E
Manti, Ut. (măn'tī)	119	39.15 N	111.40 W
Manitqueira, Serra da (Mts.), Braz. (sĕr'rä dä män-tē-kā'ē-rá)	139a	22.40 S	45.12 W
Mantova (Mantua), It. (män'tô-vä) (măn'tū-á)	170	45.09 N	10.47 E
Mantua, Cuba (män-too'ä)	132	22.20 N	84.15 W
Mantua, Ut. (măn'tū-á)	117b	41.30 N	111.57 W
Mantua, see Mantova			
Manuan (L.), Can. (mä-noo'án)	102	50.36 N	70.50 W
Manuan (R.), Can.	102	50.15 N	70.30 W
Manui, Pulau (Is.), Indon. (mä-noo'ē)	203	3.35 S	123.38 E
Manus, (I.), Pap. N. Gui. (mä'noos)	203	2.22 S	146.22 E
Manvel, Tx. (măn'vel)	123a	29.28 N	95.22 W
Manville, NJ (măn'vĭl)	110a	40.33 N	74.36 W
Manville, RI	110b	41.57 N	71.27 W
Manych (R.), Sov. Un. (mä-nĭch')	177	47.00 N	41.10 E
Manych Dep., Sov. Un.	153	46.32 N	42.44 E
Manych-Gudilo (Lake), Sov. Un.	177	46.40 N	42.50 E
Manzala L., Egypt	219b	31.14 N	32.04 E
Manzanares, Col. (män-sä-nä'rĕs)	140a	5.15 N	75.09 W
Manzanares (R.), Sp. (mänz-nä'rĕs)	169a	40.36 N	3.48 W
Manzanares, Canal del, Sp. (kä-nä'l-dĕl-män-thä-nä'rĕs)	169a	40.20 N	3.38 W
Manzanillo, Cuba (män'zä-nēl'yō)	132	20.20 N	77.05 W
Manzanillo, Mex.	128	19.02 N	104.21 W
Manzanillo, Bahía de (B.), Hai.	133	19.55 N	71.50 W
Manzanillo, Bahía de (B.), Mex. (bä-ē'ä-dĕ-män-zä-nē'l-yō)	128	19.00 N	104.38 W
Manzanillo, Punta (Pt.), Pan.	131	9.40 N	79.33 W
Manzhouli, China (män-jō-lē)	198	49.25 N	117.15 E
Manzovka, Sov. Un. (mán-zhô'f-ká)	200	44.16 N	132.13 E
Mao, Chad (mä'ô)	225	14.07 N	15.19 E
Mao, Dom. Rep.	133	19.35 N	71.10 W
Maoke, Pegunungan (Mtn.), Indon.	203	4.00 S	138.00 E
Maoming, China	199	21.55 N	110.40 E
Maoniu Shan (Mtn.), China (mou-niō shän)	198	32.45 N	104.09 E
Mapastepec, Mex. (ma-päs-tā-pĕk')	129	15.24 N	92.52 W
Mapia, Kepulauan (I.), Indon. (mä'pē-ä)	203	0.57 N	134.22 E
Mapimí, Mex. (mä-pē-mē')	122	25.50 N	103.50 W
Mapimí, Bolsón de (Des.), Mex. (bôl-sō'n-dĕ-mä-pē'mē)	122	27.27 N	103.20 W
Maple Creek, Can. (mā'p'l) (krēk)	98	49.55 N	109.27 W
Maple Grove, Can. (grōv)	93a	45.19 N	73.51 W
Maple Heights, Oh.	111d	41.25 N	81.34 W
Maple Shade, NJ (shād)	110f	39.57 N	75.01 W
Maple Valley, Wa. (văl'ē)	116a	47.24 N	122.02 W
Maplewood, Mn. (wood)	117g	45.00 N	93.03 W
Maplewood, Mo.	117e	38.37 N	90.20 W
Mapumulo, S. Afr. (mä-pä-moo'lō)	223c	29.12 S	31.05 E
Maputo (Lourenço Marques), Moz.	222	26.50 S	32.30 E
Maqueda Chan.Phil. (mä-kā'dä)	203a	13.40 N	123.52 E
Maquela do Zombo, Ang. (má-kā'lá doo zôm'boo)	222	6.08 S	15.15 E
Maquoketa, Ia. (má-kō-kē-tá)	113	42.04 N	90.42 W
Maquoketa (R.), Ia.	113	42.08 N	90.40 W
Mar, Serra do (Mts.), Braz. (sĕr'rá doo mär')	142	26.30 S	49.15 W
Maracaibo, Ven. (mä-rä-kī'bō)	140	10.38 N	71.45 W
Maracaibo, Lago de (L.), Ven. (lä'gō-dĕ-mä-rä-kī'bō)	140	9.55 N	72.13 W
Maracay, Ven. (mä-rä-käy')	141b	10.15 N	67.35 W
Marādah, Libya	221	29.10 N	19.07 E
Maradi, Niger (mà-rà-dē')	225	13.29 N	7.06 E
Marāgheh, Iran	177	37.20 N	46.10 E
Maraisburg, S. Afr.	223b	26.12 S	27.57 E
Marais des Cygnes (R.), Ks.	121	38.30 N	95.30 W
Marajó, Ilha de (I.), Braz. (mä-rä-zhō')	141	0.30 N	50.00 W
Maralal, Ken.	227	1.06 N	36.42 E
Marali, Cen. Afr. Rep.	225	6.01 N	18.24 E
Marandellas, Zimb. (mä-rán-dăl'ás)	227	18.10 S	31.36 E
Maranguape, Braz. (mä-ráŋ-gwä'pĕ)	141	3.48 S	38.38 W
Maranhão see São Luis			
Maranhão (State), Braz. (mä-rän-youN)	141	5.15 S	45.52 W
Maranoa (R.), Austl. (mä-rä-nō'ä)	212	27.01 S	148.03 E
Marano di Napoli, It. (mä-rä'nô-dē-ná'pô-lē)	169c	40.39 N	14.12 E
Marañón, Rio (R.), Peru (rē'ō-mä-rä-nyōn')	140	4.26 S	75.08 W
Marapanim, Braz. (mä-rä-pä-nē'N)	141	0.45 S	47.42 W
Maras, Tur. (mä-räsh')	177	37.40 N	36.50 W
Marathon, Can.	100	48.50 N	86.10 W
Marathon, Fl. (măr'á-thŏn)	125a	24.41 N	81.06 W
Marathon, Oh.	111f	39.09 N	83.59 W
Maravatio, Mex. (mä-rá-vä'tē-ō)	128	19.54 N	100.25 W
Marawi, Sud.	221	18.07 N	31.57 E
Marble Bar, Austl. (märb''l bär)	210	21.15 S	119.15 E
Marble Can., Az. (mär'b'l)	119	36.21 N	111.48 W
Marble Hall, S. Afr. (hâll)	219d	24.59 S	29.19 E
Marblehead, Ma. (mär'b'l-hĕd)	103a	42.30 N	70.51 W
Marburg an der Lahn, F.R.G.	164	50.49 N	8.46 E
Marca, Ponta da (Pt.), Ang.	226	16.31 S	11.42 E
Marcala, Hond. (mär-kä-lä)	130	14.08 N	88.01 W
Marche (Reg.), It. (mär'kā)	172	43.35 N	12.33 E
Marchegg, Aus.	155e	48.18 N	16.55 E
Marchena, Sp. (mär-chā'nä)	168	37.20 N	5.25 W
Marchena (I.), Ec. (ĕ's-lä-mär-chē'nä)	140	0.29 N	90.31 W
Marchfeld (Reg.), Aus.	155e	48.14 N	16.37 E
Marceline, Mo. (mär-sē-lēn')	121	39.42 N	92.56 W
Marcos Paz, Arg. (mär-kōs' päz)	139c	34.49 S	58.51 W
Marcus (I.), Asia (mär'kŭs)	204	24.00 N	155.00 E
Marcus Hook, Pa. (mär'kŭs hook)	110f	39.49 N	75.25 W
Marcy, Mt., NY (mär'sē)	109	44.10 N	73.55 W
Mar de Espanha, Braz. (mär-dĕ-ĕs-pá'nyá)	139a	21.53 S	43.00 W
Mar del Plata, Arg. (mär dĕl- plä'ta)	142	37.59 S	57.35 W
Mardin, Tur. (mär-dēn')	177	37.25 N	40.40 E
Mare (I.), N. Cal. (má-rā')	211	21.53 S	168.30 E
Maree, Loch (L.), Scot. (má-rē')	160	57.40 N	5.44 W
Marengo, Ia. (má-rĕŋ'gō)	113	41.47 N	92.04 W
Marennes, Fr. (má-rĕn')	166	45.49 N	1.08 W
Marfa, Tx. (mär'fá)	122	30.19 N	104.01 W
Marganets, Sov. Un.	173	47.41 N	34.33 E
Margarita, Pan. (mär-goo-rē'tä)	126a	9.20 N	79.55 W
Margarita, Isla de (I.), Ven. (mä-gá-rē'tá)	141b	11.00 N	64.15 W
Margate, Eng. (mär'gāt)	160	51.21 N	1.17 E
Margate, S. Afr. (mä-gāt')	223c	30.52 S	30.21 E
Margherita Pk., Afr.	227	0.22 N	29.51 E
Marguerite (R.), Can.	102	50.39 N	66.42 W
Mari (A. S. S. R.), Sov. Un. (mä'rē)	176	56.20 N	48.00 E
Maria, Can. (má-rē'á)	102	48.10 N	66.04 W
María Cleofas (I.), Mex. (mä-rē'ä klā'ô-fäs)	128	21.17 N	106.14 W
Mariager, Den. (mä-rē-ägh'ĕr)	162	56.38 N	10.00 E
María Magdalena (I.), Mex. (mä rē'ä mäg-dä-lā'nä)	128	21.25 N	106.23 W
Mariana, Braz. (mä-ryá'nä)	139a	20.23 S	43.24 W
Mariana Is., Oceania (mä-rē-ä'ná)	204	17.20 N	145.00 E
Mariana Trench, Oceania	204	12.00 N	144.00 E
Marianao, Cuba (mä-rē-ä-nä'ō)	133a	23.05 N	82.26 W
Marianna, Ar. (mā-rĭ-ăn'á)	121	34.45 N	90.45 W
Marianna, Fl.	124	30.46 N	85.14 W
Marianna, Pa.	111e	40.01 N	80.05 W
Mariano Acosta, Arg. (mä-rēä'nō-á-kōs'tä)	142a	34.28 S	58.48 W
Mariánské Lázne, Czech. (mär'yán-skĕ'läz'nyĕ)	154	49.58 N	12.42 E
Marías, Islas (Is.), Mex. (mä-rē'äs)	126	21.30 N	106.40 W
Marias R., Mt. (má-rī'áz)	115	48.15 N	110.50 W
Mariato, Punta (Pt.), Pan.	131	7.17 N	81.09 W
Maribo, Den. (mä'rē-bô)	162	54.46 N	11.29 E
Maribor, Yugo. (mä're-bôr)	170	46.33 N	15.37 E
Maricá, Braz. (mä-rē-kä')	139a	22.55 S	42.49 W
Maricaban (I.), Phil. (mä-rē-kä-bän')	203a	13.40 N	120.44 E
Marico R., S. Afr. (mä'rĭ-cō)	219d	24.53 S	26.22 E
Marie Byrd Land, Ant. (má rē'bûrd')	228	78.00 S	130.00 W
Mariefred, Swe. (mä-rē'ē-frĭd)	162	59.17 N	17.09 E
Marie Galante I., Guad. (má-rē' gá-läNt')	131b	15.58 N	61.05 W
Mariehamn, Fin. (má-rē'ē-häm''n)	162	60.07 N	19.57 E
Mariehamn, see Maarianhamina			
Mariestad, Swe. (mä-rē'ē-städ')	162	58.43 N	13.45 E
Marietta, Ga. (mā-rĭ'-ĕt'á)	110c	33.57 N	84.33 W
Marietta, Oh.	108	39.25 N	81.30 W
Marietta, Ok.	121	33.53 N	97.07 W
Marietta, Wa.	116d	48.48 N	122.35 W
Mariinsk, Sov. Un. (má-re'ĭnsk)	178	56.15 N	87.28 E
Marijampole, Sov. Un. (mä-rē-yäm-pô'lĕ)	163	54.33 N	23.26 E
Marikana, S. Afr. (mă'-rĭ-kä-ná)	219d	25.40 S	27.28 E
Marília, Braz. (mä-rē'lyá)	141	22.02 S	49.48 W
Marimba, Ang.	226	8.28 S	17.08 E
Marinduque I., Phil. (mä-rēn-doo'kä)	203a	13.14 N	121.45 E
Marine, Il. (má-rēn')	117e	38.48 N	89.47 W
Marine City, Mi.	108	42.45 N	82.30 W
Marine L., Mn.	117g	45.13 N	92.55 W
Marine on St. Croix, Mn. (äN sĕN kroo-ä)	117g	45.11 N	92.47 W
Marinette, Wi. (măr-ĭ-nĕt')	113	45.04 N	87.40 W
Maringa (R.), Zaire (mä-riŋ'gä)	226	1.15 N	20.05 E
Marinha Grande, Port. (mä-rēn'yá grän'dĕ)	168	39.49 N	8.53 W
Marion, Al. (măr'ĭ-ŭn)	124	32.36 N	87.19 W
Marion, Il.	108	37.40 N	88.55 W
Marion, In.	108	40.35 N	85.45 W
Marion, Ia.	113	42.01 N	91.39 W
Marion, Ks.	121	38.21 N	97.02 W
Marion, Ky.	124	37.19 N	88.05 W
Marion, NC	125	35.40 N	82.00 W
Marion, ND	112	46.37 N	98.20 W
Marion, Oh.	108	40.35 N	83.10 W
Marion, SC	125	34.08 N	79.23 W
Marion, Va.	125	36.48 N	81.33 W
Marion (R.), SC	125	33.25 N	80.35 W
Marion Rf., Austl.	211	18.57 S	151.31 E
Mariposa, Chile (mä-rē-pô'sä)	139b	35.33 S	71.21 W
Mariposa Cr., Ca.	118	37.14 N	120.30 W
Mariquita, Col. (mä-rē-kē'tä)	140a	5.13 N	74.52 W
Mariscal Estigarribia, Par. (mä-rēs-käl'ĕs-tē-gär-rē'byä)	141	22.03 S	60.28 W
Marisco, Ponta do (Pt.), Braz. (pô'n-tä-dô-mä-rē's-kō)	142b	23.01 S	43.17 W
Maritime Alps (Mts.), Fr.-It. (má'rĭ-tīm ălps)	167	44.20 N	7.02 E
Mariveles, Phil.	203a	14.27 N	120.29 E
Marj Uyan, Leb.	189a	33.21 N	35.36 E
Marka, Som.	219a	1.45 N	44.47 E
Marka Kul' (L.), Sov. Un.	194	49.15 N	85.48 E
Markaryd, Swe. (mär'kä-rüd)	162	56.30 N	13.34 E
Marked Tree, Ar. (märkt trē)	121	35.31 N	90.26 W
Marken, I., Neth.	155a	52.26 N	5.08 E
Market Bosworth, Eng. (bŏz'wûrth)	154	52.37 N	1.23 W
Market Deeping, Eng. (dēp'ĭng)	154	52.40 N	0.19 W
Market Drayton, Eng. (drā'tŭn)	154	52.54 N	2.29 W
Market Harborough, Eng. (här'bŭr-ô)	154	52.28 N	0.55 W
Market Rasen, Eng. (rā'zĕn)	154	53.23 N	0.21 W
Markham, Can. (märk'ám)	93d	43.53 N	79.15 W
Markham, Mt., Ant.	228	82.59 S	159.30 E
Markovka, Sov. Un. (mär-kôf'ká)	173	49.32 N	39.34 E
Markovo, Sov. Un. (mär'kô-vô)	179	64.46 N	170.48 E
Markrāna, India	190	27.08 N	74.43 E
Marks, Sov. Un.	177	51.40 N	46.40 E
Marksville, La. (märks'vĭl)	123	31.09 N	92.05 W
Markt Indersdorf, F.R.G. (märkt ēn'dĕrs-dōrf)	155d	48.22 N	11.23 E
Marktredwitz, F.R.G. (märk-rĕd'vēts)	164	50.02 N	12.05 E
Markt Schwaben, F.R.G. (märkt shvä'bĕn)	155d	48.12 N	11.52 E
Marl, F.R.G. (märl)	167c	51.40 N	7.05 E
Marlboro, NJ	110a	40.18 N	74.15 W
Marlborough, Ma.	103a	42.21 N	71.33 W
Marlette, Mi. (mär-lĕt')	108	43.25 N	83.05 W
Marlin, Tx. (mär'lĭn)	123	31.18 N	96.52 W
Marlinton, WV (mär'lĭn-tŭn)	109	38.15 N	80.10 W
Marlow, Eng. (mär'lō)	154b	51.33 N	0.46 W
Marlow, Ok.	120	34.38 N	97.56 W
Marls, The (Shoals), Ba. (märls)	132	26.30 N	77.15 W
Marmande, Fr. (mår-mäNd')	166	44.30 N	0.10 E
Marmara (I.), Tur. (mär'má-rá)	171	40.38 N	27.35 E
Marmara Denizi (Sea), Tur.	177	40.40 N	28.00 E
Marmarth, ND (mär'mårth)	112	46.19 N	103.57 W
Mar Muerto (L.), Mex. (mär-mooĕ'r-tô)	129	16.13 N	94.22 W
Marne, F.R.G. (mär'nē)	155c	53.57 N	9.01 E
Marne (R.), Fr. (märn)	166	49.08 N	3.39 E
Maroa, Ven. (mä-rō'ä)	140	2.43 N	67.37 W
Maroantsetra, Mad. (má-rō-äŋ-tsä'trá)	223	15.18 S	49.48 E
Maro Jarapeto (Mtn.), Col. (mä-rô-hä-rä-pĕ'tô)	140a	6.29 N	76.39 W
Maromokotro (Mtn.), Mad.	223	14.00 S	49.11 E
Maroni (R.), Fr. Gu.-Sur. (má-rō'nē)	141	3.02 N	53.54 W
Maro Rf., Hi.	104b	25.15 N	170.00 W
Maroua, Cam. (mär'wä)	225	10.36 N	14.20 E
Marple, Eng. (mär'p'l)	155	53.24 N	2.04 W
Marquard, S. Afr.	219d	28.41 S	27.26 E
Marquesas Is., Fr. Polynesia (mär-kē'säs)	205	8.50 S	141.00 W
Marquesas Keys (Is.), Fl. (mär-kē'zás)	125a	24.37 N	82.15 W
Marquês de Valença, Braz. (már-kĕ's-dĕ-vä-lĕ'n-sä)	139a	22.16 S	43.42 W
Marquette, Can. (mär-kĕt')	93f	50.04 N	97.43 W
Marquette, Mi.	113	46.32 N	87.25 W
Marquez, Tx. (mär-kāz')	123	31.14 N	96.15 W
Marra, Jabal (Mt.), Sud. (jĕb'ĕl mär'ä)	221	13.00 N	23.47 E
Marrakech, Mor. (mär-rä'kĕsh)	220	31.38 N	8.00 W
Marree, Austl. (măr'rē)	212	29.38 S	137.55 E
Marrero, La.	110d	29.55 N	90.06 W
Marrupa, Moz.	227	13.08 S	37.30 E
Mars, Pa. (märz)	111e	40.42 N	80.01 W
Marsabit, Ken.	227	2.20 N	37.59 E
Marsala, It. (mär-sä'lä)	170	37.48 N	12.28 E
Marsa Matrūh, Egypt	221	31.19 N	27.14 E
Marsden, Eng. (märz'dĕn)	154	53.36 N	1.55 W
Marseille, Fr. (mår-sâ'y')	166a	43.18 N	5.25 E
Marseilles, Il. (mär-sĕlz')	108	41.20 N	88.40 W
Marshall, Il. (mär'shál)	108	39.20 N	87.40 W
Marshall, Mi.	108	42.20 N	84.55 W
Marshall, Mn.	112	44.28 N	95.49 W
Marshall, Mo.	121	39.07 N	93.12 W
Marshall, Tx.	123	32.33 N	94.22 W
Marshall Is., Pac. Is. Trust Ter.	204	10.00 N	165.00 E
Marshalltown, Ia. (mär'shál-toun)	113	42.02 N	92.55 W
Marshallville, Ga. (mär'shál-vĭl)	124	32.29 N	83.55 W
Marshfield, Ma. (märsh'fēld)	103a	42.06 N	70.43 W
Marshfield, Mo.	121	37.20 N	92.53 W
Marshfield, Wi.	113	44.40 N	90.10 W
Marsh Harbour, Ba.	132	26.30 N	77.00 W
Mars Hill, In. (märz'hĭl')	111g	39.43 N	86.15 W
Mars Hill, Me.	102	46.34 N	67.54 W
Marstrand, Swe. (mär'stränd)	162	57.54 N	11.33 E
Marsyaty, Sov. Un. (märs'yá-tĭ)	180a	60.03 N	60.28 E
Mart, Tx. (märt)	123	31.32 N	96.49 W
Martaban, G. of, Bur. (mär-tŭ-bän')	202	16.34 N	96.58 E
Martapura, Indon.	202	3.19 S	114.45 E
Marthas Vineyard (I.), Ma. (mär'tház vĭn'yárd)	105	41.25 N	70.35 W
Martí, Cuba (mär-tē')	132	23.00 N	80.55 W
Martigny, Switz. (mår-tē-nyē')	164	46.06 N	7.00 E
Martigues, Fr.	166a	43.24 N	5.05 E
Martin, Tn. (mär'tĭn)	124	36.20 N	88.45 W
Martin (R.), Al.	124	32.40 N	86.05 W
Martina Franca, It. (mär-tē'nä fräŋ'kä)	171	40.43 N	17.21 E
Martinez, Ca. (mär-tē'nĕz)	116b	38.01 N	122.08 W
Martinez, Tx.	117d	29.25 N	98.20 W
Martinique, N. A. (mår-tē-nēk')	127	14.50 N	60.40 W
Martin Pt., Ak.	105	70.10 N	142.00 W
Martinsburg, WV (mär'tĭnz-bûrg)	109	39.30 N	78.00 W
Martins Ferry, Oh. (mär'tĭnz)	108	40.05 N	80.45 W
Martinsville, In. (mär'tĭnz-vĭl)	108	39.25 N	86.25 W
Martinsville, Va.	125	36.40 N	79.53 W
Martos, Sp. (mär'tōs)	168	37.43 N	3.58 W
Martre, Lac la (L.), Can. (läk la märtr)	94	63.24 N	119.58 W
Marugame, Jap. (mä'roo-gä'mā)	201	34.19 N	133.48 E
Marungu (Mts.), Tan.	227	7.50 S	29.50 E
Marve (Neigh.), India	191b	19.12 N	72.43 E
Marvín, Sp. (mär-vē'n)	168	42.24 N	8.40 W
Mary, Sov. Un.. (mä'rē)	174	37.45 N	61.47 E
Mar'yanskaya, Sov. Un. (mär-yän'ská-yá)	173	45.04 N	38.39 E
Maryborough, Austl. (mā'rĭ-bŭr-ô)	212	25.35 S	152.40 E
Maryborough, Austl.	212	37.00 S	143.50 E
Maryland (State), U. S. (mĕr'ĭ-lănd)	107	39.10 N	76.25 W
Mary's R., Nv. (mā'rĭz)	114	41.25 N	115.10 W
Marystown, Can. (mâr'ĭz-toun)	103	47.11 N	55.10 W
Marysville, Can.	102	45.59 N	66.35 W
Marysville, Ca.	118	39.09 N	121.37 W
Marysville, Ks.	121	39.49 N	96.38 W

318 Marysville – Mekong

PLACE (Pronunciation)	PAGE	Lat. °'	Long. °'
Marysville, Oh.	108	40.15 N	83.25 W
Marysville, Wa.	116a	48.03 N	122.11 W
Maryūt (L.), Egypt	219b	31.09 N	30.10 E
Maryville, Il. (mā'rĭ-vĭl)	117e	38.44 N	89.57 W
Maryville, Mo.	121	40.21 N	94.51 W
Maryville, Tn.	124	35.44 N	83.59 W
Mārzuq, Libya	221	26.00 N	14.09 E
Marzūq, Idehan (Dunes), Libya	221	24.30 N	13.00 E
Masai Steppe (Plat.), Tan.	227	4.30 S	36.40 E
Masaka, Ug.	227	0.20 S	31.44 E
Masalasef, Chad	225	11.43 N	17.08 E
Masalembo-Besar (I.), Indon.	202	5.40 S	114.28 E
Masan, Kor. (mä-sän')	200	35.10 N	128.31 E
Masangwe, Tan.	227	5.28 S	30.05 E
Masasi, Tan. (mä-sä'sē)	227	10.43 S	38.48 E
Masatepe, Nic. (mä-sä-tě'pě)	130	11.57 N	86.10 W
Masaya, Nic. (mä-sä'yä)	130	11.58 N	86.05 W
Masbate, Phil. (mäs-bä'tā)	203a	12.21 N	123.38 E
Masbate (I), Phil.	203a	12.19 N	123.03 E
Mascara, Alg. (mäs'kä-rä) (màs-kà-rà')	220	35.25 N	0.08 E
Mascarene Is., Mauritius	228	20.20 S	56.40 E
Mascot, Tn. (măs'kŏt)	124	36.04 N	83.45 W
Mascota, Mex. (mäs-kō'tä)	128	20.33 N	104.45 W
Mascota (R.), Mex.	128	20.33 N	104.52 W
Mascouche, Can. (màs-kōōsh')	93a	45.45 N	73.36 W
Mascouche (R.), Can.	93a	45.44 N	73.45 W
Mascoutah, Il. (măs-kū'tā)	117e	38.29 N	89.48 W
Maseru, Leso. (măz'ēr-ōō)	222	29.09 S	27.11 E
Mashhad, Iran	192	36.17 N	59.30 E
Mashra'ar-Ragg, Sud.	221	8.28 N	29.15 E
Masi-Manimba, Zaire	226	4.46 S	17.55 E
Masindi, Ug. (mä-sēn'dē)	221	1.44 N	31.43 E
Masjed Soleymān, Iran	192	31.45 N	49.17 E
Mask, Lough (B.), Ire. (lŏk måsk)	160	53.35 N	9.23 W
Maslovo, Sov. Un. (mäs'lô-vô)	180a	60.08 N	60.28 E
Mason, Mi. (mā'sŭn)	108	42.35 N	84.25 W
Mason, Oh.	111f	39.22 N	84.18 W
Mason, Tx.	122	30.46 N	99.14 W
Mason City, Ia.	113	43.08 N	93.14 W
Masquaro (L.), Can.	103	50.34 N	60.40 W
Massa, It. (mäs'sä)	170	44.02 N	10.08 E
Massachusetts (State), U. S. (măs-á-chōō'sĕts)	107	42.20 N	72.30 W
Massachusetts B., Ma.	102	42.26 N	70.20 W
Massafra, It. (mäs-sä'frä)	170	40.35 N	17.05 E
Massa Marittima, It.	170	43.03 N	10.55 E
Massapequa, NY	110a	40.41 N	73.28 W
Massaua, see Mesewa			
Massena, NY (mă-sē'nå)	109	44.55 N	74.55 W
Masset, Can. (măs'ĕt)	94	54.02 N	132.09 W
Masset Inlet, Can.	96	53.42 N	132.20 E
Massif Central (Plat.), Fr. (må-sēf' säN-tràl')	166	45.12 N	3.02 E
Massillon, Oh. (măs'ĭ-lŏn)	108	40.50 N	81.35 W
Massinga, Moz. (mä-sĭn'gä)	222	23.18 S	35.18 E
Massive, Mt., Co. (măs'ĭv)	119	39.05 N	106.30 W
Masson, Can. (măs-sŭn)	93c	45.33 N	75.25 W
Masuda, Jap. (mä-sōō'dä)	201	34.42 N	131.53 E
Masuria (Reg.), Pol.	165	53.40 N	21.10 E
Matadi, Zaire (mä-tä'dē)	226	5.49 S	13.27 E
Matagalpa, Nic. (mä-tä-gäl'pä)	130	12.52 N	85.57 W
Matagami (L.), Can. (mă-tä-gä'mē)	95	50.10 N	78.28 W
Matagorda B., Tx. (măt-á-gôr'då)	123	28.32 N	96.13 W
Matagorda I., Tx.	123	28.13 N	96.27 W
Matam, Senegal (mä-täm')	224	15.40 N	13.15 W
Matamoros, Mex. (mä-tä-mō'rōs)	122	25.32 N	103.13 W
Matamoros, Mex.	123	25.52 N	97.30 W
Matandu (R.), Tan.	227	8.55 S	38.35 E
Matane, Can. (må-tân')	102	48.51 N	67.32 W
Matanzas, Cuba (mä-tän'zäs)	132	23.05 N	81.35 W
Matanzas (Prov.), Cuba	132	22.45 N	81.20 W
Matanzas, Bahía (B.), Cuba (bä-ē'ä)	132	23.10 N	81.30 W
Matapalo, Cabo (C.), C. R. (kà'bō-mä-tä-pä'lō)	131	8.22 N	83.25 W
Matapédia, Can. (mă-tà-pā'dē-à)	102	47.58 N	66.56 W
Matapédia (L.), Can.	102	48.33 N	67.32 W
Matapédia (R.), Can.	102	48.10 N	67.10 W
Mataquito (R.), Chile (mä-tä-kē'tō)	139b	35.08 S	71.35 W
Matara, Sri Lanka (mä-tä'rä)	191	5.59 N	80.35 E
Mataram, Indon.	202	8.45 S	116.15 E
Mataró, Sp. (mä-tä-rō')	169	41.33 N	2.27 E
Matatiele, S. Afr. (mä-tä-tyā'lā)	223c	30.21 S	28.49 E
Matawan, NJ	110a	40.24 N	74.13 W
Matawin (R.), Can. (măt á-wĭn)	102	46.46 N	73.25 W
Matehuala, Mex. (mä-tå-wä'lä)	128	23.38 N	100.39 W
Matera, It. (mä-tå'rä)	170	40.42 N	16.37 E
Mateur, Tun. (må-tûr')	157	37.09 N	9.43 E
Mātherān, India	191b	18.58 N	73.16 E
Matheson, Can.	101	48.35 N	80.33 W
Mathews, L., Ca. (măth ūz)	117a	33.50 N	117.24 W
Mathura, India (mu-tōō'rŭ)	190	27.39 N	77.39 E
Matias Barbosa, Braz. (mä-tē'äs-bär-bô-sä)	137a	21.53 S	43.19 W
Matillas, Laguna (L.), Mex. (lä-gōō'nä-mä-tē'l-yäs)	129	18.02 N	92.36 W
Matina, C. R. (mä-tē'nä)	131	10.06 N	83.20 W
Matiši, Sov. Un. (mä'tē-sē)	163	57.43 N	25.09 E
Matlalcueyetl, Cerra, Mex. (sĕ'r-rä-mä-tläl-kwĕ'yĕtl)	128	19.13 N	98.02 W
Matlock, Eng. (măt'lŏk)	154	53.08 N	1.33 W
Matochkin Shar, Sov. Un. (mä'tŏch-kĭn)	178	73.57 N	56.16 E
Mato Grosso, Braz. (mät'ōō grōs'ōō)	141	15.04 S	59.58 W
Mato Grosso (State), Braz.	141	14.38 S	55.36 W
Mato Grosso, Chapada de (Plain), Braz. (shä-pä'dä-dě)	141	13.39 S	55.42 W
Matosinhos, Port.	168	41.10 N	8.48 W
Matrah, Om. (må-trä')	192	23.36 N	58.27 E
Matsubara, Jap.	201b	34.34 N	135.34 E
Matsudo, Jap. (mät'sōō-dô)	201a	35.48 N	139.55 E
Matsue, Jap. (mät'sōō-ĕ)	201	35.29 N	133.04 E
Matsumoto, Jap. (mät'sōō-mō'tô)	201	36.15 N	137.59 E
Matsuyama, Jap. (mät'sōō-yä'mä)	201	33.48 N	132.45 E
Matsuzaka, Jap. (mät'sōō-zä'kä)	201	34.35 N	136.34 E
Mattamuskeet (R.), NC (măt-tá-mŭs'kēt)	125	35.34 N	76.03 W
Mattaponi (R.), Va. (măt'á-poni')	109	37.45 N	77.00 W
Mattawa, Can. (măt'á-wå)	101	46.15 N	78.49 W
Matternhorn (Mtn.), Switz. (mät'ēr-hôrn)	164	45.57 N	7.36 E
Matteson, Il. (mătt'ē-sŭn)	111a	41.30 N	87.42 W
Matthew Town, Ba. (măth'ū toun)	133	21.00 N	73.40 W
Mattoon, Il. (mă-tōōn')	108	39.30 N	88.20 W
Maturín, Ven. (mä-tōō-rēn')	140	9.48 N	63.16 W
Maúa, Moz	217	13.51 S	37.10 E
Mauban, Phil. (mä'ōō-bän')	203a	14.11 N	121.44 E
Maubeuge, Fr. (mô-bûzh')	166	50.18 N	3.57 E
Maud, Oh. (môd)	111f	39.21 N	84.23 W
Mauer, Aus. (mou'ēr)	155e	48.09 N	16.16 E
Mauės, Braz. (má-wě's)	141	3.34 S	57.30 W
Mau Escarpment (Cliff), Ken.	227	0.45 S	35.50 E
Maui (I.), Hi. (mä'ōō-ē)	104a	20.52 N	156.02 W
Maule (R.), Chile (má'ōō-lě)	139b	35.45 S	70.50 W
Maumee, Oh. (mô-mē')	108	41.30 N	83.40 W
Maumee (R.), In.-Oh.	108	41.10 N	84.50 W
Maumee B., Oh.	108	41.50 N	83.20 W
Maun, Bots. (mä-ōōn')	222	19.52 S	23.40 E
Mauna Kea (Vol.), Hi. (mä'ōō-nä-kā'ä)	104a	19.52 N	155.30 W
Mauna Loa (Vol.), Hi. (mä'ōō-nälō'ä)	104a	19.28 N	155.38 W
Maung Nakhon Sawan, Thai.	202	16.00 N	99.52 E
Maurepas L., La. (mō-rē-pä')	123	30.18 N	90.40 W
Mauricie, Parc Natl. de la (Natl. Pk.), Can.	102	46.46 N	73.00 W
Mauritania, Afr. (mô-rē-tā'nĭ-á)	218	19.38 N	13.30 W
Mauritius, Afr. (mô-rĭsh'ĭ-ŭs)	228	20.18 S	57.36 E
Maury, Wa. (mô'rĭ)	116a	47.22 N	122.23 W
Mauston, Wi. (môs'tŭn)	113	43.46 N	90.05 W
Maverick, (R.), Az. (mă-vûr'ĭk)	119	33.40 N	109.30 W
Mavinga, Ang.	226	15.50 S	20.21 E
Maxcanú, Mex. (mäs-kä-nōō')	129	20.35 N	89.59 W
Maxville, Can. (măks'vĭl)	93c	45.17 N	74.52 W
Maxville, Mo.	117e	38.26 N	90.24 W
Maya (R.), Sov. Un. (mä'yä)	179	58.00 N	135.45 E
Mayaguana (I.), Ba.	133	22.25 N	73.00 W
Mayaguana Passage (Str.), Ba.	133	22.20 N	73.25 W
Mayagüez, P. R. (mä-yä-gwāz')	127b	18.12 N	67.10 W
Mayarí, Cuba (mä-yä-rē')	123	20.45 N	75.40 W
Mayari (R.), Cuba	123	20.25 N	75.35 W
Mayas, Montañas (Mts.), Belize (mŏntăŋ'ās mā'ās)	130a	16.43 N	89.00 W
Mayd (I.), Som.	219a	11.24 N	46.38 E
Mayen, F.R.G. (mī'ĕn)	164	50.19 N	7.14 E
Mayenne (R.), Fr. (må-yĕn)	166	48.14 N	0.45 W
Mayfield, Ky. (mā'fēld)	124	36.44 N	88.19 W
Mayfield Cr., Ky.	125	36.54 N	88.47 W
Mayfield Heights, Oh.	111d	41.31 N	81.26 W
Mayfield Res., Wa.	114	46.31 N	122.34 W
Maykop (Maikop), Sov. Un. (mī-kôp')	177	44.35 N	40.10 E
Maykor, Sov. Un. (mī-kôr')	180a	59.01 N	55.52 E
Maymyo, Bur. (mī'myō)	194	22.14 N	96.32 E
Maynard, Ma. (mā'nård)	103a	42.25 N	71.27 W
Mayne, Can. (mān)	116d	48.51 N	123.18 W
Mayne (I), Can.	116d	48.52 N	123.14 W
Mayo, Can. (mā-yō')	94	63.40 N	135.51 W
Mayo, Fl.	124	30.02 N	83.08 W
Mayo, Md.	110e	38.54 N	76.31 W
Mayodan, NC (mā-yō'dăn)	125	36.25 N	79.59 W
Mayon (Vol.), Phil. (mä-yōn')	203a	13.21 N	123.43 E
Mayotte (I.), France (må-yôt')	223	13.07 S	45.32 W
May Pen, Jam	132	18.00 N	77.25 W
Mayraira Pt., Phil.	199	18.40 N	120.45 E
Mayran, Laguna de (L.), Mex. (lä-ōō'nä-dě-mī-rän')	122	25.40 N	102.35 W
Maysville, Ky. (māz'vĭl)	108	38.35 N	83.45 W
Mayumba, Gabon	226	3.25 S	10.39 E
Mayville, NY (mā'vĭl)	109	42.15 N	79.30 W
Mayville, ND	112	47.30 N	97.20 W
Mayville, Wi.	113	43.30 N	88.45 W
Maywood, Ca. (mā'wŏŏd)	117a	33.59 N	118.11 W
Maywood, Il.	111a	41.53 N	87.51 W
Mazabuka, Zambia (mä-zä-bōō'kä)	227	15.51 S	27.46 E
Mazagão, Braz. (mä-zá-gou'N)	141	0.05 S	51.27 W
Mazapil, Mex. (mä-zä-pēl')	122	24.40 N	101.30 W
Mazara del Vallo, It. (mät-sä'rä děl väl'lō)	170	37.40 N	12.37 E
Mazār-i-Sharīf, Afg. (má-zär'-ē-shá-rēf')	190	36.48 N	67.12 E
Mazarrón, Sp. (mä-zär-rō'n)	168	36.37 N	1.29 W
Mazaruni (R.), Guy. (mä-zä-rōō'nē)	141	5.58 N	59.37 W
Mazatenango, Guat. (mä-zä-tå-näŋ'gō)	130	14.30 N	91.30 W
Mazatla, Mex.	129a	10.30 N	99.24 W
Mazatlán (San Juan), Mex. (mä-zä-tlän') (sañ hwän')	129	17.05 N	95.26 W
Mazatlán, Mex.	128	23.14 N	106.27 W
Mažeikiai, Sov. Un. (må-zhā'kē-ĭ)	163	56.19 N	22.24 E
Mazhafah, Jabal (Mts.), Sau. Ar.	189a	28.56 N	35.05 E
Mazoe (R.), Moz.	227	16.40 S	32.50 E
Mazzarino, It. (mät-sä-rē'nō)	170	37.16 N	14.15 E
Mbabane, Swaz. (m'bä-bä'nē)	222	26.18 S	31.14 E
Mbaiki, Cen. Afr. Rep. (m'bà-ē'kē)	225	3.53 N	18.00 E
Mbakana, Montagne de (Mts.), Cam.	225	7.55 N	14.40 E
Mbakaou, Barrage de, Cam.	225	6.10 N	12.55 E
Mbala (Abercorn), Zambia	227	8.50 S	31.22 E
Mbale, Ug.	227	1.05 N	34.10 E
Mbamba Bay, Tan.	227	11.17 S	34.46 E
Mbandaka (Coquilhatville), Zaire	226	0.04 N	18.16 E
Mbanza-Ngungu, Zaire	226	5.20 S	10.55 E
Mbarara, Ug.	227	0.37 S	30.39 E
Mbasay, Chad	225	7.39 N	15.40 E
Mbeya, Tan.	227	8.54 S	33.27 E
Mbigou, Gabon (m-bē-gōō')	222	2.07 S	11.30 E
Mbinda, Con.	226	2.00 S	12.55 E
Mbogo, Tan.	227	7.26 S	33.26 E
Mbomou (Bomu) (R.), Cen. Afr. Rep.-Zaire (m'bō'mōō)	226	4.50 S	23.35 E
Mbuji-Mayi (Bakwanga), Zaire	226	6.09 S	23.28 E
Mbout, Mauritania (m'bōō')	220	16.03 N	12.31 W
Mchinji, Malawi	227	13.42 S	32.50 E
Mead, L., Az.-Nv.	119	36.20 N	114.14 W
Mead, Ks. (mēd)	120	37.17 N	100.21 W
Meade Pk., Id.	115	42.19 N	111.16 W
Meadow Lake, Can. (měd'ō lāk)	98	54.08 N	108.26 W
Meadows, Can. (měd'ōz)	93f	50.02 N	97.35 W
Meadville, Pa. (mēd'vĭl)	109	41.40 N	80.10 W
Meaford, Can. (mē'fērd)	108	44.35 N	80.40 W
Mealy Mts., Can. (mē'lē)	95	53.32 N	57.58 W
Meandarra, Austl. (mē-ăn-dă'rá)	212	27.47 S	149.40 E
Meaux, Fr. (mō)	167b	48.58 N	2.53 E
Mecapalapa, Mex. (mā-kä-pä-lä'pä)	129	20.32 N	97.52 W
Mecatina (I.), Can. (mā-kå-tē'nå)	103	50.50 N	58.33 W
Mecatina (R.), Can. (mā-kå-tē'nå)	103	50.50 N	59.45 W
Mecca, see Makkah			
Mechanic Falls, Me. (mē-kăn'ĭk)	102	44.05 N	70.23 W
Mechanicsburg, Pa. (mē-kăn'ĭks-bûrg)	109	40.15 N	77.00 W
Mechanicsville, Md. (mē-kăn'ĭks-vĭl)	110e	38.27 N	76.45 W
Mechanicville, NY (mēkăn'ĭk-vĭl)	109	42.55 N	73.45 W
Mechelen, Bel.	155a	51.01 N	4.28 E
Méchérial, Mor.	158	33.30 N	0.13 W
Mecklenburg (Reg.), G.D.R. (měk'lěn-bōōrgh)	164	53.34 N	12.18 E
Medan, Indon. (må-dän')	202	3.35 N	98.35 E
Medanosa, Punta (Pt.), Arg. (pōō'n-tä-mě-dä-nō'sä)	142	47.50 S	65.53 W
Medden (R.), Eng. (měd'ěn)	154	53.14 N	1.05 W
Médéa, Alg. (mā-dā'ä)	169	36.18 N	2.40 E
Medellín, Col. (må-dhěl-yēn')	140a	6.15 N	75.34 W
Medellín, Mex. (mě-děl-yě'n)	129	19.03 N	96.08 W
Medenine, Tun. (må-dě-něn')	158e	33.22 N	10.33 E
Medfeld, Ma. (měd'fēld)	103a	42.11 N	71.19 W
Medford, Ma. (měd'fērd)	103a	42.25 N	71.07 W
Medford, NJ	110f	39.54 N	74.50 W
Medford, Ok.	120	36.47 N	97.44 W
Medford, Or.	114	42.19 N	122.52 W
Medford, Wi.	113	45.09 N	90.22 W
Media, Pa. (mē'dĭ-á)	110f	39.55 N	75.24 W
Medias, Rom. (měd-yäsh')	165	46.09 N	24.21 E
Medical Lake, Wa. (měd'ĭ-kăl)	114	47.34 N	117.40 W
Medicine Bow Ra., Co.-Wy. (měd'ĭ-sĭn bō)	120	40.55 N	106.02 W
Medicine Bow R., Wy.	115	41.58 N	106.30 W
Medicine Hat, Can. (měd'ĭ-sĭn hăt)	98	50.03 N	110.40 W
Medicine L., Mt. (měd'ĭ-sĭn)	115	48.24 N	104.15 W
Medicine Lodge, Ks.	120	37.17 N	98.37 W
Midicine Lodge (R.), Ks.	120	37.20 N	98.57 W
Medina, NY (mē-dī'nå)	109	43.15 N	78.20 W
Medina, Oh.	111d	41.08 N	81.52 W
Medina, see Al Madīnah			
Medina del Campo, Sp. (mā-dē'nä děl käm'pō)	168	41.18 N	4.54 W
Medina de Ríoseco, Sp. (mā-dē'nä dā rē-ō-sā'kō)	168	41.53 N	5.05 W
Médina Gonassé, Sen.	224	13.08 N	13.45 W
Medina L., Tx.	122	29.36 N	98.47 W
Medina R., Tx.	122	29.45 N	99.13 W
Medina Sidonia, Sp. (sē-dō'nyä)	168	36.28 N	5.58 W
Medio (R.), Arg. (mě'dyō)	139c	33.40 S	60.30 W
Mediterranean Sea, Afr.-Asia-Eur. (měd-ĭ-tēr-ā'nē-ăn)	158	36.22 N	13.25 E
Medjerda (R.), Tun. (mě-jěr'dà)	157	36.43 N	9.54 E
Mednogorsk, Sov. Un.	178	51.27 N	57.22 E
Medvedista (R.), Sov. Un. (měd-vyě'dē tsá)	177	50.10 N	43.40 E
Medvezhegorsk, Sov. Un. (měd-vyězh'yě-gôrsk')	176	63.00 N	34.20 E
Medvezh'y (Is.), Sov. Un.	179	71.00 N	161.25 E
Medway, Ma. (měd'wā)	103a	42.08 N	71.23 W
Medyn', Sov. Un. (mě-děn')	172	54.58 N	35.53 E
Medzhibozh, Sov. Un. (měd-zhē-bōzh')	173	49.23 N	27.29 E
Meekatharra, Austl. (mē-kà-thăr'á)	210	26.30 S	118.38 E
Meeker, Co. (mēk'ēr)	119	40.00 N	107.55 W
Meelpaeg L., Can. (mēl'pá-ěg)	103	48.22 N	56.52 W
Meerane, G.D.R. (mā-rä'nē)	164	50.51 N	12.27 E
Meerbusch, F.R.G.	167c	51.15 N	6.41 E
Meerut, India (mē'rŏŏt)	190	28.59 N	77.43 E
Megalópolis, Grc. (měg-á lŏ'pō-lĭs)	171	37.22 N	22.08 E
Meganom, M.(C.), Sov. Un. (mě-gá-nôm')	173	44.48 N	35.17 E
Mégara, Grc. (měg'á-rá)	171	37.59 N	23.21 E
Megget, SC (měg'ět)	125	32.44 N	80.15 W
Meghelaya (State), India	194	25.30 N	91.30 E
Megler, Wa. (měg'lēr)	116c	46.15 N	123.52 W
Meglino (L.), Sov. Un. (må-glē'nō)	172	58.32 N	35.27 E
Meherrin (R.), Va. (mē-hěr'ĭn)	125	36.40 N	77.49 W
Mehlville, Mo.	117e	38.30 N	90.19 W
Mehsāna, India	190	23.42 N	72.23 E
Mehun-sur-Yèvre, Fr. (mē-ŭN-sür-yěvr')	166	47.11 N	2.14 E
Meiling Pass, China (mā'lĭng')	199	25.22 N	115.00 E
Meinerzhagen, F.R.G. (mī'nĕrts-hä-gĕn)	167c	51.06 N	7.39 E
Meiningen, G.D.R. (mī'nĭng-ĕn)	164	50.35 N	10.25 E
Meiringen, Switz.	164	46.45 N	8.11 E
Meissen, G.D.R.	164	51.11 N	13.28 E
Mei Xian, China (mā shyĕn)	199	24.20 N	116.10 E
Meizhu, China (mā-jōō)	196	31.17 N	119.12 E
Mejillones, Chile (mā-Kē-lyō'nås)	142	23.07 S	70.31 W
Mekambo, Gabon	226	1.01 N	13.56 E
Mekele, Eth.	221	13.31 N	39.19 E
Meknès, Mor. (měk'něs) (měk-něs')	220	33.56 N	5.44 W
Mekong (Lancang) (R.), China (län-tsäŋ)	194	24.45 N	100.31 E

ăt; finăl; rāte; senāte; ärm; àsk; sofá; fâre; ch-choose; dh-as th in other; bē; ēvent; bět; recĕnt; cratēr; g-gō; gh-guttural g; bĭt; ĭ-short neutral; rīde; K-guttural k as ch in German ich;

PRONOUNCING INDEX

Mekong R. – Międzyrzecz 319

PLACE (Pronunciation)	PAGE	Lat. °'	Long. °'
Mekong R., Thai.-Laos	202	17.53 N	103.57 E
Mékrou (R.), Afr.	225	11.35 N	2.25 E
Melaka (Malacca), Mala.	189b	2.11 N	102.15 E
Melaka (State), Mala.	189b	2.19 N	102.09 E
Melbourne, Austl. (mĕl'bŭrn)	207a	37.52 S	145.08 E
Melbourne, Eng.	154	52.49 N	1.26 W
Melbourne, Fl.	125a	28.05 N	80.37 W
Melbourne, Ky.	111f	39.02 N	84.22 W
Melcher, Ia. (mĕl'chẽr)	113	41.13 N	93.11 W
Melekess, Sov. Un. (mĕl-yĕk ĕs)	176	54.20 N	49.30 E
Melenki, Sov. Un. (mĕ-lyĕŋ'kē)	172	55.25 N	41.34 E
Melfort, Can. (mĕl'fôrt)	98	52.52 N	104.36 W
Melik, Wadi el (R.), Sud.	221	16.48 N	29.30 E
Melilla (Sp.), Afr. (mā-lēl'yä)	220	35.24 N	3.30 W
Melipilla, Chile (mā-lē-pē'lyä)	139b	33.40 S	71.12 W
Melita, Can.	99	49.11 N	101.09 W
Melitopol', Sov. Un. (mā-lē-tô'pôl-y')	173	46.49 N	35.19 E
Melívoia, Grc.	171	39.42 N	22.47 E
Melkrivier, S. Afr.	219d	24.01 S	28.23 E
Mellen, Wi. (mĕl'ĕn)	113	46.20 N	90.40 W
Mellerud, Swe. (mål'ĕ-ro͞odh)	162	58.43 N	12.25 E
Melmoth, S. Afr.	223c	28.38 S	31.26 E
Melo, Ur. (mā'lō)	142	32.18 S	54.07 W
Melocheville, Can. (mĕ-lôsh-vēl')	93a	45.24 N	73.56 W
Melozha R., Sov. Un. (myĕ'lô-zhá)	180b	56.06 N	38.34 E
Melrhir Chott (L.), Alg. (mĕl'rēr)	220	33.52 N	5.22 E
Melrose, Ma. (mĕl'rōz)	103a	42.29 N	71.06 W
Melrose, Mn.	113	45.39 N	94.49 W
Melrose Park, Il.	111a	41.54 N	87.52 W
Melsetter, Zimb. (mĕl-sĕt'ẽr)	222	19.44 S	32.51 E
Meltham, Eng. (mĕl'thăm)	154	53.35 N	1.51 W
Melton, Austl. (mĕl'tŭn)	207a	37.41 S	144.35 E
Melton Mowbray, Eng. (mō'brā)	154	52.45 N	0.52 W
Melúli (R.), Moz.	227	16.10 S	39.30 E
Melun, Fr. (mē-lŭN')	167b	48.32 N	2.40 E
Melunga, Ang.	226	17.16 S	16.24 E
Melville, Can. (mĕl'vĭl)	98	50.55 N	102.48 W
Melville, La.	117	30.39 N	91.45 W
Melville, C., Austl.	211	14.15 S	145.50 E
Melville (I.), Austl.	210	11.30 S	131.12 E
Melville (R.), Can.	95	53.46 N	59.31 W
Melville Hills, Can.	94	69.18 N	124.57 W
Melville Pen, Can.	95	67.44 N	84.09 W
Melvindale, Mi. (mĕl'vĭn-dāl)	111b	42.17 N	83.11 W
Mélykút, Hung. (mā'l'ko͞ot)	165	46.14 N	19.21 E
Memba, Moz. (mĕm'bȧ)	223	14.12 N	40.35 E
Memel, see Klaipéda			
Memel, S. Afr. (mĕ'mĕl)	219d	27.42 S	29.35 E
Memmingen, F.R.G. (mĕm'ĭng-ĕn)	164	47.59 N	10.10 E
Memo (R.), Ven. (mĕ'mō)	141b	9.32 N	66.30 W
Memphis, Mo. (mĕm'fĭs)	121	40.27 N	92.11 W
Memphis, Tn. (mĕm'fĭs)	124	35.07 N	90.03 W
Memphis, Tx.	120	34.42 N	100.33 W
Memphis (Ruins), Egypt	219b	29.50 N	31.12 E
Memphremagog (L.), Can. (mĕm'frē-mā'gŏg)	109	45.05 N	72.10 W
Mena, Ar. (mē'nȧ)	121	34.35 N	94.09 W
Mena, Sov. Un. (mē-ná')	173	51.31 N	32.14 E
Menangle, Austl.	207b	34.08 S	150.48 E
Menard, Tx. (mē-närd')	122	30.56 N	99.48 W
Menasha, Wi. (mē-năsh'ȧ)	113	44.12 N	88.29 W
Mende, Fr. (mäNd)	166	44.31 N	3.30 E
Menden, F.R.G. (mĕn'dĕn)	167c	51.26 N	7.47 E
Menderes (R.), Tur. (mĕn'dĕr-ĕs)	177	37.50 N	28.20 E
Mendes, Braz. (mĕ'n-dĕs)	142b	22.32 S	43.44 W
Mendocino, C., Ca. (mĕn'dō-sē'nō)	114	40.25 N	124.22 W
Mendota, Il. (mĕn-dō'tȧ)	113	41.34 N	89.06 W
Mendota (L.), Wi.	113	43.09 N	89.41 W
Mendoza, Arg. (mĕn-dō'sä)	142	32.48 S	68.45 W
Mendoza (Prov.), Arg.	142	35.10 S	69.00 W
Mengcheng, China (mŭŋ-chŭŋ)	196	33.15 N	116.34 E
Meng Shan (Mts.), China (mŭŋ shän)	196	35.47 N	117.23 E
Mengzi, China	194	23.22 N	103.20 E
Menindee, Austl. (mĕ-nĭn-dē)	212	32.23 S	142.30 E
Menlo Park, Ca. (mĕn'lō pärk)	116b	37.27 N	122.11 W
Menno, SD (mĕn'ō)	112	43.14 N	97.34 W
Menominee, Mi. (mē-nŏm'ĭ-nē)	113	45.08 N	87.40 W
Menominee (R.), Mi.-Wi.	113	45.37 N	87.54 W
Menominee Falls, Wi. (fôls)	111a	43.11 N	88.06 W
Menominee Ra, Mi.	113	46.07 N	88.53 W
Menomonee R., Wi.	111a	43.09 N	88.06 W
Menomonie, Wi.	113	44.53 N	91.55 W
Menongue, Ang.	226	14.36 S	17.48 E
Menorca (I.) (Minorca), Sp. (mĕ-nō'r-kä)	169	40.05 N	3.58 E
Mentana, It. (mĕn-tä'nä)	169d	42.02 N	12.40 E
Mentawai, Kepulauan (Is.), Indon. (mĕn-tä-vī')	202	1.08 S	98.10 E
Menton, Fr. (mäN-tôN')	167	43.46 N	7.37 E
Mentone, Ca. (mĕn'tōne)	117a	34.05 N	117.08 W
Mentz (R.), S. Afr. (mĕnts)	223c	33.13 S	25.15 E
Menzel Bourguiba, Tun.	157	37.12 N	9.51 E
Menzelinsk, Sov. Un. (mĕn'zyĕ-lĕnsk')	176	55.40 N	53.15 E
Menzies, Austl. (mĕn'zēz)	210	29.45 S	122.15 E
Meogui, Mex. (mā-ō'gē)	122	28.17 N	105.28 W
Meppel, Neth. (mĕp'ĕl)	161	52.41 N	6.08 E
Meppen, F.R.G. (mĕp'ĕn)	164	52.40 N	7.18 E
Merabéllou, Kólpos (G.), Grc.	170a	35.16 N	25.55 E
Meramec (R.), Mo. (mĕr'ȧ-mĕk)	121	38.06 N	91.06 W
Merano, It. (mā-rä'nō)	170	46.39 N	11.10 E
Merasheen (I), Can. (mĕ'rȧ-shēn)	103	47.30 N	54.15 W
Merauke, Indon. (mā-rou'kā)	203	8.32 S	140.17 E
Meraux, La. (mē-ro')	106d	29.56 N	89.56 W
Mercato San Severino, It. (mĕr-kä'tō sän sĕ-vĕ-rē'nō)	169c	40.34 N	14.38 E
Merced, Ca. (mẽr-sĕd')	118	37.17 N	120.30 W
Merced (R), Ca.	118	37.25 N	120.31 W
Mercedario, Cerro (Mtn.), Chile (mĕr-sā-dhä'rē-ō)	139b	31.58 S	70.07 W
Mercedes, Arg. (mĕr-sā'dhās)	142	29.04 S	58.01 W
Mercedes, Arg.	139c	34.41 S	59.26 W
Mercedes, Tx.	122	26.09 N	97.55 W
Mercedes, Ur.	139c	33.17 S	58.04 W
Mercedita, Chile (mĕr-sĕ-dē'tä)	139b	33.51 S	71.10 W
Mercer Island, Wa. (mûr'sẽr)	116a	47.35 N	122.15 W
Mercês, Braz. (mĕ-sĕ's)	139a	21.13 S	43.20 W
Merchong (R.), Mala.	189b	3.08 N	103.13 E
Merchtem, Bel.	155a	50.57 N	4.13 E
Mercier, Can.	93a	45.19 N	73.45 W
Mercier-Lacombe, Alg. (mĕr-syā' lä-kôNb)	169	35.18 N	0.11 W
Mercy, C., Can.	95	64.48 N	63.22 W
Meredith, NH (mĕr'ē-dĭth)	109	43.35 N	71.35 W
Merefa, Sov. Un. (mā-rĕf'á)	173	49.49 N	36.04 E
Merendón, Serrania de (Mts.), Hond. (sĕr-rä-nē'ä-dā mā-rĕn-dōn')	130	15.01 N	89.05 W
Mereworth, Eng. (mē-rē wûrth)	154b	51.15 N	0.23 E
Mergui, Bur. (mĕr-gē')	202	12.29 N	98.39 E
Mergui Arch, Asia	202	12.04 N	97.02 E
Meric (R.), Grc.-Tur.	162	40.43 N	26.19 E
Mérida, Mex.	130a	20.58 N	89.37 W
Mérida, Ven.	140	8.30 N	71.15 W
Mérida, Cordillera de (Mts.), Ven. (mĕ'rē-dhä)	140	8.30 N	70.45 W
Meriden, Ct. (mĕr'ĭ-dĕn)	109	41.30 N	72.50 W
Meridian, Ms. (mē-rĭd-ĭ-ăn)	124	32.21 N	88.41 W
Meridian, Tx.	123	31.56 N	97.37 W
Mérignac, Fr.	166	44.50 N	0.40 W
Merikarvia, Fin. (mä'rē-kar'vē-ä)	163	61.51 N	21.30 E
Mering, F.R.G. (mĕ'rĕng)	155d	48.16 N	11.00 E
Meriwether Lewis Natl. Mon., Tn. (mĕr'ĭ-wĕth-ẽr lo͞o'ĭs)	124	35.25 N	87.25 W
Merkel, Tx. (mûr'kĕl)	122	32.26 N	100.02 W
Merkinė, Sov. Un. (mĕr'kĭ-nĕ)	163	54.09 N	24.10 E
Merksem, Bel.	155a	51.15 N	4.27 E
Merkys R., Sov. Un. (măr'kĭs)	165	54.23 N	25.00 E
Merlo, Arg. (mĕr-lō)	142a	34.35 S	58.44 W
Merriam, Ks. (mĕr-rĭ-yăm)	117f	39.01 N	94.42 W
Merriam, Mn.	117g	44.44 N	93.36 W
Merrick, NY (mĕr'ĭk)	110a	40.40 N	73.33 W
Merrifield, Va. (mĕr'ĭ-fēld)	110e	38.50 N	77.12 W
Merrill, Wi. (mĕr'ĭl)	113	45.11 N	89.42 W
Merrimac, Ma. (mĕr'ĭ-măk)	103a	45.20 N	71.00 W
Merrimack, NH	103a	42.51 N	71.25 W
Merrimack (R.), Ma.-NH (mĕr'ĭ-măk)	109	43.10 N	71.30 W
Merrimack R., Ma.	103a	42.49 N	70.44 W
Merritt, Can. (mĕr'ĭt)	97	50.07 N	120.47 W
Merryville, La. (mĕr'ĭ-vĭl)	123	30.46 N	93.34 W
Mersa Fatma, Eth.	221	14.54 N	40.14 E
Merseburg, G.D.R. (mĕr'zĕ-bo͞orgh)	164	51.21 N	11.59 E
Mersey (R.), Eng. (mûr'zē)	154	52.52 N	2.04 W
Merseyside (Co.), Eng.	154	53.29 N	2.59 W
Mersin, Tur. (mĕr-sēn')	177	37.00 N	34.40 E
Mersing, Mala.	189b	2.25 N	103.51 E
Merta Road, India (mär'tŭ rōd)	190	26.50 N	73.54 E
Merthyr Tydfil, Wales (mûr'thẽr tĭd'vĭl)	160	51.46 N	3.30 W
Mértola Almodóvar, Port. (mĕr-tō-lȧ-äl-mō-dô'vär)	168	37.39 N	8.04 W
Méru, Fr. (mā-rü')	167b	49.14 N	2.08 E
Meru, Ken. (mā'ro͞o)	221	0.01 N	37.45 E
Meru, Mt., Tan.	227	3.15 S	36.43 E
Merume Mts., Guy. (mĕr-ü'mĕ)	141	5.45 N	60.15 W
Merwerde, Kanal (Can.), Neth.	155a	52.15 N	5.01 E
Merwin (L.), Wa. (mĕr'wĭn)	116c	45.58 N	122.27 W
Merzifon, Tur. (mĕr'ze-fōn)	177	40.50 N	35.30 E
Merzig, F.R.G. (mĕr'tsēg)	167	49.27 N	6.54 E
Mesa, Az. (mā'sȧ)	119	33.25 N	111.50 W
Mesabi Ra., Mn. (mā-sŏb'bē)	113	47.17 N	93.04 W
Mesagne, It. (mā-sän'yâ)	171	40.34 N	17.51 E
Mesa Verde Natl. Park, Co. (vẽr'dē)	119	37.22 N	108.27 W
Mescalero Ind. Res., NM (mĕs-kä-lā'rō)	119	33.10 N	105.45 W
Mesewa (Massaua), Eth.	221	15.40 N	39.19 E
Meshchovsk, Sov. Un. (myĕsh'chĕfsk)	172	54.17 N	35.19 E
Mesilla, NM (mā-sē'yä)	119	32.15 N	106.45 W
Meskine, Chad	225	11.25 N	15.21 E
Mesolóngion, Grc. (mĕ-sō-lôŋ'gē-ōn)	171	38.23 N	21.28 E
Messina, It. (mĕ-sē'nȧ)	170	38.11 N	15.34 E
Messina, S. Afr.	222	22.17 S	30.13 E
Messina, Stretto di (Str.), It. (stĕ't-tô dē)	170	38.10 N	15.34 E
Messíni, Grc.	171	37.05 N	22.00 E
Messiniakós Kólpos (G.), Grc.	171	36.59 N	22.00 E
Mesta (R.), Bul. (mĕ-stá')	171	41.42 N	23.40 E
Mestre, It. (mĕs'trā)	170	45.29 N	12.15 E
Meta (Dept.), Col. (mĕ'tä)	140a	3.28 N	74.07 W
Meta (R.), Col.	140	4.33 N	72.09 W
Métabetchouane (R.), Can. (mĕ-tȧ-bĕt-cho͞o-än')	102	47.45 N	72.00 W
Metairie, La.	123	30.00 N	90.11 W
Metán, Arg. (mĕ-tá'n)	142	25.32 S	64.51 W
Metangula, Moz.	222	12.42 S	34.48 E
Metapán, Sal. (mā-täpän')	130	14.21 N	89.26 W
Metcalfe, Can. (mĕt-käf)	93c	45.14 N	75.27 W
Metchosin, Can.	116a	48.22 N	123.33 W
Metepec, Mex. (mā-tē-pĕk')	128	18.56 N	98.31 W
Metepec, Mex.	129a	19.15 N	99.36 W
Methow R., Wa. (mĕt'hou) (mĕt hou')	114	48.26 N	120.15 W
Methuen, Ma. (mē-thū'ĕn)	103a	42.44 N	71.11 W
Metković, Yugo. (mĕt'kō-vĭch)	171	43.02 N	17.40 E
Metlakatla, Ak. (mĕt-lȧ-kăt'lȧ)	105	55.08 N	131.35 W
Metropolis, Il. (mē-trŏp'ō-lĭs)	121	37.09 N	88.46 W
Metter, Ga. (mĕt'ẽr)	125	32.21 N	82.05 W
Mettmann, F.R.G. (mĕt'män)	167c	51.15 N	6.58 E
Metuchen, NJ (mē-tŭ'chĕn)	110a	40.32 N	74.21 W
Metz, Fr. (mĕts)	167	49.08 N	6.10 E
Metztitlán, Mex. (mĕtz-tēt-län)	128	20.36 N	98.45 W
Meuban, Cam.	225	2.27 N	12.41 E
Meuse (R.), Eur. (mûz) (müz)	166	50.32 N	5.22 E
Mexborough, Eng. (mĕks'bŭr-ô)	154	53.30 N	1.17 W
Mexia, Tx. (mā-hē'ä)	123	31.32 N	96.29 W
Mexicalcingo, Mex. (mĕ-kē-käl-sēn'gō)	129a	19.13 N	99.34 W
Mexicali, Mex. (māk-sē-kä'lē)	118	32.28 N	115.29 W
Mexican Hat, Ut. (mĕk'sĭ-kăn hăt)	119	37.10 N	109.55 W
Mexico, Me. (mĕk'sĭ-kō)	102	44.34 N	70.33 W
Mexico, Mo.	121	39.09 N	91.51 W
Mexico (State), Mex. (māk'sē-kō)	126	19.50 N	99.50 W
Mexico, N. A.	92	23.45 N	104.00 W
Mexico, G. of, N. A.	126	25.15 N	93.45 W
Mexico City, Mex. (mĕk'sĭ-kō)	129a	19.28 N	99.09 W
Mexticacán, Mex. (mĕs'tē-kä-kän')	128	21.12 N	102.43 W
Meyers Chuck, Ak.	96	55.44 N	132.15 W
Meyersdale, Pa. (mī'ẽrz-dāl)	109	39.55 N	79.00 W
Meyerton, S. Afr. (mī'ẽr-tŭn)	219d	26.35 S	28.01 E
Meymaneh, Afg.	192	35.53 N	64.38 E
Mezen', Sov. Un.	176	65.50 N	44.05 E
Mezen' (R), Sov. Un.	176	65.20 N	44.45 E
Mézenc, Mt., Fr. (mĕN-mä-zĕN')	166	44.55 N	4.12 E
Mezha (R.), Sov. Un. (myā'zhá)	172	55.53 N	31.44 E
Mézieres-sur-Seine, Fr. (mā-zyâr'sür-sân')	167b	48.58 N	1.49 E
Mezőkövesd, Hung. (mĕ'zû-kû'vĕsht)	165	47.49 N	20.36 E
Mezőtúr, Hung. (mĕ'zû-to͞or)	165	47.00 N	20.36 E
Mezquital, Mex. (māz-kē-täl')	128	23.30 N	104.20 W
Mezquital (R.), Mex.	128	23.07 N	104.52 W
Mezquitic, Mex. (māz-kē-tēk')	128	22.25 N	103.43 W
Mezquitic (R.), Mex.	128	22.25 N	103.45 W
Mfangano I., Ken.	227	0.28 S	33.35 E
Mga, Sov. Un. (m'gá)	180c	59.45 N	31.04 E
Mgeni (R.), S. Afr.	223c	29.38 S	30.53 E
Mglin, Sov. Un. (m'glĕn')	172	53.03 N	32.52 W
Miacatlán, Mex. (mē'ä-kä-tlän')	128	18.42 N	99.17 W
Miahuatlán, Mex. (mē'ä-wä-tlän')	129	16.20 N	96.38 W
Miajadas, Sp. (mē-ä-hä'däs)	168	39.10 N	5.53 W
Miami, Az.	119	33.20 N	110.55 W
Miami, Fl.	125a	25.45 N	80.11 W
Miami, Ok.	121	36.51 N	94.51 W
Miami, Tx.	120	35.41 N	100.39 W
Miami (R.), Oh.	108	39.20 N	84.45 W
Miami Beach, Fl.	125a	25.47 N	80.07 W
Miami Drainage Can., Fl.	132	26.25 N	80.50 W
Miamisburg, Oh. (mī-ăm'iz-bûrg)	108	39.40 N	84.20 W
Miamitown, Oh. (mī-ăm'ĭ-toun)	111f	39.13 N	84.43 W
Mīāneh, Iran	192	37.15 N	47.13 E
Miangas, Pulau, (I.), Phil. (myä'n-gäs)	203	5.30 N	127.00 E
Miaodao Qundao (Is.), China (mĭou-dou chyo͞on-dou)	196	38.06 N	120.35 E
Miaoli, Taiwan (mē-ou'lĭ)	199	24.30 N	120.48 E
Miaozhen, China (mĭou-jŭn)	196	31.44 N	121.28 E
Miass, Sov. Un. (mī-äs')	180a	55.00 N	60.03 E
Miastko, Pol. (my-äst'kô)	164	54.01 N	17.00 E
Michalovce, Czech. (mē'ĸá-lôf'tsĕ)	165	48.44 N	21.56 E
Michel Pk., Kan.	96	53.35 N	125.25 W
Michelson, Mt. Ak. (mĭch'ĕl-sŭn)	105	69.11 N	144.12 W
Michendorf, F.R.G. (mē'ĸĕn-dôrf)	155b	52.19 N	13.02 E
Miches, Dom. Rep. (mē'chĕs)	133	19.00 N	69.05 W
Michigan (State), U. S. (mĭsh-'ĭ-găn)	107	45.55 N	87.00 W
Michigan, L., U. S.	107	43.20 N	87.10 W
Michigan City, In.	108	41.40 N	86.55 W
Michikamau (L.), Can.	95	54.11 N	63.21 W
Michipicoten (I.), Can. (mĭ-shĭ-pĭ-kō'tĕn)	113	47.49 N	85.50 W
Michipicoten (R.), Can.	113	47.56 N	84.42 W
Michipicoten Harbour, Can.	113	47.58 N	84.58 W
Michoacán (State), Mex.	128	19.15 N	101.30 W
Michurinsk, Sov. Un. (mĭ-cho͞o-rĭnsk')	172	52.53 N	40.32 E
Mico, Punta (Pt.), Nic. (po͞o'n-tä-mē'kō)	131	11.38 N	83.24 W
Midas, Nv. (mī'dȧs)	114	41.15 N	116.50 W
Middelfart, Den. (mēd''l-färt)	162	55.30 N	9.45 E
Middleburg, S. Afr. (mĭd'ĕl-bûrg)	222	31.30 S	25.00 E
Middleburg, S. Afr.	219d	25.47 S	29.30 E
Middlewit, S. Afr. (mĭd'l'wĭt)	219d	24.50 S	27.00 E
Middle (R.), Can.	96	55.00 N	125.50 W
Middle Andaman I., Andaman & Nicobar Is. (ăn-dȧ-măn')	202	12.44 N	93.21 E
Middle Bayou, Tx.	123a	29.38 N	95.06 W
Middle Bight (B.), Ba. (bīt)	132	24.20 N	77.35 W
Middlebury, Vt. (mĭd''l-bĕr-ĭ)	109	44.00 N	73.10 W
Middle Concho, Tx. (kŏn'chō)	122	31.21 N	100.50 W
Middle Loup (R.), Ne. (lo͞op)	112	41.49 N	100.20 W
Middleport, Oh. (mĭd''l-pōrt)	108	39.00 N	82.05 W
Middle River., Md.	110e	39.20 N	76.27 W
Middlesboro, Ky. (mĭd''lz-bŭr-ô)	124	36.36 N	83.42 W
Middlesbrough, Eng. (mĭd''lz-brŭ)	160	54.35 N	1.18 W
Middlesex, NJ (mĭd''l-sĕks)	110a	40.34 N	74.30 W
Middleton, Can. (mĭd''l-tŭn)	102	44.57 N	65.04 W
Middleton, Eng.	154	53.04 N	2.12 W
Middleton (I.), Ak.	105	59.35 N	146.35 W
Middletown, Ct.	109	41.35 N	72.40 W
Middletown, De.	109	39.30 N	75.40 W
Middletown, Ma.	103a	42.35 N	71.01 W
Middletown, NY	110a	41.26 N	74.25 W
Middletown, Oh.	108	39.30 N	84.25 W
Middlewich, Eng. (mĭd''l-wĭch)	154	53.11 N	2.27 W
Midfield, Al.	110h	33.28 N	86.54 W
Midi, Canal du, Fr. (kä-näl-dü-mē-dē')	169	43.22 N	1.35 E
Mid Illovo, S. Afr. (mĭd ĭl'ō-vō)	223c	29.59 S	30.32 E
Midland, Can. (mĭd'lȧnd)	109	44.45 N	79.50 W
Midland, Mi.	108	43.40 N	84.20 W
Midland, Tx.	122	32.05 N	102.05 W
Midvale, Ut. (mĭd'vāl)	117b	40.37 N	111.54 W
Midway, Al. (mĭd'wā)	124	32.03 N	85.30 W
Midway Is., Pac. O.	204	28.00 N	179.00 W
Midwest, Wy. (mĭd-wĕst')	115	43.25 N	106.15 W
Midye, Tur. (mēd'yĕ)	177	41.35 N	28.10 E
Międzyrzecz, Pol. (myăn-dzŭ'zhĕch)	164	52.26 N	15.35 E

320 Mielec – Moçâmedes

PLACE (Pronunciation)	PAGE	Lat. °′	Long. °′
Mielec, Pol. (myĕ'lĕts)	165	50.17 N	21.27 E
Mier, Mex. (myâr)	122	26.26 N	99.08 W
Mieres, Sp. (myā'rās)	168	43.14 N	5.45 W
Mier y Noriega, Mex. (myâr'ē nô-rē-ā'gä)	128	22.28 N	100.08 W
Mirgorod, Sov. Un.	173	49.56 N	33.36 E
Miguel Auza, Mex. (mē-gĕ'l-ä-o͞o'zä)	128	24.17 N	103.27 W
Miguel Pereira, Braz. (pĕ-rā'rä)	142b	22.27 S	43.28 W
Mijares (R.), Sp. (mē-hä'rās)	169	40.05 N	0.42 W
Mikage, Jap. (mē'kä-gä)	201b	34.42 N	135.15 E
Mikawa-Wan (B.), Jap. (mē'kä-wä wän)	201	34.43 N	137.09 E
Mikhaylov, Sov. Un. (mē-кäy'lôf)	172	54.14 N	39.03 E
Mikhaylovka, Sov. Un. (mē-kä'ē-laf-ka)	173	47.16 N	35.12 E
Mikhaylovka, Sov. Un.	177	50.05 N	43.10 E
Mikhaylovka, Sov. Un.	180a	55.35 N	55.57 E
Mikhaylovka, Sov. Un.	180c	59.20 N	30.21 E
Mikhnëvo, Sov. Un. (mĭk-nyô'vô)	180b	55.08 N	37.57 E
Miki, Jap. (mē'kē)	201b	34.47 N	134.59 E
Mikindani, Tan. (mē-kēn-dä'nē)	227	10.17 S	40.07 E
Mikkeli, Fin. (mēk'ē-lī)	163	61.42 N	27.14 E
Mikonos (I.), Grc.	171	37.26 N	25.30 E
Mikulov, Czech. (mĭ'ko͞o-lôf)	164	48.47 N	16.39 E
Mikumi, Tan.	227	7.24 S	36.59 E
Mikuni, Jap. (mē'ko͞o-nē)	201	36.09 N	136.14 E
Mikuni-Sammyaku (Mts.), Jap. (säm'myä-ko͞o)	201	36.51 N	138.38 E
Mikura (I.), Jap. (mē'ko͞o-rä)	201	33.53 N	139.26 E
Milaca, Mn. (mē-lăk'à)	113	45.45 N	93.41 W
Milan, Mi. (mĭ'lăn)	108	42.05 N	83.40 W
Milan, Mo.	121	40.13 N	93.07 W
Milan, Tn.	124	35.54 N	88.47 W
Milan, see Milano			
Milano (Milan), It. (mē-lä'nō)	170	45.29 N	9.12 E
Milâs, Tur. (mē'läs)	177	37.10 N	27.25 E
Milazzo, It. (mē-lät'sô)	170	38.13 N	15.17 E
Milbank, SD (mĭl'băŋк)	112	45.13 N	96.38 W
Mildura, Austl. (mĭl-do͝o'rá)	212	34.10 S	142.18 E
Miles City, Mt. (mīlz)	115	46.24 N	105.50 W
Milford, Ct. (mĭl'fērd)	109	41.15 N	73.05 W
Milford, De.	109	38.55 N	75.25 W
Milford, Ma.	103a	42.09 N	71.31 W
Milford, Mi.	111b	42.35 N	83.36 W
Milford, NH	109	42.50 N	71.40 W
Milford, Oh.	111f	39.11 N	84.18 W
Milford, Ut.	119	38.20 N	113.05 W
Miling, Austl. (mīl''ng)	210	30.30 S	116.25 E
Milipitas, Ca. (mĭl-ĭ-pĭ'tăs)	116b	37.26 N	121.54 W
Milk River, Can. (mĭlk)	97	49.09 N	112.05 W
Milk R., Can.-U.S.	115	48.25 N	108.45 W
Mill Cr., Ca.	118	40.07 N	121.55 W
Mill Cr., Can. (mĭl)	93g	53.13 N	113.25 W
Millau, Fr. (mē-yō')	166	44.06 N	3.04 E
Millbrae, Ca. (mĭl'brā)	116b	37.36 N	122.23 W
Millbury, Ma. (mĭl'bēr-ĭ)	103a	42.12 N	71.46 W
Milledgeville, Ga. (mĭl'ĕj-vĭl)	124	33.05 N	83.15 W
Mille Îles, R. des, Can. (rê-vyâr' dā mĭl'ĭl')	93a	45.41 N	73.40 W
Mille Lac Ind. Res., Mn. (mĭl lăk')	113	46.14 N	94.13 W
Mille Lacs (L.), Mn.	113	46.25 N	93.22 W
Mille Lacs, Lac des (L.), Can. (läk dē mēl läks)	113	48.52 N	90.53 W
Millen, Ga. (mĭl'ĕn)	125	32.47 N	81.55 W
Miller, SD (mĭl'ēr)	112	44.31 N	99.00 W
Millerovo, Sov. Un. (mĭl'ē-rô-vô)	173	48.58 N	40.27 E
Millersburg, Ky. (mĭl'ērz-bûrg)	101	38.15 N	84.10 W
Millersburg, Oh.	101	40.35 N	81.55 W
Millersburg, Pa.	109	40.35 N	76.55 W
Millers Ferry Lake (Res.), Al.	124	32.10 N	87.15 W
Millerton, Can. (mĭl'ēr-tŭn)	102	46.56 N	65.40 W
Millertown, Can. (mĭl'ēr-toun)	103	48.49 N	56.32 W
Millicent, Austl. (mĭl-ĭ-sĕnt)	212	37.30 S	140.20 E
Millinocket, Me. (mĭl-ĭ-nŏk'ĕt)	102	45.40 N	68.44 W
Millis, Ma. (mĭl-ĭs)	103a	42.10 N	71.22 W
Millstadt, Il. (mĭl'stăt)	117e	38.27 N	90.06 W
Millstone (R.), NJ (mĭl'stōn)	110a	40.27 N	74.38 W
Millstream, Austl. (mĭl'strēm)	210	21.45 S	117.10 E
Milltown, Can. (mĭl'toun)	102	45.13 N	67.19 W
Mill Valley, Cal. (mĭl)	116b	37.54 N	122.32 W
Millville, NJ (mĭl'vĭl)	109	39.25 N	75.00 W
Millwood Res., Ar.	121	33.00 N	94.00 W
Milly-la-Forêt, Fr. (mē-yē'-la-fô-rĕ')	167b	48.24 N	2.28 E
Milnerton, S. Afr. (mĭl'nēr-tŭn)	222a	33.52 S	18.30 E
Milnor, ND (mĭl'nēr)	112	46.17 N	97.29 W
Milo, Me.	102	44.16 N	69.01 W
Milo (I.), see Mílos			
Mílos (Milo) (I.), Grc. (mē'lŏs)	171	36.45 N	24.35 E
Milpa Alta, Mex. (mē'l-pä-ä'l-tä)	129a	19.11 N	99.01 W
Milton, Can.	93d	43.31 N	79.53 W
Milton, Fl. (mĭl'tŭn)	124	30.37 N	87.02 W
Milton, Ma.	103a	42.16 N	71.03 W
Milton, Pa.	109	41.00 N	76.50 W
Milton, Ut.	117b	41.04 N	111.44 W
Milton, Wa.	116a	47.15 N	122.20 W
Milton, Wi.	113	42.45 N	89.00 W
Milton-Freewater, Or.	114	45.57 N	118.25 W
Milvale, Pa. (mĭl'văl)	111e	40.29 N	79.58 W
Milwaukee, Wi.	111a	43.03 N	87.55 W
Milwaukee R., Wi.	111a	43.10 N	87.56 W
Milwaukee, Or. (mĭl-wô'kē)	116c	45.27 N	122.38 W
Mimiapan, Mex. (mē-myä-pán')	129a	19.26 N	99.28 W
Mimoso do Sul, Braz. (mē-mō'sō-dô-so͞o'l)	139a	21.03 S	41.21 W
Min (R.), China (mēn)	199	26.03 N	118.30 E
Min (R.), China	199	29.30 N	104.00 E
Mina (R.), Alg. (mē'ná)	169	35.24 N	0.51 E
Minago (R.), Can. (mĭ-nä'gō)	99	54.25 N	98.45 W
Minakuchi, Jap. (mē'ná-ko͞o'chē)	201	34.59 N	136.06 E
Minas, Cuba (mē'näs)	132	21.03 N	77.35 W
Minas, Indon.	189b	0.52 N	101.29 E

PLACE (Pronunciation)	PAGE	Lat. °′	Long. °′
Minas, Ur. (mē'näs)	142	34.18 S	55.12 W
Minas, Sierra de las (Mts.), Guat. (syĕr'rá dä läs mē'näs)	130	15.08 N	90.25 W
Minas Basin, Can. (mī'nás)	102	45.20 N	64.00 W
Minas Chan., Can.	102	45.15 N	64.45 W
Minas de Oro, Hond. (mē'näs-dĕ-dĕ-ō-rô)	130	14.52 N	87.19 W
Minas de Riotinto, Sp. (mē'näs dā rē-ô-tēn'tō)	168	37.43 N	6.35 W
Minas Gerais (State), Braz. (mē'näzh-zhĕ-rä'ēs)	141	17.45 S	43.50 W
Minas Nova, Braz. (mē'näzh nō'väzh)	141	17.20 S	42.19 W
Minatare (L.), Ne. (mĭn'á-târ)	112	41.56 N	103.07 W
Minatitlan, Mex. (mē-nä-tē-tlän')	129	17.59 N	94.33 W
Minatitlan, Mex.	128	19.21 N	104.02 W
Minato, Jap. (mē'ná-tô)	201a	35.13 N	139.52 E
Minch, The (Chan.), Scot.	160	58.04 N	6.04 W
Mindanao (I.), Phil. (mĭn-dä-nou')	203	7.30 N	125.10 E
Mindanao Sea, Phil.	203	8.55 N	124.00 E
Minden, F.R.G. (mĭn'dĕn)	164	52.17 N	8.58 E
Minden, La.	123	32.36 N	93.19 W
Minden, Ne.	120	40.30 N	98.54 W
Mindoro (I.), Phil. (mĭn-dō'rō)	203a	13.04 N	121.06 E
Mindoro Str., Phil.	203a	12.28 N	120.33 E
Mindyak, Sov. Un. (mēn'dyák)	180a	54.01 N	58.48 E
Mineola, NY (mĭn-ē-ō'lá)	110a	40.43 N	73.38 W
Mineola, Tx.	123	32.39 N	95.31 W
Mineral del Chico, Mex. (mē-nā-räl'dĕl chē'kō)	128	20.13 N	98.46 W
Mineral del Monte, Mex. (mē-nā-räl dĕl mōn'tá)	128	20.18 N	98.39 W
Mineral'nyye Vody, Sov. Un.	177	44.10 N	43.15 E
Mineral Point, Wi. (mĭn'ēr-ăl)	113	42.50 N	90.10 W
Mineral Wells, Tx. (mĭn'ēr-ăl wĕlz)	122	32.48 N	98.06 W
Minerva, Oh. (mĭ-nur'vá)	108	40.45 N	81.10 W
Minervino, It. (mē-nĕr-vē'nô)	170	41.07 N	16.05 E
Mineyama, Jap. (mē-nĕ-yä'mä)	201	35.38 N	135.05 E
Mingan, Can.	102	50.18 N	64.02 W
Mingechaur (R.), Sov. Un.	177	41.00 N	47.20 E
Mingenew, Austl. (mĭn'gĕ-nû)	210	29.15 S	115.45 E
Mingo Junction, Oh. (mĭŋ'gō)	108	40.15 N	80.40 W
Minho (Reg.), Port. (mēn yo͞o)	168	41.32 N	8.13 W
Minho (R.), Jam.	132	17.55 N	77.20 W
Minho, Rio (R.), Port. (rē'ō mē'n-yô)	168	41.28 N	9.05 W
Ministik L., Can. (mĭ-nĭs'tĭk)	93g	53.23 N	113.05 W
Minna, Nig. (mĭn'à)	225	9.37 N	6.33 E
Minneapolis, Ks. (mĭn-ē-ăp'ô-lĭs)	121	39.07 N	97.41 W
Minneapolis, Mn.	117g	44.58 N	93.15 W
Minnedosa, Can. (mĭn-ē-dō'sá)	99	50.14 N	99.51 W
Minneota, Mn. (mĭn-ē-ō'tá)	112	44.34 N	95.59 W
Minnesota (State), U. S. (mĭn-ē-sō'tá)	107	46.10 N	90.20 W
Minnesota (R), Mn.	112	45.04 N	96.03 W
Minnetonka (L.), Mn. (mĭn-ē-tôŋ'ká)	113	44.52 N	93.34 W
Minnie Maud Cr., Ut. (mĭn'ĭmôd')	119	39.50 N	110.30 W
Minnitaki L., Can. (mĭ'nĭ-tä'kē)	99	49.58 N	92.00 W
Minō, Jap. (mē'nō)	201b	34.49 N	135.28 E
Mino (R.), Jap.	201b	34.56 N	135.06 E
Miño (R.), Sp. (mē'nyō)	168	42.28 N	7.48 W
Minonk, Il. (mī'nŏnk)	108	40.55 N	89.00 W
Minooka, Il. (mĭ-no͞o'ká)	111a	41.27 N	88.15 W
Minorca (I.), see Menorca			
Minot, ND (mī'nŏt)	112	48.13 N	101.16 W
Minsk, Sov. Un. (mēnsk)	172	53.54 N	27.35 E
Minsk (Oblast), Sov. Un.	172	53.50 N	27.43 E
Mińsk Mazowiecki, Pol. (mēn'sk mä-zô-vyĕt'skĭ)	165	52.10 N	21.35 E
Minsterley, Eng. (mĭnstēr-lē)	154	52.38 N	2.55 W
Minto, Can.	102	46.05 N	66.05 W
Minto (L.), Can.	95	57.18 N	75.50 W
Minturno, It. (mēn-to͞or'nô)	170	41.17 N	13.44 E
Minūf, Egypt (mē-no͞of')	219b	30.26 N	30.55 E
Minusinsk, Sov. Un. (mē-no͞o-sĕnsk')	178	53.47 N	91.45 E
Min'yar, Sov. Un. (mēn'yár)	180	55.06 N	57.33 E
Miquelon (I.), St. Pierre & Miquelon, (mĭk-ē-lôn')	103	47.00 N	56.40 W
Miquelon L., Can. (mĭ'kē-lôn)	93g	53.16 N	112.55 W
Miquihuana, Mex. (mē-kē-wä'nä)	128	23.36 N	99.45 W
Mir, Sov. Un. (mēr)	165	53.27 N	26.25 E
Mira (R.), Port. (mē'rä)	168	37.29 N	8.15 W
Miracema, Braz. (mē-rä-sĕ'mä)	139a	21.24 S	42.10 W
Mirador, Braz. (mē-rá-dōr')	141	6.19 S	44.12 W
Miraflores, Col. (mē-rä-flō'rās)	140	5.10 N	73.13 W
Miraflores, Peru	140	16.19 S	71.20 W
Miraflores Locks, Pan.	126a	9.00 N	79.35 W
Miragoâne, Hai. (mē-rá-gwän')	133	18.25 N	73.05 W
Miraí, Braz. (mē-rá-ē')	139a	21.13 S	42.36 W
Mira Loma, Ca. (mĭ'rá lō'má)	117a	34.01 N	117.32 W
Miramar, Ca. (mĭr'ă-mär)	118a	32.53 N	117.08 W
Miramas, Fr.	166a	43.35 N	5.00 E
Miramichi B., Can. (mĭr'á-mē'shē)	102	47.08 N	65.08 W
Miranda, Col. (mē-rä'n-dä)	140a	3.14 N	76.11 W
Miranda, Ven.	141b	10.09 N	68.24 W
Miranda (State), Ven.	141b	10.17 N	66.41 W
Miranda de Ebro, Sp. (mē-rä'n-dä-dĕ-ĕ'brō)	168	42.42 N	2.59 W
Miranda de Ebro, Port. (mē-rän'dä do͞o-dwĕ'rō)	168	41.30 N	6.17 W
Mirandela, Port. (mē-rän-dā'lá)	168	41.28 N	7.10 W
Mirando City, Tx. (mĭr-án'dō)	122	27.25 N	99.03 W
Mira Por Vos Islets (Is.), Ba. (mē'rä pōr vōs)	133	22.05 N	74.30 W
Mira Por Vos Pass (Str.), Ba.	133	22.10 N	74.35 W
Mirbāt, Om.	192	16.58 N	54.42 E
Mirebalais, Hai. (mēr-bá-lĕ')	133	18.50 N	72.05 W
Mirecourt, Fr. (mēr-ko͞or')	167	48.20 N	6.08 E
Mirfield, Eng. (mûr'fēld)	154	53.41 N	1.42 W
Miri, Mala. (mē'rē)	202	4.13 N	113.56 E
Mirim, L., Braz.-Ur. (mē-rēɴ')	142	33.00 S	53.15 W
Mírina, Grc.	171	39.52 N	25.01 E
Miropol'ye, Sov. Un. (mē-rô-pôl'yĕ)	173	51.02 N	35.13 E

PLACE (Pronunciation)	PAGE	Lat. °′	Long. °′
Mīrpur Khās, Pak. (mēr'po͞or кäs)	190	25.36 N	69.10 E
Mirzāpur, India (mēr'zä-po͞or)	190	25.12 N	82.38 E
Misantla, Mex. (mē-sän'tlä)	129	19.55 N	96.49 W
Miscou (I.), Can. (mĭs'kō)	102	47.58 N	64.35 W
Miscou Pt., Can.	102	48.04 N	64.32 W
Miseno, C., It. (mē-zĕ'nō)	169c	40.33 N	14.12 E
Misery, Mt., St. Kitts-Nevis (mĭz'rē-ĭ)	131b	17.28 N	62.47 W
Mishan, China (mĭ'shäɴ)	200	45.32 N	132.19 E
Mishawaka, In. (mĭsh-á-wôk'á)	108	41.45 N	86.15 W
Mishina, Jap. (mē'shē-mä)	201	35.09 N	138.56 E
Misiones (Prov.), Arg. (mē-syō'nās)	142	27.00 S	54.30 W
Miskito, Cayos (Is.), Nic.	131	14.34 N	82.30 W
Miskolc, Hung. (mĭsh'kôlts)	165	48.07 N	20.50 E
Misool (I.), Pulau, Indon. (mē-so͞ol')	203	2.00 S	130.05 E
Misquah Hills, Mn. (mĭs-kwä' hĭlz)	113	47.50 N	90.30 W
Mişr al Jadīdah (Ruins), Egypt	219b	30.06 N	31.35 E
Misrātah, Libya	221	32.23 N	14.58 E
Missinaibi (R.), Can. (mĭs'ĭn-ä'ē-bē)	95	50.27 N	83.01 W
Missinaibi L., Can.	100	48.23 N	83.40 W
Mission, Ks. (mĭsh'ŭn)	117f	39.02 N	94.39 W
Mission, Tx.	122	26.14 N	98.19 W
Mission City, Can. (sĭ'tĭ)	116d	49.08 N	112.18 W
Mississagi (R.), Can.	100	46.35 N	83.30 W
Mississauga, Can.	93d	43.34 N	79.37 W
Mississinewa (R.), In. (mĭs-ĭ-sĭn'ē-wä)	108	40.30 N	85.45 W
Mississippi (State), U.S. (mĭs-ĭ-sĭp'ē)	107	32.30 N	89.45 W
Mississippi (L.), Can.	109	45.05 N	76.15 W
Mississippi (R.), U. S.	107	31.50 N	91.30 W
Mississippi Sd., Ms.	124	34.16 N	89.10 W
Missoula, Mt. (mĭ-zo͞o'lá)	115	46.25 N	114.00 W
Missouri (State), U. S. (mĭ-so͞o'rē)	107	38.00 N	93.40 W
Missouri (R.), U. S.	107	40.40 N	96.00 W
Missouri City, Tx.	123a	29.37 N	95.32 W
Missouri Coteau, (Plat.), U. S.	106	47.30 N	101.00 W
Missouri Valley, Ia.	112	41.35 N	95.53 W
Mist, Or. (mĭst)	116c	46.00 N	123.15 W
Mistassibi (R.), Can. (mĭs-tá-sĭ'bē)	102	49.44 N	69.58 W
Mistassini, Can. (mĭs-tá-sĭ'nē)	102	48.56 N	71.55 W
Mistassini (L.), Can. (mĭs-tá-sĭ'nē)	95	50.48 N	73.30 W
Mistassini (R.), Can.	102	50.02 N	72.38 W
Mistelbach, Aust. (mĭs'tĕl-bäk)	164	48.34 N	16.33 E
Misteriosa, L., Mex. (mēs-tē-ryō'sä)	130a	18.05 N	90.15 W
Mistretta, It. (mē-strĕt'tä)	170	37.54 N	14.22 E
Mita, Punta de (Pt.), Mex. (po͞o'n-tä-dĕ-mē'tä)	128	20.44 N	105.34 W
Mitaka, Jap. (mē'tä-kä)	201a	35.42 N	139.34 E
Mitchell, Il. (mĭch'ĕl)	117e	38.46 N	90.05 W
Mitchell, In.	108	38.45 N	86.25 W
Mitchell, Ne.	112	41.56 N	103.49 W
Mitchell, SD	112	43.42 N	98.01 W
Mitchell (R.), Austl.	211	15.30 S	142.15 E
Mitchell, Mt., NC	125	35.47 N	82.15 W
Mīt Ghamr, Egypt	219b	30.43 N	31.20 E
Mitilíni, Grc.	171	39.09 N	26.35 E
Mitla P., Egypt	189a	30.03 N	32.40 E
Mito, Jap. (mē'tō)	201	36.20 N	140.23 E
Mitsu, Jap. (mēt'so͞o)	201	34.21 N	132.49 E
Mittelland (Can.), G.D.R. (mĭt'ĕl-lănd)	164	52.18 N	10.42 E
Mittenwalde, G.D.R. (mē'tĕn-väl-dĕ)	155b	52.16 N	13.33 E
Mittweida, G.D.R. (mĭt-vī'dä)	164	50.59 N	12.58 E
Mitumba, Monts (Mts.), Zaire	227	10.50 S	27.00 E
Mityayevo, Sov. Un. (mĭt-yä'yĕ-vô)	180a	60.17 N	61.02 E
Miura, Jap.	201a	35.08 N	139.37 E
Mius (R.), Sov. Un. (mē-o͞os')	173	47.30 N	38.48 W
Miwa, Jap. (mē'wä)	201b	34.32 N	135.51 E
Mixico, Guat. (mēs'kō)	130	14.37 N	90.37 W
Mixquiahuala, Mex. (mēs-kē-wä'lä)	128	20.12 N	99.13 W
Mixteco (R.), Mex. (mēs-tā'kō)	128	17.45 N	98.10 W
Miyake, Jap. (mē'yä-kā)	201b	34.35 N	135.34 E
Miyake (I.), Jap. (mē'yä-kā)	201	34.06 N	139.21 E
Miyakonojō, Jap. (mē'yá-kô'nô-jô)	201	31.42 N	131.03 E
Miyazaki, Jap. (mē'yá-zä'kē)	201	31.55 N	131.27 E
Miyoshi, Jap. (mē-yō'shē')	201	34.48 N	132.49 E
Mizdah, Libya (mēz'dä)	158	31.29 N	13.09 E
Mizil, Rom. (mē'zēl)	171	45.01 N	26.30 E
Mizonokuchi, see Takatsu			
Mizoram (Union Ter.), India	190	23.25 N	92.45 E
Mjölby, Swe. (myûl'bü)	162	58.20 N	15.09 E
Mjörn (L.), Swe.	162	57.55 N	12.22 E
Mjösa, Nor. (myûsä)	162	60.41 N	11.25 E
Mkalama, Tan.	222	4.07 S	34.38 E
Mkomazi (R.), S. Afr.	223c	30.10 S	30.30 E
Mkushi, Zambia	227	13.40 S	29.20 E
Mkwaja, Tan.	227	5.47 S	38.51 E
Mladá Boleslav, Czech. (mlä'dä bô'lĕ-slaf)	164	50.26 N	14.52 E
Mlala Hills, Tan.	227	6.47 S	31.45 E
Mlanje Mts., Malawi	227	15.55 S	35.30 E
Mława, Pol. (mwä'vá)	165	53.07 N	20.25 E
Mlazi (R.), S. Afr.	223c	29.52 S	30.42 E
Mljet (I.), Yugo. (mlyĕt)	171	42.40 N	17.45 E
Mo (R.), Togo	224	9.05 N	0.55 E
Moa, Pulau, (I.), Indon.	203	8.30 S	128.30 E
Moa (R.), S. L.	224	7.40 N	11.15 W
Moab, Ut. (mō'ăb)	119	38.35 N	109.35 W
Moanda, Gabon	222	1.37 S	13.09 E
Moapa River Ind. Res., Nv. (mō-ăp'á)	118	36.44 N	115.01 W
Moar L., Can. (môr)	99	52.00 N	95.09 W
Mobaye, Cen. Afr. Rep. (mô-bä'y')	226	4.19 N	21.11 E
Mobayi-Mbongo, Zaire	221	4.14 N	21.11 E
Moberly, Mo. (mō'bēr-lĭ)	121	39.24 N	92.25 W
Moberly (R.), Can.	97	55.40 N	121.15 W
Mobile, Al. (mô-bēl')	124	30.42 N	88.03 W
Mobile (R.), Al.	124	31.15 N	88.00 W
Mobile B., Al.	124	30.26 N	87.56 W
Mobridge, SD (mō'brĭj)	112	45.32 N	100.26 W
Moca, Dom. Rep. (mō'kä)	133	19.25 N	70.35 W
Moçambique, Moz. (mō-säɴ-bē'kĕ)	227	15.03 S	40.42 E
Moçâmedes, Ang. (mô-zá-mĕ-dĕs)	226	15.10 S	12.09 E

ăt; finăl; rāte; senăte; ärm; ȧsk; sofá; fâre; ch-choose; dh-as th in other; bē; ēvent; bĕt; recĕnt; cratēr; g-gō; gh-guttural g; bĭt; ĭ-short neutral; rīde; к-guttural k as ch in German ich;

PRONOUNCING INDEX

Moçâmedes – Moore Res. 321

PLACE (Pronunciation)	PAGE	Lat. °'	Long. °'
Moçâmedes (Reg.), Ang.	222	16.00 S	12.15 E
Mocha, Yemen (mō'kä)	192	13.11 N	43.20 E
Mochitlán, Mex. (mō-chē-tlän')	128	17.10 N	99.19 W
Mochudi, Bots. (mō-chōō'dē)	222	24.13 S	26.07 E
Mocímboa da Praia, Moz. (mô-sē'ĕm-bō-ȧ prä'ēä)	227	11.20 S	40.21 E
Moclips, Wa.	114	47.14 N	124.13 W
Môco, Serra (Mts.), Arg.	226	12.25 S	15.10 E
Mococa, Braz. (mō-kô'kȧ)	139a	21.29 S	46.58 W
Moctezuma, Mex. (môk'tā-zōō'mä)	128	22.44 N	101.06 W
Mocuba, Moz.	227	16.50 S	36.59 E
Modderfontein, S. Afr.	223b	26.06 S	28.10 E
Modena, It. (mô'dē-nä)	170	44.38 N	10.54 E
Modesto, Ca. (mô-dĕs'tō)	118	37.39 N	121.00 W
Modica, It. (mô'dē-kä)	157	36.50 N	14.43 E
Mödling, Aust. (mûd'lĭng)	155e	48.06 N	16.17 E
Moelv, Nor.	162	60.55 N	10.40 E
Moengo, Sur.	141	5.43 N	54.19 W
Moenkopi, Az.	119	36.07 N	111.13 W
Moers, F.R.G. (mûrs)	167c	51.27 N	6.38 E
Moffat Tun., Co. (môf'ăt)	120	39.52 N	106.20 W
Mogadore, Oh. (mŏg-ȧ-dōr')	111d	41.04 N	81.23 E
Mogaung, Bur. (mō-gä'ōōng)	194	25.30 N	96.52 E
Mogi das Cruzes, Braz. (mô-gē-däs-krōō'sĕs)	139a	23.33 S	46.10 W
Mogi-Guaçu (R.), Braz. (mô-gē-gwä'sōō)	139a	22.06 S	47.12 W
Mogilëv, Sov. Un. (mô-gē-lyôf')	172	53.53 N	30.22 E
Mogilëv (Oblast), Sov. Un. (mô-gē-lyôf')	172	53.28 N	30.15 E
Mogilëv-Podol'skiy, Sov. Un. (mô-gē-lyôf) (pô-dôl'skĭ)	173	48.27 N	27.51 E
Mogilno, Pol. (mô-gēl'nô)	165	52.38 N	17.58 W
Mogi-Mirim, Braz. (mô-gē-mē-rē'N)	139a	22.26 S	46.57 W
Mogincual, Moz.	227	15.35 S	40.25 E
Mogok, Bur. (mô-gōk')	194	23.14 N	96.38 E
Mogollon, NM (mō-gô-yōn')	119	33.25 N	108.45 W
Mogollon, Plat., Az. (mō-gô-yōn')	119	34.26 N	111.17 W
Mogol R., S. Afr. (mô-gŏl)	219d	24.12 S	27.55 E
Moguer, Sp. (mô-gĕr')	168	37.15 N	6.50 W
Mohács, Hung. (mô'häch)	165	45.59 N	18.38 E
Mohale's Hoek, Leso.	223c	30.09 S	27.28 E
Mohall, ND (mō'hôl)	112	48.46 N	101.29 W
Mohammadia, Alg.	169	35.35 N	0.05 E
Mohave (L.), Nv. (mô-hä'vā)	118	35.23 N	114.40 W
Mohawk (R.), NY (mō'hôk)	109	43.15 N	75.20 W
Mohe, China (mwo-hŭ)	195	53.33 N	122.30 E
Moheli (I.), Comoros (mô-ȧ-lē') (mô-hä'lē)	223	12.23 S	43.38 E
Mohenjo-Dero (Ruins), Pak.	190	27.20 N	68.10 E
Mõisaküla, Sov. Un. (mẽē'sȧ-kü'lȧ)	163	58.07 N	25.12 E
Moisie (R.), Can. (mwȧ-zē')	103	50.35 N	66.25 W
Moissac, Fr. (mwä-sȧk')	166	44.07 N	1.05 E
Moita, Port. (mô-ē'tȧ)	169b	38.39 N	9.00 W
Mojave, Ca.	118	35.06 N	118.09 W
Mojave (R.), Ca. (mô-hä'vä)	118	34.46 N	117.24 W
Mojave Desert, Ca.	118	35.05 N	117.30 W
Mokelumne (R.), Ca. (mō-kē-lŭm'nē)	118	38.30 N	120.17 W
Mokhotlong, Leso.	223c	29.18 S	29.06 E
Mokp'o, Kor. (môk'pō')	200	34.50 N	126.30 E
Moksha (R.), Sov. Un. (môk-shä')	176	54.40 N	43.20 E
Mol, Bel.	155a	51.21 N	5.09 E
Molat (I.), Yugo. (mô'lät)	170	44.15 N	14.40 E
Moldavia (Reg.), Rom.	165	47.20 N	27.12 E
Moldavian S. S. R., Sov. Un.	174	48.00 N	28.00 E
Molde, Nor. (môl'dē)	162	62.44 N	7.15 E
Moldova R., Rom.	165	47.17 N	26.27 E
Moldoveanu (Mtn.), Rom.	171	45.33 N	24.38 E
Molepolole, Bots. (mō-lȧ-pô-lō'lȧ)	222	24.15 S	25.33 W
Molfetta, It. (môl-fĕt'tä)	170	41.11 N	16.38 E
Molina, Chile (mŏ-lē'nä)	139b	35.07 S	71.17 W
Molina de Aragón, Sp. (mô-lē'nä dē ä-rä-gô'n)	168	41.40 N	1.54 W
Molina de Segura, Sp. (mô-lē'nä dē sĕ-gōō'rä)	168	38.03 N	1.07 W
Moline, Il. (mô-lēn')	113	41.31 N	90.34 W
Moliro, Zaire	227	8.13 S	30.34 E
Moliterno, It. (môl-ē-tĕr'nō)	170	40.13 N	15.54 W
Mollendo, Peru (mô-lyĕn'dō)	140	17.02 S	71.59 W
Moller, Port, Ak. (pōrt mōl'ĕr)	105	56.18 N	161.30 W
Mölndal, Swe. (mûln'däl)	162	57.39 N	12.01 E
Molochnaya (R.), Sov. Un. (mô-lôch'nȧ-yȧ) (rĕ-kä')	173	47.05 N	35.22 E
Molochnoye, Ozero (L.), Sov. Un. (ô'zĕ-rô mô-lôch'nô-yĕ)	173	46.35 N	35.32 E
Molodechno, Sov. Un. (mô-lô-dĕch'nô)	172	54.18 N	26.57 E
Molodechno (Oblast), Sov. Un.	172	54.27 N	27.38 E
Molody Tud, Sov. Un. (mō-lō-dō'ē tōō'd)	180b	55.17 N	37.31 E
Mologa (R.), Sov. Un. (mô-lô'gȧ)	172	58.05 N	35.43 E
Molokai (I.), Hi. (mō-lô kä'ē)	104a	21.15 N	157.05 E
Molokcha R., Sov. Un. (mô'lôk-chä)	180b	56.15 N	38.29 E
Molopo (R.), S. Afr. (mō-lō-pô)	222	27.45 S	20.45 E
Molson L., Can. (mōl'sŭn)	99	54.12 N	96.45 W
Molteno, S. Afr. (môl-tā'nô)	223c	31.24 S	26.23 E
Moma, Moz.	227	16.44 S	39.14 E
Mombasa, Ken. (mōm-bä'sȧ)	227	4.03 N	39.40 E
Mombetsu, Jap. (môm'bĕt-sōō')	200	44.21 N	142.48 E
Momboyo (R.), Zaire	226	0.20 S	19.20 E
Momence, Il. (mô-mĕns')	111a	41.09 N	87.40 W
Momostenango, Guat. (mô-mōs-tā-näŋ'gô)	130	15.02 N	91.25 W
Momotombo, Nic.	130	12.25 N	86.43 W
Mompog Pass, Phil. (mŏm-pŏg')	203a	13.35 N	122.09 E
Mompos, Col. (mōm-pŏs')	140	8.05 N	74.30 W
Møn (I.), Den. (mûn)	162	54.54 N	12.30 E
Monaca, Pa. (mō-nȧ'kō)	111e	40.41 N	80.17 W
Monaco, Eur. (mŏn'ȧ-kō)	157	43.43 N	7.47 E
Monaghan, Ire. (mō'ȧ-găn)	160	54.16 N	7.20 W
Mona Pass, N.A. (mō'nä)	127	18.00 N	68.10 W
Monarch Mtn., Can. (mŏn'ērk)	96	51.41 N	125.53 W
Monashee Mts., Can. (mŏ-nă'shē)	97	50.30 N	118.30 W
Monastir, Tun. (mōn-ȧs-tēr')	157	35.49 N	10.56 E
Monastir, see Bitola			
Monastyrishche, Sov. Un. (mô-nȧs-tē-rēsh'chȧ)	173	48.57 N	29.53 E
Monastyrshchina, Sov. Un. (mô-nȧs-tērsh'chĭ-nȧ)	172	54.19 N	31.49 E
Monçao, Braz. (mon-souN')	141	3.39 S	45.23 W
Moncayo (Mtn.), Sp. (môn-kä'yō)	168	41.44 N	1.48 W
Monchegorsk, Sov. Un. (mōn'chē-gôrsk)	176	69.00 N	33.35 E
Mönchengladbach, F.R.G. (mûn'κĕn glăd'bäκ)	167c	51.12 N	6.28 E
Moncique, Serra de (Mts.), Port. (sĕr'rä dä môn-chē'kĕ)	168	37.22 N	8.37 W
Monclova, Mex. (môn-klō'vä)	122	26.53 N	101.25 W
Moncton, Can. (mŭŋk'tŭn)	102	46.06 N	64.47 W
Mondego, Cabo (C.), Port. (kȧ'bō môn-dā'gōō)	168	40.12 N	8.55 W
Mondêgo (R.), Port. (mōn-dĕ'gō)	168	40.10 N	8.36 W
Mondombe, Zaire (mōn-dôm'bȧ)	222	0.45 S	23.06 E
Mondoñedo, Sp. (môn-dô-nyā'dō)	168	43.35 N	7.18 W
Mondoví, It. (mōn-dô'vē')	170	44.23 N	7.53 E
Mondovi, Wi. (mŏn-dō'vĭ)	113	44.35 N	91.42 W
Monee, Il. (mō-nĭ)	111a	41.25 N	87.45 W
Monessen, Pa. (mō'nĕs'sen)	111e	40.09 N	79.53 W
Monett, Mo. (mô-nĕt')	121	36.55 N	93.55 W
Monforte de Lemos, Sp. (môn-fôr'tä dē lĕ'môs)	168	42.30 N	7.30 W
Monga, Chad	225	4.12 N	22.49 E
Mongala R., Zaire (mōn-gál'ȧ)	221	3.20 N	21.30 E
Mongalla, Sud.	221	5.11 N	31.46 E
Monghyr, India (mōn-gēr')	190	25.23 N	86.34 E
Mongo (R.), S.L.	224	9.50 N	11.50 W
Mongolia, Asia (mŏŋ-gō'lĭ-ȧ)	188	46.00 N	100.00 E
Mongos, Chaîne des (Mts.), Cen. Afr. Rep.	221	8.04 N	21.59 E
Mongoumba, Cen. Afr. Rep. (mŏŋ-gōōm'bȧ)	226	3.38 N	18.36 E
Mongu, Zambia (mŏŋ-gōō')	226	15.15 S	23.09 E
Monkey Bay, Malawi	227	14.05 S	34.55 E
Monkey River, Belize (mŭŋ'kĭ)	130a	16.22 N	88.33 W
Monkland, Can. (mŭngk-lănd)	93c	45.12 N	74.52 W
Monkoto, Zaire (môn-kō'tô)	226	1.38 S	20.39 E
Monmouth, Il. (mŏn'mŭth)(mŏn'mouth)	121	40.54 N	90.38 W
Monmouth Junction, NJ (mŏn'mouth jŭngk'shŭn)	110a	40.23 N	74.33 W
Monmouth Mtn., Can. (mŏn'mŭth)	96	51.00 N	123.47 W
Mono (L.), Can. (mō'nō)	118	38.04 N	119.00 W
Mono (R.), Togo	224	7.20 N	1.25 E
Monon, In. (mō'nŏn)	108	40.55 N	86.55 W
Monongah, WV (mô-nŏŋ'gȧ)	109	39.25 N	80.10 W
Monongahela, Pa. (mô-nŏn-gȧ-hē'lȧ)	111e	40.11 N	79.55 W
Monongahela (R.), WV	109	39.30 N	80.10 W
Monopoli, It. (mô-nô'pô-lē)	171	40.55 N	17.17 E
Monóvar, Sp. (mô-nō'vär)	169	38.26 N	0.50 W
Monreale, It. (mōn-rā-ä'lā)	170	38.04 N	13.15 E
Monroe, Ga. (mŭn-rō')	124	33.47 N	83.43 W
Monroe, La.	123	32.30 N	92.06 W
Monroe, Mi.	108	41.55 N	83.25 W
Monroe, NY	110a	41.19 N	74.11 W
Monroe, NC	125	34.58 N	80.34 W
Monroe, Ut.	119	38.35 N	112.10 W
Monroe, Wa.	116a	47.52 N	121.58 W
Monroe, Wi.	113	42.35 N	89.40 W
Monroe (L.), Fl.	125	28.50 N	81.15 W
Monroe City, Mo.	121	39.38 N	91.41 W
Monroeville, Al. (mŭn-rō'vĭl)	124	31.33 N	87.19 W
Monrovia, Ca. (mōn-rō'vĭ-ȧ)	117a	34.09 N	118.00 W
Monrovia, Lib.	224	6.18 N	10.47 W
Mons, Bel. (môN')	161	50.29 N	3.55 E
Monson, Me. (mŏn'sŭn)	102	45.17 N	69.28 W
Mönsterås, Swe. (mŭn'stĕr-ôs)	162	57.04 N	16.24 E
Montagh Ata (Mt.), China	194	38.26 N	75.23 E
Montagne Tremblante Prov. Pk., Can.	107	46.30 N	75.51 W
Montague, Can. (mŏn'tȧ-gū)	103	46.10 N	62.39 W
Montague, Mi.	108	43.30 N	86.25 W
Montague (I.), Ak.	105	60.10 N	147.00 W
Montalbán, Ven. (mōnt-äl-bän)	141b	10.14 N	68.19 W
Montalcone, It. (môn-täl-kō'nē)	170	45.49 N	13.30 E
Montalegre, Port. (mōn-tä-lā'grĕ)	168	41.49 N	7.48 W
Montana (State), U.S. (mŏn-tăn'ȧ)	106	47.10 N	111.50 W
Montánchez, Sp. (môn-tän'chāth)	168	39.18 N	6.09 W
Montargis, Fr. (môN-tár-zhē')	166	47.59 N	2.42 E
Montataire, Fr. (môN-tá-târ)	167b	49.15 N	2.26 E
Montauban, Fr. (môN-tô-băN')	166	44.01 N	1.22 E
Montauk, NY	109	41.03 N	71.57 W
Montauk Pt., NY (mŏn-tôk')	109	41.05 N	71.55 W
Montbanch, Sp. (mônt-băn'ch)	169	41.20 N	1.08 E
Montbard, Fr. (môN-bár')	166	47.40 N	4.19 E
Montbéliard, Fr. (môN-bā-lyár')	167	47.32 N	6.45 E
Mont Belvieu, Tx. (mŏnt bĕl'vū)	123a	29.51 N	94.53 W
Montbrison, Fr. (môN-brē-zoN')	166	45.38 N	4.06 E
Montceau, Fr. (môN-sō')	166	46.39 N	4.22 E
Montclair, NJ (mŏnt-klâr')	110a	40.49 N	74.13 W
Mont-de-Marsan, Fr. (môN-dē-már-săN')	166	43.54 N	0.32 W
Montdidier, Fr. (môN-dē-dyā')	166	49.42 N	2.33 E
Monte, Arg. (mŏ'n-tĕ)	139c	35.25 S	58.49 W
Monteagudo, Bol. (mōn'tā-ä-gōō'dhō)	140	19.49 S	63.48 W
Montebello, Ca. (mŏn-tē-bĕl'ō)	117a	34.01 N	118.06 W
Montebello, Can.	93c	45.40 N	74.56 W
Monte Bello (Is.), Austl.	210	20.30 S	114.10 E
Monte Caseros, Arg. (mŏ'n-tĕ-kä-sĕ'rôs)	142	30.16 S	57.39 W
Mont Ecillos, Cord. de (Mts.), Hond. (kôr-dĕl-yĕ'rä dĕ mô'nt ĕ-sē'l-yōs)	130	14.19 N	87.52 W
Monte Cristi, Dom. Rep. (mô'n-tĕ-krē's-tē)	133	19.50 N	71.40 W
Montecristo, I. di, It. (mōn'tā-krēs'tō)	170	42.20 N	10.19 E
Monte Escobedo, Mex. (mōn'tā ĕs-kô-bā'dhō)	128	22.18 N	103.34 W
Monteforte Irpino, It. (môn-tē-fô'r-tē ē'r-pē'nō)	169c	40.39 N	14.42 E
Montefrío, Sp. (mōn-tā-frē'ō)	168	37.20 N	4.02 W
Montego Bay, Jam. (mŏn-tē'gō)	132	18.30 N	77.55 W
Monte Grande, Arg. (mô'n-tē grän'dĕ)	142a	34.34 S	58.28 W
Montelavar, Port. (mōn-tē-lȧ-vär')	169b	38.51 N	9.20 W
Montélimar, Fr. (môN-tā-lē-mär')	166	44.33 N	4.47 E
Montellano, Sp. (mōn-tā-lyä'nō)	168	37.00 N	5.34 W
Montello, Wi. (mŏn-tĕl'ō)	113	43.47 N	89.20 W
Montemorelos, Mex. (mōn'tā-mō-rā'lōs)	122	25.14 N	99.50 W
Montemor-o-Novo, Port. (môN-tē-mōr'ōō-nō'vōō)	168	38.39 N	8.11 W
Montenegro (Reg.), **see Crna Gora**			
Montepuez, Moz.	227	13.07 S	39.00 E
Montepulciano, It. (mōn'tā-pōōl-chä'nō)	170	43.05 N	11.48 E
Montereau-faut-Yonne, Fr. (môN-t'rō'fō-yôn')	166	48.24 N	2.57 E
Monterey, Ca. (mŏn-tĕ-rā')	118	36.36 N	121.53 W
Monterey, Tn.	124	36.06 N	85.15 W
Monterey B., Ca.	118	36.48 N	122.01 W
Monterey Park, Ca.	117a	34.04 N	118.08 W
Montería, Col. (mōn-tā-rä'ä)	140	8.47 N	75.57 W
Monteros, Arg. (mōn-tĕ'rôs)	142	27.14 S	65.29 W
Monterotondo, It. (mōn-tē-rō-tô'n-dō)	169d	42.03 N	12.39 E
Monterrey, Mex. (mōn-tĕr-rā')	122	25.43 N	100.19 W
Monte Sant' Angelo, It. (mô'n-tē sän ä'n-gzhē-lō)	170	41.43 N	15.59 E
Montesano, Wa. (mŏn-tē-sä'nō)	114	46.59 N	123.35 W
Montes Claros, Braz. (môn-tēs-klä'rôs)	141	16.44 S	43.41 W
Montevallo, Al. (mōn-tē-văl'ō)	124	33.05 N	86.49 W
Montevarchi, It. (mōn-tā-vär'kē)	170	43.30 N	11.45 E
Montevideo, Ur. (mōn'tā-vē-dhā'ō)	139c	34.50 S	56.10 W
Monte Vista, Co. (mŏn'tē vĭs'tȧ)	119	37.35 N	106.10 W
Montezuma, Ga. (mŏn-tē-zōō'mȧ)	124	32.17 N	84.00 W
Montezuma Castle Natl. Mon., Az.	119	34.38 N	111.50 W
Montfoort, Neth.	155a	52.02 N	4.56 E
Montfort, Fr. (môN-fôr)	166	48.09 N	1.58 W
Montfor-l'Amaury, Fr. (môN-fôr'lä-mō-rē')	167b	48.47 N	1.49 E
Montgomery, Al. (mŏnt-gŭm'ēr-ĭ)	124	32.23 N	86.17 W
Montgomery, WV	108	38.10 N	81.25 W
Montgomery City, Mo.	121	38.58 N	91.29 W
Monticello, Ar. (mŏn-tĭ-sĕl'ō)	121	33.38 N	91.47 W
Monticello, Fl.	124	30.32 N	83.53 W
Monticello, Ga.	124	33.00 N	83.11 W
Monticello, Il.	108	40.05 N	88.35 W
Monticello, In.	108	40.40 N	86.50 W
Monticello, Ia.	113	42.14 N	91.13 W
Monticello, Ky.	124	36.47 N	84.50 W
Monticello, Me.	102	46.19 N	67.53 W
Monticello, Mn.	113	45.18 N	93.48 W
Monticello, NY	109	41.35 N	74.40 W
Monticello, Ut.	119	37.55 N	109.25 W
Montijo, Port. (môn-tē'zhō)	169b	38.42 N	8.58 W
Montijo, Sp. (môn-tē'hō)	168	38.55 N	6.35 W
Montijo, Bahía (B.), Pan. (bä-ē'ä môn-tē'hō)	131	7.36 N	81.11 W
Mont-Joli, Can. (môN zhô-lē')	102	48.35 N	68.11 W
Montluçon, Fr. (môN-lü-sôN')	166	46.20 N	2.35 E
Montmagny, Can. (môN-mán-yē')	93b	46.59 N	70.33 W
Montmorency, Fr. (môN'mô-răN-sē')	167b	48.59 N	2.19 E
Montmorency (R.), Can. (mŏnt-mô-rĕn'sĭ)	93b	47.30 N	71.10 W
Montmorillon, Fr. (môN'mô-rē-yôN')	166	46.26 N	0.50 E
Montone (R.), It. (môn-tô'nē)	170	44.03 N	11.45 E
Montoro, Sp. (môn-tō'rō)	168	38.01 N	4.22 W
Montpelier, In. (mŏnt-pēl'yēr)	108	40.35 N	85.20 W
Montpelier, Id.	115	42.19 N	111.19 W
Montpelier, Oh.	108	41.35 N	84.35 W
Montpelier, Vt.	109	44.20 N	72.35 W
Montpellier, Fr. (môN-pē-lyā')	166	43.38 N	3.53 E
Montréal, Can. (mŏn-trē-ôl')	93a	45.30 N	73.35 W
Montreal L., Can.	98	54.20 N	105.40 W
Montreal (R.), Can.	100	47.15 N	84.20 W
Montreal (R.), Can.	101	47.50 N	80.30 W
Montréal-Nord, Can.	93a	45.36 N	73.38 W
Montreux, Switz. (môn-trû')	164	46.26 N	6.52 E
Montrose, Ca. (mŏnt-rōz)	117a	34.13 N	118.13 W
Montrose, Co. (mŏn-trōz')	119	38.30 N	107.55 W
Montrose, Oh.	111d	41.08 N	81.38 W
Montrose, Pa. (mŏnt-rōz')	109	41.50 N	75.50 W
Montrose, Scot.	160	56.45 N	2.25 W
Mont-Royal, Can.	93a	47.31 N	73.39 W
Monts, Pointe des (Pt.), Can. (pwăNt' dā môN')	102	49.19 N	67.22 W
Mont St. Martin, Fr. (môN săN mär-tăN')	167	49.34 N	6.13 E
Montserrat, N.A. (mŏnt-sē-răt')	127	16.48 N	63.15 W
Montvale, NJ (mŏnt-văl')	110a	41.02 N	74.01 W
Monywa, Bur. (mŏn'yōō-wȧ)	202	22.02 N	95.16 E
Monza, It. (mōn'tsä)	170	45.34 N	9.17 E
Monzón, Sp. (mōn-thōn')	169	41.54 N	0.09 E
Moody, Tx. (mōō'dĭ)	123	31.18 N	97.20 W
Mooi (R.), S. Afr. (mōō'ĭ)	219d	26.34 S	27.03 E
Mooi (R.), S. Afr.	223c	29.00 S	30.15 E
Mooirivier, S. Afr.	223c	29.14 S	29.59 E
Moolap, Austl.	207a	38.11 S	144.26 E
Moonta, Austl. (mōōn'tȧ)	212	34.05 S	137.42 E
Moora, Austl. (mōōr'ȧ)	210	30.35 S	116.12 E
Moorcroft, Wy. (mōr'krôft)	115	44.17 N	104.59 W
Moore (L.), Austl. (mōr)	210	29.50 S	128.12 E
Moorenweis, F.R.G. (mō'rĕn-vīz)	155d	48.10 N	11.05 E
Moore Res., Vt.-NH	109	44.20 N	72.10 W

ng-sing; ŋ-baŋk; N-nasalized n; nŏd; cŏmmit; ōld; ôbey; ôrder; oi-boil; fōōd; fŏŏt; ou-out; s-soft; sh-dish; th-thin; pūre; ûnite; ûrn; stŭd; circŭs; ü-as in French tu; '-indeterminate vowel.

PLACE (Pronunciation)	PAGE	Lat. °′	Long. °′
Moorestown, NJ (morz'toun)	110f	39.58 N	74.56 W
Mooresville, In. (mōrz'vĭl)	111g	39.37 N	86.22 W
Mooresville, NC	125	35.34 N	80.48 W
Moorhead, Mn. (mōr'hĕd)	112	46.52 N	96.44 W
Moorhead, Ms.	124	33.25 N	90.30 W
Moorland (Plain), see Landes			
Moose (L.), Can. (mo͞os)	94	54.14 N	99.28 W
Moose (R.), Can.	95	51.01 N	80.42 W
Moose Creek, Can.	93c	45.16 N	74.58 W
Moosehead, Me. (mo͞os'hĕd)	102	45.37 N	69.15 W
Moose I., Can.	99	51.50 N	97.09 W
Moose Jaw, Can. (mo͞os jô)	98	50.23 N	105.32 W
Moose Jaw (Cr.), Can.	98	50.34 N	105.17 W
Moose Lake, Can.	99	53.40 N	100.28 W
Moose Mtn., Can.	99	49.45 N	102.37 W
Moose Mtn. Cr., Can.	98	49.12 N	102.10 W
Moosilauke (Mtn.), NH (mo͞o-sĭ-lă'kē)	109	44.00 N	71.50 W
Moosinning, F.R.G. (mō'zē-nēng)	155d	48.17 N	11.51 E
Moosomin, Can. (mo͞o'sô-mĭn)	99	50.07 N	101.40 W
Moosonee, Can. (mo͞o'sô-nē)	95	51.20 N	80.44 W
Mopti, Mali (mŏp'tē)	224	14.30 N	4.12 W
Moquegua, Peru (mô-kā'gwä)	140	17.15 S	70.54 W
Mór, Hung. (mōr)	165	47.51 N	18.14 E
Mora, India	191b	18.54 N	72.56 E
Mora, Mn. (mō'rá)	113	45.52 N	93.18 W
Mora, NM	120	35.58 N	105.17 W
Mora, Sp. (mô-rä)	168	39.42 N	3.45 W
Mora, Swe. (mō'rä)	162	61.00 N	14.29 E
Morādābād, India (mō-rä-dā-bäd')	190	28.57 N	78.48 E
Morales, Guat. (mô-rä'lĕs)	130	15.29 N	88.46 W
Moramanga, Mad. (mō-rä-mäŋ'gä)	223	18.48 S	48.09 E
Morant Pt., Jam. (mô-rănt')	133	17.55 N	76.10 W
Morata de Tajuña, Sp. (mô-rä'tä dā tä-ho͞o'nyä)	169a	40.14 N	3.27 W
Moratuwa, Sri Lanka	191	6.35 N	79.59 E
Morava (Moravia) (Prov.), Czech. (mô'rä-vä)(mō-rā'vĭ-á)	165	49.21 N	16.57 E
Morava R., Czech.	164	49.53 N	16.53 E
Moravia, see Morava			
Morawhanna, Guy. (mô-rá-hwä'ná)	141	8.12 N	59.33 W
Moray Firth, Scot. (mŭr'â)	160	57.41 N	3.55 W
Mörbylånga, Swe. (mûr'bü-lôŋ'gá)	162	56.32 N	16.23 E
Morden, Can. (môr'dĕn)	99	49.11 N	98.05 W
Mordialloc, Austl. (môr-dĭ-ăl'ŏk)	207a	38.00 S	145.05 E
Mordvin, (A.S.S.R.), Sov. Un.	176	54.18 N	43.50 E
More, Ben (Mtn.), Scot. (bĕn môr)	160	58.09 N	5.01 W
Moreau (R.), SD (mô-rō')	112	45.13 N	102.22 W
Moree, Austl. (mō'rē)	212	29.20 S	149.50 E
Morehead, Ky.	108	38.10 N	83.25 W
Morehead City, NC (mōr'hĕd)	125	34.43 N	76.43 W
Morehouse, Mo. (mōr'hous)	121	36.49 N	89.41 W
Morelia, Mex. (mô-rā'lyä)	128	19.43 N	101.12 W
Morella, Sp. (mō-rāl'yä)	169	40.38 N	0.07 W
Morelos, Mex. (mô-rā'lōs)	128	22.46 N	102.36 W
Morelos, Mex.	122	28.24 N	100.51 W
Morelos, Mex.	129a	19.41 N	99.29 W
Morelos, R., Mex.	122	25.27 N	99.35 W
Morena, Sierra (Mt.), Ca. (syĕr'rä mō-rā'nä)	116b	37.24 N	122.19 W
Morena, Sierra (Mts.), Sp. (syĕr'rä mô-rā'nä)	168	38.15 N	5.45 W
Morenci, Az. (mô-rĕn'sĭ)	119	33.05 N	109.25 W
Morenci, Mi.	108	41.50 N	84.50 W
Moreno, Arg. (mô-rĕ'nō)	142a	34.25 S	58.47 W
Moreno, Ca.	117a	33.55 N	117.09 W
Mores (I.), Ba. (mōrz)	132	26.20 N	77.35 W
Moresby (I.), Can. (môrz'bĭ)	116b	48.43 N	123.15 W
Moresby I., Can.	94	52.50 N	131.55 W
Moreton (I.), Austl. (môr'tŭn)	212	26.53 S	152.42 E
Moreton B., Austl. (môr'tŭn)	212	27.12 S	153.10 E
Morewood, Can. (môr'wo͝od)	93c	45.11 N	75.17 W
Morgan, Mt. (môr'găn)	115	48.55 N	107.56 W
Morgan, Ut.	115	41.04 N	111.42 W
Morgan City, La.	123	29.41 N	91.11 W
Morganfield, Ky. (môr'găn-fēld)	108	37.40 N	87.55 W
Morgan's Bay, S. Afr.	223c	32.42 S	28.19 E
Morganton, NC (môr'găn-tŭn)	125	35.44 N	81.42 W
Morgantown, WV (môr'găn-toun)	109	39.40 N	79.55 W
Morga Ra, Afg.	193a	34.02 N	70.38 E
Morgenzon, S. Afr. (môr'gănt-sŏn)	219d	26.44 S	29.39 E
Moriac, Austl.	207a	38.15 S	144.12 E
Morice L., Can.	96	54.00 N	127.37 W
Moriguchi, Jap. (mō'rē-go͞o'chē)	201b	34.44 N	135.34 E
Morinville, Can. (mō'rĭn-vĭl)	93g	53.48 N	113.39 W
Morioka, Jap. (mō'rē-ō'ká)	200	39.40 N	141.21 E
Morkoka (R.), Sov. Un. (môr-kô'ká)	179	65.35 N	111.00 E
Morlaix, Fr. (mŏr-lĕ')	166	48.36 N	3.48 W
Morley, Can. (mŏr'lē)	93e	51.10 N	114.51 W
Mormant, Fr.	167	48.35 N	2.54 E
Morne Diablotin, Mt., Dominica (mōrn dē-á-blō-tăN')	131b	15.31 N	61.24 W
Morne Gimie, Mt., St. Lucia (mōrn' zhē-mē')	131b	13.53 N	61.03 W
Mornington, Austl.	207a	38.13 S	145.02 E
Morobe, Pap. N. Gui.	203	8.03 S	147.45 E
Morocco, Afr. (mō-rŏk'ō)	218	32.00 N	7.00 W
Morogoro, Tan. (mō-rō-gō'rō)	227	6.49 S	37.40 E
Moroleón, Mex. (mō-rō-lā-ōn')	128	20.07 N	101.15 W
Morombe, Mad. (mo͞o-ro͞om'bā)	223	21.39 S	43.34 E
Morón, Arg. (mo-rō'n)	142a	34.24 S	58.37 W
Morón, Cuba (mō-rōn')	132	22.05 N	78.35 W
Morón, Ven. (mô-rŏ'n)	141b	10.29 N	68.11 W
Morondava, Mad. (mō-rōn-dá'vá)	223	20.17 S	44.18 E
Morón de la Frontera, Sp. (mō-rōn'dā lăf rōn-tā'rä)	168	37.08 N	5.20 W
Morongo Ind. Res., Ca. (mō-rōŋ'gō)	118	33.54 N	116.47 W
Moroni, Comoros	222	11.41 S	43.16 E
Moroni, Ut. (mō-rō'nĭ)	119	39.30 N	111.40 W
Morotai (I.), Indon. (mō-rō-tä'ē)	203	2.12 N	128.30 E
Moroto, Ug.	227	2.32 N	34.39 E
Morozovsk, Sov. Un.	177	48.20 N	41.50 E
Morrill, Ne. (mŏr'ĭl)	112	41.59 N	103.54 W
Morrilton, Ar. (mŏr'ĭl-tŭn)	121	35.09 N	92.42 W
Morrinhos, Braz. (mô-rēn'yōzh)	141	17.45 S	48.56 W
Morris, Can. (mŏr'ĭs)	99	49.21 N	97.22 W
Morris, Il.	108	41.20 N	88.25 W
Morris, Mn.	112	45.35 N	95.53 W
Morris (R.), Can.	99	49.30 N	97.30 W
Morrison, Il. (mŏr'ĭ-sŭn)	113	41.48 N	89.58 W
Morris Plains, NJ (mŏr'ĭs pláns)	110a	40.49 N	74.29 W
Morris Res., Ca.	117a	34.11 N	117.49 W
Morristown, NJ (mŏr'rĭs-toun)	110a	40.48 N	74.29 W
Morristown, Tn.	124	36.10 N	83.18 W
Morrisville, Pa. (mŏr'ĭs-vĭl)	110f	40.12 N	74.46 W
Morro do Chapéu, Braz. (môr-o͞o do͞o-shä-pĕ'o͞o)	141	11.34 S	41.03 W
Morrow, Oh. (mŏr'ō)	111f	39.21 N	84.07 W
Morshansk, Sov. Un. (môr-shánsk')	177	53.25 N	41.35 E
Mors (I.), Den.	162	56.46 N	8.38 E
Mortara, It. (môr-tä'rä)	170	45.13 N	8.47 E
Morteros, Arg. (môr-tĕ'tôs)	142	30.47 S	62.00 W
Mortes, Rio das (R.), Braz. (rē'o-däs-mô'r-tĕs)	139a	21.04 S	44.29 W
Morton Ind. Res., Mn. (môr'tŭn)	113	44.35 N	94.48 W
Mortsel, Bel. (môr-sĕl')	155a	51.10 N	4.28 E
Morvan (Mts.), Fr. (môr-väN')	166	47.11 N	4.10 E
Morzhovets (I.), Sov. Un. (môr'zhô-vyĕts')	176	66.40 N	42.30 E
Mosal'sk, Sov. Un. (mō-zálsk')	172	54.27 N	34.57 E
Moscow, Id. (mŏs'kō)	114	46.44 N	116.57 W
Moscow, see Moskva			
Moscow Can., see Imeni Moskvy, Kanal			
Mosel R., F.R.G. (mō'sĕl) (mô-zĕl)	164	49.49 N	7.00 E
Moses Lake, Wa.	114	47.08 N	119.15 W
Moses L., Wa. (mō'zĕz)	114	47.09 N	119.30 W
Moses R., S. Afr.	219d	25.17 S	29.04 E
Moshchnyy (Is.), Sov. Un. (môsh'chnĭ)	163	59.56 N	28.07 E
Moshi, Tan. (mō'shē)	227	3.21 S	37.20 E
Mosjøen, Nor.	156	65.50 N	13.10 E
Moskva, (Moscow), Sov. Un. (mŏs-kvä')	180b	55.45 N	37.37 E
Moskva (Oblast), Sov. Un.	172	55.38 N	36.48 E
Moskva (R.), Sov. Un.	172	55.50 N	37.05 E
Mosonmagyaróvár, Hung.	165	47.51 N	17.16 E
Mosquitos, Costa de, Nic. (kôs-tä-dĕ-mōs-kē'tō)	131	12.05 N	83.49 W
Mosquitos, Gulfo de los (G.), Pan. (go͞o'l-fô-dĕ-lôs-mōs-kē'tōs)	131	9.17 N	80.59 W
Moss, Nor. (môs)	162	59.29 N	10.39 E
Moss Beach, Ca. (môs bēch)	116b	37.32 N	122.31 W
Mosselbaai, S. Afr. (mô'sul bā)	222	34.06 S	22.23 E
Mossendjo, Con.	226	2.57 S	12.44 E
Mossley, Eng. (môs'lĭ)	154	53.31 N	2.02 W
Mossoró, Braz. (mō-sô-ro͞o')	141	5.13 S	37.14 W
Moss Point, Ms. (môs)	124	30.25 N	88.32 W
Most, Czech. (môst)	164	50.32 N	13.37 E
Mostaganem, Alg. (mŏs'tä-gá-nĕm')	220	36.04 N	0.11 E
Mostar, Yugo. (môs'tär)	171	43.20 N	17.51 E
Móstoles, Sp. (môs-tō'lās)	169a	40.19 N	3.52 W
Mostoos Hills, Can. (mŏs'to͞os)	98	54.50 N	108.45 W
Mosvatnet, Nor.	162	59.55 N	7.50 E
Motagua R., Guat. (mô-tä'gwä)	130	15.29 N	88.39 W
Motala, Swe. (mô-tô'lä)	162	58.34 N	15.00 E
Motherwell, Scot. (mŭdh'ēr-wĕl)	160	55.45 N	4.05 W
Motril, Sp. (mô-trēl')	168	36.44 N	3.32 W
Motul, Mex. (mō-to͞o'l)	130a	21.07 N	89.14 W
Mouchoir Bk., Ba. (mo͞o-shwár')	133	21.35 N	70.40 W
Mouchoir Passage (Str.), Ba.	133	21.05 N	71.05 W
Moudon, Switz.	167	46.40 N	6.47 E
Moudjéria, Mauritania	224	17.53 N	12.20 W
Mouila, Gabon	226	1.52 S	11.01 E
Mouille Pt., S. Afr.	222a	33.54 S	18.19 E
Moulins, Fr. (mo͞o-lăN')	166	46.34 N	3.19 E
Moulmein, Bur. (mōl-mān')	202	16.30 N	97.39 E
Moulouya, Oued (R.), Mor. (mo͞o-lo͞o'yá)	158	34.07 N	3.27 W
Moultrie, Ga. (mōl'trĭ)	124	31.10 N	83.48 W
Moultrie (Dam), SC	125	33.12 N	80.00 W
Mound City (mound), Il.	121	37.06 N	89.13 W
Mound City, Mo.	121	40.08 N	95.13 W
Mound City Group Natl. Mon., Oh.	108	39.25 N	83.00 W
Moundon, Chad	225	8.34 N	16.05 E
Moundsville, WV (moundz'vĭl)	108	39.50 N	80.50 W
Mount, C., Lib.	224	6.47 N	11.20 W
Mountain Brook, Al. (moun'tĭn bro͝ok)	110h	33.30 N	86.45 W
Mountain Creek L., Tx.	117c	32.43 N	97.03 W
Mountain Grove, Mo. (grōv)	121	37.07 N	92.16 W
Mountain Home, Id. (hōm)	114	43.08 N	115.43 W
Mountain Park, Can. (pärk)	97	52.55 N	117.14 W
Mountain View, Ca. (moun'tĭn vū)	116b	37.25 N	122.07 W
Mountain View, Mo.	121	36.59 N	91.46 W
Mount Airy, NC (âr'ĭ)	125	36.28 N	80.37 W
Mount Athos (Reg.), see Áyion Óros			
Mount Ayliff, S. Afr. (ā'lĭf)	223c	30.48 S	29.24 E
Mount Ayr, Ia. (âr)	113	40.43 N	94.06 W
Mount Carmel, Il. (kär'mĕl)	108	38.25 N	87.45 W
Mount Carmel, Pa.	109	40.50 N	76.25 W
Mount Caroll, Il.	113	42.05 N	89.55 W
Mount Clemens, Mi. (klĕm'ĕnz)	111b	42.36 N	82.52 W
Mount Desert (I.), Me. (dē-zûrt')	102	44.15 N	68.08 W
Mount Dora, Fl. (dō'rá)	125a	28.45 N	81.38 W
Mount Duneed, Austl.	207a	38.15 S	144.20 E
Mount Eliza, Austl.	207a	38.11 S	145.05 E
Mountevideo, Mn. (mōn'tá-vē-dhā'ō)	112	44.56 N	95.42 W
Mount Fletcher, S. Afr. (flĕ'chēr)	223c	30.42 S	28.32 E
Mount Forest, Can. (fŏr'ĕst)	108	44.00 N	80.45 W
Mount Frere, S. Afr. (frâr')	223c	30.54 S	29.02 E
Mount Gambier, Austl. (găm'bēr)	212	37.30 S	140.53 E
Mount Gilead, Oh. (gĭl'ēăd)	108	40.30 N	82.50 W
Mount Healthy, Oh. (hĕlth'ē)	111f	39.14 N	84.32 W
Mount Holly, NJ (hŏl'ĭ)	110f	39.59 N	74.47 W
Mount Hope, Can.	93d	43.09 N	79.55 W
Mount Hope, NJ (hōp)	110a	40.55 N	74.32 W
Mount Hope, WV	108	37.55 N	81.10 W
Mount Isa, Austl. (ī'zá)	210	21.00 S	139.45 E
Mount Kisco, NY (kĭs'kō)	110a	41.12 N	73.44 W
Mountlake Terrace, Wa. (mount lāk tĕr'ĭs)	116a	47.48 N	122.19 W
Mount Lebanon, Pa. (lĕb'á-nŭn)	111e	40.22 N	80.03 W
Mount Magnet, Austl. (măg-nĕt)	210	28.00 S	118.00 E
Mount Martha, Austl.	207a	38.17 S	145.01 E
Mount Morgan, Austl. (môr-găn)	211	23.42 S	150.45 E
Mount Moriac, Austl.	207a	38.13 S	144.12 E
Mount Morris, Mi. (mŏr'ĭs)	108	43.10 N	83.45 W
Mount Morris, NY	109	42.45 N	77.50 W
Mt. Nimba Natl. Pk., Gui.-Ivory Coast	224	7.35 N	8.10 W
Mount Olive, NC (ŏl'ĭv)	125	35.11 N	78.05 W
Mount Peale, Ut.	119	38.26 N	109.16 W
Mount Pleasant, Ia. (plĕz'ănt)	113	40.59 N	91.34 W
Mount Pleasant, Mi.	108	43.35 N	84.45 W
Mount Pleasant, SC	125	32.46 N	79.51 W
Mount Pleasant, Tn.	124	35.31 N	87.12 W
Mount Pleasant, Tx.	121	33.10 N	94.56 W
Mount Pleasant, Ut.	119	39.35 N	111.20 W
Mount Prospect, Il. (prŏs'pĕkt)	111a	42.03 N	87.56 W
Mount Rainier Natl. Park, Wa. (rá-nēr')	114	46.47 N	121.17 W
Mount Revelstoke Natl. Park, Can. (rĕv'ĕl-stōk)	94	51.22 N	120.15 W
Mount Savage, Md. (săv'āj)	109	39.45 N	78.55 W
Mount Shasta, Ca. (shăs'tá)	114	41.18 N	122.17 W
Mount Sterling, Il. (stûr'lĭng)	121	39.59 N	90.44 W
Mount Sterling, Ky.	108	38.05 N	84.00 W
Mount Stewart, Can. (stū'ărt)	113	46.22 N	62.52 W
Mount Union, Pa. (ūn'yŭn)	109	40.25 N	77.50 W
Mount Vernon, Il. (vûr'nŭn)	108	38.20 N	88.50 W
Mount Vernon, In.	108	37.55 N	87.50 W
Mount Vernon, Mo.	121	37.09 N	93.48 W
Mount Vernon, NY	110a	40.55 N	73.51 W
Mount Vernon, Oh.	108	40.25 N	82.30 W
Mount Vernon, Va.	110e	38.43 N	77.06 W
Mount Vernon, Wa.	116a	48.25 N	122.20 W
Moura, Braz. (mō'rá)	141	1.33 S	61.38 W
Moura, Port.	168	38.08 N	7.28 W
Mourenx, Fr. (mo͞o-rän)	166	43.24 N	0.40 W
Mourne, Mts., N. Ire. (môrn)	160	54.10 N	6.09 W
Moussoro, Chad	225	13.39 N	16.29 E
Moûtiers, Fr. (mo͞o-tyâr')	167	45.31 N	6.34 E
Mowbullan, Mt., Austl. (mō'bo͞o-lán)	212	26.50 S	151.34 E
Moyahua, Mex. (mô-yä'wä)	128	21.16 N	103.10 W
Moyale, Ken. (mô-yä'lā)	221	3.28 N	39.04 E
Moyamba, S.L. (mô-yäm'bä)	224	8.10 N	12.26 W
Moyen Atlas (Mts.), Mor.	158	32.49 N	5.28 W
Moyeuvre-Grande, Fr.	167	49.15 N	6.26 E
Moyie R., Id. (moi'yē)	114	48.50 N	116.10 W
Moyobamba, Peru (mô-yō-bäm'bä)	140	6.12 S	76.56 W
Moyuta, Guat. (mô-ē-o͞o'tä)	130	14.01 N	90.05 W
Moyyero (R.), Sov. Un.	179	67.15 N	104.10 E
Mozambique, Afr. (mō-zăm-bēk')	218	20.15 S	33.53 E
Mozambique Chan., Afr. (mō-zăm-bek')	223	24.00 S	38.00 E
Mozdok, Sov. Un. (môz-dôk')	177	43.45 N	44.35 E
Mozhaysk, Sov. Un. (mô-zhäysk')	172	55.31 N	36.02 E
Mozhayskiy, Sov. Un. (mô-zhäy'skĭ)	180c	59.42 N	30.08 E
Mozyr', Sov. Un. (mô-zür')	173	52.03 N	29.14 E
Mpanda, Tan.	227	6.22 S	31.02 E
Mpika, Zambia	227	11.54 S	31.26 E
Mpimbe, Malawi	227	15.18 S	35.04 E
Mporokoso, Zambia ('m-pō-rō-kō'sō)	227	9.23 S	30.05 E
Mpwapwa, Tan. ('m-pwä'pwä)	227	6.21 S	36.29 E
Mqanduli, S. Afr. ('m-kän'do͞o-lē)	223c	31.50 S	28.42 E
Mragowo, Pol. (mräŋ'gô-vô)	165	53.52 N	21.18 E
M'sila, Alg. (m'sē'lá)	220	35.47 N	4.34 E
Msta (R.), Sov. Un. (m'stá')	172	58.33 N	32.08 E
Mstislavl', Sov. Un. (m'stē-slävl')	172	54.01 N	31.42 E
Mtakataka, Malawi	227	14.12 S	34.32 E
Mtamvuna (R.), S. Afr.	223c	30.43 S	29.53 E
Mtata (R.), S. Afr.	223c	31.48 S	29.03 E
Mtsensk, Sov. Un. (m'tsĕnsk)	172	53.17 N	36.33 E
Mtwara, Tan.	227	10.16 S	40.11 E
Muang Khon Kaen, Thai.	202	16.37 N	102.41 E
Muang Lamphum, Thai.	202	18.40 N	98.59 E
Muar (R.), Mala.	189b	2.18 N	102.43 E
Mubende, Ug.	227	0.35 N	31.23 E
Mubi, Nig.	225	10.18 N	13.20 E
Mucacata, Moz.	227	13.20 S	39.59 E
Much, F.R.G. (mo͞oK)	167c	50.54 N	7.24 E
Muchinga Mts., Zambia	227	12.40 S	30.50 E
Much Wenlock, Eng. (mŭch wĕn'lŏk)	154	52.35 N	2.33 W
Muckalee Cr., Ga. (mŭk'á lē)	124	31.55 N	84.10 W
Muckleshoot Ind. Res., Wa. (mŭck'l-sho͞ot)	116a	47.21 N	122.04 W
Mucubela, Moz.	227	16.55 S	37.52 E
Mucugê, Braz. (mo͞o-ko͞o-zhĕ')	141	13.02 S	41.19 W
Mud (L.), Mi. (mŭd)	113	46.12 N	84.32 W
Mud (L.), Nv.	118	40.28 N	119.11 W
Mudan (R.), China (mo͞o-dän)	198	45.30 N	129.40 E
Mudanjiang, China (mo͞o-dän-jyäŋ)	198	44.28 N	129.38 E
Muddy (R.), Nv. (mŭd'ĭ)	118	36.56 N	114.42 W
Muddy Boggy Cr., Ok. (mud'ĭ bŏg'ĭ)	121	34.42 N	96.11 W
Muddy Cr., Ut. (mŭd'ĭ)	119	38.45 N	111.10 W
Mudgee, Austl. (mŭ-jē)	212	32.47 S	149.10 E
Mudjatik (R.), Can.	98	56.23 N	107.40 W
Mufulira, Zambia	227	12.33 S	28.14 E
Muğla, Tur. (mo͞og'lä)	177	37.10 N	28.20 E
Mühldorf, F.R.G. (mül-dôrf)	164	48.15 N	12.33 E
Mühlhausen, G.D.R. (mül'hou-zĕn)	164	51.13 N	10.25 E
Muhu (I.), Sov. Un. (mo͞o'ho͞o)	163	58.41 N	22.55 E
Mui Ron, C., Viet.	199	18.05 N	106.45 E
Muir Woods Natl. Mon., Ca. (mûr)	118	37.54 N	123.22 W

ăt; finăl; rāte; senâte; ärm; ȧsk; sofá; fâre; ch-choose; dh-as th in other; bē; ēvent; bĕt; recĕnt; cratēr; g-gō; gh-guttural g; bĭt; ĭ-short neutral; rīde; K-guttural k as ch in German ich;

PRONOUNCING INDEX
Muizenberg – Nanam 323

PLACE (Pronunciation)	PAGE	Lat. °′	Long. °′
Muizenberg, S. Afr. (mwĭz-ĕn-bûrg')	222a	34.07 S	18.28 E
Mukachëvo, Sov. Un. (mōō-ká-chyô'vô)	165	48.25 N	22.43 E
Mukhtuya, Sov. Un. (mōōk-tōō'yá)	179	61.00 N	113.00 E
Mukilteo, Wa. (mū-kĭl-tā'ō)	116a	47.57 N	122.18 W
Muko, Jap. (mōō'kô)	201b	34.57 N	135.43 E
Muko (R.), Jap. (mōō'kô)	201b	34.52 N	135.17 E
Mukutawa (R.), Can.	99	53.10 N	97.28 W
Mukwonago, Wi. (mū-kwō-ná'gō)	111a	42.52 N	88.19 W
Mula, Sp. (mōō'lä)	168	38.05 N	1.12 W
Mulde R., G.D.R. (mŏŏl'dĕ)	164	50.30 N	12.30 E
Muleros, Mex. (mōō-lā'rōs)	128	23.44 N	104.00 W
Muleshoe, Tx.	120	34.13 N	102.43 W
Mula, Al. (mŭl'gá)	110h	33.33 N	86.59 W
Mulgrave, Can. (mŭl'grāv)	103	45.37 N	61.23 W
Mulgrave (I.), Austl.	211	10.08 S	142.14 E
Mulhacén, (Mtn.), Sp.	168	37.04 N	3.18 W
Mülheim, F.R.G. (mül'hīm)	167c	51.25 N	6.53 E
Mulhouse, Fr. (mü-lōōz')	167	47.46 N	7.20 E
Muling, China (mōō-lĭŋ)	198	44.32 N	130.18 E
Muling (R.), China	198	44.40 N	130.30 E
Mull, I. of, Scot. (mŭl)	160	56.40 N	6.19 W
Mullan, Id. (mŭl'ăn)	114	47.26 N	115.50 W
Müller, Pegunungan (Mts.), Indon. (mül'ĕr)	202	0.22 N	113.05 E
Mullingar, Ire. (mŭl-ĭn-gär)	160	53.31 N	7.26 W
Mullins, SC (mŭl'ĭnz)	125	34.11 N	79.13 W
Mullins River, Belize	130a	17.08 N	88.18 W
Multān, Pak. (mōō-tän')	190	30.17 N	71.13 E
Multnomah Chan., Or. (mŭl nō má)	116c	45.41 N	122.53 W
Mulumbe, Monts (Mts.), Zaire	227	8.47 S	27.20 E
Mulvane, Ks. (mŭl-vān')	121	37.30 N	97.13 W
Mumbwa, Zambia (mōōm'bwä)	227	14.59 S	27.04 E
Mumias, Ken.	227	0.20 N	34.29 E
Muna, Mex. (mōō'ná)	130a	20.28 N	89.42 W
München (Munich), F.R.G. (mün'kĕn)	155d	48.08 N	11.35 E
Muncie, In. (mŭn'sĭ)	108	40.10 N	85.30 W
Mundelein, Il. (mŭn-dē-lĭn')	111a	42.16 N	88.00 W
Mundonueva, Pico de (Pk.), Col. (pē'kō-dĕ-mōō'n-dô-nwĕ'vä)	140a	4.18 N	74.12 W
Muneco, Cerro (Mtn.), Mex. (sĕ'r-rô-mōō-nĕ'kō)	129a	19.13 N	99.20 W
Mungana, Austl. (mŭn-găn'á)	211	17.15 S	144.18 E
Mungbere, Zaire	227	2.38 N	28.30 E
Munger, Mn. (mŭn'gĕr)	117h	46.48 N	92.20 W
Mungindi, Austl. (mŭn-gĭn'dē)	212	32.00 S	148.45 E
Munhall, Pa. (mŭn'hôl)	111e	40.24 N	79.53 W
Munhango, Ang. (mōōn-häŋ'gá)	222	12.15 S	18.55 E
Munich, see München			
Munising, Mi. (mū'nĭ-sĭng)	113	46.24 N	86.41 W
Munku Sardyk (Mtn.), Sov. Un.-Mong. (mōōn'kōō sär-dĭk')	178	51.45 N	100.30 E
Muñoz, Phil. (mōōn-nyōth')	203a	15.44 N	120.53 E
Münster, F.R.G. (mün'stĕr)	167c	51.57 N	7.38 E
Munster, In. (mŭn'stĕr)	111a	41.34 N	87.31 W
Munster, Ire. (mŭn-stĕr)	160	52.30 N	9.24 W
Muntok, Indon. (mōōn-tŏk')	202	2.05 S	105.11 E
Munzi Freire, Braz. (mōō-nĕ'z-frâ'rĕ)	139a	20.29 S	41.25 W
Muong Sing, Laos (mōō'ông-sĭng')	202	21.06 N	101.17 E
Muping, China (mōō-pĭŋ)	196	37.23 N	121.36 E
Muqdisho, Som.	219a	2.08 N	45.22 E
Muqui, Braz. (mōō-kōō'ē)	139a	20.56 S	41.20 W
Muradiye, Tur. (mōō-rä'dē-yĕ)	177	39.00 N	43.40 E
Murat, Fr. (mü-rä')	166	45.05 N	2.56 E
Murat (R.), Tur. (mōō-rät')	177	38.50 N	40.40 E
Murchison (R.), Austl. (mûr'chĭ-sŭn)	210	26.45 S	116.15 E
Murcia, Sp. (mōōr'thyä)	168	38.00 N	1.10 W
Murcia (Reg.), Sp.	168	38.35 N	1.51 W
Murdo, SD (mûr'dō)	112	43.53 N	100.42 W
Mureş R., Rom. (mōō'rĕsh)	165	46.02 N	21.50 E
Muret, Fr. (mü-rĕ')	166	43.28 N	1.17 E
Murfreesboro, Tn. (mûr'frēz-bŭr-ō)	124	35.50 N	86.19 W
Murgab (R.), Sov. Un. (mōōr-gäb')	141	37.07 N	62.32 E
Muriaé, Braz. (mōō-ryá-ĕ')	139a	21.10 S	42.21 W
Muriaé (R.), Braz.	139a	21.20 S	41.40 W
Murino, Sov. Un. (mōō'rĭ-nô)	180c	60.03 N	30.28 E
Müritz (L.), G.D.R. (mür'its)	164	53.20 N	12.33 E
Murku Sardyk (Pk.), Sov. Un.-Mong.	194	51.56 N	100.21 E
Murmansk, Sov. Un. (mōōr-mänsk')	176	69.00 N	33.20 E
Murom, Sov. Un. (mōō'rôm)	176	55.30 N	42.00 W
Muroran, Jap. (mōō'rô-rän)	200	42.21 N	141.05 E
Muros, Sp. (mōō'rōs)	168	42.48 N	9.00 W
Muroto-Zaki (Pt.), Jap. (mōō'rô-tō zä'kē)	201	33.14 N	134.12 E
Murphy, Mo. (mŭr'fĭ)	117e	38.29 N	90.29 W
Murphy, NC	124	35.05 N	84.00 W
Murphysboro, Il. (mŭr'fĭz-bŭr-ō)	121	37.46 N	89.21 W
Murray, Ky. (mŭr'ĭ)	124	36.39 N	88.17 W
Murray, Ut.	117b	40.40 N	111.53 W
Murray (R.), Can.	97	55.00 N	121.00 W
Murray (R.), SC (mŭr'ĭ)	125	34.07 N	81.18 W
Murray Bridge, Austl.	212	35.10 S	139.35 E
Murray Harbour, Can.	102	46.00 N	62.31 W
Murray Reg., Austl. (mŭ'rē)	211	33.20 S	142.30 E
Murray R., Austl.	212	34.20 S	142.21 W
Mur R., Aus. (mōōr)	164	47.10 N	14.08 E
Murrumbidgee (R.), Austl. (mŭr-ŭm-bĭd'jē)	212	34.30 S	145.20 E
Murrupula, Moz.	227	15.27 S	38.47 E
Murshidābād, India (mōōr'shē-dä-bäd')	190	24.08 N	87.11 E
Murska Sobota, Yugo. (mōōr'skä sô'bô-tä)	170	46.40 N	16.14 E
Muruasigar (Mtn.), Ken.	227	3.08 N	35.02 E
Murwāra, India	190	23.54 N	80.23 E
Murwillumbah, Austl. (mŭr-wĭl'lŭm-bŭ)	212	28.15 S	153.30 E
Mürz R., Aus. (mürts)	164	47.30 N	15.21 E
Murzzuschlag, Aus. (mürts'tsōō-shlägh)	164	47.37 N	15.41 E

PLACE (Pronunciation)	PAGE	Lat. °′	Long. °′
Mus, Tur. (mōōsh)	177	38.55 N	41.30 E
Musala (Mtn.), Bul.	171	42.05 N	23.24 E
Musan, Kor. (mōō'sän)	200	41.11 N	129.10 E
Musashino, Jap. (mōō-sä'shē-nō)	201a	35.43 N	139.35 E
Muscat, Om. (mŭs-kăt')	192	23.23 N	58.30 E
Muscat & Oman, see Oman			
Muscatine, Ia. (mŭs-ká-tēn)	113	41.26 N	91.00 W
Muscle Shoals, Al. (mŭs''l shōlz)	124	34.44 N	87.38 W
Musgrave Ra., Austl. (mŭs'grāv)	210	26.15 S	131.15 E
Mushie, Zaire (mŭsh'ē)	222	3.04 S	16.50 E
Mushin, Nig.	225	6.32 N	3.22 E
Musi (Strm.), Indon. (mōō'sē)	202	2.40 S	103.42 E
Musinga, Alto (Ht.), Col. (ä'l-tô-mōō-sē'n-gä)	140a	6.40 N	76.13 W
Muskego L., Wi. (mŭs-kē'gō)	111a	42.53 N	88.10 W
Muskegon, Mi. (mŭs-kē'gŭn)	108	43.15 N	86.20 W
Muskegon (R.), Mi.	108	43.20 N	85.55 W
Muskegon Heights, Mi.	108	43.10 N	86.20 W
Muskingum (R.), Oh. (mŭs-kĭŋ'gŭm)	108	39.45 N	81.55 W
Muskogee, Ok. (mŭs-kō'gē)	121	35.44 N	95.21 W
Muskoka (L.), Can. (mŭs-kō'ká)	109	45.00 N	79.30 W
Musoma, Tan.	227	1.30 S	33.48 E
Mussau I., Pap. N. Gui. (mōō-sä'ōō)	203	1.30 S	149.32 E
Musselshell R., Mt. (mŭs''l-shĕl)	115	46.25 N	108.20 W
Mussende, Ang.	226	10.32 S	16.05 E
Mussuma, Ang.	226	14.14 S	21.59 E
Mustafakemalpasa, Tur.	177	40.05 N	28.30 E
Mustang Bayou, Tx.	123a	29.22 N	95.12 W
Mustang Cr., Tx. (mŭs'tăng)	120	36.22 N	102.46 W
Mustang I., Tx.	123	27.43 N	97.00 W
Mustique I., St. Vincent (müs-tēk')	131b	12.53 N	61.03 W
Mustvee, Sov. Un. (mōōst'vĕ-ĕ)	163	38.50 N	26.54 E
Musu Dan (C.), Kor. (mōō'sōō dán)	195	40.51 N	130.00 E
Musu Dan (Pt.), Kor. (mōō'sōō dán)	200	40.48 N	129.50 E
Muswellbrook, Austl. (mŭs'wŭnl-brŏŏk)	212	32.15 S	150.50 E
Mutombo Mukulu, Zaire (mōō-tôm'bō mōō-kōō'lōō)	222	8.12 S	23.56 E
Mutsu Wan (B.), Jap. (mōōt'sōō wän)	200	41.20 N	140.55 E
Mutton Bay, Can. (mŭt''n)	103	50.48 N	59.02 W
Mutum, Braz. (mōō-tōō'm)	139a	19.48 S	41.24 W
Muyun-Kum, Peski (Des.), Sov. Un. (mōō-yōōn'kōōm')	178	44.30 N	70.00 E
Muzaffargarh, Pak.	190	30.09 N	71.15 E
Muzaffarpur, India	190	26.13 N	85.20 E
Muzon, C., Ak.	96	54.41 N	132.44 W
Muzquiz, Mex. (mōōz'kēz)	122	27.53 N	101.31 W
Muztagata (Mtn.), China	194	38.20 N	75.28 E
Mvomero, Tan.	227	6.20 S	37.25 E
Mvoti (R.), S. Afr.	223c	29.18 S	30.52 E
Mwanza, Tan. (mwän'zä)	227	2.31 S	32.54 E
Mwaya, Tan. (mwä'yä)	222	9.19 S	33.51 E
Mwenga, Zaire	227	3.02 S	28.26 E
Mweru (L.), Zaire-Zambia	227	8.50 S	28.50 E
Mwingi, Ken.	227	0.56 S	38.04 E
Mya R., Alg. (myä')	158	29.26 N	3.15 E
Myingyan, Bur. (myĭng-yŭn')	194	21.37 N	95.26 E
Myitkyina, Bur. (myĭ'chē-nà)	194	25.33 N	97.25 E
Myjava, Czech. (mûē'yá-vä)	165	48.45 N	17.33 E
Mynämäki, Fin.	163	60.41 N	21.58 E
Myohyang San (Mtn.), Kor. (myō'hyang)	200	40.00 N	126.12 E
Mýrdalsjökull (Gl.), Ice. (mür'däls-yû'kōōl)	156	63.34 N	18.04 W
Myrtle Beach, SC (mûr't'l)	125	33.42 N	78.53 W
Myrtle Point, Or.	114	43.04 N	124.08 W
Mysen, Nor.	162	59.32 N	11.16 E
Myshikino, Sov. Un. (mēsh'kē-nô)	172	57.48 N	38.21 E
Mysore, India (mī-sōr')	191	12.31 N	76.42 E
Mysovka, Sov. Un. (mē' sôf-ká)	163	55.11 N	21.17 E
Mystic, Ia. (mĭs'tĭk)	113	40.47 N	92.54 W
Mytishchi, Sov. Un. (mē-tēsh'chi)	180b	55.55 N	37.46 E
Mziha, Tan.	227	5.54 S	37.47 E
Mzimba, Malawi ('m-zĭm'bä)	227	11.52 S	33.34 E
Mzimkulu (R.), S. Afr.	223c	30.12 S	29.57 E
Mzimvubu (R.), S. Afr.	223c	31.22 S	29.20 E
Mzuzu, Malawi	227	11.30 S	34.10 E

N

PLACE (Pronunciation)	PAGE	Lat. °′	Long. °′
Naab R., F.R.G. näp)	164	49.38 N	12.15 E
Naaldwijk, Neth.	155a	52.00 N	4.11 E
Naalehu, Hi.	104a	19.00 N	155.35 W
Naantali, Fin. (nän'tá-lē)	163	60.29 N	22.03 E
Nabberu (L.), Austl. (năb'ēr-ōō)	210	26.05 S	120.35 E
Nabeul, Tun. (nā-bûl')	220	36.34 N	10.45 E
Nabiswera, Ug.	227	1.28 N	32.16 E
Naboomspruit, S. Afr.	219d	24.32 S	28.43 E
Nābulus, Jordan	189a	32.13 N	35.16 E
Nacala, Moz. (nă-ká'lá)	227	14.34 S	40.41 E
Nacaome, Hond. (nä-kä-ō'mā)	130	13.32 N	87.28 W
Naceur, Bou Mt., Mor.	158	33.50 N	3.55 W
Na Cham, Viet. (nä chäm')	199	22.02 N	106.30 E
Naches R., Wa. (năch'ĕz)	114	46.51 N	121.03 W
Náchod, Czech. (näk'ôt)	164	50.25 N	16.08 E
Nacimiento (R.), Ca. (ná-sĭ-myĕn'tō)	118	35.50 N	121.00 W
Nacogdoches, Tx. (năk'ō-dō'chĕz)	123	31.36 N	94.40 W
Nadadores, Mex. (nä-dä-dō'räs)	122	27.04 N	101.36 W

PLACE (Pronunciation)	PAGE	Lat. °′	Long. °′
Nadiād, India	190	22.45 N	72.51 E
Nadir, Vir. Is. (U.S.A.)	127c	18.19 N	64.53 W
Nădlac, Rom.	171	46.09 N	20.52 E
Nad Nisou, see Jablonec			
Nad Váhom, see Nové Mesto			
Nadvornaya, Sov. Un. (näd-vōōr'ná-yá)	165	48.37 N	24.35 E
Nadym (R.), Sov. Un. (ná'dĭm)	178	64.30 N	72.48 E
Naestved, Den. (nĕst'vĭdh)	162	55.14 N	11.46 E
Nafada, Nig.	225	11.08 N	11.20 E
Nafishah, Egypt	219c	30.34 N	32.15 E
Nafūd ad Dahy (Des.), Sau. Ar.	193	22.15 N	44.15 E
Nag, Co (L.), China	190	31.38 N	91.18 E
Naga, Phil. (nä'gä)	203a	13.37 N	123.12 E
Naga (I.), Jap.	201	32.09 N	130.16 E
Nagahama, Jap. (nä'gä-hä'mä)	201	33.32 N	132.29 E
Nagahama, Jap.	201	35.23 N	136.16 E
Nagaland (State), India	194	25.47 N	94.15 E
Nagano, Jap. (nä'gä-nô)	201	36.42 N	138.12 E
Nagaoka, Jap. (nä'gá-ō'ká)	201	37.22 N	138.49 E
Nagaoka, Jap.	201b	34.54 N	135.42 E
Nāgappattinam, India	191	10.48 N	79.51 E
Nagarote, Nic. (nä-gä-rô'tē)	130	12.17 N	86.35 W
Nagasaki, Jap. (nä'gá-sä'kē)	201	32.48 N	129.53 E
Nāgaur, India	190	27.19 N	73.41 E
Nagaybakskiy, Sov. Un. (ná-gây-bäk'skĭ)	180a	53.33 N	59.33 E
Nagcarlan, Phil. (näg-kär-län')	203a	14.07 N	121.24 E
Nāgercoil, India	191	8.15 N	77.29 E
Nagorno Karabakh (Reg.), Sov. Un. (nu-gôr'nŭ-kŭ-rŭ-bäk')	177	40.10 N	46.50 E
Nagoya, Jap. (nä'gō'yá)	201	35.09 N	136.53 E
Nāgpur, India (näg'pōōr)	190	21.12 N	79.09 E
Nagua, Dom. Rep. (ná'gwä)	133	19.20 N	69.40 W
Nagykanizsa, Hung. (nôd'y'kô'nē-shô)	164	46.27 N	17.00 E
Nagykōrōs, Hung. (nôd'y'kŭ-rŭsh)	165	47.02 N	19.46 E
Naha, Jap. (nä'hä)	195	26.02 N	127.43 E
Nahanni Natl. Pk., Can.	94	62.10 N	125.15 W
Nahant, Ma. (ná-hănt)	103a	42.26 N	70.55 W
Nahariyya, Isr.	189a	33.01 N	35.06 E
Nahr al Khābur (R.), Syr.	177	35.50 N	41.00 E
Nahuel Huapi (L.), Arg. (nä'wĕl wä'pē)	142	41.00 S	71.30 W
Nahuizalco, Sal. (nä-wē-zäl'kō)	130	13.50 N	89.43 W
Naic, Phil. (nä-ēk)	203a	14.20 N	120.46 E
Naica, Mex. (nä-ē'kä)	122	27.53 N	105.30 W
Naiguatá, Ven. (nī-gwä-tá')	141b	10.37 N	66.44 W
Naiguata, Pico (Mtn.), Ven. (pē'kô)	141b	10.32 N	66.44 W
Naihāti, India	190a	22.54 N	88.25 E
Nain, Can. (nīn)	95	56.29 N	61.52 W
Nairn, Scot. (nârn)	160	57.35 N	3.54 W
Nairobi, Ken. (nī-rō'bē)	227	1.17 S	36.49 E
Naivasha, Ken. (nī-vä'shá)	223	0.47 S	36.29 E
Najd (Des.), Sau. Ar.	192	25.18 N	42.38 E
Naj 'Ḩammādī, Egypt (näg'hä-mä'dē)	219b	26.02 N	32.12 E
Najin, Kor. (nä'jĭn)	200	42.04 N	130.35 E
Najran (Des.), Sau. Ar. (nŭj-rän')	192	17.29 N	45.30 E
Naju, Kor. (nä'jōō')	200	35.02 N	126.42 E
Najusa (R.), Cuba (nä-hōō'sä)	132	21.55 N	77.55 W
Nakadorishima (I.), Jap. (nä'kä'dô'rē-shē'mä)	198	33.00 N	128.20 E
Nakatsu, Jap. (nä'käts-ōō)	201	33.34 N	131.10 E
Nakhichevan, Sov. Un. (ná-kē-chĕ-ván')	177	39.10 N	45.30 E
Nakhodka, Sov. Un. (nŭ-ĸôt'kŭ)	179	43.03 N	133.08 E
Nakhon Ratchasima, Thai.	202	14.56 N	102.14 E
Nakhon Sawan, Thai.	202	15.42 N	100.06 E
Nakhon Si Thammarat, Thai.	202	8.27 N	99.58 E
Nakskov, Den. (näk'skou)	162	54.51 N	11.06 E
Nakło nad Notecia, Pol. (näk'wō näd nō-tĕ'chōɴ)	165	53.10 N	17.35 E
Naktong (R.), Kor. (näk'tŭng)	200	36.10 N	128.30 E
Nal'chik, Sov. Un. (nál-chēk')	177	43.30 N	43.35 E
Nalón (R.), Sp. (nä-lōn')	168	43.15 N	5.38 W
Nālūt, Libya (nä-lōōt')	220	31.51 N	10.49 E
Namak, Daryacheh-ye (L.), Iran	192	34.58 N	51.33 E
Namakan (L.), Mn. (nă'má-kán)	113	48.20 N	92.43 W
Namakzār-e Shāhdād (L.), Iran (nŭ-mŭk-zär')	192	31.00 N	58.30 E
Namangan, Sov. Un. (ná-mán-gän')	178	41.08 N	71.59 E
Namao, Can.	93g	53.43 N	113.30 W
Namatanai, Pa. N. Gui. (nä'mä-tá-nä'ē)	203	3.43 S	152.26 E
Nambe Pueblo Ind. Res., NM (näm'bā pwĕb'lō)	119	35.52 N	105.39 W
Nambour, Austl. (năm'bōōr)	212	26.48 S	153.00 E
Nam Co (L.), China (näm tswo)	190	30.30 N	91.10 E
Nam Dinh, Viet. (näm dĕnĸ')	202	20.30 N	106.10 E
Nametil, Moz.	227	15.43 S	39.21 E
Namhae (I.), Kor. (näm'hī')	200	34.23 N	128.05 E
Namib (Des.), Namibia (nä-mēb')	222	18.45 S	12.45 E
Namibia, Afr.	218	19.30 S	16.13 E
Namoi (R.), Austl. (năm'oi)	212	30.10 S	148.43 E
Namous, Oued en (R.), Alg. (ná-mōōs')	158	31.48 N	00.19 W
Nampa, Id. (năm'pá)	114	43.35 N	116.35 W
Namp'o, Kor.	198	38.47 N	125.28 E
Nampuecha, Moz.	227	13.59 S	40.18 E
Nampula, Moz.	227	15.07 S	39.15 E
Namsos, Nor. (näm'sōs)	156	64.28 N	11.14 E
Namu, Can.	96	51.03 N	127.50 W
Namuli, Serra (Mts.), Moz.	227	15.05 S	37.05 E
Namur, Bel. (ná-mür')	161	50.29 N	4.55 E
Namutoni, Namibia (nä-mōō-tō'nē)	222	18.45 S	17.00 E
Nan (R.), Thai	202	18.11 N	100.29 E
Nanacamilpa, Mex. (nä-nä-kä-mē'l-pä)	129a	19.30 N	98.33 W
Nanaimo, Can. (ná-nī'mō)	96	49.10 N	123.56 W
Nanam, Kor. (nä'nän')	200	41.38 N	129.37 E

ng-sing; ŋ-baŋk; ɴ-nasalized n; nŏd; cŏmmit; ōld; ôbey; ôrder; oi-boil; fōōd; fŏŏt; ou-out; s-soft; sh-dish; th-thin; pūre; ûnite; ûrn; stŭd; circŭs; ü-as in French tu; '-indeterminate vowel.

PLACE (Pronunciation)	PAGE	Lat. °′	Long. °′
Nanao, Jap. (nä'nä-ō)	201	37.03 N	136.59 E
Nan'ao Dao, China (nän-ou dou)	199	23.30 N	117.30 E
Nanchang, China (nən-chäŋ)	199	28.38 N	115.48 E
Nanchangshan Dao (I.), China (nän-chäŋ-shän dou)	196	37.56 N	120.42 E
Nancheng, China (nän-chäŋ)	199	26.50 N	116.40 E
Nanchong, China (nän-chôŋ)	199	30.45 N	106.05 E
Nancy, Fr. (näɴ-sē')	167	48.42 N	6.11 E
Nancy Cr., Ga. (năn'cē)	110c	33.51 N	84.25 W
Nanda Devi (Mt.), India (nän'dä dā'vē)	190	30.30 N	80.25 E
Nānded, India	190	19.13 N	77.21 E
Nandurbār, India	190	21.29 N	74.13 E
Nandyāl, India	191	15.54 N	78.09 E
Nanga Parbat, Pak.	190	35.20 N	74.35 E
Nangi, India	190a	22.30 N	88.14 E
Nangis, Fr. (näɴ-zhē')	167b	48.33 N	3.01 E
Nangong, China (nän-gôŋ)	196	37.22 N	115.22 E
Nangweshi, Zambia	226	16.26 S	23.17 E
Nanhuangcheng Dao (I.), China (nän-hŭäŋ-chŭŋ dou)	196	38.22 N	120.54 E
Nanhui, China	197b	31.03 N	121.45 E
Nani Dinh, Viet.	199	20.25 N	106.08 E
Nani Hu (L.), China (näɴ'yi' hōō)	196	31.12 N	119.05 E
Nanjing, China (nän-jyĭŋ)	196	32.04 N	118.46 E
Nanjuma (R.), China (nän-jyōō-mä)	196	39.37 N	115.45 E
Nanle, China (nän-lŭ)	196	36.03 N	115.13 E
Nanliu (R.), China (nän-lĭô)	199	22.00 N	109.18 E
Nan Ling (Mts.), China	199	25.15 N	111.40 E
Nannine, Austl. (nă-nēn')	210	25.50 S	118.30 E
Nanning, China (nän'nĭng')	199	22.56 N	108.10 E
Nanpan (R.), China (nän-pän)	199	24.50 N	105.30 E
Nanping, China (nän-pĭŋ)	199	26.40 N	118.05 E
Nansei-shotō (Ryukyu Islands), Jap.	195	27.30 N	127.00 E
Nansemond, Va. (năn'sē-mŭnd)	110g	36.46 N	76.32 W
Nansemond R., Va.	110g	36.50 N	76.34 W
Nantai Zan (Mtn.), Jap. (nän-täē zän)	201	36.47 N	139.28 E
Nantes, Fr. (näɴt')	166	47.13 N	1.37 W
Nanteuil-le-Haudouin, Fr. (näɴ-tû-lē-ō-dwăɴ')	167b	49.08 N	2.49 E
Nanticoke, Pa. (năn'tĭ-kōk)	109	41.10 N	76.00 W
Nantong, China (nän-tôŋ)	196	32.02 N	120.51 E
Nantong, China	196	32.08 N	121.06 E
Nantucket (I.), Ma. (năn-tŭk'ĕt)	109	41.15 N	70.05 W
Nantwich, Eng. (nănt'wĭch)	154	53.04 N	2.31 W
Nanxiang, China (nän-shyäŋ)	197b	31.17 N	121.17 E
Nanxiong, China (nän-shôŋ)	199	25.10 N	114.20 E
Nanyang, China	198	33.00 N	112.42 E
Nanyang, Hu (L.), China (nän-yäŋ hōō)	196	35.14 N	116.24 E
Nanyuan, China (nän-yüän)	198a	39.48 N	116.24 E
Naolinco, Mex. (nä-o-lēŋ'kō)	129	19.39 N	96.50 W
Náousa, Grc. (nä'ōō-sȧ)	171	40.38 N	22.05 E
Naozhou Dao (I.), China (nou-jō dou)	199	20.58 N	110.58 E
Napa, Ca. (năp'ȧ)	118	38.20 N	122.17 W
Napanee, Can. (năp'ȧ-nē)	109	44.15 N	77.00 W
Naperville, Il. (nā'pēr-vĭl)	111a	41.46 N	88.09 W
Napier, N.Z. (nā'pĭ-ēr)	213	39.30 S	177.00 E
Napierville, Can. (nā'pĭ-ē-vĭl)	93a	45.11 N	73.24 W
Naples, Fl. (nā'p'lz)	125a	26.07 N	81.46 W
Naples, see Napoli			
Napo (R.), Peru (nä'pō)	140	1.49 S	74.20 W
Napoleon, Oh. (nȧ-pō'lē-ŭn)	108	41.20 N	84.10 W
Napoleonville, La. (nȧ-pō'lē-ŭn-vĭl)	123	29.56 N	91.03 W
Napoli (Naples), It. (nä'pō-lē)	169c	40.37 N	14.12 E
Napoli, Golfo de (G.), It. (gôl-fō-dē)	169c	40.29 N	14.08 E
Nappanee, In. (năp'ȧ-nē)	108	41.30 N	86.00 W
Nara, Jap. (nä'rä)	201b	34.41 N	135.50 E
Nara, Mali	220	15.09 N	7.27 W
Nara (Pref.), Jap.	201b	34.36 N	135.49 E
Nara (R.), Sov. Un.	172	55.05 N	37.16 E
Naracoorte, Austl. (nȧ-rȧ-kōōn'tē)	212	36.50 S	140.50 E
Naraspur, India	191	16.32 N	81.43 E
Narashino, Jap.	201a	35.41 N	140.01 E
Narberth, Pa. (när'bûrth)	110f	40.01 N	75.17 W
Narbonne, Fr. (nȧr-bôn')	166	43.12 N	3.00 E
Nardò, It. (när-dô')	171	40.11 N	18.02 E
Nare, Col. (nä'rĕ)	140a	6.12 N	74.37 W
Narew R., Pol. (när'ĕf)	165	52.43 N	21.19 E
Narmada (R.), India	190	22.17 N	74.45 E
Naroch' (L.), Sov. Un. (nä'rôch)	172	54.51 N	27.00 E
Narodnaya, Gora (Mtn.), Sov. Un. (nȧ-rôd'nȧ-yȧ)	176	65.10 N	60.10 E
Naro-Fominsk, Sov. Un. (nä'rō-mēnsk')	172	55.23 N	36.43 E
Narrabeen, Austl. (năr-ȧ-bĭn)	207b	33.44 S	151.18 E
Narragansett, RI (năr-ă-găn'sĕt)	110b	41.26 N	71.27 W
Narragansett B., RI	109	41.20 N	71.15 W
Narrandera, Austl. (nȧ-rȧn-dē'rȧ)	212	34.40 S	146.40 E
Narrogin, Austl. (năr'ō-gĭn)	210	33.00 S	117.15 E
Narva, Sov. Un. (nȧr'vȧ)	172	59.24 N	28.12 E
Narvacan, Phil. (när-vä-kän')	203a	17.27 N	120.29 E
Narva Jõesuu, Sov. Un. (nȧr'vȧ ōō-ô-ă'sōō-ōō)	172	59.26 N	28.02 E
Narvik, Nor. (när'vēk)	156	68.21 N	17.18 E
Narvskiy Zaliv (B.), Sov. Un. (nȧr'vskĭ zä'lĭf)	163	59.35 N	27.25 E
Nar'yan-Mar, Sov. Un. (när'yȧn mär')	176	67.42 N	53.30 E
Naryilco, Austl. (năr-ĭl'kō)	212	28.40 S	141.50 E
Narym, Sov. Un. (nä-rēm')	178	58.47 N	82.05 E
Naryn (R.), Sov. Un. (nŭ-rĭn')	193	41.46 N	73.00 E
Naseby, Eng. (nāz'bĭ)	154	52.23 N	0.59 W
Nashua, Mo. (năsh'ŭ-ȧ)	117f	39.18 N	94.34 W
Nashua, NH	103a	42.47 N	71.23 W
Nashville, Ar. (năsh'vĭl)	121	33.56 N	93.50 W
Nashville, Ga.	124	31.12 N	83.15 W
Nashville, Il.	121	38.21 N	89.42 W
Nashville, Mi.	108	42.35 N	85.50 W
Nashville, Tn.	124	36.10 N	86.48 W
Nashwauk, Mn. (năsh'wôk)	113	47.21 N	93.12 W
Našice, Yugo. (nä'shē-tsĕ)	171	45.29 N	18.06 E
Nasielsk, Pol. (nä'syĕlsk)	165	52.35 N	20.50 E
Näsijärvi (L.), Fin. (nĕ'sē-yĕr'vē)	176	61.42 N	24.05 E
Nāsik, India (nä'sĭk)	190	20.02 N	73.49 E
Nāşir, Sud. (nä-zēr')	221	8.30 N	33.06 E
Nāşir, Buharyrat, see Nasser, L.			
Nasirābād, Bngl.	190	24.48 N	90.28 E
Nasirabād, India	190	26.13 N	74.48 E
Naskaupi (R.), Can. (näs'kô-pĭ)	95	53.59 N	61.10 W
'Nasondoye, Zaire	226	10.22 S	25.06 E
Nass (R.), Can. (năs)	96	55.00 N	129.30 W
Nassau, Ba. (năs'ô)	132	25.05 N	77.20 W
Nassenheide, G.D.R. (nä'sĕn-hī-dĕ)	155b	52.49 N	13.13 E
Nasser, L., (Nāşir, Buḩayrat), Egypt	219b	23.50 N	32.50 E
Nässjö, Swe. (nĕs'shû)	162	57.39 N	14.39 E
Nasugbu, Phil. (nȧ-sōōg-bōō')	203a	14.05 N	120.37 E
Nasworthy L., Tx. (năz'wûr-thē)	122	31.17 N	100.30 W
Natá, Pan. (nä-tȧ')	131	8.20 N	80.30 W
Natagaima, Col. (nä-tä-gī'mä)	140a	3.38 N	75.07 W
Natal, Braz. (nä-täl')	141	6.00 S	35.13 W
Natal (Prov.), S. Afr. (nȧ-täl')	222	28.50 S	30.07 E
Natashquan, Can. (nä-täsh'kwän)	103	50.11 N	61.49 W
Natashquan (R.), Can.	103	50.35 N	61.35 W
Natchez, Ms. (năch'ĕz)	124	1.35 N	91.20 W
Natchitoches, La. (năk'ĭ-tŏsh)(nȧch-ĭ-tŏsh')	123	31.46 N	93.06 W
Natick, Ma. (nā'tĭk)	103a	42.17 N	71.21 W
National Area (Reg.), Sov. Un.	179	66.30 N	170.30 E
National Bison Ra. (Mts.), Mt. (năsh'ŭn-ăl bī's'n)	115	47.18 N	113.58 W
National City, Ca.	118a	32.38 N	117.01 W
Natitingou, Benin	224	10.19 N	1.22 E
Natividade, Braz. (nä-tē-vē-dä'dĕ)	141	11.43 S	47.34 W
Natron, L., Tan. (nā'trŏn)	227	2.17 S	36.10 E
Natrona Hts., Pa. (nā'trŏ nā)	111e	40.38 N	79.43 W
Naţrūn, Wādī an, Egypt	219b	30.33 N	30.12 E
Natuna Besar (I.), Indon.	202	4.00 N	106.50 E
Natural Bridges Natl. Mon., Ut. (năt'ū-răl brĭj'ĕs)	119	37.20 N	110.20 W
Naturaliste, C., Austl. (năt-ū-rȧ-lĭst')	210	33.30 S	115.10 E
Naucalpan, Mex. (nä'ōō-käl-pȧ'n)	129a	19.28 N	99.14 W
Nauchampatepetl (Mtn.), Mex. (näōō-chäm-pä-tē'pĕtl)	129	19.32 N	97.09 W
Nauen, G.D.R. (nou'ĕn)	155b	52.36 N	12.53 E
Naugatuck, Ct. (nô'gȧ-tŭk)	109	41.25 N	73.05 W
Naujan, Phil. (nä-ōō-hän')	203a	13.19 N	121.17 E
Naumburg, G.D.R. (noum'bōōrgh)	164	51.10 N	11.50 E
Nauru, Oceania	204	0.30 S	167.00 E
Nautla, Mex. (nä-ōōt'lä)	129	20.14 N	96.44 W
Nava, Mex. (nä'vä)	122	28.25 N	100.44 W
Nava del Rey, Sp. (nä-vä dĕl rā'ē)	168	41.22 N	5.04 W
Navahermosa, Sp. (nä-vä-ĕr-mō'sä)	168	39.39 N	4.28 W
Navajas, Cuba (nä-vä-häs')	132	22.40 N	81.20 W
Navajo Ind. Res., Az.-NM (năv'ȧ-hō)	119	36.31 N	109.24 W
Navajo Natl. Mon., Az.	119	36.43 N	110.39 W
Navajo Res., NM	119	36.57 N	107.26 W
Navalcarnero, Sp. (nä-väl'kär-nā'rō)	169a	40.17 N	4.05 W
Navalmoral de la Mata, Sp. (nä-väl'mōräl' dā lä mä'tä)	168	39.53 N	5.32 W
Navan, Can. (nă'vȧn)	93c	45.25 N	75.26 W
Navarino, (I.), Chile (nȧ-vä-rē'nō)	142	55.30 S	68.15 W
Navarra (Reg.), Sp. (nä-vär'rä)	168	42.40 N	1.35 W
Navarro, Arg. (nä-vȧ'r-rō)	139c	35.00 S	59.16 W
Navasota, Tx. (năv-aȧ-sō'tȧ)	123	30.24 N	96.05 W
Navasota R., Tx.	123	31.03 N	96.11 W
Navassa (I.), N.A. (nȧ-văs'ȧ)	133	18.25 N	75.15 W
Navia (R.), Sp. (nä-vē'ä)	168	43.10 N	6.45 W
Navidad, Chile (nä-vē-dä'd)	139b	34.57 S	71.51 W
Navidad Bk., Ba. (nä-vē-dädh')	133	20.05 N	69.00 W
Navidade do Carangola, Braz. (nȧ-vē-dä'dō-kȧ-rän-gô'la)	139a	21.04 S	41.58 W
Navojoa, Mex. (nä-vō-kô'ä)	126	27.00 N	109.40 W
Nàvplion, Grc.	171	37.33 N	22.46 E
Nawābshāh, Pak. (nȧ-wäb'shä)	190	26.20 N	68.30 E
Náxos (I.), Grc. (nȧk'sōs)	171	37.15 N	25.20 E
Nayarit (State), Mex. (nä-yä-rēt')	126	22.00 N	105.15 W
Nayarit, Sierra de (Mts.), Mex. (sē-ĕ'r-rä-dĕ)	128	23.20 N	105.07 W
Naye, Senegal	224	14.25 N	12.12 W
Naylor, Md. (nā'lōr)	110e	38.43 N	76.46 W
Nazaré, Braz. (nä-zä-rĕ')	141	13.04 S	38.49 W
Nazaré, Port. (nä-zä-rā')	168	39.38 N	9.04 W
Nazaré da Mata, Braz. (dä-mä-tä)	141	7.46 S	35.13 W
Nazas, Mex. (nä'zäs)	122	25.14 N	104.08 W
Nazas, R., Mex.	122	25.08 N	104.20 W
Nazerat, Isr.	189a	32.43 N	35.19 E
Nazilli, Tur. (nȧ-zĭ-lē')	177	37.40 N	28.10 E
Naziya R., Sov. Un. (nȧ-zē'yȧ)	180c	59.48 N	31.18 E
Nazko (R.), Can.	96	52.35 N	123.10 W
Ndali, Benin	225	9.51 N	2.43 E
Ndélé, Cen. Afr. Rep. (n'dā-lā')	221	8.21 N	20.43 E
Ndikiniméki, Cam.	225	4.46 N	10.50 E
Ndjamena (Fort-Lamy), Chad (lȧ-mē')	225	12.07 N	15.03 E
Ndjolé, Gabon (n'dzhō-lā')	222	0.15 S	10.45 E
Ndola, Zambia (n'dō'lä)	227	12.58 S	28.38 E
Ndoto Mts., Ken.	227	1.55 N	37.05 E
Ndrhamcha, Sebkha de (L.), Mauritania	224	18.50 N	15.15 W
Nduye, Zaire	227	1.50 N	29.01 E
Neagh Lough (L.), N. Ire. (lŏk nā)	160	54.40 N	6.47 W
Néa Páfos, Cyprus	189a	34.46 N	32.27 E
Neapean (R.), Austl.	207b	33.40 S	150.39 E
Neápolis, Grc. (nā-ŏp' ō-lĭs)	171	36.35 N	23.08 E
Neápolis, Grc.	170a	35.17 N	25.37 E
Near Is., Ak. (nēr)	105a	52.20 N	172.40 E
Neath, Wales (nēth)	160	51.41 N	3.50 W
Nebine Cr., Austl. (nĕ-bēne')	212	27.50 S	147.00 E
Nebit-Dag, Sov. Un. (nyĕ-bēt'däg')	177	39.30 N	54.20 E
Nebraska (State), U.S. (nē-brăs'kȧ)	106	41.45 N	101.30 W
Nebraska City, Ne.	121	40.40 N	95.50 W
Nechako Plat., Can. (nĭ-chă'kō)	96	54.00 N	124.30 W
Nechako Ra., Can.	96	53.20 N	124.30 W
Nechako Res., Can.	96	53.25 N	125.10 W
Nechako (R.), Can.	96	52.45 N	124.55 W
Neches R., Tx. (nĕch'ĕz)	123	31.03 N	94.40 W
Neckar R., F.R.G. (nĕk'är)	164	49.16 N	9.06 E
Necker I., Hi.	104b	24.00 N	164.00 W
Necochea, Arg. (nā-kō-chā'ä)	142	38.30 S	58.45 W
Nedrigaylov, Sov. Un. (nĕ-drĭ-gī'lôf)	173	50.49 N	33.52 E
Needham, Ma. (nēd'ăm)	103a	42.17 N	71.14 W
Needles, Ca. (nē'd'lz)	118	34.51 N	114.39 W
Neenah, Wi. (nē'nȧ)	113	44.10 N	88.30 W
Neepawa, Can.	99	50.13 N	99.29 W
Nee Res., Co. (nē̄)	120	38.26 N	102.56 W
Negareyama, Jap. (nā'gä-rā-yä'mä)	201a	35.52 N	139.54 E
Negaunee, Mi. (nē-gô'nē)	113	46.30 N	87.37 W
Negeri Sembilan (State), Mala. (nā'grē-sĕm-bē-län')	189b	2.46 N	101.54 E
Negev (Des.), Isr. (nĕ'gĕv)	189a	30.34 N	34.43 E
Negombo, Sri Lanka	191	7.39 N	79.49 E
Negotin, Yugo. (nĕ'gō-tēn)	171	44.13 N	22.33 E
Negro (R.), Arg.	142	39.50 S	65.00 W
Negro, Rio (R.), Braz. (rĕ'ō nā'grōō)	140	0.18 S	63.21 W
Negro, Cerro (Mt.), Pan. (sĕ'r»rō-nā'grō)	131	8.44 N	80.37 W
Negro (R.), Ur.	139c	33.17 S	58.18 W
Negro R., Nic.	130	13.01 N	87.10 W
Negros (I.), Phil. (nā'grōs)	202	9.50 N	121.45 E
Neguá, Col. (nā-gwȧ')	140a	5.51 N	76.36 W
Nehalem R., Or. (nē-hăl'ĕm)	114	45.52 N	123.37 W
Nehaus an der Oste, F.R.G. (noi'houz)(ōz'tē)	155c	53.48 N	9.02 E
Nehe, China (nŭ-hŭ)	198	48.23 N	124.58 E
Neheim-Hüsten, F.R.G. (nĕ'hīm)	167c	51.28 N	7.58 E
Neiba, Dom. Rep. (nā-ē'bä)	133	18.30 N	71.20 W
Neiba, Bahai de (B.), Dom. Rep. (bȧ-ä'ē-dĕ)	133	18.10 N	71.00 W
Neiba, Sierra de (Mts.), Dom. Rep. (sē-ĕr'rä-dĕ)	133	18.40 N	71.40 W
Neihart, Mt. (nī'hȧrt)	115	46.54 N	110.39 W
Neijiang, China (nā-jyäŋ)	199	29.38 N	105.01 E
Neillsville, Wi. (nēlz'vĭl)	113	44.35 N	90.37 W
Nei Monggol (Inner Monglia)(Aut. Reg.), China (nā-mŭŋ-gol)	194	40.15 N	105.00 E
Neiqiu, China (nā-chyō)	196	37.17 N	114.32 E
Neira, Col. (nā'rä)	140a	5.10 N	75.32 W
Neisse (R.), Pol. (nēs)	164	51.30 N	15.00 E
Neiva, Col. (nā-ē'vä)(nā'vä)	140a	2.55 N	75.16 W
Neixiang, China (nā-shyäŋ)	198	33.00 N	111.38 E
Nekemte, Eth.	221	9.09 N	36.29 E
Nekoosa, Wi. (nē-kōō'sȧ)	113	44.19 N	89.54 W
Neksø, Den. (nĕk'sû)	162	55.05 N	15.05 E
Neligh, Ne. (nē'lĭg)	112	42.06 N	98.02 W
Nel'kan, Sov. Un. (nĕl-kän')	179	57.45 N	136.36 E
Nellore, India (nĕl-lōr')	191	14.28 N	79.59 E
Nel'ma, Sov. Un. (nĕl-mä')	200	47.34 N	139.05 E
Nelson, Can. (nĕl'sŭn)	97	49.29 N	117.17 W
Nelson, Eng.	154	53.50 N	2.13 W
Nelson, N.Z.	213	41.15 S	173.22 E
Nelson (I.), Ak.	105	60.38 N	164.42 W
Nelson, C., Austl.	212	38.29 S	141.20 E
Nelson (R.), Can.	99	56.50 N	93.40 W
Nelson Cr., Nv.	118	40.22 N	114.43 W
Nelsonville, Oh. (nĕl'sŭn-vĭl)	108	39.30 N	82.15 W
Néma, Mauritania (nā'mä)	224	16.37 N	7.15 W
Nemadji R., Wi. (nĕ-măd'jē)	117h	46.33 N	92.16 W
Neman, Sov. Un. (ŋĕ'-mȧn)	163	55.02 N	22.01 E
Neman R., Sov. Un.	165	53.28 N	24.45 E
Nembe, Nig.	225	4.35 N	6.26 E
Nemeiban L., Can. (nĕ-mē'bȧn)	98	55.20 N	105.20 W
Nemirov, Sov. Un. (nyā-mē'rôf)	173	48.56 N	28.51 E
Nemours, Fr.	166	48.16 N	2.41 E
Nemuro, Jap. (nā'mōō-rō)	200	43.13 N	145.10 E
Nemuro Str., Jap.	200	43.07 N	145.10 E
Nen (R.), China (nŭn)	195	47.07 N	123.28 E
Nen (R.), Eng. (nĕn)	154	52.32 N	0.19 W
Nenagh, Ire. (nē'nȧ)	160	52.50 N	8.05 W
Nenana, Ak. (nā-nä'nȧ)	105	64.28 N	149.18 W
Nenikyul', Sov. Un. (nĕ-nyē'kyûl)	180c	59.26 N	30.40 E
Nenjiang, China (nŭn-jyäŋ)	198	49.02 N	125.15 E
Neodesha, Ks. (nē-ō-dē-shô')	121	37.24 N	95.41 W
Neosho, Mo.	121	36.51 N	94.22 W
Neosho (R.), Ks. (nē-ō'shō)	121	38.07 N	95.40 W
Nepal, Asia (nĕ-pôl')	188	28.45 N	83.00 E
Nephi, Ut. (nē'fī)	119	39.40 N	111.50 W
Nepisiguit (R.), Can. (nĭ-pĭ'sĭ-kwĭt)	102	47.25 N	66.28 W
Nepomuceno, Braz. (nĕ-pô-mōō-sĕ'no)	139a	21.15 S	45.13 W
Nera (R.), It. (nā'rä)	170	42.45 N	12.54 E
Nérac, Fr. (nā-rȧk')	166	44.08 N	0.19 E
Nerchinsk, Sov. Un. (nyĕr' chēnsk)	179	51.47 N	116.17 E
Nerchinskiy Khrebet (Mts.), Sov. Un.	179	50.30 N	118.30 E
Nerchinskiy Zavod, Sov. Un. (nyĕr'chēn-skĭzȧ-vôt')	179	51.35 N	119.46 E
Nerekhta, Sov. Un. (nyĕ-rĕĸ'tȧ)	172	57.29 N	40.34 E
Neretva (R.), Yugo. (nĕ'rĕt-vȧ)	171	43.08 N	17.50 E
Nerja, Sp. (nĕr'hä)	168	36.45 N	3.53 W
Nerl' (R.), Sov. Un. (nyĕrl)	172	56.59 N	37.57 E
Nerskaya R., Sov. Un. (nyĕr'skȧ-yȧ)	180b	55.31 N	38.46 E
Nerussa (R.), Sov. Un. (nyā-rōō'sȧ)	172	52.24 N	34.20 E
Ness, Loch (L.), Scot. (lŏĸ nĕs)	160	37.23 N	4.20 W
Ness City, Ks. (nĕs)	120	38.27 N	99.55 W
Nesterov, Sov. Un. (ŋĕs'-tzhyé-rôf)	165	50.03 N	23.58 E
Nesterov, Sov. Un. (nyĕs-tă'rôf)	163	54.39 N	22.38 E
Néstos (R.), Grc. (nās'tōs)	171	41.25 N	24.12 E
Nesvizh, Sov. Un. (nyĕs'vēsh)	172	53.13 N	26.44 E
Netanya, Isr.	189a	32.19 N	34.52 E
Netcong, NJ (nĕt'cŏnj)	110a	40.54 N	74.42 W
Netherlands, Eur. (nĕdh'ēr-lăndz)	152	53.01 N	3.57 E
Netherlands Guiana, see Suriname			
Nettilling (L.), Can.	95	66.30 N	70.40 W
Nett Lake Ind. Res., Mn. (nĕt lāk)	113	48.23 N	93.19 W
Nettuno, It. (nĕt-tōō'nô)	169d	41.28 N	12.40 E

ăt; finăl; rāte; senāte; ärm; ȧsk; sofȧ; fâre; ch-choose; dh-as th in other; bē; ēvent; bĕt; recĕnt; cratēr; g-gō; gh-guttural g; bĭt; ĭ-short neutral; rīde; ĸ-guttural k as ch in German ich;

PRONOUNCING INDEX

Neubeckum – Nimba 325

PLACE (Pronunciation)	PAGE	Lat. °′	Long. °′
Neubeckum, F.R.G. (noi'bĕ-kōōm)	167c	51.48 N	8.01 E
Neubrandenburg, G.D.R. (noi-brän'dĕn-bōōrgh)	164	53.33 N	13.16 E
Neuburg, F.R.G. (noi'bōōrgh)	164	48.43 N	11.12 E
Neuchâtel, Switz. (nû-shȧ-tĕl')	164	47.00 N	6.52 E
Neuchatel, Lac de (L.), Switz.	164	46.48 N	6.53 E
Neuenhagen, G.D.R. (noi'ĕn-hä-gĕn)	155b	52.31 N	13.41 E
Neuenrade, F.R.G. (noi'ĕn-rä-dĕ)	167c	51.17 N	7.47 E
Neufchâtel-en-Bray, Fr. (nû-shä-tĕl'ĕɴ-brā')	166	49.43 N	1.25 E
Neulengbach, Aus.	155e	48.13 N	15.55 E
Neumarkt, F.R.G. (noi'märkt)	164	49.17 N	11.30 E
Neumünster, F.R.G. (noi'münstēr)	164	54.04 N	10.00 E
Neunkirchen, Aust. (noin'kĭrκ-ĕn)	164	47.43 N	16.05 E
Neunkirchen, F.R.G.	167	49.21 N	7.20 E
Neuquén, Arg. (nĕ-ōō-kān')	142	38.52 S	68.12 W
Neuquen (Prov.), Arg.	142	39.40 S	70.45 W
Neuquén (R.), Arg.	142	38.45 S	69.00 W
Neuruppin, G.D.R. (noi'rōō-pēn)	155b	52.55 N	12.48 E
Neuse (R.), NC (nūz)	125	36.12 N	78.50 W
Neusiedler See (L.), Aus. (noi-zēd'lēr)	164	47.54 N	16.31 E
Neuss, F.R.G. (nois)	167c	51.12 N	6.41 E
Neustadt, F.R.G. (noi'shtät)	164	49.21 N	8.08 E
Neustadt bei Coburg, F.R.G. (bī kō'bōōrgh)	164	50.20 N	11.09 E
Neustadt in Holstein, F.R.G.	164	54.06 N	10.50 E
Neustrelitz, G.D.R. (noi-strĕ'lĭts)	164	53.21 N	13.05 E
Neutral Hills, Can. (nū'trăl)	98	52.10 N	110.50 W
Neu Ulm, F.R.G. (noi ōō lm')	164	48.23 N	10.01 E
Neuville, Can. (nū'vĭl)	93b	46.39 N	71.35 W
Neuwied, F.R.G. (noi'vēdt)	164	50.26 N	7.28 E
Neva (R.), Sov. Un. (nyĕ-vä')	180c	59.49 N	30.54 E
Nevada, Ia. (nē-vä'dȧ)	113	42.01 N	93.27 W
Nevada, Mo.	121	37.49 N	94.21 W
Nevada (State), U.S. (nē vȧ'dȧ)	106	39.30 N	117.00 W
Nevada, Sierra (Mts.), Sp. (syĕr'rä nä-vä'dhä)	168	37.01 N	3.28 W
Nevada, Sierra (Mts.), U.S. (sē-ĕ'r-rä nē-vä'dȧ)	106	39.20 N	120.05 W
Nevada City, Ca.	118	39.16 N	120.01 W
Nevado, Cerro el (Mtn.), Col. (sĕ'r-rô-ĕl-nē-vä'dô)	140a	4.02 N	74.08 W
Nevado de Colima (Mtn.), Mex. (nȧ-vä'dhô dā kô-lē'mä)	128	19.34 N	103.39 W
Neva Stantsiya, Sov. Un. (nyĕ-vä' stän'tsĭ-yȧ)	160c	59.53 N	30.30 E
Neve, Serra da (Mts.), Ang.	226	13.40 S	13.20 E
Nevel', Sov. Un. (nyĕ'vĕl)	172	56.03 N	29.57 E
Neveri (R.), Ven. (nĕ-vĕ-rē)	141b	10.13 N	64.18 W
Nevers, Fr. (nē-vâr')	166	46.59 N	3.10 E
Nevesinje, Yugo. (nĕ-vĕ'sēn-yĕ)	171	43.15 N	18.08 E
Nevis, Ben (Mtn.), Scot. (bĕn)	160	56.47 N	5.00 W
Nevis I., St. Kitts-Nevis (nē'vĭs)	131b	17.05 N	62.38 W
Nevis Pk., St. Kitts-Nevis	131b	17.11 N	62.33 W
Nevşehir, Tur. (nĕv-shĕ'hĕr)	177	38.40 N	34.35 E
Nev'yansk, Sov. Un. (nĕv-yänsk')	180a	57.29 N	60.14 E
New (R.), Va. (nū)	125	37.20 N	80.35 W
Newala, Tan.	227	10.56 S	39.18 E
New Albany, In. (nû ôl'bȧ-nĭ)	111h	38.17 N	85.49 W
New Albany, Ms.	124	34.28 N	39.00 W
New Amsterdam, Guy. (ăm'stēr-dăm)	141	6.14 N	57.30 W
New Amsterdam (I.), Ind. O.	228	37.52 S	77.32 E
Newark, Ca. (nū'ērk)	116b	37.32 N	122.02 W
Newark, De. (nōō'ärk)	109	39.40 N	75.45 W
Newark, Eng. (nū'ērk)	154	53.04 N	0.49 W
Newark, NJ (nōō'ûrk)	110a	40.44 N	74.10 W
Newark, NY (nū'ērk)	109	43.05 N	77.10 W
Newark, Oh.	108	40.05 N	82.25 W
Newaygo, Mi. (nū'wā-go)	108	43.25 N	85.50 W
New Bedford, Ma. (bĕd'fērd)	109	41.35 N	70.55 W
Newberg, Or. (nū'bûrg)	108	45.17 N	122.58 W
New Bern, NC (bûrn)	125	35.05 N	77.05 W
Newbern, Tn.	124	36.05 N	89.12 W
Newberry, Mi. (nū'bĕr-ĭ)	113	46.22 N	85.31 W
Newberry, SC	125	34.15 N	81.40 W
New Boston, Mi. (bôs'tŭn)	111b	42.10 N	83.24 W
New Boston, Oh.	108	38.45 N	82.55 W
New Braunfels, Tx. (nū broun'fĕls)	122	29.43 N	98.07 W
New Brighton, Mn. (brī'tŭn)	117g	45.04 N	93.12 W
New Brighton, Pa.	111e	40.34 N	80.18 W
New Britain, Ct. (brĭt''n)	109	41.40 N	72.45 W
New Britain (I.), Pap. N. Gui.	203	6.45 S	149.38 E
New Brunswick, NJ (brŭnz'wĭk)	110a	40.29 N	74.27 W
New Brunswick (Prov.), Can.	95	47.14 N	66.30 W
Newburg, In.	108	38.00 N	87.25 W
Newburg, Mo.	121	37.54 N	91.53 W
Newburgh, NY	109	41.30 N	74.00 W
Newburgh Heights, Oh.	111d	41.27 N	81.40 W
Newbury, Eng. (nū'bĕr-ĭ)	160	51.24 N	1.26 W
Newbury, Ma.	103a	42.48 N	70.52 W
Newburyport, Ma. (nū'bĕr-ĭ-pōrt)	103a	42.48 N	70.53 W
New Caledonia, Oceania	211	21.28 S	164.40 E
New Canaan, Ct. (kā-nȧn)	110a	41.06 N	73.30 W
New Carlisle, Can. (kär-līl')	102	48.01 N	65.20 W
Newcastle, Austl. (nū-kȧs''l)	212	33.00 S	151.55 E
Newcastle, Can.	102	47.00 N	65.34 W
New Castle, De.	109	39.40 N	75.35 W
Newcastle, Eng. (nû-kȧs''l) (nū-käs''l)	154	53.01 N	2.14 W
New Castle, In.	108	39.55 N	82.25 W
New Castle, Oh.	108	40.20 N	82.10 W
New Castle, Pa.	108	41.00 N	80.25 W
Newcastle, Tx.	120	33.13 N	98.44 W
Newcastle, Wy.	112	43.51 N	104.11 W
Newcastle upon Tyne, Eng.	160	55.00 N	1.45 W
Newcastle Waters, Austl. (wô'tērz)	210	17.10 S	133.25 E
Newcomerstown, Oh. (nū'kŭm-ērz-toun)	108	40.15 N	81.40 W
New Croton Res., NY (krō'tŏn)	110a	41.15 N	73.47 W
New Delhi, India (dĕl'hī)	190	28.43 N	77.18 E
Newell, SD (nū'ĕl)	112	44.43 N	103.26 W
New England Ra., Austl. (nû ĭŋ'glănd)	211	29.32 S	152.30 E
Newenham, C., Ak. (nū-ĕn-hăm)	105	58.40 N	162.32 W
Newfane, NY (nū-fān)	111c	43.17 N	78.44 W
Newfoundland (Prov.), Can. (nū-fŭn'lănd') (nū'fŭnd-lănd) (nû'found-lănd')	95a	48.15 N	56.53 W
Newgate, Can. (nû'gāt)	97	49.01 N	115.10 W
New Georgia (I.), Sol. Is. (jôr'jĭ-ȧ)	211	8.08 S	158.00 E
New Glasgow, Can. (glȧs'gō)	113	45.35 N	62.36 W
New Guinea (I.), Asia (gĭne)	203	5.45 S	140.00 E
Newhalem, Wa. (nū hă'lŭm)	114	48.44 N	121.11 W
New Hampshire (State), U. S. (hămp'shĭr)	107	43.55 N	71.40 W
New Hampton, Ia. (hămp'tŭn)	113	43.03 N	92.20 W
New Hanover, S. Afr. (hăn'ôvēr)	223c	29.23 S	30.32 E
New Hanover (I.), Pap. N. Gui.	203	2.37 S	150.15 E
New Harmony, In. (nū här'mô-nĭ)	108	38.10 N	87.55 W
New Haven, Ct. (hā'vĕn)	109	41.20 N	72.55 W
Newhaven, Eng.	161	50.45 N	0.10 E
New Haven, In. (nū hāv''n)	108	41.05 N	85.00 W
New Holland, Eng. (hŏl'ănd)	154	53.42 N	0.21 W
New Holland, NC	125	35.27 N	76.14 W
New Hope Mtn., Al. (hōp)	110h	33.23 N	86.45 W
New Hudson, Mi. (hŭd'sŭn)	111b	42.30 N	83.36 W
New Iberia, La. (ī-bē'rĭ-ȧ)	123	30.00 N	91.50 W
Newington, Can. (nū'ĕng-tŏn)	93c	45.07 N	75.00 W
New Ireland (I.), Pap. N. Gui. (īr'lănd)	203	3.15 S	152.30 E
New Jersey (State), U. S. (jûr'zĭ)	107	40.30 N	74.50 W
New Kensington, Pa. (kĕn'zĭng-tŭn)	111e	40.34 N	79.35 W
Newkirk, Ok. (nū'kûrk)	121	36.52 N	97.03 W
New Lenox, Il. (lĕn'ŭk)	111a	41.31 N	87.58 W
New Lexington, Oh. (lĕk'sĭng-tŭn)	108	39.40 N	82.10 W
New Lisbon, Wi. (lĭz'bŭn)	113	43.52 N	90.11 W
New Liskeard, Can.	101	47.30 N	79.40 W
New London, Ct. (lŭn'dŭn)	109	41.20 N	72.05 W
New London, Wi.	113	44.24 N	88.45 W
New Madrid, Mo. (măd'rĭd)	121	36.34 N	89.31 W
Newman (L.), Fl.	125	29.41 N	82.13 W
Newman's Grove, Ne. (nū'mȧn grōv)	112	41.46 N	97.44 W
Newmarket, Can. (nū'mär-kĕt)	109	44.00 N	79.30 W
New Martinsville, WV (mär'tĭnz-vĭl)	108	39.35 N	80.50 W
New Meadows, Id.	114	44.58 N	116.20 W
New Mexico (State), U. S. (mĕk'sĭ-kō)	106	34.30 N	107.10 W
New Mills, Eng. (mĭlz)	154	53.22 N	2.00 W
New Munster, Wi. (mŭn'stēr)	111a	42.35 N	88.13 W
Newnan, Ga. (nū'năn)	124	33.22 N	84.47 W
New Norfolk, Austl. (nôr'fŏk)	212	42.50 S	147.17 E
New Orleans, La. (ôr'lē-ănz)	110d	30.00 N	90.05 W
New Philadelphia, Oh. (fĭl-ȧ-dĕl'fĭ-ȧ)	108	40.30 N	81.30 W
New Plymouth, N. Z. (plĭm'ŭth)	213	39.04 S	174.13 E
Newport, Ar. (nū'pōrt)	121	35.35 N	91.16 W
Newport, Austl.	207b	33.39 S	151.19 E
Newport, Eng. (nū-pôrt)	160	50.41 N	1.25 W
Newport, Eng.	154	52.46 N	2.22 W
Newport, Ky.	111f	39.05 N	84.30 W
Newport, Me.	102	44.49 N	69.20 W
Newport, Mn.	117g	44.52 N	92.59 W
Newport, NH	109	43.20 N	72.10 W
Newport, Or.	114	44.39 N	124.02 W
Newport, RI	110b	41.29 N	71.16 W
Newport, Tn.	124	35.55 N	83.12 W
Newport, Vt.	109	44.55 N	72.15 W
Newport, Wales	160	51.36 N	3.05 W
Newport, Wa.	114	48.12 N	117.01 W
Newport Beach, Ca. (bēch)	117a	33.36 N	117.55 W
Newport News, Va.	110g	36.59 N	76.24 W
New Prague, Mn. (nū prāg)	113	44.33 N	93.35 W
New Providence (I.), Ba. (prŏv'ĭ-dĕns)	132	25.00 N	77.25 W
New Richmond, Oh. (rĭch'mŭnd)	108	38.55 N	84.15 W
New Richmond, Wi.	113	45.07 N	92.34 W
New Roads, La. (rōds)	123	30.42 N	91.26 W
New Rochelle, NY (rū-shĕl')	110a	40.55 N	73.47 W
New Rockford, ND (rŏk'fōrd)	112	47.40 N	99.08 W
New Ross, Ire. (rôs)	164	52.25 N	6.55 W
New Sarepta, Can.	93g	53.17 N	113.09 W
New Siberian Is., see Novosibirskiye O-va			
New Smyrna Beach, Fl. (smûr'nȧ)	125	29.00 N	80.57 W
New South Wales (State), Austl. (wālz)	211	32.45 S	146.14 E
Newton, Can. (nū'tŭn)	93f	49.56 N	98.04 W
Newton, Eng.	154	53.27 N	2.37 W
Newton, Il.	108	39.00 N	88.10 W
Newton, Ia.	113	41.42 N	93.04 W
Newton, Ks.	121	38.03 N	97.22 W
Newton, Ma.	103a	42.21 N	71.13 W
Newton, Ms.	124	32.18 N	89.10 W
Newton, NJ	110a	41.03 N	74.45 W
Newton, NC	125	35.40 N	81.19 W
Newton, Tx.	123	30.47 N	93.45 W
Newtonsville, Oh. (nū'tŭnz-vĭl)	111f	39.11 N	84.04 W
Newtown, ND (nū'toun)	112	47.57 N	102.25 W
Newtown, Oh.	111f	39.08 N	84.22 W
Newtown, Pa.	110f	40.13 N	74.56 W
Newtownards, Ire. (nu-t'n-ardz')	160	54.35 N	5.39 W
New Ulm, Mn. (ŭlm)	113	44.18 N	94.27 W
New Waterford, Can. (wô'tēr-fērd)	103	46.15 N	60.05 W
New Westminster, Can. (wĕst'mĭn-stēr)	116d	49.12 N	122.55 W
New York, NY (yôrk)	110a	40.40 N	73.58 W
New York (State), U. S.	107	42.45 N	78.05 W
New Zealand, Oceania (zē'lănd)	211a	42.00 S	175.00 E
Nexapa (R.), Mex. (nĕks-ä'pä)	128	18.32 N	98.29 W
Neya-gawa, Jap. (nā'yä gä'wä)	201b	34.47 N	135.38 E
Neyshābūr, Iran	192	36.06 N	58.45 E
Neyva R., Sov. Un. (nĕy'vȧ)	180a	57.39 N	60.37 E
Nezhin, Sov. Un. (nyĕzh'ēn)	173	50.03 N	31.52 E
Nez Perce, Id. (nĕz' pûrs')	114	46.16 N	116.15 W
Ngami (R.), Bots. (n'gä'mē)	222	20.56 S	22.31 E
Ngangerabeli Pln., Ken.	227	1.20 S	40.10 E
Ngangla Ringco (L.), China (ŋäŋ-lä rĭŋ-tswo)	190	31.42 N	82.53 E
Ngaoundéré, Cam. (n'gōn-dā-rā')	225	7.19 N	13.35 E
Ngarimbi, Tan.	227	8.28 S	38.36 E
Ngoko (R.), Afr.	226	1.55 N	15.53 E
Ngol-Kedju Hill, Cam.	225	6.20 N	9.45 E
Ngong, Ken. ('n-gông)	223	1.27 S	36.39 E
Ngounié (R.), Gabon	226	1.15 S	10.43 E
Ngoywa, Tan.	227	5.56 S	32.48 E
Ngqeleni, S. Afr. ('ng-kĕ-lā'nē)	223c	31.41 S	29.04 E
Nguigmi, Niger ('n-gēg'mē)	225	14.15 N	13.07 E
Ngurore, Nig.	225	9.18 N	12.14 E
Nguru, Nig. ('n-gōō'rōō)	220	12.53 N	10.26 E
Nguru Mts., Tan.	227	6.10 S	37.35 E
Nha-trang, Viet. (nyä-träng')	202	12.08 N	108.56 E
Niafounke, Mali	220	16.03 N	4.17 W
Niagara, Wi. (nī-ăg'ȧ-rȧ)	113	45.45 N	88.05 W
Niagara Falls, Can.	111c	43.05 N	79.05 W
Niagara Falls, NY	111c	43.06 N	79.02 W
Niagara-on-the-Lake, Can.	93d	43.16 N	79.05 W
Niagara R., U. S.-Can.	111c	43.12 N	79.03 W
Niakaramandougou, Ivory Coast	224	8.40 N	5.17 W
Niamey, Niger (nē-ä-mā')	225	13.31 N	2.07 E
Niamtougou, Togo	224	9.46 N	1.06 E
Niangara, Zaire (nē-äŋ-gȧ'rȧ)	227	3.42 N	27.52 E
Niangua (R.), Mo. (nī-ăŋ'gwȧ)	121	37.30 N	93.05 W
Nias, Pulau (I.), Indon. (nē'äs')	202	0.58 N	97.43 E
Nibe, Den. (nē'bĕ)	162	56.57 N	9.36 E
Nicaragua, N. A. (nĭk-ȧ-rä'gwȧ)	126	12.45 N	86.15 W
Nicaragua, Lago de (L.), Nic. (lä'gô dĕ)	130	11.45 N	85.28 W
Nicastro, It. (nē-käs'trō)	170	38.39 N	16.15 E
Nicchehabin, Punta (Pt.), Mex. (pōō'n-tä-nĕk-chĕ-ä-bē'n)	130a	19.50 N	87.20 W
Nice, Fr. (nēs)	167	43.42 N	7.21 E
Nicheng, China (nē-chŭŋ)	197b	30.54 N	121.48 E
Nichicun (L.), Can. (nĭch'ĭ-kŭn)	95	53.07 N	72.10 W
Nicholas Chan., Ba. (nĭk'ô-lȧs)	132	23.30 N	80.20 W
Nicholasville, Ky. (nĭk'ô-lȧs-vĭl)	108	37.55 N	84.35 W
Nicobar Is., Andaman & Nicobar Is. (nĭk-ô-bär')	202	8.28 N	94.04 E
Nicolai Mtn., Or. (nē-cō lī')	116c	46.05 N	123.27 W
Nicolás Romero, Mex. (nē-kô-lä's rô-mē'rô)	129a	19.38 N	99.20 W
Nicolet, L., Mi. (nĭ'kō-lĕt)	117k	46.22 N	84.14 W
Nicolls Town, Ba.	132	25.10 N	78.00 W
Nicols, Mn. (nĭk'ĕls)	117g	44.50 N	93.12 W
Nicomeki (R.), Can.	116d	49.04 N	122.47 W
Nicosia, Cyprus (nē-kô-sē'ȧ)	159	35.10 N	33.22 E
Nicoya, C. R. (nē-kō'yä)	130	10.08 N	85.27 W
Nicoya, Golfo de (G.), C. R. (gôl-fô-dĕ)	130	10.03 N	85.04 W
Nicoya, Pen. de, C. R.	130	10.05 N	86.00 W
Nidaros, see Trondheim			
Nidzica, Pol. (nē-jĕt'sȧ)	165	53.21 N	20.30 E
Niedere Tauern (Mts.), Aus.	164	47.15 N	13.41 E
Niederkrüchten, F.R.G. (nē'dĕr-krük-tĕn)	167c	51.12 N	6.14 E
Niederösterreich (Lower Austria) (State), Aus.	155e	48.24 N	16.20 E
Niedersachsen (Lower Saxony) (State), F.R.G. (nē'dĕr-zäκ-sĕn)	164	52.52 N	8.27 E
Niélé, Ivory Coast	224	10.12 N	5.38 W
Niellim, Chad	225	9.42 N	17.49 E
Nienburg, F.R.G. (nē'ĕn-bōōrgh)	164	52.40 N	9.15 E
Niénokoué, Mont (Mtn.), Ivory Coast	224	5.26 N	7.10 W
Nietverdiend, S. Afr.	219d	25.02 S	26.10 E
Nieuw Nickerie, Sur. (nē-nē'kĕ-rē')	141	5.51 N	57.00 W
Nieves, Mex. (nyā'vȧs)	128	24.00 N	102.57 W
Niğde, Tur. (nĭg'dĕ)	177	37.55 N	34.40 E
Nigel, S. Afr. (nī'jĕl)	219d	26.26 S	28.27 E
Niger, Afr. (nī'jēr)	218	18.02 N	8.30 E
Niger (R.), Afr.	225	5.33 N	6.33 E
Niger Delta, Nig.	225	4.45 N	5.20 E
Nigeria, Afr. (nī-jē'rĭ-ȧ)	218	8.57 N	6.30 E
Nihoa (I.), Hi.	104b	23.15 N	161.30 W
Nii (I.), Jap. (nē)	201	34.26 N	139.23 E
Niigata, Jap. (nē'ē-gä'tȧ)	200	37.47 N	139.04 E
Niihau (I.), Hi. (nē'ē-ha'ōō)	104a	21.50 N	160.05 W
Niimi, Jap. (nē'mē)	201	34.59 N	133.28 E
Niiza, Jap.	201a	35.48 N	139.34 E
Nijmegen, Neth. (nī'mä-gĕn)	161	51.50 N	5.52 E
Nikaidō, Jap. (nē'ki-dô)	201b	34.36 N	135.48 E
Nikitinka, Sov. Un. (nē-kĭ'tĭn-kȧ)	172	55.33 N	33.19 E
Nikkō, Jap. (nĕk'kō)	201	36.44 N	139.35 E
Nikolayev, Sov. Un. (nē-kô-lä'yĕf)	173	46.58 N	32.02 E
Nikolayev (Oblast), Sov. Un. (ôb'lȧst)	173	47.27 N	31.25 E
Nikolayevka, Sov. Un.	200	48.37 N	134.09 E
Nikolayevka, Sov. Un. (nē-kô-lä'yĕf-kȧ)	180c	59.29 N	29.48 E
Nikolayevskiy, Sov. Un.	177	50.00 N	45.30 E
Nikolayevsk-na-Amure, Sov. Un.	179	53.18 N	140.49 E
Nikol'sk, Sov. Un. (nē-kôlsk')	176	59.30 N	45.40 E
Nikol'skoye, Sov. Un. (nē-kôl'skô-yĕ)	180c	59.27 N	30.00 E
Nikopol, Bul. (nē'kô-pŏl')	171	43.41 N	24.52 E
Nikopol', Sov. Un.	173	47.36 N	34.24 E
Nikšić, Yugo. (nēk'shĕch)	171	42.45 N	18.57 E
Nīl, Nahr an-, see Nile (R.)			
Nilahue (R.), Chile (nē-lȧ'wĕ)	139b	36.36 S	71.50 W
Nile (R.), Afr. (nīl)	221	19.15 N	32.30 E
Niles, Mi. (nīlz)	108	41.50 N	86.15 W
Niles, Oh.	108	41.15 N	80.45 W
Nileshwar, India	191	12.08 N	74.14 E
Nilgiri Hills, India	191	17.05 N	76.22 E
Nilópolis, Braz. (nē-lô'pō-lēs)	142b	22.48 S	43.25 W
Nimach, India	190	24.32 N	74.51 E
Nimba, Mont (Mtn.), Ivory Coast (nĭm'bȧ)	220	7.40 N	8.33 W

326 Nimba Mts. – Northwood

PLACE (Pronunciation)	PAGE	Lat. °′	Long. °′
Nimba Mts., Gui.-Ivory Coast	224	7.30 N	8.35 W
Nîmes, Fr. (nēm)	166	43.49 N	4.22 E
Nimrod Res., Ar. (nĭm'rŏd)	121	34.58 N	93.46 W
Nimule, Sud. (nē-mo͞o'lå)	221	3.38 N	32.12 E
Ninda, Ang.	226	14.47 S	21.24 E
Ninety Mile Bch., Austl.	212	38.20 S	147.30 E
Nineveh (Ruins), Iraq (nĭn'ē-vȧ)	177	36.30 N	43.10 E
Ning'an, China (nĭŋ-än)	198	44.20 N	129.20 E
Ningbo, China (nĭŋ-bwo)	199	29.56 N	121.30 E
Ningde, China (nĭŋ-dŭ)	199	26.38 N	119.33 E
Ninghai, China (nĭng'hī')	199	29.20 N	121.20 E
Ninghe, China (nĭŋ-hŭ)	196	39.20 N	167.50 E
Ningjin, China (nĭŋ-jyĭn)	196	37.39 N	116.47 E
Ningjin, China	196	37.37 N	114.55 E
Ningming, China	199	22.22 N	107.06 E
Ningwu, China (nĭng'wo͞o')	198	39.00 N	112.12 E
Ningxia (Aut. Reg.), China (nĭŋ-shyä)	194	37.10 N	106.00 E
Ningyang, China (nĭng'yäng')	196	35.46 N	116.48 E
Ninh Binh, Viet. (nēn bĕnk')	199	20.22 N	106.00 E
Ninigo Group (Is.), Pap. N. Gui.	203	1.15 S	143.30 E
Ninnescah (R.), Ks. (nĭn'ĕs-kä)	120	37.37 N	98.31 W
Nioaque, Braz. (nēō-ȧ'-kē)	141	21.14 S	55.41 W
Niobrara (R.), Ne. (nī-ō-brâr'ȧ)	112	42.46 N	98.46 W
Niokolo Koba, Parc Natl. du (Natl. Pk.), Senegal	224	13.05 N	13.00 W
Nioro du Sahel, Mali (nē-ō'rō)	224	15.15 N	9.35 W
Nipawin, Can.	98	53.22 N	104.00 W
Nipe, Bahía de (B.), Cuba (bä-ē'ä-dĕ-nē'pä)	133	20.50 N	75.30 W
Nipe, Sierra de (Mts.), Cuba (sē-ĕ'r-rä-dē)	133	20.20 N	75.50 W
Nipigon, Can. (nĭp'ĭ-gŏn)	108	48.58 N	88.17 W
Nipigon (L.), Can.	100	49.37 N	89.55 W
Nipigon B., Can.	113	48.56 N	88.00 W
Nipisiguit (R.), Can. (nĭ-pĭ'sĭ-kwĭt)	102	47.26 N	66.15 W
Nipissing (L.), Can. (nĭp'ĭ-sĭng)	101	45.59 N	80.19 W
Niquero, Cuba (nē-kä'rō)	132	20.00 N	77.35 W
Nirmali, India	190	26.30 N	86.43 E
Niš, Yugo. (nēsh)	171	43.18 N	21.55 E
Nisa, Port. (nē'sȧ)	168	39.32 N	7.41 W
Nišava (R.), Yugo. (nē'shȧ-vȧ)	171	43.17 N	22.17 E
Nishino (I.), Jap. (nēsh'ē-nô)	201	36.06 N	132.49 E
Nishinomiya, Jap. (nēsh'ē-nô-mē'yȧ)	201 b	34.44 N	135.21 E
Nishinoomote, Jap. (nēsh'ē-nô-mō'tō)	201	30.44 N	130.59 E
Nishio, Jap. (nēsh'ē-ô)	201	34.50 N	137.01 E
Niska L., Can. (nĭs'kȧ)	98	55.35 N	108.38 W
Nisko, Pol. (nēs'kô)	165	50.30 N	22.07 E
Nisku, Can. (nĭs-kū')	93 g	53.21 N	113.33 W
Nisqually R., Wa. (nĭs-kwôl'ĭ)	114	46.51 N	122.33 W
Nissan (R.), Swe.	162	57.06 N	13.22 E
Nisser (L.), Nor. (nĭs'ĕr)	162	59.14 N	8.35 E
Nissum Fd., Den.	162	56.24 N	7.35 E
Niterói, Braz. (nē-tĕ-rô'ĭ)	142 b	22.53 S	43.07 W
Nith (R.), Scot. (nĭth)	160	55.13 N	3.55 W
Nitra, Czech. (nē'trȧ)	165	48.18 N	18.04 E
Nitra R., Czech.	165	48.13 N	18.14 E
Nitro, WV (nī'trō)	108	38.25 N	81.50 W
Niue, Oceania (nĭ'o͞o)	205	19.50 S	167.00 W
Nivelles, Bel. (nē'vĕl')	161	50.33 N	4.17 E
Nixon, Tx. (nĭk'sŭn)	123	29.16 N	97.48 W
Nizāmābād, India	190	18.48 N	78.07 E
Nizhne-Angarsk, Sov. Un. (nyēzh'nyĭ-ŭngärsk')	179	55.49 N	108.46 E
Nizhne-Chirskaya, Sov. Un. (nyĭ-ŭn-gärsk')	177	48.20 N	42.50 E
Nizhne-Kolymsk, Sov. Un. (kô-lēmsk')	179	68.32 N	160.56 E
Nizhneudinsk, Sov. Un. (nēzh'nyĭ-o͞odēnsk')	178	54.58 N	99.15 E
Nizhniye Sergi, Sov. Un. (nyēzh' nyē sĕr'gē)	180 a	56.41 N	59.19 E
Nizhniye Serogozy, Sov. Un. (nyēzh'nyĭ sĕ-rô-gô'zĭ)	173	46.51 N	34.25 E
Nizhniy Tagil, Sov. Un. (tŭgēl')	180 a	57.54 N	59.59 E
Nizhnyaya Kur'ya, Sov. Un. (nyē'zhnyȧ-yȧ koŏr'yȧ)	180 a	58.01 N	56.00 E
Nizhnyaya Salda, Sov. Un. (nyē'zhnya'ya säl'da')	180 a	58.05 N	60.43 E
Nizhnyaya Taymyra (R.), Sov. Un.	178	72.30 N	95.18 E
Nizhnyaya (Lower) Tunguska (R.), Sov. Un. (to͞on-go͞os'kȧ)	178	64.13 N	91.30 E
Nizhnyaya Tura, Sov. Un. (to͞o'rȧ)	180 a	58.38 N	59.50 E
Nizhnyaya Us'va, Sov. Un. (o͞os'vȧ)	180 a	59.05 N	58.53 E
Nízke Tatry (Mts.), Czech.	165	48.57 N	19.18 E
Njombe, Tan.	227	9.20 S	34.46 E
Njurunda, Swe. (nyo͞o-ro͞on'dȧ)	162	62.15 N	17.24 E
Nkala Mission, Zambia	227	15.55 S	26.00 E
Nkandla, S. Afr. ('n-känd'lä)	223 c	28.40 S	31.06 E
Nkawkaw, Ghana	224	6.33 N	0.47 W
Noākhāli, Bngl.	190	22.52 N	91.08 E
Noatak, Ak. (nō-ȧ'tȧk)	105	67.22 N	163.28 W
Noatak (R.), Ak.	105	67.58 N	162.15 W
Nobeoka, Jap. (nō-bā-ō'kȧ)	201	32.36 N	131.41 E
Noblesville, In. (nō'bl'z-vĭl)	108	40.00 N	86.00 W
Nobleton, Can. (nō'bl'tŭn)	93 d	43.54 N	79.39 W
Nocera Inferiore, It. (ĕn-fē-ryō'rĕ)	169 c	40.30 N	14.38 E
Nochistlán, Mex. (nō-chēs-tlän')	128	21.23 N	102.52 W
Nochixtlón (Asunción), Mex. (ä-so͞on-syōn')	129	17.28 N	97.12 W
Nogales, Az. (nō-gä'lĕs)	119	31.20 N	110.55 W
Nogales, Mex. (nŏ-gä'lĕs)	129	18.49 N	97.09 W
Nogales, Mex.	126	31.15 N	111.00 W
Nogal Val., Som. (nō'gäl)	219 a	8.30 N	47.50 E
Nogaysk, Sov. Un. (nō-gīsk')	173	46.43 N	36.21 E
Nogent-le-Roi, Fr. (nŏ-zhŏN-lĕ-rwä')	167 b	48.39 N	1.32 E
Nogent-le-Rotrou, Fr. (rō-tro͞o')	166	48.22 N	0.47 E
Noginsk, Sov. Un. (nô-gēnsk')	180 b	55.52 N	38.28 E
Noguera Pallares (R.), Sp.	169	42.18 N	1.03 E
Noirmoutier, Île de (I.), Fr. (nwär-mo͞o-tyā')	166	47.03 N	3.08 W
Nojimā-Zaki (Pt.), Jap. (nō'jē-mä zä-kē)	201	35.54 N	139.48 E
Nokomis, Il. (nō-kō'mĭs)	108	39.15 N	89.10 W
Nola, It. (nô'lä)	169 c	40.41 N	14.32 E
Nolinsk, Sov. Un. (nō-lēnsk')	176	57.32 N	49.50 E
Noma Misaki (C.), Jap. (nō'mä mē'sä-kē)	201	31.25 N	130.09 E
Nombre de Dios, Mex. (nôm-brĕ-dĕ-dyô's)	128	23.50 N	104.14 W
Nombre de Dios, Pan. (nô'm-brĕ)	131	9.34 N	79.28 W
Nome, Ak. (nōm)	105	64.30 N	165.20 W
Nonacho (L.), Can.	94	61.48 N	111.20 W
Nong'an, China (nōŋ-än)	198	44.25 N	125.10 E
Nongoma, S. Afr. (nōn-gō'mȧ)	222	27.48 S	31.45 E
Nooksack, Wa. (no͝ok'săk)	116 d	48.55 N	122.19 W
Nooksack (R.), Wa.	116 d	48.54 N	122.31 W
Noordwijk aan Zee, Neth.	155 a	52.14 N	4.25 E
Noordzee, Kanal, (Can.), Neth.	155 a	52.27 N	4.42 E
Nootka (I.), Can. (no͞ot'kȧ)	94	49.32 N	126.42 W
Nootka Sd., Can.	96	49.33 N	126.38 W
Nóqui, Ang. (nô-kē')	226	5.51 S	13.25 E
Nor (R.), China (nou')	200	46.55 N	132.45 E
Nora, In. (nō'rä)	111 g	39.54 N	86.08 W
Nora, Swe.	162	59.32 N	14.56 E
Noranda, Can.	101	48.15 N	79.01 W
Norbeck, Md. (nôr'bĕk)	110 e	39.06 N	77.05 W
Norborne, Mo. (nôr'bôrn)	121	39.17 N	93.39 W
Norco, Ca. (nôr'kō)	117 a	33.57 N	117.33 W
Norcross, Ga. (nôr'krôs)	110 c	33.56 N	84.13 W
Nord, Riviere du, Can. (rēv-yĕr' dü nōr)	93 a	45.45 N	74.02 W
Nordegg, Can. (nûr'dĕg)	97	52.28 N	116.04 W
Norden, F.R.G. (nôr'dĕn)	164	53.35 N	7.14 E
Norderney I., F.R.G. (nōr'dĕr-nĕy)	164	53.45 N	6.58 E
Nord Fd., Nor. (nô'fyôr)	162	61.50 N	5.35 E
Nordhausen, G.D.R. (nôrt'hau-zĕn)	164	51.30 N	10.48 E
Nordhorn, F.R.G. (nôrt'hôrn)	164	52.26 N	7.05 E
Nordland, Wa. (nôrd'lȧnd)	116 a	48.03 N	122.41 W
Nördlingen, F.R.G. (nûrt'lĭng-ĕn)	164	48.51 N	10.30 E
Nord-Ostsee Kan. (Kiel) Can., F.R.G. (nōrd-ōzt-zā) (kēl)	164	54.03 N	9.23 E
Nordrhein-Westfalen (North Rhine-Westphalia) (State), F.R.G. (nōrd'hīn-vĕst-fä-lĕn)	164	50.50 N	6.53 E
Nordvik, Sov. Un. (nôrd'vĕk)	179	73.57 N	111.15 E
Nore R., Ire. (nōr)	160	52.34 N	7.15 W
Norfield, Ms. (nôr'fēld)	124	31.24 N	90.25 W
Norfolk, Ma. (nôr'fŏk)	103 a	42.07 N	71.19 W
Norfolk, Ne.	112	42.10 N	97.25 W
Norfolk, Va.	110 g	36.55 N	76.15 W
Norfolk, Oceania	204	27.10 S	166.50 E
Norfork, L., Ar.	121	36.25 N	92.09 W
Noria, Mex. (nō'rē-ȧ)	128	23.04 N	106.20 W
Noril'sk, Sov. Un. (nô rēlsk')	178	69.00 N	87.11 E
Normal, Il. (nôr'mȧl)	108	40.35 N	89.00 W
Norman, Ok. (nôr'mȧn)	121	35.13 N	97.25 W
Norman, L., NC	125	35.30 N	80.53 W
Norman (R.), Austl.	211	18.27 S	141.29 E
Normandie (Reg.), Fr. (nōr-mäN-dē')	166	49.02 N	0.17 E
Normandie, Collines de (Hills), Fr. (kō-lēn'dĕ-nōr-män-dē')	166	48.46 N	0.50 W
Normanton, Austl. (nôr'mȧn-tŭn)	211	17.45 S	141.10 E
Normanton, Eng.	154	53.40 N	1.21 W
Norman Wells, Can.	94	65.26 N	127.00 W
Nornalup, Austl. (nôr-năl'ŭp)	210	35.00 S	117.00 E
Norra Dellen (L.), Swe.	162	61.57 N	16.25 E
Nørresundby, Den. (nû-rē-so͞on'bü)	162	57.04 N	9.55 E
Norris, Tn. (nŏr'ĭs)	124	36.09 N	84.05 W
Norris (R.), Tn.	124	36.17 N	84.10 W
Norristown, Pa. (nŏr'ĭs-town)	110 f	40.07 N	75.21 W
Norrköping, Swe. (nôr'chûp'ĭng)	162	58.37 N	16.10 E
Norrtälje, Swe. (nôr-tĕl'yĕ)	162	59.47 N	18.39 E
Norseman, Austl. (nôrs'mȧn)	210	32.15 S	122.00 E
Norte, Punta (Pt.), Arg. (po͞o'n-tä-nōr'tĕ)	139 c	36.17 S	56.46 W
Norte, Serra do (Mts.), Braz. (sĕ'r-rä-dô-nôr'te)	141	12.04 S	59.08 W
North C., Can.	103 c	47.02 N	60.25 W
North Adams, Ma. (ăd'ămz)	109	42.40 N	73.05 W
Northam, Austl. (nôr-dhăm)	210	31.50 S	116.45 E
Northam, S. Afr. (nôr'thăm)	219 d	24.52 S	27.16 E
North America (ȧ-mĕr'ĭ-kȧ)	92		
North American Basin, Atl. O. (ȧ-mĕr'ĭ-kȧn)	127	23.45 N	62.45 W
Northampton, Austl. (nôr-thămp'tŭn)	210	28.22 S	114.45 E
Northampton, Eng. (nôrth-ămp'tŭn)	160	52.14 N	0.56 W
Northampton, Ma.	109	42.20 N	72.45 W
Northampton, Pa.	109	40.45 N	75.30 W
Northamptonshire (Co.), Eng.	154	52.25 N	0.47 W
North Andaman I., Andaman & Nicobar Is. (ăn-dȧ-măn')	202	13.15 N	93.30 E
North Andover, Ma. (ăn'dō-vẽr)	103 a	42.42 N	71.07 W
North Arm, Can. (ärm)	116 d	49.13 N	123.01 W
North Atlanta, Ga. (ăt-lăn'tȧ)	110 c	33.52 N	84.20 W
North Attleboro, Ma. (ăt''l-bŭr-ô)	110 b	41.59 N	71.18 W
North Baltimore, Oh. (bôl'tĭ-môr)	108	41.10 N	83.40 W
North Basque, Tx. (băsk)	122	31.56 N	98.01 W
North Battleford, Can. (băt''l-fẽrd)	98	52.47 N	108.17 W
North Bay, Can.	101	46.13 N	79.26 W
North Bend, Or. (bĕnd)	114	43.23 N	124.13 W
North Berwick, Me. (bûr'wĭk)	102	43.18 N	70.46 W
North Bight, Ba. (bīt)	132	24.30 N	77.40 W
North Bimini (I.), Ba. (bĭ'mĭ-nē)	132	25.45 N	79.20 W
North Borneo (Reg.), see Sabah			
Northborough, Ma. (nôrth'bûr-ô)	103 a	42.19 N	71.39 W
Northbridge, Ma. (nôrth'brĭj)	103 a	42.09 N	71.39 W
North C., N.Z.	213	34.31 S	173.02 E
North Caicos (I.), Turks & Caicos (kī'kōs)	133	21.55 N	72.00 W
North Carolina (State), U. S. (kăr-ô-lī'nȧ)	107	35.40 N	81.30 W
North Cascades Natl. Pk., Wa.	97	48.50 N	120.50 W
North Cat Cay (I.), Ba.	132	25.35 N	79.20 W
North Chan (B.), Can. (chăn)	108	46.10 N	83.20 W
North Chan, N. Ire.-Scot.	160	55.15 N	7.56 W
North Charleston, SC (chärlz'tŭn)	125	32.49 N	79.57 W
North Chicago, Il. (shĭ-kô'gō)	111 a	42.19 N	87.51 W
North College Hill, Oh. (kŏl'ĕj hĭl)	111 f	39.13 N	84.33 W
North Concho, Tx. (kŏn'chō)	122	31.40 N	100.48 W
North Cooking Lake, Can. (ko͝ok'ĭng lăk)	93 g	53.28 N	112.57 W
North Dakota (State), U. S. (dȧ-kō'tȧ)	106	47.20 N	101.55 W
North Downs, Eng. (dounz)	160	51.11 N	0.01 W
North Dum-Dum, India	190 a	22.38 N	88.23 E
Northeast C., Ak. (nôrth-ēst)	105	63.15 N	169.04 W
Northeast Pt., Ba.	133	21.25 N	73.00 W
Northeast Pt., Ba.	133	22.45 N	73.50 W
Northeast Providence Chan., Ba. (prŏv'ĭ-dĕns)	132	25.45 N	77.00 W
Northeim, F.R.G. (nôrt'hīm)	164	51.42 N	9.59 E
North Elbow Cays (Is.), Ba.	132	23.55 N	80.30 W
Northern Cheyenne Ind. Res., Mt.	115	45.32 N	106.43 W
Northern Dvina (R.), see Severnaya Dvina			
Northern Ireland, U. K. (īr'lănd)	160	54.48 N	7.00 W
Northern Land (Is.), see Severnaya Zemlya			
Northern Territory, Austl.	210	18.15 S	133.00 E
Northfield, Mn. (nôrth'fēld)	113	44.28 N	93.11 W
North Flinders, Ra., Austl. (flĭn'dẽrz)	212	31.55 S	138.45 E
North Foreland, Eng. (dōr'lȧnd)	161	51.20 N	1.30 E
North Franklin Mt., Tx. (frăŋ'klĭn)	122	31.55 N	106.30 W
North Frisian Is., Den.	162	55.16 N	8.15 E
North Gamboa, Pan. (gäm-bô'ä)	126 a	9.07 N	79.40 W
North Gower, Can. (gō̇w'ẽr)	93 c	45.08 N	75.43 W
North Hollywood, Ca. (hŏl'ē-wo͝od)	117 a	34.10 N	118.23 W
North I., Ca.	118 a	32.39 N	117.14 W
North I., N. Z.	213	37.20 S	173.30 E
North Judson, In. (jŭd'sŭn)	108	41.15 N	86.50 W
North Kamloops, Can. (kăm'lo͞ops)	97	50.41 N	120.22 W
North Kansas City, Mo. (kăn'zȧs)	117 f	39.08 N	94.34 W
North Kingstown, RI	110 b	41.34 N	71.26 W
North Little Rock, Ar. (lĭt''l rŏk)	121	34.46 N	92.13 W
North Loup (R.), Ne. (lo͞op)	112	42.05 N	100.10 W
North Manchester, In. (măn'chĕs-tẽr)	108	41.00 N	85.45 W
Northmoor, Mo. (nôth'mo͞or)	117 f	39.10 N	94.37 W
North Moose L., Can.	99	54.09 N	100.20 W
North Mount Lofty Ranges, Austl.	212	33.50 S	138.30 E
North Ogden, Ut. (ŏg'dĕn)	117 b	41.18 N	111.58 W
North Ogden Pk., Ut.	117 b	41.23 N	111.59 W
North Olmsted, Oh. (ōlm-stĕd)	111 d	41.25 N	81.55 W
North Pease (R.), Tx. (pēz)	120	34.19 N	100.58 W
North Pender (I.), Can. (pĕn'dẽr)	116 d	48.48 N	123.16 W
North Plains, Or. (plānz)	116 c	45.36 N	123.00 W
North Platte, Ne. (plăt)	112	41.08 N	100.45 W
North Platte, (R.), U. S.	106	41.20 N	102.40 W
North Pt., Mi.	108	45.00 N	83.20 W
North Pt., Barb.	131 b	13.22 N	59.36 W
Northport, Al. (nôrth'pōrt)	124	33.12 N	87.35 W
Northport, NY	110 a	40.53 N	73.20 W
Northport, Wa.	114	48.53 N	117.47 W
North Reading, Ma. (rĕd'ĭng)	103 a	42.34 N	71.04 W
North Rhine-Westphalia (State), see Nordrhein-Westfalen			
North Richland Hills, Tx.	117 c	32.50 N	97.13 W
Northridge, Ca. (nôrth'rĭdj)	117 a	34.14 N	118.32 W
North Ridgeville, Oh. (rĭj-vĭl)	111 d	41.23 N	82.01 W
North Royalton, Oh. (roi'ăl-tŭn)	111 d	41.19 N	81.44 W
North St. Paul, Mn. (sănt pôl')	113 g	45.01 N	92.59 W
North Saskatchewan (R.), Can. (săn-kăch'ē-wän)	98	52.40 N	106.45 W
North Sea, Eur.	156	56.09 N	3.16 E
North Skunk (R.), Ia. (skŭnk)	113	41.39 N	92.46 W
North Stradbroke I., Austl. (străd'brōk)	211	27.45 S	154.18 E
North Sydney, Can. (sĭd'nē)	103	46.13 N	60.15 W
North Taranaki Bight, N. Z. (tȧ-rȧ-nä'kĭ bīt)	213	38.40 S	174.00 E
North Tarrytown, NY (tăr'ĭ-toun)	110 a	41.05 N	73.52 W
North Thompson (R.), Can.	97	50.50 N	120.10 W
North Tonawanda, NY (tŏn-ȧ-wŏn'dȧ)	111 c	43.02 N	78.53 W
North Truchas Pks. (Mts.), NM (tro͞o'chäs)	201	37.18 N	137.03 E
North Twillingate (I.), Can. (twĭl'ĭn-găt)	119	35.58 N	105.37 W
North Uist (I.), Scot. (û'ĭst)	160	57.37 N	7.22 W
Northumberland Str., Can. (nôr thŭm'bẽr-lȧnd)	102	46.25 N	64.20 W
Northumberland, NH	109	44.30 N	71.30 W
Northumberland, Is., Austl.	211	21.42 S	151.30 E
North Umpqua R., Or. (ŭmp'kwȧ)	114	43.20 N	122.50 W
North Vancouver, Can. (văn-ko͞o'vẽr)	116 d	49.19 N	123.04 W
North Vernon, In. (vûr'nŭn)	108	39.05 N	85.45 W
Northville, Mi. (nôrth-vĭl)	111 b	42.26 N	83.28 W
North Wales, Pa. (wālz)	110 f	40.12 N	75.16 W
North West C., Austl. (nôrth'wĕst)	210	21.50 S	112.25 E
Northwest Cape Fear, (R.), NC (cāp fēr)	125	34.34 N	79.46 W
North West Gander (R.), Can. (găn'dẽr)	103	48.40 N	55.15 W
Northwest Highlands, Scot.	160	56.50 N	5.20 W
Northwest Providence Chan., Ba. (prŏv'ĭ-dĕns)	132	26.15 N	78.45 W
Northwest Territories, Can. (tĕr'ĭ-tō'rĭs)	94	64.42 N	119.09 W
Northwich, Eng. (nôrth'wĭch)	161	53.15 N	2.31 W
North Wilkesboro, NC (wĭlks'bûrō)	125	36.08 N	81.10 W
Northwood, Ia. (nôrth'wo͝od)	113	43.26 N	93.13 W
Northwood, ND	112	47.44 N	97.36 W

ăt; finȧl; rāte; senåte; ärm; ȧsk; sofȧ; fâre; ch-choose; dh-as th in other; bē; ēvent; bĕt; recĕnt; cratẽr; g-gō; gh-guttural g; bĭt; ĭ-short neutral; rīde; K-guttural k as ch in German ich;

PRONOUNCING INDEX

North Wood Cr. – Obitochnaya 327

PLACE (Pronunciation)	PAGE	Lat. °′	Long. °′
North Wood Cr., Wy.	115	44.02 N	107.37 W
North Yamhill (R.), Or. (yăm' hĭl)	116c	45.22 N	123.21 W
North York Moors, Eng. (yôrk mōōrz')	160	54.20 N	0.40 W
North York, Can.	93d	43.47 N	79.25 W
North Yorkshire (Co.), Eng.	154	53.50 N	1.10 W
Norton, Ks. (nôr'tŭn)	120	39.40 N	99.54 W
Norton, Ma.	110b	41.58 N	71.08 W
Norton, Va.	125	36.54 N	82.36 W
Norton B., Ak.	105	64.22 N	162.18 W
Norton Res., Ma.	110b	42.01 N	71.07 W
Norton Sd., Ak.	105	63.48 N	164.50 W
Norval, Can. (nôr'vǎl)	93d	43.39 N	79.52 W
Norwalk, Ca. (nôr'wôk)	117a	33.54 N	118.05 W
Norwalk, Ct.	110a	41.06 N	73.25 W
Norwalk, Oh.	108	41.15 N	82.35 W
Norway, Eur. (nôr'wā)	152	63.48 N	11.17 E
Norway, Me.	102	44.11 N	70.35 W
Norway, Mi.	113	45.47 N	87.55 W
Norway House, Can.	99	53.59 N	97.50 W
Norwegian Sea, Eur. (nôr-wē'jăn)	156	66.54 N	1.43 E
Norwell, Ma. (nôr'wĕl)	103a	42.10 N	70.47 W
Norwich, Ct. (nôr'wĭch)	109	41.20 N	72.00 W
Norwich, Eng.	161	52.40 N	1.15 E
Norwich, NY	109	42.35 N	75.30 W
Norwood, Ma. (nôr'wood)	103a	42.11 N	71.13 W
Norwood, NC	125	35.15 N	80.08 W
Norwood, Oh.	111f	39.10 N	84.27 W
Nose Cr., Can. (nōz)	93e	51.09 N	114.02 W
Noshiro, Jap. (nō'shē-rō)	200	40.09 N	140.02 E
Nosovka, Sov. Un. (nô'sôf-kà)	173	50.54 N	31.35 E
Nossob (R.), Namibia (nô'sŏb)	222	24.15 S	19.10 E
Noteć R., Pol. (nô'tĕcn)	164	52.50 N	16.19 E
Noto, It. (nô'tô)	157	36.49 N	15.08 E
Notodden, Nor. (nōt'ôd'n)	162	59.35 N	9.15 E
Noto-Hantō (Pen.), Jap. (nô'tô hän'tō)	201	37.18 N	137.03 E
Notre Dame, Monts (Mts.), Can.	102	46.35 N	70.35 W
Notre Dame B., Can. (nō't'r dám')	103	49.45 N	55.15 W
Notre-Dame-du-Lac, Can.	102	47.37 N	68.51 W
Nottawasaga B., Can. (nŏt'à-wà-sä'gà)	108	44.45 N	80.35 W
Nottaway (R.), Can. (nôt'à-wā)	95	50.58 N	78.02 W
Nottingham, Eng. (nŏt'ĭng-ăm)	154	52.58 N	1.09 W
Nottingham I., Can.	95	62.58 N	78.53 W
Nottinghamshire (Co.), Eng.	154	53.03 N	1.05 W
Nottoway, (R.), Va. (nôt'à-wā)	125	36.53 N	77.47 W
Notukeu Cr., Can.	98	49.55 N	106.30 W
Nouadhibou, Mauritania	220	21.02 N	17.09 W
Nouakchott, Mauritania	224	18.06 N	15.57 W
Nouamrhar, Mauritania	224	19.22 N	16.31 W
Noumea, N. Cal. (nōō-mā'ä)	211	22.18 S	166.48 E
Nouvelle, Can. (nōō-vĕl')	102	48.09 N	66.22 W
Nouvelle-France, Cap de (C.), Can.	95	62.03 N	74.00 W
Nouzonville, Fr. (nōō-zôN-vēl')	166	49.51 N	4.43 E
Nova Cruz, Braz. (nō'vá-krōō'z)	141	6.22 S	35.20 W
Nova Freixo, Moz.	227	14.49 S	36.33 E
Nova Friburgo, Braz. (frē-bōōr'gōō)	139a	22.18 S	42.31 W
Nova Gaia, Ang.	226	10.09 S	17.31 E
Nova Iguaçu, Braz. (nō'vä-ē-gwä-sōō')	142b	22.45 S	43.27 W
Nova Lima, Braz. (lē'mä)	139a	19.59 S	43.51 W
Nova Lisboa, see Huambo			
Nova Mambone, Moz. (nō'vá-mám-bō'nē)	222	21.04 S	35.13 E
Novara, It. (nô-vä'rä)	170	45.24 N	8.38 E
Nova Resende, Braz.	139a	21.12 S	46.25 W
Nova Scotia (Prov.), Can. (skō'shá)	95	44.28 N	65.00 W
Nova Varoš, Yugo. (nō'vá vä'rôsh)	171	43.24 N	19.53 E
Novaya Ladoga, Sov. Un. (nô'vá-ya là-dô-gá)	163	60.06 N	32.16 E
Novaya Lyalya, Sov. Un. (lyá'lyá)	180a	59.03 N	60.36 E
Novaya Odessa, Sov. Un. (ô-dĕs'ä)	173	47.18 N	31.48 E
Novaya Praga, Sov. Un. (prä'gá)	173	48.34 N	32.54 E
Novaya Sibir (I.), Sov. Un. (sē-bēr')	179	75.42 N	150.00 E
Novaya Vodolaga, Sov. Un. (vō-dôl'á-gá)	173	49.43 N	35.51 E
Novaya Zemlya (I.), Sov. Un. (zĕm-lyá')	178	72.00 N	54.46 E
Nova Zagora, Bul. (zä'gô-rá)	171	42.30 N	26.01 E
Novelda, Sp. (nō-vĕl'dä)	169	38.22 N	0.46 W
Nové Mesto nad Váhom, Czech. (nō'vĕ myĕs'tō)	165	48.44 N	17.47 E
Nové Zámky, Czech. (zám'kē)	165	47.58 N	18.10 E
Novgorod, Sov. Un. (nôv'gô-rŏt)	172	58.32 N	31.16 E
Novgorod (Oblast), Sov. Un.	172	58.27 N	31.55 E
Novgorod-Severskly, Sov. Un.	173	52.01 N	33.14 E
Novi, Mi. (nō'vī)	111b	42.29 N	83.28 W
Novigrad, Yugo. (nō'vĭ grád)	170	44.09 N	15.34 E
Novi Ligure, It. (nô'vē)	170	44.43 N	8.48 E
Novinger, Mo. (nŏv'ĭn-jēr)	121	40.14 N	92.43 W
Novi Pazar, Bul. (pá-zär')	171	43.22 N	27.26 E
Novi Pazar, Yugo. (pá-zär')	171	43.08 N	20.30 E
Novi Sad, Yugo. (säd')	171	45.15 N	19.53 E
Novoasbest, Sov. Un. (nô-vô-äs-bĕst')	180a	57.43 N	60.14 E
Novoaydar, Sov. Un. (nô'vô-ī-där')	173	48.57 N	39.01 E
Novocherkassk, Sov. Un. (nô'vô-chĕr-kàsk')	173	47.25 N	40.04 E
Novogrudok, Sov. Un. (nô-vô-grōō'dôk)	165	53.35 N	25.51 E
Novo-Kazalinsk, Sov. Un. (nô-vŭ-kŭ-zá-lyĕnsk')	174	45.47 N	62.00 E
Novokuznetsk (Stalinsk), Sov. Un. (nō'vô-kōō'z-nyĕ'tsk) (stá'lĕnsk)	178	53.43 N	86.59 E
Novoladozhskiy Kanal (Can.), Sov. Un. (nô-vô-lä'dôzh-skĭ ká-näl')	180c	59.54 N	31.19 E
Novo Mesto, Yugo. (nôvô mās'tô)	170	45.48 N	15.13 E
Novomirgorod, Sov. Un. (nô'vô-mēr'gô-rôt)	173	48.46 N	31.44 E
Novomoskovsk, Sov. Un. (nô'vô-môs-kôfsk')	172	54.06 N	38.08 E
Novomoskovsk, Sov. Un.	173	48.37 N	35.12 E
Novonikol'skiy, Sov. Un. (nô'vô-nyĭ-kôl'skĭ)	180a	52.28 N	57.12 E
Novo Redondo, Ang. (nô'vōō rā-dôn'dōō)	226	11.13 S	13.50 E
Novorossiysk, Sov. Un. (nô'vô-rô-sĕsk')	173	44.43 N	37.48 E
Novorzhev, Sov. Un. (nô'vô-rzhĕv')	172	57.01 N	29.17 E
Novo-Selo, Bul. (nô'vô-sĕ'lô)	171	44.09 N	22.46 E
Novosibirsk, Sov. Un. (nô'vô-sē-bērsk')	178	55.09 N	82.58 E
Novosibirskiye O-va (New Siberian Is.), Sov. Un. (no'vŭ-sĭ-bĭr'skē-ē)	179	76.45 N	140.30 E
Novosil', Sov. Un. (nô'vô-sĭl)	172	52.58 N	37.03 E
Novosokol'niki, Sov. Un. (nô'vô-sô-kôl'nē-kē)	172	56.18 N	30.07 E
Novotatishchevskiy, Sov. Un. (nô'vô-tá-tyĭsh'chĕv-skĭ)	180a	53.22 N	60.24 E
Novoukrainka, Sov. Un.	173	48.18 N	31.33 E
Novouzensk, Sov. Un. (nô-vô-ōō-zĕnsk')	177	50.40 N	48.08 E
Novozybkov, Sov. Un. (nô'vô-zĕp'kôf)	172	52.31 N	31.54 E
Nový Jičín, Czech. (nô'vē yē'chēn)	165	49.36 N	18.02 E
Novyy Bug, Sov. Un. (bōōk)	173	47.43 N	32.33 E
Novyy Oskol, Sov. Un. (ôs-kôl')	173	50.46 N	37.53 E
Novyy Port, Sov. Un. (nô'vē)	178	67.19 N	72.28 E
Nowa Sól, Pol. (nô'vá sūl')	164	51.49 N	15.41 E
Nowata, Ok. (nô-wä'tá)	121	36.42 N	95.38 W
Nowra, Austl. (nou'rá)	212	34.55 S	150.45 E
Nowy Dwór Mazowiecki, Pol. (nô'vĭ dvōōr mä-zo-vyĕts'ke)	165	52.26 N	20.46 E
Nowy Sacz, Pol. (nô'vē sôNch')	165	49.36 N	20.42 E
Nowy Targ, Pol. (tärk')	165	49.29 N	20.02 E
Noxon Res., Mt.	114	47.50 N	115.40 W
Noxubee (R.), Ms. (nŏks'ū-bē)	124	33.20 N	88.55 W
Noya, Sp. (no'yä)	168	42.46 N	8.50 W
Noyes I., Ak. (noiz)	96	55.30 N	133.40 W
Nozaki, Jap. (nō'zä-kē)	201b	34.43 N	135.39 E
Nqamakwe, S. Afr. ('n-gä-mä'kwā)	223c	32.13 S	27.57 E
Nqutu, S. Afr. ('n-kōō'tōō)	223c	28.17 S	30.41 E
Nsawam, Ghana	224	5.50 N	0.20 W
Nsukka, Nig.	225	6.52 N	7.24 E
Ntshoni (Mtn.), S. Afr.	223c	29.34 S	30.03 E
Ntwetwe Pan (Salt Flat), Bots.	222	20.00 S	24.18 E
Nu (Salween) (R.), China (nōō)	194	30.08 N	96.38 E
Nubah, Jibāl an-(Mts.), Sud.	221	12.22 N	30.39 E
Nubian Des., Sud. (nōō'bĭ-ăn)	221	21.13 N	33.09 E
Nudo Coropuna (Mt.), Peru (nōō'dô kō-rō-pōō'nä)	140	15.53 S	72.04 W
Nudo de Pasco (Mt.), Peru (dĕ pàs'kô)	140	10.34 S	76.12 W
Nueces R., Tx. (nû-ā'sās)	122	28.20 N	98.08 W
Nueltin (L.), Can. (nwĕl'tin)	94	60.14 N	101.00 W
Nueva Armenia, Hond. (nwā'vä är-mä'nē-à)	130	15.47 N	86.32 W
Nueva Esparta (State), Ven. (nwĕ'vä ĕs-pä'r-tä)	141b	10.50 N	64.35 W
Nueva Gerona, Cuba (kĕ-rô'nä)	132	21.55 N	82.45 W
Nueva Palmira, Ur. (päl-mē'rä)	139c	33.53 S	58.23 W
Nueva Rosita, Mex. (nōōĕ'vä rô-sē'tä)	106	27.55 N	101.10 W
Nueva San Salvador (Santa Tecla), Sal. (sän' säl-vá-dōr) (sän'tä tĕ'klä)	130	13.41 N	89.16 W
Nueve de Julio, Arg. (nwā'vā dā hōō'lyô)	139c	35.26 S	60.51 W
Nuevitas, Cuba (nwā-vē'täs)	132	21.35 N	77.15 W
Nuevitas, Bahía de, Cuba (bä-ē'ä dĕ nwā-vē'täs)	132	21.30 N	77.05 W
Nuevo, Ca. (nwā'vō)	117a	33.48 N	117.09 W
Nuevo Laredo, Mex. (lä-rā'dhō)	122	27.29 N	99.30 W
Nuevo Leon (State), Mex. (lå-ōn')	126	26.00 N	100.00 W
Nuevo San Juan, Pan. (nwĕ'vô sän kōō-ä'n)	126a	9.14 N	79.43 W
Nugumanovo, Sov. Un. (nû-gû-mä'nô-vô)	180a	55.28 N	61.50 E
Nulato, Ak. (nōō-lä'tō)	105	64.40 N	158.18 W
Nullagine, Austl. (nŭ-lă'jēn)	210	22.00 S	120.07 E
Nullarbor Plain (Reg.), Austl. (nŭ-lär'bôr)	210	31.45 S	126.30 E
Numabin B., Can. (nōō-mä'bĭn)	98	56.30 N	103.08 W
Numansdorp, Neth.	155a	51.43 N	4.25 E
Numazu, Jap. (nōō'mä-zōō)	201	35.06 N	138.55 E
No. 1, Canal, Arg.	139c	36.43 S	58.14 W
No. 9, Canal, Arg.	139c	36.22 S	58.19 W
No. 12, Canal, Arg.	139c	36.47 S	57.20 W
Numfoor, Pulau (I.), Indon.	203	1.20 S	134.48 E
Nun (R.), Nig.	225	5.05 N	6.10 E
Nuneaton, Eng. (nŭn'ē-tŭn)	154	52.31 N	1.28 W
Nunivak (I.), Ak. (nōō'nĭ-văk)	105	60.25 N	167.42 W
Nunkiní, Mex. (nōōn-kē-nē')	130a	20.19 N	90.14 W
Nunyama, Sov. Un. (nûn-yä'má)	105	65.49 N	170.32 W
Nuoro, It. (nwô'rō)	170	40.29 N	9.20 E
Nura (R.), Sov. Un. (nōō'rä)	178	49.48 N	73.54 E
Nurata, Sov. Un. (nōōr'ät'á)	178	40.33 N	65.28 E
Nürnberg, F.R.G. (nürn'bĕrgh)	164	49.28 N	11.07 E
Nurse Cay (I.), Ba.	133	22.30 N	75.50 W
Nusabyin, Tur. (nōō'sī-bĕn)	177	37.05 N	41.10 E
Nushagak (R.), Ak. (nū-shă-găk')	105	59.28 N	157.40 W
Nushan Hu (L.), China (nü'shän hōō)	196	32.50 N	117.59 E
Nushki, Pak. (nŭsh'kē)	193	29.30 N	66.02 E
Nuthe R., G.D.R. (nōō'tĕ)	155b	52.15 N	13.11 E
Nutley, NJ (nŭt'lē)	110a	40.49 N	74.09 W
Nutter Fort, WV (nŭt'ēr fôrt)	109	39.15 N	80.15 W
Nutwood, Il. (nŭt'wood)	117e	39.05 N	90.34 W
Nuwaybi 'al Muzayyinah, Egypt	189a	28.59 N	34.40 E
Nuweland, S. Afr.	222a	33.58 S	18.28 E
Nyack, NY (nī'ăk)	110a	41.05 N	73.55 W
Nyaiqêntanglha Shan (Mts.), China (nyä-ĭn-chyūn-täŋ-lä shän)	194	29.55 N	88.08 E
Nyakanazi, Tan.	227	3.00 S	31.15 E
Nyala, Sud.	221	12.00 N	24.52 E
Nyanga (R.), Gabon	226	2.45 S	10.30 E
Nyanza, Rw.	227	2.21 S	29.45 E
Nyasa, L. (Malawi, L.), Afr. (nyä'sá)	227	10.45 S	34.30 E
Nyazepetrovsk, Sov. Un. (nyä'zĕ-pĕ-trôvsk')	180a	56.04 N	59.38 E
Nyborg, Den. (nü'bôr'')	162	55.20 N	10.45 E
Nybro, Swe. (nü'brô)	162	56.44 N	15.56 E
Nyeri, Ken.	227	0.25 S	36.57 E
Nyika Plat, Malawi	227	10.30 S	35.50 E
Nyíregyháza, Hung. (nyē'rĕd-y'hä'zä)	165	47.58 N	21.45 E
Nykøbing, Den. (nü'kû-bĭng)	162	56.46 N	8.47 E
Nykøbing, Den.	162	54.45 N	11.54 E
Nykøbing Sjaelland, Den.	162	55.55 N	11.37 E
Nyköping, Swe. (nü'chû-pĭng)	162	58.46 N	16.58 E
Nylstroom, S. Afr. (nĭl'strōm)	219d	24.42 S	28.25 E
Nymagee, Austl. (nī-má-gē')	212	32.17 S	146.18 E
Nymburk, Czech. (nĕm'bōōrk)	164	50.12 N	15.03 E
Nynäshamn, Swe. (nü-nĕs-häm'n)	162	58.53 N	17.55 E
Nyngan, Austl. (nĭŋ'gán)	212	31.31 S	147.25 E
Nyong (R.), Cam. (nyông)	225	3.40 N	10.25 E
Nyou, Upper Volta	224	12.46 N	1.56 W
Nyrány, Czech. (nĕr-zhä'nē)	164	49.43 N	13.13 E
Nysa, Pol. (nē'sá)	165	50.29 N	17.20 E
Nystad, see Uusikaupunki			
Nytva, Sov. Un.	176	58.00 N	55.10 E
Nyungwe, Malawi	227	10.16 S	34.07 E
Nyunzu, Zaire	227	5.57 S	28.0[illegible]
Nyuya (R.), Sov. Un. (nyōō'yá)	179	60.30 N	111.45 E
Nzega, Tan.	227	4.13 S	33.11 E
Nzérékoré, Gui.	224	7.45 N	8.49 W
Nzi (R.), Ivory Coast	224	7.00 N	4.27 W

O

PLACE (Pronunciation)	PAGE	Lat. °′	Long. °′
Oahe Dam, SD (ō-á-hē)	112	44.28 N	100.34 W
Oahe Res., SD	112	45.20 N	100.00 W
Oahu (I.), Hi. (ō-ä'hōō) (ō-ä'hū)	104a	21.38 N	157.48 W
Oak Bay, Can.	96	48.27 N	123.18 W
Oak Bluff, Can. (ōk blŭf)	93f	49.47 N	97.21 W
Oak Creek, Co. (ōk krēk')	115	40.20 N	106.50 W
Oakdale, Ca. (ōk'dāl)	118	37.45 N	120.52 W
Oakdale, Ky.	108	38.15 N	85.50 W
Oakdale, La.	123	30.49 N	92.40 W
Oakdale, Pa.	111e	40.24 N	80.11 W
Oakengates, Eng. (ōk'ĕn-gāts)	154	52.41 N	2.27 W
Oakes, ND (ōks)	112	46.10 N	98.50 W
Oakfield, Me. (ōk'fēld)	102	46.08 N	68.10 W
Oakford, Pa. (ōk'fērd)	110f	40.08 N	74.58 W
Oak Grove, Or. (grōv)	116c	45.25 N	122.38 W
Oakham, Eng. (ōk'ăm)	154	52.40 N	0.38 W
Oakharbor, Oh. (ōk'här'bēr)	108	41.30 N	83.05 W
Oak Harbor, Wa.	116a	48.18 N	122.39 W
Oakland, Ca. (ōk'lănd)	116b	37.48 N	122.16 W
Oakland, Ne.	112	41.50 N	96.28 W
Oakland City, In.	108	38.20 N	87.20 W
Oaklawn, Il. (ōk'lôn)	111a	41.43 N	87.45 W
Oakleigh, Austl. (ōk'lå)	207a	37.54 S	145.05 E
Oakley, Id. (ōk'lĭ)	115	42.15 N	135.53 W
Oakley, Ks.	120	39.08 N	100.49 W
Oakman, Al. (ōk'măn)	124	33.42 N	87.20 W
Oakmont, Pa. (ōk'mōnt)	111e	40.31 N	79.50 W
Oak Mtn., Al.	110h	33.22 N	86.42 W
Oak Park, Il. (pärk)	111a	41.53 N	87.48 W
Oak Point, Wa.	116c	46.11 N	123.11 W
Oak Ridge, Tn. (rĭj)	124	36.01 N	84.15 W
Oakville, Can. (ōk'vĭl)	93d	43.27 N	79.40 W
Oakville, Can.	93f	49.56 N	97.58 W
Oakville, Mo.	117e	38.27 N	90.18 W
Oakville Cr., Can.	93d	43.34 N	79.54 W
Oakwood, Tx. (ōk'wood)	123	31.36 N	95.48 W
Oatman, Az. (ōt'măn)	119	34.00 N	114.25 W
Oaxaca (State), Mex. (wä-hä'kä)	126	16.45 N	97.00 W
Oaxaca, Sierra de (Mts.), Mex. (sē-ĕ'r-rä dĕ)	129	16.15 N	97.25 W
Oaxaca de Juárez, Mex. (kōōä'rĕz)	129	17.03 N	96.42 W
Ob' (R.), Sov. Un.	178	62.15 N	67.00 E
Oba, Can. (ō'bá)	100	48.58 N	84.09 W
Obama, Jap. (ō'bà-mä)	201	35.29 N	135.44 E
Oban, Scot. (ō'băn)	160	56.25 N	5.35 W
Oban Hills, Nig.	225	5.35 N	8.30 E
O'Bannon, Ky. (ō-băn'nŏn)	111h	38.17 N	85.30 W
Obatogamau (L.), Can. (ō-bà-tō'găm-ô)	101	49.38 N	74.10 W
Obbia, Som. (ŏb'byä)	219a	5.24 N	48.28 E
Oberhausen, F.R.G. (ō'bĕr-hou'zĕn)	167c	51.27 N	6.51 E
Oberlin, Ks. (o'bēr-lĭn)	120	39.49 N	100.30 W
Oberlin, Oh.	108	41.15 N	82.15 W
Oberösterreich (Prov.), Aus.	164	48.05 N	13.15 E
Oberroth, F.R.G. (ō'bĕr-rōt)	155d	48.19 N	11.20 E
Obi, Kepulauan (Is.), Indon. (ō'bē)	203	1.25 S	128.15 E
Obi, Pulau (I.), Indon.	203	1.30 S	127.45 E
Óbidos, Braz. (ō'bē-dōōzh)	141	1.57 S	55.32 W
Obihiro, Jap. (ō'bē-hē'rō)	200	42.55 N	142.50 E
Obion (R.), Tn.	124	36.10 N	89.25 W
Obion (R.), North Fk., Tn. (ō-bī'ŏn)	124	35.49 N	89.06 W
Obitochnaya, Kosa (C.), Sov. Un. (kô-sä' ō-bē-tôch'ná-yá)	173	46.32 N	36.07 E

ng-sing; ŋ-baŋk; N-nasalized n; nŏd; cŏmmit; ōld; ôbey; ôrder; oi-boil; fōōd; fŏŏt; ou-out; s-soft; sh-dish; th-thin; pūre; ûnite; ûrn; stŭd; circŭs; ü-as in French tu; '-indeterminate vowel.

328 Obitsu – Ontonagon

PLACE (Pronunciation)	PAGE	Lat. °′	Long. °′
Obitsu (R.), Jap. (ō'bĕt'sōō)	201a	35.19 N	140.03 E
Obock, Djibouti (ō-bŏk')	219a	11.55 N	43.15 E
Obol' (R.), Sov. Un. (ô-bŏl')	172	55.24 N	29.24 E
Oboyan, Sov. Un. (ô-bô-yän')	173	51.14 N	36.16 E
Obskaya Guba (B.), Sov. Un.	178	67.13 N	73.45 E
Obuasi, Ghana	224	6.14 N	1.39 W
Obukhov, Sov. Un. (ŏ'bōō-kôf)	173	50.07 N	30.36 E
Obukhovo, Sov. Un.	180b	55.50 N	38.17 E
Ocala, Fl. (ô-kä'lȧ)	125	29.11 N	82.09 W
Ocampo, Mex. (ô-käm'pō)	128	22.49 N	99.23 W
Ocaña, Col. (ô-kän'yä)	140	8.15 N	73.37 W
Ocaña, Sp. (ô-kä'n-yä)	168	39.58 N	3.31 W
Occidental, Grand Erg (Dunes), Alg.	220	29.30 N	00.45 W
Occidental, Cordillera (Mts.), Col. (kôr-dēl-yĕ'rä ôk-sē-dĕn-täl')	140a	5.05 N	76.04 W
Occidental, Cordillera (Mts.), Peru	140	10.12 S	76.58 W
Occidental, Sierra Madre (Mts.), Mex. (sē-ĕ'r-rä-mä'drĕ-ôk-sē-dĕn-tä'l)	126	29.30 N	107.30 W
Ocean Beach, Ca. (ō'shăn bēch)	118a	32.44 N	117.14 W
Ocean Bight (B.), Ba.	123	21.15 N	73.15 W
Ocean City, Md.	109	38.20 N	75.10 W
Ocean City, NJ	109	39.15 N	74.35 W
Ocean Falls, Can. (Fôls)	96	52.21 N	127.40 W
Ocean Grove, Austl.	207a	38.16 S	144.32 E
Ocean Grove, NJ (grōv)	109	40.10 N	74.00 W
Oceanside, Ca. (ō'shăn-sīd)	118	33.11 N	117.22 W
Oceanside, NY	110a	40.38 N	73.39 W
Ocean Springs, Ms. (sprĭngs)	124	30.25 N	88.49 W
Ocenele Mari, Rom.	171	45.05 N	24.17 E
Ochakov, Sov. Un. (ô-chä'kôf)	173	46.38 N	31.33 E
Ochlockonee R., Fl.-Ga. (ŏk-lō-kō'nē)	124	30.10 N	84.38 W
Ocilla, Ga. (ô-sĭl'ȧ)	124	31.36 N	83.15 W
Ockelbo, Swe. (ôk'ĕl-bô)	162	60.54 N	16.35 E
Ocmulgee (R.), Ga.	125	32.25 N	83.30 W
Ocmulgee Natl. Mon., Ga. (ôk-mŭl'gē)	124	32.45 N	83.28 W
Ocna-Sibiului, Rom. (ôck'ná-sē-byōō-lōō-ê)	171	45.52 N	24.04 E
Ocoa, Bahai de (B.), Dom. Rep. (bä-ä'ē-ô-kō'á)	133	18.20 N	70.40 W
Ococingo, Mex. (ô-kô-sē'n-gō)	129	17.03 N	92.18 W
Ocom, L., Mex. (ô-kō'm)	130a	19.26 N	88.18 W
Oconee, (R.), Ga. (ô-kō'nē)	124	32.45 N	83.00 W
Oconomowoc, Wi. (ô-kŏn'ô-mô-wŏk')	113	43.06 N	88.24 W
Oconto, Wi. (ô-kŏn'tō)	113	44.54 N	87.55 W
Oconto (R.), Wi.	113	45.08 N	88.24 W
Oconto Falls, Wi.	113	44.53 N	88.11 W
Ocós, Guat. (ô-kōs')	130	14.31 N	92.12 W
Ocotal, Nic. (ō-kô-täl')	130	13.36 N	86.31 W
Ocotepeque, Hond. (ô-kō-tā-pā'kā)	130	14.25 N	89.13 W
Ocotlán, Mex. (ô-kô-tlän')	128	20.19 N	102.44 W
Ocotlán de Morelos, Mex. (dā mô-rā'lōs)	129	16.46 N	96.41 W
Ocozocoautla, Mex. (ô-kō'zô-kwä-ōō'tlä)	129	16.44 N	93.22 W
Ocumare del Tuy, Ven. (ō-kōō-mä'ra del twē')	141b	10.07 N	66.47 W
Oda, Ghana	224	5.55 N	0.59 W
Odawara, Jap. (ō'dá-wä'rä)	201	35.15 N	139.10 E
Odda, Nor. (ôdh-á)	162	60.04 N	6.30 E
Oddur, Som.	219a	3.55 N	43.45 E
Odebolt, Ia. (ō'dē-bōlt)	112	42.20 N	95.14 W
Odemira, Port. (ō-dā-mē'rá)	168	37.35 N	8.40 W
Ödemis, Tur. (û'dĕ-mēsh)	177	38.12 N	28.00 E
Odendaalsrus, S. Afr. (ō'dĕn-däls-rûs')	219d	27.52 S	26.41 E
Odense, Den. (ō'dhĕn-sĕ)	162	55.24 N	10.20 E
Odenton, Md. (ō'dĕn-tŭn)	110e	39.05 N	76.43 W
Odenwald (For.), F.R.G. (ō'dĕn-väld)	164	49.39 N	8.55 E
Oder R., G.D.R. (ō'dēr)	164	52.40 N	14.19 E
Oderhaff (L.), G.D.R.	164	53.47 N	14.02 E
Odessa, Sov. Un. (ô-dĕs'sä)	173	46.28 N	30.44 E
Odessa, Tx. (ô-dĕs'á)	122	31.52 N	102.21 W
Odessa, Wa.	114	47.20 N	118.42 W
Odessa (Oblast), Sov. Un.	173	46.05 N	29.48 E
Odiel (R.), Sp. (ō-dē-ĕl')	168	37.47 N	6.42 W
Odienné, Ivory Coast (ō-dē-ĕn-nā')	224	9.30 N	7.34 W
Odiham, Eng. (ŏd'ē-ám)	154b	51.14 N	0.56 W
Odintsovo, Sov. Un. (ô-dēn'tsô-vô)	180b	55.40 N	37.16 E
Odiongan, Phil. (ō-dē-ôŋ'gän)	203a	12.24 N	121.59 E
Odivelas, Port. (ō-dē-vä'lyäs)	169b	38.47 N	9.11 W
Odobesti, Rom. (ō-dô-bĕsh't')	165	45.46 N	27.08 E
O'Donnell, Tx. (ō-dŏn'ĕl)	120	32.59 N	101.51 W
Odorhei, Rom. (ō-dôr-hā')	165	46.18 N	25.17 E
Odra R., Pol. (ô'drȧ)	165	50.28 N	17.55 E
Oeiras, Braz. (wā-ē-räzh')	141	7.05 S	42.01 W
Oeirás, Port. (ô-ĕ'y-rá's)	169b	38.42 N	9.18 W
Oelwein, Ia. (ōl'wīn)	113	42.40 N	91.56 W
O'Fallon, Il. (ō-făl'ŭn)	117e	38.36 N	89.55 W
O'Fallon Cr., Mt.	115	46.25 N	104.47 W
Ofanto (R.), It. (ô-fän'tō)	170	41.08 N	15.33 E
Offa, Nig.	225	8.09 N	4.44 E
Offenbach, F.R.G. (ôf'ĕn-bäk)	164	50.06 N	8.50 E
Offenburg, F.R.G. (ôf'ĕn-bŏŏrgh)	164	48.28 N	7.57 E
Ofuna, Jap. (ō'fōō-nä)	201a	35.21 N	139.32 E
Ogaden Plat., Eth.	219a	6.45 N	44.53 E
Ogaki, Jap.	201	35.21 N	136.36 E
Ogallala, Ne. (ō-gä-lä'lä)	112	41.08 N	101.44 W
Ogbomosho, Nig. (ŏg-bô-mō'shō)	225	8.08 N	4.15 E
Ogden, Ia. (ŏg'dĕn)	113	42.10 N	94.20 W
Ogden, Ut.	117b	41.14 N	111.58 W
Ogden Pk., Ut.	117b	41.11 N	111.51 W
Ogden R., Ut.	117b	41.16 N	111.54 W
Ogdensburg, NJ (ŏg'dĕnz-bûrg)	110a	41.05 N	74.36 W
Ogdensburg, NY	109	44.40 N	75.30 W
Ogeechee, (R.), Ga. (ô-gē'chē)	125	32.35 N	81.50 W
Ogies, S. Afr.	219d	26.03 S	29.04 E
Ogilvie Mts., Can. (ō'g'l-vĭ)	94	64.45 N	138.10 W
Oglesby, Il. (ō'g'lz-bĭ)	108	41.20 N	89.00 W
Oglio (R.), It. (ôl'yō)	170	45.15 N	10.19 E
Ogo, Jap. (ō'gō)	201b	34.49 N	135.06 E

PLACE (Pronunciation)	PAGE	Lat. °′	Long. °′
Ogooué (R.), Gabon	226	0.50 S	9.20 E
Ogou (R.), Togo	224	8.05 N	1.30 E
Ogudnëvo, Sov. Un. (ôg-ōōd-nyô'vô)	180b	56.04 N	38.17 E
Ogulin, Yugo. (ō-gōō-lēn')	170	45.17 N	15.11 E
Ogwashi-Uku, Nig.	225	6.10 N	6.31 E
O'Higgins (Prov.), Chile (ô-kē'gēns)	139b	34.17 S	70.52 W
Ohio, (State), U. S. (ô'hī'ō)	107	40.30 N	83.15 W
Ohio R., U. S.	108	37.25 N	88.05 W
Ohoopee (R.), Ga. (ô-hōō'pe-mc)	125	32.32 N	82.38 W
Ohře (R.), Czech. (ōr'zhĕ)	164	50.08 N	12.45 E
Ohrid, Yugo. (ō'krēd)	171	41.08 N	20.46 E
Ohrid, L., Alb.-Yugo.	171	40.58 N	20.35 E
Ōi, Jap. (oi')	201a	35.51 N	139.31 E
Oi-Gawa (Strm.), Jap. (ō'ē-gä'wá)	201	35.09 N	138.05 E
Oil City, Pa. (oil sĭ'tĭ)	109	41.25 N	79.40 W
Oirschot, Neth.	155a	51.30 N	5.20 E
Oise (R.), Fr. (wäz)	166	49.30 N	2.56 E
Oisterwijk, Neth.	155a	51.34 N	5.13 E
Oita, Jap. (ō'ē-tä)	201	33.14 N	131.38 E
Oji, Jap. (ō'jē)	201b	34.36 N	135.43 E
Ojinaga, Mex. (ō-kē-nä'gä)	122	29.34 N	104.26 W
Ojitlán (San Lucas), Mex. (ōkē-tlän') (sän-lōō'käs)	129	18.04 N	96.23 W
Ojo Caliente, Mex. (ōkō käl-yĕn'tā)	128	21.50 N	100.43 W
Ojocaliente, Mex. (ô-kô-kä-lyĕ'n-tĕ)	128	22.39 N	102.15 W
Ojo del Toro, Pico (Pk.), Cuba (pē'kô-ô-kō-dĕl-tô'rô)	132	19.55 N	77.25 W
Oka, Can. (ō-kä)	93a	45.28 N	74.05 W
Oka (R.), Sov. Un. (ô-kä')	177	52.10 N	35.20 E
Oka (R.), Sov. Un. (ō-kä')	178	53.28 N	101.09 E
Oka (R.), Sov. Un. (ô-ká')	176	55.10 N	42.10 E
Okahandja, Namibia	222	21.50 S	16.45 E
Okanagan (R.), Can. (ō'kȧ-näg'ȧn)	97	49.06 N	119.43 W
Okanagan L., Can.	97	50.00 N	119.28 W
Okano (R.), Gabon (ō'kä'nō)	220	0.15 N	11.08 E
Okanogan, Wa.	114	48.20 N	119.34 W
Okanogan R., Wa.	114	48.36 N	119.33 W
Okatibbee (R.), Ms. (ō'kä-tĭb'ē)	124	32.37 N	88.54 W
Okatoma Cr., Ms. (ô-kȧ-tō'mă)	124	31.43 N	89.34 W
Okavango (Cubango) (R.), Ang.-Namibia	222	17.10 S	18.20 E
Okavango Swp., Bots.	222	19.30 S	23.02 E
Okaya, Jap. (ō'kȧ-yȧ)	201	36.04 N	138.01 E
Okayama, Jap. (ō'kȧ-yä'mȧ)	201	34.39 N	133.54 E
Okazaki, Jap. (ō'kȧ-zä'kē)	201	34.58 N	137.09 E
Okeechobee, Fl. (ō-kē-chō'bē)	125	27.15 N	80.50 W
Okeechobee, L., Fl.	125a	27.00 N	80.49 W
Okeene, Ok. (ô-kēn')	120	36.06 N	98.19 W
Okefenokee Swp., Ga. (ō'kē-fē-nō'kē)	125	30.54 N	82.20 W
Okemah, Ok. (ô-kē'mä)	121	35.26 N	96.18 W
Okene, Nig.	225	7.33 N	6.15 E
Okha, Sov. Un. (ŭ-kä')	179	53.44 N	143.12 E
Okhotino, Sov. Un. (ô-kô'tĭ-nô)	180b	56.14 N	38.24 E
Okhotsk, Sov. Un. (ô-kôtsk')	179	59.28 N	143.32 E
Okhotsk, Sea of, Asia (ô-kôtsk')	189	56.45 N	146.00 E
Oki Guntō (Arch.), Jap. (ō'kē gōōn'tō)	201	36.17 N	133.05 E
Okinawa (I.), Jap. (ō'kē-nä'wá)	200	26.30 N	128.30 E
Okinawa Guntō (Is.), Jap. (gōōn'tō')	200	26.50 N	127.25 E
Okino (I.), Jap. (ō'kē-nō)	201	36.22 N	133.27 E
Okino Erabu (I.), Jap. (ō-kē'nō-ā-rä'bōō)	200	27.18 N	129.00 E
Oklahoma (State), U. S. (ô-klȧ-hō'mȧ)	106	36.00 N	98.20 W
Oklahoma City, Ok.	121	35.27 N	97.32 W
Oklawaha (R.), Fl. (ŏk-lȧ-wô'hô)	125	29.13 N	82.00 W
Okmulgee, Ok. (ôk-mŭl'gē)	121	35.37 N	95.58 W
Okolona, Ky. (ō-kô-lō'nȧ)	111h	38.08 N	85.41 W
Okolona, Ms.	124	33.59 N	88.43 W
Okushiri (I.), Jap. (ō'koo-shē'rē)	200	42.12 N	139.30 E
Okuta, Nig.	225	9.14 N	3.15 E
Olalla, Wa. (ō-lä'lȧ)	116a	47.26 N	122.33 W
Olanchito, Hond. (ō'län-chē'tō)	130	15.28 N	86.35 W
Öland (I.), Swe. (û-länd')	162	57.03 N	17.15 E
Olathe, Ks. (ō-lā'thē)	117f	38.53 N	94.49 W
Olavarría, Arg. (ō-lä-vär-rē'ä)	142	36.49 N	60.15 W
Oława, Pol (ô-lä'vä)	165	50.57 N	17.18 E
Olazoago, Arg. (ō-läz-kōä'gō)	139c	35.14 S	60.37 W
Olbia, It. (ô'l-byä)	170	40.55 N	9.28 E
Olching, F.R.G. (ōl'kĕng)	155d	48.13 N	11.21 E
Old Bahama Chan., N. A. (bȧ-hā'mȧ)	132	22.45 N	78.30 W
Old Bight, Ba.	133	24.15 N	75.20 W
Old Bridge, NJ (brĭj)	110a	40.24 N	74.22 W
Old Crow, Can. (crō)	94	67.51 N	139.58 W
Oldenburg, F.R.G. (ôl'dĕn-bŏŏrgh)	164	53.09 N	8.13 E
Old Forge, Pa. (fôrj)	109	41.20 N	75.50 W
Oldham, Eng. (ōld'ȧm)	154	53.32 N	2.07 W
Old Harbor, Ak. (här'bēr)	105	57.18 N	153.20 W
Old Head of Kinsale, Ire. (ōld hĕd ŏv kĭn-sāl)	160	51.35 N	8.35 W
Old R, Tx.	123a	29.54 N	94.52 W
Olds, Can. (ōldz)	97	51.47 N	114.06 W
Old Tate, Bots.	222	21.18 S	27.43 E
Old Town, Me. (toun)	102	44.55 N	68.42 W
Old Wives L., Can. (wīvz)	98	50.56 N	106.00 W
Olean, NY (ō-lē-ăn')	109	42.05 N	78.25 W
Olecko, Pol. (ô-lĕt'skô)	165	54.02 N	22.29 E
Olekma (R.), Sov. Un. (ô-lyĕk-mà')	179	55.41 N	120.33 E
Olëkminsk, Sov. Un. (ô-lyĕk-mĕnsk')	179	60.39 N	120.40 E
Olenëk (R.), Sov. Un. (ô-lyĕ-nyôk')	179	70.18 N	121.15 E
Oléron, Île, d' (I.), Fr. (ēl' dō lā-rôN')	166	45.52 N	1.58 W
Oleśnica, Pol. (ô-lĕsh-nĭ'tsá)	165	51.13 N	17.24 E
Olfen, F.R.G. (ōl'fĕn)	167c	51.43 N	7.22 E
Ol'ga, Sov. Un. (ôl'gá)	179	43.48 N	135.44 E
Ol'gi, Zaliv (B.), Sov. Un. (zä'lĭf ôl'gĭ)	200	43.43 N	135.25 E
Ol'gopol, Sov. Un. (ôl-gô-pôl'y')	173	48.11 N	29.28 E
Olhão, Port. (ôl-youN')	168	37.02 N	7.54 W
Olievenhoutpoort, S. Afr.	223b	25.58 S	27.55 E
Olifants (R.), S. Afr. (ŏl'ĭ-fănts)	222	23.58 S	31.00 E
Ólimbos, Grc.	171	40.03 N	22.22 E

PLACE (Pronunciation)	PAGE	Lat. °′	Long. °′
Ólimbos (Mtn.), Cyprus	189a	34.56 N	32.52 E
Olinalá, Mex. (ô-lē-nä-lä')	128	17.47 N	98.51 W
Olinda, Braz. (ô-lē'n-dä)	141	8.00 S	34.58 W
Oliva, Sp. (ô-lē'vä)	169	38.54 N	0.07 W
Oliva de la Frontera, Sp. (ô-lē'vä dā)	168	38.33 N	6.55 W
Olive Hill, Ky. (ŏl'ĭv)	108	38.15 N	83.10 W
Oliveira, Braz. (ô-lē-vā'rä)	139a	20.42 S	44.49 W
Olivenza, Sp. (ō-lē-vĕn'thä)	168	38.42 N	7.06 W
Oliver, Can. (ŏ'lĭ-vēr)	97	49.11 N	119.33 W
Oliver, Can.	93g	53.38 N	113.21 W
Oliver, Wi. (ŏ'lĭvēr)	117h	46.39 N	92.12 W
Oliver L., Can.	93g	53.19 N	113.00 W
Olivia, Mn. (ō-lĭv'ē-ȧ)	104	44.46 N	95.00 W
Olivos, Arg. (ôlē'vōs)	142a	34.15 S	58.29 W
Ollagüe, Chile (ô-lyä'gā)	140	21.17 S	68.17 W
Ollerton, Eng. (ôl'ēr-tŭn)	154	53.12 N	1.02 W
Olmos Park, Tx. (ōl'mŭs pärk')	117d	29.27 N	98.32 W
Olney, Il. (ŏl'nĭ)	108	38.45 N	88.05 W
Olney, Or. (ŏl'nē)	116c	46.06 N	123.45 W
Olney, Tx.	120	33.24 N	98.43 W
Olomane (R.), Can. (ō'lô mȧ'nē)	103	51.05 N	60.50 W
Olomouc, Czech. (ô'lô-mōts)	165	49.37 N	17.15 E
Olonets, Sov. Un. (ô-lô'nĕts)	163	60.58 N	32.54 E
Olongapo, Phil.	203a	14.49 S	120.17 E
Oloron, Gave d' (Strm.), Fr. (gäv-dō-lō-rôN')	166	43.21 N	0.44 W
Oloron-Ste. Marie, Fr. (ō-lô-rôNt'sàNt mȧ-rē')	166	43.11 N	1.37 W
Olot, Sp. (ô-lōt')	169	42.09 N	2.30 E
Olpe, F.R.G. (ōl'pē)	167c	51.02 N	7.51 E
Ol'shanka, Sov. Un. (ôl'shaŋ-kȧ)	173	48.14 N	30.52 E
Ol'shany, Sov. Un. (ôl'shȧn-ĕ)	173	50.02 N	35.54 E
Olsnitz, G.D.R. (ölz'nētz)	164	50.25 N	12.11 E
Olsztyn, Pol. (ôl'shtĭn)	165	53.47 N	20.28 E
Olten, Switz. (ôl'tĕn)	164	47.20 N	7.53 E
Oltenita, Rom. (ôl-tā'nĭ-tsȧ)	171	44.05 N	26.39 E
Oltul (R.), Rom.	159	44.09 N	24.40 E
Olvera, Sp. (ôl-vĕ'rä)	168	36.55 N	7.16 W
Olympia, Wa. (ô-lĭm'pĭ-ȧ)	114	47.02 N	122.52 W
Olympic Mts., Wa.	114	47.54 N	123.58 W
Olympic Natl. Park, Wa. (ô-lĭm'pĭk)	114	47.54 N	123.00 W
Olympus Mt., Wa. (ô-lĭm'pŭs)	114	47.43 N	123.30 W
Olyphant, Pa. (ŏl'ĭ-fănt)	109	41.30 N	75.40 W
Olyutorskiy, Mys (C.), Sov. Un. (ûl-yōō'tôr-skē)	179	59.49 N	167.16 E
Omae-Zaki (Pt.), Jap. (ō'mä-ā zä'kē)	201	34.37 N	138.15 E
Omagh, N. Ire. (ō'mä)	160	54.35 N	7.25 W
Omaha, Ne. (ō'mȧ-hä)	112	41.18 N	95.57 W
Omaha Ind. Res., Ne.	112	42.09 N	96.08 W
Oman, Asia	188	20.00 N	57.45 E
Oman, G. of, Asia	192	24.24 N	58.58 E
Omaruru, Namibia (ō-mä-rōō'rōō)	222	21.25 S	16.50 E
Omboué, Gabon	226	1.34 S	9.15 E
Ombrone (R.), It. (ôm-brō'nā)	170	42.48 N	11.18 E
Omdurman, see UmmDurmān			
Omealca, Mex. (ōmā-äl'kō)	129	18.44 N	96.45 W
Ometepec, Mex. (ô-mā-tā-pĕk')	128	16.41 N	98.27 W
Om Hajer, Eth.	221	14.06 N	36.46 E
Omineca (R.), Can. (ō-mĭ-nĕk'ȧ)	96	55.10 N	125.45 W
Omineca Mts., Can.	96	56.00 N	125.00 W
Ōmiya, Jap. (ō'mē-yȧ)	201a	35.54 S	139.38 E
Omoa, Hond. (ô-mō'rä)	130	15.43 N	88.03 W
Omolon (R.), Sov. Un. (ō'mō)	179	67.43 N	159.15 E
Ōmori (Kioroshi), Jap. (ō'mô-rē)(kē'ō-rō'shē)	201a	35.50 N	140.09 E
Omo R., Eth. (ō'mō)	221	5.54 N	36.09 E
Omoko, Nig.	225	5.20 N	6.39 E
Omotepe, Isla de (I.), Nic. (ē's-lä-dĕ-ō-mō-tā'pā)	130	11.32 N	85.30 W
Omro, Wi. (ŏm'rō)	113	44.01 N	89.46 W
Omsk, Sov. Un. (ômsk)	178	55.12 N	73.19 E
Ōmura, Jap. (ō'mōō-rȧ)	201	32.56 N	129.57 E
Ōmuta, Jap. (ō-mōō-tȧ)	201	33.02 N	130.28 E
Omutninsk, Sov. Un. (ō'mōō-tnēnsk)	176	58.38 N	52.10 E
Onawa, Ia. (ŏn-ȧ-wȧ)	112	42.02 N	96.05 W
Onaway, Mi.	108	45.25 N	84.10 W
Oncócua, Ang.	226	16.34 S	13.28 E
Onda, Sp. (ōn'dä)	169	39.58 N	0.13 W
Ondava (R.), Czech. (ōn'dȧ-vȧ)	165	48.51 N	21.40 E
Ondo, Nig.	225	7.04 N	4.47 E
Öndör Haan, Mong.	198	47.20 N	110.40 E
Onega, Sov. Un. (ô-nyĕ'gȧ)	176	63.50 N	38.08 E
Onega (R.), Sov. Un.	176	63.20 N	39.20 E
Onega, L., see Onezhskoye Ozero			
Oneida, NY (ō-nī'dȧ)	109	43.05 N	75.40 W
Oneida (L.), NY	109	43.10 N	76.00 W
O'Neill, Ne. (ō-nēl')	112	42.28 N	98.38 W
Onekotan (I.), Sov. Un. (ŭ-nyĕ-kŭ-tän')	179	49.45 N	153.45 E
Oneonta, NY (ō-nē-ŏn'tȧ)	109	42.25 N	75.05 W
Onezhskaja Guba (B.), Sov. Un.	176	64.30 N	36.00 E
Onezhskiy, P-Ov. (Pen.), Sov. Un.	176	64.30 N	37.40 E
Onezhskoye Ozero (Onega, L.), Sov. Un. (ô-năsh'skô-yĕ ô'zĕ-rô)	176	62.02 N	34.35 E
Ongin, Mong. (ŏn'gĭn')	194	46.00 N	102.46 E
Ongole, India	191	15.36 N	80.03 E
Onilahy (R.), Mad.	223	23.41 S	45.00 E
Onitsha, Nig. (ô-nĭt'shȧ)	225	6.09 N	6.47 E
Onomichi, Jap. (ō'nō-mē'chē)	201	34.27 N	133.12 E
Onon (R.), Sov. Un. (ō'nōn)	179	50.33 N	114.18 E
Onon Gol (R.), Sov. Un. (ō'nōn)	179	48.30 N	110.38 E
Onoto, Ven. (ō-nō'tō)	141b	9.38 N	65.03 W
Onslow, Austl. (ŏnz'lō)	210	21.53 S	115.00 E
Onslow B, NC (ŏnz'lō)	125	34.22 N	77.35 W
Ontake San (Mtn.), Jap. (ōn'tä-kā sän)	201	35.55 N	137.29 E
Ontario, Ca. (ŏn-tā'rĭ-ō)	117a	34.04 N	117.39 E
Ontario, Or.	114	44.02 N	116.57 W
Ontario (Prov.), Can.	95	50.47 N	88.50 W
Ontario, L., U. S.-Can.	107	43.35 N	79.05 W
Onteniente, Sp. (ōn-tā-nyĕn'tā)	169	38.48 N	0.35 W
Ontonagon, Mi. (ŏn-tō-năg'ŏn)	113	46.50 N	89.20 W

ăt; finăl; rāte; senāte; ärm; ȧsk; sofȧ; fâre; ch-choose; dh-as th in other; bē; ēvent; bĕt; recĕnt; cratēr; g-gō; gh-guttural g; bĭt; ĭ-short neutral; rīde; K-guttural k as ch in German ich;

PRONOUNCING INDEX

Ōnuki – Ouled-Naïl 329

PLACE (Pronunciation)	PAGE	Lat. °'	Long. °'
Ōnuki, Jap. (ō'nōō-kē)	201a	35.17 N	139.51 E
Oodnadatta, Austl. (ōōd'ná-dá'tá)	210	27.38 S	135.40 E
Ooldea Station, Austl. (ōōl-dā'ä)	210	30.35 S	132.08 E
Oologah Res., Ok.	121	36.43 N	95.32 W
Ooltgensplaat, Neth.	155a	51.41 N	4.19 E
Oostanaula (R.), Ga. (ōō-stá-nô'lá)	124	34.25 N	85.10 W
Oostende, Bel. (ōst-ĕn'dē)	161	51.14 N	2.55 E
Oosterhout, Neth.	155a	51.38 N	4.52 E
Ooster Schelde (R.), Neth.	161	51.40 N	3.40 E
Ootsa L., Can.	96	53.49 N	126.18 W
Opalaca, Sierra de (Mts.), Hond. (sē-sĕ'r-rä-dĕ-ō-pä-lä'kä)	130	14.30 N	88.29 W
Opasquia, Can. (ō-păs'kwē-á)	99	53.16 N	93.53 W
Opatow, Pol. (ô-pä'tōōf)	165	50.47 N	21.25 E
Opava, Czech. (ō'pä-vä)	165	49.56 N	17.52 E
Opelika, Al. (ŏp-ē-lī'ká)	124	32.39 N	85.23 W
Opelousas, La. (ŏp-ē-lōō'sás)	123	30.33 N	92.04 W
Opeongo (L.), Can. (ŏp-ē-ôŋ'gō)	109	45.40 N	78.20 W
Opheim, Mt. (ō-fīm')	115	48.51 N	106.19 W
Ophir, Ak. (ō'fēr)	105	63.10 N	156.28 W
Ophir, Mt., Mala.	189b	2.22 N	102.37 E
Opico, Sal. (ō-pē'kō)	130	13.50 N	89.23 W
Opinaca (R.), Can. (ŏp-ĭ-nä'kȧ)	95	52.28 N	77.40 W
Opladen, F.R.G. (ōp'lä-dĕn)	167c	51.04 N	7.00 E
Opobo, Nig.	225	4.34 N	7.27 E
Opochka, Sov. Un. (ō-pôch'kȧ)	172	56.43 N	28.39 E
Opoczno, Pol. (ō-pôch'nō)	165	51.22 N	20.18 E
Opole, Pol. (ō-pôl'ä)	165	50.42 N	17.55 E
Opole Lubelskie, Pol. (ō-pō'lä lōō-bĕl'skyĕ)	165	51.09 N	21.58 E
Oppdal, Nor. (ôp'däl)	162	62.37 N	9.41 E
Opportunity, Wa. (ŏp-ŏr tū'nĭ tĭ)	114	47.37 N	117.20 W
Oposhnya, Sov. Un. (ô-pôsh'nyá)	173	49.57 N	34.34 E
Opp, Al. (ŏp)	124	31.18 N	86.15 W
Oquirrh Mts., Ut. (ō'kwēr)	117b	40.38 N	112.11 W
Oradea, Rom. (ô-räd'yä)	165	47.02 N	21.55 E
Oran (Ouahran), Alg. (ō-rän)(ô-räN')	158	35.46 N	0.45 W
Orán, Arg. (ō-rá'n)	142	23.13 S	64.17 W
Oran, Mo. (ôr'án)	121	37.05 N	89.39 W
Oran, Sebkhan d' (L.), Alg.	169	35.28 N	0.28 W
Orange, Austl. (ŏr'ĕnj)	212	33.15 S	149.08 E
Orange, Ca.	117a	33.48 N	117.51 W
Orange, Ct.	109	41.15 N	73.00 W
Orange, Fr. (ô-raNzh')	166	44.08 N	4.48 E
Orange, NJ	110a	40.46 N	74.14 W
Orange, Tx.	120	30.07 N	93.44 W
Orange, Cabo (C.), Braz. (kȧ-bô-rȧ'n-zhĕ)	141	4.25 N	51.30 W
Orange (L.), Fl.	125	29.30 N	82.12 W
Orange (R.), Namibia-S. Afr.	222	29.15 S	17.30 E
Orangeburg, SC (ŏr'ĕnj-bûrg)	125	33.30 N	80.50 W
Orange Cay (I.), Ba. (ŏr-ĕnj kē)	132	24.55 N	79.05 W
Orange City, Ia.	112	43.01 N	96.06 W
Orange Free State (Prov.), S. Afr.	222	28.15 S	26.00 E
Orangeville, Can. (ŏr'ĕnj-vĭl)	93d	43.55 N	80.06 W
Orangeville, S. Afr.	219d	27.05 S	28.13 E
Orange Walk, Belize (wôl'k)	130a	18.09 N	88.32 W
Orani, Phil. (ō-rä'nē)	203a	14.47 N	120.32 E
Oranienburg, G.D.R. (ō-rä'nē-ĕn-bōōrgh)	155b	52.45 N	13.14 E
Oranjemund, Namibia	222	28.33 S	16.20 E
Orăştie, Rom. (ô-rûsh'tyă)	171	45.50 N	23.14 E
Oraşul-Stalin, see Braşov			
Orbetello, It. (ôr-bȧ-tĕl'lō)	170	42.27 N	11.15 E
Orbigo (R.), Sp. (ôr-bē'gō)	168	42.30 N	5.55 W
Orbost, Austl. (ôr'bŭst)	212	37.43 S	148.20 E
Orcas (I.), Wa. (ôr'kȧs)	116d	48.43 N	122.52 W
Orchard Farm, Mo. (ôr'chĕrd färm)	117e	38.53 N	90.27 W
Orchard Park, NY	111c	42.46 N	78.46 W
Orchards, Wa. (ôr'chĕdz)	116c	45.40 N	122.33 W
Orchilla, Ven. (ôr-kĭl-ȧ)	140	11.47 N	66.34 W
Ord, Ne. (ôrd)	112	41.35 N	98.57 W
Ord (R.), Austl.	210	17.30 S	128.40 E
Orda, Sov. Un. (ôr'dȧ)	180a	56.50 N	57.12 E
Ordenes, Sp. (ōr'dā-nās)	168	43.46 N	8.24 W
Ordos Des., China	198	39.12 N	108.10 E
Ord Pk., Az.	119	33.55 N	109.40 W
Ordu, Tur. (ôr'dōō)	177	41.00 N	37.50 E
Ordway, Co. (ôrd'wā)	120	38.11 N	103.46 W
Ordzhonikidze, Sov. Un. (ora ghō nī kĭd ze)	177	43.05 N	44.35 E
Örebro, Swe. (û'rē-brō)	162	59.16 N	15.11 E
Oredezh R., Sov. Un. (ō'rĕ-dĕzh)	180c	59.23 N	30.21 E
Oregon, Il.	113	42.01 N	89.21 W
Oregon (State), U.S.	106	43.40 N	121.50 W
Oregon Caves Natl. Mon., Or. (căvz)	114	42.05 N	123.13 W
Oregon City, Or.	116c	45.21 N	122.36 W
Öregrund, Swe. (û-rĕ-grōōnd)	162	60.20 N	18.26 E
Orekhov, Sov. Un. (ôr-yĕ'Kôf)	173	47.34 N	35.51 E
Orekhovo, Bul.	171	43.43 N	23.59 E
Orekhovo-Zuyevo, Sov. Un. (ôr-yĕ'kô-vô zōō'yĕ-vô)	172	55.46 N	39.00 E
Orël, Sov. Un. (ôr-yôl')	172	52.54 N	36.03 E
Orël (Oblast), Sov. Un.	172	52.35 N	36.08 E
Orel' (R.), Sov. Un.	173	49.08 N	34.55 E
Orem, Ut. (ŏ'rĕm)	119	40.15 N	111.50 W
Ore Mts., see Erzgebirge			
Orenburg, Sov. Un. (ō'rĕn-bōōrg)	177	51.50 N	55.05 E
Orense, Sp. (ô-rĕn'sā)	168	42.20 N	7.52 W
Orfanoú, Kólpos (G.), Grc.	171	40.40 N	23.55 E
Organos, Sierra de los (Mts.), Cuba (sē-ĕ'r-rȧ-dĕ-lôs-ŏ'r-gä-nôs)	132	22.20 N	84.10 W
Organ Pipe Cactus Natl. Mon., Az. (ôr'găn pīp kăk'tŭs)	119	32.14 N	113.05 W
Orgãos, Serra das (Mtn.), Braz. (sĕ'r-rä-dās-ôr-gouN's)	139a	22.30 S	43.01 W
Orgeyev, Sov. Un. (ôr-gyĕ'yĕf)	173	47.27 N	28.49 E
Orhon Gol (R.), Mong.	194	48.33 N	103.07 E
Oriental, Cordillera (Mts.), Bol. (kôr-dēl-yĕ'rä ō-rē-ĕn-täl')	140	14.00 S	68.33 W
Oriental, Cordillera (Mts.), Col. (kôr-dēl-yĕ'rä)	140a	3.30 N	74.27 W

PLACE (Pronunciation)	PAGE	Lat. °'	Long. °'
Oriental, Cordillera (Mts.), Dom. Rep. (kôr-dēl-yĕ'rä-ō-ryĕ'n-täl)	133	18.55 N	69.40 W
Oriental, Sierra Madre, (Mts.), Mex. (sē-ĕ'r-rä-mä'drĕ-ō-ryĕ'n-täl')	126	25.30 N	100.45 W
Orihuela, Sp. (ō'rē-wā'lä)	169	38.04 N	0.55 W
Orillia, Can. (ô-rĭl'ĭ-ȧ)	109	44.35 N	79.25 W
Orin, Wy.	115	42.40 N	105.10 W
Orinda, Ca.	116b	37.53 N	122.11 W
Orinoco, Rio (R.), Ven. (rē'ō-ō-rī-nō'kō)	140	8.32 N	63.13 W
Orion, Phil. (ō-rē-ōn')	203a	14.37 N	120.34 E
Orissa (State), India (ŏ-rĭs'ȧ)	190	25.09 N	83.50 E
Oristano, It. (ô-rēs-tä'nō)	170	39.53 N	8.38 E
Oristano, Golfo di (G.), It. (gôl-fô-dē-ō-rēs-tä'nō)	170	39.53 N	8.12 E
Orituco (R.), Ven. (ô-rē-tōō'kō)	141b	9.37 N	66.25 W
Oriuco, (R.), Ven. (ô-rēōō'kō)	141b	9.36 N	66.25 W
Orivesi (L.), Fin.	163	62.15 N	29.55 E
Orizaba, Mex. (ô-rē-zä'bä)	129	18.52 N	97.05 E
Orkanger, Nor.	162	63.19 N	9.54 W
Orkla (R.), Nor. (ôr'klȧ)	162	62.55 N	9.50 E
Orkney, S. Afr. (ôrk'nĭ)	219d	26.58 S	26.39 E
Orkney (Is.), Scot.	160a	59.01 N	2.08 W
Orlando, Fl. (ôr-lăn'dō)	125a	28.32 N	81.22 W
Orlando, S. Afr. (ôr-lăn-dô)	223b	26.15 S	27.56 E
Orland Park, Il. (ôr-lăn')	111a	41.38 N	87.52 W
Orleans, Can. (ôr-lā-äN')	93c	45.28 N	75.31 W
Orléans, Fr. (ôr-lā-äN')	166	47.55 N	1.56 E
Orleans, In. (ôr-lēnz')	108	38.40 N	86.25 W
Orléans, Île d' (I.), Can.	93b	46.56 N	70.57 W
Orléansville, see El Asnam			
Ormond Beach, Fl. (ôr'mŏnd)	125	29.15 N	81.05 W
Ormskirk, Eng. (ôrms'kĕrk)	154	53.34 N	2.53 W
Ormstown, Can. (ôrms'toun)	93a	45.07 N	74.00 W
Orneta, Pol. (ôr-nyĕ'tä)	165	54.07 N	20.10 E
Ornö (I.), Swe.	162	59.02 N	18.35 E
Örnsköldsvik, Swe. (ûrn'skôlts-vĕk)	156	63.10 N	18.32 E
Oro, Rio del (R.), Mex. (rē'ō dĕl ō'rō)	128	18.04 N	100.59 W
Oro, Rio del (R.), Mex.	112	26.04 N	105.40 W
Orobie, Alpi (Mts.), It. (äl'pē-ô-rô'byĕ)	170	46.05 N	9.47 E
Orocué, Col. (ō-rô-kwā')	140	4.48 N	71.26 W
Oron, Nig.	225	4.48 N	8.14 E
Orosei, Golfo di (G.), It. (gôl-fô-dē-ō-rô-sā'ē)	170	40.12 N	9.45 E
Orosháza, Hung. (ô-rôsh-hä'sô)	165	46.33 N	20.31 E
Orosi Vol., C. R. (ō-rō'sē)	130	11.00 N	85.30 W
Oroville, Ca. (ŏr'ō-vĭl)	118	39.29 N	121.34 W
Oroville, Wa.	114	48.55 N	119.25 W
Orrville, Oh. (ôr'vĭl)	108	40.45 N	81.50 W
Orsa, Swe. (ōr'sä)	162	61.08 N	14.35 E
Orsha, Sov. Un. (ôr'shȧ)	172	54.29 N	30.28 E
Orsk, Sov. Un. (ôrsk)	177	51.15 N	58.50 E
Orsova, Rom. (ôr'shô-vä)	171	44.43 N	22.26 E
Ortega, Col. (ôr-tĕ'gä)	140a	3.56 N	75.12 W
Ortegal, Cabo (C.), Sp. (kȧ'bō-ôr-tȧ-gäl')	168	43.46 N	8.15 W
Orth, Aus.	155e	48.09 N	16.42 E
Orthez, Fr. (ôr-tĕz')	169	43.29 N	0.43 W
Ortigueira, Sp. (ôr-tē-gā'ē-rä)	168	43.40 N	7.50 W
Orting, Wa. (ôrt'ĭng)	116a	47.06 N	122.12 W
Ortona, It. (ôr-tō'nä)	170	42.22 N	14.22 E
Ortonville, Mn. (ôr-tŭn-vĭl)	112	45.18 N	96.26 W
Orūmīyeh, Iran	192	37.30 N	45.15 E
Orūmīyeh, Daryacheh-ye (L.), Iran	192	38.01 N	45.17 E
Oruro, Bol. (ō-rōō'rō)	140	17.57 S	66.59 W
Orvieto, It. (ôr-vyā'tō)	170	42.43 N	12.08 E
Osa, Sov. Un. (ō'sȧ)	176	57.18 N	55.25 E
Osa, Pen. de, C. R. (ō'sä)	131	8.30 N	83.25 W
Osage, Ia. (ō'sāj)	113	43.16 N	92.49 W
Osage (R.), Mo.	121	38.10 N	93.12 W
Osage City, Ks. (ō'sāj sĭ'tĭ)	121	38.28 N	95.53 W
Ōsaka, Jap. (ō'sä-kä)	201b	34.40 N	135.27 E
Ōsaka (Pref.), Jap.	201b	34.45 N	135.36 E
Ōsaka-Wan (B.), Jap. (wän)	201	34.34 N	135.16 E
Osakis, Mn. (ô-sā'kĭs)	113	45.51 N	95.09 W
Osakis (L.), Mn.	113	45.55 N	94.55 W
Osawatomie, Ks. (ŏs-ȧ-wăt'ō-mē)	121	38.29 N	94.57 W
Osborne, Ks. (ŏz'bŭrn)	120	39.25 N	98.42 W
Osceola, Ar. (ŏs-ē-ō'lȧ)	121	35.42 N	89.58 W
Osceola, Ia.	113	41.04 N	93.45 W
Osceola, Mo.	121	38.02 N	93.41 W
Osceola, Ne.	112	41.11 N	97.34 W
Osceola, Tn.	121	35.42 N	89.58 W
Oscoda, Mi. (ŏs-kō'dȧ)	108	44.25 N	83.20 W
Osëtr (R.), Sov. Un. (ō'sĕt'r)	172	54.27 N	38.15 E
Osgood, In. (ŏz'gŏŏd)	108	39.10 N	85.20 W
Osgoode, Can.	93c	45.09 N	75.37 W
Osh, Sov. Un. (ôsh)	178	40.28 N	72.47 E
Oshawa, Can. (ŏsh'ȧ-wȧ)	109	43.50 N	78.50 W
Ōshima (I.), Jap. (ō'shē'mä)	201	34.47 N	139.35 E
Oshkosh, Ne. (ŏsh'kŏsh)	112	41.24 N	102.22 W
Oshkosh, Wi.	113	44.01 N	88.35 W
Oshmyany, Sov. Un. (ôsh-myä'nĭ)	163	54.27 N	25.55 E
Oshogbo, Nig.	225	7.47 N	4.34 E
Osijek, Yugo. (ôs'ĭ-yĕk)	171	45.33 N	18.48 E
Osinniki, Sov. Un. (ŭ-sē'nyĭ-kē)	178	53.29 N	85.19 E
Oskaloosa, Ia. (ŏs-kȧ-lōō'sȧ)	113	41.16 N	92.40 W
Oskarshamn, Swe. (ôs'kärs-häm'n)	162	57.16 N	16.24 E
Oskarström, Swe. (ôs'kärs-strûm)	162	56.48 N	12.55 E
Oskol (R.), Sov. Un. (ôs-kôl')	173	51.00 N	37.41 E
Oslo, Nor. (ŏs'lō)	162	59.56 N	10.41 E
Oslofjorden (Fd.), Nor.	162	59.03 N	10.35 E
Osmaniye, Tur.	177	37.10 N	36.30 E
Osnabrück, F.R.G. (ôs-nä-brük')	164	52.16 N	8.05 E
Osorno, Chile (ō-sō'r-nō)	142	40.42 S	73.13 W
Osøyra, Nor.	162	60.24 N	5.22 E
Osprey Reef (I.), Austl. (ŏs'prā)	211	14.00 S	146.45 E
Ossa, Mt., Austl. (ŏsȧ)	212	41.45 S	146.05 E
Osseo, Mn. (ŏs'sē-ō)	117g	45.07 N	93.24 W
Ossining, NY (ŏs'ĭ-nĭng)	110a	41.09 N	73.51 W

PLACE (Pronunciation)	PAGE	Lat. °'	Long. °'
Ossipee, NH (ŏs'ĭ-pē)	102	43.42 N	71.08 W
Ossjøen (L.), Nor. (ôs-syûĕn)	162	61.20 N	12.00 E
Ostashkov, Sov. Un. (ôs-täsh'kôf)	172	57.07 N	33.04 E
Oster, Sov. Un. (ōs'tĕr)	173	50.55 N	30.52 E
Osterdalälven (R.), Swe.	162	61.40 N	13.00 E
Øster Fd., Nor. (ûs'tĕr fyôr')	173	60.40 N	5.25 E
Östersund, Swe. (ûs'tĕr-sōōnd)	162	63.09 N	14.49 E
Östhammar, Swe. (ûst'häm'är)	162	60.16 N	18.21 E
Ostrava, Czech.	165	49.51 N	18.18 E
Ostróda, Pol. (ôs'trōōt-ȧ)	165	53.41 N	19.58 E
Ostróg, Sov. Un. (ōs-trôk')	173	50.21 N	26.40 E
Ostrogozhsk, Sov. Un. (ôs-tr-gôzhk')	173	50.53 N	39.03 E
Ostrołęka, Pol. (ôs-trô-woN'kȧ)	165	53.04 N	21.35 E
Ostropol', Sov. Un. (ôs-trô-pôl')	173	49.48 N	27.32 E
Ostrov, Sov. Un. (ôs-trôf')	172	57.21 N	28.22 E
Ostrowiec Świetokrzyski, Pol. (ôs-trō'vyĕts shvyĕN-tō-kzhĭ'ske)	165	50.55 N	21.24 E
Ostrów Lubelski, Pol. (ôs'trōōf lōō'bĕl-skĭ)	165	51.32 N	22.49 E
Ostrów Mazowiecka, Pol. (mä-zô-vyĕt'skä)	165	52.47 N	21.54 E
Ostrów Wielkopolski, Pol. (ôs'trōōf vyĕl-kō-pōl'skē)	165	51.38 N	17.49 E
Ostrzeszów, Pol. (ôs-tzhā'shōōf)	165	51.26 N	17.56 E
Ostuni, It. (ôs-tōō'nē)	171	40.44 N	17.35 E
Osum (R.), Alb. (ō'sōōm)	171	40.37 N	20.00 E
Ōsumi-Guntō (Arch.), Jap. (ō'sōō-mē gōōn'tō)	201	30.34 N	130.30 E
Ōsumi Kaikyō (Van Diemen)(Str.), Jap. (käē'kyô)(văn dē'mĕn)	201	31.02 N	130.10 E
Osuna, Sp. (ō-sōō'nä)	168	37.18 N	5.05 W
Osveya, Sov. Un. (ôs'vĕ-yȧ)	172	56.00 N	28.08 E
Oswaldtwistle, Eng. (ŏz-wȧld-twĭs''l)	154	53.44 N	2.23 W
Oswegatchie (R.), NY (ŏs-wē-găch'ĭ)	109	44.15 N	75.20 W
Oswego, Ks. (ŏs-wē'gō)	121	37.10 N	95.08 W
Oswego, NY	109	43.25 N	76.30 W
Oświęcim, Pol. (ôsh-vyăN'tsyĭm)	165	50.02 N	19.17 E
Otaru, Jap. (ō'tȧ-rōō)	200	43.07 N	141.00 E
Otavalo, Ec. (ōtä-vä'lō)	140	0.14 N	78.16 W
Otavi, Namibia (ō-tä'vē)	222	19.35 S	17.20 E
Otay, Ca. (ō'tā)	118a	32.36 N	117.04 W
Otepää, Sov. Un. (ō'tĕ-pȧ)	172	58.03 N	26.31 E
Othonoi (I.), Grc.	171	39.51 N	19.26 E
Othris, Oros (Mts.), Grc.	171	39.00 N	22.15 E
Oti (R.), Ghana	224	9.00 N	0.10 E
Otish, Mts., Can. (ō-tĭsh')	95	52.15 N	70.20 W
Otjiwarongo, Namibia (ŏt-jē-wȧ-rôn'gō)	222	20.20 S	16.25 E
Otočac, Yugo. (ō'tô-chȧts)	170	44.53 N	15.15 E
Otra (R.), Nor.	162	59.13 N	7.20 E
Otradnoye, Sov. Un. (ō-trȧ'd-nôyĕ)	180	59.46 N	30.50 E
Otranto, It. (ō'trän-tô) (ô-trän'tō)	171	40.07 N	18.30 E
Otranto, Strait of, It.-Alb.	171	40.30 N	18.45 E
Otra R., Sov. Un. (ôt'rȧ)	180b	55.22 N	38.20 E
Otsego, Mi. (ŏt-sē'gō)	108	42.25 N	85.45 W
Otsu, Jap. (ō'tsōō)	201b	35.00 N	135.54 E
Otta (L.), Nor. (ôt'tȧ)	162	61.53 N	8.40 E
Ottawa, Can. (ŏt'ȧ-wȧ)	93c	45.25 N	75.43 W
Ottawa, Il.	108	41.20 N	88.50 W
Ottawa, Ks.	121	38.37 N	95.16 W
Ottawa, Oh.	108	41.00 N	84.00 W
Ottawa (R.), Can.	95	46.05 N	77.20 W
Ottawa Is., Can.	95	59.50 N	81.00 W
Otter Cr., Ut. (ŏt'ĕr)	119	38.20 N	111.55 W
Otter Cr., Vt.	109	44.05 N	73.15 W
Otter Pt., Can.	116a	48.21 N	123.50 W
Otter Tail (L.), Mn.	112	46.21 N	95.52 W
Otterville, Il. (ŏt'ĕr-vĭl)	117e	39.03 N	90.24 W
Ottery, S. Afr. (ŏt'ĕr-ĭ)	222a	34.02 S	18.31 E
Ottumwa, Ia. (ō-tŭm'wȧ)	113	41.00 N	92.26 W
Otukpa, Nig.	225	7.09 N	7.41 E
Otumba, Mex. (ō-tŭm'bä)	129a	19.41 N	98.46 W
Otway, C., Austl. (ŏt'wā)	212	38.55 S	153.40 E
Otway, Seno (B.), Chile (sĕ'nō-ō't-wä'y)	142	53.00 S	73.00 W
Otwock, Pol. (ōt'vôtsk)	165	52.05 N	21.18 E
Ouachita, (R.), U. S.	107	33.25 N	92.30 W
Ouachita Mts., Ok. (wŏsh'ĭ-tô)	121	34.29 N	95.01 W
Ouaddaï (Reg.), Chad (wä-dī')	221	13.04 N	20.00 E
Ouagadougou, Upper Volta (wä'gȧ-dōō'gōō)	224	12.22 N	1.31 W
Ouahigouya, Upper Volta (wä-ē-gōō'yä)	224	13.35 N	2.25 W
Ouahran, see Oran			
Oualâta, Mauritania (wä-lä'tä)	220	17.11 N	6.50 W
Ouallene, Alg. (wäl-lân')	220	24.43 N	1.15 E
Ouanaminthe, Hai.	133	19.35 N	71.45 W
Ouanda Djallé, Cen. Afr. Rep. (wän'dä' jä' lā')	221	8.56 N	22.46 E
Ouarane (Dunes), Mauritania	220	20.44 N	10.27 W
Ouargla, Alg. (wär'glä)	220	32.00 N	5.18 E
Ouarkoye, Upper Volta	224	12.05 N	3.40 W
Ouassel (R.), Alg.	169	35.30 N	1.55 E
Oubangui (Ubangi) (R.), Afr. (ōō-bäŋ'gē)	226	4.30 N	20.35 E
Oude Rijn (R.), Neth.	155a	52.09 N	4.33 E
Oudewater, Neth.	155a	52.01 N	4.52 E
Oud-Gastel, Neth.	155a	51.35 N	4.27 E
Oudtshoorn, S. Afr. (outs'hōrn)	222	33.33 S	23.36 E
Oued Rhiou, Alg.	169	35.55 N	0.57 E
Oued Tlelat, Alg.	169	35.33 N	0.28 W
Oued-Zem, Mor. (wĕd-zĕm')	220	33.05 N	5.49 W
Ouellé, Ivory-Coast	224	7.18 N	4.01 W
Ouessant, I. d', Fr. (ēl-dwĕ-säN')	166	48.28 N	5.00 W
Ouesso, Con.	226	1.37 N	16.04 E
Ouest, Pt., Hai.	133	19.00 N	73.25 W
Ouezzane, Mor. (wĕ-zan')	220	34.48 N	5.40 W
Ouham (R.), Cen. Afr. Rep.-Chad	225	8.30 N	17.50 E
Ouidah, Benin (wē-dä')	220	6.25 N	2.05 E
Oujda, Mor.	220	34.41 N	1.45 W
Ouled-Naïl, Monts des, (Mts.), Alg.	158	34.43 N	2.44 E

330 Oulins – Papagayo

PLACE (Pronunciation)	PAGE	Lat. °′	Long. °′
Oulins, Fr. (o͞o-lȧN′)	167b	48.52 N	1.27 E
Oullins, Fr. (o͞o-lăN′)	166	45.44 N	4.46 E
Oulu, Fin. (ō′lo͞o)	156	64.58 N	25.43 E
Oulujärvi, (L.), Fin.	156	64.20 N	25.48 E
Oum Chalouba, Chad. (o͞om shä-lo͞o′bä)	221	15.48 N	20.30 E
Oum Hadjer, Chad.	225	13.18 N	19.41 E
Ounas (R.), Fin. (ō′nȧs)	156	67.46 N	24.40 E
Oundle, Eng. (ôn′d′l)	154	52.28 N	0.28 W
Ounianga Kébir, Chad. (o͞o-nē-äŋ′gȧ kē-bēr′)	221	19.04 N	20.22 E
Ouray, Co. (o͞o-rā′)	121	38.00 N	107.40 W
Ourinhos, Braz. (ôo͞o-rē′nyôs)	141	23.04 S	49.45 W
Ourique, Port. (ō-rē′kĕ)	168	37.39 N	8.10 W
Ouro Fino, Braz. (ōŭ-rô-fē′nō)	139a	22.18 S	46.21 W
Ouro Prêto, Braz. (ō′ro͞o prā′to͞o)	139a	20.24 S	43.30 W
Outardes, Rivière aux. (R.), Can.	103	50.53 N	68.50 W
Outer (I.), Wi. (out′ēr)	113	47.03 N	90.20 W
Outer Brass (I.), Vir. Is.(U. S. A.) (bräs)	127c	18.24 N	64.58 W
Outer Hebrides (Is.), Scot.	160	57.20 N	7.50 W
Outlook, Can.	98	51.31 N	107.05 W
Outjo, Namibia (ōt′yō)	222	20.05 S	17.10 E
Outremont, Can. (o͞o-trē-môN′)	93a	45.31 N	73.36 W
Ouyen, Austl. (o͞o-ĕn)	212	35.05 S	142.10 E
Ovalle, Chile (ō-väl′yā)	142	30.43 S	71.16 W
Ovando, Bahía de (B.), Cuba (bä-ē′ä-dĕ-ȯ-vä′n-dō)	133	20.10 N	74.05 W
Ovar, Port. (ȯ-vär′)	168	40.52 N	8.38 W
Overijse, Bel.	155a	50.46 N	4.32 E
Overland, Mo. (ō-vēr-lănd)	117e	38.42 N	90.22 W
Overland Park, Ks.	117f	38.59 N	94.40 W
Overlea, Md. (ō′vēr-lā)(ō′vēr-lē)	110e	39.21 N	76.31 W
Övertornea, Swe.	156	66.19 N	23.31 E
Ovidiopol′, Sov. Un. (ô-vė-dė-ô′pȯl′)	173	46.15 N	03.28 E
Oviedo, Dom. Rep. (ȯ-vyĕ′dō)	133	17.50 N	71.25 W
Oviedo, Sp. (ō-vė-ā′dhō)	168	43.22 N	5.50 W
Ovruch, Sov. Un. (ôv′ro͝och)	173	51.19 N	28.51 E
Owada, Jap. (ō′wä-dȧ)	201a	35.49 N	139.33 E
Owambo (Reg.), Namibia	222	18.10 S	15.00 E
Owando, Con.	226	0.29 S	15.55 E
Owasco (L.), NY (ō-wăsk′kō)	109	42.50 N	76.30 W
Owase, Jap. (ō′wä-shė)	201	34.03 N	136.12 E
Owego, NY (ō-wē′gō)	109	42.05 N	76.15 W
Owen, Wi. (ō′ĕn)	113	44.56 N	90.35 W
Owens (L.), Ca. (ō′ĕnz)	118	36.27 N	117.45 W
Owens (R.), Ca.	118	37.13 N	118.20 W
Owensboro, Ky. (ō′ĕnz-bŭr-ȯ)	108	37.45 N	87.05 W
Owen Sound, Can. (ō′ĕn)	108	44.30 N	80.55 W
Owen Stanley Ra., Pap. N. Gui (stăn′lė)	203	9.00 S	147.30 E
Owensville, In. (ō′ĕnz-vĭl)	108	38.15 N	87.40 W
Owensville, Mo.	121	38.20 N	91.29 W
Owensville, Oh.	111f	39.08 N	84.07 W
Owenton, Ky. (ō′ĕn-tŭn)	108	38.35 N	84.55 W
Owerri, Nig. (ȯ-wĕr′ė)	220	5.26 N	7.04 E
Owings Mill, Md. (ōwĭngz mĭl)	110e	39.25 N	76.50 W
Owl Cr., Wy. (oul)	115	43.45 N	108.46 W
Owo, Nig.	225	7.15 N	5.37 E
Owosso, Mi. (ȯ-wŏs′ō)	108	43.00 N	84.15 W
Owyhee Mts., Id. (ȯ-wī′hė)	114	43.15 N	116.48 W
Owyhee Res., Or.	114	43.27 N	117.30 W
Owyhee R., Or.	114	43.04 N	117.45 W
Owyhee R., South Fork, Id.	114	42.07 N	116.43 W
Oxbow, Can.	99	49.12 N	102.11 W
Oxchuc, Mex. (ȯs-cho͞ok′)	129	16.47 N	92.24 W
Oxford, Al. (ŏks′fērd)	124	33.38 N	80.46 W
Oxford, Can. (ŏks′fērd)	101	45.44 N	63.52 W
Oxford, Eng.	154b	51.43 N	1.16 W
Oxford, Ma.	103a	42.07 N	71.52 W
Oxford, Mi.	108	42.50 N	83.15 W
Oxford, Ms.	124	34.22 N	89.30 W
Oxford, NC	125	36.17 N	78.35 W
Oxford, Oh.	108	39.30 N	84.45 W
Oxford L., Can.	99	54.51 N	95.37 W
Oxfordshire (CO.), Eng.	154b	51.36 N	1.30 W
Oxkutzcab, Mex. (ȯx-ko͞o′tz-käb)	130a	20.18 N	89.22 W
Oxmoor, Al. (ŏks′mo͝or)	110h	33.25 N	86.52 W
Oxnard, Ca. (ŏks′närd)	118	34.08 N	119.12 W
Oxon Hill, Md. (ōks′ōn hĭl)	110e	38.48 N	77.00 W
Oxtotepec, Mex. (ôx-tô-tĕ′pĕk)	129a	19.10 N	99.04 W
Oyapock (R.), Braz.-Fr. Gu. (ō-yȧ-pŏk′)	141	2.45 N	52.15 W
Oyem, Gabon (ȯ-yĕm)(ȯ-yăN′)	226	1.37 N	11.35 E
Øyeren (L.), Nor. (ûĭĕrĕn)	162	59.50 N	11.25 E
Oymyakon, Sov. Un. (oi-myŭ-kôn′)	179	63.14 N	142.58 E
Oyo, Nig. (ō′yō)	225	7.51 N	3.56 E
Oyonnax, Fr. (ȯ-yȯ-nȧks′)	167	46.16 N	5.40 E
Oyster Bay, NY	110a	40.52 N	73.32 W
Oyster Bayou, Tx.	123a	29.41 N	94.33 W
Oyster Cr., Tx. (ois′tēr)	123a	29.13 N	95.29 W
Ozama (R.), Dom. Rep. (ȯ-zä′mä)	133	18.45 N	69.55 W
Ozamiz, Phil. (ȯ-zä′mėz)	203	8.06 N	123.43 E
Ozark, Al. (ō′zärk)	124	31.28 N	85.28 W
Ozark, Ar.	121	35.29 N	93.49 W
Ozarks, L. of the, Mo. (ō′zärksz)	121	38.06 N	93.26 W
Ozark Plat, Mo.	121	36.37 N	93.56 W
Ozëry, Sov. Un. (ȯ-zyô′rė)	172	54.53 N	38.31 E
Ozieri, It.	170	40.38 N	8.53 E
Ozorkow, Pol. (ȯ-zȯr′ko͝of)	165	51.58 N	19.20 E
Ozuluama, Mex. (ō′zo͞o-lo͞o-ä′mä)	129	21.34 N	97.52 W
Ozumba, Mex. (ô-zo͞o′m-bä)	129a	19.02 N	98.48 W

P

PLACE (Pronunciation)	PAGE	Lat. °′	Long. °′
Paarl, S. Afr. (pärl)	222	33.45 S	18.55 E
Paauilo, Hi. (pä-ä-o͞o′ė-lō)	104a	20.03 N	155.25 W
Pabianice, Pol. (pä-byȧ-nē′tsĕ)	165	51.40 N	19.29 E
Pacaás Novos, Massiço de (Mts.), Braz. (mä-sē′sô-dĕ-pä-kȧ′s-nô′vōs)	140	11.03 S	64.02 W
Pacaraima, Serra (Mts.), Braz.-Ven. (sĕr′rȧ pä-kä-rä-ē′mȧ)	140	3.45 N	62.30 W
Pacasmayo, Peru (pä-käs-mä′yō)	140	7.24 S	79.30 W
Pachuca, Mex. (pä-cho͞o′kä)	129	20.07 N	98.43 W
Pacific, Wa. (pȧ-sĭf′ĭk)	116a	47.16 N	122.15 W
Pacifica, Ca. (pȧ-sĭf′ĭ-kä)	116b	37.38 N	122.29 W
Pacific Beach, Ca.	118a	32.47 N	117.22 W
Pacific Grove, Ca.	118	36.37 N	121.54 W
Pacific O.,	4		
Pacific Ra., Can.	96	51.00 N	125.30 W
Pacific Rim Natl. Pk., Can.	96	49.00 N	126.00 W
Pacolet (R.), SC (pā′cō-lēt)	125	34.55 N	81.49 W
Pacy-sur-Eure, Fr. (pä-sē-sür-ûr′)	167b	49.01 N	1.24 E
Padang, Indon. (pä-däng′)	202	1.01 S	100.28 E
Padang, Palau (I.), Indon.	189b	1.12 N	102.21 E
Padang Endau, Mala.	189b	2.39 N	103.38 E
Paden City, WV (pā′dĕn)	108	39.30 N	80.55 W
Paderborn, F.R.G. (pä-dĕr-bȯrn′)	164	51.43 N	8.46 E
Padibe, Ug.	227	3.28 N	32.50 E
Padiham, Eng. (păd′ĭ-hăm)	154	53.48 N	2.19 W
Padilla, Mex. (pä-dēl′yä)	128	24.00 N	98.45 W
Padilla B., Wa. (pä-dĕl′lȧ)	116a	48.31 N	122.34 W
Padova (Padua), It. (pä′dȯ-vä)(păd′û-ȧ)	170	45.24 N	11.53 E
Padre I., Tx. (pä′drā)	123	27.09 N	97.15 W
Padua, see Padova			
Paducah, Ky. (pȧ-kū′kȧ)	124	37.05 N	88.36 W
Paducah, Tx.	120	34.01 N	100.18 W
Paektu San (Mt.), China-Kor. (pâk′to͞o-sän′)	200	42.00 N	128.03 E
Pag (I.), Yugo (päg)	170	44.30 N	14.48 E
Pagai Selatan, Pulau (I.), Indon.	202	2.48 S	100.22 E
Pagai Utara, Pulau (I.), Indon.	202	2.45 S	100.02 E
Pagasitikós Kólpos (G.), Grc.	171	39.15 N	23.00 E
Page, Az.	121	36.57 N	111.27 W
Pagosa Springs, Co. (pȧ-gō′sȧ)	121	37.15 N	107.05 W
Pahala, Hi. (pä-hä′lä)	104a	19.11 N	155.28 W
Pahang (State), Mala.	189b	3.02 N	102.57 E
Pahang R., Mala.	202	3.39 N	102.41 E
Pahokee, Fl. (pȧ-hō′kē)	125a	26.45 N	80.40 W
Paide, Sov. Un. (pī′dĕ)	163	58.54 N	25.30 E
Päijänne (L.), Fin. (pĕ′ē-yĕn-nĕ)	163e	61.38 N	25.05 E
Pailolo Chan., Hi. (pä-ė-lō′lō)	104a	21.05 N	156.41 W
Paine, Chile (pī′nĕ)	139b	33.49 S	70.44 W
Painesville, Oh. (pānz′vĭl)	108	41.40 N	81.15 W
Painted Des., Az. (pānt′ēd)	121	36.15 N	111.35 W
Painted Rock Res., Az.	121	33.00 N	113.05 W
Paintsville, Ky. (pānts′vĭl)	108	37.50 N	82.50 W
Paisley, Scot. (pāz′lĭ)	160	55.50 N	4.30 W
Paita, Peru (pä-ē′tä)	140	5.11 S	81.12 W
Pai T′ou Shan (Mts.), Korea	198	40.30 N	127.20 E
Paiute Ind. Res., Ut.	121	38.17 N	113.50 W
Pajápan, Mex. (pä-hä′pän)	129	18.16 N	94.41 W
Pakanbaru, Indon.	202	0.43 N	101.15 E
Pakhra R., Sov. Un. (päK′rá)	180b	55.29 N	37.51 E
Pakistan, Asia	188	28.00 N	67.30 E
Pakistan East, see Bangladesh			
Pakokku, Bur. (pȧ-kŏk′ko͞o)	202	21.29 N	95.00 E
Paks, Hung. (pôksh)	165	46.38 N	18.53 E
Pala, Chad.	225	9.22 N	14.54 E
Palacios, Tx. (pä-lä′syōs)	123	28.42 N	96.12 W
Palagruža (Is.), Yugo (pä′lä-gro͞o′zhä)	170	42.20 N	16.23 E
Palaiseau, Fr. (pȧ-lĕ-zō′)	167b	48.44 N	2.16 E
Palana, Sov. Un.	179	59.07 N	159.58 E
Palanan B., Phil. (pä-lä′nän)	203a	17.14 N	122.35 E
Palanan Pt., Phil.	203a	17.12 N	122.40 E
Pālanpur, India (pä′lŭn-po͞or)	190	24.08 N	73.29 E
Palapye, Bots (pȧ-läp′yĕ)	222	22.34 S	27.28 E
Palatine, Il. (păl′ȧ-tīn)	111a	42.07 N	88.03 W
Palatka, Fl. (pȧ-lăt′kȧ)	125	29.39 N	81.40 W
Palau Is., Pac. Is. Trust. Ter. (pä-lä′o͞o)	203	7.15 N	134.30 E
Palauig, Phil. (pȧ-lou′ėg)	203a	15.27 N	119.54 E
Palawan (I.), Phil. (pä-lä′wȧn)	202	9.50 N	117.38 E
Pālayankottai, India	191	8.50 N	77.50 E
Paldiski, Sov. Un. (päl′dĭ-skĭ)	163	59.22 N	24.04 E
Palembang, Indon. (pä-lĕm-bäng′)	202	2.57 S	104.40 E
Palencia, Guat. (pä-lĕn′sė-ȧ)	130	14.40 N	90.22 W
Palencia, Sp. (pä-lĕ′n-syä)	168	42.02 N	4.32 W
Palengue, Mex. (pä-lĕŋ′kā)	129	17.34 N	91.58 W
Palenque, Punta (Pt.), Dom. Rep. (po͞o′n-tä)	133	18.10 N	70.10 W
Palermo, Col. (pä-lĕr′mô)	140a	2.53 N	75.26 W
Palermo, It.	170	38.08 N	13.24 E
Palestine, Tx.	123	31.46 N	95.38 W
Palestine (Reg.), Asia (păl′ĕs-tīn)	189a	31.33 N	35.00 E
Paletwa, Bur. (pŭ-lĕt′wä)	194	21.19 N	92.52 E
Palghāt, India	191	10.49 N	76.40 E
Pāli, India	190	25.53 N	73.18 E
Palimé, Togo	224	6.54 N	0.38 E
Palín, Guat. (pä-lēn′)	130	14.42 N	90.42 W
Palisade, Nv. (păl-ĭ-sād′)	114	40.39 N	116.11 W
Palizada, Mex. (pä-lė-zä′dä)	129	18.17 N	92.04 W
Palk Str., India (pôk)	190	10.00 N	79.23 E
Palma, Braz. (päl′mä)	139a	21.23 S	42.18 W
Palma, Sp.	169	39.35 N	2.38 E
Palma, Ba, de (B.), Sp. (bä-ē′ä-dĕ)	169	39.24 N	2.37 E
Palma del Rio, Sp. (dĕl rē′ō)	168	37.43 N	5.19 W
Palmares, Braz. (päl-mȧ′rĕs)	141	8.46 S	35.28 W
Palmas, Braz. (päl′mäs)	142	26.20 S	51.56 W
Palmas, C., Lib.	224	4.22 N	7.44 W
Palma Soriano, Cuba (sȯ-ré-ä′nō)	133	20.15 N	76.00 W
Palm Beach, Fl. (päm bēch′)	125a	26.43 N	80.03 W
Palmeira dos Índios, Braz. (pä-mā′rä-dȯs-ē′n-dyȯs)	141	9.26 S	36.33 W
Palmeirinhas, Ponta das (Pt.), Arg.	226	9.05 S	13.00 E
Palmela, Port. (päl-mā′lä)	169b	38.34 N	8.54 W
Palmer, Ak. (päm′ēr)	105	61.38 N	149.15 W
Palmer, Wa.	116a	47.19 N	121.53 W
Palmerston North, N. Z. (päm′ēr-stŭn)	213	40.20 N	175.35 W
Palmerville, Austl. (päm′ēr-vĭl)	211	16.08 S	144.15 E
Palmetto, Fl. (pȧl-mĕt′ȯ)	125a	27.32 N	82.34 W
Palmetto Pt., Ba.	133	21.15 N	73.25 W
Palmi, It. (päl′mē)	170	38.21 N	15.54 E
Palmira, Col. (päl-mē′rä)	140a	3.33 N	76.17 W
Palmira, Cuba	132	22.15 N	80.25 W
Palmyra, Mo. (păl-mī′rȧ)	121	39.45 N	91.32 W
Palmyra, NJ	110f	40.01 N	75.00 W
Palmyra (I.), Oceania	205	6.00 N	162.20 W
Palmyra (Ruins), Syr.	192	34.25 N	38.28 E
Palmyras Pt., India	190	20.42 N	87.45 E
Palmyre, Syr.	153	30.35 N	37.58 E
Palo Alto, Ca. (pä′lō äl′tō)	116b	37.27 N	122.09 W
Paloduro Cr., Tx. (pā-lȯ-do͞o′rȯ)	120	36.16 N	101.12 W
Paloh, Mala.	189b	2.11 N	103.12 E
Paloma, L., Mex. (pä-lō′mä)	122	26.53 N	104.02 W
Palomo, Cerro el (Mtn.), Chile (sĕ′r-rȯ-ĕl-pä-lô′mȯ)	139b	34.36 S	70.20 W
Palos, Cabo de (C.), Sp. (kȧ′bȯ-dĕ-pä′lȯs)	169	39.38 N	0.43 W
Palos Verdes Estates, Ca. (pă′lŭs vûr′dĭs)	117a	33.48 N	118.24 W
Palouse, Wa. (pȧ-lo͞oz′)	114	46.54 N	117.04 W
Palouse Hills, Wa.	114	46.48 N	117.47 W
Palouse R., Wa.	114	47.02 N	117.35 W
Palu, Tur. (pä-loo′)	177	38.55 N	40.10 E
Paluan, Phil. (pä-lo͞o′än)	203a	13.25 N	120.29 E
Pamamushir (I.), Sov. Un.	179	50.42 N	153.45 E
Pamiers, Fr. (pȧ-myā′)	166	43.07 N	1.34 E
Pamirs (Plat), Sov. Un.	193	38.14 N	72.27 E
Pamlico R., NC (păm′lĭ-kō)	125	35.25 N	76.59 W
Pamlico Sd., NC	125	35.10 N	76.10 W
Pampa, Tx. (păm′pȧ)	120	35.32 N	100.56 W
Pampa de Castillo (Plat), Arg. (pä′m-pä-dĕ-käs-tė′l-yȯ)	142	45.30 S	67.30 W
Pampana (R.), S. L.	224	8.35 N	11.55 W
Pampanga (R.), Phil. (päm-päŋ′gä)	203a	15.20 N	120.48 E
Pampas (Reg.), Arg. (päm′päs)	142	37.00 S	64.30 W
Pampilhosa do Botão, Port. (päm-pė-lyō′sȧ-dȯ-bō-to′uN)	168	40.21 N	8.32 W
Pamplona, Col. (päm-plō′nä)	140	7.19 N	72.41 W
Pamplona, Sp. (päm-plȯ′nä)	168	42.49 N	1.39 W
Pamunkey (R.), Va. (pȧ-mŭŋ′kĭ)	109	37.40 N	77.20 W
Pana, Il. (pā′nȧ)	108	39.25 N	89.05 W
Panabá, Mex. (pä-nä-bȧ′)	130a	21.18 N	88.15 W
Panagyurishte, Bul. (pȧ-nȧ-gyo͞o′rėsh-tĕ)	171	42.30 N	24.11 E
Panaji (Panjim) India	191	15.33 N	73.52 E
Panamá, N.A. (păn-ȧ-mä′)	127	8.35 N	81.08 W
Panamá, B. de, Pan.	131	8.50 N	79.08 W
Panamá, G. de, Pan.	127	7.45 N	79.20 W
Panamá, Istmo de, Pan.	127	9.00 N	81.00 W
Panama City, Fl. (păn-ȧ mä′ sĭ′tĭ)	124	30.08 N	85.39 W
Panamint Ra., Ca. (păn-ȧ-mĭnt′)	118	36.40 N	117.30 W
Panaria (Is.), It. (pä-nä′rė-a)	170	38.37 N	15.05 E
Panaro (R.), It. (pä-nä′rȯ)	170	44.47 N	11.06 E
Panay (I.), Phil. (pä-nī′)	202	11.15 N	121.38 E
Pančevo, Yugo, (pȧn′chĕ-vȯ)	171	44.52 N	20.42 E
Panchor, Mala.	189b	2.10 N	103.43 E
Pānchur, India	190a	22.31 N	88.17 E
Panda, Zaire (pän′dä′)	222	10.59 S	27.24 E
Pandar-e Pahlavī, Iran	177	37.30 N	49.30 E
Pan de Guajaibon (Mtn.), Cuba (pän dā gwä-jȧ-bōn′)	132	22.50 N	83.20 W
Pandu, Zaire	226	5.00 N	19.15 E
Panevėžys, Sov. Un. (pä′nyĕ-vāzh′ēs)	163	55.44 N	24.21 E
Panfilov, Sov. Un. (pŭn-fē′lŏf)	178	44.12 N	79.58 E
Panga, Zaire (päŋ′gä)	227	1.51 N	26.25 E
Pangani, Tan. (pän-gä′nē)	223	5.28 S	38.58 E
Pangani (R.), Tan.	227	4.40 S	37.45 E
Pangkalpinang, Indon. (päng-käl′pė-näng′)	202	2.11 S	106.04 E
Pangnirtung, Can.	95	66.08 N	65.26 W
Panguitch, Ut. (pän′gwĭch)	121	37.50 N	112.30 W
Panimávida, Chile (pä-nē-mȧ′vē-dä)	139b	36.44 S	71.26 W
Pāninàti, India	190a	22.42 N	88.23 E
Panjim, see Panaji			
Panshi, China (pän-shē)	198	42.50 N	126.48 E
Pan Si Pan (Mtn.), Viet.	199	22.25 N	103.50 E
Pantar, Pulau (I.), Indon. (pän′tär)	203	8.40 N	123.45 E
Pantelleria (I.), It. (pän-tĕl-lȧ-rē′ä)	157	36.43 N	11.59 E
Pantepec, Mex. (pän-tȧ-pĕk′)	129	17.11 N	93.04 W
Panuco, Mex. (pä′no͞o-kȯ)	128	22.04 N	98.11 W
Pánuco, Mex. (pä′no͞o-kȯ)	128	29.47 N	105.55 W
Panuco (R.), Mex.	128	21.59 N	98.20 W
Pánuco de Coronado, Mex. (pä′no͞o-kȯ dā kō-rȯ-nä′dhō)	122	24.33 N	104.20 W
Panvel, India	191b	18.59 N	73.06 E
Panyu, China (pä-yo͞o)	197a	22.56 N	113.22 E
Panzós, Guat. (pä-zós′)	130	15.26 N	89.40 W
Pao, (R.), Ven. (pȧ′ō)	141b	9.52 N	67.57 W
Paola, Ks. (pȧ-ō′lȧ)	121	38.34 N	94.51 W
Paoli, In. (pȧ-ō′lī)	108	38.35 N	86.30 W
Paoli, Pa.	110f	40.03 N	75.29 W
Paonia, Co. (pā-ō′nyȧ)	119	38.50 N	107.40 W
Paoting, China	198	42.04 N	125.00 E
Pápa, Hung. (pä′pô)	165	47.18 N	17.27 E
Papagayo, Golfo del (G.), C. R. (gȯl-fô-dĕl-pä-pä-gȧ′yō)	130	10.44 N	85.56 W

PRONOUNCING INDEX

Papagayo – Pedro II 331

PLACE (Pronunciation)	PAGE	Lat. °′	Long. °′
Papagayo, Laguna (L.), Mex. (lä-o͞o-nä)	128	16.44 N	99.44 W
Papagayo (R.), Mex. (pä-pä-gä'yō)	128	16.52 N	99.41 W
Papago Ind. Res., Az. (pä'pä'gō)	119	32.33 N	112.12 W
Papantla de Olarte, Mex. (pä-pän'tlä dā-ô-lä'r-tĕ)	126	20.30 N	97.15 W
Papatoapan (R.), Mex. (pä-pä-tô-ā-pa'n)	129	18.00 N	96.22 W
Papenburg, F.R.G. (päp'ĕn-bo͝orgh)	164	53.05 N	7.23 E
Papinas, Arg. (pä-pē'näs)	139c	35.30 S	57.19 W
Papineauville, Can. (pä-pē-nō'vēl)	93c	45.38 N	75.01 W
Papua, Gulf of, Pap. N. Gui. (păp-o͞o-ȧ)	203	8.20 S	144.45 E
Papua New Guinea, Oceania (păp-o͞o-ȧ)(gĭne)	203	7.00 S	142.15 E
Papudo, Chile (pä-po͞o'dō)	139b	32.30 S	71.25 W
Paquequer Pequeno, Braz. (pä-kĕ-kĕ'r-pĕ-kĕ'nō)	142b	22.19 S	43.02 W
Pará, see Belém			
Pará (State), Braz. (pä-rä')	141	4.45 S	53.30 W
Pará (R.), Braz. (pä-rä')	139a	20.21 S	44.38 W
Pará, Rio do (R.), Braz. (rē'ō-dō-pä-rä')	141	1.09 S	48.48 W
Para (R.), Sov. Un.	172	53.45 N	40.58 E
Paracale, Phil. (pä-rä-kä'lā)	203a	14.17 N	122.47 E
Paracambi, Braz. (pä-rä-kȧ'm-bē)	142b	22.36 S	43.43 W
Paracatu, Braz. (pä-rä-kä-to͞o')	141	17.17 S	46.43 W
Parcel Is., China	202	16.40 N	113.00 E
Paraćin, Yugo. (pȧ'rä-chēn)	171	43.51 N	21.26 E
Para de Minas, Braz. (pä-rä-dĕ-mē'näs)	139a	19.52 S	44.37 W
Paradise (I.), Ba.	132	25.05 N	77.20 W
Paradise Valley, Ny. (păr'ȧ-dīs)	114	41.28 N	117.32 W
Parados, Cerro de los (Mtn.), Col. (sĕ'r-rō-dĕ-lōs-pä-rä'dōs)	140a	5.44 N	75.13 W
Paragould, Ar. (păr'ȧ-go͞old)	121	36.03 N	90.29 W
Paraguaçu (R.), Braz. (pä-rä-gwä-zo͞o')	141	12.25 S	39.46 W
Paraguaná, Pen. de (Pen.), Ven. (pĕ-nē'ng-so͞o-lä-dĕ-pä-rä-gwȧ-nȧ')	140	12.00 N	69.55 W
Paraguay, S. A. (păr'ȧ-gwā)	138	24.00 S	57.00 W
Paraguay, Rio (R.), S.A. (rē'ō-pä-rä-gwä'y)	141	21.12 S	57.31 W
Paraíba, see João Pessoa			
Paraíba (State), Braz. (pä-rä-ē'bä)	141	7.11 S	37.05 W
Paraíba (R.), Braz.	139a	23.02 S	45.43 W
Paraíba do Sul, Braz. (dō-so͞o'l)	139a	22.10 S	43.18 W
Paraibuna, Braz. (pä-räē-bo͞o'nä)	139a	23.23 S	45.38 W
Paraiso, Pan. (pä-rä-ē'sō)	126a	9.02 N	79.38 W
Paraíso, C. R.	131	9.50 N	83.53 W
Paraíso, Mex.	129	18.24 N	93.11 W
Paraisópolis, Braz. (pä-räē-sô'pō-lēs)	139a	22.35 S	45.45 W
Paraitinga, Braz. (pä-rä-ē-tē'n-gä)	139a	23.15 S	45.24 W
Parakou, Benim (pȧ-rȧ-ko͞o')	225	9.21 N	2.37 E
Paramaribo, Sur. (pȧ-rȧ-mȧ'rē-bō)	141	5.50 N	55.15 W
Paramatta, Austl. (păr-ȧ-măt'ȧ)	207b	33.49 S	150.59 E
Paramillo (Mtn.), Col. (pä-rä-mē'l-yō)	140a	7.06 N	75.55 W
Paramus, NJ	110a	40.56 N	74.04 W
Paramushir (I.), Sov. Un.	179	50.45 N	154.00 E
Paran (R.), Isr.	189a	30.05 N	34.50 E
Paraná, Arg. (pä-rä-nä')	142	31.44 S	60.29 W
Paraná (State), Braz.	142	24.25 S	52.00 W
Paraná, Rio (R.), Arg.	142	32.15 S	60.55 W
Paraná (R.), Braz.	141	13.05 S	47.11 W
Paranaguá, Braz. (pä-rä'nä-gwȧ')	141	25.39 S	48.42 W
Paranaíba, Braz. (pä-rä-nȧ-ē'bȧ)	141	19.43 S	51.13 W
Paranaíba (R.), Braz.	141	18.58 S	50.44 W
Parana Ibicuy (R.), Arg. (ē-bē-ko͞o'ē)	139c	33.27 S	59.26 W
Paranam, Sur.	141	5.39 N	55.13 W
Paránápanema (R.), Braz. (pä-rä'nȧ'pä-nĕ-mä)	142	22.28 S	52.15 W
Paraopeda (R.), Braz. (pä-rä-o-pĕ'dä)	139a	20.09 S	44.14 W
Parapara, Ven. (pä-rä-pä-rä)	141b	9.44 N	67.17 W
Parati, Braz. (pä-rätē)	139a	23.14 S	44.43 W
Paray-le-Monial, Fr. (pȧ-rĕ'lē-mō-nyäl')	166	46.27 N	4.14 E
Pārbati (R.), India	190	24.50 N	76.44 E
Parchim, G.D.R. (par'kīm)	164	53.25 N	11.52 E
Parczew, Pol. (pär'chĕf)	165	51.38 N	22.53 E
Pardo (R.), Braz. (pär'dō)	141	15.25 S	39.40 W
Pardo (R.), Braz.	139a	21.32 S	46.40 W
Pardubice, Czech. (pär'do͞o-bĭt-sĕ)	164	50.02 N	15.47 E
Parecis, Serra dos (Mts.), Braz. (sĕr'rȧ dōs pä-rā-sēzh')	141	13.45 S	59.28 W
Paredes de Nava, Sp (pä-rā'dās dā nä'vä)	168	42.10 N	4.41 W
Paredón, Mex.	122	25.56 N	100.58 W
Parent, Can.	101	47.59 N	74.30 W
Parent, Lac (L.), Can.	101	48.40 N	77.00 W
Pare Pare, Indon.	202	4.01 S	119.38 E
Pargolovo, Sov. Un. (pȧr-gô'lō vō)	180c	60.04 N	30.18 E
Paria, Golfo de (G.), Ven. (gōl-fō-dĕ-br-pä-rē-ä)	140	10.33 N	62.14 W
Paria (R.), Az.-Ut.	119	37.07 N	111.51 W
Paricutín, Vol., Mex. (pä-rē-ko͞o-tē'n)	128	19.27 N	102.14 W
Parida, Rio de la (R.), Mex. (rē'ō-dĕ-lä-pä-rē'dä)	122	26.23 N	104.40 W
Parima, Serra (Mts.), Braz.-Ven. (sĕr'rȧ pä-rē'mȧ)	140	3.45 N	64.00 W
Pariñas, Punta (Pt.), Peru (po͞o'n-tä-pä-rē'n-yäs)	140	4.30 S	81.23 W
Parintins, Braz. (pä-rĭn-tĭNzh')	141	2.34 S	56.30 W
Paris, Ar. (păr'ĭs)	117	35.17 N	93.43 W
Paris, Can.	108	43.15 N	80.23 W
Paris, Fr. (pȧ-rē')	167b	48.51 N	2.20 E
Paris, Il.	108	39.35 N	87.40 W
Paris, Ky.	108	38.15 N	84.15 W
Paris, Mo.	121	39.27 N	91.59 W
Paris, Tn.	124	36.16 N	88.20 W
Paris, Tx.	121	33.39 N	95.33 W
Parita, Golfo de (G.), Pan. (gōl-fô-dĕ-pä-rē'tä)	131	8.06 N	80,10 W
Park City, Ut.	115	40.39 N	111.33 W
Parker, SD (pär'kēr)	112	43.24 N	97.10 W
Parker Dam, Az.-Ca.	121	34.20 N	114.00 W
Parkersburg, WV (pär'kērz-bûrg)	108	39.15 N	81.35 W
Parkes, Austl. (pärks)	212	33.10 S	148.10 E
Park Falls, Wi. (pärk)	113	45.55 N	90.29 W
Park Forest, Il.	111a	41.29 N	87.41 W
Parkland, Wa. (pärk'lănd)	116a	47.09 N	122.26 W
Park Ra., Co.	115	40.54 N	106.40 W
Park Rapids, Mn.	113	46.53 N	95.05 W
Park Ridge, Il.	111a	42.00 N	87.50 W
Park River, ND	112	48.22 N	97.43 W
Parkrose, Or. (pärk'rōz)	116c	45.33 N	122.33 W
Park Rynie, S. Afr.	223c	30.22 S	30.43 E
Parkston, SD (pärks'tŭn)	112	43.22 N	97.59 W
Park View, NM (vū)	119	36.45 N	106.30 W
Parkville, Md.	110e	39.22 N	76.32 W
Parkville, Mo.	117f	39.12 N	94.41 W
Parla, Sp. (pär'lä)	169a	40.14 N	3.46 W
Parma, It. (pär'mä)	170	44.48 N	10.20 E
Parma, Oh.	111d	41.23 N	81.44 W
Parma Heights, Oh.	111d	41.23 N	81.36 W
Parnaguá, Braz. (pär-nä-gwȧ')	141	9.52 S	44.27 W
Parnaíba, Braz. (pär-nä-ē'bä)	141	3.00 S	41.42 W
Parnaiba (R.), Braz.	141	3.57 S	42.30 W
Parnassós (Mtn.), Grc.	171	38.36 N	22.35 E
Parndorf, Aus.	155e	48.00 N	16.52 E
Pärnu, Sov. Un. (pĕr'no͞o)	163	58.24 N	24.29 E
Pärnu (R.), Sov. Un.	163	58.40 N	25.05 E
Pärnu Laht (B.), Sov. Un. (läKt)	163	58.15 N	24.17 E
Paro, Bhu. (pä'rô)	190	27.30 N	89.30 E
Paroo (R.), Austl. (pä'ro͞o)	212	29.40 S	144.24 E
Paropamisus (Mts.), Afg.	192	34.45 N	63.58 E
Páros, Grc. (pä'rōs) (pā'rŏs)	171	37.05 N	25.14 E
Páros (I.), Grc.	171	37.11 N	25.00 E
Parow, S. Afr. (pă'rō)	222a	33.54 S	18.36 E
Parowan, Ut. (păr'ō-wăn)	119	37.50 N	112.50 W
Parral, Chile (pär-rä'l)	142	36.07 S	71.47 W
Parral, R., Mex.	122	27.25 N	105.08 W
Parramatta (R.), Aust. (păr-ȧ-măt'ȧ)	207b	33.42 S	150.58 E
Parras, Mex. (pär-räs')	122	25.28 N	102.08 W
Parrita, C. R. (pär-rē'tä)	131	9.32 N	84.17 W
Parrsboro, Can. (pärz'bŭr-ō)	102	45.24 N	64.20 W
Parry (I.), Can. (păr'ĭ)	108	45.15 N	80.00 W
Parry, Mt., Can.	96	52.53 N	128.45 W
Parry Is., Can.	92	75.30 N	110.00 W
Parry Sound, Can.	109	45.20 N	80.00 W
Parsnip (R.), Can. (pärs'nĭp)	96	54.45 N	122.20 W
Parsons, Ks. (pär's'nz)	121	37.20 N	95.16 W
Parsons, WV	109	39.05 N	79.40 W
Parthenay, Fr. (pȧr-t'nĕ')	166	46.39 N	0.16 W
Partinico, It. (pär-tē'nē-kô)	170	38.02 N	13.11 E
Partizansk, Sov. Un.	200	43.15 N	133.19 E
Parys, S. Afr. (pȧ-rīs')	219d	26.53 S	27.28 E
Pasadena, Ca. (păs-ȧ-dē'nȧ)	117a	34.09 N	118.09 W
Pasadena, Md.	110e	39.06 N	76.35 W
Pasadena, Tx.	123a	29.43 N	95.13 W
Pascagoula, Ms. (păs-kȧ-go͞o'lȧ)	124	30.22 N	88.33 W
Pascagoula (R.), Ms.	124	30.52 N	88.48 W
Paşcani, Rom. (päsh-kän')	165	47.46 N	26.42 E
Pasco, Wa. (păs'kō)	114	46.13 N	119.04 W
Pasewalk, G.D.R. (pä'zĕ-välk)	164	53.31 N	14.01 E
Pashiya, Sov. Un. (pä'shĭ-yȧ)	180a	58.27 N	58.17 E
Pashkovo, Sov. Un. (pȧsh-kô'vō)	200	48.52 N	131.09 E
Pashkovskaya, Sov. Un. (pȧsh-kôf'skȧ-yȧ)	173	45.29 N	39.04 E
Pasig, Phil.	203a	14.34 N	121.05 E
Pasión, Rio de la (R.), Guat. (rē'ō-dĕ-lä-pä-syōn')	130a	16.31 N	90.11 W
Paso de los Libres, Arg. (pä-sō-dĕ-lōs-lē'brĕs)	142	29.33 S	57.05 W
Paso de los Toros, Ur. (tŏ'rōs)	139c	32.43 S	56.33 W
Paso Robles, Ca. (pă'sō rō'blĕs)	118	35.38 N	120.44 W
Pasquia Hills, Can. (păs'kwē-ȧ)	100	53.13 N	102.37 W
Passaic, NJ (pă-sā'ĭk)	110a	40.52 N	74.08 W
Passaic R., NJ	110a	40.42 N	74.26 W
Passamaquoddy B., Can. (păs'ȧ-mȧ-kwŏd'ĭ)	102	45.06 N	66.59 W
Passa Tempo, Braz. (pä's-sä-tĕ'm-pô)	139a	21.40 S	44.29 W
Passau, F.R.G. (päs'ou)	164	48.34 N	13.27 E
Pass Christian, Ms. (pȧs krĭs'tyĕn)	124	30.20 N	89.15 W
Passero, C., It. (päs-sĕ'rō)	157	36.34 N	15.13 E
Passo Fundo, Braz. (pä'sŏ fo͞on'do͞o)	142	28.16 S	52.13 W
Passos, Braz. (pä's-sōs)	139a	20.45 S	46.37 W
Pastaza (R.), Peru (päs-tä'zä)	140	3.05 S	76.18 W
Pasto, Col. (päs'tō)	140	1.15 N	77.19 W
Pastora, Mex. (päs-tō-rä)	128	22.08 N	100.04 W
Pasuruan, Indon.	202	7.45 S	112.50 E
Pasvalys, Sov. Un. (päs-vä-lēs')	163	56.04 N	24.23 E
Patagonia (Reg.), Arg. (păt-ȧ-gō'nĭ-ȧ)	142	46.45 S	69.30 W
Pātālganga (R.), India	191b	18.52 N	73.08 E
Patapsco R., Md. (pȧ-tăps'kō)	110e	39.12 N	76.30 W
Paternò, It. (pä-tĕr-nô')	170	37.25 N	14.58 E
Paterson, NJ (păt'ēr-sŭn)	110a	40.55 N	74.10 W
Pathfinder Res., Wy. (păth'fīn-dĕr)	115	42.22 N	107.10 W
Patiāla, India (pŭt-ē-ä'lŭ)	190	30.25 N	76.28 E
Pati do Alferes, Braz. (pä-tē-dō-ȧl-fĕ'rĕs)	142a	22.25 S	43.25 W
Patna, India (pŭt'nŭ)	190	25.33 N	85.18 E
Patnanongan, Phil. (pät-nä-nōŋ'gän)	203a	14.50 N	122.25 E
Patoka (R.), Ind. (pȧ-tō'kȧ)	108	38.25 N	87.25 W
Patom Plat., Sov. Un.	179	59.30 N	115.00 E
Patos, Braz. (pä'tōzh)	141	7.03 S	37.14 W
Patos, Wa. (pä'tōs)	116d	48.47 N	122.57 W
Patos, Lago dos (L.), Braz. (lä'gō-ȧ dozh pä'tōzh)	142	31.15 S	51.30 W
Patos de Minas, Braz. (dĕ-mē'näzh)	141	18.39 S	46.31 W
Pátrai (Patras), Grc. (pä-trī') (pä-träs')	171	38.15 N	21.48 E
Patraïkós Kólpos (G.), Grc.	171	38.16 N	21.19 E
Patras, see Pátrai			
Patrocínio, Braz. (pä-trō-sē'nē-o͞o)	141	18.48 S	46.47 W
Pattani, Thai. (pät'ȧ-nē)	202	6.56 N	101.13 E
Patten, Me. (păt''n)	102	45.59 N	68.27 W
Patterson, La. (păt'ēr-sŭn)	123	29.41 N	91.20 W
Patton, Pa.	109	40.40 N	78.45 W
Patuca, Punta (Pt.), Hond. (po͞o'n-tä-pä-to͞o'kä)	131	15.23 N	84.05 W
Patuca R., Hond.	131	15.22 N	84.31 W
Patuxent (R.), Md. (pȧ-tŭk'sĕnt)	109	39.10 N	77.10 W
Pátzcuaro, Mex. (päts'kwä-rō)	128	19.30 N	101.36 W
Pátzcuaro, Lago de (L.), Mex. (lä'gô-dĕ)	128	19.36 N	101.38 W
Patzicia, Guat. (pät-zē'syä)	130	14.36 N	90.57 W
Patzún, Guat. (pät-zo͞on')	130	14.40 N	91.00 W
Pau, Fr. (pō)	166	43.18 N	0.23 W
Pau, Gave de (Strm.), Fr. (gäv-dĕ)	166	43.33 N	0.51 W
Paulding, Oh. (pôl'dĭng)	108	41.05 N	84.35 W
Paulinenaue, G.D.R. (pou'lē-nĕ-nou-ĕ)	155b	52.40 N	12.43 E
Paulis, see Isiro			
Paulistana, Braz. (pȧ'o͞o-lēs-tȧ-nä)	141	8.13 S	41.06 W
Paulo Afonso, Salto (falls), Braz. (säl-tō-pou'lo͞o äf-fôN'so͞o)	141	9.33 S	38.32 W
Paul Roux, S. Afr. (pôrl ro͞o)	219d	28.18 S	27.57 E
Paulsboro, NJ (pôlz'bē-rō)	110f	39.50 N	75.16 W
Pauls Valley, Ok. (pôlz văl'ē)	121	34.43 N	97.13 W
Pavarandocito, Col. (pä-vä-rän-dō-sē'tō)	140a	7.18 N	76.32 W
Pavda, Sov. Un. (päv'da)	180a	59.16 N	59.32 E
Pavia, It. (pä-vē'ä)	170	45.12 N	9.11 E
Pavlodar, Sov. Un. (pȧv-lô-dȧr')	178	52.17 N	77.23 E
Pavlo'f B., Ak. (păv-lōf)	105	55.20 N	161.20 W
Pavlograd, Sov. Un. (pȧv-lō-grȧt')	173	48.32 N	35.52 E
Pavlovsk, Sov. Un. (pȧv-lôfsk')	173	50.28 N	40.05 E
Pavlovsk, Sov. Un.	180c	59.41 N	30.27 E
Pavlovskiy Posad, Sov. Un. (pȧv-lôf'skĭ pô-sȧt')	180b	55.47 N	38.39 E
Pavuna, Braz. (pä-vo͞o'nȧ)	142b	22.48 S	43.21 W
Päwesin, G.D.R. (pă'vĕ-zēn)	155b	52.31 N	12.44 E
Pawhuska, Ok. (pô-hŭs'kȧ)	121	36.41 N	96.20 W
Pawnee, Ok. (pô-nē')	121	36.20 N	96.47 W
Pawnee (R.), Ks.	120	38.18 N	99.42 W
Pawnee City, Ne.	121	40.08 N	96.09 W
Paw Paw, Mi. (pô'pô)	108	42.15 N	85.55 W
Paw Paw (R.), Mi.	113	42.14 N	86.21 W
Pawtucket, RI (pô-tŭk'ĕt)	110b	41.53 N	71.23 W
Paxoi (I.), Grc.	171	39.14 N	20.15 E
Paxton, Il. (păks'tŭn)	108	40.35 N	88.00 W
Payette, Id. (pā-ĕt')	114	44.05 N	116.55 W
Payette R., Id.	114	43.57 N	116.26 W
Payette R., North Fork, Id.	114	44.35 N	116.10 W
Payette R., South Fork, Id.	114	44.07 N	115.43 W
Pay-Khoy, Khrebet (Mts.), Sov. Un.	176	68.08 N	63.04 E
Payne (L.), Can. (pān)	95	59.22 N	73.16 W
Paynesville, Mn. (pānz'vĭl)	113	45.23 N	94.43 W
Payo Obispo, see Cuidad Chetumal			
Paysandú, Ur. (pī-sän-do͞o')	142	32.16 S	57.55 W
Payson, Ut. (pā's'n)	119	40.05 N	111.45 W
Pazardzhik, Bul. (pä-zȧr-dzhek')	171	42.10 N	24.22 E
Pazin, Yugo. (pä'zēn)	170	45.14 N	13.57 E
Peabody, Ks. (pē'bŏd-ĭ)	121	38.09 N	97.09 W
Peabody, Ma.	103a	42.32 N	70.56 W
Peace (R.), Can.	97	55.40 N	118.30 W
Peace Cr., Fl. (pēs)	125a	27.16 N	81.53 W
Peace Dale, RI (dāl)	110b	41.27 N	71.30 W
Peace River, Can. (rĭv'ēr)	97	56.14 N	117.17 W
Peacock Hills, Can. (pē-kŏk' hĭlz)	94	66.08 N	109.55 W
Peak, The (Mt.), Eng. (pēk)	154	53.23 N	1.52 W
Peak Hill, Austl.	210	25.38 S	118.50 E
Pearl (R.), La.-Ms. (pûrl)	124	31.06 N	89.44 W
Pearland, Tx. (pûrl'ănd)	123a	29.34 N	95.17 W
Pearl Harbor, Hi.	104a	21.20 N	157.53 W
Pearsall, Tx. (pēr'sôl)	122	28.53 N	99.06 W
Pearse I., Can. (pērs)	96	54.51 N	130.21 W
Pearston, S. Afr. (pē'ērstŏn)	223c	32.36 S	25.09 E
Peary Land (Reg.), Grnld. (pēr'ĭ)	91	82.00 N	40.00 W
Pease (R.), Tx. (pēz)	120	34.07 N	99.53 W
Peason, La. (pēz''n)	123	31.25 N	93.19 W
Pebane, Moz. (pĕ-bȧ'nē)	227	17.10 S	38.08 E
Peć, Yugo. (pĕch)	171	42.39 N	20.18 E
Pecan Bay, Tx. (pē-kăn')	122	32.04 N	99.15 W
Peçanha, Braz. (pā-kän'yȧ)	141	18.37 S	42.26 W
Pecatonica (R.), Il. (pĕk-ȧ-tŏn-ĭ-kȧ)	113	42.21 N	89.28 W
Pechenga, Sov. Un. (pyĕ'chĕŋ-gȧ)	176	69.30 N	31.10 E
Pechora (R.), Sov. Un.	176	66.00 N	52.30 E
Pechora Basin, Sov. Un. (pyĕ-chô'rȧ)	178	67.55 N	58.37 E
Pechorskaya Guba (B.), Sov. Un.	176	68.40 N	55.00 E
Pecos, NM (pā'kōs)	119	35.29 N	105.41 W
Pecos, Tx.	122	31.26 N	103.30 W
Pecos (R.), U.S.	106	31.10 N	103.10 W
Pécs, Hung. (pāch)	165	46.04 N	18.15 E
Peddie, S. Afr.	223c	33.13 S	27.09 E
Pededze (R.), Sov. Un. (pă'dĕd-zĕ)	172	57.18 N	27.13 E
Pedley, Ca. (pĕd'lē)	117a	33.59 N	117.29 W
Pedra Azul, Braz. (pā'drä-zo͞o'l)	141	16.03 S	41.13 W
Pedreiras, Braz. (pĕ-drā'räs)	141	4.30 S	44.31 W
Pedro, Pt., Sri Lanka (pē'drō)	191	9.50 N	80.14 E
Pedro Antonio Santos (Sta. Cruz Chico), Mex. (pā'drō än-tō'nē-ō sän'tōs) (sän'tä kro͞oz' chē'kō)	130a	18.55 N	88.13 W
Pedro Betancourt, Cuba (bā-täŋ-kōrt')	132	22.40 N	81.15 W
Pedro de Valdivia, Chile (pĕ'drō-dĕ-väl-dē'vē-ä)	142	22.32 S	69.55 W
Pedro do Rio, Braz. (dō-rē'rô)	142b	22.20 S	43.09 W
Pedro Juan Caballero, Par. (ho͞oȧ'n-kä-bäl-yĕ'rō)	141	22.40 S	55.42 W
Pedro Miguel, Pan. (mē-gāl')	126a	9.01 N	79.36 W
Pedro Miguel Locks, Pan. (mē-gāl')	126a	9.01 N	79.36 W
Pedro II, Braz. (pā'dro͞o sā-go͞on'do͞o)	141	4.20 S	41.27 W

ng-sing; ŋ-baŋk; N-nasalized n; nŏd; cŏmmit; ōld; ōbey; ôrder; oi-boil; fo͞od; fo͝ot; ou-out; s-soft; sh-dish; th-thin; pūre; ūnite; ûrn; stŭd; circŭs; ü-as in French tu; '-indeterminate vowel.

PLACE (Pronunciation)	PAGE	Lat. °′	Long. °′
Peebinga, Austl. (pḗ-bĭng'ȧ)	212	34.43 S	140.55 E
Peebles, Scot. (pē'b'lz)	160	55.40 N	3.15 W
Pee Dee (R.), NC-SC (pē-dē')	125	34.01 N	79.26 W
Peekskill, NY (pēks'kĭl)	110a	41.17 N	73.55 W
Pegasus B., N.Z. (pĕg'ȧ-sŭs)	213	43.18 S	173.25 E
Pegnitz R., F.R.G. (pĕgh-nēts)	164	49.38 N	11.40 E
Pego, Sp. (pā'gō)	169	38.50 N	0.09 W
Pegu, Bur. (pĕ-gōō')	202	17.17 N	96.29 E
Peguis Ind. Res., Can.	99	51.20 N	97.35 W
Pegu Yoma (Mt.), Bur. (pĕ-gōō'yō'mä)	194	19.16 N	95.59 E
Pehčevo, Yugo. (pĕκ'chĕ-vỏ)	171	41.42 N	22.57 E
Peigan Ind. Res., Can.	97	49.35 N	113.40 W
Peipus, L., see Chudskoye Ozero			
Pekin, Il. (pē'kĭn)	108	40.35 N	89.30 W
Peking, see Beijing			
Pelagie, Isole I., It.	158	35.46 N	12.32 E
Pélagos (I.), Grc.	171	39.17 N	24.05 E
Pelahatchee, Ms. (pĕl-ȧ-hăch'ḗ)	124	32.17 N	89.48 W
Pelat, Mt., Fr. (pē-lȧ')	167	44.16 N	6.43 E
Peleduy, Sov. Un. (pyĕl-yĭ-dōō'ē)	179	59.50 N	112.47 E
Pelee, Mt. (Vol.), Mart. (pē-lā')	131b	14.49 N	61.10 W
Pelee, Pt., Can.	108	41.55 N	82.30 W
Pelee I., Can. (pē'lḗ)	108	41.45 N	82.30 W
Pelequén, Chile (pĕ-lĕ-kĕ'n)	139b	34.26 S	71.52 W
Pelew (Is.), **see Palau**			
Pelham, Ga. (pĕl'hăm)	124	31.07 N	84.10 W
Pelham, NH	103a	42.43 N	71.22 W
Pelican (L.), Mn.	113	46.36 N	94.00 W
Pelican B., Can.	99	52.45 N	100.20 W
Pelican Hbr., Ba. (pĕl'ĭ-kăn)	132	26.20 N	76.45 W
Pelican Rapids, Mn. (pĕl'ĭ-kăn)	112	46.34 N	96.05 W
Pella, Ia. (pĕl'ȧ)	113	41.25 N	92.50 W
Pell-Worm I., F.R.G. (pĕl'vỏrm)	164	54.33 N	8.25 E
Pelly (L.), Can.	94	66.08 N	102.57 W
Pelly (R.), Can.	94	62.20 N	113.26 W
Pelly B., Can. (pĕl'ĭ)	94	68.57 N	91.05 W
Pelly Crossing, Can.	105	62.50 N	136.50 W
Pelly Mts., Can.	94	61.50 N	133.05 W
Peloncillo Mts., Az. (pĕl-ỏn-sĭl'lō)	119	32.40 N	109.20 W
Peloponnisos (Reg.), Grc.	171	37.28 N	22.14 E
Pelotas, Braz. (på-lō'tăzh)	142	31.45 S	52.18 W
Pelton, Can. (pĕl'tŭn)	111b	42.15 N	82.57 W
Pelym (R.), Sov. Un.	176	60.20 N	63.05 E
Pelzer, SC (pĕl'zēr)	125	34.38 N	82.30 W
Pemanggil (I.), Mala.	189b	2.37 N	104.41 E
Pematangsiantar, Indon.	202	2.58 N	99.03 E
Pemba, Moz. (pĕm'bȧ)	227	12.58 S	40.30 E
Pemba, Zambia	222	15.29 S	27.22 E
Pemba (I.), Tan	227	5.20 S	39.57 E
Pemba Chan., Afr.	227	5.10 S	39.30 E
Pembina, ND (pĕm'bĭ-nȧ)	112	48.58 N	97.15 W
Pembina (R.), Can.	97	53.05 N	114.30 W
Pembina (R.), Can.	99	49.08 N	98.20 W
Pembroke, Can. (pĕm' brōk)	109	45.50 N	77.00 W
Pembroke, Ma. (pĕm'brōk)	103a	42.05 N	70.49 W
Pembroke, Wales	160	51.40 N	5.00 W
Pen, India	191b	18.44 N	73.06 E
Penafiel, Port. (pā-nȧ-fyĕl')	168	41.12 N	8.19 W
Penafiel, Sp. (pā-nyȧ-fyĕl')	168	41.38 N	4.08 W
Peñalara (Mtn.), Sp. (pā-nyä-lä'rä)	168	40.52 N	3.57 W
Pena Nevada, Cerro, Mex.	128	23.47 N	99.52 W
Peñaranda de Bracamonte, Sp. (pā-nyä-rän'dä dā brä-kä-mōn'tå)	168	40.54 N	5.11 W
Peñarroya-Peublonuevo, Sp. (pĕn-yär-rỏ'yä-pwĕ'blỏ-nwĕ'vỏ)	168	38.18 N	5.18 W
Peñas, Cabo de (C.), Sp. (kȧ'bỏ-dĕ-pā'nyäs)	168	43.42 N	6.12 W
Penas, Golfo de, Chile (gỏl-fô-dĕ-pĕ'n-äs)	142	47.15 S	77.30 W
Penasco R., Tx. (pā-nȧs'kō)	122	32.50 N	104.45 W
Pendembu, S. L. (pĕn-dĕm'bōō)	224	8.06 N	10.42 W
Pender, Ne. (pĕn'dēr)	112	42.08 N	96.43 W
Penderisco (R.), Col. (pĕn-dĕ-rē's-kỏ)	140a	6.30 N	76.21 W
Pendjari, Parc Natl. de la (Natl. Pk.), Dahomey	224	11.25 N	1.30 E
Pendleton, Or. (pĕn'd'l-tŭn)	114	45.41 N	118.47 W
Pend Oreille L., Id. (pŏn-dỏ-rā') (pĕn-dỏ-rĕl')	114	48.09 N	116.38 W
Pend Oreille R., Wa.	114	48.44 N	117.20 W
Penedo, Braz. (på-nā'dōō)	141	10.17 S	36.28 W
Penetanguishene, Can. (pĕn'ḗ-tăŋ-gĭ-shēn')	109	44.45 N	79.55 W
Pengcheng, China (pŭŋ-chŭŋ)	196	36.24 N	114.11 E
Penglai, China (pŭŋ-lī)	196	37.49 N	120.45 E
Peniche, Port. (pĕ-nē'chå)	168	39.22 N	9.24 W
Peninsula, Oh. (pĕn-ĭn'sū-lȧ)	111d	41.14 N	81.32 W
Penistone, Eng. (pĕn'ĭ-stŭn)	154	53.31 N	1.38 W
Penjamillo, Mex. (pĕn-hä-mēl'yō)	128	20.06 N	101.56 W
Penjamo, Mex. (pān'hä-mō)	128	20.27 N	101.43 W
Penk (R.), Eng. (pĕnk)	154	52.41 N	2.10 W
Penkridge, Eng. (pĕnk'rĭj)	154	52.43 N	2.07 W
Penne, It. (pĕn'nā)	170	42.28 N	13.57 E
Penner (R.), India (pĕn'ēr)	190	14.43 N	79.09 E
Pennines (Mts.), Eng. (pĕn-īn')	160	54.30 N	2.10 W
Pennines, Alpes (Mts.), Switz.	164	46.02 N	7.07 E
Pennsboro, WV (pĕnz'bŭr-ỏ)	108	39.10 N	81.00 W
Penns Grove, NJ (pĕnz grōv)	110f	39.44 N	75.28 W
Pennsylvania (State), U. S. (pĕn-sĭl-vā'nĭ-ȧ)	107	41.00 N	78.10 W
Penn Yan, NY (pĕn yăn')	109	42.40 N	77.00 W
Pennycutaway (R.), Can.	99	56.10 N	93.25 W
Peno (L.), Sov. Un. (pā'nỏ)	172	56.55 N	32.28 E
Penobscot (R.), Me.	102	45.00 N	68.36 W
Penobscot B., Me. (pḗ-nŏb'skŏt)	102	44.20 N	69.00 W
Penong, Austl. (pḗ-nông')	210	32.00 S	133.00 E
Penonomé, Pan. (pā-nō-nỏ-mā')	131	8.32 N	80.21 W
Penrith, Austl.	207b	33.45 S	150.42 E
Pensacola, Fl. (pĕn-sȧ-kō'lȧ)	124	30.25 N	87.13 W
Pensacola Dam, Ok.	121	36.27 N	95.02 W
Pensilvania, Col. (pĕn-sḗl-vȧ'nyä)	140a	5.31 N	75.05 W
Pentecost (I.), Vanuatu (pĕn'tḗ-kŏst)	211	16.05 S	168.28 E

PLACE (Pronunciation)	PAGE	Lat. °′	Long. °′
Penticton, Can.	97	49.30 N	119.35 W
Pentland Firth, Scot. (pĕnt'lănd)	160a	58.44 N	3.25 W
Penza, Sov. Un. (pĕn'zȧ)	177	53.10 N	45.00 E
Penzance, Eng. (pĕn-zăns')	160	50.07 N	5.40 W
Penzberg, F.R.G. (pĕnts'bĕrgh)	164	47.43 N	11.21 E
Penzhina (R.), Sov. Un. (pyĭn-zē-nŭ)	179	62.15 N	166.30 E
Penzhino, Sov. Un.	179	63.42 N	168.00 E
Penzhinskay'a Guba (B.), Sov. Un.	179	60.30 N	161.30 E
Peoria, Il. (pē-ō'rĭ-ȧ)	108	40.45 N	89.35 W
Peotillos, Mex. (på-ō-tel'yōs)	128	22.30 N	100.39 W
Peotone, Il. (pē'ŏ-tỏn)	111a	41.20 N	87.47 W
Pepacton Res., NY (pĕp-ȧc'tŭn)	109	42.05 N	74.40 W
Pepe, Cabo (C.), Cuba (kä'bỏ-pĕ'pĕ)	132	21.30 N	83.10 W
Pepperell, Ma. (pĕp'ēr-ĕl)	103a	42.40 N	71.36 W
Peqin, Alb. (pĕ-kēn')	171	41.03 N	19.48 E
Perales (R.), Sp. (pā-rä'lās)	169	40.24 N	4.07 W
Perales de Tajuña, Sp. (dā tä-hōō'nyä)	169a	40.14 N	3.22 W
Percé, Can. (pĕr'sā')	102	48.31 N	64.13 W
Perche, Collines du (Hills), Fr.	166	48.25 N	0.40 E
Perchtoldsdorf, Aus. (pĕrk'tỏlts-dôrf)	155e	48.07 N	16.17 E
Perdekop, S. Afr.	219d	27.11 S	29.38 E
Perdido, Mt., Sp. (pĕr-dē'dō)	169	42.40 N	0.00 W
Perdido (R.), Al.-Fl. (pĕr-dī'dō)	124	30.45 N	87.38 W
Perdões, Braz. (pĕr-dô'ēs)	139a	21.05 S	45.05 W
Pereira, Col. (på-rā'rä)	140a	4.49 N	75.42 W
Perekop, Sov. Un. (pĕr-å-kôp')	173	46.08 N	33.39 E
Pere Marquette, Mi.	108	43.55 N	86.10 W
Pereshchepino, Sov. Un. (på'råsh-chē'pḗ-nỏ)	173	49.02 N	35.19 E
Pereslavl'-Zalesskiy, Sov. Un. (på-rå-slåv''l zȧ-lyĕs'kĭ)	172	56.43 N	38.52 E
Pereyaslav, Sov. Un. (pĕ-rå-yäs'läv)	173	50.05 N	31.25 E
Pergamino, Arg. (pĕr-gä-mē'nō)	139c	33.53 S	60.36 W
Perham, Mn. (pēr'hăm)	112	46.37 N	95.35 W
Peribonca (R.), Can. (pĕr-ĭ-bŏŋ'kȧ)	101	49.10 N	71.20 W
Périgueux, Fr. (pā-rḗ-gû')	166	45.12 N	0.43 E
Perija, Sierra de (Mts.), Col. (sē-ĕ'r-rȧ-dĕ-pĕ-rē'κä)	140	9.25 N	73.30 W
Perkam, Tandjung (C.), Indon.	203	1.20 S	138.45 E
Perkins, Can. (pĕr'kĕns)	93c	45.37 N	75.37 W
Perlas, Arch. de Las, Pan. (är-chē-pyĕ'lä-gỏ-dĕ-läs-pĕr'läs)	131	8.29 N	79.15 W
Perlas, Laguna las (L.), Nic. (lä-gōō'nä-dĕ-läs)	131	12.34 N	83.19 W
Perleberg, G.D.R. (pĕr'lē-bērg)	164	53.06 N	11.51 E
Perm', Sov. Un. (pĕrm)	180a	58.00 N	56.15 E
Pernambuco, see Recife			
Pernambuco (State), Braz. (pĕr-näm-bōō'kō)	141	8.08 S	38.54 W
Pernik, Bul. (pĕr-nēk')	171	42.36 N	23.04 E
Péronne, Fr. (pā-rỏn')	166	49.57 N	2.49 E
Perote, Mex. (pĕ-rỏ'tĕ)	129	19.33 N	97.13 W
Perouse Str., Jap.-Sov. Un.	200	45.45 N	141.38 E
Perovo, Sov. Un. (pâ'rô-vô)	180b	55.43 N	37.47 E
Perpignan, Fr. (pĕr-pē-nyäɴ')	166	42.42 N	2.48 E
Perris, Ca. (pĕr'ĭs)	117a	33.46 N	117.14 W
Perros, Bahia (B.), Cuba (bä-ē'ä-pā'rōs)	132	22.25 N	78.35 W
Perrot Île (I.), Can. (pĕr'ŭt)	93a	45.23 N	73.57 W
Perry, Fl. (pĕr'ĭ)	124	30.06 N	83.35 W
Perry, Ga.	124	32.27 N	83.44 W
Perry, Ia.	113	41.49 N	94.40 W
Perry, NY	109	42.45 N	78.00 W
Perry, Ok.	121	36.17 N	97.18 W
Perry, Ut.	117b	41.27 N	112.02 W
Perry Hall, Md.	110e	39.24 N	76.29 W
Perryopolis, Pa. (pĕ-rḗ-ŏ'pỏ-lĭs)	111e	40.05 N	79.45 W
Perrysburg, Oh. (pĕr ĭz-bûrg)	108	41.35 N	83.35 W
Perryton, Tx. (pĕr'ĭ-tŭn)	120	36.23 N	100.48 W
Perryville, Ak. (pĕr-ĭ-vĭl)	105	55.58 N	159.28 W
Perryville, Mo.	121	37.41 N	89.52 W
Persan, Fr. (pĕr-säɴ')	167b	49.09 N	2.15 E
Persepolis (Ruins), Iran (pēr-sĕp'o-lĭs)	153	30.15 N	53.08 E
Persia, see Iran			
Persian G., Asia (pûr'zhȧn)	192	27.38 N	50.30 E
Perth, Austl. (pûrth)	210	31.50 S	116.10 E
Perth, Can.	109	44.40 N	76.15 W
Perth, Scot.	160	56.24 N	3.25 W
Perth Amboy, NJ (äm'boi)	110a	40.31 N	74.16 W
Pertuis, Fr. (pĕr-tüē')	167	43.43 N	5.29 E
Peru, Il. (pḗ-rōō')	108	41.20 N	89.10 W
Peru, In.	108	40.45 N	86.00 W
Peru, S. A.	138	10.00 S	75.00 W
Perugia, It. (pā-rōō'jä)	170	43.08 N	12.24 E
Peruque, Mo. (pĕ rō'kĕ)	117e	38.52 N	90.36 W
Pervomaysk, Sov. Un. (pĕr-vô-mīsk')	173	48.04 N	30.52 E
Pervoural'sk, Sov. Un. (pĕr-vô-ōō-rálsk')	180a	56.54 N	59.58 E
Pervyy Kuril'skiy Proliv (Str.), Sov. Un.	179	51.43 N	154.32 E
Pesaro, It. (pā'zä-rō)	170	43.54 N	12.55 E
Pescado (R.), Ven. (pĕs-kä'dō)	141b	9.33 N	65.32 W
Pescara, It. (pās-kä'rä)	170	42.26 N	14.15 E
Pescara (R.), It.	170	42.18 N	13.22 E
Peschanyy, Mys (C.), Sov. Un.	177	43.10 N	51.20 E
Pescia, It. (pā'shä)	170	43.53 N	11.42 E
Peshāwar, Pak. (pĕ-shä'wŭr)	193a	34.01 N	71.34 E
Peshtera, Bul.	171	42.03 N	24.19 E
Peshtigo, Wi. (pĕsh'tḗ-gō)	113	45.03 N	87.46 W
Peshtigo (R.), Wi.	113	45.15 N	88.14 W
Peski, Sov. Un. (pyâs'kĭ)	180b	55.13 N	38.48 E
Pêso da Régua, Port. (pā-sōō-dä-rā'gwä)	168	41.09 N	7.47 W
Pespire, Hond. (pås-pē'rå)	130	13.35 N	87.20 W
Pesqueria, R., Mex. (pås-kå-rē'ȧ)	122	25.55 N	100.25 W
Pessac, Fr.	166	44.48 N	0.38 W
Petacalco, Bahía de (B.), Mex. (bä-ē'ä-dĕ-pĕ-tä-kȧl'kỏ)	128	17.55 N	102.00 W
Petah Tiqwa, Isr.	189a	32.05 N	34.53 E
Petaluma, Ca. (pét-ȧ-lōō'mȧ)	118	38.15 N	122.38 W

PLACE (Pronunciation)	PAGE	Lat. °′	Long. °′
Petare, Ven. (pĕ-tä'rĕ)	141b	10.28 N	66.48 W
Petatlán, Mex. (pā-tä-tlän')	128	17.31 N	101.17 W
Petawawa, Can.	101	45.54 N	77.17 W
Petén, Laguna de (L.), Guat. (lä-gōō'nä-dĕ-på-tān')	130a	17.05 N	89.54 W
Petenwell Res., Wi.	113	44.10 N	89.55 W
Peterborough, Can. (pē'tēr-bŭr-ỏ)	109	44.20 N	78.20 W
Peterborough, Austl.	212	32.53 S	138.58 E
Peterborough, Eng.	154	52.35 N	0.14 W
Peterhead, Scot. (pē-tēr-hĕd')	160	57.36 N	3.47 W
Peter Pt., Can.	109	43.50 N	77.00 W
Peter Pond L., Can. (pŏnd)	98	55.55 N	108.44 W
Petersburg, Ak. (pē'tērz-bûrg)	105	56.52 N	133.10 W
Petersburg, Il.	121	40.01 N	89.51 W
Petersburg, In.	108	38.30 N	87.15 W
Petersburg, Ky.	111f	39.04 N	84.52 W
Petersburg, Va.	125	37.12 N	77.30 W
Petershagen, G.D.R. (pĕ'tĕrs-hä-gĕn)	155b	52.32 N	13.46 E
Petershausen, F.R.G. (pĕ'tĕrs-hou-zĕn)	155d	48.25 N	11.29 E
Pétionville, Hai.	133	18.30 N	72.20 W
Petitcodiac, Can. (pē-tē-kỏ-dyȧk')	102	45.56 N	65.10 W
Petite Terre I., Guad. (pē-tēt'târ')	131b	16.12 N	61.00 W
Petit Goâve, Hai. (pē-tē' gỏ-ȧv')	133	18.25 N	72.50 W
Petit Jean Cr., Ar. (pē-tḗ'zhäɴ')	121	35.05 N	93.55 W
Petit Loango, Gabon	226	2.16 S	9.35 E
Petlalcingo, Mex. (pĕ-tläl-sĕŋ'gỏ)	129	18.05 N	97.53 W
Peto, Mex. (pĕ'tỏ)	130a	20.07 N	88.49 W
Petorca, Chile (pā-tōr'kȧ)	139	32.14 S	70.55 W
Petoskey, Mi. (pḗ-tŏs-kĭ)	108	45.25 N	84.55 W
Petra, Jordan	189a	30.21 N	35.25 E
Petra Velikogo, Zaliv (B.), Sov. Un. (zä'lĭf pĕt-rä' vĕ-lĭ'kỏ-vỏ)	200	42.40 N	131.50 E
Petrich, Bul. (pā'trĭch)	171	41.24 N	23.13 E
Petrified Forest Natl. Park, Az. (pĕt'rĭ-fīd fôr'ēst)	119	34.58 N	109.35 W
Petrikovka, Sov. Un. (pyĕ'trḗ-kôf-kä)	173	48.43 N	34.29 E
Petrikov, Sov. Un. (pyĕ'trḗ-kô-v)	173	52.09 N	28.30 E
Petrinja, Yugo. (pā'trēn-yȧ)	170	45.25 N	16.17 E
Petrodvorets, Sov. Un. (pyĕ-trô-dvô-ryĕts')	180c	59.53 N	29.55 E
Petrokrepost', Sov. Un. (pyĕ'trô-krĕ-pôst)	180c	59.56 N	31.03 E
Petrolia, Can. (pḗ-trō'lĭ-ȧ)	108	42.50 N	82.10 W
Petrolina, Braz. (pĕ-trō-lē'nȧ)	141	9.18 S	40.28 W
Petronell, Aus.	155e	48.07 N	16.52 E
Petropavlovka, Sov. Un. (pyĕ'trỏ-päv'lôf-κȧ)	173	48.24 N	36.23 E
Petropavlovka, Sov. Un.	180a	54.10 N	59.50 E
Petropavlovsk, Sov. Un. (pyĕ-trỏ-päv'lôfsk)	178	54.44 N	69.07 E
Petropavlovsk-Kamchatskiy, Sov. Un. (käm-chät'skĭ)	179	53.13 N	158.56 E
Petrópolis, Braz. (på-trỏ-pỏ-lēzh')	142b	22.31 S	43.10 W
Petroşani, Rom.	171	45.24 N	23.24 E
Petrovsk, Sov. Un. (pyĕ-trôfsk')	177	52.20 N	45.15 E
Petrovskaya, Sov. Un. (pyĕ-trôf'skȧ-yȧ)	173	45.25 N	37.50 E
Petrovskoye, Sov. Un.	177	45.20 N	43.00 E
Petrovsk-Zabaykal'skiy, Sov. Un. (pyĕ-trôfskzä-bī-käl'skĭ)	179	51.13 N	109.08 E
Petrozavodsk, Sov. Un. (pyā'trỏ-zȧ-vôtsk')	163	61.46 N	34.25 E
Petrus Steyn, S. Afr. (pā'trōōs stän')	219d	27.40 S	28.09 E
Petseri, Sov. Un. (pĕt'sĕ-rḗ)	172	57.48 N	27.33 E
Pewaukee, Wi. (pĭ-wô'kḗ)	111a	43.05 N	88.15 W
Pewaukee L., Wi.	111a	43.03 N	88.18 W
Pewee Valley, Ky. (pe wē)	111h	38.19 N	85.29 W
Peza (R.), Sov. Un. (pyå'zȧ)	176	65.35 N	46.50 E
Pézenas, Fr. (pā-zē-nä')	166	43.26 N	3.24 E
Pforzheim, F.R.G. (pfôrts'hīm)	164	48.52 N	8.43 E
Phalodi, India	190	27.13 N	72.22 E
Phan-thiet, Viet. (p'hän')	202	11.30 N	108.43 E
Pharsalus, see Fársala			
Phenix City, Al. (fē'nĭks)	124	32.29 N	85.00 W
Philadelphia, Ms. (fĭl-ȧ-dĕl'phĭ-ȧ)	124	32.45 N	89.07 W
Philadelphia, Pa.	110f	40.00 N	75.13 W
Philip, SD (fĭl'ĭp)	112	44.03 N	101.35 W
Philippeville, see Skikda			
Philippines, Asia (fĭl'ĭ-pēnz)	189	14.25 N	125.00 E
Philippine Sea, Asia (fĭl'ĭ-pēn)	204	16.00 N	133.00 E
Philippine Trench, Phil.	203	10.30 N	127.15 E
Philippopolis, see Plovdiv			
Philipsburg, Pa. (fĭl'lĭps-bērg)	109	40.55 N	78.10 W
Philipsburg, Wy.	115	46.19 N	113.19 W
Phillip (I.), Austl. (fĭl'ĭp)	212	38.32 S	145.10 E
Phillip Chan., Indon.	189b	1.04 N	103.40 E
Phillipi, WV (fĭ-lĭp'ĭ)	109	39.10 N	80.00 W
Phillips, Wi. (fĭl'ĭps)	113	45.41 N	90.24 W
Phillipsburg, Ks. (fĭl'lĭps-bērg)	120	39.44 N	99.19 W
Phillipsburg, NJ	109	40.45 N	75.10 W
Phitsanulok, Thai.	202	16.51 N	100.15 E
Phnum Pénh, Kamp. (nŏm'pĕn')	202	11.39 N	104.53 E
Phoenix, Az. (fē'nĭks)	119	33.30 N	112.00 W
Phoenix, Md.	110e	39.31 N	76.40 W
Phoenix Is., Oceania	204	4.00 S	174.00 W
Phoenixville, Pa. (fē'nĭks-vĭl)	110f	40.08 N	75.31 W
Phra Nakhon Si Ayutthaya, Thai.	202	14.16 N	100.37 E
Phu Bia (Pk.), Laos	202	19.36 N	103.00 E
Phu-Quoc, Dao (I.), Kamp.	202	10.13 N	104.00 E
Phuket, Thai.	202	7.57 N	98.19 E
Pi (R.), China (bē)	196	32.06 N	116.31 E
Piacenza, It. (pyä-chĕnt'sä)	170	45.02 N	9.42 E
Pianosa (I.), It. (pyä-nō'sä)	170	42.13 N	15.45 E
Piatra Neamţ, Rom. (pyä'trȧ-nå-ämts')	165	46.54 N	26.24 E
Piauí (State), Braz. (pyou'ḗ)	141	7.40 S	42.25 W
Piauí, Serra do (Mts.), Braz. (sĕr'rȧ dōō pyou'ḗ)	141	10.45 S	44.36 W
Piave (R.), It. (pyä'vā)	170	45.45 N	12.15 E

ăt; finăl; rāte; senåte; ärm; ȧsk; sofȧ; fâre; ch-choose; dh-as th in other; bē; ḗvent; bĕt; recĕnt; cratēr; g-gō; gh-guttural g; bĭt; ĭ-short neutral; rīde; κ-guttural k as ch in German ich;

PRONOUNCING INDEX

Piazza Armerina – Pochinok 333

PLACE (Pronunciation)	PAGE	Lat. °′	Long. °′
Piazza Armerina, It. (pyät'sä är-mä-rē'nä)	170	37.23 N	14.26 E
Pibor R., Sud. (pē'bôr)	221	7.21 N	32.54 E
Pic (R.), Can. (pēk)	113	48.48 N	86.28 W
Picara Pt. (U. S. A.), Vir. Is. (pē-kä'rä)	127c	18.23 N	64.57 W
Picayune, Ms. (pĭk'ȧ yōōn)	124	30.32 N	89.41 W
Picher, Ok. (pĭch'ẽr)	121	36.58 N	94.49 W
Pichilemu, Chile (pē-chē-lĕ'mōō)	139b	34.22 S	72.01 W
Pichucalco, Mex. (pē-chōō-käl'kō)	129	17.34 N	93.06 W
Pichucalco (R.), Mex.	129	17.40 N	93.02 W
Pickerel (L.), Can. (pĭk'ẽr-ĕl)	113	48.35 N	91.10 W
Pickwick (R.), Tn. (pĭk'wĭck)	124	35.04 N	88.05 W
Pico, Ca. (pē'kō)	117a	34.01 N	118.05 W
Pico de Aneto (Mtn.), Sp. (pē'kō-dē-ä-nĕ'tō)	169	42.35 N	0.38 E
Pico I., Açores (pē'kōō)	220a	38.16 N	28.49 W
Picos, Braz. (pē'kōzh)	141	7.13 S	41.23 W
Pico Rivera, Ca.	117a	34.01 N	118.05 W
Picton, Austl. (pĭk'tŭn)	207b	34.11 S	150.37 E
Picton, Can.	101	44.00 N	77.15 W
Pictou, Can. (pĭk-tōō')	102	45.41 N	62.43 W
Pidálion, Akrotírion (C.), Cyprus	189a	34.50 N	34.05 E
Pidurutalagala Mt., Sri Lanka (pē'dōō-rōō-tä'lȧ-gä'lȧ)	191	12.27 N	80.45 E
Pie (I.), Can. (pī)	113	48.10 N	89.07 W
Piedade, Braz. (pyā-dä'dĕ)	139a	23.42 S	47.25 W
Piedmont, Al. (pēd'mŏnt)	124	33.54 N	85.36 W
Piedmont, Ca.	116b	37.50 N	122.14 W
Piedmont, Mo.	121	37.09 N	90.42 W
Piedmont, SC	125	34.40 N	82.27 W
Piedmont, WV	109	39.30 N	79.05 W
Piedrabuena, Sp. (pyā-drä-bwā'nä)	168	39.01 N	4.10 W
Piedras, Punta (Pt.), Arg. (pōō'n-tä-pyĕ'dräs)	139c	35.25 S	57.10 W
Piedras Negras, Mex. (pyā'dräs nā'gräs)	122	28.41 N	100.33 W
Pieksämäki, Fin. (pyĕk'sĕ-mĕ-kē)	163	62.18 N	27.14 E
Piemonte (Reg.), It. (pyĕ-mō'n-tĕ)	170	44.30 N	7.42 E
Pienaars R., S. Afr.	219d	25.13 S	28.05 E
Pienaarsrivier, S. Afr.	219d	25.12 S	28.18 E
Pierce, Ne. (pērs)	112	42.11 N	97.33 W
Pierce, WV	109	39.15 N	79.30 W
Piermont, NY (pēr'mŏnt)	110a	41.03 N	73.55 W
Pierre, SD (pēr)	112	44.22 N	100.20 W
Pierrefonds, Can.	93a	45.29 N	73.52 W
Piešťany, Czech. (pyĕsh'tyä-nûĭ)	165	48.36 N	17.48 E
Pietermaritzburg, S. Afr. (pē-tēr-mȧ-rĭts-bûrg)	223c	29.36 S	30.23 E
Pietersburg, S. Afr. (pē'tērz-bûrg)	219d	23.56 S	29.30 E
Piet Retief, S. Afr. (pēt rĕ-tēf')	222	27.00 S	30.58 E
Pietrosul Pk., Rom.	165	47.35 N	24.49 E
Pieve di Cadore, It. (pyā'vā dē kä-dō'rā)	170	46.26 N	12.22 E
Pigeon (R.), Can.-Mn. (pĭj'ŭn)	113	48.05 N	90.13 W
Pigeon L., Can.	97	53.00 N	114.00 W
Pigeon Lake, Can.	93f	49.57 N	97.36 W
Piggott, Ar. (pĭg-ŭt)	121	36.22 N	90.10 W
Pijijiapan, Mex. (pēkē-kē-ä'pän)	129	15.40 N	93.12 W
Pijnacker, Neth.	155a	52.01 N	4.25 E
Pikes Pk., Co. (pīks)	120	38.49 N	105.03 W
Pikeville, Ky. (pīk'vĭl)	125	37.28 N	82.31 W
Pikou, China (pē-kō)	196	39.25 N	122.19 E
Pikwitonei, Can. (pĭk'wĭ-tōn)	99	55.35 N	97.09 W
Piła, Pol. (pē'lȧ)	164	53.09 N	16.44 E
Pilansberg, S. Afr. (pē'ȧns'bûrg)	219d	25.08 S	26.55 E
Pilar, Arg. (pē'lär)	139c	34.27 S	58.55 W
Pilar, Par.	142	27.00 S	58.15 W
Pilar de Goiás, Braz. (dē-gô'yá's)	141	14.47 S	49.33 W
Pilchuck (R.), Wa.	116a	48.03 N	121.58 W
Pilchuck Cr., Wa. (pĭl'chŭck)	116a	48.19 N	122.11 W
Pilchuck Mtn., Wa.	116a	48.03 N	121.48 W
Pilcomayo (R.), Par. (pēl-cō-mī'ô)	142	24.45 S	69.15 W
Pili, Phil. (pē'lē)	203a	13.34 N	123.17 E
Pilica R., Pol. (pē-lēt'sä)	165	51.00 N	19.48 E
Pillar Pt., Can. (pĭl'ȧr)	116a	48.14 N	124.06 W
Pillar Rocks, Wa.	116c	46.16 N	123.35 W
Pilón (R.), Mex. (pē-lōn')	128	24.13 N	99.03 W
Pilot Point, Tx. (pī'lŭt)	121	33.24 N	97.00 W
Pilsen, see Plzeň			
Piltene, Sov. Un. (pĭl'tē-nē)	163	57.17 N	21.40 E
Pimal, Cerra (Mtn.), Mex. (sĕ'r-rä-pē-mäl')	128	22.58 N	104.19 W
Pimba, Austl. (pĭm'bȧ)	210	31.15 S	146.50 E
Pimville (Neigh.), S. Afr. (pĭm'vĭl)	223b	26.17 S	27.54 E
Pinacate, Cerro (Mtn.), Mex. (sĕ'r-rō-pē-nä-kä'tē)	126	31.45 N	113.30 W
Pinamalayan, Phil. (pē-nä-mä-lä'yän)	203a	13.04 N	121.31 E
Pinang, see George Town			
Pinarbaşi, Tur. (pē'när-bä'shĭ)	177	38.50 N	36.10 E
Pinar del Río, Cuba (pē-när' dĕl rē'ō)	132	22.25 N	83.35 W
Pinar del Río (Prov.), Cuba	132	22.45 N	83.25 W
Pinatubo (Mtn.), Phil. (pē-nä-tōō'bō)	203a	15.09 N	120.19 E
Pincher Creek, Can. (pĭn'chēr krēk)	97	49.29 N	113.57 W
Pinckneyville, Il. (pĭnk'nĭ-vĭl)	121	38.06 N	89.22 W
Pińczów, Pol. (pēn''chōōf)	165	50.32 N	20.33 E
Pindamonhangaba, Braz. (pē'n-dä-mōnyȧ'n-gä-bä)	139a	22.56 S	45.26 W
Pinder Pt., Ba.	132	26.35 N	78.35 W
Píndhos Oros (Mts.), Grc.	171	39.48 N	21.19 E
Pindiga, Nig.	225	9.59 N	10.54 E
Pine (R.), Can. (pīn)	96	55.30 N	122.20 W
Pine (R.), Wi.	113	45.50 N	88.37 W
Pine Bluff, At. (pīn blŭf)	121	34.13 N	92.01 W
Pine City, Mn. (pīn)	113	45.50 N	93.01 W
Pine Creek, Austl.	210	13.45 S	132.00 E
Pine Cr., Nv.	118	40.15 N	116.17 W
Pine Falls, Can.	99	50.35 N	96.15 W
Pine Forest Ra., Nv.	114	41.35 N	118.45 W
Pinega, Sov. Un. (pē-nyĕ'gȧ)	176	64.40 N	43.30 E
Pinega (R.), Sov. Un.	176	64.10 N	42.30 E
Pine Hill, NJ (pīn hĭl)	110f	39.47 N	74.59 W
Pine Is., Fl.	125a	24.48 N	81.32 W
Pine Island Sd., Fl.	125a	26.32 N	82.30 W
Pine Lake Estates, Ga. (lāk ĕs-tāts')	110c	33.47 N	84.13 W
Pinelands, S. Afr. (pīn'lănds)	222a	33.57 S	18.30 E
Pine Lawn, Mo. (lôn)	117e	38.42 N	90.17 W
Pine Pass, Can.	96	55.22 N	122.40 W
Pine Ridge Ind. Res., SD (rĭj)	112	43.33 N	102.13 W
Pinerolo, It. (pē-nā-rô'lō)	170	44.47 N	7.18 E
Pines, Lake o' the, Tx.	123	32.50 N	94.40 W
Pinetown, S. Afr. (pīn'toun)	223c	29.47 S	30.52 E
Pine View Res., Ut. (vū)	117b	41.17 N	111.54 W
Pineville, Ky. (pīn'vĭl)	124	36.48 N	83.43 W
Pineville, La.	123	31.20 N	92.25 W
Ping (R.), Thai.	202	17.54 N	98.29 E
Pingding, China (pĭŋ-dĭŋ)	198	37.50 N	113.30 E
Pingdu, China (pĭŋ-dōō)	196	36.46 N	119.57 E
Pinggir, Indon.	189b	1.05 N	101.12 E
Pinghe, China (pĭŋ-hŭ)	199	24.30 N	117.02 E
Pingle, China (pĭŋ-lŭ)	199	24.30 N	110.22 E
Pingliang, China (pĭng'lyäng')	198	35.12 N	106.50 E
Pingquan, China (pĭŋ-chyüän)	198	40.58 N	118.40 E
Pingtan, China (pĭŋ-tän)	199	25.30 N	119.45 E
Pingtan Dao (I.), China (pĭŋ-tän dou)	199	25.40 N	119.45 E
P'ingtung, Taiwan	199	22.40 N	120.35 E
Pingwu, China (pĭŋ-wōō)	198	32.20 N	104.40 E
Pingxiang, China (pĭŋ-shyäŋ)	199	27.40 N	113.50 E
Pingyi, China (pĭŋ-yē)	196	35.30 N	117.38 E
Pingyuan, China (pĭŋ-yüän)	196	37.11 N	116.26 E
Pingzhou, China (pĭŋ-jō)	197a	23.01 N	113.11 E
Pinhal, Braz. (pē-nyȧ'l)	139a	22.11 S	46.43 W
Pinhal Novo, Port. (nō vōō)	169b	38.38 N	8.54 W
Pinhel, Port. (pēn-yĕl')	168	40.45 N	7.03 W
Pini, Pulau (I.), Indon.	202	0.07 S	98.38 E
Piniós (R.), Grc.	171	40.33 N	21.40 E
Pinnacles Natl. Mon., Ca. (pĭn'ȧ-k'lz)	118	36.30 N	121.00 W
Pinneberg, F.R.G. (pĭn'ĕ-bĕrg)	155c	53.40 N	9.48 E
Pinole, Ca. (pĭ-nō'lē)	116b	38.01 N	122.17 W
Pinos-Puente, Sp. (pwān'tȧ)	168	37.15 N	3.43 W
Pinotepa Nacional, Mex. (pē-nō-tā'pä nä-syō-näl')	128	16.21 N	98.04 W
Pins, Ile des, N. Cal.	211	22.44 S	167.44 E
Pinsk, Sov. Un. (pēn'sk)	165	52.07 N	26.05 E
Pinta (I.), Ec.	140	0.41 N	90.47 W
Pintendre, Can. (pĕɴ-tänɴdr')	93b	46.45 N	71.07 W
Pinto, Sp. (pēn'tō)	169a	40.14 N	3.42 W
Pinto Butte, Can. (pĭn'tō)	98	49.22 N	107.25 W
Pioche, Nv. (pī-ō'chē)	119	37.56 N	114.28 W
Piombino, It. (pyôm-bē'nō)	170	42.56 N	10.33 E
Pioneer Mts., Mt. (pī'ô-nēr')	115	45.23 N	112.51 W
Piotrków Trybunalski, Pol. (pyōtr'kōōv trĭ-bōō-nal'skē)	165	51.23 N	19.44 E
Piper, Al. (pī'pēr)	124	33.04 N	87.00 W
Piper, Ks.	117f	39.09 N	94.51 W
Pipéri (I.), Grc. (pē'per-ē)	171	39.19 N	24.20 E
Pipe Spring Natl. Mon., Az. (pīp spring)	119	36.50 N	112.45 W
Pipestone, Mn. (pīp'stōn)	112	44.00 N	96.19 W
Pipestone Natl. Mon., Mn.	112	44.03 N	96.24 W
Pipmaucan, Rés., Can. (pĭp-mä-kän')	102	49.45 N	70.00 W
Piqua, Oh. (pĭk'wȧ)	108	40.10 N	84.15 W
Piracaia, Braz. (pē-rä-kȧ'yä)	139a	23.04 S	46.20 W
Piracicaba, Braz. (pē-rä-sē-kä'bä)	139a	22.43 S	47.39 W
Piraí, Braz. (pē-rä-ē')	139a	22.38 S	43.54 W
Piraíba (R.), Braz. (pä-rä-ē'bȧ)	139a	21.38 S	41.29 W
Piramida, Gol'tsy (Mtn.), Sov. Un.	178	54.00 N	96.00 E
Piran, Yugo. (pē-rä'n)	170	45.31 N	13.34 E
Piranga, Braz. (pē-rä'n-gä)	139a	20.41 S	43.17 W
Pirapetinga, Braz. (pē-rä-pē-tē'n-gä)	139a	21.40 S	42.20 W
Pirapora, Braz. (pē-rȧ-pō'rȧ)	141	17.39 S	44.54 W
Pirassununga, Braz. (pē-rä-sōō-nōō'n-gä)	139a	22.00 S	47.24 W
Pirenópolis, Braz. (pē-rĕ-nô'pō-lēs)	141	15.56 S	48.49 W
Pírgos, Grc.	171	37.51 N	21.28 E
Piritu, Laguna de (L.), Ven. (lä-gōō'nä-dē-pē-rē'tōō)	141b	10.00 N	64.57 W
Pirmasens, F.R.G. (pĭr-mä-zĕns')	164	49.12 N	7.34 E
Pirna, G.D.R. (pĭr'nä)	164	50.57 N	13.56 E
Pirot, Yugo. (pē'rōt)	171	43.09 N	22.35 E
Pirtleville, Az. (pûr't'l-vĭl)	119	31.25 N	109.35 W
Piru, Indon. (pē-rōō')	203	3.15 S	128.25 E
Piryatin, Sov. Un. (pēr-yä-tēn')	173	50.13 N	32.31 E
Pisa, It. (pē'sä)	170	43.52 N	10.24 E
Pisagua, Chile (pē-sä'gwä)	140	18.43 S	70.12 W
Piscataway, Md. (pĭs-kȧ-tȧ-wā)	110e	38.42 N	76.59 W
Piscataway, NJ	110a	40.35 N	74.27 W
Pisco, Peru (pēs'kō)	140	13.43 S	76.07 W
Pisco, Bahia de (B.), Peru (bä-ē'ä-dē)	140	13.43 S	77.48 W
Piseco (L.), NY (pĭ-sā'kō)	109	43.25 N	74.35 W
Pisek, Czech. (pē'sĕk)	164	49.18 N	14.08 E
Pisticci, It. (pēs-tē'chē)	170	40.24 N	16.34 E
Pistoia, It. (pēs-tô'yä)	170	43.57 N	11.54 E
Pisuerga (R.), Sp. (pē-swĕr'gä)	168	41.48 N	4.28 W
Pitalito, Col. (pē-tä-lē'tō)	140	1.45 N	75.09 W
Pitcairn, Pa. (pĭt'kârn)	111e	40.29 N	79.47 W
Pitcairn, Oceania	205	24.30 S	133.00 W
Piteå, Swe. (pē'tē-ô')	156	65.21 N	21.10 E
Pitealven (R.), Swe.	156	66.08 N	18.51 E
Pitesti, Rom. (pē-tĕsht'')	171	44.51 N	24.51 E
Pithara, Austl. (pĭt'ărȧ)	210	30.27 S	116.45 E
Pithiviers, Fr. (pē-tē-vyā')	166	48.12 N	2.14 E
Pitman, NJ (pĭt'mȧn)	110f	39.44 N	75.08 W
Pitons du Carbet, Mt., Mart.	131b	14.40 N	61.05 W
Pit R., Ca. (pĭt)	114	40.58 N	121.42 W
Pitseng, Leso.	223c	29.03 S	28.13 E
Pitt (R.), Can.	116d	49.19 N	122.39 W
Pitt I., Can.	96	53.35 N	129.45 W
Pittsburg, Ca. (pĭts'bûrg)	116b	38.01 N	121.52 W
Pittsburg, Ks.	121	37.25 N	94.43 W
Pittsburg, Tx.	121	32.00 N	94.57 W
Pittsburgh, Pa.	111e	40.26 N	80.01 W
Pittsfield, IL. (pĭts'fēld)	121	39.37 N	90.47 W
Pittsfield, Me.	102	44.45 N	69.44 W
Pittsfield, Ma.	109	42.25 N	73.15 W
Pittston, Pa. (pĭts'tŭn)	109	41.20 N	75.50 W
Piūi, Braz. (pē-ōō'ē)	139a	20.27 S	45.57 W
Piura, Peru (pē-ōō'rä)	140	5.13 S	80.46 W
Piya, Sov. Un. (pē'yȧ)	180a	58.34 N	61.12 E
Placentia, Ca. (plă-sĕn'shĭ-ȧ)	117a	33.52 N	117.50 W
Placentia, CAn.	103	47.15 N	53.58 W
Placentia B., Can.	103	47.14 N	54.30 W
Placerville, Ca. (plăs'ēr-vĭl)	118	38.43 N	120.47 W
Placetas, Cuba (plä-thā'täs)	132	22.10 N	79.40 W
Placid (L.), NY (plăs'ĭd)	109	44.20 N	74.00 W
Plain City, Ut. (plān)	117b	41.18 N	112.06 W
Plainfield, Il. (plān'fēld)	111a	41.37 N	88.12 W
Plainfield, In.	111g	39.42 N	86.23 W
Plainfield, NJ	110a	40.38 N	74.25 W
Plainview, Ar. (plān'vū)	121	34.59 N	93.15 W
Plainview, Mn.	113	44.09 N	93.12 W
Plainview, Ne.	112	42.20 N	97.47 W
Plainview, NY	110a	40.47 N	73.28 W
Plainview, Tx.	120	34.11 N	101.42 W
Plainwell, Mi. (plan'wĕl)	108	42.25 N	85.40 W
Plaisance, Can. (plē-zäɴs')	93c	45.37 N	75.07 W
Plana or Flat Cays (Is.), Ba. (plä'nä)	133	22.35 N	73.35 W
Planegg, F.R.G. (plä'nĕg)	155b	48.06 N	11.27 E
Plano, Tx. (plā'nō)	121	33.01 N	96.42 W
Plantagenet, Can. (plaɴ-täzh-nĕ')	93c	45.33 N	75.00 W
Plant City, Fl. (plănt sĭ'tĭ)	125a	28.00 N	82.07 W
Plaquemine, La. (plăk'mēn')	123	30.17 N	91.14 W
Plasencia, Sp. (plä-sĕn'thē-ä)	168	40.02 N	6.07 W
Plast, Sov. Un. (plást)	180a	54.22 N	60.48 E
Plaster Rock, Can. (plȧs'tēr rŏk)	102	46.54 N	67.24 W
Plastun, Sov. Un. (plȧs-tōōn')	200	44.41 N	136.08 E
Plata, R. de la (R.), Arg.-Urg. (dālä plä'tä)	142	34.35 S	58.15 W
Platani (R.), It. (plä-tä'nē)	170	37.26 N	13.28 E
Plateforme, Pte., Hai.	133	19.35 N	73.50 W
Platinum, Ak. (plăt'ĭ-nŭm)	105	59.00 N	161.27 W
Plato, Col. (plä'tō)	140	9.49 N	74.48 W
Platón Sánchez, Mex. (plä-tōn' sän'chĕz)	128	21.14 N	98.20 W
Platte, SD (plăt)	112	43.22 N	98.51 W
Platte (R.), Mo.	121	40.09 N	94.40 W
Platte (R.), U. S.	106	40.50 N	100.40 W
Platteville, Wi. (plăt'vĭl)	113	42.44 N	90.31 W
Plattsburg, Mo. (plăts'bûrg)	121	39.33 N	94.26 W
Plattsburg, NY	109	44.40 N	73.30 W
Plattsmouth, Ne. (plăts'mŭth)	112	41.00 N	95.53 W
Plauen, G.D.R. (plou'ĕn)	164	50.30 N	12.08 E
Playa de Guanabo, Cuba (plä-yä-dē-gwä-nä'bō)	133a	23.10 N	82.07 W
Playa de Santa Fe, Cuba (sä'n-tä-fĕ')	133a	23.05 N	82.31 W
Playas (L.), NM (plä'yȧs)	119	31.50 N	108.30 W
Playa Vicente, Mex. (vē-sĕn'tȧ)	129	17.49 N	95.49 W
Playa Vicente (R.), Mex.	129	17.36 N	96.13 W
Playgreen L., Can. (plā'grēn)	99	54.00 N	98.10 W
Pleasant (L.), NY (plĕz'ănt)	109	43.25 N	74.25 W
Pleasant Grove, Al.	110h	33.29 N	86.57 W
Pleasant Hill, Ca.	116b	37.57 N	122.04 W
Pleasant Hill, Mo.	121	38.46 N	94.18 W
Pleasanton, Ca. (plĕz'ăn-tŭn)	116b	37.40 N	121.53 W
Pleasanton, Ks.	121	38.10 N	94.41 W
Pleasanton, Tx.	122	28.58 N	98.30 W
Pleasant Plain, Oh. (plĕz'ănt)	111f	39.17 N	84.06 W
Pleasant Ridge, Mi.	111b	42.28 N	83.09 W
Pleasant View, Ut. (plĕz'ănt vū)	117b	41.20 N	112.02 W
Pleasantville, NY (plĕz'ănt-vĭl)	110a	41.08 N	73.47 W
Pleasure Ridge Park, Ky. (plĕzh'ēr rĭj)	111h	38.09 N	85.49 W
Plenty, Bay of, N. Z. (plĕn'tē)	213	37.30 S	177.10 E
Plentywood, Mt. (plĕn'tē-wōōd)	115	48.47 N	104.38 W
Ples, Sov. Un. (plyĕs)	172	57.26 N	41.29 E
Pleshcheyevo (L.), Sov. Un. (plĕsh-chā'yĕ-vô)	172	56.50 N	38.22 E
Plessisville, Can. (plĕ-sē'vēl')	102	46.12 N	71.47 W
Pleszew, Pol. (plĕ'zhĕf)	165	51.54 N	17.48 E
Plettenberg, F.R.G. (plĕ'tĕn-bĕrgh)	167c	51.13 N	7.53 E
Pleven, Bul. (plĕ'vĕn)	171	43.24 N	24.26 E
Pljevlja, Yugo. (plĕv'lyä)	171	43.20 N	19.21 E
Płock, Pol. (pwôtsk)	165	52.32 N	19.44 E
Ploërmel, Fr. (plô-ĕr-mĕl')	166	47.56 N	2.25 W
Ploieşti, Rom. (plô-yĕsht'')	171	44.56 N	26.01 E
Plomárion, Grc. (plō-mä'rĭ-ŏn)	171	38.51 N	26.24 E
Plomb du Cantal (Mt.), Fr. (plôɴ'dükäɴ-täl')	166	45.30 N	2.49 E
Plonge, Lac la (L.), Can. (plōɴzh)	98	55.08 N	107.25 W
Plovdiv (Philippopolis), Bul. (plôv'dĭf) (fĭl-ĭp-ŏp'ō-lĭs)	171	42.09 N	24.43 E
Pluma Hidalgo, Mex. (plōō'mä ē-däl'gō)	129	15.54 N	96.23 W
Plunge, Sov. Un. (plōōn'gä)	163	55.56 N	21.45 E
Plymouth, Eng. (plĭm'ŭth)	160	50.25 N	4.14 W
Plymouth, In.	108	41.20 N	86.20 W
Plymouth, Ma.	109	42.00 N	70.45 W
Plymouth, Mi.	111b	42.23 N	83.27 W
Plymouth, Montserrat	131b	16.43 N	62.12 W
Plymouth, NH	109	43.50 N	71.40 W
Plymouth, NC	125	35.50 N	76.44 W
Plymouth, Pa.	109	41.15 N	75.55 W
Plymouth, Wi.	113	43.45 N	87.59 W
Plyussa (R.), Sov. Un. (plyōō'sȧ)	172	58.33 N	28.30 E
Plzeň (Pilsen), Czech.	164	49.46 N	13.25 E
Pô, Upper Volta	224	11.10 N	1.09 W
Po (R.), It.	170	44.57 N	12.38 E
Pobé, Benin (pô-bā')	225	6.58 N	2.41 E
Pocahontas, Ar. (pō-kȧ-hŏn'tȧs)	121	36.15 N	91.01 W
Pocahontas, Ia.	113	42.43 N	94.41 W
Pocatello, Id. (pō-kȧ-tĕl'ō)	115	42.54 N	112.30 W
Pochëp, Sov. Un. (pô-chĕp')	172	52.56 N	32.27 E
Pochinok, Sov. Un. (pô-chē'nôk)	172	54.14 N	32.27 E

ng-sing; ŋ-baŋk; ɴ-nasalized n; nŏd; cŏmmit; ōld; ôbey; ôrder; oi-boil; fōōd; fŏŏt; ou-out; s-soft; sh-dish; th-thin; pūre; ûnite; ûrn; stŭd; circŭs; ü-as in French tu; '-indeterminate vowel.

334 Pochinski – Potenza

PLACE (Pronunciation)	PAGE	Lat. °′	Long. °′
Pochinski, Sov. Un.	176	54.40 N	44.50 E
Pochotitán, Mex. (pô-chô-tē-tä'n)	128	21.37 N	104.33 W
Pochutla (San Pedro), Mex. (pō-chōō'tlä) (sän pā'drō)	129	15.46 N	96.28 W
Pocomoke City, Md. (pō-kō-mōk')	109	38.05 N	75.35 W
Pocono Mts., Pa. (pō-cō'nō)	109	41.10 N	75.05 W
Poços de Caldas, Braz. (pō-sôs-dĕ-käl'das)	139a	21.48 S	46.34 W
Poder, Senegal (pô-dôr')	220	16.35 N	15.04 W
Podkamennaya (Stony) (R.) Tunguska, Sov. Un.	178	61.43 N	93.45 E
Podol'sk, Sov. Un. (pô-dôl''sk)	180b	55.26 N	37.33 E
Podvolochisk, Sov. Un.	173	49.32 N	26.16 E
Poggibonsi, It. (pôd-jē-bôn'sē)	170	43.27 N	11.12 E
Pogodino, Sov. Un. (pô-gô'dē-nô)	172	54.17 N	31.00 E
P'ohang, Kor.	200	35.57 N	129.23 E
Pointe-à-Pitre, Guad. (pwănt' à pē-tr')	131b	16.15 N	61.32 W
Pointe-aux-Trembles, Can. (pōō-ănt' ō-tränbl)	93a	45.39 N	73.30 W
Pointe Claire, Can. (pōō-ănt' klĕr)	93a	45.27 N	73.48 W
Pointe-des-Cascades, Can. (kăs-kădz')	93a	45.19 N	73.58 W
Pointe Fortune, Can. (fôr'tūn)	93a	45.34 N	74.23 W
Pointe-Gatineau, Can. (pōō-ănt'gä-tē-nō')	93c	45.28 N	75.42 W
Pointe Noire, Con.	226	4.48 S	11.51 E
Point Hope, Ak. (hōp)	105	68.18 N	166.38 W
Point Pleasant, WV (plĕz'ănt)	108	38.50 N	82.10 W
Point Roberts, Wa. (rŏb'ērts)	116d	48.59 N	123.04 W
Poissy, Fr. (pwä-sē')	167b	48.55 N	2.02 E
Poitiers, Fr. (pwä-tyā')	166	46.35 N	0.18 E
Pokaran, India (pō'kŭr-ŭn)	190	27.00 N	72.05 E
Pokrov, Sov. Un. (pô-krôf)	172	55.56 N	39.09 E
Pokrovskoye, Sov. Un. (pô-krôf'skô-yĕ)	173	47.27 N	38.54 E
Pola (R.), Sov. Un. (pō'lä)	172	54.44 N	31.53 E
Pola de Laviana, Sp. (dĕ-lä-vyä'nä)	168	43.15 N	5.29 W
Pola de Siero, Sp.	168	43.24 N	5.39 W
Poland, Eur. (pō'lănd)	152	52.37 N	17.01 E
Polangui, Phil. (pô-läŋ'gē)	203a	13.18 N	123.29 E
Polazna, Sov. Un. (pô'láz-ná)	180a	58.18 N	56.25 E
Polessk, Sov. Un. (pô'lĕsk)	163	54.50 N	21.14 E
Poles'ye (Pripyat Marshes), Sov. Un.	177	52.10 N	27.30 E
Polevskoy, Sov. Un. (pô-lĕ'vs-kô'ĭ)	180a	56.28 N	60.14 E
Polgár, Hung. (pôl'gär)	165	47.54 N	21.10 E
Policastro, Golfo di (G.), It.	170	41.00 N	13.23 E
Poligny, Fr. (pō-lē-nyē')	167	46.48 N	5.42 E
Polikhnitos, Grc.	171	39.05 N	26.11 E
Polillo, Phil. (pô-lēl'yō)	203a	14.42 N	121.56 E
Polillo Is., Phil.	203a	15.05 N	122.15 E
Polillo Str., Phil.	203a	15.02 N	121.40 E
Polist' (R.), Sov. Un. (pô'lĭst)	172	57.42 N	31.02 E
Polistena, It. (pō-lēs-tā'nä)	170	40.25 N	16.05 E
Políyiros, Grc.	171	40.23 N	23.27 E
Polkan, Gol'tsy (Mtn.), Sov. Un.	178	60.18 N	92.08 E
Pollensa, Sp. (pôl-yĕn'sä)	169	39.50 N	3.00 E
Polochic R., Guat. (pō-lō-chēk')	130	15.19 N	89.45 W
Polonnoye, Sov. Un. (pô'lô-nô-yĕ)	173	50.07 N	27.31 E
Polotsk, Sov. Un. (pô'lôtsk)	172	55.30 N	28.48 E
Polpaico, Chile (pôl-pà'y-kô)	139b	33.10 S	70.53 W
Polson, Mt. (pōl'sŭn)	115	47.40 N	114.10 W
Poltava, Sov. Un. (pôl-tä'vä)	173	49.35 N	34.33 E
Poltava (Oblast), Sov. Un.	173	49.53 N	32.58 E
Põltsamaa, Sov. Un. (pôlt'sá-mä)	172	58.39 N	26.00 E
Põltsamaa (R.), Sov. Un.	172	58.35 N	25.55 E
Polunochnoye, Sov. Un. (pô-lōō-nô'ch-nô-yĕ)	180a	60.52 N	60.27 E
Poluy (R.), Sov. Un. (pôl'wē)	178	65.45 N	68.15 E
Polyakovka, Sov. Un. (pŭl-yä'kôv-kȧ)	180a	54.38 N	59.42 E
Polyarnyy, Sov. Un. (pŭl-yär'nē)	176	69.10 N	33.30 E
Pomba (R.), Braz. (pô'm-bá)	139a	21.28 S	42.28 W
Pomerania (Reg.), Pol. (pŏm-ē-rā'nĭ-ȧ)	164	53.50 N	15.20 E
Pomeranian B., G.D.R. (pō'mē-rä-ny-ăn)	162	54.10 N	14.20 E
Pomeroy, S. Afr. (pŏm'ēr-roi)	223c	28.36 S	30.26 E
Pomeroy, Wa. (pŏm'ēr-oi)	114	46.28 N	117.35 W
Pomezia, It. (pô-mĕ't-zyä)	169d	41.41 N	12.31 E
Pomigliano d' Arco, It. (pō-mē-lyá'nô-d-ä'r-kô)	169c	40.39 N	14.23 E
Pomme de Terre, Mn. (pôm dē tĕr')	112	45.22 N	95.52 W
Pomona, Ca. (pô-mō'nȧ)	117a	34.04 N	117.45 W
Pomorie, Bul.	171	42.24 N	27.41 E
Pompano Beach, Fl. (pŏm'pȧ-nō)	125a	26.12 N	80.07 W
Pompeii Ruins, It.	169c	40.31 N	14.29 E
Pompton Lakes, NJ (pŏmp'tŏn)	110a	41.01 N	74.16 W
Pomuch, Mex. (pô-mōō'ch)	130a	20.12 N	90.10 W
Ponca, Ne. (pŏn'kȧ)	112	42.34 N	96.43 W
Ponca City, Ok.	121	36.42 N	97.07 W
Ponce, P. R. (pōn'sā)	127b	18.01 N	66.43 W
Pondicherry, India (pôn-dĭ-shĕr'ē') (pŏn-dĭ-shĕr'ē)	191	11.58 N	79.48 E
Pondicherry (State), India	191	11.50 N	74.50 E
Ponferrada, Sp. (pôn-fĕr-rä'dhä)	168	42.33 N	6.38 W
Ponoka, Can. (pŏ-nō'kȧ)	97	52.42 N	113.35 W
Ponoy, Sov. Un.	176	66.58 N	41.00 E
Ponoy (R.), Sov. Un.	176	65.50 N	38.40 E
Ponta Delgada, Açores (pôn'tȧ dĕl-gä'dȧ)	220a	37.40 N	25.45 W
Ponta Grossa, Braz. (grō'sȧ)	142	25.09 S	50.05 W
Pont-à-Mousson, Fr. (pôn'tá-mōōsôn')	167	48.55 N	6.02 E
Ponta Porã, Braz.	141	22.30 S	55.31 W
Pontarlier, Fr. (pôn'tàr-lyā')	167	46.53 N	6.22 E
Pont-Audemer, Fr. (pôn'tōd'mâr')	166	49.23 N	0.28 E
Pontcarré, Fr. (pôn-kà-rā')	167b	48.48 N	2.42 E
Pontchartrain L., La. (pŏn-shàr-trān')	123	30.10 N	90.10 W
Pontedera, It. (pōn-tå-dā'rä)	170	43.37 N	10.37 E
Ponte de Sor, Port. (pōŋ'tĕ dȧ sōr')	168	39.14 N	8.03 W
Pontefract, Eng. (pŏn'tê-frăkt)	154	53.41 N	1.18 W
Ponte Nova, Braz. (pô'n-tē-nô'vȧ)	139a	20.26 S	42.52 W
Pontevedra, Sp. (pōn-tē-vĕ-drä)	168	42.28 N	8.38 W
Ponthierville, see Ubundi			
Pontiac, Il. (pŏn'tĭ-ăk)	108	40.55 N	88.35 W
Pontiac, Mi.	111b	42.37 N	83.17 W
Pontianak, Indon. (pôn-tê-ä'nák)	202	0.04 S	109.20 E
Pontian Kechil, Mala.	189b	1.29 N	103.24 E
Pontic Mts., Turk.	177	41.20 N	34.30 E
Pontivy, Fr. (pôn-tē-vē')	166	48.05 N	2.57 W
Pont-l'Abbé, Fr. (pôn-lȧ-bā')	166	47.53 N	4.12 W
Pontoise, Fr. (pôn-twáz')	167b	49.03 N	2.05 E
Pontonnyy, Sov. Un. (pôn'tôn-nyĭ)	180c	59.47 N	30.39 E
Pontotoc, Ms. (pŏn-tō-tŏk')	124	34.11 N	88.59 W
Pontremoli, It. (pôn-trĕm'ô-lē)	170	44.21 N	9.50 E
Ponziane, Isole (I.), It. (ē'sō-lĕ)	170	40.55 N	12.58 E
Poole, Eng. (pōōl)	160	50.43 N	2.00 W
Poolesville, Md. (poolĕs-vĭl)	110e	39.08 N	77.26 W
Pooley I., Can. (pōō'lē)	96	52.44 N	128.16 W
Poopó, Lago de (L.), Bol. (lä'gô-dĕ-pō-ō-pô')	140	18.16 S	67.57 W
Popayán, Col. (pō-pä-yän')	140	2.21 N	76.43 W
Poplar, Mt. (pŏp'lēr)	115	48.08 N	105.10 W
Poplar Bluff, Mo. (blŭf)	121	36.43 N	90.22 W
Poplar Plains, Ky. (plāns)	108	38.20 N	83.40 W
Poplar Point, Can.	93f	50.04 N	97.57 W
Poplar R., Mt.	115	48.34 N	105.20 W
Poplar R., West Fork, Mt.	115	48.59 N	106.06 W
Poplarville, Ms. (pŏp'lēr-vĭl)	124	30.50 N	89.33 W
Popocatépetl Volcán (Vol.), Mex. (pô-pô-kä-tä'pĕ't'l)	129a	19.01 N	98.38 W
Popokabaka, Zaire (pō'pô-kȧ-bä'kȧ)	226	5.42 S	16.35 E
Popovka, Sov. Un. (pô'pôf-kȧ)	173	50.03 N	33.41 E
Popovka, Sov. Un.	173	51.13 N	33.08 E
Popovo, Bul. (pô'pô-vō)	171	43.23 N	26.17 E
Porbandar, India (pōr-bŭn'dŭr)	190	21.44 N	69.40 E
Porce (R.), Col. (pôr-sē)	140a	7.11 N	74.55 W
Porcher I., Can. (pôr'kēr)	96	53.57 N	130.30 W
Porcuna, Sp. (pôr-kōō'nä)	168	37.54 N	4.10 W
Porcupine (R.), Ak.	105	67.00 N	143.25 W
Porcupine (R.), Can.	94	67.38 N	140.07 W
Porcupine Cr., Mt. (pôr'kū-pīn)	115	46.38 N	107.04 W
Porcupine Cr., Mt.	115	48.27 N	106.24 W
Porcupine Hills, Can.	99	52.30 N	101.45 W
Pordenone, It. (pōr-dȧ-nō'nā)	170	45.58 N	12.38 E
Poreč, Yugo. (pô'rĕch)	170	45.13 N	13.37 E
Pori, Fin. (pô'rĭ)	163	61.29 N	21.45 E
Poriúncula, Braz. (po-rēōō'n-kōō-lä)	139a	20.58 S	42.02 W
Porkhov, Sov. Un. (pôr'kôf)	172	57.46 N	29.33 E
Porlamar, Ven. (pôr-lä-mär')	140	11.00 N	63.55 W
Pornic, Fr. (pôr-nēk')	166	47.08 N	2.07 W
Poronaysk, Sov. Un. (pô'rô-nīsk)	179	49.21 N	143.23 E
Porrentruy, Switz. (pô-răn-trüē')	164	47.25 N	7.02 E
Porsgrunn, Nor. (pôrs'grōōn')	162	59.09 N	9.36 E
Portachuelo, Bol. (pôrt-ä-chwā'lô)	140	17.20 S	63.12 W
Portage, Pa. (pôr'tāj)	109	40.25 N	78.35 W
Portage, Wi.	113	43.33 N	89.29 W
Portage Des Sioux, Mo. (dē sōō)	117e	38.56 N	90.21 W
Portage-la-Prairie, Can. (lä-prā'rĭ)	93f	49.57 N	98.25 W
Port Alberni, Can. (pōr ăl-bĕr-nē')	96	49.14 N	124.48 W
Portalegre, Port. (pôr-tä-lā'grĕ)	168	39.18 N	7.26 W
Portales, NM (pôr-tä'lĕs)	120	34.10 N	103.11 W
Port Alfred (Kowie), S. Afr. (kou'ĭ)	223c	33.36 S	26.55 E
Port Alice, Can. (ăl'ĭs)	96	50.23 N	127.27 W
Port Allegany, Pa. (ăl-ē-gā'nĭ)	109	41.50 N	78.10 W
Port Angeles, Wa. (ăn'jē-lĕs)	114	48.07 N	123.26 W
Port Antonio, Jam.	133	18.10 N	76.25 W
Portarlington, Austl.	207a	38.07 S	144.39 E
Port Arthur, Tx.	123	29.52 N	93.59 W
Port Augusta, Austl. (ô-gŭs'tȧ)	212	32.28 S	137.50 E
Port au Port B., Can. (pōr'tō pōr')	103	48.41 N	58.45 W
Port-au-Prince, Hai. (prăns')	133	18.35 N	72.20 W
Port Austin, Mi. (ôs'tĭn)	108	44.00 N	83.00 W
Port aux Basques, Can.	103	47.36 N	59.09 W
Port Blair, Andaman & Nicobar Is. (blâr)	202	12.07 N	92.45 E
Port Bolivar, Tx. (bŏl'ĭ-vár)	123a	29.22 N	94.46 W
Port Borden, Can. (bôr'dĕn)	102	46.15 N	63.42 W
Port-Bouët, Ivory Coast	220	5.24 N	3.56 W
Port-Cartier, Can.	102	50.01 N	66.53 W
Port Chester, NY (chĕs'tēr)	110a	40.59 N	73.40 W
Port Chicago, Ca. (shĭ-kô'gō)	116b	38.03 N	122.01 W
Port Clinton, Oh. (klĭn'tŭn)	108	41.30 N	83.00 W
Port Colborne, Can.	101	42.53 N	79.13 W
Port Coquitlam, Can. (kô-kwĭt'lȧm)	116d	49.16 N	122.46 W
Port Credit, Can. (krĕd'ĭt)	93d	43.33 N	79.35 W
Port-de-Bouc, Fr. (pōr-dē-bōōk')	166a	43.24 N	5.00 E
Port de Paix, Hai. (pĕ)	133	19.55 N	72.50 W
Port Dickson, Mala. (dĭk'sŭn)	189b	2.33 N	101.49 E
Port Discovery (B.), Wa. (dĭs-kŭv'ēr-ĭ)	116a	48.05 N	122.55 W
Port Edward, S. Afr. (ĕd'wērd)	223c	31.04 S	30.14 E
Port Elgin, Can. (ĕl'jĭn)	102	46.03 N	64.05 W
Port Elizabeth, S. Afr. (ē-lĭz'ȧ-bĕth)	223c	33.57 S	25.37 E
Porterdale, Ga. (pōr'tēr-dāl)	124	33.34 N	83.53 W
Porterville, Ca. (pōr'tēr-vĭl)	118	36.03 N	119.05 W
Portezuelo de Tupungato (Vol.), Arg.-Chile (pôr-tĕ-zwĕ-lō-dĕ-tōō-pōō'n-gä-tô)	142	33.30 S	69.52 W
Port Francqui, see Ilebo			
Port Gamble, Wa. (găm'bŭl)	116a	47.52 N	122.36 W
Port Gamble Ind. Res., Wa.	116a	47.54 N	122.33 W
Port-Gentil, Gabon (zhän-tē')	226	0.43 S	8.47 E
Port Gibson, Ms.	124	31.56 N	90.57 W
Port Harcourt, Nig. (här'kŭrt)	225	4.43 N	7.05 E
Port Hardy, Can. (här'dĭ)	96	50.43 N	127.29 W
Port Hawkesbury, Can.	103	45.37 N	61.21 W
Port Hedland, Austl. (hĕd'lănd)	210	20.30 S	118.30 E
Porthill, Id.	114	49.00 N	116.30 W
Port Hood, Can. (hŏŏd)	103	46.01 N	61.32 W
Port Hope, Can. (hōp)	109	43.55 N	78.10 W
Port Huron, Mi. (hū'rŏn)	108	43.00 N	82.30 W
Portici, It. (pôr'tê-chē)	169c	40.34 N	14.20 E
Portillo, Chile (pôr-tē'l-yô)	139b	32.51 S	70.09 W
Portimão, Port. (pôr-tē-mo'un)	168	37.09 N	8.34 W
Port Jervis, NY (jûr'vĭs)	110a	41.22 N	74.41 W
Port Kelang, Mala.	189b	3.00 N	101.25 E
Portland, Austl. (pōrt'lănd)	212	38.20 S	142.40 E
Portland, In.	108	40.25 N	85.00 W
Portland, Me.	102	43.40 N	70.16 W
Portland, Mi.	108	42.50 N	85.00 W
Portland, Or.	116c	45.31 N	123.41 W
Portland, Tx.	123	27.53 N	97.20 W
Portland Bight (B.), Jam.	132	17.45 N	77.05 W
Portland Can., Ak.	96	55.10 N	130.08 W
Portland Inlet, Can.	96	54.50 N	130.15 W
Portland Pt., Jam	132	17.40 N	77.20 W
Port Lavaca, Tx. (lȧ-vä'kȧ)	123	28.36 N	96.38 W
Port Lincoln, Austl. (lĭŋ-kŭn)	212	34.39 S	135.50 E
Port Ludlow, Wa. (lŭd'lō)	116a	47.26 N	122.41 W
Port Lyautey, see Kenitra			
Port Macquarie, Austl. (mȧ-kwŏ'rĭ)	212	31.25 S	152.45 E
Port Madison Ind. Res., Wa. (măd'ĭ-sŭn)	116a	47.46 N	122.38 W
Port Maria, Jam. (mȧ-rī'ȧ)	132	18.20 N	76.55 W
Port-Menier, Can. (mē-nyā')	102	49.49 N	64.20 W
Port Moody, Can. (mōōd'ĭ)	116d	49.17 N	122.51 W
Port Moresby, Pap. N. Gui. (mōrz'bē)	203	9.34 S	147.20 E
Port Neches, Tx. (nĕch'ĕz)	123	29.59 N	93.57 W
Port Nelson, Can. (nĕl'sŭn)	99	57.03 N	92.36 W
Portneuf-Sur-Mer, Can. (pôr-nûf'sür mĕr)	102	48.36 N	69.06 W
Port Nolloth, S. Afr. (nŏl'ŏth)	222	29.10 S	17.00 E
Porto, Port. (pōr'tōō)	168	41.10 N	8.38 W
Pôrto Acre, Braz. (ä'krĕ)	140	9.38 S	67.34 W
Pôrto Alegre, Braz. (ä-lā'grĕ)	142	29.58 S	51.11 W
Porto Alexandre, Ang. (à-lĕ-zhän'drĕ)	226	15.49 S	11.53 E
Porto Amboim, Ang.	226	11.01 S	13.45 E
Portobelo, Pan. (pôr'tô-bā'lô)	131	9.32 N	79.40 W
Pôrto de Pedras, Braz. (pā'dräzh)	141	9.09 S	35.20 W
Pôrto Feliz, Braz. (fĕ-lē's)	139a	23.12 S	47.30 W
Portoferraio, It. (pōr'tô-fĕr-rä'yō)	170	42.47 N	10.20 E
Port of Spain, Trin. (spān)	141	10.44 N	61.24 W
Portogruaro, It. (pōr'tô-grōō-ä'rō)	170	45.48 N	12.49 E
Portola, Ca. (pôr'tō-lȧ)	118	39.47 N	120.29 W
Pôrto Mendes, Braz. (mĕ'n-dĕs)	141	24.41 S	54.13 W
Pôrto Murtinho, Braz. (mōōr-tēn'yōō)	141	21.43 S	57.43 W
Pôrto Nacional, Braz. (nä-syô-näl')	141	10.43 S	48.14 W
Porto Novo, Benin (pōr'tō-nō'vō)	225	6.29 N	2.37 E
Port Orchard, Wa. (ôr'chērd)	116a	47.32 N	122.38 W
Port Orchard (B.), Wa.	116a	47.40 N	122.39 W
Porto Santo, Ilha de (I.), Mad. Is. (săn'tōō)	220	32.41 N	16.15 W
Pôrto Seguro, Braz. (sā-gōō'rōō)	141	16.26 S	38.59 W
Porto Torres, It. (tôr'rĕs)	170	40.49 N	8.25 E
Porto-Vecchio, Fr. (vĕk'ē-ô)	170	41.36 N	9.17 E
Pôrto Velho, Braz. (vāl'yōō)	140	8.45 S	63.43 W
Portoviejo, Ec. (pôr-tō-vyā'hō)	140	1.11 S	80.28 W
Port Phillip B., Austl. (fĭl'ĭp)	212	37.57 S	144.50 E
Port Pirie, Austl. (pĭ'rē)	212	33.10 S	138.00 E
Port Radium, Can. (rā'dē-ŭm)	94	66.06 N	118.03 W
Port Royal (B.), Jam. (roi'ăl)	132	17.50 N	76.45 W
Port Said, see Būr Sa'īd			
Port St. Johns, S. Afr. (sănt jŏnz)	223c	31.37 S	29.32 E
Port Shepstone, S. Afr. (shĕps'tŭn)	223c	30.45 S	30.23 E
Portsmouth, Dominica	131b	15.33 N	61.28 W
Portsmouth, Eng. (pôrts'mŭth)	160	50.45 N	1.03 W
Portsmouth, NH	109	43.05 N	70.50 W
Portsmouth, Oh.	108	38.45 N	83.00 W
Portsmouth, Va.	110g	36.50 N	76.19 W
Port Sudan, see Būr Sūdān			
Port Sulphur, La. (sŭl'fēr)	124	29.28 N	89.41 W
Port Susan (B.), Wa. (sū-zan')	116a	48.11 N	122.25 W
Port Tampa, Fl. (tăm'pȧ)	125a	27.50 N	82.30 W
Port Townsend, Wa. (tounz'ĕnd)	116a	48.07 N	122.46 W
Port Townsend (B.), Wa.	116a	48.05 N	122.47 W
Portugal, Eur. (pōr'tu-găl)	152	38.15 N	8.08 W
Portugalete, Sp. (pōr-tōō-gä-lā'tā)	168	43.18 N	3.05 W
Portugália, Ang.	226	7.20 S	20.47 E
Portuguese East Africa, see Mozambique			
Portuguese India, see Gôa, Daman & Diu			
Portuguese West Africa, see Angola			
Port Vendres, Fr. (pôr văn'dr')	166	42.32 N	3.07 E
Port Wakefield, Austl. (wāk'fēld)	212	34.12 S	138.10 E
Port Washington, NY (wôsh'ĭng-tŭn)	110a	40.49 N	73.42 W
Port Washington, Wi.	113	43.24 N	87.52 W
Posadas, Arg. (pō-sä'dhäs)	142	27.32 S	55.56 W
Posadas, Sp. (pō-sä-dás)	168	37.48 N	5.09 W
Poshekhon 'ye Volodarsk, Sov. Un. (pô-shyĕ'kôn-yĕ vôl'ô-dársk)	172	58.31 N	39.07 E
Poso, Danau (L.), Indon. (pō'sō)	202	2.00 S	119.40 E
Pospelokova, Sov. Un. (pôs-pyĕl'kô-vá)	180a	59.25 N	60.50 E
Possession Sd., Wa. (pŏ-zĕsh-ŭn)	116a	47.59 N	122.17 W
Possum Kingdom Res., Tx. (pŏs'ŭm kĭng'dŭm)	122	32.58 N	98.12 W
Post, Tx. (pōst)	120	33.12 N	101.21 W
Post Maurice Cortier (Bidon Cinq), Alg.	220	22.22 N	0.33 E
Postojna, Yugo. (pōs-tōyná)	170	45.45 N	14.13 E
Pos'yet, Sov. Un. (pos-yĕt')	200	42.27 N	130.47 E
Potawatomi Ind. Res., Ks. (pŏt-ȧ-wä'tō mē)	121	39.30 N	96.11 W
Potchefstroom, S. Afr. (pŏch'ĕf-strōm)	219d	26.42 S	27.06 E
Poteau, Ok. (pō-tō')	121	35.03 N	94.37 W
Poteet, Tx. (pō-tēt)	122	29.05 N	98.35 W
Potenza, It. (pô-tĕnt'sä)	170	40.39 N	15.49 E
Potenza (R.), It.	170	43.09 N	13.00 E

PRONOUNCING INDEX

Potgietersrus – Puerto Vallarta 335

PLACE (Pronunciation)	PAGE	Lat. °'	Long. °'
Potgietersrus, S. Afr. (pôt-ĸē'tĕrs-rûs)	219d	24.09 S	29.04 E
Potholes Res., Wa.	114	47.00 N	119.20 W
Poti, Sov. Un. (pô'tē)	177	42.10 N	41.40 E
Potiskum, Nig.	225	11.43 N	11.05 E
Potomac, Md. (pō-tō'măk)	110e	39.01 N	77.13 W
Potomac (R.), Va. (pō-tō'măk)	109	38.15 N	76.55 W
Potosí, Bol. (pō-tō-sē')	140	19.42 S	65.42 W
Potosi, Mo. (pō-tō'sĭ)	121	37.56 N	90.46 W
Potosí, R., Mex. (pō-tō-sē')	122	25.04 N	99.36 W
Potrerillos, Hond. (pō-trā-rēl'yōs)	130	15.13 N	87.58 W
Potsdam, G.D.R. (pôts'däm)	155b	52.24 N	13.04 E
Potsdam, NY (pŏts'dăm)	109	44.40 N	75.00 W
Potsdam (Dist.), G.D.R. (pôts'dăm)	155b	52.31 N	12.45 E
Pottenstein, Aus.	155e	47.58 N	16.06 E
Potters Bar, Eng. (pŏt'ẽz bär)	154b	51.41 N	0.12 W
Pottstown, Pa. (pŏts'toun)	109	40.15 N	75.40 W
Pottsville, Pa. (pŏts'vĭl)	109	40.40 N	76.15 W
Poughkeepsie, NY (pŏ-kĭp'sē)	109	41.45 N	73.55 W
Poulsbo, Wa. (pōlz'bōō)	116a	47.44 N	122.38 W
Poulton-le-Fylde, Eng. (pōl'tŭn-lē-fīld')	154	53.52 N	2.59 W
Pouso Alegre, Braz. (pō'zōō ä-lā'grĕ)	139a	22.13 S	45.56 W
Póvoa de Varzim, Port. (pō-vō'ȧ dā vär'zēɴ)	168	41.23 N	8.44 W
Powder River, Wy.	115	43.06 N	106.55 W
Powder R., Mt.-Wy. (pou'dẽr)	115	45.18 N	105.37 W
Powder R., Or.	114	44.55 N	117.35 W
Powder R., South Fk., Wy.	115	43.13 N	106.54 W
Powell, Wy. (pou'ĕl)	115	44.44 N	108.44 W
Powell, L., Ut.	119	37.26 N	110.25 W
Powell L., Can.	96	50.10 N	124.13 W
Powell Pt., Ba.	123	24.50 N	76.20 W
Powell Res., Ky.-Tn.	124	36.30 N	83.35 W
Powell River, Can.	96	49.52 N	124.33 W
Poyang Hu (L.), China (pwo-yän-hōō)	199	29.20 N	116.28 E
Poygan (R.), Wi. (poi'gȧn)	113	44.10 N	89.05 W
Požarevac, Yugo. (pô'zhȧ'rĕ-vȧts)	171	44.38 N	21.12 E
Poznań, Pol. (pôz'nän')	164	52.24 N	16.55 E
Pozoblanco, Sp. (pō-thō-bläŋ'kō)	168	38.23 N	4.50 W
Pozo Rica, Mex. (pô-zô-rē'kä)	129	20.32 N	97.25 W
Pozos, Mex. (pô'zōs)	128	22.05 N	100.50 W
Pozuelo de Alarcón, Sp. (pô-thwā'lō dā ä-lär-kōn')	169a	40.27 N	3.49 W
Pozzuoli, It. (pôt-swô'lē)	169c	40.34 N	14.08 E
Pra (R.), Ghana (prȧ)	224	5.45 N	1.35 W
Pra (R.), Sov. Un.	172	55.00 N	40.13 E
Prachin Buri, Thai. (prä'chēn)	202	13.59 N	101.15 E
Pradera, Col. (prä-dĕ'rä)	140a	3.24 N	76.13 W
Prades, Fr. (prȧd)	166	42.37 N	2.23 E
Prado, Col. (prädô)	140a	3.44 N	74.55 W
Prado Res., Ca. (prä'dō)	117a	33.45 N	117.40 W
Prados, Braz. (prá'dôs)	139a	21.05 S	44.04 W
Prague, see Praha			
Praha (Prague), Czech. (prä'hȧ) (präg)	164	59.05 N	14.30 E
Praia, C. V. (prä'yȧ)	220b	15.00 N	23.30 W
Praia Funda, Ponta da (Pt.), Braz. (pôn'tä-dȧ-prä'yȧ-fōō'n-dä)	142b	23.04 S	43.34 W
Prairie du Chien, Wi. (prā'rĭ dōō shēn')	113	43.02 N	91.10 W
Prairie Grove, Can. (prâr'ĭ grōv)	93f	49.48 N	96.57 W
Prairie Island Ind. Res., Mn.	113	44.42 N	92.32 W
Prairies, R. des, Can. (rē-vyâr' dā prâ-rē')	93a	45.40 N	73.34 W
Pratas (Dongsha Dao) (I.), China (dôŋ-shä dou)	199	20.40 N	116.30 E
Prato, It. (prä'tō)	170	43.53 N	11.03 E
Pratt, Ks. (prăt)	120	37.37 N	98.43 W
Prattville, Al. (prăt'vĭl)	124	32.28 N	86.27 W
Pravdinsk, Sov. Un.	163	54.26 N	20.11 E
Pravdinskiy, Sov. Un. (pràv-dĕn'skĭ)	180b	56.03 N	37.52 E
Pravia, Sp. (prä'vē-ä)	168	43.30 N	6.08 W
Pregolya (R.), Sov. Un. (prĕ-gô'lă)	163	54.37 N	20.50 E
Premont, Tx. (prē-mŏnt')	122	27.20 N	98.07 W
Prenzlau, G.D.R. (prĕnts'lou)	164	53.19 N	13.52 E
Přerov, Czech. (przhě'rôf)	165	49.28 N	17.28 E
Presa Aleman (L.), Mex. (prä'sä-lĕ-mȧ'n)	129	18.20 N	96.35 W
Presa de Infiernillo (Res.), Mex.	129	18.50 N	101.50 W
Prescot, Eng. (prĕs'kŭt)	154	53.25 N	2.48 W
Prescott, Az. (prĕs'kŏt)	119	34.30 N	112.30 W
Prescott, Ar.	121	33.47 N	93.23 W
Prescott, Can. (prĕs'kŭt)	109	44.45 N	75.35 W
Prescott, Wi. (prĕs'kŏt)	117g	44.45 N	92.48 W
Presho, SD (prĕsh'ô)	112	43.56 N	100.04 W
Presidencia Roque Sáenz Peña, Arg. (prĕ-sē-dĕ'n-sēä-rô'kĕ-sä'ĕnz-pĕ'n-yä)	142	26.52 S	60.15 W
Presidente Epitácio, Braz. (prā-sē-dĕn'tĕ ā-pē-tä'syōō)	141	21.56 S	52.01 W
Presidio, Tx. (prĕ-sĭ'dĭ-ō)	122	29.33 N	104.23 W
Presidio, Rio del (R.), Mex. (rē'ō-dĕl-prĕ-sē'dyô)	128	23.54 N	105.44 W
Prešov, Czech. (prĕ'shôf)	165	49.00 N	21.18 E
Prespa, L., Alb.-Yugo. (prĕs'pä)	171	40.49 N	20.50 E
Prespuntal (R.), Ven. (prĕs-pōōn-täl')	141b	9.55 N	64.32 W
Presque Isle, Me. (prĕsk'ēl')	102	46.41 N	68.03 W
Pressbaum, Aus.	155e	48.12 N	16.06 E
Prestea, Ghana	224	5.27 N	2.08 W
Preston, Eng. (prĕs'tŭn)	142	53.46 N	2.42 W
Preston, Id. (pres'tŭn)	115	42.05 N	111.54 W
Preston, Mn. (prĕs'tŭn)	113	43.42 N	92.06 W
Preston, Wa.	116a	47.31 N	121.56 W
Prestonburg, Ky. (prĕs'tŭn-bûrg)	108	37.35 N	82.50 W
Prestwich, Eng. (prĕst'wĭch)	142	53.32 N	2.17 W
Pretoria, S. Afr. (prē-tō'rĭ-ȧ)	223b	25.43 S	28.16 E
Pretoria North, S. Afr. (prē-tō'rĭ-ȧ nōōrd)	223b	25.41 S	28.11 E
Préveza, Grc. (prĕ'vȧ-zä)	171	38.58 N	20.44 E
Pribilof (Is.), Ak. (prĭ'bĭ-lof)	105	57.00 N	169.20 W

PLACE (Pronunciation)	PAGE	Lat. °'	Long. °'
Priboj, Yugo. (prē'boi)	171	43.33 N	19.33 E
Price, Ut. (prīs)	119	39.35 N	110.50 W
Price (R.), Ut.	119	39.21 N	110.35 W
Priddis, Can. (prĭd'dĭs)	93e	50.53 N	114.20 W
Priddis Cr., Can.	93e	50.56 N	114.32 W
Priego, Sp. (prē-ā'gō)	168	37.27 N	4.13 W
Prienai, Sov. Un. (prē-ĕn'ī)	163	54.38 N	23.56 E
Prieska, S. Afr. (prē-ĕs'kȧ)	222	29.40 S	22.50 E
Priest L., Id. (prēst)	114	48.30 N	116.43 W
Priest Rapids Dam, Wa.	114	46.39 N	119.55 W
Priest Rapids Res., Wa.	114	46.42 N	119.58 W
Priiskovaya, Sov. Un. (prī-ĕs'kô-vȧ-yȧ)	180a	60.50 N	58.55 E
Prijedor, Yugo. (prē'yĕ-dôr)	170	44.58 N	16.43 E
Prijepolje, Yugo. (prē'yĕ-pô'lyĕ)	171	43.22 N	19.41 E
Prilep, Yugo. (prē'lĕp)	171	41.20 N	21.35 E
Priluki, Sov. Un. (prē-lōō'kē)	173	50.36 N	32.21 E
Primorsk, Sov. Un. (prē-môrsk')	163	60.24 N	28.35 E
Primorsko-Akhtarskaya, Sov. Un. (prē-môr'skô äĸ-tär'skĭ-ĕ)	173	46.03 N	38.09 E
Primrose, S. Afr.	223b	26.11 S	28.11 E
Primrose L., Can.	98	54.55 N	109.45 W
Prince Albert, Can. (prĭns ăl'bẽrt)	98	53.12 N	105.46 W
Prince Albert Natl. Park, Can.	94	54.10 N	105.25 W
Prince Albert Sd., Can.	95	70.23 N	116.57 W
Prince Charles I., Can. (chärlz)	95	67.41 N	74.10 W
Prince Edward I. (Prov.), Can.	95	46.45 N	63.10 W
Prince Edward Is., S. Afr.	228	46.36 S	37.57 E
Prince Edward Natl. Park, Can. (ĕd'wẽrd)	102	46.33 N	63.35 W
Prince Edward Pen., Can.	109	44.00 N	77.15 W
Prince Frederick, Md. (prĭnce frĕdĕrĭk)	110e	38.33 N	76.35 W
Prince George, Can. (jôrj)	96	53.51 N	122.57 W
Prince of Wales (I.), Ak.	96	55.47 N	132.50 W
Prince of Wales (I.), Austl.	211	10.47 S	142.15 E
Prince of Wales, C., Ak. (wālz)	105	65.48 N	169.08 W
Prince Rupert, Can. (roo'pẽrt)	96	54.19 N	130.19 W
Princes Risborough, Eng. (prĭns'ĕz rĭz'brŭ)	154b	51.41 N	0.51 W
Princess Charlotte B., Austl. (shär'lŏt)	211	13.45 S	144.15 E
Princess Martha Coast, Ant. (mär'thȧ)	228	72.00 S	5.00 W
Princess Royal Chan., Can. (roi'ăl)	96	53.10 N	128.37 W
Princess Royal I., Can.	96	52.57 N	128.49 W
Princeton, Can. (prĭns'tŭn)	97	49.27 N	120.31 W
Princeton, Il.	108	41.20 N	89.25 W
Princeton, In.	108	38.20 N	87.35 W
Princeton, Ky.	124	37.07 N	87.52 W
Princeton, Mi.	113	46.16 N	87.33 W
Princeton, Mn.	113	45.34 N	93.36 W
Princeton, Mo.	121	40.23 N	93.34 W
Princeton, NJ	110a	40.21 N	74.40 W
Princeton, WV	125	37.21 N	81.05 W
Princeton, Wi.	113	43.50 N	89.09 W
Prince William Sd., Ak. (wĭl'yăm)	105	60.40 N	147.10 W
Príncipe (I.), Afr. (prēn'sē-pĕ)	226	1.37 N	7.25 E
Principe Chan., Can. (prĭn'sĭ-pē)	96	53.28 N	129.45 W
Prineville, Or. (prīn'vĭl)	114	44.17 N	120.48 W
Prineville Res., Or.	114	44.07 N	120.45 W
Prinzapolca, Nic. (prēn-zä-pōl'kä)	131	13.18 N	83.35 W
Prinzapolca R., Nic.	131	13.23 N	84.23 W
Prior Lake, Mn. (prī'ẽr)	117g	44.43 N	93.26 W
Priozërsk, Sov. Un. (prĭ-ô'zĕrsk)	163	61.03 N	30.08 E
Pripyat (Pripet) (R.), Sov. Un. (prē'pyät)	177	51.50 N	29.45 E
Pripyat Marshes, see Poles'ye			
Priština, Yugo. (prēsh'tĭ-nä)	171	42.39 N	21.12 E
Pritchard, Al. (prĭt'chârd)	124	30.44 N	87.04 W
Pritzwalk, G.D.R. (prēts'välk)	164	53.09 N	12.12 E
Privas, Fr. (prē-väs')	166	44.44 N	4.37 E
Privol'noye, Sov. Un. (prē'vôl-nô-yĕ)	173	47.30 N	32.21 E
Prizren, Yugo. (prē'zrĕn)	171	42.11 N	20.45 E
Procida, It. (prô'chē-dä)	169c	40.31 N	14.02 E
Procida, I. di, It.	169c	40.32 N	13.57 E
Proctor, Mn. (prŏk'tẽr)	117h	46.45 N	92.14 W
Proctor, Vt.	109	43.40 N	73.00 W
Proebstel, Wa. (prōb'stĕl)	116c	45.40 N	122.29 W
Proenca-a-Nova, Port. (prô-ān'sȧ-ä-nō'vȧ)	168	39.44 N	7.55 W
Progreso, Hond. (prô-grĕ'sô)	130	15.28 N	87.49 W
Progreso, Mex. (prô-grā'sō)	129	21.14 N	89.39 W
Progreso, Mex.	122	27.29 N	101.05 W
Prokop'yevsk, Sov. Un.	178	53.52 N	86.38 E
Prokuplje, Yugo. (prô'kōōp'l-yĕ)	171	43.16 N	21.40 E
Prome (Pye), Bur.	202	18.46 N	95.15 E
Pronya (R.), Sov. Un. (prô'nyä)	172	54.08 N	30.58 E
Pronya (R.), Sov. Un.	172	54.08 N	39.30 E
Propriá, Braz. (prō-prē-ä')	141	10.17 S	36.47 W
Prospect, Ky. (prŏs'pĕkt)	111h	38.21 N	85.36 W
Prospect Park, Pa. (prŏs'pĕkt pärk)	110f	39.53 N	75.18 W
Prosser, Wa. (prŏs'ẽr)	114	46.10 N	119.46 W
Prostějov, Czech. (prôs'tyĕ-yôf)	165	49.28 N	17.08 E
Protection (I.), Wa. (prō-tĕk'shŭn)	116a	48.07 N	122.56 W
Protoka (R.), Sov. Un. (prôt'ô-kȧ)	172	55.00 N	36.42 E
Provadiya, Bul. (prō-väd'ē-yȧ)	171	43.13 N	27.28 E
Providence, Ky. (prŏv'ĭ-dĕns)	108	37.25 N	87.45 W
Providence, RI	110b	41.50 N	71.23 W
Providence, Ut.	115	41.42 N	111.50 W
Providencia, Isla de (I.), Col.	131	13.21 N	80.55 W
Providenciales (I.), Turks & Caicos Is. (prō-vē-dĕn-sē-ä'lâs) (prō-vĭ-dĕn'shȧlz)	123	21.50 N	72.15 W
Provideniya, Sov. Un. (prô-vĭ-dä'nĭ-yȧ)	105	64.30 N	172.54 W
Provincetown, Ma.	109	42.03 N	70.11 W
Provo, Ut. (prō'vō)	119	40.15 N	111.40 W
Prozor, Yugo. (prô'zôr)	170	43.48 N	17.59 E
Prudence I., RI (prōō'dĕns)	110b	41.38 N	71.20 W
Prudhoe B., Ak.	105	70.40 N	147.25 W
Prudnik, Pol. (prōōd'nĭk)	165	50.19 N	17.34 E

PLACE (Pronunciation)	PAGE	Lat. °'	Long. °'
Prussia (Reg.), G.D.R. (prŭsh'ȧ)	164	50.43 N	8.35 E
Pruszków, Pol. (prōōsh'kōōf)	165	52.09 N	20.50 E
Prut (R.), Sov. Un. (prōōt)	173	48.05 N	27.07 E
Pryor, Ok. (prī'ẽr)	121	36.16 N	95.19 W
Prypeć (R.), Sov. Un.	177	51.50 N	25.35 E
Przasnysz, Pol.	165	51.05 N	19.53 E
Przemyśl, Pol. (pzhĕ'mĭsh'l)	165	49.47 N	22.45 E
Przheval'sk, Sov. Un. (p'r-zhĭ-välsk')	178	42.25 N	78.18 E
Psará (I.), Grc. (psä'rȧ)	171	38.39 N	25.26 E
Psël (R.), Sov. Un. (psĕl)	173	49.45 N	33.42 E
Pskov, Sov. Un. (pskôf)	172	57.48 N	28.19 E
Pskov (Oblast), Sov. Un.	172	57.33 N	29.05 E
Pskovskoye Ozero (L.), Sov. Un. (p'skôv'skô'yĕ ôzĕ-rô)	172	58.05 N	28.15 E
Pitch' (R.), Sov. Un. (p'tĕch)	172	53.17 N	28.16 E
Ptuj, Yugo. (ptōō'ē)	170	46.24 N	15.54 E
Pucheng, China (pōō'chĕng')	199	28.02 N	118.25 E
Pucheng, China (pōō-chuŋ)	196	35.43 N	115.22 E
Puck, Pol. (pōōtsk)	165	54.43 N	18.23 E
Pudog, China	194	33.29 N	79.26 E
Pudozh, Sov. Un. (pōō'dôzh)	176	61.50 N	36.50 E
Puebla, Mex. (pwā'blä)	128	19.02 N	98.11 W
Puebla (State), Mex.	128	19.00 N	97.45 W
Puebla de Don Fadrique, Sp. (pwĕ'blä dā dōn fä-drē'kā)	168	37.55 N	2.55 W
Pueblo, Co. (pwā'blō)	120	38.15 N	104.36 W
Pueblo Nuevo, Mex. (nwā'vô)	128	23.23 N	105.21 W
Pueblo Viejo, Mex. (vyā'hô)	129	17.23 N	93.46 W
Puente Alto, Chile (pwĕ'n-tĕ äl'tô)	139b	33.36 S	70.34 W
Puenteareas, Sp. (pwĕn-tä-ä-rā'äs)	168	42.09 N	8.23 W
Puentedeume, Sp. (pwĕn-tȧ-dhȧ-ōō'mȧ)	168	43.28 N	8.09 W
Puente-Genil, Sp. (pwĕn'tȧ-hȧ-nēl')	168	37.25 N	4.18 W
Puerco (R.), NM (pwĕr'kō)	119	35.15 N	107.05 W
Puerto Aisén, Chile (pwĕ'r-tō ä'y-sĕ'n)	142	45.28 S	72.44 W
Puerto Angel, Mex. (pwĕ'r-tō äŋ'hăl)	129	15.42 N	96.32 W
Puerto Armuelles, Pan. (pwe'r-tō är-mōō-ā'lyās)	131	8.18 N	82.52 W
Puerto Barrios, Guat. (pwĕ'r-tō bär'rē-ōs)	130	15.43 N	88.36 W
Puerto Bermúdez, Peru (pwĕ'r-tō bĕr-mōō'dăz)	140	10.17 S	74.57 W
Puerto Berrío, Col. (pwĕ'r-tō bĕr-rē'ō)	140a	6.29 N	74.27 W
Puerto Cabello, Ven. (pwĕ'r-tō kä-bĕl'yō)	141b	10.28 N	68.01 W
Puerto Cabezas, Nic. (pwĕ'r-tō kä-bā'zäs)	131	14.01 N	83.26 W
Puerto Casado, Par. (pwĕ'r-tō kä-sä'dō)	142	22.16 S	57.57 W
Puerto Castilla, Hond. (pwĕ'r-tō käs-tēl'yō)	130	16.01 N	86.01 W
Puerto Chicama, Peru (pwĕ'r-tō chē-kä'mä)	140	7.46 S	79.18 W
Puerto Columbia, Col. (pwĕr'tō kô-lôm'bē-ȧ)	140	11.08 N	75.09 W
Puerto Cortés, C. R. (pwĕ'r-tō kôr-tās')	131	9.00 N	83.37 W
Puerto Cortés, Hond. (pwĕ'r-tō kôr-tās')	130	15.48 N	87.57 W
Puerto Cumarebo, Ven. (pwĕ'r-tō kōō-mä-rĕ'bô)	140	11.25 N	69.17 W
Puerto de Luna, NM (pwĕr'tō dā lōō'nä)	120	34.49 N	104.36 W
Puerto de Nutrias, Ven. (pwĕ'r-tō dĕ nōō-trē-äs')	140	8.02 N	69.19 W
Puerto Deseado, Arg. (pwĕ'r-tō dā-sȧ-ä'dhō)	142	47.38 S	66.00 W
Puerto de Somport (P.), Fr.-Sp.	169	42.51 N	0.25 W
Puerto Eten, Peru (pwĕ'r-tō ĕ-tĕ'n)	140	6.59 S	79.51 W
Puerto Jimenez, C. R. (pwĕ'r-tō ĸē-mĕ'nĕz)	131	8.35 N	83.23 W
Puerto La Cruz, Ven. (pwĕ'r-tō lä krōō'z)	141b	10.14 N	64.38 W
Puertollano, Sp. (pwĕ-tôl-yä'nō)	168	38.41 N	4.05 W
Puerto Madryn, Arg. (pwĕ'r-tō mä-drĕn')	142	42.45 S	65.01 W
Puerto Maldonado, Peru (pwĕ'r-tō mäl-dō-nä'dô)	140	12.43 S	69.01 W
Puerto Mexico, see Coatzacoalcos			
Puerto Miniso, Mex. (pwĕ'r-tō mē-nē'sô)	128	16.06 N	98.02 W
Puerto Montt, Chile (pwĕ'r-tō mô'nt)	142	41.29 S	73.00 W
Puerto Natales, Chile (pwĕ'r-tō nä-tá'lĕs)	142	51.48 S	72.01 W
Puerto Niño, Col. (pwĕ'r-tō nē'n-yô)	140a	5.57 N	74.36 W
Puerto Padre, Cuba (pwĕ'r-tō pä'drä)	132	21.10 N	76.40 W
Puerto Peñasco, Mex. (pwĕ'r-tō pĕn-yä's-kô)	126	31.39 N	113.15 W
Puerto Pinasco, Par. (pwĕ'r-tō pē-nä's-kô)	142	22.31 S	57.50 W
Puerto Píritu, Ven. (pwĕ'r-tō pē'rē-tōō)	141b	10.05 N	65.04 W
Puerto Plata, Dom. Rep. (pwĕ'r-tô plä'tä)	133	19.50 N	70.40 W
Puerto Princesa, Phil. (pwĕr-tô prēn-sā'sä)	202	9.45 N	118.41 E
Puerto Rico, N. A. (pwĕr'tô rē'kō)	127	18.16 N	66.50 W
Puerto Rico Trench, N. A.	127	19.45 N	66.30 W
Puerto Salgar, Col. (pwĕ'r-tō säl-gär')	140a	5.30 N	74.39 W
Puerto Santa Cruz, Arg. (pwĕ'r-tō sän'tä krōōz')	142	50.04 S	68.32 W
Puerto Suárez, Bol. (pwĕ'r-tō swä'räz)	141	18.55 S	57.39 W
Puerto Tejada, Col. (pwĕ'r-tō tĕ-ĸä'dä)	140a	3.13 N	76.23 W
Puerto Vallarta, Mex. (pwĕ'r-tō väl-yär'tä)	128	20.36 N	105.13 W

ng-sing; ŋ-baŋk; ɴ-nasalized n; nŏd; cŏmmit; ōld; ôbey; ôrder; oi-boil; fōōd; fŏŏt; ou-out; s-soft; sh-dish; th-thin; pūre; ûnite; ûrn; stŭd; circŭs; ü-as in French tu; '-indeterminate vowel.

PLACE (Pronunciation)	PAGE	Lat. °′	Long. °′
Puerto Varas, Chile (pwĕ′r-tō vä′räs)	142	41.16 S	73.03 W
Puerto Wilches, Col. (pwĕ′r-tō vēl′c-hĕs)	140	7.19 N	73.54 W
Pugachëv, Sov. Un. (po͞o′gȧ-chyôf)	177	52.00 N	48.40 E
Puget, Wa. (pū′jĕt)	116c	46.10 N	123.23 W
Puget Sd., Wa.	114	47.49 N	122.26 W
Puglia (Apulia) (Reg.), It. (po͞o′lyä) (ä-po͞o′lyä)	170	41.13 N	16.10 E
Pukaskwa Natl. Pk., Can.	100	48.22 N	85.55 W
Pukeashun Mtn., Can.	97	51.12 N	119.14 W
Pukin (R.), Mala.	189b	2.53 N	102.54 E
Pula, Yugo. (po͞o′lä)	170	44.52 N	13.55 E
Pulacayo, Bol. (po͞o-lä-kä′yō)	140	20.12 S	66.33 W
Pulaski, Tn. (pů-lăs′kĭ)	124	35.11 N	87.03 W
Pulaski, Va.	125	37.00 N	81.45 W
Pulawy, Pol. (po͞o-wä′vĕ)	165	51.24 N	21.59 E
Pulizat (R.), India	190	13.58 N	79.52 E
Pullman, Wa. (po͝ol′măn)	114	46.44 N	117.10 W
Pulog (Mtn.), Phil. (po͞o′lôg)	203a	16.38 N	120.53 E
Pultusk, Pol. (po͝ol′to͞osk)	156	52.40 N	21.09 E
Puma Yumco (L.), China (po͞o-mä yo͞om-tswo)	190	28.30 N	90.10 E
Pumpkin Cr., Mt. (pŭmp′kĭn)	115	45.47 N	105.35 W
Punakha, Bhu. (po͞o-nŭk′ŭ)	190	27.45 N	89.59 E
Punata, Bol. (po͞o-nä′tä)	140	17.43 S	65.43 W
Pune, India	190	18.38 N	73.53 E
Punjab (State), India (pŭn′jäb′)	190	31.00 N	75.30 E
Puno, Peru (po͞o′nô)	140	15.58 S	7.02 W
Punta Arenas, Chile (po͞o′n-tä-rĕ′näs)	142	53.09 S	70.48 W
Punta de Piedras, Ven. (po͞o′n-tä dĕ pyĕ′dräs)	141b	10.54 N	64.06 W
Punta Gorda, Belize (po͞on′tä gôr′dä)	130	16.07 N	88.50 W
Punta Gorda, Fl. (pŭn′tȧ gôr′dȧ)	125a	26.55 N	82.02 W
Punta Gorda, Rio (R.), Nic. (po͞o′n-tä gô′r-dä)	131	11.34 N	84.13 W
Punta Indio, Can., Arg. (po͞o′n-tä- ē′n-dyô)	139c	34.56 S	57.20 W
Puntarenas, C. R. (po͞ont-ä-rā′näs)	131	9.59 N	84.49 W
Punto Fijo, Ven. (po͞o′n-tô fē′ĸô)	140	11.48 N	70.14 W
Punxsutawney, Pa. (pŭnk-sŭ-tô′nē)	109	40.55 N	79.00 W
Puquio, Peru (po͞o′kyô)	140	14.43 S	74.02 W
Pur (R.), Sov. Un.	178	65.30 N	77.30 E
Purcell, Ok. (pûr-sĕl′)	121	35.01 N	97.22 W
Purcell Mts., Can. (pûr-sĕl′)	97	50.00 N	116.30 W
Purdy, Wa. (pûr′dē)	116a	47.23 N	122.37 W
Purépero, Mex. (po͞o-rā′pā-rō)	128	19.56 N	102.02 W
Purgatoire (R.), Colo. (pûr-gȧ-twär′)	120	37.25 N	103.53 W
Puri, India (po͞o′rē)	190	19.52 N	85.51 E
Purial, Sierra de (Mts.), Cuba (sē-ĕ′r-rä-dĕ-po͞o-rē-äl′)	133	20.15 N	74.40 W
Purificacion, Col. (po͞o-rē-fē-kä-syōn′)	140a	3.52 N	74.54 W
Purificación, Mex. (po͞o-rē-fē-kä-syô′n)	128	19.44 N	104.38 W
Purificación (R.), Mex.	128	19.30 N	104.54 W
Purkersdorf, Aus.	155e	48.13 N	16.11 E
Puruandiro, Mex. (po͞o-ro͞o-än′dē-rō)	128	20.04 N	101.33 W
Purús (R.), Braz. (po͞o-ro͞o′s)	140	6.45 S	64.34 W
Pusan, Kor.	200	35.08 N	129.05 E
Pushkin, Sov. Un. (po͞osh′kĭn)	180c	59.43 N	30.25 E
Pushkino, Sov. Un. (po͞osh′kē-nô)	180b	56.01 N	37.51 E
Pustoshka, Sov. Un. (pûs-tôsh′kȧ)	172	56.20 N	29.33 E
Pustunich, Mex. (po͞os-to͞o′nēch)	129	19.10 N	90.29 W
Putaendo, Chile (po͞o-tä-ĕn-dô)	139b	32.37 S	70.42 W
Puteaux, Fr. (pü-tō′)	167b	48.52 N	2.12 E
Putfontein, S. Afr. (po͝ot′fŏn-tān)	223b	26.08 S	28.24 E
Putian, China (po͞o-tĭĕn)	199	25.40 N	119.02 E
Putivl′, Sov. Un. (po͞o-tēv′l′)	173	51.22 N	33.24 E
Putla de Guerrero, Mex. (po͞o′tlä-dĕ-gĕr-rĕ′rō)	129	17.03 N	97.55 W
Putnam, Ct. (pŭt′nȧm)	109	41.55 N	71.55 W
Putorana, Gory (Mts.), Sov. Un.	178	68.45 N	93.15 E
Puttalam, Sri Lanka	191	8.02 N	79.44 E
Putumayo (R.), Col.-Peru (po͞o-to͞o-mä′yō)	140	1.02 S	73.50 W
Putung, Tandjung (C.), Indon.	202	3.35 S	111.50 E
Puulavesi (L.), Fin.	163	61.49 N	27.10 E
Puyallup, Wa. (pū-ăl′ŭp)	116a	47.12 N	122.18 W
Puyang, China (po͞o-yäŋ)	196	35.42 N	114.58 E
Pweto, Zaire (pwä′tō)	222	8.29 S	28.58 E
Pyasina (R.), Sov. Un. (pyä-sē′nȧ)	178	72.45 N	87.37 E
Pyatigorsk, Sov. Un. (pyȧ-tē-gôrsk′)	177	44.00 N	43.00 E
Pye, see Prome			
Pyhäjärvi (L.), Fin.	163	60.57 N	21.50 E
Pyinmana, Bur. (pyēn-mä′nŭ)	194	19.47 N	96.15 E
Pymatuning Res., Pa. (pī-mȧ-tŭn′ĭng)	108	41.40 N	80.30 W
Pyŏnggang, Kor. (pyŭng′gäng′)	200	38.21 N	127.18 E
P′yŏngyang, Kor.	200	39.03 N	125.48 E
Pyramid (L.), Nv. (pĭ′rȧ-mĭd)	118	40.02 N	119.50 W
Pyramid Lake Ind. Res., Nv.	118	40.17 N	119.52 W
Pyramids, Egypt	219b	29.53 N	31.10 E
Pyrenees (Mts.), Fr.-Sp. (pĭr-e-nēz′)	169	43.00 N	0.05 E
Pyrzyce, Pol. (pĕzhĭ′tsĕ)	164	53.09 N	14.53 E

Q

PLACE (Pronunciation)	PAGE	Lat. °′	Long. °′
Qal′at Bishah, Sau. Ar.	192	20.01 N	42.30 E
Qallābāt, Sud.	221	12.55 N	36.12 E
Quamdo, China (chyäm-dwō)	194	31.06 N	96.30 E
Qana el Suweis (Suez Can.), Egypt	219c	30.53 N	32.21 E
Qandahār, Afg.	193	31.43 N	65.58 E
Qārah (Oasis), Egypt	159	29.28 N	26.29 E
Qareh Sū (R.), Iran	177	38.50 N	47.10 E
Qarqan (R.), China	194	38.55 N	87.15 E
Qarqan, see Qiemo			
Qārūn, Birket (L.) Egypt	219b	29.34 N	30.34 E
Qasr al-Burayqah, Libya	221	30.25 N	19.20 E
Qasr al-Farāfirah, Egypt	221	27.04 N	28.13 E
Qaşr Banī Walīd, Libya	221	31.45 N	14.04 E
Qatar, Asia (kä′tȧr)	188	25.00 N	52.45 E
Qaţţārah, Munkhafaḑ (Dep.), Egypt	221	30.07 N	27.30 E
Qāyen, Iran	192	33.45 N	59.08 E
Qeshm, Iran	192	26.51 N	56.10 E
Qeshm (I.), Iran	192	26.52 N	56.15 E
Qezel Owzan, Iran	192	37.00 N	48.23 E
Qezel Owzan, (R.), Iran	177	37.00 N	47.35 E
Qeẓi′ot, Egypt-Isr.	189a	30.53 N	34.28 E
Qianwei, China (chyĕn-wā)	196	40.11 N	120.05 E
Qi′anzhen, China (chyē-än-jŭn)	196	32.16 N	120.59 E
Qibao, China (chyē-bou)	197b	31.06 N	121.16 E
Qiblīyah, Jabal al Jalālat al (Plat.), Egypt	189a	28.49 N	32.21 E
Qiemo (Qargan), China (chyär-chyän)	194	38.02 N	85.16 E
Qifṭ, Egypt (kĕft)	219b	25.58 N	32.52 E
Qijiang, China (chyē-jyäŋ)	199	29.05 N	106.40 E
Qikou, China (chyē-kō)	196	38.37 N	117.33 E
Qilian Shan (Mts.), China (chyē-lĭĕn shän)	194	38.43 N	98.00 E
Qiliping, China (chyē-lē-pĭŋ)	196	31.28 N	114.41 E
Qinā, Egypt (kä′nȧ)	219b	26.10 N	32.48 E
Qinā, Wādī, Egypt	219b	26.38 N	32.53 E
Qindao (Tsingtao), China (chyĭn-dou)	196	36.05 N	120.10 E
Qing′an, China (chyĭŋ-än)	198	46.50 N	127.30 E
Qingcheng, China (chyĭŋ-chŭŋ)	196	37.12 N	117.43 E
Qingfeng, China (chyĭŋ-fŭŋ)	196	35.52 N	115.05 E
Qinghai (Prov.), China (chyĭŋ-hī)	194	36.14 N	95.30 E
Qinghai Hu (L.), **see Koko Nor**			
Qinghe, China (chyĭŋ-hŭ)	198a	40.08 N	116.16 E
Qingjiang, China (chyĭŋ-jyäŋ)	199	28.00 N	115.30 E
Qingjiang, China	196	33.34 N	118.58 E
Qingliu, China (chyĭŋ-lĭō)	199	26.15 N	116.50 E
Qingningsi, China (chyĭŋ-nĭŋ-sz)	197b	31.16 N	121.33 E
Qingping, China (chyĭŋ-pĭŋ)	196	36.46 N	116.03 E
Qingpu, China (chyĭŋ-po͞o)	197b	31.08 N	121.06 E
Qing Xian, China (chyĭŋ shyĕn)	196	38.37 N	116.48 E
Qingyang, China (chyĭŋ-yäŋ)	198	36.02 N	107.42 E
Qingyuan, China (chyĭŋ-yôän)	199	23.43 N	113.10 E
Qingyuan, China	198	42.05 N	125.00 E
Qingyun, China (chyĭŋ-yo͞on)	196	37.52 N	117.26 E
Qingyundian, China (chĭŋ-yo͞on-dĭĕn)	198a	39.41 N	116.31 E
Qinhuangdao, China (chyĭn-huaŋ-dou)	196	39.57 N	119.34 E
Qin Ling (Mts.), China (chyĭn lĭŋ)	189	33.25 N	108.58 E
Qin Ling (Mts.), China	198	33.35 N	108.25 E
Qinyang, China (chyĭn-yäŋ)	198	35.00 N	112.55 E
Qinzhou, China (chyĭn-jō)	199	22.00 N	108.35 E
Qionghai, China (chyôŋ-hī)	199	19.10 N	110.28 E
Qiqian, China (chyē-chyĕn)	195	52.23 N	121.04 E
Qiqihar, see Tsitsihar			
Qiryat Gat, Isr.	189a	31.38 N	34.36 E
Qiryat Shemona, Isr.	189a	33.12 N	35.34 E
Qitai, China (chyē-tī)	194	44.07 N	89.04 E
Qiu Xian, China (chyô shyĕn)	196	36.43 N	115.13 E
Qi Xian, China (chyē-shyĕn)	196	34.33 N	114.47 E
Qi Xian, China	196	35.36 N	114.13 E
Qiyang, China (chyē-yäŋ)	199	26.40 N	112.00 E
Qom, Iran	192	34.28 N	50.53 E
Quabbin Res., Ma. (kwā′bĭn)	109	42.20 N	72.10 W
Quachita, L., Ar. (kwä shĭ′tô)	121	34.47 N	93.37 W
Quadra, Boca de, Str., Ak. (bŏk′ȧ dĕ kwŏd′rȧ)	96	55.08 N	130.50 W
Quadra I., Can.	96	50.08 N	125.16 W
Quakertown, Pa. (kwā′kĕr-toun)	109	40.30 N	75.20 W
Quanah, Tx. (kwä′nȧ)	120	34.19 N	99.43 W
Quang Ngai, Viet. (kwäng n′gä′ē)	199	15.05 N	108.58 E
Quang Ngai (Mtn.), Viet.	199	15.10 N	108.20 E
Quanjiao, China (chyuän-jyou)	196	32.06 N	118.17 E
Quanzhou, China (chyuän-jō)	199	24.58 N	118.40 E
Quanzhou, China	199	25.58 N	111.02 E
Qu′Appelle Dam, Can.	98	51.00 N	106.25 W
Qu′Appelle (R.), Can.	98	50.35 N	103.25 W
Quartu Sant′ Elena It. (kwär-to͞o′ sänt a′lā-nä)	170	39.16 N	9.12 E
Quartzsite, Az.	119	33.40 N	114.13 W
Quatsino Sd, Can. (kwŏt-sē′nō)	96	50.25 N	128.10 W
Qudi, China	196	37.06 N	117.15 E
Québec, Can. (kwē-bĕk′) (kā-bĕk′)	93b	46.49 N	71.13 W
Quebec (Prov.), Can.	95	51.07 N	70.25 W
Quedlinburg, G.D.R. (kvĕd′lēn-bo͝orgh)	164	51.45 N	11.10 E
Queen Bess, Mt., Can.	96	51.16 N	124.34 W
Queen Charlotte Is., Can. (kwēn shär′lŏt)	96	53.30 N	132.25 W
Queen Charlotte Ra., Can.	96	53.00 N	132.00 W
Queen Charlotte Sd., Can.	96	51.30 N	129.30 W
Queen Charlotte Str., Can. (strāt)	96	50.40 N	127.25 W
Queen Elizabeth Is., Can. (ē-lĭz′ȧ-bĕth)	92	78.20 N	110.00 W
Queen Maud G., Can. (mäd)	94	68.27 N	102.55 W
Queen Maud Land, Ant.	228	75.00 S	10.00 E
Queen Maud Mts., Ant.	228	85.00 S	179.00 W
Queens Chan., Austl. (kwēnz)	210	14.25 S	129.10 E
Queenscliff, Austl.	207a	38.16 S	144.39 E
Queensland (state), Austl. (kwēnz′lȧnd)	211	22.45 S	141.01 E
Queenstown, Austl. (kwēnz′toun)	212	42.00 S	145.40 E
Queenstown, S. Afr.	223c	31.54 S	26.53 E
Queimados, Braz. (kā-mȧ′dôs)	142b	22.42 S	43.34 W
Quela, Ang.	226	9.16 S	17.02 E
Quelimane, Moz. (kā-lē-mä′nĕ)	212	17.48 S	37.05 E
Quelpart (I.), **see Cheju**			
Quemado de Güines, Cuba (kā-mä′dhä-dē-gwē′nĕs)	132	22.45 N	80.20 W
Quemoy (Chinmen), Taiwan	199	24.30 N	118.20 E
Quemoy (I.), Taiwan	199	24.35 N	118.45 E
Quepos, C.R. (kā′pôs)	131	9.26 N	84.10 W
Quepos, Punta (Pt.), C.R. (po͞o′n-tä)	131	9.23 N	84.20 W
Que Que, Zimb. (kwē′kwē)	222	18.49 S	29.45 E
Querétaro, Mex. (kå-rā′tä-rō)	128	20.37 N	100.25 W
Querétaro (State), Mex.	128	21.00 N	100.00 W
Quesada, Sp. (kå-sä′dhä)	168	37.51 N	3.04 W
Quesnel, Can. (kā-nĕl′)	96	52.59 N	122.30 W
Quesnel L., Can.	97	52.32 N	121.05 W
Quesnel (R.), Can.	96	52.15 N	122.00 W
Quetame, Col. (kĕ-tä′mĕ)	140a	4.20 N	73.50 W
Quetta, Pak. (kwĕt′ä)	190	30.19 N	67.01 E
Quezaltenango, Guat. (kå-zäl′tå-näŋ′gō)	130	14.50 N	91.30 W
Quezaltepeque, Guat. (kå-zäl′tå-pā′kå)	130	14.39 N	89.26 W
Quezaltepeque, Sal. (kĕ-zäl′tĕ′pĕ-kĕ)	130	13.50 N	89.17 W
Quezon City, Phil. (kā-zōn)	203a	14.40 N	121.02 E
Qufu, China (chyo͞o-fo͞o)	196	35.37 N	116.54 E
Quibdo, Col. (kēb′dō)	140a	5.42 N	76.41 W
Quiberon, Fr. (kē-bē-rôɴ′)	166	47.29 N	3.08 W
Quiçama, Parque Nacional de (Natl. Pk.), Ang.	226	10.00 S	13.25 E
Quiché, Guat. (kē-shā′)	130	15.05 N	91.08 W
Quicksborn, F.R.G. (kvēks′bōrn)	155c	53.44 N	9.54 E
Quilcene, Wa. (kwĭl-sēn′)	116a	47.50 N	122.53 W
Quilimari, Chile (kē-lē-mä′rē)	139b	32.06 S	71.28 W
Quillan, Fr. (kē-yäɴ′)	166	43.53 N	2.13 E
Quillota, Chile (kēl-yō′tä)	139b	32.52 S	71.14 W
Quilmes, Arg. (kēl′măs)	142b	34.28 S	58.16 W
Quilon, India (kwē-lōn′)	191	8.58 N	76.16 E
Quilpie, Austl. (kwĭl′pē)	212	26.34 S	149.20 E
Quilpué, Chile (kēl-po͞o ĕ′)	139b	33.03 S	71.22 W
Quimbaya, Col. (kēm-bä′yä)	140a	4.38 N	75.46 W
Quimbele, Ang.	226	6.28 S	16.13 E
Quimbonge, Ang.	226	8.36 S	18.30 E
Quimper, Fr. (kăɴ-pĕr′)	166	47.59 N	4.04 W
Quinalt R., Wa.	114	47.23 N	124.10 W
Quinault Ind. Res., Wa.	114	47.27 N	124.34 W
Quincy, Fl. (kwĭn′sē)	124	30.35 N	84.35 W
Quincy, Il.	121	39.55 N	91.23 W
Quincy, Ma.	103a	42.15 N	71.00 W
Quincy, Mi.	108	42.00 N	84.50 W
Quincy, Or.	116c	46.08 N	123.10 W
Qui-nhon, Viet. (kwĭnyôn)	202	13.51 N	109.03 E
Quinn R., Nv. (kwĭn)	114	41.42 N	117.45 W
Quintanar de la Orden, Sp. (kēn-tä-när′)	168	39.36 N	3.02 W
Quintana Roo (State), Mex. (rō′ō)	130a	19.30 N	88.30 W
Quintero, Chile (kēn-tē′rô)	139b	32.48 S	71.30 W
Quionga, Moz.	227	10.37 S	40.30 E
Quiroga, Mex. (kē-rô′gä)	128	19.39 N	101.30 W
Quiroga, Sp. (kē-rô′gä)	168	42.28 N	7.18 W
Quitman, Ga. (kwĭt′mȧn)	124	30.46 N	83.35 W
Quitman, Ms.	124	33.02 N	88.43 W
Quito, Ec. (kē′tō)	140	0.17 S	78.32 W
Quixadá, Braz. (kē-shä-dä′)	141	4.58 S	38.58 W
Qulūşanā, Egypt (ko͞o-lo͞os′nä)	219b	28.22 N	30.44 E
Qumbu, S. Afr. (ko͞om′bo͞o)	223c	31.10 S	28.48 E
Quorn, Austl. (kwôrn)	212	32.20 S	138.00 E
Qurayyah, Wādī (R.), Egypt	189a	30.08 N	34.27 E
Qūş, Egypt (ko͞os)	219b	25.53 N	32.48 E
Qutang, China (chyo͞o-täŋ)	196	32.33 N	120.07 E
Quthing, Leso.	223c	30.35 S	27.42 E
Quvea (I.), N. Cal.	211	20.43 S	166.48 E
Qu Xian, China (chyo͞o-shyĕn)	199	28.58 N	118.58 E
Qu Xian, China	199	30.40 N	106.48 E
Quzhou, China (chyoō-jō)	196	36.47 N	114.58 E
Quzvīn, Iran	192	36.10 N	49.59 E

R

PLACE (Pronunciation)	PAGE	Lat. °′	Long. °′
Raab R., Aus. (räp)	164	46.55 N	15.55 E
Raahe, Fin. (rä′ĕ)	156	64.39 N	24.22 E
Rab (I.), Yugo. (räb)	170	44.45 N	14.40 E
Raba, Indon.	202	8.32 S	118.49 E
Raba R., Hung.	165	47.28 N	17.12 E
Rabat, Mor. (rȧ-bät′)	220	33.59 N	6.47 W
Rabaul, Pap. N. Gui. (rä′boul)	203	4.15 S	152.19 E
Raccoon (R.), Ia. (ră-ko͞on′)	113	42.07 N	94.45 W
Raccoon Cay (I.), Ba.	133	22.25 N	75.50 W
Race, C., Can. (rās)	103	46.40 N	53.10 W
Rachado, C., Mala.	189b	2.26 N	101.29 E
Racibórz, Pol. (rä-chē′bo͞ozh)	165	50.06 N	18.14 E
Racine, Wi. (rȧ-sēn′)	111a	42.43 N	87.49 W
Raco, Mi. (rȧ cō)	117k	46.22 N	84.43 W
Rădăuti, Rom.′(rŭ-dŭ-o͞ots′′)	165	47.53 N	25.55 E
Radcliffe, Eng. (răd′klĭf)	154	53.34 N	2.20 W
Radevormwald, F.R.G. (rä′dĕ-fōrm-väld)	167c	51.12 N	7.22 E
Radford, Va. (răd′fērd)	125	37.06 N	81.33 W
Rādhanpur, India	190	23.57 N	71.38 E
Radium, S. Afr. (rā′dĭ-ŭm)	219d	25.06 S	28.18 E
Radom, Pol. (rä′dôm)	165	51.24 N	21.11 E
Radomir, Bul. (rä′dô-mēr)	171	42.33 N	22.58 E
Radomsko, Pol. (rä-dôm′skô)	165	51.04 N	19.27 E

PLACE (Pronunciation)	PAGE	Lat. °′	Long. °′
Radomyshl, Sov. Un. (rä-dô-mēsh′′l)	173	50.30 N	29.13 E
Radoviš, Yugo. (rä-dô-vēsh)	171	41.39 N	22.28 E
Radul′, Sov. Un. (ra′dōōl)	173	51.52 N	30.46 E
Radviliškis, Sov. Un. (rad′vē-lēsh′kēs)	163	55.49 N	23.31 E
Radwah, Jabal (Mtn.), Sau. Ar.	192	24.44 N	38.14 E
Radzyń Podlaski, Pol. (räd′zēn-y′ pŭd-lä′skĭ)	165	51.49 N	22.40 E
Raeford, NC (rā′fērd)	125	34.57 N	79.15 W
Raesfeld, F.R.G. (răz′fĕld)	167c	51.46 N	6.50 E
Raeside, Austl. (rā′sīd)	210	29.20 S	122.30 E
Rae Str., Can. (rā)	94	68.40 N	95.03 W
Rafaela, Arg. (rä-fä-ā′lä)	142	31.15 S	61.21 W
Rafah, Egypt (rä′fä)	189a	31.14 N	34.12 E
Rafaï, Cen. Afr. Rep. (rä-fī′)	221	4.59 N	23.58 E
Rafḥā, Sau. Ar.	192	29.43 N	43.13 E
Rafsanjān, Iran	192	30.45 N	56.30 E
Raft R., Id. (răft)	115	42.20 N	113.17 W
Ragay, Phil. (rä-gī′)	203a	13.49 N	122.45 E
Ragay G., Phil.	203a	13.44 N	122.38 E
Ragga, Egypt	177	36.00 N	39.00 E
Ragunda, Swe. (rä-gōōn′dä)	162	63.07 N	16.24 E
Ragusa, It. (rä-gōō′sä)	157	36.58 N	14.41 E
Ragusa, see Dubrovnik			
Rahway, NJ (rô′wā)	110a	40.37 N	74.16 W
Rāichūr, India (rä′ē-chōōr′)	191	16.23 N	77.18 E
Raigarh, India (rī′gŭr)	190	21.57 N	83.32 E
Rainbow Bridge Natl. Mon., Ut. (rān′bō)	119	37.05 N	111.00 W
Rainbow City, Pan.	126a	9.20 N	79.23 W
Rainier, Or.	116c	46.05 N	122.56 W
Rainier, Mt., Wa. (rā-nēr′)	114	46.52 N	121.46 W
Rainy (L.), Can.-Mn. (rān′ē)	99	48.43 N	94.29 W
Rainy (R.), Can.-Mn.	99	48.50 N	94.41 W
Rainy River, Can.	99	48.43 N	94.29 W
Raipur, India (rä′jŭ-bōō-rē′)	190	21.25 N	81.37 E
Raisin (R.), Mi. (rā′zĭn)	108	42.00 N	83.35 W
Raitan, NJ (rā-tăn)	110a	40.34 N	74.40 W
Rājahmundry, India (räj-ŭ-mŭn′drē)	191	17.03 N	81.51 E
Rajang (Strm.), Mala.	202	2.10 N	113.30 E
Rājapālaiyam, India	190	9.30 N	77.33 E
Rājasthān (State), India (rä′jŭs-tän)	190	31.20 N	72.00 E
Rājkot, India (räj′kôt)	190	22.20 N	70.48 E
Rājpur, India	190a	22.24 N	88.25 E
Rājshāhi, Bngl.	190	24.26 S	88.39 E
Rakhov, Sov. Un. (rä′κôf)	165	48.02 N	24.13 E
Rakh′ya, Sov. Un. (räk′ya)	180c	60.06 N	30.50 E
Rakitnoye, Sov. Un. (ra-kēt′nô-yĕ)	173	50.51 N	35.53 E
Rakovnik, Czech. (rä′kôk-nyēk)	164	50.07 N	13.45 E
Rakvere, Sov. Un. (rak′vĕ-rĕ)	172	59.22 N	26.14 E
Raleigh, NC	125	35.45 N	78.39 W
Raleigh, B., NC	125	34.50 N	76.15 W
Ram (R.), Can.	97	52.10 N	115.05 W
Rama, Nic. (rä′mä)	131	12.11 N	84.14 W
Ramallo, Arg. (rä-mä′l-yô)	139c	33.28 S	60.02 W
Ramanāthapuram, India	191	9.13 N	78.52 E
Rambouillet, Fr. (räɴ-bōō-yĕ′)	167b	48.39 N	1.49 E
Rame Hd, S. Afr.	223c	31.48 S	29.22 E
Ramenskoye, Sov. Un. (ra′mĕn-skô-yĕ)	180b	55.34 N	38.15 E
Ramlat as Sab′atayn (Reg.), Sau. Ar.	192	16.08 N	45.15 E
Ramm, Jabal (Mts.), Jordan	189a	29.37 N	35.32 E
Ramos, Mex. (rä′mōs)	128	22.46 N	101.52 W
Ramos (R.), Nig.	225	5.10 N	5.40 E
Ramos Arizpe, Mex. (ä-rēz′pā)	122	25.33 N	100.57 W
Rampart, Ak. (răm′part)	105	65.28 N	150.18 W
Rampo Mts., NJ-NY (răm′pō)	110a	41.06 N	72.12 W
Rāmpur, India (räm′pōōr)	190	28.53 N	79.03 E
Ramree I., Bur. (räm′rē′)	202	19.01 N	93.23 E
Ramsayville, Can. (răm′zē vĭl)	93c	45.23 N	75.34 W
Ramsbottom, Eng. (rămz′bŏt-ŭm)	154	53.39 N	2.20 W
Ramsey, Isle of Man (răm′zē)	160	54.20 N	4.25 W
Ramsey, NJ	110a	41.03 N	74.09 W
Ramsey L., Can.	100	47.15 N	82.16 W
Ramsgate, Eng. (rămz′′gāt)	161	51.19 N	1.20 E
Ramsjö, Swe. (räm′shû)	162	62.11 N	15.44 E
Ramu (R.), Pap. N. Gui. (rä′mōō)	203	5.35 S	145.16 E
Rancagua, Chile (rän-kä′gwä)	139b	34.10 S	70.43 W
Rance (R.), Fr. (räɴs)	166	48.17 N	2.30 W
Rānchī, India (rän′chē)	190	23.24 N	85.18 E
Rancho Boyeros, Cuba (rä′n-chô-bô-yĕ′rôs)	133a	23.00 N	82.23 W
Randallstown, Md. (răn′dalz-toun)	110e	39.22 N	76.48 W
Randers, Den. (rän′ĕrs)	162	56.28 N	10.03 E
Randfontein, S. Afr. (rănt′fŏn-tān)	223b	26.10 S	27.42 E
Randleman, NC (răn′d′l-măn)	125	35.49 N	79.50 W
Randolph, Ma. (răn′dôlf)	103a	42.10 N	71.03 W
Randolph, Ne.	112	42.22 N	97.22 W
Randolph, Vt.	109	43.55 N	72.40 W
Random I., Can. (răn′dŭm)	103	48.12 N	53.25 W
Randsfjorden (Fd.), Nor.	162	60.35 N	10.10 E
Ranérou, Senegal	224	15.18 N	13.58 W
Rangeley, Me. (ränj′lē)	102	44.56 N	70.38 W
Rangeley (L.), Me.	102	45.00 N	70.25 W
Ranger, Tx. (rān′jēr)	122	32.26 N	98.41 W
Rangia, India	190	26.32 N	91.39 E
Rangoon, Bur. (raŋ-gōōn′)	202	16.46 N	96.09 E
Rangpur, Bngl. (rŭng′pōōr)	190	25.48 N	89.19 E
Rangsang (I.), Indon. (räng′säng′)	189b	0.53 N	103.05 E
Rangsdorf, G.D.R. (rängs′dōrf)	155b	52.17 N	13.25 E
Rānīganj, India (rä-nē-gŭnj′)	190	23.40 N	87.08 E
Rankin Inlet, Can. (răŋ′kĕn)	94	62.45 N	94.27 W
Ranova (R.), Sov. Un. (rä′nô-va)	172	53.55 N	40.03 E
Ransomville, NY (răn′sum-vĭl)	111c	43.15 N	78.54 W
Rantau, Mala.	189b	2.35 N	101.58 E
Rantelkomboa, Bulu (Mtn.), Indon.	202	3.22 S	119.50 E
Rantoul, Il. (răn-tōōl′)	108	40.25 N	88.05 W
Raoyang, China (rou-yäŋ)	196	38.16 N	115.45 E
Rapallo, It. (rä-päl′lô)	170	44.21 N	9.14 E
Rapa Nui (Easter) (I.), Chile (rä′pä nōō′ē) (ēs′tēr)	205	26.50 S	109.00 W
Rapel (R.), Chile (rä-pāl′)	139b	34.05 S	71.30 W

PLACE (Pronunciation)	PAGE	Lat. °′	Long. °′
Rapid (R.), Mn. (răp′ĭd)	113	48.21 N	94.50 W
Rapid City, SD	112	44.06 N	103.14 W
Rapla, Sov. Un. (räp′la)	163	59.02 N	24.46 E
Rappahannock (R.), Va. (răp′ă-hăn′ŭk)	109	38.20 N	75.25 W
Raquette (L.), NY (răk′ĕt)	109	43.50 N	74.35 W
Rara Mazowiecka, Pol. (rä′rä mä-zō-vyĕts′kä)	165	51.46 N	20.17 E
Raritan R., NJ (răr′ĭ-tăn)	110a	40.32 N	74.27 W
Rarotonga, Cook Is. (rä′rô-tŏŋ′gă)	205	20.40 S	163.00 W
Ra′s an Naqb, Jordan	189a	30.00 N	35.29 E
Ras Dashen (Mtn.), Eth. (räs dä-shän′)	221	12.49 N	38.14 E
Raseiniai, Sov. Un. (rä-syā′nyī)	163	55.23 N	23.04 E
Ra′s Fartak (C.), P. D. R. of Yem.	192	15.43 N	52.17 E
Rashayya, Leb.	189a	33.30 N	35.50 E
Rashīd (Rosetta), Egypt (ra-shēd′) (rô-zĕt′ă)	219b	31.22 N	30.25 E
Rashîd, Masabb (R. Mth.), Egypt	219b	31.30 N	29.58 E
Rashkina, Sov. Un. (rash′kĭ-na)	180a	59.57 N	61.30 E
Rashkov, Sov. Un. (räsh′kôf)	173	47.55 N	28.51 E
Rasht, Iran	192	37.13 N	49.45 E
Raška, Yugo. (räsh′ka)	171	43.16 N	20.40 E
Ras Kuh Mt., Pak.	190	34.03 N	65.10 E
Rasskazovo, Sov. Un. (räs-kä′sô-vô)	177	52.40 N	41.40 E
Rastatt, F.R.G. (rä-shtät)	164	48.51 N	8.12 E
Rastes, Sov. Un. (ras′tĕs)	180a	59.24 N	58.49 E
Rastunovo, Sov. Un. (ras-tōō′nô-vô)	180b	55.15 N	37.50 E
Ras Uarc (C.), Mor.	168	35.28 N	2.58 W
Ratangarh, India (rŭ-tŭn′gŭr)	190	28.10 N	74.30 E
Ratcliff, Tx. (răt′klĭf)	123	31.22 N	95.09 W
Rathenow, G.D.R. (rä′tĕ-nō)	164	52.36 N	12.20 E
Rathlin I., Ire. (răth-lĭn)	160	55.18 N	6.13 W
Ratingen, F.R.G. (rä′tēn-gĕn)	167	51.18 N	6.51 E
Rat Is., Ak. (răt)	105a	51.35 N	176.48 E
Ratlām, India	190	23.19 N	75.05 E
Ratnāgiri, India	191	17.04 N	73.24 E
Raton, NM (ra-tōn′)	120	36.52 N	104.26 W
Rattlesnake Cr., Or. (răt′′l snāk)	114	42.38 N	117.39 W
Rättvik, Swe. (rĕt′vēk)	162	60.54 N	15.07 E
Rauch, Arg. (ra′ōōch)	139c	36.47 S	59.05 W
Raufoss, Nor. (rou′fôs)	162	60.44 N	10.30 E
Raúl Soares, Braz. (rä-ōō′l-sôä′rĕs)	139a	20.05 S	42.28 W
Rauma, Fin. (rä′ōō-ma)	163	61.07 N	21.31 E
Rauna, Sov. Un. (rau′na)	163	57.21 N	25.31 E
Raurkela, India	190	22.15 N	84.53 E
Rautalampi, Fin. (rä′ōō-tē-läm′pô)	163	62.39 N	26.25 E
Rava-Russkaya, Sov. Un. (rä′va rōōs′kä-ya)	165	50.14 N	23.40 E
Ravenna, It. (rä-vĕn′nä)	170	44.27 N	12.13 E
Ravenna, Ne. (ră-vĕn′ă)	112	41.20 N	98.50 W
Ravenna, Oh.	108	41.10 N	81.20 W
Ravensburg, F.R.G. (rä′vĕns-bōōrgh)	164	47.48 N	9.35 E
Ravensdale, Wa. (rā′vĕnz-dāl)	116a	47.22 N	121.58 W
Ravensthorpe, Austl. (rā′vĕns-thôrp)	210	33.30 S	120.20 E
Ravenswood, WV (rā′vĕnz-wōōd)	108	38.55 N	81.50 W
Rāwalpindi, Pak. (rä-wŭl-pēn′dē)	190	33.40 N	73.10 E
Rawāndūz, Iraq	192	36.37 N	44.30 E
Rawicz, Pol. (rä′vēch)	164	51.36 N	16.51 E
Rawlina, Austl. (rôr-lēnă)	210	31.13 S	125.45 E
Rawlins, Wy. (rô′lĭnz)	115	41.46 N	107.15 W
Rawson, Arg. (rô′sŭn)	142	43.16 S	65.09 W
Rawson, Arg.	139c	34.36 S	60.03 W
Rawtenstall, Eng. (rô′tĕn-stôl)	154	53.42 N	2.17 W
Ray, C., Can. (rā)	103	47.40 N	59.18 W
Raya, Bukit (Mtn.), Indon.	202	0.45 S	112.11 E
Raychikinsk, Sov. Un. (rī′chĭ-kēnsk)	179	49.52 N	129.17 E
Rayleigh, Eng. (rā′lē)	154b	51.35 N	0.36 E
Raymond, Can. (rā′mŭnd)	97	49.27 N	112.39 W
Raymond, Wa.	114	46.41 N	123.42 W
Raymondville, Tx. (rā′mŭnd-vĭl)	120	26.30 N	97.46 W
Ray Mts., Ak.	105a	65.40 N	151.45 W
Rayne, La. (rān)	123	30.12 N	92.15 W
Rayón, Mex. (rä-yōn′)	128	21.49 N	99.39 W
Rayton, S. Afr. (rā′tŭn)	223b	25.45 S	28.33 E
Raytown, Mo. (rā′toun)	117f	39.01 N	94.48 W
Rayville, La. (rā-vĭl)	123	32.28 N	91.46 W
Raz, Pte. du (Pt.), Fr. (pwäɴt dü rä)	166	48.02 N	4.43 W
Razdel′naya, Sov. Un. (räz-dĕl′nä-ya)	173	46.47 N	30.08 E
Razdol′noye, Sov. Un. (räz-dôl′nô-yĕ)	200	43.38 N	131.58 E
Razgrad, Bul.	171	43.32 N	26.32 E
Razlog, Bul. (räz′lôk)	171	41.54 N	23.32 E
Razorback Mtn., Can. (rā′zēr-băk)	96	51.35 N	124.42 W
Ré, Île de (I.), Fr. (ēl dē rā′)	166	46.10 N	1.53 W
Rea (R.), Eng. (rē)	154	52.25 N	2.31 W
Reaburn, Can. (rā′bûrn)	93f	50.06 N	97.53 W
Reading, Eng. (rĕd′ĭng)	154b	51.25 N	0.58 W
Reading, Ma.	103a	42.32 N	71.07 W
Reading, Mi.	108	41.45 N	84.45 W
Reading, Oh.	111f	39.14 N	84.26 W
Reading, Pa.	109	40.20 N	75.55 W
Realengo, Braz. (rĕ-ä-län-gô)	142b	23.50 S	43.25 W
Rebiana (Oasis), Libya	221	24.10 N	22.03 E
Rebun (I.), Jap. (rē′bōōn)	200	45.25 N	140.54 E
Recanati, It. (rā-kä-nä′tē)	170	43.25 N	13.35 E
Recherche, Arch. of the, Austl. (rē-shârsh′)	210	34.17 S	122.30 E
Rechitsa, Sov. Un. (ryĕ′chēt-sa)	172	52.22 N	30.24 E
Recife (Pernambuco), Braz. (rā-sē′fĕ) (pĕr-näm-bōō′kô)	141	8.09 S	34.59 W
Recife, Kapp (C.), S. Afr. (rā-sē′fĕ)	223c	34.03 S	25.43 E
Reconquista, Arg. (rā-kôn-kēs′tä)	142	29.01 S	59.41 W
Rector, Ar. (rĕk′tēr)	121	36.16 N	90.21 W
Red (R.), Can.-U. S. (rĕd)	99	49.11 N	97.18 W
Red (R.), Tn.	124	36.35 N	86.55 W
Red (R.), **North Fk.,** Tx.	120	35.20 N	100.08 W
Red (R.), U.S.	107	31.40 N	92.55 W
Red (R.), Viet.	202	22.25 N	103.50 E

PLACE (Pronunciation)	PAGE	Lat. °′	Long. °′
Red (Basin), **see Szechwan**			
Redan, Ga. (rē-dăn′) (rĕd′ăn)	110c	33.44 N	84.09 W
Red Bank, NJ (băngk)	110a	40.21 N	74.06 W
Red Bluff, Ca. (blŭf)	116	40.10 N	122.14 W
Red Bluff Res., Tx.	122	32.03 N	103.52 W
Redby, Mn. (rĕd′bē)	113	47.52 N	94.55 W
Red Cedar (R.), Wi. (sē′dēr)	113	45.03 N	91.48 W
Redcliff, Can. (rĕd′clĭf)	98	50.05 N	110.47 W
Red Cliff Ind. Res., Wi.	113	46.48 N	91.22 W
Redcliffe, Austl. (rĕd′clĭf)	203	27.20 S	153.12 E
Red Cloud, Ne. (kloud)	120	40.06 N	98.32 W
Red Deer, Can. (dēr)	97	52.16 N	113.48 W
Red Deer (R.), Can.	97	52.05 N	113.00 W
Red Deer (R.), Can.	98	52.55 N	102.10 W
Red Deer L., Can.	99	52.58 N	101.28 W
Reddick, Il. (rĕd′dĭk)	111a	41.06 N	88.16 W
Redding, Ca. (rĕd′ĭng)	114	40.36 N	122.25 W
Redenção da Serra, Braz. (rĕ-dĕn-souɴ-dä-sĕ′r-rä)	139a	23.17 S	45.31 W
Redfield, SD (rĕd′fēld)	112	44.53 N	98.30 W
Red Fish Bar, Tx.	123a	29.29 N	94.53 W
Red Indian L., Can. (ĭn′dĭ-ăn)	103	48.40 N	56.50 W
Redklinghausen, F.R.G. (rĕk′lĭng-hou-zĕn)	167c	51.36 N	7.13 E
Red Lake, Can. (lāk)	99	51.02 N	93.49 W
Red Lake (R.), Mn.	112	48.02 N	96.04 W
Red Lake Falls, Mn. (lāk fôls)	112	47.52 N	96.17 W
Red Lake Ind. Res., Mn.	112	48.09 N	95.55 W
Redlands, Ca. (rĕd′lăndz)	117a	34.04 N	117.11 W
Red Lion, Pa. (lī′ŭn)	109	39.55 N	76.30 W
Red Lodge, Mt.	115	45.13 N	107.16 W
Redmond, Wa. (rĕd′mŭnd)	116a	47.40 N	122.07 W
Rednitz R., F.R.G. (rĕd′nētz)	164	49.10 N	11.00 E
Red Oak, Ia. (ōk)	112	41.00 N	95.12 W
Redon, Fr. (rē-dôɴ′)	166	47.42 N	2.03 W
Redonda, Isla, Braz. (ē′s-lä-rē-dô′n-dä)	142b	23.05 S	43.11 W
Redonda I., Antigua (rĕ-dŏn′dă)	131b	16.55 N	62.28 W
Redondela, Sp. (rā-dhôn-dā′lä)	168	42.16 N	8.34 W
Redondo, Port. (rā-dôn′dōō)	168	38.40 N	7.32 W
Redondo, Wa. (rē-dŏn′dō)	116a	47.21 N	122.19 W
Redondo Beach, Ca.	117a	33.50 N	118.23 W
Red Pass, Can. (pas)	97	52.59 N	118.59 W
Red R., Prairie Dog Town Fk., Tx. (prā′rĭ)	120	34.54 N	101.31 W
Red R., Salt Fk., Tx.	120	35.04 N	100.31 W
Red Rock Cr., Mt.	115	44.54 N	112.44 W
Red Sea, Afr.-Asia	221	23.15 N	37.00 E
Redstone, Can. (rĕd′stōn)	96	52.08 N	123.42 W
Red Sucker L., Can. (sŭk′ēr)	99	54.09 N	93.40 W
Redwater Cr., Mt.	115	47.37 N	105.25 W
Red Willow Cr., Ne.	120	40.34 N	100.48 W
Red Wing, Mn.	113	44.34 N	92.35 W
Redwood City, Ca. (rĕd′ wōōd)	116b	37.29 N	122.13 W
Redwood Falls, Mn.	113	44.32 N	95.06 W
Ree, Lough (B.), Ire. (lŏκ′rē′)	160	53.30 N	7.45 W
Reed City, Mi. (rēd)	108	43.50 N	85.35 W
Reed L., Can.	99	54.37 N	100.30 W
Reedley, Ca. (rēd′lē)	118	36.37 N	119.27 W
Reedsburg, Wi. (rēdz′bûrg)	113	43.32 N	90.01 W
Reedsport, Or. (rēdz′pôrt)	114	43.42 N	124.08 W
Reelfoot (R.), Tn. (rēl′fōōt)	124	36.18 N	89.20 W
Rees, F.R.G. (rĕz)	167c	51.46 N	6.25 E
Reeves, Mt., Austl. (rēv′s)	212	33.50 S	149.56 E
Reform, Al. (rē-fôrm′)	124	33.23 N	88.00 W
Refugio, Tx. (rā-fōō′hyô) (rĕ-fū′jō)	123	28.18 N	97.15 W
Rega (R.), Pol. (rĕ-gä)	164	53.48 N	15.30 E
Regen R., F.R.G. (rā′ghĕn)	164	49.09 N	12.21 E
Regensburg, F.R.G. (rā′ghĕns-bōōrgh)	164	49.02 N	12.06 E
Reggane, Alg.	220	27.08 N	0.06 E
Reggio, La. (rĕg′jĭ-ō)	110d	29.50 N	89.46 W
Reggio di Calabria, It. (rĕ′jô dē kä-lä′brē-ä)	170	38.07 N	15.42 E
Reggio nell′ Emilia, It.	170	44.43 N	10.34 E
Reghin, Rom. (rā-gēn′)	165	46.47 N	24.44 E
Regina, Can. (rē-jī′na)	98	50.25 N	104.39 W
Regla, Cuba (rāg′lä)	133a	23.08 N	82.20 W
Regnitz (R.), F.R.G. (rĕg′nētz)	164	49.50 N	10.55 E
Reguengos de Monsaraz, Port. (rā-gĕŋ′gōzh dā mōn-sä-räzh′)	168	38.26 N	7.30 W
Rehoboth, Namibia	222	23.10 S	17.15 E
Rehovot, Isr.	189a	31.53 N	34.49 E
Reichenbach, G.D.R. (rī′κĕn-bäκ)	164	50.36 N	12.18 E
Reidsville, NC (rēdz′vĭl)	125	36.20 N	79.37 W
Reigate, Eng. (rī′gāt)	154b	51.12 N	0.12 W
Reims, Fr. (răɴs)	166	49.16 N	4.00 E
Reina Adelaida, Arch., Chile (är-chē′pyĕ′la-gô-rā′nä-ä-dĕ-lī′dä)	142	52.00 S	74.15 W
Reinbeck, Ia. (rīn′bĕk)	113	42.22 N	92.34 W
Reindeer (L.), Can. (rān′dēr)	94	57.36 N	101.23 W
Reindeer (R.), Can.	98	55.45 N	103.30 W
Reindeer I., Can.	99	52.25 N	98.00 W
Reindeer L., Can.	99	57.15 N	102.40 W
Reinosa, Sp. (rā-ē-nō′sä)	168	43.01 N	4.08 W
Reistertown, Md. (rēs′tēr-toun)	110e	39.28 N	76.50 W
Reitz, S. Afr.	219d	27.48 S	28.25 E
Rema, Jabal (Mtn.), Yemen	192	14.13 N	44.38 E
Rembau, Mala.	189b	2.36 N	102.06 E
Remedios, Col. (rĕ-mĕ′dyôs)	140a	7.03 N	74.42 W
Remedios, Cuba (rā-mā′dhē-ōs)	132	22.30 N	79.35 W
Remedios, Pan. (rĕ-mĕ′dyōs)	131	8.14 N	81.46 W
Remiremont, Fr. (rē-mēr-môɴ′)	167	48.01 N	6.35 E
Rempang I., Indon.	189b	0.51 N	104.04 E
Remscheid, F.R.G. (rĕm′shīt)	167c	51.10 N	7.11 E
Rena, Nor.	162	61.08 N	11.17 E
Rendova (I.), Sol. Is. (rĕn′dô-va)	211	8.38 S	156.26 E
Rendsburg, F.R.G. (rĕnts′bōōrgh)	164	54.19 N	9.39 E
Renfrew, Can. (rĕn′frōō)	109	45.30 N	76.30 W
Rengam, Mala. (rĕn′gäm′)	189b	1.53 N	103.24 E
Rengo, Chile (rĕn′gō)	139b	34.22 S	70.50 W
Reni, Sov. Un. (ran′)	173	45.26 N	28.18 E

ng-sing; ŋ-baŋk; ɴ-nasalized n; nŏd; cŏmmit; ōld; ôbey; ôrder; oi-boil; fōōd; fŏŏt; ou-out; s-soft; sh-dish; th-thin; pūre; ûnite; ûrn; stŭd; circŭs; ü-as in French tu; ′-indeterminate vowel.

338 Renmark – Roche à Bateau

PLACE (Pronunciation)	PAGE	Lat. °′	Long. °′
Renmark, Austl. (rĕn′märk)	212	34.10 s	140.50 e
Rennel (I.), Sol. Is. (rĕn-nĕl′)	211	11.50 s	160.38 e
Rennes, Fr. (rĕn)	166	48.07 n	1.02 w
Rennselaer, NY (rĕn′sē-lâr)	109	42.40 n	73.45 w
Reno, Nv. (rē′nō)	118	39.32 n	119.49 w
Reno (R.), It. (rā′nô)	170	44.10 n	10.55 e
Renovo, Pa. (rē-nō′vō)	109	41.20 n	77.50 w
Renqiu, China (rŭn-chyō)	196	38.44 n	116.05 e
Rensselaer, In. (rĕn′sē-lâr)	108	41.00 n	87.10 w
Rentchler, Il. (rĕnt′chlēr)	117e	38.30 n	89.52 w
Renton, Wa. (rĕn′tŭn)	116a	47.29 n	122.13 w
Renville, Mn. (rĕn′vĭl)	113	44.44 n	95.13 w
Repentigny, Can.	93a	45.47 n	73.26 w
Republic, Al. (rē-pŭb′lĭk)	110h	33.37 n	86.54 w
Republic, Wa.	114	48.38 n	118.44 w
Republican (R.), South Fk., Co. (rē-pŭb′lĭ-kăn)	120	39.35 n	102.28 w
Republican (R.), Ks.	121	39.40 n	97.40 w
Repulse B., Austl. (rē-pŭls′)	211	20.56 s	149.22 e
Requena, Sp. (rā-kā′nä)	168	39.29 n	1.03 w
Resende, Braz. (rĕ-sĕ′n-dĕ)	139a	22.30 s	44.26 w
Resende Costa, Braz. (kôs-tä)	139a	20.55 s	44.12 w
Reshetilovka, Sov. Un. (ryĕ′ shĕ-tē-lôf-kȧ)	173	49.34 n	34.04 e
Resistencia, Arg. (rā-sēs-tĕn′syä)	142	27.24 s	58.54 w
Reşiţa, Rom. (rā′shē-tȧ)	171	45.18 n	21.56 e
Resolute, Can. (rĕz-ô-lūt′)	92	74.41 n	95.00 w
Resolution (I.), Can. (rĕz-ō-lū′shŭn)	95	61.30 n	63.58 w
Resolution I., N.Z. (rĕz-ŏl-ûshûn)	213	45.43 s	166.20 e
Restigouche (R.), Can. (rĕs-tē-gōōsh′)	102	47.35 n	67.35 w
Restrepo, Col. (rĕs-trĕ′pô)	140a	3.49 n	76.31 w
Restrepo, Col.	140a	4.16 n	73.32 w
Retalhuleu, Guat. (rā-täl-ōō-lān′)	130	14.31 n	91.41 w
Rethel, Fr. (r-tl′)	166	49.34 n	4.20 e
Réthimnon, Grc.	170a	35.21 n	24.30 e
Retie, Bel.	155a	51.16 n	5.08 e
Retsil, Wa. (rĕt′sĭl)	116a	47.33 n	122.37 w
Reunion, Afr. (rā-ü-nyôn′)	228	21.06 s	55.36 e
Reus, Sp. (rā′ōōs)	169	41.08 n	1.05 e
Reutlingen, F.R.G. (roit′lĭng-ĕn)	164	48.29 n	9.14 e
Reutov, Sov. Un. (rĕ-ōō′ôf)	180b	55.45 n	37.52 e
Reval, see Tallinn			
Revda, Sov. Un. (ryâv′dȧ)	180a	56.48 n	59.57 e
Revelstoke, Can. (rĕv′ĕl-stōk)	97	51.59 n	118.12 w
Reventazon, R., C.R. (rā-vĕn-tä-zōn′)	131	10.10 n	83.30 w
Revere, Ma. (rē-vēr′)	103a	42.24 n	71.01 w
Revillagigedo Chan, Ak. (rē-vĭl′ȧ-gĭ-gē′dō)	96	55.10 n	131.13 w
Revillagigedo I., Ak.	96	55.35 n	131.23 w
Revillagigedo, Islas (I.), Mex. (ē′s-läs-rĕ-vēl-yä-hĕ′gĕ-dô)	126	18.45 n	111.00 w
Revin, Fr. (rē-văN)	166	49.56 n	4.34 e
Rewa, India (rā′wä)	190	24.41 n	81.11 e
Rewāri, India	190	28.19 n	76.39 e
Rexburg, Id. (rĕks′bûrg)	115	43.50 n	111.48 w
Rey, L., Mex. (rā)	122	27.00 n	103.33 w
Rey, Isla del (I.), Pan. (ē′s-lä-dĕl-rā′ē)	131	8.20 n	78.40 w
Reyes, Bol. (rā′yĕs)	140	14.19 s	67.16 w
Reyes, Pt., Ca.	118	38.00 n	123.00 w
Reykjanes (C.), Ice. (rā′kyȧ-nĕs)	152	63.37 n	24.33 w
Reykjavik, Ice. (rā′kyȧ-vēk)	156	64.09 n	21.39 w
Reynosa, Mex. (rā-ē-nō′sä)	122	26.05 n	98.21 w
Rēzekne, Sov. Un. (rā′zĕk-nĕ)	172	56.31 n	27.19 e
Rezh, Sov. Un. (rĕzh′)	180a	57.22 n	61.23 e
Rezina, Sov. Un. (ryĕzh′ĕ-nĭ)	173	47.44 n	28.56 e
Rhaetien Alps (Mts.), It.	170	46.22 n	10.33 e
Rheinberg, F.R.G. (rīn′bĕrgh)	167c	51.33 n	6.37 e
Rheine, F.R.G. (rī′nĕ)	164	52.16 n	7.26 e
Rheinland-Pfalz (Rhineland-Palatinate) (State), F.R.G.	164	50.05 n	6.40 e
Rhein R., F.R.G. (rīn)	164	50.34 n	7.21 e
Rheydt, F.R.G. (rĕ′yt)	167c	51.10 n	6.28 e
Rhine (R.), Eur.	152	50.34 n	7.21 e
Rhinelander, Wi. (rīn′lăn-dēr)	113	45.39 n	89.25 w
Rhin Kanal (Can.), G.D.R. (rēn kä-näl′)	155b	52.47 n	12.40 e
Rhin R., G.D.R. (rēn)	155b	52.52 n	12.49 e
Rhiou (R.), Alg.	169	35.45 n	1.18 e
Rhode I., RI	110b	41.31 n	71.14 w
Rhode Island (State), U.S. (rōd ī′lănd)	107	41.35 n	71.40 w
Rhodes, S. Afr. (rōdz)	223c	30.48 s	27.56 e
Rhodope Mts., Bul. (rô′dô-pĕ)	171	42.00 n	24.08 e
Rhondda, Wales (rŏn′dhȧ)	160	51.40 n	3.40 w
Rhône (R.), Fr. (rōn)	166	45.14 n	4.53 e
Rhoon, Neth.	155a	51.52 n	4.24 e
Rhum (I.), Scot. (rŭm)	160	57.00 n	6.20 w
Riachão, Braz. (rē-ä-chouN′)	141	7.15 s	46.30 w
Rialto, Ca. (rē-ăl′tō)	117a	34.06 n	117.23 w
Riau (Prov.), Indon.	189b	0.56 n	101.25 e
Riau, Kepulauan (I.), Indon.	202	0.30 n	104.55 e
Riau, Selat (Str.), Indon.	189b	0.40 n	104.27 e
Riaza (R.), Sp. (rē-ä′thä)	168	41.25 n	3.25 w
Ribadavia, Sp. (rē-bä-dhä′vē-ä)	168	42.18 n	8.06 w
Ribadeo, Sp. (rē-bä-dhā′ō)	168	37.32 n	7.05 w
Ribadesella, Sp. (rē′bä-dā-säl′yä)	168	43.30 n	5.02 w
Ribauè, Moz.	227	14.57 s	38.17 e
Ribe, Den. (rē′bĕ)	162	55.20 n	8.45 e
Ribeirão Prêto, Braz. (rē-bā-rouN-prĕ′tô)	139a	21.11 s	47.47 w
Ribera, NM (rē-bĕ′rä)	120	35.23 n	105.27 w
Riberalta, Bol. (rē-bā-räl′tä)	140	11.06 s	66.02 w
Rib Lake, Wi. (rĭb lāk)	113	45.20 n	90.11 w
Rice, Ca. (rīs)	118	34.05 n	114.50 w
Rice (L.), Can.	109	44.05 n	78.10 w
Rice L., Mn.	117g	45.10 n	93.09 w
Rice Lake, Wi.	113	45.30 n	91.44 w
Richards I., Can. (rĭch′ērds)	105	69.45 n	135.30 w
Richards Landing, Can. (lănd′ĭng)	117k	46.18 n	84.02 w
Richardson, Tx. (rĭch′ērd-sŭn)	117c	32.56 n	96.44 w
Richardson, Wa.	116a	48.27 n	122.54 w
Richardson Mts., Can.	94	66.58 n	136.19 w
Richardson Mts., N.Z.	213	44.50 s	168.30 e
Richardson Park, De. (pärk)	109	39.45 n	75.35 w
Richelieu (R.), Can. (rēsh′lyû′)	109	45.05 n	73.25 w
Richfield, Mn.	117g	44.53 n	93.17 w
Richfield, Oh.	111d	41.14 n	81.38 w
Richfield, Ut.	119	38.45 n	112.05 w
Richford, Vt. (rĭch′fērd)	109	45.00 n	72.35 w
Rich Hill, Mo. (rĭch hĭl)	121	38.05 n	94.21 w
Richibucto, Can. (rĭ-chĭ-bŭk′tō)	102	46.41 n	64.52 w
Richland, Ga. (rĭch′lănd)	124	32.05 n	84.40 w
Richland, Wa.	114	46.17 n	119.19 w
Richland Center, Wi. (sĕn′tēr)	113	43.20 n	90.25 w
Richmond, Austl. (rĭch′mŭnd)	211	20.47 s	143.14 e
Richmond, Austl.	207b	33.36 s	150.45 e
Richmond, Ca.	116b	37.56 n	122.21 w
Richmond, Can.	102	45.40 n	72.07 w
Richmond, Can.	93c	45.12 n	75.49 w
Richmond, Il.	111a	42.29 n	88.18 w
Richmond, In.	108	39.50 n	85.00 w
Richmond, Ky.	108	37.45 n	84.20 w
Richmond, Mo.	121	39.16 n	93.58 w
Richmond, Tx.	123	29.35 n	95.45 w
Richmond, S. Afr.	223c	29.52 s	30.17 e
Richmond, Ut.	115	41.55 n	111.50 w
Richmond, Va.	109	37.35 n	77.30 w
Richmond Beach, Wa.	116a	47.47 n	122.23 w
Richmond Heights, Mo.	117e	38.38 n	90.20 w
Richmond Highlands, Wa.	116a	47.46 n	122.22 w
Richmond Hill, Can. (hĭl)	93d	43.53 n	79.26 w
Richton, Ms. (rĭch′tŭn)	124	31.20 n	89.54 w
Richwood, WV (rĭch′wōōd)	108	38.10 n	80.30 w
Ridderkerk, Neth.	155a	51.52 n	4.35 e
Rideau (R.), Can.	93c	45.17 n	75.41 w
Rideau L., Can. (rē-dō′)	109	44.40 n	76.20 w
Ridgefield, Ct. (rĭj′fēld)	110a	41.16 n	73.30 w
Ridgefield, Wa.	116c	45.49 n	122.40 w
Rigeley, WV (rĭj′lē)	109	39.40 n	78.45 w
Ridgeway, Can. (rĭj′wā)	111c	42.53 n	79.02 w
Ridgewood, NJ (rĭdj′wōōd)	110a	40.59 n	74.08 w
Ridgway, Pa.	109	41.25 n	78.40 w
Riding Mtn., Can. (rīd′ĭng)	99	50.37 n	99.37 w
Riding Mountain Natl. Park, Can. (rīd′ĭng)	94	50.59 n	99.19 w
Riding Rocks (Is.), Ba.	132	25.20 n	79.10 w
Riebeek-Oos, S. Afr.	223c	33.14 s	26.09 e
Ried, Aus. (rēd)	164	48.13 n	13.30 e
Riesa, G.D.R. (rē′zȧ)	164	51.17 n	13.17 e
Rieti, It. (rē-ā′tē)	170	42.25 n	12.51 e
Rievleidam (L.), S. Afr.	223b	25.52 s	28.18 e
Rifle, Co. (rī′f′l)	119	39.35 n	107.50 w
Rīga, Sov. Un. (rē′gȧ)	163	56.55 n	24.05 e
Riga, G. of, Sov. Un.	163	57.56 n	23.05 e
Rīgān, Iran	192	28.45 n	58.55 e
Rigaud, Can. (rē-gō′)	93a	45.29 n	74.18 w
Rigby, Id. (rĭg′bē)	115	43.40 n	111.55 w
Rīgestān (Reg.), Afr.	192	30.53 n	64.42 e
Rigolet, Can. (rĭg-ō-lā′)	95	54.10 n	58.40 w
Riihimäki, Fin.	163	60.44 n	24.44 e
Rijeka (Fiume), Yugo. (rĭ-yĕ′kä)	170	45.22 n	14.24 e
Rijkevorsel, Bel.	155a	51.21 n	4.46 e
Rijswijk, Neth.	155a	52.03 n	4.19 e
Rika R., Sov. Un. (rē′kȧ)	165	48.21 n	23.37 e
Rima (R.), Nig.	225	13.30 n	5.50 e
Rimavska Sobota, Czech. (rē′māf-skä sô′bô-tä)	165	48.25 n	20.01 e
Rimbo, Swe. (rēm′bōō)	162	59.45 n	18.22 e
Rimini, It. (rē′mē-nē)	170	44.03 n	12.33 e
Rîmnicu-Sărat, Rom.	171	45.24 n	27.06 e
Rîmnicu-Vîlcea, Rom.	171	45.07 n	24.22 e
Rimouski, Can. (rē-mōōs′kē)	102	48.27 n	68.32 w
Rinc n de Romos, Mex. (rēn-kōn dā rô-mōs′)	128	22.13 n	102.21 w
Ringkøbing, Den. (rĭng′kûb-ĭng)	162	56.06 n	8.14 e
Ringkøbing Fd., Den.	162	55.55 n	8.04 e
Ringsted, Den. (rĭng′stĕdh)	162	55.27 n	11.49 e
Ringvassøya (I.), Nor. (rĭng′väs-ûĕ)	156	69.58 n	16.43 e
Ringwood, Austl.	207a	37.49 s	145.14 e
Rinjani, Gunung (Mtn.), Indon.	202	8.39 s	116.22 e
Rio Abajo, Pan. (rē′ō-ä-bä′Kō)	126a	9.01 n	78.30 w
Rio Balsas, Mex. (rē′ō-bäl-säs)	128	17.59 n	99.45 w
Riobamba, Ec. (rē′ō-bäm-bä)	140	1.45 s	78.37 w
Rio Bonito, Braz. (rē′ōō bō-nē′tōō)	139a	22.44 s	42.38 w
Rio Branco, Braz. (rē′ōō brăN′kōō)	140	9.57 s	67.50 w
Rio Branco, Ur. (rĭô brăncô)	142	32.33 s	53.29 w
Rio Branco (Ter.), Braz.	141	2.35 n	61.25 w
Rio Casca, Braz. (rē′ō-kà′s-kä)	139a	20.15 s	42.39 w
Rio Chico, Ven. (rē′ō chē′kō)	141b	10.20 n	65.58 w
Rio Claro, Braz. (rē′ōō klä′rōō)	139a	21.25 s	47.33 w
Rio Cuarto, Arg. (rē′ō kwär′tō)	142	33.05 s	64.15 w
Rio das Flores, Braz. (rē′ō-däs-flô-rĕs)	139a	22.10 s	43.35 w
Rio de Janeiro, Braz. (rē′ōō dā zhä-nā′ē-rōō)	142b	22.50 s	43.20 w
Rio de Janeiro (State), Braz.	141	22.27 s	42.43 w
Rio de Jesús, Pan. (rē′ō-dĕ-Kĕ-sōō′s)	131	7.54 n	80.59 w
Rio Dercero, Arg. (rē′ō dĕr-sĕ′rō)	142	32.12 s	63.59 w
Rio Frio, Mex. (rē′ō-frē′ō)	129a	19.21 n	98.40 w
Rio Gallegos, Arg. (rē′ō gä-lā′gōs)	142	51.43 s	69.15 w
Rio Grande, Braz. (rē′ōō grän′dĕ)	142	31.04 s	52.14 w
Rio Grande, Mex. (rē′ō grän′dā)	128	23.51 n	102.59 w
Riogrande, Tx. (rē′ō grän-dā)	122	26.23 n	98.48 w
Rio Grande (R.), Co. (rē′ōō grän′dĕ)	119	37.44 n	106.51 w
Rio Grande do Norte (State), Braz. (rē′ōō grän′dĕ dōō nôr′tĕ)	141	5.26 s	37.20 w
Rio Grande do Sul (State), Braz. (rē′ōō grän′dĕ-dô-sōō′l)	142	29.00 s	54.00 w
Ríohacha, Col. (rē′ō-ä′chä)	140	11.30 n	72.54 w
Rio Hato, Pan. (rē′ō-ä′tô)	131	8.19 n	80.11 w
Riom, Fr. (rē-ôN′)	166	45.54 n	3.08 e
Rio Muni (Prov.), Equat. Gui. (rē′ō mōō′nē)	218	1.47 n	8.33 e
Rionegro, Col. (rē′ō-nĕ′grô)	140a	6.09 n	75.22 w
Rio Negro (Prov.), Arg. (rē′ō nā′grō)	142	40.15 s	68.15 w
Rio Negro (Dept.), Ur. (rē′ō-nĕ′grō)	139c	32.48 s	57.45 w
Rio Negro, Embalse del (Res.), Ur. (ĕm-bä′l-sĕ-dĕl-rē′ō-nĕ′grō)	142	32.45 s	55.50 w
Rionero, It. (rē-ō-nā′rô)	170	40.55 n	15.42 e
Rio Novo, Braz. (rē′ō-nô′vô)	139a	21.30 s	43.08 w
Rio Pardo de Minas, Braz. (rē′ō pär′dō-dĕ-mē′näs)	141	15.43 s	42.24 w
Rio Pombo, Braz. (rē′ō pôm′bä)	139a	21.17 s	43.09 w
Rio Sorocaba, Represado (Res.), Braz. (rĕ-prĕ-sä-dô-rē′ō-sô-rō-kä′bä)	139a	23.37 s	47.19 w
Ríosucio, Col. (rē′ō-sōō′syō)	140a	5.25 n	75.41 w
Rio Verde, Braz. (vĕr′dĕ)	141	17.47 s	50.49 w
Ríoverde, Mex. (rē′ō-vĕr′dā)	128	21.54 n	99.59 w
Ripley, Eng. (rĭp′lē)	154	53.03 n	1.24 w
Ripley, Ms.	124	34.44 n	88.55 w
Ripley, Tn.	124	35.44 n	89.34 w
Ripoll, Sp. (rē-pōl″)	169	42.10 n	2.10 e
Ripon, Wi. (rĭp′ŏn)	113	43.49 n	88.50 w
Ripon (I.), Austl.	210	20.05 s	118.10 e
Ripon Falls, Ug.	221	0.38 n	33.02 e
Risaralda (Dept.), Col.	140a	6.45 s	76.00 w
Risdon, Austl. (rĭz′dŭn)	211	42.37 s	147.32 e
Rishiri (I.), Jap. (rē-shē′rē)	200	45.10 n	141.08 e
Rishon le Ziyyon, Isr.	189a	31.57 n	34.48 e
Rishra, India	190a	22.42 n	88.22 e
Rising Sun, In. (rīz′ĭng sŭn)	108	38.55 n	84.55 w
Risle (R.), Fr.	166	49.12 n	0.43 e
Risor, Nor. (rēs′ûr)	162	58.44 n	9.10 e
Ritacuva, Alto (Mtn.), Col. (ä′l-tô-rē-tä-kōō′vä)	140	6.22 n	72.13 w
Rittman, Oh. (rĭt′năn)	111d	40.58 n	81.47 w
Ritzville, Wa. (rĭts′vĭl)	114	47.08 n	118.23 w
Riva, Dom. Rep. (rē′vä)	133	19.10 n	69.55 w
Riva, It. (rē′vä)	170	45.54 n	10.49 e
Riva, Md. (rĭ′vä)	110e	38.57 n	76.36 w
Rivas, Nic. (rē′väs)	130	11.25 n	85.51 w
Rive-de-Gier, Fr. (rēv-dē-zhē-ā′)	166	45.32 n	4.37 e
Rivera, Ur. (rē-vā′rä)	142	30.52 s	55.32 w
River Cess, Lib. (rĭv′ēr sĕs)	220	5.46 n	9.52 w
Riverdale, Il. (rĭv′ēr dăl)	111a	41.38 n	87.36 w
Riverdale, Ut.	117b	41.11 n	112.00 w
River Falls, Al.	124	31.20 n	86.25 w
River Falls, Wi.	113	44.48 n	92.38 w
Riverhead, NY (rĭv′ēr hĕd)	109	40.55 n	72.40 w
Riverina (Reg.), Austl. (rĭv-ēr-ē′nä)	212	34.55 s	144.30 e
River Jordan, Can. (jôr′dăn)	116a	48.25 n	124.03 w
River Oaks, Tx. (ōkz)	117c	32.47 n	97.24 w
River Rouge, Mi. (rōōzh)	111b	42.16 n	83.09 w
Rivers, Can.	99	50.01 n	100.15 w
Riverside, Ca. (rĭv′ēr-sīd)	117a	33.59 n	117.21 w
Riverside, NJ	110f	40.02 n	74.58 w
Rivers Inlet, Can.	96	51.45 n	127.15 w
Riverstone, Austl.	207b	33.41 s	150.52 e
Riverton, Va.	109	39.00 n	78.15 w
Riverton, Wy.	115	43.02 n	108.24 w
Rivesaltes, Fr. (rēv′zält′)	166	42.48 n	2.48 e
Riviera Beach, Fl. (rĭv-ĭ-ēr′ȧ bēch)	125a	26.46 n	80.04 w
Riviera Beach, Md.	110e	39.10 n	76.32 w
Rivie′re Beaudette, Can. (bō-dĕt′)	93a	45.14 n	74.20 w
Rivière-du-Loup, Can. (rē-vyâr′ dü lōō′)	102	47.50 n	69.32 w
Rivière Que Barre, Can. (rēv-yĕr′ kē-bär)	93g	53.47 n	113.51 w
Rivière-Trois-Pistoles, Can. (trwä′pēs-tôl′)	102	48.07 n	69.10 w
Riyadh (Ar Riyāḍ), Sau. Ar.	192	24.31 n	46.47 e
Rize, Tur. (rē′zĕ)	177	41.00 n	40.30 e
Rizhao, China (rē-jou)	196	35.27 n	119.28 e
Rizzuto, C., It. (rēt-sōō′tô)	171	38.53 n	17.05 e
Rjukan, Nor. (ryōō′kän)	162	59.53 n	8.30 e
Roanne, Fr. (rō-än′)	166	46.02 n	4.04 e
Roanoke, Al. (rō′ȧ-nōk)	124	33.08 n	85.21 w
Roanoke, Va.	125	37.16 n	79.55 w
Roanoke (R.), NC-Va.	125	36.17 n	77.22 w
Roanoke (Staunton) (R.), Va.	125	37.05 n	79.20 w
Roanoke Rapids, NC	125	36.25 n	77.40 w
Roanoke Rapids, L., NC	125	36.28 n	77.37 w
Roan Plat., Co. (rōn)	119	39.25 n	108.50 w
Roatan, Hond. (rō-ä-tän′)	130	16.18 n	86.33 w
Roatan I., Hond.	130	16.19 n	86.46 w
Robbeneiland (I.), S. Afr.	222a	33.48 s	18.22 e
Robbins, Il. (rŏb′ĭnz)	111a	41.39 n	87.42 w
Robbinsdale, Mn. (rŏb′ĭnz-dāl)	117g	45.03 n	93.22 w
Robe, Wa. (rōb)	116a	48.06 n	121.50 w
Roberts, Mt., Austl. (rŏb′ērts)	211	32.05 s	152.30 e
Roberts, Pt., Wa. (rŏb′ērts)	116d	48.58 n	123.05 w
Robertson, Lac (L.), Can.	103	51.00 n	59.10 w
Robertsport, Lib. (rŏb′ērts-pōrt)	224	6.45 n	11.22 w
Roberval, Can. (rŏb′ēr-văl) (rô-bĕr-vál′)	95	48.32 n	72.15 w
Robinson, Il. (rŏb′ĭn-sŭn)	108	39.00 n	87.45 w
Robinson's, Can.	103	48.16 n	58.50 w
Robinvale, Austl. (rŏb-ĭn′văl)	212	34.45 s	142.45 e
Roblin, Can.	99	51.15 n	101.25 w
Robson, Mt., Can. (rŏb′sŭn)	97	53.07 n	119.09 w
Robstown, Tx. (rŏbz′toun)	123	27.46 n	97.41 w
Roca, Cabo da (C.), Port. (kȧ′bō-dä-rō′kȧ)	169b	38.47 n	9.30 w
Roçadas, Ang. (rô-kä′däs)	222	16.50 s	15.05 e
Rocas, Atol das (Atoll), Braz. (ä-tôl-däs-rō′käs)	141	3.50 s	33.46 w
Rocedos São Pedro E São Paulo, (I.), Braz. (rô-zĕ′dôs-souN-pĕ′drô-ĕ-souN-päōō-lô)	138	1.50 n	30.00 w
Rocha, Ur. (rō′chäs)	142	34.26 s	54.14 w
Rochdale, Eng. (rŏch′dăl)	154	53.37 n	2.09 w
Roche à Bateau, Hai. (rôsh à bá-tō′)	133	18.10 n	74.00 w

ăt; finăl; rāte; senăte; ärm; ȧsk; sofȧ; fâre; ch-choose; dh-as th in other; bē; ēvent; bĕt; recĕnt; cratēr; g-gō; gh-guttural g; bĭt; ĭ-short neutral; rīde; K-guttural k as ch in German ich;

PRONOUNCING INDEX

Rochefort – Rugby 339

PLACE (Pronunciation)	PAGE	Lat. °′	Long. °′
Rochefort, Fr. (rôsh-fŏr')	166	45.55 N	0.57 W
Rochelle, Il. (rô-shĕl')	113	41.53 N	89.06 W
Rochester, In. (rŏch'ĕs-tẽr)	108	41.05 N	86.20 W
Rochester, Mi.	111b	42.41 N	83.09 W
Rochester, Mn.	113	44.01 N	92.30 W
Rochester, NH	109	43.20 N	71.00 W
Rochester, NY	109	43.15 N	77.35 W
Rochester, Pa.	111e	40.42 N	80.16 W
Rock (R.), Il.	113	41.40 N	89.52 W
Rock (R.), Ia.	112	43.17 N	96.13 W
Rock (R.), Or.	116c	45.34 N	122.52 W
Rock (R.), Or.	116c	45.52 N	123.14 W
Rockaway, NJ (rŏck'á-wā)	110a	40.54 N	74.30 W
Rockbank, Austl.	207a	37.44 S	144.40 E
Rockcliffe Park, Can. (rok'klĭf pärk)	93c	45.27 N	75.40 W
Rock Cr., Can. (rŏk)	98	49.01 N	107.00 W
Rock Cr., Il.	111a	41.16 N	87.54 W
Rock Cr., Mt.	115	46.25 N	113.40 W
Rock Cr., Or.	114	45.30 N	120.06 W
Rock Cr., Wa.	114	47.09 N	117.50 W
Rockdale, Md.	110e	39.22 N	76.49 W
Rockdale, Tx. (rŏk'dāl)	123	30.39 N	97.00 W
Rock Falls, Il. (rŏk fôlz)	113	41.45 N	89.42 W
Rockford, Il. (rŏk'fẽrd)	113	42.16 N	89.07 W
Rockhampton, Austl. (rŏk-hămp'tŭn)	211	23.26 S	150.29 E
Rockhill, SC (rŏk'hĭl)	125	34.55 N	81.01 W
Rockingham, NC (rŏk'ĭng-hăm)	125	34.54 N	79.45 W
Rockingham For., Eng. (rok'ĭng-hăm)	154	52.29 N	0.43 W
Rock Island, Il.	113	41.31 N	90.37 W
Rock Island Dam, Wa. (ī lănd)	114	47.17 N	120.33 W
Rockland, Can. (rŏk'lănd)	93c	45.33 N	75.17 W
Rockland, Me.	102	44.06 N	69.09 W
Rockland, Ma.	103a	42.07 N	70.55 W
Rockland Res., Austl.	212	36.55 S	142.20 E
Rockmart, Ga. (rŏk'märt)	124	33.58 N	85.00 W
Rockmont, Wi. (rŏk'mŏnt)	117h	46.34 N	91.54 W
Rockport, In. (rŏk'pōrt)	108	38.20 N	87.00 W
Rockport, Ma.	103a	42.39 N	70.37 W
Rockport, Mo.	121	40.25 N	95.30 W
Rockport, Tx.	123	28.03 N	97.03 W
Rock Rapids, Ia. (răp'ĭdz)	112	43.26 N	96.10 W
Rock Sd., Ba.	133	24.50 N	76.05 W
Rocksprings, Tx. (rŏk sprĭngs)	122	30.02 N	100.12 W
Rock Springs, Wy.	115	41.35 N	109.13 W
Rockstone, Guy. (rŏk'stōn)	141	5.55 N	57.27 W
Rock Valley, Ia. (văl'ĭ)	112	43.13 N	96.17 W
Rockville, In. (rŏk'vĭl)	108	39.45 N	87.15 W
Rockville, Md.	110e	39.05 N	77.11 W
Rockville Centre, NY (sĕn'tẽr)	110a	40.39 N	73.39 W
Rockwall, Tx. (rŏk'wôl)	121	32.55 N	96.23 W
Rockwell City, Ia. (rŏk'wĕl)	113	42.22 N	94.37 W
Rockwood, Can. (rŏk-wo͝od)	93d	43.37 N	80.08 W
Rockwood, Me.	102	45.39 N	69.45 W
Rockwood, Tn.	124	35.51 N	84.41 W
Rocky Boys Ind. Res., Mt.	115	48.08 N	109.34 W
Rocky Ford, Co.	120	38.02 N	103.43 W
Rocky Hill, NJ (hĭl)	110a	40.24 N	74.38 W
Rocky Island L., Can.	100	46.56 N	83.04 W
Rocky Mount, NC	125	35.55 N	77.47 W
Rocky Mountain House, Can.	97	52.22 N	114.55 W
Rocky Mountain Natl. Park, Co.	120	40.29 N	106.06 W
Rocky Mts., N.A.	92	50.00 N	114.00 W
Rocky River, Oh.	111d	41.29 N	81.51 W
Rocky R., East Br., Oh.	111d	41.13 N	81.43 W
Rocky R., West Br., Oh.	111d	41.17 N	81.54 W
Rodas, Cuba (rō'dhàs)	133	22.20 N	80.35 W
Roden (R.), Eng. (rō'dĕn)	154	52.49 N	2.38 W
Rodeo, Ca. (rō'dēō)	116b	38.02 N	122.16 W
Rodeo, Mex. (rô-dá'ō)	122	25.12 N	104.34 W
Roderick I., Can. (rŏd'ĕ-rĭk)	96	52.40 N	128.22 W
Rodez, Fr. (rô-dĕz')	166	44.22 N	2.34 E
Rōdhos, Grc.	159	36.24 N	28.15 E
Ródhos (I.), Grc.	159	36.00 N	28.29 E
Rodniki, Sov. Un. (rôd'nē-kē)	172	57.08 N	41.48 E
Rodonit, Kep I (C.), Alb.	171	41.38 N	19.01 E
Rodosto, see Tekirdağ			
Roebling, NJ (rōb'lĭng)	110f	40.07 N	74.48 W
Roebourne, Austl. (rō'bŭrn)	210	20.50 S	117.15 E
Roebuck, B. Austl. (rō'bŭck)	210	18.15 S	121.10 E
Roedtan, S. Afr.	219d	24.37 S	29.08 E
Roeselare, Bel.	161	50.55 N	3.05 E
Roesiger (L.), Wa. (rōz'ĭ-gẽr)	116a	47.59 N	121.56 W
Roes Welcome Sd., Can. (rōz)	95	64.10 N	87.23 W
Rogachëv, Sov. Un. (rôg'á-chyôf)	172	53.07 N	30.04 E
Rogatica, Yugo. (rô-gä'tē-tsä)	171	43.46 N	19.00 E
Rogatin, Sov. Un. (rô-gä'tĭn)	165	49.22 N	24.37 E
Rogers, Ar. (rŏj-ẽrz)	121	36.19 N	94.07 W
Rogers City, Mi.	108	45.30 N	83.50 W
Rogersville, Tn.	124	36.21 N	83.00 W
Rognac, Fr. (rōn-yäk')	166a	43.29 N	5.15 E
Rogoaguado (L.), Bol. (rō'gō-ä-gwä-dō)	140	12.42 S	66.46 W
Rogovskaya, Sov. Un. (rô-gôf'skà-yà)	173	45.43 N	38.42 E
Rogózno, Pol. (rô'gôzh-nō)	164	52.44 N	16.53 E
Rogue R., Or. (rōg)	114	42.32 N	124.13 W
Rojas, Arg. (rō'häs)	139c	34.11 S	60.42 W
Rojo, Cabo (C.), Mex. (rō'hō)	129	21.35 N	97.16 W
Rojo, Cabo (C.), P. R. (rō'hō)	127b	17.55 N	67.14 W
Rokel (R.), S. L.	224	9.00 N	11.55 W
Rokkō-Zan (Mtn.), Jap. (rôk'kō zän)	201b	34.46 N	135.16 E
Rokycany, Czech. (rô'kĭ'tsà-nĭ)	164	49.44 N	13.37 E
Roldanillo, Col. (rôl-dä-nē'l-yō)	140a	4.24 N	76.09 W
Rolla, Mo.	121	37.56 N	91.45 W
Rolla, ND	112	48.52 N	99.32 W
Rolleville, Ba.	133	23.40 N	76.00 W
Roma, Austl. (rō'mà)	212	26.30 S	148.48 E
Roma, Leso.	223c	29.28 S	27.43 E
Roma (Rome), It. (rō'mä) (rōm)	169d	41.52 N	12.37 E
Romaine (R.), Can. (rô-mĕn')	103	51.22 N	63.23 W
Roman, Rom. (rō'män)	165	46.56 N	26.57 E
Romania, Eur. (rō-mā'nē-à)	152	46.18 N	22.53 E
Romano, C., Fl. (rō-mä'nō)	125a	25.48 N	82.00 W
Romano, Cayo (I.), Cuba (kä'yō-rô-mä'nō)	132	22.15 N	78.00 W
Romanovo, Sov. Un. (rô-mä'nô-vô)	180a	59.09 N	61.24 E
Romans, Fr. (rô-mäN')	166	45.04 N	4.49 E
Romblon, Phil. (rōm-blōn')	203a	12.34 N	122.16 E
Romblon I., Phil.	203a	12.33 N	122.17 E
Rome, Ga. (rōm)	124	34.14 N	85.10 W
Rome, NY	109	43.15 N	75.25 W
Rome, see Roma			
Romeo, Mi. (rō'mē-ō)	108	42.50 N	83.00 W
Romford, Eng. (rŭm'fẽrd)	154b	51.35 N	0.11 E
Romilly-sur-Seine, Fr. (rô-mē-yē'sür-sān')	166	48.32 N	3.41 E
Romita, Mex. (rō-mē'tä)	128	20.53 N	101.32 W
Romny, Sov. Un. (rôm'nĭ)	173	50.46 N	33.31 E
Rømø (I.), Den. (rûm'û)	162	55.08 N	8.17 E
Romoland, Ca. (rō'mō'lănd)	117a	33.44 N	117.11 W
Romorantin-Lanthenay, Fr. (rô-mô-räN-täN')	166	47.24 N	1.46 E
Rompin, Mala.	189b	2.42 N	102.30 E
Rompin (R.), Mala.	189b	2.54 N	103.10 E
Romsdalsfjorden (Fd.), Nor.	162	62.40 N	7.05 W
Romulus, Mi. (rom'ū lŭs)	111b	42.14 N	83.24 W
Ronaldsay, North (I.), Scot.	160	59.21 N	2.23 W
Ronaldsay, South (I.), Scot. (rŏn'ăld-s'ā)	160	59.48 N	2.55 W
Ronan, Mt. (rō'năn)	115	47.28 N	114.03 W
Roncador, Serra do (Mts.), Braz. (sĕr'rá do͞o rôn-kä-dôr')	141	12.44 S	52.19 W
Roncesvalles, Sp. (rôn-sĕs-vä'l-yĕs)	168	43.00 N	1.17 W
Ronceverte, WV (rŏn'sē-vûrt)	108	37.45 N	80.30 W
Ronda, Sp. (rōn'dä)	168	37.45 N	5.10 W
Ronda, Sierra de (Mts.), Sp.	168	36.35 N	5.03 W
Rondônia (Ter.), Braz.	140	10.15 S	63.07 W
Ronge, Lac la (L.), Can. (rōnzh)	98	55.10 N	105.00 W
Rongjiang, China (rôŋ-jyäŋ)	199	25.52 N	108.45 E
Rong Xian, China	199	22.50 N	110.32 E
Rønne, Den. (rûn'ĕ)	162	55.08 N	14.46 E
Ronneby, Swe. (rōn'ĕ-bü)	162	56.13 N	15.17 E
Ronne Ice Shelf, Ant.	228	77.30 S	38.00 W
Ront Ra. (Mts.), Co. (rŏnt)	120	40.59 N	105.29 W
Roodepoort, S. Afr. (rō'dĕ-pōrt)	223b	26.10 S	27.52 E
Roodhouse, Il. (ro͞od'hous)	121	39.29 N	90.21 W
Rooiberg, S. Afr.	219d	24.46 S	27.42 E
Roosendaal, Neth. (rō'zĕn-däl)	155a	51.32 N	4.27 E
Roosevelt, Ut. (rōz''vĕlt)	119	40.20 N	110.00 W
Roosevelt (R.), Az.	119	33.45 N	111.00 W
Roosevelt (R.), Braz. (rō'sĕ-vĕlt)	141	9.22 S	60.28 W
Roosevelt I., Ant.	228	79.30 S	168.00 W
Root R., Wi.	111a	42.49 N	87.54 W
Roper (R.), Austl. (rōp'ẽr)	210	14.50 S	134.00 E
Ropsha, Sov. Un. (rôp'shà)	180c	59.44 N	29.53 E
Roques, Islas los (Is.), Ven.	140	21.25 N	67.40 W
Roque Pérez, Arg. (rô'kĕ-pĕ'rĕz)	139c	35.23 S	59.22 W
Roraima (Ter.), Braz. (rô'rīy-mä)	140	2.00 N	62.15 W
Roraima, Mtn., Ven.-Guy. (rô-rä-ē'mä)	141	5.12 N	60.52 W
Røros, Nor. (rûr'ôs)	162	62.36 N	11.25 E
Ros' (R.), Sov. Un. (rôs)	173	49.40 N	30.22 E
Rosa, Monte (Mt.), It. (mōn'tä rō'zä)	164	45.56 N	7.51 E
Rosales, Mex. (rō-zä'läs)	122	28.15 N	100.43 W
Rosales, Phil. (rō-sä'lĕs)	203a	15.54 N	120.38 E
Rosamorada, Mex. (rō'zä-mō-rä'dhä)	128	22.06 N	105.16 W
Rosaria, Laguna (L.), Mex. (lä-go͞o'nä-rō-sà'ryä)	129	17.50 N	93.51 W
Rosario, Arg. (rô-zä'rē-ō)	139c	32.58 S	60.42 W
Rosario, Braz. (rô-zä'rē-o͞o)	141	2.49 S	44.15 W
Rosario, Mex.	128	22.58 N	105.54 W
Rosario, Mex.	122	26.31 N	105.40 W
Rosario, Phil.	203a	13.49 N	121.13 W
Rosario, Ur.	139c	34.19 S	57.24 E
Rosario, Cayo (I.), Cuba (kä'yō-rō-sä'ryō)	132	21.40 N	81.55 W
Rosário do Sul, Braz. (rô-zä'rē-o͞o-dô-so͞o'l)	142	30.17 S	54.52 W
Rosário Oeste, Braz. (ō'ĕst'ĕ)	141	14.47 S	56.20 W
Rosario Str., Wa.	116a	48.27 N	122.45 W
Rosas, Golfo de (G.), Sp. (gōl-fô-dĕ-rō'zäs)	169	42.10 N	3.20 E
Rosbach, F.R.G. (rōz'bäK)	167c	50.47 N	7.38 E
Roscoe, Tx. (rōs'kō)	122	32.26 N	100.38 W
Roseau, Mn. (rô-zō')	112	48.52 N	95.47 W
Roseau, Dominica	131b	15.17 N	61.23 W
Roseau (R.), Mn.	112	48.52 N	96.11 W
Roseberg, Or. (rōz'bûrg)	114	43.13 N	123.30 W
Rosebud (R.), Can. (rōz'bŭd)	97	51.20 N	112.20 W
Rosebud Cr., Mt.	115	45.48 N	106.34 W
Rosebud Ind. Res., SD	112	43.13 N	100.42 W
Rosedale, Ms.	124	33.49 N	90.56 W
Rosedale, Wa.	116a	47.20 N	122.39 W
Roseires Res., Sud.	220	11.15 N	34.45 E
Roselle, Il. (rō-zĕl')	111a	41.59 N	88.05 W
Rosemere, Can. (rōz'mẽr)	93a	45.38 N	73.48 W
Rosemount, Mn. (rōz'mount)	117g	44.44 N	93.08 W
Rosendal, S. Afr. (rō-sĕn'täl)	219d	28.32 S	27.56 E
Rosenheim, F.R.G. (rō'zĕn-hīm)	164	47.52 N	12.06 E
Rosetown, Can. (rōz'toun)	98	51.33 N	108.00 W
Rosetta, see Rashīd			
Rosettenville (Neigh.), S. Afr.	223b	26.15 S	28.04 E
Roseville, Ca. (rōz'vĭl)	118	38.44 N	121.19 W
Roseville, Mi.	111b	42.30 N	82.55 W
Roseville, Mn.	117g	45.01 N	93.10 W
Rosiclare, Il. (rōz'ĭ-klâr)	108	37.30 N	88.15 W
Rosignol, Guy. (rôs-ĭg-nél)	141	6.16 N	57.37 W
Roşiori-de-Vede, Rom. (rô-shōr'ē dĕ vĕ-dĕ)	171	44.06 N	25.00 E
Roskilde, Den. (rôs'kĕl-dĕ)	162	55.39 N	12.04 E
Roslavl', Sov. Un. (rôs'läv'l)	172	53.56 N	32.52 E
Roslyn, Wa. (rŏz'lĭn)	114	47.14 N	121.00 W
Rosovka, Sov. Un.	173	47.14 N	36.35 E
Rösrath, F.R.G. (rûz'rät)	167c	50.53 N	7.11 E
Ross, Oh. (rôs)	111f	39.19 N	84.39 W
Rossano, It. (rô-sä'nō)	170	39.34 N	16.38 E
Rossan Pt., Ire.	160	54.45 N	8.30 W
Ross Cr., Can.	93g	53.50 N	113.08 W
Ross Dam, Wa.	114	48.40 N	121.07 W
Rosseau (L.), Can. (rôs-sō')	101	45.15 N	79.30 W
Rossel (I.), Pap. N. Gui. (rô-sĕl')	211	11.31 S	154.00 E
Rosser, Can. (rôs'sẽr)	93f	49.59 N	97.27 W
Rossignol, L., Can.	102	44.10 N	65.10 W
Ross I., Can.	99	54.14 N	97.45 W
Rossland, Can. (rôs'lănd)	97	49.05 N	118.48 W
Rosso, Mauritania	224	16.30 N	15.49 W
Rossosh', Sov. Un. (rôs'sŭsh)	173	50.12 N	39.32 E
Rossouw, S. Afr.	223c	31.12 S	27.18 E
Ross Sea, Ant.	228	76.00 S	178.00 W
Ross Shelf Ice, Ant.	228	81.30 S	175.00 W
Rossvatnet (L.), Nor.	156	65.36 N	13.08 E
Rossville, Ga. (rôs'vĭl)	124	34.57 N	85.22 W
Rosthern, Can.	98	52.41 N	106.25 W
Rostock, G.D.R. (rôs'tŭk)	164	54.04 N	12.06 E
Rostov, Sov. Un.	172	57.13 N	39.23 E
Rostov (Oblast), Sov. Un.	173	47.38 N	39.15 E
Rostov-na-Donu, Sov. Un. (rôstôv-nä-dō-no͞o)	177	47.16 N	39.47 E
Roswell, Ga. (rŏz'wĕl)	124	34.02 N	84.21 W
Roswell, NM	120	33.23 N	104.32 W
Rotan, Tx. (rô-tăn')	120	32.51 N	100.27 W
Rothenburg, F.R.G.	164	49.20 N	10.10 E
Rotherham, Eng. (rŏdh'ẽr-ăm)	154	53.26 N	1.21 W
Rothesay, Can. (rôth'sâ)	102	45.23 N	66.00 W
Rothesay, Scot.	160	55.50 N	3.14 W
Rothwell, Eng.	154	53.44 N	1.30 W
Roti, Pulau (I.), Indon. (rō'tē)	202	10.30 S	122.52 E
Roto, Austl. (rō'tô)	212	33.07 S	145.30 E
Rotorua, N.Z.	213	38.07 S	176.17 E
Rotterdam, Neth. (rôt'ẽr-däm')	155a	51.55 N	4.27 E
Rottweil, F.R.G. (rōt'vīl)	164	48.10 N	8.36 E
Roubaix, Fr. (ro͞o-bĕ')	166	50.42 N	3.10 E
Rouen, Fr. (ro͞o-äN')	166	49.25 N	1.05 E
Rouge, R., Mi.	111b	42.30 N	83.15 W
Rouge (R.), Can.	101	46.40 N	74.50 W
Rouge (R.), Can. (ro͞ozh)	93d	43.53 N	79.21 W
Rough River Res., Ky.	108	37.45 N	86.10 W
Round Lake, Il.	111a	42.21 N	88.05 W
Round Pd., Can.	103	48.15 N	55.57 W
Round Rock, Tx.	123	30.31 N	97.41 W
Round Top (Mtn.), Or. (tŏp)	116c	45.41 N	123.22 W
Roundup, Mt. (round'ŭp)	115	46.25 N	108.35 W
Rousay (I.), Scot. (ro͞o'zà)	160a	59.10 N	3.04 W
Rouyn, Can. (ro͞on)	95	48.22 N	79.03 W
Rovaniemi, Fin. (rô'và-nyĕ'mĭ)	156	66.29 N	25.45 E
Rovato, It. (rō-vä'tō)	170	45.33 N	10.00 E
Roven'ki, Sov. Un. (rô-vĕn'kĭ)	173	48.06 N	39.44 E
Roven'ki, Sov. Un.	173	49.54 N	38.54 E
Rovereto, It. (rō-vå-rā'tô)	170	45.53 N	11.05 E
Rovigo, It. (rō-vē'gô)	170	45.05 N	11.48 E
Rovinj, Yugo. (rô'ēn')	170	45.05 N	13.40 E
Rovira, Col. (rô-vē'rä)	140a	4.14 N	75.13 W
Rovno, Sov. Un. (rôv'nô)	165	50.37 N	26.17 E
Rovno (Oblast), Sov. Un.	173	50.55 N	27.00 E
Rovnoye, Sov. Un. (rôv'nô-yĕ)	173	48.11 N	31.46 E
Rovuma (Ruvuma) (R.), Moz.-Tan.	227	10.50 S	39.50 E
Rowley, Ma. (rou'lē)	103a	42.43 N	70.53 W
Roxana, Il. (rŏks'ăn-nà)	117e	38.51 N	90.05 W
Roxas, Phil. (rô-xäs)	202	11.30 N	122.47 E
Roxboro, NC (rŏks' bŭr-ô)	125	36.22 N	78.58 W
Roxo, Cap (C.), Senegal	224	12.20 N	16.43 W
Roy, NM (roi)	120	35.54 N	104.09 W
Roy, Ut.	117b	41.10 N	112.02 W
Royal (I.), Ba.	132	25.30 N	76.50 W
Royal Can., Ire. (roi-ăl)	160	53.28 N	6.45 W
Royal Natal Natl. Pk., S. Afr. (roi'ăl)	223c	28.35 S	28.54 E
Royal Oak, Can. (roi'ăl ōk)	116a	48.30 N	123.24 W
Royal Oak, Mi.	111b	42.29 N	83.09 W
Royalton, Mi. (roi'ăl-tŭn)	108	42.00 N	86.25 W
Royan, Fr. (rwä-yäN')	166	45.40 N	1.02 W
Roye, Fr. (rwä)	166	49.43 N	2.40 E
Royersford, Pa. (rô' yẽrz-fẽrd)	110f	40.11 N	75.32 W
Royston, Ga. (roiz'tŭn)	124	34.15 N	83.06 W
Royton, Eng. (roi'tŭn)	154	53.34 N	2.07 W
Rozay-en-Brie, Fr. (rō-zā-ĕN-brē')	167b	48.41 N	2.57 E
Rozhaya R., Sov. Un. (rô'zhá-yà)	180b	55.20 N	37.37 E
Rožňava, Czech. (rôzh'nyá-vá)	165	48.39 N	20.32 E
Rtishchevo, Sov. Un. ('r-tĭsh'chĕ-vô)	177	52.15 N	43.40 E
Ru (R.), China (ro͞o)	196	33.07 N	114.18 E
Ruacana Falls, Ang.-Namibia	222	17.15 S	14.45 E
Ruaha Natl. Pk., Tan.	227	7.15 S	34.50 E
Ruapehu (Vol.), N.Z. (ro͞o-á-pā'ho͞o)	213	39.15 S	175.37 E
Rubeho Mts., Tan.	227	6.45 S	36.15 E
Rubidoux, Ca.	117a	33.59 N	117.24 W
Rubondo I., Tan.	227	2.10 S	31.55 E
Rubtsovsk, Sov. Un.	178	51.31 N	81.17 E
Ruby, Ak. (ro͞o'bē)	105	64.38 N	155.22 W
Ruby (L.), Nv.	118	40.11 N	115.20 W
Ruby Mts., Nv.	118	40.11 N	115.36 W
Ruby R., Mt.	115	45.06 N	112.10 W
Rudkøbing, Den. (ro͞odh'kûb-ĭng)	162	54.56 N	10.44 E
Rüdnitz, G.D.R. (rüd'nētz)	155b	52.44 N	13.38 E
Rudolf, L., Ken.-Eth. (ro͞o'dŏlf)	227	3.30 N	36.05 E
Rudolstadt, G.D.R. (ro͞o'dôl-shtät)	161	50.46 N	13.30 E
Rufā'ah, Sud. (ro͞o-fä'ä)	221	14.52 N	33.30 E
Ruffec, Fr. (rü-fĕk')	166	46.03 N	0.11 E
Rufiji (R.), Tan. (ro͞o-fē'jē)	227	8.00 S	39.20 E
Rufisque, Senegal (rü-fēsk')	224	14.43 N	17.17 W
Rufunsa, Zambia	227	15.05 S	29.40 E
Rufus Woods, Wa.	114	48.02 N	119.33 W
Rugao, China (ro͞o-gou)	196	32.24 N	120.33 E
Rugby, Eng. (rŭg'bē)	154	52.22 N	1.15 W
Rugby, ND	112	48.22 N	100.00 W

ng-sing; ŋ-baŋk; N-nasalized n; nŏd; cŏmmit; ōld; ôbey; ôrder; oi-boil; fo͞od; fo͝ot; ou-out; s-soft; sh-dish; th-thin; pūre; ůnite; ûrn; stŭd; circŭs; ü-as in French tu; '-indeterminate vowel.

PLACE (Pronunciation)	PAGE	Lat. °'	Long. °'
Rugeley, Eng. (rōōj'lē)	154	52.46 N	1.56 W
Rügen (Pen.), G.D.R. (rü'ghĕn)	164	54.28 N	13.47 E
Ruhnu-Saar (I.), Sov. Un. (rōōnōō-sâ'ăr)	163	57.46 N	23.15 E
Ruhr R., F.R.G. (rōōr)	164	51.18 N	8.17 E
Rui'an, China (rwā-än)	199	27.48 N	120.40 E
Ruiz, Mex. (rōōē'z)	128	21.55 N	105.09 W
Ruiz, Nevado del (Pk.), Col. (nĕ-vä'dô-dĕl-rōōē'z)	140a	4.52 N	75.20 W
Rūjiena, Sov. Un. (rōō'yĭ-ă-nȧ)	163	57.54 N	25.19 E
Ruki (R.), Zaire	226	0.05 S	18.55 E
Rukwa, L., Tan. (rōōk-wä')	227	8.00 S	32.25 E
Rum (R.), Mn. (rŭm)	113	45.52 N	93.45 W
Ruma, Yugo. (rōō'mȧ)	171	45.00 N	19.53 E
Rumbek, Sud. (rŭm'bĕk)	221	6.52 N	29.43 E
Rum Cay (I.), Ba.	133	23.40 N	74.50 W
Rumford, Me. (rŭm'fērd)	102	44.32 N	70.35 W
Rummah, Wādī ar (R.), Sau. Ar.	192	26.17 N	41.45 E
Rummānah, Egypt	189a	31.01 N	32.39 E
Runan, China (rōō-nän)	196	32.59 N	114.22 E
Runcorn, Eng. (rŭŋ'kôrn)	154	53.20 N	2.44 W
Ruo (R.), China (rwô)	194	41.15 N	100.46 E
Rupat, Palau (I.), Indon. (rōō'pät)	189b	1.55 N	101.35 E
Rupat, Selat (Str.), Indon.	189b	1.55 N	101.17 E
Rupert, Id. (rōō'pērt)	115	42.36 N	113.41 W
Rupert, Rivière de (R.), Can.	95	51.35 N	76.30 W
Ruse (Russe), Bul. (rōō'sĕ) (rōō'sĕ)	171	43.50 N	25.59 E
Rushan, China (rōō-shän)	196	36.54 N	121.31 E
Rush City, Mn.	113	45.40 N	92.59 W
Rushville, Il. (rŭsh'vĭl)	121	40.08 N	90.34 W
Rushville, In.	108	39.35 N	85.30 W
Rushville, Ne.	112	42.43 N	102.27 W
Rusizi (R.), Zaire,	227	3.00 S	29.05 E
Rusk, Tx. (rŭsk)	123	31.49 N	95.09 W
Ruskin, Can. (rŭs'kĭn)	116d	49.10 N	122.25 W
Russ (R.), Aus.	155e	48.12 N	16.55 E
Russas, Braz. (rōō's-säs)	141	4.48 S	37.50 W
Russe, see Ruse			
Russell, Ca.	116b	37.39 N	122.08 W
Russell, Can. (rŭs'ĕl)	99	50.47 N	101.15 W
Russell, Can.	93c	45.15 N	75.22 W
Russell, Ks.	120	38.51 N	98.51 W
Russell, Ky.	108	38.30 N	82.45 W
Russell Is., Sol. Is.	211	9.16 S	158.30 E
Russel L., Can.	99	56.15 N	101.30 W
Russellville, Al. (rŭs'ĕl-vĭl)	124	34.29 N	87.44 W
Russellville, Ar.	121	35.16 N	93.08 W
Russelville, Ky.	124	36.48 N	86.51 W
Russian (R.), Ca. (rŭsh'ăn)	118	38.59 N	123.10 W
Russian S. F. S. R., Sov. Un.	174	61.00 N	60.00 E
Rustenburg, S. Afr. (rŭs'tĕn-bûrg)	219d	25.40 S	26.15 E
Ruston, La. (rŭs'tŭn)	123	32.32 N	92.39 W
Ruston, Wa.	116a	47.18 N	122.30 W
Rutchenkovo, Sov. Un. (rōō-chĕn'kô-vô)	173	47.54 N	37.36 E
Rute, Sp. (rōō'tā)	168	37.20 N	4.34 W
Ruth, Nv. (rōōth)	118	39.17 N	115.00 W
Ruthenia (Reg.), Sov. Un.	165	48.25 N	23.00 E
Rutherfordton, NC (rŭdh'ēr-fērd-tŭn)	125	35.23 N	81.58 W
Rutland, Vt.	109	43.35 N	72.55 W
Rutledge, Md. (rŭt'lĕdj)	110e	39.34 N	76.33 W
Rutog, China (rōō-tô-gŭ)	190	33.42 N	79.56 E
Rutshuru, Zaire (rōōt-shōō'rōō)	227	1.11 S	29.27 E
Ruvo, It. (rōō'vô)	170	41.07 N	16.32 E
Ruvuma (Rovuma) (R.), Moz.-Tan.	227	10.50 S	39.50 E
Ruwenzori Mts., Afr. (rōō-wĕn-zō'rē)	221	0.53 N	30.00 E
Ruza, Sov. Un. (rōō'zȧ)	172	55.42 N	36.12 E
Ruzhany, Sov. Un. (rōō-zhän'ĭ)	165	52.49 N	24.54 E
Rwanda, Afr.	218	2.10 S	29.37 E
Ryabovo, Sov. Un. (ryä'bô-vô)	180c	59.24 N	31.08 E
Ryazan', Sov. Un. (ryä-zän'')	172	54.37 N	39.43 E
Ryazan' (Oblast), Sov. Un.	172	54.10 N	39.37 E
Ryazhsk, Sov. Un. (ryäzh'sk')	172	53.43 N	40.04 E
Rybachiy, P-Ov. (Pen.), Sov. Un.	176	69.50 N	33.20 E
Rybatskoye, Sov. Un. (rĭ-bät'skô-yĕ)	180c	59.50 N	30.31 E
Rybinsk, Sov. Un. (ry-bĭ'nsk)	172	58.02 N	38.52 E
Rybinskoye Vdkhr. (Res.), Sov. Un.	172	58.23 N	38.15 E
Rybnik, Pol. (rĭb'nĕk)	165	50.06 N	18.37 E
Rybnitsa, Sov. Un. (rĭb'nĕt-sȧ)	173	47.45 N	29.02 E
Ryde, Eng. (rīd)	160	50.43 N	1.16 W
Rye, NY (rī)	110a	40.58 N	73.42 W
Ryl'sk, Sov. Un. (rēl''sk)	173	51.33 N	34.42 E
Ryōtsu, Jap. (ryōt'sōō)	200	38.02 N	138.23 E
Rypin, Pol. (rĭ'pēn)	165	53.04 N	19.25 E
Ryukyu, see Nansei-shotō			
Rzeszów, Pol. (zhā-shōōf)	165	50.02 N	22.00 E
Rzhev, Sov. Un. ('r-zhĕf)	172	56.16 N	34.17 E
Rzhishchëv, Sov. Un. ('r-zhĭsh'chĕf)	173	49.58 N	31.05 E

S

PLACE (Pronunciation)	PAGE	Lat. °'	Long. °'
Saale R., G.D.R. (sä-lĕ)	164	51.14 N	11.52 E
Saalfeld, G.D.R. (säl'fĕlt)	164	50.38 N	11.20 E
Saarbrücken, F.R.G. (zähr'brü-kĕn)	164	49.15 N	7.01 E
Saaremaa (Ezel) (I.), Sov. Un. (sä'rĕ-mä)	163	58.28 N	21.30 E
Saarland (State), F.R.G.	164	49.25 N	6.50 E
Saavedra, Arg. (sä-ä-vā'drä)	142	37.45 S	62.23 W
Šabac, Yugo. (shä'bȧts)	171	44.45 N	19.49 E
Sabadell, Sp. (sä-bä-dhāl')	169	41.32 N	2.07 E
Sabah (Reg.), Mala.	202	5.10 N	116.25 E
Saba I., Neth. Antilles (sä'bä)	131b	17.39 N	63.20 W
Sabana, Arch. de, Cuba (är-chē-pyĕ'lä-gô dĕ sä-bä'nä)	132	23.05 N	80.00 W
Sabana, R., Pan. (sä-bä'nä)	131	8.40 N	78.02 W
Sabana de la Mar, Dom. Rep. (sä-bä'nä dā lä mär')	133	19.05 N	69.30 W
Sabana de Uchire, Ven. (sä-bä'nä dĕ ōō-chē'rĕ)	141b	10.02 N	65.32 W
Sabanagrande, Hond. (sä-bä'nä-grä'n-dĕ)	130	13.47 N	87.16 W
Sabanalarga, Col. (sä-bä'nä-lär'gä)	140	10.38 N	75.02 W
Sabanas Páramo (Mtn.), Col. (sä-bä'näs pá'rä-mô)	140a	6.28 N	76.08 W
Sabancuy, Mex. (sä-bäŋ-kwē')	129	18.58 N	91.09 W
Sabang, Indon. (sä'bäng)	202	5.52 N	95.26 E
Sabaudia, It. (sȧ-bou'dē-ȧ)	172	41.19 N	13.00 E
Sabetha, Ks. (sȧ-bĕth'ȧ)	121	39.54 N	95.49 W
Sabi (R.), Zimb. (sä'bē)	222	20.18 S	32.07 E
Sabile, Sov. Un. (sä'bē-lĕ)	163	57.03 N	22.34 E
Sabinal, Tx. (sȧ-bī'năl)	122	29.19 N	99.27 W
Sabinal, Cayo (I.), Cuba (kä'yō sä-bē-näl')	132	21.40 N	77.20 W
Sabinas, Mex.	126	28.05 N	102.30 W
Sabinas, R., Mex. (sä-bē'näs)	122	26.37 N	99.52 W
Sabinas, Rio (R.), Mex. (rē'ō sä-bē'näs)	122	27.25 N	100.33 W
Sabinas Hidalgo, Mex. (ē-däl'gô)	122	26.30 N	100.10 W
Sabine, Tx. (sȧ-bēn')	123	29.44 N	93.54 W
Sabine, Mt., Ant.	228	72.05 S	169.10 E
Sabine (R.), U.S.	107	31.35 N	94.00 W
Sabine L., La.-Tx.	123	29.53 N	93.41 W
Sablayan, Phil. (säb-lä-yän')	203a	12.49 N	120.47 E
Sable, C., Can. (sä'b'l)	102	43.25 N	65.24 W
Sable, C., Fl.	125a	25.12 N	81.10 W
Sables, Rivière aux (R.), Can.	101	49.00 N	70.20 W
Sablé-sur-Sarthe, Fr. (säb-lā-sür-särt')	166	47.50 N	0.17 W
Sablya, Gora (Mtn.), Sov. Un.	176	64.50 N	59.00 E
Sàbor (R.), Port. (sä-bōr')	168	41.18 N	6.54 W
Sac (R.), Mo. (sôk)	121	38.11 N	93.45 W
Sacandaga Res., NY (sä-kăn-dȧ'gȧ)	109	43.10 N	74.15 W
Sacavém, Port. (sä-kä-vĕN')	169b	38.47 N	9.06 W
Sacavém (R.), Port.	163b	38.52 N	9.06 W
Sac City, Ia. (sŏk)	113	42.25 N	95.00 W
Sachigo L., Can. (săch'ĭ-gō)	99	53.49 N	92.08 W
Sachsen (Reg.), G.D.R. (zäk'sĕn)	164	50.45 N	12.17 E
Sacketts Harbor, NY (săk'ĕts)	109	43.55 N	76.05 W
Sackville, Can. (săk'vĭl)	102	45.54 N	64.22 W
Saco, Me. (sô'kō)	102	43.30 N	70.28 W
Saco (R.), Braz. (sä'kô)	142b	22.20 S	43.26 W
Saco (R.), Me.	102	43.53 N	70.46 W
Sacra Famalia do Tinguá, Braz. (sä-krä fä-mä'lyä dō tēn-gwȧ')	142b	22.29 S	43.36 W
Sacramento, Ca. (săk-rȧ-mĕn'tō)	118	38.35 N	121.30 W
Sacramento, Mex.	122	25.45 N	103.22 W
Sacramento, Mex.	122	27.05 N	101.45 W
Sacramento (R.), Ca.	118	40.20 N	122.07 W
Şa'dah, Yemen	192	16.50 N	43.45 E
Saddle Lake Ind. Res., Can.	97	54.00 N	111.40 W
Saddle Mtn., Or. (săd''l)	116c	45.58 N	123.40 W
Sadiya, India (sŭ-dē'yä)	193	27.53 N	95.35 E
Sado (I.), Jap. (sä'dō)	200	38.05 N	138.26 E
Sado (R.), Port. (sä'dōō)	168	38.15 N	8.20 W
Saeby, Den. (sĕ'bü)	162	57.21 N	10.29 E
Saeki, Jap. (sä'å-kĕ)	201	32.56 N	131.51 E
Safford, Az. (săf'fērd)	119	32.50 N	109.45 W
Safi (Asfi), Mor. (sä'fē) (äs'fē)	220	32.24 N	9.09 W
Safid Rud (R.), Iran	177	36.50 N	49.40 E
Saga, Jap. (sä'gä)	201	33.15 N	130.18 E
Sagami-Nada (Sea), Jap. (sä'gä'mē nä-dä)	201	35.06 N	139.24 E
Sagamore Hills, Oh. (săg'ȧ-môr hĭlz)	111d	41.19 N	81.34 W
Saganaga (L.), Can.-Mn. (săg-ȧ-nä'gȧ)	113	48.13 N	91.17 W
Sāgar, India	190	23.55 N	78.45 E
Saginaw, Mi. (săg'ĭ-nô)	108	43.25 N	84.00 W
Saginaw, Mn.	117h	46.51 N	92.26 W
Saginaw, Tx.	117c	32.52 N	97.22 W
Saginaw B., Mi.	108	43.50 N	83.40 W
Sagiz (R.), Sov. Un. (sä'gēz)	177	48.30 N	56.10 E
Saguache, Co. (sȧ-wăch') (sȧ-gwä'chē)	109	38.05 N	106.10 W
Saguache Cr., Co.	109	38.05 N	106.40 W
Sagua de Tánamo, Cuba (sä-gwä dĕ tá'nä-mō)	133	20.40 N	75.15 W
Sagua la Grande, Cuba (sä-gwä lä grä'n-dĕ)	132	22.45 N	80.05 W
Saguaro Natl. Mon., Az. (säg-wä'rō)	119	32.12 N	110.40 W
Saguenay (R.), Can. (săg-ē-nā')	100	48.20 N	70.15 W
Sagunto, Sp. (sä-gōōn'tō)	169	39.40 N	0.17 W
Sahara Des., Afr. (sȧ-hä'rȧ)	218	23.44 N	1.40 W
Saharan Atlas (Mts.), Mor.-Alg.	158	32.51 N	1.02 W
Sahāranpur, India (sŭ-hä'rŭn-pōōr')	190	29.58 N	77.41 E
Sahara Village, Ut. (sȧ-hä'rȧ)	117b	41.06 N	111.58 W
Sāhiwāl, Pak.	190	30.43 N	73.04 E
Sahuayo de Dias, Mex.	128	20.03 N	102.43 W
Saïda, Alg. (sä'ē-dä)	220	34.51 N	00.07 E
Saigon, see Ho Chi Minh City			
Saijō, Jap. (sä'ē-jô)	201	33.55 N	133.13 E
Saimaa, Fin. (sä'ĭ-mä)	163	61.24 N	28.45 E
Sain Alto, Mex. (sä-ēn' äl'tō)	128	23.35 N	103.13 W
St. Adolphe, Can. (sȧnt a'dôlf) (săN' tȧ-dôlf')	93f	49.40 N	97.07 W
St. Afrique, Fr. (săN' tȧ-frēk')	166	43.58 N	2.52 E
St. Albans, Austl. (sȧnt ôl'bănz)	207a	37.44 S	144.47 E
St. Albans, Eng.	154b	51.44 N	0.20 W
St. Albans, Vt.	109	44.50 N	73.05 W
St. Albans, WV	108	38.20 N	81.50 W
St. Albert, Can. (sȧnt ăl'bērt)	93g	53.38 N	113.38 W
St. Amand-MontRond, Fr. (săN't ȧ-mäN' môN-rôN')	166	46.44 N	2.28 E
St. André, Cap (C.), Mad.	223	16.15 S	44.31 E
St. André-Est., Can.	93a	45.33 N	74.19 W
St. Andrew, B., Fl.	124	30.20 N	85.45 W
St. Andrews, Can.	102	45.05 N	67.03 W
St. Andrews, Scot.	160	56.20 N	2.40 W
St. Andrew's Chan., Can. (ăn'drōōz)	103	46.06 N	60.28 W
St. Anicet, Can. (sĕNt ä-nē-sĕ')	93a	45.07 N	74.23 W
St. Ann, Mo. (sȧnt ăn')	117e	38.44 N	90.23 W
Ste. Anne, Can. (sȧNt'ăn') (sȧnt ăn')	102	46.55 N	71.46 W
St. Anne, Il.	111a	41.01 N	87.44 W
Ste. Anne, Guad.	131b	16.15 N	61.23 W
Ste.-Anne (R.), Can.	93b	47.07 N	70.50 W
Ste. Anne-de-Beaupré, Can. (dē bō-prā')	93b	47.02 N	70.56 W
Ste. Anne-des-Plaines, Can. (dā plĕN)	93a	45.46 N	73.49 W
St. Anns B., Can. (ănz)	103	46.20 N	60.30 W
St. Ann's Bay, Jam.	132	18.25 N	77.15 W
St. Anselme, Can. (săN' tăN-sĕlm')	93b	46.37 N	70.58 W
St. Anthony, Can. (săN ăn'thō-nē)	103	51.24 N	55.35 W
St. Anthony, Id. (sȧnt ăn'thō-nē)	115	43.59 N	111.42 W
St. Antoine-de-Tilly, Can.	93b	46.00 N	71.31 W
St. Apollinaire, Can. (săN' tȧ-pôl-ē-nâr')	93b	46.36 N	71.30 W
St. Arnoult-en-Yvelines, Fr. (săN-tär-nōō'ĕN-nēv-lēn')	167b	48.33 N	1.55 E
St. Augustin-de-Québec, Can. (sĕn tō-gŭs-tēn')	93b	46.45 N	71.27 W
St. Augustin-Deux-Montagnes, Can.	93a	45.38 N	73.59 W
St. Augustine, Fl. (sȧnt ô'gŭs-tēn)	125	29.53 N	81.21 W
Ste. Barbe, Can. (sȧnt bärb')	93a	45.14 N	74.12 W
St. Barthelemy I., Guad.	131b	17.55 N	62.32 W
St. Bees Hd., Eng. (sȧnt bēz' hĕd)	160	54.30 N	3.40 W
St. Benoit, Can. (sĕN bē-nōō-ä')	93a	45.34 N	74.05 W
St. Bernard, La. (bēr-närd')	110d	29.52 N	89.52 W
St. Bernard, Oh.	111f	39.10 N	84.30 W
St. Bride Mt., Can. (sȧnt brīd)	97	51.30 N	115.57 W
St. Brieuc, Fr. (săN' brēs')	166	48.32 N	2.47 W
St. Bruno, Can. (brū'nō)	93a	45.31 N	73.40 W
St. Canut, Can. (săN' kȧ-nū')	93a	45.43 N	74.04 W
St. Casimir, Can. (kȧ-zē-mēr')	102	46.45 N	72.34 W
St. Catharines, Can. (kăth'ȧ-rĭnz)	93d	43.10 N	79.14 W
St. Catherine, Mt., Grenada	131b	12.10 N	62.42 W
St. Chamas, Fr. (săN-shä-mä')	166a	43.32 N	5.03 E
St. Chamond, Fr. (săN' shȧ-môN')	166	45.30 N	4.17 E
St. Charles, Can. (săN' shärlz')	93b	46.47 N	70.57 W
St. Charles, Il. (sȧnt chärlz')	111a	41.55 N	88.19 W
St. Charles, Mi.	108	43.20 N	84.10 W
St. Charles, Mn.	113	43.56 N	92.05 W
St. Charles, Mo.	117e	38.47 N	90.29 W
St. Charles, Lac (L.), Can.	93b	46.56 N	71.21 W
St. Clair, Mi. (sȧnt klâr)	108	42.55 N	82.30 W
St. Clair (L.), Can.-Mi.	108	42.25 N	82.30 W
St. Clair (R.), Can.-Mi.	108	42.45 N	82.25 W
Ste. Claire, Can.	93b	46.36 N	70.52 W
St. Clair Shores, Mi.	111b	42.30 N	82.54 W
St. Claude, Fr. (săN' klōd')	167	46.24 N	5.53 E
St. Clet, Can. (sȧNt' klā')	93a	45.22 N	74.21 W
St. Cloud, Fl. (sȧnt kloud')	125a	28.13 N	81.17 W
St. Cloud, Mn.	113	45.33 N	94.08 W
St. Constant, Can. (kôn'stȧnt)	93a	45.23 N	73.34 W
St. Croix I., S. Afr. (săN krwä)	223c	33.48 S	25.45 E
Saint Croix (I.), Vir. Is. (U.S.A.) (sȧnt kroi')	127b	17.40 N	64.43 W
St. Croix (R.), Can.-Me. (kroi')	102	45.28 N	67.32 W
St. Croix Ind. Res., Wi.	113	45.40 N	92.21 W
St. Croix R., Mn.-Wi. (sȧnt kroi')	113	45.00 N	92.44 W
St. Damien-de-Buckland, Can. (sȧnt dā'mē-ĕn)	93b	46.37 N	70.39 W
St. David, Can. (dā'vĭd)	93b	46.47 N	71.11 W
St. David's Hd., Wales	160	51.54 N	5.25 W
St.-Denis, Fr. (săN'dē-nē')	167b	48.26 N	2.22 E
St. Dié, Fr. (dē-ā')	167	48.18 N	6.55 E
St. Dizier, Fr. (dē-zyā')	166	48.49 N	4.55 E
St. Dominique, Can. (sĕN dō-mē-nēk')	93a	45.19 N	74.09 W
St. Edouard-de-Napierville, Can. (sĕN-tē-dōō-är')	93a	45.14 N	73.31 W
St. Elias, Mt., Can. (sȧnt ē-lī'ăs)	105	60.25 N	141.00 W
St. Étienne, Fr.	166	45.26 N	4.22 E
St. Etienne-de-Lauzon, Can. (săN' tā-tyĕn')	93b	46.39 N	71.19 W
Ste. Euphémie, Can. (sĕNt û-fē-mē')	93b	46.47 N	70.27 W
St. Eustache, Can. (săN' tû-stash')	93a	45.34 N	73.54 W
St. Eustache, Can.	93f	49.58 N	97.47 W
St. Eustatius I., Neth. Antilles (sȧnt u-stā'shŭs)	131b	17.32 N	62.45 W
Ste. Famille, Can. (săN't fȧ-mē'y')	93b	46.58 N	70.58 W
St. Félicien, Can. (săN fā-lē-syăN')	103	48.39 N	72.28 W
Ste. Felicite, Can.	102	48.54 N	67.20 W
St. Féréol, Can. (fa-rā-ôl')	93b	47.07 N	70.52 W
St. Florent-sur-Cher, Fr. (săN' flō-räN'sür-shâr')	166	46.58 N	2.15 E
St. Flour, Fr. (săN flōōr')	166	45.02 N	3.09 E
Ste. Foy, Can. (sȧNt fwä)	93b	46.47 N	71.18 W
St. Francis (R.), Ar.	121	35.56 N	90.27 W
St. Francis L., Can. (săN frăn'sĭs)	109	45.00 N	74.20 W
St. François, Can. (săN'frăN-swä')	93b	47.01 N	70.49 W
St. François de Boundji, Con.	219	1.03 S	15.22 E
St. Francois Xavier, Can.	93f	49.55 N	97.32 W
St. Gaudens, Fr. (gō-dăNs')	166	43.07 N	0.43 E
Ste. Genevieve, Mo. (sȧnt jĕn'ē-vēv)	121	37.58 N	90.02 W
St. George, Austl. (sȧnt jôrj')	212	28.02 S	148.40 E
St. George, Can. (săN jôrj')	102	45.08 N	66.49 W
St. George, Can. (săN'zhôrzh')	93d	43.14 N	80.15 W
St. George, SC (sȧnt jôrj')	125	33.11 N	80.35 W

ăt; finăl; rāte; senȧte; ärm; ȧsk; sofȧ; fâre; ch-choose; dh-as th in other; bē; ēvent; bĕt; recĕnt; cratēr; g-gō; gh-guttural g; bĭt; ĭ-short neutral; rīde; K-guttural k as ch in German ich;

PRONOUNCING INDEX

St. George – Saline 341

PLACE (Pronunciation)	PAGE	Lat. °′	Long. °′
St. George, Ut.	119	37.05 N	113.40 W
St. George (I.), Ak.	105	56.30 N	169.40 W
St. George, C., Can.	103	48.28 N	59.15 W
St. George, C., Fl.	124	29.30 N	85.20 W
St. George's, Can. (jôrj'ēs)	103	48.26 N	58.29 W
St. Georges, Fr. Gu.	141	3.48 N	51.47 W
St. Georges, Grenada	131b	12.02 N	61.57 W
St. Georges B., Can.	103	45.49 N	61.45 W
St. George's B., Can.	103	48.20 N	59.00 W
St. George's Chan., Eng.-Ire. (jôr-jĕz)	160	51.45 N	6.30 W
St. Germain-en-Laye, Fr. (săN' zhĕr-măN-äN-lā')	167b	48.53 N	2.05 E
St. Gervais, Can. (zhĕr-vĕ')	93b	46.43 N	70.53 W
St. Girons, Fr. (zhē-rôN')	166	42.58 N	1.08 E
St. Gregory, Mt., Can. (sănt grĕg'ēr-ē)	103	49.19 N	58.13 W
St. Helena, Atl. O.	218	16.01 S	5.16 W
St. Helenabaai (B.), Afr.	222	32.25 S	17.15 E
St. Helens, Eng. (sănt hĕl'ĕnz)	154	53.27 N	2.44 W
St. Helens, Or. (hĕl'ĕnz)	116c	45.52 N	122.49 W
St. Helens, Mt., Wa.	114	46.13 N	122.10 W
St. Helier, Jersey (hyĕl'yēr)	166	49.12 N	2.06 W
St. Henri, Can. (săN' hĕn'rē)	93b	46.41 N	71.04 W
St. Hubert, Can.	93a	45.29 N	73.24 W
St. Hyacinthe, Can. (săN' tē-ä-săNt') (sănt hī'ȧ-sĭnth)	109	45.35 N	72.55 W
St.-Ignace, Can.	102	46.42 N	70.30 W
St. Ignace, Mi. (sănt ĭg'nās)	113	45.51 N	84.39 W
St. Ignace (I.), Can. (săN' ĭg'nās)	113	48.47 N	88.14 W
St. Irenee, Can. (săN' tē-rā-nā')	102	47.34 N	70.15 W
St. Isidore-de-Laprairie, Can. (saN' tē-zē-dōr') (sănt ĭz'ĭ-dôr)	93a	45.18 N	73.41 W
St. Isidore-de-Prescott, Can. (săN' ĭz'ĭ-dôr-prĕs-kŏt)	93c	45.23 N	74.54 W
St. Isidore-Dorchester, Can. (dŏr-chĕs'tēr)	93b	46.35 N	71.05 W
St. Jacob, Il. (jā-kŏb)	117e	38.43 N	89.46 W
St. James, Mn. (sănt jāmz')	113	43.58 N	94.37 W
St. James, Mo.	111	37.59 N	91.37 W
St. James, C., Can.	96	51.58 N	131.00 W
St. Janvier, Can. (săN' zhän-vyā')	93a	45.43 N	73.56 W
St. Jean, Can. (săN' zhäN')	109	45.20 N	73.15 W
St. Jean, Can.	93b	46.55 N	70.54 W
St. Jean, Lac (L.), Can.	101	48.35 N	72.00 W
St. Jean-Chrysostome, Can. (krĭ-zōs-tōm')	93b	46.43 N	71.12 W
St. Jean-d'Angely, Fr. (däN-zhā-lē')	166	45.56 N	0.33 W
St. Jean-de-Luz, Fr. (dē lüz')	166	43.23 N	1.40 W
St. Jérôme, Can. (sănt jĕ-rōm') (săN zhā-rōm')	93a	45.47 N	74.00 W
St. Joachim-de-Montmorency, Can. (sănt jō'ȧ-kĭm)	93b	47.04 N	70.51 W
Saint John, Can. (sănt jŏn)	102	45.16 N	66.03 W
St. John, In.	111a	41.27 N	87.29 W
St. John, Ks.	120	37.59 N	98.44 W
St. John, ND	112	48.57 N	99.42 W
St. John (R.), Can.	102	46.39 N	67.40 W
St. John B., Can.	103	50.54 N	57.08 W
St. John, C., Can.	103	50.00 N	55.32 W
St. John I., Can.	103	50.49 N	57.14 W
St. John (I.), Vir. Is. (U.S.A.)	127b	18.16 N	64.48 W
St. John (R.), N.A.	95	45.15 N	67.40 W
St. John's, Can. (jŏns)	103	47.34 N	52.43 W
St. Johns, Az. (jŏnz)	119	34.30 N	109.25 W
St. Johns, Mi.	108	43.05 N	84.35 W
St. Johns, Antigua	131b	17.07 N	61.50 W
St. Johns (R.), Fl.	125	29.54 N	81.32 W
St. Johnsbury, Vt. (jŏnz'bĕr-ē)	109	44.25 N	72.00 W
St. Joseph, Can. (jō'zhûf)	102	46.17 N	70.52 W
St. Joseph, Mi.	108	42.05 N	86.30 W
St. Joseph, Mo. (sănt jō-sĕf)	121	39.44 N	94.49 W
St. Joseph, Dominica	131b	15.25 N	61.26 W
St. Joseph (I.), Can.	108	46.15 N	83.55 W
St. Joseph (L.), Can. (jō'zhûf)	95	51.31 N	90.40 W
St. Joseph (R.), Mi. (sănt jō'sĕf)	108	41.45 N	85.50 W
St. Joseph, B., Fl. (jō'zhûf)	124	29.48 N	85.26 W
St. Joseph-de-Beauce, Can. (sĕN zhō-zĕf'dĕ bōs)	101	46.18 N	70.52 W
St. Joseph-du-Lac, Can. (sĕN zhō-zĕf' dü läk)	93a	45.32 N	74.00 W
St. Joseph I., Tx. (sănt jō-sĕf)	123	27.58 N	96.50 W
St. Junien, Fr. (săN'zhü-nyăN')	166	45.53 N	0.54 E
Ste. Justine-de-Newton, Can. (sănt jŭs-tēn')	93a	45.22 N	74.22 W
St. Kilda (I.), Scot. (kĭl'dȧ)	160	57.10 N	8.32 W
St. Kitts (I.), St. Kitts-Nevis (sānt kĭtts)	127	17.24 N	63.30 W
St. Lambert, Can. (săN' läN-bĕr') (sănt lăm'bērt)	93a	45.29 N	73.29 W
St. Lambert-de-Lévis, Can.	93b	46.35 N	71.12 W
St. Laurent, Can. (săN'lō-rän)	93a	45.31 N	73.41 W
St. Laurent, Fr. Gu.	141	5.27 N	53.56 W
St. Laurent-d'Orleans, Can.	93b	46.52 N	71.00 W
St. Lawrence, Can. (sānt lô'rĕns)	103	46.55 N	55.23 W
St. Lawrence (I.), Ak. (sănt lô'rĕns)	105	63.10 N	172.12 W
St. Lawrence, Gulf of, Can.	103	48.00 N	62.00 W
St. Lawrence R. (Fleuve St.-Laurent), Can.-U.S.	95	48.24 N	69.30 W
St. Lazare, Can. (săN'lȧ-zȧr')	93b	46.39 N	70.48 W
St. Lazare-de-Vaudreuil, Can.	93a	45.24 N	74.08 W
St. Léger-en-Yvelines, Fr. (sȧN-lā-zhĕ'ĕN-nēv-lēn')	167b	48.43 N	1.45 E
St. Leonard, Can. (sănt lĕn'ȧrd)	102	47.10 N	67.56 W
St. Léonard, Can.	93a	45.36 N	73.35 W
St. Leonard, Md.	110e	38.29 N	76.31 W
St.-Lô, Fr. (săN'lō')	166	49.08 N	1.07 W
St. Louis, Mi. (sănt lo͞o'ĭs)	108	43.25 N	84.35 W
St. Louis, Mo. (sănt lo͞o'ĭs) (lo͞o'ē)	117e	38.39 N	90.15 W
St.-Louis, Senegal	224	16.02 N	16.30 W
St. Louis, Lac (L.), Can. (săN' lo͞o-ē')	93a	45.24 N	73.51 W
St. Louis (R.), Mn. (sănt lo͞o'ĭs)	113	46.57 N	92.58 W
St. Louis-de-Gonzague, Can. (săN' lo͞o ē')	93a	45.13 N	74.00 W
St. Louis Park, Mn.	117g	44.56 N	93.21 W
Saint Lucia, N. A.	127	13.54 N	60.40 W
St. Lucia Chan., N. A. (lū'shĭ-ȧ)	131b	14.15 N	61.00 W
St. Lucie Can., Fl. (lū'sē)	125a	26.57 N	80.25 W
St. Magnus B., Scot. (măg'nŭs)	160a	60.25 N	2.09 W
St. Malo, Fr. (săN' mȧ-lō')	166	48.40 N	2.02 W
St. Malo, Golfe de (G.), Fr. (gôlf-dĕ-sȧN-mä-lō')	166	48.50 N	2.49 W
St. Marc, Hai. (săN' mȧrk')	133	19.10 N	72.40 W
St.-Marc, Canal de (Chan.), Hai.	133	19.05 N	73.15 W
St. Marcellin, Fr. (mär-sĕ-lăN')	167	45.08 N	5.15 E
Ste. Marie, Cap (C.), Mad.	223	25.31 S	45.00 E
Ste.-Marie-aux-Mines, Fr. (sȧN'tĕ-mä-rē'ō-mēn')	167	48.14 N	7.08 E
Ste. Marie-Beauce, Can. (săNt'mȧ-rē')	102	46.27 N	71.03 W
St. Maries, Id. (sănt mā'rēs)	114	47.18 N	116.34 W
St. Margarets, Md.	110e	39.02 N	76.30 W
Ste. Martine, Can.	93a	45.14 N	73.37 W
St. Martin I., Guad.-Neth-Antilles (mär'tĭn)	131b	18.06 N	62.54 W
St. Martins, Can. (mär'tĭnz)	102	45.21 N	65.32 W
St. Martinville, La. (mär'tĭn-vĭl)	123	30.08 N	91.50 W
St. Mary (R.), Can. (mā'rē)	97	49.25 N	113.00 W
St. Mary (Res.), Can.	97	49.30 N	113.00 W
St. Mary, C., Gam.	224	13.28 N	16.40 W
St. Marys, Austl. (mā'rēz)	212	41.40 S	148.10 E
St. Marys, Can.	108	43.15 N	81.10 W
St. Marys, Ga.	125	30.43 N	81.35 W
St. Mary's, Ks.	121	39.12 N	96.03 W
St. Mary's, Oh.	108	40.30 N	84.25 W
St. Marys, Pa.	109	41.25 N	78.30 W
St. Marys, WV	108	39.20 N	81.15 W
St. Marys (R.), Ga.-Fl.	125	30.37 N	82.05 W
St. Mary's B., Can.	102	44.20 N	66.10 W
St. Mary's B., Can.	103	46.50 N	53.47 W
St. Marys Is., Can.	103	50.19 N	59.17 W
St. Marys R., Can.-U.S.	117k	46.27 N	84.33 W
St. Mathew, SC (măth'ū)	125	33.40 N	80.46 W
St. Matthew (I.), Ak.	105	60.25 N	172.10 W
St. Matthews, Ky. (măth'ūz)	111h	38.15 N	85.39 W
St. Maur-des-Fossés, Fr.	167b	48.48 N	2.29 E
St. Maurice (R.), Can. (săN' mō-rēs') (sănt mô'rĭs)	102	47.20 N	72.55 W
St. Michael, Ak. (sănt mī'kĕl)	105	63.22 N	162.20 W
St. Michel, Can. (săN'mē-shĕl')	93b	46.52 N	70.54 W
St. Michel-de-l'Atalaye, Hai.	133	19.25 N	72.20 W
St. Michel-de-Napierville, Can.	93a	45.14 N	73.34 W
St. Mihiel, Fr. (săN' mē-yĕl')	167	48.53 N	5.30 E
St. Moritz, Switz. (sănt mō'rĭts) (zäŋkt mō'rēts)	164	46.31 N	9.50 E
St. Nazaire, Fr. (săN'nȧ-zâr')	166	47.18 N	2.13 W
St. Nérée, Can. (nā-rā')	93b	46.43 N	70.43 W
St. Nicolas, Can. (ne-kō-lä')	93b	46.42 N	71.32 W
St. Nicolas, Cap (C.), Hai.	133	19.45 N	73.35 W
St. Omer, Fr. (săN'tō-mâr')	166	50.44 N	2.16 E
St. Pascal, Can. (sĕN pă-skăl')	102	47.32 N	69.48 W
St. Paul, Can. (sănt pôl')	97	53.59 N	111.17 W
St. Paul, Mn.	117g	44.57 N	93.05 W
St. Paul, Ne.	112	41.13 N	98.28 W
St. Paul (I.), Ak.	105	57.10 N	170.20 W
St. Paul (R.), Lib.	224	7.10 N	10.00 W
St. Paul I, Can.	103	47.15 N	60.10 W
St. Paul I, Ind. O.	228	38.43 S	77.31 E
St. Paul Park, Mn. (pärk)	117g	44.51 N	93.00 W
St. Pauls, NC (pôls)	125	34.47 N	78.57 W
St. Peter, Mn. (pē tēr)	113	44.20 N	93.56 W
St. Peter Port, Guernsey	166	49.27 N	2.35 W
St. Petersburg, Fl. (pē'tērz-bûrg)	125a	27.47 N	82.38 W
Ste. Pétronille, Can. (sĕNt pĕt-rō-nēl')	93b	46.51 N	71.08 W
St. Philémon, Can. (sĕN fēl-mōN')	93b	46.41 N	70.28 W
St. Philippe-d'Argenteuil, Can. (săn'fe-lēp')	93a	45.20 N	73.28 W
St. Philippe-de-Lapairie, Can.	93a	45.38 N	74.25 W
St. Pierre, Mart. (săn'pyâr')	131b	14.45 N	61.12 W
St. Pierre (I.), St. Pierre & Miquelon	103	46.47 N	56.11 W
St. Pierre, Lac (L.), Can.	102	46.07 N	72.45 W
St. Pierre & Miquelon, N. A.	103	46.53 N	56.40 W
St. Pierre-d'Orléans, Can.	93b	46.53 N	71.04 W
St. Pierre-Montmagny, Can.	93b	46.55 N	70.37 W
St. Placide, Can. (plăs'ĭd)	93a	45.32 N	74.11 W
St. Pol-de-Léon, Fr. (săN-pô'dĕ-lā-ôN')	166	48.41 N	4.00 W
St. Pölten, Aus. (zäŋkt-pûl'tĕn)	164	48.12 N	15.38 E
St. Quentin, Fr. (săN'käN-tăN')	166	49.52 N	3.16 E
St. Raphaël, Can. (rä-fȧ-él')	93b	46.48 N	70.46 W
St. Raymond, Can. (săN' rā-môN') (sănt rā'mŭnd)	102	46.50 N	71.51 W
St. Rédempteur, Can. (săN rā-dāNp-tûr')	93b	46.42 N	71.18 W
St. Rémi, Can. (sĕN rĕ-mē')	93a	45.15 N	73.36 W
St. Romuald-d'Etchemin, Can. (sĕN rŏ'mo͞o-äl)	93b	46.45 N	71.14 W
Ste. Rose, Guad.	131b	16.19 N	61.45 W
Saintes, Fr.	166	45.44 N	0.41 W
Ste. Scholastique, Can. (skō-lȧs-tēk')	93a	45.39 N	74.05 W
St. Siméon, Can.	102	47.51 N	69.55 W
St. Stanislas-de-Kostka, Can. (sĕN stä-nēs-läz' de kōst'kä)	93a	45.11 N	74.08 W
St. Stephen, Can. (stē'vĕn)	102	45.12 N	66.17 W
St. Sulpice, Can.	93a	45.50 N	73.21 W
St. Thérèse-de-Blainville, Can. (tĕ-rĕz' dĕ blĕN-vēl')	93a	45.38 N	73.51 W
St. Thomas, Can. (tŏm'ȧs)	108	42.45 N	81.15 W
St. Thomas, see Charlotte Amalie			
St. Thomas (I.), Vir. Is. (U.S.A.)	127c	18.22 N	64.57 W
St. Thomas Hbr., Vir. Is. (U.S.A.) (tŏm'ȧs)	127c	18.19 N	64.56 W
St. Timothée, Can. (tē-mô-tā')	93a	45.17 N	74.03 W
St. Tropez, Fr. (trō-pĕ')	167	43.15 N	6.42 E
St. Valentin, Can. (văl-ĕn-tīn)	93a	45.07 N	73.19 W
St. Valéry-sur-Somme, Fr. (vȧ-lā-rē')	166	50.10 N	1.39 E
St. Vallier, Can. (väl-yā')	93b	46.54 N	70.49 W
St. Veit, Aus. (zäŋKt vīt')	164	46.46 N	14.20 E
St. Victor, Can. (vĭk'tēr)	102	46.09 N	70.56 W
St. Vincent, N. A.	127	13.20 N	60.50 W
St. Vincent, G., Austl. (vĭn'sĕnt)	212	34.55 S	138.00 E
St. Vincent Pass, N. A.	131b	13.35 N	61.10 W
St. Walburg, Can.	98	53.39 N	109.12 W
St. Yrieix-la-Perche, Fr. (ē-rē-ĕ)	166	45.30 N	1.08 E
Saitama (Pref.), Jap. (sī'tä-mä)	201a	35.52 N	139.40 E
Saitbaba, Sov. Un. (sá-ĕt'bá-bȧ)	180a	54.06 N	56.42 E
Sajama, Nevada (Pk.), Bol. (nĕ-vȧ'dä-sä-hȧ'mä)	140	18.13 S	68.53 W
Sakai, Jap. (sä'kä-ē)	201b	34.34 N	135.28 E
Sakaiminato, Jap.	201	35.33 N	133.15 E
Sakākah, Sau. Ar.	192	29.58 N	40.03 E
Sakakawea, Lake, ND	112	47.49 N	101.58 W
Sakania, Zaire (sȧ-kä'nĭ-ȧ)	227	12.45 S	28.34 E
Sakarya (R.), Tur. (sȧ-kär'yȧ)	177	40.10 N	31.00 E
Sakata, Jap. (sä'kä-tä)	200	38.56 N	139.57 E
Sakchu, Kor. (säk'cho͞o)	200	40.29 N	125.09 E
Sakhalin (I.), Sov. Un. (sȧ-kȧ-lēn')	179	51.52 N	144.15 E
Šakiai, Sov. Un. (shä'kĭ-ī)	163	54.59 N	23.05 E
Sakishima-Gunto (Is.), Jap. (sä'kē-shē'ma go͞on'tō')	199	24.25 N	125.00 E
Sakmara (R.), Sov. Un.	177	52.00 N	56.10 E
Sakomet R., RI (sä-kō'mĕt)	110b	41.32 N	71.11 W
Sakurai, Jap.	201b	34.31 N	135.51 E
Sakwaso L., Can. (sȧ-kwȧ'sō)	99	53.01 N	91.55 W
Sal, Cay (I.), Ba. (kē săl)	132	23.45 N	80.25 W
Sal (R.), Sov. Un. (sȧl)	177	47.20 N	42.10 E
Sala, Swe. (sô'lä)	162	59.56 N	16.34 E
Sala Consilina, It. (sä'lä kōn-sē-lē'nä)	170	40.24 N	15.38 E
Salada, Laguna (L.), Mex. (lä-go͞o'nä-sä-lä'dä)	118	32.34 N	115.45 W
Saladillo, Arg. (sä-lä-dēl'yō)	139c	35.38 S	59.48 W
Salado, Hong. (sä-lä'dhō)	130	15.44 N	87.03 W
Salado (R.), Arg. (sä-lä'dō)	142	26.05 S	63.35 W
Salado (R.), Arg.	139c	35.53 S	58.12 W
Salado (R.), Mex. (sä-lä'dô)	129	18.30 N	97.29 W
Salado, Rio (R.), Mex. (rē'ō)	122	26.55 N	99.36 W
Salado Cr., Tx.	117d	29.23 N	98.25 W
Salado de los Nadadores Rio (R.), Mex. (dĕ-lōs-nä-dä-dō'rĕs)	122	27.26 N	101.35 W
Salal, Chad.	225	14.51 N	17.13 E
Salamá, Guat. (sä-lä'mä)	130	15.06 N	90.19 W
Salamá, Hond. (sä-lä-mȧ')	130	14.43 N	86.30 W
Salamanca, Chile (sä-lä-mä'n-kä)	139b	31.48 S	70.57 W
Salamanca, Mex.	128	20.36 N	101.10 W
Salamanca, NY (săl-ȧ-măŋ'kȧ)	109	42.10 N	78.45 W
Salamanca, Sp. (sä-lä-mä'n-kȧ)	168	40.54 N	5.42 W
Salamat, Bahr (R.), Chad. (bär sä-lä-mät')	221	10.06 N	19.16 E
Salamina, Col. (sä-lä-mē'-nä)	140a	5.25 N	75.29 W
Salamis, Grc. (săl'ȧ-mĭs)	171	37.58 N	23.30 E
Salat-la-Canada, Fr.	166	44.52 N	1.13 E
Salaverry, Peru (sä-lä-vā'rē)	140	8.16 S	78.54 W
Salawati (I.), Indon. (sä-lä-wä'tē)	203	1.22 N	130.15 E
Salawe, Tan.	227	3.19 S	32.52 E
Sala-y-Gómez (I.), Chile	205	26.50 S	105.50 W
Salcedo, Dom. Rep. (säl-sā'dō)	133	19.25 N	70.30 W
Saldaña (R.), Col. (säl-dȧ'n-yä)	140a	3.42 N	75.16 W
Saldanha, S. Afr.	222	32.55 S	18.05 E
Saldus, Sov. Un. (sȧl'do͞os)	163	56.39 N	22.30 E
Sale, Austl. (sāl)	212	38.10 S	147.07 E
Sale, Eng.	154	53.24 N	2.20 W
Salé, Mor. (sȧ-lā')	220	34.09 N	6.42 W
Sale (R.), Can. (sȧl'rē-vyâr')	93f	49.44 N	97.11 W
Salekhard, Sov. Un. (sŭ-lyĭ-kärt)	176	66.35 N	66.50 E
Salem, Il. (sā'lĕm)	108	38.40 N	89.00 W
Salem, India	191	11.39 N	78.11 E
Salem, In.	108	38.35 N	86.00 W
Salem, Ma.	103a	42.31 N	70.54 W
Salem, Mo.	121	37.36 N	91.33 W
Salem, NH	103a	42.46 N	71.16 W
Salem, NJ	109	39.35 N	75.30 W
Salem, Oh.	108	40.55 N	80.50 W
Salem, Or.	114	44.55 N	123.03 W
Salem, S. Afr.	223c	33.29 S	26.30 E
Salem, SD	112	43.43 N	97.23 W
Salem, Va.	125	37.16 N	80.05 W
Salem, WV	108	39.15 N	80.35 W
Salemi, It. (sä-lā'mē)	170	37.49 N	12.48 E
Salerno, It. (sä-lĕr'nō)	169c	40.27 N	14.46 E
Salerno, Golfo di (G.), It. (gōl-fō-dē)	170	40.30 N	14.40 E
Salford, Eng. (săl'fērd)	154	53.26 N	2.19 W
Salgir (R.), Sov. Un. (sȧl'gēr)	173	45.25 N	34.22 E
Salgótarján, Hung. (shôl'gō-tôr-yän)	165	48.06 N	19.50 E
Salida, Co. (sȧ-lī'dȧ)	120	38.31 N	106.01 W
Salies-de-Béan, Fr.	166	43.27 N	0.58 W
Salima, Malawi	227	13.47 S	34.26 E
Salina, Ks. (sȧ-lī'nȧ)	121	38.50 N	97.37 W
Salina, Ut.	119	39.00 N	111.55 W
Salina (I.), It. (sä-lē'nä)	170	38.35 N	14.48 E
Salina Cruz, Mex. (sä-lē'nä kro͞oz')	129	16.10 N	95.12 W
Salina Pt., Ba.	133	22.10 N	74.20 W
Salinas, Ca. (sȧ-lē'nȧs)	118	36.41 N	121.40 W
Salinas, Mex.	128	22.38 N	101.42 W
Salinas, P. R.	127b	17.58 N	66.16 W
Salinas (R.), Ca.	118	36.33 N	121.29 W
Salinas (R.), Mex. (sä-lē'näs)	129	16.15 N	90.31 W
Salinas, Bahia de (B.), Nic.-C. R. (bä-ē'ä-dĕ-sȧ-lē'nȧs)	130	11.05 N	85.55 W
Salinas, Cape, Sp. (sä-lēnäs)	169	39.14 N	1.02 E
Salinas Victoria, Mex. (sä-lē'näs vēk-tō'rē-ä)	122	25.59 N	100.19 W
Saline (R.), Ak. (sȧ-lēn')	121	34.06 N	92.30 W

ng-sing; ŋ-baŋk; N-nasalized n; nŏd; cŏmmit; ōld; ōbey; ôrder; oi-boil; fo͞od; fo͝ot; ou-out; s-soft; sh-dish; th-thin; pūre; ūnite; ûrn; stŭd; circŭs; ü-as in French tu; '-indeterminate vowel.

342 Saline – Sanger

PLACE (Pronunciation)	PAGE	Lat. °'	Long. °'
Saline (R.), Ks.	120	39.05 N	99.43 W
Salins-les-Bains, Fr. (sá-lăN'-lā-báN')	167	46.55 N	5.54 E
Salisbury, Can.	102	46.03 N	65.05 W
Salisbury, Eng. (sôlz'bē-rē)	160	50.35 N	1.51 W
Salisbury, Md.	109	38.20 N	75.40 W
Salisbury, Mo.	121	39.24 N	92.47 W
Salisbury, NC	125	35.40 N	80.29 W
Salisbury, Zimb.	227	17.50 S	31.03 E
Salisbury (I.), Can.	95	63.36 N	76.20 W
Salisbury Plain, Eng.	160	51.15 N	1.52 W
Sal. I., C. V. Is. (säal)	220b	16.45 N	22.39 W
Salkehatchie (R.), SC (sô-kē-hăch'ē)	125	33.09 N	81.10 W
Sallisaw, Ok. (săl'ĭ-sô)	121	35.27 N	94.48 W
Salmon, Id. (săm'ŭn)	115	45.11 N	113.54 W
Salmon (R.), Can.	96	54.00 N	123.50 W
Salmon (R.), Can.	102	46.19 N	65.36 W
Salmon (R.), Id.	114	45.30 N	115.45 W
Salmon (R.), NY	109	44.35 N	74.15 W
Salmon (R.), Wa.	116c	45.44 N	122.36 W
Salmon (R.), Middle Fork, Id.	114	44.54 N	114.50 W
Salmon (R.), South Fork, Id.	114	44.51 N	115.47 W
Salmon Arm, Can.	97	50.42 N	119.16 W
Salmon Falls (R.), Id.	114	42.22 N	114.53 W
Salmon Gums, Austl. (gŭmz)	210	33.00 S	122.00 E
Salmon River Mts., Id.	114	44.15 N	115.44 W
Salon-de-Provence, Fr. (sá-lôN-dē-prô-väNs')	167	43.48 N	5.09 E
Salonta, Rom. (sä-lôn'tä)	165	46.46 N	21.38 E
Salop (Co.), Eng.	154	52.36 N	2.45 W
Saloum (R.), Senegal	224	14.10 N	15.45 W
Salsette I., India	191b	19.12 N	72.52 E
Sal'sk, Sov. Un. (sälsk)	177	46.30 N	41.20 E
Salt, (R.), Az. (sôlt)	119	33.28 N	111.35 W
Salt (R.), Mo.	121	39.54 N	92.11 W
Salta, Arg. (säl'tä)	142	24.50 S	65.16 W
Salta (Prov.), Arg.	142	25.15 S	65.00 W
Saltair, Ut. (sôlt'âr)	117b	40.46 N	112.09 W
Salt Cay (I.), Turks & Caicos Is.	133	21.20 N	71.15 W
Salt Cr., Il. (sôlt)	111a	42.01 N	88.01 W
Saltillo, Mex. (säl-tēl'yo-mc)	122	25.24 N	100.59 W
Salt Lake City, Ut. (sôlt lāk sĭ'tĭ)	117b	40.45 N	111.52 W
Salto, Arg. (säl'tō)	139c	34.17 S	60.15 W
Salto, Ur.	142	31.18 S	57.45 W
Salto, Serra do (Mtn.), Braz. (sĕ'r-rä-dô)	139a	20.26 S	43.28 W
Salto (R.), Mex.	128	22.16 N	99.18 W
Salto Grande, Braz. (grän'dä)	141	22.57 S	49.58 W
Salton Sea, Ca. (sôlt'ŭn)	118	33.28 N	115.43 W
Saltpond, Ghana	220	5.16 N	1.07 W
Salt River Ind. Res., Az. (sôlt rĭv'ēr)	119	33.40 N	112.01 W
Saltsjöbaden, Swe. (sält'shû-bäd'ĕn)	162	59.15 N	18.20 E
Saltspring I, Can. (sält'sprĭng)	96	48.47 N	123.30 W
Saltville, Va. (sôlt'vĭl)	125	36.50 N	81.45 W
Saltykovka, Sov. Un. (sál-tē'kôf-ká)	180b	55.45 N	37.56 E
Salud, Mt., Pan. (sä-lōō'th)	126a	9.14 N	79.42 W
Saluda, SC (sá-lōō'dá)	125	34.02 N	81.46 W
Saluda (R.), SC	125	34.07 N	81.48 W
Saluzzo, It. (sä-lōōt'sō)	170	44.39 N	7.31 E
Salvador (Bahia), Braz. (säl-vä-dōr') (bä-ē'ä)	141	12.59 S	38.27 W
Salvador L., La.	123	29.45 N	90.20 W
Salvador Pt., Ba.	132	24.30 N	77.45 W
Salvatierra, Mex. (säl-vä-tyĕr'rä)	128	20.13 N	100.52 W
Salwā Baḥrī, Egypt	219b	24.43 N	32.58 E
Salween R., Bur. (săl-wēn')	194	26.46 N	98.19 E
Sal'yany, Sov. Un.	177	39.40 N	49.10 E
Salzburg, Aus. (sälts'bŏŏrgh)	164	47.48 N	13.04 E
Salzburg (State), Aus.	164	47.30 N	13.18 E
Salzwedel, G.D.R. (sälts-vä'dĕl)	164	52.51 N	11.10 E
Samālūt, Egypt (sä-mä-lōōt')	219b	28.17 N	30.43 E
Samaná, Dom. Rep. (sä-mä-nä')	133	19.15 N	69.25 W
Samana Cabo (C.), Dom. Rep. (ká'bô)	133	19.20 N	69.00 W
Samana or Atwood Cay (I.), Ba.	133	23.05 N	73.45 W
Samar (I.), Phil. (sä'mär)	203	11.30 N	126.07 E
Samara (R.), Sov. Un.	177	52.50 N	50.35 E
Samara (R.), Sov. Un. (sá-mä'rá)	173	48.47 N	35.30 E
Samarai, Pap. N. Gui. (sä-mä-rä'ē)	203	10.45 S	150.49 E
Samarkand, Sov. Un. (sá-már-känt')	178	39.42 N	67.00 E
Samba, Zaire	227	4.38 S	26.22 E
Sambalpur, India (sŭm'bŭl-pōōr)	190	21.30 N	84.05 E
Sāmbhar (R.), India	190	27.00 N	74.58 E
Sambor, Sov. Un. (säm'bôr)	165	49.31 N	23.12 E
Samborombón, Bahia (B.), Arg. (bä-ē'ä-säm-bô-rôm-bô'n)	139c	35.57 S	57.05 W
Samborombón (R.), Arg.	139c	35.20 S	57.52 W
Sambre (R.), Bel. (säNbr')	161	50.20 N	4.15 E
Sambungo, Ang.	226	8.39 S	20.43 E
Sammamish, L., Wa. (sá-măm'ĭsh)	116a	47.35 N	122.02 W
Sammamish (R.), Wa.	116a	47.43 N	122.08 W
Samoa (I.), Oceania	204	15.00 S	170.00 W
Samokov, Bul. (sä'mô-kôf)	171	42.20 N	23.33 E
Samora Correia, Port. (sä-mô'rä-kôr-rĕ'yä)	169b	38.55 N	8.52 W
Samorovo, Sov. Un. (sá-má-rô'vô)	178	60.47 N	69.13 E
Sámos (I.), Grc. (sä'mŏs)	171	37.53 N	26.35 E
Samothráki (I.), Grc.	171	40.23 N	25.10 E
Sampaloc Pt., Phil. (säm-pä'lôk)	203a	14.43 N	119.56 E
Sam Rayburn Res, Tx.	123	31.10 N	94.15 W
Samsø (I.), Den. (säm'sû)	162	55.49 N	10.47 E
Samson, Al. (săm'sŭn)	124	31.06 N	86.02 W
Samsu, Kor. (säm'sōō')	200	41.12 N	128.00 E
Samsun, Tur. (sám'sōōn')	177	41.20 N	36.05 E
Samtredia, Sov. Un. (sám'trĕ-dē)	177	42.18 N	42.25 E
Samuel (I.), Can. (săm'ū-ĕl)	116d	48.50 N	123.10 W
Samur (R.), Sov. Un. (sä-mōōr')	177	41.40 N	47.20 E
San, Mali (sän)	224	13.18 N	4.54 W
Ṣan'ā', Yemen (sän'ä)	192	15.17 N	44.05 E
Sanaga (R.), Cam. (sä-nä'gä)	225	4.10 N	10.40 E
San Ambrosio, Isla de (I.), Chile (ē's-lä-dĕ-sän äm-brō'zē-ō)	138	26.40 S	80.00 W
Sanana, Pulau (I.), Indon.	203	2.15 S	126.38 E
Sanandaj, Iran	192	36.44 N	46.43 E
San Andreas, Ca. (săn ăn'drē-ăs)	118	38.10 N	120.42 W
San Andreas (L.), Ca.	116b	37.36 N	122.26 W
San Andrés, Col. (sän-än-drĕ's)	140a	6.57 N	75.41 W
San Andrés, Mex. (sän än-drās')	129a	19.15 N	99.10 W
San Andres, Laguna de (L.), Mex.	129	22.40 N	97.50 W
San Andres, Mts., U. S. (săn ăn'drē-ăs)	106	33.00 N	106.40 W
San Andrés (L.), see Petén, Laguna de			
San Andrés de Giles, Arg. (sän-än-drĕ's-dĕ-gē'lĕs)	139c	34.26 S	59.28 W
San Andres I., Col.	131	12.32 N	81.34 W
San Andres Mts., NM	119	33.45 N	106.40 W
San Andrés Tuxtla, Mex. (sän-än-drā's-tōōs'tlä)	129	18.27 N	95.12 W
San Angelo, Tx. (săn ăn-jĕ-lō)	122	31.28 N	100.22 W
San Antioco, I. di, It. (ē'sō-lä-dē-sän-än-tyŏ'kô)	170	39.00 N	8.25 E
San Antonio, Chile (sän-án-tō'nyō)	139b	33.34 S	71.36 W
San Antonio, Col.	140a	2.57 N	75.06 W
San Antonio, Col.	140a	3.55 N	75.28 W
San Antonio, Phil.	203a	14.57 N	120.05 E
San Antonio, Tx. (săn ăn-tō'nē-ō)	117d	29.25 N	98.30 W
San Antonio (R.), Ca.	118	36.00 N	121.13 W
San Antonio, Cabo (C.), Cuba (ká'bô-sän-än-tō'nyô)	132	21.55 N	84.55 W
San Antonio Abad, Sp. (sän än-tō'nyō ä-bädh')	169	38.59 N	1.17 E
San Antonio B., Tx.	123	28.20 N	97.08 W
San Antonio de Areco, Arg. (dā ä-rā'kô)	139c	34.16 S	59.30 W
San Antonio de las Vegas, Cuba (sän än-tō'nyô-dĕ-läs-vĕ'gäs)	133a	22.07 N	82.16 W
San Antonio de los Baños, Cuba (dā lōs bän'yōs)	133a	22.08 N	82.30 W
San Antonio de los Cobres, Arg. (dā lōs kō'brās)	142	24.15 S	66.29 W
San Antônio de Pádua, Braz. (dĕ-pá'dwä)	139a	21.32 S	42.09 W
San Antonio de Tamanaco, Ven. (sän-án-tô-nyô-dĕ-tá-mä-nä'kô)	141b	9.42 N	66.03 W
San Antonio Oeste, Arg. (sän-nä-tō'nyô ô-ĕs'tā)	142	40.49 S	64.56 W
San Antonio Pk., Ca. (săn ăn-tō'nĭ-ō)	117a	34.17 N	117.39 W
San Antonio R., Tx.	122	29.00 N	97.58 W
Sanarate, Guat. (sä-nä-rä'tē)	130	14.47 N	90.12 W
San Augustine, Tx. (săn ô'gŭs-tēn)	123	31.33 N	94.08 W
San Bartolo, Mex.	122	24.43 N	103.12 W
San Bartolo, Mex. (sän bär-tō'lô)	129a	19.36 N	99.43 W
San Bartolomeo, It. (bär-tô-lô-mā'ô)	170	41.25 N	15.04 E
San Benedetto del Tronto, It. (bā'nā-dĕt'tō dĕl trōn'tō)	170	42.58 N	13.54 E
San Benito, Tx. (săn bĕ-nē'tō)	123	26.07 N	97.37 W
San Benito (R.), Ca.	118	36.40 N	121.20 W
San Bernardino, Ca. (bûr-när-dē'nō)	117a	34.07 N	117.19 W
San Bernardino Mts., Ca.	118	34.05 N	116.23 W
San Bernardo, Chile (sän bĕr-när'dô)	139b	33.35 S	70.42 W
San Blas, Mex. (sän bläs')	128	21.33 N	105.19 W
San Blas, C., Fl.	124	29.38 N	85.38 W
San Blas, Cord. de (Mts.), Pan. (kôr-dĕl-yĕ'rä-dĕ)	131	9.17 N	78.20 W
San Blas,Golfo de (G.), Pan.	131	9.33 N	78.42 W
San Blas, Punta (Pt.), Pan.	131	9.35 N	78.55 W
San Bruno, Ca. (săn brōō-nō)	116b	37.38 N	122.25 W
San Buenaventura, Mex. (bwā'ná-vĕn-tōō'rá)	122	27.07 N	101.30 W
San Carlos, Ca. (săn kär'lōs)	116b	37.30 N	122.15 W
San Carlos, Chile (sän-kä'r-lōs)	142	36.23 S	71.58 W
San Carlos, Col.	140a	6.11 N	74.58 W
San Carlos, Equat. Gui.	226	3.27 N	8.33 E
San Carlos, Mex. (sän kär'lōs)	129	17.49 N	92.33 W
San Carlos, Mex.	122	24.36 N	98.52 W
San Carlos, Nic. (sän-kä'r-lôs)	131	11.08 N	84.48 W
San Carlos, Phil.	203a	15.56 N	120.20 E
San Carlos, Ven.	140	9.36 N	68.35 W
San Carlos de Bariloche, Arg. (sän-kä'r lōs-dĕ-bä-rē' lô'chĕ)	142	41.15 S	71.26 W
San Carlos Ind. Res, Az. (săn kär'lōs)	119	33.27 N	110.15 W
San Carlos Res, Az.	119	33.05 N	110.29 W
San Carlos R., C. R.	131	10.36 N	84.18 W
San Casimiro, Ven. (kä-sē-mē'rô)	141b	10.01 N	67.02 W
San Cataldo, It. (kä-täl'dō)	170	37.30 N	13.59 E
Sánchez, Dom. Rep. (sän'chĕz)	133	19.15 N	69.40 W
Sanchez, Río de los (R.), Mex. (rē'ō-dĕ-lôs)	128	20.31 N	102.29 W
Sánchez Román (Tlaltenango), Mex. (rô-má'n) (tlä'l-tĕ-nän-gō)	128	21.48 N	103.20 W
San Clemente, Sp. (sän klā-mĕn'tā)	168	39.25 N	2.24 W
San Clemente (I.), Ca.	118	33.02 N	118.36 W
San Cristobal, Dom. Rep. (krēs-tô'bäl)	133	18.25 N	70.05 W
San Cristóbal, Guat.	130	15.22 N	90.26 W
San Cristóbal, Ven.	140	7.43 N	72.15 W
San Cristobal (I.), Ec.	140	1.05 S	89.15 W
San Cristobal (I.), Sol. Is.	211	10.47 S	162.17 E
Sancti Spíritus, Cuba (säŋk'tē spē'rē-tōōs)	132	21.55 N	79.25 W
Sancti Spiritus (Prov.), Cuba	132	22.05 N	79.20 W
Sancy, Puy de (Pk.), Fr. (pwē-dĕ-säN-sē')	166	45.30 N	2.53 E
Sand (I.), Or. (sănd)	116c	46.16 N	124.01 W
Sand (I.), Wi.	113	46.03 N	91.09 W
Sand (R.), S. Afr.	219d	28.09 S	26.46 E
Sand (R.), S. Afr.	223c	28.30 S	29.30 E
Sanda, Jap. (sän'dä)	201b	34.53 N	135.14 E
Sandakan, Mala. (sán-dä'kán)	202	5.51 N	118.03 E
Sanday (I.), Scot. (sănd'ā)	160a	59.17 N	2.25 W
Sandbach, Scot. (sănd'băch)	154	53.08 N	2.22 W
Sandefjord, Nor. (sän'dĕ-fyôr')	162	59.09 N	10.14 E
San de Fuca, Wa. (de-fōō-cä)	116a	48.14 N	122.44 W
Sanders, Az.	119	35.13 N	109.20 W
Sanderson, Tx. (săn'dēr-sŭn)	122	30.09 N	102.24 W
Sandersville, Ga. (săn'dērz-vĭl)	124	32.57 N	82.50 W
Sandhammar, C., Swe. (sänt'häm-mär)	162	55.24 N	14.37 E
Sand Hills (Reg.), Ne. (sănd)	112	41.57 N	101.29 W
Sand Hook, NJ (sănd hŏŏk)	110a	40.29 N	74.05 W
Sandhurst, Eng. (sănd'hûrst)	154b	51.20 N	0.48 W
San Diego, Ca. (săn dē-ā'gô)	118a	32.43 N	117.10 W
San Diego, Tx.	120	27.47 N	98.13 W
San Diego (R.), Ca.	118	32.53 N	116.57 W
San Diego de la Unión, Mex. (sän dē-å-gô dā lä ōō-nyōn')	128	21.27 N	100.52 W
Sandies Cr., Tx. (sănd'ēz)	123	29.13 N	97.34 W
San Dimas, Ca. (săn dē-más)	117a	34.07 N	117.49 W
San Dimas, Mex. (dē-mäs')	120	24.08 N	105.57 W
Sandnes, Nor. (sänd'nĕs)	162	58.52 N	5.44 E
Sandoa, Zaire (sän-dō'á)	222	9.39 S	23.00 E
Sandomierz, Pol. (sán-dô'myĕzh)	165	50.39 N	21.45 E
San Donà di Piave, It. (sän dô ná' dē pyä'vĕ)	170	45.38 N	12.34 E
Sandoway, Bur. (sän-dô-wī')	194	18.24 N	94.28 E
Sandpoint, Id. (sănd point)	114	48.17 N	116.34 W
Sandringham, Austl. (săn'drĭng-ăm)	207a	37.57 S	145.01 E
Sandrio, It. (sä'n-dryô)	170	46.11 N	9.53 E
Sand Springs, Ok. (sănd sprĭnz)	121	36.08 N	96.06 W
Sandstone, Austl. (sănd'stōn)	210	28.00 S	119.25 E
Sandstone, Mn.	111	46.08 N	92.53 W
Sanduo, China (sän-dwō)	196	32.49 N	119.39 E
Sandusky, Al. (săn-dŭs'kē)	110h	33.32 N	86.50 W
Sandusky, Mi.	108	43.25 N	82.50 W
Sandusky, Oh.	108	41.25 N	82.45 W
Sandusky (R.), Oh.	108	41.10 N	83.20 W
Sandwich, Il. (sănd'wĭch)	108	42.35 N	88.53 W
Sandy, Or. (sănd'ē)	116c	45.24 N	122.16 W
Sandy, Ut.	117b	40.36 N	111.53 W
Sandy (R.), Or.	116c	45.28 N	122.17 W
Sandy C., Austl.	212	24.25 S	153.10 E
Sandy Cr., Wy.	115	42.08 N	109.35 W
Sandy Hook, Ct. (hŏŏk)	110a	41.25 N	73.17 W
Sandy L., Can.	93g	53.46 N	113.58 W
Sandy L., Can.	103	49.16 N	57.00 W
Sandy L., Can.	99	53.00 N	93.07 W
Sandy Point, Tx.	123a	29.22 N	95.27 W
Sandy Pt., Wa.	116d	48.48 N	122.42 W
Sandy Springs, Ga. (springz)	110c	33.55 N	84.23 W
San Enrique, Arg. (sän-ĕn-rē'kĕ)	139c	35.47 S	60.22 W
San Estanislao, Par. (ĕs-tä-nēs-lá'ô)	142	24.38 S	56.20 W
San Esteban, Hond. (ĕs-tĕ'bän)	130	15.13 N	85.53 W
San Fabian, Phil. (fä-byä'n)	203a	16.14 N	120.28 E
San Felipe, Chile (fĕ-lē'pĕ)	139b	32.45 S	70.43 W
San Felipe, Mex. (fĕ-lē'pĕ)	128	21.29 N	101.13 W
San Felipe, Mex.	128	22.21 N	105.26 W
San Felipe, Ven. (fĕ-lē'pĕ)	140	10.13 N	68.45 W
San Felipe, Cr., Ca. (săn fĕ-lēp'ā)	118	33.10 N	116.03 W
San Felipe, Cayos de (Is.), Cuba (kä'yōs-dĕ-sän-fĕ-lē'pĕ)	132	22.00 N	83.30 W
San Felíu de Guixols, Sp. (sän fā-lē'ōō dā gē-hôls)	169	41.45 N	3.01 E
San Felix, Isla de (I.), Chile (ē's-lä-dĕ-sän fā-lēks')	138	26.20 S	80.10 W
San Fernanda, Sp. (fĕr-nä'n-dä)	168	36.28 N	6.13 W
San Fernando, Arg. (fĕr-nä'n-dô)	142a	34.11 S	58.34 W
San Fernando, Ca. (fĕr-nän'dō)	117a	34.17 N	118.27 W
San Fernando, Chile	139b	36.36 S	70.58 W
San Fernando, Mex. (fĕr-nän'dô)	122	24.52 N	98.10 W
San Fernando, Phil. (sän fĕr-nä'n-dô)	203a	16.38 N	120.19 E
San Fernando de Apure, Ven. (sän-fĕr-nä'n-dô-dĕ-ä-pōō'rā)	140	7.46 N	67.29 W
San Fernando de Atabapo, Ven. (dĕ-ä-tä-bä'pô)	140	3.58 N	67.41 W
San Fernando de Henares, Sp. (dĕ-ā-nä'rās)	169a	40.23 N	3.31 W
San Fernando R., Mex. (sän fĕr-nän'dô)	122	25.07 N	98.25 W
Sånfjället (Mtn.), Swe.	162	62.19 N	13.30 E
Sanford, Can. (săn'fērd)	93f	49.41 N	97.27 W
Sanford, Fl. (săn'fôrd)	125a	28.46 N	80.18 W
Sanford, Me. (săn'fērd)	102	43.26 N	70.47 W
Sanford, NC	125	35.26 N	79.10 W
San Francisco, Arg. (sän frän'sĭs'kô)	142	31.23 S	62.09 W
San Francisco, Ca.	116b	37.45 N	122.26 W
San Francisco, Sal.	130	13.48 N	88.11 W
San Francisco, see Ixhuatán			
San Francisco (R.), NM	119	33.35 N	108.55 W
San Francisco B., Ca. (săn frăn'sĭs'kô)	116b	37.45 N	122.21 W
San Francisco del Oro, Mex. (dĕl ō'rō)	126	27.00 N	106.37 W
San Francisco del Rincón, Mex. (dĕl rēn-kōn')	128	21.01 N	101.51 W
San Francisco de Macaira, Ven. (dĕ-mä-kī'rä)	141b	9.58 N	66.17 W
San Francisco de Macoris, Dom. Rep. (dā-mä-kō'rēs)	133	19.20 N	70.15 W
San Francisco de Paula, Cuba (dā pou'lä)	133a	23.04 N	82.18 W
San Gabriel, Ca. (săn gä-brē-ĕl') (gā'brē-ĕl)	117a	34.06 N	118.06 W
San Gabriel Chilac, Mex. (sän-gä-brē-ĕl-chē-läk')	128	18.19 N	97.22 W
San Gabriel Mts, Ca.	117a	34.17 N	118.03 W
San Gabriel Res., Ca.	117a	34.14 N	117.48 W
San Gabriel R., Ca.	117a	33.47 N	118.06 W
Sangamon (R.), Il. (săn'gá-mŭn)	121	40.08 N	90.08 W
Sanger, Ca. (săng'ēr)	118	36.42 N	119.33 W

ăt; finăl; rāte; senāte; ärm; ȧsk; sofȧ; fâre; ch-choose; dh-as th in other; bē; ēvent; bĕt; recĕnt; cratēr; g-gō; gh-guttural g; bĭt; ĭ-short neutral; rīde; K-guttural k as ch in German ich;

PRONOUNCING INDEX

Sangerhausen – Santa Cruz 343

PLACE (Pronunciation)	PAGE	Lat. °′	Long. °′
Sangerhausen, G.D.R. (săng'ĕr-hou-zĕn)	164	51.28 N	11.17 E
Sangha (R.), Afr.	225	2.40 N	16.10 E
Sangihe Pulau (I.), Indon. (säŋ'gē-ē)	203	3.30 N	125.30 E
San Gil, Col. (sän-κē'l)	140	6.32 N	73.13 W
San Giovanni in Fiore, It. (sän jô-vän'nē ēn fyō'rå)	170	39.15 N	16.40 E
San Giuseppe Vesuviano, It. (sän-zhĕōō-sĕ'p-pĕ-vĕ-sōō-vyá'nô)	169c	40.36 N	14.31 E
Sangju, Kor. (säng'jōō')	200	36.20 N	128.07 E
Sāngli, India	191	16.56 N	74.38 E
Sangmélima, Cam.	225	2.56 N	11.59 E
San Gorgonio Mt., Ca. (săn gôr-gō'nĭ-ō)	117a	34.06 N	116.50 W
Sangre De Cristo Ra., U. S. (săng'ēr-de-krēs-tō)	106	37.45 N	105.50 W
San Gregoria, Ca. (săn grĕ-gôr'ā)	116b	37.20 N	122.23 W
Sangro (R.), It. (säŋ'grō)	170	41.38 N	13.56 E
Sangüesa, Sp. (sän-gwĕ'sä)	168	42.36 N	1.15 W
Sanhe, China (sän-hŭ)	196	39.59 N	117.06 E
Sanibel I., Fl. (săn'ĭ-bĕl)	125a	26.26 N	82.15 W
San Ignacio, Belize	130a	17.11 N	89.04 W
San Ildefonso, see Villa Alta			
San Ildefonso, C. Phil. (sän-ēl-dĕ-fōn-sô)	203a	16.03 N	122.10 E
San Ildefonso o la Granja, Sp. (ō lä grän'khä)	168	40.54 N	4.02 W
San Isidro, Arg. (ē-sē'drô)	142a	34.13 S	58.31 W
San Isidro, C.R.	131	9.24 N	83.43 W
San Jacinto, Ca. (săn jȧ-sĭn'tô)	117a	33.47 N	116.57 W
San Jacinto, Phil. (sän hä-sēn'tô)	203a	12.33 N	123.43 E
San Jacinto (R.), West Fork, Tx.	123	30.35 N	95.37 W
San Jacinto R., Ca. (săn jȧ-sĭn'tô)	117a	33.44 N	117.14 W
San Jacinto R., Tx.	123	30.25 N	95.05 W
San Javier, Chile (sän-hä-vē'ĕr)	139b	35.35 S	71.43 W
San Jerónimo, Mex.	129a	19.31 N	98.46 W
San Jerónimo de Juárez, Mex. (hå-rō'nē-mô dā hwä'råz)	128	17.08 N	100.30 W
San Joaquin, Ven.	141b	10.16 N	67.47 W
San Joaquin (R.), Ca. (săn hwä-kēn')	118	37.10 N	120.51 W
San Joaquin Valley, Ca.	118	36.45 N	120.30 W
San Jorge, Golfo (G.), Arg. (gôl-fô-sän-κô'r-κĕ)	142	46.15 S	66.45 W
San José, Bol. (sän hô-sā')	141	17.54 S	60.42 W
San Jose, Ca. (săn hô-zā')	116b	37.20 N	121.54 W
San Jose, C. R. (sän hô-sā')	131	9.57 N	84.05 W
San José, Guat.	130	13.56 N	90.49 W
San Jose, Phil.	203a	12.22 N	121.04 E
San Jose, Phil.	203a	15.49 N	120.57 E
San José, Ur. (hô-sĕ')	139c	34.20 S	56.43 W
San José (Dept.), Ur.	139c	34.17 S	56.23 W
San Jose (I.), Mex. (κô-sĕ')	126	25.00 N	110.35 W
San Jose (R.), NM (săn hô-zā')	119	35.15 N	108.10 W
San José (R.), Ur. (sän-hô-sĕ')	139c	34.05 S	56.47 W
San Jose, Isla de (I.), Pan. (ē's-lä-dĕ-sän hô-sā')	131	8.17 N	79.20 W
San José de Feliciano, Arg. (dā lä ĕs-kē'nä)	142	30.26 S	58.44 W
San José de Gauribe, Ven. (sän-hô-sĕ'dĕ-gáōō-rē'bĕ)	141b	9.51 N	65.49 W
San Jose de las Lajas, Cuba (sän-κô-sĕ'dĕ-läs-lä'käs)	133a	22.13 N	82.10 W
San José Iturbide, Mex. (ē-tōōr-bē'dĕ)	128	21.00 N	100.24 W
San Juan, Arg. (hwän')	142	31.36 S	68.29 W
San Juan, Col. (hōōá'n)	140a	3.23 N	73.48 W
San Juan, Dom. Rep. (sän hwän')	133	18.50 N	71.15 W
San Juan, Phil.	203a	16.41 N	120.20 E
San Juan, P. R. (sän hwän')	127b	18.30 N	66.10 W
San Juan, see Guichicovi			
San Juan, see Mazatlán			
San Juan (Prov.), Arg.	142	31.00 S	69.30 W
San Juan, Cabezas de (C.), P. R.	127b	18.29 N	65.30 W
San Juan, Cabo (C.), Equat. Gui.	226	1.08 N	9.23 E
San Juan, Pico (Pk.), Cuba (pē'kô-sän-κōōá'n)	132	21.55 N	80.00 W
San Juan (R.), Mex. (sän-hōō-än')	129	18.10 N	95.23 W
San Juan, Rio (R.), Mex. (rē'ō-sän-hwän)	122	25.35 N	99.15 W
San Juan (R.), Ut.	119	37.10 N	110.30 W
San Juan Bautista, Par. (sän hwän' bou-tēs'tä)	142	26.48 S	57.09 W
San Juan Capistrano, Mex. (sän-hōō-än' kä-pēs-trä'nô)	128	22.41 N	104.07 W
San Juan Cr., Ca. (săn hwän')	118	35.24 N	120.12 W
San Juan de Guadalupe, Mex. (sän hwan dā gwä-dhä-lōō'pā)	122	24.37 N	102.43 W
San Juan del Norte (Greytown), Nic. (dĕl nôr-tå) (grā'toun)	131	10.55 N	83.44 W
San Juan del Norte Bahia de (B.), Nic. (bä-ē'ä-dĕ-sän hwän dĕl nôr'tå)	131	11.12 N	83.40 W
San Juan de los Lagos, Mex. (sän-hōō-än'dā los lä'gôs)	128	21.15 N	102.18 W
San Juan de los Lagos (R.), Mex. (dā lōs lä'gôs)	128	21.13 N	102.12 W
San Juan de los Morros, Ven. (dĕ-lôs-mô'r-rôs)	141b	9.54 N	67.22 W
San Juan del Rio, Mex. (dĕl rē'ô)	128	20.21 N	99.59 W
San Juan del Rio, Mex. (sän hwän del rē'ô)	122	24.47 N	104.29 W
San Juan del Sur, Nic. (dĕl sōōr)	130	11.15 N	85.53 W
San Juan de Sabinas, Mex. (dĕ-sä-bē'näs)	122	27.56 N	101.23 W
San Juan Evangelista, Mex. (sän-hōō-ä'n-ā-väŋ-kå-lēs'ta')	129	17.57 N	95.08 W
San Juan I., Wa.	116a	48.28 N	123.08 W
San Juan Is., Can. (săn hwän)	116d	48.49 N	123.14 W
San Juan Ixtenco, Mex. (ēx-tĕ'n-kô)	129	19.14 N	97.52 W
San Juan Martinez, Cuba (sän kōō ä'n-mär-tē'nĕz)	132	22.15 N	83.50 W
San Juan Mts., Co. (san hwán')	119	37.50 N	107.30 W
San Juan R., Nic.	131	10.58 N	84.18 W
San Julián, Arg. (sän hōō-lyá'n)	142	49.17 S	68.02 W
San Justo, Arg. (hōōs'tô)	142a	34.25 S	58.33 W
Sankanbiriwa (Mtn.), S. L.	224	8.56 N	10.48 W
Sankarani R., Gui.-Mali (sän'kä-rä'nē)	224	11.10 N	8.35 W
Sankt Gallen, Switz.	164	47.25 N	9.22 E
Sankuru (R.), Zaire (sän-kōō'rōō)	226	4.00 S	22.35 E
San Lazaro, C., Mex. (sän-lä'zä-rō)	126	24.58 N	113.30 W
San Leandro, Ca. (săn lē-ăn'drô)	116b	37.43 N	122.10 W
San Lorenzo, Arg. (sän lô-rĕn'zô)	139c	32.46 S	60.44 W
San Lorenzo, Ca. (săn lô-rĕn'zô)	116b	37.41 N	122.08 W
San Lorenzo, Hond. (sän lô-rĕn'zô)	130	13.24 N	87.24 W
San Lorenzo de El Escorial, Sp. (sän lôrĕn'tho dĕl ĕs-kō-rē-äl')	169a	40.36 N	4.09 W
Sanlúcar de Barrameda, Sp. (sän-lōō'kär)	168	36.46 N	6.21 W
San Lucas, Bol. (lōō'kás)	140	20.12 S	65.06 W
San Lucas, see Ojitlán			
San Lucas, C., Mex.	126	22.45 N	109.45 W
San Luis, Arg. (lōō-ēs')	142	33.16 S	66.15 W
San Luis, Col. (lōōē's)	140a	6.03 N	74.57 W
San Luis, Cuba	133	20.15 N	75.50 W
San Luis, Guat.	130	14.38 N	89.42 W
San Luis (Prov.), Arg.	142	32.45 S	66.00 W
San Luis (State), Mex.	126	22.45 N	101.45 W
San Luis de la Paz, Mex. (dā lä päz')	128	21.17 N	100.32 W
San Luis del Cordero, Mex. (dĕl kôr-dā'rô)	122	25.25 N	104.20 W
San Luis Obispo, Ca. (ô-bĭs'pō)	118	35.18 N	120.40 W
San Luis Obispo, B., Ca.	118	35.07 N	121.05 W
San Luis Potosí, Mex. (pō-tō-sē')	128	22.08 N	100.58 W
San Luis Potosí (State), Mex.	126	22.45 N	101.45 W
San Luis Rey (R.), Ca. (rā'ē)	118	33.22 N	117.06 W
San Manuel, Az. (sän măn'ū-ĕl)	119	32.30 N	110.45 W
San Marcial, NM (săn mar-shäl')	119	33.40 N	107.00 W
San Marco, It. (sän mär'kô)	170	41.53 N	15.50 E
San Marcos, Guat. (mär'kôs)	130	14.57 N	91.49 W
San Marcos, Mex.	128	16.46 N	99.23 W
San Marcos, Tx. (săn mär'kôs)	122	29.53 N	97.56 W
San Marcos de Colón, Hond. (sän-má'r-kōs-dĕ-kô-lô'n)	130	13.17 N	86.50 W
San Marcos R., Tx.	122	30.08 N	98.15 W
San Maria (Vol.), Guat. (sän-mä-rē'ä)	130	14.45 N	91.33 W
San Maria di Léuca, C., It. (dē-lĕ'ōō-kä)	171	39.47 N	18.20 E
San Marino, Ca. (săn mĕr-ē'nô)	117a	34.07 N	118.06 W
San Marino, San Marino (sän mä-rē'nô)	170	44.55 N	12.26 E
San Marino, Eur.	157	43.40 N	13.00 E
San Martín, Col. (sän mär-tē'n)	140a	3.42 N	73.44 W
San Martín, Mex. (mär-tē'n)	129	18.36 N	95.11 W
San Martin (L.), Arg.-Chile	142	48.15 S	72.30 W
San Martin Chalchicuautla, Mex. (sän mär-tē'n chäl-chē-kwä-ōō'tlä)	128	21.22 N	98.39 W
San Martin de la Vega, Sp. (sän mär ten' dā lä vā'gä)	169a	40.12 N	3.34 W
San Martín Hidalgo, Mex. (sän mär-tē'n-ē-däl'gô)	128	20.27 N	103.55 W
San Mateo, Ca. (săn mä-tā'ô)	116b	37.34 N	122.20 W
San Mateo (Etlatongo), Mex. (sän-mä-tĕ'ô) (ē-tlä-tô'n-gō)	129	16.59 N	97.04 W
San Mateo, Sp. (sän mä-tā'ō)	169	40.26 N	0.09 E
San Mateo, Ven. (sän må-tĕ'ô)	141b	9.45 N	64.34 W
San Matías, Golfo (G.), Arg. (sän mä-tē'äs)	142	41.30 S	63.45 W
Sanmen Wan (B.), China	199	29.00 N	122.15 E
San Miguel, Arg. (sän mē-gĕ'l)	142a	34.17 S	58.43 W
San Miguel, Mex. (sän mē-gāl')	129	18.18 N	97.09 W
San Miguel, Pan.	131	8.26 N	78.55 W
San Miguel, Phil. (sän mē-gĕ'l)	203a	15.09 N	120.56 E
San Miguel, Sal. (săn mē-gāl')	130	13.28 N	88.11 W
San Miguel, Ven. (sän mē-gĕ'l)	141b	9.56 N	64.58 W
San Miguel, see Sola de Vega			
San Miguel, see Talea de Castro			
San Miguel, Bahia (B.), Pan. (bä-ē'ä-sän mē-gāl')	131	8.17 N	78.26 W
San Miguel (I.), Ca.	118	34.03 N	120.23 W
San Miguel (R.), Bol. (sän-mē-gĕ'l)	140	13.34 S	63.58 W
San Miguel (R.), Co. (săn mē-gĕl')	119	38.15 N	108.40 W
San Miguel (R.), Mex. (sän mē-gāl')	129	15.27 N	92.00 W
San Miguel (Vol.), Sal.	130	13.27 N	88.17 W
San Miguel B., Phil.	203a	13.55 N	123.12 E
San Miguel de Allende, Mex. (dā ä-lyĕn'dā)	128	20.54 N	100.44 W
San Miguel el Alto, Mex. (ĕl äl'tô)	128	21.03 N	102.26 W
Sannār, Sud.	221	13.34 N	33.32 E
San Narcisco, Phil. (sän när-sē'sô)	203a	15.01 N	120.05 E
San Narcisco, Phil.	203a	13.34 N	122.33 E
San Nicolás, Arg. (sän nē-kô-lä's)	139c	33.20 S	60.14 W
San Nicolas, Phil. (nē-kô-läs')	203a	16.05 N	120.45 E
San Nicolas (I.), Ca. (săn nĭ'kô-lȧ)	118	33.14 N	119.10 W
San Nicolás (R.), Mex.	128	19.40 N	105.08 W
Sanniquellie, Ivory Coast	224	7.22 N	8.43 W
Sannūr, Wādī, Egypt	219b	28.48 N	31.12 E
Sanok, Pol. (sä'nôk)	165	49.31 N	22.13 E
San Pablo, Ca. (săn păb'lô)	116b	37.58 N	122.21 W
San Pablo, Phil. (sän-pä-blô)	203a	14.05 N	121.20 E
San Pablo, Ven. (sän-pá'blô)	141b	9.46 N	65.04 W
San Pablo B., Ca. (săn păb'lô)	116b	38.04 N	122.25 W
San Pablo Res, Ca.	116b	37.55 N	122.12 W
San Pablo R., Pan. (sän päb'lô)	131	8.12 N	81.12 W
San Pascual, Phil. (päs-kwäl')	203a	13.08 N	122.59 E
San Pedro, Arg. (sän pā'drô)	142	24.15 S	64.15 W
San Pedro, Arg.	139c	33.41 S	59.42 W
San Pedro, Ca. (săn pē'drô)	117a	33.44 N	118.17 W
San Pedro, Chile (sän pĕ'drô)	139b	33.54 S	71.27 W
San Pedro, Mex. (sän pä'drô)	129	18.38 N	92.25 W
San Pedro, Par. (sän-pĕ'drô)	142	24.13 S	57.00 W
San Pedro, Sal. (sän pä'drô)	130	13.49 N	88.58 W
San Pedro, see Amusgos			
San Pedro, see Pochutla			
San Pedro (R.), Az.	119	32.48 N	110.37 W
San Pedro (R.), Cuba (sän-pĕ'drô)	132	21.05 N	78.15 W
San Pedro, Rio de (R.), Mex. (rē'ō-dĕ-sän-pĕ'drô)	129	18.23 N	92.13 W
San Pedro, Río de (R.), Mex.	128	21.51 N	102.24 W
San Pedro (R.), Mex. (sän pä'drô)	128	22.08 N	104.59 W
San Pedro B., Ca. (săn pē'drô)	117a	33.42 N	118.12 W
San Pedro de las Colonias, Mex. (dĕ-läs-kô-lô'nyäs)	122	25.47 N	102.58 W
San Pedro de Macorís, Dom. Rep. (sän-pĕ'drō-dā mä-kô-rēs')	133	18.30 N	69.30 W
San Pedro Lagunillas, Mex. (sän pā'drô lä-gōō-nēl'yäs)	128	21.12 N	104.47 W
San Pedro R., Guat. (sän pā'drô)	130a	17.11 N	90.23 W
San Pedro R., Mex.	122	27.56 N	105.50 W
San Pedro Sula, Hond. (sän pā'drô sōō'lä)	130	15.29 N	88.01 W
San Pedro y San Pablo, see Teposcolula			
San Pietro, I. di, It. (ē'sō-lä-dē-sän pyā'trô)	170	39.09 N	8.15 E
San Quentin, Ca. (săn kwĕn-tēn')	116b	37.57 N	122.29 W
San Quintin, Phil. (sän kēn-tēn')	203a	15.59 N	120.47 E
San Rafael, Arg. (sän rä-fä-ĕl')	142	34.30 S	68.13 W
San Rafael, Ca. (săn rȧ-fĕl)	116b	37.58 N	122.31 W
San Rafael, Col. (sän-rä-fä-ĕ'l)	140a	6.18 N	75.02 W
San Rafael (R.), Ut. (săn rȧ-fĕl')	119	39.05 N	110.50 W
San Rafael, Cabo (C.), Dom. Rep. (ká'bô)	133	19.00 N	68.50 W
San Ramon, Ca. (săn rä-mōn')	116b	37.47 N	122.59 W
San Ramōn, C. R.	131	10.07 N	84.30 W
San Remo, It. (sän rā'mô)	170	43.48 N	7.46 E
San R, Pol.	165	50.33 N	22.12 E
San Roman, C., Ven. (sän-rô-mä'n)	127	12.00 N	69.45 W
San Roque, Col. (sän-rô'kĕ)	140a	6.29 N	75.00 W
San Roque, Sp.	168	36.13 N	5.23 W
San Saba, Tx. (săn sä'bȧ)	122	31.12 N	98.43 W
San Saba R., Tx.	122	30.58 N	99.12 W
San Salvador, Sal. (sän säl-vä-dōr')	130	13.45 N	89.11 W
San Salvador (I.), Ec.	140	0.14 S	90.50 W
San Salvador (Watling) (I.), Ba. (săn săl'vȧ-dôr)	133	24.05 N	74.30 W
San Salvador (R.), Ur. (sän-säl-vä-dô'r)	139c	33.42 S	58.04 W
Sansanné-Mango, Togo (sän-sȧ-nā' mäN'gō)	224	10.21 N	0.28 E
San Sebastian, Can. Is. (sän sā-bäs-tyän')	220	28.09 N	17.11 W
San Sebastián, Sp.	168	43.19 N	1.59 W
San Sebastián, Ven. (sän-sĕ-bäs-tyá'n)	141b	9.58 N	67.11 W
San Sebastián de los Reyes, Sp. (sän sā-bäs-tyän'dā lōs rā'yĕs)	169a	40.33 N	3.38 W
San Severo, It. (sän sĕ-vâ'rō)	170	41.43 N	15.24 E
Sanshui, China (sän-shwā)	195	23.14 N	112.51 E
San Simon (R.), Az. (sän sī-mōn')	119	32.45 N	109.30 W
Santa Ana, Ca. (săn'tȧ ăn'ȧ)	117a	33.45 N	117.52 W
Santa Ana, Mex. (sän'tä ä'nä)	128	19.18 N	98.10 W
Santa Ana, Sal.	130	14.02 N	89.35 W
Santa Ana Mts., Ca.	117a	33.44 N	117.36 W
Santa Ana R., Ca.	117a	33.41 N	117.57 W
Santa Anna, Tx.	122	31.44 N	99.18 W
Santa Anna, Cochilha de (Mts.), Braz. (kô-chē'lä dĕ sän-tä-nä)	142	30.30 S	56.30 W
Santa Antão (I.), C. V. Is. (sä-tä-ä'n-zhĕ-lô)	220b	17.20 N	26.05 W
Sant' Antimo, It.	169c	40.40 N	14.11 E
Santa Bárbara, Braz. (sän-tä-bá'r-bä-rä)	139a	19.57 S	43.25 W
Santa Barbara, Ca. (săn'tȧ bär'bȧ-rȧ)	118	34.26 N	119.43 W
Santa Barbara, Hond. (sän'tȧ bär'bȧ-rȧ)	130	14.52 N	88.20 W
Santa Barbara, Mex.	122	26.48 N	105.50 W
Santa Barbara (I.), Ca.	118	33.30 N	118.44 W
Santa Barbara (Is.), Ca.	118	33.45 N	119.46 W
Santa Barbara Chan., Ca.	118	34.15 N	120.00 W
Santa Branca, Braz. (sän-tä-brä'N-kä)	139a	23.25 S	45.52 W
Santa Catalina (I.), Ca.	118	33.29 N	118.37 W
Santa Catalina, Cerro de (Mt.), Pan. (sĕ'r-rō-dĕ-sän-tä-kä-tä-lē'nä)	131	8.39 N	81.36 W
Santa Catalina, G. of, Ca. (săn'tȧ kă-tȧ-lē'nȧ)	118	33.00 N	117.58 W
Santa Catarina, Mex. (sän'tä kä-tä-rē'nä)	122	25.41 N	100.27 W
Santa Catarina, see Loxicha			
Santa Catarina, see Yosonotú			
Santa Catarina (State), Braz. (sän-tä-kä-tä-rē'nä)	142	27.15 S	50.30 W
Santa Catarina (R.), Mex.	128	16.31 N	98.39 W
Santa Clara, Ca. (săn'tȧ klârȧ)	116b	37.21 N	121.56 W
Santa Clara, Cuba (sän't klä'rá)	132	22.25 N	80.00 W
Santa Clara, Mex.	122	24.29 N	103.22 W
Santa Clara, Ur.	142	32.46 S	54.51 W
Santa Clara (R.), Ca. (săn'tȧ klă'rȧ)	118	34.22 N	118.53 W
Santa Clara, (Vol.), Nic.	130	12.44 N	87.00 W
Santa Clara, Bahía de (B.), Cuba (bä-ē'ä-dĕ-sän-tä-klä-rä)	132	23.05 N	80.50 W
Santa Clara, Sierra, (Mts.), Mex. (sē-ĕ'r-rä-sän'tȧ klä'rä)	126	27.30 N	113.50 W
Santa Cruz, Bol. (sän'tȧ krōōz')	140	17.45 S	63.03 W
Santa Cruz, Braz. (sän-tä-krōō's)	142	29.43 S	52.15 W
Santa Cruz, Braz.	142b	22.55 S	43.41 W
Santa Cruz, Ca.	118	36.59 N	122.02 W
Santa Cruz, Chile	139b	34.38 S	71.21 W
Santa Cruz, C. R.	130	10.16 N	85.37 W
Santa Cruz, Mex.	122	25.50 N	105.25 W
Santa Cruz, Phil.	203a	13.28 N	122.02 E
Santa Cruz, Phil.	203a	14.17 N	121.25 E
Santa Cruz, Phil.	203a	15.46 N	119.53 E
Santa Cruz (Prov.), Arg.	142	48.00 S	70.00 W
Santa Cruz (I.), Ca. (săn'tȧ krōōz')	118	34.05 N	119.55 W

ng-sing; ŋ-baŋk; N-nasalized n; nŏd; cŏmmit; ōld; ôbey; ôrder; oi-boil; fōōd; fŏŏt; ou-out; s-soft; sh-dish; th-thin; pūre; ûnite; ûrn; stŭd; circŭs; ü-as in French tu; '-indeterminate vowel.

PLACE (Pronunciation)	PAGE	Lat. °′	Long. °′
Santa Cruz (I.), Ec. (sän-tä-kro͞o′z)	140	0.38 S	90.20 W
Santa Cruz (R.), Az. (săn′tȧ kro͞oz′)	119	32.30 N	111.30 W
Santa Cruz (R.), Arg. (sän′tä kro͞oz′)	142	50.05 S	66.30 W
Santa Cruz Barillas, Guat. (sän-tä-kro͞o′z-bä-rē′l-yäs)	130	15.47 N	91.22 W
Santa Cruz Chico, see Pedro Antonio Santos			
Santa Cruz del Sur, Cuba (sän-tä-kro͞o′s-děl-so͞o′r)	132	20.45 N	78.00 W
Santa Cruz de Tenerife, Can. Is. (sän′tä kro͞oz dā tā-nå-rē′fā)	220	28.07 N	15.27 W
Santa Cruz Is., Sol. Is.	211	10.58 S	166.47 E
Santa Cruz Mts., Ca. (săn′tȧ kro͞oz′)	116b	37.30 N	122.19 W
Santa Domingo, Cay (I.), Ba.	133	21.50 N	75.45 W
Sant′ Eufemia, Golfo di (G.), It. (gôl-fô-dē-sän-tē′o͞o-fē′myä)	170	38.53 N	15.53 E
Santa Eugenia de Ribeira, Sp. (sän-tä-ĕo͞o-hĕ′nyä-dĕ-rē-bĕ′y-rä)	168	42.34 N	8.55 W
Santa Eulalia del Rio, Sp. (sän′ta â-o͞o-lä′lē-ä dĕl rē′ô)	169	38.58 N	1.29 E
Santa Fe, Arg. (sän′tä fā′)	142	31.33 S	60.45 W
Santa Fe, Cuba (sän-tä-fĕ′)	132	21.45 N	82.40 W
Santa Fe, NM (săn′tȧ fā′)	119	35.10 N	106.00 W
Santa Fe, Sp. (sän′tä-fā′)	168	37.12 N	3.43 W
Santa Fe (Prov.), Arg. (sän′tä fā′)	142	32.00 S	61.15 W
Santa Filomena, Braz. (sän-tä-fē-lô-mĕ′nä)	141	9.09 S	44.45 W
Santa Genoveva, (Mtn.), Mex. (sän-tä-hĕ-nô-vĕ′vä)	126	23.30 N	110.00 W
Santai, China (san-tī)	199	31.02 N	105.02 E
Santa Inés, Ven. (sän′tä ē-nĕ′s)	141b	9.54 N	64.21 W
Santa Inés (I.), Chile (sän′tä ē-nās′)	142	53.45 S	74.15 W
Santa Isabel (I.), Sol. Is.	211	7.57 S	159.28 E
Santa Lucia, Cuba (sän′tȧ lo͞o-sē′ȧ)	132	21.50 N	77.30 W
Santa Lucia, Ur. (sän-tä-lo͞o-sē′ä)	139c	34.27 S	56.23 W
Santa Lucia, Ven.	141b	10.18 N	66.40 W
Santa Lucia (R.), Ur. (sän-tä-lo͞o-sē′ä)	139c	34.19 S	56.13 W
Santa Lucia B., Cuba (sän′tȧ lo͞o-sē′ȧ)	132	22.55 N	84.20 W
Santa Magarita (I.), Mex. (sän′tȧ mär-gȧ-rē′tȧ)	126	24.15 N	112.00 W
Santa Maria, Braz. (sän′tȧ mä-rē′ȧ)	142	29.40 S	54.00 W
Santa Maria, Ca. (săn-tȧ mȧ-rē′ȧ)	118	34.57 N	120.28 W
Santa Maria, It. (sän-tä mä-rē′ä)	170	41.05 N	14.15 E
Santa Maria, Phil. (sän-tä-mä-rē′ä)	203a	14.48 N	120.57 E
Santa Maria, see Huazolotitlán			
Santa Maria (R.), Mex. (sän′tȧ mä-rē′ȧ)	128	21.33 N	100.17 W
Santa Maria, C, Ba.	133	23.45 N	75.30 W
Santa Maria, Cabo de (C.), Port. (kȧ′bō-dĕ-sän-tä-mä-rē′ä)	168	36.58 N	7.54 W
Santa Maria, Cayo (I.), Cuba (kä′yō-săn′tȧ mȧ-rē′ȧ)	132	22.40 N	79.00 W
Santa María del Oro, Mex. (sän′tä-mä-rē′ä-dĕl-ô-rô)	128	21.21 N	104.35 W
Santa Maria de los Angeles, Mex. (dĕ-lôs-ä′n-hĕ-lĕs)	128	22.10 N	103.34 W
Santa María del Rio, Mex. (sän′tȧ mä-rē′ȧ dĕl rē′ō)	128	21.46 N	100.43 W
Santa Maria de Ocotán, Mex. (sän′tä-mä-rē′ä-dĕ-ô-kô-tȧ′n)	128	22.56 N	104.30 W
Santa Maria I., Açores (sän-tä-mä-rē′ä)	220a	37.09 N	26.02 W
Santa Maria Madalena, Braz. (sän-tä-mȧ-rē′ä-mȧ-dȧ-lĕ-nä)	139a	22.00 S	42.00 W
Santa Marta, Col. (sän′tȧ mär′tȧ)	140	11.15 N	74.13 W
Santa Marta, Cabo de (C.), Ang.	226	13.52 S	12.25 E
Santa Monica, Ca. (săn′tȧ mŏn′ĭ-kȧ)	117a	34.01 N	118.29 W
Santa Monica Mts., Ca.	117a	34.08 N	118.38 W
Santana (R.), Braz. (sän-tä′nä)	142b	22.33 S	43.37 W
Santander, Col. (sän-tän-dĕr′)	140a	3.00 N	76.25 W
Santander, Sp. (sän-tän-dår′)	168	43.27 N	3.50 W
Santañy, Sp. (sän-tän′yē)	169	39.21 N	3.08 E
Santa Paula, Ca. (săn′tȧ pô′lȧ)	118	34.24 N	119.05 W
Santarém, Braz. (sän-tä-rĕN′)	141	2.28 S	54.37 W
Santarém, Port.	168	39.18 N	8.48 W
Santaren Chan., Ba. (sän-tȧ-rĕn′)	132	24.15 N	79.30 W
Santa Rita, NM (săn′tȧ rē′tȧ)	119	32.45 N	108.05 W
Santa Rita do Passo Quatro, Braz. (sän-tä-rē′tȧ-dô-kwȧ′trô)	139a	21.43 S	47.27 W
Santa Rita do Sapucai, Braz. (sä-po͞o-kȧ′ē)	139a	22.15 S	45.41 W
Santa Rosa, Arg. (sän-tä-rô-sä)	142	36.45 S	64.10 W
Santa Rosa, Ca. (săn′tȧ rō′zȧ)	118	38.27 N	122.42 W
Santa Rosa, Col. (sän-tä-rô-sä)	140a	6.38 N	75.26 W
Santa Rosa, Ec.	140	3.29 S	78.55 W
Santa Rosa, Guat. (sän′tȧ rō′sȧ)	130	14.21 N	90.16 W
Santa Rosa, Hond.	130	14.45 N	88.51 W
Santa Rosa, NM (săn′tȧ rō′sȧ)	120	34.55 N	104.41 W
Santa Rosa, Ven. (sän-tä-rô-sä)	141b	9.37 N	64.10 W
Santa Rosa de Cabal, Col. (sän-tä-rô-sä-dĕ-kä-bä′l)	140a	4.53 N	75.38 W
Santa Rosa de Viterbo, Braz. (sän-tä-rô-sȧ-dĕ-vē-tĕr′-bô)	139a	21.30 S	47.21 W
Santa Rosa Ind. Res., Ca. (săn′tȧ rō′zȧ′)	118	33.28 N	116.50 W
Santa Rosalia, Mex. (sän′tȧ rô-zä′lē-ȧ)	126	27.13 N	112.15 W
Santa Rosalia, see Ciudad Camargo			
Santa Rosa Mts., Nv. (săn′tȧ rō′zȧ)	114	41.33 N	117.50 W
Santa Susana, Ca. (săn′tȧ so͞o-zä′nȧ)	117a	34.16 N	118.42 W

PLACE (Pronunciation)	PAGE	Lat. °′	Long. °′
Santa Tecla, see Nueva San Salvador			
Santa Teresa, Arg. (sän-tä-tē-rĕ′sä)	139c	33.27 S	60.47 W
Santa Teresa, Ven.	141b	10.14 N	66.40 W
Santa Vitória do Palmar, Braz. (sän-tä-vē-tō′ryä-dô-pȧl-mȧr)	142	33.30 S	53.16 W
Santa Ynez (R.), Ca. (săn′tȧ ē-nĕz′)	118	34.40 N	120.20 W
Santa Ysabel Ind. Res., Ca. (săn-tȧ ĭ-zȧ-bĕl′)	118	33.05 N	116.46 W
Santee, Ca. (săn tē′)	118a	32.50 N	116.58 W
Santee (R.), SC	125	33.27 N	80.02 W
Santiago, Braz. (sän-tyȧ′gô)	142	29.05 S	54.46 W
Santiago, Chile (sän-tē-ä′gô)	139b	33.26 S	70.40 W
Santiago, Pan.	131	8.07 N	80.58 W
Santiago, Phli. (sän-tyä′gô)	203a	16.42 N	121.33 E
Santiago, see Zacatepec			
Santiago (Prov.), Chile (sän-tyȧ′gō)	139b	33.28 S	70.55 W
Santiago, Rio Grande de (R.), Mex. (rē′o-grä′n-dĕ-dĕ-sän-tyȧ′gô)	128	21.15 N	104.05 W
Santiago (I.), Phil.	203a	16.29 N	120.03 E
Santiago de Compostela, Sp.	168	42.52 N	8.32 W
Santiago de Cuba, Cuba (sän-tyȧ′gô-dā ko͞o′bȧ)	133	20.00 N	75.50 W
Santiago de Cuba (Prov.), Cuba	133	20.20 N	76.05 W
Santiago de las Vegas, Cuba (sän-tyȧ′gô-dē-läs-vĕ′gäs)	133a	21.13 N	82.23 W
Santiago del Estero, Arg. (sän-tē-ȧ′gô-dĕl ĕs-tä′rô)	142	27.50 S	64.14 W
Santiago del Estero (Prov.), Arg. (sän-tē-ȧ′gô-dĕl ĕs-tā-rô)	142	27.15 S	63.30 W
Santiago de los Cabelleros, Dom. Rep. (sän-tyȧ′gô-dȧ lōs kȧ-bä-yȧ′rôs)	133	19.30 N	70.45 W
Santiago Mts., Tx. (sän-tē-ä′gô)	122	30.00 N	103.30 W
Santiago Res., Ca.	117a	33.47 N	117.42 W
Santiago Rodriguez, Dom. Rep. (sän-tyȧ′gô-rô-drē′gĕz)	133	19.30 N	71.25 W
Santiago Tuxtla, Mex. (sän-tyȧ′gô-to͞o′x-tlä)	129	18.28 N	95.18 W
Santiaguillo, Laguna de (L.), Mex. (lä-oô′nä-dĕ-sän-tē-ȧ-gēl′yô)	122	24.51 N	104.43 W
Santiam R., Or. (săn′tyăm)	114	44.42 N	122.26 W
Santisteban del Puerto, Sp. (sän′tē stȧ-bän′dĕl pwĕr′tô)	168	38.15 N	3.12 W
Santo Amaro, Braz. (sän′to͞o ä-mä′ro͞o)	141	12.32 S	38.33 W
Santo Amaro de Campos, Braz. (sän-tô-ä-mä′rô-dĕ-kȧm′pôs)	139a	22.01 S	41.05 W
Santo André, Braz. (sän-tô-än-drĕ′)	139a	23.40 S	46.31 W
Santo Angelo, Braz. (sän-tô-ȧ′n-zhĕ-lô)	142	28.16 S	53.59 W
Santo Antônio do Monte, Braz. (sän-tô-än-tô′nyô-dô-môn′tĕ)	139a	20.06 S	45.18 W
Santo Antonio do Zaire, Ang. (sän′to͞o än-tō′nē-o͞o)	226	6.10 S	12.25 E
Santo Domingo, Cuba (sän′tô-dōmĭŋ′gô)	132	22.35 N	80.20 W
Santo Domingo, Nic. (sän-tô-dô-mē′n-gō)	130	12.15 N	84.56 W
Santo Domingo, Dom. Rep. (sän′tô dô-mĭn′gô)	133	18.30 N	69.55 W
Santo Domingo, see Zanatepec			
Santo Domingo de la Caizada, Sp. (dā lä käl-thä′dä)	168	42.27 N	2.55 W
Santoña, Sp. (sän-tō′nyä)	168	43.25 N	3.27 W
Santos, Braz. (sän′tozh)	139a	23.58 S	46.20 W
Santos Dumont, Braz. (sän′tôs-do͞o-mô′nt)	139a	21.28 S	43.33 W
Santo Tomé, Arg. (sän-tô-tô-mĕ′)	142	28.32 S	56.04 W
Sanuki, Jap. (sä′no͞o-kē)	201a	35.16 N	139.53 E
San Urbano, Arg. (sän-o͞or-bä′nô)	139c	33.39 S	61.28 W
San Valentin, M. (Mtn.), Chile (sän-vä-lĕn-tē′n)	142	46.41 S	73.30 W
San Vicente, Arg. (sän-vē-sĕn′tĕ)	139c	35.00 S	58.26 W
San Vicente, Chile	139b	34.25 S	71.06 W
San Vicente, Sal. (sän vē-sĕn′tȧ)	130	13.41 N	88.43 W
San Vicente de Alcántara, Sp. (sän vē-thĕn′tȧ dȧ äl-kän′tä-rä)	168	39.24 N	7.08 W
San Vito al Tagliamento, It. (san vē′tô)	170	45.53 N	12.52 E
San Xavier Ind. Res., Az. (x-ä′vĭēr)	119	32.07 N	111.12 W
Sanyuanli, China (sän-yûän-lē)	198a	23.11 N	113.16 E
San Ysidro, Ca. (sän ysĭ-drō′)	118a	32.33 N	117.02 W
São Bernado do Campo, Braz. (souN-bĕr-när′dô-dô-kȧ′m-pô)	139a	23.44 S	46.33 W
São Borja, Braz. (souN-bôr-zhä)	142	28.44 S	55.59 W
São Carlos, Braz. (souN kär′lôzh)	139a	22.02 S	47.54 W
São Cristovão, Braz. (souN-krĕs-tō-vouN)	141	11.04 S	37.11 W
São Fidélis, Braz. (souN-fē-dĕ′lēs)	139a	21.41 S	41.45 W
São Francisco, Braz. (souN frăN-sĕsh′ko͞o)	141	15.59 S	44.42 W
São Francisco, Rio (R.), Braz. (rē′ō-sän-frän-sĕ′s-kō)	141	8.56 S	40.20 W
São Francisco do Sul, Braz. (souN frăN-sĕsh′ko͞o-dô-so͞o′l)	142	26.15 S	48.42 W
São Gabriel, Braz. (souN′gä-brē-ĕl′)	142	30.28 S	54.11 W
São Geraldo, Braz. (souN-zhĕ-rä′l-dô)	139a	21.01 S	42.49 W
São Gonçalo, Braz. (souN′gôŋ-sä′lo͞o)	142b	22.55 S	43.04 W
São Gonçalo do Sapucaí, Braz. (souN-gôn-sä′lô-dô-sä-po͞o-kī′)	139a	21.55 S	45.34 W
São Hill, Tan.	227	8.20 S	35.12 E
Sao Joao, Guinea-Bissau	224	11.32 N	15.26 W

PLACE (Pronunciation)	PAGE	Lat. °′	Long. °′
São João da Barra, Braz. (souN-zhôuN-dä-bȧ′rä)	142b	21.40 S	41.03 W
São João da Boa Vista, Braz. (souN-zhôuN-dä-bôä-vē′s-tä)	139a	21.58 S	46.45 W
São João del Rei, Braz. (souN zhô-ouN′dĕl-rā)	139a	21.08 S	44.14 W
São João de Meriti, Braz. (souN-zhôuN-dĕ-mĕ-rē-tē)	142b	22.47 S	43.22 W
São João do Arguaia, Braz. (souN zhô-ouN′dô-ä-rä-gwä′yä)	139	5.29 S	48.44 W
São João dos Lampas, Port. (souN′ zhô-ouN′ dōzh län-päzh′)	169b	38.52 N	9.24 W
São João Nepomuceno, Braz. (souN-zhôuN-nĕ-pô-mo͞o-sĕ-nō)	139a	21.33 S	43.00 W
São Jorge I., Açores (souN zhôr′zhĕ)	220a	38.28 N	27.34 W
São José do Rio Pardo, Braz. (souN-zhô-sĕ′dô-rē′ô-pȧ′r-dō)	139a	21.36 S	46.50 W
São José do Rio Prêto, Braz. (souN zhô-zĕ′dô-re′ô-prĕ-tô)	141	20.57 S	49.12 W
São José dos Campos, Braz. (souN zhô-zā′dōzh käN pōzh′)	139a	23.12 S	45.53 W
São Leopoldo, Braz. (souN-lĕ-ô-pôl′dô)	142	29.46 S	51.09 W
São Luis (Maranhão), Braz. (souN-lo͞oē′s-mä-rän-youN′)	141	2.31 S	43.14 W
São Luis do Paraitinga, Braz. (souN-lo͞oē′s-dô-pä-rä-ē-tē′n-gä)	139a	23.15 S	44.18 W
São Mateus, Braz. (souN mä-tä′o͞ozh)	141	18.44 S	39.45 W
São Miguel Arcanjo, Braz. (souN-mē-gĕ′l-ár-kän-zhō)	139a	23.54 S	47.59 W
São Miguel I., Açores	220a	37.59 N	26.38 W
Saona (I.), Dom. Rep. (sä-ō′nä)	133	18.10 N	68.55 W
Saône (R.), Ra. (sōn)	166	46.27 N	4.58 E
São Nicolau, Ang.	226	14.15 S	12.21 E
São Nicolau, C. V. (souN′ nē-kô-louN′)	220b	16.19 N	25.19 W
São Paulo, Braz. (souN′ pou′lo͞o)	139a	23.34 S	46.38 W
São Paulo (State), Braz. (souN pou′lo͞o)	141	21.45 S	50.47 W
São Paulo de Olivença, Braz. (souN′pou′lo͞odå ô-lē-vĕn′sȧ)	140	3.32 S	68.46 W
São Pedro, Braz. (souN-pĕ′drô)	139a	22.34 S	47.54 W
São Pedro de Aldeia, Braz. (souN-pĕ′drô-dĕ-äl-dĕ′yä)	139a	22.50 S	42.04 W
São Raimundo Nonato, Braz. (souN′ rī-mo͞o′n-do nô-nä′to͞o)	141	9.09 S	42.32 W
São Roque, Braz. (souN′ rō′kĕ)	139a	23.32 S	47.08 W
São Roque, Cabo de (C.), Braz. (kä′bo-dĕ-souN′ rō′kĕ)	141	5.06 S	35.11 W
São Salvador do Congo, Ang. (souN säl-vȧ-dôr)	226	6.30 N	14.10 E
São Sebastião, Braz. (souN sȧ-bäs-tē-ouN′)	139a	23.48 S	45.25 W
São Sebastião, Ilha de (I.), Braz. (ēl′yȧ dȧ souN′ sȧ-bäs-tē-ouN′)	139a	23.52 S	45.22 W
São Sebastião do Paraíso, Braz. (souN-sĕ-bäs-tē-ouN-dô-pä-rä-ē′sô)	139a	20.54 S	46.58 W
São Simão, Braz. (souN-sē-mouN)	139a	21.30 S	47.33 W
São Tiago I., C. V. (souN tē-ä′go͞o)	220b	15.09 N	24.45 W
São Tomé, São Tomé & Príncipe (souN tô-mā′)	226	0.20 N	6.44 E
São Tomé (I.), São Tomé & Príncipe	226	0.20 N	7.00 E
São Tomé, Cabo de (C.), Braz. (kä′bō-dĕ-souN-tô-mĕ′)	139a	22.00 S	40.00 W
Sao Tome & Principe, Afr. (prēn′sĕ-pĕ)	218	1.00 N	6.00 E
Saoura, Oued (R.), Alg.	158	29.39 N	1.42 W
São Vicente, Braz. (souN ve-se′n-tĕ)	139a	23.57 S	46.25 W
Sao Vincente I., C. V. (souN vē-sĕn′tȧ)	220b	16.51 N	24.35 W
São Vinente, Cabo de (C.), Port. (kä′bō-dĕ-sän-vē-sĕ′n-tĕ)	168	37.03 N	9.31 W
Sapele, Nig. (sä-pā′lā)	225	5.54 N	5.41 E
Sapitwa (Mtn.), Malawi	227	15.58 S	35.38 E
Sapozhok, Sov. Un. (sä-pô-zhôk′)	172	53.58 N	40.44 E
Sapporo, Jap. (säp-pō′rô)	200	43.02 N	141.29 E
Sapronovo, Sov. Un. (sȧp-rô′nô-vô)	180b	55.13 N	38.25 E
Sapucaí (R.), Braz. (sä-po͞o-kȧ-ē′)	139a	21.07 S	45.53 W
Sapucaia, Braz. (sä-po͞o-kä′yȧ)	139a	22.01 S	42.54 W
Sapucaí Mirim (R.), Braz. (sä-po͞o-kȧ-ē′mē-rĕN)	139a	21.06 S	47.03 W
Sapulpa, Ok. (sȧ-pŭl′pȧ)	121	36.01 N	96.05 W
Saquarema, Braz. (sä-kwä-rĕ-mä)	139a	22.56 S	42.32 W
Sara, Wa. (sä′rä)	116c	45.45 N	122.42 W
Sara, Bahr (R.), Chad-Cen. Afr. Rep. (bär)	221	8.19 N	17.44 E
Sarajevo, Yugo. (sä-rä-yĕv′ô) (sȧ-rä′ya-vô)	171	43.15 N	18.26 E
Sarana, Sov. Un. (sȧ-rä′nȧ)	180a	56.31 N	57.44 E
Saranac Lake, NY	109	44.20 N	74.05 W
Saranac L., NY (săr′ȧ-năk)	109	44.15 N	74.20 W
Sarandi, Arg. (sä-rän′dē)	142a	34.36 S	58.21 W
Sarandi Grande, Ur. (sä-rän′dē-grän′dĕ)	139c	33.42 S	56.21 W
Sārangpur, India	190	23.39 N	76.32 E
Saransk, Sov. Un. (sȧ-ränsk′)	176	54.10 N	45.10 E
Sarany, Sov. Un. (sȧ-rá′nĭ)	180a	58.33 N	58.48 E
Sara Pk., Nig.	225	9.37 N	9.25 E
Sarapul, Sov. Un. (sä-räpo͞ol′)	176	56.28 N	53.50 E
Sarasota, Fl. (săr-ȧ-sōtȧ)	125a	27.27 N	82.30 W
Saratoga, Tx. (săr-ȧ-tō′gȧ)	123	30.17 N	94.31 W
Saratoga, Wa.	116a	48.04 N	122.29 W

ăt; finăl; rāte; senâte; ärm; ȧsk; sofȧ; fâre; ch-choose; dh-as th in other; bē; ēvent; bĕt; recĕnt; cratẽr; g-gō; gh-guttural g; bĭt; ĭ-short neutral; rīde; K-guttural k as ch in German ich;

PRONOUNCING INDEX

Saratoga Pass – Sekenke 345

PLACE (Pronunciation)	PAGE	Lat. °′	Long. °′
Saratoga Pass, Wa.	116a	48.09 N	122.33 W
Saratoga Springs, NY (sprĭngz)	109	43.05 N	74.50 W
Saratov, Sov. Un. (så rä'tôf)	177	51.30 N	45.30 E
Saravane, Laos	199	15.48 N	106.40 E
Sarawak (Reg.), Mala. (så-rä'wäk)	202	2.30 N	112.45 E
Sárbogárd, Hung. (shär'bô-gärd)	165	46.53 N	18.38 E
Sarcee Ind. Res., Can. (sär'sē)	93e	50.58 N	114.23 W
Sardalas, Libya	220	25.59 N	10.33 E
Sardinia (I.), It. (sär-dĭn'ĭ*á*)	170	40.08 N	9.05 E
Sardis, Ms. (sär'dĭs)	124	34.26 N	89.55 W
Sargent, Ne. (sär'jĕnt)	112	41.40 N	99.38 W
Sarh (Fort-Archambault), Chad. (är-chaɴ-bō')	225	9.09 N	18.23 E
Sarikamis, Tur.	177	40.30 N	42.40 E
Sariñena, Sp. (sä-rēn-yĕ'nä)	169	41.46 N	0.11 W
Sariwŏn, Korea (sä'rē-wŭn')	198	38.40 N	125.45 E
Sark (I.), Guernsey (särk)	166	49.28 N	2.22 W
Şarkoy, Tur. (shär'kû-ē)	171	40.39 N	27.07 E
Sarmiento, Monte (Mt.), Chile (mô'n-tĕ-sär-myĕn'tō)	142	54.28 S	70.40 W
Sarnia, Can. (sär'nē-*á*)	108	43.00 N	82.25 W
Sarno, It. (sä'r-nô)	169c	40.35 N	14.38 E
Sarny, Sov. Un. (sär'nē)	165	51.17 N	26.39 E
Saronikós Kólpos (G.), Grc.	171	37.51 N	23.30 E
Saros Körfezi (G.), Tur. (sä'rôs)	171	40.30 N	26.20 E
Sárospatak, Hung. (shä'rôsh-pô'tôk)	165	48.19 N	21.35 E
Šar Planina (Mts.), Yugo. (shär plä'nē-na)	171	42.07 N	21.54 E
Sarpsborg, Nor. (särps'bôrg)	162	59.17 N	11.07 E
Sarrebourg, Fr. (sär-bo͞or')	167	48.44 N	7.02 E
Sarreguemines, Fr. (sär-gē-mēn')	167	49.06 N	7.05 E
Sarria, Sp. (sär'ē-ä)	168	42.14 N	7.17 W
Sarstun R., Guat. (särs-to͞o'n)	130	15.50 N	89.26 W
Sartène, Fr. (sär-tĕn')	170	41.36 N	8.59 E
Sarthe (R.), Fr. (särt)	166	47.44 N	0.32 W
Sárvár, Hung. (shär'vär)	164	47.14 N	16.55 E
Saryche, Mys (C.), Sov. Un. (mĭs så-rĕch')	177	44.25 N	33.00 E
Sary-Ishikotrau, Peski (Des.), Sov. Un. (sä'rē ē' shĕk-ō'trou)	178	46.12 N	75.30 E
Sarysu (R.), Sov. Un. (sä'rē-so͞o)	178	47.47 N	69.14 E
Sasarām, India (sŭs-ŭ-räm')	190	25.00 N	84.00 E
Sasayama, Jap. (sä'sä-yä'mä)	201	35.05 N	135.14 E
Sasebo, Jap. (sä'sâ-bô)	201	33.12 N	129.43 E
Sašice, Czech.	164	49.14 N	13.31 E
Saskatchewan (Prov.), Can.	94	54.46 N	107.40 W
Saskatchewan (R.), Can. (săs-kăch'ē-wän)	98	53.45 N	103.20 W
Saskatoon, Can. (săs-k*á*-to͞on')	98	52.07 N	106.38 W
Sasolburg, S. Afr.	219d	26.52 S	27.47 E
Sasovo, Sov. Un. (sås'ō-vô)	176	54.20 N	42.00 E
Saspamco, Tx. (săs-păm'cō)	117d	29.13 N	98.18 W
Sassandra, Ivory Coast	224	4.58 N	6.05 W
Sassandra (R.), Ivory Coast (sås-sän'drå)	224	5.35 N	6.25 W
Sassari, It. (säs'sä-rē)	170	40.44 N	8.33 E
Sassnitz, G.D.R. (säs'nĕts)	164	54.31 N	13.37 E
Satadougou, Mali (sä-tà-do͞o-goo')	224	12.21 N	10.07 W
Säter, Swe. (sĕ'tĕr)	162	60.21 N	15.50 E
Satilla (R.), Ga. (så-tĭl'*á*)	125	31.15 N	82.13 W
Satka, Sov. Un. (sät'kå)	180a	55.03 N	59.02 E
Sátoraljaujhely, Hung. (shä'tô-rô-lyô-o͞o'yĕl')	165	48.24 N	21.40 E
Satu-Mare, Rom. (så'to͞o-mà'rē)	165	47.50 N	22.53 E
Saturna, Can. (să-tûr'nå)	116d	48.48 N	123.12 W
Saturna (I.), Can.	116d	48.47 N	123.03 W
Sauda, Nor.	162	59.40 N	6.21 E
Saudárkrókur, Ice.	156	65.41 N	19.38 W
Saudi Arabia, Asia (så-o͞o'dĭ á-rā'bĭ-ä)	188	22.40 N	46.00 E
Sauerlach, F.R.G. (zou'ĕr-läĸ)	155d	47.58 N	11.39 E
Saugatuck, Mi. (sô'g*á*-tŭk)	108	42.40 N	86.10 W
Saugeer (R.), Can. (sô'gēr)	108	44.20 N	81.20 W
Saugerties, NY (sô'gēr-tēz)	109	42.05 N	73.55 W
Saugus, Ma. (sô'gŭs)	103a	42.28 N	71.01 W
Sauk (R.), Mn. (sôk)	113	45.30 N	94.45 W
Sauk Centre, Mn.	113	45.43 N	94.58 W
Sauk City, Wi.	113	43.16 N	89.45 W
Sauk Rapids, Mn. (răp'ĭd)	113	45.35 N	94.08 W
Sault Ste. Marie, Can.	100	46.31 N	84.20 W
Sault Ste. Marie, Mi. (so͞o sănt m*á*-rē')	117k	46.29 N	84.21 W
Saumatre, Etang (L.), Hai.	133	18.40 N	72.10 W
Saunders L., Can. (sän'dĕrs)	93g	53.18 N	113.25 W
Saurimo, Ang.	226	9.39 S	20.24 E
Sausalito, Ca. (sô-s*á*-lē'tō)	116b	37.51 N	122.29 W
Sausset-les-Pins, Fr. (sō-sĕ'lā-păɴ')	166a	43.20 N	5.08 E
Saútar, Ang.	226	11.06 S	18.27 E
Sauvie I., Or. (sô'vē)	116c	45.43 N	123.49 W
Sava (R.), Yugo. (sä'vä)	171	44.50 N	17.00 E
Savage, Md. (să'vĕj)	110e	39.07 N	76.49 W
Savage, Mn.	117g	44.47 N	93.20 W
Savalan (Mtn.), Iran	177	38.20 N	48.00 E
Savalen (L.), Nor.	162	62.19 N	10.15 E
Savalou, Benin	225	7.56 N	1.58 E
Savanna, Il. (s*á*-văn'*á*)	113	42.05 N	90.09 W
Savannah, Ga. (s*á*-văn'*á*)	125	32.04 N	81.07 W
Savannah, Mo.	113	39.58 N	94.49 W
Savannah, Tn.	124	35.13 N	88.14 W
Savannah (R.), Ga.-SC	125	33.11 N	81.51 W
Savannakhét, Indo China	202	16.33 N	104.45 E
Savanna la Mar, Jam. (så-vän'á lá mär')	132	18.10 N	78.10 W
Sávara R., Czech.	164	49.36 N	15.24 E
Savé, Benin (så-vā')	220	8.09 N	2.03 E
Save (R.), Fr.	166	43.32 N	0.50 E
Save, Rio (R.), Moz. (rē'ō-sä'vĕ)	222	21.28 S	34.14 E
Saverne, Fr. (så-vĕrn')	167	48.40 N	7.22 E
Savigliano, It. (sä-vēl-yä'nô)	170	44.38 N	7.42 E
Savigny-sur-Orge, Fr.	167b	48.41 N	2.22 E
Savona, It. (sä-nō'nä)	170	44.19 N	8.28 E
Savonlinna, Fin. (så'vôn-lĕn'nå)	163	61.53 N	28.49 E
Savran', Sov. Un. (säv-rän')	173	48.07 N	30.09 E
Sawahlunto, Indon.	202	0.37 S	100.50 E
Sawākin, Sud.	221	19.02 N	37.19 E
Sawda, Jabal as (Mts.), Libya	221	28.14 N	13.46 E
Sawhāj, Egypt	219b	26.34 N	31.40 E
Sawknah, Libya	221	29.04 N	15.53 E
Sawu, Laut (Savu Sea), Indon.	202	9.15 S	122.15 E
Sawu, Pulau (I.), Indon.	202	10.15 S	122.00 E
Sawyer, (L.), Wa. (sô'yēr)	116a	47.20 N	122.02 W
Say, Niger (sä'ē)	220	13.09 N	2.16 E
Sayan Khrebet (Mts.), Sov. Un. (sŭ-yän')	178	51.30 N	90.00 E
Şaydā (Sidon), Leb. (sä'ē-dä) (sī'dŏn)	189a	33.34 N	35.23 E
Şayhūt, P. D. R. of Yem.	192	15.23 N	51.28 E
Sayre, Ok. (sā'ēr)	120	35.19 N	99.40 W
Sayre, Pa.	109	41.55 N	76.30 W
Sayreton, Al. (sā'ēr-tŭn)	110h	33.34 N	86.51 W
Sayreville, NJ (sâr'vĭl)	110a	40.28 N	74.21 W
Sayr Usa, Mong.	194	44.15 N	107.00 E
Sayula, Mex. (sä-yo͞o'lä)	129	17.51 N	94.56 W
Sayula, Mex.	128	19.50 N	101.33 W
Sayula, Luguna de (L.), Mex. (lä-go͞o'nä-dĕ)	128	20.00 N	103.33 W
Say'un, P.D.R. of Yem.	192	16.00 N	48.59 E
Sayville, NY (sā'vĭl)	109	40.45 N	73.10 W
Sazanit (I.), Alb.	171	40.30 N	19.17 E
Sazhino, Sov. Un. (såz-hē'nô)	180a	56.20 N	58.15 E
Säffle, Swe.	162	59.10 N	12.55 E
Scandinavian Pen., Eur.	188	62.00 N	14.00 E
Scanlon, Mn. (skăn'lôn)	117h	46.27 N	92.26 W
Scappoose, Or. (skă-po͞os')	116c	45.46 N	122.53 W
Scappoose (R.), Or.	116c	45.47 N	122.57 W
Scarborough, Can. (skär'bĕr-ô)	93d	43.45 N	79.12 W
Scarborough, Eng. (skär'bŭr-ō)	160	54.16 N	0.19 W
Scarsdale, NY (skärz'dāl)	110a	41.01 N	73.47 W
Scatari I, Can. (skăt'*á*-rē)	101	46.00 N	59.44 W
Schaerbeek, Bel. (skär'bāk)	155a	50.33 N	4.23 E
Schaffhausen, Switz. (shäf'hou-z*ĕ*n)	164	47.42 N	8.38 E
Schefferville, Can.	95	54.52 N	67.01 W
Schelde, R., Bel.	161	51.04 N	3.55 E
Schenectady, NY (skĕ-nĕk'tå-dē)	109	42.50 N	73.55 W
Scheveningen, Neth.	155a	52.06 N	4.15 E
Schiedam, Neth.	155a	51.55 N	4.23 E
Schiltigheim, Fr. (shēl'tegh-hīm)	167	48.48 N	7.47 E
Schio, It. (skē'ô)	170	45.43 N	11.23 E
Schleswig, F.R.G. (shlĕs'vēgh)	164	54.32 N	9.32 E
Schleswig-Holstein (State), F.R.G. (shlĕs'vēgh-hōl'shtīn)	164	54.40 N	9.10 E
Schmalkalden, G.D.R. (shmäl'käl-dĕn)	164	50.41 N	10.25 E
Schneider, In. (schnīd'ĕr)	111a	41.12 N	87.26 W
Schofield, Wi. (skō'fēld)	113	44.52 N	89.37 W
Schönebeck, G.D.R. (shû'nē-bergh)	164	52.01 N	11.44 E
Schoonhoven, Neth.	155a	51.56 N	4.51 E
Schramberg, F.R.G. (shräm'bĕrgh)	164	48.14 N	8.24 E
Schreiber, Can.	100	48.50 N	87.10 W
Schroon (L.), NY (skro͞on)	109	43.50 N	73.50 W
Schultzendorf, G.D.R. (shōōl'tzĕn-dōrf)	155b	52.21 N	13.55 E
Schumacher, Can.	100	48.30 N	81.30 W
Schuyler, Ne. (slī'lēr)	112	41.28 N	97.05 W
Schuylkill (R.), Pa. (sko͞ol'kĭl)	110	40.10 N	75.31 W
Schuylkill-Haven, Pa. (sko͞ol'kĭl hā-vĕn)	109	40.35 N	76.10 W
Schwabach, F.R.G. (shvä'bäk)	164	49.19 N	11.02 E
Schwäbische Alb (Mts.), F.R.G. (shvă'bē-shē ălb)	164	48.11 N	9.09 E
Schwäbisch Gmünd, F.R.G. (shvă'bēsh gmünd)	164	48.47 N	9.49 E
Schwäbisch Hall, F.R.G. (häl)	164	49.08 N	9.44 E
Schwandorf, F.R.G. (shvän'dôrf)	164	49.19 N	12.08 E
Schwaner, Pegunungan Mts., Indon. (sĸvän'ĕr)	202	1.05 S	112.30 E
Schwarzwald (For.), F.R.G. (shvärts'väld)	164	47.54 N	7.57 E
Schwaz, Aus.	164	47.20 N	11.45 E
Schwechat, Aus. (shvĕk'åt)	155e	48.09 N	16.29 E
Schwedt, G.D.R. (shvĕt)	164	53.04 N	14.17 E
Schweinfurt, F.R.G. (shvīn'fo͞ort)	164	50.03 N	10.14 E
Schwelm, F.R.G. (shvĕlm)	167c	51.17 N	7.18 E
Schwerin, G.D.R. (shvĕ-rēn')	164	53.36 N	11.25 E
Schweriner See (L.), G.D.R. (shvĕ'rē-nĕr zā)	164	53.40 N	11.06 E
Schwerte, F.R.G. (shvĕr'tĕ)	167c	51.26 N	7.34 E
Schwielowsee (L.), G.D.R. (shvē'lōv zā)	155b	52.20 N	12.52 E
Schwyz, Switz. (schēts)	164	47.01 N	8.38 E
Sciacca, It. (shē-äk'kä)	170	37.30 N	13.09 E
Scilly, Isles of (Is.), Eng. (sĭl'ē)	160	49.56 N	6.50 W
Scioto (R.), Oh. (sī-ō'tō)	108	39.10 N	82.55 W
Scituate, Ma. (sĭt'ū-āt)	103a	42.12 N	70.45 W
Scobey, Mt. (skō'bē)	115	48.48 N	105.29 W
Scoggin, Or. (skō'gĭn)	116c	45.28 N	123.14 W
Scotch (R.), Can. (skŏch)	93c	45.21 N	74.56 W
Scotia, Ca. (skō'sh*á*)	114	40.29 N	124.06 W
Scotland, U. K. (skŏt'l*ă*nd)	160	57.05 N	5.10 W
Scotland, SD	112	43.08 N	97.43 W
Scotland Neck, NC (nĕk)	125	36.06 N	77.25 W
Scotstown, Can. (skŏts'toun)	109	45.35 N	71.15 W
Scott, C., Can. (skŏt)	94	50.47 N	128.26 W
Scott, Mt., Or.	114	42.55 N	122.00 W
Scott, Mt., Or.	116c	45.27 N	122.33 W
Scott Air Force Base, Il.	117e	38.33 N	89.52 W
Scottburgh, S. Afr. (skŏt'bŭr-ô)	223c	30.18 S	30.42 E
Scott City, Ks.	120	38.28 N	100.54 W
Scottdale, Ga. (skŏt'dāl)	110c	33.47 N	84.16 W
Scott Is., Ant.	228	67.00 S	178.00 E
Scott Ra., Ant.	228	68.00 S	55.00 E
Scottsbluff, Ne. (skŏts'blŭf)	112	41.52 N	103.40 W
Scotts Bluff Natl. Mon., Ne.	112	41.45 N	103.47 W
Scottsboro, Al. (skŏts'bŭro)	99	34.40 N	86.03 W
Scottsburg, In. (skŏts'bûrg)	108	38.40 N	85.50 W
Scottsdale, Austl. (skŏts'dāl)	212	41.12 S	147.37 E
Scottsville, Ky. (skŏts'vĭl)	99	36.45 N	86.10 W
Scottville, Mi.	108	44.00 N	86.20 W
Scranton, Pa. (skrăn't*ŭ*n)	109	41.45 N	75.45 W
Scugog (L.), Can. (skū'gŏg)	109	44.05 N	78.55 W
Scunthorpe, Eng. (skŭn'thôrp)	154	53.36 N	0.38 W
Scutari, see Shkodër			
Scutari, L., Alb. (sko͞o'tä-rē)	171	42.14 N	19.33 E
Sea, Is., Ga.-SC (sē)	125	31.21 N	81.05 W
Seabeck, Wa. (sē'bĕck)	126a	47.38 N	122.50 W
Sea Bright, NJ (sē brīt)	110a	40.22 N	73.58 W
Seabrook, Tx. (sē'bro͝ok)	123	29.34 N	95.01 W
Seaford, De. (sē'fērd)	109	38.35 N	75.40 W
Seagraves, Tx. (sē'grāvs)	120	32.51 N	102.38 W
Seal (R.), Can.	94	59.08 N	96.37 W
Seal Beach, Ca.	117a	33.44 N	118.06 W
Seal Cays (Is.), Turks & Caicos Is.	133	21.10 N	71.45 W
Seal Cays (Is.), Ba.	133	22.40 N	75.55 W
Seal I., S. Afr. (sēl)	222a	34.07 S	18.36 E
Sealy, Tx. (sē'lē)	123	29.46 N	96.10 W
Searcy, Ar. (sûr'sē)	121	35.13 N	91.43 W
Searles (L.), Ca. (sûrl's)	118	35.44 N	117.22 W
Searsport, Me. (sērz'pōrt)	102	44.28 N	68.55 W
Seaside, Or. (sē'sīd)	114	45.59 N	123.55 W
Seattle, Wa. (sē-ăt''l)	116a	47.36 N	122.20 W
Sebaco, Nic. (sē-bä'kô)	130	12.50 N	86.03 W
Sebago, Me. (sē-bā'gō)	102	43.52 N	70.20 W
Sebastion Vizcaino, Bahia (B.), Mex. (bä-ē'ä-sē-bäs-tyō'n-vēs-kä-ē'nō)	126	28.45 N	115.15 W
Sebastopol, Ca. (sē-bås'tō-pōl)	118	38.27 N	122.50 W
Sebderat, Eth.	221	15.30 N	36.45 E
Sébé (R.), Gabon	226	0.45 S	13.30 E
Sebeş, Rom.	171	45.58 N	23.34 E
Sebewaing, Mi. (se'bē-wăng)	108	43.45 N	83.25 W
Sebezh, Sov. Un. (syĕ'bĕzh)	172	56.16 N	28.29 E
Sebinkarahisar, Tur.	177	40.15 N	38.10 E
Sebnitz, G.D.R. (zĕb'nĕts)	164	51.01 N	14.16 E
Sebou, Oued (R.), Mor.	158	34.23 N	5.18 W
Sebree, Ky. (sē-brē')	108	37.35 N	87.30 W
Sebring, Fl. (sē'brĭng)	125a	27.30 N	81.26 W
Sebring, Oh.	108	40.55 N	81.05 W
Secchia (R.), It. (sĕ'kyä)	170	44.25 N	10.25 E
Seco (R.), Mex. (sĕ'kô)	129	18.11 N	93.18 W
Sedalia, Mo.	121	38.42 N	93.12 W
Sedan, Fr. (sē-däɴ)	166	49.49 N	4.55 E
Sedan, Ks. (sē-dăn')	121	37.07 N	96.08 W
Sedom, Isr.	189a	31.04 N	35.24 E
Sedro Woolley, Wa. (sē'drô-wo͝ol'ē)	116a	48.30 N	122.14 W
Šeduva, Sov. Un. (shĕ'do͞o-vå)	163	55.46 N	23.45 E
Seekoevlei (L.), S. Afr. (zā'ko͞of-lī)	222a	34.04 S	18.33 E
Seestall, F.R.G. (zā'shtäl)	155d	47.58 N	10.52 E
Sefrou, Mor. (sē-fro͞o')	158	33.49 N	4.46 W
Seg (L.), Sov. Un. (syĕgh)	176	64.00 N	33.30 E
Segamat, Mala. (sā'gå-måt)	189b	2.30 N	102.49 E
Segang, China (sū-gäŋ)	196	31.59 N	114.13 E
Segbana, Benin	225	10.56 N	3.42 E
Segorbe, Sp. (sĕ-gôr-bĕ)	169	39.50 N	0.30 W
Ségou, Mali (sā-go͞o')	224	13.27 N	6.16 W
Segovia, Col. (sē-gô'vēä)	140a	7.08 N	74.42 W
Segovia, Sp. (så-gō'vē-ä)	168	40.58 N	4.05 W
Segovia (R.), see Coco			
Segre (R.), Sp. (så'grā)	169	41.54 N	1.10 E
Seguam (I.), Ak. (sē'gwäm)	105a	52.16 N	172.10 W
Seguam Pass., Ak.	105a	52.20 N	173.00 W
Séguédine, Niger	225	20.12 N	12.59 E
Séguéla, Ivory Coast (sā-gā-lä')	224	7.57 N	6.40 W
Seguin, Tx. (sē-gēn')	122	29.35 N	97.58 W
Segula (I.), Ak. (sē-gū'lå)	105a	52.08 N	178.35 E
Segura (R.), Sp. (så-go͞o'rä)	169	38.07 N	0.33 W
Segura, Sierra de (Mts.), Sp. (sē-ĕ'r-rä-dĕ)	168	38.05 N	2.45 W
Segura (R.), Sp.	168	38.24 N	2.12 W
Sehwān, Pak.	190	26.33 N	67.51 E
Seibo, Dom. Rep. (sĕ'y-bō)	133	18.45 N	69.05 W
Seiling, Ok.	120	36.09 N	98.56 W
Seinäjoki, Fin. (sâ'ē-nĕ-yō'kē)	163	62.47 N	22.50 E
Seine, Baie de la (B.), Fr. (bī dĕ lä sån)	166	49.37 N	0.53 W
Seine (R.), Can. (sån)	100	49.04 N	91.00 W
Seine (R.), Can. (sån)	93f	49.48 N	96.30 W
Seine (R.), Fr.	166	49.21 N	1.17 E
Seio do Venus (Mtn.), Braz. (sē-yô-dô-vē'no͞os)	142b	22.28 S	43.12 W
Seixal, Port. (sâ-ē-shäl')	169b	38.38 N	9.06 W
Sekenke, Tan.	227	4.16 S	34.10 E

ng-sing; ŋ-baŋk; ɴ-nasalized n; nŏd; cŏmmit; ōld; ōbey; ôrder; oi-boil; fo͞od; fo͝ot; ou-out; s-soft; sh-dish; th-thin; pūre; ûnite; ûrn; stŭd; circŭs; ü-as in French tu; '-indeterminate vowel.

346 Sekondi-Takoradi – Sheffield

PLACE (Pronunciation)	PAGE	Lat. °′	Long. °′
Sekondi-Takoradi, Ghana (sē-kôn'dē tä-kô-rä'dē)	224	4.59 N	1.43 W
Sekota, Eth.	221	12.47 N	38.59 E
Selangor (State), Mala. (så-län'gōr)	189b	2.53 N	101.29 E
Selanovtsi, Bul. (sål'á-nôv-tsĭ)	171	43.42 N	24.05 E
Selaru I., Indon.	203	8.30 S	130.30 E
Selatan, Tandjung (C.), Indon. (så-lä'tän)	202	4.09 S	114.40 E
Selawik, Ak. (sē-lá-wĭk)	105	66.30 N	160.09 W
Selayar, Pulau (I.), Indon.	202	6.15 S	121.15 E
Selbusjøen (L.), Nor. (sĕl'bōō)	162	63.18 N	11.55 E
Selby, Eng. (sĕl'bē)	154	53.47 N	1.03 W
Seldovia, Ak. (sĕl-dō'vē-á)	105	59.26 N	151.42 W
Selemdzha (R.), Sov. Un. (sâ-lĕmt-zhä')	179	52.28 N	131.50 E
Selenga (R.), Sov. Un. (sĕ lĕŋ gä')	179	51.00 N	106.40 E
Selenge Gol. (R.), Mong.	194	49.04 N	102.23 E
Selennyakh (R.), Sov. Un. (sĕl-yĭn-yäk)	179	67.42 N	141.45 E
Sélestat, Fr. (sē-lē-stä')	167	48.16 N	7.27 E
Selibaby, Mauritania (så-lē-bá-bē')	220	15.21 N	12.11 W
Seliger (L.), Sov. Un. (sĕl'lē-gĕr)	172	57.14 N	33.18 E
Selizharovo, Sov. Un. (så'lē-zhä'rô-vô)	172	56.51 N	33.28 E
Selkirk, Can. (sĕl'kûrk)	99	50.09 N	96.52 W
Selkirk Mts., Can.	94	51.00 N	117.40 W
Selleck, Wa. (sĕl'ĕck)	116a	47.22 N	121.52 W
Sellersburg, In. (sĕl'ĕrs-bûrg)	111h	38.25 N	85.45 W
Sellya Khskaya, Guba (B.), Sov. Un. (sĕl-yäk'sKá-yá)	179	72.30 N	136.00 E
Selma, Al. (sĕl'má)	124	32.25 N	87.00 W
Selma, Ca.	118	36.34 N	119.37 W
Selma, NC	125	35.33 N	78.16 W
Selma, Tx.	117d	29.33 N	98.19 W
Selmer, Tn.	124	35.11 N	88.36 W
Selsingen, F.R.G. (zĕl'zĕn-gĕn)	155c	53.22 N	9.13 E
Selukwe, Zimb. (sē-lŭk'wē)	222	19.34 S	30.03 E
Selway R., Id. (sĕl'wå)	114	46.07 N	115.12 W
Selwyn (L.), Can. (sĕl'wĭn)	94	59.41 N	104.30 W
Seman (R.), Alb.	171	40.48 N	19.53 E
Semarang, Indon. (sĕ-mä'räng)	202	7.03 S	110.27 E
Semarinda, Indon.	202	0.30 S	117.10 E
Semendria, see Smederevo			
Semënovka, Sov. Un. (sĕ-myôn'ôf-ká)	173	52.10 N	32.34 E
Semeru, Gunung (Mtn.), Indon.	202	8.06 S	112.55 E
Semiahmoo Ind. Res., Can.	116d	49.01 N	122.43 W
Semiahmoo Spit, Wa. (sĕm'ĭ-á-mōō)	116d	48.59 N	122.52 W
Semichi Is., Ak. (sē-mē'chĭ)	105a	52.40 N	174.50 W
Seminoe Res., Wy. (sĕm'ĭ nô)	115	42.08 N	107.10 W
Seminole, Ok. (sĕm'ĭ-nōl)	121	35.13 N	96.41 W
Seminole, Tx.	122	32.43 N	102.39 W
Seminole Ind. Res., Fl.	125a	26.19 N	81.11 W
Seminole Ind. Res., Fl.	125a	27.05 N	81.25 W
Seminole, L., Fl.-Ga.	124	30.57 N	84.46 W
Semipalatinsk, Sov. Un. (sĕ'mē-pá-lá-tyĕnsk')	178	50.28 N	80.29 E
Semisopochnoi (I.), Ak. (sĕ-mē-sá-pôsh' noi)	105a	51.45 N	179.25 W
Semiyarskoye, Sov. Un. (sĕ'mē-yär'skô-yĕ)	178	51.03 N	78.28 E
Semliki R., Ug.-Zaire (sĕm'lē-kē)	221	0.45 N	29.36 E
Semlin, see Zemun			
Semmering P., Aus. (sĕm'ĕr-ĭng)	164	47.39 N	15.50 E
Semnān, Iran	177	35.30 N	53.30 E
Senador Pompeu, Braz. (sĕ-nä-dōr-pôm-pĕ'ōō)	141	5.34 S	39.18 W
Senatobia, Ms. (sĕ-ná-tō'bē-á)	124	34.36 N	89.56 W
Sendai, Jap. (sĕn-dī')	200	38.18 N	141.02 E
Seneca, Ks. (sĕn'ē-ká)	121	39.49 N	96.03 W
Seneca, SC	124	34.40 N	82.58 W
Seneca, Md.	110e	39.04 N	77.20 W
Seneca (L.), NY	109	42.30 N	76.55 W
Seneca Falls, NY	109	42.55 N	76.55 W
Senegal, Afr. (sĕn-ĕ-gôl')	218	14.53 N	14.58 W
Sénégal (R.), Afr.	224	16.00 N	14.00 W
Senekal, S. Afr. (sĕn'ē-kál)	219d	28.20 S	27.37 E
Senftenberg, G.D.R. (zĕnf'tĕn-bĕrgh)	164	51.32 N	14.00 E
Sengunyane (R.), Leso	223c	29.35 S	28.08 E
Senhor do Bonfim, Braz. (sĕn-yôr dô bôN-fē'N)	141	5.21 S	40.09 W
Senigallia, It. (så-nē-gäl'lyä)	170	43.42 N	13.16 E
Senj, Yugo. (sĕn')	170	44.58 N	14.55 E
Senja (I.), Nor. (sĕnyä)	156	69.28 N	16.10 E
Senlis, Fr. (säN-lēs')	167b	49.13 N	2.35 E
Sennar Dam, Sud.	221	13.38 N	33.38 E
Senneterre, Can.	95	48.20 N	77.22 W
Senno, Sov. Un. (syĕ'nô)	172	54.48 N	29.43 E
Sens, Fr. (säNs)	166	48.05 N	3.18 E
Sensuntepeque, Sal. (sĕn-sōōn-tå-pä'kå)	130	13.53 N	88.34 W
Senta, Yugo. (sĕn'tä)	171	45.54 N	20.05 E
Senzaki, Jap. (sĕn'zä-kē)	201	34.22 N	131.09 E
Seoul, see Sŏul			
Sepang, Mala.	189b	2.43 N	101.45 E
Sepetiba, Baia de (B.), Braz. (bäē'ä dē så-pā-tē'bá)	142b	23.01 S	43.42 W
Sepik (R.), Pap. N. Gui. (sĕp-ĕk')	203	4.07 S	142.40 E
Septentrional, Cordillera (Mts.), Dom. Rep. (kôr-dēl-yĕ'rä sĕp-tĕn-tryô-nä'l)	133	19.50 N	71.15 W
Septeuil, Fr. (sĕ-tû')	167b	48.53 N	1.40 E
Sept-Îles, Can. (sĕ-tēl')	102	50.12 N	66.23 W
Sequatchie (R.), Tn. (sē-kwăch'ē)	124	35.33 N	85.14 W
Sequim, Wa. (sē'kwĭm)	116a	48.05 N	123.07 W
Sequim B., Wa.	116a	48.04 N	122.58 W
Sequoia Natl. Park, Ca. (sē-kwoi'á)	118	36.34 N	118.37 W
Seraing, Bel. (sē-răN')	161	50.38 N	5.28 E
Seram (I.), Indon.	203	2.45 S	129.30 E
Serāmpore, India	190a	22.44 N	88.21 E
Serang, Indon. (så-räng')	202	6.13 S	106.10 E
Seranggung, Indon.	189b	0.49 N	104.11 E
Serbia (Reg.), **see Srbija**			
Serdobsk, Sov. Un. (sĕr-dôpsk')	177	52.30 N	44.20 E
Sered', Czech.	165	48.17 N	17.43 E
Seredina-Buda, Sov. Un. (sĕ-rå-dē'ná-bōō'dá)	173	52.11 N	34.03 E
Seremban, Mala. (sĕr-ĕm-bän')	189b	2.44 N	101.57 E
Serengeti Natl. Pk., Tan.	227	2.20 S	34.50 E
Serengeti Pln., Tan.	227	2.40 S	34.55 E
Serenje, Zambia (sē-rĕn'yē)	222	13.12 S	30.49 E
Serenli, Som. (så-rĕn'lē)	219a	2.28 N	42.15 E
Seres, see Sérrai			
Seret, Czech.	165	48.17 N	17.43 E
Seret R., Sov. Un. (sĕr'ĕt)	165	49.45 N	25.30 E
Sergeya Kirova (I.), Sov. Un. (sĕr-gyĕ'yá kē'rô-vá)	178	77.30 N	86.10 E
Sergipe (State), Braz. (sĕr-zhē'pĕ)	141	10.27 S	37.04 W
Sergiyevsk, Sov. Un.	176	53.58 N	51.00 E
Sérifos, Grc.	171	37.10 N	24.32 E
Sérifos (I.), Grc.	171	37.42 N	24.17 E
Serodino, Arg. (sĕ-rô-dē'nô)	139c	32.36 S	60.56 W
Seropédica, Braz. (sĕ-rô-pĕ'dē-kä)	142b	22.44 S	43.43 W
Serov, Sov. Un. (syĕ-rôf')	180a	59.36 N	60.30 E
Serowe, Bots. (sĕ-rō'wĕ)	222	22.18 S	26.39 E
Serpa, Port. (sĕr-pä)	168	37.56 N	7.38 W
Serpukhov, Sov. Un. (syĕr'pōō-Kôf)	172	54.53 N	37.27 E
Sérrai (Seres), Grc. (sĕr'rĕ) (sĕr'ĕs)	171	41.06 N	23.36 E
Serranias Del Burro, Mex. (sĕr-rä-nē'äs dĕl bōō'r-rô)	122	29.39 N	102.07 W
Serrinha, Braz. (sĕr-rēn'yá)	141	11.43 S	38.49 W
Serta, Port. (sĕr'tá)	168	39.48 N	8.01 W
Sertânia, Braz. (sĕr-tá'nyä)	141	8.28 S	37.13 W
Sertãozinho, Braz. (sĕr-touN-zē'n-yô)	139a	21.10 S	47.58 W
Serting (R.), Mala.	189b	3.01 N	102.32 E
Seruí, Braz. (sĕ-rōō-ē')	142b	22.40 S	43.08 W
Sese Is., Ug.	227	0.30 S	32.30 E
Sesia (R.), It. (sâz'yä)	170	45.33 N	8.25 E
Sesimbra, Port. (sĕ-sē'm-brä)	169b	38.27 N	9.06 W
Sesmyl (R.), S. Afr.	223b	25.51 S	28.06 E
Sestri Levante, It. (sĕs'trē lå-vän'tå)	170	44.15 N	9.24 E
Sestroretsk, Sov. Un. (sĕs-trô-rĕtsk)	180c	60.06 N	29.58 E
Sestroretskiy Razliv, Ozero (L.), Sov. Un. (ô'zĕ-rô sĕs-trô' rĕts-kĭ-räz'lĭf)	180c	60.05 N	30.07 E
Seta, Jap. (sĕ'tä)	201b	34.58 N	135.56 W
Séte, Fr. (sĕt)	166	43.24 N	3.42 E
Sete Lagoas, Braz. (sĕ-tĕ lä-gô'äs)	141	19.23 S	43.58 W
Setif, Alg. (så-tēf')	220	36.18 N	5.21 E
Seto, Jap. (sē'tō)	201	35.11 N	137.07 E
Seto-Naikai (Sea), Jap. (sĕ'tô nī'kī)	201	33.50 N	132.25 E
Settat, Mor. (sĕt-ät') (sē-tá')	220	33.02 N	7.30 W
Sette-Cama, Gabon. (sĕ-tĕ-kä-mä')	222	2.29 S	9.40 E
Settlement Pt., Ba. (sĕt'l-mĕnt)	132	26.40 N	79.00 W
Settlers, S. Afr. (sĕt'lĕrs)	219d	24.57 S	28.33 E
Settsu, Jap.	201b	34.46 N	135.33 E
Setúbal, Port. (så-tōō'bäl)	169b	30.32 N	8.54 W
Setúbal, B. de, Port. (bä-ē'ä)	168	38.27 N	9.08 W
Seul, Lac (L.), Can. (lák sûl)	99	50.20 N	92.30 W
Sevan (L.), Sov. Un. (syĭ-vän')	177	40.10 N	45.20 E
Sevastopol' (Akhiar), Sov. Un. (syĕ-vás-tô-pôl'') (äK'yár)	173	44.34 N	33.34 E
Seven Is., see Shichitō			
Sevenoaks, Eng. (sĕ-vĕn-ōks')	154b	51.16 N	0.12 E
Severka R., Sov. Un. (sâ'vĕr-ká)	180b	55.11 N	38.41 E
Severn (R.), Can. (sĕv'ĕrn)	95	55.21 N	88.42 W
Severna Park, Md. (sĕv'ĕrn-á)	110e	39.04 N	76.33 W
Severnaya Dvina (Northern Dvina) (R.), Sov. Un.	176	63.00 N	42.40 E
Severnaya Zemlya (Northern Land) (Is.), Sov. Un. (sĕ-vyĭr-nī'u zĭ-m'lyä')	175	79.33 N	101.15 E
Severoural'sk, Sov. Un. (sĕ-vyĭ-rŭ-ōō-rälsk')	180a	60.08 N	59.53 E
Sevier (L.), Ut. (sē-vēr')	119	38.55 N	113.10 W
Sevier R., Ut.	119	39.25 N	112.20 W
Sevier R., East Fork, Ut.	119	37.45 N	112.10 W
Sevilla, Col. (sĕ-vē'l-yä)	140a	4.16 N	75.56 W
Sevilla, Sp. (sĕ-vēl'yä)	168	37.29 N	5.58 W
Seville, Oh. (sĕ'vĭl)	111d	41.01 N	81.45 W
Sevlievo, Bul. (sĕv'lyĕ-vô)	171	41.02 N	25.05 E
Sevsk, Sov. Un. (syĕfsk)	172	52.08 N	34.28 E
Seward, Ak. (sū'ård)	105	60.18 N	149.28 W
Seward, Ne.	121	40.55 N	97.06 W
Seward Pen., Ak.	105	65.40 N	164.00 W
Sewell, Chile (sĕ'ōō-ĕl)	142	34.01 S	70.18 W
Sewickley, Pa. (sē-wĭk'lē)	111e	40.33 N	80.11 W
Seybaplaya, Mex. (sā-ē-bä-plä'yä)	129	19.38 N	90.40 W
Seychelles, Afr. (sā-shĕl')	220	5.20 S	55.10 E
Seyđisfjördur, Ice. (sä'dēs-fyûr-dōōr)	156	65.21 N	14.08 W
Seyé, Mex. (sĕ-yĕ')	130a	20.51 N	89.22 W
Seyhan (R.), Tur.	159	37.28 N	35.40 E
Seym (R.), Sov. Un. (sĕym)	173	51.23 N	33.22 E
Seymour, In. (sē'mōr)	101	38.55 N	85.55 W
Seymour, Ia.	113	40.41 N	93.03 W
Seymour, Tx.	120	33.35 N	99.16 W
Seymour, S. Afr. (sē'môr)	223c	32.33 S	26.48 E
Sezela, S. Afr.	223c	30.33 S	30.37 E
Sezze, It. (sĕt'så)	170	41.32 N	13.30 E
Sfaz, Tun. (sfäks)	220	34.51 N	10.45 E
Sfîntu-Gheorghe, Rom.	171	45.53 N	25.49 E
's-Gravenhage (The Hague), Neth. ('s Krä'vĕn-hä'Kē) (hāg)	155a	52.05 N	4.16 E
Sha (R.), China (shä)	195	33.33 N	114.30 E
Shaanxi (Prov.), China (shän-shyĕ)	194	35.30 N	109.10 E
Shabani, Zimb.	222	20.15 S	30.28 E
Shablykino, Sov. Un. (sháb-lē'kĭ-nō)	180b	56.22 N	38.37 E
Shache (Yarkand), China (shä-chŭ)	194	38.15 N	77.15 E
Shackleton Shelf Ice, Ant. (shăk''l-tŭn)	228	65.00 S	100.00 E
Shades Cr., Al. (shādz)	110h	33.20 N	86.55 W
Shades Mtn., Al.	110h	33.22 N	86.51 W
Shagamu, Nig.	225	6.51 N	3.39 E
Shāhjahānpur, India (shä-jŭ-hän'pōōr)	190	27.58 N	79.58 E
Shahrezā, Iran (shä-rä'zā)	192	31.47 N	51.47 E
Shajing, China (shä-jyĭŋ)	197a	22.44 N	113.48 E
Shaker Hts., Oh. (shā'kĕr)	111d	41.28 N	81.34 W
Shakhty, Sov. Un. (shäK'tē)	173	47.41 N	40.11 E
Shaki, Nig.	225	8.39 N	3.25 E
Shakopee, Mn. (shăk'ô-pe)	117g	44.48 N	93.31 W
Shala L., Eth. (shä'lá)	221	7.34 N	39.00 E
Shām, Jabal ash (Mtn.), Om.	192	23.01 N	57.45 E
Shambe, Sud. (shäm'bå)	221	7.08 N	30.46 E
Shammar, Jabal (Mts.), Sau. Ar. (jĕb'ĕl shŭm'ár)	192	27.13 N	40.16 E
Shamo (L.), Eth.	221	5.58 N	37.00 E
Shamokin, Pa. (shá-mō'kĭn)	109	40.45 N	76.30 W
Shamrock, Tx. (shăm'rŏk)	120	35.14 N	100.12 W
Shamva, Zimb (shäm'vá)	222	17.18 S	31.35 E
Shandī, Sud.	221	16.44 N	33.29 E
Shandon, Oh. (shăn-dŭn)	111f	39.20 N	84.13 W
Shandong (Prov.), China (shän-dôŋ)	195	36.08 N	117.09 E
Shandong, Bandao (Pen.), China (shän-dôŋ bän-dou)	198	37.00 N	120.10 E
Shangcai, China (shäŋ-tsī)	196	33.16 N	114.16 E
Shangcheng, China (shäŋ-chŭŋ)	196	31.47 N	115.22 E
Shangdu, China (shäŋ-dōō)	198	41.38 N	113.22 E
Shanghai, China (shäng'hī')	197b	31.14 N	121.27 E
Shanghai-Shi (Mun.), China (shäŋ-hī shr)	195	31.30 N	121.45 E
Shanghe, China (shäŋ-hŭ)	196	37.18 N	117.10 E
Shanglin, China (shäŋ-lĭn)	196	38.20 N	116.05 E
Shangqiu, China (shäŋ-chyô)	196	34.24 N	115.39 E
Shangrao, China (shäŋ-rou)	199	28.25 N	117.58 E
Shangzhi, China (shäŋ-jr)	198	45.18 N	127.52 E
Shanhaiguan, China	196	40.01 N	119.45 E
Shannon, Al. (shăn'ŭn)	110h	33.23 N	86.52 W
Shannon (R.), Ire. (shăn'ŏn)	160	52.30 N	9.58 W
Shanshan, China (shän'shän')	194	42.51 N	89.53 E
Shantar (I.), Sov. Un. (shän'tär)	179	55.13 N	138.42 E
Shantou (Swatow), China (shän-tō)	199	23.20 N	116.40 E
Shanxi (Prov.), China (shän-shyĕ)	195	37.30 N	112.00 E
Shan Xian, China (shän shyĕn)	196	34.47 N	116.04 E
Shaobo, China (shou-bwo)	196	32.33 N	119.30 E
Shaobo Hu (L.), China (shou-bwo hōō)	196	32.07 N	119.13 E
Shaoguan, China (shou-gŭän)	199	24.58 N	113.42 E
Shaoxing, China (shou-shyĭŋ)	199	30.00 N	120.40 E
Shapki, Sov. Un. (shäp'kĭ)	180c	59.36 N	31.11 E
Shark B., Austl. (shärk)	210	25.30 S	113.00 E
Sharon, Ma. (shăr'ŏn)	103a	42.07 N	71.11 W
Sharon, Pa.	108	41.15 N	80.30 W
Sharon Springs, Ks.	120	38.51 N	101.45 W
Sharonville, Oh. (shăr'ŏn vĭl)	111f	39.16 N	84.24 W
Sharpsburg, Pa. (shärps'bûrg)	111e	40.30 N	79.54 W
Sharr, Jabal (Mtn.), Sau. Ar.	192	28.00 N	36.07 E
Shashi, China (shä-shē)	199	30.20 N	112.18 E
Shasta, Mt., Ca.	114	41.35 N	122.12 W
Shasta L., Ca. (shăs'tá)	114	40.51 N	122.32 W
Shatsk, Sov. Un. (shátsk)	176	54.00 N	41.40 E
Shattuck, Ok. (shăt'ŭk)	120	36.16 N	99.53 W
Shaunavon, Can.	98	49.40 N	108.25 W
Shaw, Ms. (shô)	124	33.36 N	90.44 W
Shawano, Wi. (shá-wô'nô)	113	44.41 N	88.13 W
Shawinigan, Can.	95	46.32 N	72.46 W
Shawnee, Ks. (shô-nē')	117f	39.01 N	94.43 W
Shawnee, Ok.	121	35.20 N	96.54 W
Shawneetown, Il. (shô'nē-toun)	108	37.40 N	88.05 W
Shayang, China	199	31.00 N	112.38 E
Shchara (R.), Sov. Un. (sh-chä'rå)	165	53.17 N	25.12 E
Shchëlkovo, Sov. Un. (shchĕl'kô-vô)	180b	55.55 N	38.00 E
Shchëtovo, Sov. Un. (shchĕ'tô-vô)	173	48.11 N	39.13 E
Shchigry, Sov. Un. (shchē'grē)	173	51.52 N	36.54 E
Shchors, Sov. Un. (shchôrs)	173	51.38 N	31.58 E
Shchuch'ye Ozero, Sov. Un. (shchōōch'yĕ ô'zĕ-rô)	180a	56.31 N	56.35 E
Sheakhala, India	190a	22.47 N	88.10 E
Shebele R., Eth. (shā'bå-lē)	219a	6.07 N	43.10 E
Shebelle (R.), Som.	218a	1.38 N	43.50 E
Sheboygan, Wi. (shē-boi'găn)	113	43.45 N	87.44 W
Sheboygan Falls, Wi.	113	43.43 N	87.51 W
Shechem (Ruins), Jordan	189a	32.15 N	35.22 E
Shedin Pk., Can. (shĕd'ĭn)	96	55.55 N	127.32 W
Shediac, Can. (shĕ'dē-ăk)	102	46.13 N	64.32 W
Sheerness, Eng. (shēr'nĕs)	154b	51.26 N	0.46 E
Sheffield, Al. (shĕf'fēld)	124	35.42 N	87.42 W

ăt; finăl; rāte; senåte; ärm; åsk; sofá; fâre; ch-choose; dh-as th in other; bē; ēvent; bĕt; recĕnt; cratĕr; g-gō; gh-guttural g; bĭt; ĭ-short neutral; rīde; K-guttural k as ch in German ich;

PRONOUNCING INDEX Sheffield – Silvânia 347

PLACE (Pronunciation)	PAGE	Lat. °′	Long. °′
Sheffield, Can.	93d	43.20 N	80.13 W
Sheffield, Eng.	154	53.23 N	1.28 W
Sheffield, Oh.	111d	41.26 N	82.05 W
Sheffield Lake, Oh.	111d	41.30 N	82.03 W
Sheksna (R.), Sov. Un. (shĕks'nȧ)	176	59.50 N	38.40 E
Shelagskiy, Mys (C.), Sov. Un. (shĭ-läg'skē)	179	70.08 N	170.52 E
Shelbina, Ar. (shĕl-bī'nȧ)	121	39.41 N	92.03 W
Shelburn, In. (shĕl'bŭrn)	108	39.10 N	87.30 W
Shelburne, Can.	102	43.46 N	65.19 W
Shelburne, Can.	109	44.04 N	80.12 W
Shelby, In. (shĕl'bē)	111a	41.12 N	87.21 W
Shelby, Mi.	108	43.35 N	86.20 W
Shelby, Ms.	124	33.56 N	90.44 W
Shelby, Mt.	115	48.35 N	111.55 W
Shelby, NC	125	35.16 N	81.35 W
Shelby, Oh.	108	40.50 N	82.40 W
Shelbyville, Il. (shĕl'bē-vĭl)	108	39.20 N	88.45 W
Shelbyville, In.	108	39.30 N	85.45 W
Shelbyville, Ky.	108	38.10 N	85.15 W
Shelbyville, Tn.	124	35.30 N	86.28 W
Shelbyville Res., Il.	192	39.30 N	88.45 W
Sheldon, Ia. (shĕl'dŭn)	112	43.10 N	95.50 W
Sheldon, Tx.	123a	29.52 N	95.07 W
Shelekhova, Zaliv (B.), Sov. Un.	179	60.00 N	156.00 E
Shelikof Str., Ak. (shĕ'lē-kôf)	105	57.56 N	154.20 W
Shellbrook, Can.	98	53.15 N	106.22 W
Shelley, Id. (shĕl'lē)	115	43.24 N	112.06 W
Shellrock (R.), Ia. (shĕl'rŏk)	113	43.25 N	93.19 W
Shelon' (R.), Sov. Un. (shâ'lôn)	172	57.50 N	29.40 E
Shelton, Ct. (shĕl'tŭn)	109	41.15 N	73.05 W
Shelton, Ne.	120	40.46 N	98.41 W
Shelton, Wa.	114	47.14 N	123.05 W
Shemakha, Sov. Un. (shĕ-mȧ-kä')	180a	56.16 N	59.19 E
Shemakha, Sov. Un.	177	40.35 N	48.40 E
Shenandoah, Ia. (shĕn-ăn-dō'ȧ)	121	40.46 N	95.23 W
Shedandoah, Pa.	109	40.50 N	76.15 W
Shenandoah, Va.	109	38.30 N	78.30 W
Shenandoah Natl. Park., Va.	109	38.35 N	78.25 W
Shenandoah (R.), Va.	109	38.55 N	78.05 W
Shendam, Nig.	225	8.53 N	9.32 E
Shengfang, China (shengfäng)	196	39.05 N	116.40 E
Shenkursk, Sov. Un. (shĕn-ko͞orsk')	180	62.10 N	43.08 E
Shenmu, China	198	38.55 N	110.35 E
Shenqiu, China	196	33.11 N	115.06 E
Shen Xian, China (shŭn shyĕn)	196	36.14 N	115.38 E
Shen Xian, China (shŭn shyän)	196	38.02 N	115.33 E
Shenyang, China (shŭn-yäŋ)	198	41.45 N	123.22 E
Shenze, China (shŭn-dzŭ)	196	38.12 N	115.12 E
Sheopur, India	190	25.37 N	78.10 E
Shepard, Can. (shĕ'pärd)	93e	50.57 N	113.55 W
Shepetovka, Sov. Un. (shĕ-pĕ-tôf'kȧ)	173	50.10 N	27.01 E
Shepparton, Austl. (shĕp'år-tŭn)	212	36.15 S	145.25 E
Sherborn, Ma. (shûr'bŭrn)	103a	42.15 N	71.22 W
Sherbro I., S. L.	224	7.30 N	12.55 W
Sherbrooke, Can.	109	45.24 N	71.54 W
Sherburn, Eng. (shûr'bŭrn)	154	53.47 N	1.15 W
Shereshevo, Sov. Un. (shĕ-rĕ-shĕ-vô)	165	52.31 N	24.08 E
Sheridan, Ar. (shĕr'ĭ-dăn)	121	34.19 N	92.21 W
Sheridan, Or.	114	45.06 N	123.22 W
Sheridan, Wy.	115	44.48 N	106.56 W
Sherman, Tx. (shĕr'măn)	121	33.39 N	96.37 W
Sherna R., Sov. Un. (shĕr'nȧ)	180b	56.08 N	38.45 E
Sherridon, Can.	99	55.10 N	101.10 W
's Hertogenbosch, Neth. (sĕr-tō'ghĕn-bôs)	155a	51.41 N	5.19 E
Sherwood, Or.	116c	45.21 N	122.50 W
Sherwood For., Eng.	154	53.11 N	1.07 W
Sherwood Park, Can.	97	53.31 N	113.19 W
Shetland (Is.), Scot. (shĕt'lănd)	160a	60.35 N	2.10 W
Shevchenko, Sov. Un.	192	44.00 N	51.10 E
Shewa Gimira, Eth.	221	7.13 N	35.49 E
She Xian, China (shŭ shyĕn)	196	36.34 N	113.42 E
Sheyang (R.), China (she-yäŋ)	196	33.42 N	119.40 E
Sheyenne (R.), ND (shī-ĕn')	112	46.42 N	97.52 W
Shi (R.), China (shr)	196	31.58 N	115.50 E
Shi (R.), China	196	32.09 N	114.11 E
Shiawassee (R.), Mi. (shī-ȧ-wôs'ē)	108	43.15 N	84.05 W
Shibām, P. D. R. of Yem. (shē'bäm)	192	16.02 N	48.40 E
Shibīn al Kawn, Egypt (shē-bēn'ĕl kōm')	219b	30.31 N	31.01 E
Shibīn al Qanāṭir, Egypt (kȧ-nä'tēr)	219b	30.18 N	31.21 E
Shichitō (Seven Is.), Jap. (shē'chē-tō)	201	34.18 N	139.28 E
Shicun, China (shr-tso͞on)	196	33.47 N	117.18 E
Shields R., Mt. (shēldz)	115	45.54 N	110.40 W
Shifnal, Eng. (shĭf'năl)	154	52.40 N	2.22 W
Shijian, China (shr-jyĕn)	196	31.27 N	117.51 E
Shijiazhuang, China (shr-jyä-jŭäŋ)	196	38.04 N	114.31 E
Shijiu Hu (L.), China (shr-jyô ho͞o)	196	31.29 N	119.07 E
Shikārpur, Pak.	190	27.51 N	68.52 E
Shiki, Jap. (shē'kē)	201a	35.50 N	139.35 E
Shikoku (I.), Jap. (shē'kō'ko͞o)	201	33.43 N	133.33 E
Shilka (R.), Sov. Un. (shĭl'kȧ)	179	53.00 N	118.45 E
Shilla (Mt.), India	190	37.18 N	78.17 E
Shillong, India (shĕl-lông')	190	25.39 N	91.58 E
Shiloh, Il. (shī'lō)	117e	38.34 N	89.54 W
Shilong, China (shr-lôŋ)	199	23.05 N	113.58 E
Shilou, China	197a	22.58 N	113.29 E
Shimabara, Jap. (shē'mä-bä'rä)	201	32.46 N	130.22 E
Shimada, Jap. (shē'mä-dä)	201	34.49 N	138.13 E
Shimizu, Jap. (shē'mē-zo͞o)	201	35.00 N	138.29 E
Shimminato, Jap. (shĕm'mē'nä-tô)	201	36.47 N	137.05 E
Shimoda, Jap. (shē'mô-dȧ)	201	34.41 N	138.58 E
Shimoga, India	191	13.59 N	75.38 E
Shimoni, Ken.	227	4.39 S	39.23 E
Shimonoseki, Jap. (shē'mô-nô-sĕ'kē) (shē-mô-nô'sĕ-kī)	201	33.58 N	130.55 E
Shimo-Saga, Jap. (shē'mô sä'gä)	201b	35.01 N	135.41 E
Shin, Loch (L.), Scot. (lŏĸ shĭn)	160	58.08 N	4.02 W
Shinagawa-Wan (B.), Jap. (shē'nä-gä'wä wän)	201a	35.37 N	139.49 E
Shinano-Gawa (Strm.), Jap. (shē-nä'nô gä'wä)	201	36.43 N	138.22 E
Shingū, Jap. (shĭn'go͞o)	201	33.43 N	135.59 E
Shinji (L.), Jap. (shĭn'jē)	201	35.23 N	133.05 E
Shinkolobwe, Zaire	227	11.02 S	26.35 E
Shinyanga, Tan. (shĭn-yäŋ'gä)	221	3.40 S	33.26 E
Shiono Misaki (C.), Jap. (shē-ô'nô mē'sä-kē)	200	33.20 N	136.10 E
Shipai, China (shr-pī)	197a	23.07 N	113.23 E
Ship Channel Cay (I.), Ba. (shĭp chă-nĕl kē)	132	24.50 N	76.50 W
Shipley, Eng. (shĭp'lē)	154	53.50 N	1.47 W
Shippegan, Can. (shĭ'pē-găn)	102	47.45 N	64.42 W
Shippegan I., Can.	102	47.50 N	64.38 W
Shippenburg, Pa. (shĭp'ĕn bûrg)	109	40.00 N	77.30 W
Shipshaw (R.), Can. (shĭp'shô)	102	48.50 N	71.03 W
Shiqma (R.), Isr.	189a	31.31 N	34.40 E
Shirane-san (Mtn.), Jap. (shē'rä'nȧ-sän')	201	35.44 N	138.14 E
Shira Saki (C.), Jap. (shē'rä sä'kē)	200	41.25 N	142.10 E
Shirati, Tan. (shē-rä'tē)	222	1.15 S	34.02 E
Shīrāz, Iran (shē-räz')	192	29.32 N	52.27 E
Shire (R.), Malawi (shē'rȧ)	227	16.20 S	35.05 E
Shirokoye, Sov. Un. (shē'rô-kô-yĕ)	173	47.40 N	33.18 E
Shishaldin Vol., Ak. (shī-shăl'dĭn)	105a	54.48 N	164.00 W
Shively, Ky. (shīv'lē)	111h	38.11 N	85.47 W
Shivpuri, India	190	25.31 N	77.46 E
Shivta, Horvot (Ruins), Isr.	189a	30.54 N	34.36 E
Shivwits (Shebit) **Ind. Res.**, Ut. (shĭv'wĭts) (shĕ'bĭt)	119	37.10 N	113.50 W
Shivwits Plat, Az.	119	36.13 N	113.42 W
Shirley, Ma. (shûr'lē)	103a	42.33 N	71.39 W
Shiwan, China (shr-wän)	197a	23.01 N	113.04 E
Shiwan Dashan (Mts.), China (shr-wän dä-shän)	199	22.10 N	107.30 E
Shizuki, Jap. (shī'zo͞o-kē)	201	34.29 N	134.51 E
Shizuoka, Jap. (shē'zo͞o'ōkȧ)	201	34.58 N	138.24 E
Shklov, Sov. Un. (shklôf)	172	54.11 N	30.23 E
Shkodër (Scutari), Alb. (shkô'dŭr) (sko͞o'tärē)	171	42.04 N	19.30 E
Shkotovo, Sov. Un. (shkô'tô-vô)	200	43.15 N	132.21 E
Shoal Cr., Il. (shōl)	121	38.37 N	89.25 W
Shoal L., Can.	99	49.32 N	95.00 W
Shoals, In. (shōlz)	108	38.40 N	86.45 W
Shōdo (I.), Jap. (shō'dō)	201	34.27 N	134.27 E
Sholāpur, India (shō'lä-po͞or)	191	17.42 N	75.51 E
Shorewood, Wi. (shōr'wo͝od)	111a	43.05 N	87.54 W
Shoshone, Id. (shô-shōn'tē)	115	42.56 N	114.24 W
Shoshone L., Wy.	115	44.17 N	110.50 W
Shoshone R., Wy.	115	44.20 N	109.28 W
Shoshoni, Wy.	115	43.14 N	108.05 W
Shostka, Sov. Un. (shôst'kȧ)	173	51.51 N	33.31 E
Shougouang, China (shō-gŭäŋ)	196	36.53 N	118.45 E
Shou Xian, China (shō shyĕn)	196	32.36 N	116.45 E
Shpola, Sov. Un. (shpô'lȧ)	173	49.01 N	31.36 E
Shreveport, La. (shrēv'pōrt)	123	32.30 N	93.46 W
Shrewsbury, Eng. (shro͞oz'bēr-ĭ)	154	52.43 N	2.44 W
Shrewsbury, Ma.	103a	42.18 N	71.43 W
Shroud Cay (I.) (shroud), Ba.	132	24.20 N	76.40 W
Shu (R.), China (sho͞o)	196	34.47 N	118.27 E
Shuangcheng, China (shŭäŋ-chŭŋ)	198	45.18 N	126.18 E
Shuanghe, China (shŭäŋ-hŭ)	196	31.33 N	116.48 E
Shuangliao, China	195	43.37 N	123.30 E
Shuangyang, China	198	43.28 N	125.45 E
Shuhedun, China (sho͞o-hŭ-do͞on)	196	31.33 N	117.01 E
Shuiye, China (shwā-yŭ)	196	36.08 N	114.07 E
Shule (R.), China (sho͞o-lŭ)	194	40.53 N	94.55 E
Shullsburg, Wi. (shŭlz'bûrg)	113	42.35 N	90.16 W
Shumagin (Is.), Ak. (sho͞o'mȧ-gēn)	105	55.22 N	159.20 W
Shumen, Bul.	171	43.15 N	26.54 E
Shunde, China (sho͞on-dŭ)	197a	22.50 N	113.15 E
Shungnak, Ak. (shŭng'nȧk)	105	66.55 N	157.20 W
Shunut, 'Gora (Mt.), Sov. Un. (gȧ-rä sho͞o'no͞ot)	180a	56.33 N	59.45 E
Shunyi, China (sho͞on-yē)	198a	40.09 N	116.38 E
Shuqrah, P. D. R. of Yem.	192	13.32 N	46.02 E
Shūrāb (R.), Iran (sho͞o räb)	192	31.08 N	55.30 E
Shuri, Jap. (sho͞o'rē)	200	26.10 N	127.48 E
Shur R., Iran (sho͞or)	177	35.40 N	50.10 E
Shūshtar, Iran (sho͞osh'tŭr)	192	31.50 N	48.46 E
Shuswap L., Can. (sho͞os'wŏp)	97	50.57 N	119.15 W
Shuya, Sov. Un. (sho͞o'yȧ)	172	56.52 N	41.23 E
Shuyang, China (sho͞o yäng)	196	34.09 N	118.47 E
Shweba, Bur.	199	22.23 N	96.13 E
Shyaulyay, see Šiauliai			
Siak Ketjil (R.), Indon.	189b	1.01 N	101.45 E
Siaksriinderapura, Indon. (sē-äks'rī ēn'drȧ-po͞o'rä)	189b	0.48 N	102.05 E
Siālkot, Pak. (sē-äl'kōt)	190	32.39 N	74.30 E
Siátista, Grc. (syä'tĭs-ta)	171	40.15 N	21.32 E
Siau, Pulau (I.), Indon.	203	2.40 N	126.00 E
Šiauliai (Shyaulyay), Sov. Un. (shē-ou'lē-ī)	163	55.57 N	23.19 E
Sibay, Sov. Un. (sē'báy)	180a	52.41 N	58.40 E
Šibenik, Yugo. (shē-bă'nĕk)	170	43.44 N	15.55 E
Siberia (Reg.), Asia	188	57.00 N	97.00 E
Siberut, Pulau (I.), Indon. (sē'bȧ-ro͞ot)	202	1.22 S	99.45 E
Sibī, Pak.	190	29.41 N	67.52 E
Sibiti, Con. (sē-bē-tē')	226	3.41 S	13.21 E
Sibiu, Rom. (sē-bĭ-o͞o')	171	45.47 N	24.09 E
Sibley, Ia. (sĭb'lē)	112	43.24 N	95.33 W
Sibolga, Indon. (sē-bō'gä)	202	1.45 N	98.45 E
Sibsāgar, India (sēb-sŭ'gŭr)	193	26.47 N	94.45 E
Sibutu I., Phil.	202	4.40 N	119.30 E
Sibuyan (I.), Phil. (sē-bo͞o-yän')	203a	12.19 N	122.25 E
Sibuyan Sea, Phil.	202	12.43 N	122.38 E
Sichuan (Prov.), China (sz-chŭän)	194	31.20 N	103.00 E
Sicily (I.), It. (sĭs'ĭ-lē)	157	37.38 N	13.30 E
Sico R., Hond. (sē-kô)	130	15.32 N	85.42 W
Sicuaní, Peru (sē-kwä'nē)	140	14.12 S	71.12 W
Sidamo (Prov.), Eth. (sē-dä'mô)	219	5.08 N	37.45 E
Siderno Marina, It. (sē-dĕr'nô mä-rē'nä)	170	38.18 N	16.19 E
Sídheros, Ákra (C.), Grc.	170a	35.19 N	26.20 E
Sidhirókastron, Grc.	171	41.13 N	23.27 E
Sidi Aïssa, Alg.	169	35.53 N	3.44 E
Sīdī Barrānī, Egypt	221	31.41 N	26.09 E
Sidi bel Abbès, Alg. (sē'dē-bĕl ȧ-bĕs')	220	35.15 N	0.43 W
Sidi Ifni, Mor. (ēf'nē)	220	29.22 N	10.15 W
Sidley, Mt., Ant. (sĭd'lē)	228	77.25 S	129.00 W
Sidney, Can.	96	48.39 N	123.24 W
Sidney, Mt. (sĭd'nē)	115	47.43 N	104.07 W
Sidney, Ne.	112	41.10 N	103.00 W
Sidney, Oh.	108	40.20 N	84.10 W
Sidney Lanier, L., Ga. (lăn'yēr)	124	34.27 N	83.56 W
Sido, Mali	224	11.40 N	7.36 W
Sidon, see Saydā			
Sidr, Wādī (R.), Egypt	189a	29.43 N	32.58 E
Siedlce, Pol. (syĕd'-'l-tsĕ)	165	52.09 N	22.20 E
Siegburg, F.R.G. (zēg'bo͝orgh)	167c	50.48 N	7.13 E
Siegen, F.R.G. (zē'ghĕn)	167c	50.52 N	8.01 E
Sieghartskirchen, Aus.	155e	48.16 N	16.00 E
Siemiatycze, Pol. (syĕm'yä'tē-chĕ)	165	52.26 N	22.52 E
Siemionówka, Pol. (sēē-mēō'nôf-kä)	165	52.53 N	23.50 E
Siem Reap, Kamp. (syĕm'rā'ăp)	202	13.32 N	103.54 E
Siena, It. (sē-ĕn'ä)	170	43.19 N	11.21 E
Sieradz, Pol. (syĕ'rädz)	165	51.35 N	18.45 E
Sierpc, Pol. (syĕrpts)	165	52.51 N	19.42 E
Sierra Blanca, Tx. (sē-ĕ'rȧ blaŋ-kä)	122	31.10 N	105.20 W
Sierra Blanca Pk., NM (blăn'kȧ)	119	33.25 N	105.50 W
Sierra Leone, Afr. (sē-ĕr'rä lȧ-ō'nȧ)	218	8.48 N	12.30 W
Sierra Madre, Ca. (mă'drē)	117a	34.10 N	118.03 W
Sierra Mojada, Mex. (sē-ĕ'r-rä-mô-ĸä'dä)	122	27.22 N	103.42 W
Sífnos (I.), Grc.	171	36.58 N	24.30 E
Sigean, Fr. (sē-zhŏɴ')	166	43.02 N	2.56 E
Sigeurney, Ia. (sē-gûr-nĭ)	113	41.16 N	92.10 W
Sighetu Marmatiei, Rom.	165	47.57 N	23.55 E
Sighisoara, Rom. (sē-gē-shwä'rȧ)	165	46.11 N	24.48 E
Siglufjördur, Ice.	156	66.06 N	18.45 W
Signakhi, Sov. Un.	177	41.45 N	45.50 E
Signal Hill, Ca. (sĭg'năl hĭl)	117a	33.48 N	118.11 W
Sigsig, Ec. (sēg-sēg')	140	3.04 S	78.44 W
Sigtuna, Swe. (sēgh-to͞o'nȧ)	162	59.40 N	17.39 E
Siguanea, Ensenada de la (B.), Cuba (ĕn-sĕ-nä-dä-dĕ-lä-sē-gwä-nä'ä)	132	21.45 N	83.15 W
Siguatepeque, Hond. (sē-gwá'tĕ-pĕ-kĕ)	130	14.33 N	87.51 W
Sigüenza, Sp. (sē-gwĕ'n-zä)	168	41.03 N	2.38 W
Siguiri, Gui. (sē-gē-rē')	224	11.25 N	9.10 W
Sihong, China (sz-hôŋ)	196	33.25 N	118.13 E
Siirt, Tur. (sĭ-ērt')	177	38.00 N	42.00 E
Sikalongo, Zambia	227	16.46 S	27.07 E
Sikasso, Mali (sē-käs'sō)	224	11.19 N	5.40 W
Sikeston, Mo. (sīks'tŭn)	121	36.50 N	89.35 W
Sikhote Alin', Khrebet (Mts.), Sov. Un. (se-ĸô'ta a-lēn')	179	45.00 N	135.45 E
Síkinos (I.), Grc. (sĭ'kĭ-nōs)	171	36.45 N	24.55 E
Sikkim (State), India	190	27.42 N	88.25 E
Siklós, Hung. (sĭ'klōsh)	165	45.51 N	18.18 E
Sil (R.), Sp. (sē'l)	168	42.20 N	7.13 W
Silang, Phil. (sē-läng')	203a	14.14 N	120.58 E
Silao, Mex. (sē-lä'ō)	128	20.56 N	101.25 W
Silchar, India (sĭl-chär')	190	24.52 N	92.50 E
Silent Valley, S. Afr. (sī'lĕnt vă'lē)	219d	24.32 S	26.40 E
Siler City, NC (sī'lēr)	125	35.45 N	79.29 W
Silesia (Reg.), Pol. (sĭ-lē'shȧ)	165	50.58 N	16.53 E
Silifke, Tur.	177	36.20 N	34.00 E
Siling Co (L.), China	190	32.05 N	89.10 E
Silistra, Bul. (sē-lēs'trȧ)	159	44.01 N	27.13 E
Siljan (R.), Swe. (sēl'yän)	162	60.48 N	14.28 E
Silkeborg, Den. (sĭl'kĕ-bôr')	162	56.10 N	9.33 E
Sillery, Can. (sēl'-re')	93b	46.46 N	71.15 W
Siloam Springs, Ar. (sĭ-lōm)	121	36.10 N	94.32 W
Siloana Plns., Zambia	226	16.55 S	23.10 E
Silocayoápan, Mex. (sē-lô-kä-yô-ȧ'pän)	128	17.29 N	98.09 W
Silsbee, Tx. (sĭlz' bē)	123	30.19 N	94.09 W
Šilutė, Sov. Un. (shĭ-lo͞o'tȧ)	163	55.23 N	21.26 E
Silva Jardim, Braz. (sē'l-vä-zhär-dēɴ)	139a	22.40 N	42.24 W
Silvana, Wa. (sĭ-văn'ȧ)	116a	48.12 N	122.16 W
Silvânia, Braz. (sēl-vá'nyä)	141	16.43 S	48.33 W

ng-sing; ŋ-baŋk; ɴ-nasalized n; nŏd; cŏmmit; ōld; ôbey; ôrder; oi-boil; fo͞od; fo͝ot; ou-out; s-soft; sh-dish; th-thin; pūre; ûnite; ûrn; stŭd; circŭs; ü-as in French tu; '-indeterminate vowel.

348 Silvassa – Soar

PLACE (Pronunciation)	PAGE	Lat. °′	Long. °′
Silvassa, India	190	20.10 N	73.00 E
Silver (L.), Mo.	121	39.38 N	93.12 W
Silverado, Ca. (sĭl-vēr-ä'dō)	116a	33.45 N	117.40 W
Silver Bk., Ba.	133	20.40 N	69.40 W
Silver Bank Passage (Str.), Ba.	133	20.40 N	70.20 W
Silver Bay, Mn.	113	47.24 N	91.07 W
Silver City, NM (sĭl'vēr sĭ'tĭ)	119	32.45 N	108.20 W
Silver City, Pan.	131	9.20 N	79.54 W
Silver Creek, NY (crēk)	109	42.35 N	79.10 W
Silver Cr., Az.	119	34.30 N	110.05 W
Silver Cr., In.	111h	38.20 N	85.45 W
Silver Cr., Muddy Fk., In.	111h	38.26 N	85.52 W
Silverdale, Wa. (sĭl'vēr-dāl)	116a	49.39 N	122.42 W
Silver Lake, Wi. (lāk)	111a	42.33 N	88.10 W
Silver L., Wi.	111a	42.35 N	88.08 W
Silver Spring, Md. (sprĭng)	110e	39.00 N	77.00 W
Silver Star Mtn., Wa.	116c	45.45 N	122.15 W
Silverthrone Mtn., Can. (sĭl'vēr-thrōn)	96	51.31 N	126.06 W
Silverton, Co. (sĭl'vēr-tŭn)	119	37.50 N	107.40 W
Silverton, Oh.	111f	39.12 N	84.24 W
Silverton, Or.	114	45.02 N	122.46 W
Silverton, S. Afr.	223b	25.45 S	28.13 E
Silves, Port. (sēl'vĕzh)	168	37.15 N	8.24 W
Silvies R., Or. (sĭl'vēz)	114	43.44 N	119.15 W
Sim, Sov. Un. (sĭm)	180a	55.00 N	57.42 E
Simao, China (sz-mou)	194	22.56 N	101.07 E
Simba, Zaire	226	0.36 N	22.55 E
Simcoe, Can. (sĭm'kō)	109	42.50 N	80.20 W
Simcoe (L.), Can.	109	44.30 N	79.20 W
Simeulue, Pulau (I.), Indon.	202	2.27 N	95.30 E
Simferopol' (Akmechet), Sov. Un. (sĕm-fĕ-rô'pôl') (àk-mĕch'ĕt)	173	44.58 N	34.04 E
Simi (I.), Grc.	159	36.27 N	27.41 E
Similk Beach, Wa. (sē'mĭlk)	116a	48.27 N	122.35 W
Simla, India (sĭm'là)	190	31.09 N	77.15 E
Simleul-Silvaniei, Rom. (shēm-lā'ōōl-sēl-vä'nyĕ-ē)	165	47.14 N	22.46 E
Simms Pt., Ba.	132	25.00 N	77.40 W
Simojovel, Mex. (sē-mō-hō-vĕl')	129	17.12 N	92.43 W
Simonésia, Braz. (sē-mô-nĕ'syä)	139a	20.04 S	41.53 W
Simonette (R.), Can. (sĭ-mŏn-ĕt')	97	54.15 N	118.00 W
Simonstad, S. Afr.	222a	34.11 S	18.25 E
Simood Sound, Can.	96	50.45 N	126.25 W
Simplon P., Switz. (sĭm'plŏn) (săN-plôN')	164	46.13 N	7.53 E
Simpson (I.), Can.	113	48.43 N	87.44 W
Simpson Des., Austl. (sĭmp-sŭn)	210	24.40 S	136.40 E
Simrishamn, Swe. (sēm'rĕs-häm'n)	162	55.35 N	14.19 E
Sim R., Sov. Un.	180a	55.00 N	57.42 E
Sims Bayou, Tx. (sĭmz bī-yōō')	123a	29.37 N	95.23 W
Simushir (I.), Sov. Un. (se-mōō'shēr)	195	47.15 N	150.47 E
Sinaia, Rom. (sĭ-nä'yà)	171	45.20 N	25.30 E
Sinai Pen., Egypt (sī'nī)	221	29.24 N	33.29 E
Sinaloa (State), Mex. (sē-nä-lô-ä)	126	25.15 N	107.45 W
Sinan, China (sz-nän)	199	27.50 N	108.30 E
Sinanju, Kor. (sĭ'nän-jōō')	200	39.39 N	125.41 E
Sinap, Tur.	177	42.00 N	35.05 E
Sincé, Col. (sēn'sā)	140	9.15 N	75.14 W
Sincelejo, Col. (sēn-sā-lā'hō)	140	9.12 N	75.30 W
Sinclair Inlet, Wa. (sĭn-klâr')	116a	47.31 N	122.41 W
Sinclair Mills, Can.	96	54.02 N	121.41 W
Sindi, Sov. Un. (sēn'dē)	163	58.20 N	24.40 E
Sinel'nikovo, Sov. Un. (sē'nye-brl-nē'kô'vô)	173	49.19 N	35.33 E
Sines, Port. (sē'nāzh)	168	37.57 N	8.50 W
Singapore, Singapore (sĭn'gà-pōr')	189b	1.18 N	103.52 E
Singapore, Asia	189b	1.22 N	103.45 E
Singapore Str., Indon.	189b	1.14 N	104.20 E
Singu, Bur. (sĭn'gŭ)	194	22.37 N	96.04 E
Siniye Lipyagi, Sov. Un. (sēn'ē lēp'yà-gē)	173	51.24 N	38.29 E
Sinj, Yugo. (sēn')	170	43.42 N	16.39 E
Sinjah, Sud.	221	13.09 N	33.52 E
Sinking (Aut. Reg.), **see Xinjiang**			
Sin'kovo, Sov. Un. (sĭn-kô'vô)	180b	56.23 N	37.19 E
Sinnamary, Fr. Gu.	141	5.15 N	57.52 W
Sinni (R.), It. (sēn'nē)	170	40.05 N	16.15 E
Sinnūris, Egypt	219b	29.25 N	30.52 E
Sino, Pedra de (Mtn.), Braz. (pĕ'drä-dô-sē'nō)	142b	22.27 S	43.02 W
Sinoia, Zimb. (sĭ-noi'à)	227	17.22 S	30.12 E
Sint Niklaas, Bel.	155a	51.10 N	4.07 E
Sinton, Tx. (sĭn'tŭn)	123	28.03 N	97.30 W
Sintra, Port. (sēn'trà)	169b	38.48 N	9.23 W
Sint Truiden, Bel.	123a	50.49 N	5.14 E
Sinŭiju, Kor. (sĭ'nōōĭ-jōō)	200	40.04 N	124.33 E
Sinyavino, Sov. Un. (sĭn-yä'vĭ-nô)	180c	59.50 N	31.07 E
Sinyaya (R.), Sov. Un. (sēn'yà-yà)	172	56.40 N	28.20 E
Sinyukha (R.), Sov. Un. (sē'nyōō-kà)	173	48.34 N	30.49 E
Sion, Switz. (sē'ôN')	164	46.15 N	7.17 E
Sioux City, Ia. (sōō sĭ'tĭ)	112	42.30 N	96.25 W
Sioux Falls, SD (fôlz)	112	43.33 N	96.43 W
Sioux Lookout, Can.	99	50.06 N	91.55 W
Sipí, Col. (sē-pē')	140a	4.39 N	76.38 W
Siping, China (sz-pĭŋ)	198	43.05 N	124.24 E
Sipiwesk, Can.	94	55.27 N	97.24 W
Sipsey (R.), Al. (sĭp'sē)	124	33.26 N	87.42 W
Sipura, Pulau (I.), Indon.	202	2.15 S	99.33 E
Siqueros, Mex. (sē-kā'rōs)	128	23.19 N	106.14 W
Siquia, R., Nic. (sē-kē'ä)	131	12.23 N	84.36 W
Siracusa, It. (sē-rä-koo'sä)	157	37.02 N	15.19 E
Sirājganj, Bngl. (sĭ-räj'gŭnj)	190	24.23 N	89.43 E
Sirama, Sal. (Sē-rä-mä)	130	13.23 N	87.55 W
Sir Douglas, Mt., Can. (sûr dŭg'lăs)	97	50.44 N	115.20 W
Sir Edward Pellew Group (Is.), Austl. (pĕl'ū)	210	15.15 S	137.15 E
Siret, Rom.	165	47.58 N	26.01 E
Siret (R.), Rom.	165	46.10 N	27.18 E
Sirhān, Wadi (R.), Sau. Ar.	192	31.02 N	37.16 E
Síros (I.), Grc.	159	37.19 N	25.10 E
Síros (I.), Grc.	171	37.23 N	24.55 E
Sirsa, India	190	29.39 N	75.02 E
Sir Sandford, Mt., Can. (sûr sănd'fērd)	97	51.40 N	117.52 W
Sirvintos, Sov. Un. (shēr'vĭn-tôs)	163	55.02 N	24.59 E
Sir Wilfrid Laurier, Mt., Can. (sûr wĭl'frĭd lôr'yēr)	97	52.47 N	119.45 W
Sisak, Yugo. (sē'sàk)	170	45.29 N	16.20 E
Sisal, Mex. (sē-säl')	129	21.09 N	90.03 W
Sishui, China (sz-shwā)	196	35.40 N	117.17 E
Sisquoc (R.), Ca. (sĭs'kwŏk)	118	34.47 N	120.13 W
Sisseton, SD (sĭs'tŭn)	112	45.39 N	97.04 W
Sistān, Daryacheh-ye (L.), Iran-Afg.	192	31.45 N	61.15 E
Sisteron, Fr. (sēst'rôN')	167	44.10 N	5.55 E
Sisterville, WV (sĭs'tēr-vĭl)	108	39.30 N	81.00 W
Sitía, Grc. (sē'tĭ-à)	170a	35.09 N	26.10 E
Sitka, Ak. (sĭt'kà)	105	57.08 N	135.18 W
Sittingbourne, Eng. (sĭt-ĭng-bôrn)	154b	51.20 N	0.44 E
Sittwe, Bur.	202	20.09 N	92.54 E
Sivas, Tur. (sē'väs)	177	39.50 N	36.50 E
Sivash (L.), Sov. Un. (sē'vàsh)	173	45.55 N	34.42 E
Siverek, Tur. (sē'vĕ-rĕk)	177	37.50 N	39.20 E
Siverskaya, Sov. Un. (sē'vĕr-skà-yà)	163	59.17 N	30.03 E
Siwah (Oasis), Egypt (sē'wä)	221	29.33 N	25.11 E
Sixaola R., C. R. (sē-kä-ō'lä) (sēk-sà-ō'lä)	131	9.31 N	83.07 W
Si Xian, China (sz shyĕn)	196	33.29 N	116.57 E
Siyang, China (sz-yäŋ)	196	33.43 N	118.42 E
Sixth Cataract, Sud.	221	16.26 N	32.44 E
Sjaelland (I.), Den. (shĕl'lán')	162	55.34 N	11.35 E
Sjenica, Yugo. (syĕ'nē-tsà)	171	43.15 N	20.02 E
Skadovsk, Sov. Un. (skä'dôfsk)	173	46.08 N	32.54 E
Skagen, Den. (skä'ghĕn)	162	57.43 N	10.32 E
Skagerrak (Str.), Eur. (skä-ghĕ-räk')	162	57.43 N	8.28 E
Skagit B., Wa. (skăg'ĭt)	116a	48.20 N	122.32 W
Skagit R., Wa.	114	48.29 N	121.52 W
Skagway, Ak. (skăg-wā)	105	59.30 N	135.28 W
Skälderviken (B.), Swe.	162	56.20 N	12.25 E
Skalistyy, Golets (Mtn.), Sov. Un.	179	57.28 N	119.48 E
Skamania, Wa. (skà-mā'nĭ-à)	116c	45.37 N	112.03 W
Skamokawa, Wa.	116c	46.16 N	123.27 W
Skanderborg, Den. (skän-ĕr-bôr')	162	56.04 N	9.55 E
Skaneateles, NY (skăn-ĕ-ăt'lĕs)	109	42.55 N	76.25 W
Skaneateles (L.), NY	109	42.50 N	76.20 W
Skänninge, Swe. (shĕn'ĭng-ĕ)	162	58.24 N	15.02 E
Skanör-Falseterbo, Swe. (skän'ûr)	162	55.24 N	12.49 E
Skara, Swe. (skä'rà)	162	58.25 N	13.24 E
Skeena (R.), Can. (skē'nă)	96	54.10 N	129.40 W
Skeena Mts., Can.	96	56.00 N	128.00 W
Skeerpoort, S. Afr.	223b	25.49 S	27.45 E
Skeerpoort (R.), S. Afr.	223b	25.58 S	27.41 E
Skeldon, Guy. (skĕl'dŭn)	141	5.49 N	57.15 W
Skelleftea, Swe. (shĕl'ĕf-tē-a')	156	64.47 N	20.48 E
Skellefteälven (R.), Swe.	156	62.25 N	19.28 E
Skhodnya, Sov. Un. (skôd'nyà)	180b	55.57 N	37.21 E
Skhodnya R., Sov. Un.	180b	55.55 N	37.16 E
Skíathos (I.), Grc. (skē'á-thôs)	171	39.15 N	23.25 E
Skibbereen, Ire. (skĭb'ēr-ēn)	160	51.32 N	9.25 W
Skidegate Inlet, Can. (skĭ'-dē-gāt')	96	53.15 N	132.00 W
Skidmore, Tx. (skĭd'môr)	123	28.16 N	97.40 W
Skien, Nor. (skē'ĕn)	162	59.13 N	9.35 E
Skierniewice, Pol. (skyĕr-nyē-vēt'sĕ)	165	51.58 N	20.13 E
Skihist Mtn., Can.	96	50.11 N	121.54 W
Skikda (Philippeville), Alg.	158	36.58 N	6.51 E
Skilpadfontein, S. Afr.	219d	25.02 S	28.50 E
Skíros, Grc.	171	38.53 N	24.32 E
Skiros (I.), Grc.	171	38.50 N	24.43 E
Skive, Den. (skē'vĕ)	162	56.34 N	8.56 E
Skjálfandafljót (R.), Ice. (skyäl'fänd-ô)	156	65.24 N	16.40 W
Skjerstad, Nor. (skyĕr-städ)	156	67.12 N	15.37 E
Škofja Loka, Yugo. (shkôf'yà lō'kà)	170	46.10 N	14.20 E
Skokie, Il. (skō'kē)	111a	42.02 N	87.45 W
Skokomish Ind. Res., Wa. (Skō-kō'mĭsh)	116a	47.22 N	123.07 W
Skole, Sov. Un. (skô'lĕ)	165	49.03 N	23.32 E
Skópelos (I.), Grc. (skô'pā-lôs)	171	39.04 N	23.31 E
Skopin, Sov. Un. (skô'pĕn)	172	53.49 N	39.35 E
Skopje, Yugo. (skôp'yĕ)	171	42.02 N	21.26 E
Skövde, Swe. (shûv'dĕ)	162	58.25 N	13.48 E
Skovorodino, Sov. Un. (skŏ'vô-rô'dĭ-nô)	179	53.53 N	123.56 E
Skowhegan, Me. (skou-hē'găn)	102	44.45 N	69.27 W
Skradin, Yugo. (skrä'dĭn)	170	43.49 N	17.58 E
Skreia, Nor. (skrā'à)	162	60.40 N	10.55 E
Skudeneshavn, Nor. (skōō'dĕ-nes-houn')	162	59.10 N	5.19 E
Skull Valley Ind. Res., Ut. (skŭl)	119	40.25 N	112.50 W
Skuna, (R.), Ms. (skû'nà)	124	33.57 N	89.36 W
Skunk (R.), Ia. (skŭnk)	113	41.12 N	92.14 W
Skuodas, Sov. Un. (skwô'dás)	163	56.16 N	21.32 E
Skurup, Swe. (skû'rōōp)	162	55.29 N	13.27 E
Skvira, Sov. Un. (skvē'rà)	173	49.43 N	29.41 E
Skwierzyna, Pol. (skvē-ĕr'zhĭ-nà)	164	52.35 N	15.30 E
Skye, I. of, Scot. (skī)	160	57.25 N	6.17 W
Skykomish (R.), Wa. (skī'kō-mĭsh)	116a	47.50 N	121.55 W
Skyring, Seno (B.), Chile (sĕ'nô-s-krē'ng)	142	52.35 S	72.30 W
Slagese, Den.	162	55.25 N	11.19 E
Slamet, Gunung (Mtn.), Indon. (slä'mĕt)	202	7.15 S	109.15 E
Slănic, Rom. (slŭ'nĕk)	171	45.13 N	25.56 E
Slate (I.), Can. (slāt)	113	48.38 N	87.14 W
Slater, Mo. (slāt'ēr)	121	39.13 N	93.03 W
Slatina, Rom. (slä'tē-nä)	171	44.26 N	24.21 E
Slaton, Tx. (slā'tŭn)	120	33.26 N	101.38 W
Slave (R.), Can. (slāv)	94	59.40 N	111.21 W
Slavgorod, Sov. Un. (slàf'gô-rôt)	178	52.58 N	78.43 E
Slavonija (Reg.), Yugo. (slä-vô'nē-yä)	171	45.29 N	17.31 E
Slavonska Požega, Yugo. (slä-vôn'skä pô'zhĕ-gä)	170	45.18 N	17.42 E
Slavonski Brod, Yugo. (skä-vôn'skē brôd)	171	45.10 N	18.01 E
Slavuta, Sov. Un. (slá-vōō'tà)	173	50.18 N	27.01 E
Slavyansk, Sov. Un. (slàv'yänsk')	173	48.52 N	37.34 E
Slavyanskaya, Sov. Un. (slàv-yàn'skà-yà)	173	45.14 N	38.09 E
Slayton, Mn. (slā'tŭn)	112	44.00 N	95.44 W
Sleaford, Eng. (slē'fērd)	154	53.00 N	0.25 W
Sleepy Eye, Mn. (slēp'ĭ ī)	113	44.17 N	94.44 W
Slidell, La. (slĭ-dĕl')	123	30.17 N	89.47 W
Sliedrecht, Neth.	155a	51.49 N	4.46 E
Sligo, Ire. (slī'gō)	160	54.17 N	8.19 W
Slite, Swe. (slē'tĕ)	162	57.41 N	18.47 E
Sliven, Bul. (slē'vĕn)	171	42.41 N	26.20 E
Sloatsburg, NY (slōts'bŭrg)	110a	41.09 N	74.11 W
Slobodka, Sov. Un. (slô'bŏd-kà)	163	54.34 N	26.12 E
Slobodskoy, Sov. Un. (slô'bôt-skoi)	176	58.48 N	50.02 E
Sloka, Sov. Un. (slô'kà)	163	56.57 N	23.37 E
Slonim, Sov. Un. (swô'nēm)	165	53.05 N	25.19 E
Slough, Eng. (slou)	154b	51.29 N	0.36 E
Slovakia (Prov.), **see Slovensko**			
Slovenija (Reg.), Yugo. (slô-vĕ'nē-yä)	170	45.58 N	14.43 E
Slovensko (Slovakia) (Prov.), Czech. (slô-vĕn'skô) (slô-vák'ĭá)	165	48.40 N	19.00 E
Sluch' (R.), Sov. Un.	165	50.56 N	26.48 E
Slunj, Yugo. (slōōn')	170	45.08 N	15.46 E
Słupsk, Pol. (swōōpsk)	165	54.28 N	17.02 E
Slutsk, Sov. Un. (slōōtsk)	172	53.02 N	27.34 E
Slyne Head, Ire. (slīn)	160	53.25 N	10.05 W
Smackover, Ar. (smăk'ô-vēr)	121	33.22 N	92.42 W
Smederevo (Semedria), Yugo. (smĕ'de-rĕ-vô) (sē-mĕn'drĭ-á)	171	44.39 N	20.54 E
Smederevska Palanka, Yugo. (smĕ-dĕ-rĕv'skä pä-län'kä)	171	44.21 N	21.00 E
Smedjebacken, Swe. (smĭ'tyĕ-bä-kĕn)	162	60.09 N	15.19 E
Smela, Sov. Un. (smyā'là)	173	49.14 N	31.52 E
Smeloye, Sov. Un. (smyā'lô-ĕ)	173	50.55 N	33.36 E
Smethport, Pa. (smĕth'pōrt)	109	41.50 N	78.25 W
Smethwick (Warley), Eng.	154	52.31 N	2.04 W
Smiltene, Sov. Un. (smĕl'tē-nĕ)	172	57.26 N	25.57 E
Smith, Can. (smĭth)	97	55.10 N	114.02 W
Smith (I.), Wa.	116a	48.20 N	122.53 W
Smith Center, Ks. (sĕn'tēr)	120	39.45 N	98.46 W
Smithers, Can. (smĭth'ērs)	96	54.47 N	127.10 W
Smithfield, NC (smĭth'fēld)	125	35.30 N	78.21 W
Smithfield, Ut.	115	41.50 N	111.49 W
Smithland, Ky. (smĭth'lănd)	108	37.10 N	88.25 W
Smith Mountain Lake (Res.), Va.	125	37.00 N	79.45 W
Smith Point, Tx.	123a	29.32 N	94.45 W
Smith R., Mt.	115	47.00 N	111.20 W
Smiths Falls, Can. (smĭths)	101	44.55 N	76.05 W
Smithton, Austl. (smĭth'tŭn)	212	40.55 S	145.12 E
Smithton, Il.	117e	38.24 N	89.59 W
Smithville, Tx. (smĭth'vĭl)	123	30.00 N	97.08 W
Smitswinkelvlakte, S. Afr.	222a	34.16 S	18.25 E
Smoke Creek Des., Nv. (smōk crēk)	118	40.28 N	119.40 W
Smoky (R.), Can. (smōk'ĭ)	97	55.30 N	117.30 W
Smoky Hill (R.), Ks. (smōk'ĭ hĭl)	121	38.40 N	97.32 W
Smøla (I.), Nor. (smûlä)	162	63.16 N	7.40 E
Smolensk, Sov. Un. (smô-lyĕnsk')	172	54.46 N	32.03 E
Smolensk (Oblast), Sov. Un.	172	55.00 N	32.18 E
Smyadovo, Bul.	171	43.04 N	27.00 E
Smyrna, De. (smûr'nà)	109	39.20 N	75.35 W
Smyrna, Ga.	110c	33.53 N	84.31 W
Snag, Can. (snăg)	105	62.18 N	140.30 W
Snake (R.), Mn. (snāk)	113	45.58 N	93.20 W
Snake (R.), Wa.	114	46.35 N	117.20 W
Snake Ra., Nv.	119	39.20 N	114.15 W
Snake R., Henrys Fork, Id.	115	43.52 N	111.55 W
Snake River Pln., Id.	115	43.08 N	114.46 W
Snap Pt., Ba.	132	23.45 N	77.30 W
Sneffels Pk., Co. (snĕf'ĕlz)	119	38.00 N	107.50 W
Snelgrove, Can. (snĕl'grōv)	93d	43.44 N	79.50 W
Sniardwy, Jezioro (L.), Pol. (snyärt'vĭ)	165	53.46 N	21.59 E
Snöhetta (Mtn.), Nor. (snû-hĕttä)	162	62.18 N	9.12 E
Snohomish, Wa. (snô-hō'mĭsh)	116a	47.55 N	122.05 W
Snohomish (R.), Wa.	116a	47.53 N	122.04 W
Snoqualmie, Wa. (snō qwäl'mē)	116a	47.32 N	121.50 W
Snoqualmie R., Wa.	114	47.32 N	121.53 W
Snov (R.), Sov. Un. (snôf)	173	51.38 N	31.38 E
Snowdon (Mtn.), Wales	160	53.05 N	4.04 W
Snow Hill, Md. (hĭl)	109	38.15 N	75.20 W
Snow Lake, Can.	99	54.50 N	100.10 W
Snowy Mts., Austl. (snō'ē)	211	36.17 S	148.30 E
Snyder, Ok. (snī'dēr)	120	34.40 N	98.57 W
Snyder, Tx.	122	32.48 N	100.53 W
Soar (R.), Eng. (sōr)	154	52.44 N	1.09 W

ăt; finăl; rāte; senāte; ärm; àsk; sofá; fâre; ch-choose; dh-as th in other; bē; ēvent; bĕt; recĕnt; cratēr; g-gō; gh-guttural g; bĭt; ĭ-short neutral; rīde; K-guttural k as ch in German ich;

PRONOUNCING INDEX

Sobat – Spanish Town 349

PLACE (Pronunciation)	PAGE	Lat. °'	Long. °'
Sobat R., Sud. (sō'bàt)	221	9.04 N	32.02 E
Sobinka, Sov. Un. (sô-bĭŋ'kà)	172	55.59 N	40.02 E
Sobo Zan (Mt.), Jap. (sô'bô zän)	201	32.47 N	131.27 E
Sobral, Braz. (sô-brä'l)	141	3.39 S	40.16 W
Sochaczew, Pol. (sô-κä'chĕf)	165	52.14 N	20.18 E
Sochi, Sov. Un. (sôch'ĭ)	177	43.35 N	39.50 E
Society Is., Fr. Polynesia (sô-sī'ĕ-tē)	205	15.00 S	157.30 W
Socoltenango, Mex. (sô-kôl-tē-näŋ'gō)	129	16.17 N	92.20 W
Socorro, Braz. (sô-kô'r-rō)	139a	22.35 S	46.32 W
Socorro, Col. (sô-kôr'rō)	140	6.23 N	73.19 W
Socorro, NM	119	34.05 N	106.55 W
Socotra I., P. D. R. of Yem. (sô-kō'trà)	219a	13.00 N	52.30 E
Socúellamos, Sp. (sô-kōō-āl'yä-môs)	168	39.18 N	2.48 W
Soda (L.), Ca. (sō'dà)	118	35.12 N	116.25 W
Soda Pk., Wa.	116c	45.53 N	122.04 W
Soda Springs, Id. (sprĭngz)	115	42.39 N	111.37 W
Söderhamn, Swe. (sû-dĕr-häm''n)	162	61.20 N	17.00 E
Söderköping, Swe.	162	58.30 N	16.14 E
Södertälje, Swe. (sû-dĕr-tĕl'yĕ)	162	59.12 N	17.35 E
Sodo, Eth.	221	7.03 N	37.46 E
Södra Dellen (L.), Swe.	162	61.45 N	16.30 E
Soest, F.R.G. (zōst)	164	51.35 N	8.05 E
Sofia, see **Sofiya**			
Sofiya (Sofia), Bul. (sô'fē-yà) (sô'fē-à)	171	42.43 N	23.20 E
Sofiyevka, Sov. Un. (sô-fē'yĕf-kà)	173	48.03 N	33.53 E
Soga, Jap. (sô'gä)	201a	35.35 N	140.08 E
Sogamoso, Col. (sô-gä-mô'sō)	140	5.42 N	72.51 W
Sognafjorden (Fd.), Nor.	162	61.09 N	5.30 E
Sogozha (R.), Sov. Un. (sô'gô-zhà)	172	58.35 N	39.08 E
Soissons, Fr. (swä-sôɴ')	166	49.23 N	3.17 E
Sōka, Jap. (sō'kä)	201a	35.50 N	139.49 E
Sokal', Sov. Un. (sô'käl')	165	50.28 N	24.20 E
Soke, Tur. (sû'kĕ)	177	37.40 N	27.10 E
Sokodé, Togo (sô-kô-dā')	224	8.59 N	1.08 E
Sokolka, Pol. (sô-kōōl'kà)	165	53.23 N	23.30 E
Sokolo, Mali (sô-kô-lō')	220	14.51 N	6.09 W
Sokone, Senegal	224	13.53 N	16.22 W
Sokoto, Nig. (sō'kô-tō)	225	13.04 N	5.16 E
Sokotów Podlaski, Pol. (sô-kô-wōōf' pŭd-lä'skĭ)	165	52.24 N	22.15 E
Sola de Vega (San Miguel), Mex. (sō'lä dā vā'gä) (sän mē-gāl')	129	16.31 N	96.58 W
Solander, C., Austl.	207b	34.03 S	151.16 E
Solano, Phil. (sō-lä'nō)	203a	16.31 N	121.11 E
Soledad, Col. (sô-lĕ-dä'd)	140	10.47 N	75.00 W
Soledad Díez Gutierrez, Mex. (sô-lâ-dhädh'dē'äz gōō-tyā'rĕz)	128	22.19 N	100.54 W
Soleduck R., Wa. (sōl'dŭk)	114	47.59 N	124.28 W
Solentiname, Islas de (Is.), Nic. (ē's-läs-dĕ-sô-lĕn-tē-nä'mā)	130	11.15 N	85.16 W
Solihull, Eng. (sō'lĭ-hŭl)	154	52.25 N	1.46 W
Solikamsk, Sov. Un. (sô-lē-kámsk')	180a	59.38 N	56.48 E
Solimões, Rio (R.), Braz. (rē'ō-sô-lē-mô'ĕs)	140	2.45 S	67.44 W
Solingen, F.R.G. (zō'lĭng-ĕn)	167c	51.10 N	7.05 E
Sollefteå, Swe. (sôl-lĕf'tē-ô)	162	63.06 N	17.17 E
Sóller, Sp. (sō'lyĕr)	169	39.45 N	2.40 E
Sol'-Iletsk, Sov. Un.	177	51.10 N	55.05 E
Sologne (Reg.), Fr. (sô-lôn'yĕ)	166	47.36 N	1.53 E
Solola, Guat. (sô-lō'lä)	130	14.45 N	91.12 W
Solomon Is., Oceania (sŏ'lō-mŭn)	204	7.00 S	160.00 E
Solomon R., Ks.	120	39.24 N	98.19 W
Solomon R. North Fk., Ks.	120	39.34 N	99.52 W
Solomon R. South Fk., Ks.	120	39.19 N	99.52 W
Solon, China (swo-lōōn)	198	47.32 N	121.18 E
Solon, Oh. (sō'lŭn)	111d	41.23 N	81.26 W
Solothurn, Switz. (zō'lō-thōōrn)	164	47.13 N	7.30 E
Solov'etskiy (I.), Sov. Un.	176	65.10 N	35.40 E
Šolta (I.), Yugo. (shôl'tä)	170	43.20 N	16.15 E
Soltau, F.R.G. (sôl'tou)	164	53.00 N	9.50 E
Sol'tsy, Sov. Un. (sôl'tsē)	172	58.04 N	30.13 E
Solvay, NY (sŏl'vā)	109	43.05 N	76.10 W
Sölvesborg, Swe. (sûl'vĕs-bôrg)	162	56.04 N	14.35 E
Sol'vychegodsk, Sov. Un. (sôl'vē-chĕ-gôtsk')	176	61.18 N	46.58 E
Solway Firth, Eng.-Scot. (sŏl'wāfûrth')	160	54.42 N	3.55 W
Solwezi, Zambia	227	12.11 S	26.25 E
Somalia, Afr. (sō-ma'lē-ă)	218	3.28 N	44.47 E
Somanga, Tan.	227	8.24 S	39.17 E
Sombor, Yugo. (sôm'bôr)	171	45.45 N	19.10 E
Sombrerete, Mex. (sōm-brå-rā'tå)	128	23.38 N	103.37 W
Sombrero, Cayo (C.), Ven. (kä-yô-sôm-brĕ'rô)	141b	10.52 N	68.12 W
Somerset, Ky. (sŭm'ĕr-sĕt)	124	37.05 N	84.35 W
Somerset, Ma.	110b	41.46 N	71.05 W
Somerset, Pa.	109	40.00 N	79.05 W
Somerset, Tx.	117d	29.13 N	98.39 W
Somerset East, S. Afr.	223c	32.44 S	25.36 E
Somersworth, NH (sŭm'ĕrz-wûrth)	102	43.16 N	70.53 W
Somerton, Az. (sŭm'ĕr-tŭn)	118	32.36 N	114.43 W
Somerville, Ma. (sŭm'ĕr-vĭl)	103a	42.23 N	71.06 W
Somerville, NJ	110a	40.34 N	74.37 W
Somerville, Tn.	124	35.14 N	89.21 W
Somerville, Tx.	123	30.21 N	96.31 W
Somesul R., Rom. (sô-mā'shōōl)	165	47.43 N	23.09 E
Somma Vesuviana, It. (sôm'mä vā-zōō-vē-ä'nä)	169c	40.38 N	14.27 E
Somme (R.), Fr. (sŏm)	166	50.02 N	2.04 E
Sommerfeld, G.D.R. (zō'mĕr-fēld)	155b	52.48 N	13.02 E
Sommerville, Austl.	207a	38.14 S	145.10 E
Somoto, Nic. (sô-mô'tō)	130	13.28 N	86.37 W
Somuncurá, Meseta de (Plat.), Arg. (mĕ-sĕ'tä-dĕ-sô-mōō'n-kōō-rá')	142	41.15 S	68.00 W
Son (R.), India (sōn)	190	24.40 N	82.35 E
Soná, Pan. (sō'nä)	131	8.00 N	81.19 W
Sŏnchŏn, Kor. (sŭn'shŭn)	200	39.49 N	124.56 E
Sondags (R.), S. Afr.	223c	33.17 S	25.14 E
Sønderborg, Den. (sûn''ĕr-bôrgh)	162	54.55 N	9.47 E
Sondershausen, G.D.R. (zôn'dĕrz-hou'zĕn)	164	51.17 N	10.45 E
Song Ca (R.), Viet.	199	19.15 N	105.00 E
Songea, Tan. (sôn-gā'à)	227	10.41 S	35.39 E
Songhua (R.), see **Sungari**			
Songjiang, China (sôŋ-jyäŋ)	197b	31.01 N	121.14 E
Sŏngjin, Kor. (sŭng'jĭn')	200	40.38 N	129.10 E
Songkhla, Thai. (sông'κlä')	202	7.09 N	100.34 E
Songwe, Zaire	227	12.25 S	29.40 E
Sonneberg, G.D.R. (sôn'ĕ-bĕrgh)	164	50.20 N	11.14 E
Sonora, Ca. (sô-nō'rá)	118	37.58 N	120.22 W
Sonora, Tx.	122	30.33 N	100.38 W
Sonora (State), Mex.	126	29.45 N	111.15 W
Sonora (R.), Mex.	126	28.45 N	111.35 W
Sonora Pk., Ca.	118	38.22 N	119.39 W
Sonseca, Sp. (sôn-sā'kä)	168	39.41 N	3.56 W
Sonsón, Col. (sôn-sôn')	140a	5.42 N	75.28 W
Sonsonate, Sal. (sōn-sô-nä'tå)	130	13.46 N	89.43 W
Sonsorol Is., Pas. Is. Trust Ter. (sŏn-sô-rōl')	203	5.03 N	132.33 E
Sooke Basin, Can. (sŏŏk)	116a	48.21 N	123.47 W
Soo Locks, Can.-U. S. (sōō lŏks)	117	46.30 N	84.30 W
Sopetrán, Col. (sô-pĕ-trä'n)	140a	6.30 N	75.44 W
Sopot, Pol. (sô'pôt)	162	54.26 N	18.25 E
Sopron, Hung. (shŏp'rŏn)	164	47.41 N	16.36 E
Sora, It. (sô'rä)	170	41.43 N	13.37 E
Sorbas, Sp. (sôr'bäs)	168	37.05 N	2.07 W
Sordo (R.), Mex. (sô'r-dō)	129	16.39 N	97.33 W
Sorel, Can. (sô-rĕl')	101	46.01 N	73.07 W
Sorell, C., Austl.	212	42.10 S	144.50 E
Soresina, It. (sō-rā-zē'nä)	170	45.17 N	9.51 E
Soria, Sp. (sō'rē-ä)	168	41.46 N	2.28 W
Soriano (Dept.), Ur. (sô-rē-ä'nô)	139c	33.25 S	58.00 W
Sorocaba, Braz. (sô-rô-kä'bà)	139a	23.29 S	47.27 W
Soroki, Sov. Un. (sô-rō'kē)	173	48.09 N	28.17 E
Sorong, Indon. (sō-rông')	203	1.00 S	131.20 E
Sorot' (R.), Sov. Un. (sō-rō'tzh)	172	57.08 N	29.23 E
Soroti, Ug. (sō-rō'tē)	227	1.43 N	33.37 E
Sørøya (I.), Nor.	156	70.37 N	20.58 E
Sorraia (R.), Port. (sôr-rī'á)	168	38.55 N	8.42 W
Sorrento, It. (sôr-rĕn'tō)	169c	40.23 N	14.23 E
Sorsogon, Phil. (sôr-sōgōn')	203	12.51 N	124.02 E
Sortavala, Sov. Un. (sôr'tä-vä-lä)	163	61.43 N	30.40 E
Sŏsan, Korea (sŭ'sän)	198	36.40 N	126.25 E
Sosna (R.), Sov. Un. (sôs'ná)	173	50.33 N	38.15 E
Sosnitsa, Sov. Un. (sôs-nē'tsá)	173	51.30 N	32.29 E
Sosnogorsk, Sov. Un.	178	63.13 N	54.09 E
Sosnowiec, Pol. (sôs-nô'vyĕts)	165	50.17 N	19.10 E
Sosunova, Mys (Pt.), Sov. Un. (mĭs sô'sōō-nôf'à)	200	46.28 N	138.06 E
Sos'va R., Sov. Un. (sôs'vá)	180a	59.55 N	60.40 E
Sos'va (R.), Sov. Un. (sôs'vá)	176	63.10 N	63.30 E
Sota (R.), Benin	225	11.10 N	3.20 E
Sota la Marina, Mex. (sô-tä-lä-mä-rē'nä)	128	22.45 N	98.11 W
Soteapan, Mex. (sō-tå-ä'pän)	129	18.14 N	94.51 W
Soto la Marina, Rio (R.), Mex. (rē'ō-so'tō lä mä-rē'nä)	128	23.55 N	98.30 W
Sotuta, Mex. (sô-tōō'tä)	130a	20.35 N	89.00 W
Souanké, Con.	226	2.05 N	14.03 E
Soublette, Ven. (sō-ōō-blĕ'tĕ)	141b	9.55 N	66.06 W
Souflion, Grc.	171	41.12 N	26.17 E
Soufriere, St. Lucia (sōō-frē-âr')	131b	13.50 N	61.03 W
Soufriere, Mt., St. Vincent	131b	13.19 N	61.12 W
Soufrière (Vol.), Montserrat	131b	16.43 N	62.10 W
Souk Ahras, Alg. (sōōk-ä-räs')	157	36.23 N	8.00 E
Sŏul (Seoul), Kor.	200	37.35 N	127.03 E
Sounding Cr., Can. (soun'dĭng)	98	51.35 N	111.00 W
Sources, Mt. aux, Leso.-S. Afr. (môɴ'tō sōōrs')	219c	28.47 S	29.04 E
Soure, Port. (sōr-ĕ)	168	40.04 N	8.37 W
Souris, Can. (sōō'rē')	103	46.20 N	62.17 W
Souris, Can.	99	49.38 N	100.15 W
Souris (R.), Can.	99	49.10 N	102.00 W
Sourlake, Tx. (sour'lāk)	123	30.09 N	94.24 W
Sousse, Tun. (sōōs)	220	36.00 N	10.39 E
South (R.), NC	125	34.49 N	78.33 W
South Africa, Afr.	218	28.00 S	24.50 E
South Amboy, NJ (south'ăm'boi)	110a	40.28 N	74.17 W
South America	138		
Southampton, Eng. (south-ămp'tŭn)	160	50.54 N	1.30 W
Southampton, NY	109	40.53 N	72.24 W
Southampton I., Can.	95	64.38 N	84.00 W
South Andaman I., Andaman & Nicobar Is. (ăn-dà-măn')	202	11.57 N	93.24 E
South Australia (State), Austl. (ôs-trā'lĭ-ă)	210	29.45 S	132.00 E
South B., Ba.	133	20.55 N	73.35 W
South Bend, In. (bĕnd)	108	41.40 N	86.20 W
South Bend, Wa. (bĕnd)	114	46.39 N	123.48 W
South Bight (B.), Ba.	132	24.20 N	77.35 W
South Bimini (I.), Ba. (bē'mē-nē)	132	25.40 N	79.20 W
Southborough, Ma. (south'bŭr-ô)	103a	42.18 N	71.33 W
South Boston, Va. (bôs'tŭn)	125	36.41 N	78.55 W
Southbridge, Ma. (south'brĭj)	109	42.05 N	72.00 W
South Caicos (I.), Turks & Caicos (kī'kōs)	133	21.30 N	71.35 W
South Carolina (State), U. S. (kăr-ô-lī'nà)	107	34.15 N	81.10 W
South Cave, Eng. (cāv)	154	53.45 N	0.35 W
South Charleston, WV (chärlz'tŭn)	108	38.20 N	81.40 W
South China Sea, Asia (chī'nà)	202	15.23 N	114.12 E
South Cr., Austl.	207b	33.43 S	167.00 E
South Dakota (State), U. S. (dà-kō'tà)	106	44.20 N	101.55 W
South Downs, Eng. (dounz)	160	50.55 N	1.13 W
South Dum-Dum, India	190a	22.36 N	88.25 E
Southeast, C., Austl.	211	43.47 S	146.03 E
Southend-on-Sea, Eng. (south-ĕnd')	154b	51.33 N	0.41 E
Southern Alps (Mts.), N. Z. (sŭ-thûrn ălps)	213	43.35 S	170.00 E
Southern Cross, Austl.	210	31.13 S	119.30 E
Southern Indian (L.), Can. (sŭth'ĕrn ĭn'dĭ-ăn)	97	56.46 N	98.57 W
Southern Pines, NC (sŭth'ĕrn pīnz)	125	35.10 N	79.23 W
Southern Ute Ind. Res., Co. (ūt)	119	37.05 N	108.23 W
Southern Yemen, see **Yemen, People's Democratic Republic of**			
South Euclid, Oh. (ū'klĭd)	111d	41.30 N	81.34 W
South Fox (I.), Mi. (fŏks)	108	45.25 N	85.55 W
South Gate, Ca. (gāt)	117a	33.57 N	118.13 W
South Georgia (I.), Falk Is. (jôr'jä)	138	54.00 S	37.00 W
South Haven, Mi. (hāv''n)	108	42.25 N	86.15 W
South Hill, Va.	125	36.44 N	78.08 W
South Indian Lake, Can.	99	56.50 N	99.00 W
Southington, Ct. (sŭdh'ĭng-tŭn)	109	41.35 N	72.55 W
South I., N. Z.	213	42.40 S	169.00 E
South Loup (R.), Ne. (lōōp)	112	41.21 N	100.08 W
South Merrimack, NH (mĕr'ĭ-măk)	103a	42.47 N	71.36 W
South Milwaukee, Wi. (mĭl-wô'kē)	111a	42.55 N	87.52 W
South Moose L., Can.	99	53.51 N	100.20 W
South Nation (R.), Can. (nā'shŭn)	93c	45.12 N	75.07 W
South Negril Pt., Jam. (nā-grēl')	132	18.15 N	78.25 W
South Ogden, Ut. (ŏg'dĕn)	117b	41.12 N	111.58 W
South Orkney Is., B. A. T.	228	57.00 S	45.00 W
South Paris, Me. (păr'ĭs)	102	44.13 N	70.32 W
South Park, Ky. (pärk)	111h	38.06 N	85.43 W
South Pasadena, Ca. (păs-à-dē'nà)	117a	34.06 N	118.08 W
South Pease (R.), Tx. (pēz)	119	33.54 N	100.45 W
South Pender (I.), Can. (pĕn'dĕr)	116d	48.45 N	123.09 W
South Pittsburgh, Tn. (pĭs'bûrg)	124	35.00 N	85.42 W
South Platte (R.), U. S. (plăt)	106	40.40 N	102.40 W
South Porcupine, Can.	100	48.28 N	81.13 W
South Pt., Mi.	108	44.50 N	83.20 W
South Pt., Barb.	131b	13.00 N	59.43 W
Southport, Austl. (south'pōrt)	212	27.57 S	153.27 E
Southport, NC	125	35.55 N	78.02 W
Southport, Eng. (south'pôrt)	154	53.38 N	3.00 W
Southport, In.	111g	39.40 N	86.07 W
South Portland, Me. (pōrt-lănd)	102	43.37 N	70.15 W
South Prairie, Wa. (prâ'rĭ)	116a	47.08 N	122.06 W
South Range, Wi. (rānj)	117h	46.37 N	91.59 W
South River, NJ (rĭv'ĕr)	110a	40.27 N	74.23 W
South R., Ga.	110c	33.40 N	84.15 W
South St. Paul, Mn.	117g	44.54 N	93.02 W
South Salt Lake, Ut. (sôlt lāk)	117b	40.44 N	111.53 W
South Sandwich Is., Falk. Is. (sănd'wĭch)	138	58.00 S	27.00 W
South Sandwich Trench, S. A.-Ant.	138	55.00 S	27.00 W
South San Francisco, Ca. (săn frăn-sĭs'kô)	116d	37.39 N	122.24 W
South Saskatchewan (R.), Can. (sās-kach'ĕ-wän)	98	53.15 N	105.05 W
South Shetland Is., B. A. T.	228	62.00 S	70.00 W
South Shields, Eng. (shēldz)	160	55.00 N	1.22 W
South Sioux City, Ne. (sōō sĭt'ē)	112	42.48 N	96.26 W
South Taranaki Bight, N. Z. (tä-rä-nä'kē)	213	39.35 S	173.50 E
South Thompson (R.), Can. (tŏmp'sŭn)	97	50.41 N	120.21 W
Southton, Tx. (south'tŭn)	117d	29.18 N	98.26 W
South Uist (I.), Scot. (ū'ĭst)	160	57.15 N	7.24 W
South Umpqua R., Or. (ŭmp'kwà)	114	43.00 N	122.54 W
Southwell, Eng. (south'wĕl)	154	53.04 N	0.56 W
South West Africa, see **Namibia**			
Southwest Miramichi (R.), Can. (mĭr à-mē'shē)	102	46.35 N	66.17 W
Southwest Pt., Ba.	133	23.55 N	74.30 W
Southwest Pt., Ba.	132	25.50 N	77.10 W
South Yorkshire (Co.), Eng.	154	53.29 N	1.35 W
Sovetsk (Tilsit), Sov. Un. (sô-vyĕtsk')	163	55.04 N	21.54 E
Sovetskaya Gavan', Sov. Un. (sŭ-vyĕt'skī-u gä'vŭn')	179	48.59 N	140.14 E
Soviet Union, Eur.-Asia (sō-vĭ-ĕt')	188	60.30 N	64.00 E
Sow (R.), Eng. (sou)	154	52.45 N	2.12 W
Sōya Misaki (C.), Jap. (sō'yä mē'sä-kē)	200	45.35 N	141.25 E
Sozh (R.), Sov. Un. (sôzh)	172	52.17 N	31.00 E
Sozopol, Bul. (sôz'ô-pôl')	171	42.18 N	27.50 E
Spa, Bel. (spä)	161	50.30 N	5.50 E
Spain, Eur. (spān)	152	40.15 N	4.30 W
Spalding, Ne. (spôl'dĭng)	112	41.43 N	98.23 W
Spanaway, Wa. (spăn'à-wā)	116a	47.06 N	122.26 W
Spangler, Pa. (spăng'lĕr)	109	40.40 N	78.50 W
Spanish Fork, Ut. (spăn'ĭsh fôrk)	119	40.10 N	111.40 W
Spanish Town, Jam.	132	18.00 N	76.55 W

PLACE (Pronunciation)	PAGE	Lat. °′	Long. °′
Sparks, Nv. (spärks)	118	39.34 N	119.45 W
Sparrows Point, Md. (spăr'ōz)	110e	39.13 N	76.29 W
Sparta, Ga. (spär'tȧ)	124	33.16 N	82.59 W
Sparta, Il.	121	38.07 N	89.42 W
Sparta, Mi.	108	43.10 N	85.45 W
Sparta, Tn.	124	35.54 N	85.26 W
Sparta, Wi.	113	43.56 N	90.50 W
Sparta, see Spárti			
Sparta Mts., NJ	110a	41.00 N	74.38 W
Spartanburg, SC (spär'tăn-bûrg)	125	34.57 N	82.13 W
Spartel (C.), Mor. (spär-tĕl')	168	35.48 N	5.50 W
Spárti, Grc. (Sparta)	171	37.07 N	22.28 E
Spartivento, C., It. (spär-tē-vĕn'tō)	170	37.55 N	16.09 E
Spartivento, C., It.	170	38.54 N	8.52 E
Spas-Demensk, Sov. Un. (spȧs dyĕ-mĕnsk')	172	54.24 N	34.02 E
Spas-Klepiki, Sov. Un. (spȧs klĕp'ē-kē)	172	55.09 N	40.11 E
Spassk-Dal'niy, Sov. Un. (spŭsk'däl'nyē)	179	44.30 N	133.00 E
Spassik-Ryazanskiy, Sov. Un. (ryä-zän'skĭ)	172	54.24 N	40.21 E
Spátha, Ákra (C.), Grc.	170a	35.42 N	24.45 E
Spaulding, Al. (spôl'dĭng)	110h	33.27 N	86.50 W
Spear, C., Can. (spēr)	103	47.32 N	52.32 W
Spearfish, SD (spēr'fĭsh)	112	44.28 N	103.52 W
Speed, In. (spēd)	111h	38.25 N	85.45 W
Speedway, In. (spēd'wā)	111g	39.47 N	86.14 W
Speichersee (L.), F.R.G.	155d	48.12 N	11.47 E
Spencer, In. (spĕn'sẽr)	108	39.15 N	86.45 W
Spencer, Ia.	113	43.09 N	95.08 W
Spencer, NC	125	35.43 N	80.25 W
Spencer, WV	108	38.55 N	81.20 W
Spencer G., Austl. (spĕn'sẽr)	212	34.20 S	136.55 E
Sperenberg, G.D.R. (shpĕ'rĕn-bĕrgh)	155b	52.09 N	13.22 E
Sperkhiós (R.), Grc.	171	38.54 N	22.02 E
Spey (L.), Scot. (spā)	160	57.25 N	3.29 W
Speyer, F.R.G. (shpī'ẽr)	164	49.18 N	8.26 E
Sphinx (Pyramid), Egypt (sfĭnks)	219b	29.57 N	31.08 E
Spijkenisse, Neth.	155a	51.51 N	4.18 E
Spinazzola, It. (spē-nät'zō-lä)	170	40.58 N	16.05 E
Spirit Lake, Id. (spĭr'ĭt)	114	47.58 N	116.51 W
Spirit Lake, Ia. (lāk)	113	43.25 N	95.08 W
Spišská Nová Ves, Czech. (spĕsh'skä nō'vä vĕs)	165	48.56 N	20.35 E
Spitsbergen (Is.), see Svalbard			
Spittal, Aus. (shpē-täl')	164	46.48 N	13.28 E
Split, Yugo. (splēt)	170	43.30 N	16.28 E
Split L., Can.	99	56.08 N	96.15 W
Spokane, Wa. (spōkăn')	114	47.39 N	117.25 W
Spokane R., Wa.	114	47.47 N	118.00 W
Spoleto, It. (spō-lā'tō)	170	42.44 N	12.44 E
Spoon (R.), Il. (spōōn)	121	40.36 N	90.22 W
Spooner, Wi. (spōōn'ẽr)	113	45.50 N	91.53 W
Sporádhes (Is.), Grc.	171	38.55 N	24.05 E
Spotswood, NJ (spŏtz'wŏŏd)	110a	40.23 N	74.22 W
Sprague R., Or. (sprāg)	114	42.30 N	121.42 W
Spratly (I.), China (sprăt'lē)	202	8.38 N	111.54 E
Spray, NC (sprā)	125	36.30 N	79.44 W
Spree R., G.D.R. (shprā)	164	51.53 N	14.08 E
Spremberg, G.D.R. (shprĕm'bĕrgh)	164	51.35 N	14.23 E
Spring (R.), Ar.	121	36.25 N	91.35 W
Springbok, S. Afr. (sprĭng'bŏk)	222	29.35 S	17.55 E
Spring, Cr., Nv. (sprĭng)	118	40.18 N	117.45 W
Spring Cr., Tx.	123	30.03 N	95.43 W
Spring Cr., Tx.	122	31.08 N	100.50 W
Springdale, Can.	103	49.30 N	56.05 W
Springdale, Ar. (sprĭng'dāl)	121	36.10 N	94.07 W
Springdale, Pa.	111e	40.33 N	79.46 W
Springer, NM (sprĭng'ẽr)	120	36.21 N	104.37 W
Springerville, Az.	119	34.08 N	109.17 W
Springfield, Co. (sprĭng'fēld)	120	37.24 N	102.04 W
Springfield, Mn.	113	44.14 N	94.59 W
Springfield, Or.	114	44.01 N	123.02 W
Springfield, Il.	121	39.46 N	89.37 W
Springfield, Ky.	108	37.35 N	85.10 W
Springfield, Ma.	109	42.05 N	72.35 W
Springfield, Mo.	121	37.13 N	93.17 W
Springfield, Oh.	108	39.55 N	83.50 W
Springfield, Tn.	124	36.30 N	86.53 W
Springfield, Vt.	109	43.20 N	72.35 W
Springfontein, S. Afr. (sprĭng'fôn-tīn)	222	30.16 S	25.45 E
Springhill, Can. (sprĭng-hĭl')	103	45.39 N	64.03 W
Spring Mts., Nv.	118	36.18 N	115.49 W
Springs, S. Afr. (sprĭngs)	223b	26.16 S	28.27 E
Springstein, Can. (sprĭng'stīn)	93f	49.49 N	97.29 W
Springton Res., Pa. (sprĭng-tŭn)	110f	39.57 N	75.26 W
Springvale, Austl.	207a	37.57 N	145.09 E
Spring Valley, Ca.	118a	32.46 N	117.01 W
Springvalley, Il. (sprĭng-văl'ĭ)	108	41.20 N	89.15 W
Spring Valley, Mn.	113	43.41 N	92.26 W
Spring Valley, NY	110a	41.07 N	74.03 W
Springville, Ut. (sprĭng-vĭl)	119	40.10 N	111.40 W
Springwood, Austl.	207b	33.42 S	150.34 E
Spruce Grove, Can. (sprōōs grōv)	93g	53.32 N	113.55 W
Spur, Tx. (spûr)	120	33.29 N	100.51 W
Squam (L.), NH (skwôm)	109	43.45 N	71.30 W
Squamish, Can. (skwŏ'mĭsh)	96	49.42 N	123.09 W
Squamish (R.), Can.	96	50.10 N	124.30 W
Squillace, Gulfo di (G.), It. (gōō'l-fō-dē skwēl-lä'chä)	170	38.44 N	16.47 E

PLACE (Pronunciation)	PAGE	Lat. °′	Long. °′
Srbija (Serbia) (Reg.), Yugo. (sr bē-yä) (sĕr'bē-ä)	171	44.05 N	20.35 E
Srbobran, Yugo. (s'r'bô-brän')	171	45.32 N	19.50 E
Sredne-Kolymsk, Sov. Un. (s'rĕd'nyĕ kô-lēmsk')	179	67.49 N	154.55 E
Sredne Rogatka, Sov. Un. (s'red'ná-ya) (rô gär'tkȧ)	180c	59.49 N	30.20 E
Sredniy Ik (R.), Sov. Un. (srĕd'nĭ ĭk)	180a	55.46 N	58.50 E
Sredniy Ural (Mts.), Sov. Un. (ōō'rál)	180a	57.47 N	59.00 E
Śrem, Pol. (shrĕm)	165	52.06 N	17.01 E
Sremska Karlovci, Yugo. (srĕm'skē kär'lov-tsē)	171	45.10 N	19.57 E
Sremska Mitrovica, Yugo. (srĕm'skä mē'trô-vē-tsä')	171	44.59 N	19.39 E
Sretensk, Sov. Un. (s'rĕ'tĕnsk)	179	52.13 N	117.39 E
Sri Lanka (Ceylon), Asia	188	8.45 N	82.30 E
Srīnagar, India (srē-nŭg'ŭr)	190	34.11 N	74.49 E
Sroda, Pol. (shrō'dȧ)	165	52.14 N	17.17 E
Stabroek, Bel.	155a	51.20 N	4.21 E
Stade, F.R.G. (shtä'dĕ)	155c	53.36 N	9.28 E
Städjan (Mtn.), Swe. (stĕd'yän)	162	61.53 N	12.50 E
Stafford, Eng. (stăf'fẽrd)	154	52.48 N	2.06 W
Stafford, Ks.	120	37.58 N	98.37 W
Staffordshire (Co.), Eng.	154	52.45 N	2.00 W
Stahnsdorf, G.D.R. (shtäns'dôrf)	155b	52.22 N	13.10 E
Stalin, see Varna			
Stalinabad, see Dushanbe			
Stalingrad, see Volgograd			
Stalino, see Donetsk			
Stalinsk, see Novokuznetsk			
Stalybridge, Eng. (stā'lē-brĭj)	154	53.29 N	2.03 W
Stambaugh, Mi. (stăm'bô)	113	46.03 N	88.38 W
Stamford, Ct. (stăm'fẽrd)	110a	41.03 N	73.32 W
Stamford, Eng.	154	52.39 N	0.28 W
Stamford, Tx.	120	32.57 N	99.48 W
Stammersdorf, Aus. (shtäm'ẽrs-dôrf)	155e	48.19 N	16.25 E
Stamps, Ar. (stămps)	121	33.22 N	93.31 W
Stanberry, Mo. (stan'bĕr-ē)	121	40.12 N	94.34 W
Standerton, S. Afr. (stăn'dẽr-tŭn)	219d	26.57 S	29.17 E
Standing Rock Ind. Res., ND (stănd'ĭng rŏk)	112	47.07 N	101.05 W
Standish, Eng. (stăn'dĭsh)	154	53.36 N	2.39 W
Stanford, Ky. (stăn'fẽrd)	124	37.29 N	84.40 W
Stanger, S. Afr. (stăŋ-gẽr)	223c	29.22 S	31.18 E
Staniard Creek, Ba.	132	24.50 N	77.55 W
Stanislaus (R.), Ca. (stăn'ĭs-lō)	118	38.10 N	120.16 W
Stanley, Can. (stăn'lē)	102	46.17 N	66.44 W
Stanley, Falk. Is.	142	51.46 S	57.59 W
Stanley, ND	112	48.20 N	102.25 W
Stanley, Wi.	113	44.56 N	90.56 W
Stanley Pool (L.), Zaire	225	4.07 S	15.40 E
Stanley Res., India (stăn'lē)	190	12.07 N	77.27 E
Stanleyville, see Kisangani			
Stann Creek, Belize (stăn krēk)	130a	17.01 N	88.14 W
Stanovoy Khrebet (Mts.), Sov. Un. (stŭn-á-voi')	179	56.12 N	127.12 E
Stanton, Ca. (stăn'tŭn)	117a	33.48 N	118.00 W
Stanton, Ne.	112	41.57 N	97.15 W
Stanton, Tx.	122	32.08 N	101.46 W
Stanwood, Wa. (stăn'wŏŏd)	116a	48.14 N	122.23 W
Staples, Mn. (stā'p'lz)	113	46.21 N	94.48 W
Stapleton, Al.	124	30.45 N	87.48 W
Stara Planina (Balkan Mts.), Bul.	152	42.50 N	24.45 E
Staraya Kupavna, Sov. Un. (stä'rá-yȧ kû-päf'nȧ)	180b	55.48 N	38.10 E
Staraya Russa, Sov. Un. (stä'rá-yȧ rōōsȧ)	172	57.58 N	31.21 E
Stara Zagora, Bul. (zä'gō-rȧ)	171	42.26 N	25.37 E
Starbuck, Can. (stär'bŭk)	93f	49.46 N	97.36 W
Stargard Szczeciński, Pol. (shtär'gärt shchĕ-chyn'skē)	164	53.19 N	15.03 E
Staritsa, Sov. Un. (stä'rē-tsȧ)	172	56.29 N	34.58 E
Starke, Fl. (stärk)	125	29.55 N	82.07 W
Starkville, Co. (stärk'vĭl)	120	37.06 N	104.34 W
Starkville, Ms.	124	33.27 N	88.47 W
Starnberg, F.R.G. (shtärn-bĕrgh)	155d	47.59 N	11.20 E
Starnberger See (L.), F.R.G.	164	47.58 N	11.30 E
Starobel'sk, Sov. Un. (stä-rô-byĕlsk')	173	49.19 N	38.57 E
Starodub, Sov. Un. (stä-rô-drōōp')	172	52.25 N	32.49 E
Starograd Gdański, Pol. (stä'rō-grad gdĕn'skē)	165	53.58 N	18.33 E
Staro-Konstantinov, Sov. Un. (stä'rô kôn-stán-tē'nôf)	173	49.45 N	27.12 E
Staro-Minskaya, Sov. Un. (stä'rô mĭn'skȧ-yȧ)	173	46.19 N	38.51 E
Staro-Shcherbinovskaya, Sov. Un.	173	46.38 N	38.38 E
Staro-Subkhangulovo, Sov. Un. (stäro-sōōb-kan-gōō'lôvô)	180a	53.08 N	57.24 E
Staroutkinsk, Sov. Un. (stá-rô-ōōt'kĭnsk)	180a	57.14 N	59.21 E
Staroverovka, Sov. Un.	173	49.31 N	35.48 E
Start Pt., Eng. (stärt)	160	50.14 N	3.34 W
Stary Sacz, Pol. (stä-rē sôŋch')	165	49.32 N	20.36 E
Staryy Oskol, Sov. Un. (stä'rē ôs-kôl')	173	51.18 N	37.51 E
Stassfurt, G.D.R. (shtäs'fōōrt)	164	51.52 N	11.35 E
Staszów, Pol. (stä'shōōf)	165	50.32 N	21.13 E
State College, Pa. (stāt kŏl'ĕj)	109	40.50 N	77.55 W
State Line, Mn. (līn)	117h	46.36 N	92.18 W
Staten I., NY (stăt'ĕn)	110a	40.35 N	74.10 W
Statesboro, Ga. (stāts'bŭr-ō)	125	32.26 N	81.47 W
Statesville, NC (stās'vĭl)	125	34.45 N	80.54 W

PLACE (Pronunciation)	PAGE	Lat. °′	Long. °′
Staunton, Il. (stôn'tŭn)	117e	39.01 N	89.47 W
Staunton, Va.	109	38.10 N	79.05 W
Stavanger, Nor. (stä'väng'ẽr)	162	58.59 N	5.44 E
Stave (R.), Can. (stāv)	116d	49.12 N	122.24 W
Staveley, Eng. (stāv'lē)	154	53.17 N	1.21 W
Stavenisse, Neth.	155a	51.35 N	3.59 E
Stavropol', Sov. Un.	177	45.05 N	41.50 E
Stawno, Pol. (swav'nō)	164	54.21 N	16.38 E
Steamboat Springs, Co. (stēm'bōt')	120	40.30 N	106.48 W
Steblëv, Sov. Un. (styĕp'lyôf)	173	49.23 N	31.03 E
Steel (R.), Can. (stēl)	113	49.08 N	86.55 W
Steelton, Pa. (stēl'tŭn)	109	40.15 N	76.45 W
Steenbergen, Neth.	155a	51.35 N	4.18 E
Steens Mts., Or. (stēnz)	114	42.15 N	118.52 W
Steep Pt., Austl. (stēp)	210	26.15 N	112.05 E
Stefaniee, L., see Chew Bahir			
Steger, Il. (stē'gẽr)	111a	41.28 N	87.38 W
Steiermark (Styria) (State), Aus. (shtī'ẽr-märk)	164	47.22 N	14.40 E
Steinbach, Can.	94	49.32 N	96.41 W
Steinkjer, Nor. (stēĭn-kyĕr)	156	64.00 N	11.19 E
Stella, Wa. (stĕl'ȧ)	116c	46.11 N	123.12 W
Stellarton, Can. (stĕl'ár-tŭn)	102	45.34 N	62.40 W
Stendal, G.D.R (shtĕn'däl)	164	52.37 N	11.51 E
Stepanakert, Sov. Un. (styĕ'pän-á-kĕrt)	177	39.50 N	46.40 E
Stephens, Port, Austl. (stē'fĕns)	212	32.43 N	152.55 E
Stephenville, Can. (stē'vĕn-vĭl)	103	48.33 N	58.35 W
Stepnyak, Sov. Un. (styĭp-nyäk')	178	52.37 N	70.43 E
Sterkrade, F.R.G. (shtĕr'krädĕ)	167c	51.31 N	6.51 E
Sterkstroom, S. Afr.	223c	31.33 S	26.36 E
Sterling, Co. (stûr'lĭng)	120	40.38 N	103.14 W
Sterling, Il.	113	41.48 N	89.42 W
Sterling, Ks.	120	38.11 N	98.11 W
Sterling, Ma.	103a	42.26 N	71.41 W
Sterling, Tx.	122	31.53 N	100.58 W
Sterlitamak, Sov. Un. (styĕr'lē-ta-mák')	180a	53.38 N	55.56 E
Šternberk, Czech. (shtĕrn'bĕrk)	165	49.44 N	17.18 E
Stettin, see Szczecin			
Stettler, Can.	97	52.19 N	112.43 W
Steubenville, Oh. (stū'bĕn-vĭl)	108	40.20 N	80.40 W
Stevens (L.), Wa. (stē'vĕnz)	116a	47.59 N	122.06 W
Stevens Point, Wi.	113	44.30 N	89.35 W
Stevensville, Mt. (stē'vĕnz-vĭl)	115	46.31 N	114.03 E
Stewart (R.), Can. (stū'ērt)	94	63.27 N	138.48 W
Stewart I., N. Z.	213	46.56 S	167.40 E
Stewiacke, Can. (stū'wē-ăk)	102	45.08 N	63.21 W
Steynsrus, S. Afr. (stīns'rōōs)	219d	27.58 S	27.33 E
Steyr, Aus. (shtīr)	164	48.03 N	14.24 E
Stikine (R.), Can. (stĭ-kēn')	94	58.17 N	130.10 W
Stikine Ranges, Can.	94	59.05 N	130.00 W
Stillaguamish (R.), Wa.	116a	48.11 N	122.18 W
Stillaguamish (R.), South Fk. Wa. (stĭl-ȧ-gwä'mĭsh)	116a	48.05 N	121.59 W
Stillwater, Mn. (stĭl'wô-tẽr)	117g	45.04 N	92.48 W
Stillwater, Mt.	115	45.23 N	109.45 W
Stillwater, Ok.	121	36.06 N	97.03 W
Stillwater Ra., Nv.	118	39.43 N	118.11 W
Stillwater R., Mt.	114	48.47 N	114.40 W
Štip, Yugo. (shtĭp)	171	41.43 N	22.07 E
Stirling, Scot. (stûr'lĭng)	160	56.05 N	3.59 W
Stittsville, Can. (stĭts'vĭl)	93c	45.15 N	75.54 W
Stjördalshalsen, Nor. (styûr-dāls-hälsĕn)	162	63.26 N	11.00 E
Stockbridge Munsee Ind. Res., Wi. (stŏk'brĭdj mŭn-sē)	113	44.49 N	89.00 W
Stockerau, Aus. (shtô'kĕ-rou)	155e	48.24 N	16.13 E
Stockholm, Me. (stŏk'hōlm)	102	47.05 N	68.08 W
Stockholm, Swe. (stŏk'hôlm)	162	59.23 N	18.00 E
Stockport, Eng. (stŏk'pôrt)	154	53.24 N	2.09 W
Stockton, Ca. (stŏk'tŭn)	118	37.56 N	121.16 W
Stockton, Eng.	160	54.35 N	1.25 W
Stockton, Ks.	120	39.26 N	99.16 W
Stockton (I.), Wi.	113	46.56 N	90.25 W
Stockton Plat., Tx.	122	30.34 N	102.35 W
Stockton Res., Mo.	121	37.40 N	93.45 W
Stöde, Swe. (stû'dĕ)	162	62.26 N	16.35 E
Stoke-on-Trent, Eng. (stōk-ŏn-trĕnt)	154	53.01 N	2.12 W
Stokhod (R.), Sov. Un. (stō-kōd)	165	51.24 N	25.20 E
Stolac, Yugo. (stô'läts)	171	43.03 N	17.59 E
Stolbovy (Is.), Sov. Un. (stôl-bô-voi')	179	73.43 N	133.05 E
Stolin, Sov. Un. (stô'lĕn)	165	51.54 N	26.52 E
Stömstad, Swe.	162	58.58 N	11.09 E
Stone, Eng.	154	52.54 N	2.09 W
Stoneham, Can. (stōn'ȧm)	93b	46.59 N	71.22 W
Stoneham, Ma.	103a	42.30 N	71.05 W
Stonehaven, Scot. (stōn'hā-v'n)	160	56.57 N	2.09 W
Stone Mountain, Ga. (stōn)	110c	33.49 N	84.10 W
Stonewall, Can. (stōn'wôl)	93f	50.09 N	97.21 W
Stonewall, Ms.	124	32.08 N	88.44 W
Stoney Creek, Can. (stō'nē)	93d	43.13 N	79.45 W
Stonington, Ct. (stōn'ĭng-tŭn)	109	41.20 N	71.55 W
Stony Cr., Ca. (stō'nē)	118	39.28 N	122.35 W
Stony Indian Res., Can.	93e	51.10 N	114.45 W
Stony Mountain, Can.	93f	50.05 N	97.13 W
Stony Plain, Can. (stō'nē plān)	93g	53.02 N	114.00 W
Stony Plain Ind. Res., Can.	93g	53.29 N	113.48 W
Stony Point, NY	110a	41.13 N	73.58 W
Storå (R.), Den.	162	56.22 N	8.35 E
Stora Lule (R.), Swe. (stōō'rä lōō'lĕ)	176	67.00 N	19.30 E
Stora Sotra (I.), Nor.	162	60.24 N	4.35 E

ăt; finȧl; rāte; senāte; ärm; ȧsk; sofȧ; fâre; ch-choose; dh-as th in other; bē; ēvent; bĕt; recĕnt; cratẽr; g-gō; gh-guttural g; bĭt; ĭ-short neutral; rīde; ĸ-guttural k as ch in German ich;

PLACE (Pronunciation)	PAGE	Lat. °′	Long. °′
Stord (I.), Nor. (stôrd)	162	59.54 N	5.15 E
Store Baelt (Str.), Den.	162	55.25 N	10.50 E
Storfjorden (Fd.), Nor.	162	62.17 N	6.19 E
Stormberg (Mts.), S. Afr. (stôrm'bûrg)	223c	31.28 S	26.35 E
Storm Lake, Ia.	113	42.39 N	95.12 W
Stormy Pt., Vir. Is. (U.S.A.) (stôr'mē)	127c	18.22 N	65.01 W
Stornoway, Scot. (stôr'nô-wā)	160	58.13 N	6.21 W
Storozhinets, Sov. Un. (stô-rô'zhēn-yĕts)	165	48.10 N	25.44 E
Störsjo, Swe. (stôr'shû)	162	62.49 N	13.08 E
Störsjoen (L.), Nor. (stôr-syûĕn)	162	61.32 N	11.30 E
Störsjon (L.), Swe.	162	63.06 N	14.00 E
Storvik, Swe. (stôr'vĕk)	162	60.37 N	16.31 E
Stoughton, Ma. (stō'tŭn)	103a	42.07 N	71.06 W
Stoughton, Wi.	113	42.54 N	89.15 W
Stour (R.), Eng. (stour)	161	52.09 N	0.29 E
Stourbridge, Eng. (stour'brĭj)	154	52.27 N	2.08 W
Stow, Ma. (stō)	103a	42.56 N	71.31 W
Stow, Oh.	111d	41.09 N	81.26 W
Straatsdrif, S. Afr.	219d	25.19 S	26.22 E
Strabane, N. Ire. (stră-băn')	160	54.59 N	7.27 W
Straelen, F.R.G. (shtrā'lĕn)	167c	51.26 N	6.16 E
Strahan, Austl. (strā'ăn)	211	42.08 S	145.28 E
Strakonice, Czech. (strä'kô-nyē-tsĕ)	164	49.18 N	13.52 E
Straldzha, Bul. (strāl'dzhà)	171	42.37 N	26.44 E
Stralsund, G.D.R. (shrāl'sōōnt)	164	54.18 N	13.04 E
Strangford, Lough (B.), Ire. (lôĸ străng'fērd)	160	54.30 N	5.34 W
Strängnäs, Swe. (strĕng'nĕs)	162	59.23 N	16.59 E
Stranraer, Scot. (străn-rär')	160	54.55 N	5.05 W
Strasbourg, Fr. (stràs-bōōr')	167	48.36 N	7.49 E
Stratford, Can. (străt'fērd)	108	43.20 N	81.05 W
Stratford, Ct.	109	41.10 N	73.05 W
Stratford, Wi.	113	44.16 N	90.02 W
Stratford-upon-Avon, Eng.	160	52.13 N	1.41 W
Strathcona Prov. Pk., Can.	96	49.40 N	125.50 W
Straubing, F.R.G. (strou'bĭng)	164	48.52 N	12.36 E
Strausberg, G.D.R. (strous'bĕrgh)	164	52.35 N	13.50 E
Strawberry (R.), Ut.	119	40.05 N	110.55 W
Strawberry Mts., Or. (strô'bĕr'ĭ)	114	44.19 N	119.20 W
Strawn, Tx. (strôn)	122	32.38 N	98.28 W
Streator, Il. (strē'tēr)	108	41.05 N	88.50 W
Streeter, ND	112	46.40 N	99.22 W
Streetsville, Can. (strētz'vĭl)	93d	43.34 N	79.43 W
Strehaia, Rom. (strĕ-ĸä'yà)	171	44.37 N	23.13 E
Strel'na, Sov. Un. (strĕl'nà)	180c	59.52 N	30.01 E
Stretford, Eng. (strĕt'fērd)	154	53.25 N	2.19 W
Strickland (R.), Pap. N. Gui. (strĭk'lănd)	203	6.15 S	142.00 E
Strijen, Neth.	155a	51.44 N	4.23 E
Stromboli (Vol.), It. (strôm'bô-lē)	170	38.46 N	15.16 E
Stromyn, Sov. Un. (strô'mĭn)	180b	56.02 N	38.29 E
Strong (R.), Ms. (strông)	124	32.03 N	89.42 W
Strongsville, Oh. (strôngz'vĭl)	111d	41.19 N	81.50 W
Stronsay (I.), Scot. (strŏn'sā)	160a	59.09 N	2.35 W
Stroudsburg, Pa. (stroudz'bûrg)	109	41.00 N	75.15 W
Struer, Den.	162	56.29 N	8.34 E
Strugi Krasnyye, Sov. Un. (strōō'gĭ krā's-ny'yĕ)	172	58.14 N	29.10 E
Struma (R.), Bul. (strōō'mà)	171	41.55 N	23.05 E
Strumica, Yugo. (strōō'mĭ-tsà)	171	41.26 N	22.38 E
Strunino, Sov. Un.	180b	56.23 N	38.34 E
Struthers, Oh. (strŭdh'ērz)	108	41.00 N	80.35 W
Struvenhütten, F.R.G. (shtrōō'vĕn-hü-tĕn)	155c	53.52 N	10.04 E
Strydpoortberge (Mts.), S. Afr.	219d	24.08 S	29.18 E
Stryy, Sov. Un. (strē')	165	49.16 N	23.51 E
Strzelce Opolskie, Pol. (stzhĕl'tsĕ o-pōl'skyĕ)	165	50.31 N	18.20 E
Strzelin, Pol. (stzhĕ-lĭn)	165	50.48 N	17.06 E
Strzelno, Pol. (stzhāl'nô)	165	52.37 N	18.10 E
Stuart, Fl. (stū'ērt)	125a	27.10 N	80.14 W
Stuart, Ia.	113	41.31 N	94.20 W
Stuart (I.), Ak.	105	63.25 N	162.45 W
Stuart (I.), Wa.	116d	48.42 N	123.10 W
Stuart L., Can.	96	54.32 N	124.35 W
Stuart Ra., Austl.	210	29.00 S	134.30 E
Stung Treng, Kamp. (stōōng'trĕng')	202	13.36 N	106.00 E
Stupava, Czech.	155e	48.17 N	17.02 E
Stupsk, Pol. (swōōpsk)	165	54.28 N	17.02 E
Sturgeon (R.), Can.	93g	53.41 N	113.46 W
Sturgeon (R.), Mi.	113	46.43 N	88.43 W
Sturgeon Bay, Wi.	113	44.50 N	87.22 W
Sturgeon B., Can.	99	52.00 N	98.00 W
Sturgeon Falls, Can.	95	46.19 N	79.49 W
Sturgis, Ky.	108	37.35 N	88.00 W
Sturgis, Mi.	108	41.45 N	85.25 W
Sturgis, SD	112	44.25 N	103.31 W
Sturt Cr., Austl.	210	19.40 S	127.40 E
Sturtevant, Wi. (stŭr'tē-vănt)	111a	42.42 N	87.54 W
Stutterheim, S. Afr. (stŭrt'ēr-hīm)	223c	32.34 S	27.27 E
Stuttgart, Ar. (stŭt'gärt)	121	34.30 N	91.33 W
Stuttgart, F.R.G. (shtōōt'gärt)	164	48.48 N	9.15 E
Stykkishólmur, Ice.	156	65.00 N	21.48 W
Styr' R., Sov. Un. (stēr)	165	51.44 N	26.07 E
Styria, see Steiermark			
Suao, Taiwan (sōō'ou)	199	24.35 N	121.45 E
Subarnarakha (R.), India	190	22.38 N	86.26 E
Subata, Sov. Un. (sōō'bà-tà)	163	56.02 N	25.54 E
Subic, Phil. (sōō'bĭk)	203a	14.52 N	120.15 E
Subic B., Phil.	203a	14.41 N	120.11 E
Subotica, Yugo. (sōō'bô'tē-tsà)	171	46.06 N	19.41 E
Subugo (Mtn.), Ken.	227	1.40 S	35.49 E
Succasunna, NJ (sŭk'kà-sŭn'nà)	110a	40.52 N	74.37 W
Suceava, Rom. (sōō-chà-ä'và)	165	47.39 N	26.17 E
Suceava R., Rom.	165	47.45 N	26.10 E
Sucha, Pol. (sōō'ĸà)	165	49.44 N	19.40 E
Suchiapa, Mex. (sōō-chē-ä'pä)	129	16.38 N	93.08 W
Suchiapa (R.), Mex.	129	16.27 N	93.26 W
Suchitoto, Sal. (sōō-chē-tō'tō)	130	13.58 N	89.03 W
Suchow (Xuzhou), China (shōō-jō)	196	34.17 N	117.10 E
Sucia Is., Wa. (soū'sē-à)	116d	48.46 N	122.54 W
Sucio (R.), Col. (sōō'syô)	140a	6.55 N	76.15 W
Suck, Ire. (sŭk)	160	53.34 N	8.16 W
Sucre, Bol. (sōō'krā)	140	19.06 S	65.16 W
Sucre (State), Ven. (sōō'krĕ)	141b	10.18 N	65.12 W
Sud, Canal du (Chan.), Hai.	133	18.40 N	73.15 W
Sud, Rivière du, Can. (rē-vyâr'dü süd')	93b	46.56 N	70.35 W
Suda, Sov. Un. (sōō'dà)	180a	56.58 N	56.45 E
Suda (R.), Sov. Un. (sōō'dà)	172	59.24 N	36.40 E
Sudair, Sau. Ar. (sŭ-dä'ēr)	192	25.48 N	46.28 E
Sudalsvatnet (L.), Nor.	162	59.35 N	6.59 E
Sudan, Afr.	218	14.00 N	28.00 E
Sudan (Reg.), Afr. (sōō-dän')	225	15.00 N	7.00 E
Sudbury, Can. (sŭd'bĕr-ē)	95	46.28 N	81.00 W
Sudbury, Ma.	103a	42.23 N	71.25 W
Sudetes (Mts.), Czech.	164	50.41 N	15.37 E
Sudogda, Sov. Un. (sōō'dôk-dà)	172	55.57 N	40.29 E
Sudost' (R.), Sov. Un. (sōō-dôst')	172	52.43 N	33.13 E
Sudzha, Sov. Un. (sōōd'zhà)	173	51.14 N	35.11 E
Sueca, Sp. (swā'kä)	169	39.12 N	0.18 W
Suemez I., Ak.	96	55.17 N	133.21 W
Suez, see As Suways			
Suez, G. of, Egypt (sōō-ĕz')	219c	29.53 N	32.33 E
Suez Can., see Qana el Suweis			
Suffern, NY (sŭf'fērn)	110a	41.07 N	74.09 W
Suffolk, Va. (sŭf'ŭk)	110g	36.43 N	76.35 W
Sugar (Cr.), In.	108	39.55 N	87.10 W
Sugar City, Co.	120	38.12 N	103.42 W
Sugar Creek, Mo.	117f	39.07 N	94.27 W
Sugar Cr., Il. (shōōg'ēr)	121	40.14 N	89.28 W
Sugar I., Mi.	117k	46.31 N	84.12 W
Sugarloaf Pt., Austl. (sōōgēr'lôf)	212	32.19 S	153.04 E
Suggi L., Can.	99	54.22 N	102.47 W
Suhaymī, Wādī as (R.), Egypt	189a	29.48 N	33.12 E
Suhl, G.D.R. (zōōl)	164	50.37 N	10.41 E
Suichuan (Mtn.), China	199	26.25 N	114.10 E
Suide, China (swā-dü)	198	37.32 N	110.12 E
Suifenhe, China (swā-fŭn-hŭ)	179	44.47 N	131.13 E
Suihua, China,	198	46.38 N	126.50 E
Suining, China (sōō'ē-nĭng')	196	33.54 N	117.57 E
Suipacha, Arg. (swē-pä'chä)	139c	34.45 S	59.43 W
Suiping, China (swā-pĭŋ)	196	33.09 N	113.58 E
Suir R., Ire. (sūr)	160	52.20 N	7.32 W
Suisun B., Ca. (sōōē-sōōn')	116b	38.07 N	122.02 W
Suita, Jap. (sōō'ē-tä)	201b	34.45 N	135.32 E
Suitland, Md. (sōōt'lănd)	110e	38.51 N	76.57 W
Sui Xian, China (swā shyĕn)	199	31.42 N	113.20 E
Suiyüan (Reg.), China (swā-yûĕn)	194	41.31 N	107.04 E
Suizhong, China (swā-jôŋ)	196	40.22 N	120.20 E
Sukabumi, Indon.	202	6.52 S	106.56 E
Sukadana, Indon.	202	1.15 S	110.30 E
Sukagawa, Jap. (sōō'kä-gä'wà)	201	37.08 N	140.07 E
Sukarnapura, see Jayapura			
Sukhinichi, Sov. Un. (sōō'ĸē'nē-chē)	172	54.07 N	35.18 E
Sukhona (R.), Sov. Un. (sōō-ĸô'nà)	176	59.30 N	42.20 E
Sukhoy Log, Sov. Un. (sōō'kôy lôg)	180a	56.55 N	62.03 E
Sukhumi, Sov. Un. (sōō-kōōm')	177	43.00 N	41.00 E
Sukkur, Pak. (sŭk'ŭr)	190	27.49 N	68.50 E
Sukkwan I., Ak.	96	55.05 N	132.45 W
Suksun, Sov. Un. (sōōk'sōōn)	180a	57.08 N	57.22 E
Sukumo, Jap. (sōō'kōō-mô)	201	32.58 N	132.45 E
Sukunka (R.), Can.	97	55.00 N	121.50 W
Sula, Kepulauan (I.), Indon.	203	2.20 S	125.20 E
Sula (R.), Sov. Un. (sōō-lä')	173	50.36 N	33.13 E
Sulaco R., Hond. (sōō-lä'kō)	130	14.55 N	87.31 W
Sulaimān Ra., Pak. (sōō-lä-ē-män')	190	29.47 N	69.10 E
Sulak (R.), Sov. Un. (sōō-làk')	177	43.30 N	47.00 E
Sulawesi (I.), see Celebes			
Suleya, Sov. Un. (sōō-lē'ya)	180a	55.12 N	58.52 E
Sulfeld, F.R.G. (zōō'fĕld)	155c	53.48 N	10.13 E
Sulina, Rom. (sōō-lē'nà)	173	45.08 N	29.38 E
Sulitelma (Mtn.), Nor.-Swe. (sōō-lē-tyĕl'mà)	156	67.03 N	16.35 E
Sullana, Peru (sōō-lyä'nä)	140	4.57 N	80.47 W
Sulligent, Al. (sŭl'ĭ-jĕnt)	124	33.52 N	88.06 W
Sullivan, Il. (sŭl'ĭ-văn)	108	41.35 N	88.35 W
Sullivan, In.	108	39.05 N	87.20 W
Sullivan, Mo.	121	38.13 N	91.09 W
Sulmona, It. (sōōl-mō'nä)	170	42.02 N	13.58 E
Sulphur, Ok. (sŭl'fŭr)	121	34.31 N	96.58 W
Sulphur (R.), Tx.	121	33.26 N	95.06 W
Sulphur Springs, Tx. (sprĭngz)	121	33.09 N	95.36 W
Sultan, Wa. (sŭl'tăn)	116a	47.52 N	121.49 W
Sultan (R.), Wa.	116a	47.55 N	121.49 W
Sultepec, Mex. (sōōl-tà-pĕk')	128	18.50 N	99.51 W
Sulu Arch., Phil. (sōō'lōō)	202	5.52 N	122.00 E
Suluntah, Libya	159	32.39 N	21.49 E
Sulu Sea, Phil.	202	8.25 N	119.00 E
Suma, Jap. (sōō'mä)	201b	34.39 N	135.08 E
Sumas, Wa. (sū'măs)	116d	49.00 N	122.16 W
Sumatera (I.), see Sumatra			
Sumatra (Sumatera) (I.), Indon. (sōō-mä-trà)	202	2.06 N	99.40 E
Sumba (I.), Indon. (sŭm'bà)	202	9.52 S	119.00 E
Sumba, Île (I.), Zaire	226	1.44 N	19.32 E
Sumbawa (I.), Indon. (sōōm-bä'wä)	202	9.00 S	118.18 E
Sumbawa-Besar, Indon.	202	8.32 S	117.20 E
Sumbawanga, Tan.	227	7.58 S	31.37 E
Sümeg, Hung. (shü'mĕg)	165	46.59 N	17.19 E
Sumida (R.), Jap. (sōō'mē-dä)	201	36.01 N	139.24 E
Sumidouro, Braz. (sōō-mē-dō'rōō)	139a	22.04 S	42.41 W
Sumiyoshi, Jap. (sōō'mē-yō'shē)	201b	34.43 N	135.16 E
Summer L., Or. (sŭm'ēr)	114	42.50 N	120.35 W
Summerland, Can. (sŭ'mēr-lănd)	97	49.39 N	117.33 W
Summerside, Can. (sŭm'ēr-sīd)	102	46.25 N	63.47 W
Summerton, SC (sŭm'ēr-tŭn)	125	33.37 N	80.22 W
Summerville, SC (sŭm'ēr-vĭl)	125	33.00 N	80.10 W
Summit, Il. (sŭm'mĭt)	111a	41.47 N	87.48 W
Summit, N.J.	110a	40.43 N	74.21 W
Summit Lake Ind. Res., Nv.	114	41.35 N	119.30 W
Summit Pk., Co.	119	37.20 N	106.40 W
Sumner, Wa. (sŭm'nēr)	116a	47.12 N	122.14 W
Šumperk, Czech. (shōōm'pĕrk)	164	49.57 N	17.02 E
Sumrall, Ms. (sŭm'rôl)	124	31.25 N	89.34 W
Sumter, SC (sŭm'tēr)	125	33.55 N	80.21 W
Sumy, Sov. Un. (sōō'mĭ)	173	50.54 N	34.47 E
Sumy (Oblast), Sov. Un.	173	51.02 N	34.05 E
Sunburst, Mt.	115	48.53 N	111.55 W
Sunbury, Pa. (sŭn'bĕr-ē)	109	40.50 N	76.45 W
Sundance, Wy. (sŭn'dăns)	115	44.24 N	104.27 W
Sundarbans (Swp.), Bngl.-India (sōōn'dēr-bŭns)	190	21.50 N	89.00 E
Sunda Selat (Str.), Indon.	202	5.45 S	106.15 E
Sunday Str., Austl. (sŭn'dā)	210	15.50 S	122.45 E
Sundbyberg, Swe. (sōōn'bü-bĕrgh)	162	59.24 N	17.56 E
Sunderland, Eng. (sŭn'dēr-lănd)	160	54.55 N	1.25 W
Sunderland, Md.	110e	38.41 N	76.36 W
Sundsvall, Swe. (sōōnds'väl)	162	62.24 N	19.19 E
Sunflower, (R.), Ms. (sŭn-flou'ēr)	124	32.57 N	90.40 W
Sungari (Songhua) (R.), China (sôŋ-hwä)	195	46.09 N	127.53 E
Sungari Res., China	198	42.55 N	127.50 E
Sungurlu, Tur. (sōōn'gōōr-lōō')	177	40.08 N	34.20 E
Sun Kosi (R.), Nep.	190	27.13 N	85.52 E
Sunland, Ca. (sŭn-lănd)	117a	34.16 N	118.18 W
Sunne, Swe. (sōōn'ĕ)	162	59.51 N	13.07 E
Sunninghill, Eng. (sŭnĭng'hĭl)	154b	51.23 N	0.40 W
Sunnymead, Ca. (sŭn'ĭ-mēd)	117a	33.56 N	117.15 W
Sunnyside, Ut.	119	39.35 N	110.20 W
Sunnyside, Wa.	114	46.19 N	120.00 W
Sunnyvale, Ca. (sŭn-nē-văl)	116b	37.23 N	122.02 W
Sunol, Ca. (sōō'nŭl)	116b	37.36 N	122.53 W
Sun R., Mt. (sŭn)	115	47.34 N	111.53 W
Sunset, Ut. (sŭn-sĕt)	117b	41.08 N	112.02 W
Sunset Crater Natl. Mon., Az. (krā'tēr)	119	35.20 N	111.30 W
Sunshine, Austl.	207a	37.47 S	144.50 E
Suntar, Sov. Un. (sōōn-tär')	179	62.14 N	117.49 E
Sunyani, Ghana	224	7.20 N	2.20 W
Suoyarvi, Sov. Un. (sōō'ô-yĕr'vē)	163	62.12 N	32.29 E
Superior, Az. (su-pē'rĭ-ēr)	119	33.15 N	111.10 W
Superior, Ne.	120	40.04 N	98.05 W
Superior, Wi.	117h	46.44 N	92.06 W
Superior, Wy.	115	41.45 N	108.57 W
Superior, Laguana (L.), Mex. (lä-gōō'nà sōō-pā-rē-ōr')	129	16.20 N	94.55 W
Superior, L., Can.-U.S.	95	47.38 N	89.20 W
Superior Village, Wi.	117h	46.38 N	92.07 W
Sup'ung Res., Kor.-China (sōō'pōōng)	200	40.35 N	126.00 E
Suqian, China (sōō-chyĕn)	196	33.57 N	118.17 E
Suquamish, Wa. (sōō-gwä'mĭsh)	116a	47.44 N	122.34 W
Şūr (Tyre), Leb. (sōōr) (tīr)	189a	33.16 N	35.13 E
Şūr, Om.	192	22.23 N	59.28 E
Surabaya, Indon.	202	7.23 S	112.45 E
Surakarta, Indon.	202	7.35 S	110.45 E
Šurany, Czech. (shōō'rà-nû')	165	48.05 N	18.11 E
Surat, Austl. (sŭ-răt)	212	27.18 S	149.00 E
Surat, India (sōō'rŭt)	190	21.08 N	73.22 E
Surat Thani, Thai.	202	8.59 N	99.14 E
Surazh, Sov. Un. (sōō-ràzh')	172	53.02 N	32.27 E
Surazh, Sov. Un.	172	55.24 N	30.46 E
Surgères, Fr. (sür-zhâr')	166	46.06 N	0.51 W
Surgut, Sov. Un. (sōōr-gōōt')	178	61.18 N	73.38 E
Suriname, S.A. (sōō-rē-näm')	138	4.00 N	56.00 W
Surud Ad (Mtn.), Som.	219a	10.40 N	47.23 E
Suruga-Wan (B.), Jap. (sōō'rōō-gä wän)	201	34.52 N	138.36 E
Surt, Libya	221	31.14 N	16.37 E
Surt, Khalīj (G.), Afr.	159	31.30 N	18.28 E
Susa, It. (sōō'sä)	170	45.01 N	7.09 E
Susa, Jap.	201	34.40 N	131.39 E
Susak, Otok (I.), Yugo. (sōō'shak)	170	44.31 N	14.15 E
Sušak (I.), Yugo.	170	42.45 N	16.30 E
Susaki, Jap. (sōō'sä-kē)	201	33.23 N	133.16 E
Susitna, Ak. (sōō-sĭt'nà)	105	61.28 N	150.28 W
Susitna (R.), Ak.	105	62.00 N	150.28 W
Susong, China (sōō-sôŋ)	199	30.18 N	116.08 E
Susquehanna, Pa. (sŭs'kwē-hăn'à)	109	41.55 N	73.55 W
Susquehanna (R.), Pa.	109	39.50 N	76.20 W
Sussex, Wi.	111a	43.08 N	88.12 W
Sussex, Can. (sŭs'ĕks)	102	45.43 N	65.31 W
Sussex, NJ	110a	41.12 N	74.36 W
Sutherland, Austl. (sŭdh'ēr-lănd)	207b	34.02 S	151.04 E
Sutherland, S. Afr. (sŭ'thēr-lănd)	222	32.25 S	20.40 E
Sutlej (R.), Pak.-India (sŭt'lĕj)	190	30.15 N	72.25 E

ng-sing; ŋ-baŋk; ɴ-nasalized n; nŏd; cŏmmit; ōld; ôbey; ôrder; oi-boil; fōōd; fŏŏt; ou-out; s-soft; sh-dish; th-thin; pūre; ûnite; ûrn; stŭd; circŭs; ü-as in French tu; '-indeterminate vowel.

352 Sutton – Taldom

PLACE (Pronunciation)	PAGE	Lat. °'	Long. °'
Sutton, Eng. (sut''n)	154b	51.21 N	0.12 W
Sutton, Ma.	103a	42.09 N	71.46 W
Sutton Coldfield, Eng. (kōld'fēld)	154	52.34 N	1.49 W
Sutton-in-Ashfield, Eng. (ĭn-ăsh'fēld)	154	53.07 N	1.15 W
Suurberge (Mts.), S. Afr.	223c	33.15 S	25.32 E
Suwa, Jap. (sōō'wä)	201	36.03 N	138.08 E
Suwanee L., Can.	99	56.08 N	100.10 W
Suwatki, Pol. (sōō-vou'kė)	165	54.05 N	22.58 E
Suwannee (R.), Fl.-Ga. (sōō-wô'nė)	124	29.42 N	83.00 W
Suways al Ḩulwah, Tur'at as (Can.), Egypt	219c	30.15 N	32.20 E
Su Xian, China (sōō shyĕn)	196	33.37 N	117.51 E
Suzdal', Sov. Un. (sōōz'dál)	172	56.26 N	40.29 E
Suzhou, China (sōō-jō)	196	31.19 N	120.37 E
Suzu Misaki (C.), Jap. (sōō'zōō mē'sä-kē)	200	37.30 N	137.35 E
Svalbard (Spitsbergen) (Is.), Eur. (sväl'bärt) (spĭts'bûr-gĕn)	174	77.00 N	20.00 E
Svaneke, Den. (svä'nĕ-kĕ)	162	55.08 N	15.07 E
Svatovo, Sov. Un. (svä'tô-vô)	173	49.23 N	38.10 E
Svedala, Swe. (svĕ'dä-lä)	162	55.29 N	13.11 E
Sveg, Swe.	162	62.03 N	14.22 E
Svelvik, Nor. (svĕl'vĕk)	162	59.37 N	10.18 E
Svenčionys, Sov. Un.	163	55.09 N	26.09 E
Svendborg, Den. (svĕn-bôrgh)	162	55.05 N	10.35 E
Svensen, Or. (svĕn'sĕn)	116c	46.10 N	123.39 W
Sverdlovsk, Sov. Un. (svĕrd-lôfsk')	180a	56.15 N	60.36 E
Svetlaya, Sov. Un. (svyĕt'lá-yá)	200	46.09 N	137.53 E
Svilajnac, Yugo. (svē'lá-ē-náts)	171	44.12 N	21.14 E
Svilengrad, Bul. (svĕl'ĕn-grát)	171	41.44 N	26.11 E
Svir' (R.), Sov. Un.	176	60.55 N	33.40 E
Svir Kanal (Can.), Sov. Un. (ká-näl')	163	60.10 N	32.40 E
Svishtov, Bul. (svĕsh'tôf)	171	43.36 N	25.21 E
Svisloch' (R.), Sov. Un. (svēs'lôk)	172	53.38 N	28.10 E
Svitavy, Czech.	164	49.46 N	16.28 E
Svitsa (R.), Sov. Un. (svĭ-tsá)	165	49.09 N	24.10 E
Svobodnyy, Sov. Un. (svô-bôd'nĭ)	179	51.28 N	128.28 E
Svolvaer, Nor. (svôl'vĕr)	156	68.15 N	14.29 E
Svyatoy Nos, Mys (C.), Sov. Un. (svyŭ'toi nôs)	179	72.18 N	139.28 E
Swadlincote, Eng. (swŏd'lĭn-kōt)	154	52.46 N	1.33 W
Swain Rfs., Austl. (swān)	211	22.12 S	152.08 E
Swainsboro, Ga. (swānz'bŭr-ô)	125	32.37 N	82.21 W
Swakopmund, Namibia (svä'kôp-mōōnt) (swá'kôp-mōōnd)	222	22.40 S	14.30 E
Swallowfield, Eng. (swŏl'ō-fēld)	154b	51.21 N	0.58 W
Swampscott, Ma. (swômp'skŏt)	103a	42.28 N	70.55 W
Swan, I., Austl. (swŏn)	207a	38.15 S	144.41 E
Swan (R.), Austl.	210	31.30 S	126.30 E
Swan (R.), Can.	99	51.58 N	101.45 W
Swan Hill, Austl.	212	35.20 S	143.30 E
Swan Hills, Can. (hĭlz)	97	54.52 N	115.45 W
Swan L., Can.	99	52.30 N	100.45 W
Swanland (Reg.), Austl. (swŏn'lănd)	210	31.45 S	119.15 E
Swan Ra., Mt.	115	47.50 N	113.40 W
Swan River, Can. (swŏn rĭv'ēr)	99	52.06 N	101.16 W
Swan R., Mt.	115	47.50 N	113.40 W
Swansea, Wales	160	51.37 N	3.59 W
Swansea, Il. (swŏn'sē)	117e	38.32 N	89.59 W
Swansea, Ma.	110b	41.45 N	71.09 W
Swanson Res., Ne. (swŏn'sŭn)	120	40.13 N	101.30 W
Swartberg (Mtn.), S. Afr.	223c	30.08 S	29.34 E
Swartkop (Mtn.), S. Afr.	222a	34.13 S	18.27 E
Swartruggens, S. Afr.	219d	25.59 S	26.40 E
Swartspruit, S. Afr.	223b	25.44 S	28.01 E
Swatow, see Shantou			
Swaziland, Afr. (Swä'zē-lănd)	222	26.45 S	31.30 E
Sweden, Eur. (swē'dĕn)	152	60.10 N	14.10 E
Swedesboro, NJ (swēdz'bē-rô)	110f	39.45 N	75.22 W
Sweetwater, Tn. (swēt'wô-tēr)	124	35.36 N	84.29 W
Sweetwater, Tx.	122	32.28 N	100.25 W
Sweetwater (L.), ND	112	48.15 N	98.35 W
Sweetwater Res., Ca.	118a	32.42 N	116.54 W
Sweetwater R., Wy.	115	42.19 N	108.35 W
Świdnica, Pol. (shvĭd-nē'tsá)	164	50.50 N	16.30 E
Świdwin, Pol. (shvĭd'vĭn)	164	53.46 N	15.48 E
Śweibodziec, Pol. (shvyĕN-bo'jĕts)	164	52.16 N	15.36 E
Świebodzin, Pol. (shvyăN-bôd'jĕn)	164	50.51 N	16.17 E
Swiecie, Pol. (shvyăN'tsyĕ)	165	53.23 N	18.26 E
Świętokrzyskie Góry (Mts.), Pol. (shvyĕN-tō-kzhĭ'skyĕ gōō'rĭ)	165	50.57 N	21.02 E
Swift (R.), Eng.	154	52.26 N	1.08 W
Swift (R.), Me. (swĭft)	102	44.42 N	70.40 E
Swift Current, Can. (swĭft kŭr'ĕnt)	98	50.17 N	107.50 W
Swift Res., Wa.	114	46.03 N	122.10 W
Swindle I., Can.	96	52.32 N	128.35 W
Swindon, Eng. (swĭn'dŭn)	160	51.35 N	1.55 W
Swinomish Ind. Res., Wa. (swĭ-nō'mĭsh)	116a	48.25 N	122.27 W
Świnoujście, Pol. (shvĭ-nĭ-ô-wĕsh'chyĕ)	164	53.56 N	14.14 E
Swinton, Eng. (swĭn'tŭn)	154	53.30 N	1.19 W
Swissvale, Pa. (swĭs'väl)	111e	40.25 N	79.53 W
Switzerland, Eur. (swĭt'zēr-lănd)	152	46.30 N	7.43 E
Syas' (R.), Sov. Un. (syäs)	172	59.28 N	33.24 E
Sycamore, Il. (sĭk'á-mōr)	113	42.00 N	88.42 W
Sychëvka, Sov. Un. (sē-chôf'ká)	172	55.52 N	34.18 E
Sydney, Austl. (sĭd'nē)	207b	33.55 S	151.17 E
Sydney, Can.	101	46.09 N	60.11 W
Sydney Mines, Can.	101	46.14 N	60.14 W
Syktyvkar, Sov. Un. (sük-tüf'kär)	176	61.35 N	50.40 E
Sylacauga, Al. (sĭl-á-kô'gá)	124	33.10 N	86.15 W
Sylarna (Mtn.), Swe.	162	63.00 N	12.10 E
Sylt I., F.R.G. (sĭlt)	164	54.55 N	8.30 E
Sylvania, Ga. (sĭl-vā'nĭ-á)	125	32.44 N	81.40 W
Sylvester, Ga. (sĭl-vĕs'tēr)	124	31.32 N	83.50 W
Syracuse, Ks. (sĭr'á-kūs)	120	37.59 N	101.44 W
Syracuse, NY	109	43.05 N	76.10 W
Syracuse, Ut.	117b	41.06 N	112.04 W
Syr-Dar'ya (R.), Sov. Un.	174	44.15 N	65.45 E
Syria, Asia (sĭr'ĭ-á)	188	35.00 N	37.15 E
Syrian Des. (Bādiyat ash Shām), Asia (sĭr'ĭ-ăn)	192	32.03 N	39.30 E
Sysert', Sov. Un. (sĕ'sĕrt)	180a	56.30 N	60.48 E
Syso'la (R.), Sov. Un.	176	60.50 N	50.40 E
Syzran', Sov. Un. (sĕz-rän')	177	53.10 N	48.10 E
Szamotuty, Pol. (shá-mô-tōō'wĕ)	164	52.36 N	16.34 E
Szarvas, Hung. (sôr'vôsh)	165	46.51 N	20.36 E
Szczebrzeszyn, Pol. (shchĕ-bzhă'shĕn)	165	50.41 N	22.58 E
Szczecin (Stettin), Pol. (shchĕ'tsĭn) (shtĕ-tēn')	164	53.25 N	14.35 E
Szczecinek, Pol. (shchĕ'tsĭ-nĕk)	164	53.41 N	16.42 E
Szczuczyn, Pol. (shchōō'chĕn)	165	53.32 N	22.17 E
Szczytno, Pol. (shchĭt'nô)	165	53.33 N	21.00 E
Szechwan Basin (Red), China	194	30.45 N	104.40 E
Szeged, Hung. (sĕ'gĕd)	165	46.15 N	20.12 E
Székesfehérvár, Hung. (sā'kĕsh-fē'hār-vär)	165	47.12 N	18.26 E
Szekszárd, Hung. (sĕk'särd)	165	46.19 N	18.42 E
Szentendre, Hung. (sĕnt'ĕn-drĕ)	165	47.40 N	19.07 E
Szentes, Hung. (sĕn'tĕsh)	165	46.38 N	20.18 E
Szigetvar, Hung. (sĕ'gĕt-vär)	165	46.05 N	17.50 E
Szolnok, Hung. (sôl'nôk)	165	47.11 N	20.12 E
Szombathely, Hung. (sôm'bôt-hĕl')	164	47.13 N	16.35 E
Szprotawa, Pol. (shprō-tä'vä)	164	51.34 N	15.29 E
Szydłowiec, Pol. (shid-wô'vyets)	165	51.13 N	20.53 E

T

PLACE (Pronunciation)	PAGE	Lat. °'	Long. °'
Taal (L.), Phil. (tä-äl')	203a	13.58 N	121.06 E
Tabaco, Phil. (tä-bä'kō)	203a	13.27 N	123.40 E
Tabankulu, S. Afr. (tä-bän-kōō'la)	223c	30.56 S	29.19 E
Tabasara, Serrania de (Ra.), Pan. (sĕr-rä-nē'ä dā tä-bä-sä'rä)	131	8.29 N	81.22 W
Tabasco, Mex. (tä-bäs'kô)	128	21.47 N	103.04 W
Tabasco (State), Mex.	129	18.10 N	83.00 W
Taber, Can.	97	49.47 N	112.08 W
Tablas (I.), Phil. (tä'bläs)	203a	12.26 N	112.15 E
Tablas Str., Phil.	203a	12.17 N	121.41 E
Table B., S. Afr. (tā'b'l)	222a	33.41 S	18.27 E
Table Mt., S. Afr.	222a	33.58 S	18.26 E
Table Rock Lake, Mo.	121	36.37 N	93.29 W
Tabligbo, Togo	224	6.35 N	1.30 E
Taboga (I.), Pan. (tä-bō'gä)	126a	8.48 N	79.35 W
Taboguilla (I.), Pan. (tä-bō-gē'l-yä)	126a	8.48 N	79.31 W
Taboleiro (Plat.), Braz. (tä-bô-lā'rō)	141	9.34 S	39.22 W
Tábor, Czech. (tä'bôr)	164	49.25 N	14.40 E
Tabora, Tan. (tä-bō'rä)	227	5.01 S	32.48 E
Tabou, Ivory Coast (tá-bōō')	224	4.25 N	7.21 W
Tabrīz, Iran (tá-brēz')	192	38.00 N	46.13 E
Tacámbaro (R.), Mex. (tä-käm'bä-rō)	128	18.55 N	101.25 W
Tacambaro de Codallos, Mex. (dā kô-däl'yōs)	128	19.12 N	101.28 W
Tacaná (Vol.), Mex.-Guat. (tä-kä-nä')	130	15.09 N	92.07 W
Tacarigua, Laguna de la (L.), Ven. (lä-gōō'nä-dĕ-lä-tä-kä-rē'gwä)	141b	10.18 N	65.43 W
Tacheng, China (tä-chŭŋ)	194	46.50 N	83.24 E
Tachie (R.), Can.	96	54.30 N	125.00 W
Tacloban, Phil. (tä-klō'bän)	203	11.06 N	124.58 E
Tacna, Peru (täk'nä)	140	18.34 S	70.16 W
Tacoma, Wa. (tá-kō'má)	116a	47.14 N	122.27 W
Taconic Ra., NY (tá-kŏn'ĭk)	109	41.55 N	73.40 W
Tacotalpa, Mex. (tä-kô-täl'pä)	129	17.37 N	92.51 W
Tacotalpa (R.), Mex.	129	17.24 N	92.38 W
Tacuarembó, Ur. (tä-kwä-rĕm'bô)	142	31.44 S	55.56 W
Tademaït, Plat. du, Alg. (tä-dē-mä'ēt)	220	28.00 N	2.15 E
Tadio, Lagune (Lagoon), Ivory Coast	224	5.20 N	5.25 W
Tadjoura, Djibouti (tád-zhōō'rá)	219a	11.48 N	42.54 E
Tadley, Eng. (tăd'lē)	154b	51.19 N	1.08 W
Tadó, Col. (tä-dō')	140a	5.15 N	76.30 W
Tadotsu, Jap. (tä'dô-tsōō)	201	34.14 N	133.43 E
Tadoussac, Can. (tá-dōō-sák')	101	48.09 N	69.43 W
Tadzhik (S. S. R.), Sov. Un. (tát'zhĕk)	174	39.22 N	69.30 E
Taebaek Sanmaek (Mts.), Kor. (tī-bĭk' sän-mĭk')	200	37.20 N	128.50 E
Taedong R., Kor. (tī-dŏng)	200	38.38 N	124.32 E
Taegu, Kor. (tī'gōō')	200	35.49 N	128.41 E
Tafalla, Sp. (tä-fäl'yä)	168	42.30 N	1.42 W
Tafna (R.), Alg. (táf'nä)	169	35.28 N	1.00 W
Taft, Ca. (táft)	118	35.09 N	119.27 W
Tagama (Reg.), Niger	225	15.50 N	6.30 E
Taganrog, Sov. Un. (tá-gán-rôk')	173	47.13 N	38.44 E
Taganrogskiy Zaliv (B.), Sov. Un. (tá-gán-rôk'skĭ zä'lĭf)	173	46.55 N	38.17 E
Tagula (I.), Pap. N. Gui. (tä'gōō-lá)	211	11.45 S	153.46 E
Tagus (Tajo) (R.), Sp. (tā'gŭs)	168	39.40 N	5.07 W
Tagus (R.), Port.	168	39.23 N	8.01 W
Tahan, Gunong (Pk.), Mala.	202	4.33 N	101.52 E
Tahat, Mt., Alg. (tä-hät')	220	23.22 N	5.21 E
Tahiti (I.), Fr. Polynesia (tä-hē'tē) (tä'ē-tē')	205	17.30 S	149.30 W
Tahkuna Nina, Sov. Un. (tàh-kōō'ná nē'ná)	163	59.08 N	22.03 E
Tahlequah, Ok. (tă-lĕ-kwä')	121	35.54 N	94.58 W
Tahoe (L.), Ca.-Nv. (tä'hō)	118	39.09 N	120.18 W
Tahoua, Niger (tä'ōō-ä)	225	14.54 N	5.16 E
Ṭahṭā, Egypt (tä'tä)	219b	26.48 N	31.29 E
Tahtsa (L.), Can. (tŏt'-sä-pĕk)	96	53.33 N	127.47 W
Tahuya, Wa. (tá-hū-yä')	116a	47.23 N	123.03 W
Tahuya (R.), Wa.	116a	47.28 N	122.55 W
Tai'an, China (tī-än)	196	36.13 N	117.08 E
Taibai Shan (Mtn.), China (tī-bī shän)	198	33.42 N	107.25 E
Taibus Qi, China (tī-bōō-sz chyē)	198	41.52 N	115.25 E
Taicang, China (tī-tsäŋ)	197b	31.26 N	121.06 E
T'aichung, Taiwan (tī'chōōng)	199	24.10 N	120.42 E
Tai'erzhuang, China (tī-är-jŭäŋ)	196	34.34 N	117.44 E
Taigu, China (tī-gōō)	198	37.25 N	112.35 E
Taihang Shan (Mts.), China (tī-häŋ shän)	198	35.45 N	112.00 E
Taihe, China (tī-hŭ)	196	33.10 N	115.38 E
Tai Hu (L.), China (tī hōō)	196	31.13 N	120.00 E
Tailagein Khara (Reg.), Mong. (tī'lá-gān' kä'rä)	194	43.39 N	105.54 E
Tailai, China (tī-lī)	198	46.20 N	123.10 E
Tailem Bend, Austl. (tā-lĕm)	212	35.15 S	139.30 E
Taimyr, P-Ov (Pen.), see Taymyr			
T'ainan, Taiwan (tī'nan')	199	23.08 N	120.18 E
Tainaron, Akra (C.), Grc.	159	36.20 N	21.20 E
Taínaron, Ákra (C.), Grc.	171	37.45 N	22.00 E
Taining, China (tī'nĭng')	199	26.58 N	117.15 E
T'aipei, Taiwan (tī'pā')	199	25.02 N	121.38 E
Taiping, Mala.	202	4.56 N	100.39 E
Taiping, Ling (Mtn.), China (lĭŋ tī-pĭŋ)	198	47.03 N	120.30 E
Taira, see Iwaki			
Taisha, Jap. (tī'shä)	201	35.23 N	132.40 E
Taishan, China (tī-shän)	199	22.15 N	112.50 E
Tai Shan (Mtn.), China (tī shän)	196	36.16 N	117.05 E
Taishet, see Tayshet			
Taitao, Peninsula de, Chile (pĕ-nē'ng-sōō-lä-dĕ-tä-ē-tä'ō)	142	46.20 S	77.15 W
T'aitung, Taiwan (tī'tōōng')	199	22.45 N	121.02 E
Taiwan (Formosa), Asia (tī-wän) (fŏr-mō'sá)	189	23.30 N	122.20 E
Tai Xian, China (tī shyĕn)	196	32.31 N	119.54 E
Taixing, China (tī-shyĭŋ)	196	32.12 N	119.58 E
Taiyuan, China (tī-yŭän)	198	37.32 N	112.38 E
Taizhou, China (tī-jō)	196	32.23 N	119.41 E
Tajano de Morais, Braz. (tĕ-zhä'nô-dĕ-mô-rä'ēs)	139a	22.05 S	42.04 W
Tajo (R.), see Tagus			
Tajumulco (Vol.), Guat. (tä-hōō-mōōl'kô)	130	15.03 N	91.53 W
Tajuña (R.), Sp. (tä-kōō'n-yä)	168	40.23 N	2.36 W
Tājūrā', Libya	158	32.56 N	13.24 W
Tak, Thai.	202	16.57 N	99.12 E
Taka (I.), Jap. (tä'kä)	201	30.47 N	130.23 E
Takada, Jap. (tä'ká-dä)	201	37.08 N	138.30 E
Takahashi, Jap. (tä'kä'hä-shĭ)'	201	34.47 N	133.35 E
Takaishi, Jap.	201b	34.32 N	135.27 E
Takamatsu, Jap. (tä'kä'mä-tsōō')	201	34.20 N	134.02 E
Takamori, Jap. (tä'kä'mô-rē')	201	32.50 N	131.08 E
Takaoka, Jap. (ta'kä'ō-kä')	201	36.45 N	136.59 E
Takapuna, N.A.	213	36.48 S	174.47 E
Takarazuka, Jap. (tä'kä-rä-zōō'kä)	201b	34.48 N	135.22 E
Takasaki, Jap. (tä'kät'sōō-kē')	201	36.20 N	139.00 E
Takatsu (Mizonokuchi), Jap. (tä-kät'sōō) (mē'zō-nō-kōō'chē)	201a	35.36 N	139.37 E
Takatsuki, Jap. (tä'kät'sōō-kē')	201b	34.51 N	135.38 E
Takaungu, Ken. (tä'kä'ōōŋ-gōō')	191	3.41 S	39.48 E
Takayama, Jap. (tä'kä'yä'mä)	201	36.11 N	137.16 E
Takefu, Jap. (tä'kĕ-fōō)	201	35.57 N	136.09 E
Takla L., Can.	96	55.25 N	125.53 W
Takla Makan (Des.), China (mä-kän')	194	39.22 N	82.34 E
Takoma Park, Md. (tă'kōmă pärk)	110e	38.59 N	77.00 W
Takum, Nig.	225	7.17 N	9.59 E
Tala, Mex. (tä'lä)	128	20.39 N	103.42 W
Talagante, Chile (tä-lä-gä'n-tĕ)	139b	33.39 S	70.54 W
Talanga, Hond. (tä-lä'n-gä)	130	14.21 N	87.09 W
Talara, Peru (tä-lä'rä)	140	4.32 S	81.17 W
Talasea, Pap. N. Gui. (tä-lä-sä'ä)	203	5.20 S	150.00 E
Talata Mafara, Nig.	225	12.35 N	6.04 E
Talaud, Kepulauan (Is.), Indon. (tä-lout')	203	4.17 N	127.30 E
Talavera de la Reina, Sp. (tä-lä-vā'rä dā lä rå-ē'nä)	168	39.58 N	4.51 W
Talawdī, Sud.	221	10.41 N	30.21 E
Talca, Chile (täl'kä)	139b	35.25 S	71.39 W
Talca (Prov.), Chile	139b	35.23 S	71.15 W
Talca, Punta (Pt.), Chile (pōō'n-tä-täl'kä)	137b	33.25 S	71.42 W
Talcahuano, Chile (täl-kä-wä'nō)	142	36.41 S	73.05 W
Taldom, Sov. Un. (täl-dôm)	172	56.44 N	37.33 E

ăt; finăl; rāte; senāte; ärm; åsk; sofá; fâre; ch-choose; dh-as th in other; bē; ēvent; bĕt; recĕnt; cratēr; g-gō; gh-guttural g; bĭt; ĭ-short neutral; rīde; K-guttural k as ch in German ich;

PRONOUNCING INDEX

Taldy-Kurgan – Tchigai 353

PLACE (Pronunciation)	PAGE	Lat. °′	Long. °′
Taldy-Kurgan, Sov. Un. (tȧl′dĭ-ko͞or-gän′)	178	45.03 N	77.18 E
Talea de Castro (San Miguel), Mex. (tä′lā́-ä dā käs′trō)	129	17.22 N	96.14 W
Talibu, Pulau (I.), Indon.	203	1.30 S	125.00 E
Talim (I.), Phil. (tä-lēm′)	203a	14.21 N	121.14 E
Talisay, Phil. (tä-lē′sī)	203a	14.08 N	122.56 E
Talkeetna, Ak. (tȧl-kēt′nȧ)	105	62.18 N	150.02 W
Talkheh Rūd (R.), Iran	177	38.00 N	46.50 E
Talladega, Al. (tăl-ȧ-dē′gȧ)	124	33.25 N	86.06 W
Tallahassee, Fl. (tăl-ȧ-hăs′ḗ)	124	30.25 N	84.17 W
Tallahatchie (R.), Ms. (tal-ȧ hăch′ḗ)	124	34.21 N	90.03 W
Tallapoosa, Ga. (tăl-ȧ-po͞o′sȧ)	124	33.44 N	85.15 W
Tallapoosa (R.), Al.	124	32.22 N	86.08 W
Tallassee, Al. (tăl′ȧ-sḗ)	124	32.30 N	85.54 W
Tallinn (Reval), Sov. Un. (tȧl′lḗn) (rā′väl)	163	59.26 N	24.44 E
Tallmadge, Oh. (tăl′mĭj)	111d	41.06 N	81.26 W
Tallulah, La. (tă-lo͞o′lȧ)	123	32.25 N	91.13 W
Talmanca, Cord. de (Mts.), C. R. (kȯr-dēl-yĕ′rä-dĕ-täl-mä′n-kä)	131	9.37 N	83.55 W
Tal′noye, Sov. Un. (tȧl′nȯ-yĕ)	173	48.52 N	30.43 E
Talo (Mt.), Eth.	221	10.45 N	37.55 E
Taloje Budrukh, India	191b	19.05 N	73.05 E
Talpa de Allende, Mex. (täl′pä dā äl-yĕn′dā́)	128	20.25 N	104.48 W
Talsi, Sov. Un. (tal′sĭ)	163	57.16 N	22.35 E
Taltal, Chile (täl-täl′)	142	25.26 S	70.32 W
Taly, Sov. Un. (täl′ĭ)	173	49.51 N	40.07 E
Tama, Ia. (tā′mä)	113	41.57 N	92.36 W
Tama (R.), Jap.	201a	35.38 N	139.35 E
Tamale, Ghana (tä-mä′lā́)	224	9.25 N	0.50 W
Taman′, Sov. Un. (tȧ-män″)	173	45.13 N	36.46 E
Tamaná, Cerro (Mtn.), Col. (sĕ′r-rȯ-tä-mä-nȧ′)	140a	5.06 N	76.10 W
Tamanaco (R.), Ven. (tä-mä-nä′kō)	141b	9.32 N	66.00 W
Tamanrasset (R.), Alg. (tä-män-räs′sĕt)	220	22.15 N	2.51 E
Tamanrasset, Alg.	220	22.34 N	5.34 E
Tamaqua, Pa. (tȧ-mô′kwă)	109	40.45 N	75.50 W
Tamar (R.), Eng. (tā′mär)	160	50.35 N	4.15 W
Tamarite de Litera, Sp. (tä-mä-rē′tā)	169	41.52 N	0.24 E
Tamaulipas (State), Mex. (tä-mä-o͞o-lē′päs′)	128	23.45 N	98.30 W
Tamazula de Gordiano, Mex. (tä-mä-zo͞o′lä dā gôr-dḗ-ä′nȯ)	128	19.44 N	103.09 W
Tamazulapan del Progreso, Mex. (tä-mä-zo͞o-lä′päm-dĕl-prȯ-grĕ-sō)	129	17.41 N	97.34 W
Tamazunchale, Mex. (tä-mä-zo͝on-chä′lā́)	128	21.16 N	98.46 W
Tambacounda, Senegal (täm-bä-ko͞on′dä)	224	13.47 N	13.40 W
Tambador, Serra do (Mts.), Braz. (sĕ′r-rä-dȯ-täm′bä-dōr)	141	10.33 S	41.16 W
Tambelan, Kepulauan (Is.), Indon. (täm-bā́-län′)	202	0.38 N	107.38 E
Tambo, Austl. (tăm′bō)	212	24.50 S	146.15 E
Tambov, Sov. Un. (tȧm-bôf′)	177	52.45 N	41.10 E
Tambov (Oblast), Sov. Un.	172	52.50 N	40.42 E
Tambre (R.), Sp. (täm′brā)	168	42.59 N	8.33 W
Tambura, Sud. (täm-bo͞o′rä)	221	5.34 N	27.30 E
Tame (R.), Eng. (tām)	154	52.41 N	1.42 W
Tâmega (R.), Port. (tȧ-mā′gȧ)	168	41.30 N	7.45 W
Tamesí (R.), Mex. (tä-mĕ-sḗ′)	128	22.36 N	98.32 W
Tamgak, Monts (Mtn.), Niger (tam-gäk′)	225	18.40 N	8.40 E
Tamgue, Massif du (Mtn.), Gui.	224	12.15 N	12.35 W
Tamiahua, Mex. (tä-myä-wä)	129	21.17 N	97.26 W
Tamiahua, Laguna (L.), Mex. (lä-go͞o′nä-tä-myä-wä)	129	21.38 N	97.33 W
Tamiami, Can., Fl. (tă-mī-ăm′ĭ)	125a	25.52 N	80.08 W
Tamil Nadu (State), India	191	11.30 N	78.00 E
Tammisaari, see Ekenäs			
Tampa, Fl. (tăm′pȧ)	125a	27.57 N	82.25 W
Tampa B., Fl.	125a	27.35 N	82.38 W
Tampere, Fin. (tȧm′pĕ-rĕ)	156	61.21 N	23.39 E
Tampico, Mex. (täm-pē′kō)	129	22.14 N	97.51 W
Tampico Alto, Mex. (täm-pē′kō äl′tō)	129	22.07 N	97.48 W
Tampin, Mala.	189b	2.28 N	102.15 E
Tamuín, Mex. (tä-mo͞o-ḗ′n)	128	22.04 N	98.47 W
Tamworth, Austl. (tăm′wûrth)	212	31.01 S	151.00 E
Tamworth, Eng.	154	52.58 N	1.41 W
Tana (R.), Ken. (tä′nä)	227	2.00 S	40.15 E
Tana (I.), Vanuatu	211	19.32 S	169.27 E
Tana (R.), Nor.-Fin.	156	69.20 N	24.54 E
Tanabe, Jap. (tä-nä′bā)	201	33.45 N	135.21 E
Tanabe, Jap.	201b	34.49 N	135.46 E
Tanacross, Ak. (tă′nȧ-crōs)	105	63.20 N	143.30 W
Tanaga (I.), Ak. (tä-nä′gä)	105a	51.28 N	178.10 W
Tanahbala, Pulau (I.), Indon. (tȧ-nä-bä′lä)	202	0.30 S	98.22 E
Tanahmasa, Pulau (I.), Indon. (tȧ-nä-mä′sä)	202	0.03 S	97.30 E
Tanakpur, India (tăn′ăk-po͝or)	190	29.10 N	80.07 E
Tana L., Eth.	221	12.09 N	36.41 E
Tanami, Austl. (tȧ-nā′mḗ)	210	19.45 S	129.50 E
Tanana, Ak. (tă′nȧ-nô)	105	65.18 N	152.20 W
Tanana (R.), Ak.	105	64.26 N	148.40 W
Tanaro (R.), It. (tä-nä′rô)	170	44.45 N	8.02 E
Tanashi, Jap.	201a	35.44 N	139.34 E
Tanbu, China (tän-bo͞o)	197a	23.20 N	113.06 E
Tancheng, China (tän-chŭŋ)	196	34.37 N	118.22 E
Tanchŏn, Kor. (tän′chŭn)	200	40.29 N	128.50 E
Tancítaro, Mex. (tän-sē′tä-rō)	128	19.16 N	102.24 W
Tancítaro, Cerro de, Mex. (sĕ′r-rȯ-dĕ)	128	19.24 N	102.19 W
Tancoco, Mex. (tän-kō′kō)	129	21.16 N	99.45 W
Tandil, Arg. (tän-dēl′)	130	36.16 S	59.01 W
Tandil, Sierra del (Mts.), Arg.	130	38.40 S	59.40 W
Tanega (I.), Jap. (tä′nā́-gä′)	201	30.36 N	131.11 E
Tanezrouft (Reg.), Alg. (tä′nĕz-ro͝oft)	220	24.17 N	0.30 W
Tang (R.), China (täŋ)	196	33.38 N	117.29 E
Tang (R.), China	196	39.13 N	114.45 E
Tanga, Tan. (tăŋ′gȧ)	227	5.04 S	39.06 E
Tangancícuaro, Mex. (täŋ-gän-sē′kwa»um rȯ)	128	19.52 N	102.13 W
Tanganyika, L., Afr.	227	5.15 S	29.40 E
Tanger (Tangier), Mor. (tăn-jēr′)	220	35.52 N	5.55 W
Tangermünde, G.D.R. (täŋ′ĕr-mün′de)	164	52.33 N	11.58 E
Tanggu, China (täŋ-go͞o)	196	39.04 N	117.41 E
Tanggula Shan (Mts.), China (täŋ-go͞o-lä shän)	194	33.15 N	89.07 E
Tangho, China	198	32.40 N	112.50 E
Tangier, see Tanger			
Tangipahoa R., La. (tăn′jḗ-pȧ-hō′ȧ)	123	30.48 N	90.28 W
Tangra Yumco (L.), China (täŋ-rä yo͞om-tswo)	190	30.50 N	85.40 E
T′angshan, China	196	39.38 N	118.11 E
Tang Xian, China (täŋ shyĕn)	196	38.09 N	115.00 E
Tangzha, China (täŋ-jä)	196	32.06 N	120.48 E
Tanimbar, Kepulauan (Is.), Indon.	203	8.00 S	132.00 E
Tanjong (C.), Mala.	189b	1.53 N	102.29 E
Tanjong Piai (I.), Mala.	189b	1.16 N	103.11 E
Tanjong Ramunia (C.), Mala.	189b	1.27 N	104.44 E
Tanjungbalai, Indon. (tän′jông-bä′lā́)	189b	1.00 N	103.26 E
Tanjungkarand, Indon.	202	5.16 S	105.06 E
Tanjungpandan, Indon.	202	2.47 S	107.51 E
Tanjungpinang, Indon. (tän′jŏng-pē′näng)	189b	0.55 N	104.29 E
Tankābon, Iran	177	36.40 N	51.00 E
Tannu-Ola (Mts.), Sov. Un.	175	51.00 N	94.00 E
Tannūrah, Ra′s al (C.), Sau. Ar.	192	26.45 N	49.59 E
Tano (R.), Ghana	224	5.40 N	2.30 W
Tanquijo, Arrecife (Reef), Mex. (är-rĕ-sē′fĕ-tän-kḗ′kô)	129	21.07 N	97.16 W
Ţanţā, Egypt (tän′tä)	219b	30.50 N	31.00 E
Tantoyuca, Mex. (tän-tō-yo͞o′kä)	128	21.22 N	98.13 W
Tanyang, Kor.	200	36.53 N	128.20 E
Tanzania, Afr.	218	6.48 S	33.58 E
Tao (R.), China (tou)	198	35.30 N	103.40 E
Tao′an, China (tou-än)	198	45.15 N	122.45 E
Tao′er (R.), China (tou-är)	198	45.40 N	122.00 E
Taormina, It. (tä-ôr-mē′nä)	170	37.53 N	15.18 E
Taos, NM (tä′ȯs)	119	36.25 N	105.35 W
Taoudenni, Mali (tä′o͞o-dĕ-nḗ′)	220	22.57 N	3.37 W
Taoussa, Mali	224	16.55 N	0.35 W
Taoyuan, China (tou-yū́än)	199	29.00 N	111.15 E
Tapa, Sov. Un. (tȧ′pȧ)	163	59.16 N	25.56 E
Tapachula, Mex.	130	14.55 N	92.20 W
Tapajós (R.), Braz. (tä-pä-zhô′s)	141	3.27 S	55.33 W
Tapalque, Arg. (tä-päl-kĕ′)	139c	36.22 S	60.05 W
Tapanatepec, Mex. (tä-pä-nä-tĕ-pĕk)	129	16.22 N	94.19 W
Tāpi (R.), India	190	21.33 N	74.30 E
Tappi Saki (C.), Jap. (täp′pḗ sä′kḗ)	200	41.05 N	139.40 E
Tapps (L.), Wa. (tăpz)	116a	47.20 N	122.12 W
Taqātu′ Hayyā, Sud.	221	18.10 N	36.17 E
Taquara, Serra de (Mts.), Braz. (sĕ′r-rä-dĕ-tä-kwä′rä)	141	15.28 S	54.33 W
Taquari (R.), Braz. (tä-kwä′rĭ)	141	18.35 S	56.50 W
Tar (R.), NC (tär)	125	35.58 N	78.06 W
Tara, Sov. Un. (tä′rȧ)	178	56.58 N	74.13 E
Tara (I.), Phil. (tä′rä)	203a	12.18 N	120.28 E
Tara (R.), Sov. Un. (tä′rȧ)	178	56.32 N	76.13 E
Ţarābulus (Tripoli), Leb. (tȧ-rä′bo͞o-lo͞os)	189a	34.25 N	35.50 E
Tarābulus (Tripoli), Libya	221	32.50 N	13.13 E
Tarābulus (Tripolitania) (Prov.), Libya	221	31.00 N	12.26 E
Tarakan, Indon.	202	3.17 N	118.04 E
Tarancón, Sp. (tä-rän-kōn′)	168	40.01 N	3.00 W
Taranto, It. (tä′rän-tô)	170	40.30 N	17.15 E
Taranto, Golfo di (G.), It. (gȯl-fō-dē tä′rän-tô)	170	40.03 N	17.10 E
Tarapoto, Peru (tä-rä-pȯ′tō)	140	6.29 S	76.26 W
Tarare, Fr. (tȧ-rär′)	166	45.55 N	4.23 E
Tarascon, Fr. (tȧ-rȧs-kôɴ′)	166	42.53 N	1.35 E
Tarascon, Fr. (tä-räs-kôɴ)	166	43.47 N	4.41 E
Tarashcha, Sov. Un. (tä′rȧsh-chȧ)	173	49.34 N	30.52 E
Tarata, Bol. (tä-rä′tä)	140	17.43 S	66.00 W
Taravo (R.), Fr.	170	41.54 N	8.58 E
Tarazit, Massif de (Mts.), Niger	225	20.05 N	7.35 E
Tarazona, Sp. (tä-rä-thō′nä)	168	41.54 N	1.45 W
Tarazona de la Mancha, Sp. (tä-rä-zȯ′nä-dĕ-lä-mä′n-chä)	168	39.13 N	1.50 W
Tarbat Ness (Hd.), Scot. (tȧr′bȧt)	160	57.51 N	3.50 W
Tarbes, Fr. (tȧrb)	166	43.04 N	0.05 E
Tarboro, NC (tär′bŭr-ȯ)	125	35.53 N	77.34 W
Tarbū, Libya	221	26.07 N	15.49 E
Taree, Austl. (tă-rē′)	212	31.52 S	152.21 E
Tarentum, Pa. (tȧ-rĕn′tŭm)	111e	40.36 N	79.44 W
Tarfa, Wādī at, Egypt	219b	28.14 N	31.00 E
Tarfaya, Mor.	220	27.58 N	12.55 W
Tarija, Bol. (tär-rē′hä)	140	21.42 S	64.52 W
Tarīm, P. D. R. of Yem. (tȧ-rĭm′)	192	16.13 N	49.08 E
Tarim (R.), China (tȧ-rĭm′)	194	40.45 N	85.39 E
Tarim Basin, China (tȧ-rĭm′)	194	39.52 N	82.34 E
Tarks (R.), S. Afr. (tä′kȧ)	223c	32.15 S	26.00 E
Tarkastad, S. Afr.	223c	32.01 S	26.18 E
Tarkhankut, Mys (C.), Sov. Un. (mĭs tȧr-ᴋän′ko͝ot)	173	45.18 N	32.08 E
Tarkio, Mo. (tär′kĭ-ō)	121	40.27 N	95.22 W
Tarkwa, Ghana (tärk′wä)	224	5.19 N	1.59 W
Tarlac, Phil. (tär′läk)	203	15.29 N	120.36 E
Tarlton, S. Afr. (tärl′tŭn)	223b	26.05 S	27.38 E
Tarma, Peru (tär′mä)	140	11.26 S	75.40 W
Tarn (R.), Fr. (tärn)	166	44.03 N	2.41 E
Târnava Mica R., Rom. (tĕr-nä′vȧ mē′kŏ)	167	46.17 N	24.20 E
Tarnów, Pol. (tär′no͝of)	167	50.02 N	21.00 E
Taro (R.), It. (tä′rō)	170	44.41 N	10.03 E
Taroudant, Mor. (tȧ-ro͞o-dänt′)	220	30.39 N	8.52 W
Tarpon Springs, Fl. (tär′pŏn)	125a	28.07 N	82.44 W
Tarporley, Eng. (tär′pēr-lḗ)	154	53.09 N	2.40 W
Tarpum B., Ba. (tär′pŭm)	133	25.05 N	76.20 W
Tarquinia (Corneto), It. (tär-kwē′nḗ-ä) (kôr-nā′tô)	170	42.16 N	11.46 E
Tarragona, Sp. (tär-rä-gō′nä)	169	41.05 N	1.15 E
Tarrant, Al. (tăr′ănt)	110h	33.35 N	86.46 W
Tarrasa, Sp. (tär-rä′sä)	169	41.34 N	2.01 E
Tárrega, Sp. (tä rā́-gä)	169	41.40 N	1.09 E
Tarrejón de Ardoz, Sp. (tär-rĕ-ᴋȯ′n-dĕ-är-dȯz)	169a	40.28 N	3.2[illegible]
Tarrytown, NY (tär′ĭ-toun)	110a	41.04 N	73.52 W
Tarsus, Tur. (tȧr′so͞os) (tär′sŭs)	177	37.00 N	34.50 E
Tartagal, Arg. (tär-tä-gȧ′l)	142	23.31 S	63.47 W
Tartu (Dorpat), Sov. Un. (tär′to͞o) (dôr′pät)	172	58.23 N	26.44 E
Ţarţūs, Egypt	159	34.54 N	35.59 E
Tarumi, Jap. (tä′ro͞o-mḗ)	201b	34.38 N	135.04 E
Tarusa, Sov. Un. (tä-ro͞os′ȧ)	172	54.43 N	37.11 E
Tarzana, Ca. (tär-ză′ȧ)	117a	34.10 N	118.32 W
Tashauz, Sov. Un. (tŭ-shŭ-o͞os′)	153	41.50 N	59.45 E
Tashkent, Sov. Un. (tȧsh′kĕnt)	178	41.23 N	69.04 E
Tasman B., N. Z. (tăz′măn)	213	40.50 S	173.20 E
Tasmania (State), Austl. (tăz-mā′nĭ-ȧ)	212	38.20 S	146.30 E
Tasmania (I.), Austl.	211	41.28 S	142.30 E
Tasman Pen, Austl.	212	43.00 S	148.30 E
Tasman Sea, Oceania	204	29.30 S	155.00 E
Tasquillo, Mex. (täs-kē′lyō)	128	20.34 N	99.21 W
Tassili-n-Ajjer (Plat.), Alg. (tā́s′ḗ-lḗ ä′jĕr)	220	25.40 N	6.57 E
Tatar (A. S. S. R.), Sov. Un. (tȧ-tär′)	176	55.30 N	51.00 E
Tatarsk, Sov. Un. (tȧ-tärsk′)	178	55.15 N	75.00 E
Tatar Str., Sov. Un.	179	51.00 N	141.45 E
Tater Hill (Mtn.), Or. (tāt′ēr hĭl)	116c	45.47 N	123.02 W
Tateyama, Jap. (tä′tḗ-yä′mä)	201	35.04 N	139.52 E
Tatlow, Mt., Can.	96	51.23 N	123.52 W
Tatuí, Braz. (tä-to͞o-ē′)	139a	23.21 S	47.49 W
Tau, Nor.	162	59.05 N	5.59 E
Taubaté, Braz. (tou-bȧ-tā′)	139a	23.03 S	45.32 W
Tauern Tun, Aus.	164	47.12 N	13.17 E
Taung, S. Afr. (tä′o͞ong)	222	27.25 S	24.47 E
Taunton, Ma. (tän′tŭn)	110b	41.54 N	71.03 W
Taunton R., RI	110b	41.50 N	71.02 W
Taupo, L., N. Z. (tä′o͞o-pō)	213	38.42 S	175.55 E
Taurage, Sov. Un. (tou′rȧ-gā)	163	55.15 N	22.18 E
Taurus Mts., see Toros Dağlari			
Tauste, Sp. (tä-o͞os′tā́)	168	41.55 N	1.15 W
Tavda, Sov. Un. (tȧv-dȧ′)	178	58.00 N	64.44 E
Tavda (R.), Sov. Un.	176	59.20 N	63.28 E
Taverny, Fr. (tȧ-vēr-nē′)	167b	49.02 N	2.13 E
Taviche, Mex. (tä-vḗ′chĕ)	129	16.43 N	96.35 W
Tavira, Port. (tä-vē′rȧ)	168	37.09 N	7.42 W
Tavoy, Bur.	202	14.04 N	98.19 E
Tavşanli, Tur. (tȧv′shän-lĭ)	177	39.30 N	29.30 E
Tawakoni (L.), Tx.	123	32.51 N	95.59 W
Tawaramoto, Jap. (tä′wä-rä-mȯ-tȯ)	201b	34.33 N	135.48 E
Tawas City, Mi.	108	44.15 N	83.30 W
Tawas Pt., Mi. (tô′wȧs)	108	44.15 N	83.25 W
Tawitawi Group (Is.), Phil. (tä′wḗ-tä′wḗ)	202	4.52 N	120.35 E
Tawkar, Sud.	221	18.28 N	37.46 E
Taxco de Alarcón, Mex. (täs′kō dĕ ä-lär-kȯ′n)	128	18.34 N	99.37 W
Tay, Loch (L.), Scot.	160	56.25 N	5.07 W
Tay (R.), Scot.	160	56.35 N	3.37 W
Tayabas B., Phil. (tä-yä′bäs)	203a	13.44 N	121.40 E
Tayga, Sov. Un. (tī′gä)	178	56.12 N	85.47 E
Taygonos, Mys (Taigonos) (C.), Sov. Un.	179	60.37 N	160.17 E
Taylor, Tx.	123	30.35 N	97.25 W
Taylor, Mt., NM	119	35.20 N	107.40 W
Taylorville, Il. (tā′lēr-vĭl)	108	39.30 N	89.20 W
Taymā, Sua. Ar.	192	27.45 N	38.55 E
Taymyr (Taimyr) (L.), Sov. Un. (tī-mĭr′)	179	74.13 N	100.45 E
Taymyr, P-Ov (Taimyr) (Pen.), Sov. Un.	178	75.15 N	95.00 E
Tayshet (Taishet), Sov. Un. (tī-shĕt′)	178	56.09 N	97.49 E
Taytay, Phil (tī-tī)	178	10.37 N	119.10 E
Tayung, Phil. (tā-yo͞ong′)	203a	16.01 N	120.45 E
Taz (R.), Sov. Un. (tȧz)	178	67.15 N	80.45 E
Taza, Mor. (tä′zä)	220	34.08 N	4.00 W
Tazovskoye, Sov. Un.	178	66.58 N	78.28 E
Tbilisi, Sov. Un. (′tbĭl-yē′sē)	177	41.40 N	44.45 E
Tchibanga, Gabon (chḗ-bäŋ′gä)	226	2.51 S	11.02 E
Tchien, Lib.	224	6.04 N	8.08 W
Tchigai, Plat. du (Plat.), Chad-Niger	225	21.20 N	14.50 E

ng-sing; ŋ-baŋk; ɴ-nasalized n; nŏd; cŏmmit; ōld; ȯbey; ôrder; oi-boil; fo͞od; fo͝ot; ou-out; s-soft; sh-dish; th-thin; pūre; ū́nite; ûrn; stŭd; circŭs; ü-as in French tu; ′-indeterminate vowel.

PLACE (Pronunciation)	PAGE	Lat. °′	Long. °′
Tczew, Pol. (t'chĕf')	165	54.06 N	18.48 E
Teabo, Mex. (tĕ-ä'bô)	130a	20.25 N	89.14 W
Teague, Tx.	123	31.39 N	96.16 W
Teapa, Mex. (tā-ä'pä)	129	17.35 N	92.56 W
Tébessa, Alg. (tā'bĕs'ä)	220	35.27 N	8.13 E
Tebing Tinggi (I.), Indon. (teb'ĭng-tĭng'gä)	189b	0.54 N	102.39 E
Tebukbetung, Indon.	202	5.30 S	105.04 E
Tecalitlán, Mex. (tā-kä-lē-tlän')	128	19.28 N	103.17 W
Techiman, Ghana	224	7.35 N	1.56 W
Tecoanapa, Mex. (tāk-wä-nä-pä')	128	16.33 N	98.46 W
Tecoh, Mex. (tĕ-kô)	130a	20.46 N	89.27 W
Tecolotlán, Mex. (tā-kô-lô-tlän')	128	20.13 N	103.57 W
Tecolutla, Mex. (tā-kô-lōō'tlä)	129	20.33 N	97.00 W
Tecolutla (R.), Mex.	129	20.16 N	97.14 W
Tecomán, Mex. (tā-kô-män')	128	18.53 N	103.53 W
Tecómitl, Mex. (tĕ-kô'mētl)	129a	19.13 N	98.59 W
Tecozautla, Mex. (tā'kô-zä-ōō'tlä)	128	20.33 N	99.38 W
Tecpan de Galeana, Mex. (tĕk-pän' dā gä-lā-ä'nä)	128	17.13 N	100.41 W
Tecpatán, Mex. (tĕk-pä-tá'n)	129	17.08 N	93.18 W
Tecuala, Mex. (tĕ-kwä-lä)	128	22.24 N	105.29 W
Tecuci, Rom. (ta-kōōch')	165	45.51 N	27.30 E
Tecumseh, Can. (tē-kŭm'sĕ)	111b	42.19 N	82.53 W
Tecumseh, Mi.	108	42.00 N	84.00 W
Tecumseh, Ne.	122	40.21 N	96.09 W
Tecumseh, Ok.	121	35.18 N	96.55 W
Tees (R.), Eng. (tēz)	160	54.40 N	2.10 W
Tefé, Braz. (tĕf-ā')	140	3.27 S	64.43 W
Teganuna (L.), Jap. (tä'gä-nōō'nä)	201a	35.50 N	140.02 E
Tegucigalpa, Hond. (tå-gōō-sē-gäl'pä)	130	14.08 N	87.15 W
Tehachapi Mts., Ca. (tē-hă-shă'pĭ)	118	34.50 N	118.55 W
Tehentlo L., Can.	96	55.11 N	125.00 W
Tehrān, Iran (tĕ-hrän')	192	35.45 N	51.30 E
Tehuacan, Mex. (tā-wä-kän')	129	18.27 N	97.23 W
Tehuantepec (Sto. Domingo), Mex. (tå-wän-tå-pĕk') (sän-tô dô-mē'n-gô)	129	16.20 N	95.14 W
Tehuantepec, Golfo de (G.), Mex. (gôl-fô dĕ)	126	15.45 N	95.00 W
Tehuantepec, Istmo de (Isth.), Mex. (ē'st-mô dĕ)	129	17.55 N	94.35 W
Tehuantepec (R.), Mex.	129	16.30 N	95.23 W
Tehuehuetla Arroyo (R.), Mex. (tĕ-wĕ-wĕ'tlä ăr-rô-yô)	128	17.54 N	100.26 W
Tehuitzingo, Mex. (tā-wē-tzĭŋ'gō)	128	18.21 N	98.16 W
Teixeira de Sousa, Ang.	226	10.42 S	22.12 E
Tejeda, Sierra de (Mts.), Sp. (sē-ĕ'r-rä dĕ tĕ-kĕ'dä)	168	36.55 N	5.57 W
Tejúpan (Santiago), Mex. (tĕ-κōō-pä'n) (sän-tyá'gô)	129	17.39 N	97.34 W
Tejúpan, Punta (Pt.), Mex. (pōō'n-tä)	128	18.19 N	103.30 W
Tejupilco de Hidalgo, Mex. (tå-hōō-pēl'kô dā ē-dhäl'gō)	128	18.52 N	100.07 W
Tekamah, Ne. (tē-kā'mă)	112	41.46 N	96.13 W
Tekax de Alvaro Obregon, Mex. (tĕ-kä'x dĕ á'l-vä-rô-brĕ-gô'n)	130a	20.12 N	89.11 W
Tekeze (R.), Eth.	221	13.38 N	38.00 E
Tekirdağ (Rodosto), Tur. (tĕ-kĕr'dägh')	171	41.00 N	27.28 E
Tekit, Mex. (tĕ-kē't)	130a	20.35 N	89.18 W
Tekoa, Wa. (tē-kō'ă)	114	47.15 N	117.03 W
Tela, Hond. (tā'lä)	130	15.45 N	87.25 W
Tela, Bahía de (B.), Hond. (bä-ē'ä dĕ)	130	15.53 N	87.29 W
Telapa Burok, Gunong (Mt.), Mala.	189b	2.51 N	102.04 E
Telavi, Sov. Un.	177	42.00 N	45.20 E
Tel Aviv-Yafo, Isr. (tĕl-ä-vēv'jä'jă'fă)	189a	32.03 N	34.46 E
Telegraph Creek, Can. (tĕl'ē-grăf)	94	57.59 N	131.22 W
Teleneshty, Sov. Un. (tyĕ-le-nĕsht'i)	173	47.31 N	28.22 E
Telescope Pk., Ca. (tĕl'ē skōp)	118	36.12 N	117.05 W
Teles Pirex (R.), Braz. (tĕ-lĕs pĕ'rĕz)	141	8.28 S	57.07 W
Telesung, Indon.	189b	1.07 N	102.53 E
Telica (Vol.), Nic. (tå-lē'kä)	130	12.38 N	86.52 W
Télimélé, Gui.	224	10.54 N	13.02 W
Tell City, In. (tĕl)	108	38.00 N	86.45 W
Teller, Ak. (tĕl'ēr)	105	65.17 N	166.28 W
Tello, Col. (tĕ'l-yô)	140a	3.05 N	75.08 W
Telluride, Co. (tĕl'ū-rīd)	119	37.55 N	107.50 W
Telok Datok, Mala.	189b	2.51 N	101.33 E
Teloloapan, Mex. (tā'lô-lô-ä'pän)	128	18.19 N	99.54 W
Tel'pos-Iz, Gora (Mtn.), Sov. Un. (tyĕl'pŏs-ēz')	176	63.50 N	59.20 E
Telšiai, Sov. Un. (tĕl'sha'ē)	163	55.59 N	22.17 E
Teltow, G.D.R. (tĕl'tō)	155b	52.24 N	13.12 E
Telukletyak, Indon.	189b	1.53 N	101.45 E
Tema, Ghana	224	5.38 N	0.01 E
Temascalcingo, Mex. (tā'mäs-käl-sĭŋ'gō)	128	19.55 N	100.00 W
Temascaltepec, Mex. (tā'mäs-käl-tå pĕk)	128	19.00 N	100.03 W
Temax, Mex. (tĕ'mäx)	130a	21.10 N	88.51 W
Temir, Sov. Un. (tyĕ'mĕr)	177	49.10 N	57.15 E
Temir-Tau, Sov. Un.	178	50.08 N	73.13 E
Témiscaming, Can. (tĕ-mĭs'kă-mĭng)	101	46.40 N	78.50 W
Temiscouata (L.), Can. (tĕ'mĭs-kōō-ä'tä)	102	47.40 N	68.50 W
Temoaya, Mex. (tĕ-mô-a-um-yä)	129a	19.28 N	99.36 W
Temperley, Arg. (tĕ'm-pĕr-lā)	142a	34.32 S	58.24 W
Tempio Pausania, It. (tĕm'pē-ō pou-sä'nē-ä)	170	40.55 N	9.05 E
Temple, Tx. (tĕm'p'l)	123	31.06 N	97.20 W

PLACE (Pronunciation)	PAGE	Lat. °′	Long. °′
Temple City, Ca.	117a	34.07 N	118.02 W
Templeton, Can. (tĕm'p'l-tŭn)	93c	45.29 N	75.37 W
Templin, G.D.R. (tĕm-plēn')	164	53.08 N	13.30 E
Tempoal (R.), Mex. (tĕm-pô-ä'l)	128	21.38 N	98.23 W
Temryuk, Sov. Un. (tyĕm-ryōōk')	173	45.17 N	37.21 E
Temuco, Chile (tå-mōō'kō)	142	38.46 S	72.38 W
Temyasovo, Sov. Un. (tĕm-yä'sô-vô)	180a	53.00 N	58.06 E
Tenabó, Mex. (tĕ-nä-bō')	130a	20.05 N	90.11 W
Tenāli, India	191	16.10 N	80.32 E
Tenamaxtlán, Mex. (tā'nä-mäs-tlän')	128	20.13 N	104.06 W
Tenancingo, Mex. (tå-nän-sēŋ'gō)	128	18.54 N	99.36 W
Tenango, Mex. (tå-näŋ'gō)	129a	19.09 N	98.51 W
Tenasserim, Bur. (tĕn-ăs'ēr-ĭm)	202	12.09 N	99.01 E
Tenderovskaya Kosa (C.), Sov. Un. (tĕn-dĕ-fôf'ská-yá kô-sá')	173	46.12 N	31.17 E
Tenéré (Des.), Niger	225	19.23 N	10.15 E
Tenerife I., Can. Is. (tå-nå-rē'få) (tĕn-ēr-ĭf')	220	28.41 N	17.02 W
Ténés, Alg. (tā-nĕs')	157	36.28 N	1.22 E
Tengiz (L.), Sov. Un. (tyĭn-gēz')	178	50.45 N	68.39 E
Teng Xian, China (tŭŋ shyĕn)	196	35.07 N	117.08 E
Tenjin, Jap. (tĕn'jēn)	201b	34.54 N	135.04 E
Tenke, Zaire (tĕŋ'kå)	227	11.26 S	26.45 E
Tenkiller Ferry Res., Ok. (tĕn-kĭl'ēr)	121	35.42 N	94.47 W
Tenkodogo, Upper Volta (tĕŋ-kô-dō'gô)	224	11.47 N	0.22 W
Tenmile (R.), Wa. (tĕn mīl)	116d	48.52 N	122.32 W
Tennant Creek, Austl. (tĕn'ănt)	210	19.45 S	134.00 E
Tennessee (State), U. S. (tĕn-ĕ-sē')	107	35.50 N	88.00 W
Tennessee (L.), U. S.	107	35.35 N	88.20 W
Tennessee (R.), U. S.	124	35.10 N	88.20 W
Tennille, Ga. (tĕn'ĭl)	124	32.55 N	86.50 W
Teno (R.), Chile (tĕ'nô)	139b	34.55 S	71.00 W
Tenora, Austl. (tĕn-ôră)	212	34.23 S	147.33 E
Tenosique, Mex. (tā-nô-sē'kå)	129	17.27 N	91.25 W
Tenri, Jap.	201b	34.36 N	135.50 E
Tenryū-Gawa (Strm.), Jap. (tĕn'ryōō'gä'wä)	201	35.16 N	137.54 E
Tensas R., La. (tĕn'sô)	123	31.54 N	91.30 W
Tensaw (R.), Al. (tĕn'sô)	124	30.45 N	87.52 W
Tenterfield, Austl. (tĕn'tēr-fēld)	212	29.00 S	152.06 E
Ten Thousand, Is., Fl. (tĕn thou'zănd)	125a	25.45 N	81.35 W
Teocaltiche, Mex. (tā'ō-käl-tē'chå)	128	21.27 N	102.38 W
Teocelo, Mex. (tā-ô-sā'lō)	129	19.22 N	96.57 W
Teocuitatlán de Corona, Mex. (tā'ō-kwē'tä-tlän' dā kō-rō'nä)	128	20.06 N	103.22 W
Teófilo Otoni, Braz. (tē-ô'fē-lô-tô'nē)	141	17.49 S	41.18 W
Teoloyucan, Mex. (tā'ô-lô-yōō'kän)	128	19.43 N	99.12 W
Teopisca, Mex. (tā-ô-pēs'kä)	129	16.30 N	92.33 W
Teotihuacán,, Mex. (tĕ-ô-tē-wă-kă'n)	129a	19.40 N	98.52 W
Teotitlán del Camino, Mex. (tā-ô-tē-tlän' dĕl kä-mē'nô)	129	18.07 N	97.04 W
Tepalcatepec, Mex. (tā'päl-kä-tå'pĕk)	128	19.11 N	102.51 W
Tepalcatepec (R.), Mex.	128	18.54 N	102.25 W
Tepalcingo, Mex. (tā-päl-sēŋ'gô)	128	18.34 N	98.49 W
Tepatitlan de Morelos, Mex. (tā-pä-tē-tlän' dä mô-rā'los)	128	20.15 N	102.47 W
Tepeaca, Mex. (tā-pā-ä'kä)	129	18.57 N	97.54 W
Tepecoacuilco de Trujano, Mex. (tā'pā-kō'ä-kwēl'kō dā trōō-hä'nō)	128	19.15 N	99.29 W
Tepeji del Río, Mex. (tā-pā-κe' dĕl rē'ō)	128	19.55 N	99.22 W
Tepelmeme, Mex. (tā'pĕl-mā'må)	129	17.51 N	97.23 W
Tepetlaoxtoc, Mex. (tā'pā-tlä'ôs-tōk')	129a	19.34 N	98.49 W
Tepezala, Mex. (tā-pā-zä-lä')	128	22.12 N	102.12 W
Tepic, Mex. (tā-pēk')	128	21.32 N	104.53 W
Těplaya Gora, Sov. Un. (tyôp'lá-yá gô-rá)	180a	58.32 N	59.08 W
Teplice Sanov, Czech. (tĕp'lĭ-tsĕ shä'nôf)	164	50.39 N	13.50 E
Teposcolula (San Pedro y San Pablo), Mex. (tā-pôs-kô-lōō'lä) (sän pä'drō ē sän pä'blō)	129	17.33 N	97.29 W
Tequendama, Salto de (Falls), Col. (sä'l-tô dĕ tĕ-kĕn-dä'mä)	140a	4.34 N	74.18 W
Tequila, Mex. (tå-kē'lä)	128	20.53 N	103.48 W
Tequisistlán (R.), Mex. (tĕ-kē-sēs-tlá'n)	129	16.20 N	95.40 W
Tequisquiapan, Mex. (tå-kēs-kē-ä'pän)	128	20.33 N	99.57 W
Ter (R.), Sp. (tĕr)	169	42.04 N	2.52 E
Téra, Niger	224	14.01 N	0.45 E
Tera (R.), Sp. (tĕ'rä)	168	42.05 N	6.24 W
Teramo, It. (tā'rä-mô)	170	42.40 N	13.41 E
Terborg, Neth. (tĕr-bōrg)	167c	51.55 N	6.23 E
Tercan, Tur. (tĕr'jän)	177	39.40 N	40.12 E
Terceira I., Acores (tĕr-sā'rä)	220a	38.49 N	26.36 W
Terebovlya, Sov. Un. (tĕ-rā'bôv-lyá)	165	49.18 N	25.43 E
Terek (R.), Sov. Un.	177	43.30 N	45.10 E
Terenkul', Sov. Un. (tĕ-rĕn'kōōl)	180a	55.38 N	62.18 E
Teresina, Braz. (tĕr-ā-sē'nă)	141	5.04 S	42.42 W
Teresópolis, Braz. (tĕr-ā-sŏ'pō-lēzh)	142b	22.25 S	42.59 W
Teriberka, Sov. Un. (tyĕr-ē-byôr'kå)	176	69.00 N	35.15 E
Terme, Tur. (tĕr'mĕ)	177	41.05 N	42.00 E
Termez, Sov. Un. (tyĕr'mĕz)	193	37.19 N	67.20 E
Termini, It. (tĕr'mē-nē)	170	37.58 N	13.39 E
Términos, Laguna de (L.), Mex. (lä-gōō'nä dĕ ĕ'r-mē-nôs)	129	18.37 N	91.32 W
Termoli, It. (tĕr'mô-lē)	170	42.00 N	15.01 E

PLACE (Pronunciation)	PAGE	Lat. °′	Long. °′
Tern (R.), Eng. (tûrn)	154	52.49 N	2.31 W
Ternate, Indon. (tĕr-nä'tä)	203	0.52 N	127.25 E
Terni, It. (tĕr'nē)	170	42.38 N	12.41 E
Ternopol', Sov. Un. (tĕr-nō-pōl')	165	49.32 N	25.36 E
Terpeniya, Zaliv (B.), Sov. Un. (zä'lĭf tĕr-pă'nĭ-yá)	200	49.10 N	143.05 E
Terpeniya, Mys (C.), Sov. Un.	179	48.44 N	144.42 E
Terrace, Can. (tĕr'ĭs)	96	54.31 N	128.35 W
Terracina, It. (tĕr-rä-chē'nä)	170	41.18 N	13.14 E
Terra Nova Natl. Park, Can.	103	48.37 N	54.15 W
Terrebonne, Can. (tĕr-bŏn')	93a	45.42 N	73.38 W
Terrebonne B., La.	123	28.55 N	90.30 W
Terre Haute, In. (tĕr-ē hōt')	108	39.25 N	87.25 W
Terrell, Tx. (tĕr'ĕl)	123	32.44 N	96.15 W
Terrell, Wa.	116d	48.53 N	122.44 W
Terrell Hills, Tx. (tĕr'ĕl hĭlz)	117d	29.28 N	98.27 W
Terschelling (I.), Neth. (tĕr-sκĕl'ĭng)	161	53.25 N	5.12 E
Teruel, Sp. (tå-rōō-ĕl')	168	40.20 N	1.05 W
Tešanj, Yugo. (tĕ'shän')	171	44.36 N	17.59 E
Teschendorf, G.D.R. (tĕ'shĕn-dōrf)	155b	52.51 N	13.10 E
Tesecheacan, Mex. (tĕ-sĕ-chĕ-ä-kă'n)	129	18.10 N	95.41 W
Teshekpuk (L.), Ak. (tē-shĕk'pŭk)	105	70.18 N	152.36 W
Teshio Dake (Mt.), Jap. (tĕsh'ē-ō-dä'kā)	200	44.00 N	142.50 E
Teshio Gawa (R.), Jap. (tĕsh'ē-ô gä'wä)	200	44.53 N	144.55 E
Tesiin Gol (R.), Mong.	194	50.14 N	94.30 E
Teslin, Can. (tĕs-lĭn)	105	60.10 N	132.30 W
Teslin (L.), Can.	94	60.12 N	132.08 W
Teslin (R.), Can.	94	61.18 N	134.14 W
Tessalon, Can.	100	46.20 N	83.35 W
Tessaoua, Niger (tĕs-sä'ōō-ä)	220	13.53 N	7.53 E
Tessenderlo, Bel.	155a	51.04 N	5.08 E
Test (R.), Eng. (tĕst)	160	51.10 N	2.20 W
Testa del Gargano (Pt.), It. (tās'tä dĕl gär-gä'nō)	170	41.48 N	16.13 E
Tetachuck L., Can.	96	53.20 N	125.50 W
Tete, Moz. (tā'tĕ)	227	16.13 S	33.35 E
Tête Jaune Cache, Can. (tĕt'zhōn-kăsh)	97	52.57 N	119.26 W
Tetepiskaw, Lac (L.), Can.	100	51.02 N	69.23 W
Teterev (R.), Sov. Un. (tyĕ'tyĕ-rĕf)	173	50.35 N	29.18 E
Teterow, G.D.R. (tā'tĕ-rō)	164	53.46 N	12.33 E
Teteven, Bul. (tĕt'ĕ-ven')	172	42.57 N	24.15 E
Teton R., Mt. (tē'tŏn)	115	47.54 N	111.37 W
Tetouan, Mor.	220	35.42 N	5.34 W
Tetovo, Yugo. (tā'tô-vô)	171	42.01 N	21.00 E
Tetyukhe-Pristan, Sov. Un. (tĕt-yōō'κĕ prĭ-stän')	200	44.21 N	135.44 E
Tetyushi, Sov. Un. (tÿt-yōō'shĭ)	176	54.58 N	48.40 E
Teupitz, G.D.R. (toi'pētz)	155b	42.08 N	13.37 E
Tevere (Tiber) (R.), It. (tā'vå-rā) (tī'bēr)	170	42.30 N	12.14 E
Teverya, Isr.	189a	32.48 N	35.32 E
Tewksbury, Ma. (tūks'bēr-ĭ)	103a	42.37 N	71.14 W
Texada I., Can.	96	49.40 N	124.24 W
Texarkana, Ar. (tĕk-sär-kän'ă)	121	33.26 N	94.02 W
Texarkana, Tx.	121	33.26 N	94.04 W
Texas (State), U. S.	106	31.00 N	101.00 W
Texas City, Tx.	123a	29.23 N	94.54 W
Texcaltitlán, Mex. (tās-käl'tē-tlän')	128	18.54 N	99.51 W
Texel (I.), Neth. (tĕk'sĕl)	161	53.10 N	4.45 E
Texcoco, Mex. (tās-kō'kō)	129a	19.31 N	98.53 W
Texistepec, Mex. (tĕk-sēs-tā-pĕk')	129	17.51 N	94.46 W
Texmelucan, Mex. (tās-må-lōō'kän)	129a	19.17 N	98.26 W
Texoma, L., Ok. (tĕk'ō-mă)	121	34.03 N	96.28 W
Teyateyaneng, Leso.	223c	29.11 S	27.43 E
Teykovo, Sov. Un. (tĕy-kô-vô)	172	56.52 N	40.34 E
Texiutlán, Mex. (tå-zē-ōō-tlän')	129	19.48 N	97.21 W
Texontepec, Mex. (tå-zōn-tå-pĕk')	128	19.52 N	98.48 W
Texontepec de Aldama, Mex. (dä äl-dä'mä)	128	20.19 N	99.19 W
Tezpur, India	190	26.42 N	92.52 E
Tha-anne (R.), Can.	94	60.50 N	96.56 W
Thabana Ntlenyana (Mtn.), Leso.	223c	29.28 S	29.17 E
Thabazimbi, S. Afr.	219d	24.36 S	27.22 E
Thailand, Asia	188	16.30 N	101.00 E
Thailand, G. of, Asia	202	11.37 N	100.46 E
Thale Luang (L.), Thai.	202	7.51 N	99.39 E
Thame, Eng. (tām)	154b	51.43 N	0.59 W
Thames (R.), Can. (tĕmz)	108	42.40 N	81.45 W
Thames (R.), Eng.	161	51.26 N	0.54 E
Thāmit, Wadi (R.), Libya	159	30.39 N	16.23 E
Thāna, India (thä'nŭ)	191b	19.13 N	72.58 E
Thāna Cr., India	191b	19.03 N	72.58 E
Thanh-Hoa, Viet. (tän'hō'ä)	199	19.46 N	105.42 E
Thanjāvūr, India	191	10.51 N	79.11 E
Thann, Fr. (tän)	167	47.49 N	7.05 E
Thaon-les-Vosges, Fr. (tä-ôN-lā-vōzh')	167	48.16 N	6.24 E
Thargomindah, Austl. (thár'gō-mĭn'dá)	212	27.58 S	143.57 E
Thásos (I.), Grc. (thă'sōs)	171	40.41 N	24.53 E
Thatch Cay (I.), Vir. Is. (U. S. A.) (thăch)	127c	18.22 N	64.53 W
Thaya R., Aus.-Czech. (tä'yá)	164	48.48 N	15.40 E
Thayer, Mo. (thâ'ēr)	121	36.30 N	91.34 W
Thebes, see Thivai			
Thebes (Ruins), Egypt (thēbz)	219b	25.47 N	32.39 E
The Brothers (Mtn.), Wa. (brŭth'ērs)	116a	47.39 N	123.08 W
The Coteau (Hills), Can.	98	51.10 N	107.30 W

PRONOUNCING INDEX

The Dalles – Toba Inlet 355

PLACE (Pronunciation)	PAGE	Lat. °′	Long. °′
The Dalles, Or. (dălz)	114	45.36 N	121.10 W
The Father (Mtn.), Pap. N. Gui.	203	5.05 S	151.30 E
The Hague, see 's Gravenhage			
Thelum, Pak.	190	32.59 N	73.43 E
The Oaks, Austl.	207b	34.04 S	150.36 E
Theodore, Austl. (thē-ō'dōr)	212	24.51 S	150.09 E
Theodore Roosevelt Dam, Az. (thē-ō-dōr rōō-sá-vělt)	119	33.46 N	111.25 W
Theodore Roosevelt Natl. Park, ND	112	47.20 N	103.42 W
Theológos, Grc.	171	40.37 N	24.41 E
The Pas, Can. (pä)	99	53.50 N	101.15 W
The Rajah (Mtn.), Can.	97	53.15 N	118.31 W
Thermopolis, Wy. (thēr-mŏp'ō-lĭs)	115	43.38 N	108.11 W
The Round Mtn., Austl.	212	30.17 S	152.19 E
Thessalía (Reg.), Grc.	171	39.50 N	22.09 E
Thessalon, Can.	95	46.11 N	83.37 W
Thessaloníki, Grc. (thěs-sá-lô-nē'kē)	171	40.38 N	22.59 E
Thetford Mines, Can. (thět'fērd mīns)	102	46.05 N	71.20 W
The Twins (Mtn.), Leso.-S. Afr. (twĭnz)	223c	30.09 S	28.29 E
Theunissen, S. Afr.	219d	28.25 S	26.44 E
Thibaudeau, Can. (tĭ'bō-dō')	99	57.05 N	94.08 W
Thibodaux, La. (tē-bō-dō')	123	29.48 N	90.48 W
Thief (L.), Mn. (thēf)	112	48.32 N	95.46 W
Thief (R.), Mn.	112	48.18 N	96.07 E
Thief Rivers Falls, Mn. (thēf rĭv'ēr fôlz)	112	48.07 N	96.11 W
Thiers, Fr. (tyâr)	166	45.51 N	3.32 E
Thiès, Senegal (tē-ěs')	224	14.48 N	16.56 W
Thika, Ken.	227	1.03 S	37.05 E
Thimbu, Bhu.	190	27.33 N	89.42 E
Thingvallavatn (L.), Ice.	156	64.12 N	20.22 W
Thionville, Fr. (tyôN-vēl')	167	49.23 N	6.31 E
Third Cataract, Sud.	221	19.53 N	30.11 E
Thisted, Den. (tēs'tědh)	162	56.57 N	8.38 E
Thistilfjördur (Fd.), Ice.	156	66.29 N	14.59 W
Thistle (I.), Austl. (thĭs''l)	212	34.55 S	136.11 E
Thívai (Thebes), Grc.	171	38.20 N	23.18 E
Thjórsá (R.), Ice. (tyûr'sá)	156	64.23 N	19.18 W
Tholen, Neth.	155a	51.32 N	4.11 E
Thomas, Ok. (tŏm'ăs)	120	35.44 N	98.43 W
Thomas, WV	109	39.15 N	79.30 W
Thomaston, Ga. (tŏm'ăs-tŭn)	124	32.51 N	84.17 W
Thomasville, Al. (tŏm'ăs-vĭl)	124	31.55 N	87.43 W
Thomasville, NC	125	35.52 N	80.05 W
Thomlinson, Mt., Can.	96	55.33 N	127.29 W
Thompson, Can.	99	55.48 N	97.59 W
Thompson (R.), Can.	97	50.15 N	121.20 W
Thompson (R.), Mo.	121	40.32 N	93.49 W
Thompson Falls, Mt.	114	47.35 N	115.20 W
Thomson (tŏm'sŭn)	125	33.28 N	82.29 W
Thomson (R.) Austl. (tŏm-sŏn)	211	29.30 S	143.07 E
Thomson's Falls, Ken.	227	0.02 N	36.22 E
Thonon-les-Bains, Fr. (tô-nôN'lā-băN')	167	46.22 N	6.27 E
Thórisvatn (L.), Ice.	156	64.02 N	19.09 W
Thorne, Eng. (thôrn)	154	53.37 N	0.58 W
Thorntown, In. (thôrn'tŭn)	108	40.05 N	86.35 W
Thorold, Can. (thō'rōld)	93d	43.13 N	79.12 W
Thouars, Fr. (tōō-är')	166	47.00 N	0.17 W
Thousand Is., NY-Can. (thou'zănd)	109	44.15 N	76.10 W
Thrace (Reg.), Grc.-Tur. (thrās)	171	41.20 N	26.07 E
Thrapston, Eng. (thrăp'stŭn)	154	52.23 N	0.32 W
Three Forks, Mt. (thrē fôrks)	115	45.56 N	111.35 W
Three Oaks, Mi. (thrē ōks)	108	41.50 N	86.40 W
Three Points, C., Ghana	224	4.45 N	2.06 W
Three Rivers, Mi.	108	42.00 N	83.40 W
Thule, Grnld.	75	76.34 N	68.47 W
Thun, Switz. (tōōn)	164	46.46 N	7.34 E
Thunder Bay, Can.	100	48.28 N	89.12 W
Thunder B., Can. (thŭn'dēr)	113	48.29 N	88.52 W
Thunder Hills, Can.	98	54.30 N	106.00 W
Thunersee (L.), Switz.	164	46.40 N	7.30 E
Thurber, Tx. (thûr'bēr)	122	32.30 N	98.23 W
Thüringen (Thuringia) (former state or region), G.D.R. (tü'rĭng-ěn)	164	51.07 N	10.45 E
Thurles, Ire. (thûrlz)	160	52.44 N	7.45 W
Thurrock, Eng. (thŭ'rŏk)	154b	51.28 N	0.19 E
Thursday (I.), Austl. (thûrz-dā)	211	10.17 S	142.23 E
Thurso, Can. (thŭn'sô)	93c	45.36 N	75.15 W
Thurso, Scot.	160	58.35 N	3.40 W
Thurston Pen. Ant. (thûrs'tŭn)	228	71.20 S	98.00 W
Thysville, Zaire (tēs-vēl')	222	5.08 S	14.58 E
Tiandong, China (tĭĕn-dôŋ)	199	23.32 N	107.10 E
Tianjin, see T'ienching			
Tianjin Shi (Mun.), China (tĭĕn-jyĭn shr)	196	39.30 N	117.13 E
Tianmen, China (tĭĕn-mŭn)	199	30.40 N	113.10 E
Tianshui, China (tĭĕn-shwā)	198	34.25 N	105.40 E
Tiaret, Alg.	220	35.28 N	1.15 E
Tibagi, Braz. (tē'bá-zhē)	142	24.40 S	50.35 W
Tibasti, Sarir (Des.), Chad	221	24.00 N	16.30 E
Tibati, Cam.	225	6.27 N	12.38 E
Tiber (R.), see Tevere			
Tibesti Massif (Mts.), Chad	221	20.40 N	17.48 E
Tibet, Plat. of, China (tĭ-bět')	194	32.22 N	83.30 E
Tibet (Aut. Reg.), see Xizang			
Tibleşului, Munţii (Mts.), Rom	165	47.41 N	24.05 E
Tibnīn, Leb.	189a	33.12 N	35.23 E
Tiburon, Ca. (tē-bōō-rōn')	116b	37.53 N	122.27 W
Tiburon, Hai.	133	18.35 N	74.25 W
Tiburón (I.), Mex.	126	28.45 N	113.10 W
Tiburon, Cabo (C.), Pan. (ká'bô)	131	8.42 N	77.19 W
Tiburon I., Ca.	116b	37.52 N	122.26 W
Ticaco Pass, Phil. (tē-kä-kō)	203a	12.38 N	123.50 E
Ticao I., Phil. (tē-kä'ō)	203a	12.40 N	123.30 E
Tickhill, Eng. (tĭk'ĭl)	154	53.26 N	1.06 W
Ticonderoga, NY (tī-kŏn-dēr-ō'gá)	109	43.50 N	73.30 W
Ticul, Mex. (tē-kōō'l)	130a	20.22 N	89.32 W
Tidaholm, Swe. (tē'dá-hōlm)	162	58.11 N	13.53 E
Tideswell, Eng. (tīdz'wěl)	154	53.17 N	1.47 W
Tidikelt (Reg.), Alg. (tē-dē-kělt')	220	25.53 N	2.11 E
Tidjikdja, Mauritania (tē-jĭk'jä)	224	18.33 N	11.25 W
Tieling, China (tĭē-lĭŋ)	198	42.18 N	123.50 E
Tielmes, Sp. (tyâl-màs')	169a	40.15 N	3.20 W
T'ienching (Tianjin), China (tĭĕn-chĭŋ) (tĭĕn-jyĭn)	196	39.08 N	117.14 E
Tienen, Bel. (Brussels In.)	155	50.49 N	4.58 E
Tien Shan (Mts.), Sov. Un.-China	194	42.00 N	78.46 E
Tienshan Hu (L.), China (dĭän'shän'hōō)	196	31.08 N	120.30 E
Tierp, Swe. (tyĕrp)	162	60.21 N	17.28 E
Tierpoort, S. Afr.	223b	25.53 N	28.26 E
Tierra Blanca, Mex. (tyĕ'r-rä-blä'n-kä)	129	18.28 N	96.19 W
Tierra del Fuego (Reg.), Chile-Arg. (tyĕr'rä děl fwā'gō)	142	53.50 S	68.45 W
Tiétar (R.), Sp. (tē-ā'tär)	168	39.56 N	5.44 W
Tietê, Braz. (tyā-tā')	139a	23.08 S	47.42 W
Tieté, (R.), Braz.	141	20.46 S	50.46 W
Tiffin, Oh. (tĭf'ĭn)	108	41.10 N	83.15 W
Tifton, Ga. (tĭf'tŭn)	124	31.25 N	83.34 W
Tigard, Or. (tĭ'gärd)	116c	45.25 N	122.46 W
Tignish, Can. (tĭg'nĭsh)	102	46.57 N	64.02 W
Tigoda (R.), Sov. Un. (tē'gô-dá)	180c	59.29 N	31.15 E
Tigre, Arg. (tē'grē)	142	34.09 S	58.35 W
Tigre (R.), Peru	140	2.20 S	75.41 W
Tigres, Península dos (Pen.), Ang. (pě-nē'ŋ-sōō-lä-dôs-tē'grěs)	222	16.30 S	11.45 E
Tigris (R.), Asia	192	34.45 N	44.10 E
Tīh, Jabal at (Mts.), Egypt	189a	29.23 N	34.05 E
Tihuatlán, Mex. (tē-wä-tlän')	129	20.43 N	97.34 W
Tijuana, Mex. (tē-hwä'nä)	118a	32.32 N	117.02 W
Tijuca, Pico da (Mtn.), Braz. (pē'kō-dä-tē-zhōō'kä)	142b	22.56 S	43.17 W
Tikal (Ruins), Guat. (tē-käl')	130a	17.16 N	89.49 W
Tikhoretsk, Sov. Un. (tē-Kôr-yětsk')	177	45.55 N	40.05 E
Tikhvin, Sov. Un. (tēK-vēn')	172	59.36 N	33.38 E
Tikrīt, Iraq	192	34.36 N	43.31 E
Tiksi, Sov. Un. (tēk-sē')	179	71.42 N	128.32 E
Tilburg, Neth. (tĭl'bûrg)	155a	51.33 N	5.05 E
Tilemsi, Vallée du (Val.), Mali	224	17.50 N	0.25 E
Tilichiki, Sov. Un. (tyĭ-le-chĭ-kē)	179	60.49 N	166.14 E
Tiligul (R.), Sov. Un. (tē'lĭ-gûl)	173	47.25 N	30.27 E
Tillabéry, Niger (tē-yá-bā-rē')	220	14.14 N	1.30 E
Tillamook, Or. (tĭl'á-mōōk)	114	45.27 N	123.50 W
Tillamook B., Or.	114	45.32 N	124.26 W
Tillberga, Swe. (těl-běr'ghá)	162	59.40 N	16.34 E
Tillsonburg, Can. (tĭl'sŭn-bûrg)	101	42.50 N	80.50 W
Tilsit, see Sovetsk			
Tim, Sov. Un. (tēm)	173	51.39 N	37.07 E
Timaru, N.Z. (tĭm'á-rōō)	213	44.26 S	171.17 E
Timashevskaya, Sov. Un. (tēmä-shěfs-kä'yä)	173	45.47 N	38.57 E
Timbalier B., La. (tĭm'bá-lēr)	123	28.55 N	90.14 W
Timber, Or. (tĭm'bēr)	116c	45.43 N	123.17 W
Timbo, Gui. (tĭm'bō)	220	10.41 N	11.51 W
Timbuktu, see Tombouctou			
Timétrine Monts (Mts.), Mali	224	19.50 N	0.30 W
Timimoun, Alg. (tē-mē-mōōn')	220	29.14 N	0.22 E
Timiris, Cap (C.), Mauritania	224	19.23 N	16.32 W
Timis (R.), Rom.	171	45.28 N	21.06 E
Timiskaming Station, Can. (tē-mĭs'ká-mĭng)	95	46.41 N	79.01 W
Timişoara, Rom.	171	45.44 N	21.21 E
Timmins, Can. (tĭm'ĭnz)	95	48.25 N	81.22 W
Timmonsville, SC (tĭm'ŭnz-vĭl)	125	34.09 N	79.55 W
Timor (I.), Indon. (tē-mōr')	203	10.08 S	125.00 E
Timor Sea, Asia	204	12.40 S	125.00 E
Timpanogos Cave Natl. Mon., Ut. (tĭ-măn'ō-gŏz)	119	40.25 N	111.45 W
Timpson, Tx. (tĭmp'sŭn)	123	31.55 N	94.24 W
Timpton (R.), Sov. Un. (têmp'tôn)	179	57.15 N	126.35 E
Timsâh (L.), Egypt (tĭm'sä)	219c	30.34 N	32.22 E
Tina, Monte (Mtn.), Dom. Rep. (mô'n-tě-tē'nä)	133	18.50 N	70.40 W
Tina (R.), S. Afr. (tē'ná)	223c	30.50 S	28.44 E
Tinaguillo, Ven. (tē-nä-gē'l-yō)	141b	9.55 N	68.18 W
Tīnah, Khalīj at (G.), Egypt	189a	31.06 N	32.42 E
Tindouf, Alg. (tēn-dōōf')	220	27.43 N	7.44 W
Tinggi, Palau (I.), Mala.	189b	2.16 N	104.16 E
Tingi Mts., S. L.	224	9.00 N	10.50 W
Tinglin, China	197b	30.53 N	121.18 E
Tingo María, Peru (tē'ngō-mä-rē'ä)	140	9.15 S	76.04 W
Tingréla, Ivory Coast	224	10.29 N	6.24 W
Tingsryd, Swe. (tĭngs'rūd)	162	56.32 N	14.58 E
Tingtzu Wan (B.), China (dĭng'tze wän)	196	36.33 N	121.06 E
Tinguindio Paracho, Mex. (tēn'kē'n-dyō-pärä-chō)	128	19.38 N	102.02 W
Tinguiririca (R.), Chile (tē'n-gē-rē-rē'kä)	139b	36.48 S	70.45 W
Tinley Park, Il. (tĭn'lē)	111a	41.34 N	87.47 W
Tinnoset, Nor. (tēn'nôs'sět)	162	59.44 N	9.00 E
Tinnsjø, Nor. (tĭnnsyū)	162	59.55 N	8.49 E
Tinogasta, Arg. (tē-nô-gäs'tä)	142	28.07 S	67.30 W
Tínos (I.), Grc.	171	37.45 N	25.12 E
Tinrhert, Plat. du, Alg.	220	27.30 N	7.30 E
Tinsukia, India (tin-sōō'kĭ-á)	193	27.18 N	95.29 W
Tintic, Ut. (tĭn'tĭk)	119	39.55 N	112.15 W
Tio, Pic de (Pk.), Gui.	224	8.55 N	8.55 W
Tioman (I.), Mala.	189b	2.25 N	104.30 E
Tipitapa, Nic. (tē-pē-tä'pä)	130	12.14 N	86.05 W
Tipitapa R., Nic.	130	12.13 N	85.57 W
Tippah Cr., (R.), Ms. (tĭp'pá)	124	34.43 N	88.15 W
Tippecanoe (R.), In. (tĭp-ē-ká-nōō')	108	40.55 N	86.45 W
Tipperary, Ire. (tĭ-pē-râ'rē)	160	52.28 N	8.13 W
Tippo Bay, Ms. (tĭp'ō bīōō')	121	33.35 N	90.06 W
Tipton, In.	108	40.15 N	86.00 W
Tipton, Ia.	113	41.46 N	91.10 W
Tirane, Alb. (tē-rä'nä)	171	41.48 N	19.50 E
Tirano, It. (tē-rä'nō)	170	46.12 N	10.09 E
Tiraspol', Sov. Un. (tē-räs'pôl')	173	46.52 N	29.38 E
Tire, Tur. (tē'rē)	177	38.05 N	27.48 E
Tiree (I.), Scot. (tī-rē')	160	56.34 N	6.30 W
Tirgovişte, Rom.	171	44.54 N	25.29 E
Tîrgu-Jiu, Rom.	171	45.02 N	23.17 E
Tîrgu-Mureş, Rom.	165	46.33 N	24.35 E
Tîrgu Neamt, Rom.	165	47.14 N	26.23 E
Tîrgu-Ocna, Rom.	165	46.18 N	26.38 E
Tîrgu-Secuiesc, Rom.	165	46.04 N	26.06 E
Tirich Mir (Mt.), Pak.	190	36.50 N	71.48 E
Tirlyanskiy, Sov. Un. (tĭr-lyän'skĭ)	180a	54.13 N	58.37 E
Tîrnăveni, Rom.	165	46.19 N	24.18 E
Tírnavos, Grc.	171	39.50 N	22.14 E
Tirol (State), Aus. (tē-rōl')	164	47.13 N	11.10 E
Tirso (R.), It. (tēr'sō)	170	40.15 N	9.03 E
Tiruchchirāppalli, India (tĭr'ōō-chĭ-rä'pá-lĭ)	191	10.49 N	78.48 E
Tirunelveli, India	191	8.53 N	77.43 E
Tiruppur, India	191	11.11 N	77.08 E
Tisa (R.), Hung.-Yugo. (tē'sä)	171	45.50 N	20.13 E
Tisdale, Can. (tĭz'dāl)	98	52.51 N	104.04 W
Tista (R.), India	190	26.03 N	88.52 E
Titāgarh, India	190a	22.44 N	88.23 E
Titicaca, Lago (L.), Bol.-Peru (lä'gō-tē-tē-kä'kä)	140	16.12 S	70.33 W
Titiribi, Col. (tē-tē-rē-bē')	140a	6.05 N	75.47 W
Tito, Lagh (R.), Ken.	227	2.25 N	39.05 E
Titograd, Yugo.	171	42.25 N	20.42 E
Titovo Užice, Yugo. (tē'tô-vô ōō'zhē-tsě)	171	43.51 N	19.53 E
Titov Veles, Yugo. (tē'tôv vě'lěs)	171	41.42 N	21.50 E
Titterstone Clee Hill, Eng. (klē)	154	52.24 N	2.37 W
Titule, Zaire	226	3.17 N	25.32 E
Titusville, Fl. (tĭ'tŭs-vĭl)	125a	28.37 N	80.44 W
Titusville, Pa.	109	40.40 N	79.40 W
Titz, F.R.G. (tētz)	167c	51.00 N	6.26 E
Tiverton, RI (tĭv'ēr-tun)	110b	41.38 N	71.11 W
Tivoli, It. (tē'vô-lē)	169d	41.38 N	12.48 E
Tixkokob, Mex. (tēx-kō-kō'b)	130a	21.01 N	89.23 W
Tixtla de Guerrero, Mex. (tē'x-tlä-dě-gěr-rě'rō)	128	17.36 N	99.24 W
Tizard Bk. and Rf., China (tĭz'árd)	202	10.51 N	113.20 E
Tizimín, Mex. (tē-zē-mē'n)	130a	21.08 N	88.10 W
Tizi-Ouzou, Alg. (tē'zē-ōō-zōō')	220	36.44 N	4.04 E
Tiznados (R.), Ven. (tēz-nä'dōs)	141b	9.53 N	67.49 W
Tiznit, Mor. (tēz-nēt)	220	29.52 N	9.39 W
Tlacolula de Matamoros, Mex. (tlä-kō-lōō'lä dā mätä-mō'rōs)	129	16.56 N	96.29 W
Tlacotálpan, Mex. (tlä-kō-täl'pän)	129	18.39 N	95.40 W
Tlacotepec, Mex. (tlä-kō-tå-pě'k)	128	17.46 N	99.57 W
Tlacotepec, Mex.	129	18.41 N	97.40 W
Tlacotepec, Mex.	128	19.11 N	99.41 W
Tláhuac, Mex. (tlä-wäk')	129a	19.16 N	99.00 W
Tlajomulco de Zúñiga, Mex. (tlä-hô-mōō'l-ko-dě-zōō'n-yē-gä)	128	20.30 N	103.27 W
Tlalchapa, Mex. (tläl-chä'pä)	128	18.26 N	100.29 W
Tlalixcoyan, Mex. (tlä-lēs'kō-yän')	129	18.53 N	96.04 W
Tlalmanalco, Mex. (tläl-mä-nä'l-kō)	129a	19.12 N	98.48 W
Tlalnepantia, Mex. (tläl-nē-pá'n-tyä)	129a	19.32 N	99.13 W
Tlalnepantla, Mex. (tläl-nå-pän'tlä)	129a	18.59 N	99.01 W
Tlalpan, Mex. (tläl-pä'n)	129a	19.17 N	99.10 W
Tlalpujahua, Mex. (tläl-pōō-Kä'wä)	128	19.15 N	100.10 W
Tlaltenango, see Sánchez Román			
Tlapa, Mex. (tlä'pä)	128	17.30 N	98.09 W
Tlapacoyan, Mex. (tlä-pä-kō-yä'n)	129	19.57 N	97.11 W
Tlapaneco (R.), Mex. (tlä-pänĕ'kō)	128	17.59 N	98.44 W
Tlapehuala, Mex. (tlä-på-wä'lä)	128	18.17 N	100.30 W
Tlaquepaque, Mex. (tlä-kě-pä'kě)	128	20.39 N	103.17 W
Tlatlaya, Mex. (tlä-tlä'yä)	128	18.36 N	100.14 W
Tlaxcala, Mex. (tläs-kä'lä)	128	19.16 N	98.14 W
Tlaxcala (State), Mex.	128	19.30 N	98.15 W
Tlaxco, Mex. (tläs'kō)	128	19.37 N	98.06 W
Tlaxiaco Sta. Maria Asunción, Mex. (tläk-sē-ä'kō sän'tä mä-rē'ä ä-sōōn-syōn')	129	17.16 N	95.41 W
Tlayacapan, Mex. (tlä-yä-kä-pä'n)	129a	18.57 N	99.00 W
Tlemcen, Alg. (tlěm-sěn')	220	34.53 N	1.21 W
Tlevak Str., Ak.	96	53.03 N	132.58 W
Tlumach, Sov. Un. (t'lŭ-mäch')	165	48.47 N	25.00 E
Toa (R.), Cuba (tō'ä)	133	20.25 N	74.35 W
Toamasina, Mad.	223	18.14 S	49.25 E
Toana Ra. (Mts.), Nv. (tō-á-nō')	115	40.45 N	114.11 W
Toar, Cuchillas de (Mtn.), Cuba (kōō-chē'l-lyäs-dě-tô-ä'r)	133	18.20 N	74.50 W
Tobago (I.), N. A. (tô-bā'gō)	127	11.15 N	60.30 W
Toba Inlet, Can.	96	50.20 N	124.50 W

ng-sing; ŋ-baŋk; N-nasalized n; nŏd; cŏmmit; ōld; ôbey; ôrder; oi-boil; fōōd; fo͝ot; ou-out; s-soft; sh-dish; th-thin; pūre; ûnite; ûrn; stŭd; circŭs; ü-as in French tu; '-indeterminate vowel.

356 Tobarra – Trasimeno

PLACE (Pronunciation)	PAGE	Lat. °′	Long. °′
Tobarra, Sp. (tô-bär'rä)	168	38.37 N	1.42 W
Tobol (R.), Sov. Un. (tô-bôl')	178	56.02 N	65.30 E
Tobol'sk, Sov. Un. (tô-bôlsk')	178	58.09 N	68.28 E
Tocaima, Col. (tô-kä'y-mä)	140a	4.28 N	74.38 W
Tocantinópolis, Braz. (tō-kän-tē-nō'pō-lēs)	141	6.27 S	47.18 W
Tocantins (R.), Braz. (tō-kän-tēns')	141	3.28 S	49.22 W
Toccoa, Ga. (tŏk'ô-à)	124	34.35 N	83.20 W
Toccoa (R), Ga.	124	34.53 N	84.24 W
Tochigi, Jap. (tō'chē-gĭ)	201	36.25 N	139.45 E
Tocoa, Hond. (tō-kō'ä)	130	15.37 N	86.01 W
Tocopilla, Chile (tō-kô-pēl'yä)	142	22.03 S	70.08 W
Tocuyo de la Costa, Ven. (tô-kōō'yō-dĕ-lä-kôs'tä)	141b	11.03 N	68.24 W
Toda, Jap.	201d	35.48 N	139.42 E
Todmorden, Eng. (tŏd'môr-dĕn)	154	53.43 N	2.05 W
Toécé, Upper Volta	224	11.50 N	1.16 W
Tofino, Can. (tō-fē'nō)	96	49.09 N	125.54 W
Töfsingdalens (Natl. Park), Swe.	162	62.09 N	13.05 E
Tōgane, Jap. (tō'gä-nā)	201	35.29 N	140.16 E
Togian, Kepulauan (Is.), Indon.	202	0.20 S	122.00 E
Togo, Afr. (tō'gō)	218	8.00 N	0.52 E
Toguzak R., Sov. Un. (tô'gōō-zák)	180a	53.40 N	61.42 E
Tohopekaliga (L.), Fl. (tō'hô-pē'kà-lī'gà)	125a	28.16 N	81.09 W
Toijala, Fin. (toi'yà-là)	163	61.11 N	21.46 E
Toi-Misaki (C.), Jap. (toi mê'sä-kê)	201	31.20 N	131.20 E
Toiyabe Ra., Nv. (toi'yă-bē)	118	38.59 N	117.22 W
Tokachi Gawa (R.), Jap. (tō-kä'chē gä'wä)	200	43.10 N	142.30 E
Tokaj, Hung. (tô'kô-ê)	165	48.06 N	21.24 E
Tokara Guntō (Is.), Jap. (tō-kä'rä gōōn'tō')	200	29.45 N	129.15 E
Tokara Kaikyo (Str.), Jap. (tō'kä'rä kī'kyō)	200	30.20 N	129.50 E
Tokat, Tur. (tô-kät')	177	40.20 N	36.30 E
Tokelau Is., Oceania (tō-kê-lä'ōō)	204	8.00 S	176.00 W
Tokmak, Sov. Un. (tôk'mák)	178	42.44 N	75.41 E
Tokorozawa, Jap. (tô'kô-rô-zä'wä)	201a	35.47 N	139.29 E
Tokuno (I.), Jap. (tô-kōō'nō)	200	27.42 N	129.25 E
Tokushima, Jap. (tō'kōō'shē-mä)	201	34.06 N	134.31 E
Tokuyama, Jap. (tō'kōō'yä-mä)	201	34.04 N	131.49 E
Tōkyō, Jap. (tō'kē-ō)	201a	35.41 N	139.44 E
Tōkyō (Pref.), Jap.	201a	35.42 N	139.40 E
Tōkyō-Wan (B.), Jap. (tō'kyō wän)	201a	35.56 N	139.56 E
Tolbukhin, Bul.	171	43.33 N	27.52 E
Tolcayuca, Mex. (tôl-kä-yōō'kä)	128	19.55 N	98.54 W
Toledo, Ia. (tô-lē'dō)	113	41.59 N	92.35 W
Toledo, Oh.	108	41.40 N	83.35 W
Toledo, Or.	114	44.37 N	123.58 W
Toledo, Sp. (tô-lē'dô)	168	39.53 N	4.02 W
Toledo, Montes de (Mts.), Sp. (mô'n-tĕs-dĕ-tô-lĕ'dô)	168	39.33 N	4.40 W
Toledo Bend Res., La.-Tx.	107	31.30 N	93.30 W
Toliary, Mad.	223	20.16 S	43.44 E
Tolima (Dept.), Col. (tô-lē'mä)	140a	4.07 N	75.20 W
Tolima, Nevado del (Pk.), Col. (nĕ-vä-dô-dĕl-tô-lē'mä)	140a	4.40 N	75.20 W
Tolimán, Mex. (tô-lê-män')	128	20.54 N	99.54 W
Tollesbury, Eng. (tōl'z-bĕrĭ)	154b	51.46 N	0.49 E
Tolmezzo, It. (tôl-mĕt'zō)	170	46.25 N	13.03 E
Tolmin, Yugo. (tôl'mên)	170	46.12 N	13.45 E
Tolna, Hung. (tôl'nô)	165	46.25 N	18.47 E
Tolo, Teluk (B.), Indon. (tō'lō)	202	2.00 S	122.06 E
Tolosa, Sp. (tô-lō'sä)	168	43.10 N	2.05 W
Tolt (R.), Wa. (tōlt)	116a	47.13 N	121.49 W
Toluca, Il. (tô-lōō'kà)	108	41.00 N	89.10 W
Toluca, Mex. (tô-lōō'kä)	129a	19.17 N	99.40 W
Toluca, Nevado de (Mtn.), Mex. (nĕ-vä-dô-dĕ-tô-lōō'kä)	129a	19.09 N	99.42 W
Tolyatti, Sov. Un.	176	53.30 N	49.10 E
Tom' (R.), Sov. Un.	178	55.33 N	85.00 E
Tomah, Wi. (tō'mà)	113	43.58 N	90.31 W
Tomahawk, Wi. (tŏm'à-hôk)	113	45.27 N	89.44 W
Tomakovka, Sov. Un. (tô-mä'kôf-kà)	173	47.49 N	34.43 E
Tomar, Port. (tō-mär')	168	39.36 N	8.26 W
Tomashevka, Sov. Un. (tô-má'shĕf-kà)	165	51.34 N	23.37 E
Tomaszow Lubelski, Pol. (tô-mä'shōōf lōō-bĕl'skĭ)	165	50.20 N	23.27 E
Tomaszów Mazowiecki, Pol. (tô-mä'shōōf mä-zō'vyĕt-skĭ)	165	51.33 N	20.00 E
Tomatlán, Mex. (tô-mä-tlà'n)	128	19.54 N	105.14 W
Tomatlán (R.), Mex.	128	19.56 N	105.14 W
Tombadonkéa, Gui.	224	11.00 N	14.23 W
Tombador, Serra do (Mts.), Braz. (sĕr'rà dōō tōm-bä-dōr')	141	11.31 S	57.33 W
Tombigbee (R.), Al. (tŏm-bĭg'bē)	124	31.45 N	88.02 W
Tombos, Braz. (tô'm-bōs)	139a	20.53 S	42.00 W
Tombouctou (Timbuktu), Mali (tôm-bōōk-tōō')	224	16.46 N	3.01 W
Tombstone, Az. (tōōm'stōn)	119	31.40 N	110.00 W
Tomelilla, Swe. (tō'mĕ-lēl-lä)	162	55.34 N	13.55 E
Tomelloso, Sp. (tō-mâl-lyō'sō)	168	39.09 N	3.02 W
Tomini, Teluk (B.), Indon. (tō-mē'nê)	202	0.10 N	121.00 E
Tommot, Sov. Un. (tŏm-mōt')	179	59.13 N	126.22 E
Tomsk, Sov. Un. (tŏmsk)	178	56.29 N	84.57 E
Tonalá, Mex. (tō-nä-lä')	129	16.05 N	93.45 W
Tonala, Mex.	128	20.38 N	103.14 W
Tonalá (R.), Mex.	129	18.05 N	94.08 W
Tonawanda, NY (tŏn-à-wŏn'dà)	111c	43.01 N	78.53 W
Tonawanda Cr., NY	111c	43.05 N	78.43 W
Tonbei, China (tōŋ-bā)	198	48.00 N	126.48 E
Tonbridge, Eng. (tŭn-brij)	154b	51.11 N	0.17 E
Tonda, Jap. (tôn'dä)	201b	34.51 N	135.38 E
Tondabayashi, Jap. (tôn-dä-bä'yä-shē)	201b	34.29 N	135.36 E
Tondano, Indon. (tôn-dä'nō)	203	1.15 N	124.50 E
Tønder, Den. (tûn'nēr)	162	54.47 N	8.49 E
Tondlá, Mex.	129	16.04 N	93.57 W
Tone (R.), Jap. (tō'nē)	201a	35.55 N	139.57 E
Tone-Gawa (Strm.), Jap. (tô'nē gä'wa)	201	36.12 N	139.19 E
Tonga, Oceania (tŏŋ'gà)	204	18.50 S	175.20 W
Tong'an, China (tôŋ-än)	199	24.48 N	118.02 E
Tongguan, China (tôŋ-gūän)	198	34.48 N	110.25 E
Tonghe, China (tôŋ-hŭ)	198	45.58 N	128.40 E
Tonghua, China (tôŋ-hwä)	198	41.43 N	125.50 E
Tongjiang, China (tôŋ-jyäŋ)	195	47.38 N	132.54 E
Tongliao, China (tôŋ-lĭou)	198	43.30 N	122.15 E
Tongo, Cam.	225	5.11 N	14.00 E
Tongoy, Chile (tôn-goi')	142	30.16 S	71.29 W
Tongren, China (tôŋ-rŭn)	199	27.45 N	109.12 E
Tongshan, China (tôŋ-shän)	196	34.27 N	116.27 E
Tongtian (R.), China (tôŋ-tĭĕn)	194	34.11 N	96.08 E
Tongue of Arabat (Spit), see **Arabatskaya Strelka**			
Tongue of the Ocean (Chan.), Ba. (tŭng ŏv thē ōshŭn)	132	24.05 N	77.20 W
Tongue R., Mt. (tŭng)	115	45.08 N	106.40 W
Tong Xian, China (tôŋ shyĕn)	198a	39.55 N	116.40 E
Tonj R., Sud. (tônj)	221	6.18 N	28.33 E
Tonk, India (Tŏŋk)	190	26.13 N	75.45 E
Tonkawa, Ok. (tŏŋ kà-wô)	121	36.42 N	97.19 W
Tonkin, Gulf of, Viet. (tôn-kăn')	199	20.30 N	108.10 E
Tonle Sap (L.), Kamp. (tôn'lā säp')	202	13.03 N	102.49 E
Tonneins, Fr. (tô-nän')	166	44.24 N	0.18 E
Tönning, F.R.G. (tû'nĕng)	164	54.20 N	8.55 E
Tonopah, Nv. (tō-nô-pä')	118	38.04 N	117.15 W
Tönsberg, Nor. (tûns'bĕrgh)	162	59.19 N	10.25 E
Tonto (R.), Mex. (tōn'tō)	129	18.15 N	96.13 W
Tonto Cr., Az.	119	34.05 N	111.15 W
Tonto Natl. Mon., Az. (tôn'tô)	119	33.33 N	111.08 W
Tooele, Ut. (tōō-ĕl ê)	117b	40.33 N	112.17 W
Toohsien, China	199	25.30 N	111.32 W
Toowoomba, Austl. (tōō wōōm'bà)	212	23.72 S	152.10 E
Topanga, Ca. (tō'păn-gà)	117a	34.05 N	118.36 W
Topeka, Ks. (tô-pē'kà)	121	39.02 N	95.41 W
Topilejo, Mex. (tô-pē-lĕ'hô)	129a	19.12 N	99.09 W
Topock, Az.	119	34.40 N	114.20 W
Topol'čany, Czech. (tô-pôl'chä-nü)	165	48.38 N	18.10 E
Topolobampo, Mex. (tō-pō-lô-bä'm-pô)	126	25.45 N	109.00 W
Topolovgrad, Bul.	171	42.05 N	26.19 E
Toppenish, Wa. (tôp'ĕn-ĭsh)	114	46.22 N	120.00 W
Tora, Île (I.), Mauritania	224	19.50 N	16.45 W
Torbay, Can. (tôr-bā')	103	47.40 N	52.43 W
Torbay, see **Torquay**			
Torbreck, Mt., Austl. (tŏr-brĕk)	212	37.05 S	146.55 E
Torch (L.), Mi. (tôrch)	108	45.00 N	85.30 W
Töreboda, Swe. (tū'rĕ-bō'dä)	162	58.44 N	14.04 E
Torhout, Bel.	161	51.01 N	3.04 E
Toribío, Col. (tô-rē-bē'ô)	140a	2.58 N	76.14 W
Toride, Jap. (tō'rē-dä)	201a	35.54 N	104.04 E
Torino (Turin), It. (tô-rē'no) (tū'rĭn)	170	45.05 N	7.44 E
Tormes (R.), Sp. (tōr'mās)	168	41.12 N	6.15 W
Torneälven (R.), Swe.	156	67.29 N	22.05 E
Torneträsk (L.), Swe. (tôr'nē trĕsk)	150	68.10 N	20.36 E
Torngat Mts., Can.	95	59.18 N	64.35 W
Tornio, Fin. (tôr'nĭ-ô)	156	65.55 N	24.09 E
Toro, Lac (L.), Can.	102	46.53 N	73.46 W
Toronto, Can. (tô-rŏn'tō)	93d	43.40 N	79.23 W
Toronto, Oh.	108	40.30 N	80.35 W
Toronto, L., Mex. (lä'gô-tô-rô'n-tō)	122	27.35 N	105.37 W
Toropets, Sov. Un. (tô'rô-pyĕts)	172	56.31 N	31.37 E
Toros Dağlari (Taurus Mts.), Tur. (tô'rŭs)	177	37.00 N	32.40 E
Torote (R.), Sp. (tô-rō'tä)	169a	40.36 N	3.24 W
Torquay (Torbay), Eng. (tôr-kē')	160	50.30 N	3.26 W
Torra, Cerro (Mtn.), Col. (sĕ'r-rô-tô'r-rä)	140a	4.41 N	76.22 W
Torrance, Ca. (tŏr'rănc)	117a	33.50 N	118.20 W
Torre Annunziata, It. (tôr'rā ä-nōōn-tsē-ä'tä)	169c	40.31 N	14.27 E
Torreblanca, Sp.	169	40.18 N	0.12 E
Torre del Greco, It. (tôr'rā dĕl grā'kō)	169c	40.32 N	14.23 E
Torrejoncillo, Sp. (tôr'rā-hōn-thē'lyō)	168	39.54 N	6.26 W
Torrelavega, Sp. (tôr-rä'lä-vä'gä)	168	43.22 N	4.02 W
Torre Maggiore, It. (tôr'rā mäd-jō'rā)	170	40.41 N	15.18 E
Torrens, L., Austl. (tŏr-ĕns)	212	30.07 S	137.40 E
Torrente, Sp. (tôr-rĕn'tā)	169	39.25 N	0.28 W
Torreon, Mex. (tôr-rā-ōn')	122	25.32 N	103.26 W
Torres Is., Vanuatu (tôr'rĕs) (tŏr'ĕz)	211	13.18 N	165.59 E
Torres Martinez Ind. Res., Ca. (tôr'ĕz mär-tē'nĕz)	118	33.33 N	116.21 W
Torres Novas, Port. (tôr'rĕzh nō'văzh)	168	39.28 N	8.37 W
Torres Str., Austl. (tôr'rĕs)	203	10.30 S	141.30 E
Torres Vedras, Port. (tôr'rĕsh vä'dräzh)	168	39.08 N	9.18 W
Torrevieja, Sp. (tôr-rā-vyā'hä)	169	37.58 N	0.40 W
Torrijos, Phil. (tôr-rē'hōs)	203a	13.19 N	122.06 E
Torrington, Ct. (tŏr'ĭng-tŭn)	109	41.50 N	73.10 W
Torrington, Wy.	112	42.04 N	104.11 W
Torro, Sp. (tô'r-rō)	168	41.27 N	5.23 W
Torsby, Swe. (tôrs'bü)	162	60.07 N	12.56 E
Torshälla, Swe. (tôrs'hĕl-ä)	162	59.26 N	16.21 E
Tórshavn, Faer. (tôrs-houn')	156	62.00 N	6.55 W
Tortola (I.), Vir. Is. (Br.) (tôr-tō'lä)	127b	18.34 N	64.40 W
Tortona, It. (tôr-tō'nä)	170	44.52 N	8.52 W
Tortosa, Sp. (tôr-tō'sä)	169	40.59 N	0.33 E
Tortosa, Cabo de (C.), Sp. (kà'bô-dĕ-tôr-tō-sä)	169	40.42 N	0.55 E
Tortue, Canal de la (Chan.), Hai. (tôr-tü')	133	20.05 N	73.20 W
Tortue, Ile de la (I.), Hai.	133	20.10 N	73.00 W
Tortue, Rivière de la (R.), Can. (lä tōr-tü')	93a	45.12 N	73.32 W
Tortuga, Isla la (I.), Ven. (ē's-lä-lä-tôr-tōō'gä)	141b	10.55 N	65.18 W
Toruń, Pol. (tō'rōōn')	165	53.01 N	18.37 E
Tõrva, Sov. Un. (t'r'vá)	172	58.02 N	25.56 E
Torzhok, Sov. Un. (tôr'zhôk)	172	57.03 N	34.53 E
Tosa-Wan (B.), Jap. (tô'sä wän)	201	33.14 N	133.39 E
Toscana (Reg.), It. (tôs-kä'nä)	170	43.23 N	11.08 E
Tosna R., Sov. Un.	180c	59.38 N	30.52 E
Tosno, Sov. Un. (tôs'nô)	180c	59.32 N	30.52 E
Tostado, Arg. (tôs-tà'dô)	142	29.10 S	61.43 W
Tosya, Tur. (tôz'yà)	177	41.00 N	34.00 E
Totana, Sp. (tô-tä-nä)	168	37.45 N	1.28 W
Tot'ma, Sov. Un. (tôt'mà)	176	60.00 N	42.20 E
Totness, Sur.	141	5.51 N	56.17 W
Totonicapán, Guat. (tōtō-nē-kä'pän)	130	14.55 N	91.20 W
Totoras, Arg. (tô-tô'räs)	139c	32.33 S	61.13 W
Totsuka, Jap. (tōt'sōō-kä)	201	35.24 N	139.32 E
Tottenham, Eng. (tŏt'ĕn-àm)	154b	51.35 N	0.06 W
Tottori, Jap. (tô'tô-rē)	201	35.30 N	134.15 E
Touat (Oasis), Alg. (tōō'ät)	220	27.22 N	0.38 W
Touba, Ivory Coast	224	8.17 N	7.41 W
Touba, Senegal	224	14.51 N	15.53 W
Toubkal Jebel (Mtn.), Mor.	220	31.15 N	7.46 W
Tougan, Upper Volta	224	13.04 N	3.04 W
Touggourt, Alg. (tōō-gōōrt') (tōō-gōōr')	220	33.09 N	6.07 E
Touil R., Alg. (tōō-ēl')	158	34.42 N	21.6 E
Toul, Fr. (tōōl)	167	48.39 N	5.51 E
Toulnustouc (R.), Can.	102	50.23 N	67.55 W
Toulon, Fr. (tōō-lôn')	167	43.09 N	5.54 E
Toulouse, Fr. (tōō-lōōz')	166	43.37 N	1.27 E
Toungoo, Bur. (tō-ōōŋ-gōō')	202	19.00 N	96.29 E
Tourane, see **Da Nang**			
Tourcoing, Fr. (tōōr-kwàn')	166	50.44 N	3.06 E
Tournan-en-Brie, Fr. (tōōr-nän-ĕn-brē')	167b	48.45 N	2.47 E
Tours, Fr. (tōōr)	166	47.23 N	0.39 E
Touside, Pic (Pk.), Chad (tōō-sē-dā')	221	21.10 N	16.30 E
Tovdalselva (R.), Nor. (tôv-däls-ĕlvå)	162	58.23 N	8.16 E
Towanda, Pa. (tô-wän'dà)	109	41.45 N	76.30 W
Town Bluff L., Tx.	123	30.52 N	94.30 W
Towner, ND (tou'nēr)	112	48.21 N	100.24 W
Townsend, Ma. (toun'zĕnd)	103a	42.41 N	71.42 W
Townsend, Mt.	115	46.19 N	111.35 W
Townsend, Mt., Wa.	116a	47.52 N	123.03 W
Townsville, Austl. (tounz'vĭl)	141	19.18 S	146.50 E
Towson, Md. (tou'sŭn)	110e	39.24 N	76.36 W
Towuti, Danau (L.), Indon. (tô-wōō'tê)	202	3.00 S	121.45 E
Toxkan (R.), China	194	40.34 N	77.15 E
Toyah, Tx. (tô'yà)	122	31.19 N	103.46 W
Toyama, Jap. (tō'yä-mä)	201	36.42 N	137.14 E
Toyama-Wan (B.), Jap.	201	36.58 N	137.16 E
Toyohashi, Jap. (tō'yō-hä'shē)	201	34.44 N	137.21 E
Toyonaka, Jap. (tō'yō-nä'kà)	201b	34.47 N	135.28 E
Tozeur, Tun. (tô-zûr')	158	33.59 N	8.11 E
Trabzon, Tur. (tràb'zôn)	177	41.00 N	39.45 E
Tracy, Ca. (trā'sē)	118	37.45 N	121.27 W
Tracy, Can.	102	46.00 N	73.13 W
Tracy, Mn.	112	44.13 N	95.37 W
Tracy City, Tn.	124	35.15 N	85.44 W
Trafalgar, Cabo (C.), Sp. (kà'bô-trä-fäl-gä'r)	168	36.10 N	6.02 W
Trafonomby (Mtn.), Mad.	223	24.32 S	46.35 E
Trail, Can. (trāl)	97	49.06 N	117.42 W
Traisen (R.), Aus.	155e	48.15 N	15.55 E
Traiskirchen, Aus.	155e	48.01 N	16.18 E
Trakai, Sov. Un. (trá-kāy)	163	54.38 N	24.59 E
Trakiszki, Pol. (trá-kē'-sh-kê)	165	54.16 N	23.07 E
Tralee, Ire. (trà-lē')	160	52.16 N	9.20 W
Tranas, Swe. (trän'ôs)	162	58.03 N	14.56 E
Trancoso, Port. (träŋ-kō'sōō)	168	40.46 N	7.23 W
Trangan, Pulau (I.), Indon. (träŋ'gän)	203	6.52 S	133.30 E
Trani, It. (trä'nē)	170	41.15 N	16.25 E
Transcaucasia (Reg.), Sov. Un.	153	41.17 N	44.30 E
Trans Himalayas (Mts.), see **Gangdisê Shan**			
Transvaal (Prov.), S. Afr. (trăns-väl')	222	24.21 S	28.18 E
Transylvania (Reg.), Rom. (trăn-sĭl-vā'nĭ-à)	165	46.30 N	22.35 E
Transylvanian Alps (Mts.), see **Carpaţii Meridionali**			
Trapani, It. (trä'pä-nê)	170	38.02 N	12.34 E
Trappes, Fr. (tráp)	167b	48.47 N	2.01 E
Traralgon, Austl. (trá'răl-gŏn)	212	38.15 S	146.33 E
Trarza (Reg.), Mauritania	224	17.35 N	15.15 W
Trasimeno, Lago (L.), Ir. (lä'gō trä-sê-mä'nō)	170	43.00 N	12.12 E

PRONOUNCING INDEX

Trâs-os-Montes – Tupelo 357

PLACE (Pronunciation)	PAGE	Lat. °′	Long. °′
Trás-os-Montes (Mts.), Port. (träzh'ōzh môn'tāzh)	168	41.33 N	7.13 W
Traun R., Aus. (troun)	164	48.10 N	14.15 E
Traunstein, F.R.G. (troun'stīn)	164	47.52 N	12.38 E
Traverse, L., Mn.-SD (trăv'ērs)	112	45.46 N	96.53 W
Traverse City, Mi.	108	44.45 N	85.40 W
Travnik, Yugo. (träv'nēk)	170	44.13 N	17.43 E
Treasure I., Ca. (trĕzh'ēr)	116b	37.49 N	122.22 W
Trebbin, G.D.R. (trĕ'bēn)	155b	52.13 N	13.13 E
Třebíč, Czech. (t'rzhĕ'bēch)	164	49.13 N	15.53 E
Trebinje, Yugo. (trå'bēn-yĕ)	171	42.43 N	18.21 E
Trebisov, Czech. (trĕ'bē-shôf)	165	48.36 N	21.32 E
Třeboň, Czech. (t'rzhĕ'bôn')	164	49.00 N	14.48 E
Tregrosse Is., Austl. (trē-grōs')	211	18.08 S	150.53 E
Treinta y Tres, Ur. (trå-ēn'tā ē trās')	142	33.14 S	54.17 W
Trélazé, Fr. (trā-là-zā')	166	47.27 N	0.32 W
Trelew, Arg. (trē'lū)	142	43.15 S	65.25 W
Trelleborg, Swe.	162	55.24 N	13.07 E
Tremiti, Isole (Is.), It. (ê'sō-lĕ trä-mē'tē)	170	42.07 N	16.33 E
Trenčín, Czech. (trĕn'chēn)	165	48.52 N	18.02 E
Trenque Lauquén, Arg. (trĕn'kĕ-lâ'ōō-kĕ'n)	142	35.50 S	62.44 W
Trent (R.), Can. (trĕnt)	101	44.15 N	77.55 W
Trent and Mersey Can., Eng. (trĕnt) (mûr zē)	154	53.11 N	2.24 W
Trento, It. (trĕn'tô)	170	46.04 N	11.07 E
Trentino-Alto Adige (Reg.), It.	170	46.16 N	10.47 E
Trenton, Can. (trĕn'tŭn)	95	44.05 N	77.35 W
Trenton, Can.	103	45.37 N	62.38 W
Trenton, Mi.	111b	42.08 N	83.12 W
Trenton, Mo.	121	40.05 N	93.36 W
Trenton, NJ	110a	40.13 N	74.46 W
Trenton, Tn.	124	35.57 N	88.55 W
Trepassey, Can. (trē-păs'ê)	103	46.44 N	53.22 W
Trepassey B., Can.	103	46.40 N	53.20 W
Tres Arroyos, Arg. (trās'är-rō'yōs)	142	38.18 S	60.16 W
Três Coracoes, Braz. (trĕ's kō-rä-zô'ĕs)	139a	21.41 S	45.14 W
Tres Cumbres, Mex. (trĕ's kōō'm-brĕs)	129a	19.03 N	99.14 W
Três Lagoas, Braz. (trĕ's lä-gô'ås)	141	20.48 S	51.42 W
Três Marias, Represa (Res.), Braz. (rĕ-prä'sä trĕs' mä-rē'äs)	141	18.15 S	45.30 W
Tres Morros, Alto de (Mtn.), Col. (á'l-tō dĕ trĕ's mô'r-rôs)	140a	7.08 N	76.10 W
Três Pontas, Braz. (trĕ'pô'n-täs)	139a	21.22 S	45.30 W
Três Pontas, Cabo das (C.), Ang.	226	10.23 S	13.32 E
Três Rios, Braz. (trĕ's rē'ôs)	139a	22.07 S	43.13 W
Très-St. Rédempteur, Can. (săN rā-dăNp-tûr')	93a	45.26 N	74.23 W
Treuenbrietzen, G.D.R. (troi'ĕn-brē-tzĕn)	155b	52.06 N	12.52 E
Treviglio, It. (trā-vē'lyô)	170	45.30 N	9.34 E
Treviso, It. (trĕ-vē'sō)	170	45.39 N	12.15 E
Triangle, The (Reg.), Asia	194	26.00 N	98.00 E
Trichardt, S. Afr. (trĭ-Kärt')	219	26.32 N	29.16 E
Trieste, It. (trê-ĕs'tā)	170	45.39 N	13.48 E
Trigueros, Sp. (trê-gā'rōs)	168	37.23 N	6.50 W
Tríkala, Grc.	171	39.33 N	21.49 E
Trikora, Puncak (Pk.), Indon.	203	4.15 S	138.45 E
Trim Cr., Il. (trĭm)	111a	41.19 N	87.39 W
Trincomalee, Sri Lanka (trĭŋ-kō-mȧ-lē')	191	8.39 N	81.12 E
Tring, Eng. (trĭng)	154b	51.46 N	0.40 W
Trinidad, Bol. (trē-nē-dhädh')	140	14.48 S	64.43 W
Trinidad, Col. (trĭn'ĭdăd)	120	37.11 N	104.31 W
Trinidad, Cuba (trē-nē-dhädh')	132	21.50 N	80.00 W
Trinidad, Ur.	139c	33.29 S	56.55 W
Trinidad, Sierra de (Mts.), Cuba (sē-ĕ'r-rä dĕ trē-nē-dä'd)	132	21.50 N	79.55 W
Trinidad (I.), Trin. (trĭn'ĭ-dăd)	141	10.00 N	61.00 W
Trinidad and Tobago, N. A. (trĭn'ĭ-dăd) (tô-bā'gō)	127	11.00 N	61.00 W
Trinidade, Ilha da (I.), Braz. (ê'lä dä trē-nē-dä-dĕ)	138	21.00 S	32.00 W
Trinidad R., Pan.	126a	8.55 N	80.01 W
Trinitaria, Mex. (trē-nē-tä'ryä)	129	16.09 N	92.04 W
Trinité, Mart.	131b	14.47 N	61.00 W
Trinity, Can. (trĭn'ĭ-tê)	103	48.59 N	53.55 W
Trinity, Tx.	123	30.52 N	95.27 W
Trinity (Is.), Ak.	105	56.25 N	153.15 W
Trinity (R.), East Fk., Tx.	120	33.24 N	96.42 W
Trinity (R.), West Fk., Tx.	121	33.22 N	98.26 W
Trinity B., Can.	103	48.00 N	53.40 W
Trinity R., Ca.	114	40.50 N	123.20 W
Trinity R., Tx.	123	30.50 N	95.09 W
Trino, It. (trē'nô)	170	45.11 N	8.16 E
Trion, Ga. (trī'ŏn)	124	34.32 N	85.18 W
Tripoli, see Ţarābulus			
Tripoli, see Tarābulus			
Tripolis, Grc. (trĭ'pō-lĭs)	171	37.32 N	22.32 E
Tripolitania (Prov.), see Tarābulus			
Tripp, SD (trĭp)	112	43.13 N	97.58 W
Tripura (State), India	190	24.00 N	92.00 E
Tristan da Cunha Is., Alt. O. (três-tän'dä kōō'n'yä)	228	35.30 S	12.15 W
Triste, Golfo (G.), Ven. (gôl-fô trē's-tĕ)	141b	10.40 N	68.05 W
Triticus Res., NY (trĭ tĭ-cŭs)	110a	41.20 N	73.36 W
Trivandrum, India (trê-vŭn'drŭm)	191	8.34 N	76.58 E
Trnava, Czech. (t'r'nȧ-vȧ)	165	48.22 N	17.34 E
Trobriand Is., Pap. N. Gui. (trō-brē-ănd')	203	8.25 S	151.45 E
Trogir, Yugo. (trô'gēr)	170	43.32 N	16.17 E
Trois-Rivières, Can. (trwä'rê-vyâ')	95	46.21 N	72.35 W
Troitsk, Sov. Un. (trô'ētsk)	180a	54.06 N	61.34 E
Troitsko-Pechorsk, Sov. Un. (trô'ĭtsk-ô-pyĕ-chôrsk')	178	62.18 N	56.07 E
Troitskoye, Sov. Un.	173	47.39 N	30.16 E
Trollhättan, Swe. (trôl'hĕt-ĕn)	162	58.17 N	12.17 E
Trollheim (Mts.), Nor. (trôll-hĕĭm)	162	62.48 N	9.05 E
Tromsö, Nor. (trôm'sû)	156	69.38 N	19.12 E
Trona, Ca. (trō'nȧ)	118	35.49 N	117.20 W
Tronador, Cerro (Mtn.), Arg. (sĕ'r-rô trō-nä'dôr)	142	41.17 S	71.56 W
Troncoso, Mex. (trôn-kô'sō)	128	22.43 N	102.22 W
Trondheim, Nor. (trôn'hâm)	162	63.25 N	11.35 E
Trosa, Swe. (trô'sä)	162	58.54 N	17.25 E
Trout (L.), Can.	95	51.16 N	92.46 W
Trout (L.), Can.	94	61.10 N	121.30 W
Trout Cr., Or.	114	42.18 N	118.31 W
Troutdale, Or. (trout'dāl)	116c	45.32 N	122.23 W
Trout Lake, Mi.	113	46.20 N	85.02 W
Trout L., Can.	99	51.13 N	93.20 W
Trouville, Fr. (trōō-vēl')	166	49.23 N	0.05 E
Troy, Al. (troi)	124	31.47 N	85.46 W
Troy, Il.	117e	38.44 N	89.53 W
Troy, Ks.	121	39.46 N	95.07 W
Troy, Mo.	121	38.56 N	99.57 W
Troy, Mt.	114	48.28 N	115.56 W
Troy, NY	109	42.45 N	73.45 W
Troy, NC	125	35.21 N	79.58 W
Troy, Oh.	108	40.00 N	84.10 W
Troy Ruins, Tur.	171	39.59 N	26.14 E
Troyes Fr. (trwä)	166	48.18 N	4.03 E
Trst, see Trieste			
Trstenik, Yugo. (t'r'stĕ-nêk)	171	43.36 N	20.00 E
Trubchëvsk, Sov. Un. (trōōp'chĕfsk)	172	52.36 N	32.46 E
Trucial States, see United Arab Emirates			
Truckee, Ca. (trŭk'ê)	118	39.20 N	120.12 W
Truckee (R.), Ca.-Nv.	118	39.25 N	120.07 W
Truganina, Austl.	207a	37.49 S	144.44 E
Trujillo, Col. (trōō-Kê'l-yō)	140a	4.10 N	76.20 W
Trujillo, Hond. (trōō-Kēl'yō)	130	15.55 N	85.58 W
Trujillo, Peru	140	8.08 S	79.00 W
Trujillo, Sp. (trōō-Kê'l-yô)	168	39.27 N	5.50 W
Trujillo, Ven.	140	9.15 N	70.28 W
Trujillo (R.), Mex.	128	23.12 N	103.10 W
Trujin, L., Dom. Rep. (trōō-Kēn')	133	17.45 N	71.25 W
Trumann, Ar. (trōō'măn)	121	35.41 N	90.31 W
Trŭn, Bul. (trŭn)	171	42.49 N	22.39 E
Truro, Can. (trōō'rō)	102	45.22 N	63.16 W
Truro, Eng.	160	50.17 N	5.05 W
Trussville, Al. (trŭs'vĭl)	110h	33.37 N	86.37 W
Truth or Consequences, NM (trōōth ŏr kŏn'sē-kwĕn-sĭs)	119	33.10 N	107.20 W
Trutnov, Czech. (trōōt'nôf)	164	50.36 N	15.36 E
Trzcianka, Pol. (tchyän'kȧ)	164	53.02 N	16.27 E
Trzebiatow, Pol. (tchĕ-byä'tōō-v)	164	54.03 N	15.16 E
Tsaidam Basin, China (tsī-däm)	194	37.19 N	94.08 E
Tsala Apopka (R.), Fl. (tsä'lȧ ă-pŏp'kȧ)	125	28.57 N	82.11 W
Tsast Bogda Ula (Mt.), Mong.	194	46.44 N	92.34 E
Tsavo Natl. Pk., Ken.	227	2.35 S	38.45 E
Tsawwassen Ind. Res., Can.	116d	49.03 N	123.11 W
Tselinograd, Sov. Un. (tsĕ'lĕ-nô-grȧ'd)	178	51.10 N	71.43 E
Tsentral'nyy-Kospashskiy, Sov. Un. (tsĕn-träl'nyĭ-kôs-pȧsh'skĭ)	180a	59.03 N	57.48 E
Tshela, Zaire (tshā'lȧ)	226	4.59 S	12.56 E
Tshikapa, Zaire (tshê-kä'pä)	226	6.25 S	20.48 E
Tshofa, Zaire	226	5.14 S	25.15 E
Tshuapa (R.), Zaire	226	10.15 S	21.25 E
Tsiafajovona (Mtn.), Mad.	223	19.17 S	47.27 E
Tsimlyanskiy (Res.), Sov. Un. (tsym-lyă'ns-kēê)	177	47.50 N	43.40 E
Tsiribihina (R.), Mad. (tsē'rê-bē-hē-nä')	223	19.45 S	43.30 E
Tsitsa (R.), S. Afr. (tsê'tsȧ)	223c	31.28 S	28.53 E
Tsitsihar (Qiqihar), China (chyē-chyē-här)	198	47.18 N	124.00 E
Tsolo, S. Afr. (tsō'lō)	223c	31.19 S	28.47 E
Tsomo, S. Afr.	223c	32.03 S	27.49 E
Tsomo (R.), S. Afr.	223c	31.53 S	27.48 E
Tsu, Jap. (tsōō)	201	34.42 N	136.31 E
Tsuchiura, Jap. (tsōō'chê-ōō-rä)	201	36.04 N	140.09 E
Tsuda, Jap. (tsōō'dä)	201b	34.48 N	135.43 E
Tsugaru Kaikyō (Str.), Jap. (tsōō'gä-rōō kī'kyō)	200	41.25 N	140.20 E
Tsumeb, Namibia (tsōō'mĕb)	222	19.10 S	17.45 E
Tsunashima, Jap. (tsōō'nä-shē'mä)	201a	35.32 N	139.37 E
Tsuruga, Jap. (tsōō'rōō-gä)	201	35.39 N	136.04 E
Tsurugi San (Mtn.), Jap. (tsōō'rōō-gē sän)	201	33.52 N	134.07 E
Tsuruoka, Jap. (tsōō'rōō-ō'kä)	200	38.43 N	139.51 E
Tsurusaki, Jap. (tsōō'rōō-sä'kē)	201	33.15 N	131.42 E
Tsu Shima (I.), Jap. (tsōō shē'mä)	201	34.28 N	129.30 E
Tsushima Kaikyō (Str.), Asia (tsōō'shē-mä kī'kyō)	201	33.52 N	129.30 E
Tsuwano, Jap. (tsōō'wȧ-nô')	201	34.28 N	131.47 E
Tsuyama, Jap. (tsōō'yä-mä')	201	35.05 N	134.00 E
Tua (R.), Port. (tōō'ä)	168	41.23 N	7.18 W
Tualatin (R.), Or. (tōō'ȧ-lā-tĭn)	116c	45.25 N	122.54 W
Tuamoto (Low), Arch., Fr. Polynesia (tōō-ä-mō'tōō)	205	19.00 S	141.20 W
Tuapse, Sov. Un. (tōō'ȧp-sĕ)	177	44.00 N	39.10 E
Tuareg (Reg.), Alg.	220	21.26 N	2.51 E
Tubarão, Braz. (tōō-bä-rouN')	142	28.23 N	48.56 W
Tübingen, F.R.G. (tü'bĭng-ĕn)	164	48.33 N	9.05 E
Tubinskiy, Sov. Un. (tû bĭn'skĭ)	180a	52.53 N	58.15 E
Tubruq, Libya	221	32.03 N	24.04 E
Tucacas, Ven. (tōō-kä'käs)	141b	10.48 N	68.20 W
Tucker, Ga. (tŭk'ēr)	110c	33.51 N	84.13 W
Tucson, Az. (tōō-sŏn')	119	32.15 N	111.00 W
Tucumán, Arg. (tōō-kōō-män')	142	26.52 S	65.08 W
Tucumán (Prov.), Arg.	142	26.30 S	65.30 W
Tucumcari, NM (tōō'kŭm-kâr-ê)	120	35.11 N	103.43 W
Tucupita, Ven. (tōō-kōō-pê'tä)	140	9.00 N	62.09 W
Tucuruí, Braz. (tōō-kōō-tōō-ē')	141	3.34 S	49.44 W
Tudela, Sp. (tōō-dhā'lä)	168	42.03 N	1.37 W
Tugaloo (R.), Ga.-SC (tŭg'ȧ-lōō)	124	34.35 N	83.05 W
Tugela (R.), S. Afr. (tōō-gel'ȧ)	223c	28.50 S	30.52 E
Tugela Ferry, S. Afr.	223c	28.44 S	30.27 E
Tug Fork (R.), WV (tŭg)	108	37.50 N	82.30 W
Tuguegarao, Phil. (tōō-gā-gȧ-rä'ō)	203a	17.37 N	121.44 E
Tuhai (R.), China (tōō-hī)	196	37.05 N	116.56 E
Tuinplaas, S. Afr.	219d	24.54 S	28.46 E
Tujunga, Ca. (tōō-jŭŋ'gȧ)	117a	34.15 N	118.16 W
Tukan, Sov. Un. (tōō'kȧn)	180a	53.52 N	57.25 E
Tukangbesi, Kepulauan (Is.), Indon.	203	6.00 S	124.15 E
Tūkrah, Libya	221	32.34 N	20.47 E
Tuktoyaktuk, Can. (tōōk-tô-yäk'tōōk)	94	69.32 N	132.37 W
Tukums, Sov. Un. (tōō'kōōms)	163	56.57 N	23.09 E
Tukuyu, Tan. (tōō-kōō'yȧ)	222	9.13 S	33.43 E
Tukwila, Wa. (tŭk'wĭ-lȧ)	116a	47.28 N	122.16 W
Tula, Mex. (tōō'lä)	128	20.04 N	99.22 W
Tula, Sov. Un. (tōō'lä)	172	54.12 N	37.37 E
Tula (Oblast), Sov. Un.	172	53.45 N	37.19 E
Tula (R.), Mex. (tōō'lä)	128	20.40 N	99.27 W
Tulagai (I.), Sol. Is. (tōō-lä'gē)	211	9.15 S	160.17 E
Tulalip, Wa. (tū-lā'lĭp)	116a	48.04 N	122.18 W
Tulalip Ind. Res., Wa.	116a	48.06 N	122.16 W
Tulancingo, Mex. (tōō-län-sĭŋ'gō)	128	20.04 N	98.24 W
Tulangbawang (R.), Indon.	202	4.17 S	105.00 E
Tulare, Ca. (tōō-lä'rȧ) (tul-âr')	118	36.12 N	119.22 W
Tulare Basin, Ca.	118	35.57 N	120.18 W
Tularosa, NM (tōō-lȧ-rō'zȧ)	119	33.05 N	106.05 W
Tulcán, Ec. (tōōl-kän')	140	0.44 N	77.52 W
Tulcea, Rom. (tōōl'chȧ)	173	45.10 N	28.47 E
Tul'chin, Sov. Un. (tōōl'chĕn)	173	48.42 N	28.53 E
Tulcingo, Mex. (tōōl-sĭŋ'gō)	128	18.03 N	98.27 W
Tule (R.), Ca. (tōōl'lȧ)	118	36.08 N	118.50 W
Tule River Ind. Res., Ca. (tōō'lȧ)	118	36.05 N	118.35 W
Tuli, Zimb. (tōō'lê)	222	20.58 S	29.12 E
Tulia, Tx. (tōō'lĭ-ȧ)	120	34.32 N	101.46 W
Tulijá (R.), Mex. (tōō-lē-Kä')	129	17.28 N	92.11 W
Tulik Vol., Ak. (tōō'lĭk)	105a	53.28 N	168.10 W
Tūlkarm, Jordan (tōōl kärm)	189a	32.19 N	35.02 E
Tullahoma, Tn. (tŭl-ȧ-hō'mȧ)	124	35.21 N	86.12 W
Tullamore, Ire. (tŭl-ȧ-mōr')	160	53.15 N	7.29 W
Tulle, Fr. (tül)	166	45.15 N	1.45 E
Tulln, Aus. (tōōln)	155e	48.21 N	16.04 E
Tullner Feld (Reg.), Aus.	155e	48.20 N	15.59 E
Tulpetlac, Mex. (tōōl-pȧ-tlăk')	129a	19.33 N	99.04 W
Tulsa, Ok. (tŭl'sȧ)	121	36.08 N	95.58 W
Tuluá, Col. (tōō-lōō-ȧ')	140a	4.06 N	76.12 W
Tulum, Mex. (tōō-lōō'm)	130a	20.17 N	87.26 W
Tulun, Sov. Un. (tōō-lōōn')	178	54.29 N	100.43 E
Tumuacacori Natl. Mon., Az. (tōō-mä-kä'kȧ-rē)	119	31.36 N	110.20 W
Tumaco, Col. (tōō-mä'kô)	140	1.41 N	78.44 W
Tuma R., Nic. (tōō'mä)	130	13.07 N	85.32 W
Tumba, Lac (L.), Zaire (tōōm'bȧ)	226	0.50 S	17.45 E
Tumbes, Peru (tōō'm-bĕs)	140	3.39 S	80.27 W
Tumbiscatío, Mex. (tōōm-bē-skȧ-tē'ō)	128	18.32 N	102.23 W
Tumbo (I.), Can.	116d	48.49 N	123.04 W
Tumen, China (tōō-mŭn)	198	43.00 N	129.50 E
Tumen (R.), China	200	42.08 N	128.40 E
Tumeremo, Ven. (tōō-mȧ-rā'mō)	141	7.15 N	61.28 W
Tumkūr, India	191	13.22 N	77.05 E
Tumuc-Humac Mts., S. A. (tōō-mōōk'ōō-mäk')	141	2.15 N	54.50 W
Tunas de Zaza, Cuba (tōō'näs dā zä'zä)	132	21.40 N	79.35 W
Tunbridge Wells, Eng. (tŭn'brĭj welz')	160	51.05 N	0.09 E
Tundra (Reg.), Sov. Un.	178	70.45 N	84.00 E
Tunduru, Tan.	227	11.07 S	37.21 E
Tungabhadra Res., India	190	15.26 N	75.57 E
Tungpa, China (tōōng-bä)	196	35.56 N	116.19 E
Tuni, India	191	17.29 N	82.38 E
Tunica, Ms. (tū'nĭ-kȧ)	124	34.41 N	90.23 W
Tunis, Tun. (tū'nĭs)	220	36.59 N	10.06 E
Tunis, Golfe de (G.), Tun.	157	37.06 N	10.43 E
Tunisia, Afr. (tu-nĭzh'ê-ȧ)	218	35.00 N	10.11 E
Tunja, Col. (tōō'n-hȧ)	140	5.32 N	73.19 W
Tunkhannock, Pa. (tŭnk-hăn'ŭk)	109	41.35 N	75.55 W
Tunnel (R.), Wa. (tŭn'ĕl)	116a	47.48 N	123.04 W
Tuoji Dao (I.), China (twô-jyē dou)	196	38.11 N	120.45 E
Tuolumne (R.), Ca. (twô-lŭm'nē)	118	37.35 N	120.37 W
Tuostakh (R.), Sov. Un.	179	67.09 N	137.30 E
Tupã, Braz. (tōō-pȧ)	141	21.47 S	50.33 W
Tupelo, Ms. (tū'pĕ-lō)	124	34.14 N	88.43 W

ng-sing; ŋ-baŋk; N-nasalized n; nŏd; cŏmmit; ōld; ôbey; ôrder; oi-boil; fōōd; fŏŏt; ou-out; s-soft; sh-dish; th-thin; pūre; ûnite; ûrn; stŭd; circŭs; ü-as in French tu; '-indeterminate vowel.

358 Tupinambaranas – Union City

PLACE (Pronunciation)	PAGE	Lat. °′	Long. °′
Tupinambaranas, Ilha (I.), Braz. (ē'lä-tōō-pē-näɴ-bä-rä'näs)	141	3.04 S	58.09 W
Tupiza, Bol. (tōō-pē'zä)	140	21.26 S	65.43 W
Tupper Lake, NY (tŭp'ẽr)	109	44.15 N	74.25 W
Tuquerres, Col. (tōō-kĕ'r-rĕs)	140	1.12 N	77.44 W
Tura, Sov. Un. (tōōr'á)	178	64.08 N	99.58 E
Turbio (R.), Mex. (tōōr-byô)	128	20.28 N	101.40 W
Turbo, Col. (tōō'bō)	140	8.02 N	76.43 W
Turda, Rom. (tōōr'dà)	165	46.35 N	23.47 E
Turfan Depression, China	194	42.16 N	90.00 E
Turffontein (Neigh.), S. Afr.	223b	26.15 S	28.03 E
Turgay, Sov. Un. (tōōr'gī)	178	49.42 N	63.39 E
Turgayka (R.), Sov. Un. (tōōr-gī'kä)	153	49.44 N	66.15 E
Tŭrgovishte, Bul.	171	43.14 N	26.36 E
Turgutlu, Tur.	177	38.30 N	27.20 E
Türi, Sov. Un. (tü'rĭ)	163	58.49 N	25.29 E
Turia (R.), Sp. (tōō'ryä)	168	40.12 N	1.18 W
Turicato, Mex. (tōō-rē-kä'tō)	128	19.03 N	101.24 W
Turiguano (I.), Cuba (tōō-rē-gwä'nō)	132	22.20 N	78.35 W
Turin, see Torino			
Turka, Sov. Un. (tōōr'kà)	165	49.10 N	23.02 E
Turkestan, Sov. Un. (tûr-kĕ-stăn') (tōōr-kĕ-stan')	178	42.40 N	65.00 E
Turkestan (Reg.), Sov. Un.	174	43.27 N	62.14 E
Turkey, Eur.-Asia	188	38.45 N	32.00 E
Turkey (R.), Ia. (tûrk'ē)	113	43.20 N	92.16 W
Turkmen (S. S. R.), Sov. Un. (tōōrk-mĕn')	174	40.46 N	56.01 E
Turks I. Pass, Turks & Caicos Is.	133	21.15 N	71.25 W
Turks (Is.), Turks & Caicos Is. (tûrks)	127	21.40 N	71.45 W
Turku (Åbo), Fin. (tōōr'kōō) (ô'bô)	163	60.28 N	22.12 E
Turlock, Ca. (tûr'lŏk)	118	37.30 N	120.51 W
Turneffe (I.), Belize	130a	17.25 N	87.43 W
Turner, Ks. (tûr'nẽr)	117f	39.05 N	94.42 W
Turner Sd., Ba.	132	24.20 N	78.05 W
Turners Pen, S.L.	224	7.20 N	12.40 W
Turnhout, Bel. (tŭrn-hout')	155a	51.19 N	4.58 E
Turnov, Czech. (tōōr'nôf)	164	50.36 N	15.12 E
Turnu-Măgurel, Rom.	171a	43.54 N	24.49 E
Turpan, China (tōō-är-pän)	194	43.06 N	88.41 E
Turquino, Pico de (Pk.), Cuba (pē'kō dā tōōr-kē'nō)	132	20.00 N	76.50 W
Turrialba, C. R. (tōōr-ryä'l-bä)	131	9.54 N	83.41 W
Turtkul', Sov. Un. (tōōrt-kōōl')	153	41.28 N	61.02 E
Turtle (R.), Can.	99	49.20 N	92.30 W
Turtle B., Tx.	123a	29.48 N	94.38 W
Turtle Cr., SD	112	44.40 N	98.53 W
Turtle Mountain Ind. Res., ND	112	48.45 N	99.57 W
Turtle Mts., ND	112	48.57 N	100.11 W
Turukhansk, Sov. Un. (tōō-rōō-ĸänsk')	178	66.03 N	88.39 E
Turya R., Sov. Un. (tōōr'yá)	165	51.18 N	24.55 E
Tuscaloosa, Al. (tŭs-kå-lōō'sȧ)	124	33.10 N	87.35 W
Tuscarora, Nv. (tŭs-kȧ-rō'rȧ)	114	41.18 N	116.15 W
Tuscarora Ind. Res., NY	111c	43.10 N	78.51 W
Tuscola, Il. (tŭs-kō-lȧ)	108	39.50 N	88.20 W
Tuscumbia, Al. (tŭs-kŭm'bĭ-ȧ)	124	34.41 N	87.42 W
Tushino, Sov. Un. (tōō'shĭ-nô)	180b	55.51 N	37.24 E
Tuskegee, Al. (tŭs-kē'gē)	124	32.25 N	85.40 W
Tustin, Ca. (tŭs'tĭn)	117a	33.44 N	117.49 W
Tutayev, Sov. Un. (tōō-tá-yĕf')	172	57.53 N	39.34 E
Tutbury, Eng. (tŭt'bēr-ē)	154	52.52 N	1.51 W
Tuticorin, India (tōō-tē-kô-rĭn')	191	8.51 N	78.09 E
Tutitlan, Mex. (tōō-tē-tlä'n)	129a	19.38 N	99.10 W
Tutóia, Braz. (tōō-tō'yȧ)	141	2.42 S	42.21 W
Tutrakan, Bul.	171	44.02 N	26.36 E
Tuttle Creek Res., Ks.	121	39.30 N	96.38 W
Tuttlingen, F.R.G. (tōōt'lĭng-ĕn)	164	47.58 N	8.50 E
Tutwiler, Ms. (tŭt'wĭ-lẽr)	124	34.01 N	90.25 W
Tuva Aut. Oblast, Sov. Un.	178	51.15 N	90.45 E
Tuvalu, Oceania	204	5.20 S	174.00 E
Tuwayq, Jabal (Mts.), Sau. Ar.	192	20.45 N	46.30 E
Tuxedo Park, NY (tŭk-sē'dō pärk)	110a	41.11 N	74.11 W
Tuxford, Eng. (tŭks'fẽrd)	154	53.14 N	0.54 W
Tuxpan, Mex. (tōōs'pän)	128	19.34 N	103.22 W
Túxpan, Mex.	129	20.57 N	97.26 W
Túxpan (R.), Mex. (tōōs'pän)	129	20.55 N	97.52 W
Túxpan, Arrecife (Rf.), Mex. (är-rē-sē'fē-tōō'x-pä'n)	129	21.01 N	97.12 W
Tuxtepec, Mex. (tōōs-tå-pĕk')	129	18.06 N	96.09 W
Tuxtla Gutiérrez, Mex. (tōōs'tlä gōō-tyår'rĕs)	129	16.44 N	93.08 W
Tuy, Sp.	156	42.07 N	8.49 W
Tuy (R.), Ven. (tōō'ē)	141b	10.15 N	66.03 W
Tuyra R., Pan. (tōō-ē'rá)	131	7.55 N	77.37 W
Tuz Gölü (L.), Tur.	177	39.00 N	33.30 E
Tuzigoot Natl. Mon., Az.	119	34.40 N	111.52 W
Tuzla, Yugo. (tōōz'lá)	171	44.33 N	18.46 E
Tvedestrand, Nor. (tvĭ'dhĕ-stränd)	162	58.39 N	8.54 E
Tveitsund, Nor. (tvåt'sōōnd)	162	59.03 N	8.29 E
Tver, see Kalinin			
Tvertsa (L.), Sov. Un. (tvĕr'tsȧ)	152	56.58 N	35.22 E
Tweed (R.), Scot. (twēd)	160	55.32 N	2.35 W
Tweeling, S. Afr. (twē'lĭng)	219d	27.34 S	28.31 E
Twelvemile Cr., NY (twĕlv'mīl)	111c	43.13 N	78.58 W
Twenty Mile Cr., Can. (twĕn'tĭ mīl)	93d	43.09 N	79.49 W
Twickenham, Eng. (twĭk''n-ăm)	154b	51.26 N	0.20 W
Twillingate, Can. (twĭl'ĭn-gāt)	103	49.39 N	54.46 W
Twin Bridges, Mt. (twĭn brĭ-jĕz)	115	45.34 N	112.17 W
Twin Falls, Id. (fôls)	115	42.33 N	114.29 W
Twinsburg, Oh. (twĭnz'bûrg)	111d	41.19 N	81.26 W
Twitchell Res., Ca.	118	34.50 N	120.10 W
Two Butte Cr., Co. (tōō būt)	120	37.39 N	102.45 W
Two Harbors, Mn.	113	47.00 N	91.42 W
Two Prairie Bay, Ar. (prâ'rĭ bī ōō')	121	34.48 N	92.07 W
Two Rivers, Wi. (rĭv'ẽrz)	113	44.09 N	87.36 W
Tyabb, Austl.	207a	38.16 S	145.11 E
Tyachev, Sov. Un. (tyä'chĕf)	165	48.01 N	23.42 E
Tyasmin (R.), Sov. Un. (tyás-mĭn')	173	49.14 N	32.23 E
Tylden, S. Afr. (tĭl-dĕn)	223c	32.08 S	27.06 E
Tyldesley, Eng. (tĭldz'lē)	154	53.32 N	2.28 W
Tyler, Mn. (tī'lẽr)	112	44.18 N	96.08 W
Tyler, Tx.	123	32.21 N	95.19 W
Tylertown, Ms. (tī'lẽr-toun)	124	31.08 N	90.06 W
Tyndall, SD (tĭn'dál)	112	42.58 N	97.52 W
Tyndinskiy, Sov. Un.	179	55.22 N	124.45 E
Tyne (R.), Eng. (tīn)	160	54.59 N	1.56 W
Tynemouth, Eng. (tīn'mŭth)	160	55.04 N	1.39 W
Tynest, Nor. (tün'sĕt)	162	62.17 N	10.45 E
Tyngsboro, Ma. (tĭnj-bûr'ô)	103a	42.40 N	71.27 W
Tyre, see Şūr			
Tyrifjorden (Fd.), Nor.	162	60.03 N	10.25 E
Tyrone, NM (tī'rōn)	119	32.40 N	108.20 W
Tyrone, Pa.	109	40.40 N	78.15 W
Tyrrell, L., Austl. (tĭr'ĕll)	212	35.12 S	143.00 E
Tyrrhenian Sea, It. (tĭr-rē'nĭ-ȧn)	157	40.10 N	12.15 E
Tyub-Karagan, Mys (C.), Sov. Un.	177	44.30 N	50.10 E
Tyukalinsk, Sov. Un. (tyōō-kȧ-lĭnsk')	178	56.03 N	71.43 E
Tyukyan (R.), Sov. Un. (tyōōk'yán)	179	65.42 N	116.09 E
Tyuleniy (I.), Sov. Un.	177	44.30 N	48.00 E
Tyumen', Sov. Un. (tyōō-mĕn')	178	57.02 N	65.28 E
Tyura-Tam, Sov. Un.	178	46.00 N	63.15 E
Tzucacab, Mex. (tzōō-kä-kä'b)	130a	20.06 N	89.03 W

U

PLACE (Pronunciation)	PAGE	Lat. °′	Long. °′
Uarc, Ras (C.), Mor.	158	35.31 N	2.45 W
Uaupés, Braz. (wä-ōō'pās)	140	0.02 S	67.03 W
Ubá, Braz. (ōō-bá')	139a	21.08 S	42.55 W
Ubangi (Oubangui) (R.), Afr. (ōō-bäŋ'gē)	226	4.30 N	20.35 E
Ubatuba, Braz. (ōō-bå-tōō'bȧ)	139a	23.25 S	45.06 W
Ubeda, Sp. (ōō'bå-dä)	168	38.01 N	3.23 W
Uberaba, Braz. (ōō-bå-rä'bȧ)	141	19.47 S	47.47 W
Uberlândia, Braz. (ōō-bĕr-lá'n-dyä)	141	18.54 S	48.11 W
Ubombo, S. Afr. (ōō-bôm'bô)	222	27.33 S	32.13 E
Ubon Ratchathani, Thai. (ōō'bŭn rä'chätá-nē)	202	15.15 N	104.52 E
Ubort' (R.), Sov. Un. (ōō-bôrt')	173	51.18 N	27.43 E
Ubrique, Sp. (ōō-brē'kå)	168	36.43 N	5.36 W
Ubsa Nuur (L.), Mong.	194	50.29 N	93.32 E
Ubundi (Ponthierville), Zaire	227	00.21 S	25.29 E
Ucayali (R.), Peru (ōō'kä-yä'lē)	140	8.58 S	74.13 W
Uccle, Bel. (ü'kl')	155a	50.48 N	4.17 E
Uchaly, Sov. Un. (û-chä'lĭ)	180a	54.22 N	59.28 E
Uch-Aral, Sov. Un. (ōōch'á-ral')	178	46.14 N	80.58 E
Uchiko, Jap. (ōō'chē-kō)	201	33.30 N	132.39 E
Uchinoura, Jap. (ōō'chē-nō-ōō'rá)	201	31.16 N	131.03 E
Uchinskoye Vdkhr. (Res.), Sov. Un. (ōōch-ĕn'skô-yĕ vô-dô-ĸrá-nĭ'li-shchĕ)	180b	56.08 N	37.44 E
Uchiura-Wan (B.), Jap. (ōō'chē-ōō'rä wän)	200	42.20 N	140.44 E
Uchur (R.), Sov. Un. (ōō-chōōr')	179	58.27 N	131.34 E
Uda (R.), Sov. Un. (ōō'dá)	179	52.28 N	110.51 E
Uda (R.), Sov. Un.	179	53.54 N	131.29 E
Udaipur, India (ōō-dŭ'ē-pōōr)	190	24.41 N	73.41 E
Uday (R.), Sov. Un. (ōō-dī')	173	50.45 N	32.13 E
Uddevalla, Swe. (ōōd'dē-väl-á)	162	58.21 N	11.55 E
Udine, It. (ōō'dē-nå)	170	46.05 N	13.14 E
Udmurt (A. S. S. R.), Sov. Un.	178	57.00 N	53.00 E
Udon Thani, Thai.	202	17.31 N	102.51 E
Udskaya Guba (B.), Sov. Un.	141	55.00 N	136.30 E
Ueda, Jap. (wā'dä)	201	36.26 N	138.16 E
Uekermünde, G.D.R. (ü'kĕr-mün-dĕ)	164	53.43 N	14.01 E
Uele R., Zaire (wā'lå)	226	3.55 N	23.30 E
Ufa, Sov. Un. (ōō'fa)	180a	54.45 N	55.57 E
Ufa (R.), Sov. Un.	176	56.00 N	57.05 E
Ugab (R.), Namibia (ōō'gäb)	222	21.10 S	14.00 E
Ugalla (R.), Tan. (ōō-gä'lä)	227	6.15 S	32.30 E
Uganda, Afr. (ōō-gän'dä) (û-gän'dȧ)	218	2.00 N	32.28 E
Ugashik L., Ak. (ōō'gá-shĕk)	105	57.36 N	157.10 W
Ugie, S. Afr. (ōō'jē)	223c	31.13 S	28.14 E
Uglegorsk, Sov. Un. (ōō-gl-gôrsk)	179	49.00 N	142.31 E
Ugleural'sk, Sov. Un. (ōōg-lĕ-ōō-rálsk')	180a	58.58 N	57.35 E
Uglich, Sov. Un. (ōōg-lĕch')	172	57.33 N	38.19 E
Uglitskiy, Sov. Un. (ōōg-lĭt'skĭ)	180a	53.50 N	60.18 E
Uglovka, Sov. Un. (ōōg-lôf'kȧ)	172	58.14 N	33.24 E
Ugra (R.), Sov. Un. (ōōg'rá)	172	54.43 N	34.20 E
Ugŭrchin, Bul.	171	43.06 N	24.23 E
Uhrichsville, Oh. (ū'rĭks-vĭl)	108	40.25 N	81.20 W
Uíge, Ang.	226	7.37 S	15.03 E
Uiju, Kor. (ōō'ējōō)	200	40.09 N	124.33 E
Uil (R.), Sov. Un. (ōō-ēl')	177	49.30 N	55.10 E
Uinkaret Plat., Az. (û-ĭn'kâr-ĕt)	119	36.43 N	113.15 W
Uinskoye, Sov. Un. (ōō-ĭn'skô-yĕ)	180a	56.53 N	56.25 E
Uinta (R.), Ut. (û-ĭn'tȧ)	119	40.25 N	109.55 W
Uintah, Ut. (û-ĭn'tå)	117b	41.09 N	111.56 W
Uintah and Ouray Ind. Res., Ut.	119	39.55 N	109.20 W
Uitenhage, S. Afr.	223c	33.46 S	25.26 E
Uithoorn, Neth.	155a	52.13 N	4.49 E
Uji, Jap. (ōō'jē)	201b	34.53 N	135.49 E
Ujiji, Tan. (ōō-jē'jē)	227	4.55 S	29.41 E
Ujjain, India (ōō-jŭĕn)	190	23.18 N	75.37 E
Ujung Pandang (Makasar), Indon.	202	5.08 S	119.28 E
Ukerewe I., Tan.	227	2.00 S	32.40 E
Ukhta, Sov. Un.	178	63.08 N	53.42 E
Ukhta, Sov. Un. (ōōk'tȧ)	176	65.22 N	31.30 E
Ukiah, Ca. (ū-kī'ȧ)	118	35.09 N	122.12 W
Ukmerge, Sov. Un. (ōōk'mĕr-ghå)	163	55.16 N	24.45 E
Ukrainian (S. S. R.), Sov. Un.	174	49.15 N	30.15 E
Uku (I.), Jap. (ōōk'ōō)	201	33.18 N	129.02 E
Ulaan Baatar, Mong.	194	47.56 N	107.00 E
Ulaan Goom, Mong.	194	50.23 N	92.14 E
Ulanhad, see Chifeng			
Ulan-Ude, Sov. Un. (ōō'län ōō'då)	179	51.59 N	107.41 E
Ulchin, Kor. (ōōl'chĕn')	200	36.57 N	129.26 E
Ulcinj (Dulcigno), Yugo. (ōōl'tsĕn')	171	41.56 N	19.15 E
Ulhās (R.), India	191b	19.13 N	73.03 E
Ulhāsnagar, India	191b	19.10 N	73.07 E
Ulindi (R.), Zaire (ōō-lĭn'dē)	226	1.55 S	26.17 E
Ulla, Sov. Un. (ōōl'á)	172	55.14 N	29.15 E
Ulla (R.), Sov. Un.	172	54.58 N	29.03 E
Ulla (R.), Sp. (ōō'lä)	168	42.45 N	8.33 W
Ullŭng (I.), Kor. (ōōl'lōōng')	200	37.29 N	130.50 E
Ulm, F.R.G. (ōōlm)	164	48.24 N	9.59 E
Ulmer, Mt., Ant. (ŭl'mûr')	228	77.30 S	86.00 W
Ulricehamn, Swe. (ōōl-rē'sĕ-häm)	162	57.49 N	13.23 E
Ulsan, Kor. (ōōl'sän')	200	35.35 N	129.22 E
Ulster (Reg.), Ire.-N. Ire. (ŭl'stẽr)	160	54.41 N	7.10 W
Ulua R., Hond. (ōō-lōō'ȧ)	130	15.49 N	87.45 W
Ulubāria, India	190a	22.27 N	88.09 E
Uluguru Mts., Tan.	227	7.15 S	37.30 E
Ulukişla, Tur. (ōō-lōō-kēsh'lȧ)	177	36.40 N	34.30 E
Ulunga, Sov. Un. (ōō-lōōn'gȧ)	200	46.16 N	136.29 E
Ulungur (R.), China (ōō-lōōn-gûr)	194	46.31 N	149.00 E
Ulu-Telyak, Sov. Un. (ōō lōō'tĕlyăk)	180a	54.54 N	57.01 E
Ulverstone, Austl. (ŭl'vẽr-stŭn)	212	41.20 S	146.22 E
Ul'yanovka, Sov. Un. (ōō-lyä'nôf-kȧ)	180c	59.38 N	30.47 E
Ul'yanovsk, Sov. Un. (ōō-lyä'nôfsk)	176	54.20 N	48.05 E
Ulysses, Ks. (ū-lĭs'ēz)	120	37.34 N	101.25 W
Ülzen, F.R.G. (ült'sĕn)	164	52.58 N	10.34 E
Umán, Mex. (ōō-män')	129	20.52 N	89.44 W
Uman', Sov. Un. (ōō-mán')	173	48.44 N	30.13 E
Umatilla Ind. Res., Or. (ū-má-tĭl'á)	114	45.38 N	118.35 W
Umberpāda, India	191b	19.28 N	73.04 E
Umbria (Reg.), It. (ŭm'brĭ-ȧ)	170	42.53 N	12.22 E
Umeå, Swe. (ōō'mĕ-ô)	156	63.48 N	20.29 E
Umeälven (R.), Swe.	156	64.57 N	18.51 E
Umhlatuzi (R.), S. Afr. (ōōm'hlá-tōō'zĭ)	223c	28.47 S	31.17 E
Umiat, Ak. (ōō'mĭ-ăt)	105	69.20 N	152.28 W
Umkomaas, S. Afr. (ōōm-kō'mäs)	223c	30.12 S	30.48 E
Umm Durmān (Omdurman), Sud. (ŏm-dōōr-män')	221	15.45 N	32.30 E
Umnak (I.), Ak. (ōōm'nák)	105a	53.10 N	169.08 W
Umnak Pass, Ak.	105a	53.10 N	168.04 W
Umniati (R.), Zimb.	222	17.08 S	29.11 E
Umpqua R., Or. (ŭmp'kwȧ)	114	43.42 N	123.50 W
Umtali, Zimb. (ōōm-tä'lē)	222	18.49 S	32.39 E
Umtata, S. Afr. (ōōm-tä'tä)	223c	31.36 S	28.47 E
Umtentweni, S. Afr.	223c	30.41 S	30.29 E
Umzimkulu, S. Afr. (ōōm-zēm-kōō'lōō)	223c	30.12 S	29.53 E
Umzinto, S. Afr. (ōōm-zĭn'tô)	223c	30.19 S	30.41 E
Una (R.), Yugo. (ōō'ná)	170	44.38 N	16.10 E
Unalakleet, Ak. (ū-ná-lák'lēt)	105	63.50 N	160.42 W
Unalaska, Ak. (ū-ná-lăs'ká)	105a	53.30 N	166.20 W
Unare (R.), Ven.	141b	9.45 N	65.12 W
Unare, Laguna de (L.), Ven. (lä-gōō'nä-de-ōō-ná'rē)	141b	10.07 N	65.23 W
Unayzah, Sau Ar.	192	25.50 N	44.02 E
Uncas, Can. (ŭŋ'kȧs)	93g	53.30 N	113.02 W
Uncía, Bol. (ōōn'sē-ä)	140	18.28 S	66.32 W
Uncompahgre (R.), Co.	119	38.20 N	107.45 W
Uncompahgre Pk., Co. (ŭn-kŭm-pä'grē)	119	38.00 N	107.30 W
Uncompahgre Plat., Co.	119	38.40 N	108.40 W
Underberg, S. Afr. (ŭn'dẽr-bûrg)	223c	29.51 S	29.32 E
Undo, Eth.	221	6.37 N	38.29 E
Unecha, Sov. Un. (ōō-nĕ'chá)	172	32.51 N	32.44 E
Ungava B., Can. (ŭŋ-gä'vá)	95	59.46 N	67.18 W
Ungava, Péninsule d' (Pen.), Can.	95	59.55 N	74.00 W
União da Vitória, Braz. (ōō-nē-ouɴ' dä vē-tô'ryä)	142	26.17 S	51.13 W
Unije (I.), Yugo. (ōō'nē-yĕ)	170	44.39 N	14.10 E
Unimak (I.), Ak. (ōō-nē-mák')	105a	54.30 N	163.35 W
Unimak Pass, Ak.	105a	54.22 N	165.22 W
Union, Ms. (ūn'yŭn)	124	32.35 N	89.07 W
Union, Mo.	121	38.28 N	90.59 W
Union, NC	125	34.42 N	81.40 W
Union, Or.	114	45.13 N	117.52 W
Union City, Ca.	116b	37.36 N	122.01 W
Union City, Ind.	108	40.10 N	85.00 W

PRONOUNCING INDEX

Union City – Valparaíso 359

PLACE (Pronunciation)	PAGE	Lat. °′	Long. °′
Union City, Mi.	108	42.00 N	85.10 W
Union City, Pa.	109	41.50 N	79.50 W
Union City, Tn.	124	36.25 N	89.04 W
Union de Reves, Cuba (o͞o-nyō'n-dĕ-rĕ-vĕ's)	132	22.45 N	81.30 W
Union de San Antonio, Mex. (sän än-tō'nyō)	128	21.07 N	101.56 W
Union de Tula, Mex. (to͞o'lä)	128	19.57 N	104.14 W
Union Grove, Wi. (ūn-yŭn grōv)	111a	42.41 N	88.03 W
Unión Hidalgo, Mex. (ē-dä'lgô)	129	16.29 N	94.51 W
Union Point, Ga.	124	33.37 N	83.08 W
Union Springs, Al. (sprĭngz)	124	32.08 N	85.43 W
Uniontown, Al. (ūn'yŭn-toun)	124	32.26 N	87.30 W
Uniontown, Oh.	111d	40.58 N	81.25 W
Uniontown, Pa.	109	39.55 N	79.45 W
Unionville, Mo. (ūn'yŭn-vĭl)	121	40.28 N	92.58 W
Unisan, Phil. (o͞o-nē'sän)	203a	13.50 N	121.59 E
Unitas, Mts., U. S. (ū-nĭ'tās)	106	40.35 N	111.00 W
United Arab Emirates, Asia	188	24.00 N	54.00 E
United Arab Republic, see Egypt			
United Kingdom, Eur.	156	56.30 N	1.40 W
United Pueblo Ind. Res., NM (u-nīt'ĕd pōō-ĕb'lō) (pwā'blō)	119	35.30 N	107.00 W
United States, N. A.	92	38.00 N	110.00 W
Unity, Can.	98	52.27 N	109.10 W
Universal, In. (ū-nĭ-vûr'săl)	108	39.35 N	87.30 W
University City, Mo. (ū'nĭ-vûr'sĭ-tĭ)	117e	38.40 N	90.19 W
University Park, Tx.	117c	32.51 N	96.48 W
Unna, F.R.G. (o͞o'nä)	167c	51.32 N	7.41 E
Unst (I.), Scot. (o͞onst)	160a	60.50 N	1.24 W
Unterhaching, F.R.G. (o͞on'tĕr-hä-kĕng)	155d	48.03 N	11.38 E
Unye, Tur. (ün'yĕ)	177	41.00 N	37.10 E
Unzha (R.), Sov. Un. (o͞on'zhá)	176	57.45 N	44.10 E
Upa (R.), Sov. Un. (o͞o'pá)	172	53.54 N	36.48 E
Upanda, Sierra do (Mts.), Ang. (sē-ĕ'r-rä-dô-o͞o-pä'n-dä)	218	13.15 S	14.15 E
Upata, Ven. (o͞o-pä'tä)	140	7.58 N	62.27 W
Upemba, Parc Natl. de l' (Natl. Pk.), Zaire	227	9.10 S	26.15 E
Upington, S. Afr. (ŭp'ĭng-tŭn)	222	28.25 S	21.15 E
Upland, Ca. (ŭp'lănd)	117a	34.06 N	117.38 W
Upolu Pt., Hi. (o͞o-pô'lo͞o)	104a	20.15 N	155.48 W
Upper Arrow L., Can. (ăr'ō)	97	50.30 N	117.55 W
Upper Darby, Pa. (där'bĭ)	110f	39.58 N	75.16 W
Upper de Lacs (R.), ND (dĕ läk)	112	48.58 N	101.55 W
Upper Kapuas Mts., Mala.	202	1.45 N	112.06 E
Upper L., Nv. (ŭp'ēr)	114	41.42 N	119.59 W
Upper Marlboro, Md. (ûpēr mărl'bōrō)	110e	38.49 N	76.46 W
Upper Mill, Wa. (mĭl)	116a	47.11 N	121.55 W
Upper Red L., Mn. (rĕd)	113	48.14 N	94.53 W
Upper Sandusky, Oh. (săn-dŭs'kē)	108	40.50 N	83.20 W
Upper San Leandro Res., Ca. (ŭp'ēr săn lē-ăn'drō)	116b	37.47 N	122.04 W
Upper Volta, Afr. (vôl'tá)	218	11.46 N	3.18 E
Uppingham, Eng. (ŭp'ĭng-ăm)	154	52.35 N	0.43 W
Uppsala, Swe. (o͞op'sá-lä)	162	59.53 N	17.39 E
Uptown, Ma. (ŭp'toun)	103a	42.10 N	71.36 W
Uraga, Jap. (o͞o'rá-gá')	201a	35.15 N	139.43 E
Uraga-Kaikyō (Str.), Jap. (o͞o'rä-gä kī'kyō)	201a	35.11 N	139.44 W
Ural (R.), Sov. Un. (o͞o-räl'') (ū-rôl)	177	49.50 N	51.30 E
Urals (Mts.), Sov. Un.	174	56.28 N	58.13 E
Ural'sk, Sov. Un. (o͞o-rálsk')	177	51.15 N	51.10 E
Uran, India (o͞o-rän')	191b	18.53 N	72.46 E
Uranium City, Can.	94	59.34 N	108.59 W
Urawa, Jap. (o͞o'rä-wä')	201a	35.52 N	139.39 E
Urayasu, Jap. (o͞o'rä-yä'so͞o)	201a	35.40 N	139.54 E
Urazovo, Sov. Un. (o͞o-rá'zô-vô)	173	50.08 N	38.03 E
Urbana, Il. (ûr-băn'à)	108	40.10 N	88.15 W
Urbana, Oh.	108	40.05 N	83.50 W
Urbino, It. (o͞or-bē'nô)	170	43.43 N	12.37 E
Urda, Sov. Un. (o͞or'dá)	177	48.50 N	47.30 E
Urdaneta, Phil. (o͞or-dä-nā'tä)	203a	15.59 N	120.34 E
Urdinarrain, Arg. (o͞or-dē-när-rāē'n)	139c	32.43 S	58.53 W
Urdzhar, Sov. Un. (o͞ord-zhär')	178	47.28 N	82.00 E
Urfa, Tur. (o͞or'fá)	177	37.20 N	38.45 E
Urgench, Sov. Un. (o͞or-gĕnch')	153	41.32 N	60.33 E
Uritsk, Sov. Un. (o͞o'rĭtsk)	180c	59.50 N	30.11 E
Urla, Tur. (o͞or'lá)	171	38.20 N	26.44 E
Urman, Sov. Un. (o͞or'mán)	180a	54.53 N	56.52 E
Urmi (R.), Sov. Un. (o͞or'mē)	200	48.50 N	134.00 E
Uromi, Nig.	225	6.44 N	6.18 E
Urrao, Col. (o͞or-rä'ō)	140a	6.19 N	76.11 W
Urshel'skiy, Sov. Un. (o͞or-shĕl'skēē)	172	55.50 N	40.11 E
Ursus, Pol.	165	52.12 N	20.53 E
Urubamba (R.), Peru (o͞o-ro͞o-bäm'bä)	140	11.48 S	72.34 W
Uruguaiana, Braz. (o͞o-ro͞o-gwī-ä'ná)	142	29.45 S	57.00 W
Uruguay, S. A. (o͞o-ro͞o-gwī') (ū'ro͞o-gwā)	138	32.45 S	56.00 W
Uruguay, Rio (R.), Braz. (rē'ō-o͞o-ro͞o-gwī)	142	27.05 S	55.15 W
Ürümqi, China (ū-rům-chyē)	194	43.49 N	87.43 E
Urup (I.), Sov. Un. (o͞o'ro͝op')	179	46.08 N	149.00 E
Uryupinsk, Sov. Un. (o͞or'yo͞o-pēn-sk')	177	50.50 N	42.00 E
Urziceni, Rom. (o͞o-zē-chĕn'')	171	44.45 N	26.42 E
Usa, Jap.	200	33.31 N	131.22 E
Usa (R.), Sov. Un. (o͞o'sà)	176	66.00 N	58.20 E
Uşak, Tur. (o͞o'shák)	177	39.50 N	29.15 E
Usakos, Namibia (o͞o-sä'kōs)	222	22.00 S	15.40 E
Ushaki, Sov. Un. (o͞o'shá-kĭ)	180c	59.28 N	31.00 E
Ushakovskoye, Sov. Un. (o͞o-shá-kôv'skô-yĕ)	180a	56.18 N	62.23 E
Usambara Mts., Tan.	227	4.40 S	38.25 E
Usangu Flats (Pln.), Tan.	227	8.10 S	34.00 E
Ushashi, Tan.	227	2.00 S	33.57 E
Ushiku, Jap. (o͞o'shē-ko͞o)	201a	35.24 N	140.09 E
Ushimado, Jap. (o͞o'shē-mä'dō)	201	34.37 N	134.09 E
Ushuaia, Arg. (o͞o-sho͞o-ī'ä)	142	54.46 S	68.24 W
Üsküdar, Tur.	177	40.55 N	29.00 E
Usman', Sov. Un. (o͞os-mán')	172	52.03 N	39.40 E
Usol'ye, Sov. Un. (o͞o-sô'lyĕ)	180a	59.24 N	56.40 E
Usol'ye-Sibirskoye, Sov. Un. (o͞o-sô'lyĕsĭ' bĕr'skô-yĕ)	178	52.44 N	103.46 E
Uspallata P., Arg.-Chile (o͞os-pä-lyä'tä)	142	32.47 S	70.08 W
Uspanapa (R.), Mex. (o͞os-pä-nä'pä)	129	17.43 N	94.14 W
Ussel, Fr. (üs'ĕl)	166	45.33 N	2.17 E
Ussuri (R.), China (o͞o-so͞o'rē)	195	46.30 N	133.56 E
Ussuriysk, Sov. Un.	179	43.48 N	132.09 E
Ust'-Bol'sheretsk, Sov. Un.	179	52.41 N	157.00 E
Ustica, I. di, It. (ē'sō-lä-dē-o͞os'tē-kä)	170	38.43 N	12.11 E
Ústí, Czech. (o͞os'tē)	164	50.39 N	14.02 E
Ustinovka, Sov. Un. (o͞os-tē'nôf-kä)	173	47.59 N	32.31 E
Ust'-Izhora, Sov. Un. (o͞ost-ēz'hô-rà)	180c	59.49 N	30.35 E
Ustka, Pol. (o͞ost'kà)	164	54.34 N	16.52 E
Ust'-Kamchatsk, Sov. Un.	179	56.13 N	162.18 E
Ust'-Kamenogorsk, Sov. Un.	178	49.58 N	80.43 E
Ust'-Katav, Sov. Un. (o͞ost kà'tàf)	180a	54.55 N	58.12 E
Ust'-Kishert', Sov. Un. (o͞ost kē'shĕrt)	180a	57.21 N	57.13 E
Ust'-Kulom, Sov. Un. (ko͞o'lŭm)	176	61.38 N	54.00 E
Ust'-Maya, Sov. Un. (mà'yà)	179	60.33 N	134.43 E
Ust' Olenëk, Sov. Un.	179	72.52 N	120.15 E
Ust-Ordynskiy, Sov. Un. (o͞ost-ôr-dyĕnsk'ĭ)	179	52.47 N	104.39 E
Ust' Penzhino, Sov. Un.	179	63.00 N	165.10 E
Ust' Port, Sov. Un. (o͞ost'pôrt')	178	69.20 N	83.41 E
Ust'-Tsil'ma, Sov. Un. (tsĭl'mà)	176	65.25 N	52.10 E
Ust'-Tyrma, Sov. Un. (tur'mà)	179	50.27 N	131.17 E
Ust'Uls, Sov. Un. (o͞ols)	180a	60.35 N	58.32 E
Ust'-Urt, Plato (Plat.), Sov. Un. (o͞ort)	174	44.03 N	54.58 E
Ustyuzhna, Sov. Un. (yo͞ozh'nà)	172	58.49 N	36.19 E
Usu, China (ů-so͞o)	194	44.28 N	84.07 E
Usuki, Jap. (o͞o'so͞o-kē')	201	33.06 N	131.47 E
Usulutan, Sal. (o͞o-so͞o-lä-tän')	130	13.22 N	88.25 W
Usumacinta (R.), Mex. (o͞o'so͞o-mä-sēn'tō)	129	18.24 N	92.30 W
Us'va, Sov. Un. (o͞os'và)	180a	58.41 N	57.38 E
Utah (State), U. S. (ū'tô)	106	39.25 N	112.40 W
Utah (L.), Ut.	119	40.10 N	111.55 W
Utan, India	191b	19.27 N	72.43 E
Ute Mtn. Ind. Res., NM	119	36.57 N	108.34 W
Utena, Sov. Un. (o͞o'tā-nä)	163	55.32 N	25.40 E
Utete, Tan. (o͞o-tā'tā)	223	8.05 S	38.47 E
Utica, In. (ū'tĭ-kà)	111h	38.20 N	85.39 W
Utica, NY	109	43.05 N	75.10 W
Utiel, Sp. (o͞o-tyăl')	168	39.34 N	1.13 W
Utika, Mi. (ū'tĭ-kà)	111b	42.37 N	83.02 W
Utik L., Can.	99	55.16 N	96.00 W
Utikuma L., Can.	98	55.50 N	115.25 W
Utila I., Hond. (o͞o-tē'lä)	130	16.07 N	87.05 W
Uto, Jap. (o͞o'tō')	201	32.43 N	130.39 E
Utrecht, Neth. (ū'trĕkt) (ü'trĕkt)	155a	52.05 N	5.06 E
Utrera, Sp. (o͞o-trā'rä)	168	37.12 N	5.48 W
Utsunomiya, Jap. (o͞ot'so͞o-nô-mē-yà')	201	36.35 N	139.52 E
Uttaradit, Thai.	202	17.47 N	100.10 E
Uttarpara-Kotrung, India	190a	22.40 N	88.21 E
Uttar Pradesh (State), India (o͞ot-tär-prä-dēsh)	190	27.00 N	80.00 E
Uttoxeter, Eng. (ŭt-tôk'sē-tēr)	154	52.54 N	1.52 W
Utuado, P. R. (o͞o-to͞o-ä'dhō)	127b	18.16 N	66.40 W
Uusikaupunki (Nystad), Fin. (o͞o'sĭ-kou'po͞oŋ-kĭ) (nü'städh)	163	60.48 N	21.24 E
Uvalde, Tx. (ū-văl'dē)	122	29.14 N	99.47 W
Uvel'skiy, Sov. Un. (o͞o-vyĕl'skĭ)	180a	54.27 N	60.22 E
Uvinza, Tan.	227	5.06 S	30.22 E
Uvira, Zaire (o͞o-vē'rä)	222	3.28 S	29.03 E
Uvod' (R.), Sov. Un. (o͞o-vôd')	172	56.52 N	41.03 E
Uvongo Beach, S. Afr.	223c	30.49 S	30.23 E
Uwajima, Jap. (o͞o-wä'jē-mä)	201	33.12 N	132.35 E
Uxbridge, Ma. (ŭks'brĭj)	103a	42.05 N	71.38 W
Uxmal (Ruins), Mex. (o͞o'x-mä'l)	130a	20.22 N	89.44 W
Uy R., Sov. Un. (o͞oy)	180a	54.05 N	62.11 E
Uyskoye, Sov. Un. (ûy'skô-yĕ)	180a	54.22 N	60.01 E
Uyuni, Bol. (o͞o-yo͞o'nē)	140	20.28 S	66.45 W
Uyuni, Salar de (Salt Flat), Bol. (sä-lär-dē)	140	20.58 S	67.09 W
Uzbek S. S. R., Sov. Un. (o͞oz-bĕk')	174	42.42 N	60.00 E
Uzen, Bol'shoy (R.), Sov. Un.	177	49.50 N	49.35 E
Uzh (R.), Sov. Un. (o͞ozh)	173	51.07 N	29.05 E
Uzhgorod, Sov. Un. (o͞ozh'gô-rôt)	165	48.38 N	22.18 E
Uzunköprü, Tur. (o͞o'zo͞on'kû-prü)	171	41.17 N	26.42 E

V

PLACE (Pronunciation)	PAGE	Lat. °′	Long. °′
Vaal (R.), S. Afr. (väl)	222	28.15 S	24.30 E
Vaaldam (L.), S. Afr.	219d	26.58 S	28.37 E
Vaalplaas, S. Afr.	219d	25.39 S	28.56 E
Vaalwater, S. Afr.	219d	24.17 S	28.08 E
Vaasa, Fin. (vä'sà)	163	63.06 N	21.39 E
Vác, Hung. (väts)	165	47.46 N	19.10 E
Vache, Île À (I.), Hai. (väsh)	133	18.05 N	73.40 W
Vadsø, Nor. (vädh'sû)	156	70.08 N	29.52 E
Vadstena, Swe. (väd'stĭ'nà)	162	58.27 N	14.53 E
Vaduz, Liech. (vä'do͞ots)	164	47.10 N	9.32 E
Vaga (R.), Sov. Un. (va'gà)	176	61.55 N	42.30 E
Vah R., Czech. (väĸ)	165	48.07 N	17.52 E
Vaigai (R.), India	190	10.20 N	78.13 E
Vakh (R.), Sov. Un. (vàĸ)	178	61.30 N	81.33 E
Valachia (Reg.), Rom.	171	44.45 N	24.17 E
Valcartier-Village, Can. (väl-kärt-yĕ'vē-läzh')	93b	46.56 N	71.28 W
Valdai Hills, Sov. Un. (vàl-dī' gô'rĭ)	172	57.50 N	32.35 E
Valday (Valdai), Sov. Un. (vàl-dī')	172	57.58 N	33.[illegible]
Valdecañas, Embalse de (Res.), Sp.	168	39.15 N	5.30 W
Valdemārpils, Sov. Un.	163	57.22 N	22.34 E
Valdemorillo, Sp. (väl-då-mô-rēl'yō)	169a	40.30 N	4.04 W
Valdepeñas, Sp. (väl-då-pān'yäs)	168	38.46 N	3.22 W
Valderaduey (R.), Sp. (väl-dĕ-rä-dwĕ'y)	168	41.39 N	5.35 W
Valdés, Pen., Arg. (väl-dĕ's)	142	42.15 S	63.15 W
Valdez, Ak. (văl'dĕz)	105	61.10 N	146.18 W
Valdilecha, Sp. (väl-dē-lā'chä)	169a	40.17 N	3.19 W
Valdivia, Chile (väl-dē'vä)	142	39.47 S	73.13 W
Valdivia, Col. (väl-dē'vēä)	140a	7.10 N	75.26 W
Val-d' Or., Can.	101	48.03 N	77.50 W
Valdosta, Ga. (văl-dŏs'tà)	124	30.50 N	83.18 W
Valdoviño, Sp. (väl-dô-vē'nō)	168	43.36 N	8.05 W
Vale, Or. (vāl)	114	43.59 N	117.14 W
Valença, Braz. (vä-lĕɴ'sà)	141	13.43 S	38.58 W
Valença, Port.	168	42.03 N	8.36 W
Valence, Fr. (vä-lĕɴs)	166	44.56 N	4.54 E
Valencia, Sp. (vä-lĕn'thē-ä)	169	39.26 N	0.23 W
Valencia de Alcántara, Sp.	168	39.34 N	7.13 W
Valencia, Ven. (vä-lĕn'syä)	141b	10.11 N	68.00 W
Valencia (Reg.), Sp. (vä-lĕn'thē-ä)	169	39.08 N	0.43 W
Valencia, Lago de (L.), Ven.	141b	10.11 N	67.45 W
Valencia I., Ire. (vȧ-lĕn'shȧ)	160	51.55 N	10.26 W
Valenciennes, Fr. (vȧ-läɴ-syĕn')	166	50.24 N	3.36 E
Valentine, Ne. (vă lăn-tē-nyĕ')	112	42.52 N	100.34 W
Valera, Ven. (vä-lĕ'rä)	140	9.12 N	70.45 W
Valerianovsk, Sov. Un. (vȧ-lĕ-rĭ-ä'nôvsk)	180a	58.47 N	59.34 E
Valga, Sov. Un. (väl'gȧ)	172	57.47 N	26.03 E
Valhalla, S. Afr. (väl-hăl-à)	223b	25.49 S	28.09 E
Valier, Mt. (vă-lēr')	115	48.17 N	112.14 W
Valjevo, Yugo. (väl'yå-vô)	171	44.17 N	19.57 E
Valki, Sov. Un. (väl'kē)	173	49.49 N	35.40 E
Valladolid, Mex. (väl-yä-dhō-lēdh')	130a	20.39 N	88.13 W
Valladolid, Sp. (väl-yä-dhō-lēdh')	168	41.41 N	4.41 W
Vall de Uxó, Sp. (väl-dē-o͞ox-ō')	169	39.50 N	0.15 W
Valle, Arroyo del, Ca. (ä-rō'yō dĕl väl'yā)	118	37.36 N	121.43 W
Vallecas, Sp. (väl-yä'käs)	169a	40.23 N	3.37 W
Valle de Allende, Mex. (väl'yā dā äl-yĕn'dā)	122	26.55 N	105.25 W
Valle de Bravo, Mex. (brä'vō)	128	19.12 N	100.07 W
Valle de Guanape, Ven. (vä'l-yĕ-dĕ-gwä-nä'pĕ)	141b	9.54 N	65.41 W
Valle de la Pascua, Ven. (lä-pä's-ko͞oä)	140	9.12 N	65.08 W
Valle del Cauca, Col. (vä'l-yĕ del kou'kä)	140a	4.03 N	76.13 W
Valle de Santiago, Mex. (sän-tē-ä'gō)	128	20.23 N	101.11 W
Valledupar, Col. (do͞o-pär')	140	10.13 N	73.39 W
Valle Grande, Bol. (grän'dā)	140	18.27 S	64.03 W
Vallejo, Ca. (vă-yä'hō) (vă-lā'hō)	116b	38.06 N	122.15 W
Vallejo, Sierra de (Mts.), Mex. (sē-ĕ'r-rä-dĕ-väl-yĕ'ĸō)	128	21.00 N	105.10 W
Vallenar, Chile (väl-yå-när')	142	28.39 S	70.52 W
Valletta, Malta (väl-lĕt'ä)	158	35.50 N	14.29 E
Valle Vista, Ca. (väl'yā vĭs'tà)	117a	33.45 N	116.53 W
Valley City, ND	112	46.55 N	97.59 W
Valley City, Oh. (văl'ĭ)	111d	41.14 N	81.56 W
Valley Falls, Ks.	121	39.25 N	95.26 W
Valleyfield, Can. (văl'ē-fēld)	93a	45.16 N	74.09 W
Valleyfield, Can.	95	45.05 N	74.00 W
Valley Park, Mo. (văl'ē pärk)	117e	38.33 N	90.30 W
Valley Stream, NY (văl'ĭ strēm)	110a	40.39 N	73.42 W
Valli di Comácchio (L.), It. (vä'lē-dē-kô-mä'chyô)	170	44.38 N	12.15 E
Vallière, Hai. (väl-yâr')	133	19.30 N	71.55 W
Vallimanca (R.), Arg. (väl-yē-mä'n-kä)	139c	36.21 S	60.55 W
Valls, Sp. (väls)	169	41.15 N	1.15 E
Valmiera, Sov. Un. (väl'myĕ-rȧ)	163	57.34 N	25.54 E
Valognes, Fr. (vȧ-lôn'y')	166	49.32 N	1.30 W
Valona, see Vlorë			
Valparaíso, Chile (väl'pä-rä-ē'sō)	139b	33.02 S	71.32 W

360 Valparaiso – Vichuga

PLACE (Pronunciation)	PAGE	Lat. °′	Long. °′
Valparaiso, In. (văl-pȧ-rā'zō)	108	41.25 N	87.05 W
Valparaiso, Mex.	128	22.49 N	103.33 W
Valpariso (Prov.), Chile	139b	32.58 S	71.23 W
Valréas, Fr. (vàl-rà-ä')	166	45.25 N	4.56 E
Vals (R.), S. Afr.	219d	27.32 S	26.51 E
Vals, Tandjung (C.), Indon.	203	8.30 S	137.15 E
Valsbaai (False Bay), S. Afr.	222a	34.14 S	18.35 E
Valuyevo, Sov. Un. (vá-lōō'yĕ-vô)	180b	55.34 N	37.21 E
Valuyki, Sov. Un. (vá-lōō-ē'kē)	173	50.14 N	38.04 E
Valverde del Camino, Sp. (väl-vĕr-dě-děl-kä-mē'nō)	168	37.34 N	6.44 W
Vambanād (R.), India	190	10.00 N	76.03 E
Vammala, Fin.	163	61.19 N	22.51 E
Van, Tur. (vàn)	177	38.04 N	43.10 E
Van Buren, At. (văn bū'rĕn)	121	35.26 N	94.20 W
Van Buren, Me.	102	47.09 N	67.58 W
Vanceburg, Ky. (văns'bûrg)	108	38.35 N	83.20 W
Vancouver, Can. (văn-kōō'vẽr)	116d	49.16 N	123.06 W
Vancouver, Wa.	116c	45.37 N	122.40 W
Vancouver I., Can.	96	49.50 N	125.05 W
Vancouver Island Ra., Can.	96	49.25 N	125.25 W
Vandalia, Il. (văn-dā'lĭ-ȧ)	108	39.00 N	89.00 W
Vandalia, Mo.	121	39.19 N	91.30 W
Vanderbijlpark, S. Afr.	219d	26.43 S	27.50 E
Vanderhoof, Can.	96	54.01 N	124.01 W
Van Diemen (Str.), see Ōsumi Kaikyō			
Van Diemen, C., Austl. (văndē'mĕn)	210	11.05 S	130.15 E
Van Diemen G., Austl.	210	11.50 S	131.30 E
Vanegas, Mex. (vä-nĕ'gäs)	128	23.54 N	100.54 W
Vänern (L.), Swe.	162	58.52 N	13.17 E
Vänersborg, Swe. (vĕ'nĕrs-bôr')	162	58.24 N	12.15 E
Vanga, Ken. (väŋ'gä)	223	4.38 S	39.10 E
Vangani, India	191b	19.07 N	73.15 E
Van Gölü (L.), Tur.	177	38.45 N	43.00 E
Van Horn, Tx.	122	31.03 N	104.50 W
Vanier, Can.	93c	45.27 N	75.39 W
Van Lear, Ky. (văn lēr')	108	37.45 N	82.50 W
Vannes, Fr. (vàn)	166	47.42 N	2.46 W
Van Nuys, Ca. (văn nīz')	117a	34.11 N	118.27 W
Van Rees, Pegunungan (Mtn.), Indon.	203	2.30 S	138.45 E
Vantaan (R.), Fin.	163	60.25 N	24.43 E
Vanuatu, Oceania	211	16.02 S	169.15 E
Van Wert, Oh. (văn wûrt')	108	40.50 N	84.35 W
Vara, Swe. (vä'rä)	162	58.17 N	12.55 E
Varaklāni, Sov. Un.	170	56.38 N	26.46 E
Varallo, It. (vä-räl'lô)	170	45.44 N	8.14 E
Vārānasi (Benares), India	190	25.25 N	83.00 E
Varanerfjorden (Fd.), Nor.	156	70.05 N	30.20 E
Varano, Lago di (L.), It. (lä'gō-dē-vä-rä'nô)	170	41.52 N	15.55 E
Varaždin, Yugo. (vä'räzh'dĭn)	170	46.17 N	16.20 E
Varazze, It. (vä-rät'sā)	170	44.23 N	8.34 E
Varberg, Swe. (vär'bĕrg)	162	57.06 N	12.16 E
Vardar (R.), Yugo. (vär'där)	171	41.40 N	21.50 E
Vardø, Nor. (värd'û)	156	70.23 N	30.15 E
Varėna, Sov. Un. (vä-rā'nȧ)	163	54.16 N	24.35 E
Varennes, Can. (vȧ-rĕn')	93a	45.41 N	73.27 W
Varěs, Yugo. (vä'rĕsh)	171	44.10 N	18.20 E
Varese, It. (vä-rā'så)	170	45.45 N	8.49 E
Varginha, Braz. (vär-zhē'n-yä)	139a	21.33 S	45.25 W
Varkaus, Fin. (vär'kous)	163	62.19 N	27.51 E
Varlamovo, Sov. Un. (vár-lá'mô-vô)	180a	54.37 N	60.41 E
Varna (Stalin), Bul. (vär'nȧ) (stä'lĭn)	171	43.14 N	27.58 E
Varna, Sov. Un.	180a	53.22 N	60.59 E
Värnamo, Swe. (vĕr'nȧ-mô)	162	57.11 N	13.45 E
Varnsdorf, Czech. (värns'dôrf)	164	50.54 N	14.36 E
Varnville, SC (värn'vĭl)	125	32.49 N	81.05 W
Vars, Can. (värz)	93c	45.21 N	75.21 W
Varvaropolye, Sov. Un. (vár'vár'ô-pô-lyě)	173	48.38 N	38.37 E
Vasa, India	191b	19.20 N	72.47 E
Vascongadas (Reg.), Sp. (väs-kôn-gä'däs)	168	42.35 N	2.46 W
Vashka (R.), Sov. Un.	176	63.20 N	47.50 E
Vashon, Wa. (văsh'ŭn)	116a	47.27 N	122.28 W
Vashon Heights, Wa. (hītz)	116a	47.30 N	122.28 W
Vashon I., Wa.	116a	47.27 N	122.27 W
Vasil'kov, Sov. Un. (vá-sēl'-kôf')	173	50.10 N	30.22 E
Vaslui, Rom. (vás-lōō'ē)	165	46.39 N	27.49 E
Vassar, Mi. (văs'ẽr)	108	43.25 N	83.35 W
Vassouras, Braz. (väs-sō'räzh)	142b	22.25 S	43.40 W
Västerås, Swe. (vĕs'tĕr-ôs)	162	59.39 N	16.30 E
Västerdalälven (R.), Swe.	162	61.06 N	13.10 E
Västervik, Swe. (vĕs'tĕr-vēk)	162	57.45 N	16.35 E
Vasto, It. (väs'tô)	170	42.06 N	12.42 E
Vasyugan (R.), Sov. Un. (vás-yōō-gán')	178	58.52 N	77.30 E
Vatican City (Città del Vaticano), Eur. (văt'ĭ-kăn sĭt'ē) (chē-tä'del vä-tē-kä'nô)	169d	41.54 N	12.22 E
Vaticano, C., It. (vä-tē-kä'nô)	170	38.38 N	15.52 E
Vatnajökull (Gl.), Ice. (vät'nȧ-yû-kōōl)	156	64.34 N	16.41 W
Vatomandry, Mad. (vä-tōō-män'drē)	223	18.53 S	48.13 E
Vatra Dornei, Rom. (vät'rȧ dôr'nå')	165	47.22 N	25.20 E
Vättern (L.), Swe.	162	58.15 N	14.24 E
Vattholma, Swe.	162	60.01 N	17.40 E
Vaudreuil, Can. (vô-drû'y')	93a	45.24 N	74.02 W
Vaugh, Wa. (vôn)	116a	47.21 N	122.47 W
Vaughan, Can.	93d	43.47 N	79.36 W
Vaughn, NM	120	34.37 N	105.13 W
Vaupés (R.), Col. (vá'ōō-pě's)	140	1.18 N	71.14 W
Vaxholm, Swe. (väks'hôlm)	162	59.26 N	18.19 E
Växjo, Swe. (vĕks'shû)	162	56.53 N	14.46 E
Vaygach (I.), Sov. Un. (vī-gách')	176	70.00 N	59.00 E
Veadeiros, Chapadas dos (Mts.), Braz. (shä-pä'däs-dôs-vě-á-dā'rōs)	141	15.20 S	48.43 W
Vedea (R.), Rom. (vå'dyȧ)	171	44.25 N	24.45 E
Vedia, Arg. (vě'dyä)	139c	34.29 S	61.30 W
Veedersburg, In. (vē'dẽrz-bûrg)	108	40.05 N	87.15 W
Vega (I.), Nor.	156	65.38 N	10.51 E
Vega de Alatorre, Mex. (vā'gä dä ä-lä-tōr'rå)	129	20.02 N	96.39 W
Vega Real (Mts.), Dom. Rep. (vě'gä-rē-ä'l)	133	19.30 N	71.05 W
Vegreville, Can.	98	53.30 N	112.03 W
Vehār L., India	191b	19.11 N	72.52 E
Veinticinco de Mayo, Arg. (vå-ēn'tē-sēn'kō dā mä'yō)	139c	35.26 S	60.09 W
Vejer de la Frontera, Sp.	168	36.15 N	5.58 W
Vejle, Den. (vī'lĕ)	162	55.41 N	9.29 E
Velbert, F.R.G. (fĕl'bĕrt)	167c	51.20 N	7.03 E
Velebit (Mts.), Yugo. (vā'lĕ-bēt)	170	44.25 N	15.23 E
Velen, F.R.G. (fĕ'lĕn)	167c	51.54 N	7.00 E
Vélez-Málaga, Sp. (vā'lāth-mä'lä-gä)	168	36.48 N	4.05 W
Vélez-Rubio, Sp. (rōō'bē-ô)	168	37.38 N	2.05 W
Velika Kapela (Mts.), Yugo. (vě'lē-kä kä-pě'lä)	170	45.03 N	15.20 E
Velika Morava (R.), Yugo. (mô'rä-vä)	171	44.20 N	21.10 E
Velikaya (R.), Sov. Un. (vå-lē'ká-yȧ)	172	57.25 N	28.07 E
Velikiy Bychkov, Sov. Un. (vě-lē'kē bōōch-kôf')	165	47.59 N	24.01 E
Velikiye Luki, Sov. Un. (vyē-lē'-kyě lōō'ke)	172	56.19 N	30.32 E
Velikiy Ustyug, Sov. Un. (vå-lē'kĭ ōōs-tyōōg')	176	60.45 N	46.38 E
Veliko Tŭrnovo, Bul.	171	43.06 N	25.38 E
Velikoye, Sov. Un. (vå-lē'kô-yě)	172	57.21 N	39.45 E
Velikoye (L.), Sov. Un.	172	57.00 N	36.53 E
Veli Lošinj, Yugo (lô'shēn')	170	44.30 N	14.29 E
Velizh, Sov. Un. (vå'lēzh)	172	55.37 N	31.11 E
Velke Meziříčí, Czech. (vĕl'kä mĕzh'r-zhĭ-chĭ)	164	49.21 N	16.01 E
Vella (I.), Sol. Is. (väl'yä)	211	8.00 S	156.42 E
Velletri, It. (vĕl-lā'trē)	169d	41.42 N	12.48 E
Vellore, India (vĕl-lōr')	191	12.57 N	79.09 E
Vels, Sov. Un. (vĕls)	180a	60.35 N	58.47 E
Vel'sk, Sov. Un. (vĕlsk)	176	61.00 N	42.18 E
Velten, G.D.R. (fel'tĕn)	155b	52.41 N	13.11 E
Velya R., Sov. Un. (vĕl'yȧ)	180b	56.23 N	37.54 E
Venadillo, Col. (vě-nä-dē'l-yō)	140a	4.43 N	74.55 W
Venado, Mex. (vå-mä'dō)	128	22.54 N	101.07 W
Venado Tuerto, Arg. (vě-nä'dô-tōōě'r-tō)	142	33.28 S	61.47 W
Vendôme, Fr. (väN-dōm')	166	47.46 N	1.05 E
Veneto (Reg.), It. (vě-ně'tô)	170	45.58 N	11.24 E
Venëv, Sov. Un. (vĕn-ĕf')	172	54.19 N	38.14 E
Venezia (Venice), It. (vå-nāt'sē-ä)	170	45.25 N	12.18 E
Venezuela, S.A. (vĕn-ē-zwē'lȧ)	138	8.00 N	65.00 W
Venezuela, Golfo de (G.), Ven. (gôl-fô-dě)	140	11.34 N	71.02 W
Veniaminof, Mt., Ak.	105	56.12 N	159.20 W
Venice, Ca. (vĕn'ĭs)	117a	33.59 N	118.28 W
Venice, Il.	117e	38.40 N	90.10 W
Venice, see Venezia			
Venice, Gulf of (G.), It.	170	45.23 N	13.00 E
Venlo, Neth.	167c	51.22 N	6.11 E
Venta (R.), Sov. Un. (vĕn'tȧ)	163	57.05 N	21.45 E
Ventana, Sierra de la (Mts.), Arg. (sē-ĕ-rà-dĕ-lä-vĕn-tá'nä)	142	38.00 S	63.00 W
Ventersburg, S. Afr. (vĕn-tẽrs'bûrg)	219d	28.06 S	27.10 E
Ventersdorp, S. Afr. (vĕn-tẽrs'dôrp)	219d	26.20 S	26.48 E
Ventimiglia, It. (vĕn-tē-mēl'yä)	170	43.46 N	7.37 E
Ventnor, NJ (vĕnt'nẽr)	109	39.20 N	74.25 W
Ventspils, Sov. Un. (vĕnt'spēls)	163	57.24 N	21.41 E
Ventuari (R.), Ven. (vĕn-tōōá'rē)	140	4.47 N	65.56 W
Ventura, Ca. (vĕn-tōō'rȧ)	118	34.18 N	119.18 W
Venukovsky, Sov. Un. (vě-nōō'kôv-skĭ)	180b	55.10 N	37.26 E
Venustiano Carranza, Mex. (vě-nōōs-tyä'nō-kär-rä'n-zä)	128	19.44 N	103.48 W
Venustiano Carranzo, Mex. (kär-rä'n-zō)	129	16.21 N	92.36 W
Vera, Arg. (vĕ-rä)	142	29.22 S	60.09 W
Vera, Sp. (vā'rä)	168	37.18 N	1.53 W
Vera Cruz, (State), Mex. (vā-rä-krōōz')	126	20.30 N	97.15 W
Veracruz, Mex.	129	19.13 N	96.07 W
Verāval, India (vẽr'vŭ-väl)	190	20.59 N	70.49 E
Vercelli, It. (vẽr-chĕl'lē)	170	45.18 N	8.27 E
Verchères, Can. (vẽr-shâr')	93a	45.46 N	73.21 W
Verde (R.), Az. (vûrd)	119	34.04 N	111.40 W
Verde, Cap (C.), Ba.	133	22.50 N	75.00 W
Verde, Cay (I.), Ba.	133	22.00 N	75.05 W
Verde (R.), Mex.	129	16.05 N	97.44 W
Verde (R.), Mex.	128	20.50 N	103.00 W
Verde (R.), Mex.	128	21.48 N	99.50 W
Verde (I.), Phil. (vĕr'dā)	203a	13.34 N	121.11 E
Verde Island Pass., Phil. (vĕr'dē)	203a	13.36 N	120.39 E
Verdemont, Ca. (vûr'dē-mŏnt)	117a	34.12 N	117.22 W
Verden, F.R.G. (fĕr'dĕn)	164	52.55 N	9.15 E
Verdigris (R.), Ok. (vûr'dē-grēs)	121	36.50 N	95.29 W
Verdun, Can. (vĕr'dŭN')	93a	45.27 N	73.34 W
Verdun, Fr. (vår-dûN')	166	49.09 N	5.21 E
Verdun, Fr.	169	43.48 N	1.10 E
Vereeniging, S. Afr. (vĕ-rā'nĭ-gĭng)	219d	26.40 S	27.56 E
Verena, S. Afr. (vĕr-ĕn ȧ)	219d	25.30 S	29.02 E
Vereya, Sov. Un. (vĕ-rå'yȧ)	172	55.21 N	36.08 E
Vergara, Sp. (vĕr-gä'rä)	168	43.08 N	2.23 W
Verín, Sp. (vå-rēn')	168	41.56 N	7.26 W
Verkhne-Kamchatsk, Sov. Un. (vyĕrk'nyĕ kȧm-chatsk')	179	54.42 N	158.41 E
Verkhne Neyvinskiy, Sov. Un. (nā-vĭn'skĭ)	180a	57.17 N	60.10 E
Verkhne Ural'sk, Sov. Un. (ōō-ralsk')	180a	53.53 N	50.15 E
Verkhneye, Sov. Un. (vyĕrK'nĕ-yĕ)	173	48.53 N	38.29 E
Verkhniy Avzyan, Sov. Un. (vyĕrk'nyĕ ȧv-zyȧn')	180a	53.32 N	57.30 E
Verkhniye Kigi, Sov. Un. (vyĕrk'nĭ-yĕ kĭ'gĭ)	180a	55.23 N	58.37 E
Verkhniy Ufaley, Sov. Un. (ōō-fȧ'lā)	180a	56.04 N	60.15 E
Verkhnyaya Pyshma, Sov. Un. (vyĕrk'nyä-yä pōōsh'mȧ)	180a	56.57 N	60.37 E
Verkhnyaya Salda, Sov. Un. (säl'dȧ)	180a	58.03 N	60.33 E
Verkhnyaya Tunguska (Angara), (R.), Sov. Un. (tōōn-gōōs'kȧ)	178	58.13 N	97.00 E
Verkhnyaya Tura, Sov. Un. (tōō'rȧ)	180a	58.22 N	59.51 E
Verkhnyaya Yayva, Sov. Un. (yäy'vȧ)	180a	59.28 N	59.38 E
Verkhotur'ye, Sov. Un. (vyĕr-kô-tōōr'yĕ)	180a	58.52 N	60.47 E
Verkhoyansk, Sov. Un. (vyĕr-Kô-yänsk')	179	67.43 N	133.33 E
Verkhoyanskiy Khrebet (Mts.), Sov. Un. (vyĕr-Kô-yänskĭ)	179	67.45 N	128.00 E
Vermilion, Can. (vẽr-mĭl'yŭn)	97	53.22 N	110.51 W
Vermilion (L.), Mn.	113	47.49 N	92.35 W
Vermilion (R.), Can.	97	53.30 N	111.00 W
Vermilion (R.), Can.	102	47.30 N	73.15 W
Vermilion (R.), Il.	108	41.05 N	89.00 W
Vermilion (R.), Mn.	113	48.09 N	92.31 W
Vermilion Hills, Can.	98	50.43 N	106.50 W
Vermilion Ra, Mn.	113	47.55 N	91.59 W
Vermillion, SD	112	42.46 N	96.56 W
Vermillion (R.), SD	112	43.54 N	97.14 W
Vermillion B., La.	123	29.47 N	92.00 W
Vermont (State), U.S. (vẽr-mŏnt')	107	43.50 N	72.50 W
Vernal, Ut. (vûr'nȧl)	115	40.29 N	109.40 W
Verneuk Pan (L.), S. Afr. (vĕr-nŭk')	222	30.10 S	21.46 E
Vernon, Ca. (vŭr'nŭn)	117a	34.01 N	118.12 W
Vernon, Can. (vĕr-nôN')	97	50.18 N	119.15 W
Vernon, Can.	93c	45.10 N	75.27 W
Vernon, In. (vûr'nŭn)	108	39.00 N	85.40 W
Vernon, NJ	110a	39.00 N	85.40 W
Vernon, Tx.	120	34.09 N	99.16 W
Vero Beach, Fl. (vē'rō)	125a	27.36 N	80.25 W
Véroia, Grc.	171	40.30 N	22.13 E
Verona, It. (vā-rō'nä)	170	45.28 N	11.02 E
Vernonia, Or. (vûr-nō'nyȧ)	116c	45.52 N	123.12 W
Versailles, Fr. (vĕr-sī'y')	167b	48.48 N	2.07 E
Versailles, Ky. (vēr-sālz')	108	38.05 N	84.45 W
Versailles, Mo.	121	38.27 N	92.52 W
Vert, Cap (C.), Senegal	224	14.43 N	17.30 W
Verulam, S. Afr. (vĕ-rōō-lăm)	223c	29.39 S	31.08 E
Verviers, Bel. (vĕr-vyā')	161	50.35 N	5.57 E
Vesëloye, Sov. Un. (vĕ-syô'lô-yĕ)	173	46.59 N	34.56 E
Vesijärvi (L.), Fin.	163	61.09 N	25.10 E
Vesoul, Fr. (vĕ-sōōl')	167	47.38 N	6.11 E
Vestavia Hills, Al.	110h	33.26 N	86.46 W
Vesterålen (Is.), Nor. (vĕs'tĕr ô'lĕn)	156	68.54 N	14.03 E
Vestfjord, Nor.	156	67.33 N	12.59 E
Vestmannaeyjar, Ice. (vĕst'män-ä-ā'yär)	156	63.12 N	20.17 W
Vesuvio, (Mtn.), It. (vĕ-sōō'vyä)	169c	40.35 N	14.26 E
Ves'yegonsk, Sov. Un. (vĕ-syĕ-gônsk')	172	58.42 N	37.09 E
Veszprem, Hung. (vĕs'prām)	165	47.05 N	17.53 E
Vészto, Hung. (vĕs'tû)	165	46.55 N	21.18 E
Vetka, Sov. Un. (vyĕt'kȧ)	172	52.36 N	31.05 E
Vetlanda, Swe. (vĕt-län'dä)	162	57.26 N	15.05 E
Vetluga, Sov. Un. (vyĕt-lōō'gȧ)	176	57.50 N	45.42 E
Vetluga (R.), Sov. Un.	176	56.50 N	45.50 E
Vetovo, Bul. (vā'tô-vô)	171	43.42 N	26.18 E
Vetren, Bul. (vĕt'rĕn')	171	42.16 N	24.04 E
Vet R., S. Afr. (vĕt)	219d	28.25 S	26.37 E
Vevay, In. (vē'vā)	108	38.45 N	85.05 W
Veynes, Fr. (vān')	167	44.31 N	5.47 E
Vézère (R.), Fr. (vā-zer')	166	45.01 N	1.00 E
Viacha, Bol. (vēä'chȧ)	140	16.43 S	68.16 W
Viadana, It. (vē-ä-dä'nä)	170	44.55 N	10.30 E
Vian, Ok. (vĭ'ăn)	121	35.30 N	95.00 W
Viana, Braz. (vē-ä'nä)	141	3.09 S	44.44 W
Viana del Bollo, Sp. (vē-ä'nä dĕl bôl'yô)	168	42.10 N	7.07 W
Viana do Alentejo, Port. (vē-ä'nȧ dōō ä-lĕN-tā'hōō)	168	38.20 N	8.02 W
Viana do Castelo, Port. (dōō käs-tā'lōō)	168e	41.41 N	8.45 W
Viangchan, Laos	202	18.07 N	102.33 E
Viar (R.), Sp. (vē-ä'rä)	168	38.15 N	6.08 W
Viareggio, It. (vē-ä-rĕd'jô)	170	43.52 N	10.14 E
Viborg, Den. (vē'bôr)	162	56.27 N	9.22 E
Vibo Valentia, It. (vē'bô-vä-lĕ'n-tyä)	170	38.47 N	16.06 E
Vicálvaro, Sp.	169a	40.25 N	3.37 W
Vicente Lòpez, Arg. (vē-sĕ'n-tĕ-lô'pĕz)	142a	34.15 S	58.20 W
Vicenza, It. (vē-chĕnt'sä)	170	45.33 N	11.33 E
Vich, Sp. (vēch)	169	41.55 N	2.14 E
Vichuga, Sov. Un. (vē-chōō'gȧ)	172	57.13 N	41.58 E

ăt; finȧl; rāte; senåte; ärm; àsk; sofȧ; fâre; ch-choose; dh-as th in other; bē; ēvent; bĕt; recĕnt; cratẽr; g-gō; gh-guttural g; bĭt; ĭ-short neutral; rīde; K-guttural k as ch in German ich;

PLACE (Pronunciation)	PAGE	Lat. °′	Long. °′
Vichy, Fr. (vē-shē')	166	46.06 N	3.28 E
Vickersund, Nor.	162	60.00 N	9.59 E
Vicksburg, Mi. (vĭks'bûrg)	108	42.10 N	85.30 W
Vicksburg, Ms.	124	32.20 N	90.50 W
Viçosa, Braz. (vē-sô'sä)	139a	23.46 S	42.51 W
Victoria, Arg. (vēk-tô'rēä)	139c	32.36 S	60.09 W
Victoria, Cam. (vĭk-tō'rĭ-ȧ)	225	4.01 N	9.12 E
Victoria, Can. (vĭk-tō'rĭ-ȧ)	96	48.26 N	123.23 W
Victoria, Chile (vēk-tô-rēä)	142	38.15 S	72.16 W
Victoria, Col. (vēk-tô'rēä)	140a	5.19 N	74.54 W
Victoria, Hong Kong (vĭk-tō'rĭ-ȧ)	199	22.10 N	114.18 E
Victoria, Phil. (vēk-tô-ryä)	203a	15.34 N	120.41 E
Victoria, Tx. (vĭk-tō'rĭ-ȧ)	123	28.48 N	97.00 W
Victoria, Va.	125	36.57 N	78.13 W
Victoria (State), Austl.	211	36.46 S	143.15 E
Victoria (L.), Afr.	227	0.50 S	32.50 E
Victoria (R.), Austl.	210	17.25 S	130.50 E
Victoria, Mt., Bur.	194	21.26 N	93.59 E
Victoria, Mt., Pap. N. Gui.	203	9.35 S	147.45 E
Victoria de las Tunas, Cuba (vēk-tō'rē-ä dā läs tōō'näs)	132	20.55 N	77.05 W
Victoria Falls, Zambia	227	17.56 S	25.50 E
Victoria Falls, Zimb.	227	17.55 S	25.51 E
Victoria I., Can.	94	70.13 N	107.45 W
Victoria L., Can.	103	48.20 N	57.40 W
Victoria Land, Ant.	228	75.00 S	160.00 E
Victoria Nile (R.), Ug.	227	2.20 N	31.35 E
Victoria Pk., Belize (vēk-tōrĭ'ȧ)	130a	16.47 N	88.40 W
Victoria Pk., Can.	96	50.03 N	126.06 W
Victoria River Downs, Austl. (vĭc-tôr'ĭȧ)	210	16.30 S	131.10 E
Victoria Str., Can. (vĭk-tō'rĭ-ȧ)	94	69.10 N	100.58 W
Victoriaville, Can. (vĭk-tō'rĭ-ȧ-vĭl)	101	46.04 N	71.59 W
Victoria West, S. Afr. (wĕst)	222	31.25 S	23.10 E
Vidalia, Ga. (vĭ-dā'lĭ-ȧ)	125	32.10 N	82.26 W
Vidalia, La.	123	31.33 N	91.28 W
Vidin, Bul. (vĭ'dēn)	171	44.00 N	22.53 E
Vidnoye, Sov. Un.	180b	55.33 N	37.41 E
Vidzy, Sov. Un. (vē'dzĭ)	172	55.23 N	26.46 E
Viedma, Arg. (vyād'mä)	142	40.55 S	63.03 W
Viedma (L.), Arg.	142	49.40 S	72.35 W
Viejo R., Nic. (vyā'hō)	130	12.45 N	86.19 W
Vienna, Ga. (vē-ĕn'ȧ)	124	32.03 N	83.50 W
Vienna, Il.	121	37.24 N	88.50 W
Vienna, Va.	110e	38.54 N	77.16 W
Vienna, see Wien			
Vienne, Fr. (vyĕn')	166	45.31 N	4.54 E
Vienne (R.), Fr.	166	47.06 N	0.20 E
Vieques, P.R. (vyā'kās)	127b	18.09 N	65.27 W
Vieques (I.), P.R. (vyā'kās)	127b	18.05 N	65.28 W
Vierfontien, S. Afr. (vĕr'fōn-tān)	219d	27.06 S	26.45 E
Viersen, F.R.G. (fēr'zĕn)	167c	51.15 N	6.24 E
Vierwaldstätter See (L.), Switz.	164	46.54 N	8.36 E
Vierzon, Fr. (vyâr-zôN')	166	47.14 N	2.04 E
Viesca, Mex. (vē-ās'kä)	122	25.21 N	102.47 W
Viesca, Laguna de (L.), Mex. (lä-ōō'nä-dĕ)	122	25.30 N	102.40 W
Vieste, It. (vyĕs'tā)	170	41.52 N	161.0 E
Vietnam, Asia (vyĕt'näm')	202	18.00 N	107.00 E
Vigan, Phil. (vēgän)	203a	17.36 N	120.22 E
Vigevano, It. (vē-jā-vä'nô)	170	45.18 N	8.52 E
Vigny, Fr. (vēn-y'ē')	167b	49.05 N	1.54 E
Vigo, Sp. (vē'gō)	168	42.18 N	8.42 W
Vihti, Fin. (vē'tĭ)	163	60.27 N	24.18 E
Viipuri, see Vyborg			
Vijayawāda, India	191	16.31 N	80.37 E
Vijosë, (R.), Alb.	171	40.15 N	20.30 E
Viksøyri, Nor.	162	61.06 N	6.35 E
Vila, Vanuatu	211	18.00 S	168.30 E
Vila Caldas Xavier, Moz.	227	15.59 S	34.12 E
Vila de Manica, Moz. (vē'lä dā mä-nē'kȧ)	222	18.48 S	32.49 E
Vila de Rei, Port. (vē'lȧ dā rā'ĭ)	168	39.42 N	8.03 W
Vila do Conde, Port. (vē'lä dōō kōn'dĕ)	168	41.21 N	8.44 W
Vilafranca de Xira, Port. (fräŋ'kä dā shē'rä)	168	38.58 N	8.59 W
Vilaine (R.), Fr. (vē-lân')	166	47.34 N	0.20 W
Vilanculos, Moz. (vē-län-kōō'lôs)	222	22.03 S	35.13 E
Vilāni, Sov. Un. (vē'lȧ-nĭ)	172	56.31 N	27.00 E
Vila Nova de Foz Côa, Port. (nō'vȧ dā fôz-kō'ȧ)	168	41.08 N	7.11 W
Vila Nova de Gaia, Port. (vē'lȧ nō'vȧ dā gä'yä)	168	41.08 N	8.40 W
Vila Nova de Milfontes, Port. (nō'vȧ dā mēl-fôn'tāzh)	168	37.44 N	8.48 W
Vila Real, Port. (rā-äl')	168	41.18 N	7.48 W
Vila Real de Santo Antonio, Port. (vē'lä-rē-ä'l-dē-sän-tô-än-tô'nyô)	168	37.14 N	7.25 W
Vila Viçosa, Port. (vē-sō'zȧ)	168	38.47 N	7.24 W
Vileyka, Sov. Un. (vē-lā'ē-kȧ)	172	54.19 N	26.58 E
Vilhelmina, Swe.	156	64.37 N	16.30 E
Viljandi, Sov. Un. (vēl'yän-dē)	163	58.24 N	25.34 E
Viljoenskroon, S. Afr.	219d	27.13 S	26.58 E
Vilkaviškis, Sov. Un. (vēl-kȧ-vēsh'kēs)	163	54.40 N	23.08 E
Vilkija, Sov. Un. (vēl-kē'ēä)	163	55.04 N	23.30 E
Vil'kitskogo (I.), Sov. Un. (vyl-kēts-kōgō)	178	73.25 N	76.00 E
Vilkovo, Sov. Un. (vĭl-kô-vô)	177	45.24 N	29.36 E
Villa Acuña, Mex. (vēl'yä-kōō'n-yä)	122	29.20 N	100.56 W
Villa Ahumada, Mex. (ä-ōō-mä'dä)	122	30.43 N	106.30 W
Villa Alta (San Ildefonso), Mex. (äl'tä)(sän ēl-dā-fōn'sō)	129	17.20 N	96.08 W
Villa Angela, Arg. (vē'l-yä à'n-kē-lä)	142	27.31 S	60.42 W
Villa Ballester, Arg. (vē'l-yä-bàl-yĕs-tĕr)	142a	34.18 S	58.33 W
Villa Bella, Bol. (bĕ'l-yä)	140	10.25 S	65.22 W
Villablino, Sp. (vēl-yä-blē'nō)	168	42.58 N	6.18 W
Villacañas, Sp. (vēl-yä-kän'yäs)	168	39.39 N	3.20 W
Villacarrillo, Sp. (vēl-yä-kä-rēl'yō)	168	38.09 N	3.07 W
Villach, Aus. (fē'läk)	164	46.38 N	13.50 E
Villacidro, It. (vē-lä-chē'drō)	170	39.28 N	8.41 E
Villa Clara (Prov.), Cuba	132	22.40 N	80.10 W
Villa Constitución, Arg. (kōn-stē-tōō-syōn')	139c	33.15 S	60.19 W
Villa Coronado, Mex. (kō-rō-nä'dhō)	122	26.45 N	105.10 W
Villa Cuauhtémoc, Mex. (vēl'yä-kōō-äōō-tē'môk)	129	22.11 N	97.50 W
Villa de Allende, Mex. (vēl'yä'dā äl-yĕn'dā)	122	25.18 N	100.01 W
Villa de Alvarez, Mex. (vēl'yä-dē-ä'l-vä-rēz)	128	19.17 N	103.44 W
Villa de Cura, Ven. (dē-kōō'rä)	141b	10.03 N	67.29 W
Villa de Guadalupe, Mex. (dē-gwä-dhä-lōō'pā)	128	23.22 N	100.44 W
Villa Dolores, Arg. (vēl'yä dō-lō'rās)	142	31.50 S	65.05 W
Villa Escalante, Mex. (vēl'yä-ĕs-kä-làn'tē)	128	19.24 N	101.36 W
Villa Flores, Mex. (vēl'yä-flō'rās)	129	16.13 N	93.17 W
Villafranca, It. (vēl-lä-fräŋ'kä)	170	45.22 N	10.53 E
Villafranca del Bierzo, Sp. (vēl'yä-fräŋ'kä dĕl byĕr'thō)	168	42.37 N	6.49 W
Villafranca de los Barros, Sp. (vēl-yä-fräŋ'kä dā lōs bär'rōs)	168	38.34 N	6.22 W
Villafranca del Panadés, Sp. (vēl-yäfrän'kä dĕl pä-nä-dās')	169	41.20 N	1.40 E
Villa García, Mex. (gär-sē'ä)	128	22.07 N	101.55 W
Villagarcia, Sp. (vēl'yä-gär-thē'ä)	168	42.38 N	8.43 W
Villagram, Mex. (vēl-yä-gräm')	122	24.28 N	99.30 W
Villa Grove, Il. (vĭl'ȧ grōv')	108	39.55 N	88.15 W
Villaguay, Arg. (vē'l-yä-gwī)	142	31.47 S	58.53 W
Villa Hayes, Par. (vēl'yä äyās)(hāz)	142	25.07 S	57.31 W
Villahermosa, Mex. (vēl'yä-ĕr-mō'sä)	129	17.59 N	92.56 W
Villa Hidalgo, Mex. (vēl'yäē-däl'gō)	128	21.39 N	102.41 W
Villajoyosa, Sp. (vēl'yä-hô-yō'sä)	169	38.30 N	0.14 W
Villalba, Sp.	168	43.18 N	7.43 W
Villaldama, Mex. (vēl-yäl-dä'mä)	122	26.30 N	100.26 W
Villa Lopez, Mex. (vēl'yä lō'pēz)	122	27.00 N	105.02 W
Villalpando, Sp. (vēl-yäl-pän'dō)	168	41.54 N	5.24 W
Villa María, Arg. (vē'l-yä-mä-rē'ä)	142	32.17 S	63.08 W
Villamatín, Sp. (vēl-yä-mä-tē'n)	168	36.50 N	5.38 W
Villa Mercedes, Arg. (mĕr-sā'dās)	142	33.38 S	65.16 W
Villa Montes, Bol. (vē'l-yä-mô'n-tĕs)	140	21.13 S	63.26 W
Villa Morelos, Mex. (mô-rĕ'lomcs)	128	20.01 N	101.24 W
Villanueva, Col. (vē'l-yä-nōōĕ'vä)	140	10.44 N	73.08 W
Villanueva, Hond. (vēl'yä-nwä'vä)	130	15.19 N	88.02 W
Villanueva, Mex. (vēl'yä-nōōĕ'vä)	128	22.25 N	102.53 W
Villanueva de Córdoba, Sp. (vēl-yä-nwĕ'vä-dä kôr'dô-bä)	168	38.18 N	4.38 W
Villanueva de la Serena, Sp. (lä sā-rā'nä)	168	38.59 N	5.56 W
Villanueva y Geltrú, Sp. (ēkĕl-trōō')	169	41.13 N	1.44 E
Villa Obregón, Mex. (vē'l-yä-ô-brē-gô'n)	129a	19.21 N	99.11 W
Villa Ocampo, Mex. (ô-käm'pō)	122	26.26 N	105.30 W
Villa Pedro Montoya, Mex. (vēl'yä-pē'drô-môn-tô'yá)	128	21.38 N	99.51 W
Villard-Bonnot, Fr. (vēl-yär'bôn-nō')	167	45.15 N	5.53 E
Villarreal, Sp. (vēl-yär-rē-äl)	169	39.55 N	0.07 W
Villarrica, Par. (vēl-yä-rē'kä)	142	25.55 S	56.23 W
Villarrobledo, Sp. (vēl-yär-rô-blā'dhō)	168	39.15 N	2.37 W
Villa Union, Mex. (vēl'yä-ōō-nyōn')	128	23.10 N	106.14 W
Villavicencio, Col. (vē'l-yä-vē-sĕ'n-syō)	140a	4.09 N	73.38 W
Villaviciosa de Odón, Sp. (vēl'yä-vē-thē-ō'sä dā ō-dōn')	169a	40.22 N	73.38 W
Villavieja, Col. (vē'l-yä-vē-ĕ'kȧ)	140a	3.13 N	75.13 W
Villazón, Bol. (vē'l-yä-zô'n)	142	22.02 S	65.42 W
Villafranche-de-Rouergue, Fr. (dē-rōō-ĕrg')	166	44.21 N	2.02 E
Villefranche, Fr.	166	45.59 N	4.43 E
Villejuif, Fr. (vēl'zhüst')	167b	48.48 N	2.22 E
Ville-Marie, Can.	101	47.18 N	79.22 W
Villena, Sp. (vē-lyā'nä)	169	38.37 N	0.52 W
Villeneuve, Can. (vēl'nûv')	93g	53.40 N	113.49 W
Villeneuve-St. Georges, Fr. (săN-zhôrzh')	167b	48.43 N	2.27 E
Villeneuve-sur-Lot, Fr. (sür-lō')	166	44.25 N	0.41 E
Ville Platte, La. (vēl plat')	123	30.41 N	92.17 W
Villers Cotterêts, Fr. (vē-âr'kō-trĕ')	166a	49.15 N	3.05 E
Villerupt, Fr. (vēl'rüp')	167	49.28 N	6.16 E
Ville-St. Georges, Can. (vĭl-sĕN-zhôrzh')	101	46.07 N	70.40 W
Villeta, Col. (vē'l-yĕ'tä)	140a	5.02 N	74.29 W
Villeurbanne, Fr. (vēl-ûr-bän')	166	45.43 N	4.55 E
Villiers, S. Afr. (vĭl'ĭ-ērs)	219d	27.03 S	28.38 E
Villingen-Schwenningen, F.R.G.	164	48.04 N	8.33 E
Villisca, Ia. (vĭ'lĭs'kȧ)	113	40.56 N	94.56 W
Villupuram, India	191	11.59 N	79.33 E
Vilnius (Wilno), Sov. Un. (vĭl'nē-ōōs)	163	54.40 N	25.26 E
Vilppula, Fin. (vĭl'pŭ-lȧ)	163	62.01 N	24.24 E
Vilvoorde, Bel.	155a	50.56 N	4.25 E
Vilyuy (R.), Sov. Un. (vēl'yĭ)	179	65.22 N	108.45 E
Vilyuysk, Sov. Un. (vē-lyōō'ĭsk')	179	63.41 N	121.47 E
Vimmerby, Swe. (vĭm'ĕr-bü)	162	57.41 N	15.51 E
Vimperk, Czech. (vĭm-pĕrk')	164	49.04 N	13.41 E
Viña del Mar, Chile (vē'nyä dĕl mär')	139b	33.00 S	71.33 W
Vinalhaven, Me. (vī-năl-hā'vĕn)	102	44.03 N	68.49 W
Vinaroz, Sp. (vē-nä'rōth)	169	40.29 N	0.27 E
Vincennes, Fr. (văN-sĕn')	167b	48.51 N	2.27 E
Vincennes, In. (vĭn-zĕnz')	108	38.40 N	87.30 W
Vincent, Al. (vĭn'sĕnt)	124	33.21 N	86.25 W
Vindelälven (R.), Swe.	156	65.02 N	18.30 E
Vindeln, Swe. (vĭn'dĕln)	156	64.10 N	19.52 E
Vindhya Ra., India (vĭnd'yä)	190	22.30 N	75.50 E
Vineland, NJ (vīn'lănd)	109	39.30 N	75.00 W
Vinh, Viet. (vēn'y')	199	18.38 N	105.42 E
Vinhais, Port. (vēn-yä'ēzh)	168	41.51 N	7.00 W
Vinings, Ga. (vī'nĭngz)	110c	33.52 N	84.28 W
Vinita, Ok. (vĭ-nē'tȧ)	121	36.38 N	95.09 W
Vinkovci, Yugo. (vēn'kôv-tsē)	171	45.17 N	18.47 E
Vinnitsa, Sov. Un. (vē'nēt-sȧ)	173	49.13 N	28.31 E
Vinnitsa (Oblast), Sov. Un.	173	48.45 N	28.01 E
Vinogradovo, Sov. Un. (vĭ-nô-grä'do-vô)	180b	55.25 N	38.33 E
Vinson Massif (Mtn.), Ant.	228	77.40 S	87.00 W
Vinton, Ia. (vĭn'tŭn)	113	42.08 N	92.01 W
Vinton, La.	123	30.12 N	93.35 W
Violet, La. (vī'ô-lĕt)	110d	29.54 N	89.54 W
Virac, Phil. (vē-räk')	199	13.38 N	124.20 E
Virbalis, Sov. Un. (vēr'bȧ-lēs)	163	54.38 N	22.55 E
Virden, Can. (vûr'dĕn)	94	49.51 N	101.55 W
Virden, Il.	121	39.28 N	89.46 W
Virgin (R.), U.S.	119	36.51 N	113.50 W
Virginia, Mn. (vĕr-jĭn'yȧ)	113	47.32 N	92.36 W
Virginia, S. Afr.	219d	28.07 S	26.54 E
Virginia (State), U.S.	107	37.00 N	80.45 W
Virginia Beach, Va.	110g	36.50 N	75.58 W
Virginia City, Nv.	118	39.18 N	119.40 W
Virgin Is., N.A. (vûr'jĭn)	127	18.15 N	64.00 W
Viroqua, Wi. (vĭ-rō'kwȧ)	113	43.33 N	90.54 W
Virovitica, Yugo. (vē-rô-vē'tē-tsä)	170	45.50 N	17.24 E
Virpazar, Yugo. (vēr'pä-zär')	171	42.16 N	19.06 E
Virrat, Fin. (vĭr'ät)	163	62.15 N	23.45 E
Virserum, Swe. (vĭr'sĕ-rōōm)	162	57.22 N	15.35 E
Vis, Yugo. (vēs)	170	43.03 N	16.11 E
Vis (I.), Yugo.	170	43.00 N	16.10 E
Visalia, Ca. (vĭ-sā'lĭ-ȧ)	118	36.20 N	119.18 W
Visby, Swe. (vĭs'bü)	162	57.39 N	18.19 E
Viscount Mellville Sound, Can.	92	74.80 N	110.00 W
Visêgrad, Yugo. (vē'shē-gräd)	171	43.45 N	19.19 E
Vishākhapatnam, India	191	17.48 N	83.21 E
Vishera R., Sov. Un. (vĭ'shĕ-rȧ)	180a	60.40 N	58.46 E
Vishnyakovo, Sov. Un.	180b	55.44 N	38.10 E
Vishoek, S. Afr.	222a	34.13 S	18.26 E
Visim, Sov. Un. (vē'sĭm)	180a	57.38 N	59.32 E
Viskan (R.), Swe.	162	57.20 N	12.25 E
Viški, Sov. Un. (vēs'kĭ)	172	56.02 N	26.47 E
Vislinskij Zaliv (B.), Pol.	165	54.22 N	19.39 E
Visoko, Yugo. (vē'sô-kô)	171	43.59 N	18.10 E
Vistula (R.), see Wisła			
Vitebsk, Sov. Un. (vē'tyĕpsk)	172	55.12 N	30.16 E
Vitebsk (Oblast), Sov. Un.	172	55.05 N	29.18 E
Viterbo, It. (vē-tĕr'bō)	170	42.24 N	12.08 E
Vitim, Sov. Un. (vē'tĕm)	179	59.22 N	112.43 E
Vitim (R.), Sov. Un. (vē'tĕm)	179	56.12 N	115.30 E
Vitino, Sov. Un. (vē'tĭ-nō)	180c	59.40 N	29.51 E
Vitória, Braz. (vē-tō'rē-ä)	141	20.09 S	40.17 W
Vitoria, Sp. (vē-tô-ryä)	168	42.43 N	2.43 W
Vitória de Conquista, Braz. (vē-tō'rē-ä-dä-kōn-kwē's-tä)	141	14.51 S	40.44 W
Vitré, Fr. (vē-trā')	166	48.09 N	1.15 W
Vitry-le-François, Fr. (vē-trē'lē-fräN-swà')	166	48.44 N	4.34 E
Vittoria, It. (vē-tô'rē-ô)	157	37.01 N	14.31 E
Vittorio, It. (vē-tô'rē-ô)	170	45.59 N	12.17 E
Vivero, Sp. (vē-vā'rō)	168	43.39 N	7.37 W
Vivian, La. (vĭv'ĭ-ăn)	123	32.51 N	93.59 W
Vize, Tur. (vē'zĕ)	171	41.34 N	27.46 E
Vizianagaram, India	191	18.10 N	83.29 E
Vlaardingen, Neth. (vlär'dĭng-ĕn)	155a	51.54 N	4.20 E
Vladimir, Sov. Un. (vlȧ-dyē'mēr)	172	56.08 N	40.24 E
Vladimir (Oblast), Sov. Un. (vlä-dyē'mĕr)	172	56.08 N	39.53 E
Vladimiro-Aleksandrovskoye, Sov. Un. (vlȧ-dyē'mē-rô ä-lĕk-sän'drôf-skô-yĕ)	200	42.50 N	133.00 E
Vladimir-Volynskiy, Sov. Un. (vlȧ-dyē'mĕr vô-lēn'skĭ)	165	50.50 N	24.20 E
Vladivostok, Sov. Un. (vlá-dē-vôs-tôk')	179	43.06 N	131.47 E
Vlasenica, Yugo. (vlä'sĕ-nēt'sä)	171	44.11 N	18.58 E
Vlasotince, Yugo. (vlä'sô-tēn-tsĕ)	171	42.58 N	22.08 E
Vlieland (I.), Neth. (vlē'länt)	161	53.19 N	4.55 E
Vlissingen, Neth. (vlĭs'sĭng-ĕn)	161	51.30 N	3.34 E
Vlorë (Valona), Alb. (vlō'rŭ)	171	40.28 N	19.31 E
Vltava (R.), Czech.	164	49.24 N	14.18 E
Vodl (L.), Sov. Un. (vôd''l)	176	62.20 N	37.20 E
Voël (R.), S. Afr.	222	32.52 S	25.12 E
Voghera, It. (vô-gā'rä)	170	44.58 N	9.02 E
Vohimarina, Mad.	223	13.35 S	50.05 E
Voight (R.), Wa.	116a	47.03 N	122.08 W
Voinjama, Lib.	224	8.25 N	9.45 W
Voiron, Fr. (vwȧ-rôN')	169	45.23 N	5.48 E

362 Voisin – Warburton

PLACE (Pronunciation)	PAGE	Lat. °′	Long. °′
Voisin, Lac (L.), Can. (vwŏ′-zĭn)	98	54.13 N	107.15 W
Volchansk, Sov. Un. (vôl-chänsk′)	173	50.18 N	36.56 E
Volch'ya (R.), Sov. Un. (vôl-chyä′)	173	49.42 N	34.39 E
Volcán Misti (Vol.), Peru	140	16.04 S	71.20 W
Volga (R.), Sov. Un. (vôl′gä)	177	47.30 N	46.20 E
Volga, Mouths of the, Sov. Un.	177	46.00 N	49.10 E
Volgograd (Stalingrad), Sov. Un. (vŏl-gō-grä′t)(stà′lĕn-grat)	177	48.40 N	42.20 E
Volgogradskoye (Res.), Sov. Un. (vôl-gô-grad′skô-yĕ)	177	51.10 N	45.10 E
Volkhov, Sov. Un. (vôl′kôf)	172	59.54 N	32.21 E
Volkhov (R.), Sov. Un.	172	58.45 N	31.40 E
Volkovysk, Sov. Un. (vôl-kô-vēsk′)	165	53.11 N	24.29 E
Volodarskiy, Sov. Un. (vô-lô-där′skĭ)	180c	59.49 N	30.06 E
Vologda, Sov. Un. (vô′lôg-dȧ)	172	59.12 N	39.52 E
Vologda (Oblast), Sov. Un.	172	59.00 N	37.26 E
Volokonovka, Sov. Un. (vô-lô-kô′nôf-kȧ)	173	50.28 N	37.52 E
Volokolamsk, Sov. Un. (vô-lô-kôlȧmsk)	172	56.02 N	35.58 E
Vólos, Grc. (vô′lôs)	171	39.23 N	22.56 E
Volozhin, Sov. Un. (vô′lô-shĭn)	172	54.04 N	26.38 E
Vol'sk, Sov. Un. (vôl′sk)	177	52.10 N	47.00 E
Volta, La., Ghana (vôl′tȧ)	224	7.10 N	0.30 W
Volta (R.), Ghana	224	6.05 N	0.30 E
Volta Blanche (R.), Upper Volta	224	11.30 N	0.40 W
Volta Noire (Black Volta) (R.), Afr.	224	10.30 N	2.55 W
Volta Redonda, Braz. (vōl′tä-rā-dôn′dä)	139a	22.32 S	44.05 W
Volterra, It. (vôl-tĕr′rä)	170	43.22 N	10.51 E
Voltri, It. (vōl′trē)	170	44.25 N	8.45 E
Volturno (R.), It. (vôl-tōōr′nô)	170	41.12 N	14.20 E
Vólvi, Límni (L.), Grc.	171	40.41 N	23.23 E
Volzhskoye (L.), Sov. Un. (vôl′sh-skô-yĕ)	172	56.43 N	36.18 E
Von Ormy, Tx. (vŏn ôr′mē)	117d	29.18 N	98.36 W
Võõpsu, Sov. Un. (vōōp′sōō)	172	58.06 N	27.30 E
Voorberg, Neth.	155a	52.04 N	4.21 E
Voortrekkerhoogte, S. Afr.	223b	25.48 S	28.10 E
Vop' (R.), Sov. Un. (vôp)	172	55.20 N	32.40 E
Vopnafjördur, Ice.	156	65.43 N	14.58 W
Vorarlberg (Prov.), Aus.	164	47.20 N	9.55 E
Vordingborg, Den. (vôr′dĭng-bôr)	162	55.10 N	11.55 E
Voríai (Is.), Grc.	171	39.12 N	24.03 E
Vorkuta, Sov. Un. (vôr-kōō′tȧ)	176	67.28 N	63.40 E
Vormsi (I.), Sov. Un. (vôrm′sĭ)	163	59.06 N	23.05 E
Vórois Evvoïkós Kólpos (G.), Grc	171	38.48 N	23.02 E
Vorona (R.), Sov. Un. (vô-rô′na)	177	51.50 N	42.00 E
Voron'ya (R.), Sov. Un. (vô-rônyȧ)	176	68.20 N	35.20 E
Voronezh, Sov. Un. (vô-rô′nyĕzh)	173	51.39 N	39.11 E
Voronezh (Oblast), Sov. Un.	173	51.10 N	39.13 E
Voronezh (R.), Sov. Un.	172	52.17 N	39.32 E
Voronovo, Sov. Un. (vô′rô-nô-vô)	165	54.07 N	25.16 E
Vorontsovka, Sov. Un. (vô-rônt′sôv-kȧ)	180a	59.40 N	60.14 E
Voroshilovgrad, Sov. Un.	177	48.34 N	39.18 E
Voroshilovgrad (Oblast), Sov. Un.	173	49.08 N	38.37 E
Võrts-Järv (L.), Sov. Un. (vôrts yärv)	172	58.15 N	26.12 E
Võru, Sov. Un. (vô′rû)	172	57.50 N	26.58 E
Vorya R., Sov. Un. (vôr′yȧ)	180b	55.55 N	38.15 E
Vosges (Mts.), Fr. (vōzh)	167	48.09 N	6.57 E
Voskresensk, Sov. Un. (vôs-krĕ-sĕnsk′)	180b	55.20 N	38.42 E
Voss, Nor. (vôs)	162	60.40 N	6.24 E
Vostryakovo, Sov. Un.	180b	55.23 N	37.49 E
Votkinsk, Sov. Un. (vôt-kēnsk′)	176	57.00 N	54.00 E
Votkinskoye Vdkhr (Res.), Sov. Un.	176	57.30 N	55.00 E
Vouga (R.), Port. (vō′gȧ)	168	40.43 N	7.51 W
Vouziers, Fr. (vōō-zyā′)	166	49.25 N	4.40 E
Voxnan (R.), Swe.	162	61.30 N	15.24 E
Voyageurs Natl. Park, Mn.	113	48.30 N	92.40 W
Vozhe (L.), Sov. Un. (vôzh′yĕ)	176	60.40 N	39.00 E
Voznesensk, Sov. Un. (vôz-nyĕ-sĕnsk′)	173	47.34 N	31.22 E
Vrangelya (Wrangel) (I.), Sov. Un.	174	71.25 N	178.30 E
Vranje, Yugo. (vrän′yĕ)	171	42.33 N	21.55 E
Vratsa, Bul. (vrät′tsȧ)	171	43.12 N	23.31 E
Vrbas, Yugo. (v′r′bäs)	171	45.34 N	19.43 E
Vrbas (R.), Yugo.	170	44.25 N	17.17 E
Vrchlabi, Czech. (v′r′chlä-bē)	166	50.32 N	15.51 E
Vrede, S. Afr. (vrĭ′dĕ)(vrĕd)	219d	27.25 S	29.11 E
Vredefort, S. Afr. (vrĭ′dĕ-fôrt)(vrĕd′fôrt)	219d	27.00 S	27.21 E
Vreeswijk, Neth.	155a	52.00 N	5.06 E
Vršac, Yugo. (v′r′shȧts)	171	45.08 N	21.18 E
Vrutky, Czech. (vrōōt′kĕ)	165	49.09 N	18.55 E
Vryburg, S. Afr. (vrī′bûrg)	222	26.55 S	29.45 E
Vryheid, S. Afr. (vrī′hīt)	222	27.43 S	30.58 E
Vsetín, Czech. (fsĕt′yēn)	165	49.21 N	18.01 E
Vsevolozhskiy, Sov. Un. (vsyĕ′vôlô′zh-skēē)	180c	60.01 N	30.41 E
Vuelta Abajo (Mts.), Cuba (vwĕl′tä ä-bä′hō)	132	22.20 N	83.45 W
Vught, Neth.	155a	51.38 N	5.18 E
Vukovar, Yugo. (vōō′kô-vär)	171	45.20 N	19.00 E
Vulcan, Mi. (vŭl′kăn)	108	45.45 N	87.50 W
Vulcano (I.), It. (vōōl-kä′nō)	170	38.23 N	15.00 E
Vŭlchedrŭma, Bul.	171	43.43 N	23.29 E
Vyartsilya, Sov. Un. (vyȧr-tsē′lyȧ)	163	62.10 N	30.40 E
Vyatka (R.), Sov. Un. (vyȧt′kȧ)	176	58.25 N	51.25 E
Vyazemskiy, Sov. Un. (vyȧ-zĕm′skĭ)	200	47.29 N	134.39 E
Vyaz'ma, Sov. Un. (vyȧz′mȧ)	172	55.12 N	34.17 E
Vyazniki, Sov. Un. (vyȧz′nē-kē)	176	56.10 N	42.10 E
Vyborg (Viipuri), Sov. Un. (vwē′bôrk)	163	60.43 N	28.46 E
Vychegda (R.), Sov. Un. (vē′chĕg-dȧ)	176	61.40 N	48.00 E
Vym (R.), Sov. Un. (vwēm)	176	63.15 N	51.20 E
Vyritsa, Sov. Un. (vē′rĭ-tsȧ)	180c	59.24 N	30.20 E
Vyshnevolotskoye (L.), Sov. Un. (vŭy′sh-ŋē′vōlŏt′s-kô′yĕ)	172	57.30 N	34.27 E
Vyshniy Volochëk, Sov. Un. (vĕsh′nyĭ vôl-ô-chĕk′)	172	57.34 N	34.35 E
Vyskov, Czech. (vĕsh′kôf)	164	49.17 N	16.58 E
Vysoké Mýto, Czech. (vû′sô-kā mû′tô)	164	49.58 N	16.07 E
Vysokovsk, Sov. Un. (vĭ-sô′kôfsk)	172	56.16 N	36.32 E
Vytegra, Sov. Un. (vû′tĕg-rȧ)	176	61.00 N	36.20 E
Vyur, Sov. Un.	176	57.55 N	27.00 E

W

PLACE (Pronunciation)	PAGE	Lat. °′	Long. °′
W, Parcs Nationaux du (Natl. Pk.), Dahomey-Niger	225	12.20 N	2.40 E
Wa, Ghana	224	10.04 N	2.29 W
Waal (R.), Neth. (väl)	161	51.46 N	5.00 E
Waalwijk, Neth.	155a	51.41 N	5.05 E
Wabamuno, Can. (wō′bă-mŭn)	97	53.33 N	114.28 W
Wabasca, Can. (wŏ-bás′kă)	97	56.00 N	113.53 W
Wabash, In. (wô′băsh)	108	40.45 N	85.50 W
Wabash (R.), Il.-In.	108	38.00 N	88.00 W
Wabasha, Mn. (wä′bȧ-shô)	113	44.24 N	92.04 W
Wabowden, Can. (wă-bō′d′n)	99	54.55 N	98.38 W
Wąbrzeźno, Pol. (vôŋ-bzĕzh′nô)	165	53.17 N	18.59 E
Wabu Hu (L.), China (wä-bōō hōō)	196	32.25 N	116.35 E
Waccamaw (R.), SC (wăk′ȧ-mô)	125	33.47 N	78.55 W
Waccasassa B., Fl. (wă-kȧ-să′sȧ)	124	29.02 N	83.10 W
Wachow, G.D.R. (vä′κōv)	155b	52.32 N	12.46 E
Waco, Tx. (wā′kō)	123	31.35 N	97.06 W
Waconda Lake (Res.), Ks.	120	39.45 N	98.15 W
Wadayama, Jap. (wä′dä′yä-mä)	201	35.19 N	134.49 E
Waddenzee (Sea), Neth.	161	53.00 N	4.50 E
Waddington, Mt., Can. (wŏd′dĭng-tŭn)	96	51.23 N	125.15 W
Wadena, Can.	98	51.57 N	103.50 W
Wadena, Mn. (wŏ-dē′nȧ)	113	46.26 N	95.09 W
Wadesboro, NC (wādz′bŭr-ô)	125	34.57 N	80.05 W
Wādī Mūsā, Jordan	189a	30.19 N	35.29 E
Wadley, Ga. (wŭd′lē)	125	32.54 N	82.25 W
Wad Madani, Sud. (wäd mē-dä′nē)	221	14.27 N	33.31 E
Wadowice, Pol. (vȧ-dô′vēt-sē)	165	49.53 N	19.31 E
Wadsworth, Oh. (wŏdz′wûrth)	111d	41.01 N	81.44 W
Wager B., Can. (wā′jēr)	95	65.48 N	88.19 W
Wagga Wagga, Austl. (wôg′ȧ wôg′ȧ)	212	35.10 S	147.30 E
Wagoner, Ok. (wăg′ŭn-ēr)	121	35.58 N	95.22 W
Wagon Mound, NM (wăg′ŭn mound)	120	35.59 N	104.45 W
Wągrowiec, Pol. (vôŋ-grô′vyĕts)	165	52.47 N	17.14 E
Wahiawa, Hi.	104a	21.30 N	158.03 W
Wahoo, Ne (wä-hōō′)	112	41.14 N	96.39 W
Wahpeton, ND (wô′pē-tŭn)	112	46.17 N	96.38 W
Waialua, Hi. (wä′ē-ä-lōō′ä)	104a	21.33 N	158.08 W
Waianae, Hi. (wä′ē-ȧ-nä′ä)	104a	21.25 N	158.11 W
Waidhofen, Aus. (vīd′hôf-ĕn)	164	47.58 N	14.46 E
Waigeo, Pulau (I.), Indon. (wä-ē-gä′ô)	179	0.07 N	131.00 E
Waikato (R.), N.Z. (wä′ē-kä′to)	213	38.10 S	175.35 E
Waikerie, Austl. (wā′kēr-ē)	212	34.15 S	140.00 E
Wailuku, Hi. (wä′ē-lōō′kōō)	104a	20.55 N	156.30 W
Waimanalo, Hi. (wä-ē-mä′nä-lo)	104a	21.19 N	157.53 W
Waimea, Hi. (wä-ē-mā′ä)	104a	21.56 N	159.38 W
Wainganga (R.), India (wä-ēn-gŭŋ′gä)	190	20.24 N	79.41 E
Waingapu, Indon.	202	9.32 S	120.00 E
Wainwright, Ak. (wān-rīt)	105	74.40 N	159.00 W
Wainwright, Can.	97	52.49 N	110.52 W
Waipahu, Hi. (wä′ē-pä′hōō)	104a	21.20 N	158.02 W
Waiska R., Mi. (wȧ-ĭz-kȧ)	117k	46.20 N	84.38 W
Waitsburg, Wa. (wāts′bûrg)	114	46.17 N	118.08 W
Wajima, Jap. (wä′jē-mȧ)	201	37.23 N	136.56 E
Wajir, Ken.	227	1.45 N	40.04 E
Wakamatsu, Jap. (wä-kä′mät-sōō)	201	33.54 N	130.44 E
Wakami (R.), Can.	100	47.43 N	82.22 W
Wakasa-Wan (B.), Jap. (wä′kä-sä wän)	201	35.43 N	135.39 E
Wakatipu (L.), N.Z. (wä-kä-tē′pōō)	213	45.04 S	168.30 E
Wakayama, Jap. (wä-kä′yä-mä)	201	34.14 N	135.11 E
Wake (I.), Oceania (wāk)	204	19.25 N	167.00 E
Wa Keeney, Ks. (wô-kē′nē)	120	39.01 N	99.53 W
Wakefield, Can. (wāk-fēld)	93c	45.39 N	75.55 W
Wakefield, Eng.	154	53.41 N	1.25 W
Wakefield, Ma.	103a	42.31 N	71.05 W
Wakefield, Mi.	113	46.28 N	89.55 W
Wakefield, Ne.	112	42.15 N	96.52 W
Wakefield, RI	110b	41.26 N	71.30 W
Wake Forest, NC (wāk fŏr′ĕst)	125	35.58 N	78.31 W
Waki, Jap. (wä′kē)	201	34.05 N	134.10 E
Wakkanai, Jap. (wä′kä-nä′ē)	200	45.19 N	141.43 E
Wakkerstroom, S. Afr. (vȧk′ēr-strōm)(wăk′ēr-strōōm)	222	27.19 S	30.04 E
Wakonassin (R.), Can.	100	46.35 N	82.10 W
Wałbrzych, Pol. (väl′bzhûk)	164	50.46 N	16.16 E
Waldoboro, Me. (wôl′dô-bŭr-ô)	102	44.06 N	69.22 W
Waldo L., Or. (wôl′dō)	114	43.46 N	122.10 W
Waldorf, Md. (wăl′dôrf)	110e	38.37 N	76.57 W
Waldron, Mo.	117f	39.14 N	94.47 W
Waldron (I.), Wa.	116d	48.42 N	123.02 W
Wales, Ak. (wālz)	105	65.35 N	168.14 W
Wales, U.K.	160	52.12 N	3.40 W
Walewale, Ghana	224	10.21 N	0.48 W
Wałez, Pol. (välch)	164	53.61 N	16.30 E
Walgett, Austl. (wôl′gĕt)	212	30.00 S	148.10 E
Walgreen Coast, Ant. (wôl′grēn)	228	73.00 N	110.00 W
Walhalla, SC (wŭl-hăl′ȧ)	124	34.45 N	83.04 W
Walikale, Zaire	227	1.25 S	28.03 E
Walker, Mn. (wôk′ēr)	113	47.06 N	94.37 W
Walker (R.), Nv.	118	39.07 N	119.10 W
Walker, Mt., Wa.	116a	47.47 N	122.54 W
Walker L, Can.	99	54.42 N	96.57 W
Walker L., Nv.	118	38.46 N	118.30 W
Walker River Ind. Res., Nv.	118	39.06 N	118.20 W
Walkerville, Mt. (wôk′ēr-vĭl)	115	46.20 N	112.32 W
Wallace, Id. (wŏl′ās)	114	47.27 N	115.55 W
Wallaceburg, Can.	100	42.39 N	82.25 W
Wallacia, Austl.	207b	33.52 S	150.40 E
Wallapa B., Wa. (wŏl ȧ pă)	114	46.39 N	124.30 W
Wallaroo, Austl. (wŏl-ȧ-rōō)	212	33.52 S	137.45 E
Wallasey, Eng. (wŏl′ȧ-sē)	154	53.25 N	3.03 W
Walla Walla, Wa. (wŏl′ȧ wŏl′ȧ)	114	46.03 N	118.20 W
Walled Lake, Mi. (wôl′d lāk)	111b	42.32 N	83.29 W
Wallel, Tulu (Mt.), Eth.	221	9.00 N	34.52 E
Wallingford, Eng. (wŏl′ĭng-fērd)	154b	51.34 N	1.08 W
Wallingford, Vt.	109	43.30 N	72.55 W
Wallis Is., Oceania	204	13.00 S	176.10 E
Wallisville, Tx. (wŏl′ĭs-vĭl)	123a	29.50 N	94.44 W
Wallowa, Or. (wôl′ô-wȧ)	114	45.34 N	117.32 W
Wallowa Mts., Or.	114	45.10 N	117.22 W
Wallowa R., Or.	114	45.28 N	117.28 W
Wallula, Wa.	114	46.08 N	118.55 W
Walnut, Ca. (wôl′nŭt)	117a	34.00 N	117.51 W
Walnut (R.), Ks.	121	37.28 N	97.06 W
Walnut Canyon Natl. Mon, Az.	119	35.10 N	111.30 W
Walnut Creek, Ca.	116b	37.54 N	122.04 W
Walnut Cr., Tx.	117c	32.37 N	97.03 W
Walnut Ridge, Ar. (rĭj)	121	36.04 N	90.56 W
Walpole, Ma. (wôl′pōl)	103a	42.09 N	71.15 W
Walpole, NH	109	43.05 N	72.25 W
Walsall, Eng. (wôl-sôl)	154	52.35 N	1.58 W
Walsenburg, Co. (wôl′sĕn-bûrg)	120	37.38 N	104.46 W
Walter F. George Res., Al.-Ga.	124	32.00 N	85.00 W
Walters, Ok. (wôl′tērz)	120	34.21 N	98.19 W
Waltham, Ma. (wôl′thȧm)	103a	42.22 N	71.14 W
Walthamstow, Eng. (wôl′tăm-stō)	154b	51.34 N	0.01 W
Walton, NY	109	42.10 N	75.05 W
Walton-le-Dale, Eng. (lē-dāl′)	154	53.44 N	2.40 W
Walvis Bay, S. Afr. (wôl′vĭs)	222	22.50 S	14.30 E
Walworth, Wi. (wôl′wŭrth)	113	42.33 N	88.39 W
Wamba (R.), Zaire	226	5.30 N	17.05 E
Wamego, Ks. (wŏ-mē′gō)	121	39.13 N	96.17 W
Wami (R.), Tan. (wä′mē)	223	6.31 S	37.17 E
Wanapitei L., Can.	101	46.45 N	80.45 W
Wanaque, NJ (wŏn′ȧ-kū)	110a	41.03 N	74.16 W
Wanaque Res., NJ	110a	41.06 N	74.20 W
Wanda Shan (Mts.), China (wän-dä shän)	195	45.54 N	131.45 E
Wandoan, Austl.	212	26.09 S	149.51 E
Wandsbek, F.R.G. (vänds′bĕk)	155c	53.34 N	10.07 E
Wandsworth, Eng. (wŏndz′wûrth)	154	51.26 N	0.12 W
Wanganui, N.Z. (wôŋ′gȧ-nōō′ē)	213	39.53 N	175.01 E
Wangaratta, Austl. (wŏŋ′gȧ-răt′ȧ)	212	36.23 N	146.18 E
Wangeroog, I., F.R.G. (vän′gĕ-rōg)	164	53.49 N	7.57 E
Wangqing, China (wäŋ-chyĭŋ)	200	43.14 N	129.33 E
Wangqingtuo, China (wäŋ-chyĭŋ-twô)	196	39.14 N	116.56 E
Wangsi, China (wäŋ-sē)	196	37.59 N	116.57 E
Wankie, Zimb. (wă ′kē)	227	18.22 S	26.29 E
Wantage, Eng. (wŏn′tȧj)	154b	51.33 N	1.26 W
Wantagh, NY	110a	40.41 N	73.30 W
Wanzai, China (wän-dzī)	199	28.05 N	114.25 E
Wanxian, China (wän-shyĕn)	199	30.48 N	108.22 E
Wan Xian, China (wän shyĕn)	196	38.51 N	115.10 E
Wanzhi, China (wän-jr)	196	31.11 N	118.31 E
Woodoan, Austl. (wŏd′ōn)	212	26.12 S	149.52 E
Wapakoneta, Oh. (wä′pȧ-kô-nĕt′ȧ)	108	40.35 N	84.10 W
Wapawekka Hills, Can. (wŏ′pă-wē′kă-hĭlz)	98	54.45 N	104.20 W
Wapawekka L., Can.	98	54.55 N	104.40 W
Wapello, Ia. (wŏ-pĕl′ō)	113	41.10 N	91.11 W
Wapesi L., Can. (wŏ-pē′zē)	99	50.34 N	92.21 W
Wappapello Res., Mo. (wă′pȧ-pĕl-lō)	121	37.07 N	90.10 W
Wappingers Falls, NY (wŏp′ĭn-jērz)	109	41.35 N	73.55 W
Wapsipinicon (R.), Ia. (wŏp′sĭ-pĭn′ĭ-kŏn)	113	42.16 N	91.35 W
Warabi, Jap. (wä′rä-bē)	201a	35.50 N	139.41 E
Warangal, India (wŭ′răŋ-gȧl)	190	18.03 N	79.45 E
Warburton, The (R.), Austl. (wŏr′bûr-tŭn)	210	27.30 S	138.45 E

PRONOUNCING INDEX

Wardān – West Bromwich 363

PLACE (Pronunciation)	PAGE	Lat. °′	Long. °′
Wardān, Wādī (R.), Egypt	189a	29.22 N	33.00 E
Ward Cove, Ak.	96	55.24 N	131.43 W
Warden, S. Afr. (wôr'dĕn)	219d	27.52 N	28.59 E
Wardha, India (wŭr'dä)	190	20.46 N	78.42 E
War Eagle, WV (wôr ē'g'l)	108	37.30 N	81.50 W
Waren, F.R.G. (vä'rĕn)	164	53.32 N	12.43 E
Warendorf, F.R.G. (vä'rĕn-dōrf)	167c	51.57 N	7.59 E
Warialda, Austl.	212	29.32 S	150.34 E
Warley, see Smethwick			
Warmbad, Namibia (värm'bäd) (wôrm'băd)	222	28.25 S	18.45 E
Warmbad, S. Afr.	219d	24.52 S	28.18 E
Warm Beach, Wa. (wôrm)	116a	48.10 N	122.22 W
Warm Springs Ind. Res., Or. (wôrm sprĭnz)	114	44.55 N	121.30 W
Warm Springs Res., Or.	114	43.42 N	118.40 W
Warnemünde, G.D.R. (vär'nĕ-mün-dĕ)	162	54.11 N	12.04 E
Warner Ra. (Mts.), Ca.-Or.	114	41.30 N	120.17 W
Warnow R., G.D.R. (vär'nō)	164	53.51 N	11.55 E
Warracknabeal, Austl.	212	36.20 S	142.28 E
Warragamba Res., Austl.	212	33.40 S	150.00 E
Warrego (R.), Austl. (wôr'ē-gō)	211	27.13 S	145.58 E
Warren, Ar. (wŏr'ĕn)	121	33.37 N	92.03 W
Warren, Can.	93f	50.08 N	97.32 W
Warren, In.	108	40.40 N	85.25 W
Warren, Mi.	111b	42.33 N	83.03 W
Warren, Mn.	112	48.11 N	96.44 W
Warren, Oh.	108	41.15 N	80.50 W
Warren, Or.	116c	45.49 N	122.51 W
Warren, Pa.	109	41.50 N	79.10 W
Warren, RI	110b	41.44 N	71.14 W
Warrendale, Pa. (wŏr'ĕn-dāl)	111e	40.39 N	80.04 W
Warrensburg, Mo. (wŏr'ĕnz-bûrg)	121	38.45 N	93.42 W
Warrenton, Ga. (wŏr'ĕn-tŭn)	125	33.26 N	82.37 W
Warrenton, Or.	116c	46.10 N	123.56 W
Warrenton, Va.	109	38.45 N	77.50 W
Warri, Nig. (wär'ē)	220	5.33 N	5.43 E
Warrington, Eng.	154	53.22 N	2.30 W
Warrington, Fl. (wŏ'ĭng-tŭn)	124	30.21 N	87.15 W
Warrnambool, Austl. (wôr'năm-bōōl)	212	36.20 S	142.28 E
Warroad, Mn. (wôr'rōd)	113	48.55 N	95.20 W
Warrumbungle Ra., Austl. (wôr'ŭm-bŭŋ-g'l)	211	31.18 S	150.00 E
Warsaw, Il. (wôr'sô)	121	40.21 N	91.26 W
Warsaw, In.	108	41.15 N	85.50 W
Warsaw, NY	109	42.45 N	78.10 W
Warsaw, NC	125	35.00 N	78.07 W
Warsaw, see Warszawa			
Warsop, Eng. (wôr'sŭp)	154	53.13 N	1.05 W
Warszawa (Warsaw), Pol. (vår-shä'vå)	165	52.15 N	21.05 E
Warta R., Pol. (vär'tå)	164	52.35 N	15.07 E
Wartburg, S. Afr.	223c	29.26 S	30.39 E
Warwick, Austl. (wŏr'ĭk)	212	28.05 S	152.10 E
Warwick, Can.	102	45.58 N	71.57 W
Warwick, Eng.	160	52.19 N	1.46 W
Warwick, NY	110a	41.15 N	74.22 W
Warwick, RI	110b	41.42 N	71.27 W
Warwickshire (Co.), Eng.	154	52.30 N	1.35 W
Wasatch Mts., Ut. (wô'săch)	117b	40.45 N	111.46 W
Wasatch Plat., Ut.	119	38.55 N	111.40 W
Wasatch Ra., U.S.	106	39.10 N	111.30 W
Wasbank, S. Afr.	223c	28.27 S	30.09 E
Wasco, Or. (wäs'kō)	114	45.36 N	120.42 W
Waseca, Mn. (wô-sē'kȧ)	113	44.04 N	93.31 W
Wash, The (Est.), Eng. (wŏsh)	161	53.00 N	0.20 E
Washburn, Me. (wŏsh'bŭrn)	102	46.46 N	68.10 W
Washburn, Wi.	113	46.41 N	90.55 W
Washburn, Mt., Wy.	115	44.55 N	110.10 W
Washington, DC (wŏsh'ĭng-tŭn)	110e	38.50 N	77.00 W
Washington, Ga.	124	33.43 N	82.46 W
Washington, In.	108	38.40 N	87.10 W
Washington, Ia.	113	41.17 N	91.42 W
Washington, Ks.	121	39.48 N	97.04 W
Washington, Mo.	121	38.33 N	91.00 W
Washington, NC	125	35.32 N	77.01 W
Washington, Pa.	111e	40.10 N	80.14 W
Washington (State), U.S.	106	47.30 N	121.10 W
Washington, Mt., NH	109	44.15 N	71.15 W
Washington, L., Wa.	116a	47.34 N	122.12 W
Washington (I.), Wi.	113	45.18 N	86.42 W
Washington Court House, Oh.	108	39.30 N	83.25 W
Washington Park, Il.	117e	38.38 N	90.06 W
Washita (R.), Ok. (wŏsh'ĭ-tô)	120	35.33 N	99.16 W
Washougal, Wa. (wô-shōō'gál)	116c	45.35 N	122.21 W
Washougal (R.), Wa.	116c	45.38 N	122.17 W
Wasilkow, Pol. (vá-sēl'kōōf)	165	53.12 N	23.13 E
Waskaiowaka L., Can. (wŏ'skä-yō'wŏ-kä)	99	56.30 N	96.20 W
Wass L., Can. (wŏs)	99	53.40 N	95.25 W
Wassenberg, F.R.G. (vä'sĕn-bĕrgh)	167c	51.06 N	6.07 E
Wassuk Ra., Nv. (wás'sŭk)	118	38.58 N	119.00 W
Waswanipi, Lac (L.), Can.	101	49.35 N	76.15 W
Water (I.), Vir. Is. (U.S.A.) (wô'tēr)	127c	18.20 N	64.57 W
Waterberge (Mts.), S. Afr. (wôrtēr'bûrg)	219d	24.25 S	27.53 E
Waterboro, SC (wô'tēr-bûr-ō)	125	32.50 N	80.40 W
Waterbury, Ct. (wô'tēr-bĕr-ē)	109	41.30 N	73.00 W
Water Cay (I.), Ba.	133	22.55 N	75.50 W
Waterdown, Can. (wô'tēr-doun)	93d	43.20 N	79.54 W
Wateree (R.), SC (wô'tēr-ē)	125	34.40 N	80.48 W

PLACE (Pronunciation)	PAGE	Lat. °′	Long. °′
Waterford, Ire. (wô'tēr-fērd)	160	52.20 N	7.03 W
Waterford, Wi.	111a	42.46 N	88.13 W
Waterloo, Bel.	155a	50.44 N	4.24 E
Waterloo, Can. (wô-tēr-lōō')	101	43.30 N	80.40 W
Waterloo, Can.	101	45.25 N	72.30 W
Waterloo, Il.	121	38.19 N	90.08 W
Waterloo, Ia.	111	42.30 N	92.22 W
Waterloo, Md.	110e	39.11 N	76.50 W
Waterloo, NY	109	42.55 N	76.50 W
Waterton-Glacier Intl. Peace Park, Mt.-Can. (wô'ter-tŭn-glā'shûr)	94	48.55 N	114.10 W
Waterton Lakes Nat. Pk., Can.	97	49.05 N	113.50 W
Watertown, Ma. (wô'tēr-toun)	103a	42.22 N	71.11 W
Watertown, NY	109	44.00 N	75.55 W
Watertown, SD	112	44.53 N	97.07 W
Watertown, Wi.	111	43.13 N	88.40 W
Water Valley, Ms. (vàl'ē)	124	34.08 N	89.38 W
Waterville, Me.	102	44.34 N	69.37 W
Waterville, Mn.	111	44.10 N	93.35 W
Waterville, Wa.	114	47.38 N	120.04 W
Watervliet, NY (wô'tēr-vlēt')	109	42.45 N	73.54 W
Watford, Eng. (wŏt'fŏrd)	154b	51.38 N	0.24 W
Wathaman L., Can.	98	56.55 N	103.43 W
Watling (I.), see San Salvador			
Watlington, Eng. (wŏt'lĭng-tŭn)	154b	51.37 N	1.01 W
Watonga, Ok. (wŏ-tôŋ'gȧ)	120	35.50 N	98.26 W
Watsa, Zaire (wät'sä)	227	3.03 N	29.32 E
Watseka, Il. (wŏt-sē'kȧ)	108	40.45 N	87.45 W
Watson, In. (wŏt'sŭn)	111h	38.21 N	85.42 W
Watson Lake, Can.	94	60.18 N	128.50 W
Watsonville, Ca. (wŏt'sŭn-vĭl)	118	36.55 N	121.46 W
Wattenscheid, F.R.G. (vä'tĕn-shīd)	167c	51.30 N	7.07 E
Watts, Ca. (wŏts)	117a	33.56 N	118.15 W
Watts Bar (R.), Tn. (bär)	124	35.45 N	84.49 W
Waubay, SD (wô'bā)	112	45.19 N	97.18 W
Wauchula, Fl. (wô-chōō'lȧ)	125a	27.32 N	81.48 W
Wauconda, Il. (wô-kŏn'dȧ)	111a	42.15 N	88.08 W
Waukegan, Il. (wŏ-kē'găn)	111a	42.22 N	87.51 W
Waukesha, Wi. (wô'kē-shô)	111a	43.01 N	88.13 W
Waukon, Ia. (wô kŏn)	113	43.15 N	91.30 W
Waupaca, Wi. (wô-păk'ȧ)	113	44.22 N	89.06 W
Waupun, Wi. (wô-pŭn')	113	43.37 N	88.45 W
Waurika, Ok. (wô-rē'kȧ)	120	34.09 N	97.59 W
Wausau, Wi. (wô'sô)	113	44.58 N	89.40 W
Wausaukee, Wi. (wô-sô'kē)	113	45.22 N	87.58 W
Wauseon, Oh. (wô'sē-ŏn)	108	41.30 N	84.10 W
Wautoma, Wi. (wô-tō'mȧ)	113	44.04 N	89.11 W
Wauwatosa, Wi. (wô-wȧ-t'ō'sȧ)	111a	43.03 N	88.00 W
Waveney (R.), Eng. (wăv'nē)	161	52.27 N	1.17 E
Waverly, Ia. (wā'vēr-lē)	113	42.43 N	92.29 W
Waverly, S. Afr.	223c	31.54 S	26.29 E
Waverly, Tn.	124	36.04 N	87.46 W
Wāw, Sud.	221	7.41 N	28.00 E
Wawa, Can.	100	47.59 N	84.47 W
Wāw al-Kabīr, Libya	221	25.23 N	16.52 E
Wawanesa, Can. (wŏ'wŏ-nē'să)	99	49.36 N	99.41 W
Wawasee (L.), In. (wô-wô-sē')	108	41.25 N	85.45 W
Waxahachie, Tx. (wăk-sȧ-hăch'ē)	123	32.23 N	96.50 W
Waycross, Ga. (wā'krôs)	125	31.11 N	82.24 W
Wayland, Ky. (wā'lănd)	124	37.25 N	82.47 W
Wayland, Ma.	103a	42.23 N	71.22 W
Wayne, Mi.	111b	42.17 N	83.23 W
Wayne, Ne.	112	42.13 N	97.03 W
Wayne, NJ	110a	40.56 N	74.16 W
Wayne, Pa.	110f	40.03 N	75.22 W
Waynesboro, Ga. (wānz'bŭr-ō)	125	33.05 N	82.02 W
Waynesboro, Pa.	109	39.45 N	77.35 W
Waynesboro, Va.	109	38.05 N	78.50 W
Waynesburg, Pa. (wānz'bûrg)	109	39.55 N	80.10 W
Waynesville, NC (wānz'vĭl)	124	35.28 N	82.58 W
Waynoka, Ok. (wā-nō'kȧ)	120	36.34 N	98.52 W
Wayzata, Mn. (wā-zä-tȧ)	117g	44.58 N	93.31 W
Wazīrbad, Pak.	190	32.39 N	74.11 E
Weagamow L., Can. (wē'ăg-ȧ-mou)	99	52.53 N	91.22 W
Weald, The (Reg.), Eng. (wēld)	160	50.58 N	0.15 W
Weatherford, Ok. (wĕ-dhēr-fērd)	120	85.32 N	98.41 W
Weatherford, Tx.	123	32.45 N	97.46 W
Weaver (R.), Eng. (wē'vēr)	154	53.09 N	2.31 W
Weaverville, Ca. (wē'vēr-vĭl)	114	40.44 N	122.55 W
Webb City, Mo.	121	37.10 N	94.26 W
Weber R., Ut.	117b	41.13 N	112.07 W
Webster, Ma.	103a	42.04 N	71.52 W
Webster, SD	112	45.19 N	97.30 W
Webster City, Ia.	113	42.28 N	93.49 W
Webster Groves, Mo. (grōvz)	117e	38.36 N	90.22 W
Webster Springs, WV (sprĭngz)	109	38.30 N	80.20 W
Weddell Sea, Ant. (wĕd'ĕl)	228	73.00 S	45.00 W
Wedel, F.R.G. (vā'dĕl)	155c	53.35 N	9.42 E
Wedge Mtn., Can. (wĕj)	96	50.10 N	122.50 W
Wedgeport, Can. (wĕj'pōrt)	102	43.44 N	65.59 W
Wednesfield, Eng. (wĕd''nz-fēld)	154	52.36 N	2.04 W
Weed, Ca. (wēd)	114	41.35 N	122.21 W
Weenen, S. Afr. (vā'nĕn)	223c	28.52 S	30.05 E
Weert, Neth.	161	51.16 N	5.39 E
Weesp, Neth.	155a	52.18 N	5.01 E
Węgorzewo, Pol. (vôŋ-gô'zhĕ-vô)	165	54.14 N	21.46 E
Wegrow, Pol. (vôŋ'grōōf)	165	52.23 N	22.02 E
Wei (R.), China (wā)	196	35.47 N	114.27 E
Wei (R.), China (wā)	198	34.00 N	108.10 E
Weichang, China (wā-chäŋ)	198	41.50 N	118.00 E
Weifang, China	196	36.43 N	119.08 E
Weihai, China (wa'hăī')	196	37.30 N	122.05 E
Weilheim, F.R.G. (vīl'hīm')	164	47.50 N	11.06 E

PLACE (Pronunciation)	PAGE	Lat. °′	Long. °′
Weimar, G.D.R. (vī'mär)	164	50.59 N	11.20 E
Weinan, China	198	34.32 N	109.40 E
Weipa, Austl.	211	12.25 S	141.54 E
Weir River, Can. (wēr-rīv-ēr)	99	56.49 N	94.04 W
Weirton, WV	108	40.25 N	80.35 W
Weiser, Id. (wē'zēr)	114	44.15 N	116.58 W
Weiser R., Id.	114	44.26 N	116.40 W
Weishi, China (wā-shr)	196	34.23 N	114.12 E
Weissenburg, F.R.G. (vī'sĕn-bōōrgh)	164	49.04 N	11.20 E
Weissenfels, G.D.R. (vī'sĕn-fĕlz)	164	51.13 N	11.58 E
Weixi, China (wā-shyē)	195	27.27 N	99.30 E
Wei Xian, China (wā shyĕn)	196	36.59 N	115.17 E
Wejherowo, Pol. (vā-hĕ-rô'vô)	165	54.36 N	18.15 E
Welch, WV (wĕlch)	125	37.24 N	81.28 W
Weldon, NC (wĕl'dŭn)	125	36.24 N	77.36 W
Weldon (R.), Mo.	121	40.22 N	93.39 W
Weleetka, Ok. (wē-lēt'kȧ)	121	35.19 N	96.08 W
Welford, Austl. (wĕl'fērd)	212	25.08 S	144.43 E
Welkom, S. Afr. (wĕl'kŏm)	219d	27.57 S	26.45 E
Welland, Can. (wĕl'ănd)	111c	42.59 N	79.13 W
Wellesley, Ma. (wĕlz'lē)	103a	42.18 N	71.17 W
Wellesley Is., Austl.	210	16.15 S	139.25 E
Wellington, Austl. (wĕl'lĭng-tŭn)	212	32.40 S	148.50 E
Wellington, Eng.	154	52.42 N	2.30 W
Wellington, Ks.	121	37.16 N	97.24 W
Wellington, N.Z.	213	41.15 S	174.45 E
Wellington, Oh.	108	41.10 N	82.10 W
Wellington, Tx.	120	34.51 N	100.12 W
Wellington (I.), Chile (ōōĕ'lĕng-tŏn)	142	49.30 S	76.30 W
Wells, Austl. (wĕlz)	210	26.35 S	123.40 E
Wells, Can.	97	53.06 N	121.34 W
Wells, Mi.	108	45.50 N	87.00 W
Wells, Mn.	113	43.44 N	93.43 W
Wells, Nv.	114	41.07 N	115.04 W
Wellsboro, Pa. (wĕlz'bŭ-rô)	109	41.45 N	77.15 W
Wellsburg, WV (wĕlz'bûrg)	108	40.10 N	80.40 W
Wells Res., Wa.	114	48.05 N	119.45 W
Wellston, Oh. (wĕlz'tŭn)	108	39.05 N	82.30 W
Wellsville, Mo. (wĕlz'vĭl)	121	39.04 N	91.33 W
Wellsville, NY	109	42.10 N	78.00 W
Wellsville, Oh.	108	40.35 N	80.40 W
Wellsville, Ut.	115	41.38 N	111.57 W
Wels, Aus. (vĕls)	164	48.10 N	14.01 E
Welshpool, Wales (wĕlsh'pōōl)	160	52.44 N	3.10 W
Welverdiend, S. Afr. (vĕl-vēr-dēnd')	219d	26.23 S	27.16 E
Welwyn Garden City, Eng. (wĕlĭn)	154b	51.46 N	0.17 W
Wem, Eng. (wĕm)	154	52.51 N	2.44 W
Wembere (R.), Tan.	227	4.35 S	33.55 E
Wen (R.), China (wŭn)	196	36.24 N	119.00 E
Wenan Wa (Swp.), China (wĕn'än' wä)	196	38.56 N	116.29 E
Wenatchee, Wa. (wē-năch'ē)	114	47.24 N	120.18 W
Wenatchee Mts., Wa.	114	47.28 N	121.10 W
Wenchang, China (wŭn-chäŋ)	199	19.32 N	110.42 E
Wenchi, Ghana	224	7.42 N	2.07 W
Wendeng, China (wŭn-dŭŋ)	196	37.14 N	122.03 E
Wendo, Eth.	221	6.37 N	38.29 E
Wendorer, Ut.	115	40.47 N	114.01 W
Wendover, Can. (wĕn-dōv'ēr)	93c	45.34 N	75.07 W
Wendover, Eng.	154b	51.44 N	0.45 W
Wenham, Ma. (wĕn'ăm)	103a	42.36 N	70.53 W
Wenonah, NJ (wĕn'ō-nā)	110f	39.48 N	75.08 W
Wenquan, China (wŭn-chyůän)	198	47.10 N	120.00 E
Wenshan, China	199	23.20 N	104.15 E
Wenshang, China (wĕn'shäng)	196	35.43 N	116.31 E
Wensu, China (wĕn-sōō)	194	41.45 N	80.30 E
Wentworth, Austl. (wĕnt'wûrth)	212	24.03 S	141.53 E
Wenzhou, China (wŭn-jō)	199	28.00 N	120.40 E
Wepener, S. Afr. (wē'pĕn-ēr) (vā'pĕn-ĕr)	222	29.43 S	27.04 E
Werder, G.D.R. (vĕr'dĕr)	155b	52.23 N	12.56 E
Were Ilu, Eth.	221	10.39 N	39.21 E
Werl, F.R.G. (vĕrl)	167c	51.33 N	7.55 E
Werneuchen, G.D.R. (vĕr'hoi-kĕn)	155b	52.38 N	13.44 E
Werra R., F.R.G. (vĕr'ä)	164	51.16 N	9.54 E
Werribee, Austl.	207a	37.54 S	144.40 E
Werribee (R.), Austl.	207a	37.40 S	144.37 E
Wertach R., F.R.G. (vĕr'täk)	164	48.12 N	10.40 E
Weseke, F.R.G. (vĕ'zĕ-kĕ)	167c	51.54 N	6.51 E
Wesel, F.R.G. (vā'zĕl)	167c	51.39 N	6.37 E
Weser R., F.R.G. (vā'zēr)	164	53.08 N	8.35 E
Weslaco, Tx. (wĕs-lā'kō)	122	26.10 N	97.59 W
Weslemkoon (L.), Can.	101	45.02 N	77.25 W
Wesleyville, Can. (wĕs'lē-vĭl)	103	49.09 N	53.34 W
Wessel (Is.), Austl. (wĕs'ĕl)	210	11.45 S	136.25 E
Wesselsbron, S. Afr. (wĕs'ĕl-brŏn)	219d	27.51 S	26.22 E
Wessington Springs, SD (wĕs'ĭng-tŭn)	112	44.06 N	98.35 W
West, Mt., Pan.	126a	9.10 N	79.52 W
West Allis, Wi. (wĕst-ăl'ĭs)	111a	43.01 N	88.01 W
West Alton, Mo. (ôl'tŭn)	117e	38.52 N	90.13 W
West B., Tx.	123a	29.11 N	95.03 W
West Bend, Wi. (wĕst bĕnd)	113	43.25 N	88.13 W
West Bengal (State), India (bĕn-gôl')	190	23.30 N	87.30 E
West Berlin, F.R.G. (bĕr-lēn')	155b	52.31 N	13.20 E
West Blocton, Al. (blŏk'tŭn)	124	33.05 N	87.05 W
Westborough, Ma. (wĕst'bŭr-ô)	103a	42.17 N	71.37 W
West Boylston, Ma. (boil'stŭn)	103a	42.22 N	71.46 W
West Branch, Mi. (wĕst branch)	108	44.15 N	84.10 W
West Bridgford, Eng. (brĭj'fērd)	154	52.55 N	1.08 W
West Bromwich, Eng. (wĕst brŭm'ĭj)	154	52.32 N	1.59 W

ng-sing; ŋ-baŋk; ɴ-nasalized n; nŏd; cŏmmit; ōld; ôbey; ôrder; oi-boil; fōōd; fŏŏt; ou-out; s-soft; sh-dish; th-thin; pūre; ûnite; ûrn; stŭd; circŭs; ü-as in French tu; '-indeterminate vowel.

364 Westbrook – Willow Run

PLACE (Pronunciation)	PAGE	Lat. °′	Long. °′
Westbrook, Me. (wĕst'brŏŏk)	102	43.41 N	70.23 W
Westby, Wi. (wĕst'bē)	113	43.40 N	90.52 W
West Caicos (I.), Turks & Caicos (kāē'kō) (kī'kōs)	133	21.40 N	72.30 W
West Cape Howe (C.), Austl.	210	35.15 S	117.30 E
West Chester, Oh. (chĕs'tẽr)	111f	39.20 N	84.24 W
West Chester, Pa.	110f	39.57 N	75.36 W
West Chicago, Il. (chĭ-kȧ'gō)	111a	41.53 N	88.12 W
West Columbia, SC (cŏl'ŭm-bē-ȧ)	125	33.58 N	81.05 W
West Columbia, Tx.	123	29.08 N	95.39 W
West Cote Blanche B., La. (kōt blănch)	123	29.30 N	92.17 W
West Covina, Ca. (wĕst kô-vē'nȧ)	117a	34.04 N	117.55 W
West Des Moines, Ia. (dē moin')	113	41.35 N	93.42 W
West Des Moines (R.), Ia.	113	42.52 N	94.32 W
West End., Ba.	132	26.40 N	78.55 W
Westerham, Eng. (wĕ'stẽr'ŭm)	154b	51.15 N	0.05 E
Westerhörn, F.R.G. (vĕs'tĕr-hōrn)	155c	53.52 N	9.41 E
Westerlo, Bel.	155a	51.05 N	4.57 E
Westerly, RI (wĕs'tẽr-lē)	109	41.25 N	71.50 W
Western Australia (State), Austl. (ôs-trā'lĭ-ȧ)	210	24.15 S	121.30 E
Western Ghāts (Mts.), India	191	17.35 N	74.00 E
Western Port, Md. (wĕs'tẽrn pōrt)	109	39.30 N	79.00 W
Western Sahara, Afr. (sȧ-hä'rȧ)	218	23.05 N	15.33 W
Western Samoa, Oceania	204	14.30 S	172.00 W
Western Siberian Lowland, Sov. Un.	174	63.37 N	72.45 E
Westerville, Oh. (wĕs'tẽr-vĭl)	108	40.10 N	83.00 W
Westerwald (For.), F.R.G. (vĕs'tĕr-väld)	164	50.35 N	7.45 E
Westfield, Ma. (wĕst'fēld)	109	42.05 N	72.45 W
Westfield, NJ	110a	40.39 N	74.21 W
Westfield, NY (wĕst'fēld)	110	42.20 N	79.40 W
Westford, Ma. (wĕst'fẽrd)	103a	42.35 N	71.26 W
West Frankfort, Il. (frăŋk'fŭrt)	110	37.55 N	88.55 W
West Ham, Eng.	154b	51.30 N	0.00 W
West Hartford, Ct. (härt'fẽrd)	109	41.45 N	72.45 W
West Helena, Ar. (hĕl'ĕn-ȧ)	121	34.32 N	90.39 W
West Indies (Reg.), N. A. (ĭn'dēz)	127	19.00 N	78.30 W
West Jordon, Ut. (jôr'dăn)	117b	40.37 N	111.56 W
West Kirby, Eng. (kûr'bē)	154	53.22 N	3.11 W
West Lafayette, In. (lä-fā-yĕt')	108	40.25 N	86.55 W
Westlake, Oh.	111d	41.27 N	81.55 W
Westleigh, S. Afr. (wĕst-lē)	219d	27.39 S	27.18 E
West Liberty, Ia. (wĕst lĭb'ẽr-tĭ)	113	41.34 N	91.15 W
West Linn, Or. (lĭn)	116c	45.22 N	122.37 W
Westlock, Can. (wĕst'lŏk)	97	54.09 N	113.52 W
West Memphis, Ar.	121	35.08 N	90.11 W
West Midlands (Co.), Eng.	154	52.26 N	1.50 W
Westminster, Ca. (wĕst'mĭn-stẽr)	117a	33.45 N	117.59 W
Westminster, Md.	109	39.40 N	76.55 W
Westminster, SC	124	34.38 N	83.10 W
Westmount, Can. (wĕst'mount)	93a	45.29 N	73.36 W
West Newbury, Ma. (nū'bẽr-ē)	103a	42.47 N	70.57 W
West Newton, Pa. (nū'tŭn)	111e	40.12 N	79.45 W
West New York, NJ (nū yŏrk)	110a	40.47 N	74.01 W
West Nishnabotna (R.), Ia. (nĭsh-nȧ-bŏt'nȧ)	121	40.56 N	95.37 W
Weston, Ma. (wĕs'tŭn)	103a	42.22 N	71.18 W
Weston, WV	108	39.00 N	80.30 W
Westonaria, S. Afr.	219d	26.19 S	27.38 E
Weston-super-Mare, Eng. (wĕs'tŭn sū'pẽr-mā'rē)	160	51.23 N	3.00 W
West Orange, NJ (wĕst ŏr'ĕnj)	110a	40.46 N	74.14 W
West Palm Beach, Fl. (päm bēch)	125a	26.44 N	80.04 W
West Pensacola, Fl. (pĕn-sȧ-kō'lȧ)	124	30.24 N	87.18 W
West Pittsburg, Ca. (pĭts'bûrg)	116b	38.02 N	121.56 W
Westplains, Mo. (wĕst-plānz')	121	36.42 N	91.51 W
West Point Ga.	124	32.52 N	85.10 W
West Point, Ms.	124	33.36 N	88.39 W
Westpoint, Ne.	112	41.50 N	96.00 W
West Point, NY	110a	41.23 N	73.58 W
West Point, Ut.	117b	41.07 N	112.05 W
West Point, Va.	109	37.25 N	76.50 W
Westport, Ct. (wĕst'pōrt)	110a	41.07 N	73.22 W
Westport, Ire.	160	53.44 N	9.36 W
Westport, Or. (wĕst'pôrt)	116c	46.08 N	123.22 W
Westray (I.), Scot. (wĕs'trā)	160a	59.19 N	3.05 W
West Road (R.), Can. (rōd)	96	53.00 N	124.00 W
West St. Paul, Mn. (sânt pôl')	117g	44.55 N	93.05 W
West Sand Spit (I.), Ba.	133	21.25 N	72.10 W
West Schelde (R.), Neth.	161	51.25 N	3.30 E
West Slope, Or.	116c	45.30 N	122.46 W
West Tavaputs Plat., Ut. (wĕst tăv'ȧ-pŏŏts)	119	39.45 N	110.35 W
West Terre Haute, In. (tĕr-ē hōt')	108	39.30 N	87.30 W
West Union, Ia. (ūn'yŭn)	113	42.58 N	91.48 W
West University Place, Tx.	123a	29.43 N	95.26 W
Westview, Oh. (wĕst'vū)	111d	41.21 N	81.54 W
West View, Pa.	111e	40.31 N	80.02 W
Westville, Can. (wĕst'vĭl)	103	45.34 N	62.43 W
Westville, Il.	108	40.00 N	87.40 W
West Virginia (State), U.S. (wĕst vẽr-jĭn'ĭ-ȧ)	107	39.00 N	80.50 W
West Walker (R.), Ca. (wôk'ẽr)	118	38.25 N	119.25 W
West Warwick, RI (wŏr'ĭk)	110b	41.42 N	71.31 W
Westwego, La. (wĕst-wē'gō)	110d	29.55 N	90.09 W
Westwood, Ca. (wĕst'wŏŏd)	118	40.18 N	121.00 W
Westwood, Ks.	117f	39.03 N	94.37 W
Westwood, Ma.	103a	42.13 N	71.14 W
Westwood, NJ	110a	40.59 N	74.02 W
West Wyalong, Austl. (wī'alông)	212	34.00 S	147.20 E
West Yorkshire (Co.), Eng.	154	53.37 N	1.48 W
Wetar, Pulau (I.), Indon. (wĕt'ár)	203	7.34 S	126.00 E
Wetaskiwin, Can. (wĕ-tăs'kē-wŏn)	97	52.58 N	113.22 W
Wetmore, Tx. (wĕt'mōr)	117d	29.34 N	98.25 W
Wetter, F.R.G.	167c	51.23 N	7.23 E
Wetumpka, Al. (wē-tŭmp'kȧ)	124	32.33 N	86.12 W
Wetzlar, F.R.G. (vets'lär)	167	50.35 N	8.30 E
Wewak, Pap. N. Gui. (wā-wäk')	203	3.19 S	143.30 E
Wewoka, Ok. (wē-wō'kȧ)	121	35.09 N	96.30 W
Wexford, Ire. (wĕks'fẽrd)	160	52.20 N	6.30 W
Weybridge, Eng. (wā'brĭj)	154b	51.20 N	0.26 W
Weyburn, Can. (wā'bûrn)	98	49.41 N	103.52 W
Weyib (R.), Eth.	221	6.25 N	41.21 E
Weymouth, Eng. (wā'mŭth)	160	50.37 N	2.34 W
Weymouth, Ma.	103a	42.44 N	70.57 W
Weymouth, Oh.	111d	41.11 N	81.48 W
Whale Cay (I.), Ba.	132	24.50 N	77.45 W
Whale Cay Chans, Ba.	132	26.45 N	77.10 W
Wharton, NJ (hwôr'tŭn)	110a	40.54 N	74.35 W
Wharton, Tx.	123	29.19 N	96.06 W
What Cheer, Ia. (hwŏt chēr)	113	41.23 N	92.24 W
Whatcom, L., Wa. (hwät'kŭm)	116c	48.44 N	123.34 W
Whatshan L., Can. (wŏt'shăn)	97	50.00 N	118.03 W
Wheatland, Wy. (hwēt'lănd)	115	42.04 N	104.52 W
Wheaton, Il. (hwē'tŭn)	111a	41.52 N	88.06 W
Wheaton, Md.	110e	39.05 N	77.05 W
Wheaton, Mn.	112	45.48 N	96.29 W
Wheeler Pk., Nv.	119	38.58 N	114.15 W
Wheeling, Il. (hwēl'ĭng)	111a	42.08 N	87.54 W
Wheeling, WV	108	40.05 N	80.45 W
Wheelwright, Arg. (ōōē'l-rē'gt)	139c	33.46 S	61.14 W
Whidbey I., Wa. (hwĭd'bē)	116a	48.13 N	122.50 W
Whippany, NJ (hwĭp'á-nē)	110a	40.49 N	74.25 W
Whistler, Al. (hwĭs'lẽr)	124	30.46 N	88.07 W
Whitby, Can. (hwĭt'bē)	101	43.50 N	79.00 W
Whitchurch, Eng. (hwĭt'chûrch)	154	52.58 N	2.49 W
White (L.), Can.	101	45.15 N	76.35 W
White (L.), Can.	100	48.47 N	85.50 W
White (R.), Can.	100	48.34 N	85.46 W
White (R.), Ar.	121	34.32 N	91.11 W
White (R.), Co.	119	40.10 N	108.55 W
White (R.), In.	108	39.15 N	86.45 W
White (R.), SD	112	43.41 N	99.48 W
White (R.), South Fork, SD	112	43.13 N	101.04 W
White (R.), Tx.	120	36.25 N	102.20 W
White (R.), Vt.	109	43.45 N	72.35 W
White, Mt., Ca.	118	37.38 N	118.13 W
White B., Can.	103	50.00 N	56.30 W
White Bear Lake, Mn.	117g	45.05 N	93.01 W
White Bear L., Mn.	117g	45.04 N	92.58 W
White Bear Ind. Res., Can.	99	49.15 N	102.15 W
White Castle, La.	123	30.10 N	91.09 W
White Center, Wa.	116a	47.31 N	122.21 W
White Cloud, Mi.	108	43.35 N	85.45 W
Whitecourt, Can. (wĭt'côrt)	97	54.09 N	115.41 W
White Earth (R.), ND	112	48.30 N	102.44 W
White Earth Ind. Res., Mn.	112	47.18 N	95.42 W
Whiteface (R.), Mn. (whīt'fās)	113	47.12 N	92.13 W
Whitefield, NH (hwĭt'fēld)	109	44.20 N	71.35 W
Whitefish, Mt. (hwĭt'fĭsh)	115	48.24 N	114.25 W
Whitefish (B.), Mi.	113	46.36 N	84.50 W
Whitefish (R.), Mi.	113	46.12 N	86.56 W
Whitefish B., Can.	99	49.26 N	94.14 W
Whitefish Bay, Wi.	111a	43.07 N	77.54 W
White Hall, Il.	121	39.26 N	90.23 W
Whitehall, Mi. (hwĭt'hôl)	108	43.20 N	86.20 W
Whitehall, NY	109	43.30 N	73.25 W
Whitehaven, Eng. (hwĭt'hā-vĕn)	160	54.35 N	3.30 W
Whitehorn, Pt., Wa. (hwĭt'hôrn)	116d	48.54 N	122.48 W
Whitehorse, Can. (whīt'hôrs)	94	60.39 N	135.01 W
White L., La.	123	29.40 N	92.35 W
White Mts., Me.	102	44.22 N	71.15 W
White Mts., NH	109	42.20 N	71.05 W
Whitemouth (L.), Can.	112	49.14 N	95.40 W
White Nile (Abyad, Al-Bahr al-) (R.), Sud.	221	14.00 N	32.35 E
White Otter (L.), Can.	113	49.15 N	91.48 W
White P., Ak.-Can.	94	59.35 N	135.03 W
White Plains NY	110a	41.02 N	73.47 W
White River, Can.	100	48.38 N	85.23 W
White R., East Fork, In.	108	38.45 N	86.20 W
White R., Wa.	114	47.07 N	121.48 W
White River Plat., Co.	119	39.45 N	107.50 W
White Rock, Can.	116d	49.01 N	122.49 W
Whiterock Res., Tx. (hwĭt'rŏk)	117c	32.51 N	96.40 W
Whitesail L., Can. (whīt'sāl)	96	53.30 N	127.00 W
White Sands Natl. Mon., NM	119	32.50 N	106.20 W
White Sea, Sov. Un.	176	66.00 N	40.00 E
White Settlement, Tx.	117c	32.45 N	97.28 W
White Sulphur Springs, Mt.	115	46.32 N	110.49 W
White Umfolzi (R.), S. Afr. (ŭm-fô-lō'zē)	223c	28.12 S	30.55 E
Whiteville, NC (hwīt'vĭl)	125	34.18 N	78.45 W
White Volta (R.), Ghana	224	9.40 N	1.10 W
Whitewater, Wi. (whīt-wŏt'ẽr)	113	42.49 N	88.40 W
Whitewater (L.), Can.	112	49.14 N	100.39 W
Whitewater B., Fl.	125a	25.16 N	80.21 W
Whitewater Cr., Mt.	115	48.50 N	107.50 W
Whitewater L., Can.	99	49.15 N	100.20 W
Whitewater R., In.	111f	39.19 N	84.55 W
Whitewell, Tn. (hwĭt'wĕl)	124	35.11 N	85.31 W
Whitewright, Tx. (hwĭt'rīt)	121	33.33 N	96.25 W
Whitham (R.), Eng. (wĭth'ŭm)	160	53.08 N	0.15 W
Whiting, In. (hwīt'ĭng)	111a	41.41 N	87.30 W
Whitinsville, Ma. (hwĭt'ĕns-vĭl)	103a	42.06 N	71.40 W
Whitman, Ma. (hwĭt'măn)	103a	42.05 N	70.57 W
Whitmire, SC (hwĭt'mīr)	125	34.30 N	81.40 W
Whitney, Mt., Ca.	118	36.34 N	118.18 W
Whitney L., Tx. (hwĭt'nē)	123	32.02 N	97.36 W
Whitstable, Eng. (wĭt'stȧb'l)	154b	51.22 N	1.03 E
Whitsunday (I.), Austl. (hwĭt's'n-dā)	211	20.16 S	149.00 E
Whittier, Ca. (hwĭt'ĭ-ẽr)	117a	33.58 N	118.02 W
Whittlesea, S. Afr. (wĭt'l'sē)	223c	32.11 S	26.51 E
Whitworth, Eng. (hwĭt'wŭrth)	154	53.40 N	2.10 W
Whyalla, Austl. (hwī-ăl'ȧ)	212	33.00 S	137.32 E
Whymper, Mt., Can. (wĭm'pẽr)	96	48.57 N	124.10 W
Wiarton, Can. (wī'ȧr-tŭn)	100	44.45 N	80.45 W
Wichita, Ks. (wĭch'ĭ-tô)	121	37.42 N	97.21 W
Wichita (R.), Tx.	120	33.50 N	99.38 W
Wichita Falls, Tx. (fôls)	120	33.54 N	98.29 W
Wichita Mts., Ok.	160	34.48 N	98.43 W
Wick, Scot. (wĭk)	160	58.25 N	3.05 W
Wickatunk, NJ (wĭk'á-tŭnk)	110a	40.21 N	74.15 W
Wickenburg, Az.	119	33.58 N	112.44 W
Wickliffe, Oh. (wĭk'klĭf)	111d	41.37 N	81.29 W
Wicklow, Ire.	160	52.59 N	6.06 W
Wicklow Mts., Ire. (wĭk'lō)	160	52.49 N	6.20 W
Wickup Mtn., Or. (wĭk'ŭp)	116c	46.06 N	123.35 W
Wiconisco, Pa. (wĭ-kŏn'ĭs-kō)	109	43.35 N	76.45 W
Widen, WV (wī'dĕn)	108	38.25 N	80.55 W
Widnes, Eng. (wĭd'nĕs)	154	53.21 N	2.44 W
Wieden, F.R.G. (vē'dĕn)	164	49.41 N	12.09 E
Wieliczka, Pol. (vyĕ-lēch'kȧ)	165	49.58 N	20.06 E
Wieluń, Pol. (vyĕ'lōōn')	165	51.13 N	18.33 E
Wien (Vienna), Aus. (vēn) (vē-ĕn'ä)	155e	48.13 N	16.22 E
Wien (State), Aus.	155e	48.11 N	16.23 E
Wiener Neustadt, Aus. (vē'nẽr noi'shtät)	164	47.48 N	16.15 E
Wiener Wald (For.), Aus.	155e	48.09 N	16.05 E
Wieprz, R., Pol (vyĕpzh)	165	51.25 N	22.45 E
Wiergate, Tx. (wẽr'gāt)	123	31.00 N	93.42 W
Wiesbaden, F.R.G. (vēs'bä-dĕn)	164	50.05 N	8.15 E
Wiegan, Eng. (wĭg'ăn)	154	53.33 N	2.37 W
Wiggins, Ms. (wĭg'ĭnz)	124	30.51 N	89.05 W
Wight, Isle of (I.), Eng. (wīt)	160	50.44 N	1.17 W
Wilber, Ne. (wĭl'bẽr)	121	40.29 N	96.57 W
Wilburton, Ok. (wĭl'bẽr-tŭn)	121	34.54 N	95.18 W
Wilcannia, Austl. (wĭl-cān-ĭȧ)	212	31.30 S	143.30 E
Wildau, G.D.R. (vēl'dou)	155b	52.20 N	13.39 E
Wildberg, G.D.R. (vēl'bĕrgh)	155b	52.52 N	12.39 E
Wildcat Hill, Can. (wīld'kăt)	98	53.17 N	102.30 W
Wildhay (R.), Can. (wīld'hā)	97	53.15 N	117.20 W
Wildomar, Ca. (wĭl'dô-mär)	117a	33.35 N	117.17 W
Wild Rice (R.), Mn.	112	47.10 N	96.40 W
Wild Rice (R.), ND	112	46.10 N	97.12 W
Wild Rice L., Mn.	117h	46.54 N	92.10 W
Wildspitze (Mtn.), Aus.	164	46.55 N	10.50 E
Wildwood, NJ	109	39.00 N	74.50 W
Wiley, Co. (wī'lē)	120	38.08 N	102.41 W
Wilge R., S. Afr. (wĭl'jē)	219d	25.38 S	29.09 E
Wilge R., S. Afr.	219d	27.27 S	28.46 E
Wilhelm, Mt., Pap. N. Gui.	211	5.58 S	144.58 E
Wilhelmina Gebergte (Mts.), Sur.	141	4.30 N	57.00 W
Wilhelmshaven, F.R.G. (vēl-hĕlms-hä'fĕn)	164	53.30 N	8.10 E
Welhemina, Kanal (Can.), Neth.	155a	51.37 N	4.55 E
Wilkes-Barre, Pa. (wĭlks'băr-ē)	109	41.15 N	75.50 W
Wilkes Land, Ant.	228	71.00 S	126.00 E
Wilkeson, Wa. (wĭl-kē'sŭn)	116a	47.06 N	122.03 W
Wilkie, Can. (wĭlk'ē)	98	52.25 N	108.43 W
Wilkinsburg, Pa. (wĭl'kĭnz-bûrg)	111e	40.26 N	79.53 W
Willamette R., Or.	114	44.15 N	123.13 W
Willapa B., Wa.	114	46.37 N	124.00 W
Willard, Oh. (wĭl'ȧrd)	108	41.00 N	82.50 W
Willard, Ut.	117b	41.24 N	112.02 W
Willcox, Az. (wĭl'kŏks)	119	32.15 N	109.50 W
Willemstad, Neth. Antilles	140	12.12 N	68.58 W
Willesden, Eng. (wĭlz'dĕn)	154b	51.31 N	0.17 W
W. A. C. Bennett Dam, Can.	97	56.01 N	122.10 W
William Creek, Austl. (wĭl'yăm)	210	28.45 S	136.20 E
Williams, Az. (wĭl'yămz)	119	35.15 N	112.15 W
Williams (I.), Ba.	132	25.30 N	78.30 W
Williamsburg, Ky. (wĭl'yămz-bûrg)	124	36.42 N	84.09 W
Williamsburg, Oh.	111f	39.04 N	84.02 W
Williamsburg, Va.	125	37.15 N	76.41 W
Williams Lake, Can.	97	52.08 N	122.09 W
Williamson, WV (wĭl'yăm-sŭn)	108	37.40 N	82.15 W
Williamsport, Md.	109	39.35 N	77.45 W
Williamsport, Pa.	109	41.15 N	77.05 W
Williamston, NC (wĭl'yămz-tŭn)	125	35.50 N	77.04 W
Williamston, SC	125	34.36 N	82.30 W
Williamstown, WV (wĭl'yămz-toun)	108	39.20 N	81.30 W
Williamsville, NY (wĭl'yăm-vĭl)	111c	42.58 N	78.46 W
Willimantic, Ct. (wĭl-ĭ-măn'tĭk)	109	41.40 N	72.10 W
Willis, Tx. (wĭl'ĭs)	123	30.24 N	95.29 W
Willis Is., Austl.	211	16.15 S	150.30 E
Williston, ND (wĭl'ĭs-tŭn)	112	48.08 N	103.38 W
Williston, L., Can.	96	55.40 N	123.40 W
Willmar, Mn. (wĭl'mär)	97	45.07 N	95.05 W
Willoughby, Oh. (wĭl'ô-bē)	111d	41.39 N	81.25 W
Willow, Ak.	105	61.50 N	150.00 W
Willow Cr., Mt. (wĭl'ô)	115	48.45 N	111.34 W
Willow Cr., Or.	114	44.21 N	117.34 W
Willow Grove, Pa.	110f	40.07 N	75.07 W
Willowick, Oh. (wĭl'ô-wĭk)	111d	41.39 N	81.28 W
Willowmore, S. Afr. (wĭl'ô-môr)	222	33.15 S	23.37 E
Willow Run, Mi. (wĭl'ô rŭn)	111b	42.16 N	83.34 W

ăt; finăl; rāte; senâte; ärm; ȧsk; sofȧ; fâre; ch-choose; dh-as th in other; bē; ēvent; bĕt; recĕnt; cratẽr; g-gō; gh-guttural g; bĭt; ĭ-short neutral; rīde; K-guttural k as ch in German ich;

PLACE (Pronunciation)	PAGE	Lat. °′	Long. °′
Willows, Ca. (wĭl'ōz)	118	39.32 N	122.11 W
Willow Springs, Mo. (sprĭngz)	121	36.59 N	91.56 W
Willowvale, S. Afr. (wĭ-lô'vâl)	223c	32.17 S	28.32 E
Wills Point, Tx. (wĭlz point)	123	32.42 N	96.02 W
Wilmer, Tx. (wĭl'mēr)	117c	32.35 N	96.40 W
Wilmette, Il. (wĭl-mĕt')	111a	42.04 N	87.42 W
Wilmington, Austl.	212	32.39 S	138.07 E
Wilmington, Ca. (wĭl'mĭng-tŭn)	117a	33.46 N	118.16 W
Wilmington, De.	110f	39.45 N	75.33 W
Wilmington, Il.	111a	41.19 N	88.09 W
Wilmington, Ma.	103a	42.34 N	71.10 W
Wilmington, NC	125	34.12 N	77.56 W
Wilmington, Oh.	108	39.20 N	83.50 W
Wilmore, Ky. (wĭl'mōr)	108	37.50 N	84.35 W
Wilmslow, Eng. (wĭlmz'lō)	154	53.19 N	2.14 W
Wilno, see Vilnius			
Wilpoort, S. Afr.	219d	26.57 S	26.17 E
Wilson, Ar. (wĭl'sŭn)	121	35.35 N	90.02 W
Wilson, NC	125	35.42 N	77.55 W
Wilson, Ok.	121	34.09 N	97.27 W
Wilson, L., Al.	124	34.45 N	86.58 W
Wilson (R.), Al.	124	34.53 N	87.28 W
Wilson, Pt., Austl.	207a	38.05 S	144.31 E
Wilson, Mt., Ca.	117a	34.15 N	118.06 W
Wilson Pk., Ut.	115	40.46 N	110.27 W
Wilson's Prom., Austl. (wĭl'sŭnz)	212	39.05 S	146.50 E
Wilsonville, Il. (wĭl'sŭn-vĭl)	117e	39.04 N	89.52 W
Wilstedt, F.R.G. (vēl'shtĕt)	155c	53.45 N	10.04 E
Wilster, F.R.G. (vēl'stēr)	155c	53.55 N	9.23 E
Wilton, Ct. (wĭl'tŭn)	110a	41.11 N	73.25 W
Wilton, ND	112	47.09 N	100.47 W
Wiluna, Austl. (wĭ-lōō'nȧ)	210	26.35 S	120.25 E
Winamac, In. (wĭn'ȧ măk)	108	41.05 N	86.40 W
Winburg, S. Afr. (wĭm-bûrg)	219d	28.31 S	27.02 E
Winchester, Ca. (wĭn'chĕs-tēr)	117a	33.41 N	117.06 W
Winchester, Eng.	160	51.04 N	1.20 W
Winchester, Id.	114	46.14 N	116.39 W
Winchester, In.	108	40.10 N	84.50 W
Winchester, Ky.	108	38.00 N	84.15 W
Winchester, Ma.	103a	42.28 N	71.09 W
Winchester, NH	109	42.45 N	72.25 W
Winchester, Tn.	119	35.11 N	86.06 W
Winchester, Va.	109	39.10 N	78.10 W
Windber, Pa. (wĭnd'bēr)	109	40.15 N	78.45 W
Wind Cave Natl. Park, SD	112	43.36 N	103.53 W
Winder, Ga. (wīn'dēr)	119	33.58 N	83.43 W
Windermere, Eng. (wĭn'dēr-mēr)	160	54.25 N	2.59 W
Windfall, Can. (wĭnd'fôl)	97	54.11 N	116.15 W
Windham, Ct. (wĭnd'ăm)	109	41.45 N	72.05 W
Windham, NH	103a	42.49 N	71.21 W
Windhoek, Namibia (vĭnt'hŏŏk)	222	22.05 S	17.10 E
Wind L., Wi.	111a	42.49 N	88.06 W
Wind Mtn., NM	122	32.02 N	105.30 W
Windom, Mn. (wĭn'dŭm)	113	43.50 N	95.04 W
Windora, Austl. (wĭn-dō'rȧ)	212	25.15 S	142.50 E
Wind R., Wy.	115	43.17 N	109.02 W
Wind River Ind. Res., Wy.	115	43.07 N	109.08 W
Wind River Ra., Wy.	115	43.19 N	109.47 W
Windsor, Austl. (wĭn'zēr)	207b	33.37 S	150.49 E
Windsor, Can.	111b	42.19 N	83.00 W
Windsor, Can.	102	44.59 N	64.08 W
Windsor, Can.	103	48.57 N	55.40 W
Windsor, Co.	120	40.27 N	104.51 W
Windsor, Eng.	154b	51.27 N	0.37 W
Windsor, Mo.	121	38.32 N	93.31 W
Windsor, NC	125	35.58 N	76.57 W
Windsor, Vt.	102	43.30 N	72.25 W
Windward Is., N. A. (wĭnd'wērd)	127	12.45 N	61.40 W
Windward Pass, N. A.	133	19.30 N	74.20 W
Winefred L., Can.	98	55.30 N	110.35 W
Winfield, Ks.	121	37.14 N	97.00 W
Winifred, Mt. (wĭn ĭ frĕd)	115	47.35 N	109.20 W
Winisk (R.), Can.	95	54.30 N	86.30 W
Wink, Tx. (wĭŋk)	122	31.48 N	103.06 W
Winkler, Can. (wĭnk'lēr)	99	49.11 N	97.56 W
Winneba, Ghana (wĭn'ē-bȧ)	224	5.25 N	0.36 W
Winnebago, Mn. (wĭn'ē-bā'gō)	113	43.45 N	94.08 W
Winnebago, L., Wi.	113	44.09 N	88.10 W
Winnebago Ind. Res., Ne.	112	42.15 N	96.06 W
Winnemucca, Nv. (wĭn-ē-mŭk'ȧ)	114	40.59 N	117.43 W
Winnemucca (L.), Nv.	118	40.06 N	119.07 W
Winner, SD (wĭn'ēr)	112	43.22 N	99.50 W
Winnetka, Il. (wĭ-nĕtkȧ)	111a	42.07 N	87.44 W
Winnett, Mt. (wĭn'ĕt)	115	47.01 N	108.20 W
Winnfield, La. (wĭn'fēld)	123	31.56 N	92.39 W
Winnibigoshish (L.), Mn. (wĭn'ĭ-bĭ-gō'shĭsh)	113	47.30 N	93.45 W
Winnipeg, Can. (wĭn'ĭ-pĕg)	93f	49.53 N	97.09 W
Winnipeg, L., Can.	99	52.00 N	97.00 W
Winnipeg (R.), Can.	94	50.30 N	95.54 W
Winnipeg Beach, Can.	99	50.31 N	96.58 W
Winnipegosis, Can. (wĭn'ĭ-pē-gō'sĭs)	99	51.39 N	99.56 W
Winnipegosis (L.), Can.	99	52.30 N	100.00 W
Winnipesaukee (L.), NH (wĭn'ē-pē-sô'kē)	109	43.40 N	71.20 W
Winnsboro, La. (wĭnz'bŭr'ō)	123	32.09 N	91.42 W
Winnsboro, SC	125	34.29 N	81.05 W
Winnsboro, Tx.	121	32.56 N	95.15 W
Winona, Can. (wĭ-nō'nȧ)	93d	43.13 N	79.39 W
Winona, Mn.	113	44.03 N	91.40 W
Winona, Ms.	124	33.29 N	89.43 W
Winooski, Vt. (wĭ'nōōs-kē)	109	44.30 N	73.10 W
Winsen (Luhe), F.R.G. (vēn'zĕn) (lōō'hĕ)	155c	53.22 N	10.13 E
Winsford, Eng. (wĭnz'fērd)	154	53.11 N	2.30 W
Winslow, Az. (wĭnz'lō)	119	35.00 N	110.45 W
Winslow, Wa.	116a	47.38 N	122.31 W
Winsted, Ct. (wĭn'stĕd)	109	41.55 N	73.05 W
Winster, Eng. (wĭn'stēr)	154	53.08 N	1.38 W
Winston-Salem, NC (wĭn stŭn-sā'lĕm)	125	36.05 N	80.15 W
Winterberge (Mts.), S. Afr.	223c	32.18 S	26.25 E
Winter Garden, Fl. (wĭn'tēr gär'd'n)	125a	28.32 N	81.35 W
Winter Harbour, Can.	96	50.31 N	128.02 W
Winter Haven, Fl. (hā'vĕn)	125a	28.01 N	81.38 W
Wintering L., Can. (wĭn'tēr-ĭng)	99	55.24 N	97.42 W
Winter Park, Fl. (pärk)	125a	28.35 N	81.21 W
Winters, Tx. (wĭn'tērz)	122	31.59 N	99.58 W
Winterset, Ia. (wĭn'tēr-sĕt)	113	41.19 N	94.03 W
Winterswijk, Neth.	167c	51.58 N	6.44 E
Winterthur, Switz. (vĭn'tĕr-tōōr)	164	47.30 N	8.32 E
Winterton, S. Afr.	223c	28.51 S	29.33 E
Winthrop, Me. (wĭn'thrŭp)	102	44.19 N	70.00 W
Winthrop, Ma.	103a	42.23 N	70.59 W
Winthrop, Mn.	113	44.31 N	94.20 W
Winton, Austl. (wĭn-tŭn)	211	22.17 S	143.08 E
Wipperfürth, F.R.G. (vē'pĕr-fürt)	167c	51.07 N	7.23 E
Wirksworth, Eng. (wûrks'wûrth)	154	53.05 N	1.35 W
Wisconsin (State), U. S. (wĭs-kŏn'sĭn)	107	44.30 N	91.00 W
Wisconsin (R.), Wi.	113	43.14 N	90.34 W
Wisconsin Dells, Wi.	113	43.38 N	89.46 W
Wisconsin Rapids, Wi.	113	44.24 N	89.50 W
Wishek, ND (wĭsh'ĕk)	112	46.15 N	99.34 W
Wisła (Vistula) R., Pol. (vēs'wȧ) (vĭs'tŭ-lȧ)	165	52.48 N	19.02 E
Wisłoka R., Pol. (vēs-wô'kȧ)	165	49.55 N	21.26 E
Wismar, Guy. (wĭs'mȧr)	141	5.58 N	58.15 W
Wismar, G.D.R. (vĭs'mär)	164	53.53 N	11.28 E
Wisner, Ne. (wĭz'nēr)	112	42.00 N	96.55 W
Wissembourg, Fr. (vē-säN-bōōr')	167	49.03 N	7.58 E
Wister, L., Ok. (vĭs'tēr)	121	35.02 N	94.52 W
Witbank, S. Afr. (wĭt-băŋk)	219d	25.53 S	29.14 E
Witberg (Mtn.), S. Afr.	223c	30.32 S	27.18 E
Witham, Eng. (wĭdh'ăm)	154b	51.48 N	0.37 E
Witham (R.), Eng.	154	53.11 N	0.20 W
Withamsville, Oh. (wĭdh'ămz-vĭl)	111f	39.04 N	84.16 W
Withlacoochee (R.), Fl. (wĭth-lȧ-kōō'chē)	125a	28.58 N	82.30 W
Withlacoochee (R.), Ga.	124	31.15 N	83.30 W
Withrow, Mn. (wĭdh'rō)	117g	45.08 N	92.54 W
Witney, Eng. (wĭt'nē)	154b	51.45 N	1.30 W
Witt, Il. (vĭt)	108	39.10 N	89.15 W
Witten, F.R.G. (vē'tĕn)	167c	51.26 N	7.19 E
Wittenberg, G.D.R. (vē'tĕn-bĕrgh)	164	51.53 N	12.40 E
Wittenberge, G.D.R. (vĭt-ĕn-bĕr'gē)	164	52.59 N	11.45 E
Wittlich, F.R.G. (vĭt'lĭk)	164	49.58 N	6.54 E
Witu, Ken. (wē'tōō)	223	2.18 S	40.28 E
Witu Is., Pap. N. Gui.	203	4.45 S	149.50 E
Witwatersberg (Mts.), S. Afr. (wĭt-wôr-tērz-bûrg)	223b	25.58 S	27.53 E
Witwatersrand (Ridge), S. Afr. (wĭt-wôr'tērs-rănd)	219d	25.55 S	26.27 E
Wkra R., Pol. (f'krȧ)	165	52.40 N	20.35 E
Wloclawek, Pol. (vwô-tswä'vĕk)	165	52.38 N	19.08 E
Wlodawa, Pol. (vwô-dä'vä)	165	51.33 N	23.33 E
Włoszczowa, Pol. (vwôsh-chô'vä)	165	50.51 N	19.58 E
Woburn, Ma. (wōō'bŭrn) (wō'bŭrn)	103a	42.29 N	71.10 W
Woerden, Neth.	155a	52.05 N	4.52 E
Woking, Eng.	154b	51.18 N	0.33 W
Wokingham, Eng. (wô'kĭng-hăm)	154b	51.23 N	0.50 W
Wolcott, Ks. (wōl'kŏt)	117f	39.12 N	94.47 W
Wolf (I.), Can. (wōōlf)	109	44.10 N	76.25 W
Wolf (R.), Ms.	124	30.45 N	89.36 W
Wolf (R.), Wi.	113	45.14 N	88.45 W
Wolfenbüttel, F.R.G. (vôl'fĕn-büt-ĕl)	164	52.10 N	10.32 E
Wolf L., Il.	111a	41.39 N	87.33 W
Wolf Point, Mt. (wōōlf point)	115	48.07 N	105.40 W
Wolfratshausen, F.R.G. (vōlf'räts-hou-zĕn)	155d	47.55 N	11.25 E
Wolfsburg, F.R.G. (vōlfs'bōōrgh)	164	52.30 N	10.37 E
Wolfville, Can. (wōōlf'vĭl)	102	45.05 N	64.22 W
Wolgast, G.D.R. (vôl'gäst)	164	54.04 N	13.46 E
Wolhuterskop, S. Afr.	223b	25.41 S	27.40 E
Wolkersdorf, Aus.	155e	48.24 N	16.31 E
Wollaston (L.), Can. (wōōl'ȧs-tŭn)	94	58.15 N	103.20 W
Wollaston Pen., Can.	94	70.00 N	115.00 W
Wollongong, Austl. (wōōl'ŭn-gŏng)	212	34.26 S	151.05 E
Wolomin, Pol. (vô-wō'mĕn)	165	52.19 N	21.17 E
Wolseley, Can.	98	50.25 N	103.15 W
Wolstanton, Eng. (wōōl-stăn'tŭn)	154	53.02 N	2.13 W
Woltersdorf, G.D.R. (vōl'tĕs-dōrf)	155b	52.07 N	13.13 E
Wolverhampton, Eng. (wōōl'vēr-hămp-tŭn)	154	52.35 N	2.07 W
Wolwehoek, S. Afr.	219d	26.55 S	27.50 E
Wŏnsan, Kor. (wŭn'sän')	200	39.08 N	127.24 E
Wonthaggi, Austl. (wŏnt-hăg'ē)	212	38.45 S	145.42 E
Wood, SD (wŏŏd)	112	43.26 N	100.25 W
Woodbine, Ia. (wŏŏd'bīn)	112	41.44 N	95.42 W
Woodbridge, NJ (wŏŏd'brĭj')	110a	40.33 N	74.18 W
Wood Buffalo Natl. Park, Can.	94	59.50 N	118.53 W
Woodburn, Il. (wŏŏd'bûrn)	117e	39.03 N	90.01 W
Woodburn, Or.	114	45.10 N	122.51 W
Woodbury, NJ (wŏŏd'bĕr-ē)	110f	39.50 N	75.14 W
Woodcrest, Ca. (wŏŏd'krĕst)	117a	33.53 N	117.18 W
Woodinville, Wa. (wŏŏd'ĭn-vĭl)	116a	47.46 N	122.09 W
Woodland, Ca. (wŏŏd'lănd)	118	38.41 N	121.47 W
Woodland, Wa.	116c	45.54 N	122.45 W
Woodland Hills, Ca.	117a	34.10 N	118.36 W
Woodlark I., Pap. N. Gui. (wŏŏd'lärk)	203	9.07 S	152.00 E
Woodlawn Beach, NY (wŏŏd'lôn bēch)	111c	42.48 N	78.51 W
Wood Mountain, Can.	98	49.14 N	106.20 W
Wood River, Il.	117e	38.52 N	90.06 W
Woodroffe, Mt., Austl. (wŏŏd'rŭf)	210	26.05 S	132.00 E
Woodruff, SC (wŏŏd'rŭf)	125	34.43 N	82.03 W
Woods (L.), Austl. (wŏŏdz)	210	18.00 S	133.18 E
Woods, L. of the, Can.-Mn.	107	49.25 N	93.25 W
Woods Cross, Ut. (krôs)	117b	40.53 N	111.54 W
Woodsfield, Oh. (wŏŏdz-fēld)	108	39.45 N	81.10 W
Woodson, Or. (wŏŏdsŭn)	116c	46.07 N	123.20 W
Woodstock, Can. (wŏŏd'stŏk)	102	43.10 N	80.50 W
Woodstock, Can.	102	46.09 N	67.34 W
Woodstock, Eng.	154b	51.48 N	1.22 W
Woodstock, Il.	113	42.20 N	88.29 W
Woodstock, Va.	109	38.55 N	78.25 W
Woodsville, NH (wŏŏdz'vĭl)	109	44.10 N	72.00 W
Woodville, Ms. (wŏŏd'vĭl)	124	31.06 N	91.11 W
Woodville, Tx.	123	30.48 N	94.25 W
Woodward, Ok. (wŏŏd'wôrd)	120	36.25 N	99.24 W
Woolwich, Eng. (wŏŏl'ĭj)	154b	51.28 N	0.05 E
Woomera, Austl. (wŏŏm'ērȧ)	212	31.15 S	136.43 E
Woonsocket, RI (wōōn-sŏk'ĕt)	110b	42.00 N	71.30 W
Woonsocket, SD	112	44.03 N	98.17 W
Wooster, Oh. (wŏŏs'tēr)	108	40.50 N	81.55 W
Worcester, Eng. (wŏŏ'stēr)	160	52.09 N	2.14 W
Worcester, Ma. (wŏŏs'tēr)	103a	42.16 N	71.49 W
Worcester, S. Afr. (wŏŏs'tēr)	222	33.35 S	19.31 E
Worden, Il. (wôr'dĕn)	117e	38.56 N	89.50 W
Workington, Eng. (wûr'kĭng-tŭn)	160	54.40 N	3.30 W
Worksop, Eng. (wûrk'sŏp) (wûr'sŭp)	154	53.18 N	1.07 W
Worland, Wy. (wûr'lănd)	115	44.02 N	107.56 W
Worms, F.R.G. (vōrms)	164	49.37 N	8.22 E
Worona Res., Austl.	207b	34.12 S	150.55 E
Worth, Il. (wûrth)	111a	41.42 N	87.47 W
Worth L., Tx.	117c	32.48 N	97.32 W
Wortham, Tx. (wûr'dhăm)	123	31.46 N	96.22 W
Worthing, Eng. (wûr'dhĭng)	160	50.48 N	0.29 W
Worthington, In. (wûr'dhĭng-tŭn)	108	39.05 N	87.00 W
Worthington, Mn.	112	43.38 N	95.36 W
Wowoni, Pulau (I.), Indon. (wō-wō'nē)	203	4.05 S	123.45 E
Wragby, Eng. (răg'bē)	154	53.17 N	0.19 W
Wrangell, Ak. (rănōgĕl)	105	56.28 N	132.25 W
Wrangell, Mt., Ak.	105	61.58 N	143.50 W
Wrangell Mts., Ak.-Can.	105	62.28 N	142.40 W
Wrath, C., Scot. (răth)	160	58.34 N	5.01 W
Wray, Co. (rā)	120	40.06 N	102.14 W
Wreak (R.), Eng. (rēk)	139	52.45 N	0.59 W
Wreck Rfs., Austl. (rĕk)	211	22.00 S	155.52 E
Wrekin, The (Mt.), Eng. (rĕk'ĭn)	154	54.20 N	2.33 W
Wrens, Ga. (rĕnz)	125	33.15 N	82.25 W
Wrentham, Ma.	103a	42.04 N	71.20 W
Wrexham, Wales (rĕk'săm)	154	53.03 N	3.00 W
Wrights Corners, NY (rīts kôr'nērz)	111c	43.14 N	78.42 W
Wrightsville, Ga. (rīts'vĭl)	125	32.44 N	82.44 W
Wrocław (Breslau), Pol. (vrôtsläv) (brĕs'lou)	165	51.07 N	17.10 E
Wrotham, Eng. (rōōt'ŭm)	154b	51.18 N	0.19 E
Wrzesnia, Pol. (vzhăsh'nyȧ)	165	52.19 N	17.33 E
Wuchang, China (wōō-chäŋ)	199	30.32 N	114.25 E
Wuchang, China	198	44.59 N	127.00 E
Wucheng, China (wōō-chŭŋ)	196	37.14 N	116.03 E
Wuhan, China	199	30.30 N	114.15 E
Wuhu, China (wōō'hōō)	196	31.22 N	118.22 E
Wuji, China (wōō-jyī)	196	38.12 N	114.57 E
Wujiang, China (wōō-jyäŋ)	196	31.10 N	120.38 E
Wulajie, China (wōō-lä-jyĕ)	200	44.08 N	126.25 E
Wuleidao Wan (C.), China (wōō-lā-dou wän)	196	36.55 N	122.00 E
Wu Liang Shan (Mts.), China	202	23.07 N	100.45 E
Wulidian, China (wōō-lē-dĭĕn)	196	32.09 N	114.17 E
Wünsdorf, G.D.R. (vüns'dorf)	155b	52.10 N	13.29 E
Wupatki Nat'l Mon., Az.	119	35.35 N	111.45 W
Wuping, China (wōō-pĭŋ)	199	25.05 N	116.01 E
Wuppertal, F.R.G. (vŏŏp'ēr-täl)	167c	51.16 N	7.14 E
Wuqiao, China (wōō-chyou)	196	37.37 N	116.29 E
Wu R., China (wōō')	199	27.30 N	108.00 E
Würm (R.), F.R.G. (Würm)	155d	48.07 N	11.20 E
Würselen, F.R.G. (vür'zē-lĕn)	167d	50.49 N	6.09 E
Würzburg, F.R.G. (vürts'bōōrgh)	164	49.48 N	9.57 E
Wurzen, G.D.R. (vōōrt'sĕn)	164	51.22 N	12.45 E
Wushi, China (wōō-shr)	194	41.13 N	79.08 E
Wusong, China (wōō-sôŋ)	197b	31.23 N	121.29 E
Wustermark, G.D.R. (vōōs'tēr-märk)	155b	52.33 N	12.57 E
Wustrau, G.D.R. (vōōst'rou)	155b	52.15 N	12.51 E
Wuustwezel, Bel.	155a	51.23 N	4.36 E
Wuwie, China (wōō'wā')	196	31.19 N	117.53 E
Wuxi, China (wōō-shyē)	196	31.36 N	120.17 E
Wuxing, China (wōō-shyĭŋ)	199	30.38 N	120.10 E
Wuyi Shan (Mts.), China (wōō-yē shän)	199	26.38 N	116.35 E
Wuyou, China (wōō-yō)	196	33.18 N	120.15 E
Wuzhi Shan (Mtn.), China (wōō-jr shän)	199	18.48 N	109.30 E
Wuzhou, China (wōō-jō)	199	23.32 N	111.25 E
Wyandotte, Mi. (wī'ăn-dŏt)	111b	42.12 N	83.10 W
Wye, Eng. (wī)	154b	51.12 N	0.57 E

ng-sing; ŋ-baŋk; N-nasalized n; nŏd; cŏmmit; ōld; ōbey; ôrder; oi-boil; fōōd; fŏŏt; ou-out; s-soft; sh-dish; th-thin; pūre; ûnite; ûrn; stŭd; circŭs; ü-as in French tu; '-indeterminate vowel.

366 Wye – Yemen

PLACE (Pronunciation)	PAGE	Lat. °′	Long. °′
Wye (R.), Eng.	154	53.14 N	1.46 W
Wymore, Ne. (wī'mōr)	121	40.09 N	96.41 W
Wynberg, S. Afr. (wĭn'bĕrg)	222a	34.00 S	18.28 E
Wyndham, Austl. (wĭnd'ăm)	210	15.30 S	128.15 E
Wynne, Ar. (wĭn)	121	35.12 N	90.46 W
Wynnewood, Ok. (wĭn'wo͝od)	121	34.39 N	97.10 W
Wynona, Ok. (wī-nō'nȧ)	121	36.33 N	96.19 W
Wynyard, Can. (wĭn'yẽrd)	98	51.47 N	104.10 W
Wyoming, Oh. (wī-ō'mĭng)	111f	39.14 N	84.28 W
Wyoming (State), U. S.	106	42.50 N	108.30 W
Wyoming Ra., Wy.	115	42.43 N	110.35 W
Wyre For., Eng. (wīr)	154	52.24 N	2.24 W
Wysokie Mazowieckie, Pol. (vē-sô'kyĕ mä-zô-vyĕts'kyĕ)	164	52.55 N	22.42 E
Wyszkow, Pol. (vēsh'ko͞of)	164	52.35 N	21.29 E
Wytheville, Va. (wĭth'vĭl)	125	36.55 N	81.06 W
X			
Xagua, Banco (Bk.), Cuba (bä'n-kō-sä'gwä)	132	21.35 N	80.50 W
Xanten, F.R.G. (ksän'tĕn)	167c	51.40 N	6.28 E
Xánthi, Grc.	171	41.08 N	24.53 E
Xau, L., Bots.	222	21.15 S	24.38 E
Xcalak, Mex. (sä-lä'k)	130a	18.15 N	87.50 W
Xenia, Oh. (zē'nĭ-ȧ)	108	39.40 N	83.55 W
Xi (R.), China (shyē)	199	23.15 N	112.10 E
Xiajin, China (shyä-jyĭn)	196	36.58 N	115.59 E
Xiamen (I.), China (shyä-mŭn)	199	24.28 N	118.20 E
Xiamen (Amoy), China	199	24.30 N	118.10 E
Xi'an, China (shyē-än)	198	34.20 N	109.00 E
Xiang (R.), China (shyäŋ)	199	26.18 N	112.25 E
Xiangcheng, China (shyäŋ-chŭŋ)	196	33.52 N	113.31 E
Xianghe, China (shyäŋ-hŭ)	198a	39.46 N	116.59 E
Xiangtan, China (shyäŋ-tän)	199	27.55 N	112.45 E
Xianyang, China (shyĕn-yäŋ)	198	34.20 N	108.40 E
Xiao Hinggan Ling (Ra.), see Lesser Khingan			
Xiaoxingkai Hu (L.), China (shyou-shyĭŋ-kī ho͞o)	200	42.25 N	132.45 E
Xiapu, China (shyä-po͞o)	199	27.00 N	120.00 E
Xiayi, China (shyä-yē)	196	34.15 N	116.07 E
Xicotencatl, Mex. (sē-kô-tĕn-kät'l)	128	32.00 N	98.58 W
Xifeng, China (shyē-fŭŋ)	198	42.40 N	124.40 E
Xigazê, China (shyē-gä-dzŭ)	190	29.22 N	88.57 E
Xiheying, China (shyē-hŭ-yĭŋ)	196	39.58 N	114.50 E
Xiliao (R.), China (shyē-lĭou)	198	41.40 N	122.40 E
Xilitla, Mex. (sē-lē'tlä)	128	21.24 N	98.59 W
Xinchang, China (shyĭn-chäŋ)	197b	31.02 N	121.38 E
Xing'an, China (shyĭŋ-än)	199	25.44 N	110.32 E
Xingcheng, China (shyĭŋ-chŭŋ)	196	40.38 N	120.41 E
Xinghua, China (shyĭŋ-hwä)	196	32.58 N	119.48 E
Xingjiawan, China (shyĭŋ-jyä-wän)	196	37.16 N	114.54 E
Xingtai, China (shyĭŋ-tī)	196	37.04 N	114.33 E
Xingú (R.), Braz. (zhĕŋ-go͞o')	141	6.20 S	52.34 W
Xinhai, China (shyĭn-hī)	196	36.59 N	117.33 E
Xinhua, China (shyĭn-hwä)	199	27.45 N	111.20 E
Xinhuai (R.), China (shyĭn-hwī)	196	33.48 N	119.39 E
XInhui, China (shyn-hwä)	199	22.40 N	113.08 E
Xining, China (shyē-nĭŋ)	194	36.52 N	101.36 E
Xinjiang (Sinkiang) (Aut. Reg.), China (shyĭn-jyäŋ)	194	40.15 N	82.15 E
Xinjin, China (shyĭn-jyĭn)	196	39.23 N	121.57 E
Xinmin, China (shyĭn-mĭn)	198	42.00 N	122.42 E
Xintai, China (shyĭn-tī)	196	35.55 N	117.44 E
Xintang, China (shyĭn-täŋ)	197a	23.08 N	113.36 E
Xin Xian, China (shyĭn shyĕn)	196	31.47 N	114.50 E
Xin Xian, China	198	38.20 N	112.45 E
Xinxiang, China (shyĭn-shyäŋ)	196	35.17 N	113.49 E
Xinyang, China (shyĭn-yäŋ)	196	32.08 N	114.04 E
Xinye, China (shyĭn-yŭ)	198	32.40 N	112.20 E
Xinzao, China (shyĭn-dzou)	197a	23.01 N	113.25 E
Xinzheng, China (shyĭn-jŭŋ)	196	34.24 N	113.43 E
Xiongyuecheng, China (shyôŋ-yüĕ-chŭŋ)	196	40.10 N	122.08 E
Xiping, China (shyē-pĭŋ)	196	33.21 N	114.01 E
Xishui, China (shyē-shwā)	199	30.30 N	115.10 E
Xi Xian, China (shyē shyĕn)	196	32.20 N	114.42 E
XIyang, China (shyē-yäŋ)	196	37.37 N	113.42 E
Xiying, China (shyē-yĭŋ)	196	31.26 N	119.57 E
Xiyou, China (shyē-yō)	196	37.21 N	119.59 E
Xizang (Tibet) (Aut. Reg.), China (shyē-dzäŋ)	194	31.15 N	87.30 E
Xizhong Dao (I.), China (shyē-jôŋ dou)	196	39.27 N	121.06 E
Xochihuehuetlan, Mex. (sô-chē-wē-wē-tlä'n)	128	17.53 N	98.29 E
Xochimilco, Mex. (sō-chē-mēl'kō)	129a	19.05 N	99.06 W
Xuancheng, China (shyüän-chŭŋ)	199	30.52 N	118.48 E
Xuanhua, China (shyüän-hwä)	198	40.35 N	115.05 E
Xuanhuadian, China (shyüän-hwä-dĭĕn)	196	31.42 N	114.29 E
Xuchang, China (shyo͞o-chäŋ)	196	34.02 N	113.49 E
Xun (R.), China (shyo͞on)	199	23.28 N	110.30 E
Xuyi, China (shyo͞o-yē)	196	31.02 N	113.49 E
Xuzhou, see Suchow			
Y			
Ya'an, China (yä-än)	199	30.00 N	103.20 E
Yablonitskiy Pereval (P.), Sov. Un. (yȧb-lô'nĭt-skĭ pĕ-rĕ-väl')	165	48.20 N	24.25 E
Yablonovyy Khrebet (Mts.), Sov. Un. (yȧ-blô-nô-vē')	179	51.15 N	111.30 E
Yacheng, China (yä-chŭŋ)	199	18.20 N	109.10 E
Yachiyo, Jap.	201a	35.43 N	140.07 E
Yacolt, Wa. (yă'kôlt)	116c	45.52 N	122.24 W
Yacolt (Mt.), Wa.	116c	45.52 N	122.27 W
Yacona (R.), Ms. (yȧ'cō nā)	124	34.13 N	89.30 W
Yacuiba, Arg. (yȧ-ko͞o-ē'bȧ)	142	22.02 S	63.44 W
Yadkin (R.), NC (yăd'kĭn)	125	36.12 N	80.40 W
Yafran, Libya,	221	31.57 N	12.04 E
Yagotin, Sov. Un. (yä'gô-tĕn)	173	50.18 N	31.46 E
Yaguajay, Cuba (yä-guä-hä'ē)	132	22.20 N	79.20 W
Yahagi-Gawa (Strm.), Jap. (yä'hä-gē gä'wä)	201	35.16 N	137.22 E
Yahongqiao, China (yä-hôŋ-chyou)	196	39.45 N	117.52 E
Yahualica, Mex. (yä-wä-lē'kä)	128	21.08 N	102.53 W
Yajalon, Mex. (yä-hä-lōn')	129	17.16 N	92.20 W
Yakhroma, Sov. Un. (yäl'rô-ma)	180b	56.17 N	37.30 E
Yakhroma R., Sov. Un.	180b	56.15 N	37.38 E
Yakima, Wa. (yăk'ĭmȧ)	114	46.35 N	120.30 W
Yakima R., Wa. (tăk'ĭ-mȧ)	114	46.48 N	120.22 W
Yakoma, Zaire	226	4.05 N	22.27 E
Yaku (I.), Jap. (yä'ko͞o)	201	30.15 N	130.41 E
Yakut A.S.S.R., Sov. Un.	179	65.21 N	117.13 E
Yakutat, Ak. (yăk'o͞o-tăt)	105	59.32 N	139.35 W
Yakutsk, Sov. Un. (yȧ-ko͞otsk')	179	62.13 N	129.49 E
Yale, Mi.	108	43.05 N	82.45 W
Yale, Ok.	121	36.07 N	96.42 W
Yale Res., Wa.	114	46.00 N	122.20 W
Yalinga, Cen. Afr. Rep. (yȧ-lĭŋ'gȧ)	221	6.56 N	23.22 E
Yalobusha (R.), Ms. (yȧ-lô-bo͝osh'ȧ)	124	33.48 N	90.02 W
Yalong (R.), China (yä-lôŋ)	194	32.29 N	98.41 E
Yalta, Sov. Un. (yäl'tȧ)	177	44.29 N	34.12 E
Yalu (R.), China (yä-lo͞o)	200	48.20 N	122.35 E
Yalu (Amnok) (R.), China-Kor.	200	41.20 N	126.35 E
Yalutorovsk, Sov. Un. (yä-lo͞o-tô'rôfsk)	178	56.42 N	66.32 E
Yamada, Jap. (yä'mȧ-dȧ)	201	33.37 N	133.39 E
Yamagata, Jap. (yä-mȧ'gä-tä)	200	38.12 N	140.24 E
Yamaguchi, Jap. (yä-mȧ'go͞o-chē)	201	34.10 N	131.30 E
Yamal, P-ov (Pen.), Sov. Un. (yä-mäl')	178	71.15 N	70.00 E
Yamantau, Gora (Mt.), Sov. Un. (gȧ-rä' yä'man-tȧw)	180a	54.16 N	58.08 E
Yamasá, Dom. Rep. (yä-mä'sä)	133	18.50 N	70.00 W
Yamasaki, Jap. (yä'mȧ'sä-kē)	201	35.01 N	134.33 E
Yamasaki, Jap.	201b	34.53 N	135.41 E
Yamashina, Jap. (yä'mä-shē'nä)	201b	34.59 N	135.50 E
Yamashita, Jap. (yä'mä-shē'tä)	201b	34.53 N	135.25 E
Yamato, Jap.	201a	35.28 N	139.28 E
Yamato-Kōriyama, Jap.	201b	34.39 N	135.48 E
Yamato-takada, Jap. (yä'mä-tô tä'kä-dä)	201b	34.31 N	135.45 E
Yambi, Mesa de, Col. (mĕ'sä-dĕ-yȧ'm-bē)	140	1.55 N	71.45 W
Yambol, Bul. (yȧm'bôl)	171	42.28 N	26.31 E
Yamdena (I.), Indon.	203	7.23 S	130.30 E
Yamethin, Bur. (yŭ-mē'thĕn)	194	20.14 N	96.27 E
Yamhill, Or. (yăm'hĭl)	116c	45.20 N	123.11 W
Yamkino, Sov. Un. (yäm'kĭ-nô)	180b	55.56 N	38.25 E
Yamma Yamma, L., Austl. (yăm'ȧ yăm'ȧ)	212	26.15 S	141.30 E
Yamsk, Sov. Un. (yämsk)	179	59.41 N	154.09 E
Yamuna (R.), India	190	26.50 N	80.10 E
Yamzho Yumco (L.), China (yäm-jwo yo͞om-tswo)	199	29.11 N	91.26 E
Yana (R.), Sov. Un. (yä'nȧ)	179	69.42 N	135.45 E
Yanac, Austl. (yăn'ăk)	212	36.10 S	141.30 E
Yanagawa, Jap. (yä-nä'gä-wä)	201	33.11 N	130.24 E
Yanam, India (yŭnŭm')	190	16.48 N	82.15 E
Yan'an, China (yän-än)	194	36.46 N	109.15 E
Yan'an, China	198	36.35 N	109.32 E
Yanbu', Sau. Ar.	192	23.57 N	38.02 E
Yancheng, China (yän-chŭŋ)	196	33.23 N	120.11 E
Yancheng, China	196	33.38 N	113.59 E
Yandongi, Zaire	226	2.51 N	22.16 E
Yangcheng Hu (L.), China (yäŋ-chŭŋ ho͞o)	196	31.30 N	120.31 E
Yangchun, China (yäŋ-cho͞on)	199	22.08 N	111.48 E
Yang'erzhuang, China (yäŋ-är-jüäŋ)	196	38.18 N	117.31 E
Yanggezhuang, China (yäŋ-gŭ-jüäŋ)	198a	40.10 N	116.48 E
Yanggu, China (yäŋ-go͞o)	196	36.06 N	115.46 E
Yanghe, China (yäŋ-hŭ)	196	33.48 N	118.23 E
Yangjiang, China (yäŋ-jyäŋ)	199	21.52 N	111.58 E
Yangjiaogou, China (yäŋ-jyou-gō)	196	36.17 N	118.53 E
Yangquan, China (yäŋ-chyüän)	196	37.52 N	113.36 E
Yangtze (Chang) (R.), China (yäng'tse) (chäŋ)	195	30.30 N	117.25 E
Yangxin, China (yäŋ-shyĭn)	196	37.39 N	117.34 E
Yangyang, Kor. (yäng'yäng')	200	38.02 N	128.38 E
Yangzhou, China (yäŋ-jō)	195	32.24 N	119.24 E
Yanji, China (yän-jyē)	198	42.55 N	129.35 E
Yanjiahe, China (yän-jyä-hŭ)	196	31.55 N	114.47 E
Yanjin, China (yän-jyĭn)	196	35.09 N	114.13 E
Yankton, SD (yănk'tŭn)	112	42.51 N	97.24 W
Yanling, China (yän-lĭŋ)	196	34.07 N	114.12 E
Yannina, see Ioánnina			
Yanqi, see Karashahr			
Yanshan, China (yän-shän)	196	38.05 N	117.15 E
Yanshou, China (yän-shō)	198	45.25 N	128.43 E
Yantai, see Chefoo			
Yanychi, Sov. Un. (yä'nĭ-chĭ)	180a	57.42 N	56.24 E
Yanzhou, China (yäŋ-jō)	196	35.35 N	116.50 E
Yanzhuang, China (yän-jüäŋ)	196	36.08 N	117.47 E
Yao, Chad (yä'ō)	211	13.00 N	17.38 E
Yao, Jap.	201b	34.37 N	135.76 E
Yaoundé, Cam. (yȧ-o͞on-dā')	225	3.52 N	11.31 E
Yap (I.), Pac. Is. Trust Ter. (yăp)	204	11.00 N	138.00 E
Yapen, Pulau (I.), Indon.	203	1.30 S	136.15 E
Yaque del Norte (R.), (yä'kȧ dĕl nōr'tȧ)	133	19.40 N	71.25 W
Yaque del Sur (R.), Dom. Rep. (yä-kĕ-dĕl-so͞o'r)	133	18.35 N	71.05 W
Yaqui (R.), Mex. (yä'kē)	126	28.15 N	109.40 W
Yaracuy (State), Ven. (yä-rä-ko͞o'ē)	141b	10.10 N	68.31 W
Yaraka, Austl. (yȧ-răk'ȧ)	212	24.50 S	144.08 E
Yaransk, Sov. Un. (yä-ränsk')	176	57.18 N	48.05 E
Yarda (Well), Chad. (yär'dȧ)	221	18.29 N	19.13 E
Yare (R.), Eng.	161	52.40 N	1.32 E
Yarkand, see Shache			
Yarkand (R.), India (yär-känt')	190	36.11 N	76.10 E
Yarlung Zangbo (R.), **see Brahmaputra**			
Yarmouth, Can. (yär'mŭth)	102	43.50 N	66.07 W
Yaroslavka, Sov. Un. (yȧ-rô-släv'kȧ)	180a	55.52 N	57.59 E
Yaroslavl', Sov. Un. (yȧ-rô-släv''l)	172	57.57 N	39.54 E
Yaroslavl' (Oblast), Sov. Un.	172	58.05 N	38.05 E
Yarra-to (L.), Sov. Un. (yȧ'rô-tô')	176	68.30 N	71.30 E
Yartsevo, Sov. Un. (yär'tsyĕ-vô)	172	55.04 N	32.38 E
Yartsevo, Sov. Un.	178	60.13 N	89.52 E
Yarumal, Col. (yä-ro͞o-mäl')	140a	6.57 N	75.24 W
Yasel'da R., Sov. Un. (yä-syŭl'dȧ)	165	53.13 N	25.53 E
Yasinya, Sov. Un.	165	48.17 N	24.21 E
Yateras, Cuba (yä-tā'räs)	133	20.00 N	75.00 W
Yates Center, Ks. (yāts)	121	37.53 N	95.44 W
Yathkyed (L.), Can. (yăth-kī-ĕd')	94	62.41 N	98.00 W
Yatsuga-take (Mtn.), Jap. (yät'so͞o-gä dä'kä)	201	36.01 N	138.21 W
Yatsushiro, Jap. (yät'so͞o'shē-rô)	201	32.30 N	130.35 E
Yatta Plat., Ken.	227	1.55 S	38.10 E
Yautepec, Mex. (yä-o͞o-tȧ-pĕk')	128	18.53 N	99.04 W
Yavorov, Sov. Un.	165	49.56 N	23.24 E
Yawata, Jap. (yä'wä-tä)	201b	34.52 N	135.43 E
Yawatahama, Jap. (yä'wä'tä'hä-mä)	201	33.24 N	132.25 E
Ya Xian, China (yä shyĕn)	199	18.10 N	109.32 E
Yayama, Zaire	226	1.16 S	23.07 E
Yayao, China (yä-you)	197a	23.10 N	113.40 E
Yazd, Iran	192	31.59 N	54.03 E
Yazoo (R.), Ms. (yă'zo͞o)	124	32.32 N	90.40 W
Yazoo City, Ms.	124	32.50 N	90.18 W
Ye, Bur. (yā)	202	15.13 N	97.52 E
Yeadon, Pa. (yē'dŭn)	110f	39.56 N	75.16 W
Yecheng, see Karghalik			
Yecla, Sp. (yā'klä)	168	38.35 N	1.09 W
Yefremov, Sov. Un. (yĕ-frĕ'môf)	172	53.08 N	38.04 E
Yegor'yevsk, Sov. Un. (yĕ-gôr'yĕfsk)	172	55.23 N	38.59 E
Yeji, China (yŭ-jyē)	196	31.52 N	115.57 E
Yelabuga, Sov. Un. (yĕ-lä'bo͞o-gȧ)	176	55.50 N	52.18 E
Yelan, Sov. Un.	177	50.50 N	44.00 E
Yelets, Sov. Un. (yĕ-lyĕts')	172	52.35 N	38.28 E
Yelizavetpol'skiy, Sov. Un. (yĕ'lĭ-za-vĕt-pôl-skĭ)	180a	52.51 N	60.38 E
Yelizavety, Mys (C.), Sov. Un. (yĕ-lyĕ-sȧ-vyĕ'tĭ)	179	54.28 N	142.59 E
Yell (I.), Scot. (yĕl)	160a	60.35 N	1.27 W
Yellow (R.), Fl. (yĕl'ō)	124	30.33 N	86.53 W
Yellowhead Pass, Can. (yĕl'ō-hĕd)	97	52.52 N	118.35 W
Yellowknife, Can. (yĕl'ō-nīf)	94	62.29 N	114.38 W
Yellow R., see Huang			
Yellow Sea, Asia	198	35.20 N	122.15 E
Yellowstone L., Wy.	115	44.27 N	110.03 W
Yellowstone Natl. Park, Wy. (yĕl'ō-stōn)	115	44.45 N	110.35 W
Yellowstone R., Mt.	115	46.28 N	105.39 W
Yellowstone R., Clark Fk., Wy.	115	44.55 N	109.05 W
Yellowtail Res., Mt.-Wy.	115	45.00 N	108.10 W
Yel'nya, Sov. Un. (yĕl'nyȧ)	172	54.34 N	33.12 E
Yemanzhelinsk, Sov. Un. (yĕ-măn-zhâ'lĭnsk)	180a	54.47 N	61.24 E
Yemen, Asia (yĕm'ĕn)	188	15.45 N	44.30 E
Yemen, People's Democratic Republic of., Asia	188	14.45 N	46.45 E

ng-sing; ŋ-baŋk; N-nasalized n;   nŏd; cŏmmit; ōld; ȯbey; ôrder; oi-boil; fōōd; fŏŏt; ou-out;   s-soft; sh-dish;   th-thin;   pūre; ûnite; ûrn; stŭd; circŭs; ü-as in French tu;   ′-indeterminate vowel.

PLACE (Pronunciation)	PAGE	Lat. °′	Long. °′
Zaysan (L.), Sov. Un.	178	48.16 N	84.05 E
Zaza (R.), Cuba (zä′zä)	132	21.40 N	79.25 W
Zbarazh, Sov. Un. (zbä-räzh′)	165	49.39 N	25.48 E
Zbruch R., Sov. Un. (zbrŏŏch)	165	48.56 N	26.18 E
Zdolbunov, Sov. Un. (zdŏl-bŏŏ′nŏŏf)	165	50.31 N	26.17 E
Zdunska Wola, Pol. (zdŏŏn′skä vŏ′lä)	165	51.36 N	18.27 E
Zebediela, S. Afr.	219d	24.19 S	29.21 E
Zeeland, Mi. (zē′länd)	108	42.50 N	86.00 W
Zefat, Isr.	189a	32.58 N	35.30 E
Zehdenick, G.D.R. (tsä′dĕ-nĕk)	155b	52.59 N	13.20 E
Zehlendorf, G.D.R. (tsä′lĕn-dôrf)	155b	52.47 N	13.23 E
Zeila, Som. (zā′lä)	219a	11.19 N	43.20 E
Zeist, Neth.	155a	52.05 N	5.14 E
Želechów, Pol. (zhĕ-lĕ′kŏŏf)	165	51.48 N	21.55 E
Zelenogorsk, Sov. Un. (zĕ-lä′nŏ-gôrsk)	163	60.13 N	29.39 E
Zella-Mehlis, G.D.R. (tsäl′ä-mä′lĕs)	164	50.40 N	10.38 E
Zémio, Cen. Afr. Rep. (za-myō′)	221	5.03 N	25.11 E
Zemlya Frantsa Iosifa (Franz Josef Land) (Is.), Sov. Un.	174	81.32 N	40.00 E
Zempoala, Punta (Pt.), Mex. (pōō′n-tä-sĕm-pô-ä′lä)	129	19.30 N	96.18 W
Zempoatlépetl (Mtn.), Mex. (sĕm-pô-ä-tlä′pĕt′l)	129	17.13 N	95.59 W
Zemun (Semlin), Yugo. (zĕ′mŏŏn) (sĕm′lĭn)	171	44.50 N	20.25 E
Zengcheng, China (dzŭŋ-chŭŋ)	197a	23.18 N	113.49 E
Zenica, Yugo. (zĕ′nĕt-sä)	171	44.10 N	17.54 E
Zeni-Su (Is.), Jap. (zĕ′nĕ sōō)	201	33.55 N	138.55 E
Zen′kov, Sov. Un. (zĕn-kof′)	173	50.13 N	34.23 E
Žepče, Yugo. (zhĕp′chĕ)	173	44.26 N	18.01 E
Zepernick, G.D.R. (tsĕ′pĕr-nĕk)	155b	52.39 N	13.32 E
Zeravshan (R.), Sov. Un. (zä-räf-shän′)	153	40.00 N	65.42 E
Zerbst, G.D.R. (tsĕrbst)	164	51.58 N	12.03 E
Zerpenschleuse, G.D.R. (tsĕr′pĕn-shloi-zĕ)	155b	52.51 N	13.30 E
Zeuthen, G.D.R. (tsoi′tĕn)	155b	52.21 N	13.38 E
Zevenaar, Neth.	167c	51.56 N	6.06 E
Zevenbergen, Neth.	155a	51.38 N	4.36 E
Zeya, Sov. Un. (zä′yä)	179	53.43 N	127.29 E
Zeya (R.), Sov. Un.	179	52.31 N	128.30 E
Zeytun, Tur. (zā-tōōn′)	177	38.00 N	36.40 E
Zezere (R.), Port. (zĕ′zä-rĕ)	168	39.54 N	8.12 W
Zghartā, Leb.	189a	34.24 N	35.53 E
Zgierz, Pol. (zgyĕzh)	165	51.51 N	19.26 E
Zgurovka, Sov. Un. (zgōō′rôf-kä)	173	50.31 N	31.43 E
Zhang (R.), China (jäŋ)	196	36.17 N	114.31 E
Zhangbei, China (jäŋ-bā)	198	41.12 N	114.50 E
Zhang Guangcai Ling (Mts.), China (jäŋ-gŭäŋ-tsī′ lĭŋ)	198	43.50 N	127.55 E
Zhanggezhuang, China (jäŋ-gŭ-jŭäŋ)	198a	40.09 N	116.56 E
Zhangjiakou, see Kalgan			
Zhangqiu, China (jäŋ-chyō)	196	36.50 N	117.29 E
Zhangwu, China (jäŋ-wōō)	200	42.21 N	123.00 E
Zhangye, China (jäŋ-yĕ)	194	38.46 N	101.00 E
Zhangzhou, China (jäŋ-jō)	199	24.35 N	117.45 E
Zhangzi Dao (I.), China (jäŋ-dz dou)	196	39.02 N	122.44 E
Zhanhua, China (jän-hwä)	196	37.42 N	117.49 E
Zhanjiang, China (jän-jyäŋ)	199	21.20 N	110.28 E
Zhanyu, China (jän-yōō)	198	44.30 N	122.30 E
Zhao′an, China (jou-än)	199	23.48 N	117.10 E
Zhaodong, China (jou-dôŋ)	198	45.58 N	126.00 E
Zhaotong, China (jou-tôŋ)	199	27.18 N	103.50 E
Zhao Xian, China (jou shyĕn)	196	37.46 N	114.48 E
Zhaoyuan, China (jou-yüän)	196	37.22 N	120.23 E
Zhdanov, Sov. Un. (zhdä′nôf)	173	47.07 N	37.32 E
Zhecheng, China (jŭ-chŭŋ)	196	34.05 N	115.19 E
Zhegao, China (jŭ-gou)	196	31.47 N	117.44 E
Zhejiang (Prov.), China (jŭ-jyäŋ)	195	29.30 N	120.00 E
Zhelaniya, Mys (C.), Sov. Un. (zhĕ′lä-nĭ-yä)	178	75.43 N	69.10 E
Zhengding, China (jŭŋ-dĭŋ)	196	38.10 N	114.35 E
Zhengyang, China (jŭŋ-yäŋ)	196	32.34 N	114.22 E
Zhengzhou, China (jŭŋ-jō)	196	34.46 N	113.42 E
Zhenjiang, China (jŭn-jyäŋ)	196	32.13 N	119.24 E
Zhenyuan, China (jŭn-yŭän)	199	27.08 N	108.30 E
Zhigalovo, Sov. Un. (zhĕ-gä′lô-vô)	179	54.52 N	105.05 E
Zhigansk, Sov. Un. (zhĕ-gänsk′)	179	66.45 N	123.20 E
Zhijiang, China (jr-jyäŋ)	199	27.25 N	109.45 E
Zhitomir, Sov. Un. (zhĕ′tô′mĕr)	173	50.15 N	28.40 E
Zhitomir (Oblast), Sov. Un.	173	50.40 N	28.07 E
Zhizdra, Sov. Un. (zhĕz′drä)	172	53.47 N	34.41 E
Zhizhitskoye (L.), Sov. Un. (zhĕ-zhĕt′skô-yĕ)	172	56.08 N	31.34 E
Zhmerinka, Sov. Un. (zhemyĕ′rĕŋ-kä)	173	49.02 N	28.09 E
Zhongwei, China (jôŋ-wä)	198	37.32 N	105.10 E
Zhong Xian, China (jôŋ shyĕn)	199	30.20 N	108.00 E
Zhongxin, China (jôŋ-shyĭn)	197a	23.16 N	113.38 E
Zhoucun, China (jō-tsōōn)	196	36.49 N	117.52 E
Zhoukouzhen, China (jō-kō-jŭn)	196	33.39 N	114.40 E
Zhoupu, China (jō-pōō)	197b	31.07 N	121.33 E
Zhoushan Qundao (Is.), China (jō-shän-chyōōn-dou)	199	30.00 N	123.00 E
Zhou Xian, China (jō shyĕn)	196	39.30 N	115.59 E
Zhu (R.), China (jōō)	197a	23.48 N	113.36 E
Zhuanghe, China (jŭäŋ-hŭ)	198	39.40 N	123.00 E
Zhuanqiao, China (jŭäŋ-chyou)	197b	31.02 N	121.24 E
Zhucheng, China (jō-chŭŋ)	196	36.01 N	119.24 E
Zhuji, China (jōō-jyĕ)	199	29.58 N	120.10 E
Zhujiang Kou (Can.), China (jōō-jyäŋ kō)	199	22.00 N	114.00 E
Zhukovskiy, Sov. Un. (zhōō-kôf′ski)	180b	55.33 N	38.09 E
Zi (R.), China (dzē)	199	26.50 N	111.00 E
Zibo, China (dzē-bwo)	196	36.48 N	118.04 E
Ziel, Mt., Austl. (zēl)	210	23.15 S	132.45 E
Zielona Góra, Pol. (zhyĕ-lô′nä gōō′rä)	164	51.56 N	15.30 E
Zigazinskiy, Sov. Un. (zī-gazinskēĕ)	180a	53.50 N	57.18 E
Ziguinchor, Senegal	224	12.35 N	16.16 W
Zilair, Sov. Un. (zĕ′lä-ĭr)	180a	52.12 N	57.23 E
Zile, Tur. (zē-lĕ′)	177	40.20 N	35.50 E
Žilina, Czech. (zhĕ′lĭ-nä)	165	49.14 N	18.45 E
Zillah, Libya	221	28.26 N	17.52 E
Zima, Sov. Un. (zĕ′mä)	178	53.58 N	102.08 E
Zimapan, Mex. (sē-mä′pän)	128	20.43 N	99.23 W
Zimatlán de Alvarez, Mex. (sē-mä-tlän′ dä äl′vä-räz)	129	16.52 N	96.47 W
Zimba, Zambia	227	17.19 S	26.13 E
Zimbabwe (Rhodesia), Afr. (rô-dē′zhĭ-á)	218	17.50 S	29.30 E
Zimnicea, Rom. (zĕm-nē′chä)	171	43.39 N	25.22 E
Zin (R.), Isr.	189a	30.50 N	35.12 E
Zinacatepec, Mex. (zĕ-nä-kä-tĕ′pĕk)	129	18.19 N	97.15 W
Zinapécuaro, Mex. (sē-nä-pä′kwä-rô)	128	19.50 N	100.49 W
Zinder, Niger (zĭn′dĕr)	225	13.48 N	8.59 E
Zion, Il. (zī′ŭn)	111a	42.27 N	87.50 W
Zion Natl. Park, Ut.	119	37.20 N	113.00 W
Zionsville, In. (zīŭnz-vĭl)	111g	39.57 N	86.15 W
Zionz L., Can. (zī′ŏnz)	99	51.25 N	91.52 W
Zipaquirá, Col. (sē-pä-kē-rä′)	140a	5.01 N	74.01 W
Zirandaro, Mex. (sē-rän-dä′rô)	128	18.28 N	101.02 W
Zitacuaro, Mex. (sē-tä-kwä′rô)	128	19.25 N	100.22 W
Zitlala, Mex. (sĕ-tlä′lä)	128	17.38 N	99.09 W
Zittau, G.D.R. (tsĕ′tou)	164	50.55 N	14.48 E
Ziway (L.), Eth.	221	8.08 N	39.11 E
Ziya (R.), China (dzē-yä)	196	38.38 N	116.31 E
Zlatograd, Bul.	171	41.24 N	25.05 E
Zlatoust, Sov. Un. (zlä-tô-ōōst′)	180a	55.13 N	59.39 E
Zlītan, Libya	221	32.27 N	14.33 E
Złoczew, Pol. (zwô′chĕf)	165	51.23 N	18.34 E
Zlynka, Sov. Un. (zlĕŋ′kä)	172	52.28 N	31.39 E
Znamenka, Sov. Un. (znä′mĕn-kä)	173	48.43 N	32.35 E
Znamensk, Sov. Un. (znä′mĕnsk)	163	54.39 N	21.49 E
Znojmo, Czech. (znoi′mô)	164	48.52 N	16.03 E
Zoetermeer, Neth.	155a	52.03 N	4.29 E
Zoeterwoude, Neth.	155a	52.03 N	4.29 E
Zoločev, Sov. Un. (zô′lô-chĕf)	157	49.48 N	24.55 E
Zolotonosha, Sov. Un. (zô′lô-tô-nô′shá)	173	49.41 N	32.03 E
Zolotoy, Mys (C.), Sov. Un. (mĭs zô′lô-tôy′)	200	47.24 N	139.10 E
Zomba, Malawi (zôm′bä)	217	15.23 S	35.18 E
Zongo, Zaire (zôŋ′gô)	221	4.19 N	18.36 E
Zonguldak, Tur. (zôn′gōōl′däk)	177	41.25 N	31.50 E
Zonhoven, Bel.	155a	50.59 N	5.24 E
Zoquitlán, Mex. (sô-kĕt-län′)	129	18.09 N	97.02 W
Zorita, Sp. (thô-rē′tä)	168	39.18 N	5.41 W
Zossen, G.D.R. (tsô′sĕn)	155b	52.13 N	13.27 E
Zou Xian, China (dzō shyĕn)	196	35.24 N	116.54 E
Zubtsov, Sov. Un. (zōōp-tsôf′)	172	56.13 N	34.34 E
Zuera, Sp. (thwä′rä)	169	41.40 N	0.48 W
Zuger See (L.), Switz. (tsōōg)	164	47.10 N	8.40 E
Zugspitze Pk., Aus.-F.R.G.	164	47.25 N	11.00 E
Zuidelijk Flevoland (Reg.), Neth.	155a	52.22 N	5.20 E
Zújar (R.), Sp. (zōō′kär)	168	38.55 N	5.05 W
Zújar, Embalse del (Res.), Sp.	168	38.50 N	5.20 W
Zulueta, Cuba (zōō-lōō-ē′tä)	132	22.20 N	79.35 W
Zululand (Reg.), S. Afr. (zōō′lōō-länd)	222	27.45 S	31.29 E
Zumbo, Moz. (zōōm′bōō)	227	15.36 S	30.25 E
Zumbro (R.), Mn. (zŭm′brō)	113	44.18 N	92.14 W
Zumbrota, Mn. (zŭm-brō′tá)	113	44.16 N	92.39 W
Zumpango, Mex. (sōōm-päŋ-gô)	128	19.48 N	99.06 W
Zundert, Neth.	155a	51.28 N	4.39 E
Zungeru, Nig. (zōōŋ-gä′rōō)	225	9.48 N	6.09 E
Zunhua, China (dzōōn-hwä)	196	40.12 N	117.55 E
Zuni, Sov. Un., Az.-NM	119	34.40 N	109.30 W
Zuni Ind. Res., NM (zōō′nĕ)	119	35.10 N	108.40 W
Zuni Mts., NM	119	35.10 N	108.10 W
Zunyi, China	194	27.58 N	106.40 E
Zürich, Switz. (tsü′rĭk)	164	47.22 N	8.32 E
Zürichsee (L.), Switz.	164	47.18 N	8.47 E
Zushi, Jap. (zōō′shĕ)	201a	35.17 N	139.35 E
Zuwārah, Libya	221	32.58 N	12.07 E
Zuwayzā, Jordan	189a	31.42 N	35.58 E
Zvenigorod, Sov. Un. (zvä-nĕ′gô-rôt)	172	55.46 N	36.54 E
Zvenigorodka, Sov. Un. (zvä-nĕ′gô-rôt′kä)	173	49.07 N	30.59 E
Zvolen, Czech. (zvô′lĕn)	165	48.35 N	19.10 E
Zvornik, Yugo. (zvôr′nĕk)	171	44.24 N	19.08 E
Zweibrücken, F.R.G. (tsvī-brük′ĕn)	164	49.16 N	7.20 E
Zwickau, G.D.R. (tsvĭk′ou)	164	50.43 N	12.30 E
Zwolle, Neth. (zvôl′ĕ)	161	52.33 N	6.05 E
Zyradow, Pol. (zhĕ-rär′dōōf)	165	52.04 N	20.28 E
Zyryanka, Sov. Un. (zĕ-ryän′kä)	179	65.45 N	151.15 E
Zyryanovsk, Sov. Un. (zĕ-ryä′nôfsk)	178	49.43 N	83.52 E
Zywiec, Pol. (zhĭ′vyĕts)	165	49.42 N	19.14 E